THE NEW GROVE
DICTIONARY OF MUSIC AND MUSICIANS®

Volume Ten

The New GROVE Dictionary

of Music and Musicians®

EDITED BY

Stanley Sadie

10

Kern – Lindelheim

GROVE

MACMILLAN PUBLISHERS LIMITED, LONDON
GROVE'S DICTIONARIES OF MUSIC INC., NEW YORK, NY
MACMILLAN PUBLISHERS (CHINA) LIMITED, HONG KONG

© Macmillan Publishers Limited 1980

First Edition of *A Dictionary of Music and Musicians*, planned and edited by SIR GEORGE GROVE, DCL, in
four volumes, with an Appendix edited by J. A. Fuller Maitland, and an Index by Mrs Edmond
Wodehouse, 1878, 1880, 1883, 1890.
Reprinted 1890, 1900

Second Edition, edited by J. A. FULLER MAITLAND, in five volumes, 1904–10

Third Edition, edited by H. C. COLLES, in five volumes, 1927

Fourth Edition, edited by H. C. COLLES, in five volumes, with Supplementary Volume, 1940

Fifth Edition, edited by ERIC BLOM, in nine volumes, 1954; with Supplementary Volume, 1961
Reprinted 1961, 1973, 1975

American Supplement, edited by WALDO SELDEN PRATT, in one volume, 1920
Reprinted with new material, 1928; many later reprints

The New Grove Dictionary of Music and Musicians,®
edited by STANLEY SADIE, in twenty volumes, 1980

The New Grove and *The New Grove Dictionary of Music and Musicians* are registered trademarks
in the United States of Macmillan Publishers Limited, London.

Macmillan Publishers Limited, London and its associated companies are the proprietors of the trademarks
Grove's, *The New Grove*, and *The New Grove Dictionary of Music and Musicians* throughout the world.

First published 1980 in hardback edition.
Reprinted with minor corrections, 1981, 1984, 1985, 1986, 1987, 1988, 1989, 1990, 1991, 1992, 1993, 1994, 1995.
Reprinted 1995 in paperback edition.

Published by Macmillan Publishers Limited, London. Both editions are distributed outside the United
Kingdom and Europe by Macmillan Publishers (China) Limited, Hong Kong, a member of the Macmillan
Publishers Group, and by its appointed agents. In the United States of America and Canada, Macmillan
Publishers (China) Limited, Hong Kong have appointed Grove's Dictionaries of Music Inc., New York,
NY, as sole distributor.

Text keyboarded, corrected, page-made-up and filmset by
Richard Clay (The Chaucer Press) Ltd, Bungay, Suffolk, England

Illustrations originated by Fletcher & Son Ltd, Norwich, England

Music examples processed by Halstan & Co.Ltd, Amersham, England

Printed and bound in the United States of America by R. R. Donnelley & Co., Crawfordsville, Indiana

British Library Cataloguing in Publication Data

The New Grove dictionary of music and
musicians.®

A catalogue record for this book is available
from the British Library.

ISBN 0–333–23111–2 (hardback)
ISBN 1–56159–174–2 (paperback)

Library of Congress Cataloging in Publication Data
Main entry under title:

The New Grove dictionary of music and musicians.®
Includes bibliographies.
1. Music-Dictionaries.
2. Music-Bio-bibliography.
I. Grove, George, Sir, 1820–1900.
II. Sadie, Stanley.
ML100.N48 780'.3   79-26207

ISBN 0–333–23111–2 (hardback)
ISBN 1–56159–174–2 (paperback)

Contents

GENERAL ABBREVIATIONS   vii

BIBLIOGRAPHICAL ABBREVIATIONS   xi

LIBRARY SIGLA   xiv

A NOTE ON THE USE OF THE DICTIONARY   xxxii

THE DICTIONARY, VOLUME TEN:

Kern – Lindelheim   1

ILLUSTRATION ACKNOWLEDGMENTS   869

General Abbreviations

A	alto, contralto [voice]
a	alto [instrument]
AB	see BA
ABC	American Broadcasting Company; Australian Broadcasting Commission
Abt.	Abteilung [section]
acc.	accompaniment, accompanied by
AD	anno Domini
add, addl	additional
add, addn	addition
ad lib	ad libitum
Ag	Agnus Dei
all	alleluia
AM	see MA
a.m.	ante meridiem [before noon]
amp	amplified
AMS	American Musicological Society
Anh.	Anhang [appendix]
anon.	anonymous(ly)
ant	antiphon
appx	appendix
arr.	arrangement, arranged by/for
ASCAP	American Society of Composers, Authors and Publishers
attrib.	attribution, attributed to
Aug	August
aut.	autumn
B	bass [voice]
B	Brainard catalogue [Tartini]
b	bass [instrument]
b	born
BA	Bachelor of Arts
Bar	baritone [voice]
bar	baritone [instrument]
BBC	British Broadcasting Corporation
BC	British Columbia (Canada)
BC	before Christ
bc	basso continuo
Bd.	Band [volume]
Berks.	Berkshire (GB)
Berwicks.	Berwickshire (GB)
bk	book
BLitt	Bachelor of Letters/Literature
BM	British Museum
BMI	Broadcast Music Inc. (USA)
BMus	Bachelor of Music
bn	bassoon
Bros.	Brothers
Bs	Benedictus

Bte	Benedicite
Bucks.	Buckinghamshire (GB)
Bulg.	Bulgarian
BVM	Blessed Virgin Mary
BWV	Bach-Werke-Verzeichnis [Schmieder, catalogue of J. S. Bach's works]
c	circa [about]
Calif.	California (USA)
CanD	Cantate Domino
carn.	Carnival
CBC	Canadian Broadcasting Corporation
CBE	Commander of the Order of the British Empire
CBS	Columbia Broadcasting System (USA)
CBSO	City of Birmingham Symphony Orchestra
CeBeDeM	Centre Belge de Documentation Musicale
cel	celesta
CEMA	Council for the Encouragement of Music and the Arts [now the Arts Council of Great Britain]
cf	confer [compare]
c.f.	cantus firmus
CH	Companion of Honour
chap.	chapter
Chin.	Chinese
chit	chitarrone
Cie	Compagnie
cimb	cimbalom
cl	clarinet
clvd	clavichord
cm	centimetre(s)
CNRS	Centre National de la Recherche Scientifique (F)
Co.	Company; County
Cod.	Codex
col.	column
coll.	collected by
collab.	in collaboration with
comm	communion
conc.	concerto
cond.	conductor, conducted by
Conn.	Connecticut (USA)
cont	continuo
Corp.	Corporation
c.p.s.	cycles per second
Cr	Credo, Creed
CSc	Candidate of Historical Sciences
Ct	countertenor
Cz.	Czech

D	Deutsch catalogue [Schubert]; Dounias catalogue [Tartini]	GmbH	Gesellschaft mit beschränkter Haftung [limited-liability company]
d.	denarius, denarii [penny, pence]	govt.	government [district in USSR]
d	died	grad	gradual
Dan.	Danish	GSM	Guildhall School of Music and Drama, London
db	double bass		
DBE	Dame Commander of the Order of the British Empire	gui	guitar
dbn	double bassoon		
DC	District of Columbia (USA)	H	Hoboken catalogue [Haydn]; Helm catalogue [C. P. E. Bach]
Dec	December		
ded.	dedication, dedicated to	Hants.	Hampshire (GB)
DeM	Deus misereatur	Heb.	Hebrew
Dept	Department	Herts.	Hertfordshire (GB)
Derbys.	Derbyshire (GB)	HMS	His/Her Majesty's Ship
dir.	director, directed by	HMV	His Master's Voice
diss.	dissertation	hn	horn
DLitt	Doctor of Letters/Literature	Hon.	Honorary; Honourable
DMus	Doctor of Music	hpd	harpsichord
DPhil	Doctor of Philosophy	HRH	His/Her Royal Highness
DSc	Doctor of Science/Historical Sciences	Hung.	Hungarian
		Hunts.	Huntingdonshire (GB)
		Hz	Hertz [c.p.s.]
ed.	editor, edited (by)		
edn.	edition		
e.g.	exempli gratia [for example]	IAML	International Association of Music Libraries
elec	electric, electronic		
EMI	Electrical and Musical Industries	ibid	ibidem [in the same place]
Eng.	English	i.e.	id est [that is]
eng hn	english horn	IFMC	International Folk Music Council
ens	ensemble	Ill.	Illinois (USA)
esp.	especially	IMS	International Musicological Society
etc	et cetera [and so on]	Inc.	Incorporated
ex., exx.	example, examples	inc.	incomplete
		incl.	includes, including
		Ind.	Indiana (USA)
f, ff	following page, following pages	inst	instrument, instrumental
f., ff.	folio, folios	int	introit
f	forte	IPEM	Institute for Psycho-acoustics and Electronic Music, Brussels
facs.	facsimile		
fasc.	fascicle	ISCM	International Society for Contemporary Music
Feb	February		
ff	fortissimo	ISM	Incorporated Society of Musicians (GB)
fff	fortississimo	ISME	International Society of Music Educators
fig.	figure [illustration]	It.	Italian
fl .	flute		
fl	floruit [he/she flourished]		
fp	fortepiano	Jan	January
Fr.	French	Jap.	Japanese
frag.	fragment	*Jb*	Jahrbuch [yearbook]
FRAM	Fellow of the Royal Academy of Music, London	Jg.	Jahrgang [year of publication/volume]
		jr	junior
FRCM	Fellow of the Royal College of Music, London	Jub	Jubilate
FRCO	Fellow of the Royal College of Organists, London	K	Kirkpatrick catalogue [D. Scarlatti]; Köchel catalogue [Mozart; no. after / is from 6th edn.]
FRS	Fellow of the Royal Society, London		
		kbd	keyboard
Gael.	Gaelic	KBE	Knight Commander of the Order of the British Empire
Ger.	German		
Gk.	Greek	KCVO	Knight Commander of the Royal Victorian Order
Gl	Gloria		
Glam.	Glamorgan (GB)	kHz	kilohertz
glock	glockenspiel	km	kilometre(s)
Glos., Gloucs.	Gloucestershire (GB)	Ky	Kyrie
		Ky.	Kentucky (USA)

£	libra, librae [pound, pounds sterling]	Oct	October
L	Longo catalogue [D. Scarlatti]	off	offertory
Lancs.	Lancashire (GB)	OM	Order of Merit
Lat.	Latin	Ont.	Ontario (Canada)
Leics.	Leicestershire (GB)	op., opp.	opus, opera
lib	libretto	op cit	opere citato [in the work cited]
Lincs.	Lincolnshire (GB)	opt.	optional
lit	litany	orch	orchestra, orchestral
LittD	Doctor of Letters/Literature	orchd	orchestrated (by)
LlB	Bachelor of Laws	org	organ
LlD	Doctor of Laws	orig.	original(ly)
LP	long-playing record	ORTF	Office de Radiodiffusion-Télévision Fran-
LPO	London Philharmonic Orchestra		çaise
LSO	London Symphony Orchestra	OUP	Oxford University Press
Ltd	Limited	ov.	overture
M.	Monsieur	P	Pincherle catalogue [Vivaldi]
MA	Master of Arts	p.	pars (1p. = *prima pars*, etc)
Mag	Magnificat	p., pp.	page, pages
mand	mandolin	*p*	piano
mar	marimba	p.a.	per annum
Mass.	Massachusetts (USA)	PC	number of chanson in A. Pillet and H.
MBE	Member of the Order of the British		Carstens: *Bibliographie der Troubadours*
	Empire		(Halle, 1933)
Mez	mezzo-soprano	Penn.	Pennsylvania (USA)
mf	mezzo-forte	perc	percussion
mic	microphone	perf.	performance, performed (by)
Mich.	Michigan (USA)	pf	piano
Minn.	Minnesota (USA)	PhD	Doctor of Philosophy
Mlle	Mademoiselle	pic	piccolo
mm	millimetre(s)	pl.	plate; plural
Mme	Madame	p.m.	post meridiem [after noon]
MMus	Master of Music	PO	Philharmonic Orchestra
mod	modulator	Pol.	Polish
Mon.	Monmouthshire (GB)	Port.	Portuguese
movt	movement	posth.	posthumous(ly)
MP	Member of Parliament (GB)	POW	prisoner of war
mp	mezzo-piano	*pp*	pianissimo
MS	manuscript	*ppp*	pianississimo
MSc	Master of Science(s)	pr.	printed
Mt	Mount	PRO	Public Record Office, London
MusB,	Bachelor of Music	prol	prologue
MusBac		PRS	Performing Right Society (GB)
MusD,	Doctor of Music	Ps	Psalm
MusDoc		ps	psalm
MusM	Master of Music	pseud.	pseudonym
		pt.	part
		ptbk	partbook
NBC	National Broadcasting Company (USA)	pubd	published
n.d.	no date of publication	pubn	publication
NJ	New Jersey (USA)		
no.	number		
Nor.	Norwegian	qnt	quintet
Northants.	Northamptonshire (GB)	qt	quartet
Notts.	Nottinghamshire (GB)		
Nov	November		
n.p.	no place of publication	R	[in signature] editorial revision
nr.	near	R.	number of chanson in G. Raynaud: *Biblio-*
NSW	New South Wales (Australia)		*graphie des chansonniers français des*
Nunc	Nunc dimittis		*XIIIe et XIVe siècles* (Paris, 1884) and H.
NY	New York State (USA)		Spanke: *G. Raynauds Bibliographie des*
			altfranzösischen Liedes (Leiden, 1955)
		R	response
ob	oboe	R	Ryom catalogue [Vivaldi]
obbl	obbligato	*R*	photographic reprint
OBE	Officer of the Order of the British Empire	*r*	recto

RAF	Royal Air Force		T	tenor [voice]
RAI	Radio Audizioni Italiane		t	tenor [instrument]
RAM	Royal Academy of Music, London		TeD	Te Deum
RCA	Radio Corporation of America		Tenn.	Tennessee (USA)
RCM	Royal College of Music, London		timp	timpani
re	response		tpt	trumpet
rec	recorder		Tr	treble [voice]
recit	recitative		tr	tract; treble [instrument]
red.	reduction, reduced for		trans.	translation, translated by
repr.	reprinted		transcr.	transcription, transcribed by/for
Rev.	Reverend		trbn	trombone
rev.	revision, revised (by/for)			
RIdIM	Répertoire International d'Iconographie Musicale		U.	University
RILM	Répertoire International de Littérature Musicale		UHF	ultra-high frequency
			UK	United Kingdom of Great Britain and Northern Ireland
RISM	Répertoire International des Sources Musicales		unacc.	unaccompanied
RMCM	Royal Manchester College of Music		unattrib.	unattributed
RNCM	Royal Northern College of Music, Manchester		UNESCO	United Nations Educational, Scientific and Cultural Organization
RO	Radio Orchestra		unperf.	unperformed
Rom.	Romanian		unpubd	unpublished
RPO	Royal Philharmonic Orchestra (GB)		US	United States [adjective]
RSFSR	Russian Soviet Federated Socialist Republic		USA	United States of America
			USSR	Union of Soviet Socialist Republics
RSO	Radio Symphony Orchestra			
Rt Hon.	Right Honourable			
RTE	Radio Telefís Eireann (Ireland)		V	versicle
Russ.	Russian		v, vv	voice, voices
RV	Ryom catalogue [Vivaldi]		v., vv.	verse, verses
			v	verso
			va	viola
S	San, Santa, Santo, São [Saint]; soprano [voice]		vc	cello
			vcle	versicle
S.	south, southern		VEB	Volkseigener Betrieb [people's own industry]
$	dollars			
s	soprano [instrument]		Ven	Venite
s.	solidus, solidi [shilling, shillings]		VHF	very high frequency
SACEM	Société d'Auteurs, Compositeurs et Editeurs de Musique (F)		vib	vibraphone
			viz	videlicet [namely]
San	Sanctus		vle	violone
Sask.	Saskatchewan (Canada)		vn	violin
sax.	saxophone		vol.	volume
Sept	September			
seq	sequence			
ser.	series		W.	west, western
sf, sfz	sforzando, sforzato		Warwicks.	Warwickshire (GB)
sing.	singular		Wilts.	Wiltshire (GB)
SJ	Societas Jesu (Society of Jesus)		wint.	winter
SO	Symphony Orchestra		Wisc.	Wisconsin (USA)
SPNM	Society for the Promotion of New Music (GB)		WoO, woo	Werke ohne Opuszahl [works without opus number]
spr.	spring		Worcs.	Worcestershire (GB)
SS	Saints		WQ	Wotquenne catalogue [C. P. E. Bach]
Ss	Santissima, Santissimo		ww	woodwind
SSR	Soviet Socialist Republic			
St	Saint, Sint, Szent			
Staffs.	Staffordshire (GB)			
Ste	Sainte		xyl	xylophone
str	string(s)			
sum.	summer			
Sup	superius		Yorks.	Yorkshire (GB)
suppl.	supplement, supplementary			
Swed.	Swedish			
sym.	symphony, symphonic			
synth	synthesizer		z	Zimmerman catalogue [Purcell]

Bibliographical Abbreviations

All bibliographical abbreviations used in this dictionary are listed below, following the typography used in the text of the dictionary. Broadly, *italic* type is used for periodicals and for reference works; roman type is used for anthologies, series etc (titles of individual volumes are italicized).

Full bibliographical information is not normally supplied in the list below if it is available elsewhere in the dictionary. Its availability is indicated as follows: D – in the article 'Dictionaries and encyclopedias of music'; E – in the article 'Editions, historical'; and P – in the list forming §III of the article 'Periodicals' (in this case the number in that list of the periodical concerned is added, in brackets). For other items, in particular national (non-musical) biographical dictionaries, basic bibliographical information is given here; and in some cases extra information is supplied to clarify the abbreviation used.

Festschriften and congress reports are not, in general, covered in this list. Although Festschrift titles are usually shortened in the dictionary, sufficient information is always given for unambiguous identification (dedicatee; occasion, if the same person is dedicatee of more than one Festschrift; place and date of publication; and where the dedicatee has an entry the editor's name may be found); for fuller information on musical Festschriften up to 1967 see W. Gerboth: *An Index to Musical Festschriften and Similar Publications* (New York, 1969). The only congress report series listed below are those of the international and the German musicological associations; for others cited in the dictionary, sufficient information is always given for identification (society or topic; place; date of occurrence); full information may be found in J. Tyrrell and R. Wise: *A Guide to International Congress Reports in Music, 1900–1975* (London, 1979).

AcM	*Acta musicologica* P [Intl 5]
ADB	*Allgemeine deutsche Biographie* (Leipzig, 1875–1912)
AM	*Antiphonale monasticum pro diurnis horis* (Paris, Tournai and Rome, 1934)
AMe (AMeS)	*Algemene muziekencyclopedie* (and suppl.) D
AMf	*Archiv für Musikforschung* P [D776]
AMI	L'arte musicale in Italia E
AMP	Antiquitates musicae in Polonia E
AMw	*Archiv für Musikwissenschaft* P [D552]
AMZ	*Allgemeine musikalische Zeitung* P [D32, 154, 170]
AMz	*Allgemeine Musik-Zeitung* P [D203]
AnM	*Anuario musical* P [E91]
AnMc	*Analecta musicologica* (some vols. in series Studien zur italienisch-deutschen Musikgeschichte), Veröffentlichungen der Musikabteilung des Deutschen historischen Instituts in Rom (Cologne, 1963–)
AnnM	*Annales musicologiques* P [F638]
AntMI	Antiquae musicae italicae E
AR	*Antiphonale sacrosanctae romanae ecclesiae pro diurnis horis* (Paris, Tournai and Rome, 1949)
AS	*Antiphonale sarisburiense*, ed. W. H. Frere (London, 1901–25/R1967)
Baker 5, 6	*Baker's Biographical Dictionary of Musicians* (5/1958 and 1971 suppl., 6/1978) D
BAMS	*Bulletin of the American Musicological Society* P [US540]
BeJb	*Beethoven-Jahrbuch* [1953–] P [D925]
BJb	*Bach-Jahrbuch* P [D434]
BMB	Biblioteca musica bononiensis E
BMw	*Beiträge zur Musikwissenschaft* P [D1013]
BNB	*Biographie nationale* [belge] (Brussels, 1866–)
BordasD	*Dictionnaire de la musique* (Paris: Bordas, 1970–76) D
Bouwsteenen: JVNM	*Bouwsteenen: jaarboek der Vereeniging voor Nederlandsche muziekgeschiedenis* P [NL20]
BrownI	H. M. Brown: *Instrumental Music Printed before 1600: a Bibliography* (Cambridge, Mass., 2/1967)
BSIM	*Bulletin français de la S[ociété] I[nternationale de] M[usique]* [previously *Le Mercure musical*; also other titles] P [F364]
BUCEM	*British Union-catalogue of Early Music*, ed. E. Schnapper (London, 1957)
BurneyH	C. Burney: *A General History of Music from the Earliest Ages to the Present* (London, 1776–89) [p. nos. refer to edn. of 1935/R1957]
BWQ	*Brass and Woodwind Quarterly* P [US756]
CaM	Catalogus musicus E
CEKM	Corpus of Early Keyboard Music E
CEMF	Corpus of Early Music in Facsimile E
CHM	*Collectanea historiae musicae* (in series Biblioteca historiae musicae cultores) (Florence, 1953–)
CM	Le choeur des muses
CMc	*Current Musicology* P [US747]
CMI	I classici musicali italiani E
CMM	Corpus mensurabilis musicae E
CMz	*Cercetări de muzicologie* P [R29]
CS	E. de Coussemaker: *Scriptorum de musica medii aevi nova series* (Paris, 1864–76/R1963)
ČSHS	*Československý hudební slovník* D
CSM	Corpus scriptorum de musica E
CSPD	*Calendar of State Papers (Domestic)* (London, 1856–1972)
Cw	Das Chorwerk E
DAB	*Dictionary of American Biography* (New York, 1928–)
DAM	*Dansk aarbog for musikforskning* P [DK88]
DBF	*Dictionnaire de biographie française* (Paris, 1933–)
DBI	*Dizionario biografico degli italiani* (Rome, 1960–)
DBL	*Dansk biografisk leksikon* (Copenhagen, 1887–1905, 2/1933–)
DBP	*Dicionário biográfico de musicos portuguezes* D
DČHP	*Dějiny české hudby v příkladech* E
DDT	Denkmäler deutscher Tonkunst E
DHM	Documenta historica musicae E
DJbM	*Deutsches Jahrbuch der Musikwissenschaft* P [D980]
DM	Documenta musicologica E
DNB	*Dictionary of National Biography* (London, 1885–1901, suppls.)
DTB	Denkmäler der Tonkunst in Bayern E
DTÖ	Denkmäler der Tonkunst in Österreich E

EDM — Das Erbe deutscher Musik E

EECM — Early English Church Music E

EIT — *Ezhegodnik imperatorskikh teatrov* P [USSR17]

EitnerQ — R. Eitner: *Biographisch-bibliographisches Quellen-Lexikon* D

EitnerS — R. Eitner: *Bibliographie der Musik-Sammelwerke des XVI. und XVII. Jahrhunderts* (Berlin, 1877) D

EKM — English (later Early) Keyboard Music E

EL — The English Lute-songs

EM — The English Madrigalists E

EM — *Ethnomusicology* P [US664]

EMDC — *Encyclopédie de la musique et dictionnaire du Conservatoire* D

EMN — Exempla musica neerlandica E

EMS — The English Madrigal School E

ES — *Enciclopedia dello spettacolo* D

ESLS — The English School of Lutenist-songwriters E

FAM — *Fontes artis musicae* P [Intl 16]

FasquelleE — *Encyclopédie de la musique* (Paris: Fasquelle, 1958–61) D

FCVR — Florilège du concert vocal de la renaissance E

FétisB (FétisBS) — F.-J. Fétis: *Biographie universelle des musiciens* (2/1860–65) (and suppl.) D

GerberL — R. Gerber: *Historisch-biographisches Lexikon der Tonkünstler* D

GerberNL — R. Gerber: *Neues historisch-biographisches Lexikon der Tonkünstler* D

GfMKB — *Gesellschaft für Musikforschung Kongressbericht* [1950–]

GMB — *Geschichte der Musik in Beispielen*, ed. A. Schering (Leipzig, 1931) E

GR — *Graduale sacrosanctae romanae ecclesiae* (Tournai, 1938)

Grove 1(–5) — G. Grove, ed.: *A Dictionary of Music and Musicians*, 2nd–5th edns. as *Grove's Dictionary of Music and Musicians* D

Grove 6 — *The New Grove Dictionary of Music and Musicians* D

GS — *Graduale sarisburiense*, ed. W. H. Frere (London, 1894/R1967)

GS — M. Gerbert: *Scriptores ecclesiastici de musica sacra* (St Blasien, 1784/R1963)

GSJ — *The Galpin Society Journal* P [GB415]

HAM — *Historical Anthology of Music*, ed. A. T. Davison and W. Apel, i (Cambridge, Mass., 1946, rev. 2/1949); ii (Cambridge, Mass., 1950) E

HawkinsH — J. Hawkins: *A General History of the Science and Practice of Music* (London, 1776) [p. nos. refer to edn. of 1853/R1963]

HJb — *Händel-Jahrbuch* P [D712, 968]

HM — Hortus musicus

HMT — *Handwörterbuch der musikalischen Terminologie* D

HMw — Handbuch der Musikwissenschaft, ed. E. Bücken (Potsdam, 1927–) [monograph series]

HMYB — *Hinrichsen's Musical Year Book* P [GB381]

HPM — Harvard Publications in Music E

HR — *Hudební revue* P [CS80]

HRo — *Hudební rozhledy* P [CS176]

HV — *Hudební věda* P [CS204]

IIM — *Izvestiya na Instituta za muzīka* P [BG14]

IMa — Instituta et monumenta E

IMi — Istituzioni e monumenti dell'arte musicale italiana E

IMSCR — *International Musicological Society Congress Report* [1930–]

IMusSCR — *International Musical Society Congress Report* [1906–11]

IRASM — *International Review of the Aesthetics and Sociology of Music* P [Intl 32]

IRMO — S. L. Ginzburg: *Istoriya russkoy muzīki v notnīkh obraztsakh* D

IRMAS — *The International Review of Music Aesthetics and Sociology* P [Intl 32]

IZ — *Instrumentenbau-Zeitschrift* P [D806]

JAMS — *Journal of the American Musicological Society* P [US613]

JbMP — *Jahrbuch der Musikbibliothek Peters* P [D336]

JEFDSS — *The Journal of the English Folk Dance and Song Society* P [GB341]

JFSS — *Journal of the Folk-song Society* P [GB183]

JIFMC — *Journal of the International Folk Music Council* P [Intl 10]

JMT — *Journal of Music Theory* P [US683]

JRBM — *Journal of Renaissance and Baroque Music* P [US590]

JRME — *Journal of Research in Music Education* P [US665]

JVNM — see *Bouwsteenen: JVNM* P [NL20]

KJb — *Kirchenmusikalisches Jahrbuch* P [D284]

KM — *Kwartalnik muzyczny* P [PL35, 64]

LaborD — *Diccionario de la música Labor* D

LaMusicaD — *La musica: dizionario* D

LaMusicaE — *La musica: enciclopedia storica* D

LM — *Lucrări de muzicologie* P [R27]

LSJ — *The Lute Society Journal* P [GB487]

LU — *Liber usualis missae et officii pro dominicis et festis duplicibus cum cantu gregoriano* (Solesmes, 1896; many later edns., incl. Tournai, 1963)

MA — *The Musical Antiquary* P [GB240]

MAB — Musica antiqua bohemica E

MAM — Musik alter Meister E

MAP — Musica antiqua polonica E

MAS — [publications of the British] Musical Antiquarian Society E

MB — Musica britannica E

MC — Musica da camera E

MD — *Musica disciplina* P [US590]

ME — *Muzīkal'naya entsiklopediya* D

MEM — Mestres de l'escolania de Montserrat E

Mf — *Die Musikforschung* P [D839]

MGG — *Die Musik in Geschichte und Gegenwart* D

MH — Musica hispana E

MJb — *Mozart-Jahrbuch des Zentralinstituts für Mozartforschung* [1950–] P [A254]

ML — *Music and Letters* P [GB280]

MLMI — Monumenta lyrica medii aevi italica E

MM — *Modern Music* P [US488]

MMA — *Miscellanea musicologica* [Australia] P [AUS19]

MMB — Monumenta musicae byzantinae E

MMBel — Monumenta musicae belgicae E

MMC — *Miscellanea musicologica* [Czechoslovakia] P [CS191]

MME — Monumentos de la música española E

MMFTR — Monuments de la musique française au temps de la renaissance E

MMg — *Monatshefte für Musikgeschichte* P [D188]

MMI — Monumenti di musica italiana E

MMN — Monumenta musicae neerlandicae E

MMP — Monumenta musicae in Polonia E

MMR — *The Monthly Musical Record* P [GB75]

MMRF — Les maîtres musiciens de la renaissance française E

MMS — Monumenta musicae svecicae E

MO — *Musical Opinion* P [GB90]

MQ — *The Musical Quarterly* P [US447]

MR — *The Music Review* P [GB376]

MRM — Monuments of Renaissance Music E

MRS — Musiche rinascimentali siciliane E

MS — *Muzīkal'nïy sovremennik* P [USSR37]

MSD — Musicological Studies and Documents, ed. A. Carapetyan (Rome, 1951–)

MT — *The Musical Times* P [GB33]

MVH — Musica viva historica E

MVSSP — Musiche vocali strumentali sacre e profane E

Mw — Das Musikwerk E

MZ — *Muzikološki zbornik* P [YU37]

NA — *Note d'archivio per la storia musicale* P [I186]

NBJb — *Neues Beethoven-Jahrbuch* P [D636]

NBL — *Norsk biografisk leksikon* (Oslo, 1921–)

NDB — *Neue deutsche Biographie* (Berlin, 1953–)

NM — Nagels Musikarchiv E

NNBW — *Nieuw Nederlandsch biografisch woordenboek* (Leiden, 1911–37)

NÖB — *Neue österreichische Biographie* (Vienna, 1923)

NOHM — *The New Oxford History of Music*, ed. E. Wellesz, J. A. Westrup and G. Abraham (London, 1954–)
NRMI — *Nuova rivista musicale italiana* P [I 282]
NZM — *Neue Zeitschrift für Musik* P [D75, 1088]

OHM — *The Oxford History of Music*, ed. W. H. Hadow (Oxford, 1901–5, enlarged 2/1929–38)
OM — *Opus musicum* P [CS222]
ÖMz — *ÖsterreichischeMusikzeitschrift* P [A233]

PalMus — Paléographie musicale (Solesmes, 1889–) [see entry SOLESMES]
PAMS — *Papers of the American Musicological Society* P [US543]
PÄMw — Publikationen älterer praktischer und theoretischer Musikwerke E
PBC — Publicaciones del departamento de música de la Biblioteca de Catalunya E
PG — *Patrologiae cursus completus*, ii: Series graeca, ed. J.-P. Migne (Paris, 1857–1912)
PGfM — Publikationen der Gesellschaft für Musikforschung E
PIISM — Pubblicazioni dell'Istituto italiano per la storia della musica E
PL — *Patrologiae cursus completus*, i: Series latina, ed. J.-P. Migne (Paris, 1844–64)
PM — Portugaliae musica E
PMA — *Proceedings of the Musical Association* P [GB80]
PMFC — Polyphonic Music of the Fourteenth Century E
PNM — *Perspectives of New Music* P [US724]
PRM — *Polski rocznik muzykologiczny* P [PL85]
PRMA — *Proceedings of the Royal Musical Association* P [GB80]
PSB — *Polskich słownik biograficzny* (Kraków, 1935)
PSFM — Publications de la Société française de musicologie E

Quaderni della RaM — *Quaderni della Rassegna musicale* P [I 272]

Rad JAZU — *Rad Jugoslavenske akademije znanosti i umjetnosti* (Zagreb, 1867–)
RaM — *La rassegna musicale* P [I 197]
RBM — *Revue belge de musicologie* P [B126]
RdM — *Revue de musicologie* P [F462]
ReM — *La revue musicale* [1920–] P [F475]
RHCM — *Revue d'histoire et de critique musicales* [1901]; *La revue musicale* [1902–10] P [F320]
RicordiE — Enciclopedia della musica (Milan: Ricordi, 1963–4) D
RiemannL 12 — Riemann Musik Lexikon (12/1959–75) D
RIM — *Rivista italiana di musicologia* P [I 280]
RISM — *Répertoire international des sources musicales* [see entry under this title]
RMARC — R[oyal] M[usical] A[ssociation] Research Chronicle P [GB496]
RMFC — *Recherches sur la musique française classique* P [F677]
RMG — *Russkaya muzïkal'naya gazeta* P [USSR19]
RMI — *Rivista musicale italiana* P [I 84]
RMS — Renaissance Manuscript Studies E
RN — *Renaissance News* P [see US590]
RRMBE — Recent Researches in the Music of the Baroque Era E
RRMR — Recent Researches in the Music of the Renaissance E

SartoriB — C. Sartori: *Bibliografia della musica strumentale italiana stampata in Italia fino al 1700* (Florence, 1952–68)
SBL — *Svenska biografiskt leksikon* (Stockholm, 1918–)
SchmidlD (SchmidlDS) — C. Schmidl: *Dizionario dei musicisti* (and suppl.) D
SCMA — Smith College Music Archives E
SeegerL — H. Seeger: *Musiklexikon* D
SEM — [University of California] Series of Early Music E
SH — *Slovenská hudba* P [CS192]
SIMG — Sammelbände der Internationalen Musik-Gesellschaft P [Intl 2]
SM — *Studia musicologica Academiae scientiarum hungaricae* P [H49]
SMA — *Studies in Music* [Australia] P [AUS20]
SMd — Schweizerische Musikdenkmäler E
SML — *Schweizer Musiker Lexikon* D
SMM — Summa musicae medii aevi E
SMN — *Studia musicologica norvegica* P [N45]
SMP — *Słownik muzyków polskich* D
SMw — *Studien zur Musikwissenschaft* P [D536]
SMz — *Schweizerische Musikzeitung/Revue musicale suisse* P [CH4]
SOB — Süddeutsche Orgelmeister des Barock E
SovM — *Sovetskaya muzïka* P [USSR66]
STMf — *Svensk tidskrift för musikforskning* P [S46]

TCM — Tudor Church Music E
TM — Thesauri musici E
TVNM — *Tijdschrift van de Vereniging voor Nederlandse muziekgeschiedenis* P [NL26]

UVNM — Uitgaven der Vereniging voor Nederlandse muziekgeschiedenis E

VMPH — Veröffentlichungen der Musik-Bibliothek Paul Hirsch E
VMw — *Vierteljahrsschrift für Musikwissenschaft* P [D282]
VogelB — E. Vogel: *Bibliothek der gedruckten weltlichen Vocalmusik Italiens, aus den Jahren 1500 bis 1700* (Berlin, 1892); rev., enlarged, by A. Einstein (Hildesheim, 1962); further addns in AnMc, nos.4, 5, 9 and 12; further rev. by F. Lesure and C. Sartori as *Bibliografia della musica italiana vocale profana pubblicata dal 1500 al 1700* (?Geneva, 1978)

WaltherML — J. G. Walther: *Musicalisches Lexicon oder Musicalische Bibliothec* D
WDMP — Wydawnictwo dawnej muzyki polskiej E
WE — Wellesley Edition E
WECIS — Wellesley Edition Cantata Index Series E

YIFMC — *Yearbook of the International Folk Music Council* P [Intl 31]

ZfM — *Zeitschrift für Musik* P [D75]
ZHMP — Zrodla historii muzyki polskiej E
ZI — *Zeitschrift für Instrumentenbau* P [D249]
ZIMG — *Zeitschrift der Internationalen Musik-Gesellschaft* P [Intl 3]
ZL — *Zenei lexikon* D
ZMw — *Zeitschrift für Musikwissenschaft* P [D556]

Library Sigla

The system of library sigla in this dictionary follows that used in its publications (Series A) by Répertoire International des Sources Musicales, Kassel, by permission. Below are listed the sigla to be found; a few of them are additional to those in the published RISM lists, but have been established in consultation with the RISM organization. Some original RISM sigla that have now been changed are retained here.

In the dictionary, sigla are always printed in *italic*. In any listing of sources a national sigillum applies without repetition until it is contradicted. For German sigla, the intermediate *brd* and *ddr* are excluded; the list below shows in which part of Germany or Berlin each library is located.

Within each national list, entries are alphabetized by sigillum, first by capital letters (showing the city or town) and then by lower-case ones (showing the institution or collection).

A: AUSTRIA

Ee	Eisenstadt, Esterházy-Archiv
Eh	——, Haydn Museum
Ek	——, Stadtpfarrkirche
F	Fiecht, Benediktinerordensstift St Georgenberg
Gd	Graz, Diözesan Archiv
Gk	——, Hochschule für Musik und Darstellende Kunst
Gl	——, Steiermärkische Landesbibliothek am Joanneum
Gmi	——, Musikwissenschaftliches Institut der Universität
Gu	——, Universitätsbibliothek
GÖ	Furth bei Göttweig, Benediktinerstift
GÜ	Güssing, Franziskaner Kloster
H	Herzogenburg, Chorherrenstift
HE	Heiligenkreuz, Zisterzienserstift
Ik	Innsbruck, Konservatorium
Imf	——, Museum Ferdinandeum
Imi	——, Musikwissenschaftliches Institut der Universität
Iu	——, Universitätsbibliothek
Iw	——, Prämonstratenser-Chorherrenstift Wilten
KN	Klosterneuburg, Augustiner-Chorherrenstift
KR	Kremsmünster, Benediktinerstift
L	Lilienfeld, Zisterzienser-Stift
LA	Lambach, Benediktinerstift
LEx	Leoben, Pfarrbibliothek St Xaver
LIm	Linz, Oberösterreichisches Landesarchiv
LIs	——, Bundesstaatliche Studienbibliothek
M	Melk an der Donau, Benediktinerstift
MB	Michaelbeuern, Benediktinerabtei
MÖ	Mödling, Pfarrkirche St Othmar
MZ	Mariazell, Benediktiner-Priorat
N	Neuburg, Pfarrarchiv
NS	Neustift, Pfarrarchiv
R	Rein, Zisterzienserstift
Sca	Salzburg, Museum Carolino Augusteum
Sd	——, Dom-Musikarchiv
Sk	——, Kapitelbibliothek
Sm	——, Internationale Stiftung Mozarteum
Smi	——, Musikwissenschaftliches Institut der Universität
Sn	——, Nonnberg, Benediktiner-Frauenstift
Ssp	——, St Peter Benediktiner-Erzabtei
SB	Schlierbach, Stift
SCH	Schlägl, Prämonstratenser-Stift
SE	Seckau, Benediktinerabtei
SEI	Seitenstetten, Benediktinerstift
SF	St Florian, Augustiner-Chorherrenstift
SH	Solbad Hall, Franziskaner-Kloster
SL	St Lambrecht, Benediktiner-Abtei
SP	St Pölten, Diözesanarchiv
SPL	St Paul, Stift
ST	Stams, Zisterzienserstift
STE	Steyr, Stadtpfarrarchiv
TU	Tulln, Pfarrkirche St Stephan
Wd	Vienna, Stephansdom
Wdo	——, Zentralarchiv des Deutschen Ordens
Wdtö	——, Gesellschaft zur Heraugabe von Denkmälern der Tonkunst in Österreich
Wgm	——, Gesellschaft der Musikfreunde
Wh	——, Pfarrarchiv Hernals
Whb	——, Hauptverband des Österreichischen Buchhandels
Wk	——, Pfarrkirche St Karl Borromäus
Wkann	——, Hans Kann, private collection
Wkh	——, Kirche am Hof
Wkm	——, Kunsthistorisches Museum
Wl	——, Archiv für Niederösterreich (Landesarchiv)
Wm	——, Minoritenkonvent
Wmg	——, Pfarre, Maria am Gestade
Wmi	——, Musikwissenschaftliches Institut der Universität
Wmk	——, Akademie für Musik und Darstellende Kunst
Wn	——, Österreichische Nationalbibliothek, Musiksammlung
Wögm	——, Österreichische Gesellschaft für Musik
Wp	——, Musikarchiv, Piaristenkirche Maria Treu
Wph	——, Wiener Philharmoniker, Archiv und Bibliothek
Wps	——, Priesterseminar
Ws	——, Schottenstift
Wsa	——, Stadtarchiv
Wsp	——, St Peter, Musikarchiv
Wst	——, Stadtbibliothek, Musiksammlung
Wu	——, Universitätsbibliothek
Ww	——, Pfarrarchiv Währing
Wweinmann	——, Alexander Weinmann, private collection
Wwessely	——, Othmar Wessely, private collection
WAY	Waydhofen an der Ybbs, Pfarre
WE	Wels, Stift
WIL	Wilhering, Zisterzienserstift
Z	Zwettl, Zisterzienserstift

B: BELGIUM

Aa	Antwerp, Stadsarchief
Aac	——, Archief en Museum voor het Vlaamse Culturleven
Ac	——, Koninklijk Vlaams Muziekconservatorium
Ak	——, Onze-Lieve-Vrouwkathedraal
Amp	——, Museum Plantijn–Moretus
Apersoons	——, Guido Persoons, private collection
As	——, Stadsbibliotheek
Asa	——, Kerkbestuur St-Andries
Asj	——, Collegiale en Parochiale Kerk St-Jacob
Averwilt	——, F. Verwilt, private collection
AN	Anderlecht, St-Guiden Kerk
Ba	Brussels, Archives de la Ville
Bc	——, Conservatoire Royal de Musique
Bcdm	——, Centre Belge de Documentation Musicale [CeBeDeM]
Bg	——, Eglise de Ste Gudule
Bi	——, Institut de Psycho-acoustique et de Musique Electronique

Br	——, Bibliothèque Royale Albert 1er/Koninklijke Bibliotheek Albert I
Brtb	——, Radiodiffusion-Télévision Belge
Bsp	——, Société Philharmonique
BRc	Bruges, Stedelijk Muziekconservatorium
D	Diest, St Sulpitiuskerk
Gar	Ghent [Gent, Gand], Stadsarchief
Gc	——, Koninklijk Muziekconservatorium
Gcd	——, Culturele Dienst Province Ost Vlaanderen
Geb	——, St Baafsarchief med Bibliotheek Van Damme
Gu	——, Rijksuniversiteit, Centrale Bibliotheek
K	Kortrijk, St Martinskerk
Lc	Liège, Conservatoire Royal de Musique
Lu	——, Université de Liège
LIc	Lier, Conservatoire
LIg	——, St Gummaruskerk
LV	Louvain, Dominikanenklooster
LVu	——, Université de Louvain
M	Mons, Conservatoire Royal de Musique
MA	Morlanwelz-Mariemont, Musée de Mariemont
MEa	Mechelen, Archief en Stadsbibliotheek
MEs	——, Stedelijke Openbare Bibliotheek
OU	Oudenaarde, Parochiale Kerk
Tc	Tournai, Chapitre de la Cathédrale
Tv	——, Bibliothèque de la Ville
TI	Tienen, St Germanuskerk
Z	Zoutleeuw, St Leonarduskerk

BR: BRAZIL

Rem	Rio de Janeiro, Escola de Música, Universidade Federal do Rio de Janeiro
Rn	——, Biblioteca Nacional

C: CANADA

E	Edmonton, University of Alberta
Fc	Fredericton, Christ Church Cathedral
Ku	Kingston, Queens University, Douglas Library
Lu	London, University of Western Ontario, Lawson Memorial Library
Mc	Montreal, Conservatoire de Musique et d'Art Dramatique
Mfisher	——, Sidney T. Fisher, private collection [in *Tu*]
Mm	——, McGill University, Faculty and Conservatorium of Music and Redpath Libraries
On	Ottawa, National Library of Canada
Qc	Quebec, Cathédrale de la Sainte-Trinité
Qul	——, Université Laval
SAu	Sackville, Mt Allison University
SJm	St John, New Brunswick Museum
Tb	Toronto, Canadian Broadcasting Corporation
Tm	——, Royal Ontario Museum
Tolnick	——, Harvey J. Olnick, private collection
Tp	——, Toronto Public Library, Music Branch
Tu	——, University of Toronto, Faculty of Music
Vu	Vancouver, University of British Columbia Library, Fine Arts Division
W	Winnipeg, University of Manitoba

CH: SWITZERLAND

A	Aarau, Aargauische Kantonsbibliothek
AShoboken	Ascona, Anthony van Hoboken, private collection
Bchristen	Basle, Werner Christen, private collection
Bm	——, Musikakademie der Stadt
Bmi	——, Musikwissenschaftliches Institut der Universität
Bu	——, Öffentliche Bibliothek der Universität, Musiksammlung
BA	Baden, Historisches Museum (Landvogtei-Schloss)
BEk	Berne, Konservatorium
BEl	——, Schweizerische Landesbibliothek
BEms	——, Musikwissenschaftliches Seminar der Universität
BEsu	——, Stadt- und Universitätsbibliothek; Bürgerbibliothek
BI	Biel, Stadtbibliothek
C	Chur, Kantonsbibliothek Graubünden
D	Disentis, Stift
E	Einsiedeln, Benediktinerkloster
EN	Engelberg, Stift
Fcu	Fribourg, Bibliothèque Cantonale et Universitaire
Ff	——, Franziskaner-Kloster
Fk	——, Kapuziner-Kloster
Fsn	——, Kapitel St Nikolaus
FF	Frauenfeld, Thurgauische Kantonsbibliothek
Gamoudruz	Geneva, Emile Amoudruz, private collection
Gc	——, Conservatoire de Musique
Gpu	——, Bibliothèque Publique et Universitaire

GLtschudi	Glarus, A. Tschudi, private collection
Lmg	Lucerne, Allgemeine Musikalische Gesellschaft
Ls	——, Stiftsarchiv St Leodegar
Lz	——, Zentralbibliothek
LAc	Lausanne, Conservatoire de Musique
LAcu	——, Bibliothèque Cantonale et Universitaire
LU	Lugano, Biblioteca Cantonale
Mbernegg	Maienfeld, Sprecher von Bernegg, private collection
MO	Morges, Bibliothèque de la Ville
MÜ	Müstair, Frauenkloster
N	Neuchâtel, Bibliothèque Publique
R	Rheinfelden, Christkatholisches Pfarramt
S	Sion, Bibliothèque Cantonale du Valais
Sa	——, Staatsarchiv
Sk	——, Kathedrale
SA	Sarnen, Bibliothek des Kollegiums
SAf	——, Frauenkloster
SCH	Schwyz, Kantonsbibliothek
SGs	St Gall, Stiftsbibliothek
SGv	——, Stadtbibliothek
SH	Schaffhausen, Stadtbibliothek
SM	St Maurice, Bibliothèque de l'Abbaye
SO	Solothurn, Zentralbibliothek, Musiksammlung
TH	Thun, Stadtbibliothek
W	Winterthur, Stadtbibliothek
Wpeer	——, Peer private collection
Zi	Zurich, Israelitische Kulturgemeinde
Zjacobi	——, Erwin R. Jacobi, private collection
Zk	——, Konservatorium und Musikhochschule
Zma	——, Schweizerisches Musik-Archiv
Zms	——, Musikwissenschaftliches Seminar der Universität
Zp	——, Pestalozzianum
Zz	——, Zentralbibliothek
ZG	Zug, Stadtbibliothek
ZO	Zofingen, Stadtbibliothek
ZU	Zuoz, Gemeindearchiv

CO: COLOMBIA

B	Bogotá, Catedral

CS: CZECHOSLOVAKIA

Bb	Brno, Klášter Milosrdných Bratří [in *Bm*]
Bm	——, Ústav Dějin Hudby Moravského Musea, Hudebněhistorické Oddělení
Bu	——, Státní Vědecká Knihovna, Universitní Knihovna
BA	Bakov nad Jizerou, pobočka Státní Archívu v Mladé Boleslavi
BEL	Bělá pod Bezdězem, Městské Muzeum
BER	Beroun, Okresní Archív
BRa	Bratislava, Okresní Archív
BRe	——, Evanjelícka a. v. Cirkevná Knižnica
BRhs	——, Knižnica Hudobného Seminara Filosofickej Fakulty University Koménskeho
BRnm	——, Slovenské Národné Muzeum, Hudobné Oddělenie
BRsa	——, Štátny Ústredný Archív Slovenskej Socialistickej Republiky
BRsav	——, Slovenská Akadémia Vied
BRu	——, Univerzitná Knižnica
BREsi	Březnice, Děkanský Kostel Sv Ignáce
BSk	Banská Štiavnica, Farský Rímsko-Katolický Kostol, Archív Chóru
CH	Cheb, Okresní Archív
CHOd	Choceň, Děkanský Úřad
CHOm	——, Městské Muzeum
H	Hronov, Muzeum Aloise Jiráska
HK	Hradec Králové, Muzeum
HOm	Hořice, Vlastivědné Muzeum
J	Jur pri Bratislave, Okresní Archív, Bratislava-Vidick
JIa	Jindřichův Hradec, Státní Archív
JIm	——, Vlastivědné Muzeum
K	Český Krumlov, Pracoviště Státního Archívu Třeboň, Hudební Sbírka
KL	Klatovy, Okresní Archív
KO	Košice, Městsky Archív
KOL	Kolín, Děkanský Chrám
KRa	Kroměříž, Státní Zámek a Zahrady, Historicko-Umělecké Fondy, Hudební Archív
KRA	Králíky, Děkanský Úřad
KRE	Kremnica, Městsky Archív
KU	Kutná Hora, Oblastní Muzeum
KVd	Karlovy Vary, Děkanský Úřad
KVso	——, Karlovarský Symfonický Orchestr
L	Levoča, Rímsko-Katolický Farský Kostol
LIa	Česká Lípa, Okresní Archív

LIT	Litoměřice, Státní Archív
LO	Loukov, Farní Úřad
Mms	Martin, Matica Slovenská, Oddělenie Hudobných Pamiatok
Mnm	——, Slovenské Národné Muzeum, Archív
MB	Mladá Boleslav, Okresní Archív
ME	Mělník, Okresní Archív
MH	Mnichovo Hradiště, Vlastivědné Muzeum
N	Nitra, Státní Archív
ND	Nové Dvory, Farní Úřad
NM	Nové Mesto nad Váhom, Rímsko-Katolický Farský Kostol
OLa	Olomouc, Státní Oblastní Archív v Opava
OLu	——, Státní Vědecká Knihovna, Universitní Knihovna
OP	Opava, Slezské Muzeum
OS	Ostrava, Československý Rozhlas, Hudební Archív
OSE	Osek, Klášter
Pa	Prague, Státní Ústřední Archív
Pak	——, Archív Metropolitní Kapituly
Pdobrovského	——, Knihovna Josefa Dobrovského
Ph	——, Československá Církev Holešovice
Pis	——, Československo Hudební Informační Středisko
Pk	——, Archív Státní Konservatoře v Praze
Pnm	——, Národní Muzeum, Hudební Oddělení
Pp	——, Archív Pražského Hradu
Ppp	——, Památník Národního Písemnictví na Strahově
Pr	——, Československý Rozhlas, Hudební Archív Různá Provenience
Pra	——, Rodinní Archív Karla Kovařovice
Ps	——, Strahovská Knihovna [in Ppp]
Psf	——, Kostel Sv Franciscus
Psj	——, Kostel Sv Jakuba
Pu	——, Státní Knihovna ČSSR, Universitní Knihovna
PLa	Plzeň, Městsky Archív
PLm	——, Západočeské Muzeum
PLA	Plasy, Okresní Archív
POa	Poděbrady, pobočka Státní Archívu Nymburk
POm	——, Helichovo Muzeum
PR	Příbram, Okresný Muzeum
PRE	Prešov, Rímsko-Katolický Farský Kostol
RA	Rakovník, Státní Archív
RAJ	Rajhrad, Klášter [in Bm]
RO	Rokycany, Okresný Muzeum
ROZ	Rožnava, Biskupski Archív
RY	Rychnov, Muzeum Orlicka
Sk	Spišská Kapitula, Katedrálny Rímsko-Katolický Kostol, Knižnica Spišskej Kapituly
SNV	Spišská Nová Ves, Rímsko-Katolický Farský Kostol
SO	Sokolov, Státní Archív
TC	Třebíč, Městsky Archív
TN	Trenčín, Okresní Archív
TR	Trnava, Dóm Sv Mikuláša
TRB	Třebenice, Klášter
TRE	Třeboň, Státní Archív
TU	Turnov, Okresný Muzeum
VE	Velenice, Farní Úřad
VM	Vysoké Mýto, Okresný Muzeum
ZA	Zámrsk, Státní Archív

CU: CUBA

Hn	Havana, Biblioteca Nacional
Hse	——, Biblioteca de la Sociedad Económica de Amigos del País

D: GERMANY

Aa	Augsburg, BRD, Kantoreiarchiv St Annen
Af	——, Bibliothek der Fuggerschen Domänenkanzlei
Ahk	——, Dominikanerkloster Heilig-Kreuz
As	——, Staats- und Stadtbibliothek
Asa	——, Stadtarchiv
AAd	Aachen, BRD, Bischöfliche Diözesanbibliothek
AAg	——, Kaiser Karl-Gymnasium, Lehrerbibliothek
AAm	——, Domarchiv
AAst	——, Stadtbibliothek
AB	Amorbach, BRD, Fürstlich Leiningische Bibliothek, private collection
ABG	Annaberg-Buchholz, DDR, Pfarramt, Kirchenbibliothek
ABGa	——, Kantoreiarchiv St Annen
AD	Adolfseck bei Fulda, BRD, Schloss Fasanerie, Bibliothek der Kurhessischen Hausstiftung
ALa	Altenburg, DDR, Landesarchiv (Historisches Staatsarchiv)
ALs	——, Stadtarchiv

ALt	——, Bibliothek des Landestheaters
AM	Amberg, BRD, Staatliche Provinzialbibliothek
AN	Ansbach, BRD, Regierungsbibliothek
AÖ	Altötting, BRD, Kapuziner-Kloster St Konrad
ARk	Arnstadt, DDR, Kirchenbibliothek
ARsk	——, Stadt- und Kreisbibliothek
ARsm	——, Schlossmuseum
ASh	Aschaffenburg, BRD, Hofbibliothek
ASm	——, Stadtbücherei
ASsb	——, Stiftsbibliothek
B	Berlin, Staatsbibliothek Preussischer Kulturbesitz [W]
Ba	——, Amerika-Gedenkbibliothek (Berliner Zentralbibliothek) [W]; Deutsche Akademie der Künste [E]
Bch	——, Musikbücherei Charlottenburg [W]
Bdhm	——, Deutsche Hochschule für Musik Hanns Eisler [E]
Bds	——, Deutsche Staatsbibliothek (formerly Königliche Bibliothek; Preussische Staatsbibliothek; Öffentliche Wissenschaftliche Bibliothek), Musikabteilung [E]
Bdso	——, Deutsche Staatsoper [E]
Be	——, Institut für Musikerziehung der Humboldt-Universität [E]
Bgk	——, Streit'sche Stiftung [in Bs] [E]
Bhbk	——, Staatliche Hochschule für Bildende Kunst [W]
Bhesse	——, A. Hesse, private collection [E]
Bhm	——, Staatliche Hochschule für Musik und Darstellende Kunst [W]
Bim	——, Staatliches Institut für Musikforschung Preussischer Kulturbesitz [W]
Bk	——, Staatliche Museen Preussischer Kulturbesitz [W]
Bko	——, Komische Oper [E]
Blk	——, Bezirks-Lehrerbibliothek Kreuzberg [W]
Bm	——, Marienkirche [E]
Bmb	——, Internationale Musikbibliothek, Verband Deutscher Komponisten und Musikwissenschaftler [E]
Bmi	——, Musikwissenschaftliches Institut der Freien Universität [W]; Musikwissenschaftliches Institut der Humboldt-Universität [E]
Bmm	——, Märkisches Museum [E]
Bn	——, Nikolaikirche [E]
Bp	——, Pädagogisches Zentrum [W]
Br	——, Deutscher Demokratischer Rundfunk, Notenarchiv [E]
Bs	——, Berliner Stadtbibliothek [E]
Bst	——, Stadtbücherei, Hauptstelle Berlin-Wilmersdorf [W]
Btu	——, Universitätsbibliothek der Technischen Universität [W]
Btum	——, Lehrstuhl für Musikgeschichte der Technischen Universität [W]
Bu	——, Universitätsbibliothek der Freien Universität [W]
Buh	——, Universitätsbibliothek der Humboldt-Universität [E]
BAa	Bamberg, BRD, Staatsarchiv
BAf	——, Franziskaner-Kloster
BAs	——, Staatsbibliothek
BAL	Ballenstedt, DDR, Stadtbibliothek
BAR	Bartenstein, BRD, Fürst zu Hohenlohe-Bartensteinsches Archiv, private collection
BAUd	Bautzen, DDR, Domstift und Bischöfliches Ordinariat
BAUk	——, Stadt- und Kreisbibliothek
BB	Benediktbeuren, BRD, Pfarrkirche
BD	Brandenburg an der Havel, DDR, Domstift
BDH	Bad Homburg von der Höhe, BRD, Stadtbibliothek
BE	Berleburg, BRD, Fürstlich Sayn-Wittgenstein-Berleburgsche Bibliothek, private collection
BEU	Beuron, BRD, Benediktiner-Erzabtei
BEV	Bevensen, BRD, Superintendantur, Ephoratsbibliothek und Bibliothek Sursen
BFa	Burgsteinfurt, BRD, Gymnasium Arnoldinum
BFb	——, Fürstlich Bentheimsche Bibliothek [in MÜu]
BG	Beuerberg über Wolfratshausen, BRD, Pfarramt, Stiftskirche
BGD	Berchtesgaden, BRD, Katholisches Pfarramt
BH	Bayreuth, BRD, Stadtbücherei
BI	Bielefeld, BRD, Städtisches Ratsgymnasium
BIB	Bibra, DDR, Pfarrarchiv
BIR	Birstein über Wächtersbach, BRD, Fürst von Ysenburgisches Archiv und Schlossbibliothek, private collection

BIT	Bitterfeld, DDR, Kreismuseum
BK	Bernkastel-Kues, BRD, Cusanusstift
BKÖ	Bad Köstritz, DDR, Pfarrarchiv
BMek	Bremen, BRD, Bücherei der Bremer Evangelischen Kirche
BMs	——, Staats- und Universitätsbibliothek
BNba	Bonn, BRD, Beethoven-Haus und Beethoven-Archiv
BNek	——, Gemeindeverband der Evangelischen Kirche
BNms	——, Musikwissenschaftliches Seminar der Universität
BNu	——, Universitätsbibliothek
BO	——, Bollstedt, Pfarramt
BOCHb	Bochum, BRD, Bergbaumuseum
BOCHmi	——, Musikwissenschaftliches Institut der Ruhr-Universität
BOCHs	——, Stadtbibliothek, Musikbücherei
BORp	Borna, DDR, Pfarrkirche
BS	Brunswick, BRD, Stadtarchiv und Stadtbibliothek
BTH	Barth, DDR, Kirchenbibliothek
BÜ	Büdingen, BRD, Fürstlich Ysenburg- und Büdingisches Archiv und Schlossbibliothek
BW	Burgwindheim über Bamberg, BRD, Katholisches Pfarramt
Cl	Coburg, BRD, Landesbibliothek
Cm	——, Moritzkirche
Cv	——, Kunstsammlung der Veste Coburg
CA	Castell, BRD, Fürstlich Castell'sche Bibliothek
CD	Crottendorf, DDR, Kantoreiarchiv
CR	Crimmitschau, DDR, Stadtkirche St Laurentius
CZ	Clausthal-Zellerfeld, BRD, Kirchenbibliothek
CZu	——, Universitätsbibliothek
Dhm	Dresden, DDR, Hochschule für Musik Carl Maria von Weber
Dkh	——, Katholische Hofkirche
Dl	——, Bibliothek und Museum Löbau [in *Dlb*]
Dla	——, Staatsarchiv
Dlb	——, Sächsische Landesbibliothek
Dmb	——, Musikbibliothek
Ds	——, Staatstheater
DB	Dettelbach über Kitzingen, BRD, Franziskanerkloster
DEl	Dessau, DDR, Universitäts- und Landesbibliothek
DEs	——, Stadtarchiv, Rathaus
DI	Dillingen an der Donau, BRD, Kreis- und Studienbibliothek
DIp	——, Bischöfliches Priesterseminar
DIN	Dinkelsbühl, BRD, Katholisches Pfarramt St Georg
DIP	Dippoldiswalde, DDR, Evangelisch-Lutherisches Pfarramt
DL	Delitzsch, DDR, Museum und Bibliothek
DM	Dortmund, BRD, Stadt- und Landesbibliothek
DO	Donaueschingen, BRD, Fürstlich Fürstenbergische Hofbibliothek, private collection
DÖ	Döbeln, DDR, Pfarrbibliothek St Nikolai
DÖF	Döffingen über Bölingen, BRD, Pfarrbibliothek
DS	Darmstadt, BRD, Hessische Landes- und Hochschulbibliothek
DSim	——, Internationales Musikinstitut
DSk	——, Kirchenleitung der Evangelischen Kirche in Hessen und Nassau
DT	Detmold, BRD, Lippische Landesbibliothek
DÜgg	Düsseldorf, BRD, Staatliches Görres-Gymnasium
DÜha	——, Hauptstaatsarchiv
DÜk	——, Goethe-Museum
DÜl	——, Landes- und Stadtbibliothek
DÜmb	——, Stadtbüchereien, Musikbücherei
DÜR	Düren, BRD, Stadtbücherei, Leopold-Hoesch-Museum
Ek	Eichstätt, BRD, Kapuzinerkloster
Es	——, Staats- und Seminarbibliothek
Ew	——, Benediktinerinnen-Abtei St Walburg
EB	Ebrach, BRD, Katholisches Pfarramt
EBS	Ebstorf, BRD, Kloster
EF	Erfurt, DDR, Wissenschaftliche Bibliothek der Stadt
EFd	——, Dombibliothek
EFs	——, Stadt- und Bezirksbibliothek
EIa	Eisenach, DDR, Stadtarchiv
EIb	——, Bachhaus und Bachmuseum
EIl	——, Landeskirchenrat
EIHp	Eichtersheim, BRD, Pfarrbibliothek
EL	Eisleben, DDR, Andreas-Bibliothek
EM	Emden, BRD, Grosse Kirche
EMM	Emmerich, BRD, Staatliches Gymnasium
EN	Engelberg, BRD, Franziskanerkloster
ERms	Erlangen, BRD, Musikwissenschaftliches Seminar der Universität
ERu	——, Universitätsbibliothek
ES	Essen, BRD, Musikbücherei der Stadtbücherei
EU	Eutin, BRD, Kreisbibliothek
F	Frankfurt am Main, BRD, Stadt- und Universitätsbibliothek
Fkm	——, Museum für Kunsthandwerk
Fmi	——, Musikwissenschaftliches Institut der Johann Wolfgang von Goethe-Universität
Fsg	——, Philosophisch-Theologische Hochschule St Georgen
Fsm	——, Bibliothek für Neuere Sprachen und Musik
FBa	Freiberg, DDR, Stadtarchiv
FBb	——, Bergakademie, Bücherei
FBo	——, Geschwister-Scholl-Oberschule, Historische Bibliothek
FBsk	——, Stadt- und Kreisbibliothek
FF	Frankfurt an der Oder, DDR, Stadt- und Bezirksbibliothek
FG	Freyburg, DDR, Pfarrarchiv
FLa	Flensburg, BRD, Stadtarchiv
FLs	——, Staatliches Gymnasium
FRcb	Freiburg im Breisgau, BRD, Collegium Borromaeum
FRms	——, Musikwissenschaftliches Seminar der Universität
FRu	——, Universitätsbibliothek
FRIs	Friedberg, BRD, Stadtbibliothek
FRIts	——, Theologisches Seminar der Evangelischen Kirche in Hessen und Nassau
FS	Freising, BRD, Dombibliothek
FUf	Fulda, BRD, Kloster Frauenberg
FUl	——, Hessische Landesbibliothek
FUp	——, Bischöfliches Priesterseminar, Bibliothek der Philosophisch-Theologischen Hochschule
Ga	Göttingen, BRD, Staatliches Archivlager
Gb	——, Johann Sebastian Bach-Institut
Gms	——, Musikwissenschaftliches Seminar der Universität
Gs	——, Niedersächsische Staats- und Universitätsbibliothek
GA	Gaussig bei Bautzen, DDR, Schlossbibliothek
GAH	Gandersheim, BRD, Stiftsbibliothek
GAM	Gau-Algesheim, BRD, Stadtarchiv
GAR	Gars am Inn, BRD, Philosophisch-Theologische Ordenshochschule der Redemptoristen
GBB	Grossbrembach, DDR, Pfarrarchiv
GBR	Grossbreitenbach bei Arnstadt, DDR, Pfarrbibliothek
GD	Gaesdonck über Goch, BRD, Collegium Augustinianum
GE	Gelenau, DDR, Pfarrarchiv
GERk	Gera, DDR, Kirchenarchiv
GERs	——, Stadtmuseum
GERsb	——, Stadt- und Bezirksbibliothek
GEY	Geyer, DDR, Kirchenbibliothek
GF	Grossfahrer, DDR, Pfarrarchiv Starcklof-Eschenberger
GHk	Geithain, DDR, Evangelisch-Lutherisches Pfarramt
GHNa	Grossenhain, DDR, Archiv
GHNk	——, Kirche
GI	Giessen, BRD, Justus Liebig-Universität
GL	Goslar, BRD, Marktkirchenbibliothek
GLA	Glashütte, DDR, Pfarrarchiv
GM	Grimma, DDR, Göschenhaus, Johannes Sturm, private collection
GMl	——, Landesschule
GO	Gotha, DDR, Evangelisch-Lutherische Stadtkirchengemeinde
GOa	——, Augustinerkirche
GOg	——, Gymnasium
GOl	——, Forschungsbibliothek [former Landesbibliothek]
GOs	——, Stadtarchiv
GOsk	——, Stadt- und Kreisbibliothek
GÖp	Görlitz, DDR, Evangelischer Parochialverband
GÖs	——, Stadtbibliothek
GÖsp	——, Pfarramt St Peter
GOL	Goldbach bei Gotha, DDR, Pfarrarchiv
GRim	Greifswald, DDR, Institut für Musikwissenschaft
GRk	——, Konsistorialbibliothek
GRu	——, Ernst-Moritz-Arndt-Universität
GRÜ	Grünhain, DDR, Pfarramt
GÜ	Güstrow, DDR, Heimatmuseum
GZ	Greiz, DDR, Stadt- und Kreisbibliothek
GZbk	——, Staatliche Bücher- und Kupferstichsammlung

GZmb	——, Städtische Musikbibliothek
GZsa	——, Historisches Staatsarchiv
Ha	Hamburg, BRD, Staatsarchiv
Hch	——, Gymnasium Christianeum
Hhm	——, Harburg, Helmsmuseum
Hj	——, Gelehrtenschule des Johanneum
Hkm	——, Kunstgewerbemuseum
Hmb	——, Musikbücherei der Hamburger Öffentlichen Bücherhallen
Hmg	——, Museum für Hamburgische Geschichte
Hmi	——, Musikwissenschaftliches Institut der Universität
Hs	——, Staats- und Universitätsbibliothek
Hsa	——, Senatsarchiv
Hth	——, Universität, Theatersammlung
HAf	Halle an der Saale, DDR, Hauptbibliothek und Archiv der Franckeschen Stiftungen [in *HAu*]
HAh	——, Händel-Haus
HAmi	——, Institut für Musikwissenschaft der Martin-Luther-Universität
HAmk	——, Marienbibliothek
HAs	——, Stadt- und Bezirksbibliothek
HAu	——, Universitäts- und Landesbibliothek Sachsen-Anhalt
HAI	Hainichen, DDR, Heimatmuseum
HB	Heilbronn, BRD, Stadtarchiv
HCHs	Hechingen, BRD, Stiftskirche
HD	Hermsdorf, DDR, Pfarrarchiv
HEk	Heidelberg, BRD, Evangelisches Kirchenmusikalisches Institut
HEms	——, Musikwissenschaftliches Seminar der Universität
HEu	——, Universitätsbibliothek
HER	Herrnhut, DDR, Archiv der Brüder-Unität
HEY	Heynitz, DDR, Pfarrbibliothek
HG	Havelberg, DDR, Museum
HHa	Hildburghausen, DDR, Stadtarchiv
HIb	Hildesheim, BRD, Beverin's che Bibliothek
HIm	——, St Michaelskirche
HIp	——, Bischöfliches Priesterseminar
HL	Haltenbergstetten, BRD, Schloss über Niederstetten, Fürst zu Hohenlohe-Jagstberg'sche Bibliothek, private collection
HLN	Hameln, BRD, Stadtbücherei des Schiller-Gymnasiums
HN	Herborn, BRD, Evangelisches Theologisches Seminar
HO	Hof an der Saale, BRD, Jean Paul-Gymnasium
HOr	——, Stadtarchiv, Ratsbibliothek
HOE	Hohenstein-Ernstthal, DDR, Kantoreiarchiv der Christophorikirche
HOG	Hofgeismar, BRD, Predigerseminar
HOR	Horst, BRD, Evangelisch-Lutherisches Pfarramt
HR	Harburg über Donauwörth, BRD, Fürstlich Oettingen-Wallerstein'sche Bibliothek, private collection
HSj	Helmstedt, BRD, Juleum
HSk	——, Kantorat zu St Stephani [in *W*]
HSm	——, Kloster Marienberg
HSwandersleb	——, Bibliothek Pastor Wandersleb
HTa	Halberstadt, DDR, Stadtarchiv
HTd	——, Dombibliothek
HTg	——, Gleimhaus
HVh	Hanover, BRD, Staatliche Hochschule für Musik und Theater
HVk	——, Arbeitsstelle für Gottesdienst und Kirchenmusik der Evangelisch-Lutherischen Landeskirche
HVl	——, Niedersächsische Landesbibliothek
HVs	——, Stadtbibliothek
HVsa	——, Staatsarchiv
HVth	——, Technische Hochschule
HX	Höxter, BRD, Kirchenbibliothek St Nikolaus
Iek	Isny, BRD, Evangelische Kirche St Nikolai
Iq	——, Fürstlich Quadt'sche Bibliothek, private collection
ILk	Ilmenau, DDR, Kirchenbibliothek
ILs	——, Stadtarchiv
IN	Indersdorf über Dachau, BRD, Katholisches Pfarramt
Jmb	Jena, DDR, Ernst Abbe-Bücherei, Musikbücherei
Jmi	——, Musikwissenschaftliches Institut der Friedrich-Schiller-Universität
Ju	——, Universitätsbibliothek der Friedrich-Schiller-Universität
JA	Jahnsdorf bei Stollberg, DDR, Pfarrarchiv
JE	Jever, BRD, Marien-Gymnasium
Kdma	Kassel, BRD, Deutsches Musikgeschichtliches Archiv
Kl	——, Murhardsche Bibliothek der Stadt und Landesbibliothek
Km	——, Musikakademie
Ksp	——, Louis-Spohr-Gedenk- und Forschungsstätte
KA	Karlsruhe, BRD, Badische Landesbibliothek
KAsp	——, Pfarramt St Peter
KAu	——, Universitätsbibliothek
KAL	Kaldenkirchen, BRD, Pfarrbibliothek
KARj	Karl-Marx-Stadt, DDR, Jacobi-Kirche
KARr	——, Ratsarchiv
KARs	——, Stadt- und Bezirksbibliothek
KBs	Koblenz, BRD, Stadtbibliothek
KBEk	Koblenz-Ehrenbreitstein, BRD, Provinzialat der Kapuziner
KFm	Kaufbeuren, BRD, Stadtpfarrkirche St Martin
KFs	——, Stadtbücherei
KIl	Kiel, BRD, Schleswig-Holsteinische Landesbibliothek
KImi	——, Musikwissenschaftliches Institut der Christian-Albrecht Universität
KIu	——, Universitätsbibliothek
KIN	Kindelbrück, DDR, Pfarrarchiv, Evangelisches Pfarramt
KMk	Kamenz, DDR, Evangelisch-Lutherische Hauptkirche
KMl	——, Lessingmuseum
KMs	——, Stadtarchiv
KNd	Cologne, BRD, Erzbischöfliche Diözesan- und Dombibliothek
KNh	——, Staatliche Hochschule für Musik
KNhi	——, Joseph Haydn-Institut
KNmi	——, Musikwissenschaftliches Institut der Universität
KNu	——, Universitäts- und Stadtbibliothek
KÖ	Köthen, DDR, Heimatmuseum
KPk	Kempten, BRD, Kirchenbibliothek, Evangelisch-Lutherisches Pfarramt St Mang
KPs	——, Stadtbücherei
KPsl	——, Stadtpfarrkirche St Lorenz
KR	Kleinröhrsdorf über Bischofswerda, DDR, Pfarrkirchenbibliothek
KT	Klingenthal, DDR, Kirchenbibliothek
KU	Kulmbach, BRD, Stadtarchiv
KZa	Konstanz, BRD, Stadtarchiv
KZr	——, Rosgarten-Museum
KZs	——, Städtische Wessenberg-Bibliothek
Lm	Lüneburg, BRD, Michaelisschule
Lr	——, Ratsbücherei
LA	Landshut, BRD, Historischer Verein für Niederbayern
LAU	Laubach, BRD, Gräflich Solms-Laubach'sche Bibliothek
LB	Langenburg, BRD, Fürstlich Hohenlohe-Langenburg'sche Schlossbibliothek, private collection
LCH	Lich, BRD, Fürstlich Solms-Lich'sche Bibliothek, private collection
LEb	Leipzig, DDR, Bach-Archiv
LEbh	——, Breitkopf & Härtel, Verlagsarchiv
LEdb	——, Deutsche Bücherei, Musikaliensammlung
LEm	——, Musikbibliothek der Stadt
LEmh	——, Hochschule für Musik
LEmi	——, Musikwissenschaftliches Institut der Karl-Marx-Universität
LEsm	——, Museum für Geschichte der Stadt
LEt	——, Thomasschule
LEu	——, Universitätsbibliothek der Karl-Marx-Universität
LFN	Laufen an der Salzach, BRD, Stiftsarchiv
LHD	Langhennersdorf über Freiberg, DDR, Pfarramt
LI	Lindau, BRD, Stadtbibliothek
LIM	Limbach am Main, BRD, Pfarramt
LL	Langula über Mühlhausen, DDR, Pfarramt
LM	Leitheim über Donauwörth, BRD, Schlossbibliothek Freiherr von Tucher
LO	Loccum über Wunstorf, BRD, Klosterbibliothek
LÖ	Lössnitz, DDR, Pfarrarchiv
LR	Lahr, BRD, Lehrerbibliothek des Scheffel-Gymnasiums
LST	Lichtenstein, DDR, Kantoreiarchiv von St Laurentius
LÜd	Lübeck, BRD, Distler Archiv
LÜh	——, Bibliothek der Hansestadt
LUC	Luckau, DDR, Nikolaikirche
Ma	Munich, BRD, Franziskanerkloster St Anna
Mb	——, Benediktinerabtei St Bonifaz
Mbm	——, Metropolitankapitel
Mbn	——, Bayerisches Nationalmuseum
Mbs	——, Bayerische Staatsbibliothek

Mcg	——, Georgianum, Herzogliches Priesterseminar
Mdm	——, Deutsches Museum
Mh	——, Staatliche Hochschule für Musik
Ml	——, Evangelisch-Lutherisches Landeskirchenamt
Mmb	——, Städtische Musikbibliothek
Mms	——, Musikwissenschaftliches Seminar der Universität
Msl	——, Süddeutsche Lehrerbücherei
Mth	——, Theatermuseum der Clara-Ziegler-Stiftung
Mu	——, Universitätsbibliothek
Mwg	——, Wilhelms-Gymnasium, Lehrerbibliothek
MAk	Magdeburg, DDR, Kulturhistorisches Museum, Klosterbibliothek
MAkon	——, Konsistorialbibliothek
MAl	——, Landeshauptarchiv
MAs	——, Stadt- und Musikbibliothek
MB	Marbach an der Neckar, BRD, Schiller-National-museum
MBG	Miltenberg am Main, BRD, Franziskanerkloster
MCH	Maria Laach über Andernach, BRD, Benediktiner-abtei
ME	Meissen, DDR, Stadt- und Kreisbibliothek
MEIk	Meiningen, DDR, Evangelisch-Lutherische Kirchengemeinde
MEIl	——, Staatsarchiv
MEIo	——, Opernarchiv
MEIr	——, Staatliche Museen mit Reger-Archiv
MEL	Meldorf, BRD, Joachimsche Bibliothek, Dithmarsches Landesmuseum
MERa	Merseburg, DDR, Domstift
MERr	——, Regierungsbibliothek
MERs	——, Stadt- und Kreisbibliothek
MERz	——, Deutsches Zentral-Archiv, Historische Abteilung
MFL	Münstereifel, BRD, St Michael-Gymnasium
MGmi	Marburg an der Lahn, BRD, Musikwissenschaftliches Institut der Philipps-Universität
MGs	——, Staatsarchiv und Archivschule
MGu	——, Universitätsbibliothek der Philipps-Universität
MH	Mannheim, BRD, Wissenschaftliche Stadtbibliothek und Universitätsbibliothek
MHrm	——, Reiss-Museum
MHR	Mülheim, BRD, Stadtbibliothek
MI	Michelstadt, BRD, Evangelisches Pfarramt West
MK	Markneukirchen, DDR, Gewerbemuseum
MLHb	Mühlhausen, DDR, Blasiuskirche
MLHr	——, Ratsarchiv im Stadtarchiv
MMm	Memmingen, BRD, Evangelisch-Lutherisches Pfarramt St Martin
MMs	——, Stadtbibliothek
MÖ	Mölln, BRD, Evangelisch-Lutherische Kirchengemeinde St Nikolai
MOSp	Mosbach, BRD, Pfarrbibliothek
MR	Marienberg, DDR, Kirchenbibliothek
MS	Münsterschwarzach über Kitzingen am Main, BRD, Abtei
MT	Metten über Deggendorf, BRD, Abtei
MÜd	Münster, BRD, Bischöfliches Diözesanarchiv
MÜms	——, Musikwissenschaftliches Seminar der Universität
MÜp	——, Bischöfliches Priesterseminar und Santini-Sammlung
MÜrt	——, Seminar für Reformierte Theologie
MÜs	——, Santini-Bibliothek [in *MÜp*]
MÜsa	——, Staatsarchiv
MÜu	——, Universitätsbibliothek
MÜG	Mügeln, DDR, Pfarrbibliothek
MWR	Marienweiher über Kulmbach, BRD, Franziskanerkloster
MZfederhofer	Mainz, BRD, Hellmut Federhofer, private collection
MZgm	——, Gutenberg-Museum
MZgottron	——, Adam Gottron, private collection
MZmi	——, Musikwissenschaftliches Institut der Universität
MZp	——, Bischöfliches Priesterseminar
MZs	——, Stadtbibliothek und Stadtsarchiv
MZsch	——, Musikverlag B. Schotts Söhne
MZu	——, Universitätsbibliothek der Johannes-Gutenberg-Universität
Ngm	Nuremberg, BRD, Germanisches National-Museum
Nla	——, Landeskirchliches Archiv
Nst	——, Stadtbibliothek
NA	Neustadt an der Orla, DDR, Pfarrarchiv
NAUs	Naumburg, BRD, Stadtarchiv
NAUw	——, Wenzelskirche
NBsb	Neuburg an der Donau, BRD, Staatliche Bibliothek
NBss	——, Studienseminar
NEhz	Neuenstein, BRD, Hohenlohe-Zentral-Archiv
NEschumm	——, Karl Schumm, private collection
NERk	Neuenrade, BRD, Kirchenbibliothek
NEZp	Neckarelz, BRD, Pfarrbibliothek
NGp	Neckargemünd, BRD, Pfarrarchiv
NIw	Nieheim über Bad Driburg, BRD, Weberhaus
NL	Nördlingen, BRD, Stadtarchiv, Stadtbibliothek und Volksbücherei
NLk	——, Kirchenbibliothek St Georg
NM	Neumünster, BRD, Schleswig-Holsteinische Musiksammlung der Stadt [in *Kil*]
NO	Nordhausen, DDR, Humboldt-Oberschule
NS	Neustadt an der Aisch, BRD, Evangelische Kirchenbibliothek
NSg	——, Gymnasialbibliothek
NT	Neumarkt-St Veit, BRD, Pfarrkirche
NW	Neustadt an der Weinstrasse, BRD, Heimatmuseum
OB	Ottobeuren, BRD, Benediktiner-Abtei
OF	Offenbach am Main, BRD, Verlagsarchiv André
OH	Oberfrankenhain, DDR, Pfarrarchiv
OLl	Oldenburg, BRD, Landesbibliothek
OLns	——, Niedersächsisches Staatsarchiv
OLH	Olbernhau, DDR, Pfarrarchiv
ORB	Oranienbaum, DDR, Landesarchiv–Historisches Staatsarchiv
OS	Oschatz, DDR, Ephoralbibliothek
OSa	Osnabrück, BRD, Niedersächsisches Staatsarchiv
OSm	——, Städtisches Museum
Pg	Passau, BRD, Gymnasialbibliothek
Pk	——, Bischöfliches Klerikalseminar
Po	——, Bischöfliches Ordinariat
Ps	——, Staatliche Bibliothek
PA	Paderborn, BRD, Erzbischöfliche Akademische Bibliothek
PI	Pirna, DDR, Stadtarchiv
POh	Potsdam, DDR, Pädagogische Hochschule
PR	Pretzschendorf über Dippoldiswalde, DDR, Pfarrarchiv
PU	Pulsnitz, DDR, Nikolaikirche
PW	Pesterwitz bei Dresden, DDR, Pfarrarchiv
Q	Quedlinburg, DDR, Stadt- und Kreisbibliothek
QUh	Querfurt, DDR, Heimatmuseum
QUk	——, Stadtkirche
Rim	Regensburg, BRD, Institut für Musikforschung [in *Ru*]
Rp	——, Bischöfliche Zentralbibliothek
Rs	——, Staatliche Bibliothek
Rtt	——, Fürstlich Thurn und Taxis'sche Hofbibliothek, private collection
Ru	——, Universitätsbibliothek
RAd	Ratzeburg, BRD, Domarchiv
RB	Rothenburg ob der Tauber, BRD, Stadtarchiv und Rats- und Konsistorialbibliothek
RE	Reutberg bei Schaftlach, BRD, Franziskanerinnen-Kloster
REU	Reuden, DDR, Pfarrarchiv
RH	Rheda, BRD, Fürst zu Bentheim-Tecklenburgische Bibliothek [in *MH* and *MÜu*]
RIE	Riesa, DDR, Heimatmuseum
RL	Reutlingen, BRD, Stadtbücherei
RMmarr	Ramelsloh über Winsen, BRD, G. Marr, private collection
ROmi	Rostock, DDR, Institut für Musikwissenschaft der Universität
ROs	——, Stadt- und Bezirksbibliothek
ROu	——, Universitätsbibliothek
RÖ	Röhrsdorf über Meissen, DDR, Pfarrbibliothek
RÖM	Römhild, DDR, Pfarrarchiv
ROT	Rotenburg, BRD, Predigerseminar
ROTTd	Rottenburg an der Neckar, BRD, Diözesanbibliothek
ROTTp	——, Bischöfliches Priesterseminar
RT	Rastatt, BRD, Friedrich-Wilhelm-Gymnasium
RUh	Rudolstadt, DDR, Hofkapellarchiv
RUl	——, Staatsarchiv
RÜ	Rüdenhausen über Kitzingen, BRD, Fürst Castell-Rüdenhausen Bibliothek
Seo	Stuttgart, BRD, Bibliothek und Archiv des Evangelischen Oberkirchenrats
Sh	——, Staatliche Hochschule für Musik und Darstellende Kunst
Sl	——, Württembergische Landesbibliothek
SAh	Saalfeld, DDR, Heimatmuseum
SAAmi	Saarbrücken, BRD, Musikwissenschaftliches Institut der Universität

SAAu —, Universitätsbibliothek
SBg Straubing, BRD, Johannes Turmair-Gymnasium
SBj —, Kirchenbibliothek St Jakob
SBk —, Karmeliter-Kloster
SCHhv Schwäbisch Hall, BRD, Historischer Verein für Württembergisch-Franken
SCHm —, Archiv der St Michaelskirche
SCHr —, Ratsbibliothek im Stadtarchiv
SCHEY Scheyern über Pfaffenhofen, BRD, Benediktinerabtei
SCHM Schmölln, DDR, Archiv der Stadtkirche
SCHMI Schmiedeberg bei Dresden, DDR, Pfarramt
SCHWherold Schwabach, BRD, Herold collection
SCHWk —, Kirchenbibliothek
SDF Schlehdorf, BRD, Katholische Pfarrkirche
SF Schweinfurt-Oberndorf, BRD, Kirchen- und Pfarrbibliothek des Evangelisch-Lutherischen Pfarramts
SFsj —, Pfarramt St Johannis, Sakristei-Bibliothek
SGh Schleusingen, DDR, Heimatmuseum
SHk Sondershausen, DDR, Stadtkirche
SHs —, Stadt- und Kreisbibliothek
SHsk —, Schlosskirche
SI Sigmaringen, BRD, Fürstlich Hohenzollernsche Hofbibliothek, private collection
SLk Salzwedel, DDR, Katharinenkirche
SLm —, J. F. Danneil-Museum
SLmk —, Marienkirche
SNed Schmalkalden, DDR, Evangelisches Dekanat
SNh —, Heimatmuseum Schloss Wilhelmsburg
SO Soest, BRD, Stadtbibliothek im Stadtarchiv
SÖNp Schönau bei Heidelberg, BRD, Pfarrbibliothek
SPlb Speyer, BRD, Pfälzische Landesbibliothek, Musikabteilung
SPlk —, Bibliothek des Protestantischen Landeskirchenrats der Pfalz
SPF Schulpforta, DDR, Heimoberschule
SSa Stralsund, DDR, Bibliothek des Stadtarchivs
ST Stade, BRD, Predigerbibliothek [in *ROT*]
STO Stolberg, DDR, Bibliothek
SUa Sulzenbrücken, DDR, Pfarrarchiv
SUH Suhl, DDR, Stadt- und Bezirksbibliothek Martin Andersen Nexö
SWl Schwerin, DDR, Wissenschaftliche Allgemeinbibliothek [former Mecklenburgische Landesbibliothek]
SWs —, Stadt- und Bezirksbibliothek, Musikabteilung
SWsk —, Schlosskirchenchor
SWth —, Mecklenburgisches Staatstheater
SZ Schleiz, DDR, Stadtkirche
Tes Tübingen, BRD, Evangelisches Stift
Tl —, Schwäbisches Landesmusikarchiv [in *Tmi*]
Tmi —, Musikwissenschaftliches Institut der Eberhard-Karls-Universität
Tu —, Universitätsbibliothek
Tw —, Bibliothek des Wilhelmstiftes
TAB Tabarz, DDR, Pfarrarchiv, Evangelisch-Lutherisches Pfarramt
TEG Tegernsee, BRD, Pfarrkirche, Katholisches Pfarramt
TEI Teisendorf, BRD, Katholisches Pfarramt
TH Themar, DDR, Pfarramt
TIT Tittmoning, BRD, Kollegiatstift
TO Torgau, DDR, Johann-Walter-Kantorei
TOek —, Evangelische Kirchengemeinde
TOs —, Stadtarchiv
TRb Trier, BRD, Bistumarchiv und Dombibliothek
TRp —, Priesterseminar
TRs —, Stadtbibliothek
Us Ulm, BRD, Stadtbibliothek
Usch —, Von Schermar'sche Familienstiftung
UDa Udestedt über Erfurt, DDR, Pfarrarchiv, Evangelisch-Lutherisches Pfarramt
V Villingen, BRD, Städtische Sammlung
VI Viernau, DDR, Pfarramt
W Wolfenbüttel, BRD, Herzog August Bibliothek
Wa —, Niedersächsisches Staatsarchiv
WA Waldheim, DDR, Stadtkirche St Nikolai
WAB Waldenburg, DDR, Kirchenmusikalische Bibliothek von St Bartholomäus
WB Weissenburg, BRD, Stadtbibliothek
WBB Walberg, BRD, Albertus-Magnus-Akademie, Bibliothek St Albert
WD Wiesentheid, BRD, Musiksammlung des Grafen von Schönborn-Wiesentheid, private collection
WE Weiden, BRD, Pfannenstiel'sche Bibliothek, Evangelisch-Lutherisches Pfarramt

WEH Weierhof, BRD, Mennonitische Forschungsstelle
WEL Weltenburg, BRD, Benediktinerkloster
WER Wernigerode, DDR, Heimatmuseum, Harzbücherei
WERk Wertheim am Main, BRD, Evangelisches Pfarramt
WERl —, Fürstlich Löwenstein'sche Bibliothek, private collection
WEY Weyarn, BRD, Pfarrkirche [in *FS*]
WF Weissenfels, DDR, Heimatmuseum
WFg —, Heinrich-Schütz-Gedenkstätte
WGk Wittenberg, DDR, Stadtkirche
WGl —, Reformationsgeschichtliches Museum, Lutherhalle
WGp —, Evangelisches Predigerseminar
WH Windsheim, BRD, Stadtbibliothek
WIl Wiesbaden, BRD, Hessische Landesbibliothek
WILd Wilster, BRD, Stadtarchiv (Doos'sche Bibliothek)
WL Wuppertal, BRD, Wissenschaftliche Stadtbibliothek
WM Wismar, DDR, Stadtarchiv
WO Worms, BRD, Stadtbibliothek
WRdn Weimar, DDR, Deutsches Nationaltheater
WRgm —, Goethe-National-Museum
WRgs —, Goethe–Schiller-Archiv und Franz-Liszt-Museum
WRh —, Franz-Liszt-Hochschule
WRhk —, Herderkirche
WRiv —, Institut für Volksmusikforschung
WRl —, Landeshauptarchiv
WRs —, Stadtbücherei, Musikbücherei
WRtl —, Thüringische Landesbibliothek, Musiksammlung
WRz —, Zentralbibliothek der Deutschen Klassik
WS Wasserburg am Inn, BRD, Chorarchiv St Jakob, Pfarramt
WÜms Würzburg, BRD, Musikwissenschaftliches Seminar der Universität
WÜsa —, Stadtarchiv
WÜu —, Universitätsbibliothek
X Xanten, BRD, Stifts- und Pfarrbibliothek
Z Zwickau, DDR, Ratsschulbibliothek
Zmk —, Domkantorei der Marienkirche
Zsch —, Robert-Schumann-Haus
ZE Zerbst, DDR, Stadtarchiv
ZEo —, Bücherei der Erweiterten Oberschule
ZGh Zörbig, DDR, Heimatmuseum
ZGsj —, Pfarramt St Jacobi
ZI Zittau, DDR, Stadt- und Kreisbibliothek
ZIa —, Stadtarchiv
ZL Zeil, BRD, Fürstlich Waldburg-Zeil'sches Archiv, private collection
ZW Zweibrücken, BRD, Bibliotheca Bipontina, Wissenschaftliche Bibliothek am Herzog-Wolfgang-Gymnasium
ZZ Zeitz, DDR, Heimatmuseum
ZZs —, Stiftsbibliothek

DK: DENMARK

A Århus, Statsbiblioteket
Dschoenbaum Dragør, Camillo Schoenbaum, private collection
Hfog Hellerup, Dan Fog, private collection
Kc Copenhagen, Carl Claudius Musikhistoriske Samling
Kh —, Københavns Kommunes Hovedbiblioteket
Kk —, Det Kongelige Bibliotek
Kmk —, Det Kongelige Danske Musikkonservatorium
Km(m) —, Musikhistorisk Museum
Ks —, Samfundet til Udgivelse af Dansk Musik
Kt —, Teaterhistorisk Museum
Ku —, Universitetsbiblioteket 1. Afdeling
Kv —, Københavns Universitet, Musikvidenskabeligt Institut
Ol Odense, Landsarkivet for Fyen, Karen Brahes Bibliotek
Ou —, Universitetsbibliotek
Rk Ribe, Stifts- og Katedralskoles Bibliotek
Sa Sorø, Sorø Akademis Bibliotek

E: SPAIN

Ac Ávila, Catedral
Asa —, Monasterio de S Ana (Real Monasterio de Encarnación)
Ast —, Monasterio del S Tomás, Archivo de la Iglesia
AL Alquezar, Colegiata
ALB Albarracin, Colegiata
AS Astorga, Catedral
Ba Barcelona, Real Academia de Ciencias y Artes
Bac —, Corona de Aragón

Bc	——, Biblioteca de Cataluña
Bca	——, Catedral
Bcapdevila	——, Felipe Capdevila Rovira, private collection
Bcm	——, Conservatorio Superior Municipal de Música
Bih	——, Instituto Municipal de Historia (formerly Archivo Histórico de la Ciudad)
Bim	——, Instituto Español de Musicología
Bit	——, Instituto del Teatro (formerly Museo del Arte Escénico)
Boc	——, Biblioteca Orfeó Catalá
Bsm	——, S María del Mar
Bu	——, Biblioteca del Universidad
BA	Badajoz, Catedral
BUa	Burgos, Catedral
BUlh	——, Monasterio de Las Huelgas
BUm	——, Museo Arqueológico
BUp	——, Biblioteca Provincial
BUse	——, Parroquia de S Esteban
C	Córdoba, Catedral
CA	Calahorra, Catedral
CAL	Calatayud, Colegiata de S María
CAR	Cardona, Archivo Comunal
CU	Cuenca, Catedral
CUi	——, Instituto de Música Religiosa
CZ	Cádiz, Archivo Capitular
E	El Escorial, Real Monasterio de S Lorenzo
G	Gerona, Biblioteca Catedralicia
Gm	——, Museo Diocesano
Gp	——, Biblioteca Pública
Gs	——, Seminario Gerundense
GRc	Granada, Catedral
GRcr	——, Capilla Real
GU	Guadalupe, Real Monasterio de S María
H	Huesca, Catedral
J	Jaca, Catedral
JA	Jaén, Catedral
LPA	Las Palmas, Catedral de Canarias
La	León, Catedral
Lc	——, Colegiata de S Isidoro
Lp	——, Biblioteca Pública Provincial
LEc	Lérida, Catedral
LEm	——, Museo Diocesano
Ma	Madrid, Real Academia de Bellas Artes de S Fernando
Mah	——, Archivo Histórico Nacional (Real Academia de la Historia)
Mam	——, Biblioteca Musical Circulante
Mat	——, Museo-Archivo Teatral
Mc	——, Conservatorio Superior de Música
Mca	——, Casa de Alba, private collection
Mcns	——, Congregación de Nuestra Señora
Mic	——, Instituto de Cultura Hispánica, Sección de Música
Mit	——, Ministerio de Información y Turismo
Mlg	——, Fundación Lazaro Galdiano
Mm	——, Biblioteca Municipal
Mmc	——, Casa Ducal de Medinaceli, Bartolomé March Servera, private collection
Mn	——, Biblioteca Nacional
Mp	——, Palacio Real
Mpm	——, Patronato Marcelino Menéndez y Pelayo del Consejo Superior de Investigaciones Científicas
Mrt	——, Radio Nacional de España-Televisión
Msa	——, Sociedad General de Autores de España
Msi	——, Ciudad Universitaria, Facultad de Filosofía y Letras, Biblioteca de S Isidoró
MA	Málaga, Catedral
MO	Montserrat, Monasterio de S María
MON	Mondoñedo, Catedral
OL	Olot, Biblioteca Popular
OR	Orense, Catedral
ORI	Orihuela, Catedral
OS	Osma, Catedral
OV	Oviedo, Catedral Metropolitana
P	Plasencia, Catedral
PAc	Palma de Mallorca, Catedral
PAp	——, Biblioteca Provincial
PAMc	Pamplona, Catedral
PAMm	——, Museo Sarasate
PAS	Pastrana, Iglesia Parroquial
RO	Roncesvalles, Monasterio de S María
Sc	Seville, Catedral
Sco	——, Biblioteca Capitular Colombina [in *Sc*]
SA	Salamanca, Catedral
SAcalo	——, José López-Calo, private collection
SAu	——, Universidad Pontificia, Biblioteca Universitaria
SAuf	——, Universidad Pontificia, Facultad de Filosofía y Letras
SAN	Santander, Biblioteca de Menéndez y Pelayo
SC	Santiago de Compostela, Catedral
SCu	——, Biblioteca Universitaria
SD	Santo Domingo de la Calzada, Archivo
SE	Segovia, Catedral
SEG	Segorbe, Catedral
SI	Silos, Monasterio Benedictino (Abadía) de S Domingo
SIG	Sigüenza, Catedral
SIM	Simancas, Archivo General
SO	Soria, Biblioteca Pública
Tc	Toledo, Archivo Capitular
Tp	——, Biblioteca Pública Provincial y Museo de la Santa Cruz
TAc	Tarragona, Catedral
TAp	——, Biblioteca Pública
TO	Tortosa, Catedral
TU	Tudela, Colegiata (formerly Catedral) de S María
TZ	Tarazona, Catedral
U (also *SU*)	Seo de Urgel, Catedral
V	Valladolid, Catedral
Vp	——, Parroquia de Santiago
VAa	Valencia, Archivo, Biblioteca y Museos Municipales
VAc	——, Catedral
VAcm	——, Conservatorio Superior de Música
VAcp	——, Colegio y Seminario del Corpus Christi del Patriarca
VAim	——, Instituto Valenciano de Musicología
VAu	——, Biblioteca Universitaria
VI	Vich, Museo Episcopal
VIT	Vitoria, Catedral
Zac	Saragossa, Archivo de Música del Cabildo
Zcc	——, Colegio Calasanci
Zfm	——, Facultad de Medicina
Zp	——, Biblioteca Pública
Zs	——, Biblioteca Capitular de la Seo
Zsc	——, Seminario de S Carlos
Zu	——, Biblioteca Universitaria
Zvp	——, Iglesia Metropolitana [in *Zac*]
ZA	Zamora, Catedral

EIRE: IRELAND

C	Cork, University College
Da	Dublin, Royal Irish Academy
Dam	——, Royal Irish Academy of Music
Dcb	——, Chester Beatty Library
Dcc	——, Christ Church Cathedral
Dm	——, Marsh's Library
Dmh	——, Mercer's Hospital
Dn	——, National Library and Museum of Ireland
Dpc	——, St Patrick's Cathedral
Dtc	——, Trinity College
Duc	——, University College

ET: EGYPT

S	Mt Sinai

F: FRANCE

A	Avignon, Bibliothèque Municipale, Musée Calvet
Aa	——, Archives Départementales de Vaucluse
AB	Abbeville, Bibliothèque Municipale
AG	Agen, Archives Départementales de Lot et Garonne
AI	Albi, Bibliothèque Municipale
AIXc	Aix-en-Provence, Conservatoire
AIXm	——, Bibliothèque Municipale, Bibliothèque Méjanes
AIXmc	——, Maîtrise de la Cathédrale
AL	Alençon, Bibliothèque Municipale
AM	Amiens, Bibliothèque Municipale
AN	Angers, Bibliothèque Municipale
ANG	Angoulême, Bibliothèque Municipale
ANN	Annecy, Bibliothèque Municipale
APT	Apt, Cathédrale Ste Anne
AR	Arles, Bibliothèque Municipale
AS	Arras, Bibliothèque Municipale
ASO	Asnières-sur-Oise, François Lang, private collection
AU	Auxerre, Bibliothèque Municipale
AUT	Autun, Bibliothèque Municipale
AV	Avallon, Société d'Etudes d'Avallon
AVR	Avranches, Bibliothèque Municipale
B	Besançon, Bibliothèque Municipale
Ba	——, Bibliothèque de l'Archevêché
Be	——, Ecole Nationale de Musique
BD	Bar-le-Duc, Bibliothèque Municipale
BE	Beauvais, Bibliothèque Municipale
BER	Bernay, Bibliothèque Municipale

BG	Bourg-en-Bresse, Bibliothèque Municipale et Musée de l'Ain
BL	Blois, Bibliothèque Municipale
BO	Bordeaux, Bibliothèque Municipale
BOI	Boisguillaume, Musée Boieldieu
BOU	Bourbourg, Bibliothèque Municipale
BR	Brest, Bibliothèque Municipale
BS	Bourges, Bibliothèque Municipale
BSM	Boulogne-sur-Mer, Bibliothèque Municipale
C	Carpentras, Bibliothèque Inguimbertine et Musée de Carpentras
CA	Cambrai, Bibliothèque Municipale
CAc	——, Cathédrale
CAD	Cadouin, Bibliothèque de l'Abbaye
CAH	Cahors, Bibliothèque Municipale
CAL	Calais, Bibliothèque Municipale
CC	Carcassonne, Bibliothèque Municipale
CF	Clermont-Ferrand, Bibliothèque Municipale et Universitaire, Section Centrale et Section Lettres
CH	Chantilly, Musée Condé
CHA	Châteauroux, Bibliothèque Municipale
CHE	Cherbourg, Bibliothèque et Archives Municipales
CHM	Chambéry, Bibliothèque Municipale
CHR	Chartres, Bibliothèque Municipale
CN	Caen, Bibliothèque Municipale
CNc	——, Conservatoire National de Musique
CO	Colmar, Bibliothèque Municipale
COs	——, Consistoire de l'Eglise de la Confession d'Augsbourg à Colmar
COUm	Coutances, Bibliothèque Municipale
COUs	——, Grand Séminaire
CSM	Châlons-sur-Marne, Bibliothèque Municipale
CV	Charleville, Bibliothèque Municipale
Dc	Dijon, Bibliothèque du Conservatoire
Dm	——, Bibliothèque Municipale (Bibliothèque Publique)
DI	Dieppe, Bibliothèque Municipale
DO	Dôle, Bibliothèque Municipale
DOU	Douai, Bibliothèque Municipale
E	Epinal, Bibliothèque Municipale
EP	Epernay, Bibliothèque Municipale
EV	Evreux, Bibliothèque Municipale
F	Foix, Bibliothèque Municipale
G	Grenoble, Bibliothèque Municipale
Ge	——, Ecole Régionale de Musique, de Danse et d'Art Dramatique
GAP	Gap, Archives Départementales des Hautes-Alpes
H	Hyères, Bibliothèque Municipale
Lc	Lille, Conservatoire
Lfc	——, Facultés Catholiques
Lm	——, Bibliothèque Municipale
LA	Laon, Bibliothèque Municipale
LB	Libourne, Bibliothèque Municipale
LG	Limoges, Bibliothèque Municipale
LH	Le Havre, Bibliothèque Municipale
LM	Le Mans, Bibliothèque Municipale
LO	Louviers, Bibliothèque Municipale
LP	Le Puy-en-Velay, Bibliothèque Municipale
LR	La Rochelle, Bibliothèque Municipale
LV	Laval, Bibliothèque Municipale
LYc	Lyons, Conservatoire National de Musique
LYm	——, Bibliothèque Municipale
Mc	Marseilles, Conservatoire de Musique et de Déclamation
Mm	——, Bibliothèque Municipale
MAC	Mâcon, Bibliothèque Municipale
MD	Montbéliard, Bibliothèque Municipale
MEL	Melun, Bibliothèque Municipale
MH	Mulhouse, Bibliothèque Municipale
MIL	Millau, Bibliothèque Municipale
MIR	Mirecourt, Bibliothèque Municipale
ML	Moulins, Bibliothèque Municipale
MLN	Montluçon, Bibliothèque Municipale
MO	Montpellier, Faculté de Médecine de l'Université
MOv	——, Bibliothèque de la Ville et du Musée Fabre
MON	Montauban, Bibliothèque Municipale
MZ	Metz, Bibliothèque Municipale
Nd	Nantes, Bibliothèque du Musée Dobrée
Ne	——, Ecole Nationale de Musique, d'Art Dramatique et de Danse
Nm	——, Bibliothèque Municipale
NAc	Nancy, Conservatoire
NAm	——, Bibliothèque Municipale
NAR	Narbonne, Bibliothèque Municipale
NI	Nice, Bibliothèque Municipale
NIc	——, Conservatoire de Musique

NO	Noyon, Bibliothèque Municipale
NS	Nîmes, Bibliothèque Municipale
NT	Niort, Bibliothèque Municipale
O	Orleans, Bibliothèque Municipale
Pa	Paris, Bibliothèque de l'Arsenal
Pal	——, American Library in Paris
Pbf	——, Centre de Documentation Benjamin Franklin
Pc	——, Conservatoire National de Musique [in *Pn*]
Pcf	——, Comédie-Française, Bibliothèque
Pcrs	——, Centre National de la Recherche Scientifique
Pe	——, Schola Cantorum (Ecole Supérieure de Musique, Danse et Art Dramatique)
Pgérard	——, Yves Gérard, private collection
Pi	——, Bibliothèque de l'Institut
Pim	——, Institut de Musicologie de l'Université, Bibliothèque Pierre Aubry
Pis	——, Institut Supérieur de Musique Liturgique
Pm	——, Bibliothèque Mazarine
Pma	——, Musée National des Arts et Traditions Populaires
Pmeyer	——, André Meyer, private collection
Pmg	——, Musée Guimet
Pmh	——, Musée de l'Homme
Pn	——, Bibliothèque Nationale
Po	——, Bibliothèque–Musée de l'Opéra
Pphon	——, Phonothèque Nationale, Bibliothèque et Musée
Ppincherle	——, Marc Pincherle, private collection [dispersed 1975]
Ppo	——, Bibliothèque Polonaise de Paris
Prothschild	——, Germaine, Baronne Edouard de Rothschild, private collection
Prt	——, Office de Radiodiffusion-Télévision Française
Psc	——, Société des Auteurs et Compositeurs Dramatiques
Pse	——, Société des Auteurs, Compositeurs et Editeurs de Musique
Psg	——, Bibliothèque Ste Geneviève
Pshp	——, Bibliothèque de la Société d'Histoire du Protestantisme
Psi	——, Séminaire Israélite de France
Pthibault	——, Geneviève Thibault, private collection
PAU	Pau, Bibliothèque Municipale
PE	Périgueux, Bibliothèque Municipale
PO	Poitiers, Bibliothèque Municipale
POu	——, Faculté des Lettres de l'Université de Poitiers, Section de Musicologie
Rc	Rouen, Conservatoire
R(m)	——, Bibliothèque Municipale
RE	Rennes, Bibliothèque Municipale
RO	Roanne, Bibliothèque Municipale
RSc	Rheims, Bibliothèque de la Cathédrale
Sc	Strasbourg, Conservatoire
Sg(sc)	——, Grand Séminaire (Séminaire Catholique)
Sim	——, Institut de Musicologie de l'Université
Sm	——, Archives et Bibliothèque Municipale
Sn	——, Bibliothèque Nationale et Universitaire
Ssa	——, Société des Amis des Arts de Strasbourg
Ssp	——, Séminaire Protestant
SA	Salins, Bibliothèque Municipale
SAU	Saumur, Bibliothèque Municipale
SCL	St-Claude, Bibliothèque Municipale
SDE	St-Denis, Bibliothèque Municipale
SDI	St-Dié, Bibliothèque Municipale
SE	Sens, Bibliothèque Municipale
SEL	Sélestat, Bibliothèque Municipale
SERRANT	Serrant, Château
SO	Solesmes, Abbaye St-Pierre
SOI	Soissons, Bibliothèque Municipale
SQ	St-Quentin, Bibliothèque Municipale
T	Troyes, Bibliothèque Municipale
TH	Thiers, Bibliothèque Municipale
TLc	Toulouse, Conservatoire
TLd	——, Musée Dupuy
TLm	——, Bibliothèque Municipale
TO	Tours, Bibliothèque Municipale
TOgs	——, Grand Séminaire
TOul	——, Bibliothèque Universitaire, Section Lettres
TOur	——, Centre d'Etudes Supérieures de la Renaissance
TOU	Toulon, Ecole Nationale de Musique
TOUm	——, Bibliothèque Municipale
TOUs	——, Société des Amis du Vieux Toulon
TU	Tulle, Bibliothèque Municipale
V	Versailles, Bibliothèque Municipale
VA	Vannes, Bibliothèque Municipale
VAL	Valenciennes, Bibliothèque Municipale
VE	Vesoul, Bibliothèque Municipale
VN	Verdun, Bibliothèque Municipale

GB: GREAT BRITAIN

A	Aberdeen, University Library, King's College
AB	Aberystwyth, National Library of Wales
AM	Ampleforth, Abbey and College Library, St Lawrence Abbey
Bp	Birmingham, Public Libraries
Bu	——, University of Birmingham, Barber Institute of Fine Arts
BA	Bath, Municipal Library
BEas	Bedford, Bedfordshire Archaeological Society
BEcr	——, Bedfordshire County Record Office
BEp	——, Public Library Music Department
BENcoke	Bentley (Hants.), Gerald Coke, private collection
BEV	Beverley, East Yorkshire County Record Office
BO	Bournemouth, Central Library
BRb	Bristol, Baptist College Library
BRp	——, Public Libraries, Central Library
BRu	——, University of Bristol Library
Ccc	Cambridge, Corpus Christi College
Cchc	——, Christ's College
Cclc	——, Clare College
Cfm	——, Fitzwilliam Museum
Cgc	——, Gonville and Caius College
Cjc	——, St John's College
Cjec	——, Jesus College
Ckc	——, Rowe Music Library, King's College
Cmc	——, Magdalene College
Cp	——, Peterhouse
Cpc	——, Pembroke College
Cpl	——, Pendlebury Library of Music
Ctc	——, Trinity College
Cu	——, University Library
Cumc	——, University Music Club
Cus	——, Cambridge Union Society
CA	Canterbury, Cathedral
CAR	Carlisle, Cathedral
CDp	Cardiff, Public Libraries, Central Library
CDu	——, University College of South Wales and Monmouthshire
CF	Chelmsford, Essex County Record Office
CH	Chichester, Diocesan Record Office
CHc	——, Cathedral
DRc	Durham, Cathedral
DRu	——, University Library
DU	Dundee, Public Libraries
En	Edinburgh, National Library of Scotland
Enc	——, New College Library
Ep	——, Public Library, Central Public Library
Er	——, Reid Music Library of the University of Edinburgh
Es	——, Signet Library
Eu	——, University Library
EL	Ely, Cathedral
EXc	Exeter, Cathedral
EXcl	——, Central Library
EXed	——, East Devon Area Record Office
EXu	——, University Library
Ge	Glasgow, Euing Music Library
Gm	——, Mitchell Library
Gsma	——, Scottish Music Archive
Gtc	——, Trinity College
Gu	——, University Library
GL	Gloucester, Cathedral
H	Hereford, Cathedral
HAdolmetsch	Haslemere, Carl Dolmetsch, private collection
Lam	London, Royal Academy of Music
Lbbc	——, British Broadcasting Corporation
Lbc	——, British Council
Lbm	——, British Library, Reference Division (formerly British Museum) (= *Lbl*)
Lcm	——, Royal College of Music
Lco	——, Royal College of Organists
Lcs	——, Vaughan Williams Memorial Library (Cecil Sharp Library)
Ldc	——, Dulwich College
Lgc	——, Gresham College (Guildhall Library)
Lkc	——, University of London, King's College
Llp	——, Lambeth Palace
Lmic	——, British Music Information Centre
Lmp	——, Marylebone Public Library
Lpro	——, Public Record Office
Lsc	——, Sion College
Lsm	——, Royal Society of Musicians of Great Britain
Lsp	——, St Paul's Cathedral
Ltc	——, Trinity College of Music
Lu	——, University of London, Music Library

Lva	——, Victoria and Albert Museum
Lwa	——, Westminster Abbey
Lwcm	——, Westminster Central Music Library
LA	Lancaster, District Central Library
LAu	——, University Library
LEbc	Leeds, University of Leeds, Brotherton Collection
LEc	——, Leeds Public Libraries, Music Department, Central Library
LF	Lichfield, Cathedral
LI	Lincoln, Cathedral
LVp	Liverpool, Public Libraries, Central Library
LVu	——, University Music Department
Mch	Manchester, Chetham's Library
Mcm	——, Royal Northern College of Music
Mp	——, Central Public Library, Henry Watson Music Library
Mr	——, John Rylands University Library, Deansgate Branch
Mrothwell	——, Evelyn Rothwell, private collection
Mu	——, John Rylands University Library
NO	Nottingham, University Library
NW	Norwich, Central Library
NWr	——, Norfolk and Norwich Record Office
Ob	Oxford, Bodleian Library
Obc	——, Brasenose College
Och	——, Christ Church
Ojc	——, St John's College
Olc	——, Lincoln College
Omc	——, Magdalen College
Onc	——, New College
Ooc	——, Oriel College
Oqc	——, Queen's College
Ouf	——, University, Faculty of Music
Oumc	——, University Music Club and Union
P	Perth, Sandeman Music Library
R	Reading, University, Music Library
RI	Ripon, Cathedral
RO	Rochester, Cathedral
SA	St Andrews, University Library
SB	Salisbury, Cathedral
SH	Sherborne, Sherborne School Library
SHR	Shrewsbury, Shropshire County Record Office
SOp	Southampton, Public Library
SR	Studley Royal, Fountains Abbey MS 23 [in *LEc*]
STb	Stratford-on-Avon, Shakespeare's Birthplace Trust
STm	——, Shakespeare Memorial Library
T	Tenbury, St Michael's College [Toulouse–Philidor collection now largely in *F-Pn, V*]
W	Wells, Cathedral
WB	Wimborne, Minster
WC	Winchester, Chapter Library
WCc	——, Winchester College
WI	Wigan, Public Library
WO	Worcester, Cathedral
WRch	Windsor, St George's Chapter Library
WRec	——, Eton College
Y	York, Minster
Yi	——, Borthwick Institute of Historical Research

GR: GREECE

Ae	Athens, Ethnike Biblioteke tes Hellados
AT	Mt Athos, Koutloumousi Monastery
ATSch	——, Chilandari Monastery
ATSdionision	——, Dionision Monastery
ATSgreat lavra	——, Monastery of the Great Lavra
ATSiviron	——, Iviron Monastery
ATSserbian	——, Serbian Monastery
ATSvatopedi	——, Vatopedi Monastery
LA	Lavra
P	Patmos

H: HUNGARY

Ba	Budapest, Magyar Tudományos Akadémia Régi Könyvek Tára és Kézirattár
Ba(mi)	——, Magyar Tudományos Akadémia Zenetudományi Intézet Könyvtára
Bb	——, Bartók Béla Zeneművészeti Szakközépiskola Könyvtára
Bev	——, Evangélikus Országos Könyvtár
Bf	——, Belvárosi Föplébániatemplom Kottatára
Bj	——, Józsefvárosi Evangélikus Egyházközség Kottatára
Bl	——, Liszt Ferenc Zeneművészeti Föiskola Könyvtára
Bm	——, Budavári Nagyboldogasszony Templom Kottatára

Bn	——, Országos Széchényi Könyvtára
Bo	——, Állami Operaház
Bp	——, Piarista Gimnázium Könyvtára
Br	——, Ráday Gyűjtemény, Könyvtár és Levéltár
Bs	——, Központi Szemináriumi Könyvtár
Bst	——, Szent István Bazilika Kottatára
Bu	——, Egyetemi Könyvtár
BA	Bártfa, church of St Aegidius [in *Bn*]
CSg	Csurgó, Csokonai Vitéz Mihály Gimnázium Könyvtára
DR	Debrecen, Tiszántúli Református Egyházkerület Nagykönyvtára
DRm	——, Déri Múzeum
DRu	——, Kossuth Lajos Tudományegyetem Könyvtára
Ea	Esztergom, Komárom Megyei Levéltár
Efko	——, Főszékesegyházi Kottatár
Efkö	——, Főszékesegyházi Könyvtár
Em	——, Keresztény Múzeum Könyvtára
EG	Eger, Főegyházmegyei Könyvtár
EGb	——, Bazilika Kottatára
Gc	Győr, Püspöki Papnevelő Intézet Könyvtára
Gk	——, Székesgyházi Kottatár
Gm	——, Xántus János Múzeum
Gz	——, Zeneművészeti Szakközépiskola Könyvtára
GGn	Gyöngyös, Országos Széchényi Könyvtár, Bajza József Müemlékkönyvtár
GYm	Gyula, Múzeum
KE	Keszthely, Országos Széchényi Könyvtár Helikon Könyvtára
KI	Kiskunhalas, Református Egyházközség Könyvtára
KŐ	Kőszeg, Plébániatemplom Kottatára
KŐm	——, Jurisich Múzeum
MOρ	Mosonmagyaróvár, 1 sz Plébániatemplom Kottatára
NY	Nyiregyháza, Református Városi Egyházközség Könyvtára
P	Pécs, Székesgyházi Kottatár
PA	Pápa, Dunántuli Református Egyházkerület Könyvtára
PH	Pannonhalma, Szent Benedekrend Központi Főkönyvtára
Se	Sopron, Evangélikus Egyházközség Könyvtára
Sg	——, Berzsenyi Dániel Gimnázium Könyvtára
Sl	——, Liszt Ferenc Múzeum
Sp	——, Szentlélekröl és Szent Mihályról Nevezett Városplébánia Kottatára
Sst	——, Storno Gyűjtemény
SA	Sárospatak, Tiszáninneni Református Egyházkerület Nagykönyvtára
SD	Szekszárd, Balogh Ádám Megyei Múzeum
SFk	Székesfehérvár, Püspöki Könyvtár
SFm	——, István Király Múzeum
SFs	——, Székesgyházi Kottatár
SG	Szeged, Somogyi Könyvtár
SGm	——, Móra Ferenc Múzeum
SGu	——, Szegedi Orvostudományi Egyetem Könyvtára
SY	Szombathely, Püspöki Könyvtár
SYb	——, Berzsenyi Dániel Megyei Könyvtár
SYm	——, Smidt Múzeum
T	Tata, Plébániatemplom Kottatára
V	Vác, Székesgyházi Kottatár
VE	Veszprém, Püspöki Könyvtár
VEs	——, Székesegyházi Kottatár

I: ITALY

Ac	Assisi, Biblioteca Comunale
Ad	——, Cattedrale S Rufino
Af	——, S Francesco
AC	Acicatena, Biblioteca Comunale
AG	Agrigento, Biblioteca Lucchesiana
AGI	Agira, Biblioteca Comunale
AGN	Agnone, Biblioteca Emidiana
AL	Albenga, Cattedrale
ALEa	Alessandria, Archivio di Stato
ALEi	——, Istituto Musicale Antonio Vivaldi
AN	Ancona, Biblioteca Comunale
ANcap	——, Biblioteca Capitolare
ANd	——, Archivio della Cappella del Duomo
AO	Aosta, Seminario Maggiore
AP	Ascoli Picena, Biblioteca Comunale
AQ	Aquileia, Archivio della Basilica
ARc	Arezzo, Biblioteca Consorziale
ARd	——, Duomo
ASc(d)	Asti, Archivio Capitolare (Duomo)
ASi	——, Istituto Musicale Giuseppe Verdi
ASs	——, Seminario Vescovile

AT	Atri, Museo della Basilica Cattedrale, Biblioteca Capitolare
Baf	Bologna, Accademia Filarmonica
Bam	——, Biblioteca della Casa di Risparmio (Biblioteca Ambrosini)
Bas	——, Archivio di Stato
Bc	——, Civico Museo Bibliografico Musicale
Bca	——, Biblioteca Comunale dell'Arciginnasio
Bl	——, Conservatorio di Musica G. B. Martini
Bof	——, Oratorio dei Filippini
Bpm	——, Facoltà di Magistero dell'Università degli Studi, Scuola di Perfezionamento in Musicologia
Bsd	——, Convento di S Domenico
Bsf	——, Convento di S Francesco
Bsm	——, Biblioteca Conventuale S Maria dei Servi
Bsp	——, Basilica di S Petronio
Bu	——, Biblioteca Universitaria
BAca	Bari, Biblioteca Capitolare
BAcp	——, Conservatorio di Musica Nicola Piccinni
BAgiovine	——, Alfredo Giovine, private collection
BAn	——, Biblioteca Nazionale Sagarriga Visconti-Volpi
BAR	Barletta, Biblioteca Comunale Sabino Loffredo
BDG	Bassano del Grappa, Biblioteca Civica
BE	Belluno, Biblioteca del Seminario
BEc	——, Biblioteca Civica
BGc	Bergamo, Biblioteca Civica Angelo Mai
BGi	——, Civico Istituto Musicale Gaetano Donizetti
BI	Bitonto, Biblioteca Comunale Vitale Giordano
BRa	Brescia, Ateneo di Scienze, Lettere ed Arti
BRd	——, Duomo
BRi	——, Istituto Musicale A. Venturi
BRp	——, Archivio di S Maria della Pace
BRq	——, Biblioteca Civica Queriniana
BRs	——, Seminario Vescovile
BRsg	——, S Giovanni Evangelista (Cappella del Ss Sacramento)
BRsmg	——, Madonna delle Grazie
BRss	——, S Salvatore
BRE	Bressanone, Seminario Vescovile Vicentinum
BRI	Brindisi, Biblioteca Pubblica Arcivescovile Annibale de Leo
BV	Benevento, Archivio Capitolare
BVa	——, Archivio di Stato
BVam	——, Biblioteca e Archivio Storico Provinciale Antonio Mellusi
BVT	Borgo Val di Toro, Biblioteca Comunale Manara
BZa	Bolzano, Archivio di Stato
BZc	——, Conservatorio di Musica Claudio Monteverdi
BZd	——, Duomo
BZf	——, Biblioteca dei Minori Francescani
BZtoggenburg	——, Count Toggenburg, private collection
CAc	Cagliari, Biblioteca Comunale
CAcon	——, Conservatorio di Musica Giovanni Pierluigi da Palestrina
CAsm	——, Cattedrale S Maria
CAu	——, Biblioteca Universitaria
CAP	Capua, Museo Provinciale Campano
CARcc	Castell'Arquato, Chiesa Collegiata
CARc(p)	——, Archivio Capitolare (Archivio Parrochiale)
CATa	Catania, Archivio di Stato
CATc	——, Biblioteche Riunite Civica e Antonio Ursino Recupero
CATm	——, Museo Belliniano
CATss	——, Società di Storia Patria per la Sicilia Orientale
CC	Città di Castello, Duomo
CCc	——, Biblioteca Comunale
CDA	Codogna, Biblioteca Civica Popolare L. Ricca
CEb(sm)	Cesena, Badia S Maria del Monte
CEc	——, Biblioteca Comunale Malatestiana
CEN	Cento, S Biagio
CF	Cividale del Friuli, Archivio Capitolare
CFm	——, Museo Archeologico Nazionale
CHR	Chieri, Facoltà Teologica dei Gesuiti
CHT	Chieta, Biblioteca Provinciale Angelo Camillo de Meis
CHV	Chiavenna, Biblioteca Capitolare Laurenziana
CLE	Corleone, Biblioteca Comunale Francesco Bentivegna
CLO	Corlono, Chiesa della Reggia Ducale
CMac	Casale Monferrato, Archivio Capitolare
CMbc	——, Biblioteca Civica
CMs	——, Seminario Vescovile
CMI	Camogli, Biblioteca Comunale Nicolo Cueno
CMO	Camerino, Biblioteca Valentiniana e Comunale
COc	Como, Biblioteca Comunale
COd	——, Duomo

CORc	Correggio, Biblioteca Comunale
COS	Cosenza, Biblioteca Civica
CPa	Carpi, Archivio Paolo Guaitoli della Commissione di Storia Patria de Carpi
CPc	——, Biblioteca Comunale
CR	Cremona, Biblioteca Statale
CRd	——, Duomo
CRE	Crema, Biblioteca Comunale
CREi	——, Istituto Musicale L. Folcioni
CT	Cortona, Biblioteca Comunale e dell'Accademia Etrusca
CZorizio	Cazzago S Martino, Orizio private collection
DO	Domodossola, Biblioteca e Archivio dei Rosminiani di Monte Calvaro
E	Enna, Biblioteca Comunale
Fa	Florence, Ss Annunziata
Faq	——, Pius XII Institute, Graduate School of Fine Arts, Aquinas Library
Fas	——, Archivio di Stato
Fc	——, Conservatorio di Musica Luigi Cherubini
Fd	——, Duomo
Ffabbri	——, M. Fabbri, private collection
Fl	——, Biblioteca Medicea-Laurenziana
Fm	——, Biblioteca Marucelliana
Fn	——, Biblioteca Nazionale Centrale
Folschki	——, Olschki private collection
Fr	——, Biblioteca Riccardiana e Moreniana
Fs	——, Seminario Arcivescovile Maggiore
Fsa	——, Biblioteca Domenicana, Chiesa S Maria Novella
Fsm	——, Convento S Marco
Fu	——, Università degli Studi, Facoltà di Lettere e Filosofia
FA	Fabriano, Biblioteca Comunale
FAd	——, Duomo
FAN	Fano, Biblioteca Comunale Federiciana
FBR	Fossombrone, Biblioteca Civica Passionei
FEbonfigliuoli	Ferrara, Bonfigliuoli private collection
FEc	——, Biblioteca Comunale Ariostea
FEd	——, Duomo
FEmichelini	——, Bruto Michelini, private collection
FELc	Feltre, Biblioteca Comunale
FELd	——, Duomo
FELm	——, Museo Civico
FEM	Finale Emilia, Biblioteca Comunale
FERc	Fermo, Biblioteca Comunale
FERd	——, Duomo
FERl	——, Liceo Musicale Girolamo Frescobaldi
FERmichelini	——, Bruno Michelini, private collection
FOc	Forlì, Biblioteca Comunale Aurelio Saffi
FOd	——, Duomo
FOG	Foggia, Biblioteca Provinciale
FOLc	Foligno, Biblioteca Comunale
FOLd	——, Duomo
FOSc	Fossano, Biblioteca Civica
FZac(d)	Faenza, Archivio Capitolare (Duomo)
FZc	——, Biblioteca Comunale
FZsavini	——, Ino Savini, private collection
Gc	Genoa, Biblioteca Civica Berio
Gf	——, Biblioteca Franzoniana
Ggrasso	——, Lorenzina Grasso, private collection
Gi(l)	——, Conservatorio di Musica Nicolò Paganini
Gim	——, Istituto Mazziniano
Gsc	——, S Caterina
Gsmb	——, S Maria della Castagna
Gsmd	——, S Maria di Castello, Biblioteca dei Domenicani
Gu	——, Biblioteca Universitaria
GA	Ganna, Badia Benedittina
GE	Gemona, Duomo
GN	Giulianova, Biblioteca Comunale Vincenzo Bindi
GO	Gorizia, Seminario Teologico Centrale
GR	Grottaferrata, Badia Greca
GUA	Guastalla, Biblioteca Municipale Maldotti
GUBsp	Gubbio, Biblioteca Comunale Sperelliana
I	Imola, Biblioteca Comunale
IE	Iesi, Archivio Comunale
IV	Ivrea, Biblioteca Capitolare
La	Lucca, Archivio di Stato
Lc	——, Biblioteca Capitolare Feliniana
Lg	——, Biblioteca Statale
Li	——, Istituto Musicale Luigi Boccherini
Ls	——, Seminario Vescovile
LA	L'Aquila, Biblioteca Provinciale Salvatore Tommasi
LE	Lecce, Biblioteca Provinciale Nicola Bernardini
LI	Livorno, Biblioteca Comunale Labronica Francesco Domenico Guerrazzi
LOc	Lodi, Biblioteca Capitolare

LOcl	——, Biblioteca Comunale Laudense
LT	Loreto, Archivio Storico della Cappella Lauretana
LU	Lugo, Biblioteca Comunale Fabrizio Trisi
Ma	Milan, Biblioteca Ambrosiana
Malfieri	——, Trecani degli Alfieri, private collection
Mb	——, Biblioteca Nazionale Braidense
Mc	——, Conservatorio di Musica Giuseppe Verdi
Mca	——, Archivio della Curia Arcivescovile
Mcap(d)	——, Cappella Musicale del Duomo
Mcom	——, Biblioteca Comunale
Md	——, Archivio della Cappella Musicale del Duomo
Mdonà	——, Mariangelo Donà, private collection
Mr	——, Archivio Storico Ricordi (Casa Editrice)
Ms	——, Biblioteca Teatrale Livia Simoni
Msartori	——, Claudio Sartori, private collection
Mt	——, Biblioteca Trivulziana
Mvidusso	——, Carlo Vidusso, private collection
MAa	Mantua, Archivio di Stato
MAad	——, Archivio Storico Diocesano
MAav	——, Accademia Virgiliana di Scienze, Lettere ed Arti
MAc	——, Biblioteca Comunale
MAi	——, Istituto Musicale Lucio Campiani
MAp	——, Duomo S Pietro
MAs	——, Seminario Vescovile
MAC	Macerata, Biblioteca Comunale Mozzi-Borgetti
MACa	——, Archivio di Stato
MC	Monte Cassino, Biblioteca dell'Abbazia
ME	Messina, Biblioteca Universitaria
MEmeli	——, Alfonso Meli, private collection
MEnicotra	——, Arturo Nicotra, private collection
MEs	——, Biblioteca Painiana del Seminario Arcivescovile
MFc	Molfetta, Biblioteca Comunale Giovanni Panunzio
MFsr	——, Pontificio Seminario Regionale Pio XI
MFsv	——, Seminario Vescovile
MOa	Modena, Accademia Nazionale di Scienze, Lettere ed Arti
MOd	——, Duomo
MOdep	——, Deputazione di Storia Patria per le Antiche Province Modenesi
MOe	——, Biblioteca Estense
MOf	——, Archivio Ferni
MOl	——, Liceo Musicale Orazio Vecchi
MOs	——, Archivio di Stato
MTventuri	Montecatini-Terme, Antonio Venturi, private collection
MV	Montevergine, Biblioteca del Santuario
MZ	Monza, Insigne Basilica di S Giovanni Battista
MZc	——, Biblioteca Civica
Na	Naples, Archivio di Stato
Nc	——, Conservatorio di Musica S Pietro a Majella
Nf	——, Biblioteca Oratoriana dei Filippini
Nlp	——, Biblioteca Lucchesi-Palli [in Nn]
Nn	——, Biblioteca Nazionale Vittorio Emanuele III
Ns	——, Seminario Arcivescovile
Nsn	——, Società Napoletana di Storia Patria
Nu	——, Biblioteca Universitaria
NO	Novacello, Biblioteca dell'Abbazia
NON	Nonantola, Seminario Abbaziale
NOVc	Novara, Biblioteca Civica
NOVd	——, Archivio Musicale Classico del Duomo
NOVg	——, Archivio e Biblioteca di S Gaudenzio
NOVi	——, Civico Istituto Musicale Brera
NOVsg	——, Archivio Musicale di S Gaudenzio
NT	Noto, Biblioteca Comunale
Oc	Orvieto, Biblioteca Comunale Luigi Fumi
Od	——, Biblioteca dell'Opera del Duomo
OR	Oristano, Seminario Arcivescovile
ORT	Ortona, Biblioteca Comunale
OS	Ostiglia, Biblioteca Musicale Greggiati
OSI	Osimo, Biblioteca Comunale
Pbonelli	Padua, E. Bonelli, private collection
Pc	——, Biblioteca Capitolare
Pca	——, Biblioteca Antoniana, Basilica del Santo
Pci	——, Museo Civico, Biblioteca Civica e Archivio Comunale
Pi(l)	——, Istituto Musicale Cesare Pollini
Ppapafava	——, Novello Papafava dei Carreresi, private collection
Ps	——, Seminario Vescovile
Pu	——, Biblioteca Universitaria
PAac	Parma, Archivio Capitolare
PAas	——, Archivio di Stato
PAc	——, Conservatorio di Musica Arrigo Boito
PAi	——, Istituto di Studi Verdiani
PAsg	——, S Giovanni Evangelista
PAst	——, Madonna della Steccata

PAt	——, Teatro Regio
PAL	Palestrina, Biblioteca Comunale Fantoniana
PAVc	Pavia, S Maria del Carmine
PAVi	——, Civico Istituto Musicale Franco Vittadini
PAVs	——, Seminario Vescovile
PAVsm	——, S Michele
PAVsp	——, S Pietro in Ciel d'Oro
PAVu	——, Biblioteca Universitaria
PCa	Piacenza, Collegio Alberoni
PCc	——, Biblioteca Comunale Passerini Landi
PCcon	——, Conservatorio di Musica G. Nicolini
PCd	——, Duomo
PCsa	——, Biblioteca e Archivio Capitolare di S Antonino
PCsm	——, S Maria di Campagna
PEc	Perugia, Biblioteca Comunale Augusta
PEd	——, Cattedrale
PEl	——, Conservatorio di Musica Francesco Morlacchi
PEsp	——, S Pietro
PEA	Pescia, Biblioteca Comunale Carlo Magnani
PESc	Pesaro, Conservatorio di Musica Gioacchino Rossini
PEScerasa	——, Amadeo Cerasa, private collection [now *VTcerasa*]
PESd	——, Duomo
PESo	——, Biblioteca Oliveriana
PIa	Pisa, Archivio di Stato
PIarc	——, Biblioteca Arcivescovile Cardinale Pietro Maffi
PIc	——, Museo Nazionale di S Matteo
PIca	——, Biblioteca Cateriniana
PIcc	——, Archivio e Biblioteca Certosa di Calci
PIp	——, Archivio Musicale dell'Opera della Primaziale
PIr	——, Biblioteca Raffaelli
PIraffaelli	——, Raffaelli private collection
PIs	——, Fondo Simoneschi
PIst	——, Chiesa dei Cavalieri di S Stefano
PIN	Pinerolo, Biblioteca Comunale Camillo Allinudi
PLa	Palermo, Archivio di Stato
PLcom	——, Biblioteca Comunale
PLcon	——, Conservatorio Vincenzo Bellini
PLd	——, Duomo
PLi	——, Istituto di Storia della Musica, Facoltà di Lettere, Università degli Studi
PLm	——, Teatro Massimo
PLn	——, Biblioteca Nazionale
PLpagano	——, Roberto Pagano, private collection
PLs	——, Baron Pietro Emanuele Sgadari di Lo Monaco, private collection [in Casa di Lavoro e Preghiera Padre Massini]
PLsd	——, Archivio Storico Diocesano
PO	Potenza, Biblioteca Provinciale
POa	——, Archivio di Stato
POd	——, Duomo
PR	Prato, Duomo
PS	Pistoia, Cattedrale
PSc	——, Biblioteca Comunale Forteguerriana
Ra	Rome, Biblioteca Angelica
Rac	——, Accademia di Francia
Raf	——, Accademia Filarmonica Romana
Ras	——, Archivio di Stato
Rc	——, Biblioteca Casanatense
Rcg	——, Curia Generalizia dei Padri Gesuiti; Pontificio Collegio Germano-Ungarico
Rchristoff	——, Boris Christoff, private collection
Rcns	——, Archivio della Chiesa Nazionale Spagnuola
Rco	——, Congregazione dell'Oratorio
Rcsg	——, Oratorio di S Girolamo della Cantà
Rdi	——, Discoteca di Stato
Rdp	——, Archivio Doria-Pamphili, private collection
Rf	——, Archivio dei Filippini
Rgiazotto	——, Remo Giazotto, private collection
Ria	——, Istituto Nazionale di Archeologia e Storia dell'Arte
Rif	——, Istituto di Fisiologia dell'Università
Rig	——, Istituto Storico Germanico
Rims	——, Pontificio Istituto di Musica Sacra
Rla	——, Biblioteca Lancisiana
Rli	——, Accademia Nazionale dei Lincei e Corsiniana
Rlib	——, Basilica Liberiana
Rn	——, Biblioteca Nazionale Centrale Vittorio Emanuele III
Rp	——, Biblioteca Pasqualini [in *Rsc*]
Rps	——, Pio Sodalizio de Piceni
Rsc	——, Conservatorio di Musica S Cecilia
Rsg	——, S Giovanni in Laterano
Rsgf	——, Arciconfraternità di S Giovanni dei Fiorentini
Rslf	——, S Luigi de' Francesi

Rsm	——, Archivio Capitolare di S Maria Maggiore [in *Rvat*]
Rsmm	——, S Maria di Monserrato
Rsmt	——, S Maria in Trastevere
Rsp	——, Santo Spirito in Sassia
Rss	——, S Sabina (Venerabile Convento)
Rv	——, Biblioteca Vallicelliana
Rvat	——, Biblioteca Apostolica Vaticana
RA	Ravenna, Duomo
RAc	——, Biblioteca Comunale Classense
RAs	——, Seminario Arcivescovile dei Ss Angeli Custodi
REas	Reggio Emilia, Archivio di Stato
REc	——, Archivio e Biblioteca Capitolare del Duomo
REd	——, Archivio Capitolare del Duomo
REm	——, Biblioteca Municipale
REsp	——, Archivio Capitolare di S Prospero
RIM	Rimini, Biblioteca Civica Gambalunga
RO	Rosate, S Stefano
RVE	Rovereto, Biblioteca Civica Girolamo Tartarotti
RVI	Rovigo, Accademia dei Concordi
Sac	Siena, Accademia Musicale Chigiana
Sas	——, Archivio di Stato
Sc	——, Biblioteca Comunale degli Intronati
Sd	——, Archivio Musicale dell'Opera del Duomo
Smo	——, Biblioteca annessa al Monumento Nazionale di Monte Oliveto Maggiore
SA	Savona, Biblioteca Civica Anton Giulio Barrili
SAL	Saluzzo, Archivio del Duomo
SAS	Sassari, Biblioteca Universitaria
SDF	San Daniele del Friuli, Biblioteca Civica Guarneriana
SE	Senigallia, Biblioteca Comunale Antonelliana
SI	Siracusa, Biblioteca Comunale
SML	Santa Margherita Ligure, Biblioteca Comunale Francesco Domenico Costa
SO	Sant'Oreste, Collegiata di S Lorenzo
SON	Sondrio, Biblioteca Civica Pio Rajna
SPc	Spoleto, Biblioteca Comunale
SPd	——, Duomo
SPE	Spello, Collegiata S Maria Maggiore
ST	Stresa, Biblioteca Rosminiana
SUsb	Subiaco, Biblioteca S Benedetto
SUss	——, Monumenta Nazionale dell'Abbazia di S Scolastica
Ta	Turin, Archivio di Stato
Tb	——, Convento di Benevagienna
Tci	——, Biblioteca Civica Musicale Andrea della Corte
Tco	——, Conservatorio Statale di Musica Giuseppe Verdi
Td	——, Duomo
Tf	——, Accademia Filarmonica
Ti	——, Istituto Salesiano Valsalice
Tmc	——, Museo Civico
Tn	——, Biblioteca Nazionale Universitaria
Tr	——, Biblioteca Reale
Trt	——, Archivio Musicale Radiotelevisione Italiana
TE	Terni, Istituto Musicale G. Briccialdi
TEc	——, Biblioteca Comunale
TI	Termini-Imerese, Biblioteca Liciniana
TLP	Torre del Lago Puccini, Museo di Casa Puccini
TOD	Todi, Biblioteca Comunale Lorenzo Feoni
TOL	Tolentino, Biblioteca Comunale Filelfica
TRa	Trent, Archivio di Stato
TRc	——, Biblioteca Comunale
TRmd	——, Museo Diocesano
TRmn	——, Museo Nazionale
TRmr	——, Museo del Risorgimento
TRE	Tremezzo, Count Gian Ludovico Sola-Cabiati, private collection
TRN	Trani, Biblioteca Comunale G. Bovio
TRP	Trapani, Biblioteca Fardelliana
TSci(com)	Trieste, Biblioteca Civica
TScm	——, Civici Musei di Storia ed Arte
TScon	——, Conservatorio di Musica G. Tartini
TSmt	——, Civico Museo Teatrale di Fondazione Carlo Schmidl
TSsc	——, Fondazione Giovanni Scaramangà de Altomonte
TSsg	——, Archivio della Cappella della Cattedrale S Giusto
TVca(d)	Treviso, Biblioteca Capitolare (Duomo)
TVco	——, Biblioteca Comunale
Us	Urbino, Cappella del Sacramento (Duomo)
Usf	——, S Francesco [in *Uu*]
Uu	——, Biblioteca Universitaria
UD	Udine, Duomo
UDa	——, Archivio di Stato

UDc	——, Biblioteca Comunale Vincenzo Joppi
UDi	——, Istituto Musicale Jacopo Tomadini
URBc	Urbania, Biblioteca Comunale
URBcap	——, Biblioteca Capitolare (Duomo)
Vas	Venice, Archivio di Stato
Vc	——, Conservatorio di Musica Benedetto Marcello
Vcg	——, Biblioteca Casa di Goldoni
Vgc	——, Biblioteca e Istituto della Fondazione Giorgio Cini
Vlevi	——, Fondazione Ugo Levi
Vmarcello	——, Andrighetti Marcello, private collection
Vmc	——, Museo Civico Correr
Vnm	——, Biblioteca Nazionale Marciana
Vqs	——, Accademia Querini-Stampalia
Vs	——, Seminario Patriarcale
Vsf	——, Conventuale di S Francesco
Vsm	——, Procuratoria di S Marco
Vsmc	——, S Maria della Consolazione detta Della Fava
Vt	——, Teatro la Fenice
VAa	Varese, Archivio Prepositurale di S Vittore
VAc	——, Biblioteca Civica
VCc	Vercelli, Biblioteca Civica
VCd	——, Duomo (Biblioteca Capitolare)
VCs	——, Seminario Vescovile
VD	Viadana, Biblioteca Civica
VEaf	Verona, Società Accademia Filarmonica
VEas	——, Archivio di Stato
VEc	——, Biblioteca Civica
VEcap	——, Biblioteca Capitolare (Cattedrale)
VEs	——, Seminario Vescovile
VEsg	——, S Giorgio in Braida
VG	Voghera, Collegiata di S Lorenzo
VIb	Vicenza, Biblioteca Civica Bertoliana
VId	——, Duomo
VImc	——, Museo Civico
VImr	——, Museo del Risorgimento
VIs	——, Seminario Vescovile
VIGsa	Vigévano, Duomo S Ambrogio
VIGsi	——, S Ignazio
VIM	Vimercate, S Stefano
VO	Volterra, Biblioteca Guarnacci
VTc	Viterbo, Biblioteca Comunale degli Ardenti
VTcarosi	——, Attilio Carosi, private collection
VTcerasa	——, Amadeo Cerasa, private collection
VTp	——, Biblioteca Pio XII, Pontificio Seminario Regionale
VTs	——, Seminario Diocesano
VTM	Ventimiglia, Civica Biblioteca Aprosiana

IL: ISRAEL

J	Jerusalem, Jewish National and University Library
Jp	——, Patriarchal Library
S	Mt Sinai
SS	St Sabas, Monastery

IS: ICELAND

Rn	Reykjavik, National Library

J: JAPAN

Tm	Tokyo, Musashino Ongaku Daigaku
Tma(Tmc)	——, Bibliotheca Musashino Academia Musicae
Tn	——, Nanki Music Library, Ohki private collection

N: NORWAY

Bo	Bergen, Offentlige Bibliotek
Bu	——, Universitetsbiblioteket
Oic	Oslo, Norwegian Music Information Centre
Oim	——, Institutt for Musikkvitenskap, Universitet
Ok	——, Musik-Konservatoriet
Onk	——, Norsk Komponistforening
Or	——, Norsk Rikskringkastings
Ou	——, Universitetsbiblioteket
Oum	——, Universitetsbiblioteket, Norsk Musikksamling
T	Trondheim, Kongelige Norske Videnskabers Selskab
Tmi	——, Musikkvitenskapelig Institutt

NL: THE NETHERLANDS

Ad	Amsterdam, Stichting Donemus
At	——, Toonkunst-Bibliotheek
Au	——, Universiteitsbibliotheek
Avnm	——, Bibliotheek der Vereniging voor Nederlandse Muziekgeschiedenis [in *At*]
AN	Amerongen, Archief van het Kasteel der Graven Bentinck, private collection

BI	Bilthoven, Stichting Gaudeamus
D	Deventer, Stads- of Athenaeumbibliotheek
DHa	The Hague, Koninklijk Huisarchief
DHgm	——, Gemeentemuseum
DHk	——, Koninklijke Bibliotheek
DHmw	——, Rijksmuseum
G	Groningen, Universiteitsbibliotheek
Hs	Haarlem, Stadsbibliotheek
HIr	Hilversum, Radio Nederland
L	Leiden, Gemeentearchief
Lml	——, Museum Lakenhal
Lt	——, Bibliotheca Thysiana [in *Lu*]
Lu	——, Bibliotheek der Rijksuniversiteit
Lw	——, Bibliothèque Wallonne
LE	Leeuwarden, Provinciale Bibliotheek van Friesland
R	Rotterdam, Gemeentebibliotheek
'sH	's-Hertogenbosch, Archief van de Illustre Lieve Vrouwe Broederschap
Uim	Utrecht, Instituut voor Muziekwetenschap der Rijksuniversiteit
Usg	——, St Gregorius Vereniging, Bibliotheek [in *Uim*]
Uu	——, Bibliotheek der Rijksuniversiteit

NZ: NEW ZEALAND

Ap	Auckland, Public Library
Au	——, University Library
Dp	Dunedin, Public Library
Wt	Wellington, Alexander Turnbull Library

P: PORTUGAL

AN	Angra do Heroismo, Biblioteca Pública e Arquivo Distrital
AR	Arouca, Museu Regional de Arte Sacra do Mosteiro de Arouca
AV	Aveiro, Museu de Aveiro, Mosteiro de Jesus
BA	Barreiro, Biblioteca Municipal
BRp	Braga, Biblioteca Pública e Arquivo Distrital
BRs	——, Sé de Braga
C	Coimbra, Biblioteca Geral da Universidade
Cm	——, Biblioteca Municipal
Cmn	——, Museu Nacional de Machado de Castro
Cs	——, Sé Nova
Cug	——, Biblioteca Geral da Universidade
Cul	——, Faculdade de Letras da Universidade
CA	Cascais, Museu-Biblioteca Condes de Castro Guimarães
Em	Elvas, Biblioteca Púbia Hortênsia
EVc	Évora, Arquivo da Sé
EVp	——, Biblioteca Pública e Arquivo Distrital
F	Figuera da Foz, Biblioteca Pública Municipal Pedro Fernandes Tomás
G	Guimarães, Arquivo Municipal Alfredo Pimenta
La	Lisbon, Palácio Nacional da Ajuda
Laa	——, Academia de Amadores de Musica (Conservatorio Municipal)
Lac	——, Academia das Ciências
Lan	——, Arquivo Nacional de Torre do Tombo
Lc	——, Conservatorio Nacional
Lcg	——, Fundação Calouste Gulbenkian
Lf	——, Fábrica da Sé Patriarcal
Lif	——, Instituto de Franca
Ln	——, Biblioteca Nacional
Lr	——, Emissora Nacional de Radiodifusão
Ls	——, Sociedade de Escritores e Compositores Portugueses
Lt	——, Teatro Nacional de S Carlos
LA	Lamego, Biblioteca da Sé
LE	Leiria, Biblioteca Erudita e Arquivo Distrital (Biblioteca Pública)
Mp	Mafra, Palácio Nacional
Pa	Oporto, Ateneu Comercial
Pc	——, Conservatorio de Musica
Pcom	——, Biblioteca Comunale
Peh	——, Museu de Etnografia e Historia
Pf	——, Clube Fenianos Portuenses
Pm	——, Biblioteca Pública Municipal
PD	Ponta Delgada, Biblioteca Pública e Arquivo Distrital
PL	Ponte de Lima, Arquivo da Misericórdia
PO	Portalegre, Arquivo da Sé
Va	Viseu, Arquivo Distrital
Vm	——, Museu Grão Vasco
Vs	——, Arquivo da Sé
VV	Vila Viçosa, Casa da Bragança, Museu-Biblioteca

	PL: POLAND
B	Bydgoszcz, Biblioteka Miejska
BA	Barczew, Archiwum Kościoła Parafialnego
Cb	Cieszyn, Biblioteka Śląska, Oddział Cieszyn
Cp	——, Biblioteka Tschammera w Kościele Ewange-
	lickim
CZp	Częstochowa, Klasztor OO. Paulinów na Jasnej
	Górze
GD	Gdańsk, Biblioteka Polskiej Akademii Nauk
GNd	Gniezno, Archiwum Archidiecezjalne
GR	Grodzisk, Klasztor OO. Cystersów
Kc	Kraków, Biblioteka Czartoryskich
Kcz	——, Biblioteka Czapskich
Kd	——, Klasztor OO. Dominikanów
Kj	——, Biblioteka Jagiellońska
Kk	——, Kapituła Metropolitalna
Kp	——, Biblioteka Polskiej Akademii Nauk
Kpa	——, Archiwum Państwowe
Kz	——, Biblioteka Czartoryskich
KA	Katowice, Biblioteka Śląska
KO	Kórnik, Polska Akademia Nauk, Biblioteka Kórnicka
Lk	Lublin, Biblioteka Katolickiego Uniwersytetu
Lw	——, ——, Biblioteka Wojewódzka i Miejska im. H.
	Łopacińskiego
ŁA	Łańcut, Muzeum
ŁO	Łowicz, Biblioteka Seminarium
MO	Mogiła, Klasztor OO. Cystersów
OB	Obra, Klasztor OO. Cystersów
Pa	Poznań, Biblioteka Archidiecezjalna
Pr	——, Miejska Biblioteka Publiczna im. Edwarda
	Raczyńskiego
Pu	——, Biblioteka Uniwersytecka
PE	Pelplin, Biblioteka Seminarium Duchownego
PŁp	Płock, Biblioteka Towarzystwa Naukowego
R	Raków, Archiwum Kościelne
SA	Sandomierz, Seminarium Duchownego
SZ	Szalowa, Archiwum Parafialne
Tu	Toruń, Biblioteka Uniwersytecka
TA	Tarnów, Archiwum Archidiecezjalne
Wm	Warsaw, Biblioteka Muzeum Narodowego
Wn	——, Biblioteka Narodowa
Wp	——, Biblioteka Publiczna
Ws	——, Biblioteka Synodalna Ewangelicka
Wtm	——, Biblioteka Warszawskiego Towarzystwa
	Muzycznego
Wu	——, Biblioteka Uniwersytecka
WL	Wilanów, Biblioteka, Oddział Muzeum Narodowego
	Warszawy
WRol	Wrocław, Biblioteka Ossolineum Leopoldiensis
WRu	——, Biblioteka Uniwersytecka
	R: ROMANIA
Ab	Aiud, Biblioteca Documentară Bethlen
Ba	Bucharest, Biblioteca Academiei Republicii Socia-
	liste România
Bc	——, Biblioteca Centrală de Stat
BRm	Brașov, Biblioteca Municipală
Sb	Sibiu, Muzeul Brukenthal
TMt	Tîrgu Mureș, Biblioteca Documentară Teleki
	S: SWEDEN
A	Arvika, Folkliga Musikskolan
E	Enköping, Samrealskolans Arkiv
ES	Eskilstuna, Stadsbiblioteket
Gem	Göteborg, Etnografiska Museet
Ghl	——, Hvitfeldtska Högre Allmänna Läroverket
Gu	——, Universitetsbiblioteket (formerly Stadsbiblio-
	teket)
GÄ	Gävle, Vasaskolans Bibliotek
Hfryklund	Hälsingborg, D. Daniel Fryklund, private collection
	[in *Skma*]
Hs	——, Stadsbiblioteket
J	Jönköping, Per Brahegymnasiet
K	Kalmar, Stifts- och Gymnasiebiblioteket
KA	Karlstad, Stadsbiblioteket
KAT	Katrineholm, Stadsbiblioteket
KH	Karlshamn, Museums Biblioteket
L	Lund, Universitetsbiblioteket
Lbarnekow	——, Barnekow private collection
LB	Leufsta Bruk, De Geer private collection
LI	Linköping, Stifts- och Landsbiblioteket
M	Malmö, Stadsbiblioteket
N	Norrköping, Stadsbiblioteket
Ö	Örebro, Karolinska Skolans Bibliotek
ÖS	Östersund, Jämtlands Läns Bibliotek
Sdt	Stockholm, Drottningholms Teatermuseum

Sic	——, Stims Informationscentral för Svensk Musik
Sk	——, Kungliga Biblioteket
Skma	——, Kungliga Musikaliska Akademiens Bibliotek
Sm	——, Musikmuseet
Smf	——, Stiftelsen Musikkulturens Främjande
Sn	——, Nordiska Museet
Ssr	——, Sveriges Radio
St	——, Kungliga Teaterns Bibliotek
SK	Skara, Stifts- och Landsbiblioteket
STd	Strängnäs, Domkyrkobiblioteket
STr	——, Roggebiblioteket
Uifm	Uppsala, Institutionen för Musikforskning vid Upp-
	sala Universitetet
Uu	——, Universitetsbiblioteket
V	Västerås, Stadsbiblioteket
Vll	Visby, Landsarkivet
VIs	——, Stadsbiblioteket
VX	Växjö, Landsbiblioteket
	SF: FINLAND
A	Turku [Åbo], Sibelius Museum Musikvetenskapliga
	Institutionen vid Åbo Akademi, Bibliotek &
	Arkiv
Aa	——, Åbo Akademis, Bibliotek
Hko	Helsinki, Helsingin Kaupunginorkester
Hmt	——, Musiikin Tiedotuskeskus
Hr	——, Oy Yleisradio AB, Nuotisto
Hs	——, Sibelius-Akatemian Kirjasto
Hy	——, Helsingin Yliopiston Kirjasto
Hyf	——, Helsingin Yliopiston Kirjasto, Department of
	Finnish Music
TA	Tampere, Tampereen Yliopiston Kansanperinteen
	Laitos
	US: UNITED STATES OF AMERICA
AA	Ann Arbor, University of Michigan Music Library
AB	Albany, New York State Library
AL	Allentown (Penn.), Muhlenberg College, John A. W.
	Haas Library
AM	Amherst (Mass.), Amherst College, Robert Frost
	Building
ATu	Atlanta (Georgia), Emory University Library
AU	Aurora (NY), Wells College Library
AUS	Austin, University of Texas
Ba	Boston, Athenaeum Library
Bbs	——, Bostonian Society
Bc	——, New England Conservatory of Music
Bco	——, American Congregational Society, Congre-
	gational Library
Bfa	——, Fine Arts Museum
Bge	——, School of Fine Arts, General Education Library
Bh	——, Harvard Musical Association
Bhh	——, Handel and Haydn Society
Bhs	——, Massachusetts Historical Society
Bl	——, Grand Lodge of Masons in Massachusetts, A. F.
	and A. M. Library
Bm	——, University, Mugar Memorial Library
Bp	——, Public Library, Music Department
Bth	——, University, School of Theology
BAep	Baltimore, Enoch Pratt Free Library, Fine Arts and
	Music Department
BAhs	——, Maryland Historical Society
BApi	——, City Library, Peabody Institute
BAu	——, Johns Hopkins University Libraries
BAw	——, Walters Art Gallery
BAT	Baton Rouge, Louisiana State University Library
BE	Berkeley, University of California, Music Library
BER	Berea (Ohio), Baldwin-Wallace College, Ritter Lib-
	rary of the Conservatory
BETm	Bethlehem (Penn.), Archives of the Moravian
	Church in Bethlehem
BETu	——, Lehigh University, Lucy Packer Lindeman
	Memorial Library
BG	Bangor (Maine), Public Library
BK	Brunswick (Maine), Bowdoin College, Department
	of Music
BLl	Bloomington, Indiana University, Lilly Library
BLu	——, Indiana University, School of Music Library
BO	Boulder, University of Colorado Music Library
BRc	Brooklyn, Brooklyn College Music Library
BRp	——, Public Library
BU	Buffalo, Buffalo and Erie County Public Library
Charding	Chicago, W. N. H. Harding, private collection [in
	GB-Ob]
Chs	——, Chicago Historical Society Library
Cn	——, Newberry Library

Cu	——, University Music Library
CA	Cambridge, Harvard University Music Libraries
CAR	Carlisle (Penn.), Dickinson College
CDhs	Concord, New Hampshire Historical Society
CDs	——, New Hampshire State Library
CG	Coral Gables (Florida), University of Miami Music Library
CHua	Charlottesville, University of Virginia, Alderman Library
CHum	——, University of Virginia Music Library
CHH	Chapel Hill, University of North Carolina Music Library
CIhc	Cincinnati, Hebrew Union College
CIu	——, University of Cincinnati College-Conservatory of Music
CLm	Cleveland, Museum of Art, Cantatorium
CLp	——, Public Library, Fine Arts Department
CLwr	——, Western Reserve University, Freiberger Library and Music House Library
COu	Columbus, Ohio State University Music Library
CR	Cedar Rapids, Iowa Masonic Library
Dp	Detroit, Public Library, Music and Performing Arts Department
DB	Dearborn (Mich.), Henry Ford Museum and Greenfield Village
DE	Denver (Colorado), Public Library, Art and Music Division
DM	Durham (North Carolina), Duke University Libraries
DN	Denton, North Texas State University Music Library
DO	Dover (New Hampshire), Public Library
Eg	Evanston (Ill.), Garrett Theological Seminary
Eu	——, Northwestern University, Music Library
ECstarr	Eastchester (NY), Saul Starr, private collection
EXd	Exeter (New Hampshire), Phillips Exeter Academy, Davis Library
EXp	——, Public Library
FW	Fort Worth, Southwest Baptist Theological Seminary
G	Gainesville, University of Florida Library, Rare Book Collection
GA	Gambier (Ohio), Kenyon College Divinity School, Colburn Library
GB	Gettysburg, Lutheran Theological Seminary
GR	Granville (Ohio), Denison University Library
GRE	Greenville (Delaware), Eleutherian Mills Historical Library
Hhs	Hartford, Connecticut Historical Society Library
Hm	——, Case Memorial Library, Hartford Seminary Foundation
Hp	——, Public Library, Art and Music Department
Hs	——, Connecticut State Library
Hw	——, Trinity College, Watkinson Library
HA	Hanover (New Hampshire), Dartmouth College, Baker Library
HB	Harrisonburg (Virginia), Eastern Mennonite College, Menno Simons Historical Library and Archives
HG	Harrisburg, Pennsylvania State Library
HO	Hopkinton, New Hampshire Antiquarian Society
HU	Huntingdon (Penn.), Juniata College, L. A. Beechly Library
I	Ithaca (NY), Cornell University Music Library
IO	Iowa, University of Iowa Music Library
K	Kent (Ohio), Kent State University Library
Lu	Lawrence, University of Kansas Libraries
LAu	Los Angeles, University of California, Walter H. Rubsamen Music Library
LAuc	——, University of California, William Andrews Clark Memorial Library
LAusc	——, University of Southern California School of Music
LB	Lewisburg (Penn.), Bucknell University, Ellen Clark Bertrand Library
LChs	Lancaster (Penn.), Lancaster County Historical Society
LCm	——, Lancaster Mennonite Historical Library and Archives
LCts	——, Theological Seminary of the United Church of Christ
LEX	Lexington, University of Kentucky, Margaret I. King Library
LOs	Louisville (Ky.), Southern Baptist Theological Seminary, James P. Boyce Centennial Library
LOu	——, University, School of Music Library

LU	Lincoln University (Penn.), Vail Memorial Library
M	Milwaukee, Public Library, Art and Music Department
MI	Middletown (Conn.), Wesleyan University, Olin Memorial Library
MORduncan	Morgantown, Richard E. Duncan, private collection
MSp	Minneapolis, Public Library
MSu	——, University of Minnesota Music Library
MV	Mt Vernon (Virginia), Mt Vernon Ladies Association of the Union Collection
Nf	Northampton (Mass.), Forbes Library
Nsc	——, Smith College, Werner Josten Music Library
NAZ	Nazareth (Penn.), Moravian Historical Society
NBs	New Brunswick, Theological Seminary, Gardner A. Sage Library
NBu	——, Rutgers University Library
NEm	Newark (NJ), Newark Museum
NEp	——, Public Library
NH	New Haven, Yale University, School of Music Library
NORts	New Orleans, Theological Seminary
NORtu	——, Tulane University, Howard Tilton Memorial Library
NP	Newburyport (Mass.), Public Library
NYcc	New York, City College Library, Music Library
NYcu	——, Columbia University Music Library
NYfo	——, Fordham University Library
NYfuld	——, James J. Fuld, private collection
NYgo	——, University, Gould Memorial Library
NYgr	——, Grolier Club
NYhc	——, Hunter College Library
NYhs	——, New York Historical Society
NYhsa	——, Hispanic Society of America
NYj	——, Juilliard School of Music
NYlateiner	——, Jacob Lateiner, private collection
NYma	——, Mannes College of Music, Clara Damrosch Mannes Memorial Library
NYmc	——, City Museum, Theatre and Music Department
NYmm	——, Metropolitan Museum of Art, Thomas J. Watson Library
NYp	——, Public Library at Lincoln Center, Library and Museum of the Performing Arts
NYpm	——, Pierpont Morgan Library
NYq	——, Queens College of the City University, Paul Klapper Library, Music Library
NYts	——, Union Theological Seminary
OA	Oakland (Calif.), Public Library
OAm	——, Mills College, Margaret Prall Music Library
OB	Oberlin, Oberlin College Conservatory of Music
Pc	Pittsburgh, Carnegie Library
Pfinney	——, Theodore M. Finney, private collection [in *Pu*]
Ps	——, Theological Seminary, Clifford E. Barbour Library
Pu	——, University of Pittsburgh, Theodore Finney Music Library
PD	Portland, Maine Historical Society
PER	Perryville (Missouri), St Mary's Seminary
PHbo	Philadelphia, St Charles Borromeo Theological Seminary
PHbs	——, William Bacon Stevens Library
PHchs	——, American Catholic Historical Society of Philadelphia
PHci	——, Curtis Institute of Music
PHem	——, Eric Mandell Collection of Jewish Music
PHf	——, Free Library of Philadelphia
PHhs	——, Historical Society of Pennsylvania
PHkm	——, Lutheran Theological Seminary
PHlc	——, Library Company of Philadelphia
PHma	——, Musical Academy
PHphs	——, Presbyterian Historical Society
PHps	——, American Philosophical Society
PHr	——, Philip H. and A. S. W. Rosenbach Foundation
PHtr	——, Trinity Lutheran Church of Germantown
PHts	——, Westminster Theological Seminary
PHu	——, University of Pennsylvania, Otto E. Albrecht Music Library
PIlevy	——, Pikesville (Maryland), Lester S. Levy, private collection
PL	Portland (Oregon), Library Association of Portland, Music Department
PO	Poughkeepsie, Vassar College, George Sherman Dickinson Music Library
PRs	Princeton, Theological Seminary
PRu	——, University, Harvey S. Firestone Memorial Library

PROhs	Providence, Rhode Island Historical Society
PROu	——, Brown University Libraries
R	——, Rochester, University, Eastman School of Music, Sibley Music Library
RI	Richmond, Virginia State Library
Sp	Seattle, Public Library
Su	——, University of Washington Music Library
SA	Salem (Mass.), Essex Institute, James Duncan Phillips Library
SB	Santa Barbara, University of California, Library
SFp	San Francisco, Public Library, Fine Arts Department, Music Division
SFs	——, Sutro Library
SFsc	——, San Francisco State College Library, Frank V. de Bellis Collection
SHE	Sherman (Texas), Austin College, Arthur Hopkins Library
SLc	St Louis, Concordia Seminary
SLf	——, Fontbonne College
SLkrohn	——, Ernst C. Krohn, private collection
SLug	——, Washington University, Gaylord Music Library
SLC	Salt Lake City, University of Utah Library
SM	San Marino (Calif.), Henry E. Huntington Library and Art Gallery
SPmoldenhauer	Spokane (Washington), Hans Moldenhauer, private collection
STu	Stanford, University, Division of Humanities and Social Sciences, Music Library
SW	Swarthmore (Penn.), Swarthmore College Library
SY	Syracuse, University Music Library and George Arents Research Library
Tm	Toledo, Toledo Museum of Art
TA	Tallahassee, Florida State University, Robert Manning Strozier Library
U	Urbana, University of Illinois Music Library
Ufraenkel	——, Fraenkel collection
UP	University Park, Pennsylvania State University Library
Wc	Washington, DC, Library of Congress, Music Division
Wca	——, Cathedral
Wcu	——, Catholic University of America Music Library
Wgu	——, Georgetown University Libraries
Ws	——, Folger Shakespeare Libraries
Wsc	——, Scottish Rite Masons, Supreme Council
Wsi	——, Smithsonian Institution, Music Library
WA	Watertown (Mass.), Perkins School for the Blind
WC	Waco (Texas), Baylor University Music Library
WE	Wellesley (Mass.), Wellesley College Library
WELhartzler	Wellman (Iowa), J. D. Hartzler, private collection
WGc	Williamsburg (Virginia), College of William and Mary
WGw	——, Colonial Williamsburg Research Department, historical collection
WI	Williamstown (Mass.), Williams College, Chapin Library
WM	Waltham (Mass.), Brandeis University Library, Music Library, Goldfarb Library
WOa	Worcester (Mass.), American Antiquarian Society
WS	Winston-Salem (North Carolina), Moravian Music Foundation

USSR: UNION OF SOVIET SOCIALIST REPUBLICS

J	Jelgava, Muzei
Kan	Kiev, Tsentral'naya Naukova Biblioteka, Akademiya Nauk URSR
Kk	——, Biblioteka Gosudarstvennoy Konservatoriy imeni P. I. Chaykovskovo
KA	Kaliningrad, Oblastnaya Biblioteka
KAg	——, Gosudarstvennaya Biblioteka
KAu	——, Universitetskaya Biblioteka

KI	Kishinev, Biblioteka Gosudarstvennoy Konservatoriy imeni G. Muzichesku
Lan	Leningrad, Biblioteka Akademii Nauk SSSR
Lia	——, Gosudarstvenniy Tsentral'niy Istoricheskiy Arkhiv
Lil	——, Institut Russkoy Literaturï
Lit	——, Leningradsky Gosudarstvenniy Institut Teatra, Muzïki i Kinematografii
Lk	——, Biblioteka Leningradskoy Gosudarstvennoy Konservatoriy imeni N. A. Rimskovo-Korsakova
Lph	——, Muzïkal'naya Biblioteka Leningradskoy Gosudarstvennoy Filarmonii
Lsc	——, Gosudarstvennaya Ordena Trudovovo Krasnovo Znameni Publichnaya Biblioteka imeni M. E. Saltïkova-Shchedrina
Lt	——, Leningradskiy Gosudarstvenniy Teatral'nïy Muzey
Ltob	——, Tsentral'naya Muzïkal'naya Biblioteka Gosudarstvennovo Akademicheskovo Teatra Operï i Baleta imeni S. M. Kirova
LV	L'vov, Biblioteka Gosudarstvennoy Konservatoriy imeni N. V. Lysenko
Mcl	Moscow, Gosudarstvenniy Tsentral'niy Literaturniy Arkhiv
Mcm	——, Gosudarstvenniy Tsentral'niy Muzey Muzïkal'noy Kul'turï imeni M. I. Glinki
Mk	——, Gosudarstvennaya Konservatoriya imeni P. I. Chaykovskovo, Nauchnaya Muzïkal'naya Biblioteka imeni S. I. Taneyeva
Ml	——, Gosudarstvennaya Ordena Lenina Biblioteka SSSR imeni V. I. Lenina
Mm	——, Gosudarstvenniy Istoricheskiy Muzei
Mt	——, Gosudarstvennïy Teatral'nïy Muzei imeni A. Bakhrushina
MI	Minsk, Biblioteka Belorusskoy Gosudarstvennoy Konservatoriy
O	Odessa, Biblioteka Gosudarstvennoy Konservatoriy imeni A. V. Nezhdanovoy
R	Riga, Biblioteka Gosudarstvennoy Konservatoriy Latviyskoy imeni J. Vitola
TAu	Tartu, Universitetskaya Biblioteka
TAL	Tallinn, Biblioteka Gosudarstvennoy Konservatoriy
TB	Tbilisi, Biblioteka Gosudarstvennoy Konservatoriy imeni V. Saradzhisvili
V	Vilnius, Biblioteka Gosudarstvennoy Konservatoriy Litovskoy SSR

YU: YUGOSLAVIA

Bn	Belgrade, Narodna Biblioteka N. R. Srbije
Dsd	Dubrovnik, Knjižnica Samostana Dominikanaca
Dsmb	——, Franjevački Samostan Mala Braća
La	Ljubljana, Knjižnica Akademije za Glasbo
Lf	——, Knjižnica Frančiskanškega Samostana
Ls	——, Škofijski Arhiv in Biblioteka
Lsa	——, Slovenska Akademija Znanosti in Umjetnosti
Lsk	——, Arhiv Stolnega Kora
Lu	——, Narodna in Univerzitetna Knjižnica
MAk	Maribor, Glazbeni Arhiv Katedrale
MAs	——, Knjižnica Škofijskega Arhiv
NM	Novo Mesto, Knjižnica Frančiskanškega Samostana
NMc	——, Glazbeni Arhiv Katedrale
O	Ohrid, Narodno Museum
Sk	Split, Glazbeni Arhiv Katedrale
Ssf	——, Knjižnica Samostana Sv Frane
Za	Zagreb, Jugoslavenska Akademija Znanosti i Umjetnosti
Zda	——, Državni Arhiv
Zha	——, Hrvatski Glazbeni Zavod
Zk	——, Glazbeni Arhiv Katedrale
Zs	——, Glazbeni Arhiv Bogoslovnog Sjemeništa
Zu	——, Nacionalna i Sveučilišna Biblioteka

Volume Ten

Kern – Lindelheim

A Note on the Use of the Dictionary

This note is intended as a short guide to the basic procedures and organization of the dictionary. A fuller account will be found in the Introduction, vol.1, pp.xi–xx.

Abbreviations in general use in the dictionary are listed on pp.vii–x; bibliographical ones (periodicals, reference works, editions etc) are listed on pp.xi–xiii.

Alphabetization of headings is based on the principle that words are read continuously, ignoring spaces, hyphens, accents, bracketed matter etc, up to the first comma; the same principle applies thereafter. 'Mc' and 'M'' are listed as 'Mac', 'St' as 'Saint'.

Bibliographies are arranged chronologically (within section, where divided), in order of year of first publication, and alphabetically by author within years.

Cross-references are shown in small capitals, with a large capital at the beginning of the first word of the entry referred to. Thus 'The instrument is related to the BASS TUBA' would mean that the entry referred to is not '**Bass tuba**' but '**Tuba, bass**'.

Work-lists are normally arranged chronologically (within section, where divided). Italic symbols used in them (like *D-Dlb* or *GB-Lbm*) refer to the libraries holding sources, and are explained on pp. xiv–xxx; each national sigillum stands until contradicted.

K

CONTINUED

Kern (Ger.: 'kernel'). Term used by Arnold Schering and others to denote an underlying thematic idea; *see* ANALYSIS, §II, 5.

Kern, Adele (*b* Munich, 25 Nov 1901). German soprano. She studied in Munich, making her début there in 1924 as Olympia in *Les contes d'Hoffmann*. She was a member of the famous Clemens Krauss ensembles, first in Frankfurt, later in Vienna, and finally in Munich, where she performed regularly from 1937 to 1943 and again briefly after World War II. She appeared frequently at Salzburg between 1927 and 1935, as Susanna, Despina, Marzelline and Sophie; international engagements included those at the Teatro Colón, Buenos Aires (1928), and Covent Garden (1931, 1934). She possessed a light, high, silvery voice of great charm – her Zerbinetta was a highlight of the Munich summer festivals in the late 1930s. She retired in 1947.

HAROLD ROSENTHAL

Kern, Jerome (David) (*b* New York, 27 Jan 1885; *d* New York, 11 Nov 1945). American composer. He first studied the piano with his mother and in 1902 studied harmony, theory and the piano at the New York College of Music; his first published work, *At the Casino* (for piano), was written that year. In 1903 he studied music theory and composition in Heidelberg and returned through London to New York, where in 1904 he worked as a song-plugger (notably for T. B. Harms) and as a rehearsal pianist in Broadway theatres. His first significant work was providing additional songs for musical shows, including *Mr Wix of Wickham* (1904) and Ivan Caryll's *The Earl and the Girl* (1905, with Kern's song 'How'd you like to spoon with me?'). By World War I over 100 of Kern's songs had been interpolated into about 30 shows, mostly foreign operettas adapted for New York. Kern served part of his theatre apprenticeship in London around 1906 (not 1903–4 as usually stated: Leslie Stuart's song 'My little canoe' in *The School Girl*, 1903, has been falsely attributed to Kern). In March 1906 two songs with words by P. G. Wodehouse were introduced in Herbert E. Haines's musical play *The Beauty of Bath* and 'Rosalie' in Caryll's and Lionel Monckton's *The Spring Chicken*; other songs were performed and published in London about the same time.

The first scores Kern wrote on his own were failures, but he continued having success with interpolated songs, notably 'They didn't believe me', for the New York version of Paul Rubens's and Sidney Jones's British musical *The Girl from Utah* (1914). The sophisticated style of his early songs inspired imitation by Gershwin among others. In 1915–18 he composed four musicals for the Princess Theatre in New York; the theatre seated only about 300 and an orchestra of about 12 and thus demanded a small cast, limited sets and an intimate style of production. With the librettist Guy Bolton, Kern wrote a new, sophisticated type of musical show, beginning with *Nobody Home* (adapted from Rubens's musical *Mr Popple (of Ippleton)*, 1915). The second of the series and his first big success was *Very Good, Eddie* (1915), in which the songs and story were more closely integrated than in the currently popular operettas or song-and-dance musicals; it seemed a radical departure, and strongly influenced Richard Rodgers. Of the other Princess Theatre shows, *Oh Boy!* achieved greater success than its predecessors, and though *Oh Lady! Lady!* was not popular it helped further to define Kern's new techniques. He demonstrated his versatility by writing more traditional musical comedies, often containing one or more exceedingly popular songs. Among them are *Leave it to Jane* (a failure in 1917 but successfully revived in 1959), *Sally* (produced by Florenz Ziegfeld in 1920), *Sunny* (1925, including 'Who?'), *Roberta* (1933, including 'Smoke gets in your eyes') and *Very Warm for May* (his last stage show, 1939, including 'All the things you are'). His most important work, however, is *Show Boat* (1927), a musical play with words by Oscar Hammerstein II, perhaps the most successful and influential Broadway musical play ever written. At least six songs, which are integral to the characterization and story, have become standard favourites – they include 'Ol' man river', 'Can't

Jerome Kern

1

help lovin' dat man' and 'Why do I love you?' – and the work has been filmed several times and performed throughout the world; its effect on American musical theatre is inestimable, particularly in that it impelled composers of Broadway musicals to concern themselves with the whole production as opposed to writing Tin Pan Alley songs for interpolation. It was the first musical to enter an opera company's repertory (New York City Opera, 1954). From 1939 Kern lived in Hollywood and wrote only for films, producing many of his best-known songs (e.g. 'The last time I saw Paris' in Lady be Good, 'The way you look tonight' in Swing Time and 'Long ago and far away' in Cover Girl). A film biography was produced by Arthur Freed in 1946, called Till the Clouds Roll by after a song from Oh Boy!

When, after World War I, the American musical comedy replaced European operetta as the most popular stage genre, Kern's work was crucial in that it provided a bridge between the two forms. He found his first models in Europe, and his style always showed more evidence of European influence than that of most American composers of musicals; several of his New York works were also successful in London between the wars, and he wrote some specially for London. But he was the first to turn his back on European operetta; with a thorough knowledge of stage technique he combined the supremacy of lyrical song with the dramatic demands of plot and motivations of character to create the American musical play, and he was possibly America's most prolific theatre composer (Ewen credited him with over 1000 songs in 104 stage and film productions). He avoided large forms or symphonic styles except in Scenario (1941), on themes from Show Boat, and in his Mark Twain Suite (1942). Many of his most elegant, effortless melodies are characterized by held notes preceded or followed by small groups of quick notes (e.g. 'Who?'), by subtle changes of rhythm or by metric shifts (e.g. 'Look for the silver lining' in Sally; 'She didn't say yes' in The Cat and the Fiddle). In the 1920s Kern's songs began to show the influence of jazz rhythms and chords. Like most composers of musicals he had his songs orchestrated for the theatre by professional arrangers, notably Robert Russell Bennett (who has also written two concert pieces based on melodies by Kern: Symphonic Study and Variations on a Theme by Jerome Kern).

WORKS

Only stage works, whole or most of score by Kern; all are musicals performed in New York unless otherwise stated; vocal scores or selections published. Authors are indicated as (book author; lyricist).

Edition: The Jerome Kern Song Book (New York, 1955)

La belle Paree (E. Smith; E. Maddern), collab. F. Tours, 20 March 1911
The Red Petticoat (R. J. Young; P. West), 13 Nov 1912
Oh, I Say! (S. Blow and D. Hoare, after Keroul and Barré; H. B. Smith), 30 Oct 1913
90 in the Shade (G. Bolton), 15 Jan 1915
Nobody Home (Bolton and Rubens), 20 April 1915
Cousin Lucy (C. Klein; S. Green), 27 Aug 1915
Miss Information (P. Dickey and C. W. Goddard), 5 Oct 1915
Very Good, Eddie (P. Bartholomae and Bolton; S. Green), 23 Dec 1915
Have a Heart (Bolton; P. G. Wodehouse), 11 Jan 1917
Love o'Mike (T. Sidney; H. B. Smith), 15 Jan 1917
Oh Boy! (Bolton; Wodehouse), 20 Feb 1917
Leave it to Jane (Bolton, after G. Ade; Wodehouse), 28 Aug 1917
Miss 1917 (revue, Bolton; Wodehouse), collab. V. Herbert, 5 Nov 1917
Oh Lady! Lady! (Bolton; Wodehouse), 1 Feb 1918
Toot, Toot (E. A. Woolf, after R. Hughes; B. Braley), 11 March 1918
Head over Heels (Woolf, after N. Bartley), 29 April 1918
Rock-a-bye Baby (Woolf and M. Mayo; H. Reynolds), 22 May 1918
She's a Good Fellow (A. Caldwell), 5 May 1919

Night Boat (Caldwell, after A. Bisson), 2 Feb 1920
Hitchy Koo of 1920 (revue, G. MacDonough and Caldwell), 19 Oct 1920
Sally (Bolton; C. Grey), ballet music Herbert, 21 Dec 1920, film 1929
Good Morning, Dearie (Caldwell), 1 Nov 1921
The Cabaret Girl (G. Grossmith and Wodehouse), London, 19 Sept 1922
The Bunch and Judy (Caldwell and H. Ford; Caldwell), 28 Nov 1922
The Beauty Prize (Grossmith and Wodehouse), London, 5 Sept 1923
Stepping Stones (Caldwell and R. H. Burnside; Caldwell), 6 Nov 1923
Sitting Pretty (Bolton; Wodehouse), 8 April 1924
Dear Sir (E. Selwyn; H. Dietz), 23 Sept 1924
Sunny (O. Harbach and O. Hammerstein II), 22 Sept 1925, films 1930, 1941
The City Chap (J. Montgomery, after W. Smith; Caldwell), 26 Oct 1925
Criss Cross (Caldwell and Harbach), 12 Oct 1926
Lucky (Harbach; B. Kalmar), collab. H. Ruby, 22 March 1927
Show Boat (Hammerstein, after E. Ferber), 27 Dec 1927, films 1929, 1936, 1951
Blue Eyes (Bolton and G. John), London, 27 April 1928
Sweet Adeline (musical romance, Hammerstein), 2 Sept 1929, film 1935
The Cat and the Fiddle (Harbach), 15 Oct 1931, film 1933
Music in the Air (Hammerstein), 8 Nov 1932, film 1934
Roberta (Harbach, after A. D. Miller), 18 Nov 1933, films 1935, 1952
Three Sisters (Hammerstein), London, 9 April 1934
Gentlemen Unafraid (Hammerstein and Harbach, after E. Boykin), St Louis, 3 June 1938
Very Warm for May (Hammerstein), 17 Nov 1939

Films: I Dream too Much (D. Fields), 1935; Swing Time (Fields), 1936; High, Wide and Handsome (Hammerstein), 1937; When you're in Love (Fields), 1937; Joy of Living (Fields), 1938; One Night in the Tropics (Fields), 1940; You were Never Lovelier (J. Mercer), 1942; Can't help Singing (E. Y. Harburg), 1944; Cover Girl (Harburg), 1944; Centennial Summer (Hammerstein), 1946; Till the Clouds Roll by, 1946

Songs (interpolated in musicals, films), incl.: How'd you like to spoon with me? (E. Laska) in The Earl and the Girl, 1905; 8 in King of Cadonia, collab. S. Jones, 1910; 5 in The Girl from Montmartre, collab. H. Bereny, 1912; You're here and I'm here (H. B. Smith) in The Marriage Market, 1913; 8 incl. They didn't believe me (H. Reynolds) in The Girl from Utah (J. T. Tanner), 1914; 4 in Ziegfeld Follies of 1916; 4 in Theodore & Co., London, 1916; The last time I saw Paris (Hammerstein) in Lady be Good, 1941

BIBLIOGRAPHY

D. Ewen: The Story of Jerome Kern (New York, 1953)
P. G. Wodehouse and G. Bolton: Bring on the Girls (New York, 1953)
D. Ewen: The World of Jerome Kern (New York, 1960)
S. Green: The World of Musical Comedy (New York, 1960, rev. 2/1968)
D. Ewen: Popular American Composers (New York, 1962, suppl., 1972)
A. Wilder: American Popular Song (New York, 1972)
H. Fordin: Jerome Kern: the Man and his Music (Santa Monica, Calif., 1975)

RONALD BYRNSIDE, ANDREW LAMB, DEANE L. ROOT

Kern, Patricia (b Swansea, 14 July 1927). Welsh mezzo-soprano. From 1949 to 1952 she studied with Parry Jones at the Guildhall School, London, winning several prizes. She began her career with Opera for All in 1952, remaining with the company until 1955. In 1959 she joined Sadler's Wells, making her début in Rusalka; for ten seasons she was a valued and busy member of the company, her most notable achievement being her interpretations, at once mischievous and sensitive, of Rossini's Cinderella, Rosina, Isolier (Le comte Ory) and Isabella (L'italiana in Algeri). Her Iolanthe, Hansel, Cherubino, Pippo (in Rossini's La gazza ladra), Messenger (in Monteverdi's Orfeo) and Josephine (in the première of Malcolm Williamson's The Violins of St Jacques, 1966) were also much admired. She made her Covent Garden début in 1967 as Zerlina, returning as Cherubino and Suzuki, and has also appeared with the Welsh and Scottish national companies. Her American début was at Washington, DC, in 1969, the year in which she played Rossini's Isabella at the Spoleto

Festival; she has also performed in Canada. Kern possesses a smooth, creamy voice, imaginative of phrase and easily capable of negotiating Rossinian fioritura – her account of Cinderella's final Rondo is a tour de force. Her stage personality is engaging and sympathetic. She sang Hansel in the English-language record of Humperdinck's opera.

ALAN BLYTH

Kernberg, Johann Philipp. See KIRNBERGER, JOHANN PHILIPP.

Kerns, Robert (*b* Detroit, *c*1933). American baritone. He studied at the University of Michigan and made his début in 1960 at Spoleto. Engaged at Zurich, he sang in Vienna and in 1964 made his London début at Covent Garden as Billy Budd. He has also sung at the Aix-en-Provence and Salzburg festivals, at the Paris Opéra, San Francisco and the Deutsche Oper, Berlin. His repertory includes Mozart's Count Almaviva, Don Giovanni and Guglielmo; Verdi's Germont, Posa and Ford; Donner (*Rheingold*), Eugene Onegin and Marcello. A stylish singer, with a light but firmly placed voice, he excels in roles such as Rossini's Figaro, Donizetti's Sergeant Belcore, or the Barber in Strauss's *Die schweigsame Frau*, where acting ability is as important as vocal agility.

ELIZABETH FORBES

Kerpely, Jenő. Hungarian cellist, member of the WALDBAUER-KERPELY QUARTET.

Kerpen, Freiherr **Hugo Franz Karl Alexander von** (*b* ?Engers, 23 March 1749; *d* Heilbronn, 31 Dec 1802). German composer. From 1762 he lived in Mainz, where in 1779 he became a canon of the cathedral and later held the same post in nearby Worms. In Mainz he was associated with an amateur theatre, for which he composed Singspiels. These and his other compositions show that the music education of aristocratic amateurs was particularly well tended in Mainz until the second French invasion of 1797. He avoided the occupation by escaping to Heilbronn where, as in Mainz, some of his works were eventually published. His lucid style favours a series of short, comprehensible motifs, but shows no overall development; instead, Kerpen seems to have held fast to the then widespread practice of musical amateurism.

WORKS

Stage [Singspiels, lost, unless otherwise indicated]: Der Schiffbrüch, 1780; Cephalus und Procris (melodrama, after Ovid), Mainz, 1781, formerly *D-DS*; Adelheid von Ponthieu (tragic ballet), Mainz, ?1782, vocal score (Mainz, 1782); Die Räthsel (2, H. G. Schmieder), Mainz, 1790; Magnetisir-Menuet in Air de la nouvelle Contredanse (Mainz, 1794); Claudine von Villa bella (after Goethe), formerly *DS*

Other vocal: Abschieds-Ode, 1v, pf (Mainz, 1783); 6 ariettes Italienes à 3 voix (Mainz, 1792); [12] Teutsche Lieder (F. von Matthisson), i (Mainz, 1797), ii (Heilbronn, 1798)

Inst: Sonate, kbd, vn, in Betrachtungen der Mannheimer Tonschule, i/5–7 (Mannheim, 1778), probably also in 3 Sonates, hpd, vn, op.1 (Mannheim, *c*1779); 6 quatuors concertants, op.3 (Mainz, 1786); Sonate, hpd 4 hands, ?op.4 (Mainz, 1788); 7 Variationen . . . 'Wir kommen von der Küste', kbd (Heilbronn, ?1799); 6 grandes sonates, pf, vn obbl, op.8 (Heilbronn, ?1799); Grand Concert, pf, orch, op.9 (Heilbronn, ?1800); 2 trios, pf, vn, vc, ?op.9 (Offenbach, n.d.); Sym., E♭, before 1797, lost

BIBLIOGRAPHY

GerberL

A. L. Veit: *Mainzer Domherren vom Ende des 16. bis zum Ausgang des 18. Jahrhunderts in Leben, Haus und Habe* (Mainz, 1924)

M. Treisch: *Goethes Singspiele in Kompositionen seiner Zeitgenossen* (diss., Humboldt U. of Berlin, 1951)

A. Gottron: *Mainzer Musikgeschichte von 1500 bis 1800* (Mainz, 1959)

H. Unverricht: 'Musik in Mainz im Spiegel der sächsisch-thüringischen Allgemeinen Zeitschriften aus dem letzten Viertel des 18. Jahrhunderts', *Mainzer Zeitschrift*, lx–lxi (1965–6), 44, 47

H. C. Müller: *Bernhard Schott, Hofmusiktecher in Mainz: die Frühgeschichte seines Musikverlages bis 1797, mit einem Verzeichnis der Verlagswerke 1779–1797* (Mainz, 1977)

HUBERT UNVERRICHT

Kerr, Harrison (*b* Cleveland, 13 Oct 1897). American composer. His principal studies were with James H. Rogers in his home city and with Boulanger in Paris. He returned to the USA in 1921 to begin a long career as a teacher and administrator: first in Cleveland, then briefly in West Virginia and subsequently in New York, where he remained from 1928 until after World War II. It was there that he became active in several interrelated organizations, among them the American Composers' Alliance and the American Music Center. He held the post of executive secretary of both of these; in addition, he served on the editorial boards of the New Music Edition and New Music Quarterly Recordings. During the immediate postwar years he spent much time abroad as chief of the Music, Art and Exhibits Section of the Army Civil Affairs Division; he was then also a member of the music panel for UNESCO. From 1949 until 1969 he was professor and dean at the University of Oklahoma. Despite these many activities, he has composed a wide variety of scores, chiefly during the periods 1935–40 and after 1950. His most extensive work is an opera, *The Tower of Kel*. In general his musical language combines linear chromaticism, vertical dissonances built largely from triads and perfect intervals, and strong rhythms, with a feeling for classical form and gesture.

WORKS

(*selective list*)

Stage: Dance Sonata, ballet, 2 pf, perc, 1938; The Tower of Kel, opera, 1958–60

Orch: 3 syms., 1927–9, rev. 1938, 1943–5, 1953–4; Vn Conc., 1950–51, rev. 1956; Variations on a Ground Bass, 1966; Sinfonietta, 1967–8

Vocal: Notations on a Sensitized Plate, high/medium v, cl, pf, str qt, 1935; Wink of Eternity, chorus, orch, 1937; In Cabin'd Ships at Sea, chorus, orch, 1971; songs

Inst: 2 pf sonatas, 1929, 1943; 2 str qts, 1935, 1937; Trio, cl, vc, pf, 1936; Pf Trio, 1938; Suite, fl, pf, 1940–41; Ov., Arioso and Finale, vc, pf, 1944–51, arr. vc, orch, 1966–7; Sonata, vn, pf, 1956; solo pieces

Principal publishers: Bèrben, Boosey & Hawkes, Presser

MSS in American Composers' Alliance, New York

STEVEN E. GILBERT

Kersey, Eda (*b* Goodmayes, Essex, 15 May 1904; *d* Ilkley, 13 July 1944). English violinist. Her parents were keen amateur musicians, and she started to study the piano and the violin at an early age. She had lessons with various teachers of the Auer school, but the steady maturing of her art depended always on her own capacity for hard work and hard thinking. A fine interpreter of the classics, she gave also the first performance of Bax's Concerto (1943), Arthur Benjamin's Concerto for violin and viola (with Bernard Shore) and Moeran's Sonata for two violins (with Marjorie Hayward). She played in two piano trios, with Cedric Sharpe and Gerald Moore in the 1930s; and in the 1940s with James Whitehead and Kathleen Long, who was also her principal duo partner.

ROBERT ANDERSON

Kersjes, Anton (*b* Arnhem, 17 Aug 1923). Dutch conductor. He studied the violin and later conducting with

Felix Hupka and Eugène Bigot. First engaged as a violinist in the Gelderland Orchestra, he made his conducting début in 1949 in Bach's *St Matthew Passion*. After some years conducting the Tuschinski Theatre orchestra, he was appointed in 1953 to the Kunstmaandorkest, which comprised 30–40 players. Although this was gradually enlarged to a full symphony orchestra, becoming the Amsterdam PO, Kersjes succeeded in retaining the original clear quality of sound. His concerts, and several television opera productions, built his reputation for competent, reliable performances, as did many performances he conducted with the Dutch National Ballet and the Netherlands Dance Theatre. He has appeared as a guest conductor in Holland and abroad, including Leningrad, and in 1972 toured the USSR with his Dutch orchestra. He teaches conducting at the Amsterdam Muzieklyceum.

TRUUS DE LEUR

Kersters, Willem (*b* Antwerp, 9 Feb 1929). Belgian composer. He studied the piano at the Antwerp Conservatory with Eugeen Traey and composition at the Brussels Conservatory with Marcel Poot and Jan Louel; he was awarded several prizes for composition in and outside Belgium. Until 1961 he was a music teacher at the Royal Atheneum at Aarschot, and thereafter music producer with the Limburg regional station of Belgian Radio. He was appointed teacher of harmony in 1962 and from 1971 professor of composition at the Antwerp Conservatory. After he left Belgian Radio he became teacher of harmony, counterpoint and analysis at the Maastricht Conservatory. His works are notable for their classic structure and rich orchestration.

WORKS
(*selective list*)

4 symphonies, 1962–8
Ballets: Parwati, 1956; Triomphe de l'esprit, 1959; Heer Halewijn, 1973; Uilenspiegel, 1976
Orch: Sinfonietta, 1955; Suite in vorm van Franse ouverture, 1964; Capriccio, 1972; Laudes, 1973; Halewijn, 1974
Vocal: Psalmen, A, male chorus, 5 brass insts, timp, org, 1961; A Gospel Song (negro spiritual texts), 4 solo vv, chorus, orch, 1965; A Hymn of Praise (Hebrew psalm texts), reciter, vocal trio, chorus, orch, 1966
Chamber works, incl. Wind Qnt, 1954; 2 str qts, 1962, 1964; Pf qt, 1970, org pieces, pf pieces, works for chorus, songs

Principal publishers: CeBeDeM, Maurer

CORNEEL MERTENS

Kertész, István (*b* Budapest, 28 Aug 1929; *d* nr. Tel-Aviv, 16 April 1973). German conductor of Hungarian birth. He began violin and piano lessons in childhood, later studying the violin and composition at the Franz Liszt Academy, Budapest, where his teachers included Kodály and Weiner. He took further conducting instruction from Somogyi, and absorbed the influence of Klemperer (then at the Budapest Opera) and Walter in particular. Kertész became resident conductor at Györ in 1953, and two years later joined the Budapest Opera as conductor and répétiteur. He left Hungary with his family after the 1956 uprising and settled in Germany, later taking German nationality.

Kertész was general music director at Augsburg (1958–63), and at Cologne from 1964; his wide repertory there included *Tristan und Isolde*, Verdi's *Stiffelio* (the German première) and *La clemenza di Tito*. He made his British début in 1960 with the Royal Liverpool PO (and in London the same year with the LSO); his American début was in 1961 on a tour with the Hamburg RSO. In 1965 he first appeared at Covent Garden (conducting Verdi's *Un ballo in maschera*) and, after a world tour with the LSO that year, succeeded Monteux as its principal conductor (1965–8), in addition to his Cologne appointment.

At the outset of his career, Kertész acquired an unusually large and varied repertory, and his performances were characterized by direct, unexaggerated interpretations that may at times have lacked some extra quality of imagination or individuality to distinguish them. He showed a special concern for the music of Bartók, Henze, Stravinsky and Britten (introducing Britten's *War Requiem* to Vienna and his *Billy Budd* to Germany). His gramophone records include a complete cycle of Dvořák's symphonies and the first western European recordings of the full *Háry János* and *Duke Bluebeard's Castle* (all with the LSO), as well as the first complete recording of Mozart's *La clemenza di Tito* (with the Vienna Staatsoper).

BIBLIOGRAPHY
A. Blyth: 'Istvan Kertesz Talks', *Gramophone*, xlv (1968), 369

NOËL GOODWIN

Kes, Willem (*b* Dordrecht, 16 Feb 1856; *d* Munich, 21 Feb 1934). Dutch conductor and violinist. After receiving his first musical training under A. J. F. Böhme in his home city, he went to Leipzig in 1871 as a violin pupil of F. David, then to Brussels (1873) to study with Wieniawski and finally to Berlin (1875) to complete his violin studies with Joachim and to study composition under Reinecke, Kiel and Bargiel. In 1876 he played in the Park-Orkest, Amsterdam, as soloist and first concertmaster; he directed the orchestra, choir and music school in Dordrecht from 1877 to 1888, except for a year (1883) as conductor of the Park-Orkest, Amsterdam. When the Concertgebouw was opened in 1888, Kes was asked to create and conduct a permanent Concertgebouw orchestra; on 3 November he conducted its inaugural concert. Under his leadership it developed into one of the outstanding European orchestras. Kes's rehearsals were unprecedented in Holland for their thoroughness and attention to detail. He forbade audiences to converse or eat during concerts, or to enter the auditorium while the orchestra was playing. His programmes included new works by R. Strauss, Dvořák, Tchaikovsky, Chabrier, d'Indy and Chausson, and his efforts to raise and broaden the public taste became a tradition which was carried on by his successor, Willem Mengelberg. He remained in the Amsterdam post until 1895 when he succeeded George Henschel as conductor of the Scottish Orchestra in Glasgow. He was appointed conductor of the Philharmonic Society of Moscow in 1898, becoming director of its music school in 1901. He returned to Germany in 1905 and directed the orchestra and music school in Koblenz until his retirement from public life in 1926. His many compositions include lieder, choral pieces, a symphony, three concertos, chamber music and transcriptions for orchestra of piano works by Schumann and Brahms.

BIBLIOGRAPHY
R. W. Greig: *The Story of the Scottish Orchestra* (Glasgow, 1945)
S. A. M. Bottenheim: *Geschiedenis van het Concertgebouw*, i (Amsterdam, 1948)
E. Reeser: *Een eeuw Nederlandse muziek* (Amsterdam, 1950)
M. Flothuis, ed.: *Het Concertgebouworkest 75 jaar* (Amsterdam, 1963)

JAN TEN BOKUM

Kessel, Johann (*fl* 1657–72). German composer and organist. According to Eitner (*Quellen-Lexikon*), he was organist of the Schlosskirche and the Johanneskirche at Oels in Silesia (now Oleśnica, Poland). His known vocal works are three occasional pieces: a six-voice funeral work for a local dignitary (Breslau, 1657) and two works in honour of members of the ruling family of Silesia (both published Brieg, 1663). He also published a collection of three-part dances and other instrumental works in five parts, *Fünff stimmige Symphonien, Sonaten, ein Canzon; nebst Allmanden, Couranten, Balletten und Sarabanden, mit drey Stimmen* (Oels, 1672).

Kessler, Dietrich M(artin) (*b* Zurich, 21 July 1929). English string instrument maker and viol player, of Swiss origin. He was trained as a violin maker at the Schweizerische Geigenbauschule in Brienz under Adolph König, from 1946 to 1950, passing his examinations with distinction, having built a perfectly matched set of instruments. In Switzerland he made violins, violas, cellos, double basses, viols, quintons and guitars. He also studied the cello as a performer. In 1950 he moved to Haslemere, England, where he worked for the firm of Arnold Dolmetsch, making and repairing viols and studying the bass viol with Nathalie Dolmetsch. In 1952 he joined the firm of Albert Arnold Ltd and worked under C. W. Jacklin in string instrument repairing, meanwhile continuing to make viols in his spare time. Kessler began his own workshop in Welling, Kent, in September 1955, and in 1959 moved to London. During this time his instruments, particularly his viols, became increasingly popular, and he was also active as a performer, touring and recording throughout Europe and the USA at various times with the Elizabethan Consort, the English Consort of Viols and the Jaye Consort of Viols. In October 1969 he took over the London firm of Edward Withers Ltd, and continued to make and repair viols and violins.

Kessler's viols are built to the pattern of the English masters. His workmanship is very clean and the instruments are light in weight, with varnish of orange-brown or reddish hue, double purfling, closed or open or carved scrolls, and beautifully inlaid designs in the manner of Barak Norman and Maggini on the back or belly or both. The sound is clear, penetrating and rich. Kessler is one of the best modern makers of viols; his instruments bear the label 'D. M. Kessler, London 19…', though some earlier ones have 'Dietrich M. Kessler of Zurich, No…. London 19…', and others are not labelled in his own name.

MURRAY LEFKOWITZ

Kessler, Thomas (*b* Zurich, 25 Sept 1937). Swiss composer. After studying French and German in Zurich and Paris, he took composition lessons at the Berlin Musikhochschule in 1962 with Hartig, Blacher and Pepping. In 1965 he set up an electronic studio in Berlin, and from 1969 to 1971 he organized courses in the use of electronics in rock music. He taught at the Centre Universitaire International, Nancy (1971–2), and in 1972 lectured on electronic music at Zurich University; in the same year he was appointed to teach composition at the Basle Academy of Music. In 1968 he was awarded the Berlin Young Generation Arts Prize. He belonged to the Gruppe Neue Musik of Berlin (1965–9), and later to the group Musikprojekte. After a number of instrumental pieces, his ballet *Beat für Orpheus* (1967) attracted attention at its Berlin staging.

Smog was written for Globokar, and *Portrait* for the New Phonic Art Ensemble.

WORKS
(*selective list*)

Beat für Orpheus, ballet, 1967; Trio 1968, str trio, 1968; Revolutionsmusik (for stage work, C. H. Henneberg: Nationale Feiertage), 21 insts, tape, 1969; Smog, trbn, orch, 1970–71; Portrait, 4 insts, 1972; Loop, 5 insts, tape, 1973; Piano Control, pf, synth, 1974

Principal publisher: Bote & Bock

H. KUNZ

Kessler, Wendelin (*b* Kannenwurff, Thuringia; *fl* 1572–80). German poet and composer. He attended the Gymnasium in Erfurt and Jena University, after which he became a tutor to the East Prussian nobility. A further two years study in Königsberg led to the post of Kantor in Danzig. In 1572 Polykarp Leyser, pastor of Göllersdorf (Lower Austria), appointed him teacher at the school for nobility at nearby Haselbach. He succeeded Leyser as pastor a few years later, having been ordained in Wittenberg in 1580. His only known works are a wedding motet (Wittenberg, 1580), of which only the tenor part survives, and *Selectae aliquot cantiones super Evangelia* (Wittenberg, 1582, complete copy in *D-Mbs*). This is a collection of Gospel paraphrases in Latin hexameters for Advent to Easter; they are five-part motet-like arrangements which are very close to the Lassus style in their expressive handling of the text.

BIBLIOGRAPHY
H. J. Moser: *Die mehrstimmige Vertonung des Evangeliums* (Leipzig, 1931/*R*1968)
——: *Die Musik im frühevangelischen Österreich* (Kassel, 1954)

WALTER BLANKENBURG

Kestenberg, Leo (*b* Rosenberg, Hungary [now Ružomberok, Slovakia], 27 Nov 1882; *d* Tel-Aviv, 14 Jan 1962). Israeli educationist and pianist of Hungarian birth, whose main work was done in Germany. After studying the piano with Kullak and Busoni and composition with Felix Draeseke in Berlin, he made frequent appearances as a concert pianist and began teaching at the Stern and Klindworth-Scharwenka Conservatories in Berlin. From his student days his political and cultural activities had developed his ideas about the role of music in education and had also equipped him with the organizational experience to put them into practice. In 1918 he became musical adviser to the Prussian Ministry of Science, Culture and Education, becoming in 1922 director of the newly established music department of the Central Institute for Education and Teaching. The institute organized in May 1921 a school music week, the first of eight annual events held in different German towns where Kestenberg's music reforms were explained and discussed. In the same year Kestenberg's *Musikerziehung und Musikpflege* was published; the thoughts expressed in this book became gradually translated into a number of government edicts which affected every aspect of music education in Prussia from kindergarten to university level and extended even to the supervision of the qualifications of private music teachers. Up to December 1932 Kestenberg was active in the Education Ministry but with the advent of Nazism he fled to Prague in 1934. There he founded and directed the International Society for Music Education, which held three congresses in the years 1936 to 1938; in 1953 he was elected the society's honorary president. In 1938 he moved to Tel-Aviv, where he became general manager of the Palestine (now Israel Philharmonic) Orchestra. On his retirement in 1945 he concentrated his energies on teaching and founded Israel's first music-teachers' training college.

WRITINGS
Musikerziehung und Musikpflege (Leipzig, 1921, 2/1927)
'Angewandte Musikpolitik', *Berliner Tageblatt* (28 Sept 1922)
'Schulmusikpflege an den höheren Lehranstalten in Preussen', *ZMw*, vii (1924–5)
Schulmusikunterricht in Preussen (Berlin, 1927)
'Förderung, Unterstützung und Beaufsichtigung des Privatunterrichts', *ZMw*, ix (1927)
ed.: *Musik im Volk, Schule und Kirche* (Leipzig, 1927)
ed., with W. Günther: *Der Musiklehrer* (Berlin, 3/1928)
ed.: *Musikpädagogische Gegenswartsfragen* (Leipzig, 1928)
Musikpflege im Kindergarten (Leipzig, 1929)
Schulmusik und Chorgesang (Leipzig, 1930)
Jb der deutschen Musikorganisation 1931 (Berlin, 1931)
Der Privatunterricht in der Musik (Berlin, 5/1932)

BIBLIOGRAPHY
G. Braun: *Die Schulmusikerziehung in Preussen von den Falkschen Bestimmungen bis zur Kestenberg-Reform* (Kassel, 1957)
L. Kestenberg: *Bewegte Zeiten* (Wolfenbüttel, 1961) [autobiography]
H. Fischer: 'Das Reformwerk Leo Kestenberg', *Musik und Bildung in unserer Zeit*, ed. E. Kraus (Mainz, 1961), 46
H. Mersmann: 'Leo Kestenberg: 1882–1962', *Mf*, xv (1962), 209
H. Fischer: 'In Memoriam Leo Kestenberg', *Musik im Unterricht*, Ausgabe A, liii (1962), 73
U. Günther: *Die Schulmusikerziehung von der Kestenberg-Reform bis zum Ende des Dritten Reiches* (Neuwied, 1967)

Ketèlbey, Albert W(illiam) [Vodorinski, Anton] (*b* Birmingham, 9 Aug 1875; *d* Cowes, 26 Nov 1959). English composer and conductor. At the age of 11 he composed a piano sonata, which was performed at Worcester, and at 13 he won the Queen Victoria Scholarship for composition at Trinity College, London. He became organist of St John, Wimbledon, at 16, and after touring with a light opera company was appointed music director at the Vaudeville Theatre when he was 22. With a quintet for piano and wind he won the Sir Michael Costa Prize, and his early published compositions included songs, anthems and pieces for various instruments. Also, he made musical comedy selections and piano arrangements of works by various composers; some piano compositions were published under the name of Anton Vodorinski. He appeared as a solo pianist at the Queen's Hall and in the provinces, and he was also proficient on the organ, cello, clarinet, oboe and horn. In 1912 *The Phantom Melody* appeared and won a prize offered by van Biene, and in 1915 *In a Monastery Garden*, followed by other 'narrative music' that achieved enormous popularity. They were sentimental pieces characterized by broad melody and somewhat garish orchestration, but there were also pieces such as *Wedgwood Blue*, in which he displayed a lighter touch. Ketèlbey also composed a good deal of descriptive music to accompany silent films. He conducted concerts of his music not only in England but with the Amsterdam Concertgebouw and other European orchestras. The success of his compositions enabled him to spend his later years in retirement on the Isle of Wight.

WORKS
(selective list; all printed works published in London)
Light orch: The Phantom Melody 1912; In a Monastery Garden, characteristic intermezzo, 1915; In the Moonlight, poetic intermezzo, 1919; Souvenir de tendresse, légende, 1919; In a Persian Market, intermezzo scene, 1920; Wedgwood Blue, dance, 1920; Bells across the Meadows, intermezzo, 1921; Gallantry, intermezzo-romance, 1921; In a Chinese Temple Garden, oriental phantasy, 1923; Sanctuary of the Heart, méditation religieuse, 1924; Cockney Suite, 1924; Chal Romano, ov., 1924; By the Blue Hawaiian Waters, tone picture, 1927; 3 Fanciful Etchings, 1928; In the Mystic Land of Egypt, 1931; many other pieces

Other pubd works: The Wonder Worker (comic opera, 2, E. Cadman), 1900; songs, anthems, pf pieces, other solo inst music, scores for silent films, musical comedy selections, pf arrs. of works by Elgar and others

Unpubd works: Caprice, pf, orch; Concertstück, pf, orch; Dramatic Ov.; Str Qt; Qnt, ob, cl, bn, hn, pf

Principal publisher: Bosworth

ANDREW LAMB

Ketting, Otto (*b* Amsterdam, 3 Sept 1935). Dutch composer and trumpeter, son and composition pupil of PIET KETTING. He trained at the Conservatory of The Hague and was then a trumpeter in The Hague PO (1955–60). In 1961 he began to devote himself mainly to composition, though he has also taught at the conservatories of Rotterdam (1967–71) and The Hague (from 1971). His First Symphony (1957–9) was first performed by the Concertgebouw under Rosbaud in 1961, and the orchestral *Due canzoni* received the Gaudeamus Prize (1958) and an award at the 1963 Warsaw Autumn Festival. Though Ketting has written many other works for the orchestra and for unusual ensembles, he has been much associated with music for the stage and cinema. He has worked with the stage directors Richard Flink and Robert de Vries, and with the film directors Bert Haanstra (*The Human Touch*), George Sluizer (*Chemistry*), Douglas Gordon, Alan Pendry and Philip Owtram. Among the choreographers for whom he has composed scores are Jaap Flier (*Interior*, 1963), Benjamin Harkarvy (*The Last Report*, 1962), Richard Glasstone and Job Sanders. In 1974 he produced his first opera, *Dummies* (text by Bert Schierbeek), for three singers and nine instrumentalists. His music is highly individual, unconventional and well-crafted; Donemus is his main publisher.

BIBLIOGRAPHY
T. Hartsuiker: 'Otto Ketting and his Time Machine', *Sonorum speculum* (1974), no.57, p.1

MADDIE STARREVELD-BARTELS

Ketting, Piet (*b* Haarlem, 29 Nov 1905). Dutch composer, pianist and conductor. He was a pupil of Anton Averkamp in Utrecht and of Pijper (1926–32), being considered the most radical of Pijper's students. A fervent advocate of modern music, he introduced many new piano works to the Netherlands. With Johan Feltkamp and Jaap Stotijn he formed a chamber ensemble which toured throughout the world; as a conductor his main interest has been in choral music. From 1930 to 1956 he was chief teacher of choral conducting, theory and composition at the Rotterdam Conservatory, and he directed the Amsterdam Music Lyceum between 1946 and 1949. Ketting has conducted the Rotterdam Chamber Choir and Orchestra, and has organized courses for conductors in that city. His music was at first close to the late Romantics and Debussy, but under the influence of Schoenberg and Pijper his style became tougher, characterized by violent rhythms in a complex system of polymetric patterns, powerful sound combinations and the use of the extremes of instrumental capabilities. Always highly expressive, his work grew more dependent on melody after 1935, a development which paralleled an increasing concern with vocal music. *Quando conveniunt* was written for the 1969 International Choral Festival in Scheveningen.

WORKS
(selective list)
Orch: Sym. no.1, 1929; Sym. no.2, vc, orch, 1963; Concertino, bn, orch, 1968; Concertino, cl, orch, 1972; Terra con 6 variazioni, fl, orch, 1976

Inst: 3 str qts, n.d., 1927, 1929; 4 pf sonatinas, 1926–9; Trio, fl, cl, bn, 1929; Fuga, pf, 1934; Partita, 2 fl, 1936; Fantasia II, hpd, 1973

Vocal: 3 Shakespeare Sonnets, 1v, pf, 1938; Quando conveniunt, chorus, 1969; many other choruses

Principal publisher: Donemus

BIBLIOGRAPHY
H. Badings: *De hedendaagsche Nederlandsche muziek* (Amsterdam, 1936)
W. Paap: 'De componist Piet Ketting', *Mens en melodie*, xxiii (1968), 2
MADDIE STARREVELD-BARTELS

Kettledrum (Fr. *timbale*; Ger. *Pauke*; It. *timpano*). A membranophone with an egg-shaped or hemispherical body acting as a resonator. The single skin is tensioned over the open end of the body by various means. Tortoise-shells, kettle-shaped hollow tree-trunks and clay bowls covered with hide were among the musical instruments of ancient peoples. Clay was afterwards replaced by metal, although oriental kettledrums still frequently have clay bodies.

Kettledrum and cymbal players with two wrestling figures: terracotta plaque (early 2nd millennium BC) *from Larsa (British Museum, London)*

A Babylonian plaque (*c*700 BC) shows a kettledrum, considered to be of metal, in the form of a deep drum shaped like a goblet. Akkadian texts (*c*300 BC) taken from tablets at Erech (and now in the British Museum) deal with instructions for furnishing the *lilis* (plural *lilissu*), a bronze kettledrum, with a skin head. A pair of kettledrums, one giving a higher note than the other, was used in the Middle East in early Islamic times and this usage was adopted in Europe for martial music during the time of the Crusades (13th century). These drums were small and their heads were secured by lacing. This type of drum and the method of thong-tensioning are still used by various peoples in the Middle East. Kettledrums with shells fashioned from tree-trunks and with laced or pegged heads are used in Africa. In India a small thong-tensioned kettledrum constitutes the lower drum of the *tablā* (*see* INDIA, SUBCONTINENT OF, §II, 6(iii) and fig.15*d*). The first type of kettledrum to reach Europe was the Arabic NAQQĀRA. These small kettledrums were known to the French as *nacaires* and to the English as NAKERS or nakeres. The English word 'kettledrum' (possibly from Latin *catinus*) is not found before the 16th century.

Owing to the shape of the body and the consequent strengthening of certain overtones in the harmonic series a kettledrum produces a note of definite musical pitch: thus orchestral kettledrums (*see* TIMPANI) function in the harmonic structure of the orchestra.

JAMES BLADES

Keuchenthal [Küchenthal], **Johannes** (*b* Ellrich, Harz, *c*1522; *d* St Andreasberg, Harz, 1583). German clergyman and music editor. The son of a Catholic lay priest converted to Lutheranism in 1521, he was preaching the Lutheran faith at St Andreasberg by 1552. He published an important collection of Protestant church music, *Kirchen Gesenge latinisch und deudsch, sampt allen Evangelien, Episteln, und Collecten auff die Sontage und Feste nach Ordnung der Zeit durchs gantze Jhar* (Wittenberg, 1573). It contains the liturgy for each Sunday and feast day of the church year arranged in chronological order. Those parts of the Roman service in use in the Protestant Church are interspersed with German hymns, and plainsong melodies are supplied alongside the text throughout. In the preface (by the Wittenberg theologian Christoph Pezelius) it is explained that the volume was produced to meet the need for a single comprehensive Protestant collection to replace the many smaller ones already in existence, and it is indeed the most comprehensive volume of its kind in the entire 16th century. In his letter of dedication Keuchenthal named as sources the Wittenberg songbooks and Johann Spangenberg's collection of 1545. Almost nothing in his volume cannot be traced to earlier publications, and to these sources may be added the *Psalmodia* of Lucas Lossius (first published in 1553) and the songbooks of Klug (1543), Babst (1545) and the Bohemian Brethren (1566). The liturgy for the principal feast days includes a German *St Matthew Passion* based on Johann Walther's Passion of about 1550.

BIBLIOGRAPHY
O. Kade: 'Keuchenthal, Johann', *ADB*
——: *Die ältere Passionskomposition bis zum Jahre 1631* (Gütersloh, 1893), 172
K. Ameln: 'Johannes Keuchenthal', *Jb für Liturgik und Hymnologie*, iii (1957), 121
GLORIA M. TOPLIS

Keuris, Tristan (*b* Amersfoort, 3 Oct 1946). Dutch composer. He acquired his first theoretical training from van Vlijmen at the Amersfoort Music School, and then in 1963 studied composition at the Utrecht Conservatory with Ton de Leeuw (1963–9), winning the composition prize. He has already developed a daring, and at the same time controlled, style with a feeling for innovations in sound and clear formal structures.

WORKS
(selective list)

Play, cl, pf, 1968; Pf Sonata, 1970; Sax Qt, 1970; Conc., a sax, orch, 1971; Concertante muziek, cl, bn, hn, pf, str qnt, 1972–3; Sinfonia, orch, 1972–4; Muziek, cl, vn, pf, 1973; Serenade, ob, orch, 1974–6; Concertino, b cl, str qt, 1977; Pf Conc., 1977–

Principal publisher: Donemus

BIBLIOGRAPHY
E. Schönberger: 'Tonality Reconsidered', *Key Notes*, no.5 (1977), 18

Keurvels, Edward (Hubertus Joannes) (*b* Antwerp, 8 March 1853; *d* Ekeren, nr. Antwerp, 29 Jan 1916). Belgian composer and conductor. He studied the violin, piano and organ at the Vlaamse Musiekschool in Antwerp, and completed his training in harmony, counterpoint, orchestration and composition under Peter Benoit, director of the school. In 1871 he was appointed répétiteur and accompanist there; in 1882 be became conductor of the Nederlandse Schouwburg, Antwerp, and composed music for its productions. A staunch supporter of Benoit, he worked hard to promote spoken lyric drama (*see* MELODRAMA) and was closely involved in setting up in 1890 the Nederlands Lyrisch Toneel, where many of Benoit's works were introduced and for which Keurvels composed the lyric drama *Parisina*. From this theatre developed the Vlaamse Opera (1893), which he conducted for many years. His work for the theatre was prolific and included excellent translations of Wagner's operas. In 1896 he founded and conducted the well-known 'Zoo concerts', held in the Antwerp Zoological Gardens. Besides working closely with Benoit at the Vlaamse Musiekschool, he was also active in founding the Koninklijk Vlaams Conservatorium (1898) and in 1902 set up the Peter Benoit-Fonds for promoting Benoit's works. Some of Keurvels's numerous songs, choruses and cantatas are paraphrases of Flemish music.

WORKS
(*MSS in B-Ac, Aac*)

Stage: Parisina (lyric drama, F. Gittens, after Byron), Antwerp, 1890; incidental music for Hamlet, Nou

Vocal: Hooggetij (vaderlandse kindercantate, M. Sabbe), vv, orch; De dietsche tale, cantata; Hulde aan het onderwijs; In 't woud, male vv, 1884; Het kloksken van Kafarnaum, vv, 1912; Thabor, vv; Mass, vv, org; songs

Inst: Poppetjes-verdriet, pf; Spelemeien, pf; Kinderideaal, vc

BIBLIOGRAPHY

F. Celis: 'Vlaanderens rijk muziekpatrimonium: Edward Keurvels (1853–1916)', *Vlaams muziektijdschrift*, xxii (1970), 104

'Archivalia van de vlaamse muziek', *Gamma*, xxvii (1975), 7

MARIE-THÉRÈSE BUYSSENS

Keussler, Gerhard von (*b* Schwanenburg, Livonia [now Gulbene, Latvia], 5 July 1874; *d* Niederwartha bei Dresden, 21 Aug 1949). German conductor, composer and musicologist. He spent his youth in St Petersburg. In 1900 he enrolled in the Leipzig Conservatory where he studied the cello, score-reading and counterpoint; at the same time he studied musicology with Kretzschmar and Riemann at the university. From 1906 to 1918 he was active in Prague as a choral and orchestral conductor and also delivered lectures in music history and aesthetics at the Athenaeum. In 1918 he was appointed director of the Berlin Singakademie and succeeded Siegmund von Hausegger as conductor of the Berlin PO. Meanwhile he continued to make appearances as a guest conductor. In 1926 he was elected to membership of the Berlin Academy of Arts and honoured by the founding of the Keussler-Gesellschaft in Prague. In the following year he and Kurt Thomas were the first recipients of the Beethoven Prize. Keussler went in 1932 to Australia where he conducted in Melbourne and Sydney and did much to further the cause of German music. In 1936 he returned to Germany to direct the master class in composition at the Berlin Academy of Arts. He retired from public life in 1945 to devote himself to composition. Keussler was noteworthy not only as a musician but also as a philosopher, critic and poet. He set his own verse in songs and oratorios, among which *Jesus aus Nazareth* is the best known. The scope of his aesthetic and critical writings attests to his eminence as a scholar.

WORKS
(*selective list*)

Stage: Wandlungen, sym. drama, 3, 1903; Gefängnisse, sym. drama, 3, perf. 1914; Die Geisselfahrt, sym. drama, 2, perf. 1923; Der Bruder, sym. drama, inc.

Orch: Morgenländische Phantasie, 1909; Juninacht am Meer, sym. poem, n.d.; Sym. no.1, d, 1925; Sym. no.2, C, 1928; Präludium Solemne, 1934; Australia, sym. fantasy, 1935

Vocal: Auferstehung und jüngstes Gericht, speaker, orch, 1905; Jesus aus Nazareth, oratorio, 1917; Die Mutter, oratorio, 1919; An den Tod, speaker, orch, 1922; Zebaoth, oratorio, 1924; In jungen Tagen, folk oratorio, 1928; Das grosse Bündnis, A, orch, 1928; Die Burg, boys' chorus, orch, 1929; Asma, A, orch, 1931; Xenion, children's chorus, orch, 1932–3

Songs: 4 vols. (Keussler), 1902–17; 10 books [from Wandlungen]

Folksong arrs. for chorus, arrs. of Palestrina madrigals and canzonets, additions to Mozart Requiem to replace Süssmayr's work

Principal publishers: Breitkopf & Härtel, O. Junne, Peters

WRITINGS

Die Grenzen der Aesthetik (diss., U. of Leipzig, 1902)

Das deutsche Volkslied und Herder (Prague, 1915)

Händels Kulturdienst und unsere Zeit (Hamburg, 1919)

'Zur Tonsymbolik in der Messen Beethovens', *JbMP 1920*, 31

'Mozarts Requiem ohne Süssmayr', *Deutsches MusikJb*, i (1923), 210

'Sinnestäuschungen und Musikästhetik', *ZMw*, viii (1925–6), 131

Die Berufsehre des Musikers (Leipzig, 1927)

'Zur Aesthetik des Chorsatzes', *Reichsschulmusikwoche* (Darmstadt, 1927)

'Zu Bachs Choraltechnik', *BJb*, xxiv (1927), 106

'Zur Aesthetik der Vokalmusik', *ZMw*, xi (1928–9), 297

'Regeneration und Bayreuth', *Baltische Monatsschrift* (Riga, 1931)

Paul Bucaenus (Riga, 1931)

ed. E. Janetschek: 'Musik und Nationalität', *ZfM*, cxiv (1953), 453

BIBLIOGRAPHY

H. Abert: 'Geistliche und weltliche in der Musik', *Zeitschrift für Aesthetik und allgemeine Kunstwissenschaft*, xix (1925), 397

'Keussler-Heft', *Der Auftakt*, ix (Prague, 1929)

E. Siemens: 'G. von Keussler', *Musica*, iv (1950), 210

E. Kroll: 'Keussler, Gerhard von', *MGG*

CHARLOTTE ERWIN

Key (i) (Fr. *clef*; Ger. *Tonart*; It. *tonalità*). The quality of a musical composition or passage that causes it to be sensed as gravitating towards a particular note, called the key note or the tonic (*see* TONALITY). One therefore speaks of a piece as being in the key of C major or minor, etc (*see* MAJOR and MINOR). The key of a movement commonly changes during its course through the process of modulation (*see* MODULATION (i)), returning to the home key before the end.

Key can also mean pitch, in the relative or absolute sense; the expression to sing 'off key' is sometimes used to signify singing out of tune; to be 'on key' can mean to be at concert (i.e. standard) pitch.

Key (ii). In such instruments as the organ, accordion, piano or harpsichord a key is a balanced lever which when depressed by the finger either operates a valve to admit air to a pipe or reed, or mechanically energizes (strikes or plucks) a tuned string.

In mouth-blown instruments it is a mechanical device which governs a note-hole that is out of reach of, or too large for, the unaided finger. It has three elements, a padded plate or cup to close the hole, a pivoted lever, or shank, and a touchpiece for the finger. This touchpiece may be a ring surrounding a directly fingered hole. Keys when at rest may be either open or closed, and two or more simple levers may be combined to form one key. *See* KEYWORK.

PHILIP BATE

Keyboard (Fr. *clavier*; Ger. *Klaviatur*, *Tastatur*; It. *tastiera*, *tastatura*). A set of levers (keys) actuating the mechanism of a musical instrument such as the organ, harpsichord, clavichord, piano etc. The keyboard probably originated in the Greek hydraulis, but its role in antiquity and in non-European civilizations appears to have remained so limited that it may be considered as characteristic of Western music. Its influence on the development of the musical system can scarcely be over-rated. The primacy of the C major scale in tonal music, for instance, is partly due to its being played on the white keys, and the 12-semitone chromatic scale, which is fundamental to western music even in some of its recent developments, could be derived from the design of the keyboard. The arrangement of the keys in two rows, the sharps and flats being grouped by two and three in the upper row, already existed in the early 15th century.

1. History. 2. Layout. 3. Experimental keyboards.

1. HISTORY. The earliest European keyboards were simple contrivances, played with the hands rather than the fingers. Praetorius and others after him stated that some primitive organs were played with the fists, the wrists or even the knees, but there is little confirmation of this in medieval documents. The spacing between the organ keys remained that which separated the pipes, sometimes over 10 cm, until an abridgment mechanism was invented. Up to the 13th century the keyboards were usually diatonic except for the inclusion of B♭. They often showed a C as first key. This seems surprising, considering that the musical system was then based on Guido's gamut, the lowest note of which was G (*Gamma ut*). But the solmization system represented no more than a series of intervals, the theoretical compass of which had to be reduced, by transposition of some of the melodies, when played on an instrument of fixed sounds as an accompaniment to voices. The addition of the B♭ to the early diatonic keyboard was not intended merely for the playing of melodies including that note, but also permitted transpositions by which the *Gamma ut*, for instance, could be played on the apparent c key. These transpositions compressed the total compass of plainsong to less than two octaves and, so long as keyboards were used only for the playing of plainsong melodies, no wider range was needed, nor any chromatic degree other than the B♭. The medieval practice of transposition must have caused some difficulties in using the same notation for both vocal and keyboard music, since a given note on the staff may have been played at different places on the keyboard; and in fact it seems that the medieval keyboard repertory usually remained unnotated. For theoretical discussions, a special alphabetical notation was often preferred to the Guidonian terminology; this notation, which has since been dubbed 'organ notation', consisted in attributing the letters A to G to the modern C major scale.

By the beginning of the 14th century, however, the development of polyphony had caused a widening of keyboard compass and the progressive addition of chromatic keys. Jehan des Murs (first half of the 14th century) mentioned keys for f♯ and g♯, and Jacques de Liège (c1330) wrote that on the organ 'the tone is almost everywhere divided into two semitones'. The late-14th-century organ of Norrlanda in the National Historical Museum in Stockholm still possesses its manual keyboard covering one octave and a 6th, from c to a', fully chromatic, and a pedal keyboard of eight keys, probably from C to B with B♭. The chromatic keys are placed at a higher level, except for the b♭ and B♭, which are ranged among the diatonic ones, as shown in fig.1. The Robertsbridge Codex (c1320), the earliest surviving keyboard music, attests to the advanced level of keyboard playing sometimes reached in the 14th century; the rapid and flexible melodies, together with a few three-part chords, imply a highly developed finger technique. The range covered is two octaves and a 3rd, from c to e'' (fully chromatic above f). The addition of chromatic keys to the late medieval keyboards may not at first have been intended to permit transpositions other than those involving only one flat in the key signature; it seems that the added chromatic degrees may have been used primarily to gain a certain number of perfect or

1. Manual keyboard of the late 14th-century organ of Norrlanda (Musikhistoriska Museet, Stockholm); for an illustration of the complete instrument, see ORGAN, fig.30

virtually perfect 3rds in polyphony, and that this function was underlined by their being placed at a different level. The chromatic degrees were in fact sometimes tuned as pure or nearly pure 3rds to some of the diatonic ones, thus foreshadowing the mean-tone temperaments of the Renaissance (*see* TEMPERAMENTS and PYTHAGOREAN INTONATION).

Before the second half of the 15th century the lowest part of keyboard compositions was often based on plainsong, or written in plainsong style. Owing to the limited number of transpositions then performed, there was no need for chromatic degrees other than the B♭ in the bass of the keyboard. This explains why pedal or bass manual keyboards remained diatonic up to a late date. As late as the 17th century, even manual keyboards sometimes lacked the first chromatic degrees when they were provided with a short octave. In the first half of the 15th century keyboards often began at F or B. The B keyboard was only a slight extension of the medieval c one. The significance of the F keyboard is more complex. The following hypothesis provides a possible explanation: the apparent c key had sometimes been used to play the *Gamma ut*; when solmization names were given to the keys, it may have seemed more convenient to call *Gamma ut* the c key (this was feasible at a time when the pattern of raised keys was not yet complete). One note, *F fa ut*, was then added below the *Gamma ut*. The F would thus have been, in effect, a variant of the B one, producing virtually the same pitches. Later in the 15th century, however, some B keyboards were enlarged down to F, so that two types of F keyboards may then have been in existence, about a 4th apart in pitch. This difference of pitch, the origin of which could be traced in the medieval practice of transposition, survived for almost two centuries. As late as the 17th century keyboards a 4th apart were sometimes combined in a single instrument, a practice exemplified by the Ruckers transposing harpsichord.

The most common keyboard compass in the second half of the 15th century and the first half of the 16th century was from F to a'', often without F♯ or G♯. In Italy, upper limits of c''' or even f''' were common. The instruments reaching f''' were perhaps made at a lower pitch standard. The low limit was extended to C, often with short octave, in the second half of the 16th century. From then, the compass of the stringed keyboard instruments increased more rapidly than that of the organ, as the latter had a pedal and octave stops that made a wide compass less necessary. Harpsichords reached five octaves, usually from F' to f''', about 1700. Pianos attained six octaves, often from F' to f'''', by 1800 and seven octaves, from A'' to a'''', by 1900. Pianos now usually cover seven octaves and a 3rd from A'' to c''''' and some reach eight octaves. Modern organ keyboards rarely cover more than five octaves.

In the 18th and 19th centuries keyboard instruments gained a leading position in European musical practice. This led to attempts to provide all types of instruments with a keyboard mechanism. The most successful of these attempts were the harmonium and the celesta; but keyboard harps, keyboard guitars or the numerous bowed keyboard instruments have remained mere curiosities. The keys of the hurdy-gurdy and the accordion have been given the arrangement of an ordinary keyboard's keys. Similarly, makers attempted, through a rearrangement of the keys or valves, to give some wind instruments a keyboard fingering, but this usually met with no lasting success. Many electronic instruments have been provided with a keyboard.

2. LAYOUT. Both for playing comfort and aesthetic appearance, it is desirable to have all natural key heads of equal width; each head should thus have one seventh of the octave span. At the same time, it would seem desirable that the natural key tails (i.e. the parts of the natural keys between the sharps) and the sharps all be of equal width, but this is incompatible with the first requirement. Each octave may be considered as divided into two sections separated by straight lines between B and C and between E and F. The section from C to E, which includes three heads and five tails and sharps, should thus also ideally comprise three-sevenths and five-twelfths of an octave; and the section from F to B, which includes four heads and seven tails and sharps, should comprise four-sevenths and, at the same time,

2. Manual and pedal keyboards for the Halberstadt organ of 1361: woodcut from Praetorius's 'Syntagma musicum' (2/1619)

seven-twelfths of an octave. Modern keyboards offer a sophisticated solution: the keys look equal in width, but actually present minute discrepancies. In former times the discrepancies were more visible. Arnaut de Zwolle (c1440) avoided the problem by making a step in the line between the E and F keys (see HARPSICHORD, fig.2). Italian keyboards often showed a relatively wide key tail for D, while the instruments belonging to the Flemish tradition had wider tails for E and F and for B and C.

Wide keys, as in the early keyboards, suit simple and slow melodies, but make the playing of more than one part in each hand difficult. Narrow keys permit more velocity and an easier playing of chords, but require more precision on the part of the player. In order to account for possible discrepancies in the key widths, it is usual to measure keyboards in terms of the octave span (seven naturals) or the three-octave span (21 naturals). The main source of information on the measurement of medieval keyboards is Praetorius's Syntagma musicum (2/1619), which is perhaps less reliable than is often thought. Praetorius mentioned keys about 8 cm wide for the Halberstadt organ of 1361 (see fig.2). Arnaut de Zwolle, however, showed octave spans of about 18 cm. In the 16th and 17th centuries an octave span of about 16·7 cm was common, which is surprisingly close to the modern span of 16·5 cm. Narrower keys were often made in the 18th century, with octave spans of about 16 cm or sometimes even 15·5 cm. The shape of the keys varied during the Middle Ages. Some were spade-shaped, as in the Halberstadt keyboards depicted by Praetorius. Others, particularly in portative organs, were T-shaped, somewhat like the keys of the hurdy-gurdy. These forms were superseded by rectangular plates in the 15th century, when the keys were often so stubby as to be almost square, and the surface slightly convex (for illustration, see PORTATIVE ORGAN). The natural heads remained quite short, about 3·5 cm, up to the 18th century. Modern piano key heads are 5 cm, the tails and sharps 10 cm long. Short keys are particularly needed in instruments with more than one keyboard, where they facilitate shifting from one keyboard to the other. Longer keys seem preferable for playing music with many sharps or flats. The depth of touch, the height of the sharps above the naturals and, to some extent, all key measurements, depend heavily on the hand position and the finger technique used, which in turn are dependent on the type of mechanism actuated by the keys. Pianos, which call for more muscular force than harpsichords or organs, have a deeper touch. The colour of the keys is a matter of taste and usage, the only requirement being that the pattern of lower and raised keys be underlined by contrasting colours. In the past the naturals were often white and the sharps black, as they are now, but in the 17th and 18th centuries these colours were often reversed. Italian makers generally used brown boxwood naturals with black sharps, and tortoiseshell, mother-of-pearl, or rare precious woods of various colours have also been employed.

3. EXPERIMENTAL KEYBOARDS. The 'sequential keyboard', invented by William A. B. Lunn under the name of Arthur Wallbridge in 1843, aimed at reducing the supremacy of the C major scale. Each octave included six lower keys, for C♯, D♯, F, G, A and B, and six raised ones, for C, D, E, F♯, G♯ and A♯. A similar arrangement was advocated by the Chroma-Verein des Gleichstufigen Tonsystems in 1875–7. Paul von Janko's

3. Detail of the Janko keyboard of an upright piano by Decker, New York, c1890 (Smithsonian Museum, Washington, DC)

keyboard (1887–8) is a later application of the same principle. As shown in fig.3, the two rows of keys were triplicated, providing a total of six rows, each slightly higher than the other and each including six keys in the octave. This arrangement permitted the same fingering in all tonalities. Jozef Wieniawski designed a piano with reversed keyboards, patented by E. J. Mangeot in 1876, which was actually made of two superposed pianos, one with the treble at the right as usual and the other with the treble at the left. The purpose was to permit the same fingering for the same passages in both hands. This arrangement is reminiscent of some medieval representations of keyboard instruments where, for reasons that remain unclear, the treble is shown at the left. In 1907 F. Clutsam patented a keyboard with keys arranged in the shape of a fan according to a principle already conceived by Staufer and Heidinger in 1824 and supposed to facilitate playing in the extreme bass and treble. Another important group of experiments concerns the ENHARMONIC KEYBOARD. The fact that the majority of the keyboard repertory has been written for the standard keyboard militates against the success of experiments with its design.

BIBLIOGRAPHY

M. Praetorius: *Syntagma musicum*, ii (Wolfenbüttel, 1618, 2/1619/*R*1958)

G. Le Cerf and E.-R. Labande: *Instruments de musique du XVe siècle: les traités d'Henri-Arnaut de Zwolle et de divers anonymes (Ms. B. N. latin 7295)* (Paris, 1932)

F. Ernst: *Der Flügel Johann Sebastian Bachs: ein Beitrag zur Geschichte des Instrumentenbaues im 18. Jahrhundert* (Frankfurt, 1955)

F. W. Riedel: 'Klavier', *MGG*

K. Bormann: *Die gotische Orgel zu Halberstadt: eine Studie über mittelalterlichen Orgelbau* (Berlin, 1966)

J. C. Schuman: ' "Reversed" Portatives and Positives in Early Art', *GSJ*, xxiv (1971), 16

E. M. Ripin: 'The Norrlanda Organ and the Ghent Altarpiece', *Festschrift to Ernst Emsheimer* (Stockholm, 1974), 193, 286

N. Meeùs: 'Some Hypotheses for the History of Organ-pitch Before Schlick', *Organ Yearbook*, vi (1975), 42

C. Page: 'The Earliest English Keyboard: New Evidence from Boethius' *De musica*', *Early Music*, vii (1979), 308

For further bibliography *see* CLAVICHORD; HARPSICHORD; ORGAN; PIANOFORTE.

NICOLAS MEEÙS

Keyboard music. Before the mid-17th century composers made little stylistic distinction between one keyboard instrument and another, and players used whichever happened to be available or was best suited to the oc-

casion. Liturgically based works and those containing either long-sustained notes or pedal parts would be heard most often on the organ, and dances and settings of popular tunes on the harpsichord; nevertheless, much of the repertory could be shared. While a number of high Baroque composers exploited the individual characteristics of the organ, harpsichord or clavichord, it was not until the latter half of the 18th century that a distinctive style for the piano, which had been invented about 1700, began to appear: hence the main divisions of this article.

See also SOURCES OF KEYBOARD MUSIC TO 1660 (with illustrations).

I. Keyboard music to c1750. II. Organ music from c1750. III. Piano music from c1750.

I. Keyboard music to c1750. The term 'keyboard' is here understood to include not only the early string keyboard instruments (the clavichord, harpsichord, virginals etc), but also the various types of organ (the positive, regal, church organ with and without pedals etc).

1. 14th and 15th centuries. 2. 16th century. 3. 17th century. 4. The period of J. S. Bach.

1. 14TH AND 15TH CENTURIES. Although the surviving sources of keyboard music go back no further than the early 14th century, players and instruments are known to have existed long before. It therefore seems likely that the lack of an earlier repertory is due partly to the wholesale loss of the manuscripts concerned, and partly to the fact that players during the earliest period relied largely on vocal originals and improvisation.

The earliest known keyboard source by almost a century is the Robertsbridge Codex of about 1320 (*GB-Lbm* Add.28550). This incomplete two-leaf manuscript from the former priory of Robertsbridge, Sussex, is a curious hybrid, for though it may have been copied in England, it is written in a form of Old German keyboard tablature, and the music it contains is probably either French or Italian in origin. It consists of two and a half dances in the form of *estampies* and two and a half arrangements of vocal motets, two of which are found in the 14th-century *Roman de Fauvel*. Thus the two main categories of early keyboard music are already represented: namely, purely instrumental works, and works that are derived in some way from a vocal original. In the *estampies* the writing is mostly in two parts, though at cadences the texture tends to become fuller, as often happens in keyboard music. In the motet arrangements the top part of the three-voice original is decorated, or 'coloured', mainly in conjunct motion and in relatively short note values. The remaining parts are generally left unchanged, though occasionally one is omitted or an extra part added. There is no indication of the instrument for which the pieces were intended.

The bulk of the Reina Manuscript (*F-Pn* nouv.acq.fr. 6771) and the musical sections of the Faenza Manuscript (*I-FZc* 117) belong respectively to the late 14th century and the early 15th. Only a keyboard setting of Francesco Landini's ballata *Questa fanciulla* and an unidentified keyboard piece are included among Reina's otherwise exclusively vocal repertory; but the oldest part of Faenza consists entirely of keyboard pieces, though at one time it was thought they might have been intended for two non-keyboard instruments. There are arrangements of secular vocal works by Italian and French composers of the 14th and early 15th centuries (such as Landini, Jacopo da Bologna, Machaut and Pierre des Molins) and settings of liturgical chants including two Kyrie–Gloria pairs based on the plainsong Mass IV, *Cunctipotens genitor Deus* (see ex.1, the conclusion of a Kyrie verse). The Kyrie–Gloria settings are the first of countless plainsong settings designed for *alternatim* performance during the

Ex.1 Faenza MS: Conclusion of a Kyrie verse (. . . . eleison)

liturgy, in which only the alternate verses are set for organ, while the remainder are sung in unison by the unaccompanied choir. Except for a few three-part cadential chords in Faenza, the pieces in both manuscripts are all in two parts, though many of the secular vocal originals are in three.

The remaining 15th-century sources are all German, three of the most significant being Adam Ileborgh's tablature of 1448 (*US-PHci*), Conrad Paumann's *Fundamentum organisandi* of 1452 (*D-Bds* mus.40613), and the Buxheim Organbook of about 1460–70. Ileborgh's tablature is notable for its five short preludes which are the earliest known keyboard pieces (other than dances) that do not rely in any way on a vocal original. In one of them pedals are indicated; and a double pedal part seems to be required in two others, where a florid upper line crosses a pair of lower lines as they move slowly from a 5th to a 3rd and back again. Paumann's *Fundamentum* is one of several treatises that illustrate techniques used in extemporization and

composition. It provides examples of a florid part added above various patterns of bass; of decorated clausulas; of two free parts; and of two parts above a static bass. In addition, it includes a number of preludes, and of two- and three-part pieces based on both sacred and secular tenors, by Georg de Putenheim, Guillaume Legrant, Paumgartner and (presumably) Paumann himself. The Buxheim Organbook, which may also be associated with Paumann or his disciples, is the most comprehensive of all 15th-century keyboard sources. It contains over 250 pieces, of which more than half are based on either chansons or motets by German, French, Italian and English composers. They are of two main types. In the first, the whole of the original texture is used, one part being embellished while the rest are left more or less untouched, as in the Robertsbridge motets. In the second, the tenor alone is borrowed, to provide the foundation for what is otherwise a new composition. The rest of the manuscript includes liturgical plainsong pieces, preludes, and pieces based on basse-danse melodies. In the liturgical pieces the plainsong generally appears in long equal notes in one part, while the remaining parts have counterpoints in more varied rhythms. But occasionally the plainsong itself is ornamented or even paraphrased. The preludes are mostly regularly barred (unlike Ileborgh's), and often alternate chordal and florid passages in a way that foreshadows the later toccata. Most of the pieces are in three parts, although sometimes in two and occasionally in four (an innovation for keyboard music). The tenor and countertenor lines – the two lowest in the three-part pieces – have roughly the same compass; and as the countertenor was always added last, as in earlier vocal music, it constantly and often awkwardly has to cross and recross the tenor in order to find a vacant space for itself. Pedals are sometimes indicated by the sign *P* or *Pe*; apparently they could also be used elsewhere, for a note at the end of the volume explains that they should always play whichever tenor or countertenor note happens to be the lower.

2. 16TH CENTURY. Printed keyboard music began to appear during the 16th century. Liturgical plainsong pieces remained of paramount importance; but they were joined by settings of Lutheran chorales (hymn tunes) and an increasing number of secular works such as dances, settings of popular tunes, variations, preludes and toccatas. Of great significance, too, were the sectional contrapuntal forms of keyboard music derived from 16th-century vocal forms, including the contrapuntal keyboard ricercare as well as the canzona, capriccio and fantasy.

The earliest known printed volume devoted at least in part to keyboard music is Arnolt Schlick's *Tabulaturen etlicher Lobgesang und Lidlein uff die Orgel und Lauten* (Mainz, 1512). Besides lute solos and songs with lute accompaniment, it contains 14 pieces for organ with pedals. They are in either three or four parts and are almost all based on plainsong, an exception being a setting of the vernacular sacred song *Maria zart*, which foreshadows a later type of chorale prelude by echoing the phrases of the melody in the accompaniment. In Schlick's unique ten-part manuscript setting of the chant *Ascendo ad Patrem* (*I-TRa* tedesca 105) no fewer than four of the parts are assigned to the pedals.

The remaining German sources contain dances and arrangements of both sacred and secular vocal music, some being anthologies while others appear to be the work of a single composer. Although most of them are described as being for either 'Orgel', or 'Orgel oder Instrument', they are generally equally well (or even better) suited to harpsichord or spinet. The two earliest are a pair of manuscripts (*CH-Bu* F.IX.22 and F.IX.58) written by Hans Kotter between 1513 and 1532 for the use of the Swiss humanist Bonifacius Amerbach. In addition to embellished arrangements of vocal works by Paul Hofhaimer, Heinrich Isaac, Josquin Desprez and others, they include preludes and dances some of which are by Kotter himself. Typical of the latter is a *Spanioler* in which the basse danse melody *Il re di Spagna* is given to the tenor, each note being played twice in long–short rhythm, while treble and bass have more lively counterpoints. Later tablatures, some printed and others manuscript, are those of Elias Nikolaus Ammerbach (1571, 1583), Bernhard Schmid the elder (1577), Jacob Paix (1583), Christhoff Loeffelholz von Colberg (1585) and August Nörmiger (1598). A new trend is shown by the inclusion of 20 Lutheran chorales in Ammerbach's volume and over 70 in Nörmiger's. The plain melody is generally, though not invariably, given to the top part, while the remaining three parts provide simple harmony with an occasional suggestion of flowing counterpoint. A *Fundamentum* of about 1520 by Hans Buchner, similar to Paumann's but dealing with a later style of three-part counterpoint, contains the earliest known example of keyboard fingering.

The dances in the tablatures and other sources are often grouped in slow–quick pairs, such as a passamezzo and saltarello, or a pavan and galliard, in which the second dance (in triple time) may or may not be a variation of the first (in duple). Not infrequently they are based on one or other of the standard harmonic patterns known throughout western Europe, of which the *passamezzo antico* and the *passamezzo moderno* or quadran were the most common.

In Italy the printing of keyboard music began in 1517 with a book of anonymous arrangements entitled *Frottole intabulate da sonare organi*. The mainly homophonic textures of the four-part vocal originals (mostly by Bartolomeo Tromboncino) are lightly embellished to give a more flowing effect; but, as is characteristic of keyboard music, the number of parts employed at any moment depends more on the capacity of a player's hands, and the demands of colour and accent, than on the rules of strict part-writing. Similar freedom was exercised, as illustrated in ex.2, by Marco Antonio Cavazzoni, whose *Recerchari, motetti, canzoni* (1523) was the earliest keyboard publication by a named Italian composer. His brilliant son Girolamo Cavazzoni, perhaps working under the influence of the Spaniard Antonio de Cabezón (see below), developed from his father's rambling ricercares a clearly defined form in dovetailed imitative sections that became the standard pattern of such works. His two books of *intavolature* (1542) contain hymn and plainsong settings for organ and two canzonas with French titles. At least one of the latter, the lively *Il est bel et bon*, is virtually an original composition, for it uses no more than the first bar and a half of the chanson by Passereau on which it is allegedly based.

During the second half of the century the most important centre for Italian keyboard music was Venice, where Andrea Gabrieli, his nephew Giovanni Gabrieli and Claudio Merulo were numbered among the organists of St Mark's Cathedral. Andrea's keyboard works were issued posthumously between 1593 and 1605 by Giovanni, who added several of his own compositions to his uncle's. Each contributed a set of *intonazioni* in all the 'tones' or modes – short pieces used during the liturgy either as interludes, or to give the choir the pitch and mode of the music they were about to sing. Like earlier preludes, they often include some brilliant passage-work; this led by extension to the toccata, essentially a keyboard piece in several contrasted sections designed to display the varied capabilities of a player and his instrument. The toccatas of Andrea and Giovanni Gabrieli rely mainly on the contrast between sustained writing and brilliant passage-work; but Merulo enlarged the form by introducing one or more sections of imitative counterpoint. In addition to toccatas all three composers wrote ricercares, ornate chanson arrangements and original canzonas. The ricercares follow the sectional pattern established by Girolamo Cavazzoni; but those of Andrea and Giovanni Gabrieli have fewer themes (sometimes only one) and achieve variety by the use of inversion, augmentation, diminution and stretto, and by the importance given to secondary material such as a counter-subject or a new thematic tag. Canzonas tend to be lighter in feeling than ricercares, and often begin with a rhythmic formula of three repeated notes, for instance minim–crotchet–crotchet. None of the works requires pedals, and many of them are as well suited to the harpsichord as to the organ.

The earliest Italian keyboard dances are found in a small anonymous manuscript of about 1520 (*I-Vnm* Ital.IV.1227). Both here and in the anonymous *Intabolatura nova di varie sorte de balli* (1551), the melody is confined to the right hand, while the left has little more than a rhythmical chordal accompaniment. More sophisticated textures appear in the dance publications of Marco Facoli (1588) and Giovanni Maria Radino (1592), proving that the addition of simple counterpoint and right-hand embellishments can make such pieces sufficiently interesting to be played and heard for their own sake, and not merely as an accompaniment for dancing.

Ex.2 M. A. Cavazzoni: Intabulation of *Plus de regres*

Although England lagged far behind the Continent in printing keyboard music, British composers led the way in developing keyboard techniques. The broken-chord basses characteristic of later string keyboard writing appear in a manuscript of about 1520–40 (*GB-Lbm* Roy.App.58), which contains an adventurous 'Hornpype' by Hugh Aston and two anonymous pieces, *My Lady Careys Dompe* and *The Short Mesure of My Lady Wynkfylds Rownde*, which may also be by him. All three have ostinato left-hand parts. The repertory for organ (manuals only) from about the same period consists of almost 100 liturgical plainsong pieces (*GB-Lbm* Roy.App.56, Add.15233, Add.29996; and *Och* Mus.371; see *Early Tudor Organ Music*, i, ed. J. Caldwell, and ii, ed. D. Stevens, London 1966–9). The plainsong is used in various ways. It may be given to a single part in long equal notes, decorated rhythmically and/or melodically, or paraphrased so freely as to be almost unrecognizable; or again, either a single section or several sections of the melody may form the basis of an otherwise free composition. At first the most favoured plainsongs were the offertory *Felix namque* and the antiphon *Miserere mihi Domine*; but later these gave place to the antiphon *Gloria tibi Trinitas*, which, under the title *In nomine*, remained immensely popular with English composers for more than a century. The only known English setting of the Ordinary of the Mass is by Philip ap Rhys 'of St Paul's in London'. Among the remaining named composers, the two whose works are outstanding in both quality and quantity are John Redford (*d* 1547) and Thomas Preston. At first glance much of their music may seem vocal in style; but a genuine understanding of the keyboard is shown by the widely ranging parts, the skilful deployment of the hands, and the idiomatic figuration. Virtually no ornament signs are used, but written-out shakes and turns are occasionally incorporated in the text.

More of Redford's works are found in the anthology known as the Mulliner Book (*c*1550–75; *GB-Lbm* Add.30593), to which the other principal contributors were Thomas Tallis and William Blitheman. In addition to many plainsong pieces the manuscript contains simple transcriptions of Latin and English motets, secular partsongs and consort music. Most of the music was probably intended primarily, though not exclusively, for organ; but three anonymous pieces at the beginning of the manuscript, and a later pavan by Newman (no.116), have the chordal basses that distinguish string keyboard music. Similar basses are found in the Dublin Virginal Manuscript (*c*1570; *EIRE-Dtc* D.3.30), which consists almost entirely of anonymous dances. These contain a sprinkling of the double- and single-stroke ornaments and many of the varied repeats or 'divisions' that later became ubiquitous features of the virginals style.

The only surviving French sources of the 16th century are seven small books of anonymous pieces published by Pierre Attaingnant of Paris in 1530–31. Three are devoted to chanson arrangements (some of them also known in lute versions); two to *alternatim* plainsong settings of the Mass, *Magnificat*, and *Te Deum*; one to motet arrangements; and one to dances (galliards, pavans, branles and basse danses). All are described as being 'en la tablature des orgues, espinettes et manicordions'; but the dances and chanson arrangements are best suited to string keyboard instruments, and the remainder to the organ.

The most outstanding keyboard composer of the first half of the century was Antonio de Cabezón, organist to Charles V and Philip II of Spain. A number of his works (ascribed simply to 'Antonio') were included in Venegas de Henestrosa's anthology, *Libro de cifra nueva* (1557); but the principal source is the volume of Cabezón's own *Obras de música* published posthumously in 1578 by his son Hernando. Although both collections are described as being for 'tecla, arpa y vihuela' (keyboard, harp and lute), they were intended primarily for keyboard – the plainsong settings for organ, the *diferencias* (variations) for harpsichord, and the tientos (ricercares) for either instrument. Cabezón's style is severe, with textures that are generally contrapuntal and always in a definite number of parts. The tientos present a number of themes in succession, each section beginning with strict imitation and culminating in free counterpoint, often in relatively small note values. No ornament signs are used, but a favourite embellishment is a written-out shake with turn. Moreover, it seems likely that contemporary players would have added extemporary *redobles* (turns), *quiebros* (shakes, and upper or lower mordents), and glosas (diminutions), as recommended in Tomás de Santa María's treatise, *Libro llamado Arte de tañer fantasia* (1565). The *diferencias* are lighter in mood, though still strictly contrapuntal. In one of the finest, *El canto llano del caballero*, the melody is at first plainly harmonized, then given successively to soprano, tenor, alto, and again tenor, with flowing counterpoint in the remaining voices. As a member of Philip's private chapel, Cabezón visited Italy, Germany and the Netherlands in 1548–51, and the Netherlands and England in 1554–6; yet he appears to have had surprisingly little influence on the many composers he must have met in his travels.

Keyboard music from Poland survives in several manuscripts, of which the most comprehensive is the so-called Lublin Tablature, copied by Jan z Lublina during the years 1537–48 (*PL-Kp* 1716). It contains some 250 works, mostly anonymous, and includes liturgical plainsong pieces, preludes, dances (often in slow–quick pairs), and arrangements of vocal works with Latin, German, French, Italian and Polish titles. The influence of the German school is apparent throughout and extends even to the notation used.

3. 17TH CENTURY. Among the principal forms and types of keyboard music introduced during the 17th century were suites, genre or character-pieces, paired preludes and fugues, chorale preludes, and (from about 1680) sonatas. Superb organs in northern and central Germany encouraged the use of the newly independent pedal registers, thus underlining the difference between organ and string keyboard idioms. But the earlier more 'generalized' style of keyboard writing tended to persist wherever organs were less highly developed.

During the early part of the century the main advances in technique still took place in England, where the printing of keyboard music began at long last with *Parthenia or the Maydenhead of the First Musicke that Ever was Printed for the Virginalls* (1612–13). Its three contributors, Byrd, Bull and Orlando Gibbons, represented successive generations of the great school of virginalists that spanned the late 16th and early 17th centuries. The remaining sources of solo virginals music are manuscripts, however, for the apparent sequel, *Parthenia In-violata* (*c*1624), is for virginals and bass viol. The most comprehensive manuscript source is the Fitzwilliam Virginal Book (c1609–19), which provides a cross-section of the whole repertory from Tallis (c1505–1585) to Tomkins (1572–1656). Besides containing many unique texts, this remarkable anthology shows the ever-growing popularity of secular works such as dances, settings of song-tunes, variations, fantasias and genre pieces.

Typical of the virginals idiom, as developed by Byrd, are textures that range from contrapuntal imitation to plain harmony in either broken or block chords; a constantly varying number of parts; short figurative motifs; and florid decoration – particularly in the 'divisions', or varied repeats, that are often included in the text. Profuse ornamentation is a constant feature of the style, though oddly enough there is no contemporary explanation of the two signs commonly used to designate ornaments – the double and single stroke. Organ music is distinguished mainly by its liturgical function, but also by an absence of broken-chord basses and a preference for contrapuntal textures in a definite number of parts.

Ex.3 Bull: 'Walsingham' variations

Keyboard techniques were enormously extended by Bull, who was the greatest virtuoso of the day, and by Farnaby, a minor master of rare charm. Brilliant effects were achieved by figuration based on broken octaves, 6ths, 3rds and common chords, by the use of quick repeated notes and wide leaps, and even (in Bull's 'Walsingham' variations, MB, xix, no.85; see ex.3) by the crossing of hands. Farnaby's tiny piece 'For Two Virginals' (MB, xxiv, no.25), one of the earliest works of its kind, consists of no more than a plain and a decorated version of the same music played simultaneously. A clearer grasp of the true principles of duet writing is shown, however, in Tomkins's single-keyboard 'Fancy: for Two to Play' (MB, v, no.32); for though based on choral procedures, its mixture of antiphonal and contrapuntal textures neatly displays the essential individuality-cum-unity of two performers.

By the time the aged Tomkins died in 1656 younger composers were already turning towards a new style, French-influenced, in which the main thematic interest lay in the top line. The change can be seen clearly in the short, tuneful pieces of *Musicks Hand-maide* (1663), a collection of 'new and pleasant lessons for the virginals or harpsycon'. One of the few composers named in it is Matthew Locke, whose more ambitious anthology, *Melothesia* (1673), is prefaced significantly by 'certain rules for playing upon a continued-bass'. It includes seven of his own pieces (voluntaries) for organ and 'for double [i.e. two-manual] organ', and a number of suites (not so named) by himself and others, consisting gen-

erally of an almain, corant, saraband and one or more additional movements. Similar suites were written later by Blow and his pupil Purcell, the principal contributors to *The Second Part of Musick's Hand-maid* (1689); Purcell's were issued posthumously as *A Choice Collection of Lessons for the Harpsichord and Spinnet* (1696) and four of Blow's appeared two years later with the same title. All these publications were aimed at the amateur. But Purcell's harpsichord music, though small in scale, is no less masterly than his more ambitious works for theatre, court and the church; and at times it achieves a depth and poignancy – particularly in the ground basses of which he was so fond – that is quite disproportionate to its size. Blow was the more significant organ composer of the two. His 30-odd voluntaries and verses (Purcell wrote only half a dozen) are sectional contrapuntal pieces based on either one or two subjects. Two of them (nos.2 and 29 in Watkins Shaw's edition) unaccountably quote sizable passages from Frescobaldi's *Toccate e partite d'intavolatura di cimbalo* (1615) and another (no.5) is similarly indebted to one of Michelangelo Rossi's published toccatas.

More orthodox musical exchanges between the Continent and England had already taken place during the early years of the century. Arrangements of madrigals by Marenzio and Lassus and original works by Sweelinck, organist of the Oude Kerk in Amsterdam, were included in the Fitzwilliam Virginal Book; and, even more significantly, Bull, Peter Philips and other Catholic recusants found refuge in the Netherlands and elsewhere, and thus spread abroad the advanced English keyboard techniques. Sweelinck himself was much influenced by the innovations, as can be seen not only from his harpsichord works, but also from his organ variations on Lutheran chorales and his echo-fantasias that exploit the dynamic contrast between one manual and another. Although none of his keyboard works appeared in print, Sweelinck's fame as the foremost teacher in northern Europe brought him numerous pupils, particularly from the neighbouring parts of Germany. The latest techniques were thus passed on to a younger generation of composers, who in their turn carried them still farther afield.

German composers of the period may conveniently be divided into two groups: those who worked in the Protestant north and centre; and those of the Catholic south, including Austria. To the former group belong Sweelinck's pupils, Scheidt and Scheidemann. Scheidt's keyboard works were issued in two collections, the *Tabulatura nova* (1624) and the *Tabulatur-Buch hundert geistlicher Lieder und Psalmen* (1650). (In the first of these the description 'new' refers to the use of open score in place of letter notation.) The organ pieces cover a wide range, for in addition to the forms used by Sweelinck they include fugues and canons as well as plainsong settings for use during the Catholic liturgy. The later volume consists of simple four-part settings of Lutheran chorales for accompanying unison singing. One of the sets of variations for harpsichord is based on the English song *Fortune my Foe*, which was also set by Sweelinck, Byrd and Tomkins. Scheidemann's works, like those of most northerners, remained unpublished. The majority are organ settings of chorales in which the borrowed melody is either left plain, ornamented, treated in motet style, or (more rarely) used as a theme for variations. The most outstanding of all the northerners was, however, Buxtehude, who left his native Denmark in 1668 to become organist of the Marienkirche in Lübeck. His organ preludes and fugues are not unlike toccatas, for they often contain two quite distinct fugal sections in addition to brilliant flourishes and sustained passages. He also wrote numerous chorale settings of various kinds, even including a set of variations on *Auf meinen lieben Gott* in the form of a dance suite. Some of the works are for manuals only, but the majority make full use of the pedals. Although Buxtehude was primarily an organ composer, the publication in 1941 of the Ryge Manuscript (*DK-Kk* C.11.49.4°) made available his suites and variations for clavichord or harpsichord; these are so similar in style to those of Nicolas-Antoine Lebègue that the editor did not notice the inclusion of one of Lebègue's suites in the Buxtehude manuscript.

The earliest and most significant German composer of the south was Froberger, who, though born in Stuttgart, held the post of court organist in Vienna for 20 years. His ricercares, canzonas and fantasias are strongly influenced by his master, Frescobaldi, but his toccatas are less Italian in style. Although they begin with the usual sustained chords and brilliant flourishes (see ex.4), they generally include two fugal sections on

Ex.4 Froberger: Toccata no. 1

rhythmic variants of a single subject, each section being rounded off with further flourishes. His suites are in an expressive, romantic vein better suited to the clavichord than to the harpsichord. They are French in style, and are said to have been the first to establish the basic suite pattern of four contrasted national dances: i.e. an allemande (German), courante (French) or corrente (Italian), saraband (Spanish) and gigue or jig (English). In Froberger's autographs the gigue either precedes the saraband or is omitted altogether; but when the works were published posthumously (Amsterdam, 1693) the order was changed ('mis en meilleur ordre') and the gigue placed at the end. During the last ten years of his life Froberger travelled widely in Germany, France, the Netherlands and England, meeting Chambonnières and Louis Couperin in Paris and Christopher Gibbons (son of Orlando) in London; thus he too played a significant part in the cross-fertilization of national styles.

Among the lesser southerners were Alessandro Poglietti, Georg Muffat and J. C. F. Fischer. Although Poglietti was probably an Italian, he became court organist in Vienna shortly after Froberger, and in 1677 presented Leopold I and his empress with an autograph collection of his harpsichord pieces entitled *Rossignolo*. Besides a ricercare, a capriccio and an *Aria bizarra*, all based on the *Rossignolo* theme, it includes a virtuoso

'imitation of the same bird', and an *Aria allemagna* with 20 variations. Each of the latter has an illustrative title ('Bohemian Bagpipes', 'Dutch Flute', 'Old Woman's Funeral', 'Hungarian Fiddles' etc), and in number its match the age of the empress, to whom they were dedicated. Muffat's *Apparatus musico-organisticus* (1690) contains 12 organ toccatas with elementary pedal parts, and four harpsichord pieces of which the large-scale Passacaglia in G minor and the shorter Ciacona in G have a power and breadth more typical of the north than of the south. In contrast to these, the four collections by Fischer are wholly southern in their delicacy of feeling. *Les pièces de clavessin* (1696) and the *Musicalischer Parnassus* (1738) are devoted to harpsichord suites, each of which begins with a prelude of some sort and continues with a group of dances or other pieces, not always including the usual allemande, courante, saraband and gigue. The other two volumes, *Ariadne musica* (1702) and *Blumen Strauss* (1733), contain miniature preludes and fugues for organ. The *Ariadne* group interestingly foreshadows Bach's *Das wohltemperirte Clavier* in the wide range of its key scheme, and even in some of its themes (Fischer's eighth fugue in E obviously inspired Bach's ninth from book 2).

In Italy the main centre for keyboard music moved from Venice to Naples and then to Rome. From Ascanio Mayone's *Diversi capricci* (1603 and 1609) and Giovanni Maria Trabaci's *Ricercate* (1603 and 1615) it can be seen that although the Neapolitans retained the strict contrapuntal style of the Gabrielis in their ricercares, they broke new ground in toccatas by shortening the sections, increasing their number and heightening the contrast between one section and the next. The same distinction was made by Frescobaldi, who, as organist of St Peter's in Rome, was the most widely acclaimed player and keyboard composer of the day. Although he visited the Netherlands in 1607, when the 45-year-old Sweelinck was at the height of his powers, he was little influenced by the techniques of the north. His works were published during the next 35 years in a series of ten volumes of which some are revised and enlarged editions of others. The three definitive collections are *Il primo libro di capricci, canzon francese e recercari* (1626) and the *Toccate d'intavolatura di cimbalo et organo* with its sequel *Il secondo libro di toccate* (both 1637). (The first two contain important prefaces by the composer concerning interpretation.) Most of the toccatas, capriccios and canzonas in these collections are equally suited to harpsichord and organ, for though some have a primitive pedal part, it generally consists of no more than long-held notes that are already present in the left hand. The works intended primarily for harpsichord include dances (sometimes grouped in threes, with the opening balletto serving as theme for the following corrente and passacaglia), and sets of variations or partitas, a number of which are based on harmonic patterns such as the romanesca and the Ruggiero. The ricercares and plainsong pieces are essentially organ music, as in the liturgical *Fiori musicali* (1635), of which Bach possessed a manuscript copy.

One of the few 17th-century Italian publications devoted wholly to dances was Giovanni Picchi's *Intavolatura di balli d'arpicordo* (1621). Besides the customary passamezzo, saltarello and padoana (pavan), it includes imitations of alien idioms such as a 'Ballo alla polacha', a 'Ballo ongaro' and a 'Todesca'. The corantos in Michelangelo Rossi's *Toccate e correnti d'intavolatura d'organo e cimbalo* (*c*1640) are in a lighter, more tuneful style, though his toccatas are still closely related to Frescobaldi's. This new style can be seen even more clearly in the works of Bernardo Pasquini, who was among the first to apply the title 'sonata' to solo keyboard music. Originally it denoted no more than a 'sound piece' as opposed to a 'sung piece' or 'cantata', for it was applied indiscriminately to toccatas, fugues, airs, dances and suites. But Pasquini, following the example of Corelli's ensemble sonatas, also gave the title to solos in more than a single movement. Among his other works are 15 sonatas for two harpsichords, in which each part consists rather oddly of no more than a figured bass (*GB-Lbm* Add.31501). The 40-odd toccatas of Alessandro Scarlatti are of interest mainly because each contains at least one *moto perpetuo* section, thus anticipating the much later *moto perpetuo* type of toccata.

Most French keyboard music of the 17th century appeared in print while the composers were still alive; and as the title-pages generally specified either organ or harpsichord, but not both, there is rarely any doubt about the instrument intended. A manuscript dated 1618 (*GB-Lbm* Add.29486), however, contains over 100 short pieces in the church modes, all anonymous apart from G. Gabrieli's 12 *intonazioni*. They include preludes, *fugae* and *alternatim* settings of the Mass, *Magnificat* and *Te Deum*, all simple enough technically for parochial use. More sophisticated are Titelouze's *Hymnes de l'église pour toucher sur l'orgue* (1623) and *Le Magnificat ... suivant les huits tons de l'église* (1626), the first French keyboard publications devoted to the works of a single composer. The earlier volume contains settings of 12 plainsong hymns, each consisting of three or four versets for which the plainsong provides either a cantus firmus or several short themes for treatment in contrapuntal motet style. The eight *Magnificat* settings of the second volume, though also in motet style, are more adventurous harmonically. Titelouze was essentially conservative, however, and his strict polyphonic idiom attracted no immediate disciples. More typically French are the many *Livres d'orgue* issued during the second half of the century by composers such as Guillaume Nivers, Nicolas-Antoine Lebègue, Nicolas Gigault, André Raison and Jacques Boyvin. They mostly contain short pieces which, though still in the church modes and intended for use during the liturgy, are fairly simple in style and often unabashedly tuneful. As was customary in France, though not elsewhere, the registration is often indicated in the title, for instance 'Récit de nazard' or 'Basse de cromorne'. Also typical is the frequent use of contrasted manuals heard either simultaneously or in alternation. Lebègue was the first Frenchman to exploit the pedals fully, for generally they were either optional or omitted altogether.

The mid-century saw the emergence of the distinctive French harpsichord idiom that exercised a potent influence throughout Europe. In essence it was based on the richly ornamented and arpeggiated textures of lute music. The founder of the school was Chambonnières, who late in life published two books of *Pièces de clavessin* (1670) containing 60 dances grouped according to key. The commonest types are allemandes, courantes (often in sets of three) and sarabandes; occasionally a gigue or some other dance is added. More of his pieces

survive in the Bauyn Manuscript (*F-Pn* Rés.Vm⁷.674–5), which also contains almost all the compositions of his pupil Louis Couperin, the one outstanding French keyboard composer who never saw any of his own works in print. In addition to the forms used by his master, Couperin wrote a number of 'unmeasured preludes' of a type peculiar to France (*see* PRÉLUDE NON MESURÉ). Another pupil of Chambonnières was Jean-Henri d'Anglebert, whose *Pièces de clavecin* were published in 1689. The volume is unusual in two respects, for it includes five fugues for organ, and 15 of its 60 harpsichord pieces are arrangements of movements from operas by Lully. D'Anglebert's magnificent *Tombeau de Mr. de Chambonnières* is a good example for keyboard of a type of memorial composition of which French composers have always been specially fond.

4. THE PERIOD OF J. S. BACH. All the forms employed during the 17th century remained in use during the first half of the 18th; but sonatas (of other than the classical type) acquired increasing importance, and ritornello form (derived from the Neapolitan operatic aria) provided the foundation on which every concerto and many extended solo movements were built.

French keyboard composers were untouched by these developments, however, and continued to confine themselves to dances and genre pieces for harpsichord, and to short liturgical and secular works for the organ. The two outstanding figures among them were Louis Couperin's nephew François Couperin the younger and Jean-Philippe Rameau, a near-contemporary of Bach. François Couperin's four books of *Pièces de clavecin* (1713–33) are the crowning achievement of the French clavecin school. The 220 pieces range from elegant trifles to the majestic Passacaille in B minor (*ordre* no.8) and the sombre allemande *La ténébreuse* (*ordre* no.3), which is almost too intense in mood for the dance form in which it is embodied. Two organ masses, written at the age of 21, are sufficiently unlike the mature works to have been attributed at one time to his father, François the elder. Couperin's views on teaching, interpretation, ornamentation and fingering are set forth in his *L'art de toucher le clavecin* (1716–17), a fascinating treatise which nevertheless often fails to answer questions that remain puzzling. Rameau's instructions to the player are contained in two of the prefaces to his four books of harpsichord pieces issued between 1706 and 1741 (he wrote nothing for organ). The works are generally simpler in texture and less richly ornamented than Couperin's, but more adventurous harmonically and in their use of the keyboard. The composer himself noted that it would take time and application to appreciate the (harmonic) beauty of parts of the piece entitled *L'enharmonique*; and he provided fingering for the widely spaced left-hand figure in *Les cyclopes* because of its unusual difficulty. Rameau's final keyboard publication, *Pièces de clavecin en concerts* (1741), is primarily a collection of five suites for violin, bass viol and harpsichord, but it also includes a solo harpsichord version of four of the movements. This practical plan was anticipated, though in reverse, in Gaspard le Roux's *Pièces de clavecin* (1705). There the main works are suites for harpsichord solo, while the arrangements consist of selected movements for trio (instruments unspecified), and several for two harpsichords, the latter being the earliest known French works for that medium. Composers other than Couperin who wrote for both harpsichord and organ include Marchand, Clérambault, Dandrieu, Dagincour and Daquin. Most of their works are in the customary forms; but the organ volumes by Dandrieu (1715) and Daquin (1757) are devoted to sets of variations on popular Christmas melodies, entitled noëls, a type which first appeared in Lebègue's *Troisième livre d'orgue* (c1685).

One of the greatest of all harpsichord composers was the Italian Domenico Scarlatti, son of Alessandro and exact contemporary of Bach and Handel. The last 35 years of his life were spent in the service of Maria Barbara of Braganza, at first in Portugal and later in Spain; during that period he appears to have written almost all his 555 single-movement sonatas. Apart from a volume of 30 *Essercizi per gravicembalo* (1738), published under his own supervision, the main sources of his works are two contemporary manuscript collections (*I-Vnm* It.iv.199–213; and *I-PAc* AG 31406–20), the first of which was copied for his royal patron. Their contents are similar but not identical, and it has been suggested by Ralph Kirkpatrick (*Domenico Scarlatti*, Princeton, 1953) that the order of their contents is to a large extent chronological, and that more than two-thirds of the sonatas were, as the manuscripts indicate, originally grouped in pairs, or sometimes in threes, according to key (this order is retained in Kirkpatrick's facsimile edition, Philadelphia, 1972, and in Kenneth Gilbert's excellent complete edition, Paris, 1971–). Although Scarlatti rarely used any structure other than binary form, and seldom aimed at emotional extremes, he achieved an astonishing variety within those self-imposed limits. Moreover, he exploited the keyboard in ways never imagined by any of his contemporaries. In the later works he virtually abandoned his wilder flights of hand-crossing; but he never lost his command of both sparkling brilliance and an unexpected vein of reflective melancholy, his delight in technical and harmonic experiment, and his love for the sounds and rhythms of the popular music of Spain. Five of the sonatas (K254–5, 287–8 and 328) are for two-manual chamber organ without pedals, and some others are not unsuited to a single-manual organ; but by far the greater number are essentially harpsichord works. (Among the harpsichords possessed by his royal patron, however, none of those with more than two registers appear to have had the full five-octave compass required by some of the sonatas.)

Scarlatti's followers in Portugal and Spain, among whom were Seixas and Soler, wrote numerous single-movement sonatas similar in style to his own; but as an expatriate he exercised little influence on Italian composers, whose sonatas are of several different types. Those by Della Ciaia (1727) are not unlike sectional toccatas; Durante's (c1732) each contain a *studio* in imitative counterpoint followed by a brilliant *divertimento*; Marcello's (MS) are in either three or four movements; and Zipoli's (1716) include liturgical and secular pieces for organ as well as suites and variations for harpsichord. Also intended for either instrument are Martini's two volumes of sonatas (1742, 1747), the first devoted to two- and three-movement works, and the second to five-movement works that combine features of both the *sonata da camera* and the *sonata da chiesa*.

English keyboard composers during the post-Purcell period rarely rose above a level of honest competence. Tuneful airs and lessons, sometimes grouped into suites, appeared in serial anthologies such as *The Harpsichord*

Master (?1697–1728) and *The Ladys Banquet* (1704–35), among whose contributors were Jeremiah Clarke, William Croft and Maurice Greene. In addition, separate volumes were devoted to works by Philip Hart, Clarke, Thomas Roseingrave and Greene. Although Croft was not accorded that distinction, he was the most accomplished composer of the group and the only one to come within hailing distance of Purcell. Indeed, the Ground from his Suite no.3 in C minor is actually ascribed to Purcell in one source. Collections of fugues and/or voluntaries were issued by Hart, Roseingrave, Greene, Boyce and Stanley. Although described as being 'for the organ or harpsichord', these are best suited to the organ. The early voluntaries consist of a single movement, generally contrapuntal in texture, while the later tend to be in two movements (slow–fast), of which the second is often a fugue. Outstanding among them are the three volumes containing Stanley's 30 voluntaries, in some of which the number of movements is increased to three or four.

A Scarlatti cult was at one time fostered in England, first by Roseingrave's edition of *XLII suites de pièces pour le clavecin* (1739), which added 12 more Scarlatti sonatas to the 30 published a year earlier in the *Essercizi*; and secondly by Charles Avison's arrangement of a number of the sonatas as Twelve Concertos (1744) for strings and continuo.

Of far greater significance to English musical life, however, was the arrival of Handel, who settled in London in 1712 after a successful visit two years earlier. Although at first occupied mainly with Italian opera and later with oratorio, he was obliged to publish his [8] *Suites de pièces de clavecin* (1720) in order to counteract the many 'surrepticious and incorrect copies' that were circulating in manuscript. Other collections of his pieces, all unauthorized, appeared later in London and Amsterdam. Some of the suites follow the normal pattern of allemande–courante–sarabande–gigue; but more often they include Italianate allegros, andantes etc, or consist of nothing else. His keyboard works combine relaxed informality with masterly rhetoric in a way that doubtless reflects the improvisations for which he was famous; this is particularly noticeable in the 14 or 15 concertos for organ, a medium he invented for use during the intervals at his oratorio performances. In many of them the soloist is expected to improvise long sections (even whole movements) where his part is marked 'ad lib'. This would have been a perfectly simple matter for Handel himself, but it does pose problems for other players. Most of the works require an orchestra of no more than strings and oboes, and as all but one are for organ without pedals, the title-pages describe them as being 'for organ or harpsichord'. It seems likely that the appearance of the first set of six in 1738 encouraged Stanley to issue a keyboard version of the concertino parts of his Six String Concertos op.2, thus helping to acclimatize the keyboard concerto in England.

Meanwhile in Germany the way had been prepared for the greatest of all pre-classical keyboard composers, J. S. Bach. Among his many musical ancestors, other than relatives, the most significant was Buxtehude (see above), whose organ toccatas and chorale fantasias, and highly developed pedal technique, provided foundations on which Bach could build. So great was Bach's reverence for Buxtehude that in 1705 he walked the distance from Arnstadt to Lübeck in order to hear his Abendmusiken – the yearly choral and instrumental performances given on the five Sundays before Christmas. Somewhat less influential were Pachelbel, Kuhnau and Georg Böhm. Nevertheless, Pachelbel's chorale-preludes, published in 1683 and 1693, were the forerunners of one important type used by Bach. In this, each successive phrase of the borrowed melody is treated in diminution to provide the theme for a short fughetta, towards whose conclusion the phrase itself appears as a cantus firmus. The keyboard works of Kuhnau, Bach's predecessor at the Thomaskirche in Leipzig, include two notable volumes: firstly, the *Frische Clavier Früchte, oder sieben Suonaten* (1696), the earliest publication in which the title 'sonata' is given to a solo as distinct from an ensemble work; and secondly, [6] *Musicalische Vorstellungen einiger biblischen Historien* (1700), the 'musical representations of biblical stories' that provided the model for Bach's early *Capriccio sopra la lontananza del suo fratello dilettissimo* BWV992. The influence of Böhm, though conjectural, would have been earlier and more direct, for he was organist of the Johanneskirche in Lüneburg when Bach was a choirboy at the nearby Michaeliskirche. Böhm's organ partitas (variations on chorales) and sensitive suites in the French style for clavichord or harpsichord were unpublished, but the evidence of Bach's own works suggests that he must have been familiar with them as a boy.

A near-contemporary of Bach and Handel, and a friend of both, was the prolific Telemann. The admiration of the two slightly younger men for his music can best be understood by reference to works such as the *XX kleine Fugen* (1731). Although these miniature keyboard fugues are based on the church modes (which were then virtually obsolete), and though they are quite small in scale, each one establishes unerringly a mood as precise as its structure.

Comparatively few of Bach's own keyboard works were published during his lifetime. The most comprehensive collection, the *Clavier-Übung*, was issued in four parts between 1731 and 1742, of which the first, second and fourth contain compositions for both single- and double-manual harpsichord, while the third is mainly devoted to the organ.

Of Bach's total output of over 250 organ works, more than two thirds are based on chorales. They range from the early sets of *Partite diverse* BWV766–8, in the style of Böhm, to mature chorale-preludes of every type. From the Weimar period come the 46 preludes of the *Orgelbüchlein*, 'wherein the beginner may learn to perform chorales of every kind and also acquire skill in the use of the pedals'. In most of them a single, continuous statement of the melody, either plain or ornamented, is supported by an accompaniment whose figuration either symbolizes the words or intensifies the mood of the hymn concerned. They are generally small in scale; yet some of the settings, such as the richly embellished *O Mensch, bewein' dein' Sünde gross* BWV622, can be numbered among Bach's profoundest utterances. The third part of the *Clavier-Übung*, from the Leipzig period, contains 21 preludes based on catechism and other hymns, of which the six that illustrate the catechism are set twice – elaborately for two manuals and pedals, and more simply for manuals only. Four quite unconnected keyboard Duettos BWV802–5 are also included in part 3; and the whole volume is framed by the magnificent Prelude and Fugue in E♭ BWV552, known in England as the 'St Anne'. During the same period Bach

published the recondite [5] *Canonische Veränderungen über das Weynacht Lied 'Vom Himmel hoch'* BWV769, which, as Schweitzer wrote, 'pack into a single chorale the whole art of canon'. He also virtually completed the revision of 18 large-scale chorale-preludes, mostly written originally in Weimar; but failing health and eyesight forced him to abandon dictating the last of them, *Vor deinen Thron tret' ich hiermit* BWV668, whose ending luckily is known from other sources. Earlier chorale-preludes include 24 copied by his pupil Kirnberger, 28 from various other manuscripts, and a set of six published by Schübler (c1746), five of which are arrangements of movements from cantatas.

In almost all of Bach's secular organ music, none of which was published, fugue is an essential element. From the beginning of the Weimar period, or even earlier, come four immature and fairly small-scale preludes and fugues BWV531–3 and 535 and two much finer toccatas in C and D minor BWV564–5, all written under Buxtehude's influence. Increasing mastery and individuality is apparent in four later Weimar works – the preludes and fugues in F minor and A BWV534 and 536, the Fantasia and Fugue in C minor BWV537 and the Toccata and Fugue in F BWV540, with its tremendous pedal solos. The finest of all the fugal works are, however, the ten written either during or just before the Leipzig period. They include the Fantasia and Fugue in G minor BWV542, the Prelude (or Toccata) and Fugue in D minor BWV538, known as the 'Dorian', and the six magnificent preludes and fugues BWV543–8, which are Bach's crowning achievements in this form.

The great Passacaglia and Fugue in C minor BWV582 and the six trio sonatas BWV525–30 far transcend their original purpose as instructional works for Bach's eldest son, Wilhelm Friedemann. They are described merely as being 'for two manuals and pedals', so it remains uncertain whether they were intended primarily for organ or for a harpsichord fitted with a pedal-board (such as used by some organists for home practice).

Much of Bach's music for normal harpsichord and/or clavichord was also didactic in aim. The 15 two-part inventions and 15 three-part sinfonias BWV772–801 were first included in a manuscript collection of keyboard pieces for Wilhelm Friedemann dated 1720, and were described in a revision of 1723 as showing not only how 'to play clearly in two voices but also, after further progress, to deal correctly and well with three obbligato parts ... and above all to achieve a singing style in playing'. Friedemann's book also contained early versions of 11 of the preludes from the first book of *Das wohltemperirte Clavier* (1722), a more advanced collection of 24 preludes and fugues in all the major and minor keys 'for the use and profit of young musicians desiring to learn, as well as for the pastime of those already skilled in this study'. The second book, containing a further 24 preludes and fugues, was not completed until 1744. Two other manuscripts, dated respectively 1722 and 1725, were compiled for the use of Bach's second wife, Anna Magdalena. The first contains five of the six French suites BWV812–17, each consisting of the usual allemande, courante, sarabande and gigue, with one or more additional dances (*Galanterien*) following the sarabande. The six so-called 'English' suites BWV806–11 and six partitas BWV825–30 are on a larger scale, for each begins with a prelude of some sort. Those of the English suites (with the exception of no.1) are ritornello-type movements, while those of the partitas are in various forms. The partitas were published singly between 1726 and 1730, and complete in 1731 as part 1 of the *Clavier-Übung*, of which part 2 (1735) consists of the Italian Concerto BWV971 and the French Overture BWV831 (sometimes known as the Partita in B minor), both for two-manual harpsichord. Part 4 (1742), also for two-manual harpsichord, is devoted to a single work: the monumental Aria with 30 Variations BWV988, usually known as the Goldberg Variations, which Tovey described as 'not only thirty miracles of variation-form, but . . . a single miracle of consummate art as a whole composition'.

Slightly later in date is the *Musicalisches Opfer* BWV1079, a collection of fugues, canons etc for various instruments on a theme provided by Frederick the Great. It includes two ricercares for solo keyboard, of which the second, in six parts, was originally printed in open score. This was not an unusual method of presenting keyboard music when its aim was partly didactic. It was used again for Bach's posthumous treatise *Die Kunst der Fuge* BWV1080, in which the majority of the fugues are clearly intended for solo keyboard, though they have frequently been arranged for various ensembles in the 20th century.

During the Weimar period Bach made solo keyboard versions, some for organ and others for harpsichord, of 22 concertos by various composers, including Vivaldi, Marcello and Telemann. These paved the way for his later concertos for solo harpsichord and strings BWV1052–8, which were the first of their kind (and roughly contemporary with Handel's organ concertos). All seven are arrangements of earlier concertos of his own – mostly for solo violin and strings – several of which have not survived. The only original keyboard work in this form appears to be the Concerto in C for two harpsichords and strings BWV1061; the remaining two for the same medium, and those for three and four harpsichords and strings, are also arrangements of concertos originally by either Bach himself or other composers such as Vivaldi.

In its depth and range of emotion, contrapuntal skill and perfection of design, Bach's keyboard music far surpasses that of any of his contemporaries or predecessors; yet by the time of his death it was generally regarded as old-fashioned. The Baroque era had ended; the contrapuntal style was outmoded; and the harpsichord and clavichord were beginning to make way for the fortepiano, which combined the power of the one with the sensitivity of the other. The gradual change can be seen in the works of three of Bach's sons. The eldest, Wilhelm Friedemann, still wrote some fugues; but, like his polonaises and three-movement sonatas, they were in the new *empfindsamer Stil*, of which his brother Carl Philipp Emanuel was the chief exponent. Philipp Emanuel's numerous sonatas, fantasias, rondos etc, embodying the violent dynamic contrasts typical of the style, were immensely influential; and his book, *Versuch über die wahre Art das Clavier zu spielen* (1753–62), was the most important treatise of its day. The youngest brother, Johann Christian, was a less original composer; nevertheless, his Italianate sonatas and concertos in the *galant* style gained great popularity in England, where he settled in 1761. And there it was that he met and befriended the eight-year-old Mozart, when that astonishing boy visited London in 1764–5.

BIBLIOGRAPHY
LISTS OF COMPOSITIONS
B. Weigl: *Handbuch der Orgelliteratur* (Leipzig, 1931)

E. Hutchinson: *The Literature of the Piano* (New York, 1938, rev. 3/1964)
W. S. Newman: 'A Checklist of the Earliest Keyboard "Sonatas"', *Notes*, xi (1953–4), 201
J. Friskin and I. Freundlich: *Music for the Piano . . . from 1580 to 1952* (New York, 1954/R1973)
H. Alker: *Literatur für alte Tasteninstrumente: Wiener Abhandlungen zur Musikwissenschaft und Instrumentalkunde* (Vienna, 1962)
K. Wolters: *Handbuch der Klavierliteratur* (Zurich, 1967)
C. R. Arnold: *Organ Literature: a Comprehensive Survey* (Metuchen, NJ, 1973)
M. Hinson: *Guide to the Pianist's Repertoire* (Bloomington, Ind., 1973)
H. Ferguson: *Keyboard Interpretation* (London, 1975)

GENERAL SURVEYS
A. G. Ritter: *Zur Geschichte des Orgelspiels* (Leipzig, 1884/R1969)
M. Seiffert: *Geschichte der Klaviermusik* (Leipzig, 1899/R1966)
J. Wolf: 'Zur Geschichte der Orgelmusik im 14. Jahrhundert', *KJb*, xiv (1899), 14
O. Kinkeldey: *Orgel und Klavier in der Musik des 16. Jahrhunderts* (Leipzig, 1910/R1968)
A. Pirro: 'L'art des organistes', *EMDC*, II/ii (1926), 1181–359
K. G. Fellerer: *Orgel und Orgelmusik: ihre Geschichte* (Augsburg, 1929)
G. Frotscher: *Geschichte des Orgel-Spiels und der Orgel-Komposition* (Berlin, 1935–6, enlarged 3/1966)
G. Schünemann: *Geschichte der Klaviermusik* (Berlin, 1940)
W. Georgii: *Klaviermusik* (Zurich, 1941, 4/1965)
M. F. Bukofzer: *Music in the Baroque Era* (New York, 1947)
G. S. Bedbrook: *Keyboard Music from the Middle Ages to the Beginnings of the Baroque* (London, 1949/R1973)
M. Kenyon: *Harpsichord Music* (London, 1949)
L. Hoffmann-Erbrecht: *Deutsche und italienische Klavier-Musik zur Bach-Zeit* (Leipzig, 1954)
G. Reese: *Music in the Renaissance* (New York, 1954, rev. 2/1959)
A. E. F. Dickinson: 'A Forgotten Collection' [*D-Bds* Ly.A1 and A2], *MR*, xvii (1956), 97
W. Apel and K. von Fischer: 'Klaviermusik', *MGG*
F. W. Riedel: *Quellenkundliche Beiträge zur Geschichte der Musik für Tasteninstrumente in der zweiten Hälfte des 17. Jahrhunderts* (Kassel, 1960)
Y. Rokseth: 'The Instrumental Music of the Middle Ages and Early 16th Century', *NOHM*, iii (1960), 406–65
F. W. Riedel and T.-M. Laquer: 'Orgelmusik', *MGG*
W. Young: 'Keyboard Music to 1600', *MD*, xvi (1962), 115–50; xvii (1963), 163–93
A. E. F. Dickinson: 'The Lübbenau Keyboard Books' [*D-Bds* Ly.A1 and A2], *MR*, xxvii (1966), 270
F. E. Kirby: *A Short History of Keyboard Music* (New York, 1966)
W. Apel: *Geschichte der Orgel- und Klaviermusik bis 1700* (Kassel, 1967; Eng. trans., rev. 1972)
——: 'Solo Instrumental Music', *NOHM*, iv (1968), 602–708

ENGLAND
E. Walker: *A History of Music in England* (Oxford, 1907, rev. 3/1952 by J. A. Westrup)
C. van den Borren: *Les origines de la musique de clavier en Angleterre à l'époque de la Renaissance* (Brussels, 1913; Eng. trans., 1913)
W. Niemann: *Die Virginalmusik* (Leipzig, 1919)
M. Glyn: *About Elizabethan Virginal Music and its Composers* (London, 1924, enlarged 2/1934)
M.-L. Pereyra: 'Les livres de virginal de la bibliothèque du Conservatoire de Paris', *RdM*, vii (1926), 204; viii (1927), 36, 205; ix (1928), 235; x (1929), 32; xii (1931), 22; xiii (1932), 86; xiv (1933), 24
L. Neudenberger: *Die Variationstechnik der Virginalisten im Fitzwilliam Virginal Book* (Berlin, 1937)
H. M. Miller: 'Sixteenth-century English Faburden Compositions for Keyboard', *MQ*, xxvi (1940), 50
——: *English Plainsong Composition for Keyboard in the Sixteenth Century* (diss., Harvard U., 1943)
——: 'The Earliest Keyboard Duets', *MQ*, xxix (1943), 438
R. Donington and T. Dart: 'The Origin of the English In Nomine', *ML*, xxx (1949), 101
G. Reese: 'The Origin of the English "In Nomine"', *JAMS*, ii (1949), 7
D. Stevens: 'Pre-Reformation Organ Music in England', *PRMA*, lxxvii (1951–2), 1
——: 'A Unique Tudor Organ Mass', *MD*, vi (1952), 167
——: *The Mulliner Book: a Commentary* (London, 1952)
E. E. Lowinsky: 'English Organ Music of the Renaissance', *MQ*, xxxix (1953), 373, 528
T. Dart: 'New Sources of Virginal Music', *ML*, xxxv (1954), 93
J. Ward: 'Les sources de la musique pour le clavier en Angleterre', *La musique instrumentale de la Renaissance: CNRS Paris 1954*, 225
J. L. Boston: 'Priscilla Bunbury's Virginal Book', *ML*, xxxvi (1955), 365
H. J. Steele: *English Organs and Organ Music from 1500–1650* (diss., U. of Cambridge, 1958)

R. L. Adams: *The Development of Keyboard Music in England during the English Renaissance* (diss., U. of Washington, 1960)

J. A. Caldwell: *British Museum Add.MS 29996* (diss., U. of Oxford, 1965)

——: 'Keyboard Plainsong Settings in England, 1500–1660', *MD*, xix (1965), 129

H. D. Johnstone: 'An Unknown Book of Organ Voluntaries', *MT*, cviii (1967), 1003

G. Beechey: 'A New Source of 17th Century Keyboard Music', *ML*, 1 (1969), 278

A. Curtis: *Sweelinck's Keyboard Works: a Study of English Elements in Seventeenth-century Dutch Composition* (London and Leiden, 1969, 2/1972)

M. C. Maas: *Seventeenth-century English Keyboard Music: a Study of Manuscripts Rés.1185, 1186 and 1186bis of the Paris Conservatory Library* (diss., Yale U., 1969)

T. Dart: 'An Early Seventeenth-century Book of English Organ Music for the Roman Rite', *ML*, lii (1971), 27

B. A. R. Cooper: 'The Keyboard Suite in England before the Restoration', *ML*, liii (1972), 309

M. Boyd: 'Music MSS in the Mackworth Collection at Cardiff', *ML*, liv (1973), 133

J. Caldwell: *English Keyboard Music before the Nineteenth Century* (Oxford, 1973)

M. Tilmouth: 'York Minster MS M.16(s) and Captain Prendcourt', *ML*, liv (1973), 302

B. A. R. Cooper: *English Solo Keyboard Music of the Middle and Late Baroque* (diss., U. of Oxford, 1974)

GERMANY, AUSTRIA AND POLAND

F. Arnold and H. Bellermann: *Das Locheimer Liederbuch nebst der Ars organisandi von Conrad Paumann* (Wiesbaden, 1864, rev. 3/1926/R1969)

R. Eitner: 'Das Buxheimer Orgelbuch', *MMg*, xix–xx (1887–8), suppl.

M. Seiffert: 'J. P. Sweelinck und seine direkten deutschen Schüler', *VMw*, vii (1891), 145–260

A. Chybiński: 'Polnische Musik und Musikkultur des XVI. Jahrhunderts', *SIMG*, xiii (1911–12), 463–505

Z. Jachimecki: 'Eine polnische Orgeltabulatur aus dem Jahre 1548', *ZMw*, ii (1919–20), 206

P. Nettl: 'Die Wiener Tanzkompositionen in der zweiten Hälfte des 17. Jahrhunderts', *SMw*, viii (1921), 45–175

H. Schnoor: 'Das Buxheimer Orgelbuch', *ZMw*, iv (1921–2), 1

A. Scheide: *Zur Geschichte des Choralvorspiels* (Hildinghausen, 1926)

W. Merian: *Der Tanz in den deutschen Tabulaturbüchern* (Leipzig, 1927/R1968)

G. Kittler: *Geschichte des protestantischen Orgelchorals* (Ueckermünde, 1931)

W. Apel: 'Die Tabulatur des Adam Ileborgh', *ZMw*, xvi (1933–4), 193

O. A. Baumann: *Das deutsche Lied und seine Bearbeitungen in den frühen Orgeltabulaturen* (Kassel, 1934)

A. Booth: *German Keyboard Music in the 15th Century* (diss., U. of Birmingham, 1954–5)

L. Schierning: *Die Überlieferung der deutschen Orgel- und Klaviermusik aus der 1. Hälfte des 17. Jahrhunderts* (Kassel, 1961)

E. Southern: *The Buxheim Organ Book* (Brooklyn, 1963)

O. Mischiati: *L'intavolatura d'organo tedesca della Biblioteca nazionale di Torino', L'organo*, iv (1963), 1–154

J. R. White: 'The Tablature of Johannes of Lublin', *MD*, xvii (1963), 137

H. R. Zöbeley: *Die Musik des Buxheimer Orgelbuchs* (Tutzing, 1964)

G. T. M. Gillen: *The Chorale in North German Organ Music from Sweelinck to Buxtehude* (diss., U. of Oxford, 1970)

S. Wollenberg: *Viennese Keyboard Music in the Reign of Karl VI (1712–40): Gottlieb Muffat and his Contemporaries* (diss., U. of Oxford, 1975)

ITALY, SPAIN AND PORTUGAL

A. Sandberger: 'Zur älteren italienischen Klaviermusik', *JbMP 1918*, 17

H. Anglès: 'Orgelmusik der Schola Hispanica vom XV. bis XVII. Jahrhundert', *Festschrift Peter Wagner* (Leipzig, 1926/R1969), 11

K. G. Fellerer: 'Zur italienischen Orgelmusik des 17./18. Jahrhunderts', *JbMP 1937*, 70

K. Jeppesen, ed.: *Die italienische Orgelmusik am Anfang des Cinquecento* (Copenhagen, 1943, rev., enlarged 2/1960)

D. Plamenac: 'Keyboard Music of the 14th Century in Codex Faenza 117', *JAMS*, iv (1951), 179

——: 'New Light on Codex Faenza 117', *IMSCR, v Utrecht 1952*, 310

N. Pirrotta: 'Note su un codice di antiche musiche per tastiera' [*I-FZc* 117], *RMI*, lvi (1954), 333

R. Lunelli: *L'arte organaria del Rinascimento in Roma* (Florence, 1958)

J. F. Monroe: *Italian Keyboard Music in the Interim between Frescobaldi and Pasquini* (diss., U. of North Carolina, 1959)

B. Hudson: *A Portuguese Source of Seventeenth-century Iberian Organ Music* (diss., Indiana U., 1961)

H. Anglès: 'Die Instrumentalmusik bis zum 16. Jahrhundert in Spanien',

Natalicia musicologica Knud Jeppesen (Copenhagen, 1962), 143

K. Jeppesen: 'Ein altvenetianisches Tanzbuch' [*I-Vnm* Ital.IV.1227], *Festschrift Karl Gustav Fellerer* (Regensburg, 1962), 245

R. Hudson: *The Development of Italian Keyboard Variations on the Passacaglio and Ciaccona from Guitar Music in the Seventeenth Century* (diss., U. of California, Los Angeles, 1967)

M. Kugler: *Die Tastenmusik im Codex Faenza* (Tutzing, 1972)

THE NETHERLANDS, BELGIUM AND FRANCE

A. Méreaux: *Les clavecinistes de 1637 à 1790* (Paris, 1867)

C. van den Borren: *Les origines de la musique de clavier dans les Pays-Bas (nord et sud) jusque vers 1630* (Brussels, 1914)

A. Pirro: *Les clavecinistes* (Paris, 1925)

Y. Rokseth: *La musique d'orgue au XVe siècle et au début du XVIe* (Paris, 1930)

S. Clercx: 'Les clavecinistes belges', *ReM* (1939), no.192, p.11

N. Dufourcq: *La musique d'orgue française de Jean Titelouze à Jehan Alain* (Paris, 1941, 2/1949)

A. Curtis: Introduction to *Nederlandse klaviermuziek uit de 16e en 17e eeuw*, MMN, iii (1961)

T. Dart: 'Elisabeth Eysbock's Keyboard Book', *STMf*, xliv (1962), 5

E. Southern: 'Some Keyboard Basse Dances of the Fifteenth Century', *AcM*, xxxv (1963), 114

A. Curtis: *Sweelinck's Keyboard Works: a Study of English Elements in Seventeenth-century Dutch Composition* (London and Leiden, 1969, 2/1972)

FORMS

R. Eitner: 'Tänze des 15. bis 17. Jahrhunderts', *MMg*, vii (1875), suppl.

T. Norlind: 'Zur Geschichte der Suite', *SIMG*, vii (1905–6), 172–203

I. Faisst: 'Beiträge zur Geschichte der Claviersonate von ihrem ersten Auftreten an bis auf C. Ph. Bach', *NBJb*, i (1924), 7–85

O. Deffner: *Über die Entwicklung der Fantasie für Tasteninstrumente bis J.P. Sweelinck* (diss., U. of Kiel, 1927)

L. Schrade: *Die ältesten Denkmäler der Orgelmusik als Beitrag zu einer Geschichte der Toccata* (Münster, 1928)

R. Gress: *Die Entwicklung der Klavier-Variation von Andrea Gabrieli bis zu Johann Sebastian Bach* (Augsburg, 1929)

E. Valentin: *Die Entwicklung der Tokkata im 17. und 18. Jahrhundert (bis J. S. Bach)* (Munich, 1930)

A. Schering: 'Zur Alternatim-Orgelmesse', *ZMw*, xvii (1935), 19

E. Epstein: *Der französische Einfluss auf die deutsche Klavier-Suite im 17. Jahrhundert* (Würzburg, 1940)

J. L. Hibberd: *The Early Keyboard Prelude* (diss., Harvard U., 1940)

M. Reimann: *Untersuchungen zur Formgeschichte der französischen Klavier-Suite* (Regensburg, 1941)

L. Schrade: 'The Organ in the Mass of the 15th Century', *MQ*, xxviii (1942), 329, 467

R. Murphy: *Fantasia and Ricercare in the Sixteenth Century* (diss., Yale U., 1954)

S. Podolsky: *The Variation Canzona for Keyboard Instruments in Italy, Austria and Southern Germany in the Seventeenth Century* (diss., Boston U., 1954)

I. Horsley: 'The 16th-century Variation', *JAMS*, xii (1959), 118

W. S. Newman: *The Sonata in the Baroque Era* (Chapel Hill, 1959, rev. 2/1966/R1972)

F. M. Siebert: *Fifteenth-century Organ Settings of the Ordinarium Missae* (diss., Columbia U., 1961)

R. S. Douglass: *The Keyboard Ricercar in the Baroque Era* (diss., U. of North Texas, 1963)

M. C. Bradshaw: *The Origin of the Toccata*, MSD, xxviii (1972)

II. Organ music from c1750.

Notable influences on the development of organ music since the mid-18th century include changes in the liturgy, a profound respect for the music of J. S. Bach, innovations in the mechanism of the organ and a growing tendency to write for the instrument in symphonic terms. In the following account, the major schools of organ composition will be considered in this context, with particular attention to those parts of the repertory less familiar today.

1. The Bach tradition: 1750–1850. 2. The 'symphonic' organ: 1850–1920. 3. Trends in 20th-century organ music.

1. THE BACH TRADITION: 1750–1850. The period between the death of J. S. Bach in 1750 and the publication of Mendelssohn's organ works nearly a century later is regarded as one of the least productive ones in the history of organ music. Except for a small number of miscellaneous preludes by Bach's followers and the famous fantasias for mechanical organ by Mozart, few works from this period are played today. The seculariz-

ing influence of the Enlightenment, with its reaction against organized religion and its emphasis on the natural and rational, effectively removed the organ from the mainstream of musical activity. That it was not completely neglected is evident from the innumerable articles on organ building, organ playing and organ music which appeared in contemporary journals.

During the second half of the 18th century church musicians did not enjoy a high social status, and were forced by their inadequate remuneration to enter other fields of musical activity. Many became renowned as theoreticians and teachers, while others applied their abilities to secular music. In England the decline in the influence of the Chapel Royal and the cathedrals, and the growing importance of the parish church, allowed organists sufficient freedom to perform in theatres and concert rooms. The element of showmanship which naturally resulted was the first stage in the secularization of the art. In Germany a tendency to reject the established contrapuntal and fugal forms as too complicated for ordinary listeners resulted in a similar emphasis on superficial display. In the preface to his *Vierstimmige Choräle mit Vorspielen* (1803), J. C. Kittel stressed that it was the duty of the organist to play 'for the people'. In this respect, the learned manner of J. S. Bach was considered inappropriate for liturgical purposes, and was soon superseded by a more directly appealing style. This prejudice against elaborate structures persisted for many years; in *Der musikalische Kirchendienst* (1832), F. Kessler barred performances in church services of the large-scale works of Bach, Handel, J. G. Albrechtsberger, Mozart, Krebs and Johann Schneider (1702–88), on the grounds that they provided 'intellectual pleasure for the initiated listener rather than for the ordinary man'.

While the prelude and voluntary continued to play a significant part in the service, increasing importance was attached to congregational singing, and the role of the organ became more and more that of providing simple accompaniment. The extent of this development is evident in the assertion made by the Rostock organ builder Paul Schmidt, in 1789, that 'a church organ is not meant for playing all kinds of pretty pieces, but for keeping the congregation in tune'. Owing to the slow pace at which hymns, metrical psalms and chorales were sung, organists were required to improvise short interludes in the breathing-spaces between individual lines and verses. Both in England and on the Continent, innumerable anthologies were published comprising cadenzas and interludes for the purpose, and these gained particular popularity among a growing number of untrained and comparatively inexpert organists unable to improvise service music or perform technically difficult pieces. This orientation towards the amateur undoubtedly deterred the great composers of the period, many of whom were renowned for their improvisations, from publishing music for the organ.

Contemporary accounts indicate that the general standard of organ playing was affected. In Germany, Burney's high expectations were continually thwarted. After a visit to Augsburg he explained that 'the rage for crude, equivocal and affected modulation which now prevails . . . renders voluntary playing so unnatural that it is a perpetual disappointment and torture to the ear' (*The Present State of Music in Germany, the Netherlands and the United Provinces*, 1773). Composers of the period, however, did not disregard the

achievements of their predecessors, nor did the music of Bach lie forgotten until its rediscovery nearly a century later. In his history (1789), Burney stated that the organ music of Handel and Bach 'established a style for that instrument which is still respected and imitated by the greatest organists in Germany'.

That tradition continued to flourish in the northern provinces of Germany. In Berlin, J. F. Agricola, J. P. Kirnberger, F. W. Marpurg and their followers were strongly influenced by the contrapuntal style of Bach's later works. While their interest in the more technical aspects of this style often resulted in a dry and academic manner, their most sucessful compositions, inspired by chorale melodies, are equal to the best German organ music. J. L. Krebs and J. P. Kellner reveal in their large-scale works a close adherence to the traditional forms and a profound understanding of Bach's techniques. Their treatment of the organ trio deserves particular attention. While their lesser contemporaries cultivated a purely melodic style in which the thematic interest lay primarily in the upper part, Krebs, Kellner, and the latter's pupil J. E. Rembt retained the kind of motivic development and true independence of part-writing exploited by Bach in his six trio sonatas. It is curious that the trio should have retained its popularity in this period, for as the contrapuntal style gave way to the simpler and more expressive textures of the *galant*, composers began to use the pedals less systematically, and publications of organ music increasingly bore the sub-title 'für Orgel und Klavier' to provide for optional performance. G. A. Sorge's *XI Sonaten* (c1745–9) are typical of this. At first German composers were reluctant to dispense entirely with the traditional contrapuntal style, but the gradual infiltration of elements from the Italian keyboard sonata produced a tendency to use the organ simply as an expressive instrument. This weakness is apparent in C. P. E. Bach's *Preludio e sei sonate per organo*, published posthumously by Rellstab in 1790. The most original and stylistic organ compositions of the period are undoubtedly the *Grosse Präludien* of J. C. Kittel, one of J. S. Bach's most gifted pupils. As the author of the treatise *Der angehend praktische Organist* (1801–9), and as the teacher of J. C. H. Rinck and M. G. Fischer, Kittel must be regarded as the most important link between Bach and the Romantic school.

Until the mid-19th century, organs in central Europe were rarely provided with full pedal-boards. For this reason, the organ music of southern Germany, Austria and Czechoslovakia does not exhibit a breadth and complexity equal to that of the north German school. The eclectic style of Georg Muffat and his son, Gottlieb, was continued by J. E. Eberlin in his *IX toccate e fughe per l'organo*, and reached its highest point of development in the works of J. G. Albrechtsberger and his pupils Ambros Rieder and Simon Sechter. Albrechtsberger, described by a contemporary critic as 'Vienna's Johann Sebastian Bach', wrote prolifically for the organ; his independently conceived preludes and fugues are particularly diverse in style, technique and thematic material.

Most of the organ music published in England after 1750 was secular in character and, stylistically, almost indistinguishable from other English keyboard music of the time. The voluntary, a purely indigenous form, had existed during the early part of the century as a single movement in fugal style. The English preference for colourful sonorities, however, produced a type of composition in which the newly incorporated Trumpet and Cornet stops of the organ were used as solo instruments. The early experiments in this style were consolidated by the mid-18th-century composers Maurice Greene, William Boyce, William Walond and John Stanley. Their voluntaries consist for the most part of slow introductions followed by brisk movements in solo concerto style, with occasionally an additional movement. Lesser composers of the period soon deprived the form of its true vitality and used increasingly orchestral sonorities provided by the new Cremona, Bassoon and Hautboy stops. The subsequent reaction against this manner from such composers as John Keeble received great stimulus from the importation of German organ music, and resulted in a renewed ascendance of the fugue over other forms. At first, the fugal compositions of Handel and his English imitators provided the basic pattern, but the growing interest in the music of Bach, initiated by Samuel Wesley, produced a more flexible and imaginative approach to the form. Thomas Adams wrote some particularly fine voluntaries in this traditional manner, but it was the orchestral and pianistic style of his more secular organ pieces that, to the detriment of the English school, prevailed during the remainder of the 19th century. The stagnation of the school may also be attributed to the comparatively late recognition of the pedal organ, which in many instruments consisted merely of a pull-down attachment for the lowest octave of the manual compass. Even in 1884, the organ of Canterbury Cathedral had only one octave of short pedals.

While the general standard of early Romantic organ music in Germany is disappointing, the true art of organ playing was not wholly forgotten. Under the guidance of Rinck and Fischer, the Bach tradition remained a vital force and provided the basis for the organ tutors written by their pupils K. C. Kegel (1830), L. E. Gebhardi (1837), A. G. Ritter (1844) and W. Wedemann (1847). The appearance of Bach's trio sonatas as a *Praktische Orgelschule* in 1832 supports this argument. It is nonetheless surprising that of the many original compositions for organ published at that time, only a small number require a highly developed technique. Most composers did no more than publish numerous anthologies of short, simple pieces suitable for liturgical use and for the limited abilities of amateurs. The works of such composers as J. G. Schneider (1789–1864), however, belong to a different class. H. F. Chorley's impressions of Schneider's performance on a Silbermann organ in the Sophienkirche, Dresden, recounted in his *Music and Manners in France and Germany* (1841), highlights this organist's purely classical training. His published compositions, such as the fine Fantasia and Fugue in D minor op.3, were conceived entirely in terms of the classical organ with its clear sonorities, balanced manual choruses and independent pedal division. In originality and breadth of conception, compositions of this calibre clearly anticipated the organ music of Mendelssohn.

Whereas Schneider adhered to the established German tradition, G. J. Vogler and J. H. Knecht represent an entirely new school of thought in which the organ is seen as an expressive symphonic instrument. Vogler, whom Mozart described as a 'loathsome musical buffoon', toured extensively throughout Europe playing programmatic improvisations on his 900-pipe

Orchestrion. His influence was considerable. Knecht not only sanctioned and strongly advocated Vogler's descriptive effects in his *Vollständige Orgelschule* (1795–8), but also published a musical representation for organ entitled *Die durch ein Donnerwetter unterbrochene Hirtenwonne*.

In France, the secularization of organ music was carried to even greater limits. While the instrument retained its close relationship with the church, the vitality and originality of invention which had characterized classical organ literature were replaced by an empty formalism in which virtuosity was exploited for its own sake. Burney's impressions, recorded in *The Present State of Music in France and Italy* (1771), reveal the extent of this transformation: the interludes played between verses of the *Te Deum* by A.-L. Couperin at St Gervais, Paris, allowed 'great latitude' to the performer; nothing was considered 'too light or too grave' and 'all styles were admitted'. A similar lapse of musical integrity beset the music at St Roque, where C. B. Balbastre improvised 'minuets, fugues, imitations and every species of music, even to hunting pieces and jigs, without surprising or offending the congregation'. The growing popularity of these interludes, together with the vogue for mediocre noëls and meretricious storm representations, contributed to the century-long decline of the French school. The translation of Knecht's *Orgelschule* by J. P. A. Martini, and the use of the organ during the French Revolution as a means of awakening 'a holy love of the fatherland in the mind of the hearers', served merely to accentuate these tendencies. In the marches and transcriptions of L. J. A. Lefébure-Wély and A. E. Batiste, the most renowned virtuosos of the 19th century, the art of organ composition reached its lowest ebb.

The foundation of the first organ class at the Paris Conservatoire in 1819 established a more salutary trend in French organ music. A. P. F. Boëly and François Benoist (the first *titulaire*) advocated a return to the principles of classical tradition, and learnt much from their acquaintance with the music of the German school. Furthermore, relations were close with the Brussels Conservatory, where J. N. Lemmens (a pupil of A. F. Hesse) held a high regard for the music of Bach. The growing concern for the Bach tradition together with new developments in organ building provided the basis for the Romantic school of composition, whose full possibilities were first recognized by Franck in his *Six pièces pour orgue* (1860–63).

2. THE 'SYMPHONIC' ORGAN: 1850–1920. Liszt's Prelude and Fugue on B–A–C–H, dedicated to Alexander Winterberger, was originally conceived for the inauguration of the rebuilt organ at Merseburg Cathedral in 1855. Ladegast's renovation of this instrument represents a turning-point in the history of organ music, for it clearly inspired in Liszt a new approach to composition. In the same way that Ladegast incorporated the tonal concepts of the Romantic organ within a purely classical framework, Liszt reconciled Bach's formal procedures and sonorous polyphony with his own highly expressive idiom. But Liszt's most profound innovation was his application to the organ of the artistic virtuosity which he had developed in the realm of piano music. Hans von Bülow (1856) rather graphically ascribed Winterberger's abilities to the perfection he had achieved as a pianist under Liszt's direc-

tion: 'The facility which he acquired in pedal playing surpasses the feats of the organists of the old school in quietness and certainty, in energy and fluency, to the same degree that his finger execution is superior to theirs. He represents the Liszt school with both hand and foot'.

The importance of this school in the development of organ music has to a large extent overshadowed many earlier attempts to compose for the instrument in true concert style. The diverse elements which Liszt combined in his organ works had tentatively been employed by many of his predecessors. In his Six Sonatas (1845), Mendelssohn made frequent use of pianistic techniques to produce new textures and sonorities. As the first major 19th-century composer to turn to the organ, his influence was considerable, but his formal approach to organ composition belonged to a very different tradition from that of Liszt. Since the beginning of the century, a firm distinction had been drawn in Germany between organ music for recital and liturgical purposes. During the 1830s, such organists as F. K. Kühmstedt, M. Brosig, A. G. Ritter, A. F. Hesse, A. Freyer and F. G. Klauer concentrated on recital work. While their compositions rarely achieve a consistently high level of inspiration, their free rhythms, extreme dynamic contrasts, frequent manual changes and shattering pedal passages are often highly original and effective. In his *Fantasia eroica* op.29, Kühmstedt avoided the sentimentality and indiscriminate use of chromaticism which marred much of the music of the period. Though lacking in formal cohesion, this fantasia has at its climactic points a relentless drive and energy which make it a worthy precursor of Liszt's best efforts in the medium.

Liszt's influence was surprisingly short-lived; with the exception of the brilliant and colourful *Sonata on the 94th Psalm* by his pupil Julius Reubke, few works followed in this tradition. The revival of interest in early organ music during the first half of the century had in many cases produced a more conservative approach to organ composition. Ritter (a composer as well as the author of a valuable textbook on the history of organ playing and composition, *Zur Geschichte des Orgelspiels*, 1884) used his understanding of Baroque techniques to produce an entirely original cyclic sonata form, incorporating within a purely Romantic context formal elements from Buxtehude's toccatas. Less capable musicians, however, succumbed to mere pastiche. The organ music of G. A. Merkel, for example, though technically accomplished, is devoid of freshness and vitality. J. G. Rheinberger's rigorous academic training also produced a certain dryness and lack of flexibility in his early works; but as his own personality came to the fore he was able to inject new life into the traditional contrapuntal forms, and in many of his slow movements achieved a Brahmsian warmth and breadth.

Several important 19th-century composers came to the organ through the music of earlier masters, which they realized could be a living force in their own works. Schumann's Six Fugues on B–A–C–H op.60 (1845) reveal a profound respect for the music of Bach, while Brahms's 11 Chorale Preludes op.122, most of which were composed during the last year of his life, undoubtedly owed their existence to the work he did in connection with the Denkmäler Deutscher Tonkunst. To Reger, Bach's organ works were 'the beginning and end of all music'. They provided the basis for his entire

output from the early Suite in E minor op.16, 'den Manen Joh. Seb. Bach's gewidmet', to the great Fantasia and Fugue in D minor op.135*b*. Reger's organ music stands at the crossroads as the culmination of 19th-century attempts to clothe the old contrapuntal forms in a truly Romantic idiom and as a profound influence on the composers of both the new Viennese school and the school of Hindemith.

The reform in organ building brought about by the work of Aristide Cavaillé-Coll had a far-reaching influence on organ composition in France. 'The modern organ is essentially symphonic', wrote Widor, 'a new language is required for the new instrument, something very different from scholastic polyphony'. The truly symphonic tradition initiated in the works of Saint-Saëns and Franck cannot be equated, however, with the orchestral style of playing fostered in England by such organists as W. T. Best during the latter part of the century. French composers never lost sight of the organ as an instrument in its own right with its own peculiar expressive qualities. In his *Technique de l'orchestre moderne* (1904), Widor stressed that 'we must employ this expression with conscientious reserve and artistic feeling; otherwise we shall ignore the essential characteristics of the instrument and convert it into a pseudo-orchestra'.

Franck's importance in the history of organ music derived from the *Six pièces* (1860–63), the *Trois pièces* (1878) and the *Trois chorals* written shortly before his death in 1890. These few pieces foreshadowed the most significant features of modern French organ music: while the *chorals* (described by Flor Peeters as 'three monuments of unforgettable beauty') inspired the liturgical approach to composition advocated by Franck's pupil and successor at Ste Clothilde, Charles Tournemire, the *Grande pièce symphonique* (from the *Six pièces*) was the first organ symphony ever written. It illustrated the brilliant concert style of organ composition and also established the trend towards large cyclic structures as featured in the works of C.-M. Widor and Louis Vierne.

The strength of the French school arose from the highly disciplined training provided at the official institutions in Paris. As direct heirs of the Lemmens tradition, Widor and F. A. Guilmant subjected their pupils to detailed studies of form, technique and improvisation. The benefit of this approach is apparent in such substantial works as Marcel Dupré's Three Preludes and Fugues op.7. Many early compositions, however, had a scholarly rather than musical appeal. In the eight sonatas of Guilmant, for instance, where the basic material lacks originality, the interest lies completely in the elaborate thematic development and infallible formal control. This consummate mastery of technique is also evident in the ten symphonies of Widor, but here the freedom from classical tradition produces music of greater character and individuality. The pure concert style of composition which Widor developed in his early symphonies was crystallized in the works of his pupil, Vierne. While Vierne's influence on the succeeding generation of organists is considerable, his persistent use of excessive chromaticism soon rendered his music unfashionable. Nevertheless, the Second Symphony was hailed by Debussy in *Gil Blas* (25 February 1903) as a remarkable composition in which 'the most generous musical qualities are combined with ingenious innovations in the particular sonorities of the organ'.

3. TRENDS IN 20TH-CENTURY ORGAN MUSIC. During the first part of the 20th century, interest in early organ music intensified and the many limitations of the symphonic organ became evident. Because the works of the great classical composers could be fully appreciated only on appropriate instruments, there was incentive for a return to the true principles of classical organ design. The foundation of the Société des Amis de l'Orgue in Paris in 1926, and the numerous organ conferences which took place in Germany around that time, served to formulate the basic precepts of the new movement, which was to have great influence on the future development of organ music. German composers were immediately impressed by the clarity of the newly refined instrument and developed an appropriate style of composition based mainly on Baroque forms and techniques. In France, where the symphonic school remained a more vital force in contemporary music, the desire to compromise between classical and Romantic traditions of organ building produced the highly versatile instrument which inspired the music of Tournemire, Alain and Messiaen.

In England, where the new movement progressed more slowly, the Romantic tradition of organ composition persisted longer. The aesthetic which guided most composers was clearly expounded by C. H. H. Parry (1911): 'This capacity of holding indefinitely any number and any combination of notes is the source of the organ's being the mightiest of all means for tremendous effects of harmony, and this quality is essentially the most important element in organ style'. Parry's own compositions and those of his contemporary C. V. Stanford are frequently marred by this predilection for heavy and overcrowded textures, but nonetheless they are conceived for the organ in particular and thus represent a significant stylistic advance over the orchestrally conceived organ music of the previous century. In the works of their followers the musical possibilities of the traditional, texturally more sophisticated idiom were fully exploited, promoting a new approach to the instrument. In his first set of Psalm Preludes op.32, Herbert Howells cultivated a relatively polyphonic style, yielding greater lightness and transparency in texture. It is these qualities, clearly achieved in the works of Britten, P. R. Fricker, John McCabe and Kenneth Leighton, that distinguish the most successful of the contemporary school. Composers working in England have also been receptive to influences from abroad. Malcolm Williamson turned to the organ as a direct result of his encounter with the music of Messiaen; his indebtedness to the French school is evident in both *Fons amoris* and *The Vision of Christ-Phoenix*. Serial techniques of composition have also produced some highly original organ music, including Humphrey Searle's *Toccata alla passacaglia* op.31 and Nicholas Maw's *Essay*, a substantial and colourful work of five sections derived from one series of notes.

The linear contrapuntal style of Reger's later works provided the basis for the music of Hugo Distler, the central figure of the new German school, and his followers J. N. David, Heinrich Kaminski, Ernst Pepping, Helmut Bornefeld and Siegfried Reda. Motivated by the organ reform movement, these composers reacted against the excesses of late Romantic music and established a more objective approach to structure and technique. They conceived their organ music within a purely liturgical context and revived the chorale to assume its former importance as a source of musical inspiration. The contrapuntal textures of Hindemith's three organ sonatas (1937–40) are an aspect of these same principles and are therefore more effective when registered in terms of the classical organ. But it is interesting to note that in the original edition of the second sonata the composer sanctioned the use of the general crescendo and swell pedals 'to give richer colours and more dynamic expression than is suggested in the text'. This inclination away from Baroque terrace registration is more apparent in two significant works dating from 1941, Schoenberg's *Variations on a Recitative* op.40 and Ernst Krenek's Sonata (neither of which adheres to strict serial techniques). Like Frank Martin's Passacaglia, written three years later, these were conceived according to the Romantic ideal of continuous and progressive development, and in many passages the organ is forced to serve ends that it cannot meet. Significantly Martin later arranged his Passacaglia for string orchestra. In its adherence to classical formal procedures and its successful incorporation of Baroque textures into a 20th-century idiom, Carl Nielsen's *Commotio* avoids these disadvantages and poses fewer problems to the organist.

The development of the modern French school has been profoundly influenced by the importance that composers have increasingly attached to the spiritual and liturgical aspects of their work. This can be traced to the revival of interest in plainsong during the latter part of the 19th century, when Guilmant, Gigout and Widor (notably in his last two symphonies) used the ecclesiastical modes as a source of inspiration. But it was after World War I that the liturgical movement, led by Tournemire, rose to true prominence. His *L'orgue mystique* (1927–32) is a collection of 51 suites, each consisting of five movements based on the plainsong theme appropriate to the Office for which the suite was intended. Tournemire's preoccupation with the mystical qualities of plainsong inspired him to original means of expression for his highly evocative musical style and his unconventional exploitation of the organ's tonal resources. The freedom which he achieved within the limitations of his thematic material provided a point of departure for many similar compositions by his followers, including Jean Langlais' *Trois paraphrases grégoriennes*, Maurice Duruflé's *Prélude, adagio et choral varié sur le thème du Veni Creator* and the *Toccata, fugue et hymne sur Ave maris stella* by the Belgian organist Flor Peeters. Plainsong extended an influence far beyond those compositions which it directly inspired; its supple melodic contours have pervaded the language of contemporary French organ music.

The symphonic style fostered by Widor and Vierne culminated in the purely concert compositions of André Fleury, Gaston Litaize, Duruflé and Dupré, in which unprecedented demands are made on both the player's virtuosity and the capabilities of the instrument. While the more recent French school has continued to emphasize these features, virtuosity is no longer regarded as an end in itself. It has become the means to a more subjective and expressive art, the style of writing being conditioned in many cases by the composer's reactions to a chosen text or idea. The earliest manifestations of this in a purely secular form were during the first quarter of the century when such composers as Georges Jacob, Ermend Bonnal and the Belgian Joseph Jongen incorporated impressionistic techniques into their compositions. In his *Symphonie-passion* (1925), Dupré reconciled this approach with the aims of the liturgical school and established a concept of religious programme music which gave a new impetus to composers for the organ. The significant developments in form, style and rhythm exemplified in the programmatic works of Langlais, Tournemire, Jacques Charpentier, Daniel-Lesur and Grunewald have been consummated in the organ cycles of Messiaen: *L'Ascension*, *La nativité du Seigneur*, *Les corps glorieux* and *Méditations sur le mystère de la Sainte Trinité*. To Messiaen, music is an integral part of philosophy and religion; his highly disciplined approach to composition is a response to the divine order he perceives in the universe, though in the most recent cycle this preoccupation has perhaps resulted in a less communicative musical language. The rhythmic complexity which characterized Messiaen's early works and which he has subsequently enriched through his acquaintance with plainsong and Hindu music was also a feature of the works of Jehan Alain. In their originality and freedom, Alain's three dances *Joies*, *Deuils* and *Luttes* (1939) may be ranked among the most remarkable contributions to the 20th-century organ repertory.

The concept of the organ as purely a church instrument has to a large extent discouraged its use as a vehicle for extreme experimentation. Since the mid-20th century, however, several composers have begun to overcome this inhibition. György Ligeti's *Volumina* (1961–2) is an interesting experiment in changing and stationary note-clusters and derives many new effects from the unconventional use of traditional organ registers. Like Mauricio Kagel's *Improvisation ajoutée* (1961–2), this work ideally employs three performers, two of whom merely assist with the registration. Kagel also composed a *Phantasie für Orgel mit Obbligati* (1967), in which traditional sonorities are combined with tape-recorded sounds, a technique which has gained particular favour in the USA among such composers as William Bolcom, Alden Ashforth and Richard Felciano. Within a more conventional framework, some noted performers are using their experience of the classical repertory and their profound understanding of the organ's resources as a basis for some highly original music; Anton Heiller's *Tanz Toccata* is a fine example. But the most satisfying trends are furnished by the many non-organist composers who are writing for the instrument without compromising their styles. Such diverse compositions as Patrick Gowers's *Toccata* and Charles Camilleri's *Missa mundi* reveal an imaginative approach which has benefited from recent developments in organ building as well as from a growing discrimination among performers and audiences.

BIBLIOGRAPHY

GENERAL REFERENCE

Musica Sacra: Vollständiges Verzeichnis aller seit dem Jahre 1750–1867 gedruckt erschienenen Compositionen für die Orgel, Lehrbücher für die Orgel ... usw (Erfurt, 1867)
D. Buck: *The Influence of the Organ in History* (London, 1882, 2/1911)
T. Forchhammer and B. Kothe: *Führer durch die Orgel-Literatur* (Leipzig, 1890, rev. 3/1931)
L. Hartmann: *Die Orgel: gemeinverständliche Darstellung des Orgelbaus und Orgelspiels* (Leipzig, 1904, 3/1921)
C. F. A. Williams: *The Story of Organ Music* (London, 1905/R1968, 2/1916)
A. Schweitzer: *Deutsche und französische Orgelbaukunst und Orgelkunst* (Leipzig, 1906/R1962, 2/1927)
C. W. Pearce: *The Organist's Directory ... with a Full List of Voluntaries* (London, 1908)
H. C. Lahee: *The Organ and its Masters* (London, 1909)
H. H. Statham: *The Organ and its Position in Musical Art* (London, 1909)
H. Grace: *The Complete Organist* (London, 1920)
F. Sauer: *Handbuch der Orgel-Literatur: ein Wegweiser für Organisten* (Vienna, 1924)
D. E. Berg: *The Organ: Composers and Literature* (New York, 1927)
H. Westerby: *The Complete Organ Recitalist: British and American* (London, 1927)
C. M. Widor: *L'orgue moderne* (Paris, 1928)
K. G. Fellerer: *Orgel und Orgelmusik: ihre Geschichte* (Augsburg, 1929)
C. F. Waters: *The Growth of Organ Music* (London, 1931, enlarged 2/1957)
H. Westerby: *The Complete Organ Recitalist: International Repertoire Guide to Foreign, British, and American Works* (London, 1933)
A. C. D. de Brisay: *The Organ and its Music* (London, 1934)
G. Frotscher: *Geschichte des Orgel-Spiels und der Orgel-Komposition* (Berlin, 1935–6, enlarged 3/1966)
H. Klotz: *Das Buch von der Orgel* (Kassel, 1938; Eng. trans., 7/1969)
G. D. Cunningham: 'The History and Development of Organ Music', *MT*, lxxix (1938), 685, 769, 848, 924; lxxx (1939), 50, 205, 282, 366 [series of articles]
F. Münger: *Choralbearbeitungen für Orgel* (Kassel, 1952)
G. A. C. de Graaf: *Literatur over het orgel* (Amsterdam, 1957)
F. W. Riedel, W. Apel and T.-M. Langner: 'Orgelmusik', *MGG*
V. Lukas: *Orgelmusikführer* (Stuttgart, 1963)
C. Probst: *Literatur für Kleinorgel* (Zurich, 1964)
W. Gurlitt: *Musikgeschichte und Gegenwart*, i–ii, ed. H. H. Eggebrecht (Wiesbaden, 1966)
L. F. Tagliavini: 'Organo', *LaMusicaE*
A. Reichling, ed.: *Acta organologica*, i–ii (Berlin, 1967–8)
F. Jakob: *Die Orgel: Orgelbau und Orgelspiel von der Antike bis zur Gegenwart* (Berne, 1969)
Various authors: 'The Organist's Repertory', *MT*, cx (1969), 673, 1286; cxi (1970), 543, 741; cxii (1971), 177, 597, 898, 1108; cxiii (1972), 193, 395, 499, 705, 805, 1123; cxiv (1973), 1049
G. S. Rowley: *A Bibliographic Syllabus of the History of Organ Literature: the Nineteenth Century* (Iowa City, 1972)
W. M. Liebenow: *Rank on Rank: a Bibliography* (Minneapolis, 1973)

SPECIFIC STUDIES

H. F. Chorley: *Music and Manners in France and Germany* (London, 1841)
H. von Bülow: 'Alexander Winterberger und das moderne Orgelspiel', *NZM*, xlv (1856), 1; Eng. trans. in *Dwight's Journal of Music*, x (1856), 65
R. J. Voigtmann: 'Der Einfluss der neudeutschen Schule auf das Orgelspiel', *NZM*, lxv (1869), 30
H. H. Statham: 'Wanted: a Composer for the Organ', *MT*, xx (1879), 633
A. G. Ritter: *Zur Geschichte des Orgelspiels, vornehmlich des deutschen, im 14. bis zum Anfange des 18. Jahrhunderts* (Leipzig, 1884/R1969)
K.-E. von Schafhäutl: *Vogler: sein Leben, Charakter und musikalisches System: seine Werke, seine Schule* (Augsburg, 1888)
O. Dienel: *Die moderne Orgel: ihre Einrichtung, ihre Bedeutung für die Kirche und ihre Stellung zu J. S. Bachs Orgelmusik* (Berlin, 1891)
C. H. H. Parry: *Style in Musical Art* (London, 1911)
H. Keller: *Reger und die Orgel* (Munich, 1923)
Freiburger Tagung für deutsche Orgelkunst: Freiburg 1926
3. Tagung für deutsche Orgelkunst: Freiberg in Sachsen 1927
F. W. Donat: *Christian Heinrich Rinck und die Orgelmusik seiner Zeit* (diss., U. of Heidelberg, 1931)
N. Dufourcq: 'La pénétration en France de l'oeuvre d'orgue de J. S. Bach', *ReM* (1932), no.131, p.27
A. Dreetz: *Johann Christian Kittel: der letzte Bach-Schüler* (Berlin, 1932)
K. G. Fellerer: *Studien zur Orgelmusik des ausgehenden 18. und frühen 19. Jahrhunderts* (Kassel, 1932)
H. Kelletat: *Zur Geschichte der deutschen Orgelmusik in der Frühklassik* (Kassel, 1933)
H. J. Wagner: *Die Orgelmusik in Thüringen in der Zeit von 1830–1860* (diss., U. of Berlin, 1937)
N. Dufourcq: 'Panorama de la musique d'orgue française au XXe siècle', *ReM* (1938), no.184, p.369; no.185, p.35; no.186, p.120; xx (1939), no.189, p.103 [series of articles]
H. Schweiger: *Abbé G. J. Vogler's Orgellehre* (diss., U. of Freiburg, 1938)
N. Dufourcq: *La musique d'orgue française de Jean Titelouze à Jehan Alain: les instruments, les artistes et les oeuvres, les formes et les styles* (Paris, 1941, 2/1949)
M. Schneider: *Die Orgelspieltechnik des frühen 19. Jahrhunderts in Deutschland, dargestellt an den Orgelschulen der Zeit* (Regensburg, 1941, 3/1973)
H. Distler: 'Die Orgel unserer Zeit', *Musica*, i (1947), 147
C. E. Vogan: *The French Organ School of the Seventeenth and*

Eighteenth Centuries (diss., U. of Michigan, 1949)

F. Peters: 'The Belgian Organ School', *HMYB*, vi (1949–50), 270

W. Sumner: 'The French Organ School', *HMYB*, vi (1949–50), 281

A. Kalkoff: *Das Orgelschaffen Max Regers im Lichte der deutschen Orgelerneuerungsbewegung* (Kassel, 1950)

H. Bornefeld: *Orgelbau und neue Orgelmusik* (Kassel, 1952)

R. Walter: 'Die zeitgenössische deutsche Orgelmusik', *Melos*, xx (1953), 37

H. J. Moser: 'Orgel und Orgelspiel', *Die evangelische Kirchenmusik in Deutschland* (Berlin, 1954), 418–54

R. Quoika: *Albert Schweitzers Begegnung mit der Orgel* (Berlin, 1954)

W. Kolneder: 'Johann Nepomuk David und das Orgelschaffen in Österreich', *ÖMz*, xiii (1958), 262

W. Stockmeier: *Die deutsche Orgelsonate der Gegenwart* (diss., U. of Cologne, 1958)

Various authors: 'Organ Music of our Century', *MT*, cii (1961), 44, 175, 331, 723; ciii (1962), 184; civ (1963), 54, 208; cv (1964), 134, 924; cvi (1965), 374

P. Williams: *English Organ Music and the English Organ under the First Four Georges* (diss., U. of Cambridge, 1962)

R. Kremer: *The Organ Sonata since 1845* (diss., U. of Washington, 1963)

P. Williams: 'J. S. Bach and English Organ Music, 1800–35', *ML*, xliv (1963), 140

S. Vendrey: *Die Orgelwerke von Felix Mendelssohn-Bartholdy* (diss., U. of Vienna, 1964)

H. J. Seyfried: *Adolph Friedrich Hesse als Orgelvirtuose und Orgelkomponist* (diss., U. of Saarbrücken, 1965)

R. Quoika: *Die Orgelwelt um Anton Bruckner: Blicke in die Orgelgeschichte Alt-Österreichs* (Ludwigsburg, 1966)

P. Williams: *The European Organ, 1450–1850* (London, 1966)

H. H. Eggebrecht: *Die Orgelbewegung* (Stuttgart, 1967)

A. Haupt: 'Orgelkunst in Italien', *Der Kirchenmusiker*, vi (1967), 241

D. C. Johns, P. Gehring and P. M. Young: 'A Survey of Contemporary Organ Music', *Church Music*, ii (River Forest, Ill., 1967), 25

M. Rudd: *Stylistic Trends in Contemporary Organ Music: a Formal and Stylistic Analysis of post World War II Works, 1945–1965* (diss., U. of Louisiana, 1967)

H. H. Eggebrecht: *Orgel und Orgelmusik heute* (Stuttgart, 1968)

F. Högner: 'Max Reger und die deutsche Orgelbewegung', *Ars organi*, xvi (1968), 1153

E. Routley: *The Musical Wesleys* (London, 1968)

F. Douglass: *The Language of the Classical French Organ: a Musical Tradition before 1800* (London, 1969)

M. Weyer: *Die deutsche Orgelsonate von Mendelssohn bis Reger* (Regensburg, 1969)

A. J. G. Jones: *A Survey of Organ Works Based on the Motive B–A–C–H* (diss., U. of Texas, 1970)

O. Biba: 'The Unknown Organ Music of Austria', *The Diapason*, lxii (1971), 10

F. Peeters and M. Vente: *The Organ and its Music in the Netherlands* (New York, 1971)

J. Caldwell: *English Keyboard Music before the Nineteenth Century* (Oxford, 1973)

F. Routh: *Early English Organ Music from the Middle Ages to 1837* (London, 1973)

THE ORGAN AND THE LITURGY

W. Riley: *Parochial Music Corrected: Containing Remarks on … the Use of Organs and the Performance of Organists* (London, 1762)

F. W. T. Linke: *Der rechte Gebrauch der Orgeln beym öffentlichen Gottesdienste* (Altenburg, 1766)

D. G. Türk: *Von den wichtigsten Pflichten eines Organisten* (Halle, 1787/R1966, rev. 2/1838)

F. Kessler: *Der musikalische Kirchendienst* (Iserlohn, 1832)

J. H. Göroldt: *Die Orgel und deren zweckmässiger Gebrauch bei dem öffentlichen Gottesdienst* (Quedlinburg, 1835)

R. S. Candlish: *The Organ Question: For and Against the Use of the Organ in Public Worship* (Edinburgh, 1856)

R. J. Voigtmann: *Das neuere kirchliche Orgelspiel* (Leipzig, 1870)

F. Zimmer: *Die Kirchenorgel und das kirchliche Orgelspiel* (Gotha, 1891)

G. Rietschel: *Die Aufgabe der Orgel im Gottesdienst bis in das 18. Jahrhundert* (Leipzig, 1893)

W. Baumann: *Das Orgelspiel im evangelischen Gottesdienst* (Karlsruhe, 1915)

F. Blume: *Die evangelische Kirchenmusik*, HMw, x (1931, rev. 2/1965 as *Geschichte der evangelischen Kirchenmusik*; Eng. trans., enlarged, 1974, as *Protestant Church Music: a History*)

K. G. Fellerer: *Beiträge zur Choralbegleitung und Choralverarbeitung in der Orgelmusik des ausgehenden 18. und frühen 19. Jahrhunderts* (Strasbourg, 1932)

J. Petzold: *Die gedruckten vierstimmigen Choralbücher für die Orgel der deutschen evangelischen Kirche, 1785–1933* (diss., U. of Halle, 1935)

R. Lachmann: 'Das moderne Choralvorspiel als gottesdienstliche Gebrauchsmusik', *Zeitschrift für Kirchenmusiker*, xx (1938), 60

J. G. Mehl: *Die Aufgabe der Orgel im Gottesdienst der lutherischen Kirche* (Munich, 1938)

R. Haupt: *Die Orgel im evangelischen Kultraum in Geschichte und Gegenwart* (Northeim, 1954)

H. J. Moser: *Die evangelische Kirchenmusik in Deutschland* (Berlin, 1954)

M. Blindow: *Die Choralbegleitung des 18. Jahrhunderts in der evangelischen Kirche Deutschlands* (Regensburg, 1957)

H. Klotz: 'Die kirchliche Orgelkunst', *Leiturgia*, iv (1961), 759–804

III. Piano music from c1750. In the period of this survey the piano achieved a position of unrivalled popularity among keyboard instruments. Much of its enduring solo repertory derives from the work of a handful of great composers, though others wrote individual important works or contributed to the development of keyboard style. Detailed lists of works and dates are available in articles on individual composers.

1. The advent of the piano. 2. The age of the Classical sonata. 3. Versatility and virtuosity. 4. Romanticism. 5. 19th-century national trends. 6. The growth of pianism, 1900–1940. 7. After World War II.

1. THE ADVENT OF THE PIANO. The designation 'piano music' must be accepted with caution in the earlier stages: the new instrument did not perfect itself, gain acceptance, or oust its rivals overnight. Lodovico Giustini published sonatas specifically for 'cimbalo di piano e forte' in Florence as early as 1732, yet J. S. Bach, who died in 1750, never owned a piano. At Potsdam, however, Bach played on Silbermann's improved models in 1747, thus giving pianists some claim to the keyboard ricercares in the subsequent *Musicalisches Opfer*. Pianists' tacit inheritance of all earlier keyboard music has long been questioned, and the revival of authentic instruments is bound to continue. It is still a far cry from Silbermann or Stein (admired by Mozart) to the familiar iron-framed piano first patented by Babcock in 1825. Yet if the quantity and quality of sound changed, so did performing conditions and listeners' ears. When Busoni described Bach's music as the foundation of piano playing, he stated a fact. He could have cited the influence of the '48' on Beethoven, Chopin or Brahms, even though his own edition of it wrongly translated Bach's generic word 'clavier' ('keyboard') as 'clavichord'. Certainly the modern pianist who eschewed Bach or Mozart on purist grounds would lose one of his most musically rewarding legacies.

The length of the harpsichord's and clavichord's survival, and the timing of the piano's ascendancy, naturally varied a good deal from one part of Europe to another; and various phases of the change are reflected in the kinds of music composed in different countries at various times. The repertory from this period – the period between the death of Bach and Handel and the emergence of Haydn and Mozart as major figures – is larger and more diverse in style than many pianists realize, and much of it is accessible in good modern editions. Different reflections of the speed of change from harpsichord or clavichord to piano can be found in, for example, the style of the conservative French composers (like Armand-Louis Couperin or Duphly), the more nearly Classical Italian keyboard writers (Platti, Galuppi, Grazioli, Rutini), the Iberians (Soler, Seixas, Blasco de Nebra), the Germans and Bohemians (some in Germany or Austria, like C. P. E. Bach's pupil Neefe in Bonn, or Kozeluch in Vienna; others abroad, like Schobert and Eckardt in Paris or Hässler in Russia) and the English (Nares, Hook).

The influence of Bach's sons, in particular, fostered the early growth of piano music as such. Although C. P. E. Bach, writing in 1753, turned to the clavichord for expressive subtlety unobtainable on the harpsichord, his impact on Haydn and hence on the later piano sonata was vital; the keyboard style of the piano was indeed strongly influenced by the clavichord. The piano also inherits and may do justice to the chromatic inflections of W. F. Bach's fugues or polonaises; J. C. Bach in fact heralded a new era when he played the instrument in public in London in 1768. Yet the proviso 'for pianoforte or harpsichord' lingered on title-pages for commercial reasons even when works were as imperatively pianistic as Beethoven's op.31 sonatas (1802). The harpsichord, most of its glories behind it, lingered as a continuo instrument, and the clavichord, with its frail dynamic range, had a later vogue. By the time of Mozart's sonatas and Haydn's middle-period ones the piano was rapidly developing and had proved itself the instrument of the future. Though still primarily domestic, it had a capacity for eloquence that made Mozart's supreme achievements in the concerto possible. It enabled keyboard music to keep pace with dramatic developments in the symphony, the string quartet, and in opera; parallel to the symphony and the quartet the important genre was the sonata, which by 1750 had become the standard label for extended solos (or duos) in more than one movement. The Italian fast–slow–fast pattern was to become the norm but by no means the rule. The Classical sonata thrived in two, three or four movements; it was infinitely flexible, assimilating minuets or sets of variations at will. It was the new vehicle, the new stronghold of expression, and the keyboard repertory from the time rests largely upon it (*see* SONATA).

2. THE AGE OF THE CLASSICAL SONATA. Many tributes have been paid to C. P. E. Bach's harmonic and formal originality. His serious but intimate manner, attuned to the clavichord and stylistically a halfway mark, may account for his later neglect by pianists. The sonatas of J. C. Bach prefigure a true piano style, representing the *galant* style at its best, and they had a considerable influence on Mozart. Haydn's sonatas, ranging from the 1750s to 1794 or 1795, illustrate both the growth of form and the takeover of the piano. Their confused numberings were not helped by his own approval of a collection (1799) that placed the last sonata first. Hoboken's chronological catalogue (1957), listing them under the 'work-group' XVI, is now generally followed, as here. The more recent Universal edition (ed. Christa Landon, 1963–4) adopted a revised system, however, accounting for fragments and lost works and increasing the total of 52 sonatas to 62.

Haydn's earliest sonatas, originally called 'partitas' or 'divertimentos', were lightweight works in the contemporary *galant* manner of Wagenseil or Alberti. The 'Alberti bass', offering a facile alternative to the more learned contrapuntal style, proved a standby for generations of keyboard composers, even the greatest. Although Vienna was more prone to Italian than north German influence, Haydn soon acknowledged his debt to C. P. E. Bach, whose 'Prussian' sonatas he studied on the clavichord. His own deepening art produced a landmark in expression in the C minor Sonata (no.20) of 1771. It exploited, as Mozart's sonata-form movements were to do, the pathos of recapitulating a major-key

second group in the tonic minor, and its dynamic contrasts demanded the piano. Haydn's other minor-key sonatas (e.g. nos.32, 36, 44) show that humour (e.g. in the popular no.37) was only one aspect of his musical genius. His sonatas thrive on unpredictability in form and texture. The slow movement of no.19 has a low-lying melodic line akin to a cello concerto, while no.30 in A links its three movements through the drama of surprise. Haydn's later sonatas are unequal since slighter works were tailored to needs or commissions, but no.49 in E♭, written for Marianne von Genzinger, is outstanding; its increasingly ornate Adagio was again dependent on the piano's cantabile.

Later notions of sonata form were often confounded by Haydn's readiness to carry first-subject material freely into the second group, as in the first movements of nos.50 and 52, sonatas written in London. The former exploited 'open pedal' effects and, in the finale, the higher compass of English pianos (such 'long' pedal marks – cf Beethoven's op.31 no.2 and op.53 – may demand discreet half-pedalling on modern pianos). No.52 in E♭ is comparable in grandeur with Haydn's London symphonies, abounding in orchestral sonorities and harmonic moves only possible on a 'well-tempered' keyboard. Its slow movement is, astonishingly, in E major, a key touched on in the first-movement development. Dittersdorf said of Haydn that 'he has the gift of sportiveness but he never loses the dignity of art'. This is borne out by two of his best-known separate pieces: the irrepressibly sportive Fantasia in C (1789), and the F minor Variations (1793), which imbue his favourite double-variation form with a dignified pathos.

Mozart's entire life-span fell between the dates of Haydn's first and last keyboard sonatas. As a child of nine Mozart adapted sonatas by J. C. Bach as concertos, already showing his grasp of a medium in which Haydn had surprisingly little to say. Though nurtured on the harpsichord Mozart soon preferred the piano. From Augsburg in 1777 he wrote that his D major Sonata (K311/284c), last of his first set of six, 'sounds exquisite on Stein's pianoforte'. His sonatas as a whole may be felt less representative than his concertos, where the drama of give-and-take and the stimulus of public performance inspired him. Yet cross-influences were strong. The rondo of K333/315c in B♭ has concerto-like exchanges and a full-scale cadenza; the opening of K457 in C minor is not only dramatic but operatic. On its publication (1785) Mozart prefaced K457 with a Fantasy (K475) in the same key, which creates a masterly unity from a wide-ranging series of episodes exploring all registers of the available keyboard. The earlier A minor Sonata K310/300d is another fine work of tragic character, standing apart from Mozart's other 'Paris' sonatas of the time. These, however, have their own attractions: K331/300i has its popular opening variations and final 'Alla turca', in part a parody of the crisper harpsichord style; K332/300k has a heartfelt Adagio that was further ornamented for printing (a clue to the filling-in implied in parts of Mozart's unpublished concertos, e.g. K488 and K491). Two brief quotations from the first movement of K333/315c show his gift for turning limitations into assets. The upper keyboard limit of f''' forced him to modify, hence to extend and enhance, the original on its return a 4th higher (ex.5). Subsequent extensions of the keyboard have tempted some editors to 'touch up' the classics, often producing anachronisms and, at worst, nullifying masterstrokes

Ex.5. Mozart: κ333/315*c*
(a)

(b)

(which the serious player can remedy by consulting an Urtext edition).

In 1782 Baron van Swieten encouraged Mozart's interest in fugues by Bach and Handel; this resulted in his 'Handelian' Suite κ399/385*i*, the Fantasy and Fugue κ394/383*a*, and a longer-term absorption in counterpoint, for example the deceptively difficult Sonata in D κ576. Yet even sonatas like κ545 ('for beginners') have become tests of a performer's sense of style. The minor key continued to call forth Mozart's most profoundly personal works – the A minor Rondo, the B minor Adagio – but he brought craft and depth to more conventionally brilliant works. The extrovert two-piano Sonata κ448/375*a* is ideal for its medium, but Mozart's four-hand duets raised a novel form (his very early κ19*d* is the first known duet sonata for one keyboard) to the highest level of art in the F major Sonata κ497 and the G major Variations κ501. On the question of style he wrote to his father in 1777 that 'everyone is amazed that I always keep strict time', adding the famous remark about phrases that 'should flow like oil'.

Clementi, at their meeting in 1781, was impressed by Mozart's cantabile playing, though Mozart was to dismiss him as a 'mechanicus', without 'a farthing's worth of taste or feeling'. Yet Crotch called Clementi 'the father of piano music' and Beethoven is known to have admired his sonatas. A great pioneer may not be a great creative genius, and despite occasional champions (including Vladimir Horowitz) Clementi hardly retains his former appeal. His sonatas cover an even wider period than Haydn's, though most were written before the turn of the century (i.e. before he involved himself in publishing and piano making). The earliest (1770) reveal him as the virtuoso, and abound in rapid 3rds, 6ths and octaves. His virtuoso manner was handed on to many pupils (e.g. Cramer and Moscheles), and indulged in his famous collection of studies, *Gradus ad Parnassum* (1817), which also shows a preoccupation with fugue and canon. Of his later sonatas the G minor, 'Didone abbandonata', exploited the romantic pathos of a *scena tragica*. The influence of Clementi's 'through-composed' movements on Beethoven may have been underrated (see Truscott).

Clementi was not the only keyboard composer to have had short-lived importance. The sonatas of Dussek, one of the first travelling virtuosos, are rarely heard. But before the close of the 18th century he was extracting rich sonorities from the English pianos of his time (see ex.6). Remarkable prophecies of Schumann and Brahms may be found in his F minor Sonata op.77 ('L'invocation'). Also rarely heard are the works of

Hummel, a pupil of Mozart and Clementi and the teacher of Czerny, Henselt and Thalberg; his prolific output included countless rondos and sets of variations, which carried an ornate pianistic style into the new higher reaches of the keyboard, and his later works contain pianistic devices which form a tenuous link between Mozart and Chopin. The four sonatas of Weber have had more regular supporters, though ironically his most popular piano work, the *Aufforderung zum Tanze*, is best known in Berlioz's orchestration. Conversely, Schubert's piano sonatas survived a long period of neglect but are in the ascendant. In the long run, true originality and what Tovey called 'contrasted proportions' seem to have prevailed over mere innovation and facility. Beethoven turned Clementi's 3rds and 6ths to far stronger structural purpose in his early C major Sonata op.2 no.3.

Ex.6 Dussek: op.10 no.2

The Beethoven piano sonatas, out of deference to Bach's '48', were called the 'new testament' of keyboard music with good reason. One may reflect on their range of character and scale, from the modest demands of op.49 nos.1 and 2 to the grand middle-period manner of the Waldstein op.53, or 'Appassionata' op.57; or compare the intimacy of op.78 with the colossus of the Hammerklavier op.106. A vast stylistic and spiritual journey is represented by this whole series of sonatas (the familiar 'three-period' division is inevitable), aided by (and even demanding) significant development in the piano itself. Beethoven's sketches from all periods reveal the patience and willpower that gave the finished works such architectural strength, through, for example, the close interweaving of dynamics and key-relations. The earliest sonatas, discounting three (1783) from his Bonn years, are mature even when viewed from the lofty heights of the late period. Beethoven's ability to give significance to the briefest figure is apparent from the index of opening bars (e.g. op.2 nos.1–3). Some of the early slow movements are profound: op.2 no.3; op.7; op.10 no.3. This last (1798) has a tragic Largo e mesto, in which the leadback already shows a structural mastery of dynamics, including the drama of measured silence (ex.7).

The first movement of the 'Moonlight' op.27 no.2

Ex.7 Beethoven: op.10 no.3

sustains a quiet, slow melodic line against gently reiterated triplets. As with Schubert's G♭ Impromptu the balance between theme and accompaniment, both given to the same hand, was a pianistic subtlety. Yet it may be argued that Beethoven added less to the technique of pianism than Clementi and certainly less than Chopin. Though famous as a pianist and extemporizer in his earlier days, he evidently regarded the instrument as a means, not an end, and the supreme musical value of Beethoven's piano music calls for a scrupulous respect for the text. A fragment from von Bülow's edition of op.106 (ex.8b), compared with the original (ex.8a), shows the danger of carrying interpretative zeal into print.

Ex.8 Beethoven: op.106

(a)   Tempo I

(b)

Whereas the more popular sonatas (e.g. opp.13, 27 no.2, 53, 57) have long appealed to players of all schools, those from op.101 onwards present a physical and mental challenge. Beethoven's growing absorption in fugal writing reached a climax in the finale of op.106;

in op.110 he alternated recitative, arioso and fugue more introspectively. Variation form, with prolonged trills used climactically, was a feature of op.109 and op.111, the latter a two-movement work in which the turbulence of a C minor Allegro is resolved in the major-key arietta. Of Beethoven's many separate sets of variations, the 'Prometheus' op.35 and the 32 in C minor (1807) are substantial, but the largest and greatest was on a waltz by Diabelli op.120. Having been asked to contribute a single variation to a composite work (*Vaterländische Künstlerverein*) Beethoven resourcefully produced 33. This was his last important piano work. The rest of Diabelli's scheme yielded a cross-section of talents in the Viennese musical scene, from names long forgotten to the expected fluency of Hummel, Czerny and Kalkbrenner, and the distinction of Schubert and the 11-year-old Liszt. It included the Czech-born Tomášek and his pupil Voříšek, who merit a revival of interest for their other works: Tomášek's *Eclogues* and *Dithyrambs* and Voříšek's Impromptus foreshadow the shorter piano pieces of Schubert and Schumann. In this respect Beethoven's three sets of *Bagatelles* must be mentioned, as well as his Fantasy op.77, which captures the improvisatory manner of his performing days.

Schubert was the last great composer of the period to give significant attention to the piano sonata. As a master of song his approach to the larger instrumental forms has sometimes been compared unfavourably with Beethoven's. Schumann however spoke of his 'heavenly length' and Tovey of the 'artistic resource' of his tonality. The frequent digressions in his long paragraphs were often disarmingly spontaneous and poetic, and the occasionally awkward piano writing came partly from his need to be, as it were, singer and accompanist in one. The warmth of the 'little' A major Sonata D664, and the austerity of the A minor D784, show his range, and in D845 (also A minor) he achieved an original compression of first-movement contrasts. Schubert completed his last three sonatas (D958–60) two months before his death. They are all on a spacious four-movement plan, and the B♭, D960, is generally regarded as the consummation of his piano music. Yet for a long time they were overlooked in favour of his shorter pieces, the *Moments musicaux*, impromptus and the many sets of dances. The cyclic form of the 'Wanderer' Fantasy inspired Liszt to arrange it for piano and orchestra, though such a public display of virtuosity can hardly have been Schubert's intention. He sought refuge in the piano as the ideal domestic instrument, versatile and independent. Hence his large output of duets for four hands, including the F minor Fantasy and the 'Grand Duo', the latter of symphonic proportions. Only one public concert of Schubert's works was given in his lifetime. The fate of Beethoven's piano sonatas was scarcely different despite his wide acclaim. They were still 'private' music. The age of the serious public recital had yet to come, though the situation was to change rapidly.

3. VERSATILITY AND VIRTUOSITY. The public display of the classical repertory had to wait for artists like Clara Schumann, who played Beethoven's op.57 in Vienna in 1838, or for Anton Rubinstein's 'historical recitals' (1886). The piano showed its versatility in other directions. Before the turn of the century Daniel Steibelt had drawn audiences with his fantasias and 'battle-pieces', exploiting tremolando effects. The popularity of

operatic medleys and naively descriptive works, for example Kotzwara's *The Battle of Prague* (1790), was encouraged by the use of 'Turkish' pedals and other percussive devices. Their novelty faded in the light of more important strides in piano-making: the six- and then seven-octave keyboard, overstringing, Erard's double-escapement action (1822), and experiments with metal bracings leading to the iron frame (1825). The added string tension led to greater brilliance, and the studies by Clementi, Cramer, Czerny and others stressed the piano's potential. No other single instrument could match its self-sufficiency and flexible dynamic scope. 'Le concert, c'est moi' wrote Liszt from Paris in 1839, referring to a one-man programme largely of arrangements and improvisation (the familiar term 'recital' was applied on his London visit the following year). A rage for flamboyant transcriptions, variations on operatic airs, popular waltzes etc persisted throughout the Romantic era from Thalberg to Godowsky. Many of these pieces survive because of their period charm, ingenuity, and attraction for the modern virtuoso. Thalberg is credited with the ingenious device of sharing the melodic line between the hands, throwing off arpeggios to right and left in turn, a 'three hand' illusion that was adopted in more serious contexts by Mendelssohn and Liszt. There is a vast gulf in purpose between showpieces like Thalberg's 'Home, sweet home' Variations and straightforward keyboard arrangements designed to make works available to a wider public. Liszt became master of both, and the piano's value as a deputy had long been recognized. Piano scores of operas date back to Galuppi (1758) and Beethoven himself arranged his string quartet 'Grosse Fuge' for four hands.

The enthusiasm of the early 19th-century piano specialists coincided with the climax and dissolution of the Classical style. Yet as piano music became at once more personal and more public the Romantics showed their allegiance to the past in various ways. Mendelssohn, who revived Bach's *St Matthew Passion* in 1829, wrote pianistically effective Preludes and Fugues (op.35). His piano works were copious, including sonatas, fantasias and variations (the *Variations sérieuses* are the best known), but his many *Lieder ohne Worte* established a favourite miniature genre, and the light-fingered brilliance of pieces like the *Rondo capriccioso* and the E minor Scherzo (from op.16) reflected the orchestra of *A Midsummer Night's Dream*. Cross-currents continued to enrich the textures of piano writing. The piano successfully adopted the cantilena and *fioritura* of Italian opera (Rossini, Bellini). John Field, born in Dublin and exploited by Clementi, wrote 'nocturnes' before Chopin, with right-hand melodies blossoming into florid decorations (ex.9), a tendency that was to become a regular feature of Romantic piano music when used by Chopin and Liszt. Although Chopin absorbed Field's keyboard patterns

Ex.9 Field: Nocturne no.4 in A

legato

along with those of Hummel, Moscheles and Kalkbrenner, his lasting hold is unique.

4. ROMANTICISM. Chopin was the ideal specialist, exploring and mastering but never overreaching his resources. But he was far more than a 'pianist's composer': even his studies are works of art, each turning some technical purpose to poetic or dramatic ends. His pianistic mastery involved extended arpeggios, based on the 10th rather than the octave, and complex figures unthinkable on a keyboard 'without pedal'. His tunefulness, influenced both by opera and by Polish folk music, was matched by outstanding harmonic originality and a superb sense of form. He could produce consummate examples of the simplest ternary structure (e.g. the posthumous E minor Waltz); but also, displaying in his large works a mastery of development of a freer kind than that of the Classical sonata, he could devise original forms of remarkable urgency – even when conveying, as in the ballades or the barcarolle, an atmosphere of improvisation. These qualities made successes of his two maturer sonatas, op.35 and op.58, though Schumann said of the former (which includes the famous 'Funeral March'): 'he has yoked together four of his maddest children'. Although the striking character of some of Chopin's studies invited nicknames ('Revolutionary', 'Winter Wind' etc) his Romanticism did not, like Schumann's, thrive on literary images. Yet he expressed the full force of his Polish nationalism in the wide variety of his mazurkas and polonaises. In the waltzes he cultivated a 'salon' manner with no sacrifice of taste, and in the nocturnes he brought to perfection a form inherited from Field. The 24 Preludes op.28 epitomize the range of his genius. Like Mozart, Chopin developed and deepened his style within a short life, from the flamboyance of his own early 'Mozart' Variations op.2, to the exquisite restraint of the Berceuse and the profound drama of the F minor Ballade.

'Forget that you are a virtuoso' was Schumann's injunction to Clara Wieck, later his wife, on the subject of performing his *Kinderszenen*. Yet many of Schumann's earlier piano works were indeed virtuoso pieces, such as the Toccata in C (1832), the Symphonic Studies, and the Fantasy op.17. The second movement of the Fantasy is notorious for the perilous leaps in the coda. In the first movement Schumann alluded to the main theme of Beethoven's *An die ferne Geliebte*. The most 'literary' of composers, he showed his fondness for esoteric devices in the 'Abegg' Variations op.1, and further play with musical letters unified the 'scènes mignonnes' of *Carnaval* op.9, in which the passionate and dreamy sides of Schumann's own nature are reflected in the characters of Florestan and Eusebius. His large output ranged from children's pieces to sonatas, of which the G minor op.22 is generally favoured for its conciseness; his sense of 'elaborate mosaic' (Tovey) suited the more episodic forms (e.g. *Kreisleriana*, *Faschingsschwank*) or groups of short pieces (e.g. *Fantasiestücke*). Despite the virtuosity of such works as the Toccata, or of 'Paganini' in *Carnaval*, he later turned from the extravagances of the Liszt school and welcomed the young Brahms (1853).

Liszt however became a living legend and was hailed as 'a darling of the gods' even by the non-Wagnerian Hanslick. As a champion of new music and avid transcriber he arranged Berlioz's *Symphonie fantastique* as early as 1833, only a year after its completion and revision by the composer. Arguments of taste do not alter the fact that he towers above other fluent piano composers: Henselt, Litolff, Moszkowski, Lyapunov. The *Etudes d'exécution transcendante* (final version, 1852) testify to his own prodigious pianism and gift for pictorialism (e.g. *Mazeppa*, *Feux follets*), carried further in the four books of *Années de pèlerinage*, the result of his travels in Switzerland and Italy. In his Sonata in B minor (1853) Liszt subjugated extreme technical demands – rapid double octaves, scales in 3rds, complex textures – to the formal needs of a large one-movement work, providing contrast and unity by means of thematic transformation. The bravura style and extension of technique that yielded Liszt's operatic paraphrases, the popular Hungarian Rhapsodies, and brilliant concert pieces like the 'Mephisto' Waltzes, does not characterize his last piano works, harmonically advanced and prophetic, like *Nuages gris* (ex.10). For all

Ex.10 Liszt: *Nuages gris*

his contradictory elements, Liszt had a colossal impact on late Romantics (Skryabin, Rakhmaninov) and post-Romantics (Debussy, Bartók). Among neglected composers he admired was the French recluse Alkan, whose 'orchestral' treatment of the piano was reflected in the application of the terms 'symphony' and 'concerto' to solo works. The Bach revival was also welcomed by Liszt, whose piano transcriptions of Bach's organ pieces were often played for their 'effectiveness' to the exclusion of the '48'.

Brahms's devotion to Bach was of a different kind, and opponents of the New German School (exemplified by Liszt and Wagner) rallied to Brahms. His three early piano sonatas (opp.1, 2 and 5), acclaimed by Schumann, were in the grand manner, but he soon turned to classical variation form and the virtues of strict counterpoint. In his Handel Variations op.24 Brahms incorporated canonic devices and a final fugue based on solid musical thought. The two books of Studies on a Theme of Paganini op.35, also in variation form, provide a technical challenge of a special kind, sharing muscular and musical problems between the hands, as in the 'blind' octaves of no.11 in the second book (ex.11). In the Ballades op.10, Brahms foreshadowed his later groups of shorter pieces, op.76 and opp.116–19. 'Intermezzo' and 'Capriccio' became favourite titles, the former generally more intimate and songlike, the latter more brilliant or turbulent. He made a few transcriptions (of Bach, Chopin, Gluck), and composed for piano duet his popular waltzes and Hungarian Dances. The solo Schumann Variations op.9 and the duet variations on Schumann's *Letzte Gedanke* op.23 were tributes to his mentor. The later 'St Anthony' set, better known in its orchestral version, appeared in one for two pianos. Though scorned for conservatism by Wolf, Brahms was seen as 'progressive' by Schoenberg. His influence on piano music was subtler and more sobering than that of

Chopin or Liszt, and his reconciliation between Romantic feeling and Classical design may be regarded as the end of an era.

Ex.11 Brahms: op.35

Other German late Romantics became absorbed with orchestra and opera to the exclusion of the piano as a vital medium. Richard Strauss, like Wagner, wrote unimportant piano music, though Reger expanded (and inflated) a Brahmsian technique, for example in his Bach and Telemann variations. While pianists from many nations made pilgrimages to study with Liszt in Weimar, the 19th-century repertory began to gain from other sources and attitudes.

5. 19TH-CENTURY NATIONAL TRENDS. By the mid-19th century the piano's multiple role was clear. It was the soloist, the general practitioner, the standard accompanist, and the versatile substitute. The modest upright served both amateur and professional and took music into the home, while in public the virtuoso held his sway with the increasingly powerful concert grand. The market for undemanding pieces was easily met, for example by the prolific output of Stephen Heller. Greater ease of travel spread influences more rapidly, and the nationalistic parts in Liszt and Chopin bred many imitators. Musical nationalism was found appealing in an exotic as well as a patriotic sense.

In Russia pianism developed during this period, though Glinka's variations, nocturnes and polkas hardly competed in the international market, and Tchaikovsky's solo piano music, from 'characteristic pieces' to larger forms, has never approached the universality of his B♭ minor Concerto. Whereas Borodin and Rimsky-Korsakov wrote piano music – including fugues – as a matter of course, two of their compatriots produced masterworks. Musorgsky's *Pictures at an Exhibition* (1874) holds together a series of tableaux with a recurring 'promenade' with a strong folk flavour: the keyboard writing is stark but impressive, an effect somewhat softened in Ravel's opulent orchestration of the work. Balakirev's *Islamey* is uncompromisingly for the virtuoso, with its two 'oriental' themes worked up to a brilliant climax. Repeated notes and octave displacements add to its colour and its risks.

In Czechoslovakia Smetana's polkas and Dvořák's four-hand Slavonic Dances expressed national aspirations more modestly. Their more ambitious piano works (e.g. Smetana's pictorial *Macbeth and the Witches*) were no parallel to their orchestral achievements. The original departures of Janáček belong to the 20th century, as does Grieg's *Slåttar* (1902), though the charm of his *Lyric Pieces* had proved his gift as a miniaturist. His fellow Norwegian Sinding is famous for one salon piece, *Rustle of Spring*, which decks out a simple tune with the harp-like arpeggios beloved of the later Romantics. The American MacDowell, pupil of Raff, retains a place in the repertory for his picturesque suites (e.g. *Woodland Sketches, Sea Pieces*). In Finland Sibelius's early Sonata in F (1893) hardly betrayed the great symphonist, though his later *Kyllikki* (1904) are more characteristic. From Denmark, Nielsen's few piano works were to be more significant. In Britain, Sterndale Bennett, though praised by Schumann and Mendelssohn and master of an elaborate keyboard style, somehow lacked the personality to outlive his period; and the medium was only a sideline for the leaders of the 'new' renaissance, Parry, Stanford and Elgar. In Spain the folk element ruled strong, however, and the guitar continued to encourage keyboard imitation. The harpsichord had been a nearer relation (and had inspired Scarlatti and Soler) but the piano added the drama of dynamic nuance and quasi-vocal inflection. Albéniz, Granados and Falla became the new masters, and the exotic Spanish influence affected others from Glinka to Debussy and Ravel.

France was a fruitful area for the new repertory. Paris, where a host of imported styles, from the 18th-century German émigrés to Chopin and Liszt, had flourished, now produced (or absorbed) Franck, Saint-Saëns, Chabrier, Fauré, Satie. Franck, Belgian and part-German, wrote his two important piano works late in life: the Prelude, Chorale and Fugue (1884) and the Prelude, Aria and Finale (1887); the former especially succeeded in tempering a Lisztian technique and cyclic form to solemn purpose, often recalling (and almost demanding) an organ pedal-board (ex.12). The facility

Ex.12 Franck: Prelude, Chorale and Fugue

gentle resignation in subtly pianistic textures, turning more naturally to Chopin's forms (nocturnes, barcarolles). The apparently eccentric and childlike piano pieces of Satie, like *Gymnopédies* (1888), are important for their immediate influence on Debussy and Ravel and their longer-term effect on 20th-century avant-garde thought.

6. THE GROWTH OF PIANISM, 1900–1940. If the 20th century has so far produced less music for the piano than did the 19th or 18th, the range of its achievement, in terms of widening the expressive potential of the instrument, is notable. With the single exception of Bartók, no composer has contributed to the repertory to anything like the same extent as did Haydn, Mozart, Beethoven or Schubert. Nevertheless, there has been more written for the piano since 1900 than for any other solo instrument, and it is possible to chart the main lines of 20th-century musical thinking from a study of the piano music alone, particularly since a number of composers (including Debussy, Bartók, Schoenberg, Boulez and Stockhausen) have made some of their most important stylistic 'discoveries' through their keyboard works.

Although it may appear that Bartók was the most radical of the early 20th-century composers in attitude to keyboard technique, Debussy, barely a generation his senior, represents an even more fundamental secession from the 19th-century Austro-German pianistic tradition. His imaginative disregard of the essentially percussive qualities of the instrument enabled him to develop a new pianism, dependent on sonority rather than attack, on subtle dynamic shading rather than sustained cantabile. His own playing was evidently notable for its range of colour within a *pianissimo* dynamic (aided by the use of both pedals) and this is reflected in a Chopinesque notation that details every nuance of touch, as well as of dynamics and phrasing. Although precise indications of pedalling are rare, Debussy's use of sustained bass notes reveals a new awareness of the possibilities of the sustaining pedal and of the minute differences that can obtain between the total clarity of legato pedalling and the total blurring of undamped strings (see ex.13).

Ravel's more traditional virtuosity, however, marries this new 'impressionism' to a bravura inherited from

Ex.13 Debussy: *La terrasse des audiences du clair de lune*

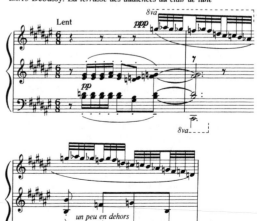

and fertility of Saint-Saëns had a far less personal imprint, and none of his solo works has matched the popularity of his concertos or, for orchestra with two-piano cooperation, his *Carnaval des animaux*. Chabrier was the paradox of a devoted Wagnerite whose own music debunked over-solemnity (e.g. the *Bourrée fantasque*, 1891). The sonata, in its former grander sense, continued to yield increasingly to lighter forms, though Dukas and d'Indy wrote isolated examples. Fauré, unique in combining lightness and depth, expressed a

Liszt, developing a characteristic brilliance of keyboard usage that was, in turn, to have as great an influence on Bartók as were Debussy's more far-reaching experiments in keyboard sonority. As early as 1911, Bartók was stressing the percussive aspect of the instrument through the use of ostinato rhythms; this 'xylophonic' approach was later extended to embrace the more vibraphone-like qualities of a *laissez vibrer* that made expressive use of the suspension and decline of a sound as well as of its initial attack. He was also to continue a Beethovenian investigation of the sharply defined contrasts possible within the instrument's wide dynamic range, and of the contrasts in sound quality suggested by its high, middle and low registers. He continued Debussy's exploration of the resonances obtainable from overlapping harmonies coloured by the sustaining pedal, which later proved equally important in the light of the instrumental techniques proposed by such composers as Messiaen, Boulez and Stockhausen.

Debussy's most important contribution to contemporary pianism resulted from his refusal to acknowledge the essentially mechanical limitations of the instrument, but Ives was to make his contribution through a disregard for the limitations of the ten fingers of the pianist, some of his chords necessitating the assistance of a third hand or of the pianist's arms. If Ives was a prophet ahead of his time, his almost exact contemporary, Rakhmaninov, while making a sizable contribution to piano literature, proved much less significant in relation to the future of both musical thought and keyboard technique. Similarly, Prokofiev's nine sonatas and numerous smaller pieces are characteristic of his own stylistic scope and Lisztian virtuosity rather than indicative of future developments. The same is true of the works of other important composers of piano music during the first three decades of the century, including those of Valen, Pijper, Dohnányi, Martinů, Casella, Skalkottas, Shostakovich and, most notably, Hindemith.

Although he was not a pianist, Schoenberg made his two most important musical 'discoveries', that of atonality and, later, of 12-note composition, through the medium of the piano. The last of the Three Pieces op.11 (his first work for solo piano) was confidently cast in a language that owed little either to the impressionistic colouring of contemporary French music or to the more Romantic, large-scale gestures of the late 19th-century Austro-German keyboard composers. The massive stretch of its atonal counterpoint, combined with the extreme contrasts of its fleeting textures and eruptive dynamics (in addition to the exploration of keyboard harmonics in the first piece) remained unique for almost 40 years, until overtaken by still more demanding techniques after World War II. Equally significant in the trend away from Romantic rhetoric, his Six Little Pieces op.19 explore the expressive qualities of the instrument (mostly at the lowest end of the dynamic range) with a restraint more typical of his friend and pupil, Webern, whose single mature work for the piano was such a major landmark. Webern's Variations op.27 renounce the grandiose technical obsessions of the recent past to return to a much earlier conception of instrumental music as an extension of, and almost indistinguishable from, vocal music. The essential simplicity of the piece becomes complex through the continual overlap of wide-ranging contrapuntal lines (and thus of the pianist's hands), demanding a new technical approach to extended part-writing, as well as to the delicate balance

between harmonic and rhythmic phrasing (see ex.14). Webern's piece, with its structural finesse and 'abstracted' *espressivo*, has cast its benevolent shadow on all subsequent composers of piano music.

Ex.14 Webern: Variations, op.27

Stravinsky's pianistic influence extends well beyond the few works he originally wrote for keyboard; not least because he was one of the first composers to establish the piano as an orchestral instrument (Symphony in Three Movements, *Petrushka*, *The Wedding*). His piano (or piano duet) versions of many of his orchestral works are, in effect, original pianistic conceptions, such was his instinctive feeling for the characteristic spacing of keyboard sonorities.

During the 1920s the American composer Henry Cowell, then regarded merely as an interesting eccentric, began to experiment with hand and arm chord clusters as a means of colouring and outlining his melodic shapes and of creating harmonic 'areas' rather than defined chords. In addition to these keyboard effects he explored the production of sounds directly from the strings themselves, either as pizzicatos; as glissandos on single strings or across the strings (as in *The Banshee*) or in conjunction with silently depressed keys (in order to produce glissando chords, as in *Aeolian Harp*); or as harmonics, produced by the simultaneous 'stopping' of relevant strings.

7. AFTER WORLD WAR II. The possibilities explored by Cowell were woven by John Cage into the aleatory fabric of his most substantial work for piano, *Music of Changes*. Cage also undertook a more radical examination of the piano as a resonating body: the accompaniment to his song, *The Wonderful Widow of Eighteen Springs*, is rendered entirely on various parts of the frame, which is made to resonate in sympathy with the strings by depressing the sustaining pedal. Moreover, he transformed the basic sound quality of the instrument by a 'prepared' extension of its timbral possibilities: by forcing certain strings to vibrate against wedges made of various materials (metal, wood, rubber etc), Cage opened up a range of keyboard sonorities limited only by the possible damage to the instrument. This, in turn, led to as many variations in the basically harp-like sound of the strings themselves. Robert Sherlaw Johnson has used timpani sticks to stunning effect (in his second sonata), as well as other types of 'beaters'; plectra of differing weights and materials have also been used (the eerie sound of a nail-file glissando in Gerhard's *Gemini* is a good example), as have wooden blocks of varying widths (used by David Bedford to produce string clusters in *Piece for Mo*). Bedford has also made

weirdly fascinating use of rotating glass milk bottles (at the end of his song *Come in here, child*). The palette of available pianistic colour has continued to be expanded and refined, notably in the chamber works of the American George Crumb, whose (gadgetless) effects are completely viable, often beautiful and never gimmicky.

It seems unlikely, however, that such methods of sound production can become established ingredients of instrumental technique unless manufacturers standardize the shape of the piano's mechanical structure. Because strings freely available on one make of instrument may be hidden or separated by crossbars on another, it is often impossible to carry out the composer's instructions to the letter. In any case, a whole new range of 'string' techniques would need to be developed and practised by the pianist. It is perhaps indicative of the lack of sophistication with regard to these techniques that the two postwar composers to have written the most substantial number of piano works, Boulez and Stockhausen, have so far ignored these more peripheral possibilities, as indeed have the majority of other important contributors to the mid-20th-century repertory, including Barber, Sessions, Copland, Feldman, Tippett, Maxwell Davies and Messiaen.

Even the most opulent of Messiaen's recent scores have a muscular background related to the kind of rhythmic counterpoint first developed in his *Mode des valeurs et d'intensité* (1949), in which the basic idea of a rhythmic ostinato was widened into an 'ostinato system' of serial control over the separate elements of duration, dynamics and attack as well as of pitch. This made almost insuperable demands on the performer (as, later, did Boulez's *Structures* for two pianos and Stockhausen's early piano pieces) since such minute degrees of expressive and rhythmic definition, within lines 'broken' by extremes of pitch, are scarcely realizable except by electronic means (see ex.15). The intellectual strictures of Messiaen's early works eventually

Ex.15 Messiaen: *Mode de valeurs et d'intensités*

merged with a freer, unmistakable pianism in his *Cantéyodjayâ* and later in the vast *Catalogue d'oiseaux*, creating a range of keyboard colour as pervasive in its influence on the works of younger composers as was that of Bartók or Stravinsky on the music of an earlier generation.

Boulez's three sonatas and Stockhausen's *Klavierstücke* (all dating from the late 1940s and 1950s) stand as models of contemporary keyboard writing, as yet unsurpassed in the variety of their neo-virtuosity or in the range of their textural contrasts and expressive sonorities. Musically they display a sharp-edged violence whose stinging contrasts require a comparably 'honed' performing technique – so that these pieces (which had at first seemed unplayable) have had the effect of enlarging the scope and the standards of virtuoso pianism. They have demanded an increase in pianistic speed and agility in order to encompass complex counterpoint (whether of lines or chords) often involving hand-crossing to an extent that even Webern would not have regarded as possible. They also require an ability to define each degree of a dynamic palette that extends from *ppp* to *fff* and beyond, in combination with as many varieties of touch or attack. In the case of Stockhausen, these controls must additionally be linked to an ability to play cluster chords of precisely defined exterior limits, whether these take the form of single attacks, arpeggiated decorations or multiple glissandos (see ex.16). Moreover, all these new technical requirements involve asymmetrical shapes that need to be mastered as thoroughly as symmetrical scales and arpeggios.

In such works, and in pieces by such stylistically diverse composers as Barraqué, Dallapiccola, Berio, Pousseur, Xenakis, Carter and Cage, pedal technique is no longer left to the good taste of the performer but must comply with the specific demands of the score. The use of the sustaining pedal has become as integral to musical expression as dynamics or phrasing; techniques such as half-pedalling, 'after'-pedalling (catching the resonance of a chord after releasing the attack) and 'flutter'-pedalling (effecting the gradual release of an attack) have become commonplace. An increasing number of works (Boulez's Sonata no.3, Stockhausen's *Klavierstücke V–XI* and Berio's *Sequenza IV*, for instance) also require the use of the centre pedal on concert instruments to free selected strings from the damping mechanism, so allowing them to vibrate in sympathy with any other notes which may be sounded. Berio's *Sequenza IV*, built on the 'ground bass' effect of such sustained notes or chords continually reinforced by the movement of the decorations superimposed on them, provides an ideal study in the use and management of the centre pedal.

See also EDITIONS, HISTORICAL, §§2–4, 6–8.

BIBLIOGRAPHY
GENERAL REFERENCE
W. Niemann: *Das Klavierbuch: Geschichte der Klaviermusik und ihre Meister* (Leipzig, 1922)

E. Blom: *The Romance of the Piano* (London, 1928)

D. F. Tovey: *Essays in Musical Analysis* (London, 1935–9)

A. Lockwood: *Notes on the Literature of the Piano* (Ann Arbor and London, 1940)

A. Loesser: *Men, Women and Pianos* (London, 1940)

W. Georgii: *Klaviermusik* (Zurich and Freiburg, 1941, 4/1965)

D. Brook: *Masters of the Keyboard* (London, 1946)

E. Hutcheson: *The Literature of the Piano* (New York, 1948, rev. 2/1964/*R*1973)

J. Friskin and I. Freundlich: *Music for the Piano ... from 1580 to 1952* (New York, 1954/*R*1973)

J. Gillespie: *Five Centuries of Keyboard Music* (Belmont, Calif., 1965/*R*1972)

F. E. Kirby: *A Short History of Keyboard Music* (New York, 1966)

K. Wolters: *Handbuch der Klavierliteratur, i* (Zurich and Freiburg, 1967)

M. Hinson: *Keyboard Bibliography* (Cincinnati, 1968)

——: *Guide to the Pianist's Repertoire*, ed. I. Freundlich (Bloomington, Ind., 1973) [comprehensive bibliography]

Ex.16 Stockhausen: Klavierstück X

Clusterglissandi schnell und leicht ohne Rücksicht auf nicht ansprechende Tasten

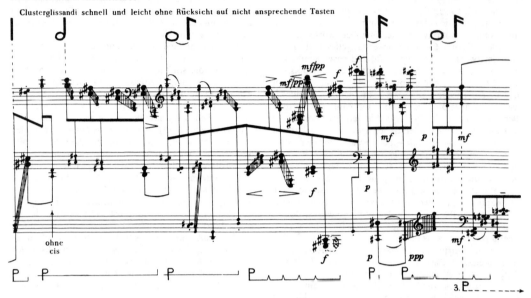

SPECIFIC STUDIES

E. J. Dent: 'The Pianoforte and its Influence on Modern Music', *MQ*, ii (1916), 271

A. Cortot: *La musique française de piano* (Paris, 1930–48; i–ii, Eng. trans., 1932)

C. Parrish: *The Early Piano and its Influence on Keyboard Technique and Composition in the Eighteenth Century* (diss., Harvard U., 1939)

J. F. Russell: 'Mozart and the Pianoforte', *MR*, i (1940), 226

N. Broder: 'Mozart and the Clavier', *MQ*, xxvii (1941), 422

E. Reeser: *De zonen van Bach* (Amsterdam, 1941; Eng. trans., 1946)

C. Parrish: 'Haydn and the Piano', *JAMS*, i/1 (1948), 27

J. Kirkpatrick: 'American Piano Music: 1900–1950', *MTNA Proceedings*, xliv (1950), 35

F. H. Garvin: *The Beginning of the Romantic Piano Concerto* (New York, 1952)

D. Stone: *The Italian Sonata for Harpsichord and Pianoforte in the Eighteenth Century* (*1730–90*) (diss., Harvard U., 1952)

A. G. Hess: 'The Transition from Harpsichord to Piano', *GSJ*, vi (1953), 75

K. Dale: *Nineteenth Century Piano Music* (London, 1954) [foreword by Myra Hess]

H. F. Wolf: *The 20th Century Piano Sonata* (diss., Boston U., 1957)

E. Blom: 'The Prophesies of Dussek', *Classics Major and Minor* (London, 1958), 88

N. Demuth: *French Piano Music* (London, 1958)

T. L. Fritz: *The Development of Russian Piano Music as Seen in the Literature of Mussorgsky, Rachmaninoff, Scriabin, and Prokofiev* (diss., U. of Southern California, 1959)

P. F. Ganz: *The Development of the Etude for Pianoforte* (diss., Northwestern U., 1960)

J. Lade: 'Modern Composers and the Harpsichord', *The Consort*, xix (1962), 128

W. S. Newman: *The Sonata in the Classic Era* (Chapel Hill, 1963, 2/1972)

E. Badura-Skoda: 'Textural Problems in Masterpieces of the Eighteenth and Nineteenth Centuries', *MQ*, li (1965), 301

T. A. Brown: *The Aesthetics of Robert Schumann in Relation to his Piano Music 1830–1840* (diss., U. of Wisconsin, 1965)

L. D. Stein: *The Performance of Twelve-tone and Serial Music for the Piano* (diss., U. of Southern California, 1965)

M. J. E. Brown: 'Towards an Edition of the Pianoforte Sonatas', *Essays on Schubert* (New York, 1966), 197

K. Heuschneider: *The Piano Sonata in the 18th Century in Italy* (Cape Town, 1966)

D. L. Arlton: *American Piano Sonatas of the Twentieth Century: Selective Analysis and Annotated Index* (diss., Columbia U., 1968)

M. K. Ellis: *The French Piano Character Piece of the Nineteenth and Early Twentieth Centuries* (diss., Indiana U., 1969)

E. Glusman: *The Early Nineteenth-century Lyric Piano Piece* (diss., Columbia U., 1969)

W. S. Newman: *The Sonata since Beethoven* (Chapel Hill, 1969, rev. 2/1972)

K. Michałowski: *Bibliografia chopinowska 1849–1969* (Kraków, 1970)

W. S. Newman: 'Beethoven's Pianos Versus his Piano Ideals', *JAMS*, xxiii (1970), 484

H. Truscott: 'The Piano Music – I', *The Beethoven Companion*, ed. D. Arnold and N. Fortune (London, 1971)

K. Michałowski: 'Bibliografia chopinowska 1970–1973', *Rocznik chopinowski*, ix (1975), 121–75

HOWARD FERGUSON (I), GLYN JENKINS (II)
DENIS MATTHEWS (III, 1–5), SUSAN BRADSHAW (III, 6–7)

Keyboard music: bibliography. This bibliography is one of a series which, taken as a whole, aims to provide a comprehensive coverage of the literature on music from the end of the classical age to about 1600. National bibliographies for the major western European areas are supplemented by general bibliographies at the ends of specific articles (e.g. PLAINCHANT). Thus the early history of keyboard music will be found in the following bibliography, but details of its relationship with other aspects of music will often also be found elsewhere, as well as in articles on specific instruments, instrumental forms and composers. This bibliography goes further than 1600 in order to include some major studies on the first half of the 17th century. This brings it into line with the lists of sources given in SOURCES OF KEYBOARD MUSIC. The bibliography is divided into two sections; the first lists the more important editions of the music, many of which are presented in short form since the full details may be found elsewhere, either in the list of historical editions (*see* EDITIONS, HISTORICAL) or under the names of individual composers. The second is concerned with writings about keyboard music: here studies of the work of a single composer have been largely excluded; this section is further subdivided to facilitate references to the music of particular areas.

I. Editions: 1. Collected editions. 2. Anthologies. II. Literature: 1. General. 2. Italy. 3. France. 4. Germany and the area using German tablature. 5. Low Countries. 6. Spain and Portugal. 7. Great Britain.

I. EDITIONS

I. 1. COLLECTED EDITIONS
Alphabetical list, excluding the article
Antiquitates musicae in Polonia (AMP) (1963–): i–x *The Pelplin*

Tablature; xv *The Organ Tablatures of Warsaw*
Archives des maîtres de l'orgue, ed. F. A. Guilmant and A. Pirro (Paris, 1898–1911/*R*1972): i Titelouze, *Oeuvres complètes*; iii Roberday, *Fugues et Caprices*; x *Liber Fratrum Cruciferorum*
Arte musicale in Italia (AMI) (1899–): iii *Composizioni per organo o cembalo secoli xvi, xvii e xviii*
Classici della musica italiana, ed. G. d'Annunzio (Milan, 1918–21): vi G. Cavazzoni, *Musica sacra*; xxvi M. A. Rossi, *Composizioni*
Classici musicali italiani (CMI) (1941–56): i Cavazzoni, *Recerchari*
Corpus mensurabilis musicae (CMM) (1947–): xx *Transcriptions of Chansons* [Attaingnant]; lvii *Keyboard Music . . . in Codex Faenza 117*
Corpus of Early Keyboard Music (CEKM) (1963–): i *Keyboard Music of the Fourteenth and Fifteenth Centuries*; ii Facoli, *Collected Works*; iii Salvatore, *Collected Keyboard Works*; iv H. Praetorius, *Organ Magnificats*; vi Jan z Lublina, *Tablature*; viii *Keyboard Dances from the Earlier 16th Century*; ix C. Antegnati, *L'Antegnata*; x *Keyboard Music from Polish Manuscripts*; xii E. Pasquini, *Collected Keyboard Works*; xiii Steigleder, *Compositions for Keyboard*; xiv *Spanish Organ Masters after . . . Cabezón*; xv M. A. Rossi, *Works for Keyboard*; xvii *The Tablature of Celle*; xviii C. Gibbons, *Keyboard Compositions*; xix *Elizabeth Rogers' Virginal Book*; xx Cima, *Ricercari et canzoni*; xxiv *Neapolitan Keyboard Composers c. 1600*; xxvi P. Cornet, *Collected Keyboard Works*; xxvii Mareschall, *Selected Works*; xxx Frescobaldi, *Keyboard Compositions . . . in MSS*; xxxii *Seventeenth-century Keyboard Music in Chigi MSS*; xxxiii Radino, *Il primo libro d'intavolatura*; xxxiv Padovano, *Works* and Anon., *Neapolitan Composers circa 1600*; xxxv Pellegrini, *Canzoni*; xxxvi Erbach, *Collected Keyboard Compositions*; xxxvii *Keyboard Music at Castell'Arquato*
Denkmäler der Tonkunst in Österreich (DTÖ) (1894–): viii, Jg.iv/1, xiii, Jg.vi/2, xxi, Jg.x/2 Froberger, *Orgel- und Klavierwerke*
Denkmäler deutscher Tonkunst (DDT), 1st ser. (1901–31): i Scheidt, *Tabulatura nova*
Denkmäler deutscher Tonkunst, 2nd ser.: Denkmäler der Tonkunst in Bayern (DTB) (1900–31): vii, Jg.iv/2 Hassler, *Werke für Orgel und Klavier*; xxxii, Jg.xxi–xxiv Kindermann, *Ausgewählte Werke*
Documenta musicologica (DM), 1st ser., *Druckschriften-Faksimiles* (1951–): xi Bermudo, *Declaración*; 2nd ser., *Handschriften-Faksimiles* (1955–): i *Das Buxheimer Orgelbuch*
Early English Church Music (EECM) (1963–): vi *Early Tudor Organ Music*, i; x *Early Tudor Organ Music*, ii
Early Keyboard Music (EKM); vols i–xxii also known as English Keyboard Music (London, 1955–): i T. Tomkins, *Nine Organ Pieces*; ii T. Tomkins, *Fifteen Dances*; iii *The Mulliner Book, Eleven Pieces*; iv Byrd, *Fifteen Pieces*; vi Locke, *Keyboard Suites*; vii Locke, *Organ Voluntaries*; viii Bull, *Ten Pieces*; ix *Clement Matchett's Virginal Book*; xi G. Farnaby, *Seventeen Pieces*; xii–xiii Morley, *Keyboard Works*; xiv Tisdall, *Complete Keyboard Works*; xv *Early Scottish Keyboard Music*; xvi *The Fitzwilliam Virginal Book, Twenty-four Pieces*; xix *Parthenia*; xxiii *Intabolatura nova di balli*; xxiv *Tisdale's Virginal Book*; xxv O. Gibbons, *Nine Organ Pieces*; xxvi O. Gibbons, *Eight Keyboard Pieces*; xxviii *Musick's Hand-maid*
Erbe deutscher Musik (EDM), 1st ser., *Reichsdenkmale* (1935–43): xxxvi, xl *Die Lüneburger Orgeltabulatur KN 208a*; xxxvii–xxxix *Das Buxheimer Orgelbuch*; liv–lv Buchner, *Fundamentum*
Exempla musica neerlandica (EMN) (1964): ii Sweelinck, *Werken . . . uit het 'Celler Klavierbuch 1662'*
Hispania schola musica sacra, ed. F. Pedrell (Barcelona, 1894–8/ *R*1971): iii–iv, vii–viii Cabezón, *Obras de música*
Historical Anthology of Music (HAM) (1946–50, rev. 2/1949)
Liber organi, ed. E. Kaller (Mainz, 1931–58): viii *Orgelmeister der Gotik*
L'organiste liturgique, ed. G. Litaize and J. Bonfils (Paris, 1953–): xiii Du Mont, *L'oeuvre pour clavier*; xviii, xxxi, lviii, lix *Les préclassiques français*; xxxiv, xxxviii, xli G. Cavazzoni, *Second livre d'orgue*; liv, lvii Trabaci, *Ricercate*
Monumenta musicae belgicae (MMBel) (1932–51, 1960–66/*R*): iv Guillet, Macque and Luython, *Werken*
Monumenta musica neerlandica (MMN) (1959–): iii *Dutch Keyboard Music*
Monumenti di musica italiana (MMI) (1961–): i/1 Merula, *Composizioni*; i/2 Frescobaldi, *Nove toccate*; i/3–4 Trabaci, *Composizioni*
Monumentos de la música española (MME) (1941–): ii Venegas de Henestrosa, *Libro de cifra nueva*; vi, xii Correa de Arauxo, *Libro de tientos*; xxvii–xxix Cabezón, *Obras de música*
Musica britannica (MB) (1951–, rev. 2/1954–): i *The Mulliner Book*; v T. Tomkins, *Keyboard Music*; xiv, xix Bull, *Complete Keyboard Works*; xx O. Gibbons, *Keyboard Music*; xxiv G. and R. Farnaby, *Keyboard Music*; xxvii–xxviii Byrd, *Keyboard music*
Musicological Studies and Documents (MSD) (1951–): x *An Early Fifteenth-century Italian Source . . . the Codex Faenza . . . 117*; xxviii Bradshaw, *The Origin of the Toccata*
Musikalische Denkmäler (Mainz, 1955–): iii *46 Choräle*
Musik alter Meister (MAM) (1954–): ii Brassicanus, *Sechs Choralbearbeitungen*; ix *Zwei Orgelstücke*

Organum, 4th ser., *Orgelmusik*, ed. M. Seiffert (Leipzig, 1925/*Rc*1960): i Scheidemann, *Fünfzehn Präludien und Fugen*; ii *Orgel-Meister I*; x *Anonymi der norddeutschen Schule*; xi Froberger, *10 Orgelwerke*; xx Siefert, *13 Fantasien à 3*; xxi *Orgel-Meister IV*
Orgel (Leipzig, 1957), 2nd ser., *Werke alter Meister*: ix *Italienische und süddeutsche Orgelstücke*; xi C. Erbach, *Drei Introitus*; xii D. Strungk, *Zwei Choralfantasien*
Orgue et liturgie, ed. N. Dufourcq and others (Paris, 1954–): iii Palestrina [attrib.], *8 Ricercari*; vi L. Couperin, *L'oeuvre d'orgue*; xlvii Bermudo, *Oeuvres d'orgue (1555)*; xlix T. de Santa María, *Arte de tañer fantasia (1565)*; lxiii, lxv Mayone, *Secondo libro*
Portugaliae musica (PM), ser. A (1959–): i, iii Rodrigues Coelho, *Flores de musica*; vii Costa de Lisboa, *Tenção*; xix *Antología de organistas do século XVI*
Publications de la Société française de musicologie (PSFM), 1st ser. (1925–44, 1947, 1952–, partial rev. 2/1965): i *Deux livres d'orgue*; v *Treize motets*
Publikationen älterer praktischer und theoretischer Musikwerke (PÄMw) (1873–1905/*R*1967): xi, Jg.x Virdung, *Musica getutscht*; xx, Jg.xxiv M. Agricola, *Musica instrumentalis deudsch*
Le pupitre: collection de musique ancienne, ed. F. Lesure (Paris, 1967–): v *Chansons françaises pour orgue vers 1550*; xviii L. Couperin, *Pièces de clavecin*; xliv Roberday, *Fugues et caprices*
Schott's Anthology of Early Keyboard Music (1950–): i *Ten Pieces by Hugh Aston and others*; ii *Twelve Pieces from Mulliner's Book*; iii *Seven Virginal Pieces from B.M. Add. 30486*; iv *Pieces from the Tomkins Manuscript*; v *Fifteen Pieces from Elizabeth Rogers's Virginal Book*
Schweizerische Musikdenkmäler (SMd) (1955–): vi–vii *Tabulaturen des XVI. Jahrhunderts*
Süddeutsche Orgelmeister des Barock (SOB) (Altötting, 1955–): vii Froberger, *Toccaten*; ix Kindermann, *Harmonica organica*
Uitgave van oudere Noord-Nederlandsche Meesterwerken (UVNM) (1869–): iii *Organ Compositions by Sweelinck and Scheidt*; xix A. van Noordt, *Tabulatuur-boeck*

I. 2. ANTHOLOGIES

Alphabetical list, excluding the article; for works of single composers see the articles for the composers concerned.

Allein Gott in der Höh sei Ehr: 20 Choralvariationen der deutschen Sweelinck-Schule, ed. H. J. Moser and T. Fedtke (Kassel and Basle, 1953)
Altenglische Orgelmusik, ed. D. Stevens (Kassel and Basle, 1953)
Altes Spielbuch aus der Zeit um 1500: Liber Fridolini Sichery, ed. F. J. Giesbert (Mainz, 1936)
Altitalienische Versetten in allen Kirchentonarten für Orgel oder andere Tasteninstrumente, ed. M. S. Kastner (Mainz, 1957)
Anne Cromwell's Virginal Book, 1638, ed. H. Ferguson (London, 1974)
Anonymi der norddeutschen Schule: sechs Praeludien und Fugen, Organum, 4th ser., x (Leipzig, 1925/*Rc*1960)
Antología de organistas clásicos españoles, ed. F. Pedrell (Madrid, 1908/*R*1968 as *Anthology of Classical Spanish Organists*)
Antología de organistas clásicos españoles, ed. L. de Villalba Muñoz (Madrid, 1914)
Antología de organistas do século XVI, PM, ser. A, xix (1969)
Antología de organistas españoles del siglo xvii, ed. H. Anglès (Barcelona, 1965–7)
Antologia di musica antica e moderna per pianoforte, ed. G. Tagliapietra (Milan, 1931–2)
Antologia organistica italiana (sec. XVI–XVII), ed. S. dalla Libera (Milan, 1957)
Balli antichi veneziani per cembalo, ed. K. Jeppesen (Copenhagen, 1962)
Buxheimer Orgelbuch, DM, 2nd ser., *Handschriften-Faksimiles*, i; EDM, xxxvii–xxxix (1958–9)
Cantantibus organis: Sammlung von Orgelstücken alter Meister, ed. E. Kraus (Kassel, 1958–)
Chansons françaises pour orgue vers 1550, Le pupitre, v (Paris, 1968)
Chansons italiennes de la fin du XVIe *siècle*, ed. A. Wotquenne-Plattel (Leipzig, n.d.)
Chansons und Tänze: Pariser Tabulaturdrucke für Tasteninstrumente aus dem Jahre 1530 von Pierre Attaingnant, ed. E. Bernoulli (Munich, 1914)
Choralbearbeitungen aus der Tabulatur Lynar A 1, ed. H. J. Moser and T. Fedtke (Kassel and Basle, 1956)
Choralbearbeitungen und freie Orgelstücke der deutschen Sweelinck-Schule, aus den Tabulaturen Lynar B 1, B 3, B 6, und Graues Kloster Ms. 52, ed. H. J. Moser and T. Fedtke (Kassel and Basle, 1955)
Classici italiani dell'organo, ed. I. Fuser (Padua, 1955)
Clavichord Music of the Seventeenth Century, ed. T. Dart (London, 1960, rev. 2/1964)
Clement Matchett's Virginal Book (1612), EKM, ix (London, 1957)
Composizioni per organo o cembalo secoli xvi, xvii e xviii, AMI, iii (n.d.)
Cravistas portuguezes, ed. M. S. Kastner (Mainz, 1935–50)
Deux livres d'orgue parus chez Pierre Attaingnant en 1531, PSFM, i

(1925)

Dublin Virginal Manuscript, WE, iii (1954, rev. 2/1964)

Dutch Keyboard Music of the Sixteenth and Seventeenth Centuries, MMN, iii (1961)

Early English Harmony from the 10th to the 15th Century, i, ed. H. E. Wooldridge (London, 1897)

Early English Keyboard Music, ed. H. Ferguson (London, 1971)

Early English Organ Music, ed. M. Glyn (London, 1939)

Early Fifteenth-century Italian Source of Keyboard Music: the Codex Faenza, Biblioteca Comunale, 117, MSD, x (1961)

Early French Keyboard Music, ed. H. Ferguson (London, 1966)

Early German Keyboard Music, ed. H. Ferguson (London, 1970)

Early Italian Keyboard Music, ed. H. Ferguson (London, 1968)

Early Keyboard Music, ed. K. Oesterle (New York, 1904)

Early Scottish Keyboard Music, EKM, xv (London, 1958)

Early Spanish Organ Music, ed. J. Muset (New York, 1948)

Early Tudor Organ Music I: Music for the Office, EECM, vi (1966)

Early Tudor Organ Music II: Music for the Mass, EECM, x (1969)

Elizabethan Virginal Music, ed. H. F. Redlich (Vienna, 1938)

Elizabeth Rogers' Virginal Book 1656, CEKM, xix (1971)

Faenza Codex: see *Early Fifteenth-century Italian Source*; *Keyboard Music of the Late Middle Ages*

Fifteen Pieces from Elizabeth Rogers's Virginal Book, Schott's Anthology of Early Keyboard Music, v (1951)

Fitzwilliam Virginal Book, ed. J. A. Fuller Maitland and W. B. Squire (Leipzig, 1899/R)

Fitzwilliam Virginal Book, Twenty-four Pieces, EKM, xvi (London, 1964)

Frühmeister der deutschen Orgelkunst, ed. H. J. Moser and F. Heitmann (Leipzig, 1930)

Harpsichord Pieces from Dr. Bull's Flemish Tablature, ed. H. F. Redlich (Wilhelmshaven, 1958)

Intabolatura nova di balli (*Venice, 1551*), EKM, xxiii (London, 1965)

Intabulatura nova (*Venedig 1551*), ed. F. Cerha (Vienna and Munich, 1975)

Italienische und süddeutsche Orgelstücke des frühen 17. Jahrhunderts, Die Orgel, 2nd ser., ix (Leipzig, 1957)

Keyboard Dances from the Earlier 16th Century, CEKM, viii (1965)

Keyboard Music at Castell'Arquato, CEKM, xxxvii (1975–)

Keyboard Music from Polish Manuscripts, CEKM, x (1965–7)

Keyboard Music of the Fourteenth and Fifteenth Centuries, CEKM, i (1963)

Keyboard Music of the Late Middle Ages in Codex Faenza 117, CMM, lvii (1972)

Klaviertänze des 16. Jahrhunderts, ed. H. Halbig (Stuttgart, 1928)

Liber Fratrum Cruciferorum, Archives des maîtres de l'orgue, x (Paris, 1909–11)

Libro de cifra nueva . . . [ed.] Luys Venegas de Henestrosa (*Alcalá . . ., 1557*), MME, ii (1944)

Locheimer Liederbuch nebst der Ars Organisandi von Conrad Paumann, ed. F. W. Arnold and H. Bellermann (Leipzig, 1926/R)

Locheimer Liederbuch und Fundamentum Organisandi des Conrad Paumann, ed. K. Ameln (Berlin, 1925) [facs.]

Lüneburger Orgeltabulatur KN 208a, EDM, xxxvi, xl (1957)

Maîtres français de l'orgue, ed. F. Raugel (Paris, 1925)

Melothesia, Keyboard Suites, ed. A. Kooiker (University Park, Penn., and London, 1968)

Mulliner Book, MB, i (1951, rev. 2/1954)

Mulliner Book, Eleven Pieces, EKM, iii (1951)

Musick's Hand-maid, EKM, xxviii (1969)

Music of Earlier Times: see *Sing- und Spielmusik aus älterer Zeit*

Musik aus früher Zeit für Klavier (*1350–1650*), ed. W. Apel (Mainz, 1934)

Neapolitan Keyboard Composers c. 1600, CEKM, xxiv (1967)

Nederlandse klaviermuziek: see *Dutch Keyboard Music*

Old Spanish Organ Music, ed. C. Reiss (Copenhagen, 1960)

Organ Compositions by Sweelinck and Scheidt, UVNM, iii (1871)

Organo italiano, 1567–1619, ed. G. Frotscher (Copenhagen, 1960)

Organ Tablatures of Warsaw, Musical Society I/200, AMP, xv (1968)

Orgel-Meister I, Organum, 4th ser., ii (Leipzig, 1925/Rc1960)

Orgel-Meister IV, Organum, 4th ser., xxi (Leipzig, 1925/Rc1960)

Orgelmeister der Gotik, Liber organi, viii (Mainz, 1938)

Orgeltabulatur von 1448 des Adam Ileborgh aus Stendal, ed. G. Most (Stendal, 1954) [facs.]

Parthenia, ed. E. F. Rimbault (London, 1847); ed. M. Glyn (London, 1927); ed. O. E. Deutsch (London, 1942) [facs.]; ed. K. Stone (New York, 1951); EKM, xix (1960, rev. 2/1962)

Parthenia In-violata, ed. T. Dart and R. J. Wolfe (New York, 1961) [facs.]

Pelplin Tablature, AMP, i–x (1963–70)

Préclassiques français, Organiste liturgique, xviii, xxxi, lviii, lix (Paris, 1957–8)

Priscilla Bunbury's Virginal Book, Sixteen Pieces, ed. J. L. Boston (London, 1962)

Seventeenth-century Keyboard Music in the Chigi Manuscripts of the Vatican Library, CEKM, xxxii (1968)

Seven Virginal Pieces from B.M.Add.30486, Schott's Anthology of Early Keyboard Music, iii (1951)

Silva ibérica de música para tecla de los siglos XVI, XVII y XVIII, ed. M. S. Kastner (Mainz, 1954–65)

Sing- und Spielmusik aus älterer Zeit, ed. J. Wolf (Leipzig, 1926, repr. New York, 1946, as *Music of Earlier Times*) [collection of exx. for Wolf, *Geschichte der Musik*]

Spanish Organ Masters after Antonio de Cabezón, CEKM, xiv (1971)

Spielbuch für Kleinorgel oder andere Tasten-Instrumente, ed. W. Auler (Leipzig, 1942)

Tablature of Celle 1601, CEKM, xvii (1971)

Tabulaturen des XVI. Jahrhunderts, SMd, vi–vii (1967–70)

Ten Pieces by Hugh Aston and others [*GB-Lbm* Roy.App.58], Schott's Anthology of Early Keyboard Music, i (1951)

Tisdale's Virginal Book, EKM, xxiv (1966)

Tomkins Manuscript, Pieces from the [*GB-Lbm* Add.29996], Schott's Anthology of Early Keyboard Music, iv (1951)

Transcriptions of Chansons for Keyboard [published by Pierre Attaingnant], CMM, xx (1961)

Treize motets et un prélude pour orgue parus chez Pierre Attaingnant en 1531, PSFM, v (1930)

Twelve Pieces from Mulliner's Book [*GB-Lbm* Add.30513], Schott's Anthology of Early Keyboard Music, ii (1951)

Twenty-five Pieces for Keyed Instruments from Cosyn's Virginal Book, ed. J. A. Fuller Maitland and W. B. Squire (London, 1923)

Two Elizabethan Keyboard Duets, ed. F. Dawes (London, 1949) [by T. Tomkins and N. Carleton (the younger)]

Zwei Orgelstücke aus einer Kärntner Orgeltabulatur des 16. Jahr., MAM, ix (1958)

II. LITERATURE

II, 1. GENERAL

BrownI

J. W. von Wasielewski: *Geschichte der Instrumentalmusik im 16. Jahrhundert* (Berlin, 1878)

A. G. Ritter: *Zur Geschichte des Orgelspiels, vornehmlich des deutschen, im 14. bis zum Anfange des 18. Jahrhunderts* (Leipzig, 1884/R1969)

M. Seiffert: 'J. P. Sweelinck und seine direkten deutschen Schüler', *VMw*, vii (1891), 145–260

——: *Geschichte der Klaviermusik*, i (Leipzig, 1899/R1966)

O. Kinkeldey: *Orgel und Klavier in der Musik des 16. Jahrhunderts* (Leipzig, 1910)

J. Wolf: *Handbuch der Notationskunde* (Leipzig, 1913–19/R1963)

A. Schering: *Studien zur Geschichte der Frührenaissance* (Leipzig, 1914)

J. Müller-Blattau: *Grundzüge einer Geschichte der Fuge* (Königsberg, 1923, 2/1931)

L. Schrade: 'Ein Beitrag zur Geschichte der Tokkata', *ZMw*, viii (1925–6), 610

A. Pirro: 'L'art des organistes', *EMDC*, II/ii (1926), 1181–374

O. Deffner: *Über die Entwicklung der Fantasie für Tasteninstrumente bis Sweelinck* (diss., U. of Kiel, 1927)

L. Schrade: *Die ältesten Denkmäler der Orgelmusik als Beitrag zu einer Geschichte der Toccata* (Münster, 1928)

K. G. Fellerer: *Orgel und Orgelmusik: ihre Geschichte* (Augsburg, 1929)

Y. Rokseth: *La musique d'orgue au XVe siècle et au début du XVIe* (Paris, 1930)

E. Valentin: *Die Entwicklung der Tokkata im 17. und 18. Jahrhundert (bis J. S. Bach)* (Münster, 1930)

J. Wolf: *Musikalische Schrifttafeln* (Bückeburg, 1930)

L. Schrade: *Die handschriftliche Überlieferung der ältesten Instrumental-Musik* (Lahr, 1931/R1968)

H. Klotz: *Über die Orgelkunst der Gotik, der Renaissance und des Barock* (Kassel, 1934)

A. Schering: 'Zur Alternatim-Orgelmesse', *ZMw*, xvii (1935), 19

G. Frotscher: *Geschichte des Orgel-Spiels und der Orgel-Komposition* (Berlin, 1935–6, enlarged 3/1966)

W. Apel: 'Neapolitan Links between Cabezón and Frescobaldi', *MQ*, xxiv (1938), 419

G. Reese: *Music in the Middle Ages* (New York, 1940)

W. Georgii: *Klaviermusik* (Zurich, 1941, 4/1965)

O. Gombosi: 'About Dance and Dance Music in the Late Middle Ages', *MQ*, xxvii (1941), 289

W. Apel: *The Notation of Polyphonic Music 900–1600* (Cambridge, Mass., 1942, 5/1953/R1961; Ger. trans., 1962)

——: *Masters of the Keyboard* (Cambridge, Mass., 1947/R1952)

——: 'Early History of the Organ', *Speculum*, xxiii (1948), 191

R. U. Nelson: *The Technique of Variation* (Berkeley, 1948)

W. Apel: 'The Early Development of the Organ Ricercar', *MD*, iii (1949), 139

G. S. Bedbrook: *Keyboard Music from the Middle Ages to the Beginnings of the Baroque* (London, 1949/R1973, with introduction by F. E. Kirby)

R. Lunelli: 'Contributi trentini alle relazioni musicali fra l'Italia e la

Germania nel Rinascimento', *AcM*, xxi (1949), 41

H. H. Eggebrecht: 'Terminus "Ricercar" ', *AMw*, ix (1952), 137

M. S. Kastner: 'Parallels and Discrepancies between English and Spanish Keyboard Music of the Sixteenth and Seventeenth Century', *AnM*, vii (1952), 77–115

H. Hering: 'Das Tokkatische', *Mf*, vii (1954), 277

M. S. Kastner: 'Rapports entre Schlick et Cabezón', *La musique instrumentale de la Renaissance: CNRS Paris 1954*, 217

G. Reese: *Music in the Renaissance* (New York, 1954, rev. 2/1959)

K. von Fischer: 'Chaconne und Passacaglia', *RBM*, xii (1958), 19

C. Parrish: *The Notation of Medieval Music* (London, 1958)

I. Horsley: 'The 16th-century Variation: a New Historical Survey', *JAMS*, xii (1959), 118

W. Apel: 'Drei plus drei plus zwei = vier plus vier', *AcM*, xxxii (1960), 29

Y. Rokseth: 'The Instrumental Music of the Middle Ages and Early Sixteenth Century', *NOHM*, iii (1960), 406–65

W. Young: 'Keyboard Music to 1600', *MD*, xvi (1962), 115–50; xvii (1963), 163–93

J. Gillespie: *Five Centuries of Keyboard Music* (Berkeley and Los Angeles, 1965/R1972)

F. E. Kirby: *A Short History of Keyboard Music* (New York, 1966)

J. Caldwell: 'The Organ in the Medieval Latin Liturgy, 800–1500', *PRMA*, xciii (1966–7), 11

W. Apel: *Geschichte der Orgel- und Klaviermusik bis 1700* (Kassel, 1967; Eng. trans., rev. 1972)

——: 'Probleme der Alternierung in der liturgischen Orgelmusik bis 1600', *Congresso internazionale sul tema Claudio Monteverdi e il suo tempo: Venezia, Mantova e Cremona 1968*, 171

——: 'Solo Instrumental Music', *NOHM*, iv (1968), 602–708

M. C. Bradshaw: *The Origin of the Toccata*, MSD, xxviii (1972)

II. 2. ITALY

SartoriB

L. Torchi: *La musica strumentale in Italia nei secoli XVI, XVII e XVIII* (Turin, 1901)

G. Pannain: *Le origini e lo sviluppo dell'arte pianistica in Italia dal 1500 al 1730 circa* (Naples, 1919)

L. Schrade: 'Tänze aus einer anonymen italienischen Tabulatur', *ZMw*, x (1927–8), 449

K. Jeppesen: *Die italienische Orgelmusik am Anfang des Cinquecento* (Copenhagen, 1943, rev. 2/1960)

F. Morel: *Gerolamo Frescobaldi* (Winterthur, 1945)

D. Plamenac: 'Keyboard Music of the 14th Century in Codex Faenza 117', *JAMS*, iv (1951), 179

A. Machabey: *Girolamo Frescobaldi Ferrarensis* (Paris, 1952)

D. Plamenac: 'New Light on Codex Faenza 117', *IMSCR, v Utrecht 1952*, 310

N. Pirrotta: 'Note su un codice di antiche musiche per tastiera' [*I-FZc* 117], *RMI*, lvi (1954), 333

K. Jeppesen: 'Eine frühe Orgelmesse aus Castell'Arquato', *AMw*, xii (1955), 187

M. S. Kastner: 'Una intavolatura d'organo italiana del 1598', *CHM*, ii (1957), 237

L. F. Tagliavini: 'Un musicista cremonese dimenticato', *CHM*, ii (1957), 413

R. Lunelli: *L'arte organaria del Rinascimento in Roma* (Florence, 1958)

W. E. McKee: *The Music of Florientio Maschera (1540–1584)* (diss., North Texas State College, 1958)

B. Becherini: *Catalogo dei manoscritti musicali della Biblioteca nazionale di Firenze* (Kassel, 1959)

W. Apel: 'Tänze und Arien für Klavier aus dem Jahre 1588', *AMw*, xvii (1960), 51

U. Prota-Giurleo: 'Giovanni Maria Trabaci e gli organisti della Real cappella di palazzo di Napoli', *L'organo*, i (1960), 185

O. Mischiati: 'Tornano alla luce i ricercari della "Musica nova" del 1540', *L'organo*, ii (1961), 73

H. C. Slim: *The Keyboard Ricercar and Fantasia in Italy, ca. 1500–1550* (diss., Harvard U., 1961)

W. Apel: 'Die handschriftliche Überlieferung der Klavierwerke Frescobaldis', *Festschrift Karl Gustav Fellerer* (Regensburg, 1962), 40

——: 'Die süditalienische Clavierschule des 17. Jahrhunderts', *AcM*, xxxiv (1962), 128

K. Jeppesen: 'Ein altvenetianisches Tanzbuch' [*I-Vnm* Ital. IV. 1227], *Festschrift Karl Gustav Fellerer* (Regensburg, 1962), 245

U. Prota-Giurleo: 'Due campioni della scuola napoletana del sec.xvii', *L'organo*, iii (1962), 115

H. C. Slim: 'Keyboard Music at Castell'Arquato by an Early Madrigalist', *JAMS*, xv (1962), 35

S. Kunze: *Die Instrumentalmusik Giovanni Gabrielis* (Tutzing, 1963)

D. Plamenac: 'A Note on the Rearrangement of Fa', *JAMS*, xvii (1964), 78

——: 'Faventina', *Liber amicorum Charles van den Borren* (Antwerp,

1964), 145

H. B. Lincoln: 'I manoscritti chigiani di musica organo-cembalistica della Biblioteca apostolica vaticana', *L'organo*, v (1964–7), 63

D. Plamenac: 'Alcune osservazioni sulla struttura del codice 117 della Biblioteca comunale di Faenza', *L'ars nova italiana del trecento II: Certaldo 1969*, 161

M. Kugler: *Die Tastenmusik im Codex Faenza* (Tutzing, 1972)

II. 3. FRANCE

A. de La Fage: *Essais de dipthérographie musicale* (Paris, 1864/R1964)

E. von Werra: 'Beiträge zur Geschichte des französischen Orgelspiels', *KJb*, xxiii (1910), 37

A. Tessier: 'Une pièce d'orgue de Charles Raquet et le Mersenne de la Bibliothèque des Minimes de Paris', *RdM*, x (1929), 275

W. Apel: 'Du nouveau sur la musique française pour orgue au XVIe siècle', *ReM* (1937), no.172, p.96

N. Dufourcq: *La musique d'orgue française de Jean Titelouze à Jehan Alain* (Paris, 1941, 2/1949)

A. C. Howell jr: 'French Baroque Organ Music and the Eight Church Tones', *JAMS*, xi (1958), 106

W. Apel: 'Attaingnant: Quatorze Gaillardes', *Mf*, xiv (1961), 361

D. Heartz: *Pierre Attaingnant: Royal Printer of Music* (Berkeley and Los Angeles, 1969)

N. Dufourcq: *Le livre de l'orgue français 1589–1789, iv: La musique* (Paris, 1972)

II. 4. GERMANY AND THE AREA USING GERMAN TABLATURE

[R. Eitner]: 'Das Buxheimer Orgelbuch', *MMg*, xx (1888), suppl.2 [incl. exx. from this MS and that of Kleber]

H. Panum: 'Melchior Schild oder Schildt', *MMg*, xx (1888), 27 [see also suppl.3, p.35 for 2 pieces]

C. Päsler: 'Fundamentbuch von Hans von Constanz', *VMw*, v (1889), 1–192

W. Nagel: 'Fundamentum Authore Johanne Buchnero', *MMg*, xxiii (1891), 71–109

J. Richter: *Katalog der Musik-Sammlung auf der Universitäts-Bibliothek in Basel* (Leipzig, 1892)

H. K. Löwenfeld: *Leonhard Kleber und seine Orgeltabulatur* (Berlin, 1897)

A. Chybiński: 'Polnische Musik und Musikkultur des 16. Jahrhunderts in ihren Beziehungen zu Deutschland', *SIMG*, xiii (1911–12), 463–505

W. Merian: *Die Tabulaturen des Organisten Hans Kotter* (Leipzig, 1916)

M. Grafczyński: *Über die Orgeltabulatur des Martin Leopolita* (diss., U. of Vienna, 1919)

Z. Jachimecki: 'Eine polnische Orgeltabulatur aus dem Jahre 1548', *ZMw*, ii (1919–20), 206

C. Mahrenholz: *Samuel Scheidt: sein Leben und sein Werk* (Leipzig, 1924/R1968)

W. Merian: *Der Tanz in den deutschen Tabulaturbüchern des 16. Jahrhunderts* (Leipzig, 1927/R1968)

H. J. Moser: *Paul Hofhaimer: ein Lied- und Orgelmeister des deutschen Humanismus* (Stuttgart, 1929, rev. 2/1965) [incl. transcr. of complete works repr. from *91 gesammelte Tonsätze Paul Hofhaimers und seines Kreises* (Stuttgart, 1929)]

——: 'Eine Trienter Orgeltabulatur aus Hofhaimers Zeit', *Studien zur Musikgeschichte: Festschrift für Guido Adler* (Vienna, 1930), 84

A. Scheide: *Zur Geschichte des Choralvorspiels* (Hildburghausen, 1930)

P. Hamburger: 'Ein handschriftliches Klavierbuch aus der ersten Hälfte des 17. Jahrhunderts', *ZMw*, xiii (1930–31), 133

G. Kittler: *Geschichte des protestantischen Orgelchorals* (Ückermünde, 1931)

F. Dietrich: *Geschichte des deutschen Orgelchorals im 17. Jahrhundert* (Kassel, 1932)

F. Feldmann: 'Ein Tabulaturfragment des Breslauer Dominikaner Klosters aus der Zeit Paumanns', *ZMw*, xv (1932–3), 241

W. Apel: 'Die Tabulatur des Adam Ileborgh', *ZMw*, xvi (1934), 193–212

O. A. Baumann: *Das deutsche Lied und seine Bearbeitungen in den frühen Orgeltabulaturen* (Kassel, 1934)

J. Handschin: 'Orgelfunktionen in Frankfurt a. M. im 15. und 14. Jahrhundert', *ZMw*, xvii (1935), 108

A. Chybiński: 'Warszawska tabulatura organowa z XVII wieku', *PRM*, ii (1936), 100

L. Schrade: 'Die Messe in der Orgelmusik des 15. Jahrhunderts', *AMf*, i (1936), 129–75

W. Apel: 'Early German Keyboard Music', *MQ*, xxiii (1937), 210

F. Feldmann: 'Mittelalterliche Musik und Musikpflege in Schlesien', *Deutsches Archiv für Landes- und Volksforschung* (1937)

F. Hirtler: 'Neu aufgefundene Orgelstücke von J. U. Steigleder und Johann Benn', *AMf*, ii (1937), 92

F. Feldmann: *Musik und Musikpflege im mittelalterlichen Schlesien* (Breslau, 1938/R1973)

G. Knoche: 'Der Organist Adam Ileborgh von Stendal: Beiträge zur Erforschung seiner Lebensumstände', *Festschrift des 600jähr. Gym-*

nasiums zu Stendal (Stendal, 1938); repr. in *Franziskanische Studien*, xxviii/1 (1941)

W. R. Nef: 'Der St. Galler Organist Fridolin Sicher und seine Orgeltabulatur', *Schweizerisches Jb für Musikwissenschaft*, vii (1938), 3–215

L. Schrade: 'The Organ in the Mass of the 15th Century', *MQ*, xxviii (1942), 329, 467

F. Welter: *Katalog der Musikalien der Ratsbücherei Lüneburg* (Lippstadt, 1950)

H. Federhofer: 'Eine Kärntner Orgeltabulatur', *Carinthia I*, cxlii (1952), 330

C. Mahrenholz: 'Aufgabe und Bedeutung der *Tabulatura nova*', *Musica*, viii (1954), 88

G. Most: *Die Orgeltabulatur von 1448 des Adam Ileborgh aus Stendal* (Stendal, 1954)

M. Reimann: 'Pasticcios und Parodien in norddeutschen Klaviertabulaturen', *Mf*, viii (1955), 265

W. Schrammek: 'Zur Numerierung im Buxheimer Orgelbuch', *Mf*, ix (1956), 298

J. H. Schmidt: *Johannes Buchner, Leben und Werk* (diss., U. of Freiburg, 1957)

J. H. van der Meer: 'The Keyboard Works in the Vienna Bull Manuscript', *TVNM*, xviii/2 (1957), 72–105

A. Basso: 'La musica strumentale del rinascimento polacco', *RaM*, xxviii (1958), 293

K. Kotterba: *Die Orgeltabulatur des Leonhard Kleber: ein Beitrag zur Orgelmusik der ersten Hälfte des 16. Jahrhunderts* (diss., U. of Freiburg, 1958)

G. Pietzsch: 'Orgelbauer, Organisten und Orgelspiel in Deutschland bis zum Ende des 16. Jahrhunderts', *Mf*, xi (1958), 160, 307, 455; xii (1959), 25, 152, 294, 415; xiii (1960), 34

A. Osostowicz: 'Nieznany motęt Diomedesa Catoni i jego utwory organowe z toruńskiej tabulatury', *Muzyka kwartalnik*, iv/3 (1959), 45

A. Sutkowski: 'Tabulatura organowa Cystersow z Pelplina', *Ruch muzyczny*, iii/1 (1959), 14

J. Gołos: 'Zaginiona tabulatura organowa Warszawskiego towarzystwa muzycznego (ca. 1580)', *Muzyka kwartalnik*, v/4 (1960), 70

F. W. Riedel: *Quellenkundliche Beiträge zur Geschichte der Musik für Tasteninstrumente in der 2. Hälfte des 17. Jahrhunderts* (Kassel and Basle, 1960)

H. Schmid: 'Una nuova fonte di musica organistica del secolo xvii', *L'organo*, i (1960), 107

A. Sutkowski: 'Nieznane polonika muzyczne z XVI i XVII wieku', *Muzyka kwartalnik*, v/1 (1960), 62

T. Göllner: *Formen früher Mehrstimmigkeit in deutschen Handschriften des späten Mittelalters* (Tutzing, 1961)

J. Gołos: 'Tabulatura Warszawskiego towarzystwa muzycznego jako źródto muzyki organowej', *Muzyka kwartalnik*, vi/4 (1961), 60

G. Golos: 'Il manoscritto I/220 della Società di musica di Varsavia, importante fonte di musica organistica cinquecentesca', *L'organo*, ii (1961), 129

B. Lundgren: 'Nikolajorganisten Johan Lorentz i Köpenhamn', *STMf*, xliii (1961), 249

L. Schierning: *Die Überlieferung der deutschen Orgel- und Klaviermusik aus der 1. Hälfte des 17. Jahrhunderts* (Kassel and Basle, 1961)

A. Sutkowski and O. Mischiati: 'Una preciosa fonte di musica strumentale: l'intavolatura di Pelplin', *L'organo*, ii (1961), 53

W. Apel: 'Neu aufgefundene Clavierwerke von Scheidemann, Tunder, Froberger, Reincken und Buxtehude', *AcM*, xxxiv (1962), 65

T. Dart: 'Elisabeth Eysbock's Keyboard Book', *STMf*, xliv (1962), 5; also in *Hans Albrecht in memoriam* (Kassel, 1962), 84

G. S. Golos: 'Tre intavolature manoscritte di musica vocale rintracciate in Polonia', *L'organo*, iii (1962), 123

A. Reichling: 'Die Präambeln der Hs. Erlangen 554 und ihre Beziehungen zur Sammlung Ileborghs', *GfMKB, Kassel 1962*, 109

L. Schierning: *Quellengeschichtliche Studien zur Orgel- und Klaviermusik in Deutschland aus der 1. Hälfte des 17. Jahrhunderts* (Kassel and Basle, 1962)

H. J. Marx: 'Der Tabulatur-Codex des Basler Humanisten Bonifacius Amerbach', *Musik und Geschichte: Leo Schrade zum 60. Geburtstag* (Cologne, 1963), 50

O. Mischiati: 'L'intavolatura d'organo tedesca della Biblioteca nazionale di Torino', *L'organo*, iv (1963), 1–154

F. W. Riedel: *Das Musikarchiv im Minoritenkonvent zu Wien*, CaM, i (1963)

E. Southern: *The Buxheim Organ Book* (Brooklyn, 1963)

——: 'Some Keyboard Basse Dances of the Fifteenth Century', *AcM*, xxv (1963), 114

A. Sutkowski and A. Osostowicz-Sutkowska: *The Pelplin Tablature: a Thematic Catalogue*, AMP, i (1963)

J. R. White: 'The Tablature of Johannes of Lublin', *MD*, xvii (1963), 137

H. R. Zöbeley: *Die Musik des Buxheimer Orgelbuchs: Spielvorgang, Niederschrift, Herkunft, Faktur* (Tutzing, 1964)

F. Blume: *Geschichte der evangelischen Kirchenmusik* (Kassel, 2/1965; Eng. trans., enlarged, 1974 as *Protestant Church Music: a History*)

F. Crane: '15th-century Keyboard Music in Vienna MS 5094', *JAMS*, xviii (1965), 237

W. Apel: 'Die Celler Orgeltabulatur von 1601', *Mf*, xix (1966), 142

W. Breig: *Die Orgelwerke von Heinrich Scheidemann* (Wiesbaden, 1967)

T. Göllner: 'Notationsfragmente aus einer Organistenwerkstatt des 15. Jahrhunderts', *AMw*, xxiv (1967), 170

G. Leonhardt: 'Johann Jakob Froberger and his Music', *L'organo*, vi (1968), 15

T. Göllner: 'Eine Spielanweisung für Tasteninstrumente aus dem 15. Jahrhundert', *Essays in Musicology: a Birthday Offering for Willi Apel* (Bloomington, 1968), 69

M. Schuler: 'Eine neu entdeckte Komposition von Adam Steigleder', *Mf*, xxi (1968), 42

C. Wolff: 'Conrad Paumanns Fundamentum organisandi und seine verschiedenen Fassungen', *AMw*, xxv (1968), 196

W. Apel: 'Der deutsche Orgelchorale um 1600', *Musa–mens–musici: im Gedenken an Walther Vetter* (Leipzig, 1969), 67

T. Göllner: 'Die Trecentonotation und der Tactus in den ältesten deutschen Orgelquellen', *L'ars nova italiana del trecento II: Certaldo 1969*, 176

C. Wolff: 'Arten der Mensuralnotation im 15. Jahrhundert und die Anfänge der Orgeltabulatur', *GfMKB, Bonn 1970*, 609

J. Stenzl: 'Un' intavolatura tedesca sconosciuta della prima metà del cinquecento', *L'organo*, x (1972), 51–82

II. 5. LOW COUNTRIES

C. van den Borren: *Les origines de la musique de clavier dans les Pays-Bas (nord et sud) jusque vers 1630* (Brussels, 1914)

——: 'Le livre de clavier de Vincentiue de la Fallle (1625)', *Mélanges de musicologie offerts à M. Lionel de La Laurencie* (Paris, 1933), 85

A. E. F. Dickinson: 'A Forgotten Collection: a Survey of the Weckmann Books', *MR*, xvii (1956), 97

T. Dart: 'John Bull's "Chapel" ', *ML*, xl (1959), 279

W. Breig: 'Der Umfang des choralgebundenen Orgelwerkes von Jan Pieterszoon Sweelinck', *AMw*, xvii (1960), 258

T. Dart: 'The Organ-book of the Crutched Friars of Liège', *RBM*, xvii (1963), 21

A. E. F. Dickinson: 'The Lübbenau Keyboard Books: a Further Note on Faceless Features', *MR*, xxvii (1966), 270

W. Breig: 'Die Lübbenauer Tabulaturen Lynar A1 und A2: eine quellenkundliche Studie', *AMw*, xxv (1968), 96, 223

A. Curtis: *Sweelinck's Keyboard Works* (London and Leiden, 1969, 2/1972)

II. 6. SPAIN AND PORTUGAL

W. Apel: 'Early Spanish Music for Lute and Keyboard Instruments', *MQ*, xx (1934), 289

M. S. Kastner: *Música hispânica: o estilo musical de Padre Manuel R. Coelho* (Lisbon, 1936)

——: *Contribución al estudio de la música española y portuguesa* (Lisbon, 1941)

——: 'Los manoscritos musicales ns. 48 y 242 de la Biblioteca Geral de la Universidad de Coimbra', *AnM*, v (1950), 78

J. Moll Roqueta: 'Músicos de la corte dal Cardenal Juan Tavera (1523–1545): Luis Venegas de Henestrosa', *AnM*, vi (1951), 156

K. Speer: 'The Organ *Verso* in Iberian Music to 1700', *JAMS*, xi (1958), 189

H. Anglès: 'Die Instrumentalmusik bis zum 16. Jahrhundert in Spanien', *Natalicia musicologica Knud Jeppesen* (Copenhagen, 1962), 143

W. Apel: 'Spanish Organ Music of the Early 17th Century', *JAMS*, xv (1962), 174

II. 7. GREAT BRITAIN

J. A. Fuller Maitland and A. H. Mann: *Catalogue of Music in the Fitzwilliam Museum, Cambridge* (London, 1893)

J. Wolf: 'Zur Geschichte der Orgelmusik im vierzehnten Jahrhundert', *KJb*, xiv (1899), 14

E. W. Naylor: *An Elizabethan Virginal Book* (London, 1905)

J. E. West: 'Old English Organ Music', *PMA*, xxxvii (1910–11), 1

C. van den Borren: *Les origines de la musique de clavier en Angleterre* (Brussels, 1913; Eng. trans., 1913)

M. Glyn: *About Elizabethan Virginal Music and its Composers* (London, 1924, enlarged 2/1934)

M.-L. Pereyra: 'Les livres de virginal de la bibliothèque du Conservatoire de Paris', *RdM*, vi (1926), 204; viii (1927), 36, 205; ix (1928), 235; x (1929), 32; xii (1931), 22; xiii (1932), 86; xiv (1933), 24

L. Neudenberger: *Die Variationstechnik der Virginalisten im Fitzwilliam Virginal Book* (Berlin, 1937)

H. M. Miller: 'Sixteenth-century English Faburden Compositions for Keyboard', *MQ*, xxvi (1940), 50

——: 'The Earliest Keyboard Duets', *MQ*, xxix (1943), 438

——: 'Pretty Wayes: for young Beginners to Looke on', *MQ*, xxxiii (1947), 543

E. H. Fellowes: 'My Ladye Nevells Book', *ML*, xxx (1949), 1

H. M. Miller: 'Fulgens Praeclara: a Unique Keyboard Setting of a Plainsong Sequence', *JAMS*, ii (1949), 97

F. Dawes: 'Nicholas Carlton and the Earliest Keyboard Duet', *MT*, xcii (1951), 542

J. Ward: 'The "Dolfull Domps" ', *JAMS*, iv (1951), 111

D. Stevens: *The Mulliner Book: a Commentary* (London, 1952)

——: 'A Unique Tudor Organ Mass', *MD*, vi (1952), 167

E. E. Lowinsky: 'English Organ Music of the Renaissance', *MQ*, xxxix (1953), 373, 528

T. Dart: 'New Sources of Virginal Music', *ML*, xxxv (1954), 93

——: 'A New Source of Early English Organ Music', *ML*, xxxv (1954), 201

J. Ward: 'Les sources de la musique pour le clavier en Angleterre', *La musique instrumentale de la Renaissance: CNRS Paris 1954*, 225

T. Dart: 'Le manuscrit pour le virginal de Trinity College, Dublin', *La musique instrumentale de la Renaissance: CNRS Paris 1954*, 237

J. Jacquot: 'Sur quelques formes de la musique de clavier élisabéthaine', *La musique instrumentale de la Renaissance: CNRS Paris 1954*, 241

J. L. Boston: 'Priscilla Bunbury's Virginal Book', *ML*, xxxvi (1955), 365

H. M. Miller: 'Forty Wayes of 2 Pts. in One of Tho[mas] Woodson', *JAMS*, viii (1955), 14

D. Stevens: 'Further Light on *Fulgens praeclara*', *JAMS*, ix (1956), 1

F. Ll. Harrison: *Music in Medieval Britain* (London, 1958, 2/1963)

H. J. Steele: *English Organs and Organ Music from 1500 to 1650* (diss., U. of Cambridge, 1958)

J. Stevens: *Music and Poetry in the Early Tudor Court* (London, 1961)

H. Ferguson: 'Repeats and Final Bars in the Fitzwilliam Virginal Book', *ML*, xliii (1962), 345

E. Apfel: 'Ostinato und Kompositionstechnik bei den englischen Virginalisten der elisabethanischen Zeit', *AMw*, xix–xx (1962–3), 29

T. Dart: 'Notes on a Bible of Evesham Abbey (ii): a Note on the Music', *English Historical Review*, lxxix (1964), 777

J. A. Caldwell: *British Museum Additional Manuscript 29996: Transcription and Commentary* (diss., U. of Oxford, 1965)

——: 'Keyboard Plainsong Settings in England, 1500–1660', *MD*, xix (1965), 129

P. le Huray: *Music and the Reformation in England, 1549–1660* (London, 1967)

G. Sargent: *A Study and Transcription of Ms. Brit. Mus. Add. 10337* (diss., Indiana U., 1968)

A. Brown: ' "My Lady Nevell's Book" as a Source of Byrd's Keyboard Music', *PRMA*, xcv (1968–9), 29

M. C. Maas: *Seventeenth-century English Keyboard Music: a Study of Manuscripts Rés. 1185, 1186 and 1186bis of the Paris Conservatory Library* (diss., Yale U., 1969)

J. Caldwell: 'The Pitch of Early Tudor Organ Music', *ML*, li (1970), 156

T. Dart: 'An Early Seventeenth-century Book of English Organ Music for the Roman Rite', *ML*, lii (1971), 27

B. A. R. Cooper: 'Albertus Bryne's Keyboard Music', *MT*, cxiii (1972), 142

J. Caldwell: *English Keyboard Music Before the Nineteenth Century* (Oxford, 1973)

F. Routh: *Early English Organ Music from the Middle Ages to 1837* (London, 1973)

JOHN CALDWELL

Keyed bugle [key bugle; Kent bugle; Royal Kent bugle; etc] (Fr. *bugle à clef, trompette à clef, cor à clef*; Ger. *Klappenhorn, Klappenflügelhorn*; It. *cornetta a chiavi*; Dutch *Klephoorn*). A conical, wide-bore, soprano brass instrument, with side-holes controlled by keys similar to those found on woodwind instruments. (*See also* REGENT'S BUGLE.)

Keyed bugles are important in the brass band movement on both sides of the Atlantic. Early examples had only five keys, but keyed bugles with up to 12 keys are found. The key closest to the bell of the instrument is the only one that remains open when the instrument is at rest. Some later instruments have a whole-tone valve in place of the E and F key. Short, double-wound models are found. Most early keyed bugles were pitched in C with a crook to B♭; later, others appeared in high E♭.

Most keyed bugles were made of copper with brass or German silver keys and fittings; instruments made of solid silver, gold and tortoiseshell also exist. Most of the fingering systems are extensions of the original concept, but the instruments made by Kersten of Dresden are

1. *Keyed bugle by Metzler & Co., London, c1820–40 (Horniman Museum, London)*

notable exceptions: here an attempt was made to divide the arrangement of six keys equally between the hands. Keyed bugle mouthpieces are similar to those used on modern flugelhorns and 19th-century cornets in that they have a deep and conical cup. The mouthpieces are made of brass or ivory and sometimes silver-plated. The rims tend to be flatter and sharper in shape than modern ones. As a result of the wide conical bore and the deep conical mouthpiece, a very mellow and woolly sound is produced, similar to but not identical with the sound of the modern flugelhorn. Because of the sonic phenomena associated with venting, the keyed bugle has a unique timbre.

The bandmaster of the Cavan Militia, Joseph Halliday, added five keys to the common military bugle in Dublin in 1810. Halliday's patent (British patent no.3334) is dated 5 May 1810. The Duke of Kent is reported to have heard Halliday perform in Dublin and to have encouraged the instrument's use in British regimental bands. Shortly after the instrument's invention, Halliday sold the patent rights to the Dublin maker Matthew Pace for £50. It must have been about this time that a sixth key was added.

One of the most famous English keyed bugle players was John Distin, whose playing may have inspired keyed bugle obbligato parts in some English operas of the period. Many English orchestral trumpeters also played the keyed bugle. Thomas Wallis of the Covent Garden Orchestra of 1818 was paid 9s. 2d. per night with an extra 5s. when required to play the keyed bugle. John Hyde, who was the first trumpet in the King's Theatre orchestra, was a fine keyed bugle player and wrote a method book for it.

Keyed bugles were commonplace in most British bands by the time of the Allied occupation of Paris in 1815. After Grand Duke Konstantin of Russia heard Distin playing with the Grenadier Guards Band, he asked the Parisian instrument maker Halary (Jean Hilaire Asté) to duplicate the English instruments. Halary's instrument (French patent no.1849, 1821) extended the idea of the keyed bugle to a whole consort of instruments, the tenor and bass members of which he called ophicleides. In 1822 a rider was attached to the original patent allowing for an even greater range of instruments, some of which were apparently never produced. Halary's instruments were approved by the Académie des Beaux-Arts, and the Athénée des Arts awarded him a medal for his achievement. This provoked a surge of keyed bugle making in London and the main European musical centres as well as in the USA. The American names of Graves and E. G. Wright and the British firms of Percival, Pace and Köhler represent a high standard of craftsmanship; many

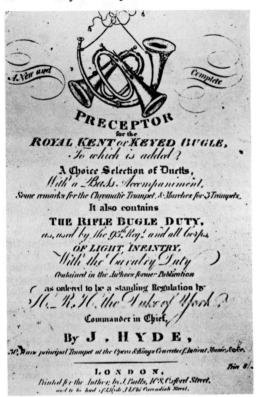

2. Title-page of J. Hyde's 'A New and Complete Preceptor for the Royal Kent or Keyed Bugle' (c1818)

beautiful instruments survive in museums and private collections.

In Germany, catalogues mention *Klappenhorn* or *Klappenflügelhorn* quite frequently among listings of military and wind music, but it appears that the keyed bugle was not considered seriously as an orchestral or solo instrument. However, the keyed bugle met with great success in the USA where famous soloists like Richard Willis (the first director of the West Point Military Academy Band), Frank Johnson (a black bandmaster in Philadelphia) and Edward ('Ned') Kendall (the last of the legendary keyed bugle soloists), performed solos and band pieces that were to establish an important band music tradition. The earliest recorded use of the keyed bugle in the USA occurred in 1815. Many performers received ornate gift or presentation bugles: Frank Johnson was given a handsome silver bugle by Queen Victoria; some performers are known only through the inscriptions on the bugles they were given.

Kendall's famous duel with the great cornet player Patrick Gilmore in 1856 has been thought to signal the demise of the popularity of the keyed bugle in the USA. Before then, however, both valved and keyed instruments co-existed in many bands. By the 1840s most bands were supplied with valved instruments. Keyed bugles were, however, still used on both sides of the Atlantic up to the mid-1860s.

Most method books for the keyed bugle contain a brief section on the instrument's technique, a fingering chart and possibly a few basic exercises followed by a selection of operatic airs and popular tunes of the day

(in solo and duet form). Band arrangements with parts for keyed bugle are common in catalogues of the period. Contemporary programmes indicate that vocal solos with keyed bugle obbligato were quite popular, but few selections were actually published in this format. An example of this type of parlour literature is a ballad by T. Phillips, entitled *The Last Bugle* (Philadelphia, 1822). The keyed bugle was assigned important parts in a number of operas including Bishop's *The Miller and his Men* (1813) and *Guy Mannering* (1816), Phillips's *The Opera of the Russian Imposter* (1822), Rossini's *Semiramide* (1823) and Kreutzer's *Ipsiboé* (1824). The parts for *trompettes à clef* in the Paris score of Rossini's *Guillaume Tell* and in Meyerbeer's *Robert le diable* were, according to Dauverné, played on valved instruments and not the keyed bugles that the score indicated. At least two substantial works for solo bugle and orchestra are known, A. P. Heinrich's *Concerto for Kent Bugle or Klappenflügel* (1834) and Joseph Küffner's *Polonaise pour le cor de signal-à-clef obligée* (1823).

BIBLIOGRAPHY

J. B. Logier: *A Complete Introduction to the Art of Playing the Keyed Bugle* (Dublin, 1813, rev. 2/c1820–23)
J. Hyde: *A New and Complete Preceptor for the Royal Kent or Keyed Bugle* (London, c1818)
E. Goodale: *The Instrumental Director* (Hallowell, 3/1829) [only this edn. has keyed bugle instructions]
Noblet: *Nouvelle méthode de bugle* (Paris, 1831)
Z. T. Purday, ed.: *Tutor for the Royal Kent Bugle* (London, c1835)
Tully: *Tutor for the Kent Bugle* (London, c1838)
Scherer: *Méthode de bugle* (Paris, 1845)
B. A. Burditt: *The Complete Preceptor for the Bugle* (Boston, c1850)
H. B. Dodworth: *Dodworth's Brass Band School* (New York, 1853)
A. Carse: *Musical Wind Instruments* (London, 1939/R1965)
——: *The Orchestra from Beethoven to Berlioz* (Cambridge, 1948)
R. Morley-Pegge: 'Key Bugle', *Grove 5*
A. Baines: *European and American Musical Instruments* (New York, 1966)
J. Wheeler: 'New Light on the Regent's Bugle, with some Notes on the Keyed-Bugle', *GSJ*, xix (1966), 65
R. Morley-Pegge: 'The Horn and Later Brass', *Musical Instruments Through the Ages*, ed. A. Baines (London, 1966)
R. E. Eliason: *Keyed Bugles in the United States* (Washington, DC, 1972)
——: *Graves & Company, Musical Instrument Makers* (Dearborn, 1975)
A. Baines: *Brass Instruments: their History and Development* (London, 1976)
R. E. Eliason: 'The Dresden Key Bugle', *Journal of the American Musical Instrument Society*, iii (1977)
R. T. Dudgeon: *The Keyed Bugle, its History, Literature and Technique* (diss., U. of California, San Diego, in preparation)
RALPH T. DUDGEON

Keyed trumpet (Fr. *trompette à clefs*; Ger. *Klappentrompete*; It. *tromba a chiavi*). A trumpet, generally with two double bends held in a horizontal plane. The keys are brought together on one side of the instrument so as to be operated by one hand only; the other hand merely holds the instrument. Austrian specimens are usually fingered with the left hand, Italian ones with the right. The keys cover soundholes, and when opened raise the pitch: the key nearest the bell by a semitone, the next by a tone, etc. Some trumpets have four, and some six keys, but five is the most common number (for illustration, see TRUMPET).

The first keyed trumpets were pitched in D and E♭. Later (c1810) they were made in G, A or A♭, with crooks for lower pitches; with the fixed position of the soundholes, this resulted in differing intonation and fingering, according to the crook employed. In Italy, where they were used in military bands, they were also constructed in families of various sizes.

The first keyed trumpet was made in Dresden in c1770 (according to information in Schubart's *Ästhetik der Tonkunst*), and in 1791–2 Nessmann built a keyed trumpet in Hamburg. This was praised by Gerber (*Neues historisch-biographisches Lexikon*, 1812–14). About 1795, ANTON WEIDINGER introduced his keyed trumpet, and in his hands it became rather successful. By 1840 it was superseded by the valve trumpet. Reconstructions of keyed trumpets have been made since 1971 by Adolf Egger (Basle) and distributed by MEINL & LAUBER.

The tone of the keyed trumpet is softer and less penetrating than that of the previously employed natural trumpet, frequently being compared with a sonorous oboe or clarinet. For this reason, it did not become popular as a solo instrument.

The keyed trumpet is not to be confused with the KEYED BUGLE, a member of the flugelhorn family, although it, too, was often called *trompette à clefs*.

BIBLIOGRAPHY
A. Carse: *Musical Wind Instruments* (London, 1939/R1965)
P. Bate: *The Trumpet and Trombone* (London, 1966)

REINE DAHLQVIST

Key note. The note by which the key of a composition, or a section thereof, is named and from which its scale starts, i.e. the FINAL of a church mode or the TONIC of the major or minor mode.

Keyrleber [Keirleber], **Johann Georg** (*b* Nürtingen, Württemberg, 27 Nov 1639; *d* ?Stuttgart, ? after 1691). German composer and theologian. He went to Tübingen University in 1657 and obtained the master's degree in 1660. Between 1662 and 1674 he taught at Güglingen, Markgröningen, Neuffen and Alpirsbach. From 1677 he lived at Frankfurt am Main and on 4 October that year he became a master at the Gymnasium. On 31 January 1678 he was appointed senior chorister at the Barfüsserkirche and soon became director of the choir school. He was dishonourably discharged on 19 April 1683 after being prosecuted for slander. After various petitions on his behalf had been rejected he earned his living from 1685 as a musician in charitable institutions and hospitals in Stuttgart. He clearly became a social outcast, and this is reflected in his fly-sheet *Dem Drey-Einigen wahren Gott ... dedicirt*, in which elements of antiquity and Christianity, humanism and theology and music and the graphic arts are all combined in an unusual way; the music consists of a perpetual canon and an arietta, both in eight parts. The sacred concerto *In festum Ascensionis* is for four voices and is specially notable for its scoring, for two violins, two cornetts, two trombones, viola da gamba, bassoon, dulcian and violone. Keyrleber is known to have written at least four works for Frankfurt and Nürtingen between 1677 and 1683 which are now lost.

WORKS
Aggratulatio musico-poetica, qua Leopoldo Imperatori romano . . . dies natalis, qui extat hujus 1691. an. 19 martij, canon (n.p., ?1691)
Dem Drey-Einigen wahren Gott, Obristen Capellmeistern . . . Regens Chori der Cherubin und Seraphin . . . eine . . . künstliche Music . . . nehmlich in dreyen Systematibus ein Canon perpetuus . . . eine Arietta . . . präsentirt und dedicirt, 8vv (n.p., n.d.); facs. in Maier, ed. in Kunz
Perpetuum mobile musico-poeticum, das ist, Immerwehrender Arbeit Ewigwehrender Gnaden-Lohn, perpetual canon, 6vv (n.p., c1691)
In festum Ascensionis, sacred concerto, 4vv, 2 cornetts, 2 trbn, 2 vn, va da gamba, bn, dulcian, vle, *D-F*

BIBLIOGRAPHY
EitnerQ; *WaltherML*
C. Valentin: *Geschichte der Musik in Frankfurt am Main vom Anfange*

des XIV. bis zum Anfange des XVIII. Jahrhunderts (Frankfurt am Main, 1906/R1972), 188ff
U. Siegele: 'Keyrleber, Johann Georg', *MGG*
H. Maier: 'Der Chemnitzer Liederblatt-Fund', *Heimatbeilage der Nürtinger Zeitung* (17 Dec 1955), no.291
E. Kunz: 'Das entschlüsselte Chemnitzer Liederblatt', *Lokalbeilage der Nürtinger Zeitung* (31 March 1956), no.76

EBERHARD STIEFEL

Keys, Ivor (Christopher Banfield) (*b* Littlehampton, Sussex, 8 March 1919). English musician and educationist. He received his schooling at Christ's Hospital where he studied the organ with C. S. Lang. In 1933 he took the ARCO, and in 1934 gained the FRCO (he was then the youngest player to do so). After studying at the Royal College of Music (1936–8), notably with Thalben-Ball, he won an organ scholarship to Christ Church, Oxford, in 1938 and became cathedral sub-organist there. He took the BA and BMus in 1940, and after war service returned to Oxford in 1946, gaining the DMus in that year. In 1947 he became a lecturer at the Queen's University, Belfast; in 1950 he was appointed reader, and in 1951 Sir Hamilton Harty Professor of Music. In 1954 he became professor of music at Nottingham University and in 1968 Peyton and Barber Professor of Music at Birmingham University. He was president of the Royal College of Organists, 1968–70. He was made CBE in 1976.

Keys's activities have always centred on music-making, whether as pianist, organist, harpsichordist or conductor. He gave series of television lectures on music in 1967 and 1976–7. Keys's writing is marked by its clarity of expression; his range of interests is catholic. Among his compositions, his Clarinet Concerto (1959) and his *Magnificat* and *Nunc dimittis* are the best known.

WRITINGS
The Texture of Music: from Purcell to Brahms (London, 1961)
'German Music', appx to *Twentieth-century German Literature*, ed. A. Closs (London, 1969), 409
Brahms Chamber Music (London, 1974)
Mozart: his Music in his Life (London, 1980)

DAVID SCOTT

Key signature. The group of sharp or flat signs placed at the beginning of a composition, immediately after the

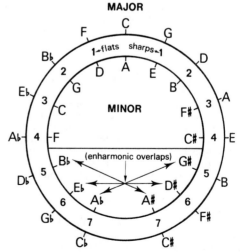

Key signatures of major and minor keys

clef, or in the course of a composition generally after a double bar. The signs affect all notes of the same names as the degrees on which they stand, and thus define the key of the composition. The illustration shows the signatures of major and minor keys (it also, in effect, shows the circle of 5ths, first described by J. D. Heinichen, in *Der General-Bass*, 1728).

The use of ♭ as a prefacing signature at the beginning of a staff is found in the earliest manuscripts using the staff (11th–12th centuries). A signature of two flats appears in the conductus *Hac in die rege nato* (*I-Fl* 29.1, f.332*r*) in both voices for six whole systems (f.333*r*); the piece begins and ends without signature. The 'partial' signature – that is, the composite one arising where different individual parts have different signatures (usually a lower one having one more flat than an upper one) – is found in the 13th century and became common in the 14th (for discussion of its significance *see* MUSICA FICTA).

The association of a signature with a definite key is a late 18th-century development. Before this pieces were often written with, in minor keys, one less flat (e.g. Bach's 'Dorian' Toccata and Fugue BWV538), or, in major keys, one less sharp (e.g. Handel's Suite in E, Set 1 no.5 for harpsichord), than would be used in the modern system. The increasingly chromatic writing of late 19th- and 20th-century music frequently led to the abandonment of key signatures.

See also ACCIDENTAL and NOTATION, §III, 3 (i), 4 (vi).

Keywork. The term used to denote collectively the various mechanical contrivances which have been devised to supplement the fingers in controlling the note-holes of wind instruments. The function of a key is to enable finger pressure applied at a convenient point to open or close a hole of any required size in any required position. Without the prior existence of established principles of keywork, some modern instruments designed following rational acoustic lines, for example the saxophone or heckelphone, could not have been realized.

1. History. 2. Key structure. 3. Covers, pads and seatings. 4. Key body and touchpiece. 5. Mountings and springs.

1. HISTORY. From very early days the need has been felt to provide wind instruments with a more extensive and musically useful scale than the mere harmonic series proper to a tube of fixed length. The process of varying the 'effective length' of a tube by means of side-holes opened and closed by the fingers has been used empirically since the time of neolithic man, as shown for example by bone pipes preserved in his burial places, but the systematic disposition of such holes seems to belong to a much later cultural stage. The oldest surviving examples of organized side-hole arrays known at present are of Sumerian origin, and date from about 2800 BC. Thereafter deliberately positioned side-holes are found in instruments of successive cultures up to the eclipse of the Roman Empire and the coming of the Dark Ages but there is no sure evidence among them of any device in the nature of a key to supplement the fingers, unless the movable rings used on some Greek *auloi* to close off unwanted holes when playing in specific modes are accepted as such (*see* MODE).

From the 12th century onwards there is some evidence of both reed pipes and flutes with six holes giving a diatonic scale of seven degrees, the octave being sounded by overblowing the lowest note. This organization also provided certain more or less satisfactory intermediate tones by the process of 'fork fingering'. In addition, the overall compass was sometimes extended by lengthening the tube and boring a further hole which could be stopped by the lowermost little finger. By the early 16th century such pipes were being made in various sizes paralleling the different ranges of the human voice and it was at this stage that practical difficulties began. The acoustic laws relating the size and position of side holes made possible the placing of the six primary holes in two fairly close-set groups of three, but this device could be carried only so far. By simple proportion the longer the tube the wider the spacing between holes necessary for reasonable intonation, soon exceeding the stretch of the normal hand. On some instruments the player can adjust the pitch of certain notes by blowing; when the limit of this ability is reached mechanical assistance becomes essential.

The first primitive keys were most likely designed to assist the little finger; the oldest surviving authoritative illustrations, by Virdung (1511) and Hans Burgkmair (before 1531), show no other arrangement. Accounts of the Duke of Burgundy for 1423 and 1439 recording the purchase of 'bombardes à clef' and 'teneurs à clef' for the court, show that keys were in fact used nearly a century earlier. Ambrogio Albonese's account of the PHAGOTUS offers some proof that a more advanced application of simple keys existed by 1539 and Praetorius in *Theatrum instrumentorum* (1619) shows keys for the thumbs on both large shawms and bassoon types. From this period on there is growing evidence of an increasing use of simple mechanism, though at the end of the 18th century it remained somewhat crude and often inefficient. As late as 1815 Gustave Vogt, professor of oboe at the Paris Conservatoire, questioned the efficiency of keys and advocated using as few as possible. At that time instrument makers in Germany and Austria were already quite generous in providing them.

At least three centuries seem to have elapsed between the invention of keys for wind instruments and their application to improve the lay-out of the primary holes. Borjon de Scellery, in a celebrated plate published with his *Traité de la musette* (1672), did show a sort of bass oboe which appears to have something of the sort and a few similar instruments are preserved in continental museums as 'basses de musette', but these are thought to have been exceptional and their history is obscure. A bass transverse flute by J. Beuker in the Paris Conservatoire collection has two jointed open keys which much improve the primary layout; the instrument has been somewhat questionably dated as late 17th century. Similar instruments employing simple second-order levers were illustrated by Diderot and d'Alembert in 1747 and were being made by Delusse of Paris in about 1760. In 1810 the London maker McGregor patented an instrument of this type and the principle was revived again by Siccama of London in 1847. These apparently unrelated recurrences of a single idea prove the difficulty of tracing clear and unbroken lines of development (if indeed such exist) with keywork as with many other features of musical instruments. There is unfortunately no authoritative instrumental historian between Agricola (published 1528 and later) and Praetorius (1619), a period rich in important developments. It is well to keep in mind that through natural conservatism or prejudice new devices were often slow to replace older, less efficient ones, and to avoid reading into slender evidence more than is warranted.

The use of keys to create a chromatic scale probably began about the last quarter of the 18th century, first with the transverse flute. Before that time fork fingering had furnished all the primary semitones except the lowest and with reed instruments, where this technique was quite satisfactory, it continued to do so for many more years; even today this process is of much service. Modern research has explained why the acoustic properties of the one-keyed flute make it more difficult to 'pull' into tune when fork fingered than was, for example, the 18th-century oboe, and no doubt this deficiency stimulated experiment with chromatic keys.

With the dawn of the 19th century a tremendous change began, and the period 1800–1850 saw rapid and brilliant progress. The ingenuity of such men as the Triéberts and Louis-Auguste Buffet in Paris, and Almenraeder, J. A. Heckel and Boehm in Germany, together with the skill of their workmen, had by mid-century established the principles of a keywork which today is completely reliable and little less responsive than the finger itself. With modern mechanism there seems at first sight to be no reason why the note-holes of all wind instruments should not be placed exactly as theory demands. This apparent ideal is, however, seldom realized, for the following reason. Most of the note-holes on the shawms, for example, and on their modified successors the true oboes, were made relatively small to compensate for the inevitable displacement imposed by the limited span of man's fingers. This applied even more to the bassoons and in turn gave rise to tonal qualities which became esteemed characteristics of these instruments and which it was found desirable to preserve. From time to time attempts have been made to design both oboes and bassoons with advanced keywork and note-holes both disposed and sized according to geometrical ideals, but the resulting departure from traditional tone quality has made these instruments unacceptable to the great majority of players. The traditional timbre of instruments can nonetheless be preserved while by the aid of suitable mechanism some of the traditional fingering problems are smoothed out. Within the last few years a movement has been started in England to introduce oboes modified in this way for school music, but the outcome is still uncertain. The greatest benefit conferred on side-hole instruments by modern keywork is that each genre now has a complete family at different pitches, all consistent as to finger technique.

2. KEY STRUCTURE. The function of a single key requires only a very simple mechanism; the highly complex equipment of many modern instruments is in fact only a combination of a number of such elements. In general a key consists of three essential parts: a plate or touch-piece for the finger; a second plate or cover for the hole, faced with some resilient material to ensure airtight closure; and a bar or shank uniting the other two parts. The shank may be in one piece or two, with an intermediate hinge, according to the action required. The whole is carried by one or two transverse pivots and is maintained in the position of rest by a spring. The mechanical principle is that of the simple lever of first, second or third order, depending on the relative disposition of the touchpiece, pivot and cover. There is

practically no limit to the size, shape or arrangement of the three parts of a key but most commonly the touch-piece and the cover are attached to the body in line with each other, with the axis of the pivot set transversely. This layout is, however, not essential and about 1830 a most useful variant appeared in which the cover and the touchpiece are attached to the two ends of a long rod or tube carried between point screws or threaded on a fixed axle. Keys of this sort are a great improvement on long levers where wide stretches have to be bridged, since they can be made more positive in action and are free from backlash; this type of key is still mechanically a simple lever. Keys are termed 'open' (fig.1e) or 'closed' (fig.1a) according to whether they open or stop the associated hole when at rest, and in identifying them it is customary to name them by the note sounded when the finger is applied, except in certain modern instruments where even the six primary holes are controlled by keys. Although it is not possible to trace unbroken lines of development in keywork generally or to assign firm dates in the earlier stages, the individual components of the simple key do show clear sequences of progress. As these changes appear to have been largely independent they will be considered separately.

3. COVERS, PADS AND SEATINGS. The cover of the earliest known key was simply a flat piece of metal, round or racquet-shaped, derived from the body of the key itself and faced with leather either sewn or cemented on. This arrangement persisted on lower-grade instruments even after improved forms had become general. The airtightness of such a key-cover depended entirely on the resilience of the facing material and little could be done to improve matters, except to flatten the tube surface around the hole (fig.1a). With the advent of the true oboes, musettes and jointed flutes which appeared in France at the end of the 17th century a considerable advance is seen. The key-heads were now either round or rectangular (fig.1b), still faced with plain leather but with the associated seatings much more strongly developed. By the end of the 18th century octagonal keys were fitted by many oboe makers who used characteristic ornament, datable by association (fig.1d). Occasionally seatings were omitted and the key itself curved to match the surface of the tube. Some makers of the early 19th century attached key-heads to the shank by a loose rivet or screw, thus allowing freer accommodation to the seating. The major objection to all plain key-leathers is their tendency to harden in use and lose their resilience. Richard Potter of London patented an ingenious solution in 1785 by which flute keys were made with conical plugs of soft pewter which fitted the holes closely, bearing either directly on the wood or on inserted metal bushes. The scheme had some success and survived on the foot keys of even superior flutes till the 1890s. The ideal solution, a resilient stopper analogous to the natural finger tip, was achieved before the middle of the 19th century with the first stuffed pads, or 'elastic plugs' as some makers called them. These were 'purses' of fine kid, filled with a ball of lamb's wool and drawn together with a thread. Such pads could accommodate themselves to any hole and even better results were obtained by providing a countersunk seating. As the pads could not easily be attached to flat cover-plates by shellac, the cement in common use, the key-heads were themselves modified to a hemispherical cup form, which also helped preserve the roundness of

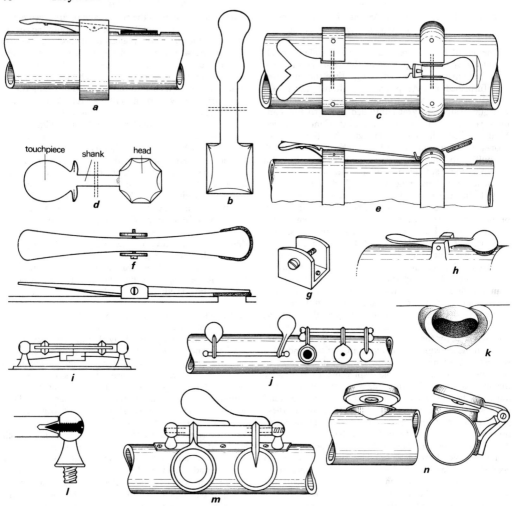

1. Examples of keywork from the 17th century to the 20th

the pad (fig.1h). Stuffed pads themselves proved to have a defect: in use, they tended to bulge and 'shade' the note-hole. The modern pad meets all requirements: it comprises a disc of card, a layer of felt and a covering of fine kid, animal membrane or waterproof plastic film, supported in a much shallower cup, closing on a raised collar in the wall of metal instruments (fig.1n); and on a conically recessed seating in non-metal instruments (fig. 1k). It is either cemented into place or retained by a tiny screw and washer and its basic construction can be modified to provide ring-pads for instruments with perforated finger-plates.

4. KEY BODY AND TOUCHPIECE. In its first form the key body was simply cut out of sheet metal as were the cover-plate and the touchpiece; the pivot was a wire passing through bent-up and perforated lugs (*see* SHAWM, fig.4). This arrangement was somewhat delicate and was provided with protecting covers of wood or metal in almost all the earliest examples. The chief disadvantage of sheet construction, its lack of stiffness when of any considerable length, was soon countered by forming the metal into a channel or flattened tubular

section (fig.1f). Cast or forged bar metal was used on the earliest clarinets (mid-18th century) for the long keys, sheet construction only for the smaller ones. Brass remained the usual metal for keywork through the early 19th century, with silver at times for superior instruments, but the advent of the white bronzes – generically known as German silver or nickel silver – in about 1830 brought many changes. These alloys, which can in different degree be cast, forged or pressed, and hard soldered, serve admirably for keywork: they polish well and can be silver- or even chrome-plated. In the later 19th century the hand production of standard-pattern keys in quantity flourished as a home industry in France, and this source of supply contributed much to the ability of French makers to sell instruments of decent quality at highly competitive prices. Exceptionally, keys have been made of hard wood and occasionally, in fairly recent times, of ivory.

The form of the touchpiece sometimes helps to date old woodwind instruments. The 'fishtail' shape may well indicate an origin before the firm adoption of 'left hand above right' in playing (fig.1c), though on oboes it survived as an ornament perhaps as late as 1830. The *d♯′* keys on early flutes are also sometimes indicative of date. Of all the forms of touchpiece, the ring surrounding an open finger-hole (fig.1*j*) has had the most influence on modern keywork. First conceived by F. Nolan in 1808, it was most fully exploited by Boehm in his flute design of 1832 and was applied to the clarinet by Sax about 1840 as the well-known 'spectacle' or *brille*; it is now used on most woodwind instruments. A device which has proved a great boon to players on the simple-system clarinet and several types of bassoon is a small ebonite or ivory roller set into the adjacent edges of a pair of touchpieces, whereby sliding the finger from one to the other is greatly facilitated.

5. MOUNTINGS AND SPRINGS. However well designed a key may be, it will soon become a nuisance if its mounting is inefficient. The wire pivots of the first sheet-metal keys were merely held in place by a staple at each end driven into the tube wall. This somewhat precarious arrangement yielded in the later 17th century to a device by which the key shank lay in a slot cut in a ring (fig.1*a* and *c*), later reduced to a block (fig.1*h*), left standing above the surface of the body tube. A small hole bored tangentially through both ring and shank carried a close-fitting pivot pin. This arrangement is in fact efficient, if inelegant, and remained in use until the early 1900s. Ring or block mountings were easily formed as part of the basic wood turning in the smaller instruments, but apparently not on the large, irregularly shaped joints of the bassoons, where they were abandoned, together with turned ornamentation, in the early 18th century; metal saddles of channel section, screwed or pinned to the joint, took their place (fig.1*g*). Saddles of this sort are often found with block mountings on oboes and clarinets and their presence has been taken to indicate additions or repairs to the original keywork. This may sometimes be so, but in many cases they were contemporary with the instrument and were adopted as a convenience in manufacture. On the other hand, wooden rings and blocks are known on oboes with as many as 12 keys, some of them interlocking and with alternative touches of modern form.

A device now fundamental to all keywork made its first appearance about 1800, on instruments of high quality. A pair of turned metal pillars is attached to a fitted metal footplate or screwed directly into the tube wall (fig.1*i*). The pivots associated with these pillars may be simple pins or more commonly, accurately made steel axles which screw into place and are capable of fine adjustment (fig.1*l*). In complicated keywork such as that of the Boehm flute several key bodies in the form of tubes can be carried on a single axle (fig.1*j*); in other cases, a solid rod is supported between point screws, one in each of the paired pillars (fig.1*m*).

The final element in efficient keywork is the return spring, which requires great accuracy of manufacture. It originally consisted of a leaf of hard brass fixed to the surface of the instrument body and pressing upwards or downwards as required against the key body. Later, springs of brass, then steel, were screwed or riveted to the key itself and, to reduce friction and wear, bore on slips of metal set into the tube. Leaf springs were effective only with lever-type keys, and were not easily applicable to those with tubular bodies; soon after these came into use the needle spring was invented, most probably by Buffet in Paris: a tempered wire of gold or steel is anchored in one of the pillars, while its free end bears on a tiny hook soldered to the key tube (fig.1*i*). The bias of such springs is very easily adjusted and they are widely used today on instruments of all sizes.

PHILIP BATE

Khachaturian, Aram Il'yich (*b* Tbilisi, 6 June 1903; *d* Moscow, 1 May 1978). Soviet composer. A bookbinder's son, he showed an early love for music but no precocious gifts. As a youth he played the tenor horn in the school band and taught himself the piano. In 1921 he moved to Moscow where his musical talent was discovered. Although lacking in professional preparation, he was admitted to the Gnesin Music Academy in 1922 and began to study the cello. His creative gifts developed rapidly and he entered the composition class of Gnesin in 1925. His earliest published compositions, *Tants* for violin and piano and *Poema* for piano (1926–7), were performed with success. In 1929 he gained admission to the Moscow Conservatory, where Myaskovsky became his composition teacher. After receiving a diploma in 1934 he continued postgraduate studies until 1937, by which time he was an established composer. His early works include the Trio for clarinet, violin and piano (1932), which Prokofiev recommended for performance in Paris, the Symphony no.1 (his diploma piece, 1935, dedicated to the 15th anniversary of the Soviet Armenian Republic), and the Piano Concerto (1936), which brought him international acclaim, followed soon by the equally successful Violin Concerto (1940). At home he secured his reputation with the patriotic cantata *Pesnya Stalina* ('Song of Stalin', 1937). He became active in the newly founded Union of Soviet Composers, first in 1937 as deputy chairman of the Moscow branch, then in 1939 as vice-president of the organizing committee.

When the directorate of the Composers' Union came under attack in 1948, Khachaturian belonged to the group of censured composers, alongside Prokofiev and Shostakovich. However, in Khachaturian's case it was mostly guilt by association, for his colourful, nationally tinged musical idiom was far removed from any modernistic excess. His major works of the 1940s included the ballet *Gayane* (1942, containing the popular 'Sabre Dance'), the Second Symphony (1943), the Cello Concerto (1946) and the *Simfoniya-poema* (1947, with 15 additional trumpets). The latter, a rather pompous *pièce d'occasion* for the 30th anniversary of the Revolution, was sharply criticized for alleged 'formalism'. Khachaturian admitted that he had become preoccupied with purely technical proficiency and apologized: 'Lately I estranged myself increasingly from my own Armenian element; I wanted to become a cosmopolitan'. For the next two years he concentrated on writing film scores, one of which was arranged into the *Traurnaya oda pamyati Vladimira Il'yicha Lenina* ('Funeral ode in memory of Lenin', 1949). In 1950 he expanded his musical activities to include orchestral conducting and composition teaching. He joined the staffs of the Gnesin Institute and the Moscow Conservatory, and he began to appear successfully as a conductor of his own works. After Stalin's death in 1953, Khachaturian was the first among prominent musicians to plead publicly for fewer bureaucratic restraints and greater creative freedom (*Sovetskaya muzïka*, 1953, no.11). In 1954 he began work on the ballet *Spartak*, which later became a major success (staged 1956, revised 1968). The score received the Lenin Prize in 1959; previously he had been awarded the Stalin Prize in 1941 for the Violin Concerto. Among his later works are the three *Kontsert-rapsodiye* for orchestra and various solo instruments of the 1960s, where he attempted a reinterpretation of the traditional concerto form. He was named People's Artist of the USSR in 1954. His wife, Nina Makarova, was also a composer.

Khachaturian's successful career represents the fulfilment of a basic Soviet arts policy: the interpenetration of regional folklorism and the great Russian tradition. His native Armenian (and, in a wider sense, trans-Caucasian) heritage is reflected in his languid melodies, stirring rhythms and the pulsating vitality of his musical idiom; yet his imagination was disciplined by an academicism based on Rimsky-Korsakov. The orientalism of a Balakirev or Borodin seems artificial beside the innate, more earthy and truly genuine fire of Khachaturian. Among earlier Armenian composers who influenced him were Komitas and Spendaryan, and he also absorbed certain traits of Ravel and Gershwin. Whenever he used folklore he reshaped it in a personal way (as, for example, in the slow movement of the Piano Concerto). His orchestra has a rich, sensuous sound, essentially post-Romantic, punctuated by colourful percussion. Not an innovator, he condemned musical experimentation; his music is straightforward and elemental in its appeal to human emotions. Shostakovich wrote in 1955:

Khachaturian's individuality – the result of his great creative gifts – reveals itself not only in his idiom, not only leaving his imprint on every bar; this individuality is broader and implies something more than musical technology alone: it comprises also the composer's outlook which is a basically optimistic, life-asserting view of our reality. . . . The national and folk idiom of his music is evident . . . in all his compositions, however different their subject may be.

Khachaturian was at his best when dealing with pictorial subjects – ballets, film, incidental music to plays. From these scores he drew a number of effective orchestral suites, and carried pictorialism into his purely orchestral works, particularly the concertos, where he combined old-fashioned virtuosity with solid workmanship. He represented socialist realism at its best.

WORKS
(*selective list*)

DRAMATIC

Ballets: Shchast'ye [Happiness], 1939; Gayane (3) [partly based on Happiness], 1942, rev. 1957; Spartak (4, N. Volkov), 1954, rev. 1968
Incidental music: Macbeth, 1934, 1955; The Widow of Valencia (Lope de Vega), 1940; Masquerade (Lermontov), 1941; King Lear, 1958; c15 others
Film scores: c25

ORCHESTRAL

Dance Suite, 1933; Sym. no.1, 1935; Pf Conc., 1936; Vn Conc., 1940; Gayane, 3 suites, 1943; Sym. no.2, 1943; Masquerade, suite, 1944; Vc Conc., 1946; Sym. no.3 (Simfoniya-poema), 1947; Traurnaya oda pamyati Vladimira Il'yicha Lenina [Funeral ode in memory of Lenin] [after film score], 1949; The Battle for Stalingrad, suite [after film score], 1952; The Widow of Valencia, suite, 1953; Concert Waltz, 1955
Spartak, suites nos.1–3, 1955–7, suite no.4, 1967; Kontsert-rapsodiya, vn, orch, 1961–2; Kontsert-rapsodiya, vc, orch, 1963; Kontsert-rapsodiya, pf, orch, 1965; 7 Marches, wind band

OTHER WORKS

Vocal: Pesnya Stalina [Song of Stalin], chorus, orch, 1937, expanded as Poema o Staline, 1938; Oda radosti [Ode of joy], chorus, orch, 1956; c40 songs; folksong arrs.; arias, 1v orch
Chamber: Tants, vn, pf, 1926; Pesnya-poema [Song-poem], vn, pf,

1929; Suite, va, pf, c1930; Sonata, vn, pf, 1932; Trio, cl, vn, pf, 1932; Double Fugue, str qt, 1932, rev. as Recitative and Fugue, 1967
Pf: Poema, 1927; Tants, 1927; Toccata, 1932; Album of Children's Pieces, 2 vols., 1946, 1964; Sonatina, 1959; Sonata, 1961
Principal publisher: Mezhkniga

BIBLIOGRAPHY

G. Abraham: *Eight Soviet Composers* (London, 1943)
G. M. Shneyerson: *Aram Khachaturian* (Moscow, 1959) [in Eng.]
G. Khubov: *Aram Khachaturian* (Moscow, 1962, 2/1966)
F. Streller: *Aram Chatschaturjan* (Leipzig, 1968)
B. Schwarz: *Music and Musical Life in Soviet Russia 1917–1970* (London, 1972)
A. Khachaturian: *Stat'i i vïskazïvaniya: sovremenniki o Khachaturiane* [Articles and opinions: contemporaries on Khachaturian] (Erevan, 1972)

BORIS SCHWARZ

Khachaturian, Karen (Surenovich) (*b* Moscow, 19 Sept 1920). Soviet composer, nephew of Aram Khachaturian. He studied under Shebalin, Shostakovich and Myaskovsky at the Moscow Conservatory, where he was later appointed senior lecturer in instrumentation. He has taken an active part in the Composers' Union, and he holds the title Honoured Art Worker of the RSFSR. His music is marked by a high degree of professionalism, sincere expressive depth and subtlety of taste. In later works, notably the oratorio *Mig istorii* ('A moment of history') dedicated to Lenin's memory, the arsenal of his methods has expanded towards greater variety, freshness and sharpness.

WORKS
(*selective list*)

Stage: Prostaya devushka [The simple girl] (operetta), 1959; Chippolino (ballet), 1973
Choral: Tsveti i zdravstvuy, molodost' [Blossom and prosper, youth] (Y. Kupala, V. Lebedev-Kumach, A. Dostal), cantata, 1948; U verbï odinokoy [By a solitary willow] (M. Pisyansky), cantata, 1950; Mig istorii [A moment of history], oratorio, reciter, chorus, orch, 1971
Orch: Sinfonietta, 1949; Molodyozhnaya uvertyura [Youth ov.], 1949; 2 syms., 1955, 1968; Druzhba [Friendship], ov., 1959; Conc., pf, chamber orch, 1974
Chamber: Sonata, vn, pf, 1947; Sonata, vc, pf, 1966; Str qt, 1969
Music for the theatre and cartoon films, children's music

BIBLIOGRAPHY

I. Nest'yev: 'K. Khachaturian i evo simfoniya', *SovM* (1955), no.9, p.43
M. Uspenskaya: *Karen Khachaturian* (Moscow, 1959)
R. Shchedrin: 'Talantivaya simfoniya', *Pravda* (25 Nov 1963)
D. Shostakovich: 'Poyot violonchel' [The cello sings], *Pravda* (25 Nov 1967)
E. Valente: 'Karen Khachaturian', *Unita* (28 March 1970)
'Nash kalendar' ' [Our calendar], *Muzïkal'naya zhizn'* (1970), no.15, p.23
E. Dolinskaya: *Karen Khachaturian* (Moscow, 1975)

GALINA GRIGOR'YEVA

Khachatur of Taron (1100–84). Abbot, hymnographer and notational reformer of the Armenian Church; *see* ARMENIAN RITE, MUSIC OF THE.

Khaikin [Khaykin], Boris (Emmanuilovich) (*b* Minsk, 26 Oct 1904; *d* Moscow, 10 May 1978). Soviet conductor. He studied at the Moscow Conservatory with Nikolay Malko and Konstantin Saradzhev (conducting) and Alexander Gedike (piano), graduating in 1928. His artistic principles as an opera conductor were formed under the influence of Stanislavsky, at whose opera theatre he was conductor (1928–35), preparing productions of *Il barbiere di Siviglia* and *Carmen*. In 1936 he replaced Samuil Samosud as principal conductor and artistic director of the Malïy Opera Theatre, Leningrad, where he followed his predecessor's example in promoting Soviet opera: he conducted (among other things) the première of Kabalevsky's *Colas*

Breugnon and the first Leningrad performance of Dzerzhinsky's *Virgin Soil Upturned*, as well as notable productions of operas by Rimsky-Korsakov, Musorgsky and Tchaikovsky. In 1943 Khaikin became principal conductor and artistic director of the Kirov Theatre, where he conducted the premières of Prokofiev's *The Duenna* and *The Tale of a Real Man*. He also staged Kabalevsky's *The Family of Taras* and Dzerzhinsky's *Knyaz'-ozero*. In 1954 Khaikin became conductor at the Bol'shoy Theatre, where he continued to champion Soviet music.

Khaikin's conducting was distinguished by fine artistry, secure taste and a sure understanding of style; and in his opera performances he used the drama inherent in the music to heighten the characterization on stage. He conducted abroad: *Khovanshchina* in Florence (1963), *The Queen of Spades* in Leipzig (1964); and he made successful appearances as an orchestral conductor (he took part in the Leningrad PO's tour of Italy in 1966). He taught at the Leningrad Conservatory (1935–53), and in 1954 became professor of conducting at the Moscow Conservatory; among his pupils were Kirill Kondrashin and Edgar Tons. He was created People's Artist of the USSR in 1972.

BIBLIOGRAPHY
K. Kondrashin: 'Velikiy master' [A great master], *SovM* (1974), no.12, p.93

I. M. YAMPOL'SKY

Khaïrat, Abu-Bakr (*b* Cairo, 10 April 1910; *d* Cairo, 25 Oct 1963). Egyptian composer and architect. As a child he had direct contact with the masters of traditional music who often visited his father's home. He began violin lessons at the age of five with a Turkish teacher, but he became more interested in the piano, which he continued to study for many years, later giving the first performance of his Piano Concerto in C minor op.10. However, architecture was his chosen profession, and after graduating from the university he received a scholarship to study this in France, where he also had private lessons in the piano, harmony and composition with Conservatoire teachers. Back in Egypt he had a successful career as an architect: he designed the complex of the Academy of Arts, comprising the ballet, cinema and drama institutes, the conservatory and the Darwish concert hall. He also continued to compose. His early works are in a romantic style without specific Egyptian features, but he then searched for a national idiom, interesting himself in some aspects of urban folk music. This resulted in, among other works, the colourful Second Symphony 'La folklorique' in G minor op.21, where in the second movement he used the tune of a 'stick dance' and in the third the 'handkerchief dance' popular at Alexandrian weddings. He came closer to the Egyptian spirit in choral orchestral works, such as *Lamma bada* (performed under Münch at the opening concert in the Darwish hall), a polyphonic version of the ancient monodic *muwashshah*.

Among Khaïrat's other nationalist compositions are the *Suite folklorique*, the Third Symphony and the overture *Isis*; works without obvious Egyptian traits include the Piano Concerto, the Lyrical Studies op.18 for piano, sonatas for piano, flute etc, the Sextet for flute and strings, and other chamber pieces. Khaïrat belonged to the first generation of Egyptian composers to draw on Western methods, a generation whose enthusiasm often

exceeded their expertise, though their role as pioneers is unquestionable. Western rhythmic and melodic influences are present in Khaïrat's style, but his melody has an obvious national flavour, particularly when it is derived from folk music. He was the first Egyptian composer to use sonata form, facing the problem of adapting a scheme to essentially lyrical oriental material; sometimes, as a result, the development section is curtailed. Founder-director of the Cairo Conservatory (1959–63), he received the state prize for composition.

SAMHA EL KHOLY

Khaml, Antonín. See KAMMEL, ANTONÍN.

Khan, Ali Akbar (*b* Shibpur, Bengal [now Bangladesh], 14 April 1922). Indian *sarod* player and composer. He is the son of Ustad Alauddin Khan and was trained by his father. His first public performance was given at the age of 14 at Allahabad, and while in his early twenties he became court musician to the Maharaja of Jodhpur. Khan first visited the USA in 1955 to perform at the Museum of Modern Art; since this date he has travelled extensively there and in Europe. Khan is credited with the creation of numerous ragas (*gouri manjari, lajwanti, mishra shivaranjani, mand, medhavi*). In 1956 he founded the Ali Akbar College of Music in Calcutta and in 1967 the Ali Akbar College of Music in Marin County, California. His many honours include the Sangeet Natak Akademi (National Academy of Music, Dance and Drama) award for Hindustani classical music (1963).

NARAYANA MENON

Khan, Vilayat (*b* Gauripur, Bengal [now Bangladesh], 28 Aug 1924). Indian sitar player and composer. He was born into a family with a long and distinguished tradition of professional musicianship and during his childhood in Calcutta was taught music by his father Ustad Enayet Khan, his mother Bashiran Begum and his maternal grandfather the singer Ustad Bande Hasan Khan, with whom he lived after his father's death (1939). Since his first major public appearance, in Bombay (1943), he has toured India, China, East Africa, Afghanistan, Nepal, Europe and the USSR and recorded extensively. His playing is distinguished by its clear line and is described in Indian musical terms as belonging to the *gayaki* (vocal) style. His compositions include several film scores, notably that for Satyajit Ray's *Jalsa Ghar* ('The Music Room'). Of his many pupils the best known are his younger brother Imrat Khan (*b* 1935), his son Sujat Husain Khan (*b* 19 May 1960), Arvind Parikh (*b* 1927) and Kalyani Roy (*b* 1931).

NARAYANA MENON

Khandoshkin, Ivan Yevstafyevich (*b* 1747; *d* St Petersburg, 29 or 30 March 1804). Russian violinist and composer. A pupil of Tito Porta, he was the finest Russian violinist of the 18th century. From 1765 he was a musician at the Russian court and taught the violin at the Academy of Fine Arts; later he was court Kapellmeister. In 1783 he was on the staff of Knipper's Free Theatre, and in 1785 was invited by Potyomkin to become director of his projected music academy at Yekaterinoslav. This enterprise failed, and in 1789 Khandoshkin returned to St Petersburg, where he continued to perform until his death. Besides three unaccompanied violin sonatas modelled on the works of Bach, Khandoshkin composed several sets of variations on Russian folktunes, which display his own extraordinary virtuosity. A viola concerto, published in 1947 and attributed to Khandoshkin, is now thought to be spurious.

WORKS
(all published in St Petersburg)

Shest' starinnïkh russkikh pesen [Six old Russian songs], with variations, vn, va (1783); 2 pol'skikh [2 polonaises], Molodka molodaya, Kak u nas vo sadochke, orch (?St Petersburg, 1786); 6 russkikh pesen [6 Russian songs], with variations, 2 vn (1794); Chansons russes variées, 2 vn, op.2 (1796); 3 sonates, vn (c1800)

BIBLIOGRAPHY

R. A. Mooser: *Annales de la musique et des musiciens en Russie*, ii (Geneva, 1951)
I. Yampol'sky: *Russkoye skripichnoye iskusstvo* [The art of the violin in Russia], i (Moscow and Leningrad, 1951)
IRMO, i (1968)

GEOFFREY NORRIS

Kharja. *See* ZAJAL.

Khar'kov. Town in the Ukrainian SSR. It was a garrison town until the mid-18th century, when it became a seat of government. After Russia conquered the Crimea and colonized the steppes, its importance steadily increased until it became the capital of the Ukrainian SSR from 1917 to 1934. Through the work of I. M. Miklashevsky some rare documents are available, although the Khar'kov archives were largely destroyed during World War II.

The flourishing college of Byelgorod was transferred to Khar'kov in 1726, with its 700 to 800 pupils. In spite of financial difficulties caused by an inadequate government subsidy, the college, which became a seminary at the end of the 18th century, contributed substantially to the development of musical life in the town. In 1773 classes in vocal and instrumental music were inaugurated, with M. Kontsevich and Artem Vedel as principal teachers. In 1780 a theatre was built and increased in importance until, in addition to plays, there were productions of operas by Mozart, Paisiello, Cimarosa, Spontini, Spohr, Cherubini and others.

After the beginning of the 19th century several piano factories opened in Khar'kov, indicating that the aristocracy as well as the bourgeoisie took an interest in music. The foundation of the university in 1805 led to development of the humanities in general and to the raising of cultural standards. Among the pioneers of instruction in music theory at the university were I. S. Ryzhsky and Gustav Hesse de Calvé, who wrote the first Russian theoretical work on music (1818–19); instrumental teachers were I. Vitkovsky and I. Lozynsky, author of an unpublished method for violin. Concert life began in the town in 1810 when Haydn's *The Seasons* was performed, followed by *The Creation* conducted by Vitkovsky, one of Haydn's pupils. Foreign musicians who worked in Khar'kov during the early 19th century included Julie Grinberg, Anton Herke, Adrien François Servais and Alexander Dreyschock; in the second half of the century the state-subsidized Khar'kov branch of the Russian Musical Association contributed greatly to the development of its musical life. P. P. Sokal'sky, equally prolific as an ethnomusicologist and as a composer, was succeeded by his nephew V. I. Sokal'sky (1863–1919), who contributed to the musical life of the city as a critic, pianist, conductor and composer.

Notable composers and teachers of Khar'kov include Serge Drimchenko (1867–1937), Boris K. Yanovsky (1875–1933), Ottomar Berndt (*b* 1896), Valentin Kostenko (*b* 1895) and P. P. Uglitzky (1892–1948); an outstanding figure was Semyon S. Bogatïryov, who in 1922 founded a school of composers at the Khar'kov Musical Institute (later the conservatory) that included Mikola O. Fomenko (1894–1961), Mikhailo D. Tits, Dmytro L. Klebaniv (*b* 1907), Vsevolod P. Rybalchenko (*b* 1904), Valentin T. Borysiv (*b* 1901), Yuly S. Meytus (*b* 1903), Andrii Y. Shtokharenko (*b* 1902) and Mikola Koliada (1907–35). David Oistrakh began his career by winning the Ukrainian Violin Competition at Khar'kov in 1930. The city has an opera company with orchestra, chorus, soloists and ballet, a symphony orchestra and several chamber music ensembles.

BIBLIOGRAPHY

P. P. Sokal'sky: *Russkaya narodnaya muzika* [Russian folk music] (Khar'kov, 1888; Ukrainian trans., 1959)
T. Karïsheva: *P. P. Sokal'sky* (Kiev, 1950)
K. Krasnopolska: 'Symfonichna muzyka kharkivskykh kompozytoriv' [The symphonic music of Khar'kov's composers], *Ukrainske muzykoznavstvo*, ii (1967), 33
I. M. Myklashevsky: *Muzychna i teatralna kultura Kharkova XVIII–XIX st.* [Musical and theatrical culture in Khar'kov in the 18th and 19th centuries] (Kiev, 1967)
I. Pyrohova: 'Iz istoriï muzykalnoho zhettva Kharkova' [From the history of musical life in Khar'kov], *Ukrainske muzykoznavstvo*, iii (1968)
——: 'Rolya pressy i rosvetok muzykalnoï kultury Kharkova' [The role of the press in the musical life of Khar'kov], *Ukrainske muzykoznavstvo*, iv (1969), 3
Y. Shcherbynin: 'Bilya dzherel muzychnoï osvity v Kharkovi' [Near the sources of music education in Khar'kov], *Ukrainske muzykoznavstvo*, vi (1971), 228

For further bibliography *see* UNION OF SOVIET SOCIALIST REPUBLICS, §X.

ARISTIDE WIRSTA

Khat-tali. Indian CLAPPERS.

Khayāl. A widespread vocal genre of north Indian classical music; *see* INDIA, SUBCONTINENT OF, §§I, 6(ii); II, 3(i), 4(ii); III, 1.

Khaykin, Boris. *See* KHAIKIN, BORIS.

Khaz. A notation of the MUSIC OF THE ARMENIAN RITE.

Khedase. An alternative spelling of *qeddasē*, a liturgical book of the Ethiopian Church, containing the anaphoras of the Eucharist; it corresponds to the Latin missal or the Byzantine euchologion; *see* ETHIOPIAN RITE, MUSIC OF THE.

Khessin, Alexander Borisovich (*b* St Petersburg, 19 Oct 1869; *d* Moscow, 3 April 1955). Russian conductor and teacher. He studied compositon under Solov'yov at the St Petersburg Conservatory, and conducting under Nikisch in Leipzig and Mottl in Karlsruhe. He was principal of the Moscow Philharmonic School (1904–5), and in 1910 became musical director and chief conductor of the Sheremetev Concert Society. From 1915 to 1917 he conducted opera at the People's House in Petrograd, and at the Mariinsky (later Kirov) Theatre (1918–19). He helped to organize the Moscow Philharmonia in 1922, and in 1924 began teaching at the Moscow Institute of Dramatic Art. From 1935 to 1941 he was director (and from 1936 to 1938 artistic adviser) of the opera studio at the Moscow Conservatory; he also taught the class in opera training, and was appointed professor in 1939. Khessin's work as director of the Soviet Opera Company of the All-

Russian Dramatic Society (1943–53) was significant; he introduced new Soviet operas to the Moscow public in concert performance (among them Prokofiev's *War and Peace*, Koval's *Sevastopol'tsï* and Kasyanov's *Foma Gordeyev*), and staged other operas not performed in the Moscow repertory, such as Gershwin's *Porgy and Bess*, Moniuszko's *The Haunted Manor*, Smetana's *Dalibor* and Taneyev's *Oresteia*. He wrote *Iz moikh vospominaniy* ('From my reminiscences', Moscow, 1959).

I. M. YAMPOL'SKY

Khierzinger. See KÜRZINGER family.

Khmer Republic. See KAMPUCHEA.

Khnes [Khness, Khnies], **Jurij.** See KNEZ, JURIJ.

Khokhlov, Pavel (Akinfiyevich) (*b* Spassky, Tambov, 2 Aug 1854; *d* Moscow, 20 Sept 1919). Russian baritone. He studied law in Moscow, also taking lessons in violin and piano, and in singing first with Yury Arnol'd (who upset his voice by making him study bass parts) and later with Alexandra Alexandrova-Kochetova. He made his début at the Moscow Bol'shoy as Valentine (3 March 1879), remaining with the company until his retirement in 1900; he also appeared at the Mariinsky in St Petersburg (1881, 1887–8), and sang in concerts in the provinces. His rich, warm voice and generous artistry quickly made an impression, and he was particularly successful as Eugene Onegin (singing the role at the first public performance, 23 January 1881, and thereafter 138 times in Moscow alone) and as Rubinstein's Demon; he also appeared in Prague (1889) in these two roles, which he virtually made his own. A scrupulous stylist, conscientious in his constantly refreshed study of a role, he was a master both of bel canto and of a more flexible declamatory style, and moreover had a fine stage presence. Various factors, including overwork and alcohol, led to an early vocal decline. Tchaikovsky, who liked and admired Khokhlov, wrote to Yuuliya Shpazhinskaya in 1886 of his singing of the Demon, 'I must tell you that your favourite Khokhlov, in spite of a more and more noticeable vocal decline, was extremely sympathetic and elegant in the interpretation of his role' (letter of 23 September/5 October 1886). His other roles included Don Giovanni, Verdi's Renato, Di Luna and Germont *père*, Wagner's Wolfram and Telramund, Meyerbeer's Nelusko and Nevers, Weber's Ottokar, and many Russian roles including Boris Godunov and Prince Igor.

BIBLIOGRAPHY
S. Durīlin: *P. A. Khokhlov 1854–1919* (Moscow and Leningrad, 1947)
V. Yakovlev: *P. A. Khokhlov* (Moscow and Leningrad, 1950)
JOHN WARRACK

Kholbio, Simon. See KOLB, SIMON.

Kholminov, Alexander Nikolayevich (*b* Moscow, 8 Sept 1925). Russian composer. He graduated from Golubev's class at the Moscow Conservatory in 1950. Secretary of the USSR Composers' Union, he holds the title Honoured Art Worker of the RSFSR and the State Prize. Operas, cantatas and songs form the bulk of his output, all of them dealing with contemporary themes. Links with the Russian tradition are evident in Kholminov's melodic breadth, his use of Russian protracted song and, in the epic, monumental quality of his work. He achieved popularity most decisively with the *Pesnya o Lenine* ('Song on Lenin'), which entered the 'golden fund' of Soviet popular song. The most significant of his operas is *Optimisticheskaya tragediya*, produced at the Bol'shoy in 1966. In this work Kholminov's characteristic closeness to the Russian popular song tradition is apparent.

WORKS
(*selective list*)
Operas: Optimisticheskaya tragediya (Kholminov, after V. Vishnevsky), 1964; Anna Snegina (A. Mashistov, after Esenin), 1966; Shinel' [The overcoat], Kolyaska [The carriage] (both after Gogol), 1971; Chapayev (Kholminov, after D. Furmanov), 1973
Orch: Geroicheskaya poema [Heroic poem], 1954; Rozhdyonnïye burey [Born in the storm], sym. poem, 1960
Cantatas: Zdravstuy, rodina! [Hail, my country] (Yu. Kamenetsky), 1960; Lenin s nami [Lenin with us] (Mayakovsky), 1967
Vocal cycles: 4 balladï, 1954; Chasï ozhidaniya [The hours of waiting] (S. Kaputikian), 1968; Bïl pervïy grom [It was the first thunder] (M. Karem), 1970
Songs: Pesnya o Lenine [Song on Lenin] (Kamenetsky), 1955; Pesnya druzhbï [Song of friendship] (Kamenetsky), 1959; Oda rodine [Ode to my country] (Yu. Polukhin), 1962; Oktyabr' 17-vo goda [October '17] (M. Matusovsky), 1964; song cycles
Inst: Pf Qnt, 1947; Detskiy al'bom [Children's album], pf, 1970
Film music

BIBLIOGRAPHY
M. Sabinina: 'Nachalo puti' [The path's beginning], *SovM* (1957), no.8, p.47
D. Kabalevsky: 'Tvorchestvo molodïkh' [The work of the young], *SovM* (1958), no.12, p.3 [on *Pesnya o Lenine*]
V. Viknogradov: 'Revolyutsionno-romanticheskaya opera', *SovM* (1966), no.5, p.44 [on *Optimisticheskaya tragediya*]
GALINA GRIGOR'YEVA

Khŏng wong. A Thai bronze gong-chime; *see* THAILAND, §2(i), and SOUTH-EAST ASIA, §§I, 3(vii); II, 4(vii).

Khrennikov, Tikhon Nikolayevich (*b* Elets, 10 June 1913). Soviet composer. He started to play the piano at the age of nine and to compose at the age of 13; his early teachers were Agarkov and Anna Vargunina. In 1929 he went to Moscow to study composition with Gnesin at the Gnesin Music School, and in 1932 he transferred to the Moscow Conservatory, where Shebalin was his teacher. He graduated with high honours in 1936. By that time he had already made his début as a composer-pianist with his Piano Concerto op.1 (1933), soon followed by the First Symphony op.4, his diploma piece; both attracted much attention. Then began his association with the Vakhtangov Theatre, for which he composed many incidental scores, notably that for *Much Ado about Nothing* (1936). His interest in the theatre led to his first opera *V buryu* ('Into the storm'), first performed in 1939. It was written in a melodious, folk-related style and appeared at a time of much controversy about Soviet opera as an expression of socialist culture. Backed by Stalin's preference, 'song opera' of this type became the accepted norm, and Prokofiev's *Semyon Kotko*, particularly, was compared unfavourably with *Into the Storm*. During the 1930s Khrennikov became known not only as a talented composer but also as an active spokesman for the young generation aiming at implementing socialist realism in music. During the 1940s he presented his Second Symphony, received two state awards for film scores (1942 and 1946) and completed his comic opera *Frol Skobeyev*. In 1948 he came suddenly to prominence during the musico-political purge which led to the condemnation of Shebalin, Prokofiev and Shostakovich and others. Khrennikov played a prominent role during the heated discussions and, backed by commissar Zhdanov, emerged as the newly elected leader of the

Soviet Composers' Union, replacing the discredited old leadership. He consolidated his position with virulent attacks against all 'formalism' in music, Russian and foreign. After the death of Stalin in 1953, he softened his hard line somewhat but remained a staunch advocate of socialist realism. Although his strong-arm rule has been criticized, he has been re-elected periodically (1974 and earlier), and has retained control of the union for over 25 years. Thanks to his political acumen, he succeeded in raising the prestige of the union and with it his own influence, so that he came to be considered the undisputed spokesman for Soviet music. In 1963 he was appointed to teach composition at the Moscow Conservatory. On his 60th birthday he was made a Hero of Socialist Labour, and in 1974 he was elected a deputy to the Supreme Soviet of the USSR.

Because of his manifold activities as a public figure, Khrennikov's creative output has remained relatively small. His great success of the 1950s was the opera *Mat'* ('Mother'), followed by an operetta and two concertos, one for violin, the other for cello. These concertos earned him the Lenin Prize for 1967, and the same award was given to him in 1974 for his Second Piano Concerto. His style has changed little over the years. In his earliest works one can discern a certain influence from the modernists of the day – Hindemith and Prokofiev in the motoric motion of the Piano Concerto op.1, and the humorous vein of Shostakovich in the First Symphony. During the later 1930s Khrennikov simplified his idiom and showed a predilection for folklike melody and traditional harmony, perhaps due to his involvement with theatre music. His skill in creating pictorial images is used most effectively in his operas, of which *Mother* is undoubtedly the most impressive. There are sections of appealing lyrical 'folksiness', alternating with conventional flag-waving patriotism. With innate theatre sense he drew on urban revolutionary songs of the period (around 1905) and shaped his own tunes in a similar idiom. In his later works (e.g. the Third Symphony) he has striven towards a more sophisticated musical language, even to the point of using a 12-note theme. However, he is not at ease with serialism (which he denounced vociferously in earlier years) and the results are unconvincing. He appears often as a soloist in his own piano concertos and is a well-known figure on European concert stages.

WORKS
(selective list)

Stage: V buryu [Into the storm], op.8 (opera, 4, A. Faiko, after N. Virta), 1936–9, rev. 1952; Frol Skobeyev, op.12 (comic opera, 4, S. Tsenin), 1945–50, rev. as Bezrodnyi zyat' (2), 1966; Mat' [Mother], op.13 (opera, 4, Faiko, after Gorky), 1952–7; 100 chertei i odna devushka [100 devils and one girl], op.15 (operetta, 3), 1962–3; Belaya noch' [White night], op.17 (musical chronicle, 3, E. Shatunovsky), 1966–7; Malchik-velikan [Boy-giant], op.18 (children's opera, 3), 1968–9; Nash dvor (ballet, 1), 1969; Lyubov'ya za lyubov [Love for Love] (ballet, 2, after Much Ado about Nothing), 1976

Orch: 2 pf concs., op.1, 1932–3, op.21, 1971; 3 syms., op.4, 1933–5, op.9, 1940–42, rev. 1944, op.22, 1973; Vn Conc., op.14, 1958–9; Vc Conc., op.16, 1964

Pf: 5 Pieces, op.2, 1933; 3 Pieces, op.5, 1934–5

Incidental music: Mik, 1934, orch suite; Much Ado about Nothing, 1936, orch suite, op.7; Don Quixote, 1941, orch suite, op.10; 9 others, also 12 film scores

Other works: songs with pf, choruses with pf and unacc.

Principal publisher: State Music Publishing House, Moscow

BIBLIOGRAPHY
L. Kaltat: *T. Khrennikov* (Moscow, 1946)
L. Sinyaver: *T. Khrennikov* (Moscow, 1947)
A. Werth: *Musical Uproar in Moscow* (London, 1949), 88ff
V. Kukharsky: *T. Khrennikov* (Moscow, 1957)
Yu. Kremlyov: *T. Khrennikov* (Moscow, 1963)
S. D. Krebs: *Soviet Composers and the Development of Soviet Music* (London, 1970), 257ff
N. Slonimsky: *Music since 1900* (New York, 4/1970), 1364ff
B. Schwarz: *Music and Musical Life in Soviet Russia, 1917–1970* (London, 1972)
D. Person: *T. N. Khrennikov: noto-bibliograficheskiy spravochnik* [musico-bibliographical catalogue] (Moscow, 1973)
I. Martinov, ed.: *Tikhon Khrennikov: stat'i o tvorchestva kompozitora* [Khrennikov: articles about his creative work] (Moscow, 1974)
BORIS SCHWARZ

Khristov, Dimiter (*b* Sofia, 2 Oct 1933). Bulgarian composer and theorist. He studied composition with Goleminov at the Sofia State Academy of Music until 1956; in 1960 he was apppointed to teach at the Bulgarian State Conservatory where he was made lecturer in polyphony in 1970. In 1963 he travelled to West Germany, France, the Netherlands and the USA on a UNESCO scholarship. He worked from 1968 at the Institute of Music of the Bulgarian Academy of Sciences, heading the department of music teaching and psychology from 1973. In 1975 he became a professor at the Bulgarian State Conservatory. He was made vice-president of the Bulgarian Composers Union in 1972, and general secretary of the International Music Council in 1975. In his compositions Khristov has drawn on Bulgarian folk music, above all on the two-part polyphonic music peculiar to the Sofia district, treating this material with novel technical means.

WORKS
(selective list)

Orch: Pf Conc., 1954; Sinfonietta, str, 1955–6; Poem, 1957; 3 syms., 1958, 1964, 1968; Ov., 1960; Sinfonichni episodi, 1962; Vn Conc., 1966; Vc Conc., 1969; Miniatures concertantes, 1970

Inst: 4 pf sonatas, 1962, n.d., n.d., 1973; Sonata, vc, 1965; Chamber Suite, 1967; Conc., 3 small drums, 5 insts, 1969; Str Qt, 1970; Qt, fl, va, harp, hpd, 1973

Principal publishers: Modern, Nauka i izkustvo

WRITINGS
Uchebnik po harmoniya (Sofia, 1963)
Sapadni horizonti [Western horizons] (Sofia, 1966)
Kompozitsionni idei v fugite na Dobre temperovanoto piano ot J. S. Bach (Sofia, 1968)
Hipoteza sa polifonichniya stroej (Sofia, 1970)
Kam teoretichnata osnova na melodikata (Sofia, 1973–)
Kompozitorat i obschtestbento sasnanie [The composer and the social sciences] (Sofia, 1975)

LADA BRASHOVANOVA

Khristov, Dobri (*b* Varna, 14 Dec 1875; *d* Sofia, 23 Jan 1941). Bulgarian composer, theoretician and choral conductor. His musical gifts were evident from early childhood when, with money collected from singing Christmas carols, he bought himself a flute and a violin. A self-taught musician by the time he completed his secondary schooling in Varna in 1894, he wrote several short pieces and conducted the school choir that he had founded as well as the choir of the music society, Gusla, which he and some of the Varna townspeople established. Up to 1900 he had earned his living by teaching music in a primary school, but with financial support from the Varna townspeople he was able to study composition with Dvořák at Prague Conservatory (1900–03). On his return to Varna he resumed music teaching and conducting, but in 1907 he moved to a secondary school post in Sofia and became choirmaster at the opera house, founded in 1908. In 1922 he joined the staff of the State Music Academy as lecturer, becoming professor (1926–33) and, for a short time, director. In 1928 he became the first Bulgarian musician to be a member of the Bulgarian Academy of Sciences. From

1935 to his death in 1941 he conducted the church choir in the Alexander Nevsky Memorial Church in Sofia.

Khristov's compositions, based on Bulgarian folk music but harmonized conventionally, are still popular in Bulgaria, especially his choral works. His theoretical study of hemiola bars (which Bartók called 'Bulgarian bars') is the first Bulgarian work on the folk music of the country.

WORKS
(selective list)

2 Balkan Suites, orch, 1903, 1914; Festive Overture 'Ivailo', 1907; Tutrakan epopoeya, orch, 1917

Choral works incl. Balkanski pesni [Balkan songs], 1912; Makedonski pesni [Macedonian songs], 1928; Dobrinka i slantseto [Dobrinka and the sun], ballad, 1931; Fugue on a Balkan Song, chorus, orch, 1933; Izvorcheto pee [The fountain sings], 375 educational songs, 1936

25 songs incl. Ergenski pesni [Bachelors' songs], n.d.; Haidushki pesni [Haiduk songs], 1914; 66 chansons populaires des bulgares macédoniens, 1931; 110 folksong arrangements

Church music incl. 2 liturgies, 1925, 1934

Folksong arrangements for chamber ensemble and for wind orch

Principal publisher: Bulgarian Academy of Sciences

WRITINGS

'Ritmichnite osnovi na narodnata ni muzika' [The rhythmic bases of Bulgarian folk music], *Sbornik za narodni umotvoreniya i narodopis*, xxvii (1913)

Tekhnicheskiyat stroezh na balgarskata narodna muzika [The technical structure of Bulgarian folk music] (Sofia, 1928, 2/1956; Russ. trans., 1959)

BIBLIOGRAPHY

S. Brashovanov: 'Dobri Christov', *Jb der Deutsch-Bulgarischen Gesellschaft* (Leipzig, 1942), 386

I. Kamburov: *Dobri Khristov* (Sofia, 1942)

V. Krastev: *Dobri Khristov* (Sofia, 1954; Russ., trans., 1960)

V. Krastev, ed.: *Muzikalno-teoretichno i publitsistichno nasledstvo na Dobri Khristov* (Sofia, 1971)

LADA BRASHOVANOVA

Khu, Emilios. *See* RIADIS, EMILIOS.

Khubov, Georgy Nikitich (*b* Kars, Turkey, 9 May 1902). Soviet musicologist and critic. After completing his studies at the Moscow Conservatory (1926–31) he worked on the editorial staff of *Pravda* as a consultant musical sub-editor (1934–57) and held various important posts on the board of the Soviet Composers' Union; he was also editor of the journal *Sovetskaya muzïka* (1952–7). He then published several significant works, which appeared after years of exhaustive research; his monographs on Bach and Khachaturian, for instance, developed essays that he had published before the war. In his books on Borodin, Musorgsky and Khachaturian he examined the oriental motifs in Russian classical and Soviet music in detail.

WRITINGS

A. P. Borodin (Moscow, 1933)

Sebast'yan Bakh (Moscow, 1936, enlarged 3/1954, 4/1964)

Aram Khachaturyan: eskiz kharakteristiki [Aram Khachaturian: a character sketch] (Moscow, 1939)

ed.: *A. N. Serov: Izbrannïye stat'i* [Selected essays] (Moscow, 1950–57)

Zhizn' A. Serova [The life of Serov] (Moscow and Leningrad, 1950)

Sovetskaya opera [Soviet opera] (Moscow, 1953)

O muzïke i muzïkantakh: ocherki i stat'i [Music and musicians: essays and articles] (Moscow, 1959)

Aram Khachaturyan (Moscow, 1962, 2/1966)

Musorgsky (Moscow, 1969)

IGOR BELZA

Khuen [Kuen], Johannes (*b* Moosach, nr. Munich, 1606; *d* Munich, 14 Nov 1675). German poet and composer. He became a student at the Jesuit school in Munich in 1623, taking the traditional courses and participating in the musical activities of the church and the court. Ordained a priest in 1630 he became a private

chaplain at the Warttenberg Chapel, Munich, the following year, and in 1634 he received a benefice at the church of St Peter there. He held these two positions for the rest of his life.

Khuen's output consists almost exclusively of religious poems, for which he also wrote music. Usually consisting of 12 stanzas and organized into cycles of 12 poems each, they appeared mainly in two large collections, the *Epithalamium Marianum* (Munich, 1636, enlarged 4/1644) and the three-part *Geistliche Schäfferey* (Munich, 1650–55). The Virgin Mary as the patron saint of Bavaria was the focus of local devotional practice. Khuen built on the tradition of a litany-like religious folksong, merging its elements with early Italian monody. His poetic style, though indulging in the imagery of flowers, jewels and music, is naive and simple and harmonizes with his use of the Bavarian idiom. His development as a composer shows the gradual abandonment of traditional traits (modality, frequent triple metre) in favour of such characteristics of early monody as major–minor tonality and more expressive, rhythmically varied melody. Although Khuen's work far surpasses any previous Catholic religious poetry in the vernacular, he had no real followers or lasting influence, mainly because of his provincialism. German Romanticism savoured this very trait, and Clemens Brentano included two of his songs in his *Des Knaben Wunderhorn* of 1808.

WORKS

Edition: *J. Khuen: Ausgewählte Texte und Melodien*, ed. R. Hirschenauer and H. Grassl (Munich, 1961)

(published in Munich)

Convivium Marianum, Freudenfest dess himmlischen Frauenzimmers, mit 12 neuen Gesänglein geziert (1637)

3 schöne neue geistliche Lieder (1637)

Epithalamium Marianum, oder Tafel Music, dess himmlischen Frauenzimmers, mit neuen geistlichen Gesänglein geziert (1636, lost; 2/1638, enlarged 4/1644)

Florilegium Marianum, der brinnendt Dornbusch (1638)

Die geistlich Turteltaub (1639)

Cor contritum et humiliatum, Engelfreud oder Bussseufftzer (1640)

Mausoleum Salomonis, der Potentaten Grabschrifft, Urlaub und Abschidt (1641)

Epithalamium Marianum, Tafel Music, Freudenfest, und Lustgarten Mariae . . . und dero gantzen himmlischen Frauenzimmer (1644)

Tabernacula pastorum, die geistliche Schäfferey (1650–55)

Munera pastorum, Hirten-Ambt, und Anweisung der geistelichen Schäfferey getreulich vorzustehn (1651)

Gaudia pastorum, Schäffer Freud, oder Triumph der geistlichen Schäfferey (1655)

Marianum Epithalamium, Tafel Music, Ehren Mahlzeit, Lust-Garten, und Bluemen-Feld (1659)

Mausoleum Salomonis, 50 Klaglieder (1665)

BIBLIOGRAPHY

B. A. Wallner: 'Johannes Kuen, Benefiziat von St. Peter', *St Peterskalender* (Munich, 1920)

C. von Faber du Faur: 'Johann Khuen', *Publications of the Modern Language Association of America*, lxiv (1949), 746 [incl. bibliography]

B. Genz: *Johannes Kuen: eine Untersuchung zur süddeutschen geistlichen Lieddichtung im 17. Jahrhundert* (diss., U. of Cologne, 1957)

TRAUTE MAASS MARSHALL

Khues [Khuess, Khüess], Jurij. *See* KNEZ, JURIJ.

Khym [Chym, Kyhm], Carl (*b* Bohemia, *c*1770; *d* after 1819). Bohemian oboist and composer. He moved as a young man to Vienna, where he spent most of his life as an oboe virtuoso and composer. On the title-page of his *Sextuor* op.9 he called himself 'Employé de sa majesté'. Khym's compositions are in a pleasant and idiomatic style that recommends them to beginners and amateurs. His known works include duets for clarinets (opp.1–2,

1798), flutes (op.6, 1800) and oboes (op.11 no.1, 1819), dances for keyboard, variations for keyboard and for strings (including a set on Mozart's 'Ein Mädchen oder Weibchen' from *Die Zauberflöte* for violin and viola, 1800), and the *Sextuor* for flute, clarinet, violin, two violas and cello (1803). He also arranged several of Beethoven's chamber works for string quintet and published songs from Dittersdorf's *Das rote Käppchen* in vocal score.

BIBLIOGRAPHY
FétisB; *GerberNL*
G. Schilling: *Encyclopädie der gesammten musikalischen Wissenschaften* (Stuttgart, 1835–42/*R*1973)
U. Rau: *Die Kammermusik für Klarinette und Streichinstrumente im Zeitalter der Wiener Klassik* (diss., U. of Saarbrücken, 1975)

based on *MGG* (xvi, 938–9) by permission of Bärenreiter
                                                ULRICH RAU

Kibkalo, Evgeny (Gavrilovich) (*b* Kiev, 12 Feb 1932). Soviet baritone. He graduated from Vladimir Politkovsky's class at the Moscow Conservatory in 1956, was engaged that year as a soloist by the Bol'shoy Theatre, then studied in Milan at La Scala opera school in 1963. His distinctive qualities are his beautiful, even voice and warm tone, his musicality, and his excellent sense of ensemble. He sang in the first Bol'shoy performances of Prokofiev's *War and Peace* (Andrey) and *The Story of a Real Man* (Alexey); his other roles include Tchaikovsky's Eletsky, Mazeppa and Onegin; Rossini's and Mozart's Figaro; and Demetrius in Britten's *A Midsummer Night's Dream*. He has performed in many countries, and was made People's Artist of the RSFSR in 1959.

                                                I. M. YAMPOL'SKY

Kichler, Johann. *See* KÜCHLER, JOHANN.

Kidson, Frank (*b* Leeds, 13 Nov 1855; *d* Leeds, 7 Nov 1926). English musical antiquary. Although of the school of William Chappell, he differed from it in accepting the validity of the oral tradition of folksong. He was an original member of the Folk Song Society in 1898 and contributed editorial annotations to its early journals; in 1906 he also contributed 30 songs and folk tales which he had himself collected in Yorkshire. Moreover, he anticipated Cecil Sharp's rediscovery of the English folkdance tradition, for as early as 1890 he published a volume, *Old English Country Dances* (tunes only), and in 1915 he wrote, in association with Mary Neal, *English Folk Song and Dance*. He was a bibliographer as well as an antiquary; an expert on old Leeds pottery – on which, with his brother, he wrote the standard book – as well as folk music. He was a contributor on a wide variety of subjects to *Grove 2–4*. His index of English songs, running to 100,000 entries, was never published but is now in the Mitchell Library, Glasgow. He published a valuable catalogue of British music publishers and engravers, and also several volumes of folksongs, of which the most important are *Songs of Britain* with piano accompaniments by Martin Shaw and *A Garland of English Folk-songs* and *English Peasant Songs*, both with accompaniments by Alfred Moffat. Leeds University gave him an honorary MA in 1923.

EDITIONS
Old English Country Dances Gathered from Scarce Printed Collections and from Manuscripts (London, 1890)
Traditional Tunes: a Collection of Ballad Airs, chiefly obtained in Yorkshire and the South of Scotland (Oxford, 1891)
The Minstrelsy of England: a Collection of 200 English Songs ... popular from the 16th Century to the middle of the 18th Century (London, 1901)
75 British Nursery Rhymes (London, 1904)
Children's Songs of Long Ago (London, 1905)
The Golden Wedding: a Yorkshire Idyll (London, 1910)
English Songs of the Georgian Period (London and Glasgow, 1911)
Dances of the Olden Time (London and Glasgow, 1912)
Songs of Britain (London and New York, 1913)
English Country Dances arranged for Children's Performance (London, 1914)
Old English Country Dance Tunes (London, 1915)
100 Singing Games, Old, New, and Adapted (London and Glasgow, 1916)
A Garland of English Folk-songs (London, 1926)
Folk Songs of the North Countrie with their Traditional Airs (London, 1927)
English Peasant Songs with their Traditional Airs (London, 1929)
The Minstrelsy of Childhood (n.p., n.d.)
Morris Tunes (London, n.d.)

WRITINGS
British Music Publishers and Engravers, London, Provincial, Scottish, and Irish, from Queen Elizabeth's Reign to George the Fourth's (London, 1900/*R*1967)
English Folk-song and Dance (Cambridge, 1915)
The Beggar's Opera: its Predecessors and Successors (Cambridge, 1922)
'Handel's Publisher, John Walsh, his Contemporaries and Successors', *MQ*, vi (1920), 430

BIBLIOGRAPHY
'Portrait of Frank Kidson by Some of His Friends', *JEFDSS*, v (1948), 127
F. Howes: *Folk Music of Britain – and Beyond* (London, 1970), 102ff
                    HERBERT THOMPSON, WILLIAM C. SMITH/
                                            FRANK HOWES

Kiefer, Bruno (*b* Baden-Baden, 9 April 1923). Brazilian composer and teacher of German birth. He studied the flute, the piano, composition and conducting at the fine arts institute of the Federal University of Rio Grande do Sul, Porto Alegre. For several years he was a flautist in the Porto Alegre SO, and he also worked with the chamber orchestra of the institute, where in 1969 he was appointed to teach history. He has also taught at the Federal University of Santa Maria. He has been an active composer since about the mid-1950s, cultivating an abstract style with neo-classical elements and some serial procedures.

WORKS
(*selective list*)
Orch: Diálogo, cl, orch, 1966; Convertimento, fl, cl, bn, str, 1970
Vocal: 5 motetos profanos, 2 female vv, eng hn, hn, 2 trbn, 1964; Missa do casamento, chorus, org, 1965; Cantata do encontro, chamber chorus, wind qnt, 1967
Chamber: Str Qt no.2, 1959; Incógnitas, cl, str trio, 1971
Pf: 2 sonatas, 1958, 1959; Terra selvagem, Prenuncios, 2 pf, 1971

WRITINGS
Elementos da linguagem musical (Porto Alegre, 1970)
História e significado das formas musicais (Porto Alegre, 1970)
                                                GERARD BÉHAGUE

Kieffer, Aldine S(illman) (*b* Saline County, Missouri, 1 Aug 1840; *d* Dayton, Virginia, 30 Nov 1904). American composer and compiler of songbooks in seven-shape notation (*see* SHAPE-NOTE HYMNODY, §4), grandson of Joseph Funk. His monthly periodical *Musical Million* (1870–1914) was a primary instrument for the promotion of shape-note gospel hymnody in the southern USA. Alone and with other composers he published 18 songbooks between 1868 and 1898.

BIBLIOGRAPHY
P. M. Hall: *The 'Musical Million': a Study and Analysis of the Periodical Promoting Music Reading through Shape-notes in North America from 1870 to 1914* (diss., Catholic U. of America, 1970)
                                                HARRY ESKEW

Kieken, Johannes. *See* PULLOIS, JOHANNES.

Kiel. City in the German Federal Republic. From 1284 to 1518 it was a member of the Hanseatic League and from 1460 to 1867 it was part of the Duchy of Holstein-Gottorp, which was under Danish rule after 1773. From 1867 it was the capital of the Prussian province of Schleswig-Holstein, and its musical significance dates from that time.

In the Middle Ages Kiel had two ecclesiastical institutions. The Franciscan monastery was dissolved in the wake of the Reformation in 1530 and under the name of Heiligengeist- or Kloster-Kirche belonged to the parish of St Nikolai. The university, founded in 1665, was housed in the old monastery buildings until 1768. The Nikolaikirche, the town church, played a decisive role in the town's musical life. From 1322 until shortly after 1526 its patrons were the Augustinian canons of Bordesholm, who were also patrons of the Lateinschule (established 1320). The Kantor, who trained the pupils in liturgical singing, was the school's headmaster; the choirs of boys and priests generally consisted of eight to 12 voices. Until the Reformation the organist was also a priest; afterwards he was appointed by the church authorities or by the town council. The separate posts of Kantor and organist were united for the first time in 1810 when they were both held by the Thuringian G. C. Apel, a pupil of J. C. Kittel. After his death (1841) the posts were again separated until 1874, when they were permanently united. Shortly before this the organist Carl Stechert had founded a choir, which did not survive, however; in 1922 the church founded the St Nikolaichor, which still has a fine reputation.

Kiel's theatrical traditions go back to the 17th century, but the city did not have a permanent theatre company until 1841, when the Stadttheater was built on the site of the demolished Opern- und Komödienhaus (1764); this theatre had an orchestra from 1907, contracted from the Verein der Musikfreunde (founded 1901). Also in 1907 a new Stadttheater was built; Fritz Stein, a pupil of Reger, became the first municipal director of music in 1925, and between the wars a high standard of opera performance was attained there. A summer theatre, the so-called 'Tivoli' theatre, was opened in 1845, but was destroyed by fire in 1870. In 1890 this theatre was re-established in a suburb of Kiel and was later renamed the Schillertheater; in 1907 it came under municipal administration as the Kleines Theater, but ceased musical productions at that time. It was renamed the Schauspielhaus in 1919, and was used for opera performances between 1945 and 1953 (as the Neues Stadttheater) while the Stadttheater was being rebuilt after destruction in World War II. From 1953 to 1957 it was used as a cinema, subsequently becoming the Schauspielhaus once more.

From the early 19th century public concerts took place in the hall of the Harmonie Gesellschaft (founded 1800), and in the great hall of the university; from 1841 the Stadttheater was used, as was the 'Tivoli' theatre from 1845 to 1870. In 1935 the hall of the trade unions' building was converted into a concert room. After World War II the newly built Ostseehalle was used temporarily for concerts, until the inauguration in 1965 of a large and a small concert hall in the castle, rebuilt in collaboration with North German Radio, which has a broadcasting station there.

Although civic musicians were responsible for the instrumental accompaniment of church music after the Reformation, the tradition of organized instrumental music originated in the private musical gatherings of students and professors. From these beginnings a Musikverein (1776–96) developed under the direction of the professor of Danish law, Holger de Fine Olivarius. A circle of accomplished amateurs gathered regularly under the direction of G. C. Apel in the family home of Otto Jahn (later the biographer of Mozart) and together with a vocal group formed the basis of the Instrumentalverein, established in 1835 and continued into the 1870s. Thereafter concert life was provided only by military musicians and private bands until 1897, when a private symphony orchestra was organized. In 1901 the Verein der Musikfreunde was founded; this established an orchestra (1907), which has since been employed for opera performances as well as symphony concerts.

Choral societies began in the 18th century, when a student collegium musicum cultivated church music. In 1820 the Singverein was formed from members of Apel's amateur circle, and was enlarged by Carl Grädener to form the Allgemeiner Gesangverein in 1841. In 1844 Grädener founded the Kieler Gesangverein, which absorbed the older group in 1871 and survived until 1914. During the industrialization of the city towards the end of the 19th century a number of workers' choral societies were founded, and from 1919 to 1929 Stein conducted an Oratorienverein which he had established. Among the popular choirs the Kieler Liedertafel (1841) is the oldest. From 1907 the theatre had its own opera chorus, the Städtischer Chor.

At the peak of its cultural life Kiel held several festivals of more than local significance. The first of the Schleswig-Holstein music festivals, arranged by Hermann Stange, took place in 1875 under the direction of Joachim, and there were five more up to 1902. Stein, besides giving performances during the Kieler Herbstwochen für Kunst und Wissenschaft, also organized the 55th Tonkünstlerfest des Allgemeinen Deutschen Musikvereins (1925), the second Handel Festival (1928) and the 18th German Bach Festival (1930).

The first classes in music at the university were given by the Kantor J. C. Oehlers (1781–1810) in the Homiletisches Seminar, established in 1775 as part of the theology department. Until 1914 this remained a duty of the Nikolaikirche Kantor or organist. Apel was appointed honorary academic director of music in 1818, a post which was formalized in 1848, when Carl Grädener was appointed. However, Grädener left Kiel a year later and the post was vacant until 1878, when Stange was appointed. The main responsibility was practical music-making, but Grädener had already given public lectures on general music theory. In 1921 Stein established a music department at the university, which became an independent institute in 1923. Under Stein's successors, Friedrich Blume (1933), Walter Wiora (1958), Walter Salmen (1966) and Friedhelm Krummacher (1976) practical music-making diminished in favour of historical, analytic and ethnological research and teaching. In 1930 H.-J. Therstappen, a lecturer in music, created in the university an Arbeitsgruppe für Neue Musik, which existed until 1936; in 1957 it was re-established as the Arbeitskreis für Neue Musik by Kurt Gudewill, and since 1959 has been one of the students' study groups.

BIBLIOGRAPHY

W. von Gersdorff: *Geschichte des Theaters in Kiel unter den Herzögen zu Holstein-Gottorp bis 1733* (Kiel, 1912)

G. Junge: *Die Geschichte des Theaters in Kiel unter der dänischen Herrschaft bis zur Errichtung einer stehenden Bühne, 1774–1841* (Kiel, 1928)

W. Danielsen: *Hundert Jahre Kieler Theater 1841–1944* (Kiel, 1961)

K. Gudewill: 'Musikpflege und Musikwissenschaft', *Geschichte der Christian-Albrechts-Universität Kiel 1665–1965*, v/1 (Neumünster, 1969), 189–244

U. Haensel: *Musikgeschichte Kiels im Mittelalter* (Bonn, 1971)

W. Pfannkuch: 'Opernaufführungen in Kiel 1780–1798', *Opernstudien: Anna Amalie Abert zum 65. Geburtstag* (Tutzing, 1975), 91

K. Stahmer: *Musik in Kiel: eine kommentierte Dokumentation zum Musikleben einer Grossstadt im Jahr 1967* (Wilhelming, 1975)

UWE HAENSEL

Kienlen, Johann Christoph (*b* Ulm, baptized 14 Dec 1783; *d* Dessau, 7 Dec 1829). German composer. He was the son of a *Stadtmusicus* at Ulm. Holzer showed that he appeared as a prodigy pianist and singer at the age of seven. With the help of some rich patrons he continued his studies at Munich (1802) and Paris (*c*1803–6, under Cherubini), and was then *Stadtmusikdirektor* in his native town for a short time. He returned to Paris in 1809 (when two sonatas were published by Naderman), travelled to Munich in 1810 (producing his *Claudine von Villa Bella*) and then to Stuttgart and Vienna. Here Schnyder von Wartensee became his pupil and followed him to Baden (near Vienna) when Kienlen was appointed music director to Baron Zinnicq, who ran a private theatre there and at Pressburg (now Bratislava). Kienlen returned to Vienna in 1815 and from 1817 lived for several years in Berlin, at first without an official appointment; in 1823 he became the singing instructor at the royal theatre. He is said to have died insane and in poverty.

WORKS

4 operas and Singspiels, 1810–16, incl.: Claudine von Villa Bella (Singspiel, 3, Goethe), Munich, 9 Sept 1810, *D-B*; Petrarca und Laura (opera, 3, E. N. Schlager), Pressburg, 1816, *B*

Incidental music for 3 plays, Berlin, 1817–23, lost

Introduction and songs for E. T. A. Hoffmann's Undine, *B*

*c*80 songs, pf acc., in 7 collections (1810–17), incl.: 12 Lieder von Goethe (Leipzig, 1810); 7 Lieder aus Goethe's Faust (Berlin, ?1817), *US-NH*

Symphony (Posen, ?1825); 2 sonates, pf (Paris, *c*1809); other pf music

BIBLIOGRAPHY

EitnerQ; *FétisB*; *FétisBS*

X. Schnyder von Wartensee: *Lebenserinnerungen* (Zurich, 1888)

E. Holzer: 'Ein vergessener schwäbischer Musiker', *Die Musik*, viii (1908–9), 145

ALFRED LOEWENBERG/DAVID CHARLTON

Kienzl, Wilhelm (*b* Waizenkirchen, Austria, 17 Jan 1857; *d* Vienna, 19 Oct 1941). Austrian composer. When he was three his family moved to Graz where he studied the piano with Johann Buwa and the violin under Ignaz Uhl. In 1872 he began piano lessons with Mortier de Fontaine, a pupil of Chopin. While a student at Graz University he studied composition with Mayer-Rémy; he also attended von Hausegger's lectures in music history and came to know Jensen, who encouraged him to pursue composition and discussed the works of Schumann and Wagner with him. In 1876 Kienzl was at Prague University where he continued his music studies with Krejči; from there he travelled to Bayreuth with Hausegger to attend the first performance of the *Ring*. This confirmed his already strong attachment to Wagner's music. In the next year he studied at Leipzig University and briefly with Liszt in Weimar, completing his formal education in Vienna. His dissertation, *Die musikalische Deklamation*, was completed in

1879 and gave expression to his ideas about opera and the history of music. In the same year he went again to Bayreuth where he spent a considerable time as a member of the close circle around Wagner. His disagreements with some of the group on musical matters soon terminated his stay, but he remained an admirer of Wagner and his music. He attended nearly every Bayreuth Festival during his lifetime as well as lecturing and writing on Wagner. His first impressions of Bayreuth are recorded in the *Miszellen* of 1886.

From 1879 to 1883 Kienzl travelled all over Europe, meeting nearly all the important musicians of the period, lecturing, and giving recitals with the violinist Richard Sahla and the singer Aglaja Orgeni. He was appointed director of the German opera in Amsterdam (1883), but soon returned to Graz where he completed his first opera, *Urvasi* (1884). Later he assumed the direction of the Steiermärkischer Musikverein there (1886), his responsibilities including the Graz Conservatory and the organization of orchestral concerts of new music, as well as the programming of Liederabende. In 1889 he conducted in Hamburg and later in Munich, where his opera *Heilmar der Narr* was first performed in 1892. Although these travels and his frequent lecturing often interrupted his residence in Graz, he still found time there and at Aussee, his summer residence, to compose. It was there that he completed his most successful opera, *Der Evangelimann*, whose immediate popularity resulted in productions all over Germany and Austria.

Kienzl remained in Graz until 1917. The essays written during these years contain important and interesting commentaries on the works of Kienzl's contemporaries. In 1917 he moved to Vienna, having exhausted the musical possibilities of a provincial city. To words by the chancellor, Renner, he composed the anthem of the first Austrian republic (1918). His first wife, Lili Hoke, a Bayreuth singer, died in 1919 and he married Henny Bauer in 1921. She wrote the texts for his last three operas and was a lifelong champion of his music. After completing these operas, Kienzl effectively gave up large-scale composition to concentrate on songs and choral music. He wrote in 1925: 'I cannot be and will not be atonal, but refuse just the same to be banal or antiquated'. His lecturing, conducting and composition continued, although he never came to understand the new music. Because of increasing illness he stopped composing in 1936 and watched with dismay as his operas disappeared from the repertory in Germany and Austria. With Humperdinck, Kienzl was responsible for the revival of Romanticism in opera, continuing the tradition of Weber, Lortzing and early Wagner. Returning to the naive elements of folk opera, he was able to develop them with music often strongly influenced by Wagner. He was at his best in the folk scenes and dialect pieces.

WORKS
(selective list)

OPERAS

Urvasi, op.20 (3, A. Gödel, after Kalidasa), 1884; Dresden, 1886; rev. 1909

Heilmar der Narr, op.40 (prelude, 3, Kienzl snr), 1891; Munich, 1892

Der Evangelimann, op.45 (musical play, 2, Kienzl, after L. F. Meissner), 1894; Berlin, 1895

Don Quixote, op.50 (3, Kienzl), 1897; Berlin, 1898

In Knecht Ruprechts Werkstatt, op.75 (Christmas fairytale, 1, H. Voigt), 1907; Graz, 1907

Der Kuhreigen, op.85 (musical play, 3, R. Batka, after R. H. Bartsch), 1911; Vienna, 1911

Das Testament, op.90 (musical comedy, 2, Kienzl), 1916; Vienna, 1916

Hassan der Schwärmer, op.100 (3, Bauer), 1921; Chemnitz, 1925

Sanctissimum, op.102 (melodramatic allegory, 1, Bauer), 1922; Vienna, 1925

Hans Kipfel, op.110 (Singspiel, 1, Bauer, after old Viennese), 1926; Vienna, 1926

CHORAL

2 Songs, op.14; 3 Pieces, op.17, male vv; 3 Songs, op.19, female 4vv; 5 Tanzweisen, op.21b, 4vv/female 4vv; Landsknechtlied, op.23 (H. Lingg), male vv, orch; Zur Trauung, op.26; 3 Songs, op.36, male vv; 3 Pieces, op.54, male vv; 5 Songs, op.58, female 4vv; 6 volkstümliche Lieder, op.59; 6 volkstümliche Männerchöre, op.60; 5 Songs, op.63, female vv, harp/pf ad lib; Wach' auf, mein Volk!, op.64 (A. A. Naaff), male vv, orch; Das Volkslied, Heerbannlied der deutschen Stämme, op.65, male vv

Fasching, op.67 (O. J. Bierbaum), T, Bar, B, male vv, orch; 4 Songs, op.68, male vv; 6 Songs, op.72, male vv, perc in 2 nos.; 8 Songs, op.76, female 4vv; 3 Pieces, op.78, male vv; 2 Geschichtsbilder, op.79 (Lingg), male vv, orch; Deutsche Ritterlieder, op.86 (H. W. Günthersberger), male vv, orch; Das Lied vom Kaiser Arnulf, op.88 (Graevell), male vv, orch; 3 Pieces, op.89, male vv; Im Schlachtendonner, op.92, male vv; Ostara, op.93 (H. Hagen), male vv, orch; Deutsch-Österreich, op.101 (national anthem, Renner), male/mixed vv

5 Pieces, op.103, male vv; Arbeiterlied, op.104, male vv; 4 Songs, op.105, male vv; 2 Pieces, op.107, male vv; 5 Songs, op.112, male vv; Spar-Hymne, op.115 (H. Giebisch), mixed vv, orch; Chor der Toten, op.118, mixed vv, orch

SONGS

(for 1v, pf unless otherwise stated)

2 Songs, op.1; 4 Songs, op.2; 2 Poems, op.4 (A. Grün); 9 Lieder im Volkston, op.6; 8 Lieder der Liebe, op.8; Liebes-frühling, op.11 (cycle, Rückert); Süsses Verzichten, op.16, cycle; Geliebt-Vergessen, op.18, cycle; 3 Albumblätter, op.24; 3 Songs, op.25; Abschied, op.27; Kuriose Geschichte, op.28; 3 Folksongs, op.31; 3 Songs, op.32; Frühlingslieder, op.33; 2 Lieder aus Osten, op.35; 2 Songs, op.37; 2 Songs, op.38; 2 Songs, op.39; 2 Songs, op.42; 4 Songs, op.44; 4 Japanese Songs, op.47; Waldmeister, op.49

6 Songs, op.55; Verwelkte Rosen, op.56, 1v, pf/harp; 4 volkstümliche Gesänge, op.57; 4 Songs, op.61; 3 Songs, op.66; 3 Songs, op.69a, 1v, pf/harmonium; Moderne Lyrik, op.71; Aus Onkels Liedermappe, op.73; Weihnacht, op.74; 5 Songs, op.81; 5 Songs, op.82; Ein Weihnachtslied, op.83, 1v, harmonium/org/pf; 3 Duets, op.84, male v, female v, pf; Nachsommerblüten, op.87; Das Lied vom Weltkrieg, op.91

7 Songs, op.94; Aus des Volkes Wunderhorn, op.96; Deutsch-Österreich, op.101 (national anthem, Renner), 1v, pf ad lib; 7 Songs, 2 Gräber [siebenbürgisch], op.106; 6 Lieder vom Glück, op.111; 6 Songs, op.114; Spar-Hymne, op.115; Vocalise-Etüde, op.116; 2 vaterländische Gesänge, op.117, unpubd; 7 Songs, op.120, unpubd; 3 Songs, op.121, unpubd; 4 Songs, op.123 (L. Fahrenkrog), unpubd; La delaissée (An den entschwundenen Geliebten) [text by Kienzl added to Chopin: Nocturne, op.27/2], unpubd

PIANO

Skizzen, op.3; Kahnszene, op.5; Bunte Tänze, op.10; Aus alten Märchen, op.12, pf/pf duet; Aus meinem Tagebuche, op.15, 3 vols.; 30 Tanzweisen, op.21, 3 vols., pf/pf duet; Scherzo, a, op.29; Kinderliebe und -leben, op.30; Romantische Blätter, op.34; Tanzbilder, op.41, 3 vols., pf/pf duet; Daheim!, op.43; Dichterreise, op.46, 2 vols.

(Kleiner) Carneval, op.51, 2 vols.; Bilder aus dem Volksleben, op.52; Abendstimmungen, op.53, pf duet; Neue Klavierstücke, op.62, 2 vols.; O schöne Jugendtage!, op.80, 3 vols.; 20 Stücke in Ländlerform, op.95, 2 vols., pf/pf duet; Variationen über das Strassburglied aus der Oper 'Der Kuhreigen', op.109b, unpubd

OTHER WORKS

Inst: 3 Phantasiestücke, op.7, vn, pf; Pf Trio, f, op.13; Str Qt no.1, b, op.22; Abendstimmungen, op.53, str orch, harp; 2 Pieces, op.69b, harmonium; Adagio (Trost in Tränen), op.69c, vc, harmonium/org/pf; 8 Chorale Preludes, op.77, 2 vols., org; Str Qt no.2, c, op.99; Waldstimmungen, op.108, 4 horns; Symphonische Variationen über das Strassburglied aus der Oper 'Der Kuhreigen', op.109a, orch; Str Qt, E, op.113; Lied ohne Worte, 2 vn, unpubd

Melodramas: Die Brautfahrt, op.9 (Eichendorff), speaker, pf/orch; 2 Melodramas, op.97 (R. Hamerling, F. K. Ginzkey), speaker, pf; Die Jungfrau und die Nonne, op.98 (Keller), speaker, choruses, orch; 3 melodramas to music by Beethoven, Schubert and Chopin; Ein Marienballade von François Villon, op.119 (De Montcorbier)

Numerous arrs. of his own and other music

Principal publishers: Bote & Bock, Breitkopf & Härtel, Forberg, Heinrichshofen, Kahnt, Kistner, Leuckart, Reibenstein, Ries & Erler, Siegel, Universal, Weinberger, Zimmermann

WRITINGS

Die musikalische Deklamation (Leipzig, 1880)

Miszellen (Leipzig, 1886) [essays]

ed.: F. Brendel: *Grosse und kleine Musikgeschichte* (Leipzig, 1886–9)

'Titus' von Mozart: Einrichtung für deutsche Bühnen (Vienna, 1893)

Die Gesamtkunst des XIX. Jahrhunderts: Richard Wagner (Vienna, 1904, 2/1908)

Aus Kunst und Leben (Berlin, 2/1904) [essays]

Im Konzert (Berlin, 1908) [essays]

Betrachtungen und Erinnerungen (Berlin, 1909) [essays]

Meine Lebenswanderung: Erlebtes, Erschautes (Stuttgart, 1926)

BIBLIOGRAPHY

H. Hagen, ed.: *Festschrift . . . Wilhelm Kienzl* (Graz, 1917)

H. Sittner: 'Aus den Kindheitsgedichten von Wilhelm Kienzl', *Die Bastei*, i (Vienna, 1946), 6

O. Wessely: 'Wilhelm Kienzl und Adolf Jensen', *Oberösterreichischer Kulturbericht* (1948), 37

K. Trambauer: *Wilhelm Kienzls Opernstoffe* (diss., U. of Vienna, 1950)

H. Kienzl: 'Kleine Begebenheiten aus einem reichen Leben', *Wiener Zeitung* (1951), 220, 225, 231, 237, 243, 249

H. Sittner: *Kienzl–Rosegger: eine Künstlerfreundschaft* (Zurich, 1953) [incl. diaries, worklist and correspondence]

H. Sittner: 'Wilhelm Kienzl', *Grosse Österreicher*, x, Neue österreichische Biographie ab 1815 (Vienna, 1957), 111

JOSEPH CLARK

Kiepura, Jan (*b* Sosnowiec, 16 May 1902; *d* Harrison, NY, 15 Aug 1966). Polish tenor. He studied in Warsaw with Leliva, making his début in Lwów as Faust in 1924. His international career began in 1926 with a very successful appearance at the Staatsoper in Vienna as Cavaradossi. He subsequently sang at La Scala in the première of *Le preziose ridicole* by Lattuada, and in Buenos Aires, Paris and Chicago. He gradually abandoned opera for films, making many in Germany and the USA, and marrying the film star and soprano Marta Eggerth in 1936. However, he sang at the Metropolitan (1938–42), and later on Broadway and on tours with his wife in *The Merry Widow*.

BIBLIOGRAPHY

R. Celletti: 'Jan Kiepura', *Le grandi voci* (Rome, 1964) [with opera discography by R. Vegeto]

LEO RIEMENS

Kiesewetter, Raphael Georg (*b* Holleschau [now Holešov, Czechoslovakia], 29 Aug 1773; *d* Baden, 1 Jan 1850). Austrian musicologist. Son of Alois Ferdinand Kiesewetter (1739–93), a doctor and writer on medicine, he studied philosophy at the University of Olomouc and then law at the University of Vienna. Leaving the university without completing his studies, he became an official in the chancellery of the imperial army, whose headquarters were in Schwetzingen; he remained there until 1801. In 1807 he became a councillor in the war office in Vienna. He was raised to the nobility in 1843 with the title 'Edler von Wiesenbrunn'. He was pensioned in 1845 and retired to Baden three years later.

As a youth Kiesewetter was taught the piano and singing; he later learnt to play the flute, and as an adult he had lessons in the bassoon and the guitar. Albrechtsberger was among his teachers in theory. From 1801 he took part as a bass singer in many public and private concerts in Vienna. From 1816, in his own house, he organized annual concerts devoted to vocal music of the 16th to 18th centuries. In connection with these concerts he formed a collection of old scores which he bequeathed to the Austrian National Library and which later provided important research material for his nephew, August Wilhelm Ambros. His continuous involvement in Viennese concert life, in particular with the Gesellschaft der Musikfreunde, earned him many honours, among them honorary membership of the Congregazione ed Accademia di S Cecilia in Rome

(1840) and in the Akademie der Künste in Berlin (1843).

Kiesewetter's pioneering achievements were in the field of musicology, which, like Fétis, he came to by way of music history and theory. In his books, many of which he had previously prepared in the form of essays for journals, he dealt with the problems of the music of non-European Mediterranean cultures and of the Ancient Greeks, as well as the history of western music from the early Middle Ages until the Viennese Classical period. His major work, the *Geschichte der europäisch-abendländischen oder unsrer heutigen Musik*, is particularly noteworthy as the last exposition of the evolutionary concept of history of the Age of Enlightenment. His studies of the music of the Netherlands established him as one of the originators of research into the history of style; his *Schicksale und Beschaffenheit des weltlichen Gesanges* was written in the early days of topographical music research and the history of genres. In compiling *Die Musik der Araber* he was the first to enlist the help of an orientalist, Joseph Freiherr von Hammer-Purgstall (1774–1856), which enabled him to base his presentation on the original Arab source material; this book was justly considered unsurpassed until the end of the 19th century. For his scholarly achievements, Kiesewetter was made a corresponding member of the Imperial Academy of Sciences, Vienna, in 1849.

WRITINGS

Geschichte der europäisch-abendländischen oder unsrer heutigen Musik (Leipzig, 1834; Eng. trans., 1848)
Ueber die Musik der neueren Griechen nebst freien Gedanken über alt-aegyptische und alt-griechische Musik (Leipzig, 1838)
Guido von Arezzo: sein Leben und Wirken (Leipzig, 1840)
Schicksale und Beschaffenheit des weltlichen Gesanges vom frühen Mittelalter bis zur Erfindung des dramatischen Styles und den Anfängen der Oper (Leipzig, 1841/R1970)
Die Musik der Araber (Leipzig, 1842)
ed.: *Der neuen Aristoxener zerstreute Aufsätze über das Irrige der musikalischen Arithmetik und das Eitle ihrer Temperaturrechnungen* (Leipzig, 1846) [incl. articles by Kiesewetter]
Catalog der Sammlung alter Musik des k.k. Hofrathes Raphael Georg Kiesewetter Edlen von Wiesenbrunn in Wien (Vienna, 1847)
Gallerie der alten Contrapunctisten: eine Auswahl aus ihren Werken in verständlichen Partituren (Vienna, 1847)
Über die Octave des Pythagoras (Vienna, 1848)

BIBLIOGRAPHY

A. Fuchs: Obituaries, *NZM*, xxxii (1850), 89, 101; *Revue et gazette musicale de Paris*, xvii (1850), 97
——: 'Raphael Georg Kiesewetter', *Blätter für Musik, Theater und Kunst*, i (1855), 155, 171, 191, 195
W. B. Squire: 'A Letter from Kiesewetter to Pearsall', *MT*, lxiii (1902), 93
H. Kier: 'Kiesewetters historische Hauskonzerte', *KJb*, lii (1968), 95
——: *Raphael Georg Kiesewetter (1773–1850): Wegbereiter des musikalischen Historismus* (Regensburg, 1968)
——: 'Musikalischer Historismus im vormärzlichen Wien', *Die Ausbreitung des Historismus über die Musik*, ed. W. Wiora (Regensburg, 1969), 55

OTHMAR WESSELY

Kiessling, Heinz [Mondstein, Christian] (*b* Nuremberg, 11 March 1926). German songwriter, arranger and pianist. He studied at the Nuremberg Conservatory (1946–9), and became a concert pianist before turning to composition in 1950. He has been most active as a television composer and arranger, but has also composed for films and written light music for orchestra, occasionally under the pseudonym Christian Mondstein. He has toured throughout the world and made recordings with his own orchestra.

Kiev. Capital of the Ukrainian SSR. Now the third

largest city of the USSR, Kiev was already a famous cultural and trading centre by the 10th century. After its official conversion to Christianity in the time of St Vladimir (baptized AD 989), the State of Kiev adopted Byzantine sacred music; Greek professional singers also came to Kiev from Byzantium. As Christianity was brought to Kiev by the Greeks and Bulgarians the liturgical chants were probably written in those two languages. However, characteristic Ukrainian music developed with its own melodies at an early date, as examples from the 11th, 12th and 13th centuries show; these were known as *Kiyevskyy rospiv*, after their origin, or *Znamennyy rospiv*, after their neumatic notation. In the second half of the 16th century the five-line staff with clef, the notation peculiar to Kiev (e.g. *Supralsky heirmologion*, 1593), was adopted, replacing the neumatic notation predominant in the Orthodox Church. Laid waste by the Tatars in the 13th and 14th centuries, Kiev had lost its political importance by that period, and it regained some musical significance only in the 16th century after the Polish–Lithuanian union of 1569, which brought the Ukrainian Church under Western influence. At the same time liturgical chant and polyphony, following Polish practice, appeared at the Kiev Academy (1615–1915); later the theorist and composer Diletsky (*c*1630–90) evolved their principles in his treatise *Musykiyskaya hramatyka* (1677). The academy maintained the tradition of sacred music and produced several generations of masters, notably Artem Vedel (1767–1806). Cantus firmus technique was employed by local composers, with the liturgical melody sounding in the tenor line, between the bass and alto. Sometimes a second tenor or bass was added, which formed the basis of the powerful choral works by the Ukrainian composers of the post-Palestrina era, such as Dmitry Bortnyansky and Maxim Berezovsky. In the Baroque era Kiev gradually lost its musical importance, and the continual drain of Ukrainian talent into Muscovy, which was assuming increasing political importance, resulted in a decline in musical activity in the Ukraine. However, two notable 18th-century symphonies on Ukrainian themes survive, one by Ovsianiko-Kulykovsky and the other anonymous.

Important 19th-century Kiev societies included the Kiev Municipal Orchestra (1704–1865), the Philharmonic Society (1833–62), a string quartet (1852), the Academy Choir (1850) and the Kijwer Gesang-Verein (1854), a choir made up of German Kiev residents. Also noteworthy was the work of the state-subsidized Kiev Russian Music Society (1863–75), which contributed greatly to the growth of musical life in Kiev; it founded a music school (1868–1912) at which the Czech violin teacher Otakar Ševčík taught from 1875 to 1893. This school provided the foundation for the later orchestral conservatory of Kiev. The Kiev Opera, which gradually became the musical focus of the Ukraine, was founded in 1867; its repertory included operas by Rossini, Tchaikovsky, Puccini and Lysenko. During this period many soloists appeared in Kiev, the best known of whom were Angelica Catalani, Ignaz Schuppanzigh, Karol Lipiński, Henryk Wieniawski, Bernhard Romberg, A. F. Servais (who wrote the play *Souvenirs de Kiev*), the guitarist M. K. Sokołowsky and Franz Liszt.

The second half of the 19th century brought a revival in Ukrainian music. Mykola Lysenko was active in Kiev as a composer, pianist, choral conductor, ethnomusicologist and teacher. His assistants Kyrylo Stetsenko, Yakiv Stepovy, M. D. Leontovich and Alexandre Koshyts made further contributions until the advent of the Soviet regime, which, through arbitrary policies, brought the group's musical acivities to an end, also causing the voluntary exile of Fyodor Akimenko, Koshyts and Nestor Horodovenko. Two outstanding composers and teachers, Levko Revutsky and Boris Lyatoshyns'ky, remained and succeeded in training a whole generation of composers at the Kiev Conservatory. In the 1970s Kiev had an outstanding Opera with a fine ballet company, the radio orchestra, the Philharmonic Orchestra, two conservatories (orchestral and operatic), a bandore ensemble, the 'Veriovka' folksong group, the 'Doumka' mixed choir and several chamber orchestras and string quartets.

BIBLIOGRAPHY

M. Stefanovych: *Kievsky derzhavny ordena Lenina teatr opery ta balety URSR imeni T. H. Shevchenka* [The Kiev T. H. Shevchenko opera and ballet theatre] (Kiev, 1960)

H. Hryhoriev: *U staromu Kievi* [In old Kiev] (Kiev, 1961)

H. Kurkovsky: 'Pedahohy-pianisty Keïvskoï konservatoriï (1913–1933)', *Ukrainske muzykoznavstvo*, ii (1967), 264

Y. Stanishevsky: *Ukraïnsky muzykalny teatr (1917–1967)* (Kiev, 1970)

P. Kozytsky: *Spiv i muzyka v Kivsky akademiïza 300 rokiv ïï isnuvannya* [Song and music at the Kiev Academy during its 300 years of existence] (Kiev, 1971)

T. Nekrasova: 'Keïvska akademiya ta ïï znachennya v rozvetku muzychnoï osvity i professionalizmu' [The Kiev Academy and the importance of musical and professional education], *Ukrainske muzykoznavstvo*, vi (1971), 238

M. Kuzmin: *Zabuti storinky muzychnoho zhettya Kieva* [Forgotten pages of the musical life of Kiev] (Kiev, 1972)

K. Shamayeva: 'Konsertne zhettya Kieva v pershi porevoliutsiyni roky' [Concerts in Kiev in the first years after the Revolution], *Ukrainske muzykoznavstvo*, viii (1973), 35

M. Hordiychuk: 'Na shlyakhu do stvorennya ukraïnskoi opery v Kievi', *Ukrainske muzykoznavstvo*, x (1975), 93

For further bibliography see UNION OF SOVIET SOCIALIST REPUBLICS, §X.

ARISTIDE WIRSTA

Kikkawa [Satō], **Eishi** (*b* Mino, nr. Hiroshima, 13 Feb 1909). Japanese musicologist. Born Eishi Satō, he changed his family name when he married Setsuko Kikkawa in 1938. In 1930 he entered Tokyo University, where he studied music history with Hisao Tanabe and aesthetics with Yoshinori Ōnishi. After graduating in 1933, he tried to become a music publisher, but returned to university in 1937 for further research into ancient documents of Japanese music. A lecturer in Japanese music history at Tokyo University (1946–69), he also held posts at Tokyo Music School (1946–9), Tokyo Geijutsu Daigaku (Tokyo National University of Fine Arts and Music) (1962–) and at Musashino College of Music (1966–). In 1949 he became one of the directors of the Society for Research in Asiatic Music, and in 1948 became responsible for many music programmes on the NHK. For his works on Japanese music he received, in 1972, the Medal of Honour with Purple Ribbon and the Broadcasting Cultural Prize.

His major contribution to musicology is his book, *Nihon ongaku no rekishi* ('A history of Japanese music', 1965), the best-documented discussion of the subject. His special field, however, is the music for *shamisen* or for *koto*, the most popular genre of Japanese music since the 17th century. He is also known for his works on Michio Miyagi, whom he knew personally.

WRITINGS

'Art of Blind Musician Miyagi', *Contemporary Japan*, xii (1943), 693–723

'Shamisen no sawari ni tsuite' [On Sawari effects of the *shamisen*], *Tanabe Festschrift* (Tokyo, 1943), 192

Nihon ongaku no seikaku [Characteristics of Japanese music] (Tokyo, 1948)

'Nihon ongaku ni oyoboboshita bungaku engeki no eikyō' [The influence of literature and drama on Japanese music], *Bigaku* (1951), no.6, p.61

Hōgaku kanshō [The Appreciation of Japanese music] (Tokyo, 1952, 2/1953)

'Nihon engeki no hōgaku ni oyoboshita eikyō' [The influence of Japanese drama on Japanese music], *Bigaku* (1953), no.13, p.27

Hōgaku kanshō techō [Notes on how to appreciate Japanese music] (Osaka, 1953)

Hōgaku meikyoku sen: nagauta [Masterpieces of Japanese music: nagauta] (Osaka, 1955)

'Sangen denrai kō' [Study on the introduction of *shamisen*]; 'An Introductory Guide to Research into the *Shamisen*', *Tōyō ongaku kenkyū*, xiv–xv (1958), 29; 52

'Hōgaku no tokushoku' [Characteristics of Japanese music], *Tōyō shisō kōza*, v (Tokyo, 1958), 183

Hōgaku kanshō nyūmon [Introduction to the appreciation of Japanese music] (Osaka, 1959, 10/1972)

Miyagi Michio den [The life of Michio Miyagi] (Tokyo, 1962, 3/1965)

Nihon ongaku no rekishi [A history of Japanese music] (Osaka, 1965, 9/1974)

'Meiji no nihon ongaku kan' [A view of Japanese music in the Meiji period], *Bigaku* (1965), no.60, p.1

'Sōkyoku to jiuta no rekishi' [A history of *koto* music and *jiuta*]; 'Rokudan' to Yatsuhashi Kengyō' [Rokudan and Yatsuhashi Kengyō]; 'Yatsuhashiryū sōkyoku ni tsuite' [On *koto* music of the Yatsuhashi school], *Sōkyoku to juita*, Tōyō ongaku sensho, iii (Tokyo, 1967), 21; 127; 115

Hogaku eno shōtai [An invitation to Japanese music] (Tokyo, 1967)

'Gagaku to kinsei hōgaku' [*Gagaku* and Japanese music of recent years], *Gagaku-kai*, xxxxviii (1968), 48

Nihon ongaku kanshō kyokushū [Examples of Japanese music] (Tokyo, 1970)

'Nihon ongaku ni okeru shōchō-giho' [The symbol-technique in Japanese traditional music], *Bigaku* (1970), no.80, p.1

'Gendai hōgaku no chichi Miyagi Michio ni oyoboshita yōgaku no eikyō' [The influence of western music on Michio Miyagi, a founder of modern Japanese music], *Musashino ongaku daigaku kiyō*, vi (1972), 18

Numerous articles in dictionaries and encyclopedias, including *Ongaku jiten* [Music dictionary] (Tokyo, 1954–7), *Sekai dai hyakka jiten* [World's great encyclopedia] (Tokyo, 1955–63), *Encyclopaedia Japponica* (Tokyo, 1967–)

BIBLIOGRAPHY

Nihon ongaku to sono shūhen: Kikkawa Eishi sensei kanreki kinen ronbun-shū [On and about Japanese music: articles to celebrate the 61st birthday of Prof. Eishi Kikkawa = *Kikkawa Festschrift*] (Tokyo, 1973) [with outline of life, p.10 (Jap. nos.) and list of works, p.17 and 26 (Jap. nos.)]

MASAKATA KANAZAWA

Kilar, Wojciech (*b* Lwów, 17 July 1932). Polish composer and pianist. He studied at the Katowice State Music School (1950–55) with Malawski (theory), Markiewiczówna (piano) and Woytowicz (piano and composition), with whom he continued his composition studies at the Kraków Conservatory (1955–8); he also had composition lessons with Boulanger in Paris. Among the awards he has received are a prize at the Festival of Youth (1955), the Lili Boulanger Foundation Award (1960) and a prize from the Polish Ministry of Culture, given in particular recognition of his film music (for which he is best known in Poland). He began his compositional career as a neo-classicist, equally at ease in writing the strict polyphony he had learned with Woytowicz and in the complex harmonic style of the Sinfonia concertante. After 1962 he began to make use of novel techniques in texture and vocal production (as in *Diphthongos* and *Upstairs-downstairs*). Apart from the film scores, he has been most unquestionably successful in his orchestral pieces.

WORKS
(selective list)

Orch: Conc., fl, str, 1953; Mała uwertura [Little ov.], 1955; Sym. no.1, str, 1955; Sinfonia concertante (Sym. no.2), pf, orch, 1956; Oda, vn, wind, perc, 1957; 2 Pf Conc., 1958; Coro, 20 wind, *c*1960; Riff 62,

1962; Générique, 1963; Springfield Sonnet, 1965; Solenne, amp S, 67 insts, 1967; Prelude and Christmas Carol, 4 ob, str, 1972; Krzesany, sym. poem, 1974; Kościelec 1909, 1976

Vocal: Kołysanki [Lullabies] (cantata, J. Czechowicz), S, 3 cl, bn, hn, harp, pf, 1957; Herbsttag (cantata, Rilke), A, str qt, 1960; Diphthongos, chorus, perc, 2 pf, str, 1964; Upstairs–downstairs (textless), 2 girls'/boys' choruses, orch, 1971; Bogurodzica [Mother of God], chorus, orch, 1975

Inst: Sonatina, fl, pf, 1951; Variations on a Theme of Paganini, pf, 1951; Pf Sonata, 1952; Sonata, hn, pf, 1954; Wind Qnt, 1954; One for Three, a sax, vib, db, 1963; Training 68, cl, trbn, vc, pf, 1968

Dramatic: Maska czarnej śmierci [The mask of the black death], ballet, after Poe, 1961; incidental music, film scores

Principal publisher: Polskie Wydawnictwo Muzyczne

BIBLIOGRAPHY
T. A. Zieliński: ' "Générique" Wojciecha Kilara', Ruch muzyczny, vii/22 (1963), 16
L. Markiewicz: 'Wojciech Kilar: en nutida komponist', Nutida musik, ix/1–2 (1965–6), 18
T. A. Zieliński: ' "Training 68" Wojciecha Kilara', Ruch muzyczny, xii/23 (1968), 10
BOGUSŁAW SCHÄFFER

Kilgen, George, & Son. American firm of organ builders. It was founded in New York in 1851 by George Kilgen (d 1902), a native of Durlach, Germany, who had been apprenticed there to an organ builder named Voijt and who went to the USA with a group of political refugees in 1848, finding employment with the Jardine firm. In 1873 Kilgen moved his company to St Louis, where it prospered. In 1886 his son, Charles Christian Kilgen (1859–1932), joined as a partner, and during his presidency one of the most noted Kilgen organs, that of St Patrick's Cathedral, New York, was built in 1928. After Charles Kilgen's death the firm was reorganized under the name Kilgen Organ Co. but, although it continued to produce many small instruments, its fortunes declined until the business was dissolved in 1960.

BARBARA OWEN

Kilian, Johann [Hans] (b 1515 or 1516; d Neuburg an der Donau, 29 Dec 1595). German composer and printer. A medal dated 1555 gives his age as 39. In early youth he went to Neuburg to the court of Count Palatine Ottheinrich, whose treasurer he was in 1544. Ottheinrich had introduced the Lutheran doctrine in 1542 and he helped Kilian to establish a publishing house for reformed literature and music which issued its first publications in 1545 but which was ravaged by war in 1546 and not reopened until 1556. In the same year Ottheinrich became Elector Palatine, had Kilian as his secretary and in 1558, just before he died, awarded him an annual payment of 200 florins 'for life'. At the same time Kilian gave up publishing. He was also interested in alchemy, and Ottheinrich left him the collection of works by Paracelsus that he had helped him assemble. Except for an isolated reference in 1594 nothing is known of his later years. Nor do we know anything of his musical education.

His four-part setting of the chorale O Herr, mein Gott was published as an appendix to Caspar Huberinus's Vom Christlichen Ritter (Neuburg, 1545). The fourth volume of Georg Forster's Frische teutsche Liedlein (Nuremberg, 1556) contains his four-part song Ach Lieb, ich muss dich lassen, which uses as bass the tenor of Isaac's Innsbruck, ich muss dich lassen; Sebastian Ochsenkun published the same song and Kilian's motet Laudate dominum in his Tabulaturbuch auff die Lauten (Heidelberg, 1558). These pieces show that Kilian was a skilful composer, who well knew how to use cantus firmus techniques. An inventory of 1544 (D-HEu Pal. Germ.318) also records some lost pieces by him: a

motet, Memor esto, and 11 different German songs (whose texts survive).

BIBLIOGRAPHY
K. Schottenloher: Pfalzgraf Ottheinrich und das Buch (Münster, 1927)
S. Hermelink: 'Ein Musikalienverzeichnis der Heidelberger Hofkapelle aus dem Jahr 1544', Ottheinrich-Gedenkschrift zur 400-jährig. Wiederkehr seiner Kurfürstenzeit (Heidelberg, 1956), 247
A. Layer: 'Pfalzgraf Ottheinrich und die Musik', AMw, xv (1958), 258
LINI HÜBSCH-PFLEGER

Killmayer, Wilhelm (b Munich, 21 Aug 1927). German composer. He had lessons in composition and conducting from von Waltershausen (1945–50) and studied at Munich University with von Ficker for musicology and Orff for composition (1953). From 1955 to 1957 he taught theory at the Trapp Conservatory in Munich, from 1961 to 1965 he was ballet conductor at the Bavarian State Opera, and in 1974 he was appointed professor of composition at the Staatliche Musikhochschule, Munich. He won the Culture Prize of Munich (1957), an Italia Prize (for Une leçon de français in 1965) and two German Rome Prizes (1958 and 1965). His creative work, influenced by Orff, has developed independently, drawing on other types of new music but retaining a direct expressive power.

WORKS
(selective list)

Stage: La buffonata (ballet-opera, T. Dorst), 1959–60, Heidelberg, 1961; La tragedia di Orfeo (after A. Poliziano), 1960–61, Munich, 1961; Yolimba, oder Die Grenzen der Magie (musical farce, 1, Dorst, Killmayer), Wiesbaden, 1964, rev., Munich, 1970; Une leçon de français, 1964, Stuttgart, 1966; Pas de deux classique, 1964, Munich, 1965; Encores (2 ballets), Munich, 1970

Orch: Pf Conc., 1955; Divertissement, 1959; Sym. no.1 'Fogli', 1968; Sym. no.2 'Ricordanze', 13 insts, 1968–9; Fin al punto, str, 1970; Sym. no.3 'Menschen-Los', 1972–3; Nachtgedanken, 1973; Paradies, 1974; The Broken Farewell, tpt, small orch, 1977; Jugendzeit, 1977; Überstehen und Hoffen, 1977–8; Verschüttete Zeichen, 1978

Choral: Canti amorosi, S, T, vv, 1953–4; Lieder, Oden und Szenen (Goethe), vv, 1962; Geistliche Hymnen und Gesänge (Racine), vv, 1964; Romantische Chorlieder (Tieck), male 3vv, harp ad lib, 1965; 7 rondeaux (d'Orléans), female vv, 1966; Lauda (Jacopone da Todi), 8vv, orch ad lib, 1968; Laudatu (St Francis), vv, 1969; Cantetto (Ungaretti), vv, 1971; Speranza, chorus 5vv, 1977

Solo vocal: Rêveries, S, pf, perc, 1953; Romanzen (Lorca), S, pf, perc, 1954; 8 Shakespeare Lieder, T, vn, cl, bn, pf, perc, 1955; Le petit savoyard (Fr. trad.), S, 7 insts, 1956; Sappho, S, small orch, 1959–60; 3 Gesänge nach Hölderlin, Bar, pf, 1965; 3 canti di Leopardi, Bar, orch, 1965; Blasons anatomiques du corps féminin, S, cl, pf trio, 1968; Altissima, S, fl, perc, 1969, orchd 1970; Preghiere (Ps lxviii), Bar, orch, 1969; Salvum me fac, Bar, pf, 1971; Tamquam sponsus, S, 7 insts, 1974

Inst: Kammermusik, jazz insts, 1958; 3 danze, ob, perc, 1959; 3 pezzi, tpt, pf, 1968; Str Qt, 1969; Per nove strumenti, 1969; The Woods so Wilde, fl, va, gui, xyl, vib, perc, 1970; Schumann in Endenich, perc ens, 1972; Paradies, pfs, 1972; Kindertage, va, pf, perc ens, 1973; Pf Qt, 1975; An John Field, 5 nocturnes, pf, 1975; Str Qt, 1975; Brahms-Bildnis, pf trio, 1976

Principal publisher: Schott

PAUL GRIFFITHS

Kilpinen, Yrjö (Henrik) (b Helsinki, 4 Feb 1892; d Helsinki, 2 May 1959). Finnish composer. He studied under Furuhjelm at the Helsinki Music Institute (1908–9, 1911–12, 1916–17), under Hofmann and Heuberger in Vienna (1910–11) and under Juon and Taubmann in Berlin (1913–14). He made several tours of Scandinavia and the rest of Europe, and was a member of the Conseil Permanent pour la Coopération International des Compositeurs. In 1948 he was elected to the Finnish Academy.

Kilpinen was essentially a composer of songs, modest pieces which found an immediate public response and gained him numerous enthusiastic admirers. Yet his standing has been contested, and some have considered his reputation to rest more on sentiment than on aesthetic judgement. The popularity of the songs may be ascribed to their treatment of homely and other familiar feelings, and also to the specifically Finnish quality that is particularly characteristic of the more ambitious numbers. Kilpinen was principally interested in giving musical expression to his reactions to Finnish scenery, and in this he expressed, to some degree, feelings and experiences common to the whole nation. The favour his songs found in Germany in the 1930s, in particular, probably resulted from his close relationship with the lied tradition and with such of its characteristic themes as death and loneliness. All his life he remained apart from any new techniques. Rather he made skilful use of the simplest materials: ostinato accompaniment figures and ideas dominated by single intervals, notably the 7th or the 9th. This excessive affection for certain intervals often leads to mannerism. 5ths, sometimes in parallel motion, also occur frequently, giving rise to a sense of emptiness and archaism that may be used to underline the text. Kilpinen's melody is founded on the semitone, tone, 4th and 5th; his line may be artlessly simple or quite free in its following the structure and sense of the text. His rhythm gradually became more straightforward and more faithful to the verse.

WORKS
(selective list)

Song cycles: Reflexer [Reflections], opp.33–4 (P. Lagerkvist), 1922; Fantasi och verklighet [Fantasy and reality] (E. Josephson), 1922; Hjärtat [The heart] (B. Bergman), 1922–3; Tunturilauluja [Songs of the fells], opp.52–4 (V. E. Törmänen), 1926; Lieder der Liebe I–II, op.59 (Morgenstern), 1928; Lieder um den Tod, op.62 (Morgenstern), 1928; Sommarsegen (A. Sergel), 1932–3; Spielmannslieder (Sergel), 1932–3; Grabstein, op.80 (H. F. von Zwehl), n.d.; Herbst, op.98 (Hesse), 1942; Lieder um eine kleine Stadt (B. Huber), 1942; Hochgebirgswinter (Hesse), 1954

Many other songs (total over 750), half unpubd

Other works: over 30 male choruses, 6 pf sonatas, other pf pieces; Sonata, vc, pf; Suite, vc; Sonata, vn, pf, inc.

Principal publishers: Breitkopf & Härtel, Finnish Broadcasting Corporation, Hansen, Musikki Fazer

BIBLIOGRAPHY

W. Legge: *The Songs of Yrjö Kilpinen* (London, 1936)
T. Karila: *Vesimaisemat Jean Sibeliuksen, Oskar Merikannon ja Yrjö Kilpisen yksinlaulujen melodiikassa* [Water-landscapes in the melodies of the solo songs of Sibelius, Merikanto and Kilpinen] (diss., Helsinki U., 1954; Helsinki, 1959)
——: *Sanat ja sävelet Yrjö Kilpisen Koskenniemi-lauluissa* (Hämeenlinna, 1956)
——: *Yrjö Kilpinen* (Borgå, 1964)
F. L. Pullano: *A Study of the Published German Songs of Yrjö Kilpinen* (diss., U. of Illinois, 1970)
B. Middaugh: 'The Lieder of Yrjö Kilpinen', *National Association of Teachers of Singing Bulletin*, xxvii/2 (1970), 2, 38

HANNU ILARI LAMPILA

Kim, Earl [Eul] (*b* Dinuba, Calif., 6 Jan 1920). American composer of Korean descent. He studied at the University of California, Los Angeles, with Schoenberg (1940–41) and with Sessions at the University of California, Berkeley (1947–52). Kim has taught at Berkeley, at Princeton and, from 1967, at Harvard. He also conducts and is an excellent ensemble pianist. His works are few and extremely delicate in style; despite Schoenberg's influence he has seldom used 12-note serial composition.

WORKS
(selective list)

Letters found near a suicide (F. Horne), S, pf, 1954; Dialogues, pf, orch, 1959; Exercises en route (Beckett): Dead Calm, They are far out, Gooseberries she said, S, fl, ob, cl, vn, vc, perc, actors, dancers, film, 1963–70; Earthlight (Beckett), romanza, coloratura S, vn, pf, lights, 1973

MICHAEL STEINBERG

Kimball, Jacob (*b* Topsfield, Mass., 22 Feb 1761; *d* Topsfield, 24 July 1826). American composer and tune book compiler. He served as a drummer boy at the outset of the War of Independence. In 1780 he graduated from Harvard College, studied law and was admitted to the Bar in New Hampshire. He was mainly occupied, however, as a singing teacher. He died in poverty. Kimball published two collections devoted almost entirely to his own music: the *Rural Harmony* (Boston, 1793) and the *Essex Harmony* (Exeter, New Hampshire, 1800). Among his 120 published compositions, some were widely known through editions of the popular *Village Harmony* (Exeter, from 1800 on).

BIBLIOGRAPHY

F. J. Metcalf: *American Writers and Compilers of Sacred Music* (New York, 1925/*R*1967)
G. Wilcox: *Jacob Kimball, Jr. (1761–1826): his Life and Works* (diss., U. of Southern California, 1957)
See also PSALMODY (ii), §II.

RICHARD CRAWFORD

Kimmerling, Robert [Johannes Evangelist] (*b* Vienna, 8 Dec 1737; *d* Oberweiden, 5 Dec 1799). Austrian composer. He was educated at the Gymnasium of the Benedictine monastery in Melk, where he also had singing and keyboard lessons and in 1751 made his début as a composer with a festival cantata. After taking vows (24 November 1754) he studied theology in Vienna, where he became a composition pupil of Joseph Haydn and independently studied the works of Graun and C. P. E. Bach. From 1761 he was choirmaster and music teacher at Melk; among his pupils were Marian Paradeiser, Cajetan Ansdorfer, Gregor Hauer, and, it is alleged, J. G. Albrechtsberger. The high points of his career came in 1764 with two concerts given at Melk (the first in the presence of the Emperor Francis I, the Crown Prince Joseph and the Archduke Leopold, and the second before the Empress Maria Theresia), and in 1770 with the performance of his biblical Singspiel *Rebekka, die Braut Isaaks*, which he had composed on the occasion of Marie Antoinette's stay at the monastery. Kimmerling spent the last 22 years of his life as a clergyman in the monastic parishes of Getsdorf (1777), Weikersdorf (from 1778) and Oberweiden (from 1781).

WORKS

Sacred: Rebekka, die Braut Isaaks (sacred Singspiel, B. Schuster), 21 April 1770 (Vienna, 1770); 3 masses, 4vv, insts, org, *A-SE*; 2 Requiem, 4vv, insts, org, *Gd*, *M*; Munera mystica Deo oblata, festal cantata, 1751, *M*; *c*30 smaller Lat. sacred works, incl. Vespers, antiphons, canticles, psalms, motets, 1–5vv, most with insts, org, *M*, Maria Taferl, *SEI*, *Wn*, titles listed in Wessely; 2 masses, formerly in *M*, smaller sacred works, lost

Other: lieder, qts, trios, duets, pf works, mentioned in Kühnel catalogue, 1802

BIBLIOGRAPHY

'Bericht über den Musikzustand des löbl. Stiftes Mölk in alter und neuer Zeit', *Allgemeine musikalische Zeitung mit besonderer Rücksicht auf den österreichischen Kaiserstaat*, ii (1818), 350
'Östreichs Prälaturen', *AMZ*, xxxi (1829), col.417, 441f
A. Fuchs: 'Beiträge zur Tonkünstler-Geschichte Österreichs. 2. Robert Kimmerling, aus dem Stifte zu Mölk', *Allgemeine Wiener Musik-Zeitung*, iii (1843), 3
F. Dworschak: 'Joseph Haydn und Karl Joseph Weber von Fürnberg', *Unsere Heimat*, v (1932), 202
O. Wessely: 'Kimmerling, Robert', *MGG*

OTHMAR WESSELY

Kincaid, William (*b* Minneapolis, 26 April 1895; *d* Philadelphia, 27 March 1967). American flautist. He began to study the flute at the age of ten. In 1911 he moved to New York, where he entered the Institute of Musical Art, studying composition and becoming the prize pupil for flute under Georges Barrère. In 1914

Walter Damrosch invited him to join the New York SO where he remained until 1918, appearing many times as soloist with the orchestra. Thereafter he returned to the IMA to take a postgraduate course, gaining the highest honours. Between 1919 and 1921 Kincaid was a member of the New York Chamber Music Society and then joined the Philadelphia Orchestra as solo flute, remaining there until 1960. He entered the faculty of the Curtis Institute of Music as one of its youngest members and became an eminent teacher and did much to enhance the institute's reputation. Kincaid was a staunch believer in the metal flute, playing latterly on one with a platinum body built by Powell of Boston in 1939. Shortly before his death he gave it to one of his most distinguished pupils, Elaine Shaffer. He also amassed a considerable collection of historic flutes.

BIBLIOGRAPHY

J. Krell: *Kincaidiana: a Flute Player's Notebook* (Culver City, Calif., 1973)

PHILIP BATE

Kind, Johann Friedrich (*b* Leipzig, 4 March 1768; *d* Dresden, 25 June 1843). German writer. He studied at the Thomasschule (1782), where he came to know Johann August Apel. He began writing poetry while pursuing his legal studies; then, settling in Dresden (1792), he published some novels and poetry, also doing much occasional writing and journalism. He was a member of the 'Dichter-Thee', later 'Liederkreis', that included Helmina von Chezy and subsequently Weber. His play *Van Dycks Landleben* was produced in Dresden in 1816, and in the same year he took on the editing, with Karl Winkler ('Theodor Hell'), of the *Abendzeitung*. Weber's triumph at the première of *Der Freischütz* (Berlin, 1821) embittered Kind, as he felt that insufficient credit was given to his libretto; a result was to stimulate him to a series of more ambitious literary projects that earned him some renown in his day. He withdrew from the *Abendzeitung* in 1826, and retired from literary life in 1832, dying in obscurity.

Kind's name survives only as the author of the text for *Der Freischütz*. Though he insisted that he found the story in a 'browning, dusty quarto' in the Leipzig Ratsbibliothek with Apel (*Unterredungen von der Reiche der Geister*, by Otto von Graben zum Stein – not a quarto), his evidence is suspect and he almost certainly took it not from there but from Apel and Laun's treatment in their popular *Gespensterbuch* (1810) and other sources. He gave his version of the events, together with the original text and much other relevant *Freischütz* material, in his *Freischützbuch* (Leipzig, 1843).

BIBLIOGRAPHY

J. G. T. Grässe: *Die Quelle des Freischütz* (Dresden, 1870)
H. A. Krüger: *Pseudoromantik: Friedrich Kind und der Dresdener Liederkreis* (Leipzig, 1904)
K. Goedeke: *Grundriss zur Geschichte der deutschen Dichtung*, ix (Dresden, 2/1910) [with complete list of writings]
H. W. von Waltershausen: *Der Freischütz: ein Versuch über die musikalische Romantik* (Munich, 1920)
F. Hasselberg: *Der Freischütz: Friedrich Kinds Operndichtung und ihre Quellen* (Berlin, 1921)
T. Cornelissen: *Weber's 'Freischütz' als Beispiel einer Operhandlung* (Berlin, 1940/R1959)
H. Schnoor: *Weber auf dem Welttheater: ein Freischützbuch* (Dresden, 1942, 4/1963)
W. Pfannkuch: 'Kind, Johann Friedrich', *MGG* [with list of works based on Kind's writings]

JOHN WARRACK

Kindermann, Hedwig Reicher-. *See* REICHER-KINDERMANN, HEDWIG.

Kindermann, Johann Erasmus (*b* Nuremberg, 29 March 1616; *d* Nuremberg, 14 April 1655). German composer and organist. His was the most imaginative and adventurous music written in Nuremberg in the 17th century: he adopted all possible means for the expressive setting of a text. He is important too in the teacher–pupil tradition in 17th-century Nuremberg that began with his teacher Johann Staden and continued through Kindermann to his foremost pupils Heinrich Schwemmer and Georg Caspar Wecker, who taught Johann Krieger and Johann Pachelbel.

Johann Erasmus Kindermann: engraving by Johann Friedrich Fleischberger after Daniel Preissler

1. LIFE. Kindermann probably attended one of the Nuremberg Latin schools, where he would have learnt singing and the rudiments of music. His lessons with Staden must have begun early, for at the age of 15 he was already receiving an annual salary of four gulden for participating in Sunday afternoon concerts at the Frauenkirche. His duties were to sing bass and play the violin (as he noted later in a letter), and he continued to do so until late in 1634 or early in 1635, when the city council gave him permission and money to visit Italy to study the new music at its source. Information about his stay in Italy is lacking. Like other Nuremberg composers before him (Hans Leo Hassler) and after him (Paul Hainlein and Johann Philipp Krieger) he probably went to Venice, where he could have studied with – or at least met – Monteverdi and Cavalli. He may also have known Carissimi, Frescobaldi and Merula, since he published music by them alongside works of his own. The Nuremberg council had given him two years' leave of absence, but after about one year, in January 1636, they called him back to take the position of second organist at the Frauenkirche.

In 1640 Kindermann was briefly employed as organist at Schwäbisch-Hall at an annual salary of 100 gulden (as well as 12 bushels of wheat, six wagon loads of wood and free housing). A few weeks after his arrival in August, however, he informed the city council that he had 'come down with a fever' and requested that Georg Dretzel (i) be given the position in his stead, to which they agreed. Kindermann's 'fever' came on shortly after the death of the organist of the Egidienkirche, Nuremberg. This is the kind of position he must have been waiting for in Nuremberg, and, having been appointed to it, he remained in it for the rest of his life; only two posts for musicians in Nuremberg were more important – those of organist of St Sebald and St Lorenz. Kindermann was much in demand as a teacher: not only Schwemmer and Wecker (as mentioned above) but also Johann Agricola and Augustin Pfleger were among his many pupils. His fame was apparently widespread, for W. C. Printz described him in his *Historische Beschreibung*, 1690, as 'a very famous Nuremberg composer and musician in his day'.

2. WORKS. Kindermann's works comprise many of the instrumental and vocal forms of his day. His instrumental music is specially noteworthy for being written with the characteristics of specific types of instrument in mind instead of being in a style adaptable to a variety of instruments and voices, as with many earlier composers. *Harmonia organica* has regard for the acoustical and technical possibilities of the organ, including an early German use of obbligato pedal, and is not adaptable to the clavier. This collection of 25 brief contrapuntal pieces, 14 of which are preludes in the seven authentic and seven plagal modes, includes a remarkable triple fugue on three chorale melodies. It is also important in the history of music printing, for along with Christian Michael's *Tabulatura* (1645) it is the last printed German organ tablature and among the earliest, if not the first, German music to be engraved. The 30 dance movements in a manuscript tablature (at *D-B*) that also includes works by Froberger, Martino Pesenti and Adam Krieger are arranged in the usual order of the keyboard suite of the time: allemande–courante–saraband. The four parts of *Deliciae studiosorum* contain 126 pieces (headed 'Symphonia', 'Sonata', 'Ritornello', 'Aria', 'Ballet', 'Intrada', etc) for three to five wind or string instruments; they are modelled on similar pieces by Johann Staden. The fourth instrumental collection, an early example of German violin music and a forerunner of Biber's sonatas, is *Canzoni, sonatae*, which contains 41 works for one to three violins, cello and continuo: 27 are designated 'canzon' and nine 'sonata', but consist of four or five short sections made independent by changes in tempo or metre, as in similar works by Frescobaldi and Massimiliano Neri. Unlike *Deliciae studiosorum* ten years earlier, *Canzoni, sonatae* is specifically conceived for violins and includes the use of scordatura, perhaps for the first time in Germany.

Most of Kindermann's output consists of vocal works, which exemplify the transitional character of German music during his generation, when the basso continuo and the concertato style were generally being adopted. There are motets with and without continuo in *Cantiones pathētikai* and *Musica catechetica*. The first two and the fourth pieces in the latter collection are in the concertato style. However, Kindermann used this style more expertly in the four manuscript cantatas

Wachet auf, Ich will singen von der Gnade des Herrn ewiglich, Lasset uns loben and *Herr Gott, dich loben wir*, which are among the earliest works in Nuremberg to show a contrast between choral and solo movements, a distinguishing trait of the cantata. Like Schütz's *Kleine geistliche Concerten* (1636–9) and first two sets of *Symphoniae sacrae* (1629–47), Kindermann's many concertos for solo voices have a sectional structure, a contrapuntal texture and little repetition of the text: the first five works in *Musicalische Friedens Seufftzer*, the first eight in *Concentus Salomonis* and the manuscript works *Turbabor sed non perturbabor* and *Befihl dem Herren deine Wege* are good examples. An interesting experiment with recitative, not found again in Nuremberg until two generations later in the music of Johann and Johann Philipp Krieger, is a work for tenor and continuo, *Dum tot carminibus*, 'in stylo recitativo': the repeated notes and unprepared dissonance are striking departures from the motet-like melodic style of his other works and those of his teacher Staden, although the work is far from the declamatory style of Monteverdi.

Of Kindermann's several dialogues, *Mosis Plag* is significant for its recitative and contemplative choruses, which did not become common features of the German oratorio until much later. Unlike the songs of his Nuremberg contemporary S. T. Staden, only four of his songs are of the old type for four voices. The 22 strophic songs in *Göttliche Liebesflamme* are for soprano and continuo. The 177 songs for one to three voices in the three parts of *Evangelische Schlussreimen* are settings, largely homophonic, of brief poetic texts written by J. M. Dilherr as closing statements of his sermons. In his *Opitianischer Orpheus* and *Musicalische Friedens Freud*, which together contain 38 songs for one or two voices, continuo and, for the ritornellos, usually two violins, Kindermann introduced to Nuremberg the type of instrumentally accompanied song associated particularly with Heinrich Albert in which an instrumental ritornello separates each stanza of the song. Considering Nuremberg's conservative, bourgeois culture in the 17th century, it is surprising that Kindermann published four humorous works, three in *Musicalischer Zeitvertreiber* (RISM 1655⁴) and one in *Intermedium musico-politicum*. One of them, a dialogue between two drunken soldiers, a Jew, and a peasant, is remarkable for the clever, simultaneous presentation of the four distinct characters by means of masterly counterpoint and an original approach to melody. Another of the four is remarkable for its title: *In honorificabilitudinationibusque*.

WORKS
(all published in Nuremberg unless otherwise stated)

Edition: *Ausgewählte Werke*, ed. F. Schreiber, DTB, xxiv, Jg.xiii; xxxii, Jg.xxi–xxiv (1913–24)

VOCAL

Cantiones [pathētikai], hoc est Ad memoriam passionis . . . Jesu Christi (motets), 3, 4vv, bc (1639)

Friedens Clag (3 motets), 3vv, bc (1640)

Concentus Salomonis, das ist Geistliche Concerten auss dem Hohen Lied dess hebräischen Königes Salomonis (Opitz), 2vv, 2 vn, bc (1642)

Dialogus, Mosis Plag, Sünders Klag, Christi Abtrag, 1–6vv, bc (1642)

[8] Musicalische Friedens Seufftzer, 3, 4vv, bc (1642)

Opitianischer Orpheus, das ist [13] Musicalischer Ergetzligkeiten (2 pts) (Opitz), 1, 2vv, 2 vn, vle/bn, bc (1642)

Dess Erlösers Christi, und sündigen Menschens heylsames Gespräch (dialogue), J. M. Dilherr), 7vv, bc (1643)

Musica catechetica, das ist Musicalischer Catechismus (12 motets), 5vv, bc (1643)

Lobgesang über den Frewdenreichen Geburtstag . . . Jesu Christi, 4vv,

sampt 1 Sinfonia, a 4 (1647)
Musicalische Friedens Freud (14 strophic songs), 1, 2vv, 3 viols, bc (1650)
Eines Christglaubigen Bekenners Hertzens Seuffzere, 2vv, 3 viols, bc (1648)
Göttliche Liebesflamme, das ist Christliche Andachten, Gebet und Seufftzer (Dilherr), S, bc (1640, text only; 2/1651)
Erster Teil J. M. Dilherrns Evangelische Schlussreimen (3 pts), 1–3vv, bc (1652)

9 occasional works (1639–54) [1 doubtful, attrib. 'J.E.K.']
4 cantatas: Wachet auf; Ich will singen; Lasset uns loben; Herr Gott, dich loben wir; 2 solo concertos: Turbabor sed non perturbabor; Befihl dem Herren: *D-B, Bds, F, Kl, Ngm, ?PL-WRu, S-Uu, ?USSR-KA*
ed.: Intermedium musico-politicum, 3, 4, 6vv (1643) [incl. 1 of his songs]; 1655[4] [incl. at least 3 of his songs]
3 works, 1v, insts (1643–5); 1 work, 5vv, insts, MS: lost

INSTRUMENTAL

Deliciae studiosorum (4 pts), a 3–5, bc (1640–43)
Harmonia organica, in tabulaturam germanicam (5 pts) (1645)
[27] Canzoni, [9] sonatae (2 pts), 1–3 vn, vc, bc (1653)
30 suite movts, kbd, ed. in HM, lxi (1950)
For lost works see *MGG*

BIBLIOGRAPHY

J. G. Doppelmayr: *Historische Nachricht von den nürnbergischen Mathematicis und Künstlern* (Nuremberg, 1730)
R. Eitner: 'Johann Erasmus Kindermann: Bibliographie', *MMg*, xv (1883), 37, 81, 137
F. Schreiber: *Der Nürnberger Organist Johannes Erasmus Kindermann (1616–1655)* (Leipzig, 1913; repr. as introduction to DTB, Jg.xiii, 1913)
H. H. Eggebrecht: 'Zwei Nürnberger Orgel-Allegorien des 17. Jahrhunderts', *Musik und Kirche*, xxvii (1957), 170
H. E. Samuel: 'Kindermann, Johann Erasmus', *MGG*
——: *The Cantata in Nuremberg during the Seventeenth Century* (diss., Cornell U., 1963)

HAROLD E. SAMUEL

Kindersley [Kennersley], **Robert** (*d* before 24 March 1634). English musician. He is first mentioned in the Lord Chamberlain's accounts for 15 July 1628, as one of the court's 'lutes and voices'. In 1631 he appears as 'basso' among the musicians for the violins. In the accounts dated 24 March 1633/4 he is said to be dead.

For Leighton's *Teares and Lamentacions of a Sorrowfull Soule* (London, 1614[7]) Kindersley wrote two settings: *O God to whom all hearts are seen*, for four voices and broken consort; and *Judge them O Lord* for five voices. Four dance compositions for lute attributed to him are in Cambridge University Library and the British Museum.

DIANA POULTON

King, Alec [Alexander] **Hyatt** (*b* Beckenham, Kent, 18 July 1911). English bibliographer and musicologist. He was educated at Dulwich College and at King's College, Cambridge (Jebb Scholar 1932), where he took a double first in classics (BA 1933). In 1934 he joined the Department of Printed Books at the British Museum, and in 1944 succeeded William C. Smith as superintendent of the Music Room. In 1948 he joined the RMA Council, edited its *Proceedings* from 1952 to 1957, became a vice-president in 1969 and was president from 1974 to 1978. In 1948 he was appointed honorary secretary of what became the *British Union-Catalogue of Early Music*; in 1951 he was elected vice-president of the International Association of Music Libraries, and from 1955 to 1959 was its president. He has been a member of the Internationale Stiftung Mozarteum since 1953. He was president of the United Kingdom branch of the RISM committee from 1953 to 1968 and vice-chairman of the committee itself from 1963. In 1970 he joined the British Academy committee of EECM.

In 1959 he became deputy keeper of the British Museum's Department of Printed Books, and in 1961

was Sandars Reader in bibliography at Cambridge. For these lectures and for *Some British Collectors of Music* he drew largely on sales catalogues, and his work in this field continued in 1973 when he began the edition of a series of reprints of music auction catalogues. At the museum he has organized many successful music exhibitions, notably the *Messiah* exhibition (1951), the Mozart exhibition (1956), the Purcell–Handel exhibition (1959), the exemplary music-printing history exhibition (1966) and the Vaughan Williams exhibition (1972).

King's writings reveal a lively mind with an unusual breadth of interests and perceptive and thorough scholarship. His contributions to Mozart studies are well known, and his bibliographical studies, as is well demonstrated in his admirable *Four Hundred Years of Music Printing*, have been thorough and valuable. As was his British Museum colleague, C. B. Oldman, he is one of the leading Mozart scholars of his generation, laying particular emphasis on bibliographical and textual studies.

WRITINGS

'The Forsytes and Music', *ML*, xxiii (1942), 24
'"Charles Auchester": a Novel of the Age of Mendelssohn', *MO*, lxviii (1944–5), 133
'Haydn's Trio for Horn, Violin and Cello', *MT*, xcvi (1945), 367
'Mountains, Music and Musicians', *MQ*, xxxi (1945), 395
'The Musical Glasses and the Glass Harmonica', *PRMA*, lxxii (1945–6), 97
'The Musical Side of Norman Douglas', *ML*, xxvii (1946), 215
'Music for the Stage', 'Schubert Bibliography', *Schubert: a Symposium*, ed. G. Abraham (London, 1946), 198, 259
Chamber Music (London, 1948)
'English Pictorial Music Title-pages: 1820–1885: their Style, Evolution and Importance', *The Library*, 5th ser., iv (1949–50), 262
'The Importance of Sir George Smart', *MT*, cvi (1950), 662
'Benjamin Goodison's Complete Edition of Purcell', *MMR*, lxxxi (1951), 63
Handel's Messiah (London, 1951) [British Museum exhibition catalogue]
with C. Humphries: *Music in the Hirsch Library Catalogue* (London, 1951)
'Paul Hirsch (1881–1951)', *MMR*, lxxxii (1952), 98
'The Music Room of the British Museum, 1753–1953: its History and Organization', *PRMA*, lxxix (1952–3), 65
'Lili Marleen: a Bibliographical Study', *British Museum Quarterly*, xvii (1952), 41
'Some Victorian Illustrated Music Titles', *Penrose Annual*, xlvi (1952), 43
'Sheet Music Covers Yesterday and Today', *Graphis*, ix (1953), 302, 330
ed. illustrations for: A. Einstein: *A Short History of Music* (London, 1953)
'Grove V and MGG', *MMR*, lxxxv (1954), 115, 152, 183
'The First Illustrated and Dated Edition of the *Marseillaise*', *British Museum Quarterly*, xx (1955–6), 1
Mozart in Retrospect: Studies in Criticism and Bibliography (London, 1955, 3/1970) [incl. King's articles on Mozart up to 1955]
Mozart in the British Museum (London, 1956, 2/1966)
'Some Notes on the Armonica', *MMR*, lxxxvi (1956), 61
'William Barclay Squire, 1855–1927, Music Librarian', *The Library*, 5th ser., xii (1957), 1
'The Royal Music Library: Some Account of its Provenance and Associations', *Book Collector*, vii (1958), 241
'Fragments of Early Printed Music in the Bagford Collection', *ML*, xl (1959), 269
'Frederick Nicolay, Chrysander and the Royal Music Library', *MMR*, lxxxix (1959), 13
'Frederick Nicolay, 1728/9–1809', *Book Collector*, ix (1960), 401
Henry Purcell 1659(?)–1695; George Frideric Handel 1685–1759 (London, 1959) [British Museum exhibition catalogue]
'An Unrecorded Song by Verdi', *British Museum Quarterly*, xxiv (1961), 1
'The Organ Tablature of Johann Woltz', *British Museum Quarterly*, xxv (1962), 61
'The History and Growth of the Catalogues in the British Museum Music Room', *Festschrift Otto Erich Deutsch zum 80. Geburtstag* (Kassel, 1963), 303
Some British Collectors of Music c. 1600–1960 (Cambridge, 1963)
Four Hundred Years of Music Printing (London, 1964, 2/1968)

'Mozart and Peter Anton Kreusser', *MR*, xxv (1964), 124

'C. G. Röder's Music-printing Business in 1885', *Brio*, ii (1965), 2

'Das neue Köchel-Verzeichnis', *Mf*, xvii (1966), 308

ed., with M. Carolan: E. Anderson: *The Letters of Mozart and his Family* (London, rev. 2/1966)

Handel and his Autographs (London, 1967)

Mozart Chamber Music (London, 1968, 2/1969)

Mozart: a Biography, with a Survey of Books, Editions and Recordings (London, 1970)

'Rastell Reunited', *Essays in Honour of Victor Scholderer* (Mainz, 1970), 213

'The Significance of John Rastell in Early Music Printing', *The Library*, 5th ser., xxvi (1971), 197

'Some Aspects of Recent Mozart Research', *PRMA*, c (1973–4), 1

'The Royal Music Library in the British Museum', *Beiträge zur Musikdokumentation: Franz Grasberger zum 60. Geburtstag* (Tutzing, 1975), 193

'The Musical Institute of London and its Successors', *MT*, cxvii (1976), 221

Mozart Wind and String Concertos (London, 1978)

'Music Circulating Libraries in Britain', *MT*, cxix (1978), 134

Printed Music in the British Museum: an Account of the Collections, the Catalogues, and their Formation, up to 1920 (London, 1979)

BIBLIOGRAPHY

F. R. Noske: 'King of the Music on his Sixtieth Birthday, 18 July 1971', *FAM*, xviii (1971), 2

O. W. Neighbour, ed.: *Music and Bibliography: Essays in Honour of Alec Hyatt King* (London, 1980)

DAVID SCOTT

King, B. B. [Riley B.] (*b* Itta Bena, Mississippi, 16 Sept 1925). American blues singer and guitarist. He was the 'Blues Boy' (hence B. B.), the host and disc jockey of a blues programme for the WDIA radio station in Memphis, and first became successful as a performer with a recording of *Three o'Clock in the Morning* (1950). He assimilated elements from jazz, gospel music and rhythm-and-blues to form his urban blues style. His guitar playing shows elements of the jazz techniques of Django Reinhardt and Charlie Christian, and of blues performers such as T-Bone Walker and Muddy Waters; his high tenor voice is outstanding among blues singers. Although he is not a performer of mainstream popular music he can sustain a lyrical melody, but he sings best in the semi-oratorical idiom of the blues, emphasizing the rhythm and inflection of the words rather than adhering to the pitches and note values of the music. In the mid-1960s, as urban blues became internationally popular, King became known to a wide audience of all races, and his music was taken as a point of departure by British rock musicians.

BIBLIOGRAPHY

C. Keil: *Urban Blues* (Chicago, 1966)

C. Gillett: *The Sound of the City* (New York, 1970)

HENRY PLEASANTS

King, Charles (*b* Bury St Edmunds, 1687; *d* London, 17 March 1748). English cathedral musician and composer. He was a chorister of St Paul's Cathedral under Blow and Jeremiah Clarke (i), to the latter of whom he was subsequently apprenticed. He married Clarke's sister, and in 1711 was responsible for the publication of his *Choice Lessons for the Harpsichord or Spinet*. He took the Oxford degree of BMus in July 1707, on which occasion it was found that no-one knew the appropriate academic dress, so long was it since anyone had proceeded to that degree, in consequence of which the dress of a bachelor of law was used. King succeeded Clarke as almoner and Master of the Choristers of St Paul's in 1707, becoming also a vicar-choral of the cathedral in 1730. Meanwhile, from 1708 until his death, he was also organist of St Benet Fink in the City of London. Among his pupils were Maurice Greene, John Alcock (i), Thomas and Joseph Baildon, Robert Wass (who sang for Handel), Robert Hudson and Jonathan Battishill.

Arnold recorded that he left a collection of church music to St Paul's, but there seems to be no trace of this now. Four of King's anthems are printed in Arnold's *Cathedral Music*, and two more in Page's *Harmonia sacra*. He is also represented in Tudway's Collection (*GB-Lbm* Harl.7341–2). He owes his niche in musical history to the remark of Greene that he was 'a very serviceable man', an allusion to the number of services he composed. Five of these were printed by Arnold, in addition to which there are two others, in B minor and D major. They are not so much bad as merely commonplace, and set a pattern of dullness in the writing of services hardly broken until the time of T. A. Walmisley and S. S. Wesley over a century later.

WATKINS SHAW

King, E. J. American composer and compiler, in 1844, of a tune-book in four-shape notation; *see* SHAPE-NOTE HYMNODY, §2.

King, James (*b* Dodge City, 22 May 1925). American tenor. After earning the MMus degree from the University of Kansas City, he began his career as a baritone. His teachers included Martial Singher and Max Lorenz. As a winner of the American Opera Auditions in Cincinnati, he was sent to Europe in 1961. His professional début was at the Teatro alla Pergola in Florence, where he sang Cavaradossi, a role he soon repeated at the Teatro Nuovo in Milan. His first resident appointment took him to the Deutsche Oper, Berlin, where his first role was the Italian Tenor in *Der Rosenkavalier* (1962). Although he continued to sing lyrical roles in Italian and French operas, he began to specialize in the more heroic repertory. Subsequent engagements took him to Salzburg (Achilles in *Iphigénie en Aulide*, 1962), Vienna (Bacchus in *Ariadne auf Naxos*, 1963), Bayreuth (Siegmund, 1965), the Metropolitan Opera (Florestan, 1966) and La Scala in Milan (Calaf, 1968). He sang the Emperor in both the Metropolitan and (1967) Covent Garden premières of *Die Frau ohne Schatten*, and in 1974, with somewhat limited success, added Verdi's Othello to his repertory at the San Francisco Opera. His bright, slender tone, easy top voice and remarkable stamina have made him particularly successful in the lighter Wagner roles such as Walther von Stolzing, Parsifal and Lohengrin.

MARTIN BERNHEIMER

King, Matthew Peter (*b* London, *c*1773; *d* London, Jan 1823). English composer and theorist. He belongs to that mysterious company of musicians about whom nothing is known beyond a catalogue of their works. He may have been a pupil of C. F. Horn, and it is likely that he was a child prodigy, as his earliest compositions appeared under the name of 'Master King'. Before 1800 he published a series of piano sonatas and other keyboard works, and around the turn of the century several theoretical treatises; in the latter King challenged the theories of A. F. C. Kollman, then living in London. About the same time King turned his attention more and more to vocal music, especially that for the stage, and in this sphere appears to have been quite successful; between 1804 and 1819 numerous stage works appeared, some written in collaboration with Kelly, Braham or Davy. The librettos were generally supplied by Kenney or S. J. Arnold. In addition King composed numerous glees, songs and the like, but he did not completely ignore more serious music. On 1 June 1816 his oratorio *The Intercession* appeared at Covent Garden; the aria 'Eve's Lamentation' had special success and was for a long time widely circulated. King was undoubtedly a talented musician, but he could not avoid the tendency towards superficiality so characteristic of lighter English music in the early 19th century. His operas were popular in their time, although the works of Bishop were already in the repertory of all theatres. The long-forgotten controversy with Kollmann gives an insight into music theory and pedagogy of the time. King's son, C. M. King, was active as a composer of songs, piano pieces and other works.

WORKS
(all printed works published in London)

DRAMATIC

(all performed in London and published in year of performance)
CG – Covent Garden   DL – Drury Lane
EO – English Opera at the Lyceum

Matrimony (comic opera, 2, J. Kenney), DL, 20 Nov 1804
Too Many Cooks (musical farce, 2, Kenney), CG, 12 Feb 1805
The Weathercock (comic opera, 2, J. T. Allingham), DL, 18 Nov 1805
False Alarms, or My Cousin (comic opera, 3, Kenney), DL, 12 Jan 1807, collab. J. Braham
Ella Rosenberg (melodrama, 2, Kenney), DL, 19 Nov 1807, *GB-Lbm*
Up all Night, or The Smuggler's Cave (comic opera, 3, S. J. Arnold), EO, 26 June 1809, Act 2 *Lbm*
Oh, This Love, or The Masqueraders (comic opera, Kenney), EO, 12 June 1810
Plots!, or The North Tower (melodramatic opera, Arnold), EO. 3 Sept 1810
The Americans (comic opera, 3, Arnold), DL company at Lyceum, 27 April 1811, collab. Braham
Timour the Tartar (melodrama, Lewis), CG, 29 April 1811
One o'clock, or The Knight and the Wood Daemon (grand romantic opera, 3, M. G. Lewis), EO, 1 Aug 1811, collab. M. Kelly
Turn Out! (musical farce, 2, Kenney), DL company at Lyceum, 7 March 1812
Love, Law and Physic (farce with songs, Kenney), CG, 20 Nov 1812
The Fisherman's Hut (melodrama, J. Tobin), DL, 20 Oct 1819, collab. J. Davy

OTHER VOCAL

4 Glees, 3–4vv (c1810)
The Harmonist, or 8 New Glees and Madrigals, 3–7vv (c1814)
Other glees, incl.: The Fortune Tellers, 3vv (c1799); The Witches' Glee ['Come, Sisters'] (Shakespeare) (c1800)
Single songs and duets, incl.: Haste, a rose wreath prepare, 1v, pf (c1785); The Smile of the Tweed, 1/2 vv, pf (c1800); The Sound of the Harps, 1v, pf (c1795); 'Tis not love, 1v, pf (c1795); Parting is such sweet sorrow (Shakespeare), autograph *Ge*
The Intercession (oratorio, after Milton: *Paradise Lost*), London, Covent Garden, 1 June 1816, *Y*; full score (1817)

INSTRUMENTAL

(partial list of extant works; numerous other works apparently lost)
op.
1   Six Sonatas, pf/hpd, vn (c1788)
2   Three Sonatas, pf/hpd, vn (c1790)
4   Six Sonatinas, pf/hpd (c1795)
5   Six Sonatas, pf/hpd, vn (c1795)
8   Cape St Vincent, a Grand Sonata, pf, vn, vc (1797)
8[?9] A Grand Duett, pf (c1800)
14   Peace, a Grand Characteristic Sonata, pf (1801)
16   Quintet, pf, fl, vn, va, vc (c1805), ?lost

The Siege of Valenciennes, military band/pf (c1794); The Princess of Wales Minuet, pf (c1797); The British March, pf (c1798); The Mary-le-Bone March, pf (c1798); The Coronation, a Grand Sonata Sinfonia, pf (1820)

WRITINGS

Thorough Bass Made Clear to every Capacity (London, c1810) [1796 according to Fétis]
A General Treatise on Music, Particularly Harmony or Thoroughbass (London, 1812) [1800 according to Fétis]

BIBLIOGRAPHY

EitnerQ; FétisB
J. Sainsbury, ed.: *A Dictionary of Musicians* (London, 2/1825/R1966)
J. D. Brown and S. S. Stratton: *British Musical Biography* (Birmingham, 1897/R1971)

The Stage Cyclopaedia (London, c1910)
W. H. Husk: 'King, Matthew Peter', Grove 5
CHARLES CUDWORTH

King, Robert (*fl* London, 1676–1728). English violinist, composer and concert promoter. Although music by King appeared in print in 1676 nothing is known about his origins or about his activities until 6 February 1680, when he was appointed to the private music of Charles II in the place left vacant by the death of John Banister (i). King retained this position under five monarchs and seems to have been particularly favoured by William and Mary. In 1689 he became their composer-in-ordinary and was granted a licence to give public concerts (*CSPD*, 25 December 1689) the terms of which suggest an exceptional degree of royal encouragement. In this venture King was associated at first with J. W. Franck. Their first concerts were probably given at the Two Golden Balls in Bow Street, but in 1691 they moved to Charles Street, Covent Garden, where a room, later known as the 'Vendu' because of the picture sales also held there, had been built for the purpose. Benefit concerts were given here twice weekly during the season and were so successful that the room very soon had to be enlarged. In 1696 King graduated MusB at Cambridge.

The last concerts given at the Vendu were in 1697. Franck had by then already left England, and the York Buildings concert room was becoming increasingly popular as a place of musical entertainment. John Banister (ii) replaced Franck as King's associate, and together they gave concerts in York Buildings in 1698; they also performed at Exeter Exchange, London: in 1699 John Walsh advertised 'a Choice Collection of new Musick, made for Mr Banister's and Mr King's Consort, performed by Gentlemen at Exeter Exchange'. King may well have been involved in the promotion of all the concerts given at York Buildings at this time: it is known that he actually lived there in 1702 and may have done so as early as 1686, when he entertained a party including Lord and Lady Exeter to dinner in the music room itself (Exeter seems to have been a patron of his).

In addition to their concert activities Banister and King were associated from 1700 to 1702 in selling music, including the works of Corelli, brought to England from publishers in Rome and Amsterdam. Scarcely anything is known about his life after 1702. He remained a member of the royal band until at least 1728 and probably died shortly after this.

King's compositions are uneven. The melodic invention in the airs he contributed to *Tripla concordia* is poor and the part-writing frequently crude and amateurish. His later music is more accomplished technically, though the melodic invention remains weak. The influence of the Italian style which superseded that of the French in England before the turn of the century is evident in such works as the violin sonata and the 'Sonetta after the Italian way'. In the preface to his *Songs for One, Two and Three Voices* King wrote: 'in some of these Compositions I have imitated the Italians in their manner of Ariettas; who for their Excellence in Vocal Music are (in my Judgement) the best Paterns'. His vocal music is perhaps more important than his instrumental, but though many of his songs are quite neatly turned they are all little more than weak reflections of those of Purcell and Blow.

WORKS

VOCAL

A Duke and no Duke, A Farce . . . with several Songs set to Music (London, 1685) with G. B. Draghi

[24] Songs for One, Two and Three Voices, org/hpd (London, 1690)

A Second Booke of Songs together with a Pastorall Elegy on the Blessed Memory . . . of Queen Mary, 1–4vv, bc (London, ?1698)

Hymn: Awake my drowsie soul, 2vv, bc in Harmonia sacra (London, 1693[1])

Anthem and hymn in The Divine Companion (London, 1701)

Songs and duets for various plays, including The Disappointment (Southerne), 1684; A Duke and no Duke (Tate), 1684; Sir Courtly Nice (Crowne), 1685; The English Friar (Crowne), 1689; The Amorous Bigotte (Shadwell), 1690; The Rape (Brady), 1692

Miscellaneous songs in Choice Ayres, Songs and Dialogues (London, 1664), Comes amoris (London, 1687[4]–93[6]), The Banquet of Musick (London, 1688[7]–90[5]), The Gentleman's Journal (London, 1692–4), Thesaurus musicus (London, 1695[12]–96[9]), Wit and Mirth, or Pills to Purge Melancholy (London, 1719–20), GB-Lbm Add.35043, Sloane 3752, Add.19759, 29397, 35043, Lcm 1119, Och 91

INSTRUMENTAL

15 airs, 2vn, bc, in Tripla concordia (London, 1677[4])

Airs, 2 rec, in Thesaurus musicus (London, 1693[8]–4[7])

Overture, rec, bc, in Airs anglois . . . livre second (Amsterdam, 1701/2)

Pièces à 3 et à 4 parties, vns, obs, recs, bc (Amsterdam, 1701/2), by King and Paisible

Some airs, 2 rec, in A Collection of Airs (London, 1703)

Prelude, vn, in Select Preludes or Volentarys (London, 1704)

13 pieces, in The Theater of Music (London, 1685[5]–7[5])

Sonatas, airs, suites and other pieces for hpd, recs, vns, str, bc in GB-Lbm Add.39569, 41205, 52363, Harl.4899, Eg.2959, D.24, Och 46, 362, Ob Mus.Sch.C.61, e 443–6, US-Pu Fi 9–12

LOST

Ode for St Cecilia's Day, 1690, O Sacred Harmony (Shadwell)

Ode for the Earl of Exeter's birthday, 1693, Once more 'tis born the happy day (Motteux)

BIBLIOGRAPHY

H. C. de Lafontaine: The King's Musick (London, 1909/R1973)

J. Pulver: A Biographical Dictionary of Old English Music (London, 1927/R1968)

R. Elkin: The Old Concert Rooms of London (London, 1955)

M. Tilmouth: 'A Calendar of References to Music in Newspapers published in London and the Provinces (1660–1719)', RMARC, i (1961/R), 10f, 22, 34, 44f, 52

MICHAEL TILMOUTH

King, Thea (b Hitchin, 16 Dec 1925). English clarinettist. She won a scholarship to the RCM, where she studied the piano with Arthur Alexander and the clarinet with Frederick Thurston. In 1956 she became principal clarinet of the London Mozart Players, and in 1964 of the English Chamber Orchestra. She has also played in the Portia Ensemble (1954–68) and the Melos Ensemble (from 1974), and has made a special study of lesser-known clarinet works of the 18th and 19th centuries. In 1961 she joined the RCM teaching staff. She gave the first performances of Searle's Suite (1956), Arnold Cooke's Sonata (1959) and Ireland's Sextet (1962), as well as many other works by British composers; Benjamin Frankel's Clarinet Quintet is dedicated to her. Her promotion of modern British works, and to a large extent her style of playing, follow in the tradition of Frederick Thurston, whom she married in 1953.

ROBERT PHILIP

King, William (b Winchester, 1624; d Oxford, 17 Nov 1680). English organist and composer. The son of George King, organist of Winchester Cathedral, William King became a clerk of Magdalen College, Oxford, on 18 October 1648 and graduated BA on 5 June 1649. During the Civil War he was one of the musicians who gathered in Oxford round the court of Charles I. He was chaplain of Magdalen College from 1652 until 25 August 1654, when he was made a probationer Fellow of All Souls College. On 10 December

1664 he became organist of New College.

The Songs and Ayres of 1668 contains King's best music and is important as an early example of the many songbooks that appeared in England with the revival of music publishing after the Restoration. His church music is of little interest. The anthem The Lord is King, still occasionally performed, may be taken as typical. In it polyphony is abandoned in favour of a largely note-against-note 'short service' style unredeemed by harmonic or other interest; it ends with a trite 'Alleluia' of the kind that later disfigured many Restoration anthems, including some by much superior composers.

WORKS

Poems of Mr. Cowley and others, composed into Songs and Ayres, 1v, bc (theorbo/hpd/b viol) (Oxford, 1668[9])

Services: Morning Service, B♭ (TeD, Jub, Lit); Morning Service, B♭ (TeD, Jub, San, Ky, Cr); Verse Whole Service, B♭ (TeD, Jub, Ky, Cr, San, CanD, DeM; not all by King); Sanctus, B♭: GB-Lbm

Anthems: Thou art gone up on high, Lcm; The Lord is King, Och, T; I will allwayes give thankes, Lbm

Verse anthems: Lord how are they increased, inc.; Now that the Lord ('For King C[harles's] Restoration'), inc.: Lbm; The Lord hath prepared, T

Airs in 3 parts, str; Duet, O blest estate: Ob

DOUBTFUL WORKS

Morning Service, B♭ (TeD, Jub); Sanctus, A: Lbm

Anthems: Lord, how are they increased; Unto thee, O Lord: Lbm

Verse anthems: My God, my God, looke upon me; Praise yee the Lord (2 settings): Lbm

Kyrie, B♭; Overture in 4 parts: Ob

BIBLIOGRAPHY

J. Pulver: A Biographical Dictionary of Old English Music (London, 1927/R1968)

MICHAEL TILMOUTH

King Cole Chamber Music Club. London music club founded in 1900; see LONDON, §VI, 4(iii).

King Musical Instruments. One of the earliest manufacturers of distinguished brass instruments in the USA. Henderson N. White (1873–1940), an instrument repairman, amateur musician and businessman, founded the firm in Cleveland, Ohio, in 1893. With Thomas King (a professional trombonist whose name was subsequently used as the company's trademark), White produced first a tenor trombone, improving the instrument's slide mechanism, bell taper and bore size; later the firm expanded and manufactured the silver cornet, tuba, baritone and trumpet.

In 1909 White moved from his original shop on 9th Street, in Cleveland's old music printing district, to a factory on Superior Avenue. Expansion after World War I included the production of metal clarinets (later discontinued) and saxophones; many of the latter are still produced by the King Co.

Family ownership was relinquished in 1965 with the sale of the firm to Nathan Dolan Associates. It was renamed King Musical Instruments, and within the same year became a subsidiary of the Seeburg Co. In 1965 King also purchased the Strasser–Marigaux–Lemaire Woodwind Co., France, which markets a complete line of wind instruments. In 1966 its offices and manufacturing plant were moved to expanded new facilities at Eastlake, Ohio.

For illustration see TUBA (i), fig.1c.

MARTIN KRIVIN

King's Band of Music. The established orchestra of the English court, from the 17th century; it declined in the early 20th century; see LONDON, §II, 2.

King's Singers. British ensemble. The original members were Nigel Perrin (*b* London, 4 Nov 1947) and Alastair Hume (*b* Edinburgh, 18 Sept 1942), countertenors; Alastair Thompson (*b* Sherborne, 28 Dec 1944), tenor; Anthony Holt (*b* Henley, 6 Nov 1940) and Simon Carrington (*b* Salisbury, 23 Oct 1942), baritones; Brian Kay (*b* Grappenhall, 12 May 1944), bass. With the exception of Holt, who was at Christ Church, Oxford, they were all choral scholars at King's College, Cambridge. Hume and Carrington were professional double bass players, the others freelance singers, before the group became established with the above personnel in January 1970 (it had made its original début in London in May 1968). In 1978 Bill (William) Ives (*b* Harleston, 15 Feb 1948) replaced Alastair Thompson as tenor. The group gained a unique reputation founded on a thorough vocal ensemble training as choral scholars. The diversity of its repertory (and consequent widespread popularity) is due in part to its extension of the distinctive Oxford and Cambridge choral sounds to vocal chamber music. More pertinently, it adapted to two very different traditions: the Renaissance consort repertory explored by pioneers like the Deller and Purcell Consorts; and the American close-harmony group repertory, derived from the barber-shop quartet, but more directly influenced by the recorded performances of such American artists as the Ink Spots, the Mills Brothers, the Four Freshmen and the Hi-Los.

The King's Singers' distinctive constitution has enabled it to produce, in association with scholars, authentic performances of 16th-century vocal music, as recordings of French Renaissance chansons and Scottish consort songs show. On the lighter side, with a judicious choice of arrangers, it has performed increasingly sophisticated versions of standard popular songs, with great verve and variety. The singers have not restricted themselves to these particular strengths but have encouraged composers to write works for them, including Penderecki, Berio, Bennett and Patterson. The group's reputation for versatility and entertaining presentation brought quick, worldwide success. They have made innumerable appearances at festivals in Britain and abroad, and on radio and television.

LESLIE EAST

King's Theatre. A leading London opera house, in the Haymarket, between 1705 and 1910; it was known as the Queen's Theatre during Anne's reign, and Her Majesty's or the Royal Italian Opera during Victoria's. *See* LONDON, §IV, 3, and figs.13 and 14.

Kinkeldey, Otto (*b* New York, 27 Nov 1878; *d* Orange, NJ, 19 Sept 1966). American musicologist and librarian. After schooling in New York he studied at the College of the City of New York (AB 1898), at the University of New York (MA 1900) and music with Edward MacDowell at Columbia University (1900–02); concurrently he was organist and choirmaster at the Chapel of the Incarnation (1898–1902) and taught in New York schools. He continued his study of music, literature and philosophy in Berlin (1902–9), with Kretzschmar at the university and Radecke at the Königliches Akademisches Institut für Kirchenmusik, taking the doctorate (a rare achievement for an American in a German university at that date) in 1909 with a dissertation on 16th-century organ and keyboard

music. During this time he was organist and choirmaster of the American church in Berlin (1903–5) and was sent by the Prussian government on a tour of the central German states (1906–7) to catalogue the music and music literature in church, ducal and civic libraries. In 1909 he was offered the posts of librarian at the Breslau Königliches Institut für Kirchenmusik and instructor in music theory and the organ at Breslau University, where he subsequently became lecturer in music history with the honorary title of professor (1912–14); he was also appointed to the board of directors of the Breslau Opera. Despite the university's offer to create an extraordinary chair for him, the outbreak and continuation of war prompted him to return to New York, where he became head of the public library's music division (1915–23) and organist of All Souls, Brooklyn; after the war (during which he served as a training officer, 1917–19) he travelled in France, Spain, Germany and Italy making purchases for the library. After a period as head of the music department at Cornell University (1923–7) he returned to the library (1927–30), but was drawn back to Cornell by the offer of the first American chair of musicology, created specially for him; he was also made university librarian (1930–46). Before his retirement in 1958 (because of increasing difficulties in hearing) he also taught at Harvard, Princeton, Texas, Illinois, Berkeley, Boston and Washington State.

Kinkeldey was the founder of American musicology. It was owing to him more than to any other individual that musicology, after a long struggle for recognition as a serious discipline, became an accepted subject in the curriculum of American universities; and it was chiefly to him that subsequent American music scholars, many of the first generation directly, and all of them indirectly, owed (and often acknowledged) their livelihood. In establishing the subject he drew on his experience of German music scholarship, and throughout his work he maintained that intellectual breadth, exacting standards and close adherence to the music itself are essential in an approach to any topic. His ability as a performing musician informed his interpretation of musical texts and history, while his wide range of interest in the humanities and comprehensive grasp of the current state of research, as well as an uncanny power of defining the essential issues with clarity, force and common sense, made him an outstanding teacher. His demanding concept of the librarian's role was evident in his statement that it necessitates a knowledge of archaeology, palaeography, art history, acoustics, economics, education and literature. He promoted his educational principles in all his own teaching and in his work as founder–president of the Music Library Association, founder–president of the American Musicological Society and a leading member of its predecessor, the Music Teachers' National Association. In his research he was similarly a pioneer: he was one of the first investigators of early keyboard music and Renaissance dance, and his *Orgel und Klavier in der Musik des 16. Jahrhunderts*, combining his characteristic attributes of breadth and thoroughness, remains a fundamental exploration.

WRITINGS
'Luzzasco Luzzaschi's Solo-Madrigale', *SIMG*, ix (1907–8), 538
Orgel und Klavier in der Musik des 16. Jahrhunderts (diss., U. of Berlin, 1909; Leipzig, 1910/*R*1968)
'Emil Bohn', *Chronologie der Königlichen Universität zu Breslau für das Jahr vom 1. Apr. 1909 bis 31. März 1910*, 1
'Die Musik in Schlesien', *Schlesische Landeskunde: Geschichtliche Arbeit*, ed. F. Kamper (Leipzig, 1913), 342

'Music in the Universities of Europe and America', *MTNA Proceedings*, x (1915), 79; see also xxix (1934), 20
'The Influence of Folk-music upon Artistic Progress', *MTNA*, x (1915), 171
'The New York Public Library and its Music Division', *Library Journal*, xl (1915), 589
'Music Education and Public Libraries', *National Education Association Journal of Proceedings*, liv (1916), 596
'The Harmonic Sense, its Evolution and its Destiny', *MTNA*, xviii (1923), 9
'Beginnings of Beethoven in America', *MQ*, xiii (1927), 217–48
'American Scholarship in Music since 1876', *MTNA*, xxiii (1928), 244
'Schubert: Dance-composer', *MQ*, xiv (1928), 610
'A Jewish Dancing Master of the Renaissance (Guglielmo Ebreo)', *Studies in Jewish Bibliography . . . in Memory of Abraham Solomon Freidus* (New York, 1929), 329–72; also pubd separately (Brooklyn, NY, 1966)
'Music and Music Printing in Incunabula', *Papers of the Bibliographical Society of America*, xxvi (1932), 89–118
'Musicology in American Colleges and Universities', *Music Educators National Conference Yearbook 1934*, 125
'The Preparation of the College Student for Graduate Study', *MTNA*, xxix (1934), 165
'Changing Relations within the Field of Musicology', *PAMS 1936*, 42; also in *MTNA*, xxxi (1936), 246
'Thomas Robinson's "Schoole of Musicke": a Lute Book of Shakespeare's Time', *BAMS*, i (1936), 7 [extract]
'The Music of the Future: a Phantasy', *BAMS*, ii (1937), 4, 14 [extract]
'Fifteenth-century Basses-danses', *BAMS*, iv (1940), 13 [extract]
'The Artist and the Scholar', *PAMS 1940*, 126; also in *MTNA*, xxxv (1940), 67
'Waldo Selden Pratt', *MQ*, xxvi (1940), 162
'Hopes and Wishes', *PAMS 1941*, 1; also in *MTNA*, xxxvi (1941), 190
'Palm Leaf Books', *William Warner Bishop: a Tribute* (New Haven, 1941), 88
'The Sapphic Ode', *BAMS*, v (1941), 14; vi (1942), 9 [extract]
'The Early Sequence: its Literary and Musical Forms', *BAMS*, vii (1943), 11 [extract]
'Thomas Mace and his Tattle de Moy', *A Birthday Offering to Carl Engel* (New York, 1943), 128
'Musical Scholarship and the University', *JRBM*, i (1946), 10
What we know about Music (Ann Arbor, 1946)
'Franchino Gafori and Marsilio Ficino', *Harvard Library Bulletin*, i/3 (1947), 379
'Johannes Wolf', *JAMS*, i (1948), 5
'The Music of the Spheres', *BAMS*, xi–xiii (1948), 30 [extract]
'The Music Teacher and the Library', *MTNA*, xlii (1948), 81
'The Term Paraphonista and its Meaning', *JAMS*, iii (1950), 158
'Oscar George Sonneck', *Notes*, xi (1953–4), 25
'Bach embellecido por si mismo' [BWV 156], *Revista de estudios musicales*, iii (1954), 271
'Dance Tunes of the Fifteenth Century', *Instrumental Music: Isham Memorial Library 1957*, 3
'Equal Voices in the "A cappella" Period', *Essays on Music in Honor of Archibald Thompson Davison* (Cambridge, Mass., 1957), 101
'Kinnor, Nebel-Cithärä, Psalterium', *The Joshua Bloch Memorial Volume* (New York, 1960), 10

EDITIONS
P. H. Erlebach: Harmonische Freude musikalischer Freunde, DDT, xlvi–xlvii (1914)

BIBLIOGRAPHY
E. J. Dent: 'Otto Kinkeldey', *MQ*, xxiv (1938), 405
G. S. Dickinson: 'Otto Kinkeldey: an Appreciation', *MQ*, xxiv (1938), 412
'Otto Kinkeldey in Honor of his Seventieth Birthday, November 27, 1948', *Notes*, vi (1948–9), 27–121 [incl. C. Sprague Smith: 'Otto Kinkeldey', 27]
E. T. Ferand: 'Otto Kinkeldey zum 80. Geburtstag am 27. November 1958', *Mf*, xii (1959), 3
P. H. Lang: 'Editorial', *MQ*, xlv (1959), 85
C. Seeger: 'Otto Kinkeldey', *AcM*, xxxi (1959), 7
'A Musicological Offering to Otto Kinkeldey upon the Occasion of his Eightieth Birthday', *JAMS*, xiii (1960), 1–269
R. Benton: 'Early Musical Scholarship in the United States', *FAM*, xi (1964), 12
Obituary: G. Reese, *JAMS*, xix (1966), 433; D. J. Grout, *AcM*, xxxix (1967), 1; P. H. Lang, *MQ*, liii (1967), 77; J. LaRue, *Mf*, xx (1967), 121

DONALD JAY GROUT

Kinloch, William (*fl c*1600). Scottish composer. There are some keyboard pieces in Duncan Burnett's Book (*GB-En*), some of which are printed in K. Elliott, ed.: *Early Scottish Keyboard Music* (London, 1958). There

is a pavan and galliard by 'Kinloughe', apparently the same composer, in *GB-Lbm* Add.30485.

The pieces in Duncan Burnett's Book include a 'Lang' pavan and a galliard which is an interesting specimen of cumulative variation. Each of the three strains of the pavan is repeated immediately in varied form. The entire scheme is then repeated as a variation. Finally, the galliard is a varied repeat of the entire pavan. His 'Fantassie' is a curious exercise in different textures and proportions.

JOHN CALDWELL

Kinner von Scherffenstein, Martin (*b* Leobschütz, Upper Silesia [now Głubczyce, Poland], 1534; *d* Baumgarten, nr. Prenzlau, 24 March 1597). German poet and composer. He matriculated at the University of Wittenberg on 12 October 1553 and took his master's degree in 1557. He then became professor of poetry and history at Wittenberg, and later was chancellor-in-chief at Leobschütz. He was a close friend of Melanchthon. As poet and composer he is known by a wedding publication, *Melodia epithalamii* (n.p., 1567), comprising three pieces, two for four voices and one for five and the posthumous *Silvulae musicae* (Hildesheim, 1605). There are also four pieces by him in a collection of German, French and Latin partsongs (*RISM* 1550²³). This collection has been only tentatively dated 1550, and the fact that Kinner was then only in his 16th year suggests that this date is rather too early.

BIBLIOGRAPHY
EitnerQ; *FétisB*; *GerberNL*
C. J. A. Hoffmann: *Die Tonkünstler Schlesiens* (Breslau, 1830)
H. Mendel and A. Reissmann: *Musikalisches Conversations-Lexikon*, vi (Berlin, 1872)
R. Eitner: 'Kinner von Scherffenstein, Martin', *ADB*

INGRID SCHUBERT

Kinnhalter (Ger.). CHIN REST.

Kinnor (Heb.). Ancient Jewish lyre; *see* JEWISH MUSIC, §I, 4(iii–iv).

Kinscella, Hazel Gertrude (*b* Nora Springs, Iowa, 27 April 1893; *d* Seattle, 14 July 1960). American music educationist. She was a piano pupil of Rafael Joseffy (1912–13) and studied at the University of Nebraska (MusB 1916, BFA 1928, BA 1931), Columbia University (MA 1934) and the University of Washington, where she took a doctorate in 1941 with the dissertation *Music in Colonial Philadelphia, 1664–1776*; she also studied composition with Rossetter G. Cole and Howard Brockway. After teaching at the University of Nebraska (1918–38) she became an instructor (1942) and professor (1947) at the University of Washington, where she remained until her retirement in 1958. In 1919 she began a series of state school piano classes in Lincoln, Nebraska; this was one of the first American experiments in state school piano teaching, and led to the publication of a series of piano books, *First [–Sixth] Steps for the Young Pianist* (New York, 1919–26). At the Anglo-American Music Conference at Lausanne (1931) she was one of the three piano consultants for the USA.

Kinscella published several anecdotal books for music appreciation classes. These include the graded series of six *Kinscella Music Appreciation Readers* (Lincoln, Nebraska, 1926–9), a book on music in the USA, *History Sings* (Lincoln, Nebraska, 1940, rev. 3/1957) and *Music and Romance* (Camden, NJ, 1930, rev. 2/1941) for junior high school. She also wrote *Music on the Air* (New York, 1934), a reference book for radio listeners, and, with Elizabeth M. Tierney, two books on music education, *Music in the Small School* (Lincoln, Nebraska, 1939) and *The Child and his Music* (Lincoln, Nebraska, 1953).

WAYNE D. SHIRLEY

Kinsky, Georg Ludwig (*b* Marienwerder, West Prussia, 29 Sept 1882; *d* Berlin, 7 April 1951). German musicologist. After a classical education in Marienwerder, he went to Berlin in 1898 and worked in a music shop and in an antiquarian bookstore. Though entirely self-taught in music, he was nevertheless made assistant to A. Klopfermann at the Prussian State Library in 1908 and in the following year became curator of the Heyer Musikhistorisches Museum at Cologne. Here, until the museum was disbanded in 1927, he catalogued and expanded the collection and organized popular lectures and concerts with historical instruments. From 1921 to 1932 he was lecturer in musicology at the University of Cologne, where he took his doctorate in 1925 with a dissertation on double reed instruments. The main fruits of these years were the valuable catalogues of the Heyer Museum, with meticulous introductions and numerous illustrations, and the *Geschichte der Musik in Bildern* (1929), which he edited together with Haas and Schnoor. After 1932 he worked privately. In 1944 his home and his private library and collection were confiscated and he was sentenced to a year of hard labour under the Nazi regime. Already a sick man, he went in 1945 to Berlin, where he worked on a thematic catalogue of Beethoven's works until his death.

Kinsky's importance lies in the example that he has given in describing and classifying instruments and in cataloguing and exploring musical manuscripts and early prints. In this way he influenced the work of associations such as the Galpin Society, the IMS and the International Association of Music Libraries, and opened new possibilities to international research in different areas of music history, especially the 19th century. His thematic catalogue of Beethoven's works has not only been fundamental to further research (such as that by Willy Hess), but has also stimulated performance of little-known works. He enriched and popularized music history through visual evidence and together with Scheurleer was a pioneer in the field of musical iconography. His example led to the formation of the Répertoire International d'Iconographie Musicale (RIdIM) in 1970.

WRITINGS

Musikhistorisches Museum von Wilhelm Heyer in Cöln: Katalog, i–ii, iv (Cologne, 1910–16) [vol.iii was not published; most of the MS is now lost]
'Musikinstrumentensammlungen in Vergangenheit und Gegenwart', *JbMP*, xxvii (1920), 47
Doppelrohrblatt-Instrumente mit Windkapsel (diss., U. of Cologne, 1925); *AMw*, vii (1925), 253
'Glucks Reisen nach Paris', *ZMw*, viii (1925–6), 551
ed.: *Glucks Briefe an Franz Kruthoffer* (Vienna, 1927)
with R. Haas and H. Schnoor: *Geschichte der Musik in Bildern* (Leipzig, 1929; Eng. trans., 1930, 2/1951)
'Beethovens Werke in Erst- und Frühausgaben: Instrumental- und Vokalmusik', *Antiquariatskatalog no. XXXVI der M. Lengfeld'schen Buchhandlung in Köln* (1929), 85
'Erst- und Frühdrucke von Werken Franz Schuberts und anderer Meister der Romantik und Neuromantik', ibid, no.xxxvii (1930), 1
'Musikbibliotheken', *Philobiblon*, vi (1933), 55
Erstlingsdrucke der deutschen Tonmeister der Klassik und Romantik (Vienna, 1934); *Philobiblon*, vii (1934), 347

'Die Erstausgaben und Handschriften der Sinfonien Beethovens', *Philobiblon*, ix (1936), 339
Die Originalausgaben der Werke Johann Sebastian Bachs (Vienna, 1937/R1968)
ed. M.-A. Souchay: *Manuskripte, Briefe, Dokumente von Scarlatti bis Stravinsky, Katalog der Musikautographen-Sammlung Louis Koch* (Stuttgart, 1951)
Das Werk Beethovens: thematisch-bibliographisches Verzeichnis seiner sämtlichen vollendeten Kompositionen (Munich and Duisburg, 1955) [completed by H. Halm]

EDITIONS

with F. Rothschild: *N. Paganini: Ausgewählte Kompositionen aus seinem Nachlass* (Vienna, 1922)
J. S. Bach: Präludium und Fuge h-moll (BWV544) (Vienna, 1923) [facs. edn.]
F. Schubert: Quartett für Flöte, Gitarre, Viola und Violoncello (Munich, 1926, 2/1931) [arrangement of a nocturne by F. Matiegka]
L. van Beethoven: 6 Menuette für 2 Violinen und Bass (WoO9) (Mainz, 1933)
F. Schubert: Ländler; J. Brahms: 11 Ländler (Mainz, 1934) [for pf duet]

BIBLIOGRAPHY

E. E. Mueller von Asow: 'Georg Kinsky', *Mf*, iv (1951), 245
H. Halm: 'Vorwort', in G. Kinsky and H. Halm: *Das Werk Beethovens* (Munich and Duisburg, 1955), ix

ALFONS OTT

Kipnis, Alexander (*b* Zhitomir, Ukraine, 1 Feb 1891; *d* Westport, Conn., 14 May 1978). American bass of Ukrainian birth. He came of a poor Jewish family, and his father died when he was 12. Supporting himself, he contrived to study music at the Warsaw Conservatory and singing in Berlin with Ernst Grenzebach. Interned as a Russian alien on the outbreak of World War I, he was soon released and began his career at Hamburg and Wiesbaden. In 1919 he joined the Berlin Charlottenburg Opera (later, Städtische Oper), remaining there as leading bass for 11 years; from 1930 he sang more often at the Staatsoper, and stayed on at first even after the Nazis had come to power. In 1934, however, he became an American citizen.

By then he had established himself everywhere as an outstanding Wagner and Mozart bass and a highly distinguished interpreter of Italian and Russian roles. He was much in demand at the Bayreuth and Salzburg festivals, as well as in the leading opera houses of the world. In England he sang often at Covent Garden (first as Marcel in *Les Huguenots*, 1927) and for one season at Glyndebourne (Sarastro, 1936). But his career took him increasingly to America, both North and South. He was particularly appreciated in Chicago, where he was a regular member of the company, 1923–32, and where his 30 roles included as many in Italian and French operas as in German. Between 1926 and 1936 he took part in six seasons at the Colón, Buenos Aires. After a surprisingly late début at the Metropolitan (in 1940 as Gurnemanz) he remained in New York until his retirement in 1946, singing his first Boris Godunov there in 1943. Pogner, King Mark, Ochs and Verdi's Philip II were among his other most successful roles. With a voice of wide range and variety of colour, as well as of unusual refinement and flexibility for a bass, he also made his mark as a lieder singer, contributing extensively and valuably to the albums of the Hugo Wolf and Brahms Song Societies. The best of his many operatic records are those made in Berlin in the early 1930s, especially Osmin's first song from *Die Entführung* and 'Il lacerato spirito' from *Simon Boccanegra*.

BIBLIOGRAPHY

A. Frankenstein, E. Arnosi and J. Dennis: 'Alexander Kipnis', *Record Collector*, xxii (1974), 53 [with discography]

DESMOND SHAWE-TAYLOR

Kipnis, Igor (*b* Berlin, 27 Sept 1930). American harpsichordist, son of Alexander Kipnis. After studying at the Westport School of Music in Connecticut and at Harvard, where he graduated in 1952, he worked for some years as musical director of a New York radio station and as a critic before taking up the harpsichord professionally. Although essentially self-taught, he was guided and encouraged by a number of musicians, notably Thurston Dart. His début as a harpsichordist was made in a radio broadcast from New York in 1959, followed by a first recital there in 1962. After extensive tours of the USA and Canada, he performed in Europe (1967, 1975), South America (1968, 1975), Israel (1969, 1976) and Australia (1971). He made his début with the New York Philharmonic under Boulez in 1975. From 1964 to 1967 he taught Baroque performing practice at the Berkshire Music Center at Tanglewood, and from 1971 to 1975 was associate professor of fine arts at Fairfield University in Connecticut, where he was appointed artist-in-residence in 1975. Kipnis's large repertory includes a representative selection of harpsichord music of every national school as well as many contemporary American works. He has edited harpsichord music and is a frequent contributor to music periodicals. His playing, while founded on a solid technique, stresses the expressive and stylistic features of the music rather than its purely instrumental qualities. His concert and recorded performances of 17th- and 18th-century music, including a number on the clavichord, are noteworthy for their bold and imaginative free ornamentation.

HOWARD SCHOTT

Király, Ernő (*b* Subotica, 16 March 1919). Hungarian composer and ethnomusicologist. He studied the trumpet at the Subotica School of Music (1939) and continued studies on his own. Until 1953 he was a member of the Subotica Municipal Theatre Orchestra and the Subotica PO; from that date he has been Hungarian folk music editor for Novi Sad broadcasting and in 1958 was appointed head of the folk music department at the Vojvodina Museum in Novi Sad. As a composer attracted by folk music he has shown a special interest in experimenting with new intonational and interpretative possibilities. He has constructed a 'citraphone' from Hungarian folk zithers of different sizes.

WORKS
(*selective list*)
Stage: A kis torkos [The little glutton] (children's opera, P. Balaž), 1962
Vocal: Vajdasági magyar népdalok [Hungarian folksongs from Vojvodina], 2–3vv, 1961; Reflections I–III, vv, tamburica orch, 1964; Vocalizzazioni, chorus, 1969; Reflections IV–V, 1v, gui, zither, 1967–70; Reflections VI, 1v, chamber orch, 1971; Four Black Horses at my Heels (K. Ladik), 1v, chamber orch, 1972; Inscription on a Balloon, speaker, fl, str orch, 1973
Inst: Tema con variazioni, str qt, 1956; 2 sonatines, pf, 1957; 3 Pieces, fl, pf, 1967; Etude II, tamburica orch, 1969; Toccata pentatonica, pf, 1972; Indications, 3 performers, tape rec, 1973

WRITINGS
Magyar népdalok [Hungarian folksongs] (Novi Sad, 1962)
'Citra narodni muzički instrument kod mađara u Jugoslaviji' [The zither as a folk instrument used by Hungarians in Yugoslavia], Rada vojvodanskih muzeja (Subotica, 1964), nos.12–13, pp.103–39
'Zajedničke crte i uzajamne veze srpskohrvatske i mađarske narodne muzike u Vojvodini' [Common traits and mutual relations of Serbo-Croatian and Hungarian folk music in Vojvodina], Združenija na folkloristite na SR Makedonija (Skopje, 1968), 443
Vajdasági magyar munkásmozgalmi dalok nyomában [Tracing the revolutionary and militant songs among Hungarians in Vojvodina] (Novi Sad, 1969)

BÁLINT SÁROSI

Kirby, F(rank) E(ugene) (*b* New York, 6 April 1928). American musicologist. He received his BA from Colorado College in 1950, and studied musicology under Leo Schrade as a graduate student at Yale, where he took his PhD in 1957. He taught at West Virginia University from 1961 to 1963, and since then has been on the faculty of Lake Forest College in Illinois.

Kirby has a wide range of scholarly interests, including German Renaissance theory, the history of keyboard music, the music of Beethoven, and such literary figures as Herder and Goethe. His *Short History of Keyboard Music*, the most complete recent survey of the subject in English, has been praised for its comprehensive and systematic coverage. His more recent *Introduction to Western Music* presents a new approach to introductory music education for college students: he uses a thorough discussion of the music of Bach, Beethoven, Wagner and Stravinsky as the basis of a history of Western music from the Baroque to the present.

WRITINGS
Harpsichord Manual (Kassel, 1960, 2/1968) [trans. of H. Neupert: Das Cembalo (Kassel, 1933, 3/1956)]
'Herman Finck on Methods of Performance', ML, xlii (1961), 212
'Herder and Opera', JAMS, xv (1962), 316
A Short History of Keyboard Music (New York, 1966)
'Beethoven and the "geselliges Lied" ', ML, xlvii (1966), 116
'Brahms and the Piano Sonata', Paul A. Pisk: Essays in his Honor (Austin, 1966), 163
An Introduction to Western Music: Bach, Beethoven, Wagner, Stravinsky (New York, 1970)
'Beethoven's Pastoral Symphony as a sinfonia caracteristica', MQ, lvi (1970), 605; reprinted in The Creative World of Beethoven, ed. P. H. Lang (New York, 1971), 103
with D. E. Lee: 'Die Rolle der Musik bei der Entstehung von Goethes West-östlichem Divan', Interpretationen zum West-östlichen Divan Goethes, ed. E. Lohner (Darmstadt, 1973), 176–227

PAULA MORGAN

Kirby, Percival (Robson) (*b* Aberdeen, 17 April 1887; *d* Grahamstown, South Africa, 7 Feb 1970). South African musicologist of Scottish birth. He studied under Terry at the University of Aberdeen, where he graduated in 1910, and under Stanford at the Royal College of Music. In 1914 he emigrated to South Africa as music organizer of the Natal Education Department. He was appointed professor of music at University College, Johannesburg (later the University of the Witwatersrand), in 1921 and held this post until his retirement in 1952. A professional timpanist from his London years, he published *The Kettledrums* in 1930. He founded and conducted the Johannesburg SO (1927) and the university orchestra (1930), for which he wrote and arranged incidental music for many university productions; he composed over 100 songs.

Kirby is best known for his work on the indigenous music of South Africa. From 1930 he engaged actively in field research, which took him on study tours of the Transvaal, Bechuanaland (Botswana), Swaziland, Vendaland and Ovamboland. He published this research in *The Musical Instruments of the Native Races of South Africa* (1934). An expedition to the Kalahari Desert in 1936 resulted in important studies of Bushman music. He was also interested in South African history and published books and papers, especially on Andrew Smith and the wreck of the *Grosvenor*. He held numerous official positions including that of president of the South African Museums Association (1951) and president of the South African Association for the Advancement of Science (1954). He was made an

FRCM (1924) and a Fellow of the Royal Anthropological Institute (1937) and received doctorates from the universities of the Witwatersrand (1931) and Grahamstown (1965).

WRITINGS

'Some Old Time Chants of the Mpumuza Chiefs', *Bantu Studies*, ii (1923), 23

'Horn Chords: an Acoustical Problem', *MT*, lxvi (1925), 811

'Some Problems of Primitive Harmony and Polyphony with special reference to Bantu Practice', *South African Journal of Science*, xxiii (1926), 951

'A Thirteenth-century Ballad Opera: an Essay on "Le Jeu de Robin et de Marion" by Adam de la Hale', *ML*, xi (1930), 163

'A Study of Negro Harmony', *MQ*, xvi (1930), 404

The Kettledrums (London, 1930)

'The Recognition and Practical Use of the Harmonics of Stretched Strings by the Bantu of South Africa', *Bantu Studies*, vi (1932), 31

'The Reed-flute Ensembles of South Africa', *Journal of the Royal Anthropological Institute*, lxiii (1933), 313–88

The Musical Instruments of the Native Races of South Africa (London, 1934, 2/1965)

'A Study of Bushman Music', *Bantu Studies*, x (1936), 205–52

'The Musical Practices of the /?Auni and ≠Khomani Bushmen', *Bantu Studies*, x (1936), 373–431

'Weber's Operas in England, 1824–1826', *MQ*, xxxii (1946), 333

'The Trumpets of Tut-Ankh-Amen and their Successors', *Journal of the Royal Anthropological Institute*, lxxvii (1947), 33

'Rossini's Overture to "William Tell" ', *ML*, xxxiii (1952), 132

'Primitive Music' and 'South Africa', *Grove 5*

'Captain Gordon, the Flute Maker', *ML*, xxxviii (1957), 250

'Buschmann- und Hottentottenmusik', *MGG*

'The Indonesian Origin of Certain African Musical Instruments', *African Studies*, xxv (1966), 3

BIBLIOGRAPHY

V. Bryer: *Professor Percival Robson Kirby . . .: a Bibliography of his Works* (Johannesburg, 1965)

P. Kirby: *Wits End* (Cape Town, 1967) [autobiography]

M. M. de Lange: *Catalogue of the Musical Instruments in the Collection of Professor Percival Kirby* (Johannesburg, 1967)

JOHN TYRRELL

Kirbye, George (*d* Bury St Edmunds, buried 6 Oct 1634). English composer. He was one of the most important contributors to East's psalter (1592). He was employed as a domestic musician at Rushbrooke Hall near Bury St Edmunds, the seat of Sir Robert Jermyn, to two of whose daughters he dedicated his single volume of madrigals (1597). Four years later he contributed *With angels face* to *The Triumphes of Oriana* (1601; in the second edition the text 'Bright Phoebus greets' was substituted). At Rushbrooke, Kirbye was only a few miles from Hengrave Hall, where Wilbye was also a resident musician, and the two men must have had personal contacts. On 16 February 1598 Kirbye married Anne Saxye at nearby Bradfield St George. Later he moved to Bury St Edmunds, living in Whiting Street. His wife was buried at St Mary's Church on 11 June 1626. During the next two years his name appears in the parish registers, evidently as churchwarden. Kirbye's own burial is recorded at St Mary's; his will reveals that he died a man of some substance.

To judge from the pieces in *GB-Ob* Mus.f.17–24 Kirbye's basic musical training had been in a pre-madrigalian style. This is shown not only in the deeply expressive Latin setting, *Quare tristis es/Convertere, anima mea*, but even more obviously in the eight secular pieces, which set mostly moralizing verse, and which are clearly viol-accompanied songs in which words have been fitted to the instrumental parts, after the style of Byrd's *Psalmes, Sonets & Songs of Sadnes and Pietie* (1588). Kirbye was, however, well acquainted with Italian music, and among his possessions at his death was a set of partbooks (now *GB-Ob* Mus.f.1–6) containing works by 16 Italian composers. All the com-

positions in the 1597 volume are genuine madrigals, yet despite an indebtedness to certain features of Morley's style, Kirbye set no light verse of the sort that had filled Morley's volumes printed during the preceding four years. All Kirbye's madrigals maintain the prevailing seriousness of pre-madrigalian English music, and all the 1597 works are in a minor mode (his Oriana madrigal, *With angels face*, alone shows how admirably he could handle a brilliant and forthright manner). His madrigalian style shows an assured consistency, with a flexible and refined response to the text, fluent harmony, a discreet yet telling use of occasional chromaticism, and admirable rhythmic plasticity. Kerman observed that 'superficially, Kirbye is one of the Englishmen most impressed with Marenzio's style', though he shows more restraint in his imagery than was typical of an Italian madrigalist. Kirbye's collection contains two settings of *Sleep now my Muse*, of which the one for six voices is a re-working of that for four voices. Just as none of Kirbye's more routine works is really weak, so neither are any of his more inventive ones as outstanding as the best madrigals of Weelkes and Wilbye. Among the English madrigalists he is the supreme master of the generalized madrigal, an impeccable craftsman of unfailing taste, possessing a musical inventiveness that lifts him far above the level of an accomplished artisan like Lichfild, yet lacking the imaginative boldness or penetrating insight that can transform talent into genius.

WORKS

SACRED

All my belief, score, *GB-T* 711

O Jesu, looke, 5vv, *Lbm* Add.29372–7

Quare tristis es (2p. Convertere, anima mea), 4vv, *Ob* Mus.f.17–19 (lacks Tr)

Vox in Rama, 6vv, *T* 807–11 (lacks B)

3 sacred contrafacta of madrigals in *Och* 750–53, 1074–7: Sleepe, restles thoughtes, 4vv (formerly Sleep now my Muse); Vayne worlde adiew, 4vv (formerly Farewell my love); Woe is me, my strength fayles, 4vv (formerly Woe am I, my hart dies)

19 contributions to The Whole Booke of Psalmes (London, 1592⁷)

SECULAR

The first set of English madrigalls, to 4. 5. & 6. voyces (London, 1597); ed. E. H. Fellowes, rev. T. Dart, EM, xxiv (Minor)/(1961)

Madrigal, 6vv, in 1601¹⁶ (later printed with the text, Bright Phoebus greets most cleerely)

8 pieces, 5vv, in *Ob* Mus.f.20–21, 23–4 (one ptbk missing)

8 madrigals, 4–6vv, *Lcm* 684 (4 ptbks only survive)

INSTRUMENTAL

Pavane, a 5, *Lbm* Add.30826–8 (lacks 2 parts)

BIBLIOGRAPHY

E. H. Fellowes: *English Madrigal Verse, 1588–1632* (London, 1920, rev., enlarged 3/1967)

——: *The English Madrigal Composers* (London, 1921, 2/1948)

J. Kerman: *The Elizabethan Madrigal: a Comparative Study* (New York and London, 1962)

C. Monson: 'George Kirbye and the English Madrigal', *ML*, lix (1978), 290

DAVID BROWN

Kirchbauer, Alphons (*fl* 1731). German composer. He was a monk at the Benedictine Abbey of Neresheim, near Dillingen. Unlike most of the German monastic composers of the early 18th century, he seems to have had a fairly successful ecclesiastical as well as musical career, having been chancellor to the Bishop of Chur.

His one known publication, *Jubileus curiae caelestis* (Augsburg, 1731), contains seven masses for four voices, two violins and organ, and is typical of the small-scale church music for parish choirs of the time. Kirchbauer was one of the earlier composers to follow the lead given by Valentin Rathgeber in writing simple, tuneful music for ordinary churches. This publication is unusual in that it does not appear to have included the optional trumpet and drum parts supplied with most publications, but it must have been popular as it was reprinted in 1740 (according to *FétisB*), a distinction which few liturgical publications received.

ELIZABETH ROCHE

Kirchentonart (Ger.). CHURCH MODE.

Kircher, Athanasius (*b* Geisa, nr. Fulda, 2 May 1601; *d* Rome, 27 Nov 1680). German polyhistorian, theologian and music theorist, resident mainly in Italy. He is important for music as the author of *Musurgia universalis*, one of the most influential of all music treatises and specially notable among those of the Baroque period.

1. LIFE. Kircher related the few known facts of his early life in an autobiography (see Seng's trans. of Langenmantel). His father, who received a doctor's degree in philosophy and theology from Mainz University, was apparently also a musician, for Kircher credited him with his first instruction in music. After starting his education in his home town he entered a Jesuit school at Fulda in 1612. On 2 October 1618 he became a novice at the Jesuit college at Paderborn, thus initiating a long period of intensive training in various Jesuit schools in both humanistic and scientific subjects. In 1622 he was forced to leave Paderborn because of the ravages of the Thirty Years War and went to Cologne to continue his studies in the physical sciences and philosophy. The following year he underwent further language training at Koblenz but was soon required to move to Heiligenstadt, near Göttingen, to teach Greek. Probably in the same year he was sent to the residence of the Archbishop of Mainz, Johann Schweikard von Kronberg at Aschaffenburg. In 1624 he began four years of theological study at Mainz, where in 1628 he was ordained. A final year of teacher training, which he pursued at Speyer, was required of him before he received his first appointment in 1629 as professor of mathematics, philosophy and oriental languages at the University of Würzburg. Two years later, when the Swedish army threatened Würzburg, he fled to France: he was sent first to Lyons and shortly afterwards to Avignon, where at a Jesuit college he took up a position similar to the one he had held at Würzburg. At Avignon he began an intensive study of the natural sciences and at this time became acquainted with Senator Nicolas Peiresc of Provence, whose similar enthusiasm for the sciences and especially for the study of ancient eastern civilizations led to a lasting friendship that soon influenced Kircher's career.

In 1633 Kircher received an appointment as court mathematician to the Emperor Ferdinand II at Vienna. He decided to travel by way of Rome, which he reached on 14 November. However, through the influence of Peiresc, who urged both Cardinal Francesco Barberini and Pope Urban VIII to keep him in Rome, he found on his arrival that he had been appointed to the Collegio Romano as professor of mathematics, physics and eastern studies. He remained there for the rest of his life except for brief visits to other parts of Italy and a longer journey, in 1637–8, to Malta as the father confessor to Landgrave Friedrich of Hessen-Darmstadt. Eventually he was released from teaching so as to be able to devote himself entirely to research and writing. In his later years he often went for reasons of health to the chapel of S Maria della Mentorella at Guadagnolo, a village near Palestrina, and after his death his heart was interred there.

2. WORKS. There has so far been no study in English evaluating Kircher's numerous contributions to knowledge. In German, however, Scharlau has summarized the content and importance of his writings on music and has also been the first to examine systematically his voluminous correspondence surviving in Rome (see also Langenmantel). Kircher wrote 30 books, several of them vast, in which he sought to embrace the entire corpus of Man's accumulated knowledge and to organize and relate it to Christian philosophy. The magnitude of his achievement precludes even a summary here. It may be noted, however, that he was one of the first to solve the meaning of Egyptian hieroglyphics, and his *Oedipus aegyptiacus* (1652–4), though often inaccurate and prone to imaginative conclusions, was in the 17th century a major source for the popularizing of ancient Egyptian culture and civilization. Like many of his contemporaries, among them Mersenne, Fludd and Kepler, Kircher often erred by failing to evaluate the accuracy of his scientific data. Nevertheless, he compiled, especially in the massive *Musurgia universalis*, a compendium of musical facts and speculation that is still essential to an understanding of 17th-century music and music theory.

Musurgia universalis, one of the really influential works of music theory, was drawn upon by almost every later German music theorist until well into the 18th

Title-page of Kircher's 'Musurgia universalis' (1650); for a further illustration from this work, see WATER ORGAN, *fig.1*

century. Its popularity was greatly aided by a German translation of a major part of it in 1662. Kircher wrote about music as an essentially conservative German rationalist, who saw it as a natural element in the Quadrivium, as part of mathematical order and, by extension, as a unique symbol of God's order expressed in number. He continued to support the essentially medieval view that the cosmos was revealed in musical ratios and that musical harmony mirrored God's harmony. This profoundly theological viewpoint of 17th-century German music theory (see Buelow) clearly extends as far as the music of Bach. Much of Kircher's contrapuntal doctrine derives from Zarlino, and in this and some other respects *Musurgia universalis* presents a synthesis of 16th- and 17th-century Italian and German compositional practices. A specifically German feature, however, is the description of the affective nature of music, in which Kircher brought the concept of *musica pathetica* into relation with the formal constructive elements of rhetorical doctrine. He examined rhetorical structure, poetic metre and musical–rhetorical figures in some detail. In this way he suggested the means for achieving an emotionally expressive yet rationally controlled musical style. His ideas concerning the classification of musical styles, based on sociological as well as national characteristics, are also original and important for the study of Baroque music (see Katz). Although he was apparently not a practising musician he was able to identify the best music composed and performed in his own (and earlier) times. In *Musurgia universalis* he quoted frequently extensive music examples from composers such as Agazzari, Gregorio Allegri, Carissimi, Froberger, Gesualdo, Kapsberger, Domenico Mazzocchi and Morales. Other aspects of his treatise that contribute to an understanding of 17th-century musical thought include the lengthy discussions of acoustics, musical instruments, the history of music in ancient cultures and the therapeutic value of music.

Kircher's insatiable curiosity about ancient cultures, the natural sciences and music, together with his extensive contacts with scholars throughout the world, led him to assemble a museum of antiquities and musical curiosities. This Museum Kircherianum was for long an attraction for visiting musicians as well as for tourists; it was eventually dispersed among various Roman museums in the 19th century. Kircher was fascinated too by all aspects of mechanics and created a composing machine – the *arca musarithmica* – that made automatic composition possible. Although frequently criticized for his attitudes which to later writers seem unscientific, and often neglected because of his difficult Latin prose, he was nevertheless one of the leading figures in the music theory of the Baroque period.

See also MICHELI, ROMANO, and NOTATION, fig.104.

WRITINGS
(only those on music)

Magnes, sive De arte magnetica (Rome, 1641, rev. 2/1643)
Ars magna lucis et umbrae (Rome, 1646)
Musurgia universalis, sive Ars magna consoni et dissoni (Rome, 1650/R1970); inc. trans. A. Hirsch as *Philosophischer Extract und Auszug aus dess Welt-berühmten teutschen Jesuiten Athanasii Kircheri von Fulda Musurgia universali* (Schwäbisch Hall, 1662)
Oedipus aegyptiacus (Rome, 1652–4)
Iter exstaticum coeleste (Rome, 1656; ed. C. Schott, Würzburg, 1671)
Organum mathematicum (Würzburg, 1668) [collab. C. Schott]
Ars magna sciendi (Amsterdam, 1669)
Phonurgia nova, sive Coniugium mechanico-physicum artis et naturae (Kempten, 1673/R1966); trans. A. Cario [Christoph Fischer] as *Neue Hall- und Thon-Kunst* (Nördlingen, 1684)
Tariffa Kircheriana (Rome, 1679)

Vita admodum reverendi P. Athanasii Kircheri SJ viri toto orbe celebratissimi (MS, c1669, incl. in Langenmantel and Seng)
Letters, see Langenmantel and Scharlau

BIBLIOGRAPHY
H. A. Langenmantel: *Fasciculus epistolarum adm. R. P. Athanasii Kircheri Soc. Jesu, viri in mathematicis et variorum idiomatum scientiis celebratissimi* (Augsburg, 1684); Ger. trans. by N. Seng in *Die Selbstbiographie des P. Athanasius Kircher* (Fulda, 1901)
C. Sommervogel: *Bibliotheca mariana de la Compagnie de Jésus*, iv (Brussels, 1893); ix (Paris, 1932)
E. Katz: *Die musikalischen Stilbegriffe des 17. Jahrhunderts* (diss., U. of Freiburg, 1926)
R. Dammann: *Der Musikbegriff im deutschen Barock* (Cologne, 1967)
U. Scharlau: *Athanasius Kircher (1601–1680) als Musikschriftsteller* (Marburg, 1969)
G. J. Buelow: 'Symposium on Seventeenth-century Music Theory: Germany', *JMT*, xvi (1972), 36

GEORGE J. BUELOW

Kirchgässner [Kirchgessner], **Marianne** [Mariane, Maria Anna] **(Antonia)** (*b* Bruchsal, 5 June 1769; *d* Schaffhausen, 9 Dec 1808). German glass harmonica player, blind from the age of 4. Having learnt the glass harmonica from J. A. Schmittbauer at Karlsruhe, she made numerous successful concert tours; on the first (1791), accompanied by the music journalist H. P. C. Bossler and his wife, she visited Munich, Salzburg, Linz and Vienna. Mozart heard her in Vienna and composed the Adagio and Rondo (K617), and the Fantasie (KAnh92/616a) for glass harmonica, flute, oboe, viola and cello, and Adagio (K356/617a) for her instrument. In London in 1794 Fröschel made her a new instrument which she used from then onwards, and Salomon wrote a sonata for her. In 1799 she retired to Gohlis, near Leipzig, but later made several concert tours, including visits to Goethe in Karlsbad in the summer of 1808. Musicians admired her playing but regretted that she failed to bring out the true qualities of the glass harmonica, through a wrong method of execution. Her death was attributed to deterioration of her nerves caused by the unusually piercing vibrations of the instrument.

BIBLIOGRAPHY
K. M. Pisarowitz: 'Zum Bizentenar einer Blinden', *Acta mozartiana*, xvi (1969), 72
H. Ullrich: *Die blinde Glassharmonikavirtuosin Mariane Kirchgessner und Wien: eine Künstlerin der empfindsamen Zeit* (Tutzing, 1971)
B. Hoffmann: 'Kirchgessner, Mariane', *MGG*

C. F. POHL/KARL MARIA PISAROWITZ

Kirchhoff, Gottfried (*b* Mühlbeck, nr. Bitterfeld, 15 Sept 1685; *d* Halle, 21 Jan 1746). German composer and organist. He was one of a family of Stadtpfeifer whose members held appointments in Weissenfels, Bitterfeld, Leipzig, Quedlinburg and other centres; Andreas Kirchhoff, an 'excellent instrumentalist' active in Copenhagen about 1670, was probably a member of the family. Along with Handel, Kirchhoff was one of Zachow's most brilliant pupils, schooled in the tradition of the Leipzig organists' and Stadtpfeifer's art. In 1709 he was Kapellmeister to the Duke of Holstein-Glücksburg (possibly through the good offices of Andreas Kirchhoff, then in Denmark) and in 1711 he was appointed organist in Quedlinburg, before moving in 1714 to Halle, where he was organist and *director musices* at the Liebfrauenkirche; the post was previously declined by J. S. Bach. In 1716 Bach, Kuhnau and Rolle came to examine the organ, newly built by Cunzius. Kirchhoff composed two cantatas on the organ's dedication and also wrote and directed the music in honour of academic festivities (1733) and the bicentenary of the Reformation in Halle (1741).

Kirchhoff's works include cantatas (two in *B-Bc*), in

the tradition of Zachow, J. S. Bach and Erdmann Neumeister, using successions of brief arioso movements and sometimes linking accompanied recitative and chorale. Ties with Bach are seen in his setting in 1717 of *Christen, ätzet diesen Tag* (cf BWV63) and in *L'ABC musical: Praeludia und Fugen aus allen Tönen* (unfortunately lost). His organ pieces and in particular chorale preludes (in *D-Bds*, *USSR-KAU*) show the influence of the Pachelbel school as well as Zachow; their characteristic features include imitative treatment of chorale melodies, free figuration, melisma and dominance of the upper voices. They do not however appear to bear out his reputation as a virtuoso organist. But his other keyboard works and his violin sonatas show that his high reputation was well founded. One of the violin sonatas appears as a five-movement sonatina in Leopold Mozart's *Notenbuch* for his son (1762).

BIBLIOGRAPHY

H. Mendel and A. Reissmann: *Musikalisches Conversations-Lexikon* (Berlin, 1870–79/R, 2/1880–83)
G. Frotscher: *Geschichte des Orgel-Spiels und der Orgel-Komposition* (Berlin, 1935–6, enlarged 3/1966)
W. Serauky: *Musikgeschichte der Stadt Halle*, ii/1 (Halle and Berlin, 1939/R1970)
H. T. David and A. Mendel, eds.: *The Bach Reader* (New York, 1945, rev. 2/1966)
H. J. Moser: *Die evangelische Kirchenmusik in Deutschland* (Berlin, 1954)

G. KRAFT

Kirchmann. See KIRCKMAN family.

Kirchner, Leon (*b* Brooklyn, NY, 24 Jan 1919). American composer, pianist and conductor. Kirchner received most of his schooling in California, where his family settled when he was nine years old. He began composing while a student at Los Angeles City College and attracted the attention of Ernst Toch, who encouraged him to study composition with Schoenberg at the University of California in Los Angeles. After obtaining a BA degree in 1940, he began graduate work at the university's Berkeley campus, where Ernest Bloch was active. Awarded the University of California's George Ladd Prix de Paris, he went to New York in 1942 for work with Roger Sessions, France being closed to him during World War II. After three years of active army service he returned to Berkeley, where he obtained both his MA degree and an appointment as lecturer (1949). Back in New York on a Guggenheim Fellowship the following year, he drew universal acclaim with his new Piano Sonata and earlier Duo. From 1950 to 1954 he served as lecturer, assistant professor and then associate professor at the University of Southern California, and in 1954 became Luther Brusie Marchant Professor at Mills College in Oakland, California. He was appointed to the Harvard faculty in 1961, and in 1966 succeeded Walter Piston as Walter Bigelow Rosen Professor of Music there.

Kirchner has distinguished himself in the USA and Europe both as a pianist and as a conductor of his own work and of the Classics, especially Mozart and Schubert. As a dynamic composer, disciplined in technique yet ranging imaginatively over a broad stylistic spectrum, he has been honoured twice by the New York Critics Circle (First and Second String Quartets), received the Naumburg Award (First Piano Concerto) and the Pulitzer Prize (Third Quartet, with electronic tape) and has received commissions from the Ford Foundation, the Fromm Foundation and the New York

Philharmonic. In 1962 he was elected to membership of both the National Institute of Arts and Letters and the American Academy of Arts and Sciences.

Stylistically, Kirchner has remained remarkably individual; earlier influences of Hindemith, Bartók and Stravinsky soon yielded to a wholehearted identification with the aesthetics, if not necessarily the specific procedures, of Schoenberg and Berg. Far from succumbing to the lures of dodecaphonic orthodoxy, Kirchner shapes his intrinsically dramatic compositions with the greatest freedom, as a rule making the most of minimal intervallic materials, especially the classic combinations of 2nds and 3rds that have dominated melodically orientated music from plainchant to Schoenberg. A growing commitment to conducting, as well as repeated attempts to come to terms with opera as a genuinely contemporary medium, may account for the gradual reduction of Kirchner's annual output. By the same token, the sublime eclecticism of *Music for Orchestra* bespeaks his complete grasp of the nature and potential of the modern orchestra no less than his profound sensitivity to the human and artistic issues of his time.

WORKS
(selective list)
ORCHESTRAL

Piece for pf and orch, 1946, unpubd
Sinfonia, 1951; New York, Jan 1952
Pf Concerto no.1, 1953; New York, 23 Feb 1956
Toccata, str, winds, perc, 1955; San Francisco, 16 Feb 1956
Concerto, vn, vc, 10 winds, perc, 1960
Pf Concerto no.2, 1963; Seattle, 29 Oct 1963
Music for orch, 1969; New York, 16 Oct 1969

CHAMBER AND INSTRUMENTAL

Duo, vn, pf, 1947; Berkeley, 1947
Pf Sonata, 1948; New York, March 1949
Little Suite, pf, 1949
Str Qt no.1, 1949; New York, March 1950
Sonata Concertante, vn, pf, 1952; New York, Nov 1952
Trio, vn, vc, pf, 1954; Pasadena, Nov 1954
Str Qt no.2, 1958
Str Qt no.3, 1966; New York, Jan 1967

VOCAL

Letter (S. Alexander), S, pf, 1943; Berkeley, 1946
The Times are Nightfall (G. Hopkins), S, pf, 1943; Berkeley, 1946
Dawn (F. Garcia-Lorca), chorus, org, 1943–6; New York, Feb 1949
Of Obedience (Whitman), S, pf, 1950; Los Angeles, 1950
The Runner (Whitman), S, pf, 1950; Los Angeles, 1950
Scenes for an Opera, 1957
Words from Wordsworth, chorus, 1968
Lily (opera, Kirchner, after S. Bellow), New York, 14 April 1977

Principal publishers: Associated, Mercury

WRITINGS

'Notes on Understanding', *Daedalus: Proceedings of the American Academy of Arts and Sciences*, xcviii/3 (1969), 739

BIBLIOGRAPHY

A. L. Ringer: 'Current Chronicle: San Francisco', *MQ*, xlii (1956), 244
——: 'Leon Kirchner', *MQ*, xliii (1957), 1

ALEXANDER L. RINGER

Kirchner, Theodor Fürchtegott (*b* Neukirchen, Saxony, 10 Oct 1823; *d* Hamburg, 18 Sept 1903). German organist and composer. He was an accomplished organist by the age of eight. In 1838 he went to Leipzig, where he studied with Julius Knorr and C. F. Becker; he also received advice from Mendelssohn and joined Schumann's circle. He went to Dresden in 1842 but returned to Leipzig the following year to study at the conservatory. Mendelssohn recommended him for the post of organist in Winterthur, and Kirchner spent his time there very successfully, teaching, composing and organizing the musical life of the town. Bülow, Liszt and Wagner admired his organ playing, and he was occasionally called upon to accompany the rehearsals of Wagner's operas. He was in touch with musical activity in Zurich, and in 1862 settled there, first assuming the direction of the subscription concerts and the leadership of a choir and later becoming organist at St Peter's. He married Maria Schmidt, a theatrical singer, in 1868.

In 1872 Kirchner took a post as music teacher to Princess Amalie in Meiningen, but he remained there only a year. He led an irregular life, often changing residence and activity: in 1873 he directed the newly founded music school in Würzburg; in 1875 he taught in Leipzig and from 1883 to 1890 he taught chamber music at the Dresden Conservatory; from 1890 he lived in Hamburg. Although he had an adequate income, his eccentric way of life led him into financial difficulties and only a collection taken up by his friends saved him from destitution. At the end of his life he was crippled and nearly blind.

Kirchner wrote about 1000 individual works for the piano and was a master of the character-piece and cyclic form. His style, which varied little, is akin to Schumann's. Among his chamber music works, his string quartets are noteworthy for their craftsmanship.

BIBLIOGRAPHY

A. Niggli: *Theodor Kirchner* (Leipzig, 1886)
O. Klauwell: *Theodor Kirchner* (Langensalza, 1909)
H. Kretzschmar: *Gesammelte Aufsätze über Musik*, i (Leipzig, 1910), 111ff
T. Kirchner: *Briefe aus den Jahren 1860–1868* (Zurich, 1949)
LUISE MARRETTA-SCHÄR

Kirckman [Kirchmann, Kirkman]. English family of harpsichord and piano makers, of Alsatian origin. Jacob Kirckman (*b* Bischweiler, 1710; *d* Greenwich, buried 9 June 1792) came to England in the early 1730s, and worked for HERMANN TABEL, whose widow he married in 1738. He took British citizenship on 25 April 1755, and in about 1770 went into partnership with his nephew, Abraham Kirckman (*b* Bischweiler, 1737; *d* Hammersmith, buried 16 April 1794). (The Jacob Kirckman who was organist of St George's, Hanover Square, at this time is probably to be identified with another of Jacob Kirckman's nephews, who died in 1812.) Abraham Kirckman in turn took into partnership his son, Joseph Kirckman (i) (dates of birth and death unknown), whose son, Joseph Kirckman (ii) (*c*1790–1877), worked with his father on their last harpsichord in 1809. The firm continued as piano makers until absorbed by Collard in 1898.

'The first harpsichord maker of the times' was Fanny Burney's description of Jacob Kirckman; but by then Shudi was dead and her father had become increasingly associated with Kirckman, judging by the correspondence with Thomas Jefferson (1786; quoted in Russell), the entries in *Rees's Cyclopaedia* and other sources. Clearly Kirckman and Shudi had a near monopoly of the English harpsichord at its apogee and various estimates have been made of how many they produced. In the event, over twice as many Kirckmans of one period or another have survived, and Hubbard's phrase 'almost mass produced', though an exaggeration, is an understandable one. It is not known how many men worked for Kirckman in any one year, nor are the details of his organization and working methods entirely clear. Burney related several anecdotes about Kirckman – about his becoming a money-lender, his wooing of Tabel's widow and his way of dealing with the competition of the 'keyed guitar' – that clung to his reputation; more pertinent to his development as a harpsichord maker are his willingness to make experimental harpsichords (such as the enharmonic instrument for Robert Smith of Trinity College, Cambridge, *c*1757), his realistic approach to new-fangled inventions (such as Walker's quasi-*Geigenwerk*, the Celestine, popular in the 1780s), his experience in related keyboard instruments (spinets, claviorgans, pianos *c*1770, square pianos *c*1775) and even his membership of the German Reformed Church of the Savoy, with which were as-

1. Harpsichord by Jacob and Abraham Kirckman, London, 1776 (Victoria and Albert Museum, London)

sociated both a musical repertory and an organ tradition much more cosmopolitan than even the most exceptional London parish churches. The fact that he sued his former worker R. Faulkner in 1771 for putting up for sale as by Kirckman a harpsichord made by somebody else (probably Faulkner, like those now in the University of Glasgow and the Russell Collection, with Kirckman nameboards) does not suggest vindictiveness; no doubt his complaint was justified and accords with other masters suing former apprentices at this period (e.g. Gottfried Silbermann and Hildebrandt).

The detailed differences and similarities of construction between a Kirckman and Shudi harpsichord are still being studied, and comparisons of their tone (based usually on restored instruments of highly questionable tonal authenticity) will remain conjectural for some years to come. What can be said is that there were three main Kirckman–Shudi harpsichord types: singles of 8′, 8′, singles of 8′, 8′, 4′ and doubles of 8′, 8′, 4′, lute. More often than not there is a buff batten (normally, but not always, for the lower 8′) after c1760, but lutes were not included on Kirckman singles; sometimes on singles, the buff was activated by a foot-lever (or 'pedal'). The machine stop, which is unlikely to date before 1765 (and then only at first for special instruments), was a registration aid whereby on being 'cocked' by a hand stop the foot could operate machinery attached to the register ends in such a way that stops could be changed without the hands needing to be removed from the keys. The standard system – though there were others – was that on, for example, the Shudi harpsichord now in the Vienna Kunsthistorisches Museum (said to have been Haydn's): on depression, the pedal changed the tutti (I 8′, I 4′ + II 8′) to a softer and different colour (I 8′ only, not coupled to II lute). On such English harpsichords, there was no coupler as such, the common 8′ row of strings being a 'dogleg' stop, that is the jacks were so shaped that they rested on the ends of both manuals' key-levers. This is today commonly regarded as a weakness of design, that the upper 8′ cannot be contrasted with the lower 8′ in two-manual play since the lower manual automatically plays it; but virtually no literature known to an English harpsichord player in the 18th century required such 'manual contrast and equality'. Either way it is unlikely that the upper manual was voiced other than as an echo. No English organ builder of 1750 was aware of the possibilities of two well-matched manuals; much the same could be said of the harpsichord makers.

The inner construction of a Kirckman was noticeably more complex, and might be thought more clumsy, than a French harpsichord of the same period, but both had developed fairly directly and clearly from the 17th-century Flemish harpsichord. Why English makers by the 1720s were so firmly committed to an idiosyncratic outward appearance to their harpsichords – veneered inside, then outside, with inlay and marquetry – is less clear; of more importance to the player, Kirckman devised an unusual keyboard and key-bed construction, whereby the keys of both manuals were placed on a three-rail frame with front rail pins, so that the key-fall is limited by a rail at the finger end of the keys, a very unpleasant system for fingers used to a French keyboard. Judging by the music written for French harpsichords in 1750, the manual coupling system, whereby the upper manual slid into and out of play with the lower manual and thus did without dogleg jacks, was not at the time understood to have the subtle advantage over

2. Portrait of a member of the Kirckman family, believed to be Abraham: pen and ink drawing, with wash (c1785), by John Nixon (private collection)

the English dogleg system for which recent authors have given it credit. By 1750, French upper manuals also were required for echoes.

Kirckman harpsichords made from c1766 may be found to have two pedals: one for the machine stop, one for the lid swell (see illustration). The latter was the name given to the device whose mechanism, operated through various types of lever by a pedal, opened a segment of the top lid along the bentside. Some kind of lid swell was incorporated in Plenius's lyrichord or lyrachord (a version of the gut-strung Geigenwerk), of which a description was published in 1755; in 1769 SHUDI patented his Venetian Swell, later adopted by Kirckman. Jefferson (in a letter dated 25 May 1786) called the device a 'machine on the top resembling a Venetian blind for giving a swell' and requested one for his commissioned Kirckman harpsichord. This was some years after Burney reported (in his travels in Italy) that the two Kirckmans he saw in Venice, and the Shudi in Naples, were 'regarded by the Italians as so many phenomena', although it is significant that the known exported Shudis (to Berlin, Vienna and Russia) had all the paraphernalia of the mature English harpsichord: machine stop, Venetian swell, four registers and a compass extended to C′. Why Kirckman should extend at least one of his harpsichords to c′′′′ is not known; perhaps in rivalry to Shudi (Kirckman's c′′′′ of 1772; Shudi's C′ for Maria Theresia, 1773) or in inspired anticipation of piano compass (Merlin, 1777, C′ to c′′′′).

It is possible that circumspect experience would suggest Shudi's harpsichords to have a more 'round' tone than Kirckman's; if so, such an opinion may be based on the more distant plucking-points reputedly given to Shudi's basic design by John Broadwood after c1770, or on the leather (or hard cowhide) plectra that details of jack design suggest to be authentic for at least some spinets and harpsichords from about 1785 or earlier. It seems to be true that Kirckman's lute registers pluck nearer the nut than Shudi's, thus pointing to a more incisive, nasal sound. So subjective is this area of study that Hubbard's considered view that such English harpsichords 'are too good. The tone . . . almost interferes with the music' could be precisely denied by others who found the tone suitably neutral for music in a very wide stylistic spectrum. All things being equal, the Venetian swells must have dulled the tone, both by interfering with its passage (even when open) and by increasing the weight of the whole structure; but there is no evidence that all things were equal, e.g. that builders did not compensate by voicing more brilliantly. Precise details of voicing and stringing, and of the materials used for both, are still imperfectly understood; the question of pitch is also difficult, since low *ton de chambre* of *a'* equal to about 415–20 Hz appears to be correct for many Shudi and Kirckman harpsichords, but perhaps not for all. At least one harpsichord from the 1770s has an apparently contemporary machine stop system whereby two foot-levers depressed in a particular order produce the 4' alone on the lower manual, thus suggesting that the voicing was meant to give the register more character of one sort or another than is usually the case today. The buff, or so-called harp, effect, produced by a batten studded with small pieces of *peau de buffle* (not felt) brought into contact with the ends of the 8' strings at the nut, is called 'guitar or harp' by Shudi in the directions on an instrument sent to Frederick the Great; but its purpose can be only conjectured, although special effects in continuo work are the most likely (e.g. in the slow movement of a flute sonata). Machine stops can produce a simulated crescendo–diminuendo effect when applied gradually, while the lid and Venetian swells change the timbre of the sound being produced as much as they do its volume. It has been suggested that, especially as the century neared its end, Kirckman and Shudi harpsichords were intended to be voiced very strongly, and Burney may well have written comparatively when he made his cryptic and unexpected remark about 'quilling, which in France is always weak'. As for the musical repertory of such harpsichords, it is probably fair to regard an enlightened English harpsichord player of *c*1770, with his interest in Scarlatti and Rameau, Handel and Corelli, J. C. Bach and Mozart, Arne and Purcell, Kirnberger and Hasse, C. P. E. Bach and Sammartini, as requiring a particularly, even uniquely, versatile instrument.

BIBLIOGRAPHY
D. H. Boalch: *Makers of the Harpsichord and Clavichord, 1440–1840* (London, 1956, rev. 2/1973) [with details of surviving Kirckman instruments]
R. Russell: *The Harpsichord and Clavichord* (London, 1959, rev. 2/1973)
F. Hubbard: *Three Centuries of Harpsichord Making* (Cambridge, Mass., 1965)
J. Barnes: 'Two Rival Harpsichord Specifications', *GSJ*, xix (1966), 49
P. Williams: 'The Earl of Wemyss' Claviorgan and its Context in Eighteenth-century England', *Keyboard Instruments*, ed. E. M. Ripin (Edinburgh, 1971), 75
DONALD HOWARD BOALCH/PETER WILLIAMS

Kirghizia. A constituent republic of the USSR; *see* CENTRAL ASIA and UNION OF SOVIET SOCIALIST REPUBLICS, §XI, 5.

Kiriac-Georgescu, Dumitru (*b* Bucharest, 18 March 1866; *d* Bucharest, 8 Jan 1928). Romanian composer, conductor and teacher. He began his musical training at the Bucharest Conservatory with Gheorghe Brătianu and Eduard Wachmann, and then studied from 1892 to 1899 in Paris, with Dubois, Bourgault-Ducoudray and Widor at the Conservatoire and with Vincent d'Indy at the Schola Cantorum. At the same time he conducted the choir of the Romanian Chapel and a French choral society, Les Enfants de Lutèce. After his return to Romania he became in 1900 a professor at the Bucharest Conservatory, and in the following year founded the 'Carmen' society, one of the most important Romanian choirs of the 20th century. In 1928 he helped to organize a library in Bucharest that was to become the Folklore Institute. With Enescu and Brăiloiu he was among the founder-members of the Society of Romanian Composers in 1920.

As a composer, Kiriac-Georgescu worked on the development of new choral and vocal genres, and as a scholar with deep knowledge of folk and church modes he created a new style of Romanian music. Use of the Locrian, Dorian and other modes underlies the harmonic structure of his music. In addition to the *Liturgia psaltică* and the *Cîntările liturgici*, he wrote many choruses and songs influenced by Romanian folklore and popular life.

WORKS
(selective list)

Edition: *D. Kiriac-Georgescu: Opere alese* [Selected works], ed. I. D. Chirescu and G. Breazul (Bucharest, 1955) [13 choruses, 2–4vv, 22 songs, 1v, pf acc.]

Coruri populare romînesti [Romanian popular choruses] (Bucharest, 1905)
Cîntările liturgici [Liturgical songs], 4vv (Tîrgu-Jiu, 1962)
Liturgia psaltică [Psalmic liturgy], 4vv (Bucharest, n.d.)
Several vols. of school choruses, collections of folktunes and folkdances

BIBLIOGRAPHY
G. Breazul: Studiu introductiv, *D. Kiriac-Georgescu: Opere alese* (Bucharest, 1955)
——: 'Kiriac, Dumitru Georgescu', *MGG*
Z. Vancea: *Creatia muzicală românească* (Bucharest, 1968)
V. Cosma: *Muzicieni români* (Bucharest, 1970)
G. Breazul: *D. G. Kiriac* (Bucharest, 1973)
ROMEO GHIRCOIAŞIU

Kiribati. From 1979 the name of the Gilbert Islands; *see* MICRONESIA, §3.

Kirk, Andy [Andrew Dewey] (*b* Newport, Ky., 28 May 1898). Black American jazz saxophonist and bandleader. He spent his childhood in Denver, where he studied the piano, singing, the alto saxophone and music theory with Wilberforce Whiteman (Paul Whiteman's father) and several others. In 1918 he joined George Morrison's orchestra as a bass saxophone and tuba player. In 1925 he moved to Dallas, where he joined Terence Holder's 'Dark Clouds of Joy' orchestra, assuming its leadership in 1929. In that year he transferred the band to Kansas City, Missouri, where it rivalled Bennie Moten's band and made its first recordings (1929–30). From 1930 he made several nationwide tours, though the band continued to be based primarily in Kansas City. The success of *Until the real thing comes along* (1936) established the band's lasting popularity. Until the group disbanded in 1948 it was constantly on tour and made many recordings; thereafter Kirk occasionally led ad hoc orchestras.

Kirk was not a soloist, and rarely played ensemble parts after the early 1930s, but made an important contribution to jazz through his leadership of the 'Clouds of Joy'. His was the only Kansas City group with a strong reputation both as jazz orchestra and commercial 'sweet' band. Its style was largely determined by the compositions and arrangements of Mary Lou Williams, the band's pianist from 1929 to 1942 and later Kirk's wife; though vigorous, her pieces were more subtly orchestrated than those of most other Midwestern bands of the period, and less dependent on riffs. Kirk's outstanding soloists included Williams and the pianist Kenny Kersey, the tenor saxophonists Dick Wilson and Don Byas, the trumpeters Harold 'Shorty' Baker, Howard

McGhee and 'Fats' Navarro, and for a brief period the alto saxophonist Charlie Parker.

BIBLIOGRAPHY

F. Driggs: 'Kansas City and the Southwest', *Jazz*, ed. N. Hentoff and A. McCarthy (New York, 1959), 189ff
—: 'Andy Kirk', *Jazz Panorama*, ed. M. Williams (New York, 1964), 119ff
B. Rust: *Jazz Records: 1897–1942* (London, 1965, rev. 2/1969)
J. Grunnet Jepsen: *Jazz Records: 1942–1967*, iv/c (Copenhagen, 1970), 360ff
A. McCarthy: *Big Band Jazz* (London, 1974), 102ff

J. R. TAYLOR

Kirkendale [née Schöttler], **Ursula (Antonie)** (*b* Dortmund, 6 Sept 1932). American musicologist of German birth. She studied musicology, art history and classical archaeology at the universities of Munich and Vienna, and took the doctorate (1961) at Bonn University with a dissertation on Caldara. She did editorial work for Knud Jeppesen in Florence during 1962; from 1964 she taught musicology at the University of Southern California, the University of California at Santa Barbara and Duke University. In 1969–70 she was visiting associate professor at Columbia University.

In her research she has concentrated on the Italian Baroque. Her book on Antonio Caldara, which deals especially with the composer's career until he became vice-Kapellmeister in Vienna in 1716, combines archival research with a wide knowledge of artistic, literary and cultural history; it provides new information on Caldara's life and places his oratorios of about 1690–1716 in the context of the Venetian style and the developing *galant* style. She has also found documentary material on Handel in the Fondo Ruspoli in the Vatican and has thereby established the chronology of about 50 cantatas between 1707 and 1711.

WRITINGS

Leben und venezianisch-römische Oratorien von Antonio Caldara (diss., U. of Bonn, 1961; Graz, 1966 as *Antonio Caldara: sein Leben und seine venezianisch-römischen Oratorien*)
'The War of the Spanish Succession Reflected in Works of Antonio Caldara', *AcM*, xxxvi (1964), 221
'The Ruspoli Documents on Handel', *JAMS*, xx (1967), 222–73, 517
'Antonio Caldara: la vita', *Chigiana*, xxvi–xxvii (1971), 223–346
'Caldara, Antonio', *MGG*
'Händel, Georg Friedrich', *RiemannL 12*
with W. Kirkendale: 'Caldara, Antonio', *DBI*
'The Source for Bach's *Musical Offering*: the Institutio oratoria of Quintilian', *JAMS*, xxxiii (1980), 88–141
with W. Kirkendale: 'Cicero, Bembo and the Ricercar' (in preparation)
'The King of Heaven and the King of France: History of a Musical Topos' (in preparation)

PAULA MORGAN

Kirkendale, (John) Warren (*b* Toronto, 14 Aug 1932). American musicologist of Canadian birth. He took the BA at the University of Toronto (1955) and continued his studies at the universities of Bonn and Berlin, taking the doctorate at the University of Vienna in 1961. After a year of research in Florence (1962), where he also did editorial work for Knud Jeppesen, he went to the USA to join the staff of the music division at the Library of Congress. From 1963 to 1967 he taught at the University of Southern California; in 1967 he became associate professor, and in 1975 professor, of musicology at Duke University. During the 1970s he studied for several years in Rome.

Kirkendale's principal areas of research are 18th-century Austrian music and music of the 16th and early 17th centuries in Italy, particularly Florence. He has a humanistic, interdisciplinary approach which takes account of liturgies, Italian literature, rhetoric, cultural history and art history. His doctoral dissertation, a thorough study of the traditions of fugue and fugato in the Rococo and Classical eras, provides models for research. In *L'Aria di Fiorenza* Kirkendale examined a harmonic bass progression which first occurred in a ballo by Emilio de' Cavalieri; he identified this version of 1589 as the prototype from which all later compositions stem, and studied the repertory of over 300 settings for a great variety of scorings.

WRITINGS

Fuge und Fugato in der Kammermusik des Rokoko und der Klassik (diss., U. of Vienna, 1961; Tutzing, 1966; Eng. trans. 1979)
'KV 405: ein unveröffentlichtes Mozart-Autograph', *MJb 1962–3*, 224
'The "Great Fugue" Op.133: Beethoven's "Art of Fugue" ', *AcM*, xxxv (1963), 14
'More Slow Introductions by Mozart to Fugues of J. S. Bach?', *JAMS*, xvii (1964), 43
'Segreto comunicato da Paganini', *JAMS*, xviii (1965), 394
'Beethovens Missa Solemnis und die rhetorische Tradition', *Beethoven-Symposion: Wien 1970*, 121–58; Eng. trans., as 'New Roads to Old Ideas in Beethoven's *Missa Solemnis*', *MQ*, lvi (1970), 665–701; repr. in *The Creative World of Beethoven* (New York, 1971), 163–99
L'Aria di Fiorenza, id est Il ballo del Gran Duca (Florence, 1972)
'Franceschina, Girometta, and their Companions in a Madrigal "a diversi linguaggi" by Luca Marenzio and Orazio Vecchi', *AcM*, xliv (1972), 181–235
'Emilio de' Cavalieri, a Roman Gentleman at the Florentine Court', *Quadrivium*, xii/2 (1971), 9
'Emilio de' Cavalieri', *DBI* (in preparation)
Archival Studies in Music: Musicians and Artists at the Court of Ferdinand I de' Medici, Grand Duke of Tuscany (1587–1609), with the Life and Letters of Emilio de' Cavalieri (in preparation)

EDITIONS

L. Marenzio, O. Vecchi, J. Eccard and M. Varotto: Madrigali a diversi linguaggi, Cw, cxxv (1975)

PAULA MORGAN

Kirkman. See KIRCKMAN family.

Kirkpatrick, John (*b* New York, 18 March 1905). American pianist and music scholar. After attending Princeton University he continued his musical studies with Nadia Boulanger at Fontainebleau during the summers from 1925 to 1928 and at the Ecole Normale de Musique in 1926 and 1927. From 1928 to 1931 he studied the piano with Louta Nouneberg. In 1942 he became chairman of the music department at Monticello College. He then taught at Mount Holyoke College from 1943 until 1946, when he was appointed to the music faculty of Cornell University; he served as chairman of the department there from 1949 to 1953 and as director of the chapel choir from 1953 to 1957. Since 1968 he has been curator of the Ives Collection at Yale University (Professor Emeritus since 1973).

Kirkpatrick has given first performances of many piano works by American composers, most notably Charles Ives's *Concord Sonata* in 1939. As a friend of the Ives family, Kirkpatrick was asked after the composer's death to catalogue his music manuscripts; this resulted in a temporary catalogue issued by Yale in 1960. He has also edited Ives's memoranda, with additional notes and appendixes, and several of his compositions.

WRITINGS

A Temporary Mimeographed Catalogue of the Music Manuscripts and Related Materials of Charles Edward Ives (New Haven, 1960)
'Performance as an Avenue to Educational Realities in Music', *College Music Symposium*, iv (1964), 39
Preface, *C. Ives: Symphony no.4* (New York, 1965)
'The Evolution of Carl Ruggles: a Chronicle Largely in his Own Words', *PNM*, vi/2 (1968), 146
Review of D.-R. de Lerma: *Charles Edward Ives, 1874–1954: a Bibliography of his Music* (Kent, Ohio, 1970), *Notes*, xxvii (1970–71), 260
ed.: *Charles E. Ives: Memos* (New York, 1972)

EDITIONS

C. Ives: Eleven Songs and Two Harmonizations (New York, 1968)
with G. Smith: *C. Ives: Psalm 90, for Mixed Chorus, Organ and Bells* (Bryn Mawr, Penn., 1970)
with G. Clarke: *C. Ives: Varied Air and Variations* (Bryn Mawr, Penn., 1971)

PAULA MORGAN

Kirkpatrick, Ralph (Leonard) (*b* Leominster, Mass., 10 June 1911). American harpsichordist, clavichordist and pianist. After studying the piano from the age of six he began to play the harpsichord in 1930 while an undergraduate at Harvard, where he took the AB in fine arts (1931) and was awarded a Paine Travelling Scholarship to study in Europe. In 1931–2 he did research at the Bibliothèque Nationale in Paris and studied the harpsichord with Landowska and theory with Boulanger. He later studied briefly with Dolmetsch, Heinz Tiessen and Günther Ramin.

Kirkpatrick first performed publicly as a harpsichordist in 1930 in Cambridge, Mass., and as a clavichordist in a radio broadcast from New York in 1946. At his European début (Berlin, 1933) he played Bach's Goldberg Variations with great success. He subsequently toured extensively in North America and Europe, first performing in Britain in 1947. His extensive repertory includes all Bach's keyboard music, a great many sonatas of Domenico Scarlatti, the 18th-century French school and some virginal music. He is also well known as an interpreter of much late 18th-century keyboard music, particularly Mozart's, on the fortepiano. His many recordings include Bach's complete keyboard works played on the harpsichord and clavichord, and the set of 60 Scarlatti sonatas which he has also edited. His playing is characterized by rhythmic vitality, stylistic authority and, where appropriate, great bravura. Perhaps in reaction to the romantic excesses of the oldest generation of modern harpsichordists, he sometimes allows a certain academic dryness to blunt his natural expressiveness.

Although in great demand as a solo harpsichordist and chamber musician Kirkpatrick continued his scholarly work. In 1937 he received a Guggenheim Fellowship for research into 17th- and 18th-century performing practice in chamber music, and began to gather material for his monumental study *Domenico Scarlatti* (Princeton and London, 1953). His editions include Bach's Goldberg Variations and, in addition to a selection of 60 sonatas, the complete keyboard sonatas of Domenico Scarlatti in facsimile. His teaching career began in 1933–4, when he held a post at the Salzburg Mozarteum. In 1940 he joined the staff of Yale University, and was professor of music, 1965–76. In 1964 he served as first Ernest Bloch Professor of Music at the University of California, Berkeley.

HOWARD SCHOTT

Kirkpatrick, William James (*b* Duncannon, Penn., 27 Feb 1838; *d* Philadelphia, 20 Sept 1921). American composer and compiler of gospel hymn collections. *See* GOSPEL MUSIC, §I.

Kirnberger [Kernberg], **Johann Philipp** (*b* Saalfeld, baptized 24 April 1721; *d* Berlin, 26 or 27 July 1783). German theorist and composer. All information relating to his career before 1754 is based on F. W. Marpurg's biographical sketch (1754), an autograph album de-

Johann Philipp Kirnberger: portrait by Schaupp after ? Christian Friedrich Reinhold Liszewiski in the Deutsche Staatsbibliothek, Berlin

scribed by Max Seiffert (1889) and comments found in letters he wrote to J. N. Forkel in the late 1770s (published in Bellermann, 1871). He received his earliest training on the violin and harpsichord at home, and attended grammar school in Coburg and possibly Gotha. He studied the organ with J. P. Kellner in Gräfenroda before 1738, and then the violin with a musician named Meil and the organ with Heinrich Nicolaus Gerber in Sondershausen in 1738. According to Marpurg, Kirnberger went in 1739 to Leipzig, where he studied composition and performance with Bach for two years (the autograph book shows that he was in Sondershausen in 1740 and Leipzig in 1741, which does not preclude his period of study with Bach). In June 1741 Kirnberger travelled to Poland, where he spent the next ten years in the service of various Polish noblemen: Baron Poninsky of Petrikau, Baron Casimir Rzewusky of Podolia and Prince Stanislaw Lubomirsky of Rufno. He also held a position as music director at the Benedictine convent at Reusch-Lemberg.

In 1751 Kirnberger returned to Germany apparently stopping at Coburg and Gotha before going to Dresden, where he studied the violin for a short time. He was then engaged by the Prussian royal chapel in Berlin as a violinist. By 1754 he had resigned that post and obtained permission to join the chapel of Prince Heinrich of Prussia, and in 1758 was given leave to enter the service of Princess Anna Amalia of Prussia. He retained this last position to the end of his life.

Kirnberger was among the most significant of a remarkable group of theorists, centred in Berlin, which included Quantz, C. P. E. Bach and Marpurg. Almost without exception his contemporaries described him as emotional and ill-tempered, but dedicated to the highest musical standards. He was criticized for being inflexible, conservative, tactless, and even pedantic, but his detractors acknowledged his devotion to students and friends. These included his employer Princess Anna Amalia (whose famous library he helped to assemble), and such eminent musicians as C. P. E. Bach, J. F. Agricola, the Graun brothers, J. A. P. Schulz (his most important pupil) and the encyclopedist J. G. Sulzer, to whose *Allgemeine Theorie der schönen Künste* he contributed articles. Most accounts agree that he was a middling performer and that his compositions were correct if uninspired. Many are in a *galant* style similar to that of C. P. E. Bach; others are in the older 'strict' style patterned after those of J. S. Bach. In neither category does Kirnberger display the harmonic or melodic imagination of his models. Although his musical knowledge was wide and profound, it was, according to his contemporaries, disorganized. He found it so difficult to express his ideas in writing that he had to call on others to edit or even rewrite his theoretical works (*Die wahren Grundsätze*, for example, was written by J. A. P. Schulz under Kirnberger's supervision). Nonetheless, even his most severe critics, such as Marpurg, considered his theoretical and didactic works to be invaluable.

All but one of Kirnberger's published works appeared after he entered the service of Princess Anna Amalia. Beginning in 1757, he issued theoretical works and music regularly, most of the latter being for solo keyboard, chamber ensembles or solo voice. His compositions appeared in many anthologies edited by others as well as in his own prints. Many unpublished compositions exist in manuscript – a large proportion in the Amalien-Bibliothek (now in *D–B*).

Kirnberger regarded J. S. Bach as the supreme composer, performer and teacher. He regretted that Bach left no didactic or theoretical works and tried through his own teaching and writing to propagate 'Bach's method'. His devotion to this cause is reflected in 14 years' intermittent effort to obtain the publication of all Bach's four-part chorale settings. Their appearance in the years immediately following Kirnberger's death was the direct result of his selfless persistence in which he offered to forgo all compensation for his share in the work. Kirnberger also edited Hassler's *Psalmen und christliche Gesänge* of 1607 and a collection of solo vocal ensembles from various operas by C. H. Graun.

Many of Kirnberger's musical publications were designed to be practical manifestations of his theoretical interests. In his *Gedanken über die verschiedenen Lehrarten in der Komposition* (1782) he observed that his works on vocal composition, his collections of dances and other works all served to complete the application of the principles set forth in his most important work, *Die Kunst des reinen Satzes* (1771–9). This juxtaposition of theory and practice is found in his *Anleitung zur Singcomposition* (1782), which contains a lengthy (but disorganized) discussion of poetic metre and its relationship to vocal composition, followed by 53 complete vocal works to illustrate the text. His *Recueil d'airs de danse caractéristiques* (c1777) contains a preface advocating the study of dances as a means of improving one's sense of metre and rhythm. The pieces in his *Clavierübungen* (1762–6) are arranged

in order of difficulty and fingered according to the principles set forth in C. P. E. Bach's *Versuch* (1753).

Kirnberger was vehemently opposed to certain aspects of Rameau's theories, yet his own works incorporated notions of chord inversion and strong and weak bass progressions. Like most of his contemporaries, he recognized the merit of older theories based on species counterpoint (Fux) but regarded them as inadequate for his purposes. *Die Kunst des reinen Satzes* is typical of the era in using the traditional ratios for constructing scales and intervals and then treating chords and their usage in a harmonic context. Only in later chapters of the work is counterpoint considered a separate discipline. The harmonic orientation of Kirnberger's thinking is further indicated by his assertion that the bass is the most important part of music. Nonetheless, he rejected Rameau's contention that harmony gives rise to melody. He also disagreed with the idea of the chord of the added 6th and with Rameau's idea of the fundamental bass. Instead he hypothesized a fundamental bass of his own that he claimed could explain certain dissonant combinations and their resolution in terms of part-writing. Thus he accounted for 9ths, 11ths and 13ths as retardations and suspensions of consonances rather than as chords formed by the sub-position of intervals below the fundamental bass. His insistence on these ideas demonstrates that his method was based on a harmonically saturated style rooted in basso-continuo practice.

WORKS

(printed works published in Berlin unless otherwise stated)

THEORETICAL WORKS

Der allezeit fertige Polonoisen- und Menuettencomponist (1757; Fr. trans., 1757)
Construction der gleichschwebenden Temperatur (1760/R1973)
'Anmerkung über das Allabreve des Herrn Kirnberger', in F. W. Marpurg: *Clavierstücke mit einem practischen Unterricht*, iii (1763)
Die Kunst des reinen Satzes in der Musik, aus sicheren Grundsätzen hergeleitet und mit deutlichen Beyspielen erläutert, i (1771/R1968; with new title-page, Berlin and Königsberg, 1774), ii (Berlin and Königsberg, 1776–9/R1968); both vols. (2/1793)
Die wahren Grundsätze zum Gebrauch der Harmonie . . . als ein Zusatz zu der Kunst des reinen Satzes in der Musik (Berlin and Königsberg, 1773/R1974, 2/1793) [written by J. A. P. Schulz under Kirnberger's supervision]
Grundsätze des Generalbasses als erste Linien zur Composition (1781/R1974)
Gedanken über die verschiedenen Lehrarten in der Komposition, als Vorbereitung zur Fugenkenntniss (1782/R1974, 2/1793)
Anleitung zur Singcomposition mit Oden in verschiedenen Sylbenmassen begleitet (1782)
Methode Sonaten aus'm Ermel zu schüddeln (1783)
Articles on music in J. G. Sulzer: *Allgemeine Theorie der schönen Künste* (1771) [A–I by Kirnberger, J–S by J. A. P. Schulz under Kirnberger's supervision]

(publications of music for didactic purposes)

Allegro für das Clavier alleine, wie auch für die Violin mit dem Violoncell zu accompagniren . . . componirt und vertheidigt (1759)
Clavierübungen mit der Bachischen Applicatur in einer Folge von den leichtesten bis zu den schwersten Stücken (1762–6)
Canons in F. W. Marpurg: *Abhandlung von der Fuge* (1753–4/R1970)

VOCAL

Lieder, songs: 3 verschiedene Versuche eines einfachen Gesanges (1760); Lieder mit Melodien (1762), 3 ed. in Borris-Zuckermann; [24] Oden mit Melodien (Danzig, 1773), 1 ed. in Borris-Zuckermann; Lied nach dem Frieden vom Herrn Claudius (c1779); Gesänge am Clavier (Berlin and Leipzig, 1780), repr. with 1773 Oden as Kleine Oden und Lieder (Berlin and Leipzig, 1789), 2 ed. in E. Lindner: *Geschichte des deutschen Liedes* (Leipzig, 1871); 3 Gesänge in Musik gesetzt (n.p., n.d.); lieder in contemporary anthologies pubd Berlin, mostly repr. in Lieder (1762)
Other vocal: Cantatas, all *D-Bds*: Ino (K. W. Ramler), S, insts, Der Fall der ersten Menschen (Bomer), S, insts (autograph), Christus ist des Gesetzes Ende, 4vv, insts; 6 motets, 4vv, insts/bc, *Bds*, *Mbs*, *SWl*, Wende dich zu mir, fugue, 4vv, pubd in *Die Kunst des reinen Satzes*; masses, lost

INSTRUMENTAL

Kbd: Clavierfuge mit dem Contrapunct in der Octava (1760); Vermischte Musikalien (1769); Diverses pièces, hpd (c1769–70); 8 fugues, hpd/org (c1777); Recueil d'airs de danse caractéristiques, hpd (c1777); chorale arrs., Bds, and in Choralvorspiele, ed. J. C. Kühnau (1790); kbd sonatas/partitas in contemporary anthologies, incl. Raccolta delle nuove composizioni, ii (1757) and Collection récréative, ii (Nuremberg, 1761), 1 partita ed. in Borris-Zuckermann; single works in anthologies pubd Berlin (1760–63), incl. Musikalisches Allerley, Musikalisches Mancherley, also in Musikalisches Vielerley, ed. C. P. E. Bach (Hamburg, 1770)

Other inst: 2 fl sonatas (c1762); Fl Sonata, Bds; 12 minuets, 8 insts, bc (1762); Sonata a tre, 2 vn, bc (1763); Musicalischer Circul, pf, vn/fl (n.d.); 2 syms., Bds, SWl; 2 ovs., A-Wn; 6 Triosonaten, 2 vn, bc, D-Bds (autograph), extracts ed. in Borris-Zuckermann; PfConc., lost

EDITIONS

C. H. Graun: Duetti, terzetti . . . ed alcuni chori, i–iv (Berlin and Königsberg, 1773–4)

H. L. Hassler: Psalmen und christliche Gesänge [1607] (Leipzig, 1777)

BIBLIOGRAPHY

GerberL

F. W. Marpurg: Historisch-kritische Beyträge zur Aufnahme der Musik, i (Berlin, 1754/R1970), 85

J. A. P. Schulz: 'Ueber die in Sulzers Theorie der schönen Künste unter dem Artikel Verrückung angeführten zwey Beyspiele von Pergolesi und Graun . . .', AMZ, ii (1799–1800), cols.257, 273

J. F. Reichardt: 'J. A. P. Schulz', AMZ, iii (1800–01), cols.153, 169, 597, 613, 629

H. M. Schletterer: J. F. Reichardt (Augsburg, 1865)

C. H. Bitter: Carl Philipp Emanuel Bach und Wilhelm Friedemann Bach und deren Brüder, ii (Berlin, 1868), 314

J. G. H. Bellermann: 'Briefe von Kirnberger an Forkel', Leipziger allgemeine musikalische Zeitung, vi (1871), cols.529, 550, 565, 614, 628, 645, 661, 677; vii (1872), cols.441, 457

M. Seiffert: 'Aus dem Stammbuche Johann Philipp Kirnbergers', VMw, v (1889), 365

C. Sachs: 'Prinzessin Amalie von Preussen als Musikerin', Hohenzollern-Jb, x (1910), 181

A. Schering: 'Johann Philipp Kirnberger als Herausgeber Bachischer Choräle', BJb, xv (1918), 141

A. Kirnberger: Geschichte der Familie Kirnberger (Mainz, 1922)

S. Borris-Zuckermann: Kirnbergers Leben und Werk und seine Bedeutung für den Berliner Musikkreis um 1750 (Kassel, 1933)

R. Sietz: 'Die Orgelkompositionen des Schülerkreises um J. S. Bach', BJb, xxxii (1935), 33–96

F. Bose: 'Anna Amalie von Preussen und Johann Philipp Kirnberger', Mf, x (1957), 129

J. Mekeel: 'The Harmonic Theories of Kirnberger and Marpurg', JMT, iv (1960), 169

P. Benary: Die deutschen Kompositionslehre des 18. Jahrhunderts (Leipzig, 1961)

W. S. Newman: 'Kirnberger's Method for Tossing off Sonatas', MQ, xlvii (1961), 517

K. Hlawiczka: 'Ze studiow na historia poloneza', Muzyka, x (1965), 41

E. E. Helm: 'Six Random Measures of C. P. E. Bach', JMT, x (1966), 139

H. T. David and A. Mendel: The Bach Reader (New York, rev. 2/1966)

M. Vogel: 'Die Kirnberger-Stimmung vor und nach Kirnberger', Colloquium amicorum: Joseph Schmidt-Görg zum 70. Geburtstag (Bonn, 1967), 441

H. Serwer: 'Marpurg versus Kirnberger: Theories of Fugal Composition', JMT, xiv (1970), 206–36

F. Sumner: 'Haydn and Kirnberger: a Documentary Report', JAMS, xxviii (1975), 530

HOWARD SERWER

Kirov Theatre. Theatre built in St Petersburg in 1833; see LENINGRAD, §2.

Kirsch, Winfried (b Dresden, 10 April 1931). German musicologist. After singing lessons with K. Forster and piano and conducting lessons with K. Thomas, he went to the University of Frankfurt in 1952 and studied musicology under Osthoff and Gennrich, with German philology and art history as subsidiary subjects; he took the doctorate at Frankfurt in 1958 with a study of Bruckner's vocal style. He was a research assistant at the university musicology institute (1962–71), where he completed his Habilitation in musicology in 1971 with a historical study of the motets of Andreas de Silva. In that year he was appointed professor of musicology at the university and in 1972 also director of the chorister's school at the Hoch Conservatory in Frankfurt.

WRITINGS

Studien zum Vokalstil der mittleren und späten Schaffensperiode Anton Bruckners (diss., U. of Frankfurt, 1958)

'Ein unbeachtetes Chorbuch von 1544 in der Österreichischen Nationalbibliothek Wien', Mf, xiv (1961), 290

Die Quellen der mehrstimmigen Magnificat- und Te Deum-Vertonungen bis zur Mitte des 16. Jahrhunderts (Tutzing, 1966)

'Die Klavier-Walzer op. 39 von Johannes Brahms und ihre Tradition', Jb des Staatlichen Instituts für Musikforschung 1969, 38–67

Die Motetten des Andreas de Silva: Studien zur Geschichte der Motette im 16. Jahrhundert (Habilitationsschrift, U. of Frankfurt, 1971; Tutzing, 1976)

'Josquin's Motets in the German Tradition', Josquin des Prez: New York 1971, 261

'Der späte Hindemith', Hindemith-Jb, ii (1972), 9

'Zur musikalischen Konzeption und dramaturgischen Stellung des Opernquartetts im 18. und 19. Jahrhundert', Mf, xxvii (1974), 186

'Prolegomena zu einer Geschichte des Opereinakters im 20. Jahrhundert', Mf, xxviii (1975), 438

'Unterterz- und Leittonklauseln als quellentypische Varianten', Formen und Probleme der Überlieferung mehrstimmiger Musik im Zeitalter Josquins Desprez: Wolfenbüttel 1976

Articles on 15th- and 16th-century vocal music in Festschriften for Osthoff (1961; 1966; 1977), AnM, xxii (1969) and in GfMKB, Kassel 1962 and GfMKB, Leipzig 1966

EDITIONS

J. Galliculus: Drei Weihnachtsmagnificat, Cw, lxxxv (1961)

Drei Te Deum-Kompositionen des 16. Jahrhunderts, Cw, cii (1967)

A. de Silva: Opera omnia, CMM, xlix/1–3 (1970)

P. Hindemith: Konzert für Violoncell und Orchester, op.3, Sämtliche Werke (Mainz, 1977)

HANS HEINRICH EGGEBRECHT

Kirshbaum, Ralph (Henry) (b Denton, Texas, 4 March 1946). American cellist. He had childhood music lessons from his father, Joseph Kirshbaum, a violinist and conductor, followed by cello lessons from Lev Aronson in Dallas, where he made his professional début with the Dallas SO as a soloist at the age of 13. He continued his studies at Yale University, with Aldo Parisot, graduating with the highest honours in music. After spending two years in Paris he won the 1969 International Cassadó Competition in Florence and the 1970 International Tchaikovsky Competition in Moscow. That year he began his adult career with a series of solo recitals in Europe including one in London. His career quickly flourished, and he has toured in Europe, North America, South Africa, the Middle East, Far East and Australia, appearing as a soloist with leading orchestras and in recitals. Kirshbaum has been widely admired for his technical skill, beauty of tone and conviction of interpretation. He plays a cello by Montagnana dated 1729 which at one time belonged to Piatti. He is a member of a piano trio with Peter Frankl and György Pauk.

Kirsten, Dorothy (b Montclair, NJ, 6 July 1917). American soprano. She first studied at the Juilliard School of Music in New York. In 1938 she received assistance from Grace Moore, who sent her to study with Astolfo Pescia in Rome. She made her début with the Chicago opera (1940) in a minor role; she then appeared in major parts with Gallo's San Carlo Opera (1942), the New York City Opera and at San Francisco. Her début at the Metropolitan was on 1 December 1945 as Mimì. She remained there singing leading French and Italian roles, including Puccini's Cio-cio-san, Tosca, Minnie and Manon Lescaut, and Nedda and Louise (which she studied with Charpentier). She has also appeared in films, including *The Great Caruso*. Kirsten has a clear but not voluminous lyric soprano that can also undertake *lirico-spinto* roles, a coolly assured voice that is employed with much security if not with overwhelming effect. She has justly earned the respect of American audiences.

MAX DE SCHAUENSEE

Kīrtana [kīrtan, kīrtanam]. Hindu devotional song genre; *see* BANGLADESH, §1, 3(i), and INDIA, SUBCONTINENT OF, §§I, 3 (iii); II, 4(iii); VI, 3.

Kirzinger. *See* KÜRZINGER family.

Kishibe, Shigeo (*b* Tokyo, 16 June 1912). Japanese musicologist. He studied oriental history at Tokyo University, receiving the bachelor's degree in 1936 and the doctorate in literature in 1961. From 1949 to 1973 he was a professor at Tokyo University; he has also given lectures at Tokyo Geijutsu Daigaku (Tokyo National University of Fine Arts and Music) since 1952, and has been research fellow at the Tokyo National Institute of Cultural Properties (1952–8). In 1957–8 he went to the USA to teach at the University of California at Los Angeles, Harvard University and the University of Hawaii. In 1961 he received the Japan Academy Prize. He went to the USA again in 1962–3, this time as a visiting professor at the University of Washington and Stanford University. He is one of the original members of the Society for Research in Asiatic Music, of which he has served as a director since 1936. He has specialized in the history of Asian music, particularly Chinese and Japanese, and has done much fieldwork in Korea, China, India, Iran and the Philippine Islands.

WRITINGS

'Tōdai ongaku bunken kaisetsu' [A short bibliography of the music of the T'ang dynasty], *Tōyō ongaku kenkyū*, i/1 (1937), 69
'Engaku meigi kō' [On the term 'Engaku'], *Tōyō ongaku kenkyū*, i/2 (1937), 9
'Shibugaku kō' [On the system of Ssu-pu-yüeh], *Shigaku zasshi*, xlix (1938), no.11, p.1; no.12, pp.1–46
'Tō no Rien' [Li-yüan of the T'ang], *Shigaku zasshi*, li/11 (1940), 1–50
'The Origin of the P'i-p'a', *Transactions of the Asiatic Society of Japan*, 2nd ser., xix (1941), 260–304
'Sōdai kyōbō no hensen oyobi soshiki' [The history and system of the chang-fang of the Sung dynasty], *Shigaku zasshi*, liv/4 (1943), 1–45
Shina ongaku-shi yō [A short history of Chinese music] (Tokyo, 1943)
'Gakugakukihan no kaihan ni tsuite' [Various printings of the Ak-hak-kwe-bun], *Tanabe Festschrift* (Tokyo, 1943), 213–44
'Saiiki shichi-chō to sono kigen' [Seven tonalities of ancient Central Asia and their origin], *Shigaku zasshi*, lvii/9 (1946), 17–80
Tōyō no gakki to sono rekishi [Musical instruments in Asia and their history] (Tokyo, 1946)
Ongaku no seiryū [Westward stream of music] (Tokyo, 1951)
'The Four Unknown Pipes of the Shō' [with L. Traynor]; 'Tōdai jubugi no seikaku' [The characteristics of the Shih-pu-chi of the T'ang dynasty], *Tōyō ongaku kenkyū*, ix (1951), 26; 113
with K. Hayashi, S. Shiba and R. Taki: 'Shōsōin gakki chōsa gaihō' [Report on the investigation of the musical instruments in the Shōsōin repository, the Imperial treasury], *Shoryōbu kiyō*, i (1951), 10; ii (1952), 28; iii (1953), 74
'The origin of the K'ung-hou' [The origin of the Chinese harp], *Tōyō ongaku kenkyū*, xiv–xv (1951), 1–51
'Saiiki-gaku tōryū ni okeru Ko gakujin raichō no igi' [Visiting musicians of Central Asia in ancient China], *Tōkyō daigaku kyōyōgakubu jinbun-kagaku-ka kiyō: rekishi*, i (1952), 67 [with Eng. outline]
'Chōan Hokuri no seikaku to katsudō' [The character and activity of Peili, the singing-girl's house in Chang-an city of the T'ang dynasty], *Tōkyō daigaku kyōyōgakubu jinbun-kagaku-ka kiyō: rekishi*, vii (1959), 25
Tōdai ongaku no rekishiteki kenkyū [A historical study of the music of the T'ang dynasty] (Tokyo, 1960–61)
'A Chinese Painting of the T'ang Court Women's Orchestra', *The Commonwealth of Music, in Honor of Curt Sachs* (New York, 1964), 104

'Tōyō Ongaku Gakkai shōshi' [A short history of the Society for research in Asiatic music], *Tōyō ongaku kenkyū*, xix (1966), 63
The Traditional Music of Japan (Tokyo, 1966, 2/1969)
'Chibetto no bukkyō geinō' [Buddhist theatricals in Tibet], *Chibetto no ongaku* (Tokyo, 1967), 23 [disc note]
'Japanese Music, Conflict or Synthesis?', *The World of Music*, ix (Basle, 1967), 11
'Sō no tsukurikata' [How to make a *koto*], *Sōkyoku to jiuta*, iii (Tokyo, 1967), 63
articles in *Tōdai no gakki* [Musical instruments in the T'ang dynasty], *Tōyō ongaku sensho*, ii (Tokyo, 1968), 9–42, 117–56, 157, 169–209, 211–40, 241, 269, 289
with M. Kishibe and Y. Suzuki: 'Yamada Kengyō no shōgai to jiseki' [The life and works of Yamada Kengyō], *Tōyō ongaku kenkyū*, xxvii–xxviii (1970), 1–67
Nihon no ongaku [Music of Japan] (Tokyo, 1971)
Nihon no ongaku no shidō [How to teach Japanese music] (Tokyo, 1973)
Shiruku-rōdo no ongaku [The music of the silk road] (Tokyo, 1973)
Tsugaru Sokyoku ikutaryu no kenkyū [Study on the Ikuta School of Koto Music in Tsugaru] (Hirosaki, 1976)
'China', §II, 'Japan', §§I and III, 2, *Grove 6*

MASAKATA KANAZAWA

Kisielewski, Stefan (*b* Warsaw, 7 March 1911). Polish composer and writer. In 1927 he entered the Warsaw Conservatory, where his teachers were Lefeld for piano (diploma 1934) and Sikorski for theory and composition (diploma 1937). He also studied Polish literature and philosophy at Warsaw University, and his music studies were continued in Paris (1938–9). From 1935 to 1937 he was secretary of *Muzyka polska*, and he has contributed criticism to that journal and also to *Ruch muzyczny* (1945–7, 1957–9). He was professor of theory at the Kraków Conservatory (1945–9), teaching composition privately thereafter. A prominent writer, he has published a novel, crime stories and essays on politics, literature and music, the last collected in several books. He is also a prolific composer, writing in all genres but showing a preference for the chamber orchestra. Though he has supported the newest developments in Polish music in his writings, his own compositions are neo-classical, melodically simple and formally straightforward. In lighter pieces, such as the Concerto for chamber orchestra (which won a prize from the Polish Ministry of Culture in 1955) and the Little Overture, he exhibits gaiety, wit and a sardonic humour. The *Dances from Rzeszów* for chorus and orchestra (1965) and other works were composed as a kind of *Gebrauchsmusik*.

WORKS
(*selective list*)

Ballets: Diabły polskie, 1957, Warsaw, 1958; System doktora Smoły i doktora Pierza [The system of Dr Pitch and Dr Feathers] (1, Kisielewski, after Poe), 1962; Wesołe miasteczko [Amusement grounds] (1, H. Kołaczkowska), 1966, Gdańsk, 1967
Orch: Ov., 1938, lost; Sym. no.1, 1939, lost; Conc., chamber orch, 1948; Rustic Rhapsody, 1950; Sym. no.2, 1951; Little Ov., 1953; Perpetuum mobile, 1955; Chamber Sym., 1956; Sym., 15 insts, 1961; Divertimento, fl, chamber orch, 1965; Le voyage dans le temps, str, 1965; Sygnały sportowe, ov., 1966; Rencontres dans un désert, 10 insts, 1969; Cosmos no.1, 1970
Chamber: Sonata no.1, vn, pf, 1932; Str Qt, 1935, lost; Trio, ob, cl, bn, *c*1940, lost; Sonata, cl, 1944; Intermezzo, cl, pf, 1953; Suite, ob, pf, 1954; Capriccio energico, vn, pf, 1956; Suite, fl, cl, 1961
Pf: Variations, 1933, lost; Sonata no.1, 1936, lost; Danse vive, 1939; Toccata, 1944; Sonata no.2, 1945; Fantasy, 1949; Dance Suite, 1951; Suite, 1955
Choral works, songs (A. Mickiewicz, K. I. Gałczyński), music for the theatre, cinema and radio

Principal publisher: Polskie Wydawnictwo Muzyczne

WRITINGS

ed. E. Kuthan: *Polityka i sztuka* [Politics and art] (Warsaw, 1949)
Poematy symfoniczne Ryszarda Straussa (Kraków, 1955)
Z muzyką przez lata [With music through the years] (Kraków, 1957)
Gwiazdozbiór muzyczny [Musical constellations] (Kraków, 1958, 2/1960)

Z muzycznej międzyepoki [From the middle epoch of music] (Kraków, 1966)
Muzyka i mózg [Music and brain] (Kraków, 1974)

BOGUSŁAW SCHÄFFER

Kiss, Lajos (*b* Zombor, Hungary [now Sombor, Yugoslavia], 14 March 1900). Hungarian ethnomusicologist. He studied aesthetics at Budapest University (graduated 1923) and composition with Albert Siklós at the Budapest Academy of Music (graduated 1925). After working as a school music teacher and conductor in Sombor, Yugoslavia (1926–39), he was deputy headmaster and choir director of the Belgrade Stanković Music School (1939–41), director of the conservatory and conductor at Ujvidék (1941–4) and director of the Győr State Conservatory (1945–50). From 1950 until his retirement in 1970 he helped edit Corpus Musicae Popularis Hungaricae and was a research fellow of the folk music research group of the Hungarian Academy of Sciences; his main interest has been in collecting Hungarian folk music.

WRITINGS

'Bitne značajke mađarskog muzičkog folklora' [The essence of Hungarian folk music], *IV kongres folklorista Jugoslavije: Varaždin 1957*, 113
'A bukovinai székelyek tánczenéje' [Dance music of Bukovina Székelys], *Tánctudományi tanulmányok* (1958), 67
'Népi verbunk-dallamainkról' [Popular *verbunkos* melodies], *Tánctudományi tanulmányok* (1959–60), 263–95
'Über den vokalen und instrumentalen Vortrag der ungarischen Volksweisen', *JIFMC*, xv (1963), 74
'Zenetörténeti emlékek a szlavóniai virrasztó énekekben' [Surviving musical history in the Hungarian funeral songs of the Slavonia region], *Ethnographia*, lxxvii (1966), 153–211
'A munkásság dalai Várpalotán és környékén' [Workmen's songs at Várpalota and its neighbourhood], *A parasztdaltól a munkásdalig*, ed. J. Katona, F. Maróthy and A. Szatmáry (Budapest, 1968), 307–448
'Bulgarische Rhythmen in Bartók's Musik', *Sbornik za pamjat V. Stoin* (Sofia, 1969), 237
'Simonffy Kálmán és a magyar népzene' [Simonffy and Hungarian folk music], *MTA nyelv- és irodalomtudományi osztályának közleményei*, xxvi (1969), 338
'Köszöntők a jugoszláviai magyar népzenében' [Rhyming greetings in Hungarian folk music in Yugoslavia], *A hungarológiai intézet tudományos közleményei*, iv (1972), 43–84
Horgosi népdalok [Folksong collection from Horgos] (Senta, 1974)

FOLKSONG EDITIONS

Lakodalom [Wedding], Corpus musicae popularis hungaricae, iii (Budapest, 1955)
Siratók [Laments], Corpus musicae popularis hungaricae, v (Budapest, 1966) [with B. Rajeczky]

BÁLINT SÁROSI

Kissing dance. See CUSHION DANCE.

Kist, Florentius Cornelis (*b* Arnhem, 28 Jan 1796; *d* Utrecht, 23 March 1863). Dutch physician and amateur musician. He was the son of Ewald Kist, a celebrated preacher. At an early age he took piano lessons and later studied the flute and horn. In 1813 he entered the University of Leiden as a medical student and in 1818 qualified as a doctor. He appeared successfully as a flautist in public; he also studied composition and singing, and was heard in concerts in The Hague, Delft and Utrecht. When he left Leiden, Kist established himself as a physician in The Hague and remained there until 1825 when he abandoned medicine to devote himself to music. He had joined in founding the society known as Diligentia in The Hague in 1821, and until 1840 was associated also with a choral group and with the Collegium Musicum in Delft.

In 1841 Kist moved to Utrecht, where he edited the *Nederlandsch muzikaal tijdschrift* until 1844, when he established the journal *Caecilia*; he edited this for the next 18 years, and developed it into the most important Dutch musical review of its time, concerned not only with contemporary music but also with historical studies of Dutch music from the 15th century. He was connected with many local organizations including Symphonie, an amateur orchestra which he started in 1847, and a singing society Duce Appoline. Fully aware of musical events in Europe generally, he was, for example, responsible for the first performance in Holland of any music by Wagner, when Kufferath conducted the *Tannhäuser* overture in Utrecht on 12 March 1853. Kist was an enterprising and influential figure in the musical life not only of Utrecht but of the country as a whole.

WORKS
(*selective list; see Fétis*)

Ernst und Freude, ov., perf. The Hague, 1842
2 cantatas; other choral works
Many romances and songs, incl. Nederland (van Isselt), op.5, Bar, pf (The Hague, ?c1825)

WRITINGS

De toestand van het protestantsche kerk-gezang in Nederland, benevens middelen tot deszelfs verbetering (Utrecht, 1840)
De levens-geschiedenis van Orland de Lassus (The Hague, 1841)
Grondtrekken van de geschiedenis der musik door Brendel (Utrecht, 1851) [trans. of K. F. Brendel: *Grundzüge der Geschichte der Musik*, Leipzig, 1848]
Articles in *Amphion*, 1820; *Nederlandsch muzikaal tijdschrift*, 1836–44; *Caecilia*, 1844–62; *Zeitschrift für Dilettanten*; *Signale*; *Teutonia Zeitschrift für Männergesangvereine*

BIBLIOGRAPHY

FétisB
Westrheene: [Appreciation], *Caecilia*, lxxvii (1920), 90

JOHN LADE

Kistler, Cyrill (*b* Grossaitingen, nr. Augsburg, 12 March 1848; *d* Bad Kissingen, 1 Jan 1907). German composer and writer on music. His family being poor, he saw in teaching the chance to earn a living and to be active in music at the same time. After attending a teachers' seminary in Lauingen he spent eight years as an assistant master in Augsburg and neighbouring villages. A patroness finally made it possible for him to study for three years at the Royal School of Music in Munich, where he was taught the organ and composition by Rheinberger, Wüllner and Franz Lachner. He became a teacher of music theory at the Fürstliche Konservatorium in Sondershausen in 1883, and two years later retired to Bad Kissingen, where he directed a private music school and lived as a freelance composer and writer.

Kistler was initially committed to Lachner's conservative attitude, but his friendship with Wagner in Bayreuth crucially affected his views. He adopted Wagner's musical language but did not develop it beyond the stage of mere imitation. Although honoured by Wagner's followers, he failed to achieve widespread and lasting recognition. His most successful work was the folk opera *Röslein im Hag*, the material for which approached his original preference for popular subjects. This inclination towards the folklike, evident in his other musical works, was also present in his writings (he was the editor of the neo-German *Musikalische Tagesfragen*), in which he expressed hostile views on everything un-German. Apart from his pedagogical works, his Wagner arrangements are particularly noteworthy.

WORKS
(*selective list*)

STAGE

Kunihild oder Der Brautritt auf Kynast (opera, 3, F. Sporck),

Sondershausen, 1884
Eulenspiegel (comic opera, 2, after Kotzebue); rev. H. Levi and L. Sauer as 1-act opera, Würzburg, 1889
Baldurs Tod (music drama, 3, von Sohlern), 1891, Düsseldorf, 1905
Im Honigmond (idyll, 1), op.112, Bad Kissingen, 1900
Arm Elslein (Christmas play, 1), op.117, Schwerin, 1902
Röslein im Hag (folk opera, 3, T. A. Kolbe), Elberfeld, 1903
Der Vogt auf Mühlstein (tragic opera, 3, B. Straub, after H. Hansjakob), Düsseldorf, 1904
Faust I. Teil (music drama, 4, Goethe: Urfaust), 1905
Die Kleinstädter (comic opera, 3, B. Luovsky)
Die Grossstädter (comic opera, 3), inc.

OTHER WORKS

Bismarck-Kantate (R. von Gottschall), T, male vv, chorus, 1885; part-songs, mixed and male vv; 5 volumes of songs, 1v, pf; other secular vocal works
Salve regina, mixed chorus; 2 settings of Pange lingua, male vv, org
Marches, etc, orch; Serenade, vn/va/vc, pf/orch
Sonatina, fantasia, numerous dances and short pieces, pf; suite, fantasias, other pieces, org/harmonium
Arrs. of excerpts from operas by Beethoven and Wagner

For complete list of published works see Pazdirek

WRITINGS

Harmonielehre (Munich, 1879)
Musikalische Elementarlehre (Chemnitz, 1880)
ed.: Musikalische Tagesfragen, i–xv (1880–81, 1884–94, 1903–6) [incl. articles by Kistler]
Chorgesangschule (Bad Kissingen, 1886)
C. Kistlers musiktheoretische Schriften (Heilbronn, 1904)

BIBLIOGRAPHY

M. Chop: 'C. Kistler', Zeitgenössische Tondichter, ii (Leipzig, 1890), 274
F. Pazdirek: Universal-Handbuch der Musikliteratur aller Zeiten und Völker (Vienna, 1904–10)
C. Kistler: 'Selbstbiographie', Musikalische Tagesfragen, xv (1906), 37
Obituary, Die Musik, vi (1907), 9
H. Ritter: 'C. Kistler', Lebensläufe aus Franken, ii, ed. A. Chroust (Würzburg, 1922), 228

HORST LEUCHTMANN

Kistner & Siegel. German firm of music publishers. It was formed in 1923 by a merger between two firms with long-standing traditions. In 1823 Heinrich Albert Probst (1791–1846) founded a music publishing firm in Leipzig which dealt primarily with French music and which was acquired in 1831 by the musical amateur Carl Friedrich Kistner (1797–1844), after whom it was named from 1836. Under his management it prospered and issued works by Schumann, Mendelssohn, Moscheles, David, Joachim, Hauptmann, Gade and Ferdinand Hiller. After his death it was managed by his brother Julius (1805–68) assisted by (among others) Carl Friedrich Ludwig Gurckhaus (1821–84), who became the sole proprietor in 1866. The firm had arrangements with Liszt, Smetana, Reinecke, Franz, Bruch and Goetz, and greatly stimulated the work of contemporary composers. In 1919 it was bought by the brothers Carl and Richard Linnemann, the proprietors of the music business of C. F. W. Siegel, which their family had owned since Siegel's death in 1869. This business had been founded by Carl Friedrich Wilhelm Siegel and Edmund Stoll in 1846, and was almost as important as the Kistner firm: it published works by Schumann, Spohr and Rubinstein and good light music, also issuing the popular collection Der Opernfreund. Under the direction of the elder Richard Linnemann (from 1870) it developed alongside the flourishing choral society movement in Germany. In 1903 Linnemann's sons bought E. W. Fritzsch's book and music publishing firm and subsequently brought out a substantial amount of Wagner literature; distinguished musicologists collaborated closely with the firm, which had issued about 30,000 items by 1943. Severe war damage led to the decline of the Leipzig firm. In 1948 the firm of Fr. Kistner & C. F. W. Siegel & Co. was founded in Lippstadt, later moving to Porz; its publications include musicological literature and choral and organ music.

BIBLIOGRAPHY

Verzeichnis des Musikalien-Verlags Fr. Kistner in Leipzig (Leipzig, 1894–1905; suppls. 1907, 1909, 1911, 1913)
R. Linnemann, ed.: Verlags-Verzeichnis von C. F. W. Siegels Musikalienhandlung (Leipzig, 1903)
R. Linnemann: Fr. Kistner 1823/1923: ein Beitrag zur Geschichte des deutschen Musik-Verlages (Leipzig, 1923)
W. Lott, ed.: Musik aus vier Jahrhunderten, 1400–1800 (Leipzig, 1932)

HANS-MARTIN PLESSKE

Kit [kytte] (Fr. poche, pochette, sourdine; Ger. Posch, Tanzmeistergeige, Taschengeige; It. canino, pochetto, sordina, sordino; Lat. linterculus). A small bowed unfretted instrument, generally with four strings, made in a great variety of shapes and played from the 16th century to the 19th. Kits can be divided into two general types: a member of the rebec family, either pear-shaped or resembling a narrow boat, with a distinctly vaulted back; or a miniature viol, violin or guitar, with a slightly arched back and a long neck. Not all have a soundpost or bass-bar; their presence depends on the size and shape of each instrument. The tuning is generally in 5ths, sometimes at the pitch of the violin, but more often a 4th or a 5th and occasionally an octave higher if there are only three strings. Surviving kits range from simple rustic instruments to the products of such makers as Joachim Tielke and Stradivari (who left working patterns for different types of kit, including the boat shape labelled 'canino' and elongated violin shapes of which the last is dated 1733).

1. Terminology. 2. History. 3. Repertory.

1. TERMINOLOGY. It has been suggested that the word 'kit' derives from kithara (itself a plucked instrument), but until real evidence is found this theory cannot be held with conviction. Perhaps more likely is the idea that it was the 'kitten' to the larger bowed instruments such as those of the violin family, which were said, however erroneously, to be strung with catgut. The term 'poche' was said by Trichet to describe the leather case in which the instrument was kept; Mersenne said that it was kept in the pockets (poches) of violinists who taught dancing. 'Taschengeige' also relates the instrument to a pocket, and 'Tanzmeistergeige' indicates its use by a dancing-master. 'Sordino' and 'sourdine' are descriptive of its small sound, and 'canino' compares it with a canine tooth. 'Linterculus' points to its resemblance to a small boat. There was considerable overlapping between the use of these names and the instruments to which they were applied; for the sake of consistency 'kit' will be used here to cover all types, except when an actual source is being quoted.

2. HISTORY. Some kits could be regarded simply as rebecs, but it is to the rebec that the name 'kit' seems first to have been applied. When this happened is uncertain, but the term was in use in England in the first quarter of the 16th century. In the Interlude of the Four Elements (c1517) Humanity says: 'This dance would do mich better yet/If we had a kit or taberet'. There is no evidence that this meant anything other than the pear-shaped rebec, an instrument which is often seen in English artistic sources of the time, and is known to have been used frequently at the court of Henry VIII. In

1. Dancing-master with a kit: engraving (1745) by Le Bas after Philippe Canot

(a)   (b)   (c)   (d)

2. Kits: (a) German or Swiss, first half of the 18th century, (b) Italian, c1700, (c) pochette d'amour by Giovanni Battista Genova, Turin, c1765, (d) by Dimanche Drouyn, Paris, late 17th century; (a), (d) Victoria and Albert Museum, London, (b), (c) Royal College of Music, London

the late 17th century Randle Holme III drew a picture of a rebec and wrote by it 'A Kit with foure bowed strings' (*GB-Lbm* Harl.2027, f.272). The French term *poche* also included instruments of the rebec shape, as indicated by several references to its similarity to the mandora. For instance, on 7 January 1625 an inventory was made of the instruments belonging to François Richomme, 'violinist in ordinary to the king, and king of the minstrels of the kingdom of France', and among its items were 'une ... poche façon de mandore'. One of Praetorius's three pictures of *Poschen* is identical to a three-stringed rebec.

During the 16th century some members of the rebec family became narrower in proportion to their length than had hitherto been usual. One of these, now in the Museo Civico at Bologna, has the inscription 'Baptista Bressano'. It is in the form of a fish, and was perhaps used for an *intermedio* or some other dramatic production. A similar instrument, though less exotic, can be seen in the woodcut 'Youth', from *The Ages of Women* by Tobias Stimmer (1539–84). By the end of the 16th century this type was firmly established in the shape of a narrow boat, still with a vaulted back, but sometimes with a clear demarcation between the body and neck, even when they were made from one piece of wood. Perhaps to compensate for its relatively simple shape, it was often lavishly decorated with inlaid wood, ivory, ebony or jewels, such as was another 'poche' from the collection of François Richomme. 'Enriched by rubies, mother-of-pearl and seed pearls', its case was furnished with a lock and key, an indication of the instrument's value. Mersenne, however, remarked that such ornamentation would not improve an instrument's musical qualities. Other kits had carved backs, a notable example being one now in the Musikhistorisk Museum, Copenhagen. Its inscription reads 'Conradus Muller 1520', but this is now held to be false and the instrument thought to date from the 17th century. A somewhat later German or Swiss kit in the Victoria and Albert Museum, London, has its back carved with animals, birds, isolated musical instruments (including a jew's harp) and cherubic dancers and instrumentalists (fig.2*a*). Although it was still being made in the early 19th century, the boat-shaped kit flourished most during the 17th, when it was described in Cotgrave's *Dictionarie of the French and English Tongues* (1611):

Poche: f. ... also, the little narrow, and long Violin (having the backe of one peece) which French dauncers, or dauncing Maisters, carrie about with them in a case, when they goe to teach their Schollers.

Late in the 17th century new shapes appeared. The body and neck became quite separate, the former resembling a viol, violin or guitar, but sometimes being a festooned hybrid (fig.2*b*). The viol form, however, was different from its prototype in that it had no frets, and also that the back was often slightly arched like that of a violin. Unlike the boat-shaped kit, this type was rarely decorated, its visual beauty being in the outer design, the wood, and the varnish. In the late 18th century Hawkins, having referred to the narrow 'poches' described by Mersenne, added 'In England this instrument is called a Kit, it is now made in the form of a violin'. By this time the influence of the viola d'amore had caused the occasional addition of sympathetic strings, resulting in the *pochette d'amour* (an example by Giovanni Battista Genova of Turin (*c*1765) is in the Royal College of Music, London; fig.2*c*).

The kit was played at all social levels. The writer of *The Christian State of Matrimony* (1543) condemned those people who came to church with 'a great noise of harpes, lutes, kyttes, lutes, basens and drommes, wherwyth they trouble the whole church, and hyndre them in matters pertayninge to God'. Drayton, in his *Poly-Olbion* (London, 1613) described the kit as being a favourite instrument of wandering fiddlers. In Cesare Negri's masque *Le gratie d'amore*, performed before Don John of Austria on 26 June 1574, the allegorical figure 'La Perseveranza' was followed onto the stage by a shepherd carrying a 'sordina'. Shepherds are also associated with kits in Monteverdi's *Orfeo* (1607), but here the instruments are described as 'violini piccoli alla

3. *Kit by Antonio Stradivari, Cremona, 1717 (Conservatoire Royale de Musique, Paris)*

Francese'. In the painting *Peasant Children* by Antoine le Nain, now in the Glasgow Art Gallery, one child plays a kit and another a pipe. His *Young Musicians* (in the private collection of Lord Aldenham) depicts a kit played in consort with a singer and guitarist. Lully's violin-shaped kit is now in the Paris Conservatoire, and at the top of the social scale the grand dauphin, eldest son of Louis XIV, had a boat-shaped kit made by Dimanche Drouyn of Paris (fig.2*d*). This ivory-backed instrument, together with its bow and leather case, is now in the Victoria and Albert Museum. Leopold Mozart wrote in his *Violinschule* (1756) that the kit was then 'almost obsolete'. However, Robert Bremner in London published among his list of wares (*c*1765):

Little Violins and Kits
Bows for small Violins & Kits

Bridges for Kits, Violins, Tenors, Viol de Gambo's and Basses
Pegs or Pins for ditto
Tail Pieces for ditto

One of his customers may have been Francis Pemberton, described by Hawkins as

a dancing master of London, lately deceased, who was so excellent a master of the Kit, that he was able to play solos on it, exhibiting in his performance all the graces and elegancies of the violin, which is all the more to be wondered at as he was a very corpulent man.

3. REPERTORY. Very little music was composed specifically for the kit so the performer generally played violin pieces or popular tunes. Hawkins wrote that the powers of the kit were 'co-extensive with those of the violin', but whether or not the performer played above the first position depended on the instrument and the manner in which it was held. A kit by James Aird of Glasgow made in about 1780, complete with a book of tunes written out by a former owner, John Hall of Ayr (1788–1862) is now in the Glasgow Museum. No instrument is specified for the music, but the dance, songs and marches in the book are playable on the violin and some are accompanied. Many of them are suitable for the kit. In 1858, when performance on the instrument was rare, Louis Clapisson acquired a kit by Stradivari, and composed a gavotte for it in his opera *Les trois Nicolas*. This instrument, violin-shaped and dated 1717 (fig.3), was originally brought to France by Luigi Tarisio, and is now in the Museum of the Paris Conservatoire (Clapisson was its first curator).

BIBLIOGRAPHY

HawkinsH

M. Praetorius: 'De organographia', *Syntagma musicum*, ii (Wolfenbüttel, 2/1619/R1958)
M. Mersenne: *Harmonie universelle* (Paris, 1636–7/R1963; Eng. trans., 1957)
P. Trichet: *Traité des instruments de musique* (Bordeaux, c1640); ed. F. Lesure (Neuilly-sur-Seine, 1957)
A. Kircher: *Musurgia universalis* (Rome, 1650/R1970)
F. W. Galpin: *Old English Instruments of Music* (London, 1910, rev. 4/1965)
G. Kinsky: *Musikhistorisches Museum von Wilhelm Heyer in Cöln* (Cologne, 1910–16)
C. Sachs: *Sammlung alter Musikinstrumente bei der Staatlichen Hochschule für Musik zu Berlin: beschreibender Katalog* (Berlin, 1913)
D. Fryklund: *Studien über die Pochette* (Sundsvall, 1917)
L. Greilsamer: 'La facture des instruments à archet', *EMDC*, II/iii (1927), 1708
N. Bessaraboff: *Ancient European Musical Instruments* (New York, 1941)
F. Lesure: 'La facture instrumentale à Paris au seizième siècle', *GSJ*, vii (1954), 11; x (1957), 87
D. D. Boyden: 'Monteverdi's *Violini Piccoli alla Francese* and *Viole da Brazzo*', *AnnM*, vi (1958–63), 387
N. and F. Gallini: *Comune di Milano: Museo degli strumenti musicali* (Milan, 1963)
L. Cervelli: *Mostra di antichi strumenti musicali* (Modena, 1963)
E. Halfpenny: 'An Eighteenth-century Trade List of Musical Instruments', *GSJ*, xvii (1964), 99
S. Marcuse: *Musical Instruments: a Comprehensive Dictionary* (New York, 1964)
D. D. Boyden: *The History of Violin Playing from its Origins to 1761* (London, 1965)
A. Baines: *European and American Musical Instruments* (London, 1966)
E. Winternitz: *Musical Instruments of the Western World* (London, 1966)
A. Baines: *Non-Keyboard Instruments*, Victoria and Albert Museum: Catalogue of Musical Instruments, ii (London, 1968)
I. Otto: *Das Musikinstrumenten-Museum Berlin* (Berlin, 1968)
C. van Leeuwen Boomkamp and J. H. van der Meer: *The Carel van Leeuwen Boomkamp Collection of Musical Instruments* (Amsterdam, 1971)
P. Frisoli: 'The *Museo Stradivariano* in Cremona', *GSJ*, xxiv (1971), 33
S. F. Sacconi: *I 'segreti' di Stradivari* (Cremona, 1972)
W. Stauder: *Alte Musikinstrumente* (Brunswick, 1973)
A. Pushman: 'A 16th-century Pochette', *The Strad*, lxxxiv (1974), 646
M. Remnant: *Musical Instruments of the West* (London, 1978)

MARY REMNANT

Kitāba daqdhām wadbāthar. A liturgical book of the Assyrian rite; *see* SYRIAN CHURCH MUSIC.

Kithara. The most important string instrument of Greco-Roman antiquity. Like the LYRE it was distinguished from most string instruments by the absence of a neck. Instead it had two arms rising vertically from its sound-chest which were crossed by a yoke near their upper extremities. Strings of equal length were stretched between the yoke and the soundbox and were tuned by varying their tension and possibly thickness. The kithara differed from the lyre in that its sound-chest was constructed from wood while that of the lyre was originally a tortoise-shell. The vertical arms are also of wood and are often hollow; this was a means of extending the sound-chest. Two shapes of sound-chest can be distinguished, the more common rectangular (illustrated here) and a somewhat smaller one with a rounded bottom referred to by historians as the 'cradle kithara' (For

Kithara player: detail from a Greek amphora (c480 BC), Attic red-figure style (attributed to the 'Brygos painter') (Museum of Fine Arts, Boston)

illustration *see* LYRE and TRIGŌNON.)

Early Greek iconography pictured the kithara, called at first the PHORMINX, with from three to five strings. Even before the classical period seven strings had become standard, a development often attributed to the shadowy 7th-century figure TERPANDER, while after the 5th century there is evidence, particularly from literary sources, that the number was often increased. Iconographic sources nevertheless continued to represent the standard number of seven strings; this is probably due to iconographic convention in dealing with mythological scenes. The kithara, larger and heavier than the lyre, was usually played while the performer was standing; it pressed against the left side of the body and was strapped to the left wrist. The lighter 'cradle kithara' was sometimes played with the performer sitting; it then rested in the lap of the player. The player's hands were held in precisely the same manner as with the lyre, that is, the left hand behind the strings, either plucking, strumming or dampening them while the right plucked them with a plectrum.

The kithara is fairly common throughout North Africa and the Near East, with Egypt, so rich in other string instruments, being the principal exception. Asia Minor seems to be the source of the Greco-Roman type as well as the Etruscan kithara, the most frequently depicted of Etruscan string instruments. In spite of its foreign origins the kithara became so thoroughly naturalized in Greece that it gained a privileged position, retaining few if any foreign or barbarous connotations. As early as in the Homeric epics it had become the indispensable accompaniment to the singing of the praises of Hellenic heroes. Together with the lyre, it was the instrument which served to symbolize that which is most Hellenic in Greek musical mythology. Apollo played it in his contest with the satyr Marsyas and Orpheus played it to charm wild beasts and mollify the guardians of the underworld.

The kithara and lyre were broadly similar in function: differences, if any, resulted from the larger instrument's adaptability to concert usage and virtuoso display. For example, the kithara was considerably more prominent in the musical *agones* at civic festivals, and during the 5th and 4th centuries BC virtuoso kithara playing was associated with the new musical trends criticized by Plato and Aristotle. In post-classical Greece and in Rome the lyre increasingly gave way to the kithara; the latter was correspondingly used in new ways. At Rome in particular it appeared in virtually every area of musical life including the theatre, the *convivium* and cult music, where at one time the tibia had been used exclusively. There were eventually a sufficient number of kithara players employed in this latter function to warrant their being organized in the *collegium fidicinum romanum*, the Roman society of string players.

BIBLIOGRAPHY

I. Henderson: 'Ancient Greek Music', *NOHM*, i (1957), 336–403
E. Winternitz: 'The Survival of the Kithara and the Evolution of the Cittern: a Study in Morphology', *Music, Libraries and Instruments*, ed. U. Sherrington and G. Oldham (London, 1961), 209
M. Wegner: *Griechenland*, Musikgeschichte in Bildern, ii/4 (Leipzig, 1963)
G. Fleischhauer: *Etrurien und Rom*, Musikgeschichte in Bildern, ii/5 (Leipzig, 1964)
J. F. Mountford and R. P. Winnington-Ingram: 'Music', *Oxford Classical Dictionary* (Oxford, 2/1970), 705

JAMES W. MᶜKINNON

Kitharode [citharode] (Gk. *kitharōdos*; Lat. *citharoedus*). In antiquity, a singer who sang to (his own) kithara accompaniment; in strict usage it is to be distinguished from a 'kitharistēs' (Lat. *citharista*, *fidicen*), meaning simply 'kithara player'.

Kitson, Charles Herbert (*b* Leyburn, Yorks., 13 Nov 1874; *d* London, 13 May 1944). English organist and music teacher. At first intending to enter the Church, he took his arts degrees at Cambridge where he was organ scholar of Selwyn College, but his music degrees at Oxford as an external student. His first important post was as organist of Christ Church Cathedral, Dublin (1913–20), and while there he became professor of music in University College, Dublin (1915). In 1920 he returned to England and joined the staff of the RCM, but the same year became also professor of music in Trinity College, Dublin, then a non-resident post, from which he retired in 1935. Though his earliest treatise, *The Art of Counterpoint*, did indeed represent a pioneering approach, albeit gingerly and cautious, all his teaching, from the elements upwards, was directed to the style then generally required for English university degrees in music. *The Evolution of Harmony*, not based on a historical process, is curiously misnamed, and his beginners' books are not inspiriting.

WRITINGS

The Art of Counterpoint and its Application as a Decorative Principle (Oxford, 1907, 2/1924)
Studies in Fugue (Oxford, 1909)
The Evolution of Harmony (Oxford, 1914, 2/1924)
Elementary Harmony (Oxford, 1920–26)
Counterpoint for Beginners (London, 1927)
Invertible Counterpoint and Canon (London, 1927)
Rudiments of Music (London, 1927)
The Elements of Fugal Construction (London, 1929)
Six Lectures on Accompanied Vocal Writing (London, 1930)
Rudiments of Music for Junior Classes (London, 1931)
Applied Strict Counterpoint (Oxford, 1931)
Contrapuntal Harmony for Beginners (London, 1931)
The Elements of Fugal Composition (London, 1936)

WATKINS SHAW

Kittel. German family of musicians.

(1) Caspar Kittel (*b* Lauenstein, 1603; *d* Dresden, 9 Oct 1639). Composer. First as a choirboy and then as a professional musician, Kittel served the Hofkapelle in Dresden from at least 23 September 1616 until his death. He was a pupil and close colleague of Schütz. In 1624 his patron, Johann Georg I, Elector of Saxony, sent him to study in Italy, where Schütz eventually joined him. They returned to Dresden in August 1629, and later that year Kittel was put in charge of four choirboys. He taught Weckmann singing during the next few years and was also capable enough on the theorbo to teach it to his brother Jonas, also a musician at the Hofkapelle. In 1632 he became instrument inspector at the court, and in 1638 Schütz left the direction of music in the Hofkapelle in Kittel's hands when he went to Denmark.

With his *Arien und Cantaten* (1638), his only known music, Kittel introduced the term 'cantata' into Germany. The collection contains 30 songs, all accompanied by continuo: five are for solo voice, ten for two voices, five for three and ten for four. The voices in each of the first three categories vary in type. All the solo arias and four duets are strophic variations, while the remaining pieces are simple strophic songs. Although he did not say so, Kittel obviously used the term 'cantata' to denote the strophic variations, just as Alessandro Grandi (i) and other Italian composers had done; he no doubt became acquainted with Italian strophic variations as cantatas when he was in Italy.

The first strophe in each case is essentially syllabic and homophonic, while the subsequent strophes are interrupted by frequent extended melismas. Two works are built on the Ruggiero bass and another on the romanesca. The bass line is altered from strophe to strophe, sometimes with considerable ornamentation, but the outline of the original bass is always clearly present. In the first solo cantata the metre changes from duple to triple for the last two strophes; in the others it is either duple or triple throughout. The seventh item has a ritornello between each strophe. In several cantatas each strophe is in binary form with the tonal scheme tonic–dominant–tonic. Bar form and the form *ABB* occur only in those arias that are not cantatas. Generally in the songs for more than one voice short passages of imitation give way to predominant homophony.

Nearly all the poems are by Martin Opitz, an exact contemporary of Kittel and possibly, through Schütz, a personal friend. They deal with pastoral love, as do so many German and other western European songs of the time. Kittel was careful to observe the correct rhetorical rhythm of the text in his cantatas, no doubt under the influence of both contemporary Italian recitative and Opitz. In a few instances there is madrigalesque word-painting.

Kittel stated in a foreword that he had written the music for his choirboys, who, he said, could learn how to sing powerfully and swiftly from the solos and duets; he promised to write a manual on how to sing in the Italian manner but did not live to do so.

(2) Christoph Kittel (*fl* Dresden, 1641–80). Like David and Christian Kittel, also musicians at the Dresden Hofkapelle, he was probably a son of (1) Caspar. He rose to become the Hofkapelle's principal organist in 1660. In the 1640s he had been one of its leaders in the absence of Schütz, who included in his *Zwölff geistliche Gesänge* (Dresden, 1657) a song by him, 'O süsser Jesu Christ', for solo voice and instruments.

(3) Johann Heinrich Kittel (*b* Dresden, 13 Oct 1652; *d* Dresden, 17 July 1682). Organist and composer, son of (2) Christoph. He succeeded Adam Krieger as second organist in the Dresden Hofkapelle in 1666 and his father as first organist by 1680. As director of the choirboys he had as pupil in 1669 Johann Kuhnau, who left after a year, however, because 'the instruction was severe'. His set of 12 keyboard preludes in successive keys, *Tabulatura Num: 12 Praeambulorum und einem Capriccio von eben 12 Variationen* (*R-BRm* Mus.808), written by 1682, is one of the earliest predecessors of Bach's '48'.

BIBLIOGRAPHY

W. Vetter: *Das frühdeutsche Lied* (Münster, 1928)

H. J. Moser: *Corydon* (Brunswick, 1933)

G. Ilgner: 'Einige klärende Nachrichten über das Leben der Musikerfamilie Kittel am Dresdener Hofe zur Schütz-Zeit', *Musik und Kirche*, x (1938), 170

J. H. Baron: 'A 17th-century Keyboard Tablature in Brasov', *JAMS*, xx (1967), 279; also R. Jackson: communication, *JAMS*, xxiv (1971), 318

JOHN H. BARON

Kittel, Johann Christian (*b* Erfurt, 18 Feb 1732; *d* Erfurt, 17 April 1809). German organist and teacher.

He studied with Jakob Adlung, organist in Erfurt, and from 1748 to 1750 was a favourite pupil of the aged J. S. Bach in Leipzig. After serving from 1751 as an organist and teacher in Langensalza he was appointed organist of Erfurt's Barfüsserkirche (1756); in 1762 he transferred to the Predigerkirche there. Despite a low salary and more favourable offers from elsewhere, he remained in Erfurt for the rest of his life, seldom undertaking concert tours and even refusing an invitation in 1790 from Duchess Anna Amalia of Weimar to travel to Italy. His fame as a virtuoso organist brought Goethe, Herder and Wieland to his evening recitals, and drew many pupils to him, of whom the most important were M. G. Fischer (his successor at the Predigerkirche), K. G. Umbreit, his nephew J. W. Hässler and J. C. H. Rinck. In 1800 he made a concert tour to Hamburg, where he remained a year while preparing his new book of chorales for Schleswig-Holstein (*Vierstimmige Choräle mit Vorspielen*, 1803).

Kittel's guiding doctrine, as expressed in his influential textbook *Der angehende praktische Organist* (1801–8), was 'grounded in the principles of Bach' and had as its aim 'to awaken, maintain and heighten feelings of devotion in the hearts of his hearers by means of music'. In keeping with his emphasis on simple forms suited to liturgical practice, his teaching centred on chorale accompaniment, which he required to be simple with inner parts capable of being sung, and on the chorale prelude, which he thought should suitably introduce the spirit and feeling of the chorale but need not adhere precisely to its melody. Although short, 'characteristic' pieces determined most of his oeuvre, he also wrote large-scale organ works, including double chorale variations which look back to the style of Bach. In the main, however, his works depart from Bach's tradition, despite their contrapuntal forms, and give sympathetic expression to contemporary idioms. The 16 *Grosse Präludien* juxtapose Bach-like counterpoint with *galant* passages in contemporary symphonic style, the whole being sustained by an emphasis on melody. In his piano sonatas (1789), his art of 'characterizing' led to a full working-out of contrasting ideas; thus, his own theoretical requirements approached the Viennese Classical style. Further character pieces for organ include his six variations on *Nicht so traurig* (1797) and, as implicit in their structure, the *Vier und zwanzig Choräle mit acht verschiedenen Bässen über eine Melodie* (1811). These works dispense with the chorale as cantus firmus and freely incorporate it into settings in the *empfindsamer Stil*. Such character pieces became decisively influential in German organ music, and in the 19th century the genre was carried even further by Kittel's own pupils.

WORKS

(*all for org, unless otherwise stated; MSS listed in Dreetz, 1932*)

6 Sonaten . . . nebst einer Fantasie, pf (Gera, 1789); 6 Veränderungen, über . . . Nicht so traurig, pf (St Petersburg, 1797); Der angehende praktische Organist, oder Anweisung zum zweckmässigen Gebrauch der Orgel bei Gottesverehrungen in Beispielen, 3 vols. (Erfurt, 1801–8; ii, 2/1808; 3/1831); Vierstimmige Choräle mit Vorspielen . . . für die Schleswig-Hollsteinischen Kirchen, 2 vols. (Altona, 1803); 24 Choräle mit 8 verschiedenen Bässen über eine Melodie, ed. J. C. H. Rinck (Offenbach, 1811); Grosse Präludien, 2 vols. (Leipzig, n.d.); 24 kurze Choralvorspiele (Offenbach, n.d.); Variationen über 2 Choräle (Leipzig, n.d.); 24 leichte Choral-Vorspiele (Bonn and Cologne, n.d.)

BIBLIOGRAPHY

A. Dreetz: *J.Chr. Kittel, der letzte Bachschüler* (Leipzig, 1932)

K. G. Fellerer: *Beiträge zur Choralbegleitung und Choralverarbeitung*

in der Orgelmusik des 18/19. Jahrhunderts (Strasbourg, 1932)
——: *Studien zur Orgelmusik des ausgehenden 18. und frühen 19. Jahrhunderts* (Kassel, 1932)
H. Kelletat: *Zur Geschichte der deutschen Orgelmusik in der Frühklassik* (Kassel, 1933)
R. Sietz: 'Die Orgelkompositionen des Schülerkreises um Johann Sebastian Bach', *BJb*, xxxii (1935), 33–97
G. Frotscher: *Geschichte des Orgelspiels und der Orgelkomposition*, ii (Berlin, 1936, enlarged 3/1966)
M. Schneider: *Die Orgelspieltechnik des frühen 19. Jahrhunderts in Deutschland* (Regensburg, 1941)
G. Fock: 'Zur Biographie des Bachschülers Johann Christian Kittel', *BJb*, xlix (1962), 97

KARL GUSTAV FELLERER

Kittl, Jan Bedřich [Johann Friedrich] (*b* Orlík nad Vltavou, 8 May 1806; *d* Lissa, Prussia [now Leszno, Poland], 20 July 1868). Czech composer. He studied law at Prague University, the piano with Tomášek's pupil Zavora and composition with Tomášek. He was employed at first by the Czech financial procurators in Prague, but in 1836, after a concert of his compositions (including a nonet, a septet and his very popular song *Wär ich ein Stern*), he devoted himself to music. He achieved European success with his second symphony (*Jagdsymphonie*), which Spohr conducted in Kassel in 1839 and Mendelssohn in Leipzig in 1840. In 1843 he succeeded D. B. Weber as director of the Prague Conservatory, which he ran on progressive lines in the spirit of the new Romantic schools; its orchestral concerts, which he conducted, included many novelties. He became friendly with Liszt and Berlioz during their visits to Prague, while Wagner wrote the libretto for his opera *Bianca und Giuseppe* (from which a march was adopted by Czech students during the 1848 Revolution). Soon after the successful première of his fourth symphony (1858), written to celebrate the 50th anniversary of the founding of the Prague Conservatory, his health and energy declined; this, together with financial embarrassments, forced him to resign from the conservatory at the end of 1865. His last years were spent in exile.

Kittl was one of the first Czech Romantics. Though his education was German and he moved in German circles, he wrote several songs and choruses in Czech, beginning in 1835 with the eight songs for Škroup's collection *Věnec ze zpěvů vlastenských* ('A garland of patriotic songs'). He was a member of the board which recommended the use of Czech in the Prague Conservatory in 1845. His impact on Prague's musical life was decisive: through his contacts with leading German musicians as well as his tactful handling of those around him, he was able to introduce the music of Berlioz and Wagner to a city which still found Beethoven modern. Among his pupils was Vilém Blodek; Smetana too benefited from the invigorating musical atmosphere which he cultivated. His compositions, always technically polished, sometimes incline to shallowness, particularly in the salon-oriented piano music and songs, but his choruses contributed to the growth of Czech choral singing in the 1860s, and his opera *Bianca und Giuseppe* was one of the most successful operas written in Bohemia before Smetana. Kittl is arguably the most substantial Czech symphonist before Dvořák. His best-known work, the *Jagdsymphonie*, has retained its melodic freshness and is still played today. It owes its title to the hunting music for four horns which, after a trumpet call, open the work, and from the movements' sub-titles, which are all connected with hunting. Though the influence of Mendelssohn is unmistak-

able, there is a distinctively Czech flavour in the second trio, and a premonition of Smetana in the march-like finale.

WORKS

OPERAS

Daphnis' Grab, Prague, 1825, lost
Bianca und Giuseppe [Die Franzosen vor Nizza] (R. Wagner), op.31, Prague, 19 Feb 1848 (Leipzig, n.d.); inc. autograph, *CS-Pk*
Waldblume (Hickel), Prague, 1852, *Pk*
Die Bilderstürmer (J. E. Hartmann), Prague, 1854, ?*Pk*

VOCAL

Choral: Mass, C, solo vv, vv, orch, 1844, Prague, 31 Oct 1844, *Pk*; Requiem, lost; Jubel-Cantate (Bayer), op.34 (Prague, 1854); unacc.: Přání: na vlast [A wish: for the fatherland], Žežulička [The cuckoo], Pro krále a pro vlast [For king and country] (V. Filípek), 1844, Společenská [A social chorus], 1846, Bergmannsleben, Schifferlied, Turnerlied, Tři sbory na slova Gustava Pflegra [3 choruses to words by G. Pfleger] (Prague, 1863), Tři sbory vlastenecké [3 patriotic choruses], op.60 (Prague, ?1863); male vv: Qt, acc. physharmonika, *Pk*, Nocturne, acc. pf, 4 hn, 1835, lost
Lieder and songs (for 1v, pf, unless otherwise stated): Wilde Rosen an Hertha (M. G. Saphir), op.3 (Vienna, n.d.); 21 lieder, op.4 (Paul, Uhland) (Vienna, n.d.), op.5 (Leipzig, n.d.), op.13 (Uhland, Birnatzky) (Leipzig, n.d.), op.21 (Prague, n.d.); 19 Gesänge, op.11 (Leipzig, n.d.), op.16 (Berlin, n.d.), op.23 (Leipzig, n.d.), op.56 (Leipzig, n.d.); 8 songs for Škroup's Věnec ze zpěvů vlastenských (Prague, 1835–9); 12 lieder, 2vv, op.35 (Prague, n.d.), op.53 (Leipzig, n.d.); Wär ich ein Stern (J. P. Richter) (Prague, n.d.); further single works, incl. opp.7, 12, 14, 15, 20

INSTRUMENTAL

Orch: 4 syms.: no.1, d, op.19, 1836 (Leipzig, n.d.), no.2, E♭, op.9, 1837 (Leipzig, n.d.) [Jagdsymphonie], no.3, D, 1841–2, op.24 (Mainz, n.d.), no.4, C, 1857, perf. Prague, 7 July 1858, *Pk*; 3 concert ovs.: D, op.22, 1841 (Leipzig, n.d.), E, *Pk*, no.3, lost; 4 marches, op.32 (Berlin, n.d.), op.33 (Prague, n.d.)
Chamber: Grand septuor, pf, wind insts, E♭, op.25, ?1832 (Leipzig, c1850); 2 fl trios, opp.11, 12, *Pk*; Trio, pf, vn, vc, op.28, ?1842–3 (Leipzig, c1842); Nonet, 1835, lost
Pf: Grande sonate, 4 hands, op.27 (Leipzig, 1847); 12 Idyllen, op.1 (Vienna, n.d.), op.2 (Prague, 1838); 3 Scherzi, op.6 (Leipzig, n.d.); 2 Romanze, op.8 (Prague, n.d.), op.10 (Leipzig, n.d.); 24 impromptus, op.17 (Berlin, n.d.), op.18, 26, 30, 38 (Leipzig, n.d.), op.59 (Prague, n.d.); Berceuse, op.39 (Prague, n.d.); 12 Aquarelles, op.42 (Leipzig, n.d.), op.44 (Leipzig, n.d.), op.45 (Prague, n.d.); Nocturne, op.53 (Prague, n.d.); Stammbuch-Blätter, op.58 (Prague, n.d.); further single works without op. nos.

THEORETICAL WORKS

Praktische Orgelschule für Präparanden (Vienna, 1861, 2/1883)

BIBLIOGRAPHY

E. Rychnovsky: *Johann Friedrich Kittl* (Prague, 1904)
J. Branberger and A. W. Ambros: *Konservatoř hudby v Praze* [The Prague Conservatory of Music] (Prague, 1911; Ger. trans., 1911)
E. Rychnovsky: 'Johann Friedrich Kittl', *Der Auftakt*, viii (1928), 71
M. Tarantová: *Jan F. Kittl* (Prague, 1948)
R. Quoika: *Die Musik der Deutschen in Böhmen und Mähren* (Berlin, 1956)
J. Burghauser: Introduction to *J. B. Kittl: Symfonie Es Dur* (Prague, 1960) [incl. full list of works and earlier bibliography]

Kiyose, Yasuji (*b* Yokkaichi, Ōita prefecture, 13 Jan 1900). Japanese composer. He studied composition privately with Kōsaku Yamada and Kōsuke Komatsu. In 1930 he took an active part in organizing the Shinkō Sakkyokuka Renmei, which later grew into the Japanese section of the ISCM. He is primarily a composer of vocal and chamber music in a style following the German Romantic tradition, though combined with French impressionist features. Besides these he has drawn on traditional Japanese music, particularly its folksongs and pentatonic scales. This tendency was inherited and developed by his most celebrated pupil, Takemitsu.

WORKS

(selective list)

Choral: Hebi-matsuri kōshin [March of the snake festival], 1954; Karasu hyakutai [100 versions of crows], 1957; Itaziki-yama no yoru [A night at Mount Itaziki], 1957; Ryūkū min'yō-shū [Folksongs from Ryūkyū], 1960; Fuyu no motekoshi [Now that winter is over], 1961; Bokura wa umi ni yuku [We are going on the ocean, or unknown soldiers], S, T, chorus, orch, 1962; To Ho no shi ni yorite [For Tu Fu's poem], 1962; Shinda shōjo [Dead girl], 1964; Tōhoku min'yō-shū [Folksongs from Tōhoku], 1965; Yoso kara kita shōjo [A foreign girl], 1972

Orch: Nihon sairei bukyoku [Japanese festival dances], 1940; Pf Conc., 1954; Nihon no sobyō [A sketch of Japan], 1963

Chamber: 3 vn sonatas, 1941, 1948, 1950; Str Trio, 1949; Str Qt, 1951; 2 pf trios, ?, 1955; Qnt, ww, harp, 1957; 2 Movts, vn, pf, 1960; Shakuhachi Trio, 1964; Suite, 8 Japanese insts, 1964; Qnt, Japanese insts, 1964; Qt, Japanese insts, 1965; Rec Qt, 1969; Duo, rec, pf, 1970; Rec Trio, 1972

Songs: Kakyoku-shū [Vocal album], nos.1–2, 1922–66; Mannyō kakyoku-shū [Songs from Mannyō], S, chamber orch, 1942

Principal publishers: Kawai Gakufu, Ongaku-no-Tomo Sha, Zen-on Gakufu

MASAKATA KANAZAWA

Kjaswa. *See* CACHUA.

Kjerulf, Halfdan (*b* Christiania, 17 Sept 1815; *d* Christiania, 11 Aug 1868). Norwegian composer and piano teacher. He studied the piano and possibly also music theory as a child, but there were no possibilities for advanced music education in Christiania at that time, nor was it his family's intention that he should become a musician. He began studying law, although his chief interest continued to be music. In 1839 he suffered a serious illness and in the summer of 1840 for health reasons went to Paris, where for the first time he experienced a rich musical life, with concert and operatic performances of Classical and early Romantic works. There, probably also for the first time, he heard performances of real artistic quality; however, as he was still an immature artist, this had no immediate effect on his composing.

Within six months of Kjerulf's return to Christiania in the autumn of 1840, his father, brother and sister died, and as the eldest surviving child he had to give up his legal studies and take up work as a journalist in order to support the family. In the autumn of 1841 his first compositions, six songs op.1, were published; later he considered these works amateurish and lacking finish, and he revised and re-published three of them. While continuing to support himself as a journalist, he studied music theory on his own, became conductor in 1845 of a newly founded male students' choral society, Den Norske Studentersangforening, and of a male voice quartet (Kjerulf's Quartet), and began teaching the piano. Kjerulf was first given formal training in composition in Christiania (1848–9) by Carl Arnold, whose recommendation helped him win a stipend to study abroad, first with Gade in Copenhagen (1849–50) and later (1850–51) at the Leipzig Conservatory, where his teachers included E. F. Richter. Returning home in 1851, he settled down as a piano teacher, his principal occupation for the rest of his life; among his several outstanding pupils were Agathe Grøndahl and Erika Nissen. His later years were marked by increasing ill-health, but he enjoyed considerable recognition as a composer; in 1863 he received a medal from King Carl XV, and in 1865 he became a member of the Swedish Royal Academy of Music.

Most of Kjerulf's works were composed after his studies in Copenhagen and Leipzig. He wrote no operatic or symphonic music, but restricted his output to smaller forms, of which his songs (about 130) are the most important, both for their intrinsic merit and for their place in the development of Norwegian music. In them influence of lieder by Schubert and Schumann is

evident, as is that of folk music, which Kjerulf knew well from published collections and from his travels throughout Norway. His settings include Norwegian, Swedish, Danish, German and French texts, and the poets include his younger brother Theodor as well as King Carl XV. Inevitably the folk influence is strongest in the Norwegian songs, especially in those set to poems by the nationalist writer Bjørnsterne Bjørnson. The flavour of folk melody is obvious in *Synnøves sang* ('Synnøve's song') op.6 no.3 and *Aftenstemning* ('Evening mood') op.14 no.1, and *Ingrids vise* ('Ingrid's song') op.6 no.4 is rhythmically and melodically modelled after the *springdans*, a characteristic Norwegian folkdance. The first phrase of *Ingrid's Song* (ex.1) shows the *springdans* rhythm with its accent on the second beat of the bar; the use of the open 5th pedal point is also a characteristic borrowed from folk music. In such other songs as *Lokkende toner* ('Enticing tunes') op.3 no.6 and *Hvile i skoven* ('Rest in the woods') op.5 no.3, both to texts by J. S. Welhaven, the specific features of folk music are less prominent, but the basic Norwegian atmosphere is still perceptible.

Kjerulf's songs are usually composed in simple or varied strophic form. In only a few examples, such as *Du kommer* ('You are coming') op.17 no.3, does the extent of strophic variation approach *Durchkomponierung* and nearly all the songs that have a folk musical colouring are simple in structure, a natural consequence of their close relation to the ubiquitous strophic style of Norwegian folksong. Kjerulf generally allowed the voice a certain predominance over the piano part, which is nevertheless carefully worked out and often has an independent prelude, interlude and postlude. The accompaniment normally depicts the general atmosphere of the text by simple means, but in the more elaborate songs it may also reflect the poem's changing moods. In his finest songs Kjerulf achieved an artistic fusion of text and music equal to the masterworks of European Romanticism.

Ex.1

Kjerulf's compositions for male chorus were the direct result of his conducting activities and the first products of his artistic maturity; two of the best known,

Halfdan Kjerulf: portrait by K. Bergslien (Kunstforeningen, Oslo)

Solvirkning ('Sun's effect') and *Brudefaerden i Hardanger* ('The bridal procession in Hardanger'), were written before 1849. In addition to about 40 original compositions, he made more than 50 arrangements of his own compositions, folksongs and other songs, which occupy an important place in the Norwegian choral repertory.

A third important group of Kjerulf's compositions, his piano works, consists largely of Romantic character pieces, such as the *Wiegenlied* from op.4 and the *Berceuse* and *Caprice* from *New Sketches* op.12. They are carefully worked out and expressive compositions, but are less interesting than the two volumes of folk arrangements, especially the *25 udvalgte norske folke-dandse* (1861), some of which point towards Grieg's *slåtter* arrangements in his op.72. Such pieces as *Hildals-halling* and *Brureslått* from the 1861 collection transform folkdances into a convincing artistic form, and show both effective writing for the piano and a bold treatment of harmony. The strong discord at the begin-

Ex.2

ning of the last bar of the passage from *Brureslått* (ex.2) is probably unique in Norwegian music of that period, consisting of a French 6th chord over an A pedal point. Another striking use of dissonance showing the influence of folk music occurs at the beginning of *Bondedans* ('Farmer's dance'), which originally belonged to op.4, but was not printed in that volume probably because the style seemed too bold to the publisher (ex.3). The dissonance in the opening chord results from a tonic pedal point played with two notes of the dominant triad. In the same example, the melodic construction of two-bar motifs is another element taken from folk music.

In certain other works the currents of German Romanticism and Norwegian folk music are more nearly fused, and Kjerulf created a stylistic synthesis of the two, but this dualism, controlled by a cultured and self-critical musical intellect, permeates his entire output and is its most prominent characteristic. He virtually created the Norwegian art song with his outstanding single achievement, the transplanting of the German lied to Norwegian soil, and laid the groundwork for Grieg and his successors.

WORKS

Editions: *H. Kjerulf: Album*, ed. Kjerulf's Quartet (Christiania, 1868) [KA]

    Samling af flerstemmige mandssange, ed. J. D. Behrens (Christiania, 1845–69) [SF]

    Sangbog for mandssangforeninger, ed. J. D. Behrens (Christiania, 1870–75) [SM]

    Firstemmig mands-sangbog, ed. J. D. Behrens (Christiania, 1876–81) [FM]

    H. Kjerulf: Sånger och visor (Stockholm, 1877–84) [KS]

(*printed works published in Stockholm unless otherwise stated*)

MALE CHORUSES

Barcarole (J. L. Heiberg), SF i; Brudefaerden i Hardanger [The bridal procession in Hardanger] (A. Munch), SF iv; Aftensang [Evening song] (Munch), Den blide dag [The mild day] (J. S. Welhaven), SF vii; Norges fjelde [Norway's mountains] (H. Wergeland), Gildesang [Banquet song] (C. Frimann), SF ix; Studenter-sommervise [Students' summer song] (P. A. Jensen), SF x; Tonernes flugt [The tone's flight] (H. Hertz), SF xii; Serenade ved strandbredden [Serenade at the shore] (C. Winther), SF xiii; Frejdigt liv [Peaceful life] (anon.), SF xv

Serenade (Hugo), Norges natur (Wergeland), SF xvi; Jaegersang [Hunter's song] (Welhaven), Morgenvandring [Morning wandering] (E. Geibel), SF xviii; I skoven [In the woods] (Geibel), SF xix; Solvirkning [Sun's effect] (Welhaven), in *Hjemmet og vandringen*, ed. P. C. Asbjørnsen (Christiania, 1847), SF xx; Unge piger og gammel vin [Young girls and old wine] (Geibel), SF xxi; Sangerhilsen til damerne [Song-greeting to the ladies] (Welhaven), SF xxv; Natten [The night] (Carl XV), Aus dem Schenkenbuch II (Geibel), KA; Kan det trøste [Can it console] (Winther), KA; Kavalierernes sang af Woodstock [The cavalier's song from Woodstock] (Scott), KA

Jubilate (Moore), KA; Livets seilads [The voyage of life] (A. Stub), KA; Jaegeres sang paa fjeldet [Hunter's song on the mountain] (Welhaven), KA; Sanger-hilsen til bruden [Song-greeting to the bride] (T. Kjerulf), KA; Serenade (T. Kjerulf), I granskoven [In the spruce forest] (J. Monrad), SM; Til Bergen [To Bergen] (Bjørnson), Ton, søde strenge [Sound, sweet string] (A. Oehlenschläger), Haev dig, vor sang [Let our song arise] (Welhaven), FM

Arrs.: Bonden i Brydlupsgaren [The peasant at the wedding] (Nor. folksong), Heimreise fraa saeteren [Journey home from the summer farm] (Nor. folksong), SF i; Pilgrimssang (anon. 12th century), SF ix; Ho Guro (Nor. folksong), SF xx; Druens pris [In praise of wine] (E. Falsen) [melody by F. L. A. Kuntzen], SF xxii; Astri, mi Astri (Nor. folksong), SF xxiii; Døl'n [Mountaineer] (Nor. folksong), KA; Paal paa Haugen [Pål on the hill] (Nor. folksong), KA; E mindes vael den gøng [I remember] (Nor. folksong), KA; Du rossignol qui chante (Fr. folksong), KA; Quand la bergère (Fr. folksong), KA

Les compagnons de la Marjolaine (Fr. folksong), KA; La pêche des moules (Fr. folksong), KA; Le célèbre menuet d'Exaudet (Fr. folksong), KA; Santa Lucia (It. folksong), KA; La gondoletta (It. folksong), KA; [9] Fredmans epistlar (nos.16, 20, 31, 48, 52, 58, 60, 64, 75) (C. M. Bellman), KA; [3] Fredmans sånger (nos.9, 28, 41) (Bellman), KA

op.   SONGS

1 Sex sange (Christiania, 1841): Nøkken [The water elf] (Welhaven), Romance (H. C. Andersen), Min skat [My treasure] (Winther), Laengsel [Longing] (Winther), Lied (A. von Platen), Violen (Oehlenschläger, after Goethe)

2 Romancer (Christiania, 1851–2): Buesnoren [The bowstring] (Welhaven), Af alfernes hvisken [From the elves' whisper] (Welhaven), Elveløbet [The torrent] (Welhaven), Paa fjeldet [In the mountains] (Welhaven), En vaarnat [A spring evening] (Welhaven), Syng, syng (T. Kjerulf), Romance af Aly og Gulhundy (Oehlenschläger), Og vil du vaere vennen min [And will you be my friend] (T. Kjerulf)

3 Sex sånger (1856): Min elskte, jeg er bunden [My beloved, I am not free] (Welhaven), Laengsel [Longing] (Winther), Du fragst mich du (Welhaven), Det var då [It was then] (J. L. Runeberg), Vidste du vei [If you knew the way] (T. Kjerulf), Lokkende toner [Enticing tunes] (Welhaven)

5 Otte sånger (1858): Chanson (Hugo), Så ensam uti natten [So lonesome in the night] (Carl XV), Hvile i skoven [Rest in the woods] (Welhaven), I søde blege kinder [You sweet pale cheeks] (T. Kjerulf), Spansk romans ur Spanisches Liederbuch (trans. P. Heyse), Framnäs (Carl XV), Liebespredigt (Rückert), I skoven [In the woods] (Winther)

6 Otte norske viser (1859): Veiviseren synger [The guide sings] (Welhaven), Ved sjøen den mørke [By the dark lake] (Wergeland), Synnøves sang (B. Bjørnson), Ingrids vise (Bjørnson), Solskins-vise [Sunshine song] (Bjørnson), Venevill (Bjørnson), Over de høie fjelde [Over the high mountain] (Bjørnson), Hjemad [Homeward] (J. Moe)

9 Sex franska romaner (1861): Quand tu dors (Hugo), Romance, from Ruy Blas (Hugo), Les rayons et les ombres (Hugo), Le retour (Hugo), Chanson (Hugo), L'attente (Richer)

11 Syv sange (1863): Naar kommer rosentiden? [When will the time of roses come?] (T. Kjerulf), Bøn for den elskede [Prayer for the beloved] (T. Kjerulf), Foraarsdigt [Spring poem] (Welhaven), Aftenstemning [Evening mood] (Welhaven), Den långa dagen [The long day] (Runeberg), Gud vet det hvar han vankar [God knows where he walks] (D. Klockhof), Albumsblad (Hoffmann von Fallersleben)

14 Fem sange (Bjørnson) (1865): Aftenstemning [Evening mood], Søvnen [Sleep], Dulgt kjaerlighed [Hidden love], Ved søen [By the lake], O, vidste du bare! [O, if you only knew!]

15 Sex sange (1866): Svundne dage [Bygone days] (Munch), Den friske sang [The gay song] (Welhaven), Taylors sang (Bjørnson), En sommersang (Welhaven), Laengsel [Longing] (T. Kjerulf), Af natten paa fjorden [Song from the night on the fjord] (Munch)

16 Sange (1867): Det var så tyst [It was so silent] (J. J. Callanan), Mit hjerte og min lyra [My heart and my lyre] (Moore), Hyrdepigens sang [The shepherdess's song] (R. M. Milnes), Serenade (Byron), Skovbaekken [The brooklet in the woods] (Burns)

17 Danske og norske sange (Copenhagen, 1867): Hvad har jeg vel andet villet [What more could I have wanted] (Winther), Ved sundet [By the sound] (Welhaven), Du kommer [You are coming] (C. Ploug), Ved afskeden [At the parting] (T. Kjerulf), Den elsktes naerhed [The nearness of the beloved] (E. Aarestrup), Paa fjellet [In the mountains] (C. Janson)

18 Tre sånger, B, pf (1868): Saknaden [The absent one] (Runeberg), Der Einsiedler (Eichendorff), Das Schiff (K. Vollheim, after C. Mackey)

19 Fyra sånger (1868): Sjömansflickan [The sailor's girl] (Runeberg), Ynglingen [The youth] (Runeberg), Modren vid vaggan [The mother by the cradle] (M. Franzén), Förställningen [The dissimulation] (Runeberg)

20 Fire sange (after Geibel) (1869): Lass Andre nur, Des Mondes Silber rinnt, Vöglein wohin so schnell?, Sehnsucht

23 Fem sange (1870): Bergens stift [Bergen's diocese] (Welhaven), I granskoven [In the spruce forest] (J. Monrad), Sangfugl fra de dunkle buske [Songbird from the dark bushes] (Bjørnson), Alfeland [Fairyland] (Welhaven), Just som jeg favned dit liv [Just as I embraced you] (Bjørnson)

25 Fyra sånger (1871): Die Schwester (after F. Hemans), Guten Morgen (Vollheim, after Mackey), Gute Nacht (Vollheim, after Mackey), Ich fuhr über Meer (Sp., trans. Heyse)

26 Sange (Moore) (1872): Gaa kun glands at vinde [Only go to win glory], Vagtskuddet [The watch's shot], Om jeg elske vil dig [Will I love you]

Täuschung (K. Beck), KS iii; Es stand ein Veilchenstrauss (Geibel), KS iii; Waldabendlust (C. Mayer), KS iii; Hjemfart [Journey home] (Welhaven), KS iii; Nachwirkung (A. Meissner), KS iii; Wie rafft ich mich auf (Platen), KS iii; Scheiden, Leiden (Geibel), KS iii; Höchstes Leben (Geibel), KS iii; Nach langen Jahren (Geibel), KS iii; Serenade (P. A. Jensen), KS iii; In der Ferne (H. Kletke), KS iii; Den hvide, røde rose [The white, red rose] (Bjørnson), KS iii; Treibe nur mit Lieben Spott (Sp., trans. Heyse), KS iii; Murmelndes Lüftchen (Sp., trans. Heyse and Geibel), KS iii; Ingen vej [No way] (T. Kjerulf), KS iii; Taushed og sang [Silence and song] (Welhaven), KS iii

OTHER VOCAL

Søcadetterne iland [The naval cadets ashore] (Wergeland), Singspiel, solo vv, chorus, orch [orchd by P. Sperati], N-Oum

Serenade ved strandbredden [Serenade at the shore] (Winther), T, SSA, pf, op.8 (1861)

Troubadouren (Welhaven), T, SATB, pf, op.17b (1868)

Duets: 4 sange, op.10, 2vv, pf (1863): Ved havet [At the sea] (Welhaven), Kein Wort und keinen Hauch (M. Harmann), Fuglekvidder [Bird warbling] (C. Richardt), Barcarole (J. L. Heiberg)

PIANO
(for 2 hands unless otherwise stated)

Intermezzo and Springdance, in Album for piano (Christiania, 1852), as op.27 (Berlin, c1870); 3 pieces, op.4 (1857); Bondedans [Farmer's dance], ed. N. Grinde (Oslo, 1961) [orig. in op.4]; 6 Sketches, op.7 (1860); [6] New Sketches, op.12 (1863); Polonaise, 4 hands, op.13 (1864); March, 4 hands, op.21 (1869); Rondino, 4 hands, op.22 (1869); 4 pieces, op.24 (1871); Scherzo, op.29 (Christiania, c1870)

Arrs.: 25 udvalgte norske folkedanse (1861); Norske folkeviser (Christiania, 1867)

BIBLIOGRAPHY

A. Grønvold: Norske musikere: Halfdan Kjerulf (Christiania, 1883)
O. M. Sandvik: 'Halfdan Kjerulf og poesien', Edda, iv (1915), 357
W. Moe, ed.: Halfdan Kjerulf: av hans efterladte papirer [Kjerulf: from his posthumous papers] (Christiania, 1917–18)
O. M. Sandvik: 'Halfdan Kjerulfs kreds i 1840-aarene' [Kjerulf's circle in the 1840s], Edda, ix (1918), 81
N. Grinde: 'En Halfdan Kjerulf-bibliografi', Norsk musikkgranskning årbok 1954–5 (Oslo, 1956)
D. Schjelderup-Ebbe: 'Modality in Halfdan Kjerulf's Music', ML, xxxviii (1957), 238
N. Grinde: 'Halfdan Kjerulfs klavermusikk', Norsk musikkgranskning årbok 1959–61 (Oslo, 1961)
D. Schjelderup-Ebbe: 'Kjerulfs fem sanger fra "Spanisches Liederbuch"', Festskrift til Olav Gurvin (Oslo, 1968), 144 [with Eng. summary]

NILS GRINDE

Klabon [Klaboni, Clabon, Claboni, Clabonius], **Krzysztof** [Christophorus] (b ?Königsberg, c1550; d in or after 1616). Polish composer, instrumentalist, lutenist and singer. As a child he was a chorister at the court of King Sigismund August at Kraków. On 6 January 1565 he was transferred to the group of instrumentalists at the royal chapel and there are records of his performing songs to the lute on festive occasions at court. In about 1576 he became director of the royal chapel, first under King Stefan Batory and then under Sigismund III. He held this post until 1601 except between 1596 and 1598. It was because Sigismund III increased the size of his chapel by appointing a number of outstanding Italian musicians that he had to give up his post: in 1596–8 he was replaced by Marenzio, and he was succeeded by G. C. Gabussi in 1601, after which he remained in charge of the Polish part of the chapel only. He accompanied the king on his travels to Sweden in 1593–4 and 1598. He is last heard of in 1616. It must be supposed that he himself composed the occasional pieces that he sang to the lute, but only one such work, to a text by Stanisław Grochowski, survives with music: *Pieśni Kalliopy Slowienskiey: na teraznieysze pod Byczyną zwycięstwo* [Songs of the Slavonic Calliope: on the recent victory at Byczyna] (Kraków, 1588; ed. Z. M. Szweykowski, *Muzyka w dawnym Krakowie*, Kraków, 1964). It is a cycle of six songs, four of which are in dance rhythms and have simple homophonic textures, and the other two are metrical pieces. A few other celebratory songs sung by Klabon, to words by Jan Kochanowski, a leading poet of the time, were printed without music (*In nuptias. . .Joanni de Zamoscio*, 1583; *Ephinicion. . . ad Stephanum Bathoreum*, 1583). Klabon also composed sacred music: one work, the five-part *Kyrie Pascale* (ed. in AMP, xv, 1968), survives complete, and of another, the *Officium Sancta Maria*, only the soprano part survives (in *PL-Kk*).

BIBLIOGRAPHY

SMP [incl. full bibliography]

Z. Jachimecki: *Wpływy włoskie w muzyce polskiej* [Italian influences in Polish music] (Kraków, 1911), 188ff

Z. M. Szweykowski: 'Rozkwit wielogłosowości w XVI wieku' [The flowering of polyphony in the 16th century], *Z dziejów polskiej kultury muzycznej, i: Kultura staropolska* [From the history of Polish musical culture, i: Early Polish culture] (Kraków, 1958)

——: 'Klabon, Krzysztof', *PSB*

A. Szweykowska: 'Przeobrażenia w kapeli królewskiej na przełomie XVI i XVII wieku' [Changes in the royal chapel in the late 16th and 17th centuries], *Muzyka*, xiii/2 (1968), 3

ZYGMUNT M. SZWEYKOWSKI

Klada, Joannes. See LAMPADARIOS, JOANNES.

Klafsky, Katharina [Katalin] (*b* Mosonszentjános, 19 Sept 1855; *d* Hamburg, 22 Sept 1896). Hungarian soprano. After singing in the chorus of the Komische Oper, Vienna, she studied briefly with Mathilde Marchesi, and in 1875 sang small parts at Salzburg. In 1876 she was engaged at Leipzig, where she studied further with Josef Sucher. She sang Waltraute (*Die Walküre*) and the Third Norn (*Götterdämmerung*) in the Leipzig première of the *Ring* (1878), Venus in *Tannhäuser* (1879) and Brangaene in the first Leipzig *Tristan und Isolde* (1882). She sang Wellgunde and Waltraute (*Die Walküre*) at Her Majesty's Theatre in the first complete London *Ring* (1882) and Sieglinde and Brünnhilde with Angelo Neumann's touring Wagner company (1882–3). After appearances in Bremen (1884) and Vienna (1885) she was engaged in Hamburg (1886), where in addition to her Wagner roles, she sang Santuzza (*Cavalleria rusticana*), Valentine (*Les Huguenots*), Norma, Agathe (*Der Freischütz*), Eglantine (*Euryanthe*), Donna Anna (*Don Giovanni*) and the Countess (*Le nozze di Figaro*). Her dramatic temperament, allied to a magnificent, full-toned voice and a secure technique acquired from Marchesi, enabled her to sing German, French and Italian roles with equal success. In 1895 she broke her contract to tour the USA with the Damrosch Opera Company, but returned to Hamburg in September 1896. She died suddenly while still in her vocal prime.

BIBLIOGRAPHY

H. Klein: *Thirty Years of Musical Life in London* (London, 1903)

L. Ordemann: *Aus dem Leben und Wirken von Katharina Klafsky* (Hameln, 1903)

A. Neumann: *Erinnerungen an Richard Wagner* (Leipzig, 1907; Eng. trans., 1909)

H. Chevalley: *100 Jahre Hamburger Stadttheater* (Hamburg, 1927)

H.-L. de La Grange: *Mahler*, i (New York, 1973)

ELIZABETH FORBES

Klage (Ger.). PLANCTUS.

Klagend (Ger.: 'plaintive', 'complaining', 'lamenting'). An expression mark used most famously by Beethoven in the finale of his op.110 Piano Sonata.

Klais, Johannes. German firm of organ builders. Johannes Klais (1852–1925) founded the existing company in Bonn in 1882, having broken with his family's farming tradition in becoming an organ builder. Some of his pupils later set up their own firms: Anton Feith, Wilhelm Furtwängler (son of the organ builder of the same name; see HAMMER-ORGELBAU) and Hans Steinmeyer. He was succeeded by his son Hans (Johannes Caspar Wilhelm Maria Klais, 1890–1965), whose own son Hans Gerd (*b* Bonn, 2 Dec 1930) directs the firm in Bonn.

The majority of Klais organs are in the Rhineland, Hesse and Westphalia, but they are also found elsewhere in Germany, Europe, and overseas; the firm's largest instrument was built for the Messehalle in Cologne in 1924 (five manuals, 130 stops). Klais initially built organs with slider-chests and tracker action; they made their first mechanical sliderless chests in 1895, their first using pneumatic action in 1897 and their first with electric action in 1906; in 1928 they built a slider wind-chest with mechanical action again, and this has been their usual type since 1948. Other works include the restoration of J. M. Stumm's organ of 1742 at Ober Lahnstein, and new instruments for the Musikakademie, Detmold (1968; four manuals, 53 stops), Würzburg Cathedral (1969; five manuals, 86 stops), the Liebfrauenkirche, Oberursel, Hesse (1970; four manuals, 52 stops), the University of Arts, Nagoya, Japan (1971; three manuals, 37 stops), Trier Cathedral (1974; four manuals, 67 stops) and St Hedwig's Cathedral, Berlin (1976; three manuals, 67 stops); organs for the minster in Ingolstadt (four manuals, 69 stops), Limburg Cathedral (four manuals, 60 stops) and Graz Cathedral (four manuals, 69 stops) were under construction in the mid-1970s.

BIBLIOGRAPHY

H. Klotz: 'Klais', *MGG*

J. Klais: 'Klais, Johannes d. Ältere', *Rheinische Musiker*, ii, ed. K. G. Fellerer (Cologne, 1962), 41

——: 'Klais, Johannes Caspar Wilhelm Maria', *Rheinische Musiker*, ii, ed. K. G. Fellerer (Cologne, 1962), 43

H. G. Klais: 'Gedanken über die Neuplanung von Orgeln', *Acta organologica*, iii (1969), 133

H. Hulverscheidt: 'Die Bonner Orgelbauanstalt Johannes Klais', *Bonner Kirchenmusik* (1970)

H. G. Klais: 'Who's Who?', *ISO Information*, iii (1970), 218

——: *Die Würzburger Domorgeln* (Frankfurt am Main, 1970)

——: *Überlegungen zur Orgeldisposition* (Frankfurt, 1973; Eng. trans., 1975)

H. Steinhaus: *Aus der Geschichte des Hauses Klais* (Bonn, 1976)

HANS KLOTZ

Klami, Uuno (Kalervo) (*b* Virolahti, 20 Sept 1900; *d* Virolahti, 29 May 1961). Finnish composer. He studied with Melartin at the Helsinki College of Music (1915–24, with interruptions), with Ravel in Paris (1924–5) and with Willner in Vienna (1928–9). A concert of his works in Helsinki in 1928 was followed by others in 1931, 1943 and 1950. He was music critic of the daily paper *Helsingin sanomat* (1932–59) and received a Finnish state pension from 1938 until 1959, when he was appointed to the Finnish Academy as Kilpinen's successor.

When Klami had completed his studies, his interests were focussed on contemporary European trends, and above all on the French school; according to his own statement, he felt at this time little sympathy with nationalist music, an attitude that was in part a reaction against the prevailing Finnish taste for decidedly Romantic nationalism in music. Works such as the *Sérénades espagnoles* (1924) and the Piano Concerto no.1 'Une nuit à Montmartre' (1925) clearly illustrate his connections with impressionism in general and his admiration for Ravel in particular. The concert waltz *Opernredoute*, written after his year in Vienna, is a homage to Johann Strauss, but through Ravel's *La valse*.

Yet in 1927 Klami had composed a *Karjalainen rapsodia* ('Karelian rhapsody') based on Finnish folk-tunes. His approach to folk music was, however, quite different from that of the older generation of nationalists, who had often contented themselves with a simple chorale-like harmonization of traditional melodies. Klami's strength was that he understood the national heritage within a wider context: he used folk music because of its appeal as music and not because of its national provenance, and so the place of the Finnish element in his work can be compared with that of the Spanishness in Ravel, or better with that of the Russian quality in early Stravinsky. The *Karelian Rhapsody* was followed by many works of the same basic orientation, notably the *Fantaisie tschérémisse* for cello and orchestra (1931).

In the early 1930s Kajanus suggested to Klami that he should write an orchestral composition on episodes from the *Kalevala*. The result was the *Kalevala sarja* ('Kalevala suite'). Its original version (1933) had four movements, and in 1943 Klami thoroughly revised the score and added a large scherzo, 'Terhenniemi'. In this form the *Kalevala Suite* has become the most widely known of his compositions. Initially planned as a ballet score, it is the work that most evidently demonstrates Klami's debt to the Stravinsky of the Russian ballets, even if its orchestration and thematic treatment also recall Sibelius and sometimes Debussy. The scoring is marked by transparency, a sense of colour and virtuoso writing, and Klami's excellent orchestral technique enabled him to throw new light on national themes and folk melodies that many earlier composers had used less convincingly. But he was not just a folklorist. In the most important works after the *Kalevala Suite* he turned away from Finnish materials. These later pieces include a most accomplished Violin Concerto of great virtuosity and the Second Piano Concerto, whose chamber-musical orchestral facture approaches neo-classical ideals. His last large-scale work, the ballet *Pyörteitä* ('Whirls'), looked back to the impressionist sonorities of his youth.

WORKS
(selective list)

Orch: Sérénades espagnoles, 1924, rev. 1944; Pf Conc. no.1 'Une nuit à Montmartre', 1925; Karjalainen rapsodia [Karelian rhapsody], 1927; Merikuvia [Sea pictures], 1928–30; Opernredoute, 1929; Symphonie enfantine, 1930; Fantaisie tschérémisse, vc, orch, 1931; Kalevala sarja [Kalevala suite], 1933, rev. 1943; Lemminkäinen, 1934; Nummisuutarit (ov. to play by A. Kivi), 1936; Suite, str,
1937; 2 syms., 1937, 1945; Suomenlinna, ov., 1940; Vn Conc., 1943, rev. 1954; King Lear (incidental music, Shakespeare), 1945; Aurora borealis, 1946; Pyöräilijä [The cyclist], 1946; Pf Conc. no.2, 1950; Pyörteitä [Whirls], ballet and 2 suites, 1960
Vocal: Psalmus (J. Cajanus), S, Bar, chorus, orch, 1935–6

BIBLIOGRAPHY
U. Klami: 'Kalevala-svitens utveckling och kompositionfaser' [The development and compositional phases of the Kalevala Suite], *Modern nordisk musik*, ed. I. Bengtsson (Stockholm, 1957), 67
O. Kauko: 'Piirteitä Uuno Klamin kuvaan' [Features to the picture of Klami], *Suomen musiikin vuosikirja 1960–61* (Helsinki, 1961), 8
U. Klami: 'Kalevala-sarjan sävellystyön', *Musiikki* (1973), nos.3–4, p.44
K. Maasalo: 'Uuno Klamin Psalmus', *Juhlakirja Erik Tawaststjernalle* (Helsinki, 1976), 363

ILKKA ORAMO

Klang (Ger.). A general term for any sound or sonority; it often occurs in compounds such as *Klangfarbe* ('tone-colour', 'timbre', *Klangideal* and *Klangwelt*. In many instances it simply means 'chord', thus *Dreiklang* ('triad') and *Klangfolge* ('chord progression').

See also DOPPELLEITTONKLANG; LEITTONWECHSELKLANG; PARALLELKLANG; WECHSELKLANG.

Klangfarbenmelodie (Ger.). A term coined by Schoenberg in his *Harmonielehre* (1911) to denote a succession of tone-colours related to one another in a way analogous to a relationship between the pitches in a melody. By this he implied that the timbral transformation of a single pitch could be perceived as equivalent to a melodic succession, that is, that one could invoke tone-colour as a structural element in composition. He had attempted this in the third of his Five Orchestral Pieces op.16 (1909), originally entitled *Farben*. Webern pursued the concept further, making the timbral structure of a work clarify as well as enhance its pitch structure; perhaps the most striking example is his orchestration of the six-part ricercare from Bach's *Musical Offering*. An important consequence of the concept of *Klangfarbenmelodie* is the serialization of timbre in atonal music, particularly in conjunction with 12-note technique and the electronic medium.

Klangschlüssel (Ger.: 'sound-clef'). A system of chordal notation invented by Hugo Riemann (*Skizze einer neuen Methode der Harmonielehre*, 1880); see NOTATION, §III, 4(viii).

Klangumwandler (Ger.). A device used in electronic music to change the frequency of a signal; *see* RING MODULATOR.

Klappenhorn [Klappenflügelhorn] (Ger.). KEYED BUGLE.

Klappentrompete (Ger.). KEYED TRUMPET.

Klatzow, Peter (James Leonard) (*b* Springs, 14 July 1945). South African composer. He started his music training in Johannesburg. After being awarded the South African Music Rights scholarship (1964) he continued his composition studies under Bernard Stevens at the RCM, London. In 1965 he won the Royal Philharmonic Prize for his Variations for Orchestra. A brief period of study in Florence (1965–6) was followed by lessons from Boulanger in Paris. On his return to southern Africa (late 1966) he took up a teaching appointment at the Rhodesian College of Music; he then worked for the South African Broadcasting Corporation as a music producer and was appointed lecturer in music at Cape Town University in 1973. In 1974 he founded the UCT Contemporary Music Society; under his guidance a large number of contemporary works have received their South African premières. His freely atonal style occasionally incorporates tonal elements. The earlier, somewhat eclectic compositions are strongly influenced by the European avant garde; in his later works the use of extremely quiet, sustained sounds is reminiscent of certain current American trends.

WORKS
(selective list)

Pf Sonata, 1969; 4 Little Pieces, pf, 1970; In memoriam N. P. van Wyk Louw, S, str orch, 1970; Interactions 1, pf, perc, chamber orch, 1971; Sym. 1972 'Phoenix', 1972; The Temptation of St Anthony, vc, orch, 1972; The World of Paul Klee, fl, va, harp, 1972; Time Structure 1, pf, 1973; Time Structure 2, orch, tape, 1974; Still Life, with Moonbeams, orch, 1975; The Garden of Memories and Discoveries, S, ens, tape, 1975; Chronogram, org, 1977; Contours and Transformations, gui, 5 insts, 1977; Night Magic II, vn, hn, pf, 1977; Str Qt, 1977

JAMES MAY

Klausenburg (Ger.). CLUJ-NAPOCA.

Klauwell, Otto (Adolf) (*b* Langensalza, 7 April 1851; *d* Cologne, 11 May 1917). German composer and writer on music. He was a pupil of Reinecke and Richter at the Leipzig Conservatory, and in 1875 was appointed to teach the piano, music history and theory at the Cologne Conservatory, of which he became deputy director in 1905. His works include two operas (*Das Mädchen vom See*, produced at Cologne, 1889, and *Die heimlichen Richter*, produced at Elberfeld, 1902), overtures, chamber music and lieder.

WRITINGS

Musikalische Gesichtspunkte (Leipzig, 1882, 2/1892 as *Musikalische Bekenntnisse*)
Der Vortrag in der Musik (Berlin and Leipzig, 1883; Eng. trans., 1890)
Die Formen der Instrumentalmusik (Leipzig and New York, 1894, rev. 2/1918 by W. Niemann)
Geschichte der Sonate (Cologne and Leipzig, 1899)
L. von Beethoven und die Variationform (Langensalza, 1901)
Theodor Gouvy (Berlin, 1902)
Studien und Erinnerungen (Langensalza, 1906)
Geschichte der Programm-Musik (Leipzig, 1910/R1968)

BIBLIOGRAPHY

R. Sietz: 'Klauwell, Otto', *Rheinische Musiker*, i, ed. K. G. Fellerer (Cologne, 1960), 136

Klavarscribo. A system of NOTATION invented in the Netherlands by Cornelis Pot in 1931. It is presented on a vertical framework, with pitch represented horizontally and time vertically, and uses white dots for notes within the diatonic scale of the piece and black ones for others. Much music has been published by the Klavarscribo Institute. (*See* NOTATION, fig.90.)

Klavecimbel (Dutch). HARPSICHORD.

Klaviatur (Ger.). KEYBOARD.

Klavier (Ger.: 'manual', 'keyboard', 'keyboard instrument'). (1) As CLAVIER, used to denote 'manual keyboard' at Rouen as early as 1386.

(2) Occasionally used for CLAVICHORD in later 18th-century central Germany (but usually 'Clavier'). Very often it is uncertain which instrument is being referred to in a source, even when a distinction is intended; Kittel used *Flügel* in 1808 to mean harpsichord when referring to J. S. Bach's music, pianoforte when referring to his own and *Klavier* to mean clavichord.

(3) Piano or Hammerklavier, especially in southern Germany and Austria.

(4) As a modern reference term or generic name,

'Klavier' usually denotes stringed keyboard instruments only; in popular usage, it normally stands for piano (*Klavierkonzert*, *Klavierspiel* etc).   PETER WILLIAMS

Klavierauszug (Ger.). A piano arrangement of ensemble music for voices, or for voices and instruments; particularly an arrangement of an opera or oratorio with the vocal parts left intact and the orchestral accompaniment reduced for piano.

Klaviergamba (Ger.). An invention of Georg Gleichmann in *c*1720; *see* SOSTENENTE PIANO, §1.

Klavier-Harmonika (Ger.). ACCORDION.

Klaviziterium (Ger). CLAVICYTHERIUM.

Klawiolin. A mechanical instrument invented by JAN JARMUSIEWICZ.

Klebe, Giselher (*b* Mannheim, 28 June 1925). German composer. He studied composition with Kurt von Wolfurt (1941–3) and with Rufer (from 1946) and Blacher (1946–51) in Berlin. In 1957 he was appointed to take a composition class at the North-west German Music Academy, Detmold.

Klebe has, together with Henze, taken a leading part in the development of opera since 1955 and in bringing the genre to a somewhat unexpected importance in the history of music since World War II. However, it was with orchestral pieces introduced at Donaueschingen, such as *Die Zwitschermaschine* (1950, after Klee), that he first came to prominence, proving himself a composer who sought to meld the achievements of the Second Viennese School in a distinctive musical language. Before this, influenced by Blacher, he had written striking, rhythmically sharp, unsentimental music whose formal clarity and resolution at once surprised and rebuked traditional expectations. The knowledge of 12-note serialism that he gained from Rufer enabled him to broaden the sound spectrum he had used hitherto; taking Berg as his example, he has always held himself open to particular expressive ideas (in which he may be compared with Fortner). Controlled freedom of this type brought with it a significant growth in expressive possibilities: his music became more fervent, highly expressive, more decisive in colour, but also clearer in gesture. At the same time his style grew simpler and developed markedly towards suspense and melancholy, so that imperceptibly he drew closer to middle-period Schoenberg. It was characteristic that a period at the Villa Massimo in Rome should have brought no evolution towards brighter colour in his music.

Klebe's inclination towards the subterranean, the dark and weighty in mood and colour, as well as the abruptness of his motivic working, were essential components of his increasing interest in dramatic music. Even his instrumental works have a clipped, fragmented character which occasionally leads to a dissolution of tension; his idealism as a composer has led him to allow formal considerations to override dramatic reality. This is particularly true in his operas, which since 1955 have become increasingly estranged from the avant garde and more accommodated to the bourgeois opera world. His subjects have always tended to be literary self-contained texts, beginning with Schiller's *Die Räuber*, which he set as a number opera; the work is technically dependent on the Second Viennese School but its model is Verdi. *Die tödlichen Wünsche* and *Die Ermordung Cäsars* emphatically demonstrate Klebe's escape from direct influence and his discovery of a personal style. *Das Märchen von der schönen Lilie* led him towards a literary symbolism and away from opera as a form requiring strict musical interpretation, but for the first time his firm reliance on literature-founded opera let him down. The danger of overvaluing detailed exposition to the detriment of dramatic vitality remains in *Ein wahrer Held* and *Das Mädchen aus Domrémy*, where the musical possibilities are no longer fully used, and where the style has become eclectic self-quotation.

WORKS
(selective list)

OPERAS

Die Räuber (Klebe, after Schiller), Düsseldorf, 1957
Die tödlichen Wünsche (Klebe, after Balzac), Düsseldorf, 1959
Die Ermordung Cäsars (Klebe, after Shakespeare), Essen, 1959
Alkmene (Klebe, after Kleist), Berlin, 1961
Figaro lässt sich scheiden (Klebe, after Horvath), Hamburg, 1963
Jacobowsky und der Oberst (Klebe, after Werfel), Hamburg, 1965
Das Märchen von der schönen Lilie (Klebe, after Goethe), Schwetzingen, 1969
Ein wahrer Held (after Synge: The Playboy of the Western World), Zurich, 1975
Das Mädchen aus Domrémy (Klebe, after Schiller), Stuttgart, 1976
Das Rendez-vous, Hanover, 1977

OTHER WORKS

Ballet: Menagerie (after Wedekind: Lulu plays), Berlin, 1958
Orch: Die Zwitschermaschine, 1950; 2 nocturnes, 1952; Sym., 42 str, 1953; Symphonie mit Mozart-Thema, 1953; Rhapsodie, 1954; Moments musicaux, 1955; Adagio und Fuge, 1962; Missa 'Miserere nobis', 18 wind, 1965; Herzschläge: Furcht, Bitte und Hoffnung, sym. scenes, rock group, orch, 1969; Sym. no.4, 1971; Orpheus, 1976
Vocal: Römische Elegien (Goethe), speaker, 3 insts, 1953; 5 Lieder, 1v, orch, 1962; 4 Vokalisen, female vv, 1963; Stabat mater, solo vv, chorus, orch, 1964; Gebet einer armen Seele, mass, chorus, org, 1966
Chamber and inst: Str Qt no.1, 1951; 2 Sonatas, vn, 1952; Vn Sonata, 1953; Elegia appassionata, pf trio, 1956; 9 duettini, fl, pf, 1962; Str Qt no.2, 1964; Introitus, aria ed alleluja, org, 1965; Pf Qnt 'Quasi una fantasia', 1967; Passacaglia, org, 1969; Fantasie und Lobpreisung, org, 1970; Nenia, vc, 1974

BIBLIOGRAPHY

W.-E. von Lewinski: 'Giselher Klebe', *Die Reihe*, iv (1958), 89; Eng. trans. in *Die Reihe*, iv (1960), 89

HANSPETER KRELLMANN

Kleber, Leonhard (*b* Göppingen, *c*1495; *d* Pforzheim, 4 March 1556). German organist. He matriculated at Heidelberg University in 1512, and was vicar-choral and organist in Horb from 1516 to 1517 and in Esslingen from 1517 to 1521. From 1521 until his death he was organist at the collegiate and parish church in Pforzheim where he also had a living. In 1541 the Margrave of Baden procured for him a benefice in the hospital church in Baden-Baden. To judge from his large number of pupils, Kleber must have been a much sought-after organ teacher.

Kleber is known chiefly for the 332-page organ tablature which he compiled between 1521 and 1524 in Pforzheim (*D-Bim* Mus.40026). Several scribes were involved in copying the 112 items, of which only a few can be identified as original compositions: in most cases they are adaptations of vocal models. Whereas the first section of the tablature contains pieces to be played on manuals, the second section contains arrangements which also use the pedals. The repertory is the normal one for tablatures of the period, and includes religious and secular song settings, arrangements of motets, some settings of dance tunes, free compositions and one didactic piece. Most pieces give no indication either of the composer or of the arranger, but vocal models for a

number of the arrangements are by Brumel, Josquin, Heinrich Finck, Hayne van Ghizeghem, Hofhaimer, Isaac, Obrecht, La Rue and Senfl. In addition there are compositions by Conrad Bruman, Hans Buchner, Othmar Luscinius, Jörg Schapf and Utz Steigleder. It is not certain whether Kleber was a composer as well as an arranger (Kotter may also have arranged some of the pieces). From a historical point of view the most interesting section of the manuscript is that containing the free compositions, for it shows an early stage in the development of independent instrumental music. Both the repertory and the method of adaptation in Kleber's organ tablature reflect the south-west German organ and keyboard style at the beginning of the Reformation.

BIBLIOGRAPHY

A. G. Ritter: *Zur Geschichte des Orgelspiels, vornehmlich des deutschen, im 14. bis zum Anfang des 18. Jahrhunderts*, ii (Leipzig, 1884) [incl. edns. of some pieces]
MMg, xx (1888), suppl., 96 [incl. edns. of some pieces]
H. Loewenfeld: *Leonhard Kleber und sein Orgeltabulaturbuch als Beitrag zur Geschichte der Orgelmusik im beginnenden XVI. Jahrhundert* (Berlin, 1897)
H. J. Moser: *Paul Hofhaimer* (Stuttgart and Berlin, 1929) [incl. edns. of some pieces]
H. J. Moser and F. Heitmann, ed.: *Frühmeister der deutschen Orgelkunst* (Leipzig, 1930)
K. Kotterba: *Die Orgeltabulatur des Leonhard Kleber* (diss., U. of Freiburg, 1958)
W. Apel: *Geschichte der Orgel- und Klaviermusik bis 1700* (Kassel, 1967; Eng. trans., rev., 1972)

MANFRED SCHULER

Klecki, Pawel. *See* KLETZKI, PAUL.

Kleczyński, Jan (*b* Janiewicze, Volïn, 8 June 1837; *d* Warsaw, 15 Sept 1895). Polish writer on music, pianist, teacher and composer. He studied the piano with Ignacy Krzyżanowski, and from 1859 studied at the Paris Conservatoire with Bazin and Carafa (theory and composition) and with Marmontel (piano). In 1866 he returned to Warsaw, and gave concerts in the capital and in other Polish towns; he taught the piano, first privately and later (1887–90) at the conservatory in Warsaw. He was also a co-founder of the Warsaw Music Society and later a member of its administrative body. He composed some piano works and songs.

Kleczyński's writings played an essential role in popularizing music in Poland. He published over 1700 reviews and articles on music in a large number of Polish journals, and from 1880 until his death was editor-in-chief of *Echo muzyczne* (later renamed *Echo muzyczne, teatralne i artystyczne*), the most respected Polish music journal of the time. As well as reviewing concerts and operas, he wrote profiles of composers, characterizing their creative work, essays on music history and studies of the Polish folk music of the Podhale (Tatra Mountains) region. A number of his writings were devoted to Chopin and his music, including discussions of interpretation and the earliest writing about his teaching methods. Kleczyński also edited a ten-volume edition of Chopin's works (Warsaw, 1882), collected and published folksongs from Podhale and translated books on music into Polish.

WRITINGS

'Szopen jako nauczyciel fortepianu' [Chopin as piano teacher], *Bluszcz* (1869), no.5, p.35
'Fryderyk Szopen' [Frederic Chopin], *Tygodnik ilustrowany* (1870), no.106, p.13; no.107, p.32; no.108, p.42
'Fortepian i jego znaczenie w historii muzyki' [The piano and its significance in music history], *Bluszcz* (1875), no.14, p.109; no.15, p.118; no.16, p.126; no.17, p.134
'Ryszard Wagner' [Richard Wagner], *Ateneum* (1876), no.2, p.517;

no.3, p.222
O wykonywaniu dzieł Szopena [On the performance of Chopin's works]
(Warsaw, 1879; Eng. trans., 1913 as *How to Play Chopin*); ed.
Z. Drzewiecki (Kraków, 1959)
'Maciej Kamieński', *Echo muzyczne* (1880), no.1, p.3; no.2, p.9; no.4,
p.25; no.5, p.33
'Kilka słów o celu i treści sztuki' [A few words on the aim and content
of the arts], *Echo muzyczne* (1880), no.18, p.142, no.19, p.149
'F. Liszt jako kompozytor' [Liszt as composer], *Echo muzyczne* (1881),
no.17, p.129; no.18, p.137; no.19, p.147; no.20, p.155; no.21,
p.162; no.23, p.178; no.24, p.185
'Ryszard Wagner' [Richard Wagner], *Echo muzyczne* (1882), no.17,
p.129; no.18, p.137; no.19, p.145; no.20, p.155; no.21, p.161;
no.22, p.169; no.24, p.185
'Józef Wieniawski', *Echo muzyczne i teatralne* (1884), no.35, p.357;
no.36, p.370
'Zakopane i jego pieśni' [The Zakopane region and its songs], *Echo
muzyczne i teatralne* (1884), no.41, p.419; no.42, p.429; no.44,
p.447; no.46, p.468
'Wycieczka po melodie' [Excursion for melodies], *Echo muzyczne i
teatralne* (1884), no.56, p.567; no.58, p.588; no.60, p.610; no.62,
p.631; no.64, p.653
Chopin w celniejszych swoich utworach [Chopin in his more important
works] (Warsaw, 1886; Eng. trans., 1896 as *Chopin's Greater
Works*)
'Franciszek Liszt', *Echo muzyczne, teatralne i artystyczne* (1886),
no.149, p.311; no.150, p.321
'Melodie Zakopiańskie i Podhalskie' [The melodies of the Zakopane and
Podhale regions], *Pamiętnik towarzystwa tatrzańskiego*, xii (1888),
39–102
'Muzyka w domu: kilka słów o technice fortepianowej' [Music in the
home: a few words on piano technique], *Echo muzyczne, teatralne i
artystyczne* (1889), no.317, p.502; no.318, p.520; no.325, p.617;
(1890), no.332, p.66; no.343, p.200
'O estetyce libretta muzycznego' [On the aesthetics of the musical
libretto], *Echo muzyczne, teatralne i artystyczne* (1892), no.478,
p.562
Słownik wyrazów używanych w muzyce [Dictionary of expressions used
in music] (Warsaw, 1893)
'Józef hrabia Wielhorski' [Józef Count Wielhorski], *Echo muzyczne,
teatralne i artystyczne* (1894), no.567, p.381; no.568, p.394; no.569,
p.406; no.570, p.419

BIBLIOGRAPHY
M. Woźna: 'Jan Kleczyński – pisarz, pedagog, kompozytor' [Jan
Kleczyński – writer, pedagogue and composer], *Szkice o kulturze
muzycznej XIX w.*, iii, ed. Z. Chechlińska (Warsaw, 1976), 130–323
[with Eng. summary]

ZOFIA CHECHLIŃSKA

Klĕdi [kĕlĕdin, kaluri, samputan]. Mouth organ of the
Dayak in central Kalimantan, Borneo. A bundle of
four to eight bamboo pipes are fitted upright into a
sealed gourd provided with a long air conduit. The reeds
inside the gourd are made of brass. Often *klĕdi* are
elaborately adorned with the plumes and occasionally
the beak of the *Rhinoplax vigil*, a sacred bird among the
Dayak. The *klĕdi* is the only instrument of its kind in the
Indonesian archipelago.

See INDONESIA, §VIII, 2 and fig.30.

ERNST HEINS

Kleen, Johan Christoph (*fl* mid-18th century). Danish
composer. He was active as an all-round freelance
musician in Copenhagen. He played the violin for a
couple of seasons in the orchestra of the Italian opera,
taught singing and music to actresses, composed and
accompanied arias which one of the dancers sang in the
ballets, and arranged and copied music for the earliest
Danish operas. It is his contribution to the latter that
has earned him a modest place in Danish musical history. An Italian opera company had been called to
Copenhagen by King Frederik V in 1747 but by 1756 it
was apparent that opera in a foreign language did not
command sufficient public support. A musically interested Norwegian dramatist in Copenhagen, Niels Krog
Bredal (1733–78), was convinced that it would be possible to use the Danish language for opera 'if only one
took sufficient care, and especially avoided the use of

foreign words'. In this venture he may have been
inspired by Giuseppe Sarti, the most successful of the
Italian composers who settled in Denmark; in any case
Bredal's first Danish opera, *Gram og Signe*, performed
by students late in 1756, used music borrowed from
various of Sarti's compositions for the arias, while the
music of the recitatives was composed by Jacob Soltau,
of whom nothing else is known. *Gram og Signe* was
repeated twice in February 1757 before an assembly of
distinguished and influential guests and met with such
encouragement that for the king's birthday on 31 March
1757 a second Danish opera by Bredal, *Eremiten* ('a
musical pastorale'), was ready for performance. This
time the arias used music by the Italians Uttini and
Galuppi, as well as Sarti, and by one native composer,
Christopher Haugsteen, who also sang in the opera. The
recitatives were by Kleen, who from this time on
became Bredal's musical collaborator. He composed the
recitatives for Bredal's subsequent intermezzos and for
Den tvivlraadige hyrde ('The confused shepherd', 1758);
he also wrote a couple of the arias, despite the fact that
'he had never seen the Tiber', as Bredal proudly boasted.
With *En musikalsk prologus* (1759) Kleen made his one
and only attempt to compose the music for a dramatic
work (by Bredal) entirely by himself. It was not a
success and the experiment with opera in Danish was
abandoned for the time being. In 1762 a tax record
refers to Kleen as a 'teacher of music', after which no
more is heard of him.

BIBLIOGRAPHY
C. Thrane: *Fra hofviolonernes tid* (Copenhagen, 1908)
T. Krogh: 'De første forsøg paa at skabe en opera i det danske sprog',
Aarbog for musik 1922, 123–58
——: 'Aeldre dansk teatermusik', *Musikhistorisk arkiv*, i (Copenhagen,
1931), 1–100

JOHN BERGSAGEL

Klega, Miroslav (*b* Ostrava, 6 March 1926). Czech
composer. He studied composition at the Prague
Conservatory (1942–4) and at the Bratislava
Conservatory under Suchoň and Cikker (1946–50).
After working as a music editor for Czech radio in
Bratislava (1950–52) he returned to Ostrava as branch
secretary of the Czech Composers' Union (1952–3) and
drama director of the opera (1953–5). He was then
professor of composition (1955–67) and director
(1967–73) of the Ostrava Conservatory. In 1973 he
was appointed music director of Czech radio in Ostrava.
As a composer he was initially influenced by dodecaphony, by Ravelian impressionism (as in the piano cycle
Zbojnické nápady) and by the concision and parody of
Stravinsky's music; this last trait is particularly evident
in the orchestral suite *Pantomima*, written for
Stravinsky's 80th birthday. In 1966 Klega attended the
Darmstadt summer courses and his later works reveal a
familiarity with avant-garde techniques: the Concerto-
partita (1965) left functional harmony behind for serial
and 'point' writing.

WORKS
(*selective list*)

Orch: Černá země [Black earth], 1951; Noční slavnosti [Nocturnal
celebrations], 1956; Sym., 1959; Pantomima, 1963; Conc.-partita,
vn, orch, 1965
Vocal: Výpověď osamělého pěšáka [The confession of a lone pede-
strian] (Klega), reciter, orch, 1969
Inst: Zbojnické nápady [Brigands' raids], pf, 1953; Concertino, str qt,
1961
Music for the theatre, cinema, radio and television

Principal publishers: Panton, State Publishing House

BIBLIOGRAPHY
ČSHS
Č. Gregor: 'Miroslav Klega', *Červený květ*, iii (1958), 194
——: 'Černá země Miroslava Klegy', *HRo*, xii (1959), 711
O. Pukl: 'Ostravští skladatelé v hudebních edicích', *Červený květ*, vi (1961), 377
M. Navrátil: 'Symfonická Pantomima', *Červený květ*, ix (1964), 185
Č. Gregor: *Miroslav Klega: tvorba 1953–1965* (Ostrava, 1966)
OLDŘICH PUKL

Kleiber, Carlos (*b* Berlin, 3 July 1930). Argentinian conductor of German birth, son of the conductor Erich Kleiber. He was taken to Buenos Aires when his parents settled there in 1935, and he began music lessons in 1950, making his début at La Plata in 1952. On the family's return to Europe, Kleiber was advised by his father against a musical career, and studied chemistry at Zurich, but he returned to music at the Theater am Gärtnerplatz, Munich, in 1953. In 1954 he was appointed conductor at Potsdam, and at the Deutsche Oper am Rhein, Düsseldorf and Duisburg (1956–64), Zurich Opera (1964–6) and the Stuttgart Staatsoper from 1966. Here he was particularly successful in Berg's *Wozzeck* (of which his father had conducted the 1925 première), and operas by Strauss, Wagner, Verdi, Bizet and Weber, whose *Der Freischütz* he first recorded in its entirety in 1973. From 1968 he made regular appearances at the Bavarian Staatsoper, Munich, and conducted *Tristan und Isolde* at his débuts at the Vienna Staatsoper in 1973, and the Bayreuth Festival in 1974, the year he first appeared at Covent Garden, in *Der Rosenkavalier*. Kleiber prefers not to hold a resident appointment, as his rigorous artistic demands restrict his frequency of appearance. A passionately eloquent conductor, he sustains strong musical and dramatic tension in an expressive range from refined lyrical poetry to frenzied ecstasy, but his instinctive approach to a work is controlled by his intellectual grasp of its character.

WOLFRAM SCHWINGER

Kleiber, Erich (*b* Vienna, 5 Aug 1890; *d* Zurich, 27 Jan 1956). Austrian conductor. He was educated in Vienna, where he studied the violin, and he was deeply impressed by performances at the Court Opera during the last years of Mahler's directorship. In 1908 he went to Prague to study philosophy and the history of the arts at the university, and music at the conservatory; his early attempts at composing were rewarded in 1911 with a prize for a symphonic poem. That year he was appointed chorus master at the German Theatre, Prague, but he moved to Darmstadt in 1912, where he conducted at the Court Theatre for seven years. Further appointments followed at Barmen-Elberfeld (now Wuppertal) in 1919, Düsseldorf in 1921 and Mannheim in 1922. An outstanding success on his Berlin début in 1923, with Frida Leider and Friedrich Schorr in *Fidelio*, led to his appointment, announced only three days later, as Generalmusikdirektor of the Berlin Staatsoper in succession to Leo Blech. Kleiber's Berlin appointment was exceptionally productive. In 1924 he conducted Janáček's *Jenůfa* in a production regarded as decisive for the composer's wider success. Krenek's *Die Zwingburg* was presented in the same year, followed in 1925 by the première, after 137 painstaking rehearsals, of Berg's *Wozzeck*. Other new works he performed included Schreker's *Der singende Teufel* (1928) and Milhaud's *Christophe Colombe* (1930), and he also conducted Wagner's *Das Liebesverbot* and various oper-

Erich Kleiber

ettas. Unwilling to compromise with the Nazi regime's cultural policy, however, he resigned from Berlin in 1934 (4 December) after the political embargo placed on such operas as Berg's *Lulu*, but he conducted the première of Berg's *Lulu* Suite at his last concert before his resignation. He did not return to Berlin until 1951.

During the 1920s and 1930s Kleiber toured widely as a guest conductor, visiting the USSR in 1927, making his American début with the New York PO in 1930 and his British début with the LSO in 1935. He was a frequent visitor to Amsterdam, Brussels and other European cities, and in 1938 appeared for the first time at Covent Garden conducting *Der Rosenkavalier* with Lotte Lehmann. Meanwhile he had begun to make a new home in Buenos Aires, where he had first appeared in 1926. He took charge of the German opera seasons at the Teatro Colón there between 1937 and 1949, and virtually made a second career as a pioneering conductor in countries like Chile, Uruguay, Mexico and Cuba. After the war he resumed his European activities, first with the London PO in 1948, and on a regular contract at Covent Garden from 1950 to 1953. There, among other operas, he conducted the first stage production in Britain of *Wozzeck* in 1952, and his presence was of crucial importance to the development of the postwar Covent Garden company. He also conducted a memorable production of *Les vêpres siciliennes* with Callas at the 1951 Maggio Musicale, Florence (his first opera in Italy), and at the same festival he gave the first performance since the 18th century of Haydn's *Orfeo ed Euridice* (also with Callas). Plans for his appointment to the Vienna Staatsoper did not materialize, and his only operatic engagement in his native city was *Der Rosenkavalier* in 1951, when the company was housed at the Theater an der Wien. His reappointment was announced to the Berlin Staatsoper, now in the eastern zone of the city, but before taking up the post in 1955 he resigned (16 March) in protest against political intrusion.

Kleiber rehearsed with an almost fanatical ardour and aimed at the utmost possible precision. He was outstanding as a conductor of Mozart, Beethoven and Richard Strauss, refusing to indulge in romantic interpretation as a means of self-projection, ignoring false performing traditions and studying the scores assiduously. He never lost his whole view of a work, and his approach was strictly non-sentimental. He won the lasting devotion of orchestral players as well as singers, and as Russell well said 'there was no such thing, to him, as an unimportant musician'. His intellect enabled him to balance structural and emotional elements in model performances, including highly regarded gramophone recordings of *Der Rosenkavalier*, *Le nozze di Figaro* and Beethoven's symphonies.

BIBLIOGRAPHY

K. Blaukopf: 'Erich Kleiber', *Grosse Dirigenten* (Teufen, 1954)
D. Webster: 'Erich Kleiber', *Tempo* (1956), no.39, p.5
J. Russell: *Erich Kleiber – a Memoir* (London, 1957)
W. Reich: 'Erich Kleiber und Alban Berg', *SMz*, xcviii (1958), 374
F. F. Clough and G. J. Cuming: 'Erich Kleiber Discography', *Gramophone Record Review*, no.74 (1959), 117

GERHARD BRUNNER

Klein, Bernhard (Joseph) (*b* Cologne, 6 March 1793; *d* Berlin, 9 Sept 1832). German composer. The son of a wine merchant who occasionally played the violin in theatre orchestras, he was essentially self-taught in music. In 1812 he was briefly in Paris, where Choron helped him but Cherubini offered him no encouragement; after six months he returned to Cologne to participate as a conductor and a composer in amateur concerts held in the cathedral. In 1816 he visited Heidelberg, where he profited from the acquaintance of Thibaut; Thibaut recognized Klein's talent but was unsuccessful in obtaining a position for him in the city. Klein was sent officially to Berlin in 1818 to observe C. F. Zelter's pedagogical methods and to apply them at Cologne Cathedral. He decided to remain in Berlin and became associated with the recently founded Institute for Church Music; he was also appointed singing teacher at the University of Berlin. After his marriage in 1824 he spent a year in Rome, where he met Santini, who helped him in his studies of earlier music. He returned to his official posts in Berlin but, numbed by the death of his wife in 1829, retired from all of them the following year.

Called 'the Palestrina of Berlin', Klein was recognized in Germany primarily as a choral composer. His works embody the musical ideals of his friend Thibaut, and his masses and oratorios draw on the style of Handel. In Berlin particularly he was known for his lieder, of which he wrote over 100; his favourite poet was Wilhelm Müller. Klein was concerned with clear prosody and set his song texts in a simple syllabic style for which he was later criticized by Schumann.

WORKS

SACRED VOCAL

Oratorios: Jephta, op.29, perf. Cologne, 1828; David, op.34, perf. Halle, 1830; others
Cantatas: Hiob (Leipzig, 1822); Johanna Sebus (Goethe), Worte des Glaubens (Schiller), both mentioned in Koch
Mixed chorus: Geistliche Musik, 4vv, pf, op.12; Magnificat, 6vv, pf, op.13; 6 Responsorien, 4–6vv, op.17; Pater noster, 2 choruses, op.18; Mass, D, 4 solo vv, chorus, orch, op.28; Stabat mater, 4vv,

org, op.30; Kyrie, 4vv, op.46; Miserere mei, 7vv (Elberfeld, 1836); Ave Maria, 4vv, pf ad lib (Leipzig, n.d.)
4 male vv: Ich danke dem Herrn, pf acc. op.4; Religiöse Gesänge, 8 bks, opp.22–7, 36–7; Salvum fac regem, op.43
Other: 4 geistliche Gesänge, 1v, pf, op.2; Salve regina, S, 2 vn, va, b, op.3; Miserere mei, S, A, pf, op.21; Ps ix, A, org, op.39; 6 geistliche Lieder (Novalis), 1v, pf, op.40; Magnificat, 1v, 2 vn, va, vc, b (Elberfeld, 1836); 5 geistliche Lieder, 1v, pf (Leipzig, n.d.)

SECULAR VOCAL

Operas: Ariadne (1 act), perf. Berlin, 1823; Dido (3, Rellstab), perf. Berlin, 1823
Choral: 5 Tafellieder, 4 male vv, op.14; Gesang der Geister über den Wassern (Goethe), 4 male vv, op.42
Other: Kinderlieder, 2vv, pf ad lib, op.35; 6 Terzette, 2 S, A, pf, op.44; *c*115 songs, 1v, pf: 9 as op.15 (Goethe), 3 as op.16 (Eichendorff), 2 as op.28, 3 as op.31 (Schwab, von Platen), 4 as op.41 (Goethe), 5 as op.46, others in collections without op. nos.

INSTRUMENTAL

Pf: 3 sonatas, opp.1, 5, 7; Fantasia, op.8; Variations, op.9; 2 variation sets without op. nos.
Other: Variations, str qt, op.38; Sonata, pf 4 hands (Bonn, 1838)

BIBLIOGRAPHY

L. Rellstab: 'Bernhard Klein', *Vossische Zeitung* (22 Sept 1832); *NZM*, iii (1835), 5
H. Truhn: 'Erinnerungen an B. Klein', *NZM*, xi (1839), 61, 65, 69
W. Neumann: *Zelter, Hummel, Klein*, Die Komponisten der neueren Zeit, xliva (Kassel, 1857)
C. Koch: *Bernhard Klein* (diss., U. of Rostock, 1902)
E. Schenk: 'Klein und die Musik des Ostens', *AMz*, lxv (1938), 699
W. Ehmann: 'Der Thibaut–Behaghel Kreis', *AMf*, iv (1939), 33
——: 'Briefe von Thibaut', *Neue Heidelberger Jb 1939*, 21
R. Sietz: 'Klein, Bernhard Joseph', *Rheinische Musiker*, ed. K. G. Fellerer, i (Cologne, 1960), 139

RICHARD D. GREEN

Klein, Henrik (*b* Rudelsdorf, Moravia, ?13 June 1756; *d* Pozsony [now Bratislava], 26 Aug 1832). Moravian composer and teacher, active in Hungary. He had his first music lessons from the *regens chori* at Röptau, then studied with Anton Hartenschneider, the cathedral organist at Olmütz (Olomouc) from 1768 to 1773. His first appointment was as Kapellmeister to Count Hodier; later he moved to Pozsony to teach music at the Convent of Our Lady. Count Ferenc Balassa arranged for a performance of his birthday cantata for Archduke Joseph Franz Leopold at the town theatre in 1799. About that time Klein began to write for the newly founded *Allgemeine musikalische Zeitung*, contributing a description of his recently perfected glass harmonica (1799) and an important anonymous article on Hungarian national dances (28 May 1800).

In 1804 Ferenc Kozma, director of a school where Klein taught for a year (1795–6), submitted two of Klein's sacred choral works to the Swedish Royal Academy of Music; these were favourably received, and Klein was elected a member of the Academy (24 July 1805). In 1807 he wrote a birthday cantata for Emperor Francis, and in 1816 he received a papal breve for a *Te Deum* celebrating the release of Pius VII from French captivity. He organized musical matinées at his home in 1816 and 1817, attracting such composers as Marschner and János Fusz.

Klein was an erudite and cultivated musician. Although he did not have close links with Hungarian music he is recognized there as an important educator of the early 19th century (his most famous pupil was Ferenc Erkel). Most of his surviving works are sacred choral compositions; three masses, a *Tantum ergo* and a *Veni Sancte Spirito* are in the library of the Bratislava College for Church Music and at the Körmöcbánya parish church.

BIBLIOGRAPHY

AMZ (1799–1821)
E. Major: 'Klein, Henrik', *ZL*

Klein, Johann Joseph (*b* Arnstadt, 24 Aug 1740; *d* Kahla, nr. Jena, 25 June 1823). German lawyer, writer on music and organist. On the title-page of his first published treatise, *Versuch eines Lehrbuchs der praktischen Musik* (Gera, 1783), he is referred to as a registered attorney to the dukes of Saxony and church organist in Eisenberg, and in 1801 he had been promoted to *Hofadvokat* and still held the post of organist. His *Versuch* is a practical treatise on basic musicianship, which discusses musical signs, melody and harmony (both separately and together), tuning, temperament, enharmonicism and continuo. It was widely read (and may have been translated into Danish; see Gerber) but lacks the depth and breadth of the principal German treatises from later in the century; at the time of Gerber's 'new' lexicon (1812) Klein was working on a revision that was never published. His second treatise, *Lehrbuch der theoretischen Musick* (written by 1798, published in Leipzig and Gera, 1801), discusses theoretical problems like sound production, resonance and the physiology of hearing, and includes illustrations of the scales and fingerings for most wind instruments then used. Klein also published an article on music theory (*AMZ*, i, 1798–9, cols.641ff), and another suggesting improvements in German singing schools (*AMZ*, i, 1798–9, cols.465ff). He edited a volume of 344 chorales (*Neues vollständiges Choralbuch zum Gebrauch bey dem Gottesdienste*, Rudolstadt, 1785, 2/1802), of which about 35 may have been of his own composition. Besides a popular setting of Gellert's *Morgengesang* (Offenbach; n.d.) no other secular compositions by him are known.

BIBLIOGRAPHY

GerberNL

H. Mendel and A. Reissmann: *Musikalisches Conversations-Lexikon* (Berlin, 1870–79, suppl. 1880, 3/1890–91/*R*1969)

J. Zahn: *Die Melodien der deutschen evangelischen Kirchenlieder* (Gütersloh, 1889–93/*R*1963)

ELLWOOD DERR

Klein, Josef (*b* Cologne, 1802; *d* Cologne, 10 Feb 1862). German composer and teacher. After a brief stay in Paris he went to Berlin to study with his stepbrother, Bernhard Joseph Klein. There he made the acquaintance of Heine, who became his lifelong friend and who later wrote the libretto for his opera *Die Batavier*. Klein then became a piano and singing teacher in Memel but, owing to ill-health, soon returned to Berlin. He spent his last years in Cologne. His chief significance as a composer of vocal music lies in his being among the first to set texts of Heine.

WORKS

Die Batavier (opera, Heine), lost, lib pubd

Choral: Hier liegt vor deiner Majestät, 4vv, orch; Die Schlacht auf Lora, 2vv, chorus, pf; Festgesang, 4 female vv, female chorus, pf; 6 Gesänge, 4 male vv

1v, pf: c75 lieder, ballads, romances, songs

Other: Die Jungfrau von Orléans, ov., orch; Grand Duo, vn, pf; Adagio und Rondeau, pf; Pf Sonata; 12 Variations, pf

BIBLIOGRAPHY

Obituary, *Kölner Zeitung* (21 Feb 1862)

R. Sietz: 'Klein, Joseph', *Rheinische Musiker*, ed. K. G. Fellerer, i (Cologne, 1960), 142 [with complete list of works]

Klein, Peter (*b* Zündorf, nr. Cologne, 25 Jan 1907). Austrian tenor of German birth. After study at the Cologne Conservatory and a season in the Cologne Opera chorus he sang at Düsseldorf, Kaiserslautern and Zurich. In 1937 he was engaged at the Hamburg Opera and in 1942 he moved to Vienna. He became a professor of opera and operetta at the Vienna Conservatory in 1956. He first sang at Covent Garden with the visiting Vienna Staatsoper in September 1947 (Jaquino); the next year he returned to sing Mime in the *Ring*, and for more than a decade he continued to be the outstanding exponent of the part. He was excellent in a host of character parts – Pedrillo and Monostatos, Blind (*Die Fledermaus*), Valzacchi (*Der Rosenkavalier*), Monsieur Taupe (*Capriccio*) – and was impressive in vital but small roles in such modern operas as *Wozzeck* and *Dantons Tod*; in 1965 he even sang Beckmesser at the Vienna Staatsoper.

PETER BRANSCOMBE

Klein, Rudolf (*b* Vienna, 6 March 1920). Austrian writer on music. He enrolled as a musicology student at Vienna University in 1938 and studied the organ privately under Louis Dité. In 1939 he emigrated to Belgium continuing his organ and theory studies at the Brussels Conservatory. He was deported to France in 1940, and after spending two and a half years in concentration camps escaped to Switzerland where he was able to resume his studies in Fribourg (1942) and to obtain his organ diploma (1946). In the same year he returned to Vienna and, in 1947, after a short period of further study at the university and the academy, he became music critic and editor for the *Wiener Kurier*, published by the American Forces of Occupation. When the newspaper ceased publication in 1955 he became an editor of the *Österreichische Musikzeitschrift* and in 1955 he also began writing programme notes for the Wiener Konzerthausgesellschaft. From 1963 to 1968 he also compiled and edited the programme notes of the Vienna Staatsoper. He organized and directed the public music academy in the Austrian pavilion at the World Fair in Brussels in 1958, and for this he was awarded the Austrian Gold Medal and the Grand Prix of the World Fair; in 1967 he received the title of professor from the Federal President. His writings include books on Frank Martin and J. N. David and topographical studies related to Beethoven and Schubert.

WRITINGS

Frank Martin (Vienna, 1960)

Johann Nepomuk David (Vienna, 1964)

Die Wiener Staatsoper (Vienna, 1967, 2/1969)

'Neues von Johann Nepomuk David', *ÖMz*, xxiii (1968), 593

Beethovenstätten in Österreich (Vienna, 1970)

'Traditionsstätten der Wiener Konzertpflege', *ÖMz*, xxv (1970), 290

'Von der Kunstwahrheit in den Analysen Johann Nepomuk Davids', *ÖMz*, xxv (1970), 165

with H. Graf and R. von Fischer: *Ernst Hess* (Zurich, 1970)

Das Symphoniekonzert: ein Stilführer (Vienna, 1971)

'Die Doppelgerüsttechnik in der Passacaglia der IV. Symphonie von Brahms', *ÖMz*, xxvii (1972), 641

Schubertstätten (Vienna, 1972)

'Die Antithese des musikalischen Pluralismus', *ÖMz*, xxviii (1973), 63

Other articles and reviews in *ÖMz*

Articles in *Grove 6*, including 'Vienna', §§5–6

WALTER SZMOLYAN

Kleine Flöte (Ger.). PICCOLO.

Kleine Trommel (Ger.). Side drum; *see* DRUM, §3.

Kleinknecht. German family of musicians. The name first appears in a collection of lute music in the Augsburg City Library and was later identified with a Protestant family in Ulm.

(1) Martin Kleinknecht (*b* Ulm, baptized 14 Oct 1665; *d* Giengen, 3 June 1730). The elder son of Hans

Conrad Kleinknecht, Martin was organist in Leipheim (near Ulm) during the late 17th century and later became a Kantor at Württemberg.

(2) Johannes Kleinknecht (*b* Ulm, baptized 7 Dec 1676; *d* Ulm, buried 4 June 1751). Younger son of Hans Conrad, he studied in Venice and from 1705 was principal violinist at Ulm Cathedral. He later also became assistant organist and devoted much of his attention to teaching and to the direction of an active Collegium Musicum.

(3) Johann Wolfgang Kleinknecht (*b* Ulm, 17 April 1715; *d* Ansbach, 20 Feb 1786). Violinist and composer, eldest son of (2) Johannes Kleinknecht. He first studied the violin with his father and apparently made an impressive début as a youthful performer. After studies at the Gymnasium in Ulm he toured several German cities with success and in 1733 became a member of the court chapel at Stuttgart. There he studied the violin with the Kapellmeister, Giuseppe Antonio Brescianello, and shortly thereafter embarked on another successful tour of many German courts. This led to an appointment as first violinist at the court of Eisenach, a position from which he soon obtained leave to serve as guest conductor at the court at Bayreuth. In 1738 he became the director at Bayreuth and in this capacity encountered many of the best performers from Berlin and Dresden, among them the violinist Franz Benda, whose style Kleinknecht thereafter adopted as a model. He returned to Eisenach briefly to fulfil his obligation to that court and to pursue his own musical studies, but after the death of his patron he again went to Bayreuth and remained until 1769, when the entire chapel moved to Ansbach.

Hiller described Johann Wolfgang as an outstanding violinist whose execution was noted for its rhythmic accuracy, energy, and beauty of tone, and claims these qualities enlivened the entire orchestra at Bayreuth. His biography first appeared in Meusel's *Miscellen* in 1782.

WORKS
(composer identified only as Kleinknecht)
6 sonatas, vn, bc (Paris, *c*1760)
3 Sonates or Duets, 2 vc/bn (London, 1774)
Lost works, listed in Brook: 7 concertos; 2 partitas, insts; sinfonia, insts; 14 trios, 2 vn, bc; 4 trios, 2 fl, bc; 6 duets, 2 fl

(4) Jakob Friedrich Kleinknecht (*b* Ulm, baptized 8 June 1722; *d* Ansbach, 11 Aug 1794). Composer and flautist, second son of (2) Johannes Kleinknecht. He studied first with his father and joined his brother in the chapel at Bayreuth as flautist in 1743. He shifted his attention to the violin in 1747, became the assistant Kapellmeister in 1748, court composer one year later and Kapellmeister in 1761. When the group moved to Ansbach in 1769, Jakob Friedrich continued as director, and it was there that most of his works were composed. His facility on both the violin and the flute is reflected in the distribution of his works between these two media. Jakob Friedrich's music, which is fluent and often original, warrants more attention and study than it has received.

WORKS
6 sonate da camera, fl, hpd/vc (Nuremberg, 1748)
3 trios, 2 fl, bc (Nuremberg, 1749)
6 Trios, 2 fl/vn, bc (London, *c*1750)
6 Trios, 2 fl/vn, bc, op.3 (Paris, 1767)
Concerto, 2 fl, orch (Paris, 1776)
2 sonatas, hpd, in Oeuvres mêlées, i, ii (Nuremberg, 1755–6)
Sinfonia concertante, kbd obbl, 2 fl, 2 ob, str, *D-Mbs*; concerto, vn, orch, *B-Bc*; Trio, 2 fl, bc, *Bc*; Sonata, 2 fl, bc, *D-KA*; Sonata, fl,

ob/vn, bc, *KA*; Sonata, fl, bc, *B*; Sonata, hpd obbl, fl/vn, *Mbs*; Sonata, hpd, *B*
Lost works, listed in Brook: 4 concertos, fl, orch; 3 trios, 2 fl, bc; 4 sonatas, 2 fl, bc; sonata, fl, kbd obbl

(5) Johann Stephan Kleinknecht (*b* Ulm, 17 Sept 1731; *d* Ansbach, after 1791). Flautist, youngest son of (2) Johannes Kleinknecht. Johann Stephan began his studies in philosophy and languages at the Gymnasium in Ulm, and at first had little interest in music. He later began to study the flute and in 1750 was sent to his two older brothers who by that time were members of the court chapel at Bayreuth. He soon became master of his instrument, spent some time in the service of the bishop of Breslau and returned to the Bayreuth court in 1754 as accompanist and musical companion to the prince. In this capacity he had the opportunity to travel and perform at courts outside Germany and soon established a reputation as one of the best flautists of the time. He moved to Ansbach with other members of the chapel in 1769. He may have contributed to some of the works for flute listed under the name of Jakob Friedrich, but no record exists of compositions under his own name. His autobiography appeared in Meusel (1782), reprinted a year later in Cramer.

(6) Christian Ludwig Kleinknecht (*b* Bayreuth, 12 Aug 1765; *d* Ansbach, 11 March 1794). Son of (4) Jakob Friedrich Kleinknecht, he was trained as a violinist, studied at Leipzig until 1788 and in 1789 was listed as a violinist and chamber virtuoso in the chapel at Ansbach.

BIBLIOGRAPHY
J. A. Hiller, ed.: *Wöchentliche Nachrichten und Anmerkungen die Musik betreffend*, i (1766), 183f
J. G. Meusel: *Miscellen artistischen Inhalts* (Erfurt, 1782)
C. F. Cramer: 'Nachrichten von einigen Virtuosen', *Magazin der Musik*, i (1783), 773
J. G. Meusel: *Teutsches Kunstlerlexikon oder Verzeichnis der jetztlebenden Künstler* (Erlangen, 1789)
J. A. Vocke: *Geburts- und Todtenalmanach Ansbachischer Gelehrten, Schriftsteller, und Künstler* (Augsburg, 1796)
C. F. D. Schubart: *Ideen zu einer Aesthetik der Tonkunst* (Vienna, 1806/R1969)
G. Schilling: *Encyclopaedie der gesammten musikalischen Wissenschaften oder Universal-Lexikon der Tonkunst* (Stuttgart, 1835–8)
R. Schaal: *Über die Ansbacher Musik* (Kassel, 1948)
B. S. Brook, ed.: *The Breitkopf Thematic Catalogues, 1762–1787* (New York, 1966)

DOUGLAS A. LEE

Kleinmichel, Richard (*b* Posen [now Poznań], 31 Dec 1846; *d* Charlottenburg, 18 Aug 1901). German pianist and composer. He received his first instruction from his father, Friedrich H. H. Kleinmichel (1827–94), a military and operatic conductor. From 1863 to 1866 he studied at the Leipzig Conservatory and then settled at Hamburg, where he published many works, mostly for his own instrument. His second symphony was given at the Gewandhaus at Leipzig with success. In that town he held for some time the post of Kapellmeister at the Städtisches Theater, and subsequently had similar appointments at Danzig and Magdeburg. His first opera, *Schloss de l'Orme*, based on Prévost's *Manon Lescaut*, was successfully produced at Hamburg in 1883, and his *Pfeifer von Dusenbach* there in 1891. He is best known for his simplified piano arrangements for vocal scores of Wagner's operas, published mostly during the 1880s, but in the last decade of his life he also made vocal scores of works by Paisiello, Mozart, Grétry, Isouard, Méhul, Cherubini, Berlioz, Lortzing and Humperdinck.

J. A. FULLER MAITLAND/R

Kleist, (Bernd) Heinrich (Wilhelm) von (*b* Frankfurt an der Oder, 18 Oct 1777; *d* Wannsee, nr. Potsdam, 21 Nov 1811). German writer. He was the great-nephew of the poet Ewald Christian von Kleist. Orphaned at an early age, he joined the army in 1792 but resigned in 1799. He travelled extensively, pausing at Dresden and Paris (1801), Berne, Königsberg (1805–6), Dresden (1807–9) and Berlin, near where he committed suicide with his incurably ill mistress.

Kleist played the flute and clarinet and, though untutored, attempted composition; yet music plays a rather small part in his literary works (one of his less successful stories is *Die heilige Cäcilie, oder Die Gewalt der Musik*). Many of his plays and stories have been used as the basis for musical compositions, with no sign of diminishing interest in the 20th century. Among these works are Marschner's incidental music for *Die Hermannsschlacht*, Wolf's incidental music to *Prinz Friedrich von Homburg* and the symphonic poem *Penthesilea*, Pfitzner's suite *Das Käthchen von Heilbronn* and *Gesang der Barden* (from *Die Hermannsschlacht*), Schoeck's opera *Penthesilea*, Henze's opera *Der Prinz von Homburg* and Egk's opera *Die Verlobung in San Domingo*.

BIBLIOGRAPHY

A. Schaefer. *Historisches und systematisches Verzeichnis sämtlicher Tonwerke zu den Dramen . . . Kleists* (Leipzig, 1886)
A. Bock: *Deutsche Dichter in ihren Beziehungen zur Musik* (Leipzig, 1893)
K. Goedeke: *Grundriss zur Geschichte der Deutschen Dichtung*, vi (Leipzig, 2/1898), 96ff
A. Mittringer: *Heinrich von Kleist: ein Beitrag zum Problem der musikalischen Dichtung* (diss., U. of Vienna, 1932)
D. P. Morgan: *Heinrich von Kleists Verhältnis zur Musik* (diss., U. of Cologne, 1940)
E. L. Stahl: *Heinrich von Kleist's Dramas* (Oxford, 1948)
H. Sembdner: *Heinrich von Kleists Lebensspuren: Dokumente und Berichte der Zeitgenossen* (Bremen, 1957, 2/1964)
H. Sembdner, ed.: *H. von Kleist: Sämtliche Werke und Briefe* (Munich, 1961, 3/1970)
K. Kanzog and H. J. Kreutzer, eds.: *Werke Kleists auf dem modernen Musiktheater* (Berlin, 1977) [incl. complete list of settings]

PETER BRANSCOMBE

Klemczyński, Julian (*b* Stare Miasto, nr. Kalisz, 1810; *d* Paris, ?1851). Polish pianist and composer. In 1831 he went to France, where he became a piano teacher at first in Meaux and later in Paris. His numerous works, mainly piano solos and duets, include pieces for violin and piano and flute and piano, the latter written in collaboration with Deneux de Varenne. His piano compositions, marked by sound craftsmanship and melodic inventiveness, were published in France, where they were popular; many were based on Polish folktunes. His works were favourably reviewed in the *Gazette musicale de Paris* (1834–7), but in 1842 H. L. Blanchard published in that journal a severe critique emphasizing Klemczyński's lack of originality; thereafter public interest in his music waned.

BIBLIOGRAPHY

FétisB
'Spis nowych dzeł muzycznych oryginalnych, w Niemczech wydanych w ostatnich czterech miesiącach 1835r.' [A list of new musical compositions, published in the last four months of 1835], *Pamiętnik muzyczny Warszawski* (1836), 107
M. Szurek-Wisti: 'Klemczyński, Julian', *PSB*

ZOFIA CHECHLIŃSKA

Klemm, Eberhardt (*b* Zwickau, 4 Sept 1929). German musicologist. He studied physics, philosophy and musicology with Bloch, Serauky, Wolff, Eller and others at Leipzig University (1949–54), taking the doc-torate there in 1966 with a dissertation on the theory of musical permutations. He was an assistant to Serauky and Besseler at the university's musicology institute (1954–65), a university lecturer (1957–66) and began freelance work in 1965. His chief interest is 20th-century music. He has published two books on Hanns Eisler, as well as numerous articles on contemporary musical theory, Mahler, Webern and Schoenberg. He has also edited various historical works on music (by Burney, Schindler, Debussy and Shaw), and has prepared editions of Mahler's Sixth Symphony (Leipzig, 1975), Debussy's piano works (Leipzig, 1968–73) and piano pieces by Gottschalk.

WRITINGS

'Notizen zu Mahler', *Festschrift Heinrich Besseler* (Leipzig, 1961), 447
'Über ein Spätwerk Gustav Mahlers', *DJbM*, vi (1961), 19
'Bemerkungen zur Zwölftontechnik bei Eisler und Schönberg', *Sinn und Form*, xvi (1964), 771
Studien zur Theorie der musikalischen Permutationen (diss., U. of Leipzig, 1966)
'Symmetrien im Chorsatz von Anton Webern', *DJbM*, xi (1966), 107
'Über Reger und Szymanowski', *Max Reger: Beiträge zur Regerforschung* (Meiningen, 1966), 82
'Zur Theorie der Reihenstruktur und Reihendisposition in Schönbergs 4. Streichquartett', *BMw*, viii (1966), 27
'Zur Theorie einiger Reihen-Kombinationen', *AMw*, xxiii (1966), 170–212
ed.: C. Burney: *Tagebuch einer musikalischen Reise* (Leipzig, 1968)
ed.: A. Schindler: *Biographie von Ludwig van Beethoven* (Leipzig, 1970)
'Der Briefwechsel zwischen Arnold Schönberg und dem Verlag C. F. Peters', *DJbM*, xv (1970), 5–66
ed.: C. Debussy: *Einsame Gespräche mit Monsieur Croche* (Leipzig, 1971)
'Hanns Eisler an Bertolt Brecht 1933 bis 1936: Briefexzerpte und Kommentare', *DJbM*, xvii (1972), 98
ed.: G. B. Shaw: *Musikfeuilletons des Corno di Bassetto* (Leipzig, 1972)
'Arnold Schönberg 1874–1974', *DJbM*, xviii (1973)
'Chronologisches Verzeichnis der Kompositionen Hanns Eislers', *BMw*, xv (1973), 93
Hanns Eisler: für sie porträtiert (Leipzig, 1973)
Hanns Eisler 1898–1962 (Berlin, 1973)
'Ernst Blochs Musikphilosophie', *Mélanges Ernst Bloch* (Paris, 1975)

HORST SEEGER

Klemm [Klemme, Klemmio, Klemmius], **Johann** (*b* Oederan, nr. Zwickau, *c*1595; *d* ?Dresden, after 1651). German composer, organist and music publisher. In 1605 he became a choirboy in the chapel of the electoral court at Dresden and in 1612 was appointed as an instrumentalist there. The following year he went to Augsburg to study at the elector's expense with the renowned organist Christian Erbach, with whom he remained until at least 1615. When he returned to Dresden, he started working at composition under Schütz; this led to a long-lasting association between the two men typical of the close ties that Schütz formed with many of his pupils. In 1625 he was appointed court organist; his duties included responsibility for the musical education of the choirboys, and in this capacity he taught the organ to Matthias Weckmann. He also became active as a music publisher, first in partnership with Daniel Weixer, later with Alexander Hering. His publications included some of his own music as well as collections by his teacher Schütz (the second set of *Symphoniae sacrae*, 1647, and the *Geistliche Chormusik*, 1648). The last reference to his activities as organist at the court chapel dates from 1651.

In 1631 Klemm brought out at his own expense in Dresden the *Partitura seu Tabulatura italica*, a collection of 36 fugues for two, three and four voices in the traditional 12 modes, suitable for organ or any other instruments. The fugues were printed in open score, a comparative novelty in Germany, where keyboard players were accustomed to reading from German organ tabulature. Klemm followed here the example of many Italian publications (hence the 'Italian Tabulature' of the alternative title), which, while perhaps more cumbersome for the performer, allowed clearer presentation of the contrapuntal structure (for ensemble performance he suggests in a postscript that individual parts can be copied out). The open-score layout, the strict modal part-writing 'abstaining from chromatic writing and diminutions' (to quote the postscript), indeed the entire nature of the work, all point to a deliberate attempt to provide a pedagogical model of instrumental *prima prattica* in line with the teachings of Schütz, stressing traditional strict counterpoint as the foundation of all compositional technique: in fact Klemm credited Schütz with instigating the work. A more progressive feature is the prevailing monothematicism, though in the handling of his subjects, as well as in other aspects of fugal writing, Klemm demonstrates a wide variety of approaches, making the collection a valuable source for the study of imitative forms current about 1630. It was apparently held in high esteem; 90 years later Mattheson still suggested that 'many a modern composer could surely learn a great many basic matters from it were he not to consider himself already too learned'.

Only one other piece by Klemm survives, the six-part *Lobe den Herren meine Seele* (*D-Z* 51, no.102, copied between 1664 and 1678). His *Teutsche geistliche Madrigalien* for from four to six voices and continuo (Freiberg, 1629) and the ten-part *Wohl dem der in Gottes Furcht steht* (formerly in an MS at the Kantoreigesellschaft, Pirna) are lost.

BIBLIOGRAPHY

J. Mattheson: *Critica musica* (Hamburg, 1722/R1964), iv, 272

R. Vollhardt: *Bibliographie der Musikwerke in der Ratsschulbibliothek zu Zwickau* (Leipzig, 1896)

A. Werner: 'Nachrichten über Johann Samuel Schein', *SIMG*, ix (1907–8), 634

L. Schierning: *Die Überlieferung der deutschen Orgel- und Klaviermusik* (Kassel, 1961), 15

W. Apel: *Geschichte der Orgel- und Klaviermusik bis 1700* (Kassel, 1967; Eng. trans., rev. 1972), 386

ALEXANDER SILBIGER

Klemm [Clemm, Clem], **Johann Gottlob** (*b* nr. Dresden, 12 May 1690; *d* nr. Bethlehem, Penn., 5 May 1762). American organ builder of Moravian birth. Klemm learnt his trade in Dresden, possibly from Gottfried Silbermann. Later he became attracted to the Moravian religious movement and moved to Count Zinzendorf's settlement at Herrnhut. In 1733 he emigrated to America, settling in Philadelphia. There in 1741 he built a three-manual organ for Trinity Church in New York City, and is known also to have made smaller organs and harpsichords. In 1745 or 1746 he moved to New York, and in 1757 settled in Bethlehem. Here, assisted by DAVID TANNENBERG, then a young apprentice, he continued to build small organs until his death.

BARBARA OWEN

Klemm & Brother(s). German importers of musical instruments and music publishers who worked in Philadelphia. John G. Klemm (*b* Neukirchen, 18 June 1795) emigrated from Saxony in 1819 to join Frederick August Klemm (*b* Neukirchen, *c*1795; *d* Philadelphia, 6 July 1876) in Philadelphia; together they formed the firm of Klemm & Brothers. From 1819 until 1879, the Klemms supplied the American musical public with wind instruments, strings and, for a time, pianos and music. Although city directories and advertisements occasionally list them as both manufacturers and importers, it appears that most of the instruments were made by their relatives George and August Klemm in Markneukirchen.

From 1819 until 1822 the firm sold imported instruments at 1 North 4th Street. From 1823 until 1832 only John G. Klemm was active. During that period he sold instruments imported from G. and A. Klemm, published music from plates purchased in 1823 from Bacon & Hart, Philadelphia publishers, and established (at 287½ High Street) a piano warehouse at which Alpheus Babcock (who came from Boston) built pianos from about 1830 to 1832. Klemm began to sell pianos in 1825, the same year he deposited a Babcock piano at the second annual exhibition of the Franklin Institute. In 1833 Frederick August Klemm returned and the firm of Klemm & Brother was established from 1833 until 1838 as a piano and musical warehouse, and from 1839 until 1879 as importers and dealers in musical instruments. Apparently F. A. Klemm ran the firm alone until the 1860s when his sons John George and Edward Meinel joined him in 1864 and 1868, respectively. The firm of Klemm & Brother does not seem to have functioned after 1879 although Frederick's two sons remained in Philadelphia for nearly two more decades.

The Klemms in Germany manufactured mostly wind and string instruments. An ornamented Klemm violin won an honourable mention at the 1851 London Exhibition. The Philadelphia Klemms supplied instruments to many military bands, especially during the Civil War. Their wind instruments can be found in major American collections; a piano made by Babcock for Klemm is at the Smithsonian Institution.

CYNTHIA ADAMS HOOVER

Klemperer, Otto (*b* Breslau, 14 May 1885; *d* Zurich, 6 July 1973). German conductor and composer of Jewish birth. After studying the piano with James Kwast and theory with Ivan Knorr at the conservatory in Frankfurt am Main, Klemperer followed Kwast to the Klindworth–Scharwenka Conservatory in Berlin, where he also studied composition and conducting with Pfitzner. In 1906 he replaced Oskar Fried at the last moment to conduct Max Reinhardt's production of Offenbach's *Orphée aux enfers* at the Neues Theater in Berlin. The previous year, on the occasion of a performance of Mahler's Symphony no.2, in which he directed the offstage orchestra, he had first encountered the composer who was to exercise a decisive influence on his career. It was on Mahler's recommendation that Klemperer was appointed chorus master and subsequently conductor at the Deutsches Landestheater in Prague in 1907 (making his début in *Der Freischütz*), and then at Hamburg from 1910 to 1912. Further appointments followed at Barmen (1913–14), Strasbourg (1914–17), where he was Pfitzner's deputy, and as musical director at Cologne (1917–24) and Wiesbaden (1924–7).

After 1918 Klemperer rapidly emerged as one of the leading German conductors of his generation (in 1923 he declined an appointment as musical director of the Berlin Staatsoper, where he felt he would have had insufficient artistic independence). His sympathy for and authoritative performances of an unusually wide range of contemporary music, as well as a less overtly emotional interpretation of the classics than had been common among older conductors, made him appear an expression of the 'new age'. He was therefore a natural choice as director when, in 1927, the Prussian Ministry of Culture set up a branch of the Berlin Staatsoper, whose special task was to perform new and recent works and repertory works in a non-traditional manner. This, the Staatsoper am Platz der Republik, played in the Kroll Theatre, from which it drew the name by which it is usually known. Klemperer's period there was of crucial significance in his career and the development of opera in the first half of the 20th century.

The Kroll Opera was an attempt to establish an institution representative of the new Weimar Republic, as the court opera Unter den Linden had represented the monarchy. It was therefore inevitably drawn into the bitter controversies that rent the republic. Growing economic distress, coupled with pressure from the Right, obliged the government to shut the Kroll Opera in July 1931 after only four seasons before it had had time to fulfil a role in opera similar to that played in 20th-century architecture by the Bauhaus (with which it had close ties). But the performance of operas, many of them for the first time, such as Stravinsky's *Oedipus rex* and *Mavra* (both produced by Klemperer), Schoenberg's *Erwartung* and *Die glückliche Hand*, Hindemith's *Cardillac* and *Neues vom Tage*, Janáček's *The House of the Dead* and Weill's *Der Jasager*, as well as the impressive list of new and recent orchestral works given at the Kroll concerts, is evidence of both bold experiment and lasting musical values. Although the vocal standards of the Kroll Opera were inevitably more modest than those of its parent house on Unter den Linden, the presence of conductors such as Klemperer (who also produced *Fidelio* and *Don Giovanni*), Alexander von Zemlinsky and Fritz Zweig ensured high musical standards; and designers such as Ewald Dülberg, Oskar Schlemmer and László Moholy-Nagy had a lasting influence on the development of operatic production after 1945. In particular, the Kroll Opera's drastically stylized production of *Der fliegende Holländer* (1929) was a decisive forerunner of Wieland Wagner's innovations at Bayreuth, after it reopened in 1951.

After the closure of the Kroll Opera, Klemperer remained with the Staatsoper, where on 13 February 1933 he conducted *Tannhäuser* on the 50th anniversary of Wagner's death. In April 1933 he emigrated, eventually going to the USA (where he had made his début in 1927). He became conductor of the Los Angeles PO (1933–9), conducted the New York PO and the Philadelphia Orchestra, and in 1937–8 played a part in the reorganization of the Pittsburgh Orchestra. In 1939 he underwent an operation for a brain tumour and his health and stability were so gravely undermined that he did little conducting for some years. His next regular engagement was at the Budapest Opera (1947–50), where he conducted an extensive repertory before leaving there because of the Communist regime's restrictive musical policies. In the early 1950s Klemperer accepted guest engagements in spite of having suffered further accidents and illnesses. But his reputation in Europe had become largely a matter of hearsay.

In 1954 a contract to conduct and make recordings with the Philharmonia Orchestra of London led to his appointment in 1955 as its principal conductor. At the age of 70 a new chapter in his life opened. By 1954 Furtwängler was dead and Toscanini retired, and

Otto Klemperer

Klemperer came to be generally accepted as the most authoritative interpreter of the Austro-German repertory from Haydn to Mahler, a reputation he retained until his retirement from public concert life in 1972. In 1961 he made his Covent Garden début, conducting and producing *Fidelio*; *Die Zauberflöte* followed in 1962, and *Lohengrin* in 1963. On his death, Klemperer's collection of annotated scores, letters and documents was given to the RAM, London. In 1973 a documentary film *Otto Klemperer's Journey through his Times*, with a soundtrack composed largely of Klemperer reminiscing in German, was made by the Dutch director Philo Bregstein.

Klemperer's performances were notable above all for their heroic dimensions and his architectural grasp. The detail revealed by his unfailingly lucid textures (prominent woodwind was a feature of his style) was always subject to his conception of a work as a whole. Yet this does justice only to the apollonian aspect of an unusually complex musical temperament. Until his later years, when his tempos became increasingly slow, his performances were also distinguished by a power and intensity that always remained subject to his grasp of structure. His interpretation of Mozart was controversial – detractors found it too plain and lacking in nimbleness, admirers praised its simplicity and directness. In Brahms he tended to emphasize what that composer owed to Beethoven rather than to Schumann, in Bruckner he realized the symphonies' monumental grandeur to a degree few conductors have equalled, and in Beethoven, a composer central to his vision, he achieved an uncontested authority. Even the characteristically unburnished Klemperer sound seemed essentially Beethovenian. But his outstanding achievement was to reveal the full extent of Mahler's genius, by rescuing his music from the rather sentimental style of interpretation that had been widely accepted.

Klemperer studied composition with Schoenberg in the mid-1930s in Los Angeles and was a prolific if spasmodic composer. His output includes an opera, a considerable number of songs (some settings of his own texts) and nine string quartets, as well as six symphonies, in a post-Mahlerian style. Not all these works have been performed. Many were extensively revised and a number were destroyed.

WORKS
(selective list)

Das Ziel, opera, 1915, rev. 1970, unperf.

Missa sacra, C, solo vv, chorus, children's chorus, org, orch, 1919; Psalm xlii, Bar, orch, 1919; Merry Waltz, orch, 1959; 6 syms. incl. no.1, 1960, no.2, 1967–9; 9 str qts, no.1 destroyed, nos.2–9, 1968–70; 17 works, 1v, orch, 1967–70; c100 songs, 1v, pf

Principal publishers: Hinrichsen, Peters, Schott, Universal

WRITINGS

Erinnerungen an Gustav Mahler (Zurich, 1960; Eng. trans., slightly enlarged, as *Minor Recollections*, London, 1964)

BIBLIOGRAPHY

R. Crichton: Obituary, *MT*, cxiv (1973), 933
P. Heyworth, ed.: *Conversations with Klemperer* (London, 1973) [with discography by M. Walker]
W. Legge: 'Otto Klemperer: Pages from an Unwritten Autobiography', *Gramophone*, li (1973–4), 1169, 1351
H. Curjel, ed. E. Kruttge: *Experiment Krolloper* (Munich, 1975)

PETER HEYWORTH

Klenau, Paul (August) von (*b* Copenhagen, 11 Feb 1883; *d* Copenhagen, 31 Aug 1946). Danish composer and conductor. He began music studies in Copenhagen in 1900 with Otto Malling (composition) and F. Hillmer (violin). With his move in 1902 to the Berlin Hochschule für Musik, where he studied composition under Bruch and the violin under Haliř, he started to enter Germanic circles, and as he did so he came to receive less recognition in Denmark. In 1904 he went to Munich as a pupil of Thuille, after whose death in 1907 he was appointed Kapellmeister to the Freiburg Opera. But he soon moved to Stuttgart, where he studied with von Schillings (1908) and took a post at the Hofoper (1909). His First Symphony had been performed at the 1908 Munich Tonkünstlerfest, and within five years it was followed by three more. Klenau was in Frankfurt in 1912 as conductor of the Bach Society; however, he returned in the next year to his position with the Freiburg Opera. By now his compositional interests had turned to dramatic music: in 1913 he completed *Sulamith*, a sacred opera on the *Song of Solomon*; *Kjarten und Gudrun*, an opera on Icelandic themes, was conducted by Furtwängler at Mannheim in 1918. Shortly after World War I he went to Schoenberg for a final period of study. The war had caused him to return to Copenhagen, where in 1920 he participated in the formation of the Danish Philharmonic Society. As conductor of that society (1920–26) he introduced much new music to Denmark, but his attempts to generate interest in Schoenberg's work at that time were unsuccessful. Feeling drawn back to German musical centres, he accepted a concurrent appointment as conductor of the Vienna Konzerthausgesellschaft (1922–30). Klenau returned in his later years to composing operas and symphonies; in his last opera, *Elisabeth von England*, his style evolved beyond the techniques of Bruckner and Strauss (these had marked most of his output) as he employed Schoenbergian atonal procedures. He remained in Vienna until advancing deafness began to limit his activities, returning finally to Copenhagen in 1940.

WORKS
(selective list)

Operas: Sulamith (after Bible), Munich, 1913; Kjarten und Gudrun (Klenau), Mannheim, 1918; Die Lästerschule (R. S. Hoffman, after Sheridan), Frankfurt, 1927; Michael Kohlhaas (Klenau, after Kleist), Stuttgart, 1933; Rembrandt van Rijn (Klenau), Berlin, 1937; Elisabeth von England (Klenau), Kassel, 1939; König Tannmor, unpubd
Ballets: Klein Idas Blumen (after Andersen: Lille Idas blomster), Stuttgart, 1916; Marion, Copenhagen, 1920
Orch: Sym. no.1, f, perf. 1908; Sym. no.2, c, perf. 1911; Sym. no.3 'Te Deum', solo vv, chorus, org, orch, perf. 1913; Sym. no.4 'Dante', perf. 1913; Jahrmarkt bei London (Bank Holiday – Souvenir of Hampstead Heath) (1922); Altdeutsche Liedersuite, small orch

(1934); Sym. no.5 'Triptikon', 1939; Sym. no.6 'Nordische', 1940; Sym. no.7 'Sturm', 1941; Vn Conc.
Vocal orch: Gespräche mit dem Tod (R. G. Binder), 6 songs, A, orch (1915); Die Weise von Liebe und Tod des Cornets Christoph Rilke (Rilke), Bar, chorus, orch, 1915
Pf: Geschichten von der Vierjährigen, 9 pieces (1915); Klein Ida Walzer [from ballet] (1916); 4 Klavierstücke (1922); 6 Präludien und Fugen (1939); other pieces
Other works: Str Qt, song collections

Principal publishers: Bote & Bock, Hansen, Schott, Universal
MSS in *DK-Kk*

WRITINGS
(see also Matthes)

'Arnold Schoenberg', *Musik* (Copenhagen, 1918), 129
'Das Wesen des Tragischen', *ZfM*, cvi (1939), 243

BIBLIOGRAPHY

R. Hove: 'Paul von Klenau', *DBL*
W. Matthes: 'Paul von Klenau', *ZfM*, cvi (1939), 237
'Paul von Klenau', *Kraks blaa bog 1944–46* (Copenhagen, 1946), 694
P. Hamburger: 'Paul von Klenau', *Aschehougs musiklexikon*, ii (Copenhagen, 1958), 36

WILLIAM H. REYNOLDS

Klencke, Helmina [Wilhelmine Christiane]. *See* CHEZY, HELMINA VON.

Klengel, August (Stephan) Alexander (*b* Dresden, 29 June 1783; *d* Dresden, 22 Nov 1852). German pianist, organist and composer. He became a pupil of Clementi in 1803, travelling extensively with him; their tour to St Petersburg in 1805 was such a success that Klengel remained there until 1811. After further tours to London, Paris and Italy, Klengel, though a Protestant, was appointed first organist at the Dresden Hofkapelle in 1817. Thereafter he travelled periodically but was decreasingly active as a pianist. His admirers included Fétis and Moscheles; Chopin reported his love of conversing with Klengel, 'from whom there is always something to be learned'.

Musically conservative, Klengel eschewed the contemporary trends of brilliance and emotionalism, favouring the Classical clarity of his teacher's generation. He was active in the Bach revival, editing *Das wohltemperirte Clavier* and performing Bach's fugues publicly as early as 1814. His chief work is a set of 48 canons and fugues, a fascinating example of neo-Baroque counterpoint. He also wrote piano concertos, chamber music, songs and other works for solo piano.

BIBLIOGRAPHY

R. Jäger: *August Alexander Klengel und seine Kanons und Fugen* (diss., U. of Leipzig, 1929)

JOEL SACHS

Klengel, Julius (*b* Leipzig, 24 Sept 1859; *d* Leipzig, 27 Oct 1933). German cellist and composer. He was brought up in a musical family (his brother was Paul Klengel) which could provide a piano quintet. He studied the cello with Emil Hegar and composition with Jadassohn. At the age of 15 he joined the Gewandhaus Orchestra, and was its principal cellist from 1881 to 1924. In 1881 he was made Royal Professor at the Leipzig Conservatory, and his pupils included Suggia, Feuermann and Piatigorsky. He toured Europe as a soloist and as a member of the Gewandhaus Quartet. He was praised for his fine sense of style and his admirable technique, particularly in Beethoven's sonatas and Bach's solo suites. He composed a great deal of music, including four cello concertos, the beautiful *Hymnus* for 12 cellos, and chamber works, but they are now of interest only to cellists. His editions of classical cello sonatas and concertos and the Bach suites are still used.

WATSON FORBES

Klengel, Paul (*b* Leipzig, 13 May 1854; *d* Leipzig, 24 April 1935). German conductor, violinist, pianist and composer, brother of Julius Klengel. He studied at the Leipzig Conservatory (1868–72) and at Leipzig University, graduating in 1876. His main activity was as a choral conductor in Leipzig (Euterpe Concerts, 1881–6), though he also had appointments in Stuttgart, and New York (1898–1902) before returning to Leipzig to conduct the Arion Society; later he joined the staff of the Leipzig Conservatory. He was a versatile musician, equally proficient as a violinist and a pianist. His compositions for violin are now rather outdated but his arrangements are still used for teaching.

WATSON FORBES

Klenovsky, Nikolay Semyonovich (*b* Odessa, 1857; *d* Petrograd, 6 July 1915). Russian conductor and composer. He graduated from the Moscow Conservatory in 1879, having studied composition with Tchaikovsky and the violin with Ivan Hřímalý. In the same year he assisted Nikolay Rubinstein in preparing the première of Tchaikovsky's *Eugene Onegin*. Besides directing the Moscow University orchestra, Klenovsky was a conductor at the Bol'shoy Theatre in Moscow (1883–93). He also composed much incidental music for plays at the Malïy Theatre. In 1893 he moved to Tiflis where, besides conducting the town's symphony concerts and taking charge of the local branch of the Russian Musical Society, he was able to develop further his interests in folk music. He had already been associated with Yuly Melgunov in harmonizing folksongs, and in 1895 he issued his own anthology, *Etnograficheskiy kontsert: sbornik pesen russkikh i inorodcheskikh* (reprinted in Moscow, 1926). From 1902 to 1906 he was deputy director of the imperial chapel in St Petersburg. As a composer, Klenovsky earned praise from Tchaikovsky, and it was in fact to Klenovsky that Vsevolozhsky (director of the imperial theatres) first offered *The Queen of Spades* as a subject for an opera; only when he failed to make any progress with the idea was the libretto passed first to Villanov and finally to Tchaikovsky. Klenovsky's three ballets were successfully mounted, but any successes among his other works were only transitory, and most of his music remains unpublished.

WORKS

Prelesti gashisha [The delights of hashish] (ballet), 1885; Svetlana (ballet), 1886; Salanga (ballet), 1900; 4 cantatas; Georgian liturgy (Moscow, n.d.); Mirazhi [Mirages], sym. picture; other orch pieces

BIBLIOGRAPHY

'Sovremennïye muzïkal'nïye deyateli: N. S. Klenovsky' [Contemporary musicians: N. S. Klenovsky], *RMG* (1900), 10

DAVID BROWN

Kleoneidēs. See CLEONIDES.

Klepalo. See SĒMANTRON; see also YUGOSLAVIA, §II, 2(v).

Klephoorn (Dutch). KEYED BUGLE.

Klerk, Albert de (*b* Haarlem, 4 Oct 1917). Dutch organist, composer and conductor, son of the Haarlem musician Joseph de Klerk. At the age of 16 he succeeded Hendrik Andriessen as organist of St Joseph in Haarlem. He then studied organ at the Amsterdam Conservatory with Anthon van der Horst and analysis with Andriessen. He graduated with honours in 1939 and was awarded the Prix d'Excellence in 1941. In 1956 he became city organist of Haarlem, and in 1964 chief organ teacher at the Amsterdam Conservatory. He has made several tours of western Europe and America and has made a reputation as a teacher and improviser. As a composer, he has written outstandingly for the organ in a conventional style of rich harmony.

WORKS

(*selective list*)

Org works incl. 2 concs., 1964, 1967; Sonata, 1942; Ricercare; Octo fantasiae; Twelve Images; Suite concertante, org, str, 1976
Missa 'Mater Sanctae laetitiae'; other sacred choral pieces
Chamber music, songs
Principal publisher: Donemus

BIBLIOGRAPHY

P. Visser: 'Albert de Klerk: Missa "Mater sanctae laetitiae", Ricercare for Organ', *Sonorum speculum*, xxiii (1965), 26

ROGIER STARREVELD

Kletzki, Paul [Klecki, Pawel] (*b* Łódź, 21 March 1900; *d* Liverpool, 5 March 1973). Swiss conductor and composer of Polish birth. He studied at the Warsaw Conservatory (composition, and the violin with Emil Młynarski) and later at the Berlin Academy. After playing in the Łódź PO, he became known as a composer and made his début at Berlin in 1923 conducting his own works. He settled there until 1933, when he went temporarily to Venice and then Milan, where he taught composition and orchestration at the Milan Scuola Superiore di Musica. After a year (1937–8) as musical director of the Khar'kov PO (USSR), he settled in Switzerland, taking Swiss nationality in 1947.

From 1945 Kletzki travelled widely as a guest conductor, making his British début with the Philharmonia Orchestra in 1947 and spending a season (1954–5) as principal conductor of the Liverpool PO. After tours in Central and South America he made his North American début in 1959 with the Philadelphia Orchestra. He was musical director of the Dallas SO (1960–63), then, in Switzerland, of the Berne SO (1964–6) and, on Ansermet's retirement, of the Suisse Romande Orchestra (1967–9). A conductor of wide experience and accomplished technique, he made a number of gramophone records which show his concern for lucidity of symphonic character and freshness of spirit. His compositions include four symphonies, violin and piano concertos, four string quartets and other chamber music and songs, but most were destroyed during World War II.

NOËL GOODWIN

Klezmer (Yiddish). A performing musician in the German ghettos and in many Jewish communities in eastern Europe. The *klezmorim* were professional musicians, generally of a high standard, who entertained at such festive occasions as weddings, circumcision feasts and social events; they were also often in demand to perform at the public festivities of their gentile neighbours. Frankfurt am Main, and in particular the Prague ghetto with its Judenstadt (1437) were centres of intense, highly professional cultural activity. The *klezmorim* also appeared at major services in the synagogues, where they performed instrumental preludes and interludes mainly on the flute, organ, violin and percussion. In the 18th and 19th centuries they often played the double bass, clarinet and trumpet. Christian authorities not only banned these competitive musicians from taking part in Christian festivities but often even prohibited them from playing at Jewish weddings inside the ghetto. It is recorded that the Archbishop of Prague in 1741 restored the right of Jewish musicians to perform. Among the most famous *klezmorim* was Michael Józef Guzikow (1806–37), a Polish flautist and player of the dulcimer and xylophone. He toured Europe, played for Mendelssohn and succeeded in arousing the admiration of many statesmen.

See also JEWISH MUSIC, §II.

SHLOMO HOFMAN

Klička, Václav (*b* Prague, 1 Aug 1882; *d* Prague, 22 May 1953). Czech harpist and composer. The son of the organist Josef Klička and brother of the harpist Helena Kličková-Nebeská, he studied the harp with Hanuš Trneček and theory and composition with Karel Knittl and Karel Stecker at the Prague Conservatory. From 1903 to 1910 he was a member of the orchestra at the Plzeň theatre, then taking up a solo career. He gave concerts in London, Hamburg, Berlin, Vienna and other European cities, and became one of the leading harpists of the day. During World War I he was active in Holland not only as a performer, but also as a propagandist for Czech music and Czech independence. After the war he returned to Prague, and in 1922 succeeded his sister as professor of harp at the conservatory, a position he held until the Nazi occupation. He continued his concert tours in Slovakia, Poland, Austria and elsewhere, and after 1945 again took a vigorous part in Czech musical life. Among his many distinguished pupils was Libuše Poupětová. His compositions, principally for the harp, consist of original works and arrangements, including fantasies on Czech and Slavonic folksongs and variations on themes of Krumpholtz and Mozart.

BIBLIOGRAPHY

ČSHS
V. Klička: Autobiographical memoir, *Sborník na paměť 125 let konservatoře hudby v Praze* [Commemorative volume for the 125th anniversary of the Prague Conservatory] (Prague, 1936), 338–75
L. Poupětová: Obituary, *HRo*, vi (1953), 459
M. Zunová-Skalska: 'Příspěvek k dějinam našeho harfového umění' [A contribution to the history of our art of playing the harp], *150 let pražské konservatoře* [150th anniversary of the Prague Conservatory] (Prague, 1961), 134
MIROSLAV K. ČERNÝ

Klien, Walter (*b* Graz, 27 Nov 1928). Austrian pianist. He studied the piano, composition and conducting in Frankfurt am Main (1939–45), in Graz (1946–9), and with Josef Dichler at the Vienna Academy of Music (1950–53), and also with Michelangeli and Hindemith (composition). He won prizes at the Bolzano Busoni Competition for pianists (1951 and 1952), the Marguerite Long–Jacques Thibaud Competition in Paris (1954) and in Vienna (1953). His tours have been in Europe, the Near and Far East, Africa and South America, and he made his début in the USA in 1969. As well as recitals, he has given concerts with many first-rank orchestras and conductors, frequently in international festivals. He is known equally for the clarity of his technique, the coolness and precision of his touch and his stylistic assurance. His many gramophone recordings include the first complete version of Brahms's works for piano solo, the complete works for piano solo and many piano concertos of Mozart, the complete piano sonatas of Schubert, several sonatas by Haydn, many works by Schumann, and music by such 20th-century composers as Stravinsky, Janáček and

Honegger. Both instrumentalists (including the violinist Wolfgang Schneiderhan) and singers (Hermann Prey, Julius Patzak) have chosen him as a partner for recordings, and he has made records of piano duets with Brendel and with his wife Beatriz.

RUDOLF KLEIN

Klimov, Mikhail Georgiyevich [Egorovich] (*b* Zavidovo, nr. Moscow, 22 Oct 1881; *d* Leningrad, 20 Feb 1937). Russian conductor, chorus master and teacher. After attending the Moscow Synodal School he studied composition with Rimsky-Korsakov and conducting with Nikolay Tcherepnin at the St Petersburg Conservatory, where he showed talent in conducting student opera productions. From 1900 to 1902 he taught choral singing and the violin at a teachers' seminary at Tambov. He was assistant teacher (1902–6) and later senior teacher (1913–17) of the court chapel choir. In addition he taught choral conducting, operatic ensemble and theory at the Petrograd Conservatory from 1908, and was appointed professor there in 1916. In 1921 he was appointed artistic director of the conservatory's opera studio, where he was responsible for many productions and for the training of such eminent singers as Vera Davidova, Alexey Ivanov and Sofiya Preobrazhenskaya. His most significant work, however, was as principal conductor of the Glinka Leningrad Academic Choir from 1919 to 1935 (including eight years as director, 1922–30); he expanded the repertory to include Western choral music, encouraged the composition of new works by Soviet composers for the choir, included women's voices from 1920, and admitted girl students to the formerly all-male choral school. In 1928 he made a successful tour with the choir to Italy, Switzerland and Germany. Klimov's scholarship and artistry embraced a wide variety of styles from Bach and Handel to Russian folksong, and under his direction the choir achieved outstanding virtuosity, enabling them to sing his vocal arrangements of instrumental works such as the waltz from *The Sleeping Beauty*, the Prelude to *Carmen* and Brahms's Hungarian Dances. Besides his choral arrangements he wrote several textbooks, including *Kratkoye rukovodstvo k izucheniyu kontrapunkta, kanona i fugi* ('A short guide to the study of counterpoint, canon and fugue', Moscow and St Petersburg, 1911).

BIBLIOGRAPHY

V. Muzalevsky: *Mikhail Georgiyevich Klimov: Ocherk tvorcheskey deyatel'nosti khorovovo dirizhora* [Sketch of the creative life of the choral conductor] (Leningrad, 1960)
D. Lokshin: *Zamechatel'nïye russkiye khorï i ikh dirizhorï* [Remarkable Russian choirs and their conductors] (Moscow, 2/1963)
I. M. YAMPOL'SKY

Klimov, Valery Alexandrovich (*b* Kiev, 16 Oct 1931). Soviet violinist. Son of the conductor Alexander Klimov, he studied with Mordkovich in Odessa before entering the Moscow Conservatory, where he was considered the most talented pupil of David Oistrakh, with whom he continued working until 1960. A prizewinner at international competitions in Paris and Prague in 1956, he was appointed a soloist with the Moscow Philharmonic in 1957; he won the 1958 Tchaikovsky Competition in Moscow. His playing is marked by stylistic authenticity, careful artistic polish and great technical mastery. He has performed widely in other countries, including the USA, Germany and Australia in the 1960s, and made his British début with the BBC

SO at the Festival Hall in 1967. He was made National Artist of the RSFSR in 1972.

I. M. YAMPOL'SKY

Klindworth, Karl (*b* Hanover, 25 Sept 1830; *d* Stolpe, nr. Oranienburg, 27 July 1916). German pianist, conductor and teacher. As a boy he learnt the violin and piano, and at the age of 17 conducted a travelling theatre company; a year later he conducted the first Hanover performance of *Le prophète*. From 1852 he was in Weimar, where he was one of a close circle of Liszt's pupils that included Bülow, Cornelius and Raff who constituted themselves 'Murls' (or anti-Philistine 'Moors') with Liszt as their Padischah, or president (see Liszt's letter to Klindworth of 2 July 1854). Liszt recommended him to Wagner as 'an excellent musician'. In 1854 Klindworth visited London, where he remained for 14 years, appearing as pianist and conductor; his playing was praised for its 'beautiful touch, fine expression and accurate reading' (*MT*, January 1855), and also in 1855 he played Henselt's Piano Concerto (with Berlioz conducting) 'in a free style, so that I was all on wires for an hour on end' (letter from Berlioz to Théodore Ritter, 3 July 1855). He organized two series of three chamber concerts in spring 1861 and 1862, and a series of three orchestral and vocal concerts, the 'Musical Art Union', in summer 1861. They were only fairly well received, being criticized for their mixture of classical and Romantic music, and were discontinued in 1862.

In 1855 Klindworth had met Wagner in England, an event he regarded as crucial to his whole career, and was entrusted with the preparation of the vocal scores of the *Ring*: these he brought out during his time as professor in Moscow, where he was appointed to the newly formed conservatory by Nikolay Rubinstein in 1868. He was an influential piano teacher though he was not popular, according to Hermann Laroche. In Russia, despite his Wagnerian views, he became friendly with Tchaikovsky, whose music he helped to introduce to Liszt and other Western musicians, though Tchaikovsky had doubts about the merits of Klindworth's versions (letter to Pyotr Jürgenson of 12 June 1882).

Returning to Germany in 1882 after Rubinstein's death, Klindworth became conductor of the Berlin Philharmonic concerts (with Joachim and Wüllner) and of the Wagner Society in Potsdam. There he played much Wagner, Liszt, Berlioz and Brahms, also giving the first local performance of Bruckner's Seventh Symphony. He founded a piano conservatory (1884), which on his retirement in 1895 was merged with Xaver Scharwenka's conservatory. He toured England and the USA in 1887–8 and retired in 1910. One of his last acts for the Wagner family was to adopt Winifred Williams; having schooled her carefully in Wagner, he introduced her to Wahnfried and to Siegfried Wagner, whom she married.

Klindworth made a number of effective arrangements (including one of Schubert's 'Great' C major Symphony for piano duet), rescored various works (including Chopin's F minor Piano Concerto), and published some original compositions and an *Elementarische Klavier-Schule*; he also made editions of Bach's *Das wohltemperirte Clavier* and of Chopin's complete works.

BIBLIOGRAPHY
D. Sasse: 'Klindworth, Karl', *MGG* [with list of pubd works, pf methods, edns., arrs. and bibliography]

JOHN WARRACK

Kling, Henri (Adrien Louis) (*b* Paris, 14 Feb 1842; *d* Geneva, 2 May 1918). Swiss horn player, teacher, conductor, organist, composer and writer of Franco-German birth. He grew up in his father's native Karlsruhe from 1844 and learnt the violin, the horn and music theory, eventually studying under the horn virtuoso Jacob Dorn. After some orchestral playing experience he went to Geneva in 1861, where he became a well known and widely influential musical figure. He took Swiss nationality in 1865. By 1862 he had become first horn at the Geneva opera and Concerts Classiques, where he played for 20 years, and in 1866 he was appointed horn professor at the Geneva Conservatory. He also taught solfège there from 1884, remaining on the staff until his death. When the city orchestra was founded in 1876 he became joint conductor for two years. In 1879 Kling became singing teacher at the Ecole Secondaire et Supérieure des Jeunes Filles, and about that time undertook conducting posts with the Landwehr band (1881–7), three local choral societies and the Kursaal orchestra (1886), as well as the post of organist of Cologny church (1881–1918).

Kling produced an exceptionally large number of textbooks, articles, reviews for periodicals in Germany (*Die Musik*, *NZM*) and France (*Le courrier musical*), original compositions and arrangements (many for various wind ensembles); he was a well-known adjudicator at brass band and *trompe de chasse* contests in different countries. His publications reflect his practical concerns, and over half the music consists of arrangements, but his original output explored many genres, including opera, of which he had four performed in Geneva. He wrote an important horn tutor and smaller tutors for other wind instruments, percussion, the mandolin and the double bass. The *Modern Orchestration and Instrumentation* includes remarks on piano reductions (he edited the Mozart clarinet and horn concertos for solo and piano), dance music, modern sound-effects and national differences in military band constitution and style.

Kling's son Otto (Marius) Kling (*b* ?Geneva, 1866 or 1867; *d* ?London, 7 May 1924) went to London in 1890, and was from 1892 manager of the English branch of Breitkopf & Härtel, and from 1915 to his death proprietor of J. & W. Chester.

WRITINGS
Populäre Instrumentationslehre (Hanover, n.d., enlarged 2/1883, further enlarged 3/1888; Eng. trans. as *Modern Orchestration and Instrumentation*, 1902, enlarged 3/1905)
Praktische Anweisung zum Transponieren (Hanover, 1885; Eng. trans., 1910)
Der volkommene Musik-Dirigent (Hanover, 1890)

BIBLIOGRAPHY
Obituary, *Schweizerische musikpädagogische Blätter* (1918), 189
Obituary, *MT*, lxv (1924), 558
E. Refardt: *Historisch-biographisches Musikerlexikon der Schweiz* (Leipzig and Zurich, 1928)
W. Tappolet: 'Kling, Henri Adrien Louis', *MGG* [with selective list of works]

DAVID CHARLTON

Klingenstein, Bernhard (*b* probably at Peiting, nr. Schongau, Upper Bavaria, between 2 March 1545 and 1 March 1546; *d* Augsburg, 1 March 1614). German composer. His gravestone in the cloister of Augsburg Cathedral gives his age at his death as 68. As a boy he was a pupil at the cathedral choir school, and later sang in the polyphonic choir as a sub-deacon. He evidently received no further musical instruction until the late

1570s, when he began to study composition with Johannes de Cleve. By this time, however, he had already been named – on 1 July 1574 – as cathedral Kapellmeister (for a portrait possibly of him in that position *see* AUGSBURG), having been preferred to the cathedral organist Jacobus de Kerle. (In June 1575 the latter was succeeded by Klingenstein's brother Christoph, who held the post until his death on 10 February 1581.) Klingenstein's duties as Kapellmeister included composing (he presented motets to the cathedral chapter in 1581, 1586 and 1601 and received remuneration), passing judgment on compositions offered by other musicians, and housing and training the choirboys under his care. He held several benefices from the cathedral and also served as Kapellmeister of the Augsburg Jesuit church, St Salvator. He seems to have been generally respected by his colleagues: for example, Gregor Aichinger, in his *Liber sacrarum cantionum* (1597), praised the cathedral chapter for entrusting its music to his 'skilful and diligent' direction.

The largest extant source of Klingenstein's music is his *Liber primus s[acrarum] symphoniarum* (a second book is not known to have been printed). It contains 34 Latin motets, most of which are scored for the customary ensembles of four, five and eight voices. Those for seven and eight voices are in Venetian *cori spezzati* style, possibly as a result of the influence of Aichinger and Hans Leo Hassler. One such work is the eight-part *Echo quae gelidas colens latebras*, in which the second choir is reserved almost exclusively for echo effects in the form of occasional chords punctuating the longer phrases of the first choir. The works in this collection are arranged by size of ensemble, from largest to smallest, an unconventional practice that gives the place of honour to the last composition, a setting of *Cantate Domino* for solo bass voice and continuo. It is the first solo vocal concerto known to have been published in Germany and is similar in style to Viadana's solo concertos for low voice in that the continuo part mostly doubles the vocal line (sometimes in a simplified version) but is occasionally independent. Klingenstein's concerto, the only piece in which he is known to have used the continuo, further indicates a close relationship with Aichinger, whose first collection of vocal concertos was published in the same year, 1607.

Rosetum Marianum comprises 33 five-part settings of German verses praising the Blessed Virgin, all of them based textually and musically on the traditional devotional song *Maria zart*. Some of the leading composers of the time in southern Germany and Austria are represented in this collection, including Rudolph and Ferdinand de Lassus, Luython, Jacob Regnart, Aichinger, Stadlmayr, Erbach, and Jakob and Hans Leo Hassler. Klingenstein's foreword describes how he distributed the verses of the poem, each composer selecting one verse. He himself chose no.12, *Maria süss, hilf dass ich büss*. The *Triodia sacra* (of which only one partbook survives) consists of 41 Latin tricinia designed, according to the title-page, 'for the use not only of novices but also of the more experienced'. Nine are by Klingenstein himself; the rest include many selected from existing sources, while others were newly composed. More than half are settings of texts from the Mass ('Crucifixus' and Benedictus) or of even-numbered *Magnificat* verses.

WORKS

Liber primus [34] s[acrarum] symphoniarum, 1–8vv (Munich, 1607)
Motet, 4vv, intabulated lute, 1586²³; 3 motets, 5, 8vv, 1590⁵ (2 repr. in 1607); litany, 8vv, 1596²; motet, 5vv, 1604⁷; 9 tricinia, 1605¹; secular song, 4vv, 1609²⁸; 4 bicinia in S. Calvisius: Biciniorum libri duo (Leipzig, 1612); 2 motets, 4vv, 1623², 1627² (both repr. from 1607, with added bc)
2 motets, 5, 6vv, *D-As*
2 motets, 4vv, *Mbs*
1 motet, 10vv, *Nst*

EDITIONS

Rosetum Marianum: unser lieben Frawen Rosengertlein . . . durch 33 beriembte Musicos . . . componirt, 5vv (Dillingen, 1604⁷), incl. 1 by Klingenstein; ed. in RRMR, xxiv–xxv (1977)
Triodia sacra . . . liber I, 3vv (Dillingen, 1605¹), incl. 9 by Klingenstein

BIBLIOGRAPHY

A. Sandberger: 'Bemerkungen zur Biographie Hans Leo Hasslers und seiner Brüder, sowie zur Musikgeschichte der Städte Nürnberg und Augsburg im 16. und zu Anfang des 17. Jahrhunderts': Introduction to DTB, v/2 (1904/R)
T. Kroyer: 'Gregor Aichingers Leben und Werke. Mit neuen Beiträgen zur Musikgeschichte Ingolstadts und Augsburgs': Introduction to DTB, x/1 (1909/R)
A. Singer: *Leben und Werke des Augsburger Domkapellmeisters Bernhardus Klingenstein (1545–1614)* (diss., U. of Munich, 1921)
R. Schaal: 'Klingenstein, Bernhard', *MGG* [incl. further bibliography]
A. Layer: *Musik und Musiker der Fuggerzeit: Begleitheft zur Ausstellung der Stadt Augsburg* (Augsburg, 1959)
WILLIAM E. HETTRICK

Klingsor. German or Hungarian poet, possibly mythical. Although Klingsor the magician in Wolfram von Eschenbach's *Parzifal* (c1200) is a fictitious character, it is possible that a poet of this name existed. The poem of the *Wartburgkrieg* (c1260) mentions him alongside more securely documented Minnesinger. Two melodies are ascribed to Klingsor in much later Meistersinger manuscripts; and indeed he was regarded by the Meistersinger as one of the 12 Old Masters (*see* MEISTERGESANG).

BIBLIOGRAPHY

H. Oppenheim: 'Klingsor', *Die deutsche Literatur des Mittelalters: Verfasserlexikon*, ed. W. Stammler, ii (Berlin, 1939)
U. Aarburg: 'Klingsor', *MGG*

For further bibliography *see* MINNESANG.

Klio. The Muse of history, represented with the kithara; *see* MUSES.

Klobásková, Libuše. *See* DOMANÍNSKA, LIBUŠE.

Klöde, Christian. *See* CLODIUS, CHRISTIAN.

Klöffler, Johann Friedrich (*b* Kassel, 20 April 1725; *d* Burgsteinfurt, 21 Feb 1790). German conductor and composer. From 1750 he was a musician and administrator at the court of the Counts of Bentheim and Steinfurt. In 1752 he founded the court orchestra, in 1753 became Konzertmeister and from 1754 was music director there; in 1757 he also took a judicial post at the court. After a concert hall was built on the grounds of the Steinfurt castle in 1770, Klöffler directed regular public concerts there. For these he composed numerous symphonies, concertos and chamber pieces (mostly for the flute) in the Mannheim style. About half of these works were published, and many were distributed in print and manuscript throughout Germany, the Netherlands, Denmark, Sweden, Finland and England. In 1773 Klöffler became a member of the 'Utili dulci' society of Stockholm. In 1777 he wrote one of his best-known works, a battle symphony in which two orchestras represent the opposing forces; the work was given in London (26 May 1783) at Almack's Rooms, sponsored by Salomon and Cramer. From 1781 to 1787 Klöffler made extended concert tours in Germany and to Copenhagen, Vienna, London, St Petersburg, Moscow and elsewhere. He retired from the Steinfurt court in 1789.

WORKS

Only those extant included; all printed works published in Amsterdam, unless otherwise stated.

ORCHESTRAL

Sinfonies périodiques: nos.iii in E♭, xv in B♭, xxiii in D (1769); no.i in D (1774); no.xxv in E♭ (1774); no.iii in F (Berlin, 1775 or 1776); no.i in C (n.d.)

Unpubd syms.: Bataille, 2 orchs, 1777, *D-BFb*, *SWl*, arr. 1 orch, *c*1781, *BFb*; 9 in *BFb*, *RH*, *Rtt*, *SWl*

Concs.: 3 for fl, 3 for 2 fl, op.1 (1765 or 1766); 3 for fl, op.2 (1767); 3 for 2 fl, op.3 (1766 or 1777); 1 for pf/hpd (1784); 1 for hpd, *c*1781, *BFb*; 8 for fl (incl. 2 for 2 fl), *BFb*, *RH*, *Rtt*, *SWl*, *DK-Kk*

CHAMBER

6 duettes, 2 fl, op.4 (1771); 6 sonatas, fl, bc, op.5 (1774); 6 sonates, pf, op.6 (1774); 6 duettes, 2 fl, op.7 (Berlin, 1780); 2 nonetto, fl, str, 1773, *D-BFb*, *SWl*; qnt, fl, str, 1773, *RH*, *DK-Kk*, *S-Skma*; qt, fl, str, *DK-Kk*; 6 qts for fl, 4 duets for fl, *D-BFb*, *DK-Kk*

BIBLIOGRAPHY

F.-H. Neumann: 'Klöffler, Johann Friedrich', *MGG*
U. Götze: *J. F. Klöffler (1725–1790)* (diss., U. of Münster, 1965) [incl. further bibliography and thematic catalogue]

URSULA GÖTZE

Klook. Nickname of KENNY CLARKE.

Klopstock, Friedrich Gottlieb (*b* Quedlinburg, 2 July 1724; *d* Hamburg, 14 March 1803). German poet. When still a schoolboy at Schulpforta he conceived the plan to write *Der Messias* which, inspired by Homer, Virgil, the Bible and Milton, occupied much of his time between the 1740s and 1773, the year in which the 20th and last canto was published. He studied theology and philosophy at Jena and Leipzig from 1745 to 1748, in which year the first three cantos of *Der Messias* appeared in the *Bremer Beiträge*. Its immense success led to invitations to Zurich (from Bodmer) and then to Copenhagen, where King Frederik V granted him an annual income and leisure to complete his great epic. In 1770, after the king's death and a change in political conditions, Klopstock moved to Hamburg, where he spent the rest of his life, with the exception of a journey to Karlsruhe during which he met Goethe and various admiring young contemporaries. Although he continued to be revered by many until the end of his life, he lost sympathy with recent developments in German literature.

Klopstock's interest in music was awakened by Gerstenberg in Copenhagen in 1764 and he became sufficiently keen to write poems to existing melodies, and to try to persuade eminent contemporary composers to set his odes. Among those who did are Telemann, C. P. E. Bach and Gluck (whom he met in 1775), Reichardt and Naumann. Later composers who set Klopstock include Beethoven, Meyerbeer, Schubert, Spohr, Schumann, Richard Strauss and Mahler (Symphony no.2). Although his poetry in many ways looks back to the Baroque era, he anticipated later developments in the intensely personal and emotional tones of much of his verse. His biblical dramas are stiff and monotonous, but the lyrical outpourings of the early cantos of *Der Messias* and the finest of the odes enable one to sense the liberating and indeed life-giving impact he had on German literature in the middle of the 18th century.

BIBLIOGRAPHY

A. Bock and A. R. C. Spindler, eds.: *F. G. Klopstock: Sämmtliche Werke* (Leipzig, 1823–30)
O. Koller: *Klopstockstudien* (Kremsier, 1889)

A. Bock: *Deutsche Dichter in ihren Beziehungen zur Musik: Klopstock* (Giessen, 1900)
K. Goedeke: *Grundriss zur Geschichte der deutschen Dichtung*, iv/1 (Dresden, 3/1916), 153ff, 1110ff
K. Viëtor: *Geschichte der deutschen Ode* (Munich, 1923)
G. Müller: *Geschichte des deutschen Liedes* (Munich, 1925)
E. A. Blackall: *The Emergence of German as a Literary Language* (Cambridge, 1959)
G. Kaiser: *Klopstock* (Gütersloh, 1963)

PETER BRANSCOMBE

Klose, Friedrich (*b* Karlsruhe, 29 Nov 1862; *d* Ruvigliana, Lugano, 24 Dec 1942). German-Swiss composer. He spent his school years in Thun and Karlsruhe, where he received instruction from Lachner and was definitively influenced by Mottl. His studies continued in Geneva with Ruthardt (Klose became a Swiss citizen in 1886) and, most importantly, with Bruckner in Vienna (1886–9). He returned to Geneva to teach at the Academy of Music and from 1891 he worked as a freelance in Vienna, Karlsruhe and Thun. After a year at the Basle Conservatory, he succeeded Thuille at the Munich Academy of Music in 1907, and in 1910 he was appointed professor. Increasing attention to his work was reflected in the Friedrich Klose Week celebrated in Munich in June 1918, but in that same year he stopped composing, and in 1919 he resigned his appointment, living in Thun until 1923, and then Tessin. His music was always written in response to pictorial or poetic ideas, and the symphonic poems contain much of his best work. The influence of Debussy is discernible in his later music, but Klose remained rooted in the Romantic tradition, particularly in the fairytale opera *Ilsebill*. He had himself written the texts for several earlier, uncompleted operatic projects. His published memoirs provide valuable insights into Bruckner's personality and into the Viennese musical life of the period, and they also contain aesthetic reflections on, for example, the conception of the 'Gesamtkunstwerk', which Klose thought might be renewed along the lines of *Carmen*.

WORKS
(selective list)

Ilsebill (opera, H. Hoffmann), perf. 1903; 9 inc. operas

Mass, d, solo vv, chorus, orch, org (1889); Die Wallfahrt nach Kevlaar (Heine), speaker, 3 choruses, orch, org (1910); Der Sonne-Geist (A. Mombert), solo vv, chorus, orch, org (1918)

Sym. poems: Elfenreigen, 1892; Das Leben ein Traum, 1896; Festzug, 1913

Prelude and Double Fugue, org, wind orch (1907)

String Quartet, E♭ (1911)

Songs incl. Verbunden (Rückert) (1892); 5 Gesänge (Bruno) (1918)

Principal publishers: Drei Masken, Kahnt, Leuckart, Luckhardt, Peters, Universal

MSS in *CH-Bu*

WRITINGS

'Über musikalische Erziehung', *Die Musik*, vii/7 (1907–8), 44

'Mein künstlerischer Werdegang', *Neue Musik-Zeitung*, xxxix/17 (1918), 235

Meine Lehrjahre bei Bruckner (Regensburg, 1927)

Bayreuth (Regensburg, 1929)

BIBLIOGRAPHY

R. Louis: *Friedrich Klose und seine symphonische Dichtung 'Das Leben ein Traum'* (Munich, 1905)
——: 'Friedrich Klose', *Die Musik*, vii/7 (1907–8), 28
H. Reinhart: *Der Sonne-Geist von Friedrich Klose* (Leipzig, 1919)
H. Knappe: *Friedrich Klose: eine Studie* (Munich, 1921)
——: *Friedrich Klose zum 80. Geburtstag* (Lugano, 1942)
F. de Quervain: 'Friedrich Klose', *SMz*, lxxxiii (1943), 221
E. Refardt: 'Der kompositorische Nachlass Friedrich Kloses', *SMz*, xciii (1953), 215
W. Zentner: 'Klose, Friedrich', *MGG*

PETER ROSS

Klosé, Hyacinthe Eléonore (*b* Corfu, 11 Oct 1808; *d* Paris, 29 Aug 1880). French clarinettist. He was notable for his collaboration with the instrument maker

Louis-Auguste Buffet in the production of a clarinet incorporating the ring-key mechanism applied to the flute by Theobald Boehm. The clarinet was exhibited in 1839 and patented in 1844 as a 'clarinet with moving rings'. In the 1860s it was given the name of Boehm clarinet. It became increasingly popular and is the system most generally in use today. Klosé came to Paris at an early age and enlisted in the band of a regiment of the Royal Guard. In 1831 he entered the Conservatoire as a pupil of Frédéric Berr, who formed such a high opinion of him that he dedicated his tutor of 1836 to him. Klosé became a bandmaster and taught at the Ecole Militaire de Musique. He played in the orchestra at the Théâtre Italien and appeared occasionally as soloist. When Berr died in 1838, Klosé succeeded him as professor at the Conservatoire and remained there for 30 years. He was a successful and much-loved teacher and had many notable pupils. Klosé wrote an admirable tutor for the Boehm clarinet which is still used extensively. He also wrote many clarinet solos and studies and three tutors adapted to different pitches of the newly invented saxophone. In 1864 he was made a Chevalier de la Légion d'Honneur.

BIBLIOGRAPHY
F. G. Rendall: *The Clarinet* (London, 1954, 3/1971)
O. Kroll: *Die Klarinette* (Kassel, 1965; Eng. trans., enlarged, 1968)
P. Weston: *Clarinet Virtuosi of the Past* (London, 1971)
PAMELA WESTON

Klose, Margarete (*b* Berlin, 6 Aug 1902; *d* Berlin, 14 Dec 1968). German mezzo-soprano. After study in Berlin with Marschalk and Bültemann she made her début at Ulm in 1927. From 1928 until 1931 she was a member of the Mannheim Opera, first coming to the notice of a wider public during the Paris Wagner season of 1930. From 1931 she was a member of the Berlin Staatsoper. In 1935 she sang Ortrud under Beecham at Covent Garden and in 1936 she began to appear at Bayreuth. She was heard in London again in 1937 (Fricka, Waltraute and Brangäne), and in 1939 she appeared in Rome for the first time. After the war she sang in North and South America, at the Salzburg Festival and in Italy, Spain, London and Vienna. In 1949 she moved from the Berlin Staatsoper to the Städtische Oper, returning to her old company in 1958. She retired in 1961. Klose's clear, rich voice and dignified stage bearing fitted her admirably for the Wagnerian mezzo roles in which she was best known; she was a distinguished Clytemnestra in *Elektra* and *Iphigénie en Aulide*, and she also appeared with success as Carmen, the Kostelnička (*Jenůfa*), Delilah and Albert's mother (*Albert Herring*), and in many of the Verdi mezzo roles.

BIBLIOGRAPHY
L. Riemens: 'Klose, Margarete', *Le grandi voci* (Rome, 1964) [with opera discography by R. Vegeto]
PETER BRANSCOMBE

Klosterneuburg. Town near Vienna with an Augustinian abbey. Founded in 1108 by the Babenberg margraves, it was originally a collegiate chapter, close to the residence of St Leopold, Margrave of Austria. Although the residence was subsequently moved to Vienna, Klosterneuburg's commanding position on the Danube near the capital enabled the canons to participate fully in the cultural life of Austria, especially during the Middle Ages. In 1133 the Augustinian canons were installed and from the first cultivated Gregorian chant, especially

psalmody. The cantor was responsible for the quality of the singing at Vespers (the musical ability of novices could apparently determine their acceptance into the convent) and during the Middle Ages he took charge of the monastery in the prelate's absence, an indication of the importance of his position. The Babenberg dukes, who had a lively interest in the abbey, secured vast estates and a valuable library for it. The large number of important manuscripts in neumatic notation includes the oldest psalter in the library (*A-KN* 987, probably 11th century) which contains two delicately neumed Gregorian settings of the Requiem and a famous miniature (David and four angels making music); it probably came from Hildesheim. The many neume manuscripts of the 12th and subsequent centuries were almost certainly written in Klosterneuburg; one of them (*A-KN* 574) contains a notable Latin Easter play from the early 13th century (the first performance was possibly in 1204), thought to be the oldest in the German-speaking area. It ends with the first verse of the hymn 'Christ ist erstanden'. The names of the abbey cantors (*regens chori* or *director musices*) can be traced only from the 15th century; until then organists, calcants (responsible for pumping the bellows of the organ) and lay choral singers were not recorded.

Wars and religious struggles during the 16th century caused a decline in cultural development. Gregorian chant was neglected in favour of polyphony and two manuscript collections of 15th- and 16th-century polyphonic music at Klosterneuburg contain works of Benedictus Ducis, Thomas Stoltzer, Finck, Stephan Mahu, Isaac, Arnold von Bruck and others. The library also contains music prints from Antwerp, including works by Philippe de Monte, George de la Hèle and Alard du Gaucquier, and a copy of Glarean's *Dodecachordon*. Early 17th-century accounts record the acquisition of musical instruments and employment of a teacher who taught the lay brothers the trombone; apparently there were also zink players, singers and organists. The great organ of the abbey church was built by J. G. Freundt of Passau between 1636 and 1642 despite the Thirty Years War. He installed some of the pipes from a Gothic organ and used pre-Baroque specifications for some of the registers; it is considered the most valuable organ in Austria.

During the Baroque period *Tafelmusik*, popular in all Austrian monasteries, was presumably fostered at Klosterneuburg, but the archives contain little secular 17th-century music; most of the church music is from the 18th and 19th centuries. The (partly Gothic) buildings were demolished during the first half of the 18th century and a new monastery, designed in the magnificent high Baroque style of Austrian contemporary architecture, was planned. Emperor Charles VI showed great interest in the plans, for he wanted a second El Escorial (as Charles III of Spain he had retreated there) created near his second residential city. The monks slowed down the construction of a castle and as the edifice was not suitable for monastic purposes and they would have been unable to afford its maintenance, they decided, on the death of the emperor, to alter the plans. The 'Austrian Escorial' remained a torso.

Emperor Charles VI, himself a trained musician and composer, influenced the music performed in Klosterneuburg. The music library contains church compositions by various court musicians including the 'Klosterneuburg Mass' attributed to Fux (the authenticity remains questionable) and works by Georg von Reutter and Caldara. M. G. Monn was a pupil and choirboy of the abbey. The library also possesses works (mainly religious) by Jommelli, Holzbauer, Joseph and Michael Haydn, Mozart, Gassmann, Gyrowetz, Dittersdorf, Salieri, Albrechtsberger, Cherubini, Weber, Schubert and others.

During the last third of the 19th century Bruckner often visited the abbey and improvised on the Freundt organ. From 1910 to 1924 Klosterneuburg accommodated the church music department of the Vienna Akademie für Musik, whose director, Vinzenz Goller, became known as a composer of church music in Catholic countries. The *regens chori*, Andreas Weissenbäck, achieved some distinction as a musicologist and composer. From 1906 onwards the use of Gregorian chant has been re-established and based on Vatican usage. A popular Roman Catholic 'liturgy in the vernacular' movement started in Klosterneuburg in the 1930s and had some influence on the development of Austrian church music.

BIBLIOGRAPHY
J. Kluger: 'Schlichte Erinnerungen an Anton Bruckner', *Jb des Stiftes Klosterneuburg*, iii (1910), 107
A. Koczirz: 'Klosterneuburger Lautenbücher', *Musica divina*, i (1913), 176
H. Pfeiffer: 'Das Klosterneuburger Österspiel', *Musica divina*, i (1913), 158
A. Weissenbäck: 'Aus dem älteren Musikleben im Stifte Klosterneuburg', *Musica divina*, i (1913), 153
H. Pfeiffer and B. Cernik: *Catalogus codicum manuscriptorum, qui in Bibliotheca Canonicorum Regularium S. Augustini Claustroneoburgi asservantur* (Vienna, 1922–31)
A. Orel: 'Zur Frage der rhythmischen Qualität in Tonsätzen des 15. Jahrhunderts', *ZMw*, vi (1923–4), 559
V. O. Ludwig: *Klosterneuburg, Stadt und Stift* (Klosterneuburg, 1927)
L. Schabek: *Alte liturgische Gebräuche in Klosterneuburg* (Klosterneuburg, 1930)
B. Cernik: *Das Augustiner-Chorherrenstift: statistische und geschichtliche Daten* (Klosterneuburg, 1936)
V. O. Ludwig: *Klosterneuburg: Kulturgeschichte eines österreichischen Stiftes* (Vienna, 1951)
E. Badura-Skoda: 'Zur musikalischen Vergangenheit Klosterneuburgs', *Festschrift Klosterneuburger Kulturtage 1959*, 41
EVA BADURA-SKODA

Klotz [Kloz]. German family of violin makers who worked in Mittenwald, Bavaria. Although members of the family have continued intermittently in the trade, the celebrated Klotz instruments date from the 18th century.

Mathias Klotz (*b* Mittenwald, 11 June 1653; *d* Mittenwald, 16 Aug 1743) was the originator of violin making in Mittenwald, and is commemorated by a statue in the centre of the town. So little is known of his life and work that much has had to be invented: visitors to Mittenwald are sometimes told that he studied violin making in Cremona, first with Amati, then with Guarneri, and finally with Stradivari himself. What is certain is that he was an apprentice with Giovanni Railich, a Paduan maker of lutes and kindred instruments, but almost certainly not of violins, and left the Railich workshop in 1678. He returned to Mittenwald and married, but his violins (now extremely rare) date from much later, and it seems that for 20 years or so he only used what he had learnt with Railich. A violin dated 1714 shows very good workmanship, more in the Italian style than after Stainer. Another from 1727 appears much more Germanic, though recognizably by the same hand. The varnish on both is excellent by Tyrolean standards.

Georg Klotz (*b* 31 March 1687; *d* 31 Aug 1737),

Sebastian Klotz (*b* 18 Jan 1696; *d* c1760) and Johann Carl Klotz (*b* 29 Jan 1709; *d* c1770) were sons of Mathias Klotz; all were born and died in Mittenwald. Sebastian was undoubtedly the best of these, as well as the most prolific. His instruments are made with delicacy and good taste, the best of them covered with a soft, glowing varnish, and have a quality of sound to match.

Aegidius Klotz (*b* Mittenwald, 1733; *d* Mittenwald, 1805) and Joseph Klotz (*b* Mittenwald, 1743; *d* Mittenwald, late 18th century) were sons of Sebastian Klotz. Each had a pleasing, individual style. By the last quarter of the 18th century violin making had become an industry in Mittenwald, employing many craftsmen whose names are for the most part little known. The term 'Klotz School' is often used to describe their instruments.

BIBLIOGRAPHY
W. L. Lütgendorff: *Die Geigen- und Lautenmacher vom Mittelalter bis zur Gegenwart* (Frankfurt am Main, 1904, 3/1922, rev. 6/1922/ R1968)
R. Vannes: *Essai d'un dictionnaire universel des luthiers* (Paris, 1932, 2/1951/R1972 as *Dictionnaire universel des luthiers*, suppl. 1959)
CHARLES BEARE

Klotz, Hans (*b* Offenbach, 25 Oct 1900). German organist and scholar. He studied the piano with W. Renner and theory with B. Sekles at the Hoch Conservatory in Frankfurt am Main (1919–22), and the organ with K. Straube, the piano with R. Teichmüller and theory with H. Grabner at the Leipzig Conservatory (1927–9). He also studied musicology at Frankfurt under M. Bauer, with philosophy and education as subsidiary subjects (1919–22, 1926–7) and took the doctorate there in 1927 with a dissertation on the acoustical aspects of notation. In 1933 he was an organ pupil of Widor in Paris. He held posts as organist, director of church music and president of the Bach Society in Aachen (1928–42), director of church music at St Nikolai, Flensburg (1946–52), instructor in organ at the Schleswig-Holstein Academy, Lübeck (1950–53), and professor of organ at the Staatliche Hochschule für Musik in Cologne (1954–66). He also taught at the summer school for organists in Haarlem (1962, 1969–71). Apart from his concerts in Europe and the USA, and his work as adviser on the construction of numerous large organs (Aachen Cathedral, Bonn University and the Beethovenhalle, the church of St Jacques, Liège, etc), Klotz has written valuable works on both historical and modern organ construction and playing. He has also composed several organ works.

WRITINGS
Über die Prägnanz akustischer Gestalten als Grundlage einer Theorie des Tonsystems (diss., U. of Frankfurt, 1927; Borna and Leipzig, 1927 as *Neue Harmoniewissenschaft*)
Über die Orgelkunst der Gotik, der Renaissance und des Barock: die alten Registrierungs- und Dispositionsgrundsätze (Kassel, 1934, 2/ 1975)
Das Buch von der Orgel: über Wesen und Aufbau des Orgelwerks, Orgelpflege und Orgelspiel (Kassel, 1938, 8/1972; Eng. trans., 1969 as *The Organ Handbook*)
'Bachs Orgeln und seine Orgelmusik', *Mf*, iii (1950), 189
'Vom rheinischen Orgelbau im 18. Jh.', *Beiträge zur Musik im Rhein-Maas-Raum*, ed. C. M. Brand and K. G. Fellerer (Cologne, 1957), 29
'Die kirchliche Orgelkunst', *Leiturgia: Handbuch des evangelischen Gottesdienstes*, ed. W. Blankenburg and K. F. Müller, iv (Kassel, 1961), 759–804
'Bauliche Beschreibung der heute anzutreffenden Orgeltypen: eine Bestandsaufnahme', *Orgel und Orgelmusik heute*, ed. H. H. Eggebrecht (Stuttgart, 1968), 105
'Die Orgel Johann Sebastian Bachs und die Wiedergabe seiner Orgelmusik', *Musik und Verlag: Karl Vötterle zum 65. Geburtstag* (Kassel, 1968), 397

'Les critères d'interprétation de la musique française sont-ils applicables à la musique d'orgue de J.-S. Bach?', *L'interprétation de la musique française aux XVIIe et XVIIIe siècles: CRNS Paris 1969*, 155

'Pour une histoire du plein-jeu', *Connaissance de l'orgue*, 2nd ser. (1971), nos.1, p.5; nos.2–3, p.6; (1973), no.4, p.8

'Aus der Geschichte der Orgeln zu Malmédy: SS Petri et Pauli', *Musicae scientiae collectanea: Festschrift Karl Gustav Fellerer* (Cologne, 1973), 263

'Die kanonischen Veränderungen in Entwurf, Reinschrift und Druck', *Die Nürnberger Musikverleger und die Familie Bach*, ed. W. Wörthmüller (Kassel, 1973)

'The Organ Works of Max Reger: an Interpretation', *Organ Yearbook*, v (1974), 66

'Romantische Registrierkunst: César Franck an der Cavaillé-Coll-Orgel', *Musik und Kirche*, xlv (1975), 217

'Erinnerungen an Charles-Marie Widor', *Ars organi*, xxiv (1976), 10

Numerous articles in *MGG*, *Neue deutsche Biographie*, *Grove 6* and other dictionaries

EDITIONS

M. Reger: Werke für Orgel, Sämtliche Werke, xv–xviii (Wiesbaden, 1956–9)

J. S. Bach: Die Orgelchoräle aus Leipziger Originalhandschrift, Neue Ausgabe sämtlicher Werke, iv/2 (Kassel, 1958); *Die einzeln überlieferten Orgelchoräle*, ibid, iv/3 (Kassel, 1958)

Orgelmeister der Gotik, Liber organi, viii (Mainz, 1958)

BIBLIOGRAPHY

W. Reindell: 'Hans Klotz en zijn artistiek werk', *De praestant*, vii (1958), 93

H. Klotz: 'Klotz, Hans', *Rheinische Musiker*, v, ed. K. G. Fellerer (Cologne, 1967) [incl. list of writings and bibliography]

HANS HEINRICH EGGEBRECHT

Klughardt, August (Friedrich Martin) (*b* Cöthen, 30 Nov 1847; *d* Rosslau, nr. Dresden, 3 Aug 1902). German conductor and composer. He studied in Cöthen and Dessau, later in Dresden. After working as a theatre conductor in Posen (1867–8), Neustrelitz (1868–9) and Lübeck (summer 1869), he became court music director at Weimar (1869), where he formed a friendship with Liszt. His compositions of these years include incidental music for theatre productions. At the première of Liszt's *Christus* in 1873 he met Wagner, to whom he dedicated his symphonic poem *Lenore*; his Symphony in F minor was composed under the impact of hearing the *Ring* at the first Bayreuth Festival in 1876. Having returned to Neustrelitz in 1873 as music director, he moved on to succeed his teacher Thiele at Dessau in 1882; he brought the ensemble to a high standard, giving the *Ring* in 1892 and 1893. His own works include the operas *Mirjam* (Weimar, 1871), *Iwein* (Neustrelitz, 1879), *Gudrun* (Neustrelitz, 1882) and *Die Hochzeit des Mönchs* (Dessau, 1886), orchestral, choral and chamber music and songs. In his operas he attempted to absorb a Wagnerian influence into number opera; his concert works also show his enthusiasm for the 'new German school' at the same time as his loyalty to classical practice. He had some success with his concertos for cello (1894) and violin (1895), and some of his chamber music was in the repertory of the Joachim Quartet; his oratorios, especially *Die Zerstörung Jerusalems*, were once widely known.

BIBLIOGRAPHY

L. Gerlach: *August Klughardt* (Leipzig, 1902)

W. Pfannkuch: 'Klughardt, August Friedrich Martin', *MGG* [with selective list of works]

JOHN WARRACK

Klukowski, Franciszek (*b* Zduny, Poznań, 1770; *d* Warsaw, 6 Feb 1830). Polish bookseller and publisher. From about 1816 he managed a music bookshop in Warsaw, which sold Polish and foreign music and also engravings of composers and virtuosos. Later he established a publishing house, at first adopting the old engraving techniques but turning gradually towards lithographic processes. He published works by many Polish composers, including Elsner, Kurpiński, Stefani and Damse, and piano miniatures, arias and opera excerpts from abroad; he also produced several educational books. After his death the firm was taken over by his nephew Ignacy Klukowski (1803–65), who directed it until 1858.

BIBLIOGRAPHY

T. Frączyk: *Warszawa młodości Chopina* [Chopin's early years in Warsaw] (Kraków, 1961), 235–74

M. Prokopowicz: 'Klukowski, Franciszek', *PSB*

KORNEL MICHAŁOWSKI

Klusák, Jan (*b* Prague, 18 April 1934). Czech composer. He graduated from the Prague Academy in 1957 as a composition pupil of Řídký and Bořkovec. Together with Libor Pešek, in 1958 he founded the Chamber Wind Ensemble, a group which took a lead in introducing new music to Prague audiences. His music has developed from a complex, tonal neo-classicism to 12-note serial writing of spontaneous invention, rhythmic freshness and imaginatively varied texture. The yearning, lyrical character of his work has something in common with the music of Berg and of Mahler, on a theme from whose Fifth Symphony he based the orchestral *Variace*. Most notable among his works is the series of *Inventions*, the second written for Darmstadt in 1962.

WORKS

(selective list)

Opera: Proces [The trial] (after Kafka), 1966

Orch: Bn Conc., 1954–5; 3 syms., D, 1956, 1959, 1959–60; Conc. grosso, wind qnt, str, 1957; Invention I, chamber orch, 1961; Variace na Mahlerovo tema, 1960–62; Invention III, str, 1962; Invention IV, 1964; Fantasie lyrique 'Hommage à Grieg', 1965

Chamber: Hudba k vodotrysku [Music for a fountain], wind qnt, 1954; Concertino, fl, str trio, 1955; 2 str qts, 1955–6, 1961–2; Obrazy [Pictures], 12 wind, 1960; Sonata, vn, wind, 1964–5; Rejdovak, b cl, va, db, 1965; 1–4–3–2–5–6–7–10–9–8–11, fl, 1965; Invention V, wind qnt, 1965; Invention VI, nonet, 1969

Choral works, vocal chamber music, songs, pf pieces

Principal publishers: Český Hudební Fond, Panton, Státní Hudební Vydavatelstvi

BRIAN LARGE

Klusen, (Karl Heinrich) Ernst (*b* Düsseldorf, 20 Feb 1909). German music educationist, musicologist and ethnomusicologist. He studied musicology with Kroyer and Bücken at Cologne University and music education at the Cologne Hochschule für Musik, taking the state teaching qualifications in 1931 and 1933; he obtained the doctorate under Schiedermair at the University of Bonn in 1938 with a dissertation on folksong in a village of the lower Rhine. In the same year he began teaching at the Gymnasium in Viersen, where he founded (1939) the Lower Rhine Folksong Archive; in 1953 he also became director of the Rhenish Folksong Archive in Bonn. Concurrently he was head of department at the Krefeld Seminar and director of the Rhenish Group for Youth and Folk Music (1952–62) before being appointed assistant professor (1962) and professor (1968) of music education at the Neuss Pädagogische Hochschule, where he has also served as dean (1970–72) and pro-dean (1972–6) as well as director of the institute for folk music research (from 1964). He is a member of several regional music commissions and chairman of the West German section of the International Folk Music Council, the working group for Rhenish music history and the folksong research committee of the German Folk Research Society. His publications include several books on folksong and on music teaching.

WRITINGS

Das Krefelder Musikleben von seinen Anfängen bis 1870 (Krefeld, 1938)

Das Volkslied im niederrheinischen Dorf: Studien zum Liedschatz der Gemeinde Hinsbeck (diss., U. of Bonn, 1938; Potsdam, 1941)

'César Franck und die Überwindung der Nationalstile im späten 19. Jahrhundert', *GfMKB, Lüneburg 1950*, 143

Der Stammescharakter in den Weisen neuerer deutscher Volkslieder (Bad Godesberg, 1953)

'Das aktuelle Lied', *Deutsche Zeitschrift für Volkskunde*, liii (1956–7), 184

'Die rheinischen Fassungen des Liedes von den 12 heiligen Zahlen im Zusammenhang der europäischen Überlieferung', *Studien zur Musikgeschichte des Rheinlands: Festschrift zum 80. Geburtstag von Ludwig Schiedermair* (Cologne, 1956), 57

'Die Melodienüberlieferung des Liedes von der Kommandantentochter', *Rheinisches Jb für Volkskunde*, viii (1957), 197

'Gustav Mahler und das böhmisch-mährische Volkslied', *GfMKB, Kassel 1962*, 246; see also *JIFMC*, xv (1963), 29

'Über gregorianisches Melodiengut im rheinischen Volkslied', *Karl Gustav Fellerer zum 60. Geburtstag* (Cologne, 1962), 103

'Beziehungen zwischen Volksliedforschung und Volksliedpflege', *Congresso internacional de etnografia: Santo Tirso 1963*, ii, 133

'Das apokryphe Volkslied', *Jb für Volksliedforschung*, x (1965), 85 ed.: *Das Bonner Gesangbuch von 1550* (Kamp-Lintfort, 1965)

'Musik zur Arbeit Heute', *Arbeit und Volksleben: Deutscher Volkskundekongress: Marburg 1965*, 306

'Gregorianischer Choral und reformatorisches Kirchenlied', *KJb*, l (1966), 75

'Über landschaftliche Volksmusikforschung: Grundsätze und Demonstrationen', *Zum 70. Geburtstag von Joseph Müller-Blattau* (Kassel, 1966), 129

'Das Gruppenlied als Gegenstand', *Jb für Volksliedforschung*, xii (1967), 21

'Zur Typologie des gegenwärtigen Jugendliedes', *Festschrift für Walter Wiora* (Kassel, 1967), 485

Rheinische Volkslieder in mehrstimmigen Sätzen: eine Zusammenstellung von Volksliedbearbeitungen (Cologne, 1968)

Volkslied: Fund und Erfindung (Cologne, 1969)

'Dokumentationsprobleme Musikalischer Volkskunde in Lichte wissenschaftlichen Selbstverständnisses', *Jb für Volksliedforschung*, xv (1970), 9

'Ingenium und Konsum: Beiträge zum Problem Komponist und Umwelt, dargestellt an der "Missa solemnis" von L. van Beethoven', *Mf*, xxiii (1970), 268

Bevorzugte Liedtypen Zehn- bis Vierzehnjähriger (Cologne, 1971)

Das Volkslied im niederrheinischen Dorf: Studien zum Lebensbereich des Volksliedes der Gemeinde Hinsbeck im Wandel einer Generation (Bad Godesberg, 1971)

Gefahr und Elend einer neuen Musikdidaktik (Cologne, 1973)

'Johann Peter Hebels Volksliedgutachten als Quelle der musikalischen Volkskunde', *Musicae scientiae collectanea: Festschrift Karl Gustav Fellerer* (Cologne, 1973), 270

Zur Situation des Singens in der Bundesrepublik Deutschland, i: *Der Umgang mit dem Lied*; ii: *Die Lieder* (Cologne, 1974–5)

Musikverständnis ohne Notenkenntnis (Berlin, 1975)

'Zwischen Symphonie und Hit: Folklore?', *Gedenkschrift für Michael Alt: Musikpädagogik heute* (Düsseldorf, 1975), 79

'Das Singen in der Schule von heute', *Handbuch der Schulmusik*, ed. H. Hopf and E. Valentin (Regensburg, 1976)

FOLKSONG EDITIONS

with H. Heeren: *Die Windmühle: Niederrheinische Volkslieder* (Bad Godesberg, 1955)

Des Dülkener Fiedlers Liederbuch, Viersen 1875 (Krefeld, 1963)

Volkslieder aus dem Kreis Kempen (Kempen, 1966)

with J. Lennards: *Lieder an Maas und Rhein* (Kempen, 1967)

with W. Hofmann: *Rheinisches Liederbuch* (Wolfenbüttel, 1967)

BIBLIOGRAPHY

E. Klusen: 'Klusen, Ernst', *Rheinische Musiker*, iv, ed. K. G. Fellerer (Cologne, 1966), 49 [with fuller list of writings to 1967 and further bibliography]

Klussmann, Ernst Gernot (*b* Hamburg, 25 April 1901). German composer and teacher. He studied in Hamburg and later (1923–5) in Munich with Haas (composition) and von Hausegger (conducting). In 1925 he was a vocal coach at the Bayreuth Festival and in the same year joined the staff of the Rheinische Musikschule and the Staatliche Musikhochschule in Cologne as a theory teacher. He returned to Hamburg in 1942 as director of the Schule für Musik und Theater and from 1950 to 1966 was professor of composition at the Hamburg Staatliche Musikhochschule. Mahler and Strauss provided the models for Klussmann's powerfully romantic early music, and their influence persisted even after he adopted a more linear, freely dissonant style that eventually led to his adoption of 12-note technique: his later works, despite their advanced tonal idiom, sometimes recall the earlier composers with respect to instrumental texture and melodic structure. Klussmann prepared the vocal scores of several operas by Strauss and Pfitzner.

WORKS
(selective list)

Orch: Epilog zu einer antiken Tragedie, 1931; 2 vc concs., 1932, 1968; Org Conc., 1933; 8 syms., 1934 rev. 1956, 1938 rev. 1957, 1939, 1941, 1946, 1964, 1967, 1970

Chamber: 2 str qts, 1927, 1940; Pf Qnt, 1925; Zenien, pf, 1945

Vocal: Hölderlin-Hymne, chorus, orch, 1932; Ultima Thule, S, male chorus, orch, 1950; Hymne an Zeus (after Aeschylus), chorus, 1954; 6 Canons, female chorus, 1955; Hamburger Lieder, 1959; Rhodope, opera, 1963; Helena, opera, 1966; lieder, choruses

Principal publisher: Tischer & Jagenberg

BIBLIOGRAPHY

E. Laaff: 'E. G. Klussmann', *ZfM*, ciii (1936), 529

F. Feldmann: 'Klussmann, Ernst Gernot', *MGG*

GEORGE W. LOOMIS

Klyuzner, Boris Lazarevich (*b* Astrakhan, 1 June 1909). Russian composer. He studied at the Leningrad Conservatory (1936–41) under Gnesin, also directing amateur choirs during this period. After war service in the army he returned to his choral work (1945–8). From 1955 to 1961 he was a member of the administration of the Soviet Composers Union Leningrad branch; he moved to Moscow in 1961. Klyuzner's first works marked him out as a lyrical composer, but he gravitated towards the expression of psychologically sharpened emotional contrasts. Accordingly his interests were centred on vocal chamber and concertante music, with a pathos, declamatory style and spontaneity of development that show signs of Mahler's influence. In time this influence was also felt in his shift towards large-scale, dramatically sophisticated vocal-symphonic works. This tendency from chamber to orchestral writing is apparent in his adaptation of the Cello Sonata (1936) into the Double Violin Concerto (1969); also, from two song sets – the Bagritsky poems (1935–6) and the English songs (1952–3) – there emerged the four-part poem *Vremena goda* ('The seasons').

The most important of Klyuzner's works, beginning with the Violin Concerto (1950), have prevailing gravity of tone, achieved through an expressive application of varied means. He has a predilection for clear polyphony, though without direct imitation of established forms or earlier music; his polyphony is often melodically fluid and economical, restrained and profound in expression. These features are particularly characteristic of his works with solo instruments, such as the Violin Concerto and the Violin Sonata, and polyphony predominates in the more concentrated, meditative episodes of other pieces. Swift and assertive movements are often linked rather with a stark, discordant Hindemithian counterpoint, as in the Piano Sonata no.2. In the climactic passages of orchestral works the polyphony at times gives birth to strong ideas accentuated by developing percussion parts, and in the Third Symphony by an additional group of electronic instruments. Alongside this, in works with extensive vocal contributions there are broad melodies, with a distinct Russian character, and a clear and expressive poetic prosody. Although Klyuzner's music is tonal in the main, he has used 12-note ideas, generally as thematic material, and also layers of free structure.

WORKS
(selective list)
Orch: Pf Conc., 1939; Vn Conc., 1950; 3 ovs., 1951, 1952, 1953; Sym. no.1, 1955; Sym. no.2, 1963; 2-Vn Conc., 1969
Vocal: Poema o Lenine (S. Davïdov), Bar, chorus, orch, 1960; Sym. no.3 (G. Yosuyosi, trans. V. Sikorsky), female chorus, children's chorus, orch, 1966; Vremena goda [The seasons] (E. Bagritsky, Shelley), S, Bar, orch, 1935–68; Sym. no.4 (Bagritsky, N. Zabolotsky, Mayakovsky), B, chorus, orch, 1972; 14 songs (Bagritsky, Blake, Burns, Keats, Pushkin, Shelley, Verkharn, Wordsworth)
Inst: Pf Preludes, 1936; 2 pf sonatas, 1935, 1966; Pf Trio, 1947

Principal publisher: Sovetskiy kompozitor

BIBLIOGRAPHY
G. Orlov: B. Klyuzner: Kontsert dlya skripki s orkestrom [Klyuzner's violin concerto] (Leningrad, 1959)
L. Rappoport: B. Klyuzner: Simfoniya (Leningrad, 1960)
GENRIKH ORLOV

Kmentt, Waldemar (b Vienna, 2 Feb 1929). Austrian tenor. He had embarked on a career as a pianist when he decided to study singing at the Vienna Academy of Music under Adolf Vogel, Elisabeth Rado and Hans Duhan. While a student he toured Holland and Belgium with an ensemble from the academy that included Walter Berry and Fritz Uhl, singing in *Die Fledermaus* and *Le nozze di Figaro*. In 1950 he sang the tenor part in Beethoven's Ninth Symphony under Böhm in Vienna, and the following year sang the Prince in Prokofiev's *The Love for Three Oranges* at the Vienna Volksoper. He was soon singing Mozart roles at the Theater an der Wien (the home of the Staatsoper until 1955) and sang Jaquino in *Fidelio* at the opening performance of the rebuilt Staatsoper. From 1955 he has sung regularly at the Salzburg Festival, where his roles have included Idamantes, Ferrando, Gabriel in Martin's *Le mystère de la Nativité*, and Tamino. In 1968 he sang Idomeneus at La Scala. He sang Walther von Stolzing at Bayreuth (1968–70) and has made guest appearances in France and Italy. Kmentt also appears regularly in concerts and as a recitalist.

HAROLD ROSENTHAL

Kmoch, František (b Zásmuky, 1 Aug 1848; d Kolín, 30 April 1912). Czech bandmaster and composer. He was the eldest of five brothers whose father was a clarinettist. He studied the violin at school in Zásmuky and Kolín and later at college in Prague. Returning to his native district as a schoolteacher in 1869, he began playing in and composing for local village ensembles. In 1873 this attention to musical activities, together with his interest in the recently formed patriotic Sokol movement, led to his suspension as a schoolmaster. He was appointed town bandmaster in Kolín, and eventually assembled a group of musicians capable of performing as a symphony orchestra, dance orchestra or wind band. As the fame of the band and of Kmoch's compositions spread, tours were made not only in Bohemia, Moravia and Silesia but also to Kraków (1884), Budapest (1886), Nizhny Novgorod (now Gorky, 1896) and Vienna (1899); later, invitations from as far as America were refused. Kmoch's output totals over 300 pieces, notably vocal marches, such as *Andulko šafářová*, *Česká muzika* and *Kolíne, Kolíne* (often built around Czech folk melodies), but also waltzes and other dances. Kmoch is esteemed as the

effective founder of the Czech band tradition, and in 1962 an annual June festival was established at Kolín, attracting bands from many countries. Kmoch was the subject of a biographical film *To byl český muzikant* (1940) and an operetta *Tak žil a hrál nám Kmoch* (by Jaroslav Jankovec).

BIBLIOGRAPHY
ČSHS
K. K. Chavalovský: *František Kmoch* (Prague, 1971)
J. Kapusta: *Dechové kapely pochod a František Kmoch* [The brass band march and František Kmoch] (Prague, 1974)
ANDREW LAMB

Knab, Armin (b Neuschleichach, Lower Franconia, 19 Feb 1881; d Bad Wörishofen, 23 June 1951). German composer and writer on music. In accordance with his father's wishes, he studied law, took his doctorate in 1904 and passed the state legal examination in 1907. At the same time he studied music theory with Max Meyer-Olbersleben, and his first compositions, some songs, were written between 1903 and 1907. From 1911 he worked as a lawyer, becoming judge in the provincial court at Würzburg in 1927. After 1920 he began to make a reputation as a composer and writer, principally in connection with the German youth music movement. He decided to devote himself to music in 1934, when he took an appointment to teach theory and composition at the Berlin Academy of Music Education and Church Music, where he was made professor in 1935. In 1943 the bombing forced him to leave Berlin, and he spent the remaining years of his life in South Germany. He was awarded the Max Reger Prize in 1940. His most important work was produced for educational purposes; his pieces range from simple songs in folksong style, with lute or piano accompaniment, to large-scale choral works.

WORKS
(selective list)
Choral: Mariae Geburt, cantata, 1921–3; Weihnachtskantate, 1931–2; Das heilige Ziel, hymns, 1935–6; Vom Bäumlein, das andere Blätter hat gewollt, cantata, 1941; Das gesegnete Jahr, oratorio, 1935–43; Vanitas mundi, cantata, 1946; Engelsgruss, cantata, 1946; Till Eulenspiegel, cantata, 1950; songs and canons
Solo songs, music for theatre and radio, inst pieces, educational arrs. of Bach, Beethoven, Bruckner, folksongs, etc

Principal publishers: Breitkopf & Härtel, Schott, Universal

WRITINGS
ed. H. Wegener: *Denken und Tun* (Berlin, 1959) [collection of essays, incl. list of works]

BIBLIOGRAPHY
H. Wegener: 'Knab, Armin', *MGG*
KLAUS L. NEUMANN

Knabe. American firm of piano makers. In 1837 William Knabe (b Kreuzburg, Berlin, 1803; d Baltimore, Maryland, 1864) established the firm in Baltimore in partnership with Henry Gaehle after training as a piano maker in Germany and emigrating to Baltimore in 1833. The firm Knabe & Gaehle advertised 'pianos of quality for genteel people of means'. When Gaehle died in 1855, Knabe continued the business under the title Knabe and Co. Knabe controlled the piano market in the majority of the southern states by 1860, but the Civil War had a disastrous effect on the firm because its market was so dependent on the South.

Knabe's sons Ernest Knabe (1827–94) and William Knabe (1841–89) were brought up in the business, and when their father died they re-established the firm's position as one of the leading piano makers in the USA. Ernest toured to arrange new agencies for the sale of

Knabe pianos in the northern and western states, and a direct agency was founded in New York in 1864. He also designed new string scales for their concert grands and upright pianos. The firm became one of the most important American piano makers, and by the turn of the century they were building about 2000 pianos annually. The Japanese government selected Knabe in 1879 to supply pianos for use in Japanese schools. The firm continued to prosper as a family concern until Ernest and William died, when it became a public company. Like other well-known American piano manufacturers (e.g. Chickering), Knabe was purchased by the American Piano Company in 1908. (William's two grandsons left the American Piano Company in 1911 to establish their own firm Knabe Brothers Company, which lasted until 1914). The firm continued to flourish, and in 1926 its pianos were officially chosen to be used at the Metropolitan Opera, New York, an association which has continued. In 1929 the firm moved to East Rochester, and since 1932 it has formed part of the Aeolian American Corporation there. In the early 1970s the firm continued to manufacture a range of grand pianos for domestic and concert use, in addition to 'console pianos', upright instruments about one metre high.

BIBLIOGRAPHY

D. Spillane: *History of the American Pianoforte* (New York, 1890/*R*1969)
A. Dolge: *Pianos and their Makers* (Covina, Calif., 1911/*R*1972)

MARGARET CRANMER

Knäfelius, Johann. *See* KNÖFEL, JOHANN.

Knape, Walter (*b* Bernburg an der Saale, 14 Jan 1906). German musicologist, conductor and composer. He studied under Kroyer, Zenck and Schultz at Leipzig University (1928–32), where he took his doctorate in 1934 with a dissertation on C. F. Abel's symphonies. He then became assistant lecturer at Leipzig and, 1948–1957, conductor of the Leipzig Sing-Akademie and the Philharmonic Choir. From 1954 he also lectured at the Berlin Hochschule für Musik. From 1957 he taught at the universities of Hamburg, Hanover and Cuxhaven. He has composed and conducted for radio, helped organize the *Generalkatalog deutscher Musik, Ost*, and arranged the archive of recordings now in Lower Saxony. He is best known for his research on C. F. Abel, of which the main product is *Carl Friedrich Abel: Kompositionen*, an edition of the complete works in 16 volumes and a thematic catalogue, published from his own press in Cuxhaven (1958–73). Of particular value is his inclusion of certain MSS destroyed in 1943. He has also produced recordings and performing editions of selected works and a study of Abel's life and music.

WRITINGS

Die Sinfonien von Karl Friedrich Abel (diss., U. of Leipzig, 1934)
'Karl Friedrich Abel – ein zu Unrecht vergessener Zeitgenosse Mozarts: zur geplanten Neuausgabe einiger seiner Sinfonien', *Musik und Gesellschaft*, viii (1957), 144
Bibliographisch-thematisches Verzeichnis der Kompositionen K. F. Abels (Cuxhaven, 1971)
Karl Friedrich Abel: Leben und Werk eines frühklassischen Komponisten (Bremen, 1973)

MURRAY R. CHARTERS

Knapp [née Byles], Janet (*b* Cobleskill, NY, 1 Sept 1922). American musicologist. She graduated from Oberlin College with a BA in 1944 and received an MA there in 1951. At Yale University she studied with Leo Schrade and took a PhD in musicology in 1961. She taught at Yale from 1958 to 1963, when she joined the faculty at Brown University. In 1971 she was appointed Mellon Professor of Music at Vassar College. Knapp specializes in medieval music, particularly the polyphonic conductus; her performing edition is a major contribution to the study of the subject.

WRITINGS

The Polyphonic Conductus in the Notre Dame Epoch: a Study of the Sixth and Seventh Fascicles of the Manuscript Florence, Biblioteca Laurenziana Pluteus 29.1 (diss., Yale U., 1961)
'Two Thirteenth-century Treatises on Modal Rhythm and the Discant', *JMT*, vi (1962), 200 [trans. of Jerome of Moravia: *Discantio positio vulgaris* and Anonymous VII: *De musica libellus*]
'Quid tu vides, Jeremia: Two Conductus in One', *JAMS*, xvi (1963), 212

EDITIONS

Thirty-Five Conductus for Two and Three Voices (New Haven, 1965)
The Polyphonic Conductus in the Manuscript Florence, Bibl. Laur. 29.1 (in preparation)

PAULA MORGAN

Knapp, J(ohn) Merrill (*b* New York, 9 May 1914). American musicologist. He received his BA from Yale University in 1936 and his MA from Columbia University in 1941. Since 1948 he has been on the staff of Princeton University, where he was appointed professor of music in 1960. He was also director of the Princeton Glee Club from 1947 to 1951 and has held administrative posts in the university. Knapp's main areas of study have been 16th-century instrumental music and the music of the 18th century, particularly opera and the works of Handel. In addition to his more scholarly works he has also written a general introduction to opera, *The Magic of Opera*.

WRITINGS

Selected List of Music for Men's Voices (Princeton, 1952)
'Handel, the Royal Academy of Music, and its First Opera Season in London (1720)', *MQ*, xlv (1959), 145
'Probleme bei der Edition von Händels Opern', *HJb 1967–8*, 113
'Handel's Giulio Cesare in Egitto', *Studies in Music History: Essays for Oliver Strunk* (Princeton, 1968), 389
'The Libretto of Handel's Silla', *ML*, l (1969), 68
with A. Mann: 'The Present State of Handel Research', *AcM*, xli (1969), 4
'Handel's Tamerlano: the Creation of an Opera', *MQ*, lvi (1970), 405
'The Autograph Manuscripts of Handel's Ottone', *Festskrift Jens Peter Larsen* (Copenhagen, 1972), 167
The Magic of Opera (New York, 1972)
'The Autograph of Handel's "Riccardo Primo"', *Studies in Renaissance and Baroque Music in Honor of Arthur Mendel* (Kassel and Hackensack, 1974), 331

EDITIONS

G. F. Handel: Amadigi, Hallische Händel-Ausgabe, ii/8 (Kassel, 1971)
G. F. Handel: Flavio, Hallische Händel-Ausgabe (in preparation)

PAULA MORGAN

Knapp, William (*b* Wareham, Dorset, 1698–9; *d* Poole, Dorset, buried 26 Sept 1768). English psalmodist. He was a glover by trade, and bought several properties at Poole, thus becoming one of its 60-odd burgesses. He was parish clerk of St James's Church, Poole, for nearly 40 years, and trained the choirs in several Dorset churches. He was a difficult personality, to judge from lines written by Henry Price (a land-waiter in Poole Quay) and quoted in *Grove 5* and also by Frost and Daniel.

Knapp compiled two collections of parish church music, both of which became widely popular: *A Sett of New Psalm-Tunes and Anthems* (eight edns., 1738–70) and *New Church Melody* (five edns., c1752–64). They contain didactic introductions, psalm tunes, hymns and parochial anthems, in four parts with the tenor leading. As well as music taken from earlier collections, they contain a good deal of Knapp's own composition. One of his psalm tunes, 'Wareham', is a classic of its period and is still well known; another, 'Spetisbury', survived at least until the second supplement to *Hymns Ancient and Modern* (1915). Many of the tunes in *New Church Melody* are of the ornate 'fuging' variety. Knapp's tunes and anthems reappeared in countless printed and MS collections, not only in many parts of England but in the American colonies also. Smith recalls that his tune for *While shepherds watched* was still being sung in Leicestershire late in the 19th century. One of his anthems, from the 1738 collection, is reprinted in Daniel. Knapp had an undoubted flair for effective melody, but was a little out of his depth in four-part counterpoint.

BIBLIOGRAPHY

H. P. Smith: 'William Knapp', *Proceedings of the Dorset Natural History & Antiquities Field Club*, xlvii (1926), 159

M. Frost, ed.: *Historical Companion to Hymns Ancient and Modern* (London, 1962), 679

R. Daniel: *The Anthem in New England before 1800* (Evanston, 1966)

P. M. Young: *A History of British Music* (London, 1967), 286f

N. Temperley: *The Music of the English Parish Church* (Cambridge, 1979), i, 159, 180f

NICHOLAS TEMPERLEY

Knappertsbusch, Hans (*b* Elberfeld, 12 March 1888; *d* Munich, 25 Oct 1965). German conductor. His parents' opposition to a musical career obliged him to study philosophy at Bonn University. Nevertheless from 1908 he also attended the Cologne Conservatory, where he was a conducting pupil of Steinbach. He conducted at the Mülheim/Ruhr theatre from 1910 to 1912; more significantly he spent the summers as assistant to Siegfried Wagner and Richter at Bayreuth. From 1913 to 1918 he was opera director at his home town of Elberfeld (and as such took part in the Wagner Festivals of 1913–14 in the Netherlands). In 1918 he went to Leipzig, in the following year to Dessau, where in 1920 he was made musical director. In this capacity he was called to Munich in 1922 as successor to Bruno Walter. He remained in Munich until 1936, when the Nazis revoked his life contract. The next nine years were spent in Vienna conducting at the Staatsoper and continuing a long association with the Vienna PO. After the war he returned to Munich, where he regained his former eminence, and was a leading conductor at the Bayreuth Festivals between 1951 and 1957.

Knappertsbusch was a large man of impressive appearance and robustly independent character. He made guest appearances in various European countries (he conducted *Salome* in the Covent Garden winter season 1936–7, although the German authorities had not allowed him to accept an invitation from Beecham for the previous summer) but was generally content to stay at home, a fact which increased his popularity in Munich even if it partly robbed him of the international fame won by more restless and ambitious colleagues. In life as in music he was a conservative in a broad sense, in his uncompromising attitude to political upstarts as in his easy-going preference for the revised editions of Bruckner symphonies over the original versions to which many conductors were returning. In the giant, unhurried stride of his conducting of Wagner and Bruckner, he appeared more and more as one of the last representatives of the old school. Orchestral players understood that his notorious dislike of rehearsals was based not on slackness or indifference but on mutual confidence and secure knowledge. He was never particularly interested in contemporary music, but during his first, long term in Munich he gave the first perfor-

mance of many operas, including *Samuel Pepys* by Albert Coates (1929) and Pfitzner's *Das Herz* (1931). Whatever his opinion of Wieland Wagner's innovations, his conducting, particularly of *Parsifal*, was probably the highest musical achievement of the postwar regime at Bayreuth (his interpretation is on record).

BIBLIOGRAPHY

F. F. Clough and G. J. Cuming: 'Hans Knappertsbusch Discography', *Gramophone Record Review* (1960), no.85, p.18

H. Hotter: 'Hans Knappertsbusch 1888–1965: in Memoriam', *Opera*, xvii (1966), 21

H. C. Schonberg: *The Great Conductors* (London, 1968)

RONALD CRICHTON

Knapton, Philip (*b* York, 20 Oct 1788; *d* York, 20 June (1833). English composer and music publisher. He was the son of Samuel Knapton, who succeeded Thomas Haxby as a music publisher and instrument maker in York about 1796. After receiving his musical education at Cambridge under Hague (though he never graduated from the university) he returned to York and joined his father's business about 1820. He was also active in local musical life and was one of the assistant conductors at the York festivals of 1823, 1825 and 1828. His published compositions consisted mostly of songs (including the popular *There be none of beauty's daughter*, *c*1818) and variations on popular airs, but according to Sainsbury he also wrote overtures, piano concertos and other works which remained in manuscript. Brown and Stratton also cited a *Collection of Tunes for Psalms and Hymns, selected as a Supplement to those now used ... in York* (York, 1810). The publishing business continued until 1829 when it passed into the hands of William Hardman, who in turn was taken over by Henry Banks; the firm is still in existence as Banks & Son.

BIBLIOGRAPHY

J. Sainsbury, ed.: *A Dictionary of Musicians* (London, 2/1825/R1966)

J. D. Brown and S. S. Stratton: *British Musical Biography* (Birmingham, 1897/R1971)

C. Humphries and W. C. Smith: *Music Publishing in the British Isles* (London, 1954, 2/1970)

PETER WARD JONES

Knarre (Ger.). RATCHET.

Knauth, Robert. See FRANZ, ROBERT.

Knecht, Justin Heinrich (*b* Biberach, 30 Sept 1752; *d* Biberach, 1 Dec 1817). German writer on music, composer and organist. He had musical instruction from local teachers, but was mainly self-taught. The writer C. M. Wieland, who lived near Biberach until 1769, was a friend and tutor of his. Knecht is said to have had his Singspiel *Kain und Abel* produced at the Biberach school when he was only 12. In 1771 he was appointed music director and organist in his native town, where he remained all his life apart from a short interlude during which he was court conductor at Stuttgart (1806–8). He enjoyed a great reputation as composer, organist and theorist of the Vogler school.

Knecht's works for the stage are mostly Singspiels in the style of Hiller. *Die Entführung aus dem Serail* (1787) is of interest as a setting of the libretto which Mozart had used five years earlier. His symphony *Le portrait musical de la nature* (*c*1784), for 15 instruments, has a printed programme which curiously anticipates the subject of Beethoven's Pastoral Symphony; in the same category, his *Die durch ein Donnerwetter unterbrochne Hirtenwonne* (1794), 'a musical portrayal for the organ', was apparently based on a famous organ improvisation by Abbé Vogler (*Spazierfahrt auf dem Rhein, vom Donnerwetter unterbrochen*).

Knecht's theoretical treatises are also indebted to Vogler, particularly his *Erklärung einiger . . . missverstandener Grundsätze aus der Voglerschen Theorie* (Ulm, 1785). His principal theoretical work, *Gemeinnütziges Elementarwerk der Harmonie und des Generalbasses* (Augsburg, 1792–8), suffers from his determination to give a complete range of the chord sequences made possible by mathematical theory (3600 being cited), without distinguishing musically significant ones from those arrived at through speculative calculation. Thus Knecht's theoretical system represents the opposite of the contemporary tendencies towards simplification which marked the development of music theory after J. F. Daube's *Generalbass in drey Akkorden* (1756). Knecht was one of the last harmonic theorists to explain chordal construction in terms of aggregations of 3rds. He also published several methods for organ, keyboard and continuo, a dictionary of music theory (Ulm, 1795), a musical catechism (Biberach, 1803), and many articles in music periodicals (including *AMZ*).

WORKS

Stage: Kain und Abel (Singspiel), c1765; Die treuen Köhler (Singspiel), 1772; Don Juan oder Das klägliche Ende eines Atheisten (incidental music), 1772; Die Entführung aus dem Serail (Singspiel), Biberach, 1787; Der Erntekranz (Singspiel), 1788; Der Schulz im Dorf (Singspiel), 1789; Der Musenchor (Singspiel), 1791; Der lahme Husar (Singspiel), 1797; Die Aeolsharfe (opera, 4, Remele), 1807; Das Lied von der Glocke (melodrama, Schiller), 1807; Feodora (Singspiel, Kotzebue), 1812

Sacred: Wechselgesang der Mirjam und Debora (F. Klopstock) (Leipzig, 1781); Lobgesang auf Gott, 4vv, insts (Hamburg, 1798), lost; Vollstimmige Sammlung . . . Choralmelodien, ed. Knecht and J. F. Christmann (Stuttgart, 1799; suppls. 1806–16); Hymnus Te Deum laudamus, 8vv, 16 insts (Offenbach, 1801); several psalms, pubd separately (c1783–95); others, incl. Magnificat, chorales, hymns, *A-Wgm, Wn, D-Bds, Dlb, USSR-KAu*

Other vocal: 3 Lieder, acc. pf/gui (Mainz, c1780); Versuch einiger zärtlichen und rührenden Stellen aus . . . Wielands Oberon, acc. kbd (Speyer, c1785); Musikalische Unterhaltungen für junge Liebhaber und Liebhaberinnen des Klaviers und Gesangs (Augsburg, n.d.)

Inst: Diverses danses, pf/(fl, gui) (Mainz, c1780); Le portrait musical de la nature, ens (Speyer, c1784); 12 variations, hpd/pf (Leipzig, c1785); 3 duos, fl (Speyer, 1791), lost; Sonates, kbd trio (Darmstadt, 1792), lost; Die durch ein Donnerwetter unterbrochne Hirtenwonne, org (Darmstadt, 1794); 4 Sonatines, pf, op.6 (Heilbronn, c1800); 48 Klavier-Vorspiele (Munich, 1802); De opstand in Jezus, prelude, org (Groningen, n.d.); many other pubd pedagogical pieces for kbd, org

BIBLIOGRAPHY

EitnerQ; *GerberL*; *GerberNL*
A. Bopp: *J. H. Knecht* (Biberach, 1917)
A. Sandberger: 'Zu den geschichtlichen Voraussetzungen der Pastoralsinfonie', *Ausgewählte Aufsätze zur Musikgeschichte*, ii (Munich, 1924/R1973), 154, 170f, 190ff
A. Bopp: *Das Musikleben der freien Reichsstadt Biberach* (Kassel, 1930)

ALFRED LOEWENBERG/KLAUS RÖNNAU

Knee-lever (Fr. *genouillère*; Ger. *Kniehebel*). Any of a variety of devices moving either horizontally or vertically, operated by the knee, and used for the production of expressive effects on a number of different types of keyboard instruments. A knee-lever was occasionally provided on reed organs to permit control of loudness, since the feet were already occupied with the pedal-operated bellows. Knee-levers preceded pedals for operating damper-lifting, muting and action-shifting mechanisms on continental pianos, and they were also used to activate the elaborate register-changing devices found on late 18th-century French harpsichords.

See also PEDAL.

EDWIN M. RIPIN

Knees [Kness], **Jurij**. *See* KNEZ, JURIJ.

Knefel, Johann. *See* KNÖFEL, JOHANN.

Kneif, Tibor (*b* Bratislava, 9 Oct 1932). German musicologist. He studied law at Budapest (1951–5, doctorate 1955) and Göttingen, where from 1959 he studied musicology under R. Stephan, philosophy under J. König and G. Patzig and Romance languages. He took his doctorate there in 1963 with a dissertation on the origins of medieval music studies. From 1963 to 1965 he was a research assistant at the Institute of Social Research in Frankfurt am Main under the directorship of T. W. Adorno. From 1967 he was research assistant at the musicology institute of the Free University in Berlin where he completed his *Habilitation* in 1971 and where he has since been active as a lecturer and (since 1973) professor of musicology. Influenced by Ernst Bloch and Georg Lukács, and in contrast to Adorno, Kneif treats music and the conception of music in modern times by considering it from the philosophico-aesthetic, socio-historical and sociological points of view.

WRITINGS

Zur Entstehung der musikalischen Mediävistik (diss., U. of Göttingen, 1963; extracts in *AcM*, xxxvi (1964), 123)
'Die geschichtlichen und sozialen Voraussetzungen des musikalischen Kitsches', *Deutsche Vierteljahrsschrift für Literatur und Geistesgeschichte*, xxxvii (1963), 22
'Forkel und die Geschichtsphilosophie des ausgehenden 18. Jahrhunderts', *Mf*, xvi (1963), 224
'Ernst Bloch und der musikalische Expressionismus', *Ernst Bloch zu ehren – Beiträge zu seinem Werk*, ed. S. Unseld (Frankfurt am Main, 1965), 277
'Gegenwartsfragen der Musiksoziologie: ein Forschungsbericht', *AcM*, xxxviii (1966), 72–118
'Das triviale Bewusstsein in der Musik', *Studien zur Trivialmusik des 19. Jahrhunderts*, ed. C. Dahlhaus (Regensburg, 1967), 29
'Historismus und Gegenwartsbewusstsein', *Die Ausbreitung des Historismus über die Musik*, ed. W. Wiora (Regensburg, 1969), 281
'Ideen zu einer dualistischen Musikästhetik', *IRMAS*, i (1970), 15
'Über funktionale und ästhetische Musikkultur', *Jb des Staatlichen Instituts für Musikforschung*, ii (Berlin, 1970), 108
'Bedeutung-Struktur-Gegenfigur: zur Theorie des musikalischen "Meinens" ', *IRMAS*, ii (1971), 213
'Die Idee der Natur in der Musikgeschichte', *AMw*, xxvii (1971), 302
'Musikästhetik', 'Musiksoziologie', *Einführung in die systematische Musikwissenschaft*, ed. C. Dahlhaus (Cologne, 1971)
Musiksoziologie (Cologne, 1971)
'Zur Entstehung und Kompositionstechnik von Bartóks Konzert für Orchester', *Mf*, xxvi (1973), 36
'Adorno und Stockhausen', *Zeitschrift für Musiktheorie*, iv/1 (1973), 34
'Anleitung zum Nichtverstehen eines Klangobjekts', *Musik und Verstehen*, ed. P. Faltin and H.-P. Reinecke (Cologne, 1974)
Die Bühnenwerke von Leoš Janáček (Vienna, 1974)
Revolutionsidee und Antisemitismus bei Richard Wagner (Munich, 1974)
'Sprachsatz und musikalischer Satz', *Musikalische Hermeneutik*, ed. C. Dahlhaus (Regensburg, 1974)
'Camille Durutte (1803–1881)', *AMw*, xxxii (1975), 226

HANS HEINRICH EGGEBRECHT

Kneller [Knöller, Knüller], **Andreas** (*b* Lübeck, 23 April 1649; *d* Hamburg, 24 Aug 1724). German composer and organist. Younger brother of the famous portrait painter Sir Godfrey Kneller, he became organist of the Jacobi- und Georgikirche, Hanover, in 1667. In 1685 he became organist of the Petrikirche, Hamburg, where he got to know Reincken and married one of his daughters. He was often asked to test new organs and organists, and was among those who examined Bach and others for the position of organist at the Jakobikirche, Hamburg, in 1720. From 1723 he received a pension. As a composer he is known by a handful of organ pieces. There are three preludes and fugues in a tablature at the church at Mylau, Saxony (one ed. M. Seiffert in *Organum*, iv/7, Leipzig, 1925, another in Shannon, ii), showing features typical of toccatas at the time. Two further works, a prelude and fugue and a praeludium (in *D-B*, both inc.), signed 'A. Kn.' and 'A. K.' respectively, are probably by him. The same source contains a set of eight variations by him on *Nun komm der Heiden Heiland*, the fourth and fifth of which appear twice in another manuscript (also in *D-B*; they are in K. Straube: *Choralvorspiele alter Meister*, Leipzig, 1907, where Kneller's first name is erroneously given as 'Anton'); the chorale melody is subjected to pleasantly varied treatment. An organ *Te Deum* in another source (in *D-Lr*) has sometimes been ascribed to Kneller, but the manuscript was compiled between 1657 and 1663 and is thus almost certainly too early to be by him. It is attributed to 'A. Kniller', and Apel believed it to be the only known work by one Anton Kniller.

BIBLIOGRAPHY
WaltherML
M. Seiffert: 'Matthias Weckmann und das Collegium musicum in Hamburg', *SIMG*, ii (1900–01), 129
——: 'Das Mylauer Tabulaturbuch von 1750', *AMw*, i (1918–19), 607
W. Stahl: 'Zur Biographie J. A. Reinken's', *AMw*, iii (1920–21), 232
F. Dietrich: *Geschichte des deutschen Orgelchorals im 17. Jahrhundert* (Kassel, 1932), 60
L. Krüger: *Die Hamburgische Musikorganisation im 17. Jahrhundert* (Leipzig, 1933), 170f
G. Frotscher: *Geschichte des Orgel-Spiels und der Orgel-Komposition* (Berlin, 1935–6, enlarged 3/1966)
H. David and A. Mendel, eds.: *The Bach Reader* (New York, 1945), 80
F. W. Riedel: *Quellenkundliche Beiträge zur Geschichte der Musik für Tasteninstrumente in der zweiten Hälfte des 17. Jahrhunderts* (Kassel, 1960)
L. Schierning: *Die Überlieferung der deutschen Orgel- und Klaviermusik aus der ersten Hälfte des 17. Jahrhunderts* (Kassel, 1961)
J. R. Shannon: *The Mylauer Tabulaturbuch: a Study of the Preludial and Fugal Forms in the Hands of Bach's Middle-German Precursors* (diss., U. of North Carolina, 1961)
W. Apel: *Geschichte der Orgel- und Klaviermusik bis 1700* (Kassel, 1967; Eng. trans., rev. 1972)
M. C. Bradshaw: *The Origin of the Toccata*, MSD, xxviii (1972)
HORACE FISHBACK

Kneller Hall. Home of the Royal Military School of Music; *see* LONDON, §VII, 4(ii).

Knepler, Georg (*b* Vienna, 21 Dec 1906). Austrian musicologist. He studied musicology with Adler, Fischer, Wellesz and Lach at the University of Vienna, where he took his doctorate in 1930 with a dissertation on form in Brahms's instrumental works; he also studied piano with Eduard Steuermann and composition and conducting with Hans Gál. He began his career as a Kapellmeister in Mannheim and was later active in Wiesbaden and Vienna; persecuted because of his political views he emigrated to England (1934), where he earned a living as a freelance conductor, accompanist and piano teacher until 1945. He also conducted various working-class choirs in London. After the war he returned to Vienna (1946) and subsequently moved to East Germany (1950), where he has remained. He was entrusted with building up a music college in East Berlin of which he was principal until 1959; from 1959 to 1970 he was professor of musicology at the Humboldt University, Berlin, and director of its musicology institute.

The principal spheres of his research are 18th- and 19th-century music history and the historiography of music. His major work, *Geschichte der Musik von der Französischen Revolution bis heute*, is in six volumes, of which the first (1960) concerns France and England, and the second (1961) Austria and Germany. In it he attempted to apply the method of historical materialism to the most important epochs of music history. His many essays, studies and articles, most of which have a strong ideological basis, chiefly concern Beethoven, contemporary music and questions of method. He is a member of the East German Academy of Science and is active in many international musicological organizations.

WRITINGS
'Die Form in den Instrumentalwerken Johannes Brahms' (diss., U. of Vienna, 1930)
'Bemerkungen zum Wandel des Bach-Bildes', *Wissenschaftliche Bachtagung der Gesellschaft für Musikforschung: Leipzig 1950*, 308
'Gustav Mahler', *Musik und Gesellschaft*, ii (1952), 7
'Das sowjetische System der Musikerziehung', *Musik und Gesellschaft*, iv (1954), 136
'Glinka und die deutsche Musikgeschichtsschreibung', *Musik und Gesellschaft*, iv (1954), 213, 253
'Motsart i sovremennost' [Mozart and the present], *SovM* (1956), no.1, p.54; no.2, p.64
'Mozart a česká lidová hudba' [Mozart and Czech folk music], *HRo*, ix (1956), 10
'Mozart: eine Gestalt der bürgerlichen Aufklärung', *Internationale Mozartkonferenz: Praha 1956*, 98
with E. H. Meyer and H. Goldschmidt: *Musikgeschichte im Überblick* (Berlin, 1956)
'Hanns Eisler und das Neue in der Musik', *Musik und Gesellschaft*, viii (1958), 344
'Die motivisch-thematische Arbeit in Händels Oratorien', *Händel-Ehrung der Deutschen Demokratischen Republik: Leipzig 1959*, 155
'Die Bestimmung des Begriffes "Romantik"', *Chopin Congress: Warszawa 1960*, 691
Geschichte der Musik von der Französischen Revolution bis heute (Berlin, 1960–)
Festrede zu Richard Wagners 150. Geburtstag (Leipzig, 1963)
'Zu Richard Wagners musikalischen Gestaltungsprinzipien', *BMw*, v (1963), 33
1000 Jahre Musikgeschichte in klingenden Beispielen, Jahrtausendwende bis 19. Jahrhundert (Berlin, 1966–70) [disc notes]
'Musikalischer Stilwandel und Geschichte', *IMSCR, x Ljubljana 1967*, 251
'Epochenstil?', *BMw*, xi (1969), 213
'Erinnerungen an Hanns Eisler', *BMw*, xi (1969), 3
'Improvisation – Komposition', *SM*, xi (1969), 241
'Das Beethoven-Bild in Geschichte und Gegenwart', *Internationaler Beethoven-Kongress: Berlin 1970*, 23
'Zu Beethovens Wahl von Werkgattungen', *BMw*, xii (1970), 308
'Čajkovskij: musicien type du XIXe siècle?', *AcM*, xliii (1971), 205
'Music Historiography in Eastern Europe', *Perspectives in Musicology*, ed. B. S. Brook, E. O. D. Downes and S. van Solkema (New York, 1972), 227
'Ein Forschungsunternehmen "19. Jahrhundert"', *BMw*, xvi (1974), 55
'Karl Kraus und die Bürgerwelt', *Sinn und Form* (Berlin, 1975)
Musikgeschichte als Weg zum Musikverständnis: Beiträge zu Theorie, Methode und Geschichte der Musikgeschichtsschreibung (Leipzig, 1976)
HORST SEEGER

Knez [Khnes, Khness, Khuess, Khüess, Khnies, Kness, Khues, Knees], **Jurij** [Georg] (*b* Vrhnika, nr. Ljubljana, mid-16th century). Singer and composer of Slovene descent. He is first mentioned as being a bass singer at the convent of Hall in the Tyrol (1582–9); he afterwards sang with the Salzburg court chapel (1589–92), dedicating his 'neu componierte Vespergesänge neben ainem musicalischen Magnificat' (now lost) to the chapter of Salzburg Cathedral. He spent periods at the courts of Munich (1588, 1590, 1592) and Stuttgart (1589, 1590); he was Kantor of the parish church at Hall (1593), a member of the Vienna royal chapel (1594–1612 and 1614–19); and was finally appointed *Provisionist* (a salaried position) in Salzburg (1620–21).

BIBLIOGRAPHY
L. von Köchel: *Die kaiserliche Hof-Musikkapelle in Wien von 1543 bis 1867* (Vienna, 1869), 50, 53
A. Sandberger: *Beiträge zur Geschichte der bayerischen Hofkapelle unter Orlando di Lasso* (Leipzig, 1895), iii, 175, 202, 283, 633

J. J. Meier: 'Archivalische Exzerpte über die herzogliche bayerische Hof-Kapelle', *KJb*, x (1895), 86

G. Bossert: 'Die Hofkantorei unter Herzog Ludwig', *Württembergische Vierteljahrshefte für Landesgeschichte*, ix (1900), 284

A. Smijers: 'Die kaiserliche Hofmusikkapelle von 1543–1619', *SMw*, vi (1919), 145

W. Senn: *Musik, Schule & Theater der Stadt Hall in Tirol* (Innsbruck, 1938), 173f

——: *Musik und Theater am Hof zu Innsbruck* (Innsbruck, 1954), 123

D. Cvetko: *Zgodovina glasbene umetnosti na Slovenskem* (Ljubljana, 1960), iii, 454

——: *Histoire de la musique slovène* (Maribor, 1967), 36

ANDREJ RIJAVEC

Kniehebel (Ger.). KNEE-LEVER.

Knight, Gerald (Hocken) (*b* Par, Cornwall, 27 July 1908; *d* London, 16 Sept 1979). English church musician. He became assistant organist at Truro Cathedral at 14, then went to Peterhouse, Cambridge (taking the MusB) and the RCM, London. He was organist of Canterbury Cathedral (1937–52) and then director of the Royal School of Church Music (1952–72). There he did much to raise the standard of Anglican choirs, to extend instruction and to make better music available; he also did much for overseas members. He was made CBE and Lambeth DMus.

STANLEY WEBB

Kniller, Anton. A 17th-century composer, almost certainly not identifiable with ANDREAS KNELLER.

Kniplová [née Pokorná], **Naděžda** (*b* Ostrava, 18 April 1932). Czech soprano. Raised in a musical family, she studied singing at the Prague Conservatory with Jarmila Vavrdová (1947–53) and at the Academy of Musical Arts with Ungrová and Otava (1954–8). After engagements at Ústí nad Labem (1957–9) and the Janáček Opera, Brno (1959–64), she became a principal of the Prague National Theatre, having won prizes at the Geneva (1958), Vienna and Toulouse (1959) competitions. From her Brno days she was noted for the dramatic force of her performances; the sonorous, metallic, dark timbre of her voice was particularly well suited to the dramatic soprano roles of Czech opera – notably Smetana's Libuše, Milada (*Dalibor*) and Anežka (*Two Widows*), and Janáček's Kostelnička and Emilia Marty. She has also sung Tosca, Aida, Senta, Ortrud, Brünnhilde and Isolde. In Brno she created splendid characterizations of Prokofiev's Renata (*The Fiery Angel*), Katerina in Martinů's *The Greek Passion*, and Shostakovich's Katerina Izmaylova. Her many international appearances, notably those at Vienna, Munich, Hamburg, San Francisco and New York, have been praised for their dramatic intensity, though some critics have commented on a certain lack of vocal purity or steadiness. In 1970 she was named Artist of Merit.

ALENA NĚMCOVÁ

Knipper, Lev Konstantinovich (*b* Tbilisi, 3 Dec 1898; *d* Moscow, 30 July 1974). Russian composer. He had no formal musical education in his early years; and it was not until 1922, after five years' military service, that he adopted music as a career and entered the Gnesin School of Music in Moscow, where he studied composition with Glier and Zhilyayev and the piano with Gnesina. During the 1921–2 season he also worked as a stage manager with the Moscow Art Theatre. He continued his compositional studies with Jarnach in Berlin and Julius Weissmann in Freiburg, returning in the mid-1920s to Moscow where he held, among other posts, that of musical adviser to the Nemirovich-Danchenko Music Theatre (1929–30). His earlier association with the armed forces was never completely dropped, however, and throughout his life Knipper held occasional posts in the music section of the Red Army. During 1932 he was music instructor to the troops of the Red Army Far Eastern Division, and he worked thereafter in the music propaganda department of the Red Army in Moscow. In 1942 and 1944 he was attached to the Red Army in Persia, and again acted as music instructor to the troops in the Ukraine in 1945 and in Buryat-Mongolia in 1946.

As a young composer in the mid-1920s Knipper aligned himself with the German-influenced avant garde. He was a member of the Association of Contemporary Music in Moscow, and under its auspices had some of his early works performed in the West. His most sophisticated composition – and his most important work historically – is the opera *Severnïy veter* ('The north wind', 1929–30). Based on Kirshon's tragic tale of the mass execution of commissars in Baku during the Civil War, the opera is in a declamatory, satirical style, musically advanced for its time. It was staged in Moscow in March 1930, but thereafter, along with Shostakovich's *The Nose* with which it has certain affinities, it was strongly criticized for its irrelevant modernism. Knipper's musical idiom underwent a radical change at the beginning of the 1930s when, in keeping with party policy, he turned to the ideals of realist music. His main achievements as a composer were his 14 symphonies (1929–54). Of these, the most famous and probably the best are the Third (1932–3), dedicated to the Far Eastern Red Army, and the Fourth (1933–4), sub-titled 'Poem about the Fighting Komsomol'. Both these works are characteristic (and perhaps the finest examples) of the Soviet song-symphony of the 1930s – a hybrid genre, of deliberate mass appeal, which combines elements of the symphony and the choral mass song. The songs were detachable, and *Meadowland* from the Fourth Symphony is among the best-known tunes of its time.

In the summer of 1930 Knipper visited the Caucasus, and he spent the following summer in the Pamir mountains of Tadzhikstan studying the local folk culture. From this period dates his lasting interest in the national musics of the outer republics of the USSR and (later) Persia. Several of his works written in the 1930s, including the orchestral suites *Stalinabad* (1931) and *Vanch* (1932) and the overture *Vakhio Bolo* (1933), are based on Tadzhik themes; of these *Vanch* is particularly successful in the integration of its material. Knipper also composed orchestral works based on Persian themes, a ballet, *Istochnik schast'ya* ('The source of happiness', 1949), on Tadzhik themes, and an opera, *Na Baykale* ('On Lake Baykal', 1946–8), on Mongolian themes. Though his symphonies are rarely heard, these more exotic works, along with his songs and his suites for children, remain in the Soviet repertory.

WORKS
(*selective list*)

DRAMATIC AND VOCAL

Operas: Severnïy veter [The north wind], 1929–30; Marya, 1936–8; Aktrisa [The actress], 1942; Na Baykale [On Lake Baykal], 1946–8; Koren' zhizni [The source of life], 1948–9

Opera-ballets: Kandida, 1926–7; Krasavitsa Angara [The beautiful
Angara], 1962
Ballets: Negritenok Sebi [The little negro Sebi], 1929, collab. L.
Polovinkin, L. Sokovnin; Istochnik schast'ya [The source of hap-
piness], 1949
Cantatas: Vesna [Spring], 1947; Druzhba nerushima [Inviolable
friendship], 1954; Podvig [The feat], 1955
Incidental music and film scores, many songs and choruses

INSTRUMENTAL
Orch: 14 syms., 1929–54; Stalinabad, 1931; Vanch, 1932; Vakhio
Bolo, ov., 1933; Na Perekonskom balu [On Perekonsky ramparts],
1940; Pesnya o konnitse [Song about the cavalry], 1942; Vn Conc.,
1943; Vc Conc., 1952; Sinfonietta no.1, 1953; Dom v Stalingrade
[The house in Stalingrad], 1955; Frontovomu drugu [To a war com-
rade], 1958; Rasskaz o Tseline [Story of the virgin soil], 1960;
Pis'ma druz'yam [Letters to friends], 1961; Sinfonietta no.2, vas, vcs,
1961; Conc.-Monologue, vc, 7 brass, timp, 1962; Little Conc., vn,
str, 1963; Saga, vc, chorus, orch, 1963; suites on Persian, Mongolian
and Tadzhik themes; suites for children; works for str
Inst: Str Qt, 1942; Sonatina, harp (1947); Concert Scherzo, vn, pf
(1964); other chamber works, pf pieces

BIBLIOGRAPHY
G. Abraham: *Eight Soviet Composers* (London, 1943), 52ff
G. Bernandt and A. Dolzhansky: *Sovetskiye kompozitorï: kratkiy bio-
graficheskiy spravochnik* [Soviet composers: concise biographical
notes] (Moscow, 1957)
B. Schwarz: *Music and Musical Life in Soviet Russia 1917–1970*
(London, 1972)

RITA McALLISTER

Knittl, Karel (*b* Polná, nr. Jihlava, 4 Oct 1853; *d*
Prague, 17 March 1907). Czech teacher and conductor.
Son of an organist, he studied at the Prague Organ
School (1872–5) and taught at private music institutes
in Prague, notably the Maydl (1872–6) and the Pivoda
(1873–83); he joined the staff of the Prague Organ
School in 1882. In 1889 he was appointed to the Prague
Conservatory, where he taught harmony and instrumentation and, as administrative director (1901–7),
reformed the teaching methods and instituted regular
student concerts. He succeeded Smetana and Bendl as
choirmaster of the Prague Hlahol choral society (1877–
90, 1897–1901), adding a permanent women's choir
and enlarging the repertory with works such as Berlioz's
Requiem, Liszt's *Christus*, Dvořák's *Stabat mater* as
well as *a cappella* pieces. An active critic writing for
Hudební listy and *Dalibor*, he sided with Pivoda in his
celebrated dispute with Smetana. His compositions,
rarely heard today, include songs, choruses, piano and
orchestral works.

WRITINGS
'O nutných reformách učební osnovy zpěvu na školách středních' [Some
necessary reforms in the singing teaching syllabus at secondary
schools], *Paedagogium*, viii (1886), 337
F. Z. Skuherský (Prague, 1894)
Nauka o skaladbě homofonní [A manual of homophonic composition]
(Prague, 1898)
Příklady pro všeobecnou nauku hudební [Examples for the general
teaching of music] (Prague, 1910)
Několik pokynů o studování sborů [Some hints on the studying of
choruses] (Prague, 2/1944)

BIBLIOGRAPHY
A. Rublič: 'O Karlu Knittlovi', *Věstník pěvecký*, ix (1904), 103
A. Piskáček: 'Karel Knittl', *Věstník pěvecký a hudební*, xxii (1907), 89
B. Kalenský: 'Karel Knittl ve světle pravdy' [Knittl in the light of truth],
Přehled, v (1907), 605
K. Stecker: 'Za Karlem Knittlem', *Přehled*, v (1907), 805
Anon.: 'Karel Knittl', *Dalibor*, xxix (1907), 214
J. Branberger: *Konservatoř hudby v Praze* [The Prague Conservatory of
Music] (Prague, 1911), 140, 150, 186
Z. Nejedlý: 'Dějiny pražského Hlaholu, iii: doba Knittlova (1877–
1890)' [History of the Prague Hlahol, iii: Knittl's era (1877–90)],
Památník zpěváckého spolku Hlahol 1861 až 1911 (Prague, 1911),
98–130
J. Fiala: 'Karel Knittl', *HRo*, vi (1953), 767

JOHN TYRRELL

Kníže, František Max (*b* Dralielčice, nr. Beroun, 7
Sept 1784; *d* Prague, 23 July 1840). Bohemian composer and conductor. He was strongly influenced by
Tomášek and may well have been one of his pupils. He
began his musical career with the Prague Estates
Theatre and held a number of posts as choirmaster in
churches there during the 1830s; during this time he
wrote several sacred works, including six masses. He
attempted unsuccessfully to gain the post of music director at St Vitus's Cathedral after the death of Vitásek
(1839).

Kníže's most important works are for the guitar and
for the voice. In addition to three major didactic publications for the guitar he wrote a number of solo works.
In vocal music he contributed greatly to the growth of a
national tradition of Czech art song, many of his songs
being written to texts by Václav Hanka, a leading Czech
nationalist poet; he was not, however, associated with
Věnec ze zpěvů vlasteneckých [Garland of patriotic
songs] (1835–44). Among his song collections, the
Patero českých písm pro jeden hlas op.21 (Prague,
*c*1820) contains the patriotic ballad *Břetislav*, his most
popular song; his songs also appeared in various
anthologies of the time. A musician of many talents, he
was also, at one time or another, a violist, bassoonist,
guitarist and singer.

PEDAGOGICAL WORKS
(*all published in Prague, n.d.*)
Vollständige Guittarschule
Fundamente für die Guittare nebst praktische Beispielen
14 Hefte verschiedener Studien für die Guitarre
Charakteristische Singübingen

BIBLIOGRAPHY
ČSHS
I. Belza: *Česká klasická hudba* (Prague, 1961)

ADRIENNE SIMPSON

Knöfel [Knäfelius, Knefel, Knöbel, Knöpflin], **Johann**
(*b* Lauban, Silesia [Lubín, Poland], 1525–30; *d*
?Prague, after 21 April 1617). German composer and
organist. Biographical details of the organist Kaspar
Krumbhorn (*b* 1542) reveal that Knöfel was Kantor at
the Valentin Trotzendorff Lateinschule, a Lutheran
institution, at Goldberg, Silesia, when he was about 30
years old and Krumbhorn was his pupil. By the time of
his marriage, on 21 June 1569, he had become
Kapellmeister to Duke Heinrich V of Liegnitz, Brieg
and Goldberg. In the preface to his *Dulcissimae cantiones* (1571), which he dedicated to the duke, he
affirmed his allegiance to the Lutheran doctrine that had
been adopted by the churches of Breslau in the earliest
years of the Reformation, and in 1575 he dedicated his
Cantus choralis – a complete setting of the Proper
chants for the festivals of the church year – to the
Breslau town council. The dedication of his mass on
Lassus's *In me transierunt* shows that by 1579 he was
Kapellmeister to the Elector Palatine Ludwig VI at
Heidelberg; he stated in the dedication to his *Cantiones
piae* (1580) that he had been appointed a short while
before. In 1583, after the death of Ludwig VI, the
Elector Johann Casimir restored Calvinism to the
palatinate, and the Lutheran Knöfel was deprived of his
post and returned to Silesia. Not long afterwards he
moved to Prague: in 1592 he wrote in the preface to his
Novae melodiae that he had already been living there for
some time. In that year he was organist and Kantor at St
Heinrich, the school of which was renowned for its
choir. Nothing further is heard of him until 1617 when
a note in the civic records at Klagenfurt confirms that he
was still alive: on 21 April that year the authorities in

Carinthia approved a payment of '30 florins to Johann Knäfelius for his dedication', which does not preclude the possibility that he continued to live in Prague.

Knöfel's musical style is modelled on that of Lassus. Except for the *Newe teutsche Liedlein* (1581) and a few hymns, which are also in German, he set only Latin texts. Apart from the one to the 1581 collection, all his prefaces too are in Latin, an indication of his humanist upbringing (at the school at Goldberg, moreover, Latin was the language of everyday conversation). It is therefore easy to understand why he was such a staunch advocate of Latin music in Protestant worship. In the preface to the *Cantus choralis* (1575) he expressed surprise at the way in which the singing of Gregorian chant was at that time 'in many places either seldom practised or else completely discontinued' and the liturgical text replaced more and more often with free hymns. He sought to counteract this development by using Gregorian melodies as the basis of the pieces in this volume. The short, choral psalm verses, which are set homophonically, are rounded off by a restatement of the material by the organ; such alternation with congregational or choral singing was a common practice in Breslau churches. The full title of the *Newe teutsche Liedlein* shows that Knöfel did not resign himself entirely to the lighthearted elegance of the secular musical world to which his duties as court Kapellmeister obliged him to pay some tribute: 'New German songs, most of which describe and unmask the way of the world, the treachery of mankind, promising much and rendering little, fine words and false hearts. With, too, some cheerful songs appropriate to collations and celebrations'. The texts are mostly of a reflective and even moral character, as were the mottoes adopted by the various branches of the palatine household. The collection also includes settings of texts that were widely known at the time, and two folktales: one is about the 'Handschuhsheimer Esel', an amusing incident from the life of the palatinate huntsmen and peasants; the other – 'Ein Gedicht, wie man der Welt kann recht tun nicht', concerning the inability of Man to do justice to the world – is in the manner of Hans Sachs and in style is close to the homophonic canzonetta. *Wunder bin ich* is in the chromatic style, then the latest fashion in madrigal composition. Though he sometimes adopted modern techniques such as *cori spezzati* writing, chromaticism and the canzonetta style, Knöfel nevertheless remained firmly entrenched in the conservative tradition of Protestant sacred music.

WORKS

Dulcissimae quaedam cantiones, numero xxxii, 5–7vv . . . tum musicis instrumentis aptae esse possint (Nuremberg, 1571); 1 (with Ger. text) ed. in *M. Praetorius: Gesamtausgabe*, v (Wolfenbüttel and Berlin, 1937)

Cantus choralis . . . 5vv . . . quo per totum anni curriculum praecipuis diebus festis in ecclesia cantari solet (Nuremberg, 1575)

Missa, 5vv, ad imitationem cantionis Orlandi 'In me transierunt' (Nuremberg, 1579)

Cantiones piae, 5, 6vv . . . quam instrumentis musicis accommodae (Nuremberg, 1580); 1 ed. F. Commer, *Musica sacra*, xix (Regensburg, 1878)

Newe teutsche Liedlein, 5vv, welche den mehrern Theil den Brauch dieser Welt beschreiben (Nuremberg, 1581); 1 ed. in *Mw*, x (1955)

Novae melodiae, 5–8vv . . . instrumentali pariter musicae accommodatae (Prague, 1592)

Christ ist erstanden, motet, 6vv, *D-Mbs*

BIBLIOGRAPHY

EitnerQ; *GerberNL*

H. A. Sander: *Geschichte des lutherischen Gottesdienstes und der Kirchenmusik in Breslau* (Breslau, 1937)

W. Scholz: 'Zu Johannes Knöfel', *AMf*, vii (1942), 228

H. Federhofer: 'Beiträge zur älteren Musikgeschichte Kärntens',

Carinthia, i: *Mitteilungen des Geschichtsvereins für Kärnten*, cxlv (1955), 372

H. J. Moser: *Die Musikleistung der deutschen Stämme* (Vienna and Stuttgart, 1957)

F. Feldmann: 'Der Laubaner Johannes Knöfel, insbesondere sein "Cantus choralis"', *Das evangelische Schlesien*, ed. G. Hultsch, vi/2: *Die schlesische Kirchenmusik im Wandel der Zeiten* (Lübeck, 1975)

LINI HÜBSCH-PFLEGER

Knöller, Andreas. See KNELLER, ANDREAS.

Knop [Knöp], **Lüder** (*b* Bremen; *d* Bremen, 5 March 1665). German composer and organist. He was the last musical member of an East Friesian family who moved to Bremen from Emden in 1584 and were active there as civic and church musicians. After briefly being assistant organist at the Ratskirche Unser lieben Frauen in 1641 he succeeded his father as organist of St Stephani and held the post until his death. He published *Erster Theil neuer Paduanen, Galliarden, Balletten, Mascaraden, Arien, Allemanden, Couranten und Sarabanden* (Bremen, 1651, inc.) for three string instruments and continuo. A second part (Bremen, 1660) is extant, for two and three instruments and continuo, and was listed as early as 1657 in catalogues of the Frankfurt and Leipzig fairs. A third, announced in 1667 as *Luderi Knopii Schwanengesang* and including pieces in up to six parts, as well as several one- and two-part pieces by the editor, Johannes Jani, Knop's successor at St Stephani, is either lost or never appeared. Knop's setting for five voices and instruments of Psalm cxxviii for the wedding of the mayor of Bremen, H. H. Meyer, on 14 December 1658 (Bremen, 1658), is also extant.

BIBLIOGRAPHY

F. Piersig: 'Die Organisten der bremischen Stadtkirchen im 17. und 18. Jahrhundert', *Bremisches Jb*, xxxv (1935), 325

——: 'Ostfriesische Musikerfamilien im bremer Musikleben des 17. Jahrhunderts', *Jb der Gesellschaft für bildende Kunst und vaterländische Altertümer zu Emden*, xxx (1950), 61

FRITZ PIERSIG

Knopf. German family of horn makers. The firm was founded by (Heinrich) August Knopf (*b* 14 June 1865; *d* 31 May 1947), whose two sons, Herbert (Fritz) Knopf (*b* 17 March 1894; *d* 26 June 1969) and (August) Kurt Knopf (*b* 4 Nov 1900; *d* 1945), worked together with their father until 1919, when Herbert set up in business under his own name. Both businesses are now carried on respectively by Kurt's son Edgar (*b* 27 Oct 1928) and Herbert's son Johannes (Fritz) (*b* 11 Dec 1929). In 1918, August senior, Kurt and Herbert began working jointly on the Prager horn (*see* HORN), a project undertaken by the firm which eventually proved abortive but which was continued even after the separation of 1919. Herbert Fritz Knopf's principal contribution to horn development, a double horn (1920–21), was extensively copied by various other manufacturers and was until recently one of the three basic models of double horn available. He also pioneered the handstopping valve on B♭ horns (which lowers the pitch by three-quarters of a tone), the ball and socket linkage for rotary valves and the double Wagner tuba in F and B♭.

BIBLIOGRAPHY

R. Morley-Pegge: *The French Horn* (London, 1960, 2/1972)

FRANK HAWKINS

Knöpflin, Johann. See KNÖFEL, JOHANN.

Knorr, Ernst-Lothar von (*b* Eitorf, 2 Jan 1896; *d* Heidelberg, 30 Oct 1973). German composer and teacher. He studied the violin, harmony and conducting at the Cologne Conservatory, and in 1909 produced his first compositions; he was awarded the Joseph Joachim Prize in 1911. After World War I he directed the violin class at the Heidelberg Academy of Music, and was at the same time the founder of the Heidelberg Chamber Orchestra, a teacher of the violin at the Mannheim Musikhochschule and leader of the Pfalz Orchestra in that city. In 1924 came his first contact with the German youth music movement, a turning-point in his professional life. He pursued a career in music education, acting as principal of Musikhochschulen and academies in Berlin, Frankfurt, Trossingen, Hanover and Heidelberg; he has also been music adviser to Lower Saxony. His works reflect his academic background.

WORKS
(selective list)

Orch: 2 conc. grossi; Little Pieces, str, 1929; Sym. Piece; Weihnachtspastorale; Conc., pf, chorus, orch; Introduction and Sym. Allegro, vc, orch; Serenadenmusik

Chamber: 3 str qts, 1929, 1930, 1970; Theme and 7 Variations, trautonium, hellertion, theremin-vox-inst, neo-Bechstein, vib. 1932; Wind Qnt, 1958; Duo, va, vc, 1961; Fantasie, cl, pf, 1970; Sonata, vc, pf, 1972

Keyboard: Suite, C, pf; 3 sonatas, C, b, G, pf; Diaphonia, 2 pf, 1971; hpd sonata; org works

Cantatas: Die heiligen drei Könige (Rilke); Würde der Frauen (Schiller); Lobe den Herrn; Werden und Vergehen (trad.); Marienleben; Von den Männern, die ihre Pflicht getan; Nun ruhen alle Wälder; Elsässisches Liederspiel; Abendmusik (A. Silesius); Unser die Sonne (Thieme); Schicksal (Barthel); Heilige Flamme (Lersch); Heraklit; Brüder, wir halten Totenwacht; Kantate zum Schulschluss (Goethe); Lob des Fleisses; Strafe der Faulheit; 2 Weihnachtskantaten, 1962; Weihnachtsbedenken über die Geburt Christi (Gryphius)

Other choral works: Hymnus des Friedens; Russische Liebeslieder; Chöre (von der Vogelweide, Morgenstern); Weinheberzyklus; Gesang im Grünen; Heiter-besinnliche Männerchöre (Busch), 1968 c30 songs, other vocal pieces, educational music

Principal publishers: Hohner, Möseler, Müller, Schott

BIBLIOGRAPHY

W. Pohl: 'Ernst-Lothar von Knorr', *Musica*, vi (1952), 182 [incl. list of works]

O. Riemer, ed.: *Ernst-Lothar von Knorr zum 75. Geburtstag* (Cologne, 1971)

O. Riemer: 'Mentor und Komponist: Ernst-Lothar von Knorr 75 Jahre', *Musica*, xxv (1971), 58   KLAUS L. NEUMANN

Knorr, Iwan (Otto Armand) (*b* Mewe, West Prussia, 3 Jan 1853; *d* Frankfurt am Main, 22 Jan 1916). German composer, teacher and writer. At the age of four he was taken to southern Russia, where he learnt the piano from his mother and grew up surrounded by Russian folk music. The Knorr family settled in Leipzig in 1868, and Iwan studied the piano with Moscheles, theory with Richter and composition with Reinecke at the conservatory. In 1874 he became a professor of music at the Imperial Institute for Noble Ladies in Khar'kov; four years later he was appointed director of the theoretical studies programme of the Khar'kov division of the Russian Imperial Musical Society. In 1877 Knorr, who was still unknown as a composer, submitted his Variations on a Ukrainian Folksong op.7 to Brahms, who much liked the work. He recommended Knorr for a teaching post at the Hoch Conservatory in Frankfurt am Main in 1883. Initially Knorr taught the piano, theory and music history there; from 1886 he also taught composition, and two years later he gave up teaching the piano in order to concentrate solely on theory and composition. He had a number of distinguished pupils, including Cyril Scott, Hans Pfitzner and Ernst Toch. In 1895 he was named royal professor, and in 1908 he succeeded Bernhard Scholz as director of the conservatory. He was made an honorary member of the American Philharmonic Academy in New York (1911). Knorr was an able and enthusiastic teacher, accord-

ing to Moritz Bauer, a colleague at the conservatory. As a composer he was gifted but not prolific: Bauer attributed this to his strong self-criticism and his interest in teaching. His music shows the influence of Ukrainian folk music and an interest in variation technique and suite forms, and much of it is extremely contrapuntal: he is often ranked with Reger as one of the greatest masters of counterpoint and fugue of his time. Some of his pedagogical works (which include tutors in fugue and harmony, and analyses of works by Bach, Brahms and Tchaikovsky) were published under the pseudonym I. O. Armand.

WORKS
OPERAS

Dunja (2, Knorr), Koblenz, 23 March 1904
Die Hochzeit, Prague, 1907, not mentioned in Bauer
Durchs Fenster (1, Knorr), Karlsruhe, 1908

OTHER WORKS

Orch: Sym., G; Sym. Fantasia; Variations on a Ukrainian Folksong, op.7; Serenade, G; 2 suites; intermezzos, fugues, other works

Chamber and pf: Pf Qt, Eb, arr. of pf qnt; 2 str qts; Variations on a Theme of Schumann, pf trio; works for vc, pf; numerous pf solos, duets and arrangements

Vocal: Marienlegende, solo vv, chorus, orch; Maria, scena, S, orch; Ukrainische Liebeslieder, 4vv, pf; c10 songs, 1v, pf; choruses, male and mixed vv

WRITINGS

P. I. Tschaikowsky, Berühmte Musiker, xi, ed. H. Riemann (Berlin, 1900)

Aufgaben für den Unterricht in der Harmonielehre (Leipzig, 1903)

Lehrbuch der Fugenkomposition (Leipzig, 1911)

Die Fugen des Wohltemperierten Klaviers in bildlicher Darstellung (Leipzig, 1912)

BIBLIOGRAPHY

M. Bauer: *Iwan Knorr: ein Gedenkblatt* (Frankfurt am Main, 1916) [with list of works]

U. Unger: *Die Klavierfuge im 20. Jahrhundert* (Regensburg, 1956)
                                                      R. J. PASCALL

Knorr von Rosenroth [Rauthner; Peganius], **Christian (Anton Philipp)** (*b* Alt-Raudten, nr. Wohlau, Silesia [now Wołow, Poland], 15 or 16 July 1636; *d* Grossalbershof, nr. Sulzbach, Upper Palatinate, 4 May 1689). German scholar and poet. He attended school in Fraustadt and Stettin, then enrolled at the University of Leipzig (1655–60), graduating with a dissertation in numismatics. From 1663 to 1666 he journeyed through the Netherlands, England and France, where he expanded his knowledge of Oriental languages and studied Hebraic sources, Christian and Jewish mystics, natural philosophy and alchemy. From 1668 on he was privy councillor to the Count Palatine Christian August of Sulzbach, who valued and used him both in a political function and for his stupendous learning in the count's areas of interest, cabala, alchemy and mysticism. Knorr's scholarship culminated in his *Kabbala denudata* (i, Sulzbach, 1677; ii, Frankfurt am Main, 1684), but he has become most popular through his *Neuer Helicon mit seinen neun Musen* (Nuremberg, 1684, 2/1699). This collection of 75 religious songs depicts the mystic's way to God. Almost half are translations, adaptations or parodies. Each song is headed 'Aria' and is provided with a setting consisting of a melody and a simple thoroughbass accompaniment. They seem not to have been written by Knorr, but the composer or composers are unknown. The Pietists cherished Knorr's songs for their mystical flavour: seven are included in the *Darmstädter Gesangbuch* of 1698; the more important *Geistreiches Gesangbuch*, edited by J. A. Freylinghausen in 1704, eventually contained 14, but only three with the original melodies.

BIBLIOGRAPHY

C. von Winterfeld: *Der evangelische Kirchengesang*, ii (Leipzig, 1845/R1966), 512ff and exx.185–7

J. Zahn: *Die Melodien der deutschen evangelischen Kirchenlieder*, v (Gütersloh, 1892/*R*1963), 433 [lists 18 melodies]

A. Fischer and W. Tümpel: *Das deutsche evangelische Kirchenlied des 17. Jahrhunderts*, v (Gütersloh, 1911/*R*1964), 494ff

K. Salecker: *Christian Knorr von Rosenroth* (Leipzig, 1931) [includes complete list of works]

TRAUTE MAASS MARSHALL

Knote, Heinrich (*b* Munich, 26 Nov 1870; *d* Garmisch, 15 Jan 1953). German tenor. He learnt singing from Kirschner in his native city, and made his début there, as Georg in Lortzing's *Der Waffenschmied*, on 7 May 1892. His long German career was almost entirely centred on Munich, where he remained for nearly 40 years, concentrating after 1900 on the heroic Wagner repertory, and making his farewell in *Siegfried* on 15 December 1931. Between 1900 and 1913 he made many successful appearances at Covent Garden, and was, if anything, even more appreciated at the Metropolitan, where he sang from 1904 to 1908, and where his performance fees were, at one time, twice those earned by Van Rooy. Knote was a superior, if typical, Wagnerian *Heldentenor*, his striking physique well matched by a clear, resonant, sympathetic voice and impressive declamation. In adddition to numerous pre-1914 recordings, mainly of Wagner, Knote made a further Wagner series as late as 1930, demonstrating an amazing endurance, even in some respects a positive improvement, of his vocal powers.

BIBLIOGRAPHY

J. H. Wagemann: *Der sechzigjährige deutsche Meistersänger Heinrich Knote in seiner stimmbildnerischen Bedeutung und im Vergleich mit anderen Sängern* (Munich, 1930)

HERMAN KLEIN/DESMOND SHAWE-TAYLOR

Knüller, Andreas. *See* KNELLER, ANDREAS.

Knüpfer, Paul (*b* Halle, 21 June 1866; *d* Berlin, 4 Nov 1920). German bass. He studied at Sondershausen where he made his début in 1885. He appeared at the Leipzig Opera from 1887 until 1898, when he was engaged by the Berlin Hofoper (later Staatsoper); there he had his greatest successes and remained until 1920. From 1901 to 1906 he took the leading bass roles at Bayreuth and from 1907 to 1914 appeared frequently at Covent Garden. He was the first Covent Garden Ochs (1913) and Gurnemanz (1914), two of his most notable roles. He was an impressive artist although in later years there was some decline in his sturdy, powerful yet flexible bass, which encompassed such contrasted roles as Osmin and King Marke. He died only six months after his retirement. His many recordings give some idea of his expressive range. He married the soprano Marie Egli.

ALAN BLYTH

Knüpfer, Sebastian (*b* Asch, Bavaria [now Aš, Czechoslovakia], 6 Sept 1633; *d* Leipzig, 10 Oct 1676). German composer. He was a distinguished Kantor of the Thomaskirche, Leipzig, and director of the city's music.

1. LIFE. Most of the biographical data about Knüpfer come from a published obituary (see Richter). He was first taught music by his father, a Kantor and organist at Asch. He also studied regularly with an unidentified tutor living near Asch, from whom he gained a solid grounding in, and lasting love for, a number of scholastic disciplines. At the age of 13 he entered the Gymnasium Poeticum at Regensburg and remained

there for eight years. During this unusually long period he became well versed in the city's musical traditions (such as the works of Andreas Raselius), studied the organ, perhaps with Augustin Gradenthaler, and mastered a number of humanistic subjects, especially the poetic arts and philology. His gifts as a student were supported by scholarships from the city of Regensburg, and he was commended by influential members of the staff of the Gymnasium and the city council, some of the latter providing him with favourable testimonials when he moved to Leipzig in 1654. It is not known why he went there, but in view of his lifelong desire to improve his mind, it was possibly because he planned to enter the university. He did not, however, do so. During his first few years at Leipzig he gave music lessons and sang as a bass in church choirs, displaying enough talent to take solo parts. He applied for the post of Thomaskantor when Tobias Michael died on 26 June 1657, and he was appointed on 17 July; the four other candidates to whom he was preferred included Adam Krieger.

In Knüpfer the Thomaskirche found a Kantor and the city of Leipzig a director of music who approached the musical and intellectual calibre of Calvisius and Schein, Michael's two predecessors. During his 19-year tenure Leipzig once again became the leading musical city in central Germany following the sharp decline resulting from the Thirty Years War, the long Swedish occupation of the city and Michael's protracted illness. Knüpfer thus initiated a final period of musical excellence in Leipzig that culminated in the careers of his three successors, Schelle, Kuhnau and Bach. Although never a student at the university, he continued the study of philosophy and philology with members of the faculty and was thought of as a member of the academic community. He was praised for his command of classical sources concerning music, which he mastered from Meibom's editions published in 1652; he studied the treatises of, among others, Guido of Arezzo, Boethius, Berno of Reichenau and Kircher. In addition to his productive career as Kantor he is known to have travelled to Halle to direct his own music for the dedication of new organs, for the Marktkirche on 15 February 1664 and the Ulrichskirche on 16 November 1675; also he directed a programme of music for the centenary of the Halle Gymnasium on 17 August 1665. His circle of musical colleagues included many men important in 17th-century German music, such as Pezel, Rosenmüller and J. C. Horn, and he may well have known Schütz. That he was regarded as one of Leipzig's leading intellectual figures is indicated by the unusual honour of his being accorded an academic funeral at the university even though he had never been officially connected with it.

2. WORKS. Knüpfer's output consisted almost entirely of sacred works to Latin or German texts. Many are lost, and of those that survive few have been published in modern editions. Most are in the traditional style and form of the 17th-century vocal concerto, incorporating many of the characteristics of similar works by Schütz – though with no traces of the latter's uniquely personal style. Large choral forms are enhanced by an orchestra of substantial size (most commonly two violins, three violas, bassoon with continuo, clarinos, trombone and timpani), which supports the choral parts as well as interjecting all manner of colourful concerted effects. The choral writing may be massively chordal or intricately

polyphonic, and there are a number of much simpler concerted passages for soloists supported only by the continuo. Knüpfer frequently based his German works on the text and melody of a chorale, and he was a master at deriving contrapuntal ideas from motivic fragmentation of the chorale. In many of these works the chorale verses are treated much as they are in slightly later German cantatas. Each verse is set separately. An opening choral movement, usually of large proportions and often repeated at the end of the work, is succeeded by movements designed for soloists. These are often ariosos or include fugal writing in which the chorale melody is passed back and forth between the voices in a duet or trio texture – a technique akin to that found in Bach's organ chorale preludes. Other movements display dramatic use of expressive recitative: there is a good example in *Wer ist, der so von Edom kömmt* (excerpt in Schering, 1926, p.162).

Knüpfer's music is primarily serious and profoundly devout, though he did publish a collection of the secular madrigals and canzonettas that he wrote for the university student with whom he worked in the collegium musicum at Leipzig. His contrapuntal mastery, the powerful drama of his thematic ideas, his brilliant instrumentation and the variety of his vocal scoring all contribute to the impression of him as a worthy predecessor of Bach, many of whose Leipzig church cantatas belong to a tradition first developed by Knüpfer.

WORKS

(all MSS in D-Dlb formerly in GMl)

LATIN SACRED VOCAL

Dies est laetitiae, 6vv, 2 vn, 3 va, 2 bn, 2 clarinos, 3 tpt, timp, 4 bombardi/3 piffari, bc, *D-Dlb*

Ecce quam bonum et quam iucundum (Ps cxxxiii), 5vv, ripieno 5vv, 2 vn, 3 va, bn, bc, *Dlb*

Justus ut palma florebit, 4vv, bc, *B*

Kyrie cum Gloria, 6vv, insts (?2 vn, 5 va), bc, *Bds*, ?lost

O benignissime Jesu, 3vv, 2 vn/cornettinos, va da gamba/bombard, bc, *Dlb*

Quare fremuerunt gentes (Ps ii), 6vv, ripieno 4vv, 2 vn, 3 va, 2 cornetts, 4 trbn, bc, *Dlb*

Quemadmodum desiderat, B solo, 5 vn, org, *Dlb*, *S-Uu*

Super flumina Babylonis (Ps cxxxvii), 4vv, ripieno 4vv, 2 vn, 3 va, bn, 2 cornettinos, 3 trbn, bc, *D-Dlb*

Surgite populi: De resurrectione et ascensione Domini, 8vv (2 choirs), 2 vn, 3 va, bn, 2 cornettinos, cornett, 5 tpt, 3 trbn, timp, bc, *Dlb*

Veni Sancte Spiritus, 5vv, 2 vn, 2 va, bn, 4 clarinos, 2 cornettinos, 3 trbn, timp, org, *Dlb*

GERMAN SACRED VOCAL

Ach Herr, lass deine lieben Engelein, 5vv, 2 vn, 2 violettas, bn, 2 clarinos, tamburi, 2 fl, org, *B*

Ach Herr, strafe mich nicht (Ps vi), 5vv, 2 vn, 2 violettas, bn, 2 clarinos, 2 fl, tamburi, org, *B*, *Dlb*; ed. in DDT, lviii–lix (1918/*R*)

Ach mein herzliebes Jesulein, 5vv, ripieno 5vv, 2 vn, 2 va, 2 cornetts, 3 trbn, vle, bc, *Dlb*

Ach, wenn kommet doch die Stunde, aria, A/T, 3 va, vle, bc, *Dlb*

Alleluja, man singet mit Freuden, 5vv, 8 insts, *Dlb*

Asche, die des Schöpfers Händ, 5vv; lost, extant in parody version by Z. Haenisch (Halle, 1665)

Der Gerechte wird grünen wie ein Palmbaum, 5vv, 2 vn, violetta, 2 va, 2 cornetts, 3 trbn, vle, bc, *Bds*, ?lost

Der Herr ist König, 8vv, vn, 5 va, 7 trbn, bc, *B*

Der Herr ist mein Hirt, B, vn, 3 va, org, *RUl*

Der Herr schaffet deinen Gränzen Friede, 3vv, 2 vn, trbn, bc, *Bds*, ?lost

Der Seegen des Herren machet reich, 5vv, 2 vn, 3 va, bc, *Bds*, ?lost

Dies ist der Tag, den der Herr macht, 5vv, ripieno 5vv, 2 va, bn, 2 clarinos, 2 trbn, *B*

Dies ist der Tag des Herrn, a 16, *Dlb*

Die Turteltaube lässt sich hören, 5vv, 2 vn, 2 va, bn, 4 clarinos, timp, bc, *Dlb*

Erforsche mich Gott, funeral motet, 14 May 1673, 8vv (2 choirs) (Leipzig, 1674), pubd version *Ju*, *WER*, *Z*; *Bds* (holograph), ?lost

Erheb dich, meine Seele, funeral motet, 1676, 4vv (Leipzig, 1676), pubd version *WER*

Erhöre, Jesulein, mein sehnlichs, S, 4 str, *Dlb*

Erstanden ist der heilge Christ, 5vv, 2 vn, 4 va, bn, bombard, 2 clarinos,

2 tpt, tamburi, bc, *B*, *Dlb* (incl. ripieno 4vv, 3 trbn)

Es haben mir die Hoffärtigen, 4vv, 2 vn, 3 va, bc, *B*

Es ist eine Stimme eines Predigers in der Wüsten, 4vv, 2 vn, 3 va, bn, bc, *B*

Es spricht der Unweisen Mund wohl, 8vv, 2 vn, 3 va, bn, 2 cornetts, 3 trbn, org, *B*; ed. in DDT, lviii–lix (1918/*R*)

Gelobet sey Gott, 5vv, 4 str, *Dlb*, ?lost

Gen Himmel zu dem Vater mein, 6vv, 2 vn, 2 clarinos, timp, 2 trbn, bn, bc, *Dlb*

Gott sei mir gnädig nach deiner Güte (Ps li), 5vv, ripieno 5vv, 4 va, bn, vle, bc, *Dlb*

Herr Christ, der einig Gottes Sohn, 5vv, 2 vn, 3 va, bn, 2 cornetts, 3 trbn, org, *B*

Herr, hilf uns, wir verderben, 4vv, 2 vn, 2 va, bn, bc, *B*

Herr, ich habe lieb die Stätte deines Hauses, 3vv, 2 vn, va, bc, *B*

Herr Jesu Christ, wahr'r Mensch, 5vv, ripieno 4vv, 2 vn, bn, bc, *S-Uu*

Herr, lehre mich thun nach deinem, 5vv, ripieno 5vv, 2 vn, 3 va, bn, bc, *D-Dlb*

Herr, lehre uns bedenken, 6vv, 2 vn, 3 va, bn, bc, *B*

Herr, strafe mich nicht (Ps xxxix), 4vv, 3 va, vle/bn, bc, *Dlb*

Herr, wer wird wohnen in deinen Hütten, 3vv, 2 cornetts, 3 va, bc, *B*

Ich freue mich in dir, 5vv, 2 vn, 2 va, 3 trbn, 2 fl, vle, bc, *B*

Ich habe dich zum Licht der Heiden gemacht, 5vv, ripieno 5vv, 2 vn, 3 va, bn, 2 cornettinos, 3 trbn, bc, *Dlb*

Ich will singen von der Gnade (Ps lxxxix), 4vv, ripieno 4vv, 2 vn, 3 va, bn, bc, *Dlb*

Jauchzet dem Herrn alle Welt (Ps c), 8vv (2 choirs), 2 vn, 3 va, bn, 2 clarinos, 2 cornettinos, tpt, 2 trbn, bc, *Dlb*

Jesu, meine Freud und Wonne, 5vv, 5 insts, *RUl*

Jesus Christus, unser Heiland, 5vv, ripieno 5vv, 2 vn, 3 va, bn, bc, *Dlb*

Komm du schöne Freudenkrone, 5vv, 2 vn, 3 violettas, violetta/bn, 2 clarinos, tamburi, 3 trbn, org, *Dlb*

Komm heilger Geist, zeuch, 4vv, ripieno 4vv, 4 va, 4 trbn, bc, *Bds*, ?lost

Lass dir gefallen, 2vv, 4 insts, *RUl*

Machet die Thore weit, 5vv, ripieno 5vv, 2 vn, 4 va, 2 cornetts/bombards, 3 trbn, bc, *Dlb*; ed. in DDT, lviii–lix (1918/*R*)

Mein Gott, betrübt ist meine Seele, funeral motet, 20 Oct 1667, a 6, org (pubd ?1667), pubd version *GOl*, *Z*

Mein Herz hält dir für dein Wort, aria, 3vv, 2 vn, bn, org, *B*

Nun dancket alle Gott, 6vv, 2 vn, 3 va, bc, *B*

Nun freut euch, lieben Christen gemein, 5vv, 2 vn, 2 va, bn, bc, *B*

Sende dein Licht (Ps xliii), 4vv, ripieno 4vv, 2 vn, 2 va, bn, bc, *Dlb*

Victoria, die Fürsten sind geschlagen, 5vv, 2 vn, 2 va, bn, 3 trbn, org, *S-Uu* (org tablature)

Vom Himmel hoch; chorus angelorum: 3 S, ripieno 3 S, 3 vn, ripieno 3 vn; coro dei pastori: 3vv, 3 bombards; coro pieno: 4vv, 2 clarinos, timp, harp, bc, *D-Dlb*

Was mein Gott will, 6vv, 2 vn, 3 va, bn, 2 cornetts, 3 trbn, *B*; ed. in DDT, lviii–lix (1918/*R*)

Was sind wir Menschen doch [Das verstimmte Orgel-Werck], funeral ode, 4vv, 22 May 1672 (Leipzig, ?1672), pubd version *Z*

Was werden wir essen, dialogue, 4vv, 4 insts, va, bc, *Bds*, ?lost

Weichet von mir, ihr Boshaftigen, funeral motet, 16 June 1661, 6vv, org (Leipzig, ?1661), pubd version *FBo*, *GOl*, *WER*

Welt Vater du! O Adam deine Kinder, aria, 2 S, 3 va, vle, *Dlb*

Wenn mein Stündlein vorhanden ist, 4vv, ripieno 4vv, 2 va, vle, bc, *Dlb*

Wer ist, der so von Edom kömmt, 5vv, 2 vn, 2 va, bn, 4 trbn, tamburi, bc, *B*, *Dlb* (incl. 2 clarinos, 2 tpt)

Wer ist, der so von Edom kömmt, 3vv, 4 va, *B*

Wir gehen nun, B, 3 insts, *RUl*

Wohl dem, der in der Gottesfurcht steht, 5vv, 2 vn, 3 va, 2 cornetts, 3 trbn, bombard, bc, *B*

O Traurigkeit, o Hertzeleid, Grab-Lied über die Begräbnis . . . Jesu Christi (J. Rist), 4vv, in G. Vopelius, Gesangbuch (Leipzig, 1682)

SECULAR

Lustige Madrigalien, 2–4vv, und Canzonetten, 1–3vv, insts (Leipzig, 1663), *CH-Zz*; 4 ed. in Moser, ii, 17ff, extracts and list of titles in Moser, i, 19ff

LOST WORKS

Cited in inventories and in lists of works bought by Leipzig council, 1677, 1686; for titles see DDT, lviii–lix (1918/*R*)

Latin sacred: 6 masses, a 4–24; 6 Magnificat, a 6–24; Historia de missione Spiritus S[anctus]; 16 motets, a 3–28

German sacred: 41 motets, a 5–20; 7 motets, a 6–23, listed in *Spezifikation derer 276 musicalischen Kirchen-Stücken, so . . . Hr. Adamus Meissner . . . Organista bey der Kirchen zu St Ulrich [Halle] in seinem Testamente gedachter Kirchen . . . vermachet 1718* (see Serauky); 2 motets written for dedication of Halle organ, 1665 (see Serauky); music written for dedication of Knauthain organ, 1674

Secular: Glück zu! Dieweil der milde Sachse Euch wiederum eröffnet Wald und Bahn, madrigal, 4vv, 5 insts (Leipzig, 1657) [for Johann Georg II]; Leipziger Kehr-Michels, i–ii; 3 madrigals; Sonata sup. Guten Abend Garten Man

BIBLIOGRAPHY

WaltherML

J. Mattheson: *Grundlage einer Ehren-Pforte* (Hamburg, 1740); ed. M. Schneider (Berlin, 1910/*R*1969)

E. Hildemann: *Geschichte der evangelischen Kirchengemeinde Asch* (Asch, 1899)

B. F. Richter: 'Zwei Funeralprogramme auf die Thomaskantoren Sebastian Knüpfer und Joh. Schelle', *MMg*, xxxiii (1901), 205

A. Schering: 'Über die Kirchenkantaten vorbachischer Thomaskantoren', *BJb*, ix (1912), 86

——: Introduction to DDT, lviii–lix (1918/*R*)

——: *Musikgeschichte Leipzigs*, ii: *Von 1650 bis 1723* (Leipzig, 1926)

H. J. Moser: *Corydon, das ist: Geschichte des mehrstimmigen Generalbassliedes und des Quodlibets im deutschen Barock* (Brunswick, 1933, 2/1960)

W. Serauky: *Musikgeschichte der Stadt Halle*, ii/1 (Halle and Berlin, 1939/*R*1970)

O. Kandmann: *Das Werk Sebastian Knüpfers im Überblick* (diss., U. of Leipzig, 1960)

W. Braun: 'Die alten Musikbibliotheken der Stadt Freyburg (Unstrut)', *Mf*, xv (1962), 123

F. Krummacher: 'Zur Sammlung Jacobi der ehemaligen Fürstenschule Grimma', *Mf*, xvi (1963), 324

GEORGE J. BUELOW

Knushevitsky, Svyatoslav Nikolayevich (*b* Petrovsk, 6 Jan 1908; *d* Moscow, 19 Feb 1963). Russian cellist. He studied at the Moscow Conservatory with Kozolupov and was soloist and principal of the Bol'shoy Theatre Orchestra from 1929 to 1943. After winning first prize in the first All Union Musicians' Competition at Moscow in 1933, he began a successful career as a soloist and chamber player. With David Oistrakh and Lev Oborin in 1940 he formed a trio which later became internationally famous; Knushevitsky made his British début with them in 1958. They made distinguished records of trios by Schubert and Beethoven, and the latter's Triple Concerto. He was a master of songlike phrasing as well as an outstanding virtuoso. His several tours abroad included Austria, Germany and the Casals Festival at Puerto Rico, and he was the dedicatee of various works, including concertos by Glier, Khachaturian, Myaskovsky and Vasilenko. A teacher at the Moscow Conservatory from 1942 until his death, he was head of the cello and double bass department there from 1954 to 1959. He received a USSR State Prize in 1950 and was made Honoured Art Worker of the RSFSR in 1955.

BIBLIOGRAPHY

T. Gaydamovich: 'Svyatoslav Knushevitsky', *SovM* (1964), no.7, p.42

L. Evgrafov: 'Pevets violoncheli' [Poet of the cello], *SovM* (1968), no.6, p.72

I. M. YAMPOL'SKY

Knussen, (Stuart) Oliver (*b* Glasgow, 12 June 1952). English composer. A son of the double bass player Stuart Knussen, he began to compose when he was six. From 1964 to 1967 he attended the Central Tutorial School for Young Musicians; he was a pupil of John Lambert (1963–9) and of Schuller at Tanglewood (1970–73). The most precocious English musical talent to emerge since Britten, Knussen was somewhat exploited by the press when he conducted his accomplished but derivative Symphony no.1 at the age of 15. Nevertheless, his subsequent development, ranging through the flexible lines of *Masks* to the massed sonorities of the Third Symphony, has proved independent and assured. The Second Symphony and *Océan de terre*, in particular, display a rare harmonic intelligence and a fine ear for complex textural blendings.

WORKS

Orch: Sym. no.1, op.1, 1966–7; Conc. for Orch, op.5, 1968–70, rev. 1976; Sym. no.2 (Trakl, Plath), op.7, S, chamber orch, 1970–71; Sym. no.3, op.18, 1973–9; Coursing, op.17, chamber orch, 1978–80

Other works: Pantomime, op.2, wind qnt, str qt, 1968, rev. 1978;

Masks, op.3, fl, 1969; Fire, capriccio, op.4, fl, str trio, 1969; 3 Little Fantasies, op.6a, wind qnt, 1970, rev. 1976; Vocalise with Songs of Winnie-the-Pooh, op.6b, S, fl, eng hn, cl, vc, pf, 1970; The Cheshire Cat, op.6c, cl, drone, 1970; Choral, op.8, wind orch, 1970–72; Turba, op.9, db, 1971; Rosary Songs, op.9, 1972; Océan de terre (Apollinaire), op.10, fl, cl, vn, vc, db, perc, pf, 1972–3, rev. 1976; Puzzle Music, after John Lloyd, op.11, fl, cl, 2 perc, harp, cel, gui, mand, 1972–3; Trumpets (Trakl), op.12, 1v, 3 cl, 1975; Ophelia Dances I, op.13, fl, eng hn, cl, hn, cel, str trio, 1975; Autumnal, op.14, vn, pf, 1976–7; Cantata, op.15, ob, str trio, 1977; Sonya's Lullaby, op.16, pf, 1977–8; Where the Wild Things are (fantasy in 2 acts, M. Sendak), 1979–80

Principal publisher: Faber

BIBLIOGRAPHY

B. Northcott: 'Oliver Knussen', *MT*, cxx (1979), 729

BAYAN NORTHCOTT

Knyff [Knyf] (*fl* *c*1425–50). Composer, presumably English, of a Credo for three voices that appears in an 'English' fascicle of *I-AO* (second layer, no.96). De Van did not include his name in his catalogue of *AO*: it has been partly cut away by the binder, but is clear enough in the index. Nothing is known of his life, unless (an extremely remote possibility) he is to be identified with the theorist RICHARD CUTELL, who was connected with St Paul's Cathedral, London, in 1394–5: in medieval Latin, *cutellus* means 'knife'.

BIBLIOGRAPHY

M. F. Bukofzer: *Geschichte des englischen Diskants und des Fauxbourdons nach den theoretischen Quellen* (Strasbourg, 1936), 141ff

F. Ll. Harrison: *Music in Medieval Britain* (London, 1958, 2/1963), 12, 113, 149f, 152, 457

B. L. Trowell: *Music under the later Plantagenets* (diss., U. of Cambridge, 1960), i, 47, 50ff; ii, 184

BRIAN TROWELL

Knyght, Thomas (*fl* *c*1525–50). English church musician and composer. Throughout his known career he was a lay vicar of Salisbury Cathedral, where he became teacher of the choristers some time between 1526 and 1529, and also organist in, or a little before, 1538 (his deed of appointment to both offices is dated 30 April 1538). He undertook 'to kepe laudablie the orgeyns according to good Musycke and armony', and to teach the choristers 'playnsonge pryckesonge Faburdon and descante'. He must be distinguished from the Thomas Knyght who was a prebendary at Salisbury; owing to the imperfect state of the cathedral's archives the musician cannot be traced there later than October 1543. But no successor is known until October 1550.

Compositions attributable to him survive for both the Latin and English rites. A five-part mass *Libera nos* survives (inc., *GB-Cu* Peterhouse 471–4); three four-part settings (of the *Alleluia, Obtine sacris*, the antiphon *Christus resurgens ex mortuis* and the Marian antiphon *Sancta Maria virgo intercede*) in *GB-Lbm* Add.17802–5 ascribed to 'Mr Knyght' are probably also by him. The best of his Latin church music shows Knyght to have been a competent and inventive composer. A vernacular *Magnificat* and *Nunc dimittis* attributed to 'Knyght' were included in John Day's *Certaine Notes* of 1565. These too may be his, for they also appear, anonymously, in the Wanley Partbooks (*Ob* Mus.Sch.E.420–22), which date from *c*1550, close to the period of Knyght's known activity.

Thomas Knyght must also be distinguished from Robert Knyght, four parts of whose five-part motet *Propterea maestum factum est cor nobis* are in *Cp* 485, 487–9. This work may be dated *c*1580–1600. Nothing is known of its composer; a second motet of his, mentioned in earlier editions of *Grove*, does not exist, but was the result of confusing Robert Knyght with Robert Whyte.

ROGER BOWERS

Knyvett, Charles (*b* ?London, 22 Feb 1752; *d* London, 19 Jan 1822). English singer. He was a chorister at Westminster Abbey and attended Westminster School. During the 1770s he became well known as an alto singer. He was a member of the Royal Society of Musicians from 4 January 1778, a Gentleman of the Chapel Royal from 6 November 1786 until 1808, and organist of that institution from 25 July 1796 until his death. He was also for many years secretary of the Noblemen's and Gentlemen's Catch Club, and was a frequent visitor to the Madrigal Society. He was one of the chief singers at the Handel Commemoration of 1784 and gave concerts until shortly before his death. He was regarded as one of the finest singers of his day, particularly in the glee and the catch. Parke called him 'perhaps the best catch singer in England, evincing in them all the genuine comedy of an Edwin'. He was also a successful composer of glees.

Knyvett embarked on various financial speculations. In 1789, with Samuel Harrison, he directed a series of oratorio performances at Covent Garden in Lent, undercutting the established Drury Lane Oratorios. In 1791 they opened the Vocal Concerts, which continued sporadically until Knyvett's death. At first they consisted entirely of vocal music, but on revival in 1801 they reverted to the more usual 'Grand Miscellaneous Selection'. Their programmes were conservative, consisting largely of excerpts from Handel's operas and oratorios, but always including some glees, in which Knyvett was a star performer. In 1800 he compiled *A Collection of Favorite Glees, Catches and Rounds*. In 1815 he published *Six Airs Harmonized for 3 and 4 Voices*. He purchased an estate at Sonning, Berkshire, which was inherited by his son Charles (1773–1852), an organist and composer.

For bibliography *see* KNYVETT, WILLIAM.

NICHOLAS TEMPERLEY

Knyvett, William (*b* London, 21 April 1779; *d* Ryde, Isle of Wight, 17 Nov 1856). English singer and composer, son of CHARLES KNYVETT. He was taught by his father and Samuel Webbe. He began singing in the Concert of Ancient Music in 1788 as a treble, and in 1795 as an alto, in which range he sang for the rest of his life. He became a Gentleman of the Chapel Royal in 1797, and soon afterwards a lay clerk at Westminster Abbey. For more than 40 years he sang at the principal concerts in London and the provinces, often as a member of a fashionable vocal trio with Harrison and Bartleman. Like his father he specialized in glee singing. He directed the Concert of Ancient Music from 1832 to 1840, the Birmingham Festival from 1834 to 1843, and the York Festival of 1835. It was maintained that 'with the exception of Sir George Smart, he was the last of the musical leaders who inherited the Handel traditions as to the method of conducting an oratorio'. His second wife, Deborah Travis (*c*1795–1876), was a well-known singer.

He assisted his father in managing the Vocal Concerts, but eventually 'impoverished himself by unsuccessful speculations'. He is said to have written 46 glees, many of which were published; one, *When the fair rose*, was awarded the Prince of Wales's Prize in 1800. He also composed songs with piano accompaniment, and some anthems, including one commissioned for the coronation of George IV in 1821 (*The King Shall Rejoice*) and another for Queen Victoria's coronation. Knyvett's compositions are smooth and competent, but show no spark of originality.

BIBLIOGRAPHY

W. T. Parke: *Musical Memoirs* (London, 1830), i, 120; ii, 77, 236
J. Burke and J. B. Burke: *The Extinct & Dormant Baronetcies of England* (London, 1838), 294
C. Mackeson: 'Vocal Concerts', *Grove 1–5*
D. Baptie: *Sketches of the English Glee Composers* (London, 1895)
——: *Descriptive Catalogue of Glees, Madrigals, Part Songs, etc.* (MS, GB-Lbm, 1897)
M. B. Foster: *Anthems and Anthem Composers* (London, 1901/R1970), 128

NICHOLAS TEMPERLEY

Kobelius, Johann Augustin (*b* Waehlitz, nr. Merseburg, 21 Feb 1674; *d* Weissenfels, 17 Aug 1731). German composer. His career was centred on his native Saxony, where he was born the son of a pastor. His mother was the daughter of Nicolaus Brause, a Weissenfels organist who became his first music teacher. Later Kobelius studied the organ with Christian Schieferdecker, Kantor and organist in Weissenfels, and, according to Gerber, composition with Johann Philipp Krieger, court Kapellmeister at Weissenfels. Gerber also stated that Kobelius travelled extensively as a student, and visited Venice. In 1702 he was appointed organist at the Holy Trinity Church in Sangerhausen and in 1703 became director of the chorus there. In 1724 he also took on the direction of choruses in the neighbouring town of Querfurt. In 1725 he was named *Landrentmeister* (land steward) for the court of Saxe-Weissenfels.

Kobelius was the last important composer to write operas during the brief but brilliant period of music at the Weissenfels court. Among his distinguished predecessors had been Keiser, Heinichen and, especially, Krieger. Kobelius was active as a composer in Weissenfels as early as 1712, but from 1715 to 1729 he served as the only regular composer of operas for performances in the royal palace, writing one score or more each year. Regrettably, all this music seems to be lost and few of the librettists have been identified.

WORKS
OPERAS
(all first performed in Weissenfels unless otherwise stated)

Der unschuldig verdammte Heinrich, Fürst von Wallis, 1715
Der Irrgarten der Liebe, oder Livia und Cleander, 1716
Der glückliche Betrug, oder Clythia und Orestes, 1717, possibly by Kobelius
Die auch im Unglück glückliche Liebe der Isabelle und Rodrigo, 1717
Die gerettete Unschuld, oder Ali und Sefira, 1717
Die bewährte und wohlbelohnte Treue, oder Cloelia und Pythias, 1718
Das doppelte Glück getreuer Liebe zwischen Fernando und Bellamira, 1719
Don Carlos und Sidonie, 1719, revived 1726
Die zwar gedrückte, doch wieder erquickte Liebe, oder Amine und Sefi, 1719
Die vom Himmel geschützte Unschuld und Tugend, oder Bellerophon, Neumeister, 1720
Damoetas und Euphrasia, Sangerhausen, 1720, possibly by Kobelius
Das durch beständige Liebe mit Persien glücklich verknüpfte Numidien, oder Achmed und Almeide, 1721
Die triumphierende Liebe, 1723
Der Triumph der Treue, oder Bellinde, 1724
Die erhabene Tugend oder Bozena, 1725
Selimone und Cloriden, 1727
Das triumphierende Glück, oder Augustas und Livia, 1727
Ismene und Menoikeus [Menalces, Menarcas], 1728
Marcus Antonius und Cleopatra, 1728, 1729
Die getreue Schäferin Doris, 1728
Meleager und Atalanta, 1729
Paris und Oenone, 1729
Theseus und Helene, 1729

BIBLIOGRAPHY

GerberL; WaltherML

A. Werner: *Städtische und fürstliche Musikpflege in Weissenfels bis zum Ende des 18. Jahrhunderts* (Leipzig, 1911)

R. Brockpähler: *Handbuch zur Geschichte der Barockoper in Deutschland* (Emsdetten, 1964)

GEORGE J. BUELOW

København (Dan.). COPENHAGEN.

Kobierkowicz [Kobierkiewicz], **Józef** [Franciszek; Antoni; ?Ignacy] (*fl c*1730–51). Polish composer and organist. He was active as a lay musician during the years 1731–5, and possibly also 1751, in the musical establishment of the monastery of the Pauline fathers in Jasna Góra in Częstochowa. It has been suggested, because his works are mentioned in a Kraków inventory in 1737, that Kobierkowicz was connected with the Jesuit chapel there, but this is conjectural. He wrote a number of pastorellas, short works connected with Christmas, on sacred texts relating the story of the shepherds, and using melodic phrases based on carols or other folktunes (including the *oberek* dance). His music is simple in style, using echo and dialogue effects and favouring parallel 3rds rather than contrapuntal imitation; it has a certain individual charm and may be regarded as representative of provincial Polish musical centres, particularly monastic ones, in the late Baroque period.

WORKS

Pastorellas, all ed. in ZHMP, xii (1968): Musae piae, S, A, T, B, 2 vn, 2 tpt, org; In pace princeps, A, T, 2 vn, 2 tpt, org; Caelum gaude, S, B, 2 vn, db, org; Dormi mei redemptio, S, 2 vn, db, org; Apparuit benignitas, S, 2 vn, db, org; Salve puelle, A, T, 2 vn, db, org; Caelo rores, S, B, 2 vn, vle, org; Caeli rores, S, B, 2 vn, vle, org; Adiuro te, S, S, 2 vn, db, org; Patris stupenda bonitas, S, A, T, B, 2 vn, 2 tpt, bn, org

Ego mater pulchrae dictionis, motet, SATB, 2 vn, db, org, ed. in WDMP, lv (1964)

Justus ut palma florebit, motet, SATB, 2 vn, 2 tpt, db, org, *PL-SA* 272/A VII, 32

LOST WORKS

2 pastorellas, S, 2 vn, bn, org, *PL-Czp* (cover only)

Confitebor, Dixit Dominus, Magnificat, Regina coeli, Salve regina, Sit tibi salus: all cited in 1737 inventory of the Jesuit society in Kraków

BIBLIOGRAPHY

SMP

A. Chybiński: *Słownik muzyków dawnej Polski* [Dictionary of early Polish musicians] (Kraków, 1949), 58, 156

W. Świerczek: 'Rękopiśmienne zabytki muzyki dawnej w bibliotece Seminarium Duchownego w Sandomierzu' [Manuscript treasures of early music in the library of the Sandomierz seminary], *Kronika diecezji Sandomierskiej* (1959), nos.7–8

Z. M. Szweykowski: 'Z zagadnień melodyki w polskiej muzyce wokalno–instrumentalnej późnego baroku' [Problems of melody in Polish vocal and instrumental music in the late Baroque], *Muzyka*, vi/2 (1961), 53

W. Świerczek: 'Katalog rękopiśmiennych zabytków muzycznych biblioteki Seminarium Duchownego w Sandomierzu' [Catalogue of manuscript music treasures in the library of the Sandomierz seminary], *Archiwa, biblioteki i muzea kościelne*, x (Lublin, 1965), 223–78

P. Podejko: 'Nieznani muzycy polscy, kompozytorzy, dyrygenci, instrumentaliści, wokaliści (1572–1820)' [Unknown Polish musicians, composers, conductors, instrumentalists, singers (1572–1820), *Z dziejów muzyki polskiej*, xi (1966), 49

Z. M. Szweykowski: 'Some Problems of Baroque Music in Poland', *Musica Antiqua Europae Orientalis I: Bydgoszcz 1966*, 294

P. Podejko: 'Na marginesie dotychczasowych wzmianek o życiu muzycznym na Jasnej Górze w Częstochowie' [Marginalia about the details of musical life in Jasna Góra Monastery in Częstochowa], *Muzyka*, xii/1 (1967), 37

——: 'Źródła do dziejów muzyki polskiej w archiwum zakonu paulinów w Częstochowie' [Sources for the history of Polish music in the archives of the Pauline monastery in Częstochowa], *Z dziejów muzyki polskiej*, xiv (1969), 38f

K. Mrowiec: *Pasje wielogłosowe w muzyce polskiej XVIII wieku* [XVIIIth-century Polish Passion music] (Kraków, 1972)

P. Podejko: *Kapela wokalno-instrumentalna zakonu paulinów na Jasnej Górze* [The vocal and instrumental establishment of the Pauline monastery of Jasna Góra] (Kraków, 1977)

MIROSŁAW PERZ

Koblenz [Coblenz]. City in the Federal Republic of Germany at the confluence of the Rhine and Mosel. It was founded in the 1st century as a Roman fort, provided with walls and fortifications towards the end of the 3rd century, and enlarged in Franconian times to make a royal residence.

Two of the three important old churches in the town, the Kastorkirche (dating from 836), the Florinkirche (900) and the Liebfrauenkirche (1180), have at various times had choral foundations with distinctive choral traditions. The Kastorkirche owns two richly illuminated graduals from the 15th and 16th centuries with staffed neumes; other manuscripts of choral music are in the library or the Görresgymnasium (formerly the Jesuits' library).

Koblenz's theatrical tradition began in 1581 at the Jesuit School; troupes of English strolling players are recorded from 1605. In 1787 an opera house, which still exists, was inaugurated with a performance of Mozart's *Die Entführung aus dem Serail* by J. H. Böhm's company, which remained in Koblenz until 1804. In 1867 the theatre was taken over by the city as the private owners were no longer able to maintain the building.

Koblenz was handed over by the Emperor Heinrich II to the archbishopric of Trier in 1018. The archbishops, who were also electors from the 13th century until the French Revolution, helped the town to prosper, and the removal of the elector's residence to Ehrenbreitstein near Koblenz at the beginning of the 17th century further stimulated the town's cultural life. The Elector Carl Caspar von der Leyen (1652–76) introduced musicians to the court in 1654, and during his reign there were 20 musicians and a dancing-master. The number of musicians was continually increased; by 1782 there were 41 instrumentalists, second only to Mannheim with 54. The lists of musicians include internationally famous names: Johann Zach, F. G. Anschuez (1711–95), Johann Peter and Philipp Dornaus, P. P. Sales, Jean Danzi, Jakob von Lindpaintner, father of the conductor P. J. von Lindpaintner, and Vincenzo Righini. The repertory was based chiefly on church music with a prevalence of works in the concertato style. The last musicians at the court included in their repertory works by Haydn, Mozart, Gluck, J. C. Bach, Pergolesi, Dittersdorf, J. A. Hasse, Salieri, Carl Stamitz and Cimarosa. In 1763 Mozart spent ten days at Koblenz, playing at the Residenz and in public concerts.

Music was fostered by the townspeople from 1760; this tradition has been continued by the Musikinstitut, founded in 1808 by J. A. Anschuez (1792–1855). Between 1865 and 1867 Max Bruch was its director and in 1866 his First Violin Concerto had its première under its auspices. Chamber music has been fostered by the Verein der Musikfreunde since 1872. Visiting virtuosos included Chopin, Ferdinand Hiller, Mendelssohn, Liszt, Paganini, Brahms and Reger. The singer Henriette Sontag was born there.

Orchestral music was provided by the bands of the military forces stationed in Koblenz until 1900, when the Stadttheater started its own orchestra; this was taken over by the town in 1913 and called the Städtisches Orchester Koblenz. In autumn 1945 the Rheinische Philharmonie was founded in Koblenz with over 80 players. Under Walter May, Carl August Vogt and Claro Mizerit it became well known in Germany and abroad and in 1973 it was adopted as a state orchestra with state support. The main concert hall is the Rhein-Mosel-Halle, built in 1962; its large concert organ, made by Kemper of Lübeck, has 72 stops. Between 1949 and 1970 the Koblenzer Sommerspiele attracted up to 120,000 visitors in June and July every year, with operettas on a floating stage on the Rhine and open-air serenade concerts in the Freilichtbühne Blumenhof of the Deutschherrenhaus (since 1955). The Koblenz Madrigal Choir, founded in 1956, is widely known and regularly participates in international festivals.

After the Musikinstitut gave up its associated school for singers and performers in 1880, a private conservatory was set up which existed until 1945 and for a time after 1906 had some 300 students under the violinist Franz Sagebiel; the staff included Bruch and Pfitzner (in 1892–3). In 1969 a college of education was established in Koblenz, which includes a course for teachers of music in primary and secondary schools, and a municipal music school was begun in 1973.

BIBLIOGRAPHY

W. J. Becker: *Forschungen zum Theaterleben von Koblenz im Rahmen der deutschen, namentlich der rheinischen Theater-Geschichte, über die Zeit bis zum Jahre 1815* (diss., U. of Bonn, 1915)
——: *Gesammelte Beiträge zur Literatur und Theatergeschichte von Coblenz* (Koblenz, 1919)
H. G. Fellmann: *Die Böhm'sche Theatergruppe und ihre Zeit* (Leipzig, 1928)
G. Reitz: *St. Kastor zu Koblenz: Kirche–Stift–Pfarrei in ihrer Geschichte* (Koblenz, 1936)
P. Schuh: *Joseph Andreas Anschuez: der Gründer des Koblenzer Musikinstituts* (Cologne, 1958)
F. Bösken: *Die Orgelbauerfamilie Stumm* (Mainz, 1960)
G. Bereths: *Die Musikpflege am kurtrierischen Hofe zu Koblenz-Ehrenbreitstein* (Mainz, 1964)
U. Baur: 'Koblenz Kulturzentrum am Mittelrhein', *1945–1970 Rheinische Philharmonie* (Mainz, 1970)
H. Bellinghausen: *2000 Jahre Koblenz* (Boppard, 1973)

HEINZ ANTON HÖHNEN

Koch. German family of organists and organ builders. Paul Koch the elder (*d* Zwickau, 1546), from St Joachimsthal (Bohemia), went to Zwickau in 1543 and there renovated the organs in the Marienkirche and the Katharinenkirche. Paul Koch the younger (buried Zwickau, 28 Sept 1580) worked as organist in Zwickau, from 1544 at St Katharinen, and from 1552 at St Marien. He renovated the organ in Weiden. Hans Koch was organist from 1563 to 1568 at the Petrikirche in Freiberg, Saxony. Stephan Koch (*d* Zwickau, 29 Dec 1590) was organist at St Dorotheen in Vienna in 1564, and later in Annaberg (Erzgebirge), where he married in 1570. From 21 July 1575 he lived as a wealthy citizen and organist and highly esteemed instrument maker in Zwickau. He completed an organ begun by Jakob Weinrebe in Bischofswerda (Christuskirche, 1571) and built instruments in Olomouc (St Mauritius, 1585), Kulmbach (1587) and Jihlava (1590). Three positive organs are ascribed to him by M. Fürstenau in the Dresden instrument inventory.

Georg Koch the elder was no doubt closely related to the Zwickau branch of the family. He built an organ in Glauchau (Georgenkirche, 1580) and from 1582 until 1585 was in Glauchau, where he owned a house and garden (though he later suffered a period of financial hardship). In 1585 he was living in Zwickau, where he remained until at least 1590. He renovated organs in Zeitz (cathedral) and Leipzig (St Nicolai) and built organs at Taus (large organ, 1572–3), Schmölln (Stadtpfarrkirche, 1583) and Brno (St Jakob, 1590). He

was assisted by his son Georg in building an organ at Waldenburg, Saxony (St Bartholomäus, 1598–9); in 1602 Georg Koch the younger made some improvements to the instrument, which had in the meantime been damaged by stormy weather. A son born to Georg Koch (the younger) and his wife Martha was baptized in Altwaldenburg on 27 October 1616.

The capable organ builders of this well-known family combined carefully planned register combinations with solid workmanship, and they are of considerable importance in the art of 16th-century organ building. Their instruments are found chiefly in Saxony, Bohemia, Moravia, Silesia and Bavaria.

BIBLIOGRAPHY

E. Herzog: *Chronik der Kreisstadt Zwickau*, ii (Zwickau, 1845)
E. Eckardt: *Chronik von Glauchau* (Glauchau, 1882)
P. Smets, ed.: *Orgeldispositionen* (Kassel, 1931)
E. Müller: 'Musikgeschichte von Freiberg', *Altertumsverein*, lxviii (1939), 80
W. Haacke: 'Orgelbauten im Zeitzer und Naumburger Dom', *AMf*, vii (1942)
R. Quoika: *Der Orgelbau in Böhmen und Mähren* (Mainz, 1966)

WALTER HÜTTEL

Koch, (Sigurd Christian) Erland von (*b* Stockholm, 26 April 1910). Swedish composer, teacher and conductor. Son of the composer SIGURD VON KOCH (1879–1919), he studied at the Stockholm Conservatory (1931–5) and then in France and Germany (1936–8) with Höffer (composition), Kraus and Gmeindl (conducting) and Arrau (piano). On his return to Sweden he concentrated on conducting, while also working as a teacher at Wohlfart's Music School, Stockholm (1939–53), and as a sound technician with Swedish radio (1943–5). In 1953 he was appointed to teach harmony at the Stockholm Musikhögskolan, where he was made professor in 1968. He was chairman of Fylkingen (1946–8) and an executive member of the Swedish Composers' Association (1947–63).

After an early neo-classical phase, typified by the popular orchestral *Dans* no.2, Koch's style matured through his studies of Grieg, Sibelius, Hindemith and Bartók, and, above all, as a result of his deep understanding of Dalecarlian folk music. His fresh, effectively scored pieces, often using folk melody, have made him one of the most popular Swedish composers abroad. With the years his treatment of tonality has broadened, and he has developed a skilful ability in the rhythmic and contrapuntal variation of peasant music, as demonstrated in the orchestral *Oxberg-trilogin*, the 12 *Skandinaviska danser* and the *Polska svedese*. In the *Impulsi-trilogin* the orchestration is heavier and there are almost 12-note melodies.

WORKS
(selective list)

ORCHESTRAL

Liten svit, chamber orch, op.1, 1933; Pf Conc. no.1, op.11, 1936; Vn Conc., op.14, 1937; Sym. no.1, op.18, 1938; Dans no.2, 1938, arr. str, 1966; Sinfonia dalecarlica (Sym. no.2), op.30, 1945; Va Conc., op.33, 1946, rev. 1966; Concertino pastorale, op.35, fl, str, 1947, rev. 1965; Sym. no.3, op.38, 1948; Serenata giocosa, op.39, 1948; Triptychon, vn, orch, op.43, 1949; Arkipelag, op.47, 1950; Vc Conc., op.49, 1951, rev. 1966; Musica malinconica, str, op.50, 1952; Sinfonia seria (Sym. no.4), op.51, 1952–3, rev. 1961; Conc., small orch, 1955

Konsertmusik, 1955; Oxberg-trilogin: Oxbergvariationer, 1956, Lapplandmetamorfoser, 1957, Dansrapsodi, 1957; Sax Conc., 1958; [12] Skandinaviska danser, 1958–60; Conc. piccolo, s sax, a sax, str, 1962; Pf Conc. no.2, 1962; Fantasia concertante, vn, orch, 1964; Impulsi-trilogin: Impulsi, 1964, Echi, 1965, Ritmi, 1966; Arioso e furioso, str, 1967; Polska svedese, 1968; Musica concertante, 8 wind, orch, 1969; Double Conc., fl, cl, str, 1970; Pf Conc. no.3, pf, wind, 1970, arr. pf, orch, 1972; Canto nordico e Rondo, ob, str orch, 1973; En Svensk i New York, 1973; Minityrsvit, str, 1973; Conc., vn, pf, orch, 1974; Festmarsch, 1974; Saxophonia, conc., 4 sax, wind orch, 1976

OTHER WORKS

Stage: Askungen, ballet, op.24, 1942; Lasse Lucidor, opera, op.27, 1943; Pelle Svanslös, children's opera, op.42, 1948; Simson och Dalila, ballet, 1965

Choral: Midsommardalen (H. Martinson), S, Bar, chorus, orch, 1960–61; 5 psalmer, chorus, org, solo inst ad lib, 1974–5; other pieces, folksongs arrs.

Chamber and inst: Str Qt no.1, op.2, 1934; Str Qt no.2, op.28, 1944; Musica intima (Str Qt no.3), op.48, 1950, arr. str orch, 1965; Conc. lirico (Str Qt no.4), 1956, arr. str orch, 1961; Str Qt no.5, 1961; Serenata espressiva (Str Qt no.6), 1963, also for str orch; 3 intermezzi concertanti, pf, 1963; Varianti virtuosi I, pf, 1965, II, vn, pf, 1969; Fantasi i vallåt och Caprice, fl, 1973; [3] Kontraster, org, 1973; Nattlig etyd, pf, 1973; Pizzicato–flageolet, vn, pf, 1973; Fantasia on 'Ack Värmeland du sköna', vn, pf, 1974; Psalm fran Älvdalen, org, 1974; Variationen über eine schwedische Volksweise, vn, 1974; Canto e danza, fl, gui, 1975; Dialogue, s sax, a sax, 1975; Monolog 2–9, various solo insts, 1975; Rytmiska bagateller, vn, pf, 1957–75; Variations II on a Swedish folksong, va, 1975; other pieces

Songs: Jungfrun i Tidlösa, 1945; Drömmen om människan [The dream of man] (Martinson), 1967–8

Principal publishers: Associated, Breitkopf & Härtel, Gehrman, Nordiska, Peer, Simrock, Southern

BIBLIOGRAPHY

'Erland von Koch svarar på frågor om sig själv' [Koch answers questions about himself], Musikvärlden (1945), no.4, p.9

I. Liljefors: 'Erland von Koch', Vår sång (1949), 8

A. Helmer: 'Erland von Koch', Musikrevy, xiii (1958), 115

Å. Brandel: 'Eine reife Generation: Larsson – Wirén – de Frumerie – von Koch', Musikrevy International (1959), 47 [Eng. trans. in Musikrevy international (1960), 61]

E. von Koch: 'Några intryck från en studieres hösten 1970' [Some impressions from a study trip autumn 1970], Kungliga musikaliska akademiens arsskrift 1970, 77

H. Connor: Samtal med tonsättare [Conversation with composers] (Stockholm, 1971), 69ff

ROLF HAGLUND

Koch, Franjo Žaver. See KUHAČ, FRANCO ŽAVER.

Koch, Friedrich E(rnst) (b Berlin, 3 July 1862; d Berlin, 30 Jan 1927). German teacher and composer. At the age of 16 he entered the Berlin Hochschule für Musik, where he studied the cello with Hausmann and composition with Bargiel (1880–81, 1883–4) and then Radecke. He was playing the cello with the Royal Orchestra in Berlin by 1882, and in 1891 he went to Baden-Baden as city Kapellmeister. After one year, however, he decided on a career in teaching and took a position as singing instructor at the municipal Lessing Gymnasium in Berlin, where he remained until 1918. The security of this appointment enabled him to give more attention to composition. His classicist pieces, with their simple, often folklike ideas, quickly found recognition, and in 1901 he was elected a full member of the Royal Academy of the Arts, Berlin (from 1902 he was a member of the senate). Nominated professor in 1900, he was active as a teacher at various conservatories; from 1911 he participated in several official examination commissions. He was a thoroughly able and gifted teacher, and in 1917 he was appointed theory teacher at the Berlin Musikhochschule, where he succeeded Humperdinck as director of the theory and composition class in 1920. His pupils included Blacher, Jacobi and Kletzki. Though the pedagogic achievements of this typical Berlin academic are unquestioned, his music was quickly forgotten.

WORKS

(selective list)

Operas: Die Halliger (2, Koch), Cologne, 1896; Die Hügelmühle, op.41 (2, after G. Gjellerup), Berlin, 1918; Die Himmelsschuhe, op.46; Lea (2, Koch), unpubd

Choral: Das Sonnenlied, op.26 (M. Bamberger: Solarliodh), solo vv, chorus, orch, org (1898); Von den Tageszeiten, op.29 (oratorio, Koch), solo vv, chorus, orch, org (1905); Die deutsche Tanne, op.30

(Koch), B, chorus, orch (1905); Die Sündflut, op.32 (Bible, Koch), solo vv, chorus, orch, org (1910); other acc. and unacc. works

Orch: Sym. no.1 'Von der Nordsee', d, op.4 (1891); Sinfonische Fuge, c, op.8 (1891); Sym. no.2, G, op.10 (1892); Deutsche Rhapsodie, D, op.31, vn, orch (1907); Romantische Suite, op.37 (1920)

Chamber works, pf pieces, songs

Principal publishers: Bote & Bock, Breitkopf & Härtel, Kahnt, Rahter

WRITINGS

Der Aufbau der Kadenz und anderes: ein Beitrag zur Harmonielehre (Leipzig, 1920)

BIBLIOGRAPHY

A. Schering: Von den Tageszeiten: Erläuterung (Leipzig, 1905)

——: Geschichte des Oratoriums (Leipzig, 1911)

H. Kretzschmar: Führer durch den Konzertsaal, i/2 (Leipzig, 4/1913); ii/1 (Leipzig, 4/1916); ii/2 (Leipzig, 3/1915)

W. Niemann: Die Musik der Gegenwart (Berlin, 1921)

Archives in D-Bhm, and Akademie der Künste

THOMAS-M. LANGNER

Koch, Heinrich Christoph (b Rudolstadt, 10 Oct 1749; d Rudolstadt, 19 March 1816). German theorist and violinist. He studied the violin and composition in Rudolstadt, and later in Berlin, Dresden and Hamburg. From 1772 he was court musician (later Konzertmeister) at Rudolstadt, but gave up the post to devote himself to writing. Various choral works, apparently lost, are attributed to him by Gerber, but these could not have equalled the importance of his Versuch einer Anleitung zur Composition (1782–93) and Musikalisches Lexikon (1802), which are the most comprehensive works of their kind in the Classic era.

The Versuch is an extensive treatment of composition, from basic harmonic principles to the construction of a symphony movement. It undoubtedly influenced the 19th-century theorists Reicha, Czerny, Choron, Marx, Lobe, Jadassohn, Prout, Riemann and Goetschius, who dealt systematically with the formal aspects of composition, and has recently received recognition as a major contribution to the theory of musical form. Koch's examples represent the style of Graun and Benda as well as the earlier Haydn and Mozart, a galant orientation addressed in its simpler terms to students and amateurs and in its complex and subtle aspects to the professional composer. The first volume begins with a description of keys and chords (later modified in the Handbuch, 1811), and concludes with instruction in counterpoint, which clearly shows his intention to teach composition in the free style. His counterpoint is based entirely on harmony, drawing its intervals from chords rather than church modes and intervallic relationships, as in the Fux tradition. Two-part counterpoint consists of a melody and bass, with frequent cadences, often including tritones and diminished 5ths, especially in modulations. Unequal counterpoint uses figuration or countermelodies in the free style, as in a Classical minuet; figured bass and fugue, the staples of the composition methods of the earlier 18th century, are ignored.

The second volume begins with a discussion of the nature of a musical composition, in which Koch set forth his aesthetic views (echoed in the Journal and the Lexikon); for him, as for many other late 18th-century writers, the principal object of music is to stir the feelings. He then described three stages in the composition of a piece of music: the Anlage (plan), in which the principal ideas of the first part or reprise are invented (late 18th-century theorists regarded two-part or two-reprise structure as standard for first movements); the Ausführung (completion of the design), which also restates some of the ideas of the first stage; and the Ausarbeitung (working-out), the finishing touches. This plan corresponds to the dispositio, elaboratio and decor-

atio of Mattheson's *Der vollkommene Capellmeister* (p.235). The rest of the second volume and all of the third deal with the 'mechanical rules of melody', probably the most valuable part of the *Versuch* and the strongest influence on later theorists. This is a detailed study of phrase and period structure and shows the influence of Riepel. The normal disposition of phrases is in groups of two and four bars. The smallest complete piece is 16 bars long, consisting of two equal reprises. Dances are given as models, including the Menuet from Haydn's Divertimento in G major, HII:1. Methods of compressing, overlapping and extending phrases are then explored in detail. The final example expands an eight-bar period in the style of a bourrée to a 32-bar reprise comparable to the exposition of a sonata, using repetitions, sequences, restatements, parentheses and cadential reinforcements.

The latter part of the third volume deals with larger genres, including recitative, aria, rondo, French overture, symphony, sonata (duet, trio, quartet) and concerto, with a final section illustrating melodic continuity in long works. Most of Koch's examples are given as melodic lines, yet underlying the arrangement of figures, phrases, periods and cadences is the premise that musical form is organized by key relationships; the form of an allegro has the outline I–V–(optional)–I.

Koch's *Lexikon*, a dictionary of musical terms, is a valuable source of information on theory and aesthetics; much of it is drawn from the *Versuch*, and Koch frequently quoted Sulzer's *Allgemeine Theorie der schönen Kunste*. The work was published in a revised version (by Arrey von Dommer) as late as 1865, and has served as the model for later non-biographical music dictionaries.

For further discussion of Koch's terminology, phrase-construction and formal models, *see* ANALYSIS, §II, 2.

WRITINGS

Versuch einer Anleitung zur Composition (Rudolstadt and Leipzig, 1782–93/R1969)
ed.: *Journal der Tonkunst* (Erfurt, 1795)
Musikalisches Lexikon, welches die theoretische und praktische Tonkunst, encyclopädisch bearbeitet, alle alten und neuen Kunstwörter erklärt, und die alten und neuen Instrumente beschrieben, enthält (Frankfurt am Main, 1802, 2/1817); abridged as *Kurzgefasstes Handwörterbuch der Musik für praktische Tonkünstler und für Dilettanten* (Leipzig, 1807)
'Über den technischen Ausdruck: Tempo rubato', *AMZ*, xxxiii (1808), cols.513ff
Handbuch bey dem Studium der Harmonie (Leipzig, 1811)
Versuch, aus den harten und weichen Tonart jeder Tonstufe der diatonisch-chromatischen Leiter vermittels des enharmonischen Tonwechsels in die Dur- und Molltonart der übrigen Stufen auszuweichen (Rudolstadt, 1812)

BIBLIOGRAPHY

H. Riemann: 'H. Chr. Koch als Erläuterer unregelmässigen Themenaufbaues', *Präludien und Studien*, ii (Leipzig, 1900)
E. Schwarzmaier: *Die Takt-und-Tonordnung Joseph Riepels* (diss., U. of Munich, 1934)
L. Ratner: 'Harmonic Aspects of Classic Form', *JAMS*, ii (1949), 159
A. Feil: *Satztechnische Fragen in den Kompositionlehren von F. E. Niedt, J. Riepel, und H. Chr. Koch* (diss., U. of Heidelberg, 1955)
L. Ratner: '18th-century Theories of Musical Period Structure', *MQ*, xlii (1956), 439
P. Benary: *Die deutsche Kompositionslehre des 18. Jahrhunderts* (Leipzig, 1961)
F. Ritzel: *Die Entwicklung der 'Sonatenform' im musiktheoretischen Schrifttum des 18. und 19. Jahrhunderts* (Wiesbaden, 1968)
R. Pečman: 'Die Musik in der Auffassung Heinrich Christoph Koch', *Sborník prací filosofické fakulty brněnské university*, xx/6 (1971)
J. Stevens: 'An 18th-century Description of Concerto First-movement Form', *JAMS*, xxiv (1971), 85
N. K. Baker: 'The Aesthetic Theories of Heinrich Christoph Koch', *IRASM*, viii (1977), 183

LEONARD G. RATNER

Koch, Helmut (*b* Wuppertal-Barmen, 5 April 1908; *d* Berlin, 26 Jan 1975). German conductor. He studied the violin, piano and conducting at Cologne, Essen and privately at Winterthur, chiefly under Max Fiedler, Fritz Lehmann and Hermann Scherchen. From 1931 he directed various workers' choirs, and his major début as a conductor was at Berlin in 1932 with Walter Gronostay's oratorio, *Mann in Beton*. He was recording manager with the Carl Lindström company from 1938 to 1945. In 1945 he founded the Berlin Chamber Orchestra, the Solistenvereinigung – a first-class vocal ensemble – and, in 1948, the Berlin Radio Choir in the German Democratic Republic. He was a regular guest conductor at the East Berlin Staatsoper from 1960, and director of the Berliner Singakademie from 1963. He made many fine recordings of pre-Classical vocal music, particularly of Handel's oratorios, as well as standard and contemporary choral works, and arranged numerous German and international folksongs. Besides touring widely, he was closely associated' with the Handel revival in East Germany, where his interpretations combined musicianly style and vitality with scholarly precision.

Koch, Jodocus. See JONAS, JUSTUS.

Koch, (Richert) Sigurd (Valdemar) von (*b* Ägnö, nr. Stockholm, 28 June 1879; *d* Stockholm, 16 March 1919). Swedish composer. He studied the piano at the Richard Andersson School and composition under Lindegren, then in Berlin (1905, 1912) and Dresden (1905). Later he worked as an accompanist and as a music critic. Painter and poet as well as composer, he ranks among the Nordic late Romantics, with a loosely rhapsodic style owing something to the French impressionists. His works include many song collections from his late years as well as violin and cello sonatas (both 1913), a piano quintet (1916), works for violin and orchestra (1914) and piano and orchestra (Ballade, 1919), incidental music and symphonic poems (including *I Pans marker*, 1917).

BIBLIOGRAPHY

F. H. Törnblom: 'Sigurd von Koch', *Ord och bild*, xlv (1936), 554
W. Seymer: 'Fyra nyromantiker', *STMf*, xxiii (1941), 61

KATHLEEN DALE/R

Kochan, Günter (*b* Luckau, 2 Oct 1930). German composer. He studied with Noetel, Wunsch and Blacher at the Berlin-Charlottenburg Musikhochschule and from 1950 to 1953 in Eisler's master class at the Academy of Arts. Between 1948 and 1951 he was attached to Berlin Radio, and in 1950 he was appointed to teach theory at the Berlin Musikhochschule.

WORKS
(*selective list*)

Orch: Vn Conc., op.1, 1952; Kleine Suite, op.13, 1956; Pf Conc., op.16, 1957; Sinfonietta 1960, op.24, 1960; Conc. for Orch, 1962; Sym., with chorus, 1964; Concertino, fl, orch, 1964; Vc Conc., 1967; Sym. no.2, 1968; Variationen über ein Thema von Mendelssohn, pf, orch, 1972; Sym. no.3, S, orch, 1972; Va Conc., 1974
Vocal: Die Welt ist jung (Wiens), cantata, chorus, orch, 1951; 3 Shakespeare Lieder, A, fl, str, 1964; Die Asche von Birkenau (St Hermlin), cantata, A, orch, 1965; Wir, unaufhaltsam (J. Schulz), Bar, speakers, chorus, orch, 1971; mass songs, youth songs
Chamber and inst: Pf Suite, op.2, 1952; Pf Trio, op.4, 1954; Divertimento, fl, cl, bn, op.12, 1956; Sonata, vc, pf, 1961; 5 Sätze, str qt, 1961; Sonata, vn, pf, 1962; Str Qt, 2 movts, 1965; Str Qt, 1973

Other works: incidental music, film scores, radio scores

Principal publisher: Peters

Kochańska, Prakseda Marcelina. *See* SEMBRICH, MARCELLA.

Kochański, Paweł (*b* Odessa, 14 Sept 1887; *d* New York, 12 Jan 1934). Polish violinist. He began lessons with Emil Młynarski when he was seven, and at 14 played first violin with the Warsaw Philharmonia. In 1903 he joined César Thomson's violin class at the Brussels Conservatory and received a *premier prix* after four months. After touring widely in Europe he returned to Poland in 1907 and taught the virtuoso class at the Warsaw Conservatory, then in 1913 succeeded Auer as professor at the Imperial Conservatory in St Petersburg. His friendship with Szymanowski brought about the composition of several violin works, notably *Mity* ('Myths', 1915) and the Concerto no.1 (1916), on both of which Kochański collaborated with the composer. He taught for two years in Kiev (1917–19); after the Revolution he left the USSR for Poland and then emigrated to the USA, where he made his début with the New York SO in 1921. He became a teacher at the Juilliard School in 1924 while continuing his concert career. Kochański wrote cadenzas to Szymanowski's concertos and made many transcriptions for violin and piano of works by Szymanowski and others, including Szymanowski's *Kurpie Song* no.9, Dance from *Harnasie* and Roxana's Song from *King Roger*, and Falla's Seven Spanish Popular Songs which he published as *Spanish Popular Suite*. He was awarded the Polish Officer Cross and made a member of the Légion d'honneur.

BIBLIOGRAPHY

I. M. Yampol'sky: 'Paweł Kochanski w Rosji', *Polsko-rosyjskie miscellanea muzyczne*, ed. Z. Lissa (Kraków, 1967)
J. Creighton: *Discopaedia of the Violin, 1889–1971* (Toronto, 1974)

MIECZYSŁAWA HANUSZEWSKA

Köchel, Ludwig (Alois Ferdinand) Ritter **von** (*b* Stein, nr. Krems, 14 Jan 1800; *d* Vienna, 3 June 1877). Austrian botanist, mineralogist and music bibliographer. Before graduating in law at Vienna University in 1827 Köchel had held several posts as tutor, of which the last and most noteworthy began in that year when, together with his friend Franz von Scharschmied, he was put in charge of the education of the four sons of Archduke Carl. In 1842 the conclusion of his services was recognized by the award of the Knight's Cross of the Order of Leopold.

As a man of private means, Köchel was able to indulge his keen interest in botany and mineralogy. He travelled much in pursuit of these studies and became a widely recognized expert in both fields. In music, too, he was an amateur who acquired a great reputation which has been secured among posterity by his total devotion to Mozart. A pamphlet, *Im Sachen Mozarts*, published anonymously in 1851 by Köchel's friend Franz Lorenz, drew attention to the very unsatisfactory state of knowledge about Mozart's music and its sources.

Köchel was thus prompted to improve the situation by compiling a chronological catalogue which provided the basis for scholarly publication. It gave the first few bars of each work (including all movements or vocal numbers) and identified it by a number; it also listed the autograph or other MS source if extant, the first edition, and added the reference to the recent biography by Jahn (to whom the catalogue was dedicated). Its compilation posed some unprecedented problems. It is true that the 176 works written by Mozart after 9 February 1784 (when he began his own, mostly dated, thematic catalogue) were simple to arrange. But many of those composed previously, to a total of nearly 450, were extremely difficult, either because the autograph was lost or, if extant, bore no date. Considering the limitation of Köchel's expertise and the scantiness of his documentary and bibliographical sources, this great catalogue, *Chronologisch-thematisches Verzeichnis sämtlicher Tonwerke Wolfgang Amade Mozarts* (1862), was a splendid achievement, the first of its scale and standard for any composer.

Subsequent editions (Leipzig, 2/1905, by P. von Waldersee; 3/1937, by Alfred Einstein; Wiesbaden, 6/1964, by Franz Giegling, Alexander Weinmann and Gerd Sievers) all added enormously to the amount of information, and have radically altered the numbering of some of the pre-1784 works for which 'K-E' or 'K6' is now increasingly found. But the initial letter of Köchel's surname and, broadly speaking, his framework have endured. Köchel also classified Mozart's works into the 24 groups that formed the scheme for the first truly complete edition (issued by Breitkopf, 1877–1905), the publication of which he instigated and subsidized with great generosity two years before his death.

WRITINGS
(*only those on music*)

Chronologisch-thematisches Verzeichnis sämtlicher Tonwerke Wolfgang Amade Mozarts (Leipzig, 1862; rev. 2/1905 by P. von Waldersee; rev. 3/1937 by A. Einstein, with suppl. 1947; rev. 6/1964 by F. Giegling, A. Weinmann and G. Sievers [see also *M Jb 1971–2*, 342–401])
Ueber den Umfang der musikalischen Produktivität W. A. Mozarts (Salzburg, 1862)
Drei und achtzig neuaufgefundene Original-Briefe Ludwig van Beethovens an den Erzherzog Rudolf (Vienna, 1865)
Die Pflege der Musik am österreichischen Hofe vom Schlusse des XV. bis zur Mitte des XVIII. Jahrhunderts (privately printed, 1866)
Die kaiserliche Hof-Musikkapelle in Wien von 1543–1867 (Vienna, 1869/R1976)
J. J. Fux Hofkompositor und Hofkapellmeister der Kaiser Leopold I, Joseph I, und Karl VI, von 1698–1740 (Vienna, 1872)

BIBLIOGRAPHY

C. F. Pohl: 'Köchel, Dr. Ludwig Ritter von', *ADB*
A. H. King: 'Köchel, Breitkopf, and the Complete Edition [of Mozart]', *Mozart in Retrospect* (London, 1955, rev. 3/1970/R1976), 55

ALEC HYATT KING

Kochem, Martin von. *See* MARTIN VON COCHEM.

Kocian, Jaroslav (*b* Ústí nad Orlicí, 22 Feb 1883; *d* Prague, 8 March 1950). Czech violinist, teacher and composer. The son of a violin teacher, he was given lessons from early childhood, later studying with Otakar Ševčík at the Prague Conservatory (1896–1901), and composition with Dvořák. He gained immediate success as a concert soloist at home and abroad from 1901, visiting Vienna, London and the USA, where he first toured in 1902. With Jan Kubelík he was regarded as an outstanding exponent of the Ševčík method and the Czech violin school, and was widely acclaimed for his warmth of tone, expressive ardour and stylistic purity. He spent two years in Russia from 1907 as professor at the Odessa Conservatory, leader of the Odessa Czech Quartet and of the Duke of Mecklenburg's private quartet at St Petersburg. In 1921 he became Ševčík's assistant at the Prague Conservatory, and in 1928 gave up concert appearances to devote himself to teaching. He was professor at the Masters' School of the Prague Conservatory from 1924 to 1943, with two years (1939–40) as rector there. His leading pupils included Alexandr Plocek, Josef Suk (ii) and Emil Zathurecky. He composed small works for violin and piano in neo-Romantic style, with some songs and choruses, and published a revision of his father's violin primer, *Počátky hry na housle* ('The beginnings of violin playing', Prague, 3/1945).

WRITINGS

'Kus svěživotopisu' [A piece of autobiography], i, *Lyra*, xix (1902)
'Preludii e intermezzi', *Sborník na památ 125 let konservatoře hudby v Praze* [Collection in memory of 125 years of conservatory music in Prague], ed. V. Blažek (Prague, 1936), 380

BIBLIOGRAPHY

ČSHS
B. Urban: *Mistr Jaroslav Kocian* (Kolín, 1926)
N. Kubát: 'Jaroslav Kocian', *Tempo*, xii (Prague, 1932–3), 275
V. Polívka: *S Kocianem kolem světa* [With Kocian round the world] (Prague, 1945)
R. Fikrle: 'K nedožitým sedmdesátinám Jaroslava Kociana' [For Jaroslav Kocian's posthumous 70th birthday], *HRo*, vi (1953), 155
C. Sychra, ed.: *Jaroslav Kocian: Sborník statí a vzpomínek* [Collection of articles and recollections] (Prague, 1953)
V. Šeft: 'Aktuální myšlenky kolem Kocianova jubilea' [Contemporary thoughts on Kocian's jubilee], *HRo*, xi (1958), 116
A. Šlajs: *Jaroslav Kocian* (Pardubice, 1958)

ALENA NĚMCOVÁ

Kocsár, Miklós (*b* Debrecen, 21 Dec 1933). Hungarian composer. After attending the Debrecen Music School he was a pupil of Farkas at the Budapest Academy of Music (1954–9). From 1963 he was director of music and conductor at the Madách Theatre, and in 1972 he was appointed to teach composition at the Budapest Conservatory. His *Lamenti* was performed at the 1968 ISCM Festival. He owes much to the examples of the modern Polish school and of Boulez and Ligeti.

WORKS
(selective list)

Vocal: Hegyi legények [Mountain lads], cantata, male chorus, brass, perc, 1957; Suhanj, szerelem [Glide away, love] (Joyce), chorus, pf, 1961; Lamenti (Lorca), S, pf, 1966–7; Évszakok zenéje [Music of the seasons] (L. Áprily), female chorus, 1967; Magányos ének [Solitary song] (cycle, A. József), S, ens, 1969; Tűz, te gyönyörű [Fire, you miracle] (L. Nagy), chorus, 1970; Liliomdal [Lily song] (Nagy), chorus, 1971; Három női kar [3 female choruses] (Nagy), 1971–2; Három Petőfi-dal [3 Petőfi songs], Bar, pf, 1973; Tűzciterák [Fire zithers] (Nagy), female vv, 1973; Kassák-dalok [Kassák songs], Mez, fl, cimb, 1976; Csili-csali nóták [7 children's choruses] (S. Weöres), 1977

Inst: Kürtverseny, hn, orch, 1957; Capriccio, orch, 1961; Dialoghi, bn, pf, 1964–5; Ungaresca, 2 ww, 1968; Variazioni, wind qnt, 1968; Serenata, str, 1957–71; Repliche, fl, zimbalo ungherese/hpd, 1971; Sextet, brass, 1972; Improvvisazioni, pf, 1972; Repliche no.2, hn, cimb, 1976; Változatok zenekarra [Variations for orch], 1977

Principal publisher: Editio Musica

BIBLIOGRAPHY

L. Somfai: 'Fiatal magyar zeneszerzők: Megjegyzések a bemutatott művekről' [Young composers: remarks on the performed compositions], *Magyar zene*, ix (1968), 165
I. Földes: *Harmincasok: Beszélgetések magyar zenezerzőkkel* [Those in their thirties: conversations with Hungarian composers] (Budapest, 1969)
Contemporary Hungarian Composers (Budapest, 1970)
G. Kroó: *A magyar zeneszerzés 25 éve* [25 years of Hungarian composition] (Budapest, 1971)
J. Kárpáti: 'Kocsár Miklós: Repliche', *Magyar zene*, xiii (1972), 190

MELINDA BERLÁSZ KAROLYI

Kocsis, Zoltán (*b* Budapest, 30 May 1952). Hungarian pianist and composer. He studied with Pál Kadosa, Ferenc Rados and György Kurtág at the Liszt Academy of Music, obtaining his diploma in 1973. As a student he caused a sensation when in 1970 he won the Hungarian Radio Beethoven Competition. The following year he made his first tour of the USA, and in 1972 appeared in London and at the Salzburg and Holland festivals. He was soon recognized as an outstanding pianist, and between 1971 and 1976 he appeared in musical centres from Tokyo to Bombay, from Helsinki to Tehran. He has an impressive technique, and his forthright, strongly rhythmic playing is nevertheless deeply felt and never mechanical. Kocsis has a natural affinity for Bach, but is also a fine exponent of contemporary music and has worked as composer with the avant-garde group the New Studio. Among his record-

ings are all Bach's concertos, and, for the complete recording of Bartók's works, the Concertos nos.1 and 2, the Sonata for two pianos, and *Contrasts*. He was awarded the Liszt Prize in 1973.

PÉTER P. VÁRNAI

Koczalski, Raoul [Raul] **(Armand Georg)** (*b* Warsaw, 3 Jan 1884; *d* Poznań, 24 Nov 1948). Polish pianist and composer. He had his first lessons with his parents and appeared at the age of four in Warsaw. He continued his studies with Chopin's pupil Mikuli in Lwów (which lends particular interest to his gramophone records) and with Anton Rubinstein. From the age of seven he toured all over Europe, and it is said that he celebrated his 1000th appearance by the time he was 12. He became renowned as one of the greatest exponents of Chopin and continued to tour widely. He lived in Germany and Sweden but after World War II returned to Poland, where he taught the master class in piano at the State High School in Poznań and later at Warsaw. His compositions include two operas, *Rymond* (Elberfeld, 1902) and *Die Sühne* (Mühlhausen, 1909), but they are otherwise mostly virtuoso piano works.

WRITINGS

Frédéric Chopin: Betrachtungen, Skizzen, Analysen (Cologne, 1936)
Über die Aufführungen Chopinscher Werke (nach Hinweisungen Mikulis) (n.p., n.d.)

BIBLIOGRAPHY

B. Vogel: *Raoul Koczalski* (Leipzig and Warsaw, 1896)
M. Paruszewska: *Biographical Sketch and the Artistic Career of Raoul Koczalski* (Poznań, 1936)

RONALD KINLOCH ANDERSON

Koczirz, Adolf (*b* Wscherowan [now Všeruby], Bohemia, 2 April 1870; *d* Vienna, 22 Feb 1941). Austrian musicologist. After studying law at Vienna University he obtained a post at the Ministry of Finance (1891), where he worked in various capacities until his retirement (1935). In his spare time he studied musicology with Guido Adler (1899–1903) and took the doctorate in 1903 at Vienna University with a dissertation on the lutenist Hans Judenkünig. For the next 20 years he lectured on lute and guitar music, particularly on tablatures, at the Vienna Musicology Institute. Through his research and his public work Koczirz fostered appreciation of the lute and guitar and the performance of their repertories, and was considered the leading authority and pioneer in this field. The principles of the transcription of lute tablature, which he drew up in 1909 in collaboration with Dent, Ecorcheville and Wolf, are still valuable. He edited two volumes of Denkmäler der Tonkunst in Österreich. Koczirz was also interested in the history of music in Vienna in the 16th century.

WRITINGS

Der Lautenist Hans Judenkünig (diss., U. of Vienna, 1903)
'Zur Geschichte der Gitarre in Wien', *Musikbuch aus Österreich*, iv (Vienna, 1907), 11
'Über die Notwendigkeit eines einheitlichen, wissenschaftlichen und instrumentaltechnischen Forderungen entsprechenden Systems in der Übertragung von Lauten-Tabulaturen', *IMusSCR*, iii *Vienna 1909*, 220; see also *ZIMG*, xi (1909–10), 235, and *RMI*, xvii (1910), 481
'Österreichische Lautenmusik zwischen 1650 und 1720', *SMw*, v (1918), 49
'Die St. Nicolai-Zeche der Spielleut zu St. Michael in Wien', *Musica divina*, viii (1920), 59, 96
'Die Fantasien des Melchior de Barberis für die siebensaitige Gitarre (1549)', *ZMw*, iv (1921–2), 11
'Über die Fingernageltechnik bei Saiteninstrumenten', *Studien zur Musikgeschichte: Festschrift für Guido Adler* (Vienna, 1930), 164
'Die Auflösung der Hofmusikkapelle nach dem Tode Kaiser Maximilians I.', *ZMw*, xiii (1930–31), 531

EDITIONS

Österreichische Lautenmusik im 16. Jahrhundert, DTÖ, xxxvii, Jg.xviii/2 (1911)

Österreichische Lautenmusik zwischen 1650 und 1720, DTÖ, l, Jg.xxv/2 (1918)

with L. Nowak and A. Pfalz: *Das deutsche Gesellschaftslied in Österreich von 1480–1550*, DTÖ, lxxii, Jg.xxvii/2 (1930)

BIBLIOGRAPHY

A. Orel: 'Ein Jubiläum Wiener musikwissenschaftlicher Arbeit', *ZMw*, vi (1923–4), 178

E. K. Blümml: 'Dr. Adolf Koczirz', *Zeitschrift für die Gitarre*, iv/5–9 (Vienna, 1925)

R. Haas and J. Zuth, eds.: *Festschrift Adolf Koczirz zum 60. Geburtstag* (Vienna, 1930)

RUDOLF KLEIN

Koczwara, František [Franz; Kotzwara, Francis] (*b* ?Prague, *c*1750; *d* London, 2 Sept 1791). Bohemian instrumentalist and composer. He seems to have been something of a vagabond, although his mature career centred on England. His music was published in London from about 1775. A catalogue issued by the publisher John Welcker in that year lists collections of trio sonatas and string quartets; a second set of trios was added to the plate about 1776. The string quartets op.3 and the trios for various combinations list the author at Bath; the first edition of op.5 gives a London address. In the late 1780s he was in Ireland. In London again he took part in the concerts of Ancient Music and in the Handel Commemoration of May 1791. At the time of his death, according to Parke, he played the double bass at the King's Theatre. According to Pohl, he had been called there from Ireland by the patentee Gallini in 1790; however, the theatre was in the process of being rebuilt that year and was not reopened until 26 March 1791 (in autumn 1790 Gallini and Giardini were producing opera at the Little Haymarket theatre). Fétis claimed to have met and performed for Koczwara while a child in his father's house in Mons, though his dating of the event (1792) is mistaken. According to Fétis, Koczwara played not only the viola and double bass, but also the piano, violin, cello, oboe, flute, bassoon and cittern.

Koczwara's programmatic *The Battle of Prague*, first published *c*1788 while he was in Dublin, had a phenomenal success and was widely reprinted in London, the USA and on the Continent. Nearly 40 issues can be found. First published with accompaniments, it also became a standard parlour piece for solo piano. In Boston it was 'indespensable to climax every concert'. Appearing shortly before widespread political upheaval in Europe, it provided the model for a host of imitations. *The Siege of Quebec*, also attributed to Koczwara, appears instead to be an arrangement by W. B. de Krifft borrowing some material from Koczwara.

According to Parke, Koczwara was adept at imitating the styles of other composers and sold to certain publishers forged works of popular continental composers such as Haydn and Pleyel. Most of his own works are light, pleasant and melodious, concocted for the pleasure of musical amateurs. There are unaccountable lacunae in the numeration of his works.

Koczwara gained special notoriety by the manner of his death, with which most early accounts of him are primarily concerned. He was reputed to have had unusual taste in his vices, and was accidentally hanged while conducting an experiment in a house of ill repute. Susan Hill, his accomplice in the experiment, was tried for murder at the Old Bailey on 16 September 1791 and was acquitted.

WORKS
(all published in London unless otherwise stated)

op.

1   3 serenades, vn, va, vc, 2 hn (Amsterdam, *c*1775)

— 6 Sonatas, 2 vn, bc (*c*1775)

3   6 Quartets, 2 vn, va, vc (*c*1775)

— 6 Sonatas (*c*1775); 3 for vn, fl, vc; 2 for 2 vn, vc; 1 for 2 va, vc, 2 hn

5   6 Trios, 2 vn, vc, 2 hn (*c*1776)

8   6 Easy Duetts, vn, fl (*c*1780)

— The Lover's Petition, 1v, hpd/pf (*c*1780)

9   6 Trios, 2 vn, vc (*c*1783)

10   A Periodical Overture in 8 parts, no.1(–4), 2 hn, str (*c*1785), Bland's catalogue also lists nos.15–18; no.1 arr. pf, vn acc. (*c*1795)

23   The Battle of Prague, programmatic sonata, pf/hpd, vn, vc, drum ad lib (Dublin, *c*1788); also pubd under other op. nos.; arr. for pf and for 2 pf

33   The Agreeable Surprise, potpourri, pf (Dublin, *c*1791)

34   3 Sonatas, hpd/pf, vn acc. (*c*1790)

35   3 Sonatas, hpd/pf, vn acc. (*c*1790)

36   3 sonatines, pf (Mannheim, *c*1790)

37   6 Easy Duetts, 2 vn (*c*1790)

— 6 Songs, 1v, pf/harp (*c*1790)

38   3 Sonatas, hpd/pf, vn acc. (*c*1791)

— 3 Solos or Sonatas, va, bc (*c*1795)

Duet in A Duett, pf/hpd (1790); 3 duets in 6 Favorite Duetts, vn, va (*c*1783); other pieces in 18th-century anthologies

BIBLIOGRAPHY

EitnerQ; FétisB; GerberL; GerberNL

Modern Propensities, or An Essay on the Art of Strangling ... Illustrated with Several Anecdotes ... with Memoirs of Susanna Hill, and a Summary of her Trial at the Old Bailey on Friday, Sept. 16, 1791, on the Charge of Hanging Francis Kotzwara at her Lodgings in Vine Street (London, *c*1792)

W. T. Parke: *Musical Memoirs* (London, 1830), i, 181

C. F. Pohl: *Mozart und Haydn in London*, ii (Vienna, 1867/*R*1970), 136

H. E. Johnson: *Musical Interludes in Boston: 1795–1830* (New York, 1943), 70

A. Loesser: *Men, Women and Pianos* (New York, 1954), 243, 449

W. S. Newman: *The Sonata in the Classic Era* (Chapel Hill, 1963), 769

RONALD R. KIDD

Kodallı, Nevit (*b* Mersin, 12 Dec 1924). Turkish composer and conductor. He studied from 1939 to 1947 at the Ankara State Conservatory with Necil Akses, and from 1948 in Paris with Honegger and Nadia Boulanger. He returned to Turkey in 1953 and, after teaching at the Ankara Conservatory for two years, was appointed conductor at the Ankara State Opera, where his two operas have been produced regularly. Since 1962 he has been a composer at the State Theatre.

Kodallı's works retain classical forms, but make use of Turkish folk music material. They include an oratorio (1950) and two operas (1955, 1963). Most of his music is published by Mills and in the editions of the Ankara State Conservatory, State Opera and Philharmonic Society.

FARUK YENER

Kodály, Zoltán (*b* Kecskemét, 16 Dec 1882; *d* Budapest, 6 March 1967). Hungarian composer, ethnomusicologist and educationist. With Bartók, he was one of the creators of a new Hungarian art music based on folk sources, and he established in Hungary a broadbased and high-level musical culture.

1. Life. 2. Music. 3. Research and education.

1. LIFE. His father, Frigyes (or Frederic, 1853–1926), worked for the Hungarian state railways as station master at Szob (1883–4), Galánta (now Galanta, Czechoslovakia, 1885–92) and Nagyszombat (now Trnava, Czechoslovakia, 1892–1910). Thus Kodály spent his first 18 years in the Hungarian countryside. At home he became acquainted with various musical instruments and with some Classical masterpieces – his father played the violin and his mother sang and played the piano – while at the elementary school in Galánta he came into contact with the unspoilt folktunes sung by

his fellows. He attended the Archiepiscopal Grammar School in Nagyszombat, a historic town of rich cultural traditions, where he passed all his examinations with distinction, showing a particular proficiency in literature and languages. Concurrently he learnt to play the piano, violin, viola and cello with very little tuition and to such a standard that he was able to take part in chamber music at home and in the performances of the school orchestra. He also sang in the church choir, and he began to compose. Some of his early pieces were performed: the Overture in D minor for full orchestra in February 1898; the Trio in E♭ major for two violins and viola in February 1899.

Kodály took the school-leaving examination in June 1900 and left Nagyszombat to read Hungarian and German at Budapest University. There, and at Eötvös College, he received a broad education, and at the same time he began studies at the Academy of Music. Taking composition with Koessler, he received diplomas in composition (1904) and teaching (1905), and in April 1906 he took a PhD for his thesis on the stanzaic structure of Hungarian folksong. He had found material for this in the existing collections and in Béla Vikár's recordings, but also in the fruits of his own collecting tours, which began in August 1905 and continued for many decades. It was in this field that there first developed a close contact between Kodály and Bartók. Their cooperation was by no means restricted to co-ordinating methods for collecting folksongs: it became a lasting friendship. Bartók was to write of Kodály in his autobiographical notes (1918): 'by his clear insight and sound critical sense he has been able to give, in every department of music, both invaluable advice and helpful warnings'. And in his radio talk 'Bartók emlékezete' ('Bartók remembered', 3 November 1955), Kodály recalled the basis and beginning of their collaboration: 'The vision of an educated Hungary, reborn from the people, rose before us. We decided to devote our lives to its realization'. Their first joint project was the publication of *Magyar népdalok* ('Hungarian folksongs', 1906), whose preface, formulated by Kodály, set out their programme.

In the same year, on 22 October, Kodály's *Nyári este* ('Summer evening') was performed at the Academy of Music diploma concert and, as a result, he received a modest scholarship for foreign study. He left in December for Berlin, moving from there to Paris the next April. The most memorable experience of his six months away – one that was to remain with him throughout his life – was the encounter with the music of Debussy. After his return to Hungary and another folksong collecting tour, Kodály was appointed professor at the Academy of Music. He lectured first on music theory and then, in 1908, took over the first-year composition students from Koessler. In spring 1910 Kodály received his first public performances. A concert was devoted to his music in Budapest on 17 March, when Bartók and the Waldbauer–Kerpely Quartet played his opp.2, 3 and 4. Some of his piano pieces were played in Paris, and in Zurich the Willem de Boer Quartet gave the First Quartet on 29 May. On 3 August of the same year Kodály married Emma Sándor (or Schlesinger), herself a talented composer, pianist, poet and translator.

The next year Kodály, Bartók and others formed the New Hungarian Music Society to ensure the careful performance of contemporary works. But within a few years the organization had ceased activities, faced with public indifference and official resistance. The publication of a collection of Hungarian folksongs foundered for the same reasons. In 1913 Kodály set out 'Az uj egyetemes népdalgyüjtemény tervezete' ('A project for a new universal collection of folksongs'), which he and Bartók submitted to the Kisfaludy Society. The plan was turned down, but the two continued work until World War I put an end to collecting tours. Kodály then carried on his work in composition and in the scientific classification of folk material, and between November 1917 and April 1919 he worked as a music critic, publishing nearly 50 reviews in the literary magazine *Nyugat* and later in the liberal daily paper *Pesti napló*. Of particular interest are his writings on the importance of folk music and his analyses of Bartók's music; the latter became the basis of aesthetics in Bartók's music.

1. Zoltán Kodály (left) with Arturo Toscanini

In 1919, after the bourgeois revolution, the Academy of Music was raised to university status, with Dohnányi as director and Kodály as his deputy. Kodály kept that post for the 133 days of the Hungarian Republic of Councils and even participated, with Bartók and Dohnányi, in the work of the music directory under Reinitz. After the fall of the republic Kodály was faced with disciplinary action which was whipped up into a campaign against him and his work, with the result that he was relieved of his post as deputy director and could not resume teaching until two years later. In addition, the war had put a stop to a promising international career. His isolation abroad and at home was broken by a contract with Universal Edition, which began to publish his scores in 1921, and by the resounding success of his *Psalmus hungaricus*. This was a setting of the translation of Psalm lv by the 16th-century preacher–poet Mihály Kecskeméti Vég, composed as a large-scale oratorio for tenor, chorus and orchestra within the space of two months. The première was conducted by Dohnányi on 19 November 1923 to mark the 50th anniversary of the union of Pest, Buda and Óbuda into Budapest, and the first performance outside Hungary took place under Andreae in Zurich on 18 June 1926. It was a turning-point in the international recognition of Kodály's art.

With the success of the *Psalmus hungaricus* Kodály had made a fresh start, and his career gained further momentum with the premières of the opera *Háry János* (Budapest, 16 October 1926) and of the six-movement suite drawn from it (Barcelona, 24 March 1927). These works consolidated Kodály's stature the world over: Toscanini and Mengelberg, Ansermet and Furtwängler were among the first to include them in their programmes. Kodály himself also appeared as the conductor of his own music after his début at Amsterdam in April 1927. Later that year he conducted the *Psalmus* in Cambridge (30 November) and London (4 December).

Increasingly frequent appearances abroad did not divert Kodály's attention from work to be done in Hungary. He extended his educational activities, giving particular attention after 1925 to the musical training of young people. For this purpose he produced singing and reading exercises and composed choruses which resuscitated the Hungarian choral movement. He gave lectures, wrote articles, conducted concerts all over the country and waged a veritable battle against musical illiteracy and semi-education. His ex-pupils were involved in the struggle, helping him as conductors, teachers or publishers. As early as the beginning of the 1930s he was able, without any official support and in the teeth of renewed press attacks, to start the Singing Youth movement on a national scale. And within ten

years the time had come for a radical change in elementary-school music education.

Meanwhile, Kodály's work as a composer and scholar was developing. In 1927 he had supplemented *Háry János* with a few new numbers, of which the *Szinházi nyitány* ('Theatre overture'), supplied with a concert ending, makes an independent piece. *Székely fonó* ('The Transylvanian spinning-room') was completed by the expansion of a scene written in 1924. This folk ballad of operatic dimensions was introduced in Budapest on 24 April 1932 and scored a considerable success at La Scala on 14 January 1933. Between 1924 and 1932 Kodály published arrangements for voice and piano of 57 folksongs and ballads in ten books under the title *Magyar népzene* ('Hungarian folk music'); and in 1930 he orchestrated the *Marosszéki táncok* ('Dances of Marosszék', composed for piano in 1927) and, encouraged by Toscanini, reworked the early *Summer Evening*. Several large-scale compositions were written to commission: the *Galántai táncok* ('Dances of Galánta') for the 80th anniversary of the Budapest Philharmonic Society (1933), the *Budavári Te Deum* for the 250th anniversary of the recapture of Buda from the Turks (1936), the orchestral variations on *Felszállott a páva* ('Fly, peacock') for the 50th anniversary of the Concertgebouw (1939) and the Concerto for Orchestra for that of the Chicago SO (1940). The last two were published by Boosey & Hawkes, since Kodály did not wish to retain his contacts with Austria after the Anschluss. Indeed, he was opposed to the shift to the

2. Zoltán Kodály

right within Hungary and, with Bartók, he was among the first to protest against the draft bill of 1938 instituting racial discrimination.

In 1927 Kodály launched the series of publications *Magyar zenei dolgozatok* ('Hungarian musical essays') to provide a forum for the emergent Hungarian musicology. He lectured for a few years from 1930 on folk music at the University of Budapest and later at the Free University. His comprehensive summary *A magyar népzene* ('Hungarian folk music') was published in 1937, having been preceded by numerous preparatory studies, and from 1934 he was engaged in the task of editing the collection of folk music, work which he had to continue alone after Bartók's emigration. At Kodály's request the ministry delegated him to work under the auspices of the Hungarian Academy of Sciences, beginning in autumn 1940. From then on he retained only a course in Hungarian folk music at the Academy of Music, continuing to teach this even after his retirement in 1942. That year, Kodály's 60th, was declared 'Kodály Year' by the Society of Hungarian Choruses; the Hungarian Ethnological Society published an album in his honour; and music journals made special issues. These expressions of respect and appreciation forced the authorities to give some tokens of recognition: the government awarded him the medium cross of the Hungarian Order of Merit, and the Academy of Sciences elected him to corresponding membership in 1943.

Kodály continued to compose during the war, notably to patriotic–revolutionary verses of Petőfi in *Csatadal* ('Battle song'), *Rabhazának fia* ('Son of an enslaved country') and *Isten csodája* ('Miracle of God'). He helped save people from persecution until he and his wife had to seek refuge in the cellar of a Budapest convent, where he completed the *Missa brevis*, a version for solo voices, chorus and orchestra of an earlier organ mass. He saw out the Battle of Budapest in the shelter of the opera house. Then, with the establishment of peace, a series of institutions invited him to take part in their work: he was elected a deputy in the national assembly and chairman of the board of directors of the Academy of Music; he was made president of the Hungarian Art Council and of the Free Organization of Musicians; and he was elected to full membership and then honorary membership of the Academy of Sciences, of which he served as president from 1946 to 1949.

After a lapse of nearly a decade Kodály made a concert tour (September 1946 to June 1947) which took him to the United Kingdom, the USA and the USSR, everywhere conducting his own works, and he again conducted in western Europe in 1948 and 1949. On 15 March 1948 the Budapest State Opera House introduced *Czinka Panna*, to a text by Balázs, and in 1951 the National Folk Ensemble gave the first performance of the *Kállai kettős* ('Kálló double dance') for chorus and orchestra. Kodály received high government decorations (1947, 1952, 1962) and three Kossuth Prizes (1948, 1952, 1957), and the Academy of Sciences issued commemorative volumes for his 70th, 75th and 80th birthdays. He was accorded honorary doctorates by the universities of Budapest (1957), Oxford (1960), East Berlin (1964) and Toronto (1966), and honorary membership of the Belgian Academy of Sciences (1957), the Moscow Conservatory (1963) and the American Academy of Arts and Sciences (1963). In addition, he was made president of the International

Folk Music Council (1961) and honorary president of the International Society of Music Education (1964). The Herder Prize was awarded to him in 1965 in recognition of his work in furthering East–West cultural relations.

Right up to his death Kodály continued to engage in a wide variety of activities. His last major compositions – which include *Zrinyi szózata* ('Hymn of Zrinyi') for baritone and chorus (1954), the Symphony (1961), *Mohács* for chorus (1965) and the *Laudes organi* for chorus and organ (1966) – show his creative powers undiminished. His wife died on 22 November 1958 and he remarried on 18 December 1959. Each year between 1960 and 1966 he travelled on long trips abroad, lecturing in English, French, German and Italian, and taking the chair at various conferences. In Hungary, thanks to the support of the cultural authorities, he lived to see the realization of his ambitious plans. The first five volumes of the Corpus Musicae Popularis Hungaricae appeared between 1950 and 1967, and daily music education according to his principles was introduced in 120 elementary schools during the same period.

2. MUSIC. Kodály's compositional career spans seven decades, from his first surviving manuscripts (1897) to his last finished work (1966), and even beyond these limits: by his own account, he began to improvise songs at the age of four; and fragments in his estate indicate that he kept on composing until his last days. This exceptionally long period of creativity is entirely devoid of spectacular turns: his individual style was already formed by 1905–7. Earlier pieces were youthful attempts conceived in the spirit of Viennese Classicism (up to 1900) or of the German Romantics, particularly Brahms (1900–04). They include some surprisingly mature compositions, such as *Este* ('Evening') for chorus (1904) and the Adagio for violin and piano (1905).

Kodály's subsequent development was profoundly influenced by his folksong experiences and by his acquaintance with the works of Debussy. Beyond this, his artistic personality was enriched by the absorption of certain specific features from Bach, Palestrina, Gregorian chant and the Hungarian *verbunkos* style. But he was never an eclectic: he possessed sufficient creative powers to bring about a synthesis of these various influences, and the prominent part played by Hungarian folk intonation throughout his career also guarded him against any heterogeneity of style. The man who knew his music best, Bartók, was to write (1921):

Kodály's compositions are characterized in the main by rich melodic invention, a perfect sense of form, a certain predilection for melancholy and uncertainty. He does not seek Dionysian intoxication – he strives for inner contemplation ... His music is not of the kind described nowadays as modern. It has nothing to do with the new atonal, bitonal and polytonal music – everything in it is based on the principle of tonal balance. His idiom is nevertheless new; he says things that have never been uttered before and demonstrates thereby that the tonal principle has not lost its raison d'être as yet.

Later (1927) Bartók added: 'Kodály ... is a great master of form and possesses a striking individuality; he works in a concentrated fashion and despises any sensation, false brilliance, any extraneous effect'. And finally, another Bartókian definition (1928) that has become something of a classic characterization:

If I were to name the composer whose works are the most perfect embodiment of the Hungarian spirit, I would answer, Kodály. His work

3. Autograph MS of the opening of Kodály's motet 'Jézus és a kufárok', composed in 1934 (private collection)

proves his faith in the Hungarian spirit. The obvious explanation is that all Kodály's composing activity is rooted only in Hungarian soil, but the deep inner reason is his unshakable faith and trust in the constructive power and future of his people.

The creative activity that lasted throughout Kodály's long life was only once interrupted: in 1921–2 he did not write anything. The reasons were both external and internal. Previously he had composed almost exclusively in the genres of song and chamber music; thereafter he contributed least in these spheres. His mature output may be divided into two major periods, with the first

dominated by lyrical elements and the second by dramatic ones, while his epic leanings were manifested time and again in both. By contrast with Bartók, Kodály was a vocally orientated composer for whom melody was always of primary importance. This he admitted in symbolic manner at the beginning and end of his career: he marked the song cycle *Énekszó* as his op.1, and in one of his last writings (1966) he declared: 'Our age of mechanization leads along a road ending with man himself as a machine; only the spirit of singing can save us from this fate'. Music and text are of a piece in Kodály's work: they breathe together. His choruses and songs – the 11 books of folksong arrangements as well as the original compositions – are difficult to translate because of their perfection in prosody. Besides this, he chose texts from those poets most Hungarian in character; the seven songs of the *Megkésett melódiák* ('Belated melodies') op.6, the Two Songs op.5 and the Three Songs op.14 sing the music of the Hungarian language, to poems both old and new. Molnár, Kodály's first biographer, justly described him as the creator of 'the genuine Hungarian art song'.

However, choruses make up the bulk of Kodály's oeuvre. Almost no other 20th-century composer showed a greater knowledge of the genre or a greater devotion to it. For Kodály, the beauty of the human voice and the charm of singing were alike inexhaustible; and in his works he contributed to choral music of all kinds. The central position is occupied by those for children: *Villő* ('Straw guy'), *Pünkösdölő* ('Whitsuntide'), *Lengyel László* and more than 50 others are marked by strict formal discipline, transparent construction, development through variation and equality of part-writing, as well as simplicity and informality. Most are folksong arrangements, but the original pieces are almost indistinguishable in style; and the same applies to the works for male, female and mixed choruses, of which the outstanding numbers are *Öregek* ('The aged'), *Akik mindig elkésnek* ('Too late'), *Norvég lányok* ('Norwegian girls') and *Jézus és a kufárok* ('Jesus and the traders'). This last is a large-scale motet: the culmination of Kodály's *a cappella* art and a masterpiece of the century's choral literature, transforming the biblical text and its emotional content into a veritable dramatic scene. The use of Baroque-like word symbolism, the alternation of homophonic and polyphonic sections, and the union of linear and vertical writing are all indicative of Kodály's rich technique, placed at the service of the expressive message.

Kodály's instrumental style was developed in solo and chamber compositions, and he was at his best in string chamber music. The two quartets, opp.2 and 10, are the works of a composer who has left Romanticism behind and found his own language. In the first, both melodic material and instrumental treatment are reminiscent of folk music, while the second demonstrates that Kodály could use the idiom of folksong as a mother tongue. At the same time, the construction of op.10 is highly accomplished, its complex form pointing forward to the quite individual structure of the *Budavári Te Deum*. The cello sonatas opp.4 (with piano accompaniment) and 8 (solo), the Duo op.7 for violin and cello, and the Serenade op.12 for two violins and viola all bear witness to Kodály's rich melodic invention and excellent sense of balance and proportion, as well as to his ability to achieve strikingly new effects through simple means.

Most of Kodály's orchestral compositions – the *Dances of Marosszék*, the *Dances of Galánta*, the *Peacock Variations* and the Concerto for Orchestra – were written in the 1930s. The first version of *Summer Evening* was a forerunner of this period and the Symphony a harmonious postscript. Of all these works the most popular has been the *Dances of Galánta*, a symphonic poem distinguished by brilliant orchestration and cast in rondo form, taking its material from 18th-century *verbunkos* music. But the *Peacock Variations* are the most revealing of the composer. The theme is drawn from the most ancient body of Hungarian folk music, that of oriental origin, and the

large-scale tripartite composition is a true apotheosis of folksong.

The same can be said of the stage works *Háry János* and *The Transylvanian Spinning-room*. It was Kodály's aim to secure a place in the opera house for Hungarian folk music in its original form, but neither work is an opera: *Háry János* is a Singspiel and *The Transylvanian Spinning-room* a scene from village life, an operatic ballad. Both are built primarily on the vocal passages, though the popularity of *Háry János* was created by the orchestral suite assembled from it. The three odd-numbered movements of the suite are exalted in tone and of folk inspiration; the three even-numbered sections have a mocking, parodistic quality. These last are also a rare expression of Kodály's full-blooded humour.

Kodály's oeuvre reached its two culminating points in the oratorios: the *Psalmus hungaricus* and the *Budavári Te Deum*. They contain no folk quotations; both, but particularly the latter, incorporate rather a wealth of foreign elements: Gregorian melodic inflections, Renaissance-like plagal harmony, choral writing in the spirit of Palestrina, Bachian polyphony, the use of the whole-tone mode, and that of the Lydian mode with a raised 5th, which might be described as a median between whole-tone and pentatonic scales (it has been termed 'heptatonia secunda' by Bárdos, who discovered this feature in Kodály's work). With regard to form, the *Psalmus hungaricus* is a classical rondo and the *Te Deum* a complex palindrome. And yet both works, from first note to last, exude the spirit of Hungarian folk music. Indeed, everything Kodály composed after Bartók's statements of the 1920s fully confirms them: he was no revolutionary innovator, but a summarizer. Nevertheless, the style he created from the folk monody of ancient, oriental extraction and from the new rich harmony of Western art music is homogeneous, individual and new.

3. RESEARCH AND EDUCATION. 'Theories become antiquated but faultlessly published material never does', wrote Kodály in the preface to the second volume of the Corpus Musicae Popularis Hungaricae (1953). That principle guided his entire work. He began with simple folksong publications in 1905 in the magazine *Ethnographia*. As a result of systematic annual collecting tours he amassed thousands of folksongs, whose analysis and classification led him to write in 1917 his first preparatory study, *Ötfokú hangsor a magyar népzenében* ('The pentatonic scale in Hungarian folk music'), a work of fundamental significance. Continued research produced two further volumes, *Kelemen Kőmies balladája* ('The ballad Kelemen the mason', 1918) and *Árgirus nótája* ('The song of Argirus', 1920). The former, by publishing 35 stanzas of the ballad in musical notation, throws light on the part played by content and atmosphere in performance and on the importance of different versions. In the second Kodály examined the connections between the histories of melody and verse. His next two publications were dedicated to saving old relics from extinction: *Erdélyi magyarság: népdalok* ('The Hungarians of Transylvania: folksongs', 1921), published jointly with Bartók, records the valuable melodic style of Székely; and *Nagyszalontai gyűjtés* ('Nagyszalonta collection', 1924) reports on the rubato performance tradition of that region. Another study of basic importance followed in *Sajátságos dallamszerkezet a cseremisz népzenében* ('The distinctive melodic structure of Cheremiss folk

music', 1934), which, through the examination of melodies built on shifting 5ths, sets out the 'dual system' principle (i.e. the unchanged reiteration of the melody in another key a 5th lower).

The achievements of 32 years of research are summarized in *A magyar népzene* (1937). Here Kodály viewed folksong as a living tradition, reviewing the characteristics of the old and new styles, and the different relations between folk and art music. It is a tersely formulated work, which laid the foundations for research into the cultural history of Hungary. After a number of publications on the history of folklore, the culmination of Kodály's scientific work came with the first issue of the Corpus Musicae Popularis Hungaricae in 1951: the project had first been drafted by Kodály and Bartók in 1913. The classification and editing of a body of folksongs had, by the 1950s, reached a total of 100,000 was guided until his death by Kodály as head of the folk music research group at the Academy of Sciences.

Folk music research constituted the bulk of Kodály's scientific activity – indeed, of his whole work. However, he also did important work in ethnology, music history, music aesthetics, music criticism, the history of literature, linguistics and language education. In size, his critical and language-educational writings stand out, but all are virtually equal in significance. Besides writing for Hungarian papers he published reviews between 1917 and 1925 in the *Musikblätter des Anbruch*, *Revue musicale*, the *Musical Courier* and *Il pianoforte*. One of his central topics was the music of Bartók, though he also wrote with unerring judgment on composers and performers past and present. From 1937 he made good use of the linguistic studies he had undertaken at university: he initiated pronunciation competitions at Budapest University (1939) in his fight against deteriorating habits of speech, and he was active in the committee for language education (from 1943) under the auspices of the Academy of Sciences.

Of pioneering value also are such works as *Néprajz és zenetörténet* ('Ethnology and music history', 1933), *Magyarság a zenében* ('The Hungarian character in music', 1939), *Népzene és műzene* ('Folk music and art music', 1941) and *Arany János népdalgyüjteménye* ('The folksong collection of János Arany', with Ágost Gyulai, 1953). Kodály was convinced that folksong was important not just as a monument of the past but also as a foundation for the future. This view fired him in organizing and popularizing activities aimed at gaining a general recognition for folk music and at creating a homogeneous musical culture. Popularization, he said, could not be 'left for amateurs and self-styled scholars to do. The best are just sufficiently good for the job'. As a scholar Kodály established up-to-date musicology in Hungary and raised it to a level comparable with that achieved in other countries; at the same time he gave a new impetus to ethnomusicology internationally.

In the field of education his work was hardly less important. He lectured on composition at the Academy of Music from 1907 to 1940, undertaking tuition in all the various subjects connected with composing – harmony, counterpoint, form, orchestration and score-reading – to ensure that his pupils developed a unified outlook. He gave particular attention in his teaching to vocal polyphony, and in every field he required an extensive knowledge of the literature. His pupils were taught to be responsible, respectful of their craft and of their public; many of his students have become internationally known composers, conductors, teachers and musicologists.

Kodály first took an interest in the education of the young in 1925. He began by writing choruses, lectures and essays, and then, starting with the book *Bicinia hungarica* (1937), extended his work to include the publication of singing and reading exercises. His series of these remained close to his heart throughout his life; he wrote hundreds of two- and three-part exercises with endless patience and resourcefulness. With the help of others he prepared the *Iskolai énekgyüjtemény* ('Song collection for schools', 1943–4) and textbooks on singing (1944–5 and 1948). His educational ideas crystallized in what has become known throughout the world as the 'Kodály method'. Its material is taken essentially from folk music and from compositions in folk style; its basic method is corporate singing, with relative solmization an important means; its aim is the creation of general musical literacy.

In order to ensure that music should become an organic part of the school curriculum and that adults should not be lost to great music, Kodály gave more and more attention, from the 1930s onwards, to the choral movement. He travelled up and down the country, giving encouragement, convinced that group singing, and not instrumental skill, was the only basis for a broad musical culture. Educational work assumed even greater importance for him after 1945, when effective state help made it possible for his efforts to bear fruit during his lifetime.

Kodály is one of the few artists in the 20th century to have achieved work of lasting value in a variety of fields. He was perhaps unique in that over many decades he worked for one principle, one ideal, uniting the many strands of his activities into an integrated whole. Since his death the values for which he strove have prospered all over the world: Kodály institutes have been established in Tokyo, Wellesley (Boston), Ottawa, Sydney and Kecskemét; international Kodály symposia have been held in Oakland, Kecskemét and Halifax; and an International Kodály Society, based in Budapest, was founded in 1975.

WORKS

STAGE

Notre Dame de Paris (incidental music for parody), small orch, 1902; Budapest, Feb 1902

Le Cid (incidental music for parody), small orch, 1903; Budapest, Feb 1903

A nagybácsi [The uncle] (incidental music), small orch, 1904; Budapest, Feb 1904

Pacsirtaszó [Lark song] (incidental music, Zs. Móricz), 1v, small orch, 1917; Budapest, 14 Sept 1917

Háry János, op.15 (Singspiel, 5 scenes, B. Paulini, Zs. Harsányi), 1925–7; Budapest, 16 Oct 1926

Székely fonó [The Transylvanian spinning-room] (lyrical play, 1, trad.), 1924–32; Budapest, 24 April 1932

Czinka Panna (Singspiel, 3, Balázs), 1946–8; Budapest, 15 March 1948

ORCHESTRAL

Overture, d, 1897; Nagyszombat, Feb 1898

Nyári este [Summer evening], 1906; Budapest, 22 Oct 1906; rev. 1929–30; New York, 3 April 1930

Régi magyar katonadalok [Old Hungarian soldiers' songs], 1917; Vienna, 12 Jan 1918; arr. vc, pf as Magyar rondo

Ballet Music (orig. for Háry János), 1925; Budapest, 16 Oct 1926

Háry János Suite, 1927; Barcelona, 24 March 1927; arr. brass band

Szinházi nyitány [Theatre Overture] (orig. for Háry János), 1927; Budapest, 10 Jan 1928

Marosszéki táncok [Dances of Marosszék] (after pf work), 1930; Budapest, 1 Dec 1930; arr. for ballet

Galántai táncok [Dances of Galánta], 1933; Budapest, 23 Oct 1933

Variations on a Hungarian Folksong 'Felszállott a páva' [The peacock], 1938–9; Amsterdam, 23 Oct 1939

Concerto for Orchestra, 1939–40; Chicago, 6 Feb 1941
Honvéd Parad March [from Háry János], brass band, 1948
Minuetto serio [enlarged from Cinka Panna], 1948–53
Symphony, C, 1930s–61; Lucerne, 16 Aug 1961

ACCOMPANIED CHORAL
(unless otherwise stated, texts are trad.)
(with orch)

Offertorium (Assumpta est), Bar, vv, orch, 1901
Psalmus hungaricus, op.13 (M. Kecskeméti Vég), T, vv, children's vv ad lib, orch, org, 1923; Budapest, 19 Nov 1923
Budavári Te Deum, S, A, T, B, vv, orch, org, 1936; Budapest, 2 Sept 1936
Missa brevis, (vv, org)/(3 S, A, T, B, vv, orch, org ad lib), 1944; Budapest, 11 Feb 1945
Vértanúk sírjánál [At the martyr's grave], vv, orch, 1945
Kállai kettős [Kálló double dance], vv, small orch, 1950
The Music Makers, an Ode (A. W. E. O'Shaughnessy), vv, orch, 1964

(with insts)

Mass, vv, org, before 1897, inc.; Ave Maria, vv, org, before 1900; 5 Tantum ergo, children's vv, org, 1928; Pange lingua, vv/children's vv, org, 1929; Katonadal [Soldier's song], male vv, tpt, side drum, 1934; Karácsonyi pásztortánc [Shepherds' Christmas dance], children's vv, rec, 1935; Ének Szent István királyhoz [Hymn to St Stephen], vv, org, 1938
Vejnemöjnen muzsikál [Vejnemöjnen makes music], high vv, harp/pf, 1944; A 114. genfi zsoltár [Geneva Psalm cxiv], vv, org, 1952; Intermezzo [from Háry János], vv, pf, 1956; Magyar mise [Hungarian Mass], unison vv, org, 1966; Laudes organi, vv, org, 1966

UNACCOMPANIED CHORAL
(unless otherwise stated, texts are trad.)
(mixed vv)

Miserere (Ps li), double chorus, 1903; Este [Evening] (P. Gyulai), S, vv, 1904; Mátrai képek [Mátra pictures], 1931; Nagyszalontai köszöntő [A birthday greeting], arr. 1931; Öregek [The aged] (S. Weöres), 1933; Székely keserves [Transylvanian lament], 1934; Jézus és a kufárok [Jesus and the traders] (Bible), 1934; Akik mindig elkésnek [Too late] (Ady), 1934; Horatii Carmen II.10 (Rectius vives), 1934; Liszt Ferenchez (Ode to Liszt) (M. Vörösmarty), 1936; Molnár Anna, 1936; A magyarokhoz [Song of faith] (D. Berzsenyi), 4-part canon, 1936
Ének Szent István királyhoz, chorus/small chorus, 1938; Norvég lányok [Norwegian girls] (Weöres), 1940; Gömöri dal [Gömör song], 1940 or 1941; Balassi Bálint elfelejtett éneke [The forgotten song of Balassi] (E. Gazdag), 1942; Első áldozás [Communion anthem] (D. Szedő), 1942; Szép könyörgés [Beseeching] (Balassa), 1943; A székelyekhez [To the Transylvanian] (Petőfi), 1943; A 121. genfi zsoltár [Geneva Psalm cxxi], 1943; Adventi ének [O come, O come, Emmanuel] (18th-century Fr. missal), 1943; Csatadal [Battle song] (Petőfi), double chorus, 1943
Sirató ének [Dirge] (P. Bodrogh), 1947; A magyar nemzet [The Hungarian nation] (Petőfi), 1947; A szabadság himnusza [La marseillaise] (trans. F. Jankovich), 1948; Naphimnusz [Adoration] (Heb. trad.), 1948; Jelige [Epigraph] (Jankovich), chorus/small chorus, 1948; Az 50. genfi zsoltár, 1948; Túrót eszik a cigány [See the gypsies], arr. 1950; Békesség óhajtás: 1801: esztendő [Wish for peace: 1801] (B. Virág), 1953; Zrinyi szózata [Hymn of Zrinyi] (M. Zrinyi), Bar, vv, 1954
Magyarország cimere [The arms of Hungary] (Vörösmarty), 1956; I will go look for death (Masefield), 1959; Media vita in morte sumus, 1960; Sik Sándor Te Deuma, 1961; Jövel, Szentlélek Uristen [Come, Holy Ghost] (A. Batizi), c1961; An Ode for Music (Collins, ?Shakespeare), 1963; Mohács (K. Kisfaludy), 1965

(high vv)

Két zoborvidéki népdal [2 folksongs from Zobor], 3 S, 3 A, vv, 1908; Hegyi éjszakák I [Mountain nights] (textless), 1923; Villő [The straw guy], 1925; Túrót eszik a cigány [See the gypsies], 1925; Gergelyjárás [St Gregory's day], 1926; Lengyel László [King László's men], 1927; Jelenti magát Jézus [The voice of Jesus], 1927; A juhász [The shepherd], 1928; A süket sógor [The deaf boatman], 1928; Cigánysirató [Gypsy lament], 1928; Isten kovácsa [God's blacksmith], 1928; Gólyanóta [The swallow's wooing], 1929; Pünkösdölő [Whitsuntide], 1929
Táncnóta [Dancing song], 1929; Uj esztendőt köszöntő [A Christmas carol], 1929; Nagyszalontai köszöntő [A birthday greeting], 1931; 4 Italian Madrigals (M. di Dino Frescobaldi, M. M. Boiardo, Gherardello da Firenze, anon. 14th-century), 1932; Vizkereszt [Epiphany] (S. Sik), 1933; Nyulacska [The leveret], 1934; Ave Maria, 1935; Harmatozzatok [Rorate], 1935; Hét könnyü gyermekkar és hat tréfás kánon (7 easy children's choruses and 6 humorous canons), 1936; A 150. genfi zsoltár (T. de Béze), 1936; Hajnővesztő [Grow, tresses], 1937; Katalinka [Ladybird], 1937
Három gömöri népdal [3 folksongs from Gömör], 1937; Ének Szent

István királyhoz, female vv, 1938; Egyetem, begyetem [Hippity, hoppity], 1938; Cú föl, lovam [Arise, my horse], 1938; Csalfa sugár [False spring] (J. Arany), 1938; Szent Ágnes ünnepére [St Agnes's Day] (Sik), 1945; A szabadság himnusza [La marseillaise] (trans. Jankovich), 2vv/3vv, 1948; Jelige [Epigraph] (Jankovich), 1948; Békedal [Song of peace] (Weöres), 1952; Árva vagyok [Orphan am I], 1953; Ürgeöntés [Gopher-flooding], 1954; Hegyi éjszakák II–IV (textless), 1955–6
Arany szabadság [Golden freedom] (Jankovich), 1957; Meghalok, meghalok [Woe is me], S, 3 A, vv, 1957; Házasodik a vakond [Mole marriage] (E. Gazdag), 1958; Méz, méz, méz [Honey], 1958; Tell me where is fancy bred (Shakespeare), 1959; Harasztosi legénynek [The lad of Harasztos], 1961; Az éneklő ifjusághoz [To the singing youth] (K. Vargha), 1962; Hegyi éjszakák V (textless), 1962

(male vv)

Stabat mater, 1898; Két férfikar [2 drinking-songs] (F. Kölcsey, anon. 17th-century), 1913–17; Karádi nóták [Songs from Karád], 1934; Kit kéne elvenni? [The bachelor], 1934; Justum et tenacem (Horace), 1935; Huszt [The ruins] (Kölcsey), 1936; Fölszállott a páva [The peacock] (Ady), 1937; Ének Szent István királyhoz, 1938; Jelenti magát Jézus [The voice of Jesus], arr. 1944; Rabhazának fia [The son of an enslaved country] (Petőfi), 1944; Isten csodája [God's miracle] (Petőfi), 1944; Élet vagy halál [Life or death] (Petőfi), 1947
Hejh Büngözsdi Bandi [Hey, Bandi Büngözsdi] (Petőfi), 1947; A szabadság himnusza [La marseillaise] (trans. Jankovich), 2vv/3vv, 1948; Jelige [Epigraph] (Jankovich), 1948; Nemzeti dal [National song] (Petőfi), 1955; Emléksorok Fáy Andrásnak [In András Fáy's album] (Vörösmarty), 1956; A nándori toronyőr [The watchman of Nándor] (Vörösmarty), 1956; A franciaországi változásokra [To the changes in France] (J. Batsányi), 1963

(children's vv)

Angyalok és pásztorok [Angels and shepherds], double chorus, 1935; Harangszó [The bells], double chorus, 1937; Angyalkert [Garden of angels], 5 plays, 1937; Ének Szent István királyhoz, boys' mixed vv, 1938; János köszöntő [Greeting on St John's Day], boys' mixed vv, 1939; Cohors generosa (Hungarian students' greeting of 1777), boys' mixed vv, 1943

(equal vv)

A csikó [The filly], 1937; Esti dal [Evening song], 1938; Semmit ne bánkodjál [Cease your bitter weeping] (A. Szkhárosi Horvát), 1939

SOLO VOCAL
(unless otherwise stated, texts are trad.)

Ave Maria, E♭, 1v, insts, 1897; Ave Maria, F, 1v, org, 1897; Ave Maria, A, 1v, org, 1898; Vadonerdő a világ [A bush the world] (Petőfi), 1v, pf, before 1900; Szeretném itthagyni a fényes világot [I should like to leave this bright world] (Petőfi), 1v, pf, 1905; Magyar népdalok [20 Hungarian folksongs], nos.11–20, 1v, pf, 1906, nos.1–10 by Bartók; Négy dal [4 songs] (Arany, A. Bálint, Móricz), 1v, pf, nos. 1–3, 1907, no.4, 1917; Énekszó [16 songs], op.1, 1v, pf, 1907–9; Himfy dal [Himfy song] (Kisfaludy), 1v, pf, 1915
Megkésett melódiák [7 songs], op.6 (D. Berzsenyi, Kölcsey, M. Csokonai Vitéz), 1v, pf, 1912–16; Két ének [2 songs], op.5 (Berzsenyi, Ady), Bar, pf/orch, 1913–16; Kádár István, 1v, pf, 1917, incorporated as no.37 in Magyar népzene; Fáj a szivem [My heart is breaking] (Móricz), 1v, small orch, 1917, incorporated as no.4 in Négy dal; Öt dal [5 songs], op.9 (Ady, Balázs), 1915–18; Három ének [3 songs], op.14 (Balassi, anon. 17th-century), 1v, pf/orch, 1924–9; Magyar népzene I–X [Hungarian folk music], 57 folksongs, 1v, pf, 1917–32
Kállai kettős [Kálló double dance], 1v, pf, 1937; Első áldozás [Communion anthem] (D. Szedő), 1v, pf, 1942; Molnár Anna, 1v, small orch, 1943, rev. 1956; Adventi ének [O come, O come, Emmanuel], 1v, org, 1943; Kádár Kata [Mother, listen], 1v, small orch, 1943; Jézus és a gyermekek [Jesus and the children] (Szedő), child's v, org, 1947; Nyolc kis duett [8 little duets], S, T, pf, 1953; Öt hegyi mari népdal [5 songs of the mountain Tcheremis], 1v, pf, 1960; Magyar népzene XI, 5 folksongs, 1v, pf, 1964
Orchestration: *B. Bartók: Öt dal, op.15*, 1962

CHAMBER AND INSTRUMENTAL

Str: Romance lyrique, vc, pf, 1898; Trio, E♭, 2 vn, va, 1899; Adagio, vn/va/vc, pf, 1905; Intermezzo, str trio, 1905; 2 str qts, op.2, 1908–9, op.10, 1916–18; Sonata, op.4, vc, pf, 1909–10; Duo, op.7, vn, vc, 1914; Sonata, op.8, vc, 1915; Capriccio, vc, 1915; Magyar rondo, vc, pf, 1917; Serenade, op.12, 2 vn, va, 1919–20; Sonatina, vc, pf, 1921–2; Exercise, vn, 1942; Feigin [arr. of Kállai kettős], vn, pf, 1958
Wind: Hivogató tábortűzhöz [Calling to camp fire], cl, 1930; Qt, c1960
Pf: pieces before 1900; Valsette, 1907; Méditation sur un motif de Claude Debussy, 1907; Zongoramuzsika [PF music] (9 pf pieces), op.3, 1909; 7 pf pieces, op.11, 1910–18; Ballet Music [arr. of orch work], 1925; Marosszéki táncok [Dances of Marosszék], 1927; Gyermektáncok [Children's dances], 1945
Org: Prelude [orig. for Pange lingua], 1931; Csendes mise [Low Mass], 1940–42, rev. as Organoedia, 1966

Bach arrs.: *Chorale Preludes* BWV743, 762, 747, vc, pf, 1924; *Fantasia cromatica*, va, 1950; *Prelude and Fugue*, E♭, from *Das wohltemperirte Clavier*, bk 1, vc, pf, 1951; *Lute Prelude*, c, BWV999, vn, pf, 1959

EDUCATIONAL

15 kétszólamú énekgyakorlat [15 2-part exercises], 1941; Énekeljünk tisztán [Let us sing correctly], 107 intonation exercises, 1941; Bicinia hungarica I–IV, 180 progressive 2-part songs, 1937–42; 333 olvasógyakorlat [333 elementary exercises in sight-singing], 1943; Iskolai énekgyűjtemény I–II [Collected songs for schools], 1943–4, ed. with G. Kerényi; 24 kis kánon a fekete billentyűkön [24 little canons on the black keys], 1945; Ötfoku zene I–IV [Pentatonic music], 1942–7; Szó-mi I–VIII, 1944–7, ed. with J. Ádám Énekeskönyv az általános iskolák I–VIII osztálya számára [Songbook for primary schools], 1947–8, ed. with Adám; 33 kétszólamú énekgyakorlat, 1954; 44 kétszólamú énekgyakorlat, 1954; 55 kétszólamú énekgyakorlat, 1954; Tricinia, 29 progressive 3-part songs, 1954; Epigrammák, 9 vocalises, 1v, pf, 1954; Kis emberek dalai [50 nursery rhymes], 1961; 66 kétszólamú énekgyakorlat, 1962; 22 kétszólamú énekgyakorlat, 1964; 77 kétszólamú énekgyakorlat, 1966

Arr.: *J. Haydn: Vn Sonata no.5: Rondo*, str orch, c1960

Principal publishers: Boosey & Hawkes, Magyar Kórus, Universal

WRITINGS

with B. Bartók: *Erdélyi magyarság: népdalok* [The Hungarians of Transylvania: folksongs] (Budapest, 1923) [with preface in Eng. and Fr.]

A magyar népzene [Hungarian folk music] (Budapest, 1937, enlarged 2/1943, enlarged with exx. by L. Vargyas 3/1952, 6/1973; Eng. trans., 1960)

with A. Gyulai: *Arany János népdalgyűjteménye* [The folksong collection of Arany] (Budapest, 1953)

ed. A. Szőllősy: *A zene mindenkié* (Budapest, 1954, 2/1975)

ed. F. Bónis: *Visszatekintés* [In retrospect], Magyar zenetudomány, v–vi (Budapest, 1964, enlarged 2/1974)

The Selected Writings of Zoltán Kodály (Budapest, 1974)

Articles in *Magyar zenei szemle* and *Zenei szemle*

BIBLIOGRAPHY

CATALOGUES AND SOURCE MATERIAL

A. Szőllősy: 'Kodály Zoltán műveinek jegyzéke' [List of Kodály's works], *Emlékkönyv Kodály Zoltán 70. születésnapjára* (Budapest, 1953), 66

L. Eősze: *Kodály Zoltán élete képekben* [Kodály's life in pictures] (Budapest, 1957, 2/1958)

L. Eősze and F. Bónis: 'Zoltán Kodálys Werke', *Zoltano Kodály octogenario sacrum* (Budapest, 1962), 11–43

D. Dille, ed.: *Documenta bartókiana*, i (Budapest, 1964), 11ff

Z. Kodály: *Mein Weg zur Musik: fünf Gespräche mit Lutz Besch* (Zurich, 1966)

L. Eősze: *Zoltán Kodály: his life in Pictures* (Budapest, 1971)

J. Ujfalussy, ed.: *Dokumentumok a Magyar Tanácsköztársaság zenei életéből* [Documents from the musical life of the Hungarian Republic] (Budapest, 1973), 499–598

MONOGRAPHS

A. Molnár: *Kodály Zoltán* (Budapest, 1936)

A. Szőllősy: *Kodály művészete* [The art of Kodály] (Budapest, 1943)

I. Sonkoly: *Kodály, az ember, a művész, a nevelő* [Kodály, the man, the artist, the educator] (Nyiregyháza, 1948)

J. Gergely: *Zoltán Kodály, musico hungaro e mestro universal* (Lisbon, 1954)

L. Eősze: *Kodály Zoltán élete és munkássága* [Kodály's life and work] (Budapest, 1956)

——: *Zoltán Kodály: his Life and Work* (London, 1962)

P. M. Young: *Zoltán Kodály: a Hungarian Musician* (London, 1964)

L. Eősze: *Kodály Zoltán*, Kis zenei könyvtár, xxxvii (Budapest, 1967)

H. Szabó: *The Kodály Concept of Music Education* (London, 1969)

L. Eősze: *Kodály Zoltán* (Budapest, 1971)

B. Szabolcsi: *Uton Kodályhoz* [Toward Kodály] (Budapest, 1972)

E. Szőnyi: *Kodály's Principles in Practice* (Budapest, 1973)

E. Hegyi: *Solfège according to the Kodály-concept* (Kecskemét, 1975)

E. Lendvai: *Bartók és Kodály harmóniavilága* [The harmonic world of Bartók and Kodály] (Budapest, 1975)

J. Breuer: *Kodály-dokumentumok*, i (Budapest, 1976)

L. Eősze: *Kodály Zoltán életének krónikája* (Kodály: chronicle of his life] (Budapest, 1977)

COLLECTIONS OF ESSAYS

Crescendo, i/3 (Budapest, 1926)

Énekszó, x/3 (1942–3)

Magyar dal, xlvii/12 (1942)

Magyar zenei szemle, ii/12 (1942)

B. Gunda, ed.: *Emlékkönyv Kodály Zoltán hatvanadik születésnapjára* (Budapest, 1943)

Uj zenei szemle, iii/12 (1952)

B. Szabolcsi and D. Bartha, eds.: *Emlékkönyv Kodály Zoltán 70. születésnapjára* (Budapest, 1953)

——: *Zenetudományi tanulmányok Kodály Zoltán 75. születésnapjára* (Budapest, 1957)

Magyar zene, iii/6 (1962)

Muzsika, v/12 (1962)

New Hungarian Quarterly, iii/8 (1962)

Zoltano Kodály octogenario sacrum (Budapest, 1962)

Tempo (1962–3), no.63

Magyar zene, viii/2 (1967)

Muzsika, x/5 (1967)

Muzsika, xv/12 (1972)

OTHER GENERAL LITERATURE

B. Bartók: 'Kodály Zoltán', *Nyugat*, xiv (1921), 235

——: 'Della musica moderna in Ungheria', *Il pianoforte*, ii/7 (Turin, 1921)

M. D. Calvocoressi: 'Zoltán Kodály', *MMR*, lii (1922), 616; repr. in Young (1964)

F. Desderi: 'Zoltán Kodály', *Il pianoforte*, vi (1925)

B. Szabolcsi: 'Kodály Zoltán', *Nyugat*, xix (1926), 670

G. Pannain: 'Zoltán Kodály', *Il pianoforte*, viii/5 (1927)

A. Tóth: 'Zoltán Kodály', *ReM*, x/9 (1929), 197

——: 'Zoltán Kodály, zu seinem 50. Geburtstag', *Musikblätter des Anbruch*, xiv (1932), 191

L. Pollatsek: 'Zoltán Kodály', *De muziek*, vii/3 (1932)

Gy. Kerényi: 'Kodály és a magyar kórus' [Kodály and Hungarian choruses], *Magyar kórus* (1932), no.8

D. Tóth: 'Un musicista ungherese: Zoltán Kodály', *Corvina*, i (Budapest, 1938)

L. Vargyas: 'Zoltán Kodály', *Ungarn*, ii/12 (Budapest, 1942)

Z. Horusitzky: 'Kodály Zoltán életutja' [Kodály's life], *A zene*, xxiv/3, 6–8 (Budapest, 1942–3)

E. Haraszti: 'Zoltán Kodály et la musique hongroise', *ReM* (1947), nos.204–5, p.93

P. Járdányi: 'Kodály, a nevelő' [Kodály, the teacher], *Válasz*, vii/2 (1947)

W. H. Mellers: 'Kodály and the Christian Epic', *ML*, xxii (1941), 155; repr. in *Studies in Contemporary Music* (London, 1947), 136

F. Wildgans: 'Zoltán Kodály, ein ungarischer Volksmusiker', *Rondo* (Vienna, 1953), no.1, p.6

A. Földes: 'Kodály', *Tempo* (1958), no.46, p.8

A. Molnár: *Irások a zenéről* [Writings on music] (Budapest, 1961), 9–119

L. Eősze: 'Zoltán Kodály, Octogenarian', *New Hungarian Quarterly*, iii/6 (1962), 3

——: 'Zoltán Kodály (1882–1967)', *Hungarian Survey*, ii (1967), 51

L. Bárdos: *Harminc irás 1929–1969* [30 studies] (Budapest, 1969), 262ff, 348–464

W. Fuchss: 'Zoltán Kodálys Beziehungen zu Zürich', *SMz*, cxii (1972), 333

J. Breuer: 'Kodály Zoltán és Franciaország' [Kodály and France], *Magyar zene*, xiv/3–4 (1973)

G. Russell-Smith: 'Zoltán Kodály: Composer, Musicologist and Educational Revolutionary', *Some Great Music Educators*, ed. K. Simpson (Borough Green, Sevenoaks, 1976), 78

STUDIES OF PARTICULAR WORKS

(stage works)

L. Pollatsek: 'Háry János', *Musikblätter des Anbruch*, ix (1927), 138

G. M. Ciampelli: 'La "Filanda magiara" di Zoltán Kodály', *Musica d'oggi*, xv/2 (1933), 81

M. D. Calvocoressi: 'Kodály's Ballet Music', *The Listener*, xviii (1937), 449

(choral works)

B. Szabolcsi: 'Die Chöre Zoltán Kodálys', *Musikblätter des Anbruch*, x (1928), 416

M. D. Calvocoressi: 'Choral Music of Kodály', *The Listener*, xv (1936), 365

B. Rajeczky: 'Kodály vallásos és egyházi művei [Kodály's sacred music], *A zene*, xix/13–14 (1938), 222

A. Szőllősy: 'Kodály kórusainak zenei szimbolikája' [The musical symbolism of Kodály's choruses], *Magyar zenei szemle*, iii/2 (1943)

G. Kerényi: 'Kodály Zoltán 25 kórusa', *Magyar dal*, xlviii/11–xlix/1 (1943–4)

A. E. F. Dickinson: 'Kodály's Choral Music', *Tempo* (1946), no.15, p.7

M. Seiber: 'Kodály: Missa brevis', *Tempo* (1947), new ser., no.4, p.3

H. Lindlar: 'Einige Kodály-Chöre', *Musik der Zeit* (Bonn, 1954), no.9

H. Stevens: 'The Choral Music of Zoltán Kodály', *MQ*, liv (1968), 147

J. Mátyás: 'Kodály: Miserere (1903)', *Muzsika*, xvi/1 (1973), 5

(other works)

B. Bartók: 'Kodály's Trio', *Musical Courier*, viii (1920)

B. Szabolcsi: 'Die Instrumentalmusik Zoltán Kodálys', *Musikblätter des Anbruch*, iv (1922), 270

O. Bie: 'Die Lieder von Zoltán Kodály', *Berliner Börsen Courier* (5 Feb 1924)

B. Szabolcsi: 'Die Lieder Zoltán Kodálys', *Musikblätter des Anbruch*, ix (1927), 283

J. S. Weissmann: 'Kodály's Later Orchestral Music', *Tempo* (1950–51), no.17, p.16; no.18, p.17

I. Kecskeméti: 'Kodály balladaköltészete' [Kodály's ballads], *Magyar zene*, viii/6–ix/1 (1967–8)

——: 'Kodály zeneszerzői műhelymunkája a "Sirfelirat" kimunkálásában' [Kodály's working method in composing his Epitaph op.11 no.41, *Magyar zenetörténeti tanulmányok*, iv (in preparation)

LÁSZLÓ EŐSZE

Kōdōn (Gk.) (1) Greek term for bell, attestable from the 5th century BC (Aeschylus, *Seven against Thebes*, ll.386, 399; ?Euripides, *Rhesus*, l.308; Aristophanes, *Frogs*, l.963). The oldest known Greek depiction of a bell, on a silver coin of Euaenetus from the Sicilian city of Catana (now Catania), has also been dated from the last third of the 5th century. Small bronze bells, termed kōdōnion, 6·2 and 8 cm long, have been excavated on Delos and in the shrine of Hera at Argos. Like other instruments in Greece bells originally served a religious (mostly apotropaic) function: a wall-painting in a Delos house shows a small bell suspended around the neck of a sacrificial pig; this was also done with other animals, particularly horses in battle. According to Aeschylus small bells were hung at the edges of soldiers' shields to avert evil and inspire fear in the enemy; Euripides compared them with the face of the Gorgon as an apotropaic symbol.

(2) An ancient Greek synonym for SALPINX; the term was occasionally used in this sense when denoting a signalling instrument.

BIBLIOGRAPHY

C. Waldstein and others: *The Argive Heraeum*, ii (Boston and New York, 1905), 299, no.2257, pl.126

G. Herzog-Hauser: 'Tintinnabulum', *Paulys Real-Encyclopädie der classischen Altertumswissenschaft*, 2nd ser., vi (Stuttgart, 1937), 1406

W. Déonna: *Le mobilier délien*, Exploration archéologique de Délos, xviii (Paris, 1938), 325, pl.92, 816

J. Liegle: 'Euainetos', *Programm zum Winckelmannsfest der archäologischen Gesellschaft zu Berlin*, ci (1941), 44, pl.12

reprinted from *MGG* (vii, 1311) by permission of Bärenreiter

MAX WEGNER

Koechlin, Charles (Louis Eugène) (*b* Paris, 27 Nov 1867; *d* Le Canadel, Var, 31 Dec 1950). French composer, teacher and musicologist. He came from a rich industrial family; his grandfather, Jean Dollfus, well known for his philanthropic and social activities, had founded the cotton textile firm of Dollfus-Mieg & Cie in Mulhouse. From his ancestors Koechlin inherited what he called his Alsatian temperament: an energy, naivety, and an absolute and simple sincerity that lie at the heart of his music and character. His father, a textile designer, moved to Paris before Koechlin was born and intended his son to become an artillery officer; but Koechlin contracted tuberculosis while at the Ecole Polytechnique and this rendered him ineligible for a military career. During his extended convalescence in Algeria in 1889 he began to study music more seriously, and he entered the Paris Conservatoire in October 1890. Here he studied harmony with Taudou and composition with Massenet. His lifelong interest in the music of J. S. Bach was stimulated by the counterpoint classes of Gédalge, and he retained an interest in modal music and folksong from the history classes of Bourgault-Ducoudray. When Dubois replaced Thomas as director in 1896, Massenet resigned, and Koechlin entered the composition class of the man who was to influence him most, Fauré. Throughout his life Koechlin strove to recapture the

classic simplicity and nobility of Fauré's style with its balance of liberty and discipline.

Koechlin's life was hard but uneventful. He lived a comfortable, rather dilettante existence until after his marriage to Suzanne Pierrard in 1903, but increasing financial problems, not assisted by the war, led to Koechlin's beginning his long career as a writer on theory in 1915, although he had started regular critical work with the *Chronique des arts* in 1909 and had increased his teaching activities at the same time.

Until the late 1920s, Koechlin was in the forefront of Parisian musical life. With fellow Conservatoire pupils Ravel and Schmitt and with the backing of Fauré, he founded the Société Musicale Indépendante in 1909 to promote new music in opposition to the Société Nationale controlled by d'Indy and the Schola Cantorum. At Debussy's request he orchestrated all but the Prelude of *Khamma* in 1913, and in 1918 Satie invited Koechlin to join a group called Les Nouveaux Jeunes together with Roussel, Milhaud and several others, although the project never materialized as originally intended and was superseded by Les Six in 1920. Between 1921 and 1924 a series of articles on Koechlin's music appeared in leading musical journals, and more of it began to be published and performed.

However, by 1932 Koechlin was already more famous as a theorist than as a composer, and organizing a festival of his major orchestral works in that year did little to change the situation, nor was his renown spread by his winning the Prix Cressent with the *Symphonie d'hymnes* in 1936, or the Prix Halphan with the First Symphony in 1937. It was not until the 1940s when the director of Belgian radio, Paul Collaer, organized performances of his works (conducted by Franz André) in Brussels that Koechlin's music began to regain public attention. But these concerts were without permanent effect: the bulk of Koechlin's music has remained neglected by publishers and performers.

Koechlin made lecturing visits to America in 1918, 1928 and 1937, and became president of the Fédération Musicale Populaire on the death of Roussel. His growing communist sympathies in the 1930s are reflected in his 'music for the people' and his work for the musical committee of the Association France–URSS, although he was never an official party member. Always abreast of the latest developments in music, he became president of the French section of the ISCM, and actively supported the music of the young at all times, provided that it did not, in his view, exploit novelty for its own sake.

Musically a late developer, Koechlin began his long composing career with a period of songwriting (1890–1909). In about 1911 Koechlin sensed himself 'capable of entering the perilous domain of chamber music', and there began a new period which ended with the Trio op.92 of 1924. During this phase Koechlin evolved his style, developing from the basis of the harmonic advances of the songs of 1905–9 (opp.28, 31 and 35) to the luminous polytonal style which characterizes his mature music. In orchestral composition, Koechlin went through an apprenticeship between 1897 and 1904. *En mer, la nuit* op.27, based on Heine's poem *La mer du Nord*, was the first symphonic work in which he found his 'inspiration was sustained by an appropriate formal development'. A period of early maturity ended with the First Symphony op.57 no.2 of 1911–16, and a second phase, which saw the composition of most of his major orchestral pieces, began with *La course de printemps* op.95.

The seven works (opp.18, 95, 159, 175 and 176) based on Kipling's *Jungle Book* stories form the core of Koechlin's orchestral output, and the composition and revision of this cycle, which lasts less than 75 minutes in performance, occupied him for over 40 years from 1899 onwards. The scores show Koechlin at his best in each period, and the music ranges from a state of demonic energy to a diaphonous luminosity which arises from chords using superposed 4ths or 5ths. His complex ideas found their most natural expression in large-scale orchestral works, and Koechlin defended the viability of the symphonic poem and the vast post-Romantic orchestra long after their vogues had faded.

Charles Koechlin

He was stimulated by a wide range of extra-musical subjects both natural and literary. A particular attraction to the forest in his early works achieved a more universal, pantheistic significance in the jungle of his later creations. Other subjects which recurringly 'imposed themselves' upon him included classical mythology, dreams and fantasy (which reflected his desire to escape from everyday reality into an 'ivory tower' within which he could compose), and the night sky, the serenity and mystery of the universe. Koechlin however was an avid self-borrower, and music 'inspired' by one subject could easily recur in a completely different context.

Koechlin's unusually wide range of musical sympathies is reflected in the eclecticism of his own works, the various styles used in each work being suggested by the subjects. His firm belief in his own imagination

resulted in an almost complete lack of self-criticism, and he rarely revised works with a view to making them more concise, excepting his earlier experimental works such as *La forêt* op.25, and in these the cuts are only optional. The spirit of freedom which pervades both his life and works often results in his larger works being extremely sectional. The juxtaposition of passages of great rhythmic complexity with others almost devoid of rhythmic interest, together with a use of long, wide-ranging and unphrased melodies, tends to make Koechlin's symphonic works sound static and uneven. For these reasons, he is really more successful as a miniaturist, particularly in the pieces he wrote while captivated by the 'insolent beauty' of the female stars of the early sound film in the mid-1930s. Lilian Harvey inspired over 100 quite beautiful cameos (opp.139, 140, 149 and 151) in which Koechlin's harmonic gift (undoubtedly his greatest) is shown to the full, although their virtues are qualified by their smaller aims. The same qualities, together with a childlike spontaneity, are revealed in his very individual piano pieces, notably the *Sonatines* (op.59), which entirely lack Satie's more adult and ironic contortions of tonality.

Koechlin described his life as a 'series of happy chances under a cloud of general misfortune'. One aspect of the silver lining was the necessity to teach, which led him to a profound study of Bach's music that considerably strengthened his own, and an increasing interest in counterpoint, as well as in modality, is evident in the compositions of the 1930s. Koechlin's polytonal music is never at all cerebral in its conception for all its skilled craftsmanship; it shows balanced concern for vertical and horizontal effect that is often lacking in Milhaud. Koechlin's influence on Milhaud has begun to be assessed; indeed, Koechlin is better remembered as a teacher (of Poulenc, Tailleferre and the Ecole d'Arcueil), theorist and orchestrator than as a composer. While he strove for recognition for his music, his own unworldly and uncompromising nature has contributed to his unjust neglect.

WORKS
(*selective list*)

STAGE

op.
36   Jacob chez Laban (pastorale biblique, 1, Koechlin), S, T, SATB, orch, 1896–1908
45   La forêt païenne [Danses antiques], ballet, 1911–16, orchd 1920–25
67   La divine vesprée, ballet, 1917, orchd 1918
158   Incidental music for the final scene of Rolland's Le 14 juillet [Liberté], orch: 2 versions, 1936
169   Alceste (Euripides, trans. H. Marchand), unison chorus, 1938
210   L'âme heureuse [from opp.205, 209], ballet, 1945–7, orchd 1947
222   Voyages: film dansé [from opp.132, 209, 214], ballet, 1947, orchestration inc.

ORCHESTRAL

2   L'épopée de l'Ecole polytechnique, narrator, orch, 1894
10   2 Pieces: Chant funèbre; Chant de fiançailles, 1894–6
—   Symphony, A, 1895–1900, inc.
20   2 Symphonic Pieces: En rêve; Au loin, 1896–1900
25   La forêt, part 1: Le jour, sym. poem, 1897–1904, orchd 1905–6
26   2 Symphonic Studies (Essays), 1896–1901, orchd 1901–4
27   En mer, la nuit, sym. poem after Heine, 1899–1904, orchd 1904
29   La forêt, part 2: La nuit, sym. poem, 1896–1907, orchd 1907
30   L'automne, sym. suite, 1896–1906
38   Nuit de walpurgis classique (Ronde nocturne), sym. poem after Verlaine, 1901–7, rev. 1915–16, orchd 1916
42/2 L'abbaye: Finale [version of op.42/10], org, orch, 1909–12, orchd 1920
43   2 Symphonic Poems: Soleil et danses dans la forêt; Vers la plage lointaine, nocturne, 1898–1909, orchd 1911, 1916

46	Etudes antiques (Suite païenne, Poèmes antiques), sym. suite, 1908–14, orchd 1913–14
46/2	Variant of the finale to op.46, 1908
—	Suite javanaise, transcriptions of gamelan music, 1910
47	2 Symphonic Poems: Le printemps, L'hiver, 1908–16, orchd 1911, 1916
48	2 Symphonic Poems (L'été): Nuit de juin, Midi en août, 1908–11, orchd 1916
49	3 Chorales: L'espérance, org, orch, 1910–12, orchd 1920; La charité, org, 1909; La foi, org, orch, 1912–16, orchd 1921
50	Ballade, 7 movts, pf, orch, 1911–15, orchd 1919
54	Suite légendaire (La nuit féerique), 1901–15, orchd 1920
57/2	Sym. no.1 [orch version of Str Qt no.2, op.57], 1911–16, orchd 1926
60/2	4 sonatines françaises [orch version of op.60], orchd 1930
62	Rapsodie sur des chansons françaises, 1911–16, orchd ?1919
65/2	Les heures persanes [orch version of op.65], orchd 1921
70/2	Poème, hn, orch [orch version of op.70], orchd 1927
76/1	3 Chorales, 1906–10 and 1919–20
76/2	2 Chorales, 1923
76/3	3 Chorales, ?1923
85/2	[orch version of Cl Sonata no.1, op.85], orchd 1946
86/2	[orch version of Cl Sonata no.2, op.86], orchd 1946
95	La course de printemps, sym. poem after Kipling, 1908–25, orchd 1926–7
106	The Bride of a God [with C. Urner], sym. poem, 1929
110	Hymne, ondes martenot, orch, 1929, orchd 1932
115/2	20 chansons bretonnes [version of op.115], vc, orch, orchd 1934
117/2	5 Chorales [from op.117], 1931, orchd 1932
121	Symphonic Fugue, 1932
127	Choral fugué, C, 1933
128	Choral fugué du style modal, org, orch, 1933, orchd 1944
129	Vers la voûte étoilée [from Nocturne, eb, pf], sym. poem, orchd 1933, rev. 1939
130	Sur les flots lointains [from song by Urner], sym. poem, 1933
148	Hymne à la jeunesse, after Gide, 1934, orchd 1935
—	Symphonie d'hymnes [compiled from opp.48/1, 69, 110, 127, 148], 1936
157/3	Marche funèbre [from opp.157/2/14], orch/wind orch, orchd 1937
159	La méditation de Purun Bhagat, sym. poem after Kipling, 1936
160	Les eaux vives, 1936, for Paris Exposition 1937
170	La cité nouvelle, rêve d'avenir, sym. poem after Wells, 1938
171	Le buisson ardent, part 2, sym. poem after Rolland, 1938
175	La loi de la jungle, sym. poem after Kipling, 1939, orchd 1940
176	Les bandar-log, sym. poem after Kipling, 1939, orchd 1940
187	Offrande musical sur le nom de BACH, 1942, orchd 1946
193	Silhouettes de comédie, 12 pieces, bn, orch, 1942–3, orchd 1943
194	2 sonatines, ob d'amore/s sax, chamber orch, 1942–3, orchd 1943
196	Symphony no.2, 5 movts [based on opp.109, 111, 114, 126, 185], 1943–4
202	Le docteur Fabricius, sym. poem after C. Dollfus, 1941–4, orchd 1946
203	Le buisson ardent, part 1 [see op.171], 1945
205	Partita, 5 movts, chamber orch, 1945, orchd 1946
214	Introduction et 4 interludes de style atonal-sériel, 1947, orchestration inc.

CHORAL

1/2	Le renouveau (d'Orléans), SATB/(S, A, T, B), 1890–94
3	La vérandah (de Lisle), S, SSAA, orch, 1893
4/1	Dans le ciel clair (de Lisle), v, female chorus, orch, 1894–5
4/2	Sous bois (Gille), v, female chorus, orch, 1897
7/4	Aux temps des fées (E. Haraucourt) [version of song], 1937
8/7	La paix (Banville) [version of song], 1898
11	La fin de l'homme (de Lisle), T, Bar, SATB, orch, 1895
12	La lampe du ciel (de Lisle), S, T, Bar/B, SA(TB ad lib), orch, 1896
15/2	Midi (de Lisle) [version of song], chorus, orch, n.d.
16	L'abbaye, part 1, S, A, chorus, org, 1899–1903
18	3 poèmes du 'Livre de la Jungle' (Kipling, trans. Fabulet and d'Humières), Mez/S, A, T, B, SAT, orch, 1899–1910
37	Chant funèbre à la mémoire des jeunes femmes défuntes (Vièrges mortes), SSAATTBB, org, orch, 1902–7
40	La chute des étoiles (de Lisle), female chorus, pf, 1905–9
42	L'abbaye, part 2, 10 movts, S, Mez, A, T, Bar, B, triple chorus, org, orch, 1905–10, orchd 1913, 1920
69	Choral (Koechlin) [finale for suite with opp.30, 47, 48], chorus, orch, 1918, orchd 1919
118	Duos, trios, quartets in modal style, 1932
138	Chant pour Thaelmann, chorus, pf/orch, 1934, orchd 1937
150	10 sacred choruses in modal style, 1935
—	Hymne à la liberté (de Lisle), chorus, band, 1936

—	Hymne à la raison (de Lisle), chorus, band, 1936
161	Requiem des pauvres bougres, 1937, inc.
225	15 motets de style archaïque, chorus, ww qt, 1949

SONGS

1/1	5 rondels (Banville): La nuit, Le thé, Le printemps, L'été, La chasse plus, 1890–94, orchd 1895
5	5 mélodies: Promenade galante (Banville), Moisson prochaine (Bouilhet), Chanson d'amour (Bouilhet), Menuet (Gregh), Si tu le veux (de Marsan), 1893–7
7	4 poèmes d'E. Haraucourt: Clair de lune, Plein eau, Dame du ciel, Aux temps des fées, 1890–95, orchd 1896–8
8	7 rondels (Banville): La pêche, L'hiver, Les pierreries, La lune, L'air, Le matin, La paix, 1891–5, orchd 1896
9	Les clairs de lune (L. de Lisle): A/S, T/Mez, pf/orch, female chorus ad lib, 1893
13	Poèmes d'automne: Déclin d'amour (Prud'homme), Les rêves morts (de Lisle), Le nénuphar (Haraucourt), fl obbl ad lib, L'astre rouge (de Lisle), 1894–9
14	9 rondels (de Banville): Le jour, Le midi, L'eau, Le vin, Les métaux, La terre, L'automne, Les étoiles, La guerre, 1896–9, orchd 1901
15	3 mélodies (de Lisle), Juin, Midi, Nox, 1897–1900, orchd 1900
17	3 mélodies: Le colibri (de Lisle), La prière de mort (de Hérédia), Epiphanie (de Lisle), 1895–1900, nos.2 and 3 orchd 1897–1900
21	2 villanelles (de Lisle), Dans l'air léger, Le temps, l'étendue et le nombre, 1900–01
22	4 mélodies: La chanson des ingénues (Verlaine), Novembre (Bourget), Mon rêve familier (Verlaine), Il pleure dans mon coeur (Verlaine), 1900–01
23	2 poèmes d'André Chénier: La jeune Tarentine, Néère, 1900–02
24	4 poèmes de 'La bonne chanson' (Verlaine): Le soleil du matin, Un jour de juin, N'est-ce pas?, Va, chanson, 1901–2
28	4 mélodies: Sur la grève (d'Humières), Automne (Samain), Accompagnement (Samain), Le vaisseau (Haraucourt), 1902–7
31	6 mélodies (Samain: Au flanc du vase): Le sommeil de Canope, Le cortège d'Amphitrite, L'île ancienne, La maison du matin, Le repas préparé, Amphise et Melitta, 1902–8, nos. 1 and 2 orchd 1913–21
35	4 mélodies (Samain): J'ai rêvé cette nuit, Améthyste, Rhodante, Soir païen, 1905–9
39	5 chansons de Bilitis (P. Louÿs): Hymne à Astarté, Pluie au matin, Chant funèbre, Hymne à la nuit, Epitaphe de Bilitis, 1898–1908
44	3 mélodies: Le paysage dans le cadre des portières (Verlaine), Des roses sur la mer (R. Vivien), Choeur des voleurs (Bonnard: Les familiers), 1900–16
56	5 mélodies (Klingsor: Shéhérazade): Chanson d'Engaddi, Paysage, La rose du rameau sec, La neige, Le ventre merveilleux, 1914–16
68	2 mélodies: Hymne à Venus (de l'Isle Adam), Dissolution (Claudel: La connaissance de l'est), 1918
84	8 mélodies (Klingsor: Shéhérazade): Dédicace, Le voyage, Le potier, La chanson des beaux amants, Chanson de flûte, L'oiseau en cage, Offrande, La chanson d'Ishak de Mossoul, 1922–3
104	2 mélodies: Infini, fais que je t'oublie (P. J. Toulet), Je suis jaloux, Psyché (Corneille), 1927–8

CHAMBER AND INSTRUMENTAL

6	Suite, 2 pf, 1896
6/2	Allegretto, vn, pf, 1898
6/3	Andante, vn, pf, 1898
10/2	Preludes, pf, 1908 [possibly incorporated in op.41]
19	Suite, 5 movts, pf duet, 1898–1901
32	4 Little Pieces, hn, vn/va, pf, 1897–1907
32/2	2 nocturnes, fl, hn, pf/harp, 1897–1907
33	Nocturne, chromatic harp, 1907
34	3 Pieces, bn, pf, 1898–1907
34/2	3 Pieces, fl, bn, pf, 1899–1907
41	24 esquisses, pf, 1905–15
51	String Quartet no.1, 1911–13
52	Flute Sonata, 1911–13
53	Viola Sonata [finale after op.28/1], 1902–15
55	Suite en quatuor, fl, vn, va, pf, 1911–15
57	String Quartet no.2, 1911–16
58	Oboe Sonata, 1911–16
59	5 sonatines, pf, 1915–16
60	4 sonatines françaises, pf duet, 1919, arr. org 1926
61a	64 exercices faciles, pf, 1919–20
61b	L'école du jeu lié, pf, 1919–20
61c	10 Easy Little Pieces, pf, 1915–16, 1919–20
61d	12 Little Pieces, pf, 1915–16, 1919–20
63	Paysages et marines, 12 pieces, pf, 1915–16
63/2	Paysages et marines, fl, cl, str qt, arr. pf 1917

64   Violin Sonata, 1915–16
65   Les heures persanes, 16 pieces, after Loti, pf, 1916–19
66   Cello Sonata, 1917
70   Horn Sonata, 1918–25
71   Bassoon Sonata, 1918–19; arr. hn, pf
72   String Quartet no.3, 1917–21
75   Sonata, 2 fl, 1918–20
75/2   Pastorale, fl, cl, pf, 1917–18
77   12 pastorales, pf, 1920
80   Quintet no.1, pf qnt, 1908, 1911, 1917–21
85   Clarinet Sonata no.1, 1923
86   Clarinet Sonata no.2, 1923
87   4 nouvelles sonatines, pf, 1923–4
91   Divertissement, 3 fl, 1923–4
92   Trio, str/ww (ob/fl, cl, bn), 1924
107   3 sonatines, org, 1928–9
115   20 chansons bretonnes sur d'anciennes chansons populaires, vc, pf, 1931–2
123   20 sonneries, hunting tpts, 1932
124   L'ancienne maison de campagne, 12 pieces, pf, 1932–3
—   Nocturne, e♭, pf, 1932–3
142   20 sonneries, hunting tpts, 1935
147/2 Tu crois à beau soleil [arr. Louis XIII song], band, 1935
153a   Quelques chorals pour des fêtes populaires, band, 1935–6
153/2 10 sonneries, hunting tpts, 1935, 1944
155a   Sonatine modale, fl, cl, 1935–6
155/2 Idylle, 2 cl/vn, va, 1936
156   Quintet 'Primavera', fl, harp. vn, va, vc, 1936
157   14 chants, fl, 1936; 157/2: arr. fl, pf, 1936
162   La belle traversée, 3 pieces, pf, 1936–7
165   Wind Septet, fl, ob, eng hn, cl, a sax, bn, hn, 1937; arr. fl, eng hn, C-cl, A-cl, basset horn, b cl, bn, hn, 1945
165/2 Finale of op.165, 14 winds, 1937
173a   4 Little Pieces, cl, bn, 1938–9
173/2 2 Pieces, cl, pf, 1939
174   Vers le soleil, 7 pieces, ondes martenot, 1939
177   Le jeu de la nativité, 9 insts, 1941
178   14 Pieces, cl, pf, 1942
179   14 Pieces, ob/ob d'amore/eng hn, pf, 1942
179/2 Chant de la résurrection [arr. op.179/14], 2 tpt, 3 trbn, pf/org/harmonium, 1942
180   15 Pieces, hn, pf, some for 4 hn, 1942
184   3 sonatines, fl, 1942
185   Suite, 3 movts, eng hn, 1942
188   15 Studies, a sax, pf, 1942–3
192   100 Themes for Organ Improvisation, 1943
195   15 Duos, 2 cl, 1943–4
197   Les chants de Kervélean, melody inst, pf, 1940, 1944
198   Les chants de nectaire, 32 pieces, after France, fl, 1944
199   Les chants de nectaire, 32 pieces, after France, fl, 1944
200   Les chants de nectaire, 32 pieces, after France, fl, 1944
201   Adagio, org, 1945, for marriage of Soizic Guieysse
206   Trio, ob, cl, bn, 1945
208   12 Very Easy Little Pieces, pf, 1946
209   15 Preludes, pf, 1946
211   Adagio, org, 1947, for marriage of Antoinette Guieysse
216   11 monodies: 1–9, cl; 10, ob d'amore/cl/s sax; 11, eng hn, 1947–8
217   In memoriam, 5 pieces, various ens, 1947
220   3 monodies, lame sonore (see Writings, 1950), 1948
221   Sonate à 7, fl, ob, hpd/harp, str qt, 1949
223   Quintet no.2, fl, harp, vn, va, vc, 1949
224   Stèle funéraire, fl (also pic, a fl), 1950
?226   2 Duos, fl, cl, ?1949
—   Adagio, org, 1950, for marriage of Colette Guieysse

CINEMA
(music written for, or suggested by, films)

132   Seven Stars' Symphony, 7 movts: Douglas Fairbanks, Lilian Harvey, Greta Garbo, Clara Bow, Marlene Dietrich, Emil Jannings, Charlie Chaplin, orch, 1933
134   L'andalouse dans Barcelone, unused score for part of film Croisières avec l'escadre, orch, 1933
139   Premier album de Lilian [Harvey], 9 pieces, S, fl, pf, cl ad lib, 1934
140   Le portrait de Daisy Hamilton, 89 sketches, 1934–8
141   Les confidences d'un joueur de clarinette (film score, Koechlin, after Erckmann-Chatrian), small orch, 1934
149   Second album de Lilian, 8 pieces, fl, ondes martenot, hpd, pf, 1935
151   7 chansons pour Gladys (Koechlin), after Lilian Harvey film Calais-Douvres, S, pf, 1935
163   5 danses pour Ginger [Rogers], no instrumentation, 1937
164   Epitaphe de Jean Harlow, fl, a sax, pf, 1937
167   Victoire de la vie, film score, dir. H. Cartier, chamber orch, 1938

MISCELLANEOUS
Many vocalises, canons, fugues [incl. 2, op.114, 1930, and 1, op.26, str qt/org, 1931, orchd as 1st movt of Sym. no.2], chorales [incl. 22, op.117, 1931], harmony and counterpoint exercises [incl. 19, op.109, 1929, and 20, op.111, 1929], pieces for sight-reading and solfège, folksong arrangements

ORCHESTRATIONS
—   G. Fauré: Pelléas et Mélisande op.80: Prélude, Andantino quasi allegretto, Sicilienne, La mort de Mélisande, 1898
—   C. Saint-Saëns: Lola, 1901
—   A. de Castillon: 6 mélodies, ?1906
—   C. Debussy: Khamma [except Prélude], 1912–13
—   C. Porter: Within the Quota, ballet, 1923
—   E. Chabrier: Bourrée fantasque, 1924
—   J. S. Bach: Chorale 'In dir ist Freude', 1933
—   F. Schubert: Fantasy, C, D760, 1933
159/2 G. Fauré: Chanson de Mélisande, 1936
—   B. Godard: Suite, 1945
—   P. Tchaikovsky: 4 Pieces, incl. Swan Lake Waltz, 1945
—   C. Urner: Suite normande (Esquisses normandes), 1945

Principal publishers: Eschig, Philippo, Salabert, Technisonor
MSS in *F-Pn* and privately owned by Y. Koechlin, Paris

WRITINGS
'La pédagogie musicale: professeurs et écoles libres', *Rapport sur la musique française contemporaine* (Rome, 1913), 139
Etude sur les notes de passage (Paris, 1922)
'La mélodie', *Cinquante ans de musique française*, ii (Paris, 1925), 1–62
'Les tendances de la musique moderne française', *EMDC*, II/i (1925), 56–145
'Evolution de l'harmonie: période contemporaine', *EMDC*, II/i (1925), 591–760
'Souvenirs de Charles Koechlin', *Cinquante ans de musique française*, ii (Paris, 1925), 387
Précis des règles du contrepoint (Paris, 1926; Eng. trans., 1927)
Gabriel Fauré (Paris, 1927; Eng. trans., 1946)
Claude Debussy (Paris, 1927)
Traité de l'harmonie (Paris, 1927–30)
Etude sur le choral d'école (Paris, 1929)
Théorie de la musique (Paris, 1934)
Etude sur l'écriture de la fugue d'école (Paris, 1934)
Pierre Maurice, musicien (Geneva, 1938)
Les instruments à vent (Paris, 1948)
'Quelques réflexions au sujet de la musique atonale', *Music Today*, ed. R. Myers (London, 1949), 26
Preface to J. Keller: *La lame sonore* (Paris, 1950)
'Etude sur Shostakovitch', *Musique russe*, ed. P. Souvtchinsky (Paris, 1953), 277
Traité de l'orchestration (Paris, 1954–9)
Numerous articles in *Contrepoints* (1946–9), *Guide du concert*, *Humanité* (1935–8), *Ménestrel* (1921–36), *Monde musicale* (1920–39), *Pensée* (1939–49), *ReM* (1921–53) and programme notes for the Concerts Colonne (1919–24)

BIBLIOGRAPHY
P. Locard: 'Boîte à musique', *Courrier musical*, iv/4 (1901), 40
——: 'Charles Koechlin', *Courrier musical*, v/19 (1902), 261
E. Oliphant: 'The Songs of Charles Koechlin', *MQ*, vii (1921), 186
E. Vuillermoz: 'Charles Koechlin', *Le temps* (14 Jan 1921; reprinted in *Musiques d'aujourd'hui* (Paris, 1923), 21ff
H. Woollett: 'Charles Koechlin', *Monde musical* (1921), Nov, 393
M. Calvocoressi: 'Charles Koechlin', *MT*, lxii (1921), 759, 830; lxiii (1922), 18
E. Royer: 'Charles Koechlin: musicien lyrique français', *ReM*, viii (1923), 114
M. Calvocoressi: 'Charles Koechlin', *Musique de chambre*, iv (1924), 10
——: 'Charles Koechlin's Instrumental Works', *ML*, v (1924), 357
M. Rousseau: 'Un entretien avec ... Charles Koechlin', *Guide du concert*, xv (1928), 215
J. Herscher-Clément: 'L'oeuvre de Charles Koechlin', *ReM*, xvii (1936), 315
G. Milhaud: 'Portrait du mois: Charles Koechlin', *Art musical populaire* (1937–8), 3
W. Mellers: 'A Plea for Koechlin', *MR*, iii (1942), 190
G. Bender: 'Un entretien avec ... Charles Koechlin', *Guide du concert*, xxviii/21–2 (1948), 227
P. Renaudin: *Notice bio-bibliographique* (Paris, 1952)
H. Sauguet: 'Charles Koechlin: poète de la jungle', *Arts*, cccxci (1952), 4
R. Myers: 'Koechlin, Charles', *Grove 5*
P. Collaer: *La musique moderne* (Brussels, 1955)
Y. Koechlin: 'Mon père', *Guitare et musique*, iii/14 (1957), 6
H. Sauguet: 'Autour d'une première audition de Charles Koechlin [Symphony no.2]', *Guitare et musique*, iii/18 (1958), 5
R. Bernard: *Histoire de la musique*, ii (Paris, 1962)

J. Roy: *Présences contemporaines: musique française* (Paris, 1962)

R. Myers: 'Charles Koechlin: some Recollections', *ML*, xlvi (1965), 217

M. Chanan: 'Charles Koechlin and the Movies', *The Listener*, lxxxii (1969), 644

R. Delage: *La musique en Alsace: hier et aujourd'hui* (Strasbourg, 1970)

R. Myers: *Modern French Music* (Oxford, 1971)

R. Orledge: 'Charles Koechlin and the Early Sound Film 1933–38', *PRMA*, xcviii (1971–2), 1

——: *A Study of the Composer Charles Koechlin (1867–1950)* (diss., U. of Cambridge, 1973)

J. E. Woodward: *The Theoretical Writings of Charles Koechlin* (diss., U. of Rochester, 1974)

T. H. McGuire: *The Piano Works of Charles Koechlin (1867–1950)* (diss., U. of North Carolina, 1975)

H. Sauget, ed.: *Oeuvres de Charles Koechlin* (Paris, 1975) [catalogue]

E. K. Kirk: *The Chamber Music of Charles Koechlin* (diss., Catholic U., Washington, DC, 1977)

——: 'A Parisian in America: the Lectures and Legacies of Charles Koechlin', *CMc* (1978), no.25, p.50

——: 'Koechlin's Neglected *Le livre de la Jungle*', *MQ*, lxiv (1978), 229

ROBERT ORLEDGE

Koeckert, Rudolf (Josef) (*b* Grosspriesen bei Aussig [now Ústí nad Labem, Czechoslovakia], 27 June 1913). German violinist. He studied with Jaroslav Kocian at the Prague Conservatory until 1938, becoming first violinist of the Prague Radio Orchestra and then the German PO in Prague, 1939–45. He became leader of the Bamberg SO, 1946–7, and from 1949 was leader of the Bavarian Radio SO in Munich. In 1952 he was appointed a professor of the violin at the Augsburg Conservatory. He has gained wider renown as the leader of the Koeckert Quartet, which he first formed in 1939 as the Sudetendeutsche String Quartet (it was also known as the Prague German String Quartet) and was renamed the Koeckert Quartet in 1947. Its other members are Koeckert's son Rudolf Joachim Koeckert, who succeeded Willi Buchner as second violin in 1965; Franz Schessl, who succeeded Oskar Riedl as viola in 1975; and Josef Merz, cello. The quartet has made international tours and given the premières of works written for it by Bialas, Ginastera, Hindemith, Krenek and Zillig, among others; later it concentrated on the standard Classical and Romantic repertory. Koeckert edited and published Bruckner's String Quartet in C minor (Vienna, 1956), which he discovered at Bamberg in 1950.

BIBLIOGRAPHY

A. Schmitt: '25 Jahre Koeckert-Quartett', *Musica*, xviii (1964), 86

J. Creighton: *Discopaedia of the Violin, 1889–1971* (Toronto, 1974)

RUDOLF LÜCK

Koellreutter, Hans Joachim (*b* Freiburg, 2 Sept 1915). German composer, teacher and conductor. He attended the Berlin Academy of Music (1934–6), where his teachers were Hindemith for composition, Thomas and Scherchen for conducting, Scheck for the flute, Martienssen for the piano and Schünemann and Seiffert for musicology; his flute studies were continued with Moysc at the Geneva Conservatory (1936–7). In 1937 he moved to Brazil, where he taught theory and composition at the Brazilian Conservatory in Rio de Janeiro (1937–52) and the São Paulo Institute of Music (1942–4). He directed the São Paulo Free Academy of Music (1952–5) and the Bahia University music department (1952–62). In these various posts he was responsible for introducing many Brazilian composers to 12-note and serial methods. He was also chief conductor of the Bahia SO (1952–62) and served as general secretary and president of the Brazilian section of the ISCM. In 1963

he left Brazil to become head of the programme department at the Munich Goethe Institute. He was then regional representative of the Goethe Institute in New Delhi (1965–9) and principal of the Delhi School of Music (1966–9), moving in 1970 to Tokyo, where he took appointments as director of the Goethe Institute, professor at the Institute of Christian Music and conductor of the Heinrich Schütz Chorale.

The only early tonal works which Koellreutter recognizes are the two flute sonatas (1937–9). These were followed by a period of strict classical 12-note serial writing, exemplified by *Música 1941* for piano and the *Noturnos* for mezzo-soprano and string quartet (1945), before he developed a more individual serial technique in such works as the orchestral *Mutações* (1953). During the 1960s he favoured a total serial organization stressing linearity, a procedure he termed 'planimetric'. He then combined serialism with graphic notation and other aleatory methods in *Tanka I* for speaker and koto (1971) and *Tanka II* for speaker and piano (1973).

WORKS
(selective list)

Orch: 4 Pieces, 1937; Variations, 1945; Música, 1947; Sinfonia de câmara, 11 inst, 1948; Mutações, 1953; Concretion, orch/chamber orch, 1960; Constructio ad synesin, chamber orch, 1962; Advaita, sitar, orch/chamber orch, 1968; Sunyata, fl, chamber orch (Western and Indian insts), tape, 1968

Vocal: Noturnos de Oneyda Alvarenga, Mez, str qt, 1945; O cafe (M. de Andrade), choral drama, 1956; 8 haikai de Pedro Xisto, Bar, fl, elec gui, pf, gongs, cymbals, woodblocks, tam tam, 1963; Cantos de Kulka, S, orch, 1964; India Report (L. Lutze), cantata, S, speaker, chamber chorus, speaking chorus, chamber orch (Western and Indian insts), 1967; Yū, S, Japanese insts, 1970; Mu-dai (Picasso), 1v, 1972; O Café (Mário de Andrade), chorus, 1975

Chamber: 2 sonatas, fl, pf, 1937, 1939; Vn Sonata, 1939; Inventions, ob, cl, bn, 1940; Música 1941, pf, 1941; Variations, fl, eng hn, cl, bn, 1941; Duo, vc, pf, 1943; Música 1947, str qt, 1947; Diaton 8, fl, eng hn, bn, harp, xyl, 1955; Tanka I, speaker, koto, 1971; Tanka II, speaker, pf, 1973

Principal publishers: Editorial Cooperativa Interamericana de Compositores, Modern, Napoleão, Southern

WRITINGS

Three Lectures on Music (Mysore, 1968)
Jazz Harmonia (São Paulo, 1969)
Ten Lectures on Music (New Delhi, 1969)
History of Western Music (New Delhi, 1970)

GERARD BÉHAGUE

Koenig. French organ builders. Joseph (*b* Luxeuil-les-Bains, 22 Feb 1846; *d* Caen, 30 July 1926) was the pupil of his brother-in-law Charles Mutin. In 1896 Mutin became the manager of the firm of Cavaillé-Coll, whereupon Joseph Koenig set up on his own in Caen. He restored a number of instruments in accordance with the Romantic trend in French organ building, including those at St Etienne, Caen (three manuals, 50 stops), Bayeux Cathedral (three manuals, 41 stops), Beuron Abbey (three manuals, 60 stops) and St Joseph, Gerleve (Westphalia). Joseph's son Paul-Marie (*b* Paris, 19 July 1887) at first carried on the business in Caen, but moved to Paris in 1929. Whereas the Cavaillé-Coll organ favoured Bombardons, Trumpets and Clairons at the expense of Mixtures and Cymbales, P.-M. Koenig strove to create an even balance between all these groups of stops, in the traditon of the classical French organ. But he departed from that tradition in the matters of resonance and volume, there following the model of Cavaillé-Coll. The organs he built on these principles include those in Beirut Cathedral (two manuals, 25 stops), St Joseph's, Beirut (two manuals, 27 stops), St Sauveur, Caen (four manuals, 58 stops), Gap Cathedral (three manuals, 62 stops), and the Basilica, Mézières (three manuals, 43 stops). He also restored a number of older organs along the same lines.

HANS KLOTZ

Koenig, Gottfried Michael (*b* Magdeburg, 5 Oct 1926). German composer and teacher. He studied church music at the Brunswick Staatsmusikschule (1946–7) and then attended the Nordwestdeutsche Musikakademie, Detmold (1947–50), as a pupil of Bialas (composition), Natermann (piano) and Maler (analysis). His education was continued at the Cologne Musikhochschule (1953–4) and Bonn University (1963–4), where he studied the construction and programming of electronic data-processing equipment. From 1954 to 1964 he worked in the Cologne electronic music studios of West German Radio; there he produced several compositions, realized works by other composers (among them Hambraeus, Kagel, Ligeti and Pousseur) and assisted Stockhausen on *Gesang der Jünglinge* and *Kontakte*. During these ten decisive years at one of the most important centres of new music, he took part in the theoretical and practical development of electronic composition, and he did important work in teaching electronic music at the Cologne Musikhochschule (1962–4), in Stockholm, Bilthoven and Essen, at the Darmstadt summer courses and at the Cologne Courses for New Music. In 1964 he was appointed artistic and scientific director of the Instituut voor Sonologie of Utrecht University, where he has worked chiefly on computer programmes for music generation. Above all he is interested in developing the use of computers in live performance, so that the music produced might be influenced in real time by composer and audience.

WORKS
(selective list)
Inst: Horae, ballet, orch, 1950; 2 Klavierstücke, 1957; Wind Qnt, 1958–9; Str Qt, 1959; Orchesterstück 1, 1960–61; Orchesterstück 2, 36 insts, 1961–2; Orchesterstück 1, 1963; Projekt 1, version 1, 1965–6, version 3, 1967; Übung, pf, 1969–70
Tape: Klangfiguren 2, 1955–6; Essay, 1957–8; Terminus 1, 1962; Terminus 2, 1966–7; Terminus X, 1967; Funktion Grün, 1967; Funktion Gelb, 1968; Funktion Orange, 1968; Funktion Rot, 1968; Funktion Blau, 1969; Funktion Indigo, 1969; Funktion Violett, 1969; Funktion Grau, 1969

Principal publishers: Peters, Tonos, Universal

COMPUTER PROGRAMMES
Projekt 1, composition programme, 1966, exists in Fortran II or Algol 60
CSP 1, sound programme, 1966, in Fortran II
Projekt 2, composition programme, in Algol 60

WRITINGS
'Studiotechnik', *Die Reihe*, i (1955), 29; Eng. trans. in *Die Reihe*, i (1958), 52
'Bo Nilsson', *Die Reihe*, iv (1958), 85; Eng. trans in *Die Reihe*, iv (1960), 85
'Henri Pousseur', *Die Reihe*, iv (1958), 18; Eng. trans. in *Die Reihe*, iv (1960), 13
'Studium im Studio', *Die Reihe*, v (1959), 74; Eng. trans. in *Die Reihe*, v (1961), 30
'Via electronica', *Movens* (Wiesbaden, 1960)
'Kommentar', *Die Reihe*, viii (1962), 73; Eng. trans. in *Die Reihe*, viii (1968), 80
Musik in ihrer technischen Rationalität (MS, *NL-BI*, 1963)
'Einführung in die elektronische Musik', *Musik im Unterricht*, lv (1964)
'The Second Phase of Electronic Music', *Congress Report 'Vision 65': New York 1966*
'Notes on the Computer in Music', *The World of Music*, ix/3 (1967), 3
'Computer-Verwendung in Kompositionsprozessen', *Musik auf der Flucht vor sich selbst*, ed. U. Dibelius (Munich, 1969), 78
'Construction and Working Methods of the Utrecht University Studio', *Electronic Music Reports*, i (1969), 61
'Project 1', *Electronic Music Reports*, ii (1970), 32
'Project 2: a Programme for Musical Composition', *Electronic Music Reports*, iii (1970)

'Emploi des programmes d'ordinateur dans la création musicale', *ReM* (1970), nos.268–9, p.89
'Serielle und aleatorische Verfahren in der elektronischen Musik', *Electronic Music Reports*, iv (1971)

BIBLIOGRAPHY
U. Stürzbecher: *Werkstattgespräche mit Komponisten* (Cologne, 1971), 19ff

MONIKA LICHTENFELD

Koenig, (Karl) Rudolf (*b* Königsberg, 26 Nov 1832; *d* Paris, 2 Oct 1901). German physicist. Although Helmholtz was his principal professor at the University of Königsberg, Koenig's research was not in acoustics. After receiving a PhD in physics, Koenig apprenticed himself to the Parisian violin maker Vuillaume. Koenig completed his apprenticeship in 1858 and set up shop at the Quai d'Anjou, where he remained for the rest of his life, making tuning-forks of great precision for his tonometer which covered the entire audible range of frequencies. He constructed remarkably precise clock tuning-forks, sirens, ingenious compound sirens, improved Helmholtz resonators and a wide variety of other apparatuses. The quality of his instruments became legendary, and they became the physics tools for university laboratories in Europe and the USA. He was commissioned by the French government to make the apparatus for establishing 'Diapason normal', $a' = 435$; and he improved Léon Scott's 'phonautograph' of 1857, the antecedent of Edison's reproducing phonograph.

Koenig's research, contained in various papers and summarized in his *Quelques expériences d'acoustique* (Paris, 1882), ranged wide, but he was interested mainly in beats among the overtones and combination tones and phase in the quality of a musical sound. For the former he criticized the use of reed harmoniums and sirens which had been Helmholtz's chief tools; Koenig believed that a proper study required the use of pure tones. Noting that the higher modes of a tuning-fork would not be harmonious, he stroked large forks with a cello bow. He studied phase relations between fundamental and overtones with special compound sirens that allowed him to introduce arbitrarily the desired phase differences. Many of Koenig's results conflicted with Helmholtz's and it is interesting to compare the work of these two men, the most important contributors to experimental musical acoustics in the 19th century.

See also PHYSICS OF MUSIC, §5, and figs. 8–9.

BIBLIOGRAPHY
S. P. Thompson: 'The Researches of Dr. R. Koenig on the Physical Basis of Musical Sounds', *Nature*, lxiii (1890–91), 199, 224, 249
D. C. Miller: *The Science of Musical Sounds* (New York, 1926)
R. S. Shankland: 'Koenig, Karl Rudolf', *Dictionary of Scientific Biography* (New York, 1970–)

JAMES F. BELL

Koering, René (*b* Andlau, 27 May 1940). French composer. At first self-taught, he attended courses given by Boulez, Maderna and Stockhausen at Darmstadt. In 1969 he was appointed to teach at the Ecole des Beaux Arts, Paris. After producing a number of serial scores he has collaborated with Butor on several projects, of which *La nuit écoute* and *Centre d'écoute* share a tape part of messages and literary descriptions from all parts of the earth, with commentary by the live musicians.

WORKS
(selective list)
Combat T 3N, pf, orch, 1961; Suite intemporelle, 1v, reciter, 6 insts, 1962; Ci-gît I, 1v, ens, 1963; Musique pour une passion, orch, 1963; Triple et trajectoires, pf, 2 orchs, 1965; Image de couloir, vn, orch, 1967; 4 extrêmes, orch, 1968; Parallèles-Distorsion, ens, tape, 1970;

Dynastie, brass, str, 1971; Centre d'écoute (Butor), female v, speaker, cl, 2 pf, tape, 1972; Oui et alors? . . ., 2 pf, 2 perc, 1972; La nuit écoute (Butor), female v, 6 str, tape, 1973; Manhattan Invention (Butor), vc, tape, 1973; Vocero, orch, 1973; Str Qt, op.19, 1973; Sym. no.1, op.21, 7 insts, b cl, 1974

Principal publisher: Editions Françaises de Musique

ANNE GIRARDOT

Koerppen, Alfred (*b* Wiesbaden, 16 Dec 1926). German composer. He studied with Kurt Thomas at the Frankfurt Musikalisches Gymnasium (1939–45) and was then active as an organist in that city. From 1948 he taught theory and composition in Hanover, first at the Landesmusikschule and after 1958 at the Staatliche Hochschule für Musik, where he was made professor in 1965. The bulk of his output is choral music, which, at its most intricate, often approaches Renaissance style in its polyphonic flow and in the treatment of the text, as the *Missa pro fidei propagatione* demonstrates. A witty and sometimes satirical spirit pervades the instrumental works, frequently polyphonically conceived and cast in older forms.

WORKS
(*selective list*)

Stage: Virgilius, der Magier von Rom, Zauberoper (1953); Arachne, ballet, 1968; Die Wettermacher, Singspiel, 1972
Choral: 4 Madrigalen (1946); Missa pro fidei propagatione (1952); Das Feuer des Prometheus, oratorio (1955); 5 Männerchöre (Eichendorff) (1959); Der Sonnenhymnus des Echnaton, 3 choruses, 1966; Invocation for Schola, chorus, insts (1967); Joseph und seine Brüder (1968); Deutsche Messe (1969); Missa in commemoratione defunctorum, 1970; Das Stadtwappen, solo vv, chorus, orch, 1973
Solo vocal: Die Vagantenballade (Villon), B-Bar, fl, pf, perc (1948); Dauer der Freude, S, vn, pf, 1967
Inst: Orpheus in Thrazien, pf (1950); Serenade, F, fl, vn, va (1952); Conc., D, str orch (1954); Der Jahrmarkt, pf (1955); Sonata, B♭, fl, pf (1957); Ob Qnt, E, A, 1959; Sonatine, vn, pf (1963); Violinterzette (1970); Transposition, fl, bn, vn, vc, pf, harps, regal, 1972; Konstellation, pf, hpd, harmonium (total 2 players), 1974

Principal publishers: Breitkopf & Härtel, Möseler

GEORGE W. LOOMIS

Koessler [Kössler], **Hans** (*b* Waldeck, 1 Jan 1853; *d* Ansbach, 23 May 1926). German composer, organist and teacher, a cousin of Reger. He trained for the teaching profession and first taught at Leonberg, but by 1871 he had been appointed organist at Neumarkt (Oberpfalz), where he remained until 1874. Then he continued his studies at the Königliche Musikschule in Munich under Rheinberger and Wüllner. In 1877 he went with Wüllner to Dresden, where he taught theory and choral singing at the conservatory until 1881. He was also, from 1879, conductor of the Dresdner Liedertafel, which won first prize at the international song festival in Cologne in 1880. As a result of this success he was invited to the conductorship of the Staatstheater in Cologne, but the atmosphere of the theatre did not suit him, and in 1882 he moved to the Budapest Academy of Music to teach the organ and choral music. The next year he succeeded Volkmann as composition teacher, and he was in charge of the composition department until his retirement in 1908. He remained in Budapest for only a short while before going on extensive travels and settling in Ansbach (1918). Between 1920 and 1925 he was back in Budapest in charge of the master school in composition at the academy, which in 1923 gave a concert of his works.

Koessler was not a composer who worked quickly; his compositions are valuable not so much for their originality of thought as for their highly accomplished technique. He was committed to the formal ideals of the classics, particularly of Brahms's music, and he had a rare feeling for the virtuoso treatment of the voice, so that his choral works are specially worthy of attention. His thorough technical knowledge and highly developed critical sense made him an outstanding teacher, and his contribution in this role to Hungarian music is indicated by the list of his pupils, which includes Bartók, Dohnányi, Kodály, Weiner and many other composers, choirmasters and writers on music.

WORKS
(*selective list*)
VOCAL

Opera: Der Münzenfranz (3, A. Schaefer), Strasbourg, 1903
Choral orch: Triumph der Liebe, oratorio; Sylvesterglocken (Kalbeck), secular requiem, solo vv, vv, orch, 1897; Dem Verklärten (Kalbeck), Trauerode, vv, orch, 1912; Hymne an die Schönheit (Gomoll), male vv, orch, 1912; Dem Vaterlande, Bar, vv, orch, 1915
Other choral works: Psalm li, 4vv, 1902; Psalm xlvi, 8 solo vv, double chorus, 1902; Lieder und Gesänge, 1912; Altdeutsche Minnelieder in Madrigal-Form, male 4vv, 1913; Letzter Wille 'Wenn einstens ist vollendet', vv, pf; Mass, female 3vv, org; other works
Songs: Kammergesänge, S/T, ob, hn, str qt, 1912; 3 Lieder, Bar, pf; Lieder und Gesänge, 3 vols., 1v, pf; Kinderlieder (Güll), 1v, pf; 3 Lieder aus des Kriegszeit, S, pf; Der kleine Rosengarten (Löns), 4 vols., 1v, pf; 5 Lieder, Bar, orch; other songs with pf

INSTRUMENTAL

Orch: Sym. Variations, c♯, 1909; Vn Conc., a, 1914; 2 syms., F, b; Vc Conc., d
Chamber: Str Qt no.1, d; Str Qt no.2, g, 1902; Str Sextet, f, 1902; Allerseelen, vn/ob/(vc, org), 1913; Str Qnt, F, 1913; Suite, a, vn, org, 1919; Trio Suite, vn, va, pf, 1922; Sonata, e, vn, pf; Deutsche Tanzweisen, vn, pf; Ungarische Tanzweisen, vn, pf; Sonata, vc, pf
Pf: Walzersuite; 5 Pf Pieces, 1913

Principal publishers; Bote & Bock, Süddeutscher Verlag

BIBLIOGRAPHY

Obituaries, *Crescendo*, i/1 (1926), 1; *Musica*, viii (1926), 159; *NZM*, xciii (1926), 434; *Nyugat*, xix/12 (1926), 1113; *Die Oberpfalz*, xx (1926), 170; *A zene*, viii/4 (1926), 69
A. Schaefer: 'Hans Kössler', *Die Tonkunst*, xxxii (1928), 295
P. Egert: 'Hans Kössler, ein vergessener Männer-Chor-Komponist', *Deutsche Sängerbundeszeitung*, xxiii (1932), 67
K. M. Pembaur: 'Hans Kössler als Dirigent der Dresdner Liedertafel', *Deutsche Sängerbundeszeitung*, xxiii (1932), 69
A. Siklós: 'Koessler János', *Az országos Magyar Királyi Liszt Ferenc Zeneművészeti Főiskola évkönyve az 1936–37-es évre* (1937), 21

VERA LAMPERT

Koetsier, Jan (*b* Amsterdam, 14 Aug 1911). Dutch composer and conductor. From 1927 to 1934 he studied at the Berlin Hochschule für Musik. After working as a conductor in Lübeck and Berlin, he was conductor of the Hague PO and second conductor of the Concertgebouw (1942–9). In 1950 he was appointed principal conductor for Bavarian Radio, and in 1966 became professor of conducting at the Munich Hochschule für Musik. He made his début with the Concertgebouw as conductor and composer in 1937 with his orchestral Suite. His work has developed under the influence of Hindemith and is characterized by craftsmanship and clear, spontaneous invention.

WORKS
(*selective list*)

Orch: Suite, 1937; Sym. no.3, 1954; Trauermusik, 1954; Conc., tpt, trbn, orch, 1965; Homage to Gershwin, 1969; Mühldorfer Serenade, 1971; Conc. capriccioso, pf, orch, 1975
Vocal: Gesang der Geister (Goethe), chorus, 7 insts, 1939, rev. 1973; Der Mann Lot, oratorio, 1940, rev. 1962; Frans Hals, opera, 1951
Chamber: Nonet, 1967; Bamberger Promenade, 2 tpt, 3 trbn, 1970; Qnt, hn, 2 tpt, trbn, tuba, 1974; Partita, trbn, org, 1976
Ballets, songs, pieces for pf, org

Principal publisher: Donemus

ROGIER STARREVELD

Koffler, Józef (*b* Stryj, 28 Nov 1896; *d* probably in Ojców or Wieliczka, 1943 or 1944). Polish composer.

He studied in Vienna with Graedener (1914–16), Schoenberg (1920–24) and Adler (1920–24), under whom he received a doctorate at the University of Vienna with his thesis *Über orchestrale Koloristik in den symphonischen Werken von Mendelssohn-Bartholdy* (1925). Subsequently he taught theory and composition at the Lwów Conservatory (1929–41), edited the monthly journals *Orkiestra* (1930–38) and *Echo* (1936–7), and served as music critic of the *Ekspres wieczorny* of Lwów. In World War I he had served in the armies of Austria and Poland; in World War II he was killed while in hiding.

The significance of Koffler's small output lies not only in the fact that he was the first Pole to employ 12-note serialism – it was no great feat, as a pupil of Schoenberg, to have introduced the new technique into a country eager for innovation and badly behind the times. Though Koffler accepted ideas from Schoenberg (the principle of permanent variation and rhythmic differentiation, as well as serialism), he was perhaps the first 12-note composer to use folk materials and, stranger still, he aligned himself with neo-classicism. Typical examples of his deployment of these seemingly opposed currents are the Piano Sonatina, the String Trio and the Second Symphony. He was unusually sensitive to colour, harmony and economy of form and technique; in this last he was close to Webern, though he lacked Webern's talent for concentration. Variation forms are frequent in his work, and he was perhaps at his best in compositions of this type, such as the *Musique quasi una sonata* for piano and the accomplished *Wariacje na temat serii dwunastotonowej* ('Variations on a 12-note series') for string orchestra. Among more straightforward pieces are the *Variations sur une valse de Johann Strauss*, a pleasant and cleverly composed piano composition. Also notable are the three symphonies, which are quite unconventional, particularly in their motivic work. In most of his successful works Koffler showed striking skill in adapting rigorous 12-note techniques to Polish folk material, and in his periodic and rather Parisian neo-classical formal methods. His achievement in fashioning an individual 12-note style retaining contact with national traditions may be compared with that of Vogel, Skalkottas or Dallapiccola. Like Skalkottas, Koffler also composed tonal folklorist pieces, among them the *Suita polska* for orchestra and the *40 polskich pieśni ludowych* ('40 Polish folksongs') for piano.

Koffler's first 12-note pieces date from the second half of the 1920s, when Schoenberg's own serial output was small. Though it is possible to accuse the pupil of epigonism, Koffler ignored some of Schoenberg's prohibitions and, above all, he did not accept his teacher's aesthetic. He was too much of an independent for that. His works were performed and understood in Poland between the wars, but, as a result of the poor knowledge there of contemporary techniques, he was relegated to the sidelines, and this perhaps impaired his natural facility. In gifts he was the equal of Woytowicz and Palester, but he died before the promise of those gifts could be fully revealed.

WORKS
(selective list)

Ballet: Alles durch M.O.W., solo vv, chorus, orch

Orch: Wariacje na temat serii dwunastotonowej [Variations on a 12-note series], str, 1933; 3 syms., incl. no.3, wind, harp, perc, 1938; Suita polska; Radosna uwertura [Gay ov.], 1941

Chamber: Str Trio, 1929; Divertimento, ob, cl, bn

Pf: 40 polskich pieśni ludowych [40 Polish folksongs], 1926; Musique de ballet, 1927; Sonatina, 1931; Variations sur une valse de Johann

Strauss, 1936; Musique quasi una sonata

Vocal: 4 poèmes (Fr. verse), 1935; Miłość [Love] (Corinthians), cantata, 1v, str trio

Principal publisher: Polskie Wydawnictwo Muzyczne

BIBLIOGRAPHY
J. Freiheiter: 'Józef Koffler', *Muzyka* (1936), nos.7–8
S. Kisielewski: 'Józef Koffler: Variations sur une valse de Johann Strauss', *Muzyka polska* (1936), no.6
T. Kaczyński: 'Józef Koffler, kompozytor nieznany' [Koffler, unknown composer], *Ruch muzyczny* (1961), no.17, p.2
B. Schäffer: *Klasycy dodekafonii* (Kraków, 1961)
M. Pluta-Kotyńska: 'Kilka uwag o życiu Józefa Kofflera' [Some notes on the life of Józef Koffler], *Ruch muzyczny* (1965), no.1, p.3
T. Kaczyński: 'A la mémoire de Józef Koffler', *Ruch muzyczny* (1968), no.17, p.11

BOGUSŁAW SCHÄFFER

Kogan, Leonid (Borisovich) (*b* Dnepropetrovsk, 14 Nov 1924). Soviet violinist. He received his first violin lessons at the age of seven. Three years later he became a pupil of Abram Yampol'sky (a disciple of Auer), first at the Central Music School in Moscow, then at the Moscow Conservatory (1943–8) and as a postgraduate (1948–51). He made his début in Moscow at the age of 17, and gave concerts throughout the USSR while still a student. In 1947 he was co-winner of the first prize at the World Festival of Democratic Youth in Prague, and in 1951 won the Queen Elisabeth Competition in Brussels. He made his débuts in London and Paris in 1955, in South America in 1956 and in the USA the following year. In 1952 he joined the teaching staff of the Moscow Conservatory. He was named People's Artist of the RSFSR in 1964 and received the Lenin Prize in 1965.

After David Oistrakh, Kogan is considered the foremost Soviet violinist, and one of the most accomplished instrumentalists of the day. Kogan's approach, however, is more objective, less emotional and could be described as more contemporary than Oistrakh's. His tone is leaner, his vibrato tighter, his temperament cooler and more controlled. His intonation is pure, his technical mastery absolute. He shows his versatility in concert series ranging from the complete Bach solo works to the Paganini Caprices. His interpretations of the great Classical concertos combine power, nobility and introspection with an admirable feeling for stylistic integrity. His avoidance of flamboyant effects and a certain reticence in his stage manners make him appeal more to the connoisseur than to the larger public.

Kogan married Elizaveta Gilels (sister of the pianist), also a concert violinist. They have appeared in violin duets, and with their son Pavel gave the first performance of the Concerto for Three Violins by Franco Mannino (1965), dedicated to them. With Gilels and Rostropovich, Kogan has given many trio performances. Among works dedicated to him are concertos by Khrennikov, Karayev, Knipper and Bunin, the Concerto-Rhapsody by Khachaturian, and sonatas by Vaynberg and Levitin. Kogan was the first Soviet violinist to play and record Berg's Violin Concerto; he is intensely interested in the modern repertory. His violin is a Guarneri 'del Gesù' dated 1726.

BIBLIOGRAPHY
W. Stewart: 'A Talk with Leonid Kogan', *The Strad*, lxix (1959), 442
L. Raaben: *Zhizn' zamechatel'nïkh skripachey* [The lives of famous violinists] (Moscow, 1967)
J. Creighton: *Discopaedia of the Violin, 1889–1971* (Toronto, 1974)

BORIS SCHWARZ

Kogoj, Marij (*b* Trieste, 27 May 1895; *d* Ljubljana, 25 Feb 1956). Yugoslav composer. He studied with

Schreker and Schoenberg in Vienna (1914–18), and was then coach and conductor at the Ljubljana Opera. Until 1932 he was also active as a music critic, but growing mental illness forced him to live in isolation. Kogoj was a pioneer of expressionism in Slovene music; the culmination of his art was in the opera *Črne maske* ('Black masks'). It is a piece that sets out to explore the inner psychic world, truly revealed only in acts of madness. The polyphonically conceived and richly orchestrated music takes Bergian liberties with strict 12-note technique, and there are parallels between this opera and *Wozzeck*, with which Kogoj was not acquainted.

WORKS
(selective list)

Večerni zvon [Evening bell], chorus, 1912; Trenutek [A moment], chorus, 1914; Istrski motiv, 1v, pf, 1919; Gazelle, 1v, pf, 1921; Mala ladja [The little ship], chorus, 1921; Pf Sonata no.1, 1921; Srce me boli [My heart is aching], chorus, 1921; Requiem, 1922; Otroške pesmi [Children's songs], chorus, 1922–3; Poljski nageljni [Carnations in the field], chorus, 1923; Double and Triple Fugue, pf, 1925; Suite, orch, 1927; Vrabci in strašilo [Sparrows and the scarecrow], chorus, 1927; Kar hočete [Twelfth night], opera, 1928; Črne maske [Black masks] (opera, L. Andrejev), 1929; Andante, vn, pf, 1930

Principal publisher: Edicije DSS

BIBLIOGRAPHY
B. Loparnik: 'Dramaturška in kompozicijska zasnova Kogojeve opere "Kar hočete"', *MZ*, ii (1966), 77
——: 'Kogojevi pogledi na slovensko narodno pesem' [Kogoj's views on Slovene folksong], *MZ*, iv (1968), 98
——: 'Prvine melodične dikcije v Kogojevih otroških pesmih' [Elements of melodic diction in Kogoj's children's songs], *MZ*, v (1969), 54
I. Klemenčič: 'Kogojeva scenska glasba "V kraljestvu palčkov"' [Kogoj's incidental music 'In the dwarfs' kingdom'], *MZ*, vii (1971), 53

ANDREJ RIJAVEC

Kohaut [Kohault, Kohout], **(Wenzel) Josef (Thomas)** (*b* Saaz [now Žatec], Bohemia, 4 May 1738; *d* Paris, ?1793). Bohemian composer. He was the son of the organist and choral director Franz Andreas Kohaut. He became a trumpeter in the Austrian army but deserted and fled to France, where he joined the private orchestra of Prince Conti and began composing and playing the lute. Kohaut was most important as a composer of *opéras comiques*; his first such work, *Le serrurier*, was performed at the Comédie-Italienne on 20 December 1764 (published in 1765; translated into Swedish, Dutch and German and revived at Prague in 1929), and was followed by *La bergère des Alpes* (libretto by Marmontel, 19 February 1766) and *Sophie, ou Le mariage caché* (4 June 1768). Scores of these works and of several separate *ariettes* were published in Paris. The opera *La closière, ou Le vin nouveau*, produced at Fontainebleau on 10 November 1770, is lost.

Six symphonies by Kohaut were published in Paris between 1760 and 1766 by La Chevardière and Venier, but are now known only from the publishers' advertisements. The *Six sonates* for harpsichord, violin and cello (1763) and eight *Trios* for the harpsichord and harp or lute with violin and cello accompaniment (1767) are Kohaut's only extant instrumental music.

BIBLIOGRAPHY
BordasD; EitnerQ
J. Branberger: 'Aufgefundene Opern von Josef Kohout', *Der Auftakt*, xi (1929), 45
R. Quoika: 'Kohaut, Wenzel Josef Thomas', *MGG*

CAMILLO SCHOENBAUM

Kohaut, Karl [Carolus Ignatius Augustinus] (*b* Vienna, baptized 26 Aug 1726; *d* Vienna, 6 Aug 1784). Austrian lute virtuoso and composer. His father, Jakob

Karl Kohaut (*b* Prague, *c*1678; *d* Vienna, 27 May 1762), was a household musician to the chief steward A. F. K. Schwarzenberg. He was not the brother of W. J. T. Kohaut as is often stated. He entered the civil service in 1758 and reached the position of secretary of the imperial chancery, in which capacity he accompanied Emperor Joseph II and Chancellor Wenzel Anton, Count of Kaunitz, on journeys abroad. While studying with Gottfried van Swieten he became acquainted with Bach's cantatas and Handel's oratorios. Hanslick referred to a public appearance of Kohaut at the Vienna Tonkünstler-Sozietät in December 1777, when a symphony and concertino for several instruments by him were performed. Kohaut was highly regarded as a lute virtuoso and composer. According to Fétis, 'of all the lutenists of his time, he was the most skilful, and the music that he composed for the instrument was also considered as the best available in its genre'. His prowess as a lutenist received similar praise from others in the 18th and 19th centuries, but his works for strings did not attract attention until the 20th. His lute trios contain rather unpretentious salon music, but his lute concertos are outstanding in the repertory.

WORKS

Inst: Divertimento primo, lute obbl, 2 vn, b (Leipzig, 1761); 3 concs., lute, 2 vn, b, *D-B*; 2 concs., lute, 4 str, *B*, 1 in *As*; 3 concs., lute, 2 vn, b, *As*; kbd conc., *A-Wgm*; 2 syms., 4 str, *Wgm*; 6 syms., sonata, 3 str, *Wgm*; 2 divertimenti, 3 syms., 3 str, *M*; 4 trietti, trio [Divertimento], lute, vn, vc, *B-Br*; trio, lute, va, vc, *Br*; 6 partitas, 3 str, *A-Wn*; sonata, 4 str, *Wn*; sonata, 3 str, *Wn*; sonata, lute solo, *D-As*; chamber works, listed in Breitkopf catalogues (1762–3, 1766–7); Simphonie périodique (Paris, n.d.), doubtful
Vocal: Applausus Mellicensis (cantata), Securitas Germaniae (cantata), 1764, *A-M*; masses, motet, *CS-Pnm*

BIBLIOGRAPHY
FétisB
E. Hanslick: 'Wiener Virtuosenkonzerte im vorigen Jahrhundert', *Jb des Vereins für Landeskunde von Niederösterreich*, i (1867)
J. Klima: 'Karl Kohaut, der letzte Wiener Lautenist', *ÖMZ*, xxvi (1971), 141 [with bibliography]

reprinted from *MGG* (xvi, 1013–14) by permission of Bärenreiter
JOSEF KLIMA

Köhler. English family of military wind instrument makers, of Hessian origin. John [Johannes, Hans] Köhler (*b* Volkenroda, nr. Kassel, *c*1735; *d* London, *c*1805) went with a regiment of Hessian mercenaries to London in about 1775, and there became bandmaster to the Lancaster Volunteers. In 1780 he set up as an instrument maker at 87 St James Street. He had no children, but sent to Germany for his nephew, John Köhler (*b* ?Volkenroda, *c*1770; *d* London, ?*c*1870), who succeeded to the family business in 1801. The younger John Köhler was appointed musical instrument maker to the Duke of York, and later to the Prince of Wales. His son and successor, John Augustus Köhler (*b* London, *c*1810; *d* London, 20 June 1878), in 1838 acquired the rights to Shaw's swivelling disc valves, which derived from Halary's invention in Paris of 1835 (*see* VALVE (i)). Soon after, he moved the business to Henrietta Street and introduced an improved version of the device called the New Patent Lever. On this he based the two-valve 'New Patent Lever French Horn', brought out for the Great Exhibition of 1851. This and other inventions by him won medals at the 1851 and 1862 exhibitions, and enjoyed some favour among military instrumentalists as late as 1890; Day's catalogue for the Royal Military Exhibition of that year gives a detailed description of Köhler's device. The disc valve, even with Köhler's improvements, proved impossible to keep airtight, and despite its initial success did not survive into the 20th century.

For instruments by the Köhler family, see CORNET(i), fig.3, FLUTE, fig.4a and POSTHORN.

HORACE FITZPATRICK

Kohler, Irene (b London, 7 April 1912). English pianist. She studied at Trinity College of Music (where she later taught), at the Royal College of Music, where she won a travelling scholarship, and with Eduard Steuermann in Vienna. In 1931 she made her début at Croydon in Rakhmaninov's Third Concerto and first appeared in London at a Promenade Concert in 1934. She was soon fulfilling concert and broadcasting engagements and undertaking tours to all parts of the world. Kohler's powerful technique enabled her to give successful performances of works more usually played by male virtuosos, her wide repertory including the Brahms–Paganini Variations, Ravel's *Gaspard de la nuit* and Albéniz's *Iberia*. She has given many first British performances including works by Hindemith, Wiéner and Goossens and has made soundtracks for several films. She holds the BMus degree of London University.

FRANK DAWES

Köhler, Johannes-Ernst (b Merano, 24 June 1910). German organist. The son of a musical director, who taught him the piano and organ, he later studied at the Staatliche Akademie für Schul- und Kirchenmusik in Berlin (1923–33), with Wolfgang Reimann (organ), Hans Beltz (piano) and Hans Chemin-Petit (theory and composition). He was organist with the Berlin PO in 1932 and 1933, playing under Pfitzner, Furtwängler and Bruno Kittel; he also recorded for Berlin radio. In 1933–4 he was organist at St Paul's in Berlin-Lichterfelde. In 1934 he was appointed organist at the Stadtkirche in Weimar and organ lecturer at the Musikhochschule there, becoming a professor and director of church music in 1950. He was awarded the East German National Prize (1955) and later the Weimar Art Prize. In 1970 he became professor of organ improvisation at the Leipzig Hochschule für Musik and at the International Music Seminar in Weimar. His many concert tours in east and west Europe have established his reputation as one of the foremost East German organists. Particularly noteworthy are his efforts to popularize organ music, both through improvisation and by 'competitions' with, for example, the Leipzig organist Robert Köbler. He has recorded music by Bach and Handel (the latter with the Leipzig Gewandhaus Orchestra).

GERHARD WIENKE

Köhler, Karl-Heinz (b Blankenhaim, Thuringia, 24 Oct 1928). German musicologist and librarian. He studied the violin with Ehlers and musicology with Münnich at the Weimar Musikhochschule (1945–50), and musicology with Besseler at Jena University, where he took the doctorate in 1956 with a dissertation on the trio sonatas of J. S. Bach's Dresden contemporaries. He worked at the Deutsche Staatsbibliothek in Berlin (1953–5) before becoming director (1956) of its music department. He was appointed lecturer at the Humboldt University in 1965 and president of the East German section of the International Association of Music Libraries in 1971. He was made a member of the Zentralinstitut für Mozartforschung, Salzburg, in 1962, and a member of the Music Council of East Germany in 1965. In 1979 he took up a post at Weimar Musikhochschule.

Köhler's research and editorial work is concerned with performance, musicology and librarianship. Both his critical and performing editions draw extensively on hitherto unavailable sources in the Deutsche Staatsbibliothek; he has concentrated on J. S. Bach and early works by Mendelssohn and is co-editor of Beethoven's writings. He has also treated these subjects analytically in monographs and articles and in a series of observations on methodology he contributed to the development of music librarianship and source material information systems.

WRITINGS

'Ein Musikalienfund in der U. B. Jena und seine Bedeutung für die musikhistorische Erschliessung der Anfänge des Jenaer "Akademischen Konzertes" ', *Wissenschaftliche Zeitschrift der Friedrich-Schiller-Universität Jena*, iv (1954–5), 155
Die Triosonate bei den Dresdener Zeitgenossen J. S. Bachs (diss., U. of Jena, 1956)
'Grundzüge eines analytischen Systems der Sachkatalogisierung der "Musica Practica" ', *Zentralblatt für Bibliothekswesen*, lxxi (1957), 267
'Zur Problematik der Violinsonaten (J. S. Bachs) mit obligatem Cembalo', *BJb*, xlv (1958), 114
'Zur Problematik der Schallplatten-Katalogisierung', *Zentralblatt für Bibliothekswesen*, lxxiv (1960), 102; Eng. trans. in *HMYB*, xi (1961), 116
'Die Musikabteilung', *Deutsche Staatsbibliothek 1661–1961* (Leipzig, 1961), 241–74
'Carl Maria von Webers Beziehungen zu Berlin', *Festschrift Heinrich Besseler* (Leipzig, 1961), 425
'Das Jugendwerk Felix Mendelssohns: die vergessene Kindheitsentwicklung eines Genies', *DJbM*, vii (1962), 18
'Die Erwerbungen der Mozart-Autographe der Berliner Staatsbibliothek: ein Beitrag zur Geschichte des Nachlasses', *MJb 1962–3*, 65
'Wilhelm Rintels "Zauberflöte", 2. Teil: ein klingendes Mozartdenkmal der Brahmszeit', *MJb 1964*, 62
Felix Mendelssohn Bartholdy (Leipzig, 1966, 2/1972)
'Mozarts Kompositionsweise: Beobachtungen am Figaro-Autograph', *MJb 1967*, 31
'Figaro-Miscellen: einige dramaturgische Mitteilungen zur Quellensituation', *MJb 1968–70*, 119
ed., with G. Heere: *Ludwig van Beethovens Konversationsheften* (Leipzig, 1968–)
'Beethovens literarische Kontakte: ein Beitrag zum Weltbild des Komponisten', *Internationaler Beethoven-Kongress: Berlin 1970*, 483
'Beethovens Gespräche: biographische Aspekte zu einem modernen Beethovenbild', *Beethoven-Symposion: Wien 1970*, 159
'Die Konversationshefte Ludwig van Beethovens als retrospektive Quelle der Mozartforschung', *MJb 1971–2*, 120
'Max Reger: Grösse und Vermächtnis als Problem für unsere Zeit', *Regerkolloquium: Meiningen 1973*, 40
'150 Jahre Musikabteilung der Deutschen Staatsbibliothek', *Beiträge zur Musikdokumentation: Franz Grasberger zum 60. Geburtstag* (Tutzing, 1975)
'Mendelssohn, Felix', *Grove 6*
Articles in *IMSCR, vii Cologne 1958* and Vetter Festschrift (1969)

EDITIONS

F. Mendelssohn: *Konzert für zwei Klaviere und Orchester E-dur*, Leipziger Ausgabe der Werke Felix Mendelssohn Bartholdys, ii/4 (Leipzig, 1960, 2/1971); *Konzert für zwei Klaviere und Orchester As-dur*, ibid, ii/5 (Leipzig, 1961, 2/in preparation); *Die beiden Pädagogen: Singspiel in einem Aufzug*, ibid, v/1 (Leipzig, 1966)

HORST SEEGER

Köhler, Siegfried (b Meissen, 2 March 1927). German composer and musicologist. At the Dresden Hochschule für Musik (1946–50) he studied composition with Finke, conducting with Hintze and the piano with MacGregor; he continued his studies at Leipzig University (1950–55) with W. Serauky (musicology) and Jahn (history of art). In 1957 he was appointed director of the International Music Library, Berlin, and in 1959 he was elected president of the German section of the UNESCO International Association of Music Libraries. He held the post of artistic director of Deutsche Schallplatten (1963–8) and then director and professor of composition at the Dresden Hochschule für Musik. His many nationalist pieces, such as the youth songs, have become widely known in East Germany. He has striven for a clear, melodic style, increasingly marked by contrast.

WORKS
(selective list)

Vocal: Reich des Menschen, oratorio, 1962; Der Richter von Hohenburg (opera, Köhler), 1963; Aspekte (Köhler), S/T, 9 insts, 1968; Dass unsre Liebe eine Heimat hat (G. Deicke), chorus, 1969; Wir – unsere Zeit (J. R. Becher), S, Bar, chorus, children's chorus, orch, 1971; Ode, T, hn, str, 1972; numerous cantatas, choruses, songs, youth songs, mass songs

Orch: Fröhliche Suite, 1956; Heiteres Vorspiel, 1956; Prolog, 1959; Sinfonie der Jugend, 1965; Concertino, cl, str, 1968; Sym. no.2, 1972; Pf Conc., 1972

Chamber: Sonata 'Rotterdam 4.5.1940', hn, pf, 1966

WRITINGS

Die Instrumentation als Mittel musikalischer Ausdrucksgestaltung (diss., Leipzig U., 1955)

'Instrumentation als Ausdruckskunst im Opernschaffen W. A. Mozarts', W. A. Mozart zum 200. Geburtstag: Sonderabdruck der Zeitschrift ... HRo, ed. J. Jiránek and P. Eckstein (Prague, 1956)

'Leoš Janáčeks Progressivität und der musikalische Modernismus in der westlichen Welt', Leoš Janáček a soudobá hudba: Brno 1958, 169

Kohlmann Quartet. Original name of the DVOŘÁK QUARTET.

Kohn, Karl (b Vienna, 1 Aug 1926). American composer, pianist and teacher of Austrian birth. After emigrating to the USA in 1939, he studied at the New York College of Music from 1940 to 1944. He served in the US Army during World War II. He attended Harvard University, studying composition with Walter Piston, Irving Fine, Randall Thompson and Edward Ballantine (gaining his BA, summa cum laude, in 1950 and MA in 1955). In 1950 he was appointed to Pomona College and Claremont Graduate School, California. For three years he was on the faculty of the Berkshire Music Center and is on the board of directors of the Monday Evening Concerts. His awards include Fulbright (1955–6) and Guggenheim (1961–2) Fellowships.

In his music he uses a chromatic and sometimes quasi-serial pitch vocabulary mixed with triadic sonorities. The resulting pitch contexts for both melodic and harmonic succession are flexible and generate powerful musical structures. Occasionally, he uses quotation or parody of pre-existing materials in his compositions, as in Introductions and Parodies (1967).

WORKS
(selective list)

Sinfonia concertante, pf, orch, 1951; Concert Music, 12 wind, 1956; 3 Scenes, orch, 1958–60; Concerto mutabile, pf, orch, 1962; Kaleidoscope, str qt, 1964; Rhapsodies, mar, vib, perc, 1968; Trio, vn, hn, pf, 1972; Encounters I–V, various insts, pf, 1965–73; Centone, orch, 1973; Innocent Psaltery, orch, 1976; pf pieces, songs

Principal publisher: Carl Fischer

BIBLIOGRAPHY

L. Morton: 'Current Chronicle', MQ, xlix (1963), 299
P. Oliveros: 'Karl Kohn: Concerto Mutabile', PNM, ii (1963–4), 87
RICHARD SWIFT

Kohout, Josef. See KOHAUT, JOSEF.

Kohoutek, Ctirad (b Zábřeh, 18 March 1929). Czech composer. He studied with Kvapil at the Brno Academy of Music (1949–53) and then remained there as a teacher of theory and composition. During the socialist realist period of the 1950s he wrote popular songs, taking an interest in folksong and composing appropriate orchestral programme works. Subsequently, however, his knowledge of the major 20th-century com-

posers and of new developments in the West, summarized in his theoretical work of 1962, led him to accept modern means of expression. 12-note serialism, in particular, appealed to his systematic nature, and he used the technique in the chamber works of the late 1950s. He also took Hindemith's linear counterpoint and free tonality as the basis for the symphony Velký přelom ('The great turning-point', 1959–60), and in the melodrama Pátý živel ('The fifth element', 1962) he was influenced by Schoenberg's A Survivor from Warsaw. His children's choral cycle Od jara do zimy ('From spring to winter', 1962) took a lead in introducing 12-note serialism to the genre which has continued to occupy the centre of his interests. In later works he has exploited the potentialities suggested in his pamphlet of 1966.

In the mid-1960s Kohoutek formally established his technique of 'project musical composition'. For each large piece he first works out a detailed graphic plan showing the architectural and proportional scheme, the dynamic course, an outline of tone-colour and any further structural elements; only then does he proceed to realization. The first piece he composed in this way was Memento 1967 for wind and percussion, a work of inventive sonorities and suggestive expressive character. In later compositions he has tended to use stratified textures; Panychida for two violas, ensemble and tape (1968), for instance, is described as 'music in two sound layers'. The culmination of his technical principles came in two big orchestral pieces, Teatro del mondo (1969) and the three-part Slavnosti světla ('Festivals of light', 1974–5), for which he received the Janáček Prize in 1975. Two years earlier he had taken the PhD at the University of Olomouc for his theoretical works.

WORKS
(selective list)

Orch: Vn Conc., 1958; Velký přelom [The great turning-point], sym., 1959–60; Symfonieta, 1963; Concertino, vc, chamber orch, 1964; Preludia, chamber orch, 1965; Memento 1967, conc., wind, perc, 1966; Teatro del mondo, 1969; Pantheon, 1970; Slavnostní prolog [Festival prologue], 1971; Slavnosti světla [Festivals of light], 1974–5

Children's choral: Od jara do zimy [From spring to winter], 3 pieces, 2–4vv, 1962; Hudební oříšky [Musical nuts] (F. Branislav), cycle, 1965; Podvečerní koncert u chaty [Evening concert at the cottage] (Branislav), cycle, vv, insts, 1969; Skalické zvony (trad.), ballad, vv, insts, 1970; Janek a Kača (trad.), cantata, vv, insts, 1973; other works and educational pieces

Other vocal works: Ukolébavka černošské mámy [Lullaby of the black mother] (J. Navrátil), A, vv, orch, 1952; Balady z povstání [Ballads from the uprising] (J. Urbánková), 2 cantatas, 1960; Za život [For life], 2 pieces, female vv, 1960; Pátý živel [The fifth element] (O. Mikulášek), reciter, small orch, 1962; other pieces for female vv

Chamber: Suite, va, pf, 1957; Suite, wind qnt, 1958–9; Str Qt, 1959; Rapsodia eroica, org, 1963; Inventions, pf, 1965; Miniatures, 4 hn, 1965, arr. str orch 1966; Panychida, 2 va, ens, tape, 1968

WRITINGS

Novodobé skladebné teorie západoevropské hudby [Modern compositional theories of western European music] (Prague, 1962, rev., enlarged 2/1965 as Novodobé skladebné směry v hudbě)

Soudobé skladebné techniky v dětských sborech [Modern compositional techniques in children's choral works] (Brno, 1966)

Projektová hudební kompozice [Project musical composition] (Prague, 1969)

Hudební styly s hlediska skladatele [Musical styles from the composer's standpoint] (Prague, 1975)

BIBLIOGRAPHY

J. Vysloužil: 'Cesta slibně započatá' [A path begun with promise], HRo, xvii (1964), 230

M. Štědroň: 'K moravskej tvorbe posledných rokov' [Moravian composition of recent years], Slovenská hudba, xv (1971), 388
ALENA NĚMCOVÁ

Kohs, Ellis (Bonoff) (*b* Chicago, 12 May 1916). American composer and teacher. He studied at the San Francisco Conservatory, at the University of Chicago with Bricken (1933–8, MA 1938), at the Juilliard School with Wagenaar (1938–9) and at Harvard with Piston, Apel and Leichtentritt (1939–41). After war service as a bandmaster in the US Army Air Force he taught at the Kansas City Conservatory (1946, 1947), Wesleyan University, Connecticut (1946–8), the College of the Pacific (1948–50), Stanford University (1950) and the University of Southern California (from 1950), serving at the last as chairman of the theory department (until 1973) and professor of music. He has also been active as an administrator. His textbook *Music Theory* (New York, 1961) has been widely used; it was followed by *Musical Form* (Boston, 1976). His compositions show an imaginative use of variation technique. The later works use newer techniques (including 12-note serialism), media and forms, but never depart from classical standards of clarity and coherence. Among the awards he has received are the Alice M. Ditson Award (1946) and the BMI Publication Award (1948).

WORKS
(*selective list*)

Opera: Amerika (Kohs, after Kafka), 1966–9
Orch: Conc. for Orch, 1941; Legend, ob, str, 1946; Sym. no.1, 1950; Sym. no.2, chorus, orch, 1957
Choral: Lord of the Ascendant (D. Allen, after Epic of Gilgamesh), 7 solo vv, chorus, orch, 8 dancers, 1955; Psalm xxiii, 4 solo vv, chorus, 1957; 3 songs from the Navajo, 1957
Chamber: Str Qt no.1, 1940; Night Watch, fl, hn, timp, 1944; Sonatina, bn, pf, 1944; Passacaglia, org, str, 1946; Sonatine, vn, pf, 1948; Str Qt no.2 'A Short Concert', 1948; Chamber Conc., va, 9 str, 1949; Sonata, vc, pf, 1951; Studies in Variation I, wind qnt, II, pf qt, III [= Pf Sonata no.2], IV [= Sonata, vn], 1962; Sonata, snare drum, pf, 1966; Duo after Kafka's 'Amerika', vn, vc, 1970
Kbd: Pf Variations, 1946; Variations on 'L'homme armé', pf, 1947; Capriccio, org, 1948; Toccata, hpd/pf, 1948; 3 Chorale Variations on Hebrew Hymns, org, 1952; 2 pf sonatas
Songs: Fatal Interview (E. St Vincent Millay), 1951; Epitaph (G. Santayana), T, pf, 1959

Principal publishers: American Composers Alliance, Associated, Gray

BIBLIOGRAPHY
Compositores de América/Composers of the Americas, ed. Pan American Union, xv (Washington, DC, 1970), 120

BARBARA HAMPTON

Koinōnikon. A short verse, usually from the psalms, which is chanted in the Orthodox liturgy when the clergy communicate.

Koizumi, Fumio (*b* Tokyo, 4 April 1927). Japanese ethnomusicologist. He graduated in aesthetics at Tokyo University in 1951 and studied music with Eishi Kikkawa. He has been assistant, then full, professor at the Tokyo National University of Fine Arts and Music since 1960. In 1967 and 1971 he visited the USA to teach at Wesleyan University in Middletown, Connecticut. In addition to his special field of Japanese folk music, he takes a broad interest in all folk traditions and has made frequent field studies, e.g. in India (1957–9), Iran (1961), Ryūkyū Islands (1963), the Near East, eastern Europe and Spain (1964).

WRITINGS
Nihon dentō ongaku no kenkyū [Study of Japanese traditional music] (Tokyo, 1958)
'Annotated Bibliography of Japanese Music', *Ongakugaku*, ix (1963), 55
'Rhythm in Japanese Folk Music', *The Japanese Music*, ed. Japanese National Committee of the International Music Council (Tokyo, 1967), 14
'Eskimō no ongaku' [Music of the Eskimo], *Nomura Festschrift* (Tokyo, 1969), 158

Warabeuta no kenkyū [Game songs of Japanese children] (Tokyo, 1969)
'Nihon ongaku no onkai to senpō' [Scales and modes of Japanese music], *Kikkawa Festschrift* (Tokyo, 1973), 179–208

MASAKATA KANAZAWA

Kókai, Rezső (*b* Budapest, 15 Jan 1906; *d* Budapest, 6 March 1962). Hungarian composer. He began his career at an early age: the Symphony in E♭ was written and performed when he was 11, and in his student years he gained recognition for his Wagnerian organ improvisations. From 1920 he was a composition pupil of Koessler and, to a certain extent influenced by Dohnányi, he composed in a Brahmsian manner. Kókai studied composition and the piano at the Budapest Academy of Music from 1925 to 1926, when his Quartet in F♯ minor won a prize that enabled him to make a study tour of Italy and France. As a condition of this competition he spent a short time collecting folksongs in Gömör county, Hungary. He started teaching in 1927, and from 1929 until his death he was a professor at the Budapest Academy, giving instruction in a range of subjects. In 1933 he took a DMus at Freiburg University as a musicology pupil of Gurlitt. Kókai was director of music for Hungarian radio from 1945 to 1948. Sketches for a divertimento, dating from 1930, show signs of an awakening interest in Debussy and Stravinsky. In 1931–2 Kókai made some Hungarian folksong arrangements, but he was averse to the new directions of Bartók and Kodály, and later in the 1930s found his own Hungarian style, connected with Liszt and 19th-century *verbunkos* music. The stage oratorio *István király* ('St Stephen') shows the achievement of this aesthetic, which was developed after World War II, sometimes using folksongs, as in the ballet *A rossz feleség* ('The bad wife'), or invented Hungarian-like melodies. Among Kókai's best works are the Violin Concerto and the orchestral *Concerto all'ungharese*.

WORKS
(*selective list*)

DRAMATIC
Zélis imádói [Adorers of Zelis] (opera buffa, 1, after Marlowe), 1931; István király [St Stephen] (stage oratorio, 2, I. Nemeth), 1938–9; A rossz feleség [The bad wife], ballet, 1942–5; A fülemile [The nightingale] (radio play, T. Barany, after J. Arany), 1950; Lészen ágyu [There will be guns] (radio play, J. Romhanyi), 1951; Hét falu kovácsa [The blacksmith of seven villages] (radio play, Z. Nadányi), 1954
Film scores: Kalandos vakáció [Adventurous holiday], 1954; Különös ismertetőjel [Recognition mark], 1955; A császár parancsára [By command of the emperor], 1956; Sóbálvány [Pillar of salt], 1958; Szegény gazdagok [Poor rich], 1959

OTHER WORKS
Orch: Sym., E♭, 1917; Romance, vn, str, 1918; Idyll, str, 1918–19; Intermezzo, str, harp, 1921–6; Suite [3rd movt identical with Intermezzo], 1926; Preludio and Scherzo, 1928–9; 2 Rondos, small orch, 1946–7; 2 Dances, 1932–49; Verbunkos szvit [Recruiting suite], small orch, 1951; Rhapsody, cl, folk orch, 1952; Kis verbunk-oszene [Short recruiting music], str, 1952; Vn Conc., 1952, rev. 1953; Márciusi induló [March of March], military band, 1952; Dances from Szék, 1952, rev. as Szék Rhapsody, 1953; Conc. all'ungharese, 1957
Chamber: Sonata, vn, pf, 1923; Sextet, cl, hn, str, 1925; Pf Qnt, 1925; Sonata, vc, pf, 1926; Str Qt, a, 1926; Str Qt, f♯, 1926; Str Qt, c, 1927; Serenade, str trio, 1932–50; Quartettino, cl, str trio, 1952
Shorter duos, pf music, songs, choruses

Principal publishers: Editio Musica, Hungarian Arts Council, Rózsavölgyi

GYÖRGY KROÓ

Kokkonen, Joonas (*b* Iisalmi, 13 Nov 1921). Finnish composer. He studied with Palmgren (harmony), Ranta (counterpoint) and Hannikainen (piano) at the Sibelius

Academy, Helsinki (diploma 1949, début recital 1950), and read musicology under Krohn at Helsinki University (MA 1948). He had no formal training in composition. He remained at the Sibelius Academy as a lecturer (1950–59) and as professor of composition (1959–63), and he has been active as a music critic. Among the central positions he has held in Finnish musical life are the chairmanships of the board of the Sibelius Academy (from 1966), of the Society of Finnish Composers (1965–70) and of the composers' copyright bureau TEOSTO (from 1968). In 1963 he was made a member of the Finnish Academy and received the music prize of the Nordic Council for the Third Symphony; he has twice won the Wihuri Foundation international prize (1961, 1973).

Essentially a symphonic composer, Kokkonen has a strong feeling for the Western tradition, particularly for the music of Bach, Brahms and Bartók, as well as a close attachment to Finnish music through his regard for Sibelius, a hearing of whose Fourth Symphony was a formative influence. His early output, mostly of chamber music, was influenced by neo-classicism, but a more individual direction was indicated by the Music for Strings (1957), where the old neo-classical elements are combined with dodecaphonic structures and chorale-like music. For a while he employed 12-note serialism (which he claims to have learnt from Bach's Inventions), but after the First Symphony and the First Quartet this gave way to a freer chromaticism including tonal features. Motivic development, however, remained his principal concern, despite an increasingly important use of orchestral colour. Often a whole work is built in sinewy architectural units from one or two motifs, and it is in this that Kokkonen shows himself an heir to Sibelius, although in other aspects his style is quite removed from that of his predecessor. He has a liking for instrumental virtuosity, notably in string writing and above all in the Cello Concerto. The choral works are much less symphonic in their quasi-Palestrinian polyphony and consonant harmony. Kokkonen's opera, Viimeiset kiusaukset ('The last temptations', 1975), commissioned by the Nordic Opera Houses, has thrown new light on his work; it has modal and even tonal elements, and in its symbolism shows the influence of Bartók, especially Bluebeard's Castle.

WORKS
(selective list)

Stage: Viimeiset kiusaukset [The last temptations] (opera, 2, L. Kokkonen), 1973–5
Orch: Music for Str, 1956–7; 4 syms., 1958–60, 1960–61, 1967, 1971; Opus sonorum, 1964; Vc Conc., 1969; Inauguratio, 1971
Choral: Missa a cappella, 1963; Laudatio Domini, 1966
Chamber: 3 str qts, 1958–9, 1964–6, 1976; Sinfonia da camera, 12 str, 1961–2; 5 Bagatelles, pf, 1968–9; Wind Qnt, 1973; Sonata, vc, pf, 1976; . . . durch einen Spiegel, 12 str, cembalo, 1977

Principal publishers: Fazer, Finnish Broadcasting Company, Muzïka (Leningrad), G. Schirmer

BIBLIOGRAPHY

E. Salmenhaara: 'Joonas Kokkonen: romantisoituva klassikko', *Suomen musiikin vuosikirja 1967–68* (Helsinki, 1968), 68ff [Swed. trans. in *Nomus nytt*, v (1969), appx p.1]
P. Heininen: 'Joonas Kokkonen', *Musiikki* (1972), no.3–4, pp.136–85
E. Tawaststjerna: 'Viimeiset kiusaukset suurtapaus' [The première of *The Last Temptations*], *Esseitä ja arvosteluja* [Essays and criticism] (Helsinki, 1976), 196

ERKKI SALMENHAARA

Kolb, Carlmann (*b* Kösslarn, Griesbach, Lower Bavaria, baptized 29 Jan 1703; *d* Munich, 15 Jan 1765). German priest, organist and composer. He

received his education and musical training in Asbach and Landshut. Later he returned to the Benedictine Abbey of Asbach where he had been a choirboy, was ordained priest in 1729 and became the permanent organist of the community. He was under the patronage of the Count of Tattenbach-Reinstein in Munich and tutored his sons.

Kolb left only two works, a Sinfonia in F for harpsichord and strings cited in a Breitkopf catalogue, and the *Certamen aonium* (Augsburg, 1733; ed. R. Walter, Altötting, 1959; another modern edn., Heidelberg, 1960). He originally intended a *secunda pars* but it was never published. Nevertheless this small collection of pieces establishes him as one of the best composers for organ of his time in southern Germany. For each of the eight church modes Kolb wrote a prelude, three verses and a cadenza. They are not firmly grounded in these modes but show many features of the diatonic and chromatic harmony of his day. South German practice implied certain limitations in organ style, particularly in the use of pedals. Kolb's preludes, on the other hand, contain many examples of brilliant passage-work for the manuals, as well as effective rests which heighten tension. In style they sometimes resemble florid harpsichord music. The verses are short fughettas which occasionally share a thematic relationship. They adopt longer and more varied subjects than much German organ music of the south. The cadenzas favour sequential treatment in the Italian style.

Kolb's modal suites owe something to predecessors such as F. X. A. Murschhauser and Gottlieb Muffat. In the fluency of their organ writing, however, his examples are models for his own time.

BIBLIOGRAPHY

E. von Werra: 'Beiträge zur Geschichte des katholischen Orgelspiels', *KJb*, xii (1897), 30
B. S. Brook, ed.: *The Breitkopf Thematic Catalogue, 1762–1787* (New York, 1966)

HUGH J. McLEAN

Kolb [Kolbanus, Kholbio], **Simon** (*b* c1556; *d* Hall [now Solbad Hall], nr. Innsbruck, 1 Sept 1614). Austrian composer, possibly of German birth. He was a choirboy in the Hofkapelle of Archduke Ferdinand II, first at Prague (1564–6) and then at Innsbruck (1566–72); during this period he was taught singing by the Kapellmeister, Wilhelm Bruneau. In 1572 he was given a scholarship for three years' study as well as an allowance to enable him to visit his parents, who were living 'nearly 100 miles away' – a hint as to where he may have been born. By 1577 at the latest he was back at Innsbruck as a tenor in the Hofkapelle, and he held this position until 1591. From 1588 payments are recorded to him for various compositions, and by 1591 he was teaching his fellow singers counterpoint (he may have taught as early as 1577, when one of his former teachers, Gerhard von Roo, identified him in his diary as a 'colleague'). From the beginning of 1592 until his death he was Kapellmeister at the royal convent at Hall. Under his leadership its Kapelle became famous for its singers, organists and cornett and trombone players. Archduke Maximilian conferred a coat-of-arms on the Kolb family on 19 July 1604. Only four works by Kolb appear to be extant: the *Missa 'Su, su non più dormir'* for six voices (in *PL-WRu*) and three five-part motets (in *RISM* 1604[7] and *D-As* and *LÜh* respectively). Another five-part motet, from his time at

Innsbruck, is known to have existed, and a set of antiphons is referred to in an inventory at Hall (1611).

BIBLIOGRAPHY

EitnerQ

W. Senn: *Aus dem Kulturleben einer süddeutschen Kleinstadt: Musik, Schule und Theater der Stadt Hall in Tirol* (Innsbruck, 1938)

——: *Musik und Theater am Hof zu Innsbruck* (Innsbruck, 1954)

E. F. Schmid: *Musik an den schwäbischen Zollernhöfen der Renaissance* (Kassel, 1962)

E. FRED FLINDELL

Kolberer, Cajetan (*b* Salzburg, 21 June 1668; *d* Andechs, 23 April 1732). German composer of Austrian birth. He entered the monastery at Andechs in 1692. He was a prolific composer of church music, but his settings of the *Magnificat* and *Dixit Dominus*, among other works, suggest that he lacked both imagination and technical skill.

WORKS

(all printed works published in Augsburg)

6 Dixit Dominus, 6 Magnificat, 4 solo vv, 4vv, 2 vn, 2 va, bc (org), partus I, op.1 (1701)

Introits, 3vv, bc, partus II, op.2 (1703)

Marian antiphons, 4vv, partus III, op.3 (1709)

Offertories, 8vv, 2 vn, bn, bc, partus IV, op.4 (1710)

Offertories, 8vv, 2 vn, bn, bc, partus V, op.5 (1719)

Vidi aquam, 4vv, bc (org), *D-Rp*; 2 masses, 4, 5vv, insts, listed in Freising court inventory, 1710

2 sacred dramas: Spiele der göttlichen Vorsicht, 1714; Eremitae walchenses, 1715: lost

ELIZABETH ROCHE

Kolberg, (Henryk) Oskar (*b* Przysucha, Opoczno district, 22 Feb 1814; *d* Kraków, 3 June 1890). Polish folklorist and composer. He was educated at the Warsaw lyceum (1822–30) and studied the piano with Vetter. He then worked in a bank, continuing his musical studies under Elsner and Dobrzyński and later in Berlin (1835–6) with Girschner and Rungenhagen. After returning from Berlin he taught the piano in Warsaw, Mitau (now Jelgava, Latvia) and Homel (Belorussia). He was also active as a composer, chiefly of songs and dances whose inspiration he drew from folk music; only a few of these were published. His cycles of *kujawiak* proved the most popular of his works. Kolberg also composed the music for two one-act stage entertainments on rural themes, Gregorowicz's *Janek spod Ojcowa* ('Johnny from Ojców'; Warsaw, 1853) and Lenartowicz's *Król pasterzy* ('The shepherd king'; Warsaw, 1859). He completed only one act of the opera *Wiesław*.

Kolberg was better known as an ethnographer. Beginning in 1838, he systematically collected folktunes, sometimes visiting villages in the Warsaw region in the company of writers, painters and other artist friends. From 1842 to 1849 he published collections of folksongs with piano accompaniment, intended for home music-making. The philosopher Libelt was critical of the 'prettifying' of authentic tunes in the accompaniments, and Chopin was still more so in a letter to Kolberg's family (19 April 1847), whom he had known in his youth. The next stage in Kolberg's output opened with *Pieśni ludu polskiego* ('Songs of the Polish people'; Warsaw, 1857); this contained 41 ballads with many regional variants, and 466 dance-songs in their original unaccompanied form. In 1861 he gave up his bank employment and, living very frugally, devoted all his energies to a series of ethnographic regional monographs under the general title of *Lud, jego zwyczaje, sposób życia, mowa, podania, przysłowia, obrzędy,* *gusła, zabawy, pieśni, muzyka i tańce* ('The people, its customs, life-style, speech, folktales, proverbs, rites, witchcraft, games, songs, music and dances'), continued as *Obrazy etnograficzne* ('Ethnographic pictures'). 33 volumes appeared between 1861 and 1890 in Warsaw and (from the fifth series onwards) in Kraków. In 1871 he moved to the estate of the Konopkas at Modlnica near Kraków, and eventually settled in Kraków in 1884. He contributed to many journals, wrote articles on the ethnography and history of Polish music, as well as entries for Orgelbrand's *Encyklopedia powszechna* ('Universal encyclopedia'). Kolberg's scholarly work won him widespread recognition, and he was nominated as a member of numerous Polish and foreign learned societies. Some of his manuscript materials were posthumously published in five volumes between 1891 and 1910, and in 1960 the State Council decreed that his collected works should be published under the aegis of the Polish Academy of Sciences, 80 volumes in all being envisaged; by the 1970s about 60 of these had appeared.

BIBLIOGRAPHY

I. Kopernicki: *Oskar Kolberg* (Kraków, 1889)

S. Lam: *Oskar Kolberg: żywot i praca* [Life and works] (Lwów, 1914)

Lud, xlii (1956) [special issue]

M. Sobieski: 'Kolberg, Henryk Oskar', *MGG*

LUDWIK BIELAWSKI

Koldofsky, Adolph (*b* London, 13 Sept 1905; *d* Los Angeles, 9 April 1951). Canadian violinist and conductor. In 1912 he moved to Toronto where he studied the violin with Harry Adaskin, Luigi von Kunits and Geza de Kresz. He also studied with Ysaÿe in Brussels (1925–8) and with Ševčík in Czechoslovakia (1929–30). In Toronto he was important in musical life as chamber player, soloist and conductor, and from 1938 to 1942 he played in the Hart House Quartet. He became leader of the Vancouver SO in 1944, and in 1946 he moved to Los Angeles where his interest in contemporary music brought him into close association with Krenek and Schoenberg; the latter composed his *Phantasy* op.47 for him. As a scholar Koldofsky was notable for bringing to light several harpsichord concertos (now in *US-BE*) by C. P. E. Bach, performances of which he conducted for the Canadian Broadcasting Corporation with Landowska as soloist in 1943. He married the Canadian pianist Gwendolyn Williams, with whom he gave many concerts.

CARL MOREY

Kolęda [*colenda*]. Polish sacred song associated with Christmas, analogous to the carol, noël and Weihnachtslied. The term derives from the Latin *calendae* and has various meanings related to the custom of calling at houses at Christmas with greetings and requests for gifts (accompanied by singing and acting) by a group of boys (*kolędnicy*), or to visits from the clergy. The term acquired musical meaning by the transference of the usual name for a visit and greeting to the song that regularly accompanied it. This probably occurred in the Middle Ages, but written evidence of the name *kolęda* is first found in a reference to music in the tablature of Jan z Lublina (written 1537–48). There, 'colenda' is used to describe several songs with melodies appropriate for Christmas. As the name of a characteristic musical style, *kolęda* is associated primarily with a repertory of melodies and texts composed in Poland in the 17th and 18th centuries under the influence of folk styles, particularly the mazurka and polonaise. It is necessary to distinguish between true *kolędy* – strophic sacred songs sung in churches and homes – and the subgroup of pastorales with texts partly or wholly secular, based on pastoral motifs and performed exclusively outside the church, mainly by carollers and at Christmas folk plays.

Evidence of songs connected with Christmas is found in Poland as early as 1124. These songs developed particularly through the spread of the Franciscan order to Poland after 1237. At first both melodies and texts belonged to an international Latin repertory, which was later supplemented, from the second half of the 14th century, with works by local composers, as shown by the Latin texts of the *kolędy* of Bartłomiej z Jasła. In the 15th century the first translations into Polish of Latin *kolędy* appeared. (Often these translations were from Czech; 10 texts of this type are extant and some of their melodies have been identified.) Some polyphonic arrangements are known, both . local (in *PL-Wn* 8054) and imported (in *Kj* 18, *Pr* 1361, and *Tm* 2015). Many melodies with Polish texts survive from the 16th century, both in manuscript Catholic hymnbooks (primarily Benedictine, in Staniątki, near Kraków, from the end of the 16th century) and printed Protestant hymnbooks (notably those of Walenty z Brzozowa 1554 and 1563, and Artomius 1587 and 1596). Three versions of a single *kolęda* are contained in the tablature of Jan z Lublina, and a large corpus of *kolędy* was published in printed leaflet form around 1550 (including one by Wacław z Szamotuł). The melodies of these pieces were largely derived from an international repertory of medieval songs, and apart from their textual association with Christmas they do not constitute a group of any distinct musical character.

Kolędy in their proper form and pastorales, their secularized variants, proliferated in the 17th and 18th centuries. These *kolędy*, as yet not fully examined, are anonymous and were the result of spontaneous popular creation. A pastoral strain is predominant, combining local rural elements, lyricism and, occasionally, crude humour, often addressed to actual situations or people. Their melodies adopt the popular folk style of their region (e.g. Mazovia or Podhale), or are of particular types like the lyrical lullaby, or, more commonly, the mazurka and the polonaise (common to the whole of Poland). It is also possible to find in them motifs from west European dances, like the moresca, saraband and minuet. In the 17th century the melodies of *kolędy* permeated ambitious artistic works (e.g. *Patrem na rotuły* by Bartłomiej Pękiel) and became the basis of choral works and staged pastorales (by S. S. Szarzyński, Józef Kobierkowicz). In the 19th century the *kolęda* took on a stylized quality. The melody of one was quoted by Chopin in the Scherzo in B minor ('Lulajże Jezuniu'). More lately attention has been concentrated on choral arrangements of *kolędy* (by Stanisław Niewiadomski, J. A. Maklakiewicz, Feliks Nowowiejski). The great popularity of the *kolęda* and the richness of its repertory have led it to its retention as a special feature of Polish Christmas customs.

Ceremonies of various names etymologically related to *kolęda* (such as the Romanian *kolenda*) form an important part of non-Christian winter solstice celebrations throughout eastern Europe, from the Baltic and Russia to Greece. These ceremonies have common characteristics, including the performance of songs wishing luck to the hearers and of rituals by masked dancers to drive away evil spirits; generally, both singers and dancers are rewarded with food, drink or money by the householders. It is possible that the Polish Christian custom originated in the assimilation of Christian symbols into such winter solstice celebrations.

See also BULGARIA, §II; CALINDA; CZECHOSLOVAKIA, §II; POLAND, §II; ROMANIA, §II; UNION OF SOVIET SOCIALIST REPUBLICS, §§VII, 2, IX, 2, X, 2; VILLANCICO, §3; and YUGOSLAVIA, §II.

BIBLIOGRAPHY
S. Dobrzycki: *Kolędy polskie i czeskie, ich wzajemny stosunek* [Polish and Czech *kolędy*, their relationship to each other] (Poznań, 1930)
H. Feicht: 'Kolęda', *MGG*
J. Prosnak: 'Melodie "Symfonii anielskich" ', *Muzyka*, vii/4 (1962), 68
B. Andrzejczak: 'Rękopis z 1721 roku – źródło do historii polskiej kolędy' [A manuscript of 1721 – source for the history of the Polish *kolędy*], *Muzyka*, xi/1 (1966), 37
K. Hławiczka: 'Vom Quempas-Singen in Polen', *Jb für Liturgik und Hymnologie*, xii (1967), 149; xiii (1968), 151
B. Kryżaniak: 'Informacje o ludowych instrumentach muzycznych w tekstach kolęd' [Information on popular musical instruments in *kolędy* texts], *Muzyka*, xvii/4 (1972), 116
T. Maciejewski: *Zasób utworów z ksiąg Archikonfraterni Literackiej w Warszawie 1668–1829* [The collection of works from the books of the Archikonfraterni Literacka in Warsaw, 1668–1829] (Warsaw, 1972)
K, Mrowiec: 'Kolędy w osiemnastowiecznych rękopisach Biblioteki klasztoru Św. Andrzeja w Krakowie' [*Kolędy* in 18th-century manuscripts in the library of St Andrzej's monastery, Kraków], *Muzyka*, xviii/3 (1973), 51

MIROSŁAW PERZ

Köler [Koler, Colerus], **David** (*b* Zwickau, *c*1532; *d* Zwickau, 13 or 25 July 1565). German composer. He came of a poor family. He attended the famous grammar school at Zwickau and matriculated at the University of Ingolstadt in 1551. From 1554 at the latest, he lived at Schönfeld, near Carlsbad, Bohemia, and probably worked as Kantor at the grammar school at nearby Schlaggenwald, since the *Zehen Psalmen Davids* that he published in June 1554 had doubtless been composed for school use. In 1556-7 he was Kantor at Joachimsthal, Bohemia, in succession to the ailing Nikolaus Herman. He then moved to Altenburg as civic Kantor. There he had to provide music for two town churches and on occasion for the Saxe-Ernestine court too. The projected establishment of a Hofkapelle at Weimar or Gotha, doubtless at his suggestion, came to nothing. In 1563 he became Kapellmeister at the court of Mecklenburg at Schwerin in the service of Duke Johann Albrecht, a post that he had declined on two earlier occasions; Nicolaus Rosthius was one of several singers who went with him from Altenburg. In 1565 he was tempted back to Zwickau as principal Kantor, but he died only four months after taking office. His main importance lies in his contribution to the early history of the Protestant motet to German words. His *Zehen Psalmen Davids*, in the manner of Thomas Stoltzer's German psalms, are the first peak of this kind of composition. Their chief stylistic features are the interplay between polyphony and homophony, and the close relationship between text and music, features that make them particularly significant for their time.

WORKS
Zehen Psalmen Davids, 5, 6vv (Leipzig, 1554); 1 ed. in *Cw*, lxxi (1959) and in *Handbuch der deutschen evangelischen Kirchenmusik*, ii/1 (Göttingen, 1935)
Rosa florum gloria, 1567[1]

Mass (on Josquin's Benedictus es coelorum regina), 7vv, inc., *D-Z*
Kyrie, Gloria, 4vv, inc., *H-Bn*
Non nobis, Domine, 5vv, inc., *H-Bn*; Te sanctum, responsory, 6vv, *D-LEu*; Veni Sancte Spiritus, 4, 5vv, inc., *H-Bn*

Ach Herr, straf mich nicht in deinem Zorn (Ps vi), 6vv, inc., *D-Dlb*; Hülf, Herr, die Heiligen haben abgenommen (Ps xii), 6vv, *Z* (anon.), ed. in Cw, lxxi (1959); Richte mich Gott (Ps xliii), 6vv, inc., *Dlb*; Eile, Gott, mich zu erretten (Ps lxx), 6vv, inc., *Z*, ed. in Cw, lxxi (1959); Wer unter dem Schirm des Höchsten sitzt (Ps xci), 6vv, inc., *Dlb*; Siehe, wie fein und lieblich (Ps cxxxiii), 6vv, inc., *Dlb*

BIBLIOGRAPHY
G. Eismann: *David Köler: ein protestantischer Komponist des 16. Jahrhunderts* (Berlin, 1956); review by K. W. Niemöller, *Mf*, xii (1959), 353
M. Ruhnke: *Beiträge zu einer Geschichte der deutschen Hofmusikkollegien im 16. Jahrhundert* (Berlin, 1963)
W. Dehnhardt: *Die deutsche Psalmmotette in der Reformationszeit* (Wiesbaden, 1971)

WALTER BLANKENBURG

Köler [Coler], Martin (*b* Danzig, *c*1620; *d* Hamburg, 1703 or 1704). German composer. By 1661 he belonged, under the name 'Musophilus', to the well-known poetic academy, the Elbschwanenorden. On 2 May 1663 he succeeded Johann Jakob Löwe as Kapellmeister at the court in Wolfenbüttel, but in April 1667 the chapel was dissolved. He may have been the Coler who was Kapellmeister in Bayreuth in May 1671 and who was succeeded by Johann Philipp Krieger a short time later. In 1675 he was temporary head of the court chapel at Gottorf, Schleswig, following the dismissal of Theile, and he remained in Schleswig until 1681. He possibly served also as Kapellmeister in Brunswick and Lüneburg.

Köler was one of the many minor composers in the Hamburg area who wrote songs to texts by Johann Rist and his disciples. He composed all the music for Rist's *Neue hochheilige Passions-Andachten* and contributed music to Georg Heinrich Weber's *Abgewechselte Liebesflammen*. He may well be the 'M.C.' who composed songs for Caspar von Stieler's *Die geharnschte Venus*; but Vetter thought it possible that two different composers with the initials 'M.C.', one of them Köler, contributed to this work, since while some pieces are subtle, expressive lieder blending text and music satisfactorily, others are simply mechanical declamations. The sacred concertos in the elder Johann Schop's *Exercitia vocis* are his most important works.

WORKS
Hochzeitliche Ehrenfackel (Hamburg, 1661)
Some songs in Die geharnschte Venus, ed. C. von Stieler (Hamburg, 1660³); 2 in Vetter
10 sacred songs in Brandanus Lange Janus (Hamburg, 1661)
A few songs, 1v, bc, in Des Elbischen Schwanen-Schäffner Hyphantes poetische Musen, ed. G. H. Weber (Glückstadt, 1661)
A few songs in Abgewechselte Liebesflammen, ed. G. H. Weber (Hamburg, 1662)
12 psalms in Sulamithische Seelen Harmoni (Hamburg, 1662)
46 songs, 1v, bc, in Neue hochheilige Passions-Andachten, ed. J. Rist (Hamburg, 1664); 18 in J. Zahn, Die Melodien der deutschen evangelischen Kirchenlieder (Gütersloh, 1883–93)
12 sacred concertos, 1v, bc, in Exercitia vocis, ed. J. Schop (i) (Hamburg, 1667⁷)
Psalm, Lobet, ihr Knechte des Herrn, 3vv, 2 vn, 2 va da gamba, bc, *D-Kl*
15 vocal pieces with various insts, MSS in *D-B* and *S-Uu*

BIBLIOGRAPHY
M. Seiffert: 'Die Chorbibliothek der St. Michaelisschule in Lüneburg', *SIMG*, ix (1907–8), 593
H. Kretzschmar: *Geschichte des neuen deutschen Liedes* (Leipzig, 1911/R1966)
W. Vetter: *Das frühdeutsche Lied* (Münster, 1928)
M. Ruhnke: 'Köler, Martin', *MGG*

JOHN H. BARON

Kolešovský, Zikmund (Michal) (*b* Prague, 2 May 1817; *d* Prague, 22 July 1868). Czech composer, choirmaster, teacher and critic. He was the son of the distinguished Prague choirmaster František Xaver Kolešovský (*b* Prague, 1781; *d* Prague, 12 June 1839), a pupil of J. A. Kozeluch. He first studied the violin with J. P. Pixis at the Prague Conservatory, and then plainsong, counterpoint, the organ and singing with B. D. Weber, Tomášek and others. He was a member of the theatre orchestra in Prague from 1835 until 1839, when he succeeded his father as choirmaster of St Stephen's and later also of St Ignatius's; in these churches he continued his father's practice of presenting music by earlier Czech masters, especially F. X. Brixi, in performances of a high standard. In the 1850s he was director of the Žofínská Akademie, an important Prague music institution with choir and school, but gave up the post to found his own school of singing and theory, where one of his pupils was Fibich. He also taught at the teachers' training institute and in other schools. In 1865 he competed unsuccessfully with Smetana and Josef Krejčí for the directorship of the Prague Conservatory. He was a respected composer of songs and sacred music, and contributed to *Dalibor* and *Slavoj*, becoming a member of the latter's editorial board. In contrast to his stylistically conservative compositions, his articles on Brixi and on Czech national style, as well as the progressive outlook shown, for example, in his reviews of Wagner's concerts, made him one of the pioneers of modern Czech music criticism. He also took a progressive stand as a member of the first committee of the Czech artists' society, Umělecká Beseda, in which Smetana was one of his colleagues.

BIBLIOGRAPHY
ČSHS
A. Hnilička: 'Z. Kolešovský', *HR*, x (1917), 345
——: *Profily české hudby z prvé poloviny 19. století* [Profiles of Czech musicians of the first half of the 19th century] (Prague, 1921), 86ff

MIROSLAV K. ČERNÝ

Kolessa, Filaret (Mykhaylovych) (*b* Tatars'kyy, Stryy district, 17 July 1871; *d* L'vov, 3 March 1947). Ukrainian ethnomusicologist. He studied in Lemberg (now L'vov) and Vienna (PhD 1918); after 1918 he studied Ukrainian folk music outside the USSR. His Western contacts included Hornbostel and Bartók. He was elected a full member of the Ukrainian Academy of Sciences in 1929. Besides several folk music collections he published basic studies outlining historical stages of Ukrainian folk music, its dialects and its relationships with traditional music of neighbouring Slavonic and non-Slavonic countries. He held that western Ukrainian traditional music was part of an all-Ukrainian corpus, that music of the Lemky on both sides of the Carpathians was one music. In 1908 he carried out a monumental expedition to record Ukrainian historical chants (*dumy*), published in meticulous musical transcriptions in 1910 and 1913, later laying the basis for asserting their folk origins by showing their relation to folk laments. His work is fundamental for comparative study of Slavonic and east European folk music.

WRITINGS
Rytmika ukrayins'kykh narodnykh pisen' [Rhythm in Ukrainian folksongs] (Lemberg, 1906–7); repr. in *Muzykoznavchi pratsi* (Kiev, 1970)
'Pro melodii haivok' [On Easter ritual song-tunes], *Melodii haivok, skhopleni na fonograf Y. Rozdol'skym*, Materialy do ukraïn'skoy etnologii, xii (Lemberg, 1909)
'Über den melodischen und rhythmischen Aufbau der ukrainischen (kleinrussischen) rezitierenden Gesänge, der sogenannten "Kosakenlieder" ', *IMusSCR*, iii *Vienna 1909*, 276
'Pro muzychnu formu dum' [On the musical form of historical chants], *Mel'odiyi ukrayins'kykh narodnykh dum* (Lemberg, 1910, rev. 2/1969)
Varianty melodiy ukrains'kykh narodnykh dum, ikh kharakterystyka i

grupovannya [Variations in melody of Ukrainian folk historical chants, their characteristics and classification] (Lemberg, 1913); also in *Mel'odiyi ukrayins'kykh narodnykh dum* (rev. 2/1969)

'Das ukrainische Volkslied, sein melodischer und rhythmischer Aufbau', *Österreichische Monatsschrift für den Orient*, xlii (1916), 218; enlarged Ukrainian version in *Muzykoznavchi pratsi* (Kiev, 1970)

Pro genezu ukrayins'kykh narodnykh dum (*ukrains'ki narodni dumy u vidnoshenni do pisen', virshiv i pokhoronnykh holosin'*) [On the origin of Ukrainian folk historical chants (*dumy* in relation to songs, religious songs and folk laments)] (Lwów, 1920–22)

'Rechytatyvni formy y ukrains'kiy narodniy poezii' [Recitative form in Ukrainian folk poetry], *Pervisne hromadyanstvo* (Kiev, 1927), nos.1–2, pp.60–113; repr. in *Muzykoznavchi pratsi* (Kiev, 1970)

'Ukrains'ka narodna pisnya v naynovishiy fazi svoho rozvytku' [Ukrainian folksong in its newest phase of development], *Yuvileynyy zbirnyk na poshanu akad. M. Hrushevs'koho* (Kiev, 1928); repr. in *Fol'klorystychni pratsi* (Kiev, 1970)

'Poryadkovannya i kharakterystychni pryznaky lemkivs'kykh pisennykh melodii' [Systematization and characteristic features of Lemky song-tunes], *Etnohrafichnyy zbirnyk*, xxxix–xl (Lwów, 1929); Ger. summary, lxi–lxxxi

'Charakterystyka ukraińskiej muzyki ludowej' [Characteristics of Ukrainian folk music], *Lud slowiański*, iii (Kraków, 1932), B34

'Karpats'kyy tsykl narodnikh pisen' (spil'nykh ukraintsyam, slovakam, chekham i polyakam)' [The 'Carpathian cycle' (folksongs common to Ukrainians, Slovaks, Moravian Czechs and Poles)], *Sborník prací*, i: *Sjezdu slovanských filologů v Praze 1929*, ii (Prague, 1932), 93; Fr. summary, 884

Sections in *Musique et chansons populaires*, ed. Société des Nations, Institut International de Coopération Intellectuelle (Paris, 1934)

'Formuly zakinchennya v ukrains'kykh narodnykh dumakh u zv'yazku z pitannyam pro naverstvuvannya dum' [Ending formulae of Ukrainian historical chants and the problems of their classification], *Zapysky naukovoho tovarystva im: Shevchenka*, cliv (Lwów, 1935), 29–67

'Virshova forma starovynnoy ukrains'koy narodnoy pisni pro Stefana voyevodu' [Verse form of an old Ukrainian folksong about Stefan Vojvoda], *Narodna tvorchist' ta etnografiya* (Kiev, 1963), no.1, p.116 [written 1939, on song collected by Blahoslav before 1571]

FOLKSONG COLLECTIONS

'Hutsul's'ki pisni' (instrumental'ni melodii ta pisni)' [Hutsul songs and instrumental tunes], in V. Shukhevich: *Hutsul'shchina*, pts.3–4 (Lemberg, 1902, 1904)

Melodii haivok, skhopleni na fonograf Y. Rozdol'skym [Easter song melodies recorded by Rozdol'sky], *Materialy do ukrain'skoy etnologii*, xii (Lemberg, 1909) [180 ritual tunes from east Galicia]

Mel'odiyi ukrayins'kykh narodnykh dum [Tunes of Ukrainian historical chants] (Lemberg, 1910–13, rev.2/1969) [1st edn. incl. Ger. introduction]

'Narodni pisni z pivdennoho Pidkarpattya' [Folksongs from southern Subcarpathia], *Naukoviy zbirnyk tovarystva 'Prosvita' v Uzhhorodi* (1923) [153 songs with tunes]

Narodni pisni z halyts'koyi Lemkivshchyny: teksty i melodiyi [Folksongs from west Galicia, Lemky country: texts and melodies] (Lwów, 1929) [624 songs with transcrs. from recordings]

'Narodni pisni z pidkarpats'koy Rusi, melodii i teksty' [Folksongs from Subcarpathian Ruthenia, melodies and texts], *Naukovyy zbirnyk tovarystva 'Prosvita' v Uzhhorodi*, xiii–xiv (1938), 49–149 [159 tunes, 178 texts]

BIBLIOGRAPHY

K. Kvitka: 'Filaret Kolessa', *Muzyka* (Kiev, 1925), nos.11–12, p.408
S. Hrytsa: *F. M. Kolessa* (Kiev, 1962)
V. Hoshovskiy: 'Akademik Filaret Kolessa', *SovM* (1971), no.9, p.106
M. Mušinka: 'Filaret Kolessa a Československo: príspevok k československo-ukrajinským etnomuzikologickým stykom' [Kolessa and Czechoslovakia: on Czechoslovak–Ukrainian ethnomusicological contact], *Slovenský národopis*, xx (Bratislava, 1972), 643

BARBARA KRADER

Kolinski, Mieczyslaw (*b* Warsaw, 5 Sept 1901). Canadian composer, ethnomusicologist and theorist of Polish origin. He received his early education in Hamburg, and appeared publicly there as piano soloist and in his own compositions (songs, piano works). He later studied the piano and composition at the Hochschule für Musik, Berlin, and musicology, psychology and anthropology at Berlin University, where he took his doctorate in 1930 with a dissertation on Malaccan and Samoan music. After serving as assistant to Erich von Hornbostel at the Staatliches

Phonogramm-Archiv in Berlin (1926–33), he moved to Prague, where he transcribed much non-Western music in association with the anthropologists Melville Herskovits and Franz Boas. Forced again to move by the advance of Nazism, in 1938 he went to Belgium where he remained for 13 years, in hiding during much of the German occupation. There he married Edith van den Berghe, daughter of the Belgian painter Frits van den Berghe. In 1951 he settled in New York, and later became an American citizen. He was general editor of the Hargail Music Press and also music therapist in a large hospital for war veterans near New York. He was co-founder (1955), and for a time president (1958–9), of the Society for Ethnomusicology. From 1966 until his retirement in 1976 he directed the course in ethnomusicology at Toronto University; he has also participated in the research programme of the Canadian Centre for Folk Culture Studies, National Museum of Man, Ottawa. He became a Canadian citizen in 1974.

In an essay from his Prague period, *Konsonanz als Grundlage einer neuen Akkordlehre*, Kolinski dealt with questions of consonance and dissonance in modern music and proposed a systematic approach to chord classification; he also patented an ingenious cardboard wheel for use in teaching the rudiments of tonality. In the 1950s and early 1960s he established widely applicable methods for analysing tonal and melodic structures, and approaches to fundamental problems of rhythm and tempo, tuning, and the study of ethnomusicology in general, which subsequently became his main field of study. Describing himself as mainly an 'armchair ethnomusicologist' (i.e. one who transcribes and analyses material gathered by others), he has made well over 2000 transcriptions from areas as diverse as Samoa, New Guinea, Surinam, West Africa, Haiti and northern-coastal British Columbia (Kwakiutl).

The originality and extraordinarily broad scholarly scope of his work in ethnomusicology has tended to obscure his continuing work as a theorist and composer. He has formulated an original method for teaching the reading of music to elementary piano students, and a comprehensive notation theory based on a staff of three lines. His ballet, *Expresszug-Phantasie*, first produced in Salzburg in 1935 by a Czechoslovak modern-dance group, had performances in Prague and several other cities in succeeding seasons. In Belgium he studied the carillon and wrote for it, and a concert of his works was given in Brussels in 1947. A number of his later chamber works and solo piano pieces have been played, broadcast and recorded in the USA and Canada.

WRITINGS

Die Musik der Primitivstämme auf Malaka und ihre Beziehungen zur samoanischen Musik (diss., Humboldt U., Berlin, 1930; *Anthropos*, xxv (1930), 585–648)

Konsonanz als Grundlage einer neuen Akkordlehre (Prague, 1936)

'Suriname Music', M. and F. Herskovits: *Suriname Folk-Lore* (New York, 1936), 489–740

'Música Europea y extraeuropea', *Revista de estudios musicales*, i (1949), 191

'A New Equidistant 12-tone Temperament', *JAMS*, xii (1959), 210

'The Evaluation of Tempo', *EM*, iii (1959), 45

'Classification of Tonal Structures', *Studies in Ethnomusicology*, i (1961), 38–76

'The Origin of the Indian 22-tone System', *Studies in Ethnomusicology*, i (1961), 3

'Consonance and Dissonance', *EM*, vi (1962), 66

Review of C. Sachs: *The Wellsprings of Music* (Leiden and The Hague, 1962), *EM*, vii (1963), 272

'The General Direction of Melodic Movement', *EM*, ix (1965), 240

'The Structure of Melodic Movement: a New Method of Analysis', *Studies in Ethnomusicology*, ii (1965), 95

'Recent Trends in Ethnomusicology', *EM*, xi (1967), 1
Barbara Allen: Tonal versus Melodic Structure', *EM*, xii (1968), 208; xiii (1969), 1–73
Review of A. Merriam: *Ethnomusicology of the Flathead Indians* (Chicago, 1967), *EM*, xiv (1970)
Review of M. Hood: *The Ethnomusicologist* (New York, 1971), *YIFMC*, iii (1971), 146
'An Apache Rabbit Dance Song Cycle, as Sung by the Iroquois', *EM*, xvi (1972), 415–64
'An Iroquois War Dance Song Cycle', *Journal of the Canadian Association of University Schools of Music*, ii (1972), 51
'A Cross-cultural Approach to Metro-rhythmic Patterns', *EM*, xvii (1973), 494
Review of B. Nettl: *Folk and Traditional Music of the Western Continents* (2/1973), *Canadian Music Educator*, xv/4 (1974), 33
'Co-ordinated Denomination and Notation of Pitch', *Journal of the Canadian Association of University Schools of Music*, vi (1976)
'Herndon's Verdict on Analysis: Tabula rosa', *EM*, xx (1976), 1
'Final Reply to Herndon', *EM*, xxi (1977), 75

FOLKSONG EDITIONS

M. Schneider: *Geschichte der Mehrstimmigkeit*, i (Berlin, 1934–5, 2/1964) [incl. 33 transcrs. of folk music from New Guinea and Samoa by Kolinski]
H. Courlander: *The Drum and the Hoe* (Berkeley, 1960), 205–313 [incl. 186 transcrs. of Haitian songs and drum rhythms by Kolinski]
——: *Negro Folk Music U.S.A.* (New York, 1963) [incl. 19 transcrs. of Negro folksongs by Kolinski]

WORKS
(selective list)

2 pf sonatas, 1919, 1946 rev. 1966; Sonata, vn, pf, 1924; Sonata, vc, pf, 1926; Lyric Sextet, S, fl, str qt, 1929, 4 pf suites, 1929–46; Str Qt, 1931; Un jour passe, pf, 1938; 4 danses en forme d'études, pf, 1938; Concertino (textless), S, str qt, pf, 1951; Dahomey Suite, fl/ob, pf/str orch, 1951; Hatikvah Variations, str qt, 1960; Dance Fantasy, str orch, 1968; Encounterpoint, org, str qt, 1973, arr. fl, cl, vn, vc, pf, 1974; Concertino, S, cl, pf, 1974
3 ballets, music for rec ens, songs, folksong arrs.

Principal publishers: Hargail, Berandol

BIBLIOGRAPHY
R. Kennedy: 'A Bibliography of the Writings of Mieczyslaw Kolinski', *CMc* (1966), no.3, p.100

JOHN BECKWITH

Kolín z Chotěřiny, Matouš. *See* COLLINUS, MATTHAEUS.

Kolisch, Rudolf (*b* Klamm am Semmering, 20 July 1896; *d* Watertown, Mass., 1 Aug 1978). American violinist of Austrian birth. An injury to his left hand in childhood, after he had begun violin lessons, compelled him to hold the violin with his right hand and the bow with his left. He graduated from the Vienna Music Academy and University in 1913 and continued to study the violin with Ševčík and theory and composition with Schreker and Schoenberg (who married Kolisch's sister Gertrud in 1924). After beginning his career as a conductor and violin virtuoso, in 1922 Kolisch formed the Kolisch Quartet, which became internationally known. Its members changed in the early years, but by 1927 consisted of Kolisch, Felix Khuner (*b* Vienna, 8 Aug 1906), Jenö Léner (Lehner) (*b* Bratislava, 5 July 1906; *d* New York, 4 Nov 1948) and Benar Heifetz (*b* Moghilev, 11 Dec 1899). This quartet toured in Europe, Africa, South America and the USA, where the members settled in 1935. The quartet was the first to insist on playing the standard repertory from memory, and made a still stronger impression as the champion of new music, particularly of works by Schoenberg, Berg and Webern. Among its important premières were Schoenberg's String Quartets nos.3 and 4, the Schoenberg–Handel Concerto for string quartet and orchestra, Berg's Lyric Suite in its original form, Webern's String Trio and String Quartet, and Bartók's Quartet no.5. Schoenberg dedicated his Quartet no.4 jointly to Elizabeth Sprague Coolidge (who commissioned it) and to 'its ideal interpreters, the

Kolisch Quartet', and wrote to the former that they were 'the best string quartet I ever heard', praising 'their virtuosity, their sonority, their understanding, their style'. Tonal richness was helped by their instruments: Kolisch played a Stradivari violin, Léner a viola by Gasparo da Salò, Heifetz an Amati cello. They disbanded in 1939 after a reorganization of membership proved ineffective. Kolisch was leader of the Pro Arte Quartet from 1942, taught at the University of Wisconsin, 1944–67, and was artist-in-residence and head of the chamber music department at the New England Conservatory of Music, Boston.

BIBLIOGRAPHY
A. Schoenberg: *Letters*, ed. E. Stein (London, 1964), esp. 164, 201, 268

BERNARD JACOBSON

Kolísek, Alois (*b* Protivanov, Moravia, 1 April 1868; *d* Brno, 25 Aug 1931). Czech writer on music. He trained for the priesthood in Brno and continued his theological studies in Rome (1892–4). From 1898 to 1918 he held a school post in Hodonín, a town in southern Moravia where the rich folk traditions often resemble those of nearby Slovakia. It was here that he acquired his interest in Slovak folksong, about which he wrote and lectured (accompanying himself on the cimbalom) both at home and abroad in Vienna, London and Cambridge. He also wrote the first account of modern Slovak music and the first monograph on the Slovak composer J. L. Bella. After the creation of the Czechoslovak Republic, he moved in 1919 to the Slovak capital of Bratislava, where he lectured in the university's theological faculty.

WRITINGS
'Slovak Popular Melodies', *Slovak Peasant Art and Melodies*, ed. R. W. S. Watson (London, 1911)
Za pisni slovenskou [In search of Slovak folksong] (n.p., 1911)
Terajší stav slovenskej hudby [The present state of Slovak music] (Prague, 1922)
J. L. Bella (Turčiansky Svätý Martin, 1923)
Pobožný spev na Slovensku [Sacred song in Slovakia] (Prague, 1923)
Introduction to *Slowakische Volkslieder*, ed. R. Felber (Zurich, 1923–31)
ed. J. Potúček: *Za slovenskú hudbu a spev* [Slovak music and song] (Bratislava, 1968)

BIBLIOGRAPHY
I. Ballo: 'Msgr. dr. Alois Kolísek', *Tempo*, xi (1931–2), 30 [obituary]
J. Tureček: 'In memoriam Dra Aloise Kolíska', *Věstník pěvecký a hudební*, xxxvi (1931), 2 [obituary]
J. Potúček: *Súpis slovenských hudobnin a literatúry o hudobníkoch* (Bratislava, 1952), 134 [bibliography]
——: *Súpis slovenských hudobnoteoretických prác* (Bratislava, 1955), 296 [bibliography and list of writings]

JOHN TYRRELL

Kollmann. German–English family of musicians.

(1) **Augustus Frederic Christopher Kollmann** (*b* Engelbostel, Hanover, 21 March 1756; *d* London, 19 April 1829). He was born into a musical family. His father was the Engelbostel organist; an uncle, Carl Christoph Hachmeister senior, composed and was organist of the Heiligen-Geist church in Hamburg; his brother, Georg Christoph Kollmann (1758–1827), became organist of St Katharine's Church, Hamburg. A. F. C. Kollmann studied with the Hanover organist Böttner and in 1779 entered the Normal School there, learning 'that methodical, and systematical manner of teaching, which has been very advantageous to him, not only for school instruction, but also in teaching music, and particularly in writing his musical treatises'. On 10 December 1781 he was appointed organist and schoolmaster of Kloster Lüne (near Lüneburg) but left and in

September 1782 became organist and schoolmaster of the Royal German Chapel in St James's Palace, London, where he remained for the rest of his life (serving also, from February 1784, as chapel-keeper). He was a member, and from 1825 a trustee, of the New Musical Fund. On 26 October 1783 he married Christina Catherina Ruel (1745–1823) at St Luke's, Chelsea; their two children are mentioned below.

As a theorist, Kollmann sought 'to rescue the science of music from the mysterious darkness in which it was wrapped' by providing a simple, natural explanatory system that accounts for each note in a 'regular' musical composition by 'as positive a rule, as it denotes a positive sound'. He divided this system into a grammatical and a rhetorical part and strove to improve each throughout his career. His *New Theory* (1806) replaced the *Essay on Musical Harmony* (1796), and in turn was superseded by the *New Theory* (2/1823), as the statement of the grammatical part; the *Essay on Practical Musical Composition* (1799, 2/1812) presented the rhetorical part.

To make his system more accessible, Kollmann wrote thoroughbass tutors that epitomize the grammatical part and composed 'theoretico-practical works', i.e. 'compositions with theoretical explanations' which illustrate particular aspects of the system. Some of these illustrations are curious (e.g. no.12 of the *Analyzed Fugues* shows that the chromatic complexity of 'regular' music can exceed that of the common practice of 1810). But Kollmann considered that he 'applied himself . . . principally to [music's] theoretical department', and it is here that his accomplishments are most noteworthy.

The structure of Kollmann's system may be summarized as follows. Equal temperament is adopted. A 'regular' composition is generable starting from a diatonic fundamental bass upon each note of which is placed, as in Kirnberger's theory, a fundamental concord (i.e. a triad whose root is the bass note) or a fundamental discord (i.e. a 7th chord whose root is the bass note). After a fundamental discord the fundamental bass must descend a 5th or ascend a 4th; between two fundamental concords the fundamental bass interval must not be a 2nd or a 7th. Next, inversions may be substituted for root position chords and notes may be omitted or doubled subject to certain counterpoint rules: the resulting chords are termed 'essential'. 'Accidental' chords now may be introduced by permitting diatonic 'forenotes' and 'afternotes' to be inserted in a portion of the time previously reserved for notes in essential chords; by permitting similar insertion of chromatic 'accidental' notes; and by permitting organ points. (Kollmann refuted Rameau's concept of chords constructed by supposition on the grounds that his explanation was simpler.) The chords thus far generated now may have their notes 'divided' into one or more musical parts, for example as an arpeggio; notes may be tied or repeated; octave doubling or octave transference may be introduced and modulation to the other mode (major or minor) or to different keys may be effected. Thus far the grammatical part. Larger-scale formal structures (as of sonata or fugue) belong to rhetoric, and Kollmann specified constraints upon total length, constituent sections, key relationships, instrumentation, text-setting, rhythm and style, that are implied by a composer's decision to write one or another type of composition.

Kollmann related German and English musical cultures. He corresponded with J. N. Forkel and gathered English contributions for Gerber's *Neues Lexikon*. He persistently advocated the music of J. S. Bach and printed in his treatises a number of Bach's compositions and in 1806 a separate edition of Bach's Chromatic Fantasy. In 1799 he proposed an edition of the '48', but after Forkel remarked on this, three European publishers proceeded to print it and Kollmann withdrew. He provided, however, the MS from which the Wesley–Horn edition of this work was prepared and lent other Bach material to Samuel Wesley when the latter's interest in Bach was roused. Kollmann translated excerpts from Forkel's life of Bach for his magazine the *Quarterly Musical Register* (1812) and may have assisted with the first complete English translation published in 1820.

WORKS

This listing is based on Kollmann's own categorization; all printed works published in London unless otherwise stated.

PRACTICAL WORKS

op.
[1] 6 geistliche Lieder mit . . . Choralmelodien, 4vv, bc (Leipzig, *c*1784)
2   4 Sonatas, hpd/pf, vn (1788)
—   A Characteristic March, pf/2fl/band (1791)
—   Charming Sally, S/fl, pf (*c*1792)
4   6 Sonatinas, pf (*c*1792)
—   New March, pf/harp/band (1795)
6   The Shipwreck, pf, with vn, vc acc. (1796)
—   Divertimento, pf, 3/1 players (1799)
—   A Hymn, with Various Harmonies, 1/4vv, pf/org (1803)
8   Concerto, pf, orch (1804); only pf printed
—   The Praise of God, oratorio, Eng./Ger., 1817, *GB-Lbm*, *T*

Minor compositions (songs, waltzes, hymns, etc) in various collections

THEORETICO-PRACTICAL WORKS

op.
3   An Introduction to the Art of Preluding and Extemporizing in Six Lessons, hpd/harp (1792)
5   The First Beginning on the Piano-Forte . . . Containing . . . Progressive Lessons and Sonatinas (1796)
7   A Symphony, pf, vn, vc, with Analytical Explanations ['Analyzed Symphony'] (1798)
9   The Melody of the Hundredth Psalm, with Examples and Directions for an Hundred Different Harmonies, 4vv (1809)
10 A Series of [12] Analyzed Fugues . . . for 2 players, pf/org (1809–10, 2/1822 as 12 Analyzed Fugues)
—   A Rondo on the Chord of the Diminished Seventh, pf (1810)
11 An Introduction to Extemporary Modulation, in Six General Lessons, pf/harp/vn/vc (1820)

THEORETICAL WORKS

An Essay on Musical Harmony (1796, 2/1817)
An Essay on Practical Musical Composition (1799/*R*1973, rev.2/1812)
A Practical Guide to Thorough-Bass (1801)
A New Theory of Musical Harmony (1806, rev.2/1823)
A Second Practical Guide to Thorough-Bass (1807; Ger. edn., 1808)

OTHER WRITINGS

Proposals for Publishing by Subscription: a New Theoretical Musical Work, Entitled An Essay on Practical Musical Composition (1798)
A. F. C. Kollmann's Vindication of a Passage in his Practical Guide to Thorough-Bass, against an Advertisement of Mr. M. P. King (1801)
'An Essay on Earl Stanhope's "Principles of the Science of Tuning Instruments with Fixed Tones" ', *La belle assemblée*, ii (1807), 321; iii (1807), 99
The Quarterly Musical Register, written and collected by A. F. C. Kollmann, 2 issues (1812)
'Bemerkungen über Hrn. J. B. Logier's sogenanntes *Neues System des Musikunterrichts*', *AMZ*, xxiii (1821), cols.769, 785, 801; 'Nachtrag zu den Bemerkungen', *AMZ*, xxiv (1822), Intelligenz-Blatt, col.9; Eng. trans. of both as *Remarks on what Mr. J. B. Logier Calls his New System of Musical Education* (1824, enlarged 2/1824)
Correspondence with J. W. Callcott, *GB-Lbm*; C. J. Smyth, *Cu*, *F-Pn*; C. Burney, *US-NH*, *B-Br*; proprietors of Biographical Dictionary of Musicians, *US-SPOma*, pr. in edited form as 'Kollman', *A Dictionary of Musicians*, ed. J. Sainsbury (London, 2/1825/*R*1966)

(2) **Jo(h)anna S(ophia) Kollmann** (*b* London, 20 July 1786; *d* London, 14 May 1849). English musician, daughter of (1) Augustus Frederic Christopher Kollmann. She first appeared publicly as a singer in the New Musical Fund concert on 13 March 1806. She

assisted her brother in his piano business and succeeded him as organist of the Royal German Chapel; on her death she was succeeded by Frederic Weber (1819–1909).

(3) **George Augustus Kollmann** (*b* London, 30 Jan 1789; *d* London, 19 March 1845). English pianist, composer and inventor, son of (1) Augustus Frederic Christopher Kollmann. He was taught by his father, of whose piano concerto he gave the first performance at his début in the New Musical Fund concert on 15 March 1804. In 1805 he accompanied Mrs Sarah Mountain on an Irish tour. In 1811 he was elected to the Royal Society of Musicians where from 1831 and 1836 he had increased responsibility as a member of the Court of Assistants and the House Committee. From 1816 he was an Associate of the Philharmonic Society. He succeeded his father in 1829 as organist, clerk and chapel-keeper of the Royal German Chapel in St James's Palace. His compositions include a set of three piano sonatas, one with violin (op.1; London, 1808), an air with variations (1808) and a set of waltzes (1812), both for piano.

In 1825 Kollmann was granted a patent for a design of pianos possessing down-striking action, an extended soundboard and a novel mechanism for tuning. He advertised grand, square and upright models in the *Musical World* in 1838 and gave a series of concerts in London in 1838–9 to demonstrate his invention. Despite favourable criticism of the instrument and admiration of Kollmann's pianistic skills, he became bankrupt in 1840. Kollmann also received two British patents relating to railways and locomotive carriages.

BIBLIOGRAPHY

J. G. Burckhardt: *Kirchen-Geschichten der deutschen Gemeinden in London* (Tübingen, 1798)
[J. N.] F[orke]l: 'Ueber den Zustand der Musik in England', *AMZ*, ii (1799), col.5
M. P. King: 'Advertisement', *A General Treatise on Music . . . a New Edition* (London, 1801), p.v
Anon.: 'On Thorough-bass', *La belle assemblée*, i (1806), 600; ii (1807), 149
Anon.: 'London', *AMZ*, xvii (1815), col.518
Anon.: 'Ueber des Zustandes der Musik in England', *AMZ*, xxi (1819), col.754
J. B. Logier: *A Short Account of the Progress of J. B. Logier's System of Musical Education in Berlin* (London, 1824)
Anon.: 'The Funeral of the Late A. F. C. Kollmann, Esq.', *Morning Post* (4 May 1829), p.3
J. Fairbairn: *Elements of Music* (Edinburgh, 1832)
Anon.: 'The Late George Augustus Kollmann', *Dramatic and Musical Review*, iv (1845), 174
H. G. Bohn: 'Kolmann', in W. T. Lowndes and H. G. Bohn: *The Bibliographer's Manual of English Literature . . . New Edition . . . Part V* (London, 1860)
Catalogue of a Valuable Collection of Music, Including an Important Selection from the Library of the Eminent Theorist A. F. C. Kollman . . . which will be Sold by Auction, by Messrs. Puttick and Simpson . . . on Tuesday, January 30, 1877 (London, 1877)
Anon.: 'Notes on an Old Music Journal: The Quarterly Musical Register', *MT*, xlviii (1907), 645
J. T. Lightwood: *Samuel Wesley, Musician* (London, 1937)
S. Godman: 'The Early Reception of Bach's Music in England', *MMR*, lxxxii (1952), 255
E. R. Jacobi: 'Augustus Frederic Christopher Kollmann als Theoretiker', *AMw*, xiii (1956), 263; Eng. trans., 'Harmonic Theory in England after the Time of Rameau', *JMT*, i (1957), 126
D. W. Beach: *The Harmonic Theories of Johann Philipp Kirnberger: their Origins and Influences* (diss., Yale U., 1974) [discusses A. F. C. Kollmann's treatises]

MICHAEL KASSLER

Kollo, René (*b* Berlin, 20 Nov 1937). German tenor, grandson of Walter Kollo. He had a successful career in light music before beginning seriously to study singing with Elsa Varena in 1958. He made his début in 1965 at Brunswick and was engaged at Düsseldorf from 1967 to 1971. At first he sang lyric roles such as Froh (*Das Rheingold*), Eisenstein (*Die Fledermaus*), Titus (*La clemenza di Tito*), Pinkerton, and the Steersman, with which he made his promising Bayreuth début in 1969. Appearing at Munich, Vienna, Berlin and Hamburg, as well as at Venice and Milan, he has gradually taken on (possibly too early because of the shortage of dramatic tenors) a heavier repertory, especially Wagner's Parsifal, Erik, Lohengrin, and Walther, which he sang at Bayreuth in 1973 and at the Salzburg Easter Festival in 1974. In 1976 he made his New York début as Lohengrin, his Covent Garden début as Siegmund, and sang Siegfried in the Bayreuth centenary *Ring*. His voice is essentially lyrical; he sings Vladimir (*Prince Igor*), Lensky (*Eugene Onegin*), Laca (*Jenůfa*), Matteo (*Arabella*), and Tamino, which he sang in a new production of *Die Zauberflöte* at Salzburg in 1974.

ELIZABETH FORBES

Kollo [Kollodzieyski], **(Elimar) Walter** (*b* Neidenburg, East Prussia, 28 Jan 1878; *d* Berlin, 30 Sept 1940). German composer. He studied music at Sondershausen Conservatory, and then took up a position as a theatre conductor in Königsberg. Already composing popular songs, he moved via Stettin to Berlin where he wrote for cabarets and, from 1908 to 1918, composed operettas and revues for the Berliner Theater. After the war he founded his own publishing company and several theatres. His most successful operetta, *Wie einst im Mai* (with Willy Bredschneider; Berliner Theater, 4 October 1913), reached the USA as *Maytime* (1917) and was later filmed; but it is chiefly as a composer of *Solang noch Untern Lindern* and other popular Berlin songs that Kollo achieved more lasting fame. His son Willi (*b* 1904) followed him as a lyricist and composer of popular songs.

BIBLIOGRAPHY
E. Nick: 'Kollo, Walter', *MGG* [incl. list of works]

ANDREW LAMB

Kolman, Peter (*b* Bratislava, 29 May 1937). Slovak composer. He studied composition and conducting in Bratislava at the conservatory and at the college of music, his principal teachers being Očenáš and Cikker. In 1961 he was appointed music adviser to Bratislava radio, and in 1965 head of the experimental studio. After a period of impressionist orientation he made a study of the Second Viennese School and began to use serial procedures, block forms and other newer trends.

WORKS
(*selective list*)

Orch: Vn Conc., 1960; 4 Pieces, 1963; Monumento per 6,000,000, 1966; Movement, wind, perc, 1971
Inst: 3 Pf Pieces, 1960; 2 časti, fl, cl, vn, pf, 1960; Partezipazioni, 12 insts, 1962; Sonata canonica, pf, b cl, 1963; Panegyrikos, fl, vib, 1965; Str Qt, 1970
Elec: D68, 1968; Omaggio a Gesualdo, 1970; Kleine Nachtmusik, 1971

Principal publisher: Slovenský Hudební Fond

LADISLAV BURLAS

Kolmarer Liederhandschrift (*D-Mbs* Cgm 4997). *See* SOURCES, MS, §III, 5.

Köln (Ger.). COLOGNE.

Kolneder, Walter (*b* Wels, Upper Austria, 1 July 1910). Austrian musicologist. During his years at the Wels

Gymnasium he was a private pupil of J. N. David (1927–9) and then studied music at the Salzburg Mozarteum (1925–35), specializing in conducting under Paumgartner; he completed the master's course in the viola under M. Strub. He taught at Graz Conservatory (1936–9), and, until 1945, at the Staatliche Hochschule für Musikerziehung in Graz-Eggenberg; he was later a conductor at Wels (1945–7). His musicological studies, begun at Vienna University (1934–5), were continued under W. Fischer at Innsbruck University (1947). He took the doctorate at Vienna in 1949 with a dissertation on vocal polyphony in the folk music of the Austrian Alps. From 1953 to 1959 he was the director of the Conservatory of Luxembourg City and organized the conservatory concerts; from 1956 he was also a *Privatdozent* at the University of Saarbrucken where, in the same year, he completed his *Habilitation* in musicology with a work on Vivaldi. He became director of the Darmstadt Academy (1959–65) and of the Hochschule für Musik in Karlsruhe (1966–72). He became *ausserplanmässiger Professor* of musicology at Karlsruhe in 1966 and the editor of *Schriften zur Musik* (Munich, 1969–).

In addition to his work on music teaching and on the history and repertory of violin playing, Kolneder has concentrated on analytical and stylistic studies of Vivaldi and Webern. He has also made performing editions of folk music from the Alpine regions, partly based on his own transcriptions, and many performing editions of instrumental music, particularly cello and violin music of the 17th and 18th centuries.

WRITINGS

Die vokale Mehrstimmigkeit in der Volksmusik der österreichischen Alpenländer (diss., U. of Innsbruck, 1949)
Antonio Vivaldi: neue Studien zur Biographie und Stilistik seiner Werke (Habilitationsschrift, U. of Saarbrücken, 1956; extracts in *Aufführungspraxis bei Vivaldi* (Leipzig, 1955, 2/1973) and in *Die Solokonzertform bei Vivaldi* (Strasbourg and Baden-Baden, 1961))
'Sind Schenkers Analysen Beiträge zur Bacherkenntnis?', *DJbM*, iii (1958), 15
Anton Webern: Einführung in Werk und Stil (Rodenkirchen, 1961)
Geschichte der Musik: ein Studien- und Prüfungshelfer (Heidelberg, 1961, 5/1973)
'Evolutionismus und Schaffenschronologie zu Beethovens Righini-Variationen', *Karl Gustav Fellerer zum 60. Geburtstag* (Cologne, 1962), 119
Musikinstrumentenkunde: ein Studien- und Prüfungshelfer (Heidelberg, 1963, 3/1972)
Singen, Hören, Schreiben: eine praktische Musiklehre in vier Lehr- und vier Übungsheften (Mainz, 1963–7)
Antonio Vivaldi: Leben und Werk (Wiesbaden, 1965; Eng. trans., 1970)
'Die "Règles de Composition" von Marc-Antoine Charpentier', *Zum 70. Geburtstag von Joseph Müller-Blattau* (Kassel, 1966), 152
ed.: C. Czerny: *Erinnerungen aus meinem Leben* (Strasbourg and Baden-Baden, 1968)
Das Buch der Violine (Zurich, 1972)
Anton Webern: Genesis und Metamorphosen eines Stils (Vienna, 1973)
Melodietypen bei Vivaldi (Zurich, 1973)
Further articles in *DJbM* and Festschriften for Schmidt-Görg (1967) and Wiora (1967)

HANS HEINRICH EGGEBRECHT

Kolophonium (Ger.). ROSIN.

Koloratur (Ger.). COLORATURA.

Kolorieren (Ger.). To introduce COLORATION.The term is often used with special reference to German organists of the late Renaissance who made extensive use (though in fact no more than others in their period) of that technique of written or improvised variation; hence *Koloristen*, composers to whom such reference is made.

Kolozsvár (Hung.). CLUJ-NAPOCA.

Kölz, Matthias. *See* KELZ, MATTHIAS (i) or (ii).

Komeda [Trzciński], **Krzysztof** (*b* Poznań, 27 April 1931; *d* Warsaw, 23 April 1969). Polish jazz composer and pianist. By profession a doctor, he adopted the pseudonym Komeda to conceal his interest in jazz, then officially discouraged in Poland. His success at the first Polish Jazz Festival (1956) was such as to make him the country's most popular musician and a figurehead for Polish youth during the period of de-Stalinization. In the 1950s and 1960s he led and composed for an avant-garde jazz quintet, drawing freely on Poland's traditional and contemporary art music; his main importance, however, lies in his scores for some 40 films, including all but one of those made in this period by his close associate Roman Polanski (*Knife in the Water*, *Cul-de-sac*, *Rosemary's Baby* etc). He visited Hollywood at Polanski's invitation from 1967 to 1969, and composed several major film scores there. His views on jazz as film music, which had a wide influence on Polish cinema, are expressed in an article in the *Polish Film Quarterly* (1961, reprinted in *Jazz Forum*, 1969, no.2).

BRADFORD ROBINSON

Komenský, Jan Ámos [Comenius, Johann Amos] (*b* Uherský Brod, 28 March 1592; *d* Naarden, 15 Nov 1670). Moravian educational reformer, theologian, historian and hymnologist. He studied at the school of the Bohemian Brethren at Prerau, and from 1611 to 1614 at Herborn (where he was a pupil of JOHANN HEINRICH ALSTED) and Heidelberg. From 1614 he was with the Bohemian Brethren as a schoolteacher, a priest (1616) and bishop (1632), first at Prerau and then, from 1618 to 1621, with the German-speaking community at Fulnek. He finally left Moravia in 1628 during the Catholic persecutions, and lived at Leszno, Poland, until 1642. In 1633 he published the most celebrated of his educational books, *Janua linguarum reserata* ('The gates of tongues unlocked'), which was translated into 15 languages, including Arabic, Persian and Turkish. He travelled to Sweden (1642, 1646), England (1642) and Hungary (1650) on educational missions. From about 1656 until his death he lived at Amsterdam.

Komenský's writings on music, scattered through his numerous publications, include remarks on musical instruments, thoroughbass and accompaniment. His *Kancionál ... kniha ... písni duchovnich* (Amsterdam, 1659) and his *Kirchen-, Haus- und Hertzens-Musica* (Amsterdam, 1661, both ed. A. Skárka, Prague, 1952) are almost the last volumes in a long series of Czech Protestant hymnals. The *Kancionál* comprises 150 psalms with 25 alternative tunes and 430 hymns. Almost all the tunes are modal; in his introduction he claimed to have composed eight of them. The collection is clearly that of an exile out of touch with Czech sources: 146 of the items arc new, but they are greatly outnumbered by those translated into Czech from German and Polish.

BIBLIOGRAPHY

K. Konrád: 'Jan Amos Komenský jako hudební skaladatel kancionálu' [Komenský as a hymnbook composer], *Cyril*, xi (1884), 42
A. Patera: 'J. A. Komenského myšlenky o novém vydání českého cancionálu' [Komenský's thoughts about a new edition of a Czech hymnbook], *Časopis Českého musea*, lxv (1891), 214
B. Štědroň: 'Komenský a hudba' [Komenský and music], *Hudební výchova*, v (1957), 28

A. Cmíral: *Hudební didaktika v duchu zásad Jana Amose Komenského* [Musical didactics in the spirit of Komenský's principles] (Prague, 1958)

J. Bužga: 'Zur musikalischen Problematik der alttschechischen Kantionalien', *Mf*, xii (1959), 13

Soupis děl J. A. Komenského v československých knihovnách archivech a musejich [Register of Komenský's works in Czechoslovak libraries, archives and museums] (Prague, 1959)

O. Settari: 'Über das Gesangbuch des Johann Amos Comenius', *Sborník prací filosofické fakulty brněnské university*, H2 (1967), 89

M. Blekastad: *Comenius* (Prague and Oslo, 1969)

O. Settari: 'J. A. Komenský ve vztahu k evropskému hudebnímu baroku' [Komenský in relation to the European musical Baroque], *OM*, i (1969), 65

V. Gregor: 'O autorství ukolébavky Komenského', *Acta Comeniana*, xxiv (1970), 86

Památce Jana Amose Komenského k 300. výročí úmrti [Commemoration of the 300th anniversary of Komenský's death] (Prague, 1970) [incl. articles by Plavec, Settari and Snížková]

J. Brambera: *Jan Amos Comenius: Geschichte und Aktualität (1670–1970)*, ii: *Eine Bibliographie des Gesamtwerkes* (Glashütten, 1971)

JOHN CLAPHAM

Komitas [Gomidas; Soghomonian, Soghomon] (*b* Kyotaya, Turkey, 8 Oct 1869; *d* Paris, 22 Oct 1935). Armenian composer, ethnomusicologist, choral conductor, singer and teacher. One of the first Armenians to have a classical Western musical education, as well as instruction in the music of his own people, he laid the foundations for a distinctive national style in his many songs and choruses, all of which are deeply influenced by the folk and church traditions of Armenia. His work on Armenian folksong is also of musicological importance.

1. LIFE. Both of his parents (his father Gevorg Soghomonian was a cobbler) had gifts for music and poetry; in 1881, however, the boy was orphaned and sent to Armenia to study at the Gevork'ian Theological Seminary in Vagharshapat (now Edjmiadsin). There his beautiful voice and his musical talents attracted notice, and under Sahak Amatuni's guidance he mastered the theory and practice of Armenian liturgical singing. He also made decisive contact with folksong, to the collection and study of which he gave himself wholeheartedly. When he had only just learnt Armenian notation he set about recording the songs of the Ararat valley peasants and, having no knowledge of European music theory, harmonized these songs for performance with a student choir at the academy. His earliest surviving collection of folk melodies dates from 1891, in which year the journal *Ararat* published a choral ode by the self-taught composer. In 1893 he made arrangements of medieval *tagher* and graduated from the academy to become a music teacher and conductor of the cathedral choir. He published his research on Armenian church melodies in 1894, and on becoming a *vardapet* (archimandrite) he adopted the name 'Komitas' (that of an important 7th-century Armenian hymn writer). In 1895 he brought out a volume of *gusan* songs from the Akn region.

The next year Komitas went to Berlin where, on Joachim's advice, he entered the private conservatory of Richard Schmidt and enrolled at the university. Apart from Schmidt his teachers included Fleischer, Bellermann and Friedlaender. He remained a student for three years, during which time he produced a setting of Psalm cxxxvii, several lieder and Armenian folksong arrangements, all far above the level of prentice work. In Berlin he was also one of the first to join the International Musical Society, and he lectured on Armenian music; the first issue of the society's journal includes an article

by him (under the name of 'Komitas Gevork'ian') on the ekphonetic transcription of Armenian church music.

On his return to Vagharshapat Komitas continued to collect songs, eventually accumulating several thousand. He also established the relationship between folk and church music, worked on deciphering the ancient *khaz* notation and made arrangements of folk and sacred songs. Some of these he recorded, and with the seminary choir he gave concerts in Vagharshapat, Erevan and Tbilisi. Of his pupils at this time, Melik'yan was to become an outstanding Armenian musician of the next generation. Already Komitas's various activities were becoming extremely important to the development of music in Armenia.

In 1906–7 Komitas gave concerts in Paris and Switzerland with other Armenian singers and with a French choir he had trained, gaining enthusiastic recognition in musical circles and from the press. He returned to Vagharshapat in autumn 1907, but the emphatically worldly nature of his activities created animosity within the conservative clergy and he was obliged to leave. From 1910 he lived in Constantinople, then one of the largest centres of Armenian culture, where he founded a large choir, Gusan. He also organized choirs in Izmir, Alexandria and Cairo, and his concerts and lectures helped to encourage a feeling of national identity among the scattered Armenians of the Near East. In 1912 he completed his last version of the *patarag*, the Armenian liturgy, besides continuing to produce lectures and articles. One of his sayings, 'The people are a great creator, learn from the people!', became something of a catch phrase.

Komitas took part in the International Musical Society congress in Paris in May–June 1914. His papers on Armenian music and a concert in the Armenian church, given under the auspices of the congress, again created great interest in Armenian music. The next year his creative work was interrupted when, on the orders of the Ottoman government, many western Armenians were annihilated and he himself was deported into the interior of the country. The experience brought about a breakdown, and from 1919 until his death he lived in a hospital in the suburbs of Paris. In 1936 his body was transferred to Erevan and interred in the Pantheon of Armenian Artists. His manuscripts, however, remained scattered and several are lost. A complete edition of compositions and musicological works is being published by the Arts Institute of the Armenian Academy of Sciences.

2. WORKS. Komitas's folksong collections are remarkable for their exactness and variety; all the poetic forms, all the dialect types, all the modal and rhythmic species are represented. One of his most valuable discoveries was that ancient types – improvisatory agricultural tunes, the *hayrenner* of the old *gusanner* (professional minstrels) and variations on medieval *tagher* – are to be found among Armenian folksongs, so that his collection includes not only a survey of folk music but also reconstructions of Armenian music from the past. He also made the first transcriptions of Kurdish melodies.

His own vocal works can be divided into two categories: those based on folk or sacred melodies and (a much smaller group) those that are freely composed. The latter are not so characteristic of Komitas, but they do show compositional mastery and directness; they include such songs as the popular lyric *Kak'avi erg*

('Song of the partridge') and choruses such as the patriotic and dramatic *Ur es gali, ay garun* ('Where are you coming, spring?'), comic scenes in recitative and the opera fragments *Anush*. The folk-based pieces are more numerous because Komitas believed a national art with popular origins could assist in arousing the national conscience of the Armenian people. His songs of this type with piano fall into many genres: love-songs and dance-songs, lullabies and pieces on the hard lot of the peasant, monologues of the *antuner* (expatriates), ancient ballads and folk parables. Emotional and picturesque, they are at the same time economical in thought and laconic in vocal narration; the harmony is fresh, the textures novel and the piano parts are unusually expressive.

Komitas's choral pieces are similarly varied in subject, including work songs, scenes of religious rites, a lament, epic-heroic pieces, landscape pictures, dance suites, comic numbers and love-songs. Here the abundance of tuneful cantilena is matched by the power of choral recitative, and emotional clarity is combined with strict narration. Unaffected in manner, Komitas was able to express joy and triumph with nobility, or to plumb grief and sorrow with manly decorum. Speech intonations are often directly imitated, so that the music contains the grandeur typical of Armenian folksong and its echoes of heathen antiquity. Moreover, his choral technique shows great variety and originality.

Also important in Komitas's output are the sacred pieces, the arrangements of ancient *sharakan*, *meghedi* and *tagher*, which emphasize the folk origins of the melodies. Outstanding here are certain numbers of the chants for unaccompanied male voices which, with some of the secular choruses, are his greatest contributions. Other works include arrangements of urban songs, often on the theme of national liberation, and popular dance-tunes for piano. Taken as a whole, Komitas's oeuvre is a vast gallery of Armenian images and a musical epic of national life.

In technique Komitas followed folk style but added original features; above all, he brought polyphonic development to a music which is essentially monodic. He did this by subordinating conventional rules of harmony and polyphony to methods originating in the folk material. In polyphony he used Armenian modes and intonations in melodically independent voices, freely allowing the occurrence of polymodality and polytonality. He also took advantage of national forms and rhythms, and the Armenian genius for antiphonal singing. Harmonically the modes proved a rich source, and Komitas also used original chords (in 4ths, 5ths etc) relating to the modes. In piano accompaniments he effectively used the pedal to shade the colour of his modal harmonies.

Komitas's work came as a culmination of the efforts of earlier Armenian composers and as a supreme expression of the yearnings of his contemporaries. He raised the standard of art music in Armenia to a level where it could create international interest, and, basing his work on Armenian material, he was able at the same time to write music in line with contemporary Western developments.

WORKS

Editions: *Hay k'nar/La lyre arménienne* (Paris, 1907) [A]

    Hay geghdjuk erger [Armenian village songs] (Leipzig, 1912) [B]

    Hay zhoghovrdakan erazhshtut'yun/Musique populaire arménienne, new ser., i–vii (Paris, 1925–37) [C]

    Pesni dlya golosa i fortepiano [Songs for voice and piano], ed. Kh. Tordzhan (Moscow and Leningrad, 1939) [D]

    Armyanskiye narodnïye pesni dlya khora bez soprovozhdeniya [Armenian folksongs for unaccompanied choir] (Moscow, 1958) [E]

    Sobraniye sochineniy [Collected works], ed. R. At'ayan (Erevan, 1960–69) [F i–iii]

    Khorovïye pesni [Choral songs] (Erevan, 1969) [G]

    Pesni dlya golosa s fortepiano (Moscow, 1969) [H]

UNACCOMPANIED CHORAL
(sacred)

Ergetsoghut'yun srboy pataragi [Chants of the sacred liturgy], male vv (Paris, 1933)

Taghk' ev aleluk' [Tagher and alleluias], mixed vv (Paris, 1946)

(secular)

First Suite of Wedding Songs, 1899–1901: Erknits, getnits [The blessing of the tree]; Merik djan, halal [The bride's farewell]; T'agvori mer, durs ari [Turning to the bridegroom's mother]; T'agvor barov [The bridegroom's blessing]; Ein dizan [The comic]; Arnem ertam im yar [Dance]; all F iii

Yel, yel [Song of the cart-driver], 1899–1901, F iii

Ay, heva, heva sirts [Tremble, O my heart], 1899–1901, F iii

Vay, le, le [Lamentation], 1899–1901, F iii

Handen gas gegh mtnis [When you return from the field], 1899–1901, F iii

Kaput k'urak hedsel em [I straddled a blue stallion], 1899–1901, F iii

Gut'an hats em berum [I am bringing bread], 1899–1901, F iii

Ur es gali, ay garun [Where are you coming, spring?], 1902, F ii

Alagyaz sarn ampel a [Alagyaz disappeared in the clouds], 1902–6, C iv, E, F ii; 2nd setting, 1907–10, F ii; 3rd setting, 1910–11, F ii, G

Khnki dsar [Incense wood], 1902–6, C iv, E, F ii; 2nd setting, 1907–10, F ii; 3rd setting, 1910–11, F ii, G

K'eler, tsoler [He walked, radiant], 1902–6, C iv, E, F ii

Dsirani dsar [Apricot wood], 1902–6, D, F ii

Loru gut'anerg [Song of the Lori ploughman], 1902–6, D, F ii

Kali erg [Song of the threshing floor], 1902–6, D, E, F ii

Sipana k'adjer [The brave men of Sipan], 1902–6, D, F ii, G; 2nd setting, 1907–10, F ii, G

Im chinari yar [My beloved is like the plane tree], 1906–7, A, F ii

Garun a, dzun a arel [Spring, though snow has fallen], 1906–7, A, E, F ii, G

Gut'anerg [Song of the ploughman], 1906–7, A, F ii, G

Andzrevn ekav [Rain fell], 1906–7, A, F ii, G

Sareri vrov gnats [He roamed the mountains], 1906–7, A, F ii, G

Yeri, yeri djan, 1906–7, A, F ii, G

Lusnakn anush [Tender moon], 1906–7, A, E, F ii, G

Shogher djan [Dear Shogher], 1906–7, A, F ii, G

Aravotun bari lus [Morning welcome], 1907–10, B, E, F ii, G

Shorora, Anush [Step lightly, Anush], 1907–10, B, E, F ii

Hov lini [Blow, cool breeze], 1907–10, B, E, F ii, G

Kuzhn ara [I took a jug], 1907–10, B, E, F ii, G

Saren elav [He went up the mountain], 1907–10, B, F ii

Gna, gna [Go, go], 1907–10, B, E, F ii, G

Oror, Adino, 1907–10, B, E, F ii

Sona yar [Beloved Sona], 1907–10, B, F ii

Khumar, 1907–10, B, E, F ii

K'aghhan [Weeding song], 1907–10, B, E, F ii, G

Nanik-nananik, 1907–10, F iii

Lusnak sari takin [The moon under the mountain], 1907–10, C vii, F iii, G

Kak'avi erg [Song of the partridge], 1908, C v, F ii

Oy, Nazan, 1908, C v, F ii, G

Akh, Maral djan [Ah, dear Maral], 1909, F ii, G

Ekek' tesek' inchn em keri [From the songs of Shrovetide], 1910–11, F iii

Kaynel es, kanchum el ches [You stand and do not call], 1910–11, F iii

Hing eds unem [I have five she-goats], 1910–11, F iii

Zar, zing, 1910–11, F iii

Esgisher, lusnak gisher [This night, moonlit night], 1910–11, F iii

Mer baghum freni dsar [There is a pomegranate in our garden], 1910–11, F iii

Kali erg ev ayl erger [Threshing and other songs], 1912, F ii

Second Suite of Wedding Songs, 1912: 1 Mer t'agvorin inch piti [Presentations to the groom]; 2 Gatsek berek t'agvoramer [Presentations of the parents]; 3 Orhnyal barerar astvads [Consecration of the wedding tree]; 4 Mer t'agvorn er khach [Extolling of the groom]; 5 En dizan [The comic]; 6 Dun halal merik [The bride's farewell]; 7 Vard, dzk'e chem siri [From the bride's songs]; 8 Eghnik [From the bride's songs]; 9 T'agvori mer, dus ari [Addressing the bridegroom's mother]; all F iii; 1–5, 9, C vii

Songs of Girls Fortune-telling, 1912: Erknk'i astgher [Stars in the sky]; Es gyul em [I am a flower]; Dsaghik unem narendji [I have an orange flower]; all in F iii

First Suite of Peasant Songs and Dance-songs, 1912: Ampel a kamar-kamar [The clouds thickened]; Erevan bagh em arel [A garden was

laid in Erevan]; Tun ari [Come home]; Horom-horom [Comic song]; Arev kayne kesor [When midday comes]; all F iii
Hov arek, sarer jan [Give coolness, dear mountains], 1913–14, F iii
Chinar es, keřanal mi [You plane tree, do not die!], 1913–14, F iii
Papuri [Dance-song], 1913–14, F iii
Inchu Bingyol mtar [Why did you come to Bingyol?], 1913–14, F iii
Susan smbul, 1913–14, F iii
Es ařun djur a gali [In the stream runs water], 1913–14, F iii
Sandï erg [Mortar song], 1913–14, F iii
Second Suite of Peasant Songs and Dance-songs, 1913–14: Yaris anun Balasan [My beloved's name is Balasan]; Aghchi, anund Shushan [The girl named Shushan]; Kaleri tjambin ketsa [I stopped on the road]; Baghi pat ddum a [Along the wall grows a pumpkin]; Putjur aghchik sevavor [The little girl in black]; Vard a yars [My beloved is like a rose]; Oy im nazani yar [O my gracious beloved]; all F iii
Third Suite of Peasant Songs and Dance-songs, 1913–14: Alagyaz acherd [Your eyes are like the Alagyaz]; Sev a chobani shun [The shepherd has a black dog]; Mi yar unem [I have a sweetheart]; Elek' tesek' dus [Go out and look]; Ay tgha mer geghedsi [Hey, the fellow from our village]; Shakhkr-shukhkr; all F iii
Fourth Suite of Peasant Songs and Dance-songs, 1913–14; Saren kuga djukht ghoch [Two rams are coming down from the mountain]; Ervum em [I'm burning]; Yar djan, ari [Come, my beloved]; Esor urbat'ē [Today it's Friday]; Djur kuga verin saren [From the mountain streams water]; Djaghats mani-mani [The windmill turns]; Ařnem ert'am en sar [I will go up to the mountain with my sweetheart]; all F iii
Fifth Suite of Peasant Songs and Dance-songs, 1913–14: Kanach art ban yeka [She worked on the green cornfield]; Nor em nor matsun merel [She prepared fresh matsun]; Haray, elli yar [You are my sweetheart]; Lusnak bak a brnel [A full moon came up]; all F iii
Sixth Suite of Peasant Songs and Dance-songs, 1913–14: Ekan Mokads harsner [Brides came from Moks]; Mer bagh dsař a [There are trees in our garden]; Im chinar yarin [To my beloved like a plane tree]; Hovn anush [The breeze is sweet]; all F iii

SONGS

(for 1v, pf unless otherwise stated)
Dsedseřnak [Swallow], 1898, D, F i, H
Akh, Maral djan [Ah, dear Maral], 1899, D, F i
Hov arek, arer djan [Give coolness, dear mountains], 1905–6, A, D, F i, H
Habrban, S, T, pf, 1905–6, A, D, F i, H
Erkink'n ampel a [The sky covered with clouds], 1905–6, A, D, F i, H
Antuni [Song of the homeless], 1905–6, A, D, F i, H
Garun a, dzun a arel [Spring, but snow has fallen], 1905–6, A, D, F i, H
Dsirani dsař [Apricot wood], 1905–6, C iv, D, F i, H
Chinar es, keřanal mi [You plane tree, do not die!], 1905–6, C ii, D, F i, H
Oror [Lullaby], 1905, C ii, D, F i
Garun [Spring], 1907, C ii, D, F i
Chem křna khagha [I cannot dance], 1907–8, C iv, D, F i, H
Kak'avi erg [Song of the partridge], 1908, C v, F i, H
K'eler, tsoler [He walked, radiant], 1908–11, B, D, F i, H
K'ele, k'ele [March, march], 1908–11, B, D, F i, H
Sar, sar [Mountains, mountains], 1908–11, B, D, F i
Kanche, křunk [You crane, sing!], 1908–11, B, D, F i
Es saren kugai [I returned from the mountains], 1908–11, B, D, F i
Zinch u zinch [What and what], 1908–11, B, D, F i
Alagyaz sarn ampel a [Alagyaz disappeared in the clouds], 1908–11, B, D, F i, H
Khnki dsař [Incense wood], 1908–11, B, D, F i, H
Al aylukhs [My scarlet kerchief], S, T, pf, 1908–11, B, D, F i, H
Kuzhn ařa [I took a jug], 1908–11, B, D, F i, H
Es ařun djur a gali [In the stream runs water], 1908–11, B, D, F i, H
Alagyaz bardzr sarin [On the high Mount Alagyaz], 1908–11, B, D, F i
Oy, Nazan [Oh, Nazan], 1908–11, B, D, F i
Ampel a kamar-kamar [The clouds thickened], 1911, C vii, F i
Es aghchik em [I am a girl], 1911, C vii, F i
Ervum em [I'm burning], 1911, C iv, D, F i
Tun ari [Come home], 1911, C vii, F i, H
Gut'an hats em berum [I am bringing bread], 1911, C vii, F i
Voghberg [Mournful song], 1911, C vii, F i
Lusnak sari takin [The moon under the mountains], 1911, C vii, F i, H
Es gisher, lusnak gisher [This night, moonlit night], 1911, F i
Křunk [The crane], 1911, C iv, D, F i, H
Djur kuga verin saren [Water streams from the mountain], 1912, F i
Shogher djan [Dear Shogher], 1912, F i, H
Mokads mirza [The Mok prince], 1914, C vii, F i, H
Le, le yaman, F i
Shakhkr, shukhkr, F i

PIANO

Dances: Erangi, Unabi, Marali, Shushiki, Et-arach, Shoror, C i
Unpubd dances: Manushaki, Shoror

FOLKSONG COLLECTIONS

Shar Akna zhoghovrdakan ergeri [Series of Akn folksongs] (Vagharshapat, 1895) [Armenian notation]

ed., with M. Abeghyan: *Hazar u mi khagh* [1001 *khagher*] (Vagharshapat, 1903–5, 2/1969) [texts only]
K'rdakan eghanakner [Kurdish melodies] (Moscow, 1904)
Zhoghovrdakan erger [Folksongs] (Erevan, 1931)
ed., with M. Abeghyan: *Zhoghovrdakan khaghikner* [Little folksongs] (Erevan, 1940) [texts only]
Hay zhoghovrdakan erger ev parerger [Armenian folksongs and dances] (Erevan, 1950)

WRITINGS

Hodvadsner ev usumnasirut'yunner [Articles and studies] (Erevan, 1941) [16 articles on Armenian secular and sacred music and on European composers]

BIBLIOGRAPHY

T. Azatyan: *Komitas* (Constantinople, 1931) [in Armenian]
S. Berberyan: *Komitas vardapet* (Bucharest, 1936; Eng. trans., 1969) [in Armenian]
G. Daian: *Komitas vardapet* (Venice, 1936) [in Armenian]
R. At'ayan: 'Printsip garmonizatsii narodnoy pesni u Komitasa' [Komitas's principle of folksong harmonization], *Izvestiya Akademii nauk Armenii*, ix (1949)
A. Shahverdyan: *Komitas i armyanskaya muzïkal'naya kul'tura* (Erevan, 1956)
R. At'ayan: 'R. A. Komitas: sobiratel' armyanskoy narodnoy pesni' [Komitas as collector of Armenian folksong], *VII Mezhdunarodnïy kongress antropologicheskikh i etnograficheskikh nauk: Moskva 1964*, 334
H. Begian: *Gomidas Vartabed: his Life and Importance to Armenian Music* (diss., U. of Michigan, 1964)
R. At'ayan and others: *Komitasakan* (Erevan, 1969) [in Armenian]
G. Geodakyan: *Komitas* (Erevan, 1969) [in Russ.]
V. Vagramyan: *Representative Secular Choral Works of Gomidas: an Analytical Study and Evaluation of his Musical Style* (diss., U. of Miami, 1973)

ROBERT AT'AYAN

Komlóssy, Erzsébet (*b* Budapest, 9 July 1933). Hungarian mezzo-soprano. After studying at the Budapest Conservatory, she joined the Szeged National Theatre in 1955, remaining there for three years. She then became a member of the Budapest State Opera, playing leading mezzo-soprano roles as well as the Mother in Szokolay's *Blood Wedding*; she has also appeared at Athens (in Casals's oratorio *El pesebre*, under the composer, 1966), Berlin, Cologne, Moscow and Vienna, and sang Azucena at Covent Garden in October 1970. Her many recordings include operas by Erkel and Kodály. A truly dramatic artist, she can create an emotionally tense atmosphere, but has also had significant success in lyrical roles.

PÉTER P. VÁRNAI

Komma, Karl Michael (*b* Asch [now Aš], Bohemia, 24 Dec 1913). German musicologist and composer. From 1932 to 1934 he studied musicology with G. Becking at the German University in Prague and composition with Fidelio Finke at the German Academy of Music; he also studied the piano and conducting. At Heidelberg University (1934) he studied musicology with Besseler, and took his doctorate in 1936 with a dissertation on Johann Zach; he then became an assistant lecturer in the musicology department. From 1940 to 1945 he was head of the music school at Liberec, Bohemia, during which time it became the State Music School. After the war he settled at Wallerstein in Bavaria where he had a successful concert career as an accompanist. He became a lecturer at the Stuttgart Musikhochschule in 1954, and has been professor of music history and composition there since 1960. He is the founder and co-editor of the *Zeitschrift für Musiktheorie* (1967). Komma specializes in the musical history of Bohemia, Baroque and pre-classical music, Hölderlin and settings of his poetry, and musical iconography. His more recent compositions include a requiem (1969), *Drei Gesänge nach F. Hölderlin* (1970), *Pfingstdiptychon* for organ

(1972), Ballade for percussion (1972) and *Tre pezzi tipici 1971/73* for piano.

WRITINGS

Johann Zach (diss., U. of Heidelberg, 1936; Kassel, 1938)
'Hölderlin und die Musik', *Hölderlin-Jb 1953*, 106; see also *Hölderlin Jb 1955–6*, 201 and *Hölderlin-Jb 1969–70*, 325
'Sprachmelodie und Musikalität der Heimatvertriebenen aus Böhmen und Mähren', *Zeitschrift für Ostforschung*, iv (1955), 66
Das böhmische Musikantentum (Kassel, 1960)
Musikgeschichte in Bildern (Stuttgart, 1961)
'Die Pentatonik in Antonín Dvořáks Werk', *Musik des Ostens*, i (1962), 63
'Das "Scherzo" der 2. Symphonie von J. Brahms', *Festschrift für Walter Wiora* (Kassel, 1967), 448
'Franz Schuberts Klaviersonate a-moll op. posth. 164', *Zeitschrift für Musiktheorie*, iii (1972), 2
Numerous articles in *MGG*, including 'Cannabich, Familie', 'Filtz, Anton', 'Marx, Karl'

EDITIONS

Gruppenkonzerte der Bachzeit, EDM, 1st ser., xi (1938/R1962)
L. van Beethoven: Klaviersonate As-Dur op.110 (Stuttgart, 1967) [facs. edn. with commentary]
Lieder und Gesänge nach Dichtungen von Friedrich Hölderlin, Schriften der Hölderlin-Gesellschaft, v (Tübingen, 1967)

HANS HEINRICH EGGEBRECHT

Kommos (Gk., from *koptein*: 'beat', 'chop', either in the sense of beating the head or breast, or in allusion to a 'choppy' rhythm). In ancient Greek tragedy an emotional and grief-laden passage set to music, divided between one leading actor on the stage and the chorus in the *orchēstra*; the term seems originally to have been synonymous with THRĒNOS. In tragedy the verse form is intermediate between dialogue and lyric poetry, the predominating measure being the dochmiac dimeter (syncopated iambic trimeter). The lines are arranged in symmetrical patterns of strophe and antistrophe, which may imply that the chorus danced. Many Greek tragedies contain a *kommos*, and some have two, at turning-points in the action.

BIBLIOGRAPHY

E. Diehl: 'Kommoi', *Paulys Real-Encyclopädie der classischen Altertumswissenschaft*, xi/1 (Stuttgart, 1921), 1195
A. Pickard-Cambridge: *The Dramatic Festivals of Athens* (Oxford, rev. 2/1968)

HECTOR THOMSON

Kōmōdoi. An ancient Greek term, dating from the time of Aristophanes, used in its normal and proper sense to signify the members of the chorus in a comedy. The term may, however, also mean the performers (actors as well as the chorus) in a comedy, or the comic performance or contest as a whole, or even comic poets and comic actors.

BIBLIOGRAPHY

A. Pickard-Cambridge: *The Dramatic Festivals of Athens* (Oxford, rev. 2/1968)

GEOFFREY CHEW

Komorous, Rudolf (*b* Prague, 8 Dec 1931). Czech composer, teacher and bassoonist. He was taught the violin and the piano by his father, and then attended the Prague Conservatory (1946–52) and Academy of Music (1952–6), where he studied the bassoon with K. Pivoňka and composition with Bořkovec. From 1952 he played in the orchestra of the Smetana Theatre in Prague; from 1959 to 1961 he taught the bassoon and chamber music at the Peking Conservatory. In Prague he worked with the Musica Viva Pragensis ensemble, of which he had been a founder, and as a soloist he devoted himself predominantly to the performance of new works. He taught theory and composition at Macalester College in St Paul, Minnesota, and in 1971 he was appointed professor of composition at the University of

Victoria, British Columbia.

Komorous's development was deeply influenced by his association with the painters Dlouhý and Vožniak and the sculptors Koblasa and Nepraš in the 'Šmidrové' group in the 1950s. Taking up ideas from the pre-war Czech avant garde, in particular from the surrealists, the group evolved an 'aesthetic of the wonderful' (Herzog). The opening of their first exhibition in 1957 was the occasion for the first public performance of a dodecaphonic piece in Prague since 1945 – the piece played was Komorous's *Glücklicher Augenblick*. This link with visual artists led Komorous to new ways of ordering sound materials: at first through geometrical graphic scores, and then, beginning with *Sladká královna* ('The sweet queen', 1964), through a 'curious, phantom-like play of tender, banal, coarse, piquant sounds, progressing in confused succession' (Herzog). In this way he has given musical expression to the group's aims: 'to push situations to the point where humour and seriousness are indistinguishable' and 'to set the paradoxical and the mysterious in play as a delight at the miraculous'. Such goals involve the employment of all manner of compositional means, even the simple, diatonic melodic shapes of *York* (1967).

WORKS
(*selective list*)

Sonatine, pf, 1955; Glücklicher Augenblick, basset hn, bn, dbn, 1957; Sladká královna [The sweet queen], harmonica, ens, 1964; Olympia, 2 players, 1964; Teufelstriller, pf, 1964; Chanson, va, gui, coilspring, 1965; Malevitschs Grabmal, tape, 1965; Mignon, str qt, 1965; York, fl, ob/tpt, bn, triangle, prepared pf, mand, db, 1967; Düstere Anmut, 11 insts, tape, 1968; Kostky [Dice], str qt, 1968; Gone, tape, 1969; Bare and Dainty, orch, 1970; Lady Whiterose, chamber opera, 1971; Lethe, orch, 1971; An Anna Blume, chorus, 1972; Untitled I–V, various insts, 1973–4; Anatomy of Melancholy, tape, 1974; Rossi, small orch, 1975; The Gentle Touch, 5 fl, 4 va, 3 vc, pf, 1977

Principal publisher: Universal (Vienna)

BIBLIOGRAPHY

E. Herzog: 'Avantgarde aus der Tschechoslowakei', Donaueschingen Festival programme book (Donaueschingen, 1968)
J. Kříž: *Šmidrové* (Prague, 1970)

CAMILLO SCHOENBAUM

Komorowski, Ignacy Marceli (*b* Warsaw, 13 Jan 1824; *d* Warsaw, 14 Oct 1857). Polish composer. He studied the piano with W. Szanior, the violin with J. Bułakowski and Jan Hornziel and the cello with Jozef Szabliński and Adam Herman. He was private music teacher to the Kretkowski family at Kamienne in the Kujawy district (1848–50), after which he returned to Warsaw, where he was cellist in the Wielki Theatre orchestra; at the same time he studied harmony and counterpoint under Freyer. In November 1856 he went to Italy for health reasons and lived for some time in Florence. At the beginning of July 1857 he returned via Paris and Ems to Warsaw, where he died of tuberculosis. Komorowski was known above all as a composer of songs, a genre in which his lyrical talent was fully evident; the most popular was *Kalina* to words by T. Lenartowicz (1846). In many of his songs he introduced Polish folkdance rhythms, for example the polonaise, mazurka and krakowiak. He also composed several piano miniatures.

BIBLIOGRAPHY

SMP
S. Barbag: 'Polska pieśń artystyczna' [Polish art songs], *Muzyka*, iv/7–9 (1927), 94

JERZY MORAWSKI

Komorzynski, Egon, Ritter von (*b* Vienna, 7 May 1878; *d* Vienna, 16 March 1963). Austrian musicologist. He was educated at the Schottengymnasium in Vienna and at the universities of Vienna, Berlin, Leipzig, Breslau, Würzburg and Munich. After studying musicology and German philology he graduated at Vienna in 1900. From 1904 until 1934 he was professor of German language and literature at the Vienna Handelsakademie, and for 40 years he was music critic of the *Österreichische Volkszeitung*.

Although his published writings cover a wide range of interests the great majority are concerned with Mozart, and especially with *Die Zauberflöte*. His first book, a study of Emanuel Schikaneder published in 1901, contains the essence of his long life's work. In it he demonstrated, against current opinion, Schikaneder's authorship, and the nature and worth, of the *Zauberflöte* libretto – a subject to which he frequently returned as fresh pieces of evidence came to light, most notably in the revised version of his Schikaneder biography in 1951. In the 1940s he published novels about Mozart and Anna Gottlieb, and about Schubert. Komorzynski's greatest virtue was his tireless search for new facts; he was perhaps less successful in presenting them, and his

'Die ägyptische "Zauberflöte" ', *ZfM*, cxii (1951), 643
'Sänger und Orchester des Freihaustheaters', *MJb 1951*, 138
'Das Urbild der "Zauberflöte" ', *MJb 1952*, 101
'Mozart und Marie Therese Paradis', *MJb 1952*, 110
' "Zauberflöte" und "Oberon" ', *MJb 1953*, 150
' "Die Zauberflöte" und "Dschinnistan" ', *MJb 1954*, 177
'Johann Baptist Henneberg, Schikaneders Kapellmeister (1768–1822)', *MJb 1955*, 243
'Ein Wiener Musikkritiker des Vormärz, Dr. Alfred Julius Becher, 1803–1848', *Jahrbuch der Grillparzer-Gesellschaft*, 3rd ser., ii (1956), 123
'Der menschliche Wunschtraum des Fliegens bei Goethe', *Jahrbuch des Wiener Goethe-Vereins*, new ser., lxvi (1962), 107
Articles in *Altwiener Kalender, Musikerziehung, Neue Wege, Österreichische Musik-Zeitschrift, Wiener Figaro, Wien und die Wiener*

BIBLIOGRAPHY
E. G.-I.: 'Ein Leben mit der "Zauberflöte" ', *Wiener Figaro*, xxi (1953), no.2, p.25 [75th birthday tribute]

PETER BRANSCOMBE

Kōmos [comus]. In Greek and Roman antiquity, a festive procession through the streets (e.g. in honour of a victor, or to the house of a friend) accompanied by music, carousing and other merrymaking. Female aulos

Kōmos: detail from the Brygos cup (attributed to the 'Brygos painter', fl c500 BC) in the Martin-von-Wagner-Museum der Universität Würzburg

writings are not free from errors. Nevertheless his place in Mozart studies is secure. He was honoured by the Viennese Mozartgemeinde, the civil authorities and university, and also by the Internationale Stiftung Mozarteum, Salzburg.

WRITINGS
Emanuel Schikaneder: ein Beitrag zur Geschichte des deutschen Theaters (Berlin, 1901, rev. 2/1951)
'Lortzing's "Waffenschmied" und seine Tradition', *Euphorion*, viii (1901), 340
'Mozarts Messen', *Die Musik*, iv (1904–5), 49
Mozarts Kunst der Instrumentation (Stuttgart, 1906)
'Grillparzers Klavier-Lehrer Johann Mederitsch, genannt Gallus', *Altwiener Kalender* (1919), 131
'Mozarts Sinfonien als persönliche Bekenntnisse', *Die Musik*, xxxiii (1940–41), 84
'Das Bühnenbild der "Zauberflöte" ', *Die Musik*, xxxiii (1940–41), 153
'Die allegorische Bedeutung der "Zauberflöte" ', *Die Musik*, xxxiii (1940–41), 265
Mozart: Sendung und Schicksal eines deutschen Künstlers (Berlin, 1941, rev. 2/1955)
'Die Vorfahren der "Meistersinger von Nürnberg" ', *Die Musik*, xxxiv (1941–2), 101
'Vorläufer des "Freischütz" ', *Die Musik*, xxxiv (1941–2), 224
'Schikaneders dramatische Erstling', *Die Musik*, xxxv (1942), 73
'Die Wiener Szenenbilder zur "Zauberflöte" ', *Neues Mozart-Jb*, iii (1943), 230
Der Vater der Zauberflöte: Emanuel Schikaneders Leben (Vienna, 1948)

players accompanied the procession through the streets; songs were sung, such as the ENCOMIUM, which was originally the song of praise to escort a victor home. Some official *kōmoi* took place in daylight; private *kōmoi* might occur at night, following a SYMPOSIUM. A famous depiction of a *kōmos* is that of the Brygos cup at Würzburg (see illustration). The earliest occurrence of the term is in the *Shield* attributed to Hesiod (actually dating from the late 6th century BC), and the *kōmos* may have developed from the increasingly important cult of Dionysus. It continued until late antiquity; attacked by St Paul (*Romans* xiii.13, *Galatians* v.21), it declined under the influence of the Church.

In late antiquity the name 'Comus' was also given to the leader of a band of revellers and is well known in this guise through *A Maske presented at Ludlow Castle, 1634* (also known as *Comus*) by Milton, which has been set to music several times – Henry Lawes, Arne (1737–8), and Hugh Wood (*Scenes from Comus*, 1965).

BIBLIOGRAPHY
H. Lamer: 'Komos', *Paulys Real-Encyclopädie der classischen Altertumswissenschaft*, xi/2 (Stuttgart, 1922), 1286

GEOFFREY CHEW

Komponium (Ger.). COMPONIUM.

Kŏmun'go. A Korean long half-tube zither related to the Chinese *ch'in* (zither); *see* KOREA, §§1(ii, v), 2(i), 3, 6(iii), 7(i), 9(ii), and fig.1. *See also* CHINA, §V, 2(i).

Komzák, Karel (i) (*b* Netěchovice, nr. České Budějovice, 4 Nov 1823; *d* Netěchovice, 19 March 1893). Czech conductor, bandmaster and composer, father of Karel Komzák (ii). It is thought that he studied at the Prague Organ School for a year before completing a teacher's course at St Henry's College in Prague (1841–2), during which time he was supported by Tomášek. At first a village teacher and organist (1842–7), he became the organist of a lunatic asylum in Prague; he also played at St Catherine's (1847–66) and directed the band of a rifle corps (1847–65). Komzák achieved his greatest fame through the orchestra which he founded and conducted in Prague (1854–65), in which Dvořák played the viola, and which, after playing for the Prague Provisional Theatre from 1862, became the official orchestra from 1865. Komzák then became a military bandmaster, travelling throughout the Austrian Empire. He retired in 1882 but returned to Austrian army service for another six years, until 1888. He wrote almost 300 works, mostly marches and dances (sometimes based on Czech folktunes), which were published in Prague, Leipzig and Hamburg.

BIBLIOGRAPHY
Obituary, *Dalibor*, xv (1893), 171
O. Šourek: *Život a dílo Antonína Dvořáka*, i (Prague, 1916, 3/1955)
F. Pilát: 'Vzpomínka na Karla Komzáka' [A memoir of Komzák], *Hudební zpravodaj*, iii/9 (1934), 12
J. Bartoš: *Prozatímní divadlo a jeho opera* (Prague, 1938), 24ff
J. Clapham: *Antonín Dvořák* (London, 1966), 5
A. Lamb: 'The Viennese Contemporaries: Karl Komzák', *Česká muzika*, i (Ashby-de-la-Zouch, 1973–4), 41, 52
JOHN TYRRELL

Komzák, Karel (ii) (*b* Prague, 8 Nov 1850; *d* Baden, nr. Vienna, 23 April 1905). Czech bandmaster and composer, son of Karel Komzák (i). He was taught first by his father and then attended the Prague Conservatory (1861–7), learning the violin with Mildner and Bennewitz. He played in his father's orchestra, became theatre conductor in Linz (1870) and then military bandmaster in Innsbruck as well as conductor of the local *Liedertafel* (1871). The places where he stayed longest were Vienna (from 1884) and Baden, as conductor of the spa orchestra (from 1893). In 1904 he directed a band at the World Exhibition in St Louis, USA. Like his father, he introduced Czech folksongs into his band arrangements, thereby attracting the hostility of the German press. Many of his dance compositions (80 polkas, 60 marches, 20 waltzes) were written in collaboration with his father. He also wrote songs and an operetta, *Edelweis*.

BIBLIOGRAPHY
A. Lamb: 'The Viennese Contemporaries: Karl Komzák', *Česká muzika*, i (Ashby-de-la-Zouch, 1973–4), 41, 52
JOHN TYRRELL

Kondakar (Russ.). A Russian liturgical book; *see* LITURGY AND LITURGICAL BOOKS, §III, 4.

Kondakarion. A Byzantine anthology of the music for all the kontakia chanted during the year. The earliest surviving copies are Slavonic and written in the enigmatic kondakarion notation. *See* KONTAKION and NEUMATIC NOTATIONS, §VI.

Kondakion. *See* KONTAKION.

Kondracki, Michał (*b* Połtawa, Ukraine, 5 Oct 1902). Polish composer. He studied with Szymanowski at the Warsaw Conservatory until 1927 and with Dukas and Boulanger at the Ecole Normale in Paris until 1931. In Paris he was secretary to the Society of Young Polish Musicians. He returned to Warsaw and then moved to Rio de Janeiro (1940) and New York (1943), where he remained as a composer and teacher; he has contributed articles on American musical life to *Ruch muzyczny*. His reputation as a composer was first established with the ballet *Metropolis* (1929) and the *Mała symfonia góralska* ('Little highlander symphony', 1930). Other early works (most of them unpublished) include a Partita for orchestra (1928), *Żołnierze* ('Soldiers on parade') and the Piano Concerto (1935) – dissonant and percussive compositions, often containing Polish folk themes; their rhapsodic expansiveness and rich romantic harmony were enriched by the influences of Roussel, Ravel and Prokofiev. During this period Kondracki was regarded as one of the most interesting younger Polish composers. In such later works as *Afrodite* for strings (1957) and the *Nokturn* for harp and strings (1951), however, he leaned towards a certain simplification of texture. After 1957 he almost gave up composing.

WORKS
(selective list)

Stage: Metropolis (ballet), 1929, lost; Popieliny (opera, after J. Kasprowicz: Marchołt), 1934, lost; Baśń krakowska [The legend of Kraków] (ballet), 1937
Orch: Partita, 1928, lost; Mała symfonia góralska [Little highlander sym.], 1930; Żołnierze [Soldiers on parade], *c*1932; Suita kurpiowska, 1933, lost; Nokturn, 1935; Pf Conc., 1935, lost; Conc. for Orch, 1936; Match, 1937, lost; Toccata, 1939; Epitafia, small orch, 1940; Sym. 'Zwycięstwa' [Victory], 1942; 2 tańce brazylijskie, 1943; Concertino, pf, chamber orch, 1944; Psalm, 1945; Nokturn, harp, str, 1951; Groteska, 1952; Pastorale, 1953; Kolęda [Christmas carol], fl, str, 1955; Afrodite, str, 1957
Choral: Cantata ecclesiastica, solo vv, chorus, orch, 1937; Hymn olimpijski, chorus, orch, 1954
Pf: Nastroje [Moods], 1956

BOGUSŁAW SCHÄFFER

Kondrashin, Kirill (Petrovich) (*b* Moscow, 6 March 1914). Soviet conductor. Born into a family of orchestral musicians, he took piano lessons, and also studied music theory under Nikolay Zhilyayev, who had a great influence on his artistic development. His conducting career began in 1931 at the Children's Theatre. From 1934 he was assistant conductor at the Nemirovich-Danchenko Music Theatre, making his début with Planquette's *Les cloches de Corneville* (25 October 1934). He studied conducting at the Moscow Conservatory with Boris Khaikin (1932–6), and was then conductor at the Malïy Theatre, Leningrad (1936–43), where he gave promising performances of Pashchenko's *Pompadour*, Puccini's *La fanciulla del West* and Cheremukhin's *Kalinki*. In 1943 he moved to the Bol'shoy Theatre, where contacts with Samosud, Pazovsky and Golovanov helped to improve his opera performances and widen his practical experience; he also staged a number of new productions.

After leaving the Bol'shoy in 1956 Kondrashin won recognition as an outstanding concert conductor and as a frequent partner of such soloists as David Oistrakh, Richter, Rostropovich, Gilels and Kogan. At the 1958 Tchaikovsky Piano Competition in Moscow he performed with Van Cliburn, and in the same year made

Kirill Kondrashin

his American and British débuts. He was artistic director of the Moscow Philharmonic c(1960–75), and this period can be regarded as his most important contribution as a performer. His experience as an opera conductor had defined his basic attitude, instilled in him a preference for programmatic interpretation of symphonic music, and given him a sound approach to musical performance; and during his years with the Moscow Philharmonic these qualities were consolidated. From 1960 he abandoned the baton, demanding that the orchestra appreciate the fluctuations of mood revealed only by the slightest movements of the hand or fingers, by mime, and mainly by the expression of the eyes. His finest work during the 1960s was his conducting of Mahler's symphonies, in which a notable restraint, characteristic of Kondrashin's interpretations, underlined the expressive tensions of the orchestra's performances. Kondrashin's repertory broadened steadily. He conducted the first performances of Shostakovich's Symphonies nos.4 and 13, and the premières of other works by Shostakovich, Khachaturian, Sviridov, Shchedrin, Boris Chaykovsky, Vaynberg and others; his repertory also includes Classical music and works by Bartók and Hindemith. Under Kondrashin's leadership the Moscow Philharmonic achieved a high standard of performance and toured many countries. In 1979 he was appointed conductor of the Concertgebouw, Amsterdam. Some of his articles on conducting were published as *O dirizhorskom iskusstve* ('The art of conducting', Leningrad and Moscow, 1972).

BIBLIOGRAPHY

R. Glezer: 'Kirill Kondrashin', *SovM* (1963), no.5, p.81
L. Grigor'yev and Ya. Platek: 'Besedï s masterami: Kirill Kondrashin' [Meetings with the masters: Kondrashin], *Muzïkal'naya zhizn'* (1969), no.8, p.6
V. Razhnikov and V. Uritsky: 'Vïsokaya missiya dirizhora: k 60-letiyu K. P. Kondrashina' [The lofty mission of a conductor: on Kondrashin's 60th birthday], *SovM* (1974), no.4, p.58
V. Yuzefovich: 'Razmïshleniya o professii dirizhora: beseda s K. P. Kondrashinïm' [Reflections on the conducting profession: a meeting with Kondrashin], *SovM* (1974), no.4, p.50

I. M. YAMPOL'SKY

Konen, Valentina Dzhozefovna [Konin, Valentine Victoria] (*b* Baku, 11 Aug 1909). Soviet musicologist. After receiving her schooling in New York, she graduated from the piano class of the Juilliard School of Music in 1929. She then studied music history with Mikhail Vladimirovich Ivanov-Boretsky and Valentin Eduardovich Ferman and piano with Mariya Veniaminovna Yudina at the Moscow Conservatory, graduating in 1938. She took her *Kandidat* degree at the Moscow Conservatory in 1940 with a dissertation on the antecedents of the Viennese classical symphony, and in 1946 was awarded a doctorate by the Moscow Institute for the History of the Arts for her work on American music. Konen has published articles as a music critic since 1932, and was the Moscow correspondent of the New York *Musical Courier* from 1934 to 1937.

Konen gave lectures on music history at the Moscow Conservatory (1939–41, 1943–9), and in 1945 was appointed senior lecturer. She also taught at the Gnesin Institute for Musical Education (1944–9) and was a professor at the Urals Conservatory in Sverdlovsk (1949–51). In 1960 she became a senior research fellow at the Institute for the History of the Arts in Moscow. Konen's academic interests cover a wide range of topics connected with the history of music in Western countries from the Renaissance to the 20th century, and she has also produced a number of critical articles on the musical life of the Soviet Union. Her writings attempt to place music history in the broader context of aesthetic problems.

WRITINGS

Ocherki po istorii amerikanskoy muzïki [Essays on the history of American music] (diss., Institut Istorii Iskusstv, Moscow, 1946)
Shubert [Schubert] (Moscow, 1957, enlarged 2/1969)
Istoriya zarubezhnoy muzïki: Germaniya, Avstriya, Italiya, Frantsiya, Pol'sha s 1789 goda do seredinï XIX veka [The history of foreign music: Germany, Austria, Italy, France and Poland, from 1789 to the middle of the 19th century] (Moscow, 1958, enlarged 2/1965, 3/1972)
Ral'f Vogan-Uyl'yams [Ralph Vaughan Williams] (Moscow, 1958)
Puti amerikanskoy muzïki [Paths of American music] (Moscow, 1961, 2/1965)
Etyudï o zarubezhnoy muzïke [Studies in foreign music] (Moscow, 1968)
Teatr i simfoniya: rol' operï v formirovanii klassicheskoy simfonii [The theatre and the symphony: the role of opera in the formation of the classical symphony] (Moscow, 1968)
'Znacheniye vneyevropeyskikh kul'tur dlya professional'nïkh kompozitorskikh shkol XX veka' [The significance of non-European cultures for 20th-century music], *SovM* (1971), no.10, p.50
'Betkhoven i evo posledovateli' [Beethoven and his successors], *Betkhoven: sbornik statey* (Moscow, 1971)
Monteverdi (Moscow, 1972)

YURY KELDÏSH

Konetzni (-Wiedmann), Anny (*b* Vienna, 12 Feb 1902; *d* Vienna, 6 Sept 1968). Austrian soprano, sister of Hilde Konetzni. She studied at the Vienna Conservatory with Erik Schmedes and made her stage début at the Volksoper in 1925 as a contralto. After provincial engagements and guest appearances in the *Ring* at Paris (1929) she joined the Berlin Staatsoper in 1931. In 1933 she appeared at Buenos Aires and soon after became a member of the Vienna Staatsoper. In 1935 she sang Brünnhilde under Beecham at Covent Garden, then returned to London in three of the next four seasons, and was invited back to sing in *Die Walküre* in the 1951 *Ring*. She also appeared at Salzburg, New York, Rome and at other leading houses. Her voice, in its prime a strong, pure dramatic soprano, was not supported by a particularly impressive stage presence. She retired in 1955 and illness obliged her to give up teaching at the Vienna Academy in 1957.

PETER BRANSCOMBE

Konetzni, Hilde (*b* Vienna, 21 March 1905; *d* Vienna, 20 April 1980). Austrian soprano, sister of Anny Konetzni. She studied at the Vienna Conservatory and made her début at Chemnitz in 1929 (Sieglinde to her sister's Brünnhilde). In 1932 she joined the German Theatre in Prague, and after a successful guest appearance as Elisabeth in *Tannhäuser* in Vienna she joined the Staatsoper in 1936. That year she first sang at Salzburg (Donna Elvira). Her Covent Garden début was in May 1938 (First Lady in *Zauberflöte* and Chrysothemis in *Elektra*); she is remembered especially for stepping into the Marschallin's clothes at a moment's notice to save the *Rosenkavalier* performance when Lehmann fell ill. She appeared in *The Bartered Bride*, *Tannhäuser*, the *Ring* and *Don Giovanni* the following season at Covent Garden, and was heard as Fidelio during the 1947 Vienna Staatsoper season. She also sang at Glyndebourne (Donna Elvira in 1938) and in the USA, and in 1955 returned to sing Sieglinde and Gutrune in the Covent Garden *Ring*. Although she and her sister both sang the Marschallin, Hilde Konetzni tended to prefer the more lyrical roles. Towards the end of her career she added to an extensive repertory a number of small character parts of the kind beloved of Viennese audiences.

PETER BRANSCOMBE

König. German family of organ builders. They were active for three generations in the region of the Eifel, the old electorate of Cologne, and in the northern Rhineland. Balthasar König (*b* c1685; *d* c1760), founder of the family firm, was resident in Münstereifel from 1711 and moved to Cologne in 1735. He established his own type of organ, and this was taken up and continued by his sons and grandsons without any significant modifications; this 'König type' remained a standard model in the German part of the Rhineland up to the second half of the 19th century. It gave prominence to the *Hauptwerk*, which was often the only manual. The second manual was a *Positiv*, and wherever possible a *Rückpositiv*. The third manual served as the 'Echo', and was equipped with flute stops. Free as well as coupled pedals frequently reached only as far as *f*, though larger instruments would extend to *c'* or *d'*. Balthasar König also showed a liking for mixture stops featuring the interval of a 3rd; the solo stops were generally distributed between the bass and the treble.

Christian Ludwig König (1717–89), son of Balthasar, studied with his father but subsequently also with Christian Müller (1690–1773) and was resident in Cologne from 1744. He frequently added to his organs characteristic stops in imitation of orchestral instruments (e.g. Viola da gamba, Flûte traversière and Hautbois).

Johann Kaspar Joseph König (1726–63), another son of Balthasar, worked mostly with his father and is on record as an independent organ builder in only five places. Johann Nicolaus König (1729–75), also a son of Balthasar, is similarly seldom mentioned as an independent organ builder. He studied with his father, and as they shared the same house in Cologne it may be

assumed that he eventually took over the business from him.

Balthasar Franz Joseph König (1744–66), a son of Johann Kaspar, was considered his father's successor; he died young, however. Carl Philipp Joseph König (1750–95), a son of Christian Ludwig, worked at first with his father and later independently. Adolph Daniel König (*b* 1768), a son of Johann Nicolaus, was the last organ builder of the König family, and is last known to have been active in 1803.

BIBLIOGRAPHY

J. van Heurn: *De orgelmaker* (Dordrecht, 1804–5)

H. Boeckeler: *Die neue Orgel im Kurhaussaal zu Aachen* (Aachen, 1876)

J. J. Merlo: *Kölnische Künstler* (Düsseldorf, 1895)

FRIEDRICH JAKOB

König, Johann Balthasar (*b* Waltershausen, nr. Gotha, baptized 28 Jan 1691; *d* Frankfurt am Main, buried 2 April 1758). German composer. He was a chorister in the city Kapelle of Frankfurt from at least 1703, at first under the direction of G. C. Strattner and from 1711 under Telemann; in 1718 Telemann became the godfather of König's son. In 1721 König was appointed director of music at the Katharinenkirche, the second most important musical post in Frankfurt. After Telemann's departure in the same year König continued to serve the Kapelle under G. C. Bodinus; he was also required to play the cello at the Barfüsserkirche, where Bodinus was Kapellmeister, and to sing in the choir without pay. After Bodinus's death (1727) König succeeded him and was made a citizen of Frankfurt in recognition of his position. He retained his post at the Katharinenkirche. When König took over from Bodinus the quality of church and public music improved; he directed several performances of works by Telemann, including the oratorio *Der königliche Prophete David* in 1733 and 1739 and, also in 1739, one of Telemann's Passions. He also seems to have been involved occasionally with opera performances.

Most of König's works were written for civic functions or for the church. He was particularly concerned with the problems of congregational singing, and as early as 1724 he presented to the city council a memorandum, *Unmassgeblicher Vorschlag wie dem übel-Singen in den Frankfurther Kirchen abzuhelfen sei*. His most important achievement was the *Harmonischer Lieder-Schatz*, a chorale book – the most comprehensive of the 18th century – containing nearly 2000 melodies with continuo, including the tunes of the entire Genevan Psalter. It reflects the general trend towards equalizing the original rhythms of the older tunes, removing the last vestiges of the church modes and supplying figured basses for new and old melodies. About 290 tunes in the collection are not known from earlier sources and may be supposed to be by König; at least two of these are still sung and are known in English hymnbooks as 'Mentzer' and 'Franconia'. König's cantatas are closely related in style to those of Telemann (though Süss credited him with a distinct musical personality). His arias are generally shorter and more concise than those of the greatest masters of his time; a prominent feature of his works is the unusually large number of choruses and chorales.

WORKS

Harmonischer Lieder-Schatz, oder Allgemeines evangelisches Choral-Buch, welches die Melodien derer . . . alten als neuen . . . Gesänge . . . in sich hält . . . dergestalt verfasset . . . dass . . . mit der Orgel oder Clavier accompagnirt werden können; ferner . . . die Melodien derer

hundert und funffzig Psalmen Davids (1913 chorale melodies), 1v, bc (Frankfurt am Main, 1738, enlarged 2/c1750) [incl. c290 probably by König]
28 cantatas, D-F (for further details see MGG), incl. Ach, Jesus geht zu seiner Pein, 4vv, chorus 4vv, 2 vn, va, vle, 2 fl, 2 ob, org (attrib. Telemann in Süss), ed. A. Adrio (Berlin, 1947)
Other cantatas, F (anon., ? by König)
18 Kaiserliche Trauer- und Freudenkantaten (occasional cantatas), mostly 1740–47, music lost
March, 3 insts [? 2 ob, bn], 1728, F
Unmassgeblicher Vorschlag wie dem übel-Singen in den Frankfurther Kirchen abzuhelfen sei, 1724, F

BIBLIOGRAPHY
E. Mentzel: 'Johann Balthasar König', *Correspondenzblatt des Evangelischen Kirchengesangsvereins für Deutschland*, xxiv/4 (1904), 37
C. Valentin: *Geschichte der Musik in Frankfurt am Main vom Anfange des XIV. bis zum Anfange des XVIII. Jahrhunderts* (Frankfurt am Main, 1906/R1970)
C. Süss: 'Die Manuskripte protestantischer Kirchenmusik zu Frankfurt am Main', *Festschrift ... Rochus Freiherrn von Liliencron* (Leipzig, 1910/R1970), 350
A. Adrio: Preface to *J. B. König: Ach, Jesus geht zu seiner Pein* (Berlin, 1947)

based on *MGG* (vii, 1358–62) by permission of Bärenreiter
WALTER BLANKENBURG

König, Johann Mattheus [Matthias] (*fl* 1778–90). German composer and government official. He was active from at least 1778 as a Prussian chamber chancellor in Ellrich (near Nordhausen) and as an amateur musician. He published three lied collections to texts mainly by his friend, the poet L. F. Günther von Göckingk; König was also in contact with two literary circles (Gleim's Dichterkreis in Halberstadt and Hölty's Hainbund in Göttingen), although he set only a few of their poems. His lieder are written in the simple folklike style of the first Berlin lied school. He also wrote two Singspiels, other lieder and a few instrumental pieces.

WORKS
Singspiels: Lilla, oder Die Gärtnerin, vocal score (Berlin, 1783); Die Execution, 1790
Lieder: [60] Lieder mit Melodien (Berlin, 1778–80); Lieder verschiedenen Inhalts (H. W. Lawätz) (Altona, 1790); 3 in *D-Bds*; 1 in Sammlung verschiedener Lieder von guten Dichtern und Tonkünstlern (Nuremberg, 1780–82)
Inst: 6 Sonatines, hpd/pf (Berlin, 1784); 12 Suiten, hpd, *Bds*; Sonata, fl, vn, b, *Bds* [doubtful]

BIBLIOGRAPHY
EitnerQ; *GerberL*; *GerberNL*
M. Friedlaender: *Das deutsche Lied im 18. Jahrhundert* (Stuttgart and Berlin, 1902/R1970)
H. Becker: 'König, Johann Mattheus', *MGG*
RAYMOND A. BARR

König, Johann Ulrich von (*b* Esslingen, Swabia, 8 Oct 1688; *d* Dresden, 14 March 1744). German poet, dramatist and librettist. He attended the Stuttgart Gymnasium and subsequently studied theology at Tübingen and law at Heidelberg. After being secretary and private tutor to a young nobleman travelling to Brabant, he settled in Hamburg in 1710. Here he rapidly achieved a leading position in the direction of the opera and began a fruitful career as librettist to many prominent German composers, including Keiser, Melchior Hoffmann, Telemann and, at Brunswick, G. C. Schürmann and C. H. Graun. He became closely associated with Brockes and Richey with whom he founded the Teutschübende Gesellschaft. In April 1716 he left Hamburg and went first to Leipzig and then to Weissenfels. In 1720 he accepted the position of court poet and private secretary at the Dresden court. He was elected a member of the Berlin Academy of Sciences in 1729, and in 1730 returned to Hamburg. In 1735, having re-established himself at the Dresden

court, he was made director of court ceremonies and court librarian. He was ennobled by the Saxon King in 1740.

König occupies an important position in the history of German opera for, as the list of settings of his opera librettos proves, he was highly respected by composers as a poet and dramatist. Mattheson, in his *Critica musica* (1722–3), extolled König as an 'incomparable poet'. Although several 19th-century writers on German opera condemned him as the untalented creator of tasteless and bombastic Baroque texts, he was, in fact, a gifted experimenter who sought to revitalize the German language and its poetry. Many of his librettos are translated and adapted from French and Italian texts, a not unusual practice for early 18th-century German opera. He subscribed to the taste of the time by retaining large numbers of arias in Italian, which created the curious mixture of languages to be found in the works of Keiser, Telemann and Schürmann. While his librettos rely on many characteristic dramatic stereotypes of the early 18th century and depend heavily on the conventions of stage decoration, machines and ballets, they are often models of straightforward, uncomplicated plot development, excelling in comedy, and with a realistic, natural and frequently folklike language. König also wrote many sacred texts including the Passion oratorio *Der zum Tode verurteilte und gecreuzigte Jesus*, which with the Brockes Passion is one of the most important oratorio texts of the 18th century.

WRITINGS
(only those relating to music)

LIBRETTOS FOR STAGE WORKS
Each libretto is followed by its first composer and year of first performance; all were performed at Hamburg unless otherwise stated; most were published.

Operas: *Die entdeckte Verstellung, oder Die geheime Liebe der Diana* (after F. Lemene: *Endimione*, 1693), R. Keiser, 1712, rev. as *Der sich rächende Cupido*, Keiser, 1724; *Die österreichische Grossmuth, oder Carolus V*, Keiser, 1712; *Die wieder-hergestellte Ruh, oder Die gekrönte Tapferkeit des Heraclius*, Keiser, 1712; *L'inganno fedele, oder Der getreue Betrug*, Keiser, 1714, abridged as *Die gekrönte Tugend*, Coronation of George I of England, 1714; *Rhea Sylvia*, M. Hoffmann, Leipzig, 1714; *Fredegunda* (after F. Silvani: *Fredegonda*, 1705), Keiser, 1715; *Die römische Grossmuth, oder, Calpurnia* (after G. Braccioli: *Calfurnia*, 1713), J. D. Heinichen, 1716; *Die durch Verachtung erlangte Gegen-Liebe, oder Zoroaster* (doubtful), Leipzig, 1717
Heinrich der Vogler, Hertzog zu Braunschweig, pt.i, G. C. Schürmann, Brunswick, 1718; *Die getreue Alceste* (after Quinault: *Alceste, ou Le triomphe d'Alcide*, 1688), Schürmann, Brunswick, 1719; *Cadmus* (trans. from Italian), J. P. Kuntze, Brunswick, 1720; *Der gedultige Socrates* (after N. Minato: *La pazienza di Socrate*, 1680), G. P. Telemann, 1721; *Heinrich der Vogler, Hertzog zu Braunschweig*, pt.ii, Schürmann, Brunswick, 1721; *Sancio, oder Die siegende Grossmuth* (after Silvani: *Il miglior d'ogni amore per il peggior d'ogni odio*, 1703), Telemann, 1727; *Die in ihrer Unschuld siegende Sinilde* (after Silvani: *Il miglior d'ogni amore per il peggior d'ogni odio*, 1703), G. H. Graun, Brunswick, 1727
Serenades: *Die gekrönte Würdigkeit*, Keiser, 1711; *Die frolockende Themse auf das höchsterfreulichster Krönungs-Fest ... Georg Ludewigs, Königs von Gross-Brittannien*, J. Mattheson, 1714; *Der Triumph des Friedens*, Keiser, 1715; *Keusche Liebe, bey dem Vietund Mohrmannischen Hochzeit-Feste*, Mattheson, 1715; *Die über die Entfernung Triumphirende Beständigkeit, bey dem Mentzer- und Wincklerischen Hochzeit-Feste*, Mattheson, 1717; *Der beglückte Zeit-wechsel*, ?Schürmann, Wolfenbüttel, 1726; *Das neu-beglückte Sachsen*, for the birthday of a prince, ?Telemann, 1730, perf. as prol to Sancio (see operas), also perf. with Herr Fähndrich Nothdurft, 1731; *Herr Fähndrich Nothdurft* (after *Melissa schernita*, 1709), ?Telemann, 1730, perf. as epilogue to Sancio (see operas), also perf. with Das neu-beglückte Sachsen, 1731

SACRED TEXTS
Each work is followed by its first composer, and place and year of first performance where known.

Tränen unter dem Kreuze Jesu, 1711, rev. as *Die gekreuzigte Liebe*, Hamburg, 1731; *Thränen und Seufzer des geängsteten Zions, aus den Klageliedern Jeremiae; Abendlied eines verfolgten Christen; Brautmesse, aus dem 23. Psalm* (oratorio), Keiser; *Brautmesse: die geistliche Vermählung der Seele mit Christo, nach Anleitung des hohen Liedes Salomons* (oratorio), Keiser, text pr. in *Theatralische, Geistliche, Vermischte und Galante Gedichte* (Hamburg and Leipzig, 1713) (see 'Other Writings'); *Die Vermählung der Klugheit mit der Tugend* (cantata), Hamburg, 1714; *Der königliche Prophete David als ein Fürbild unsers Heilandes* (*Davidische Oratorien; Die siegende David*) (oratorio), Telemann, Frankfurt, 1718; *Der willige Todesgesang des Herrn Jesu*, Hamburg; *Der zum Tode verurteilte und gecreuzigte Jesus*, Keiser, 1715, sections pubd as *Auserlesene Soliloquia* (Hamburg, 1714) and *Seelige Erlösungs-Gedancken* (Hamburg, 1715); *Die göttliche Vorsorge über alle Creaturen*, Mattheson, Hamburg, 1718

OTHER WRITINGS

Theatralische, Geistliche, Vermischte und Galante Gedichte (Hamburg and Leipzig, 1713) [incl. *Brautmesse: die geistliche Vermählung der Seele mit Christo*, see 'Sacred Texts']
'Untersuchung von dem guten Geschmack in der Dicht- und Redekunst', *R. von Canitz: Gedichte*, ed. J. U. von König (Dresden, 1727), suppl.
'Von der Vergleichung des Numerus in der Dichtkunst und Musik', *J. von Besser: Werke*, ed. J. U. von König (Leipzig, 1732), suppl.

BIBLIOGRAPHY

H. C. Wolff: *Die Barockoper in Hamburg* (Wolfenbüttel, 1957)
D. I. Lindberg: *Literary Aspects of German Baroque Opera: History, Theory and Practice* (diss., U. of California, Los Angeles, 1964)

GEORGE J. BUELOW

Königsberg (Russ. Kaliningrad). Until April 1945, the main city of the German province of East Prussia; after World War II it was renamed Kaliningrad, becoming part of the USSR in 1946. The name Königsberg originally designated a monastic castle (1255) on the river Pregel, and from 1286 also the settlement that grew up under its protection, which developed as three towns (Altstadt, Löbenicht and Kneiphof), unified in 1724. In 1525 the monastic settlement became the site of a princely court, that of the margraves of Brandenburg until 1603, and subsequently that of the electors of Brandenburg, who ruled until 1701, when Berlin became capital of Prussia.

Königsberg's remote geographical position did not prevent close cultural contact with the German Empire and other parts of Europe; the influence of the Netherlands style of Lassus and Sweelinck, of the English lute song, of Italian monody and the French *air de cour* is more apparent than in many less remote German towns and residences. Close musical connections naturally existed with Poland, too. In the 18th century, secular music flourished in Königsberg, and C. P. E. Bach and his contemporaries found an enlightened audience there. The philosophical revolution of the later 18th century was led by men born, educated or working in Königsberg: Kant, Hamann, Herder, and the writers on music J. F. Reichardt and E. T. A. Hoffmann.

Among the musical institutions of the city the three churches were the most consistently important. The cathedral already had a fine organ in the mid-15th century, and in 1587 a very large new one was installed; Heinrich Albert was organist from 1631 to 1651. The office of Kantor at the cathedral school was an esteemed position, held by such men as Johann Stobaeus and Günter Schwenkenbecher (1682–1714), as was that of the Altstadt church, held by Jonas Zornicht, Johann Weichmann, Conrad Matthaei and Georg Riedel. The growth of the Königsberg Hofkapelle is closely connected with that of the large and skilled trumpet ensemble which was a prominent feature of the town's musical life around 1525. From about 1540 the office of Hofkapellmeister was permanently established; eminent among them were Johannes Eccard (1586–1608),

Stobaeus (1627–46) and Johann Sebastiani (1661–83). Together with Albert, these figures constituted the 'Preussische Tonschule', devoting themselves chiefly to the genre of the lied, of which they composed numerous examples, generally in a serious vein. Among the resident princes, the 16th-century Margrave Albrecht was renowned as a patron and friend of musicians; this is demonstrated by his correspondence with Senfl and others, his collection of music, and the Lutheran hymns that he wrote. His successors Margrave Georg Friedrich (1578–86) and Elector Johann Sigismund (1611–19) had particularly magnificent court music at their disposal; the former brought his own orchestra from Ansbach, and the latter employed additional musicians from England.

Other important musicians employed by the Hofkapelle in the 16th century were Adrianus Petit Coclico (1547) and the trumpeters and composers Johann and Paul Kugelmann. In the 17th century the Kantors of the Altstadt church, Christoph Kaldenbach (from 1639) and Weichmann (1647–52), were important for the development of German song. Among musicians who visited Königsberg in the 16th century were the lutenists Bálint Bakfark and Matthäus Waissel, and, around 1600, the versatile Valentin Haussmann.

The Hofkapelle was disbanded in 1707, but in the course of the 17th century musical activity had become largely confined to such civic occasions as weddings, funerals and academic festivals. In the 18th century the musical life of the city was characterized by amateur concerts; in 1755 a theatre was built, although it did not have its own orchestra until 1793. Important figures of this period were the cathedral Kantor Schwenkenbecher and the Altstadt Kantor Riedel, who set to music the entire Gospel according to St Matthew, the Psalms of David and the book of Revelation.

In the 19th century Königsberg continued to maintain wide musical connections: the Kapellmeister F. E. Sobolewski corresponded with Schumann; Wagner worked at the theatre for a brief period in 1836–7; the university conferred an honorary doctorate on Liszt on 14 April 1842 (probably, however, recognizing him more as a virtuoso than as a composer); and Brahms visited the town in April 1880. Other visiting musicians were Zelter (1810), Joachim (1872), von Bülow (1890) and Busoni (1896). Otto Nicolai was born in Königsberg in 1810. Musical societies flourished, including the Singverein (1818), the Liedertafel (1824) and the Philharmonische Gesellschaft (1838). A champion of 'New Music' in Königsberg was the writer, critic and teacher Louis Köhler (1849–86), whose pupils included Adolf Jensen and Hermann Goetz. Leading conductors of the opera were Dorn (1828–9), Sobolewski (1847–53) and Max Stägemann (1875–9).

In the 20th century the critic Erwin Kroll was active in Königsberg (1924–34) and attempted to 'convert the Brahms city . . . into a Pfitzner city' (see Kroll, p.221); the Band für Neue Tonkunst, founded on 10 February 1919 and later associated with Hermann Scherchen, also encouraged contemporary composers. Prominent conductors of the early part of the century were Max Brode (*d* 1917), Ernst Wendel and Paul Scheinpflug.

The Königsberg University, founded by Albrecht in 1544 and later known as the 'Albertina', played an important part in the musical history of the city through its teaching of music and its use of music for academic ceremonies. In 1546 Thomas Horner edited a work on composition, *De ratione componendi*, for use in academic instruction, and at the beginning of the 19th century C. H. Saemann gave lectures on the history and theory of music. From 1922 musicology was taught.

Polyphonic music was first printed in Königsberg by Johann Daubmann in the mid-16th century; a century later Paschen Mense and Johann Reussner were the leading music printers. The most important library in the city was the Königliche und Universitätsbibliothek zu Königsberg in Preussen, which had the large music collection of F. A. Gotthold (*d* 1858), of which only a small portion now remains.

BIBLIOGRAPHY

A. Mayer-Reinach: 'Zur Geschichte der Königsberger Hofkapelle in den Jahren 1578–1720', *SIMG*, vi (1904–5), 32–79
G. Küsel: *Beiträge zur Geschichte der Stadt Königsberg* (Königsberg, 1923)
H. Güttler: *Königsbergs Musikkultur im 18. Jahrhundert* (Königsberg, 1925)
E. Loge: *Eine Messen- und Motettenhandschrift des Kantors M. Krüger aus der Musikbibliothek Herzog Albrechts von Preussen* (Königsberg, 1931)
M. Federmann: *Musik und Musikpflege zur Zeit Herzog Albrechts: Zur Geschichte der Hofkapelle in der Jahren 1525–1578* (Kassel, 1932)
H.-P. Kosack: *Geschichte der Laute und Lautenmusik in Preussen* (Kassel, 1935)
H. Engel: 'Königsberg', *MGG*
L. Finscher: 'Beiträge zur Geschichte der Königsberger Hofkapelle', *Musik des Ostens*, i (1962), 165
M. Ruhnke: *Beiträge zu einer Geschichte der deutschen Hofmusikkollegien im 16. Jahrhundert* (Berlin, 1963), 138ff
W. Schwarz: 'Von Musik und Musikern im deutschen Osten: Nach unveröffentlichten Briefen an R. Schumann aus den Jahren 1834–1854', *Norddeutsche und nordeuropäische Musik: Kiel 1963*, 120
F. Gause: *Die Geschichte der Stadt Königsberg*, i–iii (Cologne, 1965–71)
E. Kroll: *Musikstadt Königsberg: Geschichte und Erinnerung* (Freiburg and Zurich, 1966)
M. Geck: *Die Wiederentdeckung der Matthäuspassion im 19. Jahrhundert* (Regensburg, 1967), 107f
W. Braun: 'Mitteldeutsche Quellen der Musiksammlung Gotthold in Königsberg', *Musik des Ostens*, v (1969), 84
O. Besch: 'Erinnerung an das Königsberger Musikleben von 1900–1940', *Jb des Albertus-Universität zu Königsberg/Preussen*, xxi (1971), 435

WERNER BRAUN

Königslöw, Johann Wilhelm Cornelius von (*b* Hamburg, 16 March 1745; *d* Lübeck, 14 May 1833). German organist and composer. He first studied the piano and singing with his father Johann Christoph Burchard von Königslöw, a music teacher in Hamburg. At the age of 13 he went to Lübeck as a boy soprano in the Abendmusiken directed by the organist at the Marienkirche, A. C. Kunzen, with whom he also studied the organ, violin, composition and, perhaps, the cello. Königslöw became Kunzen's assistant (1772), then his successor as organist (1781). From 1773 he was a leading figure in Lübeck's concert life, continuing the Abendmusiken, conducting Good Friday concerts, promoting amateur concerts, performing in chamber music and organ concerts, founding a choral society and directing a series of subscription concerts of large-scale choral works by Beethoven, Graun, Handel, Homilius, Mozart and Rolle.

Most of Königslöw's compositions are oratorio-like works written for the Abendmusiken. They are firmly within the Classical tradition; apart from fugal treatment of the choral parts in passages with biblical verse and frequent tone-painting effects in the manner of Haydn, the part-writing is generally homophonic and the music is infused with Mozartian cantabile. Of less importance are his few works for orchestra and keyboard.

WORKS

(*MSS, mostly in D-LÜh*)

Oratorio, Davids Klage am Hermon, 1793; 3 cantatas, Musik fürs Gymnasium, 1779, Kirchenmusik am Neujahrstage, Johannismusik; [60] Fugen für Freunde und Liebhaber des Orgelspiels, vols.ii–v; Introduction und Fuge, G, org; Fuge, C, org; Introduction und Fuge, d, 2 org

(*lost*)

Oratorios: Des jungen Tobias Verheirathung, 1781; Die Zuhausekunft des jungen Tobias, 1782; Saras Ankunft bey Tobias, 1783; Joseph, 1784; Davids Thronbesteigung, 1785; Jojada, der Hohepriester, 1786; Esther, 1787; Der geborene Weltheiland, 1788; Die eherne Schlange, 1789; Tod, Auferstehung und Gericht, 1790; Petrus, 1791; Paulus, 1792, collab. M. A. Bauck; Saul und David im Kriege, 1800

Michaelismusik, cantata, 1801–2
Inst: Ov, orch; hpd conc., 1781; [60] Fugen für Freunde und Liebhaber des Orgelspiels, vol. i

BIBLIOGRAPHY

GerberNL
A. Schering: *Geschichte des Oratoriums* (Leipzig, 1911/*R*1966)
H. W. Stahl: *Die Lübecker Abendmusiken* (Lübeck, 1937)
J. Hennings and H. W. Stahl: *Musikgeschichte Lübecks* (Kassel and Basle, 1951–2)

GEORG KARSTÄDT

Königsperger, Marianus [Johann Erhard] (*b* Roding, nr. Regensburg, 4 Dec 1708; *d* Prüfening, nr. Regensburg, 9 Oct 1769). German composer. The son of an instrument maker, he went to the Benedictine abbey of Prüfening as a choirboy. His talent for music proved so great that he abandoned the study of theology in its favour; having entered the Benedictine order, he became organist and choirmaster at Prüfening in 1734, a post he retained for the rest of his life. On entering Prüfening he took the name Marianus, renouncing his baptismal names Johann Erhard which he never used in connection with his musical activities. From 1740 until his death he produced a steady stream of publications, most of which were church music, but which also included symphonies and keyboard pieces. With the considerable profits from the sale of nearly 40 publications Königsperger was able to finance not only the building of a new choir organ for Prüfening, but also the improvement of the main organ, the purchase of books for the abbey library and the publication of scholarly works by his fellow monks.

Königsperger was one of the most popular and prolific composers of his generation in south Germany, and his music had a very wide circulation. The Augsburg publisher J. J. Lotter, who issued most of his works, described them as the foundation stone of his firm's prosperity. Königsperger was said to have done more than any other composer to improve musical standards in Bavarian village churches. His popularity seems to have been widespread and unusually long-lasting; the last of Lotter's printed music catalogues, of 1820, lists a *Missa pastoritia* of his, when the church music of his contemporaries had long been out of print. He also had a considerable local reputation as an organist.

Königsperger belongs to the second generation of composers to write in the 18th-century Bavarian church style. This style, to be found in countless publications of liturgical music for parish choirs with limited resources, was largely developed by J. V. Rathgeber in his publications of 1721–36. Its chief characteristics were compactness combined with liturgical propriety, tunefulness, non-contrapuntal choral writing and simple solo parts. The normal scoring was solo SATB, chorus, two violins and basso continuo, with optional trumpets and drums. By the mid-1740s the style was beginning to develop in two directions. Some composers began to write more elaborate music, for well-equipped churches; those more concerned with the average parish church simplified the style even further. In much of his music Königsperger seemed uncertain which of these lines to follow, and in many ways his earliest publications, in which his style is most homogeneous, are his best. The vesper psalms op.5 show his gift for writing good, broad melodies for chorus as well as soloists, and for applying ritornello principles to a through-composed psalm setting. In his psalms of 1750 the melodic gift is less conspicuous, the sense of form and balance less assured. Expansive settings of the first few verses are often followed by a dull, perfunctory *alla breve* tutti, in which the different voices sing different words simultaneously; he made comparatively little use of ritornello techniques, and the touches of word-painting occasionally to be found in the 1743 psalms are absent.

In his masses the dichotomy between the two styles is particularly clear. In his op.15 set (1750) he followed the general trend towards greater sectionalization of the Gloria and Credo; the choral sections are short, and often dull, while the solos are usually fully developed da capo arias which make considerable demands on the singers' techniques. The same is true of a much later publication of masses, op.23 (1764), but here the divergence in style is even wider, the solos being more difficult, the choruses relying increasingly on fast repeated chords. After *c*1750, his style seems to have changed little. In these later psalms and in many of his smaller liturgical works, such as offertories, he made little or no use of the principle of solo–tutti alternation that was an important feature of the Bavarian church style in its early days and which he himself employed at the beginning of his career. On the one hand, his offertories op.12 (1748) are entirely chordal, in a four-part homophonic style of little melodic interest; on the other, the cantatas and offertories op.22 (1763) each consist of a long, difficult aria, followed by a short chorus (which the composer said may be omitted).

Little of Königsperger's secular music survives. His preludes and fugues on the eight tones suggest that he was a competent contrapuntist, but had little sense of form in instrumental music; they also indicate an interest in chromatic harmony, rare in his works for the church. His enormous reputation as a composer may have been unjustified, yet his music appears to have satisfied public demand, and it is clear that Königsperger was outstanding among south German composers who wrote for parish churches.

WORKS

(printed works published in Augsburg unless otherwise stated)

SACRED

Odeum sacrum, sive 33 cantilenae sacrae, 1v, 2 vn, org, op.1a (1733)

Decachordon sive 10 missae solemnes, quibus accesserunt . . . 2 missae pastoritiae, una cum hymno Veni Sancte Spiritus, 4vv, 2 vn, 2 tpt/hn and timp ad lib, bc, op.1b (Regensburg, 1740)

Philomela suaviter . . . 8 offertoria, 4vv, 2 vn, 2 tpt/hn ad lib, bc, op.2 (Regensburg, 1741)

Threnodia Davidica et Mariana, seu psalmus Miserere et planctus Stabat mater . . . 4vv, 2 vn, 2 hn ad lib, bc, op.3 (1743)

6 liturgiae canorae sive 6 missae praemissis 10 solemnioribus additae, 4vv, 2 vn, 2 tpt/hn and timp ad lib, bc, op.4 (1743)

Sacrificium vespertinum, 4vv, 2 vn, 2 tpt/hn and timp ad lib, bc, op.5 (1743)

Sacrae ruris deliciae, seu 6 missae rurales . . . 2 missae de requiem, 2vv, other vv ad lib, 2 tpt ad lib, vc, org, op.6 (1744)

Mariale lauretanum, complectens 6 solemnes lytanias, 4vv, 2 vn, va, 2 tpt/hn ad lib, bc, op.7 (1744)

Cymbala benesonantia, 17 offertoria, 4vv, 2 vn, 2 tpt/hn ad lib, vc, org, op.8 (1744)

Cymbala jubilationis, sive 6 missae solemniores cum . . . Te Deum, 4vv,

2 vn, va, 2 tpt/hn and timp ad lib, bc, op.10 (1747)

Luctus Marianus . . . sive 6 Stabat mater, 4vv, 2 vn, bc, op.11 (1748)

Eucharisticon complectens 4 offertoria de Ss Sacramento, 8 . . . Pange lingua, 1 offertorium . . . 1 aria de passione domini, 1 . . . Te Deum, 4vv, 2 vn, va, 2 tpt/hn and timp ad lib, bc, op.12 (1748)

Sacra ruris laetitia, sive vesperae rurales, continens omnes psalmos per annum . . . antiphonae de BVM, 2vv, other vv, 2 vn, 2 tpt and timp ad lib, vc, org, op.13 (1749)

Cythara Davidica qua psalmi vespertini, 1. pro festis Domini et dominica, 2. de BV Maria, 3. de sanctis apostolis, una cum 4 antiphonis de BVM stylo breviori . . . 4vv, 2 vn, 2 tpt/hn and timp ad lib, bc, op.14 (1750)

Jubilatio lyturgica . . . sive 6 missae solemniores cum hymno Veni Sancte Spiritus, 4vv, 2 vn, 2 tpt/hn and timp ad lib, bc, op.15 (1750)

Echo Marialis lauretani resonans 6 lytaniis solemnibus de BVM, 4vv, 2 vn, 2 tpt/hn and timp ad lib, bc, op.17 (1753)

Alauda Mariana 6 lytanias rurales et 4 arias laetis modulis, 2vv, other vv ad lib, 2 vn, 2 tpt and timp ad lib, vc, org, op.19 (1755)

Lessus ecclesiae in 2 missis de requiem et 2 Libera, 4vv, 2 vn, 2 tpt ad lib, vc, org, op.20 (1756)

Laudetur Jesus Christus sive offertorium, 4vv, 2 vn, 2 tpt/hn ad lib, vc, org (1756)

Offertorium duplicis textus, 4vv, 2 vn, vc, org (1757)

Sacrificium matutinum 6 missis solemnibus, 4vv, 2 vn, 2 tpt/hn and timp ad lib, bc, op.21 (1760)

Philomela benedictina sive 10 cantate de BVM, communi sanctorum et pro omni tempore, 4vv, 2 vn, va, 2 tpt/hn ad lib, vc, bc, op.22 (1763)

Oliva plena fructifera . . . constans 6 missis solemnibus, quarum ultima de requiem, 4vv, 2 vn, va, 2 tpt/hn and timp ad lib, bc, op.23 (1764)

VI missae solemnes quarum ultima de requiem, 4vv, 2 vn, va, 2 tpt/hn and timp ad lib, bc (1764)

Psaltes vespertinus . . . seu 2 Vesperae de dominica cum psalmis de BVM . . . quibus accedunt 4 antiphonae Marianae, 4vv, 2 vn, 2 tpt/hn and timp ad lib, bc, op.24 (1767)

Sabbathum requietionis . . . seu 2 missae . . . cum offertoriis duobus . . . una cum Te Deum, 4vv, 2 vn, 2 tpt/hn and timp ad lib, bc (org), op.25 (1767)

Il Vesperae de dominica cum psalmis de BVM . . . IV antiphonae Mariae, 4vv, 2 vn, 2 tpt/hn and timp ad lib, bc (1767)

Missa pastoritia . . . 4vv, 2 vn, 2 tpt, timp, vc, org (1769)

[III Vesperae. . .IV antiphonae], 4vv, 2 vn, org (n.p., n.d.)

SECULAR

Chordae corda trahentes, seu 12 sonatae concertantes pro missis solemnibus, vn obbl, 2 vn, va, bc, op.9 (1745)

Cibus sapidus. . .seu 10 symphoniae, 2 vn, va, 2 tpt and timp ad lib, org, op.16 (1751)

Certamen musicum complectens 6 concerta communia et 2 pastoritia, org, 2 vn, va, 2 tpt/hn and vc ad lib, op.18 (1754)

Praeambulum cum fuga [I to VIII] toni facili methodo elaboratum (1752–6, repr. 1776)

Der wohl-unterwiesene Clavier-Schüler [preludes, versets, arias], kbd (1755)

Finger-Streit oder Clavier-Übung durch ein Praeambulum und Fugen, kbd (1760)

Many Singspiels and instrumental works, lost

BIBLIOGRAPHY

P. U. Kornmuller: 'Die Pflege der Musik im Benediktiner-Orden', *Studien und Mitteilungen zur Geschichte des Benediktiner-Ordens*, ii/4 (1881), 200

E. von Werra: 'Beiträge zur Geschichte des katholischen Orgelspiels', *KJb*, xxii (1897), 32

O. Ursprung: *Die katholische Kirchenmusik*, HMw, ix (1931/*R*)

G. Frotscher: *Geschichte des Orgel-Spiels und der Orgel-Komposition* (Berlin, 1935–6, enlarged 3/1966)

K. G. Fellerer: *Geschichte der katholischen Kirchenmusik*, i (Düsseldorf, 2/1949), ii (Kassel, 1976)

F. Zwickler: *Frater Marianus Königsperger OSB (1708–1769): ein Beitrag zur süddeutschen Kirchenmusik des 18. Jahrhunderts* (diss., U. of Mainz, 1964)

ELIZABETH ROCHE

Konink [Koninck, Kooninck, Coning, Cooninck, Koning etc], **Servaas de** (*d* Amsterdam, between 9 Dec 1717 and 28 Feb 1718). Netherlands composer. He seems to have spent his whole life at Amsterdam, where he was a teacher and a member of the theatre orchestra. Like Hendrik Anders (who edited his *Hollandsche minne- en drink-liedern*), he played a significant part in the development of opera in the Dutch language. One Dutch opera, *De vrijadje van Cloris en Roosje* (1688), to

a libretto by Dirk Buysero, was so successful from both
a musical and a literary standpoint that according to
Scheurleer it was the forerunner of an important series
of similar works. Konink's reputation was not merely
local: some of his motets were published at Venice
during his lifetime, and copies of his other works
reached England and Germany.

The characteristics of Konink's music have been
clearly distinguished (Noske), in particular his use of the
French, Lullian style for vocal works and the Italian for
instrumental ones; his masterpiece is the incidental
music for Racine's *Athalie*, composed for a girls'
boarding-school at Amsterdam, incorporating many
beautiful effects obtained by simple means (choruses,
largely unison, with two instruments and continuo, and
solo music with continuo only). The mood is serious and
stately, and minor keys predominate. This same
restrained manner characterizes his motets. Konink
may be placed among the most significant Netherlands
composers of his time, as a leading representative of the
dignified, cosmopolitan style prevalent at Amsterdam at
the end of the 17th century.

WORKS

DRAMATIC

De vrijadje van Cloris en Roosje (opera, D. Buysero) (Amsterdam,
1688), music lost
Athalie (incidental music, Racine) (Amsterdam, 1697)
Pastorale (A. Alewijn), Amsterdam, 1699, music lost

VOCAL

Sacrarum armoniarum flores, 2–4vv, 2 insts, op.7 (Venice, n.d.)
Hollandsche minne- en drink-liedern, 1–3vv, insts, bc (Amsterdam,
n.d.) [corrected by H. Anders]
Motet fragments: Descendite de coelo, O quam jucunda, Stupete novum
sidus, Succurite veloces, Surge mentes: *GB-Lcm*
Airs etc, pubd in K. Sweerts, Mengelzangen en Zinnebeelden
(Amsterdam, c1695), c1695[13], 1697[4], 1697[5]

INSTRUMENTAL

Trios, fl, vn, ob, op.1 (Amsterdam, 1696)
Trios, fl, ob, vn, op.4 (Amsterdam, c1700)
Hollantsche Schouburgh, en plugge dansen vermengelt met sanghe
airen, seer bequaem om op alle instrumenten gespeelt te kunnen
werden (Amsterdam, n.d.)
XII Sonates, fl/vn/ob, bc, printed (Amsterdam, n.d.)
2 ouvertures à 4, 1700; Intrada à 3, 1700: *D-W*
Trios, opp.3 and 5; XII Sonates, 2 fl/vn, op.7: cited by Eitner

BIBLIOGRAPHY

EitnerQ; *FétisB*; *RiemannL 12*
D. F. Scheurleer: 'Het muziekleven', *Amsterdam in de zeventiende eeuw*,
iii (The Hague, 1897–1904)
E. H. Meyer: 'Die Vorherrschaft der Instrumental-Musik im niederländischen Barock', *TVNM*, xv/4 (1939), 58, 264
F. Noske: 'Une partition hollandaise d'Athalie (1697)', *Mélanges d'histoire et d'esthétique musicale offerts à Paul-Marie Masson*, ii (Paris,
1955), 105
——: 'Konink, Servaas de', *MGG*

PHILIPPE MERCIER

Koninklijke Vlaamse Opera (Flemish: 'Royal Flemish
Opera'). Company founded in ANTWERP in 1893; it was
known simply as the Vlaamse Opera until 1920.

Konitz, Lee (*b* Chicago, 13 Oct 1927). American jazz
saxophonist. After early experience with Jerry Wald he
joined Claude Thornhill in 1947 and worked briefly with
Miles Davis in 1948. He had already become closely
associated with the pianist Lennie Tristano, and it was
under Tristano's influence that his style developed,
although they made few public appearances together.
After a Scandinavian tour in November 1951, he joined
Stan Kenton the following summer, staying with the
band until late 1953. From 1954, when he formed a
quartet, he often led his own small bands, occasionally
taking part in tours abroad. He has also been active as a
teacher.

In an era dominated by Charlie Parker, Konitz successfully forged an alternative style for the alto saxophone. One of his early recordings, *Tautology* (1949),
shows the tension he could engender by combining lines
of complex harmonic implication with a near-metrono-
mic rhythmic basis, the whole executed with an austere,
incisive tone. He later broadened his expressive range,
favouring a more relaxed delivery and occasionally in-
flecting his tone. *Motion* (1961), an album featuring the
drummer Elvin Jones, was an interesting departure in
rhythmic terms, but the LP *Spirits* (1971), which
includes fascinating duets with the pianist Sal Mosca,
presents a more concentrated blend of harmonic and
rhythmic complexity and stands as a summation of his
mature powers.

BIBLIOGRAPHY

M. Harrison and M. James: 'Lee Konitz: a Dialogue', *Jazz Review*, iii
(1960), July, 10
D. Heckman: 'Lee Konitz', *Jazz Review*, iii (1960), Jan, 28
M. James: *10 Modern Jazzmen* (London, 1960), 49ff
I. Gitler: *Jazz Masters of the 40s* (New York, 1966), 226–61
M. James: 'Lee Konitz', *Jazz on Record*, ed. A. McCarthy (London,
1968), 169
L. Goddet: 'Lee Konitz', *Jazz Hot*, xxxviii (1972), Dec, 28; (1974),
July–Aug, 7
A. Morgan: 'Lee Konitz', *Modern Jazz: the Essential Records*, ed. M.
Harrison (London, 1975), 57
J. Delmas: 'Tristano et ses fils', *Jazz Hot*, xli (1976), March, 6; April, 6
MICHAEL JAMES

Konjović, Petar (*b* Čurug, 5 May 1883; *d* Belgrade, 1
Oct 1970). Yugoslav composer and writer on music.
After attending the Sombor Teachers' Training College
he went to the Prague Conservatory, where he completed his studies under Stecker in 1906. Until World
War I he worked as a music teacher and choirmaster in
Zemun and Belgrade. He returned to Sombor during the
war, and in 1917 he moved to Zagreb where, for the
first time, his music was heard in public at a concert
devoted to his works. It was also in Zagreb that his first
opera, *Ženidba Miloševa* ('Miloš's wedding', 1917), had
its première. At that time he wrote on music and the
theatre for various Yugoslav periodicals. He was appointed director of the Zagreb Opera (1921–6), where
he also conducted and produced; thereafter he directed
the national theatres in various provincial towns (1927–
33) and then that in Zagreb (1933–9). From 1939 he
lived in Belgrade, where he was a professor at the
academy of music (1939–50) and twice rector. He was
elected to full membership of the Serbian Academy in
1946, and was founder-director of its musicological
institute (1948–54). In addition, he was made a foreign
member of the Czechoslovak Academy of Sciences and
Arts in 1938.

Konjović's Prague studies had a decisive influence on
his music: acquaintance with the work of Smetana,
Novák and 'The Five' contributed to his determined
orientation towards folk music, a source which he
regarded as a 'fertilizer' of art music; he rejected any
suggestion of a cosmopolitan musical style. Following
Janáček, he consistently drew melodies from the intonation of the spoken language. In the operas that followed
the Weberian *Miloš's Wedding* he adopted the symphonic music drama form, together with what he described as 'realistic expressive recitatives'. The best of
these later operas, *Koštana*, is a powerful psychological
study, taking up south Serbian folk motifs in a style

of luxurious orchestral brilliance and great melodic richness. As with many of his works, he revised *Koštana* several times, and in 1935 made an independent 'symphonic triptych', highly various in rhythm and mood. Konjović's songs include 100 Yugoslav folksong arrangements collected as *Moja zemlja* ('My country') and a set of 24 original songs, *Lirika*, which show an impressionist treatment of voice and piano, and also a characteristically Serbian oriental feeling. His numerous choral pieces combine a modern harmonic style with an effort to create music in a popular spirit. Despite the range of influence to which he was open, there is always strong individuality in Konjović's work. He brought a new depth and contemporary awareness to Serbian music.

WORKS
(selective list)

Operas: Ženidba Miloševa [Miloš's wedding], 1917, rev. 1922; Knez od Zete [Duke of Zeta], 1929, rev. 1946; Koštana (after B. Stanković), 1931, rev. 1940, rev. 1948; Seljaci [Peasants], 1952; Otadžbina [Homeland], 1960

Orch: Serbia liberata, sym. poem, 1906; Sym., c, 1907, rev. D. Jakšić, 1955; Na selu [In the country], sym. variations, 1915, rev. 1935; Koštana, sym. triptych, 1935; Jadranski capriccio [Adriatic capriccio], vn, orch, 1937; Makar Čudra, sym. poem, 1946; 3 psalma, str, 1964

Vocal: Moja zemlja [My country], 100 folksong arrs., 1v, pf, n.d.; Lirika, 24 songs, 1v, pf, n.d.; 20 choral pieces

Chamber: 2 str qts; San letnje noći [A midsummer night's dream], suite, wind qnt; pf and vn pieces

Principal publishers: Edition Slave, Napredak, Prosveta, Srpska Akademija Nauka i Umetnosti, Udruženje Kompozitora Srbije

WRITINGS

Ličnosti [Personalities] (Zagreb, 1920)
Knjiga o muzici srpskoj i slovenskoj (Novi Sad, 1947)
Miloje Milojević (Belgrade, 1954)
Stevan Mokranjac (Belgrade, 1956)
Ogledi o muzici [Essays on music] (Belgrade, 1965)

BIBLIOGRAPHY

M. Milojević: *Muzičke studije i članci* (Belgrade, 1933)
P. Milošević: 'Petar Konjović', *Zvuk* (1933), no.2
Special issues of *Zvuk* (1963), no.58 and *Pro musica* (1968), no.37
N. Mosusova: 'O "Koštani" Petra Konjovića', *Arti musices*, ii (1971)
Spomenica posvećena preminulom akademiku Petru Konjoviću (Belgrade, 1971)

STANA ĐURIĆ-KLAJN

Konrad von Würzburg [Würzburc; Meyster Conrat von Wertzeburc] (*b* Würzburg, between 1220 and 1230; *d* Basle, 31 Aug 1287). German Minnesinger. He was of bourgeois origin, and after a thorough education he became an itinerant musician, later settling in Basle and Strasbourg; he was probably the first Minnesinger to earn his living from writing, and counted patricians, noblemen and ecclesiastical lords among his patrons. His work shows him to be the most individual poetic figure from the second half of the 13th century and suggests that his knowledge of Latin and his understanding of theology and the law were considerable. Although he was in the direct line of descent from the classic courtly poetry of Gotfrid von Strassburg, Konrad managed to develop a style that was terse in its language but at the same time exhibited a wealth of images, similes and learned arabesques. His virtuoso poetic talent, brilliant formal skill and masterly originality of formulation transcend the transitional era in which he lived.

Konrad's massive output, totalling some 85,000 lines and including all poetic genres, survives in many manuscripts. This suggests that educated society took a lively interest in his thematic range. He seems also to have had a profound effect on later generations of poets and particularly the Meistersinger who numbered him

among their 12 *alte Meister*. His lyric poetry comprises nine summer songs, nine winter songs, two dawn songs, a sacred Leich and a secular Leich (*Tanzleich*) as well as numerous *Sprüche* (*see* SPRUCH). There is also a long allegorical poem *Die Klage der Kunst* and the epics *Engelhard* (after a Latin source), *Partonopier und Meliur* and *Buoch von Troye* (unfinished); but his real strength was in the minor epic, especially the *Versnovelle*: *Herzmaere*, *Otte mit dem Barte*, *Schwanritter* and *Der Welt Lohn*. His hymn to the Virgin, *Die goldene Schmeide*, represents the culmination of the florid style.

The music for his poetry raises many questions of authenticity: the only early source for a melody by Konrad (in the Jena manuscript, *D-Ju* E1.f.101) contains music for the 'Hofton' which is only very distantly related to that in the source containing most surviving Konrad melodies (the 15th-century Colmar manuscript, *D-Mbs* cgm 4997). The survival of so much music for a 13th-century poet in a manuscript of 200 years later represents an extreme case of the fundamental problem in German song transmission: the poetic form is Konrad's, but probably not the music even though it is implicitly ascribed to him. The single melody in the Jena manuscript is much more florid and formally free than those in the Colmar manuscript.

WORKS

Editions: *Kleinere Dichtungen Konrads von Würzburg*, ed. E. Schröder, iii (Berlin, 1926, 2/1959) [standard complete text edn.]
       Die Sangesweisen der Colmarer Handschrift, ed. P. Runge (Leipzig, 1896/*R*1965) [R]
       Das Singebuch des Adam Puschman, ed. G. Münzer (Leipzig, 1906/*R*1970) [M]
       The Art of the Minnesinger, ed. R. J. Taylor (Cardiff, 1968) [T]

EARLY MELODY

'Hofton' with text Der nît sîn Vahs vil tunkel verwet, Jena MS (*D-Ju* E1.f.101), f.101, ascribed 'Meyster Conrat von Wertzeburc'; T i, 36

MELODIES IN MEISTERSINGER MSS
(late and therefore of dubious authenticity)

'Hofton' with text Waz in dem Paradys ie wart, *Mbs* cgm 4997 (Colmar MS), f.531, ascribed 'In Cunrads von Wirczburg Hoff Don'; cf different melodies in *Ju* and *PL-WRu* 356 (lost: Adam Puschman's *Singebuch*), no.63; R 128, M 63, T i, 37

'Abgespitzter Ton', with text Aus der Dieffe schrei ich zu dir; M 64

'Aspislied' with text Hoffart ist worden also gross, *D-Mbs* cgm 4997, f.506, ascribed 'In meinster Cunrades von Wirczburg Auspis', ? for text An Liuten hât diu Gotes Kraft; R 126, T i, 34

'Morgenweise' with text Ave Maria, kusche Maget stete, *D-Mbs* cgm 4997, f.512, ascribed 'In Cunradz von Wirczburg Morgenwyse', ? for text Wart ie bezzer iht vür ungemelet; R 126, T i, 35

MELODIES CONSIDERED SPURIOUS

'Blauer Ton' with text Er mac vil lîhte Witze hân, *D-Mbs* cgm 4997, f.541v, ascribed 'In Meinster Cunratz von Wirczeburg blawen Ton' but in *PL-WRu* 356 to Regenbogen; R 129, M 45, T i, 116

'Goldene Reihen' with text Wolûff ir Geist, hin über Mêr, *D-Mbs* cgm 4997, f.43, ascribed 'Meinster Cunrads guldin Reyel'; R 27, T i, 117

'Kurzer Ton' or 'Werder Ton' with text Dez soltû clein geniessen, *Mbs* cgm 4997, f.528, ascribed 'In Conratz von Wirtzburg kurczen oder im werden Don' [but the same Ton appears in *HEu* 392 ascribed 'In dem freyen Don Erenpots von Rein']; R 128, T i, 115

'Nachtweise' with text Avê, ich lob dich, reine Meit, *Mbs* cgm 4997, f.526, ascribed 'In Conrads von Wirczburg Nachtwyse; *alii dicunt esse* in Frider von Suneburg sussem Don'; R 127, T i, 115

BIBLIOGRAPHY

P. Gereke: *Textkritisches und Metrisches zu den Dichtungen Konrads von Würzburg*, Beiträge zur Geschichte der deutschen Sprache und Literatur, xxxvii–xxxviii (Halle, 1912–13)
K. H. Halbach: *Gottfried von Strassburg und Konrad von Würzburg: 'Klassik' und 'Barock' im 13. Jahrhundert*, Tübinger germanistische Arbeiten, xii (Tübingen, 1930)
E. Hartl: 'Konrad von Würzburg', *Die deutsche Literatur des Mittelalters: Verfasserlexikon*, ed. W. Stammler, ii (Berlin, 1936)
R. J. Taylor: *The Art of the Minnesinger* (Cardiff, 1968)
For further bibliography *see* MINNESANG.

BURKHARD KIPPENBERG

Konstantin. *See* PSELLUS, MICHAEL.

Konstanz [Constance]. City in the southern Federal
German Republic. Konstanz stands on the site of a
Roman fort, Constantia (*c*300 AD), named after
Emperor Constantius Chlorus. In the 6th century it
became the bishop's see of the largest German diocese,
and in 1192 the emperor raised it to a Freie Reichsstadt.
When the city joined the followers of Zwingli it was
outlawed by Emperor Charles V, and in 1548 was annexed to Austria. During the Napoleonic wars
Konstanz fell to Baden (1805), and with the dissolution
of its bishopric (1821) diminished in importance. In the
20th century industry developed in the area and a university was established, and the city again flourished.

The early medieval liturgical music of Konstanz was
probably influenced by the neighbouring Benedictine
monasteries of St Gall and Reichenau. Around 1300 the
Minnesang flourished; the Weingartner Liederhandschrift, one of the most important sources of Minnesang,
is believed to have been written in Konstanz. The
Church Council, held in Konstanz in 1414–18,
brought musicians to the city from all parts of Europe.
Episcopal, municipal and travelling minstrels played a
large part in the musical life of the medieval city. In the
early 16th century Emperor Maximilian I visited there
frequently; his musical entourage included such eminent
musicians as Isaac and Hofhaimer. In 1508, on one
such visit, Isaac was commissioned by the cathedral
chapter to compose the cycles of the Mass Propers that
appear in the second volume of the *Choralis con-
stantinus.*

During the Reformation the Konstanz reformers
Johannes Zwick and Ambrosius Blarer, with others,
published the *Nüw gsangbüchle.* Hans Kotter, a pupil of
Hofhaimer, went to Konstanz as a teacher in 1538, but
after a few months returned to Berne.

For many centuries the cathedral was the centre of
the city's musical life. The building was begun in
Romanesque style in the 11th century, and was completed in the 16th century in Gothic style. An organ was
installed in 1120–34, and the new instrument built by
Hans Schenker in 1517–20 was one of the largest of its
time; its Renaissance case survives. The provision of
choral music was originally the duty of the canons; after
the end of communal life in the mid-12th century the
task fell to the succentors. In the early 16th century the
cathedral choir consisted of nine succentors and eight
boys, and was one of the leading pre-Reformation vocal
groups in Germany. Outstanding members included
Johannes Martini in the late 15th century, and, in the
early 16th century, the composers Johannes Taiglin,
Virdung, Wolfgang Lausser, Sixt Dietrich and Siess.
Hans Buchner, a pupil of Hofhaimer, was an eminent
organist there (1512–26).

With the spread of the Reformation the bishop, cathedral chapter and many of the clergy left the city. The
cathedral choir moved to Überlingen in 1527, to
Radolfzell in 1542, finally returning to Konstanz in
1549. At the end of the 16th century, following the
decisions of the Council of Trent, the Roman breviary
was introduced. Outstanding succentors in the late 16th
century were Herpol and Geisenhof; in the 17th century
the Kapellmeisters Spiegler, Megerle, Banwart,
Steingaden and Galley were also composers, as were C.
B. Tschudi and J. A. Omlin in the 18th century. The

*Maximilian I's Hofkapelle in Konstanz cathedral: minia-
ture from 'Luzerner Bilderchronik', 1513, by Diebold
Schilling (CH-Lz S.23, f.233v)*

Kapellmeister frequently held the post of organist as
well. In the second half of the 17th century instruments
were increasingly used, and by the 18th century the
concertante style predominated in church music. The
dissolution of the bishopric of Konstanz resulted in the
disbanding of the cathedral choir (1827).

Monasteries and collegiate churches were important
centres of music in Konstanz. The Benedictine monastery of Petershausen, founded by 983, possessed an
organ before 1159. In the 17th and 18th centuries the
composers Bernard Rauchenstein, Petrus Peterle,
Alfons Albertin and Aemilian Kayser were active there.
The Capuchin monastery employed such composers as
Laurentius von Schnüffis and Theobaldus in the 17th
century, and Constantin Steingaden worked at the
Franciscan monastery. During the Baroque era the
Jesuits, who had gone to Konstanz in 1592, were influential through their presentation of musical dramas,
meditations and dialogues. The musical repertory of the
collegiate and parish church of St Stephen is typical of
sacred music of the period 1750–1850; its collection
of prints and manuscripts is one of the largest in south-
west Germany, containing sacred music of Joseph and
Michael Haydn, Mozart and Rosetti. After the dissolution of the Jesuit college in 1775, the Gymnasium
became a theatre, and travelling companies performed
operas, melodramas, operettas and plays there. In 1852
the theatre was taken over by the city; in 1949 Henze
was engaged as musical director of the ballet, but in the
following year musical productions ceased.

Konstanz's regimental band, augmented by both

amateur and professional musicians, gave symphony concerts in the 19th and early 20th centuries. Since 1932 the city has had its own orchestra, originally the Städtisches Orchester, and subsequently the Bodensee-Symphonie-Orchester (also known as the Südwestdeutsche Philharmonie). Of the city's choirs the Konstanzer Oratorienchor is outstanding; it originated in the Fidelia choral society, founded in 1842 and later known as the Bürgerverein Bodan. In 1950 an annual festival was founded, the Internationalen Musiktage Konstanz, which has brought internationally known orchestras, chamber ensembles and soloists to Konstanz.

Music printers in Konstanz have included Leonhard Straub the elder and Nikolaus Kalt (c1600); Jakob Straub, Johann Geng, David Hautt, Franz Straub and J. A. Köberle (17th century); and Leonhard Parcus (early 18th century). The city's organ builders include Anton Neuknecht (c1600), Michael Schnitzer (17th century), Elias Köberlin (c1700), J. M. Bihler (18th century), Melchior Reindl and Gottfried Maucher (c1800); in the 19th century, Benedict Grieser, Peter Nägeli and F. X. Hieber built organs and pianos in Konstanz. Violin makers of the 18th and 19th centuries include Joseph Wagner, Rudolf Abel and Conrad Nägeli.

BIBLIOGRAPHY

O. zur Nedden: 'Zur Musikgeschichte von Konstanz um 1500', *ZMw*, xii (1929–30), 449

——: *Quellen und Studien zur oberrheinischen Musikgeschichte im 15. und 16. Jahrhundert* (Kassel, 1931)

W. Salmen: 'Der Spielmannsverkehr im spätmittelalterlichen Konstanz', *Zeitschrift für die Geschichte des Oberrheins*, cvi (1958), 176

M. Schuler: 'Die Konstanzer Domkantorei um 1500', 'Der Personalstatus der Konstanzer Domkantorei um 1500', *AMw*, xxi (1964), 23, 255

——: 'Die Musik in Konstanz während des Konzils 1414–1418', *AcM*, xxxviii (1966), 150

——: 'Das Noteninventar der Kollegiat- und Pfarrkirche St. Stephan in Konstanz', *KJb*, lviii–lix (1974–5), 85

MANFRED SCHULER

Kont, Paul (*b* Vienna, 19 Aug 1920). Austrian composer. He studied the violin and piano at the Musikschule in Vienna (1938–9). During the years 1940–45 he sketched many compositions which were completed later and then attended the Vienna Music Academy (1945–8), studying composition with Lechthaler and conducting with Krips and Swarowsky. As a private pipil of Polnauer he was trained in Webernian methods of analysis and in 1952 he studied in Paris with Milhaud, Honegger and Messiaen. From that time he appeared frequently as a pianist and conductor in performances of his music. In the early 1950s he began to use 12-note methods: his triptych *Op.61* was designed to reflect his serial technique in its thesis-antithesis-synthesis structure. He received the Austrian State Prize in 1964 for *Traumleben* and has published *Antianorganikum: Beobachtungen zur neuen Musik* (Vienna, 1967).

WORKS
(selective list)

STAGE

Abälard und Heloise, Kammertanzspiel, 1951; Indische Legende, szenische Kantate, Austrian radio, 1951, stage version, Vienna, 1954; Annoncen, Kammertanzspiel, Vienna, 1956; Daphnis und Chloe, Kammertanzspiel, 1957; George und Frédéric, Kammertanzspiel, 1957; Der traurige Jäger, Kammertanzspiel, Vienna, 1958; Peter und Susanne oder die österreichische Schwermut (G. Frisch), Austrian television, 1959; Lysistrate (opera, after Aristophanes), Dresden, 1961; Traumleben (musical fairytale, J. Mauthe, after Grillparzer), Salzburg, 1963

Celestina, totales Theater, Cologne, 1966; Inzwischen, Mysterienspiel, Austrian television, 1967; Italia passata, Kammertanzspiel, Vienna, 1967; Der Sturm (stage melodrama, after Shakespeare), Vienna, 1968; Libussa, opera, 1969; Migof, choreographische Symphonie, Cologne, 1970

OTHER WORKS

Orch: Komplex E, 1956; Conc. des enfants, pf, small orch, 1958; Vc Conc., 1961; Str Sym. with Quodlibet, 1969; Conc. à la gloire de J. Ph. Rameau, 1969; Conc., brass, str, 1969; Conc. and Concertino, chamber orch, 1970; Partita, D, chamber orch, 1973; 4 kleine Symphonien, 1973; Der Raucher, vc, str, 1973; Kurzkonzert, cl, orch, 1973; 3 ernste Stücke, str, 1975; Divertimento, tpt, small orch, 1966–76

Chamber: Vn Sonata, 1947; Ww Qt, 1947; Trio, fl, vc, harp, 1948; Divertimento, str trio, 1949; Wind Qt, 1953; Op.61, 1967: Serenata a 3 in maniera materiale, fl, vn, vc; Concerto lirico in maniera pura, fl, cl, str trio; Septett in gemischter manier, fl. cl, bn, str trio, db; Diwan, pf, 1973; Duo, 2 bn, 1973; Tänze, pf, 1975; Trip, pf, 1975

Lieder, choral music, piano music, film scores

Principal publisher: Doblinger

BIBLIOGRAPHY

W. Szmolyan: 'Paul Kont', *ÖMz*, xix (1964), 591

R. Klein: 'Paul Konts Vision einer neuen Tonalität', *ÖMz*, xxvi (1971), 253

JOSEPH CLARK

Kontakion [kondakion] (Gk.: 'scroll'). A liturgical form belonging to the Byzantine Hours, originally exclusively to Matins (Ōrthros), at which it is sung immediately after the sixth ode of the KANŌN. A kontakion consists of an initial strophe, the prooimion or koukoulion, followed by some 18 to 30 strophes, the oikoi. The oikoi of a kontakion have a common metrical structure which differs from that of the prooimion.

As a form, the kontakion originated in Syria, and it is reminiscent of the poetry of St Ephraem. It may be described as a poetic homily. Its content is narrative and dramatic, and has influenced later Byzantine poetry greatly. According to legend, the Blessed Virgin Mary gave to the famous 6th-century melode Romanos a scroll on which he was divinely inspired to write his Christmas kontakion, *Hē parthenos sēmeron*. In the 6th century the kontakion was introduced into the Byzantine Hours, and not until two or three hundred years later did the new hymnodic form of the kanōn replace the kontakion and reduce the latter to its prooimion and first oikos.

While the kontakion in its full form still dominated Matins, it was recited in a simple manner. As a homily, it had to be easily understood. The people took over the refrain common to the prooimion and the oikoi of the same kontakion with great effect, as the refrain underlines the main theme of the hymn. Thus, from a theological point of view, the amputation of the many oikoi spoilt one of the most fascinating texts of the Byzantine rite. In return, the two remaining strophes were subject to melodic elaboration and became the showpiece of the solo singer, the psaltēs, as reflected in his special book, the psaltikon, of which the kontakia form the major contents. There are, however, good reasons for believing that the melismatic melodies of the kontakia derive from syllable patterns which are no longer known to us.

The classical collection of kontakion melodies covers the whole ecclesiastical year. There are two melodic traditions: one an older, short form; and the other a more recent, long form. These two differ from each other to a greater extent than the shorter and longer traditions of the allēlouïarion (*see* ALLELUIA). As an example of the short kontakion tradition, the first two lines of the prooimion of the Christmas kontakion are

Ex.1

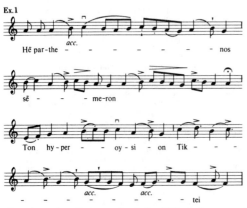

given in ex.1 as they appear in the 13th-century manuscript *I-Rvat* Ashb.64.

The festival hymn *Hē parthenos sēmeron* is similar to the famous akathistos hymn of the Annunciation of the Virgin Mary. Many manuscripts give all the oikoi of the akathistos with neumes, and the performance of this highly elaborate hymn must have lasted at least an hour. As to their melodic structure, the kontakia use almost the same material as the allēlouïarion melodies, especially the initial motifs and the cadences. This fact shows either that the kontakia depend on the allēlouïarion tradition or that the two types developed from the same simple text recitation. But while the allēlouïarion melodies afford the best example of centonization within the Byzantine repertory, the principle dominating the kontakion melodies may be better characterized as 'melody type' (as defined by Ferretti), the cadence being the principal element.

Structurally the prooimion does not differ from the oikos. Both are divided into lines which correspond to a restricted number of melody types. Most of them occur in all modes. The common kontakion tradition may be exemplified by the kontakion for All Saints (the Sunday after Pentecost). Ex.2 gives the first line of the oikos.

Ex.2

The intermodal character of the kontakion melodies has important consequences. All the eight modes are represented. However, the 1st and 3rd modes include very few melodies, and with the exception of the Christmas kontakion in the 3rd mode quoted above they are without any character of their own. There is, in fact, not sufficient melodic material for eight modes among the kontakion melodies. The tonal system tends to be a system of conjunct tetrachords, and this takes the form of either a 'low' system (ex.3a) or a 'high' one (ex.3b). This system is apparent both from an analysis of formulae and cadences that have the same interval struc-

ture but are pitched a 4th apart, and also from an analysis of the so-called 'wrong' medial signatures (i.e. signatures that seem to indicate an abnormal pitch). The ordinary melodic neumes of Byzantine notation do not show absolute pitches but rather the relative steps upwards or downwards in the Byzantine tonal system. As a result, it was common for Byzantine scribes to insert medial or reference signatures at cadence points in a melody. These generally serve to confirm the pitch reached at such a point. However, occasionally a medial signature marked an unexpected indication: D may be indicated at a point where the melody apparently stands on E; or F where the melody ostensibly stands on G. This is generally taken to mean a temporary 'transposition' of the normal diatonic system. Thus the D signature on the pitch E would cause the tetrachord E–F♯–G–A (the D tetrachord transposed up a tone) to be used in the passage following in place of E–F–G–A; similarly, an F signature on pitch G would cause an F♯ to be used below the G (E–F transposed up a tone) in place of F.

Ex.3(a)

(b)

While the psaltikon is the melody book of the soloist, the psaltēs, the asmatikon is the choirbook of a psaltēs group. In many cases the psaltikon manuscripts include part of the asmatikon repertory (a completely different style). The Byzantine sources reveal that a part of the psaltikon repertory, the hypakoai, occurs in an asmatikon version too. Furthermore, the Slavonic manuscripts from the same period as the Byzantine sources give asmatikon counterparts of the kontakia. Only the prooimia are delivered in this choral recension – possibly a relic of a practice by which the psaltēs choir sang the prooimion while one psaltēs performed the oikoi. The notation of the Slavonic manuscripts remains problematic. At any rate the kontakion melodies of this tradition seem to be less melismatic.

BIBLIOGRAPHY

P. Ferretti: *Estetica gregoriana*, i (Rome, 1934; Fr. trans., 1938), 106ff

C. Høeg, ed.: *Contacarium Ashburnhamense*, MMB, main ser., iv (1956) [incl. important introduction, pp.11ff]

E. Wellesz: *The Akathistos Hymn*, MMB, *Transcripta*, ix (1957)

A. Bugge, ed.: *Contacarium palaeoslavicum mosquense*, MMB, main ser., vi (1960)

F. Constantin: 'Das Kontakion', *Deutsche Vierteljahrsschrift für Literaturwissenschaft und Geistesgeschichte*, xxiv (1960), 84

C. Thodberg: *The Tonal System of the Kontakarium: Studies in Byzantine Psaltikon Style*, Kongelige danske videnskabernes selskab, historisk-filosofiske meddelelser, xxxvii/7 (1960)

K. Levy: 'An Early Chant for Romanus' "Contacium trium puerorum"', *Classica et mediaevalia*, xxii (1961), 172

——: 'A Hymn for Thursday in Holy Week', *JAMS*, xvi (1963), 127–75

H. Husmann: 'Modalitätsprobleme des psaltischen Stils', *AMw*, xxvii (1971), 43–72

CHRISTIAN THODBERG

Kontarsky, Alfons (*b* Iserlohn, 9 Oct 1932). German pianist, brother of Aloys Kontarsky. He studied at the Musikhochschule in Cologne with Else Schmitz-Gohr and Maurits Frank (1953–5) and in Hamburg with

Eduard Erdmann (1955–7). Since 1955 he has appeared widely with his brother. He held a seminar at the Darmstadt summer courses from 1962 to 1969, when he became responsible for a master class at the Cologne Musikhochschule. His *Pro musica nova: Studien zum Spielen neuer Musik für Klavier* (Cologne, 1973) contains original contributions by leading contemporary composers. In the mid-1960s he became rather more involved with classical music and in 1971 formed a trio with Saschko Gawriloff and Klaus Storck.

BIBLIOGRAPHY

R. Lück: *Werkstattgespräche mit Interpreten neuer Musik* (Cologne, 1971), 63ff [with discography]

RUDOLF LÜCK

Kontarsky, Aloys (*b* Iserlohn, 14 May 1931). German pianist, brother of Alfons Kontarsky. He studied at the Musikhochschule in Cologne with Else Schmitz-Gohr and Maurits Frank (1952–5) and in Hamburg with Eduard Erdmann (1955–7). In 1955 he and his brother won the first prize for piano duo at the Munich Radio International Festival. Since then the two able and adventurous musicians have been giving concerts together throughout the world and have won an international reputation, predominantly in contemporary music. Their repertory includes Mozart, Reger and Debussy, and they have given many first performances of works by Berio, Brown, Bussotti, de Grandis, Gielen, Kagel, Pousseur, Stockhausen and Zimmermann. At Darmstadt in 1966 Kontarsky gave the first complete performance of Stockhausen's *Klavierstücke I–XI*, which he also recorded and played frequently with great aplomb and precision. Known as an unorthodox interpreter of avant-garde music, he has taken part in many performances with Stockhausen's ensemble, and in the mid-1960s formed a duo with the cellist Siegfried Palm. In 1960 he began taking a seminar at the Darmstadt summer courses and in 1969 he became responsible for a master class at the Cologne Musikhochschule.

WRITINGS

'Notation für Klavier', *Darmstädter Beiträge für neue Musik*, ix (1955), 92

with Alfons Kontarsky: 'A quatre mains', *Begegnungen mit Eduard Erdmann*, ed. C. Bitter and M. Schlösser (Darmstadt, 1968), 209

BIBLIOGRAPHY

R. Lück: *Werkstattgespräche mit Interpreten neuer Musik* (Cologne, 1971), 73ff [with discography]

RUDOLF LÜCK

Kontopetrēs [Kontopetris], **Geōrgios**. Byzantine composer and *domestikos* who contributed to the AKOLOUTHIAI.

Kontrabass (Ger.). (1) DOUBLE BASS.

(2) A military and brass-band instrument; *see* BASS (iii).

Kontrafagott (Ger.). DOUBLE BASSOON.

Kontrapunkt (Ger.). COUNTERPOINT.

Kontretanz. *See* CONTREDANSE.

Kontski, de. *See* KĄTSKI family.

Konwitschny, Franz (*b* Fulnek, Northern Moravia, 14 Aug 1901; *d* Belgrade, 28 July 1962). German conductor. He was born into a family of Moravian musicians and studied at the German Musical Society's school in Brno and at the Leipzig Conservatory. While still a student he played the violin and the viola in the Leipzig Theatre Orchestra and in the Gewandhaus Orchestra (under Furtwängler). In 1925 he went to Vienna as the viola player of the Fitzner Quartet and to teach the violin and music theory at the Volkskonservatorium.

He turned to conducting in 1927, working his way up from répétiteur to chief conductor at Stuttgart (1930). He then went to Freiburg, where he was appointed musical director in 1933. He held a similar position in Frankfurt am Main from 1938 (at the Frankfurt Opera and as conductor of the Museum Concerts). Immediately after the war he worked in Hanover.

In 1949 Konwitschny was appointed conductor at the Gewandhaus in Leipzig, and he continued the great tradition of that orchestra in succession to Nikisch, Furtwängler, Walter and Abendroth. He retained this position to the end of his life, though from 1953 to 1955 he worked simultaneously as the conductor of the Dresden Staatsoper, and in 1955 was appointed musical director at the rebuilt German Staatsoper in Berlin. This placed him right at the head of East Germany's conductors.

Konwitschny's many guest appearances also won him an international reputation. In 1959 he conducted the *Ring* at Covent Garden. With the Leipzig Gewandhaus Orchestra, and the orchestras of the Berlin and Dresden Staatsopern, he travelled to the USSR, Poland, Austria, Great Britain, Japan and West Germany. He died while on a tour of Yugoslavia, during a rehearsal of Beethoven's *Missa solemnis*. He made many gramophone records.

His expansive gestures and dislike of an exact beat, as well as the markedly expressive cast of his musical personality, made him a conductor of Furtwängler's type; like Furtwängler, he was most at home with symphonic music from Beethoven to Brahms. However, his relationship with Bruckner's music had more instinctive musicianship than Furtwängler's mystically religious interpretations. He was also interested in all Slavonic music. Of Mahler's symphonies, his favourite was the Fourth. He had a special preference for the music of Reger (particularly the Mozart and the Hiller Variations). As an opera conductor he was outstanding in passionately fiery interpretations of Wagner (*Meistersinger*, *Tristan* and the *Ring* cycle), which he projected with broad dimensions and infused with great intensity. He also had a distinct affinity with the music of Richard Strauss, above all *Die Frau ohne Schatten* and the tone poems *Ein Heldenleben* and *Sinfonia domestica* (he gave notable performances at the Salzburg Festival of 1961, with the orchestra of the Dresden Staatsoper).

His natural romanticism and vital temperament drew him less to modern music; yet he repeatedly championed such contemporary composers in East Germany as Hanns Eisler, Paul Dessau (of whose *Orchestermusik 1955* he gave the first performance) and Ottmar Gerster.

BIBLIOGRAPHY

H. S. Sanders, ed.: *Vermächtnis und Verpflichtung: Festschrift für Franz Konwitschny* (Leipzig, 1961)

WOLFRAM SCHWINGER

Konya, Sandor (*b* Sarkad, 23 Sept 1923). Hungarian tenor. He studied at Budapest and, after the war, at Detmold and Milan. He made his début at Bielefeld in

1951 as Turiddu, moved in 1954 to Darmstadt and then to the Berlin Städtische Oper. His best-known role is Lohengrin, in which he made his débuts at Bayreuth in 1958, at the Metropolitan Opera in 1961 and at Covent Garden in 1963. He has sung regularly at the Metropolitan, his roles including Walther, Parsifal, Calaf, Max and Don Carlos. His clear, strong tenor lies between the lyrical and the heroic, and he is a good actor.

ALAN BLYTH

Konyus, Georgy Eduardovich (*b* Moscow, 30 Sept 1862; *d* Moscow, 29 Aug 1933). Russian musicologist and composer of French and Italian descent. He was first taught music by his father, a famous piano teacher; at the Moscow Conservatory he studied the piano with Pabst, and composition with Taneyev and Arensky. Subsequently he taught theory there (1891–9), leaving as a result of his quarrel with the director Safonov, and was professor of composition (1902–6) and director (1904–5) at the music and drama institute of the Moscow Philharmonic Society; he was also professor of composition (1902–19) and rector (1917–19) at the Saratov Conservatory, a member of the music department of the National Commissariat of Culture (1919–20) and (from 1920) professor at the Moscow Conservatory, dean of the faculty of composition (until 1929) and director of the department of analysis which he created (the first in Russia). His pupils included Skryabin, Metner, Vasilenko, Kabalevsky and Khachaturian.

Konyus's chief work was the creation and partial elaboration of an original theory of musical form, 'metrotectonism' (measured structure), which attempts to apply a sense of spacial symmetry to the temporal relationships of musical form. Konyus saw musical composition as a combination of special metrical units ('musically creative volitional statements') which in general do not coincide with the broader phrase structures; the task of analysis is to reveal these basic units (usually of different lengths) and to explain the order governing their arrangement under the one law which governs all musical styles, the 'balance of temporal values'. He rejected the traditional nomenclature for the theory of forms and often explained his analyses with sketches, reminiscent of architectural drawings. From 1922 he was head of the department of metrotectonism analysis at the State Institute of Musical Science. To popularize his theories he undertook lecture tours in Germany (1923–4) and France (1923–4, 1928–9). As a composer Konyus was representative of the Moscow school, one of the offshoots of Russian academicism of the late 19th and early 20th centuries. His works include a series of symphonic pieces, a ballet, songs and instrumental music.

WRITINGS
Sinopticheskaya tablitsa elementarnoy teorii muzïki [Synoptic table of elementary music theory] (Moscow, 1891)
Zadachnik po instrumentovke [Problems of orchestration] (Moscow, 1906–9)
Kurs kontrapunkta strogovo pis'ma v ladakh [A course of strict counterpoint in harmony] (Moscow, 1930)
Kritika traditsionnoy teorii v oblasti muzïkal'noy formï [Criticism of the traditional theory in the realm of musical form] (Moscow, 1932)
Metrotektonicheskoye issledovaniye muzïkal'noy formï [Metrotectonic research on musical form] (Moscow, 1933)
Nauchnoye obosnovaniye muzïkal'novo sintaksisa [The scientific foundation of musical syntax] (Moscow, 1935)

WORKS
(selective list)
Iz detskoy zhizni [From a child's life], op.1, suite, chorus, orch, 1891;

Kantata pamyati Alexandra III [Cantata in memory of Alexander III], op.8; Daita, op.11 (ballet, K. F. Walz, after Jap. fairy tale), 1896; Sym. Iz mira illyuziy [From the world of illusions], sym. poem, c, op.23, chorus, orch, 1902; Db Conc., op.29, 1910, unpubd; Les shumit [The forest sounds], op.30, ov, to inc. opera, after Korolenko, 1910–11

Principal publishers: Jurgenson, State Publishing House

BIBLIOGRAPHY
P. D. Krïlov: *G. E. Konyus* (Moscow, 1932)
V. Ferman: 'Pamyati G. E. Konyusa' [In memory of Konyus], *SovM* (1933), no.9, p.110
G. Golovinsky, ed.: *G. E. Konyus: stat'i, materiali, vospominaniya* [Articles, materials, reminiscences] (Moscow, 1965)
G. B. Bernandt and I. M. Yampol'sky: *Ktopisal o muzïke* [Writers on music], ii (Moscow, 1974)

L. M. BUTIR

Konzertina. (Ger.). CONCERTINA.

Konzertmeister (Ger.: 'concertmaster'). LEADER.

Konzertstück [Concertstück] (Ger.: 'concert-piece'). A work for solo instrument or instruments with orchestra, shorter than a CONCERTO and frequently in one movement (e.g. Weber's *Konzertstück* for piano and orchestra in F minor and major J 282). The term was used by many French composers for one-movement solo works with orchestra. In Germany the term is sometimes applied to works that would elsewhere be called 'concertino'.

Koole, Arend (Johannes Christiaan) (*b* Amsterdam, 22 April 1908). Dutch musicologist, conductor and pianist. He studied the piano and music theory at the Conservatory of Amsterdam and took lessons in conducting from Eduard van Beinum and Pierre Monteux. From 1933 to 1937 he studied musicology at the University of Utrecht with Smijers and graduated in 1949 with a doctoral dissertation on Locatelli. While teaching at the conservatories of Rotterdam (1938–41), Utrecht (1941–4) and Amsterdam (1946–9), he was also active as conductor and pianist. In 1945 he founded the Amsterdams Vocaal Kwartet, which specializes in unaccompanied polyphonic music. In 1949 he moved to South Africa, where he was lecturer in music at the University of the Orange Free State at Bloemfontein until 1964. He was then appointed professor of music at the University of Southern California, Los Angeles, a post he held until his retirement in 1974; he also served as visiting Fulbright professor at the University of Texas, Austin (1961–2), and Megumi Guest Professor at Kobe College, Japan (1971–2). His compositions include choral works, the ballet *De sneeuwkoningin* and incidental music for Sophocles' *Oedipus rex*.

WRITINGS
Bachs geestelijke vocale muziek (Amsterdam, 1941)
Leven en werken van Pietro Antonio Locatelli da Bergamo (diss., U. of Utrecht, 1949; Amsterdam, 1949, rev. 2/1970)
'Report on an Inquiry into the Music and Instruments of the Basutos', *IMSCR, v Utrecht 1952*, 263
Felix Mendelssohn Bartholdy (Haarlem, 1953, 2/1958)
'P. A. Locatelii', *Chigiana*, xxi (1954), 29
with A. Dunning: 'P. A. Locatelli: nieuwe bijdragen tot de kennis van zijn leven en werken', *TVNM*, xx/1–2 (1964), 52–96
EDITIONS
P. Locatelli: Opera quarta, prima parte: sei introduttioni teatrali, MMN, iv (1961)

ELLINOR BIJVOET

Kooninck, Servaas de. See KONINK, SERVAAS DE.

Kopelent, Marek (*b* Prague, 28 April 1932). Czech

composer. From 1951 to 1955 he studied composition under Řídký at the Prague Academy. He then worked as an editor of modern scores for Supraphon (1956–69). In 1969 he received a grant from the German Academy of Arts in West Berlin, and thereafter devoted his time to composition. He has been a member of the Prague New Music Group and of the Musica Viva Pragensis ensemble.

The music of Webern had a decisive influence on him when he first discovered it about 1960; his own works use serial procedures within forms and textures of great delicacy. Of Czech composers of his generation, he is one of the best-known in western Europe: his Third Quartet was performed at the 1966 ISCM Festival in Stockholm; *Snehah* received its première in Venice in 1967 and *Zátiší* was first heard at the 1968 Donaueschingen Festival.

WORKS
(selective list)

Vocal: Matka [Mother], chorus, fl, 1964; Modlitba kamene [Prayer of stone] (V. Holan), reciter, speaker, 2 chamber choruses, 3 gongs, tomtom, 1967; Snehah (oriental), S, jazz A, ens, tape, 1967; Bludný hlas [Wandering voice], actress, ens, tape, lights, film, 1970; Syllabes mouvementées, chorus, 1973; Vacillat pes meus, chorus, 1973

Inst: 4 str qts, 1954, 1955, 1963, 1967; Hommage à Vladimir Holan, 9 insts, 1965; Hra [Play], str qt, 1966; Rozjímání [Meditation], chamber orch, 1966; Bijoux de Bohème, fl, vib, hpd, 1967; Sváry [Contentions], 12 insts, orch, 1968; Zátiší [Still life], va, ens, 1968; Appassionato, pf, orch, 1970; Sonata 'Das Schweisstuch der Veronika', ens, 1973; Rondo, vor der Ankunft der liebenswürden Henker odor die dreimalige Anbetung der Hoffnung, 5 perc, 1973; A Few Minutes with an Oboist, ob, ens, 1974; Ťukáta, harp, hpd, cimb/gui, 1974; Plauderstündchen, a sax, orch, 1974–5; Capriccio, tpt, 1975; Ballade, pf, 1976

Principal publishers: Gerig, Supraphon

BIBLIOGRAPHY
ČSHS
O. Pukl: 'Marek Kopelent', *HRo*, xxiii (1970), 423
——: 'Snehah', *Konfrontace* (1970), no.4, p.19
OLDŘICH PUKL

Kopenhagene Chansonnier (*Dk-Kk* Thott 291 8°). See SOURCES, MS, §IX, 8.

Köpfer, Georges-Adam. See GOEPFERT, GEORGES-ADAM.

Kopfmotiv (Ger.). HEAD-MOTIF.

Kopfstück (Ger.). BELL (ii).

Kopïlov, Alexander Alexandrovich (*b* St Petersburg, 14 July 1854; *d* Strelna, nr. St Petersburg, 20 Feb 1911). Russian composer. He entered the court chapel in 1862, became a singing member two years later, and at the age of 12 became a soloist. During this time he studied the violin with Mayer, and was taught by Kremenetsky, who was attached to the chapel. From 1870 to 1872 he took piano lessons from Ribasov, the conductor at the Alexandrinsky Theatre. When his voice broke at the age of 18 he tried unsuccessfully to enter the St Petersburg Conservatory. But his piano teacher helped him by obtaining for him the post of violinist and pianist at the Alexandrinsky Theatre. At this time he studied harmony with Hunke. He also taught singing to the court chapel choir until 1892, replacing Rozhnov. Through his work at the chapel he met Balakirev. Kopïlov's songs (some quite attractive) may owe something to Balakirev, but some critics consider that he was more profoundly affected by Tchaikovsky. During the 1870s he took composition lessons from Lyadov and Rimsky-Korsakov. Through them he became known to Belyayev who published some of his works. Kopïlov wrote a prelude and

fugue for string quartet on B–la–F as a tribute to the Russian publisher. He composed orchestral music, several pieces for string quartet (in which his first-hand knowledge of violin technique is used to good effect), piano works and songs.

WORKS
(all published in Leipzig)

Orch: Scherzo, A, op.10; Sym., c, op.14; Concert Ov., d, op.31
Chamber: Andantino sur le thème B–la–F, str qt, op.7; Prélude et fugue sur le thème B–la–F, str qt, op.11; 4 str qts, G, op.15, F, op.23, A, op.32, C, op.33; Souvenir de Peterhof, vn, pf, op.29; Feuille d'album, vn, pf, op.45; Polka, C, for 'Les vendredis', str qt, collab. Borodin and others
Pf: 2 Mazurkas, op.3; Valse, op.6; Mazurka, op.8; Etude, op.9; 3 Fugues, op.12; 4 petits morceaux, op.13; Polka de salon sur le thème B–la–F, op.16; 4 Miniatures, op.17; 5 morceaux, op.20; 3 feuilles d'album, op.26; 2 morceaux, op.39; Musikalische Bilder aus dem Kinderleben, op.52; 2 études, op.60; 2 Mazurkas
Songs

BIBLIOGRAPHY
N. B.: 'Pamyati A. A. Kopïlova' [In memory of Kopïlov], *Narodnoye obrazovaniye* (1911), no.3, p.409
M. MONTAGU-NATHAN/JENNIFER SPENCER

Kopp, Georg (*b* ?Passau; *d* Passau, 24 Aug 1666). German composer, organist and schoolmaster. He is described as a schoolmaster in the register of deaths of the parish of St Paul, Passau. From 1637 until his death he was organist of Passau Cathedral. In 1657 he was warned by the cathedral authorities because he had composed nothing for a long time. After the great fire in the city in 1662, however, he had to 'compose music day and night for the cathedral' because its collection of music had been destroyed. His masses and other liturgical works in particular are rooted in the traditions of vocal polyphony of his time. He is particularly notable, however, for his settings of sacred texts by PROCOPIUS VON TEMPLIN, which account for all his other published music and reveal his imaginative and markedly expressive qualities as a song composer.

WORKS
(all published in Passau)

Harmonia missarum, 5, 6vv (1624)
Mariae Hülff Ehren Kräntzel, das ist himmelische Löbgesänger (1642)
Der gross-wunderthätigen Mutter Gottes Mariae Hülff Lob-Gesang, 1v, bc (org) (1659)
Eucharistiale, das ist 26 … Predigten von Fr. Procopius … mit 6 Melodien von G. Kopp, 1v, bc (1661)
Requiem, 10vv, *CS-KRa*
Benedicite omnia opera, 8vv, formerly in Breslau, Stadtbibliothek, ?*PL-WRu*
1 sonata, 2 vn, 2 va, 2 clarini, bc (org), *CS-KRa*

BIBLIOGRAPHY
W. M. Schmid: 'Zur Passauer Musikgeschichte', *ZMw*, xiii (1930–31), 289
N. Tschulik: 'Procopius von Templin und das deutsche Lied im 17. Jahrhundert', *Mf*, vi (1953), 320
A. Scharnagl: 'Geistliche Liederkomponisten des bayerischen Barock', *KJb*, xlii (1958), 81
AUGUST SCHARNAGL

Kopp, Matthaeus Adam (*fl* 1736). German composer, possibly an Augustinian monk. He was one of many south German composers who published church music for parish choirs in a simple and tuneful style, following the example of Valentin Rathgeber. His one surviving publication, *Promptuarium musico-sacrum* (Augsburg, 1736), is of interest by virtue of the unusual variety of its contents. Most contemporary liturgical publications confine themselves to one or two genres, but Kopp provided in one volume all the music which a not too ambitious parish choir would need to fulfil basic liturgical requirements: two masses, one requiem, two offertories, two litanies, two *Magnificat* and two *Salve regina* settings, all scored for four voices, two violins and organ.

ELIZABETH ROCHE

Koppel (Ger.). An ORGAN STOP (*Coppel*).

Koppel, Herman D(avid) (*b* Copenhagen, 1 Oct 1908). Danish composer and pianist of Polish parentage. The Koppels are among the foremost musical families of Denmark: Herman's younger brother Julius led the Royal Chapel Orchestra from 1939, his daughter Lone Winther became a leading soprano with the Royal Danish Opera and joined the Australian Opera in 1974, his daughter Therese studied the piano at the Copenhagen Conservatory under her father and in Paris, and became Koppel's assistant at the Conservatory, and his son Thomas is a pianist and composer, as well as the leader of the highly successful Danish rock group Savage Rose.

Herman Koppel's earliest musical impressions were received in the synagogue. He began piano studies at the age of six and became a pupil of Augusta Jürgensen at the age of ten; he began to compose while still a child. In 1926 he entered the Copenhagen Conservatory, where he studied with Bangert (music theory), Hansen (orchestration), Henrichsen (organ) and Simonsen (piano). He soon developed an abiding interest in jazz through a student friendship with Bernhard Christensen, the composer and organist. While at the conservatory Koppel attracted the attention of Nielsen, then its director, by demonstrating special skill as an accompanist for rehearsals of a Nielsen cantata. Koppel subsequently enjoyed a personal acquaintance with Nielsen and he became known as an authoritative interpreter of Nielsen's piano music. He completed the conservatory examinations in piano in 1929 and made his début as a pianist in the next year, after which he spent a year of study and travel in Berlin, London and Paris. As a recitalist he has performed throughout Scandinavia and northern Europe. He served as répétiteur for the Royal Theatre and for Danish radio in the late 1930s. Thereafter he sought practical experience through diverse employment, including performances with small ensembles and popular groups, and private teaching. In 1942 he became solo accompanist for the Tivoli Concert Hall, and in 1940 he began teaching music at the Royal Institute for the Blind, a post which he held until 1949, when he was appointed to the piano staff of the Copenhagen Conservatory. He became professor there in 1955.

From October 1943 to June 1945 Koppel and his family took refuge from the German invaders in Örebro, Sweden, where he held the title of archivist, though his work was as pianist with the Örebro SO, with which he toured Sweden as a soloist. Before his Swedish experience Koppel's style of composing, though rooted in the Nordic lyricism of Nielsen, was influenced by the music of Bartók and Stravinsky. In the early 1930s several works, including the Piano Concerto no.1, had revealed his interest in jazz. While in Sweden he produced such major works as the Third String Quartet op.38 and the Third Symphony op.39. The circumstances surrounding his flight into Sweden made a deep impression on his compositional attitudes, an impression evident in the music he wrote for the play *Niels Ebbesen*, by Kaj Munk (a martyr in the Danish underground movement), produced at the Göteborg City Theatre in 1943, and in

the score he provided for a 1944 documentary film dealing with the plight of the Danish Jews who had escaped to Sweden. Again, in 1949 he composed a major work for chorus and orchestra, *Tre-Davids-salmer* op.48, stimulated by the agony of Jewish prisoners under the Nazi regime. Vocal music had assumed only occasional importance in Koppel's output before 1949, but it now assumed importance as a medium well suited to his wish to compose to a specific purpose reflecting something of the life around him. He often chose biblical texts because of their inspirational quality. With the Fourth Piano Concerto op.69 (1960–63) and the Seventh Symphony op.70 (1960–61) he began seeking a new compositional style. He retained tonality as a basic principle, but employed serial devices within an experimentally freer tonal framework. This style has evolved to the extent that, in such a work as the Eight Variations and Epilogue op.89 for solo piano and 13 musicians (1972), he strives to present sonority and complex rhythms as primary factors, lessening the melodic and contrapuntal aspects.

WORKS
(selective list)

DRAMATIC AND ORCHESTRAL

Opera: Macbeth, op.79 (after Shakespeare), 1967–8; Copenhagen, Royal Opera, 1970
Other dramatic works: 29 film scores, 15 theatre scores, 12 radio scores
Syms.: no.1, op.5, 1929–30; no.2, op.37, 1943; no.3, op.39, 1944–5; no.4, op.42, 1946; no.5, op.60, 1955; Sinfonia breve (no.6), op.63, 1957; no.7, op.70, 1960–61
Concs.: Pf Conc. no.1, op.13, pf, chamber orch, 1931–2; Pf Conc. no.2, op.30, 1936–7; Cl Conc., op.35, 1941; Conc., op.43, vn, va, orch, 1947; Pf Conc. no.3, op.45, 1948; Vc Conc., op.56, 1952; Pf Conc. no.4, op.69, 1960–63; Ob Conc., op.82, 1970; Fl Conc., op.87, 1971

OTHER WORKS

Choral: 3 Davids-salmer, op.48, T, chorus, orch, 1949; Moses, op.76, oratorio, solo vv, chorus, orch, 1963–4; Requiem, op.78, solo vv, chorus, orch, 1965–6; Anthems (Hymns of Thanksgiving), op.93, solo vv, chorus, orch, 1974
Chamber: 5 str qts, op.2, 1928–9, op.34, 1939, op.38, 1944–5, op.77, 1964, op.95, 1975; Sextet, op.36, pf, wind, 1942; Ternio, op.53, vc, pf, 1951; Pf Qnt, op.57, 1953; Sonata, op.62, vc, pf, 1956; Variations, op.72, cl, pf, 1961; Capriccio, op.73, fl, pf, 1961; 8 Variations and Epilogue, op.89, pf, 13 insts, 1972; Divertimento, op.91, str trio, 1972; Variazione pastorale, op.94, fl, str trio, 1975; Variazione libere, op.98, 2 cl, b cl, perc, 1976
Songs: 5 Biblical Songs, op.46, 1949; 4 Love-songs, op.47, 1949; 4 Songs, op.49 (Old Testament), 1949; Psalm xlii, op.68, 1960; 3 Songs, op.96 (Bible), 1976
Pf: 10 Pieces, op.20, 1933; Suite, op.21, 1934; 2 Dances, op.31, 1937; Sonata, op.50, 1950; 15 Miniatures, op.97, 1976

Principal publishers: Hansen, Imudico, Leduc, Samfundet til Udgivelse af Dansk Musik, Skandinavisk

BIBLIOGRAPHY

G. Heerup: 'Herman D. Koppels 4. Symfoni, op.42', *Dansk musik-tidsskrift*, xxii (1947), 12
H. D. Koppel: 'Tradition og fornyelse', *Nordisk musikkultur* (1952)
——: 'Davids-salmer', *Modern nordisk musik*, ed. I. Bengtsson (Stockholm, 1957), 137
J. Müller-Marein and H. Reinhardt, eds.: *Musikalske selvportraetter* (Hamburg, 1963), 148ff
G. Colding-Jørgensen: 'Koppels "Macbeth"', *Dansk musiktidsskrift*, xliv (1969), 111
'Koppel, Herman D.', *Kraks blå bog* (Copenhagen, 1974), 582

WILLIAM H. REYNOLDS

Koppelung [Kopplung, Oktavkoppelung] (Ger.: 'coupling'). (1) In Schenkerian analysis (*see* ANALYSIS, §III) the linking of two registers an octave apart in order to distribute melodic or bass movement between two octaves or to reinforce movement in the prevailing or 'obligatory' register (*see* OBLIGATE LAGE) in another octave. In Variation 1 of the last movement of Beethoven's Piano Sonata op.109, for instance, the melodic line is centred on *b''* and the descent *b''–a''–g♯''*

in bars 9–11 is reinforced by the same progression 'coupled' to it an octave lower, as shown in ex.1; the g♯″ in the lower octave in fact gets more emphasis in bars 11–12, so that when the descent is repeated in bars 15–16 there is a sense of return to the higher octave rather

Ex.1 Beethoven: Sonata in E major op.109, 3rd movt, Var. 1

than mere emphasis of the first g♯″. As *Koppelung* involves the linking of octave registers, it is closely related to the Schenkerian concepts of HÖHERLEGUNG, the raising of a melody or bass line into a higher octave, and its counterpart TIEFERLEGUNG.

(2) A COUPLER on an organ (also *Koppel*).

WILLIAM DRABKIN

Kopřiva. Czech family of musicians.

(1) **Václav Jan Kopřiva** (*b* Brloh, nr. Citoliby, 8 Feb 1708; *d* Citoliby, 7 June 1789). Composer, organist and schoolmaster. His compositions are often found under the name Urtica (a Latin translation of the Czech word Kopřiva, meaning 'nettle'). He studied music under M. A. Kalina at Citoliby, and at Prague was an organ pupil of F. J. Dollhopf, organist of the Crusaders' Church. He was then cantor and organist at Citoliby (from 1730; definitive appointment as cantor in 1742) and Louny (1733–4). He was also secretary to Count Ernest Karl Pachta, the owner of Citoliby, at least for some time (c1754–6). In 1777 he tried to obtain a post as cantor at Louny; although he was recommended as an outstanding musician, he did not gain the post and remained in Citoliby until his death. Outstanding among his pupils were J. A. Gallina, J. Vent, J. Lokaj and his two sons.

WORKS

Principal sources: *CS-Bm*, Citoliby Church, *K, KU*, Louny, *ME, Pnm, SO*

Missa pastoralis, D [Lat. with interposed sections of Cz. text]; Sacrum pastorale integrum [Christmas mass]
Te Deum, D; Alma Redemptoris mater, D
2 offertories [Vox clamantis, In omnem terram]; 2 pastoral offertories, D, A
Litanies, C, D, E♭, A, B♭

(2) **Jan Jáchym Kopřiva** (*b* Citoliby, 17 March 1754; *d* Citoliby, 17 Aug 1792). Composer, son of (1) Václav Jan Kopřiva. He studied music with his father and succeeded him as cantor at Citoliby in 1778; in 1785 he also became church organist there as successor to his brother (3) Karel Blažej. He also taught music to Count Pachta's family. His only extant works are three masses, two *missa brevis* settings and an aria for alto (all in *CS-Pnm*).

(3) **Karel Blažej Kopřiva** (*b* Citoliby, 9 Feb 1756; *d* Citoliby, 15 May 1785). Composer and organist, son of

(1) Václav Jan Kopřiva. After studying the organ and composition (first with his father, later in Prague with J. F. N. Seger), he became church organist at Citoliby. He also taught keyboard instruments and composition. His first known work, a Requiem in C minor, was performed at Klatovy on 22 May 1774. He suffered from tuberculosis and died at 29.

The three Kopřivas were the outstanding members of a ramified Czech musical family. Thanks to their activity, and in accordance with the artistic interests of Count Ernest Karl Pachta (who had an orchestra of his own), the little village of Citoliby became a unique centre of musical life in northern Bohemia at that period. Whereas (1) Václav Jan and (2) Jan Jáchym adhered to the traditional type of Czech village music of the late Baroque and pre-Classical period, (3) Karel Blažej used an advanced Classical idiom of Mozartian character. His style is markedly individual and very expressive, with abundant chromaticism. He was also well schooled in counterpoint and his fugues are among the most remarkable of their kind in Czech organ music of the second half of the 18th century. A virtuoso organist himself, he usually treated the organ part of his church compositions in concertante manner. The demanding, florid solo parts in his vocal works are evidence of the high quality of provincial performers in Bohemia at the time.

WORKS

Principal sources: Citoliby Church, Louny, *CS-Pnm, SO*

SACRED VOCAL

4 Missa solemnis, E♭, E, F, B♭; 4 masses, C, c, e, E♭; Missa brevis, C, Requiem, c
Motets: Veni sponsa Christi, D, 4vv, ob, orch; Gloria Deo, D; Dictamina mea, D
Arias: 2 for S, B♭, E♭; Amoenitate vocum, S, chorus; Quod pia voce cano, B
Salve Regina, F

INSTRUMENTAL

Org fugues and preludes, incl.: Fugue, f, ed. C. F. Pitsch, *Museum für Orgelspieler* (Prague, 1832–4), also ed. in *Ecole classique de l'orgue*, xiii (Paris, 1900), and in MAB, xii (1953); Fugue, A♭, ed. C. F. Pitsch, *Museum für Orgelspieler* (Prague, 1832–4), also ed. in *Ecole classique de l'orgue*, xiii (Paris, 1900); Fughetta, G, 'nach Haendel', ed. C. F. Pitsch, *Museum für Orgelspieler* (Prague, 1832–4); Fuga pastorella, C; Fuga supra cognomen Debefe, d; Fugue, a: all 3 ed. in *Organistae bohemici* (Prague, 1970)
Concerto, E♭, org [1 of orig. set of 8]
12 syms., lost

BIBLIOGRAPHY

ČSHS; *EitnerQ*
G. J. Dlabacz: 'Versuch eines Verzeichnisses der vorzüglichern Tonkünstler in oder aus Böhmen', *Materialien zur alten und neuen Statistik von Böhmen*, xii, ed. J. A. Riegger (Leipzig and Prague, 1794), 248
——: *Allgemeines historisches Künstler-Lexikon* (Prague, 1815), ii, 107; iii, 314
C. von Wurzbach: *Biographisches Lexikon des Kaiserthums Oesterreich*, xii (Vienna, 1864), 445f
A. Hnilička: 'Z archivalií o hudebnících rodu Kopřivů' [Archival resources relating to musicians of the Kopřiva family], *Dalibor*, xxxvii (1920–21), 53
J. Němeček: *Nástin české hudby xviii. století* [Outline of Czech music in the 18th century] (Prague, 1955)
Letter of J. J. Kopřiva to B. J. Dlabač, 13 Jan 1788, pubd by R. Mužiková, *MMC* (1957), no.3, p.42
Z. Šesták: *Hudba citolibských mistrů 18.století* [Music of the Citoliby masters of the 18th century] (Prague, 1968) [disc notes]
——: Monograph on K. B. Kopřiva and Music at Citoliby (in preparation)

MILAN POŠTOLKA

Kopytman, Mark (*b* Kamenets-Podolsk, 6 Dec 1929). Israeli composer and musicologist of Ukrainian origin. He studied simultaneously at the music college and the medical institute in Chernovitsy, graduating from the former in 1950 and from the latter, as doctor of medicine, in 1952. His higher studies were with Simovitz at the L'vov Academy of Music (1952–5) and with Bogatïryov at the Moscow Conservatory (1955–8, PhD 1958). He immediately entered on a teaching career, becoming lecturer in theory and composition at the Moldavian State Academy of Music (1962–72) and at the same time guest doctorate-instructor at the Leningrad Conservatory. In 1972 he moved to Israel, and in 1973 was appointed to teach theory and composition at the Rubin Academy, Jerusalem. Since his move he has gradually abandoned the Russian school, to which his adherence was never strong, and produced works with a tendency towards aleatory writing and graphic notation.

WORKS
(selective list)

Stage: Kasa mare (opera, V. Telenke), 1966; Music for Ballet, 1975
Orch: Sym., f, 1954; 6 Moldavian Tunes, 1964; Pf Conc., 1971
Vocal: Songs of Captivity and Struggle, 1v, pf, 1957; Songs for Difficult Love, Mez, pf, 1964; Songs for Koder, 1965; October Sun (I. Amichai), 1v, chamber orch, 1974; Day of Memory (Amichai), 1v, chamber orch, 1975
Inst: 3 str qts, 1962, 1965, 1969; For Piano, 2 bks; Ostinati, 4 vc, 1973

Principal publisher: Israel Music Institute

BIBLIOGRAPHY
Y. W. Cohen: *Werden und Entwicklungen der Musik in Israel* (Kassel, 1976) [pt.ii of rev. edn. of M. Brod: *Die Musik Israels*]
W. Y. Elias: *The Music of Israel* (Tel-Aviv, in preparation)
WILLIAM Y. ELIAS

Kora. A 21-string plucked harp-lute (fig.1), used mainly by Mandinka and Maninka (Malinke) professional male musicians known as *jalolu* (plural of *jali*), in an area of West Africa that includes the Gambia, Senegal,

1. Mandinka kora (harp-lute)

Guinea-Bissau, the Republic of Guinea, and Mali. While the instrument is widely distributed, the Gambia River valley is one of the main centres of *kora* playing and merits consideration as the homeland of the instrument. Its origins are obscure. *Kora* players ascribe its introduction in the distant past to an unknown musician associated with the Nyencho warrior-princes of Kabu, in what has become Guinea-Bissau. Its popularization is ascribed to Koriyang Musa, a pupil of the legendary Jali Madi Wuleng who, with his pupil, served the mid-19th-century Mandinka hero Kelefa Sane. Koriyang Musa's success in popularizing the *kora* through his playing is attributed to a bargain he drove with a jinn, offering the jinn one of his sons in exchange for the jinn's virtuosity on the instrument. The legend may represent a popular account of the removal of royal or religious restrictions on the use of the *kora* in the past, and if this is so it would place the popularization of the *kora* and its music in a period during which, with the rapid demise of Mandinka traditional authority and institutions, the *kora jali* would have been hard-pressed to find new sources of patronage. Knight ('Mandinka kora') suggested that the *kora* developed from similar but smaller instruments not more than 300 years ago. This hypothesis is apparently supported by the fact that the *balo*, the Mandinka–Maninka xylophone, was noted by travellers at a considerably earlier date than the first account of the *kora* by Mungo Park in 1799. However the *kora*, traditionally associated with royalty, officialdom, the nobility and also possibly with religious practices, would not necessarily have been shown to the casual traveller.

While the *kora* is classified as a harp-lute, and Knight ('Mandinka kora') has proposed the alternative designation 'bridge harp', it is similar in certain of its general features to a number of large plucked and bowed lutes found throughout West Africa. Its fairly long neck passes diametrically through a large hemispherical gourd resonator which is covered with a leather soundtable. The strings are attached to the upper end of the neck with tuning collars and to the base of the neck by anchor strings tied to an iron anchor ring set in the neck. Distinctively, however, the *kora* has 21 strings arranged in two parallel ranks at right angles to the sound-table on either side of a vertical notched bridge, 11 strings on the left and 10 on the right. Notched bridges are found on a number of other instruments used on or near the African coast from Senegal in the north to Angola in the south (*see* MVET). The strings of the *kora* were traditionally made from leather, but more recently nylon fishing line, of different gauges to suit the different registers of the instrument, is preferred because it is stronger and more easily available and because of its brighter and more resonant sound. The two handles, the neck and the bridge are preferably of African rosewood, mahogany serving as a substitute for the handles and the neck, but not for the bridge. The leather soundtable is made from the skin of a male antelope (*Tragelophus scriptus*) or, since such game is increasingly scarce, cowhide may commonly be used. The soundtable is nailed to the back of the resonator, and the leather on the back of the resonator may be embellished with metal studs. A soundhole, usually circular or square, is cut in the top of the resonator behind the right-hand handle, allowing the *jali* to use the body of the *kora* as a receptacle for spare strings, the large iron repair needle known as *loyo*, amulets and gifts of money

accompany one or more singers, male or female; in either case a chorus may sometimes provide a refrain. If the *kora jali* is himself an indifferent vocalist, he will seek to marry, or to team up with, a woman who is acknowledged to be a good singer.

The *kora jali* today usually has some 60 or more pieces in his repertory, each piece being the traditional accompaniment for a song in honour of a specific family or clan. Each of these accompaniments is performed in a specific tuning or, more rarely, in one of two tunings; only a few pieces can be performed in any one of the three major tunings. These are known as *tomora ba* (the great *tomora*) or *sila ba* (the great road), *hardino*, which has a variant known as *sauta*, and *tomora mesengo* (the lesser *tomora*). *Tomora ba* appears to be the original *kora* tuning, and in practice the tuning from which *hardino* and *tomora mesengo* derive. Its heptatonic structure is close to that of a natural diatonic scale, as shown diagrammatically in Table 1.

The range of the *kora* is just over three octaves, and the approximate pitches of the strings when tuned to *tomora ba* are shown in relation to their positions on the bridge in fig.3. Some scholars notate the *kora* in the 'key' of F, which is probably closer to its average pitch. However its pitch is dictated by the range, and particularly the upper limits, of the voice or voices it accompanies. Thus, in practice, the pitch of the *kora* may vary by almost an octave on different instruments and between different players. Except when the *kora* is used

2. Playing technique of the kora at Kankan, Guinea, 1952

from his audiences. An ornamental cloth is almost always attached to the neck at the back of the instrument; often a woman presents this to the *jali* as a visible token of her esteem for the man and his music. A flattish metal jingle with small wire loops attached to its edges is fastened to the bridge before performance begins.

In performance the *jali* sits, holding the *kora* nearly vertical, as in fig.1, so that the base of the neck rests on the ground and the bass resonances of the instrument are amplified. Playing technique consists essentially of plucking the strings towards the player with the curved index fingers and away again with the thumbs (see fig.2). The index fingers generally produce brighter and clearer notes than the thumbs, and are often used to play the melody while the thumbs play the accompaniment. The index fingers may also be drawn across two or more adjacent strings in a strumming action, and the player obtains a staccato effect by immediately stopping a vibrating string with the index finger, or with the index finger and thumb. In certain pieces a rhythmic interruption of the melody is achieved by flicking the nail or the knuckle of the right index finger against the right handle. A rhythmic accompaniment to the *kora* is often supplied by a second musician who strikes the back of the resonator with the *loyo* repair needle. In addition, if women singers are present, they may supply a rhythmic accompaniment by striking their slit iron percussion tubes, known as *ne*, or by clicking their thumbs and middle fingers.

The *kora* is used principally to accompany narrations, recitations and songs in honour of a patron. It may, however, be used for purely instrumental performances which often consist of highly virtuoso elaborations of pieces in the accompaniment repertory. The *kora jali* may himself be the vocalist, or he may simply

TABLE 1: Tuning systems of the kora
(generalized relationships)

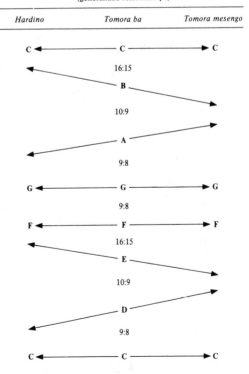

Hardino	Tomora ba	Tomora mesengo
C	C	C
	16:15	
	B	
	10:9	
	A	
	9:8	
G	G	G
	9:8	
F	F	F
	16:15	
	E	
	10:9	
	D	
	9:8	
C	C	C

(arrows indicate balanced sharpening or flattening
of the central tomora ba tuning)

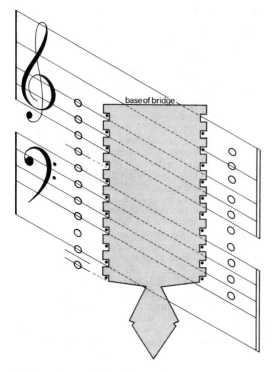

3. Approximate pitches of strings (tuned to tomora ba) in relation to their position on the bridge

by a group of players who emphasize the sharpness of the second and sixth degrees of the scale, and the flatness of the third and seventh degrees, the tuning of *tomora ba* is reasonably consistent. Though the tunings of *hardino* (with or without its *sauta* variant) and *tomora mesengo* vary more according to individual taste, their common characteristic is their symmetrical relationship to the central *tomora ba* tuning as shown in Table 1. The *sauta* variant of *hardino* involves the sharpening of the fourth degree of the scale by almost a semitone. The *hardino* and *tomora mesengo* tunings possibly originated, in pieces borrowed from other instruments, in the east or interior of the bulge of Africa. This is consistent with the division of the repertory into pieces original to the *kora*, which are of western or coastal origin and almost all played in *tomora ba* tuning, and pieces, mostly in either *hardino* or *tomora mesengo* tuning, which were borrowed from such eastern instruments as the *balo* xylophone and the *kontingo* plucked lute.

Irrespective of its regional origins, the repertory consists of three types of piece: firstly, those based on what are essentially simple melodic motifs (see ex.1) or har-

monic motifs, elaborated and varied in performance; secondly, pieces consisting of two or more balanced melodic phrases that may be elaborated or decorated but which permit little actual variation (see ex.2); thirdly, pieces which combine a first part based on a motif with a second melodic part. Each type is primarily an accompaniment to a vocal piece, and three major vocal styles or modes are employed: speech, recitation and song. The speech mode is known as *sataro* and both the remaining modes as *donkilo*. The speech mode is concerned with the narration of events connected with the patron's ancestors; it is characterized by the close-

Ex.2 *Mali sajo* (in *tomora mesengo* tuning)

ness of its intonation and rhythm to normal speech and by its higher register and faster and slightly louder delivery; it may be accompanied by any of the three types of *kora* piece, but if the third type is used the melodic second part is reserved for the songs that occur periodically in the narration. The recitation mode occurs within the speech mode, in combination with the song mode, or on its own; it is generally concerned with praises in the form of genealogies, lists of ancestors, family and clan relationships, and general observations on life; musically it is characterized by descending melodic contours, by a rather fast and even syllabic delivery, and by the use of a high and loud voice; it is accompanied in the same way as the speech mode. The song mode may occur on its own, but is usually combined with the recitation mode or occurs periodically in the speech mode; of the three modes it is the closest in style and delivery to what is normally considered strophic song; it is accompanied most commonly by the second and third types of *kora* piece, and in the latter case by the second melodic part rather than by the first part based on a motif.

BIBLIOGRAPHY

M. Park: *Travels in the Interior Districts of Africa* (London, 1799), 278f
C. A. Moloney: 'On the Melodies of the Volof, Mandingo, Ewe, Yoruba, and Houssa People of West Africa', *Journal of the Manchester Geographical Society*, v (1899), 277
J. Tiersot: 'Un instrument soudanais, la kora', *EMDC*, I/v (1922), 3224
D. Coly: 'Chant mandingue de Casamance', *Notes africaines*, xxxviii (1948), 22
R. Knight: 'Towards a Notation and Tablature for the *Kora*', *African Music*, v/1 (1971), 23
——: 'Mandinka kora: Gambie', OCR 70 [disc notes]
A. King: 'The Construction and Tuning of the *Kora*', *African Language Studies*, xiii (1972), 113
R. Knight: *Mandinka Jaliya: Professional Music of the Gambia* (diss., U. of California, Los Angeles, 1973)
A. King: 'Music: the Performance Modes', in G. Innes: *Sunjata: Three Mandinka Versions* (London, 1974), 17
——: 'Musical Tradition in Modern Africa', *Journal of the Royal Society of Arts*, cxxiii (1974), no.5221, p.15
S. G. Pevar: 'Alhaji bai konte: Kora Melodies from the Republic of the Gambia, West Africa', Rounder Records 5001 [disc notes]
'La *kora* à la conquête du monde', *Afrique nouvelle* (1975), no.1352, p. 12
ANTHONY KING

Ex.1 *Kelefa ba* (in *tomora ba* tuning)

Koran reading. A recitation (*qirā'a*) or chanting (*titāwa*) of the Koran in Arabic, moving between a kind of stylized speech and singing. It is read by the clergy or Koran readers as part of the liturgy and on other occasions, in all Islamic countries. *See* ISLAMIC RELIGIOUS MUSIC, §1(i); *see also* INDIA, SUBCONTINENT OF, §§I, 3(iii); V, 2; IRAN, §II, 2; MALAYSIA, §II, 2.

Körber, Georg (*b* Nuremberg, *c*1570; *d* Amberg, Upper Palatinate, in or after 1613). German composer and music editor. He probably attended the University of Altdorf. This was close to Nuremberg, where he is next heard of as an assistant at St Lorenz until 1598 at the latest. In that year he is recorded as Kantor at Amberg and remained in that position until the end of his life. In 1613 he held a position of trust as 'alumnorum oeconomus'. Although it could certainly have been used in worship too, he seems always to have pursued educational ends in his music, as can be assumed from his preference for small forms such as bicinia, canons and pieces for equal voices. He made a typical contribution to the small-scale dance-song forms imported from Italy about 1600. To the new edition of Balthasar Musculus's *40 schöne geistliche Gesenglein* he contributed 13 Latin pieces 'ad aequales voces' with biblical texts, and he also included 41 other pieces by various composers. Of these the best represented is Orazio Vecchi with eight pieces, and there are seven each by Gallus Dressler and Jacob Meiland; ten are anonymous.

See also MUSCULUS, BALTHASAR.

WORKS

Tyrocinium musicum (Nuremberg, 1589)
Distiche moralia, 2vv, item benedictiones et gratiarum actiones, aliaeque sacrae cantilenae, 4vv, fugis concinnatis (Nuremberg, 1590)
13 works, 1597[7]

BIBLIOGRAPHY

A. Sandberger: 'Bemerkungen zur Biographie Hans Leo Hasslers und seiner Brüder sowie zur Musikgeschichte der Städte Nürnberg und Augsburg', DTB, v (1904/*R*)
K. W. Niemöller: *Untersuchungen zu Musikpflege und Musikunterricht an den deutschen Lateinschulen vom ausgehenden Mittelalter bis um 1600* (Regensburg, 1969)
W. Dupont: *Werkausgaben Nürnberger Komponisten in Vergangenheit und Gegenwart* (Nuremberg, 1971)

WALTER BLANKENBURG

Körber, Günter (*b* 9 Jan 1922). German wind instrument maker. He is noted for his reconstructions of Renaissance and Baroque woodwind instruments. Educated in Berlin, he served as an army musician during World War II, afterwards continuing as a professional woodwind player. In 1958 he met Otto Steinkopf, and worked with him from 1959, setting up his own workshop in Berlin in 1964 when Steinkopf moved to West Germany. Körber has always aimed to improve the possibilities for performing early music, and his considerable output includes reconstructions of most varieties of early woodwind instruments, copied mainly from originals in Brussels, Berlin and Vienna. His reputation is most firmly based on wind-cap instruments, and in particular the crumhorn, which he and Steinkopf restored to active musical use.

CHRISTOPHER MONK

Korchinska, Maria (*b* Moscow, 16 Feb 1895; *d* London, 17 April 1979). Russian harpist. At the Moscow Conservatory she won the first gold medal awarded to a harpist. From 1918 to 1924 she was solo harpist in the Grand Opera of the Moscow State Theatre and during the same period taught at the conservatory. In 1926 she settled in London, where she played contemporary chamber music, especially with the Harp Ensemble and the Wigmore Ensemble. She gave the first performance of Bax's Fantasy Sonata for viola and harp, which is dedicated to her. In postwar years she devoted much time to promoting the harp as a solo instrument, making several solo and concerto records. She was regularly associated with the Dutch harpist Phia Berghout in the organization of the annual international harp weeks since their inception at Breukelen, the Netherlands, in 1960.

MARTHA KINGDON WARD/ANN GRIFFITHS

Korchmaryov, Klimenty Arkad'yevich (*b* Verkhne-Dneprovsk, 3 July 1899; *d* Moscow, 7 April 1958). Russian composer and pianist. He graduated from the Odessa Conservatory under Biber and Malïshevsky with a gold medal in 1919. From 1923 he lived in Moscow and from 1939 to 1947 in Turkmenia, where he established the first Turkmenian National Ballet and collected Turkmenian folksongs; in 1944 he was made an Honoured Art Worker of the Turkmen SSR.

WORKS
(selective list)

STAGE

Operas: Ivan-Soldat (D. Smolin), 1925–7; Desyat' dney, kotorïye potryasili mir [Ten days that shook the world] (S. Gorodetsky), 1929–31; Ditya radosti [Child of joy] (L. Cherkasinaya, A. Zhadov, after Chin. music drama The Whitehaired Girl), 1953; Bagttlï yashlïk (Schastlivaya molodost') [Happy youth] (comic opera, A. Afinogenov, R. Seidov)
Ballets: Krepostnaya balerina, Smolin, 1927; Aldar-Kose (Vesyolïy obmanshchik) [The gay impostor], N. Kholfin, K. Burunov, 1942; Devushki morya [The sea maidens], L. N. Kholfin, 1944; Yunïye patriotï [The young patriots], Abolimov, R. Zakharov, 1949; Alen'kiy tsvetochek [Alenka's flowers], L. Cherkashinaya, 1949
Operettas: Ranyaya krasavitsa (Ganna) [The early beauty (Hannah)] (S. Vetlugin, L. Oshanin), 1939; Pan-zabiyaka [Mr bully] (Ya. Galitsky, L. Cherkashinaya), 1945

ORCHESTRAL AND VOCAL ORCHESTRAL

Orch: Ivan-Soldat, suite, 1928; Vn Conc., 1937; Prazdnik na zastave [Festival day on guard], ov., 1938; Waltz, 1941; Aldar-Kose, suite, 1943; Devushki morya, suite, 1945; Raznokharakternaya syuita [Suite in different characters], 1947; Yunïye patriotï, suite, 1948
Vocal syms. for solo vv, chorus, orch: Gollandiya [Holland] (J. Last, trans. S. Berendgov), 1922–3; Oktyabr (Mayakovsky, Gorodetsky), 1931; Narodï sovetskoy stranï [Peoples of the Soviet land] (M. Ulitsky), 1935
Other vocal orch: Suite (M. Svetlov), Bar, chamber orch, 1935; 10 Chinese Songs, 1941; Svobodnïy Kitay [Free China] (cantata, M. Matusovsky), speaker, Mez, chorus, children's chorus, orch, 1950

OTHER WORKS

Chamber: Sonata, va, db, pf, 1926; Esquisse, bn, pf (1927); Sonata, vn, pf (1930); Str Qt, 1935; Concert Rondo, vn, pf (1948); Pieces, fl, pf (1949); Pieces on Turkmenian Themes, cl, pf (1949)
Pf: Improvizatsiya (1925); Vesennyaya pesn [Spring song] (1925); Revolyutsionnïy karnaval, 1926; Velikaya skorb [Great grief], 1927; Evreyskiy prazdnik [Hebrew festival], 1927
Vocal: Levïy marsh [Left march] (Mayakovsky), chorus, pf; over 50 songs, over 200 notations of Turkmenian folksongs
Incidental music, film scores

Principal publishers: Soviet State Publishing House, Universal

BIBLIOGRAPHY

E. Braudo: *Ivan Soldat* (Moscow, 1927)
D. Gojowy: *Neue sowjetische Musik der 20er Jahre* (Laaber, 1980)

DETLEF GOJOWY

Kordax. Ancient Greek solo dance, originally in honour of Artemis; it was characteristic of the comedy but also danced at banquets (*see* SYMPOSIUM), associated with drunkenness and regarded in antiquity as lascivious, in contrast to the EMMELEIA. It could be accompanied with instrumental music and choral songs, and was performed in isolation until imperial Roman times.

BIBLIOGRAPHY
A. Pickard-Cambridge: *Dithyramb Tragedy and Comedy* (Oxford, rev. 2/1962), 167
——: *The Dramatic Festivals of Athens* (Oxford, rev. 2/1968), 253, 257

GEOFFREY CHEW

Korea. An east Asian country which existed as a kingdom until 1910 when it was annexed by Japan. After World War II, Korea became divided into the Republic of Korea (South Korea) and North Korea. Since 1954 South Korea has had an area of about 98,400 sq km; in the 1975 census its population was just over 34·5 million. North Korea occupies an area of about 122,300 sq km and its population in 1975 was reckoned at about 16 million. In the discussion which follows, material from before World War II relates to Korea as a whole; material after World War II deals primarily with South Korea, because of the scarcity of information from the north.

1. History: (i) The early period (before 57 BC) (ii) Three Kingdoms period (57 BC–AD 668) (iii) Unified Silla period (668–936) (iv) Koryŏ dynasty (918–1392) (v) Early Yi dynasty (1392–1593) (vi) Late Yi dynasty (1593–1910) (vii) After 1910. 2. Instruments: (i) Chordophones (ii) Aerophones (iii) Idiophones (iv) Membranophones. 3. Notation. 4. Theory. 5. Performers: (i) Court musicians (ii) Kisaeng (iii) Kwangdae. 6. Court music: (i) Aak (ii) Tangak (iii) Hyangak. 7. Vocal art music: (i) Kagok (ii) Sijo (iii) Kasa. 8. Buddhist ritual music: (i) Chants (ii) Instrumental music and dance. 9. Folk music: (i) P'ansori (ii) Sanjo.

1. HISTORY. The literary sources of Korean musical history relate mostly to court and classical music; references to folk music are rare. There are seven distinct historical periods, marked off by conspicuous changes in musical practice as well as in the political system. Some confusion arises in the classification of Korean music since the terms used can overlap. For example, the term *aak* ('elegant music') now designates all court music genres, but originally it applied solely to court ritual music of Chinese origin. There is also overlapping between *chŏngak* ('right music'), a term which covers court music and art songs, and *sogak* ('secular music'). Table 1 shows some of the genres of Korean music on the basis of instrumentation and function. *P'ansori* is classified under both vocal folk music and theatrical music, another example of the overlap.

(i) *The early period (before 57 BC).* The earliest traceable music of the tribal states of Korea was performed at ritual festivities associated with planting the crops and harvest. According to the Chinese historical document *San-kuo chih* ('Annals of the Three States'), the earliest source for Korean music history, loud music and dance were performed for several days and nights. (The 20th-century *nongak* ('farmer's music') and *kut* (shaman ritual), relating as they do to agricultural life, probably carry on the tradition.) The same Chinese document states that an instrument resembling a Chinese *chu* was in use, but this disappeared in the influx of Chinese musical culture.

(ii) *Three Kingdoms period (57 BC–AD 668).* Music of this period shows that each state emphasized a particular instrument. Divergences in musical practice arose from both geographical and political factors. Koguryŏ (37 BC–AD 668), in north Korea, had frequent contact with China, and as early as the late 4th century AD, Chinese music and instruments were present in Korea, especially in the north, as is evident from the mural paintings in the tombs at Anak, Hwanghae province. The characteristic instrument here was a six-string zither, called *kŏmun'go* and modelled after the Chinese *ch'in* (seven-string zither) of the early 5th century. Like its Chinese counterpart, the *kŏmun'go* has always been highly esteemed and is still played. During the late 5th century a Buddhist chant, probably a type of *sutra* (see §8(i)), was introduced from China. The music of Koguryŏ was one of the repertories of the *Ch'i-pu yüeh* ('Seven kinds of music') and *Chiu-pu yüeh* ('Nine kinds of music') of the Chinese Sui dynasty (AD 581–618), and the *Shih-pu yüeh* ('Ten kinds of music') of the T'ang dynasty (AD 618–907). The instruments of the 7th century *Chiu-pu yüeh* are strikingly similar to those of the music of Hsi-liang, an area which was the north-western Chinese outpost.

Paekche (18 BC–AD 663), in the south-west, had a direct route to southern China across the Yellow Sea, and there was evident contact with Japan. Its cultural pattern was in sympathy with that of southern China. *Nihongi* ('Chronicles of Japan') recorded that, in 612, the Paekche artist Mimashi taught *gigaku* ('masked play') in Japan which he had learnt in southern China. There are several regional forms of mask dance drama performed in Korea. The music of Paekche differed from that of Koguryŏ and Silla in its emphasis on the vertical angular harp; the use of this instrument reveals a Central Asian influence by way of southern China (where it was called *k'ung-hu*, ultimately from the Persian harp, *chang*).

Because of its south-eastern position, the Silla kingdom (57 BC–AD 935) had much less contact with China and Japan in its early stages, but its progress was rapid and it conquered Koguryŏ and Paekche in the late 7th century. Early Silla music is represented by the 12-string zither called *kayago*, a modification of the Chinese 16-string zither *cheng*, and popular until quite modern times. The music of the Three Kingdoms was played at the Japanese court, the instruments used being precisely those employed in Korea. Until the unification of Korea by Silla, *komagaku* ('music of Koguryŏ') and *kudaragaku* ('music of Paekche') were more important; after unification *shiragigaku* ('music of Silla') gained in importance and this change in Japanese court music reflected the changing musical processes in newly unified Korea.

(iii) *Unified Silla period (668–936).* The expansion of the Silla dynasty, coupled with a military alliance with the T'ang dynasty, resulted for the first time in a unified Korea. The musical traditions of Paekche and Koguryŏ survived, though with a hybrid range of instruments. New types of instrument, such as the three types of transverse flute, were manufactured, a development which inevitably weakened the characteristic identity of Paekche and Koguryŏ music.

With the increasing spread of China's high Buddhist culture in Korea, attempts were made to distinguish native Korean music from that of Chinese origin. The former was called *hyangak* ('native music') and the latter *tangak* ('T'ang music'). Thereafter, these terms were used regardless of dynastic changes. Thus, 'native music' included not only native Korean music but also Chinese music which had arrived there before the T'ang dynasty. *Tangak* denoted all Chinese music imported to Korea from the T'ang dynasty and onwards. Consequently, the word *tang* became synonymous with China in a broad sense.

It was during this period that high Buddhist culture reached its peak in Korea. Artistic remains in Kyŏngju,

TABLE 1

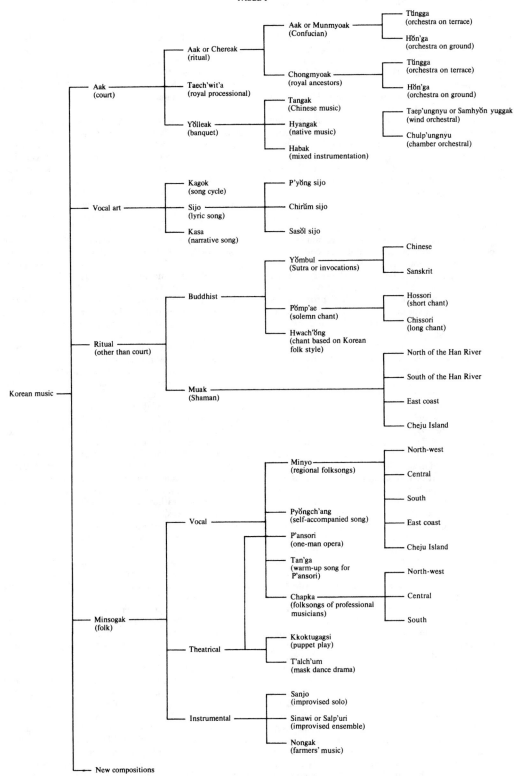

the old capital of the Silla period, reveal the strong influence of Ch'ang-an, the old T'ang dynasty capital. According to the inscription on a monument built in memory of the priest Chin'gam (774–850) and further evidence from *Nitto guho junrei gyoki* ('Diary of a pilgrimage to T'ang in search of the law') by the Japanese priest Ennin (793–864), Silla Buddhist priests not only performed archaic Buddhist chants which had developed before the T'ang dynasty as well as the new T'ang style of chant, but also created a distinct Korean style. These two records of early Korean Buddhist chants indicate that the melody was characteristically melismatic, in slow tempo, and that the text syllables were obscured. This description seems to match the present Korean Buddhist chants, particularly the *pŏm-p'ae* (see §8(i)), although it is impossible to determine whether the melodic lines correspond.

(iv) Koryŏ dynasty (918–1392). As Koryŏ was founded with Buddhism as its dynastic religion it inherited the high Buddhist culture of the preceding unified Silla period. Much of the Silla musical tradition continued in Koryŏ without pronounced modification, for example at *Yŏndŭng-hoe* (a dynastic Buddhist lantern festival held in spring) and *P'algwan-hoe* (a royal Buddhist festival held in winter). But despite official promotion of Buddhism as the dynastic religion, and frequent festivals, the sources for Koryŏ Buddhist music are more scanty than those for Silla.

One significant development in this period was the creation of *aak*, a court ritual music of Chinese origin. In 1114 a few *aak* instruments were sent to Koryŏ by the Sung dynasty, successor to the T'ang dynasty, together with instruments used at Chinese court banquets. Two years later Koryŏ received a more or less complete set of *aak* instruments for both *tŭngga* ('orchestra on the terrace') and *hŏn'ga* ('orchestra on the ground'; see figs.6, 7 and 9 below), as well as instruction in two types of ritual dance, *munmu* ('civil dance') and *mumu* ('military dance'). These orchestras and dances began to form part of various court rituals so that court music now included both *aak* and *tangak*. From the late 12th century *hyangak* was added, clearly a misuse of 'native music'. There was also the court entertainment music of the women, called *kyobangak*.

Sung dynasty court banquet music and dance were established side by side with the native Korean court banquet music and dances. *Hyangak* and *tangak* were also referred to as *ubangak* ('music of the right') and *chwabangak* ('music of the left') respectively, with reference to the position of the orchestra. *Hyangak chŏngjae* ('native court banquet dance') differed from *tangak chŏngjae* ('Chinese court banquet dance') in several respects. The song text of *hyangak chŏngjae* was written in Korean, according to *Akhak kwebŏm* ('Book of music') published in 1493, whereas *tangak chŏngjae* included a recited prologue and epilogue poem written in Chinese.

During the late Koryŏ period, *tangak* underwent modification. The angular harp disappeared and its role was probably taken over by zithers. The *tangak* orchestra by this time comprised a set of iron slabs, end-blown notched flute, transverse flute, a double-reed instrument, lute, bowed zither, large zither, hourglass drum, barrel drum and wooden clapper. This ensemble was retained until the early Yi dynasty. This compares with the *hyangak* orchestra of six-string zither, 12-string zither, five-string lute, three sizes of transverse flute, hourglass drum and wooden clapper.

Sung dynasty *tz'u* music, a rhymed form of free verse with irregular line lengths, gained popularity in Koryŏ and was included in *tangak* repertory. Only two pieces of it survive in Korea, in the form of orchestral music, but they are all the more important because musical literature from the Sung dynasty appears to have been entirely lost in China.

(v) Early Yi dynasty (1392–1593). The Yi dynasty was based on the neo-Confucianism of the theorist Chu Hsi (1130–1200), officially promulgated by the dynasty's first king, T'aejo. Koryŏ Buddhism was suppressed, but its music continued to be performed for some time before the inevitable reform took full effect. Naturally, the course of reform placed a heavy emphasis on *aak*, its instrumentation, tuning system and repertory. The fourth king, Sejong (1418–50), a devoted musicologist himself, appointed Pak Yŏn (1378–1458) to the directorship of the Chang'ak-wŏn ('Royal Music Department'). Pak Yŏn is the first genuinely attested music theorist in Korean music history and it was during this reign that the *aak* system was perfected.

The instruments were re-tuned in accordance with the cycle of 5ths based on the principal pitch of the *huang-chung*, the bronze bell of the Chinese Ming dynasty (1368–1644). This re-tuning was necessary, for each Chinese dynasty established new measurements and the numerous instruments in the Korean court had been collected during several dynasties. At the same time, steps were taken to find suitable materials for the manufacture of *aak* instruments, especially stone-chimes and bronze bells, in Korea. The *tŭngga* and *hŏn'ga* ritual orchestras began to play *yin* and *yang* keys respectively, which were required by the original sources but had been neglected until this period. *Aak* compositions of doubtful authenticity were abandoned and a new repertory was adopted from the *Taesŏng akpo* ('Music of the Confucian Shrine') of the Yüan dynasty (1260–1368) of China. To a certain extent the enthusiasm for *aak* was overdone; in 1433, for instance, *aak* was performed at a court banquet – rather inappropriate for music reserved for ritual purposes.

Hyangak flourished during this dynasty. Numerous pieces were composed with texts in *han'gŭl* (the Korean alphabetical system introduced in the reign of Sejong) employing musical elements of *koch'wi* ('processional music') and *hyangak*. Conversely, the repertory of *tangak* decreased without the further importation of Ming dynasty music. Another musical achievement during Sejong's reign was the invention of abstract mensural notation called *chŏnggan-po* ('square notation'). For the first time the pitch and metre of Korean music, especially *hyangak*, which is based on irregular note values, could be notated.

During the second half of the 15th century, by order of the seventh king, Sejo (1455–68), music for the Royal Ancestors' Shrine was arranged incorporating elements of *koch'wi* and *hyangak*. The aim was to avoid worshipping the spirits of the dead kings with music of Chinese origin. *Tangak* and *hyangak* orchestras began to be intermixed, and some of the Chinese instruments were modified to simplify playing techniques. For example, the nine holes of the *tangp'iri*, a double-reed pipe, were reduced to eight, because one hole could produce two pitches by different blowing techniques.

Two important developments marked the reign of Sŏngjong (1469–94). First, a tablature for *kŏmun'go* (six-string zither) was developed. This was modelled on the Chinese *ch'in* tablature, called *chien-tzu p'u* ('abbreviated letter notation'), which was logical enough since the instrument itself was modelled on the *ch'in*. The second achievement was the publication of the *Akhak kwebŏm* ('Book of music') completed in 1493 under the general editorship of Sŏng Hyŏn. The nine chapters are: the tonal system; arrangements of orchestras for *aak* and processional music; Chinese and Korean dances as described in the *Koryŏ-sa* (Koryŏ dynastic history, completed in 1451); contemporary Chinese dances; contemporary Korean dances; *aak* instruments; instruments of *tangak* and *hyangak*; characteristics of Chinese and Korean dances; and costumes of musicians and dancers. This document became an indispensable source for Korean musicology.

(*vi*) *Late Yi dynasty* (*1593–1910*). Extensive and long-drawn-out invasions, by the Japanese in the 16th century and by Manchuria in the early 17th century, caused a great cultural gap and destroyed much of Korea's cultural heritage, in particular its traditional court music. Because of the loss of instruments during the wars, *aak* was not played again until as late as 1645. *Tangak* and *hyangak* came to be played by a single orchestra, creating the so-called *hyangdang kyoju* ('mixed instruments of *hyangak* and *tangak*'). The use of *hyangak* instruments to perform *tangak* led to a Koreanization of the Chinese music: the beat was divided into triple metre, a typical Korean metric structure, and Korean ornamentation was added, changes which are still evident in 20th-century *tangak* pieces. From the middle of the Yi dynasty onwards, *aak* fared no better. Its performance and instruments virtually disappeared during the reign of the tyrannical ruler Yŏnsan (1494–1506), who preferred female music and dance, called *yŏak* ('female music'). Attempts to revive and reconstruct *aak* were undertaken in the late 18th century by establishing the Bureau of Instruments Construction, but the glorious days of Sejong were not to be repeated.

From the 18th century aristocratic and folk music were increasingly favoured. Traditional classical songs, such as *kagok*, *kasa* and *sijo*, appeared as the favourite vocal music of cultivated people and are still performed (see §7). With the continued domination of Confucianism, the Buddhist performing arts underwent a decline, but a handful of Buddhist artists has kept its music alive. Because it was performed in secluded temples it has resisted modification. A one-man operatic song form called *p'ansori* was a favourite musical genre of the *kwangdae*, who were itinerant professional folk musicians. In the 19th century they developed an improvised solo instrumental form called *sanjo*, which shared the same musical elements as *p'ansori*. Both forms are still popular.

(*vii*) *After 1910*. After the Japanese annexation of Korea in 1910, most *aak* performances were abolished and only Confucian ritual music survived. The distinction between *tangak* and *hyangak* mostly disappeared, being replaced by a new term *habak* ('joint music'), which mixed the instruments of *tangak* and *hyangak* but emphasized those of *hyangak*.

After the fall of the monarchical social structure in 1910, the work of the Royal Music Department was continued during the colonial period by the government-sponsored Yi Dynastic Music Department. In 1951, six years after Korea's independence, this became the National Classical Music Institute. The Institute has an attached high school for training in Korean music and numbers among its staff some folk musicians such as *p'ansori* and *sanjo* performers. In 1959, Seoul National University introduced the degree of Bachelor of Music in Korean music, and in 1963 a Master's degree. A forerunner among the world's universities in developing a full university-level curriculum for study of its own traditional music, the university's Korean music programme tries to preserve traditional music, undertakes musicological studies and encourages new compositions using traditional materials.

European music had arrived before the Japanese annexation of Korea. Western missionary hymns were introduced in the late 19th century and Western-style military bands were adopted by the Yi dynasty court in the 1900s. The 36 years (1910–45) of Japanese annexation left an indelible mark, particularly in the form of the Japanese-style nostalgic popular song. Even after independence these songs prevailed in Korea, although their performance by Korean musicians was strictly prohibited because of anti-colonial feelings. An Ethics Committee on Popular Songs was set up to censor songs in Japanese style, control the piracy of melodies, and even to restrict the use of pessimistic song texts. By contrast, the preservation and teaching of traditional Korean music is subsidized by the government, which also promotes new compositions in the Western style.

Since World War II musical activities have been manifold. Court music is performed by members of the National Classical Music Institute for ceremonies at the Confucian Shrine and Royal Ancestors' Shrine, for national events, for tourists and for the general public. There are frequent performances of folk music by various organizations or private groups. Musicological research is conducted under the auspices of the Korean Musicological Society, especially through the pilot projects initiated by Lee Hye-ku (*b* 1909) and Chang Sa-hun (*b* 1916). Rather ironically, wealthier families encourage the learning of Western instruments, mostly the piano and violin, and as a result, there are many well-known Korean pianists and violinists in Western countries. The Contemporary Music Society under its leader, Lee Sung-jae (*b* 1924), has introduced modern compositions under three broad heads: works based on re-creations of the traditional musical scheme, works in the Western tradition, and works using Korean materials in Western musical settings. Attempts have been made to transcribe traditional music in Western staff notation, but this is a hazardous procedure, for it implies that there is a definitive version of a piece, whereas there is, in fact, never a 'finished' score. The traditional method of learning and performing is by rote, the various notations that exist being in the nature of a reminder to the performer who is aware, through oral tradition, of the subtleties of the music and the possibilities of variation. Unsuccessful attempts have also been made to modify Korean instruments to compete with the sophisticated construction of Western instruments, but the 'modernized' version cannot produce the timbre of the original instrument.

2. INSTRUMENTS. Traditionally, instruments were classified in two different ways. The older system, which

originated in the Chinese court and applied mainly to instruments of court ritual music, divided them into the eight categories of metal, stone, silk, bamboo, gourd, clay, leather and wood, the essential materials for their manufacture. Its basis is the Confucian idea that the world will be in peace when these substances are in harmony. The second system grouped instruments according to the musical genre in which they were employed. This system was adopted in the *Akhak kwebŏm* and applied only to court music and not to classical and folk genres. The total number of instruments known in Korea, including those now obsolete, is more than 60, and the 44 listed here are those in modern usage.

(*i*) *Chordophones*. The *kŏmun'go*, a six-string long zither with three movable bridges and 16 convex frets, is plucked with a pencil-size bamboo stick (see fig.1). The *kayago*, or *kayagŭm* (*kayakeum*), is a 12-string long

zither with 12 movable bridges (see fig.2); its strings are either plucked by the thumb, index and middle fingers, or are flicked with the index finger of the right hand. The *yanggŭm* ('foreign zither') is a dulcimer with 14 sets of four metal strings struck with a thin bamboo stick (essentially the Persian *santur*). The *haegŭm*, a two-string fiddle, has a horsehair bow inserted between the strings; the soundbox is a small bamboo tube, the front of which is covered in paulownia wood, and the strings are tuned a 5th apart. The *ajaeng*, a seven-string long zither bowed with a rosined stick of willow wood, has seven movable bridges (see fig.3). Two other zithers are the *kŭm* and *sŭl*, identical with the Chinese *ch'in* (seven-string zither) and *se* (25-string zither) respectively (*see* CHINA, §V, 2 and 5).

(*ii*) *Aerophones*. The *taegŭm* or *chŏttae* is a long transverse bamboo flute with six finger-holes (see fig.4). The

1. *Kŏmun'go* (six-string zither)

2. *Kayago* (12-string zither)

3. *Ajaeng (seven-string bowed zither) and changgo (hourglass drum) used in Chongmyoak ritual music*

4. *Taegŭm (transverse bamboo flute)*

5. *Tangp'iri (double-reed instruments) of Chongmyoak*

mouth-hole's relatively large size allows a gradation of pitches to be produced. A smaller hole, located between the finger-holes and the mouth-hole, is covered with a thin membrane of river reed which produces the characteristic buzzing sound. The *sanjo taegŭm*, a flute slightly shorter than the usual *taegŭm*, has finger-holes and a mouth-hole which are considerably larger, thus making possible complex techniques of pitch gradation. The *tangjŏk* is a short transverse bamboo flute with six finger-holes. The *tanso* is a small end-blown notched bamboo flute with four finger-holes on the front, the lowest of which is not used, and one thumb-hole. The *t'ongso* or *t'ungso* is a larger end-blown notched bamboo flute with four finger-holes and one thumb-hole. The instrument in present use has one additional front hole covered in membrane. The *chi* is a short transverse bamboo duct flute with five finger-holes and a

mouthpiece; a cross-shaped hole at the end of the bamboo joint is stopped for certain pitches. The *yak* is an end-blown notched bamboo flute with three finger-holes. The *chŏk* is an end-blown notched bamboo flute with five finger-holes, one thumb-hole, two additional open holes near the end and a cross-shaped one at the end of the joint. The *hun* is a globular clay ocarina with a mouth-hole and five finger-holes. The *so* is a set of panpipes consisting of 16 pipes.

Double-reed instruments include the *hyangp'iri*, a small cylindrically bored pipe of river reed with seven finger-holes and one thumb-hole. The *sep'iri* has a smaller diameter but the same tuning and playing techniques. The *tangp'iri* is a double-reed instrument with a larger cylindrical bore than the *hyangp'iri*, but its black bamboo pipe is slightly shorter; it has seven finger-holes and one thumb-hole (see fig.5). The *t'aep'yŏngso* (also

6. Hŏn'ga (orchestra on ground) of aak (Confucian ritual music) showing (from left to right) chin'go (barrel drum), p'yŏnjong (bell-chime), ch'uk (pounded wooden box) and pu (clay pot)

7. Hŏn'ga (orchestra on ground) of aak (Confucian ritual music) showing p'yŏn'gyŏng (stone-chime) and ŏ (wooden scraper)

called *saenap*, *nallari* or *hojŏk*) is a double-reed instrument with seven finger-holes and one thumb-hole positioned on the back between the first and second front stops; its wooden pipe has a conical bore and a small metal air chamber attached to its narrower diameter while its wider end is extended with a cup-shaped metal bell; the reed is the joint section of a wheat straw. The *saenghwang* or *saeng* is a mouth organ with wooden air chamber and 17 bamboo pipes, one being mute. Other aerophones include the *nap'al*, a long metal trumpet, and the *nagak*, a conch trumpet.

(*iii*) *Idiophones*. The *p'yŏnjong* is a bell-chime consisting of 16 tuned bronze bells hung in a wooden frame in two lines and struck with a mallet of cow horn (see fig.6); the *p'yŏn'gyŏng* is a stone-chime of 16 tuned stones similarly hung and struck (see fig.7). The *pak* is a clapper consisting of six wooden slabs tied together at one end. The *ch'uk*, a trapeziform wooden box on a wooden base, is played by passing a stick through a hole in the top and pounding the bottom of the box. The *ŏ* is a wooden scraper in the shape of a tiger with 27 notches along its spine; a split bamboo stick is used to strike the neck and scrape the back. The *pu*, a clay pot on a wooden stand, is struck on the rim with a split bamboo stick. The *ching*, a flat bronze gong with wide rim, is struck with a soft-headed stick. The *kwaenggwari*, a small flat bronze gong with narrow rim, is struck with a wooden mallet. The *para* is a pair of cymbals.

(*iv*) *Membranophones*. The *changgo* is an hourglass drum with a wooden body; its left side, covered with cowhide, is struck with the left-hand palm and its right side, covered with horsehide, is struck with a slim bamboo stick (see fig.3 above). The *chwago* is a barrel drum with tacked wooden body hung in a wooden frame; only one end is struck, with a soft-headed stick. The *yonggŏ* is a barrel drum slung from the player's shoulder, the upper face being struck with two soft-headed sticks. The *puk* is a double-headed barrel drum with a wooden body; its right head is struck with a stick, its left head with the left palm. The *kyobanggo* is a large wooden barrel drum resting in a four-legged wooden frame; the upper head and the body are struck with two sticks. The *chŏlgo*, a barrel drum on a wooden base, is struck with a soft-headed stick. The *chin'go*, a large barrel drum raised on a four-legged wooden stand, is struck with a soft-headed stick. The *nogo* consists of two long barrel drums set atop each other at right angles in a wooden frame; only one head of each drum is played, with a soft-headed stick. The *nodo* consists of two small barrel drums similarly positioned but pierced by a wooden pole; two knotted leather cords attached to both sides of the frame of each drum strike the heads when the pole is twirled. The *sogo* is a small double-headed shallow drum with a wooden handle pierced through its narrow wooden frame. The *pŏpko* is a large barrel drum set aslant on a four-legged wooden stand and played by two players: one strikes one head and the wooden frame with two wooden sticks, the other strikes the other head with two wooden sticks.

3. NOTATION. Eight types of notation are recognized in Korean music and each performs a different function.
Yulcha-po. The 12 Chinese ideographs are used to designate absolute pitches of the scale. Introduced from China, this letter notation was used mainly for the court ritual music of Chinese origin. Examples of *yulcha-po*,

found in the 15th-century *Sillok* ('Annals') of King Sejong, show that one vertical line of characters consists of four large letters representing scale degrees and four small letters (parallel with the large letters) representing specific pitches. One line is equivalent to one bar comprising four notes of even duration. Such a letter notation without rhythmic clarification was appropriate for notating *aak* because the quadruple rhythm of each line of *aak* was fully understood on the basis of the Confucian metaphysical concept that no one note of a melody should be given a longer durational value than other notes.
Kongch'ŏk-po. This is another letter notation brought in during the 15th century from China, where it had been used mainly for operatic and secular music. In Korea it was used for the notation of court ritual music. One symbol may represent more than one pitch, so the *yulcha-po* pitch names were written alongside for clarification. This notation never gained popularity as more practical notations could readily be used instead.
Yuk-po. Employing mnemonic syllables, or 'flesh sounds' imitating the sound of the instrument, it is a useful system for memorization or for teaching by rote, but inadequate for notating pitch and rhythm. It is still popularly used, particularly in music for *kŏmun'go* (six-string long zither), *kayago* (12-string long zither) and *changgo* (hourglass drum).
Oŭmyak-po ('five-sound simplified notation'). Deriving from the reign of King Sejo (1455–68), it was aimed at notating pentatonic *hyangak* pieces. The pentatonic scale degrees are placed within a square, the centre tone being called *kung* ('palace'). One degree above that is *sangil* ('above one'), and *sango* ('above five') is an octave higher than *kung*. In the same way, one degree below the centre tone is called *hail* ('below one'), and *hao* ('below five') is an octave lower. The disadvantages are that the exact pitch of the scale degree is not clarified unless the music specifies the mode and pitch of the centre tone, and the melodic range is limited to two octaves.
Hapcha-po. This 'combined letter notation', a type of tablature specifically designed for *kŏmun'go* music (see fig.8), is modelled on the Chinese *chien-tzu p'u* ('abbreviated letters') notation for *ch'in* (zither) music and dates from the late 15th century. One symbol consists of several parts of, or whole symbols of, a Chinese ideograph. The tablature contains symbols representing the right-hand plucking and the left-hand fingering techniques, string and fret numbers. In old scores the symbols are written alongside *kŏmun'go* mnemonic syllables. This notation has no way of showing the duration of notes.
Yŏnŭm-p'yo. This is a neumatic notation used mainly for notating the classical songs.
Chŏnggan-po. Developed in the reign of King Sejong (1418–50), this is a mensural notation which indicates rhythm and metre with great precision. The notation consists of a lattice of horizontal and vertical lines, forming columns of squares. Each square represents an amount of time, and melodies are notated by inserting symbols of *yulcha-po*, *yuk-po*, *oŭmyak-po* or *hapcha-po* (see above) in rhythmically appropriate squares (see fig.8). The addition of other symbols makes it possible to include song texts, drum strokes and even choreography. The present modified version, the most popular of those in use, accommodates most of the details of melody, ornaments and complicated durational distribution by employing a series of special symbols.

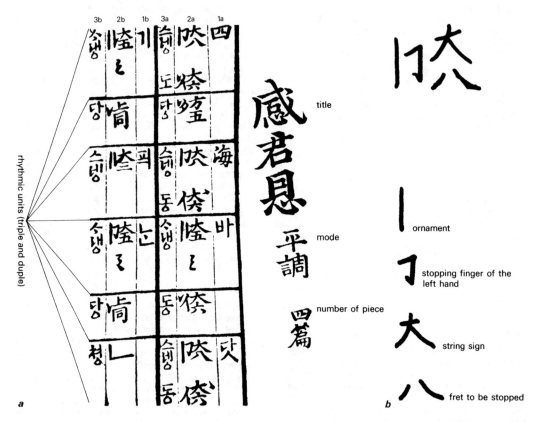

8. (a) *Two consecutive lines of hapcha-po notation for kŏmun'go music from 'Yanggŭm sinbo' ('New score of Yang's kŏmun'go music', 1610): column 1 in each line contains the text, column 2 the hapcha-po symbols in chŏnggan (squares indicating time values), and column 3 the yuk-po (mnemonic syllables in Korean script); (b) breakdown of one hapcha-po symbol*

Tongŭm-jip. A system used by Buddhist musicians in learning the melodic phrases of *chissori pŏmp'ae*, a long Buddhist chant style, it is a compilation of cross-references to similar melodic units. Each text syllable of a chant is cross-referenced to its melodically corresponding syllable in other chants. This system indicates neither pitches nor duration but can help those who already know certain *pŏmp'ae* chants to learn chants they do not know.

4. THEORY. Korean music is based on two types of mode: *p'yŏngjo* (the first, second, fourth, fifth and sixth Western degrees) and *kyemyŏnjo* (the first, third, fourth, fifth and seventh degrees) embodying different melodic and cadential patterns and implying different moods as well. Most Korean music is based on tritonic or tetratonic models, each with one or two subsidiary tones. Furthermore, the main tonal constituents of each genre of music or regional style require different emphasis to bring out the characteristics. Both in *p'yŏngjo* and *kyemyŏnjo* the centre tone (the first degree) is usually given a wide vibrato except in the case of the final note in a cadence. *P'yŏngjo* is common in court music and in the folksongs of the central area where the fourth and sixth degrees are given a downward slide. But

in the *p'yŏngjo* of *p'ansori* opera the slide is less apparent. The mode *ujo* has the same structure as *p'yŏngjo* but in a higher register. In court music or art songs *ujo* is a 4th higher than *p'yŏngjo*, but in *p'ansori* the difference between these two terms is vague and sometimes they are employed interchangeably. *Kyemyŏnjo* is more widely used than *p'yŏngjo*. In tritonic models the essential degrees are the first, fourth and fifth. Although the interval between the fourth and fifth degrees is

TABLE 2: Pitches used in Korean court music and art songs

Pitch names	Aak and tangak	Hyangak and art songs
hwangjong	C	Eb
taeryŏ	C♯	E
t'aeju	D	F
hyŏpchong	D♯	Gb
kosŏn	E	G
chungnyŏ	F	Ab
yubin	F♯	A
imjong	G	Bb
ich'ik	G♯	B
mamnyŏ	A	C
muyŏk	A♯	Db
ŭngjong	B	D

theoretically a major 2nd, in practice the fifth degree in court music is flattened slightly. In *sijo* (a genre of lyric art song: see §7) the interval between the fourth and fifth degrees is close to a minor 2nd.

In Korean music only court music and art songs require the concepts of key and absolute pitch; pitches in other genres of music are not standardized. The pitch names are those of the Chinese *lü* system, but the actual pitches implied are different for music of Chinese origin (*aak* and *tangak*) and for native Korean music (see Table 2). In notations, only the first Chinese letter of the 12 pairs of pitch names is used (e.g. *hwang*, *t'ae*, *chung*, *im* etc).

5. PERFORMERS. There are three recognized categories of professional musician: court musicians, female entertainers (*kisaeng*) and itinerant folk musicians (*kwangdae*).

(*i*) *Court musicians.* Probably with the T'ang dynasty system as its model, a court music department was first set up during the Silla dynasty. From then until the early 11th century (Koryŏ dynasty) court musicians were appointed through open competition. Their status then deteriorated drastically, the system becoming patrimonial. They were looked down on, excluded from certain privileges enjoyed by the civil service (including the civil service examinations) until their status was one of the lowest within the court hierarchy. Such a state of affairs continued until the end of the Yi dynasty, i.e. to the beginning of the 20th century.

There were two different groups of musicians in the Royal Music Department, *aksaeng* and *agong*. Aksaeng came from aristocratic families and were given higher rank than *agong*. Their main duty was to perform the court ritual music of Chinese origin, the *aak*. Agong were common people, or people put forward by aristocrats. They performed the Royal Ancestors' Shrine music and court banquet music, both of which were less respected than *aak*, but their duties were much the heavier and it was they who played the more significant role in the history of Korean music. The discrimination between these two groups illustrates the veneration felt for Chinese culture and Confucianism. The Royal Music Department, which included an Office of Music Administration and an Office of Performers, used to employ a staff of several hundred musicians. To achieve the status of a qualified regular court musician in the Office of Performers four stages of training, beginning in early youth, were required. After the Japanese annexation in 1910 and the reorganization of the Royal Music Department into the Yi Dynastic Music Department, the number of court musicians dropped significantly. On independence in 1945, the department, renamed the National Classical Music Institute in 1951, was administered by the Ministry of Culture and Information. A six-year training centre was set up in 1954, some of the graduates of the institute eventually becoming regular staff.

(*ii*) *Kisaeng.* These female entertainers attached to the court and regional governments had mostly been chosen as young girls from the common people and sent to court to learn court entertainment, which included instrumental music and songs and dances. Medicine, nursing, acupuncture and dressmaking were also taught and many *kisaeng* were also recognized prostitutes and were often chosen as concubines of the king and high officials. On reaching retirement age some were dispatched from court back to the regional governments.

Despite their low social status and insignificant family background, the contribution of the *kisaeng* to Korean music and dance was considerable. It was through the *kisaeng* that the songs and dances of the court music (called *yŏak*: 'female music') were carried beyond the palace and transmitted to the general public. Occasionally they were able to perform chamber orchestral music, but dance accompaniment was usually provided by blind musicians or by the *agong*, who were more skilled in the techniques needed for a wind orchestra. After the decline of the monarchy a handful of *kisaeng* remained, renowned for their specialized performing skills. In present society, the concept of the *kisaeng* is, of course, alien but the role of entertainer persists.

(*iii*) *Kwangdae.* These itinerant folk musicians, socially the lowest in rank, originated from the *hwarang*, young shamanistic spiritual leaders of the Silla dynasty. Although they were originally highly esteemed, social and political changes brought about a decline in their status. The prevailing Confucianism looked down upon professional entertainment as a lowly social activity. During the mid-Yi dynasty the *kwangdae* were spouses of female shamans and acted as the musical accompanists at shaman ceremonies. Eventually, *kwangdae* became a generic term for folk artists of masked dance-drama, puppet plays, acrobatics, *p'ansori* (one-man opera) and *sanjo* (type of solo instrumental music). Some of the present *p'ansori* and *sanjo* musicians are said to be descendants of shamans, but they deny such relationship because of the shaman's inferior status.

6. COURT MUSIC.
(*i*) *Aak* ('elegant music'). Originally meaning court ritual music of Chinese origin, the term was gradually limited to Confucian ritual music as the other courtly forms disappeared. The Royal Ancestors' Shrine music, a type of court ritual music established in the 15th century, is excluded from the narrow sense of *aak*, for it evolved long after in *hyangak* style. However, *aak* was to prove so important socially that the term began to be used sometimes to refer to any serious, cultivated and elegant music. In this sense, it covered *tangak* and *hyangak* as well, and even classical song.

After the arrival of the first *aak* instruments from China during the Koryŏ dynasty (early 12th century), subsequent importation of both instruments and theory allowed an expansion in the performance of the genre. But lack of systematic theoretical knowledge led to misinterpretation. The first king of the Yi dynasty had established an *aak* department but it was in the reign of King Sejong, the fourth king, that the revival gathered impetus. Much of this restoration was accomplished under the direction of Pak Yŏn, a musicologist who was concerned not only with the theoretical clarification of *aak* and the history of its origins, but also with manufacturing the necessary instruments in Korea. *Aak* orchestras expanded in size and number but the tradition was to fall out of favour in the time of King Yŏnsan (1494–1506), who disliked the music, and subsequent invasions by the Japanese and Manchurians in the 16th and 17th centuries settled its fate. The ban on *aak* performances imposed by the Japanese governor-general in 1910 led to its near extinction.

Of the several *aak* repertories, only Confucian ritual music is still practised. Performances take place twice a year in spring and autumn, during the memorial services at the Confucian shrine. The tradition seems to embrace in music the essence of Confucian doctrine; serene music reflects universal harmony by employing the eight kinds of material in its instruments: metal, stone, silk, wood, bamboo, leather, clay and gourd. Missing from modern Confucian ritual music is the mouth organ of the gourd category, and the wooden clapper is added although it was not among the original *aak* instruments. Two sets of orchestra are required for the present form of *aak* – *tŭngga* ('orchestra on the terrace'; see fig.9) and *hŏn'ga* ('orchestra on the ground'; see figs.6 and 7, p.198). Their instrumentation is shown in Table 3. Each orchestra has its own repertories which formerly had vocal parts, but are now purely instrumental. The orchestras perform alternately.

Two ritual dances are performed for the specific ritual sequences: the *munmu* ('civil dance') and the *mumu* ('military dance'). The number of dancers in each square formation depends on the spirit towards whom the worship is directed. For Confucius, 64 dancers are required in a formation of eight rows of eight. The civil dancers wear black hats; each holds a flute in the left hand and, in the right hand, a wand to which pheasant feathers are attached, symbolizing peace and prosperity. The military dancers wear red hats, and each dancer holds a shield in the left hand and a hatchet in the right hand, symbolizing glorious achievement.

The music of *aak* compositions observes strict Confucian metaphysical rules and Chinese styles. Its overall characteristics are refinement, simplicity and serenity with balanced tempo and rhythm. There is minimal embellishment, but one type which does occur in practice (though not sanctioned in any written reference) is an upward slide of about a semitone from each pitch, in a basically heptatonic melody (see the flute part of ex.1).

(*ii*) *Tangak*. Literally meaning 'music of the T'ang dynasty' in Korea, *tangak* originally indicated music of

T'ang Chinese origin used in the Korean court since the 7th century; the term was used to differentiate the music from that existing in Korea before the rise of the T'ang dynasty. In the Koryŏ dynasty, the term was extended to include all Chinese music which had come into Korea from the T'ang dynasty onwards. Because of the physical positioning of the *tangak* orchestra when performing, the term *chwabangak* ('music of the left') was used interchangeably with *tangak*; *ubangak* ('music of the right') refers to the *hyangak* orchestra.

Early *tangak* instrumentation included *tangbip'a* (short-necked, four-string lute), *tangjŏk* (transverse flute), *tangp'iri* (double-reed aerophone), *ajaeng* (seven-string long bowed zither), *saeng* (mouth organ) and *konghu* (angular harp). After undergoing some changes, *tangak* instruments of the 15th century included *panghyang* (percussion metallophone), *pak* (wooden clapper), *kyobanggo* (large barrel drum), *changgo* (hourglass drum), *wŏlgŭm* (round-bodied lute similar to the Chinese *yüeh-ch'in*), *tangbip'a* (short-necked lute), *haegŭm* (two-string fiddle), *taejaeng* (board zither corresponding to the Chinese *cheng*), *ajaeng*, *tangjŏk*, *tangp'iri*, *t'ongso* (large end-blown notched flute) and *t'aep'yŏngso* (double-reed aerophone). Some of these

Ex.1 from *aak*, Confucian ritual music (Lee Hye-ku and others, 1973)

instruments were modified and included in *hyangak* orchestras, resulting in *hyangdang kyoju* ('mixed instrumentation of *hyangak* and *tangak*'). Modern *tangak* instrumentation used by the National Classical Music Institute includes *taegŭm* (long transverse flute), *tangp'iri*, *p'yŏnjong* (bell-chime), *p'yŏn'gyŏng* (stone-chime), *chŏlgo* (barrel drum), *haegŭm*, *ajaeng* and *pak*.

The *tangak* repertory of the T'ang dynasty is no longer known. That of the Koryŏ dynasty included

9. *Tŭngga* (*orchestra on terrace*) *of aak* (*Confucian ritual music*) *with* (*front row, left to right*) *so* (*panpipes*), *three chi* (*transverse flutes*), *chŏk* (*end-blown flute*), *hun* (*ocarina*), *pak* (*wooden clapper*), *and* (*back row, left to right*) *t'ŭkchong* (*clapperless bell*), *p'yŏnjong* (*bell-chime*), *ŏ* (*wooden scraper*), *ch'uk* (*pounded wooden box*), *chŏlgo* (*barrel drum*), *p'yŏn'gyŏng* (*stone-chime*), *t'ŭkkyŏng* (*suspended stone*)

TABLE 3: Instrumentation for *tŭngga* ('orchestra on terrace') and *hŏn'ga* ('orchestra on ground')

	Tŭngga	*Hŏn'ga*	
Idiophones:	*t'ŭkkyŏng*		suspended stone struck with mallet
	t'ŭkchong		clapperless bell struck with mallet
	p'yŏn'gyŏng	*p'yŏn'gyŏng*	stone-chime
	p'yŏnjong	*p'yŏnjong*	bell-chime
	ch'uk	*ch'uk*	pounded wooden box
	ŏ	*ŏ*	wooden scraper
	pak	*pak*	wooden clapper
Aerophones:	*chi*	*chi*	short transverse bamboo flute
	yak	*yak*	end-blown notched bamboo flute
	chŏk	*chŏk*	end-blown notched bamboo flute
	hun	*hun*	globular clay ocarina
	so		panpipes
Membranophones:	*chŏlgo*		barrel drum
		chin'go	large barrel drum
		nogo	set of two long barrel drums
		nodo	set of two small barrel drums
Chordophones:	*kŭm*		seven-string zither
	sŭl		25-string zither

Chinese Sung dynasty *tz'u* music and female entertainment music. *Tangak* compositions dating from the early Yi dynasty once numbered about 100, though the musicians were familiar with only 30 of them. No more than two of these compositions exist and both originate from Chinese Sung dynasty *tz'u* music, which included vocal and instrumental music. Modern *tangak* compositions are purely instrumental. *Tangak* compositions are based on either hexatonic or heptatonic scales and on duple rhythm, typical Chinese musical elements which nevertheless underwent a stage of Koreanization. Much of the melody tends to emphasize the pentatonic scale, and the melodies are given Korean-style ornamentation. In addition, a single beat is subdivided into a triplet (ex.2), a typical metrical structure of *hyangak*.

Ex.2 from *Nagyangch' un, tangak* repertory (Lee Hye-ku and others, 1973)

STONE CHIMES

TANGP'IRI

(iii) *Hyangak*. Court music of Korean origin and Chinese music that came to Korea before the T'ang dynasty, including Central Asian acrobatics, juggling and masked play, were originally included in *hyangak*, but the term now embraces compositions of the Koryŏ and Yi dynasties as well as those of Silla. The ensemble at the time of Silla included *kayago* (12-string long zither), *kŏmun'go* (six-string long zither), *pip'a* (short-necked plucked lute), *taegŭm, chunggŭm* (medium-sized flute), *sogŭm* (short flute), *pak, taego* (large barrel drum), accompanying both dance and song. Instruments of the Koryŏ dynasty, as listed in the *Koryŏ-sa* ('Koryŏ dynastic history') of the 15th century, included the *changgo, haegŭm* and *p'iri* (bamboo oboe) of *tangak* music in addition to the Silla dynasty's own instrumentation, and were divided into two orchestras: a wind orchestra for dance accompaniment, including *chunggŭm, sogŭm, haegŭm, p'iri* and *pak*; and chamber orchestra for song accompaniment, embracing *taegŭm, kŏmun'go, kayago, pip'a* and *changgo*. During this period the *chunggŭm*, now obsolete, seems to have played an important role, but was replaced later by the *taegŭm*.

During the early Yi dynasty, a few other *tangak* instruments, such as the *tangp'iri, tangjŏk* and *tangbip'a*, were modified and adopted by *hyangak*. Late

18th-century *hyangak* orchestras, depicted in the paintings by Kim Hong-do and Sin Yun-bok, were regularly composed of two *p'iri, taegŭm, haegŭm, changgo* and *puk* (double-headed barrel drum). This type of orchestra was called *samhyŏn yuggak* and was used for accompanying dances. Modern *samhyŏn yuggak*, also called *taep'ungnyu* or *kwanak* ('wind orchestra'), have much the same range of instruments, except for employing only one *p'iri* and sometimes adding an *ajaeng*. The National Classical Music Institute has one of these orchestras, as well as a type of chamber ensemble called *chulp'ungnyu* or *hyŏnak* ('string ensemble'). This orchestra commonly includes *kŏmun'go, kayago, taegŭm, p'iri, haegŭm* and *changgo* and occasionally *yanggŭm* (dulcimer) and *tanso* (small end-blown notched flute). The *chulp'ungnyu* mainly performs chamber music or accompanies classical songs.

The 14th-century *Samguk sagi* ('Historical records of the Three Kingdoms') lists only a few titles of Silla *hyangak* compositions. As time passed, the number of works increased, the *Koryŏ-sa* recording 24. 19 compositions of Koryŏ *hyangak* are included in the *Sillok* (Yi dynastic annals covering the period 1392–1910) but they are no longer performed. Most Koryŏ *hyangak* works were performed in the early Yi dynasty. In the reign of Sejong, however, a greater number of new compositions based on *hyangak* and *koch'wi* ('processional music') appeared, reaching as many as 82 by 1434. After the 16th century, many of these compositions were lost and progressive changes took place to such effect that *hyangak* compositions now performed by National Classical Music Institute musicians are quite different although they bear the titles of the earlier music. In particular, the vocal parts of *hyangak* have been completely lost.

Court entertainment or banquet dance of Korean origin is named *hyangak chŏngjae* and is different in several respects from *tangak chŏngjae* – the *tangak* pole-bearers do not appear and Korean songs are used instead of a Chinese prologue and epilogue.

7. VOCAL ART MUSIC. Three types of art song (*kagok, sijo* and *kasa*) have been enjoyed by the literati.

(i) *Kagok. Kagok* is a type of song cycle accompanied by a chamber ensemble, in which the poems are related melodically but not textually. The present *kagok* repertory was established between the 17th and 18th centuries and consists of 27 songs, which can be divided according to mode and to the sex of the performer. 11 works belong to the *ujo* mode (which uses the first, second, third, fifth and sixth degrees); 13 to the *kyemyŏnjo* mode (using the first, third, fourth, fifth and seventh degrees), and two are based half on *ujo* and half on *kyemyŏnjo*. 13 are songs for male solo voice, an equal number for female voice and the remaining piece in the cycle is sung in duet.

The archaic form of the *kagok* poem consists of three lines, each line comprising four words, each of three to five syllables. In performance, the poem is divided into five sections in addition to the instrumental prelude or postlude (*taeyŏŭm*) and interlude (*chungyŏŭm*); the interlude is placed between the third and fourth sections. In addition, each mode of *kagok* contains a couple of special instrumental preludes in free rhythm called *tasŭrŭm*, which are different from *taeyŏŭm*. *Tasŭrŭm*, performed as a prelude to the first and the last songs of the *kagok* cycle, is usually introduced by the *kŏmun'go* (six-string long zither) but occasionally the *taegŭm* (transverse flute) is added. The *tasŭrŭm* allows the player to warm up, establishes a basic modality, and introduces the basic melodic and ornamental features, resembling in function the *netori* of Japanese gagaku or the *ālāp* of Indian raga.

The standard accompaniment includes *kŏmun'go*, *taegŭm*, *p'iri* (bamboo oboe), *haegŭm* (two-string fiddle) and *changgo* (hourglass drum) with optional *kayago* (12-string long zither) and *tanso* (end-blown flute), an ensemble similar to that for *hyangak* (native Korean court music). The part for the *kŏmun'go* places emphasis on the nuclear melody, that for the *taegŭm* and *p'iri* on elaboration, that for the *haegŭm* on sustained sound and that for the *changgo* on rhythmic punctuation. Two rhythmic cycles played on the *changgo* are used in *kagok*: the basic cycle is in 16-pulse rhythm and the condensed cycle in 10-pulse rhythm, the latter achieved by condensing the two-pulse strokes of the original cycle into one-pulse strokes as shown in ex.3. Each song comprises approximately 15 statements of one or the other rhythmic cycle.

Ex.3 Original and condensed rhythmic patterns of *kagok*; transcr. Byong Won Lee

(ii) *Sijo*. A lyric song style of the cultured tradition, *sijo* requires only the *changgo* (hourglass drum) as the standard accompaniment. If the drum is not available the singer simply simulates the rhythmic patterns by beating his knees with his bare hands. In a formal concert *p'iri*, *taegŭm* and *haegŭm* may be used in addition to *changgo*. The accompaniment of melodic instruments is not prescribed, they merely follow the vocal melody with ornaments and fill in the pauses of the vocal part. The basic style of *sijo*, called *p'yŏng sijo*, employs the same type of three-line poem as is used in *kagok*, but the song is divided into three sections, each line of text being

assigned to a section. In *sijo*, unlike *kagok*, the last three-syllable word of the last line is for some reason omitted. This does not affect the meaning of the poem, for the word is usually a verbal inflection.

Sijo contains two different rhythmic patterns within a song: one of five pulses and one of eight pulses. The common organization of central Korea's *p'yŏng sijo* rhythm is: 1st section 5–8–8–5–8, 2nd 5–8–8–5–8, 3rd 5–8–5–1. The alternation of the two different rhythmic patterns may show slight regional variations. Originally *sijo* had one basic melody, the *p'yŏng sijo*, to which any *sijo* poem could be sung. But the present *sijo* repertory contains two more styles derived from *p'yŏng sijo*: *chirŭm sijo* and *sasŏl sijo*. *P'yŏng sijo* is the standard melody in a middle register, whereas the *chirŭm sijo* is characterized by having the melody in a high register in the first section, the second and third sections being the same as in *p'yŏng sijo*. The music of *sasŏl sijo* is much longer, employing a long narrative poem with an irregular number of lines and words. The *sijo* melody is tritonic, using the first, second and fifth degrees (of a heptatonic scale). The interval between the first and second is slightly flatter than a major 2nd. This simple tonal structure, however, does not represent the essential characteristics of *sijo*. Each note is given different types of vibrato, and furthermore, *sijo* musicians distinguish the direction of vibrato, either upward or downward from the initiating pitch. Relatively simple melodic lines are aesthetically enriched by subtle dynamic changes. It is the varying combination of these two elements, directional vibrato and dynamic variation, that establishes the authenticity of the music and reflects different personal or regional styles.

(iii) *Kasa*. This is a long narrative song accompanied by the *changgo*, or by a small ensemble similar to the one used for the formal concert of *sijo*. As in *sijo* the instruments merely follow the vocal melody with ornaments. The 12 extant pieces of *kasa* are based on either strophic or through-composed forms. Hybrid elements make the mode ambiguous in *kasa* (as in other folk music). The extensive use of falsetto in *kasa* also reveals close ties with the folksong styles of the south-western and north-western regions. The rhythmic pattern of each song is based on a five- or six-pulse rhythm. Some of the text syllables of *kasa* are treated by a transformation of the original vowel sound, often into an unrelated series of vocables. Such a change, which is not found in *kagok* and *sijo*, occurs in Buddhist chants and folksongs.

8. BUDDHIST RITUAL MUSIC. Korean Buddhist ritual music varies according to its role in a given rite. A particular chant may be performed in several ways depending on the rite, the time allowed for performance and the purpose of the performance. In general, the chant has a far more important role in a rite than the instrumental music.

(i) *Chants*. Ritual chant is divided into: *sutra* (Buddhist invocation); *hwach'ŏng* (chant based on folksong style); and *pŏmp'ae* (a long solemn chant).
Sutra. The *sutra*, commonly called *yŏmbul* ('invocation'), is musically the simplest ritual chant. Two different languages are used for the texts: translations into Chinese from Sanskrit and *sutra* written in Sanskrit or phonetically transcribed into Chinese from Sanskrit. The meaning of the former type is more easily con-

veyed, since it does not require a knowledge of Sanskrit. The basic style of text setting in both types is syllabic and both types are accompanied by a *mokt'ak* (wooden gong).

Hwach'ŏng may be a title of a chant or it may be a generic term for a type of chant. This solo chant is based on the Korean vernacular, and is therefore easily understood by the laity. This fact, and the presence of folk elements in the music, suggest that the *hwach'ŏng* may have originated from an attempt to make the Buddhist religion more readily understandable to common people; this would explain why *hwach'ŏng* is often performed away from temples. These musical and literary features also contributed to its influence upon mendicant priests' songs and other traditional Buddhist folk music in Korea. *Hwach'ŏng* is sung by a solo singer who accompanies himself between the vocal sections with a small gong struck with a mallet. Another priest accompanies the chant on a *puk* (barrel drum) which is suspended on a wooden frame; he strikes the heads and the wooden body with two sticks. The singer is at liberty to select a text appropriate to the given rite; the texts commonly deal in turn with the transience of secular life, conversion to Buddhism, religious commandments, and the rewards of Buddhism. *Hwach'ŏng* is closely related to folksong in its singing style and poetic form, aesthetic technique of voice and rhythmic structure. It is usually performed in conjunction with special rites; daily services do not require *hwach'ŏng* performance.

Pŏmp'ae. A type of solemn ritual chant performed only in association with certain rites, it is considered the most important type of chant. *Pŏmp'ae* was developed as a Chinese Buddhist chant, perhaps inspired by Sanskrit Buddhist songs, in the early stage of Chinese Buddhism. Numerous historical documents agree that *pŏmp'ae* was originated by Ts'ao Chih (192–232), the third son of Emperor Ts'ao Ts'ao of China (155–220). One frequently quoted legend relates that he was inspired to create it by the supernatural sound he heard at Yusan mountain ('fish-shaped mountain') in Shantung. The word *pŏmp'ae* corresponds to the Japanese *bombai* (*see* JAPAN, §II), both derived from the Sanskrit *brahma bhan* ('sacred chanting'), but the terms have slightly different meanings in each country. *Pŏmp'ae* texts are based on the Chinese language and Chinese poetic forms, but do not observe Chinese rhyme patterns; their content is Sinicized Buddhist verse. There are seven types of *pŏmp'ae* text in Korea, each distinguished by the number of syllables and of text lines. In descending order of their frequency in the repertory these are: a four-line stanza with a five-character line; a four-line stanza with a seven-character line (divided into four plus three); a six-line stanza with a seven-character line (four plus three); a three-line stanza with a nine-character line; a three-line stanza with a six-character line (three plus three); a three-line stanza with a ten-character line (two, four and four); and lines with irregular numbers of characters. The *pŏmp'ae* as now performed in Buddhist rites is based on an extremely slow free rhythm. Because the melody of each syllable of text is greatly prolonged, the meaning of the text becomes difficult to grasp, a complication carried further by the interpolation of certain vocables. The skeletal melodies of *pŏmp'ae* are constructed out of a considerable number of stock melodic formulae, which vary slightly according to their organization in a particular composition and the style of performance.

The repertory of *pŏmp'ae* contains two different styles of chant: *hossori* ('short chant') and *chissori* ('long chant'). Some *pŏmp'ae* verses may be performed in both styles, and the musician chooses the style depending upon the duration of the given rite. Usually, a larger honorarium requires longer and more elaborate rites. In spite of their close developmental ties with Korea, Chinese and Japanese Buddhist chant have no counterpart to these two styles.

Hossori pŏmp'ae. The performance of a chant in *hossori* style usually takes two to eight minutes. A common musical structure is a binary form of *ABAB* for four lines of a complete text. Each syllable is treated either melismatically or syllabically, and vocables are interpolated between most of them. *Hossori* chant is performed solo, responsorially and chorally. One characteristic of the long melodic phrase of *hossori* is its use of repeated melodic motifs. If the motifs are repeated at the same pitch level, they can be distinguished only by their corresponding text-syllable patterns. The melodic phrase usually begins slowly, gradually accelerating for each repetition of the motif and finally ending with tempo rubato. As the tempo accelerates the repeated motifs undergo a process of rhythmic condensation (ex.4). There are also long

Ex.4 from *Ch'ohalyang, hossori pŏmp'ae* repertory; rec. and transcr. Byong Won Lee (Byong Won Lee, 1974)

eng ya   e hieng ya   e hieng ya   e hie   e hie

e hie   hi e hi ehieng ya   o   a   a

optional interpolations, some longer than the main melody, which can be inserted to extend the duration of the rites.

Hossori performance requires a small handbell which marks off the text lines, but which serves no musical function. However, when this type of *pŏmp'ae* is per-

Ex.5 *Hossori pŏmp'ae* chant; rec. and transcr. Byong Won Lee (Byong Won Lee, 1974)

♩.= 52
CHORUS

(To) To _____ a a ha hŏ

T'AEP'YŎNGSO

ŏ a e _____ i i

_____ hŭ a a ha ha o   o o (ryang) rya hŭ a _____

formed simultaneously with a ritual dance, an outdoor band (see §(ii) below) provides background accompaniment. For example, while the *Toryang-gye* is being chanted, the band constantly repeats a long melodic cycle, a *yŏmbul* ('invocation', i.e. a *sutra*), disregarding any changes in the chanted melody until the dance ends. Though there seems to be no overt melodic relationship between the instrumental accompaniment and the chanting, nor any obvious rhythmic correlation between the dance and the accompaniment, there is in fact a subtle heterophonic relationship between the band's melody and the chanted melody. Because the free rhythm of *hossori* chant is unsuitable for dancers, they follow a rhythm from the band's more animated accompaniment. In ex.5, the choral chant *Toryang-gye* is compared with the melody being played at the same time on the *t'aep'yŏngso* (double-reed aerophone) to accompany the ritual dance *nabich'um* ('butterfly dance'). Thus, the simultaneous performance (called *yojap*) of chant, instrumental accompaniment and dance contains apparently unrelated elements which actually have a place in the overall concept.

Chissori pŏmp'ae. Chissori is regarded as the most important chant style of Buddhist music and maintains one of the highest positions in the traditional vocal music of Korea. *Chissori* style uses a much longer type of melody than does *hossori*, has a different way of using melodic formulae, and has more complex vocal techniques. The performance of this highly sophisticated style of chant usually takes place at a large-scale ceremony, but such occasions and performances are becoming obsolete in Korea, and the number of Buddhist musicians who can perform in this musical style is gradually decreasing. The total *chissori* repertory is said to include 72 compositions; 56 of them are contained, in several different

versions, in the *tongŭm-jip*, collections of similar *chissori* melodic entities (see §3).

The organization of melodic phrases is important in *chissori* composition and the process is more complex than in *hossori*. For example, in one chant a certain melodic phrase may be a great portion of the entire chant, and the same phrase may appear in other chants. One characteristic of *chissori* is that certain melodic phrases are consecutively repeated several times. Sometimes a repeated melodic phrase is itself built from a series of repeated motifs. Such phrases usually begin slowly, then as the tempo gradually accelerates, the phrases and their inner motifs, together with their text syllables, are condensed. Following this there is a return to the opening tempo, and the melody tends to descend. This formula, from an aesthetic point of view, follows a pattern of tranquillity leading to tension followed by release (ex.6).

Most *chissori* textures are monophonic, performed by a chorus in unison. However, some *chissori* include one or two optional interpolations by a soloist, called *hŏdŏlp'um* ('empty style'), which may occur either at the beginning or in the middle of the choral chant. *Hŏdŏlp'um* is performed by the leader of the chorus or by a singer appointed by the leader. Musically, it is a fixed, independent melodic line set to a series of vocables. When *hŏdŏlp'um* occurs at the beginning of the composition, it does not reappear. But when it is interpolated in the middle of the chant, it may reappear any number of times (nowadays, however, usually no more than three), depending upon the leader's or singer's personal preference. One function of *hŏdŏlp'um* is to afford the leader an opportunity to demonstrate his musical virtuosity. If the *hŏdŏlp'um* precedes the main chant, it allows the singer to warm up and assists in establishing the basic mood of the chant. Finally, the interpolation of the *hŏdŏlp'um* may extend the duration of performance of the chant and thus the length of the rite.

In *hossori* each line of text is given the same amount of time and all lines of the text are performed; but in *chissori* only portions of the original text are selected and, moreover, only a few text syllables are given long melismatic treatment, others being merely recited syllabically. In a *chissori* performance, the text is either recited in a measured rhythm, or prolonged in a very slow free rhythm. The desired duration of the chant and rite determines the application of these two styles. If a *chissori* composition is assigned a short duration, more syllables will be quickly recited, and fewer be melismatically prolonged. *Chissori* style has a type of after-ornament not commonly found in *hossori*. This is produced through gradual microtonal ascent to a given pitch, followed by a sudden downward leap of an octave or more (see ex.6). If the after-ornament has to reach the note *c″* or higher, falsetto is used; otherwise the high note is reached using the 'tense throat' technique. After-ornaments appear in almost every phrase in a *chissori* composition.

Ex.6 *Porye*, process of melodic condensation and internal structure of repetitive motifs; rec. and transcr. Byong Won Lee (Byong Won Lee, 1974)

(ii) Instrumental music and dance. The outdoor Buddhist band, called *chorach'i* or *kyŏngnaech'wi*, consists of one or two *t'aep'yŏngso* (double-reed instruments), *ching* (flat bronze gong), *puk* (double-headed barrel drum), *para* (pair of cymbals), *nap'al* (long metal trumpet) and *nagak* (conch trumpet). Members of the band belong to a class of professional lay musicians, whereas most of the ritual chant singers and the dancers

are Buddhist priests.

The Buddhist ritual dances, called *chakpŏp*, are unique to Korean Buddhism (Chinese and Japanese Buddhism do not have such dances). There are four basic ritual dances: *nabich'um* ('butterfly dance', see ex.5), a prayer dance in which cherubs and angels symbolically descend from heaven; *para-ch'um* ('cymbal dance'), a prayer dance by cherubs who play a pair of large cymbals while they dance; *pŏpko-ch'um* ('drum dance'), a dance in which the beating of a huge barrel drum symbolically relieves the dead person of his tribulations; and *mogu-ch'um* ('stick dance'), in which the dancers beat on an octagonal box whose eight sides represent the eight kinds of righteousness to which one must be awakened. Each of the dances, except *mogu-ch'um*, has variants, and these share a limited number of dance movements.

9. FOLK MUSIC.
(i) *P'ansori*. This is a one-man operatic form accompanied by a *puk* (double-headed barrel drum). The singer executes all three elements: *aniri* ('dialogue' and 'narration'), *pallim* ('acting') and *sori* ('singing'). The performance of a complete *p'ansori* takes four to eight hours. The most reliable theory of its origins traces it to the early 18th century (Yi dynasty). It was originally a long dramatic form, combining a series of short songs performed at shamanistic rituals in Chŏlla province (south-western Korea). After set *p'ansori* librettos had evolved, the singers began interpolating existing folksongs appropriate to the story and mood. At first, the *p'ansori* was performed by *kwangdae*, itinerant professional entertainers who were believed to be blood relations of the shaman.

The *p'ansori* texts had been orally transmitted until the 19th century. During the reign of King Sunjo (1800–34) of the Yi dynasty 12 *p'ansori* texts were written down for the first time. Further codification of the form was undertaken by Sin Chae-hyo (1817–84); only five *p'ansori* still survive. Sin Chae-hyo initiated a reform of *p'ansori*. The first known serious scholar of *p'ansori*, he came from an aristocratic family background in Chŏlla province, which brought increased status to the genre and its musicians. He was the first to train female *p'ansori* singers, and also attempted to change the one-man operatic form into a sung drama (*ch'anggŭk*), by assigning each character's role to a different singer as in a Western opera. However, this form has not found lasting popularity, in spite of a revival during the 1950s.

The modal structure of *p'ansori* has been the aspect least investigated. Each of the various *p'ansori* modes denotes different moods, as well as implying certain melodic phrases and configurations. The most common mode is *kyemyŏnjo* which is based on three 'pillar' notes, each helping in a different way to define the mode. *Kyemyŏnjo*'s prevailing mood is elegiac, whereas the mood of *ujo*, another mode, is usually described as imperative and of heroic character. Among the three elements of *p'ansori*, singing is given prime importance by the singer and drummer. The sung section is always accompanied by one of seven rhythmic patterns suited to the text. The rhythmic patterns often convey an associative symbolism: for example, the *ŏnmori changdan*, a rhythm in 10/8 metre, always accompanies Buddhistic textual content.

P'ansori requires a heavy, hoarse vocal timbre unlike that used for any other Korean vocal music. It is obtained through long training, including shouting in remote areas until one develops a hoarse throat condition. For the proper musical effect it is necessary to be able to maintain this sort of timbre consistently while singing for long periods of time. Before a *p'ansori* performance, the singer usually warms up his voice and establishes the musical mood by performing a *tan'ga* (short epic song), which requires the same kind of vocal techniques as does *p'ansori* and contains similar melodic themes, but is easier to sing because of its non-dramatic nature. The rhythmic patterns of *tan'ga*, *chungmori* or *chungjungmori* (12/8) are performed in a moderate tempo. While performing the *p'ansori*, the singer usually stands on the performing area holding a fan and a handkerchief in each hand as symbolic props, unless the dramatic effect requires another posture. The drummer sits on the floor a short distance from the singer, and strikes the drum's left head with his left palm and its right head and the wooden frame with a stick. The drummer not only provides the required rhythmic patterns for each song but also inspires the singer by interjecting suitable exclamations at appropriate times, in such a way that they provide a link between the music of the singer and the drummer.

(ii) *Sanjo*. An improvised solo instrumental form accompanied by the *changgo* (hourglass drum), its tradition is still transmitted aurally. A complete *sanjo* performance takes 30 to 60 minutes. The earliest *sanjo* music developed from stringing together shamanistic and folk tunes of Chŏlla province. These various scattered tunes served as stock melodies for individual improvisation and as sources for the elaboration and creation of new melodies. These improvisational elements were given a formal structure by the imposition of a fixed framework of rhythm and mode. The improvisational techniques have gradually disappeared with the constraints of modern performance (e.g. the limited performance schedules of the mass media, and the teaching of music from transcription). *Sanjo* was established as a form in the second half of the 19th century by Kim Ch'ang-jo (1865–1920), who was often mistakenly referred to as its originator. There now exist several different schools of *sanjo* performance. The *kayago* (12-string long zither) was the first instrument used for *sanjo* and still remains the most popular one. Since the late 19th century other instruments, such as the *kŏmun'go* (six-string long zither) and *taegŭm* (transverse flute), have also been used to play *sanjo*.

The overall structure of *sanjo* is delineated by six independent rhythmic patterns (actually movements or sections), played without a pause in progressively faster tempos. The tempo also increases in the course of each movement. The change of movement is usually signalled by the first melodic phrase, whose rhythm suggests the basic rhythmic pattern of the *changgo*. The rhythmic patterns of each movement vary slightly each time in order to suit the subtle spontaneous changes in the melodic rhythm. The faster movements (e.g. *chajinmori* and *hwimori*) include complicated patterns with syncopation and hemiola. Each movement contains several sections which share the same tonal centre. The change of movement is usually recognized by the tonal shift. The melodic phrase consists of two or more patterns, usually built on a tetratonic model in the slow movements, or on tritonic models in the faster movements. A phrase may have a cadential pattern which ascends from an unstable vibrato, or one with a descending slide from an indeterminate pitch to the tonal centre. The stylistic characteristics of *sanjo* vary in the different schools, but in general the style is marked by subtle slides in slow movements and virtuoso rhythmic complexity in faster movements. An important aesthetic consideration is the contrast of tension and relaxation in the melodies.

BIBLIOGRAPHY
Sŏng Hyŏn, ed.: *Akhak kwebŏm* [Book of music] (Seoul, 1493/R1968)
Pak Yong-dae, ed.: *Chŭngbo munhŏn pigo* [Korean encyclopedia of documents and institutions] (Seoul, 1908/R1957)
Chosŏn wangjo sillok [Annals of the Yi dynasty] (Seoul, 1955–8)
Lee Hye-ku [Yi Hye-gu]: *Han'guk ŭmak yŏn'gu* [Studies in Korean music] (Seoul, 1957)
Chang Sa-hun: *Kugak kaeyo* [Outline of Korean music] (Seoul, 1961)
——: *Kugak non'go* [Studies of Korean music] (Seoul, 1966)
Lee Hye-ku: *Han'guk ŭmak sŏsŏl* [Topics in Korean music] (Seoul, 1967)
Han'guk ŭmak [Anthology of Korean traditional music], ed. National Classical Music Institute (Seoul, 1968–) [scores in staff notation]
Chang Sa-hun: *Han'guk akki taegwan* [Korean musical instruments] (Seoul, 1969)
Yi Tu-hyŏn: *Han'guk kamyŏn'gŭk* [Korean mask dance drama] (Seoul, 1969)
Yi Hye-gu paksa songsu kinyŏm ŭmakhak nonch'ong [Essays in eth-nomusicology: a birthday offering for Lee Hye-ku] (Seoul, 1969)
J. Levy: 'Musique bouddhique de Corée', *Vogue* LVLX 253 [disc notes; see also review, B. Smith, *EM*, xvi (1972), 560]
Pak Hŭng-su: *Kugak ŭi iron chŏgin yŏn'gu nonmunjip* [Articles on Korean music theory] (Seoul, ?1970)
The Ancient Arts of Korea, ed. Ministry of Culture and Information (Seoul, ?1970), 208ff
J. Levy: 'Korean Court Music', LL 7206 [disc notes]
——: 'Korean Social and Folk Music', LLST 7211 [disc notes; see also review, R. Garfias, *EM*, xvii (1973), 368]
Song Bang-song: *An Annotated Bibliography of Korean Music* (Providence, 1971)
Han'guk ŭmak yŏn'gu [Journal of the Korean Musicological Society] (Seoul, 1971–)
Chang Sa-hun: *Glossary of Korean Music* (Seoul, 1972)
J. Cott and D. Lewiston: 'P'ansori: Korea's Epic Vocal Art and Instrumental Music', Nonesuch Explorer H-72049 [disc notes; see also review, R. Garfias, *EM*, xvii (1973), 368]
Lee Hye-ku [Yi Hye-gu]: 'Han'guk ŭmak sŏnjip' [Selection of Korean classical music], Jigu (Chigu) Record Co., Seoul [disc notes; see also review, Song Bang-song, *EM*, xix (1975), 508]
Chang Sa-hun: *Sijo ŭmak-non* [A study of sijo] (Seoul, 1973)
Survey of Korean Arts: Traditional Music, ed. [Korean] National Academy of Arts (Seoul, 1973)
Chang Sa-hun: *Yŏmyŏng ŭi tongsŏ ŭmak* [Eastern and Western music in the early 20th century] (Seoul, 1974)
Im Tong-gwŏn: *Han'guk minyo yŏn'gu* [Studies on Korean folksong] (Seoul, 1974)
Kugak chŏnjip [Complete collection of Korean music], ed. National Classical Music Institute (Seoul, 1974–) [in Korean notation]
Byong Won Lee: *An Analytical Study of Sacred Buddhist Chant of Korea* (diss., U. of Washington, 1974)
R. C. Provine jr: 'The Treatise on Ceremonial Music (1430) in the Annals of the Korean King Sejong', *EM*, xviii (1974), 1–30
Song Bang-song: 'Supplement to an Annotated Bibliography of Korean Music', *Korea Journal*, xiv/12 (1974), 59; xv/1 (1975), 59; xv/2 (1975), 58; xv/3 (1975), 64; xv/4 (1975), 69
Chang Sa-hun: *Han'guk chŏnt'ong ŭmak ŭi yŏn'gu* [Studies in Korean traditional music] (Seoul, 1975)
R. C. Provine jr: 'The Sacrifice to Confucius in Korea and its Music', *Transactions of the Korea Branch of the Royal Asiatic Society*, 1 (1975), 43
Song Bang-song: *Kŏmun'go sanjo: an Analytical Study of a Style of Korean Instrumental Music* (diss., Wesleyan U., 1975)
Chang Sa-hun: *Han'guk ŭmak-sa* [History of Korean music] (Seoul, 1976)
——: *Kugak ch'ongnon* [Introduction to Korean music] (Seoul, 1976)
J. Condit: *Sources for Korean Music, 1450–1600* (diss., U. of Cambridge, 1976)
Lee Hye-ku: *Han'guk ŭmak nonch'ong* [Essays on Korean music] (Seoul, 1976)
K. L. Pratt: 'Music as a Factor in Sung-Koryŏ Diplomatic Relations, 1069–1126', *T'oung Pao*, lxii/4–5 (1976), 199
Song Bang-song: 'A Discography of Korean Music', *Asian Music*, viii/2 (1977), 82–121
Tongyang ŭmakhak nonch'ong [Articles on Asian music: Festschrift for Dr Chang Sa-hun] (Seoul, 1977)
Asian Music, ix/2 (1978) [Korean music issue]
J. Condit: 'A Fifteenth-century Korean Score in Mensural Notation', *Musica asiatica*, ii (1979), 1–87

BYONG WON LEE (bibliography with ROBERT C. PROVINE)

Koréh, Endre (*b* Sepsiszentgyörgy, 13 April 1906; *d* Vienna, 20 Sept 1960). Hungarian bass. He studied in Budapest under Árpád Palotay, making his début at the Budapest Opera House as Sparafucile in 1930. A naturally rich, dark bass voice soon attracted attention in Wagner roles (notably Hunding, Hagen and Fafner); an ability to undertake *basso cantante* parts also fitted him for Mozart and Verdi. In 1948, after a series of guest performances in Vienna, he became a member of the Staatsoper. He made appearances at Glyndebourne (Osmin, 1950), the Metropolitan (Ochs, 1953), and the Salzburg and Florence festivals, and was the first Caliban in Frank Martin's *The Tempest* (1956).

PÉTER P. VÁRNAI

Korev, Yury Semyonovich (*b* Moscow, 9 Aug 1928). Soviet musicologist, son of the musicologist Semyon Isaakovich Korev (1900–53). He studied music history and musicology under Yury Keldïsh at the Moscow Conservatory, graduating in 1950. He began work as a music critic in 1948, and in 1958 joined the editorial board of *Sovetskaya muzïka*, of which he became editor in 1970. From 1955 until 1958 he was a consultant to the USSR Composers' Union, and he was appointed secretary to the RSFSR Composers' Union in 1968. Korev's writings are concerned chiefly with Soviet music.

WRITINGS
Tikhon Khrennikov i evo vtoraya simfoniya [Khrennikov and his 2nd symphony] (Moscow, 1951)
Sovetskaya massovaya pesnya [Soviet mass songs] (Moscow, 1956)
Iolanta P. I. Chaykovskov [Tchaikovsky's Iolanta] (Moscow, 1957)
M. Raukhverger i evo balet Cholpon [Raukhverger and his ballet Cholpon] (Moscow, 1958)
Ocherk po istorii russkoy muzïkal'noy kul'turï [Study of the history of Russian musical culture], *Muzïkal'naya kul'tura soyuznïkh res-publik*, ii (Moscow, 1958)
'Skripichnïy kontsert T. Khrennikova' [Khrennikov's Violin Concerto], *SovM* (1959), no.12, p.18
'Tema i eyo voploshcheniye' [A theme and its realization], *SovM* (1959), no.5, p.32 [on Kabalevsky's and Ledenyov's cantatas]
'Vstrecha s geroyem Khachaturiana' [A meeting with Khachaturian's hero], *SovM* (1961), no.10, p.25
Viktor Belïy (Moscow, 1962)
Kirill Molchanov (Moscow, 1970)
'O pyatnadtsatoy simfonii D. Shostakovicha' [Shostakovich's Symphony no.15], *SovM* (1972), no.9, p.8
Muzïkal'no-kriticheskiye stat'i [Critical writings on music] (Moscow, 1974)

LEV GINZBURG

Körling, (Sven) August (*b* Kristdala, Kalmar län, 14 April 1842; *d* Ystad, 21 Oct 1919). Swedish composer and conductor. He completed his studies at the Musikaliska Akademien in Stockholm in 1861. Five years later he settled in the little town of Ystad on the south coast of Sweden, where he worked for the rest of his life as an organist, school music teacher and con-ductor of various musical ensembles. Together with the singer and viola player Salomon Smith (1853–1938) he organized many amateur musical activities there. He was elected a member of the Musikaliska Akademien in 1888.

As a composer, chiefly of vocal music in smaller forms, Körling was influenced by the national Romantic movement. Some of his solo songs became widely popular. Among his compositions for male chorus, the two ballads *Sten Sture* and *Håtunaleken* are the best known. Körling is the only composer to have been awarded first prize in the annual competition for men's choral compositions organized by the Sällskapet för Svenska Kvartettsångens Befrämjande (1886 and 1889).

FOLKE BOHLIN

Körling, (John) Felix (August) (*b* Kristdala, Kalmar län, 17 Dec 1864; *d* Halmstad, 8 Jan 1937). Swedish composer and conductor, son of August Körling. He left the Stockholm Conservatory in 1886 and worked from 1889 in Halmstad on the west coast of Sweden, dominating its musical life for many years as his father had done at Ystad. He made the Halmstad Choral Society well known throughout Scandinavia and was also one of the principal conductors of the Swedish choral association Svenska Körförbundet (founded in 1925). Many of his songs became very popular, especially those for children and young people. His gay marching song *En glad trall* is often used in community singing; its tune has also become very well known in Turkey, where it is sung to a Turkish patriotic text. Körling's other compositions include choral and orchestral works and music for the stage, among them three operettas which were performed at the Oscarsteatern in Stockholm.

His brother Sven Körling (1879–1948), also a composer, worked as an organist, conductor and music teacher in Göteborg.

FOLKE BOHLIN

Korn, Johann Daniel. German music publisher, co-founder of the firm LEUCKART.

Korn, Peter Jona (*b* Berlin, 30 March 1922). American composer and conductor of German birth. He attended the Berlin Hochschule für Musik (1932–3) and then studied composition at the Beltane School, London, with Rubbra (1934–6) and at the Jerusalem Conservatory with Wolpe (1936–8). In 1941 he moved to the USA and continued his studies under Schoenberg at the University of California at Los Angeles (1941–2). He took American citizenship in 1944. A pupil of Eisler and Toch at the University of Southern California (1946–7), he also studied composition for films with Rózsa and Dahl. He was founder-conductor of the New Orchestra of Los Angeles (1948–56), a composition teacher at the Munich Trapp Conservatory (1960–61), visiting lecturer at the University of California at Los Angeles (1964–5) and director of the Strauss Conservatory, Munich (from 1967). In addition he has been a frequent contributor to music periodicals and newspapers, including *Die Welt*.

WORKS
(selective list)

Opera: Heidi, op.35 (Korn, after J. Spyri), 1963
Orch: 3 syms., op.3, 1946, rev. 1957, op.13, 1952, op.30, 1956, rev. 1973; Tom Paine Ov., 1950; Rhapsody, op.14, ob, str, 1952; Concertino, op.15, hn, str, 1952; In media res, op.21, ov., 1953; Variations on a Tune from the Beggar's Opera, op.26, 1954; Sax Conc., op.31, 1956; Vn Conc., op.39, 1965; Semi-Sym., op.42, 1966; Diversions, 1966; Eine kleine Popmusik, 1972
Chamber: Vc Sonata, 1949; Ob Sonata, 1949; 2 str qts, op.10, 1950, op.36, 1963; Passacaglia and Fugue, 8 hn, 1952; Hn Sonata, 1953; Serenade, op.33, 4 hn, 1957; Quintettino, fl, cl, bn, vc, pf, 1964; Turandot-Variations, pf, 1973; other pf pieces
Several choral works, 8 song cycles

Principal publishers: Boosey & Hawkes, Bote & Bock, Peters, Simrock

JOSEPH CLARK

Kornauth, Egon (*b* Olmütz, 14 May 1891; *d* Vienna, 28 Oct 1959). Austrian composer and pianist. His inclination to music was coloured by a twin Austrian and Czech heritage. As a child he studied the piano, making his début at the age of 15, and he also played the flute, the clarinet, the cello and, more particularly, the organ; he formed an amateur string quartet and played in the Brno theatre orchestra. He entered Vienna University to study philology in 1909, but his interests rapidly shifted to the academy of music, where he studied theory with Fuchs, who enjoined him to an intensive study of Bach and Brahms. In 1910 he acted as accompanist to the Vienna Gesangverein on an American tour, and in 1912 he attracted public attention with the Viola Sonata op.3, which won the Austrian State Prize and was published. Differences quickly developed between Kornauth and his next teacher, Schreker, whose interest in dramatic music did not accord with his pupil's preference for composition of an essentially lyrical emphasis. After leaving Schreker, Kornauth taught himself under friendly supervision from Schmidt, and he studied musicology under Adler. For the 1916 season he was a coach at the Vienna Hofoper, and for the following two years he taught theory at the music history institute of the university.

During the 1920s Kornauth appeared as an ensemble pianist and accompanist throughout Europe. In 1926 he accepted an invitation to organize an orchestra in Medan, Sumatra, where, despite considerable difficulties, he maintained and directed the group for two years. He also founded the Vienna Trio, with which he toured Java, Celebes and Ceylon in 1928–9. Early in 1930 he returned to Vienna and received the city's Music Prize. Another tour with the Vienna Trio took him to Brazil (1933–5), and then he remained active as an accompanist in Austria until 1949. He was appointed to teach theory at the Vienna Musikhochschule in 1940, and in 1945 he was made a professor at the Salzburg Mozarteum, where he was deputy director (1946–7). He received the Austrian Staatlicher Würdigungspreis für Musik (1951) and was elected to the Kunstsenat in 1954.

WORKS
(for complete list see Müller von Asow, 1958)

Orch: Sym. Suite no.1 'Aus der Jugendzeit', op.7, 1913, rev. 1929; Burleske, op.11, fl, orch, 1914, rev. 1931; Sym. Ov. (Festliches Vorspiel), Eb, op.13, 1914, rev. 1925; Elegie auf den Tod eines Freundes, 1916; Ballade, op.17, vc, orch, 1917; Konzertstück, b, op.19, vn, chamber orch, 1917, rev. 1924; Suite (Sinfonietta), a, op.20, 1918, rev. 1922; Sym. Suite no.2, f♯, op.35, 1926–31, rev. 1937; Romantische Suite, op.40, 1932–6, rev. 1940; Suite, c♯, op.42, 1937–8
Chamber: Sonata, c♯, op.3, va, pf, 1912; Sonata, f, op.5, cl, pf, 1912–13; Sonata, e, op.9, vn, pf, 1913–14; Sonatina, D, op.13, vn, pf, 1916; Kleine Abendmusik, a, op.14, str qt, 1915; Pf Sextet, c, op.18, 1917; Str Sextet, a, op.25, 1918–19; Str Qt, g, op.26, 1920; Pf Trio, b, op.27, 1921; Sonata, e, op.28, vc, pf, 1922; Str Qnt no.1, d, op.30, 1923; Kammermusik, op.31, fl, ob, cl, hn, str qnt, 1924; Cl Qnt, f♯, op.33, 1931; Pf Qnt, f♯, op.35a, 1931; Str Qnt no.2, c♯, op.40, 1938, rev. 1947
Vocal: 6 Lieder, op.22 (Hesse), 1918–19; 3 Lieder, op.24, 1v, fl, chamber orch, 1918, rev. 1921, 1932; 4 Lieder, op.34 (Brentano), 1930–31; 8 Lieder, op.36 (Eichendorff), 1932; Lieder, op.37 (Eichendorff), 1932; 8 Lieder, op.38 (Eichendorff), 1932–3; others, opp.1, 6, 12, 21
Pf: Sonata, Ab, op.4, 1912; Fantasy, Eb, op.10, 1912–15; Kleine Suite, op.29, 1923; other pieces, opp.2, 23, 32

Principal publishers: Doblinger, Tischer & Jagenberg, Universal, Zimmermann

WRITINGS

Die thematische Arbeit in Josef Haydns Streichquartetten seit 1780 (diss., U. of Vienna, 1915)
Versuch eines Selbstbildnisses, 1944, unpubd

'Theorie und Praxis', *Wissenschaft und Praxis: Festschrift Bernhard Paumgartner* (Zurich, 1958)
Many essays in *ÖMz*

BIBLIOGRAPHY
E. H. Müller von Asow: *Verzeichnis der Werke von Egon Kornauth* (Vienna, 1937, rev. 1958)
——: *Egon Kornauth: ein Bild vom Leben und Schaffen des mährischen Komponisten* (Vienna, 1941)
E. Rieger: 'Egon Kornauth', *ÖMz*, ii (1947), 260
B. Paumgartner: 'Egon Kornauth', *ÖMz*, xii (1957), 4
                                    JOHN MORGAN

Körner, (Karl) Theodor (*b* Dresden, 23 Nov 1791; *d* Gadebusch, Mecklenburg, 26 Aug 1813). German poet. He was the son of Christian Gottfried Körner (*b* Leipzig, 2 Aug 1756; *d* Berlin, 13 May 1831), Schiller's closest friend and an aesthetician with strong musical leanings ('Über Charakterdarstellung in der Musik', *Die Horen*, v, 1795). After studying geology, philosophy and law at Freiberg, Leipzig and Berlin, Theodor Körner went to Vienna in 1811 as *Dramaturg*. He met Eichendorff, Beethoven, Weber, Moscheles and Meyerbeer and wrote a quantity of dramas and poems. He enlisted in Lützow's volunteer corps in 1813 and fell in battle. His most popular and perhaps also his best works are the soldiers' songs he wrote in the months before his death (*Lützows wilde Jagd, Du Schwert an meiner Linken, Frisch auf, mein Volk*) – lyrics that found an immediate and lasting echo, even if they would probably not have sustained quite the same impact if their creator had survived to a ripe old age. Körner composed music as well as writing texts to existing melodies. He had already discussed opera projects with Beethoven and Spohr before leaving Vienna in the year of his death, and Reichardt, Zelter, Weber, Himmel and Loewe are among those who set his songs. Schubert set 17 Körner poems and the libretto *Der vierjährige Posten* in 1815; Dvořák and Flotow both set *Alfred der Grosse* and Flotow also set *Die Bergknappen*; and a number of now forgotten composers also based operas on Körner's dramas and librettos.

BIBLIOGRAPHY
K. Streckfuss, ed.: *T. Körner: Sämtliche Werke* (Berlin, 1834)
F. Jonas: *C. G. Körner: Biographische Nachrichten über ihn und sein Haus* (Berlin, 1882)
A. Schäfer: *Historisches und systematisches Verzeichnis sämtlicher Tonwerke zu den Dramen . . . Körners* (Leipzig, 1886)
K. Goedeke: *Grundriss zur Geschichte der deutschen Dichtung*, v (Dresden, 2/1893), 499f; vii (Dresden, 2/1900), 838ff
R. Musiol: *T. Körner und seine Beziehungen zur Musik* (Ratibor, 1893)
S. Engelmann: *Der Einfluss des Volksliedes auf die Lyrik der Befreiungskriege* (diss., U. of Heidelberg, 1909)
K. Berger: *T. Körner* (Bielefeld, 1912)
W. Seifert: *Christian Gottfried Körner und seine Musikästhetik im Lichte der klassischen deutschen Ästhetik* (diss., U. of Jena, 1956)
                                    PETER BRANSCOMBE

Kornett (Ger.). (1) CORNET (i).
   (2) An ORGAN STOP (*Cornett*).

Kornfeld, Peter. *Nom de plume* of NORBERT SCHULTZE.

Korngold, Erich Wolfgang (*b* Brno, 29 May 1897; *d* Hollywood, 29 Nov 1957). American composer of Austro-Hungarian birth. He was a son of the eminent Austrian music critic Julius Korngold (1860–1945). He was a remarkable child prodigy composer. In 1907 he played his cantata *Gold* to Mahler, who pronounced him a genius and recommended that he be sent to Zemlinsky for tuition. At the age of 11 he composed the ballet *Der Schneemann*, which caused a sensation when it was first performed at the Vienna Court Opera (1910), and he followed this with a Piano Trio and a remarkable Piano Sonata in E that so impressed Schnabel that he championed the work all over Europe. Of his first orchestral works, the *Schauspiel Ouvertüre* and the Sinfonietta (1912), Strauss remarked: 'One's first reaction that these compositions are by an adolescent boy are those of awe and fear: this firmness of style, this sovereignty of form, this individual expression, this harmonic structure – it is really amazing', while Puccini was similarly impressed by his opera *Violanta* (1916). His early fame reached its height with the appearance of his operatic masterpiece, *Die tote Stadt*, composed when he was 20 and acclaimed the world over after its dual première in Hamburg and Cologne (1920). Later that decade he began teaching opera and composition at the Vienna Staatsakademie and was awarded the title professor *honoris causa* by the president of Austria. In 1928 the *Neue Wiener Tagblatt* conducted a poll whose returns named Korngold and Schoenberg as the two greatest living composers.

Max Reinhardt, with whom he had collaborated on versions of *Die Fledermaus* and *La belle Hélène*, took Korngold to Hollywood in 1934. The Anschluss prevented him from staging his fifth opera, *Die Kathrin*, and he remained in Hollywood composing some of the finest music written for the cinema; two scores, *Robin Hood* and *Anthony Adverse*, received Oscars. After the war he returned to absolute music, composing, among other things, a Violin Concerto (introduced by Heifetz), a Symphonic Serenade for strings (introduced by Furtwängler), a Cello Concerto and the Symphony in F♯.

Korngold was one of the last great Romantic composers. Over the years, however, he suffered neglect and savage criticism, largely because of changing trends and his association with Hollywood. Then in 1975 *Die tote Stadt* was revived to capacity houses in New York and the first recording was released of both this and the Symphony in F♯. His lush, late Romantic harmony, his melodic gift and the vibrant sensuousness of his music seemed to be returning to favour.

WORKS
(selective list)

OPERAS
Der Ring des Polykrates, op.7 (after H. Teweles), Munich, 28 March 1916
Violanta, op.8 (H. Muller), Munich, 28 March 1916
Die tote Stadt, op.12 (Paul Schott [E. W. and J. Korngold], after G. Rodenbach: Bruges la morte), Hamburg and Cologne, 4 Dec 1920
Das Wunder der Heliane, op.20 (Muller, after H. Kaltneker), Hamburg, 10 Oct 1927
Die Kathrin, op.28 (E. Decsey), Stockholm, 7 Oct 1939

OTHER DRAMATIC
Gold (cantata), solo vv, pf, 1907
Der Schneemann (pantomime, E. W. Korngold), Vienna, 4 Oct 1910
Much Ado about Nothing, op.11, incidental music, 1919
The Silent Serenade, op.36 (stage comedy, E. W. Korngold, H. Reisfeld), 1946

ORCHESTRAL
Schauspiel Ouvertüre, op.4, 1911; Sinfonietta, op.5, 1912; Sursum corda, op.13, sym. ov., 1921; Pf Conc., C♯, op.17, pf left hand, orch, perf. 1923; Die kleine Serenade, op.24, small orch, 1931–2; Tomorrow, op.33, sym. poem, chorus, orch, 1942; Vn Conc., D, op.35, 1945; Vc Conc., C, op.37, 1946; Sym. Serenade, B, str, op.39, perf. 1947; Sym., F♯, op.40, 1951–2; Theme and Variations, op.42, school orch

CHAMBER AND INSTRUMENTAL
Pf Sonata no.1, d, 1908; Don Quixote, pf pieces, 1908; Caprice fantastique, vn, pf, 1908; Pf Trio, D, op.1, 1909; Pf Sonata no.2, E, op.2; Märchenbilder, op.3, 7 pf pieces, 1910; Sonata, D, op.6, vn, pf; Str Sextet, D, op.10, 1917; Pf Qnt, E, op.15; Str Qt no.1, A, op.16, perf. 1924; 4 Little Caricatures, op.19, pf, unpubd; Tales of Strauss, op.21, pf; Suite, op.23, pf left hand, str, 1930; Pf Sonata no.3, C,

op.25, 1931; Str Qt no.2, E♭, op.26, 1935; Str Qt no.3, D, op.34, unpubd; Romance impromptu, vc, pf, op.posth., 1946

OTHER WORKS
Songs: Einfache Lieder, op.9; [4] Abschiedslieder, op.14; 3 Lieder, op.18 (Kaltneker); 3 Lieder, op.22 (K. Kobald), 1927; The Eternal, op.27 (E. van der Straaten), song cycle, 1935; Songs of the Clown, op.29 (Shakespeare: Twelfth Night), 1939; 5 Lieder, op.38, 1947; Sonett für Wien, op.41 (H. Kaltneker), 1952
19 film scores, 1935–54

Principal publisher: Schott (Mainz)

BIBLIOGRAPHY
R. S. Hoffman: *Erich Wolfgang Korngold* (Vienna, 1922)
L. Korngold: *Erich Wolfgang Korngold* (Vienna, 1967)
B. G. Carroll: *The Operas of Erich Wolfgang Korngold* (diss., U. of Liverpool, 1975)   B. G. CARROLL

Környei, Béla (*b* Krumau [now Krumlov, Czechoslovakia], 18 May 1875; *d* Budapest, 22 April 1925). Hungarian tenor. He sang as a bass in the chorus of the Folk Theatre, later taking solo parts at Temesvár (now Timişoara, Romania) as a baritone, and returning to the Folk Theatre in 1907 as Don José. His great success, principally in Verdi and Puccini roles, was because of the heroic power and beauty of his voice, which compensated for dramatic deficiencies. From 1915 until 1918 he was a member of the Vienna Staatsoper, where he created Bacchus in the second version of *Ariadne auf Naxos* (4 October 1916). In 1918 he returned to Budapest, where he died while still at the height of his career. Numerous acoustic and electrical recordings preserve his art. He was a life member of the Budapest Opera House.   PÉTER P. VÁRNAI

Kórodi, András (*b* Budapest, 24 May 1922). Hungarian conductor. He studied conducting with János Ferencsik and composition with László Lajtha at the Budapest Conservatory, and joined the Budapest National Opera as répétiteur in 1946. The same year he made his conducting début there with Kodály's *Háry János*, was appointed conductor, and became principal conductor in 1963. He has given several premières, including those of many Hungarian operas such as Szokolay's *Blood Wedding* (1964). He was the first Hungarian to conduct the Bol'shoy Opera when he gave *Carmen* there in 1957; that year he was appointed a professor of conducting at the Budapest Academy. He was appointed president–conductor of the Budapest PO in 1967. Kórodi's favoured repertory is the mainstream of 20th-century music and Wagner, and he has recorded some works in the complete recorded edition of Bartók. He received the Liszt Prize in 1952 and 1958, and the Kossuth Prize in 1970, and was named Artist of Merit in 1960.
                    PÉTER P. VÁRNAI

Korte, Karl (Richard) (*b* Ossining, NY, 25 Aug 1928). American composer. He studied at the Juilliard School (BS 1952, MS 1956), his teachers including Copland, Luening, Mennin, Persichetti and Petrassi. After teaching at Arizona State University (1963–4) and at the State University of New York at Binghamton (1964–70) he was appointed professor of music at the University of Texas at Austin (1971). Awards made to him include two Guggenheim Fellowships (1960, 1970) and a Gershwin Memorial Award (1957). His music shows many influences, including serialism and jazz.

WORKS
(*selective list*)
Matrix, wind qnt, sax, perc, pf, 1968; Sym. no.3, 1968; Remembrances,

fl, tape, 1971
Other works for orch, solo v, chorus, band, ens and live performer with tape

Principal publishers: Elkan-Vogel, E. C. Schirmer
                    JEROME ROSEN

Korte, Oldřich František (*b* Šala, Slovakia, 26 April 1926). Czech composer and theorist. A son of the composer František Korte, he was imprisoned in a concentration camp during World War II, and on his release he took lessons in composition with Pícha, studying later at the Prague Conservatory until 1949. He worked as a music critic for Prague daily newspapers, and also contributed essays to *Tempo, Hudební rozhledy* and *Modern Music*. His music has marked emotional vigour, and its symmetrical forms sometimes include atonal episodes. The ballet *Orbis* was performed in Prague in 1943; his response to the Nazi atrocities of the time is evident in the violent *Injuria* (1944) for piano, and in *Chvála smrti* ('Praise of death'), a suite of miniatures for piccolo and glockenspiel. Important larger works include the Sinfonietta (1949), the symphonic drama *Příběh fléten* ('Flutes' story', 1949) and the Concerto grosso for strings, trumpets and piano. His Piano Sonata (1953) received a prize at the 1966 International Busoni Competition in Bolzano. *Trubadúrské zpěvy* ('Troubadours' songs', 1965) sets medieval texts for soloists, chorus and an ensemble of old instruments. Korte's works are published by Panton and Supraphon.

BIBLIOGRAPHY
ČSHS
I. Hurník: 'Sonata pro klavír Oldřicha Korte', *HRo*, ix (1956), 885
J. Smolka: 'Korte O. F.: Sinfonietta pro velký orchestr', *HRo*, xix (1966), 501

                    OLDŘICH PUKL

Korte, Werner (*b* Münster, 29 May 1906). German musicologist. He studied mathematics, natural sciences and musicology at the universities of Freiburg and Münster (1924–6) and musicology, art history and philosophy at the University of Berlin (1926–8) where he took the doctorate under J. Wolf in 1928 with a dissertation on harmony in the early 15th century. He then became an assistant lecturer in the musicology department of Heidelberg University (1928–31) under Besseler. In 1932 he completed his *Habilitation* in musicology at the University of Münster with a study of early 15th-century Italian music; in the same year he succeeded Fellerer as director of the musicology department of Münster University. In 1937 he was appointed reader, and in 1946 professor. He had previously occupied briefly the chairs of musicology at the universities of Göttingen and Marburg.

Several of Korte's publications concern the function of musicology and educational and cultural problems in music. In his studies on Bruckner, Brahms and Stamitz, he developed a method of structural analysis which attempted, by systematic reference to symbols, to pinpoint the work of art scientifically as a unique phenomenological document.

WRITINGS
Die Harmonik des frühen 15. Jahrhunderts in ihrem Zusammenhang mit der Formtechnik (diss., U. of Berlin, 1928; Münster, 1929)
Deutsche Musikerziehung in Vergangenheit und Gegenwart (Danzig, 1932)
Studien zur Geschichte der Musik in Italien im ersten Viertel des 15. Jahrhunderts (Habilitationsschrift, U. of Münster, 1932; Kassel, 1933)
'Aufgabe der Musikwissenschaft', *Die Musik*, xxvii (1934–5), 338

'Bildungs- und Ausbildungsfragen der Musik', *Die Musik*, xxviii (1935–6), 348
J. S. Bach (Berlin, 1935)
Ludwig van Beethoven (Berlin, 1936)
Robert Schumann (Potsdam, 1937)
Musik und Weltbild (Leipzig, 1940)
'Robert Schumann in seinen Schriften', *Musik im Unterricht*, xlvii (1956), 225
'Darstellung eines Satzes von J. Stamitz', *Festschrift Karl Gustav Fellerer* (Regensburg, 1962), 282
Bruckner und Brahms: die spätromantische Lösung der autonomen Konzeption (Tutzing, 1963)
'Struktur und Modell als Information in der Musikwissenschaft', *AMw*, xxi (1964), 1
De musica: Monolog über die heutige Situation der Musik (Tutzing, 1966)
'J. S. Bach', *Johann Sebastian Bach*, ed. W. Blankenburg (Darmstadt, 1970)

HANS HEINRICH EGGEBRECHT

Kortholt (from Ger. *kurzes Holz*: 'short woodwind'). A generic term, referring to double-reed instruments from the 16th and 17th centuries with bores that double back on themselves (as in bassoons). The pitch of such instruments is thus deeper than their length would suggest. Specifically the word 'Kortholt' was used to describe four kinds of instrument: a curtal or dulzian, i.e. an early BASSOON (especially in England according to Praetorius and Galpin); a RACKET, according to various 16th-century inventories cited by Kinsky; a SORDUN, or 'Courtaut' as Mersenne called it; and a sordun with a wind cap (for details, *see* WIND-CAP INSTRUMENTS).

BIBLIOGRAPHY
M. Praetorius: *Syntagma musicum*, ii (Wolfenbüttel, 1619/*R*1958; Eng. trans., 1962)
M. Mersenne: *Harmonie universelle*, i (Paris, 1636/*R*1963; Eng. trans., 1957)
F. W. Galpin: *Old English Instruments of Music* (London, 1910, rev. 4/1965)
G. Kinsky: 'Doppelrohrblatt-Instrumente mit Windkapsel', *AMw*, vii (1925–6), 253–96

HOWARD MAYER BROWN

Kortkamp, Jakob (*b c*1620; *d c*1660). German organist and composer. He and his lifelong friend Matthias Weckmann studied with Jacob Praetorius (ii) in Hamburg about 1637. Later he was an organist in Kiel but remained in close contact with the artists in Hamburg, among whom Johann Rist called him proficient as organist and singer. He contributed four songs to Rist's *Neue himmlische Lieder* (Lüneburg, 1617), and the 16 songs initialled 'J.K.' in Jacob Schwieger's *Liebes-Grillen* (Hamburg, 1654–6) may also be his. He may also be the composer of three songs, likewise initialled 'J.K.', in Caspar von Stieler's *Die geharnschte Venus* (Hamburg, 1660/*R*). He composed a song and three dances for a wedding in 1654 which were printed as *Liebes Gespräch... Allemand, Courant, Saraband* (Hamburg, 1654). His six-verse setting for organ of the chorale *Herr Gott, dich loben wir* (*D-Lr* KN 207, incomplete in KN 209) is indebted to Jacob Praetorius (ii).

BIBLIOGRAPHY
M. Reimann: 'Kortkamp', *MGG*
K. Hortschansky: *Katalog der Kieler Musiksammlungen* (Kassel, 1963)

JOHN H. BARON

Kortkamp, Johann (*b* ?Kiel, 1643; *d* Hamburg, 20 May 1721). German organist and writer, son of Jakob Kortkamp. He studied under Weckmann from 1655 until about 1661, and later in the 1660s he served for a short time as organist at St Jacob, Hamburg, under Christoph Bernhard. His main posts – though they were not important ones – were as organist at two other Hamburg churches, the Maria-Magdalena Kloster (1669–1721) and St Gertrud (1676–1721). His only known composition is a jigg. He also arranged for organ a *Magnificat secundi toni* by Weckmann and wrote the alto and tenor parts of a cantata by Bernhard. His importance lies in his manuscript chronicle of north German music from 1291 to *c*1718, written between 1702 and 1718 (it is now in *D-Ha*). This gives invaluable accounts of north German organs and their sounds, as well as information about the lives and works of organists, clergy and Kantors, notably in the 16th and 17th centuries. The information he gave on the men whom he and his father knew personally, such as Hieronymus and Jacob Praetorius, Weckmann and Bernhard, is particularly important.

BIBLIOGRAPHY
L. Krüger: 'Johann Kortkamps Organistenchronik: eine Quelle zur Hamburgischen Musikgeschichte des 17. Jahrhunderts', *Zeitschrift des Vereins für Hamburgische Geschichte*, xxxiii (1933), 188
M. Reimann: 'Kortkamp', *MGG*

JOHN H. BARON

Koryphaios [coryphaeus]. Leader of the chorus in ancient Greek drama; he was responsible for the rhythm of the chorus and for giving the pitch of the first note or *endosimon*.

BIBLIOGRAPHY
A. Pickard-Cambridge: *The Dramatic Festivals of Athens* (Oxford, rev. 2/1968), 262

Kósa, György (*b* Budapest, 24 April 1897). Hungarian composer and pianist. At the age of ten he became a pupil of Bartók, and he studied the piano, first privately with Bartók, then from 1908 to 1915 at the Budapest Academy of Music. He continued his piano studies with Dohnányi (1915–16) and also studied composition at the academy with Herzfeld and Kodály (1908–12). In 1916–17 he was co-répétiteur at the Royal Opera House in Budapest, where he took part in the first performance of Bartók's *The Wooden Prince*. Between 1917 and 1920 he undertook concert tours in Germany, Austria, Italy and north Africa, and in 1920–21 he was a theatre conductor in Tripoli. He settled in Budapest in 1921, working first as an accompanist, then from 1927 to 1960 as professor of piano at the academy of music. In the 1920s, in conjunction with Kadosa and others, he founded the Society of Modern Hungarian Musicians. As a pianist he has devoted himself to classical as well as to modern music; each year since the 1950s he has played Bach's '48' in Budapest. He was awarded the Erkel Prize in 1955, and the Golden Order of Work in 1967. In 1963 he was created a Merited Artist and in 1972 an Honoured Artist of the Hungarian People's Republic.

In outlook, Kósa shows marked affinities with Mahler: he combines complexity with an almost childlike naivety and simplicity. Man's greatest problems stand at the centre of his work, and this preoccupation is reflected in the sub-titles of his symphonies, 'Man and the Universe', 'Joy in Nature', 'Moses', 'Atomic War', 'Salvation in Christ'. Existence, fate and men's beliefs on the one hand, and, on the other, beauty and inspiration drawn from the widest possible cultural background, embracing Greek and Chinese, Old French and Scandinavian civilizations, colour his thought. Stylistically his music is influenced neither by folk music nor by serialism. The striving gestures of a believing soul in conflict with the world characterize his type of expressionism, in which the eruptive statement of his experience appears more important than the form that the statement takes.

WORKS
(selective list)

STAGE

Operas: A király palástja [The king's cloak] (3, M. Kósa, after Andersen), 1926; Az két lovagok [Two knights] (comic opera, 3, A. Keleti), 1934; Cenodoxus (mystery opera, 3, M. Kósa, after Biedermann, Gregor), 1942; Anselmus diák [Student Anselmus] (3, G. Devecseri, after Hoffmann), 1945; Tartuffe (comic opera, 3, Molière), 1951; Pázmán lovag [Knight Pázmán] (comic opera, L. Hollós-Korvin), 1962–3; Kocsonya Mihály házassága [The marriage of Mihály Kocsonya] (comic opera, after Hung. 18th century), 1971

Ballets and pantomimes: Fehér Pierrot [White Pierrot] (ballet, L. Fodor), 1916; Phaedra (ballet, 1, V. Dienes), 1918; Mese a király-kisasszonyról [A tale of a princess] (pantomime, 1, M. Gaál), 1919; Laterna magica (pantomime, 1, A. Szederkényi), 1922; Árva Józsi három csodája [The three miracles of Józsi Árva] (pantomime, 1, J. Mohácsi, L. Márkus), 1932; Dávid király [King David] (ballet, 1, G. Kósa, after M. Rabinovszky), 1936; Ének az örök bánatról [Song about the everlasting sorrow] (ballet, Weöres), 1955

VOCAL

Oratorios: Jonah, 1931; Easter Oratorio, 1932; Saulus, 1935; Joseph, chamber oratorio, 1939; Elijah, chamber oratorio, 1940; Christus, chamber oratorio, 1943; Hajnóczy (Devecseri), 1954; Villon, 1960

Cantatas: Laodomeia (M. Babits), 1924; Job, 1933; Küldetés [Mission], 1948; Szól az úr [The Lord is saying], 1957; Amor sanctus (medieval Lat.), 1958; 2 Cantatas (J. Pilinszky), 1964; Bárányka [Lambkin], 1965; Balázsolás [St Blaise play] (Babits), 1967; Cantata humana (J. Pannonius), 1967; Orpheus, Eurydike, Hermes (Rilke), 1967; Őszikék [Autumn songs] (J. Arany), 1970; Johannes (Morgenstern), 1972; Szálkák [Splints] (Pilinszky), 1972; Perlekedő prófécia [A quarrelling prophecy] (Habbakuk), 1973; 2 Cantatas (Eliot), 1973–4; Cantata (F. Karinthy), 1974; Bikasirató [Dirge for a bull] (Devecseri), 1975; Kakasszó [Crowing of the cock] (I. Vas), 1975

Mystery: Kincses Ádám halála [The death of Ádám Kincses] (B. Szabolcsi), 1923

Works to liturgical texts: Dies irae, 1937; 2 masses, 1946, 1949; Requiem, 1949; Stabat mater, 1949; Te Deum, 1949; Biblical Mass, 1951; Requiem, 1966; De profundis, 1970

Songs: c500 (Ady, Aragon, Arany, Babits, Balassi, Csokonai Vitéz, Dehmel, Devecseri, Erdélyi, Ferch, George, Hernádi, József, Juhász, Károlyi, Kosztolányi, Molnár, Morgenstern, Petőfi, Petrarch, Pilinszky, Po-Tshu-Ye, Radnóti, Rilke, Sárközi, Sík, Silesius, Somlyó, Storm, Szabó, Szilágyi, Tagore, Á. Tóth, E. Tóth, Verlaine, Weöres, Zelk)

INSTRUMENTAL

Orch: Suite, 1915; 6 Pieces, 1919; 9 syms., 1920, 1927, 1933, 1936, 1937, 1946, 1957, 1959, 1969; Suite (Ironic Portraits), 1924; Fantasy on 3 Folksongs, 1948; Dance Suite, 1951; Conc., pf, vn, cymbals, perc, 1973

Chamber: 8 str qts, 1920, 1929, 1933, 1936, 1956, 1959, 1963, 1965; Chamber Music, 11 insts, 1928; Duo, vn, db, 1928; 6 Portraits, 6 hn, harp, 1933; Divertimento, str qt, cymbals, 1938; Qnt, fl, cl, bn, hn, harp, 1938; Trio, fl, va, vc, 1946; Trio, S, cl, vn, 1947; Duo, 2 vn, 1949; Wind Qnt, 1960; Rondo, wind qnt, 1961; Pf Trio, 1962; Duo, vn, vc, 1964; Sonata, vc, pf, 1965; 6 Intermezzos, str trio, 1969; 6 Miniatures, va, harp, 1969; Dialogus, b tuba, mar, 1975

Pf: Fantasy, 1917; Jutka, 12 pieces, 1928; Duo, 2 pf, 1933; 2 sonatas, 1941, 1947, 1956; Kis cipő [Little shoe], 1945; Jutka-ballada, 1946; 13 Bagatelles, 1947; Hommage à Béla Bartók, 1947; 2 Pieces, 1955; Divertimento, 1960; 5 Little Pieces, 1967

Principal publishers: Editio Musica, Universal

BIBLIOGRAPHY

L. Pollatschek: 'Georg Kósa', *Der Auftakt*, v (1925)
L. Fábián: 'Georg Kósa', *Musikblätter des Anbruch*, viii (1926)
M. Pándi: *Kósa György* (Budapest, 1966) [incl. list of works]

FERENC BÓNIS

Koscheluch, Johann. *See* KOZELUCH, JOHANN.

Koschovitz, Joseph. *See* KOSSOVITS, JÓZSEF.

Köselitz, Johann Heinrich. *See* GAST, PETER.

Košetický, Jiří Evermond (*b* Vlašim, 6 April 1639; *d* Prague, 20 Jan 1700). Czech folklorist. He was a Premonstratensian priest and *cantor* who made the first collection of Czech folk material, including sacred songs, lullabies, drinking songs and student and brigand songs, the majority with their melodies. His five large MS volumes, *Quodlibeticum* (1680–98), are preserved at *CS-Ps*.

BIBLIOGRAPHY

A. Podlaha: 'Rukopisný sborník Evermonda Jiřího Košetického', [Košetický's MS collection], *Sborník historického kroužku* (1901–5), 2; (1917), 4; (1923–4), 24

JOHN CLAPHAM

Kosleck, Julius (*b* Naugard, Pommern, 1 Dec 1825; *d* Berlin, 5 Nov 1905). German trumpeter. The son of poor parents, he was sent at the age of eight to a military school in Annaburg, Saxony; in 1843 he became the leading trumpeter in the band of the infantry guard regiment. From 1853 to 1893 he was a member of the Königliche Kapelle, Berlin, where from 1872 until 1903 he taught the trumpet and trombone at the Hochschule für Musik. He was well known in northern Germany as an oratorio trumpeter, although his long A trumpet does not seem to have been taken up by other players there. As a cornet soloist he travelled throughout Germany, England, Russia and the USA.

Kosleck is known for his participation as leading trumpeter in a historic performance of Bach's Mass in B minor in London on 21 March 1885, in which he played his part on the so-called BACH TRUMPET. His main interest, however, was in playing folk music on conical brass instruments; he founded the Kaiser-Kornettquartett in about 1885, expanding it in 1890 to form the Kosleck'sche Bläserbund, which won great popularity. He is also remembered for his F-trumpet method, *Grosse Schule für Cornet à piston und Trompete* (Leipzig, 1872), which was translated into English by Walter Morrow (c1907), a noted champion of that instrument. A diagram of his Bach trumpet's mouthpiece, which Kosleck carefully concealed from his English colleagues in 1885, was printed in 1934 in Menke's *History of the Trumpet of Bach and Handel*.

BIBLIOGRAPHY

H. Eichborn: *Das alte Clarinbasen auf Trompeten* (Leipzig, 1894)
W. Menke: *History of the Trumpet of Bach and Handel* (London, 1934, 2/1972)

EDWARD H. TARR

Košler, Zdeněk (*b* Prague, 25 March 1928). Czech conductor. He was first taught music by his father, an orchestral player, then studied the piano, composition and conducting at the Prague Academy, where his teachers included Karel Ančerl. His first appointments were as répétiteur for the Kühn Children's Choir and the Czech Choir (later the Prague Philharmonic Choir), and in 1948 he joined the Prague National Theatre, where he made his conducting début with *Il barbiere di Siviglia* in 1951. The same year he conducted his first major concert with the Prague SO, and he toured with the National Theatre company to Moscow in 1955 and Brussels in 1958. He won the 1956 International Conducting Competition at Besançon and the 1963 Mitropoulos Competition in New York, where he worked as assistant to Leonard Bernstein in the 1963–4 season. He was director of the Olomouc Opera (1958–62) and the Ostrava Opera (1962–6), principal conductor of the Prague SO (1966–7), and general music director of the Berlin Komische Oper in association with Felsenstein (1966–8). In 1971 he became director of the National Theatre in Bratislava and resident conductor of the Czech PO. He conducted *Salome* at the

Vienna Staatsoper in 1965, has toured in other European countries, and from 1968 has been a frequent guest conductor in Japan. His performances are deeply emotional yet balanced in character and his wide repertory includes much 20th-century music. He was named Artist of Merit in 1974.

BIBLIOGRAPHY
ČSHS
P. Vrba: 'Zblízka o Zdenkovi Košlerovi' [More about Zdeněk Košler], Slovenská hudba, vii (1963), 255
V. Pospíšil: 'Košlerovy návraty a cíle' [Košler's recoveries and aims], HRo, xvii (1964), 109
I. Jirko: 'Třikrát Zdeněk Košler' [Three times Zdeněk Košler], HRo, xxiii (1970), 195
'Košlerův nástup v Bratislavě' [Košler's appearance in Bratislava], HRo, xxv (1972), 109

ALENA NĚMCOVÁ

Kosma, Joseph (*b* Budapest, 22 Oct 1905; *d* Paris, 7 Aug 1969). French composer of Hungarian birth. After initial studies at the Budapest Academy of Music he was appointed assistant conductor at the Budapest Opera. In 1929 a scholarship enabled him to study with Eisler in Berlin, and in 1933 he settled in Paris. His life there was extremely difficult until Carné commissioned him to write the score for his film *Les enfants du paradis* (1945); the success of this was followed up in his music for *Les portes de la nuit* (1946) and for other important French films. It was Kosma's songs, however, that made his reputation, particularly those written in collaboration with the poet Jacques Prévert. Such pieces as *Les feuilles mortes, Barbara, Les enfants qui s'aiment* and *Inventaire* found enthusiastic acceptance both in French intellectual circles and by the general public, and Kosma made successful settings of poems by many of the greatest French writers of the day, including Desnos, Queneau, Aragon and Sartre. Composing in a style that retained something of Eisler's simplicity of craftsmanship, he also produced several incidental scores for the theatre and a ballet, *Le rendez-vous* (1945). Some weeks after his death the Lyons Opera mounted his satirical opera *Les hussards* (1969), a piece which indicates a development towards a more elaborate style.

DOMINIQUE AMY

Kosmas of Jerusalem [Kosmas Hagiopolïtēs, Kosmas Hierosolymïtēs, Kosmas the Monk, Kosmas of Maiuma, Kosmas the Melode] (*b* ?Jerusalem; *fl* 1st half of the 8th century). Saint, and one of the most famous Byzantine hymnographers. The epithets 'Hierosolymïtēs' and 'Hagiopolïtēs' which accompany his name in MSS and in the *Suida* (a 10th-century Byzantine compilation usually known as the '*Lexicon* of Suidas'), seem to indicate Jerusalem as his birthplace, although he may have been born elsewhere in that patriarchate. He was a monk in the Palestinian monastery of St Sabas, like his contemporary JOHN DAMASCENE. The hagiographical tradition which, in order to emphasize the relationship between the two, made Kosmas the foster-brother of John Damascene, and the latter's companion in his youthful studies and entry into the monastery, is purely legendary. Kosmas was nominated Bishop of Maiuma, near Gaza, in 742 or 743; John Damascene dedicated his work *The Source of Knowledge* to Kosmas when he was Bishop of Maiuma.

Kosmas wrote stichēra idiomela, kanōns and triōdia for the most solemn festivals of Christ and the Virgin. (*See also* KANŌN.) During the 9th century many of his hymns were introduced into Lenten services: the kanōns for Palm Sunday and Maundy Thursday, the triōdia for Monday and Wednesday of Holy Week and for Good Friday, the diōdion for Tuesday of Holy Week and the tetraōdion for Holy Saturday. Not all the hymns ascribed to 'Kosmas the Monk' or 'Kosmas Hagiopolïtēs' in the MSS can be attributed to him; a list of his works has been compiled by Efstratiadis.

The poetry of Kosmas is distinguished by its formal elegance, and his musical and metric schemes are remarkably original. Kosmas admired St Gregory Nazianzen and often imitated his writings; he wrote an extensive commentary on Gregory's poetry and composed a kanōn for his feast day.

BIBLIOGRAPHY
FACSIMILES, TRANSCRIPTIONS
W. Christ and M. Paranikas, ed.: *Anthologia graeca carminum christianorum* (Leipzig, 1871), 161–204 [text only]
H. J. W. Tillyard, ed.: *Twenty Canons from the Trinity Hirmologium*, MMB, Transcripta, iv (1952), 7ff, 18ff, 34ff, 51ff, 72ff, 90ff, 100ff
A. Ayoutanti and others, ed.: *The Hymns of the Hirmologium: I*, MMB, Transcripta, vi (1952)
A. Ayoutanti and H. J. W. Tillyard, ed.: *The Hymns of the Hirmologium: III/2*, MMB, Transcripta, viii (1956), 17ff
H. J. W. Tillyard, ed.: *The Hymns of the Pentecostarium*, MMB, Transcripta, vii (1960), 27ff

LITERATURE
A. Chappet: 'Cosmas de Maïouma', *Dictionnaire d'archéologie chrétienne et de liturgie*, iii/2 (Paris, 1914), 2993
S. Efstratiadis: 'Kosmas Hierosolymïtēs ho poïẽtis', *Nea sion*, xxviii (1933), 83, 143, 202, 257, 330, 400, 489, 530
H.-G. Beck: *Kirche und theologische Literatur im byzantinischen Reich* (Munich, 1959), 515f
For further bibliography *see* BYZANTINE RITE, MUSIC OF THE.

ENRICA FOLLIERI

Kospoth, Otto Carl Erdmann, Freiherr **von** (*b* Mühltroff, Vogtland, 25 Nov 1753; *d* Mühltroff, 23 June 1817). German composer. He attended the Ritterakademie at Leignitz. In 1776 he became chamberlain and *maître des plaisirs* at the Prussian court, where he often played the violin or cello in performances with Frederick the Great. He was also an excellent keyboard player and could play other instruments, too. In 1783 he visited Italy, spending at least six months at Venice, where he composed church works and an opera and oratorio that were performed there, probably privately. Kospoth remained a chamberlain at the court of Friedrich Wilhelm II, but in 1789 returned to his estates at Mühltroff. In 1790 he was made a Reichsgraf. Whereas earlier he had appeared a typically versatile Enlightenment figure, engaging in chemical, physical and mechanical experiments and literary activities as well as music (in June 1787 he published a biography of his friend, the composer J. H. Rolle, in *Der teutsche Merkur*), in the 1790s he turned increasingly to necromancy, alchemy, spiritualism and other eccentric pursuits with a strong megalomaniac colouring. His position in Berlin had required considerable expenditure and in the early 1790s he lavished a great deal of money on improving his estates at Mühltroff, which he eventually lost entirely, apart from the right to an apartment in the castle, and supported himself by the piecemeal sale of his furniture and collection of musical instruments. When the castle caught fire in 1817 he refused to leave it, mistakenly claiming to be impervious to fire.

Kospoth's music is agreeable and facile, qualities that helped produce his considerable success as both a dramatic and an instrumental composer (he seems to have published nothing after the late 1790s). Several of his Singspiels had long runs and manifold productions.

Gerber judged him 'among the most industrious and inventive dilettantes', and praised his serenade op.19 for its richness of ideas, while censuring his lack of economy in treating them. According to Gerber, he was working on a Singspiel on Lessing's *Emilia Galotti* in 1790, but it was never produced.

WORKS

SINGSPIELS

Der Freund deutscher Sitten (3, G. W. Burmann), Berlin, 25 Sept 1778
Adrast und Isidore, oder Die Serenate (2, C. F. Bretzner, after Molière), Berlin, 16 Oct 1779; *D-Bds*, Favourite Songs (Berlin, n.d.)
Der Irrwisch, oder Endlich fand er sie (3, Bretzner), Berlin, 2 Oct 1780; Favourite Songs (Berlin, n.d.)
Timante ed Emirene, oder Die Macht der Liebe, Venice, 1783
Karoline, oder Die Parforcejagd
Das Fest der Schäfer (divertimento), Berlin, 18 Oct 1787
Der kluge Jakob (3, J. Wetzel), Berlin, 26 Feb 1788; *Bds*
Bella und Fernando, oder Die Satyr, 1790
Der Mädchenmarkt zu Ninive, Hamburg, 1793; excerpts (Leipzig, 1795)
Il trionfo d'Arianna, *Dlb*

OTHER VOCAL

Holofernes, oratorio, Venice, 1783; Abraham, oratorio, Venice, 1787, *Dlb*
Die Macht der Harmonie, cantata, Berlin, 1783; Le beau de Nans, cantata, Berlin, 1787
Miserere, *Bds*, *Dlb*; 3 Lieder, v, pf (Brunswick, 1795)

INSTRUMENTAL

Syms.: D, E♭, F, op.1 (Berlin and Amsterdam, 1778); D, op.12 (Darmstadt and Frankfurt am Main, n.d.); C, op.13 (Darmstadt and Frankfurt am Main, 1793); G, op.22 (Brunswick and Amsterdam, 1795); A, op.23 (Brunswick and Amsterdam, 1796); D, op.24 (Brunswick, 1797); D, op.25 (Brunswick, 1798); G (n.p., n.d.)
Hpd Conc., op.6 (Offenbach, n.d.); Ob Conc. (Offenbach, n.d.), lost
Other orch: Grande sérénade, 2 vn, 2 va, 2 hn, vc, b, op.11 (Speyer, 1792); Serenata, hpd/pf, ob/fl, 2 basset hn/va, 2 bn/vc, op.19 (Offenbach, 1794); Composizioni . . . sopra il Pater noster consistenti in 7 sonate caratteristiche con un introduzione, 2 vn, 2 ob, 2 hn, bn, va, b, op.20 (Darmstadt, 1794)
Chamber: 8 qnts, 2 vn, 2 va, vc, opp.1–2 (London, n.d.); 6 qts, fl, vn, va, vc, op.5 (Offenbach, n.d.), lost; 6 str qts, op.8 (Offenbach, n.d.); 6 str qts, op.10 (Speyer, 1790); 6 sonatas, vn, vc, b, op.1 (Offenbach, n.d.); 6 sonatas, hpd, vn, op.2 (Berlin and Amsterdam, ?1784)

BIBLIOGRAPHY

GerberL
C. H. Richter: *Die Herrschaft Mühltroff und ihre Besitzer* (Leipzig, 1857)
T. M. Langner: 'Kosposth, Otto Carl Erdmann, Freiherr von', *MGG*

Kössler, Hans. *See* KOESSLER, HANS.

Kossovits, József [Koschovitz, Joseph] (*b* after 1750; *d* after 1819). Hungarian composer and cellist. He served as a musician at the court of Menyhért Szulyovszky at Rákócz, Upper Hungary, until 1794, when his employer was arrested for participating in the Jacobin uprising in Hungary; this event inspired Kossovits's Slow Hungarian Dance in C minor, published as the last of his *12 danses hongroises pour le clavecin ou pianoforte* (Vienna, c1800), which became one of the best-known dance pieces of the *verbunkos* period. Mihály Csokonai Vitéz, the most important Hungarian poet of the turn of the century, wrote his *A' reményhez* ('To Hope', 1803) to the melody of this dance, thus contributing significantly to its popularity. In 1804 Kossovits was in the service of Countess Andrássy in Kassa (now Košice, Czechoslovakia), where he remained at least until 1819. On 4 July 1818 the *Wiener allgemeine musikalische Zeitung* mentioned him as an inexhaustible composer of Hungarian dances; all his other Hungarian dances in the *verbunkos* style remain in manuscript.

BIBLIOGRAPHY

AMZ, xxi (1819), 346
B. Szabolcsi and F. Bónis: *Magyar táncok Haydn korából* [Hungarian dances from the time of Haydn] (Budapest, 1959)

FERENC BÓNIS

Kostelanetz, André (*b* St Petersburg, 22 Dec 1901; *d* Haiti, 13 Jan 1980). American conductor and arranger of Russian birth. He studied in Petrograd from 1920 to 1922, when he went to the USA; he became an American citizen in 1928. He was engaged as conductor for the CBS radio network in 1930, beginning the association with broadcasting and film work, and with the popularizing of classical music, for which he principally became known, in performances of lively and robust style. A successful guest conductor, and principal conductor of the New York PO's promenade concerts, he made a valuable contribution to musical life by commissioning works by Copland (*Lincoln Portrait*), Schuman, Hovhaness and other contemporary composers. He is the dedicatee of Walton's *Capriccio burlesco*, of which he conducted the première by the New York PO in 1968.

BERNARD JACOBSON

Kostić, Dušan (*b* Zagreb, 23 Dec 1926). Yugoslav composer. He studied at the Belgrade Academy (1947–55) with Milošević (composition) and in 1955 took conducting lessons with Scherchen at Bayreuth. He was music editor of Radio Belgrade (1957–9) and from 1964 a lecturer and later professor at the Belgrade Academy. His music takes late Romanticism as its starting-point, with the use of a harmonic idiom somewhat influenced by Hindemith and an impressionist orchestration. In his first major work, the Symphony in G, he also used elements of 12-note technique, especially in the 12-note passacaglia, as well as carefully thought-out motivic working. Two fine expressionist choral and orchestral works from 1961, *Otadžbina* ('The fatherland') and *Kragujevac*, show his use of polytonal techniques, together with a dramatic Wagnerian leitmotif structure.

WORKS

(selective list)

Opera: Majstori su prvi ljudi [Craftsmen are top people] (J. Putnik), 1962
Orch: 3 syms., 1957, 1965, 1965–6; Kontrasti, sym. poem, 1957; Crnagorska svita [Montenegro suite], 1957; Vn Conc., 1962; Svečana uvertira [Festive ov.], 1962; Pf Conc., 1962; Conc. antifonale, 1971; Divertimento, str, 1972; Conc., tpt, chamber orch, 1972
Choral and cantatas: Brod [The boat] (G. Tartalja), cantata, 1959; Morača (J. Đonović), cantata, 1959; Duž duge, duge ulice [Along the long, long street] (V. Borhert), cantata, 1959; Otadžbina [The fatherland], cantata, 1961; Kragujevac (D. Maksimović), cantata, 1962; Jama [The pit] (I. G. Kovačić), cantata, 1962; Amuleti, chorus, orch; Basne [Fables] (S. Usković), chorus, orch; short pieces, folksong arrs.
Inst: Sonata, bn, pf, 1952; Sonata amorosa, vn, pf, 1957; 2 str qts, pf pieces
Songs: Severno nebo [Northern sky] (R. Dimitrijević), Bar, pf, 1954; Pjesma gorka (D. Cesarić), Bar, pf, 1959

Principal publisher: Udruženje kompozitora Srbije

NIALL O'LOUGHLIN

Köstlin, Heinrich Adolf. German theologian and music historian, son of JOSEPHINE LANG.

Koswick, Michael (*b* in or nr. Finsterwalde, Lusatia; *fl* 1507–20). German music theorist. He matriculated at the University of Frankfurt an der Oder in 1507 and obtained the master's degree there in 1516. By 1520 he had adopted the title 'Frater'. He may have been the Michael Kosswig who was sub-deacon at Hochstift Merseburg in 1517.

In his *Compendiaria musicae artis aeditio* (Leipzig, 1516), Koswick endeavoured to present elementary music theory in a more concise form. The foreword praises the usefulness and effects of music by quoting from the Bible and ancient Greek authorities. At the centre of the first part, 'Musica choralis', is the chapter on church modes together with numerous examples and intonation formulae; the second part deals with polyphonic music and concentrates particularly on mensural theory. The treatise concludes with a chapter on counterpoint, in which Koswick made new progress in compositional theory. After surveying consonances and dissonances, Koswick gave rules for progressions in two-part settings and for the various possible effects in three-part compositions, starting with the interval between the tenor and the descant. Koswick himself admitted that he gathered the contents of his treatise from various textbooks, but he added some new points. He quoted only Gaffurius, but his prime sources are the treatises of the Cologne school: Cochlaeus, Wollick and *Anonymi introductorium musicae* (*D-LEu, c*1500; ed. H. Riemann, *MMg*, xxix (1897), 12; xxx (1898), 1).

BIBLIOGRAPHY
K. W. Niemöller: *Nicolaus Wollick und sein Musiktraktat* (Cologne, 1956), 281ff
R. Federhofer-Königs: *Johannes Oridryus und sein Musiktraktat* (Cologne, 1957)

MARTIN RUHNKE

Koszewski, Andrzej (*b* Poznań, 26 July 1922). Polish composer and musicologist. He studied composition and theory with Poradowski at the Poznań Conservatory (1946–53) and with Szeligowski at the Warsaw Conservatory (1953–8). After musicological studies with Chybiński at Poznań University he established himself as an expert on Chopin's waltzes. His best-known composition, *Muzyka fa–re–mi–do–si* for chorus (1960), is a complex score written for the sesquicentenary of the birth of Chopin, from whose name its basic motif is derived (FryDEryk CHopin). In general, his music is unpretentious and melodious. The thematic materials, particularly in early works, are derived from Polish folksong, as in the *Taniec wielkopolski* for small orchestra (1951) and the many choral pieces.

WORKS
(selective list)

Orch: Conc. grosso, str, 1947; Taniec wielkopolski, small orch, 1951; Allegro symfoniczne, 1953; Sinfonietta, 1956; Ov., 1963
Choral: Muzyka fa–re–mi–do–si, 1960; La espero, 2 choruses, 1963; Tryptyk wielkopolski, chorus, orch, 1964; Nicolao Copernico dedicatum, cantata, vocal orch, 1966; Gry [Plays], children's suite, 1968; Pastorale, 1971; Rondo, 1971; Ballata (J. Ratajczak)
Chamber: Adagio i gawot, vn, pf/hpd, 1947; Andante, 2 vn, pf/org, 1947; Pf Trio, 1950; Variations on a Choral Theme by J. S. Bach, fl, pf, 1953
Pf: Capriccio, 1947; Sonata breve, 1954; Stylizacje, 1961; Intermezzo, 1962
Songs for 1v, pf: Wokaliza, S, pf, 1953

Principal publisher: Polskie Wydawnictwo Muzyczne

WRITINGS
'Melodyka walców Chopina', *Annales Chopin* (Kraków, 1958)
'Das Walzerelement im Schaffen Chopina', *DJbM*, v (1960), 58
'Das Wienerische in Chopins Walzern', *Chopin-Jb* (1963), 27

MIECZYSŁAWA HANUSZEWSKA

Kotek, (Eduard) Yosif [Joseph] **(Yosifovich)** (*b* Kamenets-Podolsk, nr. Moscow, 6 Nov 1855; *d* Davos, 4 Jan 1885). Russian violinist and composer. He studied the violin with Hřímaly and theory with Tchaikovsky at the Moscow Conservatory, whose director Nikolay Rubinstein, recommended him as a violinist to Nadezhda von Meck. He wrote pieces for the violin

and piano which they performed together and he expressed to her his admiration for Tchaikovsky. He advised Tchaikovsky on technical problems in the solo part of his Violin Concerto, which they performed (with piano accompaniment) privately in Clarens, Switzerland, on 3 April 1878. After further lessons with Joachim in Berlin, Kotek became a violin teacher at the Berlin Hochschule für Musik (1882). His studies, duets and solo pieces for the violin were still being played at the turn of the century.

FRIEDRICH BASER

Köth, Erika (*b* Darmstadt, 15 Sept 1927). German soprano. She began her musical studies in Darmstadt in 1942 with Elsa Blank, and after an interruption resumed them in 1945, paying for them by singing with a jazz orchestra. She made her début in 1948 at Kaiserslautern as Philine in *Mignon*; engagements followed at Karlsruhe (1950–53), Munich (from 1953) and Berlin (from 1961). She first sang at Covent Garden in September 1953 with the Munich company as Fiakermilli (*Arabella*) and the Italian Soprano in *Capriccio*, its first performance in England. She appeared regularly at Salzburg, 1955–64, as the Queen of Night and Constanze, and at Bayreuth, 1965–8, as the Woodbird. It was as a coloratura singer that she established herself in Germany. Her repertory includes Lucia, Donna Elvira, Susanna, Gilda, Sophie and Zerbinetta. In 1973 she was appointed a professor of singing at the Cologne Hochschule für Musik. She was made a Bavarian Kammersängerin in 1956 and a Berlin Kammersängerin in 1970.

HAROLD ROSENTHAL

Köthen. *See* CÖTHEN.

Koto. A Japanese long zither, one of the family of east Asian zithers that includes the Chinese CH'IN, the Korean *kŏmun'go* and the Vietnamese *dan tranh*. The koto probably originated in China and was introduced to Japan around the start of the Nara period (710–84) or somewhat earlier. The term originally referred to a variety of plucked chordophones including the BIWA. The modern instrument has 13 silk or nylon strings of equal length and thickness, stretched with equal tension over 13 movable bridges. The tuning of the strings, while always pentatonic, depends on the mode of the piece. The modern koto repertory dates from the end of the 16th century. *Sōkyoku* (koto music) includes a vocal form (*kumiuta*), instrumental music (*shirabemono*) and a form based on a series of not more than six alternating songs and instrumental interludes (*jiuta* or *tegotomono*). In the *jiuta* ensemble, which includes the SHAMISEN (long-necked lute) and the SHAKUHACHI (end-blown flute), the koto plays the melody while the other instruments imitate and add variations. The koto is also included in the *tōgaku* repertory of gagaku court music. In modern Japan it is most important as a household instrument, and is considered a valuable adjunct to a refined upbringing and education.

For illustration and further discussion of the history and repertory, *see* JAPAN, §IV, 2.

Kotoński, Włodzimierz (*b* Warsaw, 23 Aug 1925). Polish composer and musicologist. He studied the piano with Klimont-Jacynowa and composition with Rytel (at the Warsaw Conservatory, 1945–51) and Szeligowski (in Poznań, 1950–51); from 1957 to 1960 he attended the Darmstadt summer courses. In addition, he did research in Polish folklore at the State Institute of Art (1951–9) and was a music adviser at the Warsaw Documentary Film Centre (1956–8). He has worked in the electronic music studios of Polish (from 1958) and West German (1967) radios, and has taught electronic music at the Warsaw Conservatory from 1967. Between 1963 and 1966 he was vice-president of the Polish Composers' Union.

The neo-Baroque style of Kotoński's early works can be exemplified by the Prelude and Passacaglia for orchestra (1953), a piece marked by linear writing and broad thematic developments. He was little influenced by his rather traditional teachers, but he was greatly interested in Polish folk music: he published a study, *Góralski i zbójnicki* ('Highlander and bandit dances'; Kraków, 1956), and used folk themes in compositions such as the *Tańce góralskie* ('Highlander dances', 1950) and the popular suite *Szkice baletowe* ('Ballet sketches', 1951), both for orchestra. At this time his stylistic model was often Szymanowski. Following his visits to Darmstadt, however, and beginning with the *Muzyka kameralna* ('Chamber music', 1958) for small orchestra, he moved gradually towards atonality and quasi-serialism. One of his major successes was the performance of the orchestral *Musique en relief* at Darmstadt in 1959. He has developed particular interests in percussion writing, publishing *Instrumenty perkusyjne we współczesnej orkiestrze* ('Percussion instruments in the modern orchestra', Kraków, 1963; Hung. trans., 1967; Ger. trans., 1968), and in complex rhythms. Kotoński was the first to experiment with electronic sounds at the Warsaw studio, his earliest tape composition being a *musique concrète* piece, *Etiuda na jedno uderzenie w talerz* ('Study on a cymbal stroke', 1959).

WORKS
(selective list)
Orch: Poemat, 1949; Tańce góralskie [Highlander dances], 1950; Szkice baletowe [Ballet sketches], 1951; Prelude and Passacaglia, 1953; Vn Conc., 1955; Muzyka kameralna, 21 insts, perc, 1958; Musique en relief, 6 orch groups, 1959; Musica per fiati e timp, 1963; Conc. per 4, harp, hpd, gui, pf, chamber orch, 1965; Music for 16 Cymbals and Str, 1969; Ob Conc., 1972; Wind Rose, 1976; Bora, 1978–9
Chamber: Quartettino, 4 hn, 1950; Romance and Toccata, harp, 1951; 5 miniatur, vn, pf, 1956; 5 miniatur, cl, pf, 1957; Trio, fl, gui, perc, 1960; Canto, ens, 1961; Pezzo, fl, pf, 1962; Selection I, a sax, t sax, elec gui, pf, 1962; Wind Qnt, 1964; A battere, gui, hpd, perc, va, vc, 1966; Pour 4, cl, trbn, vc, pf, 1968; Multiplay, 2 tpt, hn, trbn, tuba, 1971; Spring Music, fl, ob, vn, synth, 1978
Vocal: Sny o potędze [Dreams on might] (L. Staff), S, harp, str orch, 1948; Aeolian Harp, S, 4 insts, 1973
Pf: Sonata, 1948; 4 Preludes, 1952
Elec: Etiuda na jedno uderzenie w talerz [Study on a cymbal stroke], tape, 1959; Mikrostruktury, tape, 1963; Klangspiele, live elec, tape, 1967; Aela, 1970

Principal publisher: Polskie Wydawnictwo Muzyczne

BIBLIOGRAPHY
T. A. Zieliński: ' "Concerto" i "Trio" Włodzimierza Kotońskiego', *Ruch muzyczny* (1961), no.21, p.9
——: ' "Pour quatre" Włodzimierza Kotońskiego', *Ruch muzyczny* (1968), no.23, p.9
BOGUSŁAW SCHÄFFER

Kotter [Cotter, Kotther, Kotterer], **Hans** [Johannes] (*b* Strasbourg, *c*1485; *d* Berne, 1541). German organist and composer. He studied the organ with Paul Hofhaimer from 1498 until about 1500 at the expense of the Elector of Saxony. Until 1508 he was employed at the electoral court in Torgau, first as 'Meister Pauls Knabe' and later as an organist. He was probably in Basle some time after this, and met the Amerbach family. In 1514 he was appointed organist in the collegiate church of St Nikolaus in Fribourg. Because of his Protestant leanings, which he had expressed in a poem before 1522, he was expelled from Fribourg at the end of 1530. After unsuccessful attempts to find a post in Strasbourg and Basle, Kotter settled in Berne, where, at least after 1534, he earned his living as a schoolmaster. In 1538 he was appointed schoolmaster in Konstanz, but without formally taking up this post he returned to Berne in the same year.

Kotter played a considerable part in the planning and copying of three organ tablatures which belonged to the Basle humanist and lawyer Bonifacius Amerbach (1495–1562): *CH-Bu* F.IX.22, F.IX.58 and F.VI.26 (c). A large part of the first of these is in Kotter's own hand. These tablatures include some compositions of his as well as arrangements by him of vocal settings by Barbireau, Hofhaimer, Isaac, Johannes Martini, Sermisy and other composers. A further composition by Kotter is contained in Fridolin Sicher's organ tablature (*CH-SGs* 530), and it is possible that Leonhard Kleber's organ tablature contains some arrangements by him. Kotter's compositions show him to have been an accomplished musician, able to combine technical skill with musical inventiveness. His freely composed pieces merit special attention as early examples of an individual instrumental style. It is safe to assume that the three tablatures were intended primarily for the clavichord.

BIBLIOGRAPHY
LITERATURE
W. Merian: *Die Tabulaturen des Organisten Hans Kotter* (Leipzig, 1916/*R*1973) [incl. edns. of some pieces]
——: 'Bonifacius Amerbach und Hans Kotter', *Basler Zeitschrift für Geschichte und Altertumskunde*, xvi (1917), 140–206
——: 'Drei Handschriften aus der Frühzeit des Klavierspiels', *AMw*, ii (1920), 22
W. Gurlitt: 'Johannes Kotter und sein Freiburger Tabulaturbuch von 1513', *Elsass-Lothringisches Jb*, xix (1941), 216
H. J. Marx: 'Der Tabulatur-Codex des Basler Humanisten Bonifacius Amerbach', *Musik und Geschichte: Leo Schrade zum sechzigsten Geburtstag* (Cologne, 1963), 50
W. Apel: *Geschichte der Orgel- und Klaviermusik bis 1700* (Kassel, 1967; Eng. trans., rev., 1972)
M. Schuler: 'Ein Beitrag zur Biographie Hans Kotters', *Mf*, xxii (1969), 197
EDITIONS
H. J. Moser and F. Heitmann, eds.: *Frühmeister der deutschen Orgelkunst* (Leipzig, 1930)
H. J. Marx, ed.: *Tabulaturen des XVI. Jahrhunderts, I: Die Tabulaturen aus dem Besitz des Basler Humanisten Bonifacius Amerbach*, SMd, vi (1967)
MANFRED SCHULER

Kotzebue, August von (*b* Weimar, 3 May 1761; *d* Mannheim, 23 March 1819). German dramatist, diplomat and man of letters. His adventurous career included appointments as lawyer and theatre secretary, Russian court councillor and editor, poet and Russian consul. His satires, quarrels, and above all his duty to report to the Tsar of Russia on all affairs of interest in Germany and France, made him many enemies, and he was assassinated in 1819 by a student who suspected him of being a traitor and spy.

Kotzebue's immensely large output of plays includes a majority of ephemera, yet he dominated the repertory of German and Austrian (and many foreign) theatres for a considerable part of the 19th century, and the best of his comedies (including *Die deutschen Kleinstädter*, the first of a prodigious number of plays set in the self-important country town of Krähwinkel, the German equivalent of Gotham) are still effective. Beethoven wrote music for his *Die Ruinen von Athen* and *König Stephan*; Boieldieu, Gerl, Kreutzer, Lortzing, Reichardt and Spohr are among composers who set his works; and Schubert wrote two operas to Kotzebue texts: *Der Spiegelritter* (?1812, incomplete), and *Des Teufels Lustschloss* (1813–14).

BIBLIOGRAPHY
A. von Kotzebue: *Das merkwürdigste Jahr meines Lebens* (Berlin, 1801); ed. W. Promies (Munich, 1965)
A. von Kotzebue: *Sämtliche dramatische Werke* (Leipzig, 1827–9)
A. von Kotzebue: *Theater* (Vienna and Leipzig, 1840–41)
A. von Kotzebue: *Ausgewählte prosaische Schriften* (Vienna, 1842–3)
W. von Kotzebue: *A. von Kotzebue: Urtheile der Zeitgenossen und der Gegenwart* (Dresden, 1881)
K. Goedeke: *Grundriss zur Geschichte der deutschen Dichtung*, v (Dresden, 2/1893), 270ff; xv (Berlin, 2/1966), 151ff
J. Minor: *Über Kotzebue* (Vienna, 1894)
L. F. Thompson: *Kotzebue: a Survey of his Progress in France and England, preceded by a Consideration of the Critical Attitude to him in Germany* (Paris, 1928)
K.-H. Klingenberg: *Iffland und Kotzebue als Dramatiker* (Weimar, 1962)
F. Stock: *Kotzebue im literarischen Leben der Goethezeit* (Düsseldorf, 1971)

PETER BRANSCOMBE

Kotzeluch, Leopold. *See* KOZELUCH, LEOPOLD.

Kotzwara, Francis. *See* KOČZWARA, FRANTIŠEK.

Kouba, Jan (*b* Vysoké nad Jizerou, 28 July 1931). Czech musicologist. He studied musicology and history with Očadlík and Sychra at Prague University (1950–55) and took his diploma with a study of the hymns of the Union of the Bohemian Brethren (*Příspěvky ke zpěvu Jednoty bratrské*). In 1969 he took the doctorate at Prague with a dissertation on the oldest printed hymnbook (1501) from Bohemia. Subsequently he worked as assistant lecturer at the musicology department of Prague University, moving in 1965 to the Musicology Institute (now the musicology department of the Institute of the Theory and History of Art) of the Czechoslovak Academy of Sciences; in 1975 he became executive editor of *Hudební věda*. His particular areas of research are Czech hymnology and the history of Czech music in the 15th and 16th centuries.

WRITINGS
'Kancionály Václava Miřínského' [Václav Miřínský's hymnbooks], *MMC* (1959), no.8, pp.1–147
'Václav Klejch a jeho "Historia o vydání kancionálů v národu českém" ' [Klejch and his *History of the Publication of Hymnbooks in the Czech Nation*], *MMC* (1960), no.13, pp.61–203
'Blahoslavův rejstřík autorů českobratrských písní a jeho pozdější zpracování' [Blahoslav's list of the writers of Bohemian Brethren hymns and its later revision], *MMC* (1962), no.17, pp.1–175
'Zu den Liedern des Ján Sylvanus', *Jb für Liturgik und Hymnologie*, xi (1966), 169
Der älteste Gesangbuchdruck von 1501 aus Böhmen (diss., U. of Prague, 1969; extracts in *Jb für Liturgik und Hymnologie*, xiii (1968), 78–112)
with J. Bužga, E. Mikanová and T. Volek: *Průvodce po pramenech k dějinám hudby: fondy a sbírky uložené v Čechách* [Guide to the sources of music history: collections in Bohemia] (Prague, 1969)
'Jan Hus und das geistliche Lied', *Jb für Liturgik und Hymnologie*, xiv (1969), 190
'Česká hudba v období reformace a humanismu (1434–1620)' [Czech music during the Reformation and age of Humanism], *Československá vlastivěda*, ix/3, ed. M. Očadlík and R. Smetana (Prague, 1971), 53–86
'Německé vlivy v české písni 16. století' [German influences on Czech 16th-century songs], *MMC* (1975), nos.27–8, p.117–77

JOSEF BEK

Koukoulion (Gk.). The name used in Byzantine chant for the PROOIMION; *see also* BYZANTINE RITE, MUSIC OF THE, §10.

Koukouzeles [Papadopoulos], **Joannes** (*b* Dyrrachium, now Durrës, Albania, *c*1280; *d* ?Great Laura, Mount Athos, ?1360–75). Singer and composer of Byzantine chant, probably of Slavonic descent. Traditionally called 'the second source of Greek music', 'angel-voice' and 'the master', Joannes Koukouzeles is the most eminent and important composer of Byzantine church music active during the Paleologan dynasty (1261–1453). Because Koukouzeles is also a saint in the Greek Orthodox church, there is a short biography or *vita* which transmits almost all the information known about the composer's life. Since the *vita* fails to name the Byzantine emperor who was Koukouzeles' patron, the lifetime of the composer has become the subject of much dispute. Older scholars have placed his activity variously between the beginning of the 12th century and that of the 16th, but most recent research has revealed that he lived during and probably beyond the reign of Andronikos II Palaeologos (1282–1328). Direct evidence in Byzantine musical MSS indicates that his musical career was well established by about 1300, and by the end of the first third of the 14th century he was considered the leading composer in the empire. Indirect evidence in the *vita*, supported by other documents, suggests that he was born about 1280 and may have still been living as late as 1375.

Koukouzeles spent his early years in Dyrrachium. While still a boy he left to attend an imperial school in Constantinople as a protégé of the Byzantine emperor. If an episode related in the *vita* is trustworthy, 'Koukouzeles' was not the composer's real surname but only a nickname his companions at school devised after observing his difficulties with the Greek language. It was a juxtaposition of the Greek word *koukia* ('beans') and the Slavonic *zeliya* ('cabbage'). Although a few musical sources transmit Koukouzeles' surname as 'Papadopoulos', the composer was probably not from a family of Greek descent. Of his father's background nothing is known, but his mother's speech in the *vita* is Slavonic though transliterated into Greek letters.

Koukouzeles became famous in the imperial court of Constantinople for his remarkable voice, a gift which made him a favourite of the Byzantine emperor and won for him the sobriquet *angelophonos* ('angel-voice'). At the height of his fame as a singer Koukouzeles left Constantinople for some reason to lead a monastic life at the Great Laura on the southern slopes of Mount Athos. Here he sang for services in the monastery church on Sundays and on important feasts, but during the week lived outside the walls in a small chapel which he had built himself. From the nature of his life on Mount Athos described in the *vita*, Koukouzeles's monastic ideal may have fallen under the influence of Hesychasm, a mystic movement which was sweeping the peninsula during the first half of the 14th century. There is no indication that the singer-composer ever left Mount Athos once he settled near the Great Laura.

Although both the earliest extant notice of Koukouzeles as a composer and also his oldest known chants are preserved in two Heirmologia copied in 1302 and 1309, most of his music is transmitted in Akolouthiai or musical anthologies which began to proliferate during the middle of the 14th century. In the majority of these, the beginning records Koukouzeles' most famous single work, the so-called 'Schulgesang' or 'Lehrgedicht', a didactic chant whose text consists of the Greek names of Byzantine neumes. The names are graphically illustrated by the musical line, a melody which reflects the sizes of interval named in the text and reproduces corresponding inflections in the melodic line.

Studies which have compared chants of Koukouzeles with older and more traditional Byzantine liturgical melodies and with chants by Koukouzeles' contemporaries and successors have confirmed his alleged preeminence as 'the master' among Byzantine composers of the 14th and 15th centuries. Koukouzeles appears as an innovator at the beginning of the 14th century, perhaps the first to abandon an older, more conservative manner of composing for new melodic invention. In the older, traditional layer of chant before his time a simple refrain functioned as a brief cadential appendage to certain lines from the Prooemiac Psalm (Psalm ciii) in Great Vespers. (The numbering of psalms used here is that of the Greek Septuagint.) With Koukouzeles the refrain which traditionally followed the psalm text is no longer subordinate but is expanded through textual troping. Moreover, he has altered the structural emphasis in his chants for the Prooemiac Psalm by shifting the centre of musical gravity to the refrain. In two of his five chants for Psalm ciii the music for the refrain is almost twice as long as the chant for the psalm text. He also expands the text in his kalophonic settings for Psalm ii in the evening office. Kalophonic chants by his older contemporaries are all built on only a single line from the second psalm, but each of Koukouzeles' kalophonic settings incorporates at least one phase from another line of this psalm. He frequently extracts fragments from another verse, or even from other verses, and augments the basic text by weaving these phrases into the principal line from the psalm, a practice of textual expansion which leads to chants of great length.

Koukouzeles innovations in this type of expansion are paralleled by his bolder vocal concepts. Not only do the ranges of his chants either equal or exceed those of earlier traditional chants, but also ranges in the refrain portion of his chants are considerably greater than ranges from the preceding segment of psalm text. Although the melodic lines of his works are still predominantly conjunct, his chants show a substantial increase over traditional settings in the disjunct nature of their melodies since they employ leaps greater than the ascending or descending 3rd. In general Koukouzeles' melodies appear more skilfully wrought and the seams of their formulaic outlines more deftly concealed than either those of the older traditional repertory or the vast majority of chants by his contemporaries and successors. As a bridge from the older musical tradition of the 13th century, his work appears to have provided the impetus for a new repertory and new musical developments which were continued by his contemporaries and successors.

See also BYZANTINE RITE, MUSIC OF THE and RUSSIAN AND SLAVONIC CHURCH MUSIC.

BIBLIOGRAPHY
P. A. Sîrku: 'Zhitie Ioanna Kukuzelya kak' istochnik' dlya bolgarskoy istorii', *Zhurnal' Ministerstva Narodnago Prosvieshcheniya*, cclxxxii (1892), 130
S. Eustratiades: 'Iōannēs ho Koukouzelēs, ho maistōr, kai ho chronos tēs akmēs autou', *Epetēris Hetaireias Byzantinōn Spoudōn*, xiv (1938), 3–86
R. Palikarova-Verdeil: *La musique byzantine chez les Bulgares et les Russes (du IXe au XIVe siècle)*, MMB, Subsidia, iii (Copenhagen, 1953), 193
G. Dévai: 'The Musical Study of Koukouzeles in a 14th-Century Manuscript', *Acta antiqua academiae scientiarum Hungaricae*, vi (1958), 213
L. Brashovanova-Stancheva: 'Prouchvaniya vŭrkhu zhivota i deynostta na Ioan Kukuzel', *IIM*, vi (1959), 13
E. V. Williams: 'John Koukouzeles' Reform of Byzantine Chanting for Great Vespers in the Fourteenth Century' (diss., Yale U., 1968)
For further bibliography *see* BYZANTINE RITE, MUSIC OF THE.
EDWARD V. WILLIAMS

Koulsoum, Ibrahim Oum. *See* KALTHUM, IBRAHIM UM.

Kounadis, Arghyris (*b* Constantinople, 14 Feb 1924). Greek composer, conductor and pianist. A piano student of S. Farandatos at the Athens Conservatory, he graduated in 1952; he studied composition under Yannis Papaïoannou at the Hellenic Conservatory in Athens, graduating in 1956. Scholarships from the Greek and West German governments enabled him to pursue his studies at the Freiburg Hochschule für Musik, where his composition teacher was Fortner and his conducting teacher Karl Ueter. In 1963 he was appointed assistant professor to Fortner and director of the 'Musica Viva' concerts. He was one of the first composers to show an interest in *rebétiko* (a type of urban folksong), and during the period 1949–57 he composed a number of works which show the influence of this, and also that of Stravinsky and Bartók. These pieces were later rejected when Kounadis turned towards more novel techniques, including serial writing and aleatory forms, although his music has retained a strong lyrical basis. His stage works, which often display a sarcastic humour, have been successful in West Germany. Kounadis's *Chorikon* (version 1) was the first Greek work to be performed at an ISCM Festival (Cologne 1960).

WORKS
(selective list)

Stage: The Return (opera, 1, K. Cicellis and C. Clerides), 1961, rev. 1974; Der Gummisarg (opera, 1, V. Ziogas), 1962; Die verhexten Notenständer (music-theatre, 1, K. Valentin), 1969; Teresias (revue, Kounadis), 1971–2; Doctor Faustus (incidental music, Marlowe), chorus, org, ens, 1972–3; Der Ausbruch (opera, 1, W. Jens), 1974
Orch: Sinfonietta, 1951; 5 Compositions, 1957–8; Chorikon, 2 versions, 1958; Triptychon, fl, orch, 1964; Epitýmvion, 6 perc, 15 fl, 1965; Heterophonika idiomela, 1967
Inst: Moments musicaux, vn, pf, 1949–50; 5 Sketches, fl, 1959; Str Qt, 1960; Duo, fl, pf, 1961; 4 pezzi, version 1, fl, vc, pf, 1965; 'Wer Ohren hat zu hören, der höre', wind qnt, 1970; Blues [from Die verhexten Notenständer], fl, hpd, 1970; Die Sanduhr der Zeitluppe, action pieces, cl, pf, perc, tapes, 1975
Vocal: Plans for a Summer (Seferis), Bar, pf, 1949; 3 Poems (Sappho), S, fl, cel, vib, va, vc, 1959; Epigramma I (U. Thomson), chorus, 1961; 3 Poems (Cavafy), S, fl, cel, gui, vc, 1963; 4 pezzi, version 2, (Enzensberger), S, fl, vc, pf, 1965; Rhapsodia (A. Hadrian, N. Engonopoulos, Homer), S, ens, 1967; 3 Poems (M. Sachtouris, trans. T. Hensch), S/Bar, pf, 1967; Epigramma II (V. Ziogas), chorus, 1968; Epigramma III (Kounadis), chorus, 1968; Die Nachtigall, S, 10 db, 1974

Principal publishers: Bote & Bock, Modern, Tonger, Schott (Mainz)

BIBLIOGRAPHY
M. Dounias: *Moussikokritiká* (Athens, 1963), 137, 170, 223, 227f, 316
N. Slonimsky: 'New Music in Greece', *MQ*, li (1965), 231
B. Schiffer: 'Neue griechische Musik', *Orbis musicae*, i/2 (1972), 196
GEORGE S. LEOTSAKOS

Koussevitzky [Kusevitsky], Sergey (Alexandrovich) (*b* Vishny-Volotochok, Tver [now Kalinin], 26 July 1874; *d* Boston, Mass., 4 June 1951). American conductor and composer of Russian birth. He entered the Moscow Philharmonic Music School at 14, choosing the double bass as one of three instruments for which open scholarships were available, and made this his principal study, under Rambusek. After joining the double bass section of the Bol'shoy Theatre Orchestra in 1894 he began to give solo recitals from 1896 and to tour in Europe, attracting much attention in Berlin (1903) and London (1907). He wrote several small works to supplement the double bass repertory and, with some help from Glier, a concerto, of which he gave the première in Moscow in 1905. Two years later, having acquired some knowledge of conducting method from watching Nikisch, he conducted a student orchestra at the Berlin Hochschule für Musik, then engaged the Berlin PO to make his public début as a conductor in 1908. His success launched his subsequent career and was followed the same year by concerts in London with the LSO, with which he became a frequent guest conductor into the 1920s. Having acquired wealth by his marriage in 1905 to Natalia Uškov, the daughter of a tea merchant, he founded a publishing house in 1909 (its imprint appeared in the West as Editions Russes de Musique) and entered into contracts with Metner, Prokofiev, Rakhmaninov, Skryabin and Stravinsky, among others. Also in 1909 he formed his own orchestra to help propagate the works he published or admired and, besides giving concerts in leading cities, he took the orchestra by riverboat to townships along the Volga in 1910, repeating the tour in 1912 and 1914. An ardent champion of Skryabin, in particular, he conducted the première of *Prometheus* in 1910 and the same year introduced the *Poem of Ecstasy* to Britain at an LSO concert. After the 1917 Revolution, Koussevitzky left the USSR for Berlin, Rome and Paris, where he founded a concert series with another specially recruited orchestra, which gave the first performances of, among other works, Musorgsky's *Pictures at an Exhibition* in Ravel's orchestration commissioned by Koussevitzky, and Honegger's *Pacific 231*. He also conducted Paris productions of *Boris Godunov*, *Khovanshchina*, *Prince Igor* and *The Queen of Spades*, but otherwise was seldom concerned with opera.

In 1924 Koussevitzky went to the USA as conductor of the Boston SO in succession to Monteux, an appointment he retained for 25 years and in which his influence on the American musical scene rivalled, and perhaps exceeded, that of Stokowski and Toscanini. Koussevitzky transferred his enthusiasm for contemporary music to American composers, and Barber, Copland, Hanson, Harris, Piston and Schuman were among the many he commissioned and regularly performed. To mark the 50th anniversary of the Boston SO in 1931 he also commissioned Stravinsky's *Symphony of Psalms*, Ravel's Piano Concerto, Hindemith's *Konzertmusik* and works by Copland, Gershwin, Prokofiev and Roussel. After an annual series of summer concerts at Tanglewood, Massachusetts, from 1935, Koussevitzky established the Berkshire Music Center there in 1940 as a summer school of instruction with its own auditorium for public concerts. He took classes in conducting, and among his students was Bernstein, who later succeeded him in this capacity. Koussevitzky took American nationality in 1941 and, after the death of his wife the next year, he set up the Koussevitzky Music Foundation as a permanent memorial to her, the funds to be used to commission new works from composers of all nationalities. One of the first to benefit was Britten, whose *Peter Grimes* (1945) was the foundation's first commissioned opera. From 1950 a permanent endowment made the Library of Congress the repository of all scores commissioned by the foundation. In 1947 Koussevitzky married Olga Naumov, a niece of his first wife. He occasionally visited Europe and gave a series of

Sergey Koussevitzky

BBC concerts in 1935; he made his last British appearances with the LPO in 1950. His many gramophone records spread the fame of the Boston SO far and wide and greatly increased popular interest in the more colourful masterworks of the Russian and French repertory.

A flamboyant, egocentric figure, Koussevitzky never mastered idiomatic English, but never left any doubt about his meaning in conversation or in rehearsal. He rehearsed with unflagging concern for detail, and frequent titanic rages, and his performances were marked by high emotional intensity, colourful phrasing and dramatic character. He was persuasive in the contemporary works he favoured and, while his approach to the older repertory was seldom orthodox, and his treatment of Bach, Beethoven, Brahms and others untraditional, the force of his musical personality overcame most academic objections. His compositions included, besides the Double Bass Concerto, a *Humoresque*, *Valse miniature*, *Chanson triste* and similar pieces for double bass, and a Passacaglia on a Russian Theme (1934) for orchestra. Besides receiving many honorary degrees, he was appointed a Chevalier of the Légion d'honneur and received the Finnish Order of the White Rose.

BIBLIOGRAPHY

A. Lourié: *S. A. Koussevitzky and his Epoch* (New York, 1931)
M. A. DeWolfe Howe: *The Boston Symphony Orchestra, 1881–1931* (Boston, 1931)
——: *The Tale of Tanglewood* (Boston, 1946)
H. Leichtentritt: *Serge Koussevitzky, the Boston Symphony Orchestra and the New American Music* (Cambridge, Mass., 1946)
M. Smith: *Koussevitzky* (New York, 1947)
Catalog of Works Commissioned by the Koussevitzky Music Foundation (Lenox, Mass., 1958)
The Koussevitzky Music Foundation in the Library of Congress, Washington D.C. (New York, 1958)
H. C. Schonberg: *The Great Conductors* (New York, 1968), 300ff

D. Wooldridge: *A Conductor's World* (London, 1970), 137ff [with partial discography]

NOËL GOODWIN

Koutloumousi [Koutloumousiou]. Monastery on MOUNT ATHOS.

Kovačević, Krešimir (*b* Zagreb, 16 Sept 1913). Yugoslav musicologist. He studied composition at the Academy of Music in Zagreb, graduating in 1938. For a time he worked as a répétiteur at the opera houses in Zagreb and Belgrade (1936–9) and then taught music in schools in Osijek and Dubrovnik (1940–50). In 1943 he obtained his doctorate in musicology at the University of Leipzig with a dissertation on Croatian folksong. He formed the Dubrovnik City Orchestra in 1946 and was its conductor until 1950. In 1950 he became professor at the Zagreb Academy of Music (vice-dean 1961–71; dean from 1971). He was music critic of *Zvuk* from 1956 to 1966 and became music critic of the daily *Borba* in 1957. He became general editor of the second edition of *Muzička enciklopedija* in 1971 and editor of *Arti musices* in 1973.

Kovačević's main interest is the history of Croatian music of the 19th and 20th centuries. As a critic covering numerous first performances of Croatian music he has become an authoritative chronicler of its more recent trends and developments; in *Hrvatski kompozitori i njihova djela* (1960) he published analyses of all the major works of Croatian composers of the late 19th and 20th centuries.

WRITINGS

Das kroatische Volkslied aus dem Murinselgebiet (diss., U. of Leipzig, 1943)
Hrvatski kompozitori i njihova djela [Croatian composers and their works] (Zagreb, 1960)
Muzičko stvaralaštvo u Hrvatskoj 1945–1965 [Musical creativity in Croatia] (Zagreb, 1966)
'Die kroatische Musik des XVII. und XVIII. Jahrhunderts', *Musica antiqua Europae orientalis I: Bydgoszcz 1966*, 200
'Nationalism in Textbooks, Articles and General Studies in the History of Music in Yugoslavia', *Yugoslav-American Seminar on Music: Sveti Stefan 1968*, 194
'Muzička akademija u Zagrebu', *Arti musices*, i (1969), 9

BOJAN BUJIĆ

Kovách, Andor (*b* Szaszvaros, Transylvania, 21 April 1915). Hungarian composer. He studied composition with Kodály at the Budapest Academy of Music and privately with Bartók. Since graduating from the academy he has pursued a career as conductor and conservatory professor in Germany, Brazil, Belgium and Switzerland. His works include a series of operas which have brought him popular and press acclaim as 'a modern Puccini'. He was appointed professor and resident composer at Massachusetts Institute of Technology for three years from 1978.

WORKS
(*selective list*)

Operas: Meurtre dans la cathédrale (opera-oratorio, 1, after Eliot), 1957; Médée (1, after Anouilh), 1960, Saarbrücken, Stadttheater, 1967; Le rendez-vous (opéra comique, 1, after C. Arnothy), 1964, Saarbrücken, Stadttheater, 1971; Bal des voleurs (3, after Anouilh), 1970; L'Apollon de Bellac (1, after Giraudoux), 1972
Other works: 4 syms., concs., orch pieces, choral music, chamber music, songs, film scores, incidental music, folksong arrs.

WRITINGS

with R. P. Zelenka: *A magyar zsoltár* [The Hungarian psalter] (Budapest, 1941)

Kovács, Béla (*b* Budapest, 1 May 1937). Hungarian clarinettist. He studied with György Balassa at the Liszt Academy of Music, and while still a student became a member of the Budapest Opera orchestra (1956); he was later appointed a soloist. He was a founder of the Hungarian Wind Quintet, in which he played from 1961 to 1971, and is a member of the Budapest Chamber Ensemble. In 1975 he was appointed a professor at the Liszt Academy. A notable virtuoso, and Hungary's leading clarinettist, he is a fine player of both classical and contemporary music. His recordings include Mozart's concerto and quintet, Bartók's *Contrasts* and a number of contemporary Hungarian works. He was awarded the Liszt Prize in 1964 and named Artist of Merit in 1972.

PÉTER P. VÁRNAI

Kovács, Dénes (*b* Vác, 18 April 1930). Hungarian violinist. After making his début when he was six, he studied with Ede Zathureczky at the Budapest Academy, graduating in 1950, and was first violinist at the Budapest Opera, 1951–60. He won the 1955 Carl Flesch Competition in London, and in 1957 was appointed a professor at the Budapest Academy, becoming director in 1968. His crystalline tone and sense of style in a repertory from Bach to Bartók make him preeminent among Hungarian violinists; he has toured in other European countries and in China. Kovács plays a Guarneri violin of 1742, on which he has made a number of recordings, including Bartók's Concerto no.2, Rhapsodies and Solo Sonata for the complete recorded edition. He has given the first performances of several contemporary Hungarian works, most of them dedicated to him, and he was awarded the Liszt Prize in 1954 and 1958, the Kossuth Prize in 1963, and named Eminent Artist in 1970.

PÉTER P. VÁRNAI

Kovács, Sándor (*b* Budapest, 26 Jan 1886; *d* Budapest, 24 Feb 1918). Hungarian piano teacher. He studied the piano with Árpád Szendy, composition with Hans Koessler at the Budapest Academy of Music, arts at Budapest University and music history in Berlin. He took his doctorate in 1907 at Budapest University (the first music dissertation there) with a dissertation on the evolution of music and was subsequently professor at the Fodor School of Music, Budapest (1910–18). In 1911 he founded, with Bartók and Kodály, the Hungarian Society for New Music (UMZE), which later became the Hungarian section of the ISCM. Kovács was one of the first piano teachers to make use of the results of experimental psychology and to establish a systematic method of music teaching in Hungary. This method concentrated on ear training (anticipating the Leimer–Gieseking method), analysis of sound and touch, practising without the instrument and training the memory; he outlined its principles in his book *Hogyan gyakoroljunk?*. His compositions include *Petőfi-dalok* ['Petőfi lieder'] and two books of songs.

WRITINGS

Prolegomena a zene fejlődéstani történetéhez [Prolegomena to the evolution of music] (diss., U. of Budapest, 1907; Budapest 1907)
'Zeneesztétikai problémák' [Problems of music aesthetics], *Zeneközlöny* (1911)
'La jeune école hongroise', *BSIM*, vii (1911), 47
'Zur Frage der musikalischen Renaissance', *AMz*, xxix (1911)
'Introjektion, Projektion und Einfühlung', *Zentralblatt für Psychoanalyse*, ii/5–6 (1912)
Hogyan gyakoroljunk? [How to practise?] (Budapest, 1916, 3/1960)
'Hogyan kellene a gyermeket a zenébe bevezetni' [How to introduce children to music], *Népművelés* (1916)
ed. with I. Popper, O. Gombosi and A. Molnár: *Hátrahagyott zenei írásai* [Posthumous works] (Budapest, 1928)

BIBLIOGRAPHY

G. Fodor: 'Dr. Kovács Sándor', *Zenei szemle*, ii (1918)

G. Kálmán: 'Kovács Sándor', *Crescendo*, i/4 (Budapest, 1926), 9

B. Telegdi: 'Kovács Sándor', *Zenei szemle*, xii (1928), 146

I. Vitányi: 'A magyar zenetudomány kezdetei: Kovács Sándor és Molnár Antal' [Beginnings of Hungarian musicology: Sándor Kovács and Antal Molnár], *Muzsika*, xi/11 (1968), 12

IMRE FÁBIÁN

Koval, Marian Viktorovich (*b* Pristan' Vozneseniya, Olonets govt., 17 Aug 1907; *d* Moscow, 15 Feb 1971). Russian composer. He studied in Nizhny Novgorod (1918–21), in Petrograd and at the Moscow Conservatory (1925–30), where he was a pupil of Gnesin and Myaskovsky. In the 1920s he was a member of the Prokoll organization, and he began his creative career as a composer of choral pieces; from 1957 to 1961 he was artistic director of the Pyatnitsky Choir. He was also active in the Composers' Union and held the titles Honoured Art Worker of the RSFSR and Honoured Art Worker of the Lithuanian SSR, as well as the State Prize. His work is principally in choral genres, from folksong arrangements to oratorios. The most celebrated of his compositions is the monumental oratorio *Emel'yan Pugachov*, which was made into an opera. His style has its roots in folk music, with distinctively Russian, lyrical melodies.

WORKS
(selective list)

Stage: Zemlya vstayet [The earth rises] (musical-dramatic scene) (1932); Volk i semero kozilyat [The wolf and the 7 kids] (children's opera)(1938); Emel'yan Pugachov (opera, V. Kamenetsky), Moscow, 1942, rev. 1959; Sevastopol'tsï (opera), Perm, 1946, rev. 1949; Graf Nulin (comic opera), 1949; Aksyusha (ballet), 1964

Choral: Skaz o partizane [Tale of the partisan] (poem) (1935); Emel'yan Pugachov (oratorio, Kamenetsky) (1940); Narodnaya svyashchennaya voyna [National holy war] (oratorio) (1942); Chkalov (oratorio); Zvyozdï kremlya [Stars of the Kremlin] (oratorio); other pieces for chorus/children's chorus

Chamber music, pf pieces, songs, music for the theatre and cinema

BIBLIOGRAPHY

B. Yarustovsky: 'O "Emel'yane Pugachove" M. Kovalya', *SovM* (1940), no.2

M. Bruk: *Marian Koval'* (Moscow, 1950)

B. Yarustovsky: 'Novoye i staroye v "Emel'yane Pugachove" ' [Old and new in 'Emel'yan Pugachov'], *SovM* (1959), no.4

M. V. Koval': *S pesney skvoz godu* [With a song through the years] (Moscow, 1968)

G. Polyanovsky: *Marian Koval'* (Moscow, 1968)

Obituary, *SovM* (1971), no.5, p.158

GALINA GRIGOR'YEVA

Kovaříček, František (*b* Litěniny, eastern Bohemia, 17 May 1924). Czech composer. He studied composition in Prague with Hlobil at the conservatory and with Řídký at the academy, graduating in 1952. After working as music director for Czech radio in Prague (1953–8) he gave most of his time to composition, while holding external classes in composition at the academy and at the conservatory. He has also been president of the advisory committee of the music information centre in Prague. In the 1950s he composed within the folksong school, at the same time following neo-classical and constructivist models, as in the Piano Sonata no.1. A synthesis, balanced in favour of Romanticism, was achieved in the 1960s.

WORKS
(selective list)

Operas: Ukradený měsíc [The stolen moon] (lyric comic scenes, L. Aškenázy, V. Mikeš), 1966; Czech radio, 1 July 1970

Orch: Předehra [Ov.], 1951, rev. 1962; Smuteční hudba [Music of mourning], 1952; Divertimento, str, 1960; Kasace, chamber orch, 1964; Cl conc., 1964; Capriccio, chamber orch, 1970–71

Vocal: Písničky na slova lidové poesie [Songs on words from folk

poetry], 1951; Zlatá vlna června [Golden wave of June] (song cycle, M. Florian), 1957; 3 písně (J. Kainar), T, pf, 1963

Inst: 2 pf sonatas, n.d., 1968; 4 kusy [4 pieces], vn, pf, 1953; Hudba pro 13 nástrojů [Music for 13 insts], 1956–7

Principal publishers: Český Hudební Fond, Dilia, Panton

OLDŘICH PUKL

Kovařovic, Karel (*b* Prague, 9 Dec 1862; *d* Prague, 6 Dec 1920). Czech conductor and composer. He studied the clarinet, the harp and the piano at the Prague Conservatory (1873–9), and also took private lessons in singing and in composition with Fibich (1878–80). Then he worked as harpist with the Prague National Theatre (1879–85), as piano accompanist to the violinist František Ondříček and to the baritone Leopold Stropnický (1881–7), and as director and répétiteur at Pivoda's vocal school in Prague (1880–1900). Occasionally he conducted the orchestral concerts of the Umělecká Beseda artists' association (1893–4), and for the Czech Ethnographical Exhibition in Prague (1895) he established a large orchestra which he conducted. He also directed some of the first concerts of the Czech PO (1896–8).

In 1900 Kovařovic was appointed opera director of the National Theatre; he formed a new orchestra and chorus in the next year, and remained in this post until shortly before his death. His work at the National Theatre was his most important contribution to Czech musical life. He began his career there with *Dalibor* and thereafter paid particular attention to the classics of the Czech repertory – Smetana, Dvořák (including the première of *Rusalka*) and Fibich – but he also gave the first performance of operas by Ostrčil, Foerster and Novák and the first Prague performance (1916) of *Jenůfa*, which led immediately to performances in Vienna and Berlin and established Janáček's reputation. This followed his 12-year refusal to consider the work (though it had been successfully performed in Brno) and was conditional upon his revision and reorchestration of the work – in which form it is still played. He had a special sympathy with French opera and conducted Russian and German works, notably those of Wagner and Strauss. At the same time he directed the Czech PO in new orchestral works by Novák, Suk and others. He was elected to extraordinary (1901) and ordinary (1906) membership of the Czech Academy of Science and Arts, and in 1910 was made an officer of the Académie Française.

Before establishing himself as a conductor, Kovařovic had already made a reputation as a composer, at first with the opera *Ženichové* ('The bridegrooms') and the ballet *Hašiš*, both successfully performed in 1884. He had a feeling for dramatic tension and stage effect, and a refined sense of instrumental colour; his work overflows with a lyricism and elegance close to French music. The operas *Psohlavci* ('The dog heads') and *Na starém bělidle* ('At the old bleaching-house') were the most popular, their patriotic pathos proving a moral prop to the Czech people at times of oppression. The former won first prize in a competition for new Czech operas held in 1897. He is the author of *K otázce dramaturgie operní* ('On the problem of operatic dramaturgy'; Prague, 1904).

WORKS
(selective list)
OPERAS

Ženichové [The bridegrooms] (comic opera, 3, Kovařovic, after K. S. Macháček), 1880–83, Prague, 1884; Cesta oknem [The way through the window] (E. Züngl, after G. Lemoine, Scribe), 1885, rev. 1914, 1920; Crespo (Kovařovic, after Calderon), 1886–7, inc.; Armida (J. Vrchlický, after Tasso), 1888–95, inc.; Noc Šimona a Judy (comic opera, 3, K. Šípek [J. Peška], after P. d'Alarcona), 1890–91, Prague, 1892

Psohlavci [The dog heads] (3, Šípek, after A. Jirásek), 1895–7, Prague, 1898; Na starém bělidle [The old bleaching-house] (4, Šípek, after B. N. Babiček), 1898–1901, Prague, 1901, reorchd 1916; Slib (Šípek, after G. Feuillet), c1905, ov. only, orchd R. Zamrzel; Flétna (J. Kvapil), 1910, inc.

OTHER WORKS

Operetta: Edip král [Oedipus the king] (A. V. Nevšímal, after Sophocles), 1889–90, Prague, 1894

Ballets: Hašiš, 1, V. Reisinger, 1883, Prague, 1884; Pohádka o nalezeném štěstí [A tale of happiness discovered], 3, A. Berger, 1888–9, Prague, 1889; Na záletech [On excursions], ballet pantomime, 10 scenes, A. Viscusi, 1909, Prague, 1909

Incidental music: Ďáblovy pilulky [The devil's pills] (3, F. Lalone, A. Burgeois Anicet, Laurent), Prague, 1890

Orch: Comedy Ov., 1880; Pf Conc., 1887; Dramatic Ov., 1891; 2 sym. poems

3 str qts, 1878, 1887, 1894; inst pieces, songs, choruses

Principal publishers: Dilia, Hudební Matice, Otto, Umělecká Beseda, Urbánek

BIBLIOGRAPHY

J. Křička: 'Karel Kovařovic', Almanach České akademie, xxxi (1921), 124

F. Pujman: Operní sloh Národního divadla (Prague, 1933)

L. Novák: Stará garda Národního divadla (Prague, 1937)

J. Petr: Vzpomínáme Karla Kovařovice [Reminiscences of Kovařovic] (Prague, 1940)

L. Novak: Dva čeští muzikanti [Two Czech musicians] (Prague, 1941)

J. Procházka, ed.: Karel Kovařovic: první šéf Národního divadla v Praze 1900–1920 [First head of the Prague National Opera 1900–1920] (Prague, 1946)

O. Jeremiáš: 'Karel Kovařovic: tvůrce moderní hudební reprodukce' [Creator of modern musical interpretation], Národní divadlo, xxv/3 (1949–50)

A. Rektorys, ed.: Korespondence Leoše Janáčka s Karlem Kovařovicem a ředitelstvím Národního divadla (Prague, 1950)

H. Semschová: Karel Kovařovic: umělcova cesta do Národního divadla [Kovařovic's artistic journey to the National Theatre] (diss., U. of Prague, 1954)

B. Štědroň: 'Ke korespondenci a vztahu Leoše Janáčka a Karla Kovařovice' [Correspondence and relationship between Janáček and Kovařovic], Sborní filosofické fakulty brněnské university, F6 (1960), 31–69

F. Pala: Opera Národního divadla v období Otakara Ostrčila [The opera of the National Theatre at the time of Otakar Ostrčil], i (Prague, 1962)

J. Němeček: Opera Národního divadla za Karla Kovařovice (Prague, 1968–9)

MÍLAN KUNA

Kowalski, Henri (b Paris, 1841; d Bordeaux, 8 July 1916). French pianist and composer of Polish and Irish descent. He entered the Paris Conservatoire in 1853 and studied the piano under Marmontel, Prudent and Anatole Petit and composition under Carafa and Samuel David. He is also said to have studied sol-fa under Alkan at the Polish School. After experience as a chorister at La Chapelle Impériale and as pianist at the Opéra he began in 1858 a concert career which included tours of southern France (1864), Germany and Spain (1868), England, the USA and Canada (1869, 1876) and Australia (1880–82). By 1870 he had composed many songs and sacred works and over 100 piano pieces, including the celebrated Marche hongroise (1864). In 1870 he was music critic of L'Europe; his first opera, the five-act Gilles de Bretagne, was produced unsuccessfully by Vizentini at the Théâtre Lyrique in 1877. He went to Melbourne in 1880 to give a series of concerts and act as French juror at the International Exhibition, and subsequently toured country centres in Victoria and other states. He acted as overseas correspondent to Le Figaro, began work on a comic opera by the Melbourne writer Marcus Clarke and enhanced his reputation for personal generosity, charm and pianistic virtuosity. He

returned to Europe for the première of his 'Australian' opera Moustique in Brussels (1883) but in 1885 finally settled in Sydney, where he was much more appreciated (Pougin had called his A travers l'Amérique 'absolument insignificant et dénué d'intérêt'). He was appointed conductor of the Sydney Philharmonic Society (1886–9) and was co-founder with Leon Caron of Sydney's Orpheus Club (1887–91), and his activities included teaching, concert appearances (often for the benefit of Australian artists), the establishment of a French musical depot to promote his native music and polemics calling for government subsidy of his training schemes to improve theoretical and practical standards in Australia. Many of his piano pieces and songs were performed, as were his three-act lyric opera Vercingetorix (Sydney and Melbourne, 1881) and an oratorio The Future Life (Sydney, 1895), but his oncefashionable music is now forgotten and even his fame as 'the Prince of the Pianoforte' has escaped Australian music histories.

BIBLIOGRAPHY

FétisB

H. Kowalski: A travers l'Amérique: impressions d'un musicien (Paris, 1872)

O. Comettant: Au pays des kangourous et des mines d'or (Paris, 1890)

D. J. Quinn: 'Musicians and Musical Taste in Australasia; 1: Sydney', Review of Reviews (Sydney, 20 April 1895), 391

Cosmos (Sydney, 30 April 1895), 433

B. R. Elliott: Marcus Clarke (Oxford, 1958), 231, 238f

ELIZABETH WOOD

Kowalski, Július [Dominik, Alexander] (b Ostrava, Moravia, 24 Feb 1912). Czech composer and teacher. At the Prague Conservatory he studied composition with Suk and conducting with Talich. He was appointed choirmaster successively at the opera houses of Prague (1939), Salzburg (1940), Belgrade (1942) and Bratislava (1945), and also made a career as a teacher. Finally he settled in Bratislava as director of a music school. Between the wars Kowalski was allied with the Czech avant garde, but much of his later compositional activity has been in the service of amateur ensembles, many of which he has conducted.

WORKS

(selective list)

Inst: Partita, vn, $\frac{1}{4}$-note, 1936; Fantasia, vn, vc, $\frac{1}{4}$-note, 1937; Povstanie [The uprising], dramatic prelude, 1954; Str Qt no.2, 1954; 5 syms., 1954, 1957, 1959, 1970, 1974; Vn Concertino, 1955; Oslobodenie [Liberation], orch, 1955; Chamber Sym., 1958; Poema quasi una elegia, vc, orch, 1959; Serenade, fl, str orch, 1962; Str Qt no.3, 1965; Conc., vc, str, 1970; Conc., str qt, orch, 1973–4; Str Qt no.4, 1975; Concertante Symphonietta, wind qnt, orch, 1976

Vocal: Rozprávka pri praslici [Tales at the spinning wheel], opera, 1952; Lampiónová slávnosť [Chinese lantern festival], opera, 1960; many choruses

Principal publishers: Opus, Slovenský Hudobný Fond

LADISLAV BURLAS

Kowalski, Max (b Kowal, 10 Aug 1882; d London, 4 June 1956). German composer of Polish birth. In 1883 he was taken to Germany. He took a doctorate in law at the University of Marburg and studied singing with Alexander Heinemann in Berlin and composition with Sekles in Frankfurt am Main. Among his first publications was a set of songs on poems from the Giraud–Hartleben Pierrot lunaire which appeared at about the same time as Schoenberg's settings. Kowalski's songs, unlike Schoenberg's, fall within the tradition of the Romantic lied, to which he was one of the last successful contributors. In 1939, after his release from the Buchenwald concentration camp, he fled to England, where he found work as a piano tuner and synagogue singer. Later he taught singing in London and continued to compose until his death.

WORKS
(selective list)

SONGS
(all for 1v, pf)

6 Lieder, op.1 (Bierbaum, Dehmel, K. Kamlah, Verlaine) (1913); Die Sonne sinkt, op.2 (Nietzsche) (1913): 6 Gesänge, op.3 (V. Blüthgen, Dehmel, Eichendorff, Jacobsen, Su Chien-yüeh) (1913); 12 Gedichte aus Pierrot lunaire, op.4 (Giraud, trans. Hartleben) (1913); 3 Lieder, op.5 (M. Greif) (1915); 3 Balladen, op.7 (C. F. Meyer) (1914); 3 Gedichte, op.8 (Greif) (1914); 4 Gesänge, op.9 (Dehmel, E. Lissauer, Novalis, J. Vogel) (1916); 6 Lieder auf alte Gedichte, op.10 (1919); 6 Liebeslieder aus dem Rokoko, op.11 (H. C. Boie, J. W. L. Gleim, F. von Hagedorn, Kleist, Lessing) (1921)

5 Marienlieder, op.12, 1927; 6 Gedichte, op.13 (Verlaine), 1928; 5 Gedichte, op.14 (Hesse) (1931); 6 Gedichte, op.15 (Klabund), 1930; 5 Lieder, op.16 (Hebbel, Huch, Lessing, Lissauer, Nietzsche) (1931); 6 Lieder aus dem West-östlichen Divan, op.17 (Goethe) (1934); 7 Gedichte, op.18 (Hafiz), 1933; Japanische Frühling (trans. Bethge), 10 songs, 1934–8; 4 zusätzliche Lieder (Jap. verse), 1934–7; 5 Jüdische Lieder, 3 zusätzliche Jüdische Lieder, 1935–7; 12 Kinderlieder, 1936; 6 Heine-Lieder, 1938

12 Lieder (Li Tai Po), 1938–9; Ein Liederzyklus (Khayyām), 1941; 8 Lieder (Hafiz), 1948; 7 Lieder (Meyer), 1949; 6 Lieder (Hölderlin), 1950–51; 7 Lieder (Rilke), 1951; 7 Geisha-Lieder, 1951; 6 Lieder auf indischen Gedichte (trans. Bethge), 1951–2; 5 Lieder (George), 1952; 6 Lieder auf arabischen Gedichte (trans. Bethge), 1953–4

OTHER WORKS
2 Klavierstücke, op.6 (1913)

Principal publishers: Eos, Leuckart, Simrock, Universal

BIBLIOGRAPHY
H. F. Schaub: 'Max Kowalski', *ZfM*, cxiii (1952), 407
H. F. Redlich: 'Max Kowalski', *Musica*, xi (1957), 584

based on *MGG* (xvi, 1049–50) by permission of Bärenreiter
PHILIP L. MILLER

Kox, Hans (*b* Arnhem, 19 May 1930). Dutch composer. After early studies with his father, an organist and choral conductor, he attended the Utrecht Conservatory and was then a composition pupil of Badings; his piano studies were completed with Jaap Spaanderman. He was director of the Doetinchem Music School (1956–71), which he brought to a high standard, and thereafter lived in Haarlem as a freelance composer. His début had been made with a string trio performed at the Gaudeamus Foundation in 1953, and he increased his reputation with the Piano Sonata no.1 and the String Quartet. He wrote his first large orchestral work, the *Concertante muziek*, in 1956 to a commission from the Concertgebouw Orchestra. Kox's music from these early years until 1963 is marked by classical forms and by the harmonic influences of Berg, Mahler and Badings; chief among the compositions of this period are the First Symphony, the Piano Concerto and the Violin Concerto. The Symphony no.2 (1966) brought the phase to a definite close, for Kox had felt the need for greater formal freedom and the desire to apply newer techniques.

In 1964 he began the *Cyclophony* cycle, a group of short (six to ten minutes) concertante pieces of elastic structure; no.7, for example, is made up of five blocks, each with seven subdivisions which may be played simultaneously or in different successions, and each allowing improvisation around given melodic and rhythmic formulae. For the 25th anniversary of the battle of Arnhem, Kox composed *In Those Days*, an impressive piece for two choral and three instrumental groups, directed by two conductors, which won the Prix Italia in 1970. Each group has different starting-points in relation to the others, and so a fluctuating form is achieved. The *Requiem for Europe* is scored for four spatially disposed choirs with instrumental groups; some freedom is allowed to the conductor, whose choices are to be influenced by the acoustic of the hall. The work is in two parts: 'Totesfuge', a setting of Celan's poem, and 'For the Lost Hopes of Humanity', with texts by Kox and from *Deuteronomy*.

WORKS
(selective list)

VOCAL

Opera: Dorian Gray (2, Kox, after Wilde), 1973, Amsterdam, 1974, rev. 1975

Choral: Chansons cruelles (N. Louvrier, K. Merz, Rilke), 1957; De kantate van Sint Juttemis (H. Gijsbers), T, Bar, male vv, pf, 1962; Zoo (T. Fop), male vv, orch, 1964; Litania, female vv, orch, 1965; In Those Days (Old Testament, Livy, Erasmus, Churchill), 2 groups of 4vv, 3 orch groups, 1969; Requiem for Europe (Celan, Kox, Deuteronomy), 4 choruses, 2 org, orch, 1971; Puer natus est, vv, orch, 1971

Solo vocal: 3 Coplas (J. W. W. Buning), 1v, pf, 1955; Vues des anges (Rilke), 1v, pf, 1959; 3 Chinese Songs, Bar, pf, 1962; L'allegria (Ungaretti), S, orch, 1967; Gedächtnislieder, S, orch, 1972

ORCHESTRAL

Concertante muziek, hn, tpt, trbn, orch, 1956; Little Lethe Sym., 1956; Fl Conc., 1957; Conc. for Orch, 1959; Sym. no.1, str, 1959; Ballade, 1960; Spleen, ballet, 1960; Pf Conc., 1962; Vn Conc., 1963; 2 Vn Conc., 1964; Cyclophony no.1, vc, chamber orch, 1964; Cyclophony no.2, 1964; Cyclophony no.5, ob, cl, bn, 19 str, 1966; Sym. no.2, 1966; Music for Status Seekers, 1966; Cyclophony no.6, vn, tpt, pf, vib, 16 str, 1967; Vc Conc., 1969; Phobos, 1970; 6 One-act Plays, 29 insts, 1971; Conc. bandistico, 1973; Cyclophony no.9, perc, orch, 1974; A Gothic Conc., harp, chamber orch, 1975; Sinfonia concertante, vn, vc, orch, 1976

CHAMBER AND INSTRUMENTAL

3 sonatas, vn, pf, 1952, 1955, 1961; 3 str trios, 1952, 1954, 1955; 2 Pf Pieces, 1954; 2 pf sonatas, 1954, 1955; Str Qt, 1955; Sextet no.1, fl, ob, hpd, str trio, 1957; Str Qnt, 1957; Sonata miniatura, rec, hpd, 1957; Sextet no.2, str qt, hpd, pf, 1957; Suite, brass trio, 1958; 3 Pieces, vn in 31st-tones, 1958; Pf Qt, 1959; Sonata, vc, 1959; Sextet no.3, wind qnt, pf, 1959; Barcarolle, pf, 1960

3 Studies, pf, 1961; 4 Pieces, str qt in 31st-tones, 1961; Studies in Counterpoint, fl, hpd, 1962; 4 Didactic Pieces, 2 tpt, trbn, 1964; Cyclophony no.4, rec, 9 str, 1965; Serenade, 3 vn, 1968; Pf Qt, 1968; Cyclophony no.3, pf, elec, 1970; Cyclophony no.7, vn, pf, 6 perc, 1971; Cyclophony no.8, wind qnt, str trio, db, 1971; Preludes, vn, 1971; Capriccio, 2 vn, pf, 1974; The Jealous Guy Plays his Tune, vn, pf, 1975; Melancholieën, pf, 1976; Pf Trio, 1976

Principal publisher: Donemus

BIBLIOGRAPHY
W. Paap: 'De componist Hans Kox', *Mens en melodie*, xxiv (1969), 35
G. Werker: ' "In Those Days": a Musical Memory of the Battle of Arnhem', *Sonorum speculum* (1970), no.43, p.24
R. Starreveld: 'Hans Kox: Cyclophonies', *Sonorum speculum* (1973), no.52, p.28

JOS WOUTERS

Kozeluch [Koscheluch, Koželuh], **Johann Antonin** [Jan Evangelista Antonín Tomáš] (*b* Velvary, 14 Dec 1738; *d* Prague, 3 Feb 1814). Bohemian composer, Kapellmeister and music teacher, a cousin of Leopold Kozeluch. He studied music at school in Velvary, as a chorister at the Jesuit college in Březnice and in Prague with J. F. N. Seger. He then worked for a short time as Kapellmeister in Rakovník and cantor in Velvary (to March 1762). Between about 1763 and 1766 he lived in Vienna, where he studied composition with Gluck and Gassmann and recitative with Hasse. After his return to Prague he soon became renowned as a music teacher and was subsequently Kapellmeister at St Francis's Church at the Crusaders' monastery. He applied unsuccessfully for the post of *cappellae magister* at St Vitus's Metropolitan Cathedral on F. X. Brixi's death in 1771, but was appointed there on 2 March 1784 as successor to Anton Laube and held this position until his death. Among his pupils were Václav Praupner and Leopold Kozeluch; he also taught composition to his two sons, Wenzel Franz (*b* 1784, a teacher of Joseph Proksch) and Vinzenz Emanuel (1780–1839), and to his daughter Barbara, a singer and pianist.

Kozeluch was one of the most important Bohemian composers in the second half of the 18th century; his music was performed well into the 19th century. In his own day it was mainly as 'the masterly contrapuntist' that he was known; polyphonic texture is significant not only in the works of his first period (e.g. a fugue for double chorus, 1765), but also in his mature church works of about 1786 and later, in which he reduced the role of virtuoso vocal solos in favour of harmonic and contrapuntal depth. The works of his middle period show a predominantly operatic style. His operas (the first, after Mysliveček's, by a native Czech composer to be staged at Prague) are in the *opera seria* style of Jommelli, with alternating recitatives and arias in abridged da capo form. He made considerable use of accompanied recitative (especially in *Il Demofoonte*), and he used the orchestra to depict the dramatic situation and add harmonic depth to the accompaniments. Despite Italian inspiration and some traces of French *opéra comique* in the melodies, the fundamental Czech colouring of Kozeluch's idiom is unmistakable. The oratorios and other church music of his middle period are in the same operatic style; he adapted some of the opera arias for use in church. Apart from the opera and oratorio librettos nothing of his output was printed during his lifetime. His music collection at St Vitus's Cathedral (now in the archive of the Prague castle), includes 439 works by himself, F. X. Brixi, Caldara, Hasse, Michael Haydn, Leopold Hofmann, Laube, Jan Zach and others.

WORKS

Alessandro nell'Indie (3, Metastasio), Prague, spr. 1769; *A-Wn*, frag. *CS-Pnm*

Il Demofoonte (3, Metastasio), Prague, spr. 1771; holograph *Pnm*, 2 arias ed. in Němeček (1956)

Sacred: La morte d'Abel (Metastasio), Easter oratorio, Prague, Crusaders' monastery, 1776, *BREsi*; Gioas re di Giuda (Metastasio), Easter oratorio, Prague, Crusaders' monastery, 1777, only lib extant; *c*400 other works, incl. *c*45 masses, 98 offertories, 90 graduals, 60 arias, 30 motets, 10 Te Deum, 5 requiems, 2 litanies, mostly *Bm*, *Pnm*, *Pp* (see also Kouba, 1969)

Orch, *Pnm*: 4 syms., listed in Breitkopf catalogue (1774–5); 2 bn concs.; Ob Conc., ed. O. Schmid-Dresden with pf acc. (Hanover, n.d.); Cl Conc., also attrib. L. Kozeluch, ed. with pf acc. in MVH, xiv (1964)

BIBLIOGRAPHY

AMZ, ii (1799–1800), col.499; ix (1806–7), cols.67, 628

A. Podlaha: *Catalogus collectionis operum artis musicae quae in bibliotheca capituli metropolitani pragensis asservantur* (Prague, 1926), nos.548–803, pp.v, xxxi, xxxiii, xxxvi

O. Kamper: *Hudební Praha v xviii. věku* [18th-century musical Prague] (Prague, 1936), 39f, 195ff

V. Němec: *Pražské varhany* [Prague organs] (Prague, 1944), 135, 142, 149

R. Fikrle: *Jan Ev. Ant. Koželuh: život, dílo a osobnost svatovítského kapelníka* [J. E. A. Kozeluch: life, work and personality of the St Vitus Kapellmeister] (Prague, 1946) [incl. list of works]

J. Němeček: *Nástin české hudby xviii. století* [Outline of 18th-century Czech music] (Prague, 1955), 162f, 298

——: *Zpěvy xvii. a xviii. století* [17th- and 18th-century songs] (Prague, 1956), 208ff

M. Poštolka: *Leopold Koželuh: život a dílo* [L. Kozeluch: life and works] (Prague, 1964) [incl. list of works]

W. Vetter: 'Tschechische Opernkomponisten', *Sborník prací filosofické fakulty brněnské university*, F9 (1965), 353

J. Kouba, ed.: *Průvodce po pramenech k dějinám hudby* [Guide to sources of musical history] (Prague, 1969)

For further bibliography see KOZELUCH, LEOPOLD.

MILAN POŠTOLKA

Kozeluch [Kotzeluch, Koželuh], **Leopold** [Jan Antonín, Ioannes Antonius] (*b* Velvary, 26 June 1747; *d* Vienna,

7 May 1818). Bohemian composer, pianist, music teacher and publisher. He was baptized Jan Antonín, but began (not later than 1773) to use the name Leopold to differentiate himself from his older cousin of that name. He received his basic music education in Velvary and then studied music in Prague with his cousin, who probably gave him a thorough grounding in counterpoint and vocal writing, and with F. X. Dusek, whose piano and composition school prepared him mainly for writing symphonies and piano sonatas. After the success of his first ballets and pantomimes (performed in Prague, 1771–8), Kozeluch abandoned his law studies for a career as a musician. In 1778 he went to Vienna, where he quickly made a reputation as an excellent pianist, teacher and composer. By 1781 he was so well established there that he could refuse an offer to succeed Mozart as court organist to the Archbishop of Salzburg. By 1784 Kozeluch was publishing his own works; the following year he founded a music publishing house, later managed as the MUSIKALISCHES MAGAZIN by his brother Antonín Tomáš Kozeluch (1752–1805). His compositions were also published almost simultaneously by a number of other houses in various countries. Kozeluch's business contacts with English publishers, particularly John Bland, Robert Birchall, and Lewis, Houston & Hyde, are well documented by correspondence. In September 1791 he achieved success in high circles with a cantata commissioned by the Bohemian Estates for the Prague coronation of Leopold II as King of Bohemia. After the accession of Emperor Franz II he was appointed (12 June 1792) *Kammer Kapellmeister* and *Hofmusik Compositor*. From about 1804 Kozeluch's original work as a composer took second place to his arrangements of Scottish, Irish and Welsh folksongs for the Edinburgh publisher George Thomson, to teaching, and to the activities connected with his court appointment, which he held until his

Leopold Kozeluch: mezzotint by William Ridley

death. His daughter Catharina Cibbini (1785–1858) was a well-known pianist and composer of piano music during the early 19th century in Vienna.

Kozeluch was one of the foremost representatives of Czech music in 18th-century Vienna. His influence as a pianist and piano teacher was such that contemporary accounts early praised him for helping in the development of an idiomatic piano style and for discouraging the use of the harpsichord in favour of the piano. As a composer he devoted himself almost exclusively to secular music (his sacred compositions are mostly arrangements of secular works). His chief interest lay in piano music – sonatas, piano trios and concertos – but he wrote almost as much symphonic and vocal music; he also composed for the stage, though most of his ballets and all but one of his operas are lost, making his achievement difficult to assess.

Kozeluch's output falls into three main stylistic (though not chronological) divisions: except for the oratorio *Moisè in Egitto* the *galant* style of the Viennese Rococo characterizes the greater part of his vocal output of the 1780s, particularly the songs and ariettas; his piano concertos and symphonies use the normal expressive language of the Viennese Classical style at that period, and a number of piano and chamber works of the 1780s and 1790s even presage the Romantic lyricism of Schubert. Elements of Beethoven's tragic-pathetic style and (more rarely) his lyricism are most evident in works of about 1785–97 (like the piano sonatas PXII:17, 20, 27, 34, 37, and the piano trios PIX:11, 15, 33), and can also be discerned in works from the first decade of the 19th century (e.g. PXII:38–40). Romantic expression is foreshadowed in the chamber works and piano music of 1785–91 (e.g. PXII:26, 28 and PVIII:3) and above all in the *Trois caprices* for piano (PXIII:3–5, about 1797) and the piano trios using Scottish and Irish melodies (PIX:40–45, 52–4, 1798–1803). The caprices, with their novel sonorities, colourful harmony and unusual form, represent an early stage of the single-movement lyrical piano piece; the other works hint at Schubert and Weber in some stylistic traits and in the character of their melodic inspiration.

WORKS

All printed works were published in Vienna unless otherwise stated; catalogue numbers are from Poštolka (1964), which includes doubtful and lost works; editions are listed in MAB, lxxii (1969).

VOCAL

9 cantatas, XIX: 1–9: Denis Klage auf den Tod Marien Theresien (1781); Quanto è mai tormentosa (c1782); Joseph, der Menschheit Segen, perf. 1783 (1784); Cantate (K. G. Pfeffel, 'auf M. T. von Paradis', perf. 1783 (1785); Chloe, recit and aria (1783); Cantate ded. Leopold II (Meissner), perf. 1791, CS-Pk; La Galatea, 1802, Pk; In un fiero contrasto, A-Wgm; Cantata pastorale, I-Fc

7 sacred, XXV: 1–7: Mass, CS-Pnm; Tantum ergo, A-Wn; Offertory or gradual, CS-Pnm; 2 arias, Pnm; 1 aria, N; hymn (Prague, 1833)

c60 songs (1v, hpd/pf, unless otherwise stated), XXI: 1–15, XX: 1–3: 15 Lieder (1785); 12 Lieder (1785); The Happy Pair, in 6 Ballads (London, ?c1788); 12 Italian Arietts, 1v, harp/pf (London 1790); De l'arbre ces fruits (1795); march song (1796); march song (1797); 3 airs françois (1797); Hört! Maurer (Salzburg, Mainz, 1799); In questa tomba oscura, arietta (1808); 6 [12] canzonets (1815); Mein Mädchen (1811); Des Kriegers Abschied (Berlin, c1818–19); Let the Declining Damask Rose (London, n.d.); Caro bene, recit and rondo, S, orch (London, n.d.); 2 arias, A-Wgm; 1 aria, D-B

Others: Moisè in Egitto, XVI: 1, oratorio, 1787, A-Wgm; La Giuditta, XVI: 2, oratorio (G. Bertati), ?c1790–92, I-Fc; 6 notturni, XVIII: 1–6, S, A, T, B, pf, vc (1796); Non v'è nembo ne procella nò, XVII: 1, chorus, orch, A-Wgm; 27 solfeggi, XXI: C 2, CS-Pnm

Arrs., XXII: 1–2: A Select Collection of [110] Original Scottish Airs, 1v, pf, vn, vc (London, 1798); A Select Collection of [59] Original Welsh Airs, 1v, pf, vn, vc, collab. J. Haydn (London, 1809)

STAGE

6 operas, XXIII: 1–6: Gustav Wasa (3 acts), after ?1792, CS-Pk; 5

others, lost

6 ballets and pantomimes, XXIV: 1–6: La ritrovata figlia di Ottone II (ballo eroico, 5, A. Muzzarelli), Vienna, 24 Feb 1794 (1794); Arlecchino (? F. Clerico), arr. pf, A-Wgm; ballet, str, D-Bds (autograph); ballet, hpd, CS-Pnm; pantomime, hpd, Pnm; Télémaque dans l'île de Calypso (2, J. Dauberval), A-Wgm

ORCHESTRAL

11 syms., I: 1–11: D (Paris, c1786); C (Paris, c1786); D, F, g (1787), ed. in MAB, lxxii (1969); C, A, G (1787); C, D-DO; A, 'à la française', c1779–84, CS-Pnm; B♭, 'l'irresolu', Pnm

22 hpd/pf concs., IV: 1–20: F, B♭ (1784); G (1785); A, E♭ (1785); C (Paris, 1786); D (1787); F (Mainz, c1785); Concerto en rondo, C (Offenbach, 1793); Concert favori, E♭ (London, 1800); B♭ for 4 hands, listed in Breitkopf catalogue, 1785–7, CS-Pnm; D, D, Pnm; Rondo concerto, E♭, Pnm; E, Pnm (autograph); F, KRa; C, A-Wgm; C, Wn; Fantasia concertante, d, Wn; E, B-Bc; F, B♭, BR-Rn [without catalogue numbers]

Other: Sym. concertante, II: 1, E♭, perf. 1798, A-Wn; Sym. concertante, II: 2, C, Wn; Ov., III: 2, D, Wgm; 2 cl concs., V: 1–2, E♭, E♭, before 1790, CS-Pnm; 5 sets of dances, VII: 1–5, A-Wn [nos.1, 3–5 arr. pf]; march, VII: 6, lost [arr. 2vv, hpd]

CHAMBER

6 str qts, VIII: 1–6: B♭, G, E♭ (1790) [nos.2–3 arr. trios; no.3 partly arr. trio]; C, A, F (1791) [nos.4–5 arr. trios]

63 trios (sonatas), IX: 1–63, pf/hpd, vn/fl, vc: D, F, E♭ (1780) [arr. duos]; C, G, B♭ (1781); C, A, E♭ (1786) [no.8 arr. duo]; G, c, F (1787) [arr. duos]; B♭, A, g (1788); E♭, D, e (1789); B♭, C (1791); C (1792); G, E♭ (Paris, ?c1792) [arr. of str qts]; C, A, op.33 (Paris, 1793) [arr. of str qts]; D, F, G (1793); F, C, e (1795); B♭, D, G (1796) [arr. 2 vn]; F, G, D (1799); Grand Sonatas, G, B♭, F, C, A, g, 1798–9 (London, ?c1799); E♭, A, B♭, (London, 1800); D, E♭, C, 1801 (1802); B♭, D, E♭, 1803 (London, 1804); B♭, F, C, 1817 (London, n.d.); D, G, E♭, 1817 (London, n.d.); D, C, B♭, c1805–6 (London, 1800); E♭, CS-Pnm [arr. partly from str qt]

31 duos, X: 1–11, 13–24 and other (pf, vn, unless otherwise stated): E♭, C (Paris, 1785) [arr. of kbd sonatas]; G, c, F (Paris, ?c1785), [arr. of trios]; 6 sonatas, E, G, D, B♭, f, G, op.23 (Paris, n.d.); g, C, A♭ (London, ?c1788) [arr. of kbd sonatas]; f, A, E♭ (London, ?c1788) [arr. of kbd sonatas]; e, C, D, XV: 7–9, fl, vc (London, after 1792); D (London, c1820) [arr. of kbd sonata]; C (London, c1820) [arr. of kbd sonata]; Sonata, XII: 49, G (London, ?c1820); 6 [3] grands duos symphoniques, XV: 1–3, D, B♭, G, 2 vn (Paris, n.d.) [arr. of trios, no.3 arr. of La chasse, kbd]; D, XV: 6, vn, va, A-Wgm; A, CS-Pnm [arr. of trio]; D, F, E♭, Pu [arr. of trios]

Other: 2 serenades, VI: 1–2, D, E♭, vn, va, b, fl, bn, hn, op.11 (Offenbach, 1787); 16 fanfares, XV: 5, 3 hn, JIa; 2 divertimentos, VI: 9–10, E♭, E♭, pf/hpd, 2 vn, 2 ob, 2 hn, A-Wn; 3 divertimentos, VI: 4–5, 7, D, D, E♭, 2 cl, 2 hn, CS-Pnm; Nocturne, VI: 6, D, fl, vn, 2 va, vc/basset hn, Pnm; Trio XV: 4, G, fl, vn, vc, Pnm; Parthia, VI: 3, F, 2 va, fl, 2 cl, 2 bn, 2 hn, D-W; Parthia, VI: 8, F, 2 fl, 2 cl, 2 bn, 2 hn, USSR-Lsc

KEYBOARD

7 sonatas for 4 hands, XI: 1–7: F (?c1781); B♭ (1784); F (1784); B♭ (1789); C, F, D, op.12 (Paris, n.d.)

49 solo sonatas, XII: 1–48, 50: F, E♭, D (1780); B♭, A, c (1780); E♭, e, G (1784), no.3 also pubd with others, F, C (Paris, 1784) [no.5 arr. duo]; D (Amsterdam, n.d.) [arr. duo]; E♭, C (1784) [arr. duo]; g, C, A♭ (1785) [arr. duo]; f, A, E♭ (1785) [arr. duo]; F, C, d (1786); D, a, E♭ (1788); B♭, G, c (1789); F, A, g (1791); E♭, C, f (1793); G (London, ?c1797); E♭, c, d, 1803 (London, 1807); F, before 1773, USSR-Lsc; A, 1776, CS-Pnm; C, A-WLn; E♭, Wn; Grandes sonates, B♭, A, e, I-PAc; G, F, E♭, before Oct 1806 (London 1809)

Other solo works: La chasse, XIII: 2, F (1781) [arr. 2 vn]; Ov., III: 1, G (London, ?c1785); Minuet, XIV: 6 (1789); XII Menuetten, XIV: 7 (1793); XV neue deutsche Tänze, XIV: 8 (1793) [arr. of orch dances]; 6 ecossaises, XIV: 9 (?1793); 15 deutsche Tänze, XIV: 9 (?1793) [arr. of orch dances]; 6 contredanses, XIV: 5 (1795) [arr. of orch dances]; march, XIV: 10 (c1797); 3 caprices, XIII: 3–5, E♭, B♭, c (1798); 12 Pieces ... for the Use of Beginners, XIII: 6–17 (London, 1799); 12 neue deutsche Tänze, XIV: 11, A-Wn [arr. of orch dances]; andante and march, XIII: 1, 1779–80, D-B; 23 minuets, 1 polonaise, XIV: 1–4, ?1778, CS-Pnm

BIBLIOGRAPHY

G. J. Dlabacz: 'Versuch eines Verzeichnisses der vorzüglichern Tonkünstler in oder aus Böhmen', *Materialien zur alten und neuen Statistik von Böhmen*, ed. J. A. Riegger, xii (Leipzig and Prague, 1794), 249

Jb der Tonkunst von Wien und Prag (Prague, 1796/R1975), 33

G. J. Dlabacž: *Allgemeines historisches Künstler-Lexikon*, ii (Prague, 1815/R1973)

P. Weingarten: *Die Sonatenproduktion der Wiener Zeitgenossen von Haydn und Mozart von 1775–1805* (diss., U. of Vienna, 1910)

I. Pollak-Schlaffenberg: 'Die Wiener Liedmusik von 1778–89', *SMw*, v (1918), 97–139

R. Sondheimer: 'Die formale Entwicklung der vorklassischen Sinfonie', *AMw*, iv (1922), 99

H. J. Wedig: 'Beethovens Streichquartett op.18 Nr.1 und seine erste Fassung', *Veröffentlichungen des Beethovenhauses*, ii (Bonn, 1922), 8

E. Alberti-Radanowicz: 'Das Wiener Lied von 1789–1815', *SMw*, x (1923), 37–76

G. Löbl: *Die Klaviersonate bei Leopold Kozeluch* (diss., U. of Vienna, 1937)

C. Hopkinson and C. B. Oldman: 'Thomson's Collections of National Song', *Transactions of the Edinburgh Bibliographical Society*, ii (1940)

O. E. Deutsch: 'Kozeluch ritrovato', *ML*, xxvi (1945), 47

A. Weinmann: *Verzeichnis der Verlagswerke des Musikalischen Magazins in Wien* (Vienna, 1950)

K. Pfannhauser: 'Wer war Mozarts Amtsnachfolger?†', *Acta Mozartiana*, iii/3 (1956), 6

O. Wessely: 'Koželuch, Leopold Anton', *MGG*

M. Poštolka: *Leopold Koželuh: život a dílo* [Life and works] (Prague, 1964) [with thematic catalogue, bibliography; Eng. and Ger. summary]

C. Flamm: *Leopold Koželuch: Biographie und stilkritische Untersuchung der Sonaten für Klavier, Violine und Violoncello* (diss., U. of Vienna, 1968)

——: 'Ein Verlegerbriefwechsel zur Beethovenzeit', ed. E. Schenk, *Beethoven-Studien* (Vienna, 1970), 57–110

A. Weinmann: 'Supplement zum Verlagsverzeichnis des Musikalischen Magazins in Wien', *Beiträge zur Geschichte des Alt-Wiener Musikverlages*, 2nd ser., xiv (1970)

MILAN POŠTOLKA

Kozina, Marjan (*b* Novo Mesto, Slovenia, 4 June 1907; *d* Novo Mesto, 19 June 1966). Yugoslav composer and writer on music. He studied mathematics at Ljubljana University and music at the conservatory (1925–7), later continuing his compositional studies with Marx at the Vienna Academy (1927–30) and with Suk in the Prague Conservatory master classes (1930–32), where he was also a conducting pupil of Malko. On his return to Yugoslavia he worked successively as répétiteur at the Ljubljana Opera (1932–4), conductor of the Maribor Glasbena Matica and director of its music school (1934–9), teacher at the Belgrade Music Academy (1939–43, 1945–7), director of the Slovene Philharmonia (1947–50) and composition teacher at the Ljubljana Academy (1950–60). He composed in a neo-Romantic style, with touches of folksong and pictorialism.

WORKS
(selective list)

Orch: Suite, 1939; Sym. in 4 sym. poems: Ilova gora [Mt Ilova], 1947, Padlim [To the fallen], 1946, Bela Krajina, 1946, Proti morju [Towards the sea], 1949; Davnina, sym. poem, 1960

Vocal: Ekvinokcij, opera, 1946; Lepa Vida [Beautiful Vida], 3 solo vv, chorus, 1939; Balada Petrice Kerempuha, B, orch, 1946

Ballets, songs, choruses, film scores

Principal publisher: Edicije DSS

BIBLIOGRAPHY
P. Kuret: 'Marjan Kozina: prispevek za biografijo' [Kozina: a contribution to his biography], *MZ*, vii (1971), 90

ANDREJ RIJAVEC

Kozlovsky, Alexey (*b* Kiev, 15 Oct 1905; *d* Tashkent, 9 Jan 1977). Soviet composer and conductor. He began to compose at the age of six, and studied the piano and composition with Yavorsky at the Kiev Conservatory (1917–19) and the First Moscow Music Technical College. Subsequently he studied composition with Zhilyayev and Myaskovsky at the Moscow Conservatory and went to Khessin for conducting lessons. On graduating from the conservatory in 1931 he made his début as a conductor at the Stanislavsky Opera Theatre, where he worked for several years, meanwhile making himself a reputation in the USSR and the USA as a composer. In 1936 he moved to Tashkent. His activities in Uzbekistan were extremely varied: he collected and

studied examples of Uzbek and Karakalpak folk music, sometimes under the guidance of V. Uspensky (in his compositions he used only folk material recorded by himself); he composed in all genres and wrote articles on Uzbek folk music; in 1944 he began teaching composition and conducting at the Tashkent Conservatory (he was made professor in 1958); and he served as principal conductor of the Uzbek Philharmonic SO (1949–57, 1960–66). His awards included the title People's Artist of the Uzbek SSR (1955), the Order of the Badge of Honour (1944, 1952), the Order of Lenin (1959) and the Khamza State Prize (1973).

Kozlovsky was one of a number of leading Russian composers working in Uzbekistan in the 1930s who tried to achieve a creative synthesis of European and Uzbek traditions. Though he was brought up on the music of the Russian Romantics and the French impressionists, he displayed a rare insight into the essence of Asian folklore. An inventive harmonist and orchestrator, he was drawn to programmatic orchestral genres, which provided rich opportunities for imaginative sonorities, and to the musical theatre. Of his orchestral works the most popular are the suite *Lola* and the vocal-symphonic poem *Tanovar* (on a lyrical folk melody), both written shortly after his arrival in Uzbekistan. The two *Karakalpak* suites are also outstanding, while his chief opera is the heroic-historical *Ulugbek*. As a conductor he was responsible for making the Uzbek Philharmonic SO into a highly professional body; he achieved particular success in Tchaikovsky and Skryabin, Debussy and Ravel.

WORKS
(selective list)

Operas: Ulugbek (Kozlovsky, G. Gerus), 1942, rev. 1958; Afdal' (Gerus)

Ballets: Slava Oktyabryu [Hail October] (Gerus), 1947; Tanovar [The oriole] (Gerus), 1971

Orch: Sym. no.1 'Khoreograficheskaya', 1934; Sym. no.2, 1935; Lola, sym. suite, 1937; Tanovar, sym. poem, 1v ad lib, orch, 1951; Po prochtenii Ayni [On reading Ayno], sym. poem, 1952; Doston, sym. poem, 1954; Indiyskaya poema, 1955; Uzbekskaya tantseval'naya syuita [Uzbek dance suite], 1954, from the opera Ulugbek; Karakalpakskaya syuita no.1, 1956; Karakalpakskaya syuita no.2, 1962; Prazdnestvo [Celebration], sym. poem, 1964; Pamyat' gor [Memory of the mountains], sym. poem, 1973

Vocal: 2 suites, chorus, 1934; Nastavleniye mudrïm [Admonition to the wise] (Navoya), cantata, 1948; Nigorim, Tekenarish, 1v, orch, 1956; Mertsul', 1v, orch, 1962; songs, folksong arrs.

Inst: Va Sonata, 1965; 232 pf fugues, other pieces

Other works: Uzbek music dramas, collab. Uzbek composers; incidental music, film scores

Principal publishers: Gosizdat UzSSR, Gostlitizdat UzSSR, Muzïka, Sovietskiy kompozitor

BIBLIOGRAPHY
A. Kozlovsky: 'Otrazheniye tembrov uzbekskikh narodnïkh instrumentov v simfonicheskom orkestre' [The reflection of the timbres of Uzbek folk instruments in the symphony orchestra], *Voprosï muzïkal'noy kul'turï Uzbekistana* (Tashkent, 1961)

G. Vïzgo: *Alexey Kozlovsky* (Moscow, 1966)

L. M. BUTIR

Kozlovsky, Ivan Semyonovich (*b* Mar'yanovka, Kiev govt., 24 March 1900). Ukrainian tenor. He graduated from Elena Murav'yova's class at the Kiev Institute of Music and Drama in 1920 having made his début in 1918 at Poltava. He then sang in the opera houses at Khar'kov in 1924 and Sverdlovsk in 1925, and joined the Bol'shoy Theatre in 1926. He was made People's Artist of the USSR in 1940. Kozlovsky was the most popular Soviet singer of his time. The distinctive features of his singing were his clear, silvery tone and flexible upper register extending to *e''*, his warmth of manner, remarkable technique, expressive use of words and finished phrasing. A versatile artist and a fine actor, he sang such contrasting roles as Lensky, Berendey (*The Snow Maiden*), Lohengrin, and the Simpleton (*Boris Godunov*), a role that he sang in the film of the opera (1955) with astonishing power and depth of insight. His other highly successful roles included those in Gounod and Verdi operas, Mozart (*Mozart and Salieri*), the Prince (*The Love of Three Oranges*), Almaviva and Don José. From 1938 to 1941 Kozlovsky directed his own opera company and took part in Gluck's *Orfeo ed Euridice* and Massenet's *Werther*; in his productions he aimed at strong dramatic tension. He was a distinguished recitalist, performing with exceptional artistry Russian and west European songs as well as Ukrainian and Russian folksongs. At the age of 65 he recorded some Rakhmaninov songs, his voice still firm and free.

BIBLIOGRAPHY

G. Polyanovsky: *Ivan Semyonovich Kozlovsky* (Moscow and Leningrad, 1945)

V. S. Slyotov: *I. Kozlovsky* (Moscow and Leningrad, 1951)

I. M. YAMPOL'SKY

Kozłowski, Józef (*b* Warsaw, 1757; *d* St Petersburg, 27 Feb 1831). Polish composer and conductor. He probably studied in Warsaw, and as a boy was a chorister at St John's Cathedral as well as a member of its instrumental ensemble. Later he played in the band of J. Stempkowski, governor of Łabuń in the Zasław district, and from 1775 taught music at the court of the Princes Ogiński at Guzów and Troki. He moved to Russia (?1780) and served as an officer in the Russian army (1786–91), at first under Prince Dolgoruky and later under Grigory Potyomkin, with whom he went to St Petersburg in 1791. There he was put in charge of the music in Potyomkin's house and then at Prince Narïshkin's court (1791–9). In 1799 he was appointed inspector of the imperial theatres and in 1801 promoted to the directorship. In 1819 a severe illness forced him to retire, and, apart from a short stay in Poland (1822–4), he spent the rest of his life in St Petersburg.

Kozłowski was a prolific composer. He provided music for the coronation celebrations of Paul I in 1797 (op.8, St Petersburg, 1797) and in the following year composed a mass for the funeral of Poland's last king, Stanisław August. However, most of Kozłowski's compositions are polonaises, which he introduced to Russia and popularized as a dance form. He wrote several hundred, many based on themes from popular operas of the day; they were generally written for festive occasions at the Russian court and enjoyed enormous popularity. So too did Kozłowski's songs (about 30), which occupied an important place in the development of the pre-Romantic lyrical song. He composed incidental music to Ozerov's *Oedipus in Athens* (1804) and *Fingal* (1805), Shakhovskoy's *Deborah* (1810), and Racine's *Esther* (1816), among others. He also composed choral works, including a *Te Deum* for double chorus. Many of his works were published in St Petersburg; the largest collection of his manuscripts is in the library of the Institut Teatra, Muzïki i Kinematografii, Leningrad.

BIBLIOGRAPHY

N. Findeyzen: *Ocherki po istorii russkoy muzïki v Rossii s drevneyshikh vremyon do kontsa XVIII veka* [Essays on the history of Russian music from earliest times to the end of the 18th century], ii (Leningrad, 1929)

S. Golachowski: 'Missa pro defunctis J. Kozłowskiego', *KM*, iv (1932), 671

M. S. Druskin and Yu. V. Keldïsh, eds.: *Ocherki po istorii russkoy*

muzïki 1790–1825 [Essays on the history of Russian music 1790–1825] (Leningrad, 1956)

I. Belza, ed.: *Russko-polskiye muzïkal'nïye svyazi* [Musical links between Russia and Poland] (Moscow, 1963)

L. T. Błaszczyk: *Dyrygenci polscy i obcy w Polsce działający w XIX i XX wieku* [Polish and foreign conductors working in Poland in the 19th and 20th centuries] (Kraków, 1964)

Yu. V. Keldïsh: *Russkaya muzïka XVIII veka* [18th-century Russian music] (Moscow, 1965)

O. Levashova: 'Kozlovskiy i russkiy klassitsizm', *Musica antiqua Europae orientalis III: Bydgoszcz 1972*, 825

KATARZYNA MORAWSKA

Kozolupov, Semyon Matveyevich (*b* Krasnokholmskaya, Orenburg govt., 22 April 1884; *d* Moscow, 18 April 1961). Russian cellist and teacher. He studied at the St Petersburg Conservatory with A. V. Wierzbiłłowicz and I. I. Seifert, and won the Moscow Cello Competition in 1911. A soloist of the Bol'shoy Theatre Orchestra (1908–12, 1924–31), he was also a member of the Moscow Quartet. His playing was distinguished by his virtuosity and his broad, full tone, and he became one of the founders of the Soviet school of cello playing. He taught at the Saratov Conservatory (1912–16, 1921–2) and the Kiev Conservatory (1916–20), and from 1922 until his death he was a professor at the Moscow Conservatory, where he was head of the cello department (1936–54), and where his pupils included Rostropovich and Knushevitsky. His progressive views on technique are reflected in his editions of Bach's cello suites, Davïdov's concertos, and early sonatas and studies. He was made Doctor of Arts in 1941 and People's Artist of the RSFSR in 1946.

BIBLIOGRAPHY

L. Ginzburg: *Istoriya violonchel'novo iskusstva* [The history of the art of the cello], iii (Moscow, 1965), 398–432

LEV GINZBURG

Kracher, Joseph Matthias (*b* Mattinghofen, Upper Austria, 30 Jan 1752; *d* ?Kuchl [now in Salzburg], between *c*1827 and 1830). Austrian composer. He received his first musical training from the schoolmaster in Lochen (Upper Austria), and as a boy he was a singer at the Cistercian monastery at Fürstenzell, the Jesuit seminary at Landshut and the Augustinian abbey of St Nikola at Passau. He was a capable pianist and violinist, and abandoned his plans for a university career to become a schoolmaster and organist at Lochen (from 1765), later serving at Kestendorf, Bavaria (from 6 July 1766), Teisendorf (from 1769) and Michelbeuern, near Salzburg (from 1771), where he also worked as a valet at the local Benedictine abbey. On 1 May 1772 he became the organist of the Seekirche at Salzburg and in 1807 took a post as schoolmaster at nearby Kuchl. Kracher was on friendly terms with Michael Haydn, who prompted his first attempts at composition in about 1775. As a composer he was self-taught; his compositions (apparently exclusively sacred music) follow the same traditions as those of Joseph and Michael Haydn. Although few of his works are extant, they included some 22 masses, 4 requiems, 4 litanies, a vesper service, 24 graduals, 15 offertories, 2 settings of the *Te Deum*, 6 Tenebrae motets, 20 vesper hymns and lieder.

WORKS

(*only those extant*)

Mass, *A-SEI*; mass, *Gd*; Deutsche Messe, 1817, *Gd*, *Sca*; Requiem, *KR*; litany, holograph, *Wgm*; 2 litanies, *Sca*; Vesperae de BVM, *Wn*; offertory, *Wn*; Salve regina, *Wn*; Te Deum, *Wn*

BIBLIOGRAPHY

B. Pillwein: *Biographische Schilderungen oder Lexikon Salzburgischer ... Künstler* (Salzburg, 1821), 117f

C. von Wurzbach: *Biographisches Lexikon des Kaiserthums Oesterreich*, xii (Vienna, 1865), 95f

OTHMAR WESSELY

Kradenthaler, Hieronymus. *See* GRADENTHALER, HIERONYMUS.

Krader [née Lattimer], **Barbara** (*b* Columbus, Ohio, 15 Jan 1922). American ethnomusicologist. She took the AB in music in 1942 at Vassar College, where her teachers included Ernest Krenek and George Dickinson. In 1948 she took the AM in Russian language and literature at Columbia University; she worked with George Herzog and Roman Jakobson. After a year at Prague University (1948–9) she began work for the doctorate at Radcliffe College; she took courses in Slavonic folklore, linguistics and literature under Jakobson and took the PhD in 1955. She was assistant to the chief of the music section of the Pan American Union (1957–9), a reference librarian and bibliographer in the Slavonic division of the Library of Congress (1959–63) and a lecturer in the Slavonic department of Ohio State University (1963–4). During 1965 and 1966 she worked as executive secretary of the International Folk Music Council in London; returning to the USA, she taught at Columbia University (1969) and served as foreign editor of the *American Musical Digest* (1969–70).

Krader's research has centred on Slavonic folk music and music of non-Slavonic Balkan countries; she is particularly interested in wedding ritual songs. She has made field recording expeditions to Czechoslovakia, Yugoslavia, northern Greece, Rhodes and Romania. In 1972–3 she was president of the Society for Ethnomusicology.

WRITINGS

Serbian Peasant Wedding Ritual Songs: a Formal, Semantic and Functional Analysis (diss., Harvard U., 1955)
'Bibliography of George Herzog', *Ethno-Musicology Newsletter*, vi (1956), 11
'Bibliography of André Schaeffner', *EM*, ii (1958), 27
Review of *Corpus Musicae Popularis Hungaricae*, i–iv (Budapest, 1951–9), *JAMS*, xv (1962), 232; review of vol.v (Budapest, 1966), *EM*, xi (1967), 415
'Soviet Research on Russian Folk Music since World War II', *EM*, vii (1963), 252
with B. Aaronson: 'A Partial Survey of Late 18th-century Publications of Czech Music in Western Europe', *Sborník prací filosofické fakulty brněnské university*, F9 (1965), 13
'Folk Music Archive of the Moscow Conservatory, with a Brief History of Russian Field Recording', *Folklore and Folk Music Archivist*, x (1967–8), no.2
'Viktor Mikhailovich Beliaev', *EM*, xii (1968), 86
Review of *Folk Music of Albania* [recording], *EM*, xii (1968), 298
'Bulgarian Folk Music Research', *EM*, xiii (1969), 248
'Music of Czechoslovakia', 'Folklore of Czechoslovakia', *East Central Europe: a Guide to Basic Publications*, ed. P. Horecky (Chicago, 1969), 312, 347
Review of D. Stockmann: *Der Volksgesang in der Altmark* (Berlin, 1962), *EM*, xiii (1969), 559
'The Philosophy of Folk and Traditional Music Study in the United States', *Yugoslav-American Seminar on Music, Sveti Stefan 1968*, 149
Review of A. Lomax: *Folk Song Style and Culture* (Washington, D.C., 1968), *Yearbook for Inter-American Musical Research*, vi (1970), 113
'Folk Music in Soviet Russia: Some Recent Publications', *YIFMC*, ii (1970), 148
'Russian Folk Music Records; a Review Essay', *EM*, xv (1971), 432
Review of B. Bartók: *Rumanian Folk Music* (The Hague, 1967), *JAMS*, xxv (1972), 276
'Ethnomusicology', *Grove 6*

PAULA MORGAN

Kraf, Michael (*b* Neustadt, nr. Fulda, *c*1590; *d* Altdorf, nr. Ravensburg, Swabia, 15 March 1662). German composer, organist and public and court official. Georg Reichert (see *MGG*) suggested that he completed his education at the Jesuit College at Fulda. On 4 April 1616 he was appointed composer and organist of the Benedictine abbey at Weingarten, and remained there until 1633. It appears likely that his duties consisted primarily of composing sacred music, since the abbey also employed a full-time organist. When from 1632 its musical activities were curtailed because of the Thirty Years War, Kraf became active in political affairs. After successfully negotiating the preservation of the monastery from destruction by a Protestant army he became burgomaster of Altdorf-Weingarten on 29 June 1633. In 1639 he entered the service, in non-musical capacities, of Archduke Leopold of Swabia after whose death he continued to serve his successor, Ferdinand Karl; both rulers resided at Innsbruck. Though he did not resume his musical career after 1633, Kraf did maintain his ties with the abbey at Weingarten, which bestowed upon him in perpetuity the title of 'Dominus'. With one exception, the collection of four masses and a requiem published in 1652, all of his publications date from the period of his tenure at the monastery. It is clear, according to Kriessmann, that despite the presence of a basso continuo, his masses, motets and *Magnificat* settings continue the Renaissance polyphonic traditions associated with Palestrina. Several of the masses and motets use parody technique.

WORKS

Musae nova, 8vv, bc (Dillingen, 1616)
Liber I [24] sacrorum concentuum, 2–4vv, bc (Rorschach, 1620)
Canticum Deiparae virginis, liber I, 6, 8vv, bc (Rorschach, 1620)
Augustissimae caelorum dominae virginis parentis canticum, 6–8vv, bc (Rorschach, 1620)
Canticum Deiparae virginis, liber II, 8–10vv, bc (Ravensburg, 1623)
[5] Missae, 6–12vv, bc (Ravensburg, 1623)
Liber II [21] sacrorum concentuum, 2–8vv, bc (Ravensburg, 1624)
[20] Motectae quibus Deo . . . accinuit, pars I, 6–8vv, bc (Ravensburg, 1625; 6 ptbks 1626)
Sacri litaniarum, 4–6vv, bc (Ravensburg, 1627)
Camaenopaedia sacra concertus vocant, liber III, 2–8vv, bc (Ravensburg, 1627)
Agalliama vespertinam quo maximum coelitum refinam virginum, liber III, 6–12vv, bc (Rottweil, 1627)
Opus XI musicum, seu Missae quatuor, cum una pro defunctis, 16vv, bc (Innsbruck, 1652)
Motets, psalms, *A-Kr, D-Mbs*

BIBLIOGRAPHY

EitnerQ
P. Lindner: 'Professbuch der Benediktinerabtei Weingarten', *Fünf Professbücher süddeutscher Benediktinerabteien*, ii (Munich, 1909)
A. Kriessmann: *Geschichte der katholischen Kirchenmusik in Württemberg* (Stuttgart, 1939)
W. Senn: *Musik und Theater am Hof zu Innsbruck* (Innsbruck, 1954)
A. Kellner: *Musikgeschichte des Stiftes Kremsmünster* (Kassel, 1956)

CHRISTOPHER WILKINSON

Krafft [Crafft]. South Netherlands family of composers and musicians of German descent.

(1) Jean-Laurent Krafft (*b* Brussels, 10 Nov 1694; *d* Brussels, buried 1 Jan 1768). Engraver, music publisher and composer. The son of Jean-Georges Krafft and Marie Joos, he was known mainly as an engraver on wood and copper and an etcher (his engravings include a portrait of Henri-Jacques De Croes), but was also a publisher; his publications include Joseph-Hector Fiocco's *Pièces de clavecin* op.1. He may have taught composition at the church of Notre Dame des Victoires (Sablon) in Brussels. He composed a *Passion de notre seigneur Jésus-Christ*, first performed at the Grand Théâtre in Brussels on 8 April 1727 and repeated in

1732. According to Vander Straeten, he also composed a number of harpsichord sonatas published between 1730 and 1737, but none is known, and Vander Straeten may have been misled by the fact that Krafft was a publisher.

(2) François-Joseph Krafft (*b* Brussels, baptized 22 July 1721; *d* Ghent, 13 Jan 1795). Organist, conductor and composer. The son of (1) Jean-Laurent Krafft and Marie Aubersin, he is believed to have been a chorister in St Baaf Cathedral, Ghent, and to have studied composition in Italy (perhaps under Durante), where it is claimed that he won a prize for the motet *In convertendo*. Little is known of his career: he may be the Krafft mentioned in the Brussels *Almanach nouveau . . . ou Le guide fidèle* as a composer, organist and harpsichord teacher from 1761 to 1768, but it could equally be his cousin (3) François. The same applies to the 'Kraft' named as a composition teacher in Brussels in the list of subscribers to Robson's op.4, published about 1760; this could alternatively be Jean-François (*b* 1732), François' brother. On 9 January 1768 François-Joseph married Jeanne Catherine Willems in the church of St Nicolas, Brussels; on 7 April 1769 he was appointed music director of St Baaf Cathedral in Ghent, a position he held until his resignation on 23 August 1794. In 1772 he was invited to Mechelen to sit on a jury of an organ and carillon competition.

WORKS
(all presumed lost unless otherwise stated)

Masses: d, 8vv, orch; G, vv, orch; 5vv, org, 1771; a, 5vv, org, 1776; d, 4vv, org, 1791; G, 4vv, orch, 1792
Missa da requiem, 4vv, org, 1765
3 Te Deum, 8vv, org: C, 1769, D, 1774, d, 1774, all *B-Geb*
Magnificat sesti toni
Psalms: 7 psaumes de la pénitence, 4vv, orch; Dixit Dominus, F, vv, orch, 1782, *Geb*; Dixit Dominus, C, 6vv, orch, 1789, *Geb*; Ecce panis, D, 2 solo vv, orch, 1741, *Geb*; In exitu Israel, 8vv, orch, 1794; Laetatus sum, G, 4vv, orch, 1789, *Geb*; Laudate pueri, E♭, 4vv, org, orch, 1782, *Geb*; Laudate pueri, D, 4vv, orch, 1791, *Geb*
Motets etc: Ave regina; Ave verum; Beatus vir, D, 4vv, orch, 1777, *Geb*; Commendationes animae, 1766; In convertendo, 4vv, orch; O sacrum convivium, F, 2 solo vv, orch, 1792, *Geb*; O sacrum convivium, D, 8vv, orch, 1792, *Geb*; O salutaris, F, 5vv, orch, 1792, *Geb*; Quem admodum, 2 solo vv, orch, *Bc*; Quis sicut Dominus, G, 5vv, orch, 1786, *Geb*; Super flumina Babylonis, 5vv, orch

(3) François Krafft (*b* Brussels, baptized 3 Oct 1733; *d* after 1783). Harpsichordist and composer, nephew of (1) Jean-Laurent Krafft, the third son of Jean-Thomas Krafft and Elisabeth Van Helmont. He is thought to have studied in Liège. Choron and Fayolle and, following them, Fétis, stated that he was a conductor in Brussels around 1760 – not at Notre Dame des Victoires (Sablon), where the position was held by Delhaye, but possibly at the royal chapel (as seems to be confirmed by the frontispiece to his *Sei divertimenti* op.5), probably from 1770 to 1783. During that period he was well known as a professor of harpsichord at Liège and in Germany, where he may have lived for a time. The survival of manuscripts of his religious works at the collegiate church of Sts Pierre and Guidon in Anderlecht (near Brussels) and the church of St Jacques in Antwerp may cast some light on his activities.

WORKS
(all MSS in B-Asj or St Guidon's, Anderlecht)

VOCAL

Masses, 4vv, orch: Missa Sancti Francesci, D; Missa solemnis; Missa tertia, E♭
Te Deum, 4vv, orch
Motets: Beatus vir, D, 4vv, orch; Cum invocarem, D, 4vv, orch; In convertendo, D, 5vv, orch; Litania BVM, D, 4vv, orch; Qualis turbine, 4vv, orch; Quare fremuerunt, D, 4vv, orch; Quis strepitus, 4vv,

orch; Salve regina, 4vv, 9 insts; Si consistunt adversamo, D, 4vv, orch; Super flumina, g, 4vv, orch
Arias, ariettes, duos from Le faux astrologue, arr. in *L'echo, ou Journal de musique française et italienne* (March–Aug 1759, Jan–Sept 1760)
Cori Zephiri volate, 4 vv, inst, ?lost

INSTRUMENTAL

VI Symphonies, 2 vn, va, bc, 2 hn ad lib, op.1 (Nuremberg and Liège, 1756)
12 minuets, hpd, vn, fl, ob (Augsburg, 1758)
6 sonate a tre, 2 fl, bc, op.2 (Paris, n.d.)
6 divertimenti, hpd, vn, op.5 (Brussels, n.d.), ?lost
2 sonatas, hpd, in J. U. Haffner; Raccolta musicale (Nuremberg, 1756–65)
13 pieces 'en écho', org

BIBLIOGRAPHY
EitnerQ; *FétisB*
L'echo, ou Journal de musique française et italienne (Liège, 1759–60)
Almanach nouveau . . . ou Le guide fidèle (Brussels, 1761–75)
A. Choron and F. Fayolle: *Dictionnaire historique des musiciens* (Paris, 1810–11/*R*1971)
E. Thys: *Les sociétés chorales en Belgique* (Ghent, 1855, 2/1861), 204
E. vander Straeten: *La musique aux Pays-Bas avant le XIXe siècle*, i–vi (Brussels, 1867–82/*R*1969)
X. van Elewyck: *Les anciens clavecinistes flamands* (Brussels, 1877)
F. Faber: *Histoire du théâtre français en Belgique* (Brussels, 1878–81)
E. Grégoir: *Les artistes-musiciens belges au XVIIIe et au XIXe siècle* (Brussels, 1885–90)
C. Piot: 'Krafft, Jean-Laurent', *BNB*
R. Vannes: *Dictionnaire des musiciens (compositeurs)* (Brussels, 1947)
            PAUL RASPÉ

Krafft, Georg Andreas. *See* KRAFT, GEORG ANDREAS.

Kraft. Austrian family of composers and cellists.

(1) Anton Kraft (*b* Rokycany, Czechoslovakia, 30 Dec 1749; *d* Vienna, 28 Aug 1820). The son of a brewer, he was taught by Werner (*d* 1768), the cellist of the Kreuzherren Church in Prague, and studied philosophy and jurisprudence at the University of Prague. After abandoning his university studies for a career in music he went to Vienna. There his personal connections with Werner (formerly musician to Count Morzin) and Haydn presumably helped him to obtain in 1778 the post of first cellist in the orchestra of Prince Nikolaus Esterházy, which he held until the orchestra was dissolved. About 1780 he studied composition with Haydn. From 1790 he served as cellist in the orchestra of Prince Antal Grassalkovich de Gyarak in Bratislava; after 1796 he was a member of Prince Joseph Lobkowitz's orchestra in Vienna. During this period he toured frequently as a virtuoso, both alone (Berlin, 1801; Prague, 1802) and in the company of his son (2) Nikolaus Kraft (from 1789). In the year of his death he became the leading cello teacher at the conservatory of the Gesellschaft der Musikfreunde in Vienna.

Kraft was widely appreciated for his expressive playing, not only of his own compositions, but also of Haydn's Cello Concerto in D (1781, H VIIb:2) and Beethoven's Triple Concerto, both of which were written for him. He is known to have performed Mozart's Divertimento K563 after meeting Mozart in Dresden in 1789 and in the premières (1813) of Beethoven's Seventh Symphony and *Wellingtons Sieg*. He long had a high reputation as the supposed composer of the above-mentioned cello concerto by Haydn, but his authentic works prove to be insignificant. The assumption in earlier literature that he was a member of the Schuppanzigh Quartet is to be questioned; neither is there any proof of the report that he instituted public quartet concerts after 1809.

WORKS

Vc: 6 sonatas, 3 as op.1 (Amsterdam and Berlin, 1790), 3 as op.2 (Offenbach, ?1790), 1 ed. C. Adam (New York, 1948); Conc., op.4

(Leipzig, ?1792), ed. in MVH, ii (1961); 2 duos, opp.5–6 (Vienna, n.d.); Divertissements d'une difficulté progressive, vc, db, op.7 (Leipzig, n.d.); Duett, *A-Wgm* (holograph)
Other inst: 3 grands duos concertants, vn, vc, op.3 (Leipzig, ?1792); Notturno, 4 str, 2 fl, 2 hn, listed in Traeg catalogue, 1799; trios, 2 barytons, vc, Esterházy Archive, Budapest

(2) Nikolaus Kraft (*b* Eszterháza, Hungary, 14 Dec 1778; *d* Cheb, Czechoslovakia, 18 May 1853). Son of (1) Anton Kraft. He was taught the cello by his father and at the age of 11 accompanied him on a concert tour to Vienna, Bratislava, Berlin and Dresden, where on 14 April 1789 he performed with Mozart. He attended the Josephstädter Gymnasium in Vienna from 1792 to 1795. In 1792 he performed twice for the Vienna Tonkünstler-Sozietät, the first time in a cello concerto by his father. In 1796 he joined the orchestra of Prince Joseph Lobkowitz, and at about the same time became cellist in the Schuppanzigh Quartet. Despite his already quite advanced career he went to Berlin in 1801 to study with Jean-Pierre Duport. Before returning to Vienna in 1802 he made an extended concert tour from Prague to Holland. In 1809 he became solo cellist at the Kärntnertortheater, Vienna, remaining with Prince Lobkowitz as chamber virtuoso; he also performed frequently in the city's public concerts (1807–14). He moved to Stuttgart in 1814, where until 1834 he was chamber musician to the court; in this period he arranged one or two public concerts each year in Stuttgart, and gave concerts throughout Germany. In 1838 he supposedly settled in Chemnitz. It is not known when he moved to Cheb, the place of his death.

Kraft was one of the most important cello virtuosos of the first half of the 19th century. His contemporary Bernhard Romberg found in his playing 'calmness, combined with assurance and mechanical accomplishment of the highest degree, precision and fullness of every note on this difficult instrument, and united with an intelligent and varied handling of the bow'. As a composer Kraft wrote unremarkable cello concertos in the style of Rodolphe Kreutzer as well as numerous salon pieces for his instrument.

WORKS
(*printed works published in Leipzig unless otherwise stated*)
Vc, orch: Fantasie, op.1, Polonaise, op.2, with str (Offenbach, 1808–9); 4 concs., no.1, op.3 (*c*1810), no.2, op.4 (1813), op.5 (1819), op.7, 1820, mentioned in Oberleitner; Bolero, op.6 (?1819); Scène pastorale, op.9 (?1820); Rondo à la chasse, op.11 (?1822); Pot-pourri sur des thèmes du Freyschutz, op.12 (Offenbach, ?1822); Variations, ?1822); Variations, op.13 (Hanover, ?1822)
2 vc: 8 divertissements d'une difficulté progressive, op.14 (Offenbach, ?1823); 6 duos, opp.15, 17 (Offenbach, ?1824–5)
Other inst: Potpourri, pf, orch, op.8, 1820, *A-Wst*; Divertimento, vc, harp, *D-Bds* (holograph); Andante und Polonaise, vc, kbd, op.10, 1821, see Oberleitner

(3) Friedrich Anton Kraft (*b* Vienna, 13 Feb 1807; *d* Stuttgart, 4 Dec 1874). Son of (2) Nikolaus Kraft. He was taught the cello by his father, and in 1824 became cellist of the Stuttgart court orchestra. As a soloist he appeared with his father in Vienna in 1820 and 1821, and alone in Stuttgart in 1824 and 1825.

BIBLIOGRAPHY
K. Oberleitner: *Anton Kraft: biographische Skizze* (MS, *A-Wgm*)
C. F. Pohl: *Joseph Haydn*, i–ii (Leipzig, 1878–82/*R*)
T. von Frimmel: *Beethoven-Handbuch*, i (Leipzig, 1926/*R*1968), 296f
H. Weber: *Das Violoncellokonzert des 18. und beginnenden 19. Jahrhunderts* (Tübingen, 1932), 92ff
O. Wessely: 'Kraft', *MGG* [with further bibliography]
E. Forbes, ed.: *Thayer's Life of Beethoven* (Princeton, 1964, 2/1967)
OTHMAR WESSELY

Kraft [Krafft, Crafft, von Crafft], **Georg Andreas** (*b*

Nuremberg, *c*1660; *d* Kaster an der Erft, Rhineland, 1 Dec 1726). German composer. He can be traced from 1679 at the court at Düsseldorf of the Elector Palatine Johann Wilhelm, whose reign began in that year. According to Rapparini, Johann Wilhelm sent him to Rome to further his musical studies under Corelli. As its director he contributed greatly to the improvement of the electoral orchestra at Düsseldorf. He enjoyed the close friendship of the Kapellmeister Sebastiano Moratelli and J. H. von Wilderer, for whose operas he wrote much of his music. He was appointed bailiff at Kaster before 1700 and court chamber councillor shortly afterwards. In 1711 he took part, together with the Palatine Kapelle, in the coronation of the emperor at Frankfurt am Main. He apparently gave up his composing duties not long after that, since he was not involved in Wilderer's opera *Amalasunta* in 1713; he also resigned his post as director of the orchestra. He retired to Kaster and, after the death of Johann Wilhelm in 1716, did not follow the new ruler, Karl Philipp, to Heidelberg and Mannheim, as did most of the Düsseldorf musicians. He was succeeded as bailiff at Kaster in 1722 by his son Sebastian Johannes. There is a portrait of him in Rapparini (medallion no.22). As director of the electoral orchestra, which subsequently developed into the famous orchestra of the Mannheim school, he stood at the head of a line of directors leading through Gottfried Finger and Johann Sigismund Weiss to Johann Stamitz. As a composer, Rapparini placed him on a level with Wilderer. His work, which is largely confined to overtures and ballets, bears the hallmarks of a good Italian training, though as with Moratelli and Wilderer, its thoroughly Italian style is occasionally impregnated with French elements.

WORKS
STAGE
Overtures and dance music for operas performed at Düsseldorf unless otherwise stated; all MSS in *A-Wn*.
S. Moratelli: Erminia ne' boschi, 1687; Didone, 1688; Erminia al campo, 1688; Il fabbro pittore, 1695
J. H. von Wilderer: Giocasta, 1696; La monarchia risoluta, ?1697; Q. Fabio Massimo, 1697; Il giorno di salute ovvero Demetrio in Athene, 1696, 1697; La forza del giusto, 1700; La monarchia stabilita, 1703 and 1705; Faustolo, 1706
Possibly also collab.: Festa boschereccia, 1696; Il marte romano, Heidelberg, 1702; Il pregi della rosa, Heidelberg, 1702; Tiberio imperator d'oriente, 1703; J. H. Wilderer: L'Armeno, *c*1698

INSTRUMENTAL
Sonata da camera, 2 vn, vc, bc, op.1 (Amsterdam, *c*1714), lost

BIBLIOGRAPHY
EitnerQ; *GerberNL*
G. M. Rapparini: *Le portrait du vrai mérite dans la personne serenissime de Monseigneur l'Electeur Palatin* (MS, *D-DÜl*, 1709); ed. H. Kühn-Steinhausen (Düsseldorf, 1958)
F. Walter: *Geschichte des Theaters und der Musik am kurpfälzischen Hofe* (Leipzig, 1898/*R*1968)
F. Zobeley: 'Die Musik am Hofe des Kurfürsten Johann Wilhelm von der Pfalz', *Neues Archiv für die Geschichte der Stadt Heidelberg und der Kurpfalz*, xiii (1926), 133
F. Lau: 'Die Regierungskollegien zu Düsseldorf und der Hofstaat zur Zeit Johann Wilhelms (1679–1716)', *Düsseldorfer Jb*, xxxix (1937), 228; xl (1938), 257
G. Croll: 'Musikgeschichtliches aus Rapparinis Johann-Wilhelm-Manuscript (1709)', *Mf*, xi (1958), 257
G. Steffen: *Johann Hugo von Wilderer (1670–1724), Kapellmeister am kurpfälzischen Hofe zu Düsseldorf und Mannheim* (Cologne, 1960)
GERHARD CROLL, ERNST HINTERMAIER

Kraft, Günther (*b* Suhl, 2 April 1907; *d* Weimar, 20 Sept 1977). German musicologist. He studied with Danckert and Zur Nedden (University of Jena, 1935–7) and with Schering (University of Berlin, 1937–8), taking the doctorate at Jena in 1938 with a dissertation on Johann Steuerlein's life and works. In 1940 he qualified as a secondary schoolteacher and in 1964 completed his *Habilitation* at the University of Halle with a study of the Bach family in Thuringia. After teaching in schools in Berlin and Weimar he became a lecturer (1949) and professor (1952) of musicology at the Weimar Musikhochschule, and gave lectures at the University of Jena (from 1950). He founded (1950) and directed (1950–72) the Institute for Folk Music Research at Weimar and was director of the Bach House at Eisenach (1964–71). His main research concerned the history of music in Thuringia, especially around 1600; he also wrote extensively on the Thuringian associations of Bach and his family, and on the relations between Thuringian and Russian music in the 18th and 19th centuries.

WRITINGS

Johann Steuerlein (1546–1613): Leben und Werk (diss., U. of Jena, 1938; Würzburg, 1941, as pt.ii of *Die thüringische Musikkultur um 1600*)

ed. with H. Besseler: *J. S. Bach in Thüringen* (Weimar, 1950) [incl. 'Thüringer Stadtpfeifer-Familien um Bach']

'Carl Maria von Weber und Albert Lortzing in ihren volks- und schaffensmässigen Beziehungen', *Carl Maria von Weber: eine Gedenkschrift* (Dresden, 1951)

ed.: *Festschrift zur Ehrung von Heinrich Albert (1604–1651)* (Weimar, 1954) [incl. 'Heinrich Albert und seine Zeit']

ed.: *Festschrift zur Ehrung von Heinrich Schütz (1585–1672)* (Weimar, 1954) [incl. 'Zur Schütz-Ehrung 1954']

Erfurt, Meiningen, Monographien zur thüringischen Musikgeschichte (Weimar, 1955)

Musikgeschichtliche Beziehungen zwischen Thüringen und Russland im 18. und 19. Jahrhundert (Weimar, 1955)

'Zur Entstehungsgeschichte des Hochzeitsquodlibet (BWV 524)', *BJb*, xliii (1956), 140

'Polnische Folklore im Lied der Vormärz-Bewegung in Deutschland', *Chopin Congress: Warszawa 1960*, 560

'Das Schaffen von Franz Liszt in Weimer', *Liszt–Bartók: 2nd International Musicological Conference: Budapest 1961* [*SM*, v (1963)], 193

Entstehung und Ausbreitung des musikalischen Bach-Geschlechtes in Thüringen (Habilitationsschrift, U. of Halle, 1964; extracts in *BMw*, i/2 (1959), 29–61)

'Stand und Koordinierung der wissenschaftlichen Forschung auf dem Gebiet des Arbeiterliedes in der Deutschen Demokratischen Republik', *BMw*, vi (1964), 267

'Musikgeschichte: Forschungen zur Geschichte Thüringens 1945–1965', *Wissenschaftliche Zeitschrift der Friedrich-Schiller-Universität Jena*, xvi (1967), 339

'Das mittelthüringische Siedlungszentrum der Familien Bach und Wölcken', *Musa–mens–musici: im Gedenken an Walther Vetter* (Leipzig, 1969), 153

'Eine unbekannte Lieder-Handschrift des 16. Jahrhunderts', *BMw*, xi (1969), 72

'Quellenstudien zur thematischen Konzeption des Fidelio', *Internationaler Beethoven-Kongress: Berlin 1970*, 283

with P. Michel: 'Die Musik von 1902 bis 1918', *Festschrift der Hochschule für Musik 'Franz Liszt' Weimar* (Weimar, 1972), 38

BIBLIOGRAPHY

P. Michel: 'Günther Kraft 60', *Musik und Gesellschaft*, xvii (1967), 282

HORST SEEGER

Kraft, Leo (*b* Brooklyn, 24 July 1922). American composer and teacher. He studied composition with Rathaus at Queens College of the City University of New York (BA 1945), with Randall Thompson at Princeton University (MFA 1947) and with Boulanger in Paris under a Fulbright grant (1954–5). In 1947 he joined the staff at Queens College, becoming professor and chairman of the music department (1959–61). He has also held important posts in the College Music Society, the American Society of University Composers and the American section of the ISCM, and was elected president of the American Music Center (1976–8).

Kraft's numerous music theory and ear-training texts

and his active role in the College Music Society attest to his involvement in university teaching. His pedagogical approach has been influenced by Boulanger's stress on practical musical skills and by Schenker's theories as exposed in Salzer's *Structural Hearing*. His early music is marked by the neo-classical attitudes of his teachers and the basic diatonicism of Hindemith. With his Second String Quartet (1959), however, he adopted a more chromatic and expressive idiom, and since the 1960s his work has been freely atonal, though the neo-classical influence can occasionally be heard in his rhythm.

WORKS
(*selective list*)

Orch: Conc. no.1, fl, cl, tpt, str, 1951; Variations, 1958; 3 Pieces, 1963; Conc. no.2, 13 insts, 1966, rev. 1972; Toccata, band, 1967; Conc. no.3, vc, wind qnt, perc, 1969; Music for Orch, 1975; Ciacona, band, 1976

Choral: Festival Song, SATB, 1951; Psalm xviii, SA, pf, 1954; Let me laugh, 3vv, pf, 1954; A Proverb of Solomon, SATB, orch, 1957; Thanksgiving, SATB, 1958; When Israel came forth (Ps cxiv), SATB, 1963; Psalms xl, lxxxiv, xcv, lxxxix, TB, 1963–8; Fyre and Yse, SATB, tape, 1966; 8 Choral Songs (Moses Ibn Ezra), SATB, 1974; 3 3-part Songs, SSA/TTB, 1975

Solo vocal: 4 English Lovesongs, 1v, pf, 1961; Spring in the Harbor (S. Stepanchev), S, fl, vc, pf, 1970

Chamber: 3 str qts, 1950, 1959, 1966; Short Suite, fl, cl, bn, 1951; Two's Company, 2 cl, 1957; Partita no.2, vn, vc, 1961; Ballad, cl, pf, 1963; Fantasy, fl, pf, 1963; Partita no.3, wind qnt, 1964; Trios and Interludes, fl, va, pf, 1965; Dialogues, fl, tape, 1968; 5 Pieces, cl, pf, 1969; Dualities, 2 tpt, 1970; Pentagram, a sax, 1971; Line Drawings, fl, perc, 1972; Diaphonies, ob, pf, 1975; Partita no.4, fl, cl, vn, db, pf, 1975

Kbd: Allegro giocoso, pf, 1957; Partita no.1, pf, 1958; Statements and Commentaries, pf, 1965; Short Sonata no.1, hpd, 1969; Antiphonies, pf 4 hands, tape, 1970; Sestina, pf, 1974; 10 Short Pieces, pf, 1977

Principal publishers: General Music, Presser

WRITINGS

with S. Berkowitz and G. Fontrier: *A New Approach to Sight Singing* (New York, 1960, rev. 2/1976)

A New Approach to Ear Training (New York, 1967)

'In Search of a New Pedagogy', *College Music Symposium*, viii (1968), 109

'The Music of George Perle', *MQ*, lvii (1971), 444

'Reflections on CMP 6', *College Music Symposium*, xii (1972), 84

'Retrospect: Four Pieces (1964–69)', *Contemporary Music Newsletter*, vii/2 (1973), 1

Gradus: an Integrated Approach to Harmony, Counterpoint and Analysis (New York, 1976)

BRUCE SAYLOR

Kraft, Ludwicus (*fl c*1460). German composer. He is known only through the three-voice introit, *Terribilis est locus iste*, ascribed to him in Trent Codex 90 (in *I-TRmn*). The chant melody is ornamented in the top voice, which is the only one with text. The work includes the Eastertide alleluia at the end of the antiphon but does not set the psalm verse. It is typical of the functional liturgical polyphony of the Trent MSS.

BIBLIOGRAPHY

G. Adler and O. Koller, eds.: *Trienter Codices I: geistliche und weltliche Kompositionen des XV. Jahrhunderts*, DTÖ, xiv, xv, Jg.vii (Vienna, 1900)

TOM R. WARD

Kraft, Walter (*b* Cologne, 9 June 1905). German organist and composer. He studied the piano (Rebbert) and the organ (Hannemann) in Hamburg, then composition in Berlin with Hindemith, who helped to initiate his career as a composer. He first appeared in Hamburg as a pianist in 1924 but that year took a post there as organist at the Markuskirche; in 1927 he moved to the Lutherkirche in Altona-Bahrenfeld. In 1929 he became the organist of the Marienkirche, Lübeck; the church was destroyed in 1942 but he resumed his post there after the war. In 1945 he worked temporarily at the Nikolaikirche, Flensburg. He was professor of organ at the music college in Freiburg from 1947, director of the Schleswig-Holstein Music Academy (1950–55) and later of the north German organ school in Lübeck. His activity has centred round his post at the Marienkirche, in which he continued the tradition of the Lübeck 'serenades' that goes back to 1646. He also came to the fore both as a brilliant improviser and as a composer of such oratorios as *Christus* (1942–3), *Die Bürger von Calais* (1953–4), *Lübecker Totentanz* (1954) and *Die Gemeinschaft der Heiligen* (1956–7). He was awarded the Lübeck Buxtehude Prize, the Schleswig-Holstein cultural prize and the Grand Prix du Disque for his recording of the complete Buxtehude organ works. His range of activities has produced a breadth of style and approach in which interpretation is seen as artistic re-creation.

GERHARD WIENKE

Kräftig (Ger.: 'powerful', 'vigorous'). As a tempo direction it is particularly frequent in the work of Schumann and later German composers.

Kraków (Cracow). Polish city. Probably founded in the 8th century, it was the country's capital from the 11th century to 1596, and has remained a cultural and artistic centre. It passed to Austria at the third partition (1795), became part of the Duchy of Warsaw in 1809 and the Kraków Republic in 1815, and was again incorporated into Austria in 1846; in 1918 it was returned to Poland when that country was reconstituted. Its main cultural centres were the royal castle and cathedral on the Wawel hill, where coronations took place; the Jagellonian University, founded in 1364; and the numerous churches, of which St Mary's (completed 1396) is the largest.

1. To 1596. 2. 1596–1764. 3. 1764–1815. 4. 1815–46. 5. 1846–1918. 6. 1918–45. 7. From 1945.

1. TO 1596. Krakow was an episcopal see from 1000 and the earliest liturgical music used was Benedictine chant. The *Liber ordinalis* or *Pontificale* of the Kraków bishops (11th and 12th centuries), the first rhymed Office *Dies adest celebris* by Wincenty z Kielc (mid-13th century) and other sources of the 13th and 14th centuries come from Kraków Cathedral and monasteries. Several 15th-century liturgical books have also survived, some of which are valuable works of illuminative art. There are few records of musical life at the court and in the city before the mid-14th century. The guild of musicians was granted the first royal privilege in 1549, but, as some statements of the edict show, it had existed on the strength of common laws much earlier. The earliest examples of polyphonic music of Kraków date from the 14th century (*Surrexit Christus hodie*). Two substantial collections of polyphonic music from about 1430 survive (*Pl-Wn* Kras.52 and 378); they contain compositions by Ciconia, Zacharias, Grossin, Antonius de Civitate Austrie and some Polish composers, including Nicholaus de Radom, probably a royal musician. The collections were probably for the use of the royal chapel, which then consisted of a group of singing clerks and lay instrumentalists, some of whom were soloists (*citharedae*). More detailed information on its composition is available from the mid-16th century, when it had over 30 members (at least 12 singers, six discantists and 14 instrumentalists); in addition there

was a separate group of 13 trumpeters. The vocal ensemble gradually took on a greater number of lay members. Composers active in the royal chapel in the 16th century include Heinrich Finck, Josquin Baston, Wacław z Szamotuł, Marcin Leopolita, Marcin Wartecki, Gomółka, Długoraj, Cato, Klabon, Marenzio and, among the eminent virtuosos, the lutenist Bakfark.

Kraków University, founded in 1364, flourished in the 15th century. Musical training was then based chiefly on Jehan des Murs' *Musica speculativa* and Boethius's *De institutione musica*. The first known Polish treatise on choral music was written by Szydłowita about 1414; several other anonymous treatises survive (in *PL-Kj*). In the early 16th century a number of compendiums of musical science originated in the circle of university scholars and lecturers (Sebastian z Felsztyna, Marcin Kromer and Jerzy Liban) and were all published in Kraków, some being reprinted several times; they were clearly influenced by Gaffurius and Ornithoparchus. In the 16th century some parish schools had high standards of music education, especially that of St Mary's, where Liban and Gawara worked. The Kraków printing houses of Jan Haller, Ungler, Wietor, Andrysowicz, Siebeneicher and Scharffenberg published liturgical compositions from 1505, theoretical treatises from 1514, and sacred and occasional polyphonic songs, the earliest surviving example of which dates from 1530. Among the most important publications were *Lamentationes Hieremiae prophetae* by Wacław z Szamotuł (1553), Bakfark's lute tablature *Harmoniarum musicarum* (1565) and several monophonic hymnbooks.

A number of instrument workshops thrived in Kraków in the second half of the 16th century: Dobrucki and Groblicz made violins, Kejcher chiefly woodwind instruments. The names of many 15th-century Kraków organists are known, but the earliest sources of organ music date from the 16th century: the tablature from the Holy Ghost Monastery (1548), and Jan z Lublina's tablature (1537–48). In addition to numerous anonymous compositions, they contain works of Janequin, Jacotin, Festa, Verdelot, Finck and Senfl, and Polish compositions or arrangements by Mikołaj z Chrzanowa and Mikołaj z Krakowa, and transcriptions of Polish dances. Strzeszkowski's lute tablature, written in the second half of the 16th century, presents a variety of songs and dances of the period.

2. 1596–1764. At the end of the 16th century the political and economic situation of Kraków changed; between 1596 and 1609 the court moved to Warsaw, which became the capital, and privileges were limited. In 1596 Sigismund III reorganized the royal chapel to include a group of over 20 Italian singers and instrumentalists (the ensemble thus had about 38 members, excluding trumpeters); it was active in Kraków for short periods only, but nevertheless introduced new stylistic trends. In 1604 a collection of polychoral compositions written by the members of the chapel, *Melodiae sacrae*, was printed, the last important Kraków publication of polyphonic music. Gorczyn's *Tabulatura muzyki* (1647) and Starowolski's *Musices practicae erotemata* (1650) are among the theoretical works published in Kraków in the 17th century. The traditional cultivation of leading stylistic trends was taken over by the 30-member vocal–instrumental cathedral chapel founded in 1619 and augmented by singers

from the cathedral school. The chapel was directed by a succession of fine composers: Orgas, Franciszek Lilius, Pękiel, Gorczycki and Maxylewicz. Their production characterizes the repertory of the chapel only indirectly, as no vocal–instrumental compositions earlier than the late 18th century survive in the cathedral archives.

Another group of musicians that flourished in Kraków in the 17th century was the Capella Rorantistarum, a group of nine priest–musicians who sang daily services in the chapel built for the cathedral by the last Jagellons. Its name is thought to derive from the introit *Rorate coeli* and from the Rorata (dawn masses sung during Advent) with which the choir was associated (*see* RORATE CHANTS). It was founded in 1540 by Sigismund I to sing polyphony daily 'perpetuis futuris temporibus', and was active from 1543 to the partition of Poland in 1795. The Capella excluded boys and originally confined its membership to Poles, though foreigners, notably Italians, were admitted from the early 17th century. Its repertory embraced works by leading Polish composers of the 16th and 17th centuries as well as by composers from the Netherlands, France, Italy and Spain, particularly those resident in Poland. Many transcriptions were made for the ensemble of equal men's voices (e.g. Josquin's *Missa 'Mater Patris'*). The choir's directors included Mikołaj z Poznia (1543–57), Borek (1557–74) and Orgas (1628–9). Throughout its existence the Capella played an important part in continuing in Poland the *a cappella* tradition based on 16th-century polyphony.

Of Kraków's remaining ensembles, the Jesuit chapel (founded 1637) was of great importance in the 17th and 18th centuries. It was organized as an institution of music education, developing into a focal point of the city's music in the early 18th century, when it was attended by young musicians from the chapels of rich land-owners. It had about 50 members (including pupils) and performed in the city's churches as well as at private secular functions. Its repertory included many Polish compositions, some by its members; the most outstanding of these was Jacek Szczurowski, who entered the Jesuit order in 1735. An ensemble of seven instrumentalists, recruited from members of the musicians' guild, was available after 1630 at St Mary's. Until the mid-18th century the main state celebrations, such as coronations and royal funerals, took place in the Wawel castle. On such occasions the city organized festivities that featured music by local chapels, including that performed by the chapels of magnates (e.g. Lubomirski's); in the castle itself, however, the Warsaw royal chapel was predominant. No information about the repertory of the private chapels survives.

3. 1764–1815. As the city was destroyed by the Seven Years War (1757–64), Kraków's musical life was reduced during the 1760s and 1770s to activity in a few church chapels – the Rorantists, the cathedral, St Mary's, the Jesuits (until the suppression of the order in Poland in 1773) and the academy of the collegiate church of St Anna – and music-making in the homes of a few wealthy citizens. The association known as the Kazimierz Congregation of Musicians was founded and, reminiscent of the medieval guilds, channelled its energies into competitive battles with non-professional musicians. After 1800 matters improved; musical activity in Kraków was revived through the efforts of Wacław Sierakowski, a canon and parson at Wawel

Cathedral, and Jacek Kluszewski (1761–1841), proprietor of the Kraków Theatre. Sierakowski organized public concerts in his home from 1781 to 1787 on the model of the fashionable *concerts spirituels*; cantatas by Italian composers, translated by Sierakowski himself, were performed. To support these concerts he founded a singing school (1781–7), attended by boys, most of whom subsequently became members of church chapels. The head of the school was F. K. Kratzer, cantor and conductor of the Wawel Cathedral chapel, and the first of a family of Wawel cantors. Two members of the cathedral chapel taught at the school, Jakub Gołąbek and F. M. Lang. In 1795 Sierakowski published the first volume of his work devoted to music education, *Sztuka muzyki dla młodzieży krajowej* ('The art of music for the youth of the country'), and in 1796 two further volumes appeared. Containing the rudiments of music and instructions for the performance of church music, the work is a rich source of information on 18th-century Polish music. Other centres of music education included the Jesuit boarding schools (1638–1773), the music school attached to the collegiate church of St Anna (founded 1764) and the music school of Józef Zygmuntowski (1776–81).

Kluszewski founded the first permanent public opera company in Kraków. Between 1787 and 1789, with the help of an Italian opera company and an orchestra of church and army musicians, comic operas by Paisiello, Piccinni, Salieri and others were performed in Italian; from 1789 to 1794 performances in Polish were given. After the seizure of Kraków by Austria these ceased, but began again in 1805. When the Austrians left in 1809 Wojciech Bogusławski, the 'father of Polish theatre', brought his company to the city and gave many performances there, including a number of operas. During the 1790s a number of music teachers and instrument makers moved to Kraków from Vienna, Prague and Berne, and Kraków booksellers began to deal in music.

4. 1815–46. As Kraków became more settled after the political disorganization up to 1815, there was renewed activity in the intellectual and artistic life of the city. As a result of the Vienna Congress, Kraków and the surrounding area attained the status of an independent state, the Kraków Republic. Modern concert life began with the founding of the Society of Friends of Music in 1817, headed by Sebastian Sierakowski, Wacław's brother. The society, with about 400 members, included nearly all the city's musicians and amateur players. It had its own choir (conducted by the outstanding Wawel organist Wincenty Gorączkiewicz) and a symphony orchestra of 30 players; unlike anywhere else in Poland, it organized symphony concerts at least once a month. The years 1819–24 saw the greatest development in the society and its activities, after which it gradually declined until its formal dissolution in 1844. Viennese Classical works were predominant at its concerts, and choral singing was important; the repertory included polyphonic masterpieces and works of Haydn and Mozart. The society also sponsored concerts by visiting virtuosos such as Catalani. Liszt (1843) and Lipiński gave concerts in Kraków independent of the society.

The orchestra of the National Guard was founded in 1811 as a Janissary band of percussion and wind instruments. In 1820 the orchestra of the Militia of the

The Kraków Theatre: lithograph, early 19th century

Free Town of Kraków was formed, modelled on the Austrian military orchestra, introduced to the city when the Austrian army invaded the town in 1796; it entertained at occasional tattoos and religious and national ceremonies. The theatre continued under the ownership of Jacek Kluszewski, and in the decade 1820–30 almost all the operas in the contemporary repertory were presented. Besides *L'italiana in Algeri*, *Il barbiere di Siviglia* and *La gazza ladra*, Kraków audiences saw *Die Zauberflöte* and *Der Freischütz*; Polish operas performed included almost all those of Józef Elsner; the operas of Kurpiński gained great popularity. Music teaching was private for both amateurs and professionals, and music teachers with various qualifications were often recruited from church chapels and from theatre and military orchestras. Professionals were educated at the music school at St Anna's, which was under the patronage of Society of Friends of Music from 1818 to 1841. From 1838 Franciszek Mirecki directed a private school of dramatic singing, which became the municipal School of Singing and Music in 1841; it was the first state music school in Kraków and was important for the development of secular music there. The needs of sacred music were catered for by the School of Polyphonic Chant at Wawel from 1821 to 1824.

5. 1846–1918. After the suppression of the Kraków Revolution by the Austrian army (1846) Kraków was annexed to Austria, and the musical life of the city came to a standstill, not only as the result of political developments but also because of the death of some of its leading musicians, such as Gorączkiewicz and Mirecki. Musical life did not revive until the 1860s, when Stanisław

Duniecki, Kazimierz Hofmann and Antoni Vopalka (1837–79) were active. Duniecki was conductor of the theatre, where he presented many operettas and operas, including the first of many performances in Kraków of Moniuszko's *Halka* (1866), at which the composer was present. Duniecki was succeeded at the theatre by Hofmann, who was also active from 1858 to 1878 as a teacher, pianist and impresario.

As a result of Kraków's greater autonomy various scientific, cultural and artistic societies developed from 1866. In that year the Muza (Muse) amateur music society was founded, the ideological heir to the former Society of Friends of Music. The society had a male-voice and a mixed choir, which were sometimes accompanied by a military orchestra formed from Austrian units stationed in the town. From 1870 to 1875 Vopalka was artistic director of the society, which gave over 50 concerts in its first ten years, and from 1867 supported a school of music directed by Vopalka at which Hofmann taught the piano and theory. Later the society's importance in the city's cultural life declined. A German choral society, the Liedertafel, existed from 1860 to 1871.

In 1876 the declining Muza society was transformed by a group of enthusiasts into the Music Society of Kraków, which still exists. From 1876 to 1918 it was responsible for almost all musical activity in Kraków and ran the only music school at the time, later the Conservatory of Music. Its first artistic director was a singer from the Opera at Lwów (now L'vov), Stanisław Niedzielski. During the 1880s the society had about 400 members, and soloists from the School of Music appeared. In 1886 Wiktor Barabasz (1885–1928) was appointed artistic director, a post he held until 1909; he reorganized the society's choirs, which took part in all Kraków's festivals, and through his endeavours an amateur symphony orchestra was founded in 1888. A cycle of historic concerts that he organized with this orchestra was so popular that each had to be repeated. On Barabasz's initiative the society organized popular concerts in 1903 and 1904. From 1909 to 1914 the artistic director of the society was Feliks Nowowiejski, who gave fine symphony concerts, although the choir was neglected. During World War I the society's concerts ceased, and all its income was devoted to the upkeep of the conservatory. In that period the cultural life of Kraków was maintained only by 19 exhibition days given by pupils of the conservatory.

Besides the society's concerts, there were those of Princess Marcelina Czartoryska, both in her home and in public. In 1908 a concert agency was founded by Teofil Trzciński and amateur concerts began to decline in favour of systematically managed concert enterprises. The undertaking did much to acquaint Kraków with the new music of western Europe and Poland, and brought the best foreign soloists and ensembles to the town. In a fine concert guide Trzciński informed the public of contemporary developments abroad.

The Music Society of Kraków, founded in 1876, also took over the School of Music from the Muza society. The best musicians of Kraków were engaged as teachers and the number of instrumental classes increased. A new stage in the history of the school began when the eminent composer and teacher Władysław Żeleński settled in Kraków permanently in July 1881; he appeared as a pianist and conductor, organized diverse concerts, wrote music reviews and was active above all as a composer and teacher. The period up to 1914 was the 'Żeleński era'; for 40 years he held the post of director of the school of music, which through his endeavours was renamed the Conservatory of the Music Society in Kraków in 1888. From 1891 to 1895 the composer Jan Gall taught solo singing and theory at the conservatory. In addition to the conservatory, a music institute was founded in 1908 by the pianist Klara Czop-Umlaufowa and the violinist Stanisław Giebułtowski, and was active until 1918.

In 1911 a seminar on music history and theory was initiated at Jagellonian University, the first of its kind in Poland; it later became the Musicology Institute and for many years was directed by its founder, Zdzisław Jachimecki. Two bookshops were particularly important: S. A. Krzyżanowski's was established in 1869, and included a concert bureau which sponsored Paderewski's concerts; that of Antoni Piwarski and Teodor Gieszczykiewicz was founded in 1897 and played an important role in the early 20th century, publishing works by many Polish composers.

6. 1918–45. As a result of the fall of the Austro-Hungarian Empire Kraków became free and linked to the new state of Poland. Despite postwar economic instability its musical life was no less lively than before the war. One of the factors which caused this activity was the presence of numerous composers and performers. In the period following the death of Żeleński (1921) Kraków had two outstanding Polish composers, Stanisław Lipski and Bolesław Wallek-Walewski. Among the many lesser figures, Ignacy Friedman, Artur Malawski and Bernadino Rizzi are the most notable. An important element in Kraków's musical life was the Orchestra of the Union of Professional Musicians, which fulfilled the role of a philharmonic. Its activities began in 1919 under the direction of Marian Rudnicki; it was poorly subsidized by the town authorities but survived and gave regular Sunday concerts, directed by such fine conductors as Bierdiajew, Nowowiejski and Fitelberg.

An important centre of musical life was the Opera and its associated Opera Society, the pride of which was a mixed and male-voice choir. An operetta company also prospered, under the direction of Tadeusz Pilarski. From 1924 to 1927 there was a break in the work of the Opera Society, although opera companies from Lwów, Warsaw, Katowice and Olomouc occasionally made guest appearances. The Kraków Opera was reopened on 1 September 1931. Eugeniusz Bujański's Kraków Concert Agency was also important; it was in contact with all the important musical centres in Europe from 1916 to 1936, and organized over 1000 musical events in Kraków, engaging such celebrities as Kiepura, Askenase, Rubinstein, Prokofiev, Kochański, Gimpel and Huberman. The agency also organized concerts by such composers as Szymanowski, Prokofiev and Wallek-Walewski, brought foreign chamber groups and choirs to the city and arranged lectures on music.

The creation of a radio station in 1926 facilitated wider propagation of music. The work of the Music Society was also important; after its fine achievements before the war it was less active until 1925, when Wallek-Walewski became musical director, and raised the standard of the mixed choir to a particularly high level. In 1919 an Oratorio Society was founded, the only such group in Poland. The male-voice choir Echo (founded 1919), under the direction of Wallek-Walewski, was one of the foremost choirs not only in Kraków but in Poland. The most prominent church choir was the 'Cecyliański' choir (1923) at the Franciscan Church, conducted for many years by Rizzi. Wallek-Walewski also directed other distinguished Polish choirs, including the Seminary choir, Missionary Priests and the choir of the Capuchin Church.

Music education continued at the conservatory and, from 1929, the Władysław Żeleński School of Music; private music courses also existed. The conservatory's careful selection of teaching staff drew many pupils who came to stand at the forefront of the artistic life of Kraków, both before and after World War II. The Musicology Institute continued to expand under Jachimecki's direction. In 1922 Józef Reiss began his work in musicology, followed in 1930 by Włodzimierz Poźniak. In 1931 the Association of Young Musicians was formed from graduates of the conservatory and young staff in music education, and organized concerts by composers and talented young artists, thus becoming a centre for young musicians in Kraków; it gave several hundred concerts a year.

7. FROM 1945. After its liberation from the Nazis in January 1945 Kraków became the centre of musical life in the country, bringing together the most outstanding Polish composers and performers, particularly as a result of the total destruction of Warsaw. However, after the reconstruction of Warsaw in the 1950s a considerable number of musicians moved to the capital. Nevertheless, Kraków remains the second creative centre in the country. Prominent postwar Kraków composers include Wiechowicz, Malawski, Penderecki, Bogusław

Schäffer, Moszumanska-Nazar, Krzysztof Meyer and Stachowski. On 3 February 1945 the Kraków Philharmonic was inaugurated as the first music institution in liberated Poland, and in 1962 it became the Karol Szymanowski Philharmonic. Zygmunt Latoszewski became its director followed by such excellent conductors as Bierdiajew, Skrowaczewski, Rowicki, Markowski, Czyż and Katlewicz. The Kraków PO reached a high artistic standard; it gave the premières of many works by Penderecki and others. The Philharmonic's ensembles include a symphony orchestra, mixed and boys' choirs, a string quartet and the Capella Cracoviensis. The Philharmonic gives about 700 concerts each season, including a number in schools, and is responsible for organizing such established cycles of concerts and festivals as Krakowska Wiosna Muzyki ('Kraków spring of music', from 1962), Wieczory Wawelskie ('Wawel evenings', from 1966), the international Dni Muzyki Organowej ('Days of organ music', from 1966), the organ recitals at the Benedictine abbey in Tyniec, and the Jan Kiepura Festival of Arias and Songs in Krynica (from 1967). From 1963 a music-lover's club has functioned in connection with the Philharmonic, leading a lively campaign to popularize music.

The orchestra and choir of Polish radio and television in Krakow was founded in 1948 and was directed by Jerzy Gert until 1968, when he was succeeded by Krzysztof Missona. Polish music of all periods features in its repertory, and the orchestra's main task is recording for the central tape library of Polish radio, producing a complete history of Polish music in sound. Kraków does not have an opera house, and since 1945 operas have been presented in the J. Słowacki Theatre. In the early postwar years Zygmunt Latoszewski and, later, Walerian Bierdiajew presented operas with the Association of Opera Singers. Between 1948 and 1956, when the Kraków Opera Society was formed, operas were given by visiting companies. The Municipal Music Theatre was founded in 1958, and an operetta company was soon attached to it. Kazimierz Kord, director of the theatre from 1962 to 1970, made a notable contribution to opera in Kraków. The MW2 ensemble, founded in 1962, specializes in the performance of contemporary music, under the direction of Adam Kaczynski.

Kraków's amateur music-making is primarily vocal. Particularly distinguished choirs include Echo, the Academic Choir, Lutnia Robotnicza ('Workmen's lute') and Hejnał ('Bugle call'). At the university there is a song and dance ensemble, Słowianki. Kraków has four basic music schools, three middle schools and one music high school. In addition eight civic music centres, with over 1000 pupils, operate in the city under the patronage of the Music Society of Kraków. After the war the work of the music department at the university was reestablished, and continued under Jachimecki until 1953. Subsequently the department was directed by Stefania Łobaczewska (1953–63), Włodzimierz Poźniak (1963–7), Zygmunt Szweykowski (1971–4) and Elżbieta Dziębowska (1974–). The department's main areas of research are early Polish music, the music of the 19th century and ethnomusicological research. The publisher Polskie Wydawnictwo Muzyczne, founded in 1945 by Tadeusz Ochlewski, is based in Kraków, and is the only music publisher in Poland.

An ancient tradition is preserved in the hourly sounding of the Hejnał Mariacki ('St Mary's bugle-call') from the higher tower of St Mary's Church. The triadic trumpet melody is thought to date from the 14th century, and its sudden cessation in mid-phrase supposedly commemorates a Tartar invasion in which the trumpeter was killed.

BIBLIOGRAPHY

A. Chybiński: *Materiały do dziejów królewskiej kapeli rorantystów na Wawelu Cz.I: 1540–1624* (Kraków, 1910)
——: 'Materiały do dziejów królewskiej kapeli rorantystów na Wawelu Cz.II (1624–94)', *Przegląd muzyczny*, iv/14–19 (1911)
Z. Jachimecki: 'Kilka niekompletnych kompozycji polskich z XVI wieku' [Some incomplete Polish compositions of the 16th century], *KM*, i (1911)
A. Chybiński: 'Z dziejów muzyki krakowskiej' [From the history of music in Kraków], *KM*, ii (1913), 24–62, 91
Z. Jachimecki: *Tabulatura organowa z biblioteki klasztoru Św. Ducha w Krakowie z r. 1548* (Kraków, 1913)
W. Gieburowski: *Die Musica Magistri Szidlovitae . . . und sein Stellung in der Choraltheorie des Mittelalters* (Poznań, 1915)
Z. Jachimecki: *Muzyka na dworze króla Władysława Jagiełły* (Kraków, 1915)
J. W. Reiss: *Książki o muzyce w Bibliotece Jagiellońskiej od wieku XVI do wieku XVIII* [16th- to 18th-century books and music in the Jagellonian Library] (Kraków, 1924–38)
A. Chybiński: 'Nowe materiały do dziejów królewskiej kapeli rorantystów . . . na Wawelu', *Księga pamiątkowa ku czci Oswalda Balzera* (Lwów, 1925), 133
——: 'Przyczynki do historii krakowskiej kultury muzycznej w XVII i XVIII wieku', *Wiadomości muzyczne*, i (1925), 133, 179, 218, 246; ii (1926), 2
——: *Muzycy włoscy w kapelach katedralnych krakowskich 1619–57* [Italian musicians in the Kraków cathedral chapels, 1619–57], i (Poznań, 1927)
——: 'Trzy przyczynki do historii muzyki w Krakowie w pierwszej połowie XVII wieku' [Three essays on the history of music in Kraków in the early 17th century], *Prace polonistyczne ofiarowane Janowi Łosiowi* (Warsaw, 1927), 24
J. W. Reiss: *Muzyka w Krakowie w XIX wieku* (Kraków, 1931)
——: *Jak Kraków walczył o operę?* [How did Kraków fight for opera?] (Kraków, 1934)
A. Klose: 'Die musikgeschichtliche Beziehungen zwischen Krakau und Schlesien im 15. und 16. Jahrhundert', *Deutsche Monatsheft*, vi (Poznań, 1939)
J. W. Reiss: *Almanach muzyczny Krakowa 1780–1914* (Kraków, 1939)
A. Chybiński: *Słownik muzyków dawnej Polski* [Dictionary of musicians of old Poland] (Kraków, 1949)
M. Szczepańska: 'Nieznana krakowska tabulatura lutniowa z drugiej połowy XVI stulecia' [An unknown Kraków lute tablature from the second half of the 16th century], *Księga pamiątkowa ku czci Profesora Adolfa Chybińskiego w 70-lecie urodzin* (Kraków, 1950), 198
Z. Szulc: *Słownik lutników polskich* (Poznań, 1953)
W. Bieńkowski: 'Krakowska szkoła muzyczna w latach 1841–1873', *Musikwissenschaftliche Studien*, iii (1954)
A. Szweykowska: 'Początki krakowskiej kapeli katedralnej', *Muzyka*, iv/2 (1959), 3
J. Dobrzycki: *Hejnał Krakowski* [The Kraków bugle-call] (Kraków, 1961)
75 lat Wyższej Szkoły Muzycznej w Krakowie (Kraków, 1963)
Z. M. Szweykowski: Preface to *Muzyka w dawnym Krakowie* [Music of old Kraków] (Kraków, 1964) [in Pol. and Eng.]
K. Mrowiec: 'Niewykorzystane źródło do dziejów Kapeli Akademickiej w Krakowie' [An unused source for the history of the Academic Chapel in Kraków], *Muzyka*, xii/2 (1967), 32
T. Przybylski: 'Sztuka muzyki Wacława Sierakowskiego', *Muzyka*, xiii/3 (1968), 66
A. Szweykowska: 'Przeobrażenia w kapeli królewskiej na przełomie XVI i XVII wieku' [Transformations in the royal chapel at the turn of the 16th and 17th centuries], *Muzyka*, xiii/2 (1968), 3
M. Przywecka-Samecka: *Drukarstwo muzyczne w Polsce do końca XVIII wieku* [Music printing in Poland at the end of the 18th century] (Kraków, 1969)
Z. M. Szweykowski, ed.: 'Musicalia Vetera', *Katalog tematyczny rękopiśmiennych zabytków dawnej muzyki w Polsce* [Thematic catalogue of early music manuscripts in Poland] (Kraków, 1969–)
Z. Jabłoński: 'Z dziejów teatru krakowskiego w drugiej połowie XVIII wieku' [From the history of the theatre in Kraków in the second half of the 18th century], *Rocznik biblioteki Polskiej Akademii Nauk w Krakowie*, xvi (1970), 19–49
T. Przybylski: *Kultura muzyczna Krakowa na przełomie XVIII i XIX wieku* [Kraków's musical culture at the turn of the 18th and 19th centuries] (Kraków, 1974)

ZYGMUNT M. SZWEYKOWSKI (1), MIROSŁAW PERZ (2), TADEUSZ PRZYBYLSKI (3–7)

Krakowiak (Pol.; Fr. *cracovienne*; Ger. *Krakauer Tanz*). Polish folkdance, from the Kraków region, in fast duple time (crotchet = 100–20), characterized by syncopated rhythms. The term covers a variety of dances from the area, distinguished either by the place of their origin (like the *proszowiak* from Proszowo, the *skalmierzak* from Skalmierz, etc) or by the character of their choreography.

In its origins the *krakowiak* seems to be connected with courtship ritual. It is a dance for several couples, among whom the leading male dancer sings and indicates the steps. The first pair approaches the band, and the man, tapping his heels or dancing a few steps, sings a melody from an established repertory with newly improvised words addressed to his partner; the band follows the melody, and the couples move off in file and form a circle (with the leading couple back at the band). Thereafter verses are sung and played in alternation, the couples circulating during the played verses. The dance may incorporate specific steps or movements associated with its different phases: *zapraszalny* (invitation), *mijany* (passing), *goniony* (chasing), *suwany* (shuffling), *przebiegany* (running) etc. Characteristic steps evolved, including the *galop* (an energetic run forward), the *holubiec* (a jump with heel-clicking and stamping), and the *krzesany* (a sliding motion involving stamping). The nature of the dance is closely linked to the traditional costumes, the women wearing ribbons and the men plumed caps, belts with brass buckles and boots with steel strikers.

The verse-form of the *krakowiak* is traditionally four rhyming six-syllable lines, though in the earliest examples the opening lines may be irregular. The dance is symmetrically constructed, with four bars in each half. There are two basic rhythmic patterns to the bar, *a* and *b*, which may come either as *ab* or *ba* (ex.1). The rhythm may be varied, for example by the insertion of extra notes, rests, dotted rhythms, or semiquaver movement (such as the elaboration that players might add to a sung version: ex.2). The melodic line is lively and

Ex.1

Ex.2

angular rather than lyrical and commonly begins with a rising phrase.

The earliest examples of *krakowiak* rhythm are found

in organ and lute tablatures and songbooks of the 16th and 17th centuries, with such titles as 'Chorea polnica', 'Volta polnica' or 'Polnisch Tanz' – for example in Jan z Lublina's tablature (1540, *PL-Kp*), Nörmiger's tablature (1598, formerly *D-Tu*, now lost), Fuhrmann's *Testudo gallogermanica* (1615) and Giovanni Picchi's *Intavolatura di balli d'arpicordo* (2/1621). In the early 18th century elements of *krakowiak* rhythm may occasionally be found in Telemann's Polish-influenced music and in Polish sacred and operatic works. The title 'krakowiak' did not however appear in print until the publication of *Krakowiaki ofiarowane Polkom* ('Krakowiaks offered to the women of Poland') (Warsaw, 1816), with dances transcribed for piano by F. Mirecki; it was republished four years later as *Zbiór krakowiaków ułożonych na fortepian* in which form it contains 20 dances and some verses of text. A similar collection, by Wincenty Gorączkiewicz, was issued shortly afterwards by Diabelli in Vienna, *Krakowiaki zebrane i ułożone na fortepian*, containing the same pieces with the addition of melodies from the Polish highlands (34 pieces in all).

The *krakowiak* came to be adapted for the stage, and to be regarded as the Polish national dance (although the polonaise is in fact rather older). The Austrian dancer Fanny Elssler brought it to the stages of Europe and America during the mid-19th century, and a more complex, longer, stylized version emerged: it became a three-part form, using repetition and modulation to extend the outer sections, and with a contrasting middle section and modulating links in between. Several composers have used the *krakowiak* in art music: Chopin (*Krakowiak*, rondo for piano and orchestra, op.14, 1828), I. F. Dobrzyński (Symphony 'in the spirit of Polish music', finale, 1834), Z. Noskowski (many examples in opp. 2, 5, 7 and 25, 1870s and 1880s), I. Paderewski (two each in opp. 5 and 9, piano, c1883; *Krakowiak fantazja* for piano, 1884, and in op.14; *Fantasie polonaise* for piano and orchestra, op.19, 1893 – see ex.3), R. Statkowski (*Alla cracovienne* for violin and piano, op.7, c1890) and L. Różycki (*Pan Twardowski*, ballet, op.45, 1920).

Ex.3

BIBLIOGRAPHY

SMP

F. Starczewski: 'Die polnische Tänze', *SIMG*, ii (1900–01), 673–718

Z. Kłośnik: *O tańach narodowych polskich* [On Polish national dances] (Lwów, 1907)

T. Norlind: 'Zur Geschichte der polnischen Tänze', *SIMG*, xii (1910–11), 501

T. Zygler: *Polskie tańce ludowe* [Polish folkdances] (Kraków, 1952) [exhibition guide for Ethnographic Museum, Kraków]

F. Zozula: *Tańce ludowe* [Folkdances] (Warsaw, 1952)

M. Sobieski: 'Krakowiak', *MGG*

L. Bielawski: 'Problem krakowiaka w twórczósci Chopina', *Chopin Congress: Warszawa 1960*, 100

partly based on *MGG* (vii, 1705–9) by permission of Bärenreiter

Kramář, František Vincenc. *See* KROMMER, FRANZ.

Kramer, A(rthur) Walter (*b* New York, 23 Sept 1890; *d* New York, 8 April 1969). American publisher, editor, critic and composer. He studied the violin with his father, Maximilian Kramer, and with Carl Hauser and Richard Arnold. After studying at the College of the City of New York he joined the staff of the magazine *Musical America* (1910–22) and then spent several years studying, writing and composing in Europe, and for a time worked with Malipiero. In 1927 he became music supervisor for the CBS Radio Network, and then returned as editor-in-chief to *Musical America* (1929–36); subsequently he became managing director of the Galaxy Music Corporation, music publishers (1936–56), and after his retirement continued to write and compose. He helped to found the Society for Publication of American Music (1919) and served as its president (1934–40) and on the board of directors of the American Society of Composers, Authors and Publishers (1941–56). In addition to many articles and reviews in music periodicals, Kramer published over 300 compositions, including works for full orchestra, string orchestra, string quartet, voice, chorus, piano, violin, cello and organ, as well as numerous instrumental and choral transcriptions. His compositions, which are fairly conservative, are marked by much technical refinement and understanding of the instrumental or vocal medium used.

WRITINGS

Discussion of contemporary Italian composers in *The Art of Music*, ed. D. G. Mason (New York, 1915), iii, 366–403
'The Things we Set to Music', *MQ*, vii (1921), 309
'Three Italian Modernists: Malipiero, Pizzetti, Respighi', *The Chesterian*, xiii (1931–2), 68
'Berg's *Wozzeck* has U.S. Premiere in Philadelphia', *Musical America*, li (25 March 1931), 3

BIBLIOGRAPHY

J. T. Howard: *A. Walter Kramer* (New York, 1926) [comprehensive bio-bibliography; part of biography repr. as 'A. Walter Kramer, the Early Years', *Music Journal*, xxx (1972), March, 30]
W. T. Upton: *Art-song in America* (New York and Boston, 1930/R1969), 225ff

GUSTAVE REESE/RAMONA H. MATTHEWS

Krämer, Michael. See MERCATOR, MICHAEL.

Kranichsteiner Musikinstitut. Name used by the Internationales Musikinstitut in DARMSTADT between 1949 and 1962.

Kranz, Johann Friedrich (*b* Weimar, 6 April 1752; *d* Stuttgart, 20 Feb 1810). German conductor, composer and violinist. The son of a court wigmaker Georg Kranz, he was a precociously talented violinist who studied music under the chamber musician C. G. Göpfert and the Hofkapellmeister E. W. Wolf. He had a position in the Weimar court orchestra as early as 1766, and became a chamber musician in 1778. He undertook extended journeys (1780–87) to Mannheim, Munich, Italy, Vienna and Eszterháza at the behest of Duke Carl August. In Rome in 1787 Kranz and Goethe were among the guests at a feast in the home of the painter Angelica Kauffmann; under Kranz's direction the dinner evolved into a 'brilliant concert during the most beautiful summer night'. On his tours he met Cimarosa, Paisiello and Haydn, and this led, on his return to Weimar, to his German adaptations (with the poet C. A. Vulpius) of several operas by Cimarosa, Paisiello and others, as well as his performance of *The Seasons* in 1811; he later described himself as Haydn's pupil. Besides assisting the aged Göpfert as leader of the

Hofkapelle, Kranz also became music director of the court theatres in 1791, working closely with both Goethe and Vulpius, and was awarded the position of Kapellmeister in 1799. In 1801, however, a breach with Goethe was provoked by a disagreement between Kranz and the singer Caroline Jagemann, whose wilful interpretation of *Don Giovanni* Kranz strenuously opposed. Kranz was soon suspended from his theatrical duties, but he posed such stubborn resistance that Goethe remonstrated, 'If he has the impudence to ask if his action should be forgotten, I will give him a shampooing that he will not forget to the end of his days'. Kranz eventually resigned in 1803 to accept a better position as Hofkapellmeister at Stuttgart. By 1807 his health kept him from working, although he retained the post until his death.

Although Kranz composed music for several plays, as well as keyboard variations and violin concertos (all in a Classical style), he was most significant as a conductor and director. Under his leadership the Weimar Hofkapelle became one of the best in Germany, and his contributions to the court theatres, in collaboration with Goethe, were equally valuable.

WORKS

(all stage works first performed in Weimar unless otherwise stated)

Inkle und Yarico (ballet), ?1772; scenario pubd
Incidental music in plays: Der Gross-Cophta (Goethe), 1791; Otto der Schütz (F. G. Hagemann), 1792; Die Jesuiten (J. G. L. Hagemeister), 1797; Wallensteins Lager (tragedy, F. von Schiller), 1798; chorus in Die Hussiten vor Naumburg, Leipzig, 1802
Inst: Romanze, pf (Weimar, *c*1799) [variations on Cimarosa: 'An dem schönsten Frühlingsmorgen' from Die theatralisches Abentheuer]; 2 vn concs., *D-WRl*; Va Conc., 1798, ?lost

BIBLIOGRAPHY

EitnerQ; *GerberL*; *GerberNL*
J. Wahle: *Das Weimarer Hoftheater unter Goethes Leitung* (Weimar, 1892)
C. Nisbet, ed.: *J. W. von Goethe: Annals, or Day and Year Papers* (London, 1901)
R. Krauss: *Das Stuttgarter Hoftheater* (Stuttgart, 1908)
W. Bode: *Die Tonkunst in Goethes Leben* (Berlin, 1912)

G. KRAFT

Krása, Hans (*b* Prague, 30 Nov 1899; *d* ?Auschwitz, 1944). German composer. After leaving school he took composition lessons with Zemlinsky, completing these in 1921. He then worked as accompanist at the New German Theatre in Prague, and he also made several foreign tours. His composition studies were continued at the Berlin Conservatory and under Roussel in Paris. He finally settled in Prague and, as a Jew, he was interned in Terezín when Czechoslovakia fell to the Nazis. On 16 October 1944 he was transported to Auschwitz and no more is known of him. Zemlinsky encouraged him to follow Mahler and early Schoenberg, but in the 1920s Krása was attracted by the music of Stravinsky and contemporary French composers, influences demonstrated in his mature works.

WORKS

(selective list)

Grotesques (Morgenstern: Galgenlieder), Bar, orch, 1920; Str Qt, 1923; Die Erde ist des Herrn, cantata, 1932; Verlobung in Traum (opera, after Dostoyevsky), 1933; Kammermusik, hpd, 7 insts, 1936; The Bumble Bee (children's opera, K. Hoffmeister), 1939

BIBLIOGRAPHY

M. Očadlík: 'Die Erde ist des Herrn', *Klíč*, ii (1932), 168
E. Steinhard: 'H. Krása: Die Erde ist des Herrn', *Der Auftakt*, xii (1932), 107
M. Očadlík: 'H. Krása: Zasnoubení ve snu', *Klíč*, iii (1933), 231

E. Steinhard: 'H. Krása: Verlobung in Traum', *Der Auftakt*, xiii (1933), 73

V. Helfert and E. Steinhard: *Die Musik in der Tschechoslowakischen Republik* (Prague, 1936), 175f

JOSEF BEK

Krasinsky, Ernest Louis. See MÜLLER, ERNEST LOUIS.

Krasner, Louis (*b* Cherkassy, 21 June 1903). American violinist of Russian birth. He was taken to the USA at the age of five, and graduated in 1923 from the New England Conservatory, Boston, where he studied the violin with Eugene Gruenberg and composition with Frederick Converse. Further studies in Europe, under Flesch, Capet and Ševčik, led to an active concert career there and in the USA, during which he became closely identified with 20th-century music; in 1934 he commissioned Berg's concerto, believing that the cause of serial music would be helped by an effective virtuoso work in Berg's impassioned melodic style. He gave its première at the 1936 ISCM Festival, Barcelona (and its London première less than a month later), and that of Schoenberg's concerto at Philadelphia in 1940. Both these concertos were also first recorded by him, and his other first performances included concertos by Casella (Boston, 1928) and Sessions (Minneapolis, 1946), as well as shorter works by Cowell and Harris. Krasner became leader of the Minneapolis SO under Mitropoulos (1944–9), and then moved to the University of Syracuse, where he taught the violin and chamber music until his retirement in 1972. His playing combined technical proficiency with persuasive conviction of musical character, attracting a rare testament of performance approval from Schoenberg after the première of his concerto (letter, 17 December 1940).

MICHAEL STEINBERG

Krásová, Marta (*b* Protivín, 16 March 1901; *d* Vráž u Berouna, 20 Feb 1970). Czech mezzo-soprano. She took up singing on the advice of the violinist Ševčik and studied with Olga Borová-Valoušková, Růžena Maturová and, in Vienna, Ullanovský. In 1922 she joined the Slovak National Theatre in Bratislava, where under the conductor Oskar Nedbal she changed from soprano to mezzo roles. She made her début at the Prague National Theatre as Azucena (1926) and was a member of the company from 1928 to 1966.

To her musicality, excellent technique and breath control and wide range was allied a great talent as an actress with graceful movement and a rich imagination. She was an outstanding Isabella in Fibich's *Bride of Messina*, Róza in *The Secret*, Witch in *Rusalka* and Death in Rudolf Karel's *Death the Neighbour*; her non-Czech roles included Amneris, Eboli, Carmen, Gluck's Orpheus and the Countess in *The Queen of Spades*. Her finest performance was Kostelnička in Janáček's *Jenůfa*. She regularly sang lieder, achieving her greatest success in Dvořák's Biblical Songs and in Mahler. Foerster, Novák and Jirák dedicated songs to her. She appeared as a guest in many opera houses in Europe and in the USA (1937) and made many recordings. She was made National Artist in 1958.

BIBLIOGRAPHY

V. Pospíšil: 'Písňový večer Marty Krásové' [Krásová's song evening], *HRo*, v/20 (1952), 32

——: 'Marta Krásová, laureátka státní ceny [Krásová, winner of the state prize], *HRo*, vi (1953), 357

V. Šolín: 'Být živým svědomím národa' [To be a living conscience of the nation], *HRo*, viii (1955), 872 [interview]

——: *Marta Krásová* (Prague, 1960)

L. Šíp: *Pěvci před mikrofonem* [Singers before the microphone] (Prague, 1960), 55ff

V. Pospíšil: 'Výjimečný zjev českého pěveckého umění' [An exceptional figure of Czech vocal art], *HRo*, xiv (1961), 144

J. Kozák: *Českoslovenští koncertní umělci a komorní soubory* [Czechoslovak concert artists and chamber ensembles] (Prague, 1964), 257ff

R. Fikrle: *Portréty* [Portraits] (Roztoky, nr. Prague, 1967), 4

E. Kopecký and V. Pospíšil: *Slavní pěvci Národního divadla* [Famous singers of the National Theatre] (Prague, 1968), 164ff

ALENA NĚMCOVÁ

Krasowski [Krassowski] (*fl* ?c1700). Polish composer. He may have been active in Jesuit circles and generally in southern Poland. His only known extant composition is a concerted motet, *Haec dies quam fecit ex c*, the manuscript of which, dating from the beginning of the 18th century, is in the library of the seminary at Sandomierz in south-east Poland (*PL-SA*). The 1737 inventory of the Kraków Jesuits mentions two works by him – a pastorella and a sonata – which have been lost. It is also possible that he wrote the aria and two sonatas signed with the initials A. K. that are mentioned in the 1677 inventory of the Franciscan chapel at Przemyśl, but since his first name has still not been discovered this remains only a theory.

BIBLIOGRAPHY

SMP

A. Chybiński: 'Z dziejów muzyki krakowskiej' [The history of music in Kraków], *KM* (1913), 1

——: *Słownik muzyków dawnej Polski* [Dictionary of early Polish musicians] (Kraków, 1948–9), 63

W. Świerczek: 'Rękopiśmienne zabytki muzyki dawnej w bibliotece Seminarium Duchownego w Sandomierzu' [Manuscript treasures of early music in the library of the Sandomierz seminary], *Kronika diecezji Sandomierskiej* (1959), nos.7–8

——: 'Katalog rękopiśmiennych zabytków muzycznych biblioteki Seminarium Duchownego w Sandomierzu' [Catalogue of manuscript music treasures in the library of the Sandomierz seminary], *Archiwa, biblioteki i muzea kościelne*, x (Lublin, 1965), 223–78

M. Perz: 'Inwentarz przemyski (1677)' [A Przemyśl catalogue of 1677], *Muzyka*, xix/4 (1974)

MIROSŁAW PERZ

Krasselt. German family of musicians.

(1) **(Johann) Gustav Krasselt** (*b* Kohren, 13 Oct 1846; *d* in or after 1910). Violinist. He became leader of Glauchau's city orchestra in 1869. Three years later he was appointed leader of the Baden-Baden orchestra, a post he held until 1904, though he frequently returned as a guest artist to Glauchau, where his children made their solo débuts. He was also a skilful conductor and composer; his works include an albumleaf and a concert mazurka for violin and piano and a concert mazurka for orchestra. His daughter (Clara) Jenny Krasselt (*b* Glauchau, 15 Oct 1870; *d* after 1906), who made her début with Hummel's A♭ Concerto, became a well-known pianist.

(2) **(Gustav) Alfred Krasselt** (*b* Glauchau, 3 June 1872; *d* Eisenach, 27 Sept 1908). Violinist, son of (1) Gustav Krasselt. He studied the violin with Petri and Brodsky in Leipzig and won Joachim's esteem. He was the leader of the newly founded Philharmonic Orchestra in Munich and in 1896 was made leader of the Weimar court orchestra. One of the finest German violinists of his day, he played at the courts of St Petersburg and Vienna and was admired by such conductors as Herman Levi, Hans Richter and Richard Strauss.

(3) **Rudolf Krasselt** (*b* Baden-Baden, 1 Jan 1879; *d* Andernach, 12 April 1954). Cellist, son of (1) Gustav Krasselt. He was a pupil of Julius Klengel and gave recitals in Berlin and Vienna before becoming principal

Kapellmeister at the Deutsches Opernhaus in Berlin-Charlottenburg. He was also a lecturer at the Berlin Hochschule für Musik, where he taught Robert Oboussier and Kurt Weill, and until 1943 was general music director and operatic director of the city of Hanover.

BIBLIOGRAPHY

RiemannL 6

F. Pazdírek: *Universal-Handbuch der Musikliteratur* (Vienna, c1904–10)

A. Einstein: *Das neue Musiklexikon* (Berlin, 1926)

F. Nagler: *Das klingende Land* (Leipzig, 1936)

H. Sievers: *Die Musik in Hannover* (Hanover, 1961)

D. Kämper, ed.: 'Richard Strauss und Franz Wüllner im Briefwechsel', *Beiträge zur rheinischen Musikgeschichte*, li (Cologne, 1963)

WALTER HÜTTEL

Krastev, Venelin (*b* Dupnitsa, Stanke Dimitrov, 22 Sept 1919). Bulgarian musicologist and critic. He graduated from the State Music Academy in Sofia in 1943 and carried on further studies in music history at the Institute of the History of Arts in Moscow (1948–9). Greatly influenced by Soviet musicologists of the 1930s and 1940s, Krastev returned to Sofia in 1949 to hold office in the Committee for Science, Art and Culture; for many years he was also secretary of the musicologists' section of the Union of Bulgarian Composers. Assistant lecturer (1948) and lecturer (1953) in music history at the State Music Academy in Sofia, he became professor at the Institute for Musicology of the Bulgarian Academy of Sciences in 1971. Apart from two histories of Bulgarian music, Krastev has written numerous monographs on Bulgarian composers. He is active as a concert and opera critic and regularly broadcasts on the concert life of the country.

WRITINGS

Ocherki varhu razvitieto na balgarskata musika [Studies of the development of Bulgarian music] (Sofia, 1954)

Dobri Khristov (Sofia, 1954; Russ. trans., 1960)

Petko Stainov (Sofia, 1957)

Alexander Morfov (Sofia, 1958)

Nasoki v balgarskata masova pesen [Trends in Bulgarian mass songs] (Sofia, 1958)

Svetoslav Obretenov (Sofia, 1959)

Ochertsi po istoria na balgarskata muzika [Studies in the history of Bulgarian music] (Sofia, 1970; Russ. trans., 1973)

ed.: *Muzikalno-teoretichno i publizistichno nasledstvo na Dobri Khristov* [Dobri Khristov's musical, theoretical and publicist heritage] (Sofia, 1971)

Balgarska musikalna kultura (Sofia, 1974)

Articles and reviews in *Balgarska muzika* and other periodicals

LADA BRASHOVANOVA

Kratēma. A musical unit of TERETISMATA often appended to or inserted in Byzantine hymns in order to lengthen their duration. Some are given descriptive titles such as 'bell', 'viola' or 'trumpet'.

Kratēmatarion. A collection of kratēmata arranged according to the eight Byzantine modes. *See* KRATÉMA.

Kratzer. Polish family of musicians of Austrian descent.

(1) Franciszek Ksawery Kratzer (*b* Austria, 1731; *d* Kraków, 3 Aug 1818). Bass and choir trainer. After studying in Vienna he worked in Wieliczka. From 1763 he was a singer in Kraków, and was appointed cantor of Wawel Cathedral in Kraków on 20 February 1768. From 1781 to 1797 he was in charge of the singing school founded by X. W. Sierakowski, and from 1794 to 1806 was conductor of the Wawel Cathedral choir and singing master to the boy choristers. His memoirs

and reminiscences were edited by his son (2) Kazimierz Augustyn Kratzer in 1856.

(2) Kazimierz Augustyn Kratzer (*b* Kraków, baptized 21 Feb 1778; *d* Kraków, 19 June 1860). Musician and actor, son of (1) Franciszek Ksawery Kratzer. He studied music at the Sierakowski Singing School (1781–7), and from 1787 was a singer in Wawel Cathedral. Later he was a singer and actor in the Kraków Theatre (1799–1809), and from 1806 cantor and conductor of the Wawel Cathedral choir. He was a member of the Kraków Society of Friends of Music (1817–24) and organized and conducted the Choir of the German Amateur Society in Kraków.

(3) Walenty Karol Kratzer (*b* Kraków, baptized 9 Feb 1780; *d* Warsaw, 24 April 1855). Composer, singer, actor and conductor, son of (1) Franciszek Ksawery Kratzer. He sang in the choir of Wawel Cathedral (1798–1814), was a singer and actor at the National Theatre in Warsaw (1814–21), and from 1817 was singing master at the Warsaw School of Music and Dramatic Art. In the following year he also joined the staff of the Public School of Elementary Music and the School of Dramatic Art. He taught singing at the Warsaw Conservatory (1826–31) and at the singing school attached to the Wielki Theatre (1835–41), and was also conductor of the Warsaw French and Vaudeville Theatres (1821–9). He composed incidental music and some guitar pieces.

(4) Kazimierz Julian Kratzer (*b* Kraków, 22 Feb 1844; *d* Warsaw, 4 Nov 1890). Composer and conductor, grandson of (1) Franciszek Ksawery Kratzer. After studying in Warsaw he appeared, at the age of 12, in the ballet of the Wielki Theatre. From 1864 he was accompanist and répétiteur to the soloists of the Warsaw Opera, and in 1889 was appointed deputy conductor. He composed music for melodramas, and some songs which achieved great popularity.

BIBLIOGRAPHY

T. Przybylski: 'Rodzina Kratzerów' [The Kratzer family], *Muzyka*, xiv/1 (1969), 34

TADEUSZ PRZYBYLSKI

Kraus, Alfredo (*b* Canary Islands, 1927). Spanish tenor. A pupil of Mercedes Llopart, he made his début in 1956 at Turin as Alfredo Germont, a role he repeated the following year at the Stoll Theatre, London. He then sang in Spain, at Covent Garden (1959, Edgard opposite Sutherland's Lucia), and at La Scala (1960, Elvino), where he has frequently returned. He has also appeared in the USA, particularly at the Metropolitan Opera, where he made his début in 1966 in *Rigoletto*. Kraus's voice is smooth, bright and well schooled, with an extensive top register up to *d"*. He is considered the best light, lyric tenor of his generation, while the elegance and stylishness of his singing, combined with warmth of expression and a handsome stage presence, make him the ideal interpreter of such aristocratic roles as Don Ottavio, Count Almaviva, Alfredo, the Duke of Mantua, and Massenet's Des Grieux and Werther.

BIBLIOGRAPHY

R. Celletti: 'Alfredo Kraus', *Opera*, xxvi (1975), 17

RODOLFO CELLETTI

Kraus, Egon (*b* Cologne, 15 May 1912). German music educationist. He studied English (state diploma 1935), philosophy and musicology (under Kroyer, Bücken and Fellerer) at Cologne University and music education at the Cologne Musikhochschule. He took the doctorate at Innsbruck University in 1957 under Wilhelm Fischer with a dissertation on school music education. After working as a schoolteacher in Cologne (1941–50) he was appointed lecturer at the Musikhochschule, where he held seminars on folk and youth music (1950–57). In 1957 he became professor at the Oldenburg Pädagogische Hochschule. He has served as general secretary (until 1968) and president (from 1972) of the International Society of Music Education, and as editor of its journal *International Music Educator* (from 1969) and the *International Music Education Yearbook* (from 1973). He has also edited the periodicals *Musik und Bildung* and *Musik im Unterricht* (with E. Laaff), proceedings of the Bundesschulmusikwochen and several collections of school music: *Musik in der Schule* (Wolfenbüttel, 1950; with F. Oberborbeck), *Musica instrumentalis* (Zurich, 1954–), *Europäische Lieder in den Ursprachen* (Berlin, 1956; with J. Gregor and F. Klausmeier), *Europäische Madrigale* (Zurich, 1956) and *Cantare e sonare* (Hamburg, 1957). He represents West Germany on the International Music Council, of which he is vice-president.

WRITINGS

ed.: *Musik in der deutschen Bildung* (Ratingen, 1950)
'Musikerziehung in der höheren Schule', *Handbuch der Musikerziehung*, ed. H. Fischer (Berlin, 1954), i, 257
with R. Schoch: *Der Musikunterricht: Beiträge zu einer neuen Methodik* (Wolfenbüttel, 1954–5)
Internationale Bibliographie des musikpädagogischen Schrifttums (Wolfenbüttel, 1955)
Wege der Erneuerung der Schulmusikerziehung seit 1900 (diss., U. of Innsbruck, 1957)
The Present State of Music Education in the World (Cologne, 1960)
ed.: *Comparative Music Education: ISME* iv *Vienna 1961*
Music, Music Education, Musicology (Mainz, 1962)
Studying Music in Germany (Mainz, 1962)
'The Role of International Organizations in Creating a Wider Interest in Traditional Music', *Creating a Wider Interest in Traditional Music; Berlin 1967*, 214
International Directory for Music Education Institutions (Paris, 1968)

ALFRED GRANT GOODMAN

Kraus, Ernst (*b* Erlangen, 8 June 1863; *d* Wörthsee, 6 Sept 1941). German tenor. After working in his father's brewery, he was heard by the tenor Heinrich Vogl, who recommended that he studied singing; this he did in Munich with Schimon-Regan, and later in Milan with Cesare Galliera. He made his début at Mannheim in 1893 as Tamino, and was engaged as leading *Heldentenor* at the Berlin Court Opera from 1896 to the mid-1920s. He sang regularly at Bayreuth from 1899 to 1909 as Walther, Erik, Siegmund and Siegfried. He sang the title role in the first performance in Germany of *Dalibor* (1904) and was the first London Herod in *Salome*, at Covent Garden in 1910, having already appeared there between 1900 and 1907 in the Wagnerian repertory. He appeared at the Metropolitan Opera during the 1903–4 season. After he retired he taught singing in Munich. Kraus was generally considered the finest Wagner tenor of the century until the advent of Lauritz Melchior, and his voice is said to have been one of the largest ever committed to gramophone records.

HAROLD ROSENTHAL

Kraus, Joseph Martin (*b* Miltenberg am Main, 20 June 1756; *d* Stockholm, 15 Dec 1792). German composer, conductor and writer active in Sweden. From the age of 12 he was educated in Mannheim. He studied law at the universities of Mainz (1773–4), Erfurt (1775–6) and Göttingen (1777–8); he joined the 'Göttinger Hainbund'

literary circle and met the Swedish student Carl Stridsberg, who in 1778 persuaded Kraus to accompany him to Stockholm and try his fortune at the court of Gustavus III. Two years later Kraus was elected a member of the Swedish Academy of Music, and in 1781 he became deputy conductor of the court orchestra.

Kraus's greatest work, the opera *Aeneas i Carthago* (*Dido och Aeneas*), was written to a libretto by J. H. Kellgren on an outline suggested by the king. Before embarking on it, he undertook a study journey from 1782 to 1787 at the king's expense through Germany and Austria, Italy, France and England. In Vienna he met Gluck and Haydn (Silverstolpe, 1833); 'That man has great style', Gluck remarked after seeing his scores, and Haydn declared of his C minor Symphony (1783), 'I own a symphony by him, which I preserve to the memory of one of the greatest geniuses I have met'.

In Paris in 1784, Kraus composed incidental music to Molière's *Amphitryon* at the Swedish king's request. The following year he attended the second of the Handel festivals in London, and he returned to Sweden in 1787. He succeeded Uttini as *Hovkapellmästare* at Stockholm in 1788, and during his last years was close to the Swedish poet and singer Carl Michael Bellman, with whom – along with other leading cultural figures at court, including the composers G. J. Vogler, Haeffner, Frigel, Åhlström and Wikmanson (who was also his pupil) – he formed the *diktarkretsen*, a literary and musical circle which governed Gustavian musical and literary policy. He died of tuberculosis.

Kraus was a gifted and versatile musician, and for the short period of his activity at Stockholm was the most notable composer at the brilliant court of Gustavus III. His Mannheim training and his later travels gave him a cosmopolitan outlook that is evident in much of his music. Two of the operas he wrote for Stockholm, *Proserpina* and *Aeneas i Carthago*, show a relationship with Gluck's later works, though the harmonic language is bolder. The same richness of harmony, together with the influence of the Mannheim school, is a feature of his instrumental music, and in the symphonies sometimes suggests an early Romantic feeling. He was a notable song composer, but perhaps his most individual works are the two deeply committed pieces written in response to the assassination of Gustavus III March 1792; the *Symphonie funèbre* and the *Begravingskantata*.

His friend and admirer, the diplomat F. S. Silverstolpe, collected Kraus's scores and letters, which he left to the library of the University of Uppsala.

WORKS

MSS in *S-Uu*, unless otherwise stated; catalogue (incomplete) in K. F. Schreiber, 1925

STAGE

Azire (opera, 3, C. Stridsberg), 1778, unperf.; only autograph frags. extant
Proserpina (opera, 1, J. H. Kellgren, after Gustavus III), Ulriksdal Castle, June 1781, ov., arr. pf, in *Musikaliskt allehanda* (22 Jan 1824)
Fintbergs Bröllop [Fintberg's wedding] (comic play with music, 2, C. G. Holthusen), Stockholm, Bollhuset, Jan 1788
Soliman II, eller De tre sultaninnorna (comic opera, 3, J. G. Oxenstierna, after C. S. Favart), Stockholm, Royal Opera, 22 Sept 1789; selections in *Musikaliskt tidsfördrif* (1792)
Äfventyraren [The adventurer], eller Resan till Månans ö (comic play with music, 2, J. M. Lannerstjerna), Stockholm, Munkbroteatern, 30 Jan 1791, ov., 2 scenes, final chorus by Kraus; selections, arr. pf, in *Musikaliskt tidsfördrif* (1791)
Aeneas i Carthago (Dido och Aeneas) (opera, prol, 5, Kellgren, choreography F. N. Terrade), Stockholm, Royal Opera, 18 Nov 1799; ov., arr. 2 pf, ed. F. S. Silverstolpe (Vienna, 1802; Stockholm, n.d.); 2 ovs., ed. W. Lebermann (Wiesbaden, 1956)
Fiskarena [The fishermen] (pantomime-ballet, choreography A. Bournonville), Stockholm, Royal Opera, 9 March 1789

Entr'actes and ballet for Amphitryon (tragedy, Molière), Paris, 1784; ballet for Armide (opera by Gluck, scene iii), Stockholm, 24 Jan 1787; 1 aria for Visittimman [The visiting hour] (comic play, after Poinsinet: Le cercle), in Musikaliskt tidsfördrif (1789); 1 aria for Mexikanska systrarna [The Mexican sisters] (play with songs, Sparrschöld), Stockholm, Bollhuset, 13 Oct 1789, im Musikaliskt tidsfördrif (1790); 9 choruses for Oedipe (tragedy, 3, G. G. Alderbeth), Stockholm, 10 March 1792; 2 arias, 2 trios, qt for Le bon seigneur (comic play with music); incidental music for Olympie (tragedy, Kellgren); 2 pantomimes

VOCAL

Secular, orch acc.: Cantata for the king's birthday (Gröning), 4vv, 1782–3; Begravningskantata for Gustavus III (C. G. Leopold), 4 solo vv, 4vv, 1792, vocal score (Stockholm, 1792), ed in MMS, ix (1979); Prol, for birthday of Duke Carl von Södermanland, Stockholm, 7 Oct 1791; Son pietoso, aria (Leipzig, 1797); Ma tu tremi, pubd as Plus de crainte, vocal score (Paris, n.d.); 4 small cantatas (Metastasio); concert arias

Secular, pf acc.: 5 small cantatas, 1–4vv (C. M. Bellman), incl. Elegie, in Musikaliskt tidsfördrif (1793), Fiskarstuga [The little fishing hut] (Stockholm, 1794); Atis und Camilla (G. Creutz), in Musikaliskt tidsfördrif (1793); Se källan, se bålen [See the spring, see the grove], zither acc., in Musikaliskt tidsfördrif (1794); 20 airs et chansons (Leipzig, 1797); Meersturm, AMZ, iii/3 (1801); Die Mutter bei der Wiege (Die Nase), attrib. Mozart, Cäcilia, xxv (1846); other songs in Dan., Fr., It., Lat., Swed.

Sacred: Miserere, 1775; Requiem, 1776; Missa, 1776; TeD, 1776; Motet, D, 1776; Der Tod Jesu (J. M. Kraus), oratorio, 1777; Stella coeli, motet, C, 1783; TeD-Finale, 1783; Kom, din herdestaf att bära [Come, your shepherd's crook to bear] (Bellman), cantata, 1790; Förkunnom högt [Proclaim on high], motet, C, S-Sk; other works, incl. Die Geburt Jesu (Kraus), 1776, lost

INSTRUMENTAL

Syms., incl.: Wiener Sinfonie, c, 1783 (Leipzig, 1797), ed. in MMS, ii (1960); 2 syms. (Stockholm, 1781); Symphonie funèbre (Trauer-Sinfonie), 1792, arr. pf (Stockholm, n.d.), ed. W. Lebermann (Wiesbaden, 1957); Sinfonia con fugato per la chiesa, 1789; ed. Lebermann (Wiesbaden, 1957–8); Pariser Sinfonie, 1784; Sinfonia concertante, 1780

Other orch: 3 ovs., ed. Lebermann (Wiesbaden, 1957); vn conc., C. 1777, ed. Lebermann and U. Haverkampf (Wiesbaden, 1957); [2] Polonaise (polacca), Skma

Chamber: 6 str qts (Berlin, 1784), 3 str qts, before 1778, 7 ed. A. Hoffmann (Wolfenbüttel, 1960–61); Qnt, fl, str qt, op.7, 1783 (Paris, c1799), ed. Lebermann (Wiesbaden, 1959), Hoffmann (Wolfenbüttel, 1961); 4 vn sonatas, pf acc.; Duo (Sonate), d, vn, bc; Duo (Sonate), D, fl, va, in NM, lxxvi (1931); Trio, pf, vn, vc, 1787, ed. Lebermann (Wiesbaden, 1959); Allegro, pf, vn acc.

Pf solo: 2 sonate (Stockholm, 1792), incl. 1 arr. of vn sonata, E♭, 1785; Rondo (n.p., n.d.); Scherzo con variazioni; other works

WRITINGS

Versuch von Schäfergedichten (Mainz, 1773)
Tolon (Frankfurt am Main and Leipzig, 1776) [Trauerspiel, 3 acts]
Etwas von und über Musik fürs Jahr 1777 (Frankfurt am Main, 1778)
Articles in Stockholms Posten, 1778–80
Sketches for a music dictionary, Skma
Travel diary, letters, Skma, Ub

BIBLIOGRAPHY

C. Stridsberg: Åminnelsetal öfver . . . Joseph Kraus [Memorial address] (Stockholm, 1798)
[F. S. Silverstolpe]: Biographie af Kraus (Stockholm, 1833)
B. Anrep-Nordin: 'Studier över Joseph Martin Kraus', STMf, v. (1923), 15, 55, 117; vi (1924), 16, 49–93
K. F. Schreiber: 'Verzeichnis der musikalischen Werke von Jos. Kraus', AMw, vii (1925), 477
K. Meyer: 'Ein Musiker des Göttinger Hainbundes, Joseph Martin Kraus', ZMw, ix (1926–7), 468
K. F. Schreiber: Biographie über . . . Joseph Martin Kraus (Buchen, 1928)
R. Engländer: Joseph Martin Kraus und die gustavianische Oper (Uppsala, 1943)
C. Nisser: Svensk instrumentalkomposition 1770–1830 (Stockholm, 1943)
C.-G. S. Mörner: Johan Wikmanson und die Brüder Silverstolpe (Stockholm, 1952)
R. Engländer: 'Die Gustavianische Oper', AMw, xvi (1959), 314
W. Pfannkuch: 'Sonatenform und Sonatenzyklus in den Streichquartetten von Joseph Martin Kraus', GfMKB, Kassel 1962, 190
H. C. R. Landon: 'Joseph Martin Kraus', MT, ciii (1972), 25
V. Bungardt: Joseph Martin Kraus . . . ein Meister des klassischen Klavierliedes (Regensburg, 1973) [with list of songs and bibliography]
I. Leux-Henschen: Joseph Martin Kraus in seinen Briefen (Stockholm, 1978)

C.-G. S. MÖRNER (with BERTIL VAN BOER)

Kraus, Lili (b Budapest, 4 March 1905). American pianist of Hungarian birth. She took her first piano lessons at the age of six, and two years later entered the Budapest Academy of Music where her teachers included Kodály and Bartók. In 1922 she graduated with a first-class degree, and travelled to Vienna to study with Steuermann and Schnabel at the conservatory, where she was appointed a full professor in 1925. After teaching there for six years, she embarked on a world concert tour, and rapidly established herself during the 1930s as a successful soloist. About this time a number of valuable recordings of Mozart, Haydn and Beethoven, both solos and chamber music, did much to spread her fame as an exceptionally clear and musicianly interpreter of the Classics. In 1942 at the start of another tour she was taken prisoner by the Japanese in Java, and for three years was interned. After the war she toured Australia and New Zealand, and for her 'unrelenting efforts in the aid of countries in need' was granted New Zealand citizenship. She returned to the international circuit in 1948 and then travelled widely, giving recitals and playing with leading orchestras. A pianist of considerable virtuosity and stamina, she played 25 Mozart concertos in a single series in New York in 1966–7; and the next season she gave there the complete Mozart sonatas. In 1968 she was appointed artist in residence at Texas Christian University in Fort Worth, Texas.

DOMINIC GILL

Kraus, Otakar (b Prague, 10 Dec 1909). British baritone of Czech birth. He studied with Konrad Wallerstein in Prague and Fernando Carpi in Milan, made his début at Brno in 1935 as Amonasro, then sang with the Bratislava Opera (1936–9). In 1940 he settled in England, made some wartime appearances in Sorochintsy Fair and with the Carl Rosa Opera, and joined the English Opera Group in 1946, creating Tarquinius in The Rape of Lucretia. After a season with the Netherlands Opera (1950–51), he joined the Covent Garden Opera and remained a valued member of the company until 1968. There he created Diomede in Walton's Troilus and Cressida, and King Fisher in Tippett's The Midsummer Marriage. He was also an outstanding Alberich, his Italian training having made him more lyrical than many German singers; he sang the role at Bayreuth (1960–62). In 1951 he created Nick Shadow in The Rake's Progress at Venice and he repeated the part at La Scala and at Glyndebourne. Kraus established himself as a first-rate singing actor, always a vital and striking stage figure and a master of make-up. After leaving Covent Garden he taught in London; his pupils include Lois McDonall, Gwynne Howell and Robert Lloyd.

BIBLIOGRAPHY
H. Rosenthal: 'Otakar Kraus', Opera, xxiv (1973), 1067

HAROLD ROSENTHAL

Kraus, (Wolfgang Ernst) Richard (b Berlin, 16 Nov 1902; d Walchstadt, 11 April 1978). German conductor, son of Ernst Kraus. He studied at the Stern Conservatory in Berlin. Among his teachers was Erich Kleiber. He had his first engagements in Kassel, Hanover, Stuttgart and (from 1937) as music director in Halle, where he contributed to the German revival of Handel's stage works with performances of Agrippina. He conducted Der fliegende Holländer at the Bayreuth

Festival in 1942, and at the Berlin Staatsoper in 1944. After a period in Düsseldorf, in 1947 he was appointed general music director in Cologne, where his performances of Pfitzner's *Palestrina* were particularly admired. From 1952 he had no permanent post, but conducted frequently at the Städtische Oper (now the Deutsche Oper), Berlin. He took over a conductors' class at the Musikhochschule in Berlin in 1961, and assumed the directorship of the North-west German PO at Herford in 1963. His Berlin performances of Busoni's *Doktor Faust* (1955), with Fischer-Dieskau in the title role, saw the reinstatement of an almost completely forgotten work. His sense of theatre, broad musical sympathies and reliability make him suitable for works of many different styles, but he is especially successful with the music of Wagner and Strauss.

HANS CHRISTOPH WORBS

Krause, Christian Gottfried (*b* Winzig [now Wińsko], Silesia, baptized 17 April 1719; *d* Berlin, 4 May 1770). German lawyer, music aesthetician and composer. He received instruction on the violin, keyboard and timpani from his father, a town musician also named Christian Krause, but decided upon a career in law, with music as an amateur pursuit. After juristic studies at the University of Frankfurt an der Oder (1740–45), he became a legal secretary to Count Rothenburg in Berlin by the end of 1745. With his appointment as lawyer to the municipal council in 1753 his prestige increased rapidly, and he acquired a large home in Potsdam in which he established a highly popular music salon, attracting writers, poets and philosophers as well as musicians. The performances which he held there during and after the Seven Years War were among the few concert series of serious music in Berlin. He later became Justizrat of the High Prussian Court (probably in 1762) and held that post until his death.

Although Krause composed several cantatas for private performances, some lieder, a few instrumental pieces and a Singspiel, he is most important as a writer and music compiler. His *Von der musikalischen Poesie*, written by 1747, was one of the first treatises dealing with the setting of words to music. Its publication five years later marked the beginning of a new era for the lied, and the foundation of the first Berlin lied school. In this work Krause advocated a return to folklike simplicity, in contrast to the instrument-orientated style of the Leipzig lied school led by Sperontes. He cited French folksong as an ideal (perhaps a political gesture reflecting the king's preference for French culture) and called for unornamented lieder with simple accompaniments which could be eliminated without destroying the continuity of the vocal line.

Krause soon began to compile lieder of the style he wished to encourage. He collaborated with the poet Karl Ramler in gathering and editing 31 lieder which they published as *Oden mit Melodien* (1753); a second volume followed in 1755. Neither Krause, Ramler, the poets nor the composers were named in these volumes or others Krause edited, presumably because he wished the lieder to be judged solely on their intrinsic merit. However, Friedrich Marpurg published an index to the first volume of *Oden mit Melodien* (*Historisch-kritische Beyträge*, i, 1754, p.55) which showed that Krause himself had composed five songs for it; among the other

composers represented were C. P. E. Bach, Quantz and Agricola, and the poets included Gleim, Hagedorn, Kleist and Lessing. Krause and Ramler's last and largest compilation was the four-volume *Lieder der Deutschen mit Melodien* (1767–8), which incorporated most of the lieder from their earlier collections.

WORKS

Lieder edns.: [62] Oden mit Melodien, i–ii (Berlin, 1753–5); Oden mit Melodien (Berlin, 1761) [uncertain]; [240] Lieder der Deutschen mit Melodien, i–iv (Berlin, 1767–8)

Cantatas: Gelobet sey der Herr, 4vv, orch, *D-Bds*; Unendlicher, in allen Himmeln tönt Dein Lob, 8vv, orch, *B-Bc* [uncertain]; Der Tod Jesu (K. W. Ramler), c1758, *D-Mbs* [incl. recit by Telemann]; rev. edn. of Telemann's Ino, *Bds*; 8 lost cantatas, incl. Lob der Gottheit (Schlegel), 1758 and Pygmalion (Ramler), 1768, cited in Beaujean and Becker

Other: Der lustige Schulmeister (Singspiel, F. Nicolai), Berlin, 1766, lost; 8 preussische Kriegslieder in den Feldzügen 1756 und 1757 von einem Grenadier (J. W. L. Gleim) (Berlin, 1758); lied, *Bds*; new arias for Handel's Alexander's Feast (Ramler), c1766, lost; several lieder in contemporary anthologies

Inst: 4 syms., formerly *Bds*; 2 trios, fl, vn, b, lost; 2 trios, 2 fl, b, lost; 6 sonatas, hpd, *Dlb*; a few kbd pieces in contemporary collections

WRITINGS

Lettre à Mr. le Marquis de B*** sur la différence entre la musique italienne et françoise (Berlin, 1748; Ger. trans. in F. W. Marpurg: *Historisch-kritische Beyträge*, i (Berlin, 1754/R1970), 1–40 [incl. Marpurg's notes])

Von der musikalischen Poesie (Berlin, 1752, 2/1753)

'Thusnelde, ein Singspiel', in F. W. Marpurg: *Historisch-kritische Beyträge*, i (Berlin, 1754/R1970), 93–141 [review]

Other articles in contemporary periodicals

BIBLIOGRAPHY

EitnerQ; *GerberL*; *GerberNL*

C. von Ledebur: *Tonkünstler-Lexicon Berlin's* (Berlin, 1861/R1965)

M. Friedlaender: *Das deutsche Lied im 18. Jahrhundert* (Stuttgart and Berlin, 1902/R1970)

A. Schering: 'Christian Gottfried Krause: ein Beitrag zur Geschichte des Musikästhetik', *Zeitschrift für Ästhetik und allgemeine Kunstwissenschaft*, ii (1907), 548

B. Engelke: 'Neues zur Geschichte der Berliner Liederschule', *Riemann-Festschrift* (Leipzig, 1909), 456

H. Kretzschmar: *Geschichte des neuen deutschen Liedes* (Leipzig, 1911/R1966)

J. Beaujean: *Christian Gottfried Krause: sein Leben und seine Persönlichkeit im Verhältnis zu den musikalischen Problemen des 18. Jahrhunderts als Ästhetiker und Musiker* (Dillingen an der Donau, 1930)

H. Becker: 'Krause, Christian Gottfried', *MGG*

P. F. Marks: 'The Rhetorical Element in Musical *Sturm und Drang*: Christian Gottfried Krause's *Von der musikalischen Poesie*', *IRASM*, ii (1971), 49; also in *MR*, xxxiii (1972), 93

RAYMOND A. BARR

Krause, Ernst (*b* Dresden, 28 May 1911). German music critic. He studied the violin and piano at the Frankfurt Conservatory and musicology with Gerber, Adorno and Gennrich at Frankfurt University (1932–6). He began his career as a music critic on the Frankfurt *General-Anzeiger* (1934) and then worked in Dresden, first for the *Dresdner Nachrichten* (1939–41) and later as arts editor of the *Sächsischen Zeitung* (1946–50); having moved to Berlin he joined the *Nationalzeitung* and *Sonntag*. His comments on East German musical life also appear in numerous foreign journals. His book on Richard Strauss, which has been translated into seven languages, established his reputation as a Strauss specialist in the Dresden tradition and as a writer capable of fusing scholarly insight with an essayist's fluency. His comprehensive guide to opera (*Oper von A bis Z*) has been frequently reprinted.

WRITINGS

Briefe über die Oper (Dresden, 1950)

Richard Strauss: Gestalt und Werk (Leipzig, 1955, enlarged 5/1975; Eng. trans., 1964)

Oper von A bis Z (Leipzig, 1961, 10/1978)

Opernsänger: 44 Porträts aus der Welt des Musiktheaters (Berlin,

1962, 3/1965)
Die grossen Opernbühnen Europas (Leipzig and Kassel, 1966)
Walter Felsenstein auf der Probe (Berlin, 1971)
Werner Egk: Oper und Ballett (Berlin and Wilhelmshaven, 1971)
with E. Richter: *David Oistrakh, zum 65. Geburtstag* (Berlin, 1973)
'Standpunkt und Aspekte', *Deutsche Staatsoper Berlin*, ed. W. Otto and
    W. Rösler (Berlin, 1973)
'Von alten zum neuen Ruhm', *Staatskapelle Dresden: zum 415 jährigen
    Jubilieren*, ed. E. Steindorf and D. Uhrig (Berlin, 1973)
'Revolution und Dialektik: zum 80. Geburtstag von Paul Dessau',
    Musikbühne 74: Probleme und Informationen, ed. H. Seeger (Berlin,
    1974), 59   HORST SEEGER

Krause, Tom (*b* Helsinki, 5 July 1934). Finnish baritone. Studying medicine at Helsinki he became interested in jazz and dance music, developing a talent for
singing that took him to the Vienna Academy in 1956.
He made his operatic début in Berlin (1958) and quickly
gained a reputation in opera and concert throughout
Germany and Scandinavia. His career has been based in
Hamburg, where, with the basic repertory of Mozart,
Verdi and Wagner, he also appeared in such rarities as
Rossini's *La pietra del paragone* (1963), Handel's
Jephtha (1964) and in the title role of Searle's *Hamlet*
(1967); he was awarded the rank of Kammersänger
there in 1967. The Herald in *Lohengrin* was his first
role at Bayreuth (1962) and the Count in *Capriccio* his
first in England (Glyndebourne, 1963). He sang in the
American première of Britten's *War Requiem* and made
his début at the Metropolitan Opera as Malatesta in *Don
Pasquale* (1971). From 1968, when he performed Don
Giovanni, he has appeared regularly at the Salzburg
Festival. His Paris Opéra début occurred in 1975 and
he has also sung at La Scala and Covent Garden. His
recordings include recitals of German lieder and songs
by Sibelius as well as a wide range of religious and

operatic music; all show a firm, resonant voice, a sound
technique and a power of vivid characterization.
                                          J. B. STEANE

Krauss, Clemens (*b* Vienna, 31 March 1893; *d* Mexico
City, 16 May 1954). Austrian conductor. He was the
son of the Viennese actress and singer Clementine
Krauss, and great-nephew of the soprano Gabrielle
Krauss. At the age of eight he became a treble in the
Hofkapelle. In 1912 he went to Brno as chorus director,
conducting his first opera there the following year. He
was at Riga (1913–14), Nuremberg (1915–16) and
Sczeczin (1916–21), which gave him frequent opportunities of hearing Nikisch in Berlin, before returning to
Austria in 1921 as conductor of the opera and symphony concerts at Graz. In the following year he transferred to Vienna as conductor at the Staatsoper and
director of the conducting class at the State Academy
of Music. From 1924 to 1929 he was opera Intendant at
Frankfurt am Main and director of the Museum
Concerts. In 1929 he was back in Vienna as director of
the Staatsoper; in 1930 he gave the first performance in
that city of *Wozzeck*. He became director of the Berlin
Staatsoper in 1935. The climax of his official career
came in 1937 with his appointment as Intendant of the
Munich Opera. During the war he was also active at
Salzburg with the Festivals, and with the direction and
reorganization of the Mozarteum. In 1943, after the
destruction in an air raid of the National Theatre in
Munich, Krauss left for Vienna to conduct the Vienna
PO in broadcast concerts.
   As his long association with this orchestra implies,
Krauss had no lack of success in the concert hall. Yet by
blood and temperament he was a man of the theatre, a
born opera conductor with a sharp eye for visual as well
as musical detail, and a gift for administration. The flair
he showed in his operatic career deserted him in politics.
He made no bones about his Nazi sympathies: he was
ready to take over the première of Strauss's *Arabella*
(1933) when Fritz Busch, for whom the opera was
intended, had been hounded out of Dresden; his immediate predecessors in Berlin (Kleiber) and Munich
(Knappertsbusch) had both resigned for political
reasons. Against these acts of public indiscretion must
be weighed private deeds of kindness to Jewish artists in
trouble. After the war he was forbidden to conduct until
1947, when he resumed work in Vienna, by directing
opera at the Theater an der Wien (the Staatsoper was
not yet rebuilt) and concerts with the Philharmonic. He
made many visits abroad (London included; his Covent
Garden début had been in 1934) with the Opera, with
the Philharmonic or as guest conductor. His sudden
death occurred on one of these tours.
   Krauss was closely associated with Richard Strauss
both as friend and interpreter. Apart from *Arabella*, he
gave the first performances of *Friedenstag* (Munich,
1938), *Capriccio* (Munich, 1942), of which he wrote the
libretto, and *Die Liebe der Danäe* (Salzburg, 1952). He
married the singer Viorica Ursuleac, a noted exponent
of Strauss soprano roles, whom he accompanied in
recitals. Krauss had a wide repertory, embracing the
German-Austrian Classics and much beyond. For the
music of the other Strauss, Johann, he had an exceptionally light and happy touch. The Clemens Krauss
Archive in Vienna contains his non-commercial as well
as commercial recordings.

Clemens Krauss

BIBLIOGRAPHY
J. Gregor: *Clemens Krauss: eine musikalische Sendung* (Vienna and

Zurich, 1953)
O. von Pandor: *Clemens Krauss in München* (Munich, 1955)
D. Wooldridge: *Conductor's World* (London, 1970)
E. Maschat: 'Clemens Krauss', *Recorded Sound* (1971), no.42–3, p.740 [with list of non-commercial recordings]
C. Hoslinger: 'Clemens Krauss nicht als ein Wiener Musikant', *Fonoforum*, iv (1973), 322 [with discography of commercial recordings]

RONALD CRICHTON

Krauss, Gabrielle (*b* Vienna, 24 March 1842; *d* Paris, 6 Jan 1906). Austrian soprano. She studied at the conservatory in Vienna with Mathilde Marchesi and made her concert début in Berlin (1858) in Schumann's *Das Paradies und die Peri*. She sang in Vienna (1859–67), where she was the first local Venus, and then went to Paris where she was engaged by the Théâtre Italien (1859–70). In 1875 she sang Rachel in *La juive* at the inauguration of the Opéra's new building; she remained a member of the Opéra company (except for a short period, 1885–6) until the end of 1888. She became famous for her portrayals of Meyerbeer heroines, Leonore and above all Aida and Donna Anna; she created a number of roles, including Catherine of Aragon in Saint-Saëns's *Henry VIII* (1883). At La Scala she created the title role in Gomes's *Fosca* (1873). She was acclaimed for the dramatic intensity of her performances; to her operatic roles she brought a tragédienne's grand passion and nobility. The French nicknamed her 'La Rachel chantante'. After 1888 she retired from the operatic stage and devoted herself to concerts and teaching.

BIBLIOGRAPHY
G. de Charnacé: *Les étoiles du chant* (Paris, 1868–9)
M. Strakosch: *Souvenirs d'un imprésario* (Paris, 2/1887)
H. de Curzon: 'Mme Gabrielle Krauss', *Le théâtre* (1906)
L. Riemens and R. Celletti: 'Krauss, Gabrielle', *ES*

HAROLD ROSENTHAL

Kraut, Johann. *See* BRASSICANUS, JOHANNES.

Krauze, Zygmunt (*b* Warsaw, 19 Sept 1938). Polish composer and pianist. He studied composition with Sikorski and the piano with Maria Wiłkomirska at the Warsaw Conservatory; his studies were continued with Boulanger in Paris. An outstanding performer of aleatory and graphic compositions, he has appeared as a pianist in many countries, and in 1966 he won first prize in the Utrecht Competition for Performers of New Music. In 1965 he founded the Warsztat Muzyczny (Music Workshop) ensemble. He taught the piano at Cleveland State University in 1970–71, and in 1973 he was in Berlin under a Berliner Künstlerprogramm scholarship. As a composer he is concerned primarily with form, with 'homogeneous' forms and with those depending on contrast. An example of the former is *One Piano and Eight Hands*, in which all of the sound materials are presented at the outset and fragments return repeatedly – in Krauze's words, 'there are no surprises'. His most successful work is the orchestral *Folk Music*, where folk themes from many regions of Europe are tumbled together in highly complicated textures.

WORKS
(selective list)
Malay Pantuns (Indonesian, trans. R. Stiller), A/Mez, 3 fl, 1961; Pięć kompozycji unistycznych, pf, 1964; Tryptyk, pf, 1964; Trzy kompozycje unistyczne, 30 insts, 1964; Str Qt no.1, 1965; Dyptyk, 14 str, 1967; Esquisse, pf, 1967; Entrée, cl, trbn, vc, pf + elec org, 1968; Polichromia, 4–15 performers, 1968; Space Music Composition, tape, 1968; Voices, 15 insts, 1968–72; Piece for Orch no.1, 1969, no.2, 1970; Str Qt no.2, 1970; Fallingwater, pf, 1971; Folk Music, 36 insts, 1971–2; Aus aller Welt stammende, 10 insts, 1973; One Piano and Eight Hands, 1973; Idyll, folk insts, 1974; Pf

Conc., 1974–6; Music Box Waltz, pf, 1977; Suite de danses et de chansons, hpd, orch, 1977; Ballade, pf, 1978
Principal publishers: Polskie Wydawnictwo Muzyczne, Universal

BIBLIOGRAPHY
T. Kaczyński: ' "Kwartet smyczkowy" Zygmunta Krauze', *Ruch muzyczny* (1965), no.17, p.10

MIECZYSŁAWA HANUSZEWSKA

Kraynev, Vladimir (Vsevolodovich) (*b* Krasnoyarsk, 1 April 1944). Soviet pianist. In 1962 he graduated from Anaida Sumbatian's class at the Moscow Central Music School, and in the same year joined Heinrich Neuhaus's class in the conservatory. After Neuhaus's death in 1964 Kraynev studied with his son, Stanislav Neuhaus, under whose supervision he graduated in 1967, and completed his postgraduate studies in 1969. He won second prize at the 1963 Leeds Piano Competition, and first at the 1964 Vianna da Motta Competition in Lisbon and the 1970 Tchaikovsky Competition in Moscow. A remarkable representative of the younger generation of Soviet pianists, Kraynev is a brilliant virtuoso. His performances are distinguished by his broad conception and deep understanding of the music, combined with warmth of emotion. His repertory ranges from Beethoven and Brahms to Bartók, Prokofiev and Shchedrin. His tours have included England, Portugal, the USA, Hungary and Poland.

BIBLIOGRAPHY
L. Grigor'yev and Ya. Platek: 'Vladimir Kraynev (Besedï s masterami)' [Vladimir Kraynev (Conversations with the masters)], *Muzïkal'naya zhizn'* (1971), no.1, p.6

I. M. YAMPOL'SKY

Krebbers, Herman (Albertus) (*b* Hengelo, 18 June 1923). Dutch violinist. He studied at the Amsterdam Musiklyceum with Oskar Back, and gave his first concert at the age of nine. For some years he was the leader of the Gelderland Orchestra, from 1950 leader of The Hague Residentie Orchestra, and from 1962 leader of the Concertgebouw Orchestra, Amsterdam. As a soloist he is particularly admired for his fine tone and refined and stylish interpretations as well as for vigorous attack and heroic style; he has made many tours throughout Europe and the USA. In 1963 he founded the Guarneri Trio with the pianist Danièle Dechenne and the cellist Jean Decroos, and for many years he formed a violin duo with Theo Olof. He plays a Guarneri del Gesù of 1741. His teaching at the Amsterdam Musiklyceum continues the Back tradition, and his pupils include many of the most talented young Dutch violinists. He is an Officer of the Order of Oranje Nassau.

TRUUS DE LEUR

Krebs. German family of musicians, of particular interest for their close relationship with J. G. Walther and J. S. Bach as well as for their considerable output of good instrumental music, particularly for keyboard.

(1) Johann Tobias Krebs (*b* Heichelheim, Weimar, 7 July 1690; *d* Buttstädt, Weimar, 11 Feb 1762). Composer and organist. He attended school in Weimar intending to enter the church. He must also have possessed some musical ability, for in 1710 he was invited to become organist in nearby Buttelstedt. For the next few years he travelled to Weimar twice a week to take lessons, first from J. G. Walther and later from Bach himself. His second and last appointment in 1721 was to the Michaeliskirche in Buttstädt, where he also taught at the school. None of his church music is extant. A few chorale settings for organ (*D-Bds*) show a fondness for learned contrapuntal treatment that few other pupils of Bach shared.

(2) Johann Ludwig Krebs (*b* Buttelstedt, Weimar, baptized 12 Oct 1713; *d* Altenburg, 1 Jan 1780). Composer and organist, eldest of the three sons of (1) Johann Tobias Krebs. He received his first musical instruction from his father, including organ lessons as early as his 12th year. An improvement in the family fortunes enabled him to enter the Thomasschule in Leipzig in July 1726. He learnt the lute and violin, continued with his keyboard studies, and as late as 1730 was still singing in the choir. He spent nine years there and received a warm testimonial from Bach when he left. His studies at the University of Leipzig (1735–7) did not prevent him from assisting from time to time at the Thomaskirche or from playing the harpsichord in Bach's collegium musicum.

During his long professional life Krebs held only three appointments, all in the area south of Leipzig. From 1737–43 he was organist of the Marienkirche, Zwickau. Neither the organ nor the salary was attractive, and in 1744 he moved to Zeitz as organist of the castle. During his 12 years there his beloved teacher died and Krebs applied for the position. He was unsuccessful: in organ playing he was unsurpassed, but the Thomaskirche wanted a Kantor, not a Kapellmeister. Finally in 1755 he went to the castle in nearby Altenburg to become organist at the court of Prince Friedrich of Gotha-Altenburg. The organ was better there, but the salary was scarcely so. Georg Benda, who auditioned him for the post, wrote to the consistory of the castle:

In view of the rumour that the salary of the organist at Altenburg is hardly greater than what he receives in his present position as organist in Zeitz, [Krebs] lives in the respectful hope, taking into account his wife and seven children, that he might also receive some grain or other remuneration in kind.

Contemporaries spoke well of Krebs. Charles Burney, for example, reported that 'M. Krebs of Altenburg, scholar of Sebastian Bach, has been much admired for his full and masterly manner of playing the organ'. Forkel considered his organ compositions as among the most important of their time. Others praised his expert knowledge in matters connected with organ building. Krebs may not have been the favourite in the circle of Bach's pupils, as some have suggested; in Spitta's opinion his place in the hierarchy was next to Altnikol, Bach's future son-in-law. But Bach certainly regarded him very highly, if there is any truth to the contemporary pun on 'Krebs' (crayfish) and 'Bach' (stream): 'He is the only crayfish in my stream', reported by J. F. Reichardt in the *Musikalischer Almanach* for 1796. The close association between teacher and pupil has given scholars reason to be grateful as well as perplexed. Krebs, with others in the Thomaskirche circle, found useful occupation as a copyist. His work in the period 1729–31 is particularly significant, as the parts he made then for cantatas 192, 37 and 140 are primary sources. Other compositions of Bach in his hand have prompted the speculation that Krebs had access to Bach's musical estate. Löffler, for example, whose research into Krebs's life and works was so extensive, thought that this was the case with the unique Krebs copy of Bach's Fantasia and Fugue BWV537. In fact most of the manuscript is in the hand of Tobias. Other problems concern the authenticity of works which appear in the hands of both Bach and Krebs or bear their ascrip-

tion. H.-J. Schulze has recently discovered that the Trio in C minor BWV585 was composed by neither man but by J. F. Fasch. Works such as the chorale *Wir glauben all an einen Gott* in similar four- and five-part settings still await solution. Bach's Eight Short Preludes and Fugues BWV553–60 have also been attributed to both Tobias and Ludwig; on stylistic grounds neither seems likely.

The style of Krebs's music reflects the transitional period in which he lived. Some of his pieces, like the chorale *Jesu, meine Freude* for obbligato oboe and organ, are cast in a Bachian mould; others show the leavening influence of the *galant* style. But even in his warmest melodic works he could not altogether deny the contrapuntal influence of his youth. Few of the lesser composers of the mid-century share his proclivity towards counterpoint. Some of the organ pieces are modelled on his teacher's work. Bach's Toccata in F BWV540 was undoubtedly the stimulus for Krebs's E major Toccata; the Toccata in C BWV564 for a Prelude in C; and so on. In general his fugues are thoroughly worked out but show few touches of originality. He seems to have considered them more as examples of the craftsman's art than the artist's craft. One fugue on B–A–C–H pays direct homage to his teacher. The chorales and fantasias for organ and solo instrument show a more consistent level of invention, and in the case of the fantasias have no parallel in the music of G. F. Kauffmann, J. B. Bach, G. A. Homilius and others who wrote for such combinations of instruments. Krebs's Fantasia in F minor for oboe and organ has rightly been praised by Sietz, and may well be one of his most expressive works in any form.

Unlike the organ compositions, most of Krebs's clavier works were published in his own lifetime. They range in style from the simpler settings of German chorales in the *Clavier Ubung* to sophisticated examples in the 'French and Italian taste'. It is tempting to speculate that he wished to leave a representative anthology of works in all the current idioms, which is also to say that he wished to demonstrate that he was a fluent composer in all styles. His Concerto in A minor for two harpsichords is perhaps superior to the solo pieces; he wrote it for the Dresden court where he performed in 1753. Gerber's account of his success is undoubtedly true, for Krebs's inspiration remains remarkably high, not only in the lively dialogue of the outer movements but also in the appealing slow movement; here the fusion of Baroque and *galant* is extremely well contrived. Much the same is true of Krebs's sonatas for one and two flutes and harpsichord, where again his contrapuntal skill saves him from writing music of merely empty elegance.

The bulk of the orchestral and choral music awaits modern editions. The brilliant harpsichord writing of the double concerto in B minor pays homage to Bach's Fifth Brandenburg Concerto, and the opening chorus of the cantata *Gott fähret auf* to BWV51. The five-part motet *Erforsche mich, Gott* is a strong work in the mainstream of the Bach polyphonic tradition without, however, showing any obvious derivations from Bach's own motets. On the other hand the opening of the oratorio in memory of Queen Maria Josepha of Poland promises well with a solemn and poignant chorus, but then dissolves into a succession of arias and duets. In spite of that, the writing here and in his shorter choral works was never less than competent. He was too much of a craftsman to permit even occasional pieces to become merely perfunctory gestures.

Krebs's three sons were all musicians, the eldest being (3) Johann Gottfried Krebs. Carl Heinrich Gottlieb Krebs (1747–93) was court organist in Eisenberg from 1774; no compositions by him survive. Ehrenfried Christian Traugott Krebs (1753–1804) succeeded his father as court organist at Altenburg from 1780 and published a collection of six organ chorale-preludes (Leipzig, 1787); his son, Ferdinand Traugott Krebs, was awarded the post of 'Mittelorganist' at Altenburg in 1808 but nothing further is known of him.

WORKS

Editions: *J. L. Krebs: Gesammt-Ausgabe der Tonstücke für die Orgel*, ed. C. Geissler (Magdeburg, 1847–9); inc. as noted below; where MSS are lost a primary source [GA]
    J. L. Krebs: Ausgewählte Orgelwerke, ed. K. Tittel, Die Orgel, 2nd ser., xviii, xx, xxi, xxvi (Lippstadt, 1963–75) [AO]

ORGAN

For organ alone unless otherwise stated; principal sources incl. numerous autographs: *D-B, Bds, LEm, F-Pn*, also *A-Wn, B-Bc, D-Dlb, DS* and formerly Königsberg, *GB-Lbm*, Frank A. Taft estate, Montclair, NJ, also GA.
8 preludes and fugues, 4 ed. W. Zöllner (Leipzig, 1938), 2 ed. in AO (1963); 2 toccatas and fugues, 1 ed. W. Zöllner (Leipzig, 1938); 2 fantasias and fugues; 10 free preludes/fantasias, several not in GA, 16 fugues; 14 trios, 2 ed. in AO (1963)
30 extended chorale settings, 1 not in GA, several doubtful attribs., 8 ed. in AO (1964); 9 simple chorale settings, 1 not in GA
4 fantasias, ob, org [1 also for fl, 1 also for ob d'amore], 1 ed. in AO (1966), all ed. H. McLean (London, in preparation); chorale fantasia, tpt, org; 14 extended chorale settings, 1 inst, org [most for ob or ob/tpt, some for tpt or hn], 10 ed. in AO (1966, 1975), all ed. H. McLean (London, in preparation)

OTHER KEYBOARD

Erste Piece, bestehend in 6 leichten ... Praeambulis (Nuremberg, 1740), nos.2 and 6 ed. in *Alte Meister*, nos.11–12 (c1870)
Andere Piece, bestehend in einer leichten ... Suite (Nuremberg, 1741)
Dritte Piece, bestehend in einer ... Ouverture (Nuremberg, 1741)
Vierte Piece, bestehend in einem ... Concerto (Nuremberg, 1743)
Clavier Ubung, bestehend in verschiedenen Vorspielen und Veränderungen einiger Kirchen Gesänge (Nuremberg, n.d.), ed. K. Soldan (Leipzig, 1937)
Clavier-Ubung bestehe in einer ... Suite ... zweyter Theil (Nuremberg, n.d.)
Clavier-Ubung bestehend in sechs Sonatinen ... IIIer Theil (Nuremberg, n.d.)
Exercice sur le clavessin consistant en VI suites, op.4 (Nuremberg, n.d.), part ed. K. Herrmann, *Leichte Tanzstücke* (Hamburg, 1949); nos.2 and 6 ed. in *Organum*, v/32, 34 (Lippstadt, 1965)
Sonata, in Musicalisches Magazin, in Sonaten ... bestehend, pt.2 (Leipzig, 1765)
3 sonatas cited in Breitkopf catalogue
3 partite, *D-Bds, Dlb*; Conc. 2 hpd, *LEb*, ed. B. Klein (Leipzig, 1966)

INSTRUMENTAL

[6] Trio, 2 fl/vn, bc (Nuremberg, n.d.); no.1 ed. H. Riemann, Collegium musicum, xxxi (Leipzig, c1910); no.6 ed. in NM, cix (1934), nos.2, 5 ed. H. Ruf (Wilhelmshaven, 1968); MS copies, *US-CA*
[6] Sonata da camera, hpd, fl/vn (Leipzig, 1762); ed. B. Klein as *Sechs Kammersonaten* (Leipzig, 1963)
Musikalischer und angenehmer Zeitvertreib bestehet in 2 Sonaten, hpd, fl/vn (Nuremberg, n.d.)
III sonate, fl, vn, bc, cited in Breitkopf catalogue, MS copies in *D-B*, ed. F. Nagel no.1 (Wolfenbüttel, 1975), no.2 (Heidelberg, 1975); VI soli, vn, hpd, cited in Breitkopf catalogue, autograph frag. *ALa*, MS copies of 4 sonatas *B-Bc, D-B*
2 sinfonias, 2 vn, va, bc; 2 concs., lute, str, ed. R. Chiesa (Milan, 1970–71); Conc., hpd, ob, str, ed. K. Jametzky (Heidelberg, 1976); 2 sonatas, vn, bc: all in *D-B*; Conc., vn, str; Sonata, vn, bc: both cited in Breitkopf catalogue

SACRED VOCAL
(sources: D-B, Bds, LEm)

Oratorio funebre all'occasione della morte di Maria Gioseppa Regina di Pollonia, SATB, 2 ob, str, bc, cNov 1757
Missa (F), SATB, 2 hn, str, bc, 24 June 1755; Sanctus (D), SATB, 2 hn, 2 ob, str, bc; Sanctus (D), SATB, 3 tpt, 2 ob, str, bc, timp; Magnificat deutsch (F), SATB, bc; Magnificat (D) SATB, 3 tpt, str, bc, timp
Erforsche mich, Gott (motet), SSATB, ed. in Cw, lxxxix (1963); Der Herr hat Grosses an uns getan (cantata), SATB, 2 tpt, 2 ob, str, bc, 23 Dec 1739; Gott fähret auf mit Jauchzen (cantata), SATB, 2 hn,

str, bc, 27 April 1766; Bist du noch fern (aria), S, hpd
Tröste uns Gott (motet), 8vv, lost

(3) Johann Gottfried Krebs (*b* Zwickau, baptized 29 May 1741; *d* Altenburg, 5 Jan 1814). Organist and composer, eldest son of (2) Johann Ludwig Krebs. From 1758 he discharged the duties of 'Mittelorganist' at Altenburg. On his father's death in 1780 Johann Gottfried was not permitted to audition for the vacant court organist position because 'he had associated with an unacceptable female who was a hindrance to his advancement'. Instead, he became Stadtkantor in Altenburg the following year, remaining in that post until his death. Unlike his father, who wrote very little church music, he was a prolific cantata composer; at least 71 church cantatas, two psalm settings, an oratorio, a secular cantata and a musical drama are extant (*A-Wgm, B-Bc, D-B, Bds, Dlb, F, LEm, SWl, GB-Lbm*). Several keyboard works were published in 18th-century anthologies. His music shows no evidence of Bachian influence.

BIBLIOGRAPHY

C. S. Terry: *Bach: a Biography* (London, 1928, 2/1933)
H. Löffler: 'Johann Ludwig Krebs: Mitteilungen über sein Leben und Wirken', *BJb*, xxvii (1930), 99–129
H. Kelletat: *Zur Geschichte der deutschen Orgelmusik der Frühklassik* (Kassel, 1933)
G. Frotscher: *Geschichte des Orgel-Spiels und der Orgel-Komposition* (Berlin, 1935–6, enlarged 3/1966)
R. Sietz: 'Die Orgelkompositionen des Schülerkreises um Johann Sebastian Bach', *BJb*, xxxii (1935), 49
H. Löffler: 'Johann Tobias Krebs', *BJb*, xxxvii (1940–48), 136
H. Keller: *Die Orgelwerke Bachs: ein Beitrag zu ihrer Geschichte, Form, Deutung und Wiedergabe* (Leipzig, 1948; Eng. trans., 1967)
F. Schnapp: 'The Riddle of the Bach Goblet', *HMYB*, vii (1952), 335
K. Tittel: 'Krebs', *MGG* [incl. more detailed list of works]
J. Horstman: *The Instrumental Music of Johann Ludwig Krebs* (diss., Boston U., 1959) [incl. thematic catalogue]
K. Tittel: *Die musikalischen Vertreter der Familie Krebs* (diss., U. of Marburg, 1963)
W. Neumann and H.-J. Schulze: *Bach-Dokumente*, i–iii (Leipzig and Kassel, 1963–72)
K. Tittel: 'Die Choralbearbeitungen für Orgel von Johann Ludwig Krebs', *Festschrift Hans Engel* (Kassel, 1964), 406
F. Blume: *Geschichte der evangelischen Kirchenmusik* (Kassel, 1965; Eng. trans., enlarged, 1974, as *Protestant Church Music: a History*)
B. S. Brook, ed.: *The Breitkopf Thematic Catalogue, 1762–1787* (New York, 1966)
H. Engel: *Musik in Thüringen* (Cologne, 1966)
K. Tittel: 'Welche unter J. S. Bachs Namen geführten Orgelwerke sind Johann Tobias bzw. Johann Ludwig Krebs zuzuschreiben?', *BJb*, lii (1966), 102–37
W. G. Marigold: 'The Preludes and Fugues of J. L. Krebs', *MO*, xc (1967), 337
D. Mulbery: 'Bach's Favorite Pupil: Johann Ludwig Krebs', *Music/The A.G.O Magazine*, ii (1968), 24, 48

HUGH J. McLEAN

Krebs [Miedke], Karl August (*b* Nuremberg, 16 Jan 1804; *d* Dresden, 16 May 1880). German conductor and composer. The son of A. and Charlotte Miedke of the Nuremberg Theatre company, he took, on his mother's death in 1805, the name of his adoptive father, the tenor and composer Johann Baptist Krebs (1774–1851). He first appeared as a pianist at the age of six, and he began composing the following year. He studied with Schelble, then in Vienna with Seyfried (1825). After acting as third Kapellmeister at the Kärntnertor-Theater, he went to Hamburg as Kapellmeister in 1827, remaining until 1850. He then moved to Dresden as Kapellmeister at the Court Opera in succession to Wagner; his period in this post included the staging of *Lohengrin* in 1852. He retired from the theatre in 1872 and took over the directorship of Dresden's Catholic church. He was an enthusiastic supporter of Spontini and Meyerbeer, with a taste for large choirs and orchestras. Wagner, whose early music he also championed, wrote from Hamburg over the *Rienzi* production there describing him as 'a really excellent conductor ... I could have no better conductor for my opera' (letter to Minna Wagner, 17 March 1844); later Wagner lost confidence in him (over the *Lohengrin* production describing his as 'mindless') and was affronted by his demand for an extra number in *Rienzi* for his wife. His works include church music and a number of operas (*Sylvia*, Hamburg 1830; *Herzog Albrecht*, Hamburg 1833, revised as *Agnes Bernauer*, Dresden 1858), but he is best known for his many songs, which were once very popular.

In 1850 Krebs married Aloyse Michalesi (*b* Prague, 29 Aug 1826; *d* Dresden, 5 Aug 1904), daughter of the singer Wenzel Michalesi (*d* 1836). She was a mezzo-soprano who made her début in Brno in 1843 and moved to Hamburg in 1846; at Meyerbeer's request, she went to Dresden in 1849 to sing Fidès in *Le prophète*. She retired from the stage in 1870 but continued to sing in concerts and to teach. Their daughter Mary (*b* Dresden, 5 Dec 1851; *d* Dresden, 27 June 1900) was a pianist who first appeared in Meissen at the age of 11. She toured widely in Europe and visited the USA, playing frequently in London, at the Crystal Palace (1864), Philharmonic (1874), and with especial success at the Monday Popular Concerts from 1875. She had a large repertory and a fine technique.

BIBLIOGRAPHY
O. Schmid: *Mary Krebs-Brenning* (Dresden, 1892)
A. Ehrlich: *Berühmte Sängerinnen der Vergangenheit und Gegenwart* (Leipzig, 1895)
H. von Brescius: *Die Königl. Sächs. musikalische Kapelle von Reissiger bis Schuch (1826–1898): Festschrift zur Feier des 350 jährigen Kapelljubiläums* (Dresden, 1898)
H. Chevalley: *Hundert Jahre Hamburger Stadt-Theater* (Hamburg, 1927)
P. Adolph: *Vom Hof- zum Staatstheater Dresden* (Dresden, 1932)
         JOHN WARRACK

Krebsgang (Ger.). *See* RETROGRADE.

Krehbiel, Henry (Edward) (*b* Ann Arbor, Mich., 10 March 1854; *d* New York, 20 March 1923). American critic and writer on music. He studied law at Cincinnati, but soon turned to journalism, devoting himself especially to music. He was music critic of the *Cincinnati Gazette* from 1874 to 1880 and then for the *New York Tribune*, a post he held until his death. He occupied a position of authority and influence among American critics, was one of the ablest champions of musical progress and at the same time a serious student of the Classics. He did much to advance the understanding and love of Wagner's later music dramas in the USA and was among the first to welcome and appraise discriminatingly the music of Brahms, Tchaikovsky, Dvořák and other new composers of the period. It was at least to some extent due to him that such work was made familiar in New York before it became widely known in many European capitals. In his later years however his taste was conservative.

Krehbiel's activity was by no means confined to newspaper criticism. Among the list of his writings below, the revised and completed edition of the English texts of Thayer's *Life of Beethoven* is preeminent. It was the work of his last years, and its publication was due to the efforts of the Beethoven Association of New York. He was also American adviser to *Grove 2*.

Another line of original research was his study of Negro folksong, which resulted in the publication of *Afro-American Folksong*, a book now superseded by more recent and closer research.

Krehbiel was widely known as a lecturer; for many years he accomplished useful work with the programme notes and analyses he prepared for the principal New York concerts. In 1900 he was on the jury for musical instruments at the Paris Exhibition, and in 1901 he received the Croix de la Légion d'Honneur.

WRITINGS
(all pubd in New York)
Notes on the Cultivation of Choral Music and the Oratorio Society of New York (1884)
Review of the New York Musical Season, 5 vols. (1886–90)
Studies in the Wagnerian Drama (1891)
The Philharmonic Society of New York: a Memorial published on the Occasion of the Fiftieth Anniversary of the Founding of the Philharmonic Society (1892)
How to Listen to Music (1897)
Music and Manners in the Classical Period (1898, 3/1899)
Chapters of Opera (1908, 3/1911)
A Book of Operas (1909)
The Pianoforte and its Music (1911)
Afro-American Folksongs (1914)
A Second Book of Operas (1917)
More Chapters of Opera (1919)
A. W. Thayer's *Life of Beethoven*, 3 vols. (1921) [revised, completed and published for the first time in English]

BIBLIOGRAPHY
R. Aldrich: 'Henry E. Krehbiel', *ML*, iv (1923), 266
   J. A. FULLER MAITLAND, RICHARD ALDRICH/R

Krehl, Stephan (*b* Leipzig, 5 July 1864; *d* Leipzig, 7 April 1924). German music theorist. He studied at the Leipzig and Dresden conservatories and in 1889 was appointed to teach the piano and music theory at the Karlsruhe Conservatory. From 1902 until his death he held the same post at the Leipzig Conservatory, becoming professor in 1910 and director in 1921 (in succession to H. Sitt). Krehl composed a cantata, *Tröstung*, numerous chamber and choral works and songs. As a composer he was an eclectic, chiefly following the style and technique of Brahms. As a theorist, however, he achieved a considerable reputation through textbooks on harmony, counterpoint and general music education.

WRITINGS
Musikalische Formenlehre (Leipzig, 1902–5, enlarged 2/1917–20) [many reprints]
Allgemeine Musiklehre (Leipzig, 1906, 3/1933 ed. R. Hernried)
Fuge, Erläuterung und Anleitung für Komposition derselben (Leipzig, 1908; Sp. trans., 1930, 2/1953)
Kontrapunkt (Leipzig, 1908; Sp. trans., 1930, 2/1953)
Theorie der Tonkunst und Kompositionslehre (Berlin and Leipzig, 1920–22)
Harmonielehre (Leipzig, 1921, 2/1928 [pt.i only]) [pt.i = pt.ii of *Theorie der Tonkunst und Kompositionslehre*]

BIBLIOGRAPHY
F. Reuter: *Stephan Krehl* (Leipzig, 1921)
K. Jeppesen: *Counterpoint: the Polyphonic Vocal Style of the Sixteenth Century* (New York, 1939, 2/1950), 50f
R. Schaal: 'Krehl, Stephan', *MGG* [with extensive list of works]
      ALFRED GRANT GOODMAN

Kreisler, Fritz (*b* Vienna, 2 Feb 1875; *d* New York, 29 Jan 1962). American violinist and composer of Austrian birth. He began to learn the violin at the age of four with his father, a doctor and enthusiastic amateur violinist. After lessons with Jacques Auber, he gained admission to the Vienna Conservatory at the age of seven – the youngest child ever to enter. For three years he studied the violin with Joseph Hellmesberger jr and theory with Bruckner. He gave his first performance there when he was nine and won the gold medal when he was ten – an unprecedented distinction. He then studied at the Paris Conservatoire under J. L. Massart, who had taught Wieniawski. Kreisler left the Conservatoire in 1887, sharing the *premier prix* with four other violinists, all some ten years older. From the age of 12 he had no further violin instruction.

In 1889–90 Kreisler toured the USA as assisting artist to Moriz Rosenthal, but with only moderate success. He returned to Vienna: two years at the Gymnasium and two as a pre-medical student were followed by military service. All this time, Kreisler barely touched the violin. However, once he decided on a musical career, he quickly regained his technique. In 1896 he applied to join the Vienna Opera Orchestra but failed, allegedly because of poor sightreading. Two years later he had the satisfaction of scoring a notable success with the Vienna Philharmonic, actually the same ensemble that had denied him a place. A year later, on 1 December 1899, his début with the Berlin Philharmonic under Nikisch marked the beginning of an international career. He reappeared in the USA during the 1900–01 season, then made his London début at a Philharmonic concert under Richter on 12 May 1902. In 1904 he was presented with the Philharmonic Society's gold medal. Elgar composed his Violin Concerto for Kreisler who gave its première on 10 November 1910 at Queen's Hall, with Elgar conducting.

At the outbreak of World War I Kreisler joined the Austrian Army. He was medically discharged after being wounded, and embarked for the USA (his wife's native country) in November 1914. However, anti-German feelings ran so high that he withdrew from the platform, reappearing in New York on 27 October 1919. From 1924 to 1934 he lived in Berlin. When Austria was annexed by the Nazis the French Government offered him citizenship. In 1939 he returned for good to the

USA, and became an American citizen in 1943. A traffic accident in 1941 impaired his hearing and eyesight; nevertheless, he resumed his career. He made his last Carnegie Hall appearance on 1 November 1947, though he broadcast during the 1949–50 season. After that, his interest in the violin waned; he sold his collection of instruments and kept only an 1860 Vuillaume.

Kreisler was unique. Without exertion (he practised little) he achieved a seemingly effortless perfection. There was never any conscious technical display. The elegance of his bowing, the grace and charm of his phrasing, the vitality and boldness of his rhythm, and above all his tone of indescribable sweetness and expressiveness were marvelled at. Though not very large, his tone had unequalled carrying power because his bow applied just enough pressure without suppressing the natural vibrations of the strings. The matchless colour was achieved by vibrato in the style of Wieniawski who (in Kreisler's words) 'intensified the vibrato and brought it to heights never before achieved, so that it became known as the "French vibrato"'. However, Kreisler applied vibrato not only on sustained notes but also in faster passages which lost all dryness under his magic touch. His methods of bowing and fingering were equally personal. In fact his individual style was, as Flesch said, ahead of his time, and may explain his comparatively slow rise to fame. Yet there is hardly a violinist in our century who has not acknowledged admiration of and indebtedness to Kreisler.

Kreisler was also a gifted composer. Among his original works are a string quartet, an operetta, *Apple Blossoms* (with Victor Jacobi, 1919), cadenzas to the Beethoven and Brahms concertos, and numerous short pieces (*Tambourin chinois, Caprice viennois* etc). He made many transcriptions and editions. In addition, he composed dozens of pieces in the 'olden style' which he ascribed to various 18th-century composers, such as Pugnani, Francoeur, Padre Martini, etc. When Kreisler admitted in 1935 that these pieces were a hoax, many critics (including Ernest Newman) were indignant while others accepted it as a joke. It is strange indeed that so many experts were misled by Kreisler's impersonations; at any rate, these charming pieces continue to enrich the violin repertory.

WRITINGS

Four Weeks in the Trenches (Boston and New York, 1915)

BIBLIOGRAPHY

L. P. Lochner: *Fritz Kreisler* (New York, 1950, 2/1951) [with discography and repr. of the controversy with Newman]
F. Bonavia: 'Fritz Kreisler', *MT*, ciii (1962), 179
J. Hartnack: *Grosse Geiger unserer Zeit* (Gütersloh, 1968)
J. Creighton: *Discopaedia of the Violin, 1889–1971* (Toronto, 1974)
I. Yampol'sky: *Frits Kreysler: zhizn' i tvorchestvo* (Moscow, 1975)

BORIS SCHWARZ

Fritz Kreisler in 1955

Krejčí, Iša (František) (*b* Prague, 10 July 1904; *d* Prague, 6 March 1968). Czech composer and conductor. He studied composition at the Prague Conservatory with Jirák and in Novák's master classes (1927–9). After conducting lessons with Talich, he joined the staff of the Bratislava Opera (1928–32). He was then manager of the music department of Czech radio (1934–45), chief conductor of the Olomouc Opera (1945–58) and finally artistic director of the Prague National Theatre. As a composer he had most success with his stage pieces, but his best work is in small forms. The Sonatina concertante for cello and piano, the *Kasace* ('Cassation') for winds and the Trio for clarinet, double bass and piano are highly polished pieces, demonstrating Krejčí's gift for enchanting lyricism and wit. He was the leading Czech neo-classicist during the period 1930–50, as the quartets show.

WORKS
(selective list)

Stage: Malý balet [Little ballet], 1927; Antigona (opera, 1, after Sophocles), 1933–4, rev. 1963; Pozdvižení v Efesu [Revolt in Ephesus] (opera, after Shakespeare), 1943

Orch: 4 syms.; 20 variací, 1946–7; Serenade, 1949; 14 variací na píseň 'Dobru noc' [14 variations on the song 'Goodnight'], 1951

Chamber: Kasace [Cassation], fl, cl, bn, tpt, 1925; Va Sonata, 1928–9; Cl Sonata, 1929–30; Str Qt no.1, D, 1928; Trio, ob, cl, bn, 1935; Trio, cl, db, pf, 1936; Nonet, 1937; Sonatina concertante, vc, pf, 1939; Str Qt no.2, d, 1953; Str Qt no.3, 1960

Pf pieces, songs, choral works

Principal publisher: Ceský Hudebný Fond

BIBLIOGRAPHY

J. Kasan: *Novoklasicismus v díle I. Krejča* (diss., Prague Conservatory, 1956)

BRIAN LARGE

Krejčí, Miroslav (*b* Rychnov nad Kněžnou, east Bohemia, 4 Nov 1891; *d* Prague, 29 Dec 1964). Czech composer and teacher. He came from a family of strong musical traditions and learnt the piano, the organ and theory at home. From 1910 to 1914 he studied natural history, geography and music at Prague University, also taking private composition lessons with Novák (1911–13). He taught at general secondary schools in Prague and Litoměřice (1915–53), and also taught composition at the Prague Conservatory (1943–53). In 1946 he became a member of the Czech Academy of Sciences and Art.

Krejčí composed several hundred pieces, most of which remain unpublished, in almost all genres. His style is derived from Novák's and, in his mature compositions, is notable for a fully developed polyphonic technique within a tonal harmonic framework. Eschewing the developments of the interwar avant garde, Krejčí maintained a measured, basically lyrical expressive quality, which eventually took the form of a kind of Novák–Foerster synthesis. The effect is tasteful, if unenterprising. Krejčí also wrote educational music and made arrangements of medieval and early Czech music.

WORKS
(selective list)

STAGE AND ORCHESTRAL

Operas: Léto [Summer], op.41 (after F. Šrámek), 1937, Prague, National, 4 Dec 1940; Poslední hejtman [The last hetman], op.62 (E. Klenová, after A. Jirásek: Brotherhood), 1944, Prague, National, 18 March 1948

Orch: Sym. no.1, g, op.70, 1944; Va Conc., op.72, 1947; Cl Conc., op.76, 1949; Conc. capriccio, op.83, va, wind, timp, 1950; Sym. no.2, D, op.90, 1952–4; Sym. no.3 'Pax hominibus', A, op.110, 1956–7

VOCAL

Cantatas: Českému lidu [To the Czech people], op.44 (J. Hořejš), 1939; Rodné zemi [To my homeland], op.114, 1958; Mír [Peace], op.118, 1959

Choral: Helladě [To Hellada], op.8a (J. S. Machar), female vv, 1919; Caniculae polyfonicae, op.29, 55 nos., 1928–30; Ukolébavky dvojitým kánonem [Lullabies with double canon], op.35a, children's vv, 1932–3; V okovech [In shackles], op.69a (J. Týml), male vv, 1941

Songs: Mé milé [To my love], op.14 (J. Hora), 1925; Písně o dětátku [Songs about a child], op.28a, 1v, fl, pf, 1927–9; 3 Songs, op.67a (Šrámek), 1944–5

CHAMBER AND INSTRUMENTAL

For 5–10 insts: Nonet, F, op.48, 1939–40; Octet, C, op.52, 1942; Septet, G, op.68, 1945; Pf Qnt, e, op.73, 1947–8; Wind Sextet, op.79, 1949; Decet, op.94, 1952; Wind Octet, op.108, 1956

For 3–4 insts: Str Qt no.2, G, op.7, 1918; Str Qt no.4, E, op.50, 1941;

Str Trio, a, op.58, 1942; Qt, ob, cl, tuba, pf, op.101, 1955; Str Qt no.7, C, op.106, 1955

For 1–2 insts: 3 skizzy, op.25a, cl, 1942; 2 sonatas, d, A, op.59, vc, 1943; Str Duos, op.64, va, vc, 1944, vn, va, 1945, 2 va, 1950; Črty [Sketches], op.77, harp, 1948–9

Pf: Suite, D, op.55, 1942; Variations on a Theme by Novák, op.93, 1952

Org: 3 Pieces, op.9, 1926; Chorale ovs. on early Czech sacred songs, op.71, 1946–7

Principal publishers: Barvič & Novotný (Brno), Česká Hudba, Hudební Matice, Melantrich, Melpa, Školské Nakladatelství, Státní Nakladatelství Krásné Literatury Huďby a Umění

BIBLIOGRAPHY

F. Zrno: 'Miroslav Krejčí', *Česká hudba*, xxxvii (1933–5), 62

České umění dramatické [Czech dramatic art], ii (Prague, 1941), 355ff

J. T[omášek]: 'Miroslav Krejčí', *Národni divadlo*, xviii/5 (1941–2), 6

'Miroslav Krejčí: profil se soupisem skladeb' [Krejčí: profile with list of works], *Rytmus*, viii (1942–3), 95

J. Plavec: 'Dva profily soudobých českých skladatelů: Miroslav Krejčí a Václav Kálik', *Věstník pěvecký a hudební*, li (1947), 56

B. Štědroň: 'Česká hudba za nesvobody' [Czech music during the occupation], *Musikologie*, ii (1949)

J. Plavec: 'Šedesát let Miroslava Krejčího', *HRo*, iv (1951–2), 78

J. Volek: 'Jubileum Miroslava Krejčího', *HRo*, xiv (1961), 821

OLDŘICH PUKL

Krek, Uroš (*b* Ljubljana, 21 May 1922). Yugoslav composer. He studied composition with Škerjanc at the Ljubljana Academy of Music, graduating in 1947. From 1950 to 1958 he was producer of orchestral music and director of the music programme for Ljubljana radio. He undertook research in the Ljubljana Ethnomusicological Institute (1958–67) and then took an appointment as composition teacher at the Ljubljana Academy. Krek's works are mostly in a neo-classical style, employing elements of Slovene peasant music and 12-note techniques.

WORKS
(selective list)

Sonata, vn, pf, 1946; Vn Conc., 1949; Sinfonietta, 1952; Conc., bn, chamber orch, 1954; Mouvements concertants, 1955; Hn Conc., 1960; Inventiones ferales, vn, orch, 1962; 5 Songs, pf, 1963; Pic Concertino, 1967; Staroegiptovske strofe [Ancient Egyptian verses], S/T, orch, 1967; Thème varié, trbn, pf, 1968; Episodi concertanti, wind qnt, 1970; Sonata, 2 vn, 1971; Musica per archi, 1973

Principal publisher: Edicije DSS

ANDREJ RIJAVEC

Krellmann, Hanspeter (*b* Würzburg, 11 Jan 1935). German writer on music. He studied the piano as principal subject (under Max Martin Stein) at the Düsseldorf Conservatory (1955–8; state music teachers' examination 1958). He then attended Cologne University, where he studied musicology with Fellerer, theatre studies with Rolf Badenhausen, and ancient history (1958–62). He took his doctorate at Cologne in 1966 with a dissertation on Busoni. He began writing music criticism in 1957 and has held posts as a newspaper editor in Essen (1956–6) and as business manager of a private cultural society in Düsseldorf (1966–70). From 1970 he worked in Düsseldorf as a freelance critic and writer on music. In addition to general studies of the avant garde his writings include essays on Baur, Cage, Kagel, Kelemen and Schönbach as well as Rakhmaninov and Sibelius. He has also published an Urtext edition of Brahms's chamber works (opp.25, 26, 34 and 60).

WRITINGS

Studien zu den Bearbeitungen Ferruccio Busonis (diss., U. of Cologne, 1966; Regensburg, 1966)

Ich war nie Avantgardist: Gespräche mit dem Komponisten Jürg Baur (Wiesbaden, 1968)

'Plädoyer für kurze Musik oder: Gestaltete Verwirrung: Portrait des Komponisten Milko Kelemen', *Musica*, xxiii (1969), 555

'Die verschmolzenen Melodien: zur Musik Dieter Schönbachs', *Musica*, xxiv (1970), 549

'Stockhausen's Plea for Intuition: an Interview', *World Music*, xii/2 (1970), 6
Die Avantgarde der Gegenwart (Bielefeld, 1971)
Durch mathematische Formeln zu kompositorischer Freiheit: Werkstattgespräch mit Iannis Xenakis (Bonn, 1971)
Die Symphonie, ihre Hörer und Interpreten (Hamburg, 1972)
Anton Webern in Selbstzeugnisse und Bilddokumenten (Reinbeck bei Hamburg, 1975)
Articles in *MGG* and *Grove 6*

WILFRIED BRENNECKE

Kremastē. Sign used in pairs in Greek EKPHONETIC NOTATION.

Kremberg [Krembergh], **Jakob** [James] (*b* Warsaw, *c*1650; *d* ?London, ?*c*1718). German composer, instrumentalist and poet of Polish birth, later resident in England. He was registered at the University of Leipzig in 1672. Five years later he became chamber musician at Halle to the Duke-Administrator of Magdeburg. From 1678 he spent several years as a member of the royal music at Stockholm. During the 1680s he returned to Germany; in 1691 he was a chamber and court musician in the service of the Elector of Saxony at Dresden. Between 1693 and 1695 he was associated with Kusser at the Hamburg Opera.

It is likely that Kremberg then went to Italy, for the next indication of his movements comes from the announcement in the London *Post Boy* that, 'lately come out of Italy', he would be giving 'a New Consort of Musick by very great Masters, of all sorts of Instruments, with fine Singing' on 24 November 1697. These concerts were to be a weekly event and were among the earliest given at Hickford's Dancing School, which became one of the most important London concert rooms in the 18th century. By 1706 Kremberg was 'one of the Gentlemen of Her Majestys Musick', according to the title-page of *A Collection of Easy and Familiar Aires*, published in that year. According to Chamberlayne he was a member of the royal band of '24 violins' in 1708, but for how long he held the appointment is not clear. His name disappears from Chamberlayne in the 1716 edition, although it is not dropped from Miege until after the 1718 edition. It seems likely that he died in London about this time, as no further record of his activities has survived.

The *Musicalische Gemüths-Ergötzung* is a volume of some importance in the history of German song. It includes 40 secular songs with continuo, 16 of them settings of verses by Kremberg himself. In style the collection shows Italian and French influences, as its title-page indicates, and it is also important for the instructions it contains on ornamentation and performance on bowed and plucked string instruments.

WORKS

Musicalische Gemüths-Ergötzung, 1v, bc/4 insts (Dresden, 1689); 3 ed. in Friedlaender, 1 ed. in Wolf
A Collection of Easy and Familiar Aires, 2 fl; overture, passacaille, 3 fl (London, 1706)
England's Glory: Masque for Queen Anne's birthday, 1706, lost
The Entertainment, *GB-Lcm* [overture to Act III, Bachusses Revells, only]
3 songs: Aurelia has sweet pleasing charms, 1v, vn/ob, hpd/bn; Lavinia has majestic charms, 1v, bc; Since I have seen, 1v/fl, hpd: *Och*
Concerto à tre violini senza basso continuo, *S-Uu*
Several pieces, lute, in Codex Milléran, *F-Pn*
Venus, oder Die siegende Liebe, opera, libretto, lost

BIBLIOGRAPHY

E. Chamberlayne: *The Present State of England* (London, 22/1708, 23/1710)
G. Miege: *The Present State of Great Britain* (London, 2/1711, 3/1716, 4/1718)
M. Fürstenau: *Zur Geschichte der Musik und des Theaters am Hofe zu Dresden*, i (Dresden, 1861/*R*1971), 309
W. Tappert: 'Zur Geschichte der Guitarre', *MMg*, xiv (1882), 80
M. Friedlaender: *Das deutsche Lied im 18. Jahrhundert* (Stuttgart, 1902), i, 63
J. Wolf: *Handbuch der Notationskunde*, ii (Leipzig, 1919), 128, 153, 159, 171
W. Boetticher: *Studien zur solistischen Lautenpraxis des 16. und 17. Jahrhunderts* (Berlin, 1943), 372
M. Tilmouth: 'A Calendar of References to Music in Newspapers Published in London and the Provinces (1660–1719)', *RMARC*, i (1961/*R*1968), 21

MICHAEL TILMOUTH

Kremenliev, Boris (*b* Razlog, 23 May 1911). American composer and ethnomusicologist of Bulgarian birth. He went to the USA in 1929 and studied at De Paul University, Chicago (BM 1936, MM 1938), under Hanson at the Eastman School (PhD 1942) and with Harris (composition) and Altschuler (conducting). During World War II he was music director of the South German network; later he was appointed professor of composition at the University of California at Los Angeles. He experimented with electronics and other new means, but then returned to a simpler style, colourful, rhythmically intense, terse and texturally unconventional; a shared cultural background led to some similarity with the music of Bartók. Kremenliev has received grants from the American Philosophical Society (1955), the Ford Foundation (1962) and the Creative Arts Institute (1966–7), and an annual award from ASCAP from 1967.

WORKS
(*selective list*)

Orch: Bulgarian Rhapsody, 1952; Facing West from California's Shores, sym. band, 1954; Balkan Rhapsody, 1965
Chamber: Str Qt no.2, 1966; Sonata, db, pf, 1972
Film score: Crucifixion, on paintings of Rico Lebrun, 1952

Principal publishers: Bruzzichelli, Foster, Leeds, Clayton Summy

WRITINGS

Bulgarian-Macedonian Folk Music (Berkeley and Los Angeles, 1952)
'Some Social Aspects of Bulgarian Folksongs', *Slavic Folklore*, vi (1956), 112
'Types of Bulgarian Folk Songs', *Slavonic and East European Review*, xxxiv (1956), 335–76
'Some Observations on Stress in Balkan Music', *Studies in Ethnomusicology*, ii (1965), 75
'Extension and its Effect in Bulgarian Folk Song', *Selected Reports*, i (1966), 1
'The Influence of Folklore on the Modern Czech School of Composition', *Czechoslovakia Past and Present*, ii (The Hague, 1970), 1319

BIBLIOGRAPHY

'Kompositorut Boris Kremenliev', *Slaviani*, xxv/2 (1969), 32
'Professor Boris Kremenliev', *Slaviani*, xxix/3 (1973), 28

W. THOMAS MARROCCO

Kremlyov, Yuly Anatol'yevich (*b* Essentuki, North Caucasus, 19 June 1908; *d* Leningrad, 19 Feb 1971). Soviet musicologist. From 1925 he studied piano at the Leningrad Conservatory, but was compelled by a serious illness to abandon the course in 1928. He took up his musical studies again in 1929, graduated as an external student in 1933, and in the same year became a member of the Union of Soviet Composers. At about this time he began to write a series of short monographs on Russian and Western composers, including Borodin (1934), Liszt (1935), Mozart (1935), Bizet (1935) and Meyerbeer (1936), all published in Leningrad. From the late 1950s Kremlyov held positions on the editorial staff of *Sovetskaya muzïka* and the executive committee of the Soviet Composers' Union, and from 1957 was head of the music section at the Leningrad Institute of the Theatre, Music and Cinematography, which he had joined in 1937. He also produced a series of more extensive monographs on Chopin (1949, 3/1971),

Grieg (1958), Solov'yov-Sedoy (1960), Debussy (1965), Massenet (1969) and Saint-Saëns (1970), all published in Moscow. He expressed his own views in many of his writings. He was particularly concerned with the importance of ideological contents in music, the decay of western culture in the 20th century and the struggle against modernism. He was granted his *Kandidat* degree in 1944, and his doctorate in 1963. Kremlyov composed a number of chamber works, including 14 piano sonatas.

WRITINGS

Leningradskaya Gosudarstvennaya Konservatoriya 1862–1937 [Leningrad State Conservatory] (Leningrad, 1938)

Tret'ya simfoniya A. N. Skryabina [Skryabin's Third Symphony] (Leningrad, 1941)

Fortepiannïye sonatï Betkhovena (Moscow, 1953, 2/1970)

Voprosï muzïkal'noy estetiki [Problems of musical aesthetics] (Moscow, 1953)

Russkaya mïsl' o muzïke [Russian thought on music] (Leningrad, 1954–60)

Simfonii P. I. Chaykovskovo (Moscow, 1955)

Ocherki po voprosam muzïkal'noy estetiki [Essays on the problems of musical aesthetics] (Moscow, 1957)

Esteticheskiye problemï sovetskoy muzïki [Aesthetic problems of Soviet music] (Leningrad, 1959)

Estetika prirodï v tvorchestve N. A. Rimskovo-Korsakova [The aesthetics of nature in the work of Rimsky-Korsakov] (Moscow, 1962)

'Les tendences réalistes dans l'esthétique de Debussy', *Debussy et l'évolution de la musique au XX e siècle: CNRS Paris 1962*, 189

'L'influence de Debussy: Russie', ibid, 315

Vïrazitel'nost' i izobrazitel'nost' muzïki [Expressiveness and descriptiveness of music] (Leningrad, 1962)

Poznavatel'naya rol' muzïki [The cognitive function of music] (Moscow, 1963)

Chto takoye muzïkal'naya tema [What a musical theme is] (Leningrad, 1964)

ed.: *Voprosï teorii i estetiki muzïki* [Questions of the theory and aesthetics of music] (Leningrad and Moscow, 1965) [incl. 'O ponyatiyakh formalizma i sotsialisticheskovo realizma' [On the concepts of formalism and socialist realism], iv, 29]

Esteticheskiye vzglyadï Prokof'yeva [Aesthetic views of Prokofiev] (Moscow and Leningrad, 1966)

O meste muzïki sredi iskusstv [On the place of music among the arts] (Moscow, 1966)

Natsional'nïye chertï russkoy muzïki [National features of Russian music] (Leningrad, 1968)

Proshloye i budushcheye romantizma [Past and future of Romanticism] (Moscow, 1968)

Izbrannïye stat'i i vistupleniya [Collected articles and speeches] (Leningrad, 1969) [incl. list of musicological writings]

'Ucheniye Lenina o materialisticheskoy dialektike i nekotorïye voprosï muzïkal'noy nauki' [Lenin's teaching about materialist dialectics and some questions of musicology], *Ucheniye Lenina i voprosï muzïkoznaniya* [Lenin's teaching and questions of musical knowledge] (Moscow, 1969), 77–109

'O burzhuaznoy ideologii v muzïke' [On bourgeois ideology in music], *Lenin i muzïkal'naya kul'tura* [Lenin and musical culture] (Moscow, 1970), 190

O roli razuma v vospriyatii proizvedeniya iskusstva [On the role of reason in perception of a work of art] (Moscow, 1970)

Ocherki tvorchestva i estetiki novoy venskoy shkolï [Essays on the work and aesthetics of the New Viennese School] (Leningrad, 1970)

Yosef Gaydn [Haydn] (Moscow, 1972)

Kremsier (Ger.). KROMĚŘÍŽ.

Kremsmünster. Benedictine abbey in Upper Austria. It was founded in 777 by Duke Tassilo of Bavaria to provide a Christian mission and to protect the area from the neighbouring Slavs and Hungarians. Gregorian chant was sung according to the Beneventan rite, which, along with the educational system, was modified according to the rules of Benedikt von Aniane of Aachen in 828. From that time there has been an inner and an outer school: the latter was enlarged in 1549 into an Öffentliches Gymnasium. The abbey library, the Regenterei, has a rich collection of manuscripts, one of the most important in Europe. The Millenarius Minor Manuscript, a collection of gospels dating from the end of the 9th century, contains one of the earliest examples of neumatic notation; a number of manuscripts containing sequences and tropes give evidence of musical practice from the 11th to 14th centuries. Polyphonic music found acceptance under the abbot Friedrich von Aich (abbot from 1274–1325) but contemporary manuscripts have not survived. The first organ was built before 1490; a splendid new organ was built in the abbey church by Gregor Ennser in 1515, replaced in 1623 by a more Italianate instrument. The Netherlanders (Lassus, Hassler, Regnart) were replaced by Italians who also influenced the Baroque renovation of the abbey. Alessandro Tadei (c1585–1667) became Kapellmeister in 1630; he was overshadowed by his successor Benedikt Lechler (1594–1657), who compiled four partbooks (with some of his own compositions) which give some insight into contemporary musical practices in the monastery. Under Lechler a glorious period of theatre activity began at the Stiftstheater and lasted until 1803; in 1804 the theatre was destroyed and a student hostel erected on its site. Franz Sparry (1715–1767), who became *regens chori* in 1747, had completed his musical training in Naples; his celebrated successor, Georg Pasterwiz, composed over 500 works. When the existence of the Ritterakademie, where Pasterwiz was a professor, and of the monastery itself was threatened in 1785, Pasterwiz travelled as the monastery representative to Vienna, where Haydn, Salieri and Albrechtsberger were among his friends.

A series of oratorio performances began with Haydn's *The Creation* (1800) and *The Seasons* (1802); the last of these took place in 1914 with Rheinberger's *Christophorus*. A new organ with 61 stops was built by Ludwig Mooser in 1854; it has been restored several times.

BIBLIOGRAPHY

T. Hagn: *Das Wirken der Benediktiner-Abtei Kremsmünster für Wissenschaft, Kunst und Jugendbildung* (Linz, 1848)

G. Huemer: *Pflege der Musik im Stifte Kremsmünster* (Wels, 1877)

W. Neumüller and K. Holter: *Die mittelalterlichen Bibliotheksverzeichnisse des Stiftes Kremsmünster* (Linz, 1950)

A. Kellner: *Musikgeschichte des Stiftes Kremsmünster* (Kassel, 1956)

ALTMAN KELLNER

Krenek [Křenek], Ernst (*b* Vienna, 23 Aug 1900). American composer of Austrian birth. He grew up in imperial Vienna, and in his formative years was deeply touched by its particular spirit and by its Roman Catholicism. He became appalled at the dehumanizing effects of mass production, commercialization and the vulgarizing of politics and society after 1914, and at the gap between material accomplishments and spiritual standards. At the age of 16 he began studies with Schreker, who stressed individuality and freedom from obvious popular elements. When Schreker was appointed director of the Academy of Music in Berlin, Krenek joined him and entered the circle of Busoni, Erdmann, Scherchen and others. Krenek's highly individual dissonant works date from this period, which also witnessed his gradual break with the ideals and stylistic limitations of his teacher. The comic opera *Der Sprung über den Schatten*, to his own text, integrated jazz elements into an atonal structure and foreshadowed the spectacular *Jonny spielt auf*.

During the 1920s Krenek wrote a large amount of music, some, such as the First String Quartet and the First Symphony, showing the influence of Bartók. At Christmas 1923 he began a two-year visit to Switzerland, after which he travelled to Paris. There he was fascinated by the happy equilibrium, elegance and clarity he perceived in French music, and he decided his music should be more useful and entertaining. He was also touched by Stravinsky's neo-classicism. Under this influence he composed the Second Concerto Grosso, the Concertino for flute, violin, harpsichord and strings, and many shorter works. Between 1925 and 1927 he gained valuable experience in the opera houses of Kassel and Wiesbaden as conductor and composer of incidental music, and as assistant to the director, Bekker. While at Kassel he wrote the text and music for *Jonny spielt auf*, which was first performed in Leipzig to a scandalized but enthusiastic audience. Musically, he said, he 'returned to the tonal idiom, to the cantilena of Puccini, seasoning the whole with the condiments of jazz'. The work had a huge success and was performed in over 100 cities; its text was translated into 18 languages. The financial security that *Jonny* brought him enabled him to move to Vienna.

At this time, after the dissolution of his first marriage to Anna, a daughter of Mahler, he married the prominent actress Berta Herrmann. Following the success of *Jonny* he plunged into stylistically similar operatic projects. Three one-act operas were quickly composed: *Der Diktator*, on Mussolini; a milder fairy tale, *Das geheime Königreich*; and a satire on the hero-worship of sports champions, *Schwergewicht, oder Die Ehre der Nation*. The last in this vein was the 'grand opera' *Leben des Orest*. While living in Vienna he gradually succumbed to its charm and aura, and turned to a style of Austrian romanticism. In a period of 20 days he wrote as many songs for the *Reisebuch aus den oesterreichischen Alpen* in the style of Schubert's *Winterreise*. Although he had criticized Schoenberg and the 12-note technique in a public lecture and hence alienated himself from that circle, he now came into close contact with both Berg and Webern, and he became increasingly interested in their musical credo. He grew dissatisfied with his self-imposed romantic style; he was also disappointed at the failure to perform a new opera because of the political climate in Austria and Germany.

In 1930 he met Kraus, who, in his own words, 'exercised the strongest influence' on him. He set a group of his poems, using for the first time the 12 different pitch classes within motifs, though retaining a basic tonal vocabulary. A second cycle on his own texts, *Gesänge des späten Jahres*, followed in a similar vein, but coloured by the pessimism produced by the spread of Nazism. During this period of depression Krenek was invited to write an opera for the Vienna Staatsoper, and he chose as his subject the Emperor Charles V. In the text he extolled the universalism of the Catholic empire, as opposed to the disintegrating forces he saw about him. He became a devout Catholic. As he conceived the music for *Karl V*, he decided to use the 12-note technique and immersed himself in a deep study of the scores of Schoenberg, Berg and Webern. Because of the implied political nature of the work, the Vienna rehearsals in 1934 were stopped, and the monumental work was first staged on 22 June 1938 in Prague. By then Krenek was labelled in Germany as a 'Kulturbolschewist'.

He first visited the USA in 1937 with the Salzburg Opera Guild, for which he had adapted and orchestrated *L'incoronazione di Poppea*. In the following year, as Hitler invaded Vienna, Krenek emigrated to the USA. A new phase of his life began as a teacher. He taught in Boston, and in 1939 became a teacher of composition at Vassar College. In 1942 he was appointed head of the music department in the school of fine arts at Hamline University, St Paul, Minnesota, later becoming its dean. He took American citizenship in 1945, and in 1947 moved to Los Angeles, settling in the outlying Tujunga Canyon. In 1950 he married the composer Gladys Nordenstrom; they moved to Palm Springs, California, in 1966. He has taught composition or lectured at various institutions, including the Chicago Musical College, the universities of Michigan, Wisconsin and New Mexico, and Dartmouth College. During the first part of his American period he composed prolifically, principally in strict 12-note serialism, except in the motets and the Third Piano Concerto. Significant works of the time include chamber operas and the Fourth and Fifth Symphonies (1947–9). In 1950, answering requests from many performers, he began a sequence of concertante pieces.

After resuming contacts with Europe in 1950, Krenek again wrote a full-length opera with pronounced political implications, *Pallas Athene weint* (1955). The subject matter is from Greek history: the downfall of the Athenian democracy at the end of the Peloponnesian war. At that time Krenek developed advanced serial techniques, such as were forecast in the Variations (1937), the Sixth Quartet (1937) and the *Lamentatio Jeremiae prophetae* (1941); the major work of this type was *Quaestio temporis* for chamber orchestra (1959). Serialism made him aware, on the one hand, of the dialectic of predetermination and chance, which he treated seriously in the *Sestina* for voice and ten players (1957) and humorously in the TV opera *Ausgerechnet und verspielt* (1961), and, on the other, of the mysterious significance of time. This is reflected in the operas *Der goldene Bock* (1963) – a fantastic treatment of the legend of the Argonauts, involving elements of surrealism and the absurd – and *Der Zauberspiegel* (1966),

Ernst Krenek

a play shifting from 13th-century China to the present, using ideas from science fiction. In these works, as in *Sardakai* (1969), ironic elements are increasingly noticeable, indicating a sceptical attitude to opera itself. In several orchestral works of the 1960s (e.g. *Horizon Circled* and *Perspectives*) serial techniques are used selectively, leaving some parameters open to free manipulation; in other pieces (e.g. *From Three Make Seven* and *Fibonacci Mobile*) the performers are offered various possibilities for combining fully composed materials. During the same period Krenek took an interest in electronic music, usually in combination with voices and/or conventional instruments. From 1950 he returned annually to Europe to conduct his operas and orchestral works, and to produce his short television operas. He received the Great Silver Cross of Austria and the Gold Medal of Vienna in 1960.

Krenek has been one of the most prolific composers of his generation. As a writer he has contributed valuable books and essays, as well as the texts for his operas, where he has used all manner of stage devices to great effect. In scope and style his music embraces almost all of the major trends from romantic tonality to atonality, neo-classicism, dodecaphony, serialism, jazz, aleatoricism and electronics; in whatever style, he has honed his technique to a point of virtuosity. It is Krenek's belief that the diverse aesthetic approaches displayed in his work are all deeply rooted in his personality.

For a scene from *Jonny spielt auf*, see GERMANY, fig.8; for one from *Der Sprung über den Schatten*, see OPERA, fig.46.

WORKS
OPERAS

Zwingburg, op.14 (scenic cantata, 1, Werfel), 1922; Berlin, Staatsoper, 21 Oct 1924
Der Sprung über den Schatten, op.17 (comic opera, 3, Krenek), 1923; Frankfurt, 9 June 1924
Orpheus und Eurydike, op.21 (3, Kokoschka), 1923; Kassel, 27 Nov 1926
Bluff, op.36 (musical comedy, Gribble, Levetzow), 1924–5, sketch
Jonny spielt auf, op.45 (2 parts, Krenek), 1925–6; Leipzig, 10 Feb 1927
Der Diktator, op.49 (tragic opera, 1, Krenek), 1926; Wiesbaden, 6 May 1928
Das geheime Königreich, op.50 (fairytale opera, 1, Krenek), 1926–7; Wiesbaden, 6 May 1928
Schwergewicht, oder Die Ehre der Nation (burlesque operetta, 1, Krenek), 1926–7; Wiesbaden, 6 May 1928
Leben des Orest, op.60 (grand opera, 5, Krenek), 1928–9; Leipzig, 19 Jan 1930
?, op.66, 1930, withdrawn
Karl V, op.73 (play with music, 2 parts, Krenek), 1930–33; Prague, Deutsches Theater, 22 June 1938
Cefalo e Procri, op.77 (R. Küfferle), 1933–4; Venice, 1934
Tarquin, op.90 (drama with music, E. Lavery), 1940; Cologne, 1950
What Price Confidence?, op.111 (comic chamber opera, 1, Krenek), 1945–6; Saarbrücken, 1960
Dark Waters (Krenek), 1950; Los Angeles, 1950
Pallas Athene weint (prelude, 3, Krenek), 1952–5; Hamburg, 1955
The Bell Tower (1, Krenek, after Melville), 1955–6; Urbana, Ill., 1957
Ausgerechnet und verspielt (television opera, 1, Krenek), 1961; Vienna, 1962
Der goldene Bock, op.186 (4, Krenek), 1963; Hamburg, 1964
Der Zauberspiegel (television opera, 1, Krenek), 1966; Munich, 1966
Sardakai (2 parts, Krenek), 1967–9; Hamburg, 1970

OTHER STAGE WORKS

Ballets: Mammon, op.37, 1925; Der vertauschte Cupido, op.38 [after Rameau], 1925; Eight Column Line, op.85, 1939
Incidental scores: Vom lieben Augustin, op.40 (Dietzenschmidt), 1925; Die Rache des verhöhnten Liebhabers, op.41 (Toller), 1925; Das Gotteskind, op.42, radio, 1925; La vida es sueño (Calderón), Kassel, 1925, ?destroyed; Der Triumph der Empfindsamkeit, op.43 (Goethe), 1926; A Midsummer Night's Dream, op.46 (Shakespeare), 1926; Marlborough s'en va-t-en guerre, op.52 (Achard), 1927

CHORAL

3 Pieces, op.22 (Claudius), 1923
4 Small Pieces, op.32 (Hölderlin), A, male vv, 1924
Die Jahreszeiten, op.35 (Hölderlin), 1925
4 Pieces, op.47 (Goethe), 1926

3 Pieces, op.61 (Keller), 1929
Kantate von der Vergänglichkeit des Irdischen, op.72 (Flemming, Gryphius, other 17th-century Ger.), S, mixed vv, pf, 1932
Jagd im Winter, op.74 (Grillparzer), male vv, 1933
16 folksong arrs. for Jugendliederbuch (Berlin, n.d.)
2 Pieces, op.87 (Drummond, Raleigh), female vv, 1939
Proprium missae in festo SS Innocentium, op.89, female vv, 1940
Lamentatio Jeremiae prophetae, op.93, 1941–2
Cantata for Wartime, op.95 (Melville), female vv, orch, 1943
5 Prayers (Donne), female vv, 1944
The Santa Fe Timetable, 1945
Aegrotate Ezechias, motet, female vv, pf, 1945
In paradisum, motet, male vv, 1946
O would I were, canon, 1946
4 Choruses, mixed vv, org, 1953
Proprium missae in domenica III in quadragesima, 3vv, 1954
Veni Sanctificator, motet, 3vv, 1954
Psalm Verse, 2–4vv, 1955
Ich singe wieder (von der Vogelweide), mixed vv, str, 1955–6
Guten Morgen, Amerika (Sandburg), 1956
Missa duodecim tonorum, mixed vv, org, 1957–8
6 Motetten (Kafka), 4vv, 1959
3 Madrigals, 3 Motets, children's vv, 1960
Canon [for Stravinsky's 80th birthday], 2vv, 1962
O Holy Ghost (Donne), 1964
Glauben und wissen, mixed vv, orch, 1966
Proprium missae Trinitatis, S, mixed vv, insts, 1966–7
Proprium missae for St Mary's Nativity (Catalan), 1v, mixed vv, insts, 1968
Deutsche Messe, mixed vv, insts, 1968
Messe 'Gib uns dem Frieden', solo vv, mixed vv, insts, 1970
3 Lessons, 1971
Feierstag-Kantate, Mez, Bar, speaker, chorus, orch, 1974–5

ORCHESTRAL

Sym. no.1, op.7, 1921; Conc. grosso no.1, op.10, 6 insts, str, 1921; Sym. no.2, op.12, 1922; Sym. no.3, op.16, 1922; Pf Conc. no.1, F♯, op.18, 1923; Conc. grosso no.2, op.25, 1923; Concertino, op.27, fl, vn, hpd/pf, str, 1924; Vn Conc. no.1, op.29, 1924; 7 Pieces, op.31, 1924; Symphonie pour instruments à vent et batterie, op.34, 1924–5; 3 Marches, op.44, wind, 1926; Intrada, op.51a, wind, 1927; Potpourri, op. 54, 1927; Little Sym., op.58, 1928; Theme and 13 Variations, op.69, 1931; Adagio and Fugue, op.78a, str, 1936
Campo Marzio, op.80, ov., 1937; Pf Conc. no.2, op.81, 1937; Sym. Piece, op.86, str, 1939; Little Conc., op.88, pf, org, chamber orch, 1939–40; I Wonder as I Wander, op.94 [variations on North Carolina folksong], 1942; Tricks and Trifles [arr. Hurricane Variations, pf], 1945; Pf Conc. no.3, 1946; Sym. Elegy, str, 1946; Sym. no.4, 1947; Sym. no.5, 1949; Pf Conc. no.4, 1950; Conc., vn, pf, small orch, 1950; 2 Pf Conc., 1951; Conc., harp, small orch, 1951; Brazilian Sinfonietta, str, 1952
Scenes from the West, school orch, 1952–3; Vc Conc., 1953; 11 Transparencies, 1954; Sym. 'Pallas Athene', 1954; Vn Conc. no.2, 1954; Suite, fl, str, 1954; Capriccio, vc, small orch, 1955; 7 Easy Pieces, str, 1955; Suite, cl, str, 1955; Kette, Kreis und Spiegel, 1956–7; Hexaedron, chamber orch, 1958; Quaestio temporis, small orch, 1958–9; From 3 Make 7, 1960–61; Exercises of a Late Hour, small orch, tape, 1967; Horizon Circled, 1967; Perspectives, 1967; 6 Profiles, 1968; Fivefold Enfoldment, 1969; Kitharaulos, ob, harp, small orch, 1971–2; Statisch und ekstatisch, 1972; Von Vorn Herein, small orch, pf, cel, 1974; Dream Sequence, wind band, 1975; The Dissembler, 1978; Conc, org, str, 1979

VOCAL

Wechsellied zum Tanz, op.43a [from Der Triumph der Empfindsamkeit] (Goethe), 1v, orch, 1926; 5 lieder, op.53 (17th-century Ger.), 1v, orch, 1927; Stellas Monolog, op.57 (concert aria, Goethe), 1928; Durch die Nacht, op.67a (song cycle, Kraus), 1v, orch, 1930–31; Die Nachtigall, op.68 (concert aria, Kraus), 1931; Während der Trennung, op.76 (Flemming), 2 solo vv, pf, 1933; La corona, op.91 (Donne: 7 sonnets), Mez, org, perc, 1941; The Holy Ghost's Ark, op.91a (Donne), Mez, 4 insts, 1941; Etude, coloratura S, A, 1945
Medea (dramatic monologue, R. Jeffers, after Euripides), S, orch, 1951; Spiritus intelligentiae, sanctus, 2 solo vv, tape, 1955; Sestina, S, 10 insts, 1957; Nach wie vor der Reihe nach, 2 speakers, orch, 1962; Quintina, S, 6 insts, tape, 1965; 2 Zeitlieder (Pandula), 1v, str qt, 1972
Songs for 1v, pf: Lieder, op.9 (G. H. Goering), 1921; Lieder, op.15 (Werfel), 1922; 9 Lieder, op.19 (O. Krzyzanowski), 1923; Lieder, op.30 (Goering, H. Reinhart), 1924; O Lacrymosa, op.48 (Rilke), 1926; 4 Lieder, op.52 (17th-century Ger.), 1927, orchd 1927; 3 Lieder, op.56 (Goethe), 1928; Reisebuch aus dem oesterreichischen Alpen, op.62 (Krenek), 1929; Fiedellieder, op.64 (Storm, T. Mommsen), 1930; Gesänge des späten Jahres, op.71 (Krenek), 1931; Das Schweigen, op.75 (Gemmingen), 1933; 5 Lieder, op.82 (Kafka), 1937–8; The Ballad of the Railroads (Krenek), 1944; 4 Songs (Hopkins), 1946–7; 2 Sacred Songs, 1952; The Flea (Donne), 1960;

Wechselrahmen (E. Barth), 1965; 3 Songs (Lauter), 1972; Spätlese (Krenek), 1973

CHAMBER, INSTRUMENTAL AND TAPE

Sonata, f♯, op.3, vn, pf, 1919; Serenade, op.4, cl, str trio, 1919; 7 str qts, op.6, 1921, op.8, 1921, op.20, 1923, op.24, 1923–4, op.65, 1930, op.78, 1937, op.96, 1943–4; Little Suite, op.28, cl. pf, 1924; Sonata, op.33, vn, 1924–5; Trio-Fantasy, op.63, pf trio, 1929; Suite, op.84, vc, 1939; Sonata, op.91/1, org, 1941; Sonatina, op.91/2a, fl, va, 1942, arr. op.91/2b, fl, cl, 1942; Sonata, op.91/3, va, 1942; Sonata, vn, pf, 1944–5; Trio, vn, cl, pf, 1946; 5 Pieces, str, 1948; Sonata, vn, pf, 1948; Sonata, vn, 1948

Str Trio, 1948; Parvula corona musicalis ad honorem Johannes Sebastiani Bach, str trio, 1950; Wind Qnt, 1951; Phantasiestück, vc, pf, 1953; Suite, fl, pf, 1954; Sonata, harp, 1955; Suite, cl, pf, 1955; Monologue, cl, 1956; Sonatina, ob, 1956; Pentagram, wind qnt, 1957; Suite, gui, 1957; Flötenstück neunphasig, fl, 1959; Hausmusik, various insts, 1959; Alpbach Qnt, wind qnt, perc, 1962; Toccata, accordion, 1962; Organologia, org, 1962; Fibonacci Mobile, str qt, pf duet, 1964; 4 Pieces, ob, 1966; 5 Pieces, trbn, pf, 1967; Duo, fl, db, 1970; Orga-nastro, org, tape, 1971

Choralvorspiel, org, 1973; Flaschenpost vom Paradies (Der englische Ausflug), elec, 1973; Die Vierwinde, org, 1979; Opus 231, vn, org, 1979

Tape: San Fernando Sequence, 1963; Quintona, 1965

PIANO

Double Fugue, op.1a, 1918; Dance Study, op.1b, 1920; Sonata no.1, E♭, op.2, 1919; 5 Sonatinas, op.5, 1926; Toccata and Chaconne, op.13, 1922; Little Suite, op.13a, 1922; 2 Suites, op.26, 1924; 5 Pieces, op.39, 1925; Sonata no.2, op.59, 1928; 4 Bagatelles, op.70, duet, 1931; 12 Variations, op.79, 1937; 12 Short Pieces, op.83, 1938; Sonata no.3, op.92/4, 1943; Hurricane Variations, 1944

8 Pieces, 1946; Sonata no.4, 1948; George Washington Variations, 1950; Sonata no.5, 1950; Sonata no.6, 1951; 20 Miniatures, 1954; Echoes from Austria [arr. Austrian folksongs], 1958; 6 Vermessene, 1958; Basler Massarbeit, 2 pf, 1958; Piano Piece, 1967; Doppelt beflügeltes Band, 2 pf, tape, 1969–70

Principal publishers: Bärenreiter, Schott, Universal

WRITINGS

'Problemi di stile nell'opera', RaM, vii (1934)

'Zur musikalischen Bearbeitung von Monteverdis Poppea', SMz, lxxvi (1936), 545

'The New Music and To-day's Theatre', MM, xiv (1937)

Über neue Musik: sechs Vorlesungen zur Einführung in die theoretischen Grundlagen (Vienna, 1937) [rev. as Music Here and Now (New York, 1939/R1967)]

Studies in Counterpoint (New York, 1940; Ger. trans., 1952)

'Gustav Mahler', in B. Walter: Gustav Mahler (Eng. trans., New York, 1941)

'New Developments of the 12-tone Technique', MR, iv (1943), 81

'Opera Between the Wars', MM, xx (1943)

ed.: Hamline Studies in Musicology (St Paul, Minn., 1945, 1947) [incl. essay 'The Treatment of Dissonance in Okeghem']

Selbstdarstellung (Zurich, 1948) [rev. and enlarged as 'Self Analysis', University of New Mexico Quarterly, xxiii (1953)]

Musik im goldenen Westen (Vienna, 1949)

Johannes Okeghem (New York, 1953)

De rebus prius factis (Frankfurt, 1956)

Zur Sprache gebracht (Munich, 1958) [essays]

Tonal Counterpoint (New York, 1958)

Gedanken unterwegs (Munich, 1959) [essays]

Modal Counterpoint (New York, 1959)

'Extents and Limits of Serial Techniques', MQ, xlvi (1960), 210

Komponist und Hörer (Kassel, 1964)

Prosa, Drama, Verse (Munich, 1965)

Exploring Music (London, 1966) [essays]

'Vom Geiste der geistlichen Musik', Sagittarius, iii (1970), 17

'Parvula corona musicalis', Bach, ii/4 (1971), 18; see also 'Postscript to the Parvula corona', Bach, iii/3 (1972), 21

Horizons Circled: Reflections on my Music (Berkeley, 1974)

Many other articles in Anbruch, Frankfurter Zeitung, Hamline University Bulletin, Measure (Chicago), Melos, Musica, Musical America, MQ, PNM, Prisma (Stockholm), University of New Mexico Quarterly

Autobiographical MSS in US-Wc [withheld until 15 years after Krenek's death]

BIBLIOGRAPHY

R. Erickson: 'Křenek's Later Music', MR, ix (1948), 29

W. Grandi: Il sistema tonale ed il contrappunto dodecafonia di Ernst Křenek (Rome, 1954)

W. L. Ogdon: Series and Structure: an Investigation into the Purpose of the Twelve-note Row in Selected Works of Schoenberg, Webern, Křenek and Leibowitz (diss., Indiana U., 1955)

M. J. Colucci: A Comparative Study of Contemporary Musical Theories in Selected Writings of Piston, Křenek and Hindemith (diss., U. of Pennsylvania, 1957)

F. Saathen: Ernst Křenek, Langen-Müllers kleine Geschenkbücher, xc (Munich, 1959)

——: 'Ernst Křeneks Botschaft im Wort', SMz, xcix (1959), 45

R. Stockhammer: 'Ernst Křeneks "Reisebuch aus den österreichischen Alpen" ', SMz, cii (1962), 32

F. Kaufmann: 'Ernst Křeneks "Motette zur Opferung" ', Musica sacra, lxxxiii (1963), 282

T. W. Adorno: 'Zur Physiognomik Ernst Kreneks', Moments musicaux (Frankfurt, 1964)

L. Knessl: Ernst Krenek, Österreichische Komponisten des XX. Jahrhunderts, xii (Vienna, 1967)

M. H. Wennerstrom: Parametric Analysis of Contemporary Musical Form (diss., Indiana U., 1967) [on 11 Transparencies]

A. G. Huetteman: Ernst Krenek's Theories on the Sonata and their Relations to his Six Piano Sonatas (diss., U. of Iowa, 1968)

E. Marckhl: Rede für Ernst Krenek (Graz, 1969)

W. Rogge: Ernst Kreneks Opern: Spiegel der zwanziger Jahre (Wolfenbüttel, 1970)

T. W. Adorno: Theodor W. Adorno und Ernst Křenek: Briefwechsel (Frankfurt am Main, 1974)

J. Hughes: 'Ernst Krenek Festival Concerts', MQ, lxi (1975), 464

OLIVER DANIEL

Krengel, Gregor (b Frankenstein, Silesia [now in Poland], ?1550–60; d in or after 1594). German lutenist, intabulator and composer. He matriculated at the University of Frankfurt an der Oder in the summer of 1584. He was granted citizen's rights at Frankfurt on 23 November of that year and also apparently acquired property there by marriage. He later moved to Görlitz, where he is mentioned in the civic register on 12 July 1594. A woodcut portrait of him of 1592, showing him apparently in middle age, is extant (in A-Wgm). He published Tabulatura nova continens selectissimas quasque cantiones ut sunt madrigalia, mutetae, paduanae et vilanellae, testudini sic aptatas, ut quilibet singulas duplici modo ludere et concinere possit (RISM 1584¹⁴; 3 songs ed. H. Bischoff, Alte Stücke und Weisen für doppelchörige Laute, 1924). This volume contains lute arrangements of 12 Italian madrigals and eight German songs by Jacob Regnart, two Latin motets in two partes by Lassus, two Latin hymns and four German songs by the Frankfurt Kantor, Gregor Lange, and a German song by Henning Winstman, a Frankfurt student from Hamburg, as well as seven paduanas by Krengel himself. The transcriptions are printed at two different pitches on facing pages and are for a seven-course lute with the seventh string a 4th below the sixth. Both versions permit the use together of two lutes with different tunings. Unlike other lutenists, however, Krengel did not state the difference in pitch between the two lutes. One piece even appears in four versions. The style of the paduanas, which are in duple metre and without a Nachtanz, is motet-like and highly compact and appears to be strongly influenced by vocal writing. Krengel added that any text – Italian, German or Polish – may be sung to them.

BIBLIOGRAPHY

BrownI; GerberNL

J. Dieckmann: Die in deutscher Lauten-Tabulatur überlieferten Tänze des 16. Jahrhunderts (Kassel, 1931)

H. Grimm: Meister der Renaissancemusik an der Viadrina (Frankfurt an der Oder and Berlin, 1942)

HANS RADKE

Krenn, Werner (b Vienna, 21 Sept 1943). Austrian tenor. He was a member of the Vienna Boys' Choir, but intended to become a bassoonist and was a member of the Vienna SO in that capacity from 1962 to 1966. He decided to devote himself to singing, and studied with László Somogy. His stage début was in Purcell's The Fairy Queen at the 1966 Berlin Festival, and he first appeared at the Salzburg Festival the next year, as

Aceste in Mozart's *Ascanio in Alba*. He made his British début as Jaquino with Scottish Opera in 1970, and in 1971 sang Idamantes at the Vienna Staatsoper in a new production of *Idomeneo*. His recordings include several of Mozart's early operas, as well as Don Ottavio and the title role in *La clemenza di Tito*, and several lieder recitals. His light, fluent, seamless tone is heard to greatest advantage in 18th-century music, but he is also a considerable interpreter of Schubert's more lyrical songs, including *Die schöne Müllerin*, and of Baroque music.

ALAN BLYTH

Krenz, Jan (*b* Włocławek, 14 July 1926). Polish conductor and composer. He studied the piano, conducting and composition (with Sikorski) at the State Music College in Łódź, and made his début conducting the Łódź PO in 1945, followed in 1949 by opera and concerts with the Poznań PO, with which he also made gramophone records. In 1949 he was appointed assistant conductor of the Polish RSO in Katowice, and succeeded Fitelberg as principal conductor in 1953, remaining until 1968, when he became principal conductor at the Warsaw Opera. He began to tour abroad with growing success during the 1950s, visiting Europe, Japan and Australia, and making his British début in 1961. He returned the next year with the Polish RSO for concerts at the Edinburgh Festival and a British tour including his London début (October); he was praised for his firm control, vitality of spirit and lack of sentimentality. These qualities were confirmed when he returned to conduct contemporary Polish music at the 1967 Cheltenham Festival and at the Promenade Concerts with the Polish RSO. Krenz's compositions include a cantata, *Dwa miasta* ('Dialogue between two towns', 1950), a symphony (1950) and Symphonic Dance (1951), works for small orchestra and string orchestra, chamber works and songs with piano. After 1952 his compositions became fewer and he adopted a serial idiom and aleatory techniques, as in his *Capriccio per 24 strumenti* (1962). He received a Polish State Prize in 1955 and the Union of Polish Composers' Prize in 1968.

BIBLIOGRAPHY
J. M. Chomiński: ' "Dwa miasta": kantata Jana Krenza', *Muzyka*, ii (1951), 8

BOGUSŁAW SCHÄFFER

Kresánek, Jozef (*b* Čičmany, central Slovakia, 20 Feb 1913). Slovak musicologist, teacher and composer. He studied composition at the Prague Conservatory under Karel and in Novák's master classes; in addition, he read musicology at Prague University under Nejedlý, Hutter and Zich. Kresánek began his teaching career in 1944, and as professor of musicology at Bratislava University he established himself as a leading figure in Slovak music. As a musicologist he has been concerned with phenomenological–structural studies as well as with the sociological interpretation of music. His compositions, generally in smaller forms, have been influenced by Slovak folk music, by the Russian period of Stravinsky and by Szymanowski.

WORKS
(selective list)

Vocal: Hore ho! [Ho away], cantata, 1937; folksong arrs., songs
Orch: Pochod [March], 1944; Suite no.2, 1953; Preludium and Toccata, 1960
Inst: Str Qt, 1935; 2 pf suites, 1936, 1938; Pf Trio, 1939; Pf Qnt (1976); pf miniatures

Principal publishers: Opus, Slovenský Hudební Fond, Supraphon

WRITINGS
Relácia medzi motívmi ako princíp hudobnej formy [The relation of motifs as a principle of musical form] (diss., U. of Prague, 1939)
Slovenská ľudová pieseň z hľadiska hudobného [Slovak folksong from a musical standpoint] (Bratislava, 1951)
Národný umelec E. Suchoň [The national artist Suchoň] (Bratislava, 1961)
Sociálna funkcia hudby [The social function of music] (Bratislava, 1961)

LADISLAV BURLAS

Kress, Georg Philipp (*b* Darmstadt, baptized 10 Nov 1719; *d* Göttingen, 2 Feb 1779). German violinist and composer. He was the second son of Johann Jakob and Anna Maria Kress, both of whom died when he was young. By 1744 he was first violinist in the Mecklenburg court orchestra at Schwerin. In 1748 he obtained leave to visit Plön, where he was Konzertmeister from 21 February 1748 to 1 July 1751. In 1755 Kress was again in Schwerin, but left his court post in the summer of 1767 to become Konzertmeister at the University of Göttingen; the appointment dated from 23 November 1766.

Kress was widely acclaimed as a virtuoso violinist. His compositions excited less admiration; one critic described them as 'awkward, wooden and unmelodious'. Stylistically they owe something to the works of his godfather, Georg Philipp Telemann. Despite the connection with Telemann, lexicographers have long assumed that Kress's second Christian name was Friedrich: the error arose from the fact that many of his compositions with Italian titles bear the initials 'G.F.' (Giorgio Filippo). A trio for flute, viola da gamba and continuo (*D-ROu*), often ascribed to Georg Philipp, is probably by his elder brother, Ludwig Albrecht; a set of 11 pairs of minuets for violin and continuo (*D-ROu*) is probably by a G. A. Kress, son of the Stuttgart musician, Paul Kress.

WORKS

1 solo, vn (Nuremberg, 1764), lost
2 concertos, D, g, vn/fl, vn, va, bc; 11 sonate à 4, vn/fl, vn, va, bc; 6 sonaté à 4, 2 vn, va, bc; trio, fl, va d'amore, hpd/lute; 6 sonate, fl, bc; 6 sonate, fl, bc; 4 sonatas, fl, bc: all *D-ROu*
Sinfonia à 2 cori, 2 hn, 4 vn, 2 va, 2 bc; ov., 2 ob, 2 hn, 2 vn, va, bc: both *D-SWl*

BIBLIOGRAPHY
E. Noack: *Musikgeschichte Darmstadts* (Mainz, 1967), 221ff
G. Hart: 'Georg Philipp Kress', *Mf*, xxii (1969), 328
E. Noack: 'Zu Günter Harts Aufsatz Georg Philipp Kress', *Mf*, xxiii (1970), 191

PIPPA DRUMMOND

Kress, Johann Albrecht (*b* at or nr. Nuremberg, Feb or March 1644; *d* Stuttgart, 23 July 1684). German composer and musician. On 10 June 1660 he joined the Stuttgart Hofkapelle (where his brother Paul also worked) as a musician. In 1669 he became vice-Kapellmeister and from 1676 until his death acted as director of the Kapelle, since the Kapellmeister, J. F. Magg, was no longer able to carry out his duties. His contemporaries in Stuttgart regarded him highly as a composer, and he several times received special remuneration for his compositions. He was probably on good terms with P. F. Böddecker, organist of the collegiate church, who in his *Manuductio nova* added five instrumental parts to Kress's *Jubilus Bernhardi*. His output, which is exclusively sacred, belongs to the traditions of south German church music in the second half of the 17th century.

WORKS

Ein Gespräch-Lied über ... Herrn Eberhardens, Hertzogens zu Würtemberg ... Todesfall (Stuttgart, 1675)

Musicalische Seelenbelustigung oder geistliche Concerten, 4vv, 6 insts ad lib (Stuttgart, 1681)
Der süsse Name Jesu oder teutscher Jubilus Bernhardi, 3vv (Stuttgart, 1681); repr. in P. F. Böddecker: *Manuductio nova methodico-practica bassum generalem* (Stuttgart, 1701), augmented by 5 insts
In te domine speravi, 1v, 2 cornettini, bc, *D-Bds*
Es stehe Gott auf, 1688, 5vv, 2 vn, 3 viols, vle, 4 clarini, org; Ich ruf zu dir, Herr Jesu Christ, 4vv, 4 viols, vle, bn, bc; Wohl dem, der die Gottseligkeit und Furcht des Höchsten übet, 1692, 4vv, 2 vn, 3 viols, bc: *F*
Wie der Hirsch schreyet nach frischem Wasser, 1678, 4vv, 2 vn, org, *F-Sm*

BIBLIOGRAPHY
EitnerQ; GerberNL; WaltherML
J. Mattheson: *Grundlage einer Ehren-Pforte* (Hamburg, 1740); ed. M. Schneider (Berlin, 1910/R1969), 148
J. Sittard: *Zur Geschichte der Musik und des Theaters am württembergischen Hofe*, i (Stuttgart, 1890), 58, 61f
A. Bopp: 'Beiträge zur Geschichte der Stuttgarter Stiftsmusik', *Jb für Statistik und Landeskunde 1910* (1911), 227, 239, 242, 245
U. Siegele: 'Kress', *MGG*

EBERHARD STIEFEL

Kress, Johann Jakob (*b* Walderbach, Regensburg, *c*1685; *d* Darmstadt, buried 6 Nov 1728). German composer and violinist. He was the son of Johann Georg Kress of Walderbach. The family moved to Oettingen when Kress was still young; they can be traced there from 1696 onwards. At Oettingen Kress attended the Lateinschule and received a musical education at the expense of Prince Albrecht Ernst. He then obtained a post in the court orchestra under Kapellmeister Jakob Christian Hertel. In 1712 Kress was appointed to the Darmstadt court orchestra with a salary of 400 florins and gifts in kind. By 1719 his salary was in arrears and his financial situation became increasingly precarious. On 10 November 1723 he handed in his resignation, whereupon the landgrave appointed him Konzertmeister with an additional allowance of 200 florins; he withdrew his resignation and remained at Darmstadt until his death.

Six violin concertos and six violin sonatas by him were published in his lifetime. The op.3 sonatas, which Kress engraved himself, were dedicated to the Prince of Oettingen; these unpretentious works are in four movements and mix church and chamber elements. The music is occasionally reminiscent of Handel.

Kress had five children by his marriage to Anna Maria Wöhler. Two of them, Ludwig Albrecht and GEORG PHILIPP KRESS, were also musicians. Telemann acted as godfather to Georg Philipp, who became a composer of some merit. Several of the MSS in the Stadt- und Bezirksbibliothek, Rostock, and the Mecklenburgische Landesbibliothek, Schwerin, mentioned by Eitner are signed with the initials 'G.F.' and are probably therefore by the son.

WORKS
Sei concerti a 5, vn, str orch, op.1 (Darmstadt, n.d.) [? = 6 vn concertos a 5 op.1, pubd Nuremberg, according to *GerberL*]
[6] Sonate da camera, vn, b/hpd, op.3 (Darmstadt, n.d.)
Solo a flute traversiere del Sigr. Gresh, *D-ROs*

BIBLIOGRAPHY
EitnerQ
W. Nagel: 'Zur Geschichte der Musik am Hofe von Darmstadt', *MMg*, xxxii (1900), 1, 21, 41, 59, 79
F. Noack: 'Kress, Johann Jacob', *MGG*
E. Noack: *Musikgeschichte Darmstadts* (Mainz, 1967)
G. Hart: 'Georg Philipp Kress', *Mf*, xxii (1969), 328
E. Noack: 'Zu Günter Harts Aufsatz Georg Philipp Kress', *Mf*, xxiii (1970), 191

PIPPA DRUMMOND

Kretzschmar, (August Ferdinand) Hermann (*b* Olbernhau, Saxony, 19 Jan 1848; *d* Berlin, 10 May 1924). German musicologist and conductor. He was first taught music by his father, Karl Dankegott Kretzschmar, a choirmaster and organist, and at the age of 14 went to the Dresden Kreuzschule, where he studied composition until 1867 with J. Otto. In 1868 he studied musicology at the University of Leipzig with Oscar Paul, F. Ritschl and Woldemar Voigt, taking the doctorate in 1871 with a dissertation, written in Latin, on early notation. From 1869 to 1870 he also studied at the Leipzig Conservatory with Paul, E. F. Richter and Carl Reinecke. He became a teacher at the conservatory in 1871 and was also active as a conductor of several musical societies in Leipzig, including Euterpe, the Bach-Verein, Ossian and the Singakademie; but overwork forced him to give up his post at the conservatory in 1876. For a brief period he conducted at the Metz Stadttheater before moving to Rostock (1877) to become music director at the university; from 1880 he was also town music director there. Kretzschmar returned to Leipzig in 1887 as university music director and conductor of the students' choral union. He conducted the choir founded by K. Riedel (1888–98) and played an important role as the founder of the new Bach Gesellschaft. In 1890 he initiated a series of Academic Orchestral Concerts, whose programmes emphasized historical works (1890–95). He moved to Berlin in 1904 to become professor of music at the university; he also succeeded Joachim as director of the Hochschule für Musik (1909–20) and Liliencron as general editor of the Denkmäler Deutscher Tonkunst (1912–18).

Kretzschmar was regarded as second only to Riemann in importance among German music historians. His early training at the Kreuzschule in music as a humanistic discipline, together with his practical choral experience, provided him with the foundation for his later work. He viewed music history as a history of culture and studied the interaction among the individual work of art, the circumstances of its composition and the social and cultural milieu of its time; thus he argued the case for musicology, but not as an independent discipline. He aimed to make Bach's works known to a wider audience and did much organizational and editorial work for the publication of early music. His writings range from work on Venetian opera, performing practice and Baroque *Affektenlehre* to the popular *Führer durch den Konzert-Saal*.

Kretzschmar was also the director of the Institut für Kirchenmusik in Berlin and was active as an educational adviser. He sought to remove musical education from its isolated position in the lecture hall and to make it available to a wider public; he was therefore concerned with teaching music in schools and private homes, as well as the further education of both professional and amateur musicians.

See also ANALYSIS, §II, 4.

EDITIONS
J. S. Bach: Handschrift in zeitlich geordneten Nachbildungen, Johann Sebastian Bachs Werke, xliv (Leipzig, 1894/*R*)
I. Holzbauer: Günther von Schwarzburg, DDT, viii–ix (1902/*R*)
J. E. Bach, V. Herbing: Lieder, DDT, xlii (1910/*R*)

WRITINGS
De signis musicis (diss., U. of Leipzig, 1871; Leipzig, 1871)
Führer durch den Konzert-Saal, i (Leipzig, 1887, 7/1932); ii (Leipzig, 1888, 5/1921); iii (Leipzig, 1890, 5/1939)
Johann Sebastian Bachs Werke, xlvi (Leipzig, 1889/*R*) [with thematic catalogues of vocal and instrumental works, reports and indexes]
'Die venetianische Oper und die Werke Cavallis und Cestis', *VMw*, viii (1892), 1
Musikalische Zeitfragen (Leipzig, 1903)

Gesammelte Aufsätze über Musik und anderes aus den Grenzboten (Leipzig, 1910)
Aus den Jahrbüchern der Musikbibliothek Peters (Leipzig, 1911)
Geschichte des neuen deutschen Liedes (Leipzig, 1911/R1966)
Geschichte der Oper (Leipzig, 1919/R1970)
Einführung in die Musikgeschichte (Leipzig, 1920/R1970)

BIBLIOGRAPHY

RiemannL 12
Festschrift Hermann Kretzschmar (Leipzig, 1918/R1973)
H. Abert: 'Zum Gedächtnis H. Kretzschmars', *JbMP 1924*, 9
A. Einstein: 'Hermann Kretzschmar', *ZMw*, vi (1924), 31
F. M. Gatz: *Musik-Ästhetik in ihren Hauptrichtungen* (Stuttgart, 1929)
G. Braun: *Die Schulmusikerziehung in Preussen* (Kassel and Basle, 1957)
R. Heinz: *Geschichtsbegriff und Wissenschaftscharakter der Musikwissenschaft in der zweiten Hälfte des 19. Jahrhunderts* (Regensburg, 1968)
W. Wiora, ed.: *Die Ausbreitung des Historismus über die Musik* (Regensburg, 1969)

GAYNOR G. JONES

Kreuder, Peter Paul (*b* Aachen, 18 Aug 1905). German composer. After studying at musical academies in Munich and Hamburg he was musical director for Max Reinhardt's theatre in Berlin (1928–30) and for theatres in Munich (from 1930); he spent five years in South America (1945–50). In addition to a piano concerto, the operas *Der Zerrissene* (1940) and *Der Postmeister* (1966), three operettas, three musicals and music for over 150 films, Kreuder is known for numerous popular songs. He wrote two autobiographies, *Schön war die Zeit* (Munich, 1955) and *Nur Puppen haben keine Tränen* (Percha, 1971).

Kreusser, Georg Anton (*b* Heidingsfeld, nr. Würzburg, 27 Oct 1746; *d* Aschaffenburg, 1 Nov 1810). German composer and Konzertmeister. He received his early musical education in his native town. By 1759 he had arrived in Amsterdam where he studied instrumental technique and composition under his elder brother Adam Kreusser (*b* Heidingsfeld, baptized 28 Nov 1732; *d* Amsterdam, 1791) who had been leader of the Amsterdam theatre orchestra since 1752. His first compositions were published in 1768, and from 1770 to 1771 he made a study tour of Italy and France. Returning to Amsterdam he lived as an independent composer, virtuoso and conductor. On 13 December 1773 he became deputy Konzertmeister and on 21 February 1774 Konzertmeister of the electoral chapel in Mainz. A new flowering in the musical life of Mainz began with Kreusser's appointment: for a long time he was the foremost court musician, and his works enjoyed great popularity. Only when Vincenzo Righini became Kapellmeister in 1787 did he lose his pre-eminence and something of his creative fervour. After the second occupation of Mainz by the French Kreusser left the town in the winter of 1798–9 and settled in Aschaffenburg with most of the elector's court musicians. The Kapelle was not re-formed until 1810. He lived in seclusion until his death (not, as is sometimes asserted, as leader of the theatre orchestra in Frankfurt am Main) and published only a few new compositions.

With Franz Xaver Sterkel, Kreusser is the most significant Mainz composer of the second half of the 18th century. His achievement is most outstanding in his instrumental music. His style was formed by quite varied influences, so that he cannot be ascribed to any national school and he stands somewhat apart from his contemporaries who formed the early Classical style between 1760 and 1780. The majority of his symphonies have three movements after the Italian pattern; even the earliest use a remarkably balanced three-part sonata form, and the independence of the middle parts and his increasingly skilful instrumentation were in advance of his time. His chamber music draws its inspiration more from France, and favoured the two-movement form in concertante style. In his latter years Kreusser wrote mainly vocal music, of which his most important and best known work is the oratorio *Der Tod Jesu*, after Ramler, which, like Graun's setting, was performed over a long period. Familiarity with his compositions spread far beyond his immediate circle, and they were highly regarded by such notable contemporaries as Leopold Mozart and Joseph Haydn.

WORKS

(nos. in square brackets refer to complete list of works in Peters)

Orch: 6 Syms. [1–6], op.2 (Amsterdam, 1769); Sinfonie périodique [Hummel] no.5, A [7] (Amsterdam, 1769); 6 Syms. [8–13], op.5 (Amsterdam, 1770); 6 Syms. [15–20], op.7 (Amsterdam, 1772); 6 Syms. [21–6] (Amsterdam, 1774); 6 Syms. [27–32], op.9 (Berlin, ?1774–5); Hpd Conc., C [56] (Amsterdam, *c*1775); Sinfonie périodique [Hummel], C [33] (Berlin, 1776); 6 Syms. [34–9], op.1 (Offenbach, 1777); 3 Syms. [40–42], op.13 (Berlin, 1778); Sinfonie périodique [Hummel] no.31, E♭ [43] (Amsterdam, 1780); 6 Syms. [44–9], op.18 (Mainz, 1780); Sinfonie périodique [Schott] no.1, C [50] (Mainz, 1786); Sym., f [14], *c*1770–71; 4 syms. [51–4], *c*1783; Serenade [55], D, *c*1783
Chamber: 6 Qnts [57–62], fl, vn, va, vc, bc, op.10 (Berlin, 1775); 6 Qts [63–8], fl, vn, va, vc, op.8 (Amsterdam, ?1773–4); 6 Str Qts [69–74], op.12 (Berlin, 1778); 6 Str Qts [75–80] (Paris, 1779); 3 Qts [87–9], fl, vn, va, vc, op.8 bk 2 (Bonn, 1803); 6 Trios [90–95], 2 vn, bc, op.1 (Amsterdam, 1768); 6 Trios [102–7], nos.1–3 for vn, va, vc, nos.4–6 for fl, vn, bc, op.11 (Berlin, 1777); 6 Vn Duos [108–13], op.3 (Amsterdam, 1770); Vn Sonata [114], op.6 (Amsterdam, 1771); 6 Menuette und 12 Kontretänze [115], pf (Mainz, 1785); 6 str qts [81–6], *c*1780; 6 trios [96–101], *c*1770
Vocal: Der Tod Jesu [117] (K. W. Ramler), oratorio (Mainz, 1783); 7 Lieder [116], Mez, pf (Mainz, 1802); 8 masses [118–25], *c*1785–95

Numerous lost works

BIBLIOGRAPHY

E. Peters: *Georg Anton Kreusser: ein Mainzer Instrumentalkomponist der Klassik* (Munich and Salzburg, 1975)

EDITH PETERS

Kreutzbach. Danish–German family of organ builders and instrument makers. Urban Kreutzbach (*b* Copenhagen, 24 Aug 1796; *d* Borna, nr. Leipzig, 20 Aug 1868), the son of a merchant, learnt cabinet making and travelled to Germany in about 1820. In 1830 he established himself as an organ builder in Borna. His instruments, splendid examples of the Saxon Silbermann tradition, are outstanding for their thoughtful specifications, fine voicing and strong, metallic tone. Notable ones include those at Ortmannsdorf (1856), Callenberg (1859), Glauchau-Jerisau (1860) and Dresden-Hosterwitz (1863). He invented a playing valve loop, and used a fairly high wind pressure in his instruments.

Richard Kreutzbach (*b* Borna, 27 July 1839; *d* Borna, 21 June 1903), Urban's son, continued throughout his lifetime in his father's business; he adopted pneumatic action, and built good organs without, however, ever equalling his father's mastery. He built instruments in the Stadtkirche, Johanngeorgenstadt, Erzgebirge (1872) and in Waldenburg, Saxony (1878–9). Emil Bernhard Hermann Kreutzbach (*b* Borna, 5 Dec 1843), another son, also worked in his father's business, leaving it in 1875. Other employees of the firm, which produced approximately 300 instruments, included J. G. Bärmig, H. Beygang, W. Grisard, C. Ladegast, E. Müller and H. Walcker.

Julius Urban Kreutzbach (*b* Döbeln, 29 Nov 1845; *d* Leipzig, 22 Sept 1913), another relative, founded the famous Leipzig firm of piano makers that bears his name. Emil Müller (*b* Borna, 11 Oct 1857; *d* Pillnitz bei Dresden, 4 Oct 1928), a grandson of Urban Kreutzbach, who accomplished nothing of significance in organ building, took over J. G. Bärmig's works at Werdau in 1887 and made it the largest harmonium factory in Europe.

BIBLIOGRAPHY

F. Oehme: *Handbuch über ältere und neuere Orgelwerke im Königreiche Sachsen*, iii (Dresden, 1897)

R. Fritzsche: *Werdau und seine Industrie* (Werdau, 1936)

WALTER HÜTTEL

Kreutzer. French family of musicians.

(1) Rodolphe Kreutzer (*b* Versailles, 16 Nov 1766; *d* Geneva, 6 Jan 1831). Violinist, composer and teacher.

1. Life. 2. Violin playing. 3. Works.

1. LIFE. His father, a wind player, came from Breslau about 1760 to play in the newly formed Swiss Guards of the Duke of Choiseul; he also played and taught the violin locally in Versailles, but was not in the orchestra of the royal chapel. Rodolphe was the eldest of five surviving children and received his early musical education from his father. From 1778 Anton Stamitz taught him the violin and composition; on 25 May 1780 Kreutzer performed a concerto by his teacher at the Concert Spirituel, Paris, and was received as a prodigy. In 1782–3 he heard Viotti's solo violin performances and was influenced by his style of writing and playing (although he met Viotti there is no evidence that he became his pupil). In May 1784 Kreutzer performed his own First Violin Concerto at the Concert Spirituel. After the death of his parents within three months (November 1784, January 1785) he came under the kindly influence of Marie Antoinette and the Count of Artois, who probably arranged his acceptance into the king's music during 1785. He wrote chamber music and played more of his own violin concertos, and by 1789 was a leading virtuoso; in that year he moved from Versailles to Paris.

No primary evidence has been discovered for Fétis's assertion that two operas by Kreutzer were privately produced under the queen's patronage in the closing years of the *ancien régime*. But a series of operatic works was brought out by Kreutzer from 1790, chiefly at the Théâtre Italien, alias the Théâtre Favart, or Opéra-Comique. The two pieces which established his stage reputation were *Paul et Virginie* and *Lodoïska*; the latter was preferred to Cherubini's work of the same name, also first given in 1791.

The flood of energy which characterized the musical world of the Revolutionary period brought about the Institut National de Musique (1793), forerunner of the Conservatoire (1795); Kreutzer was attached to both, as professor of violin. He was to teach at the Conservatoire until 1826, and sat as a member of its council from 1825 to 1830. The famous *42 études ou caprices* for violin (originally 40; the additional two may not be Kreutzer's) appeared initially in 1796, published by the Conservatoire.

Kreutzer made a successful concert tour of Italy in 1796: by this time he had composed at least eight violin concertos. During a second tour he was attached to Bernadotte's party on the latter's appointment as French ambassador to Vienna in February 1798; his activities included the removal of Italian manuscripts to France on Napoleon's orders. A Beethoven letter of 4 October 1804 reveals that the two men came into contact, and that Beethoven heard Kreutzer's playing. The Violin Sonata op.47 (called the 'Kreutzer' Sonata) dates however from 1802–3; the dedication to Kreutzer was made without the latter's knowledge, and the sonata was published in 1805. It is not thought that the work was ever played publicly by its dedicatee. His career in Paris from 1798 on was marked by particularly successful concert appearances at the Théâtre Feydeau and the Opéra, some of which were made jointly with Rode. When Rode departed for Russia in 1801 Kreutzer replaced him as solo violin of the Opéra; he joined Napoleon's chapel orchestra in 1802 and his private orchestra four years later.

The opera *Astyanax* (1801) was fairly successful; but it was Kreutzer's first ballet score, *Paul et Virginie* (1806), using music from the earlier opera, which appealed sufficiently to the public to hold the stage for 15 years. *Aristippe* (1808), a comedy on the popular Anacreon theme, also proved a success, and was given until 1830. The ballet *Les amours d'Antoine et Cléopatre* (1808), with its spectacular finale, was Kreutzer's third stage work to catch the public imagination. The biblical opera *Abel* (1810), though at first indifferently received, was revived (minus its second act) in 1823; Berlioz wrote an ecstatic letter of appreciation to the composer. From 1802 to 1811 Kreutzer was a partner in Le Magasin de Musique, a publishing and retail concern formed with Cherubini, Méhul, Rode, Isouard and Boieldieu.

While on holiday in 1810 he broke an arm in a carriage accident and his career as a soloist ended. Nevertheless he continued to play in ensembles and retained his official positions. After the Restoration in 1815 Kreutzer was named *Maître de la chapelle du roi*; the next year he was created second conductor of the Opéra, then chief conductor in 1817. Habeneck replaced him in this post in 1824, the year in which Kreutzer became a Chevalier de la Légion d'honneur. From 1824 to 1826 he took overall direction of music at the Opéra. In the spring of 1826 Berlioz approached him unsuccessfully with a view to having *La révolution grecque* performed at the Opéra's series of *concerts spirituels*. But by this time Kreutzer's own style could find little public favour and his last opera *Matilde* was refused by the Opéra. His health declined from 1826, when he retired from most of his public positions.

2. VIOLIN PLAYING. Spohr wrote of the Kreutzer brothers that 'of all the Parisian violinists, they are the most cultivated', and Beethoven declared of Rodolphe: 'I prefer his modesty and natural behaviour to *all the exterior* without *any interior*, which is characteristic of most virtuosos'. Together with Baillot and Rode, Kreutzer formed the founding trinity of the French violin school, which was marked by brilliance of style, objectivity of approach and lack of emphasis on the expansive type of lyricism (Spohr himself said that French slow concerto movements were regarded as mere interludes between the fast outer movements). Kreutzer, who played a Stradivari, possessed a full tone and used a predominantly legato style of bowing. Fétis praised his instinctive sense of phrase and his just intonation. Williams (1973) also noted the emphasis on legato and complete absence of spiccato bowing in Kreutzer's violin concertos, which also use neither extensive shifting of the left hand nor very high posi-

tions; moreover there is limited use of double stopping, even by comparison with Viotti's concertos. Kreutzer's numerous pupils included his brother (2) Jean Nicolas Auguste Kreutzer, Charles Lafont and Massart.

3. WORKS. Kreutzer's *42 études ou caprices* (originally 40) for unaccompanied violin occupy an almost unique position in the literature of violin studies; Kreutzer met the challenge of the modern violin by aiming partly at fluency in contraction and extension of the left hand. As Szigeti (1969) pointed out, extensions and unisons were easier on the old short-necked violin; in the 'practically unknown nineteen Etudes-Caprices . . . it is obvious that the great teacher was already conscious of the need for the "opening up" of the hand'. Owing to their fundamental musicality and approach, successive editors have brought the *42 études* up to date either by adding new fingerings and bowings or by composing their own variants. Eisenberg in his edition (1920) claimed that Kreutzer anticipated this and taught more advanced versions of his caprices than those he published.

In his violin concertos Kreutzer adhered closely to contemporary forms. Williams asserted the influence of Stamitz in the earlier works, that of Viotti at its most powerful in the concertos of the 1790s, and increasing individuality in the final eight concertos. The solo violin parts become progressively more difficult throughout the canon, and the orchestration more sophisticated.

Much of Kreutzer's chamber music dates from the 1790s and reflects the style of his teachers. Concentrating later on stage productions, he achieved a measure of originality without ever producing a work of lasting value. His harmonic language is not without variety, but too often his musical thinking does not progress beyond simple melody and accompaniment; and while the melodies themselves betray Romantic turns of phrase even in the 1790s, they are not often memorable. *Lodoiska* and *Abel* are his worthiest achievements; the former is vivid in drama and colour, and has warmth of melody. *Astyanax* contains some striking final pages depicting the Greeks leaving Troy, and in *Abel* the purely musical quality runs at a consistently higher level. Biblical subject matter was topical (cf Méhul's *Joseph*, 1807, and Le Sueur's *La mort d'Adam*, 1809); in Kreutzer's opera the devils who forge the club of human destruction are the tempters of Cain, and as an apotheosis Abel is carried heavenwards. There are pages of large-scale conception, but the opening of the original Act 3, in which an exhausted Cain prays for sleep ('Doux sommeil'), contains some of Kreutzer's best music.

WORKS

(*selective list; printed works published in Paris unless otherwise stated*)

STAGE

Unless otherwise stated, all are operas first performed in Paris and all publications are full scores; other unpublished MSS may be in Brussels or in German libraries.

Jeanne d'Arc (drame historique mêlée d'ariettes, 3, P. J. B. C. Desforges), Théâtre Favart, 10 May 1790

Paul et Virginie (opéra comique, 3, E. G. F. de Favières), Théâtre Favart, 15 Jan 1791 (*c*1791)

Le franc breton (opéra comique, 1, J. E. B. Dejaure), Théâtre Favart, 15 Feb 1791 (1803–10) [collab. Solié]

Lodoiska (opéra comique, 3, Dejaure), Théâtre Favart, 1 Aug 1791 (*c*1791)

La journée de Marathon (incidental music, J. F. Guéroult), 1792, ov. (1794)

Charlotte et Werther (opéra comique, 1, Dejaure), Théâtre Favart, 1 Feb 1792

Le siège de Lille (opéra comique, 1, L. A. B. d'Antilly), Théâtre Feydeau, 14 Nov 1792

Le déserteur ou La montagne de Ham (1, Dejaure), Théâtre Favart, 6 Feb 1793

Le congrès des rois (opéra comique, 3, A. F. E. Demaillot), Théâtre Favart, 26 Feb 1794 [collab. 11 other composers]

Le lendemain de la bataille de Fleurus (impromptu, 1), Théâtre de l'Egalité, 1794

On respire (comédie mêlée d'ariettes, 1, C. L. Tissot), Théâtre Favart, 9 March 1795, lib (*c*1795)

Le brigand (drame mêle d'ariettes, 3, F. B. Hoffman), Théâtre Favart, 25 July 1795, *F-Pc*

La journée du 10 août 1792 (opera, 4, G. Saulnier and ?Darrieux), Opéra, 10 Aug 1795

Imogène ou La gageure indiscrète (comédie mêlée d'ariettes, 3, Dejaure), Théâtre Favart, 27 April 1796

Le petit page (comédie mêlée d'ariettes, 1, R. C. G. de Pixérécourt), Théâtre Feydeau, 15 Feb 1800 (*c*1800) [collab. N. Isouard]

Flaminius à Corinthe (opera, 1, Pixérécourt, ?Lambert), Opéra, 27 Feb 1801, *Po* [collab. Isouard]

Astyanax (opera, 3, Dejaure), Opéra, 12 April 1801, *Po*

Le baiser et la quittance (opéra comique, 3, L. B. Picard, M. Dieulafoy, C. de Longchamps), Opéra-Comique, 18 June 1803, *B-Bc* [collab. Boieldieu, Isouard, Méhul]

Les surprises ou L'étourdi en voyage (2, C. A. B. Sewrin), Opéra-Comique, 2 Jan 1806

Paul et Virginie (ballet-pantomime, 3), St Cloud, 12 June 1806, *F-Po*

François I ou La fête mystérieuse (comédie mêlée d'ariettes, 2, Sewrin, A. de Chazet), Opéra-Comique, 14 March 1807 (*c*1807)

Les amours d'Antoine et Cléopatre (ballet, 3, P. Aumer), Opéra, 8 March 1808, vocal score (Vienna, ?1809), *Po*

Aristippe (comédie lyrique, 2, P. F. Giraud, M. T. Leclercq), Opéra, 24 May 1808 (*c*1808)

Jadis et aujourd'hui (opéra comique, 1, Sewrin), Opéra-Comique, 29 Oct 1808 (*c*1808)

La fête de Mars (divertissement-pantomime, 1), Opéra, 26 Dec 1809, *Po*

Abel (tragédie lyrique, 3, Hoffman), Opéra, 23 March 1810, *Po*; rev. as La mort d'Abel (2), Opéra, 17 March 1823, vocal score (*c*1824)

Le triomphe du mois de Mars (1, E. M. Dupaty), Opéra, 27 March 1811, *Po* [ceremonial drama for King of Rome's birth]

L'homme sans façon (opéra comique, 3, Sewrin), Opéra-Comique, 7 Jan 1812 (*c*1812)

Le camp de Sobieski (opéra comique, 2, Dupaty), Opéra-Comique, 21 April 1813

Constance et Théodore (opéra comique, 2), Opéra-Comique, 22 Nov 1813

L'oriflamme (opera, 1, C. G. Etienne, L. P. Baour-Lormian), Opéra, 31 Jan 1814, *Po* [collab. Berton, Méhul, Paer]

Les béarnais ou Henri IV en voyage (opéra comique, 1, Sewrin), Opéra-Comique, 21 May 1814 [collab. Boieldieu]

La perruque et la redingote (opéra comique, 3, A. E. Scribe), Opéra-Comique, 25 Jan 1815 [collab. Kreubé]

La princesse de Babylone (opera, 3, L. J. B. E. Vigée), Opéra, 30 May 1815, *Po*

L'heureux retour (ballet, 1), Opéra, 25 July 1815, *Po* [collab. Berton, Persuis]

Le carnaval de Venise (ballet, 2), Opéra, 22 Feb 1816 [collab. Persuis]; rev. in 1 act, 7 Sept 1817, *Po*

Les dieux rivaux (opera-ballet, 1, C. Briffaut, A. M. Dieulafoy), Opéra, 21 June 1816, *Po* [collab. Spontini, Persuis, Berton]

Le maître et le valet (opéra comique, 3), Théâtre Feydeau, 1816

La servante justifiée ou La fête de Mathurine (ballet villageois, 1), Opéra, 30 Sept 1818, *Po*

Clari ou La promesse de mariage (ballet-pantomime, 3), Opéra, 19 June 1820, *Po*

Blanche de Provence ou La cour des fées (3, E. G. M. Théaulon, De Ranée), Opéra, 3 May 1821, *Po* [collab. Berton, Boieldieu, Cherubini, Paer]

Le négociant de Hambourg (opéra comique, 3, J. B. C. Vial, J. A. de R. St-Cyr), Opéra-Comique, 15 Oct 1821

Le paradis de Mahomet (opéra comique, 3, Scribe, A. H. J. Mélesville), Opéra-Comique, 23 March 1822 [collab. Kreubé]

Ipsiboé (opera, 4, M. de St-Lyon), Opéra, 31 March 1824, *Po*

Pharamond (opera, 3, J. A. P. F. Ancelot, P. M. T. A. Guiraud, L. A. Soumet), Opéra, 10 June 1825, *Po* [collab. Berton, Boieldieu]

Matilde (opera, 3), *c*1826–7, unperf.

ORCHESTRAL

Vn concs. (composition and publication dates from Williams, 1973): no.1, G, op.1, 1783–4 (*c*1801); no.2, A, op.2, 1784–5 (*c*1801); no.3, E, op.3, 1785 (*c*1800); no.4, C, op.4, 1786 (up to 1808); no.5, A, op.5, 1787 (by 1808); no.6, e, op.6, *c*1788 (?); no.7, A, op.7, *c*1790 (by 1808); no.8, d, op.8, *c*1795 (by 1809); no.9, e, op.9, by 1802 (Leipzig, by 1802); no.10, d, op.10, by 1802 (Leipzig, by 1802); no.11, C, op.11, by 1802 (Leipzig, by 1802); no.12, A, op.12, 1802–3 (Leipzig, *c*1803); no.13, D, op.A, 1803 (*c*1804); no.14, E, op.B, 1803–4 (*c*1804); no.15, A, op.C, 1804 (*c*1805); no.16, e, op.D, 1804 (Leipzig and Paris, *c*1805) [on themes by Haydn]; no.17, G,

op.E, 1805 (c1807); no.18, e, op.F, 1805–9 (Offenbach, c1811); no.19, d, op.G, 1805–10 (?)
Sinfonia concertantes: no.1, F, 2 vn, c1793 (c1803); no.2, F, 2 vn, vc, c1794 (Offenbach, c1819) [?B-Bc]; no.3, E, 2 vn, 1803 (1803); no.4, F, 2 vn, F-Pc
Ouverture de la journée de marathon, ww, brass (1794)

CHAMBER

Qnt, ob/cl, str qt (between 1790 and 1799)
Str qts: 6 quatuors concertans, (c1790); 3 qts, op.2 (Offenbach, c1795); 2 qts (Leipzig, between 1790 and 1799); 6 nouveaux quatuors, op.2, pt.1 (c1798)
Trios: Premier pot-pourri, vn solo, vn, b (c1800); Trio, ob/cl, bn, va (Offenbach, c1803); 3 trios brillans, 2 vn, b (c1803) [as op.16 (Leipzig, c1804)]
Duets: Duos, vn, va (Versailles, 1783); 3 vn duos, op.11, pt.2 (Offenbach, c1800); 3 vn duos, op.3 (between 1800 and 1809); 3 duos concertans, 2 vn, op.B (Offenbach, c1820); 6 nocturnes concertans, harp, vn (c1822) [collab. C. Bochsa]
Sonatas: 3 sonatas, vn, b, op.1 (between 1790 and 1799); 3 sonatas, vn, b, op.B (between 1790 and 1799); Grande sonate, vn, pf (?Paris, 1799); 3 sonates faciles, vn, b (before 1804); 3 sonatas, vn, b, op.2 (between 1800 and 1809)
Vn solo: 42 études ou caprices (1796), 1st extant edn. (c1807) [40 studies in c1807 print; other 2 ?authentic]; 18 nouveaux caprices ou études (Leipzig, c1815) [? later pubd as 19 études]

PEDAGOGICAL

Méthode de violon (1803) [collab. P. J. J. Rode, P. M. Baillot]

(2) Jean Nicolas Auguste Kreutzer (b Versailles, 3 Sept 1778; d Paris, 31 Aug 1832). Violinist and composer, brother of (1) Rodolphe Kreutzer. Having been taught the violin by his brother Rodolphe at home, he continued as his pupil while at the Paris Conservatoire, where he won the premier prix for violin in 1801. He joined the orchestra of the Théâtre Favart in 1798 and that of the Opéra in 1800 or 1801. He also became a member of the imperial chapel orchestra (1804), remaining there in the service of the Bourbons after the 1815 Restoration until 1830. On Rodolphe Kreutzer's retirement in 1826 he took charge of his Conservatoire class, though he had already been a member of the staff. He published two violin concertos, violin duos, three violin sonatas op.1 and other violin music. His playing style was less brilliant than Rodolphe's, though expressive and stylish.

(3) Léon Charles François Kreutzer (b Paris, 23 Sept 1817; d Vichy, 6 Oct 1868). Writer on music and composer, son of (2) Jean Nicolas Auguste Kreutzer. He studied the piano and composition privately. His cultural interests and independence of thought led him to music criticism; according to Fétis he began writing for L'union in 1840, concentrating on aspects of opera and operatic history. His work also appeared in the Revue et gazette musicale de Paris, Revue contemporaine (from 1854), L'opinion publique and Le théâtre. In collaboration with Edouard Fournier he wrote the articles 'Opéra' and 'Opéra-Comique' in the Encyclopédie du XIXe siècle.

Kreutzer's compositions, which attracted favourable comment from Fétis, are for the most part unpublished. His Symphony in F minor (privately printed, c1860) shows in its first and third movements excessively close adherence to Beethoven's symphonic form and style, but the remaining two movements are marked out by the inclusion of a battery of six saxophones and five saxhorns in addition to the normal orchestral wind. The fanfares that open the second movement and recur in the finale give the music an added dimension possibly inspired by Berlioz. Kreutzer also composed two operas, a symphony in B♭, about 50 songs, four string quartets, a piano trio, three piano sonatas, and other music for the piano and the organ.

BIBLIOGRAPHY

FétisB; EitnerQ

'Nachrichten: gegenwärtiger Zustand der Musik in Paris', AMZ, ii (1799–1800), 713
'Rode, Baillot and Kreutzer's Method of Instruction for the Violin', Quarterly Musical Magazine and Review, vi (1824), 527
F. J. Fétis: Obituary [Rodolphe Kreutzer], Revue musicale (15 Jan 1831), 298
P. M. F. Baillot: L'art du violon (Paris, 1834)
L. Spohr: Selbstbiographie (Kassel and Göttingen, 1860–61; Eng. trans., 1865/R1969)
J. L. Massart: L'art de travailler les études de Kreutzer (Paris, n.d.; Eng. trans., 1926)
A. Jullien: Paris dilettante au commencement du siècle (Paris, 1884)
A. Pougin: Viotti et l'école moderne du violon (Paris, 1888)
C. Pierre: Le Magasīn de musique à l'usage des fêtes nationales et du Conservatoire (Paris, 1895)
H. Kling: Rodolphe Kreutzer (Brussels, 1898)
C. Pierre: Le Conservatoire national de musique et de déclamation (Paris, 1900)
A. Schering: Die Geschichte des Instrumental-Konzerts (Leipzig, 1905, 2/1927/R1965)
J. Hardy: Rodolphe Kreutzer (Paris, 1910)
W. J. von Wasielewski: Die Violine und ihre Meister (Leipzig, rev. 5/1910 by W. von Wasielewski)
J. G. Prodhomme: 'Napoleon, Music and Musicians', MQ, v (1921), 579
A. Moser: Geschichte des Violinspiels (Berlin, 1923, rev., enlarged 2/1966–7)
C. W. Beaumont: Complete Book of Ballets (London, 1937, rev. 2/1949, enlarged 4/1956)
H. Gougelot: La romance française sous la Révolution et L'Empire (Melun, 1937–43)
P. G. Gelrud: A Critical Study of the French Violin School 1782–1882 (diss., Cornell U., 1941)
B. Schwartz: French Instrumental Music between the Revolutions 1789–1830 (diss., Columbia U., 1950)
——: 'Beethoven and the French Violin School', MQ, xliv (1958), 431
E. Anderson, ed.: The Letters of Beethoven (London, 1961)
H. Pleasants, ed.: The Musical Journeys of Louis Spohr (New York, 1961), 226ff
B. Brook: La symphonie française dans la seconde moitié du XVIIIe siècle (Paris, 1962)
E. Forbes, ed.: Thayer's Life of Beethoven (Princeton, 1964, rev. 2/1967)
H.-J. Nösselt: 'Rodolphe Kreutzer, der klassische Violinist', Das Orchester, xiv (1966), 421
D. Cairns, ed.: The Memoirs of Hector Berlioz (London, 1969)
J. Szigeti: Szigeti on the Violin (London, 1969)
H. Unverricht: Geschichte des Streichtrios (Tutzing, 1969)
P. Citron, ed.: Hector Berlioz: Correspondance générale, i (Paris, 1972)
M. R. Williams: The Violin Concertos of Rodolphe Kreutzer (diss., Indiana U., 1973)
D. Charlton: Orchestration and Orchestral Practice in Paris 1789–1810 (diss., U. of Cambridge, 1973)
C. Pierre: Histoire du Concert spirituel 1725–1790 (Paris, 1975)

DAVID CHARLTON

Kreutzer [Kreuzer], Conradin [Conrad] (b Messkirch, Baden, 22 Nov 1780; d Riga, 14 Dec 1849). German composer and conductor. The son of a respected Swabian burgher, he received his earliest musical training from the local choirmaster, Johann Baptist Rieger. In 1789 he was sent to the Benedictine monastery of Zwiefalten, where he received instruction in theory and organ from Ernst Weinrauch and learnt to play a number of instruments. In 1798 or 1799 he became a student of law at the University of Freiburg (he called himself Conradin from 1799), but after his father's death in 1800 he turned entirely to music. While still students he and friends performed his one-act Singspiel Die lächerliche Werbung. For the next three or four years he was probably in Switzerland; in 1804 he went to Vienna, where he met Haydn and was probably a pupil of Albrechtsberger. He gave music lessons and concerts in order to maintain himself, and continued to compose. From 1810 he toured Germany and Switzerland (and perhaps France and the Netherlands) with Franz Leppich, demonstrating the latter's semi-mechanical instrument, the 'panmelodicon'. They spent the winter of 1811–12 in Stuttgart, where Kreutzer's operas *Konradin von Schwaben* and *Feodora* were staged very successfully. Following Danzi's resignation he was appointed Hofkapellmeister with effect from 10 July 1812. That autumn he married for the first time; his daughters Cäcilie and Marie (the latter from his second marriage) became singers. Although he gave up his Stuttgart post in 1816 owing to intrigues, his friendship with Uhland, the leading Swabian poet and one of Germany's foremost lyricists and ballad writers, was of far-reaching importance for his later development.

After he left Stuttgart Kreutzer spent some time at Schaffhausen before accepting an invitation to become Kapellmeister (1818–22) to Prince Carl Egon of Fürstenberg at Donaueschingen, but despite an understanding employer there, he considered himself isolated and his career hampered. He made several tours while still nominally engaged at Donaueschingen, and following the successful production of his opera *Libussa* in Vienna in December 1822 he was appointed to the post of Kapellmeister at the Kärntnertor-Theater. He held the post until 1827, and again from 1829 to 1832. Between these two spells at the Vienna Court Opera he was in Paris. In 1833 he moved to the Theater in der Josefstadt, a Viennese suburban theatre, in response to an invitation from the ambitious director Pokorny. He was Kapellmeister there from 1833 to 1835, the period that saw the first performances of his two greatest successes, *Das Nachtlager in Granada* and *Der Verschwender*. Although he was back at the Kärntnertor-Theater from 1835, the opera *Die Höhle bei Waverley* was given in the Josefstadt in 1837. In 1840 he left Vienna and accompanied his daughter Cäcilie on a concert tour of Germany. Kreutzer was city music director at Cologne from 1840 until 1842; he then appeared in Belgium and France, and from 1845 he accompanied his younger daughter Marie on her engagements in Frankfurt an der Oder, Graz and Detmold. He was mentioned in 1846 as Nicolai's likely successor at the Vienna Opera, but the negotiations came to nothing and in 1848 he moved to Riga, where his daughter Marie had an engagement. He died following a cerebral stroke that occurred a few days after his daughter had broken down during a performance.

During the 1840s a number of German theatres staged Kreutzer's operas, though these were more *succès d'estime* than triumphs: Brunswick, Wiesbaden, Darmstadt, Hamburg and (posthumously) Kassel each staged one of his new operas in the years following his final departure from Vienna, but none of these houses seems to have invited him back to mount another opera. Tastes were changing, and the esteemed master of *Das Nachtlager* and *Der Verschwender* had nothing original or new to offer a public that, a decade later, was experiencing the early operas of Wagner.

Kreutzer's music has never been entirely forgotten – some of his Uhland settings for male-voice chorus long remained popular with German and Austrian choirs, *Das Nachtlager in Granada* used to be revived occasionally in Germany and a few of the solo songs are still sometimes heard; above all, his score for Raimund's 'romantic magic tale' *Der Verschwender* continues to be performed regularly in Austria. Despite the power of some of the big numbers in *Das Nachtlager* and the sure sense of dramatic timing and instrumental colour shown in his music for Raimund's play (the beggar's song 'O

hört des armen Mannes Bitte' is, in respect of its haunting, melancholy beauty, not unworthy of Schubert; its insertion within a roistering chorus is a touch that Weber would have admired), this unpretentious and pleasing minor master of the Biedermeier epoch is at his most characteristic in simple, expressive songs, such as the beggar's 'Habt Dank, ihr guten Leute' and Valentin's 'Da streiten sich die Leut herum' from *Der Verschwender*, the once-famous romance 'Ein Schütz bin ich' from *Das Nachtlager*, or some of the atmospheric Uhland settings. His effective instrumentation and lively feeling for rhythm and local colour are shown in many of his works, probably nowhere to more telling effect than in the charming (and briefly poignant) Septet in Eb op.62 for wind and strings. Several of his chamber works and songs have recently been republished.

WORKS

Printed works were published in Vienna unless otherwise stated; principal sources for MSS and published works are *A-Wdtö*, *Wgm*, *Wn*, *Wst*; *D-DO*, *Mbs*, *Rp*.

> J – *Vienna, Theater in der Josefstadt*
> K – *Vienna, Kärntnertor-Theater*
> W – *Vienna, Theater an der Wien*

STAGE
(all publications in vocal score)

Die lächerliche Werbung (Singspiel, 1), Freiburg, c1800

Die zwei Worte, oder Die Nacht im Walde (opera, 1, after Marsollier), Stuttgart, 1808 [or ? Vienna, 1803]

Aesop in Phrygien (Aesop in Lydien) (opera, 1, P. A. Wolff), ? Vienna, 1808; rev., Stuttgart, c1816

Jery und Bätely (Singspiel, 1, Goethe), K, 19 May 1810

Panthea (opera, 3), 1810, unperf.

Konradin von Schwaben (opera, 3, B. von Guseck), 1810 or before; Stuttgart, 30 March 1812 [new text by K. R. Weitzmann]; rev. 1847 as Konradin, der letzte Hohenstaufe

Feodora (opera, 1, Kotzebue), Stuttgart, 1812 (Leipzig, n.d.)

Die Insulanerin (opera, 2, ? after Metastasio), Stuttgart, 25 March 1813; rev. as Die Insulanerinnen, K, 11 Feb 1829

Der Taucher (romantic opera, 2, S. G. Bürde, after Schiller), Stuttgart, 19 April 1813; rev. 1823 (Vienna, n.d.)

Alimon und Zaide, oder Der Prinz von Katanea (opera, 3), Stuttgart, 24 Feb 1814 (Mainz, n.d.)

Die Nachtmütze (Die Schlafmütze [des Propheten Elias]) (comic opera, Kotzebue), Stuttgart, 1814

Die Alpenhütte (opera, 1, Kotzebue), Stuttgart, 1 March 1815 (Augsburg, n.d.)

Der Herr und sein Diener (opera, 1, after Fr. orig.), Stuttgart, 30 Nov 1815

Orestes (lyric tragedy, 3), ? Prague, 1818

Cordelia [? Adele von Budoy] (lyric–tragic opera, 1, Wolff), ?Donaueschingen, 1819, K, 15 Feb 1823 (Vienna, n.d.)

Libussa (Primislav) (romantic opera, 3, J. K. Bernard), K, 4 Dec 1822 (Vienna, n.d.)

Siguna (Nordic legend, 3), W, 20 Nov 1823 (Vienna, n.d.)

Erfüllte Hoffnung (bucolic scene, 1), W, 2 Dec 1824

Die lustige Werbung (comic opera, 2, C.B. [?R.B.], after Fr. orig.), W, 27 June 1826

Der Besuch auf dem Lande (comic opera, 2, R.B.), J, 8 July 1826

Jadis et aujourd'hui (opera–vaudeville, 1, C. A. Sewrin), K, 22 Sept 1826

La folle de Glaris (comic opera, 2, T.-M.-F. Sauvage), Paris, Odéon, 21 April 1827 [? same as Cordelia]

L'eau de jouvenance (comic opera, 2, F.-A. Duvert and Xavier [X. B. Saintine]), Paris, Odéon, 13 Oct 1827; as Die Verjüngerungsessenz, K, 24 Sept 1838

Das Mädchen von Montfermeuil (Denise, das Milchmädchen) (comic opera, 5, A. Schumacher), K, 3 Oct 1829

Baron Luft (Baron Lust) (Singspiel, 1, after Fr. orig.), K, 20 Jan 1830

Die Jungfrau (romantic opera, 3, Schumacher, after Mélesville), Prague, Nov 1831

Die Hochländerin (opera, 1), 1831, unperf.

Der Lastträger an der Themse (opera, 3, H. Herzenskron), Prague, 16 Feb 1832

Melusina (romantic opera, 3, Grillparzer), Berlin, Königstädter-Theater, 27 Feb 1833

Der Ring des Glückes, oder Die Quellenfürstin im Alpentale (Zauberspiel, 3, F. K. Weidmann), J, 19 Dec 1833

Das Nachtlager in [von] Granada (romantic opera, 2, K. von Braun, after F. Kind), J, 13 Jan 1834 (Vienna, n.d.)

Der Verschwender (Zaubermärchen, 3, Raimund), J, 20 Feb 1834 (Vienna, n.d.)

Tom Rick, oder Der Pavian (comic Singspiel, 3, J. Kupelwieser, after Fr. orig.), J, 1 July 1834

Der Bräutigam in der Klemme (Singspiel, 1, Herzenskron), J, 24 June 1835

Traumleben, oder Zufriedenheit, die Quelle des Glückes (Zauberspiel, 3, F. X. Told), J, 10 Oct 1835 [parody of Grillparzer: Der Traum ein Leben]

Die Höhle bei Waverley (opera, 3, G. Ott, after Oehlenschläger), J, 6 April 1837

Fridolin, oder Der Gang nach dem Eisenhammer (romantic opera, 3, J. A. F. Reil, after Schiller), K, 16 Dec 1837

Die beiden Figaro (comic opera, 2, G. F. Treitschke, after J. F. Jünger), Brunswick, 13 Aug 1840 (Brunswick, n.d.)

Der Edelknecht (opera, 4, C. von Birch-Pfeiffer), Wiesbaden, 21 June 1842 (Brunswick, n.d.)

Des Sängers Fluch (opera, 1, E. Pasqué, after Uhland), Darmstadt, 17 May 1846

Die Hochländerin am Kaukasus (romantic opera, 3, Guseck), Hamburg, 6[?16] Nov 1846 [? connected with Die Hochländerin, 1831]

Aurelia, oder Die Prinzessin von Bulgarien (romantic opera, 3, C. Gollmick, after J. F. von Weissenthurn), Vienna, 1849

Other works: Der Apollosaal (Singspiel, 1); Zenobia, unperf. [Kreutzer's final opera]; Das Bild der Landesmutter (occasional piece); Der Eremit auf Formentera (incidental music, Kotzebue), 1800–04; Fortunat (incidental music, E. von Bauernfeld), 1835; 2 ballets, Vienna, 1814: Antonius und Kleopatra, Myrsile und Anteros; Szenen aus Goethes Faust, Donaueschingen, 4 Nov 1820, songs (Vienna, 1834); Die Höhle Soncha, oder Die vierzig Räuber (melodrama, 3, K. Treuhold), unperf. [? identical with F. Roser's work of same title, 1826]

OTHER WORKS

Vocal: Die Sendung Mosis, oratorio, Stuttgart, 1 Jan 1814; Die Friedensfeier, oratorio; masses and shorter liturgical works; occasional works, incl. hymns and cantatas; over 150 lieder; numerous partsongs

Inst: 3 pf concs., B♭, op.42 (Leipzig, ?1819), C, op.50 (Bonn, ?1822), E♭, op.65 (Leipzig, ?1825); Variations, pf, orch, op.35 (Augsburg, n.d.); chamber works for str and ww in various combinations, incl. several with pf; numerous pf pieces, 2 hands and 4 hands

BIBLIOGRAPHY

C. von Wurzbach: Biographisches Lexikon des Kaiserthums Oesterreich, xiii (Vienna, 1865), 207ff

[H. Weber]: 58. Neujahrsstück der Allgemeinen Musikgesellschaft in Zürich (Zurich, 1870)

W. H. Riehl: Musikalische Charakterköpfe, i (Stuttgart, 5/1876), 263ff

H. Riemann: Opern-Handbuch (Leipzig, 1887, 2/1893 with suppl. by F. Stieger)

R. Krauss: Das Stuttgarter Hoftheater von den ältesten Zeiten bis zur Gegenwart (Stuttgart, 1908)

A. Prümers: 'Aus Kreutzers Briefwechsel', Neue Musikzeitung, xxxiii (1912), 290

R. Rossmayer: Konradin Kreutzer als dramatischer Komponist (diss., U. of Vienna, 1928)

A. Landau: Das einstimmige Kunstlied Conradin Kreutzers und seine Stellung zum zeitgenössischen Lied in Schwaben (Leipzig, 1930/R1972)

——: 'Die Klavier-Musik Conradin Kreutzers', ZMw, xiii (1930–31), 80

A. Loewenberg: Annals of Opera (Cambridge, 1943, 2/1955)

K. Goedeke: Grundriss zur Geschichte der deutschen Dichtung, xi/2 (Düsseldorf, 2/1953)

A. Bauer: 150 Jahre Theater an der Wien (Zurich, 1952)

——: Opern und Operetten in Wien (Graz, 1955)

——: Das Theater in der Josefstadt zu Wien (Vienna, 1957)

W. Rehm: 'Kreutzer, Konrad', MGG

H. Leister: Conradin Kreutzers Lieder für Männerchor (diss., U. of Mainz, 1963)

R. Heinemann: 'Kreutzer, Konrad', Rheinische Musiker, iv, ed. K. G. Fellerer (Cologne, 1966), 59

PETER BRANSCOMBE

Kreuz (Ger.). SHARP.

Kreuzchor. The choir of the Dresden Kreuzkirche; *see* DRESDEN, §§1–2.

Kreuzer, Conradin. See KREUTZER, CONRADIN.

Kreyn, Yulian Grigor'yevich (*b* Moscow, 5 March 1913). Russian composer and musicologist. His father was the composer Grigory Abramovich Kreyn (*b* Nizhny Novgorod, 18 March 1879; *d* Komarovo, nr.

Leningrad, 6 Jan 1955) and his uncle, Alexander Abramovich Kreyn (*b* Nizhny Novgorod, 20 Oct 1883; *d* Staraya Ruza, nr. Moscow, 21 April 1951) composed the celebrated ballet *Laurensiya*. Yulian Kreyn studied composition with Dukas at the Ecole Normale in Paris, graduating in 1932, and has lived in Moscow from 1934. His compositions developed under the influence of French music, but he has also drawn on the 19th-century Russian tradition and on the innovations of Skryabin. As a result his music is complex and many-sided, its lyricism clearly expressed in melodic breadth and colourful harmony. The French connection is most evident in his orchestration, while the chamber pieces are more Romantic in style. A prolific composer and a noted musicologist, he has also appeared frequently as a pianist.

WORKS
(selective list)

Orch: Razrusheniye [Destruction], sym. prelude, 1929; Vc Conc., 1929; 3 pf concs., 1929, 1943, 1942; Galateya, ballet (1934); Vesennyaya simfoniya [Spring sym.], 1935–59; Simfonicheskaya ballada (1942); Serenade, 1943; Arkticheskaya poema, sym., 1943; Vesennyaya syuita, 1948; Serebryanoye kopïttse [The silver hoof], after P. Bazhov, 1949; Tri poemï 'Druz'yam mira' [To the friends of peace], 1953; Poema-simfoniya, 1954; Poema, vn, orch, 1956; Vn Conc., 1959; Liricheskaya oda, 1962; Skazka o rïbake i rïbke [Tale of the fisher and the fish], after Pushkin, 1970

Vocal: Rembrandt, vocal-sym. picture, 1962–9; songs

Chamber: 4 str qts, 1925, 1927, 1936, 1943; Suite, vc, pf, 1928; 2 sonatas, vn, pf, 1948, 1971; Sonata-fantasia, vc, pf, 1955; Sonata, fl, pf, 1957; Pf Trio, 1958; Sonata, cl, pf, 1961; Sonata-poema, vc, pf, 1972

Pf: 2 sonatas, 1924, 1955; Ballada, 1955; other pieces

Principal publishers: Muzïka, Sovetskiy Kompozitor, Universal

WRITINGS

Manuel' de Fal'ya (Moscow, 1960)

Simfonicheskiye proizvedeniya Kloda Debyussi (Moscow, 1962)

Simfonicheskiye proizvedeniya Morisa Ravelya (Moscow, 1962)

with N. I. Rogozhina: Alexander Kreyn (Moscow, 1964)

Kamerno-instrumental'nïye ansembli Debyussi i Ravelya (Moscow, 1966)

Stil' i kolorit v orkestre (Moscow, 1967)

BIBLIOGRAPHY

Yu. N. Tyulin: Yulian Kreyn: ocherk zhizni i tvorchestva [Kreyn: sketch of his life and work] (Moscow, 1971)

G. B. Bernandt and I. M. Yampol'sky: Kto pisal o muzïke [Writers on music], ii (Moscow, 1974) [incl. list of writings]

GALINA GRIGOR'YEVA

Křička, Jaroslav (*b* Kelč, Moravia, 27 Aug 1882; *d* Prague, 23 Jan 1969). Czech composer and teacher. He studied at the Prague Conservatory (1902–5) and became an associate of Vitězslav Novák. His education was continued in Berlin (1905–6), and then he worked in Ekaterinoslav (now Dnepropetrovsk) as a music teacher for three years. While there he composed an orchestral Elegy on the Death of Rimsky-Korsakov (1908) and formed a friendship with Glazunov and Taneyev. He also conducted concerts of Czech music and contributed articles on Russian music to Czech journals. After returning home in 1909 he worked as a choirmaster, principally with the Prague Glagol choir. With them he gave the premières of works by Novák and Janáček, and of the oratorio *Jan Hus* (1920) by Jeremiáš; and he also conducted works by J. S. Bach, Liszt, Franck and others. In 1918 he was appointed professor of composition at the Prague Conservatory. He was later made rector of the conservatory, which office he held during the difficult years of the German occupation. The title of Merited Artist was bestowed on him by the liberated Czech Republic. As a composer he drew on the music of Dvořák and on folksong, and he was also influenced by Musorgsky in his popular children's songs and choral works. A spontaneous melodic gift and a flair for musical humour are evident throughout his production most of which was in dramatic works. He was also active as a writer, and helped to popularize music through his radio broadcasts.

WORKS
(selective list)

Operas: Hyppolita, 1916; Ogari, 1918; White Man (after Wilde), 1929; The Fat Great-grandfather, Thieves and Detectives, 1932; Czech Bethlehem, 1937; King Lavra, 1939; Oživlé loutky [Revived puppets], 1943; Psaníčko na cestách [A travelling letter], 1944; Joachym and Juliana, 1947; The Cradle, 1950; The Quiet House, 1951; The Zahořany Hunt, 1953; Circus Humberto, 1955

Idyllic scherzo, orch, 1909; Modrý pták [The bluebird], orch, 1911; Adventus, sym. poem, 1912; Horácká suita [Highlander suite], orch, 1935; Sinfonietta, str orch, 1942; Sinfonietta semplice, orch, 1962; Mládí [Youth], sym., n.d.; serenades

Choral works incl. Temptation in the Desert (Bible), 1922; The Thief Jenny, 1929; Tyrol Elegies, 1930; Moravian Cantata, 1936; The Golden Spinning Wheel, 1943; Requiem, 1949; 6 masses

Chamber pieces and many songs, incl. Albatross (Balmont), n.d.

Principal publisher: Hudební matice

BIBLIOGRAPHY
ČSHS [with full work-list]
J. Dostál: *Jaroslav Křička* (Prague, 1944)

JOSEF PLAVEC

Kriegck, Johann Jacob. See KRIEGK, JOHANN JACOB.

Krieger, Adam (*b* Driesen, nr. Frankfurt an der Oder, 7 Jan 1634; *d* Dresden, 30 June 1666). German composer. From 1650 or 1651 on, Krieger lived in Leipzig as a part-time student at the university, and probably during this period he studied the organ with Scheidt at Halle. He was well known to the other students, and he no doubt composed many of his more risqué songs for them. His professional musical career began in 1655, when he succeeded Rosenmüller as organist of the Nicolaikirche, Leipzig. By 1657, when he published his *Arien*, the only collection of his secular songs to appear in his lifetime, he was already known for numerous sacred compositions more commensurate with his position. In the same year Johann Georg II, the Elector of Saxony, called him to Dresden to be his daughter's private keyboard instructor, and thereafter he was under the protection of this important patron of the arts. Also in 1657 the elector encouraged him to apply for the Kantor's position at the Thomaskirche, Leipzig, as successor to Tobias Michael. He was unsuccessful, however, since he refused to submit to the conditions of teaching children and composing on command. But he often travelled the short distance from Dresden to Leipzig to participate in musical events. From 1658 until his death Krieger also served as chamber and court organist at the electoral court. He was readily accepted by the literati assembled there, most notably by the court poet David Schirmer, with whom he sometimes collaborated. There is no evidence, however, that he had any significant contact with the aging Schütz, who had retired to nearby Weissenfels.

Although he lived only 32 years Krieger's fame as a composer of songs was well established before his death. The 110 songs in his two principal collections are his most important music, and with them he brought German song to a new peak of development, firmly establishing Italian expressiveness in a tradition hitherto dominated largely by simple strophic songs influenced by French and Dutch models. His songs are both traditional and of a newer type. The texts, several by Krieger himself, range from beautiful mythological-

pastoral love scenes to bawdy drinking-poems. Most are set for one voice with continuo, but five in the earlier collection are for two or three voices, and 15 in the 1676 volume are for two to five voices. All have instrumental ritornellos.

Although no complete copy of the 1657 *Arien* survives, most of its contents have been reconstructed, principally by Helmuth Osthoff. The tunes alone are preserved in a late 17th-century Danish collection by A. D. Foss with new, psalm texts. As far as can be ascertained, all the arias are strophic, are set syllabically, and follow the models of Opitz; a few parody songs by Rist and Schwieger.

Most of the songs in the *Neue Arien* are strophic; each strophe is in binary or bar form and is followed by a ritornello for five instruments and continuo (the ritornellos to the ten extra works in the second edition were written by Johann Wilhelm Furchheim, who with Schirmer collected the songs). They thus resemble the simple strophic songs of the 1657 set, but some, with their use of dialogue, non-strophic poems and touching expressiveness, are more typical of Italian models. *Nun sich der Tag geendet hat* is an example of the older German type; it is based on Krieger's own *Ihr schönsten Blumen in der Au* of 1656, which in turn is based on a Dutch song by Jacob Cats and ultimately on a poem by Cervantes. The duet between 'Unfriendly Mopsa' and 'Enamoured Daphnis' (no.50), on the other hand, is an Italianate, non-strophic dialogue; it begins with a symphony, and a duet refrain returns after sections of dialogue. Osthoff conjectured that some of these dramatic pieces were originally performed in stage productions, possibly operas, which had become popular in Dresden at the time. This is particularly likely in the case of the most famous lied from *Neue Arien*, *Adonis' Tod*, which is a bipartite strophic aria of intense expressiveness. Krieger's songs remained popular well into the 18th century, and some of the melodies were turned into chorales, a few of which appear in Bach's cantatas.

WORKS
SACRED

Cantatas:
  An den Wassern zu Babel, 3vv, 2 vn, bc, *D-B* mus.30215
  Der Feinde erstehet, 2vv, 6 insts, lost
  Ich lobe den Krieg, *S-Uu* Vok.mus.l.hdskr. 27:8
  Ich preise dich, Herr, 4vv, 5 insts, bc, *D-B* mus.30215
  Meister, wir wissen, T, B, chorus, vn, cornett, trbn, bc, lost
Funeral songs, 4vv:
  Kommt meine Freunde, meine Lieben (Leipzig, 1654)
  Legt ein und scharrt mich in die Erde (Leipzig, 1656)
  O ihr schnöden Eitelkeiten (Leipzig, 1659)
  Ach, meine Eltern, in Saluberrima et necessaria concio (Coburg, 1667)
Aria: Nimm hin du teurer Sohn, 2vv, 2 vn, bc (Leipzig, 1656)

SECULAR

Song, Ihr schönsten Blumen in der Au, 1v, bc, in Thomas Ritzschens verteutschte Spanische Zigeunerin (Leipzig, 1656)
[50] Arien, 1–3vv, 2 vn, vle, bc (Leipzig, 1657); excerpts ed. in Osthoff and N. Schiørring: *Det 16. og 17. Århundredes Verdslige Danske Visesang* (Copenhagen, 1950)
[50] Neue Arien in 6 Zehen eingetheilet, 2, 3, 5vv, 2 vn, 2 va, bc (Dresden, 1667, enlarged 2/1676 with 10 additional songs, and with ritornellos by J. W. Furchheim; some ed. in DDT, xix (Leipzig, 1905/R)
3 songs, *D-B*

BIBLIOGRAPHY
H. Osthoff: *Adam Krieger* (Leipzig, 1929/R1970)
——: 'Krieger, Adam', *MGG*
R. H. Thomas: *Poetry and Song in the German Baroque* (Oxford, 1963)
J. H. Baron: *Foreign Influences on the German Secular Solo Continuo Lied of the Mid-seventeenth Century* (diss., Brandeis U., 1967)
N. Schiørring: 'Wiedergefundene Melodien aus der verschollenen Adam-Krieger-Ariensammlung 1657', *Festschrift für Walter Wiora* (Kassel, 1967), 304

JOHN H. BARON

Krieger, Armando (*b* Buenos Aires, 7 May 1940). Argentinian composer, pianist and conductor. He had piano lessons with John Montés and Roberto Kinsky, attended the Buenos Aires Municipal Conservatory and studied composition with Ginastera. As a pianist he has appeared throughout the Americas, introducing solo works by Hindemith, Messiaen, Boulez, Stockhausen, Pousseur and others, and taking part in local premières of concertos by Bach and Mozart. In 1963 he won a scholarship for two years' study at the Di Tella Institute, where his teachers included Copland, Dallapiccola, Maderna, Riccardo Malipiero and Messiaen. Another scholarship enabled him to continue piano studies with Loriod at the Mozarteum Argentino (1964). From this period he has been active in the Argentinian avant garde as a composer and performer. He has directed the major orchestras of the country, is a permanent conductor at the Teatro Colón (he also conducts the Pequeña Opera de Cámara of Buenos Aires) and founded his own chamber orchestra, the Solistas de Música Contemporánea de Buenos Aires. His works have been widely performed, notably at the 1962 ISCM Festival (*Elegía II*), the 1966 Paris Biennale (String Quartet no.1) and the Fourth Interamerican Music Festival at Washington, DC, in 1968. There he took the solo part in the first performance of his *Métamorphose d'après une lecture de Kafka* as well as playing, with the composer, in Gandini's *Contrastes* for two pianos and orchestra. Among the awards he has received are two Buenos Aires municipal prizes (1962 and 1965) and the first prize at the Rome Congress for the Freedom of Culture (1964, for the Cantata II). He has taught at the Escuela San Pablo, the Catholic University of Argentina, Buenos Aires University and the Instituto Superior de Arte at the Teatro Colón.

WORKS
(*selective list*)

Orch: Sym., str, 1959; Conc., 2 pf, orch, 1963; Métamorphose d'après une lecture de Kafka, pf, 15 insts, 1968; Ängst, 1970

Choral: Cantata II, S, female vv, orch, 1963; Elegía III (Bible), chorus, 1965; Cantata III (Sábato: Heroes y tumbas), speaker, solo vv, children's chorus, chorus, orch, org, 1969

Solo vocal: Cantata I, S, b cl, tpt, pf, cel, perc, vn, vc, 1959; Elegía II, A, 2 fl, pf, vib, 5 perc, 1962; Cuaderno de verano, 1v, pf, 1965; Tensiones III, 1v, ens, 1967; Cuaderno de otoño, 1v, pf, 1968; De muertes y resurrecciones, 1v, 5 insts, 1969

Chamber: Improvisaciones, fl, ob, cl, bn, 1958; Divertimento no.1, ob, cl, bn, 1959; Divertimento no.2, 2 ob, eng hn, 1959; Qt no.1, str, 1960; Elegía I, cl, pf, 1960; Aleatoria I, 10 wind, 1961; Aleatoria II, 7 insts, 1961; Duo, cl, vc, 1961; Qt no.2, fl, a sax, vib, va, 1961; Sonatina no.2, vn, pf, 1961; Tensiones II, 12 perc, 1961; 3 poemas sin nombre, 1962; 5 nocturnales, 1964

Kbd: Sonatina no.1, pf, 1958; 60, pf, 1960; Encadenamiento, pf, 1961; Tensiones I, 2 pf, 1961; Constelaciones, org, 1969

SUSANA SALGADO

Krieger, Edino (*b* Brusque, Santa Catarina, 17 March 1928). Brazilian composer, conductor and critic. He began violin studies at an early age with his father, a composer, conductor and founder of the local conservatory. A state scholarship took him in 1943 to Rio de Janeiro, where he studied the violin with Edith Reis at the conservatory and took lessons in harmony, counterpoint, fugue and composition with Koellreutter (1944–8). He became an active member of Koellreutter's Musica Viva group, winning their prize in 1945 for the Woodwind Trio. In 1948 he won first prize at the Berkshire Music Center competition for Latin American composers. He then studied orchestration and composition with Copland, composition with Mennin

at the Juilliard School (1948–9) and the violin with Nowinsky at the Henry Street Settlement School. While in New York he had several of his works performed, and he conducted the New York PO on 11 April 1949. Back in Rio he worked as a broadcaster and as music critic of the *Tribuna da imprensa* (1950–52). He organized concerts and competitions for contemporary music, and he was musical director and assistant conductor of the National SO. In 1955 he received a fellowship from the British Council to work with Berkeley for eight months at the Royal Academy of Music. The most important of his later appointments were as director of the art-music department of the Radio Jornal do Brasil, Rio (1963–73), professor of music at the Curitiba summer course (1964–8), professor of music at the Instituto Villa-Lobos (1968), general coordinator of the first and second Guanabara festivals (1969–70) and president of the Brazilian Society of Contemporary Music (1971–3).

Krieger began composing in a late-Romantic and impressionist manner, as in the *Improviso* for flute (1944). Koellreutter's influence turned him to the 12-note technique of such works as the Woodwind Trio and *Música 1947* for string quartet, but about 1952 he abandoned serialism for a slightly nationalist, neoclassical style. The most original work of this period is *Brasiliana* (1960). His music after 1965 synthesizes the two previous styles, freely employing novel techniques together with elements characteristic of Brazilian popular music.

WORKS
(*selective list*)
ORCHESTRAL AND VOCAL

Movimento misto, 1947; Contrastes, 1949; Música 1952, str, 1952; Chôro, fl, str, 1952; Suite, str, 1954; Abertura sinfônica, 1955; Concertante, pf, orch, 1955; Andante, str, 1956; Divertimento, str, 1959; Brasiliana, va/a sax, str, 1960; Variações elementares, str, 1964; Ludus symphonicus, 1966; Toccata, pf, orch, 1967; Canticum naturale, 1972

Rio de Janeiro, stage oratorio, 1965; 3 cantos de amor e paz, chorus, orch, 1967; Fanfarras e sequências, chorus, orch, 1970

Songs: Tem piedade de mim, 1947; 3 canções de Nicolás Guillén, 1953; Tu e o vento, 1954; Desafio, 1955

CHAMBER AND INSTRUMENTAL

Improviso, fl, 1944; Trio, ob, cl, bn, 1945; Peça lenta, fl, str trio, 1946; Sonata breve, vn, 1947; Música 1947, str qt, 1947; Sonatina, fl, pf, 1947; Música de câmara, fl, tpt, timp, vn, 1948; Melopéia, S, ob, t sax, trbn, va, 1949; Str Qt no.1, 1955

Pf: Peça, 1945; Epigramas, 1947; Miniaturas, 1949; Música 1952, 1952; Sonata, duet, 1953; Sonata no.1, 1954; Preludio e fuga, 1954; Sonata no.2, 1956; Sonatina, 1947

Principal publishers: Pan American Union, Peer, Universidade de Brasilia, Vitali

BIBLIOGRAPHY

'Edino Krieger: biografia e catálogo general de obras', *Compositores de America/Composers of the Americas*, ed. Pan American Union, xiii (Washington, DC, 1967)

GERARD BÉHAGUE

Krieger [Kruger], **Johann** [Kriegher, Giovanni] (*b* Nuremberg, baptized 1 Jan 1652; *d* Zittau, 18 July 1735). German composer and organist, younger brother of Johann Philipp Krieger. The Krieger family has been traced in Nuremberg from the late 16th century to 1925, when the last descendants were still practising the family trade of rugmaking. The chief source for Johann Krieger's biography is Mattheson (1740), who stated that he began his musical training with Heinrich Schwemmer, probably as his pupil at the Lateinschule attached to the church of St Sebald. Schwemmer was also Kapellmeister at this church, and Krieger sang treble in his choir for several years; he participated in a children's ballet in 1664. From 1661 to 1668 he had keyboard lessons from G. C. Wecker (another of whose pupils at this time was Pachelbel). The early years of Krieger's career are closely connected with the fortunes of his brother, through whom he obtained most of his positions. Mattheson stated that in 1671 he studied composition with his brother at Zeitz (although civic records there do not mention either of them) and that in 1672 he followed him to Bayreuth, where Johann Philipp had been appointed court organist. He was soon promoted to Kapellmeister and Johann took over the organist's post, which he held, according to Mattheson, until 1677; this is very likely, although the scanty city and court records of Bayreuth make no mention of him. When Johann Philipp became organist at the court at Halle in 1677, Johann soon appeared on the scene: he was probably employed for a short time as a chamber musician at neighbouring Zeitz before his appointment in 1678 as Kapellmeister to Count Heinrich I at nearby Greiz.

After the count's death in 1680, he was appointed Kapellmeister of the neighbouring court of Duke Christian at Eisenberg. His last position, which he held for 53 years, was as organist of St Johannis and *director chori musici* at Zittau. He played in his first service there on 5 April 1682; according to Mattheson he played in his last on 17 July 1735, the day before he died.

Johann Krieger has been praised for his contrapuntal skill, especially for his double fugues. Mattheson wrote in his *Critica musica*: 'Of the old excellent masters, I know of no one who surpasses the Zittau Kapellmeister Johann Krieger in this [the writing of double fugues]. Of the younger composers, I have come across no one who has such a skill in this as the Kapellmeister Handel'. Handel took a copy of Krieger's *Anmuthige Clavier-Übung* with him to England; he later gave it to his friend Bernard Granville, who wrote the following note in it: 'The printed book is by one of the celebrated Organ players of Germany; Mr. Handel in his youth formed himself a good deal on his plan, and said that Krieger was one of the best writers of his time for the Organ'. In contrast to the collections of the same name by Kuhnau (1689 and 1692) and Bach, which consist chiefly of partitas, Krieger's *Clavier-Übung* (published in 1699 but written about 1680) contains preludes, ricercares, fugues, fantasias, toccatas and a chaconne, which are not grouped together by key. The fugues have what were to be the essential traits of Bach's fugues – episodes, a restriction to one subject and an individuality of subject and answer – but they lack his ambitious harmony and especially his gift for melodic invention. Krieger's skill as a contrapuntist is exemplified by no.15, a quadruple fugue, which is preceded by fugues (nos.11–14) on each of the four themes. In the ricercares the answer is always an inversion of the subject. The preludes, like those of Kuhnau (the opening movements of his suites) and J. C. F. Fischer (*Les pièces de clavessin*, 1696), are free developments of a rhythmic or a harmonic idea. Krieger's second collection of keyboard music is *Sechs musicalische Partien*, though it was published first, in 1697. To the Froberger type of suite, consisting usually of allemande, courante and sarabande and later a closing gigue, Krieger added a group of dances after the sarabande; Pachelbel, on the other hand, in his *Hexachordum Apollinis* (1699), placed the added group before the sarabande, while Bach put it

before the gigue. Although the *Musicalische Partien*, like the *Clavier-Übung*, suffers somewhat from harmonic pallor and rhythmic sluggishness, Krieger nonetheless deserves to rank with Fischer, Kuhnau and Pachelbel as one of the outstanding German keyboard composers of the generation before Bach.

Krieger's other published volume, *Neue musicalische Ergetzligkeit* (1684), is a large collection of songs for one to four voices, all to texts by CHRISTIAN WEISE. Part i contains 30 strophic sacred songs, some with instrumental ritornellos. While these are in the simple lyrical style of songs written in Nuremberg at the time, the 34 secular strophic songs of part ii have freer, more ornamented melodic lines, which are appropriate to Weise's often satirical texts. Part iii contains arias – in fact strophic songs – from five Singspiels performed during the traditional Zittau Shrovetide festival in 1683 and 1684. There also survive some texts and arias from three other dramatic works by Krieger, performed at Zittau in 1688, 1717 and 1721 respectively, and he probably wrote at least one opera for the Eisenberg court. Zittau did not have its own opera; the Singspiels were performed by the pupils of the Gymnasium.

Titles of about 235 sacred vocal works by Krieger are known, but only 33 are extant, comprising 12 German cantatas, two Latin cantatas, several settings of the Sanctus, miscellaneous motets, *Magnificat* settings and solo and choral concertos. Five of the German cantatas are, for a composer working within the orbit of the Nuremberg school, rare examples of the late madrigal and mixed madrigal types, but they were all written in 1717, and by that time recitative, da capo arias and madrigal texts – the identifying features of these types of cantata – had become common practice. Krieger was thus no innovator, but compared with those of his brother, his cantatas are distinguished for their fugal movements, such as the triple counterpoint in the final movement of *Gelobet sei der Herr*, performed at Weissenfels in 1689.

WORKS

Editions: *J. Krieger: Gesammelte Werke für Klavier und Orgel*, ed. M. Seiffert, DTB, xxx, Jg.xviii (1917) [S]
  Nuremberger Meister der zweiten Hälfte des 17. Jahrhunderts, ed. M. Seiffert, DTB, x, Jg.vi/1 (1906/R) [N]
  Johann Krieger: Präludiem und Fugen, ed. F. W. Riedel, Die Orgel, ii/3 (Leipzig, 1957) [R]

INSTRUMENTAL

Allein Gott in der Höh sei Ehr, a 4, S
6 musicalische Partien (Nuremberg, 1697), S
Anmuthige Clavier-Übung (Nuremberg, 1698), S
3 fugues, 1 fantasia, 3 preludes, 3 toccatas, *US-NH*, R; Fuga, *D-Mbs*; 13 kbd works, S

CANTATAS
(dates are of first performances at Weissenfels)

Confitebor tibi Domine, 4vv, 1686, *D-B*, *GB-Lbm*; Danket dem Herrn, 4vv, 1687, N; Danksaget dem Vater, 4vv, 1688, *D-B*; Dies ist der Tag, 4vv, 1687, B; Dominus illuminatio mea, 1v, 1690, *Dlb*, *S-Uu*; Frohlocket Gott in allen Landen, 4vv, before 1717, *D-ZI*; Gelobet sey der Herr, 4vv, 1689, N; Gott ist unser Zuversicht, 4vv, *ZI*
Halleluja, lobet den Herrn, 4vv, 1685, *ZI*; Der Herr ist mein Licht, 2vv, B, *S-Uu*; Nun dancket alle Gott, 4vv, 1717, *D-ZI*; Rühmet den Herrn, 4vv, B; Sulamith, auf, auf zum Waffen, 5vv, 1717, *ZI*; Zion jaucht mit Freuden, 1v, 1717, *ZI*

SACRED VOCAL

Also hat Gott die Welt geliebet, 4vv, insts, B; Delectare in Domino, 4vv, *GB-Lbm*; Ihr Feinde weichet weg, 4vv, 1717, *D-ZI*; In te Domine speravi, 1v, *S-Uu*; Laudate Dominum omnes gentes, 5vv, *D-Bds*, B; Laudate pueri Dominum, 3vv, insts, *Dlb*
Magnificat a 4, insts, *Bds*; Magnificat a 4, insts, B; 5 settings of Sanctus, 2, 4 vv, insts: B, Bds

ARIAS AND LIEDER

Neue musicalische Ergetzligkeit, das ist Unterschiedene Erfindungen welche Herr Christian Weise, in Zittau von geistlichen Andachten,

Politischen Tugend-Liedern und Theatralischen Sachen bisher o gesetzet hat (Frankfurt and Leipzig, 1684); 2 ed. in Eitner; incl. several
arias from operas
19 occasional songs, for weddings or funerals, pubd separately 1684–
97; 1 song, ZI

OPERAS
(all lost, except for a few arias pubd in Neue musicalische Ergetzligkeit)
Der Amandus-Tag, 1688, lib ZI; Friedrich der Weise (Zittau, 1717) [5
arias only]; Nebucadnezar, 1684; Der politische Quacksalber, 1684;
Der schwedische Regner, 1684; Die sicilianische Argenis, 1683; Der
verfolgte David, 1683; Die vierte Monarchie, 1684; Von der ver-
kehrten Welt, 1683, lib ZI; Die vormahlige Zittauische Kirchen
Reformation, 1721, lib ZI

List of c225 lost works in S

BIBLIOGRAPHY
J. Mattheson: Critica musica (Hamburg, 1722–5/R1964)
J. G. Doppelmayr: Historische Nachricht von den Nürnbergischen
Mathematicis und Künstlern (Nuremberg, 1730)
J. Mattheson: Grundlage einer Ehren-Pforte (Hamburg, 1740); ed. M.
Schneider (Berlin, 1910/R1969)
R. Eitner: 'Johann Krieger', MMg, xxvii (1895), 129 and suppl., 1–60
M. Seiffert: Introduction to DTB, x, Jg.vi/1 (1906/R) and DTB,
xxx, Jg.xviii (1917)
F. W. Riedel: Quellenkundliche Beiträge zur Geschichte der Musik für
Tasteninstrumente in der zweiten Hälfte des 17. Jahrhunderts
(Kassel, 1960)
H. E. Samuel: The Cantata in Nuremberg during the Seventeenth
Century (diss., Cornell U., 1963)

HAROLD E. SAMUEL

Krieger [Kriger, Krüger, Krugl], **Johann Philipp**
[Kriegher, Giovanni Filippo] (b Nuremberg, baptized
27 Feb 1649; d Weissenfels, 6 Feb 1725). German
composer, organist and keyboard player, elder brother
of Johann Krieger. He was one of the outstanding
German composers of his time, especially of church
cantatas, of which he wrote over 2000 (nearly all lost);
under his direction the cultivation of music at the small
court at Weissenfels rose to the highest level of German
court music.

1. LIFE. The chief sources for Krieger's biography are
Doppelmayr and Mattheson (1740), who agree on its
main events but vary in details and dates, only some of
which can be substantiated from other sources.
Mattheson told the following about his early musical
training in Nuremberg: 'In his eighth year [he] began
clavier lessons with Johann Drechsel [Dretzel], a pupil
of Froberger; he also received instruction on various
other instruments from the famous Gabriel Schütz'.
According to Doppelmayr 'he progressed so rapidly in
this [clavier lessons] that already at the age of nine he
amazed large audiences with his playing; moreover, he
was able to play any melody that was sung to him and to
perform well-made arias that he himself had written'.
At the age of 14 or 16 he went to Copenhagen to
study organ playing with the royal Danish organist
Johannes Schröder and composition with Kaspar
Förster. Declining a position as organist at Christiania
(Oslo) he returned to Nuremberg after a stay of four or
five years in Copenhagen, either from 1663 to 1667
(Doppelmayr) or from 1665 to 1670 (Mattheson),
probably the latter. He cannot have remained long in
Nuremberg, for Mattheson reported, confusingly, that
he was both at Zeitz in 1670–71 and organist and later
Kapellmeister at the court at Bayreuth between 1670
and 1672 (Doppelmayr has 1669–70 for the latter
dates). According to Werner the civic records at Zeitz
contain no mention of him or his brother, and, more
confusingly still, records at Bayreuth list his name only
in 1673, as court organist.
When Margrave Christian Ernst left the Bayreuth

court in 1673 to join the war against France, Krieger
was given permission to travel to Italy without loss of
salary. He probably stayed there for about two years.
Mattheson stated that in Venice he studied composition
with Rosenmüller and the clavier with G. B. Volpe and
that in Rome he studied composition with A. M. Abbatini and the clavier and composition with Bernardo
Pasquini. Immediately after his visit to Italy he played
for the Emperor Leopold I in Vienna, in return for
which, in a letter dated 10 October 1675, the emperor
ennobled him and all his brothers and sisters. Krieger
soon left Bayreuth for Frankfurt am Main and Kassel
and was offered positions in both cities. He apparently
refused them or held them for only a short time, for on
2 November 1677 he accepted a position as organist at
the court at Halle. When Duke August died in 1680 his
successor, Johann Adolph I, moved the court to
Weissenfels. Krieger went with him as Kapellmeister, a
position he held until his death. For a time he also acted
as musical adviser to the court at Eisenberg.
Before leaving for Weissenfels Krieger sold some
music to the Marienkirche, Halle; a list of it, including
seven of his own compositions and about 50 works by
other German and Italian composers, is extant (it is
printed in DDT, liii–liv). He compiled a more important
document during his years at Weissenfels (it is also in
DDT, liii–liv): beginning in 1684 he maintained a
catalogue of every vocal work he performed. After his
death his son Johann Gotthilf continued the catalogue
until 1732 (the company of musicians at Weissenfels
was disbanded in 1736); thus it lists the music performed at the court for almost 50 years (records for the
year 1697–8 are lacking). It includes about 2000 of his
own works, 225 by his brother Johann and 475 by
other German and Italian composers. Some of his
teachers and the musicians he met in Italy – Förster,
Rosenmüller, Carissimi, Francesco Foggia, Legrenzi
and P. A. Ziani – are represented with several works
each. Among the other Italian composers in the
catalogue are Bertali, Cazzati, Ruggiero Fedeli,
Filippini, Giannettini, Gratiani, Alessandro Melani and
Peranda. Among the German composers are Beer,
Bernhard, Capricornus, Erlebach, Kerll, Knüpfer,
Printz and Theile; there are no works by Buxtehude,
Schütz, Weckmann or Zachow. Very few 16th-century
works were performed: Palestrina is represented by
eight masses and two motets, Victoria by one mass;
there are no works by Lassus or Andrea and Giovanni
Gabrieli.

2. WORKS. Krieger provided the court at Weissenfels
with secular as well as sacred music. Two published sets
of trio sonatas – 12 for two violins and continuo (1688)
and 12 for violin, viola da gamba and continuo (1693) –
are, like Corelli's but unlike Biber's and Rosenmüller's,
for only three instruments instead of four. The six suites
of his Lustige Feld-Music (1704), for four wind
instruments, are modelled on Lully's ballet suites. Eight
'sonatas' (all lost) performed at Weissenfels between
1685 and 1717 were for a large number of instruments
(e.g. 'a 15' and 'for 3 choirs') and belong to the early
history of the German concerto grosso. Although
Krieger was a well-known performer on the clavier, only
three keyboard works have survived: a passacaglia consisting of 45 variations on a six-bar theme, an aria with
24 variations and a toccata and fugue.
Krieger is known to have written 18 operas to

German texts, of which only some librettos and two published collections of arias are extant. Although some of his operas were performed at Brunswick, Dresden, Eisenberg, Hamburg and Leipzig, most of them were written for the court at Weissenfels, where Italian opera was not allowed. His arias, like those of Boxberg, Erlebach, Löhner and Strungk, are strophic songs with a syllabic setting of the text and simple harmony and rhythms; unlike those of J. W. Franck, Keiser and Kusser, they show no influence of the more developed Italian arias, in spite of Krieger's sojourn in Italy.

By far the largest part of Krieger's output consisted of cantatas. Whereas Bach wrote about 325 and Buxtehude about 400, over 2000 by him are listed in his catalogue; only 74 are extant, 26 to Latin texts, 48 to German. As a cantata composer he is significant mainly for his adoption of madrigal verse for his texts; this has earned him the title of 'father of the new cantata'. While the so-called early German cantata uses biblical, chorale or ode texts (or combinations of all three), the 'new German cantata', modelled on the Italian secular cantata and opera, consists of a series of recitatives and arias, to which biblical verses and chorale stanzas were often later added. Texts for the new cantatas were first written by the pastor and poet ERDMANN NEUMEISTER, who in 1704 was appointed deacon at the Weissenfels court. His first yearly cycle of cantata texts, the *Geistliche Cantaten statt einer Kirchen-Music*, was not published until 1704, but Krieger had them by 1700 and began to perform his settings of them during Advent 1702. Thus he had probably encouraged Neumeister to write the texts and undoubtedly advised the young poet as to their suitability for musical setting. While the music of his early cantatas is largely in the style of solo and choral concertos, *Rufet nicht die Weisheit*, the only extant setting by him of a text by Neumeister, includes recitative and, a rare form for him, the da capo aria. In general his cantatas are characterized by forthright melodic structure and simple harmony and rhythms. If they cannot be compared with Bach's, they are not unworthy to rank with those of Buxtehude and Pachelbel.

WORKS

Editions: *J. P. Krieger: 21 ausgewählte Kirchencomposition*, ed. M. Seiffert, DDT, liii–liv (1916) [S]
    J. P. Krieger: Gesammelte Werke für Orgel und Klavier, ed. M. Seiffert, DTB, xxx, Jg.xviii (1917) [G]
    J. P. Krieger: 24 Lieder und Arien, ed. H. J. Moser, NM, clxxiv, clxxv (1930) [M]
    J. P. Krieger: Triosonate, ed. H. Osthoff, NM, cxxxv (1937) [N]
    J. P. Krieger: Partie, Sonate, ed. M. Seiffert, Organum, iii/9, 11 (Leipzig, 1925–6, 2/1951–2) [O]
    J. P. Krieger: Sonate à trois, ed. C. Crussard, Flores musicae, vii (Lausanne, 1958) [C]

INSTRUMENTAL

Lustige Feld-Music (Nuremberg, 1704); 2 ed. in Eitner, 1 in O, iii/9
12 suonate, 2 vn (Nuremberg, 1688); 1 ed. in O, iii/11
12 suonate, vn, va da gamba (Nuremberg, 1693); 2 ed. in Eitner, 1 ed. in N
Sonata, 2 vn, bc, *F-Pn*, C
Sonate, 1, 2vn, va, bn, bc, *S-Uu*
Toccata e fuga, kbd, G
Aria with 24 variations, passacaglia, G

CANTATAS
(dates are of first performances, unless otherwise stated)

Musicalischer Seelen-Friede (Nuremberg, 1697); ed. in Samuel: Ach Herr, wie ist meiner Feinde so viel, 1v, 1693; Benedicam Dominum in omni tempore, 1v, 1695; Coeli enarrant gloriam Dei, 1v, 1693; Ecce nunc benedicite Dominum, 1v, 1693; Es stehe Gott auf, 1v, 1693; Fortunae ne crede est, 1v, 1699; Freuet euch des Herrn, 1v, 1693; Gott, man lobet dich in der Stille, 1v, 1693; Herr, auf dich trau ich, 1v, 1702; Der Herr ist mein Licht, 1v, 1694; Herr, warum

trittest du so ferne, 1v, 1696; Ich harre des Herrn, 1v, 1689; Ich will den Herrn loben allezeit, 1v, 1693; Ich will in aller Noth, 1v, 1688; Lobe den Herrn, meine Seele, 1v, 1692; Meine Seele harret nur auf Gott, 1v, 1695; Quam admirabilis, quam venerabilis, 1v, 1690; Rühmet den Herrn, 1v, 1693; Singet dem Herrn alle Welt, 1v, 1690; Singet frölich Gotte, 1v, 1696

Absorta est mors in victoriam, 1v, dated 1670, *S-Uu*; Ad cantus ad sonos venite, 3vv, *D-Bds*; Attendite verbum Domini, 3vv, 1688, *Dlb*; Beati omnes qui timent Dominum, 3vv, dated 1672, *S-Uu*; Cantate Domino canticum novum, 4vv, dated 1681, *D-B, GB-Lbm, S-Uu*; Cantate Domino canticum novum, 1v, *D-Dlb*, ed. O. Krüger, Die Kantate (Stuttgart, 1960), no. 50; Christus hat ausgezogen, 4vv, 1690, *Dlb*; Cor meum atque omnia mea, 5vv, 1687, *B, GB-Lbm*; Crudelis infernus inimicus, 3vv, *D-B, Dlb*; Das ist meine Freude, 3vv, *D-F*; Diligam te Domine fortitudo mea, 3vv, dated c1670, *S-Uu*; Ecce quomodo moritur justus, 4vv, 1686, *D-Dlb*

Ein feste Burg ist unser Gott, 4vv, 1688, S; Exulta, jubila, accurre laetare, 2vv, 1694, *B, S-Uu*; Fahr hin, du schnöde Welt, 2vv, *D-B*; Die Gerechten werden weggerafft, 4vv, 1686, G; Gott, du Brunnquell aller Güte, 4vv, 1687, *B, Bds*; Haurietis aquas in gaudio, 5vv, dated 1681, *S-Uu*; Der Herr ist mein Hirt, 1v, 1690, S; Heut singt die werte Christenheit, 2vv, 1688, S, ed. in Die Kantate, no.288; Ich bin eine Blume zu Saron, 2vv, edn. in Eitner; Ich freue mich dess, das mir geredt ist, 5vv, 1688, S; Ich freue mich in dem Herrn, 5vv, *D-B*; Ich habe Lust abzuscheiden, 4vv, 1697, *Dlb*

Ich lobe die Feder, 2vv, *S-Uu*; Ich verlasse mich auf Gottes Güte, 3vv, 1689, *D-B*; Ihr Christen, freuet euch, 2vv, 1687, S; Laetare anima mea, 1v, 1690, *S-Uu*; Laudate Dominum omnes gentes, 3vv, 1688, *D-B*; Laudate Dominum omnes gentes, 5vv, 1685, *F-Ssp*; Laudate pueri Dominum, 5vv, *Ssp*; Liebster Jesu, willst du scheiden, 4vv, 1687, S; Mein Gott, dein ist das alles, 3vv, *D-Mbs*; Mein Herz dichtet ein feines Lied, 8vv, 1691, S; Mein Vater nicht wie ich will, 5vv, dated 1697, B; Nun danket alle Gott, 3vv, 1685, *S-Uu*; O Jesu, du mein Leben, 1v, 1688, S

Perfunde me gratia coelesti, 3vv, dated 1670, *S-Uu*; Preise, Jerusalem, den Herren, 4vv, S; Quis me territat quis me devorat, 3vv, 1690, *D-B, F-Pn*; Quousque dormis infelix, 1v, *S-Uu*; Rufet nicht die Weisheit, 4vv, 1699, S; Sage mir, Schönster, 2vv, S; Schaffe in mir Gott ein reines Herz, 4vv, 1718, S; Singet dem Herrn ein neues Lied, 4vv, 1687, S, ed. H. Grischkat, Die Kantate (Stuttgart, 1964), no.50; Sit laus plena sit sonora, 4vv, 1691, *D-B*; Surgite cum gaudio, 1v, 1688, *Dlb*; Surgite cum gaudio, 1v, dated 1670, *S-Uu*; Träufelt, ihr Himmel, 1v, 1696, S; Trauriges Leben, betrübte Zeit, 4vv, 1694, *D-B*

Uns ist ein Kind geboren, 3vv, S; Wacht auf, ihr Christen alle, 4vv, S; Was ist doch das Menschen Leben, 4vv, 1688, *D-B*; Die Welt kann den Geist der Wahrheit nicht empfangen, 3vv, 1688, S; Wenn du gegessen hast, 4vv, B; Wo wilt du hin, 2vv, S

SACRED VOCAL

Mass, 4vv, insts, S
Magnificat, 4vv, 1685, S
Gloria, 4vv, 1718, *D-B*
Heilig, heilig, heilig, 4vv, S; ed. H. Grischkat, Die Kantate (Stuttgart, 1959), no.2
In aeternum Domine, choral concerto, 5vv, insts, 1688, *D-B*
O Jesu, meiner Seelen, in H. G. Neuss: Heb-Opfer zum Bau der Hütten Gottes (Lüneburg, 1692)

SECULAR VOCAL

Auserlesene in denen dreyen Sing-Spielen Flora, Cetrops und Procris enthaltene Arien (Nuremberg, 1690) [incl. several arias from the operas]; 6 ed. in Eitner; M
Ander Theil (Nuremberg, 1692), lost

DRAMATIC WORKS
(apart from a few arias in 1690 song collection, known only from lib)

Die ausgesöhnte Eifersucht oder Cephalus und Procris, opera, 1689; Die bewährte Liebes-Cur, lib lost, cited in Böhme, 112ff; Cecrops mit seinen drey Töchtern, opera, 1698; Chronus, Apollo, Fortuna, Constantia, Tafelmusik, 1695; Flora, Ceres und Pomona, masquerade, 1688; Ganymedes und Juventas, Tafelmusik, 1693; Die glückselige Verbindung des Zephyrs mit der Flora, Singspiel, 1683; Der grossmütige Scipio, opera, 1690

Hercules unter denen Amazonen, opera, 1693–4; Die lybische Talestrias, opera, 1698; Mars und Irene, Tafelmusik, 1687; Schleiffers Comoedia, lost; Tafelmusik bei der Rückkehr Johann Georgens und Friderica Elisabeth aus dem Emser Bade, 1707 [with H. A. Meistern]; Unterthänigstes Freuden-Opffer, Tafelmusik, 1696; Von der gedrückten und wieder erquickten Eheliebe, tragi-comedy, 1688; Der wahrsagende Wunderbrunnen, opera, 1690; Wettstreit der Treue, Schäferspiel, 1693; Der wiederkehrenden Phöbus, Singspiel, 1592

Full catalogue of works in S

BIBLIOGRAPHY

J. Mattheson: *Critica musica* (Hamburg, 1722–5/R1964), ii, 169ff

J. G. Doppelmayr: *Historische Nachricht von den Nürnbergischen Mathematicis und Künstlern* (Nuremberg, 1730)

J. Mattheson: *Grundlage einer Ehren-Pforte* (Hamburg, 1740); ed. M. Schneider (Berlin, 1910/R1969)

R. Eitner: 'Johann Philipp Krieger', *MMg*, xxix (1897), 114; suppl., 1–128

A. Werner: *Städtische und fürstliche Musikpflege in Weissenfels* (Leipzig, 1911)

M. Seiffert: Introduction to DDT, liii–liv (1916)

R. Wagner: 'Beiträge zur Lebensgeschichte Johann Philipp Kriegers und seines Schülers Nikolaus Deinl', *ZMw*, viii (1925–6), 146

E. W. Böhme: *Musik und Oper am Hofe Herzog Christians von Sachsen-Eisenberg (1677–1707)* (Stadtroda, 1930)

H. E. Samuel: *The Cantata in Nuremberg during the Seventeenth Century* (diss., Cornell U., 1963)

F. Krummacher: 'Zur Sammlung Jacobi der ehemaligen Fürstenschule Grimma', *Mf*, xvi (1963), 324

D. E. Stout: *Four Cantatas by Johann Philipp Krieger* (diss., Indiana U., 1966)

H. Kümmerling: *Katalog der Sammlung Bokemeyer* (Kassel, 1970)

HAROLD E. SAMUEL

Kriegher, Giovanni. *See* KRIEGER, JOHANN.

Kriegher, Giovanni Filippo. *See* KRIEGER, JOHANN PHILIPP.

Kriegk [Kriegck], **Johann Jacob** (*b* Bibra, nr. Meiningen, 23 June 1750; *d* Meiningen, 24 Dec 1814). German violinist and cellist. He became a chorister and, at the age of 11, a violinist in the court Kapelle at Meiningen. In 1769, while employed by the Landgrave of Hesse-Philippsthal, he visited the Netherlands and in 1773 he was first violinist with the Dutch Opera in Amsterdam, before going to Paris with the Marquis of Taillefer. There he was persuaded by J. L. Duport to exchange the violin for the cello and to study with him for a year; Kriegk became one of the first exponents of the thumb technique developed by Duport. He entered the service of the Prince of Laval-Montmorency as a cellist, and as a result of his connections with Duport and Jarnowick he was received into the leading music circles of Paris where he quickly won a reputation as a virtuoso. In 1777 he returned to Meiningen, where he was appointed chamber musican and, in 1800 (not 1798), Konzertmeister. Among his eminent pupils were his son-in-law Gustave Knoop (*b* Meiningen, 1805; *d* Philadelphia, 25 Dec 1849) and Dotzauer, founder of the 'Dresden school' of cello virtuosos.

Kriegk's four printed sonatas for cello, op.1 (his only extant works), reveal a strong sense of melody and a preference for three-movement structure and rondo form. They combine Baroque and early Classical elements with an attempt to exploit the newly-developed playing technique. His three cello concertos, apparently published in Offenbach between 1795 and 1798, are lost.

based on *MGG* (vii, 1805–6) by permission of Bärenreiter

G. KRAFT

Kriesstein [Kriegstein], **Melchior** (*b* Basle, *c*1500; *d* Augsburg, 1572 or 1573). German printer. He was probably the son of the Georg Kriechstein cited as a printer in the Basle records of 1502. By 1525 Kriesstein had moved to Augsburg, where tax records from 1527 to 1573 list his name. After his death his son-in-law, Valentin SCHÖNIG, continued the business. Kriesstein's output was relatively small, and he is known mainly for his publication of Paul Hektor Mair's genealogy of Augsburg families, *Augsburger Geschlechterbuch* (1550), and of the collections of

sacred music, mainly motets, but also a few masses and sacred lieder, edited by SIGMUND SALMINGER and JOHANN KUGELMANN, which contain numerous first editions and *unica* by German and Netherlands composers. He also printed single works by Johannes Frosch, Ulrich Brätel and Mouton. Since Salminger edited even these items, Kriesstein himself was probably not musically trained. In addition he printed various pamphlets, including reports of military actions against the Turks.

BIBLIOGRAPHY

A. Schmid: *Ottaviano dei Petrucci . . . und seine Nachfolger im sechzehnten Jahrhunderte* (Vienna, 1845/R1968), 162

B. A. Wallner: *Musikalische Denkmäler der Steinätzkunst des 16. und 17. Jahrhunderts* (Munich, 1912)

A. Dresler: *Augsburg und die Frühgeschichte der Presse* (Munich, 1952), 24

F. Krautwurst: 'Kriesstein, Melchior', *MGG* [incl. list of publications]

MARIE LOUISE GÖLLNER

Kriger, Johann Philipp. *See* KRIEGER, JOHANN PHILIPP.

Krippellied [Krippelgesang, Krippenlied] (Ger.: 'crib song'). WEIHNACHTSLIED.

Krips, Henry (*b* Vienna, 10 Feb 1912). Australian conductor of Austrian birth, brother of Josef Krips. He studied at the Vienna Conservatory and University, and made his début in 1932 at the Burg Theatre there. In 1933 he moved to Innsbruck, then to Salzburg (1934–5), and returned to Vienna until 1938, when he emigrated to Australia. He took Australian citizenship in 1944, having formed the Krips–de Vries Opera Company there, and also served as musical director for the Kirsova Ballet formed at Sydney in 1941.

From 1947 Krips worked for the Australian Broadcasting Commission, as well as being principal conductor of the West Australia SO (Perth) from 1948, and the South Australia SO (Adelaide) from 1949. For more than 20 years he played a leading part in Australian and New Zealand musical life.

In 1972 he gave up his Australian appointments to live in London, where he had appeared as a guest conductor with the Sadler's Wells Opera from 1967, and conducted occasional concerts. His performances of light Viennese music are particularly enjoyable. His compositions include opera, ballets, numerous songs and instrumental pieces.

NOËL GOODWIN

Krips, Josef (*b* Vienna, 8 April 1902; *d* Geneva, 13 Oct 1974). Austrian conductor, brother of Henry Krips. He studied at the Vienna Academy with Mandyczewski and Weingartner, and made his concert and opera début as a conductor in 1921. He joined the Vienna Volksoper under Weingartner as chorus master and répétiteur (1921–4), and then went to the city theatres at Aussig an der Elbe (1924–5) as head of the opera department; he was then at Dortmund (1925–6) and Karlsruhe as musical director (1926–33). In 1933 he became a resident conductor at the Vienna Staatsoper, and a professor at the Vienna Academy in 1935, but lost both positions on the Nazi annexation of Austria in 1938. After a season with the Belgrade Opera and Philharmonic, his musical activities were suspended by the war.

From 1945 Krips played a leading part in reorganizing postwar musical life in Vienna, conducting the resumed performances by the Vienna Staatsoper at the

Volksoper and the Theater an der Wien, and the Vienna PO at the Musikverein. In 1946 he reopened the Salzburg Festival conducting *Don Giovanni*, and returned there on several occasions. He also toured with the Vienna Staatsoper and Vienna PO to several European countries including Britain (1947), where he was appointed principal conductor of the LSO (1950–54) and much improved its musical standing. He later held similar appointments with the Buffalo PO (1954–63), the San Francisco SO (1963–70), where he was then accorded the title of conductor emeritus, and the Cincinnati May Festival (1954–60). He conducted *Don Giovanni* for his début with the Covent Garden Opera in 1963; from 1966 he was a guest conductor at the Metropolitan, and from 1970 at the Deutsche Oper, Berlin. Frequent tours with leading orchestras in Europe and North America, and many gramophone records, enhanced his reputation as a benevolent despot in performance, whose unaffected interpretations and warmth of expressive feeling served, in particular, as ideal introductions to the Viennese Classics for a post-war generation of concert-goers.

NOËL GOODWIN

Krisanizh, Georgius. See KRIŽANIĆ, JURAJ.

Krismann, Franz Xaver. See CHRISMANN, FRANZ XAVER.

Kristiania. See OSLO.

Kristinsson, Sigursveinn (David) (*b* Fljót Skagafjördur, 24 April 1911). Icelandic teacher and composer. He studied the violin and then composition, graduating from the Reykjavík College of Music in 1954. In addition, he studied composition and conducting in Copenhagen (1950–51) and at the Deutsche Hochschule für Musik, Berlin (1956–7). After a period as a music teacher and director of music schools in Siglufjördur (1958–63) he established in 1964 the Tónskóli Sigursveins D. Kristinssonar, with himself as director. He has composed a few works in a traditional Icelandic folksong style, among them *The Pine Forest* for chorus and orchestra (text by S. G. Stephansson), the symphonic poem *Winterdream of the Ptarmigan* and the *Suite on Icelandic Rhyme Songs* for violin and piano.

BIBLIOGRAPHY
O. Kristjánsson: *Kennaratal á Íslandi*, ii (Reykjavík, 1965), 450
J. Gudhnason and P. Haraldsson: *Íslenzkir samtidharmenn*, ii (Reykjavík, 1967), 241
A. Burt: *Iceland's Twentieth-century Composers and a Listing of their Works* (Fairfax, Virginia, in preparation)
AMANDA M. BURT

Kristjánsson, Arni (*b* Grund, Eyjafjördur, 17 Dec 1906). Icelandic pianist and teacher. After studying with Anders Rachlow in Copenhagen and Moritz Mayer-Mahr in Berlin he taught at the Reykjavík College of Music, where he was associate director (1933–56) and director (1956–9). He then became music director of the Iceland State Broadcast Service (1959–74) and subsequently head of the advanced piano class at the Reykjavík College of Music. He has been active both as a solo performer and as a teacher, exerting a great influence on the best young pianists in Iceland. In addition he is an outstanding accompanist and has performed with such musicians as Busch, Fischer-Dieskau, Carmirelli, Peinemann, Betty Allen

and Erling Blöndal Bengtsson. Kristjánsson has written music articles for newspapers and periodicals, has regularly lectured on music for the Iceland State Broadcast Service and is associate editor on Iceland for the second edition of *Sohlman's Musiklexikon*. He is a member of the Order of the Icelandic Falcon and Commander of the Swedish Nordstjärnan.

BIBLIOGRAPHY
Íslenzkir Samtidharmenn, i (Reykjavík, 1965), 38
AMANDA M. BURT

Křivinka, Gustav (*b* Doubravice nad Svitavou, Moravia, 24 April 1928). Czech composer. He studied composition in Brno: from 1946 to 1950 with Kaprál and Petrželka at the conservatory, later with Kvapil at the academy. While there he acted as secretary of the local branch of the Union of Czech Composers. During the 1960s he was a music producer in the Brno studios of Czech radio and television. He committed himself to socialist realism in the 1950s, composing a number of mass choruses and *častušky* (songs to encourage party ideals) designed for the widest popularity. It was at this time that he renewed his interest in Moravian folk music, which came to be a deep influence on his style, bringing it close to that of Janáček. Later he acquainted himself with the new music of western Europe, but extended vocal compositions have remained the backbone of his oeuvre.

WORKS
(selective list)
Vocal: Travařské písně [Mowers' songs] (Moravian trad.), 2 female vv, pf, 1949; Čapajev (O. Furmanov), reciter, chorus, orch, 1958; 25.000 (cantata, O. Mikulášek), S, A, str, timp, 1960; Motýli tady nežijí [No butterflies are alive here] (oratorio, concentration camp children's poems), S, Bar, children's chorus, pf, orch, 1962; Cesta člověka [The way of man], B, vc, ens, 1970
Inst: 2 vn concs., 1950, 1952; 2 syms., 1951, 1955; Sonata, vn, 1960; Conc. grosso no.2, str qt, chamber orch, 1963
Music for the theatre, cinema, radio and television

Principal publishers: Orbis, Supraphon

BIBLIOGRAPHY
ČSHS
J. Berg: 'II. symfonie Gustava Křivinky', *HRo*, xi (1958), 105, 142
R. Cigler: 'Křivinkova sonáta pro sólové housle', *HRo*, xiv (1961), 587
J. Fukač: 'K stylovému profilu Gustava Křivinky', *HRo*, xviii (1965), 136
OLDŘICH PUKL

Križanić, Juraj [Krisanizh, Georgius; Crisanius, Georgius] (*b* Obrh, Western Croatia, 1617; *d* 1683). Croatian theologian, political philosopher and writer on music. He studied theology and law in Zagreb, Graz, Bologna and Rome. As an expert in the theology and rites of the Orthodox Church he went on two important missions to Russia, in 1647 and 1659, the first time as an emissary of the Holy See, the second on his own initiative. During his second stay in Rome (1652–7) he became acquainted with Athanasius Kircher, whose example probably inspired him to write his *Asserta musicalia* (Rome, 1656), a treatise consisting of 20 succinct critical statements on various aspects of music theory.

BIBLIOGRAPHY
A. Vidaković: *Asserta musicalia (1656) Jurja Križanića i njegovi ostali radovi s područja glazbe* [Križanić's *Asserta musicalia* and other musical works] (Zagreb, 1965; Eng. trans., 1967)
J. Andreis: *Music in Croatia* (Zagreb, 1974), 87ff
I. Golub: 'Juraj Križanić's "Asserta Musicalia" in Carmuel's Newly Discovered Autograph', *IRASM*, ix (1978), 219–78
BOJAN BUJIĆ

Křížkovský, (Karel) Pavel (*b* Kreuzendorf [now Holasovice], Silesia, 9 Jan 1820; *d* Brno, 8 May

1885). Czech composer and choirmaster. He came from that part of Silesia now belonging to Czechoslovakia, but which at the time of his childhood was strongly germanized, and whose cultural centre was Troppau (now Opava). His first contact with music came from his uncles, who were village musicians, and he acquired a rudimentary musical education from the choirmaster Alois Urbánek in the church choir at Neplachovice (near Holasovice) and later as a chorister of the monastery church at Opava. He then studied at the German Gymnasium at Opava; after leaving in 1839 he entered the philosophy faculty in Olomouc, but poverty compelled him to give up his studies. On returning to Opava he qualified as a teacher and taught Czech as an assistant schoolmaster at Jamnice from 1841 to 1843. In autumn 1843 he went to Brno to resume his study of philosophy, and with only brief interruptions he spent the rest of his life in the Moravian capital.

After settling in Brno, Křížkovský set about developing his musical talent. As a student he founded and conducted a choir and apparently studied theory with Gottfried Rieger; some of his first attempts at composition date from this time. In 1845 he joined the Augustinian monastery in Old Brno, which in the first half of the 19th century was a significant centre of musical life for the whole of Moravia. From 1846 to 1850 he studied theology, and in 1848 he took orders and was appointed choirmaster of the Augustinian church and of the monastery foundation, in which Janáček later received his first musical training. He also became a founder of the Männergesangverein (1848). Although he tried to broaden the city's musical horizons by introducing works of Michael and Joseph Haydn, Mozart, Beethoven, Mendelssohn, Cherubini and Spohr at cantata and chamber concerts (he was the violinist of a Brno string quartet), he also promoted Czech hymn singing in church, and at concerts gave works by Czech composers (including himself) in the Czech language. By this time he was a supporter of Czech cultural and political nationalism and pan-Slavism, strongly influenced by the theology professor and Moravian folksong collector František Sušil. A sign of his feelings was his reversion to the original Czech spelling of his name instead of the germanized 'Krischkowsky'. After 1848 his growing national consciousness also marked his compositions; he was especially active as a choral composer, and from 1860 to 1863 was choirmaster of the Beseda Brněnská music society. His concerts during these years took him to Prague (1861) and included a concert in Brno (1863), which celebrated the 1000th anniversary of the arrival of SS Cyril and Methodius in Moravia and was attended by leading representatives of Czech political life. The Prague concert earned him Smetana's highest appreciation (for both performance and composition), but pressure from the ecclesiastical authorities forced him to abandon secular music and devote his activities as composer and conductor to sacred music along the lines of the contemporary Cecilian reforms. His creative work had begun with promising secular choruses to Czech words but now closed with occasional church compositions on Latin and Czech texts.

Křížkovský belonged to the founding generation of Czech national music. His choral settings of folksongs from Sušil's collections typify the so-called 'ohlasy národních písní' ('folksong echoes', later developed by Janáček, Dvořák, Novák, Suk and Martinů), in which

Křížkovský generally made use of authentic folktunes with their original texts. In the first of them, the chorus *Čáry* ('Enchantment'), he set the unaltered folk melody in Classical harmony and arranged it for four voices, while retaining the simple strophic structure of the original song; later, however, he treated the folksongs more freely, reshaping their melodies and recasting them in more advanced musical forms. In *Odpadlý od srdca* ('The faithless heart'), for example, he borrowed only some characteristic intervals and rhythmic patterns from the original melody; in other compositions he avoided the characteristic Moravian melodic tendency towards the flattened 7th (used freely by Janáček), and arranged the folksongs in Classical harmonic and melodic patterns, as in the choruses *Zatoč se* ('Turn round') and the unaccompanied chorus *Odvedeného prosba* ('The recruit's prayer'). Křížkovský's 'folksong echoes' also show a formal inclination to the Classical style; from the motivic material he constructed symmetrical phrases and developed them into two- or three-section song forms, large rondos, as in the 1860 version of *Utonulá* ('The drowned maiden'), or variations, as in *The Recruit's Prayer*, *Turn Round*, *Dar za lásku* ('The love-gift') and *Výprask* ('Threshing'). His compositions are chiefly homophonic; in the larger dramatic choruses, such as *The Drowned Maiden* and *The Recruit's Prayer*, the texture becomes more animated, and only in the cantatas, such as *Sv Cyril a Metoděj* ('SS Cyril and Methodius'), does it become genuinely contrapuntal.

Although Křížkovský's secular choral idiom follows the popular *Liedertafel* tradition, imported into Moravia from Germany, 'he was able to feel the spirit of the songs he selected, and from this he let the composition grow . . . he thereby served the songs and served Czech music' (Janáček). The fact that his art songs and sacred works lack the invention and inspiration of his folk-based compositions indicates both the significance and limitations of his contribution to the rise and development of Czech national music.

WORKS

Edition: *P. Křížkovský: Skladebné dílo* [Works], i, ed. V. Steinman and J. Racek (Prague, 1949) [K]

SACRED

Stationes pro Festo SS Corporis Christi, S, A, T, B, mixed vv, orch, 1845–6
Mass, c, male vv, *c*1848
Mass 'Vokalmesse', G, male vv, org ad lib (Brno, 1911)
Vater unser, Ave Maria, male vv, *c*1848
Communionlied: Welch ein Himmel, solo vv, mixed vv, *c*1848
Salve regina, mixed vv, 1853
Christus factus est obediens, off, ?male vv, 1855
9 responsories for the Office of the Dead, mixed vv, org, 1855 (Brno, n.d.)
Svatý, svatý zpíváme [Holy, holy we sing], male vv, ?1857–9, version for mixed vv (Brno, 1904)
Te Deum, mixed vv, chamber orch, org, *c*1860
Ejhle, oltář Hospodinův září [Behold, the Lord's altar is ablaze] (J. Soukup), ? vv, org, 1863–4 [orig. title: Ejhle, sváty Velehrad už září (Behold, holy Velehrad is ablaze)]
Die Hirten von Bethlehem (L. Knopp), Liederspiel, mixed vv, harmonium/org (Vienna, 1871)
Offertorium plurimum martyrum, mixed vv, *c*1873 (Brno, 1904)
Diffusa est, grad, vv, 1874
Te Deum, mixed vv, *Cecilie*, ii (1875), suppl.
Litanie lauretanae, mixed vv, *Cecilie*, ii (1875), suppl.; iii (1876), suppl.
Dextera Domini, off, mixed vv
Haec dies, grad, mixed vv, *c*1878
Missa propria pro Sabbato Sancto, vv, org, *c*1878
Requiem, male vv, *Cecilie*, v (1878), suppl.

SECULAR CHORAL

Die Universität (L. A. Frankl), male vv, 1848, K
Utonulá [The drowned maiden] (trad.), male vv, 1848, rev. 1860 (Prague, 1861); orig. and rev. versions (Prague, 1927), K

Čáry [Enchantment] (trad.), vv, 1848, K
Prosba o převoz [A request to the ferryman] (trad.), male vv, 1848 (Brno, 1904), K [orig. title: Převozníček]
Věrný do smrti [Faithful until death], Šavlička (Šablenka) [Little sabre]: (trad.), male vv, 1848 (Brno, 1904), K
Odpadlý od srdca [The faithless heart] (trad.), 1849 (Prague, 1864), K [orig. title: Dívča (Maiden)]
Dar za lásku [The love-gift] (trad.), male vv, 1849, rev. 1855 for mixed vv (Brno, 1904), rev. 1861 for male vv (Prague, 1863), K
Sv Cyril a Methoděj [SS Cyril and Methodius] (F. Sušil), cantata, male vv, 1850 (Brno, n.d.), rev. 1861 with pf/band acc. (Prague, 1895), K
Rozchodná [Song of parting] (trad.), male vv, 1850 (Prague, 1898), K
Zatoč se [Turn round] (trad.), male vv, 1851, rev. 1860 (Brno, 1904); orig. and rev. versions (Prague, 1927), K
Odvedeného prosba [The recruit's prayer] (trad.), ?male vv, 1857–61 (Brno, 1904), rev. 1862 (Prague, 1863), K
Výprask [Threshing] (trad.), male vv, ? before 1859, rev. 1866 with T solo, pf acc. (Brno, 1904), K
Žaloba [The plaint] (trad.), vv, c1859, Dalibor, v (1881), K
Pastýř a poutníci [The shepherd and the pilgrims] (Sušil), T, Bar, mixed vv, 1865 (Brno, ?1866), K
Zahrada boží [God's garden] (trad.), male vv, ?1867 (Brno, 1867), K
Zpěv pohřební (Zpěv u hrobu) [Funeral song (Song at the grave)] (Sušil), male vv ?1868 (Brno, 1904), K
Je jaro [It's spring], male vv, 1881 (Prague, 1881), K
Vesna [Spring], male vv, Dalibor, v (1881), K

SONGS
(for 1v, pf unless otherwise stated)
Aj, vy bratři, aj, jonáci! (?Křižkovský), 1848 (Brno, 1930), K
22 písní pro školy [Songs for schools], 3vv, 1855 (Brno, 1856, 2/1858), K
Kalina [The snowball tree] (trad.), c1862 (Prague, 1890), K
Zahučaly hory [Zachučal mountains] (trad.), c1864 (Prague, 1883), K
Zábrana [Hindrance] (trad.), T, pf, c1863 (Brno, 1863), K
Klekání [The evening bell], B-Bar, pf, c1866 (Brno, 1904), K
Jeseň a máj [Autumn and maytime] (Soukup), 1870 (Prague, n.d.)

BIBLIOGRAPHY
J. Geisler: Pavel Křížkovský (Prague, 1886)
L. Janáček: 'Pavla Křížkovského význam v lidové hudbě moravské a v české hudbě vůbec' [Křížkovský's role in Moravian folk music and in Czech music generally], Český lid, xi (1902), 257
K. Eichler: Pavel Křížkovský (Brno, 1904)
E. Axman: Morava v české hudbě XIX. století [Moravia in 19th-century Czech music] (Prague, 1920), 66ff
V. Helfert: 'Pavel Křížkovský a Bedřich Smetana', Morava, ii (1926), 161
P. K. Mach: Křižkovský und der kirchliche Knabengesang (Brno, 1936)
J. Racek: Pavel Křížkovský: prameny, literatura a ikonografie [Křížkovský: sources, bibliography and iconography] (Olomouc, 1946)
B. Štědron, ed.: Janáček ve vzpomínkách a dopisech [Janáček in reminiscences and letters] (Prague, 1946; Eng. trans., 1955)
JIŘÍ VYSLOUŽIL

Križman, Frančisek Ksaver. See CHRISMANN, FRANZ XAVER.

Krob, Josef Theodor. See KROV, JOSEF THEODOR.

Kroepfl [Kröpfl], Francisco (b Szeged, 26 Feb 1931). Argentinian composer and teacher of Hungarian origin. He settled in Buenos Aires in 1932 and studied composition with Paz. From adolescence he became absorbed by the problems of new compositional developments, and in particular of electronic music. In 1950 he joined the Agrupación Nueva Música, becoming its director in 1956. He translated and provided a foreword for the Spanish edition of the electronic music issue (no.1) of Die Reihe (Buenos Aires, 1958), and in 1959 he was called upon to organize and direct the Estudio de Fonología Musical at Buenos Aires University, the first permanent electronic music studio in Argentina. He was also made director, on its creation, of the Laboratorio de Música Electrónica at the Di Tella Institute and given the title of professor. Kroepfl has also taught at the Centro de Estudios Superiores de Arte of Buenos Aires University, and he held the post of

musical assessor at the Museo Nacional de Bellas Artes, Buenos Aires.

Kroepfl is one of the most prominent composers of the Argentinian avant garde, though his output also includes music based on conventional methods. One of his major tape compositions is *Diálogos I*, planned in December 1964 and realized at the Di Tella Institute studios late in 1965. The music is made up of sine waves and filtered white noise, and it was included in a concert of tape pieces at the 1968 Interamerican Music Festival in Washington, DC. Kroepfl has also composed a good deal of instrumental and electronic music for films and audio-visual spectacles: his score for *Dimensión*, made by the film institute of Buenos Aires University, won the Bucranio di Bronzo at the 1961 Parma Festival of Artistic and Scientific Short Films, and he won first prize for his contribution to the Siam di Tella Pavilion at the National Agriculture and Industry Exhibition (1964).

WORKS
(selective list)
Inst: 3 Pf Pieces, 1948; Música para fl y cl, 1951; Música para 4 insts, 1952; Pf Variations, 1952; 2 estudios, prepared pf, 1953; Música para cl, 1956; Música para pf, 1958; Música a 6 (Móvil I), 1959; Música para 25 insts, 1960; Música para 3 perc y sonidos electronicos, 1962; Móvil II, pf, 1962; Acciones para pf (Movil III), 1962–6; Forma versus textura, 4 jazz insts, 1967; Ideas asociadas, ens, 1969
Vocal: 4 canciones de Aldo, S, fl, cl, 1952; Música para S, cl, tpt, vn, pf, 1953; 3 canciones de Mario Porro, S, ens, 1954–6; Música 1957, S, vib, gui, pf, perc, 1957; La piel de cada día (R. C. Aguirre), S, ens, 1v on tape, 1959
Tape: Ejercicio de texturas, 1960; Ejercicios con impulsos, 1961; Ejercicios de movimentos, 1962; Ejercicio con ruido coloreado, 1962; Diálogos I, 1964–5; Diálogos II, 1965; Diálogos IIb, 1966; Diálogos III, 1968; Variante, 3 tape rec, 1969
SUSANA SALGADO

Kroff, Josef Theodor. See KROV, JOSEF THEODOR.

Krogh, Torben (Thorberg) (b Copenhagen, 21 April 1895; d Copenhagen, 10 Feb 1970). Danish theatre historian. He studied at the Copenhagen Conservatory (1914–17) and, until 1919, at the University of Copenhagen, but went to German universities for further studies in music history and psychology under Wolf and Stumpf and theatre history under Max Hermann. He took his doctorate in Berlin in 1922 (and in Denmark in 1924). From 1924 to 1929 he was opera producer at the Royal Theatre in Copenhagen, lecturing on the history of music and the theatre. He also edited the theatre's programmes, and was its librarian. In 1950 he became professor of opera history and aesthetics at the University of Copenhagen, moving to the chair of theatre history and aesthetics in 1953; he retired in 1966.

Krogh was the first in Denmark to emphasize the importance of source material as a basis for theatre-history research, an attitude supported by his deep knowledge of the cultural life of Europe, especially its theatre, from classical Greece onwards. He believed that each period has its own system of theatre with a specific structure which must be analysed on the basis of lists of properties, account books, iconographical material, etc. He pursued this theory, both in his writing and in his lectures, through every topic that he dealt with.

WRITINGS
'De første forsøg paa at skabe en opera i det danske sprog' [The first attempt to create an opera in the Danish language], Aarbog for musik 1922, 123–58

'Ariearterne i det 18de aarhundrede', *Aarbog for musik 1923*, 94
Zur Geschichte des dänischen Singspiels im 18. Jahrhundert (diss., U. of Copenhagen; Copenhagen, 1924)
'Det tyske operaselskabs besøg i København under Frederik IV', *Aarbog for musik 1924*, 88–160
'Studier over de sceniske opførelser af Holbergs komedier i de første aar paa den genoprettede danske skueplads' [A study of the performances of Holberg's comedies during the first years of the rebuilt Danish theatre], *Studier fra sprog- og oldtidsforskning*, clii (1929), 1–82
'Reinhard Keiser in Kopenhagen', *Musikwissenschaftliche Beiträge: Festschrift für Johannes Wolf* (Berlin, 1929), 79
'Studier over Harlekinaden paa den danske skueplads', *Studier fra sprog- og oldtidsforskning*, clix (1931), 1–100
Danske teaterbilleder fra det 18de aarhundrede: en teaterhistorisk undersøgelse (Copenhagen, 1932)
'Hofballetten under Christian IV og Frederik III: en teaterhistorisk studie', *Studier fra sprog- og oldtidsforskning*, clxxx (1939), 1–112
Aeldre dansk teater: en teaterhistorisk undersøgelse (Copenhagen, 1940)
'Heibergs vaudeviller: studier over motiver og melodier', *Studier fra sprog- og oldtidsforskning*, clxxxix (1942), 1–132
Holberg i det Kongelige teaters aeldste regieprotokoller (Copenhagen, 1943)
'Bellman som musikalsk Digter', *Studier fra sprog- og oldtidsforskning*, cxcvi (1945), 1–144
'Skuespilleren i det 18de aarhundrede: belyst gennem danske Kilder', *Studier fra sprog- og oldtidsforskning*, ccv (1948), 1–115
ed., with S. Kragh-Jacobsen: 'Fra hofballetten over Galeottis århundrede til Bournonville', *Den Kongelige danske ballet* (Copenhagen, 1952), 1–192
'Molieres Don Juan i Komediehuset på Kongens Nytorv', *Festskrift udgivet af Københavns universitet i anledning af universitetets årsfest november 1964* (Copenhagen, 1964), 5–102

BIBLIOGRAPHY
Musik og Teater (Copenhagen, 1955) [Festschrift for Krogh's 60th birthday, contains 18 major articles and a full bibliography]
F. J. Billeskov Jansen: 'Torben Krogh', *Festskrift udgivet af Københavns universitet i anledning af universitetets årsfest november 1970* (Copenhagen, 1970), 198

NANNA SCHIØDT

Krogulski, Józef Władysław (*b* Tarnów, 4 Oct 1815; *d* Warsaw, 9 Jan 1842). Polish pianist, conductor, teacher and composer. He studied the piano with his father, the composer Michał Krogulski, and performed as a pianist in 1825 in various Polish towns and in Berlin, Dresden and Leipzig. In Warsaw he studied composition under Elsner and Kurpiński, and then devoted himself to work as a composer, teacher, performer and conductor of church choirs; he was also head of a school training singers for church choirs. He composed a number of sacred works, as well as some orchestral and instrumental music.

WORKS
(*MSS in PL-Kj, Wn, Wtm*)
Ojżoneczka [Oh my wife] (comic opera, J. H. Cogniard), Warsaw, 28 May 1833
Choral: 10 masses; Requiem; Nieszpory [Vespers]; Miserere, frag. (Warsaw, n.d.); 4 cantatas; Oratorium na Wielki piątek [Oratorio for Good Friday]; Karawana na pustyniach Arabistanu [Caravan across the Arabian desert], solo vv, chorus, orch; other choral works; solo songs
Inst: Ov., d, orch; 2 pf concs., E, 1830, b, 1831; Octet, d; 2 qts; 2 pf sonatas; La bella cracoviana, pf (Leipzig, n.d.); other pf miniatures

BIBLIOGRAPHY
SMP
J. M. Wiślicki: *Józef Krogulski jako kompozytor religijny* (Warsaw, 1843)
W. Hordyński: *Józef Władysław Krogulski: życie i twórczość fortepianowa* [Life and piano works] (diss., U. of Kraków, 1939)
L. T. Błaszczyk: *Dyrygenci polscy i obcy w Polsce działający w XIX i XX wieku* [Polish and foreign conductors working in Poland in the 19th and 20th centuries] (Kraków, 1964)
A. Nowak-Romanowicz and others, eds.: *Z dziejów polskiej kultury muzycznej* [History of Polish musical culture], ii (Kraków, 1966)

KATARZYNA MORAWSKA

Krohn, Ernst C(hristopher) (*b* New York, 23 Dec 1888; *d* Santa Fe, New Mexico, 21 March 1975). American musicologist and music bibliographer. He studied the piano with Ottmar Moll (1909–13); he was named Moll's first assistant and continued to teach with him until 1934. From 1920 he studied music history privately. He was a lecturer in music history at Washington University, St Louis (1938–53), and director of music at St Louis University (1953–63). In 1963 he was appointed honorary curator of the Gaylord Music Library of Washington University.

Krohn was noted as a chronicler of the musical history of Missouri. His *Missouri Music* is based on a series of articles originally published in 1923, and Krohn added details of the growth of musical activities in his adopted state, particularly in the St Louis area. As a piano teacher he wrote numerous compositions and articles on piano teaching; from 1910 to 1950 he was an assistant editor for the Shattinger Piano & Music Co. of St Louis.

WRITINGS
'The Bibliography of Music', *MQ*, v (1919), 231
A Century of Missouri Music (St Louis, 1924/*R*1965, with additions, as *Missouri Music*)
'Die Musikwissenschaft in Amerika', *ZMw*, viii (1925–6), 297; ix (1926–7), 365
'Alexander Reinagle as Sonatist', *MQ*, xviii (1932), 140
'Reinagle, Alexander', 'Sobolewski, Edward', 'Zach, Max Wilhelm', 'Ziehn, Bernhard', *DAB*
The History of Music: an Index to the Literature Available in a Selected Group of Musicological Publications (St Louis, 1952/*R*1958)
'Vatican Music Collections on Microfilm at St. Louis University', *Caecilia*, lxxxiv (1957), 95
'Music in the Vatican Film Library at St. Louis University', *Notes*, xiv (1956–7), 317
'Some Solo Cantatas of Alessandro Stradella', *Manuscripta*, ii (1958), 3
'The *Nova Musica* of Johannes Ciconia', *Manuscripta*, v (1961), 3
'The Development of Modern Musicology', L. Spiess and others: *Historical Musicology: a Reference Manual for Research in Music* (Brooklyn, 1963), 153
'St. Louis', 'Reinagle, Alexander', *MGG*
'Musical Festschriften and Related Publications', *Notes*, xxi (1963–4), 94
Review of A. Thayer: *Life of Beethoven*, ed. E. Forbes (Princeton, 1964), *Manuscripta*, ix (1965), 115
Review of V. Duckles, ed.: *Music Reference and Research Materials: an Annotated Bibliography* (New York, 1964), *EM*, ix (1965), 328
'Musical Mechanical Figures in Formal Gardens', *Manuscripta*, xi (1967), 151
'On Classifying Sheet Music', *Notes*, xxvi (1969–70), 473
Music Publishing in the Middle Western States before the Civil War (Detroit, 1972)

BIBLIOGRAPHY
'A Bibliography of the Writings and Compositions of Ernst C. Krohn', E. C. Krohn: *Missouri Music* (New York, 1965), 317
Obituary, *Notes*, xxxii (1975–6), 33

PAULA MORGAN

Krohn, Ilmari (Henrik Reinhold) (*b* Helsinki, 8 Nov 1867; *d* Helsinki, 25 April 1960). Finnish musicologist and composer. He studied music theory, the piano, organ and composition in Helsinki with Richard Faltin (1885–6), and continued his studies at the Leipzig Conservatory (1886–90) and at Helsinki University (MA 1894), where he took the doctorate in 1900 with a dissertation on Finnish sacred folktunes; he also had a period of study in Weimar with Baussner (1909). Having collected folk music in Finland (1886, 1890, 1897–8) and Sweden (1897) he did extensive fieldwork in central Europe (1900, 1902, 1905, 1908, 1914, 1919, 1923 and 1930). Besides his activities as a music critic, choral conductor and organist he held appointments as a lecturer in music in Helsinki at the Music Institute (1900–01, 1905, 1907, 1914–16), the Philharmonic Orchestra School (1900–01, 1904–14), the Church Music Institute (1923–30, 1933–44) and at the university (1900–18), where he became the first professor of musicology (1918–35). In 1910 he founded the Finnish section of the International Musical Society; he was the founder (1916) and chairman (1917–39) of the Finnish Musicological Society and a leading member of other music organizations, especially church music commissions. His many academic honours included an honorary doctorate of theology from Helsinki University (1955).

Krohn was the founder of Finnish musicology. His research was primarily in two areas: folk music and music theory, especially formal analysis. He published three large volumes of Finnish folk music (1893–1933) systematized according to the methods he devised. Developing the theoretical methods formulated by Riemann, he provided in his five comprehensive textbooks (1914–37) the Finnish terminology for the subject and the basis of subsequent Finnish music education. His interest in rhythmic analysis led him to evolve a hierarchy of musical forms from the smallest possible units to works on the scale of the *Ring*. Towards the end of his life he published large and detailed programmatic analyses of the symphonies of Sibelius and Bruckner, comparable to Lorenz's studies of Wagner. They have been criticized for a certain Christian-patriotic naivety, but have recently attracted interest by virtue of their hermeneutic approach. Krohn's compositions are primarily sacred and include two oratorios, *Ikiaartehet* ('Eternal treasures', 1912) and *Voittajat* ('The conquerors', 1935), a *St John Passion* (1940), the opera *Tuhotulva* ('The flood', 1918), cantatas, psalms and other church music.

WRITINGS

'La chanson populaire en Finlande', *2nd International Folk-lore Congress: London 1891*, 241

Über die Art und Entstehung der geistlichen Volksmelodien in Finnland (diss., U. of Helsinki, 1900; Helsinki, 1899)

'De la mesure à 5 temps dans la musique populaire finnoise', *Congrès international d'histoire de la musique: Paris 1900*, 241; also in *SIMG*, ii (1900–01), 142

'Melodien der Berg-Tscheremissen und Wotjaken', *SIMG*, iii (1901–2), 430

'Welche ist die beste Methode um Volks- und volksmässige Melodien nach ihrer melodischen Beschaffenheit lexikalisch zu ordnen?', *SIMG*, iv (1902–3), 634

'Über das lexikalische Ordnen von Volksmelodien'; 'Das akustische Harmonium der Universität zu Helsingfors'; 'Zweckmässige Notation von Psalmen und anderen rezitativischen Gesängen'; 'Zur Einheitlichkeit der Notenschlüssel', *IMusSCR*, ii *Basle 1906*, 66; 75; 47; 55

'Über die typischen Merkmale der finnischen Volksmelodien in der Abteilungen A I und A II'; 'Reform der Taktbezeichnung', *IMusSCR*, iii *Vienna 1909*, 230; 386

Musiikin teorian oppijakso [Principles of music theory], i: *Rytmioppi*; ii: *Säveloppi*; iii: *Harmoniaoppi*; iv: *Polyfoniaoppi*; v: *Muoto-oppi* (Porvoo, 1911–37, vol.i rev. 2/1958)

Puhdasvireisen säveltapailun opas [Guide to solfège in natural tuning] (Helsinki, 1911)

'Über die Methode der musikalischen Analyse', *IMusSCR*, iv *London 1911*, 250

'Mongolische Melodien', *ZMw*, iii (1920–21), 65

'Der metrische Taktfuss in der modernen Musik', *AMw*, iv (1922), 100

'Lohengrins formbyggnad', *STMf*, iv (1922), 1

'Erneuerung des musiktheoretischen Unterrichts I–III', *Bulletin de la Société 'Union musicologique'*, iii (1923), 2; iv (1924), 128; v (1925), 194

'Die Entwicklung der Opernform in Wagners Frühwerken', *Bayreuther Festspielführer* (1924)

'Die Kirchentonarten', *Kongressbericht: Basel 1924*, 220

'Zur Analyse des Konsonanzgehalts', *Festskrift tillägnad Hugo Pipping* (Helsinki, 1924), 303

'Methode für Ausbildung zur Melodik', *Kongressbericht: Leipzig 1925*, 190

'Puccini: Butterfly', *Gedenkboek aangeboden aan Dr. D. F. Scheurleer* (The Hague, 1925), 181

'Psalmengesang in der Volkssprache', *Festschrift Peter Wagner* (Leipzig, 1926/R1969), 118

'Die Form des ersten Stazes der Mondscheinsonate', *Beethoven-Zentenarfeier: Wien 1927*, 58

'Der tonale Charakter gregorianischer Rezitative', *Studien zur Musikgeschichte: Festschrift für Guido Adler* (Vienna, 1930/R1971), 33

'Fr. Aug. Gevaerts Stellung zum gregorianischen Gesang', *IMSCR*, ii *Liège 1930*, 156

Die Sammlung und Erforschung der Volksmusik in Finnland (Helsinki, 1933)

Die finnische Volksmusik (Griefswald, 1935)

Liturgisen sävellystyylin opas [The liturgical style of composition] (Porvoo, 1940)

Der Formenbau in den Symphonien von Jean Sibelius (Helsinki, 1942)

'Módszertani kérdések az összehasonlító népdalkutatásban' [Methods of comparative folk melody research], *Emlékkönyv Kodály Zoltán hatvanadik Születésnapjára* (Budapest, 1943), 97

Der lutherische Choral in Finnland (Åbo, 1944); also in *Festskrift til O. M. Sandvik* (Oslo, 1945), 122 as 'Den lutherske choral in Finland'

Der Stimmungsgehalt der Symphonien von Jean Sibelius (Helsinki, 1945–6)

'Einheitliche Grundzüge musikalischer Formgebung', *AcM*, xxv (1953), 20

Anton Bruckners Symphonien: Untersuchung über Formenbau und Stimmungsgehalt (Helsinki, 1955–7)

'Formale und ideelle Einheitlichkeit der Symphonien Anton Bruckners', *Kongressbericht: Wien Mozartjahr 1956*, 313

FOLKSONG EDITIONS

Suomen kansan sävelmiä [Folktunes of the Finnish people] (Helsinki and Jyväskylä, 1893–1933)

BIBLIOGRAPHY

Juhlakirja Ilmari Krohn'ille 8.XI.1927 (Helsinki, 1927)

'Ilmari Krohn zum 70. Geburtstag', *Musiikkitieto* (Helsinki, 1937), Nov [special no.]

S. Ranta: 'Ilmari Krohn', *Suomen säveltäjiä*, ed. S. Ranta (Porvoo, 1945), 273

I. Krohn: *Sävelmuistoja elämäni varrelta* [Memoirs] (Porvoo, 1951)

A. O. Väisänen: 'Ilmari Krohn 90 Jahre alt', *AcM*, xxix (1957), 53

N.-E. Ringbom: 'Ilmari Krohn 90 Jahre alt', *Mf*, xi (1958), 1

M. Hela: 'Suomen musiikin kunniavanhuksen mentyä' [The grand old man of Finnish music has passed], *Suomen musiikin vuosikirja 1959–60* (Helsinki, 1960), 8

T. Kuusisto: 'Ilmari Krohn', *Musiikkimme eilispäivää* (Porvoo, 1965), 162

E. Linnala: 'Ilmari Krohn opettajana' [Krohn as teacher], *Suomen musiikin vuosikirja 1966–67* (Helsinki, 1967), 72 [with Eng. summary]

ERKKI SALMENHAARA

Krol, Bernhard (*b* Berlin, 24 June 1920). German composer and horn player. In Berlin he studied at the Mohr Conservatory (1938), at the Internationales Institut (1940–44) and with Rufer (composition). He played in the Berlin Staatskapelle (1945–61) and the South German RSO (from 1962).

WORKS
(selective list)

Operas: Pulcinella (C. Hotzel), Kaiserslautern, 24 Jan 1971; Conc(o)urs, 1971

Orch: Conc. grosso, op.15, 1957; Corno-Conc., op.29, 1959; Magnificatvariationen, op.40, Baroque tpt, str, 1965; Invocation, op.42, 1969; Sinfoniette légère, op.48; Capriciettes, op.49, ob, str, 1970

Vocal: Klopstock-Kantate, op.11, 1963; Die heile Welt, op.14 (W. Bergengruen), Mez/Bar, pf; Horati de vino carmina, S/T, hn, pf; Missa brevis, op.18, chorus, hn qt, 1954; Hohenheimer Singmesse, 1969

Inst: Harp Septet, op.7, 1953; Sonata, op.8, vn, pf (1963); Triptychon, op.20, pf, 1956, arr. str orch, op.20a, 1958; Lassus-Variationen, op.33, va, hpd (1962); Pf Qt, op.34, 1968; Aria e tarantella, op.37, a sax, pf (1968); Cantico, op.44, hn, str qt, 1968; Moments musicaux, op.46, vn, pf (1966); Reminiscenza, op.47, fl, hpd

Principal publisher: Simrock

JOHN MORGAN

Kroll, Erwin (*b* Deutsch Eylau, west Prussia, 3 Feb 1886; *d* Berlin, 1976). German writer on music, administrator and composer. After studies in Königsberg and Munich he worked briefly as a schoolmaster, turning finally to music and music journalism in Munich in

1919. He attended Sandberger's lectures at the university, studied composition with Pfitzner and Walter Braunfels and was a répétiteur at the Munich Staatsoper under Bruno Walter (1919–24). In 1925 he returned to Königsberg to become music critic of the *Hartungsche Zeitung* but in 1934 he settled in Berlin, where he wrote for various local and foreign papers. From 1946 to 1953 he was director of music of the North-west German Radio in Berlin. His compositions include songs and choruses, piano, chamber and orchestral works, many of them based on east Prussian motifs.

WRITINGS

E. T. A. Hoffmanns musikalische Anschauungen (Königsberg, 1909)
E. T. A. Hoffmann (Leipzig, 1923)
Hans Pfitzner (Munich, 1924)
Carl Maria von Weber (Potsdam, 1934)
'Die Oper', *Atlantisbuch der Musik*, ed. F. Hamel and M. Hürlimann (Zurich, 1934), 636–738
Musikstadt Königsberg: Geschichte und Erinnerung (Freiburg, 1966)

BIBLIOGRAPHY

E. Wiechert: *Jahre und Zeiten* (Zurich, 1949), 97ff, 252
W. Bollert: 'Erwin Kroll zum 70. Geburtstag', *Musica*, x (1956), 159

Kröll, Georg (*b* Linz am Rhein, 3 May 1934). German composer. He studied composition with Martin and Zimmermann and the piano with Schmitz-Gohr at the Cologne Musikhochschule (1953–62), attended Gaudeamus Foundation analysis courses under Koenig and Brown (1959–61, 1964) and took part in the 1961 Darmstadt summer courses (composition classes with Pousseur). He then worked as a composer, pianist and private music teacher, and he prepared the piano reduction of *Die Soldaten*. In 1964 he was appointed to teach theory and aural training at the Rheinische Musikschule, Cologne. He received the composition Förderpreis of the city of Cologne (1962) and a scholarship to the Villa Massimo in Rome (1969–70). In his compositions, various in form but mainly lyrical in character, he has come to grips with structural problems of timbre, sound movement and multi-layered development (*Still-Leben*), the integration of past and present techniques (*Variationen* for orchestra after Bach's Little Preludes, *Parodia ad Perotinum*) and new possibilities of musical-linguistic articulation. A member with Humpert of the Gruppe 8, he had a hand in the collective composition *Oktabus* (1969). He has written several essays, some of them published as disc notes, on Zimmermann's music.

WORKS
(*selective list*)

Magnificat, S, 6 insts, 1958; Sonata, a fl, 1959; Canto (Pound), S, orch, 1962; Variationen, orch, 1965; Estampida, gui, 1967; Invocazioni, wind qnt, 1969; Still-Leben, orch, 1969–70; Parodia ad Perotinum, orch, 1970–71; . . . schliesslich sei ja auch DAS GEHÖR der Titel der Studie (T. Bernhard: Das Kalkwerk), 6vv, 1971; Sonata no.2, vc, pf, 1972; Das Ohr auf der Strasse, open-air music, 1972, collab. Humpert, Niehaus; The Musicians and the Drummer, eng hn, cl, tpt, vc, pf, conductor, 1973; Wir besitzen keinerlei Fähigkeit aus der Klosterneuburger Strasse wegzugehen, Mez, insts, 1973–4

Principal publishers: Ars Viva, Bosse, Modern

MONIKA LICHTENFELD

Kroll, William (*b* New York, 30 Jan 1901; *d* Boston, 10 March 1980). American violinist. He studied at the Berlin Hochschule with Marteau (1911–14), made his début in New York in 1915, and continued his studies with the violinist Franz Kneisel and the theorist P. Goetschius at the Institute of Musical Art, New York (1917–22). In spite of his fine qualities as a soloist, Kroll concentrated on chamber music in such groups as the Elshuco Trio (1922–9), the Coolidge Quartet (1936–44) and the admirable Kroll Quartet (1944–69). With these, and as a soloist, he toured extensively in the USA, Mexico, Canada and Europe. In 1958–9 he played sonatas with Arthur Balsam, mainly in Europe. In 1942 he was awarded the Coolidge Medal for services to chamber music.

Kroll taught at the Institute of Musical Art (1922–38), at the Peabody Conservatory (1947–65) and at the Cleveland Institute (1964–7). In 1943 he joined the staff of the Mannes College, New York, and in 1949 began teaching at Tanglewood. In 1969 he was appointed professor of the violin at Queens College, New York. He published works for string quartet, chamber orchestra and solo violin. Kroll's playing combined vigour and elegance. His best qualities came to the fore in chamber music where he led with great authority and temperament. He played the 'ex-Ernst' Stradivari of 1709.

BORIS SCHWARZ

Krombholc, Jaroslav (*b* Prague, 30 Jan 1918). Czech conductor. At the Prague Conservatory and the Master School (1937–42) he studied with Novák and Talich, attended Hába's quarter-tone classes and, at Prague University, Zdeněk Nejedlý's lectures. He joined the National Theatre staff in 1940 and in 1942 Talich entrusted him with the première of Bořkovec's *Satyr*. He also worked at the E. F. Burian Theatre and with the Czech PO. In 1944 he became head of the Ostrava Opera, but in 1945 returned to Prague, where he was appointed conductor and a member of the management of the National Theatre, eventually becoming one of its leading musical personalities. In 1973 he was also appointed chief conductor of the Czechoslovak Radio SO.

Central to Krombholc's career is opera. Here he displays sensitivity to drama and also the experience gained from working with the prominent Czech men of the theatre, E. F. Burian and Pujman. In 1949 and 1955 he won state prizes for his outstanding performances of *Dalibor* and *Libuše*. His interpretation of Fibich is regarded as a model. He has achieved significant success with Ostrčil's *Honza's Kingdom*, Foerster's *Eva*, Jeremiáš's *The Brothers Karamazov*, Burian's *Maryša*, Kubelík's *Veronika*, and the operas of Novák, Cikker and Suchoň. He also conducts Mozart, Musorgsky, Shostakovich, Prokofiev and a very individual *Wozzeck*. Outside Czechoslovakia he is known for his appearances at the Vienna Staatsoper, where he first conducted in 1959, Covent Garden, Budapest, Stuttgart, and at the Holland and Edinburgh festivals; as the conductor of the National Theatre company on its foreign tours; and for his many excellent recordings. Krombholc also has a wide concert repertory: his interpretations of Smetana's *Má vlast*, Ostrčil, Suk, Hindemith, Kodály, Orff, Milhaud and Schoenberg particularly give evidence of his exceptional learning. He has toured in South America, is a frequent guest in England and Vienna, and has appeared in Italy, the USSR and Germany. He has composed a symphony (1942), chamber and vocal works. In 1958 he was made Artist of Merit and in 1966 National Artist.

BIBLIOGRAPHY

bor [V. Bor]: 'Jaroslav Krombholc', *HRo*, v/19 (1952), 27
B. Karásek: 'S Jaroslavem Krombholcem' [With Jaroslav Krombholc], *HRo*, xiii (1960), 10
J. Burghauser: *Slavní čeští dirigenti* [Famous Czech conductors] (Prague, 1963), 131f
J. Kozák: *Českoslovenští koncertní umělci a komorní soubory*

[Czechoslovak concert artists and chamber ensembles] (Prague, 1964), 325ff
B. Karásek: 'Český dirigent' [The Czech conductor], *HRo*, xxi (1968), 22

ALENA NĚMCOVÁ

Kromer, Marcin (*b* Biecz, nr. Tarnów, 1512; *d* Lidzbark, north-west of Warsaw, 23 March 1589). Polish historian, theologian and music theorist. He studied at the Jagellonian University, Kraków, from 1528 to 1530, and from 1537 to 1540 in Padua and Bologna. In the interim he had been employed by the court and lived in Vilnius. From 1540, back in Poland, he embarked on an ecclesiastical career, first as rector of Biecz (1542), then as parish priest at Wiślica and Sandomierz and as canon at Kielce. He took an active part in the Counter-Reformation in Poland, being largely responsible for inviting Jesuits into the country. He was also active as a diplomat: from 1545 to 1558 he was the secretary of the king's chancellory, and during this period he travelled abroad several times, visiting Rome and Vienna. In 1570 Kromer was nominated as the coadjutor to the see of Varmia and in 1579 became its bishop, remaining in this post until his death.

Kromer's historical and literary works are of particular significance in the evolution of Polish culture, and draw heavily on knowledge gleaned during his reorganization of state archives in Kraków. His musical writings, *Musicae elementa* (Kraków, before 1542, incomplete) and *De musica figurativa* (published jointly with Sebastian z Felsztyna's *Opusculum musices noviter congestum*, Kraków, 1534) are less important. *Musicae elementa* concerns elementary principles of music, and mainly follows the usual 16th-century pattern, beginning with a long praise of music in verse ('Encomium musicae') in which the author considered, among other things, the ethical attributes of musical scales. *De musica figurativa*, devoted to mensural theory, appears to depend on the views of Tinctoris and Adam von Fulda.

BIBLIOGRAPHY
A. Chybiński: *Teoria mensuralna w polskiej literaturze muzycznej I połowy XVI wieku* [Mensural theory in Polish musical writings throughout the 16th century] (Kraków, 1911)
J. Reiss: *Książki o muzyce od XV do XVII wieku w Bibliotece Jagellońskiej* [Books on music from the 15th century to the 17th in the Jagellonian library] (Kraków, 1924)
Z. M. Szweykowski, ed.: *Z dziejów polskiej kultury muzycznej* [From the history of Polish musical culture] (Kraków, 1958)
H. Barycz: 'Kromer, Marcin', *PSB*

ELŻBIETA WITKOWSKA-ZAREMBA

Kroměříž (Ger. Kremsier). A small town in Czechoslovakia, on the Morava, a tributary of the Danube, between Olomouc (Ger. Olmütz) and Brno (Ger. Brünn). From the Middle Ages until the 19th century it was the residence of the prince-bishops of Olomouc, the former episcopal seat of the large diocese of Moravia and Silesia. Its two most important buildings are the 17th-century castle residence of the prince-bishops, which dominates the centre, and the severely restored Gothic collegiate church of St Mořic. The castle was built by Prince-Bishop Karl Liechtenstein-Kastelcorn (1624–95) on the site of the medieval residence destroyed by the Swedes towards the end of the Thirty Years War.

At various times before the era of Liechtenstein and during its long history as the residence of the Olomouc bishops, Kroměříž had known several distinguished musicians. Jacob Handl was active as an organist

and composer there, and from 1579 or 1580 to 1585 he was Kapellmeister to the Bishop of Olomouc. But it was Liechtenstein who cultivated music on the grandest scale of any of the Olomouc bishops before or since his day (music-making of any consequence seems to have been rare at Olomouc). During his 31 years as bishop, from 1664 until his death, he spent vast sums of money on buildings, formal gardens, ecclesiastical foundations – which included the establishment of a choir and a college for the choristers – and the creation of a court orchestra with as many as 30 instrumentalists. His first Kapellmeister was Biber, who took unsanctioned leave from his service in 1670 and whose successor was Liechtenstein's court trumpeter, composer and copyist, Pavel Josef Vejvanovský.

The most substantial evidence of Liechtenstein's interest in music is the large collection of music manuscripts in the Kroměříž castle residence. Antonín Breitenbacher published (in 1928) a descriptive catalogue of this collection (based on a late 17th-century inventory) and of the miscellaneous 16th- to 19th-century printed music. The Liechtenstein archive, comprising masses, motets, sonatas and ballettos, mostly in sets of parts, by over 100 17th-century composers, contains the only surviving music of composers like Tolar and Vejvanovský, and most of the surviving music by several composers who worked at Vienna. Although there are 122 composers represented, the majority of the pieces were written by a relatively small group, most of whom were associated with the court of the Emperor Leopold I at Vienna. Letters exchanged between Liechtenstein and Johann Heinrich Schmelzer, who was a Kapellmeister of the emperor and a friend of the prince-bishop, verify the provenance of a substantial number of pieces. Besides the compositions acquired for Liechtenstein, some were sent as gifts by the composers themselves, whereupon the bishop often reciprocated with local Moravian produce. Most of the extant pieces at Kroměříž are by Bertali, Biber, Poglietti, Schmelzer, Tolar and Vejvanovský; of these composers only Biber, Tolar and Vejvanovský actually worked for the prince-bishop. Most of the composers at Kroměříž and Olomouc were native Moravians and Bohemians and had never worked at Vienna. Although they used folk melodies, their music is nevertheless written in a style comparable to that of the Viennese school of Schmelzer and others from the last third of the 17th century.

The music (particularly the sonatas and ballettos) constitutes an important link in the evolution of musical styles from northern Italy at the turn of the 16th century to those in a number of transalpine musical centres at the beginning of the 18th century. Obviously the ballettos were intended for dancing or for use at court festivals and entertainments at Kroměříž or Vienna. Schmelzer's *Balletto di centauri*, for example, was composed for a festival at Schönbrunn in 1674, probably to celebrate the emperor's birthday; his *Ballo di cavalli* may have been performed in Vienna for the festivities surrounding the marriage of Leopold I to Margaretha Theresia of Spain in 1667. An anonymous *Ballo canalia* was probably first performed in Kroměříž, from a barge on one of the several canals surrounding the bishop's castle. In addition ballettos were used for the Carnival festivities for which many European courts were famous.

The majority of the sonatas in the Kroměříž collection seem to have been heard during the celebration of

Mass, either in the castle chapel or in the collegiate church. Biber's noisy *Sonata Sancti Polycarpi* was specially suitable for the feast day of St Polycarp, the early church Father and martyred Bishop of Smyrna. Many of these church sonatas have elaborate instrumentation and, though different in style, probably served the same function as the sonatas and concertos by Torelli and others for Mass at S Petronio in Bologna.

Despite the frequent use of organs in the churches and castle at Kroměříž, there is no organ music in the castle archives, and little keyboard music. The organ was used mainly to support choral music, and Czech and Austrian organists traditionally improvised when solo organ music was required. The scarcity of harpsichord music, not only at Kroměříž but in most Czech archives, reflects the preference of many court and ecclesiastical establishments for Kapellmeisters who were violinists.

After the death of Liechtenstein musical life declined in his diocese. It was only during the relatively brief tenure of Beethoven's patron the Hapsburg Archduke Rudolph, Archbishop of Olomouc (for whose enthronement Beethoven's *Missa solemnis* was intended), that there was a revival of musical interest at Kroměříž, attested by the rather modest collection of late 18th-century manuscripts and printed music in the castle library, mostly copies of instrumental pieces by Mozart and a few of his contemporaries. After the archduke's death and because of the destruction in the diocese during the Napoleonic Wars, there is no evidence of music in Moravia until the discovery of the Liechtenstein collection in the late 19th century, in the loft and steeple of St Mořic.

From 1927 Breitenbacher built up the music archive in the Kroměříž castle by acquiring the collections of the music archives of St Mořic, the music collections of the Olomouc bishops of the period up to 1831 and the music archives of the church of the Virgin Mary and the Piarist college at Kroměříž. The archive is a basic source for music of the Vienese cultural circle in the second half of the 16th century and for the period 1760–1810, and contains many works by Czech composers. (For catalogues of these collections *see* BREITENBACHER, ANTONÍN.)

Kroměříž is the home of the important Moravian choir Pěvecko-hudební Spolek Moravan v Kroměříži ('Moravian singing group in Kroměříž'), which was founded by amateurs in 1863. At first a male-voice choir, in 1871 it began to be associated with the Vlastimila, a women's choir, and the two groups merged in 1882. Its greatest period was under the choirmaster Ferdinand Vach (1886–1905), one of the most important figures in Czech choral music. The local orchestra, the Hanácká Filharmonie, was founded in 1940. The town has a Higher Music School, founded in 1949, and several teacher-training colleges.

BIBLIOGRAPHY

P. Nettl: *Beiträge zur böhmischen und mährischen Musikgeschichte* (Brno, 1927)

F. V. Peřinka: *Dějiny města Kroměřize* [History of the town of Kroměříž], iii (Kroměříž, 1948)

E. H. Meyer: 'Die Bedeutung der Instrumentalmusik am fürstbischöflichen Hofe zu Olomouc (Olmütz) in Kroměříž (Kremsier)', *Mf*, ix (1956), 388

O. Fric: *Vývoj hudebni kultury na jihovýchoni Moravě* [The development of musical culture in south-east Moravia] (Brno, 1963)

J. Sehnal: 'Ze života hudebníků kroměřížské biskupské kapely v 17. stoleti' [The lives of musicians of the Kroměříž bishop's chapel in the 17th century], *Hudebnovedné štúdie*, vii (1966), 122

——: 'Die Musikkapelle des Olmützer Bischofs Karl Liechtenstein-Castelcorn in Kremsier', *KJb*, li (1967), 79–123

D. L. Smithers: 'Music for the Prince-Bishop', *Music and Musicians*, xviii/7 (1970), 24

——: 'The Liechtenstein Music Archive on Microfilm at Syracuse', *The Courier*, ix (1972), 37

DON SMITHERS

Krommer, Franz (Vinzenz) [Kramář, František Vincenc] (*b* Kamenice u Třebíče, 27 Nov 1759; *d* Vienna, 8 Jan 1831). Czech composer. He was the son of the innkeeper and later mayor of Kamenice Georg Krommer (Jiří Kramář, 1737–1810), and the nephew of the composer and choirmaster Anton Matthias Krommer. He is often known as 'Krommer-Kramář'.

From the age of 14 until Krommer was 17 he was taught the violin and organ by his uncle in Turăn; he taught himself theory. After about 1777 Krommer was temporary organist in Turăn. In 1785 he moved to Vienna and after staying for one year found employment as a violinist in the orchestra of the Duke of Styrum in Simontornya (Hungary). Two years later he was promoted to the post of musical director. Towards the end of 1790 he became Kapellmeister of Pécs Cathedral; after 1793 he acted as Kapellmeister and composer in the service of a Duke Karolyi and later of Prince Antal Grassalkovich de Gyarak.

Returning to Vienna in 1795, Krommer presumably taught composition before being appointed Kapellmeister to Duke Ignaz Fuchs in 1798. In 1806 he applied, unsuccessfully, to join the Vienna Hofkapelle as a violinist; after 1810 he was employed as Ballett-Kapellmeister of the Vienna Hoftheater. On 14 June 1815 he was appointed *Kammertürhüter* to the emperor, and in this office accompanied Emperor Franz I to Paris and Padua in the same year, and to Verona, Milan and Venice in 1816. From 13 September 1818 until his death he succeeded Leopold Anton Kozeluch as the last official director of chamber music and court composer to the Habsburg emperors.

Krommer was one of the most successful of the many influential Czech composers in Vienna at the turn of the 18th century. His creative output comprises over 300 works, although he only began to publish them in later years. Krommer's reputation is attested by the rapid spread of his compositions in reprints and arrangements by German, Danish, French, English, Italian and American publishers, and equally by his honorary membership of the Istituto Filarmonico in Venice, the Philharmonic Society in Ljubljana, the Musikverein in Innsbruck, and the conservatories in Paris (1815), Milan (1818) and Vienna (1826). With the exception of piano works, lieder and operas, Krommer cultivated all the musical genres of his time, and was regarded (with Haydn) as the leading composer of string quartets, and as a serious rival of Beethoven. The present view, however, places his solo concertos for wind instruments as his most individual accomplishments. In his symphonies, solo concertos and chamber music he followed the style of Haydn and Mozart, and yet his modes of expression extend from the *galant* style of the earlier 18th century to Romanticism. His violin duets have proved to be his most lasting works: they were still in use at the end of the 19th century as instructive pieces for students. His violin concertos, however, are largely forgotten: they were modelled on those of Pierre Rode, and the demands of their solo parts allow some insight into Krommer's own ability on the violin; but his chamber music with piano shows a lack of familiarity with the technical possibilities of keyboard instruments. His numerous dances, marches and compositions for brass band, all within the Viennese tradition for these genres, are of special interest when compared with similar works by Beethoven.

Krommer's son August Krommer (*b* Vienna, 1807; *d* Vienna, 27 March 1842), an insurance agent in Vienna, was for a time a violinist in the orchestra of the Burgtheater, and also appeared in public as a pianist in 1833.

WORKS

ORCHESTRAL
(printed works published in Offenbach unless otherwise stated)

Syms.: op.12 (1798); op.40 (1803); op.62 (1808), autograph 1807, *A-Wgm*; op.102 (n.d.); op.105 (?1820); no.6, autograph 1823, *Wgm*; no.9, 1830, *Wn*; 2 lost
Concs.: 3 for fl, ob, vn, op.18 (1799), opp.38–9 (1803); 2 for fl, cl, vn, opp.70, 80 (Vienna, ?1808); 2 for 2 cl, op.35 (?1802), op.91 (?1815); 2 for fl, no.1, op.30 (Vienna, 1802), op.86 (Vienna, n.d.) [arr. as Cl Conc. (n.d.)]; 2 for ob, op.37 (1803), op.52 (Vienna, 1805) [arr. as Cl Conc. (n.d.)], ed. in MAB, xxvii (1956); 1 for cl, op.36 (1803), ed. in MAB, xiii (1953); 9 for vn, no.1 (Vienna, 1802), nos.2–5, opp.41–4 (Vienna, 1803), op.61 (1808), op.64 (?1808), op.81 (Vienna, after 1826), 1 in *Wgm*
Wind insts: 3 partitas a 10, op.45 (Vienna, 1803); 15 marches a 10, 6 pubd (Vienna, 1803), 6 as op.31 (n.d.), 3 as op.60 (Vienna, ?1808); Harmonie-Musik a 9, i–x (Vienna, 1808–?1810); Märsche für türkische Musik, opp.97–100 (Vienna, 1818); Volkslied (Vienna, 1827); 3 partitas a 10, *Wn*

CHAMBER
(printed works published in Vienna unless otherwise stated)

Qnts: 26 for 2 vn, 2 va, vc, 3 as op.8 (Offenbach, 1797), 3 as op.11 (Offenbach, 1798), 6 as op.25 (1802–3), 2 as opp.70, 80 (Offenbach, 1817), 3 as op.88 (?1809), 3 as op.100 (Milan, ?1822), 6 as opp.106–7 (Offenbach, *c*1825); 9 for fl, vn, 2 va, vc, op.49 (1804), op.55 (1805), op.58 (?1808), op.63 (Offenbach, ?1808), op.66 (?1809), op.92 (?1823) [2 extracts, autograph, *Wgm*], op.101 (1820), op.104 (1821), op.109 (n.d.); 1 for cl, vn, 2 va, vc, op.95 (Offenbach, n.d.)
Str qts (pubd in groups of 3 unless otherwise stated): op.1 (Offenbach, 1793), op.3 (Offenbach, 1793), op.4 (Offenbach, 1794), op.5 (Augsburg, 1796) [1 ed. in MAB, v (1949)], op.7 (Augsburg, 1797), op.10 (Offenbach, 1798), op.16 (1798), op.18 (1800), op.19 (1801), 1 as op.23 (1802), op.24 (1802), op.26 (London, *c*1800), op.34 (1803), op.48 (1804), op.50 (1804), op.53 (1804), op.54 (1805), op.56 (1805), op.68 (?1808), op.72 (Paris, n.d.), op.74 (?1808), op.85 (?1809), op.90 (?1809), op.92 (Milan, 1816), op.103 (*c*1821); 12 valses viennoises (Paris, n.d.)
Other qts: 9 for fl, str, op.13 (Offenbach, 1798), op.17 (1799), op.59 (n.d.), op.75 (?1808), op.89 (Offenbach, ?1820), op.90 (1820), opp.93–4 (Offenbach, ?1820), op.97 (Augsburg, n.d.); 5 for cl, str, 2 as op.21 (Offenbach, 1802), op.69 (Bonn, n.d.), op.82 (Offenbach, ?1816), op.83, *I-Bc*; 2 for bn, 2 va, vc, op.46 (1804); 2 for pf, str, op.95 (1817), B♭
2–3 insts: 13 pièces, 2 cl, va, op.47 (1804); Trio, pf, va, vc, op.32 (1802); 2 trios, pf, vn, vc, opp.84, 87 (?1808–9); Str Trio, op.96 (1818); 27 vn duos (pubd in groups of 3), op.2 (Offenbach, 1793), op.6 (Offenbach, 1796), op.20 (London, *c*1810), op.22 (?1800) [1 ed. in Hausmusik, clxxiii (Vienna, 1958)], op.33 (1802), op.35 (?1805), op.51 (1805), op.94 (1816), op.110 (1829); 6 sonatas, vn, pf (Offenbach, n.d.); 3 sonatas, vn, va, op.27 (n.d.), op.42 (1802), op.45 (Paris, n.d.); 2 sets of variations, vn, db, opp.9, 14 (1797); Sonata, vn, db, op.15 (1799)

OTHER WORKS
Vocal: 2 masses, 4vv, orch, org, C, op.108 (Offenbach, *c*1825), d (Florence, 1842); Ave Maria, 2 Pange lingua, 2 Tantum ergo, 4vv, insts, *A-Wn*
Arrs.: 3 pf sonatas, 4 hands (Leipzig, n.d.); 21 works, arr. 2 fl (Offenbach, n.d.); Petits airs et rondeaux, vn, pf (Offenbach, n.d.); single kbd works, incl. dances and marches, pubd Copenhagen, Mannheim, Berlin

BIBLIOGRAPHY
Anon.: 'Der Compositeur Franz Krommer', *Notizenblatt der historisch-statistischen Sektion der kais. kgl. mährisch-schlesischen Gesellschaft zur Förderung der Ackerbaues, der Natur- und Landeskunde* (Brno, 1859), 37
J. Bušek: 'František Krommer: za naši hudební minulosti' [In search of our musical past], *Hudební výchova*, xii/1 (1931), 9
H. Walter: *Franz Krommer: sein Leben und Werk mit besonderer Berücksichtigung der Streichquartette* (diss., U. of Vienna, 1932)
K. Padrta: *František Krommer a jeho orchestrální skladby* [Krommer and his orchestral compositions] (diss., U. of Brno, 1949)
J. M. Barbour: 'Franz Krammer and his Writing for Brass', *Brass Quarterly*, i (1957), 1
Z. Zouhar: *František Vincenc Kramář, 1759–1959: výběrová bibliografie* [Selective bibliography] (Brno, 1959)
O. Wessely: 'Zur Neuausgabe eines Bläsersextetts von Franz Krommer', *Mf*, xiii (1960), 194
M. Matičetov: 'Štrekljeva zapuščina in korespondenca s Francem Kramarjem: ob petdesetletnici smrti dr. Karla Štrekla' [Štrekl's inheritance in correspondence with Krommer: on the 50th anniversary of Dr Karl Štrekl's death], *Slovenski etnograf*, xv (1962), 223
K. Padrta: *František Vincenc Kramář–Krommer: studie k životopismým a slohovým otázkám* [Bibliographical and stylistic questions] (Brno, 1966)
——: 'Die Menuett-Typen im Werke des Komponisten Kramář–Krommer', *Sborník prací filosofické fakulty brněnske university*, H2 (1967), 31
——: 'Pobyt F. V. Kramare–Krommera v Mad'arsku' [Krommer's stay in Hungary], *HV*, iv (1967), 148
B. Geist: 'Nález Kramářovy 7. symfonie' [The discovery of Krommer's 7th Symphony], *HV*, v (1968), 139

OTHMAR WESSELY

Kronstadt (Ger.). BRAŞOV.

Kroó, György (*b* Budapest, 26 Aug 1926). Hungarian musicologist. He studied the violin at the Eger Music School, the Budapest National Conservatory and with Dezső Rados at the Budapest Academy, where he also studied musicology with Szabolcsi and Bartha (1951–6); he graduated in 1956 with a dissertation on Bartók's *The Wooden Prince*. In 1957 he became head of the music education section of Hungarian radio and was guest lecturer (1960), associate professor (1967), professor of musicology (1969) and head of the musicology faculty (appointed 1973) of the Budapest Academy. He took the CSc in 1964 with a dissertation on the 'rescue' opera, and was awarded the Erkel Prize in 1963. In 1960 he became the Hungarian radio representative at the annual Rostrum of Composers at UNESCO; in 1967–8 he toured the USA as a Ford scholar.

Kroó is one of the leading Hungarian musicologists of his generation. He has made important contributions to music history research, music education, music criticism and the training of young musicologists. His main subject has been the nature and development of the 'rescue' opera from French composers through Cherubini to Beethoven; he examined associated types and defined its effect on the development of the Italian *opera semiseria*. He was the first to prepare a comprehensive analysis of Bartók's stage works, regarding them as a trilogy; during his year in the USA he made valuable additions to knowledge of Bartók's life. He has written fundamental studies of 20th-century Hungarian music, and as a leading music critic has (from 1960) provided a forum for discussion in his weekly radio music reviews; he regularly reviews contemporary Hungarian works in the periodical *Elet és irodalom*.

WRITINGS
'Liszt Ferenc: Magyar arcképek' [Liszt: Hungarian historical portraits], *Uj zenei szemle*, vii (1956), 9
'Szöktetés a szerájból' [Die Entführung aus dem Serail]; 'A varázsfuvola' [Die Zauberflöte], in J. Kárpáti, G. Kroó and others: *Mozart operái: hat tanulmány* (Budapest, 1956), 25–87, 257–365
Robert Schumann (Budapest, 1958)
'Einige Probleme des Romantischen bei Chopin und Liszt', *Chopin Congress: Warszawa 1960*, 319
Hector Berlioz (Budapest, 1960)
'Duke Bluebeard's Castle', *SM*, i (1961), 251–340
'Vázlat a forradalmi opera történetéhez' [Main features of a history of revolutionary opera], *Zenetudományi tanulmányok*, ix (1961), 243 [with Ger. summary]
'Monothematik und Dramaturgie in Bartók's Bühnenwerken', *Liszt–*

Bartók: 2nd International Musicological Conference: Budapest 1961, 449; also in *SM*, v (1963), 449
Bartók Béla szinpadi müvei [Bartók's stage works] (Budapest, 1962)
Wenn Schumann ein Tagebuch geführt hätte (Budapest, 1962) [many reprs.]
A 'szabadító' opera [The 'rescue' opera] (diss., Hungarian Academy of Sciences, 1964; Budapest, 1966)
Muzsikáló zenetörténet [History of music, with supplementary discs], i, iii (Budapest, 1964, 1966)
'Zoltán Kodály in Memoriam', *American Choral Review*, x (1967), 3
Richard Wagner (Budapest, 1968)
'Bartók Concert in New York on July 2, 1944', *SM*, xi (1969), 253
'Unrealized Plans and Ideas for Projects by Bartók', *SM*, xii (1970), 11
A magyar zeneszerzés 25 éve [25 years of Hungarian composing] (Budapest, 1971)
Bartók kalauz [A guide to Bartók] (Budapest, 1971; Eng. trans., 1974)
'On the Origin of the Wooden Prince', *International Musicological Conference in Commemoration of Béla Bartók: Budapest 1971*, 97
'Gustav Mahler: Vándorlegény-dalok' [Lieder eines fahrenden Gesellen], *Miért szép századunk zenéje?* (Budapest, 1974), 7
'Kurtág, György: Bornemisza Péter mondásai Op. 7' [The Sayings of Bornemisza], ibid, 317
'Richard Strauss: Don Juan op. 20', ibid, 31
A magyar zeneszerzés 30 éve [30 years of Hungarian composing] (Budapest, 1975)
Rácz Aladár (in preparation)

ISTVÁN KECSKEMÉTI

Kropfreiter, Augustinus Franz (*b* Hargelsberg, nr. St Florian, 9 Sept 1936). Austrian composer and organist. After schooling in Linz he entered the Augustinian monastery of St Florian as a choirman. There he had his first tuition in music theory, under Johann Krichbaum; he continued his studies at the Bruckner Conservatory in Linz (1954–5) and at the Vienna Musikhochschule (1956–60: composition under Tittel, organ under Pach, conducting under Gillesberger). He then returned to St Florian as organist; in 1965 he took over the direction of the monastery choir and the instruction of the boys' choir. He has travelled extensively in western Europe as organist and improviser and has broadcast and made recordings on the Bruckner organ at St Florian. His compositions are largely traditional in manner and tend towards polytonality, drawing on Hindemithian counterpoint and sequences of triadic chords.

WORKS
(selective list)

Orch: Hpd Conc., 1960; Gui Conc., 1965; Sinfonia, str, 1975
Vocal: Geistliche Gesänge, S, org, 1961, and Bar, org, 1963; In memoriam, S, fl, va, vc, 1963; Altdorfer-Passion, A, Bar, 11 insts, 1965; Freiburger Magnificat, chorus, org, 1970; Vom Baum des Lebens (H. Hesse), A, chamber orch, 1974; motets and other sacred works
Chamber: Conc. responsoriale, hpd, org, 1966; Wind qnt, 1968; 5 Aphorismen, cl, pf, 1970; Konzertante Musik, org, 10 wind, 1974; pieces for 1 inst, org
Org: Dreifaltigkeits-Triptychon, 1959; Introduction and Passacaglia, 1961; 2 sonatas, 1961, 1967; Toccata francese, 1961; Der grimmig Tod mit seinem Pfeil, 1961; Partita on Es kommt ein Schiff geladen, 1971

Principal publisher: Doblinger

based on *MGG* (xvi, 1059–60) by permission of Bärenreiter
HANS-HUBERT SCHÖNZELER

Kropstein, Nikolaus (*b* Zwickau, *c*1492; *d* Schneeberg, 1562). German Lutheran pastor and composer. He studied in Leipzig from 1512 (but was sent down) and in Wittenberg, where he matriculated on 6 May 1513. From 1527 he was a priest in Burgstein, near Plauen, from 1534 a deacon at St Catharine's, Zwickau, and from 1539 a priest in Geyer. In 1554 he became archdeacon in Schneeberg, where he remained until his death.

With Thomas Popel, Valentin Rab and others, Kropstein belongs to the number of early Protestant composers in the Erzgebirge whose religious attitude and musical activities had received their impetus from Wittenberg, the centre of the Lutheran Reformation. He probably maintained connections with Georg Rhau and Wittenberg University established in his student days for his 13 works appear in Wittenberg sources (*RISM* 1542[12]; *D-Dlb* 1/D/3; *Z* 73; *H-BA* 22–3). The texts and dates of the compositions suggest that some were intended as comments on the religious and political events of the period 1547–50: the Schmalkalden war, Charles V's antagonism towards Protestantism, and the Augsburg and Leipzig Interims. (Two pieces are in modern editions: one in K. Ameln and C. Mahrenholz, *Handbuch der deutschen evangelischen Kirchenmusik*, i/2, Göttingen, 1942; one in EDM, 1st ser., xxi, 1942/R.)

Few works by Kropstein survive and most that do are fragments. His motet *Nimm von uns Herr*, on the cantus firmus *Aufer a nobis*, is technically accomplished, alternating full-voice sections with passages for few voices, and using imitation, declamation and rhetorical figures in a mainly polyphonic texture. Although there are no German psalm motets by Kropstein, his other German works place him close to Stoltzer's followers.

BIBLIOGRAPHY

H. Albrecht: 'Zwei Quellen zur deutschen Musikgeschichte der Reformationszeit', *Mf*, i (1948), 242–85
W. Dehnhard: *Die deutsche Psalmmotette der Reformationszeit* (Wiesbaden, 1971)
W. Steude: *Untersuchungen zu Herkunft, Verbreitung und spezifischem Inhalt mitteldeutscher Musikhandschriften des 16. Jahrhunderts* (diss., U. of Rostock, 1973)
——: *Die Musik-Sammelhandschriften des 16. und 17. Jahrhunderts in der Sächsischen Landesbibliothek zu Dresden* (Leipzig and Wilhelmshaven, 1974)

WOLFRAM STEUDE

Krosnick, Joel (*b* New Haven, Conn., 3 April 1941). American cellist. He studied with William D'Amato, Luigi Silva, Jens Nygaard and Claus Adam. In 1962 he co-founded and directed the Group for Contemporary Music at Columbia University, where he also studied. From 1963 to 1966 he was a professor at Iowa University and cellist of the university string quartet. He held a similar position at the University of Massachusetts, 1966–70, while performing with the New York Chamber Soloists and touring as a soloist to London, Berlin, Amsterdam, Hamburg and Belgrade; he made his New York solo début in 1970. From 1970 to 1974 he taught at the California Institute of the Arts and then joined the Juilliard String Quartet, succeeding his teacher Claus Adam. He is a well-known exponent of modern scores, and has given the premières of works by Ligeti, Samuels and Maxwell Davies. His recording of Carter's Cello Sonata reveals an intensely focussed though not large tone, and a degree of rhythmic agility not usually found in players of low string instruments.

RICHARD BERNAS

Kross, Siegfried (*b* Wuppertal, 24 Aug 1930). German musicologist. He studied musicology with Gurlitt at the University of Freiburg and with Schmidt-Görg at the University of Bonn, where he worked on the staff of the Beethoven Archive (1954) and took his doctorate in 1957 with a dissertation on Brahms's choral works. Later he was an assistant of the musicology institute there (1960–66), completing his *Habilitation* in 1966 with a thesis on Telemann's instrumental concertos; he was then appointed lecturer (1967) and professor

(1970). His research has been mainly concerned with music of the 18th and 19th centuries, especially that of Brahms.

WRITINGS

'Schumanns Sterbehaus und die Bonner Schumann-Tradition', *Jb des Bonner Heimat- und Geschichtsvereins*, x (1956), 180

'Brahms und der Kanon', *Festschrift Joseph Schmidt-Görg zum 60. Geburtstag* (Bonn, 1957), 175

Die Chorwerke von Johannes Brahms (diss., U. of Bonn, 1957; Berlin, 1958, 2/1963)

'Zur Frage der Brahms'schen Volksliedbearbeitungen', *Mf*, xi (1958), 15

'Rhythmik und Sprachbehandlung bei Brahms', *GfMKB, Kassel 1962*, 217

'Eine problematische Stelle in Beethovens Diabelli-Variationen', *Mf*, xvi (1963), 267; xviii (1965), 184

'Brahmsiana: der Nachlass der Schwestern Völckers', *Mf*, xvii (1964), 110

'Concerto: concertare und conserere', *GfMKB, Leipzig 1966*, 216

Das Instrumentalkonzert bei G. Ph. Telemann (Habilitationsschrift, U. of Bonn, 1966; Tutzing, 1969)

ed. with H. Schmidt: *Colloquium amicorum: Joseph Schmidt-Görg* (Bonn, 1967) [incl. 'Musikalische Strukturen als literarische Form: zu Thomas Manns Faustus-Roman', 217]

'Schaffenspsychologische Aspekte der Beethoven-Skizzenforschung', *GfMKB, Bonn 1970*, 87

ed.: *Dokumentation zur Geschichte des deutschen Liedes* (Hildesheim, 1973–)

ed.: *Max Reger in seiner Zeit* (Bonn, 1973)

'Telemann und die Aufklärung', *Musicae scientiae collectanea: Festschrift Karl Gustav Fellerer* (Cologne, 1973), 284

'Brahms, der unromantische Romantiker', *Hamburger Brahms-Studien*, i (1974), 25

EDITIONS

L. van Beethoven: *Variationen für Klavier: Diabelli-Variationen op.120*, Werke, vii/5 (Munich, 1961); *Klavierquintett und Klavierquartette*, Werke, iv/1 (Munich, 1964)

G. P. Telemann: *Zwölf Violinkonzerte*, Musikalische Werke, xxiii (Kassel, 1973)

Krotalon [krotala]. *See* CROTALUM.

Kroupezion [krupezion]. *See* SCABELLUM.

Krov [Krob, Krow, Kroff], **Josef Theodor** (*b* Nové Strašeci, 19 Dec 1797; *d* Draguignan, nr. Nice, 1 March 1859). Bohemian singer and composer. He was educated at the Piarist Gymnasium in Prague and studied philosophy and law; at the same time he studied the cello and singing and became a theory pupil of Tomášek. In 1823–4 he took part in several early Czech operas given by a circle of patriots in Prague, and later he became a professional singer. He worked in Budapest, Munich, Mainz and, after 1835, London. Poor health forced him into early retirement, and he spent his last years in Switzerland and southern France.

As a composer Krov is known particularly for his drinking-song *Těšme se blahou nadějí* ('Blissfully hoping we will enjoy'). Written between 1823 and 1825 to a text by Václav Hanka, the song grew to take on patriotic connotations; Krov's authorship fell into oblivion in his own country and for some time the tune was taken for an early Hussite hymn. As such it was anonymously printed and also transcribed for piano by Liszt. Meanwhile the song had been published by Schott (Mainz, 1831) under Krov's name and with Workinski's additional German words as *Polen wird für ewig Polen*; in this form it achieved immense popularity, which probably accounts for the extensive quotation of Krov's tune in Balfe's *The Bohemian Girl*.

BIBLIOGRAPHY

ČSHS

S. Souček: *Dvě pozdní mystifikace Hankovy* [Two late mystifications of Hanka] (Prague, 1924)

Z. Nejedlý: *B. Smetana*, iii–v (Prague, 1929–52)

GRACIAN ČERNUŠAK

Kroyer, Theodor (*b* Munich, 9 Sept 1873; *d* Wiesbaden, 12 Jan 1945). German musicologist. He initially studied theology, but changed to music, attending both the university and academy in Munich; his teachers were Sandberger and Rheinberger. After taking his doctorate at Munich in 1897 with a dissertation on chromaticism in the Italian madrigal, he became music critic to the Munich *Allgemeine Zeitung*, a post he held until 1910. In 1902 he completed his *Habilitation* at Munich with a work on Senfl and became reader in 1907. In 1920 he succeeded Hermann Abert as professor at Heidelberg, moving to Leipzig as professor in 1923. During his nine years there he founded and edited Publikationen älterer Musik which was intended as a supplement to Denkmäler deutscher Tonkunst. In 1926 he arranged the acquisition by Leipzig of the musical instruments from the Heyer collection in Cologne. In 1932 he was appointed to the newly created chair of musicology at Cologne, where he remained until his retirement in 1938.

Kroyer's work was largely concerned with 16th-century vocal music: of his many writings in the field, his work on the Italian madrigal, on Senfl and Aichinger, and his critical editions of their music was of basic importance. At the same time he was fully aware of contemporary trends in music and as a music critic in Munich was one of the earliest to recognize the importance of Reger; his books on his teacher, Rheinberger, and on his contemporary, Walter Courvoisier, remain definitive. He was also much concerned with the teaching of musicology in the university, and he did valuable work in building up the discipline at Leipzig in particular; indeed it was perhaps his strong personality and his impact as a teacher which were the greatest vehicles of his influence.

WRITINGS

Die Anfänge der Chromatik im Italienischen Madrigal des xvi. Jahrhunderts (diss., U. of Munich, 1897; Leipzig, 1902/R1968)

Ludwig Senfl und sein Motettenstil (Habilitationsschrift, U. of Munich; Munich, 1902)

'Zum Akzidentienproblem im Ausgang des 16. Jahrh.', *IMusSCR, iii Vienna 1909*, 112

'Dialog und Echo in der alten Chormusik', *JbMP 1909*, 13

Joseph Rheinberger (Regensburg and Rome, 1916)

'Die Musica speculativa des Magister Erasmus Heritius', *Festschrift zum 50. Geburtstag Adolf Sandberger* (Munich, 1918), 65–120

'Acapella oder Conserto?', *Festschrift Hermann Kretzschmar* (Leipzig, 1918), 65

'Die circumpolare Oper: zur Wagnergeschichte', *JbMP 1919*, 16

'Die Beziehungen der Musikwissenschaft zu ihren Schwestern', *JbMP 1921*, no.2, p.7

'Die threnodische Bedeutung der Quart in der Mensuralmusik', *Kongressbericht: Basle 1924*, 231

'Zur Aufführungspraxis', *Gedenkboek aangeboden an Dr. D. F. Scheurleer* (The Hague, 1925), 191

'Das Orgelbuch Cod. MS 153 der Münchener Universitäts-Bibliothek', *Kongressbericht: Leipzig 1925*, 339

'Gregor Aichinger als Politiker', *Festschrift Peter Wagner* (Leipzig, 1926), 128

'Zwischen Renaissance und Barock', *JbMP 1927*, 45

'Beethoven in seinen Symphonien', *Beethoven – Almanach der deutschen Musikbücherei* (Regensburg, 1927), 283

'Universität und Musikerziehung', *Deutsche Tonkünstler-Zeitung*, xxvii (1929), 494

Walter Courvoisier (Munich and Berlin, 1929)

'Zur Chiavetten-Frage', *Studien zur Musikgeschichte: Festschrift für Guido Adler* (Vienna, 1930), 107; see also *ZMw*, xiii (1930–31), 494

'Die authentische Bruckner-Biographie', *ZfM*, xcix (1932), 864

'Die barocke Anabasis', *ZfM*, c (1933), 899

'Das A-capella-Ideal', *AcM*, vi (1934), 152

'Von der Musica reservata des 16. Jahrhunderts', *Festschrift Heinrich Wölfflin* (Dresden, 1935), 127

EDITIONS

with A. Thürlings: *L. Senfl: Werke, I. Teil*, DTB, v, Jg.iii/2 (1903)

G. Aichinger: *Ausgewählte Werke*, DTB, xviii, Jg.x/1 (1909)

BIBLIOGRAPHY

H. Zenck and others, eds.: *Theodor Kroyer: Festschrift zum 60. Geburtstage am 9. September 1933 überreicht von Freunden und Schülern* (Regensburg, 1933)

H. Zenck: 'Theodor Kroyer', *Mf*, i (1948), 81

W. Gerstenberg: 'Kroyer, Theodor', *Rheinische Musiker*, ii, ed. K. G. Fellerer (Cologne, 1962), 49 [incl. extensive bibliography]

HUGH COBBE

Krueger, Felix (*b* Posen [now Poznań], 10 Aug 1874; *d* Basle, 25 Feb 1948). German psychologist. He studied under Theodor Lipps and H. Cornelius in Munich, where he took a doctorate in 1897 with a dissertation on *Den Begriff des absolut Wertvollen*. He then became an assistant at the Physiological Institute in Kiel and in 1903 completed his *Habilitation* under Wundt at Leipzig with a work on the consciousness of consonance; three years later he went to Buenos Aires, where he was active in organizing psychological studies (1906–8). After a short stay in Leipzig, he was appointed lecturer in Halle (1910) and then taught at Columbia University (1912–13). In 1917 he succeeded Wundt as lecturer in Leipzig, where he founded the 'Second Leipzig School' of psychologists. Although named president of Leipzig University in 1935, he was forced to retire on political grounds three years later. In 1945 he emigrated to Basle, where he remained until his death. His early works dealt with psychology and musicology; he did outstanding work on the psychology of sound and phonetics, especially in developing his much-discussed theory of consonances. His influence on the psychology of hearing and music gained wide recognition after his death.

WRITINGS

'Beobachtungen an Zweiklängen', *Philosophische Studien*, xvii (1900), 307–79, 568–664

'Über Konsonanz und Dissonanz', *IVe congrès international de psychologie: Paris 1901*, 455

'Zur Theorie der Combinationstöne', *Philosophische Studien*, xviii (1901), 185

Das Bewusstsein der Konsonanz (Habilitationsschrift, U. of Kiel, 1903; Leipzig, 1903)

'Die Theorie der Konsonanz', *Psychologische Studien*, i (1906), 305–87; ii (1906), 205–55; iv (1908), 201–82; v (1910), 274–411

'Mitbewegungen beim Singen, Sprechen und Hören', *ZIMG*, xi (1909–10), 180, 205

'Consonance and Dissonance', *Journal of Philosophy, Psychology and Scientific Method*, x (1913), 158

Über Entwicklungspsychologie, ihre historische und sachliche Notwendigkeit, i (Leipzig, 1915)

Das Wesen der Gefühle (Leipzig, 1928, 5/1936; Eng. trans. in *Feelings and Emotions: the Wittenberg Symposium* (Worcester, Mass., 1928), 58–88)

Die Lehre von dem Ganzen (Berne, 1948)

ed. E. Heuss: *Zur Philosophie und Psychologie der Ganzheit* (Berlin and Heidelberg, 1953) [collection of his most important writings, 1918–40]

BIBLIOGRAPHY

C. Stumpf: 'Differenztöne und Konsonanz', *Zeitschrift für Psychologie*, xxxix (1905), 269; lix (1911), 161

R. Odebrecht: *Gefühl und Ganzheit: der Ideengehalt der Psychologie Felix Kruegers* (Berlin, 1929)

A. Wellek: 'Die Aufspaltung der "Tonhöhe" in der Hornbostelschen Gehörpsychologie und die Konsonanztheorien von Hornbostel und Krueger', *ZMw*, xvi (1934), 481, 537

O. Klemm, Hans Volkelt, K. Graf von Dürckheim-Montmartin, eds.: 'Ganzheit und Struktur: Festschrift zum 60. Geburtstage Felix Kruegers', *Neue Psychologische Studien*, xxii (1934), 121 [contains list of writings]

O. Buss: *Die Ganzheitspsychologie Felix Kruegers* (Munich, 1934)

A. Wellek: *Das Problem des seelischen Seins: die Strukturtheorie Felix Kruegers* (Leipzig, 1941)

J. Handschin: *Der Toncharakter* (Zurich, 1948)

A. Wellek: *Die Wiederherstellung der Seelenwissenschaft im Lebenswerk Felix Kruegers* (Hamburg, 1950)

H. Husmann: *Von Wesen der Konsonanz* (Heidelberg, 1953)

A. Wellek: 'Krueger, Felix', *Encyclopedia of Philosophy*, iv (New York, 1967), 366

ALFRED GRANT GOODMAN

Krug, Arnold (*b* Hamburg, 16 Oct 1849; *d* Hamburg, 4 Aug 1904). German pianist, conductor, composer and teacher. As a child he studied music first with his father, Diederich Krug, and then with Cornelius Gurlitt, an organist, choir director and composer in Altona. He entered the Leipzig Conservatory in 1868 and in the following year became a Mozart Fellow. He completed his piano studies with Reinecke and in Berlin with Eduard Frank; there he also studied composition with Friedrich Kiel. At the age of 23 he became a piano teacher at the Stern Conservatory in Berlin, and in 1877–8 travelled as a Meyerbeer Fellow in Italy and France. He subsequently lived in Hamburg as a music teacher (from 1885 at the Conservatory), as a choir director and as conductor of the Altona Singakademie and the Hamburg Liedertafel.

Being in contact with the Classical–Romantic tradition and under the spell of the works of Brahms, Krug composed vocal music of all genres except opera, mostly with chorus or for chorus *a cappella*. He was also a versatile instrumental composer; with his String Sextet op.68 he participated in the attempt by the violin maker Alfred Stelzner to enrich the chamber music arsenal with a violotta, an instrument whose register lay between the viola and the cello, and a cellone, an instrument between the cello and the double bass.

BIBLIOGRAPHY

J. Sittard: *Geschichte des Musik- und Concertwesens in Hamburg* (Altona and Leipzig, 1890)

K. Stephenson: *Hundert Jahre Philharmonische Gesellschaft in Hamburg* (Hamburg, 1928)

——: 'Krug, Arnold', *MGG* [with complete list of works]

KURT STEPHENSON

Krug, Diederich (*b* Hamburg, 25 May 1821; *d* Hamburg, 7 April 1880). German pianist, composer and teacher, father of Arnold Krug. He was a pupil of the renowned Hamburg piano teacher Jakob Schmitt. He became well known in Germany and England primarily through his piano pieces, about 350 in number, and could adjust his style to the taste and virtuosity of the diverse circles of amateurs who played his works. Among his nine didactic works for piano, mostly for beginners, the *Schule der Technik* op.75 is the most noteworthy.

BIBLIOGRAPHY

J. Sittard: *Geschichte des Musik- und Concertwesens in Hamburg* (Altona and Leipzig, 1890)

K. Stephenson: *Hundert Jahre Philharmonische Gesellschaft in Hamburg* (Hamburg, 1928)

KURT STEPHENSON

Krüger, Eduard (*b* Lüneburg, 9 Dec 1807; *d* Göttingen, 8 Nov 1885). German writer on music and conductor. He studied philology, history and music at the universities of Göttingen and Berlin, submitting his doctoral dissertation on Greek music in Pindar's time in 1830. From 1833 until 1851 he taught at the Gymnasium in Emden (East Friesland), also conducting the local choral society which performed works by Haydn and especially Handel. On 8 November 1851 he became chief school inspector for East Friesland and transferred to Aurich. In 1859 he resigned his post due to an illness which caused temporary deafness. In 1861 he moved to Göttingen, becoming professor at the university.

Krüger's primary importance lies in his theoretical, critical and historical writings, which appeared in numerous periodicals, occasionally under various pseudonyms. He wrote several articles on church music and a chorale book (1855) and founded the journal

Siona with Herold and Schöberlein in 1876. He also made a valuable contribution in his work for the university library at Göttingen. Only a few of his compositions were published.

WRITINGS

De musicis graecorum organis circa Pindari tempora florentibus (diss., U. of Göttingen, 1830)
Grundriss der Metrik antiker und moderner Sprachen (Emden, 1838)
'*Aus Ostfriesland*', *NZM*, xii (1840), 42 [under pseud. J.R.]
'Robert Schumann: *Das Paradies und die Peri*', *AMZ*, xlvii (1845), 561, 606, 617
'Die Wiederbelebung des evangelischen Kirchengesanges', *AMZ*, xlviii (1846), 570, 585
'Eine Aufführung des Messias in Emden', *AMZ*, xlviii (1846), 778 [under pseud. Dr. P.]
Beiträge für Leben und Wissenschaft der Tonkunst (Leipzig, 1847)
'Deutsches Kriegslied', *AMZ*, l (1848), 225
'Beziehungen zwischen Kunst und Politik', *AMZ*, l (1848), 401, 481, 842
'Ueber den Zusammenhang zwischen Musik und Politik', *AMZ*, l (1848), 538 [under pseud. F. Schnell]
'Eindruck und Ausdruck', *AMZ*, l (1848), 842
System der Tonkunst (Leipzig, 1866)
Musikalische Briefe aus der neuesten Zeit (Münster, 1870)

BIBLIOGRAPHY

G. Nauenburg: 'Kritische Paraphrasen über Dr. E. Krügers Beiträge für Leben und Wissenschaft der Tonkunst', *AMZ*, xlix (1847), 753, 769, 785
F. Chrysander: 'Musikalische Briefe aus der neuesten Zeit', *AMz*, v (1870), 4
A. Prüfer, ed.: *Briefwechsel zwischen Carl von Winterfeld und Eduard Krüger* (Leipzig, 1898)
W. Serauky: *Die musikalische Nachamungsästhetik im Zeitraum von 1700 bis 1850* (Münster, 1929)
W. Boetticher: *Robert Schumann: Einführung in Persönlichkeit und Werk* (Berlin, 1941)
U. Martin: 'Ein unbekanntes Schumann-Autograph aus dem Nachlass Eduard Krügers', *Mf*, xii (1959), 405
K. Hoppenrath: *Eduard Krüger: Leben und Wirken eines Musikgelehrten zwischen Schumannscher Tradition und Neudeutscher Schule* (diss., U. of Göttingen, 1964)

GAYNOR G. JONES

Krüger [Krugl], Johann Philipp. See KRIEGER, JOHANN PHILIPP.

Kruijsen, Bernard. See KRUYSEN, BERNARD.

Krumbholz, Martin (*b* Bensen [now Benešov, nr. Děčín], Bohemia; *fl* 1600–11; *d* ?Prague). Bohemian composer. He was principal organist at St Nikolai, Prague, about 1600. In 1611, to celebrate the laying of the foundation stone of the Lutheran Salvatorkirche in Prague, he composed and directed the performance of an eight-part motet *Und da die Bauleute den Grundstein legten* (Leipzig, 1611; ed. in EDM, 2nd ser., *Böhmen und Mähren*, ii, 1940). He later became Kantor at the Salvatorkirche, serving the pastor M. Hoë von Hoenegg.

WALTER BLANKENBURG

Krummel, D(onald) W(illiam) (*b* Sioux City, Iowa, 12 July 1929). American music librarian and bibliographer. He was educated at the University of Michigan, where he received the BMus in 1951, the MMus in 1953 and the MA in library science in 1954. He was awarded the PhD, also in library science, in 1958. He taught at the University of Michigan from 1952 to 1956; from 1956 to 1961 he was a reference librarian in the music division of the Library of Congress. In 1962 he joined the Newberry Library, Chicago, first as head of the reference department, then as associate librarian. In 1970 he was appointed professor of library science and of music at the University of Illinois. He held a Guggenheim Fellowship in 1976–7, and was director of the Resources of American Music History project for the National Endowment for the Humanities 1976–9.

Krummel's principal fields of research are music printing and publishing and early American music. In his dissertation and subsequent writings he has been concerned with the dating of 18th-century music prints, particularly by American publishers; he has employed both cultural and bibliographical evidence, including graphic analysis, or the study of the printed musical page. Krummel is an active member of the Music Library Association and the International Association of Music Libraries. He was also compiler of the quarterly book list for the *Musical Quarterly* from 1957 to 1960.

WRITINGS

Philadelphia Music Engraving and Publishing, 1800–1820 (diss., U. of Michigan, 1958)
'Graphic Analysis; its Application to Early American Engraved Music', *Notes*, xvi (1958–9), 213
with J. B. Coover: 'Current National Bibliographies: their Music Coverage', *Notes*, xvii (1959–60), 375
'Late 18th Century French Music Publishers' Catalogs in the Library of Congress', *FAM*, vii (1960), 61
'Twenty Years of *Notes*: a Retrospect', *Notes*, xxi (1963–4), 56
'Observations on Library Acquisitions of Music', *Notes*, xxiii (1966–7), 5
American entries in 'Cotages d'éditeurs antérieurs à c.1850: liste préliminaire', ed. F. Lesure, *FAM*, xiv (1967), 33
Review of B. S. Brook, ed.: *The Breitkopf Thematic Catalogue, 1762–1787* (New York, 1966), *Notes*, xxiv (1967–8), 697
'The Newberry Library, Chicago', *FAM*, xvi (1969), 119
'Guide for Dating Early Music: a Synopsis', *FAM*, xviii (1971), 40
Bibliotheca Bolduaniana: a Renaissance Music Bibliography (Detroit, 1972)
Guide for Dating Early Published Music (Kassel and Hackensack, 1974)
English Music Printing, 1553–1700 (London, 1975)
Newberry Library, Chicago: Bibliographical Inventory to the Early Music (Boston, 1976)

PAULA MORGAN

Krummhorn (Ger.). (1) CRUMHORN.

(2) An ORGAN STOP (*Cromorne*).

Krumpholtz [Krumpholz]. Bohemian family of musicians.

(1) Jean-Baptiste [Johann Baptist, Jan Křtitel] **Krumpholtz** (*b* Budenice, nr. Zlonice, 3 May 1742; *d* Paris, 19 Feb 1790). Harpist, composer and instrument designer. He was born into an impoverished family which was in bond to the Bohemian counts Kinský. His father was a bandmaster to the count and taught his son the horn. With the installation of a new count in 1758 Krumpholtz was sent on a court stipend to study music in Vienna, with the understanding that he perfect his horn playing; the boy's decision to concentrate instead on the harp, his mother's instrument, later led to conflict with the count. From Vienna he went to Flanders and France with an uncle (who probably married the 'Meyer' often named as Krumpholtz's first wife), presumably as hornist in a regimental band. Returning to Prague in 1771, he met and impressed the violinist Václav Pichl and pianist F. X. Dušek, who sent him to Vienna with recommendations to Haydn and others. There in 1773, after a successful concert at the Burgtheater, Haydn took him on as a composition pupil and as solo harpist in Count Esterházy's retinue.

In 1776, with Haydn's support, Krumpholtz undertook a long concert tour of Europe. He performed in Leipzig on a 'harpe organisée', probably the earliest of his attempted improvements to the instrument (a 'harpe organisée' was later marketed by Cousineau in Paris). Arriving in Metz, he worked intensively at further improvements for six months in the workshop of the instrument maker Christian Steckler, whose 12-year-old daughter Anne-Marie became his protégée (see (3) below). In 1777 he arrived in Paris to complete his tour, taking the girl with him. After a brief marriage (1778) to Marguérite Gilbert (daughter of the Parisian harp maker C. Gilbert) which ended in his wife's death in childbirth, Krumpholtz, who had now adopted the name Jean-Baptiste, married his young pupil. Three children were born to the couple, but by 1788 Anne-Marie had taken a lover, apparently the brilliant young pianist J. L. Dussek, with whom she soon eloped to London. Krumpholtz drowned himself in the Seine in 1790.

Krumpholtz was the most gifted and acclaimed harp virtuoso of the late 18th century and a prolific composer for the instrument. He is no less important for his efforts to perfect the harp. In 1785 the Parisian firm of Nadermann built an instrument to Krumpholtz's specification (described in the preface to his sonatas op.14), with 24 strings, eight of which were metal, and with an eighth pedal that opened five shutters in the resonance box; the instrument was played by his wife before the Académie, who in 1787 wrote to Krumpholtz in recognition of its virtues. The instrument is now in the Vienna Kunsthistorisches Museum. At the same concert Krumpholtz accompanied his wife on a 'pianoforte contrabasse', or 'clavichorde à marteau', made by Erard, again from his specifications. Other improvements by him were incorporated after his death into the Erard harp at the beginning of the 19th century, the prototype of the modern double-action harp.

Krumpholtz's concertos, sonatas and variations for harp, which appeared in Paris from about 1775 (many were later reprinted in London), became staples of the repertory and are still highly respected. They contributed to the instrument's rapidly evolving technique, taking increasing advantage of the modulatory possibilities of the new pedal harp at the same time as he was perfecting its mechanism. The variations combine idiomatic harp writing with fertile invention. Many of his later sonatas are programmatic. After his death a harp method, said to have been written by him for a German baroness, was published by J. M. Plane, together with a brief autobiography, as *Principes pour la harpe* (Paris, 1800/R1977).

WORKS
(published in Paris unless otherwise stated)

Orch: 2 harp concs., op.4 (c1777); 2 harp concs., op.6 (c1777); 5me conc., harp, op.7 (c1778), ed. M. Zunovoy-Skai'ska (Moscow, 1962); 6me conc., harp, op.9 (c1785), ed. F. Schroeder (Mannheim, 1970); 2 simphonies, harp, opt. acc.: 2 vn, 2 hn, fl, b, op.11 (1787); 1 conc., arr. kbd, orch, in Storace's Collection of Original Harpsichord Music, ii (London, 1789)

Harp sonatas: 6, acc. vn, op.1 (c1775); 4, acc. vn, db, 2 hn, op.3 (c1776); 6, acc. vn/fl, op.8 (c1780); 1 in Recueil, op.10 (c1787) [see below]; 4 sonates non difficiles, opt. acc.: vn, vc, op.12 (c1787); Collection de pièces de différens genres distribuées en 6 sonates, harp/pf, opp.13–14 (c1788) [4 with vn acc.], no.6 ed. M. X. Johnstone (South Pasadena, Calif., 1955); 4 sonates en forme de scènes de différens caractères, harp/pf, op.15 (c1788), 1 ed. H. J. Zingel (Mainz, 1966); 4 sonates chantantes, opt. acc.: vn, ?b, op.16 (c1788); 3 sonates . . . dont la 1er en forme de scène, acc. vn, op.17 (c1789); 2 sonates en forme de scènes, harp/pf, op.18 (c1789)

Other: Receuil de 12 préludes et petits airs, harp, op.2 (c1776), 3 ed. F. Vernillat (Paris, 1969); 2 duos, 2 harps/(harp, kbd), op.5 (c1777), also arr. as Simphonies concertantes, harp, acc.: vn, fl, bn, 2 hn, db (c1777); Recueil contenant différens petits airs variés, 1 sonate et 1 petit duo, 2 harps, op.10 (c1787); Andante, harp, acc. vn, op.19 (c1789), arr. of J. Haydn: Sym., HI:53/II; several songs, sets of variations; pieces in several 18th-century anthologies

(2) Wenzel [Václav] **Krumpholtz** (*b* ?Budenice, nr. Zlonice, *c*1750; *d* Vienna, 2 May 1817). Violinist,

brother of (1) Jean-Baptiste Krumpholtz. After serving in the orchestra of Prince Esterházy he became one of the first violins at the court opera in Vienna (1796). His name is immortalized by his friendship with Beethoven, who is said to have laid aside much of his customary reserve with Krumpholtz. He was one of the first to recognize Beethoven's genius, and he inspired others with his own enthusiasm, as Czerny mentioned. According to Ries, Krumpholtz gave Beethoven some instruction on the violin in Vienna. He also played the mandolin, and Beethoven wrote a sonata in one movement for mandolin and piano (WoO43) for him. Beethoven must have felt his death deeply, for on the following day he composed the 'Gesang der Mönche' WoO104 (from Schiller's *Wilhelm Tell*) for three men's voices 'in commemoration of the sudden and unexpected death of our Krumpholtz'. The compositions known to be by Wenzel, including two works for the violin (*Abendunterhaltung*, Vienna, n.d.; *Eine Viertelstude für eine Violine*, Vienna and Pest, n.d.) and a lied *Das Blümchen der Liebe und Chloe*, are of limited interest.

(3) Anne-Marie Krumpholtz [née Steckler] (*b* Metz, *c*1755; *d* London, after 1824). German harpist, wife and pupil of (1) Jean-Baptiste Krumpholtz. She made her first successful appearance at the Paris Concert Spirituel late in 1779, and in the following years she regularly performed her husband's compositions there. After fleeing to London she gave her first concert at the Hanover Square Rooms on 2 June 1788; for many years she performed with great success there, appearing at her own and Salomon's concerts (1791–3), at the oratorios in Drury Lane and at Haydn's benefit concerts. She frequently played J. L. Dussek's *duos concertants* for harp and piano with the composer, who was apparently her lover in the late 1780s; he dedicated a volume of sonatas to her and Steibelt composed a harp concerto for her. She performed in public until 1803.

Mme Krumpholtz was said to be an even finer player than her husband, making the instrument sound almost like an Aeolian harp. Her contemporaries were unanimous in their praise of her sensitive and attractive playing. She published a few light harp pieces in London, as did her daughter, known as Fanny Krumpholtz Pittar (who is possibly identifiable with Anne-Marie's daughter Charlotte Esprit, *b* 28 Feb 1785).

BIBLIOGRAPHY
FétisB; GerberL; GerberNL

G. J. Dlabacż: *Allegmeines historisches Künstler-Lexikon* (Prague, 1815/R1973)

F. Ries and F. G. Wegeler: *Biographische Notizen über L. van Beethoven* (Koblenz, 1838/R1972)

C. F. Pohl: *Mozart und Haydn in London* (Vienna, 1867/R1970)

H. Tribout de Morembert: *Anne-Marie Steckler: une virtuose de la harpe au XVIIIe siècle* (Metz, 1962)

W. Kolneder, ed.: *Carl Czerny: Erinnerungen aus meinem Leben* (Strasbourg and Baden-Baden, 1968), 11ff

F. Vernillat: 'La littérature de la harpe en France au xviiie siècle', *RMFC*, ix (1969), 168

ANNA TUHÁČKOVÁ (1)
C. F. POHL/HANS J. ZINGEL (2, 3)

Krupa, Gene (*b* Chicago, 15 Jan 1909; *d* Yonkers, NY, 16 Oct 1973). American jazz drummer and band-leader. He first attracted attention as drummer for the McKenzie–Condon Chicagoans, with whom he also made his first recordings (1927–8). After playing in numerous commercial orchestras, studio and pit bands, Krupa joined Benny Goodman in 1935, and by combining extraordinary show business aptitude with hypnotically effective technical displays (often in questionable musical taste) he became a national idol of the 'swing era'. He left Goodman in 1938 and successfully led his own bands until 1951; his last 20 years were divided between teaching and touring with Jazz at the Philharmonic.

GUNTHER SCHULLER

Krusceniski [Kruszelnicka], **Salomea** (*b* Tarnopol province, 23 Sept 1872; *d* L'vov, 16 Nov 1952). Ukrainian soprano, later naturalized Italian. She studied at Leopoli and made her début at L'vov in 1892, then appeared at Kraków. In 1895 she continued her studies at Milan with Fausta Crespi and during the 1895–6 season at Cremona she appeared in Puccini's *Manon Lescaut* and in *Les Huguenots*. Until 1902 she sang mostly in Russia, but a brilliant début at the San Carlo, Naples, in 1903 inaugurated her career in the leading Italian theatres (La Scala in 1907, 1909 and 1915), Spain and Buenos Aires (1906–13). She became Italian by marriage in 1910 and retired in 1925.

A woman of singular beauty and complex personality, she had a flexible, warm and well-focussed voice. At first a fine interpreter of Meyerbeer and Verdi, she later appeared in Catalani's *Loreley*, *Madama Butterfly* (she sang the title role at Brescia in 1904, when the revised version relaunched the opera), *Adriana Lecouvreur* and, during the same period, in the works of Wagner (particularly as Brünnhilde) and of Strauss. Though passionate and vigorous in temperament, she avoided the vulgar over-exuberance of many singing actresses of the *verismo* period. She was in fact guided by original and subtle ideas about the theatre, which in some roles, such as Aida and Salome, led her to a highly stylized characterization, marked by hieratic attitudes or an enigmatic oriental languor.

BIBLIOGRAPHY

P. Levi: *Paesaggi e figure musicale* (Rome, 1913), 405

G. Monaldi: *Cantanti celebri* (Rome, 1929), 248

S. Pavlishin: 'Zamechatel'naya ukrainskaya pevitsa' [A remarkable Ukrainian singer], *SovM* (1959), no.2, p.128

R. Celletti: 'Krusceniski, Salomea', *Le grandi voci* (Rome, 1964) [with opera discography by R. Vegeto]

W. Ashbrook: *The Operas of Puccini* (New York, 1968), 114

E. Arnosi and J. Dennis: 'Salomea Krusceniski', *Record Collector*, xviii (1969), 77 [with discography by R. L. Autrey]
RODOLFO CELLETTI

Kruse, Johann Secundus (*b* Melbourne, 23 March 1859; *d* London, 14 Oct 1927). Australian violinist of German descent. He appeared in public at nine years of age, playing at the first desk in the philharmonic concerts of his native town. In 1875 he went to Berlin to study with Joachim at the Hochschule für Musik, where he was later appointed professor. He became principal violin and sub-conductor of the Berlin Philharmonic Society in 1882 and also founded a string quartet. In 1885 he visited Australia, but was called back by Joachim to relieve him of some of his work at the Hochschule, where he taught until 1891, relinquishing the post to go to Bremen as leader of the philharmonic orchestra.

In October 1892 Kruse joined the Joachim Quartet as second violin, though still resident at Bremen, where he also founded a quartet of his own. In 1897 he moved to London, where he again founded a quartet and gave concerts. In 1902 he took over two concert series, organized an orchestral series under Weingartner in 1902–3, a Beethoven festival in 1903 and a further festival in 1904. He was

involved in chamber concerts in 1921 and in 1926 reappeared as leader of a new string quartet.

W. W. COBBETT/R

Kruspe. German firm of horn makers. It was founded in Erfurt on 2 January 1864 when Eduard Kruspe, an instrument maker since 1829, purchased a brass instrument-making business from Carl Zielsdorf, and the firm still trades under the name of Ed. Kruspe. On 1 April 1893 the firm was taken over by Fritz Kruspe, who together with a nephew of the distinguished horn player Friedrich Gumbert, produced the first double horn in F and B♭ in about 1898. The association between player and craftsman is particularly strong in the history of this firm; Georg Wendler, at one time principal horn of the Boston SO, married Fritz Kruspe's daughter and took over the business in 1928. He was obliged to retire in 1955 as the result of a stroke and the affairs of the firm were managed by Rudi Schneider, an apprentice who became the owner in 1961. The Kruspe double horn is one of the three basic models until recently available to players, including both original instruments and copies. All Kruspe horns have a characteristic tone, rather less brilliant than some other makes but very popular with some players.

BIBLIOGRAPHY

R. Morley-Pegge: *The French Horn* (London, 1960, 2/1972)
FRANK HAWKINS

Kruss [Crusius], **Johann** (*fl* mid-17th century). German composer and organist. He lived in or near Hamburg. It was probably in honour of his marriage in 1633 that Peter Meier wrote a *Braut-Lied*. Kruss may have composed songs which appear with the initials 'J.K.' in Caspar von Stieler's *Die geharnschte Venus* (Hamburg, 1660) and in Jacob Schwieger's two volumes of *Liebes-Grillen* (Hamburg, 1654–6) and in his *Des Flüchtigen flüchtige Feld-Rosen* (Hamburg, 1655). Although these songs are not masterpieces they are important in the context of the 17th-century Hamburg school of song-writers for the genuinely instrumental character of the accompanying basses.

BIBLIOGRAPHY

W. Vetter: *Das frühdeutsche Lied* (Münster, 1928)
JOHN H. BARON

Kruszelnicka, Salomea. *See* KRUSCENISKI, SALOMEA.

Kruyf, Ton de (*b* Leerdam, 3 Oct 1937). Dutch composer. He was self-taught until 1966, when he studied composition with Fortner, though by that time he had already made a reputation with the orchestral *Cinq impromptus* (1958) and the chamber pieces of the following years, notably *Sgrafitti* for piano, the Flute Sonatina and the Cello Sonata. The compositions of this period are founded on dodecaphonic techniques. De Kruyf won a major success with *Einst dem Grau* for mezzo-soprano and ensemble (1964), which was performed at the 1965 ISCM Festival. The piece sets three texts by Klee, each with a different instrumental combination, and makes free use of 12-note and serial procedures; the introduction and the two instrumental intermezzos are in a strict 12-note style. *Pour faire le portrait d'un oiseau* is for similar forces. In its first movement the atmosphere of the poem is sketched instrumentally in a 'Preludium', in which the piano has a solo role, and only towards the end does the voice mingle with the ensemble in vocalization, singing and speech. The second employs Prévert's poem in 14 variations, each differently instrumented. As a whole the piece has a playful character, resulting from an attempt to write a lighter kind of dodecaphonic music. The *Sinfonia II* is strictly serial and highly complex, but, as in almost all of De Kruyf's works, there is a constant lyrical undercurrent. After 1970, or thereabouts, 12-note serialism gave place to a freer technique in which timbre has taken an increasingly important function. The music of the opera *Spinoza*, first performed at the 1971 Holland Festival, was intended to be above all decorative and atmospheric. Each of the principal characters is remarkably characterized with an individual instrumentation and, in some cases, compositional technique.

WORKS
(selective list)

Stage: Spinoza (opera, 2, D. F. Frank), 1971; Inaugurazione, monodrama, Mez, small orch, 1974

Orch: Mouvements symphoniques, 1955, rev. 1966; Sinfonietta, 1956, rev. 1965; 5 impromptus, 1958; Chronologie II, 1967; Tône aus der Ferne, chamber orch, 1967; Sinfonia II (Öxnalt Sym.), 1968; 4 pas de deux, fl, chamber orch, 1972; Echoi, ob, str, 1973

Vocal: Einst dem Grau der Nacht enttauscht (Klee), Mez, ens, 1964; Pour faire le portrait d'un oiseau (Prévert), Mez, ens, 1965; Shakespeare Sonnets, Mez, fl, vc, 1965; Quauhquauhtinchan in den vreemde (oratorio, H. Mulisch), Mez, narrator, chorus, orch, 1972; Meditations, Bar, pf, str orch, 1976

Inst: Qt, fl, bn, tpt, vn, 1959; Sgrafitti, pf, 1960; Sonatina, fl, pf, 1960; Music for Str Qt, 1962; Partita, str qt, 1962; Sonata, vc, 1964; Pas de deux, fl, pf, 1968; Serenata, fl, cl, harp, str qt, 1968; Mosaico, ob qt, 1969; Seance, perc, pf, harp, 1969; Echoi, ob, 1973; Arioso, pf 4 hands, 1975

Principal publishers: Bote & Bock, Donemus

BIBLIOGRAPHY
E. Vermeulen: 'Serenata by Ton de Kruyf', *Sonorum speculum* (1969), no.40, p.23
——: 'Ton de Kruyf's opera Spinoza', *Sonorum speculum* (1971), no.47, p.1

JOS WOUTERS

Kruysen [Kruijsen], (René) Bernard (*b* Montreux, 28 March 1933). Dutch baritone. Descended from a family of artists, he studied originally at the Academy of Design in The Hague, then from 1953 at The Hague Conservatory. A scholarship from the French government enabled him to study with Pierre Bernac. Although he made his début in opera, and is frequently sought as a soloist in oratorio and concerts, he is best known for his solo recitals, especially of French song. A fastidious artist, he has an ample, burnished tone, and holds in fine balance the detailed inflections and the fuller design of each song. In France he is recognized as one of the greatest interpreters, and several of his recordings have received awards. He has given recitals with Poulenc and Hans Henkemans, among others, and has a strong partnership with the pianist Noël Lee. In addition, he has represented his country at the world championships in spear fishing, and made underwater films with apparatus that he developed himself.

TRUUS DE LEUR

Kruzhok Russkoy Muzïki (Russ.: 'Russian Music Circle'). Moscow educational society active from 1896 to 1912; *see* MOSCOW, §3.

Kryukov, Vladimir Nikolayevich (*b* Moscow, 22 July 1902; *d* Staraya Ruza, nr. Moscow, 14 June 1960). Russian composer. He studied under Myaskovsky at the Moscow Conservatory until 1925 and worked as a broadcasting editor (1930–31, 1950–51), music director of the Theatre of the Revolution (1933–5), director of the Moscow PO (1949–50) and composition teacher

at the Gnesin Institute (1957–9). His works are moderately progressive in technique.

WORKS
(selective list)

Dramatic: Korol' na ploshchadi [The king on the place] (opera, after Blok), 1925; Stantsionnïy smotritel' [The postmaster] (opera, M. Aliger, after Pushkin), 1938–40; Lev Gurïch Sinichkin (musical comedy, E. and M. Galperin, after V. Lensky), 1945; Dmitry Donskoy (opera, K. Kristi), 1947; Razlom [Breakage] (opera, B. Lavrenyov), 1948; music for the theatre, cinema and radio

Orch: Neznakomka [The unknown], sym. prologue to Blok's play, 1923; Suite, 1929; 1920 god [The year 1920], 1930; 9 yanvarya [Jan 9], 1931; Evreyskaya uvertyura [Hebrew ov.], 1933; Simfoniya-rapsodiya, 1944; Cl Concertino, 1945; Ballade, 1951; Sinfonietta, 1951; Cheshskaya rapsodiya [Czech rhapsody], 1952; Pf Conc., 1953; Conc.-Poem, tpt, orch, 1954; Ov., folk orch, 1954; Suite on Italian Themes, 1954; Bronenosets Potyomkin [Battleship Potemkin], 1955; Hn Conc. (1957)

Chamber: Sonata, va, pf, 1919–20, rev. 1933; 4 Pieces, va/vc, pf (1930); Sonata, vn, pf, 1946; 2 Pieces, vn, pf (1950); 5 Pieces, vn/va, pf (1959)

Pf: Pieces, 1920; 3 sonatas, 1921, 1924, 1931; 4 Pieces, 1952; Sonatina, 1952; Indoneziyskiye peyzazhï [Indonesian landscapes], 1953; Rhapsody no.2 (1958)

Vocal: 2 song cycles (Blok), 1v, pf, 1926, 1935; Oktyabrskaya kantata (A. Barto), children's chorus, 1947; O Moskve [On Moscow] (song cycle, A. Lugin), 1947; other song cycles

Principal publishers: Soviet State Publishing House, Universal

WRITINGS
'Internatsionalnoye obshchestvo sovremennoy muzïki' [The ISCM], *Sovremennaya muzïka* (1925), no.8, p.43
'Kontsert dlya skripki s orkestrom G. S. Gamburga' [Hamburg's Violin Concerto], *Sovremennaya muzïka* (1926), nos.15–16, p.137

BIBLIOGRAPHY
V. Belyayev: 'Moskauer Komponisten', *Musikblätter des Anbruch*, vii (1925), 173

DETLEF GOJOWY

Krzesichleb, Piotr. *See* ARTOMIUS, PIOTR.

Krzyżanowski, Ignacy (*b* Opatów, Kielce, 24 Dec 1826; *d* Warsaw 10 Feb 1905). Polish composer and pianist. He was related to Justyna Krzyżanowska, Chopin's mother. He studied the piano with his father in Kraków and harmony with Mirecki, and later at the Paris Conservatoire with H. Colet (from 1843). He also took lessons from Chopin. As a pianist Krzyżanowski was recognized as an outstanding musician, notably by Thalberg, and his playing was marked by a light, singing, soft tone. In 1848, on Chopin's advice, he went on a concert tour to London where he had considerable success. From 1850 he lived in Warsaw, concentrating on teaching; he was quickly recognized as one of the best piano teachers in Warsaw. Krzyżanowski's compositions, apart from his songs and three youthful works for violin and for cello, consist exclusively of piano music, most of which was published in Warsaw, Germany and Russia. His style shows a marked influence of Chopin, especially in form, melody and accompaniment figuration. He also published articles on music in the Polish magazines *Ruch muzyczny*, *Echo muzyczne* and *Bluszcz*.

WORKS

Pf: Andante cantabile, E♭, op.17 (Warsaw, *c*1852–9); Scherzo, c, op.21 (Warsaw, 1858); Polonaise, A, op.37 (Berlin, *c*1874–9); Sonata, b♭, op.45 (Wrocław, *c*1880–95); other pieces
Other works: Vn Sonata; Vc Sonata; Romance, vn; songs

BIBLIOGRAPHY
SMP [contains a fuller list of works]
W. Poźniak: 'Muzyka fortepianowa po Chopinie' [Piano music after Chopin], *Z dziejów polskiej kultury muzycznej*, ii (Kraków, 1966), 522
A. Zipser: 'Krzyżanowski, Ignacy', *PSB*

ZOFIA CHECHLIŃSKA

Krzyżanowski, Stanisław Andrzej (*b* Laszki Wielkie, nr. Lwów, 15 Feb 1836; *d* Kraków, 11 Oct 1922). Polish bookseller and music publisher. From 1855 he worked in various bookshops in Lwów, Chernovtsy, Leipzig and Kraków, where in 1870 he founded his own bookshop and swiftly developed it into one of the leading Polish music firms. He specialized in publishing the music of contemporary Polish composers, including Gall, Noskowski, Szopski, Żeleński, Friedman, Niewiadomski, Świerzyński and Wroński. His bookshop also imported the latest editions from abroad, and provided a music lending library, amounting to 16,000 items in 1885. From 1879 Krzyżanowski also managed a concert bureau, organizing performances in Kraków by many prominent virtuosos, notably Anton Rubinstein (1879), Joachim and Brahms (1880), Paderewski (1883 and later), Sarasate, Hofmann, Friedman, Ysaÿe and others. The versatility of Krzyżanowski's firm was of great importance to musical life in Kraków, and his bookshop soon became an artistic centre. In 1908 the firm was taken over by his son Marian Krzyżanowski (1880–1964), who directed it to 1964, from 1950 solely as a second-hand bookshop.

BIBLIOGRAPHY
J. Reiss: *Almanach muzyczny Krakowa*, i (Kraków, 1939), 154ff
B. Łopuszański and F. Pieczątkowski: 'Krzyżanowski, Stanisław', *PSB*
J. Lechiert and F. Pieczątkowski: 'Stanisław Krzyżanowski', *Słownik pracowników książkl polskiej* (Warsaw, 1972), 479
KORNEL MICHAŁOWSKI

Ktesibios. *See* CTESIBIUS.

Kūba. Sassanid hourglass drum; *see* PERSIA, §3(ii).

Kuba, Ludvík (*b* Poděbrady, Bohemia, 16 April 1863; *d* Prague, 30 Nov 1956). Czech painter, folksong collector and writer. After studying at the Prague Organ School under Skuherský (1877–9) and at a teachers' training college in Kutná Hora (1879–83), he became a village schoolmaster for a few years. He abandoned this in 1885 to devote himself wholly to his life-work, the assembly of a vast collection of Slavonic folk music (*Slovanstvo ve svých zpěvech*), which he had begun to publish privately in 1884. His research took him all over the Slavonic world: particularly valuable for instance are his notations of Russian folk polyphony and of the south Slav duets. He was equally gifted as a painter; his works blend impressionism with realism, taking much of their subject matter from his travels. When discouraged by lack of interest in his folksong research, Kuba returned to painting and studied further in Prague (1891–3), Paris (1894–5) and Munich (1896–1904). He then lived in Vienna before returning to Prague in 1911. After the establishment of the Czechoslovak Republic in 1918, Kuba found active support from President Masaryk for his folksong collection, and the entire project was finally completed in 1929 with the appearance of the 15th volume. Official recognition followed: he received an honorary doctorate from Prague University in 1936 and was made National Artist in 1945.

WRITINGS
O písni slovanské [On Slavonic song] (Prague, 1922–3)
'Nad ukončeným sborníkem "Slovanstvo ve svých zpěvech"' [On the completion of the collection 'The Slavonic world in its songs'], *Česká hudba*, xxxiii (1930), 25
Cesty za slovanskou písní (1855–1929) [Journeys in search of Slavonic song] (Prague, 1953)
ed. V. Fiala: *Křížem krážem slovanským světem* [Criss-cross through the Slavonic world] (Prague, 1956)

EDITIONS
Slovanstvo ve svých zpěvech [The Slavonic world in its songs], i–xv (Pardubice, 1884–1929)
Nowa zběrka melodiji k hornolužiskim pěsnjam [A new collection of tunes to Lower Lusatian songs] (Budyšin, 1887)
Pjesne i napjevi iz Bosne i Hercegovine [Songs and tunes from Bosnia and Hercegovina] (Sarajevo, 1906–9)

BIBLIOGRAPHY
J. Páta: *Ludvík Kuba: stručný přhled života a díla* [Ludvík Kuba: a brief account of his life and works] (Prague, 1926)
F. Kovárna: *Ludvík Kuba* (Prague, 1936)
J. Mičko: *Národní umělec Ludvík Kuba* [Ludvík Kuba, National Artist] (Prague, 1950)
L. Janáček: 'Slovanstvo ve svých zpěvech', *Leoš Janáček: O lidové písni a lidové hudbě* [Leoš Janáček on folksong and folk music] (Prague, 1955), 121
L. Kuba: *Zaschlá paleta: paměti* [A dried-up palette: memoirs] (Prague, 1955, 2/1958)
J. Stanislav: *Ludvík Kuba* (Prague, 1963)
JOHN TYRRELL

Kubelík, Jan (*b* Michle, nr. Prague, 5 July 1880; *d* Prague, 5 Dec 1940). Czech violinist and composer, father of Rafael Kubelík. His talent was encouraged from early childhood, and he studied the violin with Otakar Ševčík, at the Prague Conservatory, as well as composition with Foerster and others. At the outset of his career in 1898 he was acclaimed as 'a second Paganini' in Vienna and other cities, including London, where he made his début in 1900 at a Richter concert in St James's Hall. He toured the USA from 1902, as well as South America, the Far East, Australia and Africa in later years. His financial rewards enabled him to support the Czech PO in a financial crisis in 1901 and to organize a British tour for it in 1902, when it performed as the Kubelík Bohemian Orchestra from Prague; that

Jan Kubelík

year he received the Royal Philharmonic Society gold
medal. Kubelík was regarded as an outstanding exponent of the Ševčík violin method, and the essence of his
art was his absolute technical mastery of a wide repertory and his depth of musical perception. He had an
active concert career of over 40 years, retiring after a
celebratory season of ten Prague concerts (1939–40),
during which he performed nearly 50 works. His last
concert was given for a student audience at the Smetana
Hall, Prague, on 8 May 1940. He played a violin by
Guarneri del Gesù, presented to him in Vienna in 1899,
and then two by Stradivari, of which the first, dated
1678, was presented to him in 1901 by Lord Walter
Palmer, and the second, dated 1715 and called the
'Emperor', was bought for him in London in 1910. As a
composer he showed more taste and sense of tone-
colour than originality in a number of works, including
a symphony, six violin concertos, and works for violin
and piano. He wrote his own cadenzas for several concertos including those by Beethoven, Brahms and
Tchaikovsky, as well as for a concerto by Foerster
which was composed for him. Among his eight children
his daughter Anita (Anna) became a violinist and his son
Rafael a conductor.

BIBLIOGRAPHY

J. Čeleda: *Jan Kubelík* (Prague, 1930)

O. Nedbal: 'Ze vzpomínek na Jana Kubelíka' [Of the memories of Jan
Kubelík], *Tempo* (1930), no.9, p.324

B. Voldan: *Skladby Jana Kubelíka* [Jan Kubelík's compositions] (Prague,
1933)

K. Hoffmeister: *Jan Kubelík* (Prague, 1941)

H. Doležil: *Mistr housli Jan Kubelík* [The master of the violin Jan
Kubelík] (Prague, 1941)

J. Dostál, ed: *Jan Kubelík* (Prague, 1942) [incl. list of works and
discography]

S. Jandík: *Čaroděj housí* [The violin wizard] (Prague, 1949)

J. Creighton: *Discopaedia of the Violin, 1889–1971* (Toronto, 1974)

GRACIAN ČERNUŠÁK/ALENA NĚMCOVÁ

Rafael Kubelík, 1969

Kubelík, Rafael (Jeronym) (*b* Býchory, nr. Kolín, 29
June 1914). Swiss conductor and composer of Czech
birth, son of Jan Kubelík. He studied composition and
conducting at the Prague Conservatory, and made his
début conducting the Czech PO in 1934. Appointed
conductor of the orchestra in 1936, he toured with it to
Britain and elsewhere in 1938. After two years as musical director of the Brno Opera (1939–41), where he
first conducted the complete *Les troyens*, he returned to
the Czech PO in charge of the national Philharmonic
organization until 1948. That year, after the country
became communist, an engagement to conduct the
Glyndebourne Opera in *Don Giovanni* at the Edinburgh
Festival enabled him to leave Czechoslovakia; he settled
first in London and later in Switzerland, taking Swiss
nationality in 1973. In 1949 he was appointed musical
director of the Chicago SO (1950–53). There he was
criticized for a narrow repertory, though he gave the
premières of Roy Harris's Symphony no.7 (1952) and
Bloch's *Suite hébraïque* (1953). After conducting a brilliant revival of Janáček's *Kát'a Kabanová* with Sadler's
Wells Opera in 1954, he was appointed musical director
of the Covent Garden Opera (1955–8). There he conducted the first London productions of Janáček's *Jenůfa* in
1956 and Berlioz's *Les troyens* in 1957, and his decision
that these and other operas should be sung in English
reflected his preference for building a national ensemble
capable of giving good performances in the vernacular.
The principle continued to have its attractions, but
Covent Garden proved hardly the place for it.

Kubelík maintained his international activities as a
symphonic conductor with the Vienna PO, the Israel PO
and other orchestras, with which he also made many
records, and in 1961 he became principal conductor of
the Bavarian Radio SO in Munich. It was a fruitful
association, bringing regular public appearances, foreign
tours and a varied output of gramophone records
(including all Mahler's symphonies, and works by
Janáček and Schoenberg). He toured widely as a guest
conductor, his repertory reflecting his predilection for
such composers as Mahler, Janáček and Britten; he once
defined their works as 'a musical language dramatic and
eloquent enough to wake in the listener an ambition to
become better'. In 1971 he was named by Göran
Gentele, the newly appointed general manager of the
Metropolitan Opera, as the first musical director in the
company's history, but Gentele died in 1972 before
Kubelík's appearance in this appointment, with the first
production there of *Les troyens* in 1973; he resigned
within a year, having continued his Bavarian post.

Kubelík's works include the operas *Veronika* (staged
at Brno in 1947) and *Cornelia Faroli* (on the life of
Titian, produced at Augsburg in 1972); a choral symphony and orchestral symphony; concertos for violin
and cello, and three requiems. At the 1975 Lucerne
Festival he conducted the première of his orchestral
Sequenzen. He has recorded his *Quattro forme per archi*
with the English Chamber Orchestra. He married the
violinist Lála (Ludmila) Bertlová in 1942, and the soprano Elsie Morison in 1963.

BIBLIOGRAPHY
'Profile – Kubelík', *The Observer* (16 Oct 1955)
H. Rosenthal: 'Pen Portrait: Rafael Kubelík', *MT*, xcviii (1957), 606
———: *Two Centuries of Opera at Covent Garden* (London, 1958), 652ff
H. Raynor: 'A Great Conductor's View of Music', *The Times* (27 Dec 1967)

ARTHUR JACOBS

Kubiak, Teresa (*b* Łódź, 26 Dec 1937). Polish soprano. She studied in Łódź, making her début there in 1965 as Halka in Moniuszko's opera. In 1970 she sang Shulamith in a concert performance of Goldmark's *Die Königin von Saba* at Carnegie Hall, New York, and the following year appeared at San Francisco, Chicago, and Glyndebourne, where she sang Lisa in *The Queen of Spades* and Juno in Cavalli's *La Calisto*. In 1972 she made her London début at Covent Garden as Cio-cio-san and the next year sang Lisa at the Metropolitan Opera, and Elsa at Vienna. Her repertory also includes Aida, Senta, Tatyana, Tosca, Ellen Orford and Jenůfa. Her strong, lyrical voice with its individual timbre is particularly well suited to Puccini, while dramatic involvement in her roles has greatly increased with the inclusion of 20th-century works in her repertory.

ELIZABETH FORBES

Kubik, Gail (Thompson) (*b* South Coffeyville, Oklahoma, 5 Sept 1914). American composer. He studied at the Eastman School (1930–34) with Rogers and Royce for composition, Belov for the violin and McHose for theory, at the American Conservatory in Chicago (1935–6) with Sowerby for composition and Scott Willits for the violin, and at Harvard University (1937–8) with Piston for composition. Also, from 1937 he benefited from contacts with Boulanger. He was a staff composer and adviser for NBC in New York (1940–41), director of music for the film bureau at the Office of War Information (1942–3) and a composer-conductor for the US Air Force Motion Picture Unit (1943–6). He has continued to compose copiously for radio, television and the cinema; this involvement with functional music has had a great influence on his independent work, which, similarly, is principally melodic, dramatic and generally simple in texture.

WORKS
(*selective list*)

Dramatic: Puck: a Legend of Bethlehem (radio score), 1940; Thunderbolt (film score), 1943–5; A Mirror for the Sky (folk opera), 1946; C-Man (film score), 1949; Boston Baked Beans (opera piccola), 1950; The Miner's Daughter (film score), 1950; Gerald McBoing-Boing (film score), 1950, concert version for narrator, 9 insts, perc, 1950; The Desperate Hours (film score), 1955; The Silent Sentinel (television score), 1958–9
Orch: American Caprice, pf, 32 insts, 1933; Suite, 1935; Vn Conc., 1941, rev. 1951; Sym. no.1, E♭, 1947–9; Sym. concertante, pf, va, tpt, orch, 1952, rev. 1953; Thunderbolt Ov., 1953; Sym. no.2, F, 1955; Sym. no.3, 1956; Scenes, 1964; Prayer and Toccata, org, chamber orch, 1968; Pastorale, 1973; Pf Conc., 1976–7
Vocal: In Praise of Johnny Appleseed (V. Lindsay), B-Bar, chorus, orch, 1938, rev. 1961; Litany and Prayer, male chorus, brass, perc, 1943–5; Memphis Belle, speaker, orch, 1944; Fables in Song (Roethke), Mez/Bar, pf, 1950–69; A Christmas Set (medieval), chamber chorus, chamber orch, 1968; A Record of our Time, cantata, narrator, chorus, orch, 1970; Scholastica, unacc., 1972
Chamber and inst: 2 Sketches, str qt, 1932; Trivialities, fl, hn, str qt, 1934; Pf Trio, 1934; Wind Qnt, 1937; Celebrations and Epilogue, pf, 1938–50; Song and Scherzo, 2 pf, 1940, rev. 1962; Pf Sonatina, 1941; Sonatina, vn, pf, 1941; Pf Sonata, 1947; Divertimento nos.1–2, ens, 1959; Intermezzo: Music for Cleveland, pf, 1967; Music for Bells, handbells, 1975

Principal publishers: Chappell, Colombo, MCA, Ricordi, Southern

Kubín, Rudolf (*b* Ostrava, 10 Jan 1909; *d* Ostrava, 11

Jan 1973). Czech composer. He studied the cello with Junek and composition with Hába at the Prague Conservatory (1924–9). In 1929 he joined the Prague RO as a cellist and from 1935 he worked alternately in Ostrava and Brno as music director of Czech Radio. After World War II he was instrumental in founding the Ostrava branch of the Czech Composers' Union, and was its first president (1949–55). He also took part in the establishment of the Ostrava Higher Music Teaching College (which he directed in 1953–4), later re-formed as the conservatory, where he was director in 1958–60. Kubín was further involved in forming the Ostrava State PO (later renamed the Janáček PO) in 1954. In recognition he received the Order of Work in 1959.

Beyond its stylistic variety Kubín's music exhibits two characteristic traits: direct, folk-like melodic invention and a concern for expressiveness that is sometimes allowed to overrule formal dictates. His early works, influenced by Hába, employed quarter-tones and also took ideas from contemporary dance music. The 1930s brought a change to a style marked by expressionism and by the work of Stravinsky, Hindemith, Honegger and Janáček. Kubín's music of this time is harsh, impulsive and rhythmically emphatic; a fine example is the *Symfonietta* (1936). His postwar works are simpler and tend to synthesize his earlier techniques; they are also touched by the socialist realist aesthetic, notably in the cycle of symphonic poems *Ostrava*.

WORKS
(*selective list*)

Operas: Letní noc [Summer night] (M. Kareš), 1931; Naši furianti [Our defiant fellows] (comic opera, L. Pohl, after L. Stroupežnický), 1949
Orch: Česká předehra [Czech ov.], 1932; Zpěv uhlí [Song of the coal], sym. ov., 1936; Symfonietta, orch, org, 1936; Koncertantní symfonie, 4 ww, orch, 1937; Trbn Conc., 1937; Cl Conc., 1939; 2 vn concs., 1940, 1960; Accordion Conc., 1950; Ostrava: Vítězství [Victory], Maryčka Magdónova, Ostrava, V Beskydách [In the Beskydy mountains], Ocelovésrdce [Steel heart], sym. poems, 1950–51; Julius Fučík, ov., 1953; Tuba Concertino, 1962; Reminiscence, sym., 1968
Cantatas: Jáma Pokrok [The 'Progress' mine] (A. Vojkůvka), 1937; Píseň o domovině [A song of the homeland] (V. Martínek), 1938; Ze tmy na světlo [From darkness to light] (V. Závada), 1949
Songs and song cycles: Ostrava (P. Bezruč), Bar, male chorus, orch, 1932; Zpěvy staré Francie [Songs of old France] (J. Tiersot), S, small orch, 1944; Zpěvy anglických havířů [Songs of the English miners] (A. L. Lloyd), 1v, pf, 1957; Zpěvy albánského lidu [Songs of the Albanian people], 1v, pf, 1958; Stojí za to žít [It's worth living for] (E. F. Burian), T, pf, 1958; Zpěvy polských horníků [Songs of the Polish miners] (A. Dygacz), 1v, pf, 1959
Inst: 2 suites, ¼-tone pf, 1925, 1927; 2 fantasies, ¼-tone pf, 1926, 1927; 5 Pieces, vc, ¼-tone pf, 1926; Pf Pieces, ¼-tone pf, 1927

Principal publishers: Panton, State Publishing House, Supraphon

BIBLIOGRAPHY
ČSHS
B. Karásek: ' "Ostrava": cyklus symfonických básní Rudolfa Kubína', *HRo*, v (1952), 12
J. Paclt: 'Kantáty o ostravských hornících', *HRo*, v (1952), 16
I. Stolařík and B. Štědroň: 'K dějínám hudby v Ostravském kraji' [History of music in the Ostrava region], *Slezský sborník*, liii (1955), 219
V. Gregor: *Rudolf Kubín* (Ostrava, 1975)

OLDŘICH PUKL

Kučera, Václav (*b* Prague, 29 April 1929). Czech composer, musicologist and administrator. In 1948 he entered Prague University to read musicology, music teaching and aesthetics; he then spent five years in Moscow (1951–6) studying composition with Shebalin at the conservatory and musicology with Gruber and Cukkerman. On his return he was appointed head of the department of foreign music at Czech Radio in Prague, moving in 1959 to take charge of the department for the study of contemporary music in the Union of Czech Composers. From 1962 to 1969 he worked in the institute for musicology of the Czechoslovak Academy of Sciences, and in 1969 he was made general secretary of the Union of Czech Composers. In 1975 he was appointed to the chair of composition at the Prague Academy of Musical Arts (AMU). During the 1950s he followed the principles of socialist realism; his music was deeply influenced by folklore and retained close links with Romanticism. He became acquainted with the new music of western Europe in the mid–1960s, and this changed his development. From that time he made considerable use of electronic means, working at the electronic music studio of Czech Radio in Plzeň. His *Obraz* ('Picture') for piano and large orchestra won the Queen Marie-José prize at Geneva in 1970; *Invariant* (one of several works written for the Due Boemi) was performed at the 1971 ISCM Festival in London.

WORKS
(selective list)

Orch: Sym., 1962; Krysař [The pied piper], fl, 2 chamber orch, 1969; Obraz [Picture], pf, orch, 1970
Inst: Dramas, 9 insts, 1961; Genesis, fl, harp, 1965; Diptychon, fl, b cl, pf, perc, 1966; Spektra, dulcimer, 1966; Duodrama, b cl, pf, 1967; Invariant, b cl, pf, tape, 1969; Panta rhei, fl, vib, perc, 1969; Scenario, fl, str trio, 1970; Argot, brass qnt, 1970; Five Letters to you, 6 perc, 1970; Tabu, b cl, pf, 1971; Diario, omaggio a Che Guevara, gui, 1972; Spring Manifesto, fl, b cl, pf, perc, 1974
Vocal: Protests, 1v, pf, timp, 1963; Amoroso, cycle, Mez, fl, harp, 1975
Tape: Labyrinth, ballet, 1968; Spirala, ballet, 1968; Kinechromie, 1969; Lidice, radio fresco, 1970

Principal publishers: Panton, Supraphon

WRITINGS

ed.: *M. P. Musorgskij: Hudba života* (Prague, 1959) [correspondence, documents, etc]
'Vývoj a obsah Asafjevovy intonačni teorie' [Development and content of Asaf'yev's intonation theory], *HV 1961*, no.4, p.7
Talent, mistrovství, světový názor [Talent, mastery, world view] (Prague, 1962)
'K problematice uměleckého obrazu v hudbě' [The problem of artistic depiction in music], *HV*, ii (1965), 553
'Variačíni proces jako transformace významových kvalit modelu', *Nové cesty hudby*, ii (1970), 183–215
with others: *Dějiny české hudební kultury 1890–1945* [History of Czech music culture 1890–1945], i (Prague, 1972)

BIBLIOGRAPHY
ČSHS
V. Bokůvková: 'O elektronickém studiu v Plzni', *OM*, iv (1972), 161
A. Koštál: 'Kučerovo "Diario" a Narciso Yepes', *HRo*, xxix (1976), 260

OLDŘICH PUKL

Kuchař [Kucharsch, Kucharz, Kucharž], **Jan Křtitel** [Johann Baptist] (*b* Choteč, nr. Jičín, 5 March 1751; *d* Prague, 18 Feb 1829). Czech organist, composer and music teacher. He acquired his basic musical education in Vrchlabí with the cantor and organist A. Tham, and continued learning the organ at the Jesuit colleges at Königgrätz (now Hradec Králové) and Jičín. He completed his musical training with J. N. Seger in Prague, and became the organist of St Henry's Church (1772–90). On 1 September 1790 he was appointed organist of the monastic church at the Premonstratensian abbey at Strahov in Prague and held this post under the choirmasters Dlabač (1788–1807) and Strniště (from 1807) until his death. From about 1791 to 1797 he was also *maestro di cappella* of the Italian Opera in Prague. He was active as a teacher of singing, the piano and composition, and as a performer on the harpsichord, piano, glass harmonica and mandolin. As an organist he performed in many public concerts, including the Prague performance of Haydn's *The Creation* (1800). His abilities as an organist were highly praised, particularly by J. G. Naumann. Kuchař's son Joseph, a

Premonstratensian at Strahov (under the name Candidus), also played the organ and piano.

Kuchař was an important adherent of W. A. Mozart in Prague, and the first to arrange vocal scores of his operas, starting with *Le nozze di Figaro* (advertised in June 1787). He also composed recitatives for an Italian version of *Die Zauberflöte* which was performed at the Prague Theatre in 1794 and probably also in Dresden and Leipzig performances that year. Despite Kuchař's contemporary esteem, his extant compositions are not above average quality for the Classical period. Only a few of the organ fantasias and preludes are notable for their hints of early Romanticism.

WORKS
(MSS mainly in CS-Bm, Pk, Pnm, Pu)

Org: Partita, *D-Bds*; Fantasia, g, ed. in MAB, xii (1953, 3/1973); Fantasia, e, ed. M. Šlechta in Oblíbené varhanní skladby (Prague, 1970); Fantasia, d, ed. in MVH, xxi (1968, 3/1974); Fantasia, Eb, 1 movt ed. in MVH, xxi (1968, 3/1974); 4 preludes, ed. C. F. Pitsch in Museum für Orgelspieler, iii (Prague, c1832–4), 1 ed. F. Bachtík and S. Jiránek in Škola na varhany (Prague, n.d.), 1 ed. Šlechta in Organistae bohemici (Prague, 1970, 2/1972); Fugue, a, ed. in Museum für Orgelspieler, iii (Prague, c1832–4), Škola na varhany (Prague, n.d.), DČHP, no.153 (1958); Pastorella, D, ed. in Organistae bohemici (Prague, 1970, 2/1972); [untitled], 1826, frag. CS-Pnm; 2 concs., A (inc.), F (doubtful); others, lost
Vocal: O salutaris hostia, motet, org concertante; 3 gratulatory cantatas, incl. Cantata Miloni abbati, CS-Pnm; Gratulatory song (B. J. Dlabač), for V. Raitolar, mayor of Nebušice, 1v; other sacred works, incl. arrs. of hymns, songs, org accs. for plainchant, some lost
Other: Balli tedeschi, orch [for A. Salieri: La grotta di Trofonio], Prague, 1785, also arr. hpd/pf; vocal scores of W. A. Mozart: Le nozze di Figaro, Il dissoluto punito (Don Giovanni) [also arr. str qt, CS-Bm], Così fan tutte, Il flauto magico (Die Zauberflöte) [with recits], La clemenza di Tito; sonatas, pf 2/4 hands, lost; others, pf/glass harmonica/mand, lost

BIBLIOGRAPHY
GerberNL
Jb der Tonkunst von Wien und Prag (Prague, 1796), 123, 151
G. J. Dlabacž: *Allgemeines historisches Künstler-Lexikon*, ii (Prague, 1815/R1974), cols.148ff; iii (1815/R1974), col.258
O. E. Deutsch and C. B. Oldman: 'Mozart-Drucke', *ZMw*, xiv (1931–2), 146
P. Nettl: *Mozart in Böhmen* (Prague, 1938), 124ff
——: 'Der erste Klavierauszug des Don Giovanni', *Mitteilungen der Internationalen Stiftung Mozarteum*, xvi (1956), June, 36
J. Bužga: 'Kucharž, Johann Baptist', *MGG*
O. E. Deutsch, ed.: *Mozart: die Dokumente seines Lebens* (Kassel, 1961), 258f, 266, 435; [Eng. trans. as *Mozart: a Documentary Biography*, 1965, 2/1966)
W. Schuh: 'Il flauto magico', *Umgang mit Musik* (Zurich, 2/1972)

MILAN POŠTOLKA

Küchenthal, Johannes. *See* KEUCHENTHAL, JOHANNES.

Küchler [Kücheler, Kichler, Kiechler], **Johann** (*b* Quedlinburg, 1738; *d* Mainz, 16 Jan 1790). German bassoonist and composer. According to Eitner, he spent seven years in France and six in the Palatinate, apparently in military bands. He was in Paris in the 1770s, and served as a composer and *musicien du roi* at the court in Versailles. In 1780 he became a supernumerary in the Hofkapelle in Bonn, receiving a post as court bassoonist there in 1781; his activity in Bonn apparently ended in 1786 (Thayer), though it was not until March 1788 that his name was removed from the court rolls (Braubach). He appeared in Paris in the 1780s, playing in the orchestra of the Concert Spirituel. On 1 January 1788 he was at the electoral court in Mainz as second bassoonist (his son Friedrich had already been first bassoonist there for two years). Küchler was a recognized instrumental composer in his own time. Although no evidence has been found linking him directly to Mannheim (see Riemann), his works lie within the stylistic range of that school. He was famous mainly as a bassoon virtuoso in the 1780s, when both C. G. Neefe (in Cramer's *Magazin der Musik*, i, 1783/*R*1971, p.386) and J. N. Forkel (*Musikalischer Almanach 1784*, p.148) praised his playing.

WORKS

Azalia [Azakia] (opera), Bonn, 1782 or 1783, cited by Eitner

Orch: 1ère sinfonie concertante, orch/str qt (Paris, n.d.), lost; 3me sinfonie concertante, B♭, orch/str qt (Paris, n.d.); 2 syms. with obbl bn, cited in *FétisB*; Concerto a violino principale (Versailles, n.d.); Bn Conc., B♭, *D-SWl*

Chamber: 6 quatuors concertante, cl, vn, va, bn/vc [op.1] (Paris, 1773); 6 quartetti concertanti, str qt, op.4 (Paris, 1774); Str Qt (Paris, 1780 or 1781), lost; 6 quatuors, cl, vn, va, bn/vc, op.4 (Paris, n.d.); 6 trios concertants, 2 vn, b, op.3 (Paris, n.d.); Str Trios, op.4 (Paris, 1777), lost; 6 Duos, 2 vn, cited in *FétisB*; 6 Duos, 2 cl, op.4 (Paris, 1774)

BIBLIOGRAPHY

EitnerQ

H. Riemann, ed.: *Mannheimer Kammermusik des 18. Jahrhunderts: 2. Teil*, DTB, xxvii–xxviii, Jg.xv–xvi (1914–15/*R*)

K. Schweickert: *Die Musikpflege am Hofe der Kurfürsten von Mainz im 17. und 18. Jahrhundert* (Mainz, 1937)

E. Forbes, ed.: *Thayer's Life of Beethoven* (Princeton, 1964, 2/1967)

M. Braubach: 'Die Mitglieder der Hofmusik unter den vier letzten Kurfürsten von Köln', *Colloquium amicorum: Joseph Schmidt-Görg zum 70. Geburtstag* (Bonn, 1967), 26–63

U. Rau: *Die Kammermusik für Klarinette und Streichinstrumente im Zeitalter der Wiener Klassik* (diss., U. of Saarbrücken, 1975)

based on *MGG* (xvi, 1064) by permission of Bärenreiter

ULRICH RAU

Kücken, Friedrich Wilhelm (*b* Bleckede, Hanover, 16 Nov 1810; *d* Schwerin, 3 April 1882). German conductor and composer. He learnt the piano at an early age and played chamber music at home before moving to Schwerin, where he studied thoroughbass with Friedrich Lührss, the piano with Aron and Rettberg as well as the violin and flute; he joined the theatre orchestra as second flautist, later becoming violist and first violinist. Due to the success of his song *Ach, wie wärs möglich dann* the Grand Duke Paul Friedrich von Mecklenburg-Schwerin invited him to court. In 1832 he went to Berlin for further instruction in counterpoint with Birnbach; he composed more songs, instrumental music and an opera *Die Flucht nach der Schweiz*, which was first performed on 26 February 1839. He studied counterpoint with Sechter in Vienna (1841–3) and was active in Switzerland before making a trip to Paris to study orchestration with Halévy and vocal writing with Bordogni. His best-known opera, *Der Prätendent*, was written in Paris and first performed in Stuttgart (1847). Kücken returned to Germany in 1847 and from 1851 until his retirement in 1861 held important conducting posts at the Stuttgart court theatre.

Kücken's reputation as a composer rests mainly on his solo songs and duets, which were performed in London, Paris and Moscow. Works such as *Das Mädchen von Juda* were especially popular in London, where his works were published by Wessel. He captured the mood of the text in the accompaniment (as in the strophic *Maurisches Ständchen*) or in folklike settings (*Herzallerliebstes Shatzerl* and *Gretelein*), other songs are characterized by more subtle harmonies (*Wasserfahrt*) or melodic simplicity (*Du bist wie eine Blume*). Besides his two operas, he also wrote choral works, piano pieces and other instrumental works.

BIBLIOGRAPHY

Obituaries, *AMz*, xvii (1882), 253, 268; *NMZ*, iii (1882), nos.9–10

R. Eitner: 'Kücken', *ADB*

GAYNOR G. JONES

Kuckertz, Josef (*b* Würseln, nr. Aachen, 24 Nov 1930). German musicologist. After a practical training at the Rheinische Musikschule in Cologne, Kuckertz studied musicology from 1957 at Cologne University, where his teachers included Marius Schneider. He took his doctorate there in 1962 with a dissertation on Romanian folk music. Subsequently he became assistant lecturer at the musicology institute at Cologne University, where he completed his *Habilitation* in musicology in 1967 with a work on south Indian music. Since then he has been lecturer and (from 1973) research fellow and professor in the department of ethnomusicology and comparative musicology in the musicology institute at the university. The focal point of his research, much of which has been done abroad (especially in south India), is the music and musical theory of the developed oriental cultures and the question of the relationship between oriental and European music.

WRITINGS

Gestaltvariation in den von Bartók gesammelten rumänischen Colinden (diss., U. of Cologne, 1962; Regensburg, 1963)

'Der Tāla in der südindischen Kunstmusik', *Jb für musikalische Volks- und Völkerkunde*, iii (1967), 85, 134

Form und Melodiebildung der karnatischen Musik Südindiens – in Umkreis der vorderorientalischen und der nordindischen Kunstmusik (Habilitationsschrift, U. of Cologne, 1967; Wiesbaden, 1970)

'Die Satztechnik in den mehrstimmigen Messordinarien des 14. Jahrhunderts', *KJb*, lii (1968), 45

'Die Melodietype der westsyrischen liturgischen Gesänge', *KJb*, liii (1969), 61–98

'Bākhām-Songs from Jammu, North India', *XVII Kongres Saveza udruženja folklorista Jugoslavije: Poreč 1970*

'Origin and Development of the Rabāb', *Sangeet Natak: Journal of the Sangeet Natak Akademi*, xv (1970), 16

'Die Kunstmusik Südindiens im 19. Jahrhundert', *Die Musikkulturen Asiens, Afrikas und Ozeaniens im 19. Jahrhundert*, ed. R. Günther (Regensburg, 1973), 97–130

'Gesänge der Toda', *Musicae scientiae collectanea: Festschrift Karl Gustav Fellerer* (Cologne, 1973), 297

'Die klassische Musik Indiens und ihre Aufnahme in Europa im 20. Jahrhundert', *AMw*, xxxi (1974), 170

'Fragen zur Übertragung einheimischer Musik in den Gottesdienst', 'Indische Musik', *Musica indigena: symposium musico-ethnologicum: Roma 1975*, 26, 87

with M. T. Massoudieh: 'Volksgesänge aus Iran', *Beiträge zur Musik des Vorderen Orients und seinen Einflussbereichen: Kurt Reinhard zum 60. Geburtstag* (Berlin, 1975)

——: *Musik in Busehr, Süd-Iran* (Munich, 1976)

'Origin and Construction of the Melodies in Baul Songs of Bengal', *YIFMC*, vii (1976)

'Drei Aufführungen der Krti "Koluvamare gada" von Tyāgarāja: zum Stil und Stilwandel der karnatischen Musik in den letzten sechzig Jahren', *Studien zur Phänomenologie der musikalischen Gestaltung: Festschrift für Marius Schneider* (Regensburg, 1977)

'Gesänge der Santal', *Neue ethnomusikologische Forschungen: Festschrift Felix Hoerburger* (Laaber, 1977)

with B. Chaitanya Deva: *Ḍaf-gāne and Related Music in Central India* (in preparation)

HANS HEINRICH EGGEBRECHT

Kuckuck (Ger.). A bird-imitating ORGAN STOP (*Vogelgesang*).

Kuczynski, Paul (*b* Berlin, 10 Nov 1846; *d* Berlin, 21 Oct 1897). German composer. He studied with Bülow and Friedrich Kiel. By profession a banker, he was friendly with a number of musicians, especially Adolf Jensen, whose personality and music influenced him; he published Jensen's letters to him, *Aus Briefen Adolf Jensens* (Berlin, 1879). His connections with Bayreuth are reflected in his *Erlebnisse und Gedanken, Dichtungen zu Musikwerken* (Berlin, 1898). His compositions include vocal and instrumental works, and he was also said to be an excellent pianist.

BIBLIOGRAPHY

A. von Hanstein, ed.: *Musiker- und Dichterbriefe von Paul Kuczynski* (Berlin, 1900)

A. Niggli: *Adolf Jensen* (Berlin, 1900)

JOHN WARRACK

Kuen, Johannes. *See* KHUEN, JOHANNES.

Kuerti, Anton (*b* Vienna, 21 July 1938). American pianist, teacher and composer. He studied at the Cleveland Institute of Music with Arthur Loesser, and at the Curtis Institute in Philadelphia with Rudolf Serkin. His first appearance with an orchestra was in 1948, with the Boston Pops Orchestra. In 1957 he played with the New York PO and the Cleveland Orchestra, and the next year with the Philadelphia Orchestra. He toured South America in 1958 and Poland in 1959, and also appeared with the RIAS Berlin Orchestra. He began to perform regularly with the Toronto SO from 1961 and the Montreal SO from 1963, and made his British début with the LSO in 1965. He has toured the German Democratic Republic, and given master classes in a number of cities. In 1965 he became professor and pianist-in-residence at the University of Toronto. He has made numerous radio and television appearances and recordings.

His main repertory comprises Beethoven, Schumann, Schubert and Skryabin, but he also plays a good deal of Canadian music, and gave the first performances of Oskar Morawetz's Piano Concerto (1963) and Suite (1968), and S. C. Eckhardt-Gramatté's Piano Concerto (1967). He has appeared at the music festivals in Prague, Dubrovnik, Aspen, Spoleto and Marlboro, and is a founder-member of the Marlboro Trio. In 1974–5 he recorded and performed in Toronto and Ottowa the complete Beethoven piano sonatas. His compositions include a symphony *Epomeo*, a violin sonata, the *Linden Suite* for piano, works for cello and piano, and two string quartets.

T. BROWN

Kufferath. German (later Belgian) family of musicians.

(1) **Johann Hermann Kufferath** (*b* Mülheim, 12 May 1797; *d* Wiesbaden, 28 July 1864). Violinist, conductor and composer. As a child he showed a natural talent for music; his father, a great music lover, gave him his first music lessons. He subsequently studied with the cellist Joseph Alexander, and later with L. Scheffer (a pupil of Spohr), Spohr and Hauptmann. He was not only a gifted violinist but also an accomplished conductor; at the age of 15 he was leader of a military band, and he subsequently conducted in Mülheim, Duisburg, Bielefeld and elsewhere. In 1823 he was made music director of Bielefeld. From 1830 to 1862 he was active as director of the Collegium Musicum in Utrecht and of the Utrechter Gesangverein, where he conducted works by Haydn, Mozart, Handel, Beethoven, Mendelssohn, Spohr and Schumann. He spent the last years of his life in Wiesbaden.

Kufferath's compositions, primarily cantatas, overtures and motets, show clearly the influence of Weber, Spohr and Mendelssohn, and originality and a sound compositional technique. But he is chiefly known for his 32 years' leadership of the musical life of Utrecht, where he reformed the concert repertory thoroughly.

(2) **Louis Kufferath** (*b* Mülheim, 10 Nov 1811; *d* St Josse-ten-Noode, nr. Brussels, 2 March 1882). Pianist, teacher, conductor and composer, brother of (1) Johann Hermann Kufferath. He received his first musical instruction from his elder brother, then studied with Johann Christian Friedrich Schneider in Dessau. He became a brilliant piano virtuoso and undertook concert tours of Germany and the Netherlands. From 1836 to 1850 he directed the music school in Leeuwarden and conducted the Euphonia-Crescendo, the Grote Zangvereniging (which he founded) and various other musical groups. He moved to Ghent in 1850, where he concentrated mainly on composition; subsequently he established himself in Brussels.

His musical work, comprising primarily piano pieces, is typical of 19th-century salon music.

(3) **Hubert-Ferdinand Kufferath** (*b* Mülheim, 10 June 1818; *d* St Josse-ten-Noode, 23 June 1896). Violinist, pianist, conductor, teacher and composer, brother of (1) Johann Hermann Kufferath. He, too, was a musical child prodigy; at scarcely the age of seven he tuned church organs, and soon afterwards appeared in public as a violinist and a pianist. His brothers gave him his first musical instruction; later he studied with F. Hartmann in Cologne and with Schneider in Dessau (1833–6). In 1839 his superb performance on the violin at a concert in Düsseldorf attracted the attention of Mendelssohn, who invited him to Leipzig. There he studied the violin with David, and afterwards studied with Mendelssohn and Hauptmann. In 1841 he conducted the Männergesangverein in Cologne for six months, and after travelling a while as a virtuoso established himself in Brussels in 1844, where he taught the piano and composition. He also conducted a choral society there and, together with Léonard and Servais, founded a series of chamber concerts by which the music of Schumann, among others, was disseminated in Belgium. His home became the meeting place of such eminent musicians as Wieniawski, Bériot and Clara Schumann. In 1872 Kufferath was made professor of counterpoint and fugue at the Brussels Conservatory, a post he held until his death. His pupils Edouard Lassen, Arthur de Greef and Edgar Tinel praised his thorough technical understanding of music.

His works, which include symphonic, choral and chamber music, songs and piano pieces, are strongly influenced by Mendelssohn. Of greater significance is his single theoretical work, *Ecole pratique du choral* (Brussels, n.d.), which was used widely in Belgium and France.

(4) **Maurice Kufferath** (*b* St Josse-ten-Noode, 8 Jan 1852; *d* Uccle, nr. Brussels, 8 Dec 1919). Writer on music, conductor and cellist, son of (3) Hubert-Ferdinand Kufferath. He had his first music lessons with his father, then studied the cello with Adrien-François Servais and François-Mathieu Servais; subsequently he studied law and art history in Brussels and Leipzig. In 1874 he became a writer on foreign politics for *Indépendance belge* and in the following year became editor of *Le guide musical*. From 1890 to 1914 he was chief proprietor of this music journal, which enabled him to defend his Wagnerian ideas. Together with Guillaume Guidé, Kufferath directed the Théâtre de la Monnaie in Brussels from 1900 to 1914. There he conducted the operas of Wagner and other German, French and Italian works, including those of Strauss (*Elektra* and *Salome*), Dukas (*Ariane et Barbe-Bleue*), Debussy (*Pelléas et Mélisande*) and Galeotti (*Dorise*). Among the operas first produced at the Théâtre de la Monnaie are Chausson's *Le Roi Arthus*, Albéniz's *Pepita Jimenez* and Blockx's *La fiancée de la mer*.

During World War I Kufferath travelled in Switzerland, where he wrote for periodicals and delivered numerous lectures on art. He returned to Brussels in 1918 and again directed the Théâtre de la Monnaie.

Today Kufferath is known chiefly for his writings on music, especially the monographs on Wagner's operas.

WRITINGS

Hector Berlioz et Robert Schumann (Brussels, 1879) [trans. of articles by Schumann on Berlioz]
Henri Vieuxtemps, sa vie et son oeuvre (Brussels, 1882)
Parsifal de Richard Wagner (Paris, 1890)
L'art de diriger (Paris, 1891, 3/1909)
Le théâtre de Richard Wagner de Tannhäuser à Parsifal (Paris and Brussels, 1891–8)
Guide thématique et analyse de Tristan et Iseult (Paris and Brussels, 1894)
Cours sur les évolutions de la musique moderne (Brussels, 1895)
Les abus de la Société des auteurs, compositeurs et éditeurs de musique (Brussels, 1897)
Les maîtres-chanteurs de Nuremberg (Brussels, 1898)
Musiciens et philosophes: Tolstoï, Schopenhauer, Nietzsche, Richard Wagner (Paris, 1899)
Salomé, poème d'O. Wilde, musique de Richard Strauss (Brussels, 1907)
Fidelio de L. van Beethoven (Paris, 1913)
En commémoration de la première représentation de Parsifal au Théâtre Royal de la Monnaie (Brussels, 1914)
La flûte enchantée de Mozart (Paris, 1914)
with E. Kastner: *Catalogue biographique et bibliographique de Richard Wagner* (MS, *B-Bc*)

(5) **Antonia Kufferath** (*b* Brussels, 28 Oct 1857; *d* Shenley, 26 Oct 1939). Soprano, sister of (4) Maurice Kufferath. She studied with Julius Stockhausen and Pauline Viardot-Garcia and made her début in Berlin in 1878. A specialist in the songs of Schumann and of Brahms (she gave the first public performances of some of them), she had faultless diction and a fine voice that won great admiration at the Schumann festival in Bonn in 1880. In 1882 she sang in England; three years later she married Edward Speyer and gave up her career.

BIBLIOGRAPHY

L. Solvay: *Notice sur Maurice Kufferath* (Brussels, 1923)
K.-U. Düwell: 'Kufferath', *Rheinische Musiker*, iii, ed. K. G. Fellerer (Cologne, 1964), 52

ANNE-MARIE RIESSAUW

Kugelmann, Barthel. German 16th-century trumpeter, son of PAUL KUGELMANN.

Kugelmann, Christoph. German 16th-century trumpeter, brother of PAUL KUGELMANN.

Kugelmann, Johann [Hans] (*b* Augsburg, *c*1495; *d* Königsberg, late July or early Aug 1542). German composer, brother of Paul Kugelmann. From 1518 to 1523 he was a trumpeter in the imperial Hofkapelle in Innsbruck, and may have been a pupil of Hofhaimer. He was employed by the Fugger family in Augsburg for a short time before going to Königsberg as a trumpeter and composer at the court of Margrave Albrecht V of Brandenburg (later Duke of Prussia). From 1534 he was first trumpeter and Kapellmeister there, and was in charge of the Kantorei until 1540. He composed pieces for two Königsberg songbooks of 1527 (both probably lost) as well as melodies and some polyphonic pieces for a manuscript collection of sacred songs by Heinrich von Miltitz (*c*1539, formerly in the Staatsbibliothek Königsberg, MS 334). Kugelmann's *Concentus novi* (Augsburg, 1540), for school and church use, was commissioned from Sylvester Raid by the Fuggers and Duke Albrecht. It contains 39 sacred pieces, 30 of which are by Kugelmann (ed. in EDM, *Sonderreihe*, ii, 1955). His musical style, though furnishing a model for Johannes

Eccard, was conservative. His technical ability is shown above all in the eight-voice setting, in the form of a canon at the 5th, of *Nun lob, mein Seel, den Herren*; the melody, an adaptation by Kugelmann of the song *Weiss mir ein Blümlein blaue*, was printed here for the first time. Three songs (one of which is doubtful) are in *DK-Kk* Gl.Kgl.Saml.1872.

BIBLIOGRAPHY

C. von Winterfeld: *Der evangelische Kirchengesang*, i (Leipzig, 1843/R1966), 205ff
J. Müller-Blattau: 'Die musikalischen Schätze der Staats- und Universitätsbibliothek zu Königsberg', *ZMw*, vi (1923–4), 215
R. Fuehrer: *Die Gesangbücher der Stadt Königsberg* (Königsberg, 1927)
F. Blume: *Die evangelische Kirchenmusik*, HMw, x (1931, rev. 2/1965 as *Geschichte der evangelischen Kirchenmusik*; Eng. trans., enlarged, 1974 as *Protestant Church Music: a History*)
M. Federmann: *Musik und Musikpflege zur Zeit Herzog Albrechts* (Kassel, 1932)
M. Ruhnke: *Beiträge zu einer Geschichte der deutschen Hofmusik-kollegien im 16. Jahrhundert* (Berlin, 1963)

HANS-CHRISTIAN MÜLLER

Kugelmann, Melchior. German 16th-century trumpeter and composer, brother of PAUL KUGELMANN.

Kugelmann, Paul (*b* Augsburg; *d* Königsberg, 1580). German composer, brother of Johann Kugelmann. He went to Königsberg, probably in 1542, after Johann's death. He is first mentioned as a trumpeter in the Hofkapelle in 1548, and was first trumpeter in 1549–53 and 1575–80. In 1558 he published in Königsberg the collection *Etliche teutsche Liedlein, geistlich und weltlich*, containing 121 polyphonic lieder, among them 88 by Kugelmann (7 ed. H. Engel, *Sieben teutsche Liedlein aus P. Kugelmanns Sammlung 1558*, Königsberg, 1937/*R*). He was a conservative musician: he frequently took the tenor straight from older lieder books, and his old-fashioned settings are not always very skilful. A six-voice *Benedicamus* by him is in *DK-Kk* Gl.Kgl.Saml.1872. He also wrote a few occasional pieces (now lost) for Duke Albrecht and his son Albrecht Friedrich.

Kugelmann's brother Melchior (*b* Augsburg; *d* Königsberg, ?1548) was a trumpeter in the Königsberg Hofkapelle from 1540 to 1548 and had perhaps studied there. Nine pieces by him were included in *Etliche teutsche Liedlein*. Another brother, Christoph (*b* Augsburg; *d* Königsberg, 1531), went to Königsberg in 1527 as a trumpeter in the Hofkapelle. Paul Kugelmann's son Barthel (*b* Königsberg) was a trumpeter in the Königsberg town watch from 1567.

BIBLIOGRAPHY

F. Spitta: 'Die Liedersammlung des Paul Kugelmann', *Riemann-Festschrift* (Leipzig, 1909/R1965), 272
For further bibliography see KUGELMANN, JOHANN.

HANS-CHRISTIAN MÜLLER

Kuh, Tobias. See KÜHN, TOBIAS.

Kuhač [Koch], **Franjo Žaver** (*b* Osijek, 20 Nov 1834; *d* Zagreb, 18 June 1911). Croatian ethnomusicologist, music critic and composer. He studied privately with Thern at Leipzig in 1856, and in the same year with Liszt at Weimar; he then studied for a short time with Czerny in Vienna. He gave piano lessons in Osijek (1858–71), then moved to Zagreb in 1871 where he was music critic for the papers *Narodne novine* and *Agramer Zeitung*. He lost this position in 1874 following the demands of the Opera management, who disliked his harsh tone. From 1872 he taught music theory and piano at the Croatian Music Institute, but left in 1876, disapproving of its pro-German orientation.

Kuhač was a pioneer of ethnomusicology in Croatia. Over a number of years he made regular excursions into various Slavonic provinces in the Balkans, both within and outside the Austro-Hungarian Empire. The folksongs he collected were first published in 1878, and by 1881 he had brought out four books containing 1600 songs. The remaining 400 songs from his collection were prepared for publication by B. Širola and V. Dukat in 1941. He displayed many shortcomings in classifying the melodies, and when adding the piano accompaniment he overlooked many special characteristic elements of the folk idiom. The collection nevertheless was the first important step in the development of ethnomusicology in Croatia and exercised a powerful influence on a whole generation of Croatian composers. He was a prolific writer, and apart from numerous studies about the nature of Croatian and south Slavonic folk music he wrote about early Croatian Romanticism and campaigned forcefully for a Croatian national style in music. He pointed out the Croatian origin of several of Beethoven's and Haydn's themes but was often carried too far by his imagination. Thus in 1880 he put forward his theory about Haydn's Croatian ancestry which even attracted some followers abroad: in England it was accepted by W. H. Hadow.

WRITINGS

'Narodna glazba Jugoslavena' [Folk music of the southern Slavs], *Vienac*, i/24–6, 28–9 (1869)
'Sachliche Einleitung zur Sammlung südslavischer Volkslieder', *Agramer Zeitung* (1873), no.49
Katekizam glazbe: prva hrvatska glazbena teorija po J.Ch. Lobeu [A musical catechism: the first Croatian music theory after Lobe] (Zagreb, 1875, enlarged 2/1890)
'Prilog za poviest glazbe južnoslavjanske: opis i poviest narodnih glazbala južnih Slavena' [Contributions to the history of music of the southern Slavs: description and history of the folk instruments of the southern Slavs], *Rad JAZU* (1877), no.38, pp.1–78; (1879), no.39, pp.65–114; no.41, pp.1–48; (1878), no.45, pp.1–49; (1879), no.50, pp.44–95; (1882), no.62, pp.134–86; no.63, pp.71–112
Južno-slovjenske narodne popievke [South Slavonic folksongs] (Zagreb, 1878–1941)
'Josip Haydn i hrvatske pučke popievke' [Haydn and Croatian folksongs], *Vienac*, xii/13–29 (1880)
'Ursprung der österreichischen Volkshymne', *Kroatische Revue* (1886), May
Vatroslav Lisinski i njegovo doba [Lisinski and his time] (Zagreb, 1887, enlarged 2/1904)
'Die Zigeuner unter den Südslaven', *Ethnologische Mittheilungen aus Ungarn*, iii (1889), 308
'Die Musik in Dalmatien und Istrien', *Die österreichisch-ungarische Monarchie in Wort und Bild* (1890), no.152
'Zadaća melografa i vriednost pučkih popievaka' [A melographer's task and the value of folksongs], *Vienac*, xxiv/5–9, 11–15, 17–19 (1892)
Ilirski glazbenici [The musicians of the Illyrian movement] (Zagreb, 1893)
'Beethoven i hrvatske narodne popievke' [Beethoven and Croatian folksongs], *Prosvjeta*, ii (1894), 17
'Hrvatsko glazbeno nazivlje' [Croatian musical terminology], *Nada*, ii (1896), 14, 29
Prva hrvatska uputa u glasoviranje [The first Croatian school of piano playing] (Zagreb, 1896–7)
'Apollonova himna od god. 278 prije Isusa' [Apollo's hymn from the year 278 BC], *Rad JAZU* (1897), no.130, pp.189–238
'Josip Tartini i hrvatska pučka glazba' [Tartini and Croatian folk music], *Prosvjeta*, vi/1–3 (1898)
'Turski živalj u pučkoj glazbi Hrvata, Srba i Bugara' [The Turkish population in the folk music of the Croats, Serbs and Bulgarians], *Glasnik Zemaljskog muzeja za Bosnu i Hercegovinu* (1898), 175–217
'Die Volksmusik in Kroatien und Slavonien', *Österreichisch-ungarische Monarchie in Wort und Bild*, iv (1901)
Moj rad [My work] (Zagreb, 1904)
'Osebine narodne glazbe, naročito hrvatske' [Characteristics of folk music, particularly that of Croatia], *Rad JAZU* (1905), no.160, pp.116–251; (1908), no.174, pp.117–236; (1909), no.176, pp.1–82

BIBLIOGRAPHY

W. H. Hadow: *A Croatian Composer: Notes toward the Study of Joseph Haydn* (London, 1897)
A. Kassowitz-Cvijić: *Franco Ž. Kuhač: stari Osijek i Zagreb* [Old Osijek and Zagreb] (Zagreb, 1924)
B. Papandopulo: 'Franjo S. Kuhač kao ideolog naših muzičko-kulturnih nastojanja' [Kuhač as an ideologist of our musical and cultural endeavours], *Ćirilometodski vjesnik*, iii (1935), 51, 72, 94
B. Širola: 'Franjo Ž. Kuhač: o stotoj obljetnici rodjenja' [On the centenary of his birth], *Zvuk* (1935), no.1, p.9; no.2, p.49
A. Dobronić: 'Franjo Ž. Kuhač, *Nova Evropa*, xxix (1936), 398
V. Žganec: 'Kuhačev život, rad i značenje za našu muzičku kulturu' [Kuhač's life, work and importance to our musical culture], *Zvuk* (1962), no.54, p.435
M. Škunca: 'Franjo Kuhač kao muzički historičar' [Kuhač as musical historian], *Rad JAZU* (1969), no.351, pp.281–324
J. Andreis: *Music in Croatia* (Zagreb, 1974)

BOJAN BUJIĆ

Kuhe, Wilhelm (*b* Prague, 10 Dec 1823; *d* London, 8 Oct 1912). Czech pianist, teacher, composer and administrator. He studied in Prague with Josef Proksch (1833–6) and Tomašek (1840–43), and had some lessons with Thalberg. In 1844–5 he made a successful concert tour throughout Germany, then visited London with the singer Pišek; there he played with success at the Musical Union in a trio by Mayseder on 13 May 1845. From 1847 he lived in England, giving an annual concert and teaching at the RAM from 1886 to 1904. He organized an enterprising festival at Brighton (1871–82), where he commissioned and performed many new works, including music by Cowen, Gounod (the scena *O happy home*), Benedict, Macfarren, J. F. Barnett, George Osborne and Prout. The first year included an ambitious performance of *Elijah* with Albani, Trebelli, Edward Lloyd and Santley. His original compositions include many piano pieces, among which are *Lieder ohne Worte* op.12, *Le carillon* op.13, *Romance sans paroles* op.17, *Le feu follet* op.38 and fantasias on the British and Austrian national anthems.

As a young man, Kuhe heard first-hand stories of Mozart and the première of *Don Giovanni* from the original orchestra, was impressed by the playing of Hummel, Kalkbrenner and Moscheles, and himself played to Metternich; he lived to hear, and often admire, virtuosos whose careers lasted into the middle of the 20th century. His book *My Musical Recollections* (London, 1896) gives a lively and entertaining picture of the many musicians with whom he had personal and professional contacts in his long career, and includes vivid accounts of many of the leading singers of the day (especially Jenny Lind) and of Tomašek, Liszt, Rossini, Bülow, Chopin, Berlioz and Rubinstein, among many others. His son Ernest (*b* Brighton, 1870; *d* London, June 1936) worked as a music critic, especially for the *Daily Telegraph*.

JOHN WARRACK

Kuhglocke (Ger.). COWBELLS.

Kuhlau, (Daniel) Friedrich [Frederik] **(Rudolph)** (*b* Uelzen, nr. Hanover, 11 Sept 1786; *d* Copenhagen, 12 March 1832). Danish composer and pianist of German birth. Together with his friend C. E. F. Weyse he was the foremost representative of the late Classical and early Romantic periods in Denmark.

Kuhlau was the son of a military bandsman and was still a child when his family moved with the regiment to Lüneburg and Brunswick. Having finished school when he was 14, he went to Hamburg to study theory and composition with C. F. G. Schwenke, the Kantor of the

Catherinenkirche and a learned scholar who had been taught by Marpurg and Kirnberger. During his stay in Hamburg his earliest known compositions, songs and works for flute and piano, were published, and from 1804 he regularly gave piano recitals. When Hamburg was invaded by Napoleon's troops in 1810 Kuhlau fled to Copenhagen and began earning a living there as a pianist and composer. In January 1811 he gave a concert at the Royal Theatre, performing among other works his C major Piano Concerto op.7, which he later dedicated to Weyse. Two years later he was appointed court chamber musician, and the following year his first stage success, the Singspiel *Røverborgen* ('The robbers' castle') was given at the Royal Theatre. He was chorus master of the Royal Theatre in 1816–17 and during this season his first opera *Trylleharpen* ('The magic harp'), on a libretto originally written for F. L. A. Kunzen, was produced, though with less success than *Røverborgen*. Kuhlau gained a wide reputation as a concert pianist in Scandinavia, especially in Sweden. He visited Göteborg several times and performed in Stockholm in 1815; through his public appearances he acquired many pupils among the Swedish nobility. He travelled to Vienna in 1821 and again in 1825, when he met Beethoven and exchanged impromptu canons with him, as shown by Beethoven's canon *Kühl, nicht lau* WoO191 and his letter to Kuhlau of 3 September 1825; the two composers spent a lively evening in each other's company. In 1828 Kuhlau was made an honorary professor. The last year of his life was embittered by a fire that swept his house and destroyed all his unpublished manuscripts, including a second piano concerto and a textbook on thoroughbass playing; the latter survives in part in a manuscript copy (in *DK-Kk*). As a result of the fire Kuhlau suffered a chest ailment from which he never recovered.

As a composer Kuhlau is perhaps best known for his piano music. His sonatas, though easy to play, show off the instrument well and have gained a lasting popularity as teaching pieces. Among the works for piano duet the sonatinas, in particular, have become classics. Among his more significant works is the Concerto, which recalls Beethoven's early concertos in several respects; Kuhlau, less conservative than Weyse as a composer, also championed Beethoven's works as a pianist.

Kuhlau's appointments and concert activity did not offer him a large income, and many of his compositions for flute were written to satisfy the demand for flute music and thereby augment his own income. Contrary to widespread statements about Kuhlau's alleged flute playing, he did not play the instrument at all, but his natural intuition about writing for the instrument was helped by a flautist in the royal orchestra. By no means, however, can all of his works for flute be viewed as mere fashionable salon music; the Quintets op.51 and the G major Sonata op.69 are among his finest instrumental compositions.

Kuhlau's dramatic and vocal music was influenced mainly by French opera but was also affected by the German Romantic movement and by Weyse's Danish art songs. His operas show an awareness of the latest European trends as represented by Paer, Cherubini, Weber, Boieldieu and Rossini. *Lulu* (1824), written to a libretto based on the same oriental fairy tale that inspired Schikaneder's *Die Zauberflöte*, must be considered his main opera; Kuhlau adapted some of

Rossini's coloratura style in the vocal parts. The incidental music to Boye's *William Shakespeare* (1826) is noteworthy for its overture and fairy scenes. But Kuhlau's most important dramatic work is his incidental music to Heiberg's national play *Elverhøj* ('The elf's hill'), first produced in 1828 and still the most frequently performed work in the repertory of the Royal Theatre. It represents the culmination of Kuhlau's interest in folksong, which was shown as early as the Hamburg period in his use of folktunes as themes for instrumental variations. The overture itself is built on several folktunes heard during the play and ends with the national hymn *Kong Christian stod ved højen mast*, to which Kuhlau gave its final form here. This overture has served as the Danish national festival music *par excellence*. While Kuhlau's stage works, despite some admirable details, have generally not held their place in the repertory (mainly on account of their weak texts), the overtures are still admired for their mastery of formal organization and orchestration.

As a composer of vocal music Kuhlau was never as renowned as Weyse, yet he left a number of fine songs to texts by Ingemann, Oehlenschlaeger, Høegh-Guldberg and several German poets. For the students' society in Copenhagen he wrote a number of male-voice quartets to Danish and German texts, many of which are published in modern collections. Kuhlau was famous for his ability to write canons, many of which were published in the *Allgemeine musikalische Zeitung*, for which he was a diligent correspondent. He also taught a number of young composers, and his influence on later Danish music was considerable.

WORKS

Catalogue: *Kompositionen von Fridr. Kuhlau: thematisch-bibliographischer Katalog*, ed. D. Fog (Copenhagen, 1977)
Not including nos.128–233 as listed in Fog, 1977; all published in Leipzig unless otherwise stated.
Edition: *Samfundet til udgivelse af dansk musik* (Copenhagen, 1872–) [S]

STAGE

op.   *(first performed at Royal Theatre, Copenhagen)*

— Røverborgen [The robbers' castle] (Singspiel, A. Oehlenschlaeger), 26 May 1814, vocal score (Copenhagen, 1815), ov., S, 3rd ser., ci

27 Trylleharpen [The magic harp] (opera, J. Baggesen), 30 Jan 1817

29 Elisa (opera, C. J. Boye), 17 April 1820, vocal score (Copenhagen, 1820)

65 Lulu (opera, C. F. Güntelberg), 29 Oct 1824, vocal score (Hamburg, 1825)

74 William Shakespeare (drama, Boye), 28 March 1826, vocal score, S, 1st ser., iii, ov., S, 3rd ser., lvii

107 Hugo og Adelheid (opera, Boye), 29 Oct 1827, vocal score (Copenhagen, 1838)

100 Elverhøj [The elf's hill] (incidental music, 5, J. L. Heiberg), 6 Nov 1828, vocal score (Copenhagen, 1838), ov., S, 3rd ser., xi, Acts 4–5, S, 3rd ser., clxiii

115 Trillingbrødrene fra Damask [The triplet brothers from Damascus] (incidental music, Oehlenschlaeger), 1 Sept 1830, vocal score (Copenhagen, ?1831), ov., S, 1st ser., xviii

ORCHESTRAL

7 Piano Concerto, C (1810), S, 3rd ser., cxxxvi

45 Concertino, f, 2 hn, orch (1821)

CHAMBER MUSIC WITHOUT FLUTE

32 Piano Quartet no.1, c (1820)

33 Violin Sonata, f (Bonn, 1820)

50 Piano Quartet no.2, A (Bonn, 1822)

79 Three Violin Sonatas, F, a, C (Copenhagen, 1827)

108 Piano Quartet no.3, g (Leipzig, 1833)

122 String Quartet, a (Leipzig, 1841)

FLUTE

10a Twelve Variations and Solos, fl (Hamburg, 1806)

10b Three Duos concertants, 2 fl (1813)

13 Three Grand Trios, D, g, F, 3 fl (1813)

38 Three Fantasias, fl (1821)

39　Three Grand Duos, e, B♭, D, 2 fl (1821)
51　Three Quintets, D, E, A, fl, vn, 2 va, vc (Bonn, 1822), no.1, S, 3rd ser., cxliii
57　Three Grand Solos, F, a, G, fl, pf ad lib (1823)
63　Variations, on a theme from Weber's Euryanthe, fl, pf (1824)
64　Flute Sonata, E♭ (1824)
68　Six Divertimentos, fl, pf ad lib (Hamburg, 1825)
69　Flute Sonata, G (Hamburg, 1825)
71　Flute Sonata, e (Bonn, 1825)
80　Three Duos, G, C, e, 2 fl (1827)
81　Three Duos, D, F, g, 2 fl (1827)
83　Three Flute Sonatas, G, C, g (Bonn, 1827)
85　Flute Sonata ('Grande sonate concertante'), a (Mainz, 1827)
86　Three Grand Trios, e, D, E♭, 3 fl (Hamburg, 1827)
87　Three Grand Duos, A, g, D, 2 fl (Mainz, 1827)
90　Grand Trio, b, 3 fl (Mainz, 1827)
94　Variations, on a theme from Onslow's Le colporteur, fl, pf (1828)
95　Three Fantasias, fl, pf ad lib (Paris, 1829)
98a　Introduction and Rondo, on 'Ah! quand il gèle' from Le colporteur, fl, pf (1829)
99　Introduction and Variations, on 'Toujours de mon jeune âge' from Le colporteur, fl, pf (1829)
101　Introduction and Variations, on a theme from Spohr's Jessonda, fl, pf (Paris, 1829)
102　Three Duos brillants, D, E, A, 2 fl (Paris, 1829)
103　Grand Quartet, e, 4 fl (1829)
104　Variations, on a Scottish folksong, fl, pf (1829)
105　Variations, on an Irish folksong, fl, pf (1829)
110　Three Duos brillants, B♭, e, D, fl, pf (Paris, 1830)
119　Grand Trio, G, 2 fl, pf (?London, 1831)

PIANO TWO HANDS

—　Six Waltzes (Altona, 1806)
1–3　Three Rondos (1809)
4　Sonata, E♭ (1809)
12　Variations, on 'Guide mes pas' from Cherubini's Les deux journées (1810)
14　Five Variations, on a Danish air (Copenhagen, 1810)
5a　Sonata, d (1811)
6a　Three Sonatas, a, D, F (Hamburg, 1811)
6b　Easy Sonata, vn ad lib (1811)
—　Ten Waltzes (Leipzig, 1811)
8a　Grand Sonata, a (1812)
—　Six New Ecossaises (Copenhagen, 1814)
15　Variations, on the Norwegian air 'God dag, Rasmus Hansen' (1815)
25　Fantasia and Variations, on Swedish airs and dances (Bonn, 1815)
—　Twelve Waltzes (Copenhagen, 1816)
18　Variations, on 'Willkommen, Purpurschale, du', from Røverborgen (Hamburg, 1817)
16　Variations, on the Danish folksong 'Kong Christian stod ved højen mast' (Copenhagen, 1818)
20　Three Sonatinas, C, G, F (1819)
22　Variations, on a Danish song (1820)
26　Three Sonatas, G, C, E♭ (Bonn, 1820)
30　Sonata, B♭ (1820)
31　Three Easy Rondos, on themes from Don Giovanni, Le nozze di Figaro and Auber's Le petit chaperon rouge (Copenhagen, 1820)
35　Variations, on a Danish folksong (Copenhagen, 1820)
34　Sonata, G (Copenhagen, 1821)
37　Divertimento, E♭ (1821)
40　Six Easy Rondos (1821)
41　Eight Easy Rondos (1821)
42　Easy Variations, on 6 Austrian folksongs (1822)
46　Three Sonatas, G, d, C (Hamburg, 1822)
48　Ten Variations, on a theme from Der Freischütz (Copenhagen, 1822)
49　Six Favourite Themes, from Der Freischütz (Copenhagen, 1822)
52　Three Sonatas, F, B♭, A (1822)
53　Variations, on 3 themes from Weber's Preciosa (1823)
54　Introduction and Variations, on Bianchi's canzonetta 'Silenzio che sento' (1823)
55　Six Sonatinas, C, G, C, F, D, C (Copenhagen, 1823)
56　Three Easy Rondos, on themes from Le nozze di Figaro (1823)
59　Three Easy Sonatas, A, F, C (Hamburg, 1824)
60　Three Sonatinas and Three Airs variés, on themes by Rossini (Hamburg, 1824)
61　Six Divertimentos 'en forme de valses' (Hamburg, 1824)
62　Variations, on 3 themes from Euryanthe (Copenhagen, 1824)
73　Three Easy Rondos, on opera arias by Auber and Rossini (Copenhagen, 1825)
84　Three Easy Rondos, on opera arias by Boieldieu and Auber (Copenhagen, 1827)
88　Four Sonatinas, C, G, a, F (Copenhagen, 1827)

91　Variations, on the old Swedish air 'Och liten Karin tjente' (1828)
92　Les charmes de Copenhague, introduction and rondeau brillant (1828)
93　Fantasia, on Swedish airs (1828)
96　Rondeau brillant, on a theme from Onslow's Le colporteur (Copenhagen, 1829)
97　Two Rondeaux brillants, on themes from Hérold's Marie (Copenhagen, 1829)
98b　Introduction and Rondo, on a theme from Le colporteur (Copenhagen, 1829)
109　Three Easy Rondos (Paris, 1830)
112　Three Airs variés, on themes by Bellini and Hummel and an Austrian air (Paris, 1830)
113　Three Rondeaux brillants, on themes by Rossini and Isouard (Paris, 1830)
116　Variations, on 2 themes from Guillaume Tell (Brunswick, 1830)
117　Souvenir de Beethoven, 3 rondolettos (Brunswick, 1830)
118　Three Easy Rondos, on themes from Fra Diavolo (Copenhagen, 1831)
120　La légèreté, rondeau brillant, on a motif by Paganini (Copenhagen, 1831)
121　La clochette, rondeau brillant, on a motif by Paganini (Copenhagen, 1831)
125　Rondeau pastoral (Copenhagen, 1831)
126　Divertimento, on themes by Mozart (Copenhagen, 1831)
127　Sonata, E♭ (Copenhagen, 1831)

PIANO FOUR HANDS

8b　Sonata, F (1810)
17　Sonatina, F (Copenhagen, 1818)
24　Eight Waltzes (1820)
28　Six Waltzes (Hamburg, 1820)
44　Three Sonatinas, G, C, F (Copenhagen, 1822)
58　Variations, on 'Deh calma o ciel' from Rossini's Otello (1823)
66　Three Sonatinas, F, C, G (Hamburg, 1824)
70　Three Rondos (Hamburg, 1825)
72a　Variations, on Beethoven's 'Herz, mein Herz' (Bonn, 1825)
75　Variations, on Beethoven's 'Der Wachtelschlag' (Hamburg, 1826)
76　Variations, on Beethoven's 'Lebensglück' (Hamburg, 1826)
77　Variations, on Beethoven's 'Sehnsucht' (Hamburg, 1826)
111　Three Rondos (Paris, 1830)
114　Three Airs variés, G, C, F (Paris, 1831)
123　Allegro pathétique (Copenhagen, 1831)
124　Adagio and Rondo (Copenhagen, 1831)

VOCAL

5b　Three Songs, 1v, pf (Hamburg, 1806)
—　Six Easy Pieces, 1v, pf (Hamburg, 1807)
—　Die Blumen, 6 songs, 1v, pf (?Hamburg, 1807)
—　Sixteen canons, AMZ, xi (1809), 199; xiii (1811), 679, 763; xv (1813), 40; xxi (1819), 832; xxiii (1821), 460, 591, 847, 867
9　Six Canzoni, 1v, pf (1813)
11a　Ten German Songs, 1v, pf (1813)
—　Three Canzonettas, 1v, pf (Leipzig, 1813)
21　Three Poems (L. Gerstenberg: Poetisches Wäldchen), 1v, pf (1820)
23　Twelve German Songs, 1v, pf (Hamburg, 1820)
36　Die Feier des Wohlwollens (Sander), cantata, 3 male vv, pf (Hamburg, 1821)
—　Thirteen Comic Canons, 3 male vv (?1821–2)
72b　Three Songs, 1v, pf (?1821–3)
67　Six Songs, 4 male vv (Copenhagen, 1824)
78　Two Poems (Castelli), 1v, pf (Hamburg, 1826)
89　Eight Songs, 4 male vv (Copenhagen, 1826)
82　Nine Songs, 4 male vv (Copenhagen, 1827)
106　Six Songs (de la Motte Fouqué) (1829)

BIBLIOGRAPHY

I. Seyfried: Beethovens Studien im Generalbass (Vienna, 1832, 2/1853/R1967)
G. Schilling: 'Kuhlau', Encyclopädie der gesammten musikalischen Wissenschaften, iv (Stuttgart, 1840/R1971), 252
C. Thrane: Danske komponister (Copenhagen, 1875), 71–192, 271ff; Ger. trans. as Friedrich Kuhlau (Copenhagen, 1886/R1973)
G. St Bricka: 'Kuhlau, Daniel Frederik Rudolph', DBL
K. Graupner: Friedrich Kuhlau (Leipzig, 1930)
K. A. Bruun: 'Kuhlau, Daniel Frederik Rudolph', DBL
N. M. Jensen: Den danske romance 1800–1850 (Copenhagen, 1964), 101ff, 223ff
J.-L. Beimfohr: Das C-Dur Klavierkonzert opus 7 und die Klaviersonaten von Friedrich Kuhlau (diss., U. of Hamburg, 1971)
D. Fog, ed.: Kompositionen von Fridr. Kuhlau: thematisch-bibliographischer Katalog (Copenhagen, 1977) [incl. extensive bibliography]

CARSTEN HATTING (text)
DAN FOG (work-list, bibliography)

Kühmstedt, Friedrich Karl (*b* Oldisleben, nr. Weimar, 20 Dec 1809; *d* Eisenach, 8 Jan 1858). German composer and teacher. He received his early musical education from Zoellner in Oldisleben, then at the Gymnasien in Frankenhausen and in Weimar, where he studied the piano with Hummel. In 1826 he went secretly to Darmstadt to study the organ and music theory with C. H. Rinck, returning to Weimar three years later. Hummel had given him the start towards a virtuoso career, but overwork led to damage to his right hand which caused a psychological crisis and extreme poverty. He turned to composition, but his first works, including an opera, *Die Schlangenkönigin*, were not very successful. With Hummel's help, Kühmstedt was appointed to the Gymnasium in Eisenach in 1836. He made a valuable contribution to music in that city, as a teacher, director of church music and Kapellmeister. He became a friend of Liszt; together they drew up a plan for the reform and improvement of musical life in Weimar. This plan lay behind the foundation of the Grossherzogliche Orchesterschule by Carl Müller-Hartung, a pupil of Kühmstedt. International recognition followed: Kühmstedt became a corresponding member of the Maatschappij tot Bevordering der Toonkunst in 1846 and to professional rank in 1847.

Kühmstedt's life spanned the post-Classical and Romantic periods, and this is reflected in his output. His technique was contrapuntal, with the music of Bach serving as a model for his preludes and fugues, chorale harmonizations and motets. He developed a parallel technique in his pedagogical works, which include organ pieces, a book of chorales, children's studies, a *Vorschule zu Sebastian Bach's Clavier- und Orgelkompositionen* and a work entitled *Das kleine wohltemperierte Clavier*. His other works include an oratorio, *Sieg des Göttlichen* (first performed by Spohr in Kassel, 1843), three symphonies, a *Missa solemnis*, a *Fantasia eroica*, ballades, choral songs and lieder. His style, which was said to have had 'inner wealth, without ostentation or affectation', is musicianly and was inspired by a wish to display 'the stirrings of the spirit to arouse corresponding feelings through sounds'; these remarks are taken from the preface to his *Theoretisch-praktische Harmonien- und Ausweichungs-Lehre* (Eisenach, 1838), a work based on the innovations in harmony and aesthetics developed by G. Weber and J. M. Fischer, and thus an early exponent of Riemann's theory of harmonic function.

BIBLIOGRAPHY

Anon.: 'Friedrich Kühmstedt: Biographisches', *Niederrheinische Musikzeitung*, vi (1858), 51, 59
Anon.: 'Friedrich Kühmstedt: eine biographische Skizze', *Niederrheinische Musikzeitung*, vi (1858), 66, 73 [see also 'Friedrich Kühmstedt als Komponist', ibid, 179]
R. Eitner: 'Kühmstedt', *ADB*
G. Frotscher: *Geschichte des Orgel-Spiels und der Orgel-Komposition*, i (Berlin, 1935, enlarged 3/1966)
C. Freyse: *Musikgeschichte der Stadt Eisenach* (MS, *D-WRiv*)
G. Kraft: *Musikgeschichte der Stadt Weimar* (MS, *WRiv*)
——: *Johann Nepomuk Hummel* (Weimar, 1973)

G. KRAFT

Kuhn, Franz. German trombone maker who worked under contract with HERBERT LÄTZSCH from 1953.

Kühn, Hellmut (*b* Chemnitz, 23 June 1939). German musicologist. He studied musicology at the universities of Kiel and Saarbrücken with Wiora, Dahlhaus, Anna Amalie Abert and Finscher, taking a doctorate at Saarbrücken in 1970 with a dissertation on Ars Nova harmony in the isorhythmic motet. After holding appointments as assistant lecturer in the musicology departments of Saarbrücken University and the Free University, Berlin (1968–73), he became professor of musicology at the Staatliche Hochschule für Musik in West Berlin (1973). Apart from his interest in 14th-century music, Kühn specializes in analytical or sociological studies of 19th- and 20th-century music.

WRITINGS

Die Harmonik der Ars nova: zur Theorie der isorhythmischen Motette (diss., U. of Saarbrücken, 1970; Munich, 1973)
'Brangänes Wächtergesang: zur Differenz zwischen dem Musikdrama und der französischen grossen Oper'; 'Hans Sachs und die "insgeheim gesellschaftliche Phantasmagorie": zur Kritik einer Idee von Theodor W. Adorno', *Richard Wagner: Werk und Wirkung*, ed. C. Dahlhaus (Regensburg, 1971), 117, 147
'Musikwissenschaft und Berufsausbildung', *Mf*, xxiv (1971), 41, 303
'Versuch über Weberns Geschichtsbegriff', *Zwischen Tradition und Fortschritt*, ed. R. Stephan (Mainz, 1973), 96
'Antike Massen: zu einigen Motiven in *Les Troyens* von Hector Berlioz', *Opernstudien: Anna Amalie Abert zum 65. Geburtstag* (Tutzing, 1975), 141

HANS HEINRICH EGGEBRECHT

Kuhn, Johann. *See* KUHNAU, JOHANN.

Kühn, Rolf (*b* Cologne, 29 Sept 1929). German jazz clarinettist. After studying the piano in Leipzig from 1938 he took up the clarinet in 1941. In 1952 he moved to West Germany, where he joined a radio big band. He soon formed his own group and became well known in Europe through radio broadcasts. From 1956 to 1962 he lived in the USA, where with the encouragement of the entrepreneur John Hammond he formed his own group and also performed with various big bands, even substituting for the ailing Benny Goodman in Goodman's own band (1957–8). After returning to Germany in 1962 he formed his own jazz orchestra and led numerous smaller combos, many of which featured his younger brother Joachim Kühn as pianist.

At first influenced by Buddy de Franco and Goodman, Kühn developed a remarkable fluency on his instrument, and became one of jazz's finest performers in the bebop and 'cool' styles. Later he adopted the innovations of 'free jazz', being perhaps the first on his instrument to do so. Although Kühn is clearly one of the most gifted musicians in jazz, the decline of the clarinet as a jazz instrument has kept him from widespread recognition.

JOACHIM E. BERENDT

Kuhn, Theodor. Swiss firm of organ builders. The firm was founded in Männedorf, near Zurich, by Johann Nepomuk Kuhn (1827–88). He was succeeded by his son, Carl Theodor Kuhn, after whose death in 1925 ownership of the company passed to family friends, who with their successors control the company. By 1876 it had built organs for such important cathedrals as St Gall and the Zurich Grossmünster, and by 1900 had exported widely, especially to France.

The company has always been noted for its progressiveness, and has patented several major technical innovations, such as the 'System Kuhn', developed in 1891 for the firm's first tubular pneumatic organ. It responded quickly to the *Orgelbewegung*, and in 1937 built its first large 'reformed' instrument with slider chests and mechanical key and stop action. In 1964 it built its last electric action organ, and since then, under the guidance of Friedrich Jakob, who became associated with Kuhn in 1963 and director in 1968, the firm has specialized in the development of modern mechanical action organs. Kuhn is noted for responsive key actions, imaginative case design, excellent reed stops and superior craftsmanship and tonal finishing. The tonal design of Kuhn organs is generally more cosmopolitan than that of other European organs, fitting them for a wide range of organ literature. Modern playing aids are utilized. Some of their notable modern organs are in St Gall Cathedral (1968), the Prediger-Kirche, Zurich (1970), and the Alice Tully Hall, Lincoln Center, New York (1974, designed in collaboration with Lawrence Phelps). Through Jakob's scholarly expertise the firm has restored important historic instruments, such as the 1735 Bommer organ in St Katharinenthal (1965–9), and constructed new organs in a specific historical style, such as the organ after Andreas Silbermann for St Leonhard, Basle (1969), created within the old Silbermann cases.

GILLIAN WEIR

Kühn [Kuh, Kün], **Tobias** (*b* c1565; *d* ?after 1615). German court musician. Originally from Halberstadt, he was appointed on 15 November 1587 to a musical post at the court in Wolfenbüttel, primarily as a singer but also as a lutenist. He can be traced in court pay records up to 1591. His compositions for the lute are few and unremarkable. The 'Pavana T. K.' in Rude's *Flores musicae* (Heidelberg, 1600⁵ᵃ) is attributed to him, as are another pavan and two galliards in Fuhrmann's *Testudo gallo-germanica* (Nuremberg, 1615²⁴), a *fuga* and the 'Gagliarda Tobie' in the lost lutebook of Joachim von Loss (formerly *D-Dlb* B 1030), and the 'Galiarda Tobiae Kuhnen' in *D-LEm* II.16.5 (the Długoraj Lutebook).

BIBLIOGRAPHY

M. Ruhnke: *Beiträge zu einer Geschichte der deutschen Hofmusikkollegien im 16. Jahrhundert* (Berlin, 1963)

E. Pohlmann: *Laute, Theorbe, Chitarrone* (Bremen, 1968, enlarged 4/1976)

H. B. LOBAUGH

Kuhnau [Kuhn, Cuno], **Johann** (*b* Geising, Erzgebirge, 6 April 1660; *d* Leipzig, 5 June 1722). German composer, keyboard player, music theorist, scholar, writer and lawyer. He was a major figure in late German Baroque music who is admired now principally for his keyboard music. He was prominent in Leipzig, where he was Bach's immediate predecessor as Kantor at the Thomasschule.

1. LIFE. Kuhnau's family had originated in Bohemia, whence they fled during the Counter-Reformation because of their Protestant faith. Their name was Kuhn. Johann seems to have adopted the form 'Kuhnau' only after arriving in Leipzig, and it was assumed too by his brothers Andreas and Gottfried, who were also musicians (Johann also briefly used the form 'Cuno' when first applying for the post of organist at the Thomaskirche, Leipzig); the other members of the family, however, retained the name Kuhn (see Münnich for the family history). According to his autobiography published in Mattheson, Kuhnau gave early evidence of his potential and also had a fine voice. About 1670, therefore, he went to Dresden to study. This exceptional educational and musical opportunity had probably been arranged by Salomon Krügner, a court musician at Dresden who, according to Mattheson, was Kuhnau's cousin. He studied briefly with Krügner but soon became a pupil of the court organist, Christoph Kittel. In February 1671 he joined his elder brother Andreas as a chorister at the Kreuzkirche, where he was taught by the organist, Alexander Heringk. His musical talents brought him to the attention of the court Kapellmeister, Vincenzo Albrici, who Kuhnau said, praised his youthful compositions highly and allowed him to mix with his own children and to attend rehearsals of the court orchestra. At this time he began to study Italian and French, the languages employed in court circles. In 1680 a plague epidemic forced him to return home. He remained at Geising only briefly, however, for towards the end of the year he accepted the invitation of Erhard Titius, formerly of the Kreuzschule, to further his education at the Johanneum, the Gymnasium at Zittau, where Titius was now Kantor. The organist of the Johanniskirche, Moritz Edelmann, died on 6 December, shortly after Kuhnau's arrival, and Titius himself died in May 1681. Until the position of Kantor was filled by Johann Krieger in the spring of 1682, Kuhnau, as *praefectus chori* (i.e. first singer of the choir), was asked to act as Kantor, and also as organist of the Johanniskirche. These musical experiences were further enriched by his close association with CHRISTIAN WEISE, Rektor of the Gymnasium; he wrote music (now lost) for some of Weise's school dramas. In 1682 he completed his schooling and (again following his brother Andreas) became a law student at the University of Leipzig. At the same time he applied for the post of organist at the Thomaskirche which had recently been vacated by Albrici. Though his application was unsuccessful, his musical talent impressed the town council. While at the university he became increasingly active as a composer and performer in Leipzig, and when the post of organist at the Thomaskirche again became vacant in 1684 he was appointed to it, and he took charge in October.

For the next four years Kuhnau continued to study law while carrying out his duties as organist, and following the publication in 1688 of his dissertation, *De juribus circa musicos ecclesiasticos*, he began to practise law. In 1689 he married; he had eight children, of whom only three daughters survived him. The next ten years or so were a happy and productive time for him: his fame as an organist grew, his legal practice was highly successful, he published all his keyboard collections, which were his most popular music, and wrote his important satirical novel, *Der musicalische Quack-Salber*. He also found time for further self-education, making himself proficient in mathematics, Hebrew and Greek, and translated into German a number of French and Italian books. Although no documents support the conjecture, it can be assumed that during this period he also wrote sacred vocal music for performance in the several churches of Leipzig, including the Thomaskirche, where the Kantor was Johann Schelle (who also came from Geising). Schelle died on 10 March 1701, and almost immediately Kuhnau was elected his successor, assuming the position in April. As Thomaskantor he reached the pinnacle of his career. He was exceptionally well qualified for the post, not only as a musician and composer but also as scholar, linguist and philosopher, and he carried out its heavy musical and teaching demands with distinction. He taught several classes in the Thomasschule, including singing, and he directed church music at both the Thomaskirche and the Nikolaikirche, where the choirs consisted of students

Johann Kuhnau: engraved title-page from his 'Neue Clavier-Übung erster Theil' (1689)

from the Thomasschule. From 1711 he also directed music at the Peterskirche and, on important holidays, at the Johanniskirche. As Thomaskantor he was also director of music for the university and responsible for the city musicians and for the care and inspection of the organs of the Thomaskirche and the Nikolaikirche.

During the last years of his life Kuhnau suffered constantly from ill-health and grew deeply dissatisfied with the deteriorating conditions at the Thomasschule. The number and quality of young voices available for the choir at the Thomaskirche declined as the students were enticed away to perform at the Leipzig opera. When the young Telemann arrived in 1701 as a law student, he immediately established a rival musical organization in the form of a collegium musicum, which attracted some of Kuhnau's pupils. Telemann managed to obtain permission from the mayor to write music for the Thomaskirche: this blatantly undermined Kuhnau's authority, and he was powerless to prevent it. Much the same privilege was granted to Melchior Hoffmann when Telemann left Leipzig in 1705. Moreover, one of Kuhnau's own pupils, J. F. Fasch, attempted to interfere further with his musical responsibilities by proposing to establish another collegium musicum in the university and by trying to take over the direction of the music at the university and the Paulinerkirche, but he managed to forestall him. In 1703, during one of his several periods of illness, the town council too annoyed Kuhnau by asking Telemann to succeed him should he die. Despite his difficulties, however, he had the satisfaction of teaching many excellent students, including Graupner and Heinichen. He was greatly esteemed by many of Germany's foremost musicians and was the last of the many-sided Thomaskantors, a man who 'displayed an element of medieval universality and mastered music,

law, theology, rhetoric, poetry, mathematics and foreign languages' (Schering, 1926). Scheibe put him alongside Handel, Keiser and Telemann as one of the major German composers before Hasse and the Grauns, and Mattheson, paying equal tribute to his musicianship and his erudition, claimed never to have known his like as composer, organist, chorus director and scholar.

2. WORKS. Kuhnau's surviving music belongs to two categories: keyboard music, nearly all published by 1700, and sacred music, mostly cantatas and all of it unpublished. His secular vocal works are all lost. His reputation as a composer rests almost entirely on the four printed sets of keyboard pieces, especially the last of them, the *Biblische Historien*. This consists of six multi-movement 'sonatas', each prefaced by a prose description of a particular incident from the Old Testament illustrated in the music: *The Fight between David and Goliath*; *Saul cured by David through Music*; *Jacob's Wedding*; *Hezekiah, Sick unto Death and Restored to Health*; *Gideon, Saviour of Israel*; and *Jacob's Death and Burial*. Kuhnau emphasized in a learned and valuable preface that this type of programme music was not new, and he referred to models by Froberger and 'other excellent authors'. His purpose was to demonstrate, among other things, how keyboard music, without the benefit of a poetic text, could capture the emotional states emanating from an action or the description of a character. The various sections of each sonata bear Italian sub-titles as clues to the particular emotional state or action being described by the music. For example, the second sonata begins with 'The sadness and the fury of the king', which is followed first by 'The calming song from David's harp' and finally by 'The tranquil and contented soul of Saul'. As with other

keyboard works by Kuhnau, these sonatas are quite simple both melodically and, on the whole, harmonically. The rather naive programmatic details are, however, sustained by a rich variety of rhythms and especially textures: massive chords, often in both hands, motivic interplay in the manner of the *style brisé*, poignant dissonances, rapid toccata-like passages, and fugal sections. Each of the two parts of the *Neue Clavier-Übung* contains seven suites, those in the first in major keys, those in the second in minor keys. The suites have the same basic series of movements. They usually begin with a prelude and continue with an allemande, courante, sarabande and gigue; in a few the gigue is omitted entirely or replaced by another dance or an aria, and no.4 of the second set begins with a ciacona. The most significant work here is a Sonata in Bb appended to the second part. Becker claimed that this was the first ever keyboard sonata, but, as more recent research has shown (see especially Newman), Kuhnau was simply following a tradition, already established in the keyboard music of other countries, in which composers used the styles and forms of the instrumental ensemble sonata. His sonata is, however, the earliest known work of its type published in Germany.

More than half of Kuhnau's known vocal compositions, of which there were originally over 100, have been lost, and of those known to be extant only a handful have been published in modern editions (see Rimbach, however, for transcriptions of almost all the church cantatas). Critical opinion, including that of Schering and Riedel (in *MGG*), has generally dismissed the cantatas as routine and uninspired, though competently composed. Such judgments are not borne out by the music itself. While Kuhnau's cantatas are to some extent modelled on those of Knüpfer and Schelle, his predecessors at the Thomaskirche, they are on the whole simpler in style, at least in their melodic and harmonic elements. But they are far from mediocre; on the contrary, most of them are strikingly beautiful and often dramatic. They show a stability of formal structure previously unknown in German cantatas that strongly anticipates the Leipzig cantatas of Bach (Kuhnau's successor as Thomaskantor). The cantatas usually begin with an instrumental introduction (designated 'sonata') followed by an alternation, in the solo works, of aria and recitative or, in the choral works, of chorus, aria and recitative in various orders. Many of the arias, though brief, have a da capo structure and are markedly more lyrical than the songlike movements found in earlier German cantatas. Some of the cantatas open and close with chorales, a few of which are given instrumental concertato settings. The chorale, however, plays only a minor role in Kuhnau's conception of the cantata, and only two of the extant works are true chorale cantatas. The most impressive elements in the cantatas with chorus are the elaborately constructed choral movements, which include frequent dramatic shifts between homophonic sections and powerful, often complex fugues; such a structure gives various kinds of rhetorical emphasis to the poetic texts (a number of which are by Neumeister). In these works Kuhnau created a musical oratory which, according to his own detailed comments regarding cantata texts (see Richter: 'Eine Abhandlung'), was uppermost in his mind in his efforts to write church music that was untainted by the tendency towards the secularism arising from the growing popularity of opera.

Kuhnau is also important for his informative, highly amusing novel, *Der musicalische Quack-Salber*, which he modelled on Weise's *Politische Quacksalber*. The story concerns the life of a pompous, ill-trained musical charlatan in 17th-century Germany. His adventures in various social settings contemporary with Kuhnau's own life prompted fascinating observations about the social status of musicians, various musical practices that Kuhnau criticized by means of satire (for example, faulty text underlay, over-elaborate thoroughbass realizations, the questionable art of the castrato and the general ignorance of singers) and musical institutions, such as a description of a collegium musicum. The book is of great value to an understanding of the musical and social history of the Baroque period in Germany.

WORKS

GERMAN SACRED VOCAL
(dates are of first known performance; some ed. in Rimbach)

Ach dass Hülfe aus Zion käme, for 1st Christmas Day 1709, *D-LEm* (text only)
Ach Herr, wie sind meiner Feinde so viel, 2vv, 2 clarinos, trbn, 2 vn, bc, *Bds*
Also hat Gott die Welt geliebet, for 2nd Pentecost Day 1711, *LEm* (text only)
Also werden die letzten die ersten sein, for Septuagesima 1710, *LEm* (text only)
Christ lag in Todesbanden, 4vv, 2 vn, 2 va, vle, 2 cornetts (ad lib), org, 1693 at latest, *B*
Daran erkennen wir, dass wir in ihm verbleiben, 5vv, 2 ob, bn, 2 clarinos, timp, 2 vn, 2 va, org, for Pentecost, Feria I, *B*
Das Alte ist vergangen, 4vv, 2 clarinos, bn, timp, 2 vn, va, bc, *B-Bc*
Der Herr, dein Gott wird selber mit dir wandeln, for 2nd Easter Day 1711, *D-LEm* (text only)
Dies ist der Tag der heiligen Dreyfaltigkeit, for Trinity Sunday 1711, *LEm* (text only)
Du Arzt in Israel, for 17th Sunday after Trinity, Leipzig Nikolaikirche Archive (text only)
Du weisst, mein Gott, dass ich dich liebe, for 3rd Christmas Day 1710, *LEm* (text only)
Du wirst, mein Heyland, aufgenommen, for Ascension Day 1711, Bibliothek des Vereins für die Geschichte Leipzigs (text only)
Ende gut und alles gut, 3vv, for 27th Sunday after Trinity 1718, *LUC*
Erschrick mein Hertz vor dir, 1v, chorus 4vv, 2 vn, violetta, org, for 14th Sunday after Trinity, before 1712, *LEm*
Es steh Gott auf, 5vv, chorus 5vv, 2 clarinos, tamburi, 3 trbn, 2 va, bc, 'ad festum Paschatos' 1703, *Dlb* (doubtful)
Fleuch, mein Freund, und sei gleich einem Reh, for Sunday after Feast of the Circumcision 1710, *LEm* (text only)
Flöss mir von deinen süssen Lehren, for 1st Sunday after Epiphany 1711, *LEm* (text only)
Fürchtet euch nicht für denen, die den Leib tödten, for 2nd Christmas Day 1709, *LEm* (text only)
Für uns ein Mensch gebohren, for 3rd Christmas Day 1720, Bibliothek des Vereins für die Geschichte Leipzigs (text only)
Gott der Vater, Jesus Christus, der Heil'ge Geist wohn uns bey, 4vv, ob (tromba di tirarsi), 2 vn, va, bc, *Bds*
Gott sei mir gnädig, 4vv, chorus 4vv, 2 vn, 2 va, bn, bc, for Quinquagesima 1705, *Dlb*; ed. in DDT, lviii–lix (1918/*R*)
Himmel, bricht der Abgrund auf? (pts.i–iii), for 1st, 2nd, 3rd Easter Days 1717, Leipzig Nikolaikirche Archive (text only)
Ich freue mich im Herrn, 4vv, 2 vn, va, bc, for 2nd Sunday after Epiphany 1712, *Dlb*; ed. in DDT, lviii–lix (1918/*R*)
Ich habe Lust abzuscheiden, 4vv, chorus 4vv, ob, bn, 2 vn, va, vc, bc, for Feast of the Purification of Mary, lost (doubtful); ed. in Organum, i/14 (Leipzig, 1928)
Ich hebe meine Augen auff, 1v, 2 vn, vle, org, *LEm* (text only) (also attrib. Telemann)
Ich ruf zu dir Herr Jesu, 4vv, 10 insts, for St Matthew's Day, lost
Ich unterrede mich mit deinem Hertzen, for 3rd Easter Day 1711, *LEm* (text only)
Ich will aufstehen und in der Stadt umhergehen, for 1st Sunday after Epiphany 1710, *LEm* (text only)
Ich will dich erhöhen, mein Gott, for Feast of the Circumcision, 1 Jan 1711, *LEm* (text only)
Ihr Himmel jubilirt von oben, 5vv, 2 fl, 3 clarinos, 2 vn, va, bc, for Ascension Day, April 1717, *LEm*
Ist denn keine Salbe in Gilead?, for 3rd Sunday after Epiphany 1710, *LEm* (text only)
Jesu, hier ist deine Stadt, for 19th Sunday after Trinity, Leipzig Nikolaikirche Archive (text only)
Kommt her und sehet an die Werke des Herrn, for Sunday after Christmas 1710, *LEm* (text only)

Kündlich gross ist das gottseelige. Geheimnis, for New Year's Day 1721, Bibliothek des Vereins für die Geschichte Leipzigs (text only)

Leite mich in Liebesseilen, for 18th Sunday after Trinity, Leipzig Nikolaikirche Archive (text only)

Lobe den Herrn meine Seele, 2vv, vn, ob, org, for 7th Sunday after Trinity 1722, *Dlb*

Lobe den Herrn meine Seele, 5vv, 2 cornetts, 3 trbn, bn, 2 vn, 2 va, bc, *B*

Lobet, ihr Himmel, den Herrn, 4vv, 2 ob, 2 clarinos, timp, 2 vn, 2 va, org, for Ascension Day, *B*

Mache dich auff, werde Licht, for Feast of Epiphany 1710, *LEm* (text only)

Mein Alter kommt, ich kann nicht sterben, 5vv, 2 vn, 2 va, bn, bc, 1696, *Dlb*

Michael, wer ist wie Gott?, for St Michael's Day, Leipzig Nikolaikirche Archive (text only)

Muss nicht der Mensch auf dieser Erden, 1v, clarino, bn, vn, org, 1715, *LUC*

Nicht nur allein am frohen Morgen, 4vv, 2 clarinos, 2 hn, timp, 2 vn, va, bc, for 2nd Christmas Day 1718, *LEm*

O heilige Zeit, wo Himmel, Erd und Lufft, 2vv, 2 ob, 2 vn, va, bc, *LEm* (doubtful)

O heilige Zeit, wo Himmel, Erd und Luft, 4vv, 2 vn, 2 va, bc, *B*

O mehr als englisches Gesichte, for 1st Christmas Day 1710, *LEm* (text only)

O süssester Jesu, o freundliches Kind, for Sunday after Epiphany, Bibliothek des Vereins für die Geschichte Leipzigs (text only)

Passion according to St Mark, for Good Friday 1721, lost, formerly *USSR-KA* (inc.)

Redet unter einander von Psalmen und Lobgesängen, for New Year's Day 1721, Bibliothek des Vereins für die Geschichte Leipzigs (text only)

Sammle dir, getreue Seele, for 1st Easter Day 1711, *LEm* (text only)

Sanffter Wind, beliebtes Brausen, for 1st Pentecost Day 1711, *LEm* (text only)

Schmücket das Fest mit Meyen, 4vv, 2 rec, 4 vn, violetta, bc, *B*

Seyd willkommen, frohe Stunden, for Sunday after New Year's Day 1721, Bibliothek des Vereins für die Geschichte Leipzigs (text only)

Siehe da, ich lege einen auserwehlten, köstlichen Edelstein, for Sunday after Christmas 1709, *LEm* (text only)

Siehe, es kommt ein Tag, der brennen soll, for 5th Sunday after Epiphany 1710, *LEm* (text only)

Siehe, ich komme, im Buch ist von mir geschrieben, for Estomihi 1710, *LEm* (text only)

Siehe, ich will meinen Engel senden, for Feast of the Purification of Mary 1710, *LEm* (text only)

Siehe, ich will mich meiner Heerde selbst annehmen, for 3rd Pentecost Day 1711, *LEm* (text only)

Singet dem Herrn ein neues Lied, 4vv, 2 tpt, bn, 2 vn, va, org, *B*

Thue mir auff, liebe Freundin, for 1st Sunday after Advent 1709, *LEm* (text only)

Träum nicht, so spricht mein Jesus, for Sunday after Feast of the Circumcision 1711, *LEm* (text only)

Um deines Tempels Willen zu Jerusalem, for Feast of Epiphany 1711, *LEm* (text only)

Und ist ein Kind geboren, for 1st Christmas Day 1720, Bibliothek des Vereins für die Geschichte Leipzigs (text only)

Und ob die Feinde Tag und Nacht, 1v, vn, org, for 23rd Sunday after Trinity, *LEm*

Vermischte Traurigkeit und Freude, for Jubilate Sunday 1711, *LEm* (text only)

Vom Himmel hoch, da komm ich her, 4vv, 2 clarinos, timp, 2 vn, va, bc, *LEm*

Was betrübst du dich meine Seele, for Sunday after Epiphany 1710, *LEm* (text only)

Weicht ihr Sorgen aus dem Hertzen, 1v, 2 vn, 2 va, org, for 7th or 15th Sunday after Trinity, *LUC*

Welt adieu, ich bin dein müde, 5vv, fl, ob, 2 hn, 2 vn, 2 va, bc, for 24th Sunday after Trinity, *LEm* (inc.)

Wenn ihr fröhlich seid an euren Festen, 5vv, chorus 5vv, 2 clarinos, 'principale', trbn, tamburi, bn, 2 vn, 2 va, org, for Easter 1716, *Dlb*; ed. in DDT, lviii–lix (1918/*R*)

Wer Ohren hat zu hören, for Sexagesima 1710, *LEm* (text only)

Wie gross ist deine Güte, Gott, for Cantate Sunday 1711, *LEm* (text only)

Wie schön leuchtet die Morgenstern, 5vv, 2 vn, 2 va, 2 hn, bc, *B*; ed in DDT, lviii–lix (1918/*R*)

Wiltu, mein Gott, diss Hertz verlassen, for 2nd Christmas Day 1710, *LEm* (text only)

Zeuch mich nach dir, so laufen wir, for 3rd Christmas Day 1709, *LEm* (text only)

LATIN SACRED VOCAL
(dates are of first known performance)

Missa, 4vv, lost, formerly *MÜG*

Missa, lost, formerly Kirchenarchiv, Mylau

Magnificat, 5vv, 2 ob, 3 clarinos, timp, 2 vn, 2 va, bc, *Bds*

Bone Jesu, chare Jesu, 1v, 2 vn, bc, for 13th Sunday after Trinity 1690, *Dlb*

In dulci jubilo, for Sunday after Christmas 1720, *LEm* (text only)

In te Domine speravi, 1v, 2 vn, 2 va, bn, bc, 23rd Sunday after Trinity, *Dlb*

Laudate pueri, 1v, 2 vn, trbn (va da gamba/vc), bc, *B*

Spirate clementes, 3vv, 2 vn, bc, *B*

Tristis est anima mea, 5vv, *Bds*

OCCASIONAL
(German; some ed. in Rimbach)

Ach Gott, wie lästu mich erstarren, aria, 5vv, bc, *ZI* [for burial of Rektor Titius, Zittau, 19 May 1681]

Der Herr erhöre dich in der Not, with Verleih uns Frieden, 2 choirs, lost [for election of Zittau town council, 1682]

Der Herr hat Zion erwehlet, *LEm* (text only) [for Leipzig University jubilee, 4 Dec 1709]

Der Herr ist Gott, der uns erleuchtet, lost [for dedication of new altar in Leipzig Thomaskirche, 25 Dec 1721]

Deutsches Te Deum, 3 choirs, tpts, timp, lost (probably by Kuhnau) [for Reformation Jubilee, 1717]

Dies ist der Tag, den der Herr gemacht hat, *LEm* (text only) [for Leipzig University jubilee, 4 Dec 1709]

Erschallt, Gott zu loben, lost [for investiture of Superintendent Deylings, Leipzig Nikolaikirche, 13 Aug 1721]

Herr, der Feinde sind zu viel, Leipzig Nikolaikirche Archive (text only) [for Leipzig Evangelische Kirche jubilee, 2 Nov 1717]

Tobet, ihr Pforten der Hölle, *LEm* (text only) [for Leipzig Evangelische Kirche jubilee, 1717]

Trauerkantate, lost [on the death of Rektor Titius, 18 April 1714]

Zion auf ermuntre dich, Leipzig Nikolaikirche Archive (text only) [for Leipzig Evangelische Kirche jubilee, 1717]

(Latin)

Confitebor tibi, lost [for ded. of new anatomical theatre, 10 Sept 1704]

Ecce quam bonum et iucundum, lost (probably by Kuhnau) [for performance before the oration of Prof. B. Mencke, 6 Aug 1707]

Hodie collaetantur coeli cives, for 1st Christmas Day 1709, *LEm* (text only) [for performance after the oration]

I, Fama, pennas indice praepetes, ode, lost [for performance after the oration of Prof. B. Mencke, 6 Aug 1707]

Non mortui laudabunt te, lost [for performance after the oration at the dedication of new anatomical theatre, 10 Sept 1704]

Oda secularis, tibi litamus, lost (probably by Kuhnau) [for Leipzig University jubilee, 4 Dec 1709]

Ode, 3 choirs, lost (probably by Kuhnau) [for wedding celebration of Elector-Prince Friedrich August and Maria Josepha of Austria, 8 Sept 1719]

Salve, theatrum, splendida funerum, ode, lost [for dedication of new anatomical theatre, 10 Sept 1704]

Summe terrarum moderator, ode, lost [for dedication of new anatomical theatre, 10 Sept 1704]

Verbum caro factum est, for 1st Christmas Day 1709, *LEm* (text only) [for performance before the oration]

KEYBOARD

Neuer Clavier-Übung, erster Theil (7 suites) (Leipzig, 1689); ed. in DDT, iv (1901/*R*)

Neuer Clavier-Übung, anderer Theil (7 suites, 1 sonata) (Leipzig, 1692); ed. in DDT, iv (1901/*R*)

Frische Clavier Früchte (7 sonatas) (Leipzig, 1696); ed. in DDT, iv (1901/*R*)

Musicalische Vorstellung einiger biblischer Historien (6 programme sonatas) (Leipzig, 1700/*R*1973); ed. in DDT, iv (1901/*R*)

Prelude, G, *US-NH*; Praeludium alla breve, *NH*; Fugue, C, *NH* (orig. version of 2nd movt, Sonata B♭, 1692); Fugue, G, Kirchenarchiv, Mylau, tablature book, 1750; Toccata, *B*: ed. in Organum, iv/19 (Leipzig, n.d.)

STAGE WORKS

Orpheus, opera, lost (mentioned in *Der musicalische Quack-Salber*) [probably for Weissenfels]

Singspiel, lost (according to Scheibe)

Music for school plays by C. Weise, lost

Dramma per musica, lost [for welcome of Elector-Prince Johann Georg, Michaelmas 1683]

WRITINGS
(only those relating to music)

Divini numinis assistentia, illustrisque jure consultorum in florentissima academia Lipsiensi (Leipzig, 1688)

Der musicalische Quack-Salber, novel (Dresden, 1700); ed. K. Benndorf (Berlin, 1900)

Letter, 8 Dec 1717, in J. Mattheson: *Critica musica*, ii (1722) [on solmization etc]

Fundamenta compositionis, 1703, *Bds*

Tractatus de tetrachordo seu musica antiqua ac hodierna, lost

De triade harmonica, lost

BIBLIOGRAPHY

WaltherML

J. A. Scheibe: *Der critische Musikus* (Hamburg, 1737–40/*R*1970)

J. Mattheson: *Grundlage einer Ehren-Pforte* (Hamburg, 1740); ed. M. Schneider (Berlin, 1910/ *R*1969)

C. F. Becker: 'Die Klaviersonate in Deutschland', *NZM*, vii (1837), 25

P. Spitta: *Johann Sebastian Bach* (Leipzig, 1873–1800, 5/1962; Eng. trans., 1884–99/*R*1951)

R. Münnich: 'Kuhnau's Leben', *SIMG*, iii (1901–2), 473

B. F. Richter: 'Eine Abhandlung Joh. Kuhnau's', *MMg*, xxxiv (1902), 147

——: 'Verzeichniss von Kirchenmusik Johann Kuhnau's aus den Jahren 1707–1721', *MMg*, xxxiv (1902), 176

A. Schering: 'Über die Kirchenkantaten vorbachischer Thomaskantoren', *BJb*, ix (1912), 86

——: *Musikgeschichte Leipzigs*, ii: *Von 1650 bis 1723* (Leipzig, 1926)

J. Martin: *Die Kirchenkantaten Kuhnaus* (diss., U. of Berlin, 1928)

S. Clercx: 'Johann Kuhnau et la sonate', *ReM*, xvi/9 (1935), 89

R. Gutmann: 'Johann Kuhnau (1660–1722)', *Zeitschrift für Hausmusik*, vii (1939), 25

W. S. Newman: 'A Checklist of the Earliest Keyboard Sonatas (1641–1738)', *Notes*, xi (1953–4), 201 [correction in *Notes*, xii (1954–5), 57]

K. Hahn: 'Johann Kuhnaus "Fundamenta Compositionis"', *GfMKB Hamburg 1956*, 103

F. W. Riedel: 'Kuhnau, Johann', *MGG*

W. S. Newman: *The Sonata in the Baroque Era* (Chapel Hill, 1959, rev. 2/1966/*R*1972)

F. W. Riedel: *Quellenkundliche Beiträge zur Geschichte der Musik für Tasteninstrumente in der 2. Hälfte des 17. Jahrhunderts (vornehmlich in Deutschland)* (Kassel, 1960)

E. Rimbach: *The Church Cantatas of Johann Kuhnau* (diss., U. of Rochester, NY, 1966) [incl. transcrs. of most of the extant cantatas]

GEORGE J. BUELOW

Kühnau, Johann Christoph (*b* Volkstädt, nr. Eisleben, 10 Feb 1735; *d* Berlin, 13 Oct 1805). German composer and conductor. He was apprenticed to a town musician in Aschersleben, then from 1753 at Klosterbergen he studied to become a teacher, and had lessons on the piano and organ from Martin Grosse. In 1763 he became a schoolmaster at the Realschule in Berlin where he founded a choir which he conducted until his death. He published for the choir a series of largely religious *Chorarien* with keyboard accompaniment. He probably had further lessons in harmony and composition from Kirnberger in the late 1770s. In 1783 he became a teacher and in 1788 Kantor and musical director at the Dreifaltigkeitskirche in Berlin. He did much to stimulate musical life there by conducting performances of large-scale choral works. Kühnau compiled several volumes of vocal and instrumental works by himself and other contemporary composers, the best known of which are the *Vierstimmige alte und neue Choralgesänge*, with a preface dated 1784. The 308 chorales, including only eight by Kühnau and others by J. S. Bach, C. P. E. Bach and other German organists, were republished from 1817 in smaller editions; up to the tenth edition (1885) the series comprised 336 chorales. Kühnau's son, Johann Friedrich Wilhelm Kühnau (*b* Berlin, 29 June 1780; *d* Berlin, 1 Jan 1848), the editor of the second to sixth editions of the chorales, was an organist at the Dreifaltigkeitskirche from 1814. In addition to writing several organ pieces and four-part chorales, he edited 86 melodies as a *Nachtrag zu [J.C.] Kühnau's vollständigem Choralbuche*, 1815 (*D-Bds*), and a volume of *Choralmelodien zu sämtlichen Liedern des Berliner Gesangbuches für evangelische Gemeinen* (Berlin, 1838).

WORKS

(MSS mostly in D-Bds; printed works published in Berlin)

Vocal: Chorarien zur Neujahrsfeier gesungen, pf acc. (1773 or 1775–1806), with various titles; Sie tönt nicht mehr, ode, 1v, pf (1778); Das Weltgericht, 4vv, bc (1784), perf. Berlin, 1783; Te Deum laudamus, 2 choruses, org, insts, *c*1784; Vierstimmige alte und neue Choralgesänge, mit Provinzial-Abweichungen, i–ii (1786–90; rev. 2–10/1817–85 as Alte und neue Choralgesänge, mostly ed. J. F. W. Kühnau), incl. works by J. S. Bach, C. P. E. Bach, C. Hauer;

Verstummen muss, ode, 1v, pf (1790); choruses, 4vv chorales, songs; oratorios, sacred cantatas, 1769–97, lost, listed in Ledebur

Inst: Praeludia, org, 1772, incl. works by others; [26] Choräle für eine Harfen-Uhr aufgesetzt, 1775, incl. some by Kirnberger; [35] Choralvorspiele, org, pf (*c*1790), incl. some by C. P. E. Bach, Kirnberger; organ works

Pedagogical: Die Anfangslehren der Tonkunst: bei dem ersten Unterricht, sowohl in der Vokal- als Instrumentalmusik, 1767

BIBLIOGRAPHY

C. von Ledebur: *Tonkünstler-Lexicon Berlin's* (Berlin, 1861/*R*1965)

G. Feder: 'Kühnau', *MGG*

J. R. MILNE/R

Kühnel, August (*b* Delmenhorst, 3 Aug 1645; *d c*1700). German viol player and composer. In 1657 or 1658 he was living at Güstrow with his father, the musician Samuel Kühnel. In 1661 he went as a gamba player to the court chapel at Zeitz. He was active there until 1686, with interruptions. During one of these, in 1665, he went to Paris to study, and he later performed at Dresden and elsewhere. In 1669, when he visited Frankfurt am Main, he was described as a 'musician of the Saxon court'. In 1680–81 he was in Munich, but he decided not to take up an appointment there that would have obliged him to change his religion. He is known to have been in London in 1682 and 1685: the *London Gazette* for 23 November 1685 announced 'some performance upon the Barritone, by Mr August Keenell, the Author of this Musick'.

In 1686 Kühnel was called from Zeitz to Darmstadt by Landgravine Elisabeth Dorothea to become gamba player and director of the instrumentalists under W. C. Briegel, the Kapellmeister, but he had to leave Darmstadt in November 1688 because of the danger of attacks by the French. He is next heard of as director of the instrumentalists at the court at Weimar, and from 1695 to 1699 he was court Kapellmeister at Kassel. His son Johann Michael is also known to have been active as a gamba player and as a violinist and lutenist too.

Kühnel was a leading performer on the viola da gamba and composer of music for it. He published a set of 14 attractive *Sonate ô partite* (Kassel, 1698), six of which are for two gambas, and eight for one, all with continuo; two of them have been listed by Einstein and three edited by C. Döbereiner (Mainz, n. d.).

BIBLIOGRAPHY

A. Einstein: *Zur deutschen Literatur für Viola da gamba im 16. und 17. Jahrhundert* (Leipzig, 1905)

M. Tilmouth: 'A Calendar of References to Music in Newspapers Published in London and the Provinces (1660–1719)', *RMARC*, i (1961/*R*1968), 7

E. Noack: *Musikgeschichte Darmstadts* (Mainz, 1967)

ELISABETH NOACK

Kühnhausen, Johann(es) Georg (*d* Celle, buried 25 Aug 1714). German composer. From the autumn of 1660 he belonged, at first on a probationary basis, to the court band at Celle, the residence of the Duchy of Brunswick-Lüneburg; he was engaged there on a permanent basis as a court musician and singer on 2 January 1661. His name is listed in the court accounts until 1663. As early as September 1661, however, after a probationary course in religion and Latin, he had (with the duke's permission) taken up the post of town Kantor, which included the duties of third teacher at the grammar school. Kühnhausen held this post for the remaining 53 years of his life. In 1668, with the school's headmaster, he set up a new organization of the choir to assist discipline. Kühnhausen married twice and had eight children.

His only known composition is *Passio Christi secundum Matthäum* (autograph in *D-Bds*; ed. in Cw, l,

1938). The main chorale of the song interludes is Ernst Christoph Homburg's 'Jesu, meines Lebens Leben', to a melody by Wolfgang Wessnitzer (organist at Celle court since 1661, town organist 1679–97). Whether it may be concluded from the restriction of the instrumental part to an organ accompaniment that this Passion, generally dated around 1700, was written before the founding of the Celle municipal band in 1676, remains uncertain.

BIBLIOGRAPHY

W. Wolffheim: 'Mitteilungen zur Geschichte der Hofmusik in Celle (1635–1706) und über Arnold M. Brunckhorst', *Festschrift . . . Rochus Freiherrn von Liliencron* (Leipzig, 1910), 421

W. Engelhardt: 'Kantor Kühnhausens Celler Passionsbuch und Karfreitags-Ordnung', *Monatschrift für Gottesdienst und kirchliche Kunst*, xxxii (1927), 49, 124

G. Linnemann: *Celler Musikgeschichte bis zum Beginn des 19. Jahrhunderts* (Celle, 1935)

A. Adrio: 'Die Matthäus-Passion von J. G. Kühnhausen (Celle um 1700)', *Festschrift Arnold Schering* (Berlin, 1937), 24

C. Meyer-Rasch: *Kleine Chronik der Kalandgasse* (Celle, 1951)

W. Braun: *Die mitteldeutsche Choralpassion im achtzehnten Jahrhundert* (Berlin, 1960)

GÜNTER THOMAS

Kuhnle, Wesley (Krehbiel) (*b* Roseville, Mich., 27 June 1898; *d* Los Angeles, 7 Nov 1962). American musicologist and pianist of German descent. He studied the piano with Richard Buhlig, and performed and taught in the Los Angeles area from 1924 until his death. In the 1940s he turned to problems in the history of keyboard performance, and began to study authentic tunings and temperaments; he worked mainly in isolation, but his friends and colleagues included such musicians as Stravinsky and Cowell. Examples of his reconstructed harpsichords and clavichords and the results of his research (manuscripts and 25 tapes) have been collected by the library of California State University at Long Beach.

BIBLIOGRAPHY

P. Yates: *An Amateur at the Keyboard* (New York, 1964) [esp. appx.1: 'Temperament and Tuning']

CLARE G. RAYNER

Kuhreigen [Kuhreihen]. *See* RANZ DES VACHES.

Kuhschelle (Ger.). COWBELLS.

Kuhse, Hanne-Lore (*b* Schwann, Mecklenburg, 28 March 1925). German soprano. She studied at Rostock and Berlin, making her début in 1951 at Gera as Leonore (*Fidelio*). Engaged at Schwerin (1952–9) and Leipzig (1959–63), she then joined the Berlin Staatsoper. She made her American début in 1967, as Isolde at Philadelphia, and her London début the same year at the Albert Hall. She appeared at the Berkshire Festival, Tanglewood, and sang the title role of Busoni's *Turandot* at Philharmonic Hall, New York. Her extensive repertory included Donna Anna, Abigaille (*Nabucco*), Lady Macbeth, Aida, all the Wagner soprano roles from Irene (*Rienzi*) to Kundry, Puccini's Tosca and Turandot, Ariadne, the Marschallin and Marie (*Wozzeck*). A fine lieder singer, she gave the first performances of several songs by Siegfried Wagner at Bayreuth (1966), repeating them at a London concert (1973). She also sang Mita in the first British performance of Siegfried Wagner's *Der Friedensengel*. Her powerful voice, a real dramatic soprano, was admirably suited to such roles as Isolde, Leonore and Turandot.

ELIZABETH FORBES

Kuijken. Belgian family of musicians, specialists in early music.

(1) **Wieland Kuijken** (*b* Dilbeek, nr. Brussels, 31 Aug 1938). Viola da gamba player and cellist. The family were musicians on both sides, connected with brass bands. He left school at 15, and began musical studies (cello and piano) at the conservatory at Bruges, where the family had moved in 1952. He also studied at the Brussels Conservatoire Royale (1957–62; *prix d'excellence*, 1962). At 18 he began teaching himself the viol. He played in the Brussels avant-garde group Musiques Nouvelles (1962), and, from 1959 to 1972, in the Alarius Ensemble, a group specializing in Baroque music, especially French. After that he played with his brothers in the Kuijken Early Music Group (from 1972), and was much involved in teaching; he has held appointments at the conservatories of Antwerp, Brussels and The Hague since the early 1970s and has conducted many master classes (including annually from 1973 in Innsbruck, in Britain in 1973 and the USA in 1974). He has appeared frequently at festivals, such as Flanders, Saintes and the English Bach Festival, and toured in Australia and New Zealand with his brothers and Gustav Leonhardt in 1979. Artists with whom he has played include Alfred Deller, Gustav Leonhardt and Frans Brüggen.

In the late 1970s Wieland Kuijken came to be regarded as the leading exponent of the bass viol, both as a continuo player, in a wide repertory of French, German, Italian and English music, and as a soloist, in Bach and particularly in the French repertory, notably Marais and Forqueray. His playing combines care over scholarly detail with a high level of musicianship; it is characterized by its tonal purity, its sense of line, its poise and restraint, and by its deep seriousness of approach.

BIBLIOGRAPHY

'Wieland Kuijken and Christopher Hogwood on the Viol', *Early Music*, vi (1978), 4

(2) **Sigiswald Kuijken** (*b* Dilbeek, nr. Brussels, 16 Feb 1944). Violinist, viol player and conductor, brother of (1) Wieland Kuijken. He began violin studies at Bruges Conservatory at the age of eight, and from 1960 studied at Brussels Conservatoire Royale under M. Raskin (*premier prix*, 1964). On the Baroque violin, which he has played since 1970, he is self-taught. His career has followed lines similar to that of his brother Wieland: he played with Musiques Nouvelles for ten years, then the Alarius Ensemble, with whom he toured, playing the viola da gamba as well as the violin. He has taught the Baroque violin at The Hague conservatory since 1971, and is a regular participant in festivals involving early music (notably Flanders and the English Bach Festival). In 1972 he was a founder of a Baroque orchestra, La Petite Bande, which he directs and which has recorded a wide range of music, including works by Corelli, Rameau and Haydn and, notably, a complete performance (in 1979) of Handel's opera *Partenope* which won much praise for its vivacity and its keen sense of style. His recordings as a violinist include a set of the Bach sonatas with Leonhardt which won a German award in 1975.

(3) **Barthold Kuijken** (*b* Dilbeek, nr. Brussels, 8 March 1949). Flautist and recorder player, brother of (1) Wieland Kuijken. He studied at the conservatories of Bruges, Brussels and The Hague, where his teachers included Franz Vester (flute) and Frans Brüggen (recorder); on the Baroque flute he is self-taught. Besides

playing with his brothers, he has been a member of the Parnassus Ensemble, the Collegium Aureum and La Petite Bande, and has toured extensively. He teaches the Baroque flute at the conservatories in The Hague and Brussels. The width of his repertory is reflected in his recordings, which range from Montéclair, Handel and Telemann (the solo flute fantasias) to Haydn and Mozart (the flute quartets). His playing is notable for its musicianly understanding of Baroque stylistic precepts, its rounded tone and its intelligent and sensitive handling of rhythm.

JULIE ANNE SADIE, STANLEY SADIE

Kujawiak. Polish folk dance, from the Kujawy region. It is in moderately fast triple time and in effect a slightly slower form of the MAZURKA type of dance (which comes from the neighbouring region of Mazowsze). The *kujawiak* is characterized by its misplaced accents, usually on the second or sometimes the third beat of the bar, and a tempo of crotchet = 120–50. Usually it is ternary: a slowish section, then a faster one, then a return to the slow but with a final accelerando as the dancers whirl. The *kujawiak* is danced by couples, in a circle, either in a flowing walk, with the dancers turning to one another and then leaning away, or in a revolving pattern (with hands either free or clasped). In art music, many works entitled 'mazurka' may in effect be *kujawiaks*. There are movements in Telemann's Polish-influenced works 'that are close to the *kujawiak*; the first collection of *kujawiaks* for piano was made (c1830) by M. Miączyński, the next by O. Kolberg (1845) and another by W. Kaczyński (1933). Nowomiejski wrote a choral *kujawiak* and Wieniawski one for violin and piano. (*See also* POLAND, §II.)

Kukulion. An alternative spelling in English usage for the Greek *koukoulion*, the name used in Byzantine chant for the PROOIMION; *see also* BYZANTINE RITE, MUSIC OF THE, §10.

Kukuzeles. *See* KOUKOUZELES, JOANNES.

Kulenkampff, Georg (*b* Bremen, 23 Jan 1898; *d* Zurich, 5 Oct 1948). German violinist. He studied at Bremen and later (1912–15) with Willy Hess at the Berlin Hochschule für Musik, where he himself taught from 1923 to 1926, and gave master classes in 1931. He toured extensively in Europe. He was exiled during World War II and succeeded Flesch at the Lucerne Conservatory in 1943. In his relatively short career Kulenkampff was specially acclaimed in Germany. His death (from spinal paralysis) robbed violin playing of a highly respected musician of individual style and personality, an outstanding performer and a distinguished teacher. His recording of Beethoven's Violin Concerto, though pre-war, is still considered very fine. Despite some technical shortcomings, it is a musician's performance suffused with a classical serenity. His memoirs were published as *Geigerische Betrachtungen* (Regensburg, 1952).

WATSON FORBES

Kulintang. A GONG-CHIME of seven to 12 (usually eight) bossed gongs in a single row. In the PHILIPPINES (*see* §II,3; with illustration), an ensemble of this instrument and three or four others also has this name.

Closely associated names (e.g. *kulintangan*) appear for instruments in Borneo (*see* MALAYSIA, §II and fig. 9), while similar forms of the instrument with different names (e.g. *bonang*, *trompong*, *reyong*) exist in Sumatra, Java, Bali and other islands of INDONESIA.

JOSÉ MACEDA

Kullak. German family of musicians.

(1) Theodor Kullak (*b* Krotoschin [now Krotoszyn, Poland], 12 Sept 1818; *d* Berlin, 1 March 1882). Pianist and teacher. Encouraged by Prince Radziwiłł he gave his first piano concert before the Prussian king in Berlin at the age of 11. In 1837, while reading medicine in Berlin, he studied music under W. J. A. Agthe, E. E. Taubert and Siegfried Dehn. In 1843 he completed his musical education in Vienna under Czerny, Sechter and Nicolai; the following year he taught music to royalty and the aristocracy in Berlin and in 1846 was appointed pianist to the Prussian court. Together with Stern and Marx, he founded the conservatory (later known as the Stern Conservatory) in Berlin. He withdrew from the direction of this enterprise in 1855 (to be succeeded by Bülow) and founded the Neue Akademie der Tonkunst, which specialized in the training of pianists and soon became the largest private institute for musical education in Germany; towards the end of Kullak's life it numbered 100 teachers and 1100 pupils. His famous pupils included Hans Bischoff, Moritz Moszkowski and Xaver and Philipp Scharwenka. Among his vast number of piano compositions the most important are the studies; his *Schule des Oktavenspiels* is still considered indispensable. After Liszt, with whom he was on friendly terms, Kullak was one of the outstanding piano teachers of the 19th century.

WORKS

(*selected from 126 op. nos.; op. 111 used twice*)

Pf: 2 études de concert, op.2 (Berlin, c1840); Grande sonate, f♯, op.7 (Berlin, c1845); Symphonie de piano, op.27 (Hamburg, c1848); Ballade, op.54 (Leipzig, c1849); Lieder aus alter Zeit, op.80 (Leipzig, c1853), op.111 (Leipzig, 1862); Im Mai, op.90 (Berlin, c1855); Deutsche Volksweisen, op.111 (Berlin, c1862); Scherzo, op.125 (Leipzig, c1873); edns./arrs. of works by Chopin, Schubert and others

Pf methods: Schule des Oktavenspiels, op.48 (Berlin, 1848, 3/1877); Schule der Fingerübungen, op.61 (Berlin, c1850); Ratschläge und Studien, op.74 (Berlin, c1852); Materialien für den Elementar-Klavierunterricht (Berlin, c1859)

Other works: 2 Lieder, op.1 (Berlin, c1840); Uno sguardo, arietta, op.10 (Berlin, c1845); Pf Conc., c, op.55 (Leipzig, c1850); Andante, op.70, vn, pf (Leipzig, c1850); 3 duos, op.76, vn, pf (Leipzig, c1852), collab. R. Wüerst; Pf Trio, e, op.77 (Leipzig, 1853)

(2) Adolph Kullak (*b* Meseritz [now Międzyrzecz, Poland], 23 Feb 1823; *d* Berlin, 25 Dec 1862). Music critic, brother of (1) Theodor Kullak. He studied philosophy in Berlin and, at the same time, studied music with A. B. Marx. Through Marx, he became co-editor of the *Berliner Musikzeitung*; he also taught at his brother Theodor's Neue Akademie der Tonkunst. His writings on music and piano method, *Die Ästhetik des Klavierspiels* (Berlin, 1861), are still of value.

(3) Franz Kullak (*b* Berlin, 12 April 1844; *d* Berlin, 9 Dec 1913). Piano teacher, son of (1) Theodor Kullak. He received his musical education at his father's Neue Akademie der Tonkunst and completed his studies in Paris under Wehle and Litolff. His career as a concert virtuoso was impeded by a nervous complaint, and he worked as a teacher at his father's academy, becoming its director after his father's death. In 1890 he was forced to close the academy for reasons of health; in

1891 he opened the Akademie für höheres Klavierspiel, but had to give it up in 1900, again on account of poor health. As a teacher, he was regarded as highly as his father. He made an important edition of Beethoven's piano concertos.

WORKS

Pf methods: Der Fortschritt im Klavierspiel (Berlin, 1892–7); Die Harmonie auf dem Klavier (Berlin, n.d.); Der erste Klavierunterricht (Berlin, n.d.); Die höhere Klaviertechnik, op.14 (Leipzig, 1900)
Other works: Ines de Castro (opera), Berlin, 1877; works for orch incl. Jubiläums-Ouvertüre (Berlin, 1912); pf pieces, incl. Scherzo, d (Berlin, 1868–73); songs; numerous edns./arrs., incl. works by Beethoven: 5 pf concs., arr. 2 pf (Leipzig, c1882–9), Bach, Mozart, Hummel

WRITINGS

Der Vortrag in der Musik am Ende des 19. Jahrhunderts (Leipzig, 1898)

(4) Ernst Kullak (b Berlin, 22 Jan 1855; d Berlin, 1914). Composer, son of (2) Adolph Kullak. He studied philosophy and philology in Berlin and Leipzig and received his musical education at his uncle's Neue Akademie der Tonkunst, where he then taught composition and the piano.

BIBLIOGRAPHY

O. Reinsdorf: Theodor Kullak und seine Neue Akademie der Tonkunst (Neusalz, 1870)
H. Bischoff: Zur Erinnerung an Theodor Kullak (Berlin, 1883)
H. von Bülow: Briefe und Schriften, ed. M. von Bülow, iii (Leipzig, 1896)
H. Riemann: Präludien und Studien, iii (Heilbronn, 1901)

HORST LEUCHTMANN

Kullman, Charles (b New Haven, Conn., 13 Jan 1903). American tenor. After singing with the Yale Glee Club and Vladimir Rosing's American Opera Company, he set sail for Europe in 1930 and secured an engagement with the Kroll Opera in Berlin. There he made his début as Pinkerton on 24 February 1931. He then appeared at the Berlin Staatsoper, Covent Garden (1934–5, 1938; Babinsky, Vladimir, Walther), in Vienna and Salzburg. He made his Metropolitan Opera début in 1935 in Gounod's Faust. For 25 seasons he sang with the company, making guest appearances elsewhere, and retired in 1960. Kullman was one of the most versatile tenors ever to sing with the Metropolitan. His lyric voice could be adapted to heavy roles through intelligence, and his repertory ranged from Fenton, Tamino and Rinuccio to Tannhäuser and Parsifal. He had an appealing vocal quality and a pleasing stage personality.

MAX DE SCHAUENSEE

Kulthum, Ibrahim Umm. See KALTHUM, IBRAHIM UM.

Kultrun. A small conical kettledrum (diameter 35–45 cm), of laurel or calabash with hide covering and containing stones, seeds or coins, used in Chile (see CHILE, §II, 1(iv), fig.1 and ex.3).

Kumer, Zmaga (b Ribnica, 24 April 1924). Yugoslav musicologist. She studied Slovene literature at the University of Ljubljana, graduating in 1948, and musicology at the Ljubljana Academy of Music, graduating in 1952. In 1955 she received the doctorate at Ljubljana University with a study of the Slovene variants of the song Puer natus in Bethlehem. Since 1949 she has been an associate of the Institute for Folk Music in Ljubljana and since 1966 has been teaching ethnomusicology at the Department of Musicology, University of Ljubljana. Most of her work has been concerned with the texts of Slovene folksongs. She has studied the interrelationship of Slovene folk music and the folk music cultures of the neighbouring Alpine regions, and has been able to demonstrate the existence of various common topics, texts and tunes, their migration and transformation.

WRITINGS

'Zur Frage der deutsch-slowenischen Wechselbeziehungen im Volkslied', Zeitschrift für Volkskunde, ii (1961), 239
'Balada o maščevanju zapuščene ljubice' [The ballad of the deserted sweetheart's revenge], Slovenski etnograf, xv (1962), 167
Balada o nevesti detomorilki [The ballad of the child murderer] (Ljubljana, 1963)
Das slowenische Volkslied in seiner Mannigfaltigkeit (Munich, 1968)
Ljudska glasba med rešetarji in lončarji v Ribniški dolini [Folk music among the potters and sieve-makers in the Valley of Ribnica] (Maribor, 1968)
'Skladnosti in razlike v južnoslovanskih variantah balade o razbojnikovi ženi' [Similarities and differences among the south Slavonic variants of the Ballad of the robber's wife], Narodno stvaralaštvo – Folklor, xxv (1968), 52
Slovenska ljudska glasbila in godci [Slovene folk instruments and players] (Maribor, 1972) [with disc]
Vsebinski tipi slovenskih pripovednih pesmi [Classfied index of Slovene narrative songs](Ljubljana, 1974)
Pesem slovenske dežele (Maribor, 1975) [with 2 discs]

BOJAN BUJIĆ

Kummer, Friedrich August (b Meiningen, 5 Aug 1797; d Dresden, 22 Aug 1879). German cellist and composer. He was the most important member of a musical family that flourished in Saxony in the 18th and 19th centuries. The son of Friedrich August Kummer (1770–1849), an oboist at the Meiningen and (from 1805) Dresden courts, he developed into a fine cellist under the supervision of Friedrich Dotzauer. Following the family tradition he also learnt the oboe, and joined the electoral court orchestra as an oboist in 1814; he did not play the cello in the orchestra until after the death of the cellist Karl W. Höckner. In 1852 he succeeded Dotzauer as principal cellist, a position he held until his retirement in 1864. Kummer lived through momentous years in the musical history of the city of Dresden under the leadership, at various times, of Weber, Marschner and Wagner. Lacking the inclination to compete with cellists internationally, he remained in Saxony except for making a few concert tours in Italy and elsewhere in Germany. In addition to playing with the court orchestra, as principal cellist and as a soloist, he gave frequent chamber music concerts, notably with the younger Franz Schubert (1808–78) and Karol Lipiński (1790–1861). He was praised for his consistent strength and beauty of tone in every playing position. His 'truly classical serenity' provided a reliable support in ensemble playing. He taught the cello both at the Dresden Conservatory and privately, and, together with Dotzauer and Friedrich Grützmacher, was responsible for the high reputation of Dresden cellists in the 19th century; Bernhard Cossmann and Julius Goltermann were among the virtuosos who owed him their training. Kummer's grandson, Alexander Karl Kummer, was a pupil of Ferdinand David at the Leipzig Conservatory and had a distinguished career as a violinist in London.

Kummer's numerous compositions served the taste and demands of his time. Only about half of his 400 works were published, most of these before 1851. They fall into four principal categories: virtuoso compositions for solo cello and orchestra (written primarily for Kummer's own use); chamber music – nearly all using the cello – written to suit the abilities of the growing number of amateurs in his day; elementary and intermediate studies for the cello; and some 200 entr'actes written for the Dresden court theatre. Of the solo cello works, only the *Concertino en forme d'une scène chantante* in D minor op.73, modelled after Spohr's 'vocal scene' violin concerto, kept a place in the repertory until the beginning of the 20th century; most of these works are variations, fantasias and potpourris on popular songs and operatic melodies. Many of the studies for the cello, particularly the *Violoncello-Schule* op.60 (Leipzig, 1839), were still in use many years after Kummer's death.

BIBLIOGRAPHY
J. W. von Wasielewski: *Das Violoncell und seine Geschichte* (Leipzig, 1889, 3/1925/*R*1970; Eng. trans., 1894/*R*1968)
H. von Brescius: *Die königliche sächsische musikalische Kapelle von Reissiger bis Schuch 1826–1898* (Dresden, 1898)
J. Eckhardt: *Die Violoncellschulen von J. J. F. Dotzauer, F. A. Kummer und B. Romberg*, Kölner Beiträge zur Musikforschung, li (Regensburg, 1968)

KURT STEPHENSON

Kümmerle, Salomon (*b* Malmsheim, nr. Stuttgart, 8 Feb 1832; *d* Samaden, 28 Aug 1896). German editor and writer on music. He held appointments as teacher and organist in various German towns and also in Nice (1861–6) and Samaden (1874–90). He is noted for his work in the revival, collection and publication of Protestant church music: he published a valuable four-volume *Encyklopädie der evangelischen Kirchenmusik* (Gütersloh, 1888–95), and his editions include *Musica sacra* (Schaffhausen, 1869–70), *Grabgesänge* (1869), *Zionsharfe* (1870–71), *Choralbuch für evangelische Kirchenchöre* (Gütersloh, 1887–9) and *Aus dem älteren Württembergischen Choralschatz*.

Kumpan, Jan. See CAMPANUS, JAN.

Kün, Tobias. See KÜHN, TOBIAS.

Kunad, Rainer (*b* Chemnitz, 24 Oct 1936). German composer. He studied at the Dresden Conservatory (1955–6) and subsequently at the Leipzig Musikhochschule under Finke and Gerster. After a year as lecturer in music theory in Zwickau, in 1960 he took a post at the Dresden Staatstheater which gave him responsibility for incidental music. His Second Symphony shares with Henze's Fifth an exciting vitality and élan; another successful work, showing a real lyric gift, is the cycle *Melodie, die ich verloren hatte*. Kunad's interest in the stage found its first important expression in *Maître Pathelin*, which shows great wit and inventive skill in linking musical, dramatic and physical gesture. Its clean textures contrast with the Concerto (1970), a work full of fantasy but marred by stylistic incongruities and a choice of instrumentation that produces some extremely unattractive sonorities. Other works, including the ambitious and complex ballet score, leave the impression of a strong and lively intellect overworking often rather undistinguished material.

WORKS
(selective list)

Dramatic: Maître Pathelin (opera, Kunad, after H. Wendler, after Fr. Renaissance comedy), Dresden, Staatsoper, 1968; Wir aber nennen Liebe lebendigen Frieden, ballet, 1970; Litanische Claviere (opera for actors, G. Wolf, after Bobrowski), 1974; Die Versuchung des Sabellicus (Kunad), Berlin, Staatsoper, 1975; Schweyk (improvisation of an opera, Kunad), 1975; many theatre and television scores
Vocal: Melodie, die ich verloren hatte (G. Deicke), S, fl, 2 vn, 2 vc, 1968; Visite bei Kleist, S/T, 1 inst ad lib, 1973; Pro nova (after Dante), chorus, 1973; Die Kitschpostille (after Gryphius), short oratorio, 1974; 3 cantatas
Inst: 2 syms., n.d., 1966–7; Conc., str, 1966; Pf Conc., 1969; Conc., hpd, pf, ionica, cel, str, perc, 1970; Org Conc., 1971; Antiphonie, 2

orchs, rhythm group, 1971; Quadrophonie, 4 str orchs, brass, timp, 1973; Duomix, vn, hpd, 1973; several chamber pieces

Principal publishers: Breitkopf & Härtel, Deutscher Verlag, Henschel

DAVID BLAKE

Kunc, Božidar (*b* Zagreb, 18 July 1903; *d* Detroit, 1 April 1964). Yugoslav composer. An accomplished pianist when still a boy, he studied at Zagreb Music Academy under Stančić (piano) and Bersa (composition). He taught the piano and from 1941 directed the opera class at the Zagreb Music Academy, leaving in 1951 to live in New York. His songs and piano miniatures show the most clearly Kunc's lyrical gift. At first influenced by impressionism, he later turned towards a more radical harmonic idiom and in his latest works an element of folk music is also to be found.

The soprano Zinka Milanov is his sister.

WORKS
(selective list)

Orch: Idila, 1926; 2 Vn Concs., 1928, 1955; 2 pf concs., 1934, 1962; Triptihon, vc, orch, 1945; 3 Episodes, pf, str, 1955
Chamber, inst: Vc Sonata, 1927; 4 pf sonatas, 1930, 1936, 1937, 1943; 5 waltzes, pf, 1940; Sonatina, vn, pf, 1941; 6 bagatelles, pf, 1944; Brief Croatian Suite, pf, 1959; 7 Album Leaves, pf, 1960; music for solo wind
Vocal: Na Nilu, S, orch, 1927; Song cycles, 1v, pf, incl. opp.6, 16, 29, Mrtva ljubav, 1941, Vigilia, 1947, 2 Songs from Serbian Poetry, 1962

BIBLIOGRAPHY
J. Andreis: 'Glasovirske skladbe Božidara Kunca', *Sv Cecilija* (1942), nos.3–4, p.104
K. Kovačević: *The History of Croatian Music of the Twentieth Century* (Zagreb, 1967)
based on *MGG* (xvi, 1067–9) by permission of Bärenreiter

KRESIMIR KOVAČEVIĆ

Kunc, Jan (*b* Doubravice, 27 March 1883; *d* Brno, 11 Sept 1976). Czech composer, teacher and administrator. He studied at the Teachers' Training Institute in Brno and graduated from the Brno Organ School (where he had studied with Janáček) in 1903; his studies were completed in Prague under Novák (1905–6). He was a lecturer in composition and theory, and for many years director, at the Brno Conservatory (1923–45). Through his purposeful and determined work, he was able to raise the standard of the institution to a high level. A music critic and publicist, he wrote the first biography of Janáček (in *Pelclovy Rozhledy*, xiv (1903–4), 491). As a composer he showed promise, though his administrative responsibilities left little time for creative work. His symphonic poem *Píseň mládí* ('Song of youth') bears witness to his training in the late-Romantic tradition; he was influenced by Dvořák and Novák (e.g. in the String Quartet) and partly by Janáček, although his cantata *70,000* was written in 1907, before Janáček's famous chorus on the same words. He achieved his finest work in the field of songs and choruses.

WORKS
(selective list)

Smutky [Sorrows], song cycle, 1905; Kačena divoká [The wild duck], male chorus, 1906; 70,000 (cantata, P. Bezruč), 1907; Str Qt, G, 1909; Slovácké jednohlasé písně [Moravian-Slovak solo songs], 1912; Ostrava, male chorus, 1913; Píseň mládí [Song of youth], sym. poem, 1916; Zahrada [The garden], female chorus, 1920; Po věčném zákonu [After the eternal law], chorus, 1920; Žermanice, male chorus, 1936

Principal publishers: Pazdírek, Hudební Matice

BIBLIOGRAPHY
J. Racek: *Leoš Janáček a současní moravští skladatelé* (Brno, 1940)
Z. Zouhar: *Skladatel Jan Kunc* (Prague, 1960)
——: 'Sborové dílo Jana Kunce', *OM*, v (1973), 233

JAN TROJAN

Kundera, Ludvík (*b* Brno, 17 Aug 1891; *d* Brno, 12 May 1971). Czech pianist, musicologist and administrator. He took state examinations in singing and the piano in Vienna (1910) and studied Czech and German at Prague University (certificate 1920); he gave his first recital in Prague in 1912. As a member of the Czech legion in Russia during World War I he took part in cultural activities and published a study of Czech music. After the war he settled in Brno, becoming secretary (1921) and then professor of piano and aesthetics (1922–41) at the conservatory. In 1925 he attended Cortot's master classes in Paris, and in the same year he gained the doctorate at Brno University under Helfert with a dissertation on the aesthetic aspects of musical reproduction, later working as Helfert's assistant on *Hudební rozhledy* (1925–8). He also pursued a career as a pianist, in Prague and Brno, Vienna (1922), Paris (1925), Cologne (1929), Moscow and Kiev (1937); as a chamber musician he appeared in piano duets with Václav Kaprál, with the Moravian and Janáček Quartets, and as an accompanist. During the occupation, when he was forcibly retired, he concentrated on writing books on teaching. After the war he was director of the Brno Conservatory (1945–6), head of the music department of the Education Faculty in Prague (1946–8) and concurrently professor of piano at the Prague Academy's Brno branch and the Brno deputy dean (1946–7). On the founding of the Brno Academy (1947) he became piano professor and dean of the music faculty (1948–50), later also serving as rector (1949–62). He was awarded the Order of Labour in 1958.

As a pianist Kundera was active in promoting new works (by Janáček, Novák and their pupils) and was responsible for the piano scores of Janáček's *Makropulos Affair* and *Glagolitic Mass*. His many writings include some educational books, early studies of Janáček's style (1924–5; 1927) and two valuable documentary Janáček studies (1948); he also wrote on Kaprál and Kvapil. With his long experience of both the Brno Conservatory and the Brno Academy (which he was chiefly responsible for establishing) he was a leading figure in music education in Brno.

WRITINGS
'Richarda Wagnera Tristan a Isolda', *HR*, vi (1912–13), 233
'R. Strauss, Ariadna auf Naxos', *HR*, vi (1912–13), 202
O muzïke chekhoslovatskovo naroda [Music of the Czechoslovak nation] (Ekaterinburg, 1919)
'Hudba v Sovětském Rusku' [Music in Soviet Russia], *HRo*, i (1924–5), 24
'Janáčkův klavírní sloh' [Janáček's piano style], *HRo*, i (1924–5), 42
'Janáčeks Stil', *Der Auftakt*, vii (1927), 279
O estetice umělecké a zvláště hudební reprodukce [The aesthetics of artistic, and in particular, musical reproduction] (diss., U. of Brno, 1925)
'Hudba a ruská legie' [Music and the Russian legion], *Tempo*, viii (1928–9), 16
'Václav Kaprál'; 'Vilém Petržela'; 'Jaroslav Kvapil'; 'Jan Kunc', *Tempo*, ix (1929–30), 318; x (1930–31), 47; xi (1932), 127, 176; xii (1932–3), 241
'Soudobá hudební Morava' [Music in present-day Moravia], *Československá vlastivěda*, ii (Prague, 1935), 558
'Hudba a revoluce' [Music and revolution], *Dějiny světové hudby*, ed. J. Branberger (Prague, 1939), 553–637
Jaroslav Kvapil (Prague, 1944)
Jak organizovati hudební výchovu v obnoveném státě [How to organize music education in the renewed state] (Brno, 1945)
Janáček a Klub přátel umění [Janáček and the Club of the Friends of Art] (Olomouc, 1948)
Janáčkova varhanická škola [Janáček's organ school] (Olomouc, 1948)
'Chopinovy vlivy ve Smetanově klavírní tvorbě' [Chopin's influence on Smetana's piano works], *Musikologie*, ii (1949), 11
Ludvík van Beethoven (Prague, 1952)
'Janáčkova tvorba klavírní' [Janáček's piano works], *Musikologie*, iii (1955), 306

'K otázce interpretace Janáčkových děl' [The interpretation of Janáček's works], *Leoš Janáček a soudobá hudba: Brno 1958*, 189; also in *Sborník Janáčkovy akademie múzických umění*, ii (1960), 3; see also *Operní dílo Leoše Janáčka: Brno 1965*, 141
'O sovětském a našem hudebním školství' [Soviet and Czech music education], *HRo*, xi (1958), 179
Introduction; 'K výchově pedagoga' [Training a teacher]; 'Aktuální problémy uměleckého školství' [Present-day problems in artistic schooling], *Sborník Janáčkovy akademie múzických umění*, i (1959), 5; 171; 181
'K interpretaci I. dílu Temperového klavíru J. S. Bacha', *Sborník Janáčkovy akademie múzických umění*, iii (1961), 3
Beethovenovy klavírní sonáty, i (Prague, 1964)
'Současnost Smetanova klavírního díla' [The relevance of Smetana's piano works today], *HRo*, xvii (1964), 139
V. Kaprál: kapitola z historie české meziválečné hudby [A chapter in the history of Czech music between the wars] (Brno, 1968)

BIBLIOGRAPHY
J. Vysloužil: *Ludvík Kundera* (Brno, 1962) [incl. list of writings, editions and recordings, and bibliography to 1962]
J. Kvapil: Obituary, *HRo*, xxiv (1971), 264

Künneke, Eduard (*b* Emmerich, 27 Jan 1885; *d* Berlin, 27 Oct 1953). German composer. In Berlin he attended university lectures on theory and was a composition pupil of Bruch at the Hochschule für Musik. In 1907 he was appointed chorus master at a Berlin operetta theatre and he was for a time conductor for Reinhardt at the Deutsches Theater. During the war he played the horn in an infantry regiment, and afterwards went to the Friedrich-Wilhelmstädtisches Theater. The success of Berté's Schubert pastiche *Das Dreimäderlhaus*, which he conducted, led him to the composition of operettas, of which he became the leading German exponent, particularly with *Der Vetter aus Dingsda* (1921). In 1924 and 1925 he composed works for the Shuberts in New York and one for the Gaiety Theatre in London. In later works he used jazz, most notably in his *Tänzerische Suite* (1929) written for radio.

WORKS
(selective list)
Over 30 comic operas and operettas incl.: Die Marmorfrau, unperf.; Robins Ende (M. Moris), Mannheim, Nationaltheater, 5 May 1909; Coeur As (E. Tschirch, after Scribe), Dresden, Hofoper, Nov 1913; Das Dorf ohne Glocke (3, A. Pasztor), Berlin, Friedrich Wilhelmstädtisches, 5 April 1919; Der Vielgeliebte (3, H. Haller, Rideamus), Berlin, Nollendorfplatz, Nov 1919; Wenn Liebe erwacht (3, Haller, Rideamus), Nollendorfplatz, Aug 1920; Der Vetter aus Dingsda (3, Haller, Rideamus), Nollendorfplatz, 15 April 1921
Lady Hamilton (3, R. Bars, L. Jacobson), Breslau, Schauspielhaus, 25 Sept 1926; Die blonde Liselott (3, R. Kessler), Altenburg, 25 Dec 1927, rev. as Liselott; Der Tenor der Herzogin (3, Kessler, after Ilgenstein), Prague, Deutsches Theater, 1929; Glückliche Reise (3, M. Bertusch, K. Schwabach), Berlin, Theater am Kurfürstendamm, 23 Nov 1932; Die lockende Flamme (3, P. Knepler, H. Welleminsky), Berlin, Theater des Westens, 25 Dec 1933; Herz über Bord (3, E. van der Becke), Zurich and Düsseldorf, 30 March 1935; Die grosse Sünderin (3, K. Stoll, H. Roemmer), Berlin, Staatsoper unter den Linden, 31 Dec 1935; Zauberin Lola (3, A. Brieger, S. Graff), Dortmund, 1937
Other works: Tänzerische Suite, jazz band, orch, 1929; orch suites, ovs., 2 pf concs., str qt, choral and vocal music, film scores
ANDREW LAMB

Künspeck, Michael. *See* KEINSPECK, MICHAEL.

Kunst, Jaap [Jakob] (*b* Groningen, 12 Aug 1891; *d* Amsterdam, 7 Dec 1960). Dutch ethnomusicologist. Both his parents were professionally trained musicians; he began studying the violin at the age of four, and in his teens became interested in the folk culture of the Netherlands, learning its songs and dances and the folk style of playing the violin. He took a degree in law at Groningen (1917) and worked in banking and the law before deciding to join a string trio (1919), which made a successful tour of the Dutch East Indies (now Indonesia). He subsequently remained in Bandung (Java) until the mid-1930s, his law degree initially securing him a government post, so that he could devote his spare time to studying and collecting the indigenous music; he had become particularly interested in the Javanese gamelan. By 1927 his outstanding work in Indonesian music began to attract notice, and in 1930 he was given an official, full-time appointment as musicologist for the Dutch government. He made long tours of the Indonesian archipelago during the next few years and, with the help of his wife Katy, established an archive of musical instruments, field recordings, books and photographs for the museum at Batavia (now Djakarta). By 1934, however, his government post had been abolished (a result of the depression), and he returned to Holland; for two years he lectured throughout Europe. His lectures, based on his 15 years' experience in Indonesia, anticipated a new respect for peoples who were then still under colonial rule. In 1936 he became curator of the Royal Tropical Institute in Amsterdam and began to amass what became one of the greatest collections in Europe. He began lecturing at the University of Amsterdam in 1953 and became a faculty member in 1958; he also made two lecture tours of the USA, the first in 1954. In 1959 he succeeded Curt Sachs as honorary president of the Society for Ethnomusicology and Vaughan Williams as president of the International Folk Music Council. Shortly before his death he was elected to membership of the Anthropological Society of Vienna.

Kunst was a founder of modern ethnomusicology. In his study of Dutch folk music and various Indonesian musical cultures he showed deep concern for the humanity of man and for the need to comprehend music in the widest possible frame of reference – social, physical and spiritual. He himself coined the term ethnomusicology on the grounds that it was more accurate than 'comparative musicology' ('vergleichende Musikwissenschaft'). His many publications relating to Indonesia are standard reference works, without which Indonesians would have lost all knowledge of some of their most valued heritage; his collection of Dutch folk music is equally important.

WRITINGS

'Over moderne Fransche kamermusiek', *Kunstkroniek*, x (1920), no.2, p.1; no.3, p.1; no.4, p.1; xi/1 (1921), 1
with R. Wiranatakoesoema: 'Een en ander over Soendaneesche muziek', *Djawa*, i (Weltevreden, 1921), 235
with C. J. A. Kunst-Van Wely: 'Over Balische muziek', *Djawa*, ii (1922), 117, 194
——: 'Over toonschalen instrumenten van West-Java', *Djawa*, iii (1923), 26
'Die muziek in den Mangkoe Nagaran', *Djawa*, iv (1924), suppl., 24
with C. J. A. Kunst-Van Wely: *De toonkunst van Bali* (Weltevreden, 1924); pt.2 in *Tijdschrift voor Indische taal-, land- en volkenkunde*, lxv (1925), 369–508
with R. Goris: *Hindoe-Javaansche muziekinstrumenten* (Batavia, 1927; rev. 2/1968 as *Hindu-Javanese Musical Instruments*)
'Een en ander over den Vorstenlandschen gamelan', *Oedaya* (1928), 130
'Over eenige Hindoe-Javaansche muziekinstrumenten', *Tijdschrift voor Indische taal-, land- en volkenkunde*, lxviii (1928), 347
'De l'origine des échelles musicales javano-balinaises', *Journal of the Siam Society*, xxiii (Bangkok, 1929), 111
with R. M. A. Koesoemadinata: 'Een en ander over pélog en sléndro', *Tijdschrift voor Indische taal-, land- en volkenkunde*, lxix (1929), 320–52
'Een overwalsche bloedverwant van den Javaanschen gamelan', *Nederlandsch Indië, oud en nieuw*, xiv (1929), 79
'Over Soendaneesche zangmuziek', *Feestbundel uitgegeven door het Koninklijk Bataviaasch Genootschap van kunsten en wetenschappen bij gelegenheid van zijn 150-jarig bestaan*, i (Weltevreden, 1929), 393

A Study on Papuan Music (Weltevreden, 1931; repr. 1967 in *Music in New Guinea*)
Musicologisch onderzoek 1930 (Batavia, 1931)
Over zeldzame fluiten en veelstemmige muziek in het Ngada- en Nagehgebied, West-Flores (Batavia, 1931)
'Quelques notes sur la musique javanaise moderne', *Art populaire*, ii (1931), 107
De toonkunst van Java (The Hague, 1934; Eng. trans., 1949, enlarged 3/1973 as *Music in Java*)
'The Music of Java', *Indian Art and Letters*, new ser., viii (1934), 3
Verslagen van den ambtenaar voor het systematisch musicologisch onderzoek in den Indischen archipel omtrent de door hem verrichte werkzaamheden (Bandung, 1934)
'A Musicological Argument for Cultural Relationship between Indonesia (probably the Isle of Java) and Central-Africa', *PMA*, lxii (1935–6), 57; in Ger. in *Anthropos*, xxxi (1936), 131
'Musicological Exploration in the Indian Archipelago', *Asiatic Review*, iv (1936), 810
'Een onbekend Javaansch muziekinstrument', *Cultureel Indië*, i (Leiden, 1939), 140
Een en ander over den Javaanschen gamelan (Amsterdam, 1940, 4/1945)
'Een merkwaardig blaasinstrument: de Maleische duivenlokfluit', *Cultureel Indië*, ii (1940), 47
De waardering van exotische muziek in den loop der eeuwen (The Hague, 1942)
Music in Flores: a Study of the Vocal and Instrumental Music among the Tribes Living in Flores (Leiden, 1942)
Music in Nias (Leiden, 1942)
'Waar komt de gong vandaan?', *Cultureel Indië*, iv (1942), 241; also in *Emlékkönyv Kodály Zoltán natvanadik születésnapjára* (Budapest, 1943), 84; Eng. trans., *Ethnos*, xii (1947), 79, 147; see also *Ethnos*, xiv (1949), 160
Een en ander over de muziek en den dans op de Kei-eilanden (Amsterdam, 1945)
Muziek en dans in de buitengewesten (Amsterdam, 1946)
De inheemsche muziek en de zending (Amsterdam, 1947)
Around von Hornbostel's Theory of the Cycle of Blown Fifths (Amsterdam, 1948)
'Musicology', *Report of the Scientific Work Done in the Netherlands on behalf of the Dutch Overseas Territories during the Period . . . 1918–1943*, ed. B. J. O. Schriede (Amsterdam, 1948), 194
'Sundanese Music', *Indian Art and Letters*, new ser., xxii (1949), 54
The Cultural Background of Indonesian Music (Amsterdam, 1949)
'The Music of Bali and its Emotional Appeal', *Britain and Holland* (London, 1949), 7
Begdja, het gamelanjongetje (Amsterdam, 1950)
De inheemsche muziek in Westelijk Nieuw-Guinea (Amsterdam, 1950); also in *De Bergpapoea's van Nieuw-Guinea en hun woongebied*, ii, ed. C. C. F. M. le Roux (Leiden, 1950); Eng. trans., 1967 in *Music in New Guinea*
'Die 2000-jährige Geschichte Süd-Sumatras gespiegelt in ihrer Musik', *GfMKB, Lüneburg 1950*, 160
Metre, Rhythm and Multipart Music (Leiden, 1950) [also in Fr. and Dutch]
Musicologica: a Study of the Nature of Ethno-musicology, its Problems, Methods and Representative Personalities (Amsterdam, 1950, enlarged 2/1955 as *Ethnomusicology*, 3/1959; suppl., 1960)
'Gamelan Music', *IMSCR*, v *Utrecht 1952*, 271
Kulturhistorische Beziehungen zwischen dem Balkan und Indoneseien (Amsterdam, 1953; Eng. trans., 1954)
Sociologische bindingen in der muziek (The Hague, 1953)
'The Origin of the Kemanak', *Bijdragen tot de taal-, land- en volkenkunde van Nederlandsch-Indië*, cxvi (The Hague, 1960), suppl.
'On Dutch Folk Dances and Dance Tunes', *Studies in Ethnomusicology*, i, ed. M. Kolinski (New York, 1961), 29
ed.: C. Sachs: *The Wellsprings of Music: an Introduction to Ethnomusicology* (The Hague, 1962)
'Fragments from Diaries Written during a Lecture Tour in the New World . . . and a Trip to Australia', *The Commonwealth of Music, in Honor of Curt Sachs* (Glencoe, 1965), 328

FOLKSONG EDITIONS

Terschellinger volksleven (Uithuizen, 1916, 3/1951)
Noord-Nederlandsche volksliederen en -dansern (Groningen, 1916–18, 2/1918–19)
Het levende lied van Nederland (Amsterdam, 1918–19, 4/1947)
Songs of North New Guinea (Weltevreden, 1931; repr. 1967 in *Music in New Guinea*)
Oude westersche liederen uit oostestersche landen (Bandung, 1934)

BIBLIOGRAPHY

Lists of writings in J. Kunst: *Ethnomusicology* (Amsterdam, 3/1959) and *Music in Java* (The Hague, 1973)
Obituary: A. Bake, *Jaarboek der Koninklijke Nederlandse akademie van wetenschappen* (1960–61), 327; E. Reeser, *TVNM*, xix/1–2 (1960), 4; A. Bake, *AcM*, xxxiii (1961), 67; H. Husmann, *Mf*, xiv

(1961), 257; F. van Lamsweerde, *Sonorum speculum*, no.6 (1961), 36; W. Paap, *Mens en melodie*, xvi (1961), 1

MANTLE HOOD

Kunst, Jos (*b* Roermond, 3 Jan 1936). Dutch composer. It was not until he was 27 that he took up the study of music systematically. He was a composition pupil of Joep Straesser from 1963 to 1966, later studying under Ton de Leeuw at the Amsterdam Conservatory, where he won the composition prize in 1970. He also studied electronic music at the Institute for Sonology of the State University in Utrecht. Since 1971 he has taught theory and contemporary music at the Amsterdam Conservatory. His works bear witness to an individual musical personality. He succeeds in making selective and convincing use of avant-garde elements, but has chosen to make his own way. Apart from his electronic pieces, there are also often refined orchestral works, such as *Arboreal*, with which he won first prize at the Gaudeamus composers' competition in 1969, and *Insects* which was awarded the AVRO prize during the 1967 Gaudeamus competition. *Elements of Logic* was written with Jan Vriend, with whom Kunst has made a study of linguistics and semiotics.

WORKS
(selective list)

Insects, 13 str, 1966; Arboreal, orch, 1968; Expulsion, tape, 1969; Exterieur, tape, 1967–70; Trajectoire, 16 solo vv, 11 insts, 1970; XVII One Way, chamber orch, 1970; Outward Bound, harp, 1971; Solo Identity I, b cl, 1971; Elements of Logic, wind, 1972; Solo Identity II, pf, 1973; No time at all, b cl, pf, 1973; No Time, 3 cl, b cl, pf, 2 perc, 1974; Any Two, 2 ww, 1975

Principal publisher: Donemus

ROGIER STARREVELD

Kunst- und Industrie-Comptoir. Austrian firm of music publishers. It was founded in Vienna in 1801 by Josef Anton Kappeller, a Tyrolean painter, and Jakob Holer, who dealt mainly in fine art, maps and music. Because of illness Kappeller had to leave the firm on 12 March 1802; the artistic direction was transferred with the deed of partnership to the writer Joseph Schreyvogel (later secretary of the Hofburg Theatre). Joseph Sonnleithner and Johann Sigmund Rizy invested in the enterprise as sleeping partners. The firm was known by its German title, as Bureau des Arts et d'Industrie, and as Contojo d'Arti e d'Industria. From 1807 Schreyvogel directed it alone, and on 16 May that year he founded a branch in Pesth, Vacznergasse, which took the name of Schreyvogel & Co. in 1808. In 1811 Jakob Holer again became a partner, with Josef Riedl.

Schreyvogel was not as effective in business as he was in artistic pursuits, and the enterprise became bankrupt (probably also partly because of Holer's unreliability) and was continued by Riedl, who was granted the concession on 18 March 1814. The firm had closed by May 1823, and the music publishing rights passed over to S. A. Steiner & Co., who from 1826 brought out editions from the old plates but with new title-pages and the mark 'S.u.C.H'.

Schreyvogel published works by many well-known composers of the time including Beethoven, Albrechtsberger, L. von Call, Eberl, Prince Louis Ferdinand of Prussia, Förster, Mauro Giuliani, Gyrowetz, Hummel, Krommer, Krufft, Méhul, Mozart, Pixis, Domenico Scarlatti, Steibelt and Vanhal.

BIBLIOGRAPHY

C. von Wurzbach: *Biographisches Lexicon des Kaiserthums Oesterreich* (Vienna, 1856–91)
E. Eitner: *Buch- und Musikalien-Händler* (Leipzig, 1904)
C. Junker: *Festschrift zur Feier des hundertjährigen Bestehens der Korporation . . . 1807–1907* (Vienna, 1907)
C. Pichler: *Denkwürdigkeiten aus meinem Leben*, i (Munich, 1914), 564
F. Gräffer: *Kleine Wiener Memoiren und Wiener Dosenstücke*, i (Munich, 1917), 294
J. Stáva: 'Jos. Ant. Kappeller als Gründer des "Kunst- und Industrie-Comptoir zu Wien" ', *Tiroler Almanach* (1926), 93
O. E. Deutsch: *Music Publishers' Numbers* (London, 1946; Ger. trans., rev., 1961)
G. Kinsky and H. Halm: *Das Werk Beethovens: thematisch-bibliographisches Verzeichnis seiner sämtlichen vollendeten Kompositionen* (Munich and Duisburg, 1955)
A. Weinmann: 'Vollständiges Verlagsverzeichnis der Musikalien des Kunst- und Industrie Comptoirs in Wien', *SMw*, xxii (1955), 217–52

ALEXANDER WEINMANN

Kuntzen. See KUNZEN family.

Kunz, Erich (*b* Vienna, 20 May 1909). Austrian bass-baritone. A pupil of Theo Lierhammer and Hans Duhan at the Vienna Music Academy, he made his début at Troppau in 1933. After various provincial engagements he became a member of the Vienna Staatsoper in 1940. In 1943 he first sang Beckmesser at Bayreuth, and he soon became a regular singer at Salzburg and other festivals. In 1953 he sang at the Metropolitan, New York, for the first time. Covent Garden heard him as Leporello and Figaro during the 1947 Vienna Staatsoper season, and in 1948 and 1950 he sang Guglielmo at Glyndebourne, where he had been a member of the chorus in 1936.

An accomplished singing actor with a fine sense of humour and a gift for timing, he excelled in such roles as Papageno, Beckmesser and Figaro. For British tastes his Leporello was found too Austrian, not Italian enough, but he was a firm favourite with Viennese audiences from the beginning, often playing small parts in operetta or Volksoper performances with consummate gusto and vocal skill. He was also an accomplished singer of popular Viennese songs.

BIBLIOGRAPHY

G. Baldini: 'Kunz, Erich', *Le grandi voci* (Rome, 1964), [with opera discography by R. Vegeto]

PETER BRANSCOMBE

Kunz, Ernst (*b* Berne, 2 June 1891). Swiss composer and conductor. He studied at Munich University and then at the Music Academy there under Klose and Kellermann. He held a number of theatre appointments in Germany (including one under Walter at Munich) before returning to Switzerland in 1918, where he worked in Zurich with Busoni; thereafter he held posts with Swiss choral groups and in music education. A prolific composer in a late Romantic style, his works include operas, numerous choral works, five symphonies (1917–66), several concertos, chamber music and songs.

Kunz, Harald (*b* Plauen, 4 July 1928). German music publisher. After attending the Thomasschule in Leipzig, he studied musicology, drama, philosophy and sinology at the universities of Cologne and Vienna (1951–4), taking his doctorate in 1954 with a dissertation on the court theatre in Vienna at the time of Maria Theresia. He became assistant editor for Schott in Mainz (1955) and then joined Bote & Bock as deputy editor and public relations manager (1956), becoming head of the publishing department in 1972. He has written numerous articles and essays about contemporary composers, as well as opera librettos for the Korean composer Isang Yun (*Die Witwe des Schmetterlings*, 1969; *Geisterliebe*, 1971; *Sim Tjong*, 1972).

WRITINGS

Höfisches Theater in Wien zur Zeit der Maria Theresia (diss., U. of Vienna, 1954; *Jb der Gesellschaft für Wiener Theaterforschung 1953–4*, 31–113)
Musikstadt Berlin zwischen Krieg und Frieden (Berlin and Wiesbaden, 1958)
with L. Höffer von Winterfeld: *Handbuch der Blockflötenliteratur* (Berlin, 1959)
125 Jahre Bote und Bock (Berlin, 1963)

ALFRED GRANT GOODMAN

Kunz, Thomas Anton (*b* Prague, 21 Dec 1756; *d* Prague, *c*1830). Czech composer, pianist and inventor. Kunz studied law and philosophy at Prague University and music with the Prague organist Joseph Prokop. Two of his Singspiels were performed in Prague: *König Wenzel* (1778) and *Die Bezauberten* (1779). The piano part of the cantata *Pygmalion* (1781) and some German songs (1807) were also published in Prague; the first edition of his German songs had appeared in Leipzig in 1799. Kunz constructed an instrument which was a combination of piano and the positive organ. He also improved the first so-called ORCHESTRION (in 1791) and designed and constructed with the Prague piano makers Johann and Thomas Still a new orchestrion from 1796 to 1798. This instrument resembled a piano with a mahogany case with sides of blue taffeta stretched in ornamentally carved frames. Two manuals with 65 keys had a compass of F to a''', and a pedal with 25 keys with a compass of C to c''. On the left side above the pedal was a mechanism for the foot operation of the bellows. 230 strings and 360 pipes, together with 21 registers, made possible 105 tonal combinations. Kunz also perfected the mechanism of Meyer's *violin piano*; he introduced extended notes and removed the unpleasant cacophony of the bow mechanism.

See also MECHANICAL INSTRUMENT.

BIBLIOGRAPHY

Beckers National-Zeitung der Teutschen (1796), 434
T. A. Kunz: 'Beschreibung des Orchestrions', *AMZ*, i (1798), 88
J. U. von Rittersberg: 'Die Tonkunst in Böhmen von den ältesten bis auf die gegenwärtigen Zeiten', *Archiv für Geschichte, Statistik, Literatur und Kunst*, xvi (1825), 51
R. Haas: 'Thomas Anton Kunz und sein Orchestrion', *Der Auftakt*, xi (1931), 43

ALEXANDR BUCHNER

Kunze, Stefan (*b* Athens, 10 Feb 1933). German musicologist. He studied musicology at the universities of Heidelberg and Munich under R. von Ficker and T. Georgiades, with Byzantine studies (under F. Dölger) and classics as secondary subjects. At the same time he attended the Trapp Conservatory in Munich where he took a performer's diploma in flute in 1955. In 1961 he received the doctorate from Munich University with a dissertation on the instrumental music of Giovanni Gabrieli, and in 1970 he completed his *Habilitation* there with a study of 18th-century Italian *opera buffa*. In 1973 he accepted the chair of musicology at Berne University. His other areas of research include instrumental music and opera from the 16th century to the 19th and questions of music historiography and analysis.

WRITINGS

Die Instrumentalmusik Giovanni Gabrielis (diss., U. of Munich, 1961; Tutzing, 1963)
'Die Entstehung des Concerto-Prinzips im Spätwerk G. Gabrielis', *AMw*, xxi (1964), 81–110
'Die Vertonungen der Arie "Non so d'onde viene" von J. Chr. Bach and von W. A. Mozart', *AnMc*, no.2 (1965), 85
Schubert: Sinfonie h-moll (Munich, 1967)
'Die Arie KV 621ᵃ von W. A. Mozart und G. von Jacquin: Satztechnik und Gattung in den Liedern von Mozart und seiner Zeit', *MJb 1968*, 205
'Über die Entstehung eines Buffo-Librettos: Don Quijote-Bearbeitungen', *DJbM*, xii (1968), 75
'Anton Reichas "Entwurf einer Phrasirten Fuge": zum Kompositionsbegriff im frühen 19. Jahrhundert', *AMw*, xxv (1968), 289
W. A. Mozart: Sinfonie g-moll KV 550 (Munich, 1968)
'Gattungen der Fuge in Bachs Wohltemperiertem Klavier', *Bach-Interpretationen: Walter Blankenburg zum 65. Geburtstag* (Göttingen, 1969), 74
Die italienische Opera buffa im 18. Jahrhundert (Habilitationsschrift, U. of Munich, 1970)
'Über Melodiebegriff und musikalischen Bau in Wagners Musikdrama, dargestellt an Beispielen aus "Holländer" und "Ring"', *Das Drama Richard Wagners als musikalisches Kunstwerk*, ed. C. Dahlhaus (Regensburg, 1970), 111–48
'Die "wirklich gantz neue Manier" in Beethovens Eroica-Variationen op.35', *AMw*, xxix (1972), 124
Don Giovanni vor Mozart: die Tradition der Don-Giovanni-Opern im italienischen Buffa-Theater des 18. Jahrhunderts (Munich, 1972)
'Werkvorstellung in neuer Musik: Anmerkungen zu Schönbergs Bläserquintett op.26', *Veröffentlichungen des Instituts für neue Musik und Musikerziehung Darmstadt*, xiii (Mainz, 1972)
'Cherubini und der musikalische Klassizismus', *AnMc*, no.14 (1974), 301
'Raumvorstellungen in der Musik: zur Geschichte des Kompositionsbegriffs', *AMw*, xxi (1974), 1

EDITIONS

W. A. Mozart: Arien, Szenen, Ensembles und Chöre mit Orchester, Neue Ausgabe sämtlicher Werke, ii/7, Bd.1–4 (Kassel, 1967–72)
G. Gazzaniga: Don Giovanni o sia Il convitato di pietra (1787) (Kassel, 1973)

HANS HEINRICH EGGEBRECHT

Kunzen [Kuntzen]. German family of musicians.

(1) Johann Paul Kunzen (*b* Leisnig, Saxony, 31 Aug 1696; *d* Lübeck, 20 March 1757). Organist and composer. His talent matured early, and according to his autobiographical sketch for Mattheson's *Grundlage einer Ehren-Pforte* he deputized for Leisnig's organist when only nine years old. He distinguished himself on the violin and on keyboard instruments while at school in Torgau (1705) and Freiberg, and from 1716 to 1718 was a student in Leipzig, where he was decisively influenced by Kuhnau and Telemann. His later polyphonic choral writing shows the effect of a rigorous training under Kuhnau, and an extant four-part organ fugue displays a thorough command of this style. A gifted singer and instrumentalist, he performed in both capacities at the opera, and stood in for the organist of the Nikolaikirche.

In 1718 Kunzen became a Kapellmeister in Zerbst and in 1719 he went to Wittenberg, where he founded a concert society. After several concert tours he took over in 1723 the direction of the opera in Hamburg, where he performed a Passion and several operas of his own composition. When his two-year contract expired he remained in Hamburg as a private music teacher. During this period he journeyed to England with his son (2) Adolph Carl in 1728–9, there meeting Pepusch and Handel. On 26 September 1732 he was appointed organist and overseer of the Marienkirche, Lübeck. He was also active as a composer and conductor in Lübeck, providing numerous wedding arias and secular cantatas for merchants' festivities, instituting a subscription series and composing oratorio-like Abendmusiken annually for Advent. In 1747 he was admitted to Mizler's music society.

Kunzen's greatest achievement apparently lay in his Abendmusiken for Lübeck, which were reported by the Kantor Caspar Ruetz (1750) to have brought the genre to its zenith; *Belsatzar* of 1739 was singled out as a masterpiece by Scheibe (*Critischer musicus*) for its large double choruses. Unfortunately, as with much of

Kuhnau's work, the music has not survived; the extant first part to the undated *Der verlorene Sohn* shows a thorough familiarity with Handel's works in the handling of choruses, the portrayal of moods in arias and its fluent and adroit recitative, though without reaching a comparable command of melody. Especially noteworthy is Kunzen's effective use of string and wind instruments in support of choral polyphony.

WORKS

(music lost unless otherwise stated)

OPERAS

Die über Eifersucht und List triumphirende beständige Liebe, Wittenberg, *c*1720

Die heldenmüthigen Schäfer Romulus und Remus (3), Hamburg, 1724 [trans. of G. Porta's opera, Numitore, with added music by Kunzen]

Cadmus (3, J. U. König), 1725 [?Brunswick, Feb 1720, cited in Sonneck]

Critique des Hamburgischen Schauplatzes, Hamburg, 1725

OTHER WORKS

Choral: 22 oratorios/Abendmusiken, 1733–56; Der verlorene Sohn, oratorio, *B-Bc*; 4 Passions; liturgical music for feasts, 1745–6; wedding serenade, 1736, *D-LÜh*; Komm Freude, wedding serenade, 4vv, orch, 1746, autograph *SWl*; 3 serenades, vv, orch, *B-Bc* [1 autograph]; further occasional works, 1 chorale book, 1748

Inst: Sinfonia, D, and ov. (suite), G, *D-SWl*; 2 hpd concs., *Dlb*; fugue, org, *B-Bc*

BIBLIOGRAPHY

J. Mattheson: *Grundlage einer Ehren-Pforte* (Hamburg, 1740); ed. M. Schneider (Berlin, 1910/R1969)

O. G. T. Sonneck: *Library of Congress: Catalogue of Opera Librettos Printed before 1800* (Washington, DC, 1914/R1967)

G. Karstädt: 'Kunzen, Johann Paul', *MGG*

H. C. Wolff: *Die Barockoper in Hamburg (1678–1738)*, i (Wolfenbüttel, 1957)

(2) Adolph Carl Kunzen (*b* Wittenberg, 22 Sept 1720; *d* Lübeck, buried 11 July 1781). Organist and composer, son of (1) Johann Paul Kunzen. He learnt the organ from his father and received training in Hamburg from W. Lustig. In 1728–9 he accompanied his father on a tour of England, and in 1744 he contributed two arias – his earliest known works – to his father's serenata for the Schonenfahrer Collegium. A year later he wrote a thoroughbass tutor (*Unterricht im Generalbass mit Exempeln*, 1745, in *D-Bds*). The first volume of his collection *Lieder zum unschuldigen Zeitvertreib* appeared in Hamburg in 1748, and in 1749 he was appointed Konzertmeister at the court of Mecklenburg-Schwerin. He was made Kapellmeister there in 1752, but disputes with the court and the orchestra compelled him to resign a year later.

From 1754 to 1757 Kunzen lived mainly in London, where he probably wrote his 12 harpsichord sonatas, dedicated to the Prince of Wales and later published there as his op.1; the third part of his lieder collection also appeared in London at this time. He returned to Lübeck in 1757 as his father's successor at the Marienkirche, and continued his father's concert series and regular production of Abendmusiken. A stroke ended his career as a conductor, but with the aid of his pupil J. W. C. von Königslöw he continued to organize and plan the programmes for these series until his death.

Kunzen's work as a composer centred on the oratorio, beginning with an early six-part Passion oratorio for Schwerin with a colourful succession of scriptural texts, chorale stanzas, allegorical figures, recitatives and arias. Of his many annual Abendmusiken for Lübeck only two have survived; they distinguish Kunzen as a noteworthy proponent of accompanied recitative and of arias and duets with solo parts for virtuoso instrumentalists. His depiction of character and mood places him in the front rank of oratorio composers in his time; his choruses show Handel's influence, and in their design go beyond those of Telemann and Mattheson. Kunzen also wrote a number of occasional works; more important than these however are his lieder which, while modelled on those of Telemann, Mattheson, Görner and many others, are lyric or comic pieces of independent style notable for ease of melody and pleasing keyboard accompaniment.

WORKS

VOCAL

Choral: 21 oratorios/Abendmusiken, 1750–80, many lost, others in *D-Bds*, *LÜh*, *SWl*; 5 Passions, 1750, 1770–71, 1777, *LÜh*, *SWl*; 7 festal cantatas, 1750–52, *SWl*; numerous occasional works, incl. cantatas, serenades, intermezzos, 1736–78, *B-Bc*, *D-ROu*, *SWl*; canons, 3vv, *ROu*

Lieder: [30] Lieder zum unschuldigen Zeitvertreib, i (Hamburg, 1748) [3 ed. in Friedlaender, i/2], 1st suppl. (Lübeck, 1754), 2nd suppl. (London, 1756) [2 ed. in Friedlaender, i/2]

INSTRUMENTAL

Orch: 16 syms., *B-Bc*, *D-Bds*, *SWl*; 5 ovs., 1750–52, *A-Wgm*, *D-SWl*; 5 concs. for pf, *B-Bc*, 21 for vn, some in *D-SWl*, 1 for vc, *SWl*, 8 for fl, 6 for ob; 6 It. arias, It. duet, with orch, *ROu*, *SWl*; Intrada, 1752, marches, *SWl*; acc. to Te Deum, tpts, timp, 1763

Chamber: 4 divertimentos, 2 vn, gui, b, *B-Bc*; 17 vn sonatas, *Bc*, *D-SWl*; XII Sonatas, hpd, op.1 (London, 1759); 6 Hpd Sonatas (Nuremberg, n.d.), lost; 6 sonatinas, kbd, *Bds*; 3 sets of variations, kbd (Naples, n.d.); further single kbd works, *B-Bc*, and in 18th-century anthologies

BIBLIOGRAPHY

M. Friedlaender: *Das deutsche Lied im 18. Jahrhundert* (Stuttgart and Berlin, 1902/R1962)

C. Meyer: *Geschichte der Mecklenburg-Schweriner Hofkapelle* (Schwerin, 1913)

H. Rentzow: *Die mecklenburgischen Liederkomponisten des 18. Jahrhunderts* (diss., U. of Berlin, 1938)

J. Hennings: 'Adolph Karl Kunzen und seine "Lieder zum unschuldigen Zeitvertreib"', *Mf*, iii (1950), 66

G. Karstädt: 'Kunzen, Adolph Carl', *MGG*

(3) Friedrich Ludwig Aemilius Kunzen (*b* Lübeck, 4 Sept 1761; *d* Copenhagen, 28 Jan 1817). Composer, son of (2) Adolph Carl Kunzen. He received his earliest musical instruction from his father, who presented him in London in 1768 as a child prodigy. In 1781 he began studies in law at the University of Kiel. There he made the acquaintance of the noted author and dilettante C. F. Cramer, who encouraged him to devote himself entirely to music. Through Cramer he met J. A. P. Schulz, who gave him a recommendation to Copenhagen; there he was a successful keyboard performer, composer and organizer of concerts from 1784 to 1789. After the failure of his opera *Holger Danske* (31 March 1789) he moved to Berlin, where he founded a music shop with Reichardt and in 1791 edited the journal *Musikalisches Wochenblatt*. In 1792 he became Kapellmeister at the theatre in Frankfurt am Main, where he performed his Singspiel *Das Fest der Winzer, oder Die Weinlese* in 1793. In 1794 he took up a similar post in Prague. He succeeded Schulz as royal Kapellmeister in Copenhagen in 1795, performing many of his own operas and Singspiels there and also directing the oratorio society Det Harmoniske Selskab.

As a composer Kunzen was particularly influenced by the style of his protector J. A. P. Schulz and, in his operas, by Mozart, whose works he often performed in Copenhagen. The lied collection *Weisen und lyrische Gesänge* (1788) uses the same folklike melody and uncomplicated form to express union with nature as characterize Schulz's songs. Artless melody with simple harmonization also distinguishes his Singspiel *Die Weinlese*. The unsuccessful *Holger Danske*, composed to Wieland's proto-Romantic *Oberon* with Schulz as consultant adviser, mixes the styles of grand opera and Singspiel: simple strophic songs, situation comedy, tone-painting of nature, janissary music, energetic dance rhythms and dramatic scenas are all combined in the work, which recalls Gluck and Mozart. The large-scale oratorios *Opstandelsen* and *Das Halleluja der Schöpfung*, whose texts probably derive from Klopstock, are surprisingly effective in their succession of solos, duets and choruses, and in renderings of such natural phenomena as earthquakes (in the former) and sunrise (in the latter). The deft handling of the solo parts, powerfully conceived choruses and sensual orchestration point to Haydn's *Creation*, which Kunzen himself directed with large forces at Copenhagen in 1801. Kunzen presents a many-sided musical personality who was well versed in the music of his time, especially in Mozart's operas, and who, in his own stage works, cantatas and oratorios, produced much that is worthy of revival.

WORKS
(printed works published in Copenhagen unless otherwise stated)

DRAMATIC
Unless otherwise stated, all were written for the Kongelige Teater, Copenhagen, and MSS are in *DK-Kk*.

Holger Danske [Ogier the Dane] (opera, 3, J. Baggesen, after C. Wieland: Oberon), 31 March 1789; vocal score (n.d.)
Das Fest der Winzer, oder Die Weinlese (Singspiel, 3, J. Ihlée), Frankfurt am Main, 3 May 1793, *D-Bds*, *Dlb*; perf. as Viinhøsten, Copenhagen, Dec 1796; vocal score (?1797)
Festen i Valhal [Festival in Valhalla] (prol, E. Falsen), 1796; vocal score (n.d.)
Hemmeligheden [The secret] (Singspiel, 1, A. G. Thoroup, after Quétant), 22 Nov 1796; vocal score (?1797)
Dragedukken [The dragon doll] (Singspiel, 4, Falsen), 14 March 1797; vocal score (n.d.)
Erik Ejegod (opera, 3, Baggesen), 30 Jan 1798; ov. (Leipzig, n.d.), vocal score (n.d.)
Naturens røst [The cry of nature] (Singspiel, 3, Falsen, after Armand), 3 Dec 1799; ov. (Leipzig, 1812)
Min bedste moder [My grandmother] (2, Falsen), 15 May 1800; aria, arr. pf (n.d.)
Hjemkomsten [The homecoming] (Singspiel, 1, T. Thaarup), 1802; vocal score (n.d.)
Gyrithe (L. Kruse), 1807; vocal score (n.d.)
Kaerlighed paa landet [Love in the country] (3, N. T. Bruun, after Weisse), 23 March 1810; excerpts in Polyhymnia
Others: Jokeyen, 1797; Eropolis, 1803; Den logerende [The lodger], 1804; Hussitterne [The Hussites], 1806; Ossians Harfe, aria (Vienna, c1806); Kapertoget [The Pirates], 1808, aria (n.d.), excerpts in Polyhymnia; Husarerne paa frieri [The hussars out courting], 1813, aria (n.d.)
Incidental music: Dannequinderne [The noblewoman], 1805; Skottekrigen, 1810; Maria af Foix, 1811; Staerkodder, 1812; Salomons Dom, 1817

VOCAL
Choral: Prolog, 1795, *DK-Kk*; Opstandelsen (Die Auferstehung) (Thaarup), oratorio, 1796, *D-LÜh*; Das Halleluja der Schöpfung (Baggesen), cantata (Zurich, ?1797); Trauergesang am Grabe des Jahrhunderts (F. Bruun), 1801, ?holograph *LÜh*; Jubilaeum (Thaarup), 1801, *DK-Kk*; Erobreren og Fredsfyrsten [The conqueror and Prince of peace] (Høeg-Guldberg), 1802, *Kk*; occasional works, incl. cantatas for the coronation of Frederik VI, 1815, chorales and funeral cantatas, *B-Bc*, *D-Bds*, *LÜh*, *SWl*, *DK-Kk*
Vocal, with pf: Viser og lyriske sange [Ballads and lyric songs] (1786); Musikalsk nyeaargave for det smukke kiøn [Musical New Year gift for the fair sex] (n.d.); Musikalsk tidfordriv for det smukke kiøn [Musical pastime for the fair sex] (n.d.); Weisen und lyrische Gesänge (Leipzig, 1788) [3 ed. in Friedlaender, i/2]; Lieder in Musik (Zurich, 1794); Hymne auf Gott (C. F. Schmidt-Phiseldeck) (Zurich, ?1795); Hymne auf die Harmonie (Gerstenberg) (Zurich, 1795); Zerstreute Kompositionen (n.d.); Gesänge am Klavier zur Bildung des Gesanges (Leipzig, 1814); Auswahl der vorzüglichsten altdänischen Volksmelodien (1816); other single works, mostly lieder, pubd Berlin and Copenhagen, and in Polyhymnia and other contemporary anthologies; lieder ed. von Norgaard, *Sange fra oplysningstiden* (Copenhagen, 1967); lied (Lenore) ed. in EDM, 1st ser., xlv (1970)

OTHER WORKS
Inst: Sym., autograph *D-Bds*; 2 ovs. (Zurich, n.d.); Ouverture nach dem

Thema der Ouverture zur Zauberflöte (Leipzig, n.d.); serenades, orch, *B-Bc*; kbd works in contemporary anthologies
ed.: Polyhymnia (?1780–90) [anthology in at least 8 vols., incl. edns. of other composers' works and lieder by Kunzen; some vols. also pubd Kiel and Leipzig]; Studien für Tonkünstler und Musikfreunde, 1792 (Berlin, 1793), ed. Kunzen and J. F. Reichardt [incl. *Musikalisches Wochenblatt* (1791–2) and *Musikalische Monatsschrift* (1792)]

BIBLIOGRAPHY
M. Friedlaender: *Das deutsche Lied im 18. Jahrhundert* (Stuttgart and Berlin, 1902/R1962)
C. A. Martienssen: 'Holger Danske', *ZIMG*, xiii (1911–12), 225
B. Friis: *Friedrich Aemilius Kunzen: sein Leben und Werk I. Bis zur Oper 'Holger Danske' (1761–1789)* (diss., U. of Berlin, 1943)
S. Lunn: 'Kunzen, Friedrich Ludwig Aemilius', *MGG*

(4) Louise Friederica Ulrica Kunzen (*b* Lübeck, 15 Feb 1765; *d* Ludwigslust, 4 May 1839). Singer, daughter of (2) Adolph Carl Kunzen. She was already taking part in private concerts in Lübeck in 1781. In 1787 she became an operatic singer at the court theatre in Ludwigslust, where in 1786 she had married Johann Friedrich Braun, an oboist and violinist in the ducal band. She achieved considerable renown over a very long career there, retiring only in 1837.

BIBLIOGRAPHY
J. Hennings and W. Stahl: *Musikgeschichte Lübecks* (Kassel, 1951–2)
GEORG KARSTÄDT

Kupferman, Meyer (*b* New York, 3 July 1926). American composer and clarinettist. A self-taught composer, he was appointed to teach composition and chamber music at Sarah Lawrence College in 1951. His aesthetic position is demonstrated in *Infinities*, a cycle of 25 works begun in 1961, all based on the same 12-note series. *Infinities 1* is an entire concert for solo flute and *Infinities 5* a concert for cello, including pieces for solo cello, cello and bass voice and cello and tape, and a concerto with jazz band. *Infinities 6* is a cantata for unaccompanied chorus and *Infinities 8* a jazz string quartet – many of the other *Infinities* pieces include jazz movements. The cantata *Dem unbekannten Gott* includes sections based on the *Infinities* series as well as passages suggestive of Lisztian Bach transcriptions. The *Symphony of the Yin-Yang* opposes tonal and atonal, thematic and athematic elements.

WORKS
(selective list)

Sym. no.4, 1955; Sonata on Jazz Elements, pf, 1958; Infinities 1–25, varied forces, 1961–, incl. The Judgement (Infinities 18) (opera, P. Freeman), 1966; Moonchild and the Doomsday Trombone (Kupferman), S, jazz ens, 1966; Fantasy Sonata, vn, pf, 1970; Dem unbekannten Gott (cantata, Nietzsche), 1971; Sym. of the Yin-Yang, 1972; Madrigal, brass qt, 1974; 4 Double Features, 2 cl, 1977
Operas, other stage works, film scores, orch music, str qts, chamber and inst pieces, choral and vocal works
Principal publishers: Chappell, General, Mercury
JEROME ROSEN

Kupka, Karel (*b* Rychvald, nr. Karviná, Moravia, 19 June 1927). Czech composer. After early studies at the Ostrava Institute of Music and Singing, he studied composition under Kvapil and Petrželka in Brno (1946–52). In 1948 he was appointed headmaster of the Karviná music school, and he occupied a similar position in Petřvald, Moravia until 1954, when he became répétiteur and conductor of the opera company at the Zdeněk Nejedlý Theatre in Ostrava. His musical style was initially influenced by Janáček and Bartók; in the later 1960s he began to make use of the sonorities of more recent music, but without losing his tendency to write in extended forms. A terse vehemence and dramatic power are combined in his music with a lyrical melodiousness which has its roots in Moravian folk-song.

WORKS
(selective list)

Stage: Taškář [Jester] (opera, after Plautus), 1955; Lysistrata (opera, after Aristophanes), 1957; Florella, ballet, after F. Lope de Vega, 1960; Cassandra, R. Rücker, ballet, 1961; Sokratova smrt [Socrates' death], opera, 1965; 5 other operas, 1 other ballet
Cantatas: Zjeveni svatého Jana [The revelation of St John], 1969; Český sen [Czech dream] (J. Kainar), 1970; 2 others
Orch: 2 pf concs., 1951, 1960; Partita, str, 1955; Suita v barokním slohu, 1956; Picassiade, 1958; Concertino da camera, vn, orch, 1968
Chamber: 4 str qts, 1956, 1958, 1963, 1969; Studies, pf, perc, 1968

Principal publisher: Panton

BIBLIOGRAPHY
ČSHS
I. Stolařík and B. Štědroň: 'K dějinám hudby v Ostravském kraji' [History of music in the Ostrava region], *Slezský sborník*, liii (1955), 221
Č. Gregor: 'Rozhovor o nové opeře' [Interview on the new opera], *Červený květ*, iii/2 (1958), 68 [*on Lysistrata*]
O. Pukl: 'O soudobé hudbě: rozhovor s K. Kupkou', *Červený květ*, v/2 (1960), 67
E. Sýkorová: 'Nová opera Karla Kupky', *Červený květ*, vii/2 (1962), 61 [*on Když tančí růže*]
J. Smolka: 'Kupkova Picassiáda', *HRo*, xix (1966), 501

OLDŘICH PUKL

Kupkovič, Ladislav (*b* Bratislava, 17 March 1936). Slovak composer and conductor. He studied the violin and conducting in Bratislava at the conservatory (1950–55) and the academy of music (1955–61). After serving as conductor of the Hungarian Folk Ensemble of Bratislava (1959–60) and playing the violin in the Slovak PO (1960–63), he worked as a freelance conductor and composer, writing music for films and television. In 1963 he founded the Hudba Dneška ensemble, which, under his direction, soon won international fame through broadcasts, recordings and concert appearances. He was a co-founder of the New Music Days at Smolenice Castle, near Bratislava (1968), and from the next year he lived in Germany, first as a stipendiary of the Deutscher Akademischer Austauschdienst in Berlin, and then from 1971 in Cologne. In 1973 he became lecturer, and in 1976 professor, of composition at the Hanover Musikhochschule. He has taken a leading part in the conception and development of new 'open' forms of concert ('macrocompositions' and 'Wandelkonzerte') and experimental performances; his most important 'works' of this kind have been *Profily* (Smolenice, 1968), *Musikalische Ausstellung* (Berlin, 1970), *Musik für das Ruhrfestspielhaus* (Recklingshausen, 1970), *Musikatlas* (Hanover, 1971) and *Klanginvasion auf Bonn* (1971). In more conventional compositions he has been concerned principally with the filtering, alienation and analytical illumination of works of the past (*Präparierte Texte*, *K-Rhapsodie*) and with reforming orchestral playing (*Dioe*, *Concours*).

WORKS
(selective list)

Mäso kríža [Flesh of the cross], trbn, 6 timp, 3 tam-tams, church bell, 1962; Rozhovor času s hmotou [Conversation between time and material], bn, 3 perc, 1965; Písmená [Letters], 8 solo vv, 1967; Dioe, orch, 1968; Präparierter Text 1 [after Brahms: Sym. no.1, 2nd movt], vn, tape, 1968; Präparierter Text 2 [after Mozart: Sym. no.41, 1st movt], fl, tpt, timp, vn, vc, db, 1968; Präparierter Text 3 [after Beethoven: Sym. no.9, 4th movt], cymbals, b drum, tape, 1968; Präparierter Text 4 [after Bach: Musikalisches Opfer, Ricercar a 6], ens, 1968, orch, 1970; Treffpunkt, wind ens, 1970
K-Rhapsodie [after Offenbach, Elgar, Sarasate and others], vn, orch, 1968–71; Monolith, 48 str, 1971; Souvenir, vn, pf, 1971; E-Musik, 4-track tape, 1972; Gespräch mit Gott, orch, 1972; R-Musik, tape, 1968–73; Das Gebet, str, 1972; Concours, any solo inst, orch, 1973; Čarovné sláčiky [Magic bows], 30 vn, low str, 1974; Rrrondo, vc, pf, 1977; Marsch, vn, orch, 1978; Scherzo, va, pf, 1978

Principal publisher: Universal

WRITINGS
'Nová náuka o harmónii?' [A new harmony treatise?], *SH*, x (1966), 400
'K interpretácii novej hudby' [On the interpretation of new music], *SH*, xi (1967), 440
'Komorná hudba zajtra' [Chamber music tomorrow], *SH*, xii (1968), 422
'Metóda skladatel'ovej práce dnes' [Composition methods today], *SH*, xii (1968), 325
'Preparované texty', *Konfrontace*, i (1969), 4
'Správa z bádania o hudbe v priestore' [Report on attempt at music in space], *OM*, i (1969), 17
'Musikalische Ausstellung', *NZM*, cxxxi (1970), 149
'Der Oberbefehlshaber erinnert sich an Bonn', *Melos*, xxxviii (1971), 535
'Musik auf der Strasse', *Melos*, xl (1973), 135
'Notwendige Veränderungen', *Musica*, xxvii (1973), 343

BIBLIOGRAPHY
M. Lichtenfeld: 'Begegnung mit Ladislav Kupkovič', *Melos*, xli (1974), 5

MONIKA LICHTENFELD

Kupper, Annelies (Gabriele) (*b* Glatz, 21 Aug 1906). German soprano. After studying in Breslau, she taught music there from 1929 until 1935, when she was heard in concert by Franz von Hoesslin, musical director of the Breslau Opera; he engaged her for Breslau that year, and she remained there until 1937. After engagements at Schwerin and Weimar, she joined the Hamburg Staatsoper, making regular appearances there until 1946; she spent the next 20 years at the Bayerische Staatsoper, Munich. In 1944 she sang Eva at Bayreuth, returning as Elsa in 1960. At Salzburg she was the Female Chorus in Britten's *The Rape of Lucretia* in 1950, two years later creating the title role in the first public performance of Strauss's *Die Liebe der Danae*. At Covent Garden she played Chrysothemis in the 1953 production of *Elektra* under Kleiber, and, in the Bayerische Staatsoper's London season that autumn, Danae. She made guest appearances throughout Europe. In addition to the Mozart and Strauss repertory, Kupper was a noted Aida, Desdemona and Tatyana. Her performances of works by Orff, Haas and other contemporary German composers, for which her musicianship, sensitiviy and feeling for words so admirably suited her, were particularly distinguished.

HAROLD ROSENTHAL

Kuppers, Johannes Theodorus. *See* CUYPERS, JOHANNES THEODORUS.

Kurath, Gertrude Prokosch (Tula) (*b* Chicago, 19 Aug 1903). American ethnomusicologist. She studied at Bryn Mawr College (BA 1922, MA in art history 1928), concurrently receiving training in music and dance in Berlin, Philadelphia, New York and Providence, Rhode Island (1922–8); she then attended the Yale School of Drama (1929–30). Later she was employed as a field research worker by the Wenner-Gren Foundation (1949–73), the American Philosophical Society (1951–65) and the National Museum of Canada (1962–5, 1969–70). Her main areas of interest have been ethnomusicology and dance ethnology, and she has made particularly substantial contributions to the study of American Indian dance (*see* NORTH AMERICA, §II,2), and to dance theory and notation. She has also taught dance and has lectured on dance history. From 1958 to January 1972 she was dance editor for the journal *Ethnomusicology*.

WRITINGS

'The Tutelo Harvest Rite: a Musical and Choreographic Analysis', *Scientific Monthly* (1953), no.76, p.153
'Chippewa Sacred Songs in Religious Metamorphosis', *Scientific Monthly* (1954), no.79, p.312
'The Tutelo Fourth Night Spirit Release Singing', *Midwest Folklore*, iv (1954), 87
Songs of the Wigwam (Ohio, 1955)
'Antiphonal Songs of Eastern Woodland Indians', *MQ*, xlii (1956), 520
'Dance Relatives of Mid-Europe and Middle America', *Journal of American Folklore*, lxix (1956), 286
'Songs and Dances of Great Lakes Indians', FE 4003 [disc notes]
'Catholic Hymns of Michigan Indians', *Anthropological Quarterly*, xxx (1957), 31
'Cochiti Choreographies and Songs', in C. H. Lange: *Cochiti* (Austin, Texas, 1959), 539
'Menomini Indian Dance Songs in a Changing Culture', *Midwest Folklore*, ix (1959), 31
'Panorama of Dance Ethnology', *Current Anthropology*, i (1960), 233
with S. Martí and N. Chilkovsky: *Dances of Anáhuac: the Choreography and Music of pre-Christian Dances* (Chicago, 1964)
Iroquois Music and Dance: Ceremonial Arts of Two Seneca Longhouses (Washington, DC, 1964)
'Dogrib Choreography and Music', *The Dogrib Hand Game*, ed. J. Helm and N. O. Lurie (Ottawa, 1966), 13
Michigan Indian Festivals (Ann Arbor, 1966)
'The Kinetic Ecology of Yaqui Dance Instrumentation', *EM*, x (1966), 28
'Dance, Drama, and Music', *Handbook of Middle American Indians*, vi, ed. M. Nash (Austin, Texas, 1967), 158–90
Dance and Song Rituals of Six Nations Reserve, Ontario (Ottawa, 1968)
with A. Garcia: *Music and Dance of the Tewa Pueblos, New Mexico* (Santa Fe, 1970)

BIBLIOGRAPHY

J. W. Kealiinohomoku and F. J. Gillis: 'Special Bibliography: Gertrude Prokosch Kurath', *EM*, xiv (1970), 114 [incl. complete list of publications to 1970]
DORIS J. DYEN

Kurdish music.

1. Introduction. 2. Music: (i) Secular music (ii) Sacred and ritual music. 3. Dance. 4. Instruments.

1. INTRODUCTION. The Kurds are an Iranian people of western Central Asia who expanded outwards from western Iran to what is now central Kurdistan, perhaps integrating there with an indigenous nationality of different origin. Without a state of their own, they have zealously maintained their cultural identity as Kurds. As a result, some archaic features as well as other distinguishing characteristics survive in their music.

1. Map showing the major territory inhabited by the Kurds

They inhabit mainly, in addition to a few isolated colonies, a strip of territory about 960 km long and 200–400 km wide. This territory is at present shared between Turkey, Iran, Iraq, Syria and the USSR (see fig.1). Kurdish society includes warrior castes, whose task is to defend the various territorial holdings of their chiefs; shepherds (nomads and semi-nomads); and agriculturalists (sedentary and semi-sedentary). The semi-nomadic people live in villages during the winter, and in summer, after the harvest, they go to the mountains. They have remained unaffected by urban culture, despite the existence nearby of Kurdish principalities with their courts and urban centres.

The most important source on Kurdish history, the *Sharaf nāmeh* ('Chronicle of Sharaf', 16th century), indicates that the Kurds did not readily assimilate the written traditions and classical culture of the Arabo-Persian ruling class, and thus did not rise to high positions of power or prestige in the Islamic empire. There were, however, small Kurdish principalities, and at the folk level the Kurds did integrate into Islamic culture. For example, the *Sharaf nāmeh* reports that the Emir of the Badlis principality strictly forbade the use of any musical instrument during the seven days of festivities for his son's marriage; in doing so he acted in conformity with Islamic religious opposition to music. But the same source also relates that at a sumptuous banquet organized by the Kurdish Emir Shah in honour of the Persian Shah Ismā'īl, singers intoned expressive and moving melodies, and musicians played softly on the 'ūd (short-necked lute) and the ṭanbūr (long-necked lute) in the maqām ('mode') 'ushshāq. It is not known whether these musicians were Kurds nor whether the music was Kurdish. But the existence of a specifically Kurdish art music seems unlikely; and urban music-making probably had little influence on Kurdish folksinging and dancing until the mid-20th century.

The Kurds speak a western Iranian language with a number of quite different dialects. The majority of Kurdish dialects are grouped under the term 'kurmānjī', and within this group are two sub-groups of dialects: the eastern and the western. The inflections of the language, the prosody of the poetry and the subjects treated have to a great extent determined the nature of Kurdish music and dance. The fundamental question of whether there is a single music tradition common to all Kurds cannot be answered without separate and thorough investigation of the many individual Kurdish traditions in Turkey, Armenia, Iraq, Iran and Syria, followed by a comparison between them. Such a comparison would probably reveal both similarities and differences, which would in turn lead to another basic question: whether the differences are due to local stylistic features or whether they relate to other factors such as dialect, tribe, economic class, etc. Unfortunately not even general studies of the Kurds have yet been made, and present knowledge of their music and dance is fragmentary and sporadic. This discussion can therefore deal only with external observations and attempt to define the most typical and common characteristics of Kurdish tradition.

2. MUSIC. Vocal music predominates and even dances are often accompanied by dance-songs. This predilection for vocal music is expressed in different ways. The bardic singer, who is usually unpaid, is greatly esteemed and is always welcomed by the chief of his clan; but instrumentalists, who are paid, are considered lower in

rank. All the terms used to indicate a musician, whether singer or instrumentalist, are related to vocal music: *danbeg* (Kurdish) or *qawwāl* (Arabic: 'he who speaks'), *kalām-khwān* ('reciter'). Kurdish singers have a distinctive vocal style, characterized by a wide vocal range, a virile and expressive voice, and rapidity and precision in the performance of epic songs, which, above all, requires that the singers know a large body of traditional songs of different categories.

(*i*) *Secular music*. The repertory of songs and dances includes a large variety of categories, forms and subjects. Among non-strophic types the epic song is greatly favoured. This type relates in poetry the exploits of heroes and their deeds in famous battles. It is performed in a colourful way, enhanced by mimetic devices, and requires a particularly skilful singer to control both the repertory and the quick parlando style with its flexible tempos. Two singers usually alternate in the performance of epic songs. Although these are often about war, they are different from the group war songs intoned by warriors in battle.

Love is the subject of many Kurdish songs. There are various types of strophic love-song and ballad, including a lively form of public dialogue in verse between a woman and a man. Work songs cover several activities such as harvest, corn-grinding, milking and hunting, the last type being characterized by yodelling. Wedding festivities, which last for three to 14 days, are marked by several ceremonies and processions. These are enhanced by songs and dances, some of which are specific to the event (e.g. the songs of young girls of the same age as the bride; the songs of old women expressing their sorrow on the young girl's departure from her parents' house; the songs and dances for the bridegroom's bath in the river; separate processional songs for women and men; humorous games, dances and songs, etc). Another widespread type of song among the Kurds is the lament, which varies according to the age and rank of the deceased.

Certain basic melody types are widespread among the Kurds and provide some common traits from which to derive more specific regional distinctions. Non-metric songs (e.g. the epic song) are often characterized by a quick, tense and animated parlando style and a rapid, somewhat melismatic melodic line (*see* IRAN, §II, ex.5). In metric songs the rhythmic structure of the piece as a whole is usually dominated by the poetic metre, creating a complex relationship between the textual metric patterns and the rhythmic patterns of the music. In some dance-songs there are repeated short melodic motifs arranged in a mosaic-like structure. Another common characteristic in Kurdish song is the insertion of meaningless syllables such as *way*, *ye*, *le*, *de* and *oy*; these are often linked to melodic progressions and frequently occur at the ends of phrases. There are also some typical opening and closing melodic motifs. The melody may begin with an ascent from the third degree above the final to the fifth, or from the second to the fourth, and then stress that for a time by means of repetition or undulation, before returning, by either a sinuous or a sequential descent in one or two segments, to the final (exx.1 and 2). In another pattern (which has many variants) the melody starts with an ascending 4th from the sub-final to the third degree above the final and returns to the final; then another ascent to the fourth degree is followed by a sinuous descent to the final (ex.3). Exx.4 and 5 show yet another type of opening, in which the melody begins on its highest note followed either by a sinuous or sequential descent, or by an immediate leap to a lower pitch. The closing motif consists in most cases of a descent from the 4th or 3rd to the final, often in the form of a long reciting tone sustained by additional nonsense syllables and divided into many small repeated notes of varying rhythmic value (exx.3 and 4, and, to some extent, 1 and 5).

The general direction of the melody in most Kurdish songs is descending. Melodic progressions consist mainly of small steps, i.e. 2nds, 3rds and (rarely) some ascending 4ths. The melodic range usually varies between a 3rd and an octave but ranges of a 4th and a 5th predominate. There are, however, some melodies whose compass is more than an octave (ex.5).

Dance-songs in particular are often performed antiphonally by two singers or by two groups. This practice gives rise to melodic overlapping, heterophony and a conscious rudimentary polyphony. Christensen, who studied this phenomenon in the singing of Turkish Kurds (1967), provided an interesting example of antiphonal singing in which polyphony in 2nds and 3rds is produced by the overlapping in the two soloists' lines (ex.6). The structure of the dance-songs is essentially strophic, with the same melodic pattern repeated for each verse, although there are often small melodic and rhythmic variations each time the melody is repeated (ex.7). There is much more variety in dance-songs than in instrumental dance melodies, many of which consist of alternating short repeated melodic motifs (exx.8 and 9).

(*ii*) *Sacred and ritual music*. The Kurds who believe their ancestors were Zoroastrians are now mostly Sunnite Muslims; other minorities include Shī'ite Muslims, Nestorian and Jacobite Christians, an ancient Kurdish Jewish community who emigrated to Israel, and heretical sects such as the Yazīdī ('followers of Yazīd') and the Ahl-i Ḥaqq ('truth-worshippers'). The Jews and the Christian sects speak Aramaic in addition to Kurdish dialects. Liturgical and para-liturgical Aramaic song differs in function and musical structure

2. Kurdish dancers accompanied by the zurna (shawm)

Ex.1 Love-song, Barzan tribe, Iraq; transcr. A. Shiloah

Ex.2 *Hayran*, a love-song, western Iran; transcr. A. Shiloah

Ex.3 *Rumi*, a ballad, Barzan tribe, Iraq; transcr. A. Shiloah

Ex.4 Lament, Syria; transcr. A. Shiloah

Ex.5 Shepherd's song, Syria; transcr. A. Shiloah

Ex.6 *Çerine* dance-song for two singers, Turkish Kurds; transcr. D. Christensen (Christensen, 1963)

Ex.7 *Dabche*, dance-song, Iraq; transcr. A. Shiloah

Ex.8 Dance played on *duzala* (double clarinet), Iran; transcr. A. Shiloah

Ex.9 Dance played on *zurna* (shawm) and *dola* (double-headed drum), Iraq; transcr. A. Shiloah

from neighbouring secular song. Aramaic song includes pure monophonic cantillation and prayer tunes, and melismatic and metrical hymns of a meditative nature. Ritual music is in general rather more typical of the various minorities than of the Sunnite majority, whose ritual music is limited to that cultivated by the mystical orders.

Perhaps the most highly developed ritual music is that found among the two heretical sects. The 60,000 to 70,000 Yazīdī are concentrated in the Mosul area of Iraq. Their doctrine includes ancient pagan and shamanistic elements, as well as Zoroastrian, Manichean, Jewish, Muslim and Christian elements. Music and dance form an essential part of their worship. Their official musicians, the *qawwālūn* ('those who speak'), are clergy of minor rank and form a guild said to number 50 men. These must take part in all religious festivals and in events in the life cycle such as circumcision and burial ceremonies. The two principal occasions are the annual pilgrimage to the tomb of their prophet, Sheikh

'Adi, and their New Year. The musicians accompany the ceremonies with flute (*nāy* or *shabbābah*) and drums, which are all considered sacred. They sing hymns and ecstatic songs, perform dances and fulfil other services. The *kochak* (dancers) serve in considerable numbers at the tomb of Sheikh 'Adi and as ministrants to the *qawwālūn*.

The Ahl-i Ḥaqq, an esoteric sect living mainly in southern Iran but with a few isolated communities in India, Pakistan and Afghanistan, number almost 500,000. Their doctrine has been influenced by ancient Mesopotamian and Iranian religions, as well as by extremist Islamic mystical orders. They believe in cycles of incarnation and in theophany, i.e. manifestations of God and angels in human form throughout history. Through music the worshippers can gain access to the mysteries of the sect, so that music constitutes a central part of their liturgy and spiritual life, and all the religious leaders are musicians. In the first theophany the king of kings is said to have possessed 900 singers, 900 frame-drum players, 900 *ṭanbūr* (long-necked lute) players and 900 *balur* (flute) players. At present the *ṭanbūr* is the only instrument used in the sect's ritual music, and it is venerated as a sacred object. The musician who plays the *ṭanbūr* and sings the sacred texts is called *kalām-khwān* ('reciter'). The repertory has two main categories: the *dastgāh* and the hymns. The 12 *dastgāh* ('apparatus' or 'organization') are pieces which have points in common with Persian art music but are not identical with it. The hymns draw their melodies from sacred and secular sources. They are integrated in the liturgy, are performed responsorially by the recitant and the worshippers to the accompaniment of the *ṭanbūr*, and are solemn and moderate in tempo. Mokri (1968, pp.448f) gave several examples of this sect's hymns.

3. DANCE. Dance plays an important role in Kurdish social life and in specific family events, and there are many varieties of dance. A dance session is usually long and the dances are performed in quick succession. Dance music (see §2(i)) may be provided by an instrumental ensemble including the *zurna* (shawm; see fig.2) and the *dola* (double-headed drum) or the *duzala* (also called *dutke* or *miṭbaj*: a double-pipe clarinet), or by a dance-song with drum, or by a dance-song alone. Dance-songs are sung by the dancers themselves, who occasionally add hand-clapping and finger-snapping. Proficient instrumentalists are remunerated. There are many correspondences between the dance music and dance patterns.

There are three common types of Kurdish dance: open-circle and line dances; solo dancing; and dancing in procession. The first type is forceful, energetic and joyful, and is danced by mixed or sexually segregated groups of 10 to 100 people. The arms of the participants are linked tightly in one of three handholds. The gestures include bounces, jumps and a strong rhythmical swinging of the arms. The step patterns are short and repetitive. Solo dancing is performed by one, two or three soloists who dance in the centre of a closed circle of seated people. Processional dancing takes place on special occasions such as weddings.

4. INSTRUMENTS. The few instruments employed by the Kurds are used to accompany dances, processions and religious ceremonies. The only chordophone is the *ṭanbūr* (long-necked lute; fig.3), which has two or

3. *Kurdish ṭanbūr (long-necked lute, also known as sāz), Syria*

4. Syrian Kurds playing zurna (shawms) and dola or dawul (double-headed drum)

three strings, plucked with the fingers, and 16 frets. There are two tunings, high and low; in each case the strings are tuned either in 5ths or in 4ths. The members of the Ahl-i Ḥaqq sect believe there is a correlation between perfect tuning and salvation.

The most important aerophone is the ZURNA (shawm), which is always coupled with the *dola* or *dawul* (see below, and fig.4). It has four separate pieces: a cylindrical wooden body, a wooden piece which fits into the top of the cylinder, a mouthpiece with a double reed, and a pirouette. It has seven finger-holes and one thumb-hole. The player's mouth covers the entire top of the mouthpiece, so that the double reed vibrates freely in the mouth cavity. The *duzala*, *dutke* or *miṭbaj* is a double-pipe clarinet, each pipe having six finger-holes and one thumb-hole. Alone or with a frame drum it is used to accompany dances and in the outdoor ceremonies of the Yazīdī sect. The NĀY, *shabbābah* or *balur* is an end-blown flute about 80 cm long, with six finger-holes and one thumb-hole. It is played by shepherds and by members of the Yazīdī sect, who consider such flutes sacred. Among the Yazīdī, flutes are played exclusively by the *qawwālūn* and are used together with frame drums, but only for the most sacred ceremonies.

Membranophones used by the Kurds include frame drums and the *dola* or *dawul*, a double-headed drum about 50 cm in diameter. The *dola* hangs over the front of the performer's right hip and is played with two beaters. Both types of drum are used in ensembles; the *dola* can also be used alone to accompany dance-songs.

See also ARAB MUSIC, §II; IRAQ; IRAN, §II.

BIBLIOGRAPHY
Komitas: *Kurdische Musik* (diss., U. of Berlin, 1899)
——: *Quelques spécimens des mélodies kourdes* (Moscow, 1904)
P. R. Olsen: 'Enregistrements faits à Kuwait et Bahrain', *Ethnomusicologie III: Wégimont V 1960*, 137–70
C. Celîl [Jalil]: *Kurdskiye narodnīye pesni: k'ilamêd cime'ta k'urda svyazannikh s pereselenyem ikh predkov v Rossiyu v 30-kh godakh XIX veka* [Heroic songs of the Yezidi Kurds on events connected with their ancestors' emigration], *Iranskaya filogiya: Leningrad 1962*
D. Christensen: 'Tanzlieder der Hakkâri-Kurden', *Jb für musikalische Volks- und Völkerkunde*, i (1963), 11–47
C. Celîl [Jalil]: *Kurdish National Popular Songs* (Erevan, 1964)
O. Celîl [Jalil]: *Diloked cime'ta k'orda* [Songs of the Kurdish people] (Erevan, 1964)
C. Celîl [Jalil]: *Kurdskiye narodnīye pesni: k'ilamêd cime'ta k'urda* [Kurdish folksongs] (Moscow, 1965)
D. Christensen: 'Kurdish Folk Music in Western Iran', FE 4103 [disc notes]
——: 'Zur Mehrstimmigkeit in kurdischen Wechselgesängen', *Festschrift für Walter Wiora* (Kassel, 1967), 571
M. Mokri: 'La musique sacrée des Kurdes "Fidèles de vérité" en Iran', *Encyclopédie des musiques sacrées*, i, ed. J. Porte (Paris, 1968), 441
J. P. Reiche: 'Stilelemente Süd-türkischer Davul-Zurna-Stücke', *Jb für musikalische Volks- und Völkerkunde*, v (1970), 9–54
E. Gerson-Kiwi: 'The Music of Kurdistani Jews', *Yuval*, ii (Jerusalem, 1971), 59

AMNON SHILOAH

Kurek, Marcin. *See* GALLINIUS, MARCIN.

Kuretzky, Josef Antonín. *See* GURECKÝ, JOSEF ANTONÍN.

Kuretzky, Václav Matyáš. *See* GURECKÝ, VÁCLAV MATYÁŠ.

Kuri-Aldana, Mario (*b* Tampico, Tamaulipas, 15 Aug 1931). Mexican composer. He studied the piano with del Castillo at the Academia Juan Sebastian Bach (1948–51) and composition with Vázquez, Tercero and Michaca at the Escuela Nacional de Música of the University of Mexico (1952–60), where he did research for a thesis, *Concepto mexicano de nacionalismo* (1963). At the Instituto Nacional de Bellas Artes (INBA) he studied conducting with Markevich and Giardino (1957–8), and he had private composition lessons with Herrera de la Fuente and Rodolfo Halffter (1961–2). A grant from the Di Tella Institute enabled him to pursue his composition studies there under Ginastera, Riccardo Malipiero, Messiaen, Maderna, Dallapiccola, Copland and Chase (1963–4), and in 1965 he had lessons from Stockhausen at the Mexico City Conservatory. He has held appointments as composition teacher at the Academia Juan Sebastian Bach, teacher of theory, harmony and counterpoint at the University of Mexico (1955–65), director of the Banda Sinfónica de la Secretaría de Educación Pública (1967–70), professor of music at the Academia de la Danza of the INBA, and honorary director of the Centro Libanés Chamber Orchestra (from 1971), which has commissioned and performed many of his works, including *Formas de otros tiempos*. In addition he has worked with enthusiasm in folk music research, being particularly interested in Spanish manuscripts as a primary source; he is a member of various folklore societies and has attended international conferences on the subject.

A traditionally orientated composer, Kuri-Aldana employs a folkloristic neo-classical style that may be traced to his teacher Halffter; but a broad and sure technique has allowed him to draw effectively on the styles of his diverse later teachers and of other composers. His versatility is shown by his ability to write songs and arrangements in an accessible manner (e.g. *María de Jésus* and *Peregrina agraciada*) as well as more sophisticated works, such as *Los cuatro bacabs* and *Candelaria*. The former resembles *mariachi* music in its insistent rhythmic formulae and characteristic parallel chords in 3rds to topical texts; *Candelaria* is a good deal more complicated, but never very adventurous in technique. Clarity and timbral contrast typify his mature works. His form tends to be non-linear, with added notes or rhythmic values enhancing the basically variation-type processes; such techniques, deployed in mosaic patterns, he learnt from Messiaen, and they have proved applicable to much Mexican Indian music. The sparse textures, extreme ranges, continual rhythmic metamorphoses and harmonic dissonances (superimposed 4ths in octave displacements) of his work make for great fluidity. In some works (e.g. *Xilofonias*, *Mascaras* and *Tres-silvestre*) he has steered a 'third-stream' middle course between his popular and cultivated styles.

WORKS
(selective list)

Orch: Suite antigua, str, 1956; Sym. no.1 'Sacrificio', 1959; Los cuatro bacabs (A. F. de Obregón), narrator, double wind orch, 1960; 3 piezas, str, ob obbl., 1960; Mascaras, mar, wind, 1962; Pasos, pf, orch, 1963; Bacab de las plegarias, chamber orch, 1966; Sym. no.2, str, 1966; Villa de reyes, chamber orch, 1968; Formas de otros tiempos, harp, str, 1971; Concierto de Santiago, fl, str orch, 2 perc, 1973; Concertino Mexicano, vn, orch, 1974; Sym. no.3 'Le Actal-1521', 1976

Choral: Peregrina agraciada, 1963; Lucero de Dios, Ave Maria (Khoury), chorus, org, 1969; Misa maronita, chorus, org, 1970, collab. G. Carrillo; In memoriam (cantable, J. Cortazar: Al Ché), Bar, chorus, band, 1971

Solo vocal: Principio de cuentas (A. Khoury), 1v, pf, 1953; Cantares para una niña muerta (Khoury), Mez, fl, gui, 1961; Estas cuatro (Khoury), 1v, pf, 1963; Aguardando su aurora (L. Cernuda), S, hn, harp, str orch, 1964; Este, ese y aquel (P. Urbina, Khoury, C. Vallejo), Mez, fl, str trio, vib, 1964; Amarillo era el color de la esperanza (secular oratorio, Khoury), Mez, narrator, jazz band, 1966; Maria de Jésus (canción ranchera, A. Kuri), 1968; Noche de Verano, S, narrator, orch, 1975; A mi hermano, Bar, chorus, orch, 1977

Inst: Suite ingenua, pf, 1953; Canto de Cinco-Flor, vc, pf, 1957; 3 nocturnos, cl, pf, 1957; 3 preludios, pf, 1958; Sonatina mexicana, vn, pf, 1959; Xilofonias, pic, ob, b cl, dbn, mar, xyl, 2 perc, 1963; Candelaria, wind qnt, 1965; Villancico, cancion y jarabe, pf, 1965; Tres-silvestre, ob, cl, bn, tpt, trbn, jazz drums, harp, vn, va, 1966; Fuga, brass, 1968; Pf Sonata, 1972

Principal publishers: Ediciones Mexicanas de Música, Editorial Argentina de Música, Música Rara, Ricordi Americana

BIBLIOGRAPHY
S. Kahan: 'El compositor Kuri-Aldana', *Carnet musical de X.E.L.A.* (Mexico City, 1963), 565

GERALD R. BENJAMIN

Kurka, Robert (Frank) (*b* Cicero, Ill., 22 Dec 1921; *d* New York, 12 Dec 1957). American composer. He studied briefly with Luening and Milhaud but was principally self-taught. Writing in a neo-classical style, he was influenced by the folk music of Czechoslovakia (his parents' birthplace), towards whose culture he felt drawn all his life. His work is most particularly characterized by its use of repeated melodic and rhythmic motifs, the appearance of dissonant elements within a tonal structure and an energetic rhythmic drive (notably in the Symphony no.2 and the Serenade). He received a Guggenheim grant (1951–2), an award from the National Institute of Arts and Letters (1952) and a Creative Arts Award from Brandeis University (1957).

WORKS
(selective list)

Opera: The Good Soldier Schweik, 2, perf. 1958; also concert suite

Orch: Sym. no.2, op.24, perf. 1958; Serenade, op.25, small orch, perf. 1954; Mar Conc., op.34, perf. 1958; several chamber concs., 4 other full orch pieces

Chamber: 5 str qts, incl. no.4, op.12, perf. 1950; 4 sonatas, vn, pf, incl. no.3, op.23, perf. 1953; Sonata, op.5, vn; Sonata, vc, pf; several small pieces

Pf: For the Piano, op.13, perf. 1951; other pieces

Vocal: few songs and choral pieces

JEFFREY LEVINE

Kurpiński, Karol Kazimierz (*b* Włoszakowice, Wielkopolska, 6 March 1785; *d* Warsaw, 18 Sept 1857). Polish composer, conductor and teacher. He first studied music with his father, Marcin Kurpiński (1744–1803), an organist at Włoszakowice. At the age of 12, he became organist at Sarnów (Wielkopolska), where his uncle Karol Wański was parish priest. In 1800 another of his mother's brothers, the cellist Roch Wański, took him to Moszków (Małopolska), the estate of Feliks

Polanowski, an amateur composer who had a private orchestra of which Wański was a member, and in which the young Kurpiński played second violin. It was probably at this time (before 1808) that he composed his first opera, *Pygmalion*, now lost. In 1808 he became resident music master to the Rastawiecki family in Lwów, and in 1810 settled in Warsaw. With the help of Elsner he became deputy conductor and from 1824 principal conductor of the Warsaw Opera, a position he held until 1840. He taught music at the schools of drama (1812 and 1817) and singing (1835–40) which he himself had founded. In 1815 he became a member of the Warsaw Society of Friends of Learning, and was also a member of many musical societies in Poland and abroad, including the Société des Enfants d'Apollon in Paris. He became Kapellmeister of the Polish royal chapel in 1819 and in the same year received a medal for his services to music. In 1820–21 he founded and edited the first Polish music periodical, *Tygodnik muzyczny* ('Music weekly'). He was decorated with the Order of St Stanisław in 1823, when he also travelled to Germany, France, Italy and Austria in the service of music. He married Zofia Brzowska (1799–1879), a singer in the Warsaw Opera.

Along with Elsner, Kurpiński was a central figure in the musical life of Warsaw, and conducted Chopin's first public concerts there. One of the most talented Polish composers before Chopin, he helped to lay the foundations of a national style and prepared the ground for Polish music of the Romantic period. Gifted with exceptional creative originality, he contributed to the development of Polish opera, introducing new musical devices and achieving an intensified dramatic expression. Programmatic tendencies and formal innovations are evident in his instrumental works. Operas and polonaises (for piano or orchestra) form the largest part of his output. His operas were successful at the time and some, for instance *Zamek na Czorsztynie* ('The castle of Czorsztyn'), have not lost their appeal. Of his 24 stage works, nine survive complete and eight in part, while the rest have been lost. Although brought up on the Viennese Classics, Kurpiński followed the spirit of his times, combining the new achievements of European music with the folklore of his own country.

WORKS
(selective list)
STAGE

Pygmalion (opera), *c*1800–08, lost

Pałac Lucypera [The palace of Lucifer] (opera, 4, A. Żółkowski), Warsaw, 9 Nov 1811, *D-Dlb*

Marcinowa w Seraju [Mistress Marcin of the harem] (comic opera, 3, W. Pękalski), Warsaw, 20 March 1812, ov. (Leipzig, 1822)

Szarlatan, czyli Wskrzeszenie umarłych [The charlatan, or The raising of the dead] (opera, 2, Pękalski), Warsaw, 23 Jan 1814, MS in Poznań theatre library

Jadwiga królowa Polska [Jadwiga, Queen of Poland] (opera, 3, J. U. Niemcewicz), Warsaw, 23 Dec 1814, *PL-Wtm*, ov. (Leipzig, 1822)

Zabobon, czyli Krakowiacy i górale, albo Nowe Krakowiaki [Superstition, or Krakovians and mountaineers, or The new Krakovians] (opera, 3, J. N. Kamiński), Warsaw, 16 June 1816, *Wtm*

Jan Kochanowski w Czarnym Lesie [Jan Kochanowski at Czarny Las] (opéra comique, 2, Niemcewicz), Warsaw, 1 Jan 1817, ov. *Wtm*

Czaromysł książę słowiański [Czaromysł the Slav prince] (opera, 1, Żółkowski), Warsaw, 27 March 1818, *Kj*, *Wn*

Nowa osada Terpsychory nad Wisłą [Terpsichore's new colony on the Vistula] (ballet, L. Thierry), Warsaw, 13 Aug 1818, extracts arr. pf (Warsaw, 1818)

Zamek na Czorsztynie, czyli Bojomir i Wanda [The castle of Czorsztyn, or Bojomir and Wanda] (opera, 2, J. W. Krasiński), Warsaw, 5 March 1819 (Kraków, 1969)

Kalmora, czyli Prawo ojcowskie Amerykanów [Kalmora, or The paternal right of the Americans] (melodrama, 2, K. Brodziński), Warsaw, 10 Feb 1820, ov. (Leipzig, 1826)

Mars i Flora [Mars and Flora] (ballet, 1, Thierry), Warsaw, 3 Aug 1820, arr. pf *Wtm*, extracts (Warsaw, 1821)

Leśniczy z Kozienickiej Puszczy [The foresters of Kozienice] (opera, 1, Krasiński), Warsaw, 28 Oct 1821, *Wn*

Trzy gracje [The three graces] (ballet, Thierry), Warsaw, 2 June 1822

Cecylia Piaseczyńska (opera, 2, L. Dmuszewski), Warsaw, 31 May 1829, extracts (Warsaw, 1829)

VOCAL

Sacred: 6 masses, incl. Msza wiejska [Country mass] (A. Feliński) (Warsaw, 1821); Oratorio, 4vv, 2 tpt, 2 trbn, db, timp, org, *Wtm*

Cantatas: Cantata on the anniversary of Napoleon's coronation, 1810; Elegia na śmierć Tadeusza Kościuszki [Elegy on the death of Tadeusz Kościuszko], 1819 (Warsaw, 1820); Cantata on the unveiling of the Copernicus monument, Warsaw, 1830

Songs: Warszawianka [The song of Warsaw] (C. Delavigne, trans. K. Sienkiewicz) (Warsaw, 1831); Litwinka [The song of the Lithuanian legionaries] (S. J. Cywiński) (Warsaw, 1831); other songs

INSTRUMENTAL

Orch: Wielka symfonia bitwę wyobrážająca [Grand battle sym.], op.15, *Kj*; Wielka fuga na temat 'Jeszcze Polska nie zginęła' [Grand fugue on the song 'Poland has not perished yet'], arr. pf (Warsaw, 1821); Potpourri, czyli Wariacje z róžnych tematów narodowych [Potpourri, or Variations on national themes], pf, orch (Warsaw, 1822); Cl Conc., *Wtm*, arr. cl, pf (Kraków, 1950); polonaises

Chamber: Fantaisie en quatuor, *Wtm*; Trio, cl, vn, vc; Dumanie nad mogiłą Wandy [Reverie over Wanda's tomb], vn, pf (Warsaw, 1820); Nocturn, hn, bn, va, op.16 (Leipzig, 1823); Paysage musical, hn, bn, op.18 (Leipzig, 1823); Cavatina, tpt/trbn, pf (Kraków, 1953)

Pf: Chwila snu okropnego [A dreadful dream] (Warsaw, 1820); Le réveil de J. J. Rousseau au printemps (Warsaw, 1821); 9 variations (Warsaw, 1821); Fantaisie, a (Leipzig, 1821); Fantaisie, op.10 (Leipzig, 1823); 6 variations (Leipzig, 1823); polonaises; mazurkas; waltzes

WRITINGS

Wykład systematyczny zasad muzyki na klawikord [Systematic exposition of the principles of music for the clavichord] (Warsaw, 1818)

Zasady harmonii tonów z dołączeniem jeneral basu praktycznego [The principles of tonal harmony and a practical guide to figured bass] (Warsaw, 1821)

Zasady harmonii wykładane w sposobie lekcji dla lubowników muzyki [The principles of harmony set out in lessons for music lovers] (Warsaw, 1844)

BIBLIOGRAPHY

SMP

A. Hedley, ed.: *Selected Correspondence of Fryderyk Chopin* (London, 1962)

T. Przybylski: *Karol Kurpiński, 1785–1857* (Warsaw, 1975)

ALINA NOWAK-ROMANOWICZ

Kurrende (from Lat. *currere*: 'to run', or *corradere*: 'to scrape together', 'to beg'). A term in use from the 16th century onwards for itinerant boys' choirs trained in the Latin grammar-schools in Germany. Its members, lacking financial support, begged alms from the townsfolk by singing in the streets and squares or from house to house; in addition, their services were engaged occasionally for special functions such as weddings and funerals. The custom is still current in Germany.

BIBLIOGRAPHY

F. Krautwurst: 'Kurrende', *MGG* [incl. extensive bibliography]

Kurt(-Deri), Melanie (*b* Vienna, 8 Jan 1880; *d* New York, 11 March 1941). Austrian soprano. She originally studied the piano with Leschetizky at the Vienna Conservatory, touring from 1897 to 1900 as a concert pianist. She had, however, begun singing lessons with Fannie Müller in 1896, and in 1902 she made her stage début in Lübeck as Elisabeth. After a season in Leipzig (1903–4) she withdrew for further study with Lilli and Marie Lehmann in Berlin. In 1905 she joined the Brunswick Staatsoper, later being engaged at Berlin (from 1908) and Charlottenburg (from 1912), and also making guest appearances at Covent Garden in 1910 (as Sieglinde and then Brünnhilde in *Die Walküre*) and 1914 (as Kundry). She sang at the Metropolitan Opera from 1914 until 1917, mostly in the Wagnerian reper-

tory – her début performance (1 February 1914) as Isolde won praise both for vocal freshness and finished artistry – but also in *Iphigénie en Tauride*, and as Beethoven's Leonore, Pamina, Santuzza and the Marschallin. When the USA entered World War I, her Metropolitan contract, and thus her American career, were terminated. In 1920 she returned to Germany and joined the Berlin Volksoper, where she sang until 1925. She taught singing in Berlin from 1925, and later in Vienna, returning to New York in 1938. She possessed a rich and powerful dramatic soprano and outstanding dramatic presence.

BIBLIOGRAPHY

L. Riemens: 'Kurt, Melanie', *Le grandi voci* (Rome, 1964) [with opera discography]

HAROLD ROSENTHAL

Kurtág, György (*b* Lugoj, Romania, 19 Feb 1926). Hungarian composer of Romanian birth. He began his studies in Timişoara with Magda Kardos (piano) and Eisikovits (composition). In 1946 he moved to Hungary (he became a citizen two years later) and entered the Budapest Academy of Music, where he studied composition with Veress and then with Farkas, the piano with Kadosa and chamber music with Weiner; he took diplomas in all three subjects in 1955. In 1957 he attended the composition classes given by Milhaud and Messiaen at the Paris Conservatoire, also studying with Marianne Stein; a scholarship enabled him to study in Berlin during 1971. Kurtág worked as coach and tutor at the Bartók Secondary Music School (1958–63) and fulfilled the same function within the National Philharmonia from 1960 to 1968, training the best young Hungarian performers. In 1967 he was appointed to the staff of the Budapest Academy of Music, first as professor of piano and then of chamber music. He has received three Erkel Prizes (1954, 1956, 1969) and the Kossuth Prize (1973).

A first and continuing influence on Kurtág's work was the piano music of Bartók; he made a study of Bartók's oeuvre while at the Budapest Academy, but his period in Paris broadened his outlook, and it is from that time that the first published works date. Earlier pieces, chief among them the *Koreai kantáta* and the Viola Concerto, were indebted to the school of Bartók and Kodály; Kurtág's op.1 shows unmistakable signs of a new orientation. The definitive experiences which shaped this change of direction were the Domaine Musical concerts in Paris, the music of Webern, Stockhausen's *Gruppen* and Kurtág's association with Ligeti. After his op.1 Kurtág composed slowly: during the period 1959–73 he published only eight works, a total of less than 90 minutes of music.

Kurtág's published output is very homogeneous: each piece is built from small-scale structures whose condensation recalls Webern, and Kurtág shares the latter's characteristic of expressivity controlled by impeccable technique. The intricate lines, the free use of octave transpositions and the disjunct prosody all form part of Webern's heritage, although the influence of Bachian or Renaissance counterpoint is also present. Kurtág has made use of Webernian serialism, but never with the purity of Webern, and only within a single movement or passage. His music also employs pitch complementarity and other non-serial 12-note procedures; his approximately 12-note themes are sometimes close to Bartók or to the 'free atonal' works of Schoenberg, Berg and

Webern. Rhythmically Kurtág has also drawn on Bartók, on Hungarian speech and on strophic peasant song, which sometimes influences his pitch structuring towards tonal polarity or pentatony. Bartókian characteristics appear too in the arch form of the String Quartet, while *Bornemisza Péter mondásai* ('The sayings of Péter Bornemisza') shows the Lisztian principle of thematic transformation. A further link with Hungary is Kurtág's predilection for the cimbalom.

The Sayings of Péter Bornemisza is one of Kurtág's major works, and an outstanding contribution to postwar Hungarian music. Described as a 'concerto' for soprano and piano, it falls into 24 short movements lasting for 37 minutes. All of Kurtág's earlier published pieces had been purely instrumental; this work reflects his interests in Hungarian literature and history, the text being taken from a 16th-century sermon. Two further vocal compositions followed: op.8 tends towards broader, lied-like melodic phrases, whereas the aphoristic op.9 is more instrumental in conception.

WORKS

Suite, pf, 1943; Klárisok (A. József), chorus, 1949; Suite, pf duet, 1950; Koreai kantáta, 1953; Va Conc., 1954

Str Qt, op.1, 1959; Wind Qnt, op.2, 1959; 8 Pieces, op.3, pf, 1960; 8 Duos, op.4, vn, cimb, 1961; Jelek [Signs], op.5, va, 1961; Cinque merrycate, op.6, gui, 1961, inc.; Bornemisza Péter mondásai [The sayings of Péter Bornemisza], op.7, S, pf, 1963–8; Egy téli alkony emlékére [In memory of a winter sunset], op.8 (P. Gulyás), S, vn, cimb, 1969; 4 capriccios, op.9 (I. Balint), S, wind qnt, harp, pf, perc, cimb, str qnt, 1971; 4 songs, op.11 (J. Pilinszky), lv, cl, hn, cimb, str trio, zither ad lib, 1973–5; Splitter, op.6c, cimb, 1975; Splitter, op.6d, pf, 1978

Incidental music: The Servant of Two Masters (Goldoni), 1956; Mandragola (Machiavelli), 1956; Hamlet (Shakespeare), 2 sets, 1956, 1962; Vihar [The tempest] (Shakespeare), 1959; Csongor és Tünde (Vörösmarty), 1962

Principal publishers: Editio musica, Universal

BIBLIOGRAPHY

I. Földes: *Harmincasok* (Budapest, 1969), 185ff, 205ff
G. Kroó: *Miért szép századunk zenéje?* [Why is 20th-century music so beautiful?] (Budapest, 1974)

GYÖRGY KROÓ

Kurth, Ernst (*b* Vienna, 1 June 1886; *d* Berne, 2 Aug 1946). Swiss musicologist of Austrian birth. He studied music history at Vienna University under Adler and privately with Robert Grund and in 1908 took the doctorate with a dissertation on Gluck's early operas up to *Orfeo*. After a short spell as conductor, he taught for a time at the Freie Schulgemeinde at Wickersdorf. In 1912 Kurth completed his *Habilitation* at Berne University with a dissertation on the theory of harmony. He was appointed reader in 1920 and from 1927 until his death held the chair of musicology. He was also the founder and editor of the *Berner Veröffentlichungen zur Musikforschung*.

Kurth was a creative thinker as well as an inspiring teacher who was able to impart to his students his deeply intuitive and dynamic approach to music. At surprisingly short intervals he published a number of works of the greatest importance, both to musicology and philosophy. His *Grundlagen des linearen Kontrapunkts* (1917), in which he examined the linear and motoric aspects of melody, made his international reputation: the book had an enormous influence not only on Bach research but on the teaching of counterpoint and composition. It was followed by *Romantische Harmonik* (1920), a work which is both a harmony textbook for advanced students and a guide to the philosophical aspects of Romantic harmony. Kurth regarded chords as 'reflexes of the unconscious', and he distin-

guished two polarized 'constructive' and 'destructive' forces in Romantic harmony; for him the first chord in *Tristan* was a symbol of the Romantic attitude of mind.

Kurth's most extensive work was that on Bruckner (1925) where in addition to providing an acute biographical study he developed his theory of musical form, which he believed was not a static pattern but a creative process. His findings are summarized in *Musikpsychologie* (1931), where, as opposed to the 'psychology of sound', music and sound are regarded as proceeding from the composer's being and not from outside. This philosophical basis of Kurth's thought stems from Schopenhauer's conception of music as the manifestation of a will that created both the world and its culture; and it was on this and on Freud's theory of the subconscious mind that Kurth founded the central idea of all his work – that of psychic energy.

See also ANALYSIS, §II, 6.

WRITINGS

Der Stil der opera seria von Gluck bis zum Orfeo (diss., U. of Vienna, 1908; 'Die Jugendopern Glucks bis Orfeo', *SMw*, i (1913), 193–277)
'Zur "Ars cantus mensurabilis" des Franko von Köln', *KJb*, xxi (1908), 39
Die Voraussetzungen der theoretischen Harmonik und der tonalen Darstellungssysteme (Habilitationsschrift, U. of Berne, 1912; Berne, 1913)
Grundlagen des linearen Kontrapunkts (Berne, 1917, 5/1956)
'Zur Motivbildung Bachs', *BJb*, xiv (1917), 80–136
Romantische Harmonik und die Krise in Wagners Tristan (Berne, 1920/R1968, 3/1923)
Bruckner (Berlin, 1925/R1971)
'Die Schulmusik und ihre Reform', *SMz*, lxx (1930), 297
Musikpsychologie (Berlin, 1931/R1969, 2/1947)

BIBLIOGRAPHY

E. Bücken: 'Kurth als Musiktheoretiker', *Melos*, iv (1924–5), 358
H. Eimert: 'Bekenntnis und Methode', *ZMw*, ix (1926–7), 99
J. Handschin: 'De différentes conceptions de Bach', *Schweizerisches Jb für Musikwissenschaft*, iv (1929), 18
W. Schuh: 'Ernst Kurth zum 60. Geburtstag', *SMz*, lxxxvi (1946), 302
K. von Fischer: 'In memoriam Ernst Kurth', *Der Musikalmanach*, viii (1948), 228
W. Kreidler: 'Ernst Kurth', *Mf*, ii (1949), 9
H. Pfrogner: *Musik: Geschichte ihrer Deutung* (Freiburg, 1954), 357ff
D. Menstell Hsu: 'Ernst Kurth and his Concept of Music as Motion', *JMT*, x (1966), 2
C. Dahlhaus: *Untersuchungen über die Entstehung der harmonischen Tonalität* (Kassel, 1967)
W. Seidel: *Über Rhythmustheorien der Neuzeit* (Berne and Munich, 1975)

KURT VON FISCHER/EDITH B. SCHNAPPER

Kurtz, Efrem (*b* St Petersburg, 7 Nov 1900). American conductor of Russian birth. He studied with Nikolay Tcherepnin and Glazunov at the St Petersburg Conservatory; he then went to Riga University and the Stern Conservatory, Berlin. He made his début at Berlin in 1921, deputizing for Nikisch in a dance programme given by Isadora Duncan. He became musical director of the Stuttgart Philharmonic, 1924–33, and also toured with Anna Pavlova in Europe, Australia and South America during the three years before her death in 1931; he made his first visit to Britain at that time. He spent eight years (1933–41) as musical director of the Ballets Russes de Monte Carlo (successor to the Dyagilev company), touring widely in Europe and the USA.

After settling in the USA, where he took American nationality in 1944, he became musical director of the Kansas City SO (1943–7) and the Houston SO (1948–54), improving the standards and prestige of both orchestras. From 1954 he was a freelance conductor, giving concerts in Leningrad and Moscow in 1966 (his first return since 1919), and with operatic engagements at Rome and Milan. His repertory was wide, though he specialized in Russian music, and he directed performances of colourful yet sensitive vitality. He was married to the flautist Elaine Shaffer.

NOËL GOODWIN

Kürtzinger. *See* KÜRZINGER family.

Kurz [Kurtz, Kurz-Bernardon, Bernardon], **(Johann) Joseph Felix von** (*b* Vienna, 22 Feb 1717; *d* Vienna, 3 Feb 1784). Austrian comic actor, singer, dramatist and theatre manager. The son of the actor–manager Felix Kurz, and godson of 'Hanswurst' Stranitzky and J. B. Hilverding, he grew up in the theatre, and by the age of 20 he was performing leading roles with the German troupe at Vienna's Kärntnertor-Theater under the direction of Stranitzky's successor, Gottfried Prehauser. From 1740 until 1744 Kurz acted, sang and danced in Germany (most notably in Frankfurt am Main and Dresden). During his second period in Vienna, 1744–53, he developed and perfected the kind of magic burlesque, generously larded with songs, choruses, ensembles and incidental music, that dominated the popular repertory in most of the southern German lands. In a lengthy series of plays, mainly of his own devising, he appeared as Bernardon, a lively, urbane, satirical comic character. After the imperial ban on extemporization, Kurz moved in 1753 to Prague, where he was Locatelli's sub-lessee and director at the 'Kotzentheater'. From 1754 until 1760 he was back in Vienna, earning notoriety for his lavish spectacles, and lasting renown for the high standard of the music offered in his company's performances (Haydn was Kurz's collaborator in *Der (neue) krumme Teufel*; earlier Ignaz Holzbauer had written a score for a comedy by Weiskern, 1746). Kurz was in Prague again in autumn 1760, and subsequently he appeared at Venice and Pressburg (now Bratislava), Munich and Nuremberg. In 1767–8 he performed in a number of German cities, moving as far north as Cologne. During this period the great Schröder was a member of the company. Kurz was in Vienna again in 1769–71, as co-lessee with Gluck; his productions included *La serva padrona* and a revival of *Der krumme Teufel*. In 1771 Kurz toured via Breslau and Danzig to Warsaw, where he directed the theatre and, after his retirement, ran a paper factory.

In 1743 Kurz married Franziska Toscani, and in 1758, three years after her death, he married Teres(in)a Morelli. Both his wives and his numerous children were members of his troupe; Teresa especially was an important artist in her own right, being chosen in 1770 to create the role of Amor in Gluck's *Paride ed Elena*. Kurz himself was a versatile singer; in one of his own comic operas he sang the three principal parts (falsetto, tenor and bass). As a comic actor he was brilliantly successful. If his extemporizations offended both Maria Theresia and Joseph von Sonnenfels (the principal figure in the Viennese Enlightenment), they continued to refer to him quite frequently. As a theatre impresario, Kurz did not ignore the growing demand for regular plays and serious operas, but he is best remembered as an inventive comic dramatist and actor, with a full and remarkably early appreciation of the role of music in the theatre; he may indeed be said to have introduced the first works that can be recognized as modern Singspiels.

BIBLIOGRAPHY

C. H. Schmid: *Chronologie des deutschen Theaters* (Leipzig, 1775); ed. P. Legband (Berlin, 1902)
O. Teuber: *Geschichte des Prager Theaters*, i (Prague, 1883)
——: *Das k.k. Hofburgtheater seit seiner Begründung* (Vienna, 1896)
F. Raab: *Johann Joseph Felix von Kurz, gennant Bernardon* (Frankfurt, 1899)
A. von Weilen: *Geschichte des Wiener Theaterwesens* (Vienna, 1899)
——: 'Johann Joseph Felix von Kurz, genannt Bernardon', *Euphorion*, vi (1899), 350
M. Pirker, ed.: *Teutsche Arien* (Vienna, 1927)
O. Rommel, ed.: *Die Maschinenkomödie* (Leipzig, 1935/R1974)
——: *Die Alt-Wiener Volkskomödie* (Vienna, 1952)
U. Birbaumer: *Das Werk des Joseph Felix von Kurz-Bernardon und seine szenische Realisierung* (Vienna, 1971)
G. Zechmeister: *Die Wiener Theater nächst der Burg und nächst dem Kärntnerthor von 1747 bis 1776* (Vienna, 1971)
P. Branscombe: 'Music in the Viennese Popular Theatre of the Eighteenth and Nineteenth Centuries', *PRMA*, xcviii (1971–2), 101
PETER BRANSCOMBE

Kurz, Selma (*b* Biala, Silesia, 15 Oct 1874; *d* Vienna, 10 May 1933). Austrian soprano. A pupil of Johannes Ress, she made her début in Hamburg on 12 May 1895 as Mignon. In 1896 she began an engagement at Frankfurt, but after three years Mahler summoned her to Vienna, where she made her first appearance, again as Mignon, on 3 September 1899. Thenceforward Vienna became the centre of her artistic and private life. Her success was very great in a wide variety of lyrical and dramatic soprano roles, including Tosca and even Sieglinde, but she soon became particularly famous in the coloratura repertory, notably as Verdi's Gilda and Oscar; as Violetta in *La traviata* she was as happily suited by the florid writing of the first act as by the lyrical cantilena and pathos of the remainder. Gifted with a soprano voice of remarkable purity, sweetness and ease, she also possessed a shake of fabulous perfection and duration, which she was accustomed to display – by no means inappropriately – in an inserted cadenza to Oscar's teasing 'Saper vorreste'. In 1904, 1905 and 1907 she dazzled Covent Garden audiences in *Rigoletto* and *Un ballo in maschera*, appearing there also as Wagner's Elisabeth, Gounod's Juliet and the page in *Les Huguenots*; her English success would perhaps have been more lasting but for the rivalry of Melba, and she did not reappear at Covent Garden until 1924, when she sang Mimì and Violetta. In 1916 she became the first Zerbinetta in the revised version of Strauss's *Ariadne auf Naxos* in Vienna, where she continued to sing until 1927. Her rare American appearances were confined to the concert room. She married in 1910; her daughter, Desi Halban, became a professional singer. Kurz's numerous records, both for HMV and for Deutsche Grammophon, rank among the most successful of their type and period; especially noteworthy are her unaccompanied 'Lockruf' from Goldmark's *Königin von Saba* and numerous versions of her *cheval de bataille*, 'Saper vorreste'.

BIBLIOGRAPHY

D. Halban and others: 'Selma Kurz', *Record Collector*, xiii (1960), 53 [with discography by A. E. Knight]
D. Halban: 'My Mother Selma Kurz', *Recorded Sound* (1973), no.49, p.128
DESMOND SHAWE-TAYLOR

Kurz, Siegfried (*b* Dresden, 18 July 1930). East German conductor and composer. At the Dresden Hochschule für Musik (1945–50) he studied composition with Finke, conducting with Hintze and the trumpet with Seifert. He was music director of the Dresden Staatstheater (1949–60) and then conductor of the Dresden Staatsoper. Both as conductor and composer he displays precision and virtuosity; his music retains a spontaneity of feeling despite its accomplished technique. His Trumpet Concerto, rhythmically lively in its use of jazz ideas, won great popularity. The String Quartet shows the influence of Bartók in its thematic concentration (an influence also detectable in other pieces), and in the symphonies Kurz made unorthodox use of 12-note procedures.

WORKS
(selective list)

Orch: Divertimento, pf, str, 1950; Heiteres Vorspiel, 1952; Konzertante Musik, 1952; Sinfonia piccola, 1953; Conc., tpt, str, 1953; Tänzerische Suite, 1954; Vn Conc., 1955; 2 syms., 1958, 1959; Orchestermusik, 1960; Chamber Conc., wind qnt, str, 1962; Pf Conc., 1964; Sonatine, 1970; Musik, brass, timp, str, 1970; Hn Conc., 1973

Chamber: Wind Qnt, 1949; Sonatine, 7 brass, 1952; Str Qt, 1957

Stage: Jeff and Andy, musical, n.d.; incidental music

Kurz, Vilém (*b* Německý Brod [now Havlíčkův Brod], 23 Dec 1872; *d* Prague, 25 May 1945). Czech pianist and teacher. He studied the piano with Julius Höger (1884–6) and Jakub Virgil Holfeld (1886–98) and theory and the organ at the Prague Organ School (1886–7); he took the state music examinations at the Prague Conservatory in 1892. During his short but highly successful career as a soloist he gave solo recitals in Prague (1895), Vienna and Berlin (1897), introducing new works by Suk and Novák (who dedicated his Ballade after *Manfred* to him); he also appeared as a chamber player in the Czech Trio (which he founded) and with the Czech Quartet. As professor of piano at Lwów Conservatory (1898–1919) he developed a new style of piano teaching which he implemented on his return to Czechoslovakia, as professor of the graduate piano classes at the Brno Conservatory (1919–20) and at the Prague Conservatory, first at its Brno branch (1920–28) and then in Prague (1928–40), where he was also rector (1936–7, 1938–9). His method, which greatly influenced Czech piano teaching and playing, combined the Czech traditions of Proksch and Holfeld with Leschetizky's method and new psychophysiological concepts, paying particular attention to touch, phrasing and pedalling and to the style and content of the piece. His pupils included Rudolf Firkušný, his daughter Ilona Kurzová and her husband Václav Štěpán, František Maxián, Ilja Hurník and Rudolf Macudzinský. He was editor-in-chief of the series *Klavírní Repertoir* (published by Hudební Matice from 1935) and edited standard classical works and studies, as well as contemporary works (e.g. Janáček's *On the Overgrown Path*), and made a much used revision of Dvořák's Piano Concerto.

WRITINGS

Postup při vyučovací hře na klavír [Scheme for teaching the piano] (Prague, 1921, rev. 2/1930, 3/1936)

O klavírních methodách starších i novějších [Piano methods, both old and new] (Brno, 1922)

Technické základy klavírní hry [The theoretical basis of playing the piano] (Prague, 1924, 8/1958)

ČSHS [with list of writings and editions, and bibliography]

Z. Böhmová-Zahradníčková: *Vilém Kurz: život, práce, methodika* [Kurz's life, work and methods] (Prague, 1954)

GRACIÁN ČERNUŠÁK/R

Kurzbach, Paul (*b* Hohndorf, Erzgebirge, 13 Dec 1902). German composer and administrator. He attended a teacher training college (1916–23) and the Leipzig Conservatory (1925–8), having studied music intensively from 1920. From 1921 to 1933, while teaching in a primary school, he conducted several workers' choirs in Chemnitz (later Karl-Marx-Stadt). Through his advocacy of Eisler's works (in 1931 he painstakingly rehearsed *Die Massnahme*, for example) he got to know the composer personally, but it was the influence of Orff, with whom he was associated between 1939 and 1943, that was of decisive significance for his own music. After 1945 he held various posts in cultural administration, including that of secretary to the Composers' Union, of which he was made a vice-president in 1968. Subsequently he supported himself as a freelance composer in Karl-Marx-Stadt, receiving commissions from factory groups and from orchestras. He has gradually toned down the Orffian percussive style of his work in favour of a consistently tonal 'friendly tendency', to use his own words.

WORKS
(selective list)

Operas: Historia de Susanna, Göttingen and Magdeburg, 1948; Thomas Müntzer, Magdeburg, 1955; Thyl Claes, Görlitz, 1958

Orch: Sym., C, 1953; Hpd Conc., 1957; Bauernmusik, 1958; Thyl Claes, musical portrait, 1961; 7 serenades, 1964–74; Concertino, pf, str, 1965; Variationen über eine Melodie von Purcell, 1968; Vn Conc., 1969

Cantatas: Brecht-Kantate, 1950; Kantate der Freundschaft, 1959; Hymnus auf die Ära freundlicher Zeiten, 1961; Alles wandelt sich (Brecht), 1971; Macht die Welt uns bunt, 1971; Portrait eines Arbeiters, 1971

Other vocal works: 6 Lieder, B, pf, 1963; 4 Lieder, Bar, orch, 1967; other songs, mass songs

Inst: 4 str qts, 1945, 1947, 1948, 1958; 3 pf sonatinas, 1947, 1947, 1963; Trio, ob, cl, bn, 1958; Sonatina, vc, pf, 1961; Sonatina, vn, pf, 1962; Wind Sextet, 1962; Pf Trio, 1968

BIBLIOGRAPHY

E. Rebling: 'Die Oper "Thomas Müntzer" von Paul Kurzbach', *Musik und Gesellschaft*, v/9 (1955), 3

P. Kurzbach: 'Bemerkungen zur Situation der Gegenwartsoper', *In eigener Sache: zehn Jahre Verband deutscher Komponisten und Musikwissenschaftler* (Berlin, 1961)

H. Brock: 'Das Freundliche, ein Wesenszug unserer Musik: zum Violinkonzert Paul Kurzbachs', *Musik und Gesellschaft*, xx (1970), 757

HELLMUT KÜHN

Kurze Oktave (Ger.). SHORT OCTAVE.

Kürzinger [Kürtzinger, Kirzinger, Kyrzinger, Khierzinger]. Bavarian family of musicians and composers in the 17th and 18th centuries.

(1) Johann Kürzinger (*b* Geisenfeld, nr. Ingolstadt, *fl* 1620–30). He was the organist at the St Nikolaus church in Passau in about 1624. His known works are *Lesbij modi. 1, 2, 3, 4 voci ... Liber primus ... ab organo* (Passau, 1624), and a four-voice motet, *Benedicite omnia opera Domini* in Victorinus's *Philomela coelestis sive ... Cantiones sacrae* (Munich, 1624).

(2) Ignaz Franz Xaver Kürzinger (*b* Rosenheim, Upper Bavaria, 30 Jan 1724; *d* Würzburg, 12 Aug 1797). Instrumentalist and composer. He was the son of J. Anton Kürzinger, principal town musician in Rosenheim. He was sent to a seminary in Innsbruck to prepare for the priesthood, but he left in 1740 to become a trumpeter in a Hungarian cuirassier regiment. During the First Silesian War he was taken prisoner and brought to Berlin, where C. H. Graun took an interest in his musical abilities and gave him composition lessons. After Kürzinger's release from prison, he travelled to Bonn, meeting the Elector Clemens August of Cologne, who took him on a journey to Italy and subsequently made him a grand master of the Teutonic Knights. In the order's chapel in Mergentheim, Württemberg, he performed many musical duties, and in 1751 he was appointed Kapellmeister. He remained in Mergentheim until 1763 when he joined the court orchestra of the Prince-bishop at Würzburg as a violinist. Shortly thereafter he became the music director of the orphanage at the Julius hospital, where his students included the Abbé Vogler. He is known to have composed a school drama with music, *Fides et Perfidia*, an oratorio, *Der sterbende Heiland*, a large amount of church music, violin and guitar pieces, and secular vocal music, most of which was lost in World War II. The only works known to be extant are a *Missa solemnis* in D (1794; *D-EB*), a cantata *Wut und Liebe* (autograph keyboard score, *Bds*), and *David et Apollo … sive VIII Symphoniae solemniores*, op.1, for orchestra (Augsburg, 1750). Of more than passing interest is his manual *Getreuer Unterricht zum Singen mit Manieren, und die Violin zu spielen* (Augsburg, 1763, 5/1821), which provides a particularly good picture of the elementary music instruction prevalent in church schools of the mid-18th century. Kürzinger's informative discussions of the various vocal ornaments employed in sacred music are important and have been little noted in musicological literature.

(3) **Fortunatus Kürzinger** (*b* 1743; *d* Freising, 31 March 1805). Singer in the chapel of the Prince-bishop of Freising as a boy and later as a tenor. From 1766 to 1783 he served as chapel prefect and acted as substitute for the Kapellmeister, Placidus Camerloher, as director of the chapel musicians.

(4) **Paul Ignaz Kürzinger** (*b* Mergentheim, Württemberg, 28 April 1750; *d* Vienna, after 1820). Composer, son of (2) Ignaz Franz Xaver, from whom he received his musical training. As a violinist he joined the orchestra of the electoral court at Munich in 1775, where in the same year his opera *La Contessina* was produced. Two years later he went to Regensburg to play in the orchestra of the Prince of Thurn and Taxis, and he directed the court opera theatre there from 1780 to 1783. While in Regensburg he wrote a number of operas and ballets. Later he moved to Vienna, where he continued to write theatrical works, including the opera *Die Illumination* for the Burgtheater in 1787. He became music director at a private school in Vienna, and remained there for the rest of his life.

WORKS
STAGE WORKS
(*all performed in Regensburg and in D-Rtt unless otherwise stated*)
La Contessina (dramma giocoso per musica, Goldoni), Munich, 1775
Das Neujahrsfest in China (ballet), c1780
Inkle und Yoriko (ballet), c1780
Hebe, Göttin der Jugend (ballet), 1780
Robert und Kalliste (comic opera, J. J. Eschenburg), 1780
Cora und Alonzo (melodrama, d'Albonico-Roland), 1781
Ulissens Rückkunft nach Ithaka (ballet), 1781
Der Bergknappen (opera), 1782
Der von der Liebe gebändigte Kriegsgott (ballet), 1783
Die Illumination (comic opera), Vienna, 1787, music lost

OTHER WORKS
6 Lieder (Vienna, 1789)
12 Deutsche Tänze (Vienna, 1792)
Hofball-Tänze, pf (Munich, 1816)
La sconfitta di sisara, cantata, solo vv, chorus, orch, *A-Wgm*; 2 Duette, 1781, 1 Quartett, 1792, solo vv, insts, *Wgm*; 3 Neujahrsprologe, vv, insts, *D-Rtt*; 4 Sinfonien, insts, *Rtt*

BIBLIOGRAPHY
EitnerQ; GerberL; GerberNL
O. Kaul: *Geschichte der Würzburger Hofmusik im 18. Jahrhundert* (Würzburg, 1924)
K. G. Fellerer: *Beiträge zur Musikgeschichte Freisings* (Freising, 1926)
O. Kaul: 'Kürzinger', *MGG*
GEORGE J. BUELOW

Kūs. Sassanid kettledrums; *see* PERSIA, §3(ii).

Kusche, Benno (*b* Freiburg, 30 Jan 1916). German bass-baritone. He studied at Karlsruhe and made his début at Koblenz in April 1938 as Fra Melitone in *La forza del destino*. The next year he was engaged at Augsburg; he was conscripted into the army in 1941 but was soon released, and returned to Augsburg, where he remained until 1944, when he was drafted into a factory. In 1946 he was engaged by the Bayerische Staatsoper, Munich, and was still a member of the company in the mid-1970s; he was appointed a Bayerischer Kammersänger in 1959. He made his Covent Garden début in 1952 as Beckmesser in the performances of *Die Meistersinger* that brought Beecham back to the Royal Opera House. The next year he appeared there with the Munich company, in the first performance in Britain of Strauss's *Capriccio*, as La Roche, a role he sang at Glyndebourne in 1964 and 1965; at Glyndebourne he also sang Leporello (1954) and Don Fernando in *Fidelio* (1963). Kusche's repertory includes Papageno (which he sang in Felsenstein's 1954 production of *Die Zauberflöte* at the Komische Oper, Berlin), Alberich, Faninal, Figaro, Don Alfonso and Gianni Schicchi. Kusche has proved himself to be one of the best character singers in postwar German opera. He married the soprano Christine Görner.   HAROLD ROSENTHAL

Kusevitsky, Sergey. See KOUSSEVITZKY, SERGEY.

Kusser, Johann Sigismund [Cousser, Jean Sigismond] (*b* Pressburg [now Bratislava], baptized 13 Feb 1660; *d* Dublin, Nov 1727). Composer of Hungarian parentage active in Germany, England and Ireland. Walther established the highly significant fact that he spent six years in Paris studying with Lully, which must have been between 1674, when he moved to Stuttgart with his father, and 1682, when he was appointed to the court at Ansbach to train the violinists of the orchestra in the French style of playing. He left Ansbach in 1683, but there is no trace of him until 1690, when he became opera Kapellmeister at the court of Brunswick-Wolfenbüttel. One could speculate that it was during these seven years that, in Walther's words, he 'travelled throughout Germany, and there would hardly be a place in which he was not known'. One also learns from Walther that 'because of his volatile and fiery temperament he was unable to remain long in one place'. At Wolfenbüttel Kusser quarrelled with F. C. Bressand, court poet and manager of the opera, who wrote the librettos for several of his works: he openly criticized both the quality of Bressand's poetry and the efficiency of his management of the opera, and this probably led to Kusser's departure from the court in 1694, when he moved to Hamburg.

In Hamburg Kusser seems almost immediately to have quarrelled with Jakob Kremberg, the manager of the opera, who denied him the opera theatre for a performance of his opera *Porus*. Kusser, with the aid of Gerhard Schott, performed his opera in competition with Kremberg's theatre, and his considerable success deepened Kremberg's animosity. When Kremberg gave up the opera management some time in 1695 Kusser apparently took over his functions, but only until 1696, when Schott became manager. Kusser quickly formed his own travelling opera company, visiting Kiel for performances. He soon began to travel more widely with his company: he is known to have performed in Nuremberg and Augsburg during the 1697–8 season, in 1698 he appeared in Stuttgart and he apparently made several more journeys from there as guest conductor and opera impresario, including one to Munich. On 17 April 1700 he was appointed Oberkapellmeister at the court at Stuttgart; he visited Italy in 1701 to find musicians for the court. New disagreements, with both the Italian musicians and the church council, led him to abandon his post at Stuttgart on 19 March 1704, and towards the end of that year or early in 1705 he arrived in London.

He spent the remaining 22 years of his career in England and Ireland, but there has been little archival research into his activities in either London or Dublin. Apparently he spent the first few years as a private tutor and wrote music for well-known singers such as Giuliana Celotti and Arabella Hunt. In 1709 he went to Dublin. According to Walsh, in 1711 he was 'Chappel-Master of Trinity College' and in 1717 became 'Master of the Musick attending his Majesty's State in Ireland'. In this position, among other musical duties he wrote music annually for the birthdays of Queen Anne and George I. On 30 October 1727 his birthday ode for George II, a *serenata theatrale* was fully staged as an opera, apparently the only such dramatic representation of Kusser's music in Ireland (see Walsh for a detailed description of the libretto).

The lack of information about the major part of Kusser's career in London and Dublin and the apparent loss of virtually all the music that he wrote from 1705 onwards, as well as of his earlier German operas (except for the arias mentioned below), make any judgment of him as a composer tentative. It is apparent that his close relationship with Lully and his considerable experience with Italian operas at Wolfenbüttel made him an exponent of the most recent developments in French and Italian music. Furthermore he learnt from Lully the superiority of French orchestral discipline, especially the brilliant violin playing for which the French court orchestra under Lully's direction was famous: not only did he teach the French style of violin playing at Ansbach, but much of his career grew out of his talent and experience as an outstanding director of opera. Mattheson (*Der vollkommene Capellmeister*, 1739, 480–81) singled him out as the supreme example of the orchestra director who combines strictness of discipline in rehearsals with open-hearted cooperation and devotion to teaching both the talented and less talented their parts.

Kusser's extant music includes four sets of orchestral suites and two collections of arias, from his operas *Erindo* and *Ariadne* respectively. Wolff is one recent writer who has claimed that Kusser brought the French operatic style to Hamburg, but this distinction must be given to Kusser's predecessor at Hamburg, J. G. Conradi. It can certainly be said, however, that Kusser consolidated and reinforced the introduction of the French style, which was already known to and probably much admired by Hamburg audiences. He was a lesser composer than his successors at the Hamburg opera, Keiser and Telemann. However, his surviving music shows sensitivity, and his simple strophic songs are often of great charm, very much in the tradition of the late 17th-century lied. He also excelled in longer arias of more dramatic appeal, with expressive vocal line and

striking harmonic strength. He was far less influenced by Italian operatic practice than one might expect: although many of his arias are in da capo form, there are, for example, few lengthy melismatic passages. Much of his music is based on French dance forms, and like Conradi he frequently employed chaconne basses, both in individual arias and in longer, climactic scenes at the end of acts. The arias from *Erindo* show his predilection for solo instrumental passages in his arias, and both collections contain a number of homophonic duets in the French style.

An important contribution that Kusser made to Hamburg musical life and to the future of opera there was to introduce operas by non-German composers, including Gianettini, Carlo Pallavicino and especially Steffani. It was this, coupled with his exceptional ability as an orchestra director, more than his own operas, that changed the course of the Hamburg opera by raising the standards of musical performance and by developing a more cosmopolitan repertory.

WORKS

STAGE
(music lost unless otherwise stated)

Julia (opera, ?F. C. Bressand), Brunswick, 1690; songs in *D-SWl* (according to *MGG*)

Cleopatra (opera, prol, 3, ?Bressand), Brunswick, 1691

La Grotta di Salzdahl (divertimento, 1, F. Parisetti), Brunswick, spr. 1691

Ariadne (opera, 5, Bressand), Brunswick, 1692; a collection of arias from this opera pubd as Heliconische Musen-Lust, 1, 2vv, insts, bc (Stuttgart, 1700)

Jason (Singspiel, 5, Bressand), Brunswick, 1692

Narcissus (opera, prol, 3, G. Fiedler), Brunswick, 4 Oct 1692, pubd lib *HAu*

Andromeda (Singspiel, 3), Brunswick, ?1692

Porus (Singspiel, 5, Bressand, after Racine), Brunswick, 1693; with title Der durch Gross-Muth und Tapfferkeit besiegete Porus (lib rev. C. H. Postel), Hamburg, 1694

Erindo, oder Die unsträfliche Liebe (pastoral play, 3, Bressand), Hamburg, 1694; [44] Arien aus der Opera Erindo (Hamburg, 1695), ed. H. Osthoff, EDM, 2nd ser., *Schleswig-Holstein und Hansestädte*, iii (1938)

Gensericus, als Rom und Karthagens Überwinder (opera, Postel), Hamburg, ?1694; also attrib. J. G. Conradi

Pyramus und Thisbe getreue und festverbundene Liebe (opera, C. Schröder), Hamburg, 1694 [possibly not performed]

Der grossmütige Scipio Africanus (opera, 3, Fiedler, after N. Minato), Hamburg, 1694

Der verliebte Wald (Singspiel, 1), Stuttgart

The Man of Mode (G. Etherege), London, Little Lincoln's Inn Fields, 9 Feb 1705

Librettos of 9 serenatas performed 1711–27, *EIRE-Dtc*, Library of the Dean and Chapter of Cashel, *GB-Ob*

OTHER WORKS
(published in Stuttgart unless otherwise stated)

Composition de musique suivant la methode françoise, contenant 6 ouvertures de théâtre accompagnées de plusieurs airs (1682)

Apollon enjoué, contenant 6 ouvertures de théâtre accompagnées de plusieurs airs (1700)

Festin des muses, contenant 6 ouvertures de théâtre accompagnées de plusieurs airs (1700)

La Cicala della cetra d'Eunomio (1700)

An Ode Elegiecal on the Death of Mrs. Arabella Hunt (?1706)

BIBLIOGRAPHY

WaltherML

F. Chrysander: 'Geschichte der Braunschweig-Wolfenbüttelschen Capelle und Oper vom 16. bis zum 18. Jahrhundert', *Jb für Musikalische Wissenschaft*, i (1863), 147–286

H. Scholz: *Johann Sigismund Kusser: sein Leben und seine Werke* (Leipzig, 1911)

H. C. Wolff: *Die Barockoper in Hamburg* (Wolfenbüttel, 1957)

M. Tilmouth: 'A Calendar of References to Music in Newspapers Published in London and the Provinces (1660–1719)', *RMARC*, i (1961/R1968), 59

T. J. Walsh: *Opera in Dublin, 1705–1797: the Social Scene* (Dublin, 1973)

GEORGE J. BUELOW

Ḳuṭb al-Dīn. *See* QUṬB AL-DĪN.

Kutev, Philipp (*b* Aitos, 13 June 1903). Bulgarian composer. After graduating from the Sofia State Academy of Music in 1929 he worked for many years as a military bandmaster, first in Burgas, then in Sofia. He was entrusted with the direction of amateur art within the army after the revolution of 1944. In 1951 he established the state folksong and dance ensemble, consisting of a chorus of 45 musically untrained peasant girls, 20 players of folk instruments and 35 dancers; with this group Kutev toured throughout Europe, North America, Japan and the Middle East. He was secretary (1947–54) and president (1954–72) of the Bulgarian Composers' Union. Kutev's chief distinction has been in the field of harmonizing and orchestrating Bulgarian folk music, in which he has been influenced by earlier Bulgarian composers, such as Khristov, although he has striven to enrich and modernize his own technique. The vocal style of his peasant singers has served as a model for many subsequent amateur folk choruses in the country.

WORKS
(selective list)

Rhapsodie, orch, 1937; Sakarska suita, orch, 1940; German, sym. poem, 1940; Pastorale, fl, orch, 1943; Deweti septemwri [The 9th of Sept], solo vv, chorus, orch, 1945–6; Sym., 1950
Hundreds of folksong arrs., few film scores

Principal publisher: Nauka i izkustvo (Sofia)

BIBLIOGRAPHY

S. Stoyanov: *Philipp Kutev* (Sofia, 1962; Russ. trans., enlarged 1965)
LADA BRASHOVANOVA

Kützialflöte (Ger.). An ORGAN STOP.

Kuula, Toivo (Timoteus) (*b* Vaasa, 7 July 1883; *d* Viipuri, 18 May 1918). Finnish composer and conductor. He studied at the Helsinki Music Institute under Nováček and Wegelius (1906–8) and Järnefelt (1906–8), and continued his education in Bologna, Leipzig and Paris (1908–10) and in Berlin (1911–12). He worked as a teacher and conductor in Vaasa (1903–5), conductor of the orchestra in Oulu (1910–11), vice-conductor of the Native Orchestra (1912–14), assistant conductor of the Helsinki town orchestra (1914–16) and conductor of the orchestra of the Viipuri friends of music (1916–18). Kuula was a representative of the national romantic movement influenced by Sibelius, though his aim at individuality led him to a certain independence; indeed, the works he produced suggest that he was the most talented Finnish composer of his generation. The folktunes of his native Ostrobothnia give his music a recognizable colour, and his melody and harmony were also touched by church modes. An influence of Debussy and Ravel, dating from his stay in Paris, remained secondary and superficial. Kuula was at his best in the vocal works, particularly in their dark and pathetic melodies; his solo and choral songs entered the standard Finnish repertory. In his orchestration he was clearly indebted to Sibelius.

WORKS
(selective list)

Orch: Eteläpohjalainen sarja [South Ostrobothnian suite] no.1, 1906–9, no.2, 1912–14; c34 shorter pieces incl. 3 incidental scores, marches, folksong arrs.
Choral: Meren virsi [The song of the sea], chorus, orch, 1909; Merenkylpijäneidot [Maids on the seashore], S, orch, 1910; Stabat mater, chorus, orch, org, 1914–17; Orjan poika, S, B, chorus, orch; Kuolemattomuden toivo [Hope of immortality], Bar, chorus, orch; c50 a cappella songs

Songs: c20 incl. Aamulaulu [Morning song], 1905; Marjatan laulu, 1908; Suutelo [The kiss], 1908; Sinikan laulu, 1909; Vanha syyslaulu [An old autumn song], 1913; Tule armaani [Come my sweetheart], 1915; Kesäilta [Summer evening], 1917
Inst: Sonata, e, vn, pf, 1907; c15 other vn pieces, c10 pf pieces, 2 org pieces

Principal publishers: Finnish Broadcasting Corporation, Hansen, Musikki Fazer

BIBLIOGRAPHY

T. Elmgren-Heinonen: *Toivo Kuula: elämäkerta* (Borgå, 1938)
T. Elmgren-Heinonen and E. Roiha: *Toivo Kuula: a Finnish Composer of Genius* (Helsinki, 1952)
J. Kokkonen: *Toivo Kuula: sävellysluettelo* [Kuula: worklist] (Helsinki, 1953)
R.-E. Hillila: *The Solo Songs of Toivo Kuula and Leevi Madetoja and their Place in 20th-century Finnish Art Song* (diss., Boston U., 1965)
HANNU ILARI LAMPILA

Kuusik, Tiyt (Ditrikh Yanovich) (*b* Pärnu, Estonia, 11 Sept 1911). Estonian baritone. He graduated from Arder's class at the Tallinn Conservatory in 1938, and that year won the Vienna International Singing Competition. In the 1940–41 season and then from 1944 he was a soloist at the Estonia Opera, Tallinn. Kuusik is outstanding among Estonian singers. Along with fine musical and dramatic talents, he had a flexible, velvety voice, and considers that learning the cello as a boy contributed to his attainment of a true cantabile. Among his best roles were Boris and Tonio, and he gave captivating, sharp performances of Petruccio (Shebalin's *The Taming of the Shrew*), Vambo and Raya (Kapp's *The Fires of Vengeance* and *The Singer of Freedom*). From 1940 (from 1947 as professor) he taught at the Tallinn Conservatory; among his pupils was Georg Ots. He has toured in many countries, and was made People's Artist of the USSR in 1954.

BIBLIOGRAPHY

E. Kurbatova: 'Tiyt Kuuzik: teatral'nïy portret' [Theatrical portrait], *Teatr* (1962), no.8
H. Kõrvits: *Tiyt Kuusik* (Tallinn, 1963)
I. M. YAMPOL'SKY

Kuusisto, Taneli (*b* Helsinki, 19 June 1905). Finnish composer and organist. In 1931 he graduated from the Helsinki Institute of Church Music. He was organist of Töölö, Helsinki (1942–63), and he worked in the Helsinki Academy as teacher of liturgical organ playing and organ music history (1948–57), head of the church music department (1955–7), vice-director (1956–9) and director (1959–71). As a composer he has his roots in the national romantic tradition, although early in his career he showed some interest in Skryabin and Schoenberg; later he developed a linear style reflecting his admiration for Bach. The best known of his works are the songs and psalm settings.

WORKS
(selective list)

Orch: Nocturne, vc, orch, 1936; Pastorale, sym. poem, 1936; Laatokka, sym. ballad, 1944
Sacred choral: Martta ja Maria, 1946; Kuinka ihanat ovat sinum asuinsijasi [How amiable are thy dwelling places], 1951; other psalms, cantatas, motets
Secular choral: Suvikuvia [Summer pictures], female vv; c20 songs, mixed vv; 10 songs, male vv
Inst: Quartettino, 1925; Sonatine, str qt, 1927; Sonatine, fl, vn, hpd, 1936; Trio, fl, vn, va, 1953; Vn Sonata, pieces for pf, org
Song cycles: Keväästä kesään [From spring to summer], 1930; Kangastuksia [Mirages], 1v, orch, 1943, arr. 1v, pf, 1945; Saunakamari [Sauna chamber], 1952; many other songs

Principal publishers: Finnish Broadcasting Corporation, Musikki Fazer
HANNU ILARI LAMPILA

Kuwait. Near-Eastern country on the north-west coast of the ARABIAN GULF.

Kuypers, Johannes Theodorus. *See* CUYPERS, JOHANNES THEODORUS.

Kuznetsov, Konstantin Alexeyevich (*b* Novocherkassk, 21 Sept 1883; *d* Moscow, 25 May 1953). Soviet musicologist. He studied law at Moscow University (1902–4, 1906–7) and philosophy at the University of Heidelberg in 1906 and completed his postgraduate studies at Moscow University in 1908. In 1916 he was awarded a doctorate of civil law by Khar'kov University. He studied music history with Wolfram and composition with Reger in Germany, and from 1921 worked at the State Institute for Music Research in Moscow. He taught music history at the Moscow Conservatory (1923–31, 1934–8, 1941–9) and was appointed professor in 1936; in 1942 he was put in charge of the department of music history, and from 1943 to 1946 directed the department of Russian music history. In 1943 he was awarded an honorary doctorate, and in 1946 he was appointed a senior research fellow at the Institute of Fine Arts. Kuznetsov wrote many articles and books (sometimes under the pseudonyms K. Alexeyev and A. K. Smis) which are distinguished by their erudition and the breadth of their historical and artistic viewpoints.

WRITINGS

Etyudï o muzïke [Studies in music] (Odessa, 1919) [incl. 'Skryabin i filosofiya iskusstva' [Skryabin and the philosophy of art], 'Programmnaya muzïka' [Programme music], 'Glinka i Dargomïzhsky', 'Rimsky-Korsakov', 'Chaykovsky']

Vvedeniye v istoriyu muzïki [Introduction to the history of music], i (Moscow and Petrograd, 1923)

Glinka i evo sovremenniki [Glinka and his contemporaries] (Moscow, 1926)

'Muzïka ulitsï v Venetsii XVIII veka' [Street music in 18th-century Venice], *SovM* (1933), no.1

'Iz istorii klavirnoy muzïki' [From the history of keyboard music], *SovM* (1935), no.1, p.50

Dargomïzhsky', 'Rimsky-Korsakov', 'Chaykovsky']

Verdi i evo Rekviyem [Verdi and his Requiem] (Moscow, 1935)

Puchchini i evo opera Bogema [Puccini and his opera *Bohème*] (Moscow, 1936)

Muzïkal'no-istoricheskiye portretï: biografii kompozitorov XVI–XVII vv. [Musico-historical portraits: biographies of composers of the 16th and 17th centuries] (Moscow, 1937)

with V. S. Kuznetsova: *Klassiki russkovo romansa* [Classics of Russian song] (Moscow, 1938)

'Zametki i violonchel'nom kontserte S.S. Prokof'yeva' [Notes on Prokofiev's cello concerto], *Sovetskoye iskusstvo* (14 Feb 1939)

Orfey, opera Glyuka: istoricheskiy i muzïkal'no-kriticheskiy ocherk [Gluck's *Orphée*: historical and critical study] (Moscow, 1939)

'Novoye i staroye v kvartetakh Shebalina' [New and old in Shebalin's quartets], *SovM* (1940), no.1, p.64

'Tvorcheskaya zhizn' S. V. Rakhmaninova' [Rakhmaninov's creative life], *SovM sbornik*, iv (1945), 25

'Muzïkal'naya Moskva v proshlom i nastoyashchem' [Musical Moscow past and present], *Sovetskoye iskusstvo* (15 Aug 1947)

with I. M. Yampol'sky: *Arkandzhelo Korelli* (Moscow, 1953)

BIBLIOGRAPHY

O. E. Levashova: 'Konstantin Alexeyevich Kuznetsov (1883–1953)', *Vïdayushchiyesya deyateli teoretiko-kompozitorskovo fakul'teta Moskovskoy konservatorii*, ed. T. F. Muller (Moscow, 1966), 121

G. B. Bernandt and I. M. Yampol'sky: *Kto pisal o muzïke* [Writers on music], ii (Moscow, 1974) [contains a list of writings]

LEV GINZBURG

Kuznetsova, Maria Nikolayevna (*b* Odessa, 1880; *d* Paris, 25 April 1966). Russian singer and dancer. She first sang at the St Petersburg Conservatory as Tchaikovsky's Tatyana and joined the Imperial Opera (1905–13) where she created the role of Fevronia in Rimsky-Korsakov's *Kitezh* (1907). In 1908 she appeared at the Paris Opéra as Elsa and Thaïs. She made her Covent Garden début in 1909 as Marguerite (*Faust*), followed by Mimì; she returned in 1910 and

1920, and in Beecham's 1914 Russian season at Drury Lane sang with Shalyapin in *Prince Igor*. At the Opéra-Comique (1910) her roles included Manon, Tosca and Violetta. At the Opéra she appeared in Chabrier's *Gwendoline* (1910) and Massenet's *Roma* (1912) (she had sung in the first performance earlier that year at Monte Carlo). There she also sang Aida and Norma and created roles in Gunsbourg's *Venise* (1913) and Massenet's *Cléopâtre* (1914). In Strauss's *Josephslegende* (Opéra, 1914) she danced the role of Potiphar's wife. Influenced by Isadora Duncan and Spanish folkdances, Kuznetsova gave dance recitals in Russia, and in 1916 at the Opéra-Comique. She sang in Chicago in 1916. From the 1920s she sang with her own Russian company in Paris, Barcelona and Latin America. During her last years she taught privately. With an expressive voice and excellent technique she was the first Russian singer after Shalyapin to attach as much importance to acting as to singing. She made 36 recordings (1905–28).

BIBLIOGRAPHY

E. Stark: *Peterburgskaya opera i evo mastera* [The St Petersburg opera and its stars] (Leningrad, 1940)

D. I. Pokhitonov: *Iz proshlovo russkoy operï* [From the past of the Russian opera] (Leningrad, 1949)

S. Yu. Levik: *Zapiski opernovo pevtsa* [Notes of an opera singer] (Moscow, 1955; rev., enlarged 2/1962)

D. C. Kinrade: 'Marija Nikolaevna Kuznecova', *Record Collector*, xii/7 (1959), 156 [with partial discography by H. Barnes]

HAROLD BARNES

Kvaethi. Faeroese ballads sometimes used to accompany dancing; *see* FAEROES.

Kvandal [Johansen], **(David) Johan** (*b* Oslo, 8 Sept 1919). Norwegian composer. A son of David Monrad Johansen, he studied the organ and conducting at the Oslo Conservatory and had composition lessons from Marx in Vienna and Boulanger in Paris. He was music critic of the Oslo paper *Morgenposten* (1958–71) and holds the post of organist at the Vålerengen Church, Oslo. In addition, he has been active in professional organizations, notably as a member of the executive committees of the Norwegian Composers' Association (from 1963) and of TONO, the Norwegian performing rights society (from 1965). His music uses contemporary developments in tonality, with folk elements contributing to the character of both melody and harmony. The later works often show some connection with Baroque concerto form, but he has also composed free rondo structures.

WORKS

Orch: Divertimento, op.3, str, 1942; Norwegian Ov., op.7, 1951; Variations and Fugue, op.14, 1954; Sym. no.1, op.18, 1958; Sym. Epic, op.21, 1962; Conc., op.22, fl, str, 1963; Skipper Worse Suite, op.28b, 1968; Sinfonia concertante, op.29, 1968; Antagonia, op.38, 2 str orch, perc, 1972

Choral: Våkn op! [Wake up!], op.13, chorus, 1951; Draumkvæde Melodies, op.15, S, chorus, org, 1955; 3 Compositions, op.20, female vv, 1960; Pleiaderne, op.25, male vv, speaking vv, 1965; 3 Motets, op.35, chorus, 1971

Solo vocal: 7 Songs, op.4, Mez, pf, 1940–41; Sang til Stella [Song to Stella], op.6, S, str, 1950; 6 Songs, op.9a, Mez, pf, 1946–8; 2 Fröding Songs, op.9b, S, pf, 1948; Solo Cantata no.1, op.10, S, orch, 1953; Benedicam Dominum, op.17, S, org, 1957; 7 Sacred Folktunes, op.23a, 1v, pf, 1963; Solo Cantata no.2, op.26a, S, org, 1966; O Domine Deus, op.26b, S, org, 1966; Solo Cantata no.3, op.33, Bar, org, 1971; Natur, op.37, Bar, vn, pf, 1972

Chamber: Str Qt no.1, op.11, 1954; Str Trio, op.12, 1950; Rondo, Capriccio and Romance, op.16, vn, pf, 1955, Romance arr. fl, pf; Duo, op.19, vn, vc, 1959; 3 Sacred Folktunes, op.23b, wind qnt, 1963; Aria, cadenza e finale, op.24, vn, pf, 1964; Str Qt no.2, op.27, 1966; Introduction and Allegro, op.30, hn, pf, 1969; Da lontano, op.32, fl, pf, c1970; Wind Qnt, op.34, 1971; Duo concertante,

2 pf, 1974; Qt, fl, vn, va, vc, 1975
Pf: 5 Little Pieces, op.1, 1940; Sonatina, op.2, 1940; 7 Pieces, op.5, 1942–7; Fantasy, op.8, 1947; 3 slåtter fantasies, op.31, 1969
Org: Toccata, op.5, no.7, c1947; Partita on 'Hvor det er godt å lande', op.36, 1971

Principal publishers: KA-WE, Musik-Huset, Norsk Musikforlag

KARI MICHELSEN

Kvapil, Jaroslav (*b* Fryšták, Gottwaldov district, 21 April 1892; *d* Brno, 18 Feb 1959). Czech composer, teacher, conductor and pianist. He was a chorister in Olomouc and a pupil of Nešvera there (1902–6). In 1909 he graduated from the Brno School of Organists under Janáček, and later studied with Reger at the Leipzig Conservatory (1911–13). He taught at the School of Organists and at the Brno Conservatory, and he was also professor of composition at the academy. Kvapil was an excellent accompanist, noted for his skill in sight reading. As the choirmaster and conductor of the Brno Beseda (1919–47) he gave the Czech premières of Bach's *St Matthew Passion* (1923), Honegger's *Judith* (1933) and Szymanowski's *Stabat mater* (1937). He received the Award of Merit in 1955. In his music Kvapil worked best in traditional forms, particularly variation form, and showed a partiality for contrapuntal textures. His romantic style included few immediate references to folk music, but he achieved a simple and direct expression. The oratorio *Lví srdce* ('The Lionheart') achieved popularity through its treatment of the struggle for Czech independence during World War I. However, it is his smaller pieces that have the most lasting value.

WORKS
(*selective list*)

Vocal: Píseň o čase, který umírá [Song of the time of dying], cantata, 1924; Lví srdce [The Lionheart], oratorio, 1931; Píseň veselé chudiny [Songs of the merry poor] (cantata, medieval trad.), 1934; Horské růže [Mountain roses] (Wolker), male chorus, 1940; Pohádka máje [A May fairytale] (opera, after V. Mrštík), 1943
Orch: 4 syms., 1914, 1921, 1927, 1943; 2 vn concs., 1928, 1952; Z těžkých dob [From the hard times], sym. variations, 1939; Ob Conc., 1954; Pf Conc., 1954; Suite, va, orch, 1956
Inst: Údolím stesku a žalu [Through a valley of grief and sorrow], pf, 1912; Sonata no.2, vn, pf, 1914; Str Qt no.4, 1945; Str Qt no.5, 1956

Principal publisher: Český Hudební Fond
MSS in *CS-Bm*

BIBLIOGRAPHY
J. Racek: *Leoš Janáček a současní moravští skladatelé* (Brno, 1944)
L. Kundera: *Jaroslav Kvapil* (Prague, 1944)

JAN TROJAN

Kvapil, Radoslav (*b* Brno, 15 March 1934). Czech pianist. He studied with Ludvík Kundera, made his début in Brno (1954) and has played in many European cities. He formed a duo in 1958 with the cellist Stanislav Apolín and in 1970 joined the Dvořák Piano Trio. He has made a complete recording of the neglected piano works of Dvořák. From Kundera, a Janáček pupil, he gained valuable insight into that composer, and took part in a biographical film about him. He also plays Smetana, Fišer, Reiner, Kohoutek, Ištvan and Piňos. His well-considered, affectionate approach, and his ability to catch the national traits of the works he plays, rank him among the leading interpreters of Czech piano music. He wrote 'Rehabilitace Dvořáka', *HRo*, xix (1966), 424.

ALENA NĚMCOVÁ

Kvernadze, Bidzina [Alexander] **Alexandrovich** (*b* Signakhi, east Georgia, 29 July 1928). Soviet composer and teacher. He graduated in 1953 from Balanchivadze's composition class at the Tbilisi Conservatory, where he was later appointed to teach orchestration. A board member of the Georgian Composers' Union, he holds the title Honoured Art Worker of the Georgian SSR (1966) and the Order of the Badge of Honour.

The endeavour to renew national traditions and extend expressive resources, characteristic of Georgian music at the end of the 1950s, is perhaps most evident in Kvernadze's first mature works. In the most significant works of this period – the Violin Concerto (1957), a series of piano pieces and, above all, the symphonic picture *Tcekva-fantazia* ('Dance fantasia', 1959) – he displayed an integrated, individual style including features new to Georgian music, attracting attention for his independence, his decisive reinterpretation of Georgian style and his emancipation from superficial nationalist stereotypes. Features which have remained characteristic of his music include a plasticity of idea, an inimitable, broad folk humour and the active development of Georgian rhythmic and stylistic qualities. The First Symphony (1961) is marked by elevated lyrical ideas, with a dramatic compression of genre writing and a poetic meditativeness overshadowed by toccata-like dynamism. In the ballet *Khoreografiuli novelebi* ('Choreographic short stories', 1964) the composer's fantasy has a wide scope in the colourful illustration of an artist's world and the ideas in his paintings. The Second Piano Concerto (1965) gave proof of Kvernadze's assimilation of new expressive means, more concentrated forms, a striving after graphically clear ideas and an increased importance of developed rhythmic structures and experiments in timbre. A further evolution is exhibited in the ballet *Berikaoba* (named after ancient Georgian harvest celebrations in song and dance), a piece saturated with thorough symphonic development.

WORKS
(*selective list*)

Stage: Khoreografiuli novelebi [Choreographic short stories] (ballet, 3, Ch. Gudiashvili, G. Meliva), Tbilisi, 1964; Tsolebi da kmrebi [Wives and husbands] (musical comedy), 1970; Berikaoba (ballet, 1, G. Alexidze), Tbilisi, 1973
Vocal: Ukvdaveba [Immortality], vocal sym. poem, 1971; 1905 tceli [The year 1905], cantata, 1955, collab. S. Nasidze
Orch: 2 pf concs., 1952, 1965; Gantiadisaken [Towards the dawn], sym. poem, 1953; Vn Conc., 1957; Tcekva-fantazia [Dance fantasia], sym. picture, 1959; 2 syms., 1961, 1963
Other works: pf pieces, songs, incidental music, film scores

Principal publishers: Muzfond Gruzii (Tbilisi), Muzgiz, Muzyka, Sovetskiy Kompozitor

BIBLIOGRAPHY
V. Belïy and V. Vanslov: 'Novoye v gruzinskom simfonizme' [Something new in Georgian symphonism], *SovM* (1954), no.9, p.9
O. Taktakishvili: 'Novïye rabotï gruzinskoy molodyozhi' [New works by young Georgians], *SovM* (1955), no.1, p.39
M. Pichkhadze: 'Novïy skripichnïy kontsert' [A new violin concerto], *SovM* (1958), no.10, p.39
T. Khuroshvili: *B. Kvernadze* (Moscow, 1959)
E. Dobrïnina: 'Zamïslï i sversheniya' [Projects and achievements], *Muzïkal'naya zhizn'* (1963), no.1, p.2
G. Ordzhonikidze: 'Znakomtes': molodost'' [Get to know each other: the young], *SovM* (1963), no.8, p.14
——: 'Kartuli simfoniya "gazapkhulidan" "gazapkhulamde"' [The Georgian symphony from one 'spring' to another], *Sabchota khelovneba* (Tbilisi, 1965), no.5, p.33
——: 'Pervaya simfoniya B. Kvernadze' [Kvernadze's First Symphony], *Sovetskaya simfoniya za 50 let*, ed. G. G. Tigranov (Leningrad, 1967), 148
B. Boyakhunov: 'Iskusstvo, bogatoye talantami' [An art rich in talents], *SovM* (1971), no.6, p.14

EVGENY MACHAVARIANI

Květ, Jan Miroslav (*b* Lenešice u Loun, Bohemia, 22 Feb 1887; *d* Prague, 23 June 1961). Czech music historian. He studied classics at Prague University and after graduating in 1910 became a schoolmaster. As a student he had also attended music lectures by Hostinský, Stecker and Nejedlý and soon became increasingly active as choirmaster, organizer and writer, filling in his practical knowledge of music with further studies, notably with Suk (1929–32), on whom he became a leading authority. Another of his interests was Dvořák and in 1929 he helped to found the Dvořák Museum. During the war he was in charge of the Prague Conservatory (1939–42) and later (1945–6) of the Theatre of the Fifth of May, the former German Theatre (from 1949 the Smetana Theatre). He made various translations from English (e.g. James Jeans's *Science and Music*) and contributed to *ČSHS*.

WRITINGS

ed.: *Čtyřicet let Českého kvarteta* [40 years of the Bohemian Quartet] (Prague, 1932)
'Život a dílo' [Life and works], *Josef Suk: život a dílo* (Prague, 1935), 7–230
Josef Suk (Prague, 1936)
Z pamětí Českého kvarteta [From the memoirs of the Bohemian Quartet] (Prague, 1936)
Školy a učitelé-hudebníci v kraji Ant. Dvořáka ('Schools and teacher-musicians from Dvořák's countryside) (Prague, 1939)
Mládí Antonína Dvořáka [Dvořák's youth] (Prague, 1945)
Jiří Herold (Prague, 1947)
Josef Suk (Prague, 1947)
Karel Hoffmann (Prague, 1947)
Oskar Nedbal (Prague, 1947)
Národní umělec Ladislav Zelenka a České kvarteto (Prague, 1948)

BIBLIOGRAPHY

A. Horejš: 'Zemřel J. M. Květ', *HRo*, xiv (1961), 621 [obituary]

JOHN TYRRELL

Kvitka, Klyment (*b* Kiev, 4 Feb 1880; *d* Moscow, 19 Sept 1953). Ukrainian ethnomusicologist, husband of the Ukrainian poet Lesya Ukrayinka (*d* 1913). He was at first a lawyer, later becoming a judge, and could devote himself wholly to music only from 1920. He was director of the Ethnomusicology Bureau at the Ukrainian Academy of Sciences (1922–33); during the 1920s his fieldwork was involved primarily with ritual songs, but also included the music of minority peoples (Bulgarians, Albanians and the Greeks along the Azov Sea), and the everyday life of professional folk musicians. In 1933 he moved to Moscow, where he founded and led the Folk Music Bureau at the Moscow Conservatory. In this period he concentrated on the study of folk instruments, continued to map the exact geographical spread of folksongs and instruments, and worked on the historical stages of calendar songs. Kvitka's song collections, published in 1917–18 and 1922, are landmarks in Ukrainian folk music scholarship, the second being among the greatest field collections covering the entire Ukraine. Many of his studies remain unpublished, but the Russian edition of his selected works, edited by Hoshovsky, contains important articles, a few never published before. His work is notable for its high scholarly standards and remarkable erudition (he knew 13 languages, including Georgian), as well as for the variety of problems considered and the methodology devised to solve them.

FOLKSONG COLLECTIONS

Narodni melodiyi z holosu Lesi Ukrayinky [Ukrainian folksongs from the voice of Lesya Ukrayinka] (Kiev, 1917–18, enlarged 2/1971 as *Narodni pisni v zapysakh Lesi Ukrayinky ta z yiyi spivu*, ed. O. I. Dey and S. Y. Hrytsa)
Ukrayins'ki narodni melodiyi [Ukrainian folk melodies] (Kiev, 1922)

WRITINGS
(complete list in Hoshovsky)

Professional'ni narodni spivtsi y muzykanty na Ukrayini: prohrama dlya doslidu yikh diyal'nosti ta pobutu [Professional folk singers and instrumentalists in the Ukraine: a programme for study of their activity and everyday life] (Kiev, 1924)
'Do pytannya pro tyurks'kyy vplyv na ukrayins'ku narodnu melodyku' [The question of Turkish influence on Ukrainian folk melody], *Yuvileynyy zbirnyk na poshanu akad. M. Hrushevs'kovo*, ii (Kiev, 1928), 866
'Le système anhémitonique pentatonique chez les peuples slaves', *II Zjazd Słowiańskich geografów i einografów: Kraków 1927*, ii, 196
'Ob oblastyakh rasprostraneniya nekotorïkh tipov belorusskikh kalendarnïkh i svadebnïkh pesen', *Belorusskiye narodnïye pesni* (Moscow and Leningrad, 1941; Ger. trans. as 'Über die Verbreitung einiger Typen belorussischer Kalendar- und Hochzeitslieder', *Sowjetische Volkslied- und Volksmusikforschung: ausgewählte Studien*, ed. E. Stockmann and others (Berlin, 1967), 309)
ed. V. Hoshovsky: *Izbrannïye trudï* [Selected works] (Moscow, 1971–3) [incl. 'Ob istoricheskom znachenii kalendarnïkh pesen' [The historical significance of calendar songs], i, 73–102; 'Pesni ukrainskikh zimnikh obryadovïkh prazdnestv' [Songs of the Ukrainian winter festivals], i, 103–60; 'Yavleniya obshchnosti v melodike i ritmike bolgarskikh narodnïkh pesen i pesen vostochnïkh slavyan' [Common features in melody and rhythm of Bulgarian folksongs and songs of the eastern Slavs], i, 191]

BIBLIOGRAPHY

L. Bachinsky: 'K. V. Kvitka', *Voprosï muzïkoznaniya*, i/2, ed. A. S. Ogolevets (Moscow, 1955), 317
A. V. Rudneva: 'Kliment Vasil'yevich Kvitka (1880–1953)', *Vïdayushchiyesya deyateli teoretiko-kompozitorskovo fakul'teta Moskovskoy konservatorii*, ed. M. F. Myuller (Moscow, 1966), 156, 206 [incl. list of writings]
B. Krader: 'Folk Music Archive of the Moscow Conservatory, with a Brief History of Russian Field Recording', *Folklore and Folk Music Archivist*, x/2 (1967–8), 13–44
P. G. Bogatïryov: Introduction to *K. Kvitka: izbrannïye trudï*, i, ed. V. Hoshovsky (Moscow, 1971), 7
V. Hoshovsky, ed.: *K. Kvitka: izbrannïye trudï* [Selected works], ii (Moscow, 1973) [incl. V. Ivanenko: 'Materiali k biografii K. V. Kvitki' [Materials for Kvitka's biography], 346; A. V. Rudneva: 'K. V. Kvitka v Moskve', 360]

BARBARA KRADER

Kwela. A Zulu word given to a popular urban musical style of southern Africa. The term means 'to climb' or 'to go up'; also 'to attempt with success', 'to go up and win', but in a wider sense the word belongs to a conceptual framework associated with social emancipation and increased intensity of life. According to the South African musicologist Elkin Sithole musical use of the term first occurred during the 1940s in connection with a new kind of Zulu vocal music known as the 'bombing style' (Kubik, 1972, p.25; Rycroft, 1957, p.33). When the leader wanted the chorus to respond, he shouted 'kwela'. In reduplicated form *kwela-kwela*, it expressed the continuous action of the responding chorus. *Kwela-kwela* is also one of several names given to the South African police van.

In the early 1950s the word *kwela* became associated with bands of penny whistle playing young boys, who had become familiar with American swing and played their versions for money around the city streets and at local dances in the townships. Whistle playing first became popular in 1950 'after the success of a locally made film called *The Magic Garden*, which featured a little penny-whistle boogie, played by a cripple boy. Before this, flute blowing had always been the traditional pastime of country herd-boys and on this account had been frowned upon in town' (Rycroft, 1958, p.55). In Johannesburg the *kwela* style is also called 'jive', which term is applied even to its more recent manifestations such as *simanje-manje*, played with electrically amplified instruments, in spite of the fact that dance movements, tunes and instruments have

Kwela flautist Donald Kachamba

changed considerably since the 1950s. Others distinguish between the dance movements of *kwela*, *phataphata* etc. Several examples of *kwela* playing can be seen in the film *Come Back Africa* (1957). Well-known *kwela* flute and saxophone players in the 1950s were Spokes Mashiyane and Lemmy Special Mabaso.

The standard ensemble, which blends African and Western elements, consisted of one or two (non-electric) guitars, one or more flutes and the one-string bass. The Western instruments are played with African techniques and the string bass, though probably introduced with American popular music, is ultimately related to the African ground bow. *Kwela* flautists push the flute relatively far into the mouth (see illustration), rotating it towards the inner side of the right cheek. The oblique embouchure guarantees that the edge and window remain open between the lips of the player and a full and round tone is obtained, much louder than if it is played in a Western manner. The flute also sounds almost exactly a semitone lower than the factory-tuned pitch. By means of their own special fingering techniques they play glides, 'blue' notes and chromatic passing notes.

Kwela was quickly exploited commercially, but what appeared on records did not always represent *kwela* as heard in the streets. In the late 1950s *kwela* had spread to the states of the Federation of Rhodesia and Nyasaland. There it gained new roots and in the 1960s was developed further in Malawi by such musicians as Daniel and Donald Kachamba (see Kubik, 1971–2, 1974). In the 1960s *kwela* traits also entered Euro-American popular music, though the original instrumentation was rarely maintained.

BIBLIOGRAPHY

D. Rycroft: 'Melodic Imports and Exports: a Byproduct of Recording in Southern Africa', *Bulletin of the British Institute of Recorded Sound*, no.3 (1956), 19
——: 'Zulu Male Traditional Singing', *African Music*, i/4 (1957)
——: 'The New "Town Music" of Southern Africa', *Recorded Folk Music*, i (1958), Sept–Oct, 54
——: 'African Music in Johannesburg: African and Non-African Features', *JIFMC*, xi (1959), 25
Y. Huskisson: *The Bantu Composers of Southern Africa* (Johannesburg, 1969)
W. Laade: *Neue Musik in Afrika, Asien und Ozeanien* (Heidelberg, 1971)
G. Kubik: 'Die Verarbeitung von Kwela, Jazz und Pop in der modernen Musik von Malawi', *Jazzforschung – Jazz research*, iii–iv (1971–2), 51–115
A. A. Mensah: 'Jazz – the Round Trip', *Jazzforschung – Jazz research*, iii–iv (1971–2), 124
G. Kubik: *The Kachamba Brothers' Band* (Vienna, 1972) [with disc]
A. Benseler: 'Beobachtungen zur Kwela-Musik 1960 bis 1963', *Jazzforschung – Jazz research*, v (1973–4), 119
G. Kubik: *The Kachamba Brothers' Band – a Study of Neo-traditional Music in Malawi* (Lusaka, 1974)

GERHARD KUBIK

Kwiatkowski, Ryszard (*b* Jaroszowo, nr. Włocławek, 27 June 1931). Polish composer. He studied composition with Szeligowski and Rudziński at the Warsaw Conservatory; he won a scholarship to Rome for further study with Petrassi. Among the awards he has received is the first prize of the New York International Composers' Competition (1968). *Muzyka polifoniczna* is the best of his works, which are distinguished by impulsive rhythms and sonorous harmonies.

WORKS
(*selective list*)

Orch: Serenade, trbn, orch, 1957; 4 syms., 1958, n.d., 1969, 1969; Barwy [Colours], 1963; Kształty [Shapes], 1963; Obrazy [Pictures], chamber orch, 1963; Światła [Lights], 1964; Musica in memoriam Johannis Ciconiae, 1966; Śpiewy Bałtyku [Baltic songs], 1966; Fotografie z księżyca [Photographs from the moon], 1967; Muzyka polifoniczna, 1967; Muzyka, ob, tpts, pf, perc, str, 1968; Music, wind, pf, perc, 1969; 4 Lyrics, 1970–72; Apoteoza Października [The apotheosis of October], 1973
Chamber: Str Qt no.2, 1966; Pf Qt, pf qt, metronome, 1968; Perc Qt no.2, 1971
Choral: Modlitwa ślepego lunatyka [Prayer of a blind somnambulist] (K.I. Gałczyński), 20 male vv, 1969

Principal publisher: Polskie Wydawnictwo Muzyczne

MIECZYSŁAWA HANUSZEWSKA

Kyhm, Carl. *See* KHYM, CARL.

Kymbalon (Gk.). CYMBALUM.

Kymbos (Gk.). CYMBALS.

Kynaston, Nicolas (*b* Morebath, Devon, 10 Dec 1941). English organist. He studied from the age of 15 with Germani at the Accademia Musicale Chigiana, Siena, then at the Conservatorio S Cecilia, Rome, and finally with Ralph Downes at the Royal College of Music, London. At 19 he was appointed organist of Westminster Cathedral. The success of his Festival Hall début in 1966 and of subsequent concerts led him to relinquish his cathedral post in 1971 in favour of recital work. Kynaston allies technical skill with keen musical insight, and his interpretations of French music, notably Franck and Messiaen, are outstanding. He played Messiaen's *Messe de la Pentecôte* and *L'ascension* in the composer's presence at the 1973 English Bach Festival and also took part in the Reger centenary celebrations in Germany. In 1974 he first toured the USA.

STANLEY WEBB

Kyōgen. A Japanese comic play sometimes inserted between the acts of a noh performance; *see* JAPAN, §§II, 2(ii), and III, 2(i). The word also refers to a comic actor; *see* JAPAN, §III, 2(iii).

Kyriakou, Rena (*b* Iráklion, 25 Feb 1918). Greek pianist. She began to play the piano when she was three, and to compose little pieces which she played at the first recital she gave in Athens when she was six. Her first serious studies were with Paul Weingarten and Richard Stohr in Vienna, and then with Isidor Philipp (piano) and Henri Büsser (composition) at the Paris Conservatoire, where at the age of 15 she won a *premier prix*. Her career then began in Europe and the USA, where she gives recitals and plays with international orchestras and conductors. Her intelligence, delicacy of touch and clarity of tone are heard in her recordings extending from the 18th-century Soler through the complete works of Mendelssohn and Chabrier, which she interprets with precision of style and efficiency, to Granados's *Goyescas*. Also in her enterprising repertory are some of the less familiar 19th-century concertos. Her compositions include a set of 20 preludes, and a piano concerto.

YVONNE TIÉNOT

Kyriale (Lat.). In the Western Christian church, a collection of chants for the Ordinary of the Mass, i.e. Kyrie, Gloria, Credo, Sanctus, Agnus Dei and *Ite* or *Benedicamus*; or a book or section of a book containing these chants.

The chants are found in medieval books from the 10th and 11th centuries onwards, usually with troped texts. A group of troped Kyries might be followed by a group of untroped melodies, then troped Glorias, untroped Glorias and so on. Credo and *Ite* settings appear separately and much less frequently. Different regions preferred different ways of grouping the melodies. Northern French books of the 11th to 14th centuries, which generally lacked other tropes, often placed the Kyrie collection together with the Gloria collection, and the Sanctus collection together with the Agnus collection, on either side of a collection of proses. German books from the 12th century onwards would often pair Kyrie with Gloria, and Sanctus with Agnus; first a series of Kyrie–Gloria pairs would be written, then the Sanctus–Agnus pairs.

The melodies were rarely rubricated and it is often uncertain now for which feast they were intended. The following are among the exceptions: *I-Ra* 123, ff.190*v*–265*v* (11th century, from Bologna, facs. in PalMus, xviii), has Proper tropes, Ordinary tropes and proses for each feast in the order in which they would be sung within the service; *I-Md* I.16 (12th century, Italian) has rubrics for its Kyrie–Gloria pairs (ff.6*r*–14*v*), Sanctus (ff.77*r*–80*v*) and Agnus (ff.80*v*–82*r*); Sarum graduals from the mid-13th century *GB-Mjr* lat.24 onwards have separate Kyrie, Gloria, Sanctus, Agnus and *Ite* or *Benedicamus* collections with rubrics (the latter often taken from Office responsory melismas and named after the melisma text; *see* NEUMA); the incipits of Kyries and Glorias are entered in several masses in a 13th-century gradual from St Bénigne de Dijon (*B-Br* II 3824). Several graduals have a marginal text incipit of the Kyrie to be used on a high feast.

The new papal and Franciscan missal of the 13th century grouped the chants in 'cycles' for use on different feasts (see Van Dijk and Walker, 1960, p.328); those cycles are the basis of the current Vatican kyriale. Other sources with cycles include *D-B* mus.40078 (12th century, Quedlinburg: 4 cycles), *D-Mbs* lat.3919 (13th century, Augsburg: 11 cycles; facs. in MGG, ix, 1961,

pl.10), *DK-Kk* S.632 (French: 8 cycles), *F-Pa* 110 and *Pn* lat.830 (13th century, from Notre Dame and St Germain-l'Auxérrois, Paris, respectively: 15 cycles). The Cistercians had two cycles (from the 12th century), the Carthusians three, the Dominicans seven.

The name 'kyriale' is a comparatively recent term analogous to *graduale* (gradual), *antiphonale* (antiphoner) and so on, and may have been invented for the title-pages of early printed graduals such as that of Francis of Bruges, a Franciscan, whose *Graduale secundum morem sancte romane ecclesie, integrum et completum videlicet dominicale sanctuarium commune et cantorinum sive kyriale* first appeared in Rome in 1499–1500. The section of the book containing the Ordinary chants has no new heading; it includes three Credo chants: the first is a mensural 'Credo maior', a reworking of the present Vatican melody no.IV (facs. in F. Tack: *Der gregorianische Choral*, Mw, xii, 1960; Eng. trans., 1960, p.50; cf the setting for two voices in *I-Sc* H.I.10: see *RISM*, B/IV/4, 1972, p.1036), followed by a less ornate mensural Credo 'de apostolis' and a non-rhythmic Credo 'de dominica' (Vatican I). Rhythmic chants are not uncommon at this period. For instance, the *Missale basiliense* printed by Wenssler of Basle in 1488 has a rhythmic Gloria at the end of its Kyrie–Gloria pairs (for the Blessed Virgin), then two rhythmic Credos; a plain Credo and the Sanctus–Agnus pairs are followed by a collection of proses.

Vatican books since the *Kyriale seu ordinarium missae* of 1905 have also included other minor Ordinary Mass chants: the *Asperges* antiphons, Gloria tones for the introit and alleluia tones for Eastertide (for introit, offertory and communion).

See also MASS, §I, 3.

BIBLIOGRAPHY

FACSIMILES, EDITIONS

W. H. Frere, ed.: *Graduale sarisburiense* (London, 1901 [dated 1894]/R1966) [p11.1*–19*; facs. of *GB-Lbm* Lansdowne 462, ? royal household chapel, late 14th century]
P. Wagner, ed.: *Kyriale sive ordinarium missae cum cantu gregoriano, quem ex vetustissimis codicibus manuscriptis cisalpinis collegit* (Graz, 1904)
Kyriale seu ordinarium missae (Rome, 1905)
Kyriale seu ordinarium missae cum cantu gregoriano ad exemplar editionis Vaticanae concinnatum et rhythmicis signis a Solesmensibus monachis diligenter ornatum (Tournai, 1905; Eng. trans., with modern note shapes and rhythmic nuance signs, Tournai, 1905)
P. Wagner: *Das Graduale der Thomaskirche zu Leipzig*, Publikationen älterer Musik, v, vii (Leipzig, 1930–32) [vii.232–49; 14th century]
Le codex VI.34 de la bibliothèque capitulaire de Bénévent (XIe–XIIe siècle): graduel de Bénévent avec prosaire et tropaire, PalMus, xv (1937–53) [ff.274r–288v]

STUDIES

M. Sigl: *Die Geschichte des Ordinarium missae in der deutschen Choralüberlieferung* (Regensburg, 1911)
A. Gastoué: *Musique et liturgie: le graduel et l'antiphonaire romains* (Lyons, 1913)
D. Catta: 'Aux origines du kyriale', *Revue grégorienne*, xxxiv (1955), 175
S. van Dijk and J. H. Walker: *The Origins of the Modern Roman Liturgy* (London, 1960)
B. Stäblein: 'Messe', §A, MGG
L. Schrade: 'The Cycle of the Ordinarium Missae', *In memoriam Jacques Handschin* (Strasbourg, 1962), 87
K. von Fischer: 'Neue Quellen zum einstimmigen Ordinariumszyklus des 14. u. 15. Jahrhunderts aus Italien', *Liber amicorum Charles van den Borren* (Antwerp, 1964), 60

DAVID HILEY

Kyrie eleison. Acclamation sung in the Latin Mass directly after the introit. The basic text, which is Greek, consists of 'Kyrie eleison' (three times), 'Christe eleison' (three times), 'Kyrie eleison' (three times): 'Lord, have mercy . . . Christ, have mercy . . . Lord, have mercy . . .'. Some form of this text was used at the Eucharist since at least the 6th century, and was provided with a wide variety of musical settings. Since (in more recent practice at least) the text did not change from day to day, the Kyrie is counted a part of the Ordinary of the Mass.

1. Sources. 2. Early history. 3. Early melodies. 4. Latin texts ('tropes').

1. SOURCES. Kyrie chants survive in manuscripts of the 10th century on; the earliest are from France and Germany, while those of the 11th–12th centuries include large numbers from other European countries. The catalogue by Melnicki includes 226 items; even so, it is not complete. The whole repertory tends to divide itself between items that have large concordances, hence were widely known and used, and items whose isolated concordances show them to be purely local products. The earliest and best-known melodies – the repertory of the 10th and 11th centuries – are very well represented among the Ordinary chants included in the *Liber usualis*; Kyries are normally identified by their numbering in this source.

The *Liber usualis* also identifies Kyrie chants by the incipit of the text formerly used with a given melody (e.g. *Lux et origo* for Kyrie I). Such texts are commonly called 'tropes' by modern scholars, and are not commonly discussed as integral parts of the Kyrie, on the assumption that being 'tropes' these texts are later additions to originally melismatic chants. To this, three objections need to be raised. (1) According to recently clarified definition, what is involved here is not a 'trope' but, if anything, 'text underlay'. (2) In many cases it may not even be that, but rather simultaneous, integral composition of text and music, since the early manuscript sources, while indeed notating Kyrie chants in both melismatic form (with the universal Greek text) and syllabic form (with the individual Latin texts), give no indication that the melismatic form represents an earlier stage of composition. (3) The early history of the Kyrie, in particular the comments by St Gregory (see §2) strongly suggest that such individual texts were so closely associated with the Kyrie as to be an integral part of it.

2. EARLY HISTORY. The liturgical use of the expression 'Kyrie eleison', especially in the Greek rite, went far beyond the one occurrence at Mass with which we are most familiar; 'Kyrie eleison' tended to be used as a ubiquitous response to other liturgical items. In the west it became associated with the various litanies, and this is in many ways its most characteristic use.

In fact the Kyrie is itself a litany, and was often so called in earlier documents. Considered by itself it is a very compact litany, consisting of an acclamatory invocation, 'Kyrie', and a petition, 'eleison'. Such invocations would normally be sung by a deacon or *cantor*, the people responding with the petitions (as St Gregory said).

So compact is 'Kyrie/eleison' that it invites elaboration in the form of more prolix invocations, comparable to those preserved in numerous Latin litanies from the 8th century on. Precisely such elaborations are mentioned by St Gregory in his famous letter: 'In daily masses, moreover, we do not say the other things usually said, but only "Kyrie eleison" and "Christe eleison", in order that we may concern ourselves with these supplications at greater length'. An idea of what these other things were can be gained from analogous

constructions in the Gloria in excelsis (using the text of the Bangor Antiphonary, *c*690, and substituting 'Kyrie' for 'Domine', 'eleison imas' for 'miserere nobis'):

Kyrie [i.e. Domine] rex coelestis, Deus Pater omnipotens.
Kyrie [i.e. Domine] Fili unigenite, Jesu Christe, Sancte Spiritus Dei, et omnes dicimus, Amen.
Kyrie [i.e. Domine] Fili Dei Patris, Agne Dei, qui tollis peccatum mundi, *eleison imas* [i.e. miserere nobis].

Gregory further said that in the Roman rite 'Christe' was said as many times as 'Kyrie'; but at that time, and for a century or two thereafter, the total number of petitions was not yet fixed. *Ordo romanus I* (??7th century) leaves the number of invocations up to the pontiff, while *Ordo IV* ('St Amand', early ?9th century) says that nine petitions shall be sung, at which time the pontiff shall give the signal to stop – an obviously redundant and now vestigial signal.

3. EARLY MELODIES. Documents of the 10th century provide composed Kyries with Latin texts for major feasts in the ninefold shape, so that by that time the number of petitions was definitely fixed. In general both texts and melodies of this early repertory seem to be the product of Frankish monasteries. Many early Kyries are of a musical complexity that suggest performance by a *schola*, not by the whole congregation. There are, admittedly, simple Kyries, and one or the other of these might represent an earlier congregation use.

More likely, the 10th–11th-century repertory includes reminiscences of earlier (pre-Carolingian) practice rather than integral melodies. Such stylized reminiscences of earlier functions can most easily be imagined in the 'eleison'. In some Kyries, for example Kyrie IV (*Cunctipotens genitor*) the syllable 'e-(leison)' has a neume of several notes, as opposed to the mostly syllabic relationship in the preceding invocation with its Latin text. Even assuming the Latin text to be underlay, it would still be striking that the whole 'melisma' was not texted, but only the part preceding 'eleison'. In this and other ways the 'eleison' is often set off from what precedes, as if it were functionally a distinct part, reflecting the earlier division into the solo invocation and the people's response. Sometimes, as in Kyrie *Rex genitor* (*Liber usualis* VI) each of the nine 'eleison' settings is identical, again suggesting a response, although such 'homeoteleuton' could be explained on other grounds (it occurs in sequences for purely musical reasons). Usually the 'eleison' is varied, but variation occurs in other litanies, too. The falling-3rd cadence on 'eleison' in Kyrie *Fons bonitatis* (Kyrie II) and elsewhere might be considered a reminiscence of the kind of recitation tone that was perhaps associated with a litany.

Ordo romanus I tells us that the Kyrie was sung until the pontiff signalled the prior of the *schola* to stop. In the Kyrie from the Mass for the Dead we might see a way in which the prior would indicate to the rest of the *schola* that the Kyries should end: all phrases save the last begin alike; the last begins abruptly with a different motif, as if the prior, singing the invocations, broke in at that point with a different melodic motif to signal that this was the last time around.

Many Kyries, early and late, have a phrase repetition within the invocation of the last Kyrie. This kind of repetition could have been at one time another means of signalling the choir (although here again the same repeated phrase structure occurs in sequences within certain couplets for the purely musical purpose of marking the climax of the melody). None of this is to be taken as argument that individual Kyries go back to the 7th or 8th centuries, only that Kyries composed in the 9th and 10th centuries might well recall, deliberately and in stylized manner, an earlier practice.

The establishment of the ninefold shape seems to have been the work of the Franks and their preoccupation with order; from that time on, the large tripartite division remained a basic feature of Kyrie construction (most visible in Kyries with the form *AAABBBCCC*), and has been used as such by modern scholars in analysing Kyrie chants. Yet the litany ingredient remained strong in the Kyrie, engendering other modes of construction that cut across the tripartite division while being no less characteristic of Frankish craft. A series of litanies has no inherent sectional structure: it goes on endlessly, perhaps rising in intensity, but not falling naturally into larger groupings unless these are imposed from outside. Many of the early Kyrie melodies show an overall ascent in pitch from start to finish; often 'Christe', and even more often the following 'Kyrie', attack a higher pitch. The Kyrie ad libitum VI, favoured for high feasts in the 10th century, shows the ascent most dramatically.

Here as elsewhere, however, the overall ascent does not proceed directly, but rather through a series of alternations: successive petitions are higher or lower, or the melodic material is arranged in some such pattern as *ABACBCDCD* (*Conditor kyrie omnium*, ad libitum V). In some respects this pattern shows an enthusiasm for interlocking musical construction comparable with northern interlace patterns in graphic arts, and as such would not be due directly to a litany model; but such interlocking design always tends to obliterate a sectional structure, thus creating the continuity characteristic of litanies (in a very artful way), and might even imitate some kind of antiphonal performance.

The most important segment of the repertory – the Kyries in widespread use during the 10th and 12th centuries – show a remarkable wealth of melodic invention and organization. There are occasional borrowings of phrases from one piece to another, and (as in other medieval categories in the process of creation and development) much reworking of individual pieces through a long series of variants. Nonetheless, the individual work is clearly perceptible in its artistic integrity, exhibiting a carefully wrought plan and detail. Most characteristic, perhaps, is the development of motivic material (sometimes of great expressiveness) to bind the ninefold shape together.

4. LATIN TEXTS ('TROPES'). Latin texts for Kyrie take the form of more prolix invocations that expand upon or replace the word 'Kyrie' (as in the two cases shown in ex.1). Whether such a text begins with the word 'Kyrie'

or not seems to be without morphological significance; *Conditor kyrie omnium* falls neatly between those that begin with 'Kyrie' and those that omit it altogether. Among early Kyries, however, the word 'eleison' is less frequently omitted, especially in French as opposed to German sources. The Latin texts, acclamatory in nature, tend to consist of epithets in apposition, without strong syntactic connections; such texts do not provide the binding force of a work, but rather its low-level articulation.

Latin texts tend to be provided for festal occasions, in some cases bordering on the function of a 'proper' text. Simple Kyries were intended in the 11th century for simple occasions, when, as Gregory said in the 6th century, the 'other things usually said' were omitted. Another possible application of Gregory's comment is to assume that a more elaborate Kyrie could be sung on feast days with its Latin text, on lesser occasions without it. Still another is to imagine that each of the nine petitions was sung twice, first with, then without its Latin text, as a reminiscence of the 18-fold antiphonal practice prescribed for festal occasions in *Ordo romanus XV*.

BIBLIOGRAPHY

J. A. Jungmann: *Missarum sollemnia* (Vienna, 1948, 5/1962; Eng. trans., 1951)

M. Landwehr-Melnicki: *Das einstimmige Kyrie des lateinischen Mittelalters* (Regensburg, 1955)

For further bibliography *see* PLAINCHANT.

RICHARD L. CROCKER

Kyrton (*fl* 1545). English composer. He is known only for an organ setting of the 13-bar plainsong antiphon *Miserere* in the earliest section of *GB-Lbm* Add.29996 (EECM, vi, no.18). Curiously, it was recopied; the second copy appears at the head of the MS in its present state.

JOHN CALDWELL

Kyrzinger. *See* KÜRZINGER family.

Kytte. *See* KIT.

Kyui, Tsezar Antonovich. *See* CUI, CÉSAR.

Kyurkchiiski, Krasimir (*b* Troyan, 22 July 1936). Bulgarian composer. In 1962 he graduated from the Sofia State Academy of Music as a composition pupil of Vladigerov. He then worked as leader of the folk orchestra of the state folksong and dance ensemble, later living as a freelance composer. His music is brilliant, coloured by national traits, and employs novel technical means.

WORKS
(selective list)

Adagio, str orch, 1959; Diafonichna studiya, orch, 1962; Kantata za partiyata [Cantata for the party], chorus, orch, 1962; Balada za Paisii [Ballad for Paisii]. chorus, orch, 1962; Sinfonie-Requiem, 1966; Balada za avtoportreta [Ballad for the self-portrait], ballet, 1967; Moite spomeni [My memories], S/T, str orch, 1969; Yula, opera, 1969; Arie, str orch, 1971; Conc., orch, 1975

Inst pieces, solo and choral songs, folksong arrs.

Principal publisher: Nauka i izkustvo

LADA BRASHOVANOVA

Ex.1

Ky- ri - e rex ge- ni- tor in - ge- ni - te ve- ra es -sen- ti - a

e- le - i -son! Or - bis factor rex e-ter-ne e - - lei - son!

L

L. See LARGAMENTE.

La. The sixth and final degree of the Guidonian HEXA-CHORD; *see also* SOLMIZATION, §I. In TONIC SOL-FA, the sharpened submediant of the prevailing key (or, if this is minor, its relative major). In French, Italian and Spanish usage, the note A; *see* PITCH NAMES.

Laban, Rudolf von (*b* Pozsony [now Bratislava], 15 Dec 1879; *d* Weybridge, 1 July 1958). Hungarian dancer, choreographer and inventor of a system of dance notation. The son of a general, he was intended for a military career but in 1900 went to study at the Ecole des Beaux Arts in Paris. He became a dancer at the Moulin Rouge, toured North Africa in a revue, and later danced in Leipzig, Dresden, Münster and, in 1907–10, Vienna. In 1910 he opened a school of modern dance in Munich, at which Mary Wigman studied. He worked in Zurich during World War I and in 1919 went to Stuttgart; there he started the Laban Dance Theatre at which Kurt Jooss joined him as a pupil, accompanying him to Mannheim in 1921–3. Laban was ballet director in Hamburg from 1923 to 1925 and founded a Choreographic Institute in Würzburg in 1926. From 1930 to 1934 he was ballet director of the Berlin Staatsoper. In 1928 his book *Schifttanz* was published, presenting his system of movement notation, Kinetography Laban, which crystallized many years of thought on the anatomy of movement. For the 1936 Berlin Olympics Laban prepared an open-air performance of 1000 dancers and singers, similar to one that he had produced in Vienna in 1929, but Goebbels banned the performance. In 1937 Laban came to England, joining Jooss and his company at Dartington; during World War II and until 1951 he worked in Manchester, applying his analysis of movement to the uses of industry, and presenting his findings in *Effort* (1947, with F. C. Lawrence). In 1953 Laban moved to Addlestone, Surrey, where his former associate Lisa Ullmann had founded an Art of Movement School, and he worked there until his death. He published his *Principles of Dance and Movement Notation* in 1954, by which time his system of dance notation was widely accepted; in 1953 it was renamed Labanotation by the Dance Notation Bureau in New York. The music staves run vertically up the left of the page, and a three-staff column with printed symbols for the choreography runs alongside it; it is read from the bottom upwards (see illustration, p.335). Laban choreographed many ballets danced in the free, plastic style of modern dance, but none survives.

WRITINGS

Die Welt des Tänzers (Stuttgart, 1920)
Choreographie (Jena, 1926)
Des Kindes Gymnastik und Tanz (Oldenburg, 1926)
Kinetographie Laban (Vienna, 1928)
Ein Leben für den Tanz (Dresden, 1935)
with F. C. Lawrence: *Effort* (London, 1947)
Principles of Dance and Movement Notation (London, 1954)

BIBLIOGRAPHY

The New Era, xl/5 (1959) [entire issue]
A. Hutchinson: *Labanotation: the System of Analyzing and Recording Movement* (London and New York, 1954, rev. 2/1970)

For further bibliography *see* DANCE, §VII.

G. B. L. WILSON

La Barre [Chabanceau de la Barre]. French family of musicians active mainly at the French court from the late 16th century to the early 18th. Many court records give their name as Chabanceau de la Barre; it seems likely that their name was originally Chabanceau but that they later adopted, and preferred to be known by, the name De La Barre.

The earliest recorded musician in the family is the organist Pierre (i), who is first mentioned as an organist in Paris in 1567 and who died on 12 January 1600. Four sons of his first marriage – Claude, Pierre (ii), Jehan and Germain – became musicians. The only child of his second marriage to do so was (1) Pierre (iii). Except for the son of Pierre (ii), Pierre (iv), and Germain's eldest child, Sébastien, all the musicians of the third generation of La Barres were children of (1) Pierre (iii): Charles Henry, (2) Anne, Benjamin, (3) Joseph and (4) Pierre (v).

A 'Monsr de la Barre organiste', who cannot otherwise be identified, copied 11 manuscripts of French music (now in *US-BE*). MS 773 contains two solo motets by him (one dated 1718), and 775 includes an *air à boire*. Curtis speculated that this La Barre composed some of the numerous *airs* printed in various 18th-century collections that are generally attributed to MICHEL DE LA BARRE.

According to Gustafson there may have been another musician named La Barre, possibly resident in England. Keyboard music attributable to him appears in several manuscripts (*D-Bds* Lynar A1, *DK-Kk* Kgl. Saml.376, *E-Mn* 1360, *F-Pc* Rés.1185, *GB-Lbm* Add.10337, *Och* Mus.378, 1177, 1236, *I-Rvat* Chigi Q IV.24, *NL-Uim* q-1, *S-Uu* Ihre 284, *US-NH* Ma 21 H 59, *NYp* Drexel 5611 and in private collections: for full details see Gustafson).

(1) Pierre de la Barre (iii) (*b* Paris, baptized 27 Jan 1592; *d* Paris, buried 31 March 1656). Keyboard player and composer, son of Pierre de la Barre (i). He had become established as an organist by 1611 and was attached to the king's chamber by 1618. By 1627 he had also become organist of the royal chapel and *maître joueur d'épinette* to the king and by 1630 organist to the queen, whom he later served as spinet player too. Both Mersenne and de Gouy (see Prod'homme) praised his excellent spinet, harpsichord and organ playing, and Mersenne (Eng. trans., 476f) printed portions of his diminutions on an *air* by Louis XIII as an example of what the 'cleverest and quickest hands are able to execute' on the organ. Highly knowledgeable about musical instruments as well, La Barre wrote to Constantijn Huygens, with whom he conducted a sustained correspondence, that he had invented a device 'to make the keyboards [of the harpsichord] move for playing in all sorts of tones and semitones'. Before 1650 he established in his house the first concerts of sacred music, in which important musicians of the time as well as three of his own children – Charles Henry, (2) Anne and (3) Joseph – took part. He was a composer of some merit, who according to de Gouy wrote both for instruments and for the voice; most of his compositions, however, have either disappeared or cannot be positively identified. His *airs de violon* written for several *ballets de cour* about 1619 are no longer extant. A courante for lute (in *RISM* 1617[26], transcr. Tiersot, 1927), sometimes ascribed to him, might equally well be by one of his half-brothers, especially Pierre (ii), who was known as a lutenist. Apel maintained that three keyboard courantes, early examples of this genre, found in the Lynar tablature A1 (in *D-Bds*) probably originated with him since the collection dates from the 1630s at the latest (but see Gustafson). Three dances (in *I-Rvat* Chigi Q IV.24, ff.47ff) signed 'Monsu della Bar' and three other manuscript pieces (in *GB-Och* 1177, 1236, ed. J. Bonfils, L'organiste liturgique, xviii, Paris, 1957, 27ff), one of which is identical with one of the Lynar tablature dances, may also be by him. A collection of his keyboard works that according to Mersenne was going to be published by Ballard seems never to have come out. (For other pieces see (3) Joseph de la Barre below.)

(2) Anne de la Barre (*b* Paris, baptized 3 July 1628; *d* before 7 March 1688). Singer, daughter of (1) Pierre de la Barre (iii). One of the leading singers at the French court, she was praised as early as 1646 by Luigi Rossi for her excellent interpretation of his music. In late 1652 or early 1653 she left for the Swedish court at the invitation of Queen Christina, staying on the way with Huygens at The Hague. She remained in Sweden, where she enjoyed enormous success, until well into 1654. She then went to serve the Queen of Denmark at Copenhagen, returning to France through Kassel in late 1655. Between 1656 and 1664 she sang frequently in court ballets, Italian operas (including Cavalli's *Ercole amante*) and church music on ceremonial occasions. She also appeared privately before the king in his chamber. When in January 1661 she was in fact appointed *ordinaire* of the king's chamber music, the announcement of her appointment praised her in terms scarcely equalled in other such documents. By 1667, when she married a bourgeois named Antoine Coquerel, her career seems to have slackened, but she remained in the royal chamber music until she was pensioned in 1686.

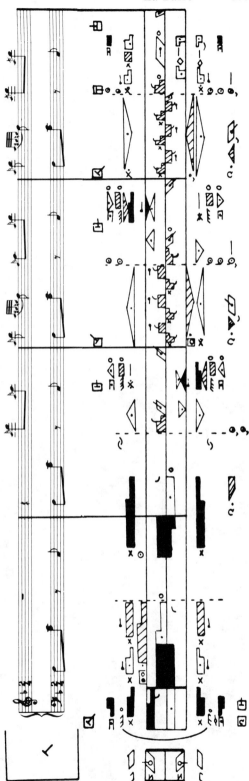

Labanotation for part of the Girl's solo from the Blue Bird pas de deux in the last act of Tchaikovsky's 'The Sleeping Beauty', choreographed by Petipa

(3) **Joseph de la Barre** (*b* Paris, baptized 21 May 1633; *d* before 6 May 1678). Organist and composer, son of (1) Pierre de la Barre (iii). He accompanied his sister, (2) Anne de la Barre, on her northern sojourn and on his father's death in 1656 succeeded him as organist of the royal chapel. His order of appointment cited both 'his capacity in the composition of music' and 'his dexterity in touching the organ'. Two of the La Barre brothers were active as instrumentalists in court ballets during the late 1650s, and the elder, who seems to have played the harpsichord, was probably either Joseph or Charles Henry. In 1674 Joseph was provided with a benefice, the Benedictine abbey of St Hilaire in the diocese of Carcassonne, and as a result he became known as 'L'abbé de la Barre'. On one occasion, in 1677, he is listed as a singer in the royal chapel. Most of his 18 two-part *airs* of 1669 are provided with *doubles*. Printing in 1678 his *Dolorosi pensieri*, a favourite of the king's, the *Mercure galant* stated that it had been circulated by some as a composition of Luigi Rossi. The Bauyn MS (in *F-Pn*) contains five harpsichord dances ascribed to a La Barre without a first name, as well as a 'gigue' assigned to Joseph that is nearly identical with one of the five dances, which is called an allemande. On the basis of stylistic similarity, a second allemande and its twin 'gigue' among these pieces can also be attributed to Joseph. The remaining dances, both courantes, may be by either Joseph or his father, (1) Pierre de la Barre (iii). One of them also reappears in the Parville MS (in

US-BE) along with seven other dances and a prelude signed 'La Barre', four of which are unique to this manuscript.

WORKS

Airs à deux parties, avec les seconds couplets en diminution (Paris, 1669)

Dolorosi pensieri, air, 3vv, b, in *Mercure galant* (Aug 1678)

Airs, ritornellos, 1665[4], 1695[5]

7 Italian arias; lost, cited in Liste de plusieurs opéras italiens (MS, *F-V* 138, ff.24–5)

2 allemandes, hpd, *Pn* Bauyn, Rés.Vm[7] 675, ff.103*v*, 104*v*; ed. J. Bonfils, L'organiste liturgique, xviii (Paris, 1957); 2 almost identical works called 'gigue', Vm[7] 674[2], ff.43*r*, 45*v*

2 courantes, hpd, *Pn* Bauyn Rés.Vm[7] 674[2], ff.40*v*, 49*r* [possibly by (1) Pierre de la Barre (iii)]; ed. J. Bonfils, L'organiste liturgique, xviii (Paris, 1957)

1 prelude, 3 allemandes [1 called 'courante'], 3 courantes, 1 sarabande, 1 gigue, hpd, *US-BE*, Parville 778, pp.15, 30–33, 35, 102–7, 171 [possibly by (1) Pierre de la Barre (iii)]

(4) **Pierre de la Barre (v)** (*b* Paris, baptized 18 Oct 1634; *d* before 18 April 1710). Instrumentalist, singer and composer, youngest child of (1) Pierre de la Barre (iii). He may have become a lutenist to the king on 31 March 1645 at the unusually early age of ten. He was probably the 'La Barre le cadet' who played the theorbo in court ballets during the 1650s and 1660s. In 1678 he belonged to the music of the queen and in 1699 to that of the Duchess of Burgundy. He seems to have sung and to have played the spinet and bass viol as well as the lute and theorbo. In 1663 he entered the royal chapel and was playing the theorbo and the 'grosse basse de violon'

1. French musicians (c1710): painting attributed to Robert Tournières in the National Gallery, London; the music on the table is by Michel de La Barre, and the standing figure is thought to be a portrait of the composer (see Huskinson)

there as late as 1708. In 1692 he was named one of nine theorbo masters in Du Pradel's *Livre commode*. On 5 July 1697 he was made a nobleman and awarded a coat-of-arms. A courante for lute in a manuscript (in *F-B* 279.152) compiled by Etienne Vaudry de Saizenay in 1699 may well be of his composition. Two Italian arias, no longer extant, ascribed to 'La Barre C' or 'La Barre le cadet' (in *F-V* Mus.138) are the only other pieces he is known to have written.

BIBLIOGRAPHY

M. Mersenne: *Harmonie universelle* (Paris, 1636–7/*R*1963; Eng. trans., 1957), 214ff, 473ff
J. Loret: *La muze historique* (Paris, 1650–65); ed. J. Ravenel and E. V. de la Pelouze (Paris, 1857–78); relevant extracts with biographical notices repr. in Y. de Brossard: 'La vie musicale en France d'après Loret et ses continuateurs: 1650–1688', *RMFC*, x (1970), 117–93
C. C. d'Assoucy: *La prison de M. Dassoucy* (Paris, 1674); repr. in *Aventures burlesques de Dassoucy*, ed. E. Colombey (Paris, 1858), 436, 439
W. J. A. Jonckbloet and J. P. N. Land, eds.: *Musique et musiciens au XVIIᵉ siècle: correspondance et oeuvres musicales de Constantin Huygens* (Leiden, 1882), pp.cxlvi ff, 17, 19ff, 55
E. Thoinan: 'La Barre et Florimont: rivaux de Molière', *Le Moliériste*, ix (1887–8), 161
M. Brenet: 'Notes sur l'histoire du luth en France', *RMI*, vi (1899), 1–44, esp. 23, 25; pubd separately (Turin, 1899/*R*1973)
——: *Les concerts en France sous l'ancien régime* (Paris, 1900/*R*1969), 55ff, 59ff
J. Ecorcheville: *Actes d'état civil de musiciens insinués au Châtelet de Paris (1539–1650)* (Paris, 1907), 23f
J. G. Prod'homme: *Ecrits de musiciens (XVᵉ–XVIIIᵉ siècles)* (Paris, 1912) [incl. letters of (1) Pierre (iii) and (2) Anne de la Barre, 174ff, and preface to J. de Gouy: *Airs à quatre parties* (Paris, 1650), 156ff]
H. Prunières: *L'opéra italien en France avant Lulli* (Paris, 1913)
T. Gérold: *L'art du chant en France au XVIIᵉ siècle* (Strasbourg, 1921/*R*1971), 117, 126ff, 149ff
J. Tiersot: 'Une famille de musiciens français au XVIIᵉ siècle: les De La Barre', *RdM*, xi (1927), 185; xii (1928), 1, 68
F. Lesure: 'La facture instrumentale à Paris au seizième siècle', *GSJ*, vii (1954), 45
P. Hardouin: 'Notes sur quelques musiciens français du XVIIe siècle: I. Les Chabanceau de la Barre', *RdM*, xxxviii (1956), 62
M. le Moël: 'Les dernières années de J. Champion de Chambonnières', *RMFC*, i (1960), 31
J. Eppelsheim: *Das Orchester in den Werken Jean-Baptiste Lullys* (Tutzing, 1961), 56ff
N. Dufourcq and M. Benoit: 'Les musiciens de Versailles à travers les minutes notariales de Lamy versées aux Archives départementales de Seine-et-Oise', *RMFC*, iii (1963), 192, 194
L. E. S. J. de Laborde: *Musiciens de Paris, 1535–1792*, ed. Y. de Brossard (Paris, 1965), 158ff
W. Apel: *Geschichte der Orgel- und Klaviermusik bis 1700* (Kassel, 1967; Eng. trans., rev., 1972), 497, 505ff, 712f, 806f
M. Jurgens: *Documents du minutier central concernant l'histoire de la musique, 1600–1650* (Paris, 1967)
A. Curtis: 'Musique classique française à Berkeley', *RdM*, lvi (1970), 123–64
M. Benoit: *Musiques de cour: chapelle, chambre, écurie, 1661–1733* (Paris, 1971)
——: *Versailles et les musiciens du roi 1661–1733* (Paris, 1971)
B. Gustafson: *The Sources of Seventeenth-century French Harpsichord Music* (diss., U. of Michigan, 1976)

JANE M. BOWERS

La Barre, Michel de (*b* *c*1675; *d* 1743 or 1744). French composer and flautist. As his first instrumental work, a set of six trio suites for violins, flutes, oboes and continuo, was published in 1694, it seems likely that he was born by *c*1675. The first reference to him as a performer dates from the year 1700 when he travelled to Spain as a player of the 'flûte allemande' for the Count of Ayen. During the same year his first *opéra-ballet*, *Le triomphe des arts*, was published, and its title-page reveals that he also played at the Académie Royale de Musique. In 1702 La Barre brought out his first book of solo suites for transverse flute and bass, the first solo pieces for flute to appear in print in any country. In May 1704 he took over Antoine Piesche's position in the Musettes et

2. Beginning of the first suite from the 'Premier livre de pièces' (1710) by Michel de La Barre

Hautbois de Poitou, and in 1705 the privilege which he received to publish his second *opéra-ballet*, *La vénitienne*, shows that he was a flautist in the royal chamber music as well. According to Claude Parfaict, he was regarded as the best flautist of his time, and was particularly celebrated for his very expressive playing.

By 1710, when La Barre brought out his second book of flute solos, he had already published three books of trios, numerous songs, and two suites for two unaccompanied flutes, a genre which he was the first in France to establish and which was to occupy him almost exclusively for the rest of his career. In 1725, when his last extant instrumental work appeared, he was still playing in the royal chamber music, although he had retired from the Académie Royale de Musique by 1721. He resigned from the Musettes et Hautbois de Poitou towards the end of 1730; nothing further is known about his activities from then until the time of his death.

The preface to his epoch-making first book of solo flute suites describes La Barre's intention of bringing his instrument to perfection, following the model of Marin Marais who had done so much for the perfection of the viol. It also contains the first information in print about slurring and ornamentation on the transverse flute. Most of the suites in this book have eight or nine movements, and each begins with a prelude and allemande pair. The other movements include dances of various types, rondeaux, airs and pieces with only names or character titles; they are arranged in no regular order. Most of the solo suites of La Barre's later two books (1710 and 1722) contain only four movements, a reduction that probably came about in response to the Italian sonata style which was sweeping France during the first decade of the 18th century.

La Barre's later duet and trio suites are likewise shorter than the earlier ones. The duets in his ninth book are called sonatas, but apart from the inclusion in one of them of an Italianate 3/2 Lentement, they resemble the four-movement suites. La Barre's trio suites are technically less advanced than either his solos or duets. They contain an abundance of short, simple dance movements as well as some slow, pathetic preludes and *plaintes*. The third book of trios also includes the first trio sonatas intended solely for transverse flutes and bass to appear in France. They conform to the following plan: slow prelude, fast fugue or gigue, moderate gavotte or rondeau, and fast fugue or gigue; and they exhibit somewhat more Italian characteristics than La Barre's other works.

La Barre's music for the flute helped make that instrument one of the most fashionable of the time. It also established a flute style that persisted until the middle of the 1720s, most notably in the works of Jacques Hotteterre le Romain. But La Barre's significance also rests upon the actual quality of his work. Though sometimes marred by excessive simplicity, much of it is imaginative, sensitively wrought and full of feeling and spirit. His vocal works are of less importance than his instrumental ones. Neither of his two *opéra-ballets* was repeated in its entirety after the year of its initial performance. Nevertheless, many melodies from *Le triomphe des arts* were copied into various 18th-century manuscript collections. Other *airs* attributed to 'M. de la Barre' appeared in collections published between 1694 and 1734. Although Curtis has suggested that some of these may have been composed by another La Barre, a 1724 collection devoted exclusively to the flautist's *airs à boire* definitely establishes his activity in this line of composition.

A group portrait attributed to Robert Tournières belonging to the National Gallery in London is thought to depict the figure of La Barre (see fig.1, p.336).

WORKS
(all printed works published in Paris)

INSTRUMENTAL

Pièces en trio, 2 vn/fl/ob, bc (1694; 2/1707 as 1er livre des trio)
Pièces en trio, 2 vn/fl/ob, bc, livre second (1700)
Pièces, fl, bc, op.4 (1702; 2/1710 as 1er livre de pièces)
3e livre des trio, 2 vn/fl/ob, bc, mêléz de sonates, 2 fl, bc (1707)
1er livre contenant une suite, 2 fl (1709); also as 1ere suitte de pièces (1709)
2e suite de pièces, 2 fl (1710)
2e livre de pièces, fl, bc (1710)
3e suite, 2 fl (1711)
4e suite, 2 fl (1711); incl. also 5e suite
5e livre contenant la 6e, et la 7e suite, 2 fl (1713)
6e livre contenant la 8e, et la 9e suite, 2 fl (1714)
7e livre contenant la 10e et la 11e suite, 2 fl (1721)
8e livre contenant 2 suites, fl, bc (1722)
9e livre contenant 2 sonates, 2 fl (1722)
10e livre contenant 2 suittes, 2 fl (1722)
12e livre contenant 2 suites, 2 fl (1725)
11th and 13th bks, presumably for 2 fl, lost

STAGE
(produced at l'Académie royale de musique)

Le triomphe des arts (ballet, A. H. de la Motte), 16 May 1700, F-Pn; as op.3 (1700)
La vénitienne (comédie-ballet, de la Motte), 26 May 1705, B-Bc, F-Pc, Pn, S-Uu

VOCAL

Recueil d'airs à boire à deux parties (1724)
Original airs and arrangements in collections: 1694[2], 1694[3], Recueils d'airs sérieux et à boire (1694[4], 1695[3], 1696[2], 1697[2], 1699[2], 1700[2], 1702-5, 1707–9, 1712), Recueil des meilleurs airs italiens (1703), Recueils d'airs sérieux et à boire (Amsterdam, 1707–9), Tendresses bacchiques, ou duo et trio mêléz de petits airs tendres et à boire (1712, 1718), Nouveau recueil de chansons choisies, ii, iv (The Hague, 1724, 1729), Meslanges de musique latine, françoise et italienne (1726–8), Nouvelles poésies spirituelles et morales (1730-31), Les parodies nouvelles et les vaudevilles inconnus (1732), Recueil d'airs ajoutéz à différents opéra depuis l'année 1698 (1734); also in F-Pc

WRITINGS

Mémoire de M. de La Barre sur les musettes et hautbois (MS, Paris, Archives Nationales 0[1] 878 no.240)

BIBLIOGRAPHY

Mercure galant (Dec 1700), 235; (Sept–Oct 1710), 229
Histoire de l'Académie royale de musique depuis son établissement, 1645, jusqu'à 1709, composée et écrite par un des secrétaires de Lully (MS, F-Po B230), 198f, 206f
Catalogue général de musique imprimée ou gravée en France (Paris, 1737), 49
'Lettre de M. l'Abbé Carbasus, à M. de ** ... sur la mode des instrumens de musique', Mercure de France, ii (1739), June, 1360
P.-L. D'Aquin: Lettres sur les hommes célèbres ... sous le règne de Louis XV (Paris, 1752), 149
C. Parfaict: Dictionnaire des théâtres de Paris (Paris, 1756), i, 382
J. B. de La Borde: Essai sur la musique ancienne et moderne (Paris, 1780/R1972), iii, 384
T. de Lajarte: Bibliothèque musicale du théâtre de l'opéra: catalogue historique, chronologique, anecdotique (Paris, 1878), i, 89f, 105
M. Brenet: 'La librairie musicale en France de 1653 à 1790, d'après les registres de privilèges', SIMG, viii (1906–7), 419, 422, 427
J.-G. Prod'homme, ed.: 'Mémoire de M. de la Barre: sur les musettes et hautbois &c.', Ecrits de musiciens (XVe–XVIIIe siècles) (Paris, 1912), 241
L. de La Laurencie: 'La musique française de Lulli à Gluck', EMDC, I/iii (1921), 1529
L. Fleury: 'The Flute and Flutists in the French Art of the Seventeenth and Eighteenth Centuries', MQ, ix (1923), 515f, 528f
S. Wallon: 'La Barre, Michel de', MGG
A. Curtis: 'Musique classique française à Berkeley', RdM, lvi (1970), 126
M. Benoit: Musiques de cour: chapelle, chambre, écurie, 1661–1733 (Paris, 1971)
J. Bowers: The French Flute School from 1700 to 1760 (diss., U. of California, Berkeley, 1971)
J. Huskinson: 'Les ordinaires de la musique du roi', RMFC, xvii (1977), 15 [in Eng.]

JANE M. BOWERS

Labarre [Berry], Théodore(-François-Joseph) (*b* Paris, 5 March 1805; *d* Paris, 9 March 1870). French harpist and composer, foster-brother of Napoleon III. He studied the harp with Bochsa, Cousineau and Nadermann, harmony with Dourlens, counterpoint with Eler and Fétis and composition with Boieldieu. In 1823 he won second prize in the Prix de Rome for his cantata *Pyramus et Thisbé* and subsequently embarked on concert tours of England, Italy and Switzerland. On his return to France in 1831 he turned his attention to the theatre, writing operas, ballets and incidental music. He also wrote music for the harp as well as romances, some of which became extremely popular (*La pauvre négresse* was one of Cornélie Falcon's great drawing-room successes). In 1837 Labarre married the singer Mlle Lambert, and from then on spent about an equal amount of time in France and England. He was a conductor at the Opéra-Comique from 1847 to 1849, and was appointed director of the imperial chapel in 1852. He succeeded Antoine Prumier as professor of harp at the Paris Conservatoire, where Léon Gatayes and Félix Godefroid were among his pupils. During the last years of his life he was music critic for *Paris illustré*. He was awarded the Légion d'honneur in 1862.

WORKS
((selective list) all first performed in Paris; printed works published in Paris)

STAGE
PO – *Opéra*   OC – *Opéra-Comique*

Les deux familles (incidental music, 3, Planard, after Corneille: Le Cid), OC, 2 Jan 1831
La révolte des femmes (ballet, 3, Taglioni), PO, 4 Dec 1833
L'aspirant de marine (opéra-comique, 1, Rochefort and Decomberousse), OC, 2 June 1834
Le ménétrier ou Les deux duchesses (opera, 3, Scribe), OC, 9 Aug 1845
Jovita ou Les boucaniers (ballet, 3 tableaux, Mazillier), PO, 11 Nov 1853
La Fonti (ballet, 6 tableaux, Mazillier), PO, 8 Jan 1855
Pantagruel (opéra-comique, 2, H. Trianon), PO, 24 Dec 1855
Graziosa (ballet, 1, Derley and L. Petipa), PO, 26 March 1861
Le roi d'Yvetot (ballet, 1, P. de Massa and Petipa), PO, 28 Dec 1865

OTHER WORKS

Fantaisie, harp, orch, op.101 (1841); Trios, harp, hn, bn, op.6; duos, harp, hn
Grand duo du couronnement, harp, pf, op.104 (1841); numerous salon pieces, harp, pf
Numerous concert works for solo harp
Romances, 1v, pf/harp
Méthode complète pour la harpe (1844)

BIBLIOGRAPHY

FétisB

Obituary, *Revue et gazette musicale* (13 March 1870)

R. Rensch: *The Harp: its History, Technique and Repertoire* (London and New York, 1969), 112ff

FRÉDÉRIC ROBERT

Labarte Keyboard Manuscript. *See* SOURCES OF KEYBOARD MUSIC TO 1660, §2(iii).

La Bassée, Adam de. *See* ADAM DE LA BASSÉE.

Labaun [Laboun]. Family of printers. Jiří Labaun had a printing works in Prague, probably from 1686 to 1708 (some authors extend the time from 1687 or 1688 to 1710 or 1713); besides prayers, sermons, disputations, calendars, legal and other documents he also printed music by such composers as Holan Rovenský and Wentzely. After his death his son Jiří Ondřej took over the business and continued to publish music, including a new edition of Holan Rovenský's *Kaple králoyska zpěvní a muzikální* and works by Brenntner and Gunther Jakob. After Jiří Ondřej's death his widow continued the business; she printed Černohorský's *Laudetur Jesus Christus* and Vaňura's *Litaniae lauretanae*. The printing works, which remained in the Labaun family until probably 1769, also produced a series of occasional songs.

BIBLIOGRAPHY

ČSHS

J. Volf: *Dějiny českého knihtiskařství do roku 1848* [History of Czech book printing to 1848] (Prague, 1926)

K. Chyba: *Slovník knihtiskařů v Československu od nejstarších dob do roku 1860* [Dictionary of printers in Czechoslovakia from early times to 1860] (Prague, 1966–)

ZDENĚK CULKA

L'abbé [Saint-Sévin]. French family of musicians.

(1) L'abbé *l'aîné* [Pierre-Philippe Saint-Sévin] (*b* ?Agen, ?c1700; *d* Paris, 15 May 1768). Cellist. While employed as *maître de musique* at the church of St Caprais in Agen, he took minor orders, thus bequeathing to his family its sobriquet 'L'abbé'. He may have reached Paris by September 1726, for a play given at the Foire St Laurent at that time (*Les amours déguisés* by Fuzelier, Le Sage and D'Orneval) had music by an 'Abbé'. In 1727 he joined the Opéra orchestra as cellist, soon promoted to the first desk where he remained until pensioned in 1767. He also was a member of the Concert Spirituel orchestra from the 1740s until 1762 and of the *musique de la chambre* at the French court from about 1753 until his death. With Blavet (flute), J.-B. Forqueray (viol) and Marella (violin) he performed Telemann's 'Paris' quartets at four sessions of the Concert Spirituel in June 1745. He was considered in part responsible for the demise of the bass viol, for Corrette, in his *Méthode de violoncelle* (Paris, 1741), wrote of 'the happy arrival of the violoncello in Paris through Messrs Batistin Stuck and L'abbé, both virtuosos. At present in the King's Music, at the Opéra, and in concerts, it is the violoncello which plays the basso continuo'.

(2) L'abbé *le cadet* [Pierre Saint-Sévin] (*b* ?Agen, ?c1710; *d* Paris, March 1777). Cellist, brother of (1) L'abbé *l'aîné*. Like his brother, he took minor orders at St Caprais in Agen, and in 1730 joined the cello section of the Paris Opéra, where he was a member of the *basses du Petit Choeur* until 1767 and the leader of the *basses du Grand Choeur* from then until pensioned in 1776. He also played at the Sainte-Chapelle from 1764 until 1777.

(3) L'abbé *le fils* [Joseph-Barnabé Saint-Sévin] (*b* Agen, 11 June 1727; *d* Paris, 25 July 1803). Composer and violinist, son of (1) L'abbé *l'aîné*. A child prodigy, he won a position in the orchestra of the Comédie-Française at the age of 11 in competition with the outstanding violinists Mangean and Branche. This feat brought him to the attention of Jean-Marie Leclair, who gave him lessons between 1740 and 1742. In the latter year L'abbé joined the Paris Opéra orchestra, in which he served for 20 years; he was then denied his pension owing to his youth, even though he had served a full term. His solo début was at the Concert Spirituel in 1741, when he performed a Leclair violin duo with the 13-year-old Gaviniès. More than three dozen solo performances at those concerts until 1754 established him as one of the finest violinists of the mid-18th century. Until the Revolution he lived in semi-retirement, teaching, composing a little, but not performing in public. During the Revolution he lost his fortune, and was forced by necessity to play in the orchestra of the Théâtre de la République et des Arts until feebleness caused his retirement on a tiny pension. He died alone, poor and forgotten.

L'abbé was an accomplished composer. His sonatas, opp.1 and 8, are in the older 'Baroque' style of Leclair, and are among the few works of the period which bear serious comparison with Leclair's sonatas. Two movements of the op.8 sonatas offer relatively rare examples of fully written-out cadenzas. His symphonies, on the contrary, are true symphonies in the modern sense, and among the earliest of the genre to appear in Paris. His collections of *airs* illustrate the lightening of taste in Paris after 1752 following the impact of the Querelle des Bouffons. The *Principes du violon* is a treatise of major importance, ranking just behind those of Leopold Mozart and Geminiani as a basic source of information on mid-18th-century violin playing. According to Wirsta (1961), the *Principes*, among its other virtues, was the earliest violin method to describe pronation, half-position, the modern fashion of holding the violin, the technique of double stops and the application of *sons filés* and arpeggios to the violin, and was the first publication since Mondonville's prefatory essay to *Les sons harmoniques* (1738) to discuss the production of harmonics.

WORKS

Orch: Premier simphonie en concert, str, bc (*c*1751); Seconde simphonie (*c*1752); 6 symphonies, str, bc, op.2 (1753); Menuet[s] de MM. Exaudet et Granier, mis en grand symphonie avec des variations, 2 vn, obs/fls, va, 2 hn, vc/bn (1764)

Chamber: 6 sonates, vn, bc, op.1 (1748); Symphonie, 2 hn, 1750, lost; Suite d'airs, 2 obs, va d'amore, va, 1754, lost; Premier [– Troisième] recueil d'airs français et italiens avec des variations (2 vn/tr viols)/(fl/ob, vn), op.3 (1756), op.4 (1757), op.5 (1758); Recueil d'airs, vn, op.6 (*c*1759), lost; Jolis airs ajustés et variés, vn, op.7 (1763); 6 sonates, vn, bc, op.8 (1763); Recueil quatrième de duos d'Opéra-Comique, 2 vn (1772)

Doubtful: Ov. to Gilles, garçon peintre, l'amoureux et rival, orch, attrib. L'abbé by Brook (1962), probably by J.-B. de La Borde

WRITINGS

Principes du violon pour apprendre le doigté de cet instrument, et les differens agremens dont il est susceptibles (Paris, 1761/*R*1961, 2/1772)

BIBLIOGRAPHY

J.-B. de La Borde: *Essai sur la musique ancienne et moderne* (Paris, 1780/*R*1972)

L. de La Laurencie: *L'école française de violon de Lully à Viotti* (Paris, 1922–4/*R*1971)

A. Wirsta: *Ecoles de violon au XVIIIème siècle* (diss., U. of Paris, 1955)

——: Introduction to facs. edn. of *Principes du violon . . . par Mr. L'abbé le fils* (Paris, 1961)

B. S. Brook: *La symphonie française* (Paris, 1962)

C. Pierre: *Histoire du Concert spirituel 1725–1790* (Paris, 1975)

NEAL ZASLAW

Labbette, Dora [Perli, Lisa] (*b* Purley, 4 March 1898). English soprano. She studied at the Guildhall School of Music, winning a gold medal, and with Lisa Lehmann on a Melba Scholarship. Boosey's Ballad Concerts and her Wigmore Hall début in 1917 led to a long recital and oratorio career with Beecham, the Hallé, the Promenade Concerts, and the Three Choirs and Delius festivals. She specialized in English songs, especially Delius's. Her involvement with opera, inspired by Dinh Gilly, began with Mimì at Covent Garden (28 September 1935); for her operatic career she assumed the name of Lisa Perli. Her voice was true, pure and youthful, and she was an outstanding actress, ideal for Gounod's heroines, Mélisande, Delius's Vreli (*A Village Romeo and Juliet*) and Verdi's Desdemona. Her many records include the first complete *Messiah*. The war cut short her London career in 1939.

ALAN JEFFERSON

La Beausse (*fl* 1420–25). French composer. He was one of a group of composers now known only through one or more of their works in *GB-Ob* 213. His single extant composition is a rondeau refrain for three voices *Or voist comme aler en porra*. Only the top voice has text. The work is rhythmically interesting, with considerable use of syncopation and coloration.

BIBLIOGRAPHY
G. Reaney, ed.: *Early Fifteenth-century Music*, CMM, xi/2 (1959), 39
For further bibliography *see* FRANCE: BIBLIOGRAPHY OF MUSIC TO 1600.

TOM R. WARD

Labey, Marcel (*b* Le Vesinet, Yvelines, 6 Aug 1875; *d* Nancy, 25 Nov 1968). French composer and conductor. It was only after studying law to doctorate level that he turned to music, entering the Schola Cantorum to study with Delaborde (piano), Lenormand (harmony) and d'Indy (composition). He was appointed professor there (1903–13), and on d'Indy's death in 1931 he became director. He also directed the César Franck School from 1935, and was elected secretary-general of the Societé National de Musique in 1901. His music is in a firmly Romantic style.

WORKS
Bérangère, opera, 1912; 4 syms.; Ouverture pour un drame, orch, 1920; Str Qt, 1911; other chamber pieces, pf works, songs
Principal publishers: Chapelier, Durand, Eschig, Sénart

BIBLIOGRAPHY
F. Raugel: 'Labey, Marcel', *MGG*

ANNE GIRARDOT

Labia, Maria (*b* Verona, 14 Feb 1880; *d* Malcesine, Lake Garda, 10 Feb 1953). Italian soprano. She studied with her mother, Cecilia Labia, making her concert débuts in 1902 in Milan, Verona and Padua. She gave concerts in Russia and Sweden in 1903–4, thereafter being engaged by the Royal Opera, Stockholm, where she made her stage début in 1905 as Mimì. In 1907 she made a great impression at the Komische Oper, Berlin, as Tosca, immediately becoming a favourite of the audience and returning subsequently as Carmen, Martha (*Tiefland*) and Salome, among other roles. Her close connection with Germany led in 1916 to her arrest in Italy and a year's imprisonment in Ancona on the charge of being a German agent. Earlier she had appeared with great success at the Manhattan Opera House, New York (1908–9), La Scala (1912) and the Paris Opéra (1913). Resuming her career after the war,

she sang Giorgetta in Rome in the first European performance of *Il tabarro* (1918), repeating the role in Buenos Aires the following summer. In the first La Scala production of Wolf-Ferrari's *I quatro rusteghi* (1922) she played Felice, a role that became her favourite and in which she continued to appear until 1936. She taught at the Warsaw Academy (1930–34), and subsequently in Rome and Siena. A slim, attractive woman, descended from the Venetian nobility, her performances in *verismo* operas were said to be impulsive and, for their day, 'shamelessly sensual'. She used her warm, not especially large voice with particular reliance on her chest register.

Her elder sister Fausta (*b* Verona, 3 April 1870; *d* Rome, 6 Oct 1935) had a relatively short career (1892–1912), which included performances as Sieglinde under Toscanini at La Scala. She retired shortly after her marriage to the tenor Emilio Perea, and together they established a school of singing in Rome. Their daughter, Gianna Perea-Labia (*b* 1908), pursued an Italian career during the 1930s and 1940s.

BIBLIOGRAPHY
R. Celletti: 'Labia, Maria', *Record News*, iii (Toronto, 1958), 32 [with discography]

HAROLD ROSENTHAL

Labitzky. Bohemian family of musicians.

(1) **Joseph Labitzky** (*b* Schönfeld [now Krásno], 3 July 1802; *d* Karlsbad [now Karlovy Vary], 19 Aug 1881). Violinist, conductor and composer. He was the son of a weaver, who in 1800 moved from Kampern in Prussian Silesia to Schönfeld and in 1802 to Petschau (now Bečov na Teplé). He studied with Karl Veit and at the age of 14 joined a travelling orchestra in Petschau. In 1820 he obtained a position as violinist in the spa orchestra at Marienbad (now Mariánské Lázně), taking other jobs during the winter months. He played in Munich (1823–4), where he took further violin lessons, and undertook a concert tour of southern Germany, visiting Regensburg, Augsburg, Ulm, Stuttgart, Würzburg and Nuremberg. In 1825 he founded his own orchestra. He visited Vienna in the winter of 1825–6, and Warsaw in 1829–30. In 1835 he became conductor of the spa orchestra at Karlsbad, where he rapidly built up a reputation for himself and his orchestra. His dance compositions began to have widespread popularity, particularly the *Paulinen-Walzer* op.33 and the *Aurora-Walzer* op.34. In 1838 he gave concerts in Pilsen (now Plzeň), and in 1839 in Prague, Vienna, Warsaw and St Petersburg (Pavlovsk). He also visited England, and several of his dances have titles with English connotations, including *Jubelklänge aus Albion* op.70, on the birth of the Princess Royal (1840), and *Eduard-Walzer* op.82, on the birth of the Prince of Wales (1841). In 1853 his son August joined him at Karlsbad, and he finally handed the orchestra over to him on 8 October 1868. He composed over 300 dances, notable more for rhythmic than melodic appeal. In the latter part of his career he was unable to challenge the supremacy of Gungl and the younger Johann Strauss as a waltz composer.

(2) **Wilhelm Labitzky** (*b* Petschau, 1829; *d* Toronto, 1871). Violinist, elder son of (1) Joseph Labitzky. He studied the violin at the Prague Conservatory (1843–9) and later settled in Toronto.

(3) **August Labitzky** (*b* Petschau, 22 Oct 1832; *d*

Reichenhall, Bavaria, 28 Aug 1903). Violinist, conductor and composer, son of (1) Joseph Labitzky. He studied the violin at the Prague Conservatory (1845–9), and then studied in Leipzig with Ferdinand David (violin) and Moritz Hauptmann (theory). He joined his father's orchestra in Karlsbad as a violinist, and finally took over from him as conductor in 1868. He composed over 50 dances, of which only *Der Traum der Sennerin* op.45 achieved any wide popularity.

For a detailed list of works by (1) Joseph and (3) August Labitzky see Pazdírek or Kaufmann.

BIBLIOGRAPHY

F. Pazdírek: *Universal-Handbuch der Musik-Literatur* (Vienna, 1904–10)
E. Rychnovsky: 'Josef Labitzky, der Walzerkönig Böhmens', *Keilberg-Jb 1909* (St Joachimsthal, 1909)
M. Kaufmann: *Josef Labitzky* (Reichenberg, 1930)

ANDREW LAMB

Lablache, Luigi (*b* Naples, 6 Dec 1794; *d* Naples, 23 Jan 1858). Italian bass. The son of an expatriate French merchant and an Irishwoman, he became the most famous bass of his generation. He entered the Conservatorio della Pietà dei Turchini, Naples, at the age of 12, and began his operatic career as a *buffo napoletano* at the Teatro S Carlino in 1812, making his first appearance in Fioravanti's *La molinara*. After further study and an engagement as *buffo* at Messina, in 1813 he became first *basso cantante* at Palermo, where he remained for several years. His reputation grew, and in 1817 he made a triumphant début at La Scala as Dandini in Rossini's *La Cenerentola*. He remained at La Scala for six seasons, and also appeared at Rome, Turin, Venice and, in 1824, Vienna, where he was a leading member of Barbaia's brilliant company. Ferdinand I of Naples, then in Vienna, appointed Lablache a singer in his royal chapel and had him engaged for the Teatro S Carlo, where for several years he appeared in new operas by Bellini and Donizetti, as well as distinguishing himself in such roles as Assur in Rossini's *Semiramide*.

On 30 March 1830, Lablache made a brilliant London début as Geronimo in Cimarosa's *Il matrimonio segreto* at the King's Theatre, where he subsequently appeared every season until 1852, except for 1833 and 1834. Lord Mount-Edgcumbe described him on his London début as 'a bass of uncommon force

Scene from the first London production of 'Don Pasquale' at Her Majesty's Theatre, 29 June 1843, with (left to right) Giovanni Mario (Ernesto), Giulia Grisi (Norina), Luciano Fornasari (Malatesta) and Luigi Lablache (Don Pasquale)

and power. His voice was not only of deeper compass than almost any ever heard, but when he chose, absolutely *stentorian*, and he was also gigantic in his person; yet when he moderated its extraordinary strength, he sang pleasingly and well'. While his reputation rested chiefly on his interpretation of comic roles, in which he excelled, he was equally impressive in serious roles such as Henry VIII in Donizetti's *Anna Bolena* and Oroveso in Bellini's *Norma*. In 1839 Wagner wrote an additional aria for this role for him, but Lablache declined to sing it. His Paris début took place on 4 November 1830 at the Théâtre-Italien, where he continued to appear regularly until 1851 and created his most important roles, including Sir George Walton in Bellini's *I puritani* (25 January 1835) and the title role in Donizetti's *Marino Faliero* (12 March 1835). *I puritani* enjoyed such success that for the next seven years this opera opened and closed each season with its original cast of Giulia Grisi, Rubini, Tamburini and Lablache. In England, Lablache appeared in opera and sang at provincial music festivals and, in 1836 and 1837, was Princess Victoria's singing teacher. He was the first Don Pasquale in Donizetti's opera (Théâtre-Italien, 3 January 1843), and his interpretation of this role, in which he displayed 'real comic genius' (Chorley), became definitive.

After the opening in 1847 of the Royal Italian Opera, Covent Garden, Lablache was one of the few artists to remain faithful to Lumley's management at Her Majesty's (formerly King's). With his readiness to take small roles without condescension he acquired a larger and more varied repertory than any other singer of comparable standing; Lumley described him as 'the greatest dramatic singer of his time'. On the closure of Her Majesty's in 1852 Lablache visited St Petersburg, and in 1854, after his return, he became a leading member of Gye's company at Covent Garden. In 1855, when he was over 60, he was still singing some of his most famous roles, including Leporello, Don Pasquale, Bartolo in *Il barbiere* and Baldassare in Donizetti's *La favorita*. His health began to deteriorate in 1856, and he retired from the stage.

Lablache wrote a *Méthode de chant* which was published in Paris but it added little to his reputation. His eldest son, Federico Lablache, was an operatic bass, and his daughter-in-law, Mme Demeric Lablache, sang for many years as a mezzo-soprano with Mapleson's company. One of his daughters, Cecchina, married the pianist Thalberg.

BIBLIOGRAPHY
Castil-Blaze: *Biographie de Lablache* (Paris, n.d.)
J. d'Ortigue: Obituary, *Le journal des débats* (Paris, 24 Feb 1858)
G. Widén: *Luigi Lablache* (Göteborg, 1897)

PHILIP ROBINSON

Labor, Josef (*b* Horovice, 29 June 1842; *d* Vienna, 26 April 1924). Bohemian pianist, organist and composer. He studied at the Vienna Conservatory. Although blind, he made the most of his considerable gifts and became chamber musician to the King of Hanover in 1863. In 1868 he settled in Vienna, where he devoted himself to teaching and composition. He edited Biber's violin sonatas for Denkmäler der Tonkunst in Österreich. His compositions include church music, a Konzertstück for piano and orchestra, chamber music for piano and strings, organ fantasies and piano pieces. Among his pupils were Julius Bittner and Arnold Schoenberg.

ERIC BLOM/R

La Borde [Delaborde], **Jean-Baptiste (Thillaie)** [Thillais, Thillaès] **de** (*b* Nevers, 9 June 1730; *d* Colancelle, late Jan 1777). French physical scientist and mathematician. He invented the first known electric-powered musical instrument. On 26 September 1745 he began his novitiate in the Society of Jesus. He taught rhetoric in Amiens around 1755, and passed his third year of novitiate at Rouen in 1762, just at the time of the suppression of the Jesuit order in France. After spending a few years in Poznań, Poland, he served as a priest in Colancelle until his death.

A competent scientist, La Borde shared the intense interest of his times in electricity. His most important publication, *Le clavessin électrique, avec une nouvelle théorie du méchanisme et des phénomènes de l'électricité* (Paris, 1761), was prompted by his invention of a keyboard instrument powered by a static charge. The 'electric harpsichord' (sometimes confused with the *clavecin chromatique* of Jean-Benjamin de La Borde) had for each pitch two bells, between which hung a clapper. Wires communicated stored charge to the bells. Depression of the appropriate key grounded one bell while cutting it off from the charge source, so that the clapper struck the charged bell and the grounded bell in rapid alternation until the key was released. By the inventor's own report, the instrument sounded like an organ's tremolo stop, and was moreover a remarkable sight in the dark on account of its production of sparks. Comment in the press was favourable, even admiring, but the instrument never became more than a curiosity. The model built by La Borde is in the Bibliothèque Nationale, Paris.

BIBLIOGRAPHY
Mémoires pour l'histoire des sciences et des beaux arts, lix (1759/R1969), 1832, 2378 [2 letters from La Borde; repr. as foreword to *Le clavessin électrique*, lxi (1761/R1969), 264]
Année littéraire, viii (1761/R1966), 169ff
Journal encyclopédique ou universel, xi (1761/R1966), 43
A. de Backer, ed.: *Bibliothèque de la Compagnie de Jésus* (Brussels, 1851–76, rev. 2/1890–1932/R1960)

FREDERIC S. MERRITT

La Borde [Laborde], **Jean-Benjamin(-François) de** (*b* Paris, 5 Sept 1734; *d* Paris, 22 July 1794). French composer, violinist and writer on music. Born to an aristocratic family, he had a political and financial career as well as an intellectual and artistic one. His friends included Voltaire and Beaumarchais, and his many publications attest to his activities in literature, the arts, geography and other topics.

La Borde was an irresponsible youth, and was nearly ruined financially more than once, although he early became a farmer-general of revenues. He entered the service of Louis XV in 1762, later becoming the king's close confidant and a *premier valet de chambre*. From 1763 to 1773 he was the acknowledged lover of Marie-Madeleine Guimard, a famous dancer. After breaking with Guimard, he travelled to Switzerland and Italy, visiting Voltaire at Ferney and Piccinni in Naples. On his return he was appointed Governor of the Louvre, but he fell out of favour at court when Louis XV died (10 May 1774). On 22 August 1774 he married Adelaide de Vismes, sister of the director of the Opéra. She went into the service of Marie-Antoinette, and was able to rehabilitate her husband at court. During the Revolution La Borde and his family left Paris to live quietly in Val St Germain, Caudebec and Rouen. In his absence his house and his large library were burnt. He was eventually sought out in Rouen, and was arrested, sentenced and guillotined.

La Borde was trained by Rameau in composition and Dauvergne on the violin. Most of his music dates from before the death of Louis XV. Beginning with *Gilles, garçon peintre*, many of his dramatic works were public successes, although the press was not always favourable. He collaborated in writing some of his opera librettos, and set many of his own chanson texts. Examples of his *Choix de chansons* are valued for their luxurious engravings by Moreau *le jeune* and others. La Borde's writings on music are probably more important than his compositions. The four-volume *Essai sur la musique ancienne et moderne* (1780), which treats of a broad range of topics, is a valuable source of information on 18th-century music. Something of a pioneer in the study of old music, La Borde published trouvère songs with the original notation and texts. With the Abbé Roussier, he was interested in ancient and allegedly ancient scales and tunings: he proposed a keyboard with 21 notes to the octave, and such a *clavecin chromatique* was built by Germain. La Borde was involved in many controversies; he attacked Rousseau's views at every opportunity, and was attacked in turn by Rousseau's disciples. Later musicians would probably agree with many of La Borde's views.

For an illustration of *Choix de chansons, see* PRINTING AND PUBLISHING OF MUSIC, fig. 16.

WORKS
(printed works published in Paris, unless otherwise stated)

STAGE

Unless otherwise stated, all are *opéras comiques*; many works for which no performance details are given were performed privately; various MSS are in *F-Pc, Po*.

PO – *Paris, Opéra*   CI – *Paris, Comédie-Italienne*
FO – *Fontainebleau*

La chercheuse d'oiseaux (Rozée), Mons, 1748 (Mons, 1748)
Le rossignol, ou Le mariage secret (1, C. Collé), Château de Berny, 18 Nov 1751, and Paris, Théâtre de Société, 1751 (The Hague, 1777)
Les trois déesses rivales, 1750s, unperf.
Gilles, garçon peintre, z'amoureux-t-et-rival (parade [burlesque scenes] and parody, 1, A. H. H. Poinsinet), for the Count of Clermont, 1757 (1758)
Annette et Lubin (pastorale, 1, Marmontel), Paris, Théâtre du Maréchal de Richelieu, 30 March 1762 (1762)
Ismène et Isménias, ou La fête de Jupiter (lyric tragedy, 3, Laujon), Choisy, 13 June 1763 (1770)
Les bons amis [Les bons compères] (1, M.-J. Sedaine), Paris, Opéra-Comique, 5 March 1761 (1761), rev. as L'anneau perdu et retrouvé, CI, 8 Aug 1764 (1764)
Le dormeur éveillé (2, Ménilglaise and La Borde), FO, 27 Oct 1764 (1764)
Les amours de Gonesse, ou Le boulanger [Le mitron et la mitronne] (1, C. S. Favart and S.-R.-N. Chamfort), CI, 8 May 1765 (?1765)
Fanny (Chamfort), 1765
Thétis et Pélée (lyric tragedy, 3, Fontenelle), FO, 10 Oct 1765 (1765) [rev. of work by Colasse]
Zénis et Almasie (ballet héroïque, 1, Chamfort and the Duke of la Vallière), FO, 2 Nov 1765 (1765), collab. de Bury
Le revenant (Desfontaines), 1766
La mandragore, 1766
Le coup de fusil, 1766
Pandore (lyric tragedy, 5, Voltaire and Chabanon), Paris, Menus-Plaisirs, 14 Feb 1767 (1767)
Amphion (ballet pastorale héroïque, Thomas), PO, 13 Oct 1767 (1767) [one act of Fragments nouveaux]
Colette et Mathurin (Desfontaines), 1767
La meunière de Gentilly (1, Lemonnier), CI, 13 Oct 1768 (1768)
Candide (Le prieur), 1768
Le chat perdu et retrouvé (1, Carmontelle), CI, 1769 (1769)
Alix et Alexis (2, Poinsinet), Choisy, 6 July 1769 (1769)
Jeannot et Colin (Desfontaines [F.-G. Fouques]), 1770
La cinquantaine (pastorale, 2, Desfontaines), CI, 8 Aug 1771 (1771)
Amadis de Gaule (lyric tragedy, 5, Quinault), PO, 4 Dec 1771, collab. P.-M. Berton [rev. of a work by Lully]
Le billet de mariage (Desfontaines), CI, 31 Oct 1772
Adèle de Ponthieu (lyric tragedy, 3, Razins de Saint-Marc), PO, 1 Dec

1772 (1772), collab. Berton
Le projet (Framéry), 1772
L'amour quêteur (Beaunoir [Robineau]), Trianon, 1779
Le marin, ou Le rival imprévu (2), unperf.
La chercheuse d'esprit (Favart)

OTHER WORKS

6 collections of chansons, solo v, vn, bc, some with harp ad lib (1763–4)
Six trios, 2 vn, bc (Paris, 1765)
Choix de chansons mises en musique, solo kbd (1772–5)
Privilège du roi, lv, small orch (1773)
Many songs and arias in various contemporary collections

WRITINGS ON MUSIC

Essai sur la musique ancienne et moderne (Paris, 1780/*R*1972)
Mémoires historiques sur Raoul de Coucy [with] *receuil de ses chansons en vieux langage, avec la traduction et l'ancienne musique* (Paris, 1781)
Mémoires sur les proportions musicales, le genre énarmonique . . . avec une lettre de l'auteur de l'Essai à M. l'Abbé Roussier (Paris, 1781)
Letter to the Académie des Sciences in *Mémoire de l'abbé Roussier sur le nouveau clavecin chromatique* (Paris, 1782)
Autobiography, in a letter to Champein, 1793, *B-Br* [bound in a copy of *Essai sur la musique*]

BIBLIOGRAPHY

Mme Latour de Franqueville [?pseud. of P. Gaviniès]: *Errata de l'Essai, . . . ou Lettre à l'auteur de cet Essai* (?Paris, 1780)
H. Chaussier: Obituary, *L'ami des arts* (Paris, 1796), 369ff
Léris: 'Notice historique', suppl. to La Borde: *Pensées et maximes* (Paris, 2/1802)
C. Mellinet: *Notice sur J.-B. de La Borde* (Nantes, 1839)
R. Pichard du Page: 'Un financier dilettante au XVIIIe siècle', *Revue de l'histoire de Versailles*, xxviii (1926), 106, 191
E. Haraszti: 'Jean-Benjamin de Laborde', *ReM*, no.158 (1935), 109
J. de Visme: *Un favori des dieux* (Paris, 1935)
E. Haraszti: 'J.-B. de La Borde et la musique hongroise', *RdM*, xix (1935), 100, 168
E. Closson: 'Les notes marginales de Grétry dans "L'essay sur la musique" de Laborde', *RBM*, ii (1948), 106
J. Warmoes: *L'exemplaire de l'"Essai sur la musique ancienne et moderne" de J.-B. de Laborde annoté par Grétry* (diss., U. of Louvain, 1956)
M. Briquet: 'La Borde, Jean-Benjamin de', *MGG*

FREDERIC S. MERRITT

Laborde Chansonnier (*US-Wc* M2.1 L25 Case). *See* SOURCES, MS, §IX, 8.

Laboun. *See* LABAUN family.

Labroca, Mario (*b* Rome, 22 Nov 1896; *d* Rome, 1 July 1973). Italian composer, music organizer and critic. He studied under Respighi and G. F. Malipiero, graduating from the Parma Conservatory in 1921. But in his work on behalf of modern music he came closer to Casella: he actively participated in the affairs of the Corporazione delle Nuove Musiche and the Italian section of the ISCM; and he showed the same zeal as director of the music division of the Direzione Generale dello Spettacolo attached to the Ministry of Popular Culture, as well as later in his post as manager of the Teatro Comunale, Florence (Maggio Musicale Fiorentino), in 1936–44. He was then artistic director of the Teatro alla Scala, Milan (1947–9) and a director of the music department of Italian radio (1949–58). In 1959 the centre of his activity shifted to Venice, where he helped to organize, for example, the Venice festivals. In the 1960s he also taught music history at the university for foreigners in Perugia.

Despite his copious activities as a critic, and as a music organizer (documented in his invaluable, partly autobiographical *L'usignolo di Boboli*), Labroca wrote a fair number of compositions, at least in the earlier part of his career. His style at first followed that of his teacher Malipiero: the Piano Suite and *Ritmi di marcia* contain unmistakably Malipierian acerbities and luminosities. Malipiero-like, too, is the vivacious First String

Quartet, although Labroca's rhythmic and formal methods are more orthodox, less wayward and improvisatory. During the 1920s Labroca was briefly associated with Massarani and Rieti in a group calling itself I Tre, in imitation of Les Six. Unlike Rieti, however, he never revealed obvious French influences in his music. In the 1930s, rather, he showed signs in some works (e.g. the sunny, ebullient Second String Quartet) of continuing to develop in parallel with Malipiero; while in others, like the rather laboured Sonata for orchestra with piano, he moved closer to Casella. These two influences fuse in the *Stabat mater*, a restrainedly moving personal statement that is probably Labroca's most important composition. Among the few works he wrote after 1940, the *Tre cantate sulla Passione* turn to a more sombre, chromatic manner; a certain sluggishness, particularly in rhythmic invention, confirms that by 1950 Labroca's creative urge had lost its former compulsiveness.

WORKS
(selective list)

Dramatic: La principessa di Perepepé (children's opera, B. Bartolazzi), Rome, 1927; Le 3 figliole di Babbo Pallino (children's opera, M. Pompei), Rome, 1928; Lamento dei mariti e delle mogli (canti carnascialeschi, Alamanni, Grazzini), 6 solo vv, small orch, Rome, 1929; 2 ballets, unperf.; incidental music; film scores

Orch: Sinfonietta, small orch, 1927; Sonata, orch, pf obbl, 1927–33

Vocal: Stabat mater, S, chorus, orch, 1933; 3 Songs (G. Vigoli), 1v, pf, 1937; 3 cantate sulla Passione di Cristo, B, chorus, orch, 1950; 8 madrigali di Tomaso Campanella, Bar, orch, 1958

Inst: Pf Suite, 1921; Ritmi di marcia, pf, 1922; 3 str qts, 1923, 1932, 1939; Sonatina, vn, pf, 1923; Suite, va, pf, 1923; Pf Trio, 1925

Principal publishers: Ricordi, Suvini Zerboni, Universal

WRITINGS

Parole sulla musica (Milan, 1954)
L'usignolo di Boboli: 50 anni di vita musicale italiana (Venice, 1959)
Other books, many articles etc

BIBLIOGRAPHY

G. Rossi-Doria: 'Giovani musicisti italiani: Labroca, Massarani, Rieti', *Il pianoforte*, v (Turin, 1924), 303
A. Casella: 'Jeunes et indépendants', *ReM*, viii/3 (1927), 62
H. Amano: *Gendai itaria ongaku* [Contemporary Italian music] (Tokyo, 1939), 133ff [list of works, 339f]
G. Calandra: 'Musicisti contemporanei: Mario Labroca', *Augustea*, xvi/3–4 (Rome, 1940), 20
J. C. G. Waterhouse: *The Emergence of Modern Italian Music (up to 1940)* (diss., U. of Oxford, 1968), 210, 215ff, 221, 670ff
F. d'Amico: 'La parte di Gatti e quella di Labroca', *NRMI*, vii (1973), 171

GUIDO M. GATTI/JOHN C. G. WATERHOUSE

Labrunie, Gérard. *See* NERVAL, GÉRARD DE.

Labunski [Łabuński], **Feliks Roderyk** (*b* Ksawerynów, 27 Dec 1892). American composer and teacher of Polish origin, brother of Wiktor Labunski. He studied with Marczewski and Maliszewski at the Warsaw Conservatory (1922–4) and with Dukas and Boulanger (composition) and Migot (musicology) at the Ecole Normale de Musique, Paris (1924–34). In 1927, together with Czapski, Perkowski and Wiechowicz, he founded the Association of Young Polish Composers in Paris. He was director of classical music for Polish radio in Warsaw from 1934 until 1936, when he moved to the USA (he took American citizenship in 1941). In 1940–41 he was professor of counterpoint and composition at Marymount College in Tarrytown (New York), and in 1945 he joined the staff of the Cincinnati College of Music. He appeared as a pianist, mostly in his own compositions, and was active as a music critic. His music is fundamentally romantic, with traits assimilated from the Paris school.

WORKS
(selective list)

Orch: Danse fantastique, 1926; Triptyque champêtre, 1931; Suite, str, 1938; Variations, 1947; Sym., D, 1954; Elegy, 1955; Xaveriana, fantasy, 2 pf, orch, 1956; Symphonic Dialogues, 1961; Canto di Aspirazione (1963); Polish Renaissance Suite (1967); Salut à Paris, ballet suite (1968); Music, pf, orch (1968); Primavera, 1974

Ballet: God's Man, 1937

Vocal: Polish Cantata (1932); Ptaki (The Birds), S, orch (1934); Song without Words, S, str (1946); There is no Death, cantata, chorus, orch, 1950; Images of Youth, cantata, 1956; songs

Inst: Str Qt no.1, 1934; Divertimento, fl, pf (1936); 3 Bagatelles, brass qt, 1955; Divertimento, fl, ob, cl, bn (1956); Diptych, ob, pf (1958); Str Qt no.2 (1962); Intrada Festiva, brass choir (1968)

Principal publishers: Polskie Wydawnictwo Muzyczne, World Library

BIBLIOGRAPHY

L. Erhardt: 'Feliks Roderyk Łabuński w Ameryce', *Ruch muzyczny* (1961), no.9, p.5

BOGUSŁAW SCHÄFFER

Labunski [Łabuński], **Wiktor** (*b* St Petersburg, 14 April 1895; *d* Kansas City, 26 Jan 1974). American pianist and composer of Polish origin, brother of Feliks Roderyk Labunski, he studied at the St Petersburg Conservatory with Nikolayeva, Blumenfeld and Safonov (piano), Vītol (theory) and Kalafati (composition); he also studied conducting with Młynarski in Poland. After directing the piano department of the Kraków Conservatory (1919–28) he moved to the USA, there he made his début as a pianist at Carnegie Hall in 1928. He taught at the Nashville Conservatory (1928–31), and was professor and director at the Memphis College of Music (1931–7) and the Kansas City Conservatory (from 1937). Well known for his lecture recitals, he had a repertory of more than 1500 works. His own compositions are in a conventional style.

WORKS
(selective list)

Orch: Pf Concertino, 1932; Sym., 1936; Pf Conc., 1939; Variations, pf, orch, 1945: Conc., 2 pf, 1957

Pf: Toccata, 1923; Variations, 1923; 2 Impromptus, 1926; Variations on a Theme of Paganini, 1943; many other pieces

Songs

Principal publisher: Polskie Wydawnictwo Muzyczne

BIBLIOGRAPHY

W. Waliszewska: 'O Wiktorze Łabuńskim', *Ruch muzyczny* (1968), no.23, p.18

BOGUSŁAW SCHÄFFER

La Casinière, Yves de (*b* Angers, 11 Feb 1897; *d* Paris, 28 Oct 1971). French composer and teacher. After war service and a short while in Tunisia, he entered the Ecole Normale de Musique, where he was a pupil of d'Ollone (composition and harmony), Boulanger (organ) and Caussade (counterpoint and fugue). He ran a small printing firm and in 1935 founded a music publishing house, the Editions du Musagète. His other activities included teaching, composing for the cinema (and for such directors as Renoir, Clair and Cavalcanti) and administrative work, in which he was involved between 1953 and 1971 as Inspecteur Principal de l'Enseignement Musical and Inspecteur de Musique (Théâtres Lyriques).

WORKS
(selective list)

Orch: Hercule et les centaures, sym. pictures after Hérédia, 1920; Sym. no.1, 1922; Persée et Andromède, sym. poem after Hérédia, 1930; Sym. no.2, pf, orch, 1930; Concerto-improvisation, org, orch, 1958

Chamber: Sonatine, vn, pf, 1923; Sonatine, vc, pf, 1923; Str Qt, 1929; Pf Qt, 1942; Pf Trio, 1944

Kbd: Pf Sonata, 1923; Preludes and Fugues, org, 1944; Chorales, org, 1950; Etudes, pf, 1950

Songs: Au clair de la lune (A. de Romain), 1921–2; Le cheval (M.

Rostand), 1921–2; Barcarolle (La Casinière); Chant du marteleur (La Casinière)

Principal publishers: Lemoine, Senart

PAUL GRIFFITHS

Lacassagne [La Cassagne; de La Cassagne], **Joseph** (*b* Ile d'Oléron, Charente-Maritime, *c*1720; *d* ?Paris, *c*1780). French theorist and teacher. He studied at the cathedral school in Marseilles, and later taught music there. He then entered the priesthood and lived in Paris, where his patrons included the dauphin and the dauphine, Marie Antoinette. His *Traité général des élémens du chant* (Paris, 1766/*R*1972), intended for beginners, is his most noteworthy publication. In it he proposed to simplify the reading of music by using only one clef (a movable G clef) and only three time signatures: 2, for simple duple metre; 3, for simple triple metre; and 2/3 for compound metre with ternary subdivisions. His supplementary *L'uni-cléfier musical* (Paris, 1768) was a response to Pascal Boyer's publication attacking the *Traité général*. Though his proposals caused some controversy they found little favour. He also wrote a *Recueil de fables mises en musique* for unaccompanied voice (1754) and an *Alphabet musical, ou Gamme de la musique* (1765), and contributed to the *Mercure de France*.

BIBLIOGRAPHY

FétisB
P. Boyer: *Lettre à Monsieur Diderot, sur le projet de l'unité de clef dans la musique* (Amsterdam and Paris, 1767)

ALBERT COHEN

Lacépède, Bernard Germain Etienne Médard de la Ville-sur-Illon, Count of (*b* Agen, 26 Dec 1756; *d* Epinay-sur-Seine, 6 Oct 1825). French naturalist, theorist and composer. He studied performance and composition at Agen and Bordeaux, and from 1775 corresponded with D'Alembert on matters of theory. Having written to Buffon and Gluck, he was cordially received by both in Paris in 1777. Gluck had just composed *Armide*, and despite his encouragement Lacépède destroyed his own setting of this text. For a short time he attempted parallel careers in science and music, reaching eminence in the former as Buffon's successor and as director of the Jardin des Plantes. He took lessons from Gossec and in 1783 his *Omphale* was accepted and rehearsed at the Opéra; the caprice of the leading singer, St Huberty, caused it to be withdrawn, and Lacépède confined his remaining dramatic and instrumental music to private performance. His *Poétique de la musique* (1785) offered an unusually serious discussion of instrumental music. He owed something to the Encyclopedist theory of imitation, and the influence of Gluck is apparent in his emphasis on the dramatic, rather than pleasurable, function of music. His descriptive instrumental music to Fénelon's *Télémaque* was intended to illustrate his ideas.

WORKS
(all lost)

Operas: Armide (tragédie lyrique, 3, Quinault), 1777; Omphale (La Motte), 1783, accepted by Opéra, not perf.; Scanderberg, before 1785; Cyrus (Paganel, after Metastasio), before 1785; Alcine (Framery), 1786, accepted by Opéra, not perf.
Incidental music to Fénelon's Télémaque, 1785
Requiem
At least 2 symphonies, 1 symphonie concertante, 2 fl, all lost, cited by Brook; 54 str sextets, 5 sets of sonatas, cited by Fétis

WRITINGS
(only those relating to music)

Réflexions sur les progrès que la musique a encore à faire (MS, Le-Archives du Lot-et-Garonne) [ed. R. P. du Page, Le Figaro (19 Dec 1925)]
La poétique de la musique (Paris, 1785, 3/1797)

BIBLIOGRAPHY

FétisB
Mahorault: *Notice sur la vie et les ouvrages de M. Lacépède* (Paris, 1825)
B. *Lacépède: Oeuvres complètes* (Paris, 1826)
G. de Cuvier: 'Eloge historique du comte de Lacépède', *Recueil des éloges*, iii (Paris, 1827)
G. le Brisoys Desnoiresterres: *La musique française au XVIIIe siècle: Gluck et Piccinni* (Paris, 1872, 2/1875/*R*1971)
E. Perrin: 'Un livre de Lacépède sur la musique', *BSIM*, iii (1907), 847
R. P. du Page: 'La vie musicale de M. de Lacépède', *Le Figaro* (19 Dec 1925)
B. S. Brook: *La symphonie française dans la seconde moitié du XVIIIe siècle* (Paris, 1962), esp. i, 334ff
O. F. Saloman: 'La Cépède's La poétique de la musique and Le Sueur', *AcM*, xlvii (1975), 144

JULIAN RUSHTON

Lacerda, Francisco (Inácio da Silveira de Sousa Pereira Forjaz) de (*b* Ribeira Seca, S Jorge, Azores, 11 May 1869; *d* Lisbon, 18 July 1934). Portuguese conductor, composer and musicologist. He studied under Vieira, Gazul, Montinho de Almeida and Soromenho at the Lisbon Conservatory, where he was made professor of piano in 1892. Three years later he went to Paris to study at the Conservatoire under Pessard, Bourgault-Ducoudray, Libert and Widor, and at the Schola Cantorum under d'Indy and Guilmant. Thereafter he established himself as a conductor in Paris, in other French cities and throughout Europe. He founded the Concerts Historiques in Nantes (1905) and the Lisbon PO (1923). A friend of Debussy and of Fauré, he numbered Ansermet among his pupils.

WORKS
(selective list)

Orch: Adamastor, sym. poem, 1902; Danse du voile, ballet, 1904; Almourol, sym. poem, 1926; La peur, ballet; Le baiser, ballet
Songs: Les morts (Richepin), 1902; 34 trovas, other pieces
Pf: Uma garrafa de cerveja, 1886; Papillons, 1896; Canção de Berço, 1896; Lusitanas, 1896
Inst: 36 histoires pour amuser les enfants d'un artiste, 1922; Serenata a una muerta, gui, 1924; Petite suite, str
Incidental music, org pieces
Edn.: Cancioneiro musical português (Lisbon, 1935–6)

BIBLIOGRAPHY

V. Nemésio: 'Cronologia biográfica de Francisco de Lacerda', *Francisco de Lacerda: exposição comemorativa do primeiro centenário do nascimento* (Lisbon, 1969)
Y. David-Peyre: 'Francisco de Lacerda à Nantes', *Actes du cinquantenaire de la création en Bretagne de l'enseignement du portugais*, ii (Rennes, 1975)

GUY BOURLIGUEUX

Lacerda, Osvaldo (Costa de) (*b* São Paulo, 23 March 1927). Brazilian composer. In his native city he studied piano with José Kliass and harmony with Ernesto Kierski (1945–7). He received his training in composition under Camargo Guarnieri (1952–62). A Guggenheim Foundation Fellowship took him in 1963 to the USA, where he studied for a year under Vittorio Giannini in New York and Copland in Tanglewood. In 1965 he participated in the Inter-American Composers Seminar held at Indiana University, and in the Third Inter-American Music Festival in Washington, DC. Actively engaged in teaching, he has been a professor at the Escola Municipal de Música (São Paulo) since 1969; he has served as president of the Comissão Estadual de Música de São Paulo (1967), and of the Sociedade Pró Música Brasileira (1961–6). In 1972 he was elected a member of the Academia Brasileira de Música.

Lacerda's music incorporates a subtle national idiom into a modern harmonic context. His intimate knowledge of Brazilian popular and folk music is best shown in the seven *Ponteios* for piano solo (1955–71) and the six suites under the title *Brasiliana* (1965–71) in which features of folksong and dance (*modinha, lundu, desafio, marcha-de-rancho*, etc) are used. His Variations and Fugue for Woodwind Quintet (1962) is based on the three main motifs of a Brazilian nursery rhyme. However, the original theme undergoes such drastic modifications as to become unrecognizable. Lacerda's best known orchestral piece is the clearly nationalist suite *Piratininga* (1962), which won him first prize in the Brazilian National Composition Competition of the same year.

WORKS

(selective list)

INSTRUMENTAL

Orch works incl. Piratininga, suite, 1962; Conc., str, 1964; Guanabara, suite, band, 1965; Invocação e ponto, tpt, str, 1965

Chamber music incl. Str Qt no.1, 1952; 8 variações sôbre um tema folclorico, vn, pf, 1954; Variations and Fugue, wind qnt, 1962; 3 estudos, perc, 1966; Trilogia, wind ens, 1968; Pf Trio, 1969; 3 dansas brasileiras antigas, vn, pf, 1972

Pf pieces incl. 15 variações sôbre 'Mulher rendeira', 1953; 7 Ponteios, 1955–71; 5 Brasilianas, 1965–71; Brasiliana no.4, duet, 1968

VOCAL

Hiroshima, meu amor, 1v, perc, 1968; Festa chinesa, 1v, fl pf, 1972

Songs incl. 4 miniaturas de Adelmar Tavares, 1955; Poema tirado de uma noticia de jornal, 1964; Murmúrio, 1965; Uma nota, uma só mão, 1967; Rotação, 1970; Cantiga de ninar escrava, 1970

Choral works incl. Ofulú lorêrê, perc ad lib, 1958; Poema da necessidade, 1967; Pequena suite coral, 1969; 3 pontos de caboclo, 1969; Fuga proverbial, 1969; Proverbios, S, B, chorus, str orch, pf, perc, 1970; 4 estudos para coro, 1971; masses, other sacred pieces

Principal publishers: Irmãos Vitale, Ricordi Brasiliana

WRITINGS

'Constancias harmônicas e polifônicas da música popular brasileira e seu approveitamento na música sacra', *Música brasileira na liturgia* (Petrópolis, 1969), 61f

'A criação do recitativo brasileiro', *Música brasileira na liturgia* (Petrópolis, 1969), 115f

BIBLIOGRAPHY

V. Mariz: *Quem é quem nas artes e nas letras do Brasil* (Rio de Janeiro, 1966), chap. 'Seção de música'

Compositores de América, xv (Washington, DC, 1969), 127f

V. Mariz: *Figuras da música brasileira contemporânea* (Brasilia, 1970)

GERARD BÉHAGUE

Lacerna, Estacio de. *See* SERNA, ESTACIO DE LA.

Lach, Robert (*b* Vienna, 29 Jan 1874; *d* Salzburg, 11 Sept 1958). Austrian musicologist and composer. He read law at the University of Vienna but entered the Austrian provincial administration in 1894 before completing his degree. At the same time he studied composition with Robert Fuchs at the Conservatory of the Gesellschaft der Musikfreunde in Vienna (1893–9) and musicology with Wallaschek, Rietsch and Adler (1896–9).

He obtained the doctorate in 1902 from the German University in Prague with a dissertation on the development of ornamented melody. The next year he was pensioned out of government service because of ill-health and lived the next few years in the south, in Istria, Dalmatia and Italy. In 1909 he returned to Vienna and in 1911 began working in the Hofbibliothek, succeeding Ferdinand Scherber as director of the music collection (1913–20). He became a lecturer at the university in 1915 and succeeded Wallaschek as lecturer in ethnomusicology, psychology and music aesthetics in 1920. From 1927 to 1939 he was professor of musicology and chairman of the Musicological Institute and from 1924 he was also professor of music history, philosophy and music aesthetics at the Vienna State Academy. He was a corresponding member of the Austrian Academy

of Sciences from 1918 and the Germany Academy from 1925. In 1954 he became general editor of the new Denkmäler der Tonkunst in Österreich.

Lach's importance was as an ethnomusicologist who, with a broad, systematic approach, attempted to explain the genesis of man's music in biological, physiological and psychological terms, an approach exemplified in his doctoral thesis. His ethnomusicological studies spilt over into general music history, where he had wide interests and a sound background as a music librarian (he carried on Mantuani's work in cataloguing the collection of music MSS in the Vienna National Library). Active as an orientologist, philosopher and aesthetician, he was also a poet and a very prolific composer. Many of his songs have been published but the majority of his works, including 8 masses, 10 symphonies, 8 string sextets, 14 string quintets, 25 string quartets and other chamber and stage music remain in MS.

WRITINGS

Studien zur Entwicklungsgeschichte der ornamentalen Melopöie (diss., German U. of Prague, 1902; Leipzig, 1913)

'Alte Weihnachts- und Ostergesänge auf Lussin', *SIMG*, iv (1902–3), 535

'Ueber einem interessanten Spezialfall von "Audition colorée"', *SIMG*, iv (1902–3), 589

'Volkslieder in Lussingrande', *SIMG*, iv (1902–3), 608–42

'Alte Kirchengesänge der ehemaligen Diözese Ossero', *SIMG*, vi (1904–5), 315–45

'Orientalistik und vergleichende Musikwissenschaft', *Wiener Zeitschrift für die Kunde des Morgenlandes*, xxix (1915), 463–501

Sebastian Sailers 'Schöpfung' in der Musik (Vienna, 1916)

'Das Kadenz- und Klauselproblem in der vergleichenden Musikwissenschaft', *Zeitschrift für die österreichischen Gymnasien*, lxvii (1916), 601–42

W. A. Mozart als Theoretiker (Vienna, 1918)

'Drei musikalische Einblattdrucke aus der Zeit des Dreissigjährigen Krieges', *AMw*, i (1918–19), 235

Zur Geschichte des Gesellschaftstanzes im 18. Jahrhundert (Vienna, 1920)

'Zur Geschichte der Beethovenschen "Prometheus"-Ballettmusik', *ZMw*, iii (1920–21), 223

'Gestaltunbestimmtheit und Gestaltmehrdeutigkeit in der Musik', *Sitzungsberichte der phil.-hist. Klasse der Akademie der Wissenschaften in Wien*, cxcvi/1 (1921), 95–149

Eine Tiroler Liederhandschrift aus dem 18. Jahrhundert (Vienna, 1923)

Zur Geschichte des musikalischen Zunftwesens (Vienna, 1923)

'Das Rassenproblem in der vergleichenden Musikwissenschaft', *Berichte des Forschungsinstitutes für Osten und Orient*, iii (1923), 107

'Der Orient in der ältesten abendländischen Musikgeschichte', ibid

'Die Musik der Natur- und orientalischen Kulturvölker', *Handbuch der Musikgeschichte*, ed. G. Adler (Frankfurt am Main, 1924, rev. 2/1930/R1961)

Die vergleichende Musikwissenschaft: ihre Methoden und Probleme (Vienna, 1924)

Das Konstruktionsprinzip der Wiederholung in Musik, Sprache und Literatur (Vienna, 1925)

Vergleichende Kunst- und Musikwissenschaft (Vienna, 1925)

'Zur Frage der Rhythmik des altfranzösischen und altprovenzalischen Liedverses', *Zeitschrift für französische Sprache und Literatur*, xlvii (1925), 35

'Die Vogelstimmenmotive in Beethovens Werken', *NBJb*, ii (1925), 7

'Sprach- und Gesangsmelos im Englischen', *Neusprachliche Studien: Festschrift für Karl Luick* (Marburg, 1925), 23

Die Bruckner-Akten des Wiener Universitätsarchivs (Vienna, 1926)

'Aus dem Handschriftenschatze der Musikaliensammlung der Wiener Nationalbibliothek', *Festschrift der Nationalbibliothek in Wien* (Vienna, 1926), 553

ed.: *Gesänge russischer Kriegsgefangener* (Vienna, 1926–52)

Geschichte der Staatsakademie und Hochschule für Musik und darstellende Kunst in Wien (Vienna, 1927)

'Die Tonkunst in den Alpen', *Die österreichischen Alpen*, ed. H. Leitmeier (Leipzig, 1928), 332–80

Das Ethos in der Musik Franz Schuberts (Vienna, 1928)

'Das Ethos in der Musik von Johannes Brahms', *Simrock-Jb*, iii (1930–34), 49–84

BIBLIOGRAPHY

L. Novak: 'Robert Lach und die Volksliedforschung', 'Verzeichnis der Arbeiten von R. Lach und Folklore', *Jb des österreichischen Volksliedwerkes*, iii (1945), 155

W. Graf, ed.: *Robert Lach: Persönlichkeit und Werk* (Vienna, 1954)

[contains complete list of writings]
W. Graf: 'Robert Lach', *ÖMz*, xiii (1958), 25
——: 'Memorial to Robert Lach', *EM*, iii (1959), 130
E. Schenk: 'Robert Lach zum Gedächtnis', *Mf*, xii (1959), 129
W. Graf: 'Die vergleichende Musikwissenschaft in Österreich seit 1896', *YIMFC*, vi (1974), 15

La Chapelle, Jacques de. *See* CHAMPION family.

Lachenet, Didier. *See* LESCHENET, DIDIER.

Lachenmann, Helmut Friedrich (*b* Stuttgart, 27 Nov 1935). German composer. He studied from 1955 to 1958 at the Stuttgart Musikhochschule, taking lessons in the piano with J. Uhde and in counterpoint with J. N. David. In addition, he attended the Darmstadt summer courses in 1957, studied with Nono in Venice (1958–60) and took part in Stockhausen's 1963–4 Cologne courses for new music. From 1966 to 1970 he taught music theory at the Stuttgart Musikhochschule, and he was appointed lecturer in music in 1970, and professor in 1972, at the Ludwigsburg Pädagogische Hochschule; in 1976 he became lecturer in composition at the Musikhochschule in Hanover. In 1972 he received the Bach Prize of the city of Hamburg. His music developed from Nono's point-like organization of notes, but Lachenmann's notion of structure arose from the sound experience of the material, rather than as a purely abstract conception (*Consolation I*). Later he went a step further in reflecting on the conditions of sound production in such pieces as *Air*, *Pression* and *Kontrakadenz*. In the last of these the means by which sounds are produced are typically freely exposed, and in later works Lachenmann simplified his forms and lessened the extent of aesthetic intervention in his material.

WORKS
(*selective list*)

5 Strophen, 9 insts, 1961; Echo andante, pf, 1961; Wiegenmusik, pf, 1961; Angelion, brass, 2 pf, 1963; Introversion, 6 insts, 1963; Introversion II, 1964; Szenario, tape, 1965; Str Trio, 1965; Interieur I, perc, 1966; Trio fluido, cl, mar, va, 1966; Consolation I, 16 solo vv, perc, 1967; Consolation II, 16 solo vv, 1968; temA, 1v, fl, vc, 1968; Notturno, vc, small orch, 1966–8; Air, perc, orch, 1968–9; Pression, vc, 1969; Guero, pf, 1970
Dal niente (Interieur III), cl, 1970; Kontrakadenz, orch, 1970; Gran Torso, str qt, 1971; Klangschatten (. . . mein Saitenspiel), 48 str, 3 pf, 1972; Fassade, orch, 1973; Consolation III–IV, 16 solo vv, insts, 1973; Schwankungen am Rand, brass, perc, str, 1974–5; Accanto, cl, orch, 1975

Principal publisher: Gerig

WRITINGS

'Klangtypen der neuen Musik', *Zeitschrift der Musiktheorie*, i (1970), 20
'Luigi Nono: Rückblick auf die serielle Musik', *Melos*, xxxviii (1971), 225

BIBLIOGRAPHY

Bach Prize booklet of the Hamburg Senat (Hamburg, 1971)
U. Stürzbecher: *Werkstattgespräche mit Komponisten* (Cologne, 1971), 95
R. Oehlschlägel: 'Zum Beispiel Helmut Lachenmann', *Musica*, xxvi (1972), 25

CLYTUS GOTTWALD

La Chevardière, Louis Balthazard de (*b* Volx, Feb 1730; *d* Verrières-le-Buisson, 8 April 1812). French music publisher. Advertisements for musical works in various periodicals in October 1758 mark the start of his activities as a music publisher. He took over the business which JEAN-PANTALÉON LE CLERC had passed on to his daughter Mme Vernadé. By December 1758 La Chevardière referred to himself as the 'successeur de M. Le Clerc'. Huberti seems to have been briefly as-

Title-page of the 'Sei sextuor' by Boccherini, published by La Chevardière in 1775 as op.15 (Boccherini's op.16)

sociated with him in 1759 for both their names appear on the title-page of Philidor's *Blaise de Savetier* ('Paris, de La Chevardière et Huberti, successeurs de M. Leclerc'). Thereafter La Chevardière worked alone until 1780. On 5 February he handed over the management of the shop to his daughter Elisabeth-Eléonore and his son-in-law Jean-Pierre Deroullède for three years; he finally sold the business to Pierre Leduc on 1 December 1784. He then retired to Verrières, where he became mayor of the municipality.

La Chevardière showed great eclecticism in the works he published: both 'fashionable' music (quadrilles, minuets, vaudevilles, rondos, ariettas, songs, and airs from *opéras comiques*) and more 'serious' compositions (chamber music, symphonies, sacred music and treatises). Haydn, J. C. Bach, Stamitz, Toeschi, Cannabich, Locatelli, Boccherini, Jommelli, Pergolesi, Gossec, Grétry, Philidor, Duni, Monsigny and La Borde are among the composers represented in his catalogues. La Chevardière was one of the first French publishers to bring out weekly music magazines and most of the symphonies he published were presented in the form of periodical publications.

BIBLIOGRAPHY

M. Brenet: 'Les débuts de l'abonnement musical', *BSIM*, ii (1906), 19
C. Hopkinson: *A Dictionary of Parisian Music Publishers 1700–1950* (London, 1954)
C. Johansson: *French Music Publishers' Catalogues of the Second Half of the Eighteenth Century* (Stockholm, 1955)
V. Fédorov: 'Louis-Balthasar de La Chevardière', *MGG*

ANIK DEVRIÈS

Lachman, Hans [Heinz] (*b* Berlin, 7 March 1906). Dutch composer, arranger and trombonist of German origin. He studied in Berlin with E. Tetzel (piano) and W. Fork (theory). He also studied mathematics, physics and the history of music at Berlin University. From 1930 he worked as a trombonist and arranger. He left Germany for the Netherlands in 1933, originally settling in The Hague and later in Amsterdam. He there became an arranger who was much in demand, and composed works for radio and films. After World War II he gave many lectures on Dutch musical life for Radio Berlin. His works are uncomplicated and conventional in manner.

WORKS
(selective list)

Sinfonia concertante, wind qnt, orch, n.d.
Radiofonische cantate over Amsterdam, 1958
Str Qts: no.1, n.d.; no.2, n.d.; no.3, 1968
Other orch, vocal and chamber pieces, film scores

ROGIER STARREVELD

Lachmann, Robert (b Berlin, 28 Nov 1892; d Jerusalem, 8 May 1939). German ethnomusicologist of Jewish descent. He studied English, French and Arabic at the universities of Berlin and London. His first contact with non-European (especially Arab) music took place during World War I when he was sent to the Wünsdorf POW camp as an interpreter; there he met Arab soldiers and made his first attempts at transcribing their songs. This work was encouraged by Erich von Hornbostel and Curt Sachs, then members of the State Phonogram Archives of Berlin. After 1918 he studied musicology under Johannes Wolf and Carl Stumpf and Semitic languages under Eugen Mittwoch at Berlin University, taking a doctorate in 1922 with a dissertation on town music in Tunisia, based on his own field recordings. In 1924 he joined the Berlin State Library and studied librarianship. After a year in Kiel (1926) he returned to the Berlin State Library in 1927 to take up a post in the music department under Wolf. Meanwhile he continued to study oriental music, mainly during several recording expeditions in North Africa. In 1925 he visited Tripoli, and in 1926 and 1929 was again in Tunisia recording fellahin and beduin music, as well as the song of the Jewish community in the Isle of Djerba.

This experience led to his appointment as head of the Phonogram Commission recording music at the Congress of Arab Music (Cairo, 1932). He selected and recorded performances of the best Arab musicians from Morocco to Iraq. At his instigation the Gesellschaft zur Erforschung der Musik des Orients was founded in 1930, and he edited its quarterly journal, Zeitschrift für vergleichende Musikwissenschaft, throughout the three years of its lifetime (1933–5).

Lachmann lost his job at the Berlin State Library under the Nazi government. In 1935, the University of Jerusalem invited him to open a Phonogram Archive for Oriental Music. His research during his last four years in Jerusalem (1935–9) marked the start of modern ethnomusicology in Israel. He brought with him his earlier recordings of Arab music (about 500 items recorded in North Africa) and made 1000 more recordings, which brought to light a number of ancient oral music liturgies preserved by oriental Jewry in Jerusalem but originating elsewhere. His new recordings also helped to perpetuate the exclusively oral music tradition of some Jewish sects (e.g. the Samaritans) and of some

eastern churches. In addition a series of recordings represents the classical art forms of Arab music as known in Iraq and Syria.

In Jerusalem Lachmann tried a new approach to the complexities of Jewish music, and in Jewish Cantillation and Song in the Isle of Djerba finally evolved a way of describing a community comprehensively through a detailed structural analysis of the recorded materials. His aim was to set the picture of oriental Jewish music against the larger background of Islamic music civilizations, thus providing the musical link with the rest of the Asiatic peoples, an idea he had already followed in his Musik des Orients on a strictly comparative basis.

Lachmann is one of the finest exponents of the early European school of comparative musicology, stressing comparative analysis of musical forms and their morphological qualities as well as the variants and parallels of one single type (e.g. women's laments, folk epics, ritual songs, etc) around the world. He deepened insight into the worldwide relationships of such basic forms. Another of his achievements was to enlarge the understanding of the intricate forms of ornamental variation and improvisation in Arab music.

WRITINGS

Die Musik in den tunesischen Städten (diss., U. of Berlin, 1922; AMw, v (1923), 136–71)
'Musik und Tonschrift des No', Kongressbericht: Leipzig 1925, 80
'Zur aussereuropäischen Mehrstimmigkeit', Beethoven-Zentenarfeier: Wien 1927, 321
with A. H. Fox-Strangways: 'Muhammedan Music', Grove 3
'Die Schubertautographen der Staatsbibliothek zu Berlin', ZMw, xi (1928–9), 109
Die Musik der aussereuropäischen Natur- und Kulturvölker (Potsdam, 1929)
'Die Weise vom Löwen und der pythische Nomos', Musikwissenschaftliche Beiträge: Festschrift für Johannes Wolf (Berlin, 1929), 97
Musik des Orients (Breslau, 1929/R1965)
'Musikalische Forschungsaufgaben im vorderen Orient', 1. Sitzung der Gesellschaft zur Erforschung der Musik des Orients: Berlin 1930, 3
'Von der Kunstmusik des Vorderen Orients', Kultur und Schallplatte, ii (1931), 164
with M. el-Hefni: Ja'qūb Ibn Ishāq al-Kindī: Risāla fi hubr tā'līf al-alhān – über die Komposition der Melodien (Leipzig, 1931)
'Die Haydn-Autographen der Staatsbibliothek zu Berlin', ZMw, xiv (1931–2), 289
with E. M. von Hornbostel: 'Das indische Tonsystem bei Bharata und sein Ursprung', Zeitschrift für vergleichende Musikwissenschaft, i (1933), 73
with E. M. von Hornbostel: 'Asiatische Parallelen zur Berbermusik', Zeitschrift für vergleichende Musikwissenschaft, i (1933), 4
'Die Vīnā und das indische Tonsystem bei Bharata', Zeitschrift für vergleichende Musikwissenschaft, ii (1934), 83 [reply to A. K. Coomaraswamy's article, p.57]
'Mustaqbal al mūsiqa l-'arabīya' [The future of Arab music], Al-kullīyat al-arabīyya, xvi (1935), 17
'Musiksysteme und Musikauffassung', Zeitschrift für vergleichende Musikwissenschaft, iii (1935), 1
At-tahdhīb al-mūsiqā fil-kullīyat al-'arabīya [Musical education in the Arab college], Al-kullīyat al-'arabīyya, xvi (1936), 193
Jewish Cantillation and Song in the Isle of Djerba (Jerusalem, 1940)
ed. E. Gerson-Kiwi: Robert Lachmann: Posthumous Works, i (Jerusalem, 1974) ['Die Musik im Volksleben Nordafrikas'; 'Orientalische Musik und Antike']
Unpubd articles, recordings and transcriptions in IL-J

BIBLIOGRAPHY

E. Gerson-Kiwi: 'Jerusalem Archive for Oriental Music', Musica hebraica, i–ii (1938), 40
——: 'Musicology in Israel: a Survey of its Historical Development', AcM, xxx (1958), 17
D. Wohlenberg: Kultmusik in Israel (Hamburg, 1967), 521
E. Gerson-Kiwi: 'Lachmann, Robert', Encyclopaedia Judaica, x (Jerusalem, 1971), 1336
——: 'Two Anniversaries: Two Pioneers in Jewish Ethnomusicology' [A. Z. Idelsohn, R. Lachmann], Orbis musicae, ii (1973–4), 17
——: 'Robert Lachmann: his Achievement and his Legacy', Yuval, iii

(1974), 100 [incl. inventory of the Lachmann Archive and complete list of published writings]

EDITH GERSON-KIWI

Lachner. German family of musicians.

(1) Theodor Lachner (*b* Rain am Lech, Upper Bavaria, 1788; *d* Munich, 23 May 1877). Composer and organist. He was court organist in Munich, a position he held until his death. He enjoyed a reputation as a composer of lieder and choral works, his quartets for men's voices being especially popular.

(2) Franz Paul Lachner (*b* Rain am Lech, 2 April 1803; *d* Munich, 20 Jan 1890). Composer and conductor, brother of (1) Theodor Lachner and the most celebrated member of the family. He received his first lessons in the piano and organ from his father, Anton Lachner, the city's organist. On his father's death in 1822, he went to Munich, where he scraped a living as an organist, music teacher and instrumentalist in the Isartor theatre orchestra. In 1823 he competed successfully for the post of organist at the Lutheran church in Vienna, where he was able to complete his musical education with Simon Sechter and the Abbé Stadler. He moved in the circle that included Schubert and Moritz von Schwind, and also came to know Beethoven. In 1827 he became assistant conductor at the Kärntnertor Theater, and in 1829 was appointed its chief conductor. After an unsuccessful attempt to establish himself in Berlin, Lachner returned to Munich in 1836, where he quickly won a position of prominence in musical life. He was appointed conductor of the Munich court opera, directed the concerts of the Musikalische Akademie and also conducted the Königliche Vokalkapelle. He directed the music festivals of Munich in 1855 and 1863, and shared in directing the Salzburg Festival in 1855 and the Aachen festivals in 1861 and 1870. In 1852 he was appointed Generalmusikdirektor and in 1862 was awarded an honorary PhD at the University of Munich. His manifold activities came to an abrupt end in 1864 with Wagner's arrival in the city. His retirement, for which he applied in 1865, was accepted at first in the form of a holiday and became effective only in 1868, when Wagner's immediate influence in Munich had long since declined; the grateful city made Lachner an honorary citizen in 1883.

Lachner was prominent in the intellectual life of his time, being a friend of David L. Strauss, Eduard Mörike and Felix Dahn. Among his most important pupils were Joseph Rheinberger and Franz Wüllner. A prolific composer, he took Beethoven and Schubert as his models but was also influenced by Spohr, Mendelssohn and Meyerbeer. He wrote many craftsmanlike works, of which the opera *Catarina Cornaro* (1841), the seventh orchestral suite (1881) and the Requiem op.146 (revised 1872) in particular had great and lasting success. His other contributions to the musical life in Munich were as conductor of the Munich Opera orchestra, which he successfully prepared for the technical demands of Wagner's operas, and in raising the standards of the public's musical taste. His performances of opera and of works by Beethoven were considered exemplary. It was impossible for Lachner to warm to Wagner's music, and personal confrontations with Wagner and his circle did not improve the relationship between the two men. Despite this antagonism, which finally deprived him of the fruits of his work in Munich, Lachner showed his magnanimity in 1873 by repeating a suggestion he had made nine years earlier, that Wagner be awarded the Royal Maximilian Order – this time successfully.

WORKS

(selective list; for complete list, see Stetter; MSS in D-Mbs)

THEATRICAL

Die Bürgschaft (opera, 3, K. von Biedenfeld, after Schiller), Budapest, 30 Oct 1828
Lanassa (incidental music), Vienna, Hofburgtheater, c1830
Alidia (opera, 3, O. Prechtler), Munich, Court Opera, 12 April 1839
Catarina Cornaro (opera, 4, H. de Saint-Georges), Munich, Court Opera, 3 Dec 1841
Benvenuto Cellini (opera, 4, H. A. Barbier and A. F. L. de Wailly), Munich, Court Opera, 7 Oct 1849
König Ödipus (incidental music, Sophocles, trans. Donner and Minkwitz), Munich, Court Opera, 18 Nov 1852
Additions to operas by Spohr, Auber, Cherubini, Lindpaintner; festival music

OTHER VOCAL

Die vier Menschenalter, cantata (J. G. Seidel), solo vv, chorus, orch, op.31 (Vienna, 1829); 2 other cantatas
Moses, oratorio (Bauernfeld), solo vv, chorus, orch, op.45, 1833
8 masses; Requiem; Stabat mater; numerous smaller sacred works
Numerous partsongs, male, female and mixed choruses; numerous songs, 2–3vv, pf; songs, 1v, hn/vc, pf; c200 songs, 1v, pf

ORCHESTRAL

8 syms.: no.1, E♭, op.32 (Vienna, 1828); no.2, F, 1833; no.3, d, op.41 (Vienna, 1834); no.4, E, 1834; no.5 'Preis-Symphonie', c, op.52 (Vienna, 1835); no.6, D, op.6 (Vienna, 1837); no.7, d, op.58, 1839; no.8, g, op.100 (Mainz, 1851)
7 suites: no.1, d, op.113 (Mainz, 1861); no.2, e, op.115 (Mainz, 1862); no.3, f, op.122 (Mainz, 1864); no.4, E♭, op.129 (Mainz, 1865); no.5, c, op.135 (Mainz, 1868); no.6, C, op.150 (Mainz, 1871); no.7, d, op.190 (Mainz, 1881)
2 harp concs.: no.1, c, 1828, no.2, d, 1833; fl conc., d, 1832
Ball-Suite, D, op.170 (Leipzig, 1874); other works

CHAMBER MUSIC WITHOUT PIANO

Nonet, F, fl, ob, cl, hn, bn, vn, va, vc, db, 1875
Andante, A♭, 4 hn, 2 tpt, 3 trbn, 1833
Octet, B♭, fl, ob, 2 cl, 2 hn, 2 bn, op.156 (Leipzig, 1850)
Septet, E♭, fl, cl, hn, vn, va, vc, db, 1824
2 qnts, fl, ob, cl, hn, bn: no.1, F, 1823; no.2, E♭, 1829
Str qnt, c, op.121, 1834 (Mainz, 1864)
6 str qts: no.1, b, op.75 (Mainz, 1843); no.2, A, op.76 (Mainz, 1843); no.3, E♭, op.77 (Mainz, 1843); no.4, d, op.120 (Mainz, 1849); no.5, G, op.169, 1849 (Mainz, 1875); no.6, e, op.173, 1850 (Mainz, 1875)
Serenade, G, 4 vc (Vienna, 1829); Elegie, f♯, 5 vc, op.160, 1834 (Leipzig, c1870)

CHAMBER MUSIC WITH PIANO

2 pf qnts: no.1, a, op.139 (Mainz, 1868), no.2, c, op.145 (Mainz, 1869)
2 trios, pf, vn, vc: no.1, E, 1828, no.2, c, 1829; trio, pf, cl, hn, B♭, 1830
Other works for vn/vc, pf; vc, pf; hn, pf

OTHER WORKS

Pf 4 hands: 2 sonatas, fantasia, variations, Momento capriccioso, Nocturne (after Weber: Oberon)
Pf solo: 3 sonatas, 3 rondos, 3 scherzos, suite, fantasia, variations, short pieces
Org: 3 sonatas (Munich, 1876); preludes and fugues
Harp: 3 Lieder ohne Worte, 1856

(3) Ignaz Lachner (*b* Rain am Lech, 11 Sept 1807; *d* Hanover, 24 Feb 1895). Composer and conductor, brother of (1) Theodor Lachner. He received his earliest musical training in Augsburg and Munich, and then went to Vienna to study with his brother (2) Franz Lachner, whom he succeeded as organist of the Lutheran church there. In 1828 he became assistant Kapellmeister of the Vienna Court Opera, moving to Stuttgart three years later to become court musical director. He moved to Munich in 1836, becoming assistant Kapellmeister of the Court Opera in 1842. He became principal Kapellmeister of the Hamburg theatre in 1853, but accepted an appointment as court Kapellmeister in Stockholm five years later. From 1861 until his retirement in 1875 he was chief conductor in

Frankfurt am Main. His most significant compositions are his chamber music and dramatic works, of which the *Alpenszenen* enjoyed considerable success in their day; a complete list of his works is not yet available.

WORKS
(selective list)

Der Geisterturm, opera, Stuttgart, 1837
Die Regenbrüder, opera (E. Mörike, H. Kurz), Stuttgart, 1839
Loreley, opera, Munich, Court Opera, 1846, vocal score (Heidelberg, c1846)
Alpenszenen (all performed Munich, Court Opera, c1850): 's letzti Fensterln (J. G. Seidel, W. von Kobell); Drei Jahrln nach'm letzten Fensterln (Seidl); Die beiden Freier; Der Freiherr als Wildschütz; Der Ju-Schroa
Deutsche Vesper, chorus, orch, org; Songs, 1v, pf
7 str qts [2 for 3 vn, va; 1 for 4 vn]; 6 pf trios; 3 sonatinas, 2/3 vn; sonata, vn, pf
7 pf sonatas; Sonata, pf 4 hands; Kindersinfonie, pf, 9 children's insts

(4) Vinzenz [Vincenz] **Lachner** (*b* Rain, 19 July 1811; *d* Karlsruhe, 22 Jan 1893). Conductor, brother of (1) Theodor Lachner. He first worked as music tutor to a Polish count in Poznań and then went to Vienna at the invitation of his brother (2) Franz Lachner. In 1834 he succeeded Franz as Kapellmeister at the Kärntnertor Theater, and took up the post of Kapellmeister in Mannheim two years later. In 1842 he directed a season of the Deutsche Operngesellschaft in London. He retired to Karlsruhe in 1872 and taught music at the conservatory there after 1884.

BIBLIOGRAPHY

F. Stetter: 'Verzeichnis der Werke von Franz Lachner', *Zeitgenössische Tondichter*, ed. M. Chop, new ser. (Leipzig, 1890)
L. K. Mayer: *Franz Lachner als Instrumental-Komponist* (diss., U. of Munich, 1922)
A. Würz: *Franz Lachner als dramatischer Komponist* (diss., U. of Munich, 1927)
F. Walter, ed.: *Briefe von Vincenz Lachner an Hermann Levi* (Mannheim, 1931)
G. Wagner: *Franz Lachner als Liederkomponist, nebst einem biographischen Teil und dem thematischen Verzeichnis sämtlicher Lieder* (diss., U. of Mainz, 1969; Giebing, 1970)
H. Federhofer: 'Briefe von Franz und Vincenz Lachner an Franz und Betty Schott', *Festschrift für einen Verleger: Ludwig Strecker* (Mainz, 1973), 149
H. Müller: *Ignaz Lachner: Versuch einer Würdigung, mit Werkverzeichnis* (Celle, 1974)

HORST LEUCHTMANN

Lachnith [Lachnitt], **Ludwig Wenzel** [Louis-Wenceslas] (*b* Prague, 7 July 1746; *d* Paris, 3 Oct 1820). Bohemian composer and horn player. He was probably the son of Franz Lachnith, a church musician in Prague, and in his youth learnt the violin, harpsichord and horn. From 1768 he was in the service of the Duke of Zweibrücken and in 1773 he received permission to travel to Paris, where he performed one of his own horn concertos at the Concert Spirituel on 28 March. Apparently he settled in Paris soon after 1780 (though remaining on the salary lists at Zweibrücken until 1786) and studied the horn with Rodolphe and composition with F. A. Philidor. From 1781 to 1783 he appeared in the *Concerts de la reine*. After being exiled during the Revolution, he returned to Paris in 1801 and became *instructeur* at the Opéra for ten months, holding that position again from 1806 to 1816.

Lachnith is remembered primarily for his stage works. His first, *L'heureuse réconciliation* (1785), was not very successful (due to its weak libretto) but merited this review: 'The music ... shows commendable aptitude. The result is sometimes laborious and painful,

but one notices in it the ideas, appropriate intentions and intelligence of a good composer' (*Mercure de France*, 26 June 1785). He later became notorious for his pasticcios. The most infamous of these is an adaptation of Mozart's *Die Zauberflöte* entitled *Les mystères d'Isis*, which acquired the nickname 'Les misères d'ici', although it was very popular with the French public. Lachnith not only cut and rearranged the score, but also incorporated music from other Mozart operas and a Haydn symphony. In his *Mémoires* Berlioz wrote a detailed account of this mutilation, ending with the statement 'Mozart was murdered by Lachnith'. Lachnith also collaborated on two pasticcio oratorios *en action* with Christian Kalkbrenner and arranged many chamber works by Haydn and Pleyel for keyboard, sometimes with accompanying instruments. His own instrumental works include symphonies, concertos, accompanied keyboard sonatas (in a severely Classical style) and string quartets. He has often been confused with the horn player and trumpeter Anton (Antoine) Lachnith (*d* Prague, c1796), who was probably related to him.

WORKS
(printed works published in Paris unless otherwise stated)

STAGE
(first performed in Paris)

L'heureuse réconciliation (comédie, 1, A. M. D. Devismes, after J. F. Marmontel), Comédie-Italienne, 25 June 1785
L' antiquaire, 1789, doubtful, cited in Grove 5
Eugénie et Linval, ou Le mauvais fils (opéra comique, 2, Devismes), Montansier, 1798
Les fêtes lacédémoniennes (opera, 3, Santerre), 1808, not perf.
Additions to or arrangements of works by others: ov., ballets in Pâris [?(P. P. Baignoux), 1784], arr. pf (n.d.), arr. 2 vn (n.d.); 7 airs in Sacchini: Oedipe à Colone, 1786, acc. hpd (n.d.); ov., airs in Salieri: Tarare, 1787, arr. hpd, vn (n.d.); ov., airs, duos in Sacchini and Rey: Arvire et Evelina, 1788, acc. hpd (c1788); ov. in Propiac: La fausse paysanne, 1789, arr. hpd (n.d.); ballets in Fontenelle: Hécube, 1800, *F-Po*; ov., airs, duos in Deux prétendus, acc. hpd (n.d.)
Pasticcios: Les mystères d'Isis (opera, 4, E. Morel, after E. Schikaneder: Die Zauberflöte), Opéra, 20 Aug 1801, music by Mozart, Haydn; Saul (oratorio mis en action, 3 pts., Morel, E. Deschamps, J. B. D. Desprès), Opéra, 6 April 1803, collab. C. Kalkbrenner, music by Cimarosa, Gossec, Haydn, Mozart, Naumann, Paisiello, Philidor, Sacchini, *Po*; Le laboureur chinois (opera, 1, Morel, Deschamps, Desprès), Opéra, 5 Feb 1813, collab. M. Berton, music by Haydn, Mozart, others; La prise de Jéricho (oratorio, 3 pts., Morel, Deschamps, Desprès), Opéra, 11 April 1805, collab. C. Kalkbrenner, music by Mozart, others

INSTRUMENTAL
(extant works only; some possibly by Anton Lachnith)

Orch: 6 Syms., op.1 (c1779); 3 Syms., op.4 (before 1782); 3 Syms., op.6 (c1782); 3 Syms., op.3 (Berlin and Amsterdam, 1784); [6] Syms., opp.11–12 (c1786); [6] Sinfonie périodique (Amsterdam, n.d.); [6] Hpd/pf Concs., opp.9–10 (c1786)
Chamber: 6 sonates, hpd/pf, vn obbl, op.2 (before 1782); 3 sonates, hpd, acc. vn, op.3 (before 1782); 6 trios, 2 vn, b, op.5 (c1782); 6 quatuors concertans, 2 vn, va, vc, op.7 (c1782); 3 sonates, hpd/pf, acc. vn, op.8 (c1782); 6 sonates concertantes, hpd/pf, vn, op.14 (c1788); 3 sonates, harp, acc. vn, op.18 (n.d.); 3 sonates, pf, vn obbl, op.20 (n.d.); 5 str qts, I-Mc; 6 sonatas, kbd, vn obbl, D-Mbs
Other: Pasticcio ou mélange d'airs, pf, acc. vn (n.d.); Recueil de walzes, pf (n.d.)

PEDAGOGICAL
Pedagogical: Méthode ou principe général du doigté pour le forte-piano (1798), with J. L. Adam, incl. arrs. of works by Cherubini, Haydn, others; Exercices préparatoires pour le piano (c1800), with J. L. Adam

BIBLIOGRAPHY

EitnerQ; *FétisB*
Babault: *Annales dramatiques ou Dictionnaire général des théâtres* (Paris, 1808–12)
A. Choron and F. Fayolle: *Dictionnaire historique des musiciens* (Paris, 1810–11/*R*1971)
H. Berlioz: *Mémoires de Hector Berlioz* (Paris, 1870; ed. and Eng. trans. by D. Cairns, 1969, 2/1970); ed. P. Citron (Paris, 1969)
G. Servières: *Episodes d'histoire musicale* (Paris, 1914), 147ff

W. Gruhn: 'Ergänzungen zur Zweibrücker Musikgeschichte', *Mf*, xxiii (1970), 173

C. Pierre: *Histoire du Concert spirituel 1725–1790* (Paris, 1975)

ETHYL L. WILL

La Clayette Manuscript (*F-Pn* n.a.fr.13521). *See* SOURCES, MS, §V, 2.

Lacombe [Trouillon-Lacombe], **Louis** (*b* Bourges, 26 Nov 1818; *d* St Vaast-la-Hougue, Manche, 30 Sept 1884). French composer, pianist and writer on music. He first studied the piano with his mother and at 11 entered the Paris Conservatoire for lessons with P.-J. Zimmermann; he won the *premier prix* within two years although he still had difficulty reaching the pedals. In 1832 he undertook a European concert tour and in 1834 he spent several months in Vienna studying the piano with Czerny, learning theory and orchestration from Sechter and Seyfried and learning some works of Beethoven. By 1840 he was back in Paris and, having decided to abandon a virtuoso's career in favour of composition, he soon published some piano pieces and chamber music. Marriage to a woman of some wealth enabled him to spend much of his time composing. In the 1850s he began writing stage works but most were performed only after his death. His best-known work, the dramatic symphony *Sapho*, was selected in a competition to be performed at the Paris World Exhibition in 1878. He contributed reviews and thoughtful, but not scholarly, articles to *La chronique musicale* and other journals. His posthumously published, aptly titled *Philosophie et musique* is a series of essays discussing aesthetics, religion and a wide range of musical topics.

Lacombe wrote hundreds of works encompassing nearly all genres. He appears to have been most at ease in light, small-scale works; his songs are sensitive and witty and few of his many piano works reflect his own virtuoso technique. His unpretentious style is appropriate to the folk-orientated plots of certain of his operas, most of which, however, lapse into exaggerated grandiosity. The large symphonic works include experimental descriptive effects in the manner of Berlioz and David. His music is characterized by inventive melodies and effective use of syncopation and hemiola, but the harmonies rarely surpass in complexity the diminished 7th (which he evidently liked) and the simple, unvaried textures become tiresome in the longer works.

Lacombe's second wife, Claudine Duclairfait (*b* Voisinlieu, Oise, 17 Jan 1831; *d* St Vaast-la-Hougue, 18 Sept 1902), was a celebrated singer at the Opéra-Comique under the name Andrée Favel. Later a highly esteemed teacher, she wrote *La science du mécanisme vocal et l'art du chant* (Paris, 1876) for which Lacombe provided the musical exercises.

WORKS
(most printed works published in Paris)

STAGE

La madone (opéra comique, 1, P. F. de Caramouche), Paris, Lyrique, 16 Jan 1861

Winkelried (opera, 4, L. Bonnemère and Moreau-Sainti), Geneva, Grand Théâtre, 17 Feb 1892, vocal score (1892)

Le tonnelier de Nuremburg (opéra comique, 2, C. Nuitter, after E. T. A. Hoffmann), perf. in Ger. as Meister Martin und seine Gesellen, Koblenz, 7 March 1897

La reine des eaux (opera, 3, Nuitter, or Lacombe and F. Barrillot), perf. in Ger. as Die Korrigane, Sondershausen, 12 or 14 March 1901

Der Kreuzritter (comic opera, 1, Clairville), Sondershausen, 21 March 1902 [? originally Le festin de fer]

5 or more other works, incl. incidental music

OTHER WORKS

Sacred: 16 or more works, incl. Mass, Petite messe, hymns, few pubd

Dramatic syms. (with solo vv, chorus, orch): Manfred (J. Barbier, de Chateau-Renaud, A. Queyroy, after Byron), 1847 (1888); Arva, ou Les hongroises (Chateau-Renaud), 1850 (1900); Sapho (Lamartine, choruses by Barrillot), 1878 (1888)

Other choral: Cimbres et teutons (Barrillot), male vv, military band, c1855; many works with orch; cantatas; works for male vv; choruses, org acc.; choruses, unacc.

Other vocal: over 100 songs, 1v, pf, incl. 80 in 3 sets, ?15 fables de La Fontaine, 8 sonnets (Barrillot); works for 1v, orch, incl. L'ondine et le pêcheur, ballade; vocalises; others

Orch: Lassan et Friss, Hung. fantasia (1890); Au tombeau d'un héros, vn, orch; ?2 concert ovs.; 4 works with speaker; others, incl. works for military band

Chamber: Grand quintette, pf, vn, ob/vn, vc, B cl/bn/vc (?c1860); Le château, str qt (n.d.); Str Qt, unpubd; 2 pf trios (n.d.); 9 or more works, vn, pf; many works for 1 inst, pf, incl. arrs.

Pf: 55 or more, incl. sets of nocturnes, études, valses, mélodies, fantasias, arrs.; works for pf 4 hands; works for 2 pf

BIBLIOGRAPHY

FétisB

E. Bourdin: *La musique et les musiciens: Louis Lacombe* (Paris, 1882)

H. Moreno: 'Louis Lacombe', *Le ménestrel*, l (1883–4), 358

H. Boyer: *Louis Lacombe et son oeuvre* (Paris, 1888)

L. Gallet: *Conférence sur Louis Lacombe et son oeuvre* (Bourges, 1891)

L. Lacombe: *Philosophie et musique*, ed. A. Lacombe [C. Duclairfait Lacombe] (Paris, 1896) [incl. detailed list of works]

E. Jongleux: *Un grand musicien méconnu, Louis Lacombe* (Bourges, 1935) [mentioned in *RiemannL 12*]

JEFFREY COOPER

Lacombe, Paul (*b* Carcassonne, 11 July 1837; *d* Carcassonne, 5 June 1927). French composer. Although he travelled widely in Europe, he resided in his native town until his death. His only formal education was acquired from a local organist and former Paris Conservatoire pupil, François Teysserre, but he attentively studied the works of established masters. He was an admirer of Bizet, with whom he corresponded from 1866, and a personal friend of Saint-Saëns. In 1901 he was elected a corresponding member of the Institut and the following year he was made a Chevalier of the Légion d'honneur.

Lacombe belonged to a generation of French composers who, inspired by the achievements of Mendelssohn and Schumann, wished to see symphonic and chamber music placed on a sound footing in France after the Franco-Prussian war. Many of his works were first performed by the Société Nationale de Musique, an organization founded in 1871 for the promotion of new French music. Although his compositions often display a superb sense of musicianship, most of them lack the originality and spontaneity necessary to escape the powerful influence of contemporary German composers. Theatrical works are notably absent from his more than 150 opus numbers. He continued to compose until after his 80th birthday, and his output consists mainly of small piano pieces, chamber music, orchestral works and approximately 120 songs. His first violin sonata was performed by Sarasate in 1869 and his Third Symphony was awarded the prize of the Société des Compositeurs de Musique in 1886. Numerous works were left in manuscript.

WORKS
(all published in Paris unless otherwise stated)

Chorus, orch: Mass; Requiem

Other vocal: c60 songs; 4 duets, incl. Nuit d'été (M. de Baure) (1902); 5 trios; c60 unpubd songs

Orch: c25 works, incl. 3 syms.; Ov. symphonique, op.22 (n.d.); Suite pastorale, op.31 (1875); Aubade printanière, op.37 (1884); Sous les étoiles, marche-nocturne, op.78 (Hamburg, 1896); Ov. dramatique; Légende symphonique; other MS works

Chamber: c15 works, incl. Pf Qt, op.101 (n.d.); 4 pf trios; 3 vn sonatas, opp.8, 17, 98; Vc Sonata, op.100 (n.d.); 3 morceaux de fantasie, op.10, vc, pf (n.d.); 4 morceaux, op.14, vn, pf (n.d.); Sérénade humoristique, pf, vn, vc, op.93 (1898)

Solo inst, orch: Divertissement, pf, op.40 (1885); Rapsodie, vn, op.51; Suite, pf, op.52; Sérénade d'automne, fl, ob, harp ad lib, str orch (n.d.); other MS works

Pf: c85 works, incl. 5 morceaux caractéristiques, op.7 (Leipzig, n.d.); 4 pièces, 4 hands, op.9 (n.d.); 2 idylles, op.11 (n.d.); Etude en forme de variations, op.18 (n.d.); Intermède de concert, op.38 (1887); Petits préludes, op.140 (1911); Marche dernière, op.150 (1917), also arr. orch (1918); Dialogue sentimental, op.151 (1917), also arr. orch (1917), vn/fl/bn/vc, pf (1917); Petite suite (New York, 1921); 2 pièces (1922); 2 berceuses; 3 suites; 7 impromptus; studies; waltzes; other MS pieces

BIBLIOGRAPHY

L. Moulin: Le romantisme musical allemand et l'âme française: un classique français du piano: Paul Lacombe (Montauban, 1915–17)
——: Paul Lacombe et son oeuvre (Paris, 1924)
G. Ferchault: 'Lacombe, Paul', MGG (with detailed list of works)
                                                        JOHN TREVITT

Lacome [Lacôme d'Estalenx], **Paul(-Jean-Jacques)** (b Le Houga, Gers, 4 March 1838; d Le Houga, 12 Dec 1920). French composer. He studied with José Puig y Absubide, organist in Aire-sur-Adour (1857–60). With an operetta, Le dernier des paladins, he won a prize in a magazine competition, and settled in Paris, where he wrote music criticism and where over 20 operettas were performed from 1870 until his return to his native Gascony at around the turn of the century. Most successful in France was Jeanne, Jeannette et Jeanneton (Folies-Dramatiques, 27 October 1876), the libretto of which had been turned down by Offenbach, but Ma mie Rosette (Folies-Dramatiques, 4 February 1890) achieved greater popularity in Britain. His most widely familiar composition is probably the 'Spanish duet' Estudiantina (no.4 of six Duos à deux voix égales) which was published in 1882 and around which Waldteufel wrote a waltz of the same name. Besides operettas and songs, Lacome composed orchestral and chamber music and piano pieces. He was a close friend of Chabrier, whose high opinion of Lacome is evident from his letters.

                                                        ANDREW LAMB

Lacorcia, Scipione (b ?Naples, ?c1585–95; d Naples, after 1620). Italian composer. On 15 March 1616 he dedicated his Secondo libro de' madrigali for five voices (Naples, 1616¹⁴) to Alessandro Miroballo, the Marchese of Bracigliano, for whom the madrigals had already been performed. On 1 October 1620 he dedicated his Terzo libro di madrigali (Naples, 1620¹⁸) to Francesco Filomarino, Count of Castello Abbate. He was a successful imitator of Gesualdo in that he avoided the obvious in order to produce the unexpected. He treated the texts in great detail and often used a literal repetition of the opening and closing phrases – features which resulted in some of the lengthiest 17th-century Neapolitan madrigals. Contrasting passages of dissonances and suspensions, fast-moving diatonic counterpoint, and chordal writing are all features of his style. He used harsh dissonances more frequently than did Gesualdo, employing augmented triads, minor triads on sharp notes and juxtapositions involving false relations. He sometimes seemed purposely to have avoided tonal coherence; for example, a group of four phrases may be repeated exactly, but for one phrase transposed down a degree and bearing no apparent tonal relation to the other three.

                                                        KEITH A. LARSON

Lacoste, Louis de (b c1675; d mid-1750s). French composer. He entered the Opéra as a chorus member in 1693, and by 1710 had assumed administrative duties; he was variously described as a 'batteur de mesure', a 'maître de musique' and an 'ordinaire' at the Académie Royale de Musique. In 1718 he was arrested (for what offence is unknown) and replaced by Blouquier at a salary of 1000 livres per annum. Two years later he and his wife, Marie-Catherine Robert, were granted the sole right for three years to produce opera in Lille, where they were then living. Lacoste was evidently back in Paris by 1725, when his opera Télégone was produced at the Opéra. Durey de Noinville listed Lacoste as a living musician in 1757, but a list of employees of the Opéra published in Les spectacles de Paris in 1754 refers to him as dead.

In the preface to his ballet, Aricie, performed at the Opéra in 1697, Lacoste stated that it was designed more to please persons of rank than those in the parterre, for he lacked the compositional skill to appeal to the latter. Apparently they agreed. After that he wrote only tragedies for the Opéra: six were given between 1705 and 1738, and two, Philomèle (parodied at the Comédie Italienne on its revival in 1723) and Créuse, seem to have been particularly successful, to judge by their several revivals.

WORKS

(all performed in Paris and published there the same year)

Aricie (opéra-ballet, prol, 5, Abbé Pic), Opéra, 9 June 1697
Philomèle (tragédie lyrique, prol, 5, P. C. Roy), Opéra, 20 Oct 1705
Bradamante (tragédie lyrique, prol, 5, Roy), Opéra, 9 May 1707
Créuse (tragédie lyrique, prol, 5, Roy), Opéra, 5 April 1712
Télégone (tragédie lyrique, prol, 5, S. J. Pellegrin), ?Opéra, 6 Nov 1725
Orion (tragédie lyrique, prol, 5, Pellegrin and J. de Lafont), ?Opéra, 17 Feb 1728
Biblis (tragédie lyrique, prol, 5, Fleury de Lyon), ?Opéra, 6 Nov 1732
Pomone (opera), lost, cited by Fétis
Airs pubd in 18th-century anthologies

BIBLIOGRAPHY

FétisB
P. F. Vente: L'état actuel de la musique de la chambre du roi et des trois spectacles de Paris (Paris, 1759)
T. Lajarte: Bibliothèque musicale du Théâtre de l'Opéra: catalogue (Paris, 1878)
E. Campardon: L'histoire de l'Académie royale de musique (Paris, 1884)
L. de La Laurencie: L'école française de violon de Lully à Viotti (Paris, 1922–4/R1971)
M. Benoit and N. Dufourcq: 'Documents du Minutier central', RMFC, ix (1969), 142
                                                        MARY HUNTER

La Court, Antoine. See DE LA COURT, ANTOINE.

La Court, Henri. See DE LA COURT, HENRI.

Lacroix [Croix], **Antoine** (b Rambouillers, nr. Nancy, 1756; d Lübeck, 18 June 1806). French violinist, composer and music dealer active in Germany. He first studied the violin and composition with Joseph-Antoine Lorenziti, maître de chapelle at Nancy Cathedral. From 1780 to 1792 Lacroix lived in Paris where he achieved considerable fame as a violin virtuoso and published his Six Sonates pour piano et violon, op.1 (1784). He left Paris in 1792 because of the Revolution, travelling via Bruges to Bremen where he evidently remained until 1794. He made several concert tours in Denmark and Germany, served for a short time as a chamber musician to the King of Prussia in Berlin, then from 22 January 1796 was a municipal musician in Lübeck. There he was also active in private concerts with the organist

J. W. C. von Königslöw. From 1799 he built up a music trade, offering the most important current works by Haydn, Zumsteeg and Pleyel, as well as his own sonatas, duos and variations for the violin. His works were praised by his contemporaries for their brilliant and effective passages for the instrument, their pleasing melodies and their straightforward structures.

WORKS
Duos: 6 sonatas, pf, vn, op.1 (Paris, 1784), lost; 3 Duos concertants, 2 vn, op.2 (Hamburg, n.d.); 3 sonatas, vn, vc, op.3 (Hamburg, n.d.); 3 for 2 vn, op.12 (Paris, 1801); 3 for 2 vn, op.14 (Paris, n.d.), lost; 3 for 2 vn, op.15 (Leipzig, n.d.), no.1 arr. as Sonate, pf, vn, op.17*b* (Leipzig, n.d.); 3 [12] for 2 vn, opp.16, 18, 20, 21 (Leipzig, n.d.); Air varié, Ah vous dirai-je, maman, 2 vn, op.19 (Leipzig, n.d.); VII variations, on O mein lieber Augustin, vn, vc (Leipzig, 1801); Air varié, vn, vc (Brunswick and Hamburg, n.d.); 12 pièces, 2 vn, mentioned in *AMZ*, v (1806); 3 Sonate, 2 vn, 1798, lost

Other: IV Angloisen, II Walzer, orch (Brunswick, n.d.); Divertissement, 1797, lost; ?3[?6] str qts, opp.5, 13 (Hamburg, n.d.), lost; 3 str qts, op.17*a* (Brunswick, n.d.); Thèmes variés, vn, op.6 (Hamburg, n.d.), lost; Thèmes variés, vn, op.19 (Vienna, n.d.), lost; Thème varié, pf, mentioned in *FétisB*; Romanze mit 4 Variationen, vn, 1795, lost; dances (Hamburg and Brunswick, n.d.), mentioned in *GerberNL*

BIBLIOGRAPHY
J. Hennings and W. Stahl: *Musikgeschichte Lübecks* (Kassel, 1951), 152
G. Karstädt: 'Lacroix, Antoine', *MGG*

                                        GEORG KARSTÄDT

La Croix [Delacroix], François de (*b* Senlis, 6 Jan 1683; *d* Paris, 8 April 1759). French priest and composer. After initial musical training at Senlis Cathedral, he probably studied under Nicolas Bernier in Paris. He was *maître de chapelle* of the royal church of St Paul from 8 September 1714 to 12 September 1726, and succeeded Bernier in the same post at the Sainte Chapelle du Palais from 18 September 1726. On 2 December 1744 he was appointed permanent chaplain of the Sainte Chapelle, succeeding P. Warnier, and on 30 January 1745 he was replaced as *maître de chapelle* by Abel-François Fanton, former *maître de chapelle* of Blois Cathedral. He composed a large number of motets, several of which were performed at the Concert Spirituel, and masses for the reopening of the Paris parliament. His surviving works consist of several airs published in Ballard's collections and one book of *Motets à une, deux et trois voix avec symphonie et sans symphonie* op.1 (Paris, 1741), which contains 14 of his motets and four posthumous motets by Bernier. La Croix's motets are distinguished by their sobriety of expression and clarity of part-writing.

Other musicians with the same name who may have been related include Abbé de La Croix, a singer at the Concert Spirituel from 1750 to 1759; Adrien de La Croix, a member of the 24 Violons in 1664 who composed an Allemande à 4 (*D-Kl*); and a Pierre La Croix a 'Maître Joueur d'Instruments' in Paris in 1724.

BIBLIOGRAPHY
EitnerQ
M. Brenet: *Les concerts en France sous l'ancien régime* (Paris, 1900/*R*1969)
——: *Les musiciens de la Sainte-Chapelle du Palais: documents inédits, recueillis et annotés par Michel Brenet* (Paris, 1910/*R*1973)
D. Launay: 'La Croix, François de', *MGG*
P. Nelson: 'Nicolas Bernier: a Résumé of his Work', *RMFC*, i (1960), 93

                                        GUY BOURLIGUEUX

La Crotte, Nicolas de. *See* LA GROTTE, NICOLAS DE.

Lacy, John (*d* Devon, *c*1865). English bass. He was a pupil of Rauzzini at Bath. After singing in London he went to Italy where he became a complete master of the Italian language and style of singing. On his return he sang at concerts and the Lenten Oratorios, but although he possessed an exceptionally fine voice and sang admirably in various styles, circumstances prevented him from taking any prominent position. In 1818 he accepted an engagement in Calcutta and, accompanied by his wife, left England, returning about 1826. Had he remained in London he would most probably have been appointed bass soloist at the Ancient Concerts on Bartleman's death in 1821.

His wife, née Jackson (*b* London, 1776; *d* London, 19 May 1858), appeared as a soprano at the Concert of Ancient Music on 25 April 1798. In 1800 she married the composer Francesco Bianchi; in 1810 they seem to have been divorced. She was married to Lacy in 1812 and sang as Mrs Bianchi Lacy until 1815. She was noted for a grand, simple style and for her perfect delivery of Italian.

BIBLIOGRAPHY
Anon.: 'Preliminary Remarks on Bass Singing', *Quarterly Musical Magazine and Review*, i (1818), 333
C. Cudworth: 'Lacy, John', *MGG*
M. Hardwick: *Emma, Lady Hamilton* (New York, 1969), 119

                                        W. H. HUSK/R

Lacy, Michael Rophino (*b* Bilbao, 19 July 1795; *d* London, 20 Sept 1867). English violinist, playwright and theatre musician. His mother was Spanish, his father an Irish merchant. A child prodigy on the violin, he performed at the age of six a concerto of Giornovichi at a concert given at Bilbao by Andreossi. In 1802 he was at college at Bordeaux and in 1803 was sent to Paris to finish his education. Kreutzer was his principal instructor in music. About the end of 1804 he performed before Napoleon at the Tuileries; he was then known as 'le petit Espagnol'. He played in the principal Dutch towns on his way to London, which he reached in October 1805. There he soon gave concerts at Hanover Square Rooms, as 'The Young Spaniard', his name not being announced until May 1807, when an engraved portrait of him by Cardon after Smart was published. He next performed at Catalani's first concert in Dublin, during a visit of Michael Kelly's opera company to Ireland, and was afterwards engaged by Corri's concerts at Edinburgh at 20 guineas per night. A few years later, at his father's insistence, he left the musical for the theatrical profession and performed genteel comedy parts at the theatres of Dublin, Edinburgh, Glasgow and other cities. In 1818 he succeeded Janiewicz as leader of the Liverpool concerts, and at the end of 1820 returned to London and was leader of the ballet orchestra at King's Theatre.

From 1827 to 1833 Lacy exercised his musical and linguistic skills in adapting to the English stage over a dozen French plays and operas, translating the words and arranging the music, and frequently taking great liberties with them, as was the contemporary practice. During the 1850s he did much of the research for Schoelcher's biography of Handel, and during his last decade produced several original dramas in London.

WORKS
THEATRICAL
All first produced, and all printed works published, in London; MS libs, all by Lacy, in *GB-Lbm*.
DL – *Drury Lane Theatre*   CG – *Covent Garden Theatre*

The Turkish Lovers (comic opera, after F. Romani: Il turco in Italia) DL, 1 May 1827; after Rossini's opera

Love in Wrinkles, or The Russian Stratagem (comic opera, after E.
    Scribe, G. Delavigne: La vieille), DL, 4 Dec 1828; after Fétis's opera
The Maid of Judah, or The Knights Templars (opera, after E. Des-
    champs, G. G. de Wailly: Ivanhoé), CG, 7 March 1829, lib pubd;
    after the Rossini pastiche
The Casket (comic opera, after Les premières amours), DL, 10 March
    1829; after Mozart's Idomeneo
Cinderella, or The Fairy Queen and the Glass Slipper (comic opera,
    after J. Ferretti), CG, 13 April 1830, vocal score pubd (1830), lib
    pubd; after Rossini's opera, incl. music from Maometto II, Armida
    and Guillaume Tell
Napoleon Buonaparte, Captain of Artillery, General and First Consul,
    Emperor and Exile (dramatic spectacle), CG, 16 May 1831, descrip-
    tion pubd
Fra Diavolo, or The Inn of Terracina (opera, 3, after Scribe), CG, 3
    Nov 1831, lib pubd; after Auber's opera
The Fiend Father, or Robert of Normandy (opera, after Scribe,
    Delavigne: Robert le diable), CG, 21 Feb 1832, lib pubd; after
    Meyerbeer's opera
The Coiners, or The Soldier's Oath (opera, after Scribe, E. J. E.
    Mazères: Le serment), CG, 23 March 1833; after Auber's opera
The Israelites in Egypt, or The Passage of the Red Sea (dramatic
    oratorio), CG, 22 Feb 1833; after Rossini's Moïse and Handel's
    Israel in Egypt
The Route of the Overland Mail to India, from Southampton to Calcutta
    (diorama, J. H. Siddons, scenery by T. Grieve, W. Telbin), Gallery of
    Illustration, 1851, lib pubd

OTHER WORKS

A set of rondos, pf, mentioned in DNB
Qnt, fl, 2 vn, va, vc, pf acc., mentioned by Fétis
Fantasies on operatic themes, pf, mentioned by Fétis
Numerous songs, pubd separately

BIBLIOGRAPHY

FétisB
V. Schoelcher: Preface to The Life of Handel (London, 1857)
E. Heron-Allen: 'Lacy, Michael Rophino', DNB
A. Nicoll: A History of English Drama, 1660–1900, iv–v (Cambridge,
    2/1955–9/R1966–7)
                                    W. H. HUSK/BRUCE CARR

Łada [Ładowski, Ładewski], **Kazimierz** (b Blizno, nr
Kalisz, 1824; d Włocławek, 5 Sept 1871). Polish violinist and composer. He had his first music lessons from
his elder brother Maciej in Włocławek. In 1837 he
moved to Warsaw where, with his brothers, he formed
the Ładowskis Quartet, in which Kazimierz was first
violin. He also gave solo performances in Poland and
Russia. From 1854 to 1857 he was in Paris, where he
studied composition with Collet and the violin with
Alard. His playing was described as melodious, lilting
and of great feeling, though technically imperfect; his
programmes consisted mainly of his own compositions
and salon pieces. In 1861 paralysis compelled him to
give up concert performance. He composed more than
40 small pieces for violin in dance and other light forms.
The most well known were the Kujawiak in D (1850),
Cygan, the Fantasy (1860) and the Caprice poétique
(1862).

WRITINGS

'Materiały do historii muzyki w Polsce', Gazeta muzyczna i teatralna
    (1866), no.19, p.4; no.20, p.3; no.21, p.5; no.22, p.2; no.23, p.3

BIBLIOGRAPHY

SMP
J. Reiss: Polskie skrzypce i polscy skrzypkowie (Warsaw, 1946), 11
                                            JERZY MORAWSKI

Ladegast, Friedrich (b Hochhermsdorf, 30 Aug 1818; d
Weissenfels, 1 July 1905). German organ builder. He
trained under his brother Christlieb in Geringswalde
and with Urban Kreutzbach in Borna, Mende in Leipzig
and Zuberbier in Dessau; his years as a journeyman
gave him first-hand knowledge of instruments by the
Silbermann family and by Cavaillé-Coll, with whom he
later held a regular exchange of ideas. He set up in
business on his own in Weissenfels in 1846. The excel-

lence of his organ at Hohenmölsen (two manuals, 25
stops; extant) led to a contract to repair and enlarge
the organ in Merseburg Cathedral. When completed in
1855, this was the largest organ in Germany (four
manuals, 81 stops); among those who played it was
Liszt, whom it inspired to compose his Prelude and
Fugue on B–A–C–H. Other major works by Ladegast
include the organs of St Nikolai, Leipzig (1858–62;
four manuals, 86 stops), Schwerin Cathedral (1866–71;
four manuals, 84 stops; extant, unaltered), and the
Gesellschaft der Musikfreunde in Vienna (1872; three
manuals, 55 stops; the case and pipes standing in the
front survive). Ladegast was in the forefront of German
organ builders of the 19th century. Unlike such master
craftsmen as Walcker and Steinmeyer, he built slider-
chests, but went over to the Kegellade chest as early as
c1875, much earlier than Ibach, Klais and Stahlhuth,
for instance. He introduced pneumatic action in 1890.
Ladegast followed the trends of German Romantic
organ building (see SCHULZE) both in tone and in the
relatively small proportion (by comparison with
Cavaillé-Coll, for instance) of reeds in the specification.
In the scale of his pipes he followed older methods in his
early instruments, employing a basic ratio of $1:2$ for
the diameters of pipes an octave apart (also used by
Bédos de Celles), but he later adopted J. G. Töpfer's
ratio (see ORGAN, §III, 1), at first for the Principal
chorus only, eventually for all stops. Ladegast was
known in professional circles as the 'Nestor of German
organ building'.

BIBLIOGRAPHY

R. Rupp: Die Entwicklungsgeschichte der Orgelbaukunst (Einsiedeln,
    1929)
W. Ellerhorst: Handbuch der Orgelkunde (Einsiedeln, 1936)
H.-G. Wauer: 'Friedrich Ladegast, ein bedeutender Orgelbauer des 19.
    Jahrhunderts', Musik und Kirche, xxv (1955), 293
E. K. Rössler: 'Ladegast', MGG
G. Beer: Orgelbau Ibach Barmen (1794–1904) (Cologne, 1975)
                                            HANS KLOTZ

Laderman, Ezra (b Brooklyn, NY, 29 June 1924).
American composer and teacher. He enjoyed early recognition with the performance of a piano concerto in
1937. Then, after war service in the US Army, resulting
in the première of his Leipzig Symphony in 1945 at
Wiesbaden, he took the BA at Brooklyn College (1946–
9), studied with Wolpe (1946–9) and took the MA at
Columbia University under Luening (1950–52). He
taught at Sarah Lawrence College (1960–61, 1965–6)
and in 1971 was appointed professor of music and composer-in-residence at the State University of New York
at Binghamton. In 1972 he was made chairman of the
Composers Commissioning Program of the National
Endowment of the Arts, and in 1973 president of the
American Music Center. He has received three
Guggenheim Awards (1955, 1958, 1964) and the
American Prix de Rome (1963). His style is intense and
romantic, traditional but with a personal vigour and
vision. Important in his career have been several works
on Jewish subjects, of which the television opera Sarah,
produced by CBS in 1959, first brought his name to
public notice.

WORKS

(selective list)

Operas: Jacob and the Indians (E. Kinoy, after S. V. Benet), 1956–7;
    Sarah, 1, 1959; Goodbye to the Clown, 1959–60; Shadows among
    us (2, N. Rostin), 1965–9
Orch: 2 pf concs., 1936, 1948; Leipzig Sym., 1945; Stanzas, chamber
    orch, 1960; Vn Conc., 1961; Sym. no.1, 1963–4; Satire: Conc. for
    Orch, 1968; Sym. no.2 'Luther', 1968; Sym. no.3 'Jerusalem','1973
Vocal: The Eagle Stirred, oratorio, 1960–61; Magic Prison, 2 nar-

rators, orch, 1966–7; The Trials of Galileo, oratorio, 1966–7; Air Raid, 1968; Priorities, 1968; From the Psalms, 1970; And David Wept, 1971; The Questions of Abraham, 1972; Columbus, B-Bar, orch, 1975; A Handful of Souls, cantata, 1976

Chamber: 2 pf sonatas, 1952, 1956; Theme and Variations, 1954; Duo, vn, vc, 1955; Fl Sonata, 1955; Cl Sonata, 1956; Wind Octet, 1957; Pf Trio, 1958; 5 str qts, 1958–9, 1964–5, 1968, 1974, 1976; Nonette, 1960; Portraits, vn, 1965; A Single Voice, va, 1969; Elegy, va, 1973; Meditations on Isaiah, vc, 1973; Momenti, 1973; Echoes in Anticipation, ob, other insts, 1975; Other Voices, 3 va, 1975; 25 Preludes, org, 1975

Songs: Songs for Eve (MacLeish), S, pf, 1962–3; Worship, song cycle, Mez, T, pf, 1976

Principal publisher: Oxford University Press

EDITH BORROFF

Ladewski [**Ładowski**], **Kazimierz.** *See* ŁADA, KAZIMIERZ.

Ladmirault, Paul (Emile) (*b* Nantes, 8 Dec 1877; *d* Kerbili en Kamoel, St Nazaire, 30 Oct 1944). French composer. He began to compose at the age of eight, and his first opera (to a libretto by his mother) was produced in Nantes on 18 May 1893. In 1895 he went to Paris where he studied harmony with Tardou, composition with Fauré and counterpoint and fugue with Gédalge. He left Paris to become professor and later director of the conservatory in his home town. A board member of the Société Nationale de Musique, Ladmirault saw many of his works first performed under its auspices. He wrote for the *Ouest-artiste* in Nantes, the *Courrier musical* and the *Revue musicale* in Paris, and the journal of the Internationale Musikgesellschaft. Debussy described Ladmirault's *Choeur des âmes de la forêt* as a work fashioned with a refined sense of poetic colour. Indeed Ladmirault is best remembered as a regionalist, whose works display the atmosphere of his native Brittany, much as Séverac's music reflects the Languedoc region. Many of Ladmirault's works remain unpublished.

WORKS

Gilles de Retz (opera, 3, L. Ladmirault), 1893
Myrdhin (opera, 4, L. Ladmirault and A. Fleury), 1899–1902 [inc., orch extracts: Suite bretonne, 1902–3; Brocéliande au matin, ov. (1908)]
La prêtresse de Korydwen, ballet, 1925
Tristan et Yseult (incidental music, J. Bédier), 1920
Orch pieces, chamber works, church music

Principal publishers: Rouart Lerolle, Leduc

BIBLIOGRAPHY

C. Debussy: 'De l'opéra et de ses rapports avec la musique', *Gil Blas* (9 March 1903)
J. Tiersot: *Un demi-siècle de musique française (1870–1917)* (Paris, 1918)
O. Séré [pseud. of J. Poueigh]: *Musiciens français d'aujourd'hui* (Paris, 2/1921)
P. Landormy: *La musique française après Debussy* (Paris, 1943)
G. Samazeuilh: *Musiciens de mon temps* (Paris, 1947)
M. Courtonne: *Un siècle de musique à Nantes et dans la région nantaise, 1850–1950* (Nantes, 1953)
G. Bender: 'Dans le souvenir de Paul Ladmirault', *Guide du concert et du disque*, xxxix (1959), 765
G. Ferchault: 'Ladmirault, Paul', *MGG*

ELAINE BRODY

La Douardière, Henri de. *See* L'ENCLOS, HENRI DE.

Ladurner, Ignace Antoine (François Xavier) [Ignaz Anton Franz Xaver/Joseph] (*b* Aldein, nr. Bolzano, 1 Aug 1766; *d* Villain, nr. Massy, 4 March 1839). French composer, pianist and teacher of Tyrolean descent, elder brother of Josef Alois Ladurner. His father, Franz Xaver (1735–82), was an organist and teacher at Aldein and later at Algund. Ignace studied music with his uncle Innozenz Ladurner (1745–1807) at the nearby monas-

tery of Benediktbeuren and became the organist at Algund on his father's death. In 1784 he went to Munich to study at the Lyceum Gregorianum, leaving the organ position to Josef Alois. He soon completed his studies and moved to Longeville, near Bar-le-Duc, with Countess Heimhausen, a distinguished pianist, who apparently employed him to play music with her. He arrived in Paris in 1788 and soon developed a reputation as an outstanding teacher. From 1797 until 1802 he taught the piano at the Conservatoire, during which time his pupils won several prizes. However, his most famous pupils, Auber and Boëly, were taught privately. When the Conservatoire was re-formed as the Ecole Royale in 1816 he was appointed to the faculty but apparently never fulfilled this role. He married Mlle Magnier de Gondreville, a talented violinist; their son, Adolphe Ladurner, became known as a painter. In 1836, disabled by paralysis, he moved to his country home in Villain.

Ladurner wrote two operas and some chamber music, but most of his compositions were for the piano. According to Saint-Foix, Ladurner was more interested in solid construction than in the flashy style of his contemporary Steibelt, and his music, characterized by good counterpoint and unusual modulations, reveals thorough knowledge of Clementi's works, but is not reactionary. He influenced his pupils, particularly Boëly, both through his interest in new ideas and his continual study of established masters.

WORKS
(all printed works published in Paris)

OPERAS

Wenzel, ou Le magistrat du peuple (drame lyrique 3, F. Pillet), Paris, Théâtre National, 10 April 1793; ov., airs, acc. pf (1795–1800)
Les vieux fous, ou Plus de peur que de mal (opéra comique, 1, J. A. de Ségur), Paris, Opéra-Comique (Feydeau), 15 or 16 Jan 1796; score, F-Pc

PIANO

12 sonatas, opp.1–2, lost, 8, 11; 3 grandes sonates avec la charge de cavalerie, op.4 (1797); 4 caprices, 3 as op.8, 1 as op.11; 3 divertissements, op.13; 3 thèmes variés, op.14; 6 airs variés, op.16, lost; Airs irlandais variés, op.17, lost; Airs des Trembleurs variés, op.18, lost; Mélange harmonique, op.3; Second mélange harmonique, op.10; Fantaisie, op.12; Gai, gai, rondo fantaisie, autograph, Pc; pieces in Etude ou Exercice de différents auteurs (1798)
Pf 4 hands: 3 sonatas, op.2 (1793), op.6 (c1804), op.12 [with Une larme sur la tombe de la plus tendre mère]

OTHER WORKS

Chamber: Sonata, pf, vn acc. in Journal de pièces de clavecin par différents auteurs (1792); 3 Sonatas, pf, vn, vc, op.1 (?1793); 9 Sonatas, pf, vn acc., 3 as op.5 (1798), 3 as op.7 (after 1804), 3 others, ?op.9; Introduction pour la sonate de Steibelt, vn, pf, Pc
Vocal: Amant cher autant qu'infidèle, romance, in Journal hebdomadaire composé d'airs d'opéras, xxiv/42 (1789); Orgie militaire, ou Gaité militaire (Pillet) (?1795)

BIBLIOGRAPHY

EitnerQ; FétisB
G. de Saint-Foix: 'Les premiers pianistes parisiens (VIII): Ignace-Antoine Ladurner (1766–1839)', *ReM*, viii/1 (1926), 13

FRÉDÉRIC ROBERT

Ladurner, Josef Alois (*b* Algund, nr. Merano, 7 March 1769; *d* Brixen [Bressanone], 20 Feb 1851). Austrian composer of Tyrolean descent, brother of Ignace Antoine Ladurner. He studied with his uncle at the monastery of Benediktbeuren, became organist at Algund in 1784, and attended the Lyceum Gregorianum at Munich where he studied theology and philosophy until 1798. He also had piano lessons and received instruction in composition and counterpoint from the *Hofclaviermeister* Josef Graetz. He became a priest in 1799, and held various positions at the prince-bishop's consistory at Brixen, including those of court chaplain from 1802 and councillor from 1816. Although he was not a professional musician, he directed choirs, gave piano lessons and participated in the activities of music societies at Innsbruck and Salzburg. His compositions, which were highly regarded by his contemporaries, include variations and fantasias for the piano, considerable church music and some pedagogical works; many of his works remain in manuscript.

WORKS

(published in Munich after 1826 unless otherwise indicated)

Sacred vocal, 4vv: Tantum ergo, op.2; Ecce sacerdos, op.3, acc. pf; Ave Maria, op.4; O salutaris hostia, op.5; other works, unpubd incl. MSS, *A-Wgm, D-LEm*

Pf: Fantaisie, ?op.1 (Mainz, before 1811); Fantasie, op.6 (*c*1835); 52 kurze Cadenzen mit variirter Modulation, op.7; Rondo all'anglaise, op.8; 16 variations on a pastoral theme, op.9; 16 variations on a Viennese waltz, op.10; Fantasia, fugue, sonata, on a theme from a fugue by Handel, op.11; Fugue, op.12; Fantasia on a theme from Mozart: ov. to Don Giovanni, op.13; 56 moderne Orgel- und Clavier-Praeludien, op.14; other works, unpubd

Pedagogical works, incl. Grundliches Lehrbuch [piano teaching method]

BIBLIOGRAPHY

FétisB

G. W. Fink, ed.: 'Joseph Aloys Ladurner', *AMZ*, xxxvii (1835), col.759

Lady Day. *See* HOLIDAY, BILLIE.

Lady Mass. One of the votive masses; *see* VOTIVE MASS, VOTIVE ANTIPHON.

Ładysz, Bernard (*b* Vilnius, 24 July 1922). Polish bass. He studied singing in Vilnius, then under the direction of Filipowicz at the Fryderyk Chopin Music School in Warsaw, and joined the Polish Army Representative Ensemble, with which he appeared at home and abroad. In 1950 he was engaged as a soloist by the Warsaw Opera. After he won the Viotti Competition in Vercelli (1956) he began to appear at many European opera houses, including Palermo, Naples (the Teatro San Carlo), Parma, and the Bol'shoy Theatre. His main roles include the Inquisitor and Philip II in *Don Carlos*, Mephistopheles in *Faust* and the title role in *Boris Godunov*; and he has sung in Szymanowski's *King Roger*, Stravinsky's *Oedipus rex* and Penderecki's *The Devils of Loudon*. He has recorded arias by Verdi and by Russian and other composers. He has a voice of wide range and considerable talent as an actor. In 1964 he received the order of Standard of Work.

MIECZYSŁAWA HANUSZEWSKA

Laet, Jean [Jan] **de** [Latius, Joannes; Latio, Giovanni] (*b* Stabroeck, *c*1525; *d* Antwerp, *c*1567). Flemish printer. He became a citizen of Antwerp in 1545 and began to print in the same year. In 1553 he registered in the Guild of St Luke under the name Jan van Stabroeck. He printed Bibles, histories, Spanish books, classical texts and, from 1554, a number of music books, either in conjunction with the Antwerp teacher and composer HUBERT WAELRANT, or on his own. Together, in the years 1554–6, Waelrant and Laet published eight books of motets and four books of chansons by various composers. Alone, Laet brought out a number of music publications including Lassus's motets in 1556, the year of the composer's visit to Antwerp; thus he was one of Lassus's first publishers. Laet was on good terms with the Antwerp printer and type cutter Ameet Tavernier. He sold books printed by Tavernier and in 1566 bought some type from him. It is likely that the elegant music type used by Laet was designed by Tavernier, for it also occurs in a book published by Tavernier's widow. After Laet's death, his widow published several music books, including a reprint of Bakfark's first book for lute.

BIBLIOGRAPHY

A. Goovaerts: *Histoire et bibliographie de la typographie musicale dans les Pays-Bas* (Antwerp, 1880/*R*1963)

Å. Davidsson: *Musikbibliographische Beiträge* (Uppsala, 1954), 15

W. Boetticher: *Orlando di Lasso und seine Zeit* (Kassel and Basle, 1958)

E. Roobaert and A. Moerman: 'Jean de Laet', *De gulden passer*, xxxiv (1961), 188

H. D. L. Vervliet: *Sixteenth Century Printing Types of the Low Countries* (Amsterdam, 1968)

S. Bain: *Music Printing in the Low Countries in the Sixteenth Century* (diss., U. of Cambridge, 1974)

SUSAN BAIN

Laetrius, Petit Jean. *See* DE LATRE, PETIT JEAN.

La Fage, (Juste-)Adrien(-Lenoir) de (*b* Paris, 30 March 1805; *d* Charenton, 8 March 1862). French composer and writer on music. He was a grandson of the celebrated architect Lenoir. Educated for the church and the army, he decided instead on a career in music, and as a harmony and counterpoint pupil of Perne made a particular study of plainsong; he was then a pupil, and later assistant, of Choron. In 1828, sent by the government to Rome, he studied for a year under Baini, and while in Italy produced a farce, *I creditori*, but he never gained any distinction in this genre. On his return to Paris (December 1829) he was appointed *maître de chapelle* of St Etienne-du-Mont, where he substituted an organ (built by John Abbey) for the harsh out-of-tune serpent previously used with the chant. At the same time he held a similar post at the church of St François-Xavier, where he restored much ancient plainchant and introduced antiphonal singing for men's and boys' choirs.

La Fage spent the years 1833–6 in Italy and while he was there his wife and son both died. On returning to Paris he published the *Manuel complet de musique vocale et instrumentale* (1836–8), of which the first chapters had been prepared by Choron, some critical works and collections of biographical and critical articles. He visited Italy again after the 1848 revolution and made copies of previously unstudied MSS; he also visited Germany and Spain, and England during the 1851 Great Exhibition. He finally settled in Paris and published the works on which his reputation rests. Overwork as an author and as general editor of *Le plainchant*, a periodical which he founded in 1859, brought on a nervous illness that ultimately led to his removal to the insane asylum at Charenton.

La Fage was a prolific composer of sacred music and also wrote some chamber music for flute, but is remembered as a historian and didactic writer. His *Cours complet de plain-chant* (1855–6) fully justifies its title. It was succeeded in 1859 by an equally valuable supplement, the *Nouveau traité de plain-chant romain* (with questions). His *Histoire générale de la musique et de la danse*, though dealing only with Chinese, Indian, Egyptian and Hebrew music, is a careful and conscientious work. His learning and method appear conspicuously in his *Extraits du catalogue critique et raisonné d'une petite bibliothèque musicale* and in his *Essais de dipthérographie musicale*, works of particular importance in that they refer to MSS and documents now lost. His substantial library was catalogued (Paris, 1862) and afterwards dispersed by auction. His unpublished works and materials including his compositions are in the Bibliothèque Nationale, to which he bequeathed all his papers, with the MSS of Choron and Baini in his possession.

WRITINGS

Manuel complet de musique vocale et instrumentale (Paris, 1836–8) [begun by A. Choron]
Séméiologie musicale (Paris, 1837)
De la chanson considérée sous le rapport musical (Paris, 1840)
Eloge de Choron (Paris, 1843)
Miscellanées musicales (Paris, 1844)
Histoire générale de la musique et de la danse (Paris, 1844)
Nicolai Capuani presbyteri compendium musicale (Paris, 1853)
De la reproduction des livres de plain-chant romain (Paris, 1853)
Lettre écrite à l'occasion d'un mémoire pour servir à la restauration du chant romain en France, par l'abbé Céleste Alix (Paris, 1853)
Cours complet de plain-chant (Paris, 1855–6)
Quinze visites musicales à l'Exposition Universelle de 1855 (Paris, 1856)
Extraits du catalogue critique et raisonné d'une petite bibliothèque musicale (Rennes, ?1857)
Nouveau traité de plain-chant romain (Paris, 1859) [suppl. to *Cours complet de plain-chant*]
De l'unité tonique et de la fixation d'un diapason universel (Paris, 1859)
Essais de dipthérographie musicale (Paris, 1864)

BIBLIOGRAPHY
R. D. Denne-Baron: *Adrien de La Fage* (Paris, 1863)
M. Cole: 'Sonata-rondo, the Formulation of a Theoretical Concept in the 18th and 19th Centuries', *MQ*, lv (1969), 180

GUSTAVE CHOUQUET/ARTHUR HUTCHINGS

La Fage, Jean de (*fl c*1518–30). Composer, probably of French birth. On stylistic grounds, and to judge from the range of manuscripts and printed volumes in which his music appears, La Fage was probably trained before the turn of the 16th century and worked in Paris. He is cited in Rabelais' list of musicians in the prologue to book 4 of *Pantagruel* and in a noël by Jean Daniel in 1530.

Over a dozen surviving motets are attributed to La Fage, one or two of which were very popular. *Elizabeth zacharie* (*RISM* 1519[1]) is in ten sources from the Medici codex (*I-Fl* 666) of 1518 onwards, and was respected enough to be attributed to Jean Mouton in two sources. In common with much of La Fage's music this motet is based on short, very rhythmic points, with occasional bursts of more melismatic writing. The harmonic structure is clearcut, and a strong pulse is always apparent. *Aspice Domine* (*RISM* 1535[3]) has few contrasts of sonority, but in other works La Fage regularly divided the four voices into two pairs. In the five-voice *Super flumina Babylonis* (*RISM* 1534[5]) the three lower voices are similarly paired with the two upper ones. One chanson by La Fage survives.

WORKS
13 motets, 3–5vv, 1519[1], 1520[2], 1521[5], 1534[5], 1534[6], 1535[3], 1541[2], 1558[4], *GB-Lbm* Add.19583
Chanson, 3vv, *I-Fn* Magl.XIX.117

STANLEY BOORMAN

La Farge, P. de (*fl* 1539–46). French or Franco–Flemish composer. Although Eitner (*EitnerS* and *EitnerQ*) considered La Farge and JEAN DE LA FAGE to be the same person, they were in fact two different composers. La Farge's music appeared only in the music publications of Jacques Moderne of Lyons and in no other source, printed or manuscript, so far as is known. Eight Latin motets and two French chansons survive, all attributed by Moderne to 'P. de la Farge'.

WORKS
A solis ortu, 5vv, 1542[5]; Ave regina caelorum, 4vv, 1539[11]; Clamabat autem mulier cananea, 5vv, 1547[2]; Cum sero factum esset, 5vv, 1542[5]; Regina celi letare, 4vv, 1539[11]; Sanctificamini hodie, 5vv, 1542[5]; Suscipiens Jesum, 4vv, 1539[11]; Virgo Maria non est tibi similis, 6vv, 1547[2]
Las que te sert, 4vv, 1543[14]; Robin avoit de la souppe, 4vv, 1544[9]

SAMUEL F. POGUE

La Faya, Aurelio. *See* DELLA FAYA, AURELIO.

La Feillée, François de (*d c*1780). French theorist. He probably lived in or near Poitiers around 1750. His reputation stands on his *Méthode nouvelle pour apprendre parfaitement les règles du plainchant et de la psalmodie*, published in Poitiers in 1748 and appearing nine times in four editions up to 1784. It advocates the 'expressive' performance of chant in accord with the doctrine of the Affections as it was then understood. La Feillée wrote: 'Expression is an image which sensitively renders the character of all that one utters in singing, and which depicts it realistically'. The use of trills and other ornamentation is recommended, and relative speeds of delivery are prescribed. The same text should be sung more slowly on a solemn feast-day than on normal days, but otherwise the immediate contents of the text should determine the manner of singing: prayers are to be sung 'devoutly and sadly', narrative texts 'without any passion but with good pronunciation'. The treatise provides a valuable sidelight on the history of chant performance, and may reflect the kinds of expressive effect that 18th-century composers of religious music may have intended. La Feillée also published *Epitome gradualis romani* (Poitiers, n.d.) and *Epitome antiphonarii romani* (Poitiers, 1746).

BIBLIOGRAPHY
K. G. Fellerer: 'Zur Neukomposition und Vortrag des gregorianischen Chorals im 18. Jahrhundert', *AcM*, vi (1934), 145

See also PLAINCHANT MUSICAL.

MARY HUNTER

L'Affilard [Laffilard, L'Affillard, La Filiade], **Michel** (*b c*1656; *d* ?Versailles, 1708). French composer, theorist and singer. On 24 March 1679 he was appointed *chantre clerc* at the Sainte-Chapelle, Paris, where he may have studied with René Ouvrard. He joined the royal chapel at Versailles in 1683 and remained there until his death. In 1696 he became an officer of the king's music and bought a coat-of-arms.

L'Affilard was the first composer to supply metronomic indications for his own music, and he was scrupulous in editing it, indicating breathing places, ornaments and *notes inégales*. His surviving music amounts to about three dozen elegant *airs de mouvement* or dance-songs, which are found in manuscript (in *F-V*), in *Recueils* published by Ballard (*RISM* 1695[3] and 1697[2], and two others of 1701 and 1705) and especially in what might be termed his 'complete works': the *Principes très-faciles pour bien apprendre la musique* (Paris, 1694, 2/1697, 3/1700 repr. 1701, 4/1702, 5/1705 repr. 1705/*R*1971, 11/1747). The last-named is a treatise on sight-singing which he seems to have used as a laboratory, for he reworked and recomposed the songs in each fresh edition up to the fifth. When he introduced metronome indications into that edition, which he issued in both sacred and secular versions, the 'complete works' reached its final form, and the six subsequent editions (two of which appeared more than once) are all based on one of the three issues of the fifth edition.

The *Principes* would be a rather ordinary self-tutor were it not for the high quality of L'Affilard's dance-songs, which are regular and can be danced to. The anthology is important for the insights it provides on questions of the tempo, articulation, phrasing, ornamentation and quality of movement of early 18th-century dance music. L'Affilard based his tempo indications on

TABLE 1

Signature	Dance	Tempo
¢	March	♩ 60*?
2	Gavotte	♩ 60
2	Rigaudon	♩ 60
2	Bourrée	♩ 60
2	Pavan	♩ 45
2	Branle	♩ 53*
3/2	Sarabande	♩ 36?
3/2	Courante	♩ 45?
3	Sarabande	♩ 43?
3	Passacaille	♩ 53
3	Chaconne	♩ 79
3	Minuet	♩. 35 (♩ 105)
3/8	Passepied	♩. 43 (♪ 129)
3/8	Gigue	♩. 58
6/4	Sarabande	♩ 67
6/4	March	♩ 75*
6/8	Canaries	♩. 53
6/8	Minuet	♩. 38 (♪ 114)
6/8	Gigue [i.e. *Gigue lent* or Loure]	♩. 50

the pendulum of JOSEPH SAUVEUR, whose scale is divided into 60th parts of a second, but he seems to have understood Sauveur's system imperfectly. Scholars who have translated his markings have misunderstood him in turn, making his tempos twice too fast. The corrected metronome indications shown in Table 1 are definitive only for his own pieces. The table can, however, serve to some extent as a guide to the choice of appropriate tempos for early 18th-century dance music. An asterisk indicates that no contemporary choreography exists, and question marks indicate tempos that are unreasonably slow.

BIBLIOGRAPHY

A. Jal: *Dictionnaire critique de biographie et d'histoire* (Paris, 1872)
M. Brenet: *Les musiciens de ·la Sainte-Chapelle du Palais* (Paris, 1910/*R*1973)
R. E. M. Harding: *The Origins of Musical Time and Expression* (London, 1938)
M. Benoit: *Musiques de cour: chapelle, chambre, écurie, 1661–1733* (Paris, 1971)
——: *Versailles et les musiciens du roi, 1661–1733* (Paris, 1971)
E. Schwandt: 'L'Affilard on the French Court Dances', *MQ*, lx (1974), 389
——: 'L'Affilard's Published Sketchbooks', *MQ*, lxiii (1977), 99
ERICH SCHWANDT

Lafitte, José White. *See* WHITE LAFITTE, JOSÉ.

Lafont, Charles Philippe (*b* Paris, 1 Dec 1781; *d* nr. Tarbes, 23 Aug 1839). French violinist and composer. His mother, a sister of the violinist Bertheaume, gave him his first violin lessons, which were continued under his uncle's guidance. At the age of 11 he was ready to accompany Bertheaume on a concert tour to Germany, where his precocious talent was much admired. On his return to Paris, Lafont resumed his studies, first under Kreutzer (with whom he worked for two years), then for a brief period with Rode. He also developed an attractive voice and appeared occasionally as a singer of French ballads. In 1801 he gave concerts in Belgium, and in 1802 was acclaimed at the Concerts Français in Paris. Soon he was recognized as one of France's leading violinists, and his pre-eminence was firmly estab-lished when Rode left for Russia in 1803. There fol-lowed successful tours in Germany, Holland, Belgium and England. In 1808 he was appointed solo violinist to the Tsar, succeeding Rode, and he remained in St Petersburg for six years. In 1815 he was named solo violinist to Louis XVIII.

Resuming his travels, Lafont had a memorable encounter with Paganini in Milan in 1816. They agreed, on Lafont's suggestion, to give a joint concert at La Scala; the programme consisted of a double concerto by Kreutzer as well as solo works by the two artists. This event is often described as a 'contest' in which Lafont was allegedly humiliated by Paganini's wizardry. In fact, in a letter, Paganini praised Lafont's artistry and even conceded his 'greater beauty of tone', but concluded, 'He plays well but he does not surprise' (see de Courcy, p.147). Lafont, angered by the persistent story of his 'defeat', published his own belated version of the encounter in the *Harmonicon* in 1830, saying: 'I was not beaten by Paganini, nor he by me' and defending the French school as 'the first in the world for the violin'. This statement was made when Paganini was at the height of his fame. Whatever the outcome of the encoun-ter, Lafont's supreme self-assurance remained unshaken, and he continued his career for more than 20 years. Spohr, who heard him in Paris in 1821, ranked him first among French violinists and admired his 'beauty of tone, the greatest purity, power, and grace', but criticized the lack of 'deeper feeling'. In the course of his career, Lafont often collaborated with prominent pian-ists, among them Kalkbrenner, Herz, Osborne and Moscheles; these partnerships produced joint compo-sitions for violin and piano in which both instruments were treated with equal brilliance. Lafont died in a carriage accident while on a concert tour in the south of France.

Lafont represented French violin playing at its best. He inherited the classical technique of the Viotti school through his teachers Kreutzer and Rode, but modern-ized it by making it more brilliant and idiomatic. Thus he stands midway between Rode and de Bériot. His encounter with Paganini came too late to influence his style and he was gradually overshadowed by the rising generation of Paganini-inspired virtuosos. As a com-poser, Lafont was of little importance: his seven violin concertos lack musical distinction, and his numerous fantasias and *airs variés* on operatic themes do not rise above the mediocre level of fashionable virtuoso music. Thanks to his pianist-collaborators, particularly Moscheles, higher musical standards are displayed in his *duos concertants*. He also composed more than 200 French ballads (romances), which for a time were very popular, and an opera, *La rivalité villageoise* (1799). Other operas mentioned by Fétis cannot be traced.

BIBLIOGRAPHY

FétisB
Obituary, *Revue et gazette musicale* (1839), no.45, p.359
L. Spohr: *Selbstbiographie* (Kassel, 1860–61; Eng. trans., 1865)
E. van der Straeten: *The History of the Violin*, i (London, 1933), 290ff
G. I. C. de Courcy: *Paganini the Genoese*, i (Norman, Oklahoma, 1957), 146ff

BORIS SCHWARZ

La Fontaine, Jean de (*b* Château-Thierry, Aisne, 8 July 1621; *d* Paris, 13 April 1695). French poet, fabulist, dramatist and librettist. He was educated at Château-Thierry and in Paris, where he finally settled in 1661, having spent months at a time there from 1658. He quickly established links with leading writers and musicians (Molière, Racine and Boileau; Michel Lambert and Lully) and with their patrons (Fouquet, Brienne and Madeleine de Scudéry). Frequenting salons such as the Hôtel de Nevers he met Mme de Sévigné, Mme de la Fayette, La Rochefoucauld and other prominent arbiters of taste. When his first patron, the Duchess of Orleans, died in 1672, he sought refuge with Mme de la Sablière, who protected him until her death in 1693. He was faithful to friends such as Fouquet and the Duchess of Bouillon even when they were disgraced. He received few formal honours and little financial reward, and not until 1684 was he elected to the Académie Française.

La Fontaine is principally renowned for his gently ironic stories (*Contes et nouvelles en vers*, 1665–6) and for the finely drawn portrait of man that emerges from his fables (*Fables choisies mises en vers*, 1668, 1679). Many composers since his day have taken tales from both volumes as the basis of both stage and concert works. But La Fontaine's love of variety and his taste for novelty led him to experiment with many other literary forms, including drama. His first published work (1654) was a translation of Terence's *Eunuchus*, and his second dramatic effort was a ballet, *Les rieurs du Beau-Richard* (the music for which is lost), performed at Château-Thierry in 1659 or 1660, about the time that he composed his comedy *Clymène*. These early works show that he was aware of the need to adapt material to prevailing tastes and that he could exploit the dramatic and comic elements latent in a situation; they also show how he found it difficult to sustain a tone for long or to keep personal interjections out of the drama.

Diversity was essential to La Fontaine's view of art, and music played an equally important role in creating those effects of charm and grace by which he judged good style. As a spectator he found such effects in the ballet *Les fâcheux*, given at Vaux in 1661. In 1671 his *Les amours de Psyché et de Cupidon* (1659) inspired *Psyché*, the *tragédie-ballet* created by Molière and Lully with the aid of Quinault and Corneille. Lully's collaboration with Quinault, which began after Molière's death in 1673, was temporarily interrupted early in 1674, and he asked La Fontaine for a libretto. He produced the pastoral *Daphne*, light in tone, lyrical and graceful. It did not please: Lully required something more heroic, more dramatically consistent. La Fontaine's characteristic lyricism and irony were indeed unsuitable for opera librettos, where drama and simplicity are demanded; furthermore his self-conscious, independent character was incompatible with Lully's taxing, temperamental demands. Despite his consequent criticism of Lully (in *Le florentin*, 1674) and of opera as a form (in a verse letter to Pierre de Nyert, 1677), he wrote the unfinished libretto *Galatée* (1682), dedicatory verses for Lully (*Amadis*, 1684, and *Roland*, 1685), and *Astrée* (1691). This last work, set to music by Pascal Collasse, received only six performances: La Fontaine had persisted in seeing Louis XIV as a lyrical Apollo rather than as a heroic Jupiter, and he had also indulged his private taste for make-believe and enchantment, showing that his gifts were more appropriate to armchair theatre than to *tragédie lyrique*.

BIBLIOGRAPHY

P. Clarac: *La Fontaine: l'homme et l'oeuvre* (Paris, 1947)
O. de Mourgues: *O muse, fuyante proie* (Paris, 1962)
M. M. McGowan: 'Le Papillon du Parnasse: a Reappraisal of La Fontaine's Experiments in Drama', *Australian Journal of French Studies*, iv (1967), 204
J.-P. Collinet: *Le monde littéraire de La Fontaine* (Paris, 1970)

MARGARET M. McGOWAN

Lagacé, Bernard (*b* St Hyacinthe, Quebec, 21 Nov 1930). Canadian organist. He studied in St Hyacinthe and Montreal with Conrad Letendre (organ), Yvonne Hubert (piano) and Gabriel Cusson (music theory). A scholarship from the Quebec government enabled him to perfect his organ technique in Paris from 1954 to 1956 under the aegis of André Marchal whose assistant he became at St Eustache; he gave his first official recital there in June 1956. He then spent a year working with Heiller at the Vienna Music Academy. In 1957 he was appointed organ professor at the Quebec Conservatory in Montreal and returned to Canada; he continued to give numerous concerts and recitals in Europe as well as in Canada and the USA. He was a prizewinner in the international competitions at Ghent and Munich and in the USA. Lagacé has exerted considerable influence both through his master classes and lectures, and through his important part in the organ revival in Canada. He has made several gramophone records, including Couperin's *Messe pour les convents*, *The Art of Fugue* and a Frescobaldi programme, combining a classical purity of style with a rigorous approach to interpretation.

JACQUES THÉRIAULT

Lagarde, John. *See* LAGUERRE, JOHN.

La Garde [Lagarde, Garde], **Pierre de** (*b* nr. Crécy-en-Brie, Seine-et-Marne, 10 Feb 1717; *d c*1792). French composer and baritone. As an *ordinaire de la chambre du roi* he was highly regarded by Louis XV, who made him responsible for the musical training of the royal children. In 1755 he shared this duty with Mion, *Maître de musique des enfants de France*, and gained the title himself two years later. He was an assistant conductor at the Opéra from 1750 to 1755 and on the resignation of François Francoeur in 1756 he became *compositeur de la chambre du roi*. Some time later he was placed in charge of the concerts given for the Count of Artois. He is also reported to have taught the harp to Marie-Antoinette. La Borde described him as having a baritone voice of wide compass and great facility.

La Garde's reputation as a composer was firmly established when his *Aeglé*, a *pastorale héroïque* in one act, was performed at Madame de Pompadour's Théâtre des Petits Cabinets in 1748; it is indebted to Rameau, particularly in its orchestral style. Two years later it was incorporated into *La journée galante* as the second act of that *opéra-ballet*; the first and last acts, of which no scores are extant, were *La toilette de Vénus* and *Léandre et Héro*. While there is no record of *La journée galante* being performed outside court circles, *Aeglé* was performed at the Opéra in 1751 and continued to be played there until 1777. Other works commissioned by Madame de Pompadour were *Silvie*, a full-length *pastorale héroïque* performed at Versailles in 1749, and *L'impromptu de la cour de marbre*, a *divertissement comique* performed in her country house at Bellevue in 1751 after the Théâtre des Petits Cabinets at Versailles had been dismantled.

La Garde's lyrical gifts were often charmingly displayed in his *airs*, cantatas and *cantatilles*. Among his collections of airs were three volumes of brunettes (1764) with harp or guitar (both much in vogue at the time) and sometimes harpsichord or violin accompaniment. The guitar was also used to accompany some of the *cantatilles* in his *Journal de musique* (1758); although such works represent a decline in the French cantata, La Garde also composed cantatas and *cantatilles* of a high artistic level: for a long time his *La musette* was attributed to Rameau. His last published works were contained in two volumes entitled *Les soirées de l'Ille Adam*, dedicated to the Prince of Conti. They contained airs (and a *cantatille*, *L'amant malheureux*) for one and two voices accompanied by violin, oboe, bassoon, horn and bass. As in the works of a number of French composers at this time the music, in both thematic and instrumental writing, was greatly influenced by the nascent Classical style. While La Garde seems to have written no compositions during the last 25 years of his life, his *airs* remained popular for many years. In 1780 La Borde stated that the composer's 'charming duets and melodious songs will always be sung with pleasure by music lovers. He is, without doubt, the finest composer in this genre'.

WORKS
(all printed works published in Paris)

Aeglé (pastorale héroïque, 1, P. Laujon), Versailles, 13 Jan 1748, vocal score (1751)
Silvie (pastorale héroïque, 3, Laujon), Versailles, 26 Feb 1749, *F-Pn, Po*
La journée galante (opéra-ballet, 3, Laujon), Versailles, 25 Feb 1750, lib pubd in Divertissemens du Théâtre des petits appartemens pendant l'hiver de 1749 à 1750 [incl. Aeglé as Act 2]
L'impromptu de la cour de marbre (divertissement comique, 1, C.-S. Favart), Bellevue, 28 Nov 1751, lost

Cantatas (1v, insts): Enée et Didon (c1751); La sonate (?1757); Le triomphe de l'Amour (?1757); Vénus retrouvée (?1757)
Cantatilles: La musette (before 1758); 12 in Journal de musique (1758); 1 in Les soirées de l'Ille Adam, ii (1766)
Airs, etc: 1re–6ème recueils d'airs, 1 or more vv (c1742–64); 1re–3me recueils de brunettes (1764); Les soirées de l'Ille Adam, i (1764), ii (1766)
Many works, arrs. in 18th-century anthologies
Other works, *Pc, Pn*

BIBLIOGRAPHY
J.-B. de La Borde: *Essai sur la musique ancienne et moderne* (Paris, 1780/R1972)
T. L'Huillier: 'Note sur quelques artistes musiciens dans La Brie', *Bulletin de la Société d'archéologie, sciences, lettres et arts de Seine et Marne* (Meaux, 1868)
N. Dufourcq: *La musique . . . de Louis XIV et de Louis XV d'après les mémoires de Sourches et Luynes 1681–1758* (Paris, 1970)
W. H. Kaehler: *The Operatic Repertoire of Madame de Pompadour's Théâtre des petits cabinets (1747–1753)* (diss., U. of Michigan, 1971)
R. Machard: 'Les musiciens en France au temps de Jean-Philippe Rameau, d'après les actes du Secrétariat de la Maison du roi', *RMFC*, xi (1971), 5–177
D. Tunley: *The Eighteenth-century French Cantata* (London, 1974)
DAVID TUNLEY

La Garsa. *See* GARSI, SANTINO.

Lagarto, Pedro de (*fl* 1490–1507). Spanish composer. In a document dated 19 June 1490 he was listed as *claustrero* (master of the boy choristers) of Toledo Cathedral. In February 1495 he competed successfully in a public contest for a singer's post in the cathedral. The winner was to be the 'most accomplished and fluent singer' and well versed in polyphonic composition. His successor as *claustrero* was named on 13 February 1507.

In the Cancionero Musical de Palacio, Lagarto is represented by one *romance*, *Quéxome de ti, ventura*, and three villancicos. The *romance* is a complaint against the rigours of Fortune. The three voices begin in characteristic anapaestic rhythm in chordal style. In *Andad, pasiones, andad* the expressive setting of an emotionally wrought text is characterized by an initial descending motif, c''–b'–g'–e', which is effectively repeated several times in slightly varied forms.

WORKS
Editions: *La música en la corte de los reyes católicos: Cancionero musical de palacio*, ed. H. Anglés, MME v, x (1947–51) [A i–ii]
Cancionero musical de los siglos XV y XVI, ed. F. Asenjo Barbieri (Madrid, 1890)

Andad, pasiones, andad, 3vv, A ii, no.279; Callen todas las galanas, 3vv, A ii, no.226; D'aquel fraire flaco, 4vv, A ii, no.255; Quéxome de ti, ventura, 3vv, A i, no.90

BIBLIOGRAPHY
M. Schneider: 'Gestaltimitation als Komposition-Prinzip im Cancionero de Palacio', *Mf*, xi (1958), 415
R. Stevenson: *Spanish Music in the Age of Columbus* (The Hague, 1960), 235ff
G. Haberkamp: *Die weltliche Vokalmusik in Spanien um 1500* (Tutzing, 1968), 186
ISABEL POPE

Lage (Ger.). (1) In string playing, position playing or position fingering. (The equivalent term in the 18th century was *Applicatur*.) *See* APPLICATION.

(2) REGISTER.

Lagidze, Revaz Il'yich (*b* Bagdadi [now Mayakovski], west Georgia, 10 July 1921). Soviet composer. He studied first in the violin class of the fourth music college in Tbilisi and then, from 1940 to 1949, played in orchestras. In 1948 he graduated from Balanchivadze's composition class at the Tbilisi Conservatory, subsequently pursuing postgraduate work with the same teacher (1949–52). He has taught chamber music at the Tbilisi Conservatory and directs the music department of the Tbilisi Institute of Education. A board member of the Georgian Composers' Union, he has served as chairman of the board of the Georgian department of the Muzïkal'nïy Fond publishing house since 1973. He is also a deputy to the Supreme Soviet of the Georgian SSR, a People's Artist of the Georgian SSR (1961) and a holder of the orders of the Badge of Honour, the Red Banner of Labour and the Rustaveli Prize (1975).

Despite the great variety of genre and theme in Lagidze's work, it is possible to detect a preponderance of song forms and of heroic–patriotic and lyrical ideas. He very rarely quotes folk themes but makes wide use of the modal, intonational and cadential characteristics of folk music; the link with national resources is apparent too on the level of ideas and emotions, and in the typical improvisatory quality of his thematic development. Outstanding among his orchestral works is *Sachidao*, named after the ancient folk instrumental music performed at athletic contests and based on developing the colouristic possibilities of an unassuming folk theme. His chamber pieces – lyrical vocal works, cello and string quartet pieces, etc – are distinguished by delicate melodic lines. The songs enjoy immense popularity throughout the USSR, having established themselves alongside original folksongs; *Tbiliso*, in particular, has become almost a musical symbol of the city. In his later cantatas emotional immediacy is combined with a symphonic treatment of song forms.

WORKS
(selective list)

Stage: Megobrebi [Friends] (musical comedy), 1951; Komble (musical comedy), 1957; Lela (opera), completed 1973, Tbilisi, 1975
Cantatas: Sakartvelo [Georgia], 1961; Melis Vardzia [Vardzia is waiting for me], 1966; Balada vazze [Ballad of the rod], 1967; Simgera samshobloze [Song about our motherland], 1967
Orch: Samshoblosatvis [For the motherland], sym. poem, 1949; Sachidao, sym. picture, 1952
Other works: songs, chamber pieces, incidental music, over 30 film scores

Principal publishers: Muzfond Gruzii (Tbilisi), Muzgiz, Muzïka, Sovetskiy Kompozitor (Moscow and Leningrad)

BIBLIOGRAPHY

G. Ordzhonikidze: 'Revaz Lagidze', *Sovetskaya muzïka* (Moscow, 1956), 284
K. Lortkipanidze: 'Sovetskiy romans', *Gruzinskaya muzïkal'naya kul'-tura* (Moscow, 1957), 369
E. Balanchivadze: 'Sakutari gzit' [By his own path], *Sabchota khelov-neba* (Tbilisi, 1966), no.7, p.27
E. Ol'khovich: 'Muzïkal'niy aktyor', *SovM* (1969), no.12, p.50
G. Toradze: 'Revaz Lagidze', *Kompozitori Gruzii* (Tbilisi, 1973)
M. Akhmetali: 'Lela: akhali karthuli opera' [Lela: the new Georgian opera], *Sabchota khelovneba* (Tbilisi, 1975), no.7, p.9

EVGENY MACHAVARIANI

Lagkhner, Daniel (*b* Marburg, Lower Styria, after *c*1550; *d* after 1607). Austrian composer. A minor master of early Protestant music, he was among the first composers born in Styria. On the title-page of his major work, *Soboles musica*, he described himself as citizen and organist of Loosdorf in Lower Austria; in his publications of 1606 and 1607 he called himself 'symphonista' and 'musurgus' of the freemen of Losenstein, founders of a notable evangelical grammar school at Loosdorf (1574–1619) in which Lagkhner probably taught. Evidence of his connection with the school is to be found in his three-part *Flores Jessaei* for boys' voices, and in his four-part *Semina florum Jessaeorum*, also set mainly for equal voices. After 1607 he may well have gone into exile on account of his Protestant sympathies. Fétis maintained that he became Kapellmeister of St Sebaldus, Nuremberg; this, however, is based on inferences wrongly drawn from the place of publication of Lagkhner's works.

The 28 motets in the *Soboles musica*, for four to eight voices, are characterized by an abundant use of contrary motion, quasi-polyphony, block harmony and by both simulated and actual double-choir textures, all suggesting strong Venetian influences. His *Neuer teutscher Lieder I. Theil* contains 23 songs for four voices, nearly all secular, with dedications to various members of the Austrian nobility who had joined together in singing them. The texts are also found in the Ambraser Songbook in settings by G. Forster, H. L. Hassler, J. Regnart, J. Eccard and others. This confirms Lagkhner's relationship with the German songwriting tradition at the time of Hassler.

WORKS

Melodia funebris, 6vv (Vienna, 1601); cited in *FétisB*
Soboles musica, 4–8vv (Nuremberg, 1602)
Flores Jessaei, 3vv (Nuremberg, 1606)
Neuer teutscher Lieder 1. Theil, 4vv (Nuremberg, 1606)
Semina florum Jessaeorum (Nuremberg, 1607)
1 galliard, *D-Rp*

BIBLIOGRAPHY

FétisB
H. J. Moser: *Die Musik im frühevangelischen Österreich* (Kassel, 1954), 44ff

HELLMUT FEDERHOFER

Lago, Giovanni del. See DEL LAGO, GIOVANNI.

Lagrange, Joseph-Louis, Comte (*b* Turin, 25 Jan 1736; *d* Paris, 10 April 1813). French mathematician and physicist. He was largely self-trained and was encouraged by Euler and d'Alembert, whose protégé he became. He held positions in Berlin (from 1766) and Paris (from 1787). He is remembered as an acoustician for his work in 1759 on the transverse vibrations of the taut, massless cord loaded by *n* weights, equally spaced. He is credited with being the first to represent the string in this way and to calculate its modes and proper frequencies, and for having established Euler's solution for the continuous monochord as being the result of taking the limit as *n* tends to infinity. In fact the discrete model was a very old one, and Lagrange's work on it is a straightforward extension of Euler's; further, as d'Alembert pointed out, Lagrange's passage to the limit is fallacious. In 1788 Lagrange showed how to determine in principle the proper frequencies and modes of any discrete system in small oscillation about a stable position of equilibrium. In acoustics, as in many other domains, Lagrange's work closely follows Euler. It is Lagrange's chief merit to have been the only man of his day to master Euler's discoveries and methods as soon as they appeared, so that he was often able to extend Euler's results.

See also PHYSICS OF MUSIC, §3.

La Grotte [La Crotte]**, Nicolas de** (*b* 1530; *d* *c*1600). French keyboard player and composer. In 1557 he was organist and spinet player at Pau to Antoine de Bourbon, King of Navarre. In October 1558 he married and, though still 'following the court' of Navarre, resided at Paris. After Antoine's death in 1562 he joined Costeley and Jean Dugué in the service of Henri de Valois, Duke of Anjou, and was appointed 'vallet de chambre et organiste ordinaire' in 1574 when the duke succeeded his brother Charles IX to become Henri III of France. In 1583 he and Claude Le Jeune were paid 600 gold crowns for serving during the festivities for the wedding of the Duke of Joyeuse in September and October 1581. In 1584 he tested a new organ at St Germain-l'Auxérrois and his playing was praised by La Croix du Maine for its 'sweetness of execution, manual delicacy' and 'musical profundity'; La Croix du Maine also quoted the poet laureate Jean Dorat, who had shared his sentiments in a Latin anagram, *Tu solus organicus*. In 1587 La Grotte petitioned the king for a sinecure, and between 1586 and 1589 made several applications to purchase land in the Corbeil district, near Paris.

His chansons reflect the contemporary preference of poets and humanists for monody; although the publication, in four partbooks, follows the standard format, the music was clearly conceived as melody and accompaniment – the three lower voices providing harmonic support – and seems more naturally suited to the arrangement for voice and lute issued under Le Roy's own name as *airs de cour* in 1571 (this includes all but the final piece of La Grotte's 1569 collection). Several of the tunes were also used in Jehan Chardavoine's monophonic *Recueil des plus excellents chansons en forme de voix de ville* (Paris, 1576). The declamatory rhythm of some of these pieces foreshadows the work of musicians in Baïf's circle and La Grotte demonstrated his interest in *musique mesurée à l'antique* by including four chansons mesurées (*Il a menty*, *La belle Aronde*, *Lesse-moy osu* (Baïf) and *Ma gente bergère*) in his 1583 collection. The distinction between *air* and chanson in the title of the collection refers only to strophic and non-strophic texts, among which are verses by Baïf and Belleau, religious texts by Desportes, du Bellay and Guéroult, two Italian poems and a long opening piece in five sections entitled *Mascarades de Pionniers*; La Grotte's own literary talent is evident in that he translated from Dorat's original Latin the prefatory verses addressed to Henri III in the 1583 volume. In view of the chronology, La Grotte seems more likely than Gombert,

Millot or Guillaume Nicolas to have written the chansons ascribed to 'Nicolas' in anthologies published between 1559 and 1578; these are generally more old-fashioned in style than the collections of 1569 and 1583, although they include a few settings of the Pléiade poets (Ronsard, Du Bellay and Belleau). In spite of his fame as an organist, only one of La Grotte's keyboard works survives – a four-part polyphonic fantasia on Rore's madrigal *Ancor che col partire*.

WORKS

CHANSONS

[16] Chansons de P. de Ronsard, Ph. Desportes et autres mises en musique par Nicolas de la Grotte, 4vv (Paris, 1569, 3/1572 with 2 added chansons); 6 ed. H. Expert, *La fleur des musiciens de P. de Ronsard* (Paris, 1923); 15 arr. in *Livre d'airs de cour miz sur le luth* par Adrian le Roy (Paris, 1571); ed. A. Mairy, L. de La Laurencie and G. Thibault, *Chansons au luth et airs de cour français* (Paris, 1934)

Premier livre d'airs et chansons (28 chansons), 3–6vv (Paris, 1583)
1 chanson, 4vv, 1569¹⁷ (attrib. 'N. la Grotte')
50 chansons, 1 canon, 3–6vv, 1559⁸, 1559¹¹, 1559¹², Livre de mes-langes (Paris, 1560), 1561⁶, 1564⁸, 1564¹¹, 1565⁵, 1572², 1578¹⁴: all attrib. 'Nicolas', possibly by La Grotte; 1 ed. F. Lesure, *Anthologie de la chanson parisienne* (Monaco, 1953)

INSTRUMENTAL

Courante, lute, 1617²⁶
Fantasia a 4 sopra 'Ancor che col partire', kbd, *A-Wn*

BIBLIOGRAPHY

A. Du Verdier and F. La Croix du Maine: *Bibliothèques françaises*, ed. R. de Juvigny (Paris, 1772), ii, 163ff
E. Droz: 'Les chansons de Nicolas de la Grotte', *RdM*, viii (1927), 133
L. de La Laurencie: 'Nicolas de la Grotte – musicista di Ronsard', *RaM*, v (1932)
——: Introduction to *Chansons au luth et airs de cour français* (Paris, 1934)
R. Lebègue: 'Ronsard corrigé par un de ses musiciens', *RdM*, xxxix (1957), 71
F. Lesure: 'La Grotte, Nicolas', *MGG*

FRANK DOBBINS

Lagudio, Paolo (*fl* 1563). Italian composer. His *Primo libro di madrigali a cinque voci* (Venice, 1563¹⁰) is dedicated from Naples. In addition to his own three madrigal pairs and a 21-stanza cycle, the book contains one madrigal by Ferrante Bucca. Such extended cycles as Lagudio's *Quel antico mio* were uncommon even in Rome, Venice and Verona where settings of entire canzoni were popular.

PATRICIA ANN MYERS

La Guerre, Elisabeth-Claude Jacquet de. *See* JACQUET DE LA GUERRE, ELISABETH-CLAUDE.

Laguerre [Lagarde, Legar, Legard, Legare, Leguar, Leguerre etc], **John** (*b* c1700; *d* London, 28 March 1748). English baritone and painter. He first appeared in Italian opera, having small roles in Handel's *Radamisto* (1720) and *Giulio Cesare* (1724). Most of his career was spent in John Rich's company, where between 1721 and 1740 he sang in pantomimes, afterpieces, ballad operas and burlesques. His most popular roles were Hob in *Flora* and Gaffer Gubbins in *The Dragon of Wantley*. He sang Corydon in the first public performance of Handel's *Acis and Galatea* in March 1731. In 1724 he married the dancer and actress Mary Rogeir; they always worked together and after her death in 1739 his career declined. In 1741 he was imprisoned for debt, but was released for a day on 23 April to sing in his benefit performance. In 1746 he was taken on by Rich as a scene painter. He had published engravings of theatrical subjects, having been trained by his father, the

French-born mural painter Louis Laguerre, who died at the theatre on John's first benefit night in 1721. 'Honest Jack Laguerre' had a reputation as a wit, a mimic and an amusing companion.

OLIVE BALDWIN, THELMA WILSON

Laguerre, Marie-Joséphine (*b* Paris, 1755; *d* Paris, 14 Feb 1783). French soprano. She joined the Opéra as a chorister in 1771–2 and in 1776 took the title roles in La Borde's *Adèle de Ponthieu* and Gluck's *Alceste*, replacing Rosalie Levasseur. A pure-voiced and expressive singer, she shared leading roles with Levasseur from 1778, having the advantage in looks, youth and agility. She created the roles of Hellé in Floquet's *Hellé* (1779), Sangaride in Piccinni's *Atys* (1780), Iphigenia in Piccinni's *Iphigénie en Tauride* (1781) and the countess in Grétry's *La double épreuve* (1782). Her early death was apparently the result of loose living, which may also have brought her the considerable wealth indicated by her legacy. In a famous incident at the second performance of Piccinni's *Iphigénie*, she was incoherent through inebriation, giving rise to the witticism (sometimes attributed to Sophie Arnould) that it was now 'Iphigénie en Champagne'. For this offence she was imprisoned in Fort-l'Evêque until the following performance.

BIBLIOGRAPHY

FétisB
H. Audiffret: 'Laguerre (Marie-Joséphine)', *Biographie universelle*, ed. L. G. Michaud (Paris, 1843–65)
D. Denne-Baron: 'Laguerre (Marie-Sophie)', *Nouvelle biographie générale*, ed. J. C. F. Hoefer (Paris, 1852–66)
C. Davillier: *Une vente d'actrice sous Louis XVI: Mlle Laguerre* (Paris, 1870)
G. Le Brisoys Desnoiresterres: *La musique française au XVIII siècle: Gluck et Piccinni* (Paris, 1872, 2/1875)

JULIAN RUSHTON

La Guerre, Michel de (*b* Paris, 1605 or 1606; *d* Paris, buried 13 Nov 1679). French organist and composer. He was the most important member of a family of musicians who flourished, especially as organists, in Paris for about 100 years from about 1630; they included Marin de la Guerre, husband of ELISABETH-CLAUDE JACQUET DE LA GUERRE. At the age of 14 Michel de la Guerre succeeded Charles Racquet as organist of St Leu, Paris. From 1633 until his death he was organist of the Sainte-Chapelle and from 1658 acted as its treasurer too. Contemporary documents also refer to him as *organiste du roi*. He was certainly active at court: his pastorale *Le triomphe de l'Amour sur des bergers et bergères* was performed before the king at the Louvre on 22 January 1655, and it was revived on 26 March 1657 as a stage work with scenery. Only the text (by Charles de Beys) has survived, in two printed editions (1654 and 1661–2), the second of which (with additions) was produced to counter the claim by Perrin that it was he and Cambert who had written the first French *comédie en musique*: their *Pastorale d'Issy* was first produced only in 1659, so La Guerre's pastorale must clearly be considered to have sown the first seeds of French opera.

BIBLIOGRAPHY

H. Quittard: 'La première comédie française en musique', *BSIM*, iv (1908), 377, 497–537
M. Brenet: *Les musiciens de la Sainte-Chapelle du Palais* (Paris, 1910/R1973)
L. de La Laurencie: 'Les pastorales en musique au XVIIᵐᵉ siècle en France avant Lully et leur influence sur l'opéra', *IMusSCR, iv London 1911*, 139
H. Prunières: *L'opéra italien en France avant Lulli* (Paris, 1913)

EDWARD HIGGINBOTTOM

Lah. The submediant of the prevailing key (or, if this is minor, the submediant of its relative major), in TONIC SOL-FA.

La Halle, Adam de. *See* ADAM DE LA HALLE.

La Harpe [Delaharpe], **Jean François de** (*b* Paris, 20 Nov 1739; *d* Paris, 11 Feb 1803). French man of letters. He wrote several tragedies, of which *Le comte de Warwick* (1763) was the most successful, but he is chiefly remembered for his didactic and critical work, including the *Cours de littérature* in 16 volumes (1799–1805) and an *Eloge de Racine* (1772). A dogmatic critic with little understanding of music, he joined with Marmontel to support the Italians against Gluck, and particularly favoured Sacchini; his virulent attack on *Armide* in the *Journal de politique et de littérature* (5 October 1777) was ridiculed by Gluck himself in the *Journal de Paris* (12 October 1777) and by La Harpe's colleague J. B. A. Suard using the pseudonym 'L'anonyme de Vaugirard'. His *Correspondance littéraire* (1774–91, published 1801–7), a manuscript periodical similar to Grimm's, though less extensive, is a valuable informal record of the period.

BIBLIOGRAPHY
G. M. Leblond, ed.: *Mémoires pour servir à l'histoire de la révolution opérée dans la musique par . . . Gluck* (Paris, 1781/*R*1967)
G. Peignot: *Recherches . . . sur la vie et les ouvrages de M. de La Harpe* (Dijon, 1820)
A. Tissier: 'La Harpe, Jean François', *ES*

JULIAN RUSHTON

La Hèle, George de. *See* HÈLE, GEORGE DE LA.

La Hire, Philippe de (*b* Paris, 18 March 1640; *d* Paris, 21 April 1718). French astronomer, mathematician and physicist. He was the son of the painter Laurent de la Hire. In 1678 he was admitted a member of the Académie Royale des Sciences in Paris, and he was a teacher of mathematics at both the Collège de France and the Académie Royale d'Architecture (of which he was a founder-member). Among the many works by this celebrated and productive scientist are several essays devoted to research into the nature of sound, which appear in the publications of the French scientific academy. The most noteworthy features of these investigations are his concerns with partial vibrations as determinants of timbre, with the acoustical differences between the vibration of cylinders and of solid bodies and with the effect on a resultant sound of such factors as the elastic quality of a vibrating body, its relative moisture content and the means by which it is set into vibration.

WRITINGS
(*only those relating to music*)
'Explication des différences des sons de la corde tendue sur la trompette marine', *Mémoires de l'Académie royale des sciences. Depuis 1666. jusqu'à 1699*, ix, 330; also issued in *Mémoires de mathématique et de physique* (Paris, 1694), 213; *Oeuvres diverses* (Paris, 1730), 500; and *Oeuvres meslées* (Amsterdam, 1759), 330
'Observation d'acoustique', *Histoire de l'Académie royale des sciences. Année 1709*, 96; reviewed in *Histoire . . . 1716*, 66
'Expériences sur le son', *Histoire de l'Académie royale des sciences. Année 1716. Avec les Mémoires*, 262; 'Continuation d'expériences sur le son', ibid, 264

BIBLIOGRAPHY
B. le B. de Fontenelle: 'Eloge', *Histoire de l'Académie royale des sciences en 1699* (Paris, 1724, and later edns.)
N. Nielsen: *Géomètres français du dix-huitième siècle* (Copenhagen and Paris, 1935), 248ff

ALBERT COHEN

Lahmer, Reuel (*b* Maple, Ont., 27 March 1912). American composer and choirmaster of Canadian origin. He took the MusB at Westminster Choir College, New Jersey, and did graduate work at Columbia and Cornell universities; his composition teachers were Bingham and Harris. He has taught at Cornell (1940–41), Carroll College, Wisconsin (1946–8), Colorado College as head of theory and composition (1948–51), the American College, Leysin, Switzerland, as composer-in-residence (1967–71) and Franklin College, Lugano, as composer-in-residence (from 1971). In addition, he has served as music director of various churches and was conductor of the Pittsburgh Madrigal Singers, as well as of other choruses and choral festivals in the USA and Europe. He has also appeared as an organ, harpsichord and American folksong recitalist in several countries. His compositions are traditional in style and often based on American folk melodies or similar patterns. Festivals devoted entirely to his music were given in Rome (1959) and on Budapest radio (1966).

WORKS
(*selective list*)
Choral: Choral Suite, 8vv, 2 pf, 1946; Folk Fun, unison vv, fl, cl, 2 pf, 1947; Folk Fantasy, unison vv, orch, 1948; Paul Bunyan, narrator, chorus, orch, 1948; The Campbells are Coming, chorus, band, 1948; Civil War Suite, chorus, 2 pf, 1956; Sing the Sweet Land, chorus, pf, wind, 1957; Glory to God, chorus, org, brass, 1960; The Passing, S, female vv, pf, 1962; Synthesis, 1973; many other pieces
Orch: Prelude and Fugal Fantasy, ww, str, 1945; Sym. Piece no.1, 1946; Theme with Variations, str, 1946; 4 Chorale Preludes, 1948; Conc. grosso, str trio, str, 1949; Sym. Piece no.2, 1954; Sym. for 9, 1963
Solo vocal: Song Universal, Mez, str qt, 1939; God be Merciful, S, ob/vn, va, vc, 1949; Folk Song Cycle, 1v, pf, 1950; The Way, song cycle, T, lute, viols, 1968; In the Beginning was the Word, T, vn, pf, 1970; many songs
Inst: Passacaglia and Fugue, cl, pf 4 hands, 1949; Suite on American Folk Hymns, vn, 1949; Variations on a Folk Hymn, cl, 1949; pieces for org, pf, band
Edn.: *Western Pennsylvania Hymn Tune Collection* (Pittsburgh, 1957)
PEGGY GLANVILLE-HICKS/BARBARA HAMPTON

Laḥn (Arabic: 'tone', 'melody'). A term equivalent to Greek *ēchos* in the MUSIC OF THE COPTIC RITE but usually signifying melody rather than mode; *see also* IRAN, §I, 1.

La Houssaye [Housset], **Pierre(-Nicolas)** (*b* Paris, 11 April 1735; *d* Paris, 1818). French violinist, conductor and composer. Originally called Housset, he studied the violin in the 1740s with J.-A. Piffet. Shortly after 1750 his brilliant performance of a Tartini sonata at a gathering of eminent violinists created the opportunity to study with Pagin, a pupil of Tartini. La Houssaye was later employed by the Count of Clermont, then by the Prince of Monaco, with whom he travelled to Italy, probably in about 1753. On arrival in Padua he received a few lessons from Tartini. He was employed briefly at the court of the infante Dom Philippe in Parma, where he studied composition with Traetta, but he soon returned to Padua for more lessons with Tartini. During his stay of about 15 years in Italy he became an excellent violinist and conductor.

In 1768 or later La Houssaye left Italy for London, probably passing through Paris. Fétis and most subsequent sources have reported that he directed the orchestra of the Italian Opera in London in the 1770s, but later research shows this to be improbable. A 'La Haussage', however, often played the violin at the King's Theatre during the 1769–70 season. By 1776 La Houssaye had returned to Paris, and in 1777 he was named conductor and leader of the Concert Spirituel under Legros. (In 1778 Mozart, after observing La Houssaye's particularly disastrous rehearsal of his symphony K297/300a, wrote that he would be tempted to remove the violin from La Houssaye's hands and conduct himself if the performance were equally bad; but the performance on 18 June was a great success.) In 1781 La Houssaye became conductor and leader of the Comédie-Italienne orchestra but remained a violinist at the Concert Spirituel until at least 1788. He also played in the highly respected Concert des Amateurs. In 1790 he shared with Puppo the position of conductor and leader at the Théâtre de Monsieur (later the Théâtre Feydeau); by 1792 he alone held this position, but in 1801, the merger of the Théâtre Feydeau and the Théâtre Favart resulted in his dismissal. After the Paris Conservatoire opened in 1795, he was appointed a violin teacher, a post he retained until 1802. Now an elderly man, he played second violin in the Opéra orchestra and taught privately until 1813, when deafness and age forced him to retire. His final five years were spent in poverty.

La Houssaye was regarded as a master of the violin by those who heard him, including Fétis and Viotti; his one remaining collection of compositions, *Sei sonate* for violin and bass, op.1 (Paris, c1774), supports this evaluation, demanding great proficiency in double stops and calling for notes in the extreme upper register. According to Fétis, La Houssaye wrote other works for the violin, the manuscripts of which are lost: 12 'church' concertos, seven books of sonatas and three books of duos. His only other known work is a comic opera, *Les amours de Courcy*, performed at the Théâtre de Monsieur on 22 August 1790.

BIBLIOGRAPHY

FétisB

A. Vidal: *Les instruments à archet* (Paris, 1876–8/R1961)

L. Pericaud: *Théâtre de Monsieur* (Paris, 1908)

L. de La Laurencie: *L'école française de violon de Lully à Viotti* (Paris, 1922–4/R1971)

The London Stage, 1660–1800 (Carbondale, Ill., 1960–68)

JEFFREY COOPER

Lai (Fr.). An extended song form cultivated particularly in the 13th and 14th centuries. The stanzas – if the poem can be divided in that way – are each in a different form and therefore have different music. Though the number of surviving examples is small compared with the total extent of medieval song these works occupy a special position for several reasons: the very irregularity of the poetic form led to large metrical and rhyming patterns that have caused the lai and its German equivalent the *Leich* to be described as the major showpieces of medieval lyric poetry; and there is much truth in Spanke's useful distinction (1938) between songs that are primarily metrical in their formal concept (i.e. nearly all medieval strophic song) and those that are primarily musical (the lai and the sequence), a distinction that almost inevitably brings with it the suggestion that the lai and related forms represent by far the earliest surviving attempts at continuous musical composition outside the liturgy. In general it is true to say that in the 13th century the form could be extremely free, with highly irregular rhyme schemes and lines of uneven length, but that in the 14th century it developed a standard pattern with each stanza following a double-versicle scheme (often refined to an apparent quadruple-versicle) and a 12-stanza form in which the first and last could be related musically or even have the same music at different pitches.

1. Terminology and origins. 2. Poetic form. 3. The lai before 1300. 4. The lai after 1300. 5. Notes on the checklist of lai music.

1. TERMINOLOGY AND ORIGINS. Many different extended forms in medieval (and later) poetry are encompassed by the word 'lai' and related words in other European languages. The form described above is more strictly called the lyric lai (or *lai lyrique*) to distinguish it from the narrative lai (or *lai breton*), a long poem normally in octosyllabic rhyming couplets and often associated with stories of the Arthurian cycle.

The narrative lai was most elegantly described by Chaucer's Franklin:

> Thise olde gentil Bretouns in hir dayes
> Of diverse aventures maden layes,
> Rymeyed in hir firste Briton tonge;
> Which layes with hir instrumentz they songe,
> Or elles redden hem for hir plesaunce.

In French this genre saw its first success with Marie de France, who apparently worked in England and whose 12 narrative lais date from the years after 1160, though she claimed they were adapted from Breton originals which are now lost; but it continued well into the 15th century: after 1415 Pierre de Nesson called his poem in that form lamenting the French defeat at Agincourt the *Lay de la guerre*. Though the narrative lai, like much other narrative verse, was evidently sung, certainly in its earlier history, no music for it survives: only the presence of empty staves above a manuscript of the *Lai de Graelent* (F-Pn fr.2168) and a lost manuscript of the lais of Marie de France (see Maillard, 1963, p.66) witness that this music may have been written down. (*See also* CHANSON DE GESTE.)

Even within the terminology 'lyric lai' there are poems that cannot be described as lais according to the definition adopted for this article. Several poems carrying the title 'lai' are found inserted in longer narratives: particularly famous examples of this category appear in the *Roman de Perceforest* and the *Roman de Tristan en prose*. For the latter there is even music, surviving in manuscripts at Paris and Vienna (listed below); but they are simple strophic songs, as is Tannhäuser's *Lude Leich* (D-Mbs cgm 4997, f.72). More difficult to classify are the two 'lais' attributed by Beck to Charles d'Anjou and described by Stäblein (1975) as merely a series of single-stanza songs.

The word itself has been traced back to the Low Latin *leudus*, found as early as Venantius Fortunatus (c550)

1. How the lady made the lover read the lai he had composed: miniature from one of the Machaut MSS (F-Pn fr.1586, f.28v)

and meaning a vernacular song in Latin metre: this is probably a latinization of a germanic word (perhaps *leuthaz*, though the German word *Leich* is thought to derive from *laik*; asterisks in this context denote hypothetical roots) and is glossed in one manuscript with the Old High German *Uuinileodos* (singer); the later Latin *laudes* and the Irish *loíd* (or *laíd*) are evidently related. The Irish word (meaning blackbird's song) can be documented from the mid-9th century and may go back further; since the 16th century it has been used to mean any poem, but particularly songs related to the epic of Finn. There is much evidence in favour of Irish origin for the form, a theory supported by Aarburg and by Maillard, who showed how the rhythmic interest of early Irish poetry may have influenced the lai ('Lai, Leich', 1973, pp.326ff); but no music survives to document this and nothing in Irish poetic structure can be linked directly with the musical form that appeared in France about 1200.

The earliest recorded French uses of the word 'lai', those of Wace in his *Roman de Brut* (*c*1155: lais et notes/lais de vieles, lais de rotes/lais de harpes et de frestels), describe instrumental melody, but this is by no means the rule for other early references: Wolf (1841, pp.4ff) showed that the word 'lai' in English or Old French often meant no more than 'song'.

Just as the word 'lai' itself had and still has several meanings beyond and around the specific musico-poetic form that is the subject of this article, so also many other words cover ranges of meaning that include that of the lyric lai.

(*i*) *Descort*. Derived from the Latin *discordia*, descort was the standard Provençal word for lai and was carried into Old French as well as into Italian, where the word *discordio* appears describing a poem of Jacopo da Lentino. There has been some disagreement as to the differences between *descort* and lai, with Wolf (1841) and Jeanroy (1901) pioneering the opinion that there was none and Stäblein (1975) suggesting that *descort* was merely a later and more sophisticated name preferred by the trouvères, perhaps because of its continental roots. (An excellent and full survey of the dispute appears in Baum, 1971; see also Bec, 1977, pp.199ff.) For musical purposes the two probably were identical since the confusion appears to lie mainly in the range of other materials encompassed by the word *descort*: though primarily designating the same form (or forms) as the lyric lai, it is also used for a poem whose stanzas disagree in some other way (e.g. Raimbaut de Vaqeiras's *descort Ara quan vei verdejar* has five isometric stanzas but their *discordia* lies in the fact that each is in a different language) and for a poem whose subject matter is discordance, disagreement or most characteristically severe disappointment in love (this last explaining the definition of the *descort* in the Provençal *Doctrina de comprendre dictatz*). In this context it might be worth noting that Konrad von Würzburg's second *Leich* (for which no music survives) repeatedly describes itself as a *Streit* ('contest').

It must be added, however, that some scholars see substantial differences between the lai and the *descort*. Maillard (1963), starting from the nomenclature found in the sources, divided the extant lyric lais into lais and *descorts*, but his efforts (pp.128ff) to define the difference are not entirely convincing. His suggestion (pp.143f) that the essence of the *descort* was in its poetical form occasionally departing from its musical form

seems questionable in view of the relative frequency of troubadour strophic songs whose musical form is at variance with their poetic form, and the extremely small number of Provençal lais (or *descorts*) with surviving music against which the theory can be tested (see also Maillard, 1971). Yet another opinion as to the difference is offered by Gennrich (1932, pp.138ff). Although the matter is still a subject of considerable dispute, this article has been prepared in the belief that these distinctions are artificial.

(*ii*) *Leich or leih*. The Middle High German word for lai. Kuhn (1952) argued that the earlier form was *laik*, a dance-song (but *see also* CAROL), and there is much evidence that the word 'leih' was originally used to denote a melody: so Browne (1956) gave examples of a *sancleich* (sung *Leich*), a *herafleih* (harp *Leich*) and a *keraleih* (sorrowful *Leich*). By the late 12th century there is some evidence that 'Leich' could mean any sacred poem, and the Monk of Salzburg used the word to describe his sequence contrafacta. But otherwise the word is perhaps the most specific of all those related to the form discussed in this article: it was not used for narrative poems and seems to have had very little currency for other purposes. Since Spanke many German philologists have preferred to form the plural artificially as *Leichs* (since *Leiche*, the more correct plural, also means 'corpse').

(*iii*) *Note, nota, notula*. One or other of these words is used by Johannes de Grocheo and in several French lais apparently describing lai form. In the title of the 'Note Martinet' (the lai *J'ai trouvé*), 'note' may be merely the designation of the melody or perhaps more particularly of the musical and poetic scheme (*see also* TON). Maillard cited several instances of its apparently referring to the melody of a lai; but sometimes it meant simply the melody of any song. The word is discussed more fully by Gennrich (1932, pp.167ff).

(*iv*) *Estampie, estampida, ostampida, stantipes, stampita*. The trouvère manuscript *GB-Ob* Douce 308 contains a group of 19 poems in lai form having the title 'estampie', but none of them has music. Among the Provençal repertory, the poem *Kalenda maia* by Raimbaut de Vaqeiras describes itself as an *estampida* but is isostrophic with each stanza following the pattern aabb¹cc¹. Instrumental pieces (perhaps dances) of the 13th and 14th centuries have the title and are in double-versicle sections with refrains at the end of each stanza and with *ouvert* and *clos* endings. The form is mentioned by Johannes de Grocheo, by the author of *Las leys d'amors* (1328) and as late as Michael Praetorius; *see* ESTAMPIE.

(*v*) *Ductia*. Another form mentioned by Johannes de Grocheo and closely related to the *estampie*: it has double-versicle sections with refrains but differs from most such forms in having isometric stanzas; *see* DUCTIA.

(*vi*) *Caribo, caribetto* (Provençal *garip*). An Italian word used primarily for instrumental versions of the form though also implying dance music. It was mentioned together with the *nota* and the *stampita* by the theorist Francesco da Barberino (1310). As a name for a kind of poem it appears in Dante's *Purgatorio* (xxxi.132), and describes a poem in lai form by Giacobo Pugliese. There is some disagreement as to whether the word derives from the Greek *charis* or from the name of an Arabic instrument. (See Appel, 1887, p.224.)

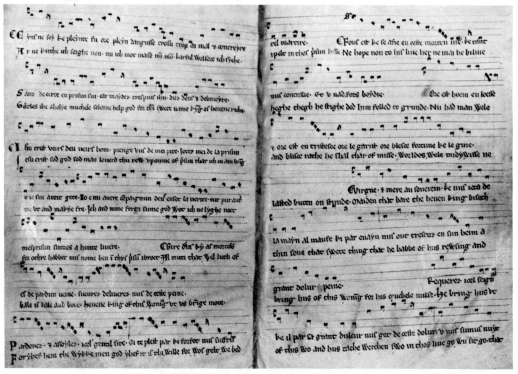

2. *Prisoner's song from 'Liber de antiquis legibus' (Corporation of London Records Office 49A, ff.160v–161r); the melody of the Latin 'Planctus ante nescia' is underlaid with the French text 'Eyns ne soy ke pleynte fu' and the English text 'Ar ne kuthe ich sorghe non'*

(vii) *Consonium*. Mentioned by Francesco da Barberino as the text for a *caribus*, a *nota* or a *stampita* (see Gennrich, 1932, p.163).

(viii) *Ensalada, ensaladilla*. Rengifo's *Arte ·poetica española* (1592) described the form in terms strikingly similar to earlier descriptions of the lai and *descort*. In surviving Portuguese and Spanish music the ENSALADA is not known before the mid-16th century; on earlier traces of the poetic form see d'Heur (1968) and G. Tavani: *Repertorio metrico della lirica galego-por-toghese*, Officina romanica, vii (Rome, 1967).

(ix) *Sequence, prose, conductus, planctus, versus*. These are the Latin forms that include material which could be described in Spanke's terms as 'musikalisch primär'. Ferdinand Wolf's theories (1841) on the substantial identity of sequence and lyric lai were totally discredited by Jeanroy and Aubry (1901), who asserted a little too absolutely that all sequences were built on an unvarying double-versicle pattern – a pattern that can rarely be seen in the 13th-century lai. Subsequent studies of the sequence (*see* SEQUENCE (i)) may not restore Wolf's original position, but they do suggest that both forms began less strict than they later became and that although the surviving history of the sequence's development belongs to a time nearly four centuries earlier than that of the lai the two have much in common and even share some music. Gautier de Coincy's *Hui enfantés* is a straight contrafactum of the Christmas sequence *Letabundus* which also served as source for the Anglo-Norman drinking-song *Or hi parra*; and it may be an evasion of the real issue to omit these works

from considerations of the lai, dismissing them as mere contrafacta. Godefroy de St Victor's *Planctus ante nescia* provided the melody and the form for the French lai *Eyns ne soy ke pleynte fu*, the English 'translation', *Ar ne kuthe ich sorghe non* (both in Corporation of London: Records Office, *Liber de antiquis legibus*, ff.160v–161v; fig.2) and the Hungarian poem *Volék sirolm tudotlan*. There are several other such examples in which the Latin original is obviously far earlier and served as a model: the fullest study is that of Spanke (1936); Handschin (1954) gave good reason for think-ing that both sequence and lai have their roots in the Celtic tradition; and Stäblein (1954, 1962) showed how a close examination of the Latin precursors can throw important light on the history of the lai.

Questions of definition are made even more difficult by the inserted 'Amen' and 'EVOVAE' phrases in lais by Ernoul de Gastinois and *Leichs* by Frauenlob, sug-gesting some liturgical origin (see Maillard, 1963, pp.310ff). Perhaps the most interesting contrafacta, however, merit inclusion on their own account: Heinrich von Laufenberg's two *Salve regina* parodies have no connection with the metrical scheme of the original because they set the melismatic melody syllab-ically.

These works all belong in a kind of no-man's-land between the lai and the sequence, but they should not allow any confusion as to the fundamental separateness of the two forms. The classic sequence has a com-pactness and clarity of design that are entirely different from either the rambling motivic dialectic of the 13th-century lai or the closely defined stanza and repetition patterns of the form in the 14th century. Certain aspects of the essence of both are more easily understood if sequence and lai are seen as the same form, but many others only make sense if the two are considered separately.

2. POETIC FORM. Maillard (1963) provided an extensive listing of extant poems in the lai form: far fewer than half of them survive with music. Since musical form was at the time almost invariably determined by poetic form and since there are some discussions of it in the poetical theory, it is in literary terms that the essential features of the form's history are most easily summarized.

Jeanroy (1901) mentioned the difficulty of being certain in identifying the stanzaic divisions of the 13th-century lyric lai: the poems are often too irregular to permit unambiguous analysis and the illuminated initials that normally begin a stanza in the manuscripts are sometimes clearly misplaced in lais, as though the early scribes were as confused as anybody. Put another way, the early lai is often a mere series of poetic lines, mostly brief and all rhyming with some other line, sometimes easily divisible into larger sections but not always giving any clear clue as to formal shape. An extreme example is the beginning of *Commencerai* by Thibaut IV (for the music, see ex.1):

Commencerai / a fere un lai / de la meillor /
forment m'esmai / que trop parai / fet de dolor, / dont mi chant
    torront a plor.
Mere virge savoree / se vos faitez demoree /
    de proier le haut segnor / bien doi avoir grant paor /
du deable, du felon / que en la noire prison /
    nos velt mener / dont nus ne peut eschaper;

Jeanroy, surveying the 30 13th-century lais known to him (a few more have since been discovered), listed a range of six to 19 stanzas, of two to 56 lines comprising two to 11 syllables but tending to favour the shorter lines that are in general a special characteristic of the lai throughout its history.

Few lais are quite as irregular as Thibaut's *Commencerai*, and one of the most prominent features of the lai is normally the principle of response, or repeated material. 'Lesser response' is the immediate or almost immediate repetition of a metrical or poetic scheme in the manner of the 'classical' double-versicle sequence: the repeated metre and rhyme scheme normally bring with them a musical repeat. But in the lai, particularly in the early stages of its history, the scheme of a single line or a couplet will often be repeated several times before new material is introduced, and this brings in its train the multifold repetition of short melodic fragments. In the 14th-century lai lesser response became customary throughout, normally in the form of regular fourfold response which was given music with alternating *ouvert* and *clos* cadences. Thus the 11th stanza of Machaut's *Le lay de l'ymage* runs:

Riens ne desir / tant com li servir / a plaisir. / Mi desir
    sont la jour et nuit,
pour desservir, / en lieu de merir, / li veir, / li oir:
    a ce Amours me duit.
Mieus vueil languir / pour li, sans mentir, / et morir / que joir
    d'autre; c'est le fruit
dont soustenir / me vueil et norir. / La metir / la querir
    vueil tout mon deduit.

'Greater response' entails repeating the scheme of a larger section later within the lai. Maillard ('Lai, Leich', 1973, p.335) gave the following formal analysis (others are possible) of the long 'Lai de l'ancien et du nouveau testament': *ABCDEFG EHIJ EHIJ EIJ EIJ E AB*. Such

greater responsion is also found in the sequence (*see* DOUBLE CURSUS). In lais of the 14th century it had reduced itself to a single case: the last stanza normally repeated the verse scheme of the first, but here the music was often transposed to another pitch, thereby both breaking the convention of the same verse scheme having the same music and also anticipating the sonata form recapitulation idea in many of its essential features by some 400 years.

Spanke (1938), in making what is still the most comprehensive attempt to analyse and categorize the 13th-century lais, was particularly reluctant to postulate any 'development' of form within the lai, asserting that the strictest poetic form in Machaut was already known in the 12th century. There was merely an extraordinarily wide range of structures, from the almost shapeless, such as Thibaut's *Commencerai*, through the heavily repetitive but rambling, such as the two lais of Ernoul de Gastinois, to the most painstakingly balanced lai with strictly paired lesser responsions, such as the 'Lai du chevrefeuille' or *Puis qu'en chantant*. On the other hand, it is also true to say that of the 46 Provençal poems and 109 Old French poems inventoried by Maillard (not all are strictly lais within the terms of this article and many are lost), remarkably few have 12 stanzas, the number favoured by Machaut and increasingly adhered to through the 14th century. So also, the earliest theorist to discuss the form at any length, Guilhem Molinier in the first version of *Las leys d'amors* (1328), was suitably vague in his definition, saying that it 'can have as many stanzas as a *vers*, that is to say five or ten, these stanzas being *singulars*, and distinct in rhyme, in music and in text; and they can each have the same metre or different metre'.

Only two of the *Roman de Fauvel* lais have 12 stanzas, but nearly all of Machaut's are in that form, later described by his nephew Eustache Deschamps (*Art de dictier*, 1392), who himself wrote 12 such poems. He described the lai as long and difficult to write ('c'est une chose longue et malaisee a faire et trouver'), having 12 double stanzas of 16, 18, 20 or 24 lines, each stanza with a different rhyme except the last, which should repeat that of the first without however repeating any of the actual rhyme words. He also said that lais were fairly common: in view of his own output and the continued cultivation of this intricate and elaborate form by Froissart (who gave a similar definition in his *Prison amoureuse*, ll.3483–514), Oton de Grandson, Christine de Pizan, Alain Chartier and Georges Chastellain, this is no surprise.

An even further increase in the rigidity of the form is apparent from the *Regles de la seconde rhetorique* (*c*1411–32) which gives a brief history of the form, according special honours to Philippe de Vitry and to Machaut (see §4 below). It describes the lai as having '12 stanzas of which the first and the last are similar in form and rhyme while the other ten are each individual in these respects; but each stanza must have four quarters'. Baudet Herenc (1432, ed. in Langlois, 1902, pp.166ff) was even more restrictive as to the length of each line and the permissible rhyme schemes.

Poetic theory on the subject in the later 15th century and after, represents a falling away at the edges. Deschamps had described and exemplified a *double lai* with 38 stanzas, but for Molinet a century later the form had become so rigid that *double lai* was merely a lai with 16 lines in the stanza rather than the 12 lines that had by

3. *'Tant me sui de dire teu', one of the 'lais' inserted in the 'Roman de Tristan en prose' (F-Pn fr.776, f.271v)*

then become almost mandatory: the 12-line form most favoured was that with the rhyme scheme *aab aab bba bba*, often called the *petit lai de contradiction* but also sometimes called *virelai* – a name that is particularly confusing in musical contexts because the form has nothing at all to do with the standard VIRELAI of the 14th century. At the same time a distinction evolved between the *petit lai* or *commun lai* with only one stanza and the full-size *grand lai*: a late example of a 'commun lay' in the *Jardin de plaisance* (Paris, *c*1501) comprises four stanzas with the same metre and rhyme scheme (that described above as 'virelai') and commends Chartier as a writer of lais. Thomas Sebillet's *Art poëtique françois* (Lyons, 2/1556) mentioned the lai and the virelai as an afterthought, declaring both to be obsolete. One particularly interesting late example of a lai (discussed in Giacchetti, 1973) is in fact a connected 'cycle' of seven poems in the following sequence of forms: rondeau,

fatras, virelai, fatras, ballade, fatras, rondeau; but it describes itself as being a lai, and is a lai in having each stanza in a different form from the last.

3. THE LAI BEFORE 1300. The earliest lai repertories with music are most simply described in terms of their manuscript sources. Peripheral to the main subject of this article are the inserts in the *Roman de Tristan en prose* (*c*1225–30, found particularly in *A-Wn* 2542); these are a series of simple stanzaic songs, very much in the musical and poetic style of the trouvère tradition at the time. Several of them are entitled 'lai' and they are the only surviving music with that title actually associated with Arthurian or narrative material: for these reasons they are included in the checklist below and must be considered in any study of the subject so long as the question of definition remains unsolved. But nothing in their poetry or their music suggests any connections

with the genre under consideration here.

The main collection of true 13th-century lais is in the Chansonnier de Noailles (*F-Pn* fr.12615) which contains 17, ten of them together. Smaller quantities of music, less clearly organized, appear in the Chansonnier du Roi (*F-Pn* fr.844), in *F-Pn* fr.845 and in the Wiener Leichhandschrift (*A-Wn* 2701). In two of the French sources the collection of chansons is followed by a group of two-voice motets after which the lais are to be found; and in the third collection a group of motets is nearby. All four sources are probably from the late 13th century but their repertories, partly anonymous, have such stylistic variety as to cause considerable disagreement on the early history of the lai form.

The Provençal *vida* of Garin d'Apchier states that he 'made the first *descort* that ever was made' ('fetz lo premier descort que anc fos faitz'), which would place the birth of the form around 1200; and while it is surely pertinent to ask how much the anonymous 14th-century biographer really understood about the subject, just as his comment raises again the question as to whether any clear distinction between the *descort* and the lyric lai was intended, it seems possible that the form appeared in the troubadour and trouvère traditions only shortly before 1200. This judgment may seem dangerous in view of the far greater antiquity of the sequence tradition, of the various discussions as to the roots of the sequence, and of the Celtic roots Handschin and others impute to the lai; nevertheless it makes sense in terms of the lyric tradition of the troubadours and trouvères as it survives, a tradition that grew up gently in the 12th century, gradually trying new formal ideas and expanding its boundaries as the century progressed.

Surveying the lais of the trouvère repertory (published almost complete in Jeanroy, Brandin and Aubry, 1901), Aubry called attention to a clear stylistic division falling approximately between those that were anonymous and those whose authors were known. The former (together with the two lais of Ernoul de Gastinois, who has even been suggested as a possible author for the others because they appear immediately after his lais in the Chansonnier de Noailles) include some extremely irregular patterns and occasional apparently incomplete musical notation on the basis of which a complete edition can require reconstruction and even guesswork. Aubry concluded that the incompletely notated lais were more improvisational and that they left hints as to possible Celtic origins for the genre; and several other scholars have pointed out that the tendency to repeat relatively brief musical phrases eight or nine times before moving on is perhaps symptomatic of some derivation from the style of the *chanson de geste*. Stäblein (1975) went further and proposed a chronology based on the assumptions that these less formalized pieces were earlier (an opinion it is difficult to endorse wholeheartedly in view of the full formalization of the substantially similar sequence form by 1100), and that the 'Lai des pucelles' (*Coraigeus*) was already written in the early 12th century when Abelard wrote his 'Planctus virginum Israel' to the same melody (for a contrary opinion see Weinrich, 1969): Stäblein suggested that all these anonymous lais may date from about 1100. He also proposed a chronology for the ascribed lais beginning with the three rather stolid pieces of Gautier de Dargies early in the 13th century, then the slightly freer works of the brothers li Vinier; the second half of the 13th century was then represented by Colin Muset,

Adam de Givenchi, Thomas Herier, Jaque de Cysoing and Ernoul de Gastinois.

Rietsch (DTÖ, xli, Jg.xx, 1913/*R*) observed many of the same characteristics in the *Leichs* of the Wiener Leichhandschrift as he found in some of the lais in the Jeanroy collection, especially those of Ernoul de Gastinois: he mentioned the short rhyming lines with no obvious scheme, rarity of clear stanza patterns and the absence of greater responsion. Similarly, Stäblein (1975, pp.172f) made an extremely interesting melodic analysis of a *Leich* by Tannhäuser, *Ich lobe ein wip*, and pointed out (p.97) that it is closely related in style to the French lais of the time. An adequate survey of the genres in the 13th century will need to view the French and German traditions together, if only because it is likely that none of the music in the French sources dates from later than about 1250 and the chronological (and stylistic) gap before the lais of the *Roman de Fauvel* is slightly closed by a consideration of the *Leich* of Herman Damen, a long rambling piece with constantly developing material, as well as those of Frauenlob with their consistently precise repetition in double versicles.

The developing melodic material just mentioned is perhaps the most absorbing characteristic of the lai as a musical form: figures and motifs carried from one section and expanded in the next are to some extent inevitable in a sectional monodic form the size of the lai, particularly if the composer has any feeling for the need to supply some shape to his work. In the opening section of *Commencerai* each unit builds on the preceding one, but the fifth unit grows anew out of the melodic material that had evolved at the end of the third and fourth units (ex.1; the texts, which have one syllable for each note or neume, are represented by only the rhyming syllable at the end of each line; for the text see §2 above).

Something similar happens in Herman Damen's *Ir kristenen*. The section of it in ex.2 contains short fragments repeated several times and representing a considerable change of pace after the more casual *aab* form that had characterized all that went before in the piece. This section is therefore transitional, setting up its own signposts, perceptibly changing character and, in the event, leading to a new section with a higher tessitura. The transitional passage treats a simple melodic figure in several different ways, finally transposing it up a tone before launching into the new section – at which point the frequency of repetition relaxes again and the melodic material for the first time in the piece has no obvious relation to that of the preceding sections.

4. THE LAI AFTER 1300. Schrade (1958) put forward tentative but persuasive arguments for suspecting that the four lais in the *Roman de Fauvel* could be the work of Philippe de Vitry, who otherwise contributed some of the most distinguished and modern music to that collection. The *Regles de la seconde rhetorique* (see Langlois, 1902, p.12) said: 'Aprez vint Philippe de Vitry qui trouva la maniere des motés, et des balades, et des lais et des simples rondeaux', and continued by praising Machaut 'le grant retthorique de nouvelle fourme, qui commencha toutes tailles nouvelles et les parfais lays d'amours'. In any case these four *Fauvel* lais are the only immediate precursors of the magnificent lais of Machaut. Their musical rhythm is clear, their sections are carefully balanced, and the repetitions have reached a regularity of form that suggests an effort to build on the basis of the 13th-century lai and crystallize it into a

4. End of the 'Lai des pucelles' and opening of 'Lai Markiol' from the 'Chansonnier de Noailles' (F-Pn fr.12615, ff.71v–72r)

Ex.1 Thibaut IV: lai *Commencerai*, opening, from *F-Pn* fr. 844, f.66

more balanced and logical shape in line with so many other innovations of the early 14th century. In these lais there is an even clearer sense of melodic progress: each section builds on the material with which the last ended, so the result is a constantly developing musical organism along the lines seen in the 13th-century lai but more continuous, more conscious of a thematic evolution.

Machaut's lais often include this feature, and in formal terms they follow the same scheme as those of the *Roman de Fauvel*. But the development of the mensural system opened new avenues: he was able to vary the pace from one section to another thereby giving this still-growing form an opportunity to become even larger, with (effective) changes of tempo giving the whole piece a sense of variety and springiness that was not found earlier. In a way this is the major importance of Machaut's lais in musical history, for none of his other works is so long as to require such full and conscious exploitation of the mensural system, using musical techniques more commonly found in the larger mass cycles of the 15th century.

Four of Machaut's lais contain polyphony written in 'successive notation'. This is clearly indicated only in *Je ne cesse de prier* where the even-numbered stanzas have the annotation 'chace' and make three-voice polyphony if performed in unison canon with the entries three perfections apart. *S'onques douleureusement* can be per-

formed in three-voice unison canon throughout. The polyphony of *Pour ce que plus proprement* is written after the manner of certain St Martial sources: the first versicle in each double-versicle stanza has different music from the second, but the two fit in excellent polyphony. Finally the music for stanzas 1, 2 and 3 in *En demantant* combines in three-voice polyphony as does that for stanzas 4–6, 7–9 and 10–12. In all these cases there is a serious question as to how the music might best be performed: if each voice was sung and texted the cumulative effect of the poem would presumably be lost, so perhaps the canonic possibilities are merely aids towards the construction of an instrumental accompaniment more carefully controlled by the composer than it was in the monophonic repertories of the preceding generation. The polyphony of Machaut's lais has been observed but not explained.

If Machaut's lais must be regarded as the highpoint of the form's history, there is little evidence that any of his successors followed this lead. That 15th-century composers seem not to have given the form their attention may perhaps be because it was still an essentially monodic form, and monophonic writing had none of the prestige it enjoyed in earlier centuries. (Securely ascribed monophonic music in the 15th century survives only from Germany.) Another reason was possibly that the composer interested in developing ex-

Ex.2 Herman Damen: Leich *Ir kristenen*, part only, from *D-Ju* (without call-number), f.113v

tended forms concentrated more on the cyclic mass which was now beginning to take its definitive form.

But two examples of later lai composition have come to light and the circumstances surrounding each suggest that they were not entirely isolated but rather examples of a larger tradition that happens to have been lost. The lai *De cuer je soupire* (*c*1400; ed. in Wright, 1974) has exact double versicles and *ouvert–clos* cadences: the nature of its melodic line and its changes of pace both clearly separate it from the sequence tradition. And if the brevity of its sections contrasts strongly with the inflated length of the unset lais of Chartier and Grandson this may be seen as the only way of keeping the form within the scope of other secular monophony in the 15th century. A similar situation exists in Hans Folz's 'Kettenton' (*c*1500), which Petzsch (1970) ingeniously identified as being in the lai form: again the sections are brief, and the continuous development of material passing from one section to the next is fully within the received tradition. If these are symptoms characteristic of a larger tradition, the size of the form in the 13th century was considerably expanded and reduced to formulae by composers in France and Germany after 1300, whereas the composers after Machaut reduced size and scope with the lai as they did with so much of their cultural heritage.

5. NOTES ON THE CHECKLIST OF LAI MUSIC. While it is clear that a study of the lai must take account of the poems and their form, it seems also that much can be learnt from a study of the music alone, and it is to this end that the appended list has been compiled. The fullest listing of texts is still that in Maillard (1963), where they are tabulated separately under lais (pp.71ff), *descorts*

(pp.119ff) and *Leichs* (pp.153ff) and much additional material is included. In the list here four categories of material have been deliberately omitted: (i) the many poems in lai form with no surviving music: it is not suggested that these are unimportant, but that the reader of this dictionary might be grateful for a listing that confines itself to what music is actually there; (ii) other text sources for lais whose music does survive: they can quickly be ascertained from Maillard and from the standard inventories of medieval literary genres; (iii) Latin pieces that might be described as in lai form: these are listed and discussed in Spanke (1936); (iv) pieces that happen to be called lais either in manuscript titles or within the poem, but show no apparent trace of lai form (examples would be Gautier de Coinci's *Entendés tuit ensemble* and Harder's 'Kôrwîse'), pieces that are in the form but are straight translations of sequences (such as Gautier's *Hui enfantés*) and pieces showing elements of lai form (see Spanke, 1936, pp.91ff).

Unresolved questions as to the strict definition of the lai and as to its pre-history have made some of the decisions in this last category extremely difficult. One category has been included even though it strictly has nothing to do with the lai as defined here: the lyric insertions in the *Roman de Tristan en prose* are listed because many are entitled 'lai' and they represent a complete independent category of material; moreover they are included as such in the major studies of Wolf (1841) and Maillard (1963), and their omission could therefore cause unnecessary confusion.

Editions listed are not necessarily the best or the most recent but merely the most convenient for obtaining an overview of the repertory. Descriptions of form are added only when unambiguous and relatively simple.

CHECKLIST OF LAI MUSIC

Editions: *Die Sangesweisen der Colmarer Handschrift und die Liederhandschrift Donaueschingen*, ed. P. Runge (Leipzig, 1896/*R*1965) [Ru]
Lais et descorts français du XIIIe siècle, ed. A. Jeanroy, L. Brandin and P. Aubry (Paris, 1901/*R*1969) [J]
Gesänge von Frauenlob, Reinmar v. Zweter und Alexander, ed. H. Rietsch, DTÖ, xli, Jg.xx (1913/*R*) [Ri]
Guillaume de Machaut: Musikalische Werke, iv: *Messe und Lais*, ed. F. Ludwig and H. Besseler (Leipzig, 1954) [L]
The Works of Guillaume de Machaut: First Part, ed. L. Schrade, PMFC, ii (1956) [S]
Der musikalische Nachlass der Troubadours: kritische Ausgabe der Melodien, ed. F. Gennrich. SMM, iii (1958) [G]
J. Maillard: *Evolution et esthétique du lai lyrique* (Paris, 1963) [M]
R. J. Taylor: *The Art of the Minnesinger* (Cardiff, 1968) [T]

PROVENÇAL LAIS

Title	Composer	Text incipit	Identification	Musical sources	Editions	Remarks
Lai nom par	—	Finamens	PC 461.122	*F-Pn* fr.844, fr.12615	G no.281	11 stanzas; music of 1 repeated for 11
Lai Markiol	—	Gent me nais	PC 461.124	*F-Pn* fr.844, fr.12615	G no.280	melody also used for Flour ne glais, for Philippe the Chancellor's 'Veritas, equitas, largitas' (*GB-Lbm* Eg.274, *I-Fl* 29.1, *F-Pn* fr.146) and for the St Martial 'Prosa virginalis'
—	Aimeric de Peguilhan	Qui la ve en ditz	PC 10.45	*F-Pn* fr.844, fr.22543	G no.182	music inc. and different in the 2 sources
—	Guilhem Augier Novella, or Peire Ramon de Tolosa or Guiraut de Calanso	Ses alegratge	PC 205.5	*F-Pn* fr.844	G no.184	discussed in Maillard: 'Structures mélodiques' (1973)
—	? Charles d'Anjou	Sill qu'es captz e quitz	PC 461.67a	*F-Pn* fr.844	G p.170, Maillard (1967), 60	ed. in G as part of Qui la ve

LYRIC LAIS IN THE ROMAN DE TRISTAN EN PROSE
(*all isostrophic*)

Title	Speaker	Text incipit	Musical sources	Editions	Remarks
	Helyas	Amors de vostre acointement	*A-Wn* 2542	—	
Lai de victoire, or Le recort de victoire	Tristan	Apres ce que je vi victoire	*A-Wn* 2542	Maillard (1969), p.1354	

Title	Speaker	Text incipit	Musical sources	Editions	Remarks
Lettre	Dame Morgan	A toi roi Artu qui signour	A-Wn 2542	—	
Lai de Kahedin	Kahedin	A vos Amors ainz qu'a nului	A-Wn 2542	—	
[lettre]	Yseut	A vous Tristan ami verai	A-Wn 2542	—	
Lai de plour	Tristan	D'amour vient mon chant	A-Wn 2542	M 198, Wolf (1841), viii	
Lai mortel	Kahedin	En mourant de si douce mort	A-Wn 2542	—	
[lettre]	Yseut	Folie n'est pas vasselage	A-Wn 2542	—	
—	Tristan	Grant tens a que je ne vi cele	A-Wn 2542	Maillard (1969), p.1360	9 lines only
—	Tristan	Ja fis canchonnetes et lais	A-Wn 2542	Wolf (1841), vii	
Lai du boivre amoureux	—	La ou je fui dedenz la mer	A-Wn 2542	Maillard (1969), p.1358	
Lai mortel	Yseut	Li solaus luist et clers	A-Wn 2542	M 188	
Lai	Roi Artus	Rien n'est qui ne viegne a	A-Wn 2542	M 201; Wolf (1841), vii	
—	Roi Marc	Salu vous nanc com je le doi faire	A-Wn 2542, F-Pn fr.776	M 200	the 2 sources have different music
—	Lamorat de Galles	Sans cuer sui et sans cuer remaing	F-Pn fr.776	M 200	
Lai voir disant	Dynadan	Tant me sui de dire teu	A-Wn 2542, F-Pn fr.776	M 189, M 189	the 2 sources have different music

FRENCH LAIS BEFORE 1300

Title	Composer	Text incipit	Identification	Musical sources	Editions	Remarks
—	Gille li Vinier	A ce m'acort	R.1928	F-Pn fr.844, fr.12615	J ix	
—		Amors m'a au laiz pris	R.1605a	F-Pn fr.845 (frag.)	Gennrich (1932), 139	melody = Lonc tens
Lai a la Vierge	Thibaut IV	Commencerai	R.73a	F-Pn fr.844, fr.846	J xiv, M 297	considered by Stäblein (1975) not to be a lai
Lai des pucelles	—	Coraigeus	R.1012	F-Pn fr.12615	J xxiii, M 262	melody also used for Abelard's 'Planctus virginum Israel' (of which the title 'Lai des pucelles' could be a trans.), I-Rvat reg.lat.288
—	Gautier de Dargies	De celi me plaing	R.1421	F-Pn fr.844, fr.12615	J iii	
—	Colin Muset	En ceste note dirai	R.74	F-Pn fr.845, n.a.fr.1050	J iv	
Lai de Notre Dame	Ernoul le vielle	En entente curieuse	R. 1017	F-Pn fr.12615	J xvii, Maillard (1964), 25	music frag.; needs heavy reconstruction
Lai d'Aelis	—	En sospirant de trop	R.1921	F-Pn fr.12615	J xxv, M 228	
—		. . . en tremblant	R.362a	F-Pn fr.845		
—	Guillaume li Vinier	Espris d'ire et d'amor	R.1946	F-Pn fr.844, fr.12615	J viii	
—	—	Eyns ne soy ke pleynte fu	—	Corporation of London: Records Office, Liber de antiquis legibus, f.160v–161v	Gennrich (1928–9), 346f	melody also used for Godefroy de St Victor's 'Planctus ante nescia' and Eng. 'Prisoner's song'
Lai de Notre Dame ['contre le lai Markiol']	—	Flour ne glais	R.192	F-Pn fr.2193, fr.12615, Wolf frag.	J xvi, Gennrich (1942), 4	melody = Gent me nais
Cantus de Domina post cantum Aaliz	—	Flur de virginite	R.476a	GB-Lbm Arundel 248	J xxx, M 235	melody appears only with Lat. text Flos pudicitie
Lai des amants	—	Ichi comans	R.635	F-Pn fr.12615	J xx	
—	Gautier de Dargies	J'ai maintes fois chanté	R.416	F-Pn fr.844, fr.12615	J i	
Note Martinet	? Martin le Beguin	J'ai trouvé	R.474	F-Pn fr.845, Mesmes (lost)	Gennrich (1932), 169	
—	? Charles d'Anjou	Ki de bons est souef	[R.165a]	F-Pn fr.844	M 285, Maillard (1967), 46	Stäblein (1975) suggested that this was merely a series of single-stanza trouvère songs in the normal aab form, although the poem is described as a lai in l.5; melody also used in same MS for Iam mundus
—	Adam de Givenchi	La doce acordance	R.205	F-Pn fr.844, fr.12615	J x	
—	Gautier de Dargies	La doce pensee	R.539	F-Pn fr.844, fr.12615	J ii	
—	? Charles d'Anjou	La plus noble emprise	[R.1623a]	F-Pn fr.844	M 290, Maillard (1967), 43	Stäblein (1975) suggested that this was merely a series of single-stanza trouvère songs
Plaintes de la Vierge au pied de la croix	—	Lasse que deviendrai gie	R.1093	F-Pn fr.12483	J xxix	same metrical scheme as Par courtoisie despuel, but different melody
Lai de la pastourelle	—	L'autrier chevauchoie	R.1695	F-Pn fr.845, Mesmes (lost)	J xxiv	melody = Lonc tens

Title	Composer	Text incipit	Identi-fication	Musical sources	Editions	Remarks
Lai des Hermins	—	Lonc tens m'ai teu	R.2060	F-Pn fr.845, Mesmes (lost)	J xxvii	melody also used for L'autrier, Amors m'a, Virge glorieuse and Philippe the Chancellor's sequence 'Ave gloriosa'; 10 stanzas; music of 1 repeated for 10
—	—	Mere de pitié	R.1094a	F-Pa 3517	see M 127	same metrical scheme as De cele me plaing
—	—	Ne flours ne glais	R.192a	F-Pa 3517	see M 79	
Lai du chevre-feuille, or Note del kievrefuel	—	Par courtoisie despuel	R.995	F-Pn fr.844 fr.12615, Wolf frag.	J xxii, Gennrich (1942), 40	11 stanzas; music of 1 repeated for 11
Lai de la rose	—	Pot s'onques mais nus hom	R.900	F-Pn fr.12615	J xxi	
—	—	Puis qu'en chantant	R.1931	F-Pn fr.846	J xxvi, M 237	9 stanzas; music of 1 repeated for 9
—	—	Qui porroit un guirredon	R.1868	F-Pn fr.846 (frag.)	M 300	inc.
Lai a la Vierge	Gautier de Coinci	Royne celestre	R.956	F-Pn n.a.fr.24541 and 10 others	J xv	3 stanzas each in form aabbccdd
—	Guillaume li Vinier	Se chans ne descors ne lais	R.193	F-Pn fr.844, fr.12615	J vii	
Lai de l'ancien et du nouveau testament	? Ernoul le Vielle	S'onques hom en lui s'asist	R.1642	F-Pn fr.12615	J xviii, Maillard (1964), 14	music frag.; needs heavy reconstruction
—	Adam de Givenchi	Trop est costumiere Amors	R.2018	F-Pn fr.844, fr.12615	J xi	
—	Thomas Herier	Un descort vaurai retraire	R.186	F-Pn fr.12615	J xiii	
—	? Gautier de Coinci	Virge glorieuse	R.1020	F-Pa 3517	J xxviii	melody = Lonc tens

LAIS IN THE ROMAN DE FAUVEL
(all anonymous and ed. only in Harrison, 1963)

Title	Text incipit	Musical sources	Remarks
Lai des Hellequines	En ce douz temps d'este	F-Pn fr.146, f.34v	called 'descort' in the text; 12 stanzas, each sung by a different character
Lai de Fortune	Je qui pooir seule ai	F-Pn fr.146, f.19	9 stanzas plus frag. of a 10th
Lai de Venus	Pour recouvrer alegiance	F-Pn fr.146, f.28b	12 stanzas; music of 1 repeated for 12
Lai de Fauvel	Talant que j'ai d'obeir	F-Pn fr.146, f.17	14 stanzas; music of 1 repeated for 14

LAIS BY GUILLAUME DE MACHAUT
(in Vg [Wildenstein Gallery, New York], A [F-Pn fr.1584], B [Pn fr.1585], C [Pn fr.1586], E [Pn fr.9221], and G [Pn fr.22546] unless otherwise stated)

Title	Text incipit	Musical sources	Editions	Remarks
Le lay des dames	Amis, t'amour me contreint		S 7, L 10	12 stanzas; music of 1 repeated up a 5th for 12
—	Amours doucement me tente		S 6, L 7	12 stanzas; music of 1 repeated up a 4th for 12
Le lay de Nostre Dame	Contre ce doulz mois de may	not in C	S 10, L 15	12 stanzas; music of 1 repeated up a 5th for 12
—	En demantant et lamentant	E only	S 18, L 24	12 stanzas; music of 1 repeated down a 4th for 12; each group of 3 stanzas combines in polyphony for 3vv, see Hasselman and Walker (1970)
	J'aim la flour de valour		S 2, L 2	7 stanzas; music of 1 repeated for 7
Le lay de la fonteinne, or Le lay de Nostre Dame	Je ne cesse de prier	not in C	S 11, L 16	12 stanzas; music of 1 repeated up a 5th for 12; even-numbered stanzas are chaces, 3vv
Le lay de bonne esperance, or Le lay d'esperance	Longuement me sui tenus		S 13, L 18	12 stanzas; music of 1 repeated up a 5th for 12
	Loyaute que point ne delay	not in E	S 1, L 1	12 stanzas, each with the same melody
Le lay de plour	Malgre Fortune et son tour	A and G only	S 14, L 19	12 stanzas; music of 1 repeated up a 5th for 12
Le lay de l'ymage	Ne say comment commencier		S 9, L 14	12 stanzas; music of 1 repeated up a 5th for 12
—	Nuls ne doit avoir		S 4, L 5	12 stanzas; music of 1 repeated up a 5th for 12
—	Par trois raisons me vueil		S 5, L 6	12 stanzas; music of 1 repeated up a 5th for 12
Un lay de consolation	Pour ce que plus proprement	E only	S 17, L 23	12 stanzas; music of 1 repeated for 12; 2vv throughout in successive notation, see Hoppin (1958)
	Pour ce qu'on puist	also in Lille, Archives du Nord, MS 134 (frag.)	S 3, L 3	12 stanzas; music of 1 repeated for 12
Le lay de la rose	Pour vivre joliement	A and G only	S 15, L 21	12 stanzas; music of 1 repeated up a 5th for 12
Le lay de plour	Qui bien aimme a tart oublie	not in G	S 16, L 22	12 stanzas; music of 1 repeated up a 5th for 12
	Qui n'aroit autre depart		S 19, Li, 93	12 stanzas; music of 1 repeated up a 5th for 12
Le lay de confort	S'onques douleureusement	not in C	S 12, L 17	12 stanzas; music of 1 repeated for 12; all stanzas canonic 3vv
Le lay mortel	Un mortel lay vueil commencier	also in Maggs	S 8, L 12	12 stanzas; music of 1 repeated for 12

LEICHS BEFORE 1300

Title	Composer	Text incipit	Musical sources	Editions	Remarks
—	Reinmar von Zweter	Got und dîn eben êwikeit	A-Wn 2701	T i, 72, Ri 62	29 stanzas; use of rhyming cadences
—	Tannhäuser	Ich lobe ein wip	D-Mbs clm 5539	Kuhn (1952), 111	
—	Alexander	Mîn trûreclîchez klagen	D-Ju	T i, 7	2 different though noticeably related melodies
			A-Wn 2701	T i, 11, Ri 83	
—	Ulrich von Winterstetten	Swer die wunne	lost Schreiber frag.	T i, 92	frag.

LEICHS AROUND 1300

Title	Composer	Text incipit	Musical sources	Editions	Remarks
Frauenleich, or Der guldin flügel	Frauenlob	Ei ich sach in dem trône	A-Wn 2701, D-Mbs cgm 4997, Mbs Mus.921, PL-WRu fr.12 (frag.), Königsberg, lost frag.	Ru 3, Ri 57	dated Nov 1318; 22 stanzas
Taugenhort, or Slosshort	? Frauenlob	In gotes schôz gesehen wart	D-Mbs cgm 4997	Ru 28	25 stanzas
—	Herman Damen	Ir kristenen alle schriet	D-Ju		
Minnekliche leich	Frauenlob	O wîp du hôher êren haft	A-Wn 2701	Ri 67	33 stanzas
Des Heylygyn Cruecysleych	Frauenlob or Regenbogen	O wundirwernder	A-Wn 2701, D-Mbs 4997	Ri 71, Ru 106	22 stanzas; music incomplete at end in Mbs 4997

LATER LEICHS

Title	Composer	Text incipit	Musical sources	Editions	Remarks
Goldenes ABC	Monk of Salzburg	Ave Balsams Creatur	D-Mbs cgm 4997, Mbs cgm 715, A-Wn 2856	Ru 145	12 stanzas
—	H. von Laufenberg	Bis grûst maget reine	F-STR 222	Wolf (1841), ix; Runge (1910)	contrafactum-paraphrase of Salve regina
Hort	Peter von Reichenbach	Got vater, sun	D-Mbs cgm 4997	Ru 53	10 stanzas
—	H. von Laufenberg	Wilcom lobes werde	F-STR 222	Runge (1910)	contrafactum-paraphrase of Salve regina

LATEST EXAMPLES

Title	Composer	Text incipit	Musical sources	Editions	Remarks
Kettenton	Hans Folz	[no surviving orig. text]	D-Nst Will III.792, WRtl fol.420.2, PL-WRu 356	Petzsch (1970)	4 double versicles and coda
		De cuer je soupire	F-Dm 2837	Wright (1974)	6 stanzas; 1st used for tenor of mass cycle in I-TRmn 89
Tageweise	Albrecht Lesch	Zuch durch die wolken	D-Mbs cgm 4997	Ru 180	see Petzsch (1975)

BIBLIOGRAPHY

F. Wolf: *Über die Lais, Sequenzen und Leiche* (Heidelberg, 1841)

C. Appel: 'Vom Descort', *Zeitschrift für romanische Philologie*, xi (1887), 212

H. R. Lang: 'The Descort in Old Spanish and Portuguese Poetry', *Beiträge zur romanischen Philologie: Festgabe für Gustav Gröber* (Halle, 1899), 484

A. Jeanroy, L. Brandin and P. Aubry: *Lais et descorts français du XIIIème siècle: texte et musique*, Mélanges de musicologie critique, iii (Paris, 1901/R1969)

E. Langlois: *Recueil d'arts de seconde rhétorique* (Paris, 1902)

G. Schläger: review of Jeanroy, Brandin and Aubry in *Literaturblatt für germanische und romanische Philologie*, xxiv (1903), 286

O. Gottschalk: *Der deutsche Minneleich und sein Verhältnis zu Lai und Descort* (diss., U. of Marburg, 1908)

P. Runge: 'Der Marienleich Heinrich Laufenbergs "Wilkom lobes werde"', *Festschrift...Rochus Freiherr von Liliencron* (Leipzig, 1910/R1970), 228

G. Hase: *Der Minneleich Meister Alexanders und seine Stellung in der mittelalterlichen Musik*, Sächsische Forschungsinstitut für neuere Philologie: altgermanistische Abteilung, i (Halle, 1921)

F. Gennrich: 'Internationale mittelalterliche Melodien', *ZMw*, xi (1928–9), 259, 321

J. Handschin: 'Über Estampie und Sequenz', *ZMw*, xii (1929–30), 1; xiii (1930–31), 113

H. Spanke: 'Eine neue Leich-Melodie', *ZMw*, xiv (1931–2), 385 [Tannhäuser's *Ich lobe ein wip*]

——: 'Über das Fortleben der Sequenzenform in den romanischen Sprachen', *Zeitschrift für romanische Philologie*, li (1931), 309

F. Gennrich: *Grundriss einer Formenlehre des mittelalterlichen Liedes als Grundlage einer musikalischen Formenlehre des Liedes* (Halle, 1932)

H. Spanke: *Beziehungen zwischen romanischer und mittellateinischer Lyrik mit besonderer Berücksichtigung der Metrik und Musik*, Abhandlungen der Gesellschaft der Wissenschaften zu Göttingen, 3rd ser., xviii (Berlin, 1936)

——: 'Sequenz und Lai', *Studi medievali*, new ser., xi (1938), 12–68

F. Gennrich: 'Zwei altfranzösische Lais', *Studi medievali*, new ser., xv (1942), 1–68

H. Spanke: *Deutsche und französische Dichtung des Mittelalters* (Stuttgart and Berlin, 1943)

G. Vecchi: 'Sequenza e lai: a proposito di un ritmo di Abelardo', *Studi medievali*, new ser., xvi (1943–50), 86

H. Kuhn: 'Ulrich von Winterstetten und der deutsche Leich', *Minnesangs Wende* (Tübingen, 1952, 2/1967), 91–142

J. Handschin: 'Trope, Sequence, and Conductus', *NOHM*, ii (1954), 128–74

B. Stäblein: 'Von der Sequenz zum Strophenlied: eine neue Sequenzenmelodie "archaischen" Stiles', *Mf*, vii (1954), 257

A. Machabey: *Guillaume de Machault 130?–1377* (Paris, 1955), i, 98–130

G. Reaney: 'The *Lais* of Guillaume de Machaut and their Background', *PRMA*, lxxxii (1955–6), 15 [incl. information on earlier lais]

R. J. Browne: *A Stylistic and Formal History of the Middle High German Leich, 1190–1290* (diss., Yale U., 1956)

R. H. Hoppin: 'An Unrecognized Polyphonic Lai of Machaut', *MD*, xii (1958), 93 [*Pour ce que pens proprement*]

J. Maillard: 'Problèmes musicaux et littéraires du "lai" ', *Quadrivium*, iii (1958), 32

G. Reaney: 'Concerning the Origins of the Medieval Lai', *ML*, xxix (1958), 343

L. Schrade: 'Guillaume de Machaut and the Roman de Fauvel', *Miscelánea en homenaje a monseñor Higinio Anglés* (Barcelona, 1958–61), ii, 843

J. Maillard: 'Le "lai" et la "note" du Chèvrefeuille', *MD*, xiii (1959), 3

U. Aarburg: 'Lai, Leich', *MGG*

B. Stäblein: 'Die Schwanenklage: zum Problem Lai–Plunctus–Sequenz', *Festschrift Karl Gustav Fellerer* (Regensburg, 1962), 491

G. A. Harrison: *The Monophonic Music in the 'Roman de Fauvel'* (diss., Stanford U., 1963)

J. Maillard: *Evolution et esthétique du lai lyrique, des origines à la fin du XIVème siècle* (Paris, 1963)

K. H. Bertau: *Sangverslyrik: über Gestalt und Geschichtlichkeit mittel-hochdeutscher Lyrik am Beispiel des Leichs*, Palaestra, ccxl (Göttingen, 1964)

J. Maillard: *Lais et chansons d'Ernoul de Gastinois*, MSD, xv (1964)

D. Poirion: *Le poète et le prince: l'évolution du lyrisme courtois de Guillaume de Machaut à Charles d'Orléans* (Grenoble, 1965), 397ff

H. Baader: *Die Lais: zur Geschichte einer Gattung der altfranzösischen Kurzerzählungen*, Analecta romanica, xvi (Frankfurt, 1966)

J. Maillard: *Roi-trouvère du XIIIème siècle: Charles d'Anjou*, MSD, xviii (1967)

J.-M. d'Heur: 'Des descorts occitans et des descordos galiciens-portugais', *Zeitschrift für romanische Philologie*, lxxxiv (1968), 323

R. Baum: 'Les troubadours et les lais', *Zeitschrift für romanische Philologie*, lxxxv (1969), 1–44 [analysis of 58 uses of the word 'lai' in Provençal]

I. Glier: 'Der Minneleich im späten 13. Jahrhundert', *Werk–Typ–Situation: Studien zu poetologischen Bedingungen in der älteren deutschen Literatur: Hugo Kuhn zum 60. Geburtstag* (Stuttgart, 1969), 161

J. Maillard: 'Lais avec notation dans le *Tristan en prose*', *Mélanges offerts à Rita Lejeune* (Gembloux, 1969), 1347 [rectifies omissions in Maillard, 1963]

L. Weinrich: 'Peter Abaelard as Musician', *MQ*, lv (1969), 295, 464

M. Hasselman and T. Walker: 'More Hidden Polyphony in a Machaut Manuscript', *MD*, xxiv (1970), 7 [*En demantant*]

C. Petzsch: 'Ein spätes Zeugnis der Lai-Technik', *Zeitschrift für deutsches Altertum*, xcix (1970), 310 [Folz's 'Kettenton']

R. Baum: 'Le descort ou l'anti-chanson', *Mélanges . . . Jean Boutière* (Liège, 1971), 75 [with extensive bibliography]

J. Maillard: 'Coblas dezacordablas et poésie d'oïl', *Mélanges . . . Jean Boutière* (Liège, 1971), 361

G. Objartel: 'Zwei wenig beachtete Fragmente Reinmars von Zweter und ein lateinisches Gegenstück seines Leichs', *Zeitschrift für deutsche Philologie*, xc (1971), *Sonderheft*, 217

C. Bullock-Davies: 'The Form of the Breton Lay', *Medium aevum*, xlii (1973), 18

A. Giacchetti: 'Une nouvelle forme du *lai* apparue à la fin du XIVe siècle', *Etudes de langue et de littérature du moyen âge offertes à Félix Lecoy* (Paris, 1973), 147

J. Maillard: 'Descort', *MGG*

——: 'Lai, Leich', *Gattungen der Musik in Einzeldarstellungen: Gedenkschrift Leo Schrade*, i (Berne and Munich, 1973), 323

——: 'Structures mélodiques complexes au moyen âge', *Mélanges de langue et de littérature médiévales offerts à Pierre le Gentil* (Paris, 1973), 523 [*Ses alegratge*]

G. Fotitch and R. Steiner: *Les lais du roman de Tristan en prose d'après le manuscrit de Vienne 2542* (Munich, 1974) [incl. complete edn.]

C. Wright: 'A Fragmentary Manuscript of Early 15th-century Music in Dijon', *JAMS*, xxvii (1974), 306 [*De cuer je soupire*]

C. Petzsch: 'Folgen nachträglich eingeführter Text-Form-Korrespondenz für Text und Lai-Technik', *Mf*, xxviii (1975), 284 [Lesch's 'Tageweise']

B. Stäblein: *Schriftbild der einstimmigen Musik*, Musikgeschichte in Bildern, iii/4 (Leipzig, 1975), 95ff, 172ff

E. Köhler: 'Deliberations on a Theory of the Genre of the Old Provençal Descort', *Italian Literature: Roots and Branches: Essays in Honor of Thomas Goddard Bergin* (New Haven and London, 1976), 1

P. Bec: *La lyrique française au moyen-âge (XIIe–XIIIe siècles): contribution à une typologie des genres poétiques médiévaux* (Paris, 1977), i, 189ff

D. Fallows: 'Guillaume de Machaut and the Lai: a New Source', *Early Music*, v (1977), 477

E. Mulder: 'Einige Bewerkungen zu Machauts "Lay de L'ymage"', *Mf*, xxxii (1979), 58

DAVID FALLOWS

Lai, François. *See* LAYS, FRANÇOIS.

Laibach (Ger.). LJUBLJANA.

Lainati, Carlo Ambrogio. *See* LONATI, CARLO AMBROGIO.

Laine, Cleo [Campbell, Clementina Dinah] (*b* Southall, Middlesex, 28 Oct 1927). British jazz, popular and concert singer. Her imaginative musicianship and often spectacular singing were first admired in the 1950s. She has made many recordings and has often appeared on television in Britain and the USA. She has an instinctive vocal command of the style and repertory of Billie Holiday, Ella Fitzgerald and Sarah Vaughan, but she has also sung *Pierrot lunaire*, songs by Ives, and other 20th-century works; several composers, notably Richard Rodney Bennett and her husband John Dankworth, have written for her. Laine's contralto voice is capable of great variety of colour, and has an extraordinary upward extension in falsetto to *c''''*, giving her a compass of four octaves. She is noted for virtuoso scat-singing accompanied by Dankworth on the alto saxophone or clarinet. She was made an OBE in 1979.

BIBLIOGRAPHY
G. Collier: *Cleo and John* (London, 1976)

HENRY PLEASANTS

Lais, Johan Dominico (*fl* 2nd half of the 16th century). Arranger and ?composer. He was the joint-author with Sixt Kargel of *Nova eaque artificiosa et valde commoda ratio ludendae cytharae* (Strasbourg, 1575), a tablature volume of 63 dances for six-course solo cittern tuned *b–G–d–g–d'–e'*. Some of the pieces use vocal models from French, Italian and German sources, including works by Lassus, Arcadelt, Berchem, Crecquillon, Didier Lupi Second, Rore and Senfl. The tablature system is Italian and the volume also contains rules in Latin and German for tuning. The 1575 edition was followed by another from the same printer (*RISM* 1578²⁶; 1 ed. in Wolf); a collection referred to by Draud as *Carmina italica, gallica et germanica ludenda cythara* (Strasbourg, 1569) may have been an earlier edition of the same work.

BIBLIOGRAPHY
BrownI
G. Draud: *Bibliotheca exotica, sive Catalogus officinalis librorum pere-grinus linguis usualibus scriptorum* (Frankfurt, rev. 2/1625), 1622
J. Wolf: *Handbuch der Notationskunde*, i (Leipzig, 1913/R1963), 141f
K. Levy: '*Susanne un jour*: the History of a 16th Century Chanson', *AnnM*, i (1953), 375–408

IAIN FENLON

Laisse. A form of stanza used primarily in French epic poetry of the Middle Ages (*see* CHANSON DE GESTE and CHANTE-FABLE). A laisse consists of a varying number of lines each having the same number of syllables and linked together by assonance. In many poems the laisse ends with a line of different length, sometimes in the form of a refrain or a meaningless series of vowels or short syllables. In a few instances such last lines are provided with notes, with no clear indication of metre or of relation to other lines in the laisse.

BIBLIOGRAPHY
F. Gennrich: *Grundriss einer Formenlehre des mittelalterlichen Liedes* (Halle, 1932), 40ff
R. Louis: 'Le refrain dans les plus anciennes chansons de geste et le sigle AOI dans le Roland d'Oxford', *Mélanges de linguistique et de littérature romanes à la mémoire d'István Frank* (Saarbrücken, 1957)

HENDRIK VANDERWERF

Laisser vibrer (Fr.: 'let vibrate'). A performing direction used for certain percussion instruments, especially cymbals.

Lajarte, Théodore (Edouard Dufaure de) (*b* Bordeaux, 10 July 1826; *d* Paris, 20 June 1890). French musicologist and composer. A pupil of Leborne at the Paris Conservatoire, he concentrated on composition during the first part of his life. His works include at least ten *opéras comiques* (among which *Le secret de l'oncle Vincent* of 1855 had notable success), two ballets, choral works and music for military band. He wrote in a facile and correct manner, but showed little orginality; he sometimes imitated 18th-century music or the 19th-century Viennese style. He is better known for his new editions of early music: *Airs à danser de Lully à Méhul* (Paris, 1876), *Chefs-d'oeuvre classiques de l'opéra français* (Paris, 1880), and vocal scores of 11 operas by Lully, two by Rameau and one by Campra (in the

Michaelis collection, 1880–82). From 1873 he worked as a librarian in the archives of the Opéra, under the direction of Charles Nuitter, and there undertook his principal achievement, the *Bibliothèque musicale du théâtre de l'Opéra*. This valuable work, with an excellent preface, gives a list of works performed at the Opéra from its origins in 1669 until 1876, providing historical and bibliographical information for each work. Lajarte wrote several other books and contributed to many periodicals. He also organized concerts of early music, particularly in south-west France.

WRITINGS
Instruments-Sax et fanfares civiles (Paris, 1867)
Bibliothèque musicale du théâtre de l'Opéra: catalogue historique, chronologique, anecdotique (Paris, 1878/R1969)
with A. Bisson: *Grammaire de la musique* (Paris, 1880, 3/1913)
——: *Petit traité de composition musicale* (Paris, 1881)
——: *Petite encyclopédie musicale* (Paris, 1881–4)
Les curiosités de l'Opéra (Paris, 1883)
Numerous articles in *Le ménestrel*, *France musicale*, *Moniteur des arts*, *Globe* and *Petit journal*

BIBLIOGRAPHY
FétisB
A. Ménetrat: 'Lajarte, Théodore-Edouard Dufaure de', *MGG* [with list of works]
                                        ELISABETH LEBEAU

Lajeunesse, Emma. *See* ALBANI, EMMA.

Lajovic, Anton (*b* Vače, Slovenia, 19 Dec 1878; *d* Ljubljana, 28 Aug 1960). Yugoslav composer. After studies at the Ljubljana Glasbena Matica music school, he was a composition pupil of Fuchs at the Vienna Conservatory (1897–1902), concurrently completing his training in law at the university. He worked as a judge in Slovenia and Croatia and was a member of the Slovene Academy of Arts and Sciences. At first influenced by Romanticism and impressionism, he later became a champion of new developments in Slovene music; his greatest contribution was in the field of vocal composition.

WORKS
(selective list)
Orch: Adagio, 1900; Andante, 1901; Capriccio, 1901; Caprice, 1922; Pesem jeseni [Autumn song], sym. poem, 1938
Vocal: Gozdna samota [Forest solitude], cantata, 1902; Album samospevov [Song album] (1956); other songs, choruses
Pf: Sanjarija [Rêverie], pf, 1900
Principal publisher: Edicize DSS

BIBLIOGRAPHY
L. M. Škerjanc: *Anton Lajovic* (Ljubljana, 1958)
                                        ANDREJ RIJAVEC

Lajtha, László (*b* Budapest, 30 June 1892; *d* Budapest, 16 Feb 1963). Hungarian composer, ethnomusicologist and conductor.

1. LIFE. He studied at the Academy of Music in Budapest under Victor Herzfeld (composition) and Árpád Szendy (pianoforte), and concurrently read law at the university, where he obtained a degree in 1913. In 1910 he became associated with the folk music movement of Bartók and Kodály and joined their collecting expeditions, which he continued independently and in the company of folklorists. On his early travels he visited Leipzig (1910), Geneva (1910–11) and Paris (1911–13), where his becoming acquainted with some of the leading musicians contributed to the widening of his experience and outlook. In 1913 he joined the staff of the ethnographical department of the Hungarian National Museum. His travels were interrupted in August 1914, when he returned to Hungary and joined the services. After the war, in 1919, he was appointed professor of composition and chamber music, subsequently also of aesthetics and theory of Magyar music, at the National Conservatory in Budapest, of

which he became honorary director after World War II and where he remained until the institute ceased to function in 1949.

In 1926 Lajtha became choirmaster of the Goudimel Choir attached to the Budapest congregation of the Calvinist church. In 1929 he won the Coolidge Prize for his Third String Quartet; from 1930 he was the musician for the Institute of Intellectual Co-operation, a League of Nations organization; and in 1932 he was appointed director of the music section of the Commission Internationale des Arts et Traditions Populaires (CIATP). He organized a chamber orchestra in 1941 and conducted its performances until 1944. After the end of hostilities he was appointed director of the music department in the Hungarian Broadcasting Service in 1945.

In the years between the wars Lajtha travelled widely in Europe, appearing frequently in Paris, the place of his most important successes. In 1947, when the CIATP held its first postwar meeting in Paris, he took part in the deliberations which resulted in the setting up of the International Folk Music Council. In the same year he visited London, where he finished his important Third Symphony and Variations for orchestra. In 1951 he was awarded the Kossuth Prize in recognition of his work on Hungarian folk music. The following year he was appointed professor and supervisor of musical folklore researches by the Budapest Academy of Music. In 1955 he became the first Hungarian to be elected a corresponding member of the Institut de France.

2. WORKS. In many respects Lajtha occupied a unique position among Hungarian composers. Like Bartók and Kodály he was not only acknowledged as a composer of distinction, but also recognized as an authority on folk music; further, again like Bartók and Kodály, his activities were not confined to creative and scientific work, but also included teaching. His main distinguishing characteristic, however, was his attachment to French, and generally to Latin, culture in sensibility and taste. In this he was one of the few nonconformists of Hungarian music history, most of whose development was affected by German influences. Superior workmanship is the most prominent and consistent feature of his music; and the principle that 'in all works of art the quality of craftsmanship is a decisive factor of evaluation' always guided his artistic consideration.

Regarding the Hungarian accent, the influence of Magyar folk music is less obvious in his works than in those of Bartók and Kodály, chiefly because Lajtha was attracted by another aspect of the traditional materials: it was their melodic shape and form, viewed primarily as an objective musical element regardless of their peculiarly national characteristics, that inspired him. This conception admitted a considerable stylistic freedom of treatment: thus the Magyar flavour succeeded in permeating equally his Italianized passages (e.g. the slow movement of the Sonatina for violin and piano and the 'Aria' from the Cello Sonata), his sectional forms (couplets, rondeaux etc) modelled on classical French prototypes, dance movements and contrapuntal textures (fugues). It also permitted him to resort to popular tunes, some of which are not strictly folktunes, often assuming the understanding of an allusive quotation, and to subject them to 'Western' treatment, i.e. elaborate harmonization and contrapuntal development (especially in the Serenade for string trio and the Sinfonietta for string orchestra). Here there is an unexpected affinity with 19th-century Romantic Hungarian composers, who also availed themselves of popular tunes and treated them in Western (mainly German) fashion, and whose style and endeavours were vehemently rejected by the generation immediately following, to which Lajtha himself belonged.

These stylistic mainstays kept in view, a survey of Lajtha's music reveals an almost unbroken continuity of development, in the early phases of which the harmonic aspects are stressed, giving place, during subsequent stages, to predominantly contrapuntal treatment and arriving at an equilibrium of craftsmanship and invention of exceptional clarity and directness. Seen from another standpoint, Lajtha's development may be characterized as a gradual assertion of melody.

The harmonic style of Lajtha's early works shows a complex idiom derived from the experimental tendencies of the first decade of the 20th century: superimposed 4ths, appoggiaturas and suspensions and other dissonant aggregates furnish the basis of chordal structure whose progression is predominantly chromatic. These are evident in his early piano works, where the specific influences of Bartók and Debussy are also discernible; in addition the part-writing of his Piano Sonata, apart from its considerable harmonic complexities, is conceived in the grand virtuoso manner of Liszt. In his subsequent works, where the contrapuntal aspect gradually gained prominence, his harmony, though not relinquishing the advanced vocabulary, is subordinated to the horizontal elements. Discords are more purposefully used, and their tension values consequently become increased. Emergence of counterpoint also led to a preoccupation with chamber combinations during a period which may be said to have started, approximately, with the years following World War I and lasted up to about the mid-1930s. The most typical works, with the points previously mentioned well in evidence, are the Third and Fourth Quartets, the Second String Trio and the Fifth Quartet, which indicates a transition to his subsequent creative period. This was characterized, as far as harmony is concerned, by a return to a chordal structure of diatonic purity, in which Lajtha rediscovered the far from exhausted potentialities of the common chord. The new harmonic conception is evident in the extended D major passages of the Capriccio and the sustained E♭ of his Third Symphony. Nevertheless, Lajtha's was fundamentally a contrapuntal temperament. Even in his early works contrapuntal passages appear frequently, and their neatness and competence of treatment, although embryonic, provide a curious contrast to his harmonic extravagance.

In Lajtha's second period horizontal elements dominate, manifesting themselves above all in the frequency of complete fugues expanding into independent movements, prolonged fugal and imitative passages, and of canonic treatment. The contrapuntal aspect is also evident in his particular treatment of figuration; though obviously instrumental in character, his invention shows a conspicuous melodic shapeliness. The primacy of horizontal values in these works also appears in the contrapuntally conditioned harmony derived from the interplay of the various polyphonic strains. In the earlier works of this period the resulting harmony is often bitonal or polytonal (e.g. the chamber music with piano, in which this treatment is particularly advantageous owing to the differentiation of colour). In later works his return to a simplified harmonic basis resulted in a more euphonious texture, as in the chamber music with harp,

the Capriccio and the Third String Trio. The vitality of his counterpoint gains a great deal from the energy of his rhythmic drive: derived from folk music impulses, Lajtha's symphonic music absorbed this element into a 'civilized' musical speech much more readily than did Bartók's or Kodály's.

In Lajtha's next period the assertion of melodic values was his main concern. Seeking to display them in a suitable formal disposition prompted him to investigate the designs of Italian and French 17th- and 18th-century composers; the titles of many of his movements – 'Aria', 'Strophes et ritournelles' etc – indicate this attitude. The conspicuous simplification of musical grammar, concurrently with and in consequence of a superior technical accomplishment, produces in these works an equilibrium between transparency of expression and range of emotional sensibility, between technique and inspiration: a classical art in the truest sense of the word (see the symphonies, especially the Third, the Sinfonietta for strings, the Third String Trio and the Second Quartet for harp, violin, viola and cello).

Lajtha's folk music investigation included the collecting of melodies from those districts which were left largely untouched by Bartók and Kodály. These explorations yielded many variants of the previously collected material which, together with not a few hitherto unknown tunes, supplemented the work of the two pioneers. Lajtha took a considerable share in the work conducted in the Ethnographical Museum of transcribing melodies from recordings: he was engaged in this almost continuously from the time of his joining the society. As a delegate of the Hungarian Ethnographical Society he took an active part in the gramophone recording scheme undertaken jointly by the society and the Hungarian Broadcasting Station in 1937. Among his numerous collecting expeditions those in the 1930s (Great Hungarian Plain and adjoining districts) and during the years 1940 to 1944 (Transylvania) were the most important. The latter resulted in a particularly rich harvest: a representative selection of it was published in a Transylvanian periodical and an important part, whose evaluation may considerably modify the current view concerning the origin and development of Magyar music, was prepared for publication in 1950. He was the editor of the series Népzenei monográfiák, in which appeared his most important ethnomusicological publications (1954–62). In the years 1958 to 1960 he gave several ethnomusicological lectures in Paris, London and Scandinavia.

Lajtha's interest in folk music led him to investigate other, related manifestations of folk art: he was a leading authority on folkdance. He also served the cause of folk music by taking part in many conferences and joining the international organizations. He participated, together with Bartók, in the first International Congress of Folk Art, held in Prague in 1928, at which their suggestions resulted in the adoption of a number of far-reaching resolutions.

As a teacher Lajtha exercised an influence necessarily less than that of the professors at the academy; yet in encouraging his pupils to study the Latin musical culture he did a great service to the indigenous development of a healthy musical life. Being a professor of theory and practice of Hungarian music, he was the first to introduce folk music into the ordinary curriculum, based partly on Bartók's book and partly on practical exercises in the Ethnographical Museum. In his composition class he insisted on the investigation of modern, especially French music. In general he did not attach great importance to an academic, prescribed course of study, but relied on the intellectual curiosity of his students, which he stimulated with his sharp-witted conversation and by allowing free discussion of controversial points.

WORKS

DRAMATIC

op.
19 Lysistrata (ballet, 1), 1933
21 Hortobágy (film score), 1935
38 Le bosquet des quatre dieux (ballet, 1), 1943
39 Capriccio (ballet, 1), 1944
44 Murder in the Cathedral (film score, Eliot), 1948
48 Shapes and Forms (film score), 1949, unpubd
51 Le chapeau bleu (opéra bouffe, 2, S. de Madariaga), 1950
—   Kövek, várak, emberek [Stones, castles, men] (film score), 1956

ORCHESTRAL

15 Violin Concerto, 1931, unpubd, lost
19a Overture and Suite, from Lysistrata, 1933
21a Suite, from Hortobágy, 1935
24 Symphony no.1, 1936
25 Divertissement, 1936
27 Symphony no.2, 1938
30 Divertissement no.2, 1939, unpubd, lost
31 Cello Concerto, 1940
33 Les soli, sym., str, harp, perc, 1941
35 In memoriam, sym. poem, 1941
37 Evasion fuite liberté, sym. poem, 1942, lost
38a Suite du ballet no.2, from Le bosquet des quatre dieux, 1943
39a Suite, from Capriccio, 1944
43 Sinfonietta, str, 1946
44 Variations, 1947, unpubd
45 Symphony no.3, 1948
48 Shapes and Forms, small orch, 1949, unpubd, lost
52 Symphony no.4 'Le printemps', 1951
55 Symphony no.5, 1952
56 Suite no.3, 1952
61 Symphony no.6, 1955
62 Sinfonietta no.2, str, 1956
63 Symphony no.7, 1957
66 Symphony no.8, 1959
67 Symphony no.9, 1961

CHORAL

16 Deux choeurs (L. Áprily), unacc., 1932: A hegylakók [The mountaineers], Esti párabeszéd [Nocturnal dialogue]
23 Deux choeurs (d'Orléans), unacc., 1936: Chanson, Rondel
29 Trois madrigaux (d'Orléans), unacc., 1939
32 Par ou est passé le chant (Áprily), unacc., 1940
50 Missa in tono phrygio, chorus, orch, 1950
54 Mass, chorus, org, 1952
60 Magnificat, female vv, org, 1954
65 Trois hymnes pour la Ste Vierge, female vv, org, 1958

SOLO VOCAL

8   Motet, 1v, pf/org, 1926
—   Vocalise étude, 1v, pf, 1930
34 Trois nocturnes, S, fl, harp, str qt, 1941
—   Ballade et chant des recruteurs, Bar, pf/orch, 1951

CHAMBER AND INSTRUMENTAL

3   String Sextet, 1921, unpubd, lost
4   Piano Quintet, 1922, unpubd
5   String Quartet no.1, 1922, unpubd
6   Piano Quartet, 1925, unpubd
7   String Quartet no.2, 1926, unpubd
9   String Trio no.1 (Sérénade), 1927, unpubd
10 Piano Trio, 1928, unpubd
11 String Quartet no.3, 1929
12 String Quartet no.4, 1930
13 Sonatina, vn, pf, 1930
17 Sonata, vc, pf, 1932
18 String Trio no.2, 1932
20 String Quartet no.5 (Cinq études), 1934
22 Trio no.1, harp, fl, vc, 1935
26 Marionettes, harp, fl, str trio, 1937
28 Sonata, vn, pf, 1939, unpubd, lost
36 String Quartet no.6 (Quatre études), 1942, unpubd
40 Serenade, wind trio, 1944, lost
41 String Trio no.3 'Soirs transylvains', 1945
42 Quatre hommages, fl, ob, cl, bn, 1946
47 Trio no.2, harp, fl, vc, 1949
49 String Quartet no.7, 1950
53 String Quartet no.8, 1951
57 String Quartet no.9, 1953
58 String Quartet no.10 (Suite transylvaine), 1953
59 Intermezzo, sax, pf, 1954
64 Sonate en concert, fl, pf, 1958
—   Deux pièces, fl, 1958
68 Sonate en concert, vn, pf, 1962

PIANO

1   Des écrits d'un musicien, 1913
2   Contes, 1915; also Contes II, 1917, unpubd, lost
—   Sonata, 1916
—   Prélude, 1918
14 Scherzo et toccata, 1930, unpubd
—   Trois berceuses, 1955–7

Principal publishers: Leduc, Universal

FOLKSONG COLLECTIONS

Szépkenyerüszentmártoni gyüjtés [Collection from Szépkenyerüszentmárton], Népzenei monográfiák, i (Budapest, 1954)
Széki gyüjtés [Collection from Szék], Népzenei monográfiák, ii (Budapest, 1954)
Kőrispataki gyüjtés [Collection from Kőrispatak], Népzenei monográfiák, iii (Budapest, 1954)
Sopronmegyei virrasztó énekek [Vigil songs of Sopron county], Népzenei monográfiák, iv (Budapest, 1956)
Dunántuli táncok és dallamok [Transdanubian dances and melodies], Népzenei monográfiák, v (Budapest, 1962–)
Numerous articles; for list see Volly (1967)

BIBLIOGRAPHY

O. Gombosi: 'Ladislas Lajtha', *Melos*, viii (1929), 231
Laszlo Lajtha (Paris, 1954)
Laszlo Lajtha: quelques oeuvres (Paris, 1961)
I. Volly: 'Lajtha László zenetudományos munkássága' [Lajtha's musicological works], *Magyar zene*, viii (1967), 65; Fr. trans., *Etudes finno-ougriennes*, v (1968), 14
H. Barraud and others: 'Hommage à László Lajtha', *Etudes finno-ougriennes*, v (1968) [special issue]
M. Berlász: 'En souvenir de László Lajtha', *SM*, xiv (1972), 11
J. S. Weissmann: 'László Lajtha: the Symphonies', *MR*, xxxvi (1975), 197

JOHN S. WEISSMANN/MELINDA BERLÁSZ

Lakatos, István [Ştefan] (*b* Zorlenţul-Mare, Caraş-Severin region, 26 Feb 1895). Romanian musicologist of Hungarian descent. He studied music in Cluj and Budapest, taking his doctorate at Cluj in 1946 with a dissertation on the Romanian folksong and its literature. He taught the violin at the Romanian Conservatory, Cluj (1919–23), and founded the active Lakatos Quartet (1920–40); he also taught music history at the Gheorghe Dima Conservatory, Cluj (1949–63). Concurrently he became known as a musicologist and music critic, writing for Hungarian journals published in Romania and in foreign periodicals; in particular he has written on the music history of Transylvania (he has a thorough knowledge of its documentary sources) and on Romanian–Magyar relations. He has delivered papers abroad (Hungary, Poland, Czechoslovakia), on the interrelation of Romanian musical culture and that of neighbouring peoples. His publications are largely of documentary material, particularly of letters by Prokofiev, Bartók, Berg, Richard Strauss and others.

WRITINGS

'Magyaros elemek Brahms zenéjében' [The Hungarian element in Brahms's music], *Erdélyi tudományos füzetek* (Cluj, 1935), no.73
'A román zene fejlődéstörténete' [The history of Romanian music], *Erdélyi tudományos füzetek* (Cluj, 1938), no.98
'A román népdal és irodalma' [Romanian folksong and its literature], *Apolló könyvtár* (Budapest, 1939), no.10
ed.: *Egy erdélyi muzsikus vallomásai: Ruzitska György emlékezései 1856 évből* [Ruzitska's memoirs from 1856] (Cluj, 1940–44)
Bibliografia az 1919–1940 között erdélyi szerzőtől önállóan megjelent magyar zenei vonatkozású munkákról [Bibliography of music 1919–40, published in Transylvania in Hungarian] (Kecskemét, 1943)
Cîntecul popular românesc şi literatura sa [Romanian folksong and its literature] (diss., U. of Cluj, 1946)
with V. Cosma: 'Erkel Ferenc élete és munkássága, mint összekötőkapocs a magyar és román zenekultura között' [Erkel's life and work in the relations between Hungarian and Romanian music cultures], *Zenetudományi tanulmányok*, ii (1952), 17
'Kolozsvári Liszt emlékek' [Memories of Liszt in Kolozsvár], *Zenetudományi tanulmányok*, iii (1955), 101

with G. Merişescu: *Legături muzicale româno-maghiare de-a lungul veacurior* (Cluj, 1957)
'Alte tschechische Musikalien in der Bibliothek der Musikhochschule von Klausenburg', *SM*, vi (1964), 143
'Enescu budapesti hangversenyei' [Enescu's concerts in Budapest], *Magyar zene*, vi (1965), 227
'Instrumente muzicale ale vechi Muzeului de Istorie Cluj' [Old musical instruments in the historical museum in Cluj], *Acta musei napocensis*, iii (Cluj, 1966), 257; Ger. trans. in *SM*, xv (1973), 336
'Deux lettres de Prokofieff', *SM*, x (1968), 163
'Ein unbekannter Alban Berg-Brief', *SM*, xii (1970), 319; also in *Melos*, xxxviii (1971), 412
'Jiří Růžička: moravský hudebník v Rumunsku' [Georg Ruzitska: Moravian composer in Romania], *OM*, iii (1971), 114
Zenetörténeti irások [Studies in music history] (Bucharest, 1971)
'Kodály művészetének romániai útja' [Kodály's music in Romania], *Magyar zene*, xiii (1972), 373; xiv (1973), 24
with A. Benkő and I. Almási: Preface to *Seprődi János válogatott zenei irásai és népzenei gyűjtése* [Seprődi's selected writings on music and his folksong collections], ed. A. Benkő (Bucharest, 1974)
A kolozsvári zenés szinpad (1792–1973) [Music-theatre in Cluj/Kolozsvár 1792–1973] (Bucharest, 1977)

BIBLIOGRAPHY

V. Cosma: *Muzicieni români* (Bucharest, 1970), 272
A. Benkő: 'Lakatos István zenei bibliográfiája (1911–1969)' [Lakatos's music bibliography 1911–69], in I. Lakatos: *Zenetörténeti irások* (Bucharest, 1971), 245–90

VIOREL COSMA

Lake George Opera Festival. A summer season of opera in English, founded in 1962 and held at Lake George, New York; the singers are drawn from American opera companies and the musicians from the Albany SO and the Syracuse SO. Workshops and courses are held in cooperation with the State University of New York. The director of the festival, since its inception, is the tenor and opera administrator David Lloyd.

RITA H. MEAD

Lākhumārā. A category of chant in the Assyrian rite; *see* SYRIAN CHURCH MUSIC.

Lakner, Yehoshua (*b* Bratislava, 24 April 1924). Israeli composer. In 1941 he settled in Palestine, where he studied composition with Partos and Boskovich, and the piano with Pelleg. After graduating from the Tel-Aviv Academy he spent the year 1952 in the USA, studying with Copland at Tanglewood. A scholarship from the Anna Frank Foundation (1959–60) enabled him to study electronic music at the West German Radio studios in Cologne with Stockhausen, Koenig and Kagel, and to work under Zimmermann at the Cologne Musikhochschule. He also attended the Darmstadt summer courses in 1959, 1960 and 1965. In 1963 he moved to Zurich, working as a teacher and restricting his composition almost exclusively to electronic music for plays, notably for the world première of Brecht's *Turandot* at the Zurich Schauspielhaus (1969). His work for the theatre gained him an award from the city of Zurich in 1970. He has also produced music for television and films, including that for *Swiss Time* for Expo 67 in Montreal. Most of Lakner's works incorporate intervals, harmonies or, more particularly, rhythms characteristic of jazz.

WORKS
(selective list)

Sonata, fl, pf, 1948; T'nu'a b'fa [Movt in F], pf, 1950; Sextet, wind, pf, 1951; Iltur [Improvisations], va, 1952; Toccata, orch, 1953; Dances, cl, pf, perc, 1956; Hexachords, orch, 1960; D'muyot [Figures], ballet, 1962; 5 Birthdays, pf, 1965; Dream of Mohamed, chorus, tape, 1968; Rabbits, speaker, perc, 2 tapes, 1973
Music for the theatre, cinema and television

Principal publishers: Israel Music Institute, Israeli Music Publications

WRITINGS
'A New Method Representing Tonal Relations', *JMT*, iv (1960), 194

BIBLIOGRAPHY
A. L. Ringer: 'Musical Composition in Israel', *MQ*, li (1965), 282
Y. W. Cohen: *Werden und Entwicklung der Musik in Israel* (Kassel, 1976) [pt.ii of rev. edn. of M. Brod: *Die Musik Israels*]
W. Y. Elias: *The Music of Israel* (in preparation) [bibliography]

WILLIAM Y. ELIAS

Laks, Szymon (*b* Warsaw, 1 Nov 1901). Polish composer. He studied mathematics for two years at Vilnius University before entering the Warsaw Conservatory, where he studied under Statkowski, Melcer and Rytel (1921–4). In 1926 he went to Paris to study with Vidal and Rabaud at the Conservatory. Arrested by the Germans in 1941, he spent three years in the concentration camps of Oświęcim and Dachau. A large quantity of his MSS was lost during the war. In 1945 he returned to Paris, promoting music in Polish émigré circles. The best of his work is in the deeply lyrical vocal music, concentrated in expression and simple in language. Many of his pieces are based on Polish folk music.

WORKS
(selective list)

Stage: L'hirondelle inattendue (opera buffa, 1, C. Aveline), 1965
Orch: Farys, sym. poem, 1924; Sym., C, 1924; Scherzo, 1925; Sinfonietta, str, 1936; 3 Warsaw Polonaises, 1947; Sym., str, 1964
Chamber: 5 str qts, 1928, 1932, 1946, 1962, 1964; Sonata, vc, pf, 1932; Polish Suite, vn, pf, 1935; Pf Trio, 1950; Conc. da camera, pf, 9 wind, perc, 1963; Dialogue, 2 vc, 1964; Concertino, wind trio, 1965; Pf Qnt on Polish Folk Themes, 1967; Suite concertante, trbn, pf, 1969; Chorale, 4 trbn, 1973
Kbd: Sonate brève, hpd, 1947; Suite dans le goût ancien, pf, 1973
Songs: 3 Songs (J. Tuwim), 1938; Passacaille-vocalise, 1946; 8 Jewish Songs, 1947; 3 Songs (W. M. Berezowska), 1960; Elegia ż ydowskich miasteczek [Elegy of the Jewish country town] (A. Słoniński), 1961; Songs (Tuwim, J. Iwaszkiewicz, M. Jastrun), 1961–3; Portrait de l'oiseau-qui-n'existe-pas (Aveline), 1964; 5 Melodies (Tuwim), 1968

TERESA CHYLINSKA

Lal, Chatur (*b* Udaipur, Rajasthan, 23 Jan 1925; *d* Delhi, 14 Nov 1965). Indian *tablā* player. His father was a well-known musician and he began his musical training when he was seven, studying first under Pandit Nathu Lalji and later with Ustad Hafiz Mian of Udaipur. In 1947 he joined All-India Radio, remaining on its staff as an accompanist and soloist until his early death. Even as a young man he accompanied some of the leading musicians of the time, particularly Ravi Shankar. In 1954 he toured the USA and Europe with Ustad Ali Akbar Khan, and he accompanied Ravi Shankar during his tour of the USA and Europe (1956) and two subsequent extensive tours; he also performed in the USSR, Australia and Romania. Besides accompanying noted musicians in their recordings, he made several records as a soloist.

NARAYANA MENON

Lalande, Desiré Alfred (*b* Paris, 5 Sept 1866; *d* London, 8 Nov 1904). French oboist. After two and a half years at the Paris Conservatoire under Georges Gillet, Lalande's first professional engagement was with Lamoureux. He came to England in 1886 to join the Hallé (in which his father was a bassoonist) where he remained for five years. After a period with the Scottish Orchestra he joined the Queen's Hall Orchestra. In 1897 Henry Wood appointed him first oboist for the third season of the Promenade Concerts in succession to Malsch.

The delicacy and refinement of Lalande's performance did much to foster appreciation of the French school of oboe playing in England at a period when in many areas German artists were predominant. Many regarded him as the finest oboist of his time in Britain. The beauty of his tone was remarkable, particularly in solos for english horn.

PHILIP BATE

Lalande [La Lande, de La Lande, Delalande], **Michel-Richard de** (*b* Paris, 15 Dec 1657; *d* Versailles, 18 June 1726). French composer, organist and harpsichordist, the leading composer of the late Baroque *grand motet*.

1. LIFE. Lalande was the 15th child of Michel Lalande, a master tailor, and Claude Dumourtiers. Most information about his early life comes from scattered notarial documents, church registers and the anecdotal preface (presumably written by Claude Tannevot) to the posthumous edition of his 40 *grands motets*.

About 1666, Lalande entered the choir of the royal church of St Germain-l'Auxerrois in Paris, where he remained until his voice changed at the age of 15. François Chaperon directed the choir, of which Marin Marais was a member. Nothing is known of Lalande's formal musical training. Tannevot related that he preferred the violin of the instruments he cultivated in his youth, but that when he was rejected by Lully for the opera orchestra he 'renounced the violin forever'. He mastered both harpsichord and organ, perhaps studying the latter with Charles Damour, organist at St Germain-l'Auxerrois. The Maréchal de Noailles, who had employed him as a harpsichord teacher for his daughter, recommended that Louis XIV should do likewise for his two daughters by Mme de Montespan, Louise-Françoise (Mlle de Nantes) and Françoise-Marie (Mlle de Blois). Tannevot said that Lalande played the organ for the king at St Germain-en-Laye but that Louis XIV thought him too young to be appointed an *organiste du roy*.

His skill as an organist was sufficient to gain him employment in four Paris churches: St Louis, where he also composed *intermèdes* and choruses (lost) for the dramatic productions of the Jesuits; the conventual church of Petit St Antoine; St Gervais where, following the death of Charles Couperin (1679), he was contracted to remain until Couperin's eldest son, François, was 18 (1686); and St Jean-en-Grève, where in 1682 he replaced Pierre Meliton until the increasing responsibilities of his court position forced his resignation in 1691.

In 1683, after Du Mont and Robert retired from the royal chapel, the king ordered a competition to be held for the four positions of *sous-maîtres* for his chapel. 35 musicians competed, and four were chosen to share the responsibility by quarters: Coupillet (January), Collasse (April), Minoret (July) and Lalande (October). According to Tannevot, Louis XIV himself intervened to assure a quarter for Lalande, thus initiating his rise as a favoured court composer. Although Tannevot described his being 'shy in public', this seems to have been no deterrent to Lalande's accumulation of most of the official positions available to a court musician. In September 1693, after the enforced retirement of Coupillet, he added the January quarter to that of October; in March 1704, on the retirement of Collasse, the king gave the April quarter to 'nostre bien amé Richard Michel de La Lande'; and after Minoret stepped down in 1714, Lalande was in total control of the royal chapel.

In January 1685 he was appointed *compositeur de la musique de la chambre*, sharing half the year with Collasse, the other half of the year being controlled by Pierre Robert. In 1700, after Robert's death, Lalande was given three-quarter control, and following Collasse's death in 1709 all charges of *compositeur de la musique* were his. In January 1689 he was appointed *surintendant de la musique de la chambre*, replacing Jean-Louis de Lully and sharing the year with Jean-Baptiste Boësset. In 1695 he became *maître de musique de la chambre*.

On 7 July 1684 Lalande married the singer Anne Rebel, daughter of Jean Rebel, *ordinaire de la musique du roy* and sister of Jean-Féry Rebel, the violinist, conductor and director of the opera. The couple had two daughters, Marie-Anne (*b* 1686) and Jeanne (*b* 1687), both of whom became well-known singers; they were rewarded for their artistry by Louis XIV, who in 1706 gave each a pension of 1000 livres. Unfortunately, both succumbed to smallpox in 1711. Lalande was not alone in his bereavement; a few months later (18 April 1712), at the request of the king, he conducted 129 musicians of the royal chapel in a memorial service for the dauphin and his wife at St-Denis.

Lalande lived comfortably as a result of royal appointments and lucrative pensions which included one of 6000 livres paid to him and his wife from the revenues of the Paris Opéra (1713). He was one of the few composers of his day to own a coach. In addition to a Paris house in the Palais-Royal quarter, he had an apartment in the Grand Commun at Versailles and a large country house in the Parc-aux-Cerfs.

After the king's death in 1715, Lalande gradually

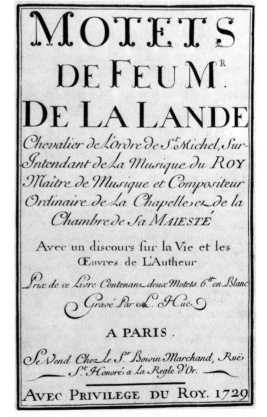

1. Title-page of Lalande's 'Motets', i (1729)

2. Michel-Richard de Lalande: engraving by Simon Henri Thomassin after Santerre

abandoned his heavy responsibilities at Versailles. In doing so he made sure that his best pupils, André-Cardinal Destouches, Collin de Blamont and Jean-François de La Porte received good positions. In February 1718 Destouches took over one of the charges of *surintendant*. He was succeeded in the same post by Collin de Blamont in November 1719. In March 1718, Làlande's brother-in-law, Jean-Féry Rebel, and La Porte succeeded him as *compositeur de la musique de la chambre*.

On 5 May 1722, Lalande's wife died. Soon afterwards Louis XV made him a Chevalier of the Order of St Michel. Late the same year, Lalande expressed his desire to remit voluntarily three-quarters of his salary at the royal chapel in order to return to the original situation of four *sous-maîtres*. Touched by the composer's request, Louis XV agreed and in January 1723 granted him an annual life pension of 3000 livres. A new generation of composers, protégés of the regent, Philip of Orleans, were quickly chosen for the three vacancies (André Campra, Nicolas Bernier, Charles-Hubert Gervais).

Lalande remarried in 1723; his bride was Marie-Louise de Cury (1692–1775), a daughter of the surgeon of the Princess of Conti. They had one daughter, Marie-Michelle (1724–81). According to Tannevot, Lalande died of pneumonia in 1726. He was buried in the church of Notre Dame de Versailles, not far from the château where he had served for 43 years.

2. WORKS. Most of Lalande's secular music was written between 1682 and 1700. Ballets, divertissements and pastorales entertained the royalty at Versailles, Marly, Fontainebleau and Sceaux. His *Ballet de la jeunesse* (1686) was an important precursor of the *opéra-ballet*. Its long poem is divided into three episodes devoted to Mercury, Pallas and Tircis respectively. The music is rich in *symphonies*, *airs*, choruses and dances. The 'Chaconne de la jeunesse' at the centre of the work, with a total of 61 variations, is specially noteworthy; the theme and 28 variations are instrumental, and the remaining music is for vocal solo, ensemble and chorus. (For illustration see DANCE, fig.13.)

Lalande extracted, and subtly varied, parts of his ballets and divertissements for use in his popular

Symphonies 'performed every 15 days during the supper of Louis XIV and Louis XV'. The copy of the *Symphonies* made in 1745 is a true manuscript *de luxe*. This collection, though based on earlier copies (1703, 1727), carefully 'orders' the suites by key (interior movements, however, are often in related keys) and numbers the supper for which each suite was performed. Suites 6 to 8 are entitled 'Caprices' or 'Caprices ou Fantaisies', and are free orchestral pieces unrelated to the dance. Suite 7, 'which the king often asked for', is in five movements designated only by tempo indications which move from slow to fast. It is imaginatively scored as an orchestral 'quartet' for violins, violas, bassoons and a continuo ('figured by M. Rebel'). The final Caprice (Suite 8) includes a fine set of free variations in concerto scoring. Contrary to normal procedures, its *tous* sections rather than its solo sections increase in complexity. Following the suites in volume i of this collection are the *Symphonies des Noëls*, settings of traditional French carol melodies, 'which were played in the king's chapel on Christmas night'.

The 'Versailles style', initiated by Veillot and Formé and nurtured by Du Mont, Lully and Robert, reached full flower in over 70 *grands motets* composed by Lalande for the royal chapel. During the 18th century they were considered to be 'masterpieces of the genre' (Rousseau). Their eloquent message touched both the favoured few who attended the king's Mass and, after 1725, the crowds who applauded them at the Concert Spirituel. Far from representing what Bukofzer called 'the most conservative spirit of the period' (*Music in the Baroque Era*, New York, 1947), they bring together totally dissimilar elements with an unprecedented depth of feeling. *Galant* 'operatic' *airs* and the pompous 'official' style of the Versailles motet stand side by side. Cantus firmus treatment of Gregorian melodies in finely wrought polyphony is found together with

Ex. 1(a) First version (after Philidor copy, *F-V*)

(b) Second version (after 1729 edn.)

Ex.2 Extract from *Pange lingua* (after 1729 edn.)   silence

weighty homophonic 'battle' choruses worthy of Lully's *Bellérophon*. Lalande was deeply imbued with the spirit of the Latin psalms he chose. The warmth of his musical language humanized the *grand motet*; for this he was dubbed the 'Latin Lully' (Collin de Blamont).

Three large collections contain most of Lalande's motets: Philidor's manuscript copy of 27 motets, made in 1689 and 1690; the 1729 printed edition of 40 motets; and the manuscript copy of 41 motets made for (or by) a Gaspard Alexis Cauvin. The Cauvin manuscript is a mid-18th-century copy, partly based on the 1729 edition and partly on earlier copies, with a changed sequence of motets and the addition of the instrumental inner parts which are missing from the printed edition. A comparison of the same motets found in the collections above gives an insight into Lalande's stylistic development and bears out Tannevot's comment that 'from the time of the former king [Louis XIV], he began to make changes in several of his earlier motets'.

These changes came partly from his increased maturity as a composer and partly from his wish to conform to the change in taste evident in the closing years of Louis XIV's reign. In general, they take the following forms: (1) the change from a loosely organized structure with elided sectional divisions to autonomous movements (solos and ensembles interspersed between choruses) that resemble the German cantata at the time of Bach; (2) the creation out of simple *récits* of elaborate concert arias or duets, often accompanied by obbligato instruments; (3) the changing of predominantly homophonic choruses into more polyphonic ones; (4) the change from an orchestra primarily doubling choral lines to one independent of the voices; and (5) greater economy in the use of some material while other material is expanded.

The 'Requiem aeternam' from the *De profundis* is a fine example of the fifth category. The Philidor version includes a *symphonie* of 14 bars, a solo *récit* of 8 bars, a second *symphonie* of 6 bars and a basically homophonic chorus of 31 bars up to the 'Et lux perpetua' (ex.1*a*). In the 1729 edition there is only one *symphonie*, of 9 bars, which merges with a 53-bar chorus up to 'Et lux perpetua'. The writing is dense, five-part polyphony of Bach-like intensity in which both instruments and voices participate (ex.1*b*).

Lalande's use of counterpoint, both melodic and rhythmic, is not pedantic. A favourite device is to present two independent motifs in the opening *symphonie* and then to combine them in a large fugal chorus (see, for example, 'Hostem repellas longius', from the *Veni Creator Spiritus*). Lalande's harmony may owe something to his exposure to the music of Charpentier and to the Italian motets he inherited as a young man from Abbé Mathieu, *curé* of St André-des-Arts. The dissonant chord of the mediant 9th with major 7th and augmented 5th, found in the music of Charpentier, is no stranger to the motets of his younger contemporary (ex. 2, bars 2 and 7). Lalande, like Rameau, found the diminished 7th chord compellingly dramatic. In ex.2, from the *Pange lingua*, his coupling this chord with an indicated 'silence' shows the care with which he chose the most effective musical setting for the text.

In the *Avertissement* to the 1729 edition, Collin de Blamont best summed up his teacher's style:

His great merit ... consisted in a wonderful choice of melody, a judicious choice of harmony, and a nobility of expression. ... Profound and learned on the one hand, simple and natural on the other ... the mind is refreshed ... by the ingenious disparities with which he ornaments his works and by the graceful melodies that serve as contrasting episodes to the most complex choral sections.

WORKS

GRANDS MOTETS

P – Motets de M. Delalande . . ., MS copied by Philidor in 1689–90, 27 motets in 10 vols., *F-V*

H – Motets de feu De La Lande ... avec un discours sur la vie et les oeuvres de l'autheur, gravé par L. Hue (Paris, 1729–33), 40 motets and shorter works in 21 vols.; lacks instrumental inner parts

C – Gaspard Alexis Cauvin's collection, MS of mid-18th century, 41 motets and shorter works in 21 vols.; i–xx, *F-V*; xxi, *Pn*

T – 9 motets in score, and (with 2 others) in partbooks, copied by Philidor in 1704 and 1706, formerly *GB-T* (now in *F-Pn* or *V*)

S – 5 motets and shorter works in Motets Delalande, To.9, M. R. Lutz's private collection, Strasbourg

Volume or MS number in parentheses

Ad te Domine clamabo, 1703, H(12), C(8)
Ad te levavi oculos, c1689, P(9)
Afferte Domino, 1683, P(6)
Audite coeli, 1689, P(5)
Beati omnes, 1698, H(6), C(18); ed. Letocart (Paris, 1928)
Beati quorum, 1683, P(2); extract: Loetamini in Domino, ed. Roussel (Sèvres, 1951)
Beatus vir qui timet, 1692, H(19), C(2); ed. Pagot (Paris, 1950)
Benedictus Dominus Deus Israel, 1702, H(18), C(19); ed. Roussel (Paris, 1955)
Benedictus Dominus Deus meus, 1695, H(1), C(7); extracts ed. F. Raugel (Paris, 1951)
Cantate Domino ... quia mirabilia, 1707, H(2), C(1); ed. Roussel (Paris, 1956–7)
Cantate Domino omnis terra, 1698, S
Cantemus Domino, 1687, P(3); ed. K. Husa (New York, 1971)
Christe redemptor, 1690, P(8); ed. Roussel (Paris, 1953)
Confitebimur tibi Deus, 1701, H(9), C(3), T; ed. Cellier (Paris, 1952)
Confitebor tibi Domine in consilio, 1699, H(1), C(4), T
Confitebor tibi Domine quoniam, 1697, H(19), C(7)
Confitemini Domino, 1705, H(7), C(6)
Credidi propter, 1697, H(13), C(13)
Deitatis majestatem, 1682, P(7); extract ed. Roussel (Paris, 1950)
De profundis, 1689, P(6), H(9), C(2), S; ed. Cellier (Paris, 1944), ed. L. Boulay (Paris, c1961)
Deus, Deus meus, 1685, P(9)
Deus in adjutorium, 1689, H(4), C(15); ed. Cellier (Paris, 1958)
Deus misereatur nostri, 1687, P(3)
Deus noster refugium, 1699, H(10), C(13)
Dies irae, 1690, S
Dixit Dominus, 1680, P(4)
Dixit Dominus, 1708, H(5), C(5); ed. Sarlit (Paris, 1950)
Domine in virtute tua, 1689, P(10), H(15), C(17); ed. Roussel (Paris, 1952)
Domine non est exaltatum, 1691 (?1690), P(2)
Dominus regit me, 1695, H(11), C(20)
Dominus regnavit, 1704, H(8), C(5); ed. Chirat (Paris, 1953)
Ecce nunc benedicite, 1686, P(6)
Eructavit cor meum, 1697, S
Exaltabo te Deus meus, 1712, H(10), C(19); ed. Boulay (Paris, 1956)

Exaltabo te Domine, 1704, H(17), C(12), T; extract: Psallite Domino, ed. Roussel (Paris, 1952)
Exaudi Deus, c1689, 1719, P(3), C(8)
Exultate justi in Domino, 1710, H(15), C(15)
Exurgat Deus, 1706, H(14), C(10)
In convertendo, 1684, P(10), H(13), C(17)
Jubilate Deo, 1689, P(8)
Judica me Deus, 1693, H(8), C(9)
Lauda Jerusalem, c1689, 1725, P(10), H(4), C(12)
Laudate Dominum, omnes gentes, 1686, P(7)
Laudate Dominum quoniam, 1700, H(20), C(9), T
Laudate pueri, 1686, P(4)
Magnus Dominus, 1701, (H, 1702), H(20), C(12)
Miserere mei Deus quoniam, 1685, P(7)
Miserere mei Deus secundum, 1687, P(1), H(3), C(4); ed. Letocart (Paris, 1927)
Nisi Dominus, 1694, (H, 1704), H(16), C(20); ed. Boulay (Paris, 1956)
Nisi quia Dominus, 1703, H(18), C(1), T
Notus in Judaea Deus, 1702, H(11), C(6)
O filii, 1698, H(2), C(14); ed. Roussel (Paris, 1952)
Omnes gentes, c1689, P(8)
Pange lingua, 1704, (H, 1689), H(14), C(16); ed. Sarlit (Paris, 1951)
Quam dilecta, 1686, P(2), T; extract: Beati qui, ed. Roussel (Paris, 1951)
Quare fremuerunt, 1706, H(17), C(18); ed. Cellier (Paris, 1949)
Quemadmodum, 1696, H(7), C(14); extract: Quando veniam, in Répertoire classique de musique religieuse (Paris, c1913)
Regina coeli, 1698, H(3), C(11); ed. S. Spycket (Paris, 1951), ed. Roussel (Paris, 1959), ed. Boulay (Paris, c1970)
Sacris solemniis, 1709, H(16), C(16); extracts ed. Roussel (Paris, 1951)
Super flumina, 1687, P(5), T
Te Deum, 1684, P(1), H(6), C(11); ed. Sarlit (Paris, 1951), ed. Boulay (Paris, c1970)
Usquequo Domine, 1692, H(5), C(10); ed. F. Gervais (Paris, 1970)
Veni Creator Spiritus, 1684, 1722, P(4), S; extracts ed. Roussel (Paris, 1953)
Venite exultemus, 1700, H(12), C(3), T; ed. Roussel (Paris, 1953)

MS, *F-A*, lists and dates most printed and MS motets, including 7 (some frags., some otherwise unknown):
Cum invocarem, 1714
Deus in nomine tuo, 1690
Domine Dominus noster, 1686
Domine quid multiplicati sunt, 1691
Exaudiat, 1688
Laetatus sum, 1693
Magnificat, 1681
Omnes gentes, 1721

MISCELLANEOUS SACRED

Messe des deffuns, 1v; O salutaris, Domine salvum, in Messes de plainchant musical, *F-Pn*
Cantemus Domino, *Pc* Rés.1899; ed. G. Morche, *Motets à une voix et basse continue* (Paris, 1975) [attrib. Lalande by Morche, formerly attrib. J. Gilles]
Cantique de Racine, 2vv, no.4 in Cantiques chantez devant le Roy, *Pn*
Domine, salvum fac regem, 3vv, *V*
5 settings of Domine salvum fac regem, Bar, *Pn*
2 settings of Domine salvum fac regem, 5vv, T
Laudate Dominum in sanctis ejus, 3vv, *V*
Laudate pueri, 3vv, *Pn*
Miserere, 1v, *Pn*
Les III leçons de Ténèbres et le Miserere à voix seule de feu M de La Lande, H(21)
O filii et filiae, 1v, *Pc*
Récits from grands motets, in Les motets à voix seule à l'usage des dames religieuses and in Récits en duo, *Pn*

STAGE

(ballets unless otherwise stated)

La sérénade (Abbé Genest), Fontainebleau, 1682, *F-Pn*
L'amour berger (pastorale), Marquis de Lomagne, Paris, Hôtel de Duras, 1683, 2 airs in *Mercure galant* (1683)
Les fontaines de Versailles (Morel), Versailles, 5 April 1683, *Pn*
Epithalame (Abbé Genest), Versailles, 25 June 1685, for marriage of the Duke of Bourbon and Mlle de Nantes, music lost
Le ballet de la jeunesse (Morel), Versailles, 28 Jan 1686, *V*
Le Palais de Flore (Ballet de Trianon), Trianon, 5 Jan 1689, *Pn*, *Pc*
Ballet de M. de La Lande, *Pn*
Ballet (or Sérénade) de M. de La Lande, Versailles, 25 Aug 1691, *Pn*
Prologue sur la Prise de Mons (or Les géants foudroyez), *V*
Adonis (divertissement), 1696, *Pn*
L'amour, fléchy par la constance (pastorale), Fontainebleau, 1697, *LYm*
Intermèdes of music and dance for comedies: Mirtil et Mélicerte (Molière, Guérin), Fontainebleau, Oct 1698, Comédie des fées, Fontainebleau, Sept 1699, *Pc*
La noce de village (Rousseau), Sceaux, 21 Feb 1700, *Pn*, *Pc*

L'hymen champestre, Marly, home of Mme de Maintenon, 1700, *Pc*
Ode à la louange du Roy (Abbé Genest), Sceaux, home of Mme de Maintenon, 24 Oct 1704, music lost
Ballet (Divertissement) de la Paix (Longepierre), Marly, home of Mme de Maintenon, July 1713, *Pc*, *Pn*
L'inconnu (T. Corneille), first ballet 'dansé par Sa Majesté dans son Palais des Tuileries' (other music by Campra, Bertin de la Doué, Destouches, Rebel), Paris, Feb 1720; L'inconnu: airs à chanter (Paris, 1720)
Les folies de Cardenio (Coypel), second ballet 'dansé par le Roy', Paris, 30 Dec 1720, *Pc*
Les éléments (opera ballet, Roy), third ballet 'dansé par le Roy', most music by Destouches, Lalande composed ov. and numbers for Prologue and Act 1, Paris, Opéra, 29 May 1725, *Pn*, selections (Paris, 1725)

AIRS

Airs in the following collections:
Nouvelles poésies morales sur les plus beaux airs de la musique françoise et italienne (Paris, 1737)
Nouvelles poésies spirituelles et morales sur les plus beaux airs de la musique françoise et italienne (Paris, 1730, 1733)
Les parodies nouvelles et les vaudevilles inconnus (Paris, 1730, 1737)
Recueil de pièces, petits airs, brunettes (Paris, c1755)
Second recueil des nouvelles poésies spirituelles et morales (Paris, 1731)
Airs de violons de l'inconnu (Paris, 1720)

INSTRUMENTAL

Les symphonies de M. de La Lande . . . copiés par . . . Philidor l'aîné . . . et par son fils aîné, l'an 1703 (10 suites and a Concert de trompettes), *Pn*
Recueil d'airs détachés et d'airs de violons de M. De la lande . . . 1727 (21 Symphonies des Noëls and 19 suites, no.19 not by Lalande), *Pn*
Symphonies de M. De La Lande . . . mises dans un nouvel ordre, et ses augmentations, recueillés en 1736 tome I, 1745 (vol. i includes 8 suites and 20 Symphonies des Noëls, vol. ii includes 18 suites, not all by Lalande), *Pn*
Symphonies des Noëls; nos.1–4, ed. Cellier (Paris, 1937); nos.1, 4, ed. Roussel (Paris, 1957); no.2, ed. Schroeder (Berlin, 1968); no.3, ed. Chirat (Paris, 1957)
Sinfonies pour les soupers du Roi; Suite 1, ed. R. Desormière (Paris, 1947); Caprices 1, 2, ed. Paillard (Paris, 1965); Suite 4, ed. Clerisse (Paris, 1954); extracts, ed. Boulay (Paris, 1965)

BIBLIOGRAPHY

M. Brenet: *La musique sacrée sous Louis XIV* (Paris, 1899)
——: *Les concerts en France sous l'ancien régime* (Paris, 1900/*R*1970)
H. Quittard: 'Notes sur Michel-Richard de Lalande', *RHCM*, ii (1902), 315
H. Leichtentritt: *Geschichte der Motette* (Leipzig, 1908/*R*1967)
A. Tessier: 'La carrière versaillaise de La Lande', *RdM*, ix (1928), 134
A. Cellier: 'Les motets de Michel-Richard de Lalande', *ReM* (1946), no.198, p.20
J. E. Richards: *The 'Grand Motet' of the Late Baroque in France as exemplified by Michel-Richard de Lalande* (diss., U. of Southern California, 1950)
N. Dufourcq: 'La musique religieuse française de 1660 à 1789', *ReM* (1953–4), nos.222–3, p.89
——: 'La place occupée par Michel-Richard Delalande dans la musique occidentale aux XVIIe et XVIIIe siècles', *3e congrès international de musique sacrée: Paris 1957*, 171
——, ed.: *Notes et références pour servir à une histoire de Michel Richard Delalande* (Paris, 1957)
——: 'Quelques réflexions sur les ballets et divertissements de Michel Delalande', *Divertissements de cour au XVIIe siècle* (Paris, 1957), 44
M. Barthélemy: 'La musique dramatique à Versailles de 1660 à 1715', *XVIIe*, xxxiv (1957), 7
L. Boulay: 'Les cantiques spirituels de Racine mis en musique au XVIIe siècle', ibid, 79
F. Raugel: 'La musique à la chapelle du château de Versailles sous Louis XIV', ibid, 19
H. Bert: 'Un ballet de Michel-Richard Delalande', ibid, 58
S. Spycket: 'De La Lande ou la noblesse intérieure', *L'art sacré* (1957), July–Aug, 22
H. A. Durand: 'Note sur la diffusion de M. R. Delalande dans les chapitres provençaux au XVIIIe siècle', *RdM*, xxxix (1957), 72
J. E. Richards: 'Structural Principles in the Grands Motets of Michel Richard de Lalande', *JAMS*, xi (1958), 119
N. Dufourcq: 'Michel-Richard de la Lande', *Revue de l'histoire de Versailles et de Seine et Oise*, liii (1959–60), 71
L. Boulay: 'Notes sur quatre motets inédits de Michel-Richard Delalande', *RMFC*, i (1960), 77
N. Dufourcq: 'Retour à Michel-Richard Delalande', *RMFC*, i (1960), 69
G. Thibault: 'Le "Te Deum" de Lalande', *FAM*, xii (1965), 162
J. R. Anthony: *French Baroque Music from Beaujoyeulx to Rameau* (London, 1973, rev. 2/1978)

L. Sawkins: 'Lalande and the Concert Spirituel', *MT*, cxvi (1975), 333
P. Oboussier: 'Lalande's Grands Motets', *MT*, cxvii (1976), 483
L. Sawkins: *The Sacred Music of Michel-Richard De Lalande (1657–1726)* (diss., U. of London, in preparation)
JAMES R. ANTHONY

La Laurencie, Comte **(Marie-Berband-)Lionel(-Jules) de** (*b* Nantes, 24 July 1861; *d* Paris, 21 Nov 1933). French musicologist. He took degrees in law and sciences at Nantes and studied at the Collège Stanislas, Paris, and the Ecole des Eaux et Forêts, Nancy (1881–3); concurrently he was taught the violin by Léon Reynier and theory by Alphonse Weingartner and studied with Bourgault-Ducoudray at the Paris Conservatoire (1891–2). He learnt the Classical repertory through regular domestic quartet playing, which he continued to the end of his life. In 1898 he abandoned a promising government administrative career to devote himself to music; he gave popular lecture courses (mainly at the Ecole des Hautes Etudes) on music history and aesthetics (1906–33), also serving as the archivist and librarian (1905–14) and vice-president (from 1914) of the Paris section of the International Musical Society. In 1917 he founded the Société Française de Musicologie, of which he became president (1924–5, 1932) and honorary president (from 1927). He succeeded Lavignac as editor of the *Encyclopédie de la musique et dictionnaire du Conservatoire* in 1919.

Although La Laurencie turned to professional musicology comparatively late, he had early served an apprenticeship in letters as the list of his writings shows. To his new career he brought a solid musical grounding and a boundless enthusiasm for a wide range of subjects to which was added precision of thought derived from legal and scientific studies. To complete his training, he acquired an unrivalled skill in archival investigation at the Ecole des Chartes. Notwithstanding an immense output he showed minute attention to detail and documentation, and yet wore his knowledge lightly enough to rivet the reader's attention.

La Laurencie's main area of study, French music from Lully to Gluck, is the theme of a well-balanced contribution to Lavignac's *Encyclopédie* which highlights the mediocre quality of the others. For the scholar he compiled a thematic index (*Fonds Blancheton*) and a library catalogue (*Bibliothèque de l'Arsenal*); other books cater for the general reader, such as *Orphée* (which views Gluck's opera from every angle) and his shorter books on Lully and Rameau. *Les luthistes* is well illustrated, but weakened by his dismissal of the important Spanish vihuela school in four pages. Of greater significance are a fascinating metaphysical study *Le goût musical* and *Les créateurs de l'opéra français*, in which the genesis of opera is traced to the ancient liturgical trope.

Many articles on miscellaneous topics reflect the tremendous musical activity in France that characterized La Laurencie's chosen period. Of special importance is the extended survey on the French symphony (in collaboration with Saint-Foix). A chronological list (1727–64) provides a motley assortment of titles which portray the utter confusion in terminology then current in Europe. The authors therefore restricted themselves to instrumental ensembles however constituted, regarding them as precursors of symphonic style, at the same time justifying the inclusion of mediocre or unknown composers in the interests of historical completeness.

L'école française de violon is La Laurencie's master-piece, the result of over 20 years' research, and dwarfs all similar works. The author's apology for a certain monotony is too modest in view of the vivid manner of presentation, the abundance of musical examples and footnotes which in themselves would constitute a book, the whole capped by an exhaustive set of appendices. The first two volumes are chronologically devoted to composers and their works, while the third deals with violin manuals, techniques, theorists and teachers, and the evolution of French instrumental music. This work and the study of the symphony, with Barry Brook's *La symphonie française* (1962), form a remarkable trilogy covering the whole spectrum of French concerted music from Lully to the Revolution.

WRITINGS

La légende de Parsifal et le drame musical de Richard Wagner (Nantes, 1888, 2/1894)
'Les primitifs du violon et l'ornementation musicale', *Courrier musical*, iii (1900), March, 1; also in *Art moderne*, xx (Brussels, 1900), 66
'Le goût musical au XVIIIe siècle: philosophes et dilettanti', *Courrier musical*, iv (1901), no.5, p.49; no.6, p.61; no.7, p.73
'L'oeuvre de Vincent d'Indy', *Durendal*, ix (Brussels, 1902), 204
'Un moment musical: notes sur l'art de Cl. Debussy', *Durendal*, x (1903), 614; repr. in *Courrier musical*, vii (1904), 141, 181
'Hector Berlioz et le public de son temps', *Courrier musical*, vii (1904), 1
'Jean-Marie Leclair l'aîné, premier symphoniste du roi, d'après des documents inédits', *SIMG*, vi (1904–5), 250
'J.-L. Leclair: une assertion de Fétis', *Revue musicale*, iv (1904), 496
'L'origine de J.-M. Leclair l'aîné, violiniste-compositeur', *Courrier musical*, vii (1904), 321
'Sur les oeuvres de Jean-Marie Leclair l'aîné', *Courrier musical*, vii (1904), 597
Le goût musical en France (Paris, 1905/*R*1971)
'Une dynastie de musiciens aux XVIIe et XVIIIe siècles: Les Rebel', *SIMG*, vii (1905–6), 253
'Un grand violiniste de l'ancien régime: les deux Jean-Baptiste Anet', *Revue musicale*, v (1905), 548, 582
'Un musicien lyonnais au XVIIIe siècle: Jean-Marie Leclair le second', *Courrier musical*, viii (1905), 393
'Un primitif français du violon: François du Val', *BSIM*, i (1905), 59
'Jacques Aubert et les premiers concertos français de violon', *BSIM*, ii (1906), 441
L'Académie de musique et le concert de Nantes à l'Hôtel de la Bourse (1727–1767) (Paris, 1906/*R*1972)
'Quelques documents sur Jean-Philippe Rameau et sa famille', *BSIM*, iii (1907), 541–614
'Les Forqueray', *BSIM*, iv (1908), 1251; v (1909), 48
'Notes sur la jeunesse d'André Campra', *SIMG*, x (1908–9), 159–259
Rameau (Paris, 1908, 2/1926)
with H. Prunières: 'La jeunesse de Lully', *BSIM*, v (1909), 234, 329
with G. de Saint-Foix: 'Contribution à l'histoire de la symphonie française vers 1750', *Année musicale*, i (1911), 1–123
'Les pastorales en musique au XVIIme siècle en France avant Lully et leur influence sur l'opéra', *IMusSCR*, iv London 1911, 139; also in *Monde musical* (15 Dec 1912), 359
Lully (Paris, 1911, 2/1919/*R*1977)
'Un émule de Lully: Pierre Gautier de Marseille', *SIMG*, xiii (1911–12), 33–69
'André Campra, musicien profane: notes biographiques', *Année musicale*, iii (1913), 153–205
'L'Amérique dans la musique française des XVIIe et XVIIIe siècles', *MQ*, vii (1921), 284
'La musique française de Lully à Gluck (1687–1789)', *EMDC*, I/iii (1921), 1362–1562
Les créateurs de l'opéra français (Paris, 1921, 2/1930)
L'école française de violon de Lully à Viotti: études d'histoire et d'esthétique (Paris, 1922–4/*R*1971)
with A. Mairy: 'Le luth', *EMDC*, II/iii (1927), 1972
Les luthistes (Paris, 1928)
Inventaire critique du Fonds Blancheton de la bibliothèque du Conservatoire de Paris (Paris, 1930–31)
'Antonio Bartolomeo Bruni musicista cunese (1751–1821)', *Richerche e studi*, ed. L. Borgo (Turin, 1931), 117–83
'G.-Ph. Telemann à Paris', *RdM*, xiii (1932), 75
'L'apparition des oeuvres d'Haydn à Paris', *RdM*, xiii (1932), 191
'Les débuts de la musique de chambre', *RdM*, xv (1934), 3
Orphée (Paris, 1934)
with A. Gastoué: *Catalogue des livres de musique de la bibliothèque de l'Arsenal* (Paris, 1936)

BIBLIOGRAPHY

Mélanges de musicologie offerts à M. Lionel de la Laurencie (Paris, 1933)

M. Pincherle: 'Lionel de La Laurencie', *RdM*, xv (1934), 3 [with complete list of writings]

H. Prunières: 'Lionel de La Laurencie', *RdM*, xv (1934), 94

B. S. Brook: 'Lionel de la Laurencie's "L'école française de violon" ', *Notes*, xxvi (1969–70), 9
G. B. SHARP

Lalli, (Benedetto) Domenico [Biancardi, Nicolò Bastiano (Sebastiano)] (*b* Naples, 27 March 1679; *d* Venice, 9 Oct 1741). Italian librettist. He fled from Naples in 1706, when he was accused of having taken money from the treasury of the brotherhood of the Annunziata, where he had been employed. He denied the charges, but left behind his wife and children. Seeking refuge in Rome in the palace of the Duke of Osseda, the Spanish ambassador to the pope, Lalli met the composer E. d'Astorga, and together they wandered throughout Italy. In Venice Lalli wrote several poems and librettos and assisted Grimani, director of two Venetian theatres (he also remarried and had more children).

In the early 1720s Lalli adapted previously written texts for the archiepiscopal court at Salzburg, and from 1727 to 1740 served as court poet to the Elector of Bavaria. During these years he made the acquaintance of Metastasio and Goldoni, and the latter often praised him for his 'poetic genius'. (Goldoni also succeeded Lalli as impresario at the Venetian S Samuele and S Giovanni Grisostomo theatres.) One of Lalli's greatest achievements was in 1711, when his text *Elisa* (with music by G. M. Ruggeri) became the first comic opera to be performed in Venice. In fact *opera buffa* had existed as early as 1706 in Naples (Faggioli's *La Cilla*), and at least one scholar considers that the text of *Elisa* may have been taken from an even earlier Neapolitan comedy by N. Amenta. Yet regardless of where Lalli acquired his understanding of the genre and despite the fact that comic opera did not flourish in Venice until later, Lalli's importance lay in the initial step he took in presenting comic opera to the Venetians.

With the exception of *Elisa* most of Lalli's texts adhered faithfully to the 18th-century convention of developing character relationships. These texts were first set to music by such composers as G. F. Gasparini, A. Paulati, F. Mancini, Vivaldi (*Ottone in villa*, 1713, *La ventà in cimento*, 1720, text in collaboration with G. Palazzi, and *Filippo re di Macedonia*, music in collaboration with G. Boniventi), Albinoni, C. F. Pollaroli, M. A. Gasparini, S. A. Fiorè, A. Scarlatti (*Cambise*, 1719), Orlandini, Caldara, L. Leo (*Pisistrato*, 1714, and *Timocrate*, 1723), Porpora (*Damiro e Pizia*, 1724), Porta, A. Pollarolo (text for one opera in collaboration with G. Boldini), P. Torri and F. Campi (text in collaboration with Boldini). Hasse and Galuppi composed music for texts by Minato, Zeno and Metastasio which Lalli had adapted. Lalli also composed texts and some music for serenades, cantatas, festive occasions, dedications, sacred works, and other works of comic and tragic nature.

BIBLIOGRAPHY

O. G. Sonneck: *The Library of Congress: Catalogue of Opera Librettos Printed before 1800*, ii (Washington, DC, 1914), 1300f

F. Walker: 'E. d'Astorga and a Neapolitan Librettist', *MMR*, lxxxi (1951), 90

M. Bogianckino: 'Lalli, Domenico', *ES* [incl. complete list of works]
WENDY N. GIBNEY

Lallouette [Lalouette], **Jean François** (*b* Paris, 1651; *d* Paris, 31 Aug 1728). French composer. He was trained at the choir school of St Eustache, Paris, and studied the violin with Guy Leclerc and composition with Lully. Lully appointed him as his secretary and as time-beater at the Opéra and asked him to fill in the inner parts of certain of his works, a task at which he became so adept that he began to attract attention. When he reportedly boasted of having written some of the best parts of Lully's *Isis* (1677) he was dismissed. *Isis*, however, displeased Louis XIV because of its thinly disguised and unflattering portrayal of Mme de Montespan in the character of Juno. The work was withdrawn, not to be performed again until 1704, and Philippe Quinault, the librettist, was dismissed. Lully came through the affair unscathed, and one must wonder if Lallouette was a scapegoat. On 18 April 1678 the duchess regent of the Savoy court at Turin appointed him composer of French music and director of the band of violins. She dismissed him in July 1679, possibly because in over a year he had produced only one composition, a three-part serenata performed on 14 May 1678. He probably returned to Paris, where he soon composed an opera; on 27 January 1681 the king's secretary wrote to a M. de la Régnie informing him that the king forbade further performances of it on the grounds that it violated Lully's privilege. Lallouette competed unsuccessfully in April 1683 for one of the four positions of *sous-maître* at the royal chapel. The post was awarded to Pascal Collasse, who had succeeded him as Lully's secretary; it is likely that Lully intervened on Collasse's behalf and against Lallouette.

Little is known of Lallouette's activities from 1683 to 1693. He paid a visit to Rome in 1689 and while he was there composed a concerto in the Italian style which was performed at least once. It is established that in 1692 he was living near St Germain-l'Auxerrois, Paris, and he may have been employed there. On 7 December 1693 he was made choirmaster of Rouen Cathedral, where he remained until 15 February 1695. There is disagreement on his whereabouts between 1695 and 1700. One source has him at St Germain-l'Auxerrois from September 1695 and busy with a four-act opera, *Europe*; another has him at Notre Dame, Versailles, in 1695–7 and at St Germain-l'Auxerrois only in 1697–8. Those that have him at St Germain-l'Auxerrois from 1693 to 1700 or maintain that he went from Rouen to Notre Dame, Paris, in 1695 are undoubtedly in error. On 17 November 1700, however, he certainly was appointed to succeed Campra as choirmaster of Notre Dame, Paris. He asked to be released in 1716, claiming fatigue, although the chapter had given him unprecedented yearly vacations and in 1706 had even employed an assistant so that he could be absent frequently. His resignation was accepted, and he was made a canon of St Jean-le-Rond. Early in 1718, however, he asked to be reinstated as choirmaster, asserting that his music was not being well performed; he resumed his duties on 5 March. He finally retired on 22 January 1727, and he was allotted a yearly pension of 400 livres.

Lallouette was in his day a respected and popular musician and teacher. His works were thought to be well composed and to display a certain originality, although the sacred music was said to suffer from his faulty knowledge of Latin. It bears witness to two influences. On the one hand Italian cantatas seem to have prompted the alternation of vocal and instrumental sections, the use of certain forms and textures (which derive also from the trio sonata) and the tendency towards stereotyped figuration; on the other hand he sometimes seems consciously to refer to the great Versailles motets of Lalande. His *Miserere* was performed at the Concert Spirituel in 1726.

WORKS

Motets livre premier, 1–3vv, bc (Paris, 1726)
Le psalme Miserere à grand choeur et l'hymne Veni Creator à 3 voix, bc, livre second (Paris, 1730)
Missa 'Veritas', 4vv (Paris, 1744)
Messe en plain chant, in Recueil de messes en plain chant musical, *F-Pn*
O cibum super omnia, motet, 2vv, bc, *Pn* (also attrib. Lully)
6 motets, 3vv, bc, *Pn* (attrib. by Brossard; also attrib. Lully)
Menuet pour le 1er dessus, in Suite de danses pour les violons et les hautbois, *Pn*

LOST

Opera, Paris, c1678–80
Concerto, probably 1689
Serenata, a 3, 1678
Ballet airs, incidental music

BIBLIOGRAPHY

Mercure galant (1677–1728)
A. du Pradel [pseud. of N. de Blégny]: *Le livre commode des adresses de Paris pour 1692* (Paris, 1692, repr. 1878)
P. Bourdelot and P. Bonnet-Bourdelot: *Histoire de la musique et de ses effets*, ed. J. Bonnet (Paris, 1715/R1969, 7/1743)
J. L. Le Cerf de la Viéville: *Comparaison de la musique italienne et de la musique françoise* (Brussels, 1704–6/R1972); repr. in P. Bourdelot and P. Bonnet-Bourdelot: *Histoire de la musique et de ses effets*, ii–iv (Amsterdam, 2/1722, 2/1743)
E. Titon du Tillet: *Le Parnasse françois* (Paris, 1732/R1971)
J.-B. de La Borde: *Essai sur la musique ancienne et moderne* (Paris, 1780/R1972)
E. de Coussemaker: *Notice sur les collections musicales de la Bibliothèque de Cambrai et des autres villes du Département du Nord* (Paris, 1843)
A. Collette and A. Bourdon: *Histoire de la maîtrise de Rouen* (Rouen, 1892)
F. L. Chartier: *L'ancien chapitre de Notre-Dame de Paris et sa maîtrise* (Paris, 1897/R1971)
S. Cordero di Pamparato: 'Alcuni appunti sul teatro melodrammatico francese in Torino', *RMI*, xxxvii (1930), 562; xxxviii (1931), 21
M. Barthélemy: *André Campra: sa vie et son oeuvre (1660–1744)* (Paris, 1957)
L. E. S. J. de Laborde: *Musiciens de Paris, 1535–1792*, ed. Y. de Brossard (Paris, 1965)
M.-T. Bouquet: 'Quelques relations musicales franco-piémontaises au XVIIe et au XVIIIe siècles', *RMFC*, x (1970), 5
M. Benoit: *Musiques de cour: chapelle, chambre, écurie, 1661–1733* (Paris, 1971)
R. M. Isherwood: *Music in the Service of the King* (Ithaca, NY, and London, 1973)
WILLIAM HAYS, ERIC MULARD

Lalo, Charles (*b* Périgueux, 24 Feb 1877; *d* Paris, 1 April 1953). French aesthetician. He studied philosophy and aesthetics in Bayonne and in Paris, where he took his doctorate in 1908 with two dissertations, on contemporary experimental aesthetics and on his own theory of musical aesthetics. After teaching philosophy at the University of Bordeaux and various leading secondary schools, he succeeded Victor Basch as lecturer in aesthetics and art history at the Sorbonne (1933–53). He was president of the Société Française d'Esthétique, and one of the directors of the *Revue d'esthétique*. Throughout his writings (which deal with sociology and logic as well as general aesthetics) he insisted that aesthetics is a scientific discipline that must be based on facts, on an examination of the mathematical, psychological, physiological and sociological aspects of the beautiful rather than on theory or criticism; and that the components of a musical (or any artistic) structure are interdependent parts of the organic whole and cannot be assessed in isolation (*see* AESTHETICS OF MUSIC, §15).

WRITINGS

Esquisse d'une esthétique musicale scientifique (diss., U. of Paris, 1908; Paris, 1908, enlarged 2/1939 as *Eléments d'une esthétique*)
L'esthétique expérimentale contemporaine (diss., U. of Paris, 1908; Paris, 1908)
Les sentiments esthétiques (Paris, 1910)
'La philosophie de la musique', *Congresso internazionale di musica: Roma 1911*, 117
Introduction à l'esthétique (Paris, 1912, rev. 4/1952 as *Notions de philosophie, notions d'esthétique*)
L'art et la vie sociale (Paris, 1921)
La beauté et l'instinct sexuel (Paris, 1922)
L'art et la morale (Paris, 1922)
L'expression de la vie dans l'art (Paris, 1933)
'Sur les valeurs culturelles et sociales des beaux-arts', *2ᵉ congrès international d'esthétique et de science de l'art: Paris 1937*, i, 358
L'art loin de la vie (Paris, 1939)
L'art et la vie (Paris, 1946–7)
'L'esthétique musicale', *La musique des origines à nos jours*, ed. N. Dufourcq (Paris, 1946, rev. enlarged 2/1959), 481–514
L'économie des passions (Paris, 1947)
Les grandes évasions esthétiques (Paris, 1947)
Articles in *Revue d'esthétique* and *Journal de psychologie*

BIBLIOGRAPHY

Revue d'esthétique, vi/2 (1953) [fasc. devoted to Lalo]
G. Ferchault: 'Lalo, Charles', *MGG*

Lalo, Edouard(-Victoire-Antoine) (*b* Lille, 27 Jan 1823; *d* Paris, 22 April 1892). French composer. His father had fought for Napoleon and although the name was originally Spanish, the family had been settled in Flanders and northern France since the 16th century. Lalo's parents at first encouraged musical studies and he learnt both the violin and the cello at the Lille Conservatory, but his more serious inclinations towards music met with stern military opposition from his father, compelling him to leave home at the age of 16 to pursue his bent in Paris. He attended Habeneck's violin class at the Paris Conservatoire for a brief period and studied composition privately with the pianist Julius Schulhoff and the composer J.-E. Crèvecoeur. For a long while he worked in obscurity, making his living as a violinist and teacher. He became friendly with Delacroix and played in some of Berlioz's concerts. He was also composing and two early symphonies were apparently destroyed. In the late 1840s he published some *romances* in the manner of the day and some violin pieces; his inclination was, unfashionably, towards chamber music. By 1853 he had composed two piano trios, a medium almost entirely neglected in France at the time. The revival of interest in chamber music in France in the 1850s owed much to Lalo, for he was a founder-member of the Armingaud Quartet, formed in 1855 with the aim of making better known the quartets of Haydn, Mozart, Beethoven and also of Mendelssohn and Schumann; Lalo played the viola and later second violin. His own string quartet dates from 1859.

A period of discouragement then ensued and Lalo wrote little until 1866 when, at the age of 43, he embarked on an opera in response to a competition set up by the Théâtre-Lyrique. His *Fiesque*, a grand opera in three acts to a libretto by Charles Beauquier after Schiller's play *Fiesko*, was not awarded the prize, and despite interest shown by both the Paris Opéra and the Théâtre de la Monnaie, Brussels, it was never performed. Lalo was embittered by these refusals and had the vocal score published at his own expense. He valued the work highly and drew on it for numerous later compositions, including the scherzo of the Symphony in G minor, the two *Aubades* for small orchestra, the *Divertissement*, *Néron* and other works.

Lalo's fame as a composer was greatly widened in the 1870s by the performance of a series of important instrumental works. The formation of the Société Nationale and the support of Pasdeloup, Lamoureux, Colonne, Sarasate and others gave Lalo an opportunity to pursue his ambitions as a composer of orchestral music in an essentially German tradition. The F major violin concerto was played by Sarasate in 1874 and the *Symphonie espagnole*, also by Sarasate, the following year. His cello concerto was played by Fischer in 1877 and the *Fantaisie norvégienne* in 1878. The *Concerto russe* for violin was first played by Marsick in 1879.

Edouard Lalo

Despite this highly productive period devoted to orchestral music, the composition of *Fiesque* had satisfied Lalo that he should continue to seek success in the theatre, and in 1875 he began work on a libretto by Edouard Blau based on a Breton legend, *Le roi d'Ys*. By 1881 it was substantially completed and extracts had been heard in concerts. But no theatre accepted it, and the Opéra, perhaps as consolation for turning it down, asked Lalo instead for a ballet ('a genre that I know nothing about', he admitted) to be completed in four months. *Namouna* was composed in 1881–2 (when Lalo suffered an attack of hemiplegia Gounod helped with the orchestration) and played at the Opéra the following year. The production was beset with intrigue and survived only a few performances. Lalo's music was variously criticized as that of a symphonist or a Wagnerian or both, but the more discerning critics appreciated its freshness and originality. Debussy, then a student at the Conservatoire, remained an enthusiastic admirer of the score, and it became popular in the form of a series of

orchestral suites.

More orchestral works followed, notably the symphony and the piano concerto, but Lalo's main attention was given to the production of his masterpiece *Le roi d'Ys*, finally mounted at the Opéra-Comique on 7 May 1888. It was an overwhelming success, and for the remaining four years of his life Lalo finally enjoyed the general acclaim he had sought for so long. Although he worked on two more stage works, the pantomime *Néron* staged at the Hippodrome in 1891 and *La jacquerie*, an opera of which he completed only one act, both drew almost entirely on earlier compositions; his productive life was essentially over. In 1865 Lalo had married one of his pupils, Julie de Maligny – a singer of Breton origin; their son was Pierre Lalo.

Although Lalo's fame has rested, in France at least, on *Le roi d'Ys*, his instrumental music must be accorded a more prominent historical importance, for it represents a decisively new direction in French music at that period, taken more or less simultaneously by César Franck and Saint-Saëns. Outside France the *Symphonie espagnole*, a violin concerto in five movements using Spanish idioms and whimsically entitled symphony, has remained his most popular work; the freshness of its melodic and orchestral language is imperishable. The cello concerto is on the whole a stronger and more searching work, with a central movement that combines slow movement and scherzo as Brahms was wont to do, and a forward momentum, especially in the first movement, of exceptional power. In his Symphony it is the two central movements, a scherzo and an adagio (both drawn from earlier music) which carry the weight of the argument. The piano concerto is disappointing, but the string quartet, composed in 1859 and revised in 1880, and the second piano trio are both works that deserve to be heard more frequently.

The opera *Fiesque* is encumbered with a libretto laden with absurdities and awkward stage manoeuvres, belonging in spirit to the age of Scribe. Yet for a first opera the music is extraordinarily deft and varied, occasionally pompous but never dull, and full of brilliantly successful numbers. The *Divertissement*, drawn from the opera, is one of Lalo's most effective orchestral pieces. *Le roi d'Ys* is a fine opera too, with some borrowing of the conventional scenes of grand opera, such as the offstage organ with ethereal voices. Margared is well characterized, especially in her expressions of anxiety or horror, and Rozenn has music of winning tenderness. The choral music is less convincing, for Lalo seems inadequate to the task of collective characterization except when the chorus are being conventionally decorative, as for example in the exquisite wedding scene. The opera has considerable dramatic force and a real individuality of style.

Many of Lalo's songs were written for his wife's contralto voice. They form a more sentimental and genuinely lyrical part of his output in notable contrast to the instrumental music. His gift in this area was already evident in the *Six romances populaires* of 1849 and the Hugo settings of 1856.

Lalo's music has strong melodic and rhythmic elements, but virtually no counterpoint. His harmony is piquant and chromatic, but not at all like Wagner's, for his melodies are generally diatonic. His favourite harmonic colour is the so-called French 6th, which is almost overused, but he did turn harmonic progression to fine effect as a source of forward momentum. His orchestration is noisy but ingenious; *Namouna* is a particularly skilful score. He had an evident fondness for scherzo movements in 6/8, 3/8 and even 3/16. Another hallmark is a recurring emphatic chord (often an octave), *fortissimo*, commonly on an unexpected beat of the bar; in his orchestral music this mannerism can be brusque or crude in effect. His temperament was naturally tuned to the styles of Mendelssohn and Schumann on which he superimposed a variety of colours, sometimes drawn from folk idioms of Scandinavia, Russia, Brittany or Spain. All his music has a vigour and energy that place it in striking contrast to the music of Franck's pupils on the one hand and the impressionists on the other. His kinship is more with the Russians, especially Borodin, and with Smetana, than with composers of his own country, although it is not difficult to find traces of his influence in Dukas and Debussy and perhaps more distinctly in Roussel.

WORKS
(all printed works published in Paris unless otherwise stated)

STAGE

Fiesque (opera, 3, C. Beauquier, after Schiller), 1866–7, unperf., vocal score (1873), full score (c1875)
Namouna (ballet, 2, C. Nuitter, H. Blaze de Bury, M. Petipa), 1881–2, Paris, Opéra, 6 March 1882 (1882)
Le roi d'Ys (opera, 3, E. Blau), 1875–88, Paris, Opéra-Comique, 7 May 1888, vocal score (1888), full score (n.d.)
Néron (pantomime with chorus, 3, P. Milliet), 1891, Paris, Hippodrome, 28 March 1891, *F-Pn* [drawn from Fiesque and other works]
La jacquerie (opera, 4, Blau, S. Arnaud), 1891–2, Monte Carlo, 9 March 1895 (1894), [Act 1 only, completed by A. Coquard]

VOCAL

Choral: Litanies de la sainte Vierge, org/pf acc. (1876); O salutaris, female vv, org, op.34 (1884)
Collections: 6 romances populaires (P. J. de Béranger) (1849): 1 La pauvre femme, 2 Beaucoup d'amour, 3 Le suicide, 4 Si j'étais petit oiseau, 5 Les petits coups, 6 Le vieux vagabond; 6 mélodies (V. Hugo), op.17 (1856): 1 Guitare, 2 Puisqu'ici bas, 3 L'aube naît, 4 Dieu qui sourit et qui donne, 5 Oh! quand je dors, 6 Chanson à boire [2 settings]; 3 mélodies (A. de Musset) (?c1870): 1 A une fleur, 2 Chanson de Barberine, 3 La Zuecca; 5 Lieder (Mainz, 1879): 1 Prière de l'enfant à son réveil (Lamartine), 2 A celle qui part (A. Silvestre), 3 Tristesse (Silvestre), 4 Viens (Lamartine), 5 La chanson de l'alouette (V. de Laprade); 3 mélodies (1887): La fenaison (Stella), L'esclave (T. Gautier), Souvenir (Hugo)
Songs (all pf acc.): Adieu au désert (A. Flobert) (1848); L'ombre de Dieu (A. Lehugeur) (?1848); Le novice (H. Stupuy), op.5 (1849); Ballade à la lune (de Musset) (1860); Humoresque (Beauquier) (?1867); Aubade (V. Wilder) (1872); Chant breton (A. Delpit), acc. fl/ob, op.31 (1884); Marine (A. Theuriet), op.33 (1884); Dansons, S, Mez, op.35 (1884) [arr. from Namouna]; Au fond des halliers (Theuriet), S, T (1887) [arr. from Fiesque]; Le rouge-gorge (Theuriet) (1887); Veni, Creator, d'après un thème bohème, A, pf/org (n.d.)

ORCHESTRAL

2 symphonies, early, destroyed by Lalo
2 aubades, 10 insts/small orch, 1872 (n.d.) from Fiesque: 1 Allegretto, 2 Andantino
Divertissement, 1872 (c1872), ballet music from Fiesque, incl. the 2 aubades
Violin Concerto, F, op.20, 1873 (1874)
Symphonie espagnole, vn, orch, op.21, 1874 (1875)
Allegro appassionato, vc, orch, op.27 (1875), arr. of op.16; also orchd as Allegro symphonique (n.d.)
Cello Concerto, d, 1877 (Berlin, 1877)
Fantaisie norvégienne, vn, orch, 1878 (Berlin, 1880)
Rapsodie norvégienne, 1879 (Berlin, 1881), portions arr. from Fantaisie norvégienne
Romance-sérénade, vn, orch, 1879 (Berlin, 1879)
Concerto russe, vn, orch, op.29, 1879 (Mainz, 1883)
Fantaisie-ballet, vn, orch, 1885 (n.d.), from Namouna
Andantino, vn, orch, from Namouna
Sérénade, str, from Namouna
Symphony, g, 1886 (?1887)
Piano Concerto, f, 1888–9 (1889)

CHAMBER

op.
1   Fantaisie originale, vn, pf, c1848 (c1850)
2   Allegro maestoso, vn, pf, c1848 (c1850)
4   Deux impromptus, vn, pf, c1848 (c1850): 1 Espérance, 2 Insouciance
–   Arlequin, esquisse caractéristique, vn/vc, pf, c1848 (c1850); also orchd
7   Piano Trio no.1, c, c1850 (n.d.)
8   Pastorale and Scherzo alla Pulcinella, vn, pf, c1850 (n.d.)
–   Piano Trio no.2, b (?1852)
12 Violin Sonata, 1853 (1855); originally Grand duo concertant
14 Chanson villageoise, Sérénade, vn/vc, pf (1854)
16 Allegro, vc, pf (?1856); arr. vc, orch as op.27, and again as Allegro symphonique (n.d.)
18 Soirées parisiennes, vn, pf, 1856 (c1860), collab. C. Wehle: 1 Ballade, 2 Menuet, 3 Idylle
–   Cello Sonata, 1856 (n.d.)
19 String Quartet, Eb, 1859 (Leipzig, n.d.); rev. as op.45
26 Piano Trio no.3, a, 1880 (1881); Scherzo orchd 1884
28 Guitare, vn, pf (1882)
45 String Quartet, Eb, 1880 (1886); rev. of op.19
—   Valse, vc, pf
—   Piano Quintet, Ab, *F-Pn*
—   Adagio, 2nd fantaisie-quintette, pf, str qt, *F-Pn*

PIANO

Sérénade (1864)
La mère et l'enfant, pf 4 hands, op.32, 1873 (c1873): 1 Romance, 2 Sérénade

BIBLIOGRAPHY

H. Imbert: *Nouveaux profils de musiciens* (Paris, 1892)
A. Pougin: 'Edouard Lalo', *Le ménestrel*, lviii (1892), 139
G. Servières: *La musique française moderne* (Paris, 1897)
A. Bruneau: *Musiques de Russie et musiciens de France* (Paris, 1903)
M. Dufour: *Edouard Lalo* (Lille, 1908)
G. Servières: 'La musique de chambre d'Edouard Lalo', *Guide musical*, lvi (1910), 711
O. Seré [J. Poueigh]: *Musiciens français d'aujourd'hui* (Paris, 1911, 8/1921) [incl. bibliography to 1921]
J. Tiersot: *Un demi-siècle de musique française* (Paris, 1918, 2/1924)
G. Servières: 'Une lettre inédite de Ch. Gounod sur Edouard Lalo', *ReM*, ii/8 (1921), 285
H. Malherbe: *Edouard Lalo, conférence prononcée . . . 23 décembre, 1920* (Paris, 1921)
P. Dukas: 'Edouard Lalo', *ReM*, iv/5 (1923), 97
A. Jullien: 'Quelques lettres inédites de Lalo', *ReM*, iv/5 (1923), 108
P. Lalo: 'La vie d'Edouard Lalo', *ReM*, iv/5 (1923), 118
G. Servières: *Edouard Lalo* (Paris, 1925)
M. Pincherle: *Musiciens peints par eux-mêmes* (Paris, 1939)
E. Lockspeiser: *The Literary Clef* (London, 1958)
G. Schulz: 'A Northern Legend', *Opera News*, xxiv (1960), 12
K. R. Brachtel: 'Edouard Lalo zum 75. Todestag am 22 April', *Musica*, xxi (1967), 130

HUGH MACDONALD

Lalo, Pierre (*b* Puteaux, 6 Sept 1866; *d* Paris, 9 June 1943). French music critic, son of Edouard Lalo. He was a brilliant student of literature, classics, philosophy and, at the Ecole de Chartes and the Ecole Polytechnique, modern languages. From 1896 he contributed for some time to the *Journal des débats* before making his mark as a music critic with an article on d'Indy's *Fervaal* in the *Revue de Paris* (15 May 1898); this secured him the post of critic of *Le temps* (in succession to J. Weber) which he held from October 1898 until 1914. Lalo's articles in that paper, and in *Courrier musical* and *Comoedia*, are characterized by conservatism, wit, astuteness and a linguistic finesse which occasionally turned to virulence: his diatribes against 'Debussyism' (*Le temps*, 21 Feb 1906) were heavily sarcastic and his preoccupation with the supposed influence of Debussy on Ravel (see the review of *Histoires naturelles* entitled 'Maurice Ravel et le Debussysme', *Le temps*, 19 March 1907) was an important feature of the journalistic *cause célèbre* that largely caused the strained relations between the two men. Lalo was later a member of the governing bodies of the Conservatoire and the Radiofusion.

WRITINGS

La musique (Paris, 1898–9) [collection of articles]
Richard Wagner ou le Nibelung (Paris, 1933)

De Rameau à Ravel: portraits et souvenirs (Paris, 1947) [posthumous selection of articles]

JOHN TREVITT

Lalouette, Jean François. See LALLOUETTE, JEAN FRANÇOIS.

Laloy, Louis (*b* Gray, Haute-Saône, 18 Feb 1874; *d* Dôle, 4 March 1944). French musicologist and critic. He was a pupil at the Ecole Normale (1893), an agrégé des lettres (1896) and docteur ès lettres (1904); he also studied at the Schola Cantorum with d'Indy, Bordes and others (1899–1905). He contributed as editor-in-chief ('without title', as he said later) to Combarieu's *Revue musicale* from 1901, and in 1905 founded, with Jean Marnold, the *Mercure musical* which Ecorcheville later transformed into the *Bulletin français de la S.I.M.* He was also co-founder of the short-lived *L'année musicale* (1911–13) and an influential music critic of the *Grande revue*, the *Gazette des beaux-arts* and (from 1930) the *Revue des deux mondes*. In 1906–7 he lectured on music history at the Sorbonne while Romain Rolland was on leave. He served as secretary general of the Opéra from 1914 and was professor of music history at the Conservatoire (1936–41).

Laloy was a cultured man whose interests included the music of ancient Greece (discussed in his dissertation) and that of the Far East: he lectured on Chinese music at the Sorbonne from 1921 and wrote the libretto for Roussel's *Padmâvatî*. Though his work at the Schola Cantorum led to a book on Rameau, Laloy was a noted defender of contemporary French music and was a close friend of, and mediator between, Ravel and Debussy, with whom he collaborated on some unrealized stage works; he was also the author of the first major work (and the first in the French language) on Debussy.

WRITINGS

Aristoxène de Tarente et la musique de l'antiquité (diss., Ecole Normale Supérieure, Paris, 1904)
'Notes sur la musique cambodgienne', *IMusSCR, ii Basle 1906*, 61
Jean-Philippe Rameau (Paris, 1908, 3/1919)
Claude Debussy (Paris, 1909, 2/1944)
Richard Wagner (Leipzig, 1910) [trans. of G. Adler: *Richard Wagner*, Leipzig, 1904]
The Future of Music (London, 1910)
La musique chinoise (Paris, ?1912)
La danse à l'Opéra (Paris, 1927)
La musique retrouvée, 1902–1927 (Paris, 1928)
Une heure de musique avec Beethoven (Paris, 1930)
Comment écouter la musique (Paris, 1942)

JOHN TREVITT

Lamalle, Pierre (*b* c1648; *d* Liège, 28 July 1722). South Netherlands composer. He entered the cathedral of St Lambert at Liège as a *duodenus*, and he spent his life there as musician and priest. On 26 September 1664 he received a *bursa toledana* – an award that enabled choristers whose voices had broken to continue their studies – and on the same day in 1688 the chapter made him another award so that he could continue his studies at the seminary. The following year he offered the chapter a mass he had composed, and its success is confirmed by that of a *simphonia* by him which was heard at High Mass in the cathedral on two consecutive Sundays in January 1671. The political troubles and wars that racked Liège between 1672 and 1715 also affected the cathedral and probably hindered Lamalle's output and success. Nonetheless on 30 April 1672 the *maître de chant*, Lambert Pietkin, who taught him composition, drew the chapter's attention to his talent as a composer, and he was appointed second succentor. Piet-

kin's retirement in 1674 and the death seven years later of the first succentor made it possible for Lamalle to become director of the cathedral choir school on 3 September 1681. However, the title of *phonascus* and the revenue from the post were not accorded him until 1688; in his plea to the chapter to obtain this delayed nomination he pointed out that he had *de facto* been carrying out the duties of *maître de chant* for years without being paid to do so and also that he had been composing works for the cathedral in the Italian style.

From 1688, as *maître de chant*, he set about reorganizing the school, which by 1699 consisted of 30 performers. He encouraged the performance of Italian music, and the Italianate tradition that he established persisted throughout the 18th century. From this time onward the canons sent their best young musicians to Rome to perfect their talents. Lamalle himself set them the highest artistic standards. The chapter accepted his resignation on 2 September 1713; in doing so they specifically stated that he should hand over to them all the works that he had composed for the cathedral, a common practice in Liège that unfortunately led to the disappearance of MS works of several centuries composed by the *maîtres de chant* of St Lambert. Lamalle's lost works include the mass and *simphonia* already referred to and also two other masses. Of a four-part *Salve regina* only the continuo part survives (in *B-Lc* Fonds Terry). The same source contains his only surviving complete work, a six-part mass with two obbligato instruments, bassoon and continuo, composed in 1672. The brilliant style of this work, in which the soloists, chorus and instrumentalists partake in a lively dialogue, probably characterized his more mature works too. Free imitation, duets in 3rds, rapid melismas at the ends of phrases and the judicious distribution of the text between the voices are features of a work whose quality explains the high esteem that the canons of St Lambert felt for Lamalle.

BIBLIOGRAPHY

A. Auda: *La musique et les musiciens de l'ancien pays de Liège* (Liège, 1930)
R. Vannes: *Dictionnaire des musiciens (compositeurs)* (Brussels, 1947)
J. Quitin: 'Pierre Lamalle ... 1648(?)–1722', *Bulletin de la Société royale Le vieux Liège*, v (1958)
——: 'Lamalle, Pierre', *BNB*

JOSÉ QUITIN

La Marre, de (*b* c1630; *d* after 1666). French dancer, instrumentalist and composer. His first name is unknown. He regularly performed in court ballets from 1653, when he was mentioned as playing the role of 'une assez laide bourgeoise' in *Le ballet de la nuit*, to 1666, when he danced as a muse in *Le ballet des Muses*. He was a *maître joueur d'instruments*. His only known music is a collection of *Chansons pour danser et pour boire* (Paris, 1650) for one and two voices without continuo. The dedication, to Prévost, one of Louis XIV's dancing-masters, singles out the king's ability as a dancer and recommends him as an example to others.

BIBLIOGRAPHY

M.-F. Christout: *Le ballet de cour de Louis XIV, 1643–1672* (Paris, 1967)

MARGARET M. McGOWAN

Lamartine, Alphonse(-Marie-Louis Prat) de (*b* Mâcon, 21 Oct 1790; *d* Paris, 28 Feb 1869). French poet. 'Declamation is not designed to be sung, nor music to be declaimed. Each should keep to its own sphere'. These words of Lamartine's sum up his suspicion of vocal music, though he enjoyed instrumental music free of 'the heterogeneous alliance with poetry, drama, declamation, decoration and faded finery'. He made an exception for religious music and was a great admirer of Mozart's Requiem.

The musical character of his own poetry, and the mood of noble idealism, often tinged with melancholy, attracted a number of composers from Niedermeyer, whose setting of *Le lac* was regarded by the poet as the single exception proving the rule of the incompatibility of words and music, to Liszt, who described his symphonic poem *Les préludes* as 'after Lamartine', although in fact the music was originally conceived for a male-voice chorus and piano setting of *Les quatre éléments* by Joseph Autran.

MARTIN COOPER

La Martoretta [Martoretta, Il Martoretta], **Giandominico** (*b* Calabria; *fl* 1544–66). Italian composer. Before 1554 he had travelled to the Holy Land. On his return he spent some time in Cyprus where he enjoyed the hospitality of the nobleman Piero Singlitico. Einstein wrote that La Martoretta was 'apparently an ecclesiastic'. In 1552 he was referred to as a 'Dottor in musica'. Jan Nasco is known to have supplied the Accademia Filarmonica at Verona with some five-voice madrigals by La Martoretta, but these are now lost. The second of his four-part madrigal books is entitled 'madrigali cromatici', which signifies that they were written under the new common-time mensuration. The third book contains a setting of a Greek text, *O pothos isdio*, which he probably took back to Venice after his stay in Cyprus.

WORKS
(all published in Venice)
[34] Madrigali, 4vv (1548)
Il secondo libro di [29] madrigali cromatici, 4vv (1552)
Il terzo libro de [28] madrigali, 4vv (1554) [incl. 5 repr. from 1548 book]
Sacrae cantiones liber I, 5vv (1566)
Madrigals in 1544[16], G. Scotto: Il secondo libro delle muse, 3vv (1562)

BIBLIOGRAPHY
A. Einstein: *The Italian Madrigal* (Princeton, 1949/*R*1971)
J. Haar: 'The *Note nere* Madrigal', *JAMS*, xviii (1965), 22

DON HARRÁN

Lamas, José Ángel (*b* Caracas, 2 Aug 1775; *d* Caracas, 9 Dec 1814). Venezuelan composer. Records exist for his baptism, his burial, the marriage to Maria Josefa Sumosa (1 July 1802) and the birth of three children (1808, 1810, 1812). According to the Caracas Cathedral records he became a soprano in the cathedral choir in 1789–90 and in 1796 was promoted to bassoonist. His appointment and promotion coincide with those of Cayetano Carreño and were probably due to Carreño's influence. The association with Carreño also suggests that Lamas received his musical training at Padre Sojo's school. Lamas, unlike other colonial composers, took no part in the independence war. Nevertheless, during the 19th century several biographical legends grew around him; these have been dispelled by Juan Plaza's researches.

Lamas's works are religious compositions in the style of the Classical motets of the late 18th century. He normally employed two oboes, two horns, strings and a chorus of three or four voices. His choral writing is largely homophonic with little or no imitation. In the three-voice works the bass is invariably provided by the

orchestra. Instruments are treated simply but independently, without excessive doubling of vocal parts. The wind usually have sustained tones, the lower strings provide the harmonic foundation and rhythmic pulse and the violins have the main melodies or simple figurations. The violin writing is so careful and idiomatic as to suggest that Lamas also played the violin. Choral sections are contrasted with short solos for one or another of the voices. In these passages the instrumental writing *colla parte* increases considerably. Although Lamas's music is simple, it shows delicate melodic sensibility and a perfect sense of formal balance. The *Popule meus* is his best-known work; the Mass in D, *Miserere* and *Ave maris stella* in D minor are also notable.

WORKS
(all for vv, orch; MSS in Escuela Superior de Música, Caracas)
Mass, D, 1810
30 motets, 1 doubtful, 1 inc., incl.: Popule meus, 1801, ed. in Archivo de música colonial venezolana, vii (Montevideo, 1943); En premio, 1802; Sepulto Domino, 1805; Salve regina, 3vv, 1808, ed. in Archivo de música colonial venezolana, v (Montevideo, 1943); 2 Ave maris stella, E♭, 1808, d, 1814; 3 lessons for the Office of the Dead, ed. in Archivo de música colonial venezolana, ii (Montevideo, 1943); Miserere, 4vv
7 tonos (3 doubtful)

BIBLIOGRAPHY
J. B. Plaza: 'Music in Caracas during the Colonial Period (1770–1811)', *MQ*, xxix (1943), 198
——: 'José Angel Lamas', *Revista nacional de cultura*, c (1953), 21
J. A. Calcaño: *La ciudad y su música* (Caracas, 1958)

ALEJANDRO ENRIQUE PLANCHART

Lamb, Benjamin (*fl* 1700–33). English church musician. He succeeded John Walters as teacher of the choristers of Eton College in 1704 and as organist in 1708; there are indications that he acted as organist in Walters's last years. He himself disappeared from the Eton accounts in 1733. At St George's Chapel, Windsor, he deputized for John Golding as Master of the Choristers and for John Pigott as Master of the Choristers and probably also as organist. He was a very minor composer of church music, represented in Tudway's collection (*GB-Lbm* Harl.7341–2), and wrote a few songs. He also copied music for Eton College, where some of his transcripts survive.

BIBLIOGRAPHY
R. Williams: 'Manuscript Organ Books in Eton College Library', *ML*, xli (1960), 358

WATKINS SHAW

Lamb, Joseph (Francis) (*b* Montclair, NJ, 6 Dec 1887; *d* Brooklyn, 3 Sept 1960). American composer and pianist. He had no formal musical training, but wrote songs during his college years and by 1907 was composing ragtime. His *Sensation: a Rag* (1908, not to be confused with Scott Joplin's *Sensation Rag* of the same year) was published by John Stark with the encouragement of Joplin. In the next decade Lamb wrote *American Beauty Rag* (1913), *The Ragtime Nightingale* (1915), *Patricia Rag* (1916) and *Top Liner Rag* (1916, also known as *Cottontail Rag*). He ceased composing in the 1920s but was rediscovered by Rudi Blesh and Harriet Janis, resumed composing, and in 1959 was recorded for the first time. Lamb was altogether anomalous among the better ragtime composers: he was neither black nor from the Midwest, and although a pianist he never played professionally (he was employed in textile imports for 44 years from *c*1901). Despite the small number of his published works, however, his reputation as a ragtime composer is clearly exceeded only by Joplin's. While Lamb's work is more conventional in form than Joplin's, the two had an almost equal sense of lyricism.

BIBLIOGRAPHY

R. Blesh and H. Janis: *They all played Ragtime* (New York, 1950, rev. 4/1971)

D. Jasen: *Recorded Ragtime* (New York, 1973)

W. Shafer and J. Riedel: *The Art of Ragtime* (Baton Rouge, 1973), 11ff

J. R. TAYLOR

Lambach. Benedictine abbey in Upper Austria. It was founded in 1056 and sanctioned by the emperor in 1061, taking its name from the fortress built by the Frankish counts of Wels-Lambach in the 9th century. The first monks came from the monastery of Münster-Schwarzach near Würzburg, and as early as 1089 requested the consecration of their new church.

By the 12th century there was a school for scribes (presumably established earlier), from which several important illuminated manuscripts survive. The famous frescoes in the west chancel of the church date from the same period: they depict the Three Kings, also the subject of the famous *Dreikönigsspiel* performed at Lambach. This was written down in neumatic notation, but only a fragment of the manuscript has survived. An abbey school was founded in the late 12th century; in accordance with the Rule of St Benedict young oblates were trained in monastic duties and studied many subjects including singing and music theory. Liturgical manuscripts in neumatic notation indicate considerable activity in sacred music. Secular music was also cultivated at Lambach. A 14th-century manuscript of songs by Hermann, Monk of Salzburg (*A-Wn* 4696), originated in Lambach; it contains the well-known 'Martin's Canon', which represents a transition to the early polyphonic style of German-speaking countries, as do the songs of the Mondsee Liederhandschrift (*A-Wn* 2856). The tradition of Christmas, Epiphany and Easter plays also continued to be cultivated. A document of 1409 states that every year the story of St Achatzius was to be sung on his feast day (22 June). In the 15th century the Gothic church was altered and extended to contain two naves, and there is evidence of a choir and an organ built by Hans Reicher in 1469; a second organ was built in 1581. Peasants' wars and the upheaval caused by the Reformation influenced Lambach's cultural life adversely until the 18th century; however a musical culture continued to thrive. A new horn-organ was built in the gate-tower by the Passau organ builder Andreas Putz in 1639, and in 1657 a second one was built for the new Baroque collegiate church. The famous Passau organ builder Johann Freundt built a positive organ for the abbey. For the emperor's visit to Passau in 1676, the bishop there requested the abbot of Lambach to send a tenor, a soprano and an alto as well as one or more violinists, proving the monastery's widespread acclaim. Lambach composers included the monk Roman Weichlein (*d* 1706).

During the 17th and 18th centuries there was much interest in the theatre and small-scale operas: Abbot Schickmayer built a new theatre in 1770. Under Abbot Maximilian Pagl (1705–25) music at the monastery flourished: the organist and *regens chori*, responsible for training the choirboys, were also expected to compose music for use at the monastery. The cathedral organist J. B. Hochreiter was an active composer there in the early 18th century and wrote several masses dedicated to the abbot. His successor was Maximilian Röll, some of whose compositions are in the music archive. Most of

the works commissioned by the abbot from composers outside Lambach (e.g. B. A. Aufschnaiter of Passau and Franz Sparry of Kremsmünster) have been lost. One of the Lambach monks, Maurus Lindemayr (1723–83), wrote the text of comedies set by Michael Haydn (*Rebecca als Braut*, 1766) and probably Joseph Haydn (*Die reisende Ceres*, ?1768/9); Mozart evidently knew Lindemayr's *Der ernsthafte Spass*, for he gave part of it to his pupil Süssmayr to set as an exercise. Michael Haydn's wife Maria Magdalena Haydn-Lipp often sang in the abbey theatre; he himself played the organ and violin there, and the music archive contains several of his instrumental works, including a unique copy of the D major flute concerto. Mozart and his father visited the abbey and presented two symphonies to the library.

The choirboys' hostel was rebuilt in the 19th century and the choir directors were once more encouraged to compose (principally sacred music). A catalogue (1823) records numerous musical works, most of which have been destroyed. After 1950 strict liturgical Cecilian church music became prevalent, probably because early in the 20th century a *regens chori* was appointed who had been trained in Regensburg (where the movement started). The Lambach church choir has remained active.

BIBLIOGRAPHY

P. Schmieder: *Breve chronicon monasterii Beatae Mariae Virginis lambacensis* (Linz, 1865)

A. Eilenstein: *Die Benediktinerabtei Lambach in Österreich ob der Enns und ihre Mönche* (Linz, 1936)

W. Luger: *Die Benediktinerabtei Lambach* (Linz, 1952)

S. Leidinger: *900 Jahre Lambach* (Lambach, 1956)

W. Luger: 'Beiträge zur Musikgeschichte des Stiftes Lambach vom Mittelalter bis zum Barock', *Oberösterreichische Heimatblätter*, xv (1961), 1, 102

EVA BADURA-SKODA

Lambardi, Camillo (*b* Naples, *c*1560; *d* Naples, November 1634). Italian organist and composer. He spent nearly all his musical career at the church of the Annunziata in Naples. He served there from 1569 as a high treble and was taught by Nola, the *maestro di cappella*; he had become a tenor by February 1579. After having deputized for Nola on several occasions in 1588 and 1591, he took up the appointment of *maestro di cappella* on 5 May 1592, working under the condition that he perform only works by Stella and Macque, the organists of the Annunziata. This condition was relaxed, however, on 24 May 1595. He supplemented his income by providing music for such occasions as the funerals of members of the Monte della Misericordia in 1612 and 1630. When he retired in 1631 his monthly wage was 15 ducats.

Lambardi's sacred works were all dedicated to the governors of the Annunziata. His responsories are for double chorus but, unlike Gesualdo's, they have through-composed responds. The two-part motets of 1613, mainly for soprano and bass, include three pieces that may be arrangements of motets from Tartaglino's book of 1574. The three-part motets of 1628, many with high alto parts, use a great deal of repetition in the last half of each work. His first book of madrigals for four voices has none of the strong dissonances and contrasts characteristic of the *seconda prattica* and used in some madrigals of the second book.

Camillo Lambardi's sons were FRANCESCO LAMBARDI, Andrea (*b* Naples, 1590–?95; *d* Naples, 1629) who in 1604 was a soprano at the Annunziata and later a tenor at the royal chapel, and Giacinto (*b* Naples, 1585–?90; *d* Naples, *c*1650) who composed the music (now lost) for G. B. Basile's mascherata *Monte Parnaso* of 1630. Giacinto aided Francesco as organist of the royal chapel from 1636 and succeeded him in that post in 1642. Gennaro Lambardi, possibly another son of Camillo, was an alto at the Annunziata in 1604 and in 1614 an alto-tenor in the royal chapel. Filippo Lambardi, whose relationship with the rest of the family is unknown, received six ducats on 29 January 1627 for organizing the music for the funeral of a member of the Accademia degli Annoverati in Naples.

WORKS

SACRED

Responsorii della Settimana Santa con il Miserere, Benedictus et Christus factus est, 2 choirs (Naples, 1592)
Il secondo libro di [26] motetti, 2vv, bc (org) (Naples, 1613) [contains 2 by Tartaglino, 1 by Animuccia]
Il secondo libro di [22] motetti, 3vv, bc (org), op.10 (Naples, 1628)
Masses, vespers; lost, cited by C. Tutino (MS, *I-Nn* Brancacciana VII B3, f.245)

SECULAR

Il primo libro di [18] madrigali, 4vv (Naples, 1600[13])
Secondo libro de [19] madrigali ariosi, 4vv (Naples, 1609[22])
Madrigal, 5vv, 1609[16]

BIBLIOGRAPHY

S. Cerreto: *Della prattica musica* (Naples, 1601), 156
G. Filangieri: *Documenti per la storia le arti e le industrie delle provincie napoletane* (Naples, 1891), vi, 68f
N. D'Arienzo: 'Salvator Rosa musicista e lo stile monodico da camera (delle origini della musica moderna)', *RMI*, i (1894), 395
S. di Giacomo: *Il Conservatorio di Sant'Onofrio a Capuana e quello di S. M. della Pieta dei Turchini* (Palermo, 1924), 310f
U. Prota-Giurleo: 'La musica a Napoli nel Seicento', *Samnium*, i/4 (1928), 77, 82
G. Pannain: *L'oratorio dei Filippini e la scuola musicale di Napoli*, IMi, v (1934), xxvi–xxvii
F. Nicolini: 'Notizie storiche tratte dai giornali copiapolizze dell'antico Banco della Pietà', *Banco di Napoli bollettino dell'Archivio storico*, iii (1951), nos.2322, 2629
U. Prota-Giurleo: 'Aggiunte ai "Documenti per la storia dell'arte a Napoli"', *Il fuidoro*, ii (1955), 275
F. Strazzulo: 'Inediti per la storia della musica a Napoli', *Il fuidoro*, ii (1955), 106
U. Prota-Giurleo: 'Giovanni Maria Trabaci e gli organisti della real cappella di palazzo di Napoli', *L'organo*, i (1960), 188
W. P. Stalnaker, jr: *The Beginnings of Opera in Naples* (diss., Princeton U., 1968), 46–54, 65–84

KEITH A. LARSON

Lambardi, Francesco (*b* Naples, *c*1587; *d* Naples, 25 July 1642). Italian composer and son of Camillo Lambardi. After serving as a treble in 1599 and an alto in 1600 at the Annunziata, he served the royal chapel as a tenor in 1607 and, from 1615 until his death, as organist. He was *maestro di cappella* of the Pietà dei Turchini conservatory from 1626 to 1630, and of S Maria della Nova in 1628. He gave private music lessons to Maria Ruffo, Princess of Scilla, in 1612, provided entertainment music at Posillipo in 1614, and opened a singing school in 1623. His arias are among the earliest Neapolitan pieces to specify the use of a basso continuo. One two-part piece *Vita mia di te privo* from the 1607 publication, although titled 'madrigal', is stylistically no different from the arias for two voices that make up the rest of the publication, and is partly modelled on Nenna's madrigal for five voices to the same text from his first 1603 publication. Only the 1614 arias use *gorgia* and *sprezzatura* effects. The villanellas in the 1614 and 1616 books are mostly in two sections and make much use of smooth triple metre enlivened by syncopation.

WORKS

Villanelle et arie, libro primo, 3–5vv (Naples, 1607)
Il secondo libro de [22] villanelle . . . con alcune à modo di dialoghi, & 2 arie nel fine, 3–5vv (Naples, 1614)

Canzonette con alcune arie per cantar solo nella parte del tenore, libro terzo, 1, 3–5vv (Naples, 1616[15])
Madrigals in 1609[16], 1609[22], 1612[12], 1616[14], 1620[14]; ed. in Stalnaker 4 works, kbd, *GB-Lbm* Add.30491

For bibliography *see* CAMILLO LAMBARDI.

KEITH A. LARSON

Lambardi [Lambardo], **Girolamo** (*b* Venice; *fl* 1586–1623). Italian composer. On the title-pages of his publications he described himself as a canon regular of S Spirito, Venice; he appears not to have held a specific musical post and probably spent his life in Venice. Giovanni Croce's *Magnificat* of 1605 is dedicated to him and describes him as a pupil of Zarlino, and Gaspari and Eitner maintained that he studied under Palestrina. All his works belong to the tradition of 16th-century sacred polyphony, even the later ones that include continuo. His settings of the antiphoner consist of short motets with controlled imitative sections; each piece is well suited to its liturgical function. Lambardi probably acquired a chiefly local reputation; he was well respected in Venice, for Monteverdi bought some of his music, together with works by Lassus, Palestrina and Soriano, for the library of St Mark's, for performance on ferial days.

WORKS

(all published in Venice)

Sacra cantica B. Mariae Virginis cuiusvis toni, 4vv (1586)
Psalmi ad tertiam, una cum missa, 8vv (1594)
Antiphonarium vespertinum dierum festorum totius anni . . . nunc nuper . . . exornatum atque auctum . . . in tres partes distributum, 8vv (1597)
Antiphonae omnes . . . pro totius anni dominicis diebus in primis, & secundis vesperis nunc primum . . . exornatae . . . atque in duas partes coactae, 4vv (1600)
Missae quattuor . . . liber primus, 4, 5vv (1601)
Psalmodia vespertina omnium solemnitatum cum cantico Beatae Mariae Virginis . . . liber secundus, 8vv, org (1605)
Vespertina omnium solemnitatum psalmodia . . . cum cantico Beatae Mariae Virginis, 6vv, bc (1612)
Vespertina omnium solemnitatum totius anni psalmodia . . . cum duobus canticis Beatae Mariae Virginis, 3, 5vv, bc (1613)
Psalmodia ad vespertinas omnium solemnitatum horas . . . cum duobus canticis Beatae Mariae Virginis, 5vv, bc (1613)
Contrapunta in introitus missarum, 4vv (1617)
Vespertina omnium psalmodia solemnitatum, 3vv (1623)
2 motets, 4vv, *I-Af* (probably from printed vols.)

BIBLIOGRAPHY

EitnerQ
G. Gaspari: *Catalogo della biblioteca del Liceo musicale di Bologna*, ii (Bologna, 1892/*R*1961)

JUDITH NAGLEY

Lambe (*fl c*1400). English composer. His name is attached to a Sanctus in the Old Hall Manuscript (no.97), a descant setting in score with Sarum 2 in the middle voice. The manuscript has been trimmed so as to leave open the possibility that his name may have been longer. He might, for instance, be the Lambertus to whom a SQUARE in *I-Rvat* Reg.lat.1146 is ascribed. It has also been suggested that he may have been the LAMPENS of the lost Strasbourg Manuscript.

BIBLIOGRAPHY

T. Dart: 'Une contribution anglaise au manuscrit de Strasbourg?', *RBM*, viii (1954), 122

For further bibliography and edition *see* OLD HALL MS and ENGLAND: BIBLIOGRAPHY OF MUSIC TO 1600.

MARGARET BENT

Lambe, Walter (*b* ?1450–51; *d* after Michaelmas 1499). English composer. He may be identifiable with the Walter Lambe born in Salisbury and aged 15 on 15 August 1466, who was elected scholar of Eton College on 8 July 1467. On 5 January 1479 he was admitted clerk of the choir of St George's Chapel, Windsor. At

Michaelmas 1479 he and William Edmunds were appointed joint *Informatores*, replacing Thomas Gossyp, who with several other members of the chapel had died of plague during the summer. Lambe's motet *Stella caeli*, the text of which is an invocation for relief from plague, was perhaps written at this time. Lambe became sole *Informator* from Christmas 1479 until he left the chapel in 1484 or 1485. On 1 July 1492 he resumed his clerkship at Windsor but was not reappointed *Informator*. He remained at Windsor at least until Michaelmas 1499, but his subsequent career has not been traced.

Lambe was a popular and esteemed composer. Only John Browne contributed more compositions to the Eton Choirbook, and of the Eton Choirbook composers only William Cornysh, Richard Davy, John Dunstable and Robert Fayrfax are represented in as many surviving sources. Lambe was an extremely accomplished and resourceful exponent of the florid choral style which came to maturity during his lifetime and which English composers continued to cultivate until the 1530s. He wrote with complete assurance in as many as six parts, creating sonorous and animated polyphonic textures while respecting each voice as a melodic entity. His motets in five and six parts are most characteristic, encompassing a total of 21, 22 or 23 notes and contrasting fully-scored sections with more elaborately decorated passages for a reduced number of voices. Stylistic differentiation is not so marked in the four-voice motets, which contain a larger proportion of music in full scoring and use an overall compass of 14 or 15 notes.

Lambe's cantus firmus technique is an interesting blend of current and retrospective practice. *O Maria plena gratia* illustrates contemporary English techniques in its use of a plainsong unconnected with the motet text mainly in long note values in the tenor of the fully-scored sections. The fragmentary six-part *O regina caelestis gloriae* displays an adventurous extension of this, being written on a double cantus firmus of two simultaneously stated plainsongs, a technique that seems to have no English precedent; one of the very few comparable foreign works is *Missa 'Ecce ancilla'/'Ne timeas'* by Johannes Regis (d 1485). In *Ascendit Christus, Nesciens mater* and *Salve regina*, however, Lambe maintained an earlier 15th-century English tradition of using the plainsongs proper to the texts. His treatment of these in a technique which combines paraphrase, migration and conventional tenor cantus firmus emphasizes Lambe's important transitional role in the history of later 15th-century English music.

WORKS

Edition: *The Eton Choirbook*, ed. F. Ll. Harrison, MB, x–xii (1956–61) 2/1969–73) [H]

Magnificat, 5vv, H xii, 88 (on 8th tone, faburden)
Ascendit Christus, 4vv, H xii, 37
Gaude flore virginali, 5vv (indexed in Eton Choirbook but now missing)
Gaude flore virginali, 4vv, H xii, 42
Nesciens mater, 5vv, H xii, 10
Nunc dimittis (lost; mentioned in *GB-Ckc* inventory, 1529)
O Maria plena gratia, 6vv, H x, 31
O regina caelestis gloriae, inc., 6vv, H xii, 161
O regina caelestis gloriae, 5vv (indexed in Eton Choirbook but now missing; an anon. medius, *GB-Lbm* Harl.1709, is perhaps from this motet)
O virgo virginum, 4vv (indexed in Eton Choirbook but now missing)
Salve regina, 5vv, H x, 131
Stella caeli, 4vv, H xii, 32
Virgo gaude gloriosa, 5vv (indexed in Eton Choirbook but now missing)

BIBLIOGRAPHY

F. Ll. Harrison: 'The Eton Choirbook: its Background and Contents', *AnnM*, 1 (1953), 151
——: *Music in Medieval Britain* (London, 1958, 2/1963)

NICHOLAS SANDON

Lambeg drum. A large double-headed drum associated with the Ulster Orange Order, measuring approximately 90 cm in diameter, 75 cm in depth and weighing about 20 kg, traditionally used for accompanying fife tunes in Orange processions. Among the many myths about its origin is one that it was introduced by Duke Schomberg's troops at the time of the Battle of the Boyne (1690). However, its name probably derives from the first use of such a drum at a demonstration about 1894 in the village of Lambeg near Belfast. The 'Lambeg', as it is colloquially known, is beaten with bamboo canes: earlier drums were smaller and beaten with boxwood drumsticks.

Although the fife-and-drum bands, playing reel, jig or hornpipe tunes in march time, have largely been replaced by brass bands in the towns, the drum and its playing art have been preserved, mainly as a sport or hobby, and the Lambeg still accompanies certain processions in country districts and in Ballymena. Lambeg drumming contests are held regularly during the summer in which solo drummers display the good tone or 'ring' of their drums and their skill in maintaining and ornamenting traditional rhythms. Each district of Ulster has its own march-rhythm dialects based on traditional dance rhythms. Some are based on popular songs. Ex.1 illustrates the relationship between a Lambeg rhythm and its fife tune.

Ex.1 *Boyne Water*, transcr. F. Scullion

Two families, Johnson and Hewitt, have traditionally been responsible for the manufacture and maintenance of Lambeg drums, though the hard-wearing oak shells need little attention; many drummers have learnt to recover their own shells with the traditional goatskin. Before World War II occasional 'stick-ins' were held in which champion drummers, often representing rival families, faced each other in a test of endurance and strength, playing for up to nine hours at a time as the one attempted to outlast the other or to confuse his rhythm.

FIONNUAGHLA SCULLION

Lambert, (Leonard) Constant (*b* London, 23 Aug 1905; *d* London, 21 Aug 1951). English composer, conductor and writer on music. His parents (the father was a painter) had come to England from Australia. Lambert was a delicate child, and in later life, though there was little in his striking appearance except a limp to betray it, he was plagued by ill-health. He was educated at Christ's Hospital from 1915 until 1922 when he won a scholarship at the Royal College of Music. His teachers there included Vaughan Williams and Morris. An interest in French and Russian music and in ballet declared itself early. At this impressionable period he made friends with, among others, the Sitwells, his contemporary Walton, with Heseltine, Gray and Van Dieren. He took part as co-reciter with Edith Sitwell in one of the early public performances of Walton's *Façade* (Chenil Galleries, Chelsea, 1926); the work is dedicated to Lambert, who was the composer of the opening 11 bars of 'Four in the Morning'. By then he had been introduced to Dyagilev and had been invited by him to write for the Ballets Russes. Lambert thus became the first English composer to have a work performed by the famous company, beating Berners and his *Triumph of Neptune* by a matter of months. Lambert's *Romeo and Juliet* had a difficult birth at Monte Carlo in 1926. Dyagilev had changed his mind about the designing, replacing the English painter Christopher Wood with the surrealists Ernst and Miró, and insisting on alterations in the choreography. Lambert had a row with the all-mighty impresario, threatened to withdraw his score, but was forcibly prevented from doing so. His action won the sympathy of the choreographer, Nizhinska, who asked him to write a second ballet (*Pomona*, 1926) for the company she was directing at the Teatro Colón in Buenos Aires. *Romeo and Juliet* was largely taken from a student work, a dance suite called *Adam and Eve*, which also provided one number for *Pomona* (the ballet called *Adam and Eve*, given by the Camargo Society in 1932, used the score of *Romeo and Juliet*). Both these early ballets consist of separate numbers mainly in dance forms, with French, Italian or archaic English titles. Outwardly they belong to the Parisian world of neo-classical pastiche, but already, and especially in *Pomona*, there is a hint of independence.

Lambert's activity was not confined to ballet. Between 1926 and 1929 he wrote several delicate songs on words by the Chinese poet Li-Po. Music for Orchestra is a one-movement work of the 'introduction and allegro' type. Lambert was becoming increasingly absorbed in jazz, his addiction being stimulated by two London Pavilion shows, *Dover Street to Dixie* (1923) and *Blackbirds* (1926), both featuring black musicians and dancers, both starring Florence Mills, who died prematurely; Lambert's tribute to her, the *Elegiac Blues* (1927) was the first fruit of his infatuation. It was followed by *The Rio Grande*, which was broadcast by the BBC in 1928, and had its first public performances in 1929 by the Hallé Orchestra at Manchester and London on consecutive evenings, the composer conducting, and with Harty as soloist. This setting for solo piano, chorus, strings, brass and percussion of a poem by Sacheverell Sitwell became and remained Lambert's best-known work, winning a success that put him with Walton at the head of the young generation of English composers. Though he was to write music which went further into human experience, he never surpassed this balance of fantasy with form, of spontaneity with finely judged proportions, sifting Latin American habaneras, Negro jazz, Delius and Duke Ellington through his own sensibility. His response to jazz, more emotional than

Constant Lambert

cerebral, also colours two important works that followed shortly after, but now the starry-eyed rapture of *The Rio Grande* is soured with gall. In the bravura writing and restless rhythms of the Piano Sonata (1928–9) there is Lisztian sulphur as well as exotic spice. The Concerto for solo piano and nine players (1930–31) became a memorial for Heseltine, whose death in 1930 depressed Lambert profoundly. The combination of aggressiveness with blues melancholy disconcerted those hoping for new ventures in the balmy climate of *The Rio Grande*, and the Concerto has been neglected. The crowning work of this, the most prolific phase of Lambert's creative career, ought to have been *Summer's Last Will and Testament*, a masque for orchestra, chorus and baritone solo to words from Nashe's 'pleasant comedy' of that name. The subject of pestilence, nudging Elizabethan roistering with black thoughts about death, was calculated to appeal to him – autumn was his favourite season. In scope if not in actual duration this is his largest work. But though it contains choral numbers with false-relation harmony sensitively used, whiplash orchestral writing in the Lisztian scherzo 'King Pest', and an impressively mournful saraband finale, the score as a whole just fails to get off the ground. In the Sonata and Concerto, pressure of subjective emotion seems to blur the focus. In the masque (which took three years, 1932–5, to write) there are signs of over-elaboration, and Lambert's usually distinct musical personality sometimes merges into English eclecticism.

By now he was facing the dilemma of composers who are talented performers and need to perform to earn a living. In 1930 he became conductor for the newly founded Camargo Society, a private organization which gathered the talent available in England after the death of Dyagilev and the disbanding of the Ballets Russes.

The experience was valuable, and when in 1931 the Vic–Wells (later Sadler's Wells, still later Royal) Ballet started operations, Lambert was the obvious choice for musical director. He remained in the post until his resignation in 1947, but continued to make guest appearances as conductor, was made an artistic director in 1948, and took part in 1949 in the company's first American tour. As a ballet conductor his respect for the score coupled with detailed knowledge of the general and particular needs of dancers enabled him to project his authority from the pit to the stage – by his support he could enhance a dancer's performance. With the flair, judgment and knowledge he showed during his long, selfless and energy-absorbing stint for the Ballet, he was able to play a major role in English cultural life. He threw himself into the work, touring under wartime conditions, acting as one of the two pianists when there was no orchestra. The strain on his health was as severe as the drain on his composing time. The life aggravated his sense of frustration and his heavy drinking. That he should have written little music during these years was to be expected. Yet the ballet *Horoscope* (1937) has greater certainty of touch than *Summer's Last Will and Testament*. It is his most accomplished if not his most ambitious theatre score. The *Dirge from Cymbeline* for male voices and strings (1940) is another example of his attraction to images of decay. *Aubade héroïque*, a short, fastidious orchestral piece written in 1942, reflects his experience with the Ballet during the German invasion of the Netherlands. The pentatonic piano duets, *Trois pièces nègres pour les touches blanches*, recapture much of the old liveliness. His last work was another ballet. *Tiresias* is a tart mythological comedy laid out for a large company and scored for full orchestra without upper strings. Lambert was in poor health (much of the orchestration was written out under his direction by colleagues) and the muted reception of the music at the Covent Garden première in July 1951 did not help. He died six weeks later, one of the causes of death being undiagnosed diabetes. He was nearly 46. *Tiresias*, in a version shortened by Lutyens, remained in the repertory for a few seasons. It is unpublished. Especially in the second of the three scenes, it contains some excellent music, and Lambert's fingerprints are present. The initial theme of the ballet is a gaunt descendant of the fanfare figures occurring in earlier works (e.g. the chorus entry in *The Rio Grande*) deriving, according to Angus Morrison (quoted in Shead) from the black-minstrel shows referred to above. There is a dance for Tiresias-woman in the siciliana rhythm he loved, and there are springy uneven metres, and syncopations which relate both to jazz and to English madrigal.

As a man Lambert stood in vivid relief against the background of English musical life. His musical tastes were unconventional; he had wide-ranging interests in the visual arts and in literature. There were black moods, and they grew more frequent, but at his best there would pour out a stream of verbal effervescence compounded of memories, gossip or limericks, evidence of his ravenous appetite for the strange, absurd or comic, peppered with spluttering indignation against things that annoyed or depressed him. In music he was an independent, rejecting English provincialism and the German slant that had partly caused it, yet discriminating among the newer orthodoxies of the inter-war period, whether they came from Paris or Vienna. But however cool he was in general about neo-classicism or serial music, he would make willing exception for individual works by, say, Stravinsky or Berg that appealed to him. He was not concerned with fashion. His admiration for Chabrier, for instance, may have echoed the taste of his Parisian contemporaries, but few of them shared his enthusiasm for Puccini. In 1934 there appeared his book *Music ho!* (sub-titled *A Study of Music in Decline*) whose almost insolent ease of writing and width of reference remain stimulating reading. Acumen is shot through with prejudice: consciously or no, Lambert wrote less as critic than as composer, with a composer's subjective attitude to other music, but a more than average articulateness. From 1930 he wrote on music for the *Nation and Athenaeum*, from 1931 for the *Sunday Referee*; he also contributed characteristically lively articles to other publications. An evident gift for conducting opera was limited to works by two favourite composers, Purcell and Puccini: *Dido and Aeneas* at Sadler's Wells (1931), *Manon Lescaut* (1937) and *Turandot* (1939 and 1947) at Covent Garden. In 1946 he conducted the first postwar production at Covent Garden, *The Fairy Queen*, in a version prepared by himself in association with Dent. Though his regular work left him little time for guest appearances at home or abroad, he took part in a Festival of British Music at Bad Homburg in 1930 and in the London–Oxford ISCM Festival of 1931, directed performances of Weill's *Die sieben Todsünden* (under the title *Anna-Anna*) for the London season of Les Ballets 1933, and made a number of broadcasts. In 1945 and 1946 he was associate conductor of the Proms. After 1947 he appeared as guest conductor with the Hallé and Scottish orchestras, and in the 1949 ISCM Festival in Palermo. The inauguration of the BBC Third Programme in 1946 gave Lambert a perfect opportunity to conduct the kind of music in which he excelled. In the few years left to him he made well over 50 broadcasts, including little-known music by Liszt, the first performance in England of Satie's *Socrate* and, finally, two memorial concerts for Berners, an old friend who predeceased him by one year. Lambert also broadcast talks, and continued to recite, inimitably, in Walton's *Façade* and in the Berners ballet *A Wedding Bouquet*. He made numerous recordings. Writing in 1946, Dent described him as 'the best all-round musician we have in this country'. His versatility was no doubt one reason why his initial promise as a composer was not consistently fulfilled, but without the many-sidedness he would have been a different sort of composer. He edited eight symphonies and three overtures by Boyce. Of his arrangements, the majority were done for the Sadler's Wells Ballet. He was expert at making a selection providing a danceable and theatrically effective score while also drawing attention to a favourite composer. Among those so treated were Boyce, Chabrier, Liszt, Meyerbeer and Purcell.

WORKS

BALLETS

Romeo and Juliet, 2 tableaux, 1924–5; cond. M.-C. Scotto, Monte Carlo, 4 May 1926

Pomona, 1, 1926; cond. A. Lieti, Buenos Aires, Colón, 9 Sept 1927

Horoscope, 1, 1937; cond. Lambert, London, Sadler's Wells, 27 Jan 1938

Tiresias, 3 scenes, 1950–51; cond. Lambert, London, Covent Garden, 9 July 1951

Arrs.: Mars and Venus [after D. Scarlatti], part of incidental music for Jew Süss; Hommage aux belles viennoises [after Schubert], London, Old Vic, 19 Dec 1929; Les rendezvous [after Auber: L'enfant prodigue], London, Sadler's Wells, 5 Dec 1933; Apparitions [after Liszt], selected Lambert, orchd Jacob, London, Sadler's Wells, 11 Feb 1936, unpubd; Les patineurs [after Meyerbeer: Le prophète,

L'étoile du nord], London, Sadler's Wells, 16 Feb 1937, suite pubd; Harlequin in the Street [after Couperin], selected Lambert, orchd Jacob, London, Sadler's Wells, 10 Nov 1938, unpubd; Dante Sonata [after Liszt], pf, orch, London, Sadler's Wells, 23 Jan 1940, unpubd; The Prospect before us [after Boyce], London, Sadler's Wells, 4 July 1940, unpubd; Comus [after Purcell], London, New Theatre, 14 Jan 1942; Ballabile [after Chabrier], selected Lambert, orchd Chabrier, R. Irving, Lambert, Mottl, London, Covent Garden, 5 May 1950

CHORAL AND ORCHESTRAL

The Bird Actors [originally for pf 4 hands], ov., 1925, reorchd 1927; cond. Lambert, London, 5 July 1931; unpubd
Champêtre, chamber orch, 1926; cond. G. Warrack, London, Aeolian Hall, 27 Oct 1926; used as Intrada of Pomona, arr. pf as Pastorale, unpubd in original form
Elegiac Blues, 1927, also for pf
Music for Orchestra, 1927; cond. L. Heward, BBC, 14 June 1929
The Rio Grande (S. Sitwell), pf, chorus, orch, 1927; cond. Lambert, BBC, 27 Feb 1928
Concerto, pf, fl, 2 cl, b cl, tpt, trbn, perc, vc, db, 1930–31; Benjamin, cond. Lambert, London, Aeolian Hall, 18 Dec 1931
Summer's Last Will and Testament (Nashe), Bar, chorus, orch, 1932–5; cond. Lambert, London, Queen's Hall, 29 Jan 1936
Dirge from Cymbeline (Shakespeare), T, Bar, male chorus, str/pf, 1940; Cambridge, Caius College, Nov 1940 [with pf]; cond. Lambert, BBC, 23 March 1947 [with str]
Aubade héroïque, 1942; cond. Lambert, London, Golders Green, 21 Feb 1943

OTHER WORKS

Songs: 8 Poems of Li-Po, 1v, pf/8 insts, 1926–9; O. de Foras, cond. Lambert, London, Aeolian Hall, 30 Oct 1929 [inst version]
Pf: Pastorale, 1926, unpubd; Elegiac Blues, 1927; Sonata, 1928–9, G. Bryan, London, Aeolian Hall, 30 Oct 1929; Elegy, 1938; Trois pièces nègres pour les touches blanches, 4 hands, 1949
Incidental music: Jew Süss (A. Dukes, after Feuchtwanger), ?1929, cond. Lambert, London, Duke of York's, 19 Sept 1929; Salome (Wilde), completed 1931, cond. Lambert, London, Gate, 27 May 1931; Hamlet (Shakespeare), 1944, London, New Theatre, 11 Feb 1944, unpubd
Film scores: Merchant Seamen, 1940, orch suite arr. 1943, cond. Lambert, Norwich, Royal, 15 May 1943, suite pubd; Anna Karenina, 1947, unpubd
Arrs.: Caprice péruvien [after Berners: Le carrosse du St Sacrement], orch; 8 Syms. [edn. of Boyce], str orch, wind ad lib; 3 Ovs. [edn. of Boyce: The Power of Music, The Cambridge Ode, Pan and Syrinx], str orch, wind ad lib; Conc., pf, small orch [after Handel: Org Concs. nos.2 and 6]; The Fairy Queen [edn. of Purcell], collab. Dent, unpubd

Principal publishers: Chester, Oxford University Press

WRITINGS

Music Ho! a Study of Music in Decline (London, 1934, 3/1966)

BIBLIOGRAPHY

H. Foss: 'Constant Lambert', *MT*, xcii (1951), 449
D. Webster: 'Constant Lambert – an Appreciation', *Opera*, ii (1951), 656
A. Morrison: Obituary, *RCM Magazine* (1951), Nov, 107
R. Buckle: *The Adventures of a Ballet Critic* (London, 1953), 220
M. Clarke: *The Sadler's Wells Ballet* (London, 1955)
R. Irving: 'Constant Lambert', *Decca Book of Ballet*, ed. D. Drew (London, 1958), 184
R. McGrady: 'The Music of Constant Lambert', *ML*, li (1970), 242
C. Palmer: 'Constant Lambert – a Postscript', *ML*, lii (1971), 173
R. Shead: *Constant Lambert* (London, 1973) [with bibliography, detailed list of works, discography, etc]

RONALD CRICHTON

Lambert, Herbert. English clavichord maker, active in Bath; his instruments served as models for those built by THOMAS GOFF.

Lambert, Johann Heinrich (*b* Mulhouse, 29 Aug 1728; *d* Berlin, 25 Sept 1777). German scientist. From 1748 to 1758 he was tutor to the children of a noble family; in 1765 he managed to obtain a post at the Akademie der Wissenschaften in Berlin. He was one of those universal scientists characteristic of the 17th and 18th centuries, and was a figure of particular importance in several subjects mainly connected with physics and mathematics. He determined very precisely the frequencies of the first eight overtones of a bar in its clamped-free modes, correcting and extending Euler's results; the results of Rayleigh and others, a century or more later, were less conclusive. Lambert projected a musical instrument, the 'musique solitaire', whereby a person might enjoy music through his teeth without awakening sleepers.

See also PHYSICS OF MUSIC, §3.

BIBLIOGRAPHY

G. J. Scriba: 'Lambert, Johann Heinrich', *Dictionary of Scientific Biography* (New York, 1970–)

Lambert, John (Arthur Neill) (*b* Maidenhead, 15 July 1926). English composer. He studied composition at the RAM and the RCM (1943–50) and privately with Boulanger in Paris (1950–53). He was director of music at the Old Vic Theatre (1958–62) and was appointed professor of composition at the RCM in 1963. His development has been decisively influenced by his work in the theatre and by contact with student composers; by his own account he has progressed from an academic adolescence to an experimental middle-age, and certainly his most interesting music dates from the later period. Such pieces as '... but then face to face' and *Formations and Transformations* (commissioned for the 1972 Proms) exploit contrasting sonorities and great layers of sound in dramatic juxtaposition, features comparable with the work of Lutosławski and, more particularly, Ligeti.

WORKS

(selective list)

Orch: Variations for Dancing, 1952; Ricercare no.1, str, 1955; Formations and Transformations, 1969; 'From the Nebula', vc, str, 1971
Choral: Mass, D, chorus, wind, 1950; Mass, C, chorus, bc, 1952; O How Amiable are thy Dwellings, chorus, 1962
Vocal: On the Birth of Jesus, S/T, harp, 1951; 3 Songs of Baudelaire, Bar, pf, 1956; The Golden Sequence, 2 solo vv, str, org, 1966; Jubilatio, 1v, 4 perc, 1968; Orpheus Cycle I, experimental film, vv, perc, 1969–70; '... but then face to face', 1v, org, 10 gui, 1971; For a While (Dowson), S, ens, 1973–4; 5 songs of Po Chii-i, Bar, pf, 1974; Antiphons, chorus, org, 1976
Inst: Sonata, fl, pf, 1953; Fantasy Sonata, pf, 1953–4; Ricercare no.2, org, 1956; Org Mass, 1964–8; Orpheus Cycle II, ob, hpd, 1970; 'Tread Softly ...', 4 gui, 1971; Persona, 4 gui, 1975, rev. 1976; Str Qt 'Consider the lilies ...', 1976
Incidental music, edn. of H. Purcell: The Tempest

Principal publishers: Chappell, Chester
MSS in *GB-Lmic*

WRITINGS

'Educating the Student Ear', *Composer* (1967), no.23, p.13
'Whither Music, Whither?', *Composer* (1968), no.28, p.9

RICHARD COOKE

Lambert, Juan Bautista (*b* Barcelona, 1884; *d* Barcelona, 4 May 1945). Spanish conductor and composer. He studied at the Barcelona Municipal Music School and privately with Pedrell and Morera (composition) and Pellicer and Malats (piano). In Barcelona he conducted the bands of the Mozos de Escuadra (1928), the Casa de Caridad and the Municipal Music School. He was also choirmaster and organist at various churches and colleges, and censor of sacred music for the bishopric (1940–45). One of the foremost representatives of the Catalan school of religious music, he composed three masses (*Missa brevis, Misa de San Gregorio* and a Requiem), hymns, motets and organ pieces; his other works include orchestral pieces, three operas, five zarzuelas, chamber music and piano pieces.

A. MENÉNDEZ ALEYXANDRE

Lambert, Michel (*b* Champigny-sur-Veude, nr. Loudun, 1610; *d* Paris, 29 June 1696). French composer, singer and singing teacher. He was a choirboy at Champigny and then a page in the chapel in Paris of Gaston of Orleans, the elder brother of Louis XIII. While there he attracted the attention of Etienne Moulinié, whom Gaston appointed his *chef de la musique* in 1628. From 1634 to 1649 Moulinié served in the same capacity for Gaston's daughter, Mlle de Montpensier, and it was undoubtedly he who was responsible for Lambert's appointment as singer and member (later director) of Mlle de Montpensier's 'six violons'. Lambert was still serving her in 1652, when Loret (*La muze historique*) commented on the pleasure that she received from his performances of dialogues with his sister-in-law and pupil, Hilaire Dupuy. Between 1651 and 1663 he sang and danced in several court ballets. On 10 March 1659 he received a 20-year royal privilege for the printing of his music. In May 1661 he succeeded Cambefort as *Maître de musique de la chambre du Roi*, a position that he held until his death. On 24 July 1662 Lully married Lambert's daughter Madeleine, and during the next three years he collaborated with Lully on the music for three ballets.

Lambert had been recognized since 1636 as an important singer and singing teacher. In the dedication of his first book of *airs* to Pierre de Nyert in 1660, he praised the 'beautiful manner of singing' introduced by Nyert after his sojourn in Italy and said that he was indebted to him for 'all the best I know'. His singing and teaching were widely, even extravagantly, praised. The singer Anne de la Barre wrote to Constantijn Huygens that he was 'the best singing teacher in Paris' (letter of 31 July 1648); Perrin called him the 'Amphion of our days'; according to Le Cerf de la Viéville he was 'the best master to have appeared in centuries'; and Titon du Tillet described the 'charming concerts' in his country home at Puteau-sur-Seine in which he accompanied himself on the theorbo. His popularity at court is a matter of record: the 'Compte de la maison du Roi' for July 1688 shows that 1200 livres were given to him as soloist for the king. Some idea of his method may be obtained from a reading of the *Remarques curieuses sur l'art de bien chanter* (1668; Eng. trans., 1968) of Bacilly, who directed his readers to several *airs* by Lambert for illustrations.

Although most of Lambert's collections of *airs* are lost (the *Mercure galant* numbered them at 20 in 1668), his position as the most important French composer of *airs* in the second half of the 17th century can be confirmed by a study of the more than 300 *airs* by him that remain in printed and MS sources. Quinault and Benserade were among the poets who supplied him with texts. The commonest form in the *airs* is a short binary structure followed by a *double* familiar from the *air de cour*. There are also examples of rounded binary *airs* (e.g. *Mes yeux, que vos plaisirs*) and *airs en rondeau* (*Ah! qui voudra desormais s'engager*); some *airs* border on recitative (*Ombre de mon amant*); others borrow the rhythmic organization of dances such as sarabands (*D'un feu secret*) or are built over chaconne basses (*Ma bergère*); and some are organized as dialogues (*Loin de vos yeux*). In general Lambert's *airs* are models of elegance and grace in which careful attention is paid to correct declamation. In most of his *doubles* he did not allow melismatic writing to destroy the shape of the original melodies (see ex.1) and rarely wrote the sort of purely abstract melodic patterns that mar some of the *airs* even of Guédron. Ex.2 illustrates his control of

Ex.1 *Inutiles pensers* and *double* (*Les airs de Monsieur Lambert*, 1666 edn.)

Ex.2 *Mes yeux, que vos plaisirs* (*Airs*, 1689)

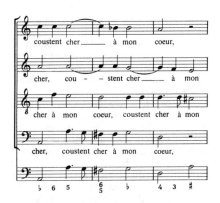

H. Quittard: 'La première comédie française en musique', *BSIM*, iv (1908), 497

A. Arnheim: 'Ein Beitrag zur Geschichte des einstimmigen weltlichen Kunstliedes in Frankreich im 17. Jahrhundert', *SIMG*, x (1908–9), 399

J. Ecorcheville: 'Lully gentilhomme et sa descendance', *BSIM*, vii (1911), 1

T. Gérold: *L'art du chant en France au XVIIᵉ-siècle* (Strasbourg, 1921/*R*1971)

H. Prunières: 'Un maître de chant au XVIIᵉ siècle: Bénigne de Bacilly', *RdM*, iv/8 (1923), 156

L. de La Laurencie: *Les créateurs de l'opéra français* (Paris, 1930)

L. Maurice-Amour: *Benserade, M. Lambert et Lulli*, Cahiers de l'Association Internationale des Études Français, ix (Paris, 1957)

E. Millet: 'Le musicien Michel Lambert (1610–1696) était de Champigny-sur-Veude', *Bulletin des Amis du vieux Chinon*, vii (1968), 186

J. Anthony: *French Baroque Music from Beaujoyeulx to Rameau* (London, 1973, rev. 2/1978)

JAMES R. ANTHONY

variation techniques: a three-part instrumental statement is followed by solo and ensemble settings, and all are based on the same melodic and harmonic materials.

Through his dialogues and some of his more dramatic *récits* Lambert influenced French opera composers. Ménestrier (*Des représentations en musique anciennes et modernes*, Paris, 1681) quoted the text of a dialogue by him between Silvie and Tircis to show how such 'petites chansons' had served as models for what he called 'musique d'action et de Théâtre'.

WORKS

SECULAR VOCAL

Les airs de Monsieur Lambert [20 airs with doubles] (Paris, 1660); 1 ed. in La Borde; 1 facs. edn. from 3/1669 in Ecorcheville

Nouveau livre d'airs (Paris, 1661) [doubtful, probably by B. de Bacilly, see Prunières]

[60] Airs, a 1–4, bc (Paris, 1689); 1 ed. in La Borde; 1 ed. in Quittard; 1 ed. in Gérold

Airs de Monsieur Lambert non imprimez, 75 simples, 50 doubles, *c*1710, *F-Pa*, *Pn*; 1 ed. in Mw, xvi (1958; Eng. trans., 1958)

Airs in 1656³, 1658², 1658³, 1659⁴, 1 ed. in Gérold, 1660¹, 1662⁵, 1662⁶, 1678³, 1679³, 1682², 1683², 1685³, 1687², 1691¹, 1695³; Airs spirituels des meilleurs autheurs (Paris, 1701), 2, ed. F. Delsarte, Archives du chant, iv, xvi (Paris, 1856–61); Brunètes ou petits airs tendres (Paris, 1704), 5 ed. H. Expert, Chants de France et d'Italie, i (Paris, 1910), 1 ed. J. Weckerlin, Echos du temps passé, i (Paris, 1857); Parodies spirituelles en forme des cantates (Paris, 1717), 2 ed. H. Prunières, Les maîtres du chant, iv/1 (Paris, 1924); Meslanges de musique latine, françoise et italienne, divisez par saisons (Paris, 1725); Nouveau recueil de chansons choisies, iv (The Hague, 1729); Nouvelles poésies morales sur les beaux airs de la musique française et italienne (Paris, 1737); Journal de la Haye, ou Choix d'airs français dédié aux dames (The Hague and Amsterdam, *c*1785)

Airs in *Pn* Vm⁷501, Rés Vma 854, Vm⁷651, Rés Vm⁷583–4, Vm⁷513, Vm⁷4822, Rés 89ter

STAGE MUSIC

1 récit, 3 dialogues, in Ballet des arts, Paris, Palais Royal, 8 Jan 1663, *F-Pn*, *V* [with Lully and Benserade]

1 dialogue, in Ballet des amours déguisés, Paris, Palais Royal, 13 Feb 1664, *Pn* [with Lully and Benserade]

1 dialogue, in Ballet de la naissance de Vénus, Paris, Palais Royal, 26 Jan 1665, *Pn* [with Lully and Benserade]

SACRED MUSIC

Leçons de ténèbres pour la semaine sainte, 1689, *Pn* Rés 585, 588 [2 versions]

Miserere mei Deus, 3vv, *Pn* Rés 586

BIBLIOGRAPHY

J. L. le Cerf de la Viéville: *Comparaison de la musique italienne et de la musique françoise* (Brussels, 1704–6/*R*1972)

E. Titon du Tillet: *Le Parnasse françois* (Paris, 1732/*R*1971)

J.-B. de La Borde: *Essai sur la musique ancienne et moderne* (Paris, 1780/*R*1972)

G. Tallemant des Réaux: *Historiettes*, ed. L. J. N. Monmerqué et P. Paris (Paris, rev. 3/1854–60)

E. J. Bertrand: 'Michel Lambert: vie d'un musicien au XVIIᵉ siècle', *Revue et gazette musicale* (1859), 9–156

Lambert, Pierre-Jean (*fl* 1749). French composer and harpsichordist, known only through two works, *Pièces de clavecin* and a *cantatille*, *L'aurore* (both in *F-Pn*), as well as a privilege dated 1 April 1749. The harpsichord pieces are dedicated to the Marquise de Thybouto, Comtesse de Mongommery, a pupil. Their indebtedness to earlier music is naively apparent – a hunting divertissement is modelled on Dandrieu, a variation of *Les sauterelles* on Rameau's *Les niais de Sologne*. The *cantatille* is later than the harpsichord pieces (its title includes an advertisement for them); it is for voice, one obbligato line marked 'violons & flûtes' and basso continuo, and divided into four movements. A romance and a set of contredanses and waltzes were published under the name of Lambert during the Empire.

DAVID FULLER

Lambert Ferri. See FERRI, LAMBERT.

Lambertini. Portuguese firm of piano makers. Luigi Gioacchino Lambertini (*b* Bologna, 17 March 1790; *d* Lisbon, 13 Nov 1864) was a fellow student of Rossini at the Liceo Filarmonico, Bologna. He emigrated to Lisbon for political reasons in 1836, and started his piano-making business, receiving a prize for his instruments in 1838. In 1860, under the direction of his sons Evaristo and Ermete Lambertini, the firm became Lambertini Filhos & Ca., selling and publishing music as well as making pianos. The firm later became Lambertini & Irmão. Evaristo's son, Michel' Angelo Lambertini, was a fine pianist and founded the Grande Orchestra Portuguesa in 1906. The firm closed in 1922.

MARGARET CRANMER

Lambertini, Giovan Tomaso (*b* Bologna; *fl* 1545–73; *d* ?Rome). Italian composer and singer. He was appointed *mansionario* (beneficed priest) at S Petronio, Bologna, in November 1545. The archives record a payment to him in December 1546 for copying a book of music by the *maestro del canto*, Michele Cimatore. In 1548 he entered the choir of the basilica and was registered as singer and scribe. His name disappeared from the record of payments after September 1568 but reappeared in a notice of his expulsion from his benefice in March 1573. Although he was reinstated two months later, he was in Rome in September of the same year: apparently Cardinal Otto von Truchsess von Waldburg, to whom he had dedicated his *Septem psalmi poenitentiales* (1569), invited him to serve him there. The statement by Eitner that he was a singer at S Petronio until 1628 is incorrect, as is the one by Fétis that he was vice-*maestro di cappella* at S Lorenzo, Venice, in 1560.

Lambertini's compositions, all for four voices, display a rich harmonic language that exploits the interplay of major and minor sonorities. His part-writing is non-imitative, and his vocal lines tend to lack distinct melodic shape. However, since he wrote excellent counterpoint and maintained a happy balance between linear and chordal passages, the humanistic text declamation is neither monotonous nor artlessly obvious.

WORKS

Il primo libro de madregali, 4vv (Venice, 1560)
Septem psalmi poenitentiales (Venice, 1569)
1 work, 1559¹⁹; ed. G. Vecchi (Bologna, 1953)

BIBLIOGRAPHY

EitnerQ; FétisB
G. Gaspari: 'Continuazione delle Memorie biografiche e bibliografiche sui musicisti bolognesi del XVI secolo', *Atti e memorie della R. Deputazione di storia patria per le provincie della Romagna*, 2nd ser., i (1875); repr. in *Musica e musicisti a Bologna* (Bologna, 1970), 179ff

FRANK TIRRO

Lambertus, Magister [Pseudo-Aristoteles] (*fl c*1270). Music theorist. His *Tractatus de musica* made an important contribution to the theory of measured music between Johannes de Garlandia and Franco of Cologne. All that is known of his life or nationality is that he evidently spent time in Parisian musical circles. Apart from the treatise itself, the only information about him derives from the comments of three other theorists: the St Emmeram or Sowa Anonymous, Johannes de Grocheo and Jacques de Liège. The St Emmeram Anonymous, writing in 1279, mentioned Lambertus by name and several times made strenuous objections to his notational ideas. At the end of the 13th century Grocheo mentioned him as an advocate of a system of nine rhythmic modes rather than the six modes of Johannes de Garlandia or the five of Franco of Cologne. Jacques de Liège in the 14th century cited him three times along with Franco as a respected and eminent authority, but Jacques referred to him by the name Aristotle rather than Lambertus – an error that probably arose as a result of one anonymous copy of Lambertus's treatise following a work ascribed to Aristotle.

Lambertus's *Tractatus de musica* (ed. in *CS*, i, 251–81) dates from the third quarter of the 13th century, most probably from the late 1260s or early 1270s. The first two-thirds of the treatise deals with the traditional topics of speculative music and of practical rudiments needed by performers; the more important last portion discusses measured music and its notation. After statements on the definitions, etymology and invention of music, there is a section dealing with the notes of the gamut, the hexachord system, the staff, B♭ and B♮ and mutation. Lambertus allowed 12 musical intervals from the unison to the octave, deliberately excluding the tritone. Like Johannes de Garlandia, he subdivided consonant and dissonant intervals into perfect, medial and imperfect, although his formulation differs in its details. This section concludes with an explanation of the ecclesiastical modes and a fairly extensive tonary with musical examples.

In his discussion of measured music Lambertus shows himself to be the most important polyphonic theorist between Johannes de Garlandia and Franco of Cologne. His doctrine, though heavily indebted to Garlandia, nonetheless reveals a shift in emphasis that

prepared the way for the fully mensural system set out by Franco in about 1280. Lambertus's work indicates that by about 1270 the old modal rhythms and melismatic successions of ligatures were of necessity giving way to mensural techniques in the syllabically texted motet. (For an alternative interpretation of the chronology, *see* FRANCO OF COLOGNE.)

After the classification of the categories of *musica mensurabilis* as discant, 'hokettus' and organum, there is an extensive discussion of discant, followed by several paragraphs on hocket (organum is mentioned only in passing). Lambertus did not begin with a discussion of mode and ligature patterns but with an exposition of single note forms: the perfect long, the imperfect long, the *brevis recta* and *brevis altera*, the *semibrevis major* and *minor*, and later, the duplex long. The most significant innovation proved to be his insistence on the priority of the perfect long of three tempora as the fount and origin of all other note values. Here he directly contradicted Johannes de Garlandia, who regarded the long of two tempora as the 'correct' long and the basis of the rhythmic system; Lambertus's perfect long was in Garlandia's teaching the long 'beyond measure'. Lambertus dwelt at length on the concept of perfection and imperfection, explaining how perfections are formed by various combinations of longs and breves and quoting musical examples from the motet repertory. He also specified that the *brevis recta* divides into three equal or two unequal semibreves.

Lambertus next considered ligatures of two to five notes and their rhythmic interpretation. For him the shape of a ligature, not its position in an additive modal series, was the most significant factor as regards its rhythm; the propriety of a ligature is determined purely by the presence or absence of a descending stroke on the left side. Lambertus was also precise about the length of the symbols for rests of different durations.

His last major topic, presented in poetic form, is a consideration of the RHYTHMIC MODES, of which he is unique in listing nine. In accordance with his concept of the primacy of the perfect long, his 1st mode is Johannes de Garlandia's 5th, and he stated that all other modes can be resolved or reduced to this mode. His 2nd to 5th modes are equivalent to Garlandia's 1st to 4th modes and his 7th is Garlandia's 6th. The 6th, 8th and 9th modes are Lambertus's additions; all three feature semibreves, and in the motets quoted as musical examples, each semibreve has its own syllable of text. Thus his added modes reflect the new divisive rhythms and more rapid declamation of text fashionable in the motet during the last third of the 13th century.

The dozen or more motets which Lambertus cited are found mostly in the Montpellier and Bamberg manuscripts (*F-MO* H 196 and *D-BAs* Ed.IV.6), although several appear also in the La Clayette and Las Huelgas manuscripts (*F-Pn* fr.13521 and *E-BUlh*), and other sources, including the musical appendix in the 13th-century manuscript which is the most important source of the *Tractatus* itself (*F-Pn* lat.11266). Lambertus's notational ideas find their best representation in the motets of this short collection appended to his treatise, but his doctrine is also partly reflected in the notation of the Bamberg manuscript. By providing Franco of Cologne with the fruitful concepts of perfection, the perfect long and the imperfect long, Lambertus helped to set the stage for the next several centuries of the mensural system.

BIBLIOGRAPHY

P. Aubry: *Cent motets du XIIIe siècle, publiés d'après le manuscrit Ed. IV. 6 de Bamberg* (Paris, 1908)

H. Sowa: *Ein anonymer glossierter Mensuraltraktat 1279* (Kassel, 1930)

W. G. Waite: *The Rhythm of Twelfth-century Polyphony: its Theory and Practice* (New Haven, 1954)

R. Bragard, ed.: *Jacobi Leodiensis Speculum musicae*, CSM, iii (1955)

G. Reaney: 'Lambertus', *MGG*

J. Smits van Waesberghe, P. Fischer and C. Maas: *The Theory of Music from the Carolingian Era up to 1400*, RISM, B/III/1–2 (Munich and Duisburg, 1961–8)

R. Crocker: 'Discant, Counterpoint, and Harmony', *JAMS*, xv (1962), 1

G. Reaney: 'The Question of Authorship in the Medieval Treatises on Music', *MD*, xviii (1964), 7

——: *Manuscripts of Polyphonic Music: 11th–Early 14th Century*, RISM, B/IV/1 (Munich and Duisburg, 1966)

F. Reckow: 'Proprietas und Perfectio', *AcM*, xxxix (1967), 115

A. Seay, ed. and trans.: *Johannes de Grocheo: Concerning Music* (Colorado Springs, 1967, 2/1974)

M. Huglo: *Les tonaires: inventaire, analyse, comparaison* (diss., U. of Paris, 1969; Paris, 1971)

W. Frobenius: 'Zur Datierung von Francos *Ars cantus mensurabilis*', *AMw*, xxvii (1970), 122

E. Rohloff: *Die Quellenhandschriften zum Musiktraktat des Johannes de Grocheio* (Leipzig, 1972)

E. Reimer, ed.: *Johannes de Garlandia: De mensurabili musica* (Wiesbaden, 1972)

G. A. Anderson: 'Magister Lambertus and Nine Rhythmic Modes', *AcM*, xlv (1973), 57

M. Ralph: *The 'Tractatus de musica' of Lambertus: Edition, Translation, Commentary* (diss., New York U., in preparation)

REBECCA A. BALTZER

Lambeth Choirbook (*GB-Llp* 1). *See* SOURCES, MS, §IX, 19.

Lambranzi, Gregorio (*fl* early 18th century). Italian ballet-master. He wrote one of the most interesting 18th-century books on dance: *Neue und curieuse theatrialische Tantz-Schul* (Nuremberg, 1716/*R*1975, ed. K. Petermann, with Eng. trans. by M. Talbot); Lambranzi's original MS is in Munich Staatsbibliothek (facsimile edition, New York, 1972). It contains 101 plates beautifully engraved by J. G. Puschner, showing costumed dancers in typical positions in an appropriate stage setting. Above the figures, a few lines of music are given, and below are suggestions for the steps and the manner of performance. The subjects of the dances are varied, ranging from *commedia dell'arte* to sport, including dances for two tennis players, peasants, fishermen, soldiers, flag- and arms-bearers, as well as gymnastic exercises. Lambranzi was a very ingenious choreographer, and although he said in his preface that he came from Venice and had performed such dances on the principal stages of France, Germany and Italy it has not been possible to trace his name in contemporary archives or in theatrical literature.

A Giovanni Battista Lambranzi [Lambranci, Lambranti, Lanfranchi] worked as a scenographer at Venice, 1669–95; whether he was related to Gregorio Lambranzi is unknown.

BIBLIOGRAPHY

B. Oskar: *Der Tanz* (Berlin, 1906)

F. Derra de Moroda: 'Auffindung des Gregorio Lambranzi Manuscript', *Die Musik*, xxxiv/8 (1942), 260

FRIDERICA DERRA DE MORODA

Lambuleti, Johannes. French composer. He was active in the 14th century and his name appears near the end of the second voice of the Kyrie of the so-called Sorbonne Mass (edn. in CMM, xxix, 6, 59, 123, 131, 138). He may have been the composer of the complete mass setting, which includes a two-voice *Benedicamus*

Title-page, with a portrait of Gregorio Lambranzi and an example of his dance notation for the loure, from 'Neue und curieuse theatrialische Tantz-Schul' (1716); see also FOLIA

Domino, since there are relationships between the movements of the mass, and since also the movements are all based on mass settings in *I-IV* (with the exception of the *Benedicamus Domino*). The Gloria and Sanctus are incomplete, and the Credo is missing.

BIBLIOGRAPHY

J. Chailley: 'La messe de Besançon', *AnnM*, ii (1954), 93 [with facs. and partial transcr.]

L. Schrade: 'A Fourteenth Century Parody Mass', *AcM*, xxvii (1955), 13

R. Jackson: 'Musical Interrelations between Fourteenth Century Mass Movements', *AcM*, xxix (1957), 54

H. Stäblein-Harder: *Fourteenth-Century Mass Music in France*, MSD, vii (1962), 13, 24f, 48f, 71ff, 77f, 98, 108

GILBERT REANEY

Lamellaphone. A musical instrument whose sound is produced essentially by the vibration of thin lamellae (Lat. *lamella*, from *lamina*: 'a thin plate or layer') or tongues (hence the term 'linguaphone') of metal, wood or other material. Here, however, the term 'lamellaphone' is not used for free-reed aerophones such as the JEW'S HARP, ACCORDION or the European MOUTH ORGAN, nor for the European MUSICAL BOX, but for another type of 'plucked' idiophone found throughout many regions of sub-Saharan Africa and in Latin America, where Africans have introduced it.

Various European terms have been applied to this instrument, for example thumb piano, hand piano and linguaphone ('glottophone' might also be appropriate).

Some common African names are *mbira*, *kalimba*, *likembe* and *sanza* or *kisaanji*. Following the lead of Montandon many musicologists have preferred *sanza* as a generic term though variants of this name are generally to be found only in Zaïre and neighbouring territories.

1. General. 2. Marimba types. 3. Mbira types. 4. Likembe types. 5. West Africa. 6. Latin America.

1. GENERAL. Though construction details vary greatly, the African lamellaphone consists basically of a set of tuned metal, bamboo or other vegetable tongues fitted to a box or calabash resonator or a plain board so that one end of each tongue can vibrate freely. Most board types are usually further resonated during play by holding or propping them inside or on top of a section of a gourd or a bowl of some kind. The timbre of most lamellaphones is frequently modified by means of shell or metal rattling devices attached to the board or the resonator, or both, or by means of small metal sleeves which vibrate freely at the base of the tongues. Sometimes the desired buzzing sound is produced by a mirliton fitted over a small hole in the instrument.

The term 'plucked idiophone', though frequently used, is not strictly accurate, for the lamellae are not plucked; their free ends are depressed and released by the player, who may use his thumbs and fingers, or more rarely, just one or two of his fingers. The tuning arrangement of the keys is important in distinguishing between some instrumental types, but generally the keyboard is arranged to facilitate the production of the desired sound pattern when its notes are divided between the two hands. The lamellaphone is commonly used to accompany song; it is often played solo by a singer, or in small groups to accompany a singer who again is usually one of the players. In some cases, however, it appears that the music is purely instrumental, as in the case of the Nsenga *kalimba*, the sound patterns of different melodies being produced by similar motor patterns. These patterns are often based on separate rhythms common to the music of the particular society.

In several parts of Africa, xylophones and lamellaphones are linked by terminology, and it has been suggested by Nurse that this results from the similar shape of the sounding agents. Jones suggested that lamellaphones are the portative equivalents of xylophones, and, in those societies where one name is used for both types of instrument, lamellaphones are often distinguished by the use of a diminutive prefix, or by adding an adjective. Thus, in Zanzibar xylophones are called *marimba*, and lamellaphones are called *marimba madogo* ('small marimba').

In central, southern and eastern Africa three sets of names for lamellaphones are notable for their frequent appearance and wide distribution, though Laurenty's survey of 467 instruments collected in Zaïre shows a far greater variety of types and terminology for that country alone, including another large category of calabash-resonated board instruments most often called *kakolondondo*. The first set of names, found in an extensive area of eastern and south-east Africa, uses the stem *rimba* or *limba* ('r' and 'l' are one phoneme in many Bantu dialects) with a variety of prefixes as, for instance, in *cilimba*, *kalimba* and *marimba*. The form *marimba* is preferred in this article for referring to instruments of this group. A second set of names is found in the Zimbabwe or lower Zambezi culture area, where the instrument is commonly termed *mbira* or *mbila*, a term to which extensions of various kinds may be added, as in *mbira dza vadzimu*, *mbira dza vaNdau* and *mbila deza*, to indicate the specific instrument. However, the word *mbira* (*mbila*) also occurs with various plural prefixes to indicate xylophones, as in *timbila*, *dimbila* and *mambira*, as well as with reduplication as in *mambirira*. Nevertheless, the word 'mbira' will be used in this article for referring to the Zimbabwe and lower Zambezi group of lamellaphones. A third set of names comprises those based on the stem *kembe*, as in *dikembe*, *ikembe*, *likembe* and *lukeme*. The members of this group are small, box-resonated instruments that are generally of Zaïrean origin. In this article the term 'likembe' is preferred for referring to the members of this group.

2. MARIMBA TYPES. The term 'marimba', with a variety of prefixes, is used by many Bantu societies in wide areas of eastern and south-east Africa and in parts of the Angola–Zaïre region to denote both xylophones and lamellaphones. The singular form usually denotes a one-note xylophone (*see* XYLOPHONE). In such languages in Malawi as Cewa and Yao the term *limba* conveys the notion of a flattish object sticking out (Nurse). In the wide inland region of Tanzania the term 'marimba' or 'malimba' is used exclusively for lamellaphones.

The largest instruments occur among the Gogo of the Central Province of Tanzania: their marimba consists of a rectangular soundbox which is not made from one piece of hollowed-out wood (as are the box-resonated lamellaphones in Central Africa) but of top and side parts nailed or glued together. The box has two soundholes, one at the back for the left middle finger to generate vibrato effects, the other in the centre of the soundboard, which is covered with a membrane from a spider's web that produces a humming or droning effect, particularly when deep notes are sounded. Gogo instruments vary in size and have 19 to 36 lamellae. They are usually decorated with brass nails, beads and pieces of animal skin and are played either solo or in groups of two to three, sometimes in combination with

1. Malimba of the Zimba people of southern Malawi

other instruments (*see* TANZANIA, §5). Large lamella-phones called *malimba* also occur in southern Malawi and central Mozambique, particularly in the Lower Shire–Zambezi valley. They are played by Sena, Zimba and Phodzo musicians (see fig.1). These instruments have a bell-shaped body and usually 26 notes arranged in two ranks. The body is propped inside a large calab-ash with two sticks or pieces of river reed. Pieces of shells are attached to the gourd resonator to give a buzzing sound quality. The playing technique entails using both thumbs and the right index finger, the latter sounding certain notes in upward movement. In playing techniques and organology the Shire–Zambezi lamella-phones are related to the *mbira* types.

Among the Pangwa, Kinga, Bena, Kisi and Nyakyusa of south-western Tanzania the name 'malimba' is given to a small box-resonated instrument with eight lamellae made of umbrella ribs. This instrument is similar to the *likembe* types but lacks the characteristically cut-out section of the top of the *likembe* and the metal sleeves. Instead a chain of beads or metal links lies across the keyboard to give the desired buzzing sound. Further-more, the Pangwa *malimba* is not made from one piece of wood but from two; a trough-shaped resonator is covered with a separate board nailed or glued to it. At the back of the body is a soundhole which the left middle finger alternately covers and opens to produce 'timbre-melodies'. This technique is highly developed among Pangwa and Kisi musicians. This instrument (see fig.2) is often used during long walks in the Livingstone mountains and on the Njombe plateau.

Virtually the same instrument is called *kalimba* by the Tumbuka of Malawi, the diminutive prefix *ka-* refer-ring to the smallness of the instrument. The *kalimba* of the Nsenga of Zambia is, however, quite different. It is also very small, but has a shovel-shaped soundboard which is played over a small gourd. Its 14 notes are laid out in two ranks and a hole made in the middle of the soundboard is covered by a spider's-web mirliton. Blacking (1961) reported the Nsenga *kalimba* as an instrument for youths who would often play it when walking alone or with friends; he found certain recur-rent patterns of 'fingering'.

3. MBIRA TYPES. In the singular the term 'mbira' is used for several types of large gourd-resonated lamellaphones found in the Zimbabwe and lower Zambezi culture region of south-east Africa. In north-eastern Zambia and southern Zaïre the same term denotes single-note xylophones. When used for lamellaphones the word has a plural significance meaning 'the notes' of a single instrument or, as in the case of the Phodzo *malimba*, a certain section of the keyboard only.

The name 'mbira' was first reported in João dos Santos's *Ethiopia oriental* (1609). Dos Santos was a Dominican priest who arrived on the Mozambique coast in 1586 and travelled up the Zambezi river to the trading posts of Sena and Tete. He wrote extensively about music in Mozambique and described instruments called *ambira*, referring to gourd-resonated xylophones and to lamellaphones 'all made of irons about a palm in length, tempered in the fire so that each has a different sound'.

(*i*) *Mbira dza vadzimu*. This instrument is considered to be an ancient form of lamellaphone played by the Shona-speaking peoples in southern Africa. It is used mainly for religious ceremonies for ancestors; the terms

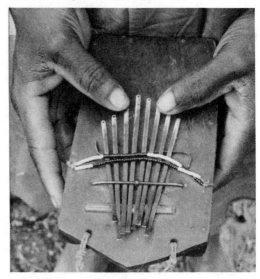

2. *Malimba of the Kisi people of south-western Tanzania*

'mbira dza vadzimu' (in the Zezuru dialect) or 'mbira dze midzimu' (Karanga) mean 'notes of the ancestral spirits'. It is closely related to the *hera* or *matepe*, another type of large lamellaphone which is also played for the *vadzimu* by Korekore, by Sena–Tonga musicians of Zimbabwe and by the Tavara and Nyungwe of Mozambique. The instrument is large, usually with 22 or 23 metal lamellae. Two distinguishing features of this type are its tray-shaped body and the hole in the lower right-hand corner of the soundboard; the hole enables the player to hold his instrument by hooking the little finger of his right hand into it (see fig.3). The instrument is wedged inside a calabash with two pieces of river reed or stick which are placed on the lamellae just above the straining bar and wedged tightly under the lip of the calabash. The calabash is called *deze*, a name which is also often used for the instrument itself. Another distinc-tive characteristic is the arrangement of the keys; all the treble notes are on the right-hand side and all the bass notes on the left (A. Tracey, 1963). On the left-hand side the notes are arranged in two ranks. The tuning plan is also distinctive, the keys being tuned to a nearly equidis-tant heptatonic scale. Tracey suggested a close relation-ship in the tuning pattern between the *mbira dza vad-zimu* and the eight-note *kalimba* which occurs north of the Zambezi; he wrote, 'at the centre of the *mbira dza vadzimu* there is a *kalimba*'. This would account for a certain irregularity in the tuning pattern of the former. On the *mbira dza vadzimu* (see fig.4) the *kalimba* layout is, however, reversed left to right.

In 1872 Carl Mauch, a German traveller and geologist, saw a *mbira dze midzimu* of a Karanga musician at Pika's village near Zimbabwe. In a diary note of 13 March he described the instrument and its music, gave a sketch of its tuning (see fig.5) and notated some melodies. This tuning is identical to a tuning observed 88 years later by A. Tracey in the Salisbury area (Tracey, 1963; Kubik, 1971). The *mbira dza vadzimu* is played with the two thumbs and the right-hand index finger. The playing action is described by Zezuru musicians as *kukwenya* ('to scratch', 'to strike').

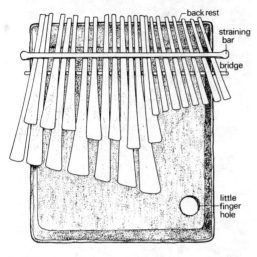

3. *Mbira dza vadzimu*

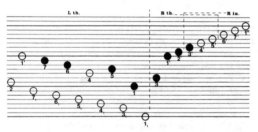

4. *Tuning pattern of the mbira dza vadzimu (the kalimba core is shown in black)*

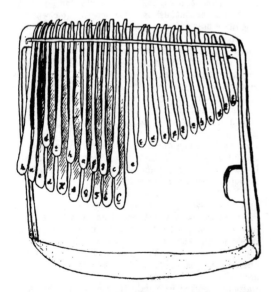

5. *Carl Mauch's sketch (1872) of the mbira dze midzimu of a Karanga musician, Zimbabwe*

The thumbs play in the normal manner while the right index finger 'scratches' the six reeds of its playing area (outer right) in an upward movement. Zezuru songs for the *mbira dza vadzimu* are all the same length with 48 elementary pulses making up the total pattern for this form. The music is based on chord sequences, the most important regulative feature in Shona *mbira* music (A. Tracey, 1963). The *mbira dza vadzimu* is often a duet instrument. Two or more players form a group, and rattles known to the Zezuru as *hosho* are played with the *mbira* ensemble in ancestor-cult rituals, in which rattles stress the three-pulse rhythm. A full performance includes various voices, used in three or four different styles and pitches, including *kuhongera* ('singing the bass'), humming and *kunguridzira* ('yodelling'). The first part of the music is called *kushaura* ('to start', 'to lead') and is usually played by the junior musician. Any following part is called *kutsinhira* ('to sing a refrain', 'to exchange notes'). In the 1930s there were few players of the *mbira dze midzimu*, and in the Karanga-speaking area it has been replaced by the *njari*, another type of large lamellaphone, imported from the Sena–Nyungwe group of peoples at Tete, Mozambique. However, the *mbira dze midzimu* survived among the Zezuru, who live in the area around Salisbury, and there are now a great number of players, some of them organized into *mbira* clubs.

(*ii*) *Venda types*. The *mbila dza madeza* of the Venda in northern Transvaal, South Africa, is similar to the Zezuru *mbira dza vadzimu*. It also occurs among the Lemba and was probably imported into Vendaland. This large calabash-resonated instrument is heptatonic and has 27 notes. It is often used to accompany songs at beer parties and is also played by men other than Lemba. Three instruments are often played together. Another Venda type is called the *mbila tshipai*. It has 11 to 18 lamellae and a pentatonic tuning. According to some oral traditions, both the instrument and its tuning pattern were borrowed from the Tsonga who live to the south of the Venda. This small *mbila* is usually played by boys (see Blacking, 1965).

(*iii*) *Mbira dza vaNdau*. There are three major types among the Ndau: the *tomboji* or 'highland type', found around the Mozambique border to the south of the town of Umtali, and played mostly by older people; the *danda*, a development of the older *tomboji*, the most common type and played by young people; and the *utee*, characterized by soft, flexible, deep notes. Ndau lamellaphones differ from the Shona types both in tuning and in layout of the notes; furthermore, they are not used in religious contexts. The tuning pattern shows two very small and four very large intervals within a hexatonic division of the octave.

(*iv*) *South-eastern types*. Other closely related kinds of lamellaphone in south-eastern Africa include the *njari huru* of the Chikunda, the *hera* of the Korekore, the *malimba* of the Zimba and Phodzo, the *mana embudzi* (also called the *mbira dza vaTonga*) and the *nyonga-nyonga*. Tracey believes that the ten or more types of lamellaphone that occur in this region are, like the *mbira dza vadzimu*, all descended from one instrument, the eight-note *kalimba*.

4. LIKEMBE TYPES. *Likembe* (plural *makembe*) is the most common form of a name given to a distinctive type of box-resonated lamellaphone of Zaïrean (Congolese) origin. Members of some language groups give other

prefixes to the stem, for example *dikembe* and *ikembe*, or omit the prefix, as in the *kembe* played by the Mpyemo of the Central African Republic. Speakers of Sudanic or Nilotic languages deformed even the word stem when they adopted the instrument, e.g. *lukeme* in Acooli (northern Uganda); others have given it an entirely different name. This instrument is also often referred to by the generic term '-sanji' (*esanji, chisanji, chisanzi* etc). Among Ngangela, Luchazi, Mbwela and Mbunda speakers of south-eastern Angola and north-western Zambia the full term 'chisandzi cha likembe' is often used. This establishes that *chisandzi* is the generic and *likembe* a specific term in these languages.

The *likembe* is a distinct kind of lamellaphone; the origin and etymology of the word are uncertain. 162 specimens of this type form the most important group out of a total of 467 lamellaphones collected during the years 1904–58 for the Musée Royal de l'Afrique

are burnt into the body of the *likembe*, one in the end closest to the player's body, the other in the back. By alternately opening and closing the back hole with the middle finger of the left hand the musician produces timbre modifications, vibrato and 'wow' effects. This is regarded as the most difficult part of the playing technique, as the middle finger often moves in a counter-rhythm to the motor patterns of the thumbs. The lamellae, straining bar and bridge of the *likembe* are of forged iron. Eight to 12 lamellae are commonly used and, in contrast to some other types of lamellaphone, the width of each does not vary throughout its length. The ends are filed smooth in order not to hurt the player's thumbs. A strong straining bar is stitched to the projecting section of the soundboard and holds the lamellae down between bridge and backrest. The latter, a piece of hard wood, is held in place solely by the pressure of the lamellae. Layout of the lamellae and tuning plan vary

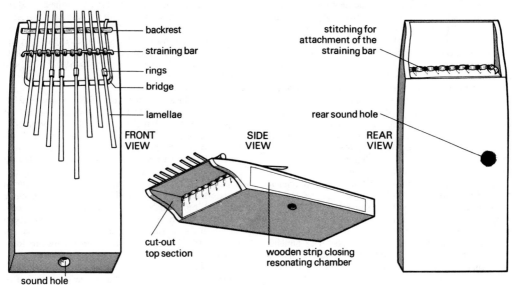

backrest
straining bar
rings
bridge
lamellae

FRONT VIEW

stitching for attachment of the straining bar

rear sound hole

REAR VIEW

SIDE VIEW

cut-out top section

wooden strip closing resonating chamber

sound hole

6. *Front, side and rear views of a likembe*

Central in Tervuren, Belgium. They indicate how popular *likembe* may have been during the first half of the 20th century in the vast Congo region. In the 1970s the *likembe* was known all over Zaïre, in the Republic of the Congo, various parts of the Central African Republic, the south-east corner of Cameroon, north-western Zambia, eastern and south-eastern Angola, the southern Sudan, most parts of Uganda, parts of Ruanda and Burundi and in border areas of western Tanzania.

(*i*) *Construction.* The *likembe* (see fig.6) has a distinctive cut-out section projecting from one end of the hollowed-out box. Instrument makers usually begin by cutting out this top section from a log of hard, dry wood (in southern Zaïre, Zambia and Angola the wood most frequently used is *Pterocarpus angolensis*); the box is then hollowed out, usually from the left side, but in some areas from both. Before closing the resonating chamber with a thin strip of wood the maker usually inserts a few small pieces of glass, one or two bottle-tops or small stones to create additional vibration when the instrument is played. The wooden strip, sometimes made from eucalyptus, is glued in place with wax. Two soundholes

from region to region but one arrangement seems to be particularly widespread: the lower-pitched, longer lamellae are in the centre, but a further bass note with a long lamella is added at the extreme right (see fig.6). Buzzing metal rings, which are usually threaded on to the lower-pitched keys, are another important feature. Musicians often aim at obtaining an accentuation of certain notes and note patterns by their careful distribution of such buzzing devices.

(*ii*) *History and social context.* Montandon called the *likembe* 'type Bangala et du Bas-Congo', associating it with Lingala-speaking peoples of the Lower Congo. Maes called this *sanza* the 'type fluvial' and confirmed that it was already in existence among the Ngala before the arrival of the Belgians, though he could not say whether it originated there or in the Lower Congo. Coquilhat, the first Belgian agent in this territory, described the *likembe* in his writings about the Upper Congo (1888). Laurenty wrote that the Kongo and the Ngala probably carried this type of *sanza* across the Congo. In the decade before World War I the *likembe* was well established along the Congo River (among the

Kongo, Mfinu and Teke peoples) and as far up as Kisangani (formerly Stanleyville). It was known among the Loi and Mbuja and had also already spread along the Ubangi River, where it was collected several times from Ngbaka musicians in the years 1911–13, and from the Ngbandi. In the south it was known in the Kasai region at that time.

Evidence suggests that the *likembe* is a relatively recent offshoot of the lamellaphone family, and has become widespread in many territories only since the late 19th century. In Zaïre it was played mainly for personal diversions during long journeys on foot; its melodic motor patterns combined with the rhythm of walking to sustain the traveller for long distances. Being thus favoured by porters, workers and servants it quickly spread across the continent during the period of European exploration and colonization. The process quickened with the onset of vast labour migrations, as men travelled to the mines and the new industrial and agricultural centres. There were two processes: in the first, workers who came from *likembe*-playing societies introduced the instrument into a new region; in the second, workers from societies not playing the *likembe* adopted the instrument at their place of work and later introduced it to their home areas.

A chronology of the recent spread of the *likembe* can be reconstructed from the still abundant oral traditions of central and east Africa. For example, one independent Ganda informant, Ephraim Bisase (*b* 1912; see Kubik, 1976), related that the instrument was played in his youth by the Alur, a Nilotic people settled in north-western Uganda, who had adopted it from the Congo. The Alur went to Buganda as porters and agricultural workers, playing and singing to their lamellaphones in the Luganda tongue, 'Maria, jangu, tugende Kongo' ('Maria, come, let us go to Congo'). Consequently people in Buganda named the new instrument *kongomaria*. Bisase first heard this expression in Mengo (Buganda) as a schoolboy in 1924. The Alur lamellaphones were small, and when the Soga, a Bantu-speaking people living to the east of the Ganda, adopted these instruments from the Alur, they called them *budongo* (plural of *kadongo*). This term derives from the word 'ndongo', the name the Ganda and Soga use for the bowl lyre, an instrument well established in this area, and the diminutive prefix *ka*. In Busoga it is used as a group instrument: a *kadongo* ensemble often comprises three to five lamellaphones of different sizes and a flat container rattle. In northern Uganda, among the Acooli, Labwor and Lango peoples, the *lukeme* is also played in ensembles, sometimes with as many as 20 instruments of three different sizes. In 1929 Tucker found the *likembe* firmly established among the Azande of southern Sudan; again, it was associated with porters. Later it spread further north to the town of Wau and north-east to the Ethiopian border. After 1945 the *likembe* lost much of its popularity in Zaïre when the guitar appeared and began to assume a similar social role, being often used on journeys. In Kinshasa in the 1950s the *likembe* was sometimes combined with the guitar in small dance bands playing rumba music but it disappeared from modern Congolese bands with the introduction of electrically amplified instruments.

The spread of the *likembe* has not halted everywhere. In the remote south-eastern parts of Angola it is still advancing and has been played by Mbwela and Luchazi musicians only since the 1950s. Young workers who travelled north to work on Portuguese plantations adopted it from the Cokwe and Lwena; hence many of their songs are in one of these languages.

5. WEST AFRICA. Although both the box- and the gourd-resonated lamellaphones are found in west Africa, the distribution of the instrument is not as widespread as in Bantu-speaking Africa. Lamellaphones in this part of Africa include the Tikar *mboton* and the Vute *timbrh* in Cameroon; the Yoruba *agidigbo*, the Edo *akpata* and the Igbo *ubo* in Nigeria; the Songhay *jidiga* in Niger; the Ashanti *prempensua* in Ghana; the Kpelle *gbelee* and *bonduma* and the Vai *kongoma* in Liberia; and the *kondi* and *kongoma* in Sierra Leone. These instruments may have spread into the west African coastal zone via Cameroon. With a few exceptions, like the Edo *akpata* and some of the larger instruments such as the *kongoma* of Sierra Leone and Liberia, used in ensembles, the lamellaphone is used for personal music-making, and is sometimes considered merely a child's instrument. On the whole, it is overshadowed by the historical, social and religious significance of other instruments (*see* ASHANTI MUSIC; CAMEROON; GUINEA; IVORY COAST; NIGERIA; SONGHAY MUSIC).

6. LATIN AMERICA. During the 19th century lamellaphones were taken by African slaves to various parts of the New World. Ewbank reported its great popularity among Africans in Rio de Janeiro in 1856 and described a calabash-resonated instrument similar to that in fig.1. The instrument has also been reported in Louisiana and as far south as Montevideo, Uruguay, where in the 1950s it was still known as *quisanche*, which is the Zaïrean 'chisanji'. Variants of the name 'marimba', reported by Ewbank as in common use in Brazil by Africans of Mozambique origin, have been reported in the Caribbean; there the instrument is still very popular, whereas in South America it appears to be obsolescent.

Ortiz's survey (1952–5) of Afro-Cuban instruments mentions the small type, commonly held in the lap of seated performers. But by the 1970s the large box-resonated instrument, the size and shape of a small suitcase, was apparently much more popular. Thompson described its manufacture and use in the Caribbean area in some detail. He reported that in Haiti and Dominica the instruments usually have three or four steel tongues, whereas in Cuba and Puerto Rico they have ten or more. They are usually made from lengths of discarded gramophone spring, but clock springs and saw- or knife-blades have also been used. The player sits on the instrument, reaching down to sound the keys with the fingers of one hand while beating out sometimes complex rhythms on the sides and front of the box with the other hand. The *marimbula* (a common name-variant in this area) serves as a rhythmic and harmonic bass instrument in folk and commercial popular dance ensembles, the keyboard being divided from the centre so that two sets of notes (each sounding, for example, the tonic, supertonic and dominant degrees of a scale) provide tolerable bass harmony for two or more different tonalities, keeping the need for extreme changes of hand position to a minimum. Used in this manner the instrument serves as a robust and portable 'poor man's string bass' (Thompson).

In Jamaica, where it is known as the 'rumba-box', the

instrument is also used in the ensembles of religious groups such as the Rastafarians. Like the *prempensua* in Ghana it serves to replace drums.

BIBLIOGRAPHY

J. dos Santos: *Ethiopia oriental e varia historia de cousas notaveis do Oriente* (Evora, 1609, 2/1891)

T. Ewbank: *Life in Brazil* (London, 1856), 111f

D. and C. Livingstone: *Narrative of an Expedition to the Zambesi and its Tributaries – 1858–64* (London, 1865)

C. Coquilhat: *Sur le Haut-Congo* (Paris, 1888), 364

G. Montandon: 'La généalogie des instruments de musique et les cycles de civilisation', *Archives suisses d'anthropologie générales*, iii/1 (1919), 1–95

J. Maes: 'La sanza du Congo belge', *Congo*, ii (1921), 542–72

H. P. Junod: 'The Mbila or Native Piano of the Tshopi Tribe', *Bantu Studies*, iii (1929), 275

P. R. Kirby: *The Musical Instruments of the Native Races of South Africa* (London, 1934, 2/1965)

J. Kunst: 'A Musicological Argument for Cultural Relationship between Indonesia – Probably the Isle of Java – and Central Africa', *PMA*, lxii (1935–6), 57

F. Ortiz: *Los instrumentos de la música Afrocubana* (Havana, 1952–5)

K. P. Wachsmann: 'The Sound Instruments', in M. Trowell and K. P. Wachsmann: *Tribal Crafts of Uganda* (London, 1953)

F. J. de Hen: *Beitrag zur Kenntnis der Musikinstrumente aus Belgisch Kongo und Ruanda-Urundi* (Tervuren, 1960)

J. Blacking: 'Patterns of Nsenga Kalimba Music', *African Music*, ii/4 (1961), 26

H. Tracey: 'A Case for the Name Mbira', *African Music*, ii/4 (1961), 17

G. Kubik: 'The Phenomenon of Inherent Rhythms in East and Central African Instrumental Music', *African Music*, iii/1 (1962), 33 [see also corrigenda, *African Music*, iv/4 (1970), 136]

J. S. Laurenty: *Les Sanza du Congo* (Tervuren, 1962)

A. Tracey: 'Three Tunes for "Mbira dza vadzimu" ', *African Music*, iii/2 (1963), 23

A. M. Jones: *Africa and Indonesia: the Evidence of the Xylophone and other Musical and Cultural Factors* (Leiden, 1964, 2/1970)

G. Kubik: 'Generic Names for the Mbira', *African Music*, iii/3 (1964), 25; iii/4 (1965), 72 [see also corrigenda, *African Music*, iv/4 (1970), 136]

J. Blacking: 'The Role of Music in the Culture of the Venda of Northern Transvaal', *Studies in Ethnomusicology*, ii (1965), 20–53

M. Dias: 'Os instrumentos musicais de Moçambique', *Geográphica: revista da Sociedade de geografia de Lisboa*, ii/6 (1966), 2

G. Kubik: 'Ethno-musicological Research in Southern Parts of Malawi', *Society of Malawi Journal*, xxi/1 (1968), 20

F. O. Bernhard, trans.: *The Journals of Carl Mauch: his Travels in the Transvaal and Rhodesia* (Salisbury, 1969)

H. Tracey: 'The Mbira Class of African Instruments in Rhodesia (1932)', *African Music*, iv/3 (1969), 78

G. Kubik: *Natureza e estrutura de escalas musicais africanas* (Lisbon, 1970)

G. T. Nurse: 'Cewa Concepts of Musical Instruments', *African Music*, iv/4 (1970), 32

R. Garfias and D. A. Maraire: 'The African Mbira: Music of the Shona People of Rhodesia', H 72043 [disc notes]

P. Kazadi: 'Congo Music: Africa's Favorite Beat', *Africa Report*, xvi/4 (1971), 24

G. Kubik: 'Carl Mauch's Mbira Musical Transcriptions of 1872', *Review of Ethnology*, iii/10 (1971), 73

D. Thompson: 'The *Marimbula*, an Afro-Caribbean Sanza', *Yearbook for Inter-American Musical Research*, vii (1971), 103

A. Tracey: 'The Original African Mbira?', *African Music*, v/2 (1972), 85

J. Blacking: *How Musical is Man?* (Seattle and London, 1973)

C. van Oven: 'The Kondi of Sierra Leone', *African Music*, v/3 (1973–4), 77

G. Kubik: 'Uganda Music of the Past: an Interview with Ephraim Bisase', *African Music*, vi/1 (1976)

ROBERT A. KAUFFMAN (1), GERHARD KUBIK (2–4)
ANTHONY KING (5), PETER COOKE (6)

Lame musicale (Fr.). SAW, MUSICAL.

Lament. A term for a variety of musical and poetic forms related to or inspired by mourning rites for the dead or ritual leave-taking, as in the case of bridal laments. These forms include: the once universal domestic funeral lament, the main concern of this article; instrumental laments which, in Scotland for example, make up a notable part of the repertory of the highland bagpipe (*see* SCOTLAND, §II, 7), but are known else-where, particularly in eastern Europe among shepherd communities; and numerous creations of Western art composers, some in commemoration of the death of famous people or personal friends, others for theatrical purposes. (For discussion of these *see also* APOTHÉOSE; DÉPLORATION; DIRGE; DUMP; ELEGY; EPICEDIUM; LAMENTO; NENIA; PLAINTE; PLANCTUS; THRENODY; and THRENOS.)

1. Introduction. 2. Antiquity. 3. 20th-century domestic practice.

1. INTRODUCTION. The domestic sung lament still flourishes in many parts of Europe and elsewhere. Despite its importance as an example of music and poetry produced spontaneously under the pressure of deep emotion, it has not been studied comprehensively. While such a study could say much about the nature and purpose of art the lament is also utilitarian: it serves firstly as a technique of mourning, to ease the mind of its grief; secondly as a lyrical expression of regard for the dead person; and thirdly as a ritual aid to reconcile the dead to their new condition and to persuade them not to return to trouble the living. Beyond any therapeutic role, the funeral lament is a part of the rites of transition and incorporation into the world of the dead, taking on a ceremonial form that raises it from the level of a mere sequence of cries of grief and despair. In this form, remarkably consistent through the ages and across the globe, two kinds of expression are balanced – the almost involuntary cry of grief (which will henceforth be referred to as the 'planctus') and the more or less deliberate framing of a message (the 'discourse'). 'Planctus' and 'discourse' may be said to represent moments of crisis and order respectively, the planctus being a paroxysmic utterance (sometimes accompanied by the self-infliction of physical pain), whereas the discourse is a relatively rational communication and a lyrical resolution of suffering. The ritual sense asserts itself artistically, by turning the planctus into a refrain that punctuates the discourse at fairly regular intervals, so that a relatively shapely composition evolves.

It is hard to determine to what extent the process is deliberate. Wherever the custom of ritual lament is found, the performers tend initially to break into cries of despair, and only gradually to introduce more and more 'message-laden' phrases in a singing tone of voice, until finally a form emerges that perceptibly follows the traditional rules of the locality. The planctus consists of stereotyped exclamations of grief such as 'oi, ioi, ay, jaj, hej, och, ohone, of, mu, mamo, alas, alalu', which become converted into periodic refrains in the course of the ritualization of the lament, along with apostrophes such as 'Oh, my father!', 'Ah, brother!', 'Ay, little sister!' or the repeated invocation of the dead person's name.

However long the keen may last (a single lament of half an hour's duration is not uncommon), the discourse usually consists of a sequence of short lines – metrical or not – each preceded or followed by a planctus refrain. The discourse is sung solo, while the refrain may be sung either by the soloist or, nowadays more rarely, by the group of those present. Ex.1 is a classic example of the alternation of discourse and planctus.

2. ANTIQUITY. References to ritual lament, for the passing of gods and heroes and for natural or military disasters as well as for ordinary people, abound in the literature of this period. The laments to Osiris in Egypt, Attis in Asia Minor and Adonis in Syria are particularly

Ex.1 from a lament, Lezhë district, north Albania; coll. and transcr.
A. Lloyd

A ça pas-ke pritë me ba? O mi-ku je-me,
Ej hej, ej hej! Pas-ke my-lle goj' e sy. O
mi-ku je-me, Ej hej, ej hej!...

What has come over you? *O my friend, ej hej!*
You've closed your mouth and your eyes. *O my friend, ej hej!* ...

well known and are discussed along with Babylonian laments by Gaster (pp.30ff). The famous Assyrian lament of Egi-me is quoted by Langdon (p.215). Plato, Solon and Plutarch are among Greek writers whose works contain references to the custom (see Leipoldt, Reiner). In ancient Rome funeral song was known as *nenia*. Gregory of Nissa, Ambrose, Tertullian, Origen and John Chrysostom are among the fathers of the early Christian church who describe and deplore the custom. Something is even known of the tone of voice in which laments were sung in ancient Mesopotamia, a kind of quasi-musical utterance known as *sasu*, shared alike by keeners, town criers and speakers in the tribune. The solo lament was doubtless always common at a domestic level, but documents suggest that the responsorial type was also frequently performed in the ancient world. The combination of solo discourse and group planctus is found in descriptions such as that in the *Iliad* (xxii, 474–515), when Hector's body was brought on a mule-cart to the gates of Troy and in turn Andromache, Hecuba and Helen led the lament 'while the women wailed in chorus'. Likewise Xerxes' lament at the end of *The Persians* gives a fairly vivid illustration of the relationship between keener and chorus in Aeschylus's time, although here the dirge is for a military disaster, not an individual death.

Numerous as the reports are, however, the writings of the ancient world give only indirect and fragmentary impressions of lament performances, comprehensible only in the light of modern survivals. They testify to the eloquence of the keeners (and folklorists have reported modern peasant laments that do not fall below the great models of the past in poetic force), but since their concern was literary or moral, they usually present only the discourse of the laments; the planctus aspects were to them redundant, regrettable crudities, or even (for some Greek city writers) dubious practices from Asia. The antiphonal planctus occupied a more important place than is generally shown in Greek literature. The same is true of the Old Testament, where the discourses of lamentations appear frequently, but only on rare occasions, such as in David's lament for Abner in *2 Samuel* iii.32–4, are the planctus responses of the onlookers indicated. Yet the custom of combining individual lament with group planctus was so popular that in the time of Jesus it appeared in a children's game. A passage in *St Matthew* xi.16–18, none too clear in the Authorized Version, yields its sense immediately if it is translated as: '[The present generation] is like unto children sitting in the market place calling to their playmates and saying: We sang to

you and you did not dance, we intoned the lament and you did not cry the responses'. As De Martino observed, 'an individual lament without the periodic reply of the planctus seemed to the evangelist an absurdity as evident as the Jews' resistance to the preachings of the Baptist'. Where musical (and poetic) form is concerned, the combination of discourse and planctus has been of great importance. Indeed the very origin of antiphon and of refrain may lie in the lament. Probably the frequency with which the discourse was punctuated by planctus cries depended considerably on the social and cultural level of the mourners. Among the traditionally minded peasants the laments were doubtless improvised amid a profusion of unbridled emotive refrains, whereas among the educated classes of the cities of the Near East and Mediterranean, the dirges would to some extent be prepared in advance and even written down (as is suggested in *2 Chronicles* xxxv.25), and the interjections would be fewer and more subdued, until the laments for people of rank ceased to be sung and were instead recited, ultimately becoming simply funeral orations, delivered in a speaking voice only slightly heightened musically.

3. 20TH-CENTURY DOMESTIC PRACTICE. In Europe the sung lament is still to be heard in parts of the Iberian peninsula and it flourishes most vigorously in certain Mediterranean islands (e.g. Corsica), southern Italy and throughout the Balkans. In Central Europe, Hungary is probably its grandest home, as Finland is in the north. It was still possible to record ceremonial keening in Ireland (*see* CAOINE) and northern Russia (*see* UNION OF SOVIET SOCIALIST REPUBLICS, §IX, 2) in the 1950s, but the informants were few and old.

Where music and poetry are concerned, in Europe, three kinds of lament are distinguishable: firstly an extemporized melopoeia, a kind of musical prose, with an improvised text but no attempt at versification; secondly a melodic recitative, with numerous repetitions of the same motif in improvised variations according to the metre of the text, which is more or less versified (in extempore fashion) but entirely irregular in strophe; and thirdly a more songlike (i.e. arioso-like) performance, in which the melody and the basic text are known in advance and the extempore element is merely a matter of adapting certain established poetic formulae to fit the particular circumstances (e.g. 'O my father [mother, brother, friend], as fire burns, so burns my heart. You were a good ploughman [housewife, shepherd, cobbler], and now you've vanished behind the cross...). Inevitably the first category contains a far higher proportion of planctus to discourse than the third category. It is hard to say which is older: both kinds appear to have existed since ancient times. In any case the most common and perhaps most classic kind of lament is that in the second category, in which planctus and discourse are likely to be well balanced, and the equilibrium between what is already in the memory and what is made up on the spur of the moment may be delicately maintained. Katsarova remarked (p.183): 'Each utterance of the lament is a fragment of a melodic and poetic whole, which before taking actual musical shape has been living and echoing in the keener's consciousness in countless variations, and which continues to dominate her thoughts after it has been uttered in the form of a song'.

In Albania the emotional outpouring is called 'lament by tears' and the more formal, relatively controlled keen is called 'lament by voice'. In actual performance it often happens that as the wailer becomes more and more immersed in the expression of her grief and more and more inspired, what began as a chaotic 'lament by tears' gradually becomes formalized into a nearly metrical melody, carrying an almost regularly syllabic set of text lines, although at any time excessive grief may break the pattern. A talented Bulgarian keener, Pena Grozeva, remarked in 1954: 'A lament is a song. But with a song, you know the tune, you know the words. With laments you know neither words nor tune; you just shed your tears, and arrange the words and tune as they come into your head. . . . It's something quick-firing and true; it comes straight from your soul, and you can never exactly repeat what you've once sung' (Katsarova, p.179). Ex.2 shows the beginning of Pena Grozeva's lament for her mother, a dirge whose text reached classic heights of eloquence.

Ex.2 Opening of Pena Grozeva's lament for her mother, Dermantsi, Bulgaria (Katsarova, 1969)

Mu, dear little mother, you are separated from the white world. *Mu mamo mu mamo,* I couldn't find you alive. *Mu mamo, mu, little mother,* you are still warm. *Mu mamo mu, dear little mother, mo mamo ma,* mother who gave me birth, *mamo, mamo, mamo, mu, little mother . . .*

Lament melodies usually have a narrow compass, confined within the range of a tetra- or pentachord. In some places, however, notably Hungary, a form with a wider compass, extending to an octave or more, can be found. If ex.2 may be taken as being typical of a large class of Balkan lament melodies, the main Hungarian type, according to Rajeczky, is a descending minor pentatonic tune, cadencing on 5, 4, ♭3 and 1, and distinguishable from similarly constructed Hungarian folksongs mainly by its unrhymed prose-like text, by its variety of line length and by its free recitative character (as in ex.3). The lament of southern Italy shows some similarities to Balkan models. A typical example from Lucania was given by De Martino (see ex.4). Each short

Ex.3 from a Hungarian lament, Nitra district, Czechoslovakia; transcr. Z. Kodály (Rajeczky, 1966)

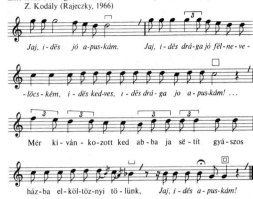

Oh, my own father! Oh you dear good man who brought me up. My dear, my kind father! Why did you want to go away from us into that sad dark house? Oh, my own father!

line is followed by a planctus refrain, and is sung to a melody traditional for laments in the locality. In essence the melody is formed by a descending pentatonic series with a range of a 5th, each line beginning with an explosive upward slide of a semitone before tumbling downward. Here, as elsewhere, the laments are marked by the constant reiteration of a simple melodic formula, by rubato, by occasional accelerations punctuated by agonized vocal outbursts and by sobs, sighs and moans (usually omitted by transcribers). In modern Europe group participation seldom occurs and the Italian laments are no exception. But judging from the structure of the Lucanian laments and the regular occurrence of the refrains, it seems likely that the ritual leader–chorus pattern was present in the territory, and perhaps not so very long ago.

Ceremonial laments performed by men are not unknown, but as a rule the task is entrusted to women, most often the close relatives of the dead person; sometimes, however, specialist keeners are invited to mourn. They may be regarded, in some degree, as professionals. Generally they are women of prestige in the village, with a known talent for keening, who are invited to funerals to lead or augment the lamenting. If they are paid at all, it is likely to be in kind, rarely in money. Sometimes

Ex.4 from a lament, Ferrandina, southern Italy; coll. E. de Martino and D. Carpitella (de Martino, 1958)

these specialists rely on a ready-made repertory of versified laments, sung to songlike melodies, but the admired keeners are those with a ready gift of poetic inspiration, which at times shows itself on a massive scale. 30,000 lines of lament were recorded from the Russian keener Irina Fedosova, and when Maxim Gorky heard her performing at the Nizhni Novgorod fair he found her improvisations 'of a sincerity and power no longer to be found among book poets nowadays'.

Among modern city-dwellers the personal ritual lament is transformed at best into the funeral oration by priest or minister. By personally and ritually articulating their grief, members of the societies discussed above find relief and help with the problem of bereavement. Often, in her heart, the keener is not only lamenting the dead, but is also giving expression to the sorrows of her own life and finding solace thereby. Rajeczky reported a Hungarian peasant woman's remark: 'I look forward to lamenting as one would to a shower of rain'.

BIBLIOGRAPHY

S. Langdon: *The Babylonian Epic of Creation* (Oxford, 1923), 215
E. Mahler: *Die russische Totenklage* (Leipzig, 1935)
Z. Kodály: *A magyar népzene* [Hungarian folk music] (Budapest, 1937, enlarged 2/1943, enlarged with exx. 3/1952, 6/1973; Eng. trans., 1960, rev. 2/1971)
C. Brăiloiu: *Bocete din Oaş* [Laments from Oaş] (Bucharest, 1938)
E. Reiner: 'Die rituelle Totenklage der Griechen', *Tübinger Beiträge zur Altertumswissenschaft*, xxx (1938)
J. Leipoldt: *Der Tod bei Griechen und Juden* (Leipzig, 1942)
Y. Sokolov: *Russian Folklore* (New York, 1950)
E. de Martino: *Morte e pianto rituale nel mondo antico* (Turin, 1958)
T. H. Gaster: *Thespis, Ritual Myth and Drama in the Ancient Near East* (New York, 1961)
B. Rajeczky, ed.: *Siratók* [Laments], Corpus musicae popularis hungaricae (Budapest, 1966)
R. Katsarova: 'Oplakvane na pokoynitsi' [Funeral laments], *IIM*, xiii (1969), 177 [with Fr. summary]
M. Alexiou: *The Ritual Lament in Greek Tradition* (London, 1974)

A. L. LLOYD

Lamentations. The Old Testament verses of mourning of the prophet Jeremiah (*Threni, Lamentationes*), portions of which are sung in the Roman Catholic liturgy as lessons for the first Nocturn of Matins on Maundy Thursday, Good Friday and Holy Saturday. Along with the great responsories, the Lamentations are musically the most important texts of TENEBRAE and were set polyphonically by major composers as early as the 15th century.

1. Structure of chant. 2. Polyphonic Lamentations to 1600. 3. Settings after 1600.

1. STRUCTURE OF CHANT. Until the 16th century the number and selection of Lamentations verses used as lessons for the *triduum sacrum* varied considerably, but the Council of Trent succeeded in establishing an ordered system. Since then the division has essentially been as shown in Table.1. The first lesson begins with

TABLE 1

	Lesson I	Lesson II	Lesson III
Maundy Thursday	i.1–5	i.6–9	i.10–14
Good Friday	ii.8–11	ii.12–15	iii.1–9
Holy Saturday	iii.22–30	iv.1–6	v.1–11

the words 'Incipit lamentatio Jeremiae prophetae' (or 'De lamentatione'), the third lesson on Holy Saturday with 'Incipit oratio Jeremiae prophetae'. A distinguishing feature is the appearance of Hebrew letters (Aleph,

Beth, Ghimel) at the beginning of each verse, indicating that in the original Hebrew the five chapters of laments were largely an alphabetical acrostic. Each lesson ends with the line 'Jerusalem, Jerusalem, convertere ad Dominum Deum tuum', which is not from Jeremiah but is freely adapted from *Hosea* xiv.1.

Like the Passion, the Lamentations receive particular emphasis in the readings of the Holy Week liturgy and are distinguished by special lesson chants. Those that survive from the Middle Ages are in part simple recitation formulae and in part more individual settings that attempt to express the content of the text (ex.1). Since

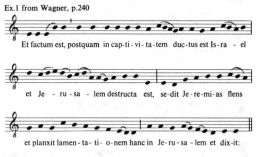

Ex.1 from Wagner, p.240

Et factum est, postquam in cap-ti-vi-ta-tem duc-tus est Is-ra - el

et Je - ru - sa - lem destructa est, se-dit Je-re-mi-as flens

et planxit lamen-ta-ti-o-nem hanc in Je-ru-sa-lem et dix-it:

the Council of Trent a specific *tonus lamentationum*, related structurally to the 6th psalm tone, has been officially prescribed in the Roman liturgy (ex.2). For the *Oratio Jeremiae* (third lesson on Holy Saturday) a melodically rich, ornamented *tonus lamentationum* of Spanish provenance can be used.

Ex.2 *LU*, 631

A - leph   Quomodo sedet sola civitas ple-na   po-pu-lo:
fa-cta est quasi vidua   Do-mi-na Gen-ti-um:

2. POLYPHONIC LAMENTATIONS TO 1600. The history of polyphonic Lamentations can be traced only as far back as the middle of the 15th century. Like contemporary polyphony for the Passion, the earliest settings intended to serve liturgically as lessons for the *triduum sacrum* were organum-like with strictly syllabic declamation and frequent parallel movement. Such settings may be distinguished, however, from a smaller group of motet-like works based on single verses. The best-known example is Dufay's three-voice lament on the fall of Constantinople (1453), which has a French text ('O tres piteulx') in the upper voice and the Roman *tonus lamentationum* with the text 'Omnes amici ejus sprever-unt eam' (*Lamentations* i.2) in the tenor. Other 'Lamentation motets' of the late 15th century are Johannes Cornago's *Patres nostri peccaverunt* and Compère's *O vos omnes*.

A large, two-volume collection of polyphonic Lamentations printed by Petrucci in 1506 illustrates the extent to which composers of the Josquin generation were interested in works of this genre. These composers were Alexander Agricola, Marbrianus de Orto, Johannes de Quadris, Gaspar van Weerbeke, Erasmus Lapicida, Tinctoris, Tromboncino and Bernhard Ycart. A characteristic of the works of this collection, and of Lamentations generally in the first half of the 16th century, is that individual composers treated a varied selection of *Lamentations* chapters. They also differ greatly in the number of verses they set, as well as in the way they grouped them in the course of the lesson. In melodic substance the majority of the Lamentations in Petrucci's collection bear the stamp of the Roman *tonus lamentationum*, which is clearly recognizable as a cantus firmus in places and more freely worked in others. The setting of Tromboncino is peculiar in that the opening is set to an original theme, the individual motifs of which are repeated in the same or a different order as the text progresses. The Lamentations of Quadris are also notable for their strophic-like form, similar in structure to settings of the *Magnificat* c1500.

The flowering of polyphonic Lamentations that began with the Petrucci edition lasted for the whole of the 16th century. Netherlands, French, Italian and Spanish composers were first and foremost in this field, English and German being less in evidence. For the first half of the century the main sources are *Liber decimus: Passiones* (Paris, 1534; *RISM* 1535²); *Selectae harmoniae* (Wittenberg, 1538¹); *Lamentationes Hieremiae Prophetae* (Nuremberg, 1549¹); and *Piissimae ac sacratissimae lamentationes* (Paris, 1557⁷). These publications include Lamentations by Arcadelt, Crecquillon, Festa, Antoine de Févin, Johannes Gardano, Isaac, La Rue, Stephan Mahu and Claudin de Sermisy. Carpentras must rank as the most prolific composer of the genre at this time; his Lamentations, which had appeared in an individual edition in Avignon in 1532, enjoyed special favour with the popes and were regularly sung in St Peter's until 1587.

Lamentations in the first half of the 16th century adhered more rigidly to the Roman *tonus lamentationum* than those of earlier composers, which means that most were in the same mode (F Ionian). Stylistically they are similar to the contemporary motet; four-part writing is clearly the rule and the spectrum of contrapuntal possibilities is quite varied. The Lamentations of Carpentras and Crecquillon, in particular, are often highly imitative and rhythmically complex, whereas La Rue preferred a more homorhythmic texture reminiscent of the French chanson. Expressive devices are not more highly developed or more frequently used than in other genres despite the strongly expressive nature of the text.

In the second half of the 16th century the most significant settings are those of Morales (Venice, 1564), Victoria (Rome, 1581), Lassus (Munich, 1585), Asola (Venice, 1585), Handl (in *Opus musicum*, iii, Prague, 1587) and Palestrina (five books from 1564 on, only the first of which was printed in Rome in 1588). Palestrina's Lamentations, along with works of other composers, replaced those of Carpentras in the papal chapel from 1587. Stylistically they are close to his *Improperia* and *Stabat mater* and belong among his most mature works. In contrast to settings from the first half of the century, they reveal a stronger tendency to homorhythmic texture in order to obtain a clear declamation of the text (this is also true of the Lamentations of Lassus and Handl, but not of Morales and Victoria). In Palestrina's compositions only the Hebrew letters are melodically and rhythmically ornate, rather like illuminated initials. Adherence to the Roman *tonus lamentationum* was no longer as prevalent nor as strict; this is generally true of other settings of his time. The only complete setting of the Lamentations from 16th-century England, which

appears anonymously in the British Museum (Roy. App.12–16), does occasionally paraphrase the chant tone in the upper voice, but the Lamentations of Byrd, Tallis and White appear to dispense with it altogether. In contrast, Palestrina's Spanish contemporaries made striking use of a Spanish *tonus lamentationum*: a setting by Morales, in which this lesson tone appears as a cantus firmus, was transcribed into tablature for lute and solo voice by Miguel de Fuenllana in 1554, anticipating to some extent the early monodic Lamentations of the next century.

3. SETTINGS AFTER 1600. The stylistic innovations of the early 17th century influenced the Lamentations slowly. Among the numerous settings in the *stile antico* are those of Giovanni Croce (Venice, 1603 and 1610), Karl Luython (Prague, 1604), Viadana (Venice, 1609) and Gregorio Allegri (1641). The Lamentations of Allegri partly superseded those of Palestrina in the papal chapel. But monodic Lamentations with basso continuo began to be written in Italy as early as the end of the 16th century. According to a report by G. B. Doni, Vincenzo Galilei of the Florentine Camerata had been moved to attempt composition by the Lamentations and by the songs of sorrow in Dante's *Divina commedia*, and performed his own monodic Lamentations 'molto soavemente . . . sopra un concerto di viole' (*Trattato della musica scenica*, chap.9). Any settings that Galilei may have written down, however, have not survived. The Lamentations by Cavalieri may have been written in collaboration with Galilei, but must also be seen in connection with the religious aspirations of the Congregazione dell'Oratorio. Probably performed in 1599 in the Oratorio della Vallicella in Rome, Cavalieri's setting is transitional in its alternation of parts for soloist and chorus; it remained as much a phenomenon as the Lamentations of Annibale Gregori for solo voice and basso continuo printed in Siena in 1620. Not until the middle of the century do the sources for monodic Lamentations become more common, principally in Italy. Among those printed are works by A. B. della Ciaia (1650), Pietro Cesi (1653), C. D. Cossoni (1668), Cazzati (1668), Francesco Cavanni (1689) and G. P. Colonna (1689); manuscripts surviving from this period include Lamentations by Carissimi, Frescobaldi, M. Marazzoli, G. F. Marcorelli, Carlo Rainaldi, Stradella, Gaetano Veneziano and others. The only Lamentations from Germany in this period, those of Rosenmüller, were completely under the influence of Italian art.

The texts of these composers conform to the basic criteria of a liturgical Lesson (Hebrew letters, 'Jerusalem' line, and occasionally even traces of the Roman *tonus lamentationum*). Musically, however, they depart dramatically from the traditional reserve of the *stile antico*. The Lamentations text, in places very moving, gave the composers of the 17th century a number of welcome opportunities for text expression (chromaticism, free use of dissonance etc), and the pathos thus achieved, reinforced by a tendency to arioso form, brought the monodic Lamentations of this period into the immediate domain of the *lamento* in opera, oratorio and cantata. Interest in the setting of Lamentation texts waned noticeably in 18th-century Italy, but remained relatively high in Naples. Many representatives of the so-called Neapolitan school composed such works: Alessandro Scarlatti, Durante, Francesco Feo, Porpora, Leonardo Leo, David Perez, Jommelli, Alessandro Speranza and, in the 19th century, N. A. Zingarelli.

Apart from Italy, only France played an important part in the history of the Lamentations in the 17th and 18th centuries. There, more than 100 years after the collected edition of Lamentations of Le Roy & Ballard (1557), a new development began that culminated in the extensive *leçons de ténèbres* of Michel Lambert (1689) and Charpentier (?c1670–95). The most important characteristics of these settings, apart from the expressiveness of the Italian arioso style, are highly melismatic writing which shows to the full the French practice of diminution, and the frequent use of the Roman *tonus lamentationum* as a melodic foundation. In fact, the *leçons de ténèbres* are unique, contrasting both with the French motet and with contemporary Italian Lamentations. The *leçons* not only served a liturgical function but were also performed in the courtly presentations of Louis XIV. The Lamentations for chorus by Guillaume Nivers (1689) were a specifically French phenomenon inspired by the exceptionally successful masses 'en plain chant' of Henri Du Mont. In the 18th century the published settings of François Couperin (?1714), Brossard (1721) and Lalande (1730) must be counted among the most noteworthy French church music of their time; their influence was felt even outside France, particularly in the Lamentations of J.-H. Fiocco, who was active in Brussels. French appreciation of the Lamentations at this time is reflected in literature, as in Diderot's reference to the Lamentations of Jommelli (*Le neveu de Rameau*).

For the most part, the continuing development of the Lamentations drew to a close at the end of the 18th century and not until the middle of the 20th century did the genre experience a short revival. Krenek's *Lamentatio* (first performed in 1958) is based on the complete text of the nine lessons and the music combines modern serial techniques with formal and stylistic devices of the late Middle Ages to produce an original choral style of great forcefulness. In contrast, Stravinsky's *Threni* of 1958 for soloists, chorus and orchestra is a pure 12-note work, in which the composer expressly avoided both liturgical and historical connotations.

Special cases in the history of the Lamentations are the German solo songs of the Neumarkt Cantional (c1480), non-biblical songs of mourning using the Hebrew letters and Jerusalem line. Finally, Haydn's Symphony no.26 ('Lamentatione') may be mentioned in this context as a unique work, one in which the Gregorian tone is used as a motif as well as a cantus firmus.

BIBLIOGRAPHY

G. Vale: 'Le lamentazioni de Geremia ad Aquileia', *Rassegna gregoriana*, viii (1909), 105
P. Bohn: 'Die Lamentation des Propheten Jeremias', *Gregorius-Blatt*, xxxviii (1913), 100
P. Wagner: *Einführung in die gregorianischen Melodien*, iii: *Gregorianische Formenlehre* (Leipzig, 1921/R1962)
G. Prado: *Cantus lamentationum pro ultimo Triduo Hebdomadae majoris juxta Hispanos Codices* (Paris, Tournai and Rome, 1934)
A. Schmitz: 'Ein schlesisches Cantional aus dem 15.Jahrhundert', *AMf*, i (193⸗, 385–423
A. E. Sch⸗   ⸗erstemmige muziek op de Lamenties van Jeremia tot het einde der 16de eeuw (diss., U. of Louvain, 1948)
——: 'Les origines des Lamentations polyphoniques au XVᵉ siècle dans les Pays-Bas', *IMSCR*, v Utrecht 1952, 352
G. E. Watkins: *Three Books of Polyphonic Lamentations of Jeremiah*,

1549–1564 (diss., U. of Rochester, 1953)
G. Massenkeil: 'Zur Lamentationskomposition des 15. Jahrhunderts', *AMw*, xviii (1961), 103
——: 'Eine spanische Choralmelodie in mehrstimmigen Lamentationskompositionen des 16. Jahrhunderts', *AMw*, xix–xx (1962–3), 230
——: *Mehrstimmige Lamentationen aus der ersten Hälfte des 16. Jahrhunderts*, Musikalische Denkmäler der Akademie der Wissenschaften und der Literatur in Mainz, vi (Mainz, 1965)
T. Käser: *Die 'Leçon de ténèbres' im 17. und 18. Jahrhundert*, Publikationen der Schweizerischen musikforschenden Gesellschaft, ii/12 (Berne, 1966)
A. A. Ross: *A Study of 'Hieremiae Prophetae Lamentationes' of Orlando di Lasso*, i (diss., Indiana U., 1968)
E. R. Thomas: *Two Petrucci Prints of Polyphonic Lamentations 1506* (diss., U. of Illinois, 1970)
C. W. Warren: 'The Music of Royal Appendix 12–16', *ML*, li (1970), 357
H. T. David: 'Hebrew Letters in Polyphonic Settings by Christian Composers', *Bach*, ii/2 (1971), 6
P. Ludwig: 'Lamentations notées dans quelques manuscrits bibliques', *Etudes grégoriennes*, xii (1971), 127
H. J. Marx: 'Monodische Lamentationen des Seicento', *AMw*, xxviii (1971), 1

GÜNTHER MASSENKEIL

Lamento (It.: 'lament'). Usually, a vocal piece based on a mournful text, often built over a descending tetrachord ostinato (*see* GROUND, §3) and common in cantatas and operas of the Baroque period.

Originating in ancient Greek drama and further developed in Latin poetry, the lament topos enjoyed a privileged status in European literature. Set apart as an exceptional moment of emotional climax of particularly intense expression, it provided an occasion for special formal development and for the display of expressive rhetoric and of affective imagery.

Madrigals designated 'lamento' appeared occasionally during the 16th century; Stefano Rossetto's *Lamento di Olimpia* (1567) and B. S. Nardò's *Lamento di Fiordeligi* (1571), for example, each set appropriately dramatic stanzas from Ariosto's *Orlando furioso*. The genre assumed musical importance around the turn of the 17th century as a focus of the theoretical justifications of the new monodic style. Indeed, in defining the cathartic purpose of that style, theorists such as Giacomini, Mei and Galilei singled out the lament; because it expressed a height of emotional intensity, it was the type of text best calculated to move an audience to pity, thereby purging them of strong passions.

Librettists and composers of early opera acknowledged the special dramatic position and affective responsibility of the *lamento*, distinguishing it from the narrative flow of its context: librettists imposed greater formality through using more strongly metred and rhymed texts in which particularly affective lines often recurred as refrains; and composers interpreted these texts with greater freedom, repeating or otherwise enhancing specially affective words or phrases with melodic sequence, dissonance or textural conflicts, often imposing an overall tonal coherence to create structural self-sufficiency.

One of the most effective and clearly the most influential of early 17th-century *lamenti* was Monteverdi's *Lamento d'Arianna* from his opera to a libretto by Ottavio Rinuccini, performed in Mantua in 1608. The musical isolation of this *lamento* from its context was recognized immediately in contemporary descriptions of the opera's performance and confirmed by the publication of monodic Ariadne laments by Severo Bonini (1613), Possenti (1623) and F. A. Costa (1626) and, most conclusively, by Monteverdi's own reworking of the piece as a madrigal (1614), the publication of the monodic version (1623) and his adaptation of the madrigal to a sacred text (1640). His madrigal publication may well have inspired the madrigal laments of Ariadne published by Claudio Pari and Antonio Il Verso in 1619.

Monteverdi's monodic *lamento*, though self-contained, is not a closed form. Its organization develops out of the internal exigencies of its text: no super-imposed formal structure determines its shape. It is not an aria, for arias, by definition, were fixed, predetermined musical structures and therefore inappropriate to the expression of uncontrolled passion in a lament. Clear distinctions between laments and arias persisted for some time. Claudio Saracini's second and fifth monody books (1620 and 1624) each contain one lengthy dramatic piece entitled 'lamento', in addition to madrigals and pieces marked 'aria'. Sigismondo d'India's fourth and fifth books of *Musiche* (1621 and 1623), in addition to a large number of 'arias', characterized by strophic structure and simple rhythmic and melodic style, contain a total of five monodic 'lamenti in stile recitativo', highly expressive, irregular settings of lengthy dramatic texts by the composer himself. The tradition of the extended, dramatic recitative *lamento* persisted until nearly the middle of the century and is exemplified in such works as Peri's *Lamento d'Iole* (1628), Abbatini's *Pianto di Rodomonte* (1633) and Rovetta's *Lagrime d'Erminia* (1649).

At the same time a new stage in the development of the Baroque *lamento* was achieved in Monteverdi's *Amor*, generally known as the *Lamento della ninfa*, published in his eighth book of madrigals (1638). The central section of a dramatic scene 'in stile recitativo', *Amor* is constructed over a descending tetrachord ostinato. Although probably anticipated by other tetrachord laments – including the *Lamento di Madama Lucia* published in 1628 under the name 'Il Fasolo' and almost certainly by Francesco Manelli – its full exploitation of the affective implications of the pattern asserted a relationship between tetrachord and lament that soon became fundamental to the genre.

In the Venetian opera repertory of the 1640s a definitive association between lament and tetrachord became explicit. Cavalli's 27 operas, the most comprehensive surviving musical documentation of Venetian opera from 1640 to 1660, confirm this association. Cavalli's earliest *lamenti*, like those of Monteverdi's operas, are in continuous recitative style, heightened by dissonance and affective text repetition and structured primarily by refrains. But after Apollo's *lamento* from *Gli amori di Apollo e di Dafne* (1640), partly in free recitative, partly based on the descending tetrachord, Cavalli began to employ the bass pattern consistently in *lamenti*, which initially occupied a specific position at the dramatic climax immediately preceding the resolution of the plot. Characterized by a slow tempo, highly accented triple metre and usually accompanied by strings, they use the tetrachord in a variety of ways, ranging from strict ostinato treatment of the simple pattern to freer treatment of one of its variants, such as a chromatic or inverted version. All these *lamenti* exploit the tetrachord as a source of harmonic, melodic and rhythmic dissonance created by suspensions, syncopation and overlapping phrases between the voice and the bass.

The popular success of such arias is indicated by their proliferation – accompanied by a loss of specific dramatic function – during the 1650s and 1660s, to the point where some operas contain as many as four *lamenti* spread over their three acts (e.g. Cavalli's *Statira*, 1655, and *Eliogabalo*, 1667). Similar *lamenti*, many either partly or entirely based on the descending tetrachord, occur frequently in aria and cantata collections from the 1640s onwards by such composers as Benedetto Ferrari, Luigi Rossi, Carissimi and Cesti. Although a few were written for specific occasions (e.g. Rossi's *Lamento della Regina di Svetia*) most are settings of pastoral texts involving the amorous trials of nymphs and shepherds.

Pathetic lament arias, many of them associated with some form of the tetrachord bass, continued to occur in operas, oratorios and cantatas of the late 17th and early 18th centuries; indeed, with the development of other aria types, they tended to reassume their former specific dramatic position. Purcell's *Dido and Aeneas* and *The Fairy Queen* each contains a lament based on a chromatically descending tetrachord just before the resolution of the plot, and several Handel operas, such as *Orlando* (1733), contain similarly placed laments in which the tetrachord bass plays a significant role.

The term 'lamento' also appeared in conjunction with instrumental music of a programmatic nature in the late 17th and early 18th centuries. Froberger's Suite in C (1656) bears the title *Lamento sopra la dolorosa perdita della Real Maestà di Ferdinando IV*; several sets of sonatas including Biber's Mystery (or Rosary) Sonatas (*c*1676) and Kuhnau's Biblical Sonatas (1700) contain occasional 'lamento' movements; and Bach's Capriccio in B♭ (*c*1704) 'sopra la lontananza del suo fratello dilettissimo' contains an 'allgemeines Lamento der Freunde'. Although the term generally refers to the expressive musical language and dramatic intentions of these movements, in Bach's capriccio it also refers to the descending tetrachord on which the movement is based.

The persistence of an association between lament and descending tetrachord in the 19th century is attested by Jérôme-Joseph de Momigny (*Cours complet d'harmonie*, Paris, 1803–5). In his analysis of Mozart's Quartet in D minor K421/417*b*, which opens with a descending tetrachord in the bass, Momigny applied to the first violin part the text of a lament of Dido (*see* ANALYSIS, §II, 2).

See also PLANCTUS.

BIBLIOGRAPHY

T. Kroyer: 'Dialog und Echo in der alten Chormusik', *JbMP 1909*, 13

E. Wellesz: 'Cavalli und der Stil der venezianischen Oper 1640–1660', *SMw*, i (1913), 38

L. Propper: *Der Basso Ostinato als technisches und formbildendes Prinzip* (diss., Friedrich-Wilhelms U., Berlin, 1926)

P. Epstein: 'Dichtung und Musik in Monteverdis "Lamento d'Arianna" ', *ZMw*, x (1927–8), 216

L. Walther: *Die Ostinato-Technik in den Chaconne- und Arienformen des 17. und 18. Jahrhunderts* (Würzburg, 1940)

J. A. Westrup: 'Monteverdi's "Lamento d'Arianna" ', *MR*, i (1940), 48

N. Fortune: 'Sigismondo d'India: an Introduction to his Life and Works', *PRMA*, lxxxi (1954–5), 29

W. Osthoff: 'Die frühesten Erscheinungsformen der Passacaglia in der italienischen Musik des 17. Jahrhunderts', *Congresso internazionale di musiche popolari mediterranee: Palermo 1954*, 275

——: 'Monteverdi-Funde', *AMw*, xiv (1957), 267

K. von Fischer: 'Chaconne und Passacaglia: ein Versuch', *RBM*, xii (1958), 19

W. Osthoff: Preface to *Claudio Monteverdi: 12 composizioni vocali profane e sacre* (Milan, 1958)

——: 'Antonio Cestis "Alessandro vincitor di se stesso" ', *SMw*, xxiv (1960), 29

——: *Das dramatische Spätwerk Claudio Monteverdis* (Tutzing, 1960), 77ff, 114ff
C. Gallico: 'I due pianti di Arianna di Claudio Monteverdi', *Chigiana*, xxiv (1967), 29
G. Barblan: 'Un ignoto "Lamento d'Arianna" mantovano', *RIM*, ii (1967), 217
D. Arnold: 'Monteverdi: some Colleagues and Pupils', *The Monteverdi Companion*, ed. D. Arnold and N. Fortune (London, 1968), 119ff
N. Fortune: 'Monteverdi and the Seconda Prattica, i: Monody', *The Monteverdi Companion*, ed. D. Arnold and N. Fortune (London, 1968), 203ff
L. Galleni-Luisi: 'Il lamento d'Arianna di Severo Bonini (1613)', *Convegno internazionale sul tema Claudio Monteverdi e il suo tempo: Venezia, Mantova e Cremona 1968*, 573
N. Pirrotta: 'Early Opera and Aria', *New Looks at Italian Opera: Essays in Honor of Donald J. Grout* (Ithaca, 1968), 39–107
T. Walker: 'Ciaccona and Passacaglia: Remarks on their Origin and Early History', *JAMS*, xxi (1968), 300
P. E. Carapezza: Introduction to *Claudio Pari Borgognone: Il lamento d'Arianna: Quarto libro dei madrigali a 5 voci*, MRS, i (1970)
E. Ferrari Barassi: ' "La Luciata" di Francesco Manelli: considerazioni su una perduta stampa della Biblioteca Municipale di Breslavia, l'esemplare di un manoscritto berlinese, e un componimento del "Fasolo"', *2° incontro con la musica italiana e polacca: Bologna 1970*, 211
R. Hudson: 'Further Remarks on the Passacaglia and Ciaccona', *JAMS*, xxiii (1970), 302   ELLEN ROSAND

Lamm, Pavel Alexandrovich (*b* Moscow, 27 July 1882; *d* Moscow, 5 May 1951). Russian editor and musicologist. He graduated from N. E. Shishkin's piano class at the Moscow Conservatory in 1912, and in the years before World War I participated in chamber music concerts and was an accompanist in vocal recitals. In 1912 he became an artistic adviser in the Russian Music Publishing House. After the Revolution he took up a teaching post as a director of chamber music at the Moscow Conservatory, and he continued this work for the rest of his life. In 1923 he was one of the founders of the progressive Association of Contemporary Music in Moscow, and between 1922 and 1930 he was an active member of the music department of the State Academy of Artistic Studies. Lamm is best known for his restoration work on important 19th-century Russian scores which had suffered from the later 'emendations' of Rimsky-Korsakov and others. In 1928 he became general editor of the Soviet complete edition of Musorgsky, and was responsible for the first publication of the original version of *Boris Godunov*. He also produced authentic editions of Borodin's chamber music, songs and *Prince Igor*, Dargomïzhsky's *Rusalka* (1947), Tchaikovsky's *Voyevoda*, Taneyev's E minor and D minor symphonies, Rakhmaninov's early songs and collected piano works, and the vocal works of Schubert, Liszt, Wolf and Grieg. He was a contemporary and close friend of Myaskovsky and Prokofiev, and in their latter years acted as their musical amanuensis.

BIBLIOGRAPHY
V. Kiselyov: 'Pamyati P. A. Lamma' [In memory of P. A. Lamm], *SovM* (1951), no.6, p.90   RITA McALLISTER

Lammers, Gerda (*b* Berlin, 25 Sept 1915). German soprano. She studied in Berlin with Lula Mysz-Gmeiner and Margret Schwedler-Lohmann. After 15 years as a concert singer, when she established herself as one of Germany's leading Bach interpreters, she sang Ortlinde at the 1955 Bayreuth Festival; that autumn she joined the Kassel Opera, making her début as Marie in *Wozzeck*, and singing there until 1968 in such roles as Alcestis, Medea, Isolde, Brünnhilde and Electra. In this last role she made an unheralded London début at Covent Garden in 1957, scoring a personal triumph, singing Strauss's fiendishly individual music as if em-

barking on a lieder programme, never forcing her voice or making an unpleasant sound. In 1958 she sang Purcell's Dido at Ingestre Hall, Staffordshire, and in 1959 Kundry at Covent Garden. Her only American appearances were as Electra at the Metropolitan Opera, 1961–2. In spite of many invitations she preferred to remain a member of the Kassel ensemble, and to regard concerts as her main activity.

HAROLD ROSENTHAL

La Moeulle [La Mole, La Moulaz, La Mule], Guillaume de (*b* Geneva, *c*1485; *d* Geneva, September 1556). Swiss composer, instrumentalist and singer. He was secretary to the last bishop of Geneva, Pierre de la Baume, and acquired a reputation as a fiddler (*barbitonsor*). The new republic granted him citizenship in January 1517. In 1545 he was an instrumentalist in Lyons (Lyons, Municipal Archives, CC 40). He may have lived in Lyons for some years before that time, for Jacques Moderne printed seven of his chansons between 1538 and 1543. On 12 October 1553, Calvin and his council appointed La Moeulle singer at St Peter's Cathedral, Geneva, in succession to Loys Bourgeois who had moved to Lyons the previous year. Despite ill health and poverty, La Moeulle set a number of psalms, canticles and *chansons spirituelles* for four voices. The tenor melodies were printed by Dubosc and Guéroult in 1554; those of the *chansons spirituelles* are identical with those by Didier Lupi published in Lyons by the Beringen brothers in 1548. In April 1555 and February 1556, the consistory reprimanded La Moeulle for playing his rebec for dancing, and rejected a petition to allow violins and other instruments to accompany psalm singing. The six chansons resemble the contemporary Parisian genre in their clear form and careful matching of textual and musical rhythm. They are, however, unusual in their use of passing chromatic harmonies, and in their unstable tonality; only one, *Le mien désir*, ends in the opening mode and three have mixolydian closes.

WORKS
(all for 4vv)

Premier livre de pseaumes, cantiques et chansons spirituelles (Geneva, 1554)

J'ay veu que j'estois franc et maistre, 1543[14]; Je l'ayme tant qu'elle m'en aymera, 1540[16]; Le mien désir qui longtemps a chassé, 1540[17]; Les encaveux qui sont en l'herberie, 1541[7]; Licite m'est endurer pour mon mieulx, 1538[16] (intabulated for viols in 1546[31]); Si je maintiens ma vie seullement, 1538[15]
Vous semblet-il, 1547[27] (lute intabulation)

BIBLIOGRAPHY
P. Pidoux: *Le Psautier Huguenot* (Kassel, 1962)
F. Dobbins: *The Chanson at Lyons in the Sixteenth Century* (diss., U. of Oxford, 1971), i, 146ff; ii, nos.8–13a
FRANK DOBBINS

La Monaca, Riccardo. Italian composer, possibly identifiable with MICHELE MALERBA.

Lamond, Frederic(k Archibald) (*b* Glasgow, 28 Jan 1868; *d* Stirling, 21 Feb 1948). Scottish pianist and composer. In 1882 he entered the Raff Conservatory at Frankfurt am Main where his teachers were Schwarz (piano), Heermann (violin) and Urspruch (composition). He also studied under Bülow and Liszt. He made his Berlin début on 17 November 1885 and appeared shortly thereafter in Vienna and Glasgow. At his recital on 15 April 1886 at St James's Hall, London, Liszt was in the audience. Lamond was mainly active in Germany, but he visited England regularly. He lived in Berlin from 1904 until his opposition to the Nazi regime caused him to make his home in Britain. Although he also played Brahms, Liszt and Saint-Saëns, he was particularly known as an exponent of Beethoven, several of whose most popular works he recorded. He published *Beethoven: Notes on the Sonatas* (Glasgow, 1944) and left fragments of an autobiography, *The Memoirs of Frederic Lamond* (Glasgow, 1949). It deals with the early part of his career, is valuable for closely observed pen-portraits of Brahms, Bülow and Anton Rubinstein among others, and shows Lamond to have been a musician of wide sympathies. Fuller Maitland considered it 'due to his all-round musical interest and cultivation that all his life he impressed his audiences as a musician first and as a pianist only incidentally' (*Grove 5*). Lamond's compositions include a symphony, a concert overture *From the Scottish Highlands* and a piano trio.

FRANK DAWES

Lamoninary, Jacques-Philippe (*b* Maroilles, 14 July 1707; *d* Boulogne, 29 Oct 1802). French violinist and composer. He is first mentioned as an apprentice musician in Valenciennes in 1723. He remained there until 1779, playing the violin and composing; by 1768 he was one of the town's most affluent citizens. At various times he was engaged by the St Pierre chapel, Valenciennes; many of his compositions were performed in the chapel's richly endowed *maîtrise*. In 1779 he moved to Boulogne, where he gave singing and violin lessons, but died in poverty at the age of 95.

Lamoninary dedicated his compositions to his generous patron, the Marquis of Cernay. These works, which demand the fluent technique for which Lamoninary was famous, comprise 18 trio sonatas for two violins and bass) in three sets – opp.1–2 (Paris, 1749) and op.3 (Paris, 1755) – and a set of *quatuors en simphonie* op.4 (Paris, ?1765–6) for string orchestra and organ. The somewhat archaic style of these pieces probably reflects the taste of Lamoninary's patron; an Italian influence is also suggested. Some of the first movements have a development and recapitulation and are bithematic, while the third (final) movements are almost invariably entitled 'Minuetto amoroso'. The compositions are characterized by a diversity of thematic structures, a primarily homophonic texture and a lack of tonal variation, both within and among movements.

BIBLIOGRAPHY

L. de La Laurencie: *L'école française de violon de Lully à Viotti* (Paris, 1922–4/R1971)

B. S. Brook: *La symphonie française dans la seconde moitié du XVIIIᵉ siècle* (Paris, 1962)

JEFFREY COOPER

La Montaine, John (*b* Chicago, 17 March 1920). American composer. He studied composition with Rogers and Hanson at the Eastman School (1938–42), with Wagenaar at the Juilliard School and with Boulanger at Fontainebleau. Subsequently he was pianist with the NBC SO (1950–54) and taught at the Eastman School (1964–5). He has received numerous awards and commissions, including two Guggenheim fellowships and a Pulitzer Prize (1959, for the Piano Concerto). A growing interest in the sounds of nature has led him to include them in several pieces, such as *Birds of Paradise*, the *Missa naturae*, *Wilderness Journal* and *De rebus naturae*, the last a result of a three-week sojourn in Africa gathering bird and animal sounds. He writes in a quite consonant 12-note style.

WORKS
(*selective list*)

Dramatic: Novellis, novellis, op.31 (Christmas pageant opera), 1961; The Shepardes Playe, op.38 (Christmas opera), 1967; Erode the Greate, op.40 (Christmas opera), 1969; Be glad then America (opera), perf. 1976

Orch: Pf Conc., op.9, 1958–9; Passacaglia and Fugue, op.21a, str; Birds of Paradise, op.34, pf, orch; Incantation, op.39, jazz band

Vocal: Wonder Tidings, op.23, Christmas carols, chorus, org, harp, perc; Fragments from the Song of Songs, op.29, S, orch; Songs of the Rose of Sharon, op.29, S, pf/orch; Missa naturae, op.37, narrator, chorus, orch

Chamber: Str Qt, op.16, 1960; Woodwind Qt, op.24a

Principal publishers: Broude Brothers, Galaxy, G. Schirmer

W. THOMAS MARROCCO

Lamote de Grignon, Juan (*b* Barcelona, 7 July 1872; *d* Barcelona, 11 March 1949). Spanish composer, teacher and conductor. He studied at the Barcelona Conservatory, where he was appointed professor in 1890 and director in 1917. In 1911 he founded the Barcelona SO, in 1914 he was made conductor of the municipal band of Barcelona and in 1943 he established the Valencia Municipal Orchestra, which he directed until his death. His compositions include the trilogy *Hispánicas* and other orchestral pieces, the oratorio *La nit de Nadal* (performed at Barcelona in 1902), the opera *Hesperia* (staged in the same city in 1907), a mass for two voices and organ, motets, piano pieces and about 150 songs. He also published *Musique et musiciens français à Barcelone: musique et musiciens catalans à Paris* (Barcelona, 1935).

His son Ricardo Lamote de Grignon y Ribas (*b* Barcelona, 23 Sept 1899; *d* Barcelona, 5 Feb 1962) was also a composer and conductor. Among his works are an opera, *La cabeza del dragón* (text by R. del Valle Inclán), and *Enigmas* for chorus and orchestra (1951) on words from the Apocalypse.

GUY BOURLIGUEUX

Lamotte [La Motte], **Antoine Houdar** [Houdart, Houdard] **de** (*b* Paris, 15 Jan 1672; *d* Paris, 26 Dec 1731). French dramatist, librettist, theorist and poet. Educated by the Jesuits for the Bar, the roles he took at school in comedies of Molière fired Lamotte with such enthusiasm for the theatre that when his first effort, the farce *Les originaux*, failed miserably in 1693 he fled to a Trappist monastery: a desperate self-punishment for a stagestruck and gregarious young man. By 1697 he was back in mufti and in Paris, the author of a great success, the *opéra-ballet L'Europe galante* with music by Campra. This proved the first of many librettos supplied to composers like Colasse, Dauvergne, Rebel, Francoeur, La Barre and, especially, Destouches (as well as, posthumously, to Rameau). Nor was his brief essay at the religious life wholly without fruit: he also took to versifying Old Testament stories into cantata texts which were eventually set to music by Elisabeth Jacquet de la Guerre and Clérambault. Elected in 1710 to the Académie Française as successor to Thomas Corneille (a seat furiously coveted by Rousseau), Lamotte turned to nobler concerns than the musical theatre, to tragedies in verse or prose, theoretical writings and, in 1714, a polemical version of the *Iliad* condensed and adapted to the taste of the time. The latter work revived and exacerbated the 'querelle des Anciens et des Modernes', which thereupon once more became a subject of passionate debate in the new coffee houses and the salons. A subsequent controversy pitted Lamotte, partisan of tragedy in prose and opponent of the iron rule of the three unities, against Voltaire, who owed too much to Corneille and Racine to be anything but traditionalist when it came to the theatre. Blind and lame in the last third of his life, Lamotte continued his activity, visiting the salons and dictating to a nephew not only his literary works but also the 'correspondance galante' of his last fling, presumably chiefly epistolary, with the likewise aging Duchesse de Maine.

A mediocre versifier but effective dramatist, what Lamotte offered his composers was the means to loosen the straitjacket of French dramatic conventions, to freshen their mythological subjects with a touch of unpedantic fantasy, to go on embellishing their spectacles with ballets but now in a more integrated manner than before. His aesthetic influence was on the whole salutary and progressive. He criticized as insufficient and unilluminating the contemporary notions of art as no more than an imitation of nature. Not everything in nature, he argued, is worthy of imitation, so one must have recourse to a 'nature choisie'. Nor is it just a matter of selection, because imitation becomes an absurdity unless restricted to those things appropriate to the effect aimed at. In deciding on the choices most likely to 'touch' other men, the author must rely on the 'natural judgment' of the human heart. Unabashedly subjective, Lamotte 'proved' that he did not himself operate without rules or guidelines: his measuring rod, he assured us, 'is what it pleases me to call natural' – a notion that was to enjoy great fortune among the Romantics and is still far from extinct. Be that as it may, Lamotte did his part to further the claims of 'reason' and 'free choice', and this was a matter of as much consequence to music, and especially French opera still under the spell, or incubus, of Lully, as it was to literature and the political dilemma of France under the Regency and the young Louis XV. For music historians he is particularly notable as the addressee of the letter of 25 October 1727 in which Rameau defined his own aesthetic bases and goals.

LIBRETTOS
(all performed and published in Paris unless otherwise stated)

Tragédies lyriques, each with prol and 5 acts: *Amadis de Grèce*, Destouches, 1699, pubd; *Marthésis, première reine des Amazones*, Destouches, Fontainebleau, 1699, pubd; *Canente*, Collasse, 1700, pubd; *Dauvergne*, 1760, text rev. de Cury; *Omphale*, Destouches, 1701, pubd; *Alcione*, Marais, 1706, 1719, 1730, all pubd; *Sémélé*, Marais, 1709, pubd; *Scanderberg* (collab. La Serre), Rebel and Francoeur, 1735, pubd, revived 1763

Pastorales héroïques: *Issé* (prol and 3 acts, later 5 acts), Destouches, 1697, pubd, revived 1698; *Titon et l'aurore* (prol only, the 3 acts by La Marre and Voisenon), Dauvergne, 1735, pubd

Opéra-ballets: *L'Europe galante* (4 acts), Campra, 1697, pubd; *Le triomphe des Arts* (5 acts), de La Barre, 1700, pubd; last act of the preceding as *Pygmalion*, Rameau, 1748, text rev. Ballot de Sovot

Comédies-ballets: *Le carnaval et la folie* (prol, 4 acts), Destouches, 1704, pubd; *Le ballet des ages* (prol, 4 entrées), usually attrib. Fuzelier; *Le ballet des fées* (3 acts), 1737; *Le vénitienne* (prol, 3 acts), La Barre, 1705, pubd; the same reduced to 3 acts, Dauvergne, 1768; *Le professeur de folie* (divertissement based on Act 3 of *Le vénetienne*), 1706, pubd

37 sacred cantata texts: 12 set by E. Jacquet de la Guerre in her Cantates françoises; *Abraham*, Clérambault (1715); *Sémélé*, Destouches (1719)

Odes and chansons: *Le désir* (anacreontic ode), anon. setting in Ballard's *Recueil d'airs sérieux et à boire* (1707); various settings of song texts in Rousseau's *Les consolations* (1781) and La Borde's *Choix de chansons* (1773)

WRITINGS
(only those relevant to music)

Réflexions sur la critique (Paris, 1715, 2/1716)

'Suite de réflexions sur la tragédie', *Oeuvres de théâtre*, iv (1730), and *Oeuvres complètes*, iii (1754)

'Discours sur la tragédie', *Oeuvres de théâtre*, iv (1730), and *Oeuvres complètes*, iv (1754)

BIBLIOGRAPHY
A. de Lamotte: *Oeuvres de théâtre* (Paris, 1730, 2/1765 as *Pièces de théâtre*)
E. Titon du Tillet: *Le Parnasse français* (Paris, 1732/R1971), 635
Abbé Trublet: 'Lettre sur M. H. de La Motte et ses ouvrages', *Mercure de France* (Jan 1732), 62
A. de Lamotte: *Oeuvres complètes* (Paris, 1754/R1971)
Abbé Trublet: *Mémoires pour servir à l'histoire de la vie et des oeuvres de M. de Fontenelle et de M. de La Motte* (Amsterdam, 1759)
A. de Lamotte: *Oeuvres choisies* (Paris, 1811)
A. Jal: *Dictionnaire critique de biographie et d'histoire* (Paris, 1867)
P. Dupont: *Un poète philosophe au commencement du dix-huitième siècle, Houdar de La Motte* (Paris, 1898)
G. Dost: *Houdar de La Motte als Tragiker und dramatischer Theoretiker* (diss., U. of Weida-Thüringen, 1909; Leipzig, 1929)
H. Goldschmidt: *Die Musikästhetik des 18. Jahrhunderts* (Zurich and Leipzig, 1915)
M. Beaufils: *Par la musique vers l'obscur* (Marseilles, 1942)
R. G. Saisselin: *Taste in Eighteenth-century France: Critical Reflections on the Origins of Aesthetics, or An Apology for Amateurs* (Syracuse, NY, 1965)
R. Finch: *The Sixth Sense* (Toronto, 1966)

ROBERT ERICH WOLF

Lamotte, Franz (*b* ?1751; *d* ?The Hague, ?1781). Violinist and composer, probably of South Netherlands origin. According to Burney he was Flemish (although his name appears to come from the French-speaking, Walloon, part of the South Netherlands) and received lessons on the violin from Felice Giardini in London, which is probably why he was often dubbed 'the young Englishman'. On 29 December 1766 he performed in the Burgtheater, Vienna; he so impressed the Viennese court that in 1767 he was given financial support to undertake a long concert tour. He appeared in Prague and Leipzig (where he performed with J. A. Hiller), and in 1768 in Padua and Venice. Leopold Mozart referred to a lengthy stay in Naples, but by 1769 Lamotte was performing in competition with the violinist G. M. Giornovichi in Paris. In 1770 or 1772 he returned to Vienna and joined the Hofkapelle of Empress Maria Theresia as a first violinist, though he continued to make concert tours. In 1775 he appeared at the Paris Concert Spirituel, and in 1776 gave concerts in London, where he may have given several subscription concerts with Rauzzini in 1778–9 (Loewenberg). He seems to have left London hurriedly in about 1780, probably because of criminal offences, but it remains unclear to what extent the resulting suspicions and reports of scandal are justified. According to Viotti he was dead by 1782.

Even in his youth, Lamotte was regarded as a virtuoso of the first rank whose double stopping was particularly remarkable. In 1767 he caused a stir in Prague by performing at sight a violin concerto in F♯ or C♯ major by the Prince of Fürstenberg's secretary, Bablizeck (Choron and Fayolle claimed that he tuned his violin a semitone higher and ignored the sharps in accomplishing this feat). His bowing technique was also admired and, according to Mozart, his staccato playing was long remembered in Vienna. He composed concertos, sonatas and airs for the violin.

WORKS
(printed works published in Paris unless otherwise stated)

Concerto, vn, orch (1775); IIe concerto, vn, orch (1775); IIIe concerto, vn, orch (1775); vn conc., D, *D-W*
Sonate, vn, b (hpd/vc), op.5 (*c*1770); 3 sonatas, vn, b (kbd) in 6 sonate (London and Paris, ?1776)
6 airs mis en variation, vn, b (1775)
Marche des 2 avares, 2 tr insts (n.p., n.d.)
Duetti, vn, va (n.d.)

BIBLIOGRAPHY
GerberL
C. Burney: *The Present State of Music in Germany, the Netherlands and United Provinces* (London, 1773, 2/1775); ed. P. Scholes as *Dr. Burney's Musical Tours* (London, 1959)

J. F. Reichardt: *Briefe eines aufmerksamen Reisenden*, i (Frankfurt am Main and Leipzig, 1774/*R*), 162

F. A. Ernst: 'Anekdote', *AMZ*, ii (1799–1800), col.315f

A. Choron and F. Fayolle: *Dictionnaire historique des musiciens* (Paris, 1810–11/*R*1971)

P. M. Baillot: *Notice sur J. B. Viotti* (Paris, 1825)

E. Hanslick: *Geschichte des Concertwesens in Wien* (Vienna, 1869), 107f

J. Schmidt: 'Voltaire und Maria Theresia', *Mitteilungen des Vereins für Geschichte der Stadt Wien*, xi (1931), 92

A. Loewenberg: 'Lamotte, Franz', *Grove 5*

OTHMAR WESSELY

La Moulaz, Guillaume de. *See* LA MOEULLE, GUIL-
LAUME DE.

Lamoureux, Charles (*b* Bordeaux, 28 Sept 1834; *d*
Paris, 21 Dec 1899). French conductor and violinist.
The son of a café owner, he began studying the violin
with Baudoin, who sent him to Paris at his own expense
to enrol in Girard's class at the Conservatoire. There he
took a *premier prix* for the violin in 1852, a *second* in
1853 and another *premier* in 1854, and studied harmony under Tolbecque, counterpoint and fugue under
Leborne and composition with Chauvet. From 1850 he
earned his living playing in the orchestra of the Théâtre
du Gymnase, leaving it for a position at the Opéra. He
also played in the orchestra for young performers
recently formed by Pasdeloup and eventually joined the
Société des Concerts du Conservatoire. In 1860 he
founded the Séances Populaires de Musique de
Chambre with Colonne, Adam and Pilet; this society,
whose partners changed several times, gave numerous
concerts that were particularly interesting for their
inclusion of new and seldom-performed works. From
1872 a quartet formed by Lamoureux with Coblain,
Adam and Tolbecque gradually became a chamber
orchestra, and, with the addition of singers, began to
perform important works including Bach's keyboard
concertos and excerpts from his cantatas and even a
whole cantata, *Der Streit zwischen Phöbus und Pan*.

Lamoureux had travelled in England and Germany
and was anxious to emulate the performances of large-
scale choral works he had heard at the great festivals
organized by Hiller and Costa. After his marriage, he
found himself in possession of a large fortune, and
when the committee of the Société des Concerts du
Conservatoire, where he had been assistant conductor
since 26 May 1872, refused his request to organize one
or two performances of oratorios, Lamoureux resigned
from the Société and decided to finance the performances himself. He produced Handel's *Messiah* in
December 1873, followed by the *St Matthew Passion*,
performed three times in March and April 1874 with
such success that he founded the Société Française de
l'Harmonie Sacrée (1874) and under its auspices
presented *Judas Maccabaeus* and *Alexander's Feast* by
Handel, Gounod's *Gallia* and Massenet's *Eve*. The
Société was obliged to break off its activities owing to
lack of funds, but Lamoureux had made his mark as a
conductor. In 1876 he joined the Opéra-Comique, then
under the direction of Carvalho, but stayed only six

*Charles Lamoureux: engraving by Rous-
seau after Guth*

months, resigning after an argument during a rehearsal. In 1877 he was appointed to the Opéra, but only stayed there until December 1879, leaving for London, after a disagreement with the director Vaucorbeil over Mozart's *Don Giovanni*, to organize a festival of French music, which took place in 1881 and was a great success. He then submitted a memorandum demanding the restoration of the Théâtre-Lyrique and an annual subsidy of 600,000 francs to make it into an 'opéra populaire', but this project came to nothing.

It was at this point that Lamoureux decided to sign a contract with the Théâtre du Château d'Eau to give weekly symphony concerts. The Société des Nouveaux-Concerts (also called the Concerts Lamoureux) gave its first concert on 23 October 1881; it had an immediate and well-deserved success because of the high quality of the performances, whose precision and firmness, but also expressiveness, were Lamoureux trademarks. Almost at once he began the struggle to introduce the music of Wagner, which he carried on to the end of his career. He first performed single acts from *Lohengrin* and *Tristan* in concerts and then went to Bayreuth, where it seems that Wagner finally authorized him to produce *Lohengrin*. This he did in 1887 at the Eden-Théâtre, where he had established himself two years before. However the anti-Wagner extremists, using a border incident with Germany as a pretext, staged a street demonstration to protest against the performance, calling it an unpatriotic act. Lamoureux was intimidated and, though the government had not insisted on his doing so, gave up the venture before the second performance and was held responsible for the financial loss incurred. At least his nomination as Officier of the Légion d'honneur was a source of some consolation at this time. He devoted himself once more to his weekly concerts and also directed the stage music at the Théâtre de l'Odéon. In 1891, the Opéra produced *Lohengrin* and Lamoureux was made the musical director. He was replaced by Colonne at the beginning of 1892 on the occasion of a change of management.

In 1893 Lamoureux made a tour of Russia; from 1896 he brought his orchestra to London yearly, and in May 1899 he took part with Sir Henry Wood in a festival in the Queen's Hall where the two conductors directed their respective orchestras alternately. In 1897 Lamoureux decided to give up the direction of his orchestra and chose Camille Chevillard, his son-in-law, to succeed him as permanent conductor. It was in order to give more time to the theatre that he curtailed his conducting, but his projects were not successful and he never built the French Bayreuth of his dreams. He did, however, finally succeed in producing *Tristan und Isolde* on 28 October 1899 at the Nouveau-Théâtre.

BIBLIOGRAPHY
H. Imbert: *Portraits et études* (Paris, 1894)
A. Jullien: 'Charles Lamoureux', *RMI*, vii (1900), 153
R. Rolland: *Musiciens d'aujourd'hui* (Paris, 1908, 8/1947; Eng. trans., 1914)

ELISABETH BERNARD

Lampadarios [Klada], **Joannes** (*fl c*1400). Composer of Byzantine chant. Joannes Klada, with his predecessors Joannes Koukouzeles and Xenos Koronis, is one of the three most important and prolific composers of Byzantine church music active during the 14th and 15th centuries. Klada is generally equated with the composer frequently cited in Byzantine music MSS as Joannes Lampadarios or simply as Lampadarios. Although nothing is yet known of the composer's life beyond his citation as 'Lampadarios of the holy imperial clergy', the office of 'Lampadarios' identifies him as the leader of singers in the left-hand choir of a Byzantine church. The designation 'of the holy imperial clergy' further reveals that he held this position in the imperial church of Hagia Sophia in Constantinople. The title of the office had become identified with its holder, hence Klada is referred to in the MSS as Joannes Lampadarios.

Chants by Lampadarios first appear in MSS of Akolouthiai copied towards the end of the 14th century and become even more numerous in sources from the first half of the 15th century. With this evidence and with his citation as the last of five major Byzantine composers of kalophonic Kontakia mentioned in a mid-15th-century treatise by Manuel Chrysaphes, the activity of Lampadarios can be placed securely within the first half of the 15th century, immediately before the career of Chrysaphes himself.

In MSS of Akolouthiai from the first half of the 15th century, chants by Lampadarios appear in almost all musical repertories for the liturgies and offices of the Byzantine rite. In the process of bringing these musical sources up to date as they were re-copied, scribes replaced many earlier settings by 14th-century composers with chants recently composed by Lampadarios. Unlike settings for the Prooimiac Psalm (Psalm ciii of the Greek Septuagint) in Great Vespers by his 14th-century predecessors, the ten chants attributed to Lampadarios in this repertory undergo no migration to other lines of the psalm in the course of their transmission from one source to another. They remain attached to their original lines of psalm text at a time when chants by Koukouzeles and Koronis were still being adapted to new verses. The simple refrain *Doxa soi O Theos* ('Glory to Thee O God'), sung after each line from the Prooimiac Psalm, is a Doxology which Koukouzeles had first troped with restraint in the 14th century. In the settings of Lampadarios, however, this refrain attains considerable length and even more structural importance through such a trope as the following: 'Glory to Thee unbegotten Father; Glory to Thee begotten Son; Glory to Thee Holy Spirit which proceed from the Father and repose in the Son; Glory to Thee Holy Trinity; Glory to Thee O God'.

Chants by Lampadarios show a marked preference both for greater proportions and for wider vocal ranges when compared with settings by the 14th-century composers. He extended his chants through chains of melodic clichés and repetitions of melodic patterns, either at the same pitch or in sequential movement. Even more than his 14th-century predecessors, the vocal line of Lampadarios relies upon descending two-note couplets (e.g. *b-a, b-a, a-g, a-g, g-f, g-f, f-e, f-e*, etc), a melodic pattern which Lampadarios carried to great lengths in his kalophonic Kratemata. He also used percussive lines of repeated notes which alternate between pitch levels at the distance of a perfect 5th. In comparison with melodies by Koukouzeles and other 14th-century Byzantine composers, the chants of Lampadarios are more sequential in their melodic construction and vocally less focussed and more effusive.

BIBLIOGRAPHY
G. I. Papadopoulos: *Symbolai eis tēn historian tēs par' hēmin ekklēsiastikēs mousikēs* (Athens, 1890), 274f
L. Tardo: *L'antica melurgia bizantina* (Grottaferrata, 1938), 82f, 234ff
K. Levy: 'A Hymn for Thursday in Holy Week', *JAMS*, xvi (1963), 127–75

M. Velimirović: 'Byzantine Composers in MS. Athens 2406', *Essays presented to Egon Wellesz* (Oxford, 1966), 7

For further bibliography *see* BYZANTINE RITE, MUSIC OF THE.

EDWARD V. WILLIAMS

Lampadius, Auctor (*b* Brunswick, *c*1500; *d* Halberstadt, 1559). German theorist and composer. Between 1532 and 1535 he left a teaching post at Goslar to become Kantor at the Johannisschule at Lüneburg, newly opened after the Reformation, where Lossius also taught. In 1537 Lampadius's children died of the plague and he and his wife left Lüneburg. In a letter to the Lüneburg council written from Wernigerode on 27 November 1537, he still described himself as Lüneburg Kantor. Shortly afterwards he entered the service of the Count of Stolberg at Wernigerode, as schoolmaster and court chaplain. At Easter 1541 he was appointed pastor at the Martinikirche, Halberstadt, where he remained until his death. In the winter of 1541–2 he matriculated at Leipzig University and, on 6 June 1542, he was accepted 'ad licentiam recipiendi doctoratus insignia'. In 1546, in a request for an increase in salary, he pleaded that he needed the money because the University had offered him a doctorate. In the 1550s he took an active part in the exchanges between leading Protestant theologians, including Flacius Illyricus.

Though a Kantor for only a few years, Lampadius was occupied with music throughout his life. In 1556, 19 years after becoming a pastor, he described himself, in a letter sent to a friend with a new composition, as 'musician and confessor of Christ', and stated that he would shortly be composing a mass; however, his only known musical works are two bicinia (in *RISM* 1546[16]). His treatise *Compendium musices tam figurati quam plani cantus* (Berne, 1537) was written during his period as Kantor at Lüneburg. The first two parts of the *Compendium* are devoted to *musica plana* and *musica figurata* and provide the traditional material for teaching singing; here Lampadius relied heavily on Ornithoparchus and Rhau. The third part, described in the title as an appendix (*De compositione cantus compendium*), is a significant contribution to the theory of composition in the 16th century. Josquin's works are presented in general terms as models worthy of imitation, and their style is aptly described. In them Lampadius found the realization of his ideals of 'suavitas', 'subtilitas' and 'simplicitas'; he specially praised the 'most melodious and varied clausulas', 'embellishment' by means of imitation, the technique of paired imitation and the euphony of the simple yet skilfully formed chords. On the other hand, he turned sharply against those who composed 'without skill and order'. Lampadius was one of the few theoreticians to comment on how a composer wrote down a polyphonic composition. For the instruction of beginners, he advocated the usual ten-line staff with bar-lines after every two semibreve beats; for vocal music pupils had to write out the individual voices on this staff. According to Lampadius, the great masters did not use a ten-line staff; older composers were supposed to have used wooden or stone 'tabulae' but by the time of Josquin and Isaac it was usual to write the parts in score. (For a page from *Compendium musices*, *see* SCORE, fig.2.)

BIBLIOGRAPHY

E. Jacobs: 'Zwei harzische Musiktheoretiker des 16. und 17. Jahrhunderts', *VMw*, vi (1890), 91
G. Pietzsch: 'Zur Pflege der Musik an den deutschen Universitäten bis zur Mitte des 16. Jahrhunderts', *AMf*, iii (1938), 320
E. Lowinsky: 'On the Use of Scores by Sixteenth-century Musicians', *JAMS*, i (1948), 17
G. Reichert: 'Martin Crusius und die Musik in Tübingen um 1590', *AMw*, x (1953), 187
M. Bukofzer: 'Nachwort', *A. Coclico: Compendium musices*, DM, 1st ser., *Druckschriften-Faksimiles*, ix (1954)
S. Hermelink: *Dispositiones modorum* (Tutzing, 1960)
H. Walter: *Musikgeschichte der Stadt Lüneburg* (Tutzing, 1967)

reprinted from *MGG* (viii, 150) by permission of Bärenreiter

MARTIN RUHNKE

Lampe, Charles John Frederick (*b* ?London, ?1739; *d* ?London, ?1769). English composer and organist. He was the son of John Frederick Lampe and the singer Isabella Young, who were married in 1738. In 1758 he succeeded his grandfather, Charles Young, as organist at All Hallows, Barking, and held the post until 1769. On 7 May 1763 he married a singer called Miss Smith, and in 1764 he published *Six English Songs as sung by Mr Lowe & Mrs Lampe Junr at Mary-bone Gardens*. They are competent but unadventurous; two have words by 'Mr S. Boyce', who may have been the well-known composer's son. Lampe's only other published compositions were some catches and a song called *Britannia's Invitation to her sons, to partake of the Glory of the intended Expedition*. He may be the Lampe who played in the Covent Garden orchestra in 1760–61 (*The London Stage 1747–1776*, Carbondale, Ill., 1962).

ROGER FISKE

Lampe, Isabella [Mrs Lampe]. English soprano; *see* YOUNG family.

Lampe, Johann Friedrich (*b* Wolfenbüttel, 1744). German composer and singer. After being musical director of the Hamburg theatre (1773–7) he apparently stayed on as a singer. In 1788 he was a member of the court theatre at Schwedt (Pomerania). He wrote symphonies (lost), songs, incidental music for the stage and *Das Mädchen in Eichthale*, a German adaptation of Bickerstaffe's *Love in a Village* and Burgoyne's *The Maid of the Oaks*, performed at Hanover (1776), Hamburg, Berlin and elsewhere (score in *D-Bdhm*).

ALFRED LOEWENBERG

Lampe, John Frederick (*b* Saxony, *c*1703; *d* Edinburgh, 25 July 1751). German composer and bassoonist who spent most of his life in Britain; the title-page of his textbook on thoroughbass describes him as 'sometime Student at Helmstad' (sic). Lampe arrived in London about 1724 and was soon playing the bassoon in one of the London theatres. He seems to have composed very little before the 1730s, and it is strange that in 1726 Henry Carey included him in his series of short poems about London composers, calling him 'my learned friend'.

In 1732 Arne's father organized a number of 'English Opera' productions partly to launch his son's career and partly to break the Italian monopoly in opera. Lampe did more of the composing than anyone, even though he is not known to have had any previous theatre experience. In just under 12 months three full-length operas by him were staged, all said to be 'after the Italian manner', and they were followed nine months later by a fourth on a rather different model. All four operas failed. Only two songs from *Amelia* were published, and nothing at all from the others. *Amelia* had a libretto by Carey that aped all the worst characteristics of Italian librettos without adding anything distinctive. The libretto of *Britannia* was by Thomas Lediard, who devised unusual 'transparent' scenery for it which he described in detail in the libretto; his architectural stage set was reproduced as a pull-out frontispiece. Arne's future wife, Cecilia Young, made her debut in the title role. Of *Dione* not even the libretto survives. It was based on an uninteresting 'pastoral tragedy' by John Gay, written in heroic couplets and never acted. Someone must have cut it down, added lyrics for the set pieces, and (perhaps) given it a happy ending to accord with convention.

Lampe's fourth opera had a confusing origin. Thomas Arne had just set Eliza Hayward's revision of Fielding's *Tragedy of Tragedies*, and it was staged at the Little Theatre in May 1733 as *The Opera of Operas*. It proved popular enough to merit revival after the summer break, but by then, as a result of a disagreement, half the Drury Lane company had left and offered their services to the Little Theatre; the less distinguished of those already there found themselves displaced, and Arne had to recast his burlesque, cutting it down to an afterpiece. Meanwhile Drury Lane found itself with the original Huncamunca (Mrs Mason) and Grizzle (Waltz) but no music. Lampe was commissioned to prepare another score as quickly as possible, and it was staged in November, just over a week after Arne's revision; but in spite of Mrs Clive as Dollalolla there were only three performances.

Engraving of a song by Lampe from Bickham's 'The Musical Entertainer' (i, 96), with a scene from 'The Dragon of Wantley'

Later that season Lampe wrote music for a Drury Lane pantomime, *Cupid and Psyche*; from the following season onwards it was known by its alternative title, *Columbine Courtezan*. None of the vocal music survives, but the Comic Tunes that accompanied the mimed scenes were published with the overture in keyboard arrangement. This was the second of the new-style 'medley' overtures (the first, according to Hawkins, was written by Charke). They seem always to have been associated with pantomimes, and were not medleys in the modern sense but sophisticated patterns of tune fragments, some of them in the bass or even in a middle part; quite often two were played at the same time. As the tunes were all well known, the result was like a musical quiz. Lampe drew on at least five Handel operas, as well as combining in double counterpoint *Butter'd Peas* and *Over the Hills and Far Away*; he identified his tunes in the keyboard arrangement, though not always helpfully. The overture was also published in parts, and republished about 1760 by Walsh in a set of six Medley Overtures; presumably they were still being played in front of later pantomimes or at concerts.

Burlesque was Lampe's métier, and in 1737 he had his greatest success with *The Dragon of Wantley*. Carey's dedicatory preface tells how he and 'Jack' Lampe had spent

many joyous hours ... chopping and changing, lopping, ekeing out and coining Words, Syllables, and Jingles, to display in *English* the Beauty of Nonsense, so prevailing in the Italian Operas ... Your Musick is as grand and pompous as possible, by which Means the *Contrast* is the stronger.

It is also surprisingly charming in places, but there are some good satirical touches, aimed mainly at Handel, and the extreme banality of the words is often very funny. The unheroic hero, Moore of Moore Hall near Rotherham, was got up ridiculously to look like Farinelli, then in London (see Bickham's engravings in *The Musical Entertainer*, i, 96, 100). *The Dragon* enjoyed a number of revivals later in the century, but its sequel, *Margery, or A Worse Plague than the Dragon*, had only a one-season success. Both were published in full score, in two volumes, one for the songs and one for the orchestral items and ensembles. Neither includes the recitatives, but a set for *The Dragon* is extant (*GB-Lcm*).

The Licensing Act of 1737 had at first the effect of limiting the Little Theatre to isolated concerts, and Rich was able to take over the entire production of *The Dragon* for Covent Garden at very little trouble to himself. He was now very sparing indeed with new productions, but in 1740 he staged one that is hard to categorize. *Orpheus and Euridice* started as a short opera with four pantomime interludes, but, as the libretto reveals, the vocal scenes were much cut before the first night. Lampe's songs were not published, but some of his Comic Tunes appeared. Rich later accepted a 'comic masque' and a 'mock opera' from him. No libretto was published for *The Sham Conjurer* (1741), which failed; a full score was published without recitatives, and it includes an undistinguished Grand Concerto for oboes, horns and strings that presumably served as the overture. *Pyramus and Thisbe* was more successful. The libretto, adapted from one Leveridge had set in 1716, consisted of an all-sung opera (the play-within-a-play in *A Midsummer Night's Dream*, Act 5) in a framework of spoken dialogue about operatic foibles of the day. Though the music has too much of the then-fashionable snap rhythm, it entertainingly mocks such operatic stupidities as having characters sing about the necessity for quick action without doing anything about it. *Pyramus and Thisbe* had its first modern revival in London in 1971.

Lampe's Little Theatre operas do not survive sufficiently for a description. One was called an 'operetta'; the term seems not to have been used before in Britain. In 1745 Lampe celebrated the failure of the rebellion with a large-scale but uninteresting anthem published in full score with both English and German words; the first and perhaps only performance was on 9 October 1746 at the Protestant-Lutheran-German Church in the Savoy, London. In 1748 the Lampes went to Dublin for two years, and then to Edinburgh.

Margery, the heroine in *The Dragon*, had been sung by Isabella Young, Mrs Arne's sister, and in 1738 Lampe married her; they had one son. Attracted to Methodism, they became close friends of Charles Wesley, the prolific hymn writer, and in 1746 Lampe published a considerable volume of hymns he had written to Charles's words; they sound rather secular with their numerous appoggiaturas. Charles Wesley always deplored Lampe's involvement with theatre music, but honoured his memory with a hymn when he died.

WORKS
(all printed works pubd in London unless otherwise indicated)
CG—Covent Garden   DL—Drury Lane   LT—Little Theatre

OPERAS
Amelia, English opera (Carey), LT, 13 March 1732; 2 songs pubd
Britannia, English opera (Lediard), LT, 16 Nov 1732; music unpubd
Dione (Gay and others), LT, 23 Feb 1733, lost
The Opera of Operas, or Tom Thumb the Great, burlesque (Hayward, after Fielding), DL, 7 Nov 1733; airs (c1733)
The Dragon of Wantley, burlesque (Carey), LT, 10 May 1737; full score without recits (1738), score with recits GB-Lcm
Margery, or A Worse Plague than the Dragon, burlesque, sequel to preceding (Carey), CG, 9 Dec 1738; full score (c1739), recits lost
The Sham Conjurer, comic masque, CG, 19 April 1741; full score (1741), no lib
The Queen of Spain, or Farinelli at Madrid (?Ayres), LT, 19 Jan 1744; unpubd, no lib
The Kiss Accepted & Returned, operetta (Ayres), LT, 16 April 1744; unpubd, no lib
Pyramus and Thisbe, mock opera (after Shakespeare), CG, 25 Jan 1745; full score (c1745), no recits; lib Ob, add. acc. recit Lbm

PANTOMIMES
Cupid and Psyche, or Columbine Courtezan, DL, 4 Feb 1734; Comic Tunes, lib, ov. (c1734); 1 song pubd
Orpheus and Euridice, with The Metamorphoses of Harlequin (Theobald), CG, 12 Feb 1740; Comic Tunes (1740)

MISCELLANEOUS
Wit Musically Embellish'd . . . Forty New English Ballads (1731)
British Melody (1739) [about a quarter of the songs by Lampe, probably none from his operas]
The Cuckoo Concerto, fl, str (c1740)
Lyra Britannica: a Collection of Favourite English Songs (c1745)
Hymns on the Great Festivals (1746); texts by Charles Wesley
Thanksgiving Anthem . . . for the Suppression of the Rebellion, str, winds, perc (1746); full score Lbm
Cantata and Four English Songs, 1v, bc (1748)
Ladies' Amusement, songs, 1v, opt. treble inst, bc (Dublin, 1748)
Single songs

WRITINGS
A Plain and Compendious Method of Teaching Thorough Bass (London, 1737)
The Art of Musick (London, 1740) [a short book on harmony]

BIBLIOGRAPHY
BurneyH; HawkinsH
R. Fiske: *English Theatre Music in the Eighteenth Century* (London, 1973)
                                                ROGER FISKE

Lampens. Composer, probably Flemish, active in the 15th century. His name is known only from *F-Sm* 222 (no.182), where a three-voice Credo is ascribed to him. The piece is notated in minor prolation, and survives only in Coussemaker's copy. *See also* LAMBE, WALTER.
For bibliography *see* SOURCES, MS.
                                        KURT VON FISCHER

Lamperti, Francesco (*b* Savona, 11 March 1813; *d* Cernobbio, nr. Como, 1 May 1892). Italian singing teacher. He studied in Lodi with Pietro Rizzi and then at the Milan Conservatory. After working as co-director with Masini of the Teatro Filodrammatico, Lodi, he returned to Milan and taught at the conservatory from 1850 to 1875; his pupils included Albani, Aldighieri, Artôt, Barbacini, Campanini, Lagrange, Teresa Stolz and Waldmann. He published several vocal studies and a treatise on the art of singing. His elder son, Giuseppe (*b* Milan, 1834; *d* Rome, 1899), was an impresario who worked at La Scala, Milan (1883–8), the Teatro Apollo, Rome, and the Teatro S Carlo, Naples. His younger son, Giovanni Battista (*b* Milan, 24 June 1839; *d* Berlin, 18 March 1910), was also a singing teacher; he studied at the Milan Conservatory and taught in Milan, Dresden and Berlin. His pupils included Abendroth, Bispham, Buls, Nachbaur, Schumann-Heink, Sembrich and Stagno.

BIBLIOGRAPHY
W. E. Brown: *Vocal Wisdom: Maxims of Giovanni Battista Lamperti* (New York, 1931)
                                        ELIZABETH FORBES

Lampugnani, Giovanni Battista (i) (*b* Florence; *fl* 1690–98). Italian writer. In 1690–96 he was in Warsaw in the service of the nuncio Andrea Santa Croce, in 1697 in Vienna in the same role and in 1698 in London as a correspondent of the Tuscan court, a post he held from 1693. He may have been related to Giovanni Battista Lampugnani (ii). Two of his *drammi per musica* are known: *Per goder in amor ci vuol costanza* (1691; music by Viviano Augustini) and the pastoral *Amor vuol il giusto* (1694; composer unknown). They were written for the weddings of King Jan Sobieski's children. Lampugnani also wrote two oratorio texts in the manner of Arcangelo Spagna: *Il transito di San Casimiro* (1695; composer unknown) and *La caduta d'Aman* (1697; music by Raniero Borrini).

BIBLIOGRAPHY
S. Ciampi: *Bibliografia critica* (Florence, 1834), i, 222; ii, 99
W. Roszkowska and T. Bienkowski: 'Polski przekład opery G. B. Lampugnaniego "Amor vuol il giusto" ', *Archiwum literackie*, xvi (1972), 297–345
                                        ANNA SZWEYKOWSKA

Lampugnani, Giovanni Battista (ii) (*b* Milan, 1706; *d* ?Milan, after autumn 1786). Italian composer, possibly a son of GIOVANNI BATTISTA LAMPUGNANI (i). No information is available about his activities before the 1730s. For most of this decade it seems that he worked in Milan, where his earliest heroic operas, *Candace* (1732) and *Antigono* (1736), were performed. He first acquired commissions for operas in other cities about 1737, and thereafter became a popular operatic composer, especially in north Italy. In 1743 he was invited to London to become resident composer for a season at the King's Theatre. His first London opera production was *Rossane* (15 November). Some confusion still exists about this work, which was advertised in the press as by Handel (it could not have been a new work by Handel, who had given up composing operas by this date). Some commentators have accepted the opera as an original work by Lampugnani, but it was probably a pasticcio with music by Handel included. Two further operas that Lampugnani produced in London during the early months of 1744, *Alfonso* and *Alceste*, were certainly his own. By January 1746, at the latest, he was back in Italy. Of his subsequent operas just two received first performances abroad: *Vologeso* (Barcelona, 1753) and *Siroe re di Persia* (London, 1755). Whether he went in person to Barcelona and London to supervise these productions is unknown. Torrefranca asserted that the composer 'lived long in Germany', but gave no evidence in support. About 1758 Lampugnani finally settled in Milan where he became well known as a singing teacher and where, for the first time, he concerned himself with the composition of comic opera. He also became attached to the Milan opera house as harpsichordist in the orchestra. He gave up composing for the stage probably about 1769, but continued for many years after to play in operas by other composers. He helped to rehearse Mozart's *Mitridate, re di Ponto* (produced Milan 26 December 1770), played second harpsichord during the first three performances of the work (while Mozart led at the first harpsichord), and in later performances led the orchestra himself. He was still playing at the Milan opera as late as 1786, for he is mentioned as harpsichordist in the libretto of Cimarosa's *Il marito disperato* produced at La Scala in the autumn of that year. His death is not recorded, but must have occurred either that autumn or later.

In spite of popular approval Lampugnani's music gained only lukewarm acclaim from 18th-century critics. He acquired a reputation for providing his arias with over-energetic orchestral accompaniments; Arteaga, in particular, accused him of giving all his attention to them. The best-considered judgment of his music was passed by Burney in his *General History*. Writing about his *Alfonso* (1744), Burney commented on the large amount of bravura in the arias for the leading singer Monticelli, thought the work lacked dignity, but conceded nonetheless that 'there is a graceful gaiety in the melody of his quick songs, and an elegant tenderness in the slow, that resemble no other composer's works of that time'. In fact the arias of Lampugnani's early heroic operas contain many of the usual melodic formulae of the period. Not so usual however is the curious combination within several arias of elaborate melodic ornamentation, usual in heroic opera, on the one hand and a catchy tunefulness and a light, buoyant style, suitable for comic opera, on the other. The gay and elegant qualities that Burney noticed in *Alfonso* are present in his last extant opera, and incidentally his only comic opera surviving, *L'amor contadino* (1760). In this work Lampugnani minimized the comical, grotesque nature of the characters and relied on tunefulness to gain his effects. Unlike his earlier heroic operas, in which the da capo form is preferred for the arias, he here adopted a variety of different forms for his vocal items, and never used an exact da capo. The ensembles, consisting of several sections in differing time signatures and speeds, may owe something to the example of the Venetian composer Galuppi, who during the 1750s constructed ensembles in a similar way.

Lampugnani's instrumental music was occasionally confused with that of other composers, including G. B. Sammartini, who was his contemporary and, like him, Milanese. Lampugnani is not as important a figure as Sammartini in the history of the development of the Classical symphony and chamber music. His early instrumental compositions are nonetheless not without interest, especially the early trio sonatas (published in London in the 1740s), some of which contain first movements exhibiting a primitive extended binary form (the forerunner of the later Classical first-movement sonata form) with a clear recapitulatory final section and some elementary division of material into first and second subject groups. The music, with its embroidered, closely textured style, is only of moderate quality, but it does suggest that Lampugnani played a small role in popularizing the newly emerging first-movement sonata form that later became the norm.

WORKS
(all printed works published in London unless otherwise stated)

OPERAS
(all drammi per musica unless otherwise stated)

Candace (D. Lalli, after F. Silvani: I veri amici), Milan, Ducale, 26 Dec 1732
Antigono (G. Marizoli), Milan, Ducale, 26 Dec 1736
Ezio (Metastasio), Milan, 1736, according to Münster; (B. Vitturi), Venice, S Angelo, aut. 1737, according to Petrobelli
Demofoonte (Metastasio), Piacenza, Ducale, carn. 1738, according to Münster; (Vitturi), according to Petrobelli
Artaserse (Metastasio), Milan, Ducale, Jan 1738
Angelica (C. Vedoa), Venice, S Samuele, 11 May 1738
Didone abbandonata (Metastasio), Padua, Obizzi, June 1739; rev. Naples, 20 Jan 1753; 2 acts in *E-Mn*
Adriano in Siria (Metastasio), Vicenza, Delle Grazie, May 1740
Semiramide riconosciuta (Metastasio), Rome, Delle Dame, carn. 1741; without recits in *I-Nc*
Arsace (A. Salvi), Crema, fiera 1741; with revs. by Gluck, Milan, Ducale, 1744; 1 act in *I-Fc*
Ezio (Metastasio), Venice, S Samuele, Ascension 1743 [according to Petrobelli, a different opera from Ezio, 1737]
Alfonso (P. A. Rolli), London, King's, 3 Jan 1744; 6 arias in The Favourite Songs in the Opera call'd Alfonso (*c*1744)
Alceste (Rolli, after Metastasio), London, King's, 28 April 1744; 6 arias in The Favourite Songs in the Opera call'd Alceste (*c*1744)
Semiramide o Nino, written for Padua, Obizzi, 1745, not perf., according to Petrobelli
Il gran Tamerlano (A. Piovene), Milan, Ducale, 20 Jan 1746
Tigrane (Goldoni, after Vitturi), Venice, S Angelo, 10 May 1747; (Goldoni, after Silvani), according to O. Sonneck, *Catalogue of Opera Librettos Printed Before 1800* (Washington, 1914)
L'Olimpiade (Metastasio), Florence, Pergola, carn. 1748
Andromaca (Salvi), Turin, Regio, 1748, according to Münster; carn. 1749, according to Petrobelli
Alessandro sotto la tenda di Dario (G. Riviera), Piacenza, Ducale, spr. 1751
Vologeso (Zeno: Lucio Vero, rev.), Barcelona, 1753
Siroe re di Persia (after Metastasio), London, King's, 14 Jan 1755; 6 arias in The Favourite Songs in the Opera call'd Siroe (*c*1755)
Il re pastore (Metastasio), Milan, Ducale, April 1758
Le cantatrici (dramma giocoso), Milan, Ducale, aut. 1758; as La scuola delle cantatrici, Modena, 1761
La contessina (dramma giocoso, Goldoni), Milan, Ducale, aut. 1759
Il conte Chicchera (dramma giocoso, Goldoni), Milan, Ducale, aut. 1759
L'amor contadino (dramma giocoso, Goldoni), Venice, S Angelo, 11 Nov 1760; without ov. in *GB-Cfm*, modern copy *US-Wc*
Enea in Italia (? after G. Bussani), Palermo, 1763
L'illustre villanella (dramma giocoso), Turin, Regio, 1769
Pasticcios with 1 or more arias by Lampugnani; all perf. London, King's, and pubd in collections of Favourite Songs shortly after perf. unless otherwise stated: Alessandro in Persia (? F. Vanneschi), 31 Oct 1741; Meraspe o L'Olympiade (Metastasio), 20 April 1742; Gianguir (Zeno), 2 Nov 1742, unpubd; Rossane o Alessandro nell' Indie (Rolli), 15 Nov 1743, unpubd [? music by Handel and Lampugnani]; La finta schiava (Silvani), Venice, S Angelo, Ascension 1744, unpubd; Alessandro nell'Indie (Metastasio), 15 April 1746; Annibale in Capua (Vanneschi), 4 Nov 1746; Catone, Rome, 1747–8, according to Petrobelli, unpubd; L'ingratitudine punita, London, Little Theatre, Haymarket, 12 Jan 1748, 1 aria in Le delizie dell' opere, v (London, *c*1750); Semiramide (Metastasio), 7 May 1748, 1 aria in Le delizie dell'opere, v (London, *c*1750); Didone (Metastasio), 26 March 1748, according to Münster; Ipermestra (after Metastasio), 9 Nov 1754; Andromaca (after Salvi: Astianatte), 11 Nov 1755; Tito Manlio (M. Noris), 10 April 1756; ?La finta schiava, Milan, Ducale, 26 Dec 1760; Le pescatrici (Goldoni), 29 April 1761, according to Münster; The Summer's Tale (R. Cumberland), London, Covent Garden, 6 Dec 1765, 1 aria in The Summer's Tale (*c*1765)

OTHER VOCAL
Il passaggio per Ferrara della Sacra Reale Maestà di Maria Amalia (serenata, 2, G. Melani), Ferrara, Scrofa, 5 June 1738
Serenata per lo felicissimo giorno natalizio dell'Imperiale Real Maestà di Maria Teresa d'Austria (serenata, 1, C. Frugoni), Reggio, May 1748

1 aria in Venetian Ballads compos'd by Sigr Hasse and all the Celebrated Italian Masters (c1754); 17 arias/songs arr. in Farinelli's Celebrated Songs &c collected from Sig Hasse, Porpora, Vinci and Veracini's Operas, fl/vn/hpd, i–ii (before c1755); pieces in A Collection of Marches and Airs, vns/fls/obs, vc/hpd (Edinburgh, 1761)

Salve Pater Salvatoris, cantata, S, str, bc; Quid te angis fata, cantata, S, str, bc; Minax crudelis tempestas, aria, B, 2 tpt, timp, str, bc: all *A-LA, D-DO*

Over 100 arias, pezzi teatrali, etc, most from operas, in various European libraries

INSTRUMENTAL

6 Sonatas . . . compos'd by Sigr Giov. Battista Lampugnani and St. Martini of Milan (A, B♭, A, D, E♭, G), 2 vn, bc, op.1 (Walsh, c1744) [2/c1748 attrib. all 6 sonatas to Lampugnani]; no.1 in *GB-T, S-Skma*; no.2 in *L, Skma*; no.5 in *Skma* [2 copies] and Breitkopf catalogue (1762), all attrib. Brioschi; no.6 in *L*

Sonatas nos.2, 4, 6 (G, C, D), in 6 Sonatas . . . compos'd by Sigr Gio. Battista Lampugnani and St. Martini of Milan, 2 vn, bc, op.2 (Walsh, c1744); no.6 arr. kbd in *GB-Lbm* attrib. 'Lanpongniar'

6 Sonatas (G, A, B♭, A, D, A), 2 vn, bc, op.1 (Simpson, ?1745) [also (Thomson, ?1765)]; nos.1–4 are same as nos.6, 3, 2, 1, of 6 Sonatas . . . op.1 (Walsh)

Sonatas in Sinfonie . . . dei più celebri autori d'Italia recueillis per M. Estien, 2 vn, bc, Premier recueil (Paris, c1747)

6 sinfonias listed in Breitkopf catalogue (1762): no.1 (A), str, lost; no.2 (D), 2 hn, str, bc, in *F-AG* Fonds d'Aguillon, attrib. Lampugnani in *CH-Bu* Sarasin collection, attrib. Galimberti, and in *F-Pc* Fonds Blancheton, anon.; no.3 (A), 2 ob, str, bc, in *S-Skma*, formerly in *D-DS*, attrib. Bernasconi by Brook (1962); no.4 (D), 2 hn, str, lost; no.5 (D), 2 ob, 2 tpt, str, lost; no.6 (D), 2 hn, str, lost

Sinfonia (D), 2 hn, str, bc, *D-DS*; Sinfonia (B♭), str, bc, *S-L, Skma*; Sinfonia (G), 2 hn, str, bc, attrib. Sammartini by Torrefranca, *D-KA*

3 sonatas (E♭, A, F), 2 vn, bc, *GB-T*

2 sinfonias (D, D), 2 hn, str, bc; 3 concs. (B♭, C, F), kbd, orch; 2 sonatas (E♭, A), 2 vn, bc: all formerly *D-DS*

BIBLIOGRAPHY

BurneyH; GerberL

C. Burney: *The Present State of Music in France and Italy* (London, 1771)

J. G. Sulzer: *Allgemeine Theorie der schönen Künste*, iii (Leipzig, c1774), 646

S. Arteaga: *Le rivoluzioni del teatro musicale italiano*, ii (Venice, 2/1785), 256f

A. Paglicci Brozzi: *Il Regio ducal teatro di Milano nel secolo xviii* (Milan, 1894)

P. Cambiasi: *La Scala 1778–1906: note storiche e statistiche* (Milan, 1906)

F. Piovano: 'Un opéra inconnu de Gluck', *SIMG*, ix (1907–8), 231

F. Torrefranca: 'Le origini della sinfonia', *RMI*, xx (1913), 291

P. Petrobelli: 'Lampugnani, Giovanni Battista', *ES*

R. Münster: 'Lampugnani, Giovanni Battista', *MGG*

B. S. Brook: *La symphonie française dans la seconde moitié du XVIII* *siècle* (Paris, 1962)

——, ed.: *The Breitkopf Thematic Catalogue, 1762–1787* (New York, 1966)

MICHAEL F. ROBINSON

La Mule, Guillaume de. *See* LA MOEULLE, GUILLAUME DE.

Lamy, Alfred Joseph (*b* Mirecourt, 8 Sept 1850; *d* Paris, 1919). French bow maker. Lamy learnt his craft in Mirecourt with Charles Claude Husson from 1862 to 1868. He then took up a position with the firm of Gautrot at Château-Thierry, but his career was firmly established when he went to Paris to be assistant to F. N. Voirin. With exceptional gifts of hand and eye he copied every detail of his master's work, and it is difficult to tell their bows apart. He may have made certain of Voirin's bows unaided, but on Voirin's death in 1885 Lamy was employed by his widow for some years, and Voirin's brand continued in use. By 1889, when he won a gold medal at the Paris exhibition, Lamy was working on his own account, at premises at 24 rue Poissonnière. His brand-mark was 'A. Lamy à Paris'. He never varied from his teacher's style, with the characteristic small, elegant head and mostly round sticks. Generally his bows have a little more weight than Voirin's average, a feature particularly appreciated by cellists. His output

was quite large. His bows are highly regarded and the value of well-preserved examples has risen constantly.

BIBLIOGRAPHY

R. Vannes: *Essai d'un dictionnaire universel des luthiers* (Paris, 1932, 2/1951/R1972 as *Dictionnaire universel des luthiers*, suppl. 1959)

J. Roda: *Bows for Musical Instruments of the Violin Family* (Chicago, 1959)

E. Vatelot: *Les archets français* (Nancy, 1976)

CHARLES BEARE

Lamy, Bernard (*b* Le Mans, baptized 29 June 1640; *d* Rouen, 29 Jan 1715). French philosopher, mathematician and philologist. He first studied at Le Mans at the Congrégation de l'Oratoire, an order that he later joined. After further studies in Paris and Saumur he taught grammar, rhetoric and philosophy at Vendôme and Juilly. He became a Jansenist. In 1667 he was ordained priest and later taught philosophy at Saumur and Angers. His teaching, based on the novel doctrines of Michael Baius and Descartes, became a centre of controversy. He was formally denounced in 1675 and sent to the seminary in Grenoble, where he remained until 1686. He was then recalled to the seminary of St Magloire, Paris, and in 1689 retired to Rouen, where he remained until his death. In his writings he attempted to develop a methodology to reconcile the humanistic and religious doctrines of his time with those based on the new mechanistic approach to scientific investigation, leading to a universal wisdom. His contributions to music are contained in studies devoted to biblical history, mathematics and especially rhetoric, in which he explained music as a phenomenon of language and laid an important theoretical basis for the later development of a doctrine of the passions.

WRITINGS
(*only those on music*)

L'art de parler (Paris, 1675, Eng. trans., 1676, 2/1708; 3/1688 as *La rhétorique ou L'art de parler*; 4/1699/R1969, rev. 1741)

'Traité de la proportion harmonique', *Les éléments des mathématiques ou Le traité de la grandeur*, viii (Paris, 3/1704), suppl.

'De Levitis cantoribus, eorum divisione, classibus: de Hebraeorum canticis, musica, instrumentis', *De tabernaculo foederis, de sancta civitate Jerusalem et de templo eius*, vii (Paris, 1720), 1173

BIBLIOGRAPHY

F. Girbal: *Bernard Lamy (1640–1715): étude biographique et bibliographique* (Paris, 1964)

F. Girbal and P. Clair: introduction to edn. of B. Lamy: *Entretiens sur les sciences* (Paris, 1966)

A. Cioranescu: *Bibliographie de la littérature française du dix-septième siècle*, ii (Paris, 1966), 1177ff

W. G. Waite: 'Bernard Lamy, Rhetorician of the Passions', *Studies in Eighteenth-century Music: a tribute to Karl Geiringer* (New York and London, 1970), 388

ALBERT COHEN

Lamy, Fernand (*b* Chauvigny, Vienne, 8 April 1881; *d* Paris, 18 Sept 1966). French composer and conductor. His first musical studies were at the Poitiers Conservatory; later he studied in Paris with Bleuzet, Caussade and Dukas, and finally with Ropartz. For a time he conducted a military band, and then was appointed conductor at the Théâtre des Champs Elysées, where he was responsible for the Paris première of Fauré's *Pénélope* and for the first performance in French of *Boris Godunov*. He left this position in order to direct the Vallencienne Conservatory (1914–43), and in 1951 he became inspector general for the arts and literature.

WORKS

La barque au crépuscule, 1v, orch, 1905; Impromptu (Adolphe Rettés), 1v, pf (1912); 4 ballades (Fort), 1v, pf (1917–22); choral pieces

Rustique, ob, orch/pf (1921); Cantabile et scherzo, hn, orch/pf (1947); Pastorales variées, ob, orch/pf (1951–2); other orch works

Principal publishers: Leduc, Durand, Salabert

WRITINGS

Guy Ropartz: l'homme et l'oeuvre (Paris, 1948)

BIBLIOGRAPHY

M. Frémiot: 'Lamy, Fernand', *MGG*

ANNE GIRARDOT

Lanari, Alessandro (*b* S Marcello di Iesi, 1790; *d* Florence, 3 Oct 1862). Italian impresario. His first appointment as impresario was at Lucca in 1821. For the next 40 years he was active in various cities of central and northern Italy, sometimes controlling several theatres simultaneously. He was associated mainly with the Teatro della Pergola in Florence, which he managed in 1823–8, 1830–35, 1839–48 and 1860–62. With Barbaia, Merelli and Jacovacci, he was among the leading impresarios of 19th-century Italy and in general was the best liked of the four. His breadth of vision and skilful use of resources earned him the nickname (shared according to some sources with Merelli) 'the Napoleon of the impresarios', and he was warmly praised by Donizetti and Mercadante. His career was not free from reverses: the theatre at Senigallia burnt down under his management; he lost a lawsuit against the famous mezzo-soprano Giuditta Grisi; and in Rome he was ousted successively from the Apollo and Argentina theatres by Jacovacci. Because of financial difficulties he resigned from the direction of the Teatro della Pergola shortly before his death. His unpublished letters in the Biblioteca Nazionale, Florence, shed an interesting light on the theatrical conditions of the time and also on the career of Giuseppina Strepponi, whom he managed for several years. Important premières given under his direction were Bellini's *I Capuleti ed i Montecchi* (Venice, 1830), *Norma* (Milan, 1831), *Beatrice di Tenda* (Venice, 1833), Donizetti's *L'elisir d'amore* (Milan, 1832), *Pia de' Tolomei* (Venice, 1837), *Maria di Rudenz* (Venice, 1848), Verdi's *Attila* (Venice, 1846) and *Macbeth* (Florence, 1847). Lanari also mounted the first Italian performances of Meyerbeer's *Robert le diable* (1840) and Weber's *Der Freischütz* (1843) at the Pergola theatre.

BIBLIOGRAPHY

Jarro [pseud. of G. Piccini]: *Memorie di un impresario fiorentino* (Florence, 1892)

G. Monaldi: *Impresari celebri del secolo XIX* (Rocca S Casciano, 1918)

U. Morini: *La R. Accademia degli Immobili ed il suo teatro 'La Pergola'* (*1649–1925*) (Pisa, 1926)

A. de Angelis: *La musica a Roma nel secolo XIX* (Rome, 1935)

A. Cametti: *Il Teatro di Tordinona poi di Apollo* (Tivoli, 1938)

JULIAN BUDDEN

Lancashire sol-fa. A traditional solmization system; *see* FASOLA.

Lancers. 19th-century square dance, which was a variant of the quadrille with an elaborate final figure ('Grand Chain'). Even more than the quadrille, the music used for the dance was almost invariably derived from popular songs and stage works. The Lancers flourished alongside the quadrille in the last quarter of the 19th century and even outlived the latter into the early 20th century.

The name 'Lancers' was derived from the *Quadrille des lanciers*, which was introduced in Dublin in 1817 by the dancing-master John Duval. It consisted of the following five figures: 'La Dorset' (music by Spagnoletti); 'Lodoïska' (music by Rodolphe Kreutzer); 'La Native' ('If the heart of a man' from *The Beggar's Opera*); 'Les Graces' ('Pretty Maiden' from Storace's *The Haunted Tower*); and 'Les Lanciers' (music by Janiewicz). The *Quadrille des lanciers* achieved international popularity during the 1850s after being introduced to Paris by the dancing-master Laborde, but had virtually died out by 1870 except in England where it achieved new life with new sets of music as the Lancers. The five figures of the *Quadrille des lanciers* were known in France as 'Les Tiroirs', 'Les Lignes', 'Les Moulinets', 'Les Visites' and 'Les Lanciers', and in Germany (where the whole dance was alternatively known as 'Quadrille à la Cour') as 'La Dorset', 'La Victoire', 'Les Moulinets', 'Les Visites' and 'Les Lanciers' or 'Finale à la Cour'.

BIBLIOGRAPHY

J. S. Richardson: *The Social Dances of the Nineteenth Century in England* (London, 1960)

ANDREW LAMB

Lanchbery, John (Arthur) (*b* London, 15 May 1923). English conductor. He studied at the Royal Academy of Music, and became musical director of the Metropolitan Ballet (1948–50), then of Sadler's Wells Theatre Ballet (1951) and, in 1960, principal conductor of the Royal Ballet, touring widely throughout the world. He worked in television opera, and has composed incidental music for films, television and radio; his popular orchestral arrangements include the film score for *The Tales of Beatrix Potter* (1971). He has made new performing versions of various ballet scores, including *La fille mal gardée* and *The Dream* for the Royal Ballet, and *Don Quixote*, *Giselle*, *Les sylphides* and *The Tales of Hoffmann* for companies in Britain, Austria, Sweden and USA. In 1972 he was appointed musical director of the Australian Ballet, and decided not to take up the additional appointment, announced at the same time, of principal guest conductor of the Royal Ballet.

NOËL GOODWIN

Lanciani, Flavio Carlo (*b* Rome, *c*1655; *d* Rome, 1724). Italian composer. He probably came into close contact about 1685 with Benedetto Pamphili, a music-loving cardinal for whose musical academies he wrote cantatas and arias. From 1689 to 1702 he was in the service of Cardinal Pietro Ottoboni. As a harpsichordist, violinist, copier and composer he was one of the pillars of Ottoboni's orchestra, which was directed by Corelli. In 1702 he went to the church of S Maria in Trastevere, Rome, becoming *maestro di cappella* there two years later. He occupied the same position at S Agostino from 1704. Between 1683 and 1706 he wrote ten oratorios for the Confraternità del Crocifisso. A large proportion of the music he composed, even after leaving Ottoboni's service, must have been written for the academies in the Palazzo Cancelleria. His vocal style is above all bland and grateful to the singers. His instrumental style may be considered as three-part writing, with clear stylistic affinities with Corelli. No thorough research has yet been undertaken on his voluminous work.

WORKS

ORATORIOS

(all lost unless otherwise stated)

Excidium Abimelech, 1683, Rome; S Dimna, 1687, Modena, *I-MOe*; S Stefano, 1687, Rome; Constantia fidei et haeresis coecitas, 1689, Rome; Judith, 1689, Rome; La gioia del seno d'Abramo, 1689, Rome; L'Absalone ribello, 1691, Rome; Gesta Josue, 1693, Rome; Innocentiae de hypocrisi triumphus, 1696, Rome; Vox succisa, 1700, Rome; Dilectionis portentum, 1702, Rome; Santa Clotilde, 1702, Bologna, *F-Pn*; Abimelech amor et poena, 1704, Rome; Pharaonis poena, 1705, Rome; Pudicitia ab innocentia vindicata, 1706, Rome; Il martirio di S Eustachio, Pn; S Maria Egiziaca

OPERAS
(all lost unless otherwise stated)

Il visir amante geloso, 1685, Todi; La forza del sangue, 1686, Rome; L'amante del suo nimico, 1688, Rome; Amore e gratitudine, 1691, Rome, D-Hs

OTHER WORKS

1 serenade, 3vv, 2 vn, tpt, I-MOe
Cantatas, arias, Fc, MOe, Nc, Vnm, D-MÜs

HANS JOACHIM MARX

Lanclos, Henri de. See L'ENCLOS, HENRI DE.

Lanctin, Charles François Honoré. See DUQUESNOY, CHARLES.

Landaeta, Juan José (b Caracas, 10 March 1780; d Cumaná, 16 Oct 1814). Venezuelan composer. He studied in the school of Father Sojo, who left him in his will 50 pesos, a violin and a viola. As a black man Landaeta could not be employed by the Church, which may explain his small sacred output. In 1805 he sought to establish a school for black children; he conducted the opera season in 1808, and participated in the 1810 conspiracy for independence. He died in the Cumaná massacre of 1814. The song Gloria al bravo pueblo, which became the Venezuelan national anthem, has been attributed to Lino Gallardo (c1770–1837), but Landaeta is now officially considered the composer. J. B. Plaza published an official edition in three versions (Caracas, 1947), and also edited a Salve regina in Archivo de Música Colonial Venezolana, xi (Montevideo, 1943). Landaeta's manuscripts, including five motets, a Spanish tonos and two songs, are in the Caracas school of music.

BIBLIOGRAPHY

J. B. Plaza: 'Music in Caracas during the Colonial Period (1770–1811)', MQ, xxix (1943), 198
J. A. Calcaño: La ciudad y su música (Caracas, 1958)
ALEJANDRO ENRIQUE PLANCHART

Landauer, Erich. See LEINSDORF, ERICH.

Landi, Giuseppe (b Bologna; fl late 18th and early 19th centuries). Italian composer and double bass player. In 1792 he became a member, in 1801 a principe, of the Accademia Filarmonica in Bologna. He may be the Landi who performed in Gluck's Alceste in 1778 at the Teatro Comunale in Bologna, or the Giuseppe Landi who in 1798 was primo violino dei balli at the Teatro degli Intrepidi in Florence. In 1791 and 1793 he conducted performances of his Sanctus Deus, sanctus fortis at S Francesco in Bologna. His sacred works are in the style of Stanislao Mattei, in which concertante elements in the style of contemporary opera are combined with older contrapuntal techniques. He is one of the last representatives of the Italian oratorio cantata.

WORKS

Requiem e Kyrie da morto, 4vv; Responsorio del beato Leonardo, 3vv, insts; Mulier, ecce filius tuus, 2vv, str; Sitio, 2vv, str; Domine ad adjuvandum, 4vv, insts, ripieni; Sanctus Deus, sanctus fortis, 4vv, insts, ripieni; Ecce nunc, 4vv, 1792, insts, ripieni: all I-Bc
Gloria Patri, 2vv, vn, b, Baf
Instrumentation for L. Gibelli's O gloriosa virginum and Quam terra pontus, and G. A. Perti's Confitebor: Bc

BIBLIOGRAPHY

EitnerQ
L. Bignami: Cronologia di tutti gli spettacoli al Teatro Comunale di Bologna (Bologna, 1882), 29
C. Ricci: I teatri di Bologna (Bologna, 1888), 654
SIEGFRIED GMEINWIESER

Landi, Stefano (b Rome, 1586 or 1587; d Rome, 28 Oct 1639). Italian composer, singer and teacher. He is one of the most important figures in the early history of opera and a leading Roman composer of his day.

1. LIFE. The best information on Landi's date of birth is a little-known document of 5 May 1630, translated by Haberl, in which Landi is said to have been 43 years old. The fact that he was regularly described as 'romano' indicates that he was born in Rome, but his grandfather came from Padua, a city to which Landi later returned.

On 8 May 1595 Landi entered the Collegio Germanico, Rome, as a boy soprano. Here he was presumably taught by Asprilio Pacelli, who was appointed maestro di cappella in the same year, and took minor orders on 28 October 1599. On 25 February 1602, on the recommendation of Princess Beatrice Caetana and of her son, Cardinal Cesis, he entered the Seminario Romano, where he studied rhetoric and philosophy until 1607. The maestro di cappella there was Agostino Agazzari, whose opera Eumelio was performed at the seminary in 1606. During April and May 1610 Landi was organist of S Maria in Trastevere, and he was a singer at the Oratorio del Ss Crocifisso in 1611, and he was presumably still in Rome in 1616, when his first published composition appeared in an anthology of Roman motets.

By 1 February 1618, however, Landi had been appointed maestro di cappella to Marco Cornaro, Bishop of Padua, to whom he dedicated his book of five-part madrigals, and it was from Padua, on 1 June 1619, that he dedicated his first opera, La morte d'Orfeo, to Alessandro Mattei, a familiaris of Pope Paul V. It is possible that the work was performed on the marriage that year of Marcantonio Borghese and Camilla Orsini: the only surviving copy (in GB-Lbm) stems from the Borghese library and Landi later served Cardinal Scipione Borghese – he sent him a 'compositione allegra' for three voices from Ancona on 19 December 1619.

Landi soon returned to Rome and apparently remained there for the rest of his life. On 1 June 1620 he dedicated his first book of Arie to Paolo Savello, Prince of Albano, and in 1621 he composed some music for the Arciconfraternità del Ss Crocifisso. He is said to have served the Borghese family again in 1623, and apart from helping with the music at S Eustachio he was, according to the title-page of his Psalmi integri (1624), both a 'clericus beneficiatus' of St Peter's and maestro di cappella of the church of the Madonna ai Monti. His Psalmi were dedicated to Cardinal Maurizio of Savoy, whom he continued to serve, on and off, until at least 19 March 1636, and his second book of Arie (1627) to the cardinal's sister-in-law, the Princess of Piedmont. The statement that his pupil, Angelo Ferrotti, would be going to Turin to sing the songs to her indicates that Landi was by then a teacher. His pupils in 1629–30 included Francesco Manelli and five boys aged 7–17, all of whom lived with Landi, his aunt and two servants, and in February 1630 Landi was also paid as 'mastro di dozzena del putto musico' by Cardinal Francesco Barberini.

Landi was closely associated with the Barberini family in the late 1620s and 1630s. His Missa in benedictione nuptiarum (1628) was probably composed for the wedding in 1627 of Taddeo Barberini and Anna Colonna and was dedicated to Pope Urban VIII, and it

Set, probably designed by Gian Lorenzo Bernini, for Act 1 scene 5 of Landi's 'Il Sant'Alessio', first performed in Rome in 1632: engraving by F. Collignon from the libretto (1634); see also OPERA, fig.25

was probably on the recommendation of the Barberini that Landi joined the papal choir on 29 November 1629 as an alto on half-salary, the other half going to Gregorio Allegri. In 1630 he helped with the music for the feast of the Visitation of the Virgin (2 July) at the church of S Maria d'Aquiro, the title-church of Cardinal Antonio Barberini, and he may have been the 'Don Stefano' who, with Marco Marazzoli and probably Filippo Vitali, accompanied the cardinal to Urbino in 1631.

In April of that year, apparently on Maundy Thursday, some responsories by Landi were sung by the papal choir at the request of their protector, Cardinal Biscia. Most of the choir disapproved of the settings, because they were evidently composed according to the *seconda* rather than the *prima prattica*, and although Landi beseeched Francesco Barberini to order a second performance the following year, it seems that they were never revived. Despite this, Landi was one of four papal singers who on Easter Sunday 1631 provided music for a Vespers service in the pope's apartments.

Landi's most important work, his sacred opera *Il Sant'Alessio*, was performed at the Palazzo Barberini on 21 February 1632 and repeated there in a revised form before Prince Alexander Charles of Poland in 1634. In June 1632 Landi was paid by Francesco Barberini for the purchase of strings for a harp and a Spanish guitar; this, together with the letter notation found in his books of *Arie*, suggests that he played the guitar and may have performed his songs to his own accompaniment. According to Baini he was one of several musicians commissioned by the pope in 1634 to prepare the new edition of hymns which was published at Antwerp in 1643 but appears now to be lost, while in 1635 he set to music Ottaviano Castelli's play *I pregi di primavera*, which was performed on 1 May at Castel Gandolfo and later at the Quirinal. His respect for Urban VIII is summed up in his only authenticated literary work, an undated eulogy in Latin distiches.

Landi appears to have done less for the papal choir and the Barberini after 1636, owing partly to ill-health. Nevertheless, during the last two years of his life he published no fewer than four more books of *Arie*, the last consisting entirely of duets, and one of masses. His fifth book of *Arie* (1637) was dedicated to Prince Gian

Carlo of Tuscany, and his sixth (1638) to the Prince von Ecchembergh who had seen *Il Sant'Alessio* in 1632. His seventh and eighth books (both 1639) are known only from Pitoni and appeared shortly before his death. Although he had lived in the parish of S Stefano in Piscinula from 1629, he was buried at S Maria in Vallicella (Chiesa Nuova), presumably in the communal tomb for members of the papal choir.

2. WORKS. *Il Sant'Alessio* was the first opera on a historical subject, the first on the inner life of a human character and one of the earliest about a saint. Having renounced the world for a religious life, Alexis returns incognito to his family home. He is ridiculed by pages and tempted by demons but remains true to his calling and eventually is rewarded in Heaven. The moral of this legend was underlined by spectacular sets and machines, including the engulfing of the Devil in the flames of Hell and the descent of Religion in a *carro* of clouds. The opera also had a social message. The two pages and the nurse not only alleviate the solemnity of the subject but also point up the nobility of the main characters and their conduct. They reflect the influence of the *commedia dell'arte* and were the prototypes for similar comic characters in countless later operas.

Il Sant'Alessio exhibits a strong interest in formal patterning comparable to that in Monteverdi's *Orfeo*. The Prologue and Acts 2 and 3 are each preceded by a sinfonia, Acts 1 and 3 begin with a chorus, and each act ends with a chorus and dancing. The sinfonias – substantial canzonas for three violins, harps, lutes, theorbos and harpsichords – are the first real 'overtures' in the history of opera. The first is in four sections and anticipates the form of the *sonata da chiesa*; the other two, which are in three sections, foreshadow the Italian overture of the later 17th century. The choruses of slaves and servants are in six parts, the demons in four and the angels in eight – a hierarchy of some significance. The dances at the ends of Acts 2 and 3 arise naturally from the action; that at the end of Act 1 was apparently added (like the part of the Second Page) between 1632 and 1634, yet it contributes to the development of the story and serves a formal function. The recitative is typical of the earlier 17th century. There are striking harmonic progressions and melodic leaps, and Religion has some florid ornamentation straight out of the papal chapel. The few distinct solo arias are mostly in triple time and are settings of strophic texts. The verses of Alexis's two 'ariettas' are separated by instrumental ritornellos. The comic duet (also marked 'arietta') in which the pages ridicule Alexis is justly famous. Perhaps the most expressive piece is the lament – a chromatic madrigal without continuo – sung on his death by his wife and parents; it is in three sections separated by recitatives and is thus another example of Landi's use of an ensemble to shape a scene. The same tendency is evident in *La morte d'Orfeo*, each act of which ends with a large scene-complex involving solos and choral ensembles. Most of the finales here, however, are only loosely related to the action and are more like *intermedi*. Ritornellos are for two (rather than three) violins and continuo, but otherwise the opera resembles *Il Sant'Alessio* in marrying the monodic and polyphonic styles.

The same two styles are also evident in Landi's music for chamber and church. His five-part madrigals are well within the bounds of 16th-century style, whereas his solo songs reflect the decline of the madrigal in the early 17th century and the rise of the aria and cantata. His first book of *Arie* is a substantial set containing 12 long arias in four to six *partes* (including one setting over the romanesca), two through-composed madrigals and six strophic songs. The arias are in strophic-variation form and look ahead to the strophic-bass cantata: the bass usually moves in crotchets and is almost unvarying. The vocal line is constantly varied, but mechanical ornamentation and phrase repetition too often act as substitutes for real melodic invention, a lack that is also apparent in the strophic songs.

The second book, unlike the first, is dominated by eleven strophic airs, with only two madrigals and one sonnet setting, while the fifth and sixth books, which are indistinguishable in style, consist entirely of arias, of which the texts are all ascribed. The bulk of the settings are in triple time, but there are almost as many in common time and several that embrace changes of time and style (e.g. arioso, recitative). Landi's first book of church music, which contains settings of the Vespers psalms and *Magnificat*, is in the new concertato style, but his two masses are in the *stile antico* and epitomize the conservatism of papal music in the age of the Counter-Reformation. Indeed, the formal and stylistic variety displayed in Landi's works as a whole seems typical of Roman vocal music in the early 17th century.

WORKS

DRAMATIC

La morte d'Orfeo, tragicommedia pastorale, ?Rome, 1619, op.2 (Venice, 1619); lib ed. in A. Solerti: *Gli albori del melodramma*, iii (Milan, 1904/*R*1969), 293ff; music extracts ed. in Goldschmidt, 188ff

Il Sant'Alessio, dramma musicale (G. Rospigliosi), Rome, ?1631 (Rome, 1634/*R*1970); lib ed. in A. della Corte: *Drammi per musica dal Rinuccini allo Zeno*, i (Turin, 1958), 195ff; music extracts ed. in Goldschmidt, 202ff; AMI, v, 43ff; Riemann, 253ff; HAM, ii, 47ff; 1 sinfonia ed. in Mw, xxiv (1964; Eng. trans., 1964), 37; 1 recit ed. in Mw, xxxi (1968; Eng. trans., 1968), 40ff

SACRED

Psalmi integri, 4vv, [bc] (Rome, 1624); ed. in Leopold, ii, 31ff
Missa in benedictione nuptiarum, 6vv (Rome, 1628); ed. in Leopold, ii, 73ff
Messa, 5vv, [bc], *I-Rsmt*; ed. in Leopold, ii, 137ff
Motets, 1616[1], 1621[3], 1625[1]

SECULAR

[18] Madrigali . . . libro primo, 5vv, bc (Venice, 1619); 1 ed. in Fortune (1954), appx iv, 30ff; 4 ed. in Leopold, ii, 9
Arie, 1v, [bc] (Venice, 1620); 1 ed. C. MacClintock: *The Solo Song*

1580–1730: a Norton Music Anthology (New York, 1973), 48ff
Il secondo libro d'arie musicali, 1v, [bc] (Rome, 1627)
Il quinto libro d'arie, 1v, bc (Venice, 1637)
Il sesto libro d'arie, 1v, [bc] (Venice, 1638)
2 arias, 1621[15], 1621[16]; duet, 1629[9]
2 works in P. Quagliati: La sfera armoniosa (Rome, 1623); ed. in SCMA, xiii (1957), 57ff
Dialogues, S, bc, *I-Baf*
Cantata, T, bc, *MOe*, ed. in Leopold, ii, 27f; aria, S, bc, 4 duets, 2vv, bc, *Ru* (1 of the duets probably = 1 formerly in F. Manelli: Ciaccone et arie, 1629, inc.)
6 inst works, formerly in Heyer collection, Cologne, now *I-Rn* (authenticity doubtful; see Sartori)

LOST WORKS

Poesie diverse in musica (Rome, 1628), cited in Pitoni, Fétis and *RiemannL 11*
Il quarto libro di arie, 1v, [bc] (Rome, 1629), cited in Pitoni
Responsories (1631)
I pregi di primavera (1635)
Il libro 7. dell'arie, 1v, [bc] (Rome, 1639), cited in Pitoni
Il libro 8. d'arie, 2vv, [bc] (Rome, 1639), cited in Pitoni
Il primo libro delle messe, 4, 5vv (Rome, 1639), cited in Adami, Baini, Gerbert and Fétis

(authenticity doubtful)
Il primo libro di madrigali, 4vv (Venice, 1619), cited in Fétis and *Grove 5*
Madrigali, 5vv (Rome, 1625), cited in Fétis and *Grove 5*

BIBLIOGRAPHY

EitnerQ; FétisB

A. Adami: *Osservazioni per ben regolare il coro dei cantori della Capella pontificia* (Rome, 1711), 197
G. O. Pitoni: *Notitia de contrapuntisti e de compositori di musica* (MS, *I-Rvat* C. G., I/1, *c*1725), 566f; ed. in Leopold (1976), i, 79f
M. Gerbert: *De cantu et musica sacra* (St Blasien, 1774), ii, 333f
G. Baini: *Memorie storico-critiche della vita e delle opere di G. P. da Palestrina* (Rome, 1828/*R*1966), ii, 217ff
C. Ricci: *I teatri di Bologna nei secoli XVII e XVIII* (Bologna, 1888/*R*1965), 331
A. Ademollo: *I teatri di Roma nel secolo decimosettimo* (Rome, 1888/*R*1969), 7ff
F. X. Haberl: 'Giovanni Maria Nanino: Darstellung seines Lebensganges und Schaffens auf Grund archivalischer und bibliographischer Dokumente', *KJb*, vi (1891), 88
H. Goldschmidt: *Studien zur Geschichte der italienischen Oper im 17. Jahrhundert*, i (Leipzig, 1901/*R*1967), 39ff, 188ff
R. Rolland: 'La première représentation du *San Alessio* de Stefano Landi en 1632, à Rome, d'après le journal manuscrit de Jean Jacques Bouchard', *RHCM*, ii (1902), 29, 74
G. Canevazzi: *Di tre melodrammi del secolo XVII* (Modena, 1904)
E. Celani: 'I cantori della Cappella pontificia nei secoli XVI–XVII', *RMI*, xiv (1907), 782
A. Salza: 'Drammi inediti di Giulio Rospigliosi', *RMI*, xiv (1907), 480
E. Schmitz: 'Zur Frühgeschichte der lyrischen Monodie Italiens im 17. Jahrhundert', *JbMP 1910*, 35, 41
A. Bonaventura: *Saggio storico sul teatro musicale italiano* (Livorno, 1913), 111ff
H. Botstiber: *Geschichte der Ouvertüre und der freien Orchesterformen* (Leipzig, 1913), 18f, 30
H. Prunières: *L'opéra italien en France avant Lulli* (Paris, 1913), 2f, 8ff
E. Schmitz: *Geschichte der weltlichen Solokantate* (Leipzig, 1914, rev. 2/1955), 61f
H. Kretzschmar: *Geschichte der Oper* (Leipzig, 1919), 77f
G. Pavan: 'Un dramma musicale a Roma nel 1634: il S. Alessio di Stefano Landi', *Musica d'oggi*, iii (1921)
H. Riemann: *Handbuch der Musikgeschichte*, ii/2 (Leipzig, rev. 2/1922/*R*1972 by A. Einstein)
R. Haas: *Die Musik des Barocks*, HMw (1928), esp. 70ff, 89f
S. Cordero di Pamparato: 'I musici alla corte di Carlo Emanuele I di Savoia', *Biblioteca della Società storica subalpina*, cxxi (1930), 131
U. Rolandi: 'Un tricentario contestato – l'apertura del teatro Barberini (18 febbraio 1632)', *Rassegna dorica*, iii/4 (1932)
R. Casimiri: ' "Disciplina musicae" e "mastri di capella" dopo il Concilio di Trento nei maggiori istituti ecclesiastici di Roma: Seminario romano – Collegio germanico – Collegio inglese (sec. XVI–XVII)', *NA*, xv (1938), 231
F. Vatielli: 'Operisti-librettisti dei secoli XVII–XVIII', *RMI*, xliii (1939), 5
M. F. Bukofzer: *Music in the Baroque Era* (New York, 1947), 62
D. J. Grout: *A Short History of Opera* (New York, 1947, rev. 2/1965), 62, 64ff
N. Fortune: 'Italian Secular Monody from 1600 to 1635: an Introductory Survey', *MQ*, xxxix (1953), 187
A. A. Abert: *Claudio Monteverdi und das musikalische Drama* (Lippstadt, 1954), 169f, 176ff
N. Fortune: *Italian Secular Song from 1600 to 1635: the Origins and*

Development of Accompanied Monody (diss., U. of Cambridge, 1954)

N. Castiglioni: 'Landi, Stefano', *ES*

S. A. Carfagno: *The Life and Dramatic Music of Stefano Landi with a Transliteration and Orchestration of the Opera Sant'Alessio* (diss., U. of California, Los Angeles, 1960)

S. Reiner: 'Collaboration in *Chi soffre speri*', *MR*, xxii (1961), 265

H. Wessely-Kropik: *Lelio Colista* (Vienna, 1961), 26, 28

D. J. Grout: 'The Chorus in Early Opera', *Festschrift Friedrich Blume* (Kassel, 1963), 160

P. Kast: 'Biographische Notizen zu römischen Musikern des 17. Jahrhunderts', *AnMc*, no.1 (1963), 48

E. Barassi: 'Il "S. Alessio" di Stefano Landi', *Musica università*, ii (Rome, 1964)

H.-W. Frey: 'Die Gesänge der Sixtinischen Kapelle an den Sonntagen und hohen Kirchenfesten des Jahres 1616', *Mélanges Eugène Tisserant* (Vatican City, 1964), 395–437

J. Racek: *Stilprobleme der italienischen Monodie* (Prague, 1965)

M. F. Robinson: *Opera before Mozart* (London, 1966, 2/1972), 75f

H. Hucke: 'Palestrina als Autorität im 17. Jahrhundert', *Congresso internazionale sul tema Claudio Monteverdi e il suo tempo: Venezia, Mantova, Cremona 1968*, 255

I. Küffel: *Die Libretti Giulio Rospigliosis: ein Kapitel frühbarocker Operngeschichte in Rom* (diss., U. of Vienna, 1968)

N. Pirrotta: 'Early Opera and Aria', *New Looks at Italian Opera: Essays in Honor of Donald J. Grout* (Ithaca, 1968), 87, 94, 99

A. Ziino: ' "Contese letterarie" tra Pietro della Valle e Nicolò Farfaro sulla musica antica e moderna', *NRMI*, iii (1969), 109

T. D. Culley: *Jesuits and Music, i: A Study of the Musicians connected with the German College in Rome during the 17th Century and of their Activities in Northern Europe* (Rome, 1970)

M. K. Murata: *Operas for the Papal Court with Texts by Giulio Rospigliosi* (diss., U. of Chicago, 1975)

C. Sartori: 'Stefano Landi uno e due. Ma di chi sono le canzoni strumentali?', *NRMI*, ix (1975), 3

S. Leopold: *Stefano Landi: Beiträge zur Biographie: Untersuchungen zur weltlichen und geistlichen Vokalmusik* (Hamburg, 1976)

COLIN TIMMS

Landini, Francesco [Landino, Franciscus; Magister Franciscus de Florentia; Magister Franciscus Cecus Horghanista de Florentia; Francesco delgli orghany; Cechus de Florentia] (*b* ? Fiesole or Florence, *c*1325; *d* Florence, 2 Sept 1397). Italian composer, poet, organist, singer and instrument maker of the second generation of Italian trecento composers.

1. Life. 2. Survival of works. 3. Musical style. 4. Poetry.

1. LIFE. Only a few dates relating to Landini's life can be established with any certainty. There is no record of his date of birth, which Fétis gave as *c*1325 and Pirrotta as *c*1335. Fiesole was stated as his place of birth, but by only one authority: the Florentine humanist Cristoforo Landino (1429–98), Landini's great-nephew, in his *Elegia de suis majoribus*. Further biographical information derives from Filippo Villani's *Liber de civitatis Florentiae famosis civibus*. The chapter of that work which concerns certain of the trecento composers (Bartholus, Giovanni, Lorenzo and Jacopo) was written after 1381 but still within Landini's lifetime. The name Landini (Landino), according to Pirrotta, descends from Francesco's grandfather, Landino di Manno, who can be traced in Pratovecchio (Casentino) from 1289 onwards. However that may be, Francesco's name is nowhere specified as 'Landini' in musical manuscripts.

Francesco Landini was the son of the painter Jacopo Del Casentino (*d* 1349), who was one of the school of Giotto and a co-founder of the Florentine guild of painters (in 1339). Francesco lost his sight in childhood during an attack of smallpox. As a result, he turned to music early in life. He mastered several instruments in addition to the organ; he sang, played and wrote poetry. He worked also as organ builder, organ tuner and instrument maker. According to Villani, he is supposed to have devised a string instrument called 'Serena Serenarum'. Villani's chronicle, and also Cristoforo

Landino's Dante commentary, mention Francesco's concern also with philosophical, ethical and astrological matters. As an adherent to the teaching of William of Occam he wrote an extended poem in praise of this philosopher's logic. With this, and the verses 'in contumeliam Florentinae juventutis effeminatae', referred to by Villani, Landini took issue in the political and religious strife of his day. In view of all this, it is quite likely that several of the texts he set to music were in fact his own (see Taucci, p.152). Villani reported the crowning of the poet–musician with the 'corona laurea' by the King of Cyprus in Venice (*c*1360–68). Doubts have been cast upon this event by E. Li Gotti. Nonetheless, it is highly probable that the composer spent at least some time in northern Italy before 1370, presumably in Venice itself. Evidence for this comes not only from the style and texts of some of the early works, but perhaps also from a single surviving voice of a motet *Principium nobilissime*, in which (as Plamenac has pointed out) the writer describes himself as 'Franciscus peregre canens'. This piece is addressed to the Doge Andrea Contarini (doge from 1368 to 1382). It is possible, too, that a motet *Marce Marcum imitaris* addressed to Marcus Cornaro, who was elected doge in 1365, may be by Landini. There is, at least, nothing to rule out the possibility that this work, which perhaps owes something to the three-part madrigal style of Jacopo da Bologna, is an early work of Francesco's, despite the objections which Ursula Günther has raised. Further possible associations of the composer with northern Italy are the name Anna, hidden in the text as a so-called Senhal, in the madrigal *Non AN NArcisso* (cf madrigals by Giovanni, Jacopo and Piero), and the possibility that the madrigal *Una colomba candida* was written for the marriage of Gian Galeazzo Visconti and Caterina Visconti (1380).

Recent research by D'Accone and by Gallo has produced evidence of Landini as organist at the monastery of Santa Trinità in 1361, and as *cappellanus* at the church of S Lorenzo from 1365 until his death. That Landini was on good terms with the Florentine chancellor of state and humanist Coluccio Salutati is indicated by a letter of recommendation for Landini addressed to the Bishop of Florence and dated 10 September 1375. Also, in the late 1370s there is a clear and strong association between Landini and the composer ANDREAS DE FLORENTIA. In 1379 Landini was involved in the building of the new organ in the church of the Ss Annunziata, where he is also known to have been organ tuner. In the same year he received a payment from Andreas 'pro quinque motectis': 'motecti' are probably not to be understood here as motets, but rather, in the wider sense of the word, as songs. In 1387 Landini was involved in planning the new organ for Florence Cathedral. A vivid portrayal of his activities in Florentine society was painted by Giovanni da Prato in his narrative poetic account of Florence in 1389, *Il paradiso degli Alberti*. The poet–composer emerges there as singer and organetto player, and takes part in erudite conversations and discussions of philosophical and political matters.

Landini died in Florence on 2 September 1397, and was buried there on 4 September in the church of S Lorenzo. His tombstone, which was discovered in Prato in the 19th century, and which is now back in S Lorenzo (in the second side-chapel to the right), shows the blind composer with his organetto. A similar illustration is to be found on f.121*v* of the Squarcialupi Manuscript (in *I-Fl*), in which Landini is depicted with

Francesco Landini wearing the 'corona laurea' and playing the organetto: miniature from the Squarcialupi MS, 15th century (I-Fl 87, f.121v)

the 'corona laurea' referred to by Villani.

The composer's fame was proclaimed by Cino Rinuccini (1350–1417) and C. Landino (1446). Landini's name does not occur again until 1589; it was cited by Michael Poccianti (*Catalogus scriptorum Florentiae*), and taken up by Walther in 1732 and A. M. Bandini in 1748. As a composer he was rediscovered by Fétis (*Revue musicale*, i, 1827).

2. SURVIVAL OF WORKS. 154 works can be attributed with certainty to Landini: 90 ballate for two voices, 42 for three voices, and eight which survive in both two-part and three-part versions (though in three of these cases the contratenor is probably not by Landini); one French virelai; nine madrigals for two or three voices; one canonic madrigal for three voices; and one caccia. To these must be added (as works of doubtful authenticity) two or perhaps three ballate for two voices; and four motets, of which three survive only as fragmentary single voices. The music for at least one further text by Sacchetti is lost. Landini's extant works represent about a quarter of the entire known repertory of secular music from the trecento.

The manuscripts of Landini's music are confined exclusively to Italy and, in a few cases, southern Germany. The source which is central to Landini's work, and with which he was probably directly concerned, is *I-Fn 26*. Numerically speaking, the largest collection of Landini's works – 145 pieces – is the Squarcialupi Manuscript (*see* SOURCES, MS). Three works are known in instrumental versions from the early 15th century. There are sacred contrafacta in two south German sources. In addition, at least 15 ballata texts known through Landini's settings were poetically recast as *laude spirituali*. To what extent the music of the prototypes was retained for these recast poems, or indeed whether it was retained at all, we cannot be sure. With a syllabic piece such as *Ecco la primavera*, the use of the same music for the *lauda* version, *Preghian Gesù con*

lieta cera, is quite conceivable throughout. To do the same thing for a melismatic piece such as *Donna, s'i' t'ò fallito* in its *lauda* version *Donna, s'i' son' partito da Cristo per peccare* is more questionable. The ballata *Questa fanciulla* must have been particularly popular, for it survives in at least six different forms: the original ballata, an instrumental intabulation, and four contrafacta (a Kyrie, an Agnus, an *Est illa* and a lauda *Creata fusti, O Vergine Maria*). Moreover, Oswald von Wolkenstein used the piece for his lied *Mein hertz das ist versert* (see Göllner). Seven Landini works are cited in Prudenzani's *Liber Saporecti* (Orvieto, c1410–20), and one in a treatise by Anonymous V (*CS*, iii, pp.395f).

The notation of Landini's works exhibits certain French scribal practices which were of increasing importance in Italy towards the end of the 14th century. This is particularly evident in cases where a piece was apparently originally composed in *divisio duodenaria* or *octonaria* but has been written down in augmented form, in *modus perfectus* or *imperfectus*.

3. MUSICAL STYLE. Landini's style has many facets. It ranges from the simple dance-song to the highly stylized piece with canonic or isorhythmic structure. It stretches from the Italian style of his precursors Jacopo and Lorenzo, across the infiltration of French influences, to an ultimate synthesis of French and Italian elements of style. Most immediate in its impression is Landini's gift for melody – distinctively shaped and at the same time expressive. At phrase-ends the under-3rd cadence (the so-called LANDINI CADENCE) figures frequently in the upper voices (see ex.1).

Ex. 1 Ballata, *Gram piant'agli ochi*

Very little can be said with certainty about the development of Landini's style. The texts offer very scanty clues on which to date works. Schrade's belief that the order of the pieces as written in *I-Fn 26* reflects their chronological order is unsubstantiated. Some precision of dating arises from the known dates of three ballata texts by Sacchetti. The pieces in question are *Non creder, donna* (1368–70), *Perché virtù* (1374) and *Altri n'arà* (after 1384); we may assume that their musical setting followed in each case not too long after the writing of the poems. The ballata *Or su, gentili spiriti*, referred to in *Paradiso degli Alberti*, was presumably a newly composed work of Landini's at the time of writing (1389). Furthermore, the pieces which have a possible connection with the Occamist-inclined Florentine studio – the madrigal *Tu che l'oper'altrui* and the ballata *Contemplar le gran cose* – date presumably from about 1380. The madrigal *Per lanfluença di Saturn'e Marte* centres on a historical event: but whether its subject is the events of the 1370s or those of the late 1360s remains an open question. The madrigals *Musica son* and *Mostrommi amor* are to be construed autobiographically, and perhaps also the two ballate *I' fu tuo servo amore* and *I' piango, lasso*.

On the basis of known datings, and of considerations of style, the following picture emerges of the separate categories of composition.

The two-voice madrigals, which accord with the older trecento practice in always setting text to both voices, in placing melismas on the initial and penultimate syllables of the line, and in effecting a change of mensuration in the ritornello, follow the models of Giovanni, Jacopo and others. Despite this, they are not all to be assigned to the composer's youth. The criteria for early date of composition seem to be: parallel open 5ths (a pointer to the connection of madrigal style with the earlier style of organum), simultaneous declamation of syllables, and untexted linking phrases, for one voice alone, between individual lines of verse (as in ex.2), on the model of Jacopo.

Ex.2 Madrigal, *Non an Narcisso*

As his style developed, these linking phrases came to be texted. At corresponding points in the later works imitative entries become a regular feature. There also seems to have been, during the course of Landini's stylistic development, a growing tendency towards a certain tonal cohesion. *Non an Narcisso*, for example, an early work, has its stanza beginning on E and ending on A, and the ritornello ending on C; the ends of the lines cadence on C, G, A, D and C. *Una colomba candida* (?1380), on the other hand, has its stanza beginning and ending on G, the ritornello ending on C, the lines cadencing on A, G, G, A, C.

The three-voice madrigals exhibit a fusion of Italian with French techniques of composition. *Musica son* is a triple-texted madrigal, perhaps modelled on Jacopo's *Aquil'altera*. *Si dolce non sonò* is constructed isorhythmically (see Fischer, 1975). *Dè, dimmi tu* is canonic in structure. His only caccia, *Cosi pensoso*, is, judging from its style, an early work possibly composed in northern Italy.

In the realm of the polyphonic ballata, a form which was scarcely to be found in Florence before the 1360s, Landini appears to have been a pioneer. Of his 91 two-voice ballate, no fewer than 82 follow the pattern of the madrigal in having text for both voices. With two exceptions, these pieces lack the first- and second-time endings with two *piedi* (ouvert–clos, or verto–chiuso) so characteristic of the French virelai (the French form corresponding to the ballata). Moreover, among the ballate with text in both voices, the majority have predominantly Italian mensurations (*duodenaria, octonaria, senaria perfecta* – admittedly in most cases converted into French notation). All of this points to a rather early date of composition, at least for a proportion of the two-voice ballate. Only very rarely in these

pieces does the concluding phrase of the *piede* mirror melodically that of the *ripresa* (as it does for example in *Vaga fanciulla*, a work which, with its *senaria imperfecta*, its texting of only the upper voice, and in other respects as well, displays French influence). The placing of melisma on first and penultimate syllables of a line is a feature taken over from the madrigal. In contrast to the madrigal, on the other hand, the two sections (*ripresa/volta* and *piedi*) are not rhythmically differentiated. Also the ballate show a generally stronger tonal cohesion than do the madrigals; approximately half of the two-voice ballate begin and end on the same pitch. (For illustration *see* SOURCES, MS, fig.36.)

The influence of the French chanson style is more apparent in the three-voice ballate. Of the total of 49 single-texted pieces, as many as 27 have text in only the top voice; a further 12 in the top voice and tenor; and only 10 have the full text in all three voices. Furthermore, about a third of all the three-voice ballate are in *senaria imperfecta* (= *senaria gallica*). *Verto* and *chiuso* endings occur in 31 pieces. Significant for Landini's style is the fact that nine out of the ten pieces that have text in all voices, in the Italian manner, do not have this double ending. French influence can however be suspected wherever in place of smooth flowing lines and small regularly sequential passages the melodic style gives way to much tinier motifs and more frequent syncopations. Similarly, the greater amount of melodic parallelism at the ends of *ripresa* and *piede* to be found in the three-voice ballate (e.g. *Lasso! di donna*) is to be put down to French influence.

From all of this, it follows that the three-voice ballate must belong primarily to the middle or later period of Landini's career. The unified tonality of these works points to the same conclusion. About half of them begin and end the *ripresa* on the same pitch; moreover, in 14 cases the *piede* ends on the same pitch as the *ripresa*.

Particularly revealing for Landini's style is his treatment of the contratenor. In about half of the three-voice ballate there is – in contrast to French practice – no crossing of parts between tenor and contratenor. In 20 cases, even the contratenor moves in the same range as the superius. As in the three-voice madrigals of Jacopo and Lorenzo, and in a manner reminiscent of the caccia, the contratenor in such cases functions as a secundus cantus, as in ex.3.

Ex. 3 Ballata, *Guard'una volta*

The remaining three-voice ballate do have, in French fashion, crossing of parts between tenor and contratenor. Above them the superius voice moves mostly in shorter note values (see ex.4).

One type of composition, possibly created by Landini, and cultivated in particular by Paolo da Firenze, is a mixed Italian–French type (found only in Italy) in which the superius and tenor are texted while the contratenor forms an untexted, instrumental middle voice. One or two of the three-voice ballate (such as *Amar si li*

Ex. 4 Ballata, *Amor c'al tuo sugetto*

A - mor__ c'al tuo su - get - to_o -

- mai __ da'__ le - - -

Ex. 5 Ballata, *Partesi con dolore*

[co] - - - - - - - - - - - re.____

alti and *Partesi con dolore*), pieces which can be considered late works, have a distinctly melodic top voice, and underlying harmonies which occasionally come close to fauxbourdon, as in ex.5.

If one were to apply an extremely hypothetical scheme of dating to the various facets of style within Landini's work, a pattern such as the following would emerge: up to *c*1370 (including the earliest ballate), assimilation of the older trecento style; *c*1370–80/85,

French influence, notably upon the three-voice ballate; *c*1385–97, a synthesis of Italian and French features, and an increase of vertical harmonic effect. In these late works Landini points towards the music of the 15th century.

4. POETRY. With the exception of the verses about Occam mentioned above, and a poem composed in Latin and Italian in the same manuscript, there is scarcely a poem to which Landini's authorship can be securely attached. Nonetheless, the texts of the clearly autobiographical pieces at least presumably come from him, and some of the ballate named by Taucci, too. These, along with the texts that he set by Cino Rinuccini and Bindo d'Alesso Donati, belong to the tradition of the Italian *dolce stil novo* and the poetic triumvirate of Dante, Boccaccio and Petrarch.

WORKS

Editions: *The Works of Francesco Landini*, ed. L. Ellinwood (Cambridge, Mass., 1939, 2/1945) [E]

Der Squarcialupi-Codex Pal. 87 der Biblioteca medicea laurenziana zu Florenz, ed. J. Wolf (Lippstadt, 1955) [W]; see K. von Fischer: 'Zu Johannes Wolfs Uebertragung des Squarcialupi-Codex', *Mf*, ix (1956), 77, and L. Schrade: 'Der Squarcialupi-Codex', *Notes*, xiii (1955–6), 683

The Works of Francesco Landini, ed. L. Schrade, PMFC, iv (1958) [S]

Editions of poetry: S. Prudenzani: *Liber Saporecti*, ed. S. Debenedetti, 'Il "Sollazzo" e il "Saporetto" con altre rime di Simone Prudenzani d'Orvieto', *Giornale storico della letteratura italiana*, suppl.15 (1913); pubd separately as *Il 'Sollazzo'* (Turin, 1922) [Pr]

Poesie musicali del trecento, ed. G. Corsi (Bologna, 1970) [incl. texts of *laude*] [Co]

Incipit	No. of vv	E	S	W	Remarks
				VIRELAI	
Adiu, adiu, dous dame	3	169	192	298	
				BALLATE	
Abbonda di virtu	2	39	90	279	
A lle' s'andrà lo spirt' (2 versions)	3, 2	40	166	227	Senhal: 'Sandra' or 'Alexandra'
Altera luc'ed angelic'aspetto	2	42	91	281	
Altri n'arà la pena	2	43	68	239	Text: Sacchetti; lauda contrafactum: 'Preghian la dolce vergine'
Ama, donna, chi t'ama	2	44	24	298	Text: ?Landini; lauda contrafactum: 'Ami ciascun cristian'; Pr no.48
Amar si li alti	3	171	176	280	'Ballata per Mona marsilia di manetto davanzati'; Co no.48
Amor c'al tuo sugetto (2 versions)	3, 2	174	183	241	Senhal: ?'Lena'
Amor con fede seguito	2	46	56	218	
Amor, in te spera'	3	176	141	—	
Amor in uom gentil	3	178	153	270	
Angelica biltà	2	48	54	204	
Ara' tu pietà mai	2	291	69	240	Text inc.; laude contrafacta: 'Merzé con gran pietà', ?'Volgi li occhi tuoi in qua'
Benché crudele siate	2	49	59	228	
Benché la bionda treça	2	292	88	271	Text incomplete
Bench'ora piova	2	50	93	284	
Cara mie donna	3	180	188	291	
Caro signor, palesa	3	183	126	295	See Co no.145
Che fai? che pensi?	2	51	92	283	
Che pena è quest'al cor (2 versions)	3, 2	188	162	218	Instrumental version, *I-FZc* 117
Chi più le vuol sapere	2	52	55	208, 304	
Chi pregio vuol	2	53	30	282	
Com'al seguir	2	55	45	274	
Con gli occhi assai	2	56	46	282	Text: C. Rinuccini; Pr no.34
Contemplar le gran cose	3	191	177	273	Text: ?Landini
Conviens'a fede	3	193	150	271	
Cosa nulla più fe'	3	196	158	221	Senhal: 'Cosa'
D'amor mi biasmo	2	58	10	253	
Da poi che va mie donna	2	60	94	285	
Da poi che vedi 'l mie fedel	2	61	81	264	
Dappo' c'a te rinasce	2	62	84	268	
Debba l'anim'altero	3	198	186	254	Text incomplete
Dè, che mi giova	2	64	79	262	
Dè, non fugir da me	2	65	40	250	
Dè, pon' quest'amor	2	67	4	250	Senhal: 'Cosa'; text: ?Landini; Pr no.34
De sospirar sovente	2	69	80	263	Lauda contrafactum: 'Batista da Dio amato'
Dè, volgi gli occhi	2	70	31	255	?Lauda

Incipit	No. of vv	E	S	W	Remarks
Divennon gli ochi	3	200	172	—	
Dolcie signiore	2	71	35	—	
Donna, che d'amor senta	2	72	82	265	Lauda contrafactum: 'Laudan Giesù piatoso'; ?Pr no.35; quoted by Anonymous V (*CS*, iii, p.396)
Donna, con vo' rimane	2	74	72	249	
Donna, i' prego amor	3	202	152	252	
Donna, laguir mi fay	2	78	78	262	
Donna, la mente mia	2	75	36	—	
Donna, la mie partença	2	77	83	267	
Donna, l'animo tuo	2	79	9	269	
Donna, 'l tuo partimento (2 versions)	3, 2	204	106	268	Ct by ?Landini
Donna, perché mi spregi	2	294	73	251	Text incomplete
Donna, per farmi guerra	3	206	160	255	
Donna, se 'l cor t'ò dato	2	80	21	274	Text: ?Landini
Donna, s'i' t'ò fallito	2	81	1	284	Lauda contrafactum: 'Donna, s'i' son' partito'; Pr no.48
Donna, tu prendi sdegno	2	83	75	256	
Duolsi la vita	2	84	74	252	
Ecco la primavera	2	85	58	228	Lauda contrafactum: 'Preghian Gesù con lieta cera'
El gran disio (2 versions)	3, 2	209	146	257	Text: Malatesta
El mie dolce sospir	3	212	123	259	
Fatto m'à serv'amore	2	86	77	260	
Fior di dolceça	2	88	76	260	
Fortuna ria (2 versions)	2, 3	89	27	158	3-part version *E-Sco* 25, no.2a/b; Ct and alius T by ?Landini
Gentil aspetto	3	214	134	223	
Già d'amore sperança	2	91	97	289	
Già ebbi liberate	2	92	43	—	
Già non biasim'amor	3	218	170	311	
Già perch'i' penso	2	94	2	310	
Giovine donna vidi star	2	95	98	290	
Giovine vaga, (i') non senti'	2	97	96	288	
Giunta vaga biltà	3	220	124	289	
Gli occhi che in prima	2	98	20	261	Text: ?Landini
Gram piant'agli ochi	3	222	128	224	Pr no.34
Guard'una volta	3	224	110	292	
I' fu tuo servo amore	2	99	47	301	Text: ?Landini
Il sùo bel viso	2	100	44	243	
I' non ardisco	2	102	42	—	Text: Rinuccini
In somm'alteça	2	103	103	312	
I' piango, lasso	2	105	61	230	Text: ?Landini
I' priego amor (2 versions)	3, 2	226	190	293	
I vegio ch'a natura	2	106	63	231	
La bionda treçça	2	107	18	209	Laude contrafacta: 'Or che non piangi', 'O Gesù Cristo padre'
La dolce vista (2 versions)	3, 2	229	108	265	Ct by ?Landini
L'alma leggiadra	2	109	34	378	
L'alma mie piange	3	232	148	219	Pr no.34
La mala lingua	2	111	70	240	
La mente mi riprende	3	236	132	266	
L'antica fiamma	2	112	12	278	
L'aspetto è qui	2	114	86	268	
Lasso! di donna	3	238	138	222	Contrafactum: 'Dilectus meus misit', *F-Sm* 222
Lasso! per mie fortuna	3	240	180	220	
L'onesta tuo biltà	2	116	89	277	
Ma' non s'andrà	2	118	50	242	Senhal: 'Sandra'
Muort'oramai, dè	3	242	178	216	
Nella mi vita	3	245	120	308	
Nella partita pianson	2	120	48	237	
Nella più cara parte	2	121	102	310	
Nella tuo luce	2	123	57	227	
Né 'n ciascun mie pensiero	3	247	168	238	
Nessun ponga speranza	3	249	174	294	
Nessun provò giamma	2	124	95	286	
Non avrà mai pietà	3	252	144	225	Text: B. d'Alesso Donati; inst version, *I-FZc* 117
Non creder, donna	2	126	6	232	Text: Sacchetti; laude contrafacta 'Preghian la dolce vergine', 'Ciascun che 'l regno di Gesù disia'
Non dò la colp'a te	3	255	122	226	
Non per fallir	2	128	14	306	
Ochi dolenti mie	2	130	60	229	
O fanciulla giulia	3	257	154	287	Text: ?Landini; written for the wife of Cavalcante Cavalcanti
Ognor mi trovo	2	131	62	230	
Or è tal l'alma mia	2	132	23	242	Senhal: 'Oretta' (?Lauretta)
Or su, gentili spiriti	3	260	184	244	Text: ?Landini; Senhal: 'Petra' (? = 'Cosa')
Oymè 'l core!	2	134	71	244	
Partesi con dolore	3	262	136	276	Text incomplete, possibly French ballade form
Per allegreçça del parlar	2	136	17	286	Laude contrafacta: 'Per l'alegreza del nostro Signore', 'Ciascun fedel cristian per riverenza'
Perché di novo sdegno/Vendetta far dovrei/Perché tuo servo	3	265	142	297	Triple ballata
Perché virtù	2	137	42	—	Text: Sacchetti
Per la belleça	2	138	99	299	
Per la mie dolçe piaga	3	268	185	247	
Per seguir la sperança	3	271	112	302	
Per servar umiltà	2	140	8	309	
Per un amante	2	141	100	303	
Più bella donn'al mondo	2	143	52	—	

Incipit	No. of vv	E	S	W	Remarks
Po' ch'amor ne' begli ochi	2	145	26	307	
Po' che di simil	2	296	66	236	Text incomplete
Po' che partir convienmi	3	273	118	300	Lauda contrafactum: 'Po' che da morte nessun si ripara'
Poi che da te mi convien	2	147	16	246	Laude contrafacta: 'Po' che v'ho posto', 'Ciascun che 'l regno di Gesù disia'
Posto che dall'aspetto	3	276	156	275	
Quanto più caro fai	3	279	130	248	Name of Bartolino erased in F-Pn 568
Quel sol che raggia	3	282	114	236	
Questa fanciulla, Amor	3	285	116	234	Inst version, F-Pn 6771; contrafacta: 'Kyrie', D-Mbs 3232a; 'Agnus', Guardiagrele, S Maria Maggiore MS 1, f.192v, see Cattin etc, 1972; 'Est illa', F-Sm 222 [lost]; lauda contrafactum: 'Creata fusti, O Vergine Maria' (used by Oswald von Wolkenstein for 'Mein hertz das ist versert'; see Göllner, 1964)
S'andray sança merçe	2	149	37	304	Senhal: 'Sandra'
Se la nimica mie	2	151	101	306	
Se la vista soave	2	153	64	233	
Selvagia, fera di Diana	3	287	182	232	
Se merçe, donna	2	155	38	—	
Sempre girò caendo	2	298	104	314	Text incomplete
Se pronto non sarà	2	157	32	313	
Sia maladetta l'or	2	159	19	314	
S'i' fossi certo	3	289	140	235	
S'i' ti son stato	2	161	22	246	Lauda contrafactum: 'Sempre laudata e benedetta sia'
Tante belleçe	2	162	67	238	
Vaga fanciulla	2	163	29	300	
Va' pure, Amore	2	165	25	315	Lauda contrafactum: 'O falso amore privato di paçe'
Viditi, donna, già vaga	2	166	105	316	
Vita non è più miser'	2	167	28	305	Lauda contrafactum: 'Vita, chi t'ama in pace morto sia'; text mentioned in Giovanni Sercambi's Novelle

MADRIGALI

Incipit	No. of vv	E	S	W	Remarks
Dè, dimmi tu	3	22	216	206	Canon T–Ct
Fa metter bando	2	3	192	200	
Lucea nel prato	2	5	204	210	
Mostrommi amor	2	7	200	204	Text: ?Landini
Musica son che mi dolgo/Già furon/Ciascun vuol	3	26	213	197	Triple madrigal
Non an Narcisso	2	9	198	205	Senhal: 'Anna'
O pianta vaga	2	11	196	212	
Per lanfluença	2	13	202	208	
Si dolce non sonò	3	31	210	201	Isorhythmic
Somma felicità	2	15	206	211	Text: Sacchetti
Tu che l'oper'altrui	2	17	194	199	Text: ?Landini
Una colomba candida	2	19	208	215	

CACCIA

Incipit	No. of vv	E	S	W	Remarks
Cosi pensoso	3	35	219	213	Pesca

CANZONETTA

Incipit	No. of vv	E	S	W	Remarks
Né te né altra voglio amar	?	—	—	—	Lost. Text: Sacchetti – MS of poem mentions Landini as composer; for the 4 laude contrafacta, see Corsi, 1959

DOUBTFUL WORKS

MOTETS

Incipit	No. of vv	E	S	W	Remarks
Principium nobilissime	?3	—	222	—	Only 1v extant (see Plamenac, 1955)
Florencia, mundi speculum	?3	—	—	—	Biblioteca Egidi, Montefiore dell'Aso; only 1v extant
Leonarde, pater inclite	?3	—	—	—	Biblioteca Egidi, Montefiore dell'Aso; only 1v extant
Marce Marcum imitaris	3	—	—	—	Biblioteca dell'Abbazia, Grottaferrata, 197; see Günther (1970)

BALLATE

Incipit	No. of vv	E	S	W	Remarks
Acburr'uomo	2	—	—	—	Landini's name erased in F-Pn 568 (see Günther, 1966); ed. in PMFC, xi
Io son'un pellegrin	2	—	—	—	?Pr no.25 (see, CMM, viii/3, p.iii); ed. in PMFC, xi, and CMM, viii/3, p.51
Mort'è la fè	2	—	—	—	Landini's name erased in F-Pn 568 (see Günther, 1966); ed. in PMFC, xi

The two French ballades De Narcissus and Phiton, beste très venimeuse are not by Landini.

BIBLIOGRAPHY

RiemannL 12

A. M. Bandinius: Specimen literaturae Florentiae saeculi XV, i (Florence, 1748)

G. C. Galletti, ed.: Philippi Villani Liber de civitatis Florentiae famosis civibus (Florence, 1847)

A. de La Fage: Essais de diphtérographie musicale (Paris, 1864/R1964)

A. Wesselofsky, ed.: Giovanni da Prato: Il paradiso degli Alberti (Bologna, 1867/R1968)

C. Guasti: 'Della sepoltura di Francesco Cieco de' Landini', Belle arti (Florence, 1874), 95

R. Gandolfi: 'Una riparazione a proposito di Francesco Landini', Rassegna nazionale, x (1888), 58

P. H. Horne: 'A Commentary upon Vasari's Life of Jacopo dal Casentino', Rivista d'arte, vi (Florence, 1909), 95, 165

R. Taucci: 'Fra Andrea dei Servi organista e compositore del trecento', Studi storici sull'ordine dei Servi di Maria, ii (Rome, (1934–5), 73, 152

E. Li Gotti and N. Pirrotta: Il Sacchetti e la tecnica musicale del trecento italiano (Florence, 1935)

L. Ellinwood: 'Francesco Landini and his Music', MQ, xxii (1936), 190

A. von Königslöw: Die italienischen Madrigalisten des Trecento (Würzburg-Aumühle, 1940)

E. Li Gotti: La poesia musicale italiana del secolo XIV (Palermo, 1944)

——: 'Una pretesa incoronazione di Francesco Landini', Restauri trecenteschi (Palermo, 1947), 91

M. Johnson: 'A Study of Conflicting Key-signatures in Francesco Landini's Music', Hamline Studies in Musicology, ii (1947), 27

H. Nolthenius: 'Een autobiografisch madrigaal van F. Landino', TVNM, xvii/4 (1955), 237

D. Plamenac: 'Another Paduan Fragment of Trecento Music', JAMS, viii (1955), 165

H. Nolthenius: *Renaissance in Mei: Florentijns leven rond F. Landino* (Utrecht, 1956)

K. von Fischer: *Studien zur italienischen Musik des Trecento und frühen Quattrocento* (Berne, 1956)

G. Corsi: 'Madrigali e ballate inedite del trecento', *Belfagor*, xiv (1959), 329

N. Pirrotta: 'Landini (Landino), Francesco', *MGG*

K. von Fischer: 'On the Technique, Origin, and Evolution of Italian Trecento Music', *MQ*, xlvii (1961), 41

M. Schneider: 'Das gestaltpsychologische Verfahren in der Melodik des Francesco Landino', *AcM*, xxxv (1963), 2

K. von Fischer: 'Neue Quellen zur Musik des 13., 14. und 15. Jahrhunderts', *AcM*, xxxvi (1964), 79

T. Göllner: 'Landinis "Questa fanciulla" bei Oswald von Wolkenstein', *Mf*, xvii (1964), 393

U. Günther: 'Die "anonymen" Kompositionen des Ms. Paris BN, fonds ital, 568 (Pit)', *AMw*, xxiii (1966), 73

K. von Fischer: 'Ein Versuch zur Chronologie von Landinis Werken', *MD*, xx (1966), 31

U. Günther: 'Quelques remarques sur des feuillets récemment découverts à Grottaferrata', *L'ars nova italiana del trecento II: Certaldo 1969*, 315

C. Schachter: 'Landini's Treatment of Consonance and Dissonance', *Music Forum*, ii (New York, 1970), 130

F. D'Accone: 'Music and Musicians at the Florentine Monastery of Santa Trinità, 1360–3', *Quadrivium*, xii (1971), 131

G. Cattin, O. Mischiati and A. Viino: 'Composizioni polifoniche del primo quattrocento nei libri corali di Guardiagrele', *RIM*, vii (1972), 153

K. von Fischer: 'Zum Wort-Ton Problem in der Musik des italienischen Trecento', *Festschrift Arnold Geering* (Berne, 1972), 53

——: 'Philippe de Vitry in Italy: an Homage of Francesco Landini to Philippe', *L'ars nova italiana del trecento III: Certaldo 1975*, 225

F. A. Gallo: 'Lorenzo Masini e Francesco degli Organi in San Lorenzo', *Studi musicali*, iv (1975), 57

D. Baumann: *Die dreistimmige Satztechnik bei Francesco Landini* (Baden-Baden, 1978)

For further bibliography *see* ITALY: BIBLIOGRAPHY OF MUSIC TO 1600.

KURT VON FISCHER

Landini cadence [Landino 6th] (Ger. *Landinoklausel, Landinosext*). A name often used for a cadential formula in which the sixth degree of the scale is interposed between the leading note and its resolution on the tonic or final degree (ex.1). Many examples appear in the work of Francesco Landini (exx.2 and 3), but it is particularly common in polyphony of the 15th and early 16th centuries.

Ex.1

Ex.2

Ex.3

The pattern is perhaps inevitable because contrapuntal theory of the Middle Ages required that a cadence should include two voices moving outwards to an octave (or perhaps a 5th), and composers were driven to add variety by embellishing the progression: several different kinds of embellishment pattern can be found in the music of that time, most of them giving prominence to the sixth degree which had the advantage of giving a perfect 5th with the lower voice in all such cadences. Exx.4–6 show the three most common types of the cadence, all taken from the songs of Binchois.

Ex.4

Ex.5

Ex.6

In general the term has been used with extreme caution in scholarly writing: it is normal to put it in quotes, to qualify it as 'the so-called Landini cadence', or to find a synonym such as 'under-third cadence'. But the name, though it has no medieval authority, may not be entirely inappropriate: certainly the examples of it from earlier music that are occasionally more quoted are usually more easily explained in other ways, and it seems that Landini was the first composer to use the pattern at all systematically in the manner described above.

A. G. Ritter (*Zur Geschichte des Orgelspiels*, Leipzig, 1884, p.5) gave what seems to be the earliest description of such a cadence as being characteristic of Landini: he felt that Landini's reputation as an organist merited a place in the history of organ music but he had access to only one work by the composer, the ballata *Non avrà mai pietà*, printed in Kiesewetter's influential and pioneering *Schicksale und Beschaffenheit* (1841). On the basis of that piece alone Ritter attempted to describe Landini's musical style and drew attention to the cadence in ex.1. His book had such success, in terms of both subsequent editions and its influence on other handbooks, that the label has remained current, though evidence of that currency must be sought in the more transitory literature rather than in the standard scholarly works.

DAVID FALLOWS

Landis, Clericus de. French composer. He was active in the 14th century but is known only from a composition in *NL-Uu* 37, in which he is described as 'bone memorie'. The composition is a three-voice rondeau, *Des dont que part*, with text in the top voice only (edited in CMM, liii/1, 38). It is noteworthy for use of syncopation in c time, as well as for the use of imitation between top voice and tenor at the opening of the two principal sections.

GILBERT REANEY

Ländler (Ger.). A folkdance in slow 3/4 time which in regional variants is highly popular in Austria, south Germany (Bavaria, Swabia) and German Switzerland, and which was also danced by the German settlers in Transylvania (Siebenbürgen) and the Carpathian Ukraine. The name, though seemingly denoting 'country dance', derives from 'Landl' or 'Land ob der Enns' which was the old description of Upper Austria. The title is first encountered (as 'Länderli') in a lute manuscript compiled by J. S. von Hallwill in the 17th century (now in *A-KR*). The first mention of its modern name is in the 'Zwölf Ländler' for guitar composed by Leonhard von Call in about 1800 (manuscript in *A-Wgm*).

The Austrian court traditionally staged popular feasts called 'Wirtschaften', 'Königreiche' and 'Bauernhochzeiten' – dramatic representations of scenes from peasant life in which members of the imperial family appeared in costumes of peasants and hunters. These entertainments were in the nature of *bals champêtres* with folksongs and folkdances. Ex.1 shows a 'Brader' dance (after the Prater, one of Vienna's largest pleasure gardens) contrasted with a true ländler, both from the 17th century. Composers such as J. H. Schmelzer wrote ballet suites containing ländlers for these festive occasions, and later neither Haydn nor Mozart considered it beneath his dignity to write *Teutsche* or German Dances for the masked balls given by the court during Carnival at the Redoutensaal in the Hofburg.

Ex.1

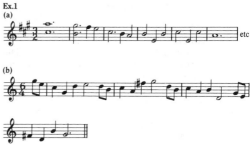

The ländler is a round dance for individual couples, and, depending on the kind of figures executed by the dancers and the region where it was favoured, it bears different names such as 'Dreher', 'Weller', 'Spinner', 'Schleifer', 'Wickler' (Salzburg), 'Steirer' (Styria) and 'Scheiben' (Lower Austria). When transferred to the opera or the ballroom it became stylized and took on French titles like 'Tyrolienne' and 'Styrienne'. The ländler is an outdoor dance, with hopping and stamping as consistent features. The two partners hold each other by the waist and from time to time pass under each

Ländler: engraving by Binde

other's arms and often perform such difficult movements as throwing the female over the male dancer's shoulder. It is usually danced on a rostrum outside an inn (as in Berg's *Wozzeck*, Act 2 scene iv) or on the village green. The male partner traditionally wore heavy hob-nailed shoes or boots which partly accounted for the slow and robust character of the rustic dance. With the opening of urban ballrooms with parquet floors towards the end of the 18th century, the heavy footwear was replaced by lighter shoes and the dance became quicker and confined itself to a gliding and rotating movement. This marked the birth of the WALTZ, which gradually ousted the ländler as the favourite dance form. It is noteworthy that, while Joseph Lanner still called his first waltzes 'Ländler' and 'Deutsche' (*Neue Wiener Ländler* op.1; *Krönungsdeutsche* op.5) and even later wrote the *Zauberhornländler* op.31 and the *Steirische Tänze* op.165, Johann Strauss (i) had already named his op.1 'Täuberlwalzer'.

The choreographic pattern of the ländler is left–right–left on the three crotchets of a bar, with every beat accented; in certain regions it is accompanied by 'Paschen' or rhythmic hand-clapping. The music consists of two strains eight or 16 bars long, with each period repeated at least once. It is nearly always in a major key, is markedly diatonic, and the melody shows the influence of Alpine folksong in its tendency towards arpeggio figures. The ländler can be entirely instrumental, and is then usually played by two violins and a double bass or harp; or it can be wholly vocal, as in Silcher's *Ännchen von Tharau*; or it can alternate between normal singing and yodelling as in ex.2, a folksong from the Tyrol. Individual ländlers are sometimes gathered together to form a ländler chain, examples of which are provided by Schubert's dances for piano D145, 366, 681 and 734. In Upper Austria there is also a ländler in common time (see Gielge). In Styria the dancing couple first sing a 'Schnadahüpfl' ('hopping of the mower') or a quatrain with which they indicate to the band the key and character of the dance melody. Typical of Bavaria, the Tyrol and Salzburg is the 'Schuhplattler', in which the two partners dance opposite each other, holding their arms crossed and stamping with their feet. By tradition the ländler music is played from memory, yet most players have a 'Partien' or 'Schnoasn', a notebook in which they enter various ländlers in a much abbreviated form and according to key. These musical 'stenographs' are never complete and, moreover, do not contain rhythmic variants and embellishments. The practice is still alive today. Zoder is said to have possessed a collection of over 11,000 ländler melodies.

The ländler was used by such Austrian symphonists as Haydn, Mozart, Bruckner and Mahler, whose minuet or scherzo movements are frequently ländler-like. The Carinthian tune in Berg's Violin Concerto is a true ländler melody, as is the waltz in Act 1 of Weber's *Der Freischütz*. Some of Brahms's songs are in ländler style, including *Der Schmied*, *Sonntag*, *Wiegenlied* and *Vergebliches Ständchen*.

BIBLIOGRAPHY

F. M. Böhme: *Geschichte des Tanzes in Deutschland* (Leipzig, 1886)

E. Binder: *Oberösterreichische Original-Ländler aus älterer Zeit* (Vienna, 1909)

H. Dondl: *Der Ländler* (Munich, 1912)

R. Zoder: 'Die melodische-stychische Anordnung von Ländlermelodien', *Das deutsche Volkslied*, xvi (1914), 87

H. Gielge: 'Der geradtaktige Ländler – ein musikalischer Eigenbrötler', *Das deutsche Volkslied*, xlii (1940), 21

P. Nettl: *The Story of Dance Music* (New York, 1947/R1961)

MOSCO CARNER

Lando, Stefano (*b* Naples, *c*1530; *d* Naples, April 1571). Italian composer. Cerreto mentioned him as one of 'the excellent composers from the city of Naples, now no longer living'. In 1559 he was appointed keeper of the vihuelas at the royal palace of Naples, and was also chamber musician to the Duke of Alcalà, Viceroy of Naples. His *Il primo libro de madrigali a quattro voci* (Venice, 1558) contains 39 madrigals, and five more for three voices appeared in contemporary collections (*RISM* 1566⁹, 1566¹⁰, 1570¹⁸).

BIBLIOGRAPHY

S. Cerreto: *Della pratica musica vocale, et strumentale* (Naples, 1601/R1969)

PIER PAOLO SCATTOLIN

Landolfi, Carlo Ferdinando (*fl c*1750–*c*1775). Italian violin maker. He worked in Milan, where he may have started as an assistant to one of the Testores (perhaps Paolo Antonio) but was more likely associated with G. B. Guadagnini, who went there in 1749. His instruments draw much more from the Guadagnini workshop than from the earlier Milanese makers. By the mid-1750s he was producing his best violins, elegant in design and neat in workmanship, though with strong personal character. The varnish is rich in appearance, sometimes the deep red of the Venetians but more often a lighter orange-brown. His violins are desirable tonally, but mostly not in the same class as those of Guadagnini. Equally interesting are his violas, varying in size from a minute 38·1 cm body length, to a good 38·9 cm model and an occasional splendid pattern just over 40·6 cm. Landolfi cellos are invariably small, though good instruments.

Landolfi's main pupils were Pietro Giovanni Mantegazza, who was independent before 1760, and his son Pietro Antonio Landolfi (*fl c*1760–*c*1785). Some of Pietro's instruments were spoilt by their rather high build and a harder varnish than that used by his father. His influence is increasingly noticeable in the Landolfi instruments after 1760, but his enthusiasm for the craft seems to have waned from 1770.

BIBLIOGRAPHY

W. L. von Lütgendorff: *Die Geigen- und Lautenmacher vom Mittelalter bis zur Gegenwart* (Frankfurt am Main, 1904, 6/1922/R1968)

O. Möckel: *Die Kunst des Geigenbaues* (Leipzig, 1930, rev. 2/1954)

R. Vannes: *Essai d'un dictionnaire universel des luthiers* (Paris, 1932, 2/1951/R1972 as *Dictionnaire universel des luthiers*; suppl. 1959)

H. Hamma: *Meisterwerke italienischer Geigenbaukunst* (Stuttgart, 1933)

CHARLES BEARE

Ex.2

Landon [née Fuhrmann], **Christa** (*b* Berlin, 23 Sept 1921; *d* Funchal, Madeira, 19 Nov 1977). Austrian musicologist. She studied the piano and organ with Bruno Seidlhofer, theory with Joseph Marx and Alfred Uhl and the harpsichord with Isolde Ahlgrimm at the Vienna Academy of Music and had private lessons in analysis with Webern. After passing the final harpsichord examination (1948), she worked for the Haydn Society in Boston and Vienna (1949–58), collaborating with H. C. Robbins Landon, then her husband, on publications and working as his research partner in libraries, monasteries and private collections. In 1959 she began working as a freelance editor, specializing in editions of Haydn (symphonies and cassations), Mozart (serenades) and Bach (Brandenburg Concertos, etc). With Walther Dürr and Arnold Feil she was general editor of the new Schubert edition, contributing herself two volumes, containing symphonies and the piano music for four hands. In the course of her editorial work she discovered about 50 sheets of hitherto unknown Schubert autographs in Vienna; she published two rediscovered songs *Vollendung* and *Die Erde* (Kassel, 1970). With Alexander Weinmann she also discovered a proof copy of Beethoven's Piano Sonata op.111 with corrections in the composer's hand.

WRITINGS
'Neue Schubert-Funde', *ÖMz*, xxiv (1969), 299; Eng. trans. in *MR*, xxxi (1970), 215
'Ein neuer Schubert-Brief', *ÖMz*, xxxii (1977), 545

EDITIONS
J. Haydn: *Messen Nr. 5–8*, Werke, xxiii/2 (Munich and Duisburg, 1958) [with K. H. Füssl and H. C. R. Landon]; *Klaviersonaten*, i–iii (Vienna, 1963–6); *Sinfonia concertante Hob. I: 105* (Zurich, 1968)
F. Schubert: *Symphonien Nr. 1–3*, Neue Ausgabe sämtlicher Werke, v/1 (Kassel, 1967) [with A. Feil]; *Werke für Klavier zu vier Händen*, ibid, vii/1/iv (Kassel, 1972), vii/1/ii (Kassel, 1978)

BIBLIOGRAPHY
J. LaRue: 'Christa Landon (1921–1977)', *MQ*, lxiv (1978), 104
RUDOLF KLEIN

Landon, H(oward) C(handler) Robbins (*b* Boston, 6 March 1926). American musicologist. After studying music theory with Alfred Swan, composition with Harl McDonald and English literature with W. H. Auden at Swarthmore College (1943–5), and music with Karl Geiringer and Hugo Norton at Boston University (1945–7, MusB 1947), he worked as a music critic for American papers in England, France, Holland and Austria (1947–9). In 1949 he founded the Haydn Society, of which he became secretary general (1949–51), and which planned a complete edition of Haydn's works; he has also held appointments as professor of music at Queens College, New York (1969), and regis professor at the University of California at Davis (1970).

Landon started publishing material on Haydn and critical editions of his music in the late 1940s. This culminated in his book on the symphonies, which discusses new chronologies and new texts, setting the works in the broad context of 18th-century music and of Haydn's output as a whole; it represents one of the most substantial products of postwar musical scholarship and a major landmark in Haydn studies. Landon drew fresh public and scholarly attention to other Haydn works, notably the masses and operas, several of which he published in new critical editions, thereby stimulating performances and provoking a reappraisal of Haydn as a dramatic composer. He has also contributed to Mozart scholarship and has done much work on the sources of Austrian 18th-century music in general. Some of his work has been directed to a broader public; he has been a prolific writer of magazine articles, sleeve notes and reviews, and has broadcast and appeared on television. Some of his work (particularly on composers slightly outside his specialist field, for example J. C. Bach and Beethoven) has been criticized for lacking the scholarly precision that distinguished his earlier research, particularly that on Haydn.

WRITINGS
'On Haydn's Quartets of Opera 1 & 2: Notes and Comments on Sondheimer's Historical and Psychological Study', *MR*, xiii (1952), 181
'Die Verwendung gregorianischer Melodien in Haydns Frühsymphonien', *ÖMz*, ix (1954), 119
'The Original Versions of Haydn's First "Salomon" Symphonies', *MR*, xv (1954), 1–32
'Haydn and Authenticity: some New Facts', *MR*, xvi (1955), 138
The Symphonies of Joseph Haydn (London, 1955; suppl., 1961)
'La crise romantique dans la musique autrichienne vers 1770: quelques précurseurs inconnus de la Symphonie en sol mineur (KV 183) de Mozart', *Les influences étrangères dans l'oeuvre de Mozart: CNRS Paris 1956*, 27
'Symphonien: ihr geistiger und musikalischer Ursprung und ihre Entwicklung', *Mozart-Aspekte*, ed. P. Schaller und H. Kühner (Olten and Freiburg, 1956), 39
ed. with D. Mitchell: *The Mozart Companion* (London and New York, 1956, 2/1965) [incl. 'Concertos: their Musical Origin and Development', 234–82]
The Preclassical Symphony (London, 1956)
The Viennese Classical Mass: the Circumstances of Mozart's Requiem, Analytical and Descriptive Notes (New York and London, 1956) [disc notes]
'Doubtful and Spurious Quartets and Quintets Attributed to Haydn', *MR*, xviii (1957), 213
'Eine aufgefundene Haydn-Messe', *ÖMz*, xii (1957), 183 [*Missa Rorate coeli desuper*]
'Mozart fälschlich zugeschriebene Messen', *MJb 1957*, 85
'Problems of Authenticity in Eighteenth-century Music', *Instrumental Music: Isham Memorial Library 1957*, 31
The Unknown Haydn (London, 1958)
'Survey of the Haydn Sources in Czechoslovakia', *Internationale Konferenz zum Andenken Joseph Haydns: Budapest 1959*, 69
ed.: *The Collected Correspondence and London Notebooks of Joseph Haydn* (London, 1959)
'Haydn's Marionette Operas and the Repertoire of the Marionette Theatre at Esterház Castle', *Haydn Yearbook*, i (1962), 111–97 [with thematic catalogue, list of marionette operas and marionette productions at Eszterháza 1773–83]
ed.: *Haydn Yearbook* (1962–70)
Haydn Symphonies (London, 1966, 2/1968)
Foreword to C. S. Terry: *Johann Christian Bach* (London, 2/1967)
'Haydniana', *Haydn Yearbook*, iv (1968), 199 [*Missa Rorate coeli desuper*, authenticity of concertos, letters to L. Polzelli, Viotti]; vii (1970), 307 [letters to Mme Pointer, Artaria, Sieber]
'Haydn's Newly Discovered Responsorium ad Absolutionem, "Libera me, Domine" ', *Haydn Yearbook*, iv (1968), 140 [with facs. and modern edn.]
Beethoven: a Documentary Study (London, 1970; in Ger., 1970 as *Beethoven: sein Leben und seine Welt in zeitgenössischen Bildern und Texten*)
ed. with R. E. Chapman: *Studies in Eighteenth-century Music: a Tribute to Karl Geiringer* (New York and London, 1970)
Essays on the Viennese Classical Style: Gluck, Haydn, Mozart, Beethoven (London and New York, 1970)
'A New Authentic Source for "La fedeltà premiata" by Haydn', *Soundings*, ii (1971–2), 6
'Due nuovi ritratti di Mozart', *NRMI*, v (1971), 669
'Haydns erste Erfahrungen in England: von der Ankunft in London bis zum ersten Salomon-Konzert', *Jb für österreichische Kulturgeschichte*, i/2: *Beiträge zur Musikgeschichte des 18. Jahrhunderts* (1971), 154
'Two Research Lacunae of the Classic Period', *Perspectives in Musicology*, ed. B. Brook (New York, 1972), 136
'Opera in Italy and the Holy Roman Empire: the Operas of Haydn', *NOHM*, vii (1973), 172
'Haydns Oper "La fedeltà premiata": eine neue authentische Quelle', *Beiträge zur Musikdokumentation: Franz Grasberger zum 60. Geburtstag* (Tutzing, 1975), 213
Haydn: Chronicle and Works (London, 1976–)

EDITIONS

J. Haydn: Symphonies, nos.82–7, Kritische Gesamtausgabe, 1st ser., ix (Leipzig, 1950); *Symphonies, nos.88–92*, ibid, 1st ser., x (Leipzig, 1951); *Messen Nr.5–8*, Werke, xxiii/2 (Munich and Duisburg, 1958) [with K. H. Füssl and C. Landon]; Critical Edition of the complete symphonies in pocket score, with foreword and notes to each symphony (Vienna, 1963–8); also critical edns. of numerous other works

W. A. Mozart: Symphonien, K.V.543, 550, 551, Neue Ausgabe sämtlicher Werke, iv/11/9 (Kassel, 1957); *Mauerische Trauermusik*, ibid, x/53 (1956)

Landormy, Paul (Charles René) (*b* Issy-les-Moulineaux, 3 Jan 1869; *d* Paris, 17 Nov 1943). French musicologist and composer. He was an agrégé des lettres of the Ecole Normale and taught philosophy in Roanne and Bar-le-Duc; he later wrote on Socrates and Descartes. He began to study music in Paris in 1892, taking singing lessons from Sbriglia and Plançon whose niece, a pianist, he married in 1897. From 1902 he worked with Romain Rolland organizing courses in music history at the Ecole des Hautes Etudes, where he also founded and directed the acoustics laboratory (1904–7). Landormy was a regular contributor to *Le temps* and in 1918 was appointed music critic of *Le victoire*. He also served as secretary of the music section of the Paris International Exhibition (1937) and as editor-in-chief of the series Collection des Chefs d'Oeuvre de la Musique Expliqués, to which he contributed a volume on Gounod's *Faust*. His compositions include piano pieces and songs.

WRITINGS

'Des moyens d'organiser en France une ligue pour la protection et le développement de l'art musical', *Congrès international d'histoire de la musique: Paris 1900*, 246

Les philosophes Socrate (Paris, 1901)

Descartes (Paris, 1902)

Commentaire au 'Discours de la méthode' (Paris, n.d.)

Histoire de la musique (Paris 1910, rev. 2/1911, 3/1923)

'La musique de chambre', *Congresso internazionale di musica: Roma 1911*, 103

Brahms (Paris, 1920)

Bizet (Paris, 1924)

Schumann (Paris, n.d.)

La vie de Schubert (Paris, 1928)

Albert Roussel (Paris, 1938)

Gluck (Paris, 1941)

Gounod (Paris, 1942)

La musique française, i: *La musique française de Franck à Debussy*; ii: *La musique française après Debussy*; iii: *La musique française de 'La Marseillaise' à la mort de Berlioz* (Paris, 1943–4)

JOHN TREVITT

Landowska, Wanda (*b* Warsaw, 5 July 1879; *d* Lakeville, Conn., 16 Aug 1959). Polish keyboard player, a champion of 17th- and 18th-century music, and the leading figure in the 20th-century revival of the harpsichord. Her date of birth has been variously given, but on her passport is 5 July 1879.

She played the piano from the age of four; her first teachers were Jan Kleczyński and then, at the Warsaw Conservatory, Alexander Michałowski, both Chopin specialists. In 1896 she went to Berlin and studied composition under Heinrich Urban, but was, in her own words, 'refractory to rules'. She had already shown an enthusiasm for Bach (then played mostly in transcriptions), and was beginning to make a reputation as a pianist. In 1900 she moved to Paris, married Henry Lew (an authority on Hebrew folklore, killed in a car accident in 1919) and with his help threw herself energetically into research on every aspect of 17th- and 18th-century music and its interpretation. She played Bach concertos (on the piano) at the Schola Cantorum,

with which she was associated for the next decade, but became increasingly convinced that only the harpsichord was really appropriate to this period. She first played the harpsichord in public in 1903 and subsequently made concert tours in Europe, at the same time assiduously writing what she herself later recognized as 'belligerent' articles to overcome the resistance widely shown towards the harpsichord, largely on account of the feeble tone of the available instruments. In 1909 she published her book *Musique ancienne*, and three years later at the Breslau Bach Festival triumphantly introduced a large new two-manual harpsichord built to her own specification by Pleyel. In 1913 she began a harpsichord class at the Hochschule für Musik in Berlin, where she and her husband were detained as civil prisoners on parole during World War I.

Wanda Landowska at the harpsichord

Immediately after the war Landowska played a harpsichord continuo in the *St Matthew Passion* – for the first time this century – in Basle, where she held master classes before returning to Paris, where she made her home; she lectured at the Sorbonne and gave classes at the Ecole Normale. With four Pleyel harpsichords, she made her first visit to the USA in 1923, appearing with the Philadelphia Orchestra under Stokowski and making her first gramophone records (she had made some piano rolls in 1905); she also toured extensively in other countries. In 1925 she settled at St-Leu-la-Forêt (north of Paris) where she founded an Ecole de Musique Ancienne which attracted students from all over the world to private and public courses; the summer concerts held in its concert hall (built 1927) were to become celebrated. When the Germans approached Paris in 1940 she had to abandon the school, her library of over 10,000 volumes and her valuable collection of in-struments; after several months at Banyuls-sur-mer, in the Pyrenees, she went to the USA, where she was rapturously received for her performance of the Goldberg Variations. She toured widely, performing and teaching, and found a new home in Lakeville, Connecticut. At the age of 70 she recorded the complete Bach '48'.

Decorated by both the French and Polish govern-ments, Landowska was also held in the highest esteem by the entire musical world. Concertos were written for her by Falla and Poulenc (*Concert champêtre*); many of her pupils later became eminent harpsichordists, and she exercised an even wider influence through her numerous writings and recordings. She developed modern harp-sichord technique, particularly in matters of fingering, and laid emphasis on good touch and on the acquisition of a true legato and of variety of articulation. Her own playing was characterized by its vigour and sparkling vitality, which contrasted with her seemingly frail figure and the unobtrusive way she glided on to a platform, although she radiated a deep and serene confidence. She gave spirit precedence over letter; and if her regi-strations, in her many recordings, appear over-coloured for later taste, these arise partly from the nature of the instrument she used and, like the vehemence of many of her writings, seemed necessary at the time to counter objections to the 'bloodlessness' of the harpsichord.

Her writings reveal the thoroughness of preparation and the imaginative insight she brought to her perform-ances; an extensive selection of these (many of them re-workings of previous material) is to be found in *Landowska on Music* (London, 1965), edited by her disciple Denise Restout. It includes a list of her com-positions and a discography (which is complete except for the Mozart and Poulenc items issued by the International Piano Library, IPL 106–7).

BIBLIOGRAPHY

A. Schaeffner: 'Wanda Landowska et le retour aux "humanités" de la musique', *ReM*, viii/3 (1927), 254

N. Dufourcq: *Le clavecin* (Paris, 1948), chap.9

R. Gelatt: *Music Makers* (New York, 1953), 254

B. Gavoty and R. Hauert: *Wanda Landowska* (Geneva, 1957)

R. Subin: 'And so I am going on . . .', *American Record Guide*, xxvi (1959), 239 [with discography by I. Kipnis]

T. Bainbridge: 'Wanda Landowska and her Repertoire: a Note', *Early Music*, iii (1975), 39

R. Dyson: 'Bend the Finger at All Three Joints: a First-hand Record of Landowska's Teaching Methods', *Early Music*, iii (1975), 240

H. Schott: 'Wanda Landowska', *Early Music*, vii (1979), 467

LIONEL SALTER

Landowski, Marcel (*b* Pont L'Abbé, Finistère, 18 Feb 1915). French composer and administrator. He studied the piano with Marguerite Long and in 1934 entered the Paris Conservatoire, where he was a pupil of Noël Gallon for fugue, Büsser for composition and Gaubert for orchestral conducting. Monteux performed two of his early orchestral works and also gave the young composer further tuition in his summer classes at Paux de Provence. Later, after military service (1939–40), he benefited from the advice of Honegger. He lived in Boulogne-sur-Seine after the war, eventually taking the post of director of the conservatory there (1959–62). His next appointment was as music director for the Comédie Française (1962–5), and he then became inspector-general for music education (1965) and music director for the Ministry of Cultural Affairs (1966).

In his works Landowski has sought a middle path between conservatism and the avant garde; perhaps the closest stylistic comparison might be with Honegger, though in the stage works this influence is married with the dramatic realism of Menotti. The orchestral and choral pieces, however, show an involvement with metaphysical thought, often that of the East or of the neo-Platonists. Landowski's intentions are revealed in his statement that 'the future will, like the past, belong to works which are clear and direct, and which issue from the heart of the artist to be understood by the hearts of all'.

WORKS
(selective list)

STAGE

Le rire de Nils Halerius (opera-ballet-oratorio, 3, G. Caillet, Landowski), 1944–8; Mühlhausen, 1951; Act 1 (opera), Act 2 as Les jeux du monde (ballet), Act 3 (oratorio) may be perf. separately

Le fou (opera, 3, Landowski), 1949–54; Nancy, 1956

Le ventriloque (opera, 1, P. Arnold, Landowski), 1954–5; Le Mans, 1956

Die Tiefe (ballet); Essen, 1959

Les adieux (drame lyrique, 1, Landowski), 1960

L'opéra de poussière (drame lyrique, Caillet, Landowski), 1958–62; Avignon, 1962

ORCHESTRAL

Clairs obscurs, 1938, unpubd; Poème (Pf Conc. no.1), 1938–40; Vc Conc., 1944–5; Edina, sym. poem, 1946; Le petit poucet, sym. suite, 1946; Sym. no.1 'Jean de la peur', 1949; 3 histoires de la prairie, 1950; Conc., ondes martenot, str, perc, 1954; Bn Conc., 1957; La passante, sym. poem, 1958; L'orage, sym. poem after Giorgione, 1960; Pf Conc. no.2, 1963; Sym. no.2, 1963; Sym. no.3 'Des espaces', 1964; Conc., fl, str, 1968; Tpt Conc., 1976

VOCAL

Les sept loups (Goethe), female vv, orch (1937); Les sorcières, SA, orch, 1937, unpubd; 3 mélodies, 1938; Rythmes du monde, oratorio, speaker, solo vv, vv, orch, 1939–41; Desbat du cuer et du corps, S, T, 3 insts, 1943; La quête sans fins, oratorio, speaker, Bar, vv, orch, 1943–4, unpubd; Brumes, speaker, orch, 1944; Cantique d'action de grâce, S, vv, 1945; 3 révérences à la mort (Tagore), S, orch, 1946

Cantata no.1 'Jésus es-tu là?' (A. Marc), vv, orch, 1948; Le lac d'Un-deneur, A, pf, 1949; 5 chants d'innocence, female vv, 1952; Espoir, speaker, vv, orch, 1959; Chant de solitude, 4 female vv, orch, 1960; Notes de nuit, children's speaking vv, chamber orch, 1961; Cantata no.6 'Aux mendiants du ciel', S, orch, 1966

OTHER WORKS

Inst: Sonatine, pf, 1940; Le petit poucet, 6 easy pieces, pf, 1946; Trio, hn, tpt, pf, 1954; 4 préludes, perc, pf, 1963

Many film scores, incidental music

Principal publisher: Choudens

WRITINGS

with L. Aubert: *L'orchestre* (Paris, 1951)

Honegger (Paris, 1957)

with G. Morançon: *Louis Aubert: musicien français* (Paris, 1967)

BIBLIOGRAPHY

A. Goléa: *Marcel Landowski* (Paris, 1969)

Landré, Guillaume (*b* The Hague, 24 Feb 1905; *d* Amsterdam, 6 Nov 1968). Dutch composer. He was one of the most prominent pupils of Pijper, with whom he studied composition concurrently with his law studies at Utrecht University. Earlier he had been taught by his father, Willem Landré, and by Zagewijn. After completing his law course he worked for many years in Amsterdam as a teacher of commercial law and music critic. Later he held various important posts in Dutch musical life, including the chairmanships of the BUNA (the Dutch music copyright society, 1947–58), the Dutch section of the ISCM and the Society of Dutch Composers, and the secretaryship of the Dutch Arts Council. Among the prizes he received were the Willem Pijper Prize (1958 for the Quartet no.2), the Van der

Leeuw Prize (1962 for the *Permutazioni simfoniche*) and the Sweelinck Prize (1965).

Landré's first compositions, the chamber pieces of 1925–30, were strongly influenced by Pijper. With the First Symphony, performed at the 1933 ISCM Festival, he came to international notice, and this first period closed with the comic opera *De snoek* (1934). It is a surrealist piece, containing a number of humorous, shrewdly typified scenes in a colourful, polytonal idiom. A change of style is apparent in the Suite for string orchestra (1936): the short motifs characteristic of the Pijper style are replaced by broad, expressive melodies, and there is a notable lyrical feeling, particularly in the middle movement, dedicated to the memory of Queen Astrid of Belgium. The tendency towards lyricism and a freer, livelier music-making was further developed in the orchestral works composed up to 1956. One of the most striking compositions of this period is the *Piae memoriae pro patria mortuorum* for chorus and orchestra (1942), written in remembrance of those who fell in the German invasion of 1940. The liturgical Requiem text with which the work opens is, towards the end, interwoven with and finally superseded by a Dutch folksong.

An elegiac, 'in memoriam' tone is present in many of Landré's works. The *Sinfonia sacra in memorium patris* (1948), for example, is a meditation on his father's *Requiem in memoriam uxoris*, quoting fragments of the original and at certain points merging the styles of father and son. In the Symphony no.3, a memorial to a friend, the valedictory character is most pronounced in the outer movements. The work's theme, from which all other melodic ideas are derived, is a 12-note one, but its development is non-serial. A striking deployment of the orchestra marks the Fourth Symphony: the first and fifth movements are for the full ensemble, the second for strings and harp, the third for woodwinds and horn, and the fourth for brass and low strings. Two concertos, for clarinet and for bass clarinet (1958–9), exploit jazz effects and complicated rhythmic patterns; the shorter post-1956 orchestral pieces are all based on variation techniques, often applied to a 12-note theme, though, again, serial methods are not prominent. These last years also saw the composition of two operas, of which *La symphonie pastorale* was first performed during the Gide celebrations at Rouen in 1968.

WORKS
(selective list)

ORCHESTRAL

Sym. no.1, 1932; Suite, str, pf, 1936; 4 Pieces, 1937; Vc Conc., 1940; Sinfonietta, vn, orch, 1941; Sym. no.2, 1942; Sym. Music, fl, orch, 1948; Sinfonia sacra in memoriam patris, 1948; 4 mouvements symphoniques, 1949; Sym. no.3, 1951; Sym., chamber orch, 1952; Sonata festiva, chamber orch, 1953; Sym. no.4, 1955; Caleidoscopio, 1956; Permutazioni simfoniche, 1957; Cl Conc., 1958; Concertante, b cl, orch, 1959; Anagrammen, 1960; Conc. da camera, 1961; Variazioni senza tema, 1967; La symphonie pastorale, interludes, 1967

VOCAL AND CHAMBER

Operas: De snoek (3, E. van Lockhorst), 1934, Amsterdam, 1938; Jean Lévecq (1, G. Smit, after Maupassant), 1963, Holland Festival, 1963; La symphonie pastorale (prologue, 3, epilogue, C. Rostand, after Gide), 1964, Rouen, 1968

Other vocal works: Egidius waer bestu bleven, chorus, 1929; Piae memoriae pro patria mortuorum, chorus, orch, 1942; Groet der martelaren, Bar, orch, 1944

Chamber: Sonata, vn, pf, 1927; 4 str qts, 1927, 1943, 1950, 1966; Wind Qnt, 1930; 4 Miniaturen, cl, str, 1950; Sextet, fl, cl, str qt, 1959; Quartetto piccolo, 2 tpt, hn, trbn, 1961

Principal publisher: Donemus

BIBLIOGRAPHY

H. Badings: 'Guillaume Landré', *De hedendaagse nederlandse muziek* (Amsterdam, 1936), 87

J. Wouters: 'Guillaume Landré: Symphonic Permutations', *Sonorum speculum* (1961), no.8, p.10

——: 'Guillaume Landré: Symphony no.III', *Sonorum speculum* (1964), no.20, p.34

W. Paap: 'In memoriam Guillaume Landré', *Sonorum speculum* (1968), no.37, p.1

C. Rostand: 'La symphonie pastorale: Opera by Guillaume Landré', *Sonorum speculum* (1968), no.34, p.1

J. Wouters: 'Guillaume Landré', *Dutch Composers' Gallery* (Amsterdam, 1971), 88

JOS WOUTERS

Landré, Willem [Guillaume] **(Louis Frédéric)** (*b* Amsterdam, 12 June 1874; *d* Eindhoven, 1 Jan 1948). Dutch composer and critic of French origin. After studies in theory and composition with Bernard Zweers in Amsterdam, he worked as a music critic from 1898 to 1937 in Haarlem, The Hague and in Rotterdam (for the *Nieuwe Rotterdamsche courant*). He had great influence in turning attention to the innovations in French music (including those of Debussy) at a time when Dutch musical life was still strongly German-orientated. His music is related to that of Diepenbrock, for the most part harmonically, and generally has an introverted, elegiac character, as in his best work, the *Requiem in memoriam uxoris*.

WORKS
(selective list)

Operas: De roos van Dekama, 1897; Beatrijs (F. Rutten), 1925

Orch: Nocturne, small orch, 1921; In memoriam matris, 1923; Romantisch pianoconcert, 1935

Choral: Requiem in memoriam uxoris, 1931, rev. G. Landré, 1954

Incidental music, chamber works, choruses, songs, pf pieces

Principal publisher: Donemus

BIBLIOGRAPHY

W. Paap: 'In memoriam Willem Landré', *Mens en melodie*, iii (1948), 19

P. Nissing: 'De componist Willem Landré', *Mens en melodie*, iii (1948), 40

——: 'Herdenking Willem Landré', *Mens en melodie*, xiii (1958), 34

ROGIER STARREVELD

Landsberg, Ludwig (*b* Breslau, 1807; *d* Rome, 6 May 1858). German musician and collector. After beginning his career as a tenor in the chorus of the Royal Theatre in Berlin, he settled in Rome and lived there for 24 years. He studied the piano and organized successful amateur concerts. He also devoted himself intensively to the study of early music and musical literature. His wide knowledge helped him to amass a valuable library, drawn from all over Italy and Germany. At his death, his heirs conveyed part of the collection to Breslau and part to Berlin, and catalogues were prepared to enable it to be acquired by music lovers. But many of the choicest items appear to have vanished (this statement is derived from Fétis, who seems to have known Landsberg by correspondence and received from him a manuscript catalogue on which he based his comparisons). Nevertheless, some of the greatest treasures, including a number of Beethoven sketchbooks, found their way into the Königliche Bibliothek (later called the Preussische Staatsbibliothek) in Berlin; most of them remain in the collections of the Deutsche Staatsbibliothek and the Staatsbibliothek der Stiftung Preussischer Kulturbesitz in Berlin.

ALEC HYATT KING

Landshoff, Ludwig (*b* Stettin [now Szczecin], 3 June 1874; *d* New York, 20 Sept 1941). German musicologist and conductor. He studied music with Thuille, Urban and Reger and musicology with Friedlaender and Fleischer at Berlin University and with Sandberger at the University of Munich, where he took the doctorate in 1900 with a dissertation on Johann Rudolf Zumsteeg. He was subsequently an opera conductor at the theatres in Aachen (1902–4), Kiel (1912–13), Breslau (1913–15) and Würzburg (1915–20), and music director of the Munich Bach-Verein (1918–28), where he performed a wide variety of music, including that of Bach's sons, Pergolesi, Hasse and Jommelli as well as contemporary works. When the municipal subsidy was stopped in 1928 he moved to Berlin; his activity there was confined to occasional broadcasts, lectures at the Lessing Hochschule and library research. He emigrated to Italy in 1936 and later to Paris (1938) and to New York (1941).

Landshoff's reputation rests chiefly on his research into the vocal music of the 17th and 18th centuries. His most important work was his Alte Meister des Bel Canto, a collection in five volumes that printed for the first time (and furnished with comprehensive bibliographical and historical notes) vocal works by Carissimi, Luigi Rossi, Mario Savioni and others. He made many other editions of vocal and instrumental works by Domenico Gabrielli, J. S. Bach, J. C. Bach, C. P. E. Bach, Vivaldi, Zelter, Zumsteeg, Fasch, Haydn and Rossini. In his studies of the problems of accompaniment and performance he aimed at reaching a wide audience while attempting to give an authentic representation of the original style.

WRITINGS

Johann Rudolf Zumsteeg: ein Beitrag zur Geschichte des Liedes und der Ballade (diss., U. of Munich, 1900; Berlin, 1902)
'Über das vielstimmige Accompagnement und andere Fragen des Generalbass-spiels', *Festschrift zum 50. Geburtstag Adolf Sandberger* (Munich, 1918), 189
Introduction to *Wolfgang Amadeus Mozart: Nekrolog von Friedrich Schlichtegroll* (Munich, 1924)
'Die Aufführungspraxis Bachscher Chorwerke', *Die Musik*, xxi (1928–9), 81

EDITIONS

J. R. Zumsteeg: Ausgewählte Lieder (Leipzig, 1907)
Alte Meister des Bel Canto, i–v (Frankfurt and New York, 1912–27)
I classici del bel canto (Leipzig, 1927)
C. F. C. Fasch: Ariette mit 14 Variationen, Andantino mit 7 Variationen für Cembalo oder Klavier, NM, xxxviii (1929)

BIBLIOGRAPHY

A. Einstein: 'In memoriam Ludwig Landshoff', *MQ*, xxviii (1942), 241
ALFRED GRANT GOODMAN

Lane, Burton [Kushner, Morris Hyman] (*b* New York, 2 Feb 1912). American songwriter. He studied the piano under Simon Bucharoff and in 1927 became a staff composer and pianist for Remick music publishers in New York. He wrote songs for revues before going to Hollywood in 1933. In two decades there he composed songs for over 35 films, but his occasional New York shows were his most successful works. He wrote Al Jolson's last musical, *Hold on to your Hats* (1940, E. Y. Harburg), a comedy *Laffing Room Only* (1944, Lane), *Finian's Rainbow* (1947, Harburg) and *On a Clear Day You Can See Forever* (1965, A. J. Lerner). *Finian's Rainbow*, considered one of the best musicals of the century, is a fantasy based on Irish legend and deals with American social problems in a satirical, somewhat sentimental way; it includes the songs 'Look to the Rainbow', 'Old Devil Moon' and 'How are things in Glocca Mora?'. He was president of ASCAP, 1957–64.

BIBLIOGRAPHY

S. Green: *The World of Musical Comedy* (New York, 1960, 3/1974)
R. D. Kinkle: *The Complete Encyclopedia of Popular Music and Jazz 1900–1950* (New Rochelle, NY, 1974)
DEANE L. ROOT

Laneare [Laneer]. *See* LANIER family.

La Neuville, Martin Joseph. *See* ADRIEN, MARTIN JOSEPH.

Lanfranco, Giovanni Maria (*b* Terenzio, nr. Parma, *c*1490; *d* Parma, late Nov 1545). Italian theorist. He studied with the organist Lodovico da Milano and possibly with Nicolaus Burtius. He probably took minor orders before 1528, when he became *maestro di cappella* at Brescia Cathedral. There he published his *Scintille di musica* and *Rimario*. He evidently wrote another treatise, *Musica terentiana*, which has not survived. He became *maestro di cappella* in Verona about 1536 but left in 1538, perhaps because of an indiscretion with a choirboy, and entered an Augustinian monastery near Bergamo. In 1540 he became *maestro di cappella* at S Maria della Steccata in Parma, where he died and is buried.

Lanfranco's *Scintille di musica* is notable for its clear, detailed presentation of basic theoretical concepts. With its numerous rules and suggestions for exercises, it is a textbook well suited to beginners; thus it differs from most other 16th-century treatises. Another unusual feature is Lanfranco's list of earlier writers used as sources. Of the four books in the treatise, the first presents the gamut, solmization and notation of plainsong. Book 2 is devoted to mensural notation. Its description of the *tactus* is especially clear, while its rules for text underlay are the earliest known, antedating those of Zarlino by 25 years. An extended section on proportions is the only part of the treatise not always related to musical practice. The presentation of the modes in the third book is conventional. Book 3 begins with rules for counterpoint and then presents tunings. The tuning for a keyboard approaches equal temperament in its departures from just intervals, while the tunings for plucked and bowed string instruments are the first published in Italy.

WRITINGS

Rimario di tutti le voci usate dal Petrarca nel fine de versi (Brescia, 1531)
Scintille di musica (Brescia, 1533/*R*; Eng. trans. in Lee)
2 letters, *I-Rvat* Vat.Lat.5318, f.192r, 254r

BIBLIOGRAPHY

C. Palisca: 'Lanfranco, Giovanni Maria', *MGG*
B. Lee: *Giovanni Maria Lanfranco's 'Scintille di Musica' and its Relation to 16th-Century Music Theory* (diss., Cornell U., 1961) [includes translation of *Scintille di musica*]
D. Harran: 'New Light on the Question of Text Underlay prior to Zarlino', *AcM*, xlv (1973), 24–56
PETER BERGQUIST

Lang, Benjamin (Johnson) (*b* Salem, Mass., 28 Dec 1837; *d* Boston, Mass., 3 April 1909). American pianist, conductor, organist and teacher. His father was a well-known piano teacher at Salem, and he began his studies under him, continuing them under Francis G. Hill of Boston. By the time he was 15 years old he held a post as organist of a Boston church. In 1855 he went to Europe to study composition in Berlin and elsewhere in Germany, and the piano with Alfred Jaell; he also met Liszt.

On his return to Boston, Lang made his first public appearance as a pianist in 1858. His début as a conductor was in Boston in May 1862, when he gave the first performance there of Mendelssohn's *Walpurgisnacht*. The next year he shared with Carl Zerrahn the direction of the music at the jubilee concert in honour of President Lincoln's Emancipation Proclamation, and from then onwards he figured more and more extensively at Boston as a conductor. He was appointed conductor of the Apollo Club, a men's singing society, on its formation in 1871 and remained until 1901. He was also conductor of Caecilia, a mixed choir, from its establishment in 1874, and of the Handel and Haydn Society for two seasons from 1895 to 1897. He gave several complete performances of Wagner's *Parsifal* in concert form.

In the early 1860s Lang became prominent as a concert pianist at Boston, playing frequently at the concerts of the Harvard Musical Association, at chamber concerts of his own and with the Mendelssohn Quintet Club. He was less important as a composer than as an interpreter; yet he left an oratorio, *David*, symphonies, overtures, chamber music, piano pieces, church music and many songs, mostly in MS. In 1903 Yale University granted him an MA.

RICHARD ALDRICH

Lang, Eddie [Massaro, Salvatore] (*b* Philadelphia, 25 Oct 1902; *d* New York, 26 March 1933). American jazz guitarist. He studied the violin formally for 11 years and learnt the guitar from his father, a guitarist and instrument maker. He formed a successful and long-lived partnership with the jazz violinist Joe Venuti, his former schoolmate in Philadelphia, and performed with him in the early 1920s in Atlantic City. By 1924, when he recorded with the Mound City Blue Blowers, he had moved to New York. There he performed and recorded frequently with, among others, Red Nichols, Jean Goldkette, Frank Trumbauer, the Dorsey brothers, Paul Whiteman and above all Venuti, with whom he made a series of duet recordings in 1926–7 including the noteworthy *Stringin' the Blues*, their recomposition of *Tiger Rag*. After playing with Whiteman in 1929–30 he became Bing Crosby's accompanist. Lang was the first well-known solo jazz guitarist and, from the mid-1920s, was widely influential. His career coincided with the development of recording techniques suitable to the acoustic guitar, which partly through his influence supplanted the banjo as a jazz instrument. He was highly regarded for his single-string solos and his accompaniments, which usually interspersed chords and single-string lines in the middle register. Although some contemporary black guitarists were better soloists, Lang's accompaniments resulted in interesting textures (but with rather undirected lines at times); he was a good rhythm guitarist with a fine technique and attained a consistently high level of performance.

BIBLIOGRAPHY
N. Shapiro and N. Hentoff, eds.: *Hear me Talkin' to ya* (New York, 1955), 246ff
R. Hadlock: *Jazz Masters of the 20s* (New York, 1965), 239ff
B. Rust: *Jazz Records: 1897–1942* (London, 1965, rev. 2/1969)
A. McCarthy: *Jazz on Record* (London, 1968), 174f
——: *Big Band Jazz* (London, 1974), 172ff

JAMES DAPOGNY

Láng, István (*b* Budapest, 1 March 1933). Hungarian composer. He studied composition with Viski and later Szabó at the Budapest Academy of Music (1950–58). In 1966 he was appointed musical director of the State Puppet Theatre, and in 1973 he went to the University of Colorado as guest lecturer and joined the Budapest Academy as a lecturer. He has received two Erkel Prizes (1968, 1975).

A leading representative of the generation of Hungarian composers born in the 1930s, Láng has not followed any fashionable trend but has established a closely defined, individual style which is up-to-date without being eclectic. During the last years of his studies he was already exciting interest by his compositions. In the 1960s his creative activity was determined by the stage: he produced three important dramatic pieces, *Mario és a varázsló* ('Mario and the magician'), *Hiperbola* and *A gyáva* ('The coward'), related to each other in plot, and the influence of the theatre – in terms of character and gesture – can be detected in such works as *Monodia* for clarinet, which is designed for stage or concert performance.

Another of Láng's preoccupations has been cyclic form. His early pieces (e.g. the Concertino, the Chamber Cantata and the *Variazioni ed allegro*) are typically in two movements, but later he came to cast his music in sequences of short movements constructed from small motifs, or 'micro-organisms'. This is shown in the two wind quintets and the String Quartet no.2. In several works the proportions of the movements are determined by mathematical series – for example, the Fibonacci-type series in *Gyász-zene* ('Funeral music', 3–4–7–11–18–29) and *Laudate hominem* (5–6–11–17–28). Other features of his work are an individually interpreted 12-note technique, the careful balancing of free and strict parts in those works which employ aleatory writing, the extreme, yet always musical, exploitation of instrumental possibilities in chamber pieces, and a careful consideration of genre and function (as, for example, in the Symphony no.2, a three-movement work which attempts to renew the classical model through modern means).

WORKS
(*selective list*)

Stage: Mario és a varázsló [Mario and the magician] (dance drama, A. Pernye, Láng, after Mann), 1962; Hiperbola (ballet, I. Eck), 1963; A gyáva [The coward] (opera, Láng, after I. Sarkadi), 1964–8; Csillagra-török [Starfighters] (ballet-cantata, I. Ágh), 1971
Orch: Xyl Concertino, 1961, rev. 1967; Variazioni ed allegro, 1965; Gyász-zene [Funeral music], 1969; Impulsioni, ob, inst groups, 1969; Három mondat a Rómeó és Júliából [3 sentences from Romeo and Juliet], str, 1969–70; Conc. bucolico, hn, orch, 1969–70; Sym. no.2, 1972–4
Cantatas: Chamber Cantata, S, cl, vc, perc, pf, 1962; Laudate hominem, 1968; In memoriam N. N., 1971
Chamber: Duo, 2 fl, 1963; 3 wind qnts, 1963–4, 1966, 1975; Str Qt no.2, 1966; Cassazione, brass sextet, 1971; Duo, 2 trbn, 1972; Rhymes, fl, cl, pf, va, vc, 1972; Constellations, ob qt, 1974–5; Hullámok [Waves], S, vib, 1975
Solo inst: Sonata, vc, 1960; Monodia, cl, 1965; Dramma breve, a fl, 1970; Intermezzi, pf, 1972; Villanások [Flashes], vn, 1973; Improvizáció, cimb, 1973; Monologue, hn, 1974; Solo, 6 fl, 1975
Elec: Surface Metamorphosis, 1974, realized M. Maros, 1975

Principal publisher: Editio Musica

ANTAL BORONKAY

Lang, Johann Georg (*b* Svojšín, 1722; *d* Ehrenbreitstein, 17 July 1798). German composer of Bohemian descent. As a youth he studied the keyboard and violin in Bohemia. In 1746 he began service in the orchestra of the Prince-Bishop of Augsburg. After mid-1749 he embarked on a three-year trip to Italy and for a year studied counterpoint at Naples with Francesco Durante and Girolamo Abos. By 1758 he was Konzertmeister of the prince-bishop's orchestra. In 1768 Clemens Wenzeslaus, Elector of Trier, succeeded to the bishopric of Augsburg and took over the orchestra, moving some of its personnel to Ehrenbreitstein, his electoral residence; Lang was made Konzertmeister there in 1769 and remained even after the elector moved across the Rhine into the new palace at Koblenz in 1786. Lang's official duties included leading the strings and advising the elector's *Musikintendant*, Baron von Thünnefeld, on orchestral administration. In 1794 the elector abandoned both his residences because of the advancing French Republican forces, but Lang remained at Ehrenbreitstein. He was buried in the Kreuzkirche.

Lang's orchestral output consists mainly of keyboard concertos and symphonies. One of his early concertos has been erroneously attributed to Haydn and several symphonies to J. C. Bach and others. Among his instrumental pieces are many ensemble sonatas with obbligato keyboard and quartets with obbligato flute. Lang's larger vocal works are mostly sacred, including masses, litanies and *Te Deum* settings. The stylistic evolution of the keyboard concertos shows the changing musical taste at Koblenz between 1769 and 1784; particularly after 1775 greater textural flexibility, slower harmonic rhythm, and more broadly arched melodies become clearly characteristic. A parallel development occurred in the symphonies (mostly from the late 1750s and 1760s), which were praised by a correspondent to Baron von Eschstruth's *Musicalische Bibliothek* (5 June 1784) as 'fluent and in accord with the rules'.

WORKS

(lost works mostly listed in catalogues: see Brook, 1972)

ORCHESTRAL

29 hpd concs.: 2 as opp.4–5 (Offenbach, 1776); 1 (London, c1785); 1 in *D-B*, falsely attrib. J. Stamitz (London, c1783), and Haydn, *CH-E*; Concerto da caccia, *D-B*, *Rtt*; 24 others, incl. 13 in *B*, 2 in *Dlb*, 2 in *SWl*, 1, E♭, in *B*, doubtful, 8 lost

8 other concs.: 3 for fl, *Rtt*; 1 for fl, lost; 1 for vn, *HR*; 3 vn, *A-Wmi*

38 syms.: 6 (Augsburg, 1760); 3 (Speier, 1782); 29 others: incl. 12 in *D-Rtt*, 10 in *DO* (incl. 2 falsely attrib. 'Bilz'), 9 in *A-Wmi*, 6 in *ST*, 3 in *KR*, 3 in *CH-FF*, 3 in *Zz*, 3 in *CS-Pnm*, 3 in *D-B*, 2 in *Pnm*, 2 in *D-Mbs*, 1 in *CS-Pnm* (falsely attrib. Körgle [?Körzl] in *A-GÖ*, and Ordoñez in Brook, no.194); 4 falsely attrib. [J.C.] Bach in *A-Wgm*; 1 falsely attrib. Gispi [?Bach], lost

CHAMBER

9 qts, kbd, fl, str: 6 as op.3 (Offenbach, 1775), no.6 arr. solo hpd, *GB-Lbm*; 1 as Concertino, G, *D-Mbs*; 2 lost

25 acc. sonatas (kbd, str, unless otherwise stated): 6 (London, 1774); 6 as op.6 (Offenbach, 1779); 2 short works (Speier, 1782); 4 as op.7 (Offenbach, 1782–3), no.4 hpd/pf 4 hands, vn, vc; 3 as op.9 (Speier, 1783); 1 in *Dlb*; 3 lost

21 works for kbd solo: 4 sonatas (Nuremberg, 1758–63); Fuga prima a 3, org (Nuremberg, 1764); 3 sonatas, sonata movt, *B-Bc*; Sonata, *CS-Pnm*; 5 short works (Speier, 1782–3); 6 works, as Divertimento, *D-B*

5 others: 2 sonatas, vn, vc (London, c1775); 3 trios, 2 vn, b, lost

VOCAL

3 masses, *D-TRb*; Mass, *CS-Pnm*; Mass, lost; Tantum ergo, lost; 1 (?2) litany, 1 litany of Loreto, 1 Te Deum, all lost

1 secular song (Bayreuth, c1788), doubtful; 2 songs and MS collection mentioned in *EitnerQ*; song(s) in Melodien zum Taschenbuch für Freunde des Gesanges (Stuttgart, 1796), spurious

BIBLIOGRAPHY

GerberL

P. von Stetten: *Kunst-, Gewerb- und Handwerksgeschichte der Reichsstadt Augsburg*, i (Augsburg, 1779), 546

Hof-Musik-Intendanz-Protokoll (MS, 1783–93, *D-KBs*)

H. A. von Eschstruth, ed.: *Musicalische Bibliothek für Künstler und Liebhaber*, ii (Marburg and Giessen, 1785), 248

F. J. Lipowsky: *Baierisches Musik-Lexikon* (Munich, 1811/*R*1971)

G. J. Dlabač: *Allgemeines historisches Künstler-Lexikon* (Prague, 1815/*R*1973)

J. J. Wagner: *Coblenz-Ehrenbreitstein: biographische Nachrichten* (Koblenz, 1925)

G. Bereths: *Die Musikpflege am kurtrierischen Hofe zu Koblenz-Ehrenbreitstein* (Mainz, 1964)

J. Schmidt-Görg: 'Ein Wappenbrief für den kurfürstlich-trierschen Konzertmeister Johann Georg Lang', *Festschrift Hans Engel* (Kassel, 1964), 326

H. Grappenbach: 'Lang, Johann Georg', *Rheinische Musiker*, v, ed. K. G. Fellerer (Cologne, 1967), 104

S. G. Davis: *The Keyboard Concertos of Johann Georg Lang (1722–1798)* (diss., New York U., 1971)

A. Gottron: 'Böhmische Musiker des 18. Jahrhunderts am Mittelrhein', *Symbolae historiae musicae: Hellmut Federhofer zum 60. Geburtstag* (Mainz, 1971), 131

B. S. Brook: *Thematic Catalogues in Music: an Annotated Bibliography* (Hillsdale, NY, 1972)

S. Davis: 'J. G. Lang and the Early Classical Keyboard Concerto', *MQ*, lxvi (1980), 21–52

SHELLEY DAVIS

Lang, Josephine (Caroline) (*b* Munich, 14 March 1815; *d* Tübingen, 2 Dec 1880). German composer. She was the granddaughter of the coloratura soprano Sabina Hitzelberger (née Renk), and daughter of the soprano Regina Hitzelberger-Lang (*b* Würzburg, 15 Feb 1788; *d* Munich, 10 May 1827) and the court director of music Theobald Lang (1783–1839); her maternal aunts were the pianist and contralto Catharina Elisabeth Hitzelberger, the soprano Kunigunde Hitzelberger and the contralto Johanna Hitzelberger. She studied with her mother, also learning theory with Mendelssohn, whom she greatly impressed in the course of his visits to Munich in 1830 and 1831. He described her gifts, and no less her personal charm, enthusiastically and at length in a letter to his family: 'she has the gift of composing and singing songs in a manner I have never heard anything to match' (6 October 1831); the impression she made on his susceptibilities is confirmed in subsequent letters, including one of 15 December 1841 on her betrothal to congratulate her future husband Christian Reinhold Köstlin (1813–56), a lawyer and music theoretician who sometimes wrote under the name C. Reinhold. In Tübingen, where they settled, her house was a meeting-place for many artists and intellectuals. She published several books of songs (more than 30 opus numbers), which were highly praised in the *Allgemeine Musikalische Zeitung*, and won the admiration of her contemporaries for their literary sensibility and their Schumann-influenced lyricism. She taught in Munich and also sang in the Hofkapelle. Köstlin's early death obliged her to struggle hard for the support of their six children. These included Heinrich Adolf Köstlin (*b* Tübingen, 4 Sept 1846; *d* Cannstatt, 4 June 1907), a theologian who wrote on the history of music, especially on evangelical church music, and left a memoir of his mother; and Maria Fellinger (*d* Zehlendorf, 1925), in whose Vienna house Brahms found warm hospitality in his last years.

BIBLIOGRAPHY

F. Hiller: *Aus dem Tonleben unseres Zeit*, ii (Leipzig, 1868), 116ff

H. A. Köstlin: 'Josephine Lang', *Sammlung musikalischer Vorträge*, iii, ed. P. Waldersee (Leipzig, 1881), 49–104

E. Friedrichs: 'Josephine Lang', *Neue Musikzeitung*, xxvii/10 (1905)

JOHN WARRACK

Lang, Matthäus (*b* Augsburg, 1468; *d* Salzburg, 30 March 1540). German cardinal and patron. After studying at the universities of Ingolstadt, Vienna and Tübingen, he became a politician in the Habsburg imperial chancellory in 1493 and was made first privy councillor to Maximilian I in 1501. After 1500 he also carried out spiritual duties and, although a layman, was Bishop of Gurk from 1505 to 1522, was named a cardinal in 1511 by Pope Julius II, became Prince-Archbishop of Salzburg in 1519 and Primate of Germany in 1529. On his appointment to Salzburg he was finally ordained, and soon afterwards he established a court chapel. Of the many musicians employed by him Wilhelm Waldner was Kapellmeister, Nicolaus Lescallier, Paul and Thomas Hofhaimer and Gregor Peschin were organists, and Heinrich Finck was a composer. Trumpeters, fifers, drummers, fiddlers and lutenists also belonged to Lang's retinue. Among other works the collection *Liber selectarum cantionum* (*RISM* 1520⁴) and Paul Hofhaimer's *Harmoniae poeticae* (Nuremberg, 1539) were dedicated to him.

BIBLIOGRAPHY

F. P. Dotterer: *Des Cardinals und Erzbischofs von Salzburg Matthäus Lang Verhalten zur Reformation* (Freising, 1890)

H. Spies: 'Aus der musikalischen Vergangenheit Salzburgs bis 1634', *Musica divina*, ii (Vienna, 1914)

C. Schneider: *Geschichte der Musik in Salzburg* (Salzburg, 1935), 44ff

H. Spies: 'Beiträge zur Musikgeschichte Salzburgs im Spätmittelalter und zu Anfang der Renaissancezeit', *Mitteilungen der Gesellschaft für Salzburger Landeskunde*, lxxxi (1941), 41

OTHMAR WESSELY

Lang, Paul Henry [Láng, Pál] (*b* Budapest, 28 Aug 1901). American musicologist of Hungarian birth. He studied at the Budapest Academy of Music, graduating in 1922. His teachers there were Kodály (composition), Hans Koessler (counterpoint), Leó Weiner (chamber music) and Wieschendorf (bassoon). On leaving the academy he was appointed assistant conductor at the Budapest Opera and played the bassoon in several orchestras. In 1924, encouraged by Kodály and Bartók, he decided to study musicology. As Budapest did not offer courses in this field he enrolled at the University of Heidelberg, where he became a pupil of Kroyer; he also studied comparative literature with Ernst R. Curtius and Friedrich Gundolf. The last two were responsible for starting him on the path of cultural history which he followed throughout his career. In the autumn of the same year he transferred to the Sorbonne, from which he received a degree in literature (1928); his chief teachers were Pirro (musicology), Henri Focillon (art history), Fernand Baldensperger, Félix Gaiffe (literature) and Victor Basch (aesthetics). During his four years in Paris, Lang also played the bassoon professionally, conducted choral societies, served as accompanist to singers and assisted Prunières in editing the *Revue musicale*. In the spring of 1928 he was named a Junior Scholar to the United States by the Rockefeller Foundation and taught music for a year at Vassar College (1930–31). This was followed by an appointment to Wells College (1931–3), and while teaching there he worked on a doctoral dissertation in French literature and philology (*A Literary History of French Opera*, 1934) under James Frederick Mason at Cornell University. He also continued his studies in musicology with Kinkeldey.

Lang, who became an American citizen in 1934, took an active and influential part in the musical life of his adopted country. In 1933 he began to teach at Columbia University, where from 1939 to 1969 he was full professor of musicology and trained several genera-

tions of musical scholars. His monumental *Music in Western Civilization*, which appeared in 1941, is one of the outstanding 20th-century contributions to cultural history and probably his major achievement. In it he lucidly expounded the history of music by placing it firmly in its artistic, social and political contexts. As editor of the *Musical Quarterly* (1945–73) he continued the development of this journal of international importance with literary as well as scholarly contributions, and he opened its pages to contemporary music, notably in the feature called 'Current Chronicle'. He also served from 1954 to 1963 as chief music critic of the *New York Herald Tribune* and brought to this task a historical knowledge rare in American journalism. He held many positions of importance: in 1934 he was one of the founders of the American Musicological Society and from 1955 to 1958 president of the International Musicological Society. He has received degrees in music and letters from Temple and Northwestern universities, the University of Western Ontario and the New England Conservatory of Music; he is also a fellow of the American Academy of Arts and Sciences.

WRITINGS

'Haydn and the Opera', *MQ*, xviii (1932), 274

'The Place of Musicology in the College Curriculum', *MTNA Proceedings*, xxix (1934), 144

'Ecce Criticus', *American Scholar*, vii (1938), 478

'The Future of Opera', *Columbia University Quarterly*, xxx (1938), 1

'The So-called Netherlands School', *MQ*, xxv (1939), 48

Music in Western Civilization (New York, 1941)

'The Department of Music and its Functions', *MTNA Proceedings*, xxxv (1941), 259

'The Formation of the Lyric Stage at the Confluence of Renaissance and Baroque', *A Birthday Offering to Carl Engel* (New York, 1943), 143

Review of L. Schrade: *Beethoven in France: the Growth of an idea* (New Haven and London, 1942), *Romantic Review*, xxxv (1944), 73

'The Influence of Political Thought on the History of Music', *PAMS 1940*, 108

'The Equipment of the Musical Journalist', *Music and Criticism: a Symposium*, ed. R. F. French (Cambridge, Mass., 1948), 137

'Music and the Liberal Arts College', *MTNA Proceedings*, xlii (1950), 32

Five chapters on Renaissance national schools, *Music and Western Man*, ed. P. Garvie (London, 1958) [originally CBC radio scripts]

with O. L. Bethmann: *A Pictorial History of Music* (New York, 1960)

'Mozart after 200 Years', *JAMS*, xiii (1960), 197

ed.: *Problems of Modern Music* (New York, 1960) [originally pubd in *MQ*, xlvi (1960), 145–259]

ed.: *One Hundred Years of Music in America* (New York, 1961) [incl. 'Portrait of a Publishing House' (Schirmer)]

'Objectivity and Construction in the Vocal Music of the Fifteenth and Sixteenth Centuries', *Natalicia musicologica Knud Jeppesen* (Copenhagen, 1962), 115

'Palestrina across the Centuries', *Festschrift Karl Gustav Fellerer* (Regensburg, 1962), 294

'Handel, Churchman or Dramatist?', *Festschrift Friedrich Blume* (Kassel, 1963), 214

ed.: *Stravinsky: a New Appraisal of his Work* (New York, 1963) [originally pubd in *MQ*, xlviii (1962), 287–384]

ed.: *The Creative World of Mozart* (New York, 1963) [originally pubd in *MQ*, xlii (1956), 145–229]

'Aggiornamento in Sacred Music', *Sacred Music*, xcii (1965), 11

ed., with N. Broder: *Contemporary Music in Europe: a Comprehensive Survey* (New York, 1965) [originally pubd in *MQ*, li (1965), 1–297]

George Frideric Handel (New York, 1966)

'The Patrimonium musicae sacrae and the Task of Sacred Music Today', *Sacred Music*, xciii (1966), 119

'The Enlightenment and Music', *Eighteenth-century Studies*, i (1967), 93

'Diderot as Musician', *Diderot Studies*, x (1968), 95

'Musicology and Musical Letters', *Musik und Verlag: Karl Vötterle zum 65. Geburtstag* (Kassel, 1968), 403

'The Composer', *Man versus Society in Eighteenth-century Britain*, ed. J. L. Clifford (Cambridge, 1968), 85

Review of D. Sices: *Music and the Musician in 'Jean-Christophe'* (New Haven, 1968), *Romantic Review*, xl (1969), 312

ed.: *The Concerto 1800–1900* (New York, 1969) [anthology]

ed.: *The Symphony 1800–1900* (New York, 1969) [anthology]

ed.: *The Creative World of Beethoven* (New York, 1970) [originally

pubd in *MQ*, lvi (1970), 505–793]
Critic at the Opera (New York, 1971; Eng. edn., 1973 as *The Experience of Opera*) [collected reviews]
'French Opera and the Spirit of the Revolution', *Studies in Eighteenth-century Culture*, ii (Cleveland and London, 1972), 97
'Musicology and Related Disciplines', *Perspectives in Musicology*, ed. B. S. Brook, E. O. D. Downes and S. van Solkema (New York, 1972), 185

BIBLIOGRAPHY
'18th-century Studies in Honor of Paul Henry Lang', *CMc* (1969), no.9, p.47–189 [incl. O. Fellow: 'Paul Henry Lang: an Enlightened Critic of the French Enlightenment', 84]
CARLETON SPRAGUE SMITH

Lang, Walter (*b* Basle, 19 Aug 1896; *d* Baden, canton of Aargau, 17 March 1966). Swiss pianist and composer. After studies in Basle he became in 1913 a pupil of Jaques-Dalcroze in Hellerau and then in Geneva, where he taught for a time at the Jaques-Dalcroze Institute. He also had lessons with Klose in Munich and with Andreae and Frey in Zurich. As a piano teacher he worked at the Zurich Conservatory (1922–41) and, from 1949 to 1964, at the conservatories of Basle and Berne and the Zurich Musikakademie. He appeared as a solo pianist and with the Lang Trio, and he was a pianist and conductor for Radio Monte Ceneri, Lugano (1942–8). A late-Romantic disciple of Bartók (particularly in his teaching works for the piano), he was also at home in a neo-Baroque style.

WORKS
(selective list)
Stage: Leggende del Ticino, Festspiel, 1944
Orch: Sonata festiva, op.25, chamber orch, 1935; Scherzo fugato, op.30, str, 1929; Fantasie, op.40, vn, vc, orch, 1941; Pf Conc., op.34, 1940; Sym., op.45, 1946; Concertino, op.51, 1947; Vc Conc., op.60, 1951; Konzertante Suite, op.65, 2 pf, str, 1954; Divertimento, op.69, str, 1957
Chamber: Pf Qt, op.52, 1947; several other pieces
Pf: 12 Konzertetüden, op.26, 1935; Tagebuch, op.43, 1943; Klangskizze, op.47, 1947; Der Baumeister, op.50, 1947; many other works
Org: 2 Orgelfantasien, op.73, 1961
Choral music, songs

Principal publisher: Hug

BIBLIOGRAPHY
W. Bertschinger: 'Klavierwerke von Walter Lang', *SMz*, lxxxix (1949), 378
——: 'Walter Lang zum 60. Geburtstag', *SMz*, xcvi (1956), 295
E. Graf: 'Walter Langs Unterrichtswerke', *SMz*, civ (1964), 307
E. Tobler: 'Walter Lang', *SMz*, cvi (1966), 169
FRITZ MUGGLER

Langa, Francisco Soto de. *See* SOTO DE LANGA, FRANCISCO.

Langdon, Michael (*b* Wolverhampton, 12 Nov 1920). English bass. He joined the Covent Garden chorus in 1948, graduated to small roles in 1950–51, and sang the Grand Inquisitor in Visconti's production of *Don Carlos* in 1958. His main parts have included Baron Ochs, Fafner, Hagen and Hunding, Don Basilio, Rocco, Kecal, Varlaam and Waldner (*Arabella*). Outside Great Britain he has become best known for his Ochs, an authentic portrayal since he studied the part in Vienna with Jerger; he has sung it at the Metropolitan Opera, the Paris Opéra, the Vienna Staatsoper and the main German houses, more than 100 times in all. He has also sung Osmin with considerable success on the Continent, and with Scottish Opera in 1972 he added Don Pasquale to his repertory. For television he sang a memorable Claggart in *Billy Budd*. Langdon has a voluminous, slightly dry voice, which he adapts with equal success for evil or good humour. He is a master of

character and make-up. In 1977 he announced his retirement from the stage.

BIBLIOGRAPHY
H. Rosenthal: 'Michael Langdon', *Opera*, xxvi (1975), 1111
ALAN BLYTH

Langdon, Richard (*b* Exeter, *c*1729; *d* Exeter, 8 Sept 1803). English organist and composer. He came of a family long connected with the music of Exeter Cathedral, and was probably the grandson of Tobias Langdon, a priest vicar-choral there. He himself became lay vicar-choral and organist of Exeter Cathedral in June 1753 and also Master of the Choristers in 1762. In 1761 he took the Oxford degree of BMus. He resigned his posts at Exeter in October 1777 and in November of that year was appointed organist of Ely Cathedral, moving thence to Bristol Cathedral in 1778 and to Armagh Cathedral in 1782. He left Armagh in poor health in 1794 and appears to have retired to Exeter, where he died. In June 1784 one Richard Langdon was appointed organist of Peterborough Cathedral but it is apparent that he did not take up duty there.

WORKS
(published in London)
10 Songs and a Cantata, op.1 (*c*1754)
A Collection of Songs, op.2 (*c*1755)
Cupid and Chloe, cantata (*c*1755)
6 Sonatas, hpd, op.3 (1765)
12 Songs and 2 Cantatas, op.4 (*c*1770)
Divine Harmony [psalms, anthems etc] ... by the Most Eminent Masters, op.5 (1774)
12 Glees, 3–4vv, op.6 (*c*1780)
Songs pubd separately

WATKINS SHAW

Lange, Aloysia. German soprano; *see* WEBER family.

Lange, de. Dutch family of organists and composers.

(1) Samuel de Lange (i) (*b* Rotterdam, 9 June 1811; *d* Rotterdam, 15 May 1884). He studied the organ and the piano with Pruys and van Bree and became organist of several Rotterdam churches, the Lutherse Kerk from 1827, the Waalse Kerk from 1833, the Zuiderkerk from 1854 and, finally, the St Laurenskerk from 1864, where he became celebrated for his regular series of recitals. He taught at the newly founded school of the Rotterdam Maatschappij tot Bevordering der Toonkunst from 1844 and was also the city's carillonist. His compositions, in the style of Mendelssohn, include sonatas, fantasias, variations on the Dutch national hymn and transcriptions of popular parts of symphonies and oratorios, all for organ, as well as chamber music and songs.

(2) Samuel de Lange (ii) (*b* Rotterdam, 22 Feb 1840; *d* Stuttgart, 7 July 1911). Son of (1) Samuel de Lange (i). He studied with his father, J. F. Dupont and Verhulst. During a concert tour as pianist with his brother Daniel as cellist, he took lessons (1859) in Vienna from Winterberger, a Liszt pupil. The two brothers continued their travels through Romania and Galicia, and in Lwów they taught for a time at the music school, where Samuel also studied with Mikuli. They returned to Rotterdam in 1862, where Samuel was appointed teacher at the (Toonkunst) Maatschappij music school, director of the society's choir and organist of the Waalse Kerk. He became known for his influential part in the Dutch Bach renaissance, organizing and conducting orchestral concerts of Bach's music, as well as performing as organist and as pianist in both solo and chamber music; he also promoted the organ works of Muffat, Frescobaldi, Liszt and Brahms. In 1874 he went to Basle and in 1876 to Paris; from 1877 to 1884 he lived in Cologne where he was organ teacher at the conservatory and also a choral conductor. He returned to Holland in 1884 and assumed the directorship of the (Toonkunst) Maatschappij music school of The Hague, but in 1893 he left for good to teach at the Stuttgart Conservatory, which he directed from 1900 to 1908. His compositions include an oratorio *Mozes*, several symphonies and concertos, choruses, songs and numerous works for organ and for piano. He also published an edition of Muffat's *Apparatus musico-organisticus* (Leipzig, 1888).

(3) **Daniël de Lange** (*b* Rotterdam, 11 June 1841; *d* Point Loma, Calif., 31 Jan 1918). Brother of (2) Samuel de Lange (ii). He likewise first studied with his father, Dupont and Verhulst. He studied the cello in Rotterdam with Ganz, continuing in 1855 with A. F. Servais at the Brussels Conservatory, where he was also in Damcke's composition class. In 1858 he toured eastern Europe with his brother Samuel, returning to Rotterdam in 1863 to teach the cello at the (Toonkunst) Maatschappij music school. He lived in Paris as an organist and choir conductor from 1864 until the outbreak of the Franco-Prussian War in 1870 when he settled in Amsterdam and taught at the music school of the (Toonkunst) Maatschappij section. He conducted the Caecilia orchestra from 1886 to 1889, and from 1895 to 1913 was director of the Amsterdam Conservatory in succession to its first director, Frans Coenen. After the founding of the Leiden section of the (Toonkunst) Maatschappij in 1875, he became a member of its general committee (1876–1909), and also served on the board of the Vereeniging voor Nederlandsche Muziekgeschiedenis (1881–1913). In 1914 he became director of the music department of the Isis Conservatory of Art, Music and Drama in Point Loma, California.

Lange's chief importance lies in his championship of early Netherlands polyphony. In 1881 he founded in Amsterdam a choir of ten soloists with which he toured the Netherlands, and in 1885 it gave a concert of polyphonic music at the International Inventions Exhibition in London. In 1892 he was invited to Vienna where he directed another *a cappella* choir which he had assembled, this time with 18 soloists, at the Internationale Ausstellung für Musik- und Theaterwesen. An extended, successful concert tour of western Europe followed. His performances won great acclaim for their technical polish. He also promoted contemporary and oriental music. From 1876 he wrote music criticism for the newspaper *Nieuws van den Dag*. His other writings include books about the Galin-Paris–Chevé music-teaching method, Dutch folksong, and music theory; he contributed the article on Indonesian music to the Lavignac *Encyclopédie* (Paris, 1913–31). He also edited the *St Matthew Passion* ascribed to Obrecht for the Vereeniging voor Nederlandsche Muziekgeschiedenis (1894). His own compositions include symphonies, cantatas, choruses, songs, chamber and piano works, as well as an unperformed opera *De val van Kuilenberg*.

BIBLIOGRAPHY

H. Viotta: *Onze hedendaagsche toonkunstenaars* (Amsterdam, 1894)
A. Averkamp: *Levensbericht van Daniël de Lange* (Leiden, 1918)
J. D. C. van Dokkum: *Honderd jaar muziekleven in Nederland* (Amsterdam, 1929)
E. Reeser, ed.: *De Vereeniging voor Nederlandsche Muziekgeschiedenis 1868–1943, Gedenkboek* (Amsterdam, 1943)
J. G. A. ten Bokum: *Johannes Gijsbertus Bastiaans 1812–1875* (diss., U. of Utrecht, 1972) [with Eng. summary]

JAN TEN BOKUM

Lange, Francisco [Franz] **Curt** [Kurt] (*b* Eilenburg, 12 Dec 1903). Uruguayan musicologist of German origin. He studied at Leipzig, Berlin, Munich and Bonn universities, taking an architect's diploma at Munich (1927) and the doctorate at Bonn (1929) with a dissertation on the polyphony of the Netherlands; his teachers included Nikisch, Sandberger, Bücken, van den Borren, Oeser, Hornbostel and Sachs. In 1930 the Uruguayan government invited him to help organize the country's musical life and he settled in Montevideo, adopting Uruguayan citizenship and working energetically on a variety of projects. He was a founder of the State Broadcasting System (SODRE) and the State Record Library, and was SODRE's music adviser (1930–48); he introduced musicological studies at the Instituto de Estudios Superiores (1933), and in Montevideo started the 'Americanismo musical' movement to promote music and musicians of the Americas: the first Ibero-American Music Festival (Bogotá, 1938) and Inter-American Conference in the Field of Music (Washington, DC, 1939) were organized under its auspices. For several years he worked on music organization and education in Argentina, Brazil, Peru and Colombia. In 1935 he began to publish the *Boletín latino-americano de música*, dealing with the various musical traditions of the Americas. He also founded the Instituto Interamericano de Musicología (1938) at Montevideo, which published some 66 works by Latin American composers under the auspices of Editorial Cooperativa Interamericana de Compositores (1941–56). In connection with this, he published with Hans J. Koellreutter the short-lived review *Música viva* (Rio de Janeiro, 1940–41), and under the institute's auspices and in collaboration with Juan Bautista Plaza the *Archivo de música colonial venezolana* (1941–2), the first organized Latin American historical collection (12 volumes). In 1948 Lange was invited to establish the department of musicology at the National University of Cuyo in Mendoza, Argentina, where he founded and edited the *Revista de estudios musicales* (1949–56) and a series of contemporary Latin American music.

Lange's main contribution to musicological research has been his extensive exploration of colonial archives in Argentina and Brazil, supported by grants from over 20 foundations and governments. In Minas Gerais he discovered a particularly rich 18th-century musical culture, developed exclusively by mulattos, and edited many scores of its religious music for his Monumenta Musicae Brasiliae; further volumes of valuable documentation resulted from his work on Brazilian archives. This research has been amplified by further study in Spain and Portugal. Between 1933 and 1970 he organized hundreds of concerts of this music throughout South America, the USA and Europe, and has thus contributed more than any other individual to the dissemination of Latin American music. He has also been active in disseminating European and North American culture in South America: he mounted many concerts of new music from the USA in Montevideo and Rio de Janeiro, and to extend Latin American knowledge of international bibliography translated numerous studies into Spanish. As a visiting lecturer he has taught throughout Europe and the USA, and he is the Latin

American representative of most European and north American musicological organizations.

WRITINGS

Über die Mehrstimmigkeit der Niederländischen Motetten (diss., U. of Bonn, 1929)

'Organización musical en el Uruguay: La Ossodre', *Boletín latino-americano de música*, i (1935), 111

'Villa-Lobos, un pedagogo creador', *Boletín latino-americano de música*, i (1935), 189

'Americanismo musical', *Boletín latino-americano de música*, ii (1936), 117

'La difusión radio-eléctrica como medio de educación de las masas y como factor de difusión cultural y científica', *Boletín latino-americano de música*, ii (1936), 131

'Sistemas de investigación folklórica y el empleo del acervo folklórico en la música artística', *Boletín latino-americano de música*, ii (1936), 143

'León Ribeiro', *Boletín latino-americano de música*, iii (1937), 519

'Los estudios musicales de la América Latina publicados últimamente', *Handbook of Latin American Studies*, iii (1937), 527

'El compositor argentino Juan Carlos Paz', *Boletín latino-americano de música*, iv (1938), 799

'El festival Ibero-Americano de Música', *Boletín latino-americano de música*, iv (1938), 55

'Guillermo Espinosa y la Orquesta Sinfónica Nacional', *Boletín latino-americano de música*, iv (1938), 23

'Guillermo Uribe Holguín', *Boletín latino-americano de música*, iv (1938), 757

'Juan Bautista Massa', *Boletín latino-americano de música*, iv (1938), 665

'Colonial Music in Latin American Lands', *Musical America*, lix/14 (1939), 8

Programs of Latin American Music (Washington, DC, 1939)

'La educación musical infantil en el Uruguay: una nueva orientación', *Boletín latino-americano de música*, v (1941), 619

'Suma de las relaciones interamericanas en el campo de la música', *Boletín latino-americano de música*, v (1941), 11

ed.: *Latin-American Art Music for the Piano by Twelve Contemporary Composers* (New York, 1942)

'La música en Minas Gerais, un informe preliminar', *Boletín latino-americano de música*, vi (1946), 409

'La vida musical en la Argentina', *Asomante*, iii/2 (1947), 57

'A manera de prólogo', *Revista de estudios musicales*, i/1 (1949), 13

'Estudios brasileños (Mauricinas) I: manuscritos de la biblioteca nacional de Rio de Janeiro', *Revista de estudios musicales*, i/3 (1950), 99

'Vida y muerte de Louis Moreau Gottschalk en Rio de Janeiro (1869): el ambiente musical en la mitad del segundo imperio', *Revista de estudios musicales*, ii (1950–51), no.4, p.43; nos.5–6, p.97

ed.: *Archivo de música religiosa de la 'Capitanía Geral das Minas Gerais' siglo XVIII* (Mendoza, 1951)

'Huellas de la música eclesiástica durante la dominación hispánica', *Buenos Aires musical*, no.117 (1952), 4

'La música eclesiástica argentina en el período de la dominación hispánica (una investigación), i: (Humahuaca-Jujuy)', *Revista de estudios musicales*, iii/7 (1954), 15

'Órganos y organeros en los conventos franciscanos de la Argentina en el período de la dominación hispánica', *Meridiano 66*, i/2 (1955), 1

La música eclesiástica en Córdoba durante la dominación hispánica (Córdoba, 1956)

'La música en Minas Gerais durante el siglo XVIII', *Estudios americanos*, no.57–8 (1956), 1

La música religiosa en el área de Rosario de Santa Fe y en el convento San Carlos de San Lorenzo, durante el período aproximado de 1770 a 1820 (Rosario, 1956)

'Die Musik von Minas Gerais', *Musica*, xi (1957), 375

'La música eclesiástica en Santa Fe y Corrientes durante la dominación hispánica', *Universidad*, no.34 (Santa Fe, 1957), April, 23

'A música barroca', *História da civilização brasileira*, i/2, ed. S. Buarque de Holanda (São Paulo, 1960), 121

'La ópera y las casas de ópera en el Brasil colonial', *Boletín interamericano de música*, no.44 (1964), 3

'Organeros y órganos durante el período colonial argentino', *Boletín interamericano de música*, no.50 (1965), 3

'Os compositores na Capitania Geral de Minas Gerais', *Estudos históricos*, nos.3–4 (1965), 33

'Sobre las difíciles huellas de la música antigua del Brasil: la "Missa abreviada" del Padre José Mauricio Nunes Garcia', *Yearbook, Inter-American Institute for Musical Research*, i (1965), 15

'A música em Sabará', *Estudos históricos*, no.5 (1966), 97

A organização musical durante o período colonial brasileiro (Coimbra, 1966)

'A música erudita na regência e no império', *Historia da civilização brasileira*, ii/3, ed. S. Buarque de Holanda (São Paulo, 1967), 369

'La música en Villa Rica, Minas Gerais, siglo XVIII', *Revista musical chilena* (1967), no.102, 8; (1968), no.103, 77

'Erdmann Neuparth: ein deutscher Musiker in Brasilien', *Staden-Jb*, xv (1967), 163

'Os irmãos músicos da Irmandade de São José dos Homens Pardos de Villa Rica', *Yearbook, Inter-American Institute for Musical Research*, iv (1968), 110

'Pesquisas esporádicas de musicologia no Rio de Janeiro', *Revista do Instituto de estudos brasileiros*, no.4 (1968), 99

'As danças coletivas públicas no período colonial brasileiro e dança das corporações de oficios em Minas Gerais', *Barroco*, i (1969), 15

Historia de la música colonial argentina (?Buenos Aires, 1972–3)

'Der Fall Domenico Zipoli: Verlauf und Stand einer Berichtigung', *Musicae scientiae collectanea: Festschrift Karl Gustav Fellerer* (Cologne, 1973), 327

Historia de la música colonial cordobesa, i (Córdoba, 1977)

Articles in *Die Musik Latein-Amerikas im 19. Jahrhundert*, ed. R. Günther (Regensburg, 1977)

História da música nas Irmandades de Vila Rica, i– (Belo Horizonte, 1979–)

BIBLIOGRAPHY

G. Chase: 'Linking the Americas', *Musical America*, lix/3 (1939), 224

——: 'Francisco Curt Lange and "Americanismo musical" ', *Inter-American Monthly*, ii/5 (Washington, 1943), 33

G. Espinosa: 'Un explorador musical uruguayo', *Américas*, i/2 (1949), 25

F. Bose: 'Südamerikanische Musikforschung', *AcM*, xxix (1957), 43

A. G. Pérez: 'Discovery in Minas Gerais: on the Trail of 18th Century Musical Sources', *Américas*, xiii/1 (1961), 24

G. Chase: 'An Anniversary and a New Start', *Yearbook, Inter-American Institute for Musical Research*, i (1965), 1

'Curt Lange, o descobridor', *Suplemento literário*, viii (Minas Gerais, 1973), nos.355–6, 1

P. S. Urtubey: *Las obras colectivas de Francisco Curt Lange* (Buenos Aires, 1974)

GERARD BÉHAGUE

Lange, Gregor [Langius, Hieronymus Gregorius] (*b* Havelberg, Brandenburg, *c*1540; *d* Breslau [now Wrocław], ? 1 May 1587). German composer. He matriculated at the University of Frankfurt an der Oder in 1573 and in 1574 became the university Kantor. He appears to have contracted an incurable disease about 1580, since shortly afterwards he was obliged to relinquish his position; in the last dedication he wrote, in 1585, he stated that his hands and feet were completely paralysed. From 1583 he lived at Breslau, where he was supported by the town council; he spent the final period of his life in the Hieronymus Hospital there.

Lange was highly esteemed by his contemporaries, who ranked him with Lassus and Lechner, and his reputation endured until the 19th century. The influence of Lassus on him is evident in the swiftly developing structures and penchant for modulation in his music; the motet *Vae misero mihi* from the 1584 collection, for example, is remarkable for its unusual chromatic modulations. In other respects, however, his work was outmoded, particularly in its rapid alteration of vocal groupings and the brevity of its themes. His Latin motets, 45 of which were published in his collections of 1580 and 1584, enjoyed considerable favour. His three-voice German songs are less attractive than those of Regnart, for they are somewhat stiff and lacking in melody, but they were popular enough for the first book (1584) to be reprinted four times and the second (1586) twice before the end of the 16th century; and in 1615 they reappeared with sacred texts by Henning Dedekind and in arrangements for five voices by Christoph Demantius that are of greater musical merit.

WORKS

Edition: *G. Lange: Eine ausgewählte Sammlung Motetten*, 4, 5, 6, 8vv, ed. R. Starke, PÄMw, xxv (1901/R1966) [24 motets]

SACRED VOCAL

[19] Cantiones aliquot novae, 5, 6vv (Frankfurt an der Oder, 1580)

Liber secundus [26] cantionum sacrarum, 4–6, 8vv, cum adjuncto in fine dialogo, 10vv (Nuremberg, 1584)

4 sacred works, 1646[3]; 2 motets intabulated for lute, 1584[14]

SECULAR VOCAL

Neuer deutscher Lieder . . . der erste Theil, 3vv (Breslau, 1584) [arr. 5vv by Demantius (Leipzig, 1614)]

Der ander Theil neuer deudscher Lieder, 3vv (Breslau, 1586) [arr. 5vv by Demantius (Leipzig, 1615)]

4 songs, intabulated for lute, 1584[14]

OCCASIONAL

Gamedion (Audi dulcis amica mea) in honorem Adami Bolforosii, 5vv (Frankfurt, 1574)

Cantiones due, quarum altera in honorem nuptiarum D . . . Martini Nosleri . . . et Evae D. Basilij Mehlhornij . . . altera in eiusdem gratiam & honorem . . . composita est, 6vv (Frankfurt, 1582)

Nuptiis . . . Henrici Schmid . . . et Catharinae . . . Christophori . . . cantio gratulatoria composita (Breslau, 1584)

Bekentnis der Sünden, und Gebet umb gnedige Linderung der vorstehenden Not und Gefahr . . . der . . . Stadt Bresslau, 4vv (Breslau, 1585)

Prudens simplex, simplex prudens: symbolum Francisci Virlingi Diaconi, 5vv (Breslau, 1585), lost (cited in Starke, 1889)

Epithalamion melos . . . Iohanni Hennmanno, medicinae doctori, ac . . . eius sponsae Mariae, 5vv (Breslau, 1586)

Wedding work, 5vv, in J. Belitz: Epithalamia (Frankfurt, 1581)

For MS works incl. 2 masses, Lat. motets, Ger. sacred and secular works, see EitnerQ and Starke (1899)

BIBLIOGRAPHY

R. Starke: 'Hieronymus Gregorius Lange Havelbergensis', MMg, xxxi (1899), 101

H. J. Moser: Geschichte der deutschen Musik, i (Stuttgart, 1920, 5/1930)

F. Blume: Die evangelische Kirchenmusik, HMw, x (1931, rev. 2/1965 as Geschichte der evangelischen Kirchenmusik; Eng. trans., enlarged, 1974 as Protestant Church Music: a History)

A. A. Abert: Die stilistischen Voraussetzungen der Cantiones sacrae von Heinrich Schütz (Wolfenbüttel, 1935)

N. Hampel: Deutschsprachige protestantische Kirchenmusik Schlesiens bis zum Einbruch der Monodie (diss., U. of Breslau, 1937)

H. Grimm: Meister der Renaissancemusik an der Viadrina (Frankfurt an der Oder and Berlin, 1942)

H. J. Moser: Die evangelische Kirchenmusik in Deutschland (Berlin, 1954)

W. Boetticher: Orlando di Lasso und seine Zeit (Kassel, 1958)

I. Gallwitz: Die Neuen deutsche Lieder von 1584 und 1586 des Gregorius Langius und deren Bearbeitung durch Christoph Demantius und Henning Dedekind (diss., U. of Vienna, 1960)

H. Osthoff: Das deutsche Chorlied vom 16. Jahrhundert bis zur Gegenwart (Cologne, 1960)

based on MGG (viii, 184–5) by permission of Bärenreiter

BERNHARD STOCKMANN

Lange, Johann Caspar (fl Hildesheim, 1688). German writer on music. He was Kantor at the Protestant Gymnasium at Hildesheim, according to the title-page of his only known work, an instruction manual for use in his own teaching entitled Methodus nova & perspicua in artem musicam, das ist: Recht gründtliche Anweisung wie die edle Music mit allen zugehörigen Stücken auffs allerleichteste und gewisseste nach heutiger neuesten Art fähigen Subjectis in kurtzer Zeit beyzubringen sey (Hildesheim, 1688). The text is brief and concerned with basic elements of music: notation, scales, intervals, elementary principles of singing. There is a glossary of terms most often used in music and a set of music examples giving melodies for the practice of singing in canon.

GEORGE J. BUELOW

Langeleik. A folk zither of Norway fitted with one melody and several drone strings and a fretted fingerboard, and played with a plectrum. It is related to the langspil of Iceland and the hommel and similar zithers of the Low Countries. See NORWAY, §II, 4 and fig.2.

Lange-Müller, Peter Erasmus (b Frederiksberg, 1 Dec 1850; d Copenhagen, 26 Feb 1926). Danish composer. He came from a wealthy and musical family of scientists, clergymen and academics and was taught the piano from an early age by Gottfred Matthison-Hansen. After leaving school in 1870 he enrolled at Copenhagen University (to read political science) and at the conservatory, where he was taught the piano by Edmund Neupert, but ill-health soon forced him to give up his studies. Throughout his life he suffered from constant headaches, which affected both his personal relations and his musical development. He was largely self-taught, and his isolation meant that he could more readily develop the original and untraditional characteristics of his music; he withdrew from official musical life except between 1879 and 1883, when he was conductor of the Koncertforening that he had helped to found. Shortly after his marriage in 1892 he moved to a beautiful country estate in northern Zealand, and the surroundings there deeply influenced his creative work.

Lange-Müller was a Romantic by temperament and artistic inclination. His style was strongly influenced by the music of his countrymen Hartmann and Heise and by that of Schumann, but he evolved an individual late Romantic style built around emotionally concentrated tonal effects on a dark harmonic background, reminiscent of Brahms and contemporary French developments – an expression of nostalgia that was not directly followed up in Danish music. His substantial output is dominated by vocal music. The Piano Trio op.53 is one of his best instrumental pieces, but his lack of technical training becomes apparent in the sometimes awkward orchestration of his larger works. As a composer of songs he had no equal among his Danish contemporaries; his wide choice of texts and acute sensitivity to the mood of each poem enabled him to create a vocal style whose subtlety was without precedent in Danish music. He found a source of sympathetic inspiration in his friend, the poet Thor Lange, whose varied imagery and reworkings of Russian and other Slav folk poetry influenced Lange-Müller's musical expression. He hoped for success as a composer of opera, as is shown by his numerous efforts in that genre, but his most ambitious work, the opera Vikingeblod, was also his greatest disappointment; the critics found the style and subject outdated, and this judgment may partly account for the decline in his output after 1900 and its virtual cessation by 1910. By that time, however, his songs with piano and works such as the Madonnasange op.65 and the music for Der var engang ('Once upon a time') op.25 had secured the widespread acceptance and popularity of his music. The younger generation of Danish composers regarded him with respect and veneration.

WORKS

Edition: P. E. Lange-Müller: Sange (Copenhagen, 1911–12)

(all printed works published in Copenhagen; MSS in DK-Kk)

STAGE

(first performed at Copenhagen, Royal Theatre, unless otherwise stated)

op.

7   Tove (Singspiel, 2, Lange-Müller), 1878, abridged vocal score (1879)

13 I Mester Sebalds have [In Master Sebald's garden] (incidental music, S. Bauditz), 1880, abridged vocal score (1881)

15 Fulvia (incidental music, H. V. Kaalund), 1881, abridged vocal score (1881)

22 Spanske studenter (opera, 2, V. Faber), 1883, vocal score (1883)

25 Der var engang [Once upon a time] (incidental music, H. Drachmann), 1887, abridged vocal score (1887)

30 Fru Jeanna (tragic opera, 4, E. von der Recke), composed 1886; 1891, vocal score (1891)

32 Gildet paa Solhaug [The Feast at Solhaug] (incidental music, Ibsen), composed 1888; Christiania, 1897, abridged vocal score (1888), songs (1894)

41 Ved Bosporus [At the Bosporus] (incidental music, Drachmann), 1891, abridged vocal score (1893)

42 Peter Plus (incidental music, E. Christiansen), 1891, 2 songs (1891)

43 Die schlimmen Brüder (incidental music, P. Heyse), Weimar, 1891, serenade, vn, pf (1922)

44 Hertuginden af Burgund [The Duchess of Burgundy] (incidental music, von der Recke), abridged vocal score (1892)

48 Letizia (incidental music, Christiansen), Copenhagen, Dagmar, 1898, songs (1893–8)

50 Vikingeblod (opera, 4, Christiansen), composed before 1897; 1900, vocal score (1897)

51 Sommernat paa sundet [Summer night on the sound] (O. Benzon), 1894 [prelude to Anna Bryde]

55 Middelalderlig [Medieval] (melodrama, Drachmann), 1896, abridged vocal score (1903)

59 Renaissance (melodrama, Drachmann), 1901, vocal score (1903)

CHORAL

op.
5 Tonernes flugt [The tones' flight] (H. Hertz), Novemberstemning [November mood] (H. Høst), both for mixed vv, 1876, acc. pf 4 hands (1913), with orch acc. (1914–15)

9 Niels Ebbesen (C. Gandrup), Bar, male vv, orch (1878), rev. 1924

10 Tolv kor- og kvartetsange, male vv (1879)

21 Tre salmer, mixed vv, orch (1883)

29 Zwei Madonnalieder (P. Heyse, after Sp. orig.), Mez, female vv, orch (1895)

36 Kantate ved universitetets fest, June 1888 (H. Drachmann), mixed vv, orch, vocal score (1911)

60 1848 (E. von der Recke), cantata, Bar, male vv, wind, vocal score (1919)

62 Arion (Recke), T, mixed vv, orch, perf. 1899, vocal score (n.d.)

65 Tre Madonnasange (T. Lange), mixed vv (1900)

71 H. C. Andersen-kantate (Recke), solo vv, mixed vv, orch (1906)

73 Agnete og havmanden [Agnete and the merman] (E. Blaumüller), chorus, orch, vocal score (1910)

SONGS

5 sange af Sulamith og Salomon (B. S. Ingemann), op.1 (1874); Menuet og marsch (H. V. Kaalund, F. Paludan-Müller), 2 songs, low v, op.2 (1874); 3 digte (V. Bergsøe), op.4 (1875); 8 sange (Ingemann), op.6 (1876); 6 sange efter det russiske (T. Lange), op.11 (1879); Fem danske sange (C. F. K. Molbech, C. Hauch, Kaalund), op.14 (1882); 5 norske sange (Bjørnson, Ibsen, Welhaven), op.16 (1882); 6 folkeviser (trans. Lange), op.18 (1883); Naar sol gaar ned [At sunset] (Lange), 4 songs, op.19 (1883); Skumring [Twilight] (Lange, after Tolstoy), 4 songs, op.20 (1883); Bjørnen, hinden, junkeren [The bear, the hind, the squire], op.23 (1884)

7 sange (Recke), op.24 (1884); 6 ernste Lieder (Heine, Heyse), op.27 (1895); 6 anciennes chansons d'amour, op.28 (1885); 4 digte (C. Richardt, Molbech, Kaalund), op.31 (1887); 8 folkeviser (trans. Lange), op.34 (1888); 5 Romanzen und Balladen (L. Uhland), op.35 (1889); 3 sange (Lange, after Pol. and Russ. orig.), op.38 (1890); 6 sange af Min kaerligheds bog (K. Gjellerup), op.40 (1890); 5 Sange ved havet [Songs by the sea] (Drachmann), op.54 (1896); 4 sange af Cosmus (E. Christiansen), op.57 (1898); 4 sange (L. Holstein), op.61 (1899); 17 viser og sange (Lange), op.64 (1899); 3 digte (Jacobsen), op.74 (1908); 9 sange (Recke), op.75 (1908); [5] Vandringsmandens sange [Songs of travel] (C. Bahnson), op.77 (1910); 12 smaasange (1901)

INSTRUMENTAL

Orch: Sym. 'Efteraar' [Autumn], op.17, 1879–81, arr. pf 4 hands (1881); Sym., d, op.33, 1889, rev. 1915; 2 suites, I Alhambra, op.3 (1875) and Weyerburg, op.47, arr. pf 4 hands (1894); Romance, vn solo, op.63 (1899); Vn Conc., C, op.69 (1904)

Chamber: Pf Trio, F, op.53 (1898); 3 fantasistykker, vn, pf, op.39 (1891); works for pf 2 hands, incl. 12 klaverstykker, op.8 (1877), Danse og intermezzi, op.49 (1894), 7 skovstykker [Forest pieces], op.56 (1898), En efteraarsfantasi [An autumn fantasia], op.66 (1900), Daempede melodier [Soft melodies], op.68 (1904), Smaa klaverstykker for børn [Little pf pieces for children] (1911); Meraner-Reigen, pf 4 hands, op.26 (1886)

BIBLIOGRAPHY

Fortegnelse over P. E. Lange-Müller's kompositioner (Copenhagen, 1910) [catalogue]

P. E. Lange-Müller: Autobiography, Illustreret tidende (27 Nov 1910)

G. Lynge: 'P. E. Lange-Müller', Danske komponister i det 20. aarhundredes begyndelse (Århus, 1916, 2/1917), 170ff

E. Abrahamsen: 'Lange-Müller, Peter Erasmus', DBL

J. Clausen: P. E. Lange-Müller (Copenhagen, 1938)

H. Bonnén: P. E. Lange-Müller (Copenhagen, 1946) [incl. list of works]

K. A. Brunn: 'P. E. Lange-Müller', Dansk musiks historie, ii (Copenhagen, 1969), 243–79

NIELS MARTIN JENSEN

Langenfeld, Friedrich Spee von. See SPEE VON LANGENFELD, FRIEDRICH.

Langer, Susanne K(atharina) (b New York, 20 Dec 1895). American philosopher. After studying philosophy at Radcliffe College (PhD 1926) and (briefly) at the University of Vienna, she taught at various institutions between 1927 and 1954, when she was appointed professor at Connecticut College, where she has been a research scholar since her retirement in 1962. Between 1940 and 1960 her publications centred on a philosophy of art derived from a theory of musical meaning which in turn exemplified a general philosophy of mind. According to this 'philosophy in a new key' (1942), all the modes of understanding characteristic of mankind are forms of symbolic transformation: that is, we understand any phenomenon by constructing an object analogous to it or referring to it. The structural principles embodied in these constructed objects are amenable to logical analysis, which it is the mission of philosophy to perform. In this context, Langer used music as paradigm of a symbol system whose symbols are presentational rather than discursive, having meaning but not asserting anything. Her interpretation hinges on the fact that although music has generally been thought to express feeling, the history of music is always written in terms of its formal development. She suggested that this is because the principles of musical form are structurally the same as those of the patterns of human feelings. This identity is what makes musical forms interesting, though music need not describe or express or evoke anyone's actual feelings. Her later work (1953, 1957) generalizes this account into a theory of all the fine arts, whose formal patterns she found to be variously isomorphic with specific aspects of human experience which they thereby render intelligible. She subsequently (1967) suggested that because of this isomorphism the vocabulary of art criticism might form the basis for the development of an independent conceptual apparatus for the biological and behavioural sciences, which they have hitherto lacked.

Many aestheticians hold that Langer's basic contentions were decisively refuted by Nagel (1943). Others maintain that Nagel's rebuttal rests on misunderstandings induced by an unargued acceptance of traditional terminologies and theories of meaning.

WRITINGS

The Practice of Philosophy (New York, 1930)

Introduction to Symbolic Logic (Boston, 1937)

Philosophy in a New Key (Cambridge, Mass., 1942, 3/1957)

Feeling and Form (New York, 1953)

Problems of Art (New York, 1957)

Philosophical Sketches (Baltimore, 1962)

Mind: an Essay in Human Feeling (Baltimore, 1967–72)

BIBLIOGRAPHY

E. Nagel: Review of Philosophy in a New Key, Journal of Philosophy, xl (1943), 323

L. A. Reid: Review of Philosophy in a New Key, Mind, lv (1945), 73

M. Schoen: 'On Musical Expression', JRME, ii (1954), 57

W. Sargent: 'Profiles: Philosopher in a New Key', New Yorker, xxxvi (1960), 67–100

B. Lang: 'Langer's Arabesque and the Collapse of the Symbol', Review of Metaphysics, xvi (1962), 349

A. Bertocci: 'Susanne Langer, or the Symbol Abstracted', Philological Quarterly, xlviii (1969), 261

P. A. Bertocci: 'Susanne K. Langer's Theory of Feeling and Mind', Review of Metaphysics, xxiii (1970), 527

F. E. SPARSHOTT

Langford, Samuel (b Manchester, 1863; d Manchester, 8 May 1927). English music critic. He was the son of a nursery gardener (and himself wished to be remembered as a cultivator of flowers rather than as a music critic); he showed early talent for music and was sent to study under Carl Reinecke in Leipzig (1896–1900). As music critic of the *Manchester Guardian* from 1905 to 1927, in succession to Ernest Newman and under C. P. Scott, he far exceeded in scope and depth the contemporary expectations of music journalism. His prose was individual, copious, detailed, allusive and to the point. His knowledge was immense, and he never indulged in technical analysis without relating it to aesthetic implications. As a writer about pianists he has not been excelled. His perceptions were often in advance of his time; he was one of the first English critics to understand Debussy and Mahler and to appreciate Wolf. A selection of his *Manchester Guardian* pieces was edited by Neville Cardus as *Samuel Langford: Musical Criticisms* (London, 1929).

NEVILLE CARDUS

Langgard, Rued [Rud] **(Immanuel)** (*b* Copenhagen, 28 July 1893; *d* Ribe, 10 July 1952). Danish composer and organist. His mother, Emma Foss, was a pianist and his father, Siegfried, a pianist, composer and teacher at the Royal Academy of Music, Copenhagen. Before Langgard went to school he had lessons from his parents and from Gustav Helsted (organ), Christian Petersen (violin) and C. F. E. Horneman (theory). He produced his first compositions at the age of seven, and in 1905 his début as an organist and improviser attracted wide notice. In 1908 a public performance of the cantata *Musae triumphantes* (1906) caused astonishment at the precocious development of his technique. He was able to write an accomplished late Romantic First Symphony (1908–11) which, though declared unplayable in Copenhagen, was given in Berlin in 1913 together with other of his works, including the orchestral *Sphinx*. The music he wrote before 1918 was influenced mainly by Liszt, Wagner, Bruckner and Mahler, the composers most in favour in his home background (his father had been a pupil of Liszt). In succeeding works, however, his attitude became more adventurous: he was influenced by Nielsen and, beginning with the Symphony no.6 (1919), he developed an atonal polyphonic style that foreshadowed the Hindemith of the early 1920s. His *Sfaerernes musik* (1918) opens with a dense string cluster and proceeds in an amorphous manner with precipitous stylistic changes reminiscent of Ives, although in other respects it accords with Langgard's earlier work. Indeed, both periods are linked by the constancy of Langgard's symbolist aesthetic and his deep religious feelings.

Such attitudes brought Langgard into conflict with the European mainstream after World War I; he was totally opposed to the anti-metaphysical objectivity of neo-classicism, and reacted by abandoning his more experimental writing for a Romantic style based on Gade and Wagner. The Seventh Symphony (1925–6) is a pure echo of Gade; Wagner's influence is less frequently evident, though *Parsifal* was clearly the foundation for Langgard's biblical opera *Antikrist*, composed and recomposed in three stages between 1916 and 1936. This stylistic retreat, accompanied by violent attacks on the state of Danish musical life, quickly made Langgard an isolated figure. His society Klassisk Musikforening, founded in 1927, was short-lived and, despite his outstanding qualities as an organist, he was passed over for every Copenhagen post for which he applied. Only in 1940 was he appointed cathedral organist in the small town of Ribe, where he considered himself something of an exile. Nevertheless, he continued to compose extensively. His appointment led him to write a number of short, romantic character pieces for organ, related to scriptural passages and designed for liturgical use. Outstanding among his other instrumental works are the Third Quartet (1924), a piece that looks forward to Bartók's middle quartets, and the piano sonata *Afgrundsmusik* (1921).

WORKS
(*selective list*)

Orch: Sphinx, 1909; Sym. no.1 'Klippepastoraler', 1908–11; Sym. no.2 'Vaarbrud', 1912–13; Sym. no.4 'Løvfald', 1916; Sym. no.6 'Det himmelrivende', 1919; Sym. no.7, 1925–6; Vn Conc., 1943–4; Sym. no.11 'Ixion', 1944; Sym. no.13 'Undertro', 1947; Sym. no.16 'Syndflod af sol', 1951

Vocal: Musae triumphantes, solo vv, chorus, orch, 1906; Lenau-sentiments, Mez, str qt, 1917; Sfaerernes musik, S, chorus, orch, 1918; A Poet's Dream, incidental music, *c*1925; Antikrist (Fortabelsen, Kremasco) (opera, Langgard after Revelation), 1916–36; choral motets, many songs

Inst: Aubade, vn, pf, 1907; Fjeldblomster, vn, pf, 1908; 6 str qts incl. no.1, 1914, no.3, 1924; Den store Mester kommer, sonata, vn, pf, 1920; Afgrundsmusik, sonata, pf, 1921; Flammekamrene, after Dante, pf, 1930; Messis I–III, org, 1934–7; Italian Scherzo, str qt, 1950; short pf and org pieces, org arrs.

Principal publishers: Hansen, Samfundet til Udgivelse af Dansk Musik, Skandinavisk Musikforlag

BIBLIOGRAPHY

G. Lynge: *Danske komponister i det 20. aarhundredes begyndelse* (Århus, 1916, 2/1917), 321ff
G. Skjerne: 'Rued Langgard', *Musik*, i (1917)
J. Brincker: 'Langgards 6. symfoni: et forsøg på eksegese', *Dansk musiktidsskrift*, xliii (1968), 183
B. Wallner: 'Om Rued Langgard og Sfaerernes musik', *Dansk musiktidsskrift*, xliii (1968), 174
——: *Vår tids musik i Norden* (Stockholm, 1968), 46ff

BO MARSCHNER

Langhans, (Friedrich) Wilhelm (*b* Hamburg, 21 Sept 1832; *d* Berlin, 9 June 1892). German writer, composer and violinist. He showed an inclination to be a performer at an early age and was enrolled at the Leipzig Conservatory from 1849 to 1852, studying the violin with David and composition with Hauptmann and Richter. Subsequently he played in the Gewandhaus Orchestra, Leipzig, from 1852 to 1856, during which time he also took further violin instruction from Alard in Paris. He was appointed Konzertmeister at Düsseldorf in 1857; the following year he married Louise Japha, a pianist from Hamburg with whom he gave joint recitals. He was active as a violinist and teacher in Hamburg (1860), Paris (1863) and Heidelberg (1869), where he received the doctorate in 1871. He moved to Berlin in 1871, teaching music history and theory at Kullak's Neue Akademie der Tonkunst from 1874, then at Scharwenka's newly founded conservatory from 1881.

Langhans's published compositions, including the Concert Allegro for violin and orchestra, violin studies, a sonata, string quartet and songs, are mainly forgotten. His major contribution was as a writer on music; he was a critic for the *Neue Berliner Musikzeitung*, a correspondent for the *Neue Zeitschrift für Musik*, the editor of the Berlin music journal *Echo* (1873–9) and contributor to Mendel's *Musikalisches Conversationslexikon*. Many of his writings are coloured by his admiration for Wagner. He recommended reforms in music education, advocating that music be given a status comparable with other disciplines in the Gymnasium, and was a champion of academic freedom in the secondary educational system, which he felt should be run on similar lines to those of the university. His contribution to Italian music was recognized by honorary memberships in musical academies in Florence, Rome and Bologna.

WRITINGS

Das musikalische Urtheil und seine Ausbildung durch die Erziehung (Berlin, 1872, 2/1886)

Die Königliche Hochschule für Musik zu Berlin (Leipzig, 1873)

Zum dritten Male die Königliche Hochschule (Berlin, 1874)

Die Musikgeschichte in zwölf Vorlesungen (Leipzig, 1878, 2/1879; Eng. trans., 1886)

Die Geschichte der Musik des 17., 18. und 19. Jahrhunderts in chronologischem Anschlusse an die Musikgeschichte von A. W. Ambros (Leipzig, 1881–7)

I lavori di Riccardo Wagner considerati dal lato pedagogico (Florence, 1887)

Friedrich Chopin als Mensch und als Musiker (Leipzig, 1890) [trans. of F. Niecks: *Frederick Chopin as a Man and Musician* (London, 1888)]

Der Endreim in der Musik (Leipzig, 1892)

BIBLIOGRAPHY

Review in *MMR*, xvi (1886), 15

Obituary: *Neue Berliner Musikzeitung*, xlvi (1892), 322

A. von Hanstein: *Musiker- und Dichterbriefe* (Berlin, n.d.)

GAYNOR G. JONES

Langhedul. Flemish family of organ builders. Active about 1475 to 1635, they were one of the prominent families in Ieper during that period, and particularly significant in the early development of the French Baroque organ.

Victor (*d* ?1513) was one of the great organ builders at the turn of the 16th century, as can be concluded from the importance of the churches for which he worked (Courtrai, St Omer and Lille). After his death his clients were taken over by Matthijs de Wulf [Matthieu le Leup] (*fl* 1515–22), husband of one of his four daughters.

Michiel the elder, Victor's son, went to England in his youth, probably to allow Matthijs de Wulf to work unhindered; while there he improved and enlarged the organ at Trinity Chapel, Salisbury Cathedral (1530–31). Apparently Michiel returned to Ieper after the early death of his brother-in-law and continued the family business from 1534 to *c*1570. His name is linked with a great number of organs, including many which he built new, though all are within the narrow geographical range of south-west Flanders and surroundings: Ieper, Courtrai (1534, 1546, 1570), Bruges (1535), Veurne (1536, 1557), St Omer (1546), Bergues (1548, 1557), Nieuwpoort (1553, 1557), Dunkirk (1555, 1559), Poperinghe (1569). And as very many village churches in the 16th century had organs, a large number in west Flanders must naturally be ascribed to Michiel. Towards the end of his life he was particularly occupied with the restoring of organs destroyed during the religious troubles of 1566.

Jan (*d* Ghent, 6 Feb 1592), son of Michiel the elder, was active at first in the same area (Courtrai, Ieper), but war, the temporary regime of the Calvinists and economic confusion forced him to move, in 1583 to Lille, and in 1585 to Paris. His Paris organ restorations (St Benoît, the Sainte-Chapelle, Couvent des Augustines, St Eustache) and the new instrument he built in St Jacques-de-la-Boucherie show several important innovations: a balanced *plein jeu*, a progressive Cornet of four, five and six ranks, and a rich complement of reed stops. He received the title 'Organ Builder to the King of France' for his work in the Sainte-Chapelle, part of the royal palace. Jan left Paris sometime after 15 October 1590 and returned to Ieper; his last works are found especially in Ghent and were produced in partnership with Guillames [Guillaume] (*fl* Ghent, 1590–95), probably his son. Jan is buried in the Dominican Church, the only church in Ghent whose organ survived the religious uprisings.

Guillames' methods are especially known from a pair of plans for a new organ in St Baaf Cathedral, Ghent (*c*1590), which he submitted but which were not realized. They closely resemble the instruments constructed by his father in Paris.

Matthijs [Mattheus, Matthieu, Mateo], (*b* Ieper; *d* Brussels, 1635–6), son of Jan, was perhaps the most important organ builder of the family. It is likely that he was with his father during the latter's Paris years; when Jan decided to return to Flanders, Matthijs went to Spain. From 1592 to 1599 he was the organ tuner (*templador*) for the Spanish court. From mid-1599 to mid-1605 he was again in Paris, where his family's reputation brought him immediate work: restoration of organs in St Jean-en-Grève, Saints-Innocents, Hôpital de St Esprit-en-Grève, St Benoît, Chapelle St Leu and St Jacques-de-la-Boucherie, and provision of a new *Rückpositiv* organ and a modernized great organ for St Eustache (1604–5). Matthijs's most important organ was the new one he built for St Gervais (1601–2), which provided the basis for the later instrument of the Couperin family. This organ still contains an amount of important pipework by Matthijs, including some with his signature.

It was Jan and Matthijs, together with CRESPIN CARLIER, who laid the groundwork for the classic French organ of the 17th and 18th centuries. In 1605 Matthijs returned to Ieper, from where he built the organ in Hondschoote (1611), the *Rückpositiv* of which is still preserved. About 1613 he settled in Brussels and became court organ builder to the Archdukes Albertus and Isabella. While there, he built organs in a wide radius including St Omer, Antwerp and Tongeren, as well as one for the Spanish court at Madrid.

Other family members are: Michiel the younger, son of Michiel the elder, resident of Ieper, organ builder and organist, mentioned in 1610 as organist at Hazebrouck; and two other Jans. One was choirmaster of the Church of Our Lady at Antwerp about 1570. Another was city magistrate at Ieper, and though himself a Calvinist was able to save the organs of the main church there (certainly products of his family) from destruction during the Calvinist interregnum of 1578. He was a signatory of the Union of Utrecht (1579); after the restoration of Catholicism in 1584, he fled to England, where he died in Norwich.

BIBLIOGRAPHY

E. Grégoir: *Historique de la facture et des facteurs d'orgues* (Antwerp, 1865)

E. vander Straeten: *La musique aux Pays-Bas avant le XIXe siècle* (Brussels, 1867–88/*R*1969), i, 160f; ii, 9, 309f; viii, 400ff

M. A. Vente: 'Figuren uit Vlaanderens orgelhistorie: het geslacht Langhedul', *De schalmei*, i (1946), July, 2; Sept, 2

B. de Keyzer: 'Charles Blanquaert en Guillames Langhedul in de St. Baafs-kathedraal te Gent', *De schalmei*, iii (1948), 2

A. Deschrevel: 'Het orgel in de St. Maartenskathedraal te Ieper', *De schalmei*, iii (1948), 68

M. A. Vente: *Proeve van een repertorium van de archivalia betrekking hebbende op het Nederlandse orgel en zijn makers tot omstreeks 1630* (Brussels, 1956)

N. Dufourcq: 'Recent Researches into French Organ-building from the Fifteenth to the Seventeenth Century', *GSJ*, x (1957), 66

A. Deschrevel: 'Historische terugblik op het orgel in West-Vlaanderen, Ieper, international centrum van orgelbouw en orgelcultuur', *West-Vlaanderen*, xi (1962), 23

M. Vanmackelberg: *Les orgues d'Arras* (Arras, 1963), 20

G. Moortgat: *Oude orgels in Vlaanderen*, ii (1965), 11f

M. Jurgens: *Documents du minutier central concernant l'histoire de la musique, 1600–1650* (Paris, 1967), 787ff

N. Dufourcq and J. Krug-Basse: 'A propos de l'orgue dit "Des Couperin"', *Mélanges François Couperin* (Paris, 1968), 72

F. Douglas: *The Language of the Classical French Organ* (New Haven and London, 1969), 60f

N. Dufourcq: *Les sources*, i: *Le livre de l'orgue francais 1589–1789* (Paris, 1969)

P. Hardouin: 'A propos de l'orgue dit des Couperin', *Renaissance de l'orgue* (1969), no.4, p.27

——: 'Facteurs d'orgues flamands en France sous Henri IV', *Renaissance de l'orgue* (1970), no.8, p.8; *Connaissance de l'orgue* (1973), no.4, p.18

MAARTEN ALBERT VENTE

Langhveldt, Joris van. *See* MACROPEDIUS, GEORGIUS.

Langius, Hieronymus Gregorius. *See* LANGE, GREGOR.

Langlais, Jean (*b* La Fontenelle, 15 Feb 1907). French organist and composer. At the Institution des Jeunes Aveugles, Paris, he studied the piano with Blazy, harmony with Mahaut and the organ with Marchal, who prepared him for Dupré's class at the Conservatoire, where he won a *premier prix* in 1930. His composition teacher was Dukas, for whom he nurtured great admiration and of whom he was, with Messiaen, one of the last pupils. His lessons with Tournemire at this period were decisive. In 1932 he won a *premier prix* for composition, took the first prize of the Amis de l'Orgue for interpretation and improvisation, and was appointed organist of St Pierre de Montrouge. He also joined the staff of the Institution des Jeunes Aveugles, teaching composition and organ and conducting the choir in music by Palestrina, Bach and Josquin. In 1945 he followed Franck and Tournemire as organist of Ste Clotilde. He made his first visit to the USA in 1952, and has repeatedly returned for concerts and teaching: many of his works have been written for Americans. Langlais' organ music follows the tradition of Tournemire. A quarter of his work is based on Gregorian themes, treated with great inventiveness and enhanced by rich polymodal harmonies. Almost all of his music is intended as an expression of his religious faith, although he has written important secular works. The Mass 'Salve regina' was first sung at Notre Dame, Paris, at Christmas 1954 and the Solemn Mass 'Orbis factor' received its first performance in Washington (DC) in 1969.

WORKS
(selective list)

Org: 3 poèmes évangéliques, 1932; 3 paraphrases grégoriennes, 1934; 24 pieces, 1933–9; Sym. no.1, 1942; 9 pieces, 1943; Suite brève, 1947; Suite médiévale, 1947; Suite française, 1948; Incantation, 1949; 4 postludes, 1950; Hommage à Frescobaldi, 1951; Suite folklorique, 1952; 8 pièces modales, 1956; Organ Book, 1956; Triptyque, 1957; 3 characteristic pieces, 1957; Office pour la Sainte Famille, 1957; Office pour la Sainte Trinité, 1958; American Suite, 1959; 3 méditations, 1962; 12 petites pièces, 1962; Essai, 1962; Homage to Jean-Philippe Rameau, 1963; Livre oecuménique, 1968; 3 voluntaries, 1969; 3 implorations, 1970; 5 chorales, 1971; Offrande à Marie, 1972; Supplication, 1972; Suite baroque, 1973; 5 méditations sur l'apocalypse, 1974; 8 chants de Bretagne, 1975; 3 esquisses romanes, 1976; Mosaïque, 1977; Sym. no.2, 1977; 3 esquisses gothiques, 1977; Progression, 5 pièces, 1979

With org: Qt, org, str trio, 1936; 3 concs., 1949, 1961, 1971; 7 chorales, tpt/ob/fl, org/pf, 1973; 73 pièces, tpt/ob/fl, org/pf, 1973

Vocal: Messe solennelle, 1951; Missa in simplicitate, chorus, org, 1953; Mass 'Salve regina', 3 solo vv, unison chorus, 2 org, 8 brass, 1954; 3 psalms, 4 solo vv, chorus, org, brass, timp, 1965; Canticle of the Sun, S, Mez, org, 1968; Solemn Mass 'Orbis factor', SATB, org, 1969; Festival Alleluia, SATB, org, 1971; 3 oraisons, 1 solo v/unison chorus, org, fl/vn, 1974

Inst: Sonatine, tpt, pf, 1978

Principal publishers: Bornemann, Costallat, Durand, Elkan-Vogel, Philippo

BIBLIOGRAPHY

P. Giraud: 'Le thème grégorien dans les oeuvres pour orgue de Jean Langlais', *Orgue* (1967), nos.122–3, p.220

R. T. Nyquist: *The Use of Gregorian Chant in the Organ Music of Jean Langlais* (diss., Indiana U., 1968)

J. Langlais: 'Quelques souvenirs d'un organiste d'église', *Orgue* (1971), no.137, p.4

XAVIER DARASSE

Langlé, Honoré (François Marie) (*b* Monaco, 1741; *d* Villiers-le-Bel, nr. Paris, 20 Sept 1807). French composer, singing teacher and theorist. A scholarship from Prince Honoré III of Monaco paid for his musical education at the Conservatorio della Pietà dei Turchini in Naples from 1756 to 1764. After managing the theatre and the noblemen's concerts in Genoa from 1764 to 1768, he made a career as a teacher and composer in Paris where his first works were performed at the Concert Spirituel. Drawn by the theatre, he wrote several stage works, but only two of them were performed: *Antiochus et Stratonice* and *Corisandre*. He was appointed professor of singing at the Ecole Royale de Chant et de Déclamation at its founding in 1784 and kept his appointment through its reorganization in 1791 and again in 1795, when it became the Conservatoire. From about 1797 he also served as librarian there until his retirement to Villiers-le-Bel in 1802. During the early years of the Revolution he was an *éditeur-musicien* in the Parisian National Guard.

Langlé's compositions were far less successful than his theoretical and didactic works, through which he is largely remembered today. He had a receptive mind and wide knowledge which led him to be nicknamed 'the Fontenelle of music'.

WORKS

STAGE

Antiochus et Stratonice (opera), Versailles, 1786; score, *F-Pn*

Corisandre, ou Les fous par enchantement (comédie-opéra, de Linières, A. F. Lebailly, after Voltaire: Pucelle), Paris, Opéra, 8 March 1791; score (Paris, 1791), *Po*

Other dramatic works, unperf., scores in *Pn*: Oreste et Tyndare, 1783; Soliman et Eromine, 1792, also known as Mahomet II; L'auberge des volontaires, 1793; Le choix d'Alcide, 1800; Médée; Tancrède; Les vengeances

OTHER WORKS

[6] Symphonies militaires, wind insts, op.1 (Paris, 1776)

Motets, 1774–6: Dies irae, De profundis, Pater noster, Cantate Domino, Te Deum

La mort de Lavoisier (hiérodrame, C. Desaudroy), Paris, Lycée des Arts, 1794; score, *Pn*

Déclaration des droits de l'homme et du citoyen (Mentelle), 1v, b (Paris, 1794)

Romance sur la liberté des hommes de couleur (d'Auguste), 1v, bc, in Musique à l'usage des fêtes nationales, ii (Paris, 1794)

Hymne à Bara et Viala, 1v, bc, in Musique à l'usage des fêtes nationales (Paris, c1795); ed. in Pierre (1899)

Hymne à la liberté (Desorgues), !v, b, in Musique à l'usage des fêtes nationales (Paris, 1795), ed. in Pierre (1899)

Hymne à l'éternel (Lebrun), 1v, ww insts, in Recueil des époques (Paris, c1798); ed. in Pierre (1899)

6 duos en canon (Metastasio), 2vv (Paris, n.d.)

6 noturni op. petits duos italiens, 2vv, hp/pf ad lib (Paris, n.d.)

6 romances in Journal anacréontique (Paris, n.d.); other pieces in contemporary anthologies

Romance d'Alix et d'Alexis, Monologue de Sapho, other scenes and airs, *F-Pn*

THEORETICAL AND PEDAGOGICAL WORKS

Traité d'harmonie et de modulation (Paris, 1795, 2/1797)

Traité de la basse sous le chant précédé de toutes les règles de la composition (Paris, c1798)

Annotations to T. de Iriarte: *La musique* (Fr. trans., Paris, 1799)

with others: *Principes élémentaires de musique* (Paris, c1800)

——: *Solfèges pour servir à l'étude dans le Conservatoire* (Paris, 1801)

Nouvelle méthode pour chiffrer les accords (Paris, 1801)

ed.: B. Mengozzi: *Méthode de chant du Conservatoire* (Paris, 1804, 2/c1815)

Traité de la fugue (Paris, 1805)

BIBLIOGRAPHY

EitnerQ; *FétisB*; *GerberL* ('Angle'); *GerberNL*

F. Fayolle: *Eloge de Langlé* (Paris, 1808)

A. Adam: *Souvenirs d'un musicien* (Paris, 1857)

C. Pierre: *Musique des fêtes et cérémonies de la Révolution française* (Paris, 1899)

M. Brenet: *Les concerts en France sous l'ancien régime* (Paris, 1900)

C. Pierre: *Le Conservatoire nationale de musique* (Paris, 1900)

——: *Les hymnes et chansons de la Révolution* (Paris, 1904)

L. Canis: 'Honoré-François-Marie-Langlé, compositeur monégasque', *Le petit monégasque* (5 Aug 1923), 1

R. Valette: 'A propos d'Honoré Langlé', *Le petit monégasque* (12 Aug 1923), 1

J. Tiersot: *Lettres de musiciens*, i (Turin, 1924)

L. de Castro: 'Notice sur le musicien Honoré Langlé', *Annales du Comté de Nice*, iv/17, 3ème trimestre (1935), 89

G. Favre: *Histoire musicale de la principauté de Monaco* (Paris, 1974)

PAULE DRUILHE

Langreder, Martin (*b* Hildesheim; *d* Suben am Inn, Upper Austria, before 1602). German writer of contrafacta. He was a canon regular at the Augustinian canonry at Suben. He is known by a five-voice occasional motet, published in Passau in 1602, and by seven six-part *Magnificat* settings, all of them contrafacta, published by MICHAEL HERRER in his *Canticum gloriosae deiparae Virginis Mariae ... super varia (ut vocant) madrigalia* (Passau, 1602). Herrer explained that he had taken them from the 'vast treasure' of contrafacta that Langreder had left behind at his sudden death. He listed the titles but not the composers of the models: *Mentr'io compai contento, Leggiadrissima, Voi ch'ascoltate, Nel più fiorito aprile, Un pastor, Tiridola, non dormire* and *Exaudiat te Dominus*.

HORST LEUCHTMANN

Langridge, Philip (Gordon) (*b* Hawkhurst, Kent, 16 Dec 1939). English tenor. From 1958 he studied the violin at the RAM, playing professionally for a short period until 1964; in 1962 he began singing lessons with Bruce Boyce, continuing later with Celia Bizony. One of the most versatile of younger British singers, he has a large concert repertory that extends from Monteverdi, through Rameau (appearances in concert performances of the *tragédies lyriques*) and the 18th- and 19th-century oratorios, to first performances of works by Bennett, Goehr, Holliger, Lutyens and Milner, to all of which he brings meticulous musicianship, clear diction and an attractively astringent timbre. His opera roles include Handel's Scipio and Lurcanio (*Ariodante*) for the Handel Opera Society, Idomeneus and Rossini's Almaviva, and, in June 1976, the creation of the leading role in Thomas Wilson's *Confessions of a Justified Sinner*, for Scottish Opera.

MAX LOPPERT

Langsam (Ger.: 'slow'). A tempo mark, the German equivalent of *adagio*, *lento* or *largo*; it was used as early as the 17th century by Schütz in his madrigal *Itzt blicken durch des Himmels Saal*. Wagner's *Tristan* opens with the direction *langsam und schmachtend*.

Langsflöte (Ger.). RECORDER.

Langspil. An Icelandic bowed zither. *See* ICELAND, §II, 1 and fig.2.

Langue des durées. French method of teaching rhythmic notation to beginners. It was introduced by Aimé Paris (1798–1866) as part of the GALIN-PARIS-CHEVÉ METHOD of teaching sight-singing. The method gives to notes and groups of notes names which, when spoken aloud, reproduce the rhythmic effects concerned (see illustration). The system was later adapted for English

Table illustrating the 'langue des durées' introduced by Aimé Paris as part of the Galin–Paris–Chevé method of teaching sight-singing, from 'Méthode élémentaire de musique vocal' (1844) by Emile Chevé; the tailless dot implies an extension of the value of the preceding note

use by John Curwen (1811–80) and incorporated into the tonic sol-fa method under the name of 'French time names'.

BERNARR RAINBOW

Langveld, Joris van. *See* MACROPEDIUS, GEORGIUS.

Langwill, Lyndesay G(raham) (*b* Portobello, Midlothian, 19 March 1897). Scottish organologist. He studied at the University of Edinburgh and from 1922 was in private practice as a chartered accountant in Edinburgh. His lifelong interest in music centred first on the cello, which he began to play when he was 14, and then on the bassoon, which he took up in 1931 and of which he wrote a standard history. He has also studied waits and barrel organs. His main contribution to organology has been a pioneering index of wind instrument makers, a standard work of reference in which the holdings of all known collections and all known related literature appear under the makers' names. His other publications include contributions to *Grove 5* and to various musical journals. He was a founder member of the Galpin Society and its treasurer until 1968. He was awarded the OBE (1968) and an honorary MA by the University of Edinburgh (1964).

WRITINGS

'Notes on Three Bassoons in the National Museum of Antiquities of Scotland', *Proceedings of the Society of Antiquities of Scotland*, lxvii (1932–3), 335

'Alto-fagotto, Misnamed Tenoroon: its Original, the Caledonica and their Inventor', *Musical Progress and Mail*, iv (1934), 165

'The Curtal, 1550–1750: a Chapter in the Evolution of the Bassoon', *MT*, lxxviii (1937), 305

'The Bassoon', *PMA*, lxvi (1939–40), 1

'The Waits', *HMYB*, vii (1952), 170

Index of Wind Instrument Makers (Edinburgh, 1960, rev., enlarged 4/1977)

The Bassoon and Contrabassoon (London, 1965)

with N. Boston: *Church and Chamber Barrel-organs* (Edinburgh, 1967, enlarged 2/1970)

'Barrel Organ', *Grove 6*

WILLIAM WATERHOUSE

Lanier [Laniere, Laneare, Laneer, Lanyer, Lenear etc].
English family of musicians of French descent. John (i)
(*d* 29 Nov 1572) and Nicholas (i) (*d* 1612) came
originally from Rouen but settled in London in 1561,
becoming musicians to Queen Elizabeth. Nicholas was
the father of at least 11 children: John (ii) (*d* 1616),
Alfonso (*d* 1613), Andrea (*d* 1660), Clement (*d* 1661),
Innocent (*d* 1625) and Jerome (*d* 1657), all of whom
were wind players in the royal band, and five daughters,
two at least of whom were married to musicians –
Katherine to Daniel Farrant and Ellen to Alfonso
Ferrabosco (ii). Of this generation John (ii) had seven
children who survived to maturity, including (1) John
Lanier (iii) and (2) Nicholas Lanier (ii). Clement had
nine children and Jerome 11, one of whom, William
(1618–*c*1660), served in the royal music. Andrea had
eight children; a son, Thomas (1633–*c*1686), was in the
royal band, as was Henry (*d* 1633), the son of Alfonso.
(For further details see *Grove 5*, suppl.)

(1) John Lanier (iii) (*d* London, 1650). English tenor
and composer, son of John (ii) and brother of (2)
Nicholas Lanier (ii). He served as musician for the lutes
and voices in the King's Musick from 1625 to 1642. He
sang the part of Irene in Shirley's *Triumph of Peace*
(1634) and is mentioned in Richard Lovelace's *Lucasta*
(1649) as having set some of the songs. But neither these
nor any others appear to have survived.

(2) Nicholas Lanier (ii) (*b* London, baptized 10 Sept
1588; *d* London, buried 24 Feb 1666). English composer, singer, lutenist and artist, son of John (ii) and
brother of (1) John Lanier (iii). As a child he was no
doubt surrounded by music in his family, but he was
indentured to the Earl of Salisbury for a period up to
1607 and his name occurs in the Cecil family and estate
papers at Hatfield House as a recipient of various payments between 1605 and 1613. He may even have gone
to Italy in 1610 to join the earl's son, William Cecil, who
wrote to his father asking for Lanier to be sent 'into
Italy with me by reason of a desire to learn the viol
while I am there'. Such protection and patronage must
have been valuable to him at the start of his career.
Although he was not appointed to the King's Musick as
a lutenist until 1616 he had already made his mark at
court, for in 1613 he composed and sang the song
'Bring away this sacred tree' in Campion's masque for
the marriage of Robert Carr, Earl of Somerset, and
Lady Frances Howard.

Lanier composed the music for Ben Jonson's masque
Lovers Made Men (1617) and in doing so was described
by Jonson in the printed text of 1640 as introducing
'stylo recitativo' into England; in the absence of the
music this claim must be accepted guardedly. Not only
did Lanier sing in the masque, he also designed the
scenery. He wrote music for three further masques by
Jonson: *The Vision of Delight* (1617), *The Gypsies
Metamorphosed* (1621) with Robert Johnson, and *The
Masque of Augurs* (1622) with Alfonso Ferrabosco (ii).
He was appointed Master of the Musick to Prince
Charles in 1618 at a salary of £200 a year, and
when Charles acceded Lanier became, in effect, Master
of the King's Musick. The office may therefore be
said to date from 1625 although not officially established. Early in the new reign, his knowledge of
the art of painting had been turned to account, when
Charles I and the Duke of Buckingham sent him to Italy
to buy pictures. He seems to have made three visits

*Nicholas Lanier: portrait by Anthony van Dyck (1599–
1641) in the Kunsthistorisches Museum, Vienna*

between 1625 and 1628, arranging, with the help of
Daniel Nys in Venice, for the purchase of the Duke of
Mantua's collection of pictures at a cost of more than
£25,000. Some of these pictures are still in the royal
collection at Hampton Court, but the rest were
dispersed during the Commonwealth period and are
now at the National Gallery (London), the Louvre, the
Prado, the Uffizi etc; about half are probably still identifiable (a list is given by Spink in *ML*). In addition he
bought many master drawings; dozens survive bearing
his mark (a small star), 34 of them at Windsor Castle,
although many have disappeared.

On 6 February 1629 Lanier was arrested with his
brother John and uncles Andrea, Clement and Jerome
for disorderly behaviour in the street; the affair caused
quite a stir, and an angry exchange of letters between the
City and the court ensued. In 1630 he set to music
Herrick's poem on the birth of Prince Charles. In 1646
he was in the Low Countries – 'old, unhappye in a
manner in exile, plundered not only of his fortune, but of
all his musicall papers, nay, almost of his witts and
vertue', as he described himself in a letter to Constantijn
Huygens. He was also in France at one stage, for
William Sanderson in *Graphice* (1658) said: '*Laniere* in
Paris, by a cunning way of tempering his colours with
Chimney Soote, the painting becomes duskish, and
seems ancient; which done, he roules up and thereby it
crackls, and so mistaken for an old Principall, it being
well copied from a good hand'. In 1656 Lanier pub-
lished a book of etchings from drawings by
Parmigianino, *Prove prime fatti a l'aqua forte da N:
Lanier a l'età sua giovanile di sessanta otto Anni 1656.*
A similar set from drawings by Parmigianino and
Giulio Romano is entitled *Maschere delineato di Julio
Romano ex Collne NLanier* (n.d.). Several portraits
(including sketches) of him are known, among them Van
Dyck's (reproduced here) in the Kunsthistorisches

Museum, Vienna, possibly painted at Genoa and said to have been what prompted Charles I to invite Van Dyck to England (where he stayed with Lanier's brother-in-law Edward Norgate).

Although it is apparent that much of his output has not survived – indeed he implied as much in the letter cited above – Lanier was one of the most important English songwriters of his time, particularly as an innovator. 'Bring away this sacred tree' (1613) is one of the earliest declamatory ayres, a type that Henry and William Lawes, John Wilson, Charles Coleman and Lanier himself developed between 1620 and 1660. The accompaniment is chordal, anticipating a true continuo style, although the bass is not figured. The effect is of a heroic kind of declamation, almost completely unmelodic though strongly tonal and in harmony with the sumptuous Baroque qualities of Inigo Jones's scenery, and other features of the Jacobean masque. On his return from Italy Lanier composed his long recitative *Hero and Leander* ('Nor com'st thou yet'), which is very different in style from his declamatory ayres and closer to true recitative; it was surely inspired by Italian laments. The various moods of Hero's soliloquy – her agonies and near-delirium as she awaits Leander and her final grief at his death – are expressed with amazing force. Another Italian form that Lanier may have imported was the strophically varied aria over a repeated bass: he set Carew's *No more shall meades be decked with flowers* in this way.

WORKS
Edition: *English Songs 1625–1660*, ed. I. Spink, MB, xxxiii (1971) [S]
      Nicholas Lanier: Six Songs, ed. E. Huws Jones (London, 1976) [H]

STAGE
(surviving songs listed below)

Maske . . . at the Marriage of . . . the Earle of Somerset (T. Campion), London, 1613; collab. G. Coprario
Lovers Made Men (B. Jonson), London, 1617, inc.; see Sabol (1963)
The Vision of Delight (Jonson), London, 1617
The Gypsies Metamorphosed (Jonson), London, 1621; collab. R. Johnson (ii)
The Masque of Augurs (Jonson), London, 1622; The Beares Dance, *GB-Lbm* Add.10444; collab. A. Ferrabosco (ii)

VOCAL
Bring away this sacred tree (Campion), S [same music as Weep no more]
Colin say why sit'st thou so, *GB-Eu* Dc.1.69, *Lbm* Add.11608, 29396, *Ob* d.238, *US-NYp* Drexel 4041
Come, thou glorious object of my sight (Killigrew), H
Do not expect to hear of all thy good (Jonson), *GB-Lbm* Add.11608
Fire, lo here I burn (Campion), S
I prithee keep my sheep for me (Yong), 1652[8]
I was not wearier when I lay (Jonson), *Lbm* Eg.2013
I wish no more thou should'st love me, 1652[8]
In guilty night, *Lbm* Add.22100 [authorship questionable; probably by Robert Ramsay]
Like hermit poor (?Raleigh), S, H
Love and I of late did part, S
Mark how the blushful morn (Carew), S, H
Neither sighs, nor tears, nor mourning, S
No, I tell thee, no, 1669[5]
No more shall meads (Carew), S
Nor com'st thou yet (Hero and Leander), S
Of thee, kind boy, I ask no red and white (Suckling), *US-NYp* Drexel 4257, 4041
Shepherd, in faith, I cannot stay, 1652[8]
Silly heart, forbear, S
Stay, silly heart, and do not break, S
Sweet, do not thus destroy me, *GB-Och* 17
Tell me shepherd, dost thou love, S
Thou art not fair for all thy red and white (Campion), 1652[8], H
Though I am young (Jonson), 1652[8], H
Weep no more my wearied eyes, S [same music as Bring away]
White though ye be (Herrick), 1669[5]
Young and simple though I am (Campion), 1652[8], H

Amorosa pargoletta, *Och* 17
Miser pastorella, *Och* 17
Qual musico gentil, *Lbm* Add.11608

O amantissime Domine, motet, 1v, *Ob* Mus.Sch.C.11

INSTRUMENTAL
2 symphonia, a 3, *Och* Mus.379–81
Almand and sarabande, cornetts, *Cfm* 734

BIBLIOGRAPHY
L. Cust: 'The Lanier Family', *Miscellanea genealogica et heraldica*, 5th ser., vi (1926–8), 375
A. Sabol, ed.: *Songs and Dances for the Stuart Masque* (Providence, Rhode Island, 1959, rev. and enlarged 2/1978)
I. Spink: 'Lanier in Italy', *ML*, xl (1959), 242
——: 'English Cavalier Songs', *PRMA*, lxxxvi (1959–60), 61
McD. Emslie: 'Nicholas Lanier's Innovations in English Song', *ML*, xli (1960), 13
A. J. Sabol: Introduction to *A Score for 'Lovers Made Men': a Masque by Ben Jonson* (Providence, Rhode Island, 1963)
V. Duckles: 'English Song and the Challenge of Italian Monody', in V. Duckles and F. B. Zimmerman: *Words to Music* (Los Angeles, 1967), 3–42
F. L. Graham: *The Earlier Life and Work of Nicholas Lanier . . . Collector of Paintings and Drawings* (diss., Columbia U., 1967)
R. Charteris: 'Jacobean Musicians at Hatfield House, 1605–1613', *RMARC*, xii (1974), 115
I. Spink: *English Song: Dowland to Purcell* (London, 1974), 45ff, 100ff
For bibliography relating to the activities in painting of (2) Nicholas Lanier (ii), see *Grove 5*, suppl.

IAN SPINK

Lanier, Sidney (Clopton) (*b* Macon, Georgia, 3 Feb 1842; *d* Lynn, North Carolina, 7 Sept 1881). American poet, theorist, flautist and composer. He was descended from the Laniers active as musicians at the English court in the 16th and 17th centuries. He graduated from Oglethorpe University in 1860, served in the Confederate Army during the Civil War and then spent several years in various business ventures; torn between music and poetry throughout his life, from 1873 he devoted his time entirely to literary and musical pursuits. As a writer he is best known for his sensitive poetry, some of which has been set to music by G. W. Chadwick, H. K. Hadley and others, but he also produced numerous books and scholarly essays, a translation of *Das Rheingold*, a libretto for D. Buck's *The Centennial Meditation of Columbia* (1876), and gave lectures. He was a highly respected flautist, being first flautist with the Peabody Orchestra, Baltimore, and he arranged music and wrote several idiomatic pieces (most are still in manuscript) for the instrument. Much of his work dealt with a systematic study of the relation between poetry and music: he developed a technique of describing poetic metre through musical notation and compared the phonetic structure of poetry with the timbre of music. His principal publications on the subject were *The Science of English Verse*, an important study of English prosody, *The English Novel* and *Music and Poetry*.

WORKS
(most MSS unlocated)

Sacred Memories, perf. 1868; Field Larks & Blackbirds, 1873; Swamp Robin, 1873; Longing, 1874; Wind-Song, 1874, MS facs. in Starke (1933), 184: all for fl unacc.
Danse des Moucherons, op.1, fl, pf, 1873, *US-BAu*
The Song of Love and Death (Tennyson), 1862; Little Ella (Lanier) (Montgomery, Alabama, 1866); Love that Hath us in the Net (Tennyson) (New Orleans, 1884); My Life is like a Summer Rose (H. Wilde), lost: all 1v, pf
Arrangements: Labitzsky: Huldigung der britischen Nation, 3 fl, *c*1862, MS facs. in Mims (1905), 134; Fürstenau: Nocturne, 3 fl, *c*1862, MS facs. in Starke (1933), 44; Verdi: Il balen, fl, pf (New York, 1888)
Projected works: Choral Symphony; Symphony of Life; Symphony of the Plantation

WRITINGS
The Science of English Verse (New York, 1880)
The English Novel (New York, 1883)
Music and Poetry (New York, 1899)
ed. C. R. Anderson: *The Centennial Edition of the Works of Sidney Lanier* (Baltimore, 1945)
Reviews for Baltimore newspapers (1876–81)

BIBLIOGRAPHY
E. Mims: *Sidney Lanier* (Boston, Mass., 1905)
T. E. Dewey: *Poetry in Song* (Kansas City, 1907)
E. Mims: 'Lanier, Sidney', *DAB*
A. H. Starke: *Sidney Lanier* (Chapel Hill, 1933)
——: 'Sidney Lanier as a Musician', *MQ*, xx (1934), 384
G. Chase: *America's Music* (New York, 1955, rev. 2/1966), 341ff
J. W. Hendren: *Time and Stress in English Verse* (Houston, 1959)
DOUGLAS A. LEE

Lankveld, Joris van. *See* MACROPEDIUS, GEORGIUS.

Lanner, Joseph (Franz Karl) (*b* Vienna, 12 April 1801; *d* Oberdöbling, nr. Vienna, 14 April 1843). Austrian dance composer and violinist. The son of a glove maker and virtually self-taught, he became a violinist at the age of 12 in the dance orchestra of Michael Pamer in which Johann Strauss (i) was a young violist. Pamer (1782–1827) was also well known as a composer of ländler and waltzes and thus was one of the immediate forerunners of Lanner and Strauss. In 1818 Lanner left Pamer and with the two brothers Drahanek formed a trio consisting of two violins and a guitar that in the next year was augmented by Strauss as the violist and in 1820 by a cello. It was Lanner's quintet which Schubert must often have heard on his visits to the Café Rebhuhn in the inner city. In 1824 Lanner enlarged his ensemble into a string band and then into a full orchestra of Classical size which played in city taverns, coffee-houses and in the Prater, Vienna's great amusement park, where the orchestra is said to have given the city's first open-air concerts. His popularity and consequent demand were so great that Lanner was forced to divide his orchestra, making Strauss conductor of the other half. Quarrels of a professional nature – Strauss accused Lanner of introducing some of his own compositions under Lanner's name – led to a separation commemorated by Lanner in his amusingly programmatic *Trennungs-Walzer* op.19. Vienna had now two renowned dance bands, each with its own enthusiasts and partisans; Lanner and Strauss were the idols of their public and, in Hanslick's opinion, other nations might well have envied Austria two such brilliant musicians who intoxicated Vienna with their insinuating and irresistible music in 3/4 time. But Hanslick could not refrain from adding that this dance music, together with the prevalence of Italian opera and the cult of the virtuoso, made the Vienna audiences increasingly unfit for loftier and more intellectual musical fare. Unlike Strauss, Lanner hardly ever travelled outside the Austrian empire but confined his tours to provincial capitals (Budapest, Graz and Pressburg) and to the coronation of Ferdinand II in Milan. He died of typhus at the height of his career.

Together with the elder Strauss, Lanner laid the foundations of the classical Viennese waltz. Taking Weber's *Aufforderung zum Tanze* as his principal model, Lanner reduced the considerable number of waltzes still found in Schubert to an average of five, prefaced the set with a slow introduction often having a programmatic character and concluded it with a coda usually made up of reminiscences of the previous waltzes. Lanner's early waltzes were still ländler-like in essence (slow of gait, with every beat of the 3/4 bar emphasized and yodelling figures in the melody) and in name (his first set of published dances bore the title *Neue Wiener Ländler*) whereas Strauss's op.1 was already called *Täuberlwalzer*. In his later dances he also cultivated the more rustic variety, as for instance in *Die Zauberhornländler* op.31 and the *Steyrische Tänze* op.165. From these

dances a direct line of evolution runs to the *G'schichten aus dem Wienerwald* by the younger Johann Strauss and *Dorfschwalben aus Osterreich* by his brother Josef.

Lanner's special gift was a coaxing, almost Schubertian lyricism, while Strauss's strength was his fiery rhythmic invention. The Viennese expressed this difference by saying: 'With Lanner it's "Pray, dance! I beg you;" with Strauss, "You must dance, I command you!" '. A remarkable sweep and shapeliness of line matched by a sense of Romantic harmonic colour in which his rival Strauss was comparatively rather deficient characterize Lanner's masterly late waltzes such as *Die Pesther* op.93, *Die Schwimmer* op.99, *Die Werber* op.103, *Die Romantiker* op.167 and *Die Schönbrunner* op.200. Sometimes Lanner would introduce a Hungarian flavour, as in *Die Pesther* and *Die Werber*; on other occasions he turned tunes from popular operas into waltzes, a custom dating at least as far back as Mozart's *Figaro*, as in *Die Mozartisten* op.196, based on themes from *Don Giovanni* and *Die Zauberflöte*. Many waltz melodies of Lanner and Strauss have a violinistic character because both were excellent fiddlers who alternated in their performances between conducting with the bow and joining the orchestra on their instrument; this procedure has become a tradition in concerts of Viennese light music.

Of Lanner's three children, August (*b* Vienna, 1834; *d* Vienna, 1855) followed in his father's footsteps as a conductor and dance composer, but died of tuberculosis at the age of 21. His daughter Katti (Katharina) (*b* Vienna, 1829; *d* Vienna, 1904) became a celebrated ballet dancer and was called the 'Taglioni of the North'. She made her début at the Vienna Hofoper in 1845 and appeared in many theatres outside the Austrian empire including the Drury Lane Empire and Crystal Palace in London.

WORKS

All works were published in Vienna for solo piano; most works also appeared simultaneously in arrangements for orchestra, piano 4 hands, violin and piano, 3 violins and double bass and for solo flute; principal MS sources are A-Wgm, Wn and Wst.

Editions: J. Lanner: Werke: neue Gesamtausgabe, ed. E. Kremser (Leipzig, 1889–91/R1973), solo pf [K]
J. Lanner: Ländler und Walzer, ed. A. Orel, DTÖ, lxv, Jg.xxxiii/2 (1926), orch [O]

WALTZES

Aufforderung zum Tanze, op.7 (?1826), K i; Terpsichore-Walzer, op.12 (?1827), K i, O; Trennungs-Walzer, op.19 (?1828), K i; Katharinen-Tänze, op.26 (?1829), K i, O; Fortsetzung der Catharinen-Tänze, op.41 (?1830), K i; Annen-Einladungs-Walzer, op.48 (?1830), K i; Die Ein-und-Dreissiger, op.55 (1831), K i; Die Badner Ring'In, op.64 (?1883), K i, O; Lock-Walzer, op.80 (1883), K i; Die Abenteurer, op.91 (1834), K ii; Die Humoristiker, op.92 (1834), K ii; Pesther-Walzer, op.93 (1834), K ii, O; Dampf-Walzer, op.94 (1835), K ii; Abschied von Pesth, Monument-Walzer, op.95 (1835), K ii

Die Schwimmer, op.99 (1835), K ii; Walzer, Anna Maria Carolina, Kaiserin von Österreich (etc) gewidmet, op.101 (1835), K ii; Die Werber, op.103 (1835), K ii, O; Amors Flügel, op.120 (1837), K iii; Prometheus-Funken, Grätzer Soirée-Walzer, op.123 (1837), K iii; Die Aelpler, op.124 (1837), K iii; Die Kosenden, op.128 (1838), K iii; Walzer-Fluth, oder 20 Jahre in 20 Minuten, Grosses Walzer-Potpourri, op.129 (1838), K iii; Die Flotten, op.140 (1839), K iii; Marien-Walzer, op.143 (1839), K iii

Liebesträume, Brünner Walzer, op.150 (1839), K iv; Die Pressburger Comité-Ball-Tänze, op.155 (1840), K iv; Hoffnungs-Strahlen, op.158 (1840), K iv; Nacht-Violen, op.160 (1840), K iv; Hofball-Tänze, op.161 (1840), K iv; Die Romantiker, op.167 (1841), K iv, O; Kammerball-Tänze, op.177 (1841), K iv; Abendsterne, op.180 (1841), K iv; Ideale: Künstler-Ball-Tänze, op.192 (1842), K iv; Die Vorstädtler, op.195 (1842), K v; Die Mozartisten, op.196 (1842), K v; Die Schönbrunner, op.200 (1842), K v, O; 77 other waltz sets

OTHER WORKS

28 galops, incl. Sommernachtstraum-Galoppe, op.90 (1834), K vii; Panorama der beliebtesten Galoppe: 1 Italienische Galoppe, 2

Spanische Galoppe, 3 Ungarische Galoppe, 4 Englisch Galoppe, op.97 (1835); Panorama der beliebtesten Galoppe, no.2: a Der Zapfenstreich, K vii, b Galoppe nach Beatrice di Tenda, op.108 (?1836); 3. Panorama der beliebtesten Galoppe: Gartenfest-, Huguenotten-, Champagner-Knall-Galoppe, op.114 (?1836); 4. Panorama der beliebtesten Galoppe: 3 Galoppe nach [Adam's] Postillon von Lonjumeau, op.122 (1837)

25 ländler, incl. Neue Wiener Ländler mit Coda, op.1 (1825); Dornbacher Ländler, op.9 (?1826), K vi, O; Zauberhorn-Ländler, op.31 (1829), K vi/14; Steyrische Tänze, op.165 (1841), K vi, O

8 mazurkas, incl. Der Uhlane (Le Lancier), op.76 (1833), K vi; Sehnsuchts-Mazur, op.89 (1834), K vi

6 marches, incl. 3 Märsche des 2. Wiener Bürgerregimentes [i], op.130 (1838), K viii; 3 Märsche des 2. Wiener Bürger Regimentes, ii, op.157 (1840), K viii

Miscellaneous dances, incl. 10 Quadrilles; 3 Polkas; Bolero, op.209 (1845), K viii [last work]

Ov. to fairy tale Der Preis einer Lebenstunde, op.106 (1835), K viii

BIBLIOGRAPHY

H. Sachs: *Josef Lanner* (Vienna, 1889)

F. Rebay and O. Keller: *Josef Lanner* (Vienna, 1901)

F. Lange: *Josef Lanner und Johann Strauss* (Vienna, 1904, 2/1919)

M. Carner: *The Waltz* (London, 1948)

A. Weinmann: *Verzeichnis der im Druck erschienen Werke von Joseph Lanner* (Vienna, 1948)

MOSCO CARNER

Lannis, Johannes de. *See* HILLANIS, JOHANNES.

Lantins, de. Several composers and musicians of the early 15th century bearing this name may well have been related. All are thought to have come from the diocese of Liège.

(1) Berthold de Lantins alias de Bolsée. Cantor at the church of St Jean, Liège, from 1379 to 1413.

(2) Ray. de Lan(tins). Composer of *Ut queant laxis* (two voices with fauxbourdon) in *D-Mbs* Mus.Ms.3224. The manuscript otherwise contains works of Dunstable, Dufay, Christopherus de Feltro and Bartolomeus Brollo. He is possibly to be identified with the Reynaldus Tenorista at Treviso Cathedral from 2 February 1438 to 25 December 1439.

(3) Johannes de Lotinis. Dedicatee of Tinctoris's *Expositio manus* (*CS*, iv, 1; *c*1475).

(4) Arnold [Arnoldo, Arnoldus] **de Lantins** [Lantinis, Latinis] (*fl c*1430). Franco-Flemish composer. The majority of his works are in north Italian manuscripts dating from around 1430, and later sources contain no new works. Annotations in *GB-Ob* 213 (*Se ne prenés* and *Quant je mire*) indicate that he was in Venice in March 1428. In November 1431 he was listed as a singer in the papal choir under Pope Eugene IV along with Dufay and the newly joined Malbecque; but he stayed only six months. The ballade *Puisque je suy cypriané* may perhaps have been written for the arrival of Anne of Cyprus and her retinue in Italy.

The esteem in which Arnold was held around 1430 can be assessed from the extremely wide distribution of his Marian motet *Tota pulchra es* as also from the equal status with Dufay, Binchois and Ciconia afforded him in the tenor partbook to *GB-Ob* 213 in *F-Pn* n.a.fr.4379 (see Schoop). Further indication of this is in the composite mass at the beginning of *I-Bc* Q15: the tenors of the introit, Kyrie, Sanctus and Agnus are all based on the appropriate chant (Vatican IX, with northern French variants in the Sanctus; see P. J. Thannabaur: *Das einstimmige Sanctus*, Munich, 1962); the mass is completed by a Gloria with the Marian trope 'Spiritus et alme' and a Credo, both by Ciconia.

Instead of the unified setting of the movements, this composite cycle adopts the tonal sequence of Mass IX; but in Arnold's full cyclic mass, liturgical uniformity appears to be of equal importance with the musical unity achieved through the same *finalis* and the use of the same head-motif or motto in the top voice. The Kyrie trope 'Verbum incarnatum' and the Sanctus trope 'Qui hominem limo' point to Advent and Lent, as do the chants used in the Sanctus and Agnus (Vatican XVII). The short introductory canon in the Gloria is supported by a 'tuba' part.

Arnold's music is characterized by frequent octave-leap cadences and a tendency towards fauxbourdon style (e.g. the 6-3 and 5-3 parallels in the Credo of his full cyclic mass). Besides tonality and mensuration (see Hamm), a short head-motif in one or all of the voices links the three mass pairs. The paired movements in *I-Bu* 2216 are further united by the use of identical music in their opening sections and again at the mensuration changes ('Qui tollis'; 'secundum scripturas').

The two Marian motets and the *lauda In tua memoria* (which falls into short sections) contain rhythmically simple three-voice writing with a melodic top voice and largely syllabic texting. Several of his chansons open with a discantus figure descending stepwise through a complete octave with similar rhythm (see L 5–8).

WORKS
(all 3vv; doubtful works listed under Hugo)

Editions: *Polyphonia sacra*, ed. C. van den Borren (Burnham Wood, 1932, rev. 2/1962) [P]
Pièces polyphoniques profanes de provenance liégeoise (XVe siècle), ed. C. van den Borren, Flores musicales belgicae, i (Brussels, 1950) [L]

MASS ORDINARY

Missa 'Verbum incarnatum', P 1–5
Introitus, Kyrie, Sanctus, Agnus [Gl and Cr by Ciconia complete the cycle], *I-Bc* Q15, nos.2, 3, 8, 9
Gloria–Credo, *I-Bc* Q15, nos.43, 44
Gloria–Credo, *I-Bc* Q15, nos.55, 56
Gloria–Credo, *I-Bu* 2216, pp.46–52

SMALLER SACRED PIECES

In tua memoria, lauda, P 42
O pulcherrima mulierum, P 43
Tota pulchra es [Cantus II in *I-Bc* Q15 seems to be a later addition], P 41

BALLADES

Puisque je suy cyprianés, L 8
Tout mon desir et mon voloir, L 7

RONDEAUX

Amour servir et honnourer, L 3
Ce jour de l'an belle je vous supplye, L 5
Certes belle quand de vous partiray, L 1
Esclave a dueil et forain de liesse, L 4
Helas emy ma dame et ma mestresse, L 13
Las pouray je mon martire celer, L 10
Mon doulx espoir mon souvenir [ascribed Ar. Lantins in *I-Bc* Q15, Hugo in *GB-Ob* 213], L 23
Ne me vueilliés belle oblier, L 2
Or voy je bien que je moray martir, L 14
Puis que je voy belle que ne m'amés, L 6
Quant je mire vos doulce portraiture [dated in MS Venice, March 1428], L 12
Sans desplaisir et sans esmay, L 9
Se ne prenés de moy pité [dated in MS Venice, March 1428], L 11

(5) Hugo [Hugho, Ugho, Ugo] **de Lantins** [Lantinis, Latinis] (*fl* 1420–30). Franco-Flemish composer. His works appear in the same manuscripts as those of (4) Arnold de Lantins. His motet *Christus vincit* praises Doge Francesco Foscari (Doge from 1423) in accordance with a twice-yearly Venetian custom. Further indication of his activity in Italy is in the ballata *Tra quante regione*, praising Sparta, the Eastern Roman Empire and Cleofe Malatesta, who married Theodore Palaiologos, Prince of Sparta, in 1421. Dufay's motet *Vasilissa ergo gaude* is also addressed to Cleofe, but since Theodore is not named in either work, neither is likely to have been for the wedding itself (cf Pirrotta). The rondeau *Mirar non posso* contains a reference to the

Colonna family which was connected to the Malatesta family by the wedding celebrated in Dufay's ballade *Resveilliés vous*. From the way Hugo's motet *Celsa sublimatur/Sabine presul* is linked with Dufay's motet *O gemma lux/Sacer pastor barensium* in a common dedication to St Nicholas of Bari, it is possible that they spent a short time together in that town; in any case a close connection with Dufay is indicated.

The openings of the paired Gloria and Credo are identical in all three voices; both repeat their tenor pattern several times (three in the Gloria and four in the Credo), and both reflect material from the tenor in the other parts (cf Gossett). The Gloria printed in CMM, i/4, and ascribed to both Hugo and Dufay is paired with a Credo by Dufay, though not very closely linked to it musically; but there is some stylistic justification for Hamm's attribution of the Gloria to Dufay.

Ave gemma claritas is articulated with the form AA^1BC: the first two sections are in three voices, after which a fourth voice is added. In this and in *O lux et decus* another structural feature is the change of mensuration. The form of the three ballate is unusual in the way the *volta* is sung as a newly composed third section rather than the more customary repeat of the music for the refrain.

Imitation not only distinguishes the work of Hugo de Lantins from that of Arnold, but also appears more consistently in his work than in that of any other composer of the time. In the Gloria P 15 nearly every new phrase of text is introduced by imitation, perhaps following the example of Ciconia. The Gloria P 17 (with *tempus perfectum diminutum* and set for low voices) has the two upper voices in canon. The Gloria P 16 deviates from Hugo's methods in the sparsity of its imitation as also in the varied distributions of the text among all three voices; so the contrary ascription to Dufay may be correct. Imitation is particularly common in the rondeaux, with the single exception of the rhythmically intricate *Je suy exent*. For this reason the doubtful works *Chanter ne scay* and *Un seul confort* are probably his, whereas the more homophonic *Mon doulx espoir* belongs rather to Arnold.

WORKS
(*3vv unless otherwise stated*)

Editions: *Polyphonia sacra*, ed. C. van den Borren (Burnham Wood, 1932, rev. 2/1962) [P]

Pièces polyphoniques profanes de provenance liégeoise (XVᵉ siècle), ed. C. van den Borren, Flores musicales belgicae, i (Brussels, 1950) [L]

MASS ORDINARY
Gloria–Credo, *I-Bc* Q15, nos.86, 87 [tenors ed. in Gossett; ascribed to Forest in *D-Mbs* 14274]
Gloria [Hugo in *I-Bc* and *AO*, Dufay in *GB-Ob* 213], ed. in CMM, i/4 (1962), 15
Gloria, P 15
Gloria [ascribed in index of *GB-Ob* 213 to Dufay, but in body of MS to Hugo], P 16
Gloria, P 17

MOTETS
Ave gemma claritas, 4vv [St Catharine], *I-Bc* Q15
Ave verum, 4vv, *I-Bc* Q15
Celsa sublimatur/Sabine presul, 4vv or 3vv [isorhythmic motet for St Nicholas of Bari], P 32 [contrary to Van den Borren's statement, the motet is correct in 4vv except for the rests; tenor and contratenor then combine to form a *solus tenor*]
Christus vincit, ed. in Gallo
O lux et decus [St James], *I-Bc* Q15

RONDEAUX
A ma damme playsant et belle, L 15
Ce j'eusse fait ce que je pence, L 21
Chanter ne scay ce poyse moy [contrary ascription to Arnold de Lantins], L 27
Grant ennuy m'est tres douce simple et coye, L 18

Helas amour que ce qu'endure, L 19
J'ay ma joye ben perdue, L 16
Je suy espris d'une damme amoureuse, L 20
Je suy exent entre aman pour amour, L 25
Joly et gay je me tenray, 2vv, L 24
Mon doulx espoir mon souvenir [contrary ascription to Arnold de Lantins], L 23
Plaindre m'estuet de ma damme jolye [acrostic: PVTAIN DE MERDE], L 22
Pour resioyr la compaignie, L 26
Prendre convint de tout en gré, L 17
Un seul confort pour mon cuer resjoir [ascribed only 'de L'], L 28

BALLATE
Io sum tuo servo, L 31
Per amor de costey, L 29
Tra quante regione el sol si mobele [for Cleofe Malatesta, ?1421], L 32

ITALIAN ?RONDEAU
Mirar non posso ni conçerner dona, L 30

BIBLIOGRAPHY
J., J. F. R. and C. Stainer, eds.: *Dufay and his Contemporaries* (London, 1898/*R*1963)
C. van den Borren: 'Hugo et Arnold de Lantins', *Annales de la Fédération archéologique et historique de Belgique*, xxix (1932), 263
A. Pirro: *Histoire de la musique de la fin du XIVe siècle à la fin du XVIe* (Paris, 1940)
W. Apel: *The Notation of Polyphonic Music, 900–1600* (Cambridge, Mass., 1942, rev. 5/1961)
G. de Van: 'Inventory of Manuscript Bologna, Liceo Musicale, Q15 (olim 37)', *MD*, ii (1948), 231
G. D'Alessi: *La cappella musicale del Duomo di Treviso* (Treviso, 1954)
G. Reaney: 'The Manuscript Oxford, Bodleian Library, Canonici Misc. 213', *MD*, ix (1955), 73–104
W. Rehm: 'Lantins', *MGG*
R. Bockholdt: *Die frühen Messenkompositionen von Guillaume Dufay* (Tutzing, 1960)
F. A. Gallo: 'Musiche veneziane nel Ms. 2216 della Biblioteca universitaria di Bologna', *Quadrivium*, vi (1964), 107
C. Hamm: 'The Reson Mass', *JAMS*, xviii (1965), 5
P. Gossett: 'Techniques of Unification in Early Cyclic Masses and Mass Pairs', *JAMS*, xix (1966), 205
N. Pirrotta: 'On Text Forms from Ciconia to Dufay', *Aspects of Medieval and Renaissance Music: a Birthday Offering to Gustave Reese* (New York, 1966), 673
F. A. Gallo, ed.: *Il codice musicale 2216 della Biblioteca universitaria di Bologna* (Bologna, 1968)
G. Reaney: 'The Italian Contribution to the Manuscript Oxford, Bodleian Library, Canonici Misc. 213', *L'ars nova del trecento II: Certaldo 1969*, 443
H. Schoop: *Entstehung und Verwendung der Handschrift Oxford, Bodleian Library, Canonici misc. 213* (Berne, 1971)
G. Chew: 'The Early Cyclic Mass as an Expression of Royal and Papal Supremacy', *ML*, liii (1972), 254

HANS SCHOOP

Lantos. *See* TINÓDI, SEBESTYÉN.

Lanyer. *See* LANIER family.

Lanza. Italian family of musicians.

(1) Francesco Giuseppe Lanza (*b* Naples, *c*1750; *d* ?Naples, after 1812). Composer and singing teacher. He probably moved to London in 1793, where he was employed by the Duke of Abercorn. On returning to Naples in 1812 he was appointed singing teacher at the Reale Collegio di Musica (now the Conservatorio di S Pietro a Majella) and at the Pensionato Reale dei Miracoli.

WORKS
(*printed works published in London unless otherwise stated*)

Comic operas: L'ingannatrice; Le nozze per fanatismo
Ballets: Don Quichotte; The Calif
Vocal: Il pianto delle virtù, cantata, 1780; Stabat mater, 2 S, op.12 (*c*1795); Canzonette, duetti e trio, op.6 (*c*1796); other trios, op.8 (*c*1798), op.13 (*c*1800); other duos, op.5 (1794), op.7 (*c*1797), op.11 (1800); 6 arie notturne, 1v, gui, vn ad lib (Naples, 1792); ariettas, op.1 (1794), op.4 (?1794), op.10 (1800)
Instrumental: duos, fl, pf; sonatas, pf solo

(2) Gesualdo Lanza (*b* Naples, 1779; *d* London, 12 March 1859). Composer and singing teacher, son of (1)

Francesco Giuseppe Lanza. As a child he went with his father to London, where he became well known as a singing teacher.

WORKS
(printed works published in London)

Stage: The Deserts of Arabia (1806); Spirits of Dew (masque, 3)

Vocal and instrumental: Gran messa di gloria, 2 S, T, B, chorus, orch (c1840); Britannia weeps, funeral monody (1805); ballads, canzonas, songs, 1v, pf; pf solo works

Didactic: The Elements of Singing (1809); Studii elementari di canto (c1830); New Method of Teaching Class Singing (1843)

(3) **Francesco Lanza** (*b* Naples, 1783; *d* Naples, 1862). Pianist and composer, son of (1) Francesco Giuseppe Lanza, and the most celebrated member of the family. At a very early age he was taken to London by his father, where he became a pupil of Field and studied theory with Fenaroli; he then began teaching the piano. In 1803 during a short visit to Naples he made a mark as a concert artist. After another stay in London he returned to Naples permanently in 1808, opened a private piano school and also taught at the court. He was made a piano teacher at the Naples Conservatory on 4 April 1827 and taught there for 33 years; his pupils included Costantino Palumbo and Michele Ruta.

Francesco Lanza is regarded as the founder of the Neapolitan piano school. As a pupil of Field he was thus a descendant of Clementi; his piano works, which include sonatas, études and a tutor, are endowed with harmonic subtlety and melodic elegance, and clearly show Clementi's influence.

(4) **Giuseppe Lanza** (*b* London; *d* Naples). Singing teacher and composer, son of (1) Francesco Giuseppe Lanza. After being employed as a music teacher by the Duke of Abercorn, he returned to Naples in 1819, where he opened a singing school with his daughter. He composed ariettas, canzonets, duos and terzets.

A fourth son, a singer whose name is unknown, was born in London and finished his studies there. At the age of about 20 he moved to Paris, where he lived for some years. In 1838 he taught singing in Lille, and in 1841 he settled in the USA.

BIBLIOGRAPHY

EitnerQ; *FétisB*; *SchmidlD*

J. Sainsbury, ed.: *A Dictionary of Musicians* (London, 2/1825/R1966)
F. Florimo: *La scuola musicale di Napoli e i suoi conservatorii* (Naples, 1880–82/R1969)
L. A. Villanis: *L'arte del pianoforte in Italia* (Turin, 1907)
S. Martinotti: *Poetiche e presenze nel pianismo italiano dell'ottocento*, Quaderni della rassegna musicale, iii (Turin, 1965)
——: *Ottocento strumentale italiano* (Bologna, 1973)

FRANCESCO BUSSI

Lanza, Alcides (*b* Rosario, 2 June 1929). Argentinian composer, conductor, pianist and teacher. His early studies were in Buenos Aires with Ruwin Erlich (piano), Julian Bautista (composition) and Roberto Kinsky (conducting). Thereafter he attended courses given by Loriod, Messiaen, Maderna and Ginastera at the Di Tella Institute, where he worked intensively in electronic composition. He also studied electronic engineering at the Escuela Industrial de la Nación, Rosario. From 1959 to 1965 he was artistic coordinator at the Teatro Colón, and then a Guggenheim Fellowship enabled him to work as instructor at the Columbia-Princeton Electronic Music Center (1966–70); at that time he also lectured on music appreciation at the New York City Community College. In 1971 he was appointed associate professor of composition and electronic music at McGill University, and he received a Deutscher Akademischer Austauschdienst grant to live in Berlin in 1972–3. While in Europe he toured as associate music director of the Composer/Performers Group; he also directs the Composers' Group for International Performance and is a member of the Asociación Música Viva of Buenos Aires, which, from 1960, has given first performances of avant-garde compositions in Argentina and elsewhere in Latin America. In addition he has, from youth, travelled extensively in the Americas as a pianist, lecturer, composer and conductor. His major preoccupation has been electronic music – its composition, notation, recording and so on. *Eidesis II*, first performed at Tanglewood in 1967, has, in Lanza's words, 'masses of sound in motion, with an enormous charge of sensuality, resolved in several "orgasms of sound" '. The piece employs quarter-tone tuning, special coloured lights and contact microphones for the strings.

WORKS
(selective list)

Toccata, pf, 1957; Sonata, 2 pf, 1958; Sonata, vn, pf, 1959; Desplazamientos, fl, cl, tpt, vn, db, 1961; Cuarteto II, fl, cl, bn, pf/vib, 1962; Plectros I, 1/2 pf, 1962; Eidesis sinfónica, orch, 1963; Pf Conc., 1964; Cuarteto IV, 4 tpt, 1964; Interferencias I, wind, tape, 1966; Plectros II, pf, tape, 1966; Eidesis II, 13 insts, 1967; Strobo I, db, perc, lights, tape, 1967

Ekphonesis II (Lanza), 1v, pf, tape, elec, 1968; Ekphonesis III, insts, tape, elec, 1969; Penetrations II, insts, tape, elec, 1969; Penetrations III, mixed-media, 1969; Penetrations V, mixed-media, 1970; Acúfenos II, 4 insts, tape, 1971; Eidesis III, 1/2 orch, tape, 1971; Mantis I, 1972; Hip'nes I, 1973; Kron'ikelz 75, 1975

BIBLIOGRAPHY

Composers of the Americas, xvii (Washington, DC, 1971)

SUSANA SALGADO

Lanzetti, Domenico. Italian cellist and composer, possibly related to SALVATORE LANZETTI.

Lanzetti, Salvatore (*b* Naples, c1710; *d* Turin, c1780). Italian cellist and composer. He studied at the Naples Conservatorio di S Maria di Loreto. For a short time he was a member of the court chapel in Lucca and in 1727 entered the service of Vittorio Amedeo II in Turin, a post he retained despite numerous tours in northern Europe. At the end of the 1730s he was in London, where he seems to have lived until at least 1754. He had great success there and, according to Burney, helped to establish a taste for the cello. In May 1751 he gave concerts in Frankfurt am Main. He returned to Italy about 1760 and rejoined the royal chapel in Turin, of which he probably remained a member until his death.

A generation before Boccherini, Lanzetti anticipated his full emancipation of the cello from its bass function. The technical demands of his cello writing, particularly for bowing, are almost on a level with those of the Venetian violin concertos. From this there arises a conception of the sonata close to that of the solo concerto: three-movement form, intensity of expression in the slow middle movement, well-characterized themes in the fast ones. This can well explain his influence on the English school, mentioned by Burney.

The cellist and composer Domenico Lanzetti was perhaps related to Salvatore. Two of his cello sonatas and five concertos are extant (*D-B*). Six concertos, mentioned by Eitner, were formerly in the same library.

WORKS

Inst: 12 sonate, vc, bc, op.1 (Amsterdam, 1736); 6 Solos, 2 vc, bc (hpd) (London, 1740; 2/c1745 as 6 solos, 2 vc/fl, b, op.2); 6 Solos, 2 vc/fl, b (London, c1745) [same title-page as op.2, different contents]; 6 Solos after an Easy & Elegant Taste, vc, bc (hpd) (London, c1760); Sonata intitolata Porto Maone, vc, va, vn, b, op.5, *D-B* [vn, b pts. only]; Sonates, vc, bc, op.5, ?unpubd, *F-Pn*; Sonates, vc, bc, op.7, ?unpubd, *Pn*

Pedagogical: *Principes ou l'application de violoncelle par tous les tons* (Amsterdam, before 1770)

BIBLIOGRAPHY
J. W. von Wasielewski: *Das Violoncell und seine Geschichte* (Leipzig, 1889, enlarged 3/1925/*R*1970; Eng. trans., 1894/*R*1968)
B. Weigl: *Handbuch der Violoncell-Literatur* (Vienna, 1911, rev., enlarged 3/1929)
L. Forino: *Il violoncello, il violoncellista ed i violoncellisti* (Milan, 1930)
K. Stephenson: 'Lanzetti, Salvatore', *MGG*

GUIDO SALVETTI

Lanzi, Francesco (*fl* 1696–1712). Italian organist, instrumentalist, singing teacher and composer. A member of the clergy, he was from 1696 at the latest organist of S Maria della Steccata, Parma, and from 1706 until at least 1712 organist of Parma Cathedral, where he also played the horn. His only known composition consists of adjustments made to the opera *Il Pertinace* (originally given at Venice in 1689 with music by Paolo Biego) for a performance at the Teatro Ducale, Parma, in 1699; only the published libretto survives (in *I-Bc* and elsewhere). Lanzi was the teacher of FRANCESCA CUZZONI.

BIBLIOGRAPHY
GerberL
N. Pelicelli: 'Musicisti in Parma nel sec. XVIII', *NA*, xi (1934), 32

THOMAS WALKER

Laos. Country in south-east Asia. The population is mostly Lao, who have a common origin with the Siamese and Shan in southern China. They at present occupy the flat ricelands on both banks of the Mekong River in Laos and north-east Thailand, the latter having been a Khmer stronghold earlier. There are various groups living in the mountainous regions of Laos, including the Pootai, Miao and Yao. Before its partition into the princedoms of Luang Prabang, Wiangjun (Vientiane) and Champasak about 1700, the 14th-century kingdom of Lan Sang ('Million Elephants') was an important power in south-east Asia. After 1827 when the Siamese armies defeated the Lao and sacked Wiangjun, the Korat plateau came under the control of Bangkok. Lacking the relative prosperity of Thailand, Laos's population of roughly three million remains culturally more conservative than the 13 million Lao-Thai living in the 16 provinces of north-east Thailand.

1. Vocal music. 2. Theatrical traditions. 3. Instruments. 4. Other peoples.

1. VOCAL MUSIC. Lao singing cannot be understood without reference to the Lao language, whose tonal inflections tend to create melodic patterns. A speaker's tonal inflections may follow one of two anhemitonic pentatonic scale patterns, D–F–G–A–C or C–D–F–G–A. In reciting various literary forms, ritualists exaggerate these tonal inflections, creating clear melodic styles. Although Buddhist monks may chant non-tonal Pali texts on a monotone, the inflections inherent in the Lao alphabet often intrude, expanding the recitation to three or four pitches, for example D falling to C and rising to F and G. Sermons (*tet*) read to common people are usually in Lao, allowing the reader even greater pitch variation. At the Boon Prawet festival in February talented monks recite the *Jataka* of Prince Wetsundawn, the penultimate incarnation of Buddha, in cantillation which varies from three pitches to highly embellished versions, whose scale (D–F–G–A–C–D) and range may exceed a 10th. In *sookwun*, a Brahmanistic rite, a male ritualist called *pram* (from 'Brahman') recites (*soot*) texts in Lao to summon the *kwun*, the 'spiritual essence' of a person which tends to flee during crises, rites of passage

and extended journeys (see Tambiah). The reading of versified *Jataka* and local stories (*nitan pün müang*) from palmleaf manuscripts (*nungsü pook*) at funeral wakes, called *an nungsü* ('reading a book'), bears a clear relationship to singing (ex.1). Another influence on Lao singing, although itself spoken, has been the *pa-nyah*, an old courtship custom in which boys and girls test each other's wit in a poetic dialogue replete with simile and metaphor.

Ex.1 *An nungsü*, from *Sio Sawut*; rec. and transcr. T. Miller (Miller, 1977)

But nee___ juk glao gae___ Sio Sa-wut tet__ nah__

un tee lao boo han   bat boon blaeng wai___

Lao singing is inseparable from Lao literature, largely derived from or modelled on Buddhist *Jataka* (tales of Buddha's 547 former lives). The primary poetic form, *glawn* or *gawn yawn*, consists of four-line stanzas with seven or more syllables to the line, in which certain words have prescribed tonal signs. Although *glawn* for singing (*glawn lum*) allows rhyme between lines, literary *glawn* exploits interior rhyme and alliteration. *Glawn* is best exemplified in Bang-kum's epic poem *Sung Sin-sai* of about 1650, a story whose significance for the Lao is like that of the *Rāmāyana* for the Siamese, Malay and Indonesians. Of less importance is *gap* or *gawn dut* in which the last word of each seven-syllable line rhymes with the third of the following. While *gap* may be encountered within *glawn lum* texts, it is best known in *süng bungfai*, a kind of leader-chorus singing heard at the rocket festival in May. Both traditional Lao poetry and Pali texts were scratched with a stylus on narrow strips of palmleaf and highlighted with lamp black, the Pali texts written in the *tam* alphabet and Lao poetry in *tai noi* or old Lao.

The verbs describing various recited forms differ from those for 'singing'. A *pram* performs *soot* ('formula'), Buddhist monks *kata* chants and *tet* sermons, boys and girls *wao* ('speak') *pa-nyah*, and literate men *an* ('read') *Jataka* tales at funeral wakes. Two words distinguish singing: the less common word *hawng* connotes a fixed melody to which word-tones must be adjusted; *lum* (*kup* in northern Laos) connotes melody generated from word-tones. Singers are called *mawlum*, *maw* meaning 'skilled person'. In Laos *mawlum* tend to be amateurs, however skilled, seldom singing for money, while in north-east Thailand many are professionals, demanding sizable fees. Many performers turn to farming during the Buddhist fast, which coincides with rice planting, a time of few performances. There are two primary scale patterns in Lao singing. The first, called the *lum hai fung* scale, is C–D–F–G–A, and the second, called *yao an nungsü*, is D–F–G–A–C.

Although Lao on both banks of the Mekong River have a common language and culture, their musical differences are considerable. Laos, relatively isolated and lacking the improved communications of north-east Thailand and stimulation from prosperous Bangkok retains more conservative musical styles. Although these conclusions must be qualified as tentative, at least 11 regional styles can be distinguished in Laos, seven south of the 18th parallel and four to the north. In the north

are: (1) *kup toom luang prabang* (from Luang Prabang);
(2) *kup ngüm*, referring to the Ngüm River area about 64
km north of Vientiane; (3) *kup siang kuang* (Xieng
Khouang); and (4) *kup sum nüa* (Sam Neua). The styles
of southern Laos are: (5) *lum see-tun-dawn* (Sithandone)
along the Mekong near the Cambodian border; (6) *lum
som* in the same area, especially at Müang Khong; (7)
lum sarawun (Saravane) in the interior between the 15th
and 16th parallels; (8) *lum ban sawk* (Ban Xok) a few
kilometres south-east of Savannakhet; (9) *lum dung-wai*
(Tang-vay) 100 km south-east of Savannakhet; (10) *lum
kawn-sawun* in Savannakhet province; and (11) *lum
mahasai* (Mahaxay) 40 km east of Thakhek.

Each style uses only one scale: in four styles (1, 5,
10, 11) this is the *lum hai fung* scale; in the others (2–4,
6–9) *yao an nungsü*. In at least two styles (2, 10) the
female participant speaks *pa-nyah* but in one (3) she
chants *pa-nyah* using four pitches. The *kaen* (a bamboo
mouth organ) accompanies five styles (2–6) while ensembles of three or more of the following instruments
accompany the other styles (1, 7–11): *kaen, look bee
kaen* (flute), *sing* (finger cymbals), drum, *pin* (lute), *saw*
(two-string fiddle) and *mai bok baek* (notched stick). In
five styles (5–8, 11) the rhythmical ostinato accompaniment contrasts sharply with the free rhythm of the
singer. Additional research is needed to establish the
relationships between these diverse styles.

In north-east Thailand styles can be classified more
clearly according to the number of singers. The most
archaic style, now nearly extinct, is *lum pün* ('tale')
which is closely related to *tet, an nungsü* and *lum som*.
In *lum pün* a single singer accompanied by *kaen* sings
Jataka and local stories of epic proportions such as
Jumba-seedon ('Four jumba trees'), *Prince Galaget,
Prince Sooriwong*, and historical stories describing such
events as Wiangjun's fall to Bangkok in 1827. Though
each tale requires from one to three nights, all consist of
memorized *glawn* poetry. A related form called *lum
lüang* differs from *lum pün* only in that the singer
impersonates the different characters by changing
articles of clothing and position. Though some *mawlum
pün* use the scale C–D–F–G–A, the traditional pattern
is hexatonic, D–E–F–G–A–C–D.

The most widespread non-theatrical form in north-
east Thailand is *lum glawn*. Performed at temple fairs,
Red Cross fairs, merit-making events at homes, and
Buddhist festivals, *lum glawn* consists of alternating
male and female singers plus *kaen* players (fig.1). At
about 9 p.m. the first singer begins by introducing himself in a style called *lum tang sun* ('short style', see ex.2),
sung in a steady duple metre, and asks about his partner's family background and marital status. After a

*1. Lum glawn singers with a kaen (*mouth organ*), north-
east Thailand*

Ex.2 *Lum tang sun* singing style; rec. and transcr. T. Miller (Miller, 1977)
♩ = 96

nang   oi   sao   ben   jung   sun   dawk   dee   lü   dee

ai   wa   baw   ngam,   lü   paw   mae   sa   la

kü   nawng   ham   hai   lang   wa   sun   dai

solo introduction, the *kaen* player follows the singer's
part in unison, heterophonically, or with repeated patterns. He also plays solo interludes. The poetry is
previously memorized, but the order is improvised to
accommodate the situation, and the melody generated
according to the principles of *lum*. The most usual scale
is the *lum hai fung* scale, but modulations to *yao an
nungsü* occur for emotional passages called *dün dong*
('walking in the forest'). Shortly before dawn when the
singers have theoretically fallen in love and must part,
they begin *lum tang yao* ('long style') or *lum la* ('farewell')
which is in free rhythm and uses a plaintive pentatonic
scale (*yao an nungsü*). After about 15 minutes the rhythm
becomes steady again as they begin *lum döi*. *Döi* ('to
court') is of three types: *döi kong* (Mekong River); *döi
pama* (Burma); and *döi tumadah* ('ordinary'). The origin
of *döi* is unclear, but it became a part of *lum glawn* only
after World War II. Throughout a *mawlum* performance singers often perform a graceful dance called
fawn.

Lum glawn singers tend to classify themselves according to two regional styles, Ubon and Khon Kaen,
cities at opposite ends of the Chi River whose course
through north-east Thailand defines the area of greatest
musical activity. This distinction is most apparent in
lum tang sun; in both *lum tang yao* and *lum döi* it can
hardly be seen. While a search for singers with a 'pure'
style would be futile since characteristics of both have
influenced today's singers, each had a different origin.
Khon Kaen style originated in *lum jot*, a kind of *lum
glawn* in which two singers of either sex challenged each
other with questions and riddles concerning Buddhism,
history, literature or geography. Difficult words of Pali-
Sanskrit origin did not fit readily into *glawn* poetry,
giving Khon Kaen style singing an uneven quality as
poetic patterns yielded to prose and the *kaen* player
stopped. Ubon style, however, relied almost exclusively
on *glawn gio* ('courting poems') and *dün dong* whose even
phrases contributed to a more lyrical quality. Such love-
poetry may be quite erotic, but this aspect often has

been overemphasized. Most Lao styles also rely upon *glawn giio*.

Of lesser importance is *lum ching choo* ('competing for a lover') in which two male singers vie for the affections of a female; *lum gup gep* in which a lone singer accompanies himself with pairs of woodblocks (*gup gep*); and *lum pee fah* ('sky spirit'). In the last of these, old women intercede with the *pee fah*, a powerful but benevolent spirit, on behalf of someone made ill by lesser spirits, either malevolent or merely capricious. *Tet lae*, a kind of art singing practised by talented Buddhist monks, although an outgrowth of ordinary *tet* in its most embellished form, is more closely related to *mawlum*, since the monk sings memorized *glawn* poems.

2. THEATRICAL TRADITIONS. Though Laos lacks a musical theatre, two principal forms flourish in north-east Thailand, *mawlum moo* ('group') and *mawlum plün* ('spontaneous'). Two earlier forms combined to create these, *mawlum lüang* (*lum pün*) and Siamese *likay* theatre (*see* SOUTH-EAST ASIA, §II, 4, iv). The latter, whose instruments and vocal styles are Siamese and whose popularity is centred in Korat (now Nakhon Ratchasima), appeared in the north-east as early as the 1920s, spawning a number of locally isolated imitations. *Likay lao* played by north-easterners varied from close imitations to versions in which Lao stories, instruments and singing styles predominated. While *likay lao* became well known in Khon Kaen province, another variation called *mawlum moo maeng dup dao* appeared in Roi Et province in about 1937, when a troupe began performing the story of Prince Kooloo using only Lao singing and instruments, in addition to the bawdy song *Maeng dup dao* (the name of an insect) which gave the form its name.

Mawlum plün began in 1950 in Ubon province when a group of amateurs began performing the story *Gaeo na mah* ('Horse-faced girl'). *Mawlum moo*, under the direct influence of *likay* and *lum lüang*, began independently in Khon Kaen province about 1952. The early forms were performed at night on the ground before a white backdrop using simple costumes, but in the later 1950s stages, painted scenery cloths and colourful costumes borrowed from *likay* appeared, and in the 1960s came electric lighting and amplification. Gradually both forms came to resemble each other, leaving virtually no visual differences. While both rely heavily on *Jataka* stories performed from newly versified scripts, *lum plün*'s best known tale is *Koon chang koon paen*, a Siamese story. For instrumental accompaniment *mawlum moo* relies exclusively on the *kaen* but *mawlum plün* also requires a *pin*. Both forms now begin with an hour of Western popular music accompanying dancing-girls in mini-skirts, a trend which is now intruding upon the play itself.

Lum plün differs from *lum moo* in several respects including its more light-hearted mood and contrasting vocal styles. Whereas *lum moo* relies almost exclusively on *lum tang yao*, though more highly embellished than in *lum glawn*, *lum plün* alternates between a stylized form of *lum tang yao* and a pulsating *lum tang sun* whose scale, however, remains *yao an nungsü*. *Lum plün* is accompanied by a set of Western drums and sung at breakneck pace. *Lum moo* may also use *döi hua non dan* (a place name) whose origin is evidently *lum kawnsawun* from southern Laos. Neither form displays much dramatic acting since the performers are primarily sin-

gers and action must take place around the immovable microphone.

A troupe usually has about 20 members although it varies from 15 to 45. Because plots vary little from play to play, each troupe maintains at least eight stock characters: a leading male (*pra ek*), a leading female (*nang ek*), secondary leading roles (*pra lawng* and *nang lawng*), king–queen or father–mother figures (*paw payah* and *mae payah*), a foil for the lead (*poo lai*), and a joke man (*dua dalok*) who may improvise. There may be in addition servants, soldiers, monks, ghosts and giants. While many troupes are professional, most are amateurs from a single village or family who hire a teacher, buy a script, costumes, scenery, and join a *mawlum* association which acts as a booking agent. Estimates as to the total number of troupes operating vary from hundreds to more than a thousand. Performances take place at temples or homes, occasioned by the same events as *mawlum glawn*, and similarly last all night. Whereas *lum moo* began to displace *lum glawn* in the 1960s, *lum plün* came to replace it during the 1970s.

Nung daloong (shadow theatre) from southern Thailand came to Ubon province, Thailand, as early as 1926, when amateur troupes began performing the *Ramakien* story with home-made puppets accompanied by drum, *ching* (finger cymbals) and the Siamese *ranāt* (xylophone). Today's troupes also perform Lao stories, usually adding *mawlum* and *kaen* to increase their appeal. About 17 troupes are known to operate in the provinces along the Chi River.

2. *Kaen baet* (*mouth organ with 16 pipes*) *player near Roi Et, Thailand*

3. INSTRUMENTS. Of at least 25 sound-producing instruments which may be listed, the *kaen* is by far the most significant. The remainder include eight aerophones, four chordophones, four membranophones, six idiophones, and two extinct instruments whose classification is unknown. Old Lao literature is full of references to instruments and ensembles called *pinpat*, but these are described as they fit the poetry, and no clear picture of their musical practice can be gained.

The *kaen* is a bamboo mouth organ in raft form (fig.2) whose free reeds of copper and silver are mounted in the pipe walls inside a carved wooden windchest called *dao* ('gourd'). *Kaen* are made in four sizes, *kaen hok* ('six'), a child's toy with six pipes, *kaen jet* ('seven') with 14 pipes, *kaen baet* ('eight') with 16 pipes, and *kaen gao* ('nine') with 18 pipes. By the 1970s *kaen baet* were nearly universal, measuring approximately one metre in length, although instruments measuring two to three metres were common in the 1920s. Although made throughout north-east Thailand, *kaen* making is centred in Roi Et province and especially in the subdistrict town of See-gaeo. Most makers in Laos came from Thailand. *Kaen* are properly held tilted to the left or right with the hands cupped over the windchest. The 16 pipes of the *kaen baet* play 15 pitches (one doubled at the unison) within a range of two octaves consisting of semitones and whole tones averaging 100 and 200 cents respectively. Although there is certainly no Western influence, the pitches parallel the piano's naturals from *a* to *a''*, but their physical arrangement follows no recognizable pattern. Instead the pipes have been arranged to facilitate fingering and to avoid the technical problem of playing three consecutive pipes. Inhaling and exhaling produce identical pitches, but pipes sound only when finger-holes are covered.

The *kaen* is related to other free-reed aerophones distributed in Asia from Japan to Thailand and from Bangladesh to Borneo. Best known is the Chinese *sheng* (Japanese *shō*) whose metal or wooden bowl was formerly a gourd and whose circular form superseded the earlier raft form. The Miao in Laos and southern China use a mouth organ with six tubes, each with a metal reed set into a carved wooden windchest, while both Tibeto-Burman and Mon-Khmer upland groups on the mainland and certain tribes in Borneo use similar instruments with gourd windchests. Buffalo horns with a metal free reed on the concave side are found chiefly among the Karen of Burma, but they are also known to the Lao and Khmer. Lastly, side-blown reed flutes with and without gourd windchests are widespread, the latter found chiefly in Burma, the former in northern Thailand, among the Miao and Pootai.

Whether playing solo or accompanying a singer, *kaen* players, who are always male, have at their disposal five mode positions called *lai*, each an anhemitonic pentatonic scale. They are called *sootsanaen* (G–A–C–D–E), *bo sai* (C–D–F–G–A), *soi* (D–E–G–A–B), *yai* (A–C–D–E–G) and *noi* (D–F–G–A–C). Each *lai* requires certain drones produced by closing the finger-holes either with a finger or a piece of beeswax. Notes are played singly, in octaves, or in combination with other notes, usually as 4ths or 5ths (see ex.3). *Kaen* players may accompany the *lum hai fung* scale with *sootsanaen*, *bo sai* or *soi*, and the *yao an nungsü* scale with *yai* or *noi* depending on the singer's range. Besides the five basic improvisations in each *lai*, there are others

3. Pin or süng (lute), Maha Sarakham, Thailand

known to all competent players, for example *Maeng poo dawm dawk* ('Bees around the flowers'), *Lom put chai kao* ('The wind through the hills'), and *Lai rot fai* (an imitation of a steam engine). Modern players also imitate the many styles of Lao singing and invent new pieces, but all remain within the five *lai*. While *kaen* players in Laos use the same *lai*, they are not known as systematically as in Thailand. The *kaen wong* ('ensemble') of six or more instruments commonly encountered in schools is of recent origin and plays only the classical songs of central Thailand.

Ex.3 *Kaen piece in bo sai*; rec. and transcr. T. Miller (Miller, 1977)

The aerophones include, besides the *kaen*, the *look bee kaen* (a single-tubed reed flute), the *sung* (conch trumpet), *bee tae* (an oboe formerly used to signal the time), *klui* or *khlui* (a bamboo fipple flute more typical of central Thailand), *bee sanai* (a buffalo horn fitted with a metal free reed), *wot* (circular panpipes for children), and *bee goo füang* and *bee bai dawng glui* (children's toys made from rice or banana stalks).

The chordophones include the *pin* or *süng*, a plucked lute with two to four metal strings over five to eight frets (fig.3); *saw mai pai*, a two-string fiddle with a coconut body similar to the Siamese *saw oo*; *saw bip*, a fiddle with a metal body (made from a discarded kerosene can; fig.4); and *sanoo*, a musical bow mounted on a large kite and sounded by the wind. In music played on the *pin* one string may parallel the melody string in 5ths while the others sound a drone. Few men besides beggars play the fiddles, whose repertory is derived from that of the *kaen*.

Three of the four membranophones are also known in central Thailand: the single-headed *glawng yao* ('long

4. Saw bip (fiddle) player near Roi Et, Thailand

6. Gaeng (mouth organ) of the Miao people

5. Kaw law (vertical 12-keyed xylophone), near Kalasin, Thailand

drum'); *glawng dün*, a large frame drum also called *ramana lum dut*; and *ton*, a small goblet-shaped single-headed drum. *Glawng sing* (drums) are beaten in pairs in competition to attain the highest pitch. Idiophones include *sing* (*ching* in Siamese), metal finger cymbals; larger cymbals called *saeng* (*chap yai* in Siamese); *mawng*, a large metal gong; and the *mai bok baek*, a notched stick rubbed over a stone, known chiefly to the Pootai. The *hoon*, a bamboo jew's harp, is also played. Of little significance, in spite of publicity, is the *kaw law* (or *bong lang*), a vertical 12-keyed xylophone (fig.5) of 20th-century origin in Kalasin province, Thailand.

Although dominating most published literature on Lao music, the court music at Luang Prabang was borrowed directly from Bangkok and Phnom Penh and does not represent Lao musical culture. Although *kaen* may be added to the ensembles of Siamese instruments used in this music, the *sep noi* (or *mahōrī*) and *sep yai*, neither the tunings nor the repertories correspond. *Kon* (masked mime) and *lakon nai* (female dance-drama), classical forms identified with the Bangkok court, also dominated the Lao court where *mawlum* and *kaen* playing were little known (*see* SOUTH-EAST ASIA, §II, 4, vii).

4. OTHER PEOPLES. Relatively little is known of the music of upland Tai groups living in Laos, but that of the Pootai is doubtless the most significant. While most Pootai live in southern Laos, many have migrated into parts of north-east Thailand where they perform a kind of *lum* related to several Laotian styles. *Lum pootai*, which restricts itself to the *yao an nungsü* scale, may be accompanied by an ensemble which at its fullest consists of *kaen, saw bip, pin, look bee kaen, mai bok baek, saeng* and *sing*. Pootai also perform a *kaen* solo called *Fawn pootai* which is identical to the north-eastern solo *Lom put chai kao*.

Similarly, little is known of the musical cultures of the Tibeto-Burman, Miao-Yao and upland Mon-Khmer ethnic groups living within Laos. Those of the mountain-dwelling Miao, Akha and Lahu are most accessible. The best-known Miao instrument is the *gaeng* (fig.6), a mouth organ with six tubes, which accompanies dancing for both religious and secular occasions. Miao also play small metal jew's harps and reed flutes. Agnew and Graham have described their unaccompanied ballad singing in some detail. Both Akha (Ekaw) and Lahu (Musur) use a mouth organ called *naw* whose five short tubes fit into a gourd windchest. The *naw* accompanies both dance and song, although both groups also have unaccompanied singing. Because these groups are continuously migrating and isolate themselves from the lowland Lao, there is little if any musical contact between them. Lowland Khmer living in north-east Thailand, however, have adopted the *kaen* and perform singing called *jariang*, which resembles *mawlum* although the language is non-tonal. Chinese opera from Bangkok and central Thai *likay* theatre are presented in north-eastern cities and have had a noticeable influence on *mawlum moo*.

See also THAILAND.

BIBLIOGRAPHY

P. Lefèvre-Pontalis: *Chansons et fêtes du Laos*, Collection de contes et chansons populaires, xxii (Paris, 1896)
H. W. Smyth: *Five Years in Siam, from 1891–1896* (London, 1898)
J. Brengues: 'Les Mo Lâm: la chanson au Laos', *Revue indo-chinoise*, ii (1904), 588
G. Knosp: 'Rapport sur une mission officielle d'étude musicale en Indochine', *International Archiv für Ethnographie*, xx (1912), 121, 165, 217; xxi (1913), 1, 49
R. G. Agnew: 'The Music of the Ch'uan Miao', *Journal of the West China Border Research Society*, xi (1939), 9
G. de Gironcourt: 'Recherches de géographie musicale en Indochine', *Bulletin de la Société des études indochinoises*, new ser., xvii/4 (1942), 3–174
H. A. Bernatzik: *Akha und Meau: Probleme der eingewandten Völkerkunde in Hinterindien* (Innsbruck, 1947; Eng. trans., 1970)
D. C. Graham: *Songs and Stories of the Ch'uan Miao* (Washington, DC, 1954)
R. de Berval, ed.: 'Présence du royaume Lao', *France-Asie*, xii (1956), 703–1153; Eng. trans., 1959 as *Kingdom of Laos* [incl. Souvanna-Phouma: 'La musique', 777; T. Kene: 'Le fabricant de *khène*', 897]
A. Daniélou: *La musique du Cambodge et du Laos* (Pondicherry, 1957)
D. Yupho: *Khrŭang dontri thai* [Thai musical instruments] (Bangkok, 1957, 2/1967; Eng. trans., 1960), 76f
Oobalee-koonoo-bamajan: *Rüang kaen* [The story of the *kaen*] (Bangkok, 1964)
J. Brandon: *Theatre in Southeast Asia* (Cambridge, Mass., 1967)
S. Tambiah: *Buddhism and the Spirit Cults in North-east Thailand* (London, 1970)
A. M. Gagneux: 'Le khene et la musique Lao', *Bulletin des Amis du royaume Lao*, vi (1971), 175
T. and T. A. Stern: ' "I Pluck my Harp": Musical Acculturation among the Karen of Western Thailand', *EM*, xv (1971), 186–219
Jarernchai Chonpairot: *Kaen Wong* [The *kaen* ensemble] (Mahasarakam, Thailand, 1972)
K. Ratanavong: *Learn to Play the Khene* (Vientiane, 1973)
T. Miller: *Kaen Playing and Mawlum Singing in Northeastern Thailand* (diss., Indiana U., 1977)

TERRY E. MILLER

Laparra, Raoul (*b* Bordeaux, 13 May 1876; *d* Suresnes, 4 April 1943). French composer. He was a pupil of Gédalge, Fauré, Lavignac and Diemer at the Paris Conservatoire (1890–1903). His cantata *Ulysse* won him the Prix de Rome in 1903, but it was not until 1937, when he resigned from his post as critic for *Le matin*, that he devoted himself entirely to composition. A deep interest in Basque and Spanish folk music marked his work.

WORKS

Peau d'âne, opera, 1899; La habanera, opera, 3, 1908; La jota, opera, 2, 1911; Le joueur de viole, opera, 1926; Las torreras, zarzuela, 1929
Un dimanche basque, pf, orch, n.d.; other instrumental works

WRITINGS

'La musique et la danse populaire en Espagne', *EMDC*, I/iv (1920), 2353–2400
Bizet et l'Espagne (Paris, 1934)

ANNE GIRARDOT

Lapicida, Erasmus (*b* ?1440–45; *d* Vienna, 19 Nov 1547). Composer. According to an entry in Johann Rasch's *Schottencloster ... Stiftung und Prelaten ...*

zu Wienn (1586), he reached at least 100 years of age; he himself claimed in 1544 that he was in extreme old age. There is no evidence to support Fétis's theory, based on Lapicida's name, that he was originally a stonemason. Rasch's statement that Lapicida was Kapellmeister to the emperors Friedrich III and Maximilian I and to the Hungarian kings Matthias Corvinus and Lajos II has been disproved. Lapicida was a priest, and from Whitsun 1510 until about 1521 he was a singer in the Elector Ludwig V's Hofkapelle in Heidelberg. During this period he met Ornithoparchus, who included Lapicida in his list of recognized composers in *Musicae activae micrologus* (Leipzig, 1517). He seems also to have formed connections with the Habsburgs at this time, for in 1514 he dedicated a Latin poem and a motet to Maximilian I's secretary, Bernhard von Cles. Probably in 1521 (not in 1519, as some authorities claimed) Archduke Ferdinand of Austria granted Lapicida a benefice in the Schottenkloster, Vienna, where he remained until his death. Some time between 1527 and 1534 he met Johann Zanger, who recorded a dispute on music theory between Lapicida, Arnold von Bruck and Stephan Mahu in his *Practicae musicae praecepta* (Leipzig, 1554). Lapicida was still composing in his old age: in 1536 he received payment for dedicating several motets (now lost) to Ferdinand I. He made his last public appearances on 26 and 27 June 1539 at the funeral of Isabella of Portugal in St Stephen's, Vienna. From 1 December 1544 he was in financial straits and drew a gratuity from the Lower Austrian Vizedomamt. Sebastianus Solidus published a Latin poem in his *Necrophilia, seu funerum libri duo* (Vienna, 1549), mourning Lapicida's death.

Lapicida began composing early in the second half of the 15th century and continued probably for seven or eight decades. His longevity explains not only the varied character but also the numerous different styles of his works. More than half of his few surviving works are secular, but he may have written more sacred pieces in his capacity as a priest. His polyphonic adaptations of German folksongs and *Hofweisen* are outstanding; their frottola-like traits and flowing melodic lines suggest that he had some contact with Italian influences.

WORKS
SACRED

Ave regina caelorum, 4vv, *I-Fn* Magl.XIX.58; Benedictus Dominus, 4vv, 1506²; Efferor ad manus, 4vv, *D-Rp* Perner; Lamentatio Jeremiae, 3vv, 1506²; Nativitas tua, Dei genitrix, 4vv, 1505²; Veni electa mea, 4vv, 1538⁸, ed. in G. Rhau: *Musikdrucke*, iii (1959); Veni Sancte Spiritus, 4vv, 1505²

SECULAR

German songs, 4vv: Ach edles N.; Die mich erfreut; Es lebt mein Hertz; Gut Ding muss haben weil; Ich hoff es sey vast wol müglich; Nie grösser Lieb; O hertzigs S.; 1539²⁷, all ed. in DTÖ, lxxii, Jg.xxxvii/2 (1930/R), EDM, 1st ser., xx (1942/R); Tandernaken, 3vv, 1504³, ed. in DTÖ, lxxii, Jg.xxxvii/2 (1930/R)
Sacerdos et pontifex, 4vv, *I-TRa*
La pietà ha chiuso le porte, frottola, 4vv, 1509²

BIBLIOGRAPHY

L. Nowak: 'Das deutsche Gesellschaftslied in Österreich von 1480 bis 1550', *SMw*, xvii (1930), 21–52
H. Federhofer: 'Biographische Beiträge zu Erasmus Lapicida und Stephan Mahu', *Mf*, v (1952), 37
O. Wessely: 'Ein unbekannter Brief von Erasmus Lapicida', *Musik-Erziehung*, viii (1954–5), 38
——: 'Neues zur Lebensgeschichte von Erasmus Lapicida', *Anzeiger der phil.-hist. Klasse der Österreichischen Akademie der Wissenschaften*, xcii (1955), 85
——: 'Neue Beiträge zur Lebensgeschichte von Erasmus Lapicida', *KJb*, xli (1957), 16
G. Pietzsch: 'Quellen und Forschungen zur Geschichte der Musik am kurpfälzischen Hof zu Heidelberg bis 1622', *Abhandlungen der*

geistes- und sozialwissenschaftlichen Klasse der Heidelberger Akademie der Wissenschaften und der Literatur, 6th ser., vi (1963), 674

OTHMAR WESSELY

La Pierre, Louis-Maurice de (*b* Versailles, 17 Feb 1697; *d* Lunéville, 1 Jan 1753). French composer. He is first heard of as composer of an air published in the Ballard collection of 1722 and of two books of cantatas dated 1728. From 1729 he was in the service of Stanislas, the Duke of Lorraine and exiled King of Poland, at Chambord, and in 1737 he became Stanislas's *surintendant de la musique* in Lorraine. He married Thérèse Salcenska, lady-in-waiting to the Queen of Poland, in Lunéville in February 1744. They had a son in May 1749; La Pierre died four years later and was buried in the Capuchin church at Lunéville.

Besides cantatas and *cantatilles*, La Pierre wrote a motet, some instrumental pieces and two stage works, divertissements for the celebration for the name days of the King and Queen of Poland. His music, characterized by graceful melodies and competent workmanship, has a certain surface charm. The cantatas show the influence of Lully.

WORKS
Stage: Divertissement pour le jour de la fête du Roy de Pologne, duc de Lorraine et de Bar (de Solignac), before 1740, music lost; Pastorale pour le jour de la feste de la Reine de Pologne, duchesse de Lorraine et de Bar (divertissement, de Solignac), solo vv, 4vv, insts, bc, 24 Nov 1740, *F-Pc*

Vocal: En amour la ruze est permise, air, 1v, bc, in Recueil d'airs serieux et à boire (Paris, 1722); Cantates françaises, 1–2vv, insts, bc, 2 bks, 1728, formerly H. Prunières' private collection; 4 cantatilles, 1v, insts: L'amant vainqueur (Paris, 1748), L'inconstance (Paris, 1748), Danaé (Paris, n.d.), La pudeur (Paris, n.d.); Veni creator spiritus, motet, solo vv, 4vv, insts, bc, April 1752, *F-Pc*

Inst: Conc., G, 4 insts; Sonata, a, 2 vn, bc; Sonata, G, 2 fl, bc: all formerly H. Prunières' private collection; Prélude, menuet, musette, tambourin, 1743, lost

BIBLIOGRAPHY
Mercure de France (1740), Dec; (1743), March
H. Prunières: 'Notes sur un musicien oublié, Louis-Maurice de la Pierre', *RdM*, ii (1920–21), 71
M. Antoine: 'Notes sur les violonistes Anet', *RMFC*, ii (1962), 81
D. Tunley: *The Eighteenth Century French Cantata* (London, 1974)

VIVIEN LO

La Pierre, Paul de (*b* Avignon, baptized 7 Jan 1612; *d* ?Turin, after 1690). French composer, violinist and dancing master. In 1640 he appeared in the *Ballet du bureau des adresses* performed before the Duke of Enghien at Dijon. From 1644 to 1661 he was in charge of the violin band of the consuls of Montpellier and in 1654 appeared together with Molière in the *Ballet des incompatibles*. In 1660 he was in Turin taking part in Princess Margherita's marriage celebrations with the violin band from Avignon. He settled in Turin in 1662 and became dancing master to Carlo Emanuele II, Duke of Savoy, and then director of the duke's band of 24 violins when it was formed in 1671. Between 1662 and 1690 he composed most of the dance tunes for ballets and operas performed at the court of Savoy, most notably for *L'amore vendicato* (1688) and *Silvio, re degli Albane* (1689). He had several children from his second marriage, some of whom were also musicians in Turin.

BIBLIOGRAPHY
J. Robert: 'Une famille de joueurs de violon avignonnais au XVIIᵉ siècle, les de La Pierre', *RMFC*, iv (1964), 54
M.-T. Bouquet: 'Musique et musiciens à Turin de 1648 à 1775', *Memorie dell'Accademia delle scienze di Torino*, ser.4a, xvii (1968)

JEAN ROBERT

Lapis, Santo (*fl* 1725–65). Italian composer. Little is known of his life beyond what can be deduced from his works. He and B. Cordans wrote the opera *La generosità di Tiberio* for Venice in 1729, and the following year he partly reset C. F. Gasparini's *L'amor generoso* for Venetian production under the title *La fede in cimento*. In 1738 he was in Prague, where his opera *Tigrane* was given and his op.1, a set of trio sonatas published in Augsburg, may date from that period. He lived in Holland from about 1752 to 1756 and several of his works for harpsichord, flute, etc, were published in Amsterdam. The score of his opera *L'infelice avventurato* (?Amsterdam, 1754) was once in Breitkopf's possession. Lapis was probably in London in 1758–60 when his opp.15 to 17, consisting successively of cello solos, songs, and harpsichord and guitar pieces, were published there by or for 'the author', as the title-pages show. The last record of him was in Edinburgh, as harpsichordist of a visiting Italian intermezzo company which performed Pergolesi's *La serva padrona* in June 1763, and he may have gone with the same company to York in October 1763 and to Dublin in the spring of 1764.

ALFRED LOEWENBERG/MICHAEL F. ROBINSON

La Popelinière, Alexandre-Jean-Joseph Le Riche de. *See* LA POUPLINIÈRE, ALEXANDRE-JEAN-JOSEPH LE RICHE DE.

Laporte, André (*b* Oplinter, Limburg, Belgium, 12 July 1931). Belgian composer. He studied with Peeters and de Jong at the Lemmens Institute, Mechelen, where he won the Lemmens-Tinel Award for organ and composition in 1958. He attended the Darmstadt summer courses from 1960 and also took part in the 1964 and 1965 Cologne courses for new music. In 1963 he was appointed producer of contemporary music for Belgian radio, and he has taught new composition techniques at the Brussels Conservatory. He received the Koopal Award from the Belgian Ministry of Culture in 1971. Laporte's music shows an awareness of contemporary trends, even to the extent of including pop elements in *Story*, together with a feeling for balance and instrumentation. He has written about *La vita non è sogno* in the June–July issue of *Vlaams muziektijdschrift* (1972).

WORKS
(*selective list*)
Jubilus, brass, perc, 1966; Story, vn, va, vc, hpd, 1967; Ascension, pf, 1967; Inclinations, fl, 1968; Le morte chitarre (Quasimodo), T, fl, str, 1969; Reflections, cl, 1970; Nachtmusik, orch, 1970; La vita non è sogno (Quasimodo, Marinetti), narrator, T, B, chorus, orch, 1972

Principal publishers: Tonos, Chester, Gerig

BIBLIOGRAPHY
H. Heughebaert: 'Ontmoetingen met Vlaamse komponisten: André Laporte', *Vlaams muziektijdschrift* (1970), Aug–Sept
H. Sabbe: 'De Vlaamse componist André Laporte: overzicht van een evolutie', *Mens en melodie*, xxvii (1972)

CORNEEL MERTENS

Laporte, Joseph de (*b* Belfort, 1713; *d* Paris, 19 Dec 1779). French writer. He left the Jesuit order, in which he was educated, and devoted himself to the literature, theatre, and opera of Paris. He wrote a few minor plays and librettos, translated the works of Pope, edited literary periodicals and contributed to the *Mercure de France*; his published work consists chiefly of anthologies and chronicles of the Paris theatres, with valuable details of plays and operas, authors, performers and receipts.

WRITINGS

(only those relating to music included)

Almanach historique et chronologique de tous les spectacles de Paris, i (1752); *Calendrier historique de théâtres de l'Opéra et des Comédies Française et Italienne et des Foires*, ii (1753); *Les spectacles de Paris, ou Suite du Calendrier historique et chronologique des théâtres*, iii–xxvii (1754–78) [continued after 1778 by Duchesne and others]

with J. B. A. Suard: *Nouveaux choix de pièces tirées des anciens Mercures et des autres journeaux*, lx–cviii (Paris, 1762–4)

L'esprit de l'"Encyclopédie" ou Choix des articles les plus curieux (Geneva and Paris, 1768)

with J. M. B. Clément: *Anecdotes dramatiques contenant toutes les pièces de théâtres . . . jusqu'en 1775* (Paris, 1775)

with S. R. N. Chamfort: *Dictionnaire dramatique contenant l'histoire des théâtres et les règles du genre dramatique* (Paris, 1776)

2 libs for J.-M. Leclair: *Le danger des épreuves*, 1749; *Apollon et Climène*, 2nd entrée in Les amusements lyriques, 1750

BIBLIOGRAPHY

FétisB

L. G. Michaud: 'Porte (L'Abbé Joseph de la)', *Biographie universelle*, xxxiv (Paris, n.d.)

M. Briquet: 'Laporte, Joseph de', *MGG*

JULIAN RUSHTON

La Pouplinière [La Popelinière], **Alexandre-Jean-Joseph Le Riche de** (*b* Chinon, Limousin, 26 July 1693; *d* Paris, 5 Dec, 1762). French patron of music, art and literature. The son of a financier, he became a lawyer and later *fermier général*. The many poets, artists and musicians he befriended include Voltaire, Marmontel, the Van Loos and La Tours, Rameau and Rousseau. From about 1731 he held frequent concerts in his Paris mansion (opposite what is now the Bibliothèque Nationale) and his country estate at Passy. Up to 1753 La Pouplinière's excellent orchestra performed Rameau's own compositions under his direction, as well as those of Mondonville, and other Frenchmen and Italians; La Pouplinière developed a particular fondness for these last. J. W. A. Stamitz and Gossec later assumed the direction of the orchestra. Though not an accomplished performer, La Pouplinière played the vielle and guitar and composed airs (some incorporated by Rameau; see Cucuël, 288f). A portrait of him by Carle Van Loo shows him seated holding a flute. Rameau's 'La La Poplinière' from his *Pièces de clavecin en concerts* (1741) pays tribute either to his devoted friend and patron or to his patron's first wife, Thérèse Des Hayes, an accomplished harpsichordist and pupil of Rameau.

BIBLIOGRAPHY

G. Cucuël: *La Pouplinière et la musique de chambre au XVIIIᵉ siècle* (Paris, 1913)

C. Girdlestone: *Jean-Philippe Rameau: his Life and Work* (London, 2/1969)

MARY CYR

Lappi, Pietro (*b* Florence, *c*1575; *d* Brescia, 1630). Italian composer. He became a member of the Congregazione Fiesolana, a religious order, and spent his working life as *maestro di cappella* at S Maria delle Grazie, Brescia, from about 1593 until his death. His works, whether vocal or instrumental, are all for church use. They span the period of transition from the polyphonic to the concertato style, though he tended to adhere to the former, and only one or two of his collections include motets for the more intimate scorings of the new style. Working in Brescia he was in contact with the school of instrumental musicians and instrument makers that flourished in that city, and he produced a volume of canzonas in 1616 as well as three others by which he is represented in an anthology of 1608. Like several composers at this period he sought to demonstrate his mastery of both old and new styles in the same

publication: the masses of 1613 comprise two which can be sung without organ and three 'concertate a voci sole nell'organo'. The latter have more quaver movement, chordal writing and dotted rhythms in melismatic solos. The motets of 1614 show that Lappi was concerned with problems of musical form, trying out ternary and rondo schemes, with alternating solos and tuttis. But the hymns of 1628 hark back to the previous century: he set alternate verses only and paraphrased the plainsong in a polyphonic idiom, and only the last verse of each setting is in a simple chordal style in triple time.

WORKS

(all except anthologies published in Venice)

Sacra omnium solemnitatum vespertina psalmodia cum 3 BVM canticis, 8vv, bc (1600)

Missarum, 8vv, liber I (1601; 2/1607 with bc) [contains 2 motets]

Regis Davidis psalmi ad Vesperas, 5vv, ut hymnus Gloria . . . 9vv ad lib, regiae virginis deiparae cantica alternis choris, 9–10vv (1605)

La terza con il Te Deum e letanie della beata vergine et santi, 8vv (1607)

[5] Missarum, 8, 9vv, liber II (1608)

[5] Missarum, 4–6vv, bc (org), liber I (1613)

[10] Sacrae melodiae, 1–6vv, bc (org), liber I (1614, enlarged 2/1621, further enlarged 3/1622)

Canzoni da suonare, a 4–13, libro I, op.9 (1616)

Salmi, 8vv (1616)

Salmi a 3 e 4 chori, bc (org), op.12 (1621; 2/1626 as Compieta a 3 e 4 chori) [includes 1 Magnificat]

Concerti sacri, 1–7vv, bc, libro II, op.13 (1623)

Messe secondo libro, 4–6vv, op.14 (1624)

Missa et responsorii, op.15 (1625)

Letanie della beatae virgine, 4–8vv, bc ad lib, libro II, op.17 (1627)

Salmi concertati, 5vv, bc (org), op.18 (1627)

[30] Hymni per tutto l'anno, 4vv, bc (org) (1628)

Rosario musicale: una messa a 2 cori con terzo coro aggiunto, salmi, litanie, motetti, canzone (1629)

Salmi spezzati, 4vv, bc, op.22 (1630)

5 masses in 1618², 1628²; 2 motets in 1612², 1623²; several pieces in Tripartus SS. concentuum fasciculus (Frankfurt am Main, 1621); 3 canzonas in 1608²⁴

Motets, *D-Bds*, *USSR-KA*; MS fragments, *D-Mbs*

BIBLIOGRAPHY

J. L. A. Roche: *North Italian Liturgical Music in the Early 17th Century* (diss., U. of Cambridge, 1968)

JEROME ROCHE

Lappish music. *See* SAMISH MUSIC.

Lara, Agustin (*b* Tlacotaplan, Veracruz, 30 Oct 1900; *d* Mexico City, 6 Nov 1969). Mexican composer. One of the best-known Mexican composers of popular music, he wrote over 600 songs, many of which achieved international celebrity; among these were *Granada*, *Maria Bonita* and *Solamente una vez*. In 1966 Franco accorded him honorary Spanish citizenship.

JUAN A. ORREGO-SALAS

Lara, Manuel Manrique de. *See* MANRIQUE DE LARA, MANUEL.

Larchet, John F(rancis) (*b* Dublin, 13 July 1884; *d* Dublin, 10 Aug 1967). Irish composer and teacher. After he had studied with Esposito at the Royal Irish Academy of Music, his enthusiasm for Irish traditional music led to his appointment as musical director of the Abbey Theatre (1907–34), where he worked with the leading Irish literary figures of the time. He took the MusB (1915) and MusD (1917) at Dublin University, and was professor of composition at the RIAM (1920–55). As professor of music at University College, Dublin, he established his subject as a university discipline in the newly founded Irish state, and through his teaching he founded a flourishing school of Irish composers. Active also as an adviser and organizer, he was closely concerned with every aspect of Dublin musical life. He received an honorary DMus from the National University of Ireland in 1953. Larchet's compositions reveal an elegant craftsmanship; the harmonies are tinged with modality and his melody shows the influence of old Irish tunes.

WORKS
(selective list)

Orch: Lament for Youth, 1939; Dirge of Oisín, str, 1940; By the Waters of Moyle, 1957
Choral: The Legend of Lough Rea, 1920; c30 folksong arrs.
Songs: Padraic the Fiddler, 1919; An Ardglass Boat Song, 1920; The Stranger, 1939; The Cormorant, 1947; Wee Hughie, 1947

Principal publishers: Boosey & Hawkes, Irish Government, Novello, Stainer & Bell

BIBLIOGRAPHY
E. Deale, ed.: *Catalogue of Contemporary Irish Composers* (Dublin, 1968)

ANTHONY HUGHES

Larchier, Federicus (*fl* ?1543). Composer who may be identifiable with JEAN LARCHIER.

Larchier, Jean (*fl* ?1543, 1544–55). French or Franco-Flemish composer. His works appeared in collections published in Antwerp and Louvain. He may be identifiable with Federicus Larchier, or related to him.

WORKS

Motets in 1547[6], 1553[15], 1554[10]
Chansons in 1543[14] (attrib. Federicus Larchier), 1544[13], 1545[14], 1550[14], 1553[24], 1555[5]

SAMUEL F. POGUE

Lardenois, Antoine (*b* Paris; *d* ?Dax, 1672 or later). French composer. He lived at Nîmes at least from 1651 to 1653, possibly to about 1658; he figures in the records of the consistory there. On 14 August 1652 he abjured Catholicism and in spite of his quarrelsome nature received financial aid from his protectors there towards a journey to Geneva in March and April 1653 to arrange for the publication of a volume of music. In November 1653 he sought but was not appointed to the dual post of janitor of the college and singer at the little temple at Nîmes. In 1657, with support from the Protestants at Nîmes, he offered his solmization method to the Protestants of La Rochelle. Lardenois continued his career as a musician in Paris, where on 27 January 1660 he abjured the reformed faith. He later became choirmaster of Dax Cathedral. His name appears for the last time in the chapter records in 1672, when it was recorded that he had been troubling his colleagues with 'grandes injures at autres emportements'.

Lardenois devised a simplified solmization method that he adapted to the Protestant psalter to make it easier to read and use. His method reduces the notation to a single system, with a single (C) clef and a signature of one flat and with a fixed *doh*, starting on *fa* (= *ut*); it freely makes use of the note *si* but places it at the interval *mi–fa*. The first edition of his *Les psaumes de David, mis en rime française par Clément Marot et Théodore de Bèze, réduits tout nouvellement à une bonne et facile méthode pour apprendre le chant ordinaire de l'église* (Geneva, 1651) is lost (2/1657, with a slightly different title-page and a sheet of music illustrating his method; subsequent edns., 1659 and 1662, and others later in the 17th century). At this period the *Paraphrase des pseaumes de David, en vers françois* by Antoine Godeau was becoming known to the public in settings by Louis XIII, Jacques de Gouy and Aux Cousteaux. This version received a warm welcome,

above all from Protestants who could sing it without running the risk involved with using Marot's paraphrases. Lardenois in his turn took it up and at his own expense (or perhaps that of the church at Nîmes) published his *Paraphrase . . . de Godeau, nouvellement mise en musique* (Paris, 1655, 2/1658/R1668). The chronicler Loret in *La muze historique* for 31 January 1660 reported that Lardenois' settings were being sung by Protestants throughout France. The melodies that he adapted for them are for the most part derived from those used in the Huguenot Psalter.

BIBLIOGRAPHY
O. Douen: *Clément Marot et le psautier huguenot* (Paris, 1878–9)
H. Charnier: 'La musique du chapitre de Dax dans la deuxième moitié du XVIIème siècle', *Bulletin trimestriel de la Société de Borda, Dax* (1955), no.1
D. Launay: '*La paraphrase des pseaumes de Godeau et ses musiciens*', *RdM*, l (1964), 30
——: 'Les musiciens de Godeau', *Colloque Godeau: Grasse 1972*

DENISE LAUNAY

Laredo, Jaime (Eduardo) (*b* Cochabamba, 7 June 1941). American violinist of Bolivian birth. His family moved to the USA when he was seven to enable him to further his musical training, and he was taught by Ivan Galamian at the Curtis Institute, Philadelphia. After making his professional début at the age of 11 with the San Francisco SO, he toured Latin America on a number of occasions. In 1959 he became the youngest winner of the Queen Elisabeth Competition, Brussels, and the same year he appeared with the Philadelphia and Cleveland Orchestras. A series of Bolivian airmail stamps issued in his honour bore his portrait and the notes A, D and C (La-re-do). His career as an adult violinist began with a much-praised Carnegie Hall recital in October 1960; he also received the New York City Handel Medallion that year. Laredo has performed throughout the USA and Europe, and made his London début at the Albert Hall in 1961. He is a frequent visitor to the Marlboro Festival, and his recording of Beethoven's Triple Concerto with Serkin, Parnas and the Marlboro Festival Orchestra well represents his style. Laredo is an aristocratic and predominantly lyrical performer; he is not as demonstrative as other Galamian pupils, but his clean intonation and meticulous phrasing make him valuable as an ensemble player (he is a member of the Chamber Music Society of Lincoln Center). He owns a 1717 violin by Stradivari known as the 'Ex-Gariel'; he married the pianist Ruth Meckler.

RICHARD BERNAS

Largamente (It.: 'broadly', 'generously'). Though strictly the adverb from LARGO, this word is rather different in its uses. It is used as an expression mark to denote a more stately manner of playing; or it can be an instruction to slow down the tempo. In this second sense it was a particular favourite of Elgar who found it so indispensable that in some of his works he even abbreviated it to *L* (together with *A* for *accelerando* and *R* for *ritardando*); see especially the scores of the Second Symphony and *The Kingdom*.

See also TEMPO AND EXPRESSION MARKS.

DAVID FALLOWS

Large (Lat. *larga, maxima*). The longest note value of medieval and Renaissance music. It is first found in late 13th-century music. Its value was twice or three times that of a long, and it was usually shown as in ex.1a. Its

Ex.1

(a)   (b)

rest was usually shown as in ex.1*b*, the choice of form depending on whether the mensuration of the long was binary or ternary. The large survived into the period of 'white' or 'void' notation (post-1450), although its use in the Renaissance was restricted mainly to the notation of tenor parts and other cantus firmi. It is mentioned in writings as late as Christopher Simpson's *Compendium of Practical Musick* (1667), although by this date its existence was purely theoretical. Indeed, Simpson stated that 'The *Large* and *Long* are now of little use, being too long for any Voice, or Instrument (the Organ excepted) to hold out to their full length'. Some sources use the term 'duplex longa' as an alternative term for the large.
See also NOTE VALUES.

JOHN MOREHEN

Larghetto (It.: 'rather wide'; diminutive of *largo*). A tempo mark indicating a rather more lighthearted *largo*. 'Handel's Largo' ('Ombra mai fù' from *Serse*) is marked *larghetto*, as are many other movements in the same opera; 'Comfort ye' from *Messiah* is marked *larghetto e piano*. The word seems to have come into use early in the 18th century: Brossard (1703) did not mention it; but Rousseau (1768, article 'Mouvement') gave it as one of the main adjustments of tempo (though not of mood) and described it (article 'Largo') as being 'a little less slow than *largo*'. Koch (1802) said it was 'normally the same as *andante*'.
For bibliography *see* TEMPO AND EXPRESSION MARKS.

DAVID FALLOWS

Largo (It.: 'large', 'broad'). A tempo mark, considered by many theorists of the 18th century to be the slowest of all: Rousseau (1768) listed it as the slowest of his five main degrees of movement in music, and many other writers agreed with him; but there is no overall consistency of opinion among earlier writers about its relation to such designations as *adagio*, *lento* and *grave*. 19th-century usage seems to have been more consistent in placing it somewhere between *adagio* and *andante*: it was surely in this sense that Bach had used it for the opening fugue of his B minor Mass and the final fugue in book 1 of the '48'; and Vivaldi had used the direction *largo ma più tosto andante* (P211/RV227).
    Largo appeared relatively often in music from the beginning of the 17th century, though normally to indicate a contrast in tempo within a faster movement. Caccini (*Le nuove musiche*, 1601/2) included an instruction 'escla con misura più larga'; Frescobaldi (*Partite e toccate*, 1615) recommended a *tempo largo* for runs and embellishments; and a similar usage in Giovanni Scipione (1650) endorses the conclusion that for them, at least, *largo* was already more a tempo than an affect. Praetorius (*Syntagma musicum*, iii, 2/1619) gave the equation *adagio: largo: lento: langsam*. In the late 17th and early 18th centuries the term was commonly applied to third movements, in 3/2 time and saraband rhythm, of *sonate da chiesa*.
    In England *largo* may have had a firmer position similar to that of *andante* in later centuries. Purcell, in the preface to his *Sonnata's of III Parts* (1683), gave *largo*, along with *presto largo* and *poco largo* as the moderate tempo between *adagio* and *allegro*; and the

anonymous *A Short Explication* (London, 1724) gave the progression *adagio, grave, largo, vivace, allegro, presto*.
    Brossard's *Dictionaire* (1703), followed by J. G. Walther's *Musicalisches Lexicon* (1732), gave an interesting description of *largo*:

Very slowly as though expanding the beat, and often marking the major accents unusually, etc. This happens above all in the *Recitative* of the Italians, in which one often does not make the beats equal because it is a kind of declamation in which the actor must follow the movement of the passion which affects him and which he wishes to express instead of following that of an equal and regulated beat.

For bibliography *see* TEMPO AND EXPRESSION MARKS.

DAVID FALLOWS

Larigot (Fr.). An ORGAN STOP.

La Roche, François de (*d* Vaux, 23 Dec 1676). French composer and singer. He was a 'chantre ordinaire de la musique' to the Duke of Orléans. An exponent of the four-part *air*, he produced 100 such pieces in five sets (Paris, 1648–9, 1652, 1655, 1658); only the tenor part is extant. A solo *air* by him is contained in the collection *Airs de cour et airs à boire* (*F-Pn* French MSS dated 1645–80).

BIBLIOGRAPHY
T. L'Huillier: 'Les anciens registres paroissiaux de Maincy', *Bulletin de la Société d'archéologie, sciences, lettres et arts de Seine et Marne* (1868)
L. E. S. J. de Laborde: *Musiciens de Paris, 1535–1792*, Vie musicale sous les rois Bourbons, ed. Y. de Brossard, xi (Paris, 1965)

DAVID TUNLEY

Laroche, Herman [Larosh, German Avgustovich] (*b* St Petersburg, 25 May 1845; *d* St Petersburg, 18 Oct 1904). Russian music critic. After studying under Dubuque, he attended the St Petersburg Conservatory (1862–6) and showed early promise as a composer. He taught for some years at the Moscow Conservatory and subsequently at the St Petersburg Conservatory. A prolific writer, Laroche contributed regularly to the Russian press. His critical outlook was cosmopolitan and conservative, and his articles, though often perceptive and always entertaining, are sometimes marred by blind prejudice. He was an unwavering opponent of the composers of the 'New Russian School', whom he considered to be limited and even barbaric, but he was a lifelong champion of Tchaikovsky, a fellow student at the conservatory. Under the pen name L. Nelyubov, Laroche wrote literary criticism, in which he attacked the work of the 'realist' writers Dobrolyubov and Pisarev. He also composed some vocal and instrumental pieces.

WRITINGS
Glinka i evo znacheniye v istorii muzïki [Glinka and his significance in music history] (Moscow, 1867)
Introduction to A. D. Ulïbïshev: *Novaya biografiya Motsarta* [A new biography of Mozart] (Moscow, 1890)
Muzïkal'no-kriticheskiye stat'i [Critical articles on music] (St Petersburg, 1894)
with N. D. Kashkin: *Na pamyat' o P.I. Chaykovskom* [In memory of Tchaikovsky] (Moscow, 1894)
O muzïkal'no-prekrasnom (Moscow, 1895) [trans. of E. Hanslick: *Vom Musikalisch-Schönem*, Leipzig, 1870]
ed.: N. D. Kashkin and V. Yakovlev: *Sobraniye muzïkal'no-kriticheskikh statey* [Collection of critical articles on music] (Moscow, 1913–24)
ed.: S. I. Levit: *Izbrannïye stat'i o Glinke* [Selected articles on Glinka] (Moscow, 1953)

BIBLIOGRAPHY
E. Bogoslovsky: 'G. A. Larosh', *Muzïka* (1911)
V. G. Val'ter: 'German Avgustovich Larosh', *Russkaya mïsl'* (1914), no.5
V. Belyayev: 'Bibliografiya', *Muzïka* (1914), 305

'Govoryat klassiki', *SovM* (1948), no.1, pp.29–59

A. S. Ogolevets: *Materialï i dokumentï po istorii russkoy realisticheskoy muzïkal'noy estetiki* [Materials and documents on the history of the Russian aesthetics of realism in music] (Moscow, 1954–6)

M. Sabinina: 'Larosh i Chaykovsky', *SovM* (1954), no.10, p.67

Yu. A. Kremlyov: *Russkaya mïsl o muzïke: ocherki istorii russkoy muzïkal'noy kritiki i estetiki XIX veka* [Russian thinking on music: essays on the history of Russian music criticism and aesthetics in the 19th century], ii (Leningrad, 1958), 297ff; iii (Leningrad, 1960), 129ff

S. Levit: 'Laroche, Hermann Awgustowitsch', *MGG*

G. B. Bernandt and I. M. Yampol'sky: *Kto pisal o muzïke* [Writers on music], ii (Moscow, 1974) [contains a list of writings]

JENNIFER SPENCER

La Rochelle. French town, site of the Rencontres Internationales d'Art Contemporain and the Concours Messiaen; *See* ROYAN FESTIVAL.

Larrauri, Antón (*b* Bilbao, 30 April 1932). Spanish composer and critic. He studied music privately in his home city where he also graduated in philosophy and arts, and his music career has developed alongside his activities as a classics teacher. In 1960 he was appointed music critic of the *Correo español* of Bilbao, holding that post until 1971 when he decided to give his time to composition. He has carried out studies on the relationships between sound and the sense of smell, and has developed these to some extent in his music. His works are few, but each is a thorough exploration of a particular compositional problem. The early pieces show the evolution of an individual style within the avant garde; his mature work incorporates philosophical concepts. *Espatadantza* has been much admired for its successful union of the basic elements of Basque folk music with avant-garde processes.

WORKS
(selective list)

Dédalo, orch, 1961; Apokatástasis, orch, 1965; Fluctuante no.1, 1v, ens, 1967; Contingencias, orch, 1971; Espatadantza, chorus, orch, 1972; Munduak, 1v, tape, 1973

BIBLIOGRAPHY

A. Fernández-Cid: *La música española en el siglo XX* (Madrid, 1973)

TOMÁS MARCO

Larrivée, Henri (*b* Lyons, 9 Jan 1737; *d* Paris, 7 Aug 1802). French baritone. While employed as a *perruquier* he met François Rebel, a director of the Opéra, who engaged him for the Opéra chorus. His career as a soloist began in 1755, when he played a priest in Rameau's *Castor et Pollux*; later he took the role of Jupiter and finally of Pollux. Apart from other roles in operas of Rameau and Lully, he created Ricimer in Philidor's *Ernelinde* (1767) and the title role in Gossec's *Sabinus* (1773). For Gluck he sang Agamemnon (in *Iphigénie en Aulide*), Hercules (in *Alceste*), Ubalde (in *Armide*) and Orestes (in *Iphigénie en Tauride*); he also played Orestes in Piccinni's *Iphigénie*, Grétry's *Andromaque* and Lemoyne's *Electre*. Larrivée venerated Gluck (despite difficulty in pleasing him as an actor) and for his sake refused to sing in Sacchini's *L'olympiade* in 1777. He overcame a lack of sympathy with Piccinni to sing Roland with such success as to give rise to Framery's 'Epître à M. Larrivée' (*Journal de Paris*, 4 February 1778), to which he made a rejoinder the next day. Subsequently he created Danaus in Salieri's *Les Danaïdes* (1784). After his final return to the stage in 1797 he was granted a sinecure for two well-received performances in Gluck's *Iphigénie en Aulide*. He had a good figure and a flexible voice with a wide range, which, according to Fétis and others, became nasal on high notes.

Larrivée's wife, Marie Jeanne Larrivée (née Le Mière) (*b* Sedan, Ardennes, 29 Nov 1733; *d* Paris, Oct 1786), was a soprano who appeared at the Opéra from 1750, mostly in minor roles. Her career was overshadowed by that of Sophie Arnould, but she created the title role of Philidor's *Ernelinde* (written for Arnould, 1767) and Eponine in Gossec's *Sabinus* (1773). She also sang at the Concert Spirituel.

JULIAN RUSHTON

Larrocha (y de la Calle), Alicia de (*b* Barcelona, 23 May 1923). Spanish pianist. She gave a public concert when she was five, became a student of Frank Marshall in Barcelona, and made her concerto début at the age of 12 with Fernandez Arbós and the Madrid SO. In 1947 she began touring outside Spain, but limited her engagements for some years because of family commitments. Her British début was in 1953 (Wigmore Hall, London), and her American début in 1955 with the Los Angeles PO. She formed a duo in 1956 with the cellist Gaspar Cassadó, and together they gave numerous concerts in Spain and elsewhere. In 1959 Larrocha became director of the Marshall Academy at Barcelona (where her husband, the pianist Juan Torra, also teaches), and during the 1960s she was a juror at several international piano competitions. She was awarded the Paderewski Memorial Medal in London in 1961. Her reputation was advanced at this time by several gramophone records, those of piano works by Granados and Albéniz being awarded international prizes. They reflect the balance of lively attack and poetic shading which is characteristic of her concert performances, achieving a distinctive blend of keyboard colour and expression in Romantic works, and a more formal elegance in Mozart and other classics.

BIBLIOGRAPHY

M. Smith: 'Legend Comes to Light', *Records and Recording*, xiii/7 (1970), 36

A. Blyth: 'Alicia de Larrocha talks', *Gramophone*, li (1973), 605, 654

R. Crichton: 'Lady of Spain', *Records and Recording*, xvii/1 (1973), 30

NOËL GOODWIN

Larsen, Jens Peter (*b* Copenhagen, 14 June 1902). Danish musicologist. He studied mathematics (1920–21) and musicology at Copenhagen University and between Hammerich's retirement (1922) and Abrahamsen's appointment there (1924) had private tuition in organ playing from Wöldike and music history from Laub, taking the organ examination at the Royal Danish Conservatory (1923); subsequently he resumed his study of musicology at the university (MA 1928). He then began a distinguished teaching career there, being appointed lecturer (1939), professor (1945) and director of the institute of musicology (1949–65); he retired in 1970. He was also visiting professor at the University of California at Berkeley (1961) and Herbert F. Johnson Professor at the University of Wisconsin (1971–2).

Larsen's first main interest was Haydn, and for more than 40 years he has occupied a leading position in Haydn scholarship. In his *Die Haydn Überlieferung* (1939), for which he received the doctorate of Copenhagen University, he meticulously investigated questions of authenticity and established a canon on which subsequent research and the publication of a Haydn edition were based. He was general editor of the Haydn Society edition (1949–51) and the collected edition prepared under the auspices of the Joseph-Haydn-

Institut, Cologne (1955–60), as well as chairman of the International Haydn Conference in Washington, DC (1975). In *Handel's 'Messiah'* (1957) he again considered the problem of authenticity and, by a careful identification of copyists' handwriting and other palaeographical evidence, made a valuable contribution to the ordering of Handelian sources. Several of his later essays on Handel were collected and issued in English translation by the American Choral Foundation (1972). He has served on the board of directors of the Halle G.-F. Händel-Gesellschaft (from 1955) and the council of the Göttingen Händel-Gesellschaft (from 1967), and was awarded the City of Halle Handel Prize (1965) and the gold medal of the Göttingen Händel-Gesellschaft (1972). He has also worked on Mozart and on general issues, particularly to do with changes of form and style between the Baroque and Classical periods.

In the field of Danish music Larsen has written about and edited music by C. E. F. Weyse (e.g. *Tolv sange for lige stemme*, 1929), but his most important achievements have been on behalf of church music: he was organist of Vangede Church (1930–45) and lecturer on church music at the Pastoral Seminary (1933–71); his work as an editor, with Wöldike and others, includes a number of publications of liturgical music for use in Danish churches, the music of the standard Danish hymnbook, *Den danske koralbog* (1954, 2/1973), and the *Nordisk koralbog* (1961).

WRITINGS

'Den gregorianske sang', *Kirken: tidsskrift for kirkelig orientering* (1929), 324

'Händel og vor tid', *Dansk musiktidsskrift*, iv (1929), 41

'6 nye sange af Weyse', *Dansk musiktidsskrift*, iv (1929), 103

'Om Laubs folkevise-rekonstruktioner', *Dansk musiktidsskrift*, vi (1931), 197

'Laub og dansk kirkesang', *Kirken: tidsskrift for kirkelig orientering* (1932), 66

'Haydn und das "kleine Quartbuch" ', *AcM*, vii (1935), 111; see also viii (1936), 22, 149 and ix (1937), 38

'Kirkesalme og kirkemelodi', *Tidskrift för kyrkomusik och svenskt gudstjänstliv*, x (1935), 145

ed.: *Messetoner efter gammel kirkelig tradition* (1935, 3/1965)

'Joseph Haydn: nogle problemer og synspunkter', *Dansk musiktidsskrift*, xi (1936), 224

Die Haydn-Überlieferung (diss., U. of Copenhagen, 1939; Copenhagen, 1939)

Drei Haydn-Kataloge in Faksimile: mit Einleitung und ergänzenden Themenverzeichnissen (Copenhagen, 1941, rev. 2/1979)

Weyses sange: deres betydning for sangen i hjem, skole og kirke (Copenhagen, 1942)

'Forslag til en dansk højmesseliturgi, iii: Bemærkninger om forslagets musikalske udformning og udførelse', *Dansk kirkesangs årsskrift* (1943), 33

'Thomas Laub og den danske sang', *Tidsskriftet Danmark* (1944), 15

'Laubs Melodiredaktioner og ord-tone-problemer', *Dansk kirkesangs årsskrift* (1945–6), 28

'Litaniet i den danske kirke', *Dansk kirkesangs årsskrift* (1948–9), 18

'Bach – den universelle', *Dansk musiktidsskrift*, xxv (1950), 237

'Zur Gesamtausgabe der Werke Joseph Haydns', *ÖMz*, v (1950), 48

'The Text of Handel's Messiah', *MQ*, xl (1954), 21

'Ein Händel-Requiem: die Trauerhymne für Königin Caroline (1737)', *GfMKB Hamburg 1956*, 15

'The Symphonies', *The Mozart Companion*, ed. H. C. R. Landon and D. Mitchell (London, 1956, 2/1965), 156–99

'Zu Haydns künstlerischer Entwicklung', *Festschrift Wilhelm Fischer* (Innsbruck, 1956), 123

'Eine bisher unbeachtete Quelle zu Haydns frühen Klavierwerken', *Festschrift Joseph Schmidt-Görg zum 60. Geburtstag* (Bonn, 1957), 188

Handel's 'Messiah': Origins, Composition, Sources (Copenhagen, 1957, rev. 2/1972)

'Haydn und Mozart', *ÖMz*, xiv (1959), 216

'Tempoprobleme bei Händel, dargestellt am "Messias" ', *Händel-Ehrung der Deutschen Demokratischen Republik: Leipzig 1959*, 141

'En Haydn gådekanon', *STMf*, xliii (1961), 215

'Handel Traditions and Handel Interpretations', *DAM*, i (1961), 38

'Et notationsproblem i Hans Thomissøns Psalmebog (1569)', *Natalicia musicologica Knud Jeppesen* (Copenhagen, 1962), 131

'Probleme der chronologischen Ordnung von Haydns Sinfonien', *Festschrift Otto Erich Deutsch* (Kassel, 1963), 90

'Sonatenform-Probleme', *Festschrift Friedrich Blume* (Kassel, 1963), 221

'Some Observations on the Development and Characteristics of Vienna Classical Instrumental Music', *SM*, ix (1967), 115

'Tendenzen der kirchengesanglichen Erneuerungsbewegung in Dänemark und den anderen skadinavischen Ländern', *Musik und Kirche*, xxxvii (1967), 63

'Zur Geschichte der "Messias"-Aufführungstraditionen', *HJb 1967–8*, 13

'Der musikalische Stilwandel um 1750 im Spiegel der zeitgenössischen Pariser Verlagskataloge', *Musik und Verlag: Karl Vötterle zum 65. Geburtstag* (Kassel, 1968), 410

'A Challenge to Musicology: the Viennese Classical School', *CMc* (1969), no.9, p.105

'Schütz und Dänemark', *Sagittarius*, ii (1969), 9; see also *BMw*, xiv (1972), 215

'Zu Schuberts Vertonung des Liedes "Nur wer die Sehnsucht kennt" ', *Musa-mens-musici: im Gedenken an Walther Vetter* (Leipzig, 1969), 277

'Der Stilwandel in der österreichischen Musik zwischen Barock und Wiener Klassik', *Der junge Haydn: Internationale Arbeitstagung des Instituts für Aufführungspraxis: Graz 1970*, 18

'Händels Weg zum Oratorium und sein "Messias" '; '*Esther* und Entstehung der Händelschen Oratorien-Tradition'; '45 Jahre Göttinger Händel-Bewegnung'; 'Oratorium versus Oper: Wandlungen der Oratoriumspflege durch die Jahrhunderte', *50 Jahre Göttinger Händel-Festspiele: Festschrift: Göttingen 1970*, 21; 40; 57; 113

'Kammermusik und Sinfonie', *Musica bohemica et europaea: Brno V 1970*, 349

'Zur Frage der Porträtähnlichkeit der Haydn-Bildnisse', *SM*, xii (1970), 153

'Epochenstil – Generationsstil', *HJb 1971*, 25

'Traditionelle Vorurteile bei der Betrachtung der Wiener klassischen Musik', *Symbolae historiae musicae: Hellmut Federhofer zum 60. Geburtstag* (Mainz, 1971), 194

Handel Studies (New York, 1972)

'Towards an Understanding of the Development of the Viennese Classical Style', *IMSCR*, xi *Copenhagen 1972*, 23

'Über Echtheitsprobleme in der Musik der Klassik', *Mf*, xxv (1972), 4

'Bemerkungen zum Aufführungsstil der Barockmusik', *Festschrift für Ernst Hermann Meyer* (Leipzig, 1973), 237

'Die Triosonaten von Johann Joseph Fux im Wiener Musikleben um 1740', *Musicae scientiae collectanea: Festschrift Karl Gustav Fellerer* (Cologne, 1973), 356

'To slags Weyse-stil', *Festschrift Gunnar Heerup* (Egtved, 1973), 197

'A Haydn Contract', *MT*, cxvii (1976), 737

Articles on Haydn in *Sohlmans musiklexicon* (Stockholm, 1948–52), *MGG* [with H. C. R. Landon], *Grove 6* [with G. Feder], *Histoire de la musique*, ii, ed. Roland-Manuel (Paris, 1963)

BIBLIOGRAPHY

N. Schiørring, H. Glahn and C. E. Hatting, eds.: *Festskrift Jens Peter Larsen: studier udgivet af Musikvidenskabeligt institut ved Københavns universitet* (Copenhagen, 1972) [incl. C. E. Hatting and N. Krabbe: 'Bibliografi', 1]

JOHN BERGSAGEL

Larsén-Todsen, Nanny (*b* Hagby, 2 Aug 1884). Swedish soprano. She studied in Stockholm, Berlin and Milan, and made her début with the Stockholm Opera in 1906 as Agathe in *Der Freischütz*. She remained a regular member of this company until 1923, first in lyric, later in heavy Wagnerian, roles. She sang at La Scala under Toscanini (1923–4), at the Metropolitan (1925–7), in Amsterdam, Vienna, Munich, Berlin, London and other centres. From 1927 to 1931 she sang at Bayreuth as Isolde, Kundry and Brünnhilde. She had a voice of great volume, with a slow beat which would strike some listeners as a tremolo, more noticeable in her records than on the stage. After she retired she taught in Stockholm.

LEO RIEMENS

Larsson, Lars-Erik (Vilner) (*b* Åkarp, Skåne, 15 May 1908). Swedish composer. After taking the organist's examination in Växjö (1924) he studied at the Stockholm Conservatory (1925–9) with Ernst Ellberg for composition and Olallo Morales for conducting.

While still a student he attracted attention with *En spelmans jordafärd* (1928) and his First Symphony (1927–8), and in 1929 he received a state composer's grant. In 1929–30 he made a study trip to Vienna and Leipzig, taking lessons from Berg and Fritz Reuter, and in 1930–31 he was a coach at the Royal Theatre, Stockholm. He then taught music in Malmö and Lund, and was music critic of the *Lund dagblad* (1933–7). His Sinfonietta, performed at the 1934 ISCM Festival, brought him international recognition and contributed to his growing reputation in the 1930s. He worked for Swedish radio as a conductor, composer and producer (1937–43); from 1945 to 1947 he was supervisor of the radio orchestras, and he remained conductor of the chamber orchestra until 1953. He was also professor of composition at the Stockholm Conservatory (1947–59) and later director of music at Uppsala University (1961–6). In 1971 he retired to Helsingborg.

As a composer Larsson has continually oscillated between Nordic Romanticism, neo-classicism and more unconventional styles (serialism and polytonality). His first works are Sibelian, but his year abroad (1929–30) brought a change: the Ten Two-part Piano Pieces (1932) include the first examples of 12-note serialism in Swedish music, and a string quartet fragment of the same period is in a harsh tonal style reminiscent of Hindemith. Of much greater importance, however, is the Sinfonietta for strings (also 1932), a quite un-Romantic, contrapuntal piece with neo-Baroque motivic work in the outer movements; for a composer of Larsson's gentle lyrical disposition it is a work of biting aggressiveness. It was followed by a series of successful and entertaining pieces in an increasingly warm, elegant neo-classical style, the Concert Overture no.2 (1934), the Saxophone Concerto (1934), the Little Serenade for strings (1934), the Divertimento no.2 (1935) and the much performed Piano Sonatina no.1 (1936). Works on a larger scale met with less success: both the Second Symphony (1936–7) and the monumental opera *Princessen av Cypern* ('The princess from Cyprus', 1930–37) were criticized for their mixture of styles, lack of originality and weak ideas, and they were withdrawn, though the symphony was performed again after revision in the 1970s.

Larsson's appointment to the radio service brought another change, and until the mid-1940s he concentrated exclusively on music for broadcasting, the theatre and films. Together with Hjalmar Gullberg and Pontus Boman he developed a new type of radio programme, the 'lyrical suite', consisting of poetry readings interspersed with music. His works in this form included *Dagens stunder* (1938), from which the *Pastoralsvit* was compiled for concert performance, *Senhöstblad* (1938), which produced the *Intima miniatyrer* for string quartet, and *Förklädd gud* ('The disguised god', 1940), a more cantata-like piece. In all of these, and particularly in the slower sections, there is a warm Scandinavian Romanticism, though the lively movements still show the airy, witty elegance of Larsson's neo-classicism. The war years found him writing works of contemporary relevance, most notably the *Obligationsmarschen* (1940), which, in a Norwegian version, played a part in encouraging the resistance movement in Norway.

A return to substantial independent composition came with the First String Quartet (1944) and the withdrawn Third Symphony (1944–5). In the Cello Concerto (1947) there was another change of direction, best demonstrated in the *Musik för orkester* (1948–9),

one of Larsson's weightiest works. It represents an unconscious approach to Hindemith: there are polytonal tendencies, thematic metamorphosis is used without schematicism on an extended scale, and the ideas have a new depth and tension. This direction was continued in the Violin Concerto (1952) and in the 12 concertinos for solo instrument and strings (1953–7), a group designed for skilled amateurs and comparable with Larsson's neo-classical works.

In the late 1950s, composing nothing, Larsson again reviewed his style. There had been 12-note suggestions in the Kyrie of his *Missa brevis* (1954), and he now developed his own 12-note technique, based not on series but on 'interval piles' (four of three notes separated by a major 3rd, or three of four notes separated by a minor 3rd). The few works written in this manner, including the Adagio for strings (1960), the Three Orchestral Pieces (1960) and the Orchestral Variations (1962–3), display an introspective, austere character. Larsson then moved in the opposite direction with the colourful cantata *Soluret och urnan* ('The sundial and the urn', 1966) and the *Lyrisk fantasi* for orchestra (1966). He returned again to neo-classicism in a series of lesser chamber pieces, and in the orchestral *Due auguri* (1971) and *Råå-rokoko* (1973) he brought together learning and humour in subtle musical witticism.

WORKS
(*selective list*)
DRAMATIC

op.

—	Princessen av Cypern [The princess from Cyprus] (opera, 4), 1930–37; Stockholm, 1937; withdrawn
—	Arresten på Bohus [The arrest on Bohus] (opéra bouffe, 2), 1938–9
46	Linden (ballet), 1957–8; Stockholm, 1958
	Numerous scores for the theatre, cinema and radio

ORCHESTRAL

2	Symphony no.1, D, 1927–8
4	Concert Overture no.1, 1929
5	Symfonisk skiss, 1930
7	Divertimento no.1, chamber orch, 1932
10	Sinfonietta, str, 1932
12	Little Serenade, str, 1934
13	Concert Overture no.2, 1934
14	Concerto, sax, str, 1934
15	Divertimento no.2, small orch, 1935
—	Drei Opernbilder [from Princessen av Cypern]
[17]	Symphony no.2, 1936–7, withdrawn except for 3rd movt, Ostinato, op.17
18	En vintersaga, 1937–8
19	Pastoralsvit [from lyrical suite Dagens stunder], 1938
22	Festmusik (Hyllningsmusik), 1939
23	Jorden sjunger, 1940
28	Gustaviansk svit [from film score Kungajakt], fl, hpd, str, 1944
32	Two Pieces, 1944
[34]	Symphony no.3, 1944–5, withdrawn except for 4th movt, Concert Overture, op.34
37	Cello Concerto, 1947
40	Musik för orkester, 1948–9
42	Violin Concerto, 1952
45	Concertinos, 1 inst, str: no.1, fl, 1955; no.2, ob, 1955; no.3, cl, 1957; no.4, bn, 1955; no.5, hn, 1955; no.6, tpt, 1953; no.7, trbn, 1955; no.8, vn, 1956; no.9, va, 1956; no.10, vc, 1956; no.11, db, 1957; no.12, pf, 1957
48	Adagio, str, 1960
49	Three Orchestral Pieces, 1960
50	Orchestral Variations, 1962–3
54	Lyrisk fantasi, 1966
62	Due auguri, 1971
64	Råå-rokoko, 1973

VOCAL
(*choral*)

—	De nakna trädens sånger, male vv, 1932
24	Förklädd gud [Disguised God], speaker, S, Bar, vv, orch, 1940
25	Väktarsånger [Songs of the guardian], speaker, Bar, vv, orch, 1940
43	Missa brevis, 3vv, 1954
51	Intrada solemnis, vv, brass, org, 1963

| 53 | Soluret och urnan [The sundial and the urn], cantata, Bar, vv, orch, 1966 |
| 59 | Tre citat, vv, 1969 |

(solo)

—	En spelmans jordafärd, 1v, pf, 1928, orchd
—	Two Songs (E. Lindorm), 1v, pf, 1945
—	Nine Songs (H. Gullberg), 1v, pf, 1946
52	Eight Songs, 1964

CHAMBER AND INSTRUMENTAL

3	Sonatina, vn, pf, 1928
6	Duo, vn, va, 1931
—	Ten Two-part Piano Pieces, 1932
16	Piano Sonatina no.1, 1936
20	Intima miniatyrer [from lyrical suite Senhöstblad], str qt, 1938
31	String Quartet no.1, d, 1944
38	Croquiser, pf, 1946–7
39	Piano Sonatina no.2, 1947
41	Piano Sonatina no.3, 1950
44	String Quartet no.2 (Quartetto alla serenata), 1955
47	12 Little Piano Pieces, 1960
55	Quattro tempi, divertimento, wind qnt, 1968
56–8	Easy Pieces, Five Pieces, Seven Little Fugues with Preludes pf, 1969
60	Sonatina, vc, pf, 1969
61	Three Pieces, cl, pf, 1970
63	Aubade, ob, str trio, 1972
65	String Quartet no.3, 1975

Principal publisher: Gehrman

BIBLIOGRAPHY

B. Wallner, H. Blomstedt and F. Lindberg: *Lars-Erik Larsson och hans concertinor* (Stockholm, 1957)

GÖRAN BERGENDAL

LaRue, (Adrian) Jan (Pieters) (*b* Kisaran, Sumatra, Indonesia, 31 July 1918). American musicologist. He took the SB at Harvard in 1940. He began graduate work at Princeton, where he studied with Roger Sessions and Oliver Strunk and received the MFA in 1942. Returning to Harvard for additional studies, he took courses from Walter Piston, A. Tillman Merritt and Archibald T. Davison; he received the PhD from Harvard in 1952. He taught at Wellesley College from 1942 to 1943 and 1946 to 1957. Since then he has been a professor in the music department at New York University; he was appointed chairman in 1971.

LaRue has done research in both ethnomusicology and historical musicology. He has studied the native vocal and instrumental music of Okinawa and wrote his dissertation on this subject. His more recent interests include late 18th-century music, style analysis and tools of research, including watermark analysis, study of publisher's catalogues and computer applications in musicology. He has sought to combine and relate these interests through such projects as computer-aided preparation of thematic catalogues and use of the computer for problems of analysis. His examinations of 18th-century publisher's catalogues have furnished information concerning dating of publications, musical tastes and the speed with which music prints became available throughout Europe. His book on style analysis provides both a methodology and a system of analytical symbols for the student. LaRue's professional activities have included a period as president of the American Musicological Society (1966–8); he was co-editor of the Deutsch 80th birthday Festschrift, the Reese Festschrift and the eighth IMS congress report.

See ANALYSIS, §§II, 8; III, 6.

WRITINGS

'Native Music on Okinawa', *MQ*, xxxii (1946), 157
'The Okinawan Notation System', *JAMS*, iv (1951), 27
The Okinawan Classical Songs: an Analytical and Comparative Study (diss., Harvard U., 1952)
'Bifocal Tonality: an Explanation for Ambiguous Baroque Cadences', *Essays on Music in Honor of Archibald Thompson Davison* (Cambridge, Mass., 1957), 173

'Abbreviated Description for Watermarks', *FAM*, iv (1957), 26
'A System of Symbols for Formal Analysis', *JAMS*, x (1957), 25
'Harmonic Rhythm in the Beethoven Symphonies', *MR*, xviii (1957), 8
'Major and Minor Mysteries of Identification in the 18th-century Symphony', *JAMS*, xiii (1960), 181
'Watermarks and Musicology', *AcM*, xxxiii (1961), 120
'Significant and Coincidental Resemblances between Classical Themes', *JAMS*, xiv (1961), 224
'Two Problems in Musical Analysis: the Computer Lends a Hand', *Computers in Humanistic Research*, ed. E. A. Bowles (Englewood Cliffs, NJ, 1967), 194
with M. Cobin: 'The Ruge-Seignelay Catalogue: an Exercise in Automated Entries', *Elektronische Datenverarbeitung in der Musikwissenschaft*, ed. H. Heckmann (Regensburg, 1967), 41
'Computer Aids to Musicology: Future Technological Directions', *IMSCR, x Ljubljana 1967*, 457
Revue of L. von Köchel: *Chronologisch-thematisches Verzeichnis sämtlicher Tonwerke Wolfgang Amadé Mozarts*, ed. F. Giegling, A. Weinmann and G. Sievers (Wiesbaden, 6/1964), *JAMS*, xx (1967), 495
'Mozart Listings in Some Rediscovered Sale-Catalogues, Breslau 1787–1792', *MJb 1967*, 46
'The Bydgoszcz Festival Celebrating Poland's Thousand Years', *Notes*, xxiii (1966–7), 455
'Ten Rediscovered Sale-catalogues: Leuckart's Supplements Breslau 1787–1792', *Musik und Verlag: Karl Vötterle zum 65. Geburtstag* (Kassel, 1968), 424
'The Mapping of Musical Classicism, a Little-known and Dangerous Period', *CMc* (1969), no.9, p.113
with J. B. Holland: 'The Sharp Manuscript, London, 1759–ca.1793: a Uniquely Annotated Music Catalogue', *New York Public Library Bulletin*, lxxiii (1969), 147
'Fundamental Considerations in Style Analysis', *Notes*, xxv (1968–9), 447
Guidelines for Style Analysis (New York, 1970)
'New Directions for Style Analysis', *Musicology and the Computer*, ed. B. S. Brook (New York, 1970), 194
with H.-R. Dürrenmatt and M. Gould: 'Die Notierung thematischer Incipits auf "Mark-Sense-Cards" ', *FAM*, xvii (1970), 15
'Specialized Lights for Watermark Readers', *Notes*, xxvi (1969–70), 479
with H. LaRue: 'Trade Routes and Time Lag in the Export of Late Eighteenth-century Opera', *A Musical Offering: Essays in Honor of Martin Bernstein* (New York, 1977)
'Mozart Authentication by Activity Analysis', *MJb 1978–9*, 209
'Japan', §VI, 2, 'Symphony', §I, *Grove 6*

PAULA MORGAN

La Rue, Pierre de (*b* ?Tournai, *c*1460; *d* Courtrai, 20 Nov 1518). Flemish composer. He stands alongside Josquin, Obrecht, Weerbeke, Isaac, Agricola, Compère and Brumel as one of the leading Flemish composers of the period, and is particularly significant for the extent and diversity of his work, as well as for its quality and individuality. His name occurs in extremely varied forms in contemporary documents: apart from the different forms of his christian name (Pierre, Petrus, Perchon, Pierchon, Pierson, Pirson, Pierrazon etc), he is also known by the various forms and translations of La Rue (Peteren van Straeten, Petrus Platensis or de Platea, Piero delapiazza, Petrus de Vico, de Vito or la Vic, Petrus Vicanus, Petrus de Robore etc).

1. LIFE. La Rue was the son of Jehan de la Rue and Gertrud de la Haye. Biographical statements (by Ambros and Pinchart) for 1477 and 1485 have no factual basis, and the first accurate record of him is from May and June 1482 and from March 1483 to March 1485 as a tenor at Siena Cathedral. From June 1489 to March 1492 he was a tenor at 's-Hertogenbosch Cathedral. In 1492–3 he also joined the Marian Brotherhood there and was described as 'Cantor Romanorum regis', which implies that he was a singer in Maximilian's Burgundian Hofkapelle. Continuous archival references show that after Maximilian was elected emperor in 1493 La Rue remained a member of the Grande Chapelle, now under Philip the Fair. After Philip's death in Spain in 1506, La Rue remained there for a time in the service of Philip's widow Juana. He

does not appear to have returned to the Netherlands until 1508, although he had held livings in Courtrai (and temporary ones elsewhere) since 1501. He became a singer in Mechelen at the court of the art-loving Marguerite of Austria. She evidently held La Rue in high esteem and her personal recommendation enhanced his reputation with Maximilian. La Rue then served in Archduke Karl's private Kapelle from 1514 until early 1516. He seems to have retired to Courtrai at the beginning of 1516; he drew up his will there on 16 June of that year and died in 1518.

La Rue's close link with the Burgundian and Netherlands courts naturally enabled him not only to take part in important historical events, which were often celebrated with musical festivities (for details see Rubsamen, *MGG*), but also to make several extensive journeys through Europe. His two journeys to Spain with Philip the Fair in 1501–3 and 1506 are particularly important; on them he met composers working in France and in German lands – Isaac, Robert de Févin and presumably Josquin. An epitaph formerly in St Catharine's Chapel of Notre Dame, Courtrai, but now lost, also referred to La Rue's knowledge of Europe, stating that the canonicus La Rue 'Pannonos reges coluit, Gallos et Hiberos' (there is in fact no proof that he actually served at the Hungarian or French courts).

2. WORKS.

(*i*) *General.* The frequent references to La Rue in 16th-century theoretical literature indicate that his compositions occupied a prominent position: together with Obrecht, Isaac, Agricola, Brumel and others of the Netherlands school, he emerges as one of the most important masters of Josquin's generation. The range and quality of his surviving work confirms this assessment. It is accordingly strange that scholars have so little concerned themselves with his compositions that there is still no sufficient bibliographical basis for study, in spite of the work of Davison and Picker on the motets and the chansons. The masses have not been sufficiently investigated and there is no complete discussion of the composer's style. Rubsamen's work provided many valuable starting-points, but these have hardly been taken up. As a result, it is difficult to make more than guarded remarks about La Rue's musical style.

(*ii*) *Sources and chronology.* The recent discovery that La Rue was active in Siena in 1482 and 1483–5 is important primarily because he was always believed to be one of the few Netherlands composers who did not visit Italy and whose works lacked any sign of Italian influence. It is of interest, too, in that no sources containing works clearly ascribable to La Rue date from this period. The early sources for his music are mostly from Netherlands areas (those copied by Alamire are particularly important) and they did not begin to appear until shortly before 1500. Both they and the Spanish sources can be related to La Rue's residence in those two areas. The Italian sources first appear only in the 1520s and 1530s (apart from some chansons printed about 1500 and a little later and the masses printed by Petrucci in 1503 and 1508). The inference must be that La Rue did not compose during his stay in Italy; consequently the period of composition of all his works seems to be restricted to the last 20 or so years of his life. This narrow span of activity makes an accurate chronological ordering of his compositions almost impossible.

(*iii*) *Masses.* The core of La Rue's work lies in his settings of the Mass: 31 (or perhaps 33) mass cycles, two Kyries and five isolated Credos survive. He preferred plainchant to secular models; as is normal with the Netherlands composers of the period, the liturgically correct chants (e.g. *Missa paschalis, Missa de feria, Missa pro defunctis*) are used less than those taken from elsewhere (e.g. *Missa 'Conceptio tua'* and others).

The form of the masses corresponds to the norm about 1500 in that they are composed for four or five voices (six parts are rare) and follow the usual patterns in the distribution of text and of sections for fewer voices. La Rue treated his model in various ways. The borrowed melody is often found as the cantus firmus, presented once in every movement. In the five-voice masses in particular he seems to have had a decided predilection for using a cantus firmus tenor part arranged in this manner. A second technique is the adaptation of a brief initial motif or excerpt from his model which is then repeated as an ostinato (e.g. *Missa 'Cum iucunditate', Missa 'Sancta Dei genetrix'*). Thirdly, a number of masses use a cycle of chants, a different one for each movement. Such an arrangement, found typically when the composer chose a cycle from the Ordinary of the Mass (e.g. *Missa paschalis*, in which, moreover, he used correct chants and ones from elsewhere in the liturgy simultaneously), gains its unity from the liturgical unity of the borrowed models, and not from any inherent musical feature. A similar arrangement of a sequence of cantus firmi also occurs in the *Missa de septem doloribus*. On occasion La Rue was content to achieve cyclic unity with head-motifs, for example in the *Missa 'Ave Maria'*. He placed strikingly little emphasis on the parody mass: the only known examples are the admittedly large-scale six-voice *Missa 'Ave sanctissima Maria'* and an isolated eight-voice Credo *'Angeli archangeli'*.

Almost certainly this reluctance to use parody technique can be attributed to the attraction that canonic forms had for La Rue, for the possibilities for canonic writing would have been reduced in parody compositions. In addition to the frequent two-part canons found in individual sections of a mass, there are also several complete canon masses in which, for example, one part yields four voices (*Missa 'O salutaris hostia'*) or three parts six voices (*Missa 'Ave sanctissima Maria'*). These are perhaps the clearest examples of the constructivist element that is often emphasized in the literature on the composer.

Another characteristic feature is La Rue's predilection for simple two-voice sections: pairs of voices are time and again used for contrast, either initially or during a movement. His proximity to Josquin is apparent not only in his skilful mastery of canonic settings but also in this tendency. In some (possibly later) works this preference leads to an arrangement of, as it were, two alternating choirs (e.g. the six-voice Credo) which may also be marked with a decidedly declamatory and homophonic style at variance with the composer's much-lauded constructivism. Although imitation is almost totally absent from these works, it is normally an important feature of La Rue's music, frequently and elegantly permeating all the voices, both at the beginning and in the course of a movement. His masses show a tendency to be subdivided by clausulas predictably and quite audibly into sections. Finally, La Rue possessed the fascinating ability to give each individual part a linear flow, allowing it to retain a plastic quality; this is frequently inspired by his fresh treatments of musical ideas presented earlier, a process that can also be seen in the repetition of the cantus firmus.

(*iv*) *Motets.* Davison has shown that a number of two- and three-voice motet settings by La Rue (found in German post-Reformation bicinium literature) are sections from his masses provided with new texts (contrafacta). When these works and those of dubious authenticity are subtracted from the total, the number of sacred compositions outside the mass repertory amounts to a little over 30. Of these, an almost complete *Magnificat* setting, a corpus of *Salve regina* settings and a fairly lengthy setting from the book of *Lamentations* are of major significance.

La Rue's adherence to four-voice writing is even more pronounced in these works than in his masses; there are practically no works for five voices and only a few isolated six-part works. In many ways they follow the pattern found in the masses, ranging from formally constructed works with distinctive cantus firmi (as in the *Magnificat* and *Salve regina* settings) to works with a perfect balance between the voices (*Delicta iuventutis*) and very homophonic settings (*O salutaris hostia*). Although imitation is used abundantly it rarely appears at the opening of four-voice works (see Davison). Canonic writing is also common, while in some motets there seems to be little relationship to the pre-existing melody (e.g. *Ave regina*). Further aspects of his mass style reappear – ostinato, sequence and a predictable breaking-up of the flow by cadences – and he was also able to sustain the interest by continually varied treatment of his material.

(*v*) *Chansons.* Six chansons long believed to be by La Rue on the strength of their attribution to Pietrequin are by another composer of that name. There appear to be approximately 30 authenticated chansons. In addition Picker has suggested that some anonymous chansons (in *B-Br* 228) may be by La Rue, in many cases on good grounds but without factual proof.

Although La Rue occasionally used three, five and six voices in his chansons, his standard setting was for four. His chanson style changed freely; thus there are typical late Burgundian chansons with vocal upper part and textless lower parts and, at the other extreme, typical 16th-century settings with vocal parts of equal design. The characteristic features of the masses and the motets are evident, *mutatis mutandis*, in the chansons. Within the context of the *formes fixes* then common in chanson composition, La Rue's arrangements are free but formally balanced and are clear in structure as a result of the clausulas frequently used at the end of each line of text. They also show his marked predilection for setting pairs of voices either at the beginning or within a composition, and for imitation (though only rarely does this develop into genuine canonic writing). Many of his chansons appear to have been written while he was with Marguerite of Austria, and these in particular show the way in which his melodic lines flow independently, while often skilfully developing earlier material.

(*vi*) *Assessment.* In the present state of research on La Rue, it is impossible to assess accurately the place of the composer in his time, either from a stylistic or from a historical point of view. However, an attempt at assessment is important, for the available biographical data show that he was exposed to an extremely varied field of

influence: as a member of the Burgundian Hofkapelle, he would have been familiar with the work of colleagues such as Agricola, Champion, Divitis, Weerbeke and Orto; as a result of his travels, he knew Robert de Févin and Isaac, and presumably also Hofhaimer and very probably Josquin. It is unlikely that he was a pupil of Ockeghem, as might be inferred from Jean Molinet's *Déploration de Johan. Okeghem*, for La Rue's compositional style, punctuated with clear cadential points, would tend to contradict such an assumption. There is no clearly discernible reflection in his music of his early years in Italy: there are no settings of Italian texts, as with Josquin and particularly Isaac, nor definite traces of the rich-sounding, largely homophonic style such as appears in the works of Josquin, Weerbeke or Compère during and after their years in Milan. Literature on La Rue has occasionally overemphasized the constructivist element in his works (explained as a specifically Netherlands trait), but this general stylistic feature can best be explained if it is assumed that he decided to turn to composition only after returning to the Netherlands from Italy, and patently southern influences are therefore absent. The influence, in his masses, of Spanish music (Anchieta, Peñalosa and others; pointed out by Rubsamen, 1937) seems to be overestimated.

It thus seems that La Rue's music is probably closest to Josquin's. However, he seems to have been reluctant to follow Josquin's developments in using the sense of the text as the basis of greater expressiveness in the setting; he appears, on the contrary, to have preferred to use musical means to reinforce the implications of the text, for example by condensing the setting or by carefully controlling the rate of movement. The technical constructivist aspects, most apparent in the use of canon, never detract from the flexibility of his work; this may well reflect on his relatively late start as a composer. These aspects rarely, as sometimes with Obrecht, generate a static approach to form. There seems on the other hand to be a certain stylistic affinity with Isaac. Together with Josquin and Brumel, La Rue probably influenced the succeeding generation, particularly such men as Richafort, Manchicourt and Gascongne. His reputation lasted well into the 16th century, and he was cited repeatedly by theorists as an excellent composer.

WORKS

For full sources see Rubsamen (*MGG*) and Robyns (1954); only additional sources listed.
Editions: *P. de La Rue: Liber missarum*, ed. A. Tirabassi (Kassel and elsewhere, 1941) [T]
        M. Picker: *The Chanson Albums of Marguerite of Austria* (Berkeley and Los Angeles, 1965) [P]

MASSES

Missa 'Alleluia', 5vv
Missa almana [Missa 'Pourquoy non', 'Sexti ut fa'], 4vv, *I-Rvat* C.S.45
Missa 'Assumpta est Maria', 4vv, ed. in Musica divina, xviii (Regensburg, 1966)
Missa 'Ave Maria', 4vv, *I-CMac* M, ed. in MMRF, viii (1898/R)
Missa 'Ave sanctissima Maria' [Missa de beata virgine], 6vv, T and ed. in Documenta polyphoniae liturgicae, 1st ser. B, i (Rome, 1950)
Missa 'Conceptio tua', 5vv, T
Missa 'Coronata', see Missa de beata virgine, 4vv
Missa 'Cum iucunditate', 4vv
Missa de beata virgine [Missa 'Salve sancta parens', 'Coronata'], 4vv, ed. in MMBel, viii (1960)
Missa de beata virgine, see Missa 'Ave sanctissima Maria'
Missa de doloribus, see Missa de septem doloribus
Missa de feria, 5vv, T
Missa de Sancta Anna [Missa Felix Anna], 4vv, ed. in MMBel, viii (1960)
Missa de sancta cruce [Missa 'Nos autem gloriari'], 5vv, T
Missa de Sancto Antonio [Missa 'O sacer Anthoni'], 4vv, *I-CF* 59, *VEcap* DCCLVI (as Missa 'Agnosce o vicenti'), Ky ed. in GMB
Missa de Sancto Job [Missa 'Floruit egregius'], 4vv

Missa de septem doloribus [Missa de doloribus], 5vv, T
Missa de virginibus [Missa 'O quam pulchra est'], 4vv, ed. in MMBel, viii (1960)
Missa Felix Anna, see Missa de Sancta Anna
Missa 'Floruit egregius', see Missa de Sancto Job
Missa 'Incessament' [Missa 'Sic Deus'], 5vv, Ky ed. A. Smijers, *Van Ockeghem tot Sweelinck* (Amsterdam, 1939, 2/1951)
Missa 'Inviolata', 4vv
Missa 'Ista est speciosa', 5vv, T
Missa 'Iste confessor', 4–6vv
Missa 'Jesum liate' (?lost; in MS belonging to Mary of Hungary: see vander Straeten, viii, 379)
Missa 'L'homme armé' (i), 4vv, ed. in Cw, cxiv (1972)
Missa Margaretha, see Missa 'O gloriosa Domina'
Missa 'Nos autem gloriari', see Missa de sancta cruce
Missa 'Numque fue pena maior', 4vv, D-F 2
Missa 'O gloriosa Domina' [Missa Margaretha], 4vv, F 2
Missa 'O quam pulchra est', see Missa de virginibus
Missa 'O sacer Anthoni', see Missa de Sancto Antonio
Missa 'O salutaris hostia', 4vv
Missa paschalis [Missa 'Resurrexi'], 5vv, T
Missa 'Pourquoy non', see Missa almana
Missa pro defunctis, 4vv, ed. in Cw, xi (1931/R)
Missa 'Puer est natus', 4vv, F 2
Missa quarti toni, see Missa 'Sub tuum praesidium'
Missa 'Resurrexi', see Missa paschalis
Missa 'Salve sancta parens', see Missa de beata virgine
Missa 'Sancta Dei genetrix', 4vv
Missa 'Sexti ut fa', see Missa almana
Missa 'Sic Deus', see Missa 'Incessament'
Missa [sine nomine] (i), 4vv
Missa 'Sub tuum praesidium' [Missa quarti toni], 4vv
Missa 'Tandernaken', 4vv
Missa 'Tous les regretz', 4vv, San ed. A. W. Ambros, *Geschichte der Musik*, v (Leipzig, rev. 2/1882 by O. Kade)

Doubtful: Missa 'L'homme armé' (ii), 4vv; Missa [sine nomine] (ii), 4vv, Ju 12

MASS SECTIONS

Kyrie in festo Paschae, 4vv
Kyrie paschale, 5vv
Credo 'Angeli archangeli', 8vv
Credo de villagiis, 4vv
Credo 'L'amour de moy', 4vv
Credo, 4vv
Credo, 6vv, E-B 681

MAGNIFICAT AND LAMENTATIONS

Magnificat primi toni, 3–6vv
Magnificat secundi toni, 2–4vv
Magnificat quarti toni, 3–4vv
Magnificat quinti toni, 2–4vv
Magnificat sexti toni, 3–5vv, ed. in Trésor musical, xix (Brussels, 1883); xxix (Brussels, 1893)
Magnificat septimi toni, 3–4vv
Magnificat octavi toni, 4vv
Lamentationes Hieremiae, 4vv, ed. in Musikalische Denkmäler, vi (Mainz, 1965)

MOTETS

2- and 3-voice contrafacta of mass and Magnificat sections identified by Rubsamen (*MGG*) and Davison (1962) are not listed.

Ave regina caelorum, 4vv, ed. in Cw, xci (1962); Considera Israel, 4vv, ed. in Cw, xci (1962); Da pacem, 4vv; Delicta iuventutis, 4vv, ed. in Cw, xi (1931/R); Doleo super te [= 4p. of Considera Israel]; Domini est terra, 4vv; Frange esurienti, 2vv (?contrafactum); Gaude virgo mater, 4vv, ed. in Trésor musical, xvii (Brussels, 1882)
Lauda anima mea, 4vv, ed. in Cw, xci (1962); Laudate Dominum omnes gentes, 4vv, ed. in Cw, xci (1962); Ne temere quid loquaris, 2vv (?contrafactum); Num stultum est mortem, 3vv (?contrafactum); O Domine Jesu Christe, 4vv; O salutaris hostia, 4vv (may replace Osanna in Missa de Sancta Anna), B-Br IV 922
Pater de caelis, 6vv; Quis dabit pacem, 4vv, 1p. ed. W. Osthoff, *Theatergesang und darstellende Musik in der italienischen Renaissance* (Tutzing, 1969); Regina caeli, 4vv; Salve mater Salvatoris, 4vv; Salve regina (i), 4vv, ed. in Trésor musical, xix (Brussels, 1883), xxix (Brussels, 1893); Salve regina (ii), 4vv; Salve regina (iii), 4vv; Salve regina (iv), 4vv; Salve regina (v), 4vv, ed. in Trésor musical, xviii (Brussels, 1882); Salve regina (vi), 4vv
Sancta Maria virgo, 3vv, 1538⁹ (1p. only); Vexilla Regis, 4vv, ed. A. Smijers, *Van Ockeghem tot Sweelinck* (Amsterdam, 1939, 2/1951); Virga tua, 4vv (?contrafactum)

Doubtful: Ave sanctissima Maria, 6vv (?Verdelot); Magnificat quarti toni, 4vv (? Agricola, Brumel, Josquin); 2p. of Sancta Maria virgo (?Craen); Te decet laus, 5vv; Si dormiero, 3vv (?Agricola)
Spurious: Salva nos, 4vv, by Isaac

SECULAR

Au feu d'amour, 4vv, ed. H. Riemann, *Musikgeschichte in Beispielen* (Leipzig, 1912); Autant en emporte, 4vv, ed. in Cw, iii (1929/R); A vous non autre, 3vv, P; Carmen in la, see Secretz regretz; Carmen in re, see Leal scfray; Ce n'est pas jeu, 4vv, P; Dedans boutons, 4vv; De l'oeil de la fille, 4vv, P; Dictes moy bergère, 3vv; Dung aultre aymer, 6vv; Dung desplaisir, 4vv
En espoir vis, 4vv; Forsseulement (i), 4vv, ed. F. J. Giesbert, *Ein altes Spielbuch* (Mainz, 1936); Forsseulement, 5vv, ed. in Gombosi; Il est bien heureux, 4vv, P; Jam sauche, 4vv; Il faut morire, 6vv; Il viendra le jour, 4vv, P; Incessament mon povre cueur, 5vv, ed. A. Smijers, *J. Desprez: Wereldlijke werken*, i/1, fasc.3 (Amsterdam and Leipzig, 1925); Las que plains, 4vv; Leal scfray (Carmen in re), 4vv
Ma bouche rit, 4vv; Mijn hert heeft altijt, 4vv, P; Plorer gemir/ Requiem, 4vv; Pourquoy non, 4vv, P; Pourquoy tant me fault, 4vv, P; Pour ung jamais, 3vv, P; Puis que je suis, 4vv, P; Secretz regretz (Carmen in la), B-Br 228, P; Si le changer, 4vv; Tant que nostre argent, 4vv; Tous les regretz, 4vv, D-Bds 40026, P; Tous nobles cueurs, 3vv, P; Trop plus de secretz, 4vv, Bds 40026, P

Doubtful: Ach hulff mich leid, 4vv (? Bauldeweyn, Josquin); Cent mille regretz, 5vv (?Josquin); Cueurs desolez, 5vv; Een vrolic wesenn, 4vv (?Pipelare); Elle a bien, 4vv (?Sermisy); En l'amour, 1v (frag.); Forsseulement (ii), 4vv (?Pipelare); Il me fait mal, 3vv; Ma mère hellas, 4vv; Quant il survient, 4vv
Spurious (by Pietrequin): Adieu florens la yolye, 4vv; En desirant, 3vv; Mais que ce fust secretement, 3vv; Mes douleurs, 3vv; Quen dictez vous, 3vv; Sans y penser, 3vv

BIBLIOGRAPHY

A. W. Ambros: *Geschichte der Musik*, iii (Breslau, 1868)
A. Pinchart: *Archives des arts, sciences et lettres*, iii (Ghent, 1881)
L. de Burbure: 'Etude sur un manuscrit du XVIe siècle', *Académie royale des sciences, des lettres et des beaux-arts de Belgique: mémoires couronnés et autres mémoires*, xxxii (1882)
E. vander Straeten: *La musique aux Pays-Bas avant le XIXe siècle*, vii–viii (Brussels, 1885–8/R1969)
G. Caullet: *Musiciens de la collégiale Notre-Dame à Courtrai d'après leur testaments* (Courtrai, 1911)
A. Hocquet: 'Un musicien tournaisien dit courtraisien', *Revue tournaisienne* (1911), Sept; repr. in *Gazette musicale de Belgique*, iii/69 (15 Aug 1936)
P. Wagner: *Geschichte der Messe*, i (Leipzig, 1913/R1963)
M. Bruchet and E. Lancien: *L'itinéraire de Marguerite d'Autriche* (Lille, 1934)
G. van Doorslaer: 'La chapelle musicale de Philippe le Beau', *Revue belge d'archéologie et d'histoire de l'art*, iv (1934), 21–57, 139
L. K. J. Feininger: *Die Frühgeschichte des Kanons bis Josquin des Prez* (Emsdetten, 1937)
W. H. Rubsamen: *Pierre de la Rue als Messen-Komponist* (diss., U. of Munich, 1937)
J. Schmidt-Görg: 'Die Acta Capitularia der Notre-Dame-Kirche zu Kortrijk als musikgeschichtliche Quelle', *Vlaamsch jaarboek voor muziekgeschiedenis*, i (1939), 21–78
R. B. Lenaerts: 'The 16th-century Parody Mass in the Netherlands', *MQ*, xxxvi (1950), 410
G. Reese: *Music in the Renaissance* (New York, 1954, rev. 2/1959)
J. Robyns: *Pierre de la Rue (circa 1460–1518): een bio-bibliographische studie* (Brussels, 1954)
——: 'Pierre de la Rue als overgangsfiguur tussen Middeleeuwen en Renaissance', *RBM*, ix (1955), 122
R. B. Lenaerts: 'Niederländische polyphone Musik in der Bibliothek von Montserrat', *Festschrift Joseph Schmidt-Görg zum 60. Geburtstag* (Bonn, 1957), 196
M. Picker: 'The Chanson Albums of Marguerite of Austria', *AnnM*, vi (1958–63), 145–285
L. Hoffmann-Erbrecht: 'Ein Frankfurter Messenkodex', *AMw*, xvi (1959), 328
W. Rubsamen: 'La Rue, Pierre de', *MGG*
N. Davison: 'The Motets of Pierre de la Rue', *MQ*, xlviii (1962), 18
G. Pietzsch: *Quellen und Forschungen zur Geschichte der Musik am kurpfälzischen Hof zu Heidelberg* (Wiesbaden, 1963)
E. H. Sparks: *Cantus Firmus in Mass and Motet* (Berkeley and Los Angeles, 1963)
M. Picker: *The Chanson Albums of Marguerite of Austria* (Berkeley and Los Angeles, 1965)
M. Rosenberg: 'Symbolic and Descriptive Text Settings in the Work of Pierre de la Rue (c1460–1518)', *MMA*, i (1966), 225
C. Maas: 'Josquin–Agricola–Brumel–de la Rue: een authenticiteits probleem', *TVNM*, xx/4 (1967), 120
M. Staehelin: 'Pierre de la Rue in Italien', *AMw*, xxvii (1970), 128

MARTIN STAEHELIN

Laruette [Ruette, La], **Jean-Louis** (*b* Paris, 7 March 1731; *d* Paris, 10 Jan 1792). French composer and tenor. In 1752 he made his début at the Opéra-Comique, playing lovers' roles. Later, because of his homely appearance, he played old men's roles, in spite of his light tenor voice. His reputation became so great that comic roles of fathers, bankers etc came to be written for high voices (until the second half of the 19th century, when they were given to basses) and are still known as 'laruettes'.

As a composer, Laruette participated actively in the early development of the *opéra comique*, and thus has a historical significance far surpassing his actual talent. His first works, *Le plaisir et l'innocence* and *Le boulevard* (both 1753), involved the introduction of new tunes among vaudevilles. Next he combined Italian ariettas with new librettos in his *pastiches*, *Le diable à quatre* (1756) and *La fausse aventurière* (1757). Finally, by progressively replacing the vaudevilles and Italian *ariettes* with new music, he became, with Duni, the creator of the *opéra comique* in the form which it eventually retained – a characteristic mixture of original music and spoken text – and thus the precursor of Monsigny and F.-A. Philidor. After *Le docteur Sangrado*, in which he collaborated with Duni in 1758, he devoted himself almost exclusively to the new genre. It soon won favour at the Opéra-Comique and later at the Comédie-Italienne, where his major works, *Le dépit généreux* (1761) and *Le guy de chesne* (1763), were produced. He joined the Comédie-Italienne when it combined with the Opéra-Comique in 1762, and soon became a shareholder and one of the musical representatives to its committee. His last opera, *Les deux compères* (1772), was a failure. Poor health forced him to leave the theatre in 1779, at the time when the Italians were dismissed and the committee was turning the Comédie-Italienne into the real Opéra-Comique Theatre to which Laruette had devoted his life. He continued to perform solo parts at concerts until 1785 and was a member of the Société Académique des Enfants d'Apollon. Laruette's wife, Marie-Thérèse (née Villette) (*b* Paris, 6 March 1744; *d* Paris, 16 June 1837), performed at the Opéra and the Comédie-Italienne from 1758 to 1777, often playing the roles of girls and soubrettes. She had a pretty voice, and her reputation was helped by her husband after their marriage in 1763. After his death she married the Count of Aurignac.

WORKS
All are stage works, first performed in Paris; all printed works published in Paris.

FL – Opéra-Comique, Théâtre de la Foire St Laurent

Le plaisir et l'innocence (opéra comique based on vaudevilles, 1, Parmentier), FL, 14 Aug 1753 (1753)

Le boulevard (opéra comique based on vaudevilles, 1, L. Anseaume), FL, 24 Aug 1753 (1753)

Les amans trompés (pastiche, 1, Anseaume), FL, 26 July 1756 (1756), ?spurious

Le diable à quatre, ou La double métamorphose (pastiche with some new music, 3, M. J. Sedaine), FL, 19 Aug 1756 (1757), collab. F.-A. Philidor

La fausse aventurière (pastiche with some new music, 2, Anseaume, P. A. L. de Marcouville), Foire St Germain, 22 March 1757 (1757)

Le docteur Sangrado (opéra comique, 1, Anseaume, J. B. Lourdet de Santerre), Foire St Germain, 13 Feb 1758 (1758), collab. E. Duni

L'heureux déguisement, ou La gouvernante supposée (opéra comique, 2, Marcouville), FL, 7 Aug 1758, excerpts in Recueil d'ariettes (1758) and Nouveau Théâtre de la Foire, iv (1763)

Le médecin de l'amour (opéra comique, 1, Anseaume, Marcouville), FL, 22 Sept 1758 (1758)

Cendrillon (opéra comique, 1, Anseaume), Foire St Germain, 21 Feb 1759

L'ivrogne corrigé, ou Le mariage du diable (opéra comique, 2, Anseaume, Lourdet de Santerre), FL, 24 July 1759 (1759)

Le dépit généreux (opéra comique, 2, Anseaume, A.-F. Quétant),

Comédie-Italienne, 16 July 1761, *F-Pn*

Le guy de chesne, ou La fête des druides (opéra comique, 1, J.-B. de Junquières), Comédie-Italienne, 26 Jan 1763 (1763), excerpts in Supplément aux parodies du Théâtre Italien, ii (1765)

Les deux compères (opéra comique, 2, Lourdet de Santerre), Comédie-Italienne, 4 Aug 1772, air in *La muse lyrique*, ii/45 (1772)

BIBLIOGRAPHY
J.-B. de La Borde: *Essai sur la musique ancienne et moderne*, iii (Paris, 1780/*R*1972)

A. Choron and F. Fayolle: *Dictionnaire historique des musiciens* (Paris, 1810–11/*R*1971)

G. Cucuel: *Les créateurs de l'opéra comique français* (Paris, 1914)

P. Letailleur: 'Jean-Louis Laruette: chanteur et compositeur', *RMFC*, viii (1968), 161; ix (1969), 145; x (1970), 57–86

PAULETTE LETAILLEUR

Larway, J. H. English firm of music publishers, taken over by EDWIN ASHDOWN.

LaSalle Quartet. American string quartet. It was formed in 1949 by students from the Juilliard School of Music in New York. The first violinist, Walter Levin (*b* Berlin, 6 Dec 1924), studied under Ivan Galamian at the Juilliard School; the second violinist, Henry Meyer (*b* Dresden, 29 June 1923), studied at the Prague Music Academy, in Paris with Enescu and Rene Benedetti, and with Galamian at the Juilliard School; the violist, Peter Kamnitzer (*b* Berlin, 27 Nov 1922), studied at the Manhattan School of Music in New York and at the Juilliard School; the cellist, Lee Fiser (*b* Portland, Oregon, 26 April 1947), who joined the quartet in 1975 (replacing Jack Kirstein, a member from 1955), studied at the Cleveland Institute and was a member of the Cincinnati SO up to 1975. The ensemble was quartet-in-residence at Colorado College (1949–53) and at the College Conservatory of Music, University of Cincinnati (1953), where all four members became professors. The quartet made its European début in 1954 and has toured extensively in the USA and abroad. It performs works of all periods but is best known for its performances and recordings of Schoenberg, Berg and Webern and the late quartets of Beethoven. Among the many composers who have written music for the quartet are Hans Erich Apostel, Herbert Brün, Earle Brown, Henri Pousseur, Wolf Rosenberg, Kagel, Ligeti, Penderecki and Lutosławski. In 1958 the quartet acquired a matched set of Amati instruments: two violins by Nicolo (1648 and 1682), a viola by Antonio and Girolamo (1619) and a cello by Nicolo (1670). Although the LaSalle Quartet is associated mainly with 20th-century music, its playing of it is not archetypally 'modern'. Rather it is compounded of tonal richness (with pronounced vibrato), broad tempos and, at all times, linear clarity. In its famous performances and recordings of the works of the Second Viennese School, the quartet is able to project the essence of the music's 'modernity' while at the same time exposing its roots in 19th-century Romanticism.

HERBERT GLASS

Lascarini, Francesco Maria. See RASCARINI, FRANCESCO MARIA.

Lascelles, George Henry Hubert. See HAREWOOD.

Lasceux, Guillaume (*b* Poissy, 3 Feb 1740; *d* Paris, ?1831). French organist and composer. He began his career as an organist in the nearby village of Chevreuse at the age of 18. He went to Paris in 1762 and spent five years studying composition with the organist Charles

Noblet, who was also harpsichordist of the Opéra. In 1769 he became supernumerary organist to Claude-Nicolas Ingrain at St Etienne-du-Mont and took over the post in 1774. Other positions which he held simultaneously were at the Mathurins (from 1769, succeeding Noblet), St Aure (from 1769), Minimes de la Place Royale (from 1779), Collège de Navarre and Séminaire St Magloire. As a result of the Revolution he lost his patronage and most of his organ positions and then, in order to support himself, played for the services of the Theophilanthropists in St Etienne-du-Mont (renamed Temple de la Piété-filiale). When St Etienne-du-Mont was restored to Roman Catholic worship in 1803 he resumed his former duties until he retired on 2 January 1819.

Lasceux was known as a virtuoso organist, and was particularly celebrated for his improvisations depicting the Last Judgement. He composed in many genres, including *opéras comiques*, accompanied keyboard sonatas, sacred organ pieces and made keyboard arrangements of popular songs. The novelty of his works gained them some success, particularly with amateurs.

WORKS
(*printed works published in Paris unless otherwise stated*)

Vocal: Les epoux réconciliés (comédie lyrique, 1), ?1789, B-Bc; 3 opéras comiques, 1789, cited in Choron and Fayolle; Messe, chorus, orch (1804); 2 motets au Saint Sacrement, 3vv, org (Charleville, 1836); Ariettes et petits airs, 1v, hpd/pf/harp (?c1775); romances pubd singly, incl. Hommage à l'amour (1767), Absence et retour (n.d.), Les adieux de la violette (n.d.)

Org: Journal de pièces d'orgue, contenant des messes, Magnificat et noëls (1771–2); Nouveau journal [Nouvelle suite] . . . des messes, Magnificat et noëls (c1782–4); Messes des grands solennels (1783); Te Deum (1786), lost; Nouvelle suite (1810): 1. Messe des annuels et grands solennels, 2. Hymnes, proses et répons de l'office de la Fete-Dieu, 3. Messe des solennels mineurs [no.3 lost]; Annuaire de l'organiste, 1819; 12 fugues, 1820

Other inst: [12] Sonates, hpd, vn ad lib (1768–72); Quatuor, hpd/pf, 2 vn, b, op.4 (1775); Potpuri d'airs connus, hpd, op.9 (1783); many pubd kbd arrs. of ovs. and songs from stage works, incl. some in 18th-century anthologies

Pedagogical: Essai théorique et pratique sur l'art de l'orgue, 1809

BIBLIOGRAPHY
FétisB; *GerberL*

A. Choron and F. Fayolle: *Dictionnaire historique des musiciens* (Paris, 1810–11/R1971)

G. Servières: *Documents inédits sur les organistes français des XVIIe et XVIIIe siècles* (Paris, ?1922)

G. Favre: 'Guillaume Lasceux', *RdM*, xxxi (1952), 38

EILEEN MORRIS GUENTHER

Laschi [Mombelli], Luisa (*b* Florence, 1760s; *d* c1790). Italian soprano. She made her Viennese début on 24 September 1784 in Cimarosa's *Giannina e Bernardone*. The *Wiener Kronik* said:

Mlle Laschi sang with the greatest success. She is still very young, and has a beautiful clear voice, which in time will become rounder and fuller; she is very musical, sings with more expression than the usual opera singers and has a beautiful figure! Madam Fischer (Storazi [i.e. Nancy Storace]) has only more experience, and is otherwise in no way superior to Dem Laschi, who from all points of view is a fine acquisition for Vienna.

On 21 January 1785 Laschi sang Rosina in Paisiello's *Il barbiere di Siviglia* 'very well, and was much applauded' (Zinzendorf). On 11 February she sang in a concert for her benefit, and on 13 February in another where Mozart played his Piano Concerto in Bb κ456. Emperor Joseph II grudgingly released her for an engagement in Naples – where she met her future husband, the tenor Domenico Mombelli (1751–1835) – for the 1785 season, but secured her again from Easter 1786, and she sang at the Viennese court opera during its finest period. There, on 1 May 1786, she created the role of the Countess in *Le nozze di Figaro*, in which she

was very well received; Nancy Storace sang Susanna. She had a further success on 15 May in Anfossi's *Il trionfo delle donne*. On 1 August she appeared, probably for the first time in Vienna with Mombelli, in Sarti's *I finti eredi*. On 29 September the emperor wrote to his chamberlain Count Rosenberg, with a jocular reference to *Figaro*: 'The marriage between Laschi and Mombelli may take place without waiting for my return, and I cede to you *le droit de Seigneur*'.

On 17 November 1786 she was billed as Mme Mombelli in Martín y Soler's *Una cosa rara*. Casts for the Vienna repertory of this period are not specifically recorded, but it may be assumed that she appeared regularly. On 1 October 1787 she sang Amore in Martín y Soler's *L'arbore di Diana*. She appeared half as a man, half as a woman, 'travesti en femme' according to Zinzendorf. An anonymous commentator wrote that it was 'very unsuitable to let Amor appear on the stage as a man naked down to his nipples, and later as a woman enveloped right up to her neck'. But the *Kritische Theaterjournal von Wien* described her as 'Grace personified. Mombelli's Amor; O, who would not be enchanted by it, what painter could adequately depict her mischievous smile, what sculptor the grace of all her movements, what singer would be capable of following her melting zephyr-like singing allied to simplicity, with the proper warm feeling?'.

On 8 January 1788 she sang in Salieri's *Axur rè d'Ormus*, and on 7 May she sang Zerlina in the first Vienna performance of Mozart's *Don Giovanni*. Mozart specially composed a new duet, 'Per queste due manine' κ540b, for Leporello and Zerlina, to be sung by Benucci and Mombelli. She was already seven months pregnant, and continued singing until the day before her confinement at the beginning of July. She reappeared only four weeks later in *Axur* on 4 August, because, according to the *Wiener Zeitung*, 'her endeavour has always been to fulfil her duty and serve the goodwill of a highly respected public'. But during 1788 there were difficulties between the Italian company and the management; on 30 May the emperor wrote to Count Rosenberg: 'I think you have done well to let the Mombellis go and finally make a clean sweep'. It appears that they objected, however, and later in the year the emperor gave them notice personally. On 10 September 1788 Luisa appeared in Salieri's *Il talismano*, which was probably her last new production in Vienna.

Nothing further seems to be known about Luisa Mombelli, but it appears that Domenico Mombelli became a widower and in 1791 married the ballerina Vincenza Viganò, by whom he had 12 children. Possibly Luisa died in childbirth.

BIBLIOGRAPHY
O. E. Deutsch: 'Mozart in Zinzendorfs Tagebüchern', *SMz*, cii (1962), 211

O. Michtner: *Das alte Burgtheater als Opernbühne* (Vienna, 1970)

CHRISTOPHER RAEBURN

Laserna, Blas de (*b* Corella, Navarre, baptized 4 Feb 1751; *d* Madrid, 8 Aug 1816). Spanish composer. At 23 he began his career as a theatrical composer in Madrid and by 1776 his fame was such that the impresario Eusebio Ribera contracted him to write 63 *tonadillas* every year. In 1773 he married the daughter of the Madrid organist Vicente Adán. Widowed in 1795, he next married the singer María Pupillo, who died in 1809. In 1790 he succeeded Esteve as conductor at the Teatro de la Cruz, remaining there until 1808.

Despite being one of the most prolific composers of his time, he was constantly underpaid and after 1800 had to resort to menial copying and teaching to secure a livelihood.

Laserna's speciality was the *tonadilla* or skit for one to four actors, of which he wrote at least 700, some to his own texts. 684 of these along with 78 *sainetes* are in the Biblioteca Municipal in Madrid, and several were circulated as far as Lima and Mexico City. Usually showing piquant scenes from contemporary middle and low life, these genre pieces lasted no more than 20 minutes and were inserted between acts of a play or opera. Although *El majo y la italiana fingida* (1778; ed. in Subirá, 1930) involves a girl who, to pose as an Italian, sings in Italian operatic style, Laserna's early *tonadillas* on the whole were exempt from the influence of bel canto (in 1790 he even proposed founding a school to preserve authentic Spanish traditions). In his last period, however, he had to adopt the Italian vogue in order to have his pieces produced. Laserna also wrote the music for eight *melólogos* (1791–7) and for several zarzuelas, as well as instrumental pieces and prologues. Two excerpts from his *melólogos* are edited in Subirá (1950) and five vocal selections appear in Joaquín Nin's *Classiques espagnols du chant* (Paris, 1926).

BIBLIOGRAPHY

J. Gómez García: *Don Blas de Laserna: un capítulo de la historia del teatro lírico español visto en la vida del último tonadillero* (diss., U. of Madrid, 1916; extracts in *Revista de la Biblioteca, Archivo y Museo del Ayuntamiento de Madrid*, ii–iii, 1925–6)

J. Subirá: *La tonadilla escénica*, iii (Madrid, 1930), 69ff [117–45]

——: *El compositor Iriarte (1750–1791) y el cultivo español del melólogo*, ii (Barcelona, 1950), 265f, 272ff, 422ff

J. Gómez, J. L. de Arrese and E. Aunós: *El músico Blas de Laserna* (Corella, 1952)

J. Subirá: 'Laserna, Blas de', *ES*

——: *Catálogo de la Sección de música de la Biblioteca municipal de Madrid* (Madrid, 1965), i, 105ff, 337ff

R. Stevenson: *Renaissance and Baroque Musical Sources in the Americas* (Washington, DC, 1970), 113

ROBERT STEVENSON

Laserna, Estacio de. *See* SERNA, ESTACIO DE LA.

Las Huelgas Manuscript. *See* SOURCES, MS, §V, 2.

Laskaris, Joannēs [Laskaris Pigonitis; Joannēs Laskaris tou Syrpaganou] (*b* ?Constantinople; *fl* Crete, 1st half of 15th century). Byzantine composer and theorist. *See* BYZANTINE RITE, MUSIC OF THE.

BIBLIOGRAPHY

M. Velimirović: 'Two Composers of Byzantine Music: John Vatatzes and John Laskaris', *Aspects of Medieval and Renaissance Music: a Birthday Offering to Gustave Reese* (New York, 1966), 818

C. J. Bentas: 'The Treatise on Music by John Laskaris', *Studies in Eastern Chant*, ii (1971), 21

Laskine, Lily (*b* Paris, 31 Aug 1893). French harpist. She studied with Alphonse Hasselmans and Georges Marty at the Paris Conservatoire, gaining a *premier prix* in 1905. From 1909 to 1926 she was a member of the Paris Opéra orchestra and subsequently played with many other orchestras, notably those of the Koussevitzky concert series (from 1921), the Lamoureux Association (1921–40 and 1943–5) and the National Radio Orchestra (from 1934). Her international career began with appearances at Donaueschingen in 1934, followed by concerts in London, Rome, Brussels and Amsterdam. Laskine was professor of the harp at the Paris Conservatoire, 1948–58. She was awarded the Cross of the Légion d'honneur in 1936 and made a Chevalier in 1958. In later years she recorded many interesting works by lesser composers, for example the hitherto neglected Concerto no.1 in E minor (op.15) by N.-C. Bochsa. She is the dedicatee of Roussel's only work for solo harp, his Impromptu op.86.

ANN GRIFFITHS

Laskovsky, Ivan Fyodorovich (*b* St Petersburg, 1799; *d* St Petersburg, 1855). Russian composer. His father was of Polish descent, his mother a native Russian. After serving as an officer in the Preobrazhensky Regiment from 1817 until 1832 he took a post in the war office. He was a pupil of John Field and became a fine pianist; he is remembered particularly for his valuable contributions to the piano repertory during the first half of the 19th century. Some of his compositions, a march, two waltzes and a polonaise, were published in an *Album musical* in 1826, and thereafter his pieces appeared frequently in annual albums and journals. A nocturne and several dance pieces were published in the supplement to the *Liricheskiy al'bom na 1832 god* ('Album of lyrical songs for 1832', St Petersburg) which Laskovsky produced himself in collaboration with the composer Norov; Glinka included a number of Laskovsky's pieces in his *Sobraniye muzïkal'nïkh pyes* ('Collection of musical pieces', St Petersburg, 1839), and Balakirev, who was a great admirer of Laskovsky's works, prepared an edition of them, *Oeuvres complètes pour piano de Jean Laskowsky* (St Petersburg, 1858).

Laskovsky's piano compositions show a considerable technical advance on the pieces of earlier Russian composers, such as Genishta, Alexander Gurilyov and Esaulov, and in many respects are the precursors of the piano works of Tchaikovsky, Balakirev and other composers in the second half of the century. His mazurkas and waltzes show a certain stylistic affinity with Chopin, whose works he knew well and often performed at concerts. He also composed two sets of variations on Russian folk melodies, one of which is the *Kamarinskaya*, on which Field had based a set of keyboard variations and on which Glinka composed his Fantasia. Laskovsky's most notable extended pieces are a Nocturne in B♭ minor/major and a Ballade in F♯ minor; both make extensive use of the piano's range, and skilfully exploit its ability to provide dramatic contrasts between lyrical and percussive sounds. Besides writing solo piano music Laskovsky completed three string quartets, in E minor, G major and G minor, the last of which has been published in a modern edition (Leningrad and Moscow, 1947).

BIBLIOGRAPHY

L. A. Barenboym and V. I. Muzalevsky: *Khrestomatiya po istorii fortepiannoy muzïki v rossii* (Moscow and Leningrad, 1949) [incl. Nocturne in B♭ minor/major and Ballade in F♯ minor]

V. I. Muzalevsky: *Russkaya fortepiannaya muzïka* (Moscow and Leningrad, 1949), 237ff

C. Cui: *Izbrannïye stat'i* [Collected articles] (Leningrad, 1952), 246ff

L. N. Raaben: *Instrumental'nïy ansambl' v russkoy muzïke* (Moscow, 1961), 134ff

GEOFFREY NORRIS

Lasos of Hermione. *See* LASUS OF HERMIONE.

Lassen, Eduard (*b* Copenhagen, 13 April 1830; *d* Weimar, 15 Jan 1904). Belgian composer of Danish origin, active in Germany. He studied at the Brussels Conservatory, receiving prizes for piano (1844) and composition (1847), and winning the Belgian Prix de Rome (1851), which enabled him to tour Germany and

Rome and meet Spohr and Liszt. Returning to Brussels in 1855, he was unable to secure a performance of his five-act opera *Le roi Edgard*, but this was successfully produced under Liszt in Weimar in 1857. He was offered the position of music director at Weimar and in 1858 succeeded Liszt as court music director, a post he held until his retirement in 1895. He was awarded an honorary doctorate by the University of Jena.

Lassen's operas *Frauenlob* and *Der Gefangene* did not have lasting success, though his music to Goethe's *Faust* gained popularity and was praised by Liszt. His solo songs and duets show a variety of treatment from the folklike *Sei nur ruhig, lieber Robin* or the songs with dance rhythms to the through-composed *Abendlandschaft* (with its more interesting modulations and accompaniment) to the rhapsodic and improvisatory *Ich hab im Traum geweinet*. Many of his songs, for instance *Vöglein wohin so schnell*, were translated into both English and French and were popular at the end of the 19th century.

WORKS
(many MSS in D-WRdn)

Operas: Le roi Edgard, 1855, perf. as Landgraf Ludwigs Brautfahrt, Weimar, 1857; Frauenlob, Weimar, 1860; Der Gefangene, perf. as Le captif, Brussels, 1865

Incidental music: Triumph der Empfindsamkeit (Goethe); Pandora (Goethe); König Ödipus; Faust I and II (Goethe); Die Göttin Diana (after Heine); Nibelungen (Hebbel); Über allen Zauber Liebe (Calderón)

Orch: 2 syms., D, C; Vn Conc.; Festmarsch; Festouverture; Beethovenouverture; 11 Characterstücke

Vocal: cantatas, choruses; many solo songs with pf or inst acc.

BIBLIOGRAPHY

La Mara, ed.: *Briefwechsel zwischen Franz Liszt und Hans von Bülow* (Leipzig, 1898)
A. Bartels: *Chronik des Weimarer Hoftheaters 1817–1907* (Weimar, 1908)
L. Schrickel: *Geschichte des Weimarer Theaters von seinen Anfangen bis heute* (Weimar, 1928)
N. Del Mar: *Richard Strauss*, ii (London, 1969)
E. Perényi: *Liszt: the Artist as Romantic Hero* (Boston, 1974)
GAYNOR G. JONES

Lasser, Johann Baptist (*b* Steinkirchen, 12 Aug 1751; *d* Munich, 21 Oct 1805). Austrian composer, singer, violinist and conductor. He studied at Linz before moving to Vienna, where he probably continued his studies but also taught. In 1781 (Wurzbach) or 1782 (Lipowsky) he married the singer Johanna Roithner (who continued to sing at the Munich Opera until at least 1811). The couple were at Brünn (now Brno) in 1783 as members of Waizhofer's company, and in 1785 they moved on to Linz, where Lasser directed the company in the 1786–7 season. In 1788, after a brief season as director at Eszterháza, he rejoined Waizhofer, then at Graz. In 1791 the Lassers went to Munich, where he distinguished himself at court by singing arias in all four registers, and by playing a violin concerto. Apart from a successful guest appearance as singer and violinist in Berlin in 1797 he remained in Munich for the remainder of his life, well loved and respected as both man and musician.

Despite the vocal feat of his Munich court concert it is difficult to reconcile the opinions of Lipowsky and Wurzbach that he was a tenor with statements in later books that he was a bass. Apart from a *Vollständige Anleitung zur Singkunst* (Munich, 1798) that was published in several editions and revisions, he achieved some renown with a series of compositions: several masses, some of them published, and a handful of Singspiels dating mainly from his Graz years. His two sons Joseph Lasser (*b* Vienna, 7 Nov 1782) and

Emanuel Lasser (*b* Brünn, 20 Jan 1784) achieved some distinction as musicians, the former as a pianist (successful début in Vienna in 1794), the latter as a court singer in Munich.

WORKS

Cora und Alonzo (opera), ? Munich, after 1791

Singspiels: Die kluge Witwe, Brünn, 1782; Die glückliche Maskerade, Graz, 1788; Das wüthende Heer (C. F. Bretzner), Graz, 1789; Die Modehändlerin (F. Ebert), Graz, 1790; Der Kapellmeister (J. C. Bock), ?Graz, 1789, and Vienna, Freihaus, 2 July 1790; Die unruhige Nacht (after Goldoni), Vienna, Kärntnertor, 28 May 1790; Die Huldigung der Töne [?Treue] (W. von Bube), ? Graz, c1790; Der Jude, Graz, 1791

Other works: 3 missae, op.1 (Augsburg, 1795); 6 missae, op.2 (Augsburg, 1801); Duetti e solfeggi, *A-Wgm*

BIBLIOGRAPHY

EitnerQ
F. J. Lipowsky: *Baierisches Musik-Lexikon* (Munich, 1811/R1971)
C. d'Elvert: *Geschichte des Theaters in Mähren und Oesterreichisch Schlesien* (Brno, 1851)
C. von Wurzbach: *Biographisches Lexikon des Kaiserthums Oesterreich*, xiv (Vienna, 1865), 173
C. d'Elvert: *Geschichte der Musik in Mähren und Oesterr.-Schlesien* (Brno, 1873)
F. Grandaur: *Chronologie des königlichen Hof- und Nationaltheaters in München* (Munich, 1878)
H. Mendel and A. Reissmann: *Musikalisches Conversations-Lexikon*, vi (Berlin, 1881/R), 254
J. Kürschner: 'Lasser, Johann Baptist', *ADB*
A. Rille: *Die Geschichte des Brünner Stadttheaters* (Brno, 1885)
F. Fuhrich: *Theatergeschichte Oberösterreichs im 18. Jahrhundert*, Theatergeschichte Österreichs, i/2 (Vienna, 1968)
PETER BRANSCOMBE

Lasson, Mathieu (*d* before 1595). French cleric and composer at Nancy, Lorraine. He was sometimes confused with Roland de Lassus. He was treasurer and canon of St Georges, Nancy, in 1528, and also *maître de chapelle* to the Duke of Lorraine. In 1543 he became rector at the hospital of Nôtre-Dame in Pont à Mousson. The records of St Georges include an obituary for him from 1595. Lasson composed five four-voice motets which were printed and reprinted not only in Paris but also in Italy and Germany. One of them, *Virtute magna*, was used as a model for parody masses by Clemens non Papa and Palestrina. The motets maintain a balance, typical of the period, between imitative and homophonic writing. Four chansons by Lasson survive; the best known, *En l'ombre d'ung buyssonet*, was intabulated for lute solo by Hans Gerle in 1533.

WORKS
(all 4vv)

Edition: *Treize livres de motets parus chez Pierre Attaingnant en 1534 et 1535*, ed. A. Smijers and A. T. Merritt (Monaco, 1934–64) [S]

Anthoni, pater inclyte, S viii; Congratulamini mihi, 1539[13]; In manibus tuis, S xi; Quem dies vidi fugiens, 1549[16]; Virtute magna, S xiii (attrib. Verdelot in 1538[8] and A. de Silva in *D-Bds* Landsberg 321, almost certainly erroneously)

En l'ombre d'ung buysonnet, ed. A. Seay: *Thirty Chansons for Three and Four Voices from Attaingnant's Collections* (New Haven, Conn., 1960); La grant doulceur, 1534[14]; L'oeil a plaisir, 1534[14]; Pour satisfaire a l'esperit tourmenté, 1534[14]

BIBLIOGRAPHY

G. Reese: *Music in the Renaissance* (New York, 1954; rev. 2/1959)
F. Lesure: 'Some Minor French Composers of the 16th Century', *Aspects of Medieval and Renaissance Music: a Birthday Offering to Gustave Reese* (New York, 1966), 538
CAROLINE M. CUNNINGHAM

Lassu (Hung.). The slow introductory section of the VERBUNKOS dance form.

Lassus [Lasso]. Franco-Flemish family of composers.

(1) Orlande [Roland] **de Lassus** [Orlando di Lasso] (*b* Mons, Hainaut, 1532; *d* Munich, 14 June 1594). He was one of the most prolific and versatile of 16th-century composers, and in his time the best-known and most widely admired musician in Europe.

1. Early years. 2. Munich. 3. Letters. 4. Masses. 5. Passions. 6. Magnificat settings and other liturgical works. 7. Motets. 8. Madrigals. 9. Chansons. 10. German lieder. 11. Lassus and Palestrina.

1. EARLY YEARS. Lassus was born at Mons in Hainaut, a Franco-Flemish province notable for the number of distinguished musicians born and trained there during the Renaissance. Nothing definite is known of his parents, nor is there any solid proof that he was a choirboy at the church of St Nicholas – much less for the legend that he was three times abducted because of the beauty of his voice. The first known fact about him, attested to by his contemporary and earliest biographer, Samuel Quickelberg, is that at about the age of 12 he entered the service of Ferrante Gonzaga, a cadet of the Mantuan ducal house and a general in the service of Charles V. Gonzaga was in the Low Countries in summer 1544; when he headed south the boy Lassus presumably accompanied him. After a stop near Paris Gonzaga returned to Italy, where he visited Mantua before proceeding to Sicily late in 1545. Thus Lassus's first Italian experience was at the Mantuan court. From Palermo, Gonzaga went to Milan, where Lassus apparently spent the years 1547–9. It is likely that at this time he met other musicians in the service of the Gonzaga, particularly Hoste da Reggio, a madrigalist who headed whatever musical establishment Ferrante Gonzaga maintained.

According to Quickelberg, Lassus next went to Naples, where he entered the service of Constantino Castrioto and lived in the household of G. B. d'Azzia della Terza, a man of letters who introduced him into the Accademia de' Sereni. It is thought that Lassus began to compose while in Naples, and that the villanellas printed in Antwerp in 1555 may have been written at this time. From Naples he went to Rome; after a period in the household of Antonio Altoviti, Archbishop of Florence but then resident in Rome, he became *maestro di cappella* at St John Lateran in spring 1553 (succeeding Animuccia and preceding, by two years, Palestrina). Though young and as yet not well known as a composer – at least in print – Lassus must by this time have acquired a certain reputation as a musician in order to get a post such as this.

A little over a year later Lassus left Rome, for a visit to his parents who were ill, but he found them dead on his arrival. His whereabouts for a short period after this are unknown, and it has been claimed, though not proved (he himself never spoke of it), that he visited France and England in the company of the singer–diplomat–adventurer G. C. Brancaccio. Early in 1555 Lassus was in Antwerp. Although he is not known to have held any official post, he seems to have made friends quickly here, and with helpful people such as the printers Tylman Susato and Jean de Laet. In that year Susato printed what has been called Lassus's 'op.1', a collection of 'madrigali, vilanesche, canzoni francesi e motetti' for four voices; meanwhile Antonio Gardane in Venice had issued Lassus's first book of five-part madrigals. In 1556 the first book of five- and six-part motets appeared in Antwerp; it seems that Lassus had waited to publish his music until he had accumulated a substantial number of pieces. How much other music he had written up to this time we do not know; but it is probable that some of the madrigals appearing in

Antonio Barrè's Roman anthologies of the late 1550s date from Lassus's stay in Rome, that at least one mass, the *Missa 'Domine secundum actum meum'*, was written before 1556, and that the *Sacrae lectiones novem ex propheta Iob*, though not printed until 1565, belong to this period. The *Prophetiae Sibyllarum*, a collection of highly chromatic settings of humanistic Latin texts that was not published until after Lassus's death although it had periods of notoriety during his lifetime – including the amazed response of Charles IX of France in 1571 – may also belong to Lassus's Italian years (it survives in a manuscript containing a portrait of the composer at the age of 28).

2. MUNICH. In 1556 Lassus received and accepted an invitation to join the court of Duke Albrecht V of Bavaria in Munich. The circumstances of this appointment are not clear, but it is evident that Dr Seld, the imperial vice-chancellor at Brussels, played a part in the negotiations (having first recommended Philippe de Monte for the post). Lassus was engaged as a tenor in a chapel headed by Ludwig Daser; a half-dozen other newly engaged Flemish singers also arrived in Munich in 1556–7, the result of a deliberate plan to 'netherlandize' a chapel which had perhaps come to seem too provincially German in character (Albrecht V's ambitions to revitalize his chapel may have been spurred by news of the dissolution of Charles V's chapel in 1555).

During the next few years Lassus's salary began to rise, but as late as 1568 he was still referred to in the chapel records as 'cantor' and 'tenor 2us'. On the other hand the title-pages of prints such as the *Libro quarto de madrigali* for five voices of 1567 referred to him as *maestro di cappella* of the Bavarian court. Whether for musical reasons or political and religious ones (Daser was a Protestant and Albrecht V, who had for some time tolerated and even encouraged reformers in Bavaria, had turned back to Catholicism, sending a representative to the Council of Trent in 1563), Lassus, who appears to have remained Catholic though he was no Counter-Reformation zealot, took over the leadership of the chapel when Daser was pensioned in 1563, a position he was to hold for 30 years. During this period the make-up of the chapel changed as more and more Italians were recruited. There was much fluctuation in numbers of singers and instrumentalists, the highpoint being reached in 1569 at the time of the young Duke Wilhelm's marriage, the low occurring after the latter's accession to the throne in 1579. But Lassus's position ended only with his death, and so firm was his hold on it that it could be inherited by his two sons in turn; in 1629 a grandson still represented the family in the chapel.

Lassus's duties included a morning service, for which polyphonic masses, elaborate or simple as the occasion required, were prepared. Judging from his enormous output of *Magnificat* settings, Vespers must have been celebrated solemnly a good deal of the time. It is less clear for what services much of the repertory of motets was created, though many could have fitted into celebrations of the Mass and Offices. Music for special occasions was provided by the ducal chapel; this included state visits, banquets for which 'Tafelmusik' was customary and hunting parties. Indeed Albrecht's love of musical display and his munificence towards musicians was much criticized in some court quarters. In addition Lassus supervised the musical education of the choirboys; he saw to copying of manuscripts and perhaps to

1. Orlande de Lassus: woodcut from his 'Livre de chansons nouvelles' (1571)

the collection of printed music for the ducal library; and he became a friend and companion to the duke and especially to his heir, the future Wilhelm V.

In 1558 Lassus married Regina Wäckinger, the daughter of a Bavarian court official. Among their children two sons, (2) Ferdinand (*b* c1560) and (3) Rudolph (*b* c1563), were to become musicians. He settled into what seems to have been a stable and comfortable existence, apparently one that he never seriously considered changing. This was varied by journeys undertaken at ducal behest. Thus in 1560 he went to Flanders to recruit singers; in 1562 he was in Frankfurt for the coronation of the Emperor Maximilian II; Andrea Gabrieli joined Lassus's chapel for this visit, and may have remained in Munich for a year or two thereafter. In 1567 Lassus was in northern Italy, visiting Ferrara and Venice – and reminding Italians that, as he said in the dedication to his fourth book of five-part madrigals, good Italian music could be written even in far-off 'Germania'.

Lassus's fame was steadily growing, at home and abroad. He began, perhaps at the duke's request, to collect and put in order his own compositions, particularly the motets. The Venetian and Flemish printers who published his first works continued to issue madrigals, chansons and sacred music; in the 1560s Berg in Munich, Montanus and Neuber in Frankfurt, and Le Roy & Ballard in Paris began to print individual works, then series of volumes devoted to the music of the man becoming known as 'princeps musicorum' and the 'divin Orlande'.

In 1569 Lassus played an important part in the festivities for the wedding of Wilhelm V with Renée of Lorraine; in addition to composing music and supervising performances he is said to have performed the role of a 'magnifico' in Italian comedies. He was becoming something of a genuine 'magnifico': in 1570 Maximilian II conferred upon him a patent of nobility; in 1571 and again in 1573 and 1574 he visited the French court at the invitation of Charles IX; in 1574 he was made a Knight of the Golden Spur by Pope Gregory XIII. Such

honours were rarely bestowed on musicians. Still, Lassus was content to remain in Munich; there seems to be no proof that in 1574 he seriously thought of moving to France, and turned back only on hearing of the death of Charles IX.

In the period 1574–9 Lassus made a number of journeys, visiting Vienna, Trent, Ferrara, Mantua, Bologna and Rome. His Cecilian motet *Cantantibus organis* was awarded the prize at Evreux in 1575. He may have had as a pupil Giovanni Gabrieli, who was in Munich during the 1570s. From these years a charming correspondence between the composer and Duke Wilhelm, Albrecht's son and heir, survives; these letters, and some correspondence between Wilhelm and his father, are proof of the high regard felt by both men for Lassus. Before his death, Albrecht V provided that the composer was to receive his salary for the rest of his life. The five magisterial volumes of sacred works called *Patrocinium musices* (see fig.2) appeared during these years, and numerous reprints of his earlier music testify to Lassus's continuing popularity all over Europe.

On the accession of Wilhelm V in 1579 the ducal chapel was much reduced in size. Whatever Lassus may have felt about this, he did not consider leaving. Refusing an invitation (1580) to succeed Scandello in Dresden, he wrote to the Duke of Saxony that he did not want to leave his house, garden and other good things in Munich, and that he was now beginning to feel old. His activity as a composer did not diminish, however; the years 1581–5 are marked by a number of new publications, of masses, *Magnificat* settings, motets, psalms and German lieder. In 1584 Ferdinand Lassus took over some of his father's duties, and the next year Lassus made a pilgrimage to Loreto. On this journey he visited Verona and Ferrara, where he heard new Italian music of an advanced style. The conservatism of his own later music was the result of deliberate choice, viewed by the composer himself with some wryness, and not because of ignorance of what was happening in Italy.

Although Lassus's final years were marked by some poor health and by a 'melancholia hypocondriaca' for which he sought the help of a physician, Thomas Mermann, he was occasionally active, accompanying Wilhelm V to Regensburg in 1593; and he continued to write music, if only intermittently. Shortly before his death he dedicated to Pope Clement VIII his last cycle of compositions, the *Lagrime di S Pietro*, adding to it a seven-voice motet, *Vide homo quae pro te patior*.

3. LETTERS. A series of letters from Lassus to Duke Wilhelm, son and heir of Albrecht V, survives. The letters, dated between 1572 and 1579 and for the most part written from Munich to the duke's establishment at Landshut, are celebrated for their mixture of languages, passing back and forth from a playful, half-macaronic Latin to Italian, French and German. A few are partly in doggerel verse, strengthening the supposition that Lassus wrote some of his own texts for occasional and humorous pieces. The tone of these letters and their amusing signatures ('Orlando Lasso col cor non basso'; 'Orlandissimo lassissimo, amorevolissimo'; 'secretaire publique, Orlando magnifique') show Lassus to have been on terms of easy familiarity with Wilhelm. Occasionally there is a reference to music, as in a letter of 22 March 1576, when he wrote: 'I send a copy of *Io son ferito*; if it seems good to you, I will hope to hear my work at Landshut or elsewhere' (this must refer to

Lassus's mass written on Palestrina's well-known madrigal and published in 1589). Wilhelm apparently knew a good deal about music and liked to talk about it; thus Lassus could send him a letter (11 March 1578; see fig.3) entirely made up of musical puns and jokes, mentioning other composers such as Rore, Clemens and Arcadelt, and referring jokingly to musical terms, as in the description of 'una baligia senza pause, coperta di passagi di molte cadenze fatte in falso bordone a misura di macaroni' ('a valise without rests, covered with passage-work of many cadences made from *falsibordoni* the size of macaroni'). These letters suggest that Lassus had read Italian epistolary writers such as Pietro Aretino and Antonfrancesco Doni; and they confirm his reputation as – when the occasion required and perhaps when the mood was on him – an amusing friend and boon companion.

4. MASSES. The earliest surviving printed volume of masses by Lassus, issued by Claudio Merulo in Venice in 1570, is a 'volume two'; an earlier first volume must have existed. Some of Lassus's masses belong to the first years of his residence in Munich in the late 1550s; the latest, a five-voice mass based on Gombert's *Triste depart*, was written as a kind of valedictory gesture near the end of his life. The 60 or so masses known to be authentic (there are a number of doubtful works in this genre) make up a not inconsiderable part of his oeuvre. Since their publication in the new Lassus edition, the traditional view that Lassus's masses are of peripheral importance in his work, and indeed of largely perfunctory character, has been modified. Certainly they were not considered of negligible value during the late 16th and early 17th centuries. Although no single mass attained the popularity of some of the more celebrated motets, many were reprinted during and after his lifetime; several groups were included in the *Patrocinium musices*; and Le Roy & Ballard's resplendent *Missae variis concentibus ornatae ab Orlando de Lassus* of 1577–8 suggests that the Parisian publishers planned (although they did not carry out) a complete edition of his masses.

Most of Lassus's settings are parody masses, based on motets (chiefly his own), French chansons (by Gombert, Willaert, Monte and members of the Parisian school), or Italian madrigals (by Sebastiano Festa, Arcadelt, Rore and Palestrina). They provide a highly instructive anthology of the techniques of parody. His rearrangement and recomposition of his own music, as in the *Missa 'Locutus sum'*, show Lassus's technical prowess; his striking transformation of a rather simple model, such as Daser's motet for the *Missa 'Ecce nunc benedicite'*, illustrates his ability to raise the level of music of his lesser contemporaries. More remarkable still is the sensitivity he displayed in adapting secular models as diverse as Arcadelt's *Quand'io pens'al martire*, the densely polyphonic texture of Gombert's chansons, and the supple and subtle flow of Rore's madrigals. The masses based on these pieces are reminiscent of their models in style yet show no musical incongruity or technical strain. A work like the *Missa 'Qual donna attende'*, based on Rore's distinguished madrigal, must have provided a rich treat for connoisseurs of this genre.

At the other extreme in Lassus's masses are the short, syllabic *missae breves*. Some of these are parodies of works, like Sermisy's *La la maistre Pierre*, themselves in concise syllabic style. The shortest of all these works

is the 'Jäger' Mass or *Missa venatorum*, a work designed for a brief service on days the court spent hunting. Some of the masses based on plainchant are of this succinct type; an exception is the impressive five-voice *Missa pro defunctis* with its curious bass intonations. Whether or not because they fit post-Tridentine ideas about music for the Mass (Lassus is known to have been stubborn about changing things at Munich to conform with new ideas coming from Rome), some of the shortest and simplest of Lassus's masses were among his most popular works in the genre. It should be stressed, however, that these works do not represent him fully or entirely characteristically as a composer of masses.

5. PASSIONS. Lassus's four Passions are responsorial and of the kind cultivated by north Italian composers throughout most of the 16th century. In two of them (the *St Matthew* and *St John*) the words of the turbae and of the various individuals are set polyphonically, the first group for five-part chorus and the second for solo duos and trios; the words of Christ and the evangelists' narrative are to be chanted. The Passions according to St Mark and St Luke are shorter works in which chordal polyphony is provided only for the turbae. In the *St Matthew Passion*, first published in 1575, a clear stylistic distinction is made between the music of the turbae – chordal successions with ponderously decorated cadences – and the supple imitative style of the duos and trios used for the words of Peter, Judas and other characters. This work enjoyed great and lasting popularity.

2. Title-page of Lassus's 'Patrocinium musices: missae aliquot' (Munich: Adam Berg, 1589)

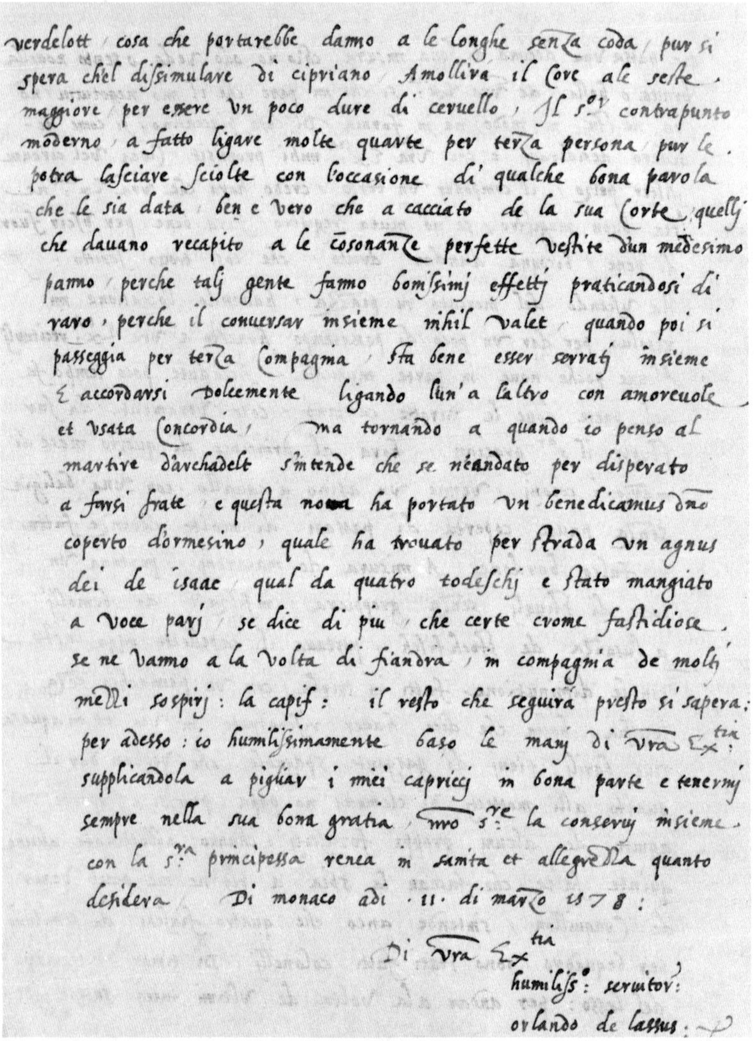

verdelott / cosa che portarebbe danno a le longhe senza coda / pur si
spera chel dissimulare di cipriano Amolliva il core ale seste .
maggiore per essere vn poco dure di ceruello , s s.r contrapunto
moderno a fatto ligare molte quarte per terza persona pur le .
potra lasciare sciolte con l'occasione di qualche bona parola
che le sia data ben e vero che a cacciato de la sua corte quelli
che dauano recapito a le consonanze perfette vestite dun medesimo
panno / perche tali gente fanno bonissimi effetti praticandosi di
raro , perche il conuersar insieme nihil valet / quando poi si
passeggia per terza compagnia / sta bene esser serrati insieme
& accordarsi dolcemente ligando lun'a laltro con amoreuole
et vsata concordia /   ma tornando a quando io penso al
martire darchadelt s'intende che se neandato per disperato
a farsi frate e questa noua ha portato vn benedicamus dno
coperto dormesino , quale ha trouato per strada vn agnus
dei de isaac qual da quatro todeschi e stato mangiato
a voce pari se dice di piu che certe cvome fastidiose .
se ne vanno a la volta di fiandra / in compagnia de molti
melli sospiri : la capisi : il resto che seguira presto si sapera :
per adesso : io humilissimamente baso le mani di vra Ex.tia
supplicandola a pigliar i miei capricci in bona parte e tenermi
sempre nella sua bona gratia nro s.re la conserui insieme .
con la s.ra principessa renca in sanita et allegrezza quanto
desidera   Di monaco adi . 11 . di marzo 1578 :

Di vra Ex.tia
humiliss: seruitor:
orlando de lassus .

3. Part of an autograph
letter (11 March 1578)
from Lassus to Duke
Wilhelm (D-Mbs Galli.
942, Brief 37)

Various later Passions borrowed from it, and a manuscript dated 1743, complete with added thoroughbass part, shows that it was still performed 150 years after its composition. The other three Passions survive only in manuscript, with convincing though not absolutely definitive attribution to Lassus.

6. MAGNIFICAT SETTINGS AND OTHER LITURGICAL WORKS. Lassus's 101 settings of the *Magnificat*, collected in a posthumous edition (1619) by his son Rudolph, far outnumber those of any other 16th-century composer (Palestrina, for example, wrote 35). Their wide circulation in print and manuscript is testimony to their lasting popularity; only those of Morales had anything like this success. All but a few are *alternatim* settings of the even verses, leaving the odd verses to be chanted, as was customary, or perhaps played on the organ.

In 1567 Lassus published three cycles each containing a six-verse setting for all eight tones. He went on to write two more such cycles; all are based on the appropriate chant tones of the *Magnificat*, with widely varied use of cantus firmus technique. Some 60 settings use the

psalmodic tones; a number of others have monophonic tunes used as cantus firmi. He respected the *Magnificat* tones in his choice of mode, and tended not to embellish the cantus firmus when using it intact; but no brief description could do justice to the flexible virtuosity with which the time-honoured device of the cantus firmus is used in these works. There is of course much integration of cantus firmus with other voices through melodic paraphrase and contrapuntal imitation.

A *Magnificat* parodying Rore's celebrated madrigal *Ancor che col partire* was published in the collection of 1576. Some 25 of the *Magnificat* settings appearing in subsequent years are parody works; Lassus was the first to make consistent use of parody technique in this genre, and he seems to have liked using the procedure almost as much as he did in the masses. His own motets (and an occasional chanson) were favoured sources, but he ranged widely through 16th-century literature, from Josquin (whose *Praeter rerum seriem* served as model for a magnificently elaborate six-voice work) to Striggio and Vecchi, from motets to madrigals. As in the masses, parody technique is used here in almost bewilderingly varied fashion, and with a sure instinct for blending the style of the model with that of the 'copy'.

Lassus's settings of the *Magnificat* vary greatly in length and complexity, from concise settings resembling *falsibordoni* to resplendently contrapuntal works over 200 bars long. His tendency generally to write more compact, harmonically conceived works in his later years may be seen in these pieces, but not in any easily predictable way. The opening and closing verses are generally closer to their melodic or contrapuntal models, the middle verses correspondingly freer. All voices respect to some degree the bipartite structure of the psalm verses.

There are a large number of liturgical and quasi-liturgical works in other genres. Some were printed in the composer's lifetime: the Offices for Christmas, Easter and Pentecost in the third volume of the *Patrocinium musices* (1574); the Christmas Lessons of volume iv (1575) in that series; the Lamentations of Jeremiah, some of which were printed in 1585; the Lessons from Job (two sets, printed in 1565 and 1582); and the seven *Psalmi Davidis poenitentiales* (printed in 1584 but composed much earlier). Posthumously published works include 12 litanies (1596; two others survive in manuscript copies). None of these works was included in the *Magnum opus musicum* and none therefore appears in Haberl's edition. Only the penitential psalms have been much studied.

An important category of Office polyphony in Lassus's works is the *Nunc dimittis*. 12 settings survive, none of them ever printed: four, based on chant, date from about 1570, and eight (not all confirmed as genuine), of which five are known to be parody works based on motets and madrigals, from the last period of his life. Still other groups of liturgical pieces survive only in manuscript and were apparently never printed (they were perhaps considered in a way the private property of the Bavarian court chapel): these include a group of *falsibordoni*, an important hymn cycle (c1580) and a group of responsories (1580s). These have been described briefly (by Boetticher), but await publication and thorough investigation.

7. MOTETS. Difficult to assess simply by reason of their enormous number, the motets of Lassus as they appear in Haberl's edition pose an additional problem: they are printed in the order assigned to them by Rudolph and Ferdinand Lassus in the *Magnum opus musicum* of 1604, and thus arranged by number of voices rather than in chronological order of publication (the new Lassus edition is fortunately proceeding on quite different principles). Studies of Lassus's music based on chronology have been made (Boetticher), but much remains to be done. It is not easy to be sure about relative composition dates for much of this music; the publication date is of course not an infallible guide, sometimes not even a useful one. Details of stylistic growth and change can probably be seen and analysed, but the criteria for such a study have yet to be fully developed.

In motet composition, as in the writing of madrigals, Lassus began by assimilating the styles fashionable in Italy in his youth. Cipriano de Rore and the Roman school around Barrè seem the two most important of these influences, as seen in the carefully conceived declamatory rhythms in all voice parts. The bold yet tonally controlled chromaticism of motets such as *Alma nemes*, and the use of distinctive, finely chiselled thematic material in *Audi dulcis amica mea* (both printed in 1555), certainly show that Lassus knew Rore's work. The motets of the Roman and Antwerp years, and also those of the first decade in Munich, are dazzlingly virtuoso in invention and the handling of vocal textures. *Videntes stellam*, a two-section motet for five voices printed in 1562, is a good example of Lassus's brilliant early style. The melodic material, distantly derived from a *Magnificat* antiphon for Epiphany week, transforms gentle hints in the chant into dramatically descriptive motifs that rocket through the texture, a texture that is constantly varied but always clear, and always well grounded harmonically. It is no wonder that the composer of pieces such as this rapidly won for himself first place at the Bavarian court and an international reputation soon to surpass that of all his contemporaries.

Imitation plays a large role in the contrapuntal technique of Lassus's early work, as does voice pairing; he did not of course observe these techniques as strictly as did Josquin's generation, but neither did he favour the thick texture and close-set imitation cultivated by Gombert. Everywhere there is harmonic clarity and solidity, equally apparent in pieces such as the *Prophetiae Sibyllarum*, which use the chromatic vocabulary fashionable in the 1550s, as in completely diatonic works.

It has been said that Lassus made little use of canon or other constructivist elements. This is true in a statistical sense, but when he chose he could show off Netherlands skills; for example, the seven-part *In omnibus requiem quaesivi* (published 1565) has a three-part canon, with one of the voices in contrary motion. Cantus firmus writing is rarer in Lassus than in Palestrina, but on occasion Lassus could revert to the kind of cantus firmus procedure used by Josquin and Obrecht; *Homo cum in honore esset* (six voices; published 1566) has a *soggetto cavato* as cantus firmus on the text 'Nosce te ipsum', heard successively in breves, semibreves and minims. In this eclectic revival of earlier techniques, and in many individual passages where archaisms like fauxbourdon or use of outmoded long notes are seen, Lassus may have been using elements of an older Netherlands style for expressive reasons, making a musical allusion to support the meaning of a phrase of text.

Like all Lassus's music, the motets are immensely varied in musical invention and expressive detail. Nonetheless a recognizable stylistic 'set' may be observed in all the motets of the period c1555–70: thematic originality is blended with a contrapuntal fluidity that in less distinguished pieces approaches formula; there is plenty of chordal declamation, always marked by strength and clarity of harmony; expressive word-painting abounds but does not dominate or upset the equilibrium of a piece; and a certain succinctness – the economy of utterance that was to become increasingly evident in Lassus's later works – is noticeable (the famous six-part *Timor et tremor*, published 1564, is as surprising for brevity as it is celebrated for expressive power). Lassus's capacity for obtaining iridescent changes of colour in the plainest of diatonic palettes through skilful vocal scoring, a trait very marked in his later works, is present in his early motets; it is indeed one of the most characteristic of his stylistic traits (see ex.1, the opening of *O Domine salvum me fac*, published 1562).

Ex.1 *O Domine salvum me fac*

In his motets of the 1570s and 1580s, as in other works of this period, Lassus made much use of chordal declamation on short note values, varied by quickly alternating points of imitation of rather neutral melodic character. This 'villanella' style (see Boetticher) may indicate a desire for a more up-to-date vocabulary on Lassus's part. If so, that is about as far as he went; the works of the last decade are less markedly declamatory, more complex in texture and marked by a certain denseness and concentration of style that is not so much progressive as it is highly individual, a final style seen to good advantage in the six-part *Musica Dei donum optimi* (published 1594), a moving tribute to the composer's art (this text was also set by other 16th-century composers).

Although they cannot be categorized in any very neat way, Lassus's motets can be divided roughly under a few general headings.

(i) *Didactic works.* The 24 duos of 1577 and many of the pieces for three voices must have been intended for students. In this the duos are particularly interesting. When compared with other famous 16th-century collections of duos such as those of Gero or of Lupacchino – both of them sets that were reprinted so often as to leave no doubt about their pedagogical usefulness – Lassus's psalm settings and textless bicinia are surprising in their individuality of style: they are not generic counterpoint but rather illustrations of his own contrapuntal practice. They were popular enough to be reprinted and even to be 'modernized' (in a Parisian reprint of 1601 with an added third voice), but they did not rival Gero's in longevity of use; they have about them too much of the finished and idiosyncratic composition, too little of the contrapuntal exercise. For Lassus's own pupils they

must have been of great value since the writing of duos was probably the most important part of a 16th-century composer's training. It may be noted that the two-part pieces illustrate the D, E, F and G modes but not those on A and C; this supports the remark of Lechner, Lassus's pupil, that his teacher used only the traditional eight modes.

(ii) *Ceremonial motets.* There are a surprising number of pieces written for special occasions or to honour rulers and dignitaries; these are mostly grouped together in the *Magnum opus musicum*, near the beginning or end of the divisions by number of voices. Some of them provide clues to the composer's life; thus the five-part *Te spectant Reginalde Poli* (published 1556) may indicate that Lassus knew the English Cardinal Pole in Rome in the 1550s. Many occasional pieces honouring the Habsburgs and various secular and religious potentates throughout Germany were doubtless commissioned by the Bavarian court. By far the largest number of these are addressed to Albrecht V, to his eldest son (the future Wilhelm V) and to other members of the ducal family (one of these, *Unde revertimini*, started its existence under a slightly different name as a work in praise of Henri d'Anjou, the future Henri III of France). They vary in length and scoring (from three to ten voices) but as a matter of course are uniformly bright and festive in nature. Some, like the nine-section *Princeps Marte potens, Guilelmus*, are little more than a series of acclamations (in this instance addressed to Wilhelm V, his bride, and members of the imperial and ducal families); others are in full polyphonic style. A distinguishing feature of Lassus's ceremonial pieces honouring the Wittelsbachs is their personal tone, evident proof of the composer's close relationship with his employers. This is seen in *Multarum hic resonat*, addressed to Wilhelm on his name day in 1571, and in *Haec quae ter triplici*, the dedicatory piece of a collection of motets for three voices (1577) honouring Albrecht's three sons, on a text ending 'Lassus mente animoque dicat' ('Lassus' set to the composer's musical signature of *la-sol*). Most appealingly personal of all is *Sponsa quid agis*, for five voices, thought to have been composed for Lassus's marriage in 1558; here the colouristic harmony on the words 'Non me lasciviae veneris', in an otherwise diatonic framework, is a charming bit of musical allusion.

(iii) *Humorous motets.* Pieces with texts ranging from playfulness to burlesque are to be found among the works with Latin texts. Their music is appropriate and often witty in itself, but almost never broadly farcical; Lassus, rather like Mozart, tended to clothe his verbal jokes in exquisite musical dress. One exception is the travesty of 'super flumina Babylonis', beginning 'SU-su-PER-per' and proceeding haltingly and confusedly through both text and music, perhaps mocking the efforts of inexpert singers. Of a similar nature is *Ut queant laxis*, for five voices, in which the tenor sings the isolated notes of the hexachord between snatches of four-voice polyphony. In many apparently serious motets the tone-painting of individual words is so literal that one suspects a half-humorous intent, and occasionally one is sure of it: the concertato performance of motets is parodied in *Laudent Deum cythara*, in which five instrumental families are named, to music characteristic for each, in the space of a dozen bars (the total length of the piece).

There are drinking-songs in Latin in his output, as

there are in German and French. These may be elaborate, as in the eight-part double chorus *Vinum bonum*. Perhaps the most amusing is the macaronic *Lucescit jam o socii*, whose independently rhymed series of alternating Latin and French lines sounds so much like some of the composer's letters to Duke Wilhelm that Lassus must surely be author of both text and music.

(*iv*) *Classical and classicistic texts*. The ceremonial motets are full of classical phrases. Other pieces setting either classical texts (Virgil, Horace) or humanistic 16th-century verse are to be found; there is a whole group of these near the end of the five-part section of the *Magnum opus musicum*. Lassus made his contribution to the list of Renaissance composers who set Dido's lament *Dulces exuviae*; his version is in correctly quantitative declamatory chords with little ornament, a style not far from that used for classical choruses (as in Andrea Gabrieli's music for *Edippo tiranno*). Most of these pieces are less academic in character, closer to the composer's normal motet style. There are, however, examples of almost completely literal quantitative settings; the five-voice setting of *Tragico tecti syrmate coelites* looks very much like the settings of Horatian odes used in German schools, a genre with which Lassus was evidently familiar. Related to this genre are the *Prophetiae Sibyllarum*, famous for their chordal chromaticism but also showing careful declamatory exactness in setting the curious half-Christian, half-pagan humanistic verse.

(*v*) *Religious works*. There are hints of ordering within the liturgical calendar in sections of the *Magnum opus musicum* (examples are the four-part offertories, roughly nos.124–68 in Haberl's edition, and the section in the five-part motets beginning with the Christmas antiphon *Angelus ad pastores*, no.192; the six-part motets also show traces of liturgical sequence). The collection also has groupings by category such as hymns, Marian antiphons, Gospel or Epistle motets etc, which are convenient for study but of little help in determining liturgical usage. As Lassus's sons included in their huge anthology a good many pieces which are motets only by virtue of being contrafacta of secular works, their methods of assemblage and editing appear too arbitrary to serve as the basis for study of the religious function of their father's motets.

A large proportion of the motets must of course have been used in performance of the Mass and Offices in the court chapel. The number of settings of Marian antiphons, some of which are very elaborate, suggest that portions of the Office were sung with great solemnity. This is also true of settings of the *Pater noster*, the *Ave Maria*, and hymns included in the *Magnum opus musicum*; the six-part settings of *Veni Creator Spiritus* and *Veni Sancte Spiritus* are particularly resplendent. When one recalls that many of Lassus's motet prints carried the rubric 'apt for voices and instruments' it is easy to imagine concerted performances of motets using some of the forces depicted in Hans Mielich's miniature, which shows the court chapel as assembled for chamber performance (see fig.4). Among the motets appearing in tablatures, chiefly of German origin, are a group in Johannes Rühling's keyboard book (1583) which are arranged in liturgical order for Sundays and great feast days throughout the year, and thus are clearly intended for use in the liturgy.

Whether motets on religious texts were used as liturgical works, for private devotional purposes or in concert is hard to determine. Marian antiphons, for example, could certainly have been used as devotional pieces. Style may offer some clue; the Gospel motets (six voices, nos.549–58) are severely conservative and thus 'sound' liturgical whereas the Epistle motets adjacent to them are highly expressive (*Cum essem parvulus*, nos.570–71, with its touching delineation of the cardinal virtues and especially of charity, is one of the composer's most moving works in any genre) and thus appear devotional in character. The many psalm settings, some of them free compilations from various psalms (the celebrated *Timor et tremor* is among them), are difficult to judge in this regard. A thorough study of the liturgical practices at Munich might help to place many works whose function is now not clear.

The motets of Lassus were admired in their own day not only for their beauty and technical perfection but also for their rhetorical power – their ability to move the affections through the use of rhetorical devices transferred into musical idioms. Joachim Burmeister's celebrated rhetorical analysis of *In me transierunt* (published 1562) in his *Musica poetica* (1606; an expanded version of the *Musica autoschediastikou*, 1601) compares the motet to a classically ordered speech. 40 years earlier Quickelberg had praised Lassus's ability to 'describe an object almost as if it were before one's eyes'. One has only to think of the many striking, sharply individualized openings of motets – the *exordia* of classical rhetoric – in Lassus's work to see that both expressiveness and the rhetorician's trick of catching attention can hardly be missed in this music. Whether the composer proceeded as deliberately, even pedantically, as Burmeister would have it may be doubted. But if one recalls Lassus's carefully precise declamation of classical texts it becomes clear that he knew something of the German didactic tradition linking music with the study of classical metres; it is not a large step from this to assume that he also knew how classical rhetoric was studied in the schools. The 'speaking' quality of much of this music cannot be a fortuitous property; it is not only expressive in a general sense but affective in a precise way, clearly perceptible to the composer's contemporaries.

8. MADRIGALS. In the mixed print issued in Antwerp by Susato in 1555 and often referred to as Lassus's 'op.1', there are seven madrigals for four voices showing the composer's grasp of the genre as a result of his Italian, particularly his Roman, years. His poetic tastes – a quatrain and a canzone stanza of Petrarch, an ottava by Ariosto, a Sannazaro poem and a pastoral in sestina (a form he particularly liked) – are typical of the period. *Del freddo Rheno*, a complete sestina rather in the style of the cyclic madrigals of Arcadelt and Berchem, opens the group on a note of simple tunefulness (this piece was popular with intabulators); in other madrigals the style varies from Willaert-like seriousness (*Occhi piangete*), through supple contrapuntal writing resembling Rore (*Per pianto la mia carne*), to the chordal declamation typical of the Roman *madrigale arioso* (*Queste non son più lagrime*). A certain clarity and succinctness of utterance are Lassus's personal stamp; in other respects this collection is highly eclectic. These madrigals, together with a few others including the chanson-like *Appariran per me le stell'*, reappeared in Lassus's first book of four-part madrigals, published by Dorico in Rome and then by Gardane in Venice, both in 1560. The strong

resemblance of Lassus's early madrigals to those of his contemporaries may be illustrated by the fact that one piece in this volume, *Non vi vieto*, credited to Lassus and included in Sandberger's edition, is actually the work of Hoste da Reggio, part of a cycle in the latter's second book for four voices (1554). Lassus's volume was a popular one, reprinted a dozen times over the next 30 years and supplying favourite materials for lutenists' intabulations. Other early four-part madrigals appeared in Barrè's Roman anthologies of *madrigali ariosi*.

Also highly successful, to judge by the frequency with which they were reprinted, were the first book for

4. *The Bavarian court chapel assembled for chamber music: miniature by Hans Mielich from the Mielen Codex, 16th century (D-Mbs Mus.Ms.AII, f.187); Lassus is at the keyboard, surrounded by musicians playing viola da gamba, viole da braccia, bass recorder, flute, trombone, cornetts, racket and lute*

five voices, first issued by Gardane in Venice in 1555, and the second, printed by Barrè in Rome in 1557 after having long been held in private hands (so says the dedicatory letter of G. B. Bruno, who is known to have been in Rome in 1554). These madrigals and, in all probability, most of those in the third book for five voices (brought out by Barrè in Rome in 1563 after, says the publisher, a diligent search for works by Orlande) must have been written before Lassus's departure from Rome in 1555. Petrarch dominates the first volume and is well represented in the others, with a six-section canzone cycle (*Standomi un giorno*) in a 'narrative', vibrantly declamatory style opening the second book.

The Petrarchan sonnets receive on the whole the most serious treatment, with sharply expressive thematic material in the tradition of Rore (see ex.2, the opening of *Sol'e pensoso*). Other forms such as the sestina, cyclic or in individual stanzas, are given lighter polyphonic dress; and the chordal declamation of the arioso madrigal may be seen (Bernardo Tasso's *Vostro fui vostro son*). Some works, particularly a group near the end of the second book, are clearly in an easy, 'popular' style. Even the most ambitious Petrarchan settings, however, are marked by Lassus's ever-present clarity of tonal palette and attractiveness of melody. These madrigals are distinguished by free use of material (there is little exact imitative writing) and by much variety of speed and character in declamation, despite the fact that the *misura cromatica* (C) is used in only a few pieces. They do not perhaps equal the work of Rore in intensity but they do rival the older master in variety of mood and seamless technical perfection – no mean achievement for a man in his twenties. The frequent choice of texts in which the word 'lasso' appears (in six pieces scattered through the three volumes), and the invariable *la–sol* setting it receives, suggest a youthful desire to 'sign' his works; Lassus as a young Roman clearly wanted the world to know who he was.

From the first decade in Munich come the contents of the fourth book for five voices, written to show, in the composer's words, that the Muses were cherished and could flourish in 'Germania' as well as in Italy. Lassus visited Venice in May 1567; while there (when he was described in a letter as 'lively and a good companion') he saw to the printing of this fourth book, which he dedicated to Duke Alfonso II d'Este and then took to Ferrara to present to him. Lassus's inclination towards the cyclic madrigal is again seen here; there is a complete sestina by Petrarch at the beginning, sonnets in two parts, and another sestina (*Qual nemica fortuna oltra quest'Alpe*) that seems to combine local Ferrarese reference (the Po river) with a laboured geography-of-love image.

Lassus's madrigal output slowed down after this. He contributed to the anthologies of Bavarian court madrigals assembled by Troiano (1569) and Bottegari (1575); the recent discovery in Dublin of the long-missing tenor partbook of the 1569 volume (*RISM* 1569[19]) will allow publication and study of these works. Whether a true 'middle period' in stylistic terms can be seen in these and other individual pieces appearing in various anthologies of the 1570s remains to be demonstrated.

In 1585 Lassus was again in Italy; the dedication of his volume of five-part madrigals printed in Nuremberg in that year (reissued in Venice in 1587 as the *Libro*

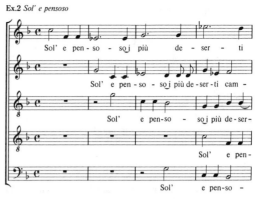

Ex.2 *Sol' e pensoso*

quinto) is to the great Veronese patron Mario Bevilacqua, whose *ridotto* the composer may have visited at this time. Here serious Petrarchan texts alternate with religious sonnets by Gabriel Fiamma. In style these madrigals, separated from the fourth book by nearly 20 years, show definite awareness of the newer Italian madrigal: not that of the chromaticists but rather that of Marenzio, with brief contrast motifs, declamation on short note values and counterpoint that is chiefly figured chordal progressions (*Io che l'età più verde* is an example). Lassus's older style is not completely absorbed by these novelties, and in a few pieces his earlier madrigals are recalled (the sestina *Quando il giorno*). How well he could write in a newer style is demonstrated by the amusing *La non vol esser più mia* (published 1584), a work in fully-fledged canzonetta idiom.

The madrigals for four, five and six voices dedicated to Lassus's friend the physician Thomas Mermann (Nuremberg, 1587) show some of the traits seen in the volume of 1585 but are more varied in style (at least one, *Pensier dicea*, is an older work), often suggesting the compression and individuality of his late motet style. In this volume a five-section religious cycle to text by Beccuti ('il Copetta'), *Signor le colpe mie*, has been shown (see Boetticher) to be missing its first stanza, *Di terrena armonia*, a piece for some reason printed separately in *Continuation du mellange* issued by Le Roy & Ballard in 1584.

At the very end of his life Lassus set the 21 ottava stanzas of Tansillo's *Lagrime di S Pietro*. This cycle of seven-voice spiritual madrigals is one of the most remarkable artistic testaments in the history of music. Deliberately restrained in mood and character, planned as a magnificent tonal arch covering the whole range of 16th-century sound, the work is at once musically unified and expressively varied. Lassus's lifelong habits of concision and balance, subordinating vivid declamation and rhetorical power to inexorable musical clarity, are here given their definitive statement. The transcendentally synthetic quality of this music, blending styles as diverse as the *Prophetiae Sibyllarum* and the late madrigals, stands in the sharpest possible contrast to what was in other hands already becoming the drily academic *stile antico*.

Among Lassus's most popular Italian-texted works are the six four-voice villanellas in the 'op.1' of 1555 (these pieces are often found in anthologies of lute intabulations) and the contents of the *Libro de villanelle, moresche, et altre canzoni* for four, five, six and eight voices (Paris, 1581), a volume said by the composer to have been written in his old age when he should have known better. The famous *Matona mia cara* may serve as an example of pieces to be found in this volume, although some of the other pieces are equally amusing. All are reworkings of older material, following the time-honoured principle of using pre-existing melodies in this genre; the most outrageous texts receive elegant if simple musical setting, in its own way a final statement about this sub-species of the madrigal.

9. CHANSONS. Fewer in number than his madrigals, Lassus's chansons, about 150 in all, are nonetheless considerable in bulk and, more important, highly characteristic of the composer, who never entirely left off being a Frenchman. He wrote a number of chansons in his youth and did not by any means stop when he moved to Munich; French was in common use at the court, and chansons of various types were evidently in demand from his patrons as well as from his publishers.

To judge by their dates of publication, Lassus wrote chansons from the 1550s into the 1580s; a greater proportion than of most other categories are early works. Just as the madrigals were brought out for the most part by Roman and Venetian printers, so the chansons were published chiefly in the Netherlands (Phalèse, Susato, Laet) and in Paris (Le Roy & Ballard, Du Chemin). Their wide popularity can be seen from the frequent reprints and from their appearance in print in Lyons, La Rochelle, Strasbourg and London (Vautrollier, 1570). Some of the later reprints bear the proud description of the composer as 'Prince des musiciens de nostre temps'. The chansons were much in favour with keyboard, cittern and especially lute intabulators; the *Theatrum musicum* of Phalèse and Bellère (*RISM* 1568²³, 1571¹⁶) is particularly rich in Lassus's works. The English translation of Le Roy's lute tutor (London, 1574) contains 11 chansons by Lassus. A very large number of chansons, including some of the bawdiest, were 'spiritualized' in French and German religious collections (Pasquier, 1576; Berg, 1582). The bulk of Lassus's chanson output was collected in two volumes of 'meslanges' issued by Le Roy & Ballard (1576, 1584). Of the chansons not included in these volumes or in the important *Livre de chansons nouvelles* issued by Phalèse in 1571, some have not survived complete; among these are a set of religious chansons on texts by Guy du Faur de Pibrac, published in 1581. Fortunately two of these pieces, illustrating the sobriety of Lassus's late chanson style, have been reassembled through the discovery (by Bernstein) of a set of manuscript parts in Edward Paston's library (in *GB-Cfm*).

Lassus turned to some of the most famous of 16th-century French poets for texts: Marot, Ronsard, Du Bellay and Baïf. The fact that he often set texts already known in musical settings is reflected in his occasional choice of Mellin de Saint-Gelais, a favourite poet among composers of the preceding generation, and also in his fondness for light verse from popular anthologies such as *La fleur de poesie francoyse* (1542). Occasional choice of much earlier poetry (Chartier, Villon) can also be seen. The subject matter ranges from dignified nature-poetry (Du Bellay) and Petrarchesque lyrics (Ronsard), through sententious and moralizing texts, to the familiar drinking-songs, some macaronic texts, and Rabelaisian amorous and bawdy narratives; no one wrote more amusing chansons of this last type (*En un chasteau* and *Il esteoit une religieuse* are excellent examples). There are also biblical and religious texts (the famous *Susanne un jour*, for example) – these apart from the contrafacta imposed by other hands on nearly all the secular chansons. There are a few real love-lyrics, some occasional pieces, and isolated soundings of familiar chanson-like themes such as 'faulte d'argent' (in *Je suis quasi prest d'enrager*).

In musical style the chansons are more varied than the usual blanket description given them – as either 'Parisian' patter chansons or motet-like serious pieces – would suggest. Lassus could and often did write chansons, usually light narratives or dialogues, in the classically clear and succinct style made popular in Attaingnant's anthologies. How directly and economically he went about this can be seen in a work such as *Un advocat dit à sa femme* (ex.3). These pieces are usually for four voices, but Lassus, who in all genres preferred five-part texture, could manage 'Parisian' style just as easily in five voices (*La terre les eaux*, for example). He could even write a piece that resembles, paradoxically, an instrumental *canzona alla francese* transcribed for voices (*Si pour moy avez du souci*). The light chansons are not always written in 'Parisian' fashion; the Italian patter style infecting so much of Lassus's work in his middle years may also be seen here (there is

Ex.3 *Un advocat dit à sa femme*

5. *Autograph MS of the alto part of Lassus's chanson 'Quand mon mary vient', 1564 (PL-GD E.2165)*

one outright 'villanelle', to Baïf's *Une puce j'ay dedans l'oreill'*).

Many chansons begin, as do so many of the lieder, with a contrapuntal *exordium*, sharply delineating the character of the piece through distinctive melodic shapes; then follow patter chords or lightweight texture in which short motifs are constantly thrown back and forth among the voices. Sometimes the music changes character with every flicker of meaning in the text, as in the setting of Marot's *Qui dort icy*. The declamation in all the lively chansons is good; in some it is extraordinarily vivid – Marot's *Bon jour et puis quelles nouvelles* is given a setting of such conversational immediacy that on hearing it all barriers separating us from the 16th century seem to drop away.

The more serious chansons resemble the reflective, affective madrigals of Rore and his successors more than they do motets. Chansons such as *Le temps passé* (with its 'soupir' figures), *Mon coeur ravi d'amour* and *Comme la tourterelle* (with its madrigalian chromaticism) are madrigals in all but their very Gallic declamatory diction. Use of madrigalian style is sometimes but not always influenced by the text; thus Ronsard's *J'espère et crains*, with its laboured Petrarchan oxymora, is given a quite restrained setting, while *Vray dieu disoit une fillette*, a very French text, is given such Italian touches as a long final pedal point. In a category by themselves are pieces such as *La nuict froide et sombre* (Du Bellay), set as an expansive, colouristic tone poem in style even though characteristically brief in actual duration.

German schoolmasters would not have picked chansons by Lassus as examples of rhetorical organization and affective power; the genre was not sufficiently grand. Many of the chansons would nevertheless make good examples of the musician as rhetorician; Marot's *Fleur de quinze ans*, for instance, is in Lassus's hands a seduction speech of extraordinarily tight organization and persuasive musical diction.

10. GERMAN LIEDER. For Lassus, French by birth and Italian by musical training, composition in a German vein must have posed problems. He published no lieder until 1567; by that time he was surely fluent in setting German texts, enough for him to have written for private use, at the court, pieces Duke Albrecht liked too well to allow to circulate in print (preface to the 1567 collection). But the native tradition was very strong in Munich, where Senfl had worked until his death (1542–3); the song collections of Ott, Forster and others remained popular, and the need for new works was correspondingly less great during Lassus's early years at the Bavarian court.

The lieder are few in number only by the standards of Lassus's prolific output in other genres; if one counts the German psalms for three voices (1588) there are over 90 compositions, including several multipartite six-part sacred compositions larger in scale than most of the motets. Many of the secular pieces were famous in the composer's time and are among his best-known works today (*Audite nova*, for example). The proportion of sacred pieces among the lieder is high, even without counting the volume of psalms; this suggests that the German collections were intended for a somewhat different audience from that for the madrigals and the chansons.

In the preface to the third book of five-part lieder (1576), Lassus contrasted the Italian and German styles, emphasizing (and defending) the roughness of the latter. He evidently tried to cultivate a specifically German style. The results were good, certainly; but his position in the history of the lied has been described (by Osthoff) as that of an innovator who discarded German tradition, that of the Tenorlied, in favour of a style mixing elements of the madrigal, the villanella and the chanson. This is true primarily of the secular lieder; the sacred works use traditional melodies in, on the whole, as strict an adherence to cantus firmus writing as Lassus showed in any genre.

In some respects Lassus was conservative as a composer of lieder. He chose texts for the most part already known in sacred and secular songbooks (one exception is the setting of Hans Sachs's *Ein Körbelmacher in ein Dorff*), and inclined towards folklike ones. His German settings are rhythmically lively and correct in declamation, but not exaggeratedly so; nor are there experiments in chromaticism in the lieder. His preference for five-part texture (which he felt he had to justify as a novelty in the preface to the 1567 collection) was merely carrying over into the lieder a general preference typical of his generation.

The sacred lieder use texts and melodies common to Lutheran and Catholic songbooks (the Ulenberg psalm translations are, however, Catholic and even anti-Protestant in intent), with Luther's *Vater unser im Himmelreich* opening the first collection. The psalm settings range from the rather simple tricinia of the 1588 collection (where they alternate with similar settings by his son Rudolph) to the great six-part psalm-motets such as *Ich ruff zu dir*, using paraphrased and cantus firmus versions of the borrowed melodies, in the French–German volume of 1590.

Among the secular texts chosen by Lassus are drinking-songs and lieder in which the bad effects of liquor are lamented (*Mein Fraw hilgert*); possibly the constantly expressed preference for wine over beer was a personal one. Comic rustic narrative encounters (*Baur, was tregst im Sacke?*) are among the most famous of the lieder. There are also melancholy and satirical pieces (*Die zeit, so jetz vorhanden ist*), some love-songs of narrative character, and a few songs of nature-love. The traditional vein of elegiac introspection seen in the lied from Hofhaimer to Senfl was on the whole avoided by Lassus.

Many lieder begin with an imitative *exordium* followed by lively patter. Relationships to the villanella and lighter madrigal may of course be seen (Lassus knew the celebrated German villanella collections of Regnart), and the presence of chanson-like rhythms is frequent. The combination is a natural and convincing one; Lassus did not so much break with German tradition as simply set texts in his own style, a somewhat eclectic one in every genre. In any event the triumphantly German character of the best lieder is proof enough that he mastered the lied in his own way.

11. LASSUS AND PALESTRINA. If one were to attempt a comparison of Lassus with Palestrina, certain similarities could be cited: each possessed a flawless technique, and each revelled in its use; both were conservative musicians, perhaps by temperament but certainly in accord with the demands of the positions they held. Many stylistic details, such as frequent use of imitative

melismas based on cambiata figures, are common to both men's work. What sets them apart are Lassus's greater variety of style and genre, his greater economy of utterance (occasionally verging on the perfunctory, but nearly always effective aesthetically by its very brevity), his liking for highly individual opening subjects and his preference for clearcut and strongly directed chordal harmony.

WORKS

Editions: *O. de Lassus: Sämtliche Werke*, ed. F. X. Haberl and A. Sandberger (Leipzig, 1894–1926) [S]
    O. de Lassus: Sämtliche Werke: neue Reihe, ed. S. Hermelink and others (Kassel, 1956–) [H]

Il primo libro di madrigali, 5vv (Venice, 1555) [1555a]
Il primo libro dove si contengono madrigali, vilanesche, canzoni francesi, e motetti, 4vv (Antwerp, 1555[29]) [1555b]
Il primo libro di mottetti, 5, 6vv (Antwerp, 1556) [1556]
Secondo libro delle muse, madrigali . . . con una canzone del Petrarca, 5vv (Rome, 1557[22]) [1557]
Il primo libro di madrigali, 5vv (Venice, 1560) [enlarged edn. of 1555a] [1560a]
Liber decimus quintus ecclesiasticarum cantionum . . . ex omnibus tonis, 5, 6vv (Antwerp, 1560) [enlarged edn. of 1556] [1560b]
Tiers livre des chansons, 4–6vv (Louvain, 1560) [1560c]
[25] Sacrae cantiones, 5vv (Nuremberg, 1562) [1562]
Il terzo libro delli madrigali, 5vv (Rome, 1563[11]) [1563]
Le premier livre de chansons, auquel sont ving et sept chansons nouvelles, 4vv (Antwerp, 1564) [1564a]
Primus liber concentuum sacrorum, 5, 6vv (Paris, 1564) [1564b]
Quatriesme livre des chansons, 4, 5vv (Louvain, 1564) [1564c]
Dixhuictieme livre des chansons, 4, 5vv (Paris, 1565) [1565a]
Modulorum . . . modulatorum secundum volumen, 4–8, 10vv (Paris, 1565) [1565b]
Quinque et sex vocibus perornatae sacrae cantiones . . . liber secundus, 5, 6vv (Venice, 1565) [1565c]
Sacrae lectiones novem ex propheta Iob, in officiis defunctorum cantari solitae, 4vv (Venice, 1565) [1565d]
Liber missarum . . . liber primus, 4–6vv (Venice, 1566[1]), lost [1566a]
Sacrae cantiones . . . liber secundus 5, 6vv (Venice, 1566) [1566b]
Sacrae cantiones . . . liber tertius 5, 6vv (Venice, 1566) [1566c]
Sacrae cantiones . . . liber quartus 6, 8vv (Venice, 1566) [1566d]
Libro quarto de madrigali, 5vv (Venice, 1567) [1567a]
Magnificat octo tonorum, 4–6vv (Nuremberg, 1567) [1567b]
Neue teütsche Liedlein, 5vv (Munich, 1567) [1567c]
Selectissimae cantiones, 6 and more vv (Nuremberg, 1568) [1568a]
Selectissimae cantiones, 4, 5vv (Nuremberg, 1568) [1568b]
Cantiones aliquot, 5vv (Munich, 1569) [1569a]
Liber secundus sacrarum cantionum, 4vv (Louvain, 1569) [1569b]
Disieme livre de chansons, 4vv (Paris, 1570[9]) [1570a]
Mellange d'Orlande de Lassus, contenant plusieurs chansons, tant en vers latins qu'en ryme francoyse, 4, 5vv (Paris, 1570) [1570b]
Praestantissimorum divinae musices auctorum missae decem, 4–6vv (Louvain, 1570[1]) [1570c]
Premier livre des chansons, 4, 5vv (Louvain, 1570[5]) [1570d]
Quinque missae suavissimis modulationibus refertae . . . liber secundus, 4, 5vv (Venice, 1570) [1570e]
Second livre des chansons, 4, 5vv (Louvain, 1570[6]) [1570f]
Selectiorum aliquot cantionum sacrarum, 6vv, fasciculus adiunctis in fine tribus dialogis, 8vv (Munich, 1570) [1570g]
Viginti quinque sacrae cantiones, 5vv (Nuremberg, 1570) [enlarged edn. of 1562] [1570h]
Livre de chansons nouvelles, 5vv, avec 2 dialogues, 8vv (Paris, 1571) [1571a]
Moduli nunquam hactenus editi, 5vv (Paris, 1571) [1571b]
Der ander Theil teutscher Lieder, 5vv (Munich, 1572) [1572a]
Moduli, 4, 8vv (Paris, 1572) [1572b]
Moduli, 6, 7, 12vv (Paris, 1573) [1573a]
Patrocinium musices . . . cantionum . . . prima pars, 4–6vv (Munich, 1573) [1573b]
6 cantiones latinae, 4vv, adiuncto dialogo, 8vv: 6 teutsche Lieder, 4vv, sampt einem Dialogo, 8vv: 6 chansons françoises nouvelles, 4vv, avecq un dialogue, 8vv: 6 madrigali nuovi, 4vv, con un dialogo, 8vv (Munich, 1573) [1573c]
Patrocinium musices . . . missae aliquot, secunda pars, 5vv (Munich, 1574) [1574a]
Patrocinium musices . . . officia aliquot, de praecipuis festis anni . . . tertia pars, 5vv (Munich, 1574) [1574b]
Patrocinium musices . . . passio, 5vv, idem lectiones Iob, et lectiones matutinae de nativitate Christi, 4vv, quarta pars (Munich, 1575) [1575]
Der dritte Theil schöner, neuer, teutscher Lieder, sampt einem zu End gesetzten frantzösischen frölichen Liedlein, 5vv (Munich, 1576) [1576a]

Les meslanges . . . contenantz plusieurs chansons, tant en vers latins qu'en ryme francoyse, 4–6, 8, 10vv (Paris, 1576, earlier edn. 1570, lost, repr. with sacred contrafacta, London, 1570) [1576b]

Patrocinium musices . . . Magnificat aliquot, quinta pars, 4–6, 8vv (Munich, 1576) [1576c]

Thresor de musique . . . contenant . . . chansons, 4–6vv (Geneva, 1576) [1576d]

Liber mottetarum, 3vv (Munich, 1577) [1577a]

Missae variis concentibus ornatae . . . cum cantico beatae Mariae octo modis variato, 4–6, 8vv (Paris, 1577–8) [1577b]

Moduli, 4–9vv (Paris, 1577) [1577c]

Novae aliquot et ante hac non ita usitatae cantiones suavissimae, 2vv (Munich, 1577) [also incl. 12 textless bicinia] [1577d]

Altera pars selectissimarum cantionum, 4, 5vv (Nuremberg, 1579) [1579]

Liber missarum, 4, 5vv (Nuremberg, 1581) [1581a]

Libro de villanelle, moresche, et altre canzoni, 4–6, 8vv (Paris, 1581) [1581b]

Fasciculi aliquot sacrarum cantionum, 4–6, 8vv (Nuremberg, 1582) [1582a]

Lectiones sacrae novem, ex libris Hiob excerptae, 4vv (Munich, 1582) [1582b]

Missa ad imitationem moduli (Quand'io penso al martire), 4vv (Paris, 1582) [1582c]

Mottetta typis nondum uspiam excusa, 6vv (Munich, 1582) [1582d]

Sacrae cantiones, 5vv (Munich, 1582) [1582e]

Neue teutsche Lieder, geistlich und weltlich, 4vv (Munich, 1583) [1583a]

Teutsche Lieder, zuvor unterschiedlich, jetzund aber . . . inn ein Opus zusammen getruckt, 5vv (Nuremberg, 1583) [1583b]

Continuation du mellange, 3–6, 10vv (Paris, 1584) [1584a]

Psalmi Davidis poenitentiales, modis musicis redditi . . . his accessit psalmus Laudate Dominum de coelis, 5vv (Munich, 1584/R1970) [1584b]

Cantica sacra, recens numeris et modulis musicis ornata, 6, 8vv (Munich, 1585) [1585a]

Hieremiae prophetae lamentationes, et aliae piae cantiones, 5vv (Munich, 1585) [1585b]

Madrigali novamente composti, 5vv (Nuremberg, 1585) [1585c]

Sacrae cantiones . . . recens singulari industria compositae, 4vv (Munich, 1585) [1585d]

Madrigali novamente composti, 4–6vv (Nuremberg, 1587) [1587a]

Missa ad imitationem moduli Beatus qui intelligit, 6vv (Paris, 1587) [1587b]

Missa ad imitationem moduli Locutus sum, 6vv (Paris, 1587) [1587c]

Patrocinium musices: Beatissimae deiparaeque Virginis Mariae canticum Magnificat, ad imitationem cantilenarum quarundam, 4–6vv (Munich, 1587) [1587d]

Missae . . . liber primus, 4, 5vv (Milan, 1588⁴) [1588a]

Tertium opus musicum, continens lectiones Hiob et motectas seu cantiones sacras, 4–6vv (Nuremberg, 1588⁸) [1588b]

Teutsche Psalmen: geistliche Psalmen, 3vv (Munich, 1588¹²) [1588c]

Patrocinium musices: missae aliquot, 5vv (Munich, 1589) [1589]

Neue teutsche, unnd etliche frantzösische Gesäng, 6vv (Munich, 1590) [1590]

Cantiones sacrae, 6vv (Graz, 1594) [1594]

Lagrime di S Pietro . . . con un mottetto nel fine, 7vv (Munich, 1595) [1595]

Musica nuova dove si contengono madrigali, sonnetti, stanze, canzoni, villanelle et altri compositioni, 3vv (Munich, 1595), lost

Cantiones ab Orlando di Lasso et huius filio Ferdinando di Lasso compositae, 5vv (Munich, 1597³) [1597]

Prophetiae Sibyllarum . . . chromatico more singulari confecatae, 4vv (Munich, 1600) [1600]

Liber primus cantiones sacrae Magnificat vocant, 5, 6vv (Paris, 1602¹) [1602]

Magnum opus musicum . . . complectens omnes cantiones, 2–10, 12vv (Munich, 1604) [1604]

Missa ad imitationem moduli Dixit Joseph, 6vv (Paris, 1607) [1607a]

Missa ad imitationem moduli Or sus à coup, 4vv (Antwerp, 1607) [1607b]

Missae posthumae, 6, 8vv (Munich, 1610) [1610]

Iubilus beatae virginis, hoc est centum Magnificat, 4–8, 10vv (Munich, 1619) [1619]

Further printed works, 1555³⁰, 1557²⁰, 1558¹³, 1559¹², 1559¹³, 1560¹⁴, 1561⁵, 1561¹⁰, 1562⁷, 1563³, 1564¹, 1564², 1564³, 1564⁴, 1564⁵, 1566², 1566¹⁷, 1567³, 1567¹³, 1567¹⁶, 1568², 1568⁴, 1568⁵ 1569¹⁸, 1569¹⁹, 1570¹⁵, 1575¹¹, 1576⁵, 1579², 1583², 1583⁷, 1583⁸, 1583¹⁵, 1584⁴, 1585¹⁷, 1594⁶, 1596², 1601³

MASSES
(for manuscript sources see edition)

Alleluia, 5vv, frag. (T only of Kyrie and Gloria); H xii, 155

Alleluia, 5vv, frag. (B only of Kyrie and Gloria); H xii, 157

Amar donna [Chi passa; Amor donna; Donna chi bella], 5vv, 1589; H vi, 23

Amor ecco colei, 6vv, 1610; H viii, 93

Beatus qui intelligit, 6vv, 1587b (on own motet); H vii, 195

Bell'Amfitrit'altera, 8vv, 1610; H viii, 55

Benedicam Dominum, 5vv, MS c1670 (on own motet); H xi, 3

Cantorum, 4vv (inc.); H xii, 3

Certa fortiter, 6vv, 1610 (on own motet); H viii, 131

Confundantur superbi, 5vv, MS c1564 (on own motet); H ix, 3

Congratulamini mihi, 6vv, 1570c (on own motet); H vii, 137

Credidi propter, 5vv, 1574a (on own motet); H iii, 249

De feria, 4vv, 1577b; H iv, 87

De feria in Quadragesima, 4vv, MS 1566; H ix, 43

De feria in Septimana Sancta, 4vv, MS 1566; H ix, 51

Deus in adjutorium, 6vv, 1610 (on own motet); H viii, 211

Deus misereatur, 8vv (doubtful, possibly by A. Grothusius) (on Lassus's motet); H xii, 99

Dittes maistresse, 5vv, 1589 (on Monte's chanson); H vi, 3

Dixit Joseph, 6vv, 1607a (on own motet); H iii, 3

Domine Dominus noster, 6vv, MS 1577 (on own motet); H x, 41

Domine secundum actum meum, 5vv, 1570c (on Jacquet of Mantua's motet); H vii, 49

Doulce memoire, 4vv, 1577b (on Sandrin's chanson); H iv, 3

Ecce Maria, 5vv (inc.) (on own motet); H xii, 51

Ecce nunc benedicite, 6vv, 1610 (on L. Daser's motet); H viii, 173

Entre vous filles, 5vv, 1581a (on Clemens's chanson); H v, 159

Frère Thibault [Sine nomine], 4vv, 1570e (on Certon's chanson); H iii, 75

Il me suffit [Beschaffens-Glück], 4vv, 1581a (on Sermisy's chanson); H v, 139

In die tribulationis, 5vv, 1589 (on Jacquet of Mantua's motet); H vi, 71

In me transierunt, 5vv, frag. (T only of Kyrie and Gloria) (on own motet); H xii, 154

In principio, 6vv (inc.) (on own motet); H xii, 65

In te Domine speravi, 6vv, 1566a (on own motet); H v, 51

Io son ferito ahi lasso, 5vv, 1589 (on Palestrina's madrigal); H vi, 105

Ite rime dolenti, 5vv, 1574a (on Rore's madrigal); H iii, 133

Jäger [Venatorum], 4vv, 1577b; H iv, 73

Je ne mange poinct de porcq, 4vv, 1570e; H iii, 3

Je prens en gres, 4vv, MS 1572 (on Clemens's chanson); H ix, 77

Je suis desheritée, 4vv, MS 1583 (on J. Lupi's chanson); H x, 93

Jesus ist ein süsser Nam, 6vv, MS c1592; H x, 145

La la maistre Pierre [Ad placitum], 4vv, 1570e (on Sermisy's chanson); H iii, 27

Laudate Dominum omnes gentes, 4vv, 1588a; H vii, 3

Le berger et la bergère, 5vv, 1570e (on Gombert's chanson); H iii, 97

Locutus sum, 6vv, 1587c (on own motet); H vii, 89

Mon coeur se recommende à vous, 5vv, MS 1579 (doubtful, possibly by J. Eccard) (on Lassus's chanson); H xi, 233

Octavi toni, 5vv (doubtful, possibly by Neuner); H xii, 306

Officium mortuorum, 6vv (doubtful, possibly by J. de Kerle); H xi, 263

On me l'a dict, 4vv, MS c1570 (on Certon's chanson); H ix, 61

O passi sparsi, 4vv, 1577b (on S. Festa's madrigal); H iv, 49

Or sus à coup, 4vv, 1607b (doubtful, ? by J. Lockenburg) (on Crecquillon's chanson); H xi, 91

Osculetur me, 8vv, MS after 1582 (on own motet); H x, 187

Paschalis, 5vv, MS 1576; H ix, 131

Pilons pilons lorge [Quinti toni], 4vv, 1570e (on Sermisy's chanson); H iii, 51

Pro defunctis, 4vv, 1577b; H iv, 95

Pro defunctis, 5vv, 1589; H vi, 135

Puisque i'ay perdu, 4vv, 1577b; H iv, 23

Qual donna attende à gloriosa fama, 5vv, 1589 (on Rore's madrigal); H vi, 43

Quand'io pens'al martire, 4vv, 1582d (on Arcadelt's madrigal); H vii, 25

Qui la dira, 5vv, MS 1576 (on Willaert's madrigal); H x, 3

Requiem, 4vv (inc.); H xii, 326

Rompi de l'empio cor, 6vv, MS c1570 (on Willaert's madrigal); H xi, 45

Scarco di doglia, 5vv, 1574a (on Rore's madrigal); H iii, 175

Se salamandre, 4vv, MS c1570 (doubtful, possibly by Lockenburg) (on Crecquillon's chanson); H xi, 113

Sesquialtera, 4vv, MS 1579; H x, 69

Sidus ex claro, 5vv, 1574a (on own motet); H iii, 217

Si me tenez, 6vv, MS c1560 (doubtful, possibly by J. Vaet) (on Crecquillon's chanson); H xi, 179

Si rore aenio, 5vv, MS 1572; H ix, 101

Surge propera, 6vv, 1577b (on own motet); H iv, 157

Surrexit Pastor bonus (i), 5vv, MS c1576 (doubtful, possibly by Ivo de Vento) (on Lassus's motet); H xi, 135

Surrexit Pastor bonus (ii), 5vv (on own motet); H xii, 15

Susanne un jour, 5vv, 1577b (on own chanson); H iv, 121

Tempus est ut revertar, 6vv, frag. (B only of Kyrie and Gloria) (on own motet); H xii, 159

Tous les regretz, 6vv, 1577b (on Gombert's chanson); H v, 3

Triste depart, 6vv, MS 1592 (on Gombert's chanson); H x, 115

Veni in hortum meum, 5vv, 1581a (on own motet); H v, 185

Vinum [Verbum] bonum, 8vv, 1577b (on own motet); H v, 105

PASSIONS

Passio Domini nostri Jesu Christi secundum Mattheum, 5vv, 1575; H ii, 3

Passio Domini nostri Jesu Christi secundum Marcum, 4vv, MS 1582; H ii, 27

Passio Domini nostri Jesu Christi secundum Lucam, 4vv, MS 1582; H ii, 37

Passio Domini nostri Jesu Christi secundum Johannem, 5vv, MS 1580; H ii, 47

MAGNIFICAT SETTINGS

Alma real se come fide stella (octavi toni), 5vv, 1619 (on Rore's madrigal)

Amor ecco colei (septimi toni), 6vv, 1587d

Ancor che col partire (quarti toni), 5vv, 1576c (on Rore's madrigal)

Aria di un sonetto (octavi toni), 5vv, 1587d (on D. Ortiz's Aria di Ruggiero)

Aurora lucis rutilat (octavi toni), 10vv, 1619 (on own motet)

Beau le cristal (sexti toni), 4vv, 1619 (on own chanson)

Benedicta es caelorum regina (octavi toni), 6vv, 1602 (on Josquin's motet)

Dalle belle contrade (sexti toni), 5vv, 1619 (on Rore's madrigal)

Dessus le marché d'Arras (primi toni), 6vv, 1587d (on own chanson)

Deus in adjutorium (septimi toni), 5vv, 1587d (on own motet)

Dies est laetitia (sexti toni), 6vv, 1602

D'ogni gratia e d'amor (septimi toni), 6vv, 1619 (on Striggio's madrigal)

Ecco ch'io lasso il core (secundi toni), 6vv, 1587d (? on Striggio's madrigal)

Erano capei d'oro (septimi toni), 5vv, 1619 (on G. M. Nanino's madrigal)

Hélas j'ai sans merci (septimi toni), 5vv, 1619 (on own chanson)

Il est jour (secundi toni), 4vv, 1587d (on Sermisy's chanson)

Las je n'iray plus (secundi toni), 5vv, 1619 (on own chanson)

Mais qui pourroit (secundi toni), 6vv, 1587d (on own chanson)

Margot labouréz les vignes (septimi toni), 4vv, 1619 (on own chanson)

Memor esto (secundi toni), 6vv, 1619 (on own motet)

Mort et fortune (tertii toni), 5vv, 1587d (on Gombert's chanson)

O che vezzosa aurora (secundi toni), 6vv, 1619 (on Vecchi's madrigal)

Omnis enim homo (primi toni), 6vv, 1587d (on own motet)

Omnis homo primum bonum vinum ponit (sexti toni), 6vv, 1602 (on Wert's motet)

O s'io potessi (secundi toni), 4vv, 1619 (on Berchem's madrigal)

Pange lingua gloriosa (septimi toni), 4vv, 1619

Praeter rerum seriem (secundi toni), 6vv, 1602 (on Josquin's motet)

Quando lieta sperai (quarti toni), 6vv, 1587d (on Rore's madrigal)

Quanti in mille anni il ciel (secundi toni), 6vv, 1587d (on Nollet's madrigal)

Recordare Jesu pie (septimi toni), 6vv, 1619 (on own motet)

S'io credessi per morte (tertii toni), 4vv, 1619 (on A. de Reulx's madrigal)

S'io esca vivo (septimi toni), 6vv, 1619 (on own madrigal)

Si par souhait (primi toni), 4vv, 1587d (on own chanson)

Si vous estes m'amie (sexti toni), 6vv, 1619 (on own chanson)

Susanne un jour (primi toni), 6vv, 1587d (on Lupi's chanson)

Tant vous allez doux (sexti toni), 6vv, 1619 (on Ebran's chanson)

Ultimi miei sospiri (secundi toni), 6vv, 1619 (on Verdelot's madrigal)

Vergine bella (primi toni), 5vv, 1619 (on Rore's madrigal)

Vola vola pensier [Aeria a la italiana] (octavi toni), 5vv, 1602

Vous perdez temps (septimi toni), 5vv, 1619 (on Sermisy's chanson)

Primi toni, 4vv, 1576c; Primi toni (i), 5vv, 1619; Primi toni (ii), 5vv, 1619; Primi toni (iii), 5vv, 1619

Secundi toni (i), 5vv, 1619; Secundi toni (ii), 5vv, 1619; Secundi toni, 6vv, 1619

Tertii toni, 5vv, 1619

Quarti toni (i), 5vv, 1619; Quarti toni (ii), 5vv, 1619; Quarti toni (iii), 5vv, 1619; Quarti toni, 8vv, 1619

Quinti toni, 5vv, 1619; Quinti toni, 6vv, 1619

Sexti toni (i), 5vv, 1619; Sexti toni (ii), 5vv, 1619; Sexti toni (iii), 5vv, 1619; [Sexti toni], 5vv, MS c1582, D-Mbs; Sexti toni, 8vv, 1576c

Septimi toni (i), 5vv, 1619; Septimi toni (ii), 5vv, 1619; Septimi toni, 7vv, 1619; Septimi toni, 8vv, 1576c; Septimi toni, 8vv, 1619

Octavi toni (i), 5vv, 1619; Octavi toni (ii), 5vv, 1619; Octavi toni, 6vv, 1619; Octavi toni (i), 8vv, 1619; Octavi toni (ii), 8vv, 1619

8 settings, octo tonorum, 6vv, 1567b; 8 settings, octo tonorum, 5vv, 1567b; 8 settings (i), octo tonorum, 4vv, 1567b; 8 settings (ii), octo tonorum, 4vv, 1576b

OFFICES
(all printed works in 1574b)

Asperges me (i), 5vv

Asperges me (ii), 5vv

Cibavit eos (Officium corporis Christi), 5vv

Puer natus est (Officium natalis Christi), 5vv

Resurrexit (Officium paschale), 5vv

Spiritus Domini (Officium pentecostes), 5vv

Vidi aquam, 5vv

Officium in purificatione Beatae Mariae Virginis, 4vv, c1583–5, Mbs

LESSONS

Sacrae lectiones ex propheta Iob, 4vv, 1565d; ed. H. J. Therstappen, *Die Klagen des Hiob* (Berlin, 1948)

Lectiones matutinae de nativitate Christi, 4vv, 1575

Lectiones sacrae novem ex libris Hiob, 4vv, 1582b

LAMENTATIONS

9 Lamentationes Hieremiae, 4vv, c1588, *Mbs*

9 Lamentationes Hieremiae, 5vv, 1585b; ed. in *Musica sacra*, xii (Berlin, 1867)

LITANIES
(all printed works in 1596²; for some edns. see Boetticher)

De gloriosissima Dei genitrice, 4vv

De gloriosissima Dei genitrice (i), 5vv

De gloriosissima Dei genitrice (ii), 5vv

De gloriosissima Dei genitrice (iii), 5vv

De gloriosissima Dei genitrice (iv), 5vv

De gloriosissima Dei genitrice, 6vv

De gloriosissima Dei genitrice, 8vv

De gloriosissima Dei genitrice, 9vv

De gloriosissima Dei genitrice, 9vv, c1590, *D-Mbs*

De gloriosissima Dei genitrice, 10vv, c1580, *Mbs*

De nomine Jesu, 5vv

De omnibus sanctis, 4vv

De omnibus sanctis, 5vv

De omnibus sanctis, 7vv

NUNC DIMITTIS
(all MSS in D-Mbs)

Come havran fin, 4vv, c1592

Heu mihi Domine, 5vv, c1592

Io son si stanco, 5vv, c1592

Oculi mei semper ad Dominum, 6vv, c1592

S'el mio sempre per voi, 4vv, c1592

Secundi toni, 4vv, c1570

Quarti toni, 4vv, c1570

Quarti toni, 5vv, c1592

Septimi toni, 4vv, c1570

Octavi toni, 4vv, c1570

[without title], 5vv, c1592

[without title], 7vv

FALSIBORDONI
(all in D-Mbs, c1578)

Advena (primi toni), 5vv

Donec ponam (primi toni stravaganti), 5vv

Donec ponam (sexti toni), 5vv

Nisi Dominus (quinti toni), 5vv

Quoniam confortavit (septimi toni), 5vv

Sit nomen Domini (secundi toni), 5vv

Stantes erant pedes nostri (tertii toni), 5vv

[textless] (quarti toni), 4vv

[textless] (sexti toni), 5vv

[textless] (octavi toni), 5vv

HYMNS
(all in D-Mbs, c1580)

Aurem benignam protinus, 4vv; Beata quoque agmina, 4vv; Colladaumus venerantes, 4vv; Cuius corpus sanctissimum, 4vv; Gloria Deo per immensa, 4vv; Hic nempe mundi, 4vv; Hic nempe mundi, 4vv; Hi sunt quos retinens, 4vv; Ibant magi quam, 5vv; Illustre quiddam cernimus, 4vv; Janitor coeli doctor, 4vv; Maria soror Lazari, 4vv; Nova veniens ex coelo, 4vv; Nuntius celso veniens, 4vv; Pange lingua gloriosi, 5vv; Procul recedant somnia, 4vv; Quae te vicit clementia, 4vv; Qui condolens interitu, 5vv; Qui mane junctum, 4vv; Qui paracletus diceris, 5vv; Qui pascis inter lilia, 4vv; Qui pius prudens, 4vv; Quo volneratus insuper, 4vv; Respice clemens solio, 4vv; Scrutator alme cordium, 4vv; Sermone blando angelus, 4vv; Sit trinitatis sempiterna, 4vv; Sumen illud ave, 4vv; Te mane laudum, 4vv; Tu lumen tu splendor, 5vv; Vos prima Christi victima, 4vv; Vos secli justi, 4vv

RESPONSORIES

In nativitate Domini, 5vv, ?1580–85, *Mbs*

Pro Triduo sacro in nocturno II et III, 4vv, ?1580–85, *Mbs*

MOTETS

Accipe qua recrees (2p. Quo fers), 6vv, 1604; S xi, 101

Ad Dominum cum tribularer (2p. Heu mihi), 6vv, 1594; S xvii, 49

Adoramus te Christe (i), 3vv, 1604; S i, 57

Adoramus te Christe (ii), 3vv, 1604; S i, 57

Adoramus te Christe, 4vv, 1604; S i, 112

Adoramus te Christe, 5vv, 1604; S v, 63

Adorna thalamum, 4vv, 1585d; S i, 91

Ad primum morsum, 6vv, 1594; S xix, 74

Ad te Domine levavi (2p. Vias tuas), 5vv, 1556; S ix, 150

Ad te levavi animam meam, 6vv, 1582d; S xvii, 121

Ad te levavi oculos meos (2p. Miserere nostri), 6vv, 1570g; S xvii, 125

Ad te perenne gaudium, 3vv, 1604; S i, 60

Adversum me loquebantur, 5vv, 1562; S ix, 40

Agimus tibi gratias, 3vv, 1604; S i, 59

Agimus tibi gratias, 4vv, 1604; S i, 131

Agimus tibi gratias, 5vv, 1576d; S v, 98

Agimus tibi gratias, 5vv, 1579; S v, 100

Agimus tibi gratias, 6vv, 1573b; S xiii, 103

Alleluja laus et gloria, 4vv, 1604; S i, 68

Alma nemes quae sola [Alme Deus qui cuncta tenes], 4vv, 1555b; S iii, 93

Alma parens dilecta Deo (2p. Qua sina coelestis; 3p. Nos pia turba; 4p. Tu modo diva; 5p. Aspicient invictos), 5vv, 1604; S v, 128

Alma Redemptoris mater, 5vv, 1597; S v, 102

Alma Redemptoris mater, 6vv, 1582d; S xiii, 105

Alma Redemptoris mater, 6vv, 1604; S xiii, 108

Alma Redemptoris mater, 8vv, 1604; S xxi, 14

Alma Venus [Christe Patris verbum] (2p. Nunc elegos divae [Tu poteris]), 5vv, 1560b; S v, 37

Amen dico vobis, 4vv, 1564⁵; S i, 119

Andreas Christi famulus, 6vv, 1585a; S xv, 1

Angelus ad pastores iat, 5vv, 1562; S iii, 139

Angelus Domini descendit (2p. Nolite timere), 6vv, 1585a; S xiii, 1

Angelus Domini locutus est, 5vv, 1571b; S v, 51

Anima mea liquefacta, 5vv, 1582e; S ix, 42

Animam meam dilectam (2p. Congregamini), 5vv, 1565b; S v, 29

Anna mihi dilecta veni [Christe Dei soboles] (2p. Accipe daque), 4vv, 1579; S iii, 3

Anni nostri sicut, 6vv, 1566d; S xv, 53

Ante me non est formatus, 6vv, 1573b; S xi, 131

Audi benigne conditor (2p. Multum quidem), 5vv, 1568²; S vii, 86

Audi dulcis [filia] amica mea, 4vv, 1555b; S i, 99

Audi tellus (2p. Ubi Plato; 3p. Ubi David), 6vv, 1566d; S xv, 44

Auris bona est, 5vv, 1582e; S vii, 56

Aurora lucis rutilat, 10vv, 1604; S xxi, 119

Ave color vini clari [Ave decus coeli; Ave Christe] (2p. O quam flagrans), 5vv, 1568b; S xi, 11

Ave Jesu Christe [Maria] alta stirps, 4vv, 1579; S i, 102

Ave Maria gratia plena, 5vv, 1604; S v, 118

Ave mater matris Dei, 4vv, 1604; S i, 132

Ave regina coelorum, 3vv, 1577a; S i, 25

Ave regina coelorum, 4vv, 1604; S i, 79

Ave regina coelorum, 5vv, 1604; S v, 104

Ave regina coelorum, 6vv, 1582d; S xiii, 111

Ave regina coelorum, 6vv, 1604; S xiii, 114

Ave verum corpus, 6vv, 1582d; S xiii, 66

Beati omnes qui timent (2p. Ecce sit benedicetur), 3vv, 1577a; S i, 49

Beati omnes qui timent (2p. Ecce sit benedicetur), 5vv, 1565b; S vii, 136

Beati pauperes (2p. Beati pacifici), 4vv, 1572b; H i, 11

Beatus homo cui donatum est, 6vv, 1594; S xvii, 99

Beatus homo qui invenit, 2vv, 1577d; S i, 1

Beatus ille qui procul (2p. Ergo aut adulta; 3p. Libet jacere), 5vv, 1569a; S xi, 22

Beatus Nicolaus, 8vv, 1604; S xxi, 23

Beatus qui intelligit (2p. Dominus opem), 6vv, 1565b; S xvii, 105

Beatus vir qui in sapientia, 2vv, 1577d; S i, 1

Beatus vir qui inventus est, 5vv, 1582e; S ix, 117

Beatus vir qui non abiit, 6vv, 1568a; S xv, 159

Beatus vir qui timet, 4vv, 1568b; S iii, 50

Benedicam Dominum, 4vv, 1585d; S iii, 73

Benedicam Dominum, 5vv, 1562; S ix, 174

Benedic anima mea, 4vv, 1585d; S i, 152

Benedic anima mea Domine (2p. Qui replet; 3p. Non secundum; 4p. Recordare; 5p. Benedicite Domino), 6vv, 1570g; S xv, 169

Benedic Domine domum istam, 8vv, 1588b; S xix, 160

Benedicite gentes, 4vv, 1585d; S i, 157

Benedicite omnia opera (2p. Benedicite ignis; 3p. Benedicite montes; 4p. Benedicite sacerdotes), 5, 6vv, 1565b; S ix, 93

Benedictio et claritas, 6vv, 1582d; S xi, 139

Benedictus Dominus Deus Israel (i), 9vv, MS 1580s, *Mbs*

Benedictus Dominus Deus Israel (ii), 9vv, MS 1580s, *Mbs*

Benedictus Dominus Deus Israel (iii), 9vv, MS 1580s, *Mbs*

Benedictus es Domine (i), 4vv, 1585d; S iii, 49

Benedictus es Domine (ii), 4vv, 1585d; S iii, 65

Benedixisti Domine, 5vv, 1582e; S ix, 179

Bestia curvafia pulices [Bestia stultus homo], 5vv, 1576b; S xi, 44; H i, 67

Bone Jesu verbum patris, 8vv, 1604; S xix, 154

Bonitatem fecisti, 5vv, 1565b; S ix, 15

Caligaverunt populi mei, 5vv, 1562; S ix, 182

Cantabant canticum Moysi (2p. Quis non timet), 6vv, 1594; S xvii, 131

Cantantibus organis (2p. Fiat Domine), 5vv, 1582e; S v, 164

Cantate Domino canticum novum (2p. Cantate ... et benedicite), 3 vv, 1577a; S i, 42

Cantate Domino canticum novum, 5vv, 1565c; S vii, 142

Cantate Dominum canticum novum (2p. Viderunt omnes), 6vv, 1582e; S xix, 14

Cernere virtutes, 5vv, 1568b; S iii, 114

Certa fortiter, 6vv, 1582e; S xv, 82

Christus resurgens ex mortuis, 3vv, 1577d; S i, 23

Christus resurgens ex mortuis, 5vv, 1582e; S v, 54

Circumdederunt me dolores mortis, 6vv, 1604; S xv, 106

Clamaverunt ad Dominum, 6vv, 1570g; S xvii, 29

Clare sanctorum senatus (2p. Thoma), 5vv, 1562; S v, 144

Cognoscimus Domine (2p. Vita nostra), 5vv, 1564⁴; S vii, 147

Cognovi Domine (2p. Veniant mihi), 4vv, 1565b; S i, 147

Concupiscendo concupiscit (2p. Exaltabo te), 6vv, 1565c; S xvii, 145

Confirma hoc Deus, 6vv, 1583²; S xvii, 96

Confisus Domino (2p. Inde tuo si quis), 5vv, 1564⁴; S vii, 92

Confitebor tibi Domine, 4vv, 1585d; S iii, 16

Confitebor tibi Domine, 6vv, 1594; S xix, 20

Confitebor tibi Domine, 8vv, 1564¹; S xxi, 56

Confitemini Domino (2p. Narrate omnia), 5vv, 1562; S vii, 131

Confitemini Domino (2p. Ipse castigavit), 6vv, 1573b; S xvii, 79

Confortamini et jam nolite, 4vv, 1585d; S iii, 89

Confundantur superbi (2p. Fiat cor meum), 5vv, 1562; S ix, 155

Congratulamini mihi (2p. Tulerunt), 6vv, 1566d; S xiii, 10

Congregati sunt, 5vv, 1597; S ix, 186

Conserva me Domine (2p. Sancti qui sunt), 6vv, 1594; S xvii, 101

Conveniens homini est, 6vv, 1585a; S xv, 92

Creator omnium Deus, 6vv, 1556; S xiii, 68

Credidi propter (2p. Vota mea), 5vv, 1569a; S ix, 21

Cum essem parvulus (2p. Nunc cognosco), 6vv, 1582d; S xv, 72

Cum invocarem exaudibit me (2p. Sacrificate; 3p. Signum est), 6vv, 1570g; S xvii, 43

Cum natus esset (2p. At illi; 3p. Et ecce stella), 6vv, 1566d; S xi, 141

Cum rides mihi (2p. Data est), 5vv, 1577c; H i, 23

Custodi me Domine, 4vv, 1585d; S iii, 88

Da pacem Domine, 5vv, 1588b; H i, 62

Da pacem Domine (i), 6vv, 1582d; S xiii, 72

Da pacem Domine (ii), 6vv, 1556; S xiii, 74

Da pater antique, 5vv, 1569a; S v, 84

Decantabat populus Israel, 7vv, 1564²; S xix, 91

Deficiat in dolore vita mea, 6vv, 1594; S xvii, 22

Delitiae Phoebi, 5vv, 1556; S xi, 81

De ore prudentis, 5vv, 1565c; S vii, 38

Descendit sicut pluvia (2p. Coram illo), 5vv, 1571b; S v, 3

Deus canticum novum (2p. Quia delectasti), 5vv, 1565c; S vii, 164

Deus in adjutorium meum intende, 6vv, 1582d; S xvii, 160

Deus iniqui insurrexerunt, 6vv, 1594; S xvii, 113

Deus in nomine tuo (2p. Ecce enim Deus), 4vv, 1565c; S iii, 44

Deus judex justus (2p. Et in eo paravit), 5vv, 1571b; S ix, 61

Deus meus in simplicitate, 6vv, 1582d; S xvii, 156

Deus misereatur nostri, 8vv, 1566d; S xxi, 35

Deus noster refugium, 5vv, 1565b; S ix, 131

Deus qui bonum vinum [Deus qui non vis mortem], 4vv, 1565a; S iii, 97

Deus qui sedes super thronum, 5vv, 1562; S ix, 12

Deus tu conversus, 5vv, 1582e; S ix, 46

Deus tu scis, 3vv, 1577a; S i, 40

Dextera Domini, 4vv, 1585d; S i, 158

Dic mihi quem portas, 8vv, 1570g; S xix, 133

Diligam te Domine, 3vv, 1577a; S i, 48

Diligam te Domine fortitudo, 6vv, 1594; S xvii, 67

Dilige solitudinem, 5vv, 1583²; S vii, 35

Diliges proximum (2p. Quoniam qui talia; 3p. Fructus autem), 4vv, 1582b; S i, 113

Dixi custodiam vias meas, 8vv, 1577c; S xxi, 48

Dixi ergo in corde meo (2p. Possedi servos; 3p. Et omnia), 5vv, 1585b; S vii, 107

Dixit Dominus, 8vv, 1570g; S xxi, 27

Dixit Joseph undecim fratribus suis (2p. Nunciaverunt), 6vv, 1564¹; S xv, 76

Dixit Martha, 9vv, 1577c; S xxi, 98

Dominator Domine, 5vv, 1571b; S v, 96

Domine ad adjuvandum me, 4vv, 1585d; S iii, 32

Domine clamavi (2p. Cum hominibus; 3p. Dissipata sit), 5vv, 1573b; S ix, 140

Domine convertere, 4vv, 1585d; S iii, 17

Domine da nobis auxilium, 6vv, 1585a; S xvii, 19

Domine deduc me (2p. Sepulchrum patens), 6vv, 1566d; S xvii, 24

Domine Deus fortissime, 5vv, 1585b; S vii, 83

Domine Deus meus, 3vv, 1577a; S i, 34

Domine Deus salutis meae, 4vv, 1585d; S iii, 91

Domine Dominus noster, 6vv, 1604; S xvii, 39

Domine exaudi orationem meam, 4vv, 1585d; S iii, 33

Domine fac mecum, 4vv, 1585d; S iii, 63

Domine in auxilium, 4vv, 1585d; S iii, 92

Domine Jesu Christe pastor bone, 5vv, 1585b; S v, 167

Domine Jesu Christe qui cognoscis (2p. Averte Domine), 5vv, 1604; S v, 91

Domine labia mea, 4vv, 1585d; S iii, 66

Domine non est exaltatum (2p. Sicut ablactatus), 3vv, 1577a; S i, 30

Domine non est exaltatum (2p. Sicut ablactatus), 5vv, 1556; S vii, 152

Domine non est exaltatum (2p. Sicut ablactatus), 5vv, 1585a; S xvii, 117

Domine probasti me (2p. Ecce Domine), 5vv, 1556; S ix, 34

Domine quando veneris, 4vv, 1555b; S iii, 107

Domine quando veneris, 5vv, 1568[4]

Domine quid multiplicati sunt, 6vv, 1582d; S xvii, 110

Domine quid multiplicati sunt (2p. Ego dormivi), 12vv, 1604; S xxi, 135

Domine secundum actum meum, 4vv, 1573c; S iii, 13

Domine vivifica me, 4vv, 1582b; S iii, 81

Dominus mihi adjutor (2p. Bonum est confidere), 6vv, 1566d; S xvii, 58

Dominus scit cogitationes, 5vv, 1556; S ix, 128

Dulces exuviae (2p. Urbem praeclaram), 5, 6vv, 1570h; S xi, 57

Dulci sub umbra, 5vv, 1597; S xi, 49

Ecce Maria genuit (2p. Ecce Agnus Dei), 5vv, 1568b; S v, 15

Ecce nunc benedicite, 7vv, 1604; S xix, 114

Ecce quam bonum, 8vv, 1604; S xxi, 52

Edite Caesareo Boiorum (2p. Obscura sub nocte), 8vv, 1568a; S xix, 146

Ego cognovi, 6vv, 1594; S xv, 41

Ego dixi Domine (2p. Convertere Domine), 3vv, 1577a; S i, 55

Ego sum panis vivus, 5vv, 1582e; S v, 71

Ego sum pauper (2p. Laudabo nomen), 3vv, 1577a; S i, 44

Ego sum pauper, 5vv, 1582e; S ix, 159

Ego sum qui sum (2p. Ego dormivi), 6vv, 1570g; S xiii, 4

Ego sum resurrectio, 3vv, 1577a; S i, 22

Emendemus in melius, 5vv, 1571b; S vii, 32

Ergo rex vivat, 8vv, 1604; S xix, 129

Eripe me de inimicis, 4vv, 1573c; S i, 150

Eripe me de inimicis, 4vv, 1585d; S iii, 60

Estote ergo misericordes, 7vv, 1564[2]; S xix, 87

Evehor invidia pressus (2p. Rumpere livor), 5vv, 1582e; S xi, 53

Exaltabo te Domine, 4vv, 1582b; S iii, 59

Exaltabo te Domine (2p. Domine eduxisti), 6vv, 1594; S xvii, 136

Exaudi Deus orationem (2p. Contristatus sum), 3vv, 1577a; S i, 52

Exaudi Deus orationem meam, 4vv, 1585d; S iii, 20

Exaudi Domine preces, 5vv, 1573b; S ix, 56

Exaudi Domine vocem meam (2p. Ne avertas), 5vv, 1562; S vii, 158

Exaudi me Domine, 3vv, 1577a; S i, 46

Expectans expectavi Dominum, 4vv, 1585d; S iii, 72

Expectans expectavi Dominum (2p. Et immisit os), 5vv, before 1560, *Mbs*

Expectatio justorum, 2vv, 1577d; S i, 3

Exultate justi, 4vv, 1568b; S iii, 2

Exultet coelum mare, 5vv, 1571b; S iii, 144

Exurgat Deus, 4vv, 1604; S iii, 1

Exurgat Deus (2p. Cantate ei; 3p. Deus in loco), 5vv, 1573b; S ix, 105

Facta est Judaea sanctificatio, 4vv, 1581, *Mbs*

Factus est Dominus, 4vv, 1585d; S iii, 85

Fallax gratia, 4vv, 1573c; S i, 143

Feci judicium, 5vv, 1582e; S ix, 120

Fertur [vertur] in conviviis vinus [Tristis ut Euridicen Orphaeus ab orco] (2p. Volo inter omnia; 3p. Potatores incliti), 4vv, 1564b; S iii, 99

Fili quid fecisti nobis sic, 5vv, 1564[4]; S vii, 14

Flemus extremos (2p. Regiam Christi), 6vv, 1604; S xix, 40

Forte soporifera, 5vv, 1566[17]; S xi, 98

Fratres gaudete in Domino (2p. Petitiones vestrae), 6vv, 1585a; S xv, 97

Fratres nescitis, 6vv, 1594; S xv, 95

Fratres qui gloriatur, 6vv, 1604; S xv, 126

Fratres sobrii, 4vv, 1569b; S i, 129

Fremuit spiritus Jesus (2p. Videns Dominus), 6vv, 1556; S xv, 23

Fulgebunt justi, 2vv, 1577d; S i, 6

Gaudent in coelis, 4vv, 1573b; S i, 133

Genuit puerpera regem, 6vv, 1594; S xi, 164

Gloriamur in tribulationibus, 6vv, 1604; S xv, 144

Gloria Patri et Spiritui Sancto, 6vv, 1565c; H i, 71

Gratia soli Dei pie (2p. Legitimo ergo; 3p. Res mira), 5, 6vv, 1569a; S iii, 117

Gressus meos dirige, 4vv, 1585b; S iii, 70

Gustate et videte (2p. Divites eguerunt), 5vv, 1556; S v, 73

Haec est vera fraternitas, 6vv, 1585a; S xiii, 167

Haec quae ter triplici, 3vv, 1577a; S i, 20

Heroum soboles, 6vv, 1556; S xi, 122

Heu mihi Domine quia peccavi, 5vv, 1556; S ix, 6

Heu quantus dolor, 5vv, 1562; S xi, 51

Heu quis armorum furor (2p. Jam satio longo), 6vv, 1594; S xix, 44

Heu quos dabimus miseranda (2p. Mens male), 6vv, 1604; S xix, 48

Heu quos dabimus miseranda (2p. Mens male), 7vv, 1568a; S xix, 116

Hispanum ad coenam (2p. Mox importuno), 5vv, 1569a; S xi, 90

Hodie completi sunt (2p. Misit eos), 6vv, 1582d; S xiii, 32

Homo cum in honore esset, 6vv, 1566d; S xv, 90

Honorabile est [Inter omnes], 4vv, 1573c; S i, 123

Huc ades, 6vv, 1585a; S xi, 105

Huc me sidero (2p. De me solus), 6vv, 1568a; S xi, 180

Illumina oculos meos, 4vv, 1604; S i, 107

Illustra faciem (2p. Quam multa multitudo), 5vv, 1562; S ix, 77

Immittet angelus, 4vv, 1582b; S iii, 69

Improperium expectavit, 4vv, 1585d; S iii, 21

Impulsus eversus sum (2p. Vox exultationis), 5vv, 1562; S ix, 114

Inclina Domine, 4vv, 1555b; S iii, 26

Inclina Domine, 9vv, 1604; S xxi, 106

In conspectu angelorum, 8vv, 1570d (doubtful)

In convertendo Dominus (2p. Convertere Domine), 8vv, 1565b; S xxi, 63

In dedicatione templi, 6vv, 1594; S xv, 121

In Deo salutarem meum (2p. Sperate in eo), 6vv, 1573b; S xvii, 140

In exitu Israel, 6vv, c1581, *Mbs*

Infelix ego (2p. Solus igitur; 3p. Ad te igitur), 6vv, 1566d; S xiii, 95

In hora ultima, 6vv, 1604; S xv, 151

In illo tempore, 6vv, 1604; S xv, 20

In me transierunt, 5vv, 1562; S ix, 49

In monte Oliveti, 6vv, 1568a; S xi, 187

In omnibus requiem quaesivi, 7vv, 1565b; S xix, 101

In pace in idipsum, 3vv, 1604; S i, 59

In principio erat verbum (2p. Fuit homo missus; 3p. In propria venit), 6vv, 1566d; S xv, 8

In quoscumque locos, 5vv, 1597; S xi, 17

In religione homo vivit, 6vv, 1585a; S xv, 66

In te Domine speravi (2p. Quonium fortitudo mea), 6vv, 1564[1]; S xvii, 87

Intende voci, 4vv, 1585d; S iii, 19

Inter natos mulierum, 4vv, 1571b; S v, 150

In te speravi Domine, 4vv, 1582c; S iii, 82

Iste flos Allemannorum, 4vv, 1604; S i, 141

Jam lucis orto (2p. Qui ponit aquam), 8vv, 1564[1]; S xxi, 84

Jam non dicam vos (2p. Accipite Spiritum), 6vv, 1573a; S xiii, 38

Jerusalem plantavis (2p. Gaude et laetare), 5vv, 1562; S xiii, 134

Jesu corona virginum (2p. Quocumque pergis; 3p. Te deprecamur; 4p. Laus honor), 6vv, 1565c; S xiii, 174

Jesu nostra redemptio (2p. Inferni claustra; 3p. Ipsa te cogat; 4p. Tu esto nostrum gaudium), 6vv, 1567[3]; S xiii, 18

Johannes est nomen, 4vv, 1604; S i, 136

Jubilate Deo omnis terra, 4vv, 1585d; S iii, 62

Jubilate Deo omnis terra (2p. Populus eius), 6vv, 1565b; S xvii, 149

Jubilemus singuli (2p. Inter animalia), 6vv, 1570g; S xi, 151

Junior fui, 6vv, 1566d; S xv, 101

Justi tulerunt, 2vv, 1577d; S i, 4

Justorum animae, 5vv, 1582e; S v, 139

Justus cor suum, 2vv, 1577d; S i, 2

Justus es Domine et rectum, 3vv, 1577a; S i, 35

Laetatus sum (2p. Jerusalem; 3p. Quia illic; 4p. Propter fratres), 3vv, 1577a; S i, 36

Laetentur coeli (2p. Tunc exultabunt), 4vv, 1569b; S iii, 76

Lauda anima mea Dominum, 4vv, 1573b; S iii, 75

Lauda anima mea Dominum, 6vv, 1594; S xiii, 34

Laudabit usque ad mortem, 8vv, 1604; S xxi, 41

Lauda Jerusalem Dominum (2p. Qui emittit; 3p. Emittit verbum; 4p. Non fecit taliter), 6vv, 1565c; S xvii, 70

Lauda mater ecclesia, 5vv, 1597; S v, 171

Lauda mater ecclesia (2p. Aegra currit; 3p. Surgentem cum victoria), 6vv, 1582d; S v, 3

Lauda Sion salvatorum (2p. Dies enim; 3p. Quod non capis; 4p. Ecce panis), 6vv, 1577c; H i, 75

Laudate Dominum de coelis (2p. Laudate Dominum de terra; 3p. Juvenes et virgines; 4p. Laudate eum), 5vv, 1565b; S ix, 161

Laudate Dominum omnes gentes, 6vv, 1604; S xv, 156

Laudate Dominum omnes gentes, 12vv, 1573a; S xxi, 152

Laudate Dominum quoniam bonus est (2p. Magnus Dominus; 3p. Praecinite; 4p. Non in fortitudine), 7vv, 1568a; S xix, 106

Laudate pueri Dominum, 7vv, 1568a; S xix, 94

Laudavi igitur, 6vv, 1604; S xv, 154

Laudent Deum cythara, 4vv, 1604; S iii, 58

Legem pone mihi (2p. Da mihi intellectum), 5vv, 1562; S ix, 73

Levabo oculos meos, 4vv, 1582c; S iii, 29

Levabo oculos meos, 8vv, 1566d; S xxi, 71

Libera me Domine, 6vv, 1585a; S xv, 109

Locutus sum in lingua mea (2p. Fac mecum signum), 6vv, 1568a; S xvii, 62

Lucescit jam o socii (see 'Chansons')

Lucesit jam pariter, 4vv, 1584a (doubtful)

Luxuriosa res vinum, 6vv, 1594; S xv, 85

Martini festum celebremus (2p. Plebs igitur), 5vv, 1573b; S v, 153

Media vita in morte sumus (2p. Sancte Deus), 6vv, 1573b; S xiii, 90

Meditabor in mandatis, 4vv, 1582b; S iii, 83

Memento peccati tui, 5vv, 1597; S vii, 58

Memor esto, 6vv, 1585a; S xvii, 32

Mirabile mysterium, 5vv, 1556; S v, 18

Mira loquor, 10vv, 1604; S xxi, 126

Miserere mei Deus, 9vv, MS 1580s, *Mbs*

Miserere mei Domine, 4vv, 1585d; S iii, 31

Misericordias Domini, 5vv, 1573b; S ix, 9

Missus est angelus (2p. Ne timeas Maria; 3p. Dixit autem; 4p. Dixit autem), 5, 6vv, 1565c; S vii, 16

Momenta quaevis temporis, 6vv, 1604; S xix, 58

Mors tua mors Christi (2p. Quisquid erit), 5vv, 1585b; S vii, 43

Mortalium jucunditas, 5vv, 1597; S xi, 20

Multarum hic resonat, 5vv, 1571b; S iii, 112

Multe tribulationes, 6vv, 1604; S xv, 65

Multifariam multisque modis, 6vv, 1594; S xi, 161

Musica Dei donum optimi, 6vv, 1594; S xix, 63

Nectar et ambrosiam, 6vv, 1594; S xi, 109

Ne derelinquas amicus, 6vv, 1604; S xv, 134

Ne reminiscaris, 4vv, 1577c; S i, 109

Ne reminiscaris, 7vv, 1577c; S xix, 78

Nisi Dominus (2p. Cum dederit), 5vv, 1562; S ix, 66

Noli regibus o Lamuel (2p. Date siceram), 5vv, 1571b; S vii, 47

Non des mulieri, 6vv, 1604; S xv, 139

Non vos me elegistis, 5vv, 1562; S v, 141

Nos qui sumus in hoc mundo, 4vv, 1573b; S i, 139

Nunc gaudere licet [Or sus, esgaions nous], 6vv, 1568a; S xix, 66

Nuntium vobis fero (2p. Thus, Deo), 5vv, 1571b; S v, 9

Nuptiae factae sunt (2p. Dixit mater; 3p. Et dicit ei Jesu; 4p. Omnis homo), 6vv, 1566d; S xv, 30

Nuptias clares (2p. Viribus magni), 5vv, 1597; S xi, 7

O altitudo divitiarum (2p. Quis enim cognovit), 6vv, 1582d; S xi, 133

O bone Jesu o piissime Jesu (2p. O bone Jesu si merui; 3p. O misericordissime), 4vv, 1582b; S i, 69

O crux splendidior (2p. Dulce lignum), 6vv, 1568a; S xi, 167

Oculi mei semper, 6vv, 1585a; S xvii, 15

Oculi omnium (2p. Justus Dominus), 5vv, 1573b; S vii, 122

Oculus non vidit, 2vv, 1577d; S i, 2

O decus celsi genus, 6vv, 1582d; S xi, 156

O Domine salvum me fac (2p. Non moriar), 5vv, 1562; S ix, 26

O gloriosa domina (2p. Tu regis), 6vv, 1582d; S xiii, 139

O gloriosa domina, 6vv, 1573b; S xiii, 145

O Maria clausus hortus, 3vv, 1577a; S i, 29

Omnes de Saba venient, 8vv, 1604; S xxi, 1

Omnia quae fecisti, 5vv, 1562; S vii, 127

Omnia tempus habent (2p. Tempus amplexandi), 8vv, 1585a; S xxi, 77

Omnis enim homo, 6vv, 1585a; S xv, 58

Omnium deliciarum, 6vv, 1604; S xv, 132

O mors quam amara (2p. O mors bonum est), 6vv, 1564b; S xv, 67

O peccator, 6vv, 1604; S xiii, 163

O quam suavis, 6vv, 1568a; S xiii, 61

O sacrum convivium, 5vv, 1582e; S v, 68

O salutaris hostia, 5vv, 1582e; S v, 79

Osculetur me osculo, 8vv, 1582a; S xxi, 9

Pacis amans (2p. Te nunc laetetur), 6vv, 1570g; S xi, 125

Pater Abraham miserere (2p. Fili recordare), 5vv, 1571b; S vii, 1

Pater noster, 4vv, 1573b; S i, 104

Pater noster (2p. Panem nostrum), 6vv, 1585a; S xiii, 77

Pater noster, 6vv, 1565b; S xiii, 81

Pater peccavi (2p. Quanti mercenarii), 5vv, 1564b; S vii, 24

Pauper sum ego, 4vv, 1573b; S iii, 79

Peccantem me quotidie, 4vv, 1555b; S i, 159

Peccata mea Domine, 5vv, 1582e; S ix, 3

Peccavi quid faciam, 5vv, 1556; S vii, 100

Peccavit David, 6vv, 1604; S xv, 129

Perfice gressus meos, 4vv, 1585d; S iii, 86

Popule meus (2p. Numquid redditur), 5vv, 1582e; S v, 34

Populum humilem, 4vv, 1585d; S iii, 67

Praesidium Sara, 4vv, 1570a; H i, 7

Precatus est Moyses, 4vv, 1585d; S iii, 23

Princeps Marte potens, Guilelmus (2p. Gloria pontificum Ernestus; 3p. Magnanimus princeps; 4p. Matronarum decus; 5p. Virginitatis honos; 6p. Luna velut; 7p. Nec minus effulget Salome; 8p. Princeps egregius; 9p. Vive Pater patriae), 4, 8vv, 1604; S i, 61

Proba me Deus, 4vv, 1579; S iii, 35

Prolongati sunt dies mei (2p. Inveterata sunt; 3p. Si ergo fas), 6vv, 1594; S xvii, 1

Pronuba Juno tibi [Gratia summi; Qui regit astra], 4vv, 1570a; H i, 3

Prophetiae Sibyllarum (1p. Virgine matre; 2p. Ecce dies venient; 3p. Non tardat; 4p. In teneris; 5p. Ecce dies nigras; 6p. Jam mea; 7p. Dum meditor; 8p. Ipsa Deum; 9p. Virginis aeternum; 10p. Verax ipse; 11p. Cerno Dei; 12p. Summus erit), 4vv, 1600; ed. in Cw, xlviii (1937/R)

Providebam Dominum, 7vv, 1604; S xix, 98

Psalmi Davidis poenitentiales (1p. Domine ne in furore tuo . . . miserere; 2p. Beati quorum remissae sunt; 3p. Domine ne in furore tuo . . . quoniam; 4p. Miserere mei Deus; 5p. Domine exaudi . . . non avertas; 6p. De profundis; 7p. Domine exaudi . . . auribus percipe), 5vv, 1584b/R1970; ed. W. Bäuerle (Leipzig, 1905)

Pulvis et umbra sumus, 4vv, 1573b; S i, 127

Quam benignus es (2p. O beatum hominem), 4vv, 1562; S ix, 30

Quam bonus Israel Deus (2p. Quia non est respectus), 6vv, 1594; S xix, 12

Quam magnificata sunt (2p. Beatus homo), 6vv, 1564³; S xvii, 7

Quam pulchra es (2p. Guttur tuam), 6vv, 1585a; S xiii, 149

Quare tristis es anima mea, 4vv, 1573c; S i, 154

Quare tristis es anima mea, 6vv, 1564b; S xvii, 12

Quasi cedrus, 4vv, 1564⁵; S i, 93

Quemadmodum desiderat cervus, 6vv, 1569a; S xix, 18

Quem dicunt homines (2p. Tu es Christus), 5vv, 1567³; S vii, 6

Quem vidistis pastores, 5vv, 1569a; S v, 1

Quia vidisti me, 4vv, 1563³; S i, 137

Quicumque vult salvus esse (2p. Alia est enim; 3p. Et tamen; 4p. Haec est fides), 5vv, 1577c; H i, 32

Qui cupit, 4vv, 1564⁵; S i, 125

Quid estis pusillanimes, 4vv, 1573c; S i, 121

Quid facies, 4vv, 1582b; S iii, 100

Quid gloriaris (2p. Propterea Deus), 5vv, 1566c; S ix, 81

Quid prodest homini (2p. Futurum est), 5vv, 1571b; S vii, 70

Quid prodest stulto, 5vv, 1564b; S vii, 41

Quid tamen [Sponsa quid agis] (2p. Non me lasciviae), 5vv, 1571b; S xi, 64

Quid trepidas (2p. Gaudeat exultetque), 6vv, 1570g; S xi, 111

Quid vulgo memorant, 8vv, 1604; S xix, 122

Qui moderatur sermones suos, 6vv, 1604; S xv, 142

Qui novus aethereo, 5vv, 1569a; S v, 80

Qui patiens est, 6vv, 1604; S xv, 137

Qui sequitur me, 2vv, 1577d; S i, 3

Quis est homo, 5vv, 1567³; S ix, 53

Quis mihi det lacrimis, 5vv, 1573b; S v, 44

Quis mihi quis te rapuit [Quid tibi quidnam] (2p. Me miserum; 3p. Nunc juvat immensi), 5vv, 1565b; S xi, 30

Qui sunt hi sermones (2p. Tu solus peregrinus), 5vv, 1582e; S vii, 9

Quis valet eloquio, 5vv, 1565b; S xi, 78

Qui timet Deum, 6vv, 1594; S xv, 56

Qui tribulant me (2p. Unam petii), 4vv, 1582b; S i, 145

Qui vult venire, 2vv, 1577d; S i, 5

Quocumque loco fuero (2p. Jam quod quae sivi), 5vv, 1585b; S v, 65

Quod licet id libeat, 5vv, 1604; S xi, 16

Quo properas facunde, 10vv, 1565b; S xxi, 112

Rebus in adversis, 5vv, 1569a; S vii, 68

Recordare Jesu pie, 6vv, 1594; S xv, 112

Regina coeli laetare (2p. Resurrexit sicut dixit), 4vv, 1604; S i, 81

Regina coeli laetare, 5vv, 1604; S v, 106

Regina coeli laetare (2p. Resurrexit sicut dixit), 5vv, 1604; S v, 109

Regina coeli laetare (2p. Resurrexit sicut dixit), 5vv, 1604; S v, 112

Regina coeli laetare (2p. Resurrexit sicut dixit), 6vv, 1585a; S xiii, 118

Regina coeli laetare (2p. Resurrexit sicut dixit), 6vv, 1604; S xiii, 122

Regina coeli laetare (2p. Resurrexit sicut dixit), 7vv, 1604; S xix, 84

Regnum mundi, 6vv, 1573b; S xiii, 170

Res neque ab internis, 5vv, 1569a; S xi, 69

Resonet in laudibus (2p. Hodie apparuit; 3p. Manum nomen Domini), 5vv, 1569a; S iii, 148

Respexit Elias, 5vv, 1582e; S v, 158

Respicit Dominus vias hominis, 6vv, 1594; S xvii, 37

Rumpitur invidia, 5vv, 1571b; S xi, 72

Salve festa dies (2p. Felices), 5vv, 1568b; S xi, 1

Salve regina mater (2p. Et Jesum benedictum), 5vv, 1597; S v, 115

Salve regina mater, 6vv, 1582d; S xiii, 125

Salve regina mater, 6vv, 1604; S xiii, 128

Salve regina mater, 8vv, 1604; S xxi, 18

Salve regina misericordiae, 4vv, 1573b; S i, 83

Salve regina misericordiae (2p. Et Jesum benedictum), 4vv, 1604; S i, 89

Sancta et immaculata, 3vv, 1577a; S i, 27

Sancta Maria (i), 4vv, 1604; S iii, 110

Sancta Maria (ii), 4vv, 1604; S iii, 110

Sancta Maria (iii), 4vv, 1604; S iii, 111

Sancta Maria, 5vv, 1585b; S v, 135

Sancti mei, 2vv, 1577d; S i, 4

Scapulis suis, 4vv, 1582b; S iii, 12

Scio enim quod Redemptor, 4vv, 1568b; S iii, 105

Serve bone, 2vv, 1577d; S i, 6

Si ambulavero in medio, 5vv, 1556; S ix, 18

Si bene perpendi, 5vv, 1579; S xi, 37

Si bona suscepimus, 5vv, 1571b; S ix, 87

Si coelum et coeli coelorum, 6vv, 1594; S xv, 115

Sic sua virtutum (2p. Tu maxime rerum), 5vv, 1604; S xi, 4

Sicut mater consolator, 5vv, 1562; S vii, 97

Sicut rosa, 2vv, 1577d; S i, 7

Sidus ex claro veniet (2p. Qui maris terrae), 5vv, 1569a; S iii, 153

Si qua tibi obtulerint, 6vv, 1556; S xi, 118

Si quid vota valent, 5vv, 1571b; S xi, 124

Sperent in te omnes, 4vv, 1585d; S i, 155

Sponsa quid agis: see Quid tamen 1582e

Stabat mater dolorosa, 8vv, 1585a

Stabunt justi (2p. Hic sunt quos habuimus), 5vv, 1571b; S vii, 61

Stet quicumque volet (2p. Si cum transilierint), 5vv, 1556; S xi, 44

Super flumina Babylonis, 4vv, 1585d; S iii, 25

Surgens Jesus, 5vv, 1562; S v, 60

Surge propera amica mea et veni (2p. Surge . . . speciosa), 6vv, 1566b; S xiii, 158

Surrexit Dominus (2p. Allueluja; 3p. Dum transisset; 4p. Maria Magdalena; 5p. Ut venientes; 6p. Et valde mane; 7p. Gloria Patri),

6vv, 1592, *Mbs*
Surrexit Pastor bonus, 5vv, 1562; S v, 57
SU-su-PER-per (2p. IL-il-LIC-lic), 5vv, 1567[13]; S ix, 133
Taedet animam, 5vv, 1562; S vii, 103
Te decet hymnus, 4vv, 1564[1]; S iii, 37
Te Deum laudamus, 6vv, 1568a; S xix, 24
Te merito Daniel, 5vv, 1604; S v, 160
Tempus est ut revertar (2p. Nisi ego abiero), 6vv, 1566d; S xiii, 25
Te spectant Reginalde Poli, 5vv, 1556; S iii, 127
Tibi laus tibi gloria, 4vv, 1604; S i, 67
Tibi laus tibi gloria (2p. Da gaudiorum), 5vv, 1564[4]; S iii, 130
Tibi progenies (2p. Tu quae versat; 3p. Tu nostros Deus; 4p. Dum nos Erebi; 5p. Tu multa), 5vv, 1604; S xi, 40
Tibi progenies (2p. Tu quae versat; 3p. Dum nos Erebi), 6vv, 1604; S xix, 35
Timor Domini gloria, 6vv, 1604; S xv, 147
Timor Domini principium, 6vv, 1594; S xv, 89
Timor et tremor (2p. Exaudi Deus), 6vv, 1564[3]; S xix, 6
Tityre tu patule (2p. O Meliboee), 6vv, 1560b; S xix, 68
Tota pulchra es, 4vv, 1604; S i, 96
Tragico tecti syrmate coelites, 5vv, 1597; S xi, 75
Tragico tecti syrmate coelites (2p. Hic belligeras), 6vv, 1604; S xix, 53
Tribulationem et dolorem (2p. Convertere anima), 4vv, 1572b; S iii, 8
Tribus miraculis, 5vv, 1565c; S v, 25
Tristis est anima mea, 5vv, 1565b; S v, 48
Tu Domine benignus es (2p. Respice me), 5vv, 1565b; S v, 87
Tui sunt coeli, 8vv, 1604; S xxi, 5
Ubi est Abel, 5vv, 1567[1]; S vii, 80
Unde revertimini, 8vv, 1573c; S xix, 138
Unus Dominus una fides, 6vv, 1604; S xv, 124
Ut queant laxis, 5vv, 1582c; S v, 152
Ut radios edit rutilo, 5vv, 1565b; S xi, 85
Veni Creator Spiritus (2p. Tu septiformis muner; 3p. Hostem repellas), 6vv, 1568a; S xiii, 43
Veni dilecte mi (2p. Videamus si), 5vv, 1571b; S v, 124
Veni Domine et noli tardare, 5vv, 1583[2]; S ix, 1
Veni Domine et noli tardare, 6vv, 1570g; S xvii, 84
Veni in hortum meum, 5vv, 1562; S v, 120
Veni Sancte Spiritus, 6vv, 1582d; S xiii, 53
Venite ad me omnes, 5vv, 1571b; S vii, 52
Venite filii audite me (2p. Diverte a malo), 5vv, 1604; S vii, 75
Verba mea auribus percipe (2p. Quoniam ad te), 5vv, 1571b; S vii, 116
Verbum caro factum est, 6vv, 1564[1]; S xi, 158
Verbum caro panem verum, 3vv, 1604; S i, 58
Verbum caro panem verum, 4vv, 1604; S i, 111
Vere Dominus est, 6vv, 1594; S xv, 118
Vexilla regis prodeunt (2p. Impleta sunt; 3p. Beata cuius; 4p. O crux ave), 6vv, 1565c; S xi, 172
Vide homo quae pro te patior, 7vv, 1595; S xix, 82
Videntes stellam magi (2p. Et apertis), 5vv, 1562; S v, 22
Vidi calumnias (2p. Rursum contemplatus), 6vv, 1594; S xvii, 53
Vidi impium, 5vv, 1569a; S ix, 125
Vincenti dabo edere (2p. Qui viderit), 6vv, 1594; S xiii, 56
Vinum bonum et suave, 8vv, 1570g; S xxi, 91
Voce mea ad Dominum clamavi, 6vv, 1604; S xix, 10
Vos quibus rector, 6vv, 1601[3]; S xix, 60
Vulnerasti cor meum, 6vv, 1582d; S xiii, 154
Zachaei festinans descende, 5vv, 1565c; H i, 56

12 textless bicinia, a 2, 1577d; S i, 13–24

MADRIGALS

A che tenderm'amor, 4vv, 1570f; S viii, 59
Ad altre le voi dare, 4vv, 1581b; S x, 77
Al dolce suon (Minturno), 5vv, 1569[19]
Al gran Guglielmo nostro, 5vv, 1584a; H i, 147
Allala la pia calia, 4vv, 1581b; S x, 104
Alma cortese (2p. Ch'udirai), 5vv, 1555a; S ii, 12
Alma real dignissima d'impero, 4vv, 1564c; S viii, 44
Amor che ved'ogni pensier (Petrarch), 5vv, 1563; S iv, 48
Amor mi strugge 'l cor (Petrarch), 5vv, 1563; S iv, 26
Appariran per me le stell'in cielo, 4vv, 1560a; S viii, 27
Ardo sì ma non t'amo (Tasso), 5vv, 1585[17]; S viii, 144, 147 (2 versions)
Arse la fiamma e consumò, 4vv, 1587a; S vi, 83
A voi Guglielmo invitto, 5vv, 1584a; H i, 143
Bella guerriera mia (Bembo) (2p. Ma se con l'opr'), 5vv, 1563; S iv, 38
Ben convenne madonna (G. Manrique) (2p. Solo n'andrò), 5vv, 1569[19]
Ben mi credea passar mio tempo (Petrarch), 5vv, 1555a; S ii, 67
Ben sono i premi tuoi (Fiamma) (2p. Poi che sì grand'), 6vv, 1587a; S vi, 137
Ben veggio di lontan' (Petrarch), 4vv, 1562[7]; S viii, 37
.Bianca neve è il bel collo (Ariosto), 4vv, 1573c; S viii, 78
Candid'albor del ciel, 5vv, 1557; S ii, 144
Canta Giorgia canta, 6vv, 1581b; S x, 125
Cantai hor piango (Petrarch) (2p. Tengan dunque), 5vv, 1555a; S ii, 1
Canzon la doglia e 'l pianto, 4vv, 1587a; S vi, 90
Canzon se l'esser meco (Petrarch), 4vv, 1584a; H i, 131

Cathalina apra finestra (2p. Andar a valezza), 6vv, 1581b; S x, 112
Che fai alma (Petrarch), 7vv, 1569[18]; S x, 23
Che fai che pensi (Petrarch) (2p. Deh non rinovellar), 5vv, 1567a; S iv, 90
Che giova posseder (Bembo), 5vv, 1587a; S vi, 110
Che più d'un giorno (Petrarch), 5vv, 1567a; H i, 140
Chi chilichi, 6vv, 1581b; S x, 120
Chi è fermato di menar sua vita (Petrarch), 4vv, 1584a; S vi, 82
Chi no'l sa di ch'io vivo (Petrarch), 5vv, 1576[5]; S viii, 123
Chi non sa come spira (2p. Ma quel ch'una), 5vv, 1587a; S vi, 113
Come la cera al foco (Fiamma), 6vv, 1585c; S vi, 66
Come la notte ogni fiamella (Ariosto), 5vv, 1584a; H i, 136
Come lume di notte (Petrarch), 4vv, 1584a; H i, 134
Come pianta (2p. Perche qual peregrin), 4vv, 1587a; S vi, 87
Come va 'l mondo (Petrarch) (2p. Ma 'l cieco amor), 5vv, 1567a; S iv, 101
Con lei fuss'io (Petrarch), 5vv, 1555a; S ii, 63
Così cor mio vogliate (Ariosto), 4vv, 1587a; S vi, 80
Crudel acerba inesorabil morte (Petrarch), 5vv, 1555a; S ii, 44
Dappoi che sott'il ciel (Petrarch), 5vv, 1584a; H i, 172
Deh hor foss'io co'l vago (Petrarch), 4vv, 1558[13]; S viii, 26
Deh lascia anima homai (Fiamma), 4vv, 1587a; S vi, 85
Deh perche voglio anco (Ariosto) (2p. Dunque fia ver), 5vv, 1584a; H i, 183
Deh sol che sei si chiaro, 4vv, 1570f; S viii, 61
Del auro crin de la Tassinia bella (2p. Con le stell'), 5vv, 1570f; S viii, 112
De l'eterne tue sante (Fiamma) (2p. Per questa), 5vv, 1585c; S vi, 1
Del freddo Reno (2p. Ch'il credera; 3p. Rotava ed è pur ver; 4p. Si fe cristallo; 5p. Et io qual; 6p. Hor su la nuda terra), 4vv, 1555b; S viii, 3
Dicesi che la morte (A. Marsi), 5vv, 1563; S iv, 22
Di pensier in pensier (Petrarch), 6vv, 1579[2]; S x, 3
Di persona era tanto ben formata (Ariosto), 4vv, 1573c; S viii, 72
Di qua di là (Ariosto), 5vv, 1584a; H i, 176
Ditemi vita mia, 7vv, 1584[4]; S x, 30
Di terrena armonia (Beccuti) (2p. Signor le colpe mia; 3p. Padre rivolgi; 4p. Stanco di lagrimar; 5p. Voi che di prave; 6p. Fugga), 5vv, 1584a [repr. without 1st stanza as Signor le colpe mie, 1587a]; H i, 179
Ecco che pur vi lasso, 5vv, 1587a; S vi, 92
Ecco la ninph'ebraica chiamata, 4vv, 1581b; S x, 76
Evro gentil se d'amoroso ardore (G. B. d'Azzia) (2p. Et in sembiante), 5vv, 1557; S ii, 121
Fiera stella s'el ciel ha forza (Petrarch) (2p. Ma tu prendi), 5vv, 1555a; S ii, 50
Già mi fu co'l desir (Petrarch), 5vv, 1555a; S ii, 14
Guarda 'I mio stat'a le vaghezze (Petrarch), 5vv, 1555a; S ii, 6
Hai Lucia buona cosa, 4vv, 1581b; S x, 86
Hor ch'a l'albergo de monton (Fiamma), 6vv, 1587a; S vi, 105
Hor che la nuova e vaga primavera, 10vv, 1575[11]; S x, 43
Hor qui son lasso e voglio esser (Petrarch), 5vv, 1555a; S ii, 22
Hor vi riconfortate (Petrarch), 5vv, 1585c; S vi, 14
Hor vi riconfortate (Petrarch), 6vv, 1584a; S x, 14
Il grave de l'età (Fiamma) (2p. Alma tu che 'l furor), 6vv, 1587a; S vi, 126
Il tempo passa e l'hore (Petrarch), 5vv, 1567a; S iv, 92
In dubbio di mio stato (Petrarch), 4vv, 1560c; S viii, 35
In dubbio di mio stato (Petrarch), 4vv, 1562[7]; S viii, 42
In qual parte del ciel (Petrarch) (2p. In divina bellezza), 5vv, 1557; S ii, 134
Io che l'età più verde (Fiamma) (2p. Ma conven), 5vv, 1585c; S vi, 6
Io ho più tempo (2p. Almen nel suo fuggir), 5vv, 1575[11]; S viii, 117
Io non sapea di tal vista (Petrarch), 5vv, 1585c; S vi, 33
Io son si stanco sotto il fascio antico (Petrarch), 5vv, 1585c; S vi, 45
Io son si stanco sotto il grave peso (Guidiccioni) (2p. Hora per far), 5vv, 1557; S ii, 139
Io ti vorria contar, 4vv, 1581b; S x, 85
I vo piangendo i miei passati tempi (Petrarch) (2p. Si che s'io vissi), 5vv, 1567a; S iv, 116
La cortesia voi donne predicate, 4vv, 1555b; S x, 66
Lagrime di S Pietro (Tansillo), 7vv, 1595; ed. in Cw, xxxiv, xxxvii, xli (1935–6/R)
L'alto signor, dinanzi a cui (Petrarch), 5vv, 1563; S iv, 3
L'altr'hier sul mezzo giorno, 5vv, 1555a; S ii, 79
La non vol esser più mia, 5vv, 1584a; H i, 152
La notte che segui l'horribil (Petrarch) (2p. Riconosci; 3p. Come non conosch'io), 5vv, 1561[10]; S viii, 88
La ver' i'aurora (Petrarch) (2p. Temprar potess'io; 3p. Quante lagrime; 4p. Huomini e Dei; 5p. All'ultimo bisogno; 6p. Ridon hor), 5vv, 1567a; S vi, 65
La vita fugge (Petrarch), 5vv, 1563; S iv, 44
Le voglie e l'opre mie (Fiamma), 5vv, 1585c; S vi, 17
Lucia celu hai biscamia, 4vv, 1581b; S x, 97
Madonna mia pietà, 4vv, 1555b; S x, 61
Madonna sa l'amor, 5vv, 1576b; H i, 156
Malvaggio horrido gelo, 4vv, 1570f; S viii, 63
Matona mia cara, 4vv, 1581b; S x, 93

Mentre che 'l cor da gl'amorosi vermi (Petrarch) (2p. Quel fuoco), 5vv, 1555a; S ii, 27
Mentre fioriv'amor (2p. Così aspettando), 5vv, 1557; S ii, 111
Mia benigna fortun'e 'l viver lieto (Petrarch), 5vv, 1555a; S ii, 37
Mi me chiamere, 5vv, 1581b; S x, 108
Miser qui speme in cose mortal pone (Petrarch), 5vv, 1567a; S iv, 90
Misera che farò, 5vv, 1576[5]; S viii, 129
Mostran le braccia sue (Ariosto), 4vv, 1573c; S viii, 81
Nessun visse giamai (Petrarch), 5vv, 1584a; S viii, 137
No giorno t'haggio havere, 4vv, 1555b; S x, 65
Non ha tante (2p. In sonno eterno; 3p. Secchi vedransi; 4p. Io vo fuggendo; 5p. Deh che fuss'io; 6p. Ma sarò spento), 3, 5, 6vv, 1563; S iv, 6
Non s'incolpi 'l desire, 5vv, 1563; S iv, 53
Non vi vieto per questo (Ariosto), 4vv, 1560a (by Hoste da Reggio); S viii, 29
O bella fusa, 4vv, 1581b; S x, 89
O beltà rara, 5vv, 1567a; S iv, 82
Occhi piangete accompagnate il core (Petrarch), 4vv, 1555b; S viii, 19
O d'amarissime onde, 5vv, 1561[10]; S viii, 97
O dolci parolette (Cassola), 5vv, 1564c; S viii, 107
O fugace dolcezza (Petrarch), 5vv, 1584a; S vi, 127
Ogni giorno m'han ditt', 4vv, 1581b; S x, 91
O invidia nemica di virtute (Petrarch) (2p. Ne però), 5vv, 1555a; S ii, 39
O là o che bon eccho, 8vv, 1581b; S x, 140
O Lucia miau, 3vv, 1560[14]; S x, 70
O occhi manza mia, 4vv, 1581b; S x, 103 [previously pubd 1557[20], 3vv (inc.)]
Ornando come suole, 6vv, 1587a; S vi, 154
O tempo o cielo (Petrarch) (2p. E sarebbe hora), 5vv, 1585c; S vi, 11
Ov'è condott'il mio amoroso stile (2p. O noiosa mia vita), 4vv, 1562[7]; S viii, 38
Ove d'altra montagn' ombra tocchi, 4vv, 1567[16]
Ove le luci giro, 5vv, 1576b; H i, 163
Ove sei vita mia (2p. Come sei stat' o ciel), 5vv, 1561[10]; S viii, 102
Parch'hai lasciato, 4vv, 1581b; S x, 82
Passan vostri trionfi (Petrarch), 10vv, 1584a; S x, 53
Pensier dicea che 'l cor (Ariosto), 5vv, 1569[19]; S vi, 123
Per aspro mar di notte (Fiamma) (2p. Non hanno tante; 3p. Errai scorrendo; 4p. Ma quel gran re; 5p. Così quel che m'avanza; 6p. O voi già stanchi), 4vv, 1587a; S vi, 179
Perchè sempre nimica mia, 5vv, 1555a; S ii, 83
Perch'io veggio (Petrarch), 4vv, 1555b; S viii, 23
Per pianto la mia carne (Sannazaro), 4vv, 1555b; S viii, 13
Pien d'un vago pensier (Petrarch), 5vv, 1555a; S ii, 75
Più volte un bel desio (Fiamma) (2p. Hor a cantar), 6vv, 1587a; S vi, 132
Poi che 'l camin m'è chiuso (Petrarch), 5vv, 1555a; S ii, 25
Poi che 'l'iniquo e fero mio destino (2p. Diviso m'ha), 5vv, 1555a; S ii, 32
Poi che'l mio largo pianto (Petrarch), 4vv, 1583[15]; S viii, 84
Pon fren' al gran dolor (Petrarch), 5vv, 1555a; S ii, 46
Prendi l'aurata lira (Fiamma), 6vv, 1587a; S vi, 158
Qual nemica fortuna (2p. Lasso che; 3p. Sol'io quanto; 4p. Tal hor dico; 5p. Talhor parmi la luce; 6p. Re de gli altri), 5, 6vv, 1567a; S iv, 128
Quando fia mai quel giorno, 4vv, 1570f; S viii, 65
Quando il giorno da l'onde (Fiamma) (2p. Non hebbe; 3p. Hor come i rai; 4p. Parmi che sempre sian'; 5p. Il mondo muta; 6p. Poggi, valli), 5vv, 1585c; S vi, 39
Quando io penso al fuggir (Fiamma) (2p. Vedi gli dico), 5vv, 1585c; S vi, 39
Quando la sera scaccia (Petrarch), 5vv, 1555a; S ii, 35
Quando 'l voler (Petrarch) (2p. Onde come colui), 5vv, 1555a; S ii, 17
Quanto il mio duol, 4vv, 1560a; S viii, 31
Quant'invidia ti porto avara terra (Petrarch) (2p. Quant'invidia), 5vv, 1563; S iv, 18
Quant'invidia vi port'aure (C. Besalio), 5vv, 1563; S iv, 32
Quel chiaro sol (2p. Che se la ver'), 5vv, 1557; S ii, 116
Quel rossignuol che si soave piagne (Petrarch) (2p. O che lieve è), 5vv, 1567a; S iv, 85
Queste non son più lagrime (Ariosto), 4vv, 1555b; S viii, 15
Questi ch'inditio fan (Ariosto), 5vv, 1557; S ii, 132
Questi son lasso de la mia spem', 5vv, 1563; S iv, 28
Saccio 'na cosa, 4vv, 1581b; S x, 8
Scorgo tant'altro il lume (Tansillo), 5vv, 1563; S iv, 57
Se ben l'empia mia sorte, 4vv, 1555b; S viii, 51
Se ben non veggion gl'occhi, 4vv, 1570f; S viii, 67
Seguì già le speranze (Petrarch), 5vv, 1584a; S viii, 141
Se si alto pon gir mie stanche rime (Petrarch), 5vv, 1563; S iv, 59
Si come'al chiaro giorno (2p. O sempre vagh'; 3p. Tal ch'io possa; 4p. Al'hor nel; 5p. Già senz'affan'; 6p. Altri non vedrà), 4vv, 1566[2]; S viii, 46
Si com'i fiori da l'ardente sole, 5vv, 1570[15]; H i, 168
Signor da l'alto trono, 5vv, 1584a; H i, 150

Signor le colpe mie: see Di terrena armonia
Signor se la tua grazia è fuoco (Tansillo) (2p. Queste contrarie tempre), 5vv, 1567a; S iv, 106
Silen di rose ha 'l volto (C. Camilli), 6vv, 1594[6]; S x, 18
S'io esca vivo (Petrarch), 6vv, 1579[2]; S x, 9
S'io fusse siaul', 4vv, 1581b; S x, 92
S'io tal'hor muovo gli occhi (F. Ronconi) (2p. Al'hor lasso), 5vv, 1555a; S ii, 58
S'io ti vedess'una sol volt'il giorno, 4vv, 1581b; S x, 102
S'io ve dico, 4vv, 1581b; S x, 75
Soleasi nel mio cor (Petrarch) (2p. Que piangon), 5vv, 1576b; S viii, 131
Sol'e pensoso i più deserti campi (Petrarch) (2p. Si ch'io mi credo), 5vv, 1555a; S ii, 71
Sotto duo negri e sottilissimi archi (Ariosto), 4vv, 1573c; S viii, 74
Sotto quel sta (Ariosto), 4vv, 1573c; S viii, 76
Spent'è d'amor (Minturno) (2p. Ma che morta), 5vv, 1569[19]
Spesso in poveri alberghi (Ariosto), 4vv, 1573c; S viii, 83
Standomi un giorno (Petrarch) (2p. Indi per altro ; 3p. In un boschetto; 4p. Chiara fontana; 5p. Una strana fenice; 6p. All fin vidd'io), 5vv, 1557; S ii, 89
Sto core mio se fosse di diamante, 4vv, 1555b; S x, 69
S'una fede amorosa (Petrarch), 8vv, 1573c; S x, 36
Tanto e quel ben eterno amor (Fiamma) (2p. E puro bene), 6vv, 1587a; S vi, 149
Tra verdi rami (2p. Questo e disceso), 6vv, 1587a; S vi, 160
Tu sai madonna mia, 4vv, 1555b; S x, 63
Tu traditora, 4vv, 1555b; S x, 68 [also pubd 1555[30], 3vv (inc.)]
Tutto 'l dì mi dici, 4vv, 1581b; S x, 79
Tutto 'l dì mi dici, 8vv, 1581b; S x, 130
Tutto 'l dì piango (Petrarch) (2p. Lasso che par), 5vv, 1567a; S iv, 122
Un dubbio verno (Petrarch), 4vv, 1585c; S vi, 23
Valle profonda, 10vv, 1584[4]; S x, 50
Vatene lieta homai coppia d'amici, 4vv, 1555b; S viii, 121
Vedi l'aurora (Petrarch), 5vv, 1584a; S vi, 120
Veggio se al vero apre ragion (Fiamma) (2p. Al'hor mi desto), 6vv, 1587a; S vi, 143
Vieni dolc'hymeneo (2p. Indi gl'acuti strali), 4vv, 1570f; S viii, 69
Vivo sol di speranza (Petrarch), 4vv, 1560a; S viii, 33
Voi ch'ascoltate in rime (Petrarch) (2p. Ma ben veggi' hor), 5vv, 1567a; S iv, 111
Volgi cor mio la tua speranza (F. Spira) (2p. Ed a noi restare), 5vv, 1557; S ii, 127
Vostro fui vostro son (B. Tasso), 5vv, 1557; S ii, 114
V' son gl'ingegni (Fiamma) (2p. Ahi che la forza), 5vv, 1585c; S vi, 30
Zanni piasi patro, 8vv, 1581b; S x, 135

CHANSONS

A ce matin [L'avare veut avoir], 4vv, 1564a; S xii, 28
Amour donne-moy pays (Ronsard), 5vv, 1571a; S xvi, 75
Amour ne veult user, 5vv, 1570d (doubtful)
Ardant amour souvent, 4vv, 1564c; S xii, 25
Ardant amour souvent [Divin amour; La ferme foi], 5vv, 1560c; S xiv, 84
A toy je crie, 5vv, 1583b; S xvi, 118
Au feu venez-moy [au feu las] (2p. A l'eau jettes-toy [A l'eau de grace vistement]) (M. de Saint-Gelais), 5vv, 1564c; S xiv, 92
Au temps jadis, 5vv, 1560c; S xiv, 100
Avec vous [Dieu] mon amour finira, 4vv, 1555b; S xii, 37
Beau le cristal, 4vv, 1576d; S xii, 94
Bon jour et puis quelles nouvelles [Bon coeur amis] (C. Marot), 5vv, 1571a; S xvi, 53
Bon jour mon coeur (Ronsard) [Christ est mon Dieu], 4vv, 1564a; S xii, 100
Ce faux amour [Satan], 4vv, 1564a; S xii, 103
Célébrons sans cesse, 4vv, 1576d; S xvi, 102
Ce qui tu peux maintenant (G. du Faur de Pybrac), 4vv, 1583[7] [previously pubd 1581, now lost]; ed. in Bernstein, 320
C'estoit en ton jeune age, 5vv, 1584a; S xvi, 123
Chanter je veux la gente [l'heur de l'ame], 5vv, 1569[19]; S xiv, 50
Comme la tourterelle (2p. Où t'attend ta maistresse [De l'éternelle liesse]), 5vv, 1565a; S xiv, 120
Comme un qui prend (Ronsard) [Que malheureuse est la troupe], 5vv, 1571a; S xvi, 3
D'amours me va (Marot) [Le monde va tout à rebours], 5vv, 1571a; S xvi, 100
De plusieurs choses, 5vv, 1571a; S xvi, 72
Dessus le marché d'Arras, 6vv, 1584a; S xvi, 152
De tout mon coeur (G. Crétin), 5vv, 1564b; S xiv, 33
De vous servir, 4vv, 1570a; S xii, 69
Dis-moy mon coeur, 8vv, 1573c; S xiv, 150
Dix ennemies [Mes vains desirs] tous désarmés, 5vv, 1576b; S xiv, 59
Du corps absent, 4vv, 1564a; S xii, 55
Du fond de ma pensée (Marot), 4vv, 1564a; S xvi, 159
Elle s'en va de moy [Elle périt ma chair] (Marot), 5vv, 1560c; S xiv, 105
En espoir vis et crainte, 4vv, 1555b; S xii, 52

En m'oyant chanter (Marot), 4vv, 1564a; S xii, 106

En un chasteau, madame [L'homme mortel contemplant], 4vv, 1570b; S xii, 14

En un lieu [En ce monde] (Saint-Gelais), 4vv, 1564a; S xii, 83

Est-il possible à moy [Est-il possible en ce monde], 5vv, 1560c; S xiv, 112

Et d'où venez vous [Que devenez-vous], 5vv, 1564c; S xiv, 68

Fleur de quinze ans (Marot), 4vv, 1564a; S xii, 43

Fuyons tous d'amour [Fuyons de vices] le jeu, 4vv, 1564a; S xii, 80

Gallans qui par terre (Villon), 4vv, 1584a; S xvi, 111

Guérir ma douleur, 4vv, 1584a; S xvi, 106

Hâtez-vous [Haste-toi de me faire], 4vv, 1567[11]; S xii, 81

Hélas j'ai sans merci, 5vv, 1584a; S xvi, 132

Hélas mon Dieu, 5vv, 1571a; S xvi, 46

Hélas quel jour, 4vv, 1560c; S xii, 47

Heureux qui met en Dieu (du Faur de Pybrac), 4vv, 1583[7] [previously pubd 1581, now lost]; ed. in Bernstein, 322

Holà Caron (O. de Magny), 8vv, 1571a; S xvi, 81

Il esteoit une religieuse [Si j'estoi où mon ame], 4vv, 1565a; S xii, 74

J'aime la pierre précieuse, 5vv, 1584a; S xvi, 121

J'attends le tems, 5vv, 1560c; S xiv, 48

J'ay cherché la science [J'ay du ciel la science] (Saint-Gelais), 4vv, 1564a; S xii, 57

J'ay de vou voir (Du Bellay), 4vv, 1584a; S xvi, 113

Je l'ayme bien [J'aime mon Dieu et l'aimerai], 4vv, 1555b; S xii, 41

J'endure un tourment (2p. Mais à quel propos [Mais de quoi me sert]), 5vv, 1564c; S xiv, 38

Je ne veux plus que chanter, 5vv, 1565a; S xiv, 88

Je ne veux rien qu'un baiser [que deux mots], 4vv, 1564a; S xii, 98

J'espère et crains (Ronsard) (2p. Plus que me pique), 5vv, 1571a; S xvi, 12

Je vous donne en conscience (Marot), 5vv, 1571a; S xvi, 70

Je suis quasi prest d'enrager [de mourir], 4vv, 1570b; S xii, 54

La mort est [Les dez, c'est] jeu pire (Marot), 4vv, 1564a; S xii, 58

La nuict froide et sombre (Du Bellay), 4vv, 1576d; S xii, 34

La peine dure, 4vv, 1584a; S xvi, 104

Las je n'iray plus, 5vv, 1576a; S xvi, 126

Las me fault-il, 5vv, 1560c; S xiv, 76

Las voulez-vous, 4vv, 1555b; S xii, 3

La terre les eaux (Ronsard) [La terre son Dieu va louant], 5vv, 1564c; S xiv, 7

Le départir [Partir d'ici, c'est un departement], 5vv, 1564c; S xiv, 116

Le rossignol plaisant, 5vv, 1560c; S xiv, 107

Le sage fils est du père, 4vv, 1583[7]

Le temps passé (B. d'Auriol) [Le tems perdu je souspire], 4vv, 1567[11]; S xii, 49

Le temps peut bien, 4vv, 1564a; S xii, 76

Le vray amy (Saint-Gelais) [Le vertueux ne s'estonne de rien], 4vv, 1564a; S xii, 62

L'heureux amour [plaisir qui esleve], 4vv, 1576b; S xii, 5

L'homme se plaint, 4vv, 1583[7] [previously pubd 1581, now lost]

Lucescit jam o socii, 4vv, in Vingtquatrieme livre d'airs et chansons (Paris, 1578); H i, 121

Mais qui pourroit, 3vv, 1584a; S xvi, 107

Mais qui pourroit (2p. Si mon gentil; 3p. Hélas mon Francin), 6vv, 1584a; S xvi, 137

M'amie a bien le regard, 4vv, 1584a; S xvi, 102

Margot labouréz, 4vv, 1564a; S xii, 102

Mes pas semés [Mes pas Seigneur tant esgarez], 4vv, 1564a; S xii, 87

Mon coeur ravi d'amour, 5vv, 1564c; S xiv, 22

Mon coeur se recommande (Marot) [Mon coeur se rend à toi; Qui laboure champ ou vigne], 5vv, 1560c; S xiv, 15

Monsieur l'abbé (Marot) [Maistre Robbin], 4vv, 1564a; S xii, 16

Noblesse gist au coeur, 5vv, 1570b; S xiv, 3

O comme heureux, 4vv, 1564c; S xvi, 160

O doux parler (Ronsard), 8vv, 1571a; S xvi, 89

O foible esprit (Du Bellay), 5vv, 1571a; S xvi, 34

O mère des amours Ciprine (2p. Tu suis o gentille; 3p. Or cesse doncques), 4vv, 1584a; S xvi, 109

On doit le fer battre, 4vv, 1583[8]; S xvi, 100

Ores que je suis dispos (Ronsard), 5vv, 1571a; S xvi, 24

Orsus filles (R. Belleau) [Sus, je vous pri], 4vv, 1576b; S xii, 63

O temps divers [Maudit peché qui me deffens], 4vv, 1559[12]; S xii, 67

O vin en vigne [Bonté divine, vien et monstre], 4vv, 1570b; S xii, 36

Paisible domaine [Qu'est-ce que Dieu donne], 5vv, 1571a; S xvi, 50

Parens sans amis, 5vv, 1571a; S xvi, 40

Père qui habites les cieux, 5vv, 1584a; S xvi, 115

Petite folle [Troupe fidele, es-tu pas], 4vv, 1564a; S xii, 78

Pour courir en poste (Marot) (2p. Pour mettre; 3p. Pour desbaucher; 4p. Pour faire), 5vv, 1571a; S xvi, 61

Puisque fortune [Peché infame; Puis que peché à moi], 5vv, 1564c; S xiv, 125

Puisque vivre en servitude (Saint-Gelais), 4vv, 1584a; S xvi, 103

Quand me souvient [Sentant l'effort et la triste], 5vv, 1570b; S xiv, 128

Quand mon mary vient [Quand l'homme honneste], 4vv, 1564a; S xii, 23

Quand un cordier (Chartier), 4vv, 1573c; S xii, 108

Que dis-tu (Ronsard), 8vv, 1576b; S xiv, 142

Que gaignez vous [D'où vient cela], 5vv, 1570d; S xvi, 166

Qui bien se mire, 4vv, 1573c; S xii, 65

Qui dort icy [en nous] (Marot), 4vv, 1564a; S xii, 19

Qui veult d'amour (Bouchet) [Qui de peché veut savoir], 5vv, 1576b; S xiv, 133

Rends-moi mon coeur (Ronsard), 5vv, 1561[5]; S xiv, 18

Sais-tu dire l'Avé [Sais-tu dire bien], 4vv, 1573c; S xii, 66

Sauter danser faire les tours, 4vv, 1576d; S xii, 10

Secourés moy [Assiste moy Seigneur] (Marot), 5vv, in Livre de meslanges, contenant six vingtz chansons, des plus rares (Paris, 1560); S xvi, 163

Si du malheur [De ce malheur], 4vv, 1573c; S xii, 50

Si froid et chault, 4vv, 1564a; S xii, 96

Si je suis brun, 4vv, 1573c; S xii, 30

Si le long temps (P. du Val), 4vv, 1559[12]; S xii, 7

Si le mal ennuyeux, 4vv, 1583[7] [previously pubd 1581, now lost]

S'il y a compagnons [Il n'y a que douleur], 5vv, 1576b; S xiv, 65

Si par souhait je vous [te] tenoit, 4vv, 1570d; S xiv, 64

Si pour moy avez du souci (Marot) [Quand mon coeur a quelque souci], 4vv, 1576b; S xii, 85

Si vous estes m'amie, 6vv, 1584a; S xvi, 147

Si vous n'estes en bon point (Marot), 4vv, 1564a; S xii, 60

Soufflons d'autant amis [Cherchons ailleurs], 5vv, 1571a; S xvi, 30

Soyons joyeux, 4vv, 1564c; S xii, 20

Sur tous regretz, 5vv, 1560c; S xiv, 26

Susanne un jour (G. Guérault), 5vv, 1560c; S xiv, 29

Ton [Mon] feu s'esteint, 4vv, 1559[13]; S xii, 109

Ton nom que mon vers (Ronsard), 5vv, 1571a; S xvi, 6

Toutes les nuitz (Marot), 5vv, 1563; S xiv, 130

Trop endurer sans avoir [de peché], 4vv, 1555b; S xii, 70

Un advocat dit à sa femme [L'homme de bien dit à son ame], 4vv, 1570b; S xii, 8

Un bien petit (Marot), 5vv, 1571a; S xvi, 18

Une puce j'ay dedans l'oreill' (Baïf), 5vv, 1576b; S xiv, 114

Ung doulx nenny (Marot) [Ta voix, ô Dieu, avec ton doux], 4vv, 1560c; S xii, 45

Un jeune moine [Quitte le monde], 4vv, 1573c; S xii, 89

Un jour concluz, 4vv, 1583[7] [previously pubd 1581, now lost]

Un jour l'amant, 8vv, 1570b; S xiv, 136

Un jour vis un foulon [On ne peut le fol amour], 4vv, 1570b; S xii, 39

Un mesnagier, 5vv, 1570b; S xiv, 54

Un [Mon] triste coeur rempli, 5vv, 1560c; S xiv, 80

Veux-tu ton mal [Puis qu'en mon mal], 5vv, 1559[12]; SS xiv, 71

Vignon vignon vignette, 6vv, 1584a; S xvi, 144

Vive sera et toujours perdurable, 5vv, 1570f; S xiv, 11

Voir est beaucoup, 4vv, 1559[13]; H i, 126

Vous qui aymez les dames, 5vv, 1560c; S xiv, 45

Vray dieu disoit une fillette [une ame sainte], 4vv, 1555b; S xii, 72

(German contrafacta)

Al mein Anfang (= Le temps peut bien); Auss tiefer Not (= Si le long temps); Bewar mich Herr (= Ton feu s'esteint); Das sawer Tranck (= La mort est jeu pire); Frölich und frey (= Quand mon mary vient); Gott ist mein Schütz (= A ce matin); Gross Angst und Not (= Trop endurer); Gunst geht für gspunst (= Soyons joyeux); Herr Jesu Christ (= Le vray amy); Hilff uns, o Herr (= Si froid et chault); Ich rieff zu dir Herr Jesu Christ (= Au feu verez-moy); Ich ruff zu dir, hilff mir (= Monsieur l'abbé); Id quid? fit, sit, Wie kann ich dirs abschlagen (= Je ne veux rien); Kein Lieb noch treu ist (= En un lieu); Laetamini in Domino und singt in dulci jubilo (= Je l'ayme bien); Mein aininger Trost (= Petite folle); Mein Hoffnung (= Fleur de quinze ans); Merck schönes (= Hélas quel jour); O Herre Gott mein Not (= Bon mon coeur); O trewer Gott (= Ung doulx nenny); Seit frisch (= Margot labouréz); Thue dich, o Herr (= Du corps absent); Vor Zeiten was ich lieb gehalten (= Hâtez-vous); Wenn wir recht thun betrachten (= Du fond de ma pensée); Wer singen wil (= En m'ovant chanter); Wer sucht der findt (= Qui dort icy); Wolauff gut Gsellen (= Un jeune moine); Zu aller Stund (= Ardant amour souvent)

LIEDER

Am Abent spat, beim khiellen Wein, 5vv, 1567c; S xviii, 33

Annelein, du singst fein, 4vv, 1573c; S xx, 46

Audite nova Der Bawr von Eselsskirchen, 4vv, 1573c; S xx, 51

Auff dich, mein heber Herr und Gott (Ulenberg), 3vv, 1588c; S xx, 63

Auss gutem Grundt, 4vv, 1573c; S xx, 47

Auss härtem Weh, 6vv, 1590; S xx, 99

Auss meiner sünden Tieffe (2p. Wann sich ein grimmer zoren; 3p. Allein Gott; 4p. Von Gott kein Mensch), 4vv, 1583a; S xx, 17

Baur, was tregst im Sacke?, 4vv, 1583a; S xx, 29

Christ ist erstanden, 4vv, 1583a; S xx, 3

Der Herr erhöre deine Klag (Ulenberg), 3vv, 1588c; S xx, 68

Der König wirdt seyn Wolgemut (Ulenberg) (2p. Du hast ihm geben; 3p. Dann eh er's hat begert), 6vv, 1590; S xx, 128

Der Meye bringt uns der Blümlein vil (J. Klieber), 5vv, 1572a; S xviii, 75

Der starcke Gott im Himmelreich (Ulenberg), 3vv, 1588c; S xx, 80
Der Tag der ist so frewdenreich, 5vv, 1572a; S xviii, 71
Der Wein, der schmeckt mir also, 5vv, 1567c; S xviii, 11
Der Welte Pracht ist hoch geacht, 5vv, 1576a; S xviii, 147
Die Fassnacht ist ein schöne Zeit, 5vv, 1567c; S xviii, 6
Die Gnad kombt oben her (2p. Wer Gott vertrauen thut; 3p. Wir armes Volck; 4p. Das Volck von Israel; 5p. Joseph verkauffet; 6p. Als Holophernes; 7p. Darauff hat Gott gesandt; 8p. Daniels Knaben drey; 9p. Daniel geworfen war; 10p. Darumb, o frommer Gott; 11p. Wer diss Lied hat gemacht; 12p. Hierauf sey nun gepreiset), 4vv, 1583a; S xx, 4
Die Thoren sprechen wohl (Ulenberg), 3vv, 1588c; S xx, 66
Die Welt und all ir Reichethumb (Ulenberg), 3vv, 1588c; S xx, 70
Die Zeit, so jetzt vorhanden ist, 5vv, 1567c; S xviii, 14
Ein Esel und das Nüssbawmholtz, 4vv, 1573c; S xx, 45
Ein guten Raht wil geben ich (2p. In Glück und Frewd), 6vv, 1590; S xx, 83
Ein guter Wein ist Lobens werd, 5vv, 1567c; S xviii, 44
Ein Körbelmacher in eim Dorff (H. Sachs), 6vv, 1590; S xx, 124
Einmal ging ich spatzieren (2p. Das Meidlein), 5vv, 1572a; S xviii, 65
Ein Meidlein zu dem Brunnen gieng (2p. Ich sprach o Fraw; 3p. Die Fraw gantz höflich; 4p. So danck ich Gott), 5vv, 1572a; S xviii, 82
Erzürn dich nicht o frommer Christ (L. Hätzer), 5vv, 1572a; S xviii, 65
Es jagt ein Jeger vor dem Holtz, 5vv, 1572a; S xviii, 88
Es sind doch selig alle die (M. Greiter), 5vv, 1572a; S xviii, 77
Es thut sich als verkeren, 4vv, 1573c; S xx, 49
Es zeugen des gottlosen Wercke (Ulenberg), 3vv, 1588c; S xx, 75
Fraw ich bin euch von hertzen Hold, 5vv, 1567c; S xviii, 31
Frölich und frey on alle Rey, 5vv, 1576a; S xviii, 149
Frölich zu sein ist mein Manier, 5vv, 1567c; S xviii, 38
Gott ist auf den wir immer hoffen (Ulenberg), 3vv, 1588c; S xx, 79
Gott nimbt und geit zu jeder Zeit, 5vv, 1576a; S xviii, 130
Gross ist der Herr im heilgen Thron (Ulenberg), 3vv, 1588c; S xx, 79
Halt mich o Herr in deiner Hut (Ulenberg), 3vv, 1588c; S xx, 66
Herr der du meine Stercke bist (Ulenberg), 3vv, 1588c; S xx, 67
Herr Gott mein Hort (Ulenberg), 3vv, 1588c; S xx, 72
Hilff lieber Herr die heilig Frommen (Ulenberg), 3vv, 1588c; S xx, 65
Hort zu ein news Gedicht (2p. So fundt man; 3p. Der g'winnen will), 5vv, 1576a; S xviii, 124
Ich armer Mann was hab ich than, 5vv, 1576a; S xviii, 113
Ich hab dich lieb das weist du wol (2p. Und wann du freundlich bist), 5vv, 1572a; S xviii, 93
Ich hab ein Mann (2p. Wann er auffsteht; 3p. Nach dem Frühmal; 4p. Umb fünffe hin; 5p. Ich armes Weib; 6p. Bald ich von Gelt; 7p. Wann ich dann sag; 8p. Nun wars umb mich), 4vv, 1583a; S xx, 31
Ich harre auff Gott (Ulenberg), 3vv, 1588c; S xx, 76
Ich ruff zu dir mein Herr und Gott (Ulenberg) (2p. Wann du Herr wolltest; 3p. Ich harr auf Gott; 4p. Mein Hoffnung steht; 5p. Dann bey dem Herren), 6vv, 1590; S xx, 88
Ich sprich wan ich nit leuge, 5vv, 1576a; S xviii, 159
Ich weiss ein hübsches Frawelein, 5vv, 1572a; S xviii, 91
Ich weiss nur ein Meidlein, 4vv, 1583a; S xx, 28
Ich will auss gantzem Hertzen mein (Ulenberg), 3vv, 1588c; S xx, 64
Ich will dich Herr gebürlich loben (Ulenberg), 3vv, 1588c; S xx, 73
Ich will Gott unaufhörlich preisen (Ulenberg), 3vv, 1588c; S xx, 74
Im Lant zu Wirtenberg (2p. Da das der Herr; 3p. Der richter lacht), 5vv, 1567c; S xviii, 19
Im Mayen hört man die Hanen krayen, 5vv, 1567c; S xviii, 24
In viel Trübsal (2p. Derhalben dann nichts), 6vv, 1590; S xx, 116
Ist keiner hie, der sprich zu mir, 5vv, 1567c; S xviii, 8
Kombt her zu mir spricht Gottes Son (G. Grünwald), 5vv, 1572a; S xviii, 73
Man sieht nun wol wie stet du bist, 5vv, 1572a; S xviii, 81
Maria voll Genad (2p. Der Herr, der ist mit dir; 3p. Du best genbenedeyd; 4p. Gebenedeyt auch), 6vv, 1590; S xx, 108
Mein Fraw hilgert (2p. Mein Fraw unmilt; 3p. Mein Fraw unrein; 4p. Do ich lang stilt; 5p. Sie raufft jr gnug), 5vv, 1576a; S xviii, 132
Mein Gott, mein heber trewer Gott (Ulenberg), 3vv, 1588c; S xx, 69
Mein Mann, der ist in Krieg (2p. Was soll ich euch; 3p. In wölches Hauss; Wolstu mich), 5vv, 1572a; S xviii, 51
Mit Lust thet ich aussreitten (2p. Das ein das Annelein; 3p. Da lagens), 5vv, 1576a; S xviii, 124
Nun grüss dich Gott, 8vv, 1573c; S xx, 54
Nur närrisch seyn ist mein Monier, 5vv, 1572a; S xviii, 62
O Herr, ich klag es dir (Ulenberg), 3vv, 1588c; S xx, 62
O Mensch gedenck (2p. Dort aber wirdt), 6vv, 1590; S xx, 102
O selig dem der trewe Gott (Ulenberg), 3vv, 1588c; S xx, 74
Schaff mir Herr nicht in Eiffermut (Ulenberg), 3vv, 1588c; S xx, 71
Selig ist der auff Gott sein Hoffnung, 4vv, 1583a; S xx, 42
Selig zu preisen ist der Mann (Ulenberg), 3vv, 1588c; S xx, 61
So trincken wir alle, 5vv, 1576a; S xviii, 145
Straff mich Herr nicht in Eiffermut (Ulenberg), 3vv, 1588c; S xx, 76
Susannen frumb, 5vv, 1576a; S xviii, 109
Tritt auf en Rigel von der Thür, 5vv, 1567c; S xviii, 35
Vater unser im Himmelreich (Luther), 5vv, 1567c; S xviii, 1
Vernimb Herr meine Wort (Ulenberg), 3vv, 1588c; S xx, 62

Von Gott wil ich nit lassen (2p. Wann sich der Menschen Hulde; 3p. Auff ihn wil ich vertrawen), 6vv, 1590; S xx, 134
Von Morgens frü mit Gottes Lob, 4vv, 1583a; S xx, 27
Vor Zeiten was ich Lieb und Werd, 5vv, 1567c; S xviii, 16
Wach auff o Menschenkind (2p. Ist doch Gott gar), 4vv, 1583a; S xx, 24
Was heut soll sein, 4vv, 1583a; S xx, 23
Was kann uns kommen an für Not (A. Knöpken), 5vv, 1572a; S xviii, 68
Welt, Gelt, dir wird einmal (2p. Gelt, Welt, dir wird; 3p. Welt, Gelt, dir wird), 5vv, 1576a; S xviii, 117
Wem soll man jetzund trawen, 4vv, 1573c; S xx, 50
Wie ein hirsch gierlich schreien thut (Ulenberg), 3vv, 1588c; S xx, 77
Wie lang, o Gott, in meiner Not, 5vv, 1567c; S xviii, 27
Willig und trew on alle Rew, 5vv, 1572a; S xviii, 80
Wir haben Herr mit unsern Oren (Ulenberg), 3vv, 1588c; S xx, 78
Wohl kombt der May, 4vv, 1583a; S xx, 40

(2) Ferdinand de Lassus (*b* Munich, *c*1560; *d* Munich, 27 Aug 1609). Singer and composer, eldest son of (1) Orlande de Lassus. He entered the Bavarian court chapel in 1584; in 1585 he was in the service of Friedrich von Hohenzollern-Sigmaringen, but at the beginning of 1590 he was again in Munich and Landshut. In 1602 he succeeded Johann à Fossa as Kapellmeister at Munich. In 1585 he married; eight children were born of this marriage (including Ferdinand, 1592–1630, who became a musician, studied in Rome, and was Kapellmeister in Munich, 1616–29). His music where different in style from his father's shows some turn-of-the-century characteristics.

WORKS

Cantiones sacrae, 6vv (Graz, 1587)
Apparatus musicus, 8vv, bc (org) (Munich, 1622)
Works in 1583², 1585¹⁷, 1588⁸, 1596², 1597³, 1602¹, 1604⁷, 1616², 1623², 1624¹, *D-Mbs*

(3) Rudolph de Lassus (*b* Munich, *c*1563; *d* Munich, 1625). Organist and composer, second son of (1) Orlande de Lassus. He entered the Bavarian court chapel in 1585, becoming first organist there in 1589 and remaining in that post until his death. In 1609 he became court composer to the duke. He married some time before 1590 and had four children. Together with his brother (2) Ferdinand he assembled and published the *Magnum opus musicum* (1604), the enormous if incomplete corpus of his father's motets. Rudolph established himself as a composer through his share, one half, of the Ulenberg psalm settings published in 1588 (Rudolph's contributions alternate regularly with those of Orlande in this volume). His father's influence remained important; several of Rudolph's *Magnificat* settings are parodies of works by Orlande. He went so far, however, as to write some works making use of thoroughbass and of soprano duets in the style of the early 17th century. Rudolph was a fairly prolific composer and may deserve study aside from the matter of his father's influence.

WORKS

Teutsche Psalmen: geistliche psalmen, 3vv (Munich, 1588¹²); ed. W. Lipphardt (Kassel, 1928/R1952)
Cantiones sacrae, 6vv (Munich, 1601³)
Selectae aliquot cantiones, 4vv (Munich, 1606)
Circus symphoniacus commissi in arenam Phonomachi, 9, 11, 12vv (Munich, 1607)
Triga musica qua missae odaeque Marianae triplice fugantur: in Viadanae modo, 4–6vv (Munich, 1612)
Virginalia Eucharistica, 2–8vv (Munich, 1615)
Ad sacrum convivium modi sacri, 2–6vv (Munich, 1617)
Alphabetum Marianum triplici cantionum, 2–4vv, bc (org) (Munich, 1621)
Cygnaeum melos, 2–4vv, una cum litaneis, 4vv cecinit (Munich, 1626)
Missae (Ingolstadt, n.d.), lost
Works in Pantheon musicum (Paris, 1600), 1585¹⁷, 1590¹, 1596², 1604⁷, *c*1610¹⁸, 1616², 1622², 1623², 1624¹, 1627², 1628³, *A-Wn*, *D-Mbs*

BIBLIOGRAPHY

FasquelleE

R. Eitner: 'Chronologisches Verzeichniss der gedruckten Werke von H. L. Hassler und Orlandus de Lassus', *MMg*, v, vi (1874), suppls.

C. van den Borren: *Orlande de Lassus* (Paris, 1920/*R*1975)

A. Sandberger: *Ausgewählte Aufsätze zur Musikgeschichte* (Munich, 1921), 1–168

E. Lowinsky: *Das Antwerpener Motettenbuch O. di Lasso's und seine Beziehungen zum Motettenschaffen der niederländischen Zeitgenossen* (The Hague, 1937)

H. Osthoff: *Die Niederländer und das deutsche Lied* (Berlin, 1938/*R*1967), 139ff

A. Einstein: *The Italian Madrigal* (Princeton, 1949/*R*1971), 477ff

K. Levy: ' "Susanne un jour": the History of a 16th Century Chanson', *AnnM*, i (1953), 375–408

B. Meier: 'Alter und neuer Stil in lateinisch textierten Werken von Orlando di Lasso', *AMw*, xv (1958), 51

W. Boetticher: *Orlando di Lasso und seine Zeit, 1532–1594* (Kassel, 1958)

H. Leuchtmann: *Die musikalische Wortausdeutungen in den Motetten des Magnum opus musicum von Orlando di Lasso* (Strasbourg, 1959)

W. Boetticher: 'Lasso, Orlando di', *MGG* [incl. detailed bibliography to c1958]

W. Frei: 'Die bayerische Hofkapelle unter Orlando di Lasso: Ergänzungen und Berichtigungen zur Deutung von Mielichs Bild', *Mf*, xv (1962), 359

W. Boetticher: *Aus Orlando di Lassos Wirkungskreis* (Kassel, 1963)

——: 'Wortausdeutung und Tonalität bei Orlando di Lasso', *KJb*, xlvii (1963), 75

R. Ears: 'Zur Deutung von Mielichs Bild der bayerischen Hofkapelle', *Mf*, xvi (1963), 364

S. Hermelink: 'Jägermesse: Beitrag zu einer Begriffsbestimmung', *Mf*, xviii (1965), 29

W. Boetticher: 'Über einige neue Werke aus Orlando di Lassos mittlerer Madrigal- und Motettenkomposition (1567–1569)', *AMw*, xxix (1965), 12

——: 'New Lasso Studies', *Aspects of Medieval and Renaissance Music: a Birthday Offering to Gustave Reese* (New York, 1966), 17

K. Morawska: 'Kompozycje Orlanda di Lasso w repertuarze instrumentalnym', *Muzyka*, xiii/3 (1968), 3

W. Boetticher: 'Weitere Beiträge zur Lasso-Forschung', *Renaissancemuziek 1400–1600: donum natalicium René Bernard Lenaerts* (Louvain, 1969), 61

S. Hermelink: 'Die Gegenquintsprungkadenz, ein Ausdrucksmittel der Satzkunst Lassos', *GfMKB, Bonn 1970*, 435

D. Kämper: 'Studien zur instrumentalen Ensemblemusik des 16. Jahrhunderts', *AnMc*, no.10 (1970)

H. Leuchtmann: 'Lassos Huldigungsmotette für Henri d'Anjou 1573', *Mf*, xxiii (1970), 165

W. Mitchell: 'The Prologue to Orlando di Lasso's *Prophetiae Sibyllarum*', *Music Forum*, ii (1970), 264

C. V. Palisca: '*Ut oratoria musica*: the Rhetorical Basis of Musical Mannerism', *The Meaning of Mannerism*, ed. F. W. Robinson and S. G. Nichols (Hanover, New Hampshire, 1972), 37

H. Leuchtmann: 'Orlando di Lasso in München', *Oberbayerisches Archiv*, xcvii (1973), 1

J. Bernstein: 'Lassus in English Sources: Two Chansons Recovered', *JAMS*, xxvii (1974), 315

B. Meier: *Die Tonarten der klassischen Vokalpolyphonie* (Utrecht, 1974)

M. Ruhnke: 'Lassos Chromatik und die Orgelstimmung', *Convivium musicorum: Festschrift Wolfgang Boetticher* (Berlin, 1974), 291

W. Boetticher: 'Anticipations of Dramatic Monody in the Late Works of Lassus', *Essays on Opera and English Music in Honour of Sir Jack Westrup* (Oxford, 1975), 84

J. Erb: *Parody Technique in the Magnificats of Orlando di Lasso* (diss., Harvard U., 1975)

J. Haar: 'A Madrigal Falsely Ascribed to Lasso', *JAMS*, xxviii (1975), 526

H. Leuchtmann: *Orlando di Lasso* (Wiesbaden, 1976)

G. R. Hoekstra: 'An Eight-voice Parody of Lassus: An Introduction and the Complete Music of André Pevernage's "Bon jour mon coeur"', *Early Music*, vii (1979), 367

JAMES HAAR

Lasus [Lasos] **of Hermione** (*b* Hermione [now Kastri], Argolis; *fl c*530–20 BC). Greek lyric poet and the earliest music theorist. According to Herodotus (vii, chap.6, §3), Lasus was at Athens at some time between 527 and 514 BC. A brief fragment of the text of one of his compositions has survived, the beginning of a hymn to Demeter (frag.1, ed. Edmonds). During his lifetime he was famous chiefly as a composer of dithyrambs; Aristophanes (*Wasps*, l.1410) referred to a competition

between him and Simonides, and in the late classical period dithyrambs were spuriously attributed to him.

The original (wrongly emended) text of the Byzantine *Suda* lexicon and a brief reference by Pseudo-Plutarch (*De musica*, chap.xxix, §1141c) credit him with a radical innovation: the introduction of dithyrambic rhythm and tempo (*agōgē*, actually a broader concept; see Privitera, p.75n., on Rossi) into other forms of composition. Music sung to the kithara would thus have become more like music sung to aulos accompaniment: for example, the diatonic whole tone may have been subdivided into microtones (modern theorizing about semitones and quarter-tones seems anachronistic). Lasus cannot, however, be termed a forerunner of the dithyrambists associated with the 'New Music' movement; it is significant that Pherecrates did not list him among the ravishers of *Mousikē*.

Aristotle's famous pupil Aristoxenus wrote in the *Harmonics* (p.3, ed. Meibom; p.7, ll.18–23, ed. da Rios) that Lasus did research in acoustics, and three centuries later Theon of Smyrna (p.59, ll.4ff, ed. Hiller) made a similar reference, associating him with Pythagorean inquiry. The link here between practice and theory, if genuine, is unusual.

Research has broadly confirmed the *Suda* statement that Lasus 'was the first to write a treatise *On Music*'. His ideas and gnomic sayings were considered subtle and profound at an early period – Aristophanes parodied one of them in the *Wasps* (l.1411) – and he was sometimes numbered among the Seven Sages. In the 5th century AD Martianus Capella (*De nuptiis*, ix, §936; text in Wille) claimed that originally (*primo*) Lasus distinguished the harmonic, rhythmic and metrical aspects of music; his claim echoes a tradition believed to go back through Aristides Quintilianus and perhaps Varro to an original source. From the 5th century BC Lasus's theories were evidently heeded and remembered, whether or not he ever wrote them down.

BIBLIOGRAPHY

J. M. Edmonds, ed. and trans.: *Lyra graeca*, i (London and Cambridge, Mass., 1922–7, 2/1928–40); ii (1924, 5/1964), 222ff

H. Abert: 'Lasos (2)', *Paulys Real-Encyclopädie der classischen Altertumswissenschaft*, xii/1 (Stuttgart, 1924), 887

A. W. Pickard-Cambridge: *Dithyramb, Tragedy and Comedy* (Oxford, 1927, rev. 2/1962 by T. B. L. Webster), 12ff, 23f

F. Lasserre, ed.: *Plutarque: De la musique* (Olten and Lausanne, 1954), 34ff

L. Richter: *Zur Wissenschaftslehre von der Musik bei Platon und Aristoteles* (Berlin, 1961), 14f

D. L. Page, ed.: *Poetae melici graeci* (Oxford, 1962), 364ff

G. A. Privitera: *Laso di Ermione nella cultura ateniese e nella tradizione storiografica*, Filologia e critica, ed. B. Gentili, 1 (Rome, 1965); reviewed by E. K. Borthwick, *Classical Review*, new ser., xvii (1967), 146

G. Wille: *Musica romana* (Amsterdam, 1967), 645f

WARREN ANDERSON

László, Ferenc (*b* Cluj, 8 May 1937). Romanian-Hungarian music critic and flautist. He graduated from the Academy of Music in Cluj (now Cluj-Napoca) in 1959 and then became flautist in the Philharmonic Orchestra in Sibiu (1959–65), chamber music instructor at the Cluj Music School (1966–70) and senior assistant in the chamber music department of the Bucharest Academy of Music (appointed 1970). From 1970 to 1973 he organized the music pages of the weekly journal *A het*; he is also active in the Hungarian-language transmissions of Romanian radio and television. As a chamber musician he has made concert tours in Romania and abroad. His writings have included studies of Mozart and Bartók.

WRITINGS

'Zur Tätigkeit Philipp Caudellas in Hermannstadt', *Forschungen zur Volks- und Landeskunde*, no.1 (Bucharest, 1965), 91

ed.: *Bartók-könyv 1970–1971* [Bartók book 1970–1971] (Bucharest, 1971)

'Untersuchungen zu Mozarts zweiten Opus 1 Nr. 1', *MJb 1971–2*, 149

'Contribuţiuni la studiul formei de sonată la Mozart', *Studii de muzicologie*, ix (1973), 481

ed.: *Bartók-dolgozatok* [Essays about Bartók] (Bucharest, 1974) [incl. 'Széljegyzetek egy Bartók-kézirat margójára' [Notes on a Bartók MS], 29]

ed.: *Bartók-levél* [99 letters of Bartók] (Bucharest, 1974)

'Geneza trioului cu pian la Mozart' [History of the origin of Mozart's piano trios], *Studii de muzicologie*, x (1974), 302

ANDRÁS BENKŐ

Lászlò, Magda (*b* Marosvásárhely, 1919). Hungarian soprano. She studied at the Liszt Academy of Music, Budapest, and with Irene Stowasser. Prevented by the war from taking up a scholarship for further study in Italy, she instead joined the Budapest Opera (1943–6), singing, among other roles, Elisabeth, Lauretta, and Amelia (*Simon Boccanegra*). In 1946 she settled in Italy where she was engaged by Italian radio to sing in several studio opera performances, as Isolde, Strauss's Daphne, and the Mother in Dallapiccola's *Il prigioniero*. This last she created, and subsequently repeated in the opera's first stage performance at the 1950 Florence Maggio Musicale. Her intelligent musicianship gained her many parts in contemporary Italian works by Malipiero, Ghedini, Casella and Lualdi. At Glyndebourne she appeared in the title role in Gluck's *Alceste* (1953–4), also as Dorabella (1954) and Monteverdi's Poppaea (1962–3). Her 1954 creation at Covent Garden of Cressida in Walton's *Troilus and Cressida* won her praise for charm of acting and stage presence, though her enunciation in English was often indistinct. Other roles in her repertory included Marie (*Wozzeck*), Busoni's Turandot, Senta and Norma. Despite her concentration on contemporary music, she also sang Bach, Mozart and Handel in concert; recordings of Bach and *arie antiche* display her distinguished musicianship and voice of great beauty.

HAROLD ROSENTHAL

Lateiner, Jacob (*b* Havana, 31 May 1928). American pianist. From 1934 to 1940 he studied in Havana with Jascha Fischermann, and in 1940 he went to the Curtis Institute in Philadelphia and studied with Isabelle Vengerova. He also worked in the chamber music classes of Primrose and Piatigorsky. He made his début in 1945 with the Philadelphia Orchestra under Ormandy, as winner of the Philadelphia Youth Competition. In 1947 he was engaged by Koussevitzky for the Tanglewood Summer Festival and he made his New York recital début the following year. By this time he had already made many appearances in the USA and had toured Australia. After service in the US Army he continued his career and from 1954 he played throughout the USA and made a number of appearances in Europe. Lateiner has been associated particularly with Beethoven and with contemporary American music. In 1967 he gave, with the Boston SO under Leinsdorf, the first performance of Elliott Carter's Piano Concerto and in 1968 of Sessions's Third Piano Sonata. He has frequently played and recorded chamber music with Heifetz and Piatigorsky.

RONALD KINLOCH ANDERSON

Latere, Petit Jean de. *See* DE LATRE, PETIT JEAN.

Lates, James (*b* ?*c*1740; *d* Oxford, 21 Nov 1777). English composer and violinist. He was a son of David Francisco Lates, who taught modern languages at Oxford University. According to Sainsbury, he studied in Italy. He played in the Oxford music-room orchestra and in other concerts in the vicinity of Oxford (including Henley and Banbury) from about 1759 until his death, and was connected with the Duke of Marlborough's musical establishment at Blenheim. His earliest known works, the op.1 violin duets, have a rhythmic life rare in his more *galant* later music, even the flute duets of op.2. In the op.3 violin solos there is occasional Baroque-style instrumental figuration within a primarily *galant* idiom; in spite of pallid slow movements, a feature of nearly all Lates's music, these are among the most interesting English violin solos of the period. The op.4 trio sonatas, each in three movements, are marked by their leisurely, languishing style of *galant* melody; the writing is generally homophonic, and the single movement marked 'Fuga' is not a real fugue. The op.5 sonatas, dedicated to the Duke of Marlborough, 'for whose private amusement they were principally composed' (according to the dedication), are for the rare combination in English music of violin, cello and basso continuo, no doubt following the example of C. F. Abel's op.9 (*c*1770); they are each in two movements, the first usually in a moderate tempo, the second a minuet. Lates's music is old-fashioned for its date, but there is a gentle, relaxed charm to his melodic lines, and a sureness of general technique, which make his opp.4 and 5 among the most interesting products of the late flowering of the trio sonata in England.

Lates's name is sometimes given as John James, which may be due to confusion with his son of that name. Another son, Charles (1771–*c*1810), was a professional pianist and organist, and published keyboard music and songs; in 1793, when he graduated BMus at Oxford, he was organist of Gainsborough, Lincs.

WORKS

(all published in London)

op.

1   6 Duets, 2 vn (1761)
2   6 Duets, 2 fl (1761)
3   6 Solos, vn, bc (*c*1765)
4   6 Sonatas, 2 vn, bc (*c*1768)
5   6 Sonatas, vn, vc, bc (*c*1775)

BIBLIOGRAPHY

J. Sainsbury, ed.: *A Dictionary of Musicians* (London, 2/1825/*R*1966)

J. H. Mee: *The Oldest Music Room in Europe* (London, 1911)

S. J. Sadie: *British Chamber Music, 1720–1790* (diss., U. of Cambridge, 1958)

STANLEY SADIE

Latham, Peter (Morton Sturges) (*b* London, 17 Nov 1894; *d* London, 14 May 1970). English musical scholar and lecturer. He was educated at Rugby where he took a classical scholarship, and Balliol College, Oxford. His studies were interrupted in 1914 by war service in India and Palestine but resumed in 1919. He left Oxford with the MA and took the Oxford BMus in 1934. In 1919–20 he studied at the RAM, where he gained the Charles Lucas Prize for orchestral composition. In 1921 he became a university extension lecturer for Oxford and Cambridge, and later also for London University. He was appointed professor of harmony and counterpoint at the RAM in 1938 and lecturer in musical history and appreciation at the GSM in 1948. From 1941 to 1964 he was Gresham Professor of Music.

WRITINGS

'Beethoven', *Lives of the Great Composers*, ed. A. L. Bacharach (London, 1935), 45; repr. in *The Music Masters*, ed. A. L. Bacharach (London, 1957–8), i, 51

Brahms (London, 1948, 2/1962)

ERIC BLOM/PETER PLATT

Latilla, Gaetano (*b* Bari, 12 Jan 1711; *d* Naples, 15 Jan 1788). Italian composer. As a boy he sang in the choir of Bari Cathedral. He then moved to Naples where, in March 1726, he enrolled as a student in the conservatory S Maria di Loreto. The chief music masters there were Francesco Mancini and Giovanni Veneziano, one of whom must have been responsible for Latilla's training during his late adolescence. Latilla began his professional career in 1732 by composing a comic opera, *Li marite a forza*, for the Fiorentini Theatre in Naples, and he wrote other comic operas for that theatre during the next five years.

His first successes outside Naples occurred around 1738 when he obtained commissions for comic operas at several Roman theatres and for a serious opera, *Demofoonte*, at the S Giovanni Grisostomo Theatre in Venice. These works set the seal on his popularity throughout Italy, and from then until about 1755 he was constantly in demand as an opera composer. He is known to have held three appointments not involving work in opera houses. The first was that of assistant *maestro* at the Roman basilica S Maria Maggiore, where he worked from 31 December 1738 until April 1741. On 14 December 1753 he was engaged as *maestro di coro* at the Venetian conservatory Della Pietà; for reasons unspecified in the documents this appointment was terminated on 14 March 1766. In March 1762 he was also made assistant *maestro* at St Mark's under Galuppi; he was still in this post in 1770 when Charles Burney met him in Venice and obtained much useful information from him on the history and constitution of the Venetian conservatories. Burney remarked that he seemed 'in great indigence', and in fact his popularity among opera audiences had dwindled by this time. Later, Burney reported a rumour that Latilla finally fell foul of the Venetian state authorities and was thrown into prison there. He had left Venice and was in Naples again by 1774, where he spent the last years of his life writing a few compositions and teaching. One of his composition pupils during this period was Thomas Attwood, who later took lessons from Mozart in Vienna.

Because Latilla's official posts were all with religious or charitable foundations, it is likely that he composed a quantity of church music. Few such works have survived. He composed some religious music while serving at the Pietà, where there were several gifted female solo singers among the pupils; Latilla's surviving *Miserere* (*GB-Lbm*) contains the kind of highly elaborate vocal writing that was specially suited to these singers. No-one has yet established what music he wrote for S Maria Maggiore or St Mark's. His chief extant instrumental compositions are six quartets published in London. Only six of his three-act operas and two of his short operas (both adaptations of larger works) remain intact. The earliest, the comic opera *Angelica ed Orlando* of 1735, dates from the same period as the operas of his almost exact contemporary Pergolesi, though its music bears less resemblance to Pergolesi's than to that of another Neapolitan, Leonardo Leo. Over the following decades Latilla changed his style considerably in conformity with new tastes. The lyrical items of his heroic opera *Antigono* of 1775, the last of his compositions that has survived, are characterized by longer melodic lines and heavier accompaniments than those of his earlier works, and the racier and less lilting style he adopted seems to have been an attempt to come to terms with the latest music of Niccolò Piccinni, Antonio Sacchini and others among the new generation of Neapolitan composers.

WORKS

STAGE

(music lost unless otherwise stated)

Li marite a forza (comic opera, 3, B. Saddumene), Naples, Fiorentini, spr. 1732

L. Ottavio (comic opera, 3, G. A. Federico), Naples, Fiorentini, wint. 1733

Gl'Ingannati (comic opera, 3, Federico), Naples, Fiorentini, wint. 1734

Angelica ed Orlando (comic opera, 3, T. Fonsaconico [F. A. Tullio]), Naples, Fiorentini, aut. 1735, *GB-Lbm*, modern copy *US-Wc*

Gismondo (comic opera, 3, Federico), Naples, Fiorentini, sum. 1737; rev. as La finta cameriera (3, text rev. G. Barlocci), Rome, Valle, spr. 1738, *B-Bc*, modern copy *US-Wc*; rev. as Don Calascione (3), London, King's, 21 Jan 1749, Favourite Songs pubd (London, 1749); rev. as La finta cameriera (intermezzo, 2), Paris, Opéra, 1752, *F-Po*; rev. as La giardiniera contessa (1), *B-Bc*

Polipodio e Rocchetta (intermezzo, 2), Rome, Argentina, carn. 1738

Demofoonte (heroic opera, 3, Metastasio), Venice, S Giovanni Grisostomo, carn. 1738

Madama Ciana (comic opera, 3, Barlocci), Rome, Pallacorda, Feb 1738; rev. as Gli artigiani arricchiti (intermezzo, 2), Paris, Opéra, 25 Sept 1753, *F-Po*

[?] Romolo (heroic opera, 3), Rome, Delle Dame, carn. 1739, attrib. Latilla and Terradellas; ov. and 20 vocal items *D-Dlb*

Siroe (heroic opera, 3, Metastasio), Rome, Delle Dame, carn. 1740, *A-Wgm*, modern copy *US-Wc*

Olimpia nell'isola di Ebuda (heroic opera, 3, A. Trabucco), Naples, S Carlo, 20 Jan 1741

La vendetta generosa (comic opera, 3), Naples, Fiorentini, aut. 1742

Zenobia (heroic opera, 3, Metastasio), Turin, Royal, aut. 1742, 4 arias *D-Dlb*

La gara per la gloria (comic opera, 3, B. Vitturi), Venice, S Moisè, carn. 1744

Amare e fingere (comic opera, 3), Naples, Nuovo, carn. 1745

Il concerto (comic opera, 3, Partenio Chriter [P. Trinchera]), Naples, Nuovo, spr. 1746

Catone in Utica (heroic opera, 3, Metastasio), Rome, Capranica, carn. 1747

Il vecchio amante (comic opera, 3, Barlocci), Turin, Carignano, carn. 1747

Il barone di Vignalunga (comic opera, 3, A. Palomba), Naples, Nuovo, 1747

Adriano in Siria (heroic opera, 3, Metastasio), Naples, S Carlo, 19 Dec 1747

Ciascheduno ha il suo negozio (comic opera), Madrid, Buen ritiro, 1747

La Celia (comic opera, 3, A. Palomba), Naples, Fiorentini, aut. 1749

L'astuzia felice (comic opera, 3, C. Goldoni), Turin, Carignano, spr. 1750

Amore in Tarantola (comic opera, 3, Abate Vaccina), Venice, S Moisè, aut. 1750

La Maestra (comic opera, 3, G. Palomba), Naples, Fiorentini, carn. 1751, collab. G. Cocchi and G. Cordella

L'opera in prova alla moda (comic opera, 3, G. Fiorini), Venice, S Moisè, carn. 1751

Urganostocar ('tragedia tragichissima di lieto fine', 3, Fiorini), Venice, S Moisè, carn. 1751, perf. with L'opera in prova alla moda

La pastorella al soglio (serious opera, 3, G. C. Pagani), Venice, S Moisè, Ascension 1751

Griselda (heroic opera, 3, Zeno), Venice, S Cassiano, aut. 1751, ?4 arias *D-Dlb*

Gl'impostori (comic opera, 3), Venice, S Moisè, aut. 1751

L'isola d'amore (comic opera, 3, A. Rigo), Venice, S Moisè, carn. 1752

Olimpiade (heroic opera, 3, Metastasio), Venice, S Cassiano, aut. 1752, 6 arias *D-Dlb*

Alessandro nell'Indie (heroic opera, 3, Metastasio), Venice, S Cassiano, carn. 1753, collabs. unknown

Antigona (heroic opera, 3, G. Roccaforte), Modena, Court, 1753

Venceslao (heroic opera, ?3, Zeno), Barcelona, 1754

Il protettor del poeta (intermezzo, 2, G. Piccinelli), Rome, Valle, carn. 1754

Il giuoco de'matti (comic opera, 3, A. Palomba), Naples, Nuovo, sum. 1754

La finta sposa (comic opera, 3), Bologna, Formagliari, 1755

Ezio (heroic opera, 3, Metastasio), Naples, S Carlo, 10 July 1758, *US-CA*

L'amore artigiano (comic opera, 3, Goldoni), Venice, S Angelo, wint. 1761

Merope (heroic opera, 3, Zeno), Venice, S Benedetto, carn. 1763
La buona figliuola supposta vedova (comic opera, 3, A. Bianchi), Venice, S Cassiano, carn. 1766
Il maritato fra le disgrazie (comic opera, 3, G. Palomba), Naples, Fiorentini, aut. 1774
Antigono (heroic opera, 3, Metastasio), Naples, S Carlo, 13 Aug 1775, *I-Nc*
I sposi incogniti (comic opera, 3, P. Mililotti), Naples, Nuovo, 1779
Il Temistocle (heroic opera, 3, Metastasio), n.d., *A-Wgm*, modern copy *US-Wc*

SACRED VOCAL
(music lost unless otherwise stated)
Sanctorum Patrum in Abrahae sinu expectatio (cantata, 2), Venice, Pietà, 1755
Carmina Sacra, Venice, Pietà, 1756
Judith triumphans (oratorio), Venice, Pietà, 1757
Modulamina sacra (motet), Venice, Pietà, 1760
Miserere, Eb, SATB, 2 hn, str, bc, Venice, Pietà, c1760, *GB-Lbm*
Omnipotenza e misericordia divina [characters Omnipotenza, Umanità, Misericordia, Lucifero] (oratorio), 4vv, *D-MÜs*
Messa in pastorale, 2vv, org, *I-Nc*
Salve regina, SA, str, bc, *GB-Lbm*
Bonum est confiteri (motet)
Matutino, dum surgit (cantata), cited by Mondolfi
Motets ?written for Pietà, Venice, all in *I-Vc*: Aurum voluptas, per Ellena, S, bc; Ave Regina, per Ellena, S, bc; Ave Regina, per Gregoria, A, bc; Furen furens hostis, per Josepha, S, bc; Mormorate, per Ellena, S, bc; Non timeo, per Josepha, S, bc; Regina celi, per Ellena, S, bc; Regina celi, per Iseppa, S, bc; Regina celi, per Marina, S, bc; Surge aurora luminosa, per Ellena, S, bc; Ut errant, per Josepha, S, bc

OTHER WORKS
Various arias and ensembles, vv, insts, *B-Bc*, *D-B*, *GB-Lbm*, *I-Gi(l)*, *US-Wc*
6 Quartettos, 2 vn, va, vc obbl (London, n.d.)
Trio, fl, v, bc, *I-Gi(l)*
Sinfonia, 2 vn, 2 ob, 2 hn, bc, *B-Bc*
Sinfonia a 8, D, *D-B*
Sinfonia, G, *B*

BIBLIOGRAPHY
BurneyH
G. G. Ferrari: *Aneddoti piacevoli e interessanti occorsi nella vita di G. G. F. da Roveredo* (London, 1830); ed. S. Di Giacomo (Milan, 1929)
F. Florimo: *La scuola musicale di Napoli e i suoi conservatorii*, ii, iv (Naples, 1881–2)
T. Wiel: *I teatri musicali veneziani del settecento* (Venice, 1897)
M. Bellucci La Salandra: 'Saggio cronologico delle opere teatrali di Gaetano Latilla', *Japigia*, v (1935), 310
A. Loewenberg: 'Latilla, Gaetano', *Grove 5*
P. Scholes, ed.: *Dr. Burney's Musical Tours in Europe*, i (London, 1959)
A. Mondolfi: 'Latilla, Gaetano', *MGG*
D. Arnold: 'Orphans and Ladies: the Venetian conservatories (1680–1790)', *PRMA*, lxxxix (1962–3), 46
S. H. Hansell: 'Sacred Music at the Incurabili in Venice at the Time of J. A. Hasse, pt 2', *JAMS*, xxiii (1970), 505
MICHAEL F. ROBINSON

Latin America. The countries constituting Latin America present cultural traits mainly inherited from the Iberian peninsula, but their folk music traditions have generally preserved less of that heritage than North American folk music has kept of British lore. Many parts of what is called 'Latin America' are virtually devoid of any Latin cultural elements. Some tropical-forest Amerindian cultures, for example, and some Indian groups of the Bolivian highlands, are still relatively untouched by European traditions. Moreover, in many cases the prevailing cultural influences have been more African than European. The study of folk and traditional music in individual countries or territories is inevitably somewhat artificial, although there are common cultural traits in very large geographical areas, such as that formerly in the Inca empire, extending from western Argentina to the highlands of northern Ecuador, or the areas inhabited by Afro-American populations in Brazil, Trinidad, Cuba, western Colombia, Ecuador and Venezuela, with their analogous developments.

In Bolivia, where about 70% of the population is of Indian descent, the music of the highland area is essentially indigenous (Aymara, Quechua), but the music of the valleys and the eastern provinces is typical mestizo (culturally and racially mixed) folk music, characterized by mestizo tunes and words, using Indian or European instruments and accompanying dances of Indian and European origin. It is not uncommon to find rather isolated highland Indian groups using string instruments clearly of Spanish descent, such as the *charango* (an instrument with five double strings, made in its most rustic form out of an armadillo shell) and the harp. In contrast to Indian music of tropical-forest cultures (Mato Grosso, Upper Amazon), Indian music of the Andean countries is a dominant ingredient of the folk music traditions of the area. In the transfer of Hispanic or African material to the Americas, syncretism accounts for the creation of certain forms and the preservation or rejection of others.

The history of a country must also be considered in accounting for specific stylistic traits; a case in point would be a comparative historical study of Haiti, Jamaica and Trinidad. While all three countries have a majority of population of African descent, they were at various periods of their history under the political and cultural domination of Spain, France and Great Britain. In the case of Trinidad, although never dominated by France, French influence has been strong because of immigration. West African cultures transferred to Caribbean areas were quite diverse: Ewe (Benin) in the case of Haiti, mostly Yoruba (Nigeria) and Ashanti (Ghana) in Jamaica and Trinidad. Other ethnic groups, such as the East Indians in Trinidad, Guyana and Surinam and the Javanese in Surinam must also be taken into account.

Latin American traditional music presents a complex picture and a macroscopic exposition alone will be presented here, giving a few illustrations of what is found rather than a survey of all the types of song, dance and instrument. (For more detailed discussion, *see* entries on the individual countries.)

I. Indian music. II. Folk music. III. Afro-American music. IV. Popular music.

I. Indian music

1. South America: (i) The social context (ii) Song texts (iii) Musical resources and style (iv) Genres (v) Instruments. 2. Central America: (i) Introduction (ii) Pre-Columbian instruments (iii) 20th-century aboriginal music (iv) Changes in aboriginal music.

1. SOUTH AMERICA. South American Indians may be grouped in three categories according to their economic system: nomadic hunters, fisherfolk and gatherers who, as they become sedentary, cultivate rudimentary crops; agriculturists and shepherds, who also hunt, fish and gather; and agriculturists, shepherds and craftsmen of superior culture. According to Steward's *Handbook of South American Indians*, 'Andean civilizations' make up the peoples in the third economic group; the remaining tribes, marginal, tropical-forest and circum-Caribbean, fall into the first and second economic groups. The music of the peoples in the first group is chiefly discussed here, including some anthropological aspects of their music, its manifestations and styles, and the use of particular instruments. The map overleaf shows the location of some of the different tribes in South America.

(i) *The social context.* The Indians seek to establish contact with superior forces through music. Song, however, is inseparable from text, and often from the dance

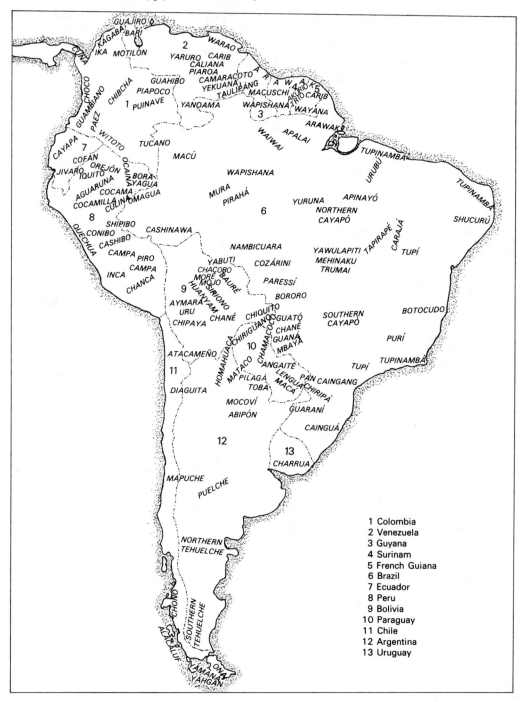

Map of South America showing the location of the principal tribes discussed below.

and a complex ceremony also involving the playing of instruments. Tribal gatherings always have a ritual basis. Among the Sanema of Venezuela the Pijiguao feast takes place when the palm-tree fruits are ripe, but different ceremonies with a mythical background are combined in the same feast: the cremation, pulverization, cooking (with the food) and ingestion of the bones of the dead to acquire the vital energy supposedly within them;

a mock warrior attack, with a battle of clubs; the exorcism of adverse spirits by fire, etc (Barandiarán, p.8). The Piaroa (also of Venezuela) perform a complex initiation feast which includes impressive flute and trumpet music. The Mapuche Indians organize a general annual prayer to ask their god Gnechen for health, food and well-being throughout the year; this includes a sequence of songs and instrumental pieces, dances and other rites such as sacrifices of sheep and circling around the sacred cinnamon tree. The Chocó Indians in Colombia gather to 'sing chicha' in a multiple ceremony consisting of 'an act of reconciliation with the spirits of predatory animals, who participate in the chicha feast together with the ancestral spirits' (chicha is a drink made of sugar, molasses, etc). The ceremony also serves 'to reaffirm the social cohesion of the group', as Reichel Dolmatoff pointed out (1960, pp.132, 135).

According to many Indians and their shamans, music and text are composed by spirits. The Yaruro of Venezuela believe, for example, that the shamans receive instructions during hallucinations induced by taking special powders. The non-Christian Guaraní say that man receives song from the divinity. The more songs a Guaraní knows, the more he is respected.

Music is learnt by ear and practice, but this does not imply the absence of instructors. In many tribes, witch-doctors and shamans are in charge of teaching the songs to novices. Roberto Pineda Giraldo described how among the Guajiro of Colombia the piache maestra (shaman teacher) transmits her knowledge to her disciple over an extended period. The girl is taught, among other things, how to invoke spirits with 'movements, attitudes, prayers and songs' and how to handle the ceremonial maraca (p.15). The Warao of Venezuela train the apprentice 'in the control of the diaphragm and breathing to provoke snoring sounds characteristic of communication with the supernatural force called hebu. Lastly the apprentice is instructed in the hebu vocabulary, incomprehensible to the common Warao' (Suárez, p.161).

Among the Piaroa the piache acts as doctor, magician and chronicler or historian in charge of passing on to the tribe, in sung oral tradition, the tales, legends and laws. He is the tribe's educator and initiates boys in all the required knowledge such as the songs, the playing of instruments and the sacred dances or pantomimes which represent the creation of the world (Baumgartner, p.163). Among the Tucano of the mouth of the Vaupes (Brazil) the boy to be initiated is taken to the forest where he must learn to distinguish the sounds of various instruments from far away (Ypiranga Monteiro, p.37). Among the Sanema of Venezuela messages are learnt and transmitted by means of song. The old men teach them to the messengers, then verify that they have been learnt properly. When a messenger delivers his message, the village chief and the old men answer him with the same song (Barandiarán). Reichel Dolmatoff (1949–50, pp.37, 74) noted that among the Kogi of Colombia

the great majority of myths, tribal traditions, descriptions of ceremonies and other topics are sung and learnt by means of these songs . . . [and] the status system is based solely on the individual's competence with regard to texts sung or at least recited in a ceremonial manner . . . Sometimes an individual will spend hours alone singing in this way with the sole purpose of learning a song correctly.

Some Cuna Indians of Colombia and Panama learn the basic framework of a melody with its text and then improvise from this.

(ii) Song texts. A salient feature of song texts among primitive Latin American Indians is the use of expressive syllables which, although once perhaps significant, have often lost all meaning in ordinary speech. The Wapishana, for example, repeat the syllables hai-ya; according to Farabee, their musical resources are extremely limited. Métraux wrote that the Aweikoma-Caingang sing meaningless syllables to a single note (Steward, i, p.468).

The texts are generally related to myths and beliefs. The shaman, man or woman, carries in his songs the full mythical heritage of the tribe. He must attract the good spirits and drive away evil ones in order to cure illnesses, help the sun overcome night, dissipate thunder, initiate youths into their adult lives, etc. Sometimes a shaman will attract adverse spirits to bring harm to someone. The shaman achieves his aim by means of complex ritual, the language of which may be incomprehensible to others. The Mapuche, for example, have songs with texts from which María Ester Grebe was able to reconstruct the already forgotten myths of the tribe.

Hunting and fishing give rise to three types of song: one before setting out, propitiatory in character; another to help catch or trap the prey; the third, a festive song of thanks. The first and last types are sung in groups, and the second type is sung individually, usually consisting of imitations of the hunted animal's cries and noises to attract it.

Songs to ensure the increase of plants and animals are found among sedentary tribes. Jívaro women, for instance, sing to the stems and souls of plants and to mother earth. Songs may also express events from daily life, as in a Taulipáng song from the Great Savanna of Venezuela, translated by Baltasar de Matallana (p. 661):

El arrendajo hizo su nido
el conoto hizo su nido
le cortaron la rama
fué el raton.

The mocking-bird made his nest
The conoto made his nest
His branch was cut
The mouse did it.

Some Indians sing work songs, as in an example collected by Hornbostel (1955–6, p.150) among Macuschí women:

u(a) lála pukatá
apí meliké
a 'yutón kétané

Go hunt the tortoise
little brother
I'm baking you a cake
grating the yucca

In certain tribes there is a kind of shaman who must not only communicate with spirits and gods, but also act as the community's intermediary and therefore recount his supernatural communications from them. To this end he uses responsorial songs, the texts of which include a refrain or simple repeated words. During the rainy season the Tapirapé (who belong to the Tupí-Guaraní group, according to Wagley and Galvão), sing in two groups; the first, led by a 'guide', introduces the verse while the second group (which includes women) sings the refrain (Steward, iii, 175).

Another type of song text, found among warlike peoples, recounts the exploits of chiefs and ancestors. The Abipón of Paraguay recite epic songs during victory celebrations, enumerating in a regulated number of verses, and in great detail, their past military deeds (Steward, i, 339). There are also songs dedicated to the dead. The Guajiro of the border between Venezuela and Colombia enact dramas in which each group is led by a minstrel who improvises a narration of events, adapting the text to a traditional melody.

There are poets among Indians of more advanced culture. The Incas called a poet or maker of verses haravec ('one who invents'). Examples of their poems were collected by the earliest chroniclers of Peru, The

Quechua and other Andean Indians sing verses differing in form and content from Spanish or European poetry, indicating a rich poetic tradition. This poetry circulates in oral, not written, form and is generally allied to music.

(iii) Musical resources and style. The salient characteristics of South American indigenous music as discussed by Ramón y Rivera (1966) serve as the basis of this analysis.

Acculturation has occurred, and continues to occur, among many peoples. It takes place in various ways: by the assimilation of musical elements from other Indian groups, without affecting the original style, as in the case of the Andean pentatonic scale, which was diffused to Araucania and the remotest groups in the Amazonian jungle; by contact with European musical elements which, when imposed rather than assimilated, as in the case of missionary music, often results in the gradual loss of indigenous musical idioms; by the gradual assimilation and adaptation of European, African and Arabic elements (this last in the case of Guajiro music, highly individual among the aboriginal styles in South America); and by the fusion of aboriginal and European elements to constitute a new musical style, as in the mestizo music of Bolivia, Peru and Ecuador, often equal in popularity to the Andean music of pre-Columbian origin.

Among the more primitive peoples, the three most common forms of expression are cries, recitations and cantillation. The Yanoama of Venezuela have a wide repertory of rhythmic cries which may pass momentarily into song, as in their *regateo* (bargaining) songs. They use cantillation in their 'welcome' songs: these consist of singing in imprecise pitch, interpolating imitations of barking. Cantillation is also common among the Yuruna of the Xingu river (they sing in loose unison with oscillations of a semitone), among the Shucarramai of Brazil (agriculturists) and among the Ona and Alacaluf of the extreme south (whose cantillation, characterized by imprecision of pitch, alternates with recitation on one, two or three principal notes). Strong accents may result in a periodic rhythm, or emphasis may be marked by an audible expiration on each note, as described by Hornbostel (1948, p.67). Guevara mentioned the *huepin* (emphatic speech) style among the Mapuche (p.287). Colbacchini and Albisetti noted recitation on a single note among the eastern Bororo of the Mato Grosso in Brazil (p.352).

The songs of primitive cultures are characterized by great freedom of intonation, in which both tempered and untempered intervals may occur, as well as quartertones and oscillations, sometimes moving over a single note or two or three notes, sometimes embracing a wide tessitura ranging from the very high range of women's falsetto to the lowest register of a bass voice. Heterophony, or the combination of independent voices singing a known melody in different versions and beginning at different points in time, may also be noted (ex.1). This manner of singing differs from the type of choral song in which everyone sings the same melody in unison, octaves or even parallel 5ths depending on the tessitura of the voices. Other types of singing are responsorial (solo and chorus) and dialogue (two solos) (*see* VENEZUELA, §II, ex.2).

Primitive song also makes free use of vocal resources and ornaments, such as various kinds of rising or falling

Ex.1 Music of the Motilones (Ramón y Rivera, 1965)

slurs or glissandos – a characteristic element of Mapuche song. The method of breathing is also important: the performer may fill his lungs with air and sing until out of breath (Mapuche, Guajiro) or he may aspirate certain syllables while singing (Shucarramai of Peru). According to Reichel Dolmatoff (1949–50, p.72):

The Kogi sing in a very particular manner. The singer aspirates forcefully and contracts the abdominal muscles, then lets the air escape slowly through the half-open lips, holding the note until the air in his lungs is entirely used up. Violently and noisily he aspirates once more and the breath is again spent, all this with great physical effort and muscular tension. Among the Kogi the art of singing consists of retaining the air for the longest possible period and sustaining a note or certain modulations of it for a long time without breathing again. Not only is the note varied, but the volume changes as well. Sometimes it is almost inaudible, growing slowly and then waning, depending on the rhythm of the song or the motion of the body accompanying it. Generally the song is nasalized and intoned in a high falsetto, which is characteristic not only of singing but of all ceremonial conversation. Eventually an octave descent from the falsetto is made, later to rise or sing the melody proper.

Intonation may rise gradually, as noted by Aretz among the Guahibo of Venezuela and Colombia, as far as the Orinoco (recordings in the Instituto Nacional de Folklore). Gusinde (p.918) showed a fluctuation in tonality among the Yámana. Conversely, a song may start each repetition in a lower register. Koch-Grünberg recorded examples of this type on wax cylinders among tribes between the Roraima and Orinoco rivers (copies of the recordings are in the archives of INIDEF in Caracas). The Angaité of Paraguay sing a long initial note; an elongation of the last sound of the last word in each sentence was noted by Guevara in Mapuche speeches (p.287). Another feature is the raising of the culminating notes of a theme in the second part of the song, as among the Yabuti of Mato Grosso (Schneider, p.159). According to Hornbostel rhythm may be faster among more 'lively' Indians (Yekuana) and slower among others (Taulipáng, Macuschí). He noted that 'tempo' of a people could be an important anthropological concept as yet unexploited (1955–6, p.15).

Songs that begin *pianissimo* with a gradual crescendo to *fortissimo* may be found among the Guahibo, Warao,

Tupinambá, Shipibo and Conibo. Another common dynamic resource, noted above in the discussion of rhythm, is the use of strong accents as practised by the Conibo, Macuschí, Taulipáng, Yekuana, Chaco and especially the Mataco, who are considered 'noisy' Indians.

When pitch is precise and organized into short motifs repeated many times with slight variations, the term 'melody' may be used. The Chaco of Argentina, Paraguay and Bolivia employ simple phrases in a tritonic scale (equivalent to a perfect major chord), in a tetratonic or pentatonic scale, or wandering around these notes without exactly defining the pitch (thus remaining closer to cantillation). Sometimes both precise and imprecise pitch may occur in a single song (Yuruna, Sanema and others). These songs do not use a simple repeated motif as in the Indian song of the extreme south; instead they consist of a sequence of lines or phrases which, beginning on a high pitch, descends with repetitions of notes and intervals until the lowest note is reached, as in the Warao song shown in ex.2.

Ex.2 *Hobisanuka*, Warao song; transcr. Ramón y Rivera (Suárez, 1968)

Scales may be considered 'fixed' when the entire repertory of a group belongs to a single scale type. This seems to occur among sedentary cultures. In South America three basic pre-Columbian scale types may be noted. The tritonic scale is used primarily by the descendants of the Diaguita-Calchaquí of Argentina and Chile, the Chanca of central Peru, the Aguaruna, Shipibo and Conibo of the Peruvian tropical forests and the Jívaro of the Peruvian and Ecuadorian mountains. This scale

Ex.3 *Wigudu*, war song, Jívaro Indians (I. Muriel, 1970)

usually consists of a major 3rd with a minor 3rd above, as in a major triad (ex.3), although the reverse is also found. The tetratonic scale is used primarily by the Indians of the Paraguayan Chaco (ex.4). The pentatonic scale, proper to the people of the Andean range from Jujuy in Argentina to Colombia, is strongly characterized by the preference for certain intervals and figures, fitted to specific rhythms and phrase forms, shown in ex.5. The pentatonic scale is widely diffused as far as Araucania, Calchaquí, Chaco and the jungles of Brazil, Bolivia, Peru, Ecuador, Colombia and Venezuela. But among the peoples in this area the scale appears sporadically, as a product of acculturation, and the melodies generally retain a style particular to each

Ex.4 *Canto angaité*, song of the Paraguayan Chaco; transcr. I. Aretz

Ex.5 *Huayno*, social dance, Bolivia; transcr. I. Aretz (Aretz, 1952)

Ex.6 Nambicuara melody (Halmos, 1965)

Ex.7 Bari song, transcr. Ramón y Rivera (Ramón y Rivera, 1965)

tribe. There are in addition many scales, natural and altered, which are not exclusive to one group.

Primitive dance, with the rhythm marked by the feet and by the use of rattles and rhythm sticks, may result in regular rhythmic emphasis, as among the Chaco, Wapishana and others. Sometimes polyrhythm results from rhythmic beats independent of the melody, as among the Amazonian Yuruna. But rhythm is often not regular, or even periodic, since indigenous song may be free in structure despite accents. A song may consist of stanzas which are clear and articulate but vary in the formation of the individual lines, as described by Halmos (1964, p.319) in Nambicuara melodies, which are clearly articulated, with cadences particularly marked either by trills from the flutes or by rhythmical barking cries from the voices (ex.6). In other groups, such as the Mapuche, phrases are clearly outlined and cadences marked by rising vocal glissandos or slight, also rising, instrumental ornaments. Ramón y Rivera (1965, p.157) noted in Bari music the beginnings of

rhythmic symmetry and semi-structured phrases that are variants of phrases with clearer structures (ex.7). Other typical rhythmic figures are small groupings of two or three beats (e.g. quavers) or similar figurations, constructing a short motif which is combined with others to constitute a true melodic phrase. This is repeated an indefinite number of times to accompany dances and songs.

(iv) *Genres*. A genre common among many Indian groups is the song imitating birds, often in order to attract them while hunting, sometimes to acquire their 'powers'. Among the Mataco and Pilagá of Argentina young men go to the forest seeking a revelation of song. A study of birdsongs from the tropical forests and continental south, comparing them with Indian songs, shows that birds sing precise pitches, some even giving the pentatonic scale (such as the tropical-forest *Nictibeo grisaceo*, which then sings beautiful variations enriching the scale). The Colombian Motilón commonly imitate the toucan and other birds. The Huanyam of Mato Grosso sing a mimetic song to communicate with birds.

The Yanoama of Venezuela imitate the croaking of frogs (associated with rain), sometimes accompanying the voices of real frogs. Among the Yukpa of Perija imitations of the roar of the mountain tiger, puma and deer are performed in direct relation to the powers the Indian wishes to acquire, whether to tame the natural and animistic world or simply to hunt the animals. Among the mimetic cries used in hunting and fishing are those of the Caliana and Camaracoto of the Venezuelan jungles, and the Chamacoco of the Gran Chaco, who also imitate storms. Dancers of the Carajá and Gavae in Araguaia, Brazil, sing a plaintive melody to celebrate luck in hunting, fishing or other events. This melody ends with cadences reminiscent of the roaring of beasts (Sekelj, p.102). Among the eastern Bororo song is preceded by cries imitating ancestral animals and the voices of the souls of the dead (Colbacchini and Albisetti, p.395).

Many peoples sing laments for the dead, but the lament proper alternates with sung motifs in which the *llorona* (lamenter) recalls episodes in the life of the dead man. Laments have been described and recorded among the Guaraní, the Shipibo of Peru, the Carajá and Gavae of Araguaia, Brazil, the Sanema, Piaroa, Yekuana, Piapoco, Warao and Guajiro of Venezuela and Colombia, and other groups.

Shamans, who acquire powers in trance, sing a form of cantillation or recitation accompanied by cries, calls, snorts, snoring sounds from the diaphragm, guttural modifications of the voice and other effects which may increase as the shaman believes he has made contact with spirits coming to his aid. This kind of singing (shown in ex.8) is usually accompanied by a maraca. There are instances among the Sanema, Yanoama, Shucarramai, Macuschí, Guajiro and Mapuche, but many other tribes also practise them. The accent in the vocal melody usually coincides with a strong maraca beat. Among the Fuegians the accent may fall on each quaver (Hornbostel, 1948, p.67).

(v) *Instruments*. In spite of some assertions to the contrary (Izikowitz, p.411) all South American Indians use some form of rhythmic accompaniment or elementary instrument: the feet, a stick beaten on the ground (stamping tubes), a branch shaken by the hand, or rattles

Ex.8 Curative song, Mapuche shaman's cantillation; transcr. I. Aretz (Aretz, 1970)

tied to the body in the form of bracelets and necklaces of seeds, claws, teeth and small shells, shaken rhythmically in the dance. According to Izikowitz, the most important indigenous instruments were flutes and rattles. Among different Brazilian tribes the sound of the bullroarer has an extramusical magical function. The wooden drums of the tropical-forest Indians may be combined in groups of four or five to send different signals. Songs and dances are accompanied by maracas, used by shamans everywhere; water-drums with a skin head tied over the opening and struck with a mallet, as played by the Chaco; wooden drums or concave plates containing pebbles which the Mapuche shamans shake and strike; and *tinyas* (double-headed frame drums) used by all the Andean tribes from Calchaquí to Colombia. Simple trumpets of clay, bark or bamboo are used as megaphones or voice disguisers, while conch shells are used for signals and sometimes for dance accompaniment. Trumpets of bone, bamboo or wood with resonators, polyglobular trumpets made from clay or gourd, and many other varieties are used by the Indians in their rites. Aerophones include flutes and whistles of bone, reed or wood, which may be combined in ensembles of two or more; ocarinas with finger-holes, often used to imitate birds; transverse flutes, with both ends stopped or opened; and transverse nose flutes without finger-holes. The *quena* (notched flute), with varying numbers of holes, is common in Bolivia and Peru, but is also found among other peoples of more primitive culture. Fipple flutes, which are usually made with a wax stopper, although wooden stoppers are also used, may be played alone or in groups of two or three and usually have finger-holes. The flutes of the Jujuy and Chaco in Argentina constitute an intermediate stage between notched and fipple flutes, since added to the notch there is a prolongation of the rim which is covered by the player's lips. Flutes and whistles with attached air ducts are also found (Izikowitz, pp.372ff).

Panpipes, according to Izikowitz, are found only in South America, the most northern example being the Cuna panpipe, and may be played singly or in pairs, organized in one or two rows of tubes either open at the bottom or stopped, and tuned in 3rds to form a complete scale. The instruments may be duplicated in larger sets, at one or two octaves, as in the *sicuri* 'bands' of the Aymara in northern Argentina, Bolivia and southern Peru. Although panpipes are most common in the Andean region, they are also found in Brazil and Venezuela, among descendants of the Caribs, and among the Panamanian Cuna (*see* PANAMA, fig.1) who play them in pairs. Idioglott and heteroglott clarinets, possibly of post-Columbian origin, are used by different tribes. The former appear in Chaco, northern Argentina, southern Bolivia and Guyana. The Guajiro play clarinets with four finger-holes and some with attached gourd bells. The heteroglott clarinets are used by the Warao and Waiwai.

Many of these instruments have magic significance: the stamping tubes and pellet-bell rattles used in initiation dances; the maraca, the outstanding shamanic instrument, containing pebbles which represent gods or spirits; the clarinet of the Brazilian Cozárini, identified with the serpent of evil; the bullroarers used by many Brazilian tribes to divert storms or when walking in the forest at night; and many other instruments used to drive away evil spirits.

Among the Mojo and Bauré of Bolivia the 'jaguar-shaman' plays a special flute to make contact with the jaguar whose strength and form he wishes to possess. The tribesmen dance around him all night until dawn, striking a drum. Also sacred are the bark trumpets of the Tupí-Witoto and the trumpets which the Piaroa divide into male and female. The huge *cuhay* trumpets of the Puinave sound like bellowing bulls, and are taken by women for devils (Wilbert, pp.107f). The Tucano shamans of the Rio Negro classify instruments according to size by zoological analogy, using names of animals and birds; they are all played to call on spirits to make the trees and plantations fruitful (Ypiranga Monteiro, p.37). The sacred instruments are usually kept in special huts, to which women have no access.

Every instrument is played according to a particular acquired technique. The wooden drums of the tropical-forest Indians are played in pairs so that each produces two sounds of different quality and pitch (Witoto of Colombia); or, as among the Tupí, the instruments may be strategically placed over a kilometre away from one another to transmit the vibrations, the second drum answering so that the first drum receives the echo (Steward, iii, 679).

In the simpler trumpets the hand regulates the escape of air to modulate pitch. But it is mostly in the instruments capable of producing melodies that the Indians use special techniques of performance or construction, such as partially stopping the finger-holes to obtain semitones and microtones; overblowing to obtain the harmonics in flutes and trumpets; shortening tubes and modifying or stopping holes with wax; narrowing the mouthpiece of a flute with a small leaf; or dividing the melody between two similar instruments, as on the panpipes (ex.9).

Pieces may be played in parallel 5ths or 4ths on two instruments; or diaphony may result, as shown in ex.10. A drone may be played to accompany a melody, as noted among the Amorua (Guahibo of Venezuela and Colombia). Various instruments are often played together in large ensembles, as among the Yanoama and Piaroa of Venezuela and the Mapuche of Chile.

Archives of South American Indian music may be

Ex.9 Panpipe melody (Vega, 1946)

Ex.10 Flute melody of the Kágaba Indians, Santa Marta, Colombia
(Bose, 1958)

found in Caracas (INIDEF) and the Archives of Traditional Music, Bloomington, Indiana.

2. CENTRAL AMERICA.

(i) *Introduction.* The oldest circum-Caribbean cultures are in the area extending from Panama to the lowlands of Nicaragua and Honduras; further north, descendants of the Mopán-Maya, the Kekchi, Poconchi, Quiché, Cackchiquel, Tzutujil, Pocomán and the Maya have undergone acculturation with *ladinos* (creoles). Other Panamanian and Central American aboriginal groups survive who have been influenced by western civilization, for example, the black Caribs of Honduras and the Miskito, who have mixed with both blacks and whites from North America and the Caribbean. The Guaymíe of Panama have a well-preserved indigenous culture, incorporating Maya-Quiché and Carib-Arawak traits.

Most research on Central American Indians has been archaeological, concentrating on musical instruments, dances portrayed in large murals of the Maya region, descriptions in post-Conquest chronicles and famous books of mythical narrative (compiled shortly after the Conquest) such as the *Popol Vuh* and the *Books of Chilam Balám.* Both contain important musical references. Information, including tape recordings, about surviving pre-Columbian cultures can be found in the institutions of the various countries.

The music of the Maya area was first studied and notated by Jesús Castillo in Guatemala and María de Baratta in El Salvador. In 1927 Franz Termer made cylinder recordings of oboe and drum music in the district of Huehuetenango in north-western Guatemala (transcribed by Wilhelm Heinitz; see Aretz, 1972). Henrietta Yurchenco has also published recordings from western Guatemala.

No study of Central American Indian music would be complete without research on pre-Columbian instruments, and the chronicles and codices that refer to music and dance. Understanding this music is impossible without knowing its myths and related rituals.

In the *Popol Vuh*, the book of the Quiché, an account is given of the divine origin of music, and of how it became a profession. Humbatz and Hunchogüen, spirits who preside over the arts, were great musicians and singers, and from earliest times the pipe and tabor were instruments that led the dance. The dance and theatre which were performed then survive in modern times among descendants of the Quiché and Maya. The *Books of Chilam Balám* by Chumayel (the magician who interpreted books and wishes of the gods) describe propitiatory ceremonies for the hunt in the month of Ceh ('deer') and ceremonies imploring the mercy of the sun during drought. The *Memorial of Tecpan Atitlán* (the place of origin of the Cackchiquele) mentions other dances such as those of the heart of the mountain Gaxanul and of the sacrifice of Tolcom. These dances survived the Conquest, since the chroniclers discuss them in conjunction with 'much music of melancholy flutes, kettledrums, pipes and conches ...', and with songs intoned in 'discordant and sad voices' (D. Vela: 'Danzas y primeras manifestaciones dramaticas del indígena maya-quiché', 1972). Pre-Conquest dance spectacles depicted mythological and historical themes, and contained 'garlands of words' and 'pantomimic gestures'.

Each ethnic group of the area retains music related to mythical beliefs, and particularly healing ceremonies. Healing music was the responsibility of the shaman, with or without participation of the social group, for example, the song for the dead and the lamentations of the Miskito.

Agricultural life has its own folklore expressed in songs, dances and ceremonies related to ancient myths. Among Guatemalan Indians 'the dance of the snake, in its ancient form, contains a myth of fertility, and is used to pray to the world god that the seed-time shall be favourable, and yield good harvests' (D. Vela: 'Música tradicional y folklórica en América central', 1972). The dance of *Quetzal* (basket dance) 'is also intimately connected with agrarian life, since it tells the story of the loss of the maize and the means used for its recovery' (Paret Limardo de Vela). In addition, 'these dances still preserve their autochthonous character', such as the stag dance, in which 'permission is sought of the world god for the hunt' (ibid, p.7).

(ii) *Pre-Columbian instruments.* Archaeological evidence reveals considerable difference between instruments earlier than the time of Columbus and those now in use. Pre-Columbian instruments include whistles and ocarinas in the shape of men, birds and animals, with holes for pitch modification. Ocarinas produce a variety of scales. They are found throughout the area, as well as to the north and south. But each culture had its own characteristic ceramic style. In the Brunca area on the Pacific coast to the south of Costa Rica, for example, the pottery as the well as the silver and gold artefacts show links with Chibcha items. A decorated cup-shaped ceramic drum of the Diquis tribe is similar to Talamanca and Chiriqui drums mentioned by Izikowitz. It also resembles drums of the Chorotega area in north-western Costa Rica and even African drums. The polychrome ceramics on the drum, a dark coffee colour, show stylized animals. Ocarinas have also been found in the Huetar area, at one time inhabited by southern Indians of circum-Caribbean origin. One in the shape of a lobster (preserved in the Museo Nacional de Costa Rica) shows the technical skills of these Indians. This ocarina has a duct and six holes permitting production of all chromatic pitches from c' to f''.

In Nicaragua, El Salvador, Honduras and Guatemala ocarinas and whistles were used to accompany prayers. The Tegucigalpa (Honduras) Instituto de Antropología e Historia has a large collection of Maya whistles discovered in the valley of Comayagua. In the shape of men, animals and birds, some have a duct and produce a great variety of sounds.

The pre-Cortesian frescoes at Bonampak provide valuable evidence about the playing of ancient Maya instruments, including playing a *tunkul* (vertical drum), scraping a turtle-shell, shaking gourd rattles and blowing twin trumpets, the conductor of this ensemble marking the beat with ocarina and rattle. Another fresco shows a ceremonial dancer representing a bird with extended wings and shaking a rattle in one hand. These instruments were all seen and described in chronicles after the Conquest. Landa (p.38) described small kettledrums struck with the hand; kettledrums made from hollowed wood, producing a heavy sound, and played with a long thin stick tipped with latex from a tree; long, thin trumpets of hollowed wood, with long, twisted gourds on the ends; whistles made from deer bones; large conches; reed flutes; and a turtle-shell struck with the palm of the hand, producing a lugubrious sound. These instruments are still used by isolated groups.

(iii) 20th-century aboriginal music. The music of the Cuna, Chocó, Guaymíe, Guatuso, Cubécar, Miskito and Aguacatán has undergone varying degrees of acculturation. The Cuna Indians inhabit islands off the Atlantic coast of Panama; others live in mainland jungles along the rivers. Their healing songs are in a secret language, and the *inatuledis* (healers) use *nuchu* (wooden idols). Illness, they believe, is caused by loss of the *purba* (soul), which the *nia* (Devil) usurps. If healing fails, they turn for help to the *nele* (seer). Other Cuna songs are used for events of the life cycle: birth, girls' puberty, marriage and death. Garay gave an account of his visit to the Cuna of San Blas. Other Cuna were recorded in 1924 by Frances Densmore in Washington, where they were taken for an exhibition. Densmore found that the Cuna musicians were professionals, playing for money on demand. Apprentices learnt basic melodies and words, and then improvised, making no attempt to sing every rendition in the same way. Other musicians were amateur and did not sing in public. Women sang to accompany their daily tasks or the men's plantation work. Densmore also learnt that in Cuna villages the chief, the shaman and the musicians were the most important people. Their voices, she said, are hard, 'with a pinched, forced quality not pleasing to our ears and impossible to describe. It is an artificial tone . . . There are no contrasts in volume' (p.4); and they rarely accent a note.

The Cuna possess a rich musical culture, shown in the variety of skilfully constructed instruments and in the wide range of song melodies. Most melodies transcribed by Garay are descending, and use a scale of three, four or five pitches (such as A–G–F–E–D). According to Densmore, Cuna intonation is never precise. (She found quarter-tones in one healing song, but not in others.)

Instrumental pieces are rhythmically varied. Musical instruments include panpipes (*camburgüe*), played in pairs, the two performers sitting face to face. The Cuna of Uala also use paired aerophones, both male and female *tolo* and male and female *süpe*. These flutes have a feather-tube mouthpiece fixed to the flute with black wax. According to Garay the Indians of San Blas played on the four-holed female *tolo* 'smooth sounds that cover more than an octave in range', and the performer 'sought with his fingers, placed over the holes of the pipe, to achieve effects of vibrato similar to those obtained by the violinist by movement of his finger on the strings'. The male *tolo* is similar to the female, but has only one hole and produces two heavy sounds that function as a kind of harmonic pedal. The Kantule of the archipelago of San Blas also play maracas and the *kamu*, a type of flute that can be blown as a flute or as a trumpet. Cuna Indians wear a great assortment of necklaces, including ones made of pelican bones, each representing a flute.

In the 20th century the traditional culture of the Cuna in the native reserve of El Bayano survives and, according to Tejeira Jaen, the Cuna of San Blas are actively concerned with preservation of their folklore. From 1970 onwards they have organized competitions, including the Nuga Cope-Camburgüe (drinking from the calabash cup and playing on the flute). Tejeira Jaen (pp.141f) described the dances and the ensembles as follows:

> The musical group is usually made up of six men and six women, who play six pairs of maracas and six panpipes, called *camu, cambur,* or *camburgüe.*
>
> Besides the instruments that appear in the folkloric ensembles at Ustupo, there are others which are played within the Cuna settlements, but which do nót appear in the dance ensembles of the San Blas district. These include the following: the *tolo,* a long panpipe with a pelican feather at one end; the *tede,* an instrument made from the bone of an animal that digs the ground, and from whose bone, placed inside a *camu,* music is produced; the *pati,* made from the shell of a box turtle in the shape of a hoop; and the *suara,* a long flute with a single tube.
>
> The dances are all performed in a similar manner. The couples form an irregular circle and cross past each other, bending their knees as they leap, playing the flute or maracas.

The dances include *Puna lola* ('I am a girl'), *Ulukukupuriwat* (children's toy boats), *Tule machi* ('Son of a Cuna'), *Tule machi purriwat* (imitating the young Cuna playing the flute), *Tule machi kuichi* ('young Cuna dancing'), *Kulikama guadargae* (explaining the myth of the origin of dance), *Neten neten* ('No, no'), *Mugamboe* (a lament) and *Nuga werque* (for the fight against evil spirits). The Cuna also sing songs inspired by the songs and flight of birds.

The Panamanian Chocó Indians come from the area adjacent to the Chocó of Colombia, and live along most of the rivers that flow into the Gulf of Darien. They are Perichibcha in origin but not in language. They believe that the soul is stolen by powers of the lower world and that the songs of the witch-doctor can restore the soul to its body.

The Guaymíe derive from the Maya-Quiché and the Caribe-Arahuaca. They inhabit a large area in the province of Chiriquí, Panama, and extend from the Pacific coast, southern Costa Rica. Guaymíe perform on many instruments, often in orchestral ensembles which accompany them as they process to the site of their athletic games. According to Garay (p.118), their instruments include ocarinas with two or three holes, vertical bamboo flutes, turtle-shells, bulls' horns, bell-shaped trumpets, seashells and drums made from tree-trunks. At a festival Garay heard an Indian play the *toleró* with deep feeling. The *toleró* (vertical reed flute) has five holes; six principal pitches are produced, as well as harmonics obtained by overblowing. Another vertical flute, the *ñora kragrogó*, is made of deer bone, has only four holes, but also produces six pitches and their corresponding harmonics, the sixth being obtained by the simultaneous opening of two holes. The Guaymíe perform both instrumental and vocal music, including dance music, love-songs and work songs. Songs occasionally use heterophony. Guaymíe also play the *dobo drué* (clay flute) at funerals.

Costa Rican Indian groups include the Guatuso or Maleku, who live to the north in the province of Alajuela; the Nicoya (Chorotega), in the province of Guanacaste; the Cubécar, who live between the Atlantic and Pacific near the centre of the country; the Bribri, who mix with the Cubécar, living more to the south, and with the Quitirrisi from the province of San José; the Boruca or Brunka; and the Térraba, who live in Puntarenas. More mobile Indian groups are the Teribe and the Guaymíe, who come from Panama, and the Miskito, or Sambos Mosquitos, from Nicaragua.

Guatuso Indian music has been recorded by Doris Stone and transcribed and analysed by Ramón y Rivera (1969). The repertory includes ritual ceremonial songs, funeral songs and laments, work songs, and songs for enjoyment and for dancing. Instruments include reed pipes and drums, played with the hand (similar to African drums).

Cubécar Indians inhabit the valley of the Chirripó river and also the neighbouring countryside along the Caribbean. Jones divided Chirripó music into six categories: *jawa*, songs of *sukia* (shamans) in special dialect; *bulsiqué*, dance-songs that accompany the chicha festival held when a new hut is completed (*chicha* is a strong drink); *dule tie*, drum music performed by immigrants from Talamanca where these drums were very popular; *dzaba pable*, tender lullabies sung by mothers and grandmothers; *dulacleiwa cse tse*, lovesongs (joyful and varied, but very secretive); and work songs, sung by women as they hull maize or by men at work in the fields. Cubécar song style is known as 'terrace' style, descending from a high to a low pitch. Scales are often tetratonic, sung with a strident, nasal tone, irregular rhythm and accent. But each category, according to Jones, has its own particular characteristics.

Approximately 5000 Bribri Indians live in the region of Lower Talamanca, south of Costa Rica. The Bribri language is related to the Chibcha tongue. Doris Stone has recorded their music, including maize songs, water-jaguar hunting-songs, cradle songs, love-songs and dance-songs.

Miskito culture has been studied in the region lying between the Patuca and Wans Coco (or Segovia) rivers on the east coast of Honduras. Miskito music reflects their acculturation with North Americans and with negroes from the islands of Belice and the Caribbean. *Tyun* songs, for example, are now sung with guitar accompaniment. *Inanka* (laments) and *sukya* songs (*sukya lawana*), however, are sung in connection with traditional myths and their corresponding rites. Because of the impact of Christianity, especially from Moravia,

some Miskito dances are acculturated; for example, the *Krismis* (Christmas) dance. Traditional dances are also preserved, such as the *Kati tilwan* (full moon dance).

The indigenous peoples of Guatemala speak 23 languages and dialects belonging to the Chalchitec, Maya, Quiché and Caribe families (there are others still unclassified). Indigenous groups have combined traditional culture with outside influences. They maintain some aboriginal rites, performed by magicians, soothsayers and priests, together with Christian practices as imposed by Catholic and Protestant missionaries.

Some dances of pre-Columbian origin survived the Conquest in new forms: the *Rabinal achí* or *Tun* dance, basket dance (*Quetzal*), snake dance (which includes à fertility rite) and the stag dance (symbolizing the sun and vitality). Other dances are of post-Columbian origin but contain indigenous elements, for instance, the dance of the Conquest. Others are predominantly European, such as the dance of Moors and Christians and the Twelve Peers of France. McArthur explained that the Aguacatán Indian dancers from near Huehuetenango believe that 'only death awaits the one who does not dance, because the *mam* [religious leader] burns our names in the copal fire' (p.499). They believe furthermore that the dead who are imprisoned are liberated by the complex rite of the dance. Every fourth year, in the course of their great annual festival Nim Kiej, some Aguacatán Indians dance the *Tz'unum* (sparrow dance), which the *ladinos* (creoles) know as the *Tum* or *Tun* dance. (The *tun* is the *teponaztli* drum used by Maya and Aztec groups.) Another group from Aguacatán, the Muxtec, perform the same dance, but one year later, to prolong the lives of the dancers and their families. The characters involved indicate that the modern dance is post-Columbian, but the origins of the dance are reputedly much older. The dance is performed to the accompaniment of *tun*, trumpet and turtle-shell, the trumpet leading the dance (see McArthur).

In San Antonio Ilotenango, the Quiché Indians play the marimba and the *chinchin* (gourd rattle) to accompany the snake dance, and the pipe and drum to accompany the stag dance. In San Juan Ixcoy, Huehuetenango, inhabited by Mam-speaking Indians, the *Tilux* and the *Tun* dances are accompanied by polytonal marimbas; and in Cubulco, Lower Verapaz, there are a variety of dances, including the dance of the Conquest, with Kekchi text. African marimbas are now common in Guatemala and other countries of Central America; they are played both by young Indians and by *ladinos*, even at traditional festivals. Marimba pieces that have been recorded show no traces of pre-Columbian music, but there is indigenous music played on a European trumpet.

Music of the Maya area, and instruments used for its performance, are sometimes Spanish or European and sometimes purely indigenous. Indigenous instruments include the *teponaztli* (two-keyed slit-drum), the *huehuetl* (cylindrical upright drum), reed whistles, clay ocarinas, trumpets and turtle-shells played with antlers (*ayotl*).

(iv) Changes in aboriginal music. The aboriginal musical repertory has incorporated foreign musical forms, such as children's songs, entertainment songs and new dances; traditional instruments (in Central America at least) have become interspersed with drums and marimbas of African origin and guitars, flutes, oboes, trumpets and timbrels from Europe, particularly Spain.

Indigenous ethnic groups all continue to use their own language in songs. Often the Indians translate texts from the surrounding culture into their own dialect; at other times, they preserve in their ritual songs a language not in general use in the group (as, for example, among the Cuna).

The disappearance of aboriginal music is due to several factors. These include the destruction of musical instruments at the time of the Conquest, and also of the codices containing the cultural history of the community (as in the case of the Maya area). Moreover, prohibitions and penalties were imposed by the conquerors on the playing of all music of pre-Hispanic origin. This situation is confirmed by many written accounts, the most important and best known being that of Landa. Missionaries taught new music and introduced new instruments, and ample evidence of missionary influence is found in the living oral tradition; the oboes and medieval trumpets still in use in different parts of Latin America, for example, and the flutes with wooden keys are clearly of European origin. Furthermore, as a result of close daily contact with black slaves and many other immigrants musical acculturation occurred. Examples of acculturation include the adoption of the African marimba, both the name and the instruments, the *caramba* or *quijongo* (a large musical bow), certain drums and many instruments of the Spanish guitar family. Music played on these adopted instruments is neither aboriginal nor African. The music for flutes and oboes used in dramatic representations is largely Spanish; but occasionally one can hear melodic shapes or phrases of pre-Columbian origin. Indians who lived in isolation from the Europeans continued to perform traditional ceremonies with traditional music using flutes, kettledrums, pipes and conches.

The process of the Conquest was peaceful in some areas. Paret Limardo de Vela (quoting José Milla) described how the Dominicans managed to conquer the province of Tezulutlán (now Verapaz) by teaching four Indians the Catholic religion, using songs in Quiché. The music was European, but the accompaniment was provided by aboriginal instruments, which spread abroad 'that strange music ... accompanied by the rough teponaztle'. Acculturation, therefore, has varied from group to group, resulting in the rich diversity of musical styles of Central American Indians in the 20th century.

BIBLIOGRAPHY

SOUTH AMERICA

T. Guevara: *Antropolojía araucana*, i: *Historia de la civilización de Araucanía* (Santiago de Chile, 1898)

M. Gusinde: *Die Selk'nam*, i: *Die Feuerland Indianer* (Mödling, 1931)

K. G. Izikowitz: *Musical and Other Sound Instruments of the South American Indians* (Göteborg, 1934/R1970)

F. Baltasar de Matallana: 'La música indígena taurepán', *Boletín latinoamericano de música*, iv (1938), 649

P. A. Colbacchini and P. C. Albisetti: *Os Boróros orientais* (Brasil, 1942)

C. Vega: *Los instrumentos musicales aborígenes y criollos de la Argentina* (Buenos Aires, 1946)

R. Pineda Giraldo: 'Aspectos de la Magia en la Guajira', *Revista del Instituto etnológico nacional*, iii/1 (1947), 1–163

E. M. von Hornbostel: 'The Music of the Fuegians', *Ethnos*, xiii (1948), 61–102

T. Sekelj: 'Excursión a los indios del Araguaia (Brasil)', *Runa*, i (1948), 97

G. Reichel Dolmatoff: 'Los Kogi', *Revista del Instituto etnológico nacional*, iv/1–2 (1949–50), 1–319

I. Aretz: 'Músicas pentatónicas en Sudamérica', *Archivos venezolanos de folklore*, i/2 (1952), 283

M. Schneider: 'Contribución a la música indígena de Matto Grosso, Brasil', *AnM*, vii (1952), 159

J. Baumgartner: 'Apuntes de un médico-indigenista sobre los Piaroa de Venezuela', *Boletín indigenista venezolano*, ii (1954), 111

E. M. von Hornbostel: 'La música de los Makuschí Taulipang y Yekuana', *Archivos venezolanos de folklore*, iii/4 (1955–6), 137

F. Bose: 'Die Musik der Chibcha und ihrer heutigen Nachkommen', *International Archives of Ethnography*, xlviii (1958), 149–98

L. P. Ramón y Rivera: 'Música indígena de Venezuela', *Boletín del Instituto de folklore*, iii (1960), 333

G. Reichel Dolmatoff: 'Notas etnográficas sobre los indios del Chocó', *Revista colombiana de antropología*, ix (1960), 73–158

M. Ypiranga Monteiro: 'Cariamã, Pubertätsritus der Tucano-Indianer', *Zeitschrift für Ethnologie*, lxxxv (1960), 37

J. H. Steward, ed.: *Handbook of South American Indians* (New York, 1963)

I. Halmos: 'Melody and Form in the Music of the Nambicuara Indians, Mato Grosso, Brazil', *SM*, vi (1964), 317–56

———: 'Das Verhältnis von Instrument, Stimmung und Tonart in Langsflöten-Melodien der Nambikuara-Indianer', *Abhandlungen und Berichte des Staatlichen Museums für Völkerkunde Dresden*, xxiv (1965), 49

L. P. Ramón y Rivera: 'Música de los motilones', in O. d'Empaire: *Introducción al estudio de la cultura Barí* (diss., Central U. of Venezuela, Caracas, 1965), 156

———: 'Introducción a un curso de etnomusicología', *Folklore americas*, xxvi/1 (1966), 9

J. Wilbert: *Indios de la región Orinoco-Ventuari* (Caracas, 1966)

M. M. Suárez: *Los Warao: indígenas del delta del Orinoco* (Caracas, 1968)

D. de Barandiarán: 'La fiesta del pijiguao entre los indios "Waikas"', *Natura*, xxxvi (1969), 8

I. Aretz: 'Cantos araucanos de mujeres', *Revista venezolana de folklore*, 2nd ser., no.3 (1970), 73–104

I. Muriel: *Beitrag zur Musikkultur der Jíbaro-Indianer in Ekuador* (diss., U. of Leipzig, 1970)

CENTRAL AMERICA

D. de Landa: *Relation des choses de Yucatan* (Paris, 1864) [with Sp. text]

F. Densmore: *Music of the Tule Indians of Panama* (Washington, DC, 1926)

N. E. Garay: *Tradiciones y cantares de Panama: ensayo folklórico* (Brussels, 1930)

W. Heinitz: 'Chirimía- und Tambór-Phonogramme aus Nordwest-Guatemala', *Vox*, xix/1–2 (1933), 4

K. G. Izikowitz: *Musical and Other Sound Instruments of the South American Indians* (Göteborg, 1934/R1970)

J. Castillo: *Música Maya-Quiché* (Quezaltenango, 1941)

A. Prado Quesada: *Apuntes sintéticos sobre la historia y producción musical de Costa Rica* (San José, Costa Rica, ?1941)

R. González Sol: *Fiestas cívicas, religiosas y exhibiciones populares de El Salvador* (San Salvador, 1945, 2/1947)

J. Fonseca: 'La música folklórica de Costa Rica', *Revista de estudios musicales*, i/3 (1950), 75

M. de Baratta: *Cuzcatlán típico: ensayo sobre etnofonía de El Salvador* (San Salvador, 1952)

H. Yurchenco: 'Taping History in Guatemala', *American Record Guide*, xxv/4 (1958), 228, 282

L. Paret Limardo de Vela: 'Folklore musical de Guatemala', *Congreso internacional de folklore: Buenos Aires 1960*, no.176

M. A. Guzman Anleu: *Danzas de Guatemala*, Folklore de Guatemala, i (Guatemala City, 1965)

R. Toledo Palomo: *Los bailes del Tum en los siglos XVI y XVII*, Folklore de Guatemala, i (Guatemala City, 1965)

G. Aguilar Machado: 'La ocarina huetar y su técnica musical', *Artes letras*, i/10 (1969), 25

L. F. Ramón y Rivera: 'Formaciones escalísticas en la etnomúsica latinoamericana', *YIFMC*, i (1969), 200

I. Aretz: 'Colecciones de cilindros y trabajos de musicología comparada realizados en Latinoamérica durante los primeros treinta años del siglo XX', *Revista venezolana de folklore*, 2nd ser., no.4 (1972), 49

H. S. McArthur: 'Los bailes de Aguacatán y el culto de los muertos', *América indígena*, xxxii/2 (1972), 491

E. Tejeira Jaen: 'El festival de danzas Cunas en Ustupo', *América indígena*, xxxii/1 (1972), 139

D. Vela: 'Danzas y primeras manifestaciones dramáticas del indígena maya-quiché', *América indígena*, xxxii/2 (1972), 515

———: 'Música tradicional y folklórica en América central', *Guatemala indígena*, vii/1–2 (1972), 227

R. Velasquez and T. Agerkop: *Charla sobre la Mosquitia: la OEA en Honduras* (1973) [unpublished lecture]

R. Galbis: 'Métodos de curación entre los Cunas y los Otomí: estudio comparativo', *América indígena*, xxxiv/4 (1974), 939

P. K. Jones: 'Una breve descripción de la cultura musical Chirripó', *América indígena*, xxxiv/2 (1974), 427

E. Lopez de Piza: 'Xirinachs de Zent, una comunidad Cabécar de Costa Rica', *América indígena*, xxxiv/2 (1974), 439

B. and J. Nietschmann: 'Cambio y continuidad: los indígenas Rama de Nicaragua', *América indígena*, xxxiv/4 (1974), 905

II. Folk music

1. South America: (i) Songs (ii) Dances (iii) The Andean area (iv) Afro-Hispanic folk music. 2. Central America and the Caribbean.

1. SOUTH AMERICA.

(i) *Songs.* Examples of independent folksong genres are relatively few in South American folk music since, in most of the repertory, song is used as an accompaniment to dancing. Throughout the continent there are many types of song that derive from the old Spanish *romance*, a narrative song form dating back to the early Renaissance, typically based on eight-syllable lines and four-line stanzas. Under different local names *romances* have been preserved, sometimes in their original form (as in Colombia) and sometimes with significant variations. The *copla*, a ballad type derived from the *romance*, is common throughout Colombia, the Andean countries and Argentina. *Romances* and *coplas* usually describe in a lyrical manner famous historical events of a region or episodes of everyday life. Other folksongs, such as the Argentinian and Chilean *tonadas* and *tonos*, have maintained other old Spanish literary forms. The *glosa* and the *décima*, for example, consist of two parts, the first a quatrain which sets the basic subject, the second a development of it in a stanza of ten octosyllabic lines. This structure is found in Chilean, Peruvian, Ecuadorian and Colombian *décimas*, Argentinian *estilos* and *cifras*, and in many other genres, such as the *guabina* of Colombia or the *romances* and *xácaras* of Brazil. The classical rhyme scheme of the Spanish *décima*, *abbaaccddc*, prevails in most of the types of folksong mentioned. Ex.11 shows two versions

Ex.11 *La esposa difunta o la Aparición*, two versions (Romero, 1952)

of a traditional *romance* known in Lima, Peru. Entitled *La esposa difunta o la Aparición*, its origin has been traced to 16th-century Spain. The regular two- and four-bar phrases and their isometric structure are characteristic of Spanish folksong. Literary versions of this same *romance* have been collected in New Mexico, California, Mexico, Nicaragua, Cuba, the Dominican Republic, Puerto Rico, Venezuela, Ecuador and several provinces of Argentina, which attests to the wide diffusion of the *romance* tradition in Latin America.

Iberian folk melodies still sung in Spain and Portugal are, however, rarely found in Latin America. Children's songs are the notable exceptions, for many remain basically the same in both areas. While texts are frequently Iberian in origin, tunes sung in Latin America were generally either composed in Latin America in the styles brought from Europe, or brought from Europe with the Conquest, but so changed by the process of oral tradition that the tunes originally related to them in Europe can no longer be recognized (or perhaps it is the European tunes that have undergone change). This situation is not identical in the minority groups living in South America – Germans, east Europeans, Italians – for although they have preserved many songs brought from Europe, they have not created much new material in traditional styles.

A recent study by Grebe (1967) of the Chilean *verso*, a traditional genre of sung poetry, has shown that it has stylistic similarities to Spanish medieval and Renaissance genres (*cantigas*, *villancicos*), especially in its modality and cadences. Such archaic elements are also found in Brazil in some types of folk melody associated with the *desafio* (literally 'challenge'), with texts consisting of questions and answers, performed by two singers, often having an antiphonal musical structure with instrumental guitar interludes between the vocal sections. The most common literary form of *desafio* in Brazil is the six-line heptasyllabic stanza, common in Portuguese popular poetry. The *desafio* and a related form, the *embolada*, together with praise songs (*louvações*), form the bulk of the folksong repertory of northeastern Brazil. This particular folk music tradition, known in Brazil as the *caboclo* tradition (with traits inherited from the Portuguese and some local Amerindian cultures), consists mainly of modal melodies, frequently the F and G modes. Song genres similar to the *desafio* are found widely in South America, variously called *contrapunto* and *cifra* in Argentina, *payas* in Chile, or *porfias* in Venezuela.

Lyrical love-songs abound in South American folk music. Known as *tonadas* in the Spanish-speaking countries and *toadas* in Brazil, they are generally in four-, five- or ten-line stanzas, sometimes incorporating a refrain. The Argentine *estilo* will serve as an example. According to Aretz (1952) the *estilo* incorporated two melodic ideas, the 'theme' and a somewhat faster strain known as *alegre*. The form is ternary, *ABA* (see ex.12). In the Cuyo province of Argentina, as well as in Chile, the *estilo* is known as *tonada*, and in the northern provinces it is called *verso* or *décima*. The *estilo* is also common in Uruguay.

An interesting example of the sources and development of folksong in South America is the Brazilian *modinha*. *Modinha* became part of the Brazilian folk music repertory only in the latter part of the 19th century, when it gradually lost its original Italian operatic flavour and became a simple sentimental song. As it was popularized its structure became simpler (*ABACA*, or a refrain and a stanza). With its art music origin, the *modinha* illustrates the transplanting of European musical culture into the popular music of Brazil.

A fairly important body of folksongs comes from popular religious customs accompanying the liturgical calendar of the Catholic church. Here again, the repertory shows a close relationship with songs of the Iberian peninsula. The hymns and songs of praise brought to the New World by Spanish missionaries are known as *alab-*

Ex.12 *Estilo* (Aretz, 1952)

Ex.13 *Aguinaldo*. Venezuela (Aretz, 1962)

lancicos and *aguinaldos* are in 2/4, 6/8 or 3/4, with regular phrases of two- and four-bar lengths, major and minor mode or bimodality, melodies in parallel 3rds with a range not exceeding a 6th, almost total absence of modulation and chromaticism, and syllabic setting of the text. All these features are also found in the Spanish Christmas repertory. But most *aguinaldos* differ from the Spanish villancico in their complex rhythmic accompaniment, provided by an ensemble consisting of *cuatro* (a small four-string guitar) and various percussion instruments, based on the alternation of binary and ternary rhythmic figures common in mestizo dances such as the *merengue*. The melodies of the Venezuelan *aguinaldos* tend also to be more syncopated than the Spanish villancico. Ex.13 shows some of the features of the *aguinaldo*.

ados and *alabanzas*. Most of them are prevailingly modal and follow the traditional pattern of hymn singing, with an alternation of *estribillo* ('refrain'), sung by a chorus, and *copla* ('stanza'), sung by a soloist. In the Chocó province of Colombia the *alabado* is also used at wakes to pay tribute to the dead person, the text being an improvised account of his life. Most religious folksongs are associated with the Christmas season. The traditional Spanish villancico has developed into many folksong genres, such as *aguinaldo*, *adoración*, *coplas de Navidad* and *esquinazo*, in the various countries of Latin America. While most of them obviously relate to their Spanish counterpart, they also show many mestizo or creole characteristics. For example, the Venezuelan vil-

(*ii*) *Dances*. Many Latin American Christmas songs are associated with popular dramatizations of the Nativity and the journey of the Three Kings, as well as with processions of various kinds. Such festivities, of which dance forms an integral part, are found throughout the continent and are variously called *posadas*, *auto sacramental* or *pastoris*.

Rituals associated with the Roman Catholic feasts of the Lord and the commemoration of saints' days often constitute cycles of syncretic feasts. Carnival is the most popular. Many folkdances and folksongs belong to the summer and winter feast cycles (such as St John's day or feasts of the Virgin), in which there is often syncretism with African deities. In Brazil, for example, there are many dramatic dances with a religious central subject. Most of them appeared during the colonial period as a result of Hispanic religious instruction. The *congada*, a dramatic dance known throughout Brazil, combines elements of the popular religious theatre of the Iberian peninsula with Afro-Brazilian traditions and customs. The songs accompanying the cortège, which is led by the main characters, show traits typical of Portuguese folksongs.

Many Latin American secular folk and popular dances originated in the Iberian peninsula and, while they have undergone considerable changes in the New World, choreographic traits specific to much Spanish folkdance remain, such as shoe-tapping and finger-snapping. An example is the Argentinian *chacarera* whose exact origin is still not known. The name of the dance is apparently derived from *chacra* ('farm'; from Quechua *chagra*: 'cornfield'); thus it is believed that the *chacarera* was probably created by the farmers of the plains in the province of Buenos Aires, although it is performed in almost all Argentine provinces. The choreography includes foot-stamping and finger-snapping. Spanish ancestry is shown among other features in the hemiola rhythm (alternation of 6/8 and 3/4 metres) of the instrumental introduction, which is generally six or eight bars long. The *chacarera* also appears in exclusively instrumental versions; the instruments used are harp, guitar in *punteado* ('picked') style, violin or accordion, with a drum accompaniment.

One of the most important creole dances of the Argentine countryside is the *gato*. Not only is it widespread but other dances derive from it. Its Spanish heritage is reflected in dance figures which include shoe-tapping steps performed by women, who lift their long skirts to show the agility of their foot movements, and the *escobillado* (or *escobilleo*), a very fast foot movement performed by men, consisting of swinging one foot after the other, scraping the ground. The *gato* is accompanied by a guitarist who also sings. The Spanish guitar technique, *guitarra rasgueada* (strumming), is used here consistently in 6/8 metre. Picked guitar is used only in the prelude and interludes. The rhythmic formula of the *gato* alternates between 6/8 and 3/4 metres (the hemiola rhythm again). Generally, the sung *gato* has four melodic phrases, repeated with minor variants in the following order (prelude and interludes are instrumental): prelude, *AABB*, interlude, *AB*, interlude, *CD*. When it is sung in duet parallel 3rds prevail, a characteristic of Iberian folk polyphony.

The *zamba* is one of the many Argentine couple-dances. Like the *aires* and the *lorencita*, it is a *danza de pañuelo* ('scarf dance'), the use of the scarf having symbolic significance. The history of the *zamba* is obscure. An old colonial Peruvian dance known as *zamacueca* or *zambacueca* (now called *marinera*) was introduced into Argentina during the first half of the 19th century. The *zamba* and the *cueca* both derive from the *zambacueca*. The *cueca* became one of the most familiar dances of Chile and Bolivia. In the western provinces of Argentina the name *chilena* was used to designate the Chilean *cueca*. Thus the three names *zamba*, *cueca* and *chilena* now have specific meanings. Choreographically, *zamba* and *cueca* differ considerably. While the basic figures are similar, the *cueca* allows extemporized shoe-tapping, whereas the *zamba* adheres to more traditional figures. Musically, both dances have the same general form and

prevailing 6/8 metre but have different melodic types.

In older *zamba* melodies major and minor 3rds often alternate; the melodic minor scale also appears. More recent melodies are in the major mode, as are *cueca* melodies, which tend, however, to end on the 5th degree of the scale. In rhythmic structure the *cueca* differs intrinsically from the *zamba* and, while the *zamba* is mainly instrumental, the *cueca* is essentially vocal.

Many Brazilian folksongs and folkdances also retain European elements. For example, the round-dances used in the fandangos of southern Brazil are often of Portuguese derivation. These fandangos are popular rural revelries in which regional dances such as the *tirana*, *tatu*, *balaio* and *recortado* are performed. A frequent feature of these dances is shoe-tapping; another, in the state of Rio Grande do Sul, is the use of castanets. Thus fandango was transformed in Brazil into a generic term, which suggests that the Spanish dance of the same name was once popular there, as it was in Portugal. The numerous designations of these dances derive from the song texts. The singing, in which stanza and refrain alternate and which is always in parallel 3rds or 6ths, is typically performed by the guitar players.

(iii) The Andean area. In Bolivia, Peru and Ecuador Spanish culture was influenced by Indian culture. Spanish and Indian styles combined throughout the area of the former Inca empire (in contrast with the lack of musical acculturation between English and Indian styles in North America). In his study of instruments used by the Incas and their predecessors, Stevenson (1968) claimed that the Andean peoples had, at the time of the Conquest, the most refined musical culture of the American continent. Not only did they play five- and six-hole flutes with unequal finger-holes, 14- and 15-tube *antaras* (panpipes made of clay), double-row panpipes and transverse flutes, but also their instrument making shows their intent to use predetermined pitches. In the Andean area most villages and towns (even in the Spanish-speaking villages) now have a traditional music with Indian elements. The widespread use of pre-Columbian instruments, such as the panpipe (called *sicu* by the Aymara and *antara* by the Quechua) and vertical flute (*pincollo*, *pincullo*), attests to that influence. The ubiquitous *quena* (end-blown notched flute) is used together with European types of drums in processions for Catholic saints, and in social dances, together with post-Columbian indigenous instruments such as the *charango*. In Andean music, elements of Indian origin are difficult to separate from those of the European tradition. Acculturation began in the 16th century and was fostered by Catholic missionaries, who realized that the survival of Christianity depended in part on its absorption of native elements. The elements of the two cultures combined inseparably. Tunes are essentially European but often have much repetition and use tetratonic and pentatonic scales. The introduction of diatonic scales in modern times required adjustments in instrument making, and now six- and seven-hole *quenas* are more common than those with three or four holes. In addition, European string instruments (violin, guitar, lute, harp) have influenced highland Indian music. For example, European harmonic patterns have been added to a music that was probably essentially monodic.

Out of some 200 Quechua melodies collected in the highlands and analysed, the majority have a descending progression and are in the anhemi-pentatonic scale G–E–D–C–A, where the highest note tends to act as a dominant. Mestizo melodies also abound, many of them based in part on the European diatonic scale. But all tunes retain some modal features, a prevailing descending tendency, large intervals and few modulations. Rhythmically, Indian traits also prevail. Duple metres, with binary and ternary divisions, are most frequent, especially a dactylic formula for percussion accompaniment. Syncopated melodic lines are also common in song genres, such as the *yaraví*, and in dance types, such as the *huayno*. Syncopation is particularly important (ex.14). The same syncopation occurs in most Afro-

Ex.14 Rhythmic formulas of Andean music (d'Harcourt, 1925)

American music of Latin America but here the resulting effect is different, partly because the first note of each beat tends to be strongly accented. Another rhythmic trait of many Andean melodies is the emphasis of shorter note values when they occur at the beginning of a beat. Also common are 6/8 metres, frequently used in alternation with 3/4 metres. Triple metres are found in mestizo music, in which Spanish elements appear more clearly, but in song forms of Indian descent, such as the *yaraví*, the melodies are also often in triple metre. Many Indian and mestizo song melodies are nonmensural. Typical Andean rhythmic accompaniment consists for the most part of a repetition of simple patterns. In addition to the dactylic rhythm in 2/4, the percussive accompaniment uses the figures shown in ex.15.

Ex.15

In some genres, such as the *cachua* (or *kashua*) dance of the Aymara of Bolivia, the percussion accompaniment is a simple continuous drum roll. String accompaniment, whether with harp, *charango* or guitar, also presents distinctively Andean features, in particular a series of arpeggios based on an octave with its 5th, with roots a minor 3rd apart, in the rhythm shown in ex.16. This is the basic accompaniment of many dances, such as the *huayno*, *carnaval*, *pandilla* and *pampeña*. Much Quechua and Aymara music is in strophic form. Simple types of variation are also fairly common, and improvisation occurs but does not play a major role. Mestizo songs or tunes are usually binary or ternary structures, with parallel 3rds. Aymara instrumental

Ex.16 Accompanimental patterns of Andean dance music (d'Harcourt, 1925)

ensembles, however, often double the melody at the 4th and the octave, especially in *sicus* ensembles.

Many indigenous dances of the Aymara and Quechua Indians, including pantomime dances, have become traditional for celebrating both Catholic religious feasts and Indian rituals. For example, the dance of *kena-kena* (or *uturunku*) is used for the feast of the Holy Cross; the *wipfala* is associated with the agrarian rituals (to the deity of the earth, Pachamama) and is preferably performed during the harvest season and on 15 August (Assumption day). The Quechua and Aymara also have dramatic dances, as in the rest of Latin America, depicting Christians and Moors, but reminiscent of events from the Conquest period, or of the glory of the past. For example, the *chunchus-collas* dance of Peru involves two sides representing Spanish soldiers and Indians, and the well-known Quechua and Aymara *baile del Inca* commemorates Atahualpa's cruel death.

Among the principal social dances of the Andes is the *huayno*, popular from northern Argentina to Ecuador where it is known as *sanjuanito*. An Indian dance, it has been adopted by highland mestizos as their own. The Aymara and Quechua *huayno* combines aboriginal Indian traits with Spanish features in both music and texts. The Indian *huayno*, for example, is generally sung in the native language, although texts in both Spanish and Quechua are not uncommon. Most *huayno* are in lively duple metre and binary form consisting of two phrases of equal length repeated ad lib. Most tunes associated with the dance use the anhemi-pentatonic scale G–E–D–C–A. Ex.17 shows a typical *huayno*.

Ex.17 Typical *huayno kaypipas*, Cuzco, Peru; coll. C. P. Galdo, transcr. R. Holzmann (Pagaza Galdo, 1967)

(iv) Afro-Hispanic folk music. The Afro-American tradition, resulting in the fusion of African and Hispanic styles, is particularly important in Brazil, Venezuela and Colombia and, to a lesser extent, in Uruguay, Argentina and the coastal regions of Peru and Ecuador.

The special character of Brazilian folk music is largely due to the importance of the black communities which maintain their own musical traditions that are often very close to African styles (see §III below). Moreover, the folk music of the Brazilian mestizos and whites in many instances cannot be distinguished from that of the Afro-Brazilians, since both result from basically identical syntheses. Afro-Brazilian components are the driving rhythms, the particular performance practices and the explicit importance of percussion instruments. The emphasis on dancing can also be interpreted as a result of the same syntheses. The number of Brazilian folkdance forms of Luso-African derivation is striking. Among these, the best known are *batuque*, *samba*, *jongo*, *côco*, *lundu*, *baiano* and some purely urban types, such as the *samba de morro*, *maracatu*, *maxixe* and *chôro*. All Afro-Brazilian folkdances include specific choreographic traits: tapping, marked movement of the hips and the shoulders, and *umbigada*, the touching of the couple's navels. When there is no *umbigada* in a given dance, the dance generally belongs to the *caboclo* folklore or has a Hispanic origin.

Afro-American musical traits are prominent in Venezuelan and Colombian folk music. Black musical influence in these countries is strongest in the coastal regions that belong to the circum-Caribbean area. The most authentically African drumming and dancing in Venezuela comes from the states of Zulia and Trujillo, along Lake Maracaibo. Among the various percussion instruments of African origin are three types of drum: the *mina* (or *tambor grande*), about 2 metres tall, with a single head fastened by ropes and wedges; the *curbata*, of the same family but smaller; and the *tambor redondo* ('round drum', also called *culepuya*), double-headed and always played in a battery of three. Bamboo stamping tubes, called *quitiplás*, are also part of the African heritage of Venezuela. Most percussion instruments are used almost exclusively for accompaniment. That a significant body of Afro-Venezuelan folk music is used in connection with Catholic feasts (for example, the feasts of St John and St Benedict) is again indicative of the strong local cultural blending.

One of the most typical dances and songs of Venezuela is the *joropo*. The urban *joropo*, which has also penetrated the rural regions, is a fast, composed dance in triple time, with a strongly syncopated accompaniment and frequent hemiola effect. Its choreography (for a solo couple) seems analogous to that of the Colombian *pasillo* and *bambuco*. The *bambuco*, with its alternating 3/4 and 6/8 metres, is one of the most representative dances of the Colombian mestizo. Its text, Spanish-derived, consists of four octosyllabic lines with an occasional refrain, and its accompaniment calls for Spanish folk instruments, such as the *tiple* (small guitar) and the *bandola* (mandolin). In the Pacific lowlands the *bambuco* is related to the *currulao*, a specifically Afro-American dance (see §III, 4(ii)).

2. CENTRAL AMERICA AND THE CARIBBEAN.

Mexican folk music is largely in the Spanish tradition and, while the Mexican Indians retain to some extent their native musical styles, there seems to have been less influence of the Indian styles on the Spanish-derived folk music here than in the Andean countries. The basic difference, therefore, between the Inca and the Aztec areas is that whereas Inca folk music could be considered the result of Hispanic influence on an indigenous foundation, Aztec folk music appears to reveal an indigenous influence on a Hispanic foundation. The Hispanic foundation is manifested in Mexico mainly in the melody types of

mestizo folksongs, the Spanish-derived choreography in numerous mestizo folkdances, and the widespread adoption of Hispanic instruments, even among rather isolated Indian groups. But one large difference between Spanish and Central American folk music is the greater importance of instruments in Central America. According to the testimony of early Spanish missionaries and conclusions based on archaeological studies, the Spaniards found sophisticated musical instruments in Mexico at the time of the Conquest (percussion instruments, flutes, multiple flutes and ocarinas) and a refined melodic system.

Early missionaries in Mexico evidently tried to suppress native Indian musical culture. They did not entirely succeed, but as a result of their efforts much Spanish folk music found its way into the culture of Mexican Indian groups. Mendoza collected songs of the Otomí Indians of northern Mexico that show the characteristic triplets of Spanish folksong and have elements of major tonality emphasizing tonic and 3rd. Other Otomí songs give even greater evidence of European influence in their parallel 3rds and 6ths, rarely found in aboriginal Indian music. This is not to say that these songs are simply Spanish songs by Indians; their style, with short melodies, few notes and small range, differs from the Spanish. More likely they are songs composed by Indians who had contact with Hispanic folk music in Mexico. The most typical mestizo musical forms likewise result from local adoption and gradual adaptation of both Spanish and Indian material throughout post-Conquest Mexican history. Almost never has an entire Spanish folksong form or dance been adopted. For example, the Spanish *romance* was transformed in Mexico and some Caribbean countries into the *corrido*, although its general character remained closely identifiable with the *romance*. The *corrido* continued to be essentially a narrative song, with a four-line stanza or a *décima* form but with a repetitive melodic structure and many regional sub-types. *Corridos* often dealt with current events, crimes and love stories, much as the English broadside ballads tell of sensational happenings; new ones are still being composed. Art songs are also sometimes reshaped into *corridos* through oral tradition.

The *jarabe*, *jarana*, *huapango*, *son*, *canción* and *valona* are among the numerous kinds of mestizo songs and dances. The *jarabe* is one of the oldest folkdances of Mexico, popular among Indians, rural and urban mestizos, and whites. It is predominantly in triple metre, occasionally alternating with 6/8, and follows a binary form. Each section has its own *son* (melody). Similar to the *jarabe* is the *jarana*, the most popular dance in Yucatán. The music has the same lively character as that of the *jarabe*, but the dance is generally accompanied not by singing but by an ensemble composed of *jaranas* (small guitars), drums, cornets and sometimes *güiro* (scraper).

The *huapango* is a well-known folkdance from the Gulf coast province of Veracruz and the central region of Huasteca. Musical characteristics, noted by Stevenson (1968), are the rapid shift from 3/4 to 6/8; the rapid gait of the beats and alternation of accents; a frequent sharp accent on the last quaver in a measure; and the frequent harmonic use of interior tonic pedals. In the modern *huapango* (e.g. *La bamba*) the typical instrumental accompaniment includes a violin, two *guitarrones* (large five-string bass instruments with convex bodies) and a *jarana*, although the *huapango* ensemble

Ex.18 Characteristic rhythmic patterns of Mexican *sones* (Bowles, 1941)

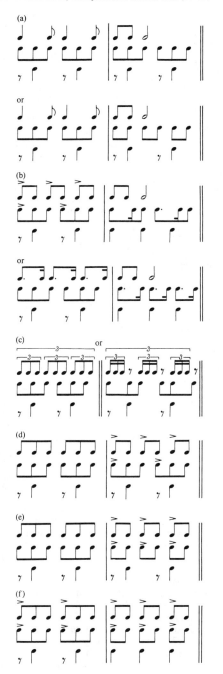

(a)

or

(b)

or

(c)

(d)

(e)

(f)

also uses harps and *jabalinas* (similar to the *guitarrón*).

Son has several meanings in Mexican music. The word sometimes refers to individual sections of *jarabes* and *huapangos*, and at other times to any song or portion of a song. *Son* also designates a separate choreographic genre. But the precise meaning of *son* also depends on association with a particular region or state: *son huasteco*, *son jarocho*, *son jaliciense*. The *son* is associated with the *mariachi*, an instrumental group compris-

ing violins, guitars, *jaranas* and *guitarrón*, and sometimes harp. In the mid-20th century brass instruments have been added to the traditional ensemble. Rhythmic vigour and the alternating or simultaneous use of 3/4 and 6/8 metre characterizes the *son*. Often units of three notes and two notes are combined to produce a 5/8 metre. Ex.18 shows six characteristic rhythmic patterns for *sones* from the Jalisco region.

The *canción* is a typical song that has assimilated many characteristics of 19th-century Italian opera. It is not restricted to any given metre or rhythm, but its form is generally binary, consisting of the song and an instrumental ritornello. The *valona* (or *balona*) is a declamatory genre whose poetic form follows the *décima* model.

The most typical performance characteristics of Mexican folk music include a high tension in the voice, producing a vigorous incisive effect; a slight continuous nasalizing of the voice and a preference for high pitch, frequently passing into falsetto; and a frequent practice of beginning instrumental pieces in a slower tempo than is used in the main body of the piece, with a gradual acceleration to the desired tempo, which is then maintained rigorously until the final cadence. Improvisation is not emphasized in Mexican music, and melismatic ornamentation, of the Andalusian *cante hondo* type, is largely absent (as it is throughout Latin America).

The states of Central America, from Guatemala to Panama, have varied musical traditions that combine a Hispanic foundation (as in Mexican folk music), aboriginal Indian music and black musical influence. For example, although the most popular dance of Guatemala, the *son chapín*, has European traits, the national instrument of the country is the marimba, a xylophone of African origin. Similarly the *sique*, the most characteristic folkdance of Honduras is closely related to the Spanish jota. But it is also in Honduras and Nicaragua that black Carib settlements are found. (Black Caribs are descendants of Arawak and Carib Indian tribes and former African slaves.) Black Carib culture and music combine West African traits with the ceremonial dancing of tropical-forest Indians.

Panama's musical traditions clearly reflect its ethnohistory. Traditional music is found among Indian groups, such as the Cuna and the Guaymíe; Hispanic music is represented by various folksong genres and dances, especially the *mejorana* or *socavón*; and African-derived music is represented by *tamborito* dances. In the *mejorana*, hemiola rhythm between the voice and the accompaniment on guitar or *mejoranera* is quite common. The singing style involves a harsh penetrating voice (without tremolo), with frequent alternation of falsetto and normal voice, extending the range to more than two octaves. The *mejorana* uses traditional Spanish choreography divided into two parts: *zapateo* (foot figures) and *paseo* (promenade as in the squaredance).

The most typical example of Afro-Panamanian singing and dancing is the *tamborito*, danced by mixed couples but sung exclusively by women (both solo and chorus). Generally a short phrase is sung alternately by soloist and chorus, although there are other forms. The dance is in duple metre and is accompanied by handclapping and drums. The drums are played in a battery of three, in complex rhythmic combinations.

In general terms the Hispanic tradition and the African tradition are the basis of music in Hispanic

Caribbean islands such as Cuba, Puerto Rico and the Dominican Republic. The *punto* and the *guajira* sung by Cuban peasants (*guajiros*) of Oriente province and the interior of the island have the same stylistic traits as most Spanish-related folk music of Latin America. The *punto*, spread throughout the Caribbean, is found in Puerto Rico, the Dominican Republic, Colombia, Venezuela and Panama.

Afro-Cuban music, in addition to cult music (discussed in §III, 4), includes such important dance forms as the *conga* and the rumba, and other hybrid forms, such as the *son*, the *danzón*, the *guaracha*, the habanera and the bolero. Together with the various types of drum associated with cult music, the typical Afro-Cuban instrumental ensembles include maracas, güiros, claves (clappers), bongo drums, and *tres* and *cuatro* (small three- and four-string guitars). Ex.19 illustrates the fun-

Ex.19 Rhythmic figures of Afro-Cuban music (G. Agüero y Barreras: 'El aporte africano a la música popular cubana', *Estudios Afrocubanos*, 1946)

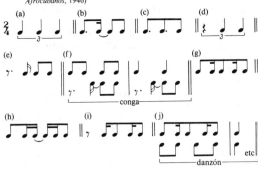

damental rhythmic figures of Afro-Cuban music. The first figure, called *tresillo* in Cuba, is often notated as a simple triplet (*a*), but in performance sounds as in (*b*) or (*c*). The second figure, notated as in (*d*) but performed as in (*e*), is further complicated in the basic *conga* rhythm by tying together the first two notes of that rhythmic cell (*f*). The third figure (*g*) is perhaps the most characteristic formula of Cuban folk and popular music. It is known as *cinquillo* and possibly results from a contraction of the rhythm (*h*), which is African in its symmetry. It also forms the basis of much ritual drumming of the Haitian *vodun*, as well as the *merengue*, a Caribbean dance found in Haiti and the Dominican Republic. It sometimes appears as (*i*), and it generates the basic rhythm of the Cuban *danzón* (*j*). The last two models show the typical figures, in duple and triple metres, associated with the claves in almost all Afro-Caribbean dances. The first bar of the duple-metre example is the habanera rhythmic formula.

BIBLIOGRAPHY

R. and M. d'Harcourt: *La musique des Incas et ses survivances* (Paris, 1925)

Handbook of Latin American Studies (1935–)

J. I. Perdomo Escobar: *Historia de la música en Colombia* (Bogotá, 1938, 4/1975)

P. Bowles: 'On Mexico's Popular Music', *Modern Music*, xviii/4 (1941), 225

C. Vega: *Los instrumentos musicales aborígenes y criollos de la Argentina* (Buenos Aires, 1946)

O. Alvarenga: *Música popular brasileira* (Rio de Janeiro, 1950)

V. T. Mendoza: 'Música indígena otomí', *Revista de estudios musicales*, ii/5–6 (1950–51), 527

I. Aretz: *El folklore musical argentino* (Buenos Aires, 1952), 144

L. F. Ramón y Rivera: *El joropo: baile nacional de Venezuela* (Caracas, 1952)

E. Romero: *El romance tradicional en el Perú* (Mexico, 1952)

R. Stevenson: *Music in Mexico: a Historical Survey* (New York, 1952)

S. Martí: *Instrumentos musicales precortesianos* (Mexico City, 1954, rev. 2/1968)

R. Tavares de Lima: *Melodia e ritmo no folclore de São Paulo* (São Paulo, 1954)

V. T. Mendoza: *Panorama de la música tradicional de México* (Mexico City, 1956)

M. and R. d'Harcourt: *La musique des Aymara sur les hauts plateaux boliviens* (Paris, 1959)

V. T. Mendoza: *La canción mexicana* (Mexico City, 1961)

I. Aretz: *Cantos navideños en el folklore venezolano* (Caracas, 1962)

G. Chase: *A Guide to the Music of Latin America* (Washington, DC, 1962)

A. M. Araújo: *Folclore nacional*, i (São Paulo, 1964), 216

V. Chenoweth: *The Marimbas of Guatemala* (Lexington, Ky., 1964)

G. P. Kurath and S. Martí: *Dances of Anahuac* (Chicago, 1964)

C. L. Boilès: 'The Pipe and Tabor in Mesoamerica', *Yearbook of the Inter-American Institute for Musical Research*, ii (1966), 43–74

I. Aretz: *Instrumentos musicales de Venezuela* (Cumaná, 1967)

M. E. Grebe: *The Chilean Verso: a Study in Musical Archaism* (Los Angeles, 1967)

C. Pagaza Galdo: *Cancionero andino sur* (Lima, 1967)

R. Stevenson: *Music in Aztec and Inca Territory* (Berkeley and Los Angeles, 1968)

III. Afro-American music

1 The colonial period: (i) Spanish America (ii) Brazil (iii) West Indies. 2. Independence to *c*1900. 3. 20th century. 4. Folk music: (i) Religious music (ii) Secular ceremonial music.

1. THE COLONIAL PERIOD.

(*i*) *Spanish America.* The first negroes came with the conquistadores; one of Cortés's gunners was a negro and another, named Juan Garrido, was the first to sow wheat in Mexico. After Bartolomé de Las Casas (1474–1566) suggested substituting negro for Indian labour to save the less hardy Indians from extermination, they arrived in increasing numbers. On 4 May 1553 the Viceroy, Luis de Velasco, urged Charles V to stop the influx, since the 20,000 negroes in Mexico far exceeded the number of Spaniards. In 1580 Mexico had less than 15,000 Spaniards, whereas the negro population was more than 18,500, with another 1500 registered as mulattos. In Mexico City untill 1569 the negroes' favourite diversion was playing and dancing around the famous Aztec calendar stone (carved before 1481 for King Axayacatl). The stone was buried after Velasco issued a decree (2 January 1569) confining their dancing in the main plaza to Sundays and feast-day afternoons, from noon to six p.m. By 1598 negro drums were so much better known in Mexico than the pre-Conquest *tlapanhuehuetl* that an Indian historian, Alvarado Tezozomoc, had to explain the dread death drum of his ancestors by calling it the same as the 'drum used by the negroes who now dance in the plazas'.

In the 17th century negroes throughout Mexico organized public dances, taught music and dancing, directed 'oratorios', and managed what would now be called musical comedy theatres. In 1624, for example, in the Pánuco area north of Veracruz, a pre-Conquest dance, the *payà*, was led by a negro slave, Lucas Olola, who put on an Indian costume and headed a cult which freely mixed Aztec *teponaztli* (slit-drum) with African *bambalos* (tomtoms). Joseph Chamorro, a free negro, taught dancing and guitar playing at Oaxaca in 1682. In 1669 in Puebla and again in 1684 in the Cuernavaca area, negroes and mulattos were cited as directing 'oratorios' although these had been forbidden by a printed edict issued at Mexico City on 5 December 1643. This edict defined an 'oratorio' as a nocturnal musical party (held in an interior patio as a rule), with dancing, music and refreshments, all ostensibly in honour of the Holy Cross, Our Lady or some saint, and recurring nightly nine times with different guests each night. The entertainment included a monologue by a dramatic reader accompanied by harp or guitar. Two such oratorios, given in Puebla in May 1669, were managed by negroes. Chorillo (also known as Melchor), nicknamed 'the Virgin's singer', led a combination of 'many harps and guitrs' and his companion Cervantes gave readings to the accompaniment of these instruments.

These lively negro entertainments became so popular with the ruling classes that complaints of irreverence and indecency were overlooked. On 2 May 1651 Fabián Ximeno, *maestro de capilla* of Mexico City Cathedral (1648–54), complained to his superiors that a choir under a negro took the bread out of the mouths of his own cathedral singers. According to Ximeno, the negro's choir sang in 'an indecent manner' but managed to get more paid engagements. At Guadalajara in 1746, in the afternoons, small bands of negroes playing trumpets and drums would visit the wine shops to advertise the night's musical entertainment and dancing in their small musical-comedy houses where (said a complainant) 'the greatest disorder' prevailed.

In Peru, the other New World viceroyalty, negro musicians were noted from the mid-16th century. On 31 August 1551 the Lima *cabildo* (town council) hired negro drummers to welcome the Viceroy, Antonio de Mendoza, paying to have their big drums draped in vermilion, the Inca colour. 12 years later, the Lima *cabildo* confined negro dancing and drumming in the public streets to the public plaza or the plaza of Nicolás de Ribera *el mozo*. The act of 13 August 1563 imposed further limits, because negro dancing and music were interfering with beasts of burden. To welcome Lope García de Castro, the Lima *cabildo* again called on negro drummers, and Indians were amazed at the size of the drums they played. In the Quito area, however, the blacks were surprised to find that the Indians themselves already used huge drums for signalling across great distances in the mountains (see Rocha).

Negroes who had been brought to Lima from the Congo and the coasts of Guinea and Senegal numbered several thousand in 1628, and by 1748 had reached 10,000. In *El lazarillo de ciegos caminantes* (1773) Bustamante listed the instruments used by the blacks in Buenos Aires to accompany dancing as an ass's dried jawbone scraped vigorously with another dry bone or hard stick, and a drum carried on top of one negro's head, while another following behind 'hit the leather drumhead with two claw-shaped sticks'. In 1791 Rossi y Rubí described the music of negroes in Lima, who still spoke only their native African tongues:

Their principal instrument is the drum, the skin of which they stretch over a hollow cylindrical log or over a clay frame. They play it not with mallets but with their hands. They also favour small nose flutes. They make dried horses' or asses' jawbones into a clattering instrument, with the teeth knocking against each other. They also make a sort of music with striated wooden blocks rubbed against each other. Their most melodious instrument is the marimba, fashioned of wooden slabs which serve as keys of different sizes. Beneath the slabs they adjust dried hollow gourds, also of different sizes, to serve as resonators. Slabs and resonators are together mounted on an arched wooden frame. They play the marimba with two small sticks, like Bohemian psalteries. The diameter of the gourds is graduated with the ascending scale, and the sound that is emitted at times pleases the most fastidious ear.

The prominent role played by blacks in the musical life of colonial Altoru (modern Bolivia) is attested as early as 12 June 1568, when Juan de la Peña Madrid contracted with a married mulatto, Hernán García, to open a school in the capital of the Audiencia de Charcas, where they would teach respectively singing and dancing, and playing and dancing (documents in Sucre, Bolivia, National Archive, Escrituras Públicas, Águila 1568, f.226v, Bravo 1569, ff.29v, 148v, 156). Throughout the 18th century blacks (or sometimes actors made up as blacks) continued as leading entertainers in all districts of Peru. Torre described a *mogiganga* with 30 performers held in Potosí on Sunday, 26 April 1716, led by a 'King and Queen of Angola', both of 'midnight hue'.

Probably the earliest picture of negro musicians is to be found in a miscellany of local curiosities collected in northern Peru between 1782 and 1785 by Baltasar Jaime Martínez Compañón (1737–97) and sent between 1788 and 1790 to Madrid, where the collection survives (*E-Mp* 90/344). It includes a coloured picture of 'negroes playing marimba and dancing' (E142), another of a negro pair doing a handkerchief dance to the tune supplied by a negro drum and fife player (E140). The marimba is diatonic; two negroes are playing it while four more dance. Another instrument mentioned as a favourite of Peruvian blacks around 1800 was the *bandurria* (*bandore*, a flat-backed lute). In Lima in the 1790s a negro named Galindo, who could neither read nor write, sang in the streets, improvising witty topical verses (*Correo Peruano*, 6 November 1845).

The system of *cofradías* and *hermandades* (confraternities and brotherhoods) fostered among negroes by missionaries and local clergy was fundamental to the preservation of negro identity in Spanish America throughout the colonial period. It sprang up the more readily because of Andalusian precedents: the first negro *cofradía* with its own chapel at Seville was inaugurated in 1403. At Cádiz a negro *cofradía* dedicated to Nuestro Señor de los Reyes and at Jaén one endowed by the negro, Juan Cobo, were both in existence before 1600. Apart from eleemosynary activities, these Andalusian negro *cofradías* sponsored dances, pageants, floats and other festival entertainments, and also regularly provided funds to pay both singers and instrumentalists. In 1600, for instance, the Jaén negro confraternity hired singers from San Andrés church for 28 reales and two players of the guitar or vihuela for 6 reales.

Spanish as well as Spanish American writers responded to the omnipresence of negroes with characters such as the black Luis in Cervantes's *El celoso extremeño*, who loved music so violently that he was willing to risk life itself if only he could study with someone able to teach him the *guitarra*, *clavicímbano*, *órganos* or *harpa*. Francisco de Quevedo y Villegas (1590–1645) advised writers who wished to imitate negro dialect to show their knowledge of the Guinea tongue 'by changing "r" into "l"', thus *Francisco = Flancisco*, *primo = plimo*'. The ambivalence of 'r' and 'l' in Twi, Fanti, Guan, Ga and Mende accords with this, and confirms what is known from other sources, namely that the earliest slaves came from West Africa.

The villancicos written in both Spain and Spanish America to negro-dialect texts were called *negros*. The earliest *negros* catalogued (in John IV's *Primeira parte do Index*, 1649) were set by Philippe Rogier and Géry de Ghersem, court composers at Madrid. But according to the catalogue the most prolific composers of *negros* in the Iberian peninsula were Francisco de Santiago and

Gabriel Dias. The earliest surviving *guineos*, *negros*, *negrillas* and *negritos* in a Spanish American manuscript were composed by Gaspar Fernandes (*d* 1629), appointed *maestro de capilla* (Guatemala) on 16 July 1599 and at Puebla (Mexico) on 15 September 1606. A 284-folio autograph discovered at Oaxaca Cathedral in 1966 contains over a dozen 'black' works under his name. The first *guineo* from this Oaxaca manuscript to be published (Stevenson, *MQ*, 1968) begins with a tenor solo answered by the second alto and then by a five-part chorus singing a refrain 'sarabanda tenge que tenge'. Together with the abundant colonial *negros* in archives in Bogotá, Cuzco, Guatemala City, Puebla and Sucre, the 'black' pieces already published by Fernandes, Juan Gutiérrez de Padilla, Antonio de Salazar, Juan de Vaeza Saavedra and Juan de Araujo all share certain identifying traits: a preference for 6/8 time with constant hemiola shifts to 3/4, the prevalence of what would now be called the 'key' of F major; and a texture governed by the solo voice or soloists answered by chorus. A. M. Jones's transcriptions of clapping patterns from the Yoruba, Bemba and Lala include a Gankogui 'standard pattern' for Ewe drumming that closely resembles the fast hemiola triple movement recurrent in all New World *negros*. As in Spain, the *negro* texts written in the New World mix genders, suppress final sibilants, change 'll' to 'y' and 'r' to 'l', alter all words with the 'th' ('z') sound, repeat words such as 'gulungú, gulungú', 'gurumbé, gurumbé, gurumbá', 'he, he, he, cambulé', 'tumba la-lá-la, tumba la-lé-le' and mention the names of places in Africa.

Throughout the Americas, the Spanish encouraged the memory of places in Africa from which the blacks had emigrated, and which could reinforce black pride (Sofala, for example, the prosperous capital of Mozambique, and Ethiopia where 'Prester John' ruled, are mentioned in *negro* texts set by Araujo and Fernandes). The *cofradías* or *sociedades* in the larger Spanish American capitals also fostered African pride. Among the seven at Buenos Aires at the close of the colonial period, at least three took their names from African areas to which members could trace their ancestry: the Sociedades Angola, Bangala (Benguela) and Conga. On 31 October 1795 two chiefs of the Nación Conga at Buenos Aires petitioned the incoming Viceroy, Pedro de Portugal y Villena, for permission to celebrate his formal entry with dances preserving pure regional style, such dances to continue thereafter every Sunday and feast-day afternoon. In December 1802 one clubhouse of the blacks in the Concepción parish of Buenos Aires was called 'Casa y sitio del tango' ('House and site of the tango'). In Montevideo in 1808 the citizens petitioned the governor to prohibit negroes from dancing their 'tangos' within city limits, and in 1816 again asked that black 'dances known as tangos be prohibited inside city limits and permitted outside only on feast-day afternoons until sunset'.

The earliest purely instrumental black dances intabulated in New World manuscripts are a *portorrico de los negros* (f.20 of a *Método de Cítara* written at Puebla by Sebastián de Aguirre, *c*1650) and a *zarambeque* preceded by *cumbees* (items 21 and 22 in an anonymous 94-folio collection of five-course guitar music compiled *c*1750 at León, Guanajuato, Mexico).

(*ii*) *Brazil*. Like the rest of Latin America, Brazil had many negro and mulatto composers long before 1900. In Bahia, formalized music instruction was given to negroes as early as 1610, when a Frenchman from Provence taught 20 or 30 negroes how to play and sing, having been hired for this purpose by João Furtado de Mendonça (governor of Angola, 1594–1602), on whose estate he lived. The private orchestra he trained established a custom (followed by other wealthy South Americans during the next two centuries) of maintaining ensembles of slaves trained to play European music. In the next century free blacks visited Portugal for musical instruction. In 1749 Manuel de Almeida Botelho (*b* Recife, 1721) migrated to Lisbon, 'where the court honoured him with the highest marks of favour – not allowing his dusky colour to diminish by an iota the deference due his gifts, virtues, and ingenuous deportment' (*P-Ln* F.G. 873, pp.394f). Botelho's success at court soon inspired another Recife-born mulatto, Luiz Álvares Pinto (1719–89) to visit Lisbon. His 43-page treatise *Arte de solfejar* (1761; *P-Ln* F.G. 2265) is the earliest extant treatise on music by anyone born in the Americas. At S Pedro dos Clérigos, the church in Recife served by Pinto on his return to Brazil, an interracial St Cecilia's confraternity was founded with royal approval in 1789. Pinto's orchestrally accompanied *Te Deum* shows that he had thoroughly mastered the methods of his Lisbon teacher, Henrique de Silva Negrão. Another notable contemporary was José Joaquim Emerico Lôbo de Mesquita, a 'dark mulatto' who worked successively at Diamantina (1780–98), Villa Rica (approximately two years), and Rio de Janeiro (until his death in 1805), and whose Latin works entitle him to first rank among a school of composers of African descent at work in Minas Gerais.

Louis Antoine de Bougainville (1729–1811) described how Metastasio operas were being sung by a mulatto troupe led by a mulatto priest in June 1767 at Rio de Janeiro, the capital of Brazil after 1763. At Cuyabá on 31 August 1791 in the midst of a gold rush, a new governor was welcomed by an all-male mulatto operatic troupe singing *Ezio in Roma* (the composer was not specified, but was probably Jommelli). At São Paulo, a mulatto named António Manso da Mota (*b* 1732) became *mestre de capela* in 1768 and at once tried to produce operas, much to the resentment of the bishop installed in 1771.

The most prolific and certainly the most gifted of Brazilian composers of African descent of any period was José Maurício Nunes Garcia (1767–1830), who had a classical training. According to Balbi, upon the arrival of King John VI, who transferred the Portuguese court to Rio de Janeiro (1808–21), a royal residence at nearby Santa Cruz became a conservatory for negroes. In 1812 'negroes studying in this conservatory' delighted the newly arrived Marcos Portugal, who compared them favourably with the best European operatic performers.

(*iii*) *West Indies*. The first negro dance-song with a wholly African text was transcribed in Jamaica in 1688 for Hans Sloane (1660–1753). Published in 1707, it is in the west African 'Koromanti' language, according to Sloane. It begins: 'Meri bombo mich langa meri wá langa'. For a correct transcription of this and other songs he employed the 'best Musician' on the island, a 'Mr. Baptiste', who took down both melody and text during 'one of the festivals when a great many of the Negro Musicians were gathered together'. To perform it properly, 'You must clap your Hands when the Base [drum] is plaid and cry, *Alla Alla*'. Part of the melody of this song from Benin is shown in ex.20. Sloane's Plate III (after his p.154; facs. in *MQ*, lix (1973), 74) illustrates

Ex.20 *Meri bombo*, song from Benin (Sloane, 1707)

*missing in original
†altered time value in original

the African instruments used in Jamaica during his visit in 1688. He described as still in use African 'Lutes made of small gourds fitted with Necks, strung with Horse hairs, or the picked stalks of climbing Plants or Withs' (p.48). Duarte Lopes had already described similar un-fretted plucked instruments popular at the Congo court in Mbanza (1568–87). Besides being instruments on which 'they can declare with their hande in touching and striking ... every thing almost which may be explained with the tongue' these Congo 'lutes' had been similarly played to stimulate dancing and clapping.

After Sloane, the next to describe Jamaican negro instruments was Charles Leslie, who was surprised by the 'indecent' *calenda* dance. The banjo he called 'ban-gil', and two jagged sticks rubbed together a 'rookaw'. The practice called 'jengkoving' he explained as 'clap-ping their Hands on the Mouth of Two Jars'. William Beckford, after 12 years in Jamaica (1755–77), listed among other instruments popular with island blacks 'Caramantee-flutes about a yard in length, and of nearly the thickness of the upper part of a bassoon, made from porous branches of the trumpet-tree ... a cotter, upon which they beat with sticks, a gomba, which they strike with their hands ... a box filled with pebbles, which they shake with their wrists; and ... the jaw-bone of an animal'. On 18 March 1802 the wife of the British governor of Jamaica wrote in her *Journal* that 'the Coromantee flute is a long black reed ... played with the nose', making a 'plaintive' sound. But by 1788 town-bred negroes in Jamaica were relinquishing their African instruments in favour of fiddles, which they played to accompany minuets. Three years later sophis-ticated blacks on St Vincent (Windward Islands) danced the minuet and a dance not unlike a Scotch reel to the sound of 'two excellent fiddles'. Meanwhile country blacks on the same estate played 'an African *balafo*, an instrument composed of pieces of hardwood of different diameters, laid on a row over a sort of box: they beat on one or the other so as to strike out a good musical tune'. On this xylophone 'they played two or three African

tunes' enticing 'about a dozen girls' from the slave huts to begin 'a curious and most lascivious dance with much grace as well as action', according to the owner of the estate, Sir William Young.

Philip Young, a 'resident of Jamaica' and a former Crotch pupil, was the first to compile a collection of West Indian melodies and negro tunes. The 'negro beat' which he mentioned is an accented graced quaver on the second half of each first beat in a duple measure, preceded by a quaver rest. The tunes, given such titles as *Mountain Busha, Guinea-Corn, Dolly Caboca, Liz me nega, Man-a-war Buckra, Corn-Tick* and *Massa Tommy*, look on paper no more 'African' than *Emmit's* [D. D. Emmett's] *Celebrated Negro Melodies* (London, 1843–4). Accompanied by the ostinato 'negro beat', *Guinea-Corn* divides into two four-bar repeats (see ex.21). Earlier 'negro' songs published in London and America include John Mounds's *The Negro Boy* (Boston, 1796), Charles Dibdin's *Negro Philosophy* (London, 1796), John Ross's *The Negro Mother*, J. Ambrose's *The Negro's Revels*, W. Howard's *The Negro Lamentation* and G. G. Ferrari's *African Song*, the last four undated but antedating 1830 (copies are found in *GB-Lbm*).

Ex.21 *Guinea-Corn* (Young, ?1822)

In Paris, Nicolas Alexandre Dezède (c1740–92) professed to recapture the flavour of Haitian music with an 'air nègre' sung by a Cap Haitien slave at the begin-ning of his one-act comedy *Les nègres* (1783). A diver-tissement danced by blacks closes the comedy, but noth-ing specifically African distinguishes Dezède's pub-lished music.

2. INDEPENDENCE TO c1900. The first American-born black to become a European musical celebrity was Joseph Boulogne, Chevalier de Saint-Georges (1739–99). Equally famous as violinist and composer, he was born in Guadeloupe and trained in Santo Domingo Island (Hispaniola); he studied the violin with the black Joseph Platon. The Cuban-born negro violinist and composer José White (1835–1918) was equally suc-cessful in Paris, where on 26 February 1867 in Herz Hall he gave the première of an original three-movement concerto. In America he made his début with the New York Philharmonic on 22 January 1876. After touring western South America he made his first public appear-ance in Buenos Aires in the Teatro Colón on 4 June 1879. White settled in Rio de Janeiro, where in the same year he founded the Sociedade de Concertos Clássicos. In 1894 he went to Paris, where he published as his op.30 one of his rare virtuoso pieces for violin and piano, modelled on a folkdance of negro derivation, the *zamacueca* (*zambacueca*, a couple-dance of Chile and Peru). Its popularity inspired a solo piano version published at Valparaíso by E. Niemeyer & Inghirami.

The internationally famous black Cuban violinist, Claudio José Domingo Brindis de Salas (1852–1911), followed White to Paris, studying there at the Conservatoire with Dancla, David and Sivori. The Emperor Wilhelm II made him a baron and from 1880 to 1900 he lived in Berlin. His accompanist at his first performance in Buenos Aires on 21 August 1889 was the black Argentinian pianist Zenón Rolón (1856–1902). Both men were prominent in racial activities throughout their careers. Brindis de Salas returned to Cuba in 1903 for a Black Congress. Rolón began his advocacy with a stirring manifesto whose Spanish title can be translated as 'A few words to my racial brothers' published on 20 June 1878 in the Buenos Aires periodical, *La Juventud*. Two years later the Buenos Aires première of Rolón's first symphony was reviewed in the 29 April 1880 issue of *La Nación*. During the next two decades Rolón continued to be one of the most productive of Argentine composers, with new operas and zarzuelas, salon, military and religious works constantly pouring from his pen, while at the same time he founded and directed the Club Social for middle-class blacks in the capital and led the concerts patronized by them in the Jardín Florida.

Rolón was only one of many Argentine black or mulatto conductors active before 1900: Bernardo Pintos (*fl* 1804–16) directed small orchestras; Remigio Navarro (*fl* 1829–39) was the chief composer of salon dances in his day, and published *valses*, *minués*, variations and songs; Gregorio Marradas (*d* 1884) was another composer of salon dances; Federico Espinosa (1820–72) studied piano with the negro Tiburcio Silbarrios, greatly impressed Thalberg when the latter visited Buenos Aires in 1855, and during the next eight years published a series of popular polkas, mazurkas, marches and *valses*. Espinosa's *Los Miriñaques* (Buenos Aires, 1856) was republished in Vicente Gesualdo (vol. ii, pp.418f). But his music, like that of every other Latin American black composer before 1900, fails to reveal any traits that ethnologists today would classify as peculiarly 'African'.

3. 20TH CENTURY. Such folk songs and dances as the Brazilian *batuque*, *candomblé*, *capoeira* and *xango*, the Cuban *conga*, the Panamanian *cumbia*, the Colombian *currulao* and the Haitian *moundongue* show African influences either overtly, in their percussive, ostinato rhythmic substructures, or in their solo-chorus patterns. An example of a Kêtu (Queto) cult song from Bahia, Brazil, sung by Adrovaldo Martins dos Santos, the black cult leader, in 1937, was collected by Camargo Guarnieri (see ex.22). It is entitled *Canto de Ogum* (Ogum, son of the Yoruba goddess Yemanjá, taught fighting with iron weapons). In 1932 Ramos published transcriptions of typical accompanying drum rhythms, remarking that the drumming induced possession. In his classic study of Africanisms in Cuban music (1950), Ortiz revealed that negro singers in Cuba, as in Brazil, improvised collectively. In such literary contests as the *puya*, *managua* or *makagua*, he noted that these remarkable improvisers competed with one another on given themes, and that in their 'songs of sanction' they chastised any breaker of the black ethical code. Among

the African dances surviving on the island into the 1920s he mentioned some (such as the *rumba brava*) which included navel-to-navel contact (*vacunao*). The rest of the principal dances (except the religious ones) can be traced to Bantu origins – the *yuka*, *caringa* (*calenda*) and also probably the *danse de mani* (incorporating fighters' movements that recall the Bahian *capoeira*). The musical instruments of African origin, variously called *ashanti*, *arara*, *congos*, *lucumi* and *abakua*, range from knocking sticks to drums. Although some Ewe and Yoruba influence can also be detected, Bantu influence predominates in the black folk music of both Cuba and Haiti.

Among Brazilian black popular singers, Jorge Ben (Jorge Lima Menezes, *b* 1940) recorded *Banzo: funeral dum rei nagô* ('Banzo, funeral of a Nagô king'), Elza Soares (*b* 1937) *Tributo a Martin Luther King*, and Dorval Caymmi (*b* 1914) *E doce morrer no mar*. It was the subject matter rather than any distinctively African stylistic features that made such songs specifically black. Jair Rodrigues de Oliveira (*b* 1939) and Wilson Simonal (*b* 1939) are among the black Brazilian singers who have sought to reach a wider audience rather than isolated black groups.

4. FOLK MUSIC. Defining 'black' folk music in Latin America is an extremely complex matter, since the term 'Afro-American' is not as unequivocal there as in North America, in either its ethnic or cultural connotations. In Central and South America there are some black groups who have virtually no sense of belonging to an African culture, such as the Caribs of Honduras and Nicaragua, who are black representatives of an Indian culture. Conversely, important non-black groups have borrowed African-related cultural traits, such as the East Indians of Trinidad, Guyana and Surinam or the Cayapa Indians of western Ecuador. In many areas of Latin America there has been considerable acculturation between negro and other ethnic groups both pure and mixed, producing a remarkably homogeneous 'black' culture. Race, then, is not the only criterion in discussing Afro-American musical styles in Latin America (as already seen in the discussion of black art music, §III,1 above). Although Africanisms are being stressed here, it should be borne in mind that Afro-American music cuts across ethnic lines.

(*i*) *Religious music.* Black music in Latin America is found in both sacred and secular contexts, but generally more African musical elements are preserved in sacred contexts. Various cults in Cuba, Haiti, Jamaica, Trinidad and Brazil involve deities (called *orixás*, *voduns*, saints etc) that have been transferred from west Africa. West African religions as developed in the Americas are animistic and involve a pantheon of greater and lesser deities, each worshipped with characteristic ceremonies, songs and drum rhythms. The music of Christian Revivalist cult groups in the West Indies, however, is similar to black Protestant music of the southern USA, mixing various types of traditional Protestant hymnody with an important body of 19th-century gospel hymns. The distinguishing feature of Revival cult music is the constant presence of harmonized choruses; its accompanying rhythmic patterns are substantially less African than in Cuban, Haitian or Brazilian cults. The call-and-response practice in Jamaican revivalist music could be considered a retention of an African feature.

Ex.22 *Canto de Ogum*, Kêtu cult song, Bahia; coll. C. Guarnieri

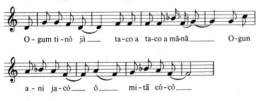

O - gum ti - nô já___   ta - co a ta - co a mã - nã___   O - gun

a - ni ja - có___ ô___   mi - tã cô - cô___

Protestant-related cults excepted, the most obvious stylistic trait common to the cult musics of Latin America is the predominant use of call-and-response patterns. The leader or solo singer may be either a woman or a man, but the chorus is usually composed of women. The chorus sings monophonically, but occasionally individual singers deviate from the main melodic line. Among the most acculturated groups (Abakuá in Cuba, Caboclo and Umbanda in Brazil) heterophony is common. Sometimes soloist and chorus overlap. Scales are usually anhemi-pentatonic, though diatonic scales are used in many songs. Tempo varies considerably from one cult group to another and within the same cult, in accordance with the choice of song cycle. Gradual acceleration in songs or in drum music is fairly frequent, depending on the particular ritual function. Ranges of melodies are not uniform; for example, the Gêgê cult of Bahia has songs with wide range (most exceed an octave), while those of the Jesha cult in the same area average less than an octave. Melodic contours are generally descending, but frequent pendulum-like movements are also characteristic, as in the series of songs to the deity Exú in the Bahian Kêtu cult. Melodic intervals are often large. Whenever there is leader-chorus alternation the melodic phrases tend to be short, but with solo songs or duets the melodic line is longer and more complex. The form, within the framework of the leader-chorus alternation, is frequently based on repetition of a single phrase, with variation through ornamentation. The soloist is likely to present a theme with variations as the basis of his tune. The chorus often uses the same tune; occasionally it uses material from the last portion of the soloist's line. Most songs are strophic. Ex.20 illustrates some of these characteristics in Afro-Bahian cult songs. The singing styles of most Afro-American cults are essentially like the relaxed, open manner of singing common in west Africa. Female voices present a characteristically hard, metallic quality, with a preference for the upper range of the voice. Falsetto is often used by both soloists and chorus.

The song repertories of Afro-American religions have not been fully classified, but we know that songs attributed to a deity form the bulk of the repertories. Cycles of songs are performed in a traditional ritual order. Song texts appear in various languages, from Yoruba (Nago), Fon and various Congo dialects to Spanish and Portuguese, Haitian Creole, or a combination of all these. Typically, song texts are simple praise or imprecation addressed to the gods; sometimes they refer to specific events in the lives of deities or to their remarkable feats, following west African mythology as reinterpreted in the New World through the influence of popular Christianity.

Although most song repertories are traditional, stylistic changes occur and new repertories are created. According to cult leaders in Salvador, Bahia, many songs attributed to specific deities have disappeared from the repertory, and new songs are being incorporated. These are not, in general, songs composed by the priest or priestess of a cult house; they are spontaneously created when a new member, in a state of possession, sings his (or her) song to the orixá. Such songs are apparently remembered afterwards. Especially among the Congo-Angola and the Caboclo cults, these 'new' songs frequently include elements from folk music or urban musical culture (such as Carnival street music), foreign to the tradition but familiar to the songmakers.

The single most important ritual and musical element in Afro-American cults is drumming. Complex ritual involving drums is essential since they alone are thought to have the power of communicating with deities. Drums are considered sacred instruments; they undergo ritual baptism by means of animal sacrifices and offerings of food. Some Cuban Abakuá drums have an exclusively symbolic function and are never played. In most cults drums are played in a battery of three, together with an iron gong or a rattle. In different cults they vary in size and shape, but are always of three sizes. The largest drum (called *rum* in the Kêtu of Bahia, *iya* among the Lucumi of Cuba, *maman* in the Vodun cult, *mama* or *bemba* in the Shango of Trinidad) is played by the master drummer. The medium sized drum (known in these same cults as *rumpí*, *itótele*, *seconde* and *congo* respectively) and the smallest one (respectively *lê*, *okónkolo*, *bébé* and *oumalay*) usually repeat a single steady rhythm. In contrast, the largest and lowest drum varies its beats, producing some of the complex and exciting rhythms typical of Afro-American styles. The bell (variously called *agogó*, *gan*, *ogan* or *ekon* in Brazil and Cuba) or the rattle generally sets the fundamental beat; the drums join in a few seconds later. As Herskovits has pointed out, the melody of the song is merely accompaniment to the rhythm of the drums. This emphasis on rhythm is an obvious African heritage, and each cult, dance, ceremony or deity has its characteristic rhythms on which the master drummer improvises. There is also much drum music without song, whose main function is to 'call' the gods and to induce 'possession', also to provide accompaniment for the many ritual dances. Cross-rhythms and polyrhythms predominate (for music examples, *see* HAITI and BRAZIL, §II).

Metres are usually duple but often triple, and the typically African hemiola rhythm is also common. There is no evidence of any retention of African talking-drum techniques in Latin America, but it is believed that some ritual drum patterns (those attributed to the different deities) were originally rhythmic renderings of the melodic shape of phrases in Yoruba, a tone language. Such renderings would have been learnt, memorized and transmitted by use of onomatopoeia.

Within the social structure of Afro-American cults, women have a particularly important position. In the Afro-Bahian cults most leaders are women. The leaders, referred to in Bahia as 'Pai' or 'Mãe-de-santo', in Cuba as 'Padrino' or 'Madrina', represent the leading spiritual and temporal authority of the cult house, and determine its degree of orthodoxy. They are usually leading singers, responsible for transmitting knowledge of their vast repertory and for supervising instruction in music and dancing in the house. Drummers have an exalted position. They go through a series of tests before they are allowed to perform in ritual ceremonies, and their acceptance in the cult is publicly signified by a 'confirmation' ceremony. A drummer can become a master drummer only after years of experience, and under certain circumstances, for it is considered a special privilege.

(ii) *Secular ceremonial music.* In Latin American black culture, music plays a focal role in what might be termed 'secular rituals'. The *currulao* (marimba dance) of south-west Colombia and north-west Ecuador is an example of such a ritual, a social occasion incorporating symbolic behavioural patterns. The music of the marimba dance preserves many African patterns. It requires an ensemble of six to seven male musicians, two of whom play the marimba and the others drums. The marimba may have 20 to 28 hardwood keys (each with bamboo resonators), and it provides both melody and harmony. The player called *bordonero* is in charge of the melody, on the lower half of the instrument; the *tiplero*, on the upper half, plays the counterpoint and harmony. The tuning of the marimba is not uniform. As in religious cult music, solo-chorus alternation predominates in the *currulao*; female singers (*respondedoras*) participate in the chorus. The leading male musician is the *glosador*; his function is to lead the singing, to give the shouts and to indicate to the women what part of the repertory should be sung at a given time. Accompaniment is provided by two *bombos* (large double-headed drums), two *cununos* (single-headed, cone-shaped drums played with the hands) and rattles (maracas and *guasás*, the latter being bamboo tubes filled with seeds into which hardwood nails are driven).

The relationship of religious cult music to secular (social) dance and song is always close. Reasons for this are various: some of the Haitian and Afro-Bahian ceremonial music, for example, has lost its religious significance and become part of the social side of musical life. This is also true of the *candombe*, an Afro-Uruguayan ritual dance performed at the time of the Mardi Gras Carnival in Montevideo. The characters who dance in the parade probably represent figures from the earlier time of slavery and from the period after emancipation, when African cults and tribal rivalries dominated the life of the urban Negro community.

Among the Afro-Bahians, a secular form of singing and dancing not entirely dissociated from the sacred context is a type of athletic game known as *capoeira angola*. In spite of its name, this game was apparently invented in Brazil by former slaves, and must have been, in its original form, a simple kind of fight. The modern game is a simulated fight, preserving stylized steps (strokes). The *capoeira* uses a small instrumental ensemble, including the *berimbau* (musical bow, also called *urucungo*), and various percussion instruments. A distinctive characteristic of the *capoeira* song is that it is in the form of a dialogue between the *capoeira* singer and some abstract, imagined character. Fernando Ortiz has observed the same thing in Cuba as well as in other Afro-American areas of Latin America. Strikingly similar genres are found in widely separated areas; for example, the stick-fight game of Trinidad associated with the *kalinda* and accompanied by drum music has its equivalent in the Bahian *maculelê*.

While the ceremonial music (sacred and secular) of the Latin American and Caribbean black communities is its most prominent and most African form of musical expression, there are other genres: work songs, social dance-songs, narrative songs of various sorts and love-songs. The calypso, reminiscent of African satirical songs, probably originated in Trinidad and spread rapidly throughout the Caribbean. A product of racial tensions, it combines African, North American negro and Spanish popular styles (*see* TRINIDAD AND TOBAGO). Jamaican negroes sing spirituals and sea shanties with words of English and North American origin but with the African call-and-response form, though this may have been reinforced by similar forms in English sea shanties. Similarly, Afro-Cuban, Afro-

Brazilian, Afro-Colombian and Afro-Venezuelan urban popular music has patterns that can be attributed to several stylistic origins.

BIBLIOGRAPHY

D. Lopes: *A Report of the Kingdom of Congo* (London, 1597), 182f
R. Jobson: *The Golden Trade: or, a Discovery of the River Gambra, and the Golden Trade of the Aethiopians* (London, 1623), 105ff
R. Ligon: *A True and Exact History of the Island of Barbados* (London, 1657), 46ff
J. Baptiste Du Tertre: *Histoire générale des Antilles habitées par les françois*, ii (Paris, 1667), 526f
D. A. Rocha: *Tratado único* (Lima, 1681/R1891), 39
H. Sloane: *A Voyage to the Islands Madera, Barbados, Nieves, S. Christophers, and Jamaica* (London, 1707), 48, 51, 153f
J. de la Torre: *Aclamacion festiva* (Lima, 1716), 26
C. Leslie: *A New History of Jamaica* (London, 1740), 310
D. Diderot: 'Calinda', 'Nègres', 'Bamboula', *Encyclopédie, ou dictionnaire raisonné des sciences, arts et des métiers* (Paris, 1751–80), ii, 474; xi, 80; xv, 874
W. Beckford: *A Descriptive Account of the Island of Jamaica* (London, 1790), 215ff, 387
J. Rossi y Rubí: 'Idea de las congregaciones públicas de los *negros bozales*', *Mercurio peruano*, no.49 (1791), 112, 122
M. L. E. Moreau de Saint-Méry: *Description topographique, physique, civile, politique et historique de la partie française de l'isle Saint-Domingue*, i (Philadelphia, 1797), 44
B. Edwards: *The History, Civil and Commercial, of the British West Indies*, iii (London, 4/1807), 256ff
J. Grainger: 'The Sugar-Cane', *The Works of the English Poets, from Chaucer to Cowper*, ed. A. Chalmers, xiv (London, 1810), 478–511
A. Balbi: *Essai statistique sur le royaume de Portugal et d'Algarve*, ii (Paris, 1822), 213f
P. Young: *West-India Melodies; or Negro Tunes* (London, ?1822)
J. Hunter and J. Stevenson, eds.: *Boucher's Glossary of Archaic and Provincial Words* (London, 1832), p.BAN
A. Dessalles: *Histoire générale des Antilles*, iii (Paris, 1847), 296f
R. Almeida: *História da música brasileira* (Rio de Janeiro, 1926, 2/1942), 9ff, 137ff, 156ff
I. Castellanos: *Instrumentos musicales de los afrocubanos* (Havana, 1927)
A. Ramos: 'Os instrumentos musicaes dos candomblés da Bahia', *Bahia médica*, iii/7 (1932), 194
——: 'A sobrevivencia da dança e da música', *O folclore negro do Brasil* (Rio de Janeiro, 1935, rev. 2/1954), 118
H. Courlander: *Haiti Singing* (Chapel Hill, 1939)
A. Ramos: 'The Negro in Music', *The Negro in Brazil* (Washington, DC, 1939), 116ff
D. Pierson: 'The Candomblé', *Negroes in Brazil* (Chicago, 1942), 275–317
M. J. Herskovits: 'Drums and Drummers in Afrobrazilian Cult Life', *MQ*, xxx (1944), 477 [also pubd in *The New World Negro: Selected Papers in Afroamerican Studies* (Bloomington, Ind., 1966), 183ff]
R. Nettel: 'Historical Introduction to La Calinda', *ML*, xxvii (1946), 59
F. Ortiz: *La africania de la música folklórica de Cuba* (Havana, 1950)
——: *Los bailes y el teatro de los negros en el folklore de Cuba* (Havana, 1951)
R. A. Waterman: 'African Influence on the Music of the Americas', *Acculturation in the Americas: XXIXth International Congress of Americanists* (Chicago, 1952), 207
F. Ortiz: *Los instrumentos de la música afrocubana* (Havana, 1952–5)
A. M. Jones: *Studies in African Music*, i (Oxford, 1959), 212f
H. Courlander: *The Drum and the Hoe: Life and Lore of the Haitian People* (Berkeley, 1960)
V. Gesualdo: *Historia de la música en la Argentina* (Buenos Aires, 1961), i, 543ff; ii, 861ff
F. C. Lange: *Os compositores na Capitania Geral das Minas Gerais* (Marília, 1965)
B. Nettl: *Folk and Traditional Music of the Western Continents* (Englewood Cliffs, NJ, 1965, 2/1973)
R. Bastide: *Les amériques noires: les civilisations africaines dans le Nouveau Monde* (Paris, 1967; Eng. trans., 1971), 41b, 83, 118, 137, 174, 178, 224
F. C. Lange: *La música en Villa Rica, Minas Gerais, siglo XVIII* (Santiago, 1968)
R. Stevenson: 'The Afro-American Musical Legacy to 1800', *MQ*, liv (1968), 475
——: *Music in Aztec and Inca Territory* (Berkeley, Los Angeles and London, 1968)
E. Southern: *The Music of Black Americans: a History* (New York, 1971)
——: *Readings in Black American Music* (New York, 1971)
J. W. Work: 'African Music in British and French America', *MQ*, lix (1973), 61

IV. Popular music. The term 'popular music' is understood here to represent musical repertories and genres emanating primarily from urban areas, and disseminated through sheet music, radio and television and commercial recordings. Implicit in urban popular music are commercial promotion of composers and performers, the orientation of genres to particular social groups, and the relative sophistication of musical arrangements. Popular music is used primarily for entertainment, but it may also involve socio-political participation and criticism. Rather than going through ephemeral fashion cycles, popular music should be considered as changing more rapidly than other repertories because of the complexity and heterogeneity of urban cultures and the ready exchange of information among practitioners.

As an urban phenomenon Latin American popular music evolved during the first part of the 19th century when art music traditions had been firmly established, mostly in the major cities. After independence and the abolition of slavery, interaction between urban and rural areas facilitated the development of popular music genres that were often urban renditions of folk genres. This trend can be seen in the 20th century in most Latin American countries: almost all important folkdances have had their urban counterpart. Since few genres originated in cities before World I, a clear distinction between folk and popular music is particularly difficult to establish in Latin America. In most cases the distinguishing feature is in performance characteristics rather than in the contents of urban popular forms.

European and other foreign influences are important to Latin American popular music. In the 19th century fashionable European dances such as the waltz, mazurka, polka, schottische, contredanse and others were adopted in Central and South America and became 'creolized', that is, transformed by local characteristics. For example, the waltz had local versions with different names in most countries. Likewise European salon music of the 19th century provided an important source for many popular genres of the early 20th century, and the Romantic character of many popular genres stems from that tradition. Later in the 20th century North American popular music influenced local genres in hybrid forms such as *Inca-fox*, *ruba-fox* and *samba-fox*. The big jazz band era in the USA during the 1930s and 1940s also left its imprint on the performing practice of most classical Latin urban popular forms. Finally in the 1950s there was an attempt to develop Latin American expressions of jazz (for example, the 'samba jazz' in Brazil), and during the 1960s local adaptations of international pop music (especially rock music) gave rise to innovations in local popular music.

1. Mexico and the Caribbean. 2. The Andean area. 3. Argentina, Uruguay and Brazil.

1. MEXICO AND THE CARIBBEAN. Much Mexican popular music shows the influence of European salon music. For example, the first Mexican popular composer to gain international recognition was the Indian Juventino Rosas (1868–94), author of the set of waltzes, *Sobre las olas* ('Over the waves', 1891). The melody of the first section of the set (ex.23) has been known internationally since the beginning of the 20th century. Considered in Mexico to be very national in character, it is apparent that this melody follows the international style of salon music of the time in its eight-bar phrases, symmetry, contours and sectionalized form. Another tune

Ex.23 Juventino Rosas: *Sobre las olas*, 1891 (Campos, 1930)

popular in Mexico since about 1865 is *La golondrina*, composed in 1862 by Narciso Serradell (1843–1910); it is a song of farewell and has the same salon music characteristics.

The popular genres that most influenced the Mexicanization of European dances were the *jarabe* and the *danza mexicana*. The *jarabe*, a type of dance dating from the late colonial period, became the most popular dance and song of the revolutionary war of independence in the early 19th century. Since then it has been cultivated by most salon musicians and popular musicians. *Jarabes* printed during the second half of the 19th century generally have fast tempos, 6/8 and 3/4 metres, 8, 16 or 24 bars for each *son* (tune), frequent syncopation of the melodic line, parallel 3rds and 6ths and simple harmonic accompaniments that stress tonic–dominant relationships. These pieces were generally printed for solo piano, but in practice were performed by bands, especially *mariachi* ensembles, during the late 19th century. While many *jarabes* in 6/8 metre stressed syncopation (usually the repeated pattern of a semiquaver followed by a quaver), those in 3/4 could easily be transformed into a fast-tempo waltz, as is *Cielieto lindo*, believed to have been written by a Quirino F. Mendoza during the Mexican Revolution in the second decade of the 20th century (ex.24). The *jarabe*

Ex.24 *Cielieto lindo, jarabe*

Ex.25 M. Ramón Ortiz: *La sandunga* (Campos, 1930)

also influenced *La sandunga* by Máximo Ramón Ortiz (1816–55). While *sandungas* were waltz-like pieces, this one is in 6/8 metre with the same syncopation of the melodic line as the 6/8 *jarabe* (ex.25). The Mexican *danza* originated from the *contradanza*, itself transformed by the Andalusian tango and the Cuban habanera. Their characteristic rhythm (see ex.27a) gave rise to a series of Latin American popular dances; the basic dotted rhythm is almost always superimposed on regularly running semiquavers. In Mexico the *danza* was cultivated by composers such as Ernesto Elorduy, Felipe Villanueva and, later, Miguel Lerdo de Tejada. Many popular pieces, at first intended as simple songs (*canciones*), were performed as *danzas*, the most conspicuous examples being *La paloma*, written in Cuba by the Spaniard Sebastián Yradier (and known in Mexico since about 1866), and *La cucaracha*, popularized during the Mexican revolution.

The *canción mexicana*, considered the epitome of Mexican popular music, was derived from European popular lyrical tunes of the early 19th century, particularly the Spanish *coplas* and *romances*. The melody of the *canción* is typically in binary form with eight-bar phrases preceded by an instrumental introduction; some have an additional refrain. Since the beginning of the 20th century the *canción* has been influenced by other popular song genres, especially the bolero. The special type known as *canción ranchera*, introduced to the urban scene from folk tradition, has a distinctive Mexican character. It appeared in the 1920s, was cultivated especially as a genre accompanying sound films, and became popular during the 1930s. One of the first was *Mano a mano* by Lorenzo Barcelata, written for the film of the same title (1932). *Canciones* and boleros have been written since the beginning of the 20th century, the most popular composer being Agustín Lara (1897–1970); his song, *Granada*, was an international hit. Other well-known composers of *canciones* are Tata Nacho (Ignacio Fernández Esperón, 1894–1968), author of some 200 songs (among which *Que sí, que no*, *La borrachita*, *Serenata ranchera* and others won international acclaim), and Guty Cárdenas (1905–32), immortalized among Mexicans by his songs *Rayito de sol*, *Nunca* and *Caminante del Mayab*.

During the period from 1931 to 1941, often considered the 'golden age' of the romantic *canción mexicana*, musicians such as Emilio de Nicolás, María Grever, Manuel Esperón, the brothers Pablo and Carlos Martínez Gil, Luis Arcaraz and Gonzalo Curiel were active. At the same time the first regular recording firms were established in Mexico, stimulating the development of popular music. The Victor Talking Machine Company opened its Mexican factory in 1935, followed several years later by Columbia Records. During the 1940s and 1950s many boleros, *canciones*, *fox canciones* and *corridos* were composed as well as more recent genres such as beguines, blues, *danzón*, *guaracha* and *huapango*. The *corrido*, the folk ballad of Mexico, became popular during the revolution, but composers began to pay attention to it in the 1940s. The *huapango*, a folkdance of rhythmic intricacy and vitality, also began to be urbanized in the 1940s. Typical characteristics of the *huapango* are alternation of rhythms in 6/8 and 3/4 metres, the frequent falsetto singing and vocal duets and trios. José Alfredo Jiménez (*b* 1926) has been particularly successful as a composer of *huapangos* and especially *ranchera* music, that is, music with a strong Mexican flavour. During the 1950s with the penetration of rock and roll Jiménez came to symbolize the Mexican reaction against what many considered a foreign intrusion in national popular music.

Particularly important for modern Mexican and other Latin American popular dances has been the simple two-step march (similar to the Spanish *paso doble*). Innumerable genres derive from it, from the 19th-century *galopa* to modern *corridos* whose melodies are often accompanied by a regular duple metre, performed by a *mariachi* ensemble. Modern *rancheras* are also often performed as simple marches.

No Latin American country has been the source of so many influential popular genres as Cuba, from the habanera, *danza cubana* and bolero, to the *mambo*, rumba, *conga* and cha cha cha. Most of what is characterized as Afro-Cuban music (*see* CUBA, §II, 3) is applicable to Cuban popular music forms. The most typical forms

have a predominantly binary metre, with dotted rhythmic figures and syncopations. As in most dance music, isometric figures prevail. The Cuban habanera has been influential throughout Latin America; Eduardo Sánchez de Fuentes's piece entitled *Tu* (published in 1894) is a typical example (ex.26). A dotted figure (ex.27a) appears consistently as rhythmic accompaniment. The four-bar introduction shows a Cuban rhythm known as *cinquillo* (ex.27b), often reduced to a *tresillo* (ex.27c). The melodic line is also fairly consistent in its reliance on the dactylic figure (ex.27d), on anacrusis and on melodic sequence. The descending melody is also characteristic (ex.26). The Cuban bolero and rumba also have systematic syncopations in both accompaniment and melody. Rhythmic figures found in some typical boleros by Ernesto Lecuona and other popular com-

Ex.26 Eduardo Sánchez de Fuentes: *Tu*, habanera (Grenet, 1939)

Ex.27 Rhythmic patterns
(a) syncopated habanera pattern

(b) *cinquillo*

(c) *tresillo*

(d) melodic figure

(e) *bolero*

(f) *bolero*

posers (ex.27e and f) recur in numerous Latin American dances. Some Cuban popular genres such as the *criolla* have the Spanish-related rhythm of 6/8 figures against 3/4 accompaniments (creating hemiola effects) that is so typical of many Caribbean dances, such as the Colombian *bambuco* or the Venezuelan *joropo*.

The *merengue*, popular throughout the Caribbean and South America in the 1940s and 1950s, originated in the Dominican Republic, but it is also known in Haiti (*méringue*), Puerto Rico, Venezuela and Colombia. The Dominican *merengue* is a fairly fast dance in duple metre that relies, like so many other Caribbean dances, on syncopation of both melodic (vocal) line and accompaniment. The *merengue* has an instrumental introduction (generally of eight bars) called the *paseo*, followed by the vocal part, generally in two sections of 16 bars each. Instrumental *jaleos* (interludes) alternate between the first and second vocal parts. The *jaleos* may be four or eight bars long. Isometric figures predominate in the accompaniment. Numerous *merengues* have been written in the Caribbean and Central America, primarily for solo voice with piano accompaniment, but in performance they became part of the standard repertory of popular bands, from simple village bands to urban night-club bands. Besides the urbanized versions of folk-dances and folksongs Central American popular music includes local renditions of European and other Latin American popular forms.

2. THE ANDEAN AREA. In Colombia the most popular forms were the *bambuco*, the *porro* and then the *cumbia*. The popular *bambuco* is identical in form and general characteristics to the folk *bambuco* of the highlands. It combines rhythmic figures in 3/4 and 6/8 metres and is accompanied by an ensemble of *tiples* (treble guitars), *bandolas* (flat-backed lutes) and guitars. Urban renditions of *bambucos* often have vocal duets singing in parallel 3rds. During the 1940s the folkdance known as *porro* was adopted by many dance bands in Colombia and the Caribbean (Xavier Cugat and his orchestra popularized it after World War II) and transformed into a foxtrot-like rhythmic accompaniment. No dance form, however, has had the lasting popularity in Latin America of the *cumbia*, originally an Afro-Panamanian and Colombian folkdance. In its urbanization the *cumbia* lost some of its choreographic traits, particularly the typical hip movement. But musically the characteristics are very similar: prevailing duple metre, steady tempo, percussion accompaniment and syncopated melodic line. The popular *cumbia* or *cumbia de salón* also provided dance bands with an important part of their repertory. Whether in the ballroom or salon context, it is generally sung in a responsorial fashion. Another widespread popular dance in Colombia is the *pasillo*, often known as *el vals del país* ('the waltz of the country'). It is a moderately slow waltz-like dance, sung by either solo voice or duet (in parallel 3rds, the voices being referred to as *primo* and *segundo*), and accompanied by piano in the context of the salon or by *tiple* and guitar supplemented by tambourines and 'spoons' (used like Spanish castanets), or by an *estudiantina* (string ensemble) in the popular context. The repertory of *pasillos* composed during the 20th century is even more voluminous than that of the popular *bambuco*. The Colombian *pasillo* was widely popularized in Central America (especially Nicaragua and El Salvador) and has been adopted in Ecuador.

Ecuadorian popular music consists essentially of urbanized renditions of folksongs and folkdances. Those transformed genres include particularly the *sanjuanito*, the *pasillo* and the *cachullapi*. Much like the Peruvian *huayno*, the *sanjuanito* is a dance in duple metre, with syncopated melodies frequently in the minor mode. Pentatonic tunes are found in the popular music of Ecuador as often as diatonic tunes. The Ecuadorian *pasillo* is somewhat slower than its Colombian counterpart. It is usually strictly instrumental, especially in the highlands. The *quena* (end-blown notched flute) and the *pingullo* (small fipple flute) often carry the melody, the accompaniment being provided by guitars, double bass and *bombo* (drum). Many *pasillos* from the coastal area are sung. The dance genre known as *cachullapi* frequently appears as the concluding section of the *yaraví*, a sentimental love-song. As in other Latin American countries Ecuadorian composers have always adopted fashionable 20th-century popular dances. The American foxtrot of the 1930s became popular in the form called *fox incaico*. Later Caribbean, Brazilian and American dances are now favourites of urban middle-class young people.

Since the early 19th century Peru has produced many composers of salon music who later developed an interest in local fashionable song and dance genres. These genres include the popular *huayno*, similar to its folk counterpart but performed by urban bands with an instrumentation foreign to folk tradition; the *marinera*,

also like its folk counterpart; and the *vals peruano* or *criollo*, popular among the working and middle classes particularly in the coastal area and the urban centres, especially Lima. The *vals peruano* or *criollo* is generally sung by more than one voice, accompanied by guitar, *bandurria* or mandolin and an instrument of the lute type; the rhythm section of the accompanying ensemble includes also a *cajón* (drum), castanets, hand-clapping and shoe-tapping. From the beginning of the 20th century the *vals* has been used for serenades and cultivated by many composers including Felipe Pinglo Alva, Laureano Martínez, Carlos Saco, Filomeno Ormeño, Chabuca Granda and Alicia Maguiña. Like the Argentine tango, the Brazilian *samba canção* and the urban samba, the Peruvian *vals* texts symbolize the psychology of the Peruvian people at different times. *Vals* lyrics reveal the cultural personality of the Peruvian people and express the conflicts, attitudes and value systems resulting from the people's reaction to their social conditions.

Bolivian popular composers have also cultivated the *huayno popular*, the *cueca*, the *yaraví* and the *taquirari*. The Bolivian *cueca*, similar to the original Chilean *cueca*, combines 6/8 and 3/4 metres, and includes a short introduction and two sections generally of equal length. The *cuecas* for piano written by Simeón Roncal (1870–1953) are still popular among Bolivian pianists. The *yaraví*, a sentimental love-song, is often used in Bolivia to express melancholy. The *taquirari* is a dance with song which originated in the eastern provinces of Beni and Santa Cruz; it is in duple metre with a typical dactylic accompanimental figure throughout the dance and a moderately syncopated vocal line. The singing almost invariably has parallel 3rds or 6ths. In the cities and towns of the Bolivian plateau the *bailecito*, similar to the *cueca*, has also been cultivated. The *carnavalito*, found throughout the country, is a characteristic popular dance in which the rhythmic hemiola effect prevails, with the simultaneous use of 3/4 and 6/8.

Apart from the adaptation of international forms of popular music, Chilean music consists primarily of such popular forms as the *cueca* and urban versions of *tonadas*, *tristes*, *carnaval* and *tiranas*. The Chilean *cueca* is a dance with song, alternating rhythmic figures in 6/8 and 3/4 metres. It is generally accompanied by a flute (*quena* or *pingullo*), guitar, *charango* (small guitar) and *bombo*; the instrumentalists are often the singers as well. During the Allende regime in the late 1960s and early 1970s, several composers of popular music turned to song genres akin to folk music as homage to the people of Chile and the socialist reforms; the songs of Angel Parra in particular had wide repercussions in Latin America.

3. ARGENTINA, URUGUAY AND BRAZIL. The tango is by far the most important popular musical genre that originated in Argentina and Uruguay. Not only is it internationally popular, but it also epitomizes basic aspects of the social and cultural history of Argentina and Uruguay since the late 19th century. It symbolizes the hopes, successes and failures of the millions of immigrants who were concentrated in the big cities, particularly in the *arrabal* ('ghettos'). The origin of the term 'tango' is disputed. According to Rossi (1926) it was the name that black slaves gave their drums during the colonial period. From this the term may have been used generically to designate dancing, the accompanying in-

struments and the locale of the dancing. The coastal *milonga*, a dance of Afro-Argentine and Uruguayan folk tradition in duple metre and syncopated rhythm, probably contributed to the development of the tango of the River Plate area. As a dance the tango is in part a local adaptation of the Andalusian tango, the Cuban *danzón* and habanera and, to a lesser extent, the European polka and schottische. The tango followed the habanera rhythmic pattern in duple metre (2/4) up to about 1915, when 4/8 metre became more frequent; after about 1955 new rhythmic complexities were added. There are three types of tango: the strongly rhythmic instrumental *tango-milonga* for popular orchestras, the instrumental or vocal *tango-romanza* with a more melodic and romantic character, and the accompanied vocal *tango-canción* ('tango-song'), which is strongly lyric and sentimental. The texts of the *tango-canción* tend to express views of love and life in pessimistic and at times pathologically dramatic terms. Tango reflects a complex state of mind peculiar to the cultural area including Buenos Aires, Montevideo, La Plata, Córdoba, Rosario and southern Brazil. It is performed by embracing couples, with the obvious symbolic domination of the male over the female.

The first ensembles performing tangos were *tercetos* (trios), generally including violin, guitar and flute, with accordion frequently replacing the guitar. When the tango was introduced to middle-class ballrooms and homes, numerous pieces were written for the piano. About 1900 the new trio included piano, violin and *bandoneón* (accordion). The first recording of Vicente Greco's ensemble was made in 1911, with two violins, two *bandoneones*, guitar and flute. After that larger bands were formed, including up to four *bandoneones*, a sizable string section, with violins, a cello and a double bass, and a piano. These constituted what came to be called *orquestas típicas*; numerous such ensembles gained popularity, particularly those of Juan Maglio ('Pacho'), Roberto Firpo, Francisco Canaros and Eduardo Arolas. Some of the best-known bands included the Orquesta Típica 'Select', established in 1919, the Orquesta Típica 'Victor' (1925), exclusively for recording purposes, the Orquesta Típica 'Novel' (1934), and the Orquesta Típica 'Los Provincianos', under the famous *bandoneón* player and tango composer Ciríaco Ortiz (*b* 1908).

The internationalization of the tango took place during the early 20th century. Carlos Gardel (1887–1935), a popular idol in the 1920s, was particularly important in making it fashionable throughout Europe and the western hemisphere. Gardel's major contribution was to transform the tango from a dance form into a song type of social and cultural significance. Besides his own recordings of well-known tangos, his best-known compositions include *El día que me quieras*, *Mi Buenos Aires querido*, *Por una cabeza*, *Volver*, *Silencio* and *Cuesta abajo*. Perhaps the most successful tango ever written was Gerardo Matos Rodríguez's *La cumparsita* (1917), written in Montevideo. Other representative successful pieces are Julio César Sanders's *Adiós muchachos* (1928), Enrique Santos Discépolo's *Yira, yira* (1930), Angel Villoldo's *El choclo* (1905), Juan Carlos Cobián's *Nostalgias*, Francisco Canaro's *Adiós, pampa mía* and Edgardo Donato's *A media luz*. Although the tango lost some of its earlier popularity in the 1940s and 1950s it was revived in the 1960s and 1970s.

In the 1950s and 1960s Argentina, like most other Latin American countries, had its own local adaptations of international pop music. The 'new wave', as it was called, was a trend involving local renditions of rock and roll at first and later of rock music. In the early 1960s its most popular figures included, among others, Ramón Bautista Palito Ortega and Violeta Rivas. The 'new wave' produced a reaction that promoted the revival of the tango of the 1930s and 1940s, in which the Uruguayan Julio María Sosa (1926–64) was very influential.

Brazilian popular music began to gain stylistic originality during the last 30 years of the 19th century. The MODINHA and the *lundu*, cultivated in the salons since the period of independence, were popularized. Local adaptation of European urban dances, particularly the polka, gave rise to new genres such as the MAXIXE and the *tango brasileiro*, whose first composers were Joaquim Antonio da Silva Callado, Francisca Gonzaga and Ernesto Nazareth. The CHORO first appeared as a manner of improvisation of fashionable dances, such as the polka. The improvising ensembles included guitars, *cavaquinhos* and flutes, later reinforced by other wind or brass instruments. The *choros* of about 1900 show a virtuoso concern for solo performance.

Popular music in Brazil has been stimulated above all by Carnival, first organized on a regular basis during the last years of the 19th century. At first simple marches, polkas and waltzes were used, but the most typical Carnival genre that evolved, especially in Rio de Janeiro, was the urban samba, which appeared during the second decade of the 20th century. As a Carnival dance the urban samba incorporated figures such as *requebros* (hip movements). It also took the fast tempo of the *maxixe* which it eventually replaced. The Carnival samba appeared primarily as a stylization of *samba de morro* rhythms by popular composers, particularly José Barbosa da Silva, nicknamed 'Sinhô' (1888–1930), who was considered the 'king of samba' (*see* SAMBA). His first important pieces were *Jura*, *Não quero saber mais dela* and *Que vale a 'nota' sem o carinho da mulher*. From the time of the first successful Carnival samba to be recorded (*Pelo telefone* by Donga, 1917), the new genre was cultivated by composers. Through recordings and radio programmes the samba of the 1920s soon became the foremost national popular dance. Among the most sucessful composers were José Luís de Morais (1883–1961), nicknamed 'Caninha', who wrote *Essa nêga qué me dar*, *É batuoada* and *O, que vizinha danada!* and Alfredo Rocha Viana Filho (1898–1973), nicknamed 'Pixinguinha', a flautist, saxophonist and organizer of important bands, such as Os Oito Batutas (1922), Grupo da Velha Guarda (1932) and the famous Orquestra Típica Pixinguinha-Donga (1928). Pixinguinha's compositions – *Samba de nêgo*, *Pé de mulata*, *Promessa*, *Festa de branco* – were hits in their time, but he was most influential as a performer and a band-leader. Other important composers of the 'golden phase' of the urban samba were Ary Barroso (1907–64) who won international acclaim with such sambas as *Aquarela do Brasil*, *Faceira*, *É luxo só* and *Na baixa do sapateiro*; Noel Rosa (1910–37), who wrote *Com que roupa*, *Feitiço da vila*, *Palpite infeliz* and *Fita amarela*; Lamartine Babo (1904–63), particularly successful as a composer of Carnival marches (e.g. *O teu cabelo não nega, mulata*) and sambas (e.g. *A tua vida é um segredo*); and Carlos Ferreira Braga (*b* 1907), nicknamed 'João de Barro'.

Around 1928 two significant new developments affected the samba: the creation of the 'samba schools' and the advent of the genre *samba-canção*. The samba schools were Carnival associations whose members came down from the hill slums of the city to parade in the streets, dancing and singing sambas which often alluded to national or local events. The first group was Deixa Falar (1928), followed in 1930 by Estação I de Mangueira, Vai Como Pode (later known as Portela), Cada Ano Sai Melhor and others. At first the female dancers wore typical Bahian costumes, used in a stylized fashion by the singer Carmen Miranda (1909–55) in her many Hollywood appearances. After about 1952 several samba schools joined with other organizations and were transformed into clubs or societies. The *samba-canção* was created primarily for the urban middle class and was strongly reminiscent melodically and textually of the older *modinha*; rhythmically and harmonically it was influenced in the 1940s and 1950s by boleros and the 'fox-blues'. One of the most popular singers of *samba-canções* was Francisco Alves (1898–1952).

Other important popular genres are the *frevo*, a fast-tempo march with complex choreography, associated primarily with the Carnival of Pernambuco; the *baião*, also from the north-eastern area, popularized during the 1940s especially by Luis Gonzaga and Humberto Teixeira; and urbanized folksong and folkdance genres such as the *moda-de-viola*. The Bahian composer-singer Dorival Caymmi (*b* 1914) has been successful in writing in a semi-folk style. The advent of BOSSA-NOVA in the late 1950s, and the *jovem guarda* movement in the early 1960s under the leadership of Roberto Carlos, provided Brazilian popular music with new stylistic currents and a dynamic vitalization that brought about highly sophisticated groups such as the Tropicalia.

BIBLIOGRAPHY

MEXICO AND THE CARIBBEAN

R. M. Campos: *El folklore musical de las ciudades* (Mexico, 1930)
E. Grenet: *Popular Cuban Music* (Havana, 1939)
D. Castañeda: *Balance de Agustín Lara* (Mexico, 1941)
H. Menéndez Peña: *Monografías y cantares huastecos* (Mexico, 1944)
M. Talavera: *Miguel Lerdo de Tejada* (Mexico, n.d.)
A. Carpentier: *La música en Cuba* (Mexico, 1946)
V. T. Mendoza, ed.: *Canciones mexicanas – Mexican Folk Songs* (New York, 1948)
V. T. Mendoza: *El corrido de la revolución mexicana* (Mexico, 1956)
J. Sesto: *La bohemia de la muerte* (Mexico, 1958)
V. T. Mendoza: *La canción mexicana* (Mexico, 1961)
R. Ayala: *Musicosas* (Mexico, 1962)
A. de María y Campos: *La revolución mexicana a través de los corridos populares* (Mexico, 1962)
H. de Grial: *Músicos mexicanos* (Mexico, 1965)
G. Baqueiro Fóster: *La canción popular de Yucatán* (Mexico, 1970)
J. S. Garrido: *História de la música popular en México (1896–1973)* (Mexico, 1974)

THE ANDEAN AREA

N. Garay: 'Folklore musical colombiano', *Revista gris* (1894), 240
P. Humberto Allende: 'La musique populaire chilienne', *1er congrès international des arts populaires: Praha 1928*, 118
C. Raygada: *Panorama musical del Perú* (Lima, 1936)
L. Sandoval: *Selección de canciones populares chilenas* (Santiago, 1937)
A. Acevedo Hernández: *Canciones populares chilenas* (Santiago, 1939)
T. Vargas: *Aires nacionales de Bolivia* (La Paz, 1940)
P. Garrido: *Biografía de la cueca* (Santiago, 1943)
C. Vega: 'La forma de la cueca chilena', *Revista musical chilena*, nos.20–21 (1947), 7; nos.22–3 (1947), 15
——: *Las danzas populares argentinas* (Buenos Aires, 1952)
Panorama de la música tradicional del Perú, ed. Escuela Nacional de Música y Danzas Folklóricas (Lima, 1966)
Cancionero Andino Sur, ed. Escuela Nacional de Música y Danzas Folklóricas (Lima, 1967)
S. Zapata Agurto: 'Psicoanálisis del vals peruano', *Revista de ciencias psicológicas y neurológicas*, v/1–2 (1968), 5
E. Pereira Salas: *Guía bibliográfica para el estudio del folklore chileno* (Santiago, n.d.)

ARGENTINA, URUGUAY AND BRAZIL

V. Rossi: *Cosas de negros* (Córdoba, 1926)
O. Barbosa: *Samba* (Rio de Janeiro, 1933)
C. Vega: *Danzas y canciones argentinas* (Buenos Aires, 1936)
M. Lira: *Brasil sonoro* (Rio de Janeiro, 1938)
R. Almeida: *História da música brasileira* (Rio de Janeiro, 1942)
I. Aretz: *El folklore musical argentino* (Buenos Aires, 1952)
C. Vega: *Las danzas populares argentinas*, i (Buenos Aires, 1952)
L. Ayestarán: *La música en el Uruguay*, i (Montevideo, 1953)
V. Mariz: *A canção brasileira* (Rio de Janeiro, 1959)
L. Rangel: *Sambistas e chorões* (Rio de Janeiro, 1962)
A. Vasconcelos: *Panorama da música popular brasileira* (São Paulo, 1964)
C. Vega: 'Las pespecies homónimas y afines de "los orígenes del tango argentino" ', *Revista musical chilena*, no.101 (1967), 49
F. García Jiménez: *Estampas de tango* (Buenos Aires, 1968)
H. Ferrer: *El libro del tango* (Buenos Aires, 1970)
B. Matamoro: *Carlos Gardel* (Buenos Aires, 1971)
——: *Historia del tango* (Buenos Aires, 1971)
J. Ramos Tinhorão: *Música popular, de indios, negros e mestiços* (Petrópolis, 1972)
——: *Pequena história da música popular* (Petrópolis, 1974)

ISABEL ARETZ (I)
GERARD BÉHAGUE (II; III, 4; IV)
ROBERT STEVENSON (III, 1–3)

Latin secular song, early. *See* EARLY LATIN SECULAR SONG.

Latio, Giovanni [Latius, Joannes]. *See* LAET, JEAN.

La Tombelle, (Antoine Louis Joseph Gueyrand) Fernand (Fouant) de (*b* Paris, 3 Aug 1854; *d* Château de Fayrac, Dordogne, 13 Aug 1928). French organist and composer. He first studied music with his mother, a pupil of Liszt and Thalberg. At the Paris Conservatoire he studied the organ with Guilmant and composition with Théodore Dubois. When the Trocadéro organ concerts began in 1878 he became an active associate of Guilmant, and also made successful recital tours. From 1885 to 1898 he was Dubois' assistant at the Madeleine. When the Schola Cantorum was founded by Bordes, d'Indy and Guilmant (1894) La Tombelle devoted much time to realizing the aims of its revised programme, the improvement and enlarging of the organ repertory and the foundation of a modern school of church music. From 1896 to 1904 he was professor, and later inspector, of harmony at the Schola Cantorum, and collaborated in the production of the *Répertoire moderne de musique religieuse*. He also contributed articles to *La tribune de St Gervais*, the magazine of the Schola, which began in 1895.

Before turning to sacred works La Tombelle composed much secular music, including orchestral pieces, songs, choral music, two operettas, *Un bon numéro* and *Un rêve au pays du bleu* (both 1892), piano solos and duets, a violin sonata and a trio op.35 (1894). He was also a prolific composer of sacred music: masses, oratorios, motets, canticles, hymns and organ and harmonium pieces. Ferchault stressed the traditional form and language of most of La Tombelle's music. He published a book *L'oratorio et la cantate* (Paris, 1911) and a *Méthode d'harmonium*.

BIBLIOGRAPHY

A. Gastoué: Obituary, *La tribune de St Gervais*, v (1928), 170
G. Ferchault: 'La Tombelle, Fernand de', *MGG* [with list of works]

E. BORREL/DAVID CHARLTON

Latorre, Gerónimo (*d* Saragossa, early 18th century). Spanish organist and composer. He has previously been thought to be the Jerónimo de la Torre who was second organist at Valencia Cathedral from 3 April 1645 to 16 May 1665, but this cannot be so. Latorre, called 'the cripple', was probably a pupil of Andrés de Sola. He became second organist at the Cathedral of La Seo in Saragossa on 20 September 1674. In August 1677 he was appointed organist at El Pilar in that city and remained so until his elevation to *maestro de capilla* on 5 March 1695. He retired on 13 October 1699 to the monastery of S Ildefonso, Saragossa, and presumably died there some years later. It was probably Latorre who in addition to his musical activities wrote *Gozos de las virtudes y milagros del Seráphico y gran Patriarcha S. Bruno* (Barcelona, 1702).

WORKS

The music usually attributed to Jerónimo de la Torre is probably by Latorre:

Missa 7° tono, Missa 8° tono, *E-Zac*; Lamentatio, 8vv, bc, *J*; Letania a Nuestra Señora, 5vv, *Ac*; sacred villancico, Aquel sol, 3vv, bc, *GU*
Traidor corazón, ¿qué tienes?, 4vv; Para divertir a filis, 4vv; Loco estoy, 1v, bc, *Bc*; tonadillas and letrillas, *Mn*; 12 secular pieces in Música antiqua, *Mn*
12 organ versos for the Mass, *J*

BIBLIOGRAPHY

J. Climent: 'Organistas valencianos de los siglos XVII y XVIII: Organistas de la catedral', *AnM*, xvii (1962), 179
L. Siemens Hernández: 'La Seo de Zaragoza, destacada escuela de órgano en el siglo XVII', ii, *AnM*, xxiii (1968), 129

BARTON HUDSON

Latour, Francis Tatton. One of the original partners in the music-publishing firm of CHAPPELL.

Latre, Petit Jean de. *See* DE LATRE, PETIT JEAN.

Latrobe [La Trobe], Christian Ignatius (*b* Fulneck, Leeds, 12 Feb 1758; *d* Fairfield, nr. Liverpool, 6 May 1836). English composer. His family was originally of Huguenot descent; his father, Benjamin Latrobe, was superintendent of the Moravian Brethren in England and moved in the highest political and intellectual circles. He was educated among the United Brethren at Niesky, Upper Lusatia (1771–84), became a minister in the Moravian Church on his return and secretary of the Unity of the Brethren in England in 1795. He took part in various missions, including one to South Africa in 1815–16, and published accounts of his own and other Moravian missionary activities.

Latrobe was never a professional musician and was apparently self-taught, yet his achievement was considerable. His first compositions were instrumental, including three piano sonatas (London, *c*1790) dedicated to Haydn, with whom he was on friendly terms. It was Graun's *Tod Jesu* and Haydn's *Stabat mater* (according to his own account) that 'first gave him the idea of the powers of vocal music, in the expression of every feeling of which a devotional mind is capable'. He composed and edited much church music for both Moravian and general use, and a few pieces of Anglican cathedral music. His most important Moravian publication was *Anthems for One or More Voices Sung in the Church of the United Brethren* (London, 1811), which is indispensable to the study of Moravian music. It includes a dozen of his own compositions. He also edited the first English collection of Moravian hymn tunes (London, 1790), which remained in use for a century and more; the tunes were chiefly drawn from Gregor's *Choralbuch* (Leipzig, 1784). In 1828 he published a collection of his own sacred music.

A publication of wider influence was Latrobe's six-volume *Selection of Sacred Music* (London, 1806–26), in which was introduced to the British public for the first time the church music of such European composers as Graun, Hasse, Pergolesi, Haydn and Mozart (see *Grove 1–3*, 'Latrobe'). The music was published in vocal score with fully written out accompaniments, some of them with the original text, others in translation. This pioneering work opened an entirely new realm of music, most of it Catholic in origin, to English musicians. It anticipated Novello's publications in which Latrobe also played an acknowledged part. Although he disapproved of opera, Latrobe delighted in the operatic style in church music. He was the first English composer to use the style of Haydn's later masses with confidence and skill. His settings of the canticles are markedly more expressive and dramatic than those of contemporary Anglican composers (they are probably too long, however, for normal cathedral use). In such works as his cantata *The Dawn of Glory* (London, 1803/*R*1968) operatic recitative and aria are successfully adapted to sacred English words, with sensitive attention to word-setting and with richly varied accompaniments.

One of Latrobe's sons, John Antes Latrobe (1799–1878), named after the distinguished Moravian composer John Antes, took orders in the Church of England, and was incumbent of St Thomas's, Kendal (1840–65); he wrote a number of books on music, the most important of which, *The Music of the Church Considered in its Various Branches, Congregational and Choral* (London, 1831), gives an excellent picture (though in stilted language) of Anglican church music before the Oxford Movement.

WORKS

(all published in London)

Original Anthems . . . Adapted for Private Devotion or Public Worship (1828) [incl. Morning and Evening Service, G, 1817; Dies irae, 1823; Magnificat, D, 1823; Evening Service, G, 1828; 2 Agnus Dei; 9 anthems; 2 duets; 8 arias, ariettas; *c*17 hymn tunes]
2 other anthems: Anthem for . . . the Jubilee of George III (1809); Miserere mei (1814)
2 cantatas: The Dawn of Glory (C. I. Latrobe), solo vv, chorus, pf (1803); In Memory of a Beloved Sister (J. A. Latrobe), 1v, pf (1826)
6 Airs, the Words on Serious Subjects (Cowper, H. More), 1v, pf (*c*1812)
3 pf sonatas, op.3 (*c*1790)

EDITIONS

The Hymn-tunes of the Church of the Brethren (London, 1790)
A Selection of Sacred Music from the Work of Some of the Most Eminent Composers of Germany and Italy (London, 1806–26)
Anthems for One or More Voices Sung in the Church of the United Brethren (London, 1811) [incl. 12 of Latrobe's compositions]

BIBLIOGRAPHY

J. Sainsbury, ed.: *A Dictionary of Musicians* (London, 2/1825/*R*1966)
E. Holmes: 'The Rev. Christian Ignatius Latrobe', *MT*, iv (1851), 249
Brief Notices of the Latrobe Family (London, 1864)
J.C. Haddon: 'Latrobe, Christian Ignatius'; 'Latrobe, John Antes', *DNB*
C. E. Stephens: *The Musical Works of Christian Ignatius Latrobe* (diss., U. of North Carolina, 1971)

NICHOLAS TEMPERLEY

Lattuada, Felice (*b* Caselle di Morimondo, Milan, 5 Feb 1882; *d* Milan, 2 Nov 1962). Italian composer. He studied with Ferroni at the Milan Conservatory, graduating in 1912. From 1935 until his death he was director of the Milan Civic School of Music. As a composer he was tied to traditional forms and, in particular, to the passionate *verismo* operatic style. He wrote scores for films directed by his son, Alberto Lattuada, and he published an autobiography, *La passione dominante* (Bologna, 1951).

WORKS

(selective list)

Operas: La tempesta (A. Rossato, after Shakespeare), Milan, 1922; Sandha (F. Fontana), Genoa, 1924; Le preziose ridicole (Rossato, after Molière), Milan, 1929; Don Giovanni (Rossato, after J. Zorilla), Naples, 1929; La caverna di Salamanca (V. Piccoli, after Cervantes), Genoa, 1938; Caino (F. L. and G. Zambianchi, after Byron), Milan, 1957
Other works: orch and vocal orch pieces, choral music, chamber music

ALBERTO PIRONTI

Latvia. A constituent republic of the USSR; *see* UNION OF SOVIET SOCIALIST REPUBLICS, §VI.

Lätzsch, Herbert (*b* Störmthal, nr. Leipzig, 23 Dec 1917). German maker of brass instruments. He learnt to play the trumpet as a youth, and studied with Schopper, a master craftsman of metal wind instruments, in Leipzig (1933–6). After his qualifying examination (1936) he served in the navy. At the end of World War II he rebuilt the firm of Riedel in Bremen with violin maker Fritz Riedel, and in 1949 he founded his own firm (taking his master's examination in Hamburg in 1954). His work has been considerably influenced by the distinguished trombone maker Franz Kuhn of Langenberg, who began working under contract with Lätzsch in February 1953 after he lost his own workshop and sold the remainder of his tools to the firm of Monke (Cologne). Lätzsch was able to continue making the 'Alschausky–Kuhn' trombone as the 'Lätzsch–Kuhn' model, and developed the 'Kuhn' trombone, which has won worldwide esteem for its good, delicate tone, particularly well suited to interpreting German Classical and Romantic compositions.

Lätzsch has built trombones in five sizes and thus continues the German tradition, which is also distinguished from English and American practice in that the instruments have longer slides and shorter bodies. A particular feature of his instruments is that the normal rounded tube at the upper end of the body may be replaced by a tube that lowers the horn by a 4th when its valve is opened, thus making it a B♭/F instrument. (When C. F. Sattler first developed this concept in 1839, the additional tubing was a permanent fixture; *see* TROMBONE.) Lätzsch's firm also makes trumpets and flugelhorns.   ARMIN ROSIN

Lau, Heinz (*b* Stettin, 8 Sept 1925; *d* Berlin, 21 June 1975). German composer. He studied with Ernst Gernot Klussman, Jarnach, Wilhelm Keller and Wilhelm Maler, and also, from 1954 to 1957, with Hindemith. In 1963 he was appointed lecturer in improvisation and harmony at the Pädagogische Hochschule in West Berlin, where he was made professor in 1971; in addition, he became editor of music education programmes for Radio Free Berlin in 1973. In the same year he was made a member of the Amriswil Academy, Switzerland. His work was important to the German youth music movement from 1950, and he made his reputation in the field of music education, particularly through his method of improvisation.

WORKS
(selective list)

Choral: Anbetung des Kindes (Weinheber), 1951; O Musica (after Peuerl), 1951; Die Weihnachtsgeschichte, chorus, insts, 1952, rev. 1957; Die Himmel erzählen, 1952; Lob des Tanzes, 1953; Mein Lied für Europa (Forestier), 1953; Dona nobis pacem, 1954; Die helle Sonne, chorus, insts, 1955; Regenkantate, chorus, insts, 1958; Die Weihnachtsgeschichte, 1961; Olympische Ode (Pindar), chorus, insts, 1963; Missa brevis canonica, solo vv, chorus, 1968; Klangstudien, children's vv, insts, tape, 1970; Die Weihnachtsgeschichte, improvisation for children, 1972

Requiem für eine Verfolgte – in memoriam Anne Frank (Eich, Celan, etc), T, str qt, 1961; Competition, org, solo vv, insts, tape, 1971

Disputation, orch, 1972

Many songs and short choral pieces, chamber works, film and radio music

Principal publishers: Möseler, Pelikan (Zurich)

KLAUS L. NEUMANN

Laub, Ferdinand (*b* Prague, 19 Jan 1832; *d* Gries, nr. Bolzano, 18 March 1875). Czech violinist and composer. His father taught him the violin as a child of four

and he began to appear publicly when he was six; in 1841 Ole Bull praised his virtuoso playing. He was accepted straight into the second year at the Prague Conservatory, where he studied from 1843 to 1846 under Mořic Mildner, in his last year attracting the attention of H. W. Ernst (who later dedicated to Laub one of his *Mehrstimmige Studien*) and of Berlioz, who invited him to Paris. In December 1846 he went on a concert tour of Austria and Germany but was prevented from going to Paris by the 1848 Revolution. From 1848 to 1850 he worked in Vienna as a soloist with the orchestra of the Theater an der Wien and studied counterpoint with Sechter. At the end of 1850 he was invited by Balfe to take part in the national concerts at Her Majesty's Theatre in London (March to August 1851); he also appeared in Berlin, Paris and St Petersburg. In 1853 he succeeded Joachim as Konzertmeister in Weimar, where he came to know Liszt and played chamber music with him. From 1855 to 1857 he was violin professor at the Stern Conservatory in Berlin, and in 1856 was appointed chamber virtuoso to the Prussian king.

Between 1858 and 1865 Laub's performing career was at its peak. He appeared as soloist in all the major European cities and organized quartet evenings in Berlin (1858–62) at which he systematically performed all the Beethoven quartets; in Vienna (1862–6) he was made chamber virtuoso (1863) and organized successful chamber evenings in competition with Hellmesberger. He appeared with his most eminent contemporaries, including Clara Schumann and Bülow (Berlin, 1858), Rubinstein and Leschetizky (St Petersburg, 1859), Smetana (Göteborg, 1860), Patti and Jaëll (England, 1862) and Joachim (London, 1862). In 1866 he accepted the post of violin professor at the conservatory in Moscow, where he was acclaimed as soloist, chamber player and conductor and was much in demand as a teacher. He made deep friendships with the foremost Russian artists and contributed significantly to the high standard of the city's musical life; Tchaikovsky dedicated his Third String Quartet op.30 to Laub's memory in gratitude for the performances of his first two quartets (as leader of the Russian Musical Society's quartet). A year before his death Laub went for treatment to Bohemia, where he appeared in public for the last time in August 1874.

In his time Laub was renowned for his beautiful tone, his technical virtuosity and his unfailing sense of style. His wide repertory embraced such virtuoso works as the concertos of Mendelssohn, Joachim, Ernst, Paganini and Spohr, and his interpretation of the Beethoven concerto was particularly celebrated. He was one of the first violinists to perform the Bach sonatas. His instruments included an Amati, a 1706 Guarneri and a 1727 Stradivari. He composed a number of technically demanding violin pieces and some vocal works. His son Váša (Václav) Laub (*b* Berlin, 31 Dec 1857; *d* Khabarovsk, 23 Nov 1911) studied under his father in Moscow, in Prague under Karel Bendl (1875) and at the organ school (1879). He was a choirmaster and piano teacher in Moscow, military conductor in Port Arthur (from 1900) and the composer of numerous piano and orchestral pieces, songs and choruses.

BIBLIOGRAPHY

ČSHS

V. V. Mareš: 'Ferdinand Laub', *Lumír*, viii (1858), 467

J. W. von Wasielewski: *Die Violine und ihre Meister* (Leipzig, 1869), 353

A. Kalvoda: *O českém houslistovi Ferdinandu Laubovi* [On the Czech

violinist Laub] (Křivoklát, 1912)
K. Hůlka: 'Ferdinand Laub', *HR*, vi (1912–13), 24
A. Moser: *Geschichte des Violinspiels* (Berlin, 1923, rev., enlarged 2/1966–7)
A. HniliČka: 'Ze styků Ferdinanda Lauba s Chrudimí' [Laub's contact with Chrudim], *Vlastivědný sborník východočeský*, iv (1929), 63ff
J. Čeleda: *Paganini a Praha* (Prague, 1940), 167ff
F. Žídek: *Přehledné dějiny českého houslového umění* [Survey of the history of Czech violin playing] (Vyškov, 1940), 45ff
——: *Ferdinand Laub* (Prague, 1946)
L. S. Ginzburg: *Ferdinand Laub* (Moscow and Leningrad, 1951)
B. Šich: *Ferdinand Laub* (Prague, 1951) [with list of works]
                                    ALENA NĚMCOVÁ

Laub, Thomas (Linnemann) (*b* Langaa, Fyn, 5 Dec 1852; *d* Gentofte, nr. Copenhagen, 4 Feb 1927). Danish church musician and composer. After taking his matriculation examination in 1871 he first studied theology, but from 1873 to 1876 he attended the Copenhagen Conservatory, where he was taught by the distinguished theorist J. C. Gebauer. It was probably due to Gebauer's influence that during these years he became interested in the Cecilian movement within church music. On a trip to Italy in 1882–3 he became acquainted with classical vocal polyphony, and he saw the reform movement for himself in Germany in 1886. He then began his life's work for a revival of Danish ecclesiastical music, work which also came to embrace the medieval Danish ballad and popular song. From 1884 to 1891 he was organist at Helligåndskirken in Copenhagen, following Gebauer, and in 1891 he succeeded Gade as organist at Holmens Kirke, a position he held until two years before his death. The commotion this appointment aroused showed clearly how far he had already departed from the 19th-century tradition of ecclesiastical music in Denmark. From the first Laub put his energies into purifying what he saw as the corrupt tradition of 18th- and 19th-century psalmody. For him, Gregorian chant was unsurpassed as a melodic basis for ecclesiastical vocal music, and the chorale was the most beautiful expression of devotional music. He strove to re-create this tradition by restoring the melody, rhythm and harmony of the hymns to their original form and by composing anew in the old spirit. He also put his views in writings, as well as in arrangements and his own compositions, of which the most important is the collection *Dansk kirkesang* (1918). His untiring work and valuable artistic achievements aroused much debate and great opposition during his life, but his efforts have left a deep mark on 20th-century Danish church music. In 1922 the Danish Hymn Society was founded to spread his ideas, and 'Laubianismen' became a strong movement within Danish ecclesiastical musical practice.

Laub also wanted to restore the medieval ballad, whose melodies are known mainly from copies made in the 19th century, to what he saw as its genuine form on a foundation of Gregorian chant and modal melody. But although his attempts at restoration, particularly his polyphonic arrangements, hold many beauties, they represent a view of art music on a popular substratum that has been abandoned in the light of research into the ballad genre. Laub shared his interest in popular community singing with other contemporary composers in the years after 1900. In his efforts to re-create a simple song tradition with models in, among others, J. A. P. Schulz, he joined with Nielsen and also with Oluf Ring and Thorvald Aagaard to publish the most popular collection of tunes of the time, *Folkehøjskolens melodibog* (1922), containing some of the most beautiful of Laub's own secular melodies, which, as Nielsen ex-

pressed it, are 'never at any point self-assertive, but continuously, lovingly, both adorn and subserve the songs'.

WORKS
(selective list)
SACRED

80 rytmiske koraler (Copenhagen, 1888)
Kirkemelodier, firstemmig udsatte (Copenhagen, 1888–90)
Salmemelodier i kirkestil (Copenhagen, 1896–1902)
Forspil og melodier: forsøg i kirkestil (Copenhagen, 1909)
Dansk kirkesang: gamle og nye melodier (Copenhagen, 1918, suppl. 1930)
Aandelige sange (Copenhagen, 1925)
24 salmer og 12 folkeviser, ed. M. Wöldike (Copenhagen, 1928)
Liturgisk musik, ed. M. Wöldike (Copenhagen, 1937)

SECULAR

10 gamle danske folkeviser (Copenhagen, 1890)
Danske folkeviser med gamle melodier (Copenhagen, 1899–1904, 2/1930)
with C. Nielsen: En snes danske viser (Copenhagen, 1915–17)
Ti Aarestrupske ritorneller (Copenhagen, 1920)
Tolv viser og sange af danske digtere (Kolding, 1920, 2/1938)
with C. Nielsen, O. Ring and T. Aagaard: Folkehøjskolens melodibog (Copenhagen, 1922, suppl. 1927)
30 danske sange for 3 og 4 lige stemmer (Copenhagen, 1922)
Faerøske og danske folkevisemelodier udsatte for mandskor af Henrik Rung og Thomas Laub, ed. K. Clausen (Copenhagen, 1942)
Danske folkeviser, ed. M. Wöldike and A. Arnholtz (Copenhagen, 1948)
Sange med klaver, ed. H. Glahn and M. Wöldike (Copenhagen, 1957)

WRITINGS

Vor musikundervisning og den musikalske dannelse (Copenhagen, 1884)
Om kirkesangen (Copenhagen, 1887)
'Studier over vore folkevisemelodiers oprindelse og musikalske bygning', *Dania*, ii (1892–3), 1, 149–79
'Vore folkevisemelodier og deres fornyelse', *Danske studier*, i (1904), 177–209
Musik og kirke (Copenhagen, 1920, 2/1938)

BIBLIOGRAPHY

C. Nielsen: *Levende musik* (Copenhagen, 1925)
P. Hamburger: *Bibliografisk fortegnelse over Thomas Laubs litteraere og musikalske arbejder* (Copenhagen, 1932)
J. P. Larsen: 'Thomas Laub', *DBL*
P. Hamburger: *Thomas Laub: hans liv og gerning* (Copenhagen, 1942)
E. Dal: *Nordisk folkeviseforskning siden 1800* (Copenhagen, 1956), 89ff
——: 'Vore folkevisemelodier: Thomas Laubs synspunkter og deres revision', *Dansk kirkesangs årsskrift*, xiv (1957), 7
M. Wöldike: 'Erindringer om Laub og Carl Nielsen', *Dansk kirkesangs årsskrift*, xx (1967–8), 11
J. I. Jensen: 'Musikalisk isolation og gudstjenstligt faellesskab i Thomas Laubs to tidlige skrifter', *Dansk kirkesangs årsskrift*, xxii (1971–2), 34
                                    NIELS MARTIN JENSEN

Laube, Anton (*b* Brüx [now Most], Bohemia, 13 Nov 1718; *d* Hradčany, Prague, 24 Feb 1784). Bohemian composer and choirmaster. His letter of application in 1771 for the position of choirmaster at St Vitus Cathedral in Prague reveals that he was a composer and choirmaster at St Gallus Church. On 29 October 1771 he was appointed F. X. Brixi's successor as *capellae magister* of St Vitus and held this post until his death.

Laube wrote both sacred and secular music in an early Classical idiom similar to Brixi's. His church compositions have a homophonic texture of striking simplicity. They were performed throughout Bohemia during his lifetime, but soon after his death objections were raised to their almost complete lack of counterpoint. As a composer of instrumental music, Laube was known both in Bohemia and abroad (some of his works were listed in the Breitkopf catalogues, 1763–71). His symphonies, the earliest of which probably date from about 1750, are mostly in three movements, though some follow the Classical four-movement arrangement. The movements in sonata form have distinctly marked secondary themes. Apparently none of Laube's music has been printed. His identity with the composer of several Singspiels performed in Berlin in 1776 (titles cited by Graf) has not been established.

WORKS

Inst: 6 syms., *CS-Bm*, 1 doubtful; 1 sym., *Pnm*; 9 syms., *Bu* (8 microfilm); Bn Conc., C, *Pnm*; Bn Conc., d, listed in Breitkopf catalogue (1766); Concertino, F, eng hn, *Pnm*; 11 serenades, 2 ob, 2 hn, 2 bn, *Pnm*; Sonata, C, fl, vn, vc, listed in Breitkopf catalogue (1763); 2 trios, E, C, 2 vn, vc, listed in Breitkopf catalogue (1771); Trio, 2 vn, vc, *D-Mbs*

Vocal: 12 songs, S, pf, *B-Br*; Die thränende und versöhnte Magdalena, Easter oratorio, *CS-Bb*; masses, TeD, Requiem, other sacred works, mostly *Bm*, *Pnm*, *Pp*, see Podlaha (1926), Kouba (1969)

BIBLIOGRAPHY

ČSHS

G. J. Dlabacz: 'Versuch eines Verzeichnisses der vorzüglichern Tonkünstler in oder aus Böhmen', *Materialien zur alten und neuen Statistik von Böhmen*, ed. J. A. Riegger, xii (Leipzig and Prague, 1794), 253

——: *Allgemeines historisches Künstler-Lexikon*, ii (Prague, 1815), 182

C. von Wurzbach: *Biographisches Lexikon des Kaiserthums Oesterreich*, xiv (Vienna, 1865), 192f [bibliography]

A. Podlaha: *Tumbarius S. Metropolitanae ecclesiae pragensis* (Prague, 1916), 48f

——: *Catalogus collectionis operum artis musicae quae in bibliotheca capituli metropolitani pragensis asservantur* (Prague, 1926), pp.iv f, xxviii, xxxi, nos.804–36

H. Graf: *Das Repertoire der öffentlichen Opern- und Singspielbühnen seit dem Jahr 1771* (Berlin, 1934)

O. Kamper: *Hudebni Praha v xviii.věku* [18th-century musical Prague] (Prague, 1936), 34, 184, 189

R. Quoika: 'Zur Geschichte der Musikkapelle des St. Veitsdomes in Prag', *KJb*, xlv (1961), 102, 109

B. S. Brook, ed.: *The Breitkopf Thematic Catalogue, 1762–1787* (New York, 1966)

J. Kouba, ed.: *Průvodce po pramenech k dějinám hudby* [Guide to sources of musical history] (Prague, 1969)

J. Havlik: *Symfonie J. Bárty a A. Laubeho* (diss., U. of Prague, 1974)

MILAN POŠTOLKA

Laubenthal [Neumann], **Horst (Rüdiger)** (*b* Eisfeld, Thuringia, 8 March 1939). German tenor. He studied in Munich and with the tenor Rudolf Laubenthal and his wife Erika Steinhausen, adopting the name of his teacher for professional purposes. After seven years of study he made his début at the Würzburg Mozart Festival in 1967 as Don Ottavio. Engagements followed at the Württembergische Staatsoper, Stuttgart (1967–73), the Deutsche Oper, Berlin (from 1973), and at leading festivals including Salzburg, Aix-en-Provence, Munich and Glyndebourne, mainly in the Mozart repertory (Belmonte, Tamino, Ferrando) in which he has specialized. In Berlin he scored great successes as Lensky in *Eugene Onegin* and in the title role of Pfitzner's *Palestrina*. He appeared at Bayreuth in 1970. Laubenthal's training in lieder and oratorio led to engagements by Karl Richter as the Evangelist in both Bach's Passions and in the Christmas Oratorio, and to lieder recordings with Erik Werba. His stage performances, although somewhat stiff dramatically, are notable for intrinsic musicianship and for well-schooled, supple singing.

HAROLD ROSENTHAL

Laubenthal, Rudolf (*b* Düsseldorf, 18 March 1886; *d* Pöcking, Starnbeger See, 2 Oct 1971). German tenor. He studied with Lilli Lehmann in Berlin, and made his début in 1913 at the Deutsche Oper, where he remained until 1923. He was a member of the Metropolitan Opera (1923–33) where he sang in the first American performances of *Jenůfa*, *Die aegyptische Helena* and *Schwanda the Bagpiper*. He sang at Covent Garden (1926–30) as Erik, Siegfried, Tristan and Walther von Stolzing. He continued to appear in Munich, Vienna and other European theatres until 1937. His repertory further included Arnold in *Guillaume Tell*, Hoffmann, and John of Leyden in *Le prophète*. A handsome man and intelligent actor, he was considered by many to be the best Siegfried and Tristan of the mid-1920s, even surpassing Melchior; his voice was heroic but somewhat lacking in lyric beauty.

HAROLD ROSENTHAL

Lauchery, Etienne (*b* Lyons, Sept 1732; *d* Berlin, 5 Jan 1820). French ballet-master and teacher, an influential figure in the history of the *ballet d'action*. He was a pupil of his father, Laurentius (1713–83), ballet-master in Mannheim; he studied in Paris, and held various appointments in Mannheim (1756–64), Kassel (1764–72), Mannheim and Munich (1772–81), Kassel again (1781–6) and finally Berlin (1788–1813), where he was ballet-master at the royal theatre and also the Académie de Danse. Lauchery produced many *ballets d'action*, some of which are recorded in his *Recueil de ballets* (Kassel, 1768); others survive in Kassel (*D-Kl*) and Munich (Theatre Museum). His work in Berlin was continued by his son and pupil Albert (1779–1853).

BIBLIOGRAPHY

R. Klöiber: *Die dramatischen Ballette von Christian Cannabich* (diss., U. of Munich, 1928)

FRIDERICA DERRA DE MORODA

Lauclos, Henri de. See L'ENCLOS, HENRI DE.

Laúd (Sp., from Arabic *el 'ūd*). Spanish term for the lute, from 'la ud'; it was introduced to Spain by Arabs during the 13th century.

Lauda Sion (Lat.: 'praise, O Sion'). The sequence for Corpus Christi (*Liber usualis*, p.945); the text is by Thomas Aquinas, set to a melody originally used for several of Adam of St Victor's sequences, resembling most closely that of *Laudes crucis*. It was one of the four sequences retained by the Council of Trent (1543–63). There are settings by Brumel (an *alternatim* paraphrase of the plainsong) as well as by Lassus, Victoria and Palestrina (three) (*see* SEQUENCE (i), §10). Among more recent settings is the imaginative work by Edmund Rubbra, for double chorus with soprano and baritone soloists.

JOHN CALDWELL

Lauda [laude] **spirituale** (pl. *laude* [*laudi*] *spirituali*) (It.: 'spiritual praise'). The principal form of non-liturgical religious song in Italy during the Middle Ages and Renaissance, remaining part of popular Italian religious music into the 19th century. Because of its longevity as a form, the *lauda* is an important source of popular tunes from late medieval and Renaissance Italy.

1. Monophonic. 2. Polyphonic.

1. MONOPHONIC. During the period from about 1250 to about 1400 the *lauda* was a popular religious song, monophonic, mainly vernacular, congregational and usually anonymous. The polyphonic *lauda* of the 15th century, surviving largely in early 16th-century printed collections, ousted the monophonic form from favour as art music for a cultured élite, but not, it appears, from popular circulation. In the absence of other surviving monophony to Italian words, the *lauda spirituale* is a phenomenon of particular interest.

Fraternities of *lauda* singers (*laudesi*) certainly

existed in Italy before the *lauda* proper developed as a musico-poetic genre in the second half of the 13th century. A guild of *Laudesi della Beata Vergine*, whose members were upper-class laymen, existed in Florence in 1233. The members worshipped together, singing the 'lauds' of God and his saints, engaged in works of mercy and observed the rules of their company (D'Ancona, De Bartholomaeis). It is not clear whether these 'lauds' were the liturgical Office, Lauds of the Blessed Virgin (the 'Little Office of Our Lady' is of the 10th century), or an act of vernacular worship related to the Office (such as a litany or processional song) or something less formal. The earliest surviving *lauda* texts include *Raina potentissima*, addressed to the Virgin, and the acclamation of a certain 'frater J.', *Benedictu, laudatu et glorificatu lu Patre* (Liuzzi, i, 13). Even earlier than these texts is the famous 'Canticle of the Sun' by St Francis of Assisi (1182–1226), *Altissimu, onnipotente bon Signore / tue so le laude, la gloria et l'onore* (*I-Af* 338, with empty music staves). St Francis was described as one who went about 'cantando e laudando magnificamente Iddio'. The continuous connection of the *lauda* with the Franciscan friars underlines the fact that its origins were not solely institutional (in the confraternities). The *lauda* also embodied Franciscan missionary zeal: profane songs were to be replaced by godly ones. Those who sang *laude* were indeed 'God's minstrels' (*joculatores Dei*).

In the mid-13th century the *lauda* was swept up in a wave of extraordinary religious hysteria. In an attempt to atone for the sins of the age, to expiate the guilt of internecine war, civil corruption and savage pestilence, the inhabitants of cities in north Italy, Provence and Germany (*see* GEISSLERLIEDER) were seized by a penitential frenzy. A chronicler, Bartolomeo Scriba, related that in 1260 in the city of Perugia 'men began to go around the town naked, lashing themselves with whips, both grown-ups and children' (they were called variously *disciplinati*, *flagellanti* and *battuti*). The end of the world seemed to be at hand. When the hysteria abated, it was again the guilds who kept the spirit of Franciscan fervour alive. In Perugia alone there were perhaps 40 fraternities, and they spread throughout Umbria and Tuscany. Their strength and popularity can be gauged from the fact that no fewer than 200 manuscript collections of *lauda* texts survive. Most *laude* are anonymous. But one poet of stature, a Franciscan, wrote *laude* – JACOPONE DA TODI. The *lauda* is also seminal for Italian drama (*see* MEDIEVAL DRAMA, §III, 3, iv).

Musical sources are unfortunately scarce. There are only two substantial collections (*laudarii*), at Cortona (*I-CT* 91, late 13th century, containing 46 *laude* and one with empty staves) and Florence (*I-Fn* Magl.II.I.122, BR18, containing 89 *laude* plus several with empty staves and some sequences). There are four other *laudario* fragments in libraries at Cambridge, London, New York and Worcester, Massachusetts, possibly all from a single manuscript.

The principal religious themes of the *lauda* are the praise of the Virgin, the birth, Passion and Resurrection of Christ, the saints, including St Francis, the Holy Spirit, the Divine Love and the approach of death. These familiar topics are treated in a familiar way – familiar in the sense that each text is a tissue of commonplaces, and familiar also in tone, which is easy, natural and unforced. The *ripresa* and first two stanzas of *Altissima luce* (*I-CT* 91, f.17v) demonstrate these points and also

show the standard metrical pattern; the rhyme scheme produced is *ab/cccb/dddb*, with internal rhymes in *c* and *d*:

Ripresa: Altissima luce col grande splendore,
   in voi, dolçe amore, agiam consolança.

1: Ave, regina, pulçell'amorosa,
 stella marina ke non stai nascosa,
 luce divina, virtù gratiosa;
 belleça formosa, di Dio se' semblança.

2: Templo sacrato, ornato vasello
 annunciato da san Gabriello;
 Cristo incarnato nel tuo ventre bello,
 fructo novello cum gran delectança.

To describe the poetical form is also to describe the musical. Musically the *lauda* is related to the Italian *ballata*, the French *virelai* and the English *carol*. The initial *ripresa* (not unlike the burden in carol terminology) is repeated after each verse, and there is generally a musical link between *ripresa* and verse. The wide range of forms found in the Cortona manuscript alone includes *ABccab* (*O Maria, d'omelia se' fontana*), *ABcc'db'* (*Altissima luce*), *ABCdedeabc* (*Ciascun ke fede sente*) and *ABCDefc'dghc''d'* (*Christo è nato*). Formally the *laude* of the Florence manuscript are only slightly more elaborate. But stylistically the Florence manuscript, the later of the two, shows in certain pieces a degree of elaboration that suggests professional performance.

The musical style of the monophonic *lauda* allows a considerable amount of variation. The repertory of the two main manuscripts overlaps; they have 20 texts but only ten melodies in common. *Altissima luce* (ex.1) is in

Ex.1 *Altissima luce, I-CT* 91, ff.17–18 (*ripresa* transposed up a 3rd)

both. It is an example of the simplest *lauda* style: the melodic movement is mostly conjunct (no leap larger than a 3rd within a phrase); the range is small, especially in individual phrases; the tonality (assuming that the Florence version is correct and the Cortona a 3rd too low) is major; the word-setting is syllabic (no syllable has more than two notes in the Cortona version, three notes in the Florence). Ex.2, *Nat'e in questo mondo l'altissima regina*, is characteristic of the highly melismatic melodies that occur only in the Florence manuscript. In general style such a melody is not unlike the more elaborate courtly products of troubadour and trouvère art (cf in particular the religious songs of Guiraut Riquier). The subtle elaboration of the basic

Ex.2 *Nat'e in questo mondo, I-Fn* Magl.II.I.122 (BR 18), ff.39–40

ripresa

Na - - t'e in ques-to mon - do

l'al - - tis - si - ma re - gi - na

per dar a no - i doc - tri - na

di nos - tro sal - va - men-to

stanza

La vir - - go in - pe - ri - a - le

2. in ques-to mon - do e na - ta

3. pri-ma san - cti - fi - ca - ta

4. da - re ce - les - ti - a - le

5. dal - le pe - ne in - fer - na - le

6. la gien-ta li - be - ra - ta

7. la qual fu e pro-fe - ta - ta

8. per lun-go tem-po - ra - le

9. che l'al - to di - e e - ter - na - le

10. l'a - ve - a pro-ve - du - to

11. di man - dar - ci sa - lu - to

12. al nos-tro per - di - men-to

AAB form of the stanza is analogous to the procedures by which French composers diversified *canzo*/chanson form (also *AAB*). The melodic ornamentation in each case is, moreover, quite unrelated to the general sense or particular meanings of the words; it exists for its own sake.

Finally, the rhythm of the monophonic *laude* is problematic. They appear to belong to the main tradition of early medieval monophonic music (*see* TROUBADOURS, TROUVÈRES). The *laude* of the Florence and Cortona manuscripts are notated in square black notation, normally on a four-line stave. The notes and ligatures are the familiar ones of Gregorian chant notation – *virga, punctum, ligatura binaria, ternaria* and so on. No mensural indications are given. Published transcriptions of *laude* tend to follow one of three methods. Riemann's theory of *Vierhebigkeit* is applied in Liuzzi's transcriptions: each melody is arranged in 4/4 units, the time-value of the ligatures being extended or compressed as required. The results are often very unhappy, especially in melismatic songs. J. B. Beck and Pierre Aubry applied modal rhythms, choosing one of the six triple-rhythm 'rhythmic modes' of contemporary polyphony on grounds of poetic metre. More recently, Anglès (1968) developed his own system based on a comparison between *lauda* and CANTIGA notation. In this 'modified mensural' approach all single notes and groups of two or three notes occupy a single beat, groups of four or five, notes two beats and so on. The beats are then themselves arranged in 'bars' of irregular length. The results are attractive but seem to have no specific warrant. (In the musical examples given here an isochronous method of transcription has been used, based on the assumed approximate equal length of each syllable.)

Also important during the *trecento* was the *lauda* with a Latin text. The most important source of these works is in Turin (*I-Tn* Bobbiese F.I.4); it contains 13 Latin monophonic *laude*, mostly ballatas in form, that seem to have been destined for clerical (or monastic) use rather than for the secular fraternities.

2. POLYPHONIC. The earliest polyphonic *laude* were apparently composed during the 14th century. The Florence manuscript (*I-Fn* Magl.II.I.122, BR18), in addition to being one of the two major sources of the monophonic *lauda* in the vernacular, contains at the end several Latin *laude* with added (possibly instrumental) tenor parts. Polyphonic *laude* with Italian texts are also found at this time. Among these are Niccolò del Proposto's *Dio mi guardi di peggio* and Jacopo da Bologna's *Nel mio parlar di questa donn'eterna*, both ballatas. The latter work, significantly, is Jacopo's only work in ballata form (the typical verse type of the *lauda*), and both are simpler in melodic style than the composers' purely secular works.

Traces of the later *travestimenti spirituali*, or the substitution of spiritual texts in secular works, are also found from the Ars Nova. Thus Niccolò's *Ciascun faccia per se* is documented as having been copied in 1384 with the text *Ogni uom con pura fè*, and Landini's famous *La bionda treccia* became *Or che non piangi, o miser peccatore*. The number of semi-professional singers employed by the Florentine companies of *laudesi* suggests strongly that *lauda* performances were polyphonic (see D'Accone's studies).

In the period immediately after the Ars Nova, the *lauda* continued to flourish. Both Latin- and Italian-texted examples are included in the major Italian manuscripts from about 1430 to 1490 (among these are *I-Bu* 2216; *I-Bc* Q15; *I-PAVu* Aldini 361; *I-Vnm* It.Cl.IX.145; and *US-Wc* ML 171 J6, formerly in a private collection at Brescia). The *laude* of this time are generally for two or three voices, although there are some four-voice ones and several monophonic examples. In strong contrast to the contemporary works of northern musicians in Italy, these two- and three-part *laude* are exceedingly simple in style: the settings are mostly syllabic; each poetic line has its own melody; the voices cadence simultaneously; and the parts are written in a homorhythmic style. *Cum autem venissem* (from *I-PAVu* c1450) is typical (ex.3). This work shows the

Ex.3 *Cum autem venissem*

longevity of many *laude*, for as late as 1563 it was included in Serafino Razzi's first book of *laude* with the phrase 'the words and music are very old'. On the other hand, many *laude* show vestigial traces of the typical melismas of the *trecento* in the superius; *Con desiderio io vo' cercando* (from *I-Bu* 2216) has such a melisma on the penultimate syllable of the word 'cercando' (ex.4).

Ex.4 *Con desiderio*

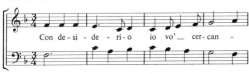

Many polyphonic *laude* seem to be elaborations of originally monophonic works. The melody of *El nome del bon Jhesù* (from the Turin manuscript cited above, c1350) is used in several polyphonic *laude* over the next 150 years: it appears with the text *Verbum caro factum est* in *I-RAc* Montis Libani as the *superius* in a two-part setting; as tenor of a three-part version in *I-Bu* 2216; as bassus in a two-part setting in *I-Vnm* Cl.IX.145; and as tenor of a four-part setting by Innocentius Dammonis in Petrucci's first book of *laude* (1508).

During the 15th century the Italian *lauda* began to use text forms other than the ballata, these being the simpler ones found in the later frottola. Thus, *Con desiderio io vo cercando* cited above is a *barzelletta*,

Dilecto cortesia (from *I-Bc* Q15) is a *strambotto*, and *Se gratia per gratia* (*I-Vnm* Cl.IX.145) is a *capitolo*.

During the time of the frottola (1490–1530), the *lauda* reached a height of popularity and influence. In north Italy the chief sources of the genre are Petrucci's *Laude, libro primo* (Venice, 1508), his *Laude, libro secondo* (1507/8), and the Cape Town manuscript (Grey 3.b.12 of the South African Public Library); this was listed as lost by Jeppesen ('Lauda', *MGG*) but was found by F. Alberto Gallo (see Cattin, 1973).

Petrucci's first book is entirely devoted to the works of Innocentius Dammonis, an otherwise unknown member of the Congregazione di Salvatoriani in Venice. Of the 66 pieces in the book 51 have Italian texts and 15 Latin. Petrucci's second book, on the other hand, is devoted largely to *laude* by the composers of the north Italian frottola, such as Tromboncino, Cara and Lurano. Only 23 of its texts are Italian; 31 are Latin, and two are macaronic. These works are for four voices with functional bass parts and are generally homorhythmic.

The *laude* of Petrucci's time also furnished a strong impetus towards the 'new' style of sacred music by major composers of the motet and mass in Italy, such as Josquin, Gaspar van Weerbeke, and Compère. Lowinsky has shown that, under the influence of the *lauda*, these composers began to set sections and sometimes whole works in the homorhythmic style of the *lauda*, instead of in the more involved, often imitative, style of the north. The first *pars* of Josquin's homorhythmic motet *Tu solus qui facis mirabilia* is included in Petrucci's second book of *laude* with the text *O mater Dei et hominis*, and a part of Weerbeke's *Panis angelicus* is included in the same publication with the text *Ave, panis angelorum*.

The *lauda* also flourished in Florence during the years 1480–1520, partly because of the Dominican monk Girolamo Savonarola (1452–97), who condemned other figural music. In Florence, a large number of books were published containing *lauda* texts by such poets as Feo Belcari, Lorenzo de' Medici, Lucrezia de' Medici (Lorenzo's mother) and Savonarola himself. Although relatively little music for these *laude* is extant, the settings can be reconstructed, as most were sung to popular melodies. In the prints of *lauda* texts, these are marked 'cantasi come', and their models are both popular French chansons and carnival songs of Florence. Thus the *lauda Signor Jesù, tu sia lo ben venuto* is sung to the music of *Seigneur Lyon, vous soyez le bien venu*, and *Iesù, Iesù, Iesù, ognun chiami Iesù* to *Visin, visin, visin chi vuol spazzar camin*. Other *laude* carry a more general designation, such as 'sung like the *strambotti*', and some carry the rubric 'this *lauda* has its own melody'.

Laude had several different functions during this period. First, they were sung by the semi-professional singers employed by the companies of *laudesi*. D'Accone has documented the names, tenures and duties of these singers throughout the 15th century and early 16th. These documents reveal that *laude* were sung both on ferial and feast days and that instrumentalists as well as singers were employed.

Second, *laude* were also sung by the professional singers who were members of church and cathedral choirs. Thus when the chapel of Florence Cathedral was reconstituted in 1501, four years after the death of Savonarola, the choir was instructed to 'sing figural music in the chapel [situated] between the two front doors; and *laude* in the same chapel on the evenings of all feast days, as they have begun to do and as is customary' (D'Accone, 1971).

Third, *laude* were sung by monks and nuns in monastic exercises. As mentioned above, Innocentius Dammonis, the author of Petrucci's first book of *laude*, was a cleric in Venice, and he dedicated the book to the leader of his order there. Cattin, moreover, believes that the newly discovered Grey manuscript was used by the Benedictine order in north Italy.

Fourth, *laude* were used as the musical portions of *rappresentazioni sacre*, plays based on sacred topics that reached their highest development in 15th- and 16th-century Florence. Here, most of the text was intoned to melodic formulae, but *laude* were also sometimes used to add musical interest. In Feo Belcari's *Rappresentazione di Abramo ed Isac*, for example, 'Isaac carries the knife in his hand and, praising God, goes down from the mountain, singing as follows: "Tutto se' dolce, Iddio Signore eterno" '. At the end of the same drama, as accompaniment to a final dance, all were to sing the *lauda Chi serve a Dio con purità di core*.

After Petrucci's books of 1508, no printed collection of *laude* was issued until 1563. Further, collections of *lauda* texts declined sharply in number (although less dramatically) after 1520. In spite of this apparent lacuna, the singing of *laude* continued throughout the second quarter of the 16th century. *Rappresentazioni sacre* continued to be written, Florentine churches such as the Ss Annunziata continued to employ singers for the performance of *laude*, and many of the texts of Razzi's 1563 *lauda* print were written by Dominican monks from the monastery of S Marco, Florence (Savonarola's monastery), during the period 1525–63.

With the advent of the Counter-Reformation, *laude* grew greatly in popularity and collections of them were published all over Italy – in Venice, Rome, Genoa, Turin, Ferrara and Naples. The first two books to be printed were both issued in 1563, Razzi's *Libro primo delle laudi spirituali* in Venice (by Rampazetto for the Giunta of Florence) and Giovanni Animuccia's *Il primo libro delle laudi* in Rome (by Dorico). Razzi was a Dominican priest who entered S Marco, Florence, in 1549. In addition to the first book of 1563, he compiled four manuscript books of *laude* (*I-Fn* Pal.173) and published the *Santuario di laudi o vero Rime spirituali* (Florence, 1609). Razzi was apparently himself a composer, but his *laude* books are more important for their transmission of the music and texts of earlier *laude*. *Cum autem venissem* has been cited above, but the books also contain the *travestimenti spirituali* of such carnival songs as Lorenzo de' Medici's *Quant'è bella la giovinezza* (with the text *Quant'è grande la bellezza di te, Vergin santa e pia*) and of his *Siam galanti di Valenza* (with the text *O maligno e duro core*). Further, Razzi's texts are often those of the period 1480–1520, for the works of such poets as Belcari, Poliziano, Benevieni and Savonarola are included, in addition to those of Razzi himself.

Animuccia's first book of *laude* began a long series of such prints written and published for Filippo Neri's Congregazione dell'Oratorio in Rome, one of the most important and influential spiritual groups in the Counter-Reformation. Animuccia himself published another book of *laude* in 1570, which in turn was followed by 11 further books (including reprints). Most of these later books were edited by Francisco Soto de Langa and by Giovenale Ancina. A small percentage of these *laude* had narrative or dramatic texts and thus influenced the beginnings of the *oratorio volgare* of the early Baroque period (a genre that was intimately related to Neri's Congregazione dell'Oratorio).

The beginnings of the *laude filippine*, as the Roman *laude* are called, were, however, not Roman but Florentine. Like many of those chosen by Razzi, the great majority of the texts of Animuccia's first print are by Florentine poets who wrote during the years 1480–1520. Thus Animuccia's *Laudate Dio* not only uses a text by Belcari but also elaborates the tune of Poliziano's May song *Ben venga maggio*.

The style of the *lauda* of the Counter-Reformation remains essentially that of the time of Petrucci, although many are for only three voices instead of four. Razzi's *laude* are particularly simple, in strict note-against-note style, and those of the Congregazione del'Oratorio are only slightly more involved. Animuccia, in his second book (1570), wrote that he had made the selections more ornate because the services were then being attended by 'prelates and important gentlemen'; but the third book (1577) returned to a simpler style so that the *laude* could be 'sung by all'. The *lauda* texts also remained simple in both form and content. During the early Counter-Reformation they were still the verse types of the frottola; in the later Counter-Reformation, they were generally simple, free, strophic forms.

With the end of the 16th century and the rise of the oratorio, the *lauda* decreased in importance, although *lauda* prints were still issued, and the tradition of *travestimenti spirituali* continued into the 18th century and the early 19th. Matteo Coferati's *Corona di sacre laudi* (1675; rev. 1689 and 1710) includes approximately 140 secular melodies with spiritual texts for each. For example, *Tu mondo ingannatore* is sung to the tune of the *Aria di Clorindo, ovvero Levasi la mattina*, and *Andiamo al cielo* to *Amor fals'ingrato, ovvero Ballo di Mantova*.

BIBLIOGRAPHY

G. C. Galletti: *Laude spirituali di Feo Belcari, di Lorenzo de' Medici, di Francesco d'Albizzo, di Castellano Castellani e di altri, comprese nelle quattro più antiche raccolte* (Florence, 1863)

A. d'Ancona: *La poesia popolare italiana* (Livorno, 2/1906)

D. Alaleona: 'Le laudi spirituali italiane nei secoli XVI e XVII, e il loro rapporto coi canti profani', *RMI*, xvi (1909), 1–54

E. J. Dent: 'The Laudi Spirituali in the XVIth and XVIIth Centuries', *PMA*, xlii (1916–17), 63–95

G. Monti: *Bibliografia della laude* (Florence, 1925)

F. Liuzzi: *La lauda e i primordi della melodia italiana* (Rome, 1934)

K. Jeppesen and V. Brøndal: *Die mehrstimmige italienische Laude um 1500* (Leipzig, 1935/R1971)

V. de Bartholomaeis, ed.: *Laude drammatiche e rappresentazioni sacre* (Florence, 1943/R1967)

B. Becherini: 'La musica nelle "sacre rappresentazioni fiorentine" ', *RMI*, liii (1951), 193–241

F. Ghisi: 'L' "Aria di Maggio" et le travestissement spirituel de la poésie musicale profane en Italie', *Musique et poésie au XVIe siècle: CNRS Paris 1953*, 267

——: 'Strambotti e laude nel travestimento spirituale della poesia musicale del Quattrocento', *CHM*, i (1953), 45–78

B. Becherini: 'Musica italiana a Firenze nel XV secolo', *RBM*, viii (1954), 109

F. Ghisi: 'La persistance du sentiment monodique et l'évolution de la polyphonie italienne du XIVe au XVe siècle', *L'ars nova: Wégimont II 1955*, 217

G. Vecchi: 'Tra monodia e polifonia: appunti da servire alla storia della melica sacra in Italia nel secolo XIII e al principio del XIV', *CHM*, ii (1957), 447

G. Cattin: 'Contributi alla storia della lauda spirituale', *Quadrivium*, ii (1958), 45–75

C. Garboli: 'Lauda', *ES*

G. Cattin: 'Il manoscritto Vente. Marc. Ital. IX, 145', *Quadrivium*, iv (1960), 1–61

F. Ghisi: 'Gli aspetti musicali della lauda fra il XIV e il XV secolo, prima metà', *Natalicia musicologica Knud Jeppesen* (Copenhagen, 1962), 51

P. Damilano: 'Fonti musicali della lauda polifonica intorno alla metà del secolo XV', *CHM*, iii (1963), 59–90

——: 'Laudi latine in un antifonario bobbiese del Trecento', *CHM*, iii (1963), 15–57

E. E. Lowinsky: 'Scholarship in the Renaissance: Music', *RN*, xvi (1963), 255

F. Ghisi: 'Antiche canzoni popolari nella "Corona di sacre laudi" di Matteo Coferati (1689)', *Liber amicorum Charles van den Borren* (Antwerp, 1964), 69

N. Bridgman: 'Un manuscrit milanais (Biblioteca Nazionale Braidense. Cod. AD. XIV. 49)', *RIM*, i (1966), 237

S. Kenney: 'In Praise of the Lauda', *Aspects of Medieval and Renaissance Music: a Birthday Offering to Gustave Reese* (New York, 1966), 489

B. J. Blackburn: 'Te matrem Dei laudamus: a Study in the Musical Veneration of Mary', *MQ*, liii (1967), 53

G. Cattin: 'Le composizioni musicali del Ms. Pavia Aldini 361', *L'ars nova italiana del trecento I: Certaldo 1967*, 1

W. Rubsamen: 'The Music for "Quant'è bella la giovinezza" and other Carnival Songs by Lorenzo de' Medici', *Art, Science, and History in the Renaissance*, ed. C. S. Singleton (Baltimore, 1967), 163

J. Stevens and others: 'The English Carol', *IMSCR*, x *Ljubljana 1967*, 284 [esp. 294ff]

H. Anglès: 'The Musical Notation and Rhythm of the Italian Laude', *Essays in Musicology: a Birthday Offering for Willi Apel* (Bloomington, 1968), 51

G. Cattin: 'Polifonia quattrocentesca italiana nel codice Washington, Library of Congress, ML 171 J6', *Quadrivium*, ix (1968), 87

A. Ziino: *Strutture strofiche nel laudario di Cortona* (Palermo, 1968)

W. Osthoff: *Theatergesang und darstellende Musik in der italienischen Renaissance (15. und 16. Jahrhundert)* (Tutzing, 1969)

H. E. Smither: 'Narrative and Dramatic Elements in the Laude Filippine, 1563–1600', *AcM*, xli (1969), 186

F. D'Accone: 'Le compagnie dei laudesi in Firenze durante l'Ars Nova', *L'ars nova italiana del trecento II: Certaldo 1969*, 253

K. von Fischer: 'Quelques remarques sur les relations entre les laudesi et les compositeurs florentins du Trecento', *L'ars nova italiana del trecento II: Certaldo 1969*, 247

F. D'Accone: 'The Musical Chapels at the Florentine Cathedral and Baptistry during the First Half of the 16th Century', *JAMS*, xxiv (1971), 1–50

A. Ziino: 'Frammenti di laudi nell'Archivio di Stato di Lucca', *Cultura Neolatina*, xxxi (1971), 295

G. Cattin: 'Nuova fonte italiana della polifonia intorno al 1500 (MS. Cape Town, Grey 3.b.12)', *AcM*, xlv (1973), 165–221

A. Ziino: 'Adattamenti musicali e tradizione manoscritta nel repertorio laudistico del Duecento', *Scritti in onore di Luigi Ronga* (Milan and Naples, 1973), 653

F. D'Accone: 'Alcune note sulle compagnie fiorentine dei laudesi durante il Quattrocento', *RIM*, ix (1975), 86

J. Jaenecke: 'Eine unbekannte Laudensammlung des 15. Jahrhunderts', *Renaissance-Studien: Helmuth Osthoff zum 80. Geburtstage* (Tutzing, 1977)

H. E. Smither: *A History of the Oratorio, i: The Oratorio in the Baroque Era: Italy, Vienna, Paris* (Chapel Hill, 1977)

A. Ziino: 'Laudi e miniature fiorentine del primo trecento', *Studi musicali*, vii (1978), 39–83

JOHN STEVENS (1), WILLIAM F. PRIZER (2)

Lauder, Sir Harry (Maclennan) (*b* Portobello, nr. Edinburgh, 4 Aug 1870; *d* Strathaven, 26 Feb 1950). Scottish baritone music-hall singer and composer. As a young man he won prizes at local singing contests and gained attention at concert parties, and after deciding to become a professional entertainer in 1894 he toured Scotland with the violinist Mackenzie Murdoch.

Lauder's most successful years as a singer coincided with the most popular years of the music hall, between 1900 and World War I. During this time he became known not only in the best London music halls but also, through concert tours, in Europe and North America. During both world wars he was an ardent recruiter, and was knighted for his efforts (1919). He performed at Buckingham Palace and for several American presidents. Later he made many gramophone recordings for the Victor label.

Lauder's stage personality was a stereotyped Scotsman, with a kilt and a generalized brogue. He often included an interlude of patter before the final verse of a song, sometimes ending with a jolly laugh; he preferred the sentimental appeal of love-songs and images of his home country, and usually ended his performances in a serious vein with *Rocked in the Cradle of the Deep* or *The End of the Road*. Lauder composed many of his own songs, of which more than 90 have been published, including a comedy sketch with four songs, *The Night Before*; the two major published collections of his works are *Harry Lauder's Songs* (arr. C. Greenwood, London, 1942) and *Francis & Day's Album* issued in five volumes (London, 1907–c1930). All the songs follow accepted popular formulae, and have little in common with Scottish folk music except for the occasional use of bagpipe effects in the accompaniment or a hexatonic scale. They usually have an instrumental introduction, two or more verses and a chorus. Most are firmly in the major mode, with diatonic melodies built on the repetition or sequential use of symmetrical two- or four-bar triadic phrases. Some of Lauder's tunes have become internationally known in oral tradition (*A Wee Deochan'-Doris*, *The End of the Road*, *I Love a Lassie* and *Roamin' in the Gloamin'*). The principal publishers of his works were Francis, Day & Hunter (London) and T. B. Harms (New York). He published ten books of stories and memoirs, notably *Roamin' in the Gloamin'* (London, 1927) and *Ticklin' Talks* (London, 1934).

BIBLIOGRAPHY

G. Malvern: *Valiant Minstrel: the Story of Sir Harry Lauder* (New York, 1943)

Obituary, *The Times* (27 Feb 1950)

I. Brown: 'Lauder, Sir Harry', *DNB*

G. Irving: *Great Scot: the Life Story of Sir Harry Lauder* (London, 1968)

DEANE L. ROOT

Laudes regiae. A set of acclamations sung initially in honour of, and in the presence of, the king or emperor. The oldest set dates from the 8th century; a variety of forms were used in several different contexts throughout the Middle Ages.

In its most characteristic form (found in a Frankish MS *c*796–800, with text only), the Laudes regiae include (1) the triadic acclamation 'Christus vincit, Christus regnat, Christus imperat' ('Christ conquers, Christ reigns, Christ commands'), the most distinctive element of the Laudes; (2) several acclamations for pope, emperor, and others, each introduced by the 'hail' formula 'Exaudi Christe' ('Hear, O Christ!'); these acclamations are interspersed among (3), invocations to each of a list of saints, with the response 'tu illum adiuva' ('help him!' – 'him' being the pope, emperor, or other personage just acclaimed in the 'Exaudi'); (4) a series of attributes of Christ ('King of kings . . .') each followed by the triad 'Christus vincit . . .'; (5) doxologies addressed to Christ; (6) 'Christe audi nos/Kyrie eleison', as at the end of litanies; (7) congratulatory wishes, in particular the ancient imperial acclamation 'multos annos' ('long life').

The whole series was chanted by precentors and responded to either by a *schola* or by all those present. The chant (first preserved in 10th-century MSS) is syllabic with more or less frequent two-note neumes, depending on the version. It uses formulae that are hard to locate stylistically with reference to those of the Roman chant; the Laudes formulae come closest to some of the lection tones (not the psalm tones), but more likely they represent a Frankish adaptation of a Gallican, Visigoth, or Byzantine tone of some kind. The reciting note, flanked by whole tones, leaping up a minor 3rd and dropping a 4th, is either *a* or *d*, or *g* with a *b♭* above. This 'subtonal' tone is cognate with the older prayer and lection tones of the first millennium.

The Laudes regiae show contact with litanies on one hand (especially the Litany of the Saints) and with military hails for the Roman emperor on the other. Both elements might be traced far back in Roman culture; but it should be noted that the litanies in question are not at all characteristic of Gregorian chant and liturgy, being (apparently) instead the products of Irish or insular devotions and liturgies of the 8th century. And the imperial formulae of pagan Rome had never been put together in such a developed form – a form that gives every sign of Frankish origin, reflecting Carolingian syncretism as well as the desire to adopt imperial customs. The Laudes regiae were the most forceful expression of a tendency towards sets of loosely connected, highly stylized exclamations; this tendency reappeared in many different ways in Frankish chant, contributing to its individuality with regard to the Gregorian repertory.

Originally destined (it would seem) for Charlemagne himself, the Laudes formulae were eventually adapted for bishops or popes, and were perhaps used on a wide variety of occasions even apart from the reception of a princely personage. Some early sources indicate use at Easter or Pentecost, perhaps simply as a festival observance.

BIBLIOGRAPHY

E. Kantorowicz: *Laudes regiae: a Study in Medieval Ruler Worship and Liturgical Acclamations* (Berkeley, 1946)

For further bibliography *see* PLAINCHANT.

RICHARD L. CROCKER

Laudi, Victorino (*b* Alcara [now Alcara li Fusi], province of Messina; *fl* 1597). Italian composer. Schmidl's statement that he was born at Alcama is incorrect. He was *maestro di cappella* at Messina Cathedral; his only extant work is *Il primo libro de madrigali con dialogo* (Palermo, 1597), for five and eight voices. According to Mongitore, he contributed some pieces to a five-voice anthology, now lost, entitled *Madrigali di diversi autori siciliani* (Palermo, 1603).

BIBLIOGRAPHY

SchmidlD

A. Mongitore: *Biblioteca Sicula*, ii (Palermo, 1714/*R*1971), 272f

P. E. Carapezza: 'I *duo* della scuola siciliana', introduction to MRS, ii (1971), p.xi

PIER PAOLO SCATTOLIN

Laudis, Francesco (*d* Venice, ?Aug or Sept 1600). Italian instrumentalist and composer. He came from a family of instrumentalists. He was a musician at the Bavarian court at Munich under Lassus from 1572 onwards and contributed to an anthology of madrigals by composers working there, published in 1575. It is not known exactly when he left, but it was probably during a general exodus of musicians after the death of Duke Albrecht V in 1579. He was active in Venice in the later 1580s as a freelance cornett player and trombonist. At an unknown date he became one of the salaried musicians of St Mark's, Venice; he was replaced in the late summer of 1600, presumably because he had died.

BIBLIOGRAPHY

W. Boetticher: *Orlando di Lasso und seine Zeit* (Kassel and Basle, 1958)

DENIS ARNOLD

Lauds (from Lat. *laudes*: 'praises'). One of the services of the DIVINE OFFICE, traditionally sung during the gradual brightening of the sky that precedes sunrise. Sometimes called 'matutina laus' or 'matutini', Lauds begins with five selections of biblical poetry joining the praise of God and that of the new light. Each of the five is prefaced and followed by an antiphon, often a Proper one linking the theme of the day with that of the hour. The five selections for most Sundays and feasts are as follows (the numbering of the psalms given here is that of the Vulgate): Psalm xcii, *Dominus regnavit*; Psalm xcix, *Jubilate Deo*; Psalms lxii, *Deus, Deus meus*; and lxvi, *Deus misereatur nostri*, together; the Old Testament canticle *Benedicite omnia opera* (*Song of the Three Young Men*, Daniel iii. 35–68 and 34 in the numbering of the Common Bible); and the psalms sometimes themselves called 'laudes', cxlviii–cl, *Laudate Dominum de caelis*, *Cantate Domino canticum novum* and *Laudate Dominum in sanctis eius*. On weekdays the first psalm is Psalm lix, *Miserere mei, Deus*. The second and fourth of the selections change from day to day in an ordinary week according to the following scheme: Monday, Psalm v, *Verba mea*, the canticle *Confitebor tibi, Domine* (Isaiah xii, 1–6, the Canticle of Isaiah); Tuesday, Psalm xlii, *Judica me, Deus*, the canticle *Ego dixi* (Isaiah xxxviii, 10–20, the Canticle of Ezekiel); Wednesday, Psalm lxiv, *Te decet hymnus*, the canticle *Exultavit cor meum* (1 Samuel ii, 1–10, the Canticle of Hannah); Thursday, Psalm lxxxix, *Domine refugium*, the canticle *Cantemus Domino* (Exodus xv, 1–19, the Canticle of Moses); Friday, Psalm cxlii, *Domine exaudi*, the canticle *Domine audivi* (Habakkuk iii, 2–19, the Canticle of Habakkuk); and Saturday, Psalm xci, *Bonum est confiteri*, the canticle *Audite caeli* (Deuteronomy xxxii, 1–43, the Canticle of Moses). (This was the plan in use during the Middle Ages. In the reformed breviary of Pius X, 1911, substantial changes were made, among them the inclusion of a second complete series of canticles.)

A short lesson follows, the chapter; it is followed in the monastic cursus by a short responsory and a hymn, in the Roman cursus by a hymn only. On Sundays this is *Aeterne rerum conditor*. A different hymn is prescribed for each ordinary weekday; there are also some Proper hymns for Lauds of feast days. A short versicle and response follow. Lauds reaches its climax in the chanting of the New Testament canticle *Benedictus Dominus Deus* (Luke i, 68–79, the Canticle of Zechariah). The association of this text with daybreak seems particularly felicitous: in it Zechariah spoke of his new-born son, John the Baptist, as one who will 'go before the Lord to prepare his ways', and said that 'the day shall dawn upon us from on high to give light to those who sit in darkness and in the shadow of death, to guide our feet into the way of peace'. The antiphon for this canticle is often marked 'in evangelio' in the MSS. The term indicates the source of the canticle, and also refers to the fact that the text of the antiphon itself is frequently taken from or based on the gospel read in the Mass of the day. This can be seen, for example, in the Sundays after Epiphany. In some MSS a series of antiphons is given for each of these Sundays (see *I-IV* CVI, f.15*v*, and LXIV, ff.41*v*–43*r*; and *Corpus antiphonalium officii*, i and ii, ed. R. Hesbert, Rome, 1963–5, nos.26, 33–5). They are in different modes, and sometimes overlap in their retelling of the Gospel lesson; thus the additional antiphons must have been intended as substitutes for the first (perhaps for the days following the Sunday).

The music for Lauds thus consists of a simple formula for the versicle and response, the tones to which the psalms and canticles are chanted, the hymn, the antiphons and, in the monastic cursus, the short responsory. For a few feasts in some MSS of the 12th and later centuries, a prosa is substituted for the hymn; and in place of the versicle there appears another prosa (H. Villetard, *Office de Pierre de Corbeil*, Paris, 1907, 102f, 153ff), or an alleluia verse prosula, sometimes with the same basic text as the versicle (*F-Pn* lat.17296, ff.37*v*, 42*r*; lat.12044, ff.15*r*, 18*v*, 39*r*; *F-LA* 263, f.96*r*; see D. Hughes, 'Music for St. Stephen at Laon', *Words and Music: The Scholar's View . . . in Honor of A. Tillman Merritt*, Cambridge, Mass., 1972, 150). The concluding formula for Lauds, 'Benedicamus Domino–Deo gratias', may be replaced by a poem in two strophes of accentual verse ending with these phrases (see AS, 53f).

For bibliography *see* DIVINE OFFICE.

RUTH STEINER

Laufenberg [Loufenberg], **Heinrich** [?Henricus; ?Heinricus de Libero Castro] (*b* ?Laufenburg, *c*1390; *d* Strasbourg, 31 March 1460). South German-Swiss poet, theologian and musician. He was chaplain at the minster of Freiburg from 1429 to 1445. He probably lived also in Zofingen (Switzerland) for a while. In 1445 he returned to Strasbourg, to the house of the Knights Hospitallers, where he remained until his death. Laufenberg was closely connected with the popular religious movement of the 15th century in southern Germany. Numerous sacred poems by him are known, as well as German translations and contrafacta of Latin hymns and sequences, and also theological and scientific writings.

It is no accident that Laufenberg's name is associated with *F-Sm* 222, for this is an Alsatian–south-west German source containing a large number of references to contrafacta. Laufenberg may have been the compiler of the MS, but the matter is in some doubt, as too is the identification of the poet with the composer Heinricus de Libero Castro (i.e. Freiburg). Two three-voice compositions by the latter survive: a Sanctus (possibly a contrafactum) and a motet *Virgo dulcis* with 'Contratenor tube'; there is also a textless tenor part (*F-Sm* 222, nos.2, 55, 138 – for transcriptions, see van den Borren).

There are three works in the same MS ascribed to 'Henrici'. Of these, the two monophonic songs *Bis gruest, Maria* (no.207) and *Sunt festa* (no.208) are both probably by Laufenberg, while the three-voice *Sonorum varietas* (no.13*bis*), written *c*1400 in the French style must remain in doubt as to its authorship. It could conceivably be by HENRICUS HESSMAN DE ARGENTORATO.

See also CONTRAFACTUM.

BIBLIOGRAPHY

P. Wackernagel: *Das deutsche Kirchenlied von den ältesten Zeiten bis zum Anfang des 17. Jahrhunderts* (Leipzig, 1863–77), ii, nos.701–98
E. R. Müller: *Heinrich Laufenberg: eine litterar-historische Untersuchung* (diss., U. of Strasbourg, 1888; Berlin, 1888)
C. van den Borren: 'La musique pittoresque dans le manuscrit 222 C 22 de la Bibliothèque de Strasbourg (XVᵉ siècle)', *Kongressbericht: Basel 1924*, 88
F. Ludwig, ed.: *Guillaume de Machaut: musikalische Werke* (Leipzig, 1926–54/*R*1968), ii, 37
L. Boll: *Heinrich Loufenberg: ein Lieddichter des 15. Jahrhunderts* (diss., U. of Cologne, 1934)
J. Müller-Blattau: 'Heinrich Laufenberg: ein oberrheinischer Dichtermusiker des späten Mittelalters', *Elsass-Lothringisches Jb*, xvii (1938), 143
L. Denecke: 'Heinrich Laufenberg', *Die deutsche Literatur des Mittelalters*, iii (Berlin, 1943), 27
W. Salmen: 'Laufenberg, Heinrich', *MGG*

For further bibliography *see* SOURCES, MS.

KURT VON FISCHER

Lauffensteiner, Wolff Jacob (*b* Steyr, baptized 28 April 1676; *d* Munich, 26 March 1754). Austrian lutenist. He was the son of Wolff Jacob Lauffensteiner, towerkeeper in Steyr, and Anna Susanna Werfferin. By 1709 he had settled in Graz as a lutenist. From 1712 he was a valet and lutenist in the service of the Bavarian court, and was in the service of the Bavarian princes during their internment in Graz; he taught them the lute and other instruments. In 1715 he went with the prince's retinue to Munich, entering the private service of the prince, Duke Ferdinand; as valet he accompanied his master in the field and on his travels. In 1739, on the duke's death, he was granted a pension. For his services to the electoral House of Bavaria Duke Clemens August, Archbishop of Cologne, appointed him chamber counsellor (*Hofkammerrat*).

Lauffensteiner was an excellent lutenist-composer and stood high in the esteem of his contemporaries; Baron said that he wrote much attractive music. In the solo pieces for the lute with 11, 12 or 13 courses, he still sometimes used the *style brisé*, but most often a more cantabile style.

WORKS

CONCERTOS, SONATAS

Concerto, g, lute, 2 vn, vc, *B-Br* II.4089; 2 Concertos, B♭, F, *P-Wu* Mf.2006, only lute part extant; Concerto, F, *A-Su* M.III.25, only lute part extant; Sonata, A, 2 lutes or lute, vn, va da gamba, vc, *D-As* Tonk.2°, fasc.III, no.5, vc part lost, ed. H. Neeman (Berlin, 1927)

PARTHIEN, SUITE MOVEMENTS

Parthie, F, lute, vn, b, *A-Su* M.III.25, only lute part extant; 4 Parthien, D, b/D, F, A, lute, *GÖ*, ed. in Musik alter Meister, xxx (Graz, 1973); Parthie, D/b, lute, *KR* L.77; Parthie, c, lute, *CS-Bm* A.13.268, ed. in Musik alter Meister, xxx (Graz, 1973); 2 menuets, Bourée, B♭, 2 menuets, Gay, A, Sarabande, E, Aria, g, lute, *D-Mbs* 5362; Bourée, lute, B♭, *CS-POm*; Menuet, d, lute, *D-KNu* 1.P.56; 3 preludes, lute, d, *A-Wgm* 7763/92, 2 ed. in Musik alter Meister, xxx (Graz, 1973)

BIBLIOGRAPHY

GerberL
E. G. Baron: *Historisch-theoretisch und practische Untersuchung des Instruments der Lauten* (Nuremberg, 1727), 76
H. Federhofer: 'Die Grazer Stadtpfarrmatrikeln als musikgeschichtliche Quelle', *Zeitschrift des Historischen Vereins für Steiermark*, xlv (Graz, 1954), 163
R. Flotzinger: 'Rochus Berhandtzky und Wolff Jacob Lauffensteiner. Zum Leben und Schaffen zweier Lautenisten in kurbayerischen Diensten', *SMw*, xxvii (1966), 212

HANS RADKE

Laugier, Abbé Marc-Antoine (*b* Manosque, Basses-Alpes, 25 July 1713; *d* Paris, 7 April 1769). French writer. He was educated by Jesuits and spent many years in Germany as an ambassador's secretary. A man of wide cultural interests, he wrote a 12-volume history of the Venetian republic and works on painting and architecture. His *Apologie de la musique française contre M. Rousseau* (Paris, 1754), a 78-page essay written during the Querelle des Bouffons, took issue with Rousseau's severe criticisms of French music and his theory of a close association between a nation's music and the character of its language. Laugier argued that French and Italian music alike had faults and positive qualities, but that in each case it was the genius of the individual composer, rather than national characteristics, which was the essential factor. He showed an appreciative knowledge of the works of Lully, Clérambault,

Campra and Lalande, and analysed their capacity for provoking feelings beyond the merely pleasurable responses expounded by Rousseau. He agreed with Rousseau's comments about the failings of French performers, which arose largely from taking liberties with the printed score; but his essential point was to defend the undoubted achievements and unrivalled expressive powers of the best French music against Rousseau's extravagant assertion that French music as such did not even exist.

BIBLIOGRAPHY
H. Goldschmidt: *Die Musikästhetik des 18. Jahrhunderts* (Zurich, 1915)
L. Richebourg: *Contribution à l'histoire de la 'Querelle des Bouffons'* (Paris, 1937)
A. R. Oliver: *The Encyclopedists as Critics of Music* (New York, 1947)
A. M. Whittall: *La Querelle des Bouffons* (diss., U. of Cambridge, 1963)

ARNOLD WHITTALL

Launay, Denise (*b* Paris, 7 Oct 1906). French musicologist and librarian. She studied musicology with Pirro and Masson at the Sorbonne, counterpoint and fugue with Caussade and the organ with Dupré at the Paris Conservatoire (also with André Marchal and Gaston Litaize) and qualified as a teacher at the Ecole Normale de Musique in 1936. Subsequently she was a librarian at the Bibliothèque Nationale for over 30 years (1939–71), including seven (1960–67) when she was seconded to the CNRS; she has also been organist at Notre Dame de Lorette, Paris (from 1943), and a lecturer at the musicology institute of the University of Paris (from 1970). Her research, informed by her experience as a librarian and organist, is concerned with the 17th and 18th centuries in France, especially sacred music. She has produced several editions of French music both sacred (for example works by Du Caurroy, Courbes, J. Mauduit, N. Formé, A. Pèchon, H. Du Mont, Bouzignac, Charpentier, Gaillard and Moulinié) and secular (court airs by Boësset), which complement her writings. Her articles include many contributions, mainly on French musicians of the 17th and 18th centuries, for major dictionaries and encyclopedias.

WRITINGS
'G. Bouzignac', *Musique et liturgie*, xxi (1951), 3
'La "Fantaisie" [instr.] en France jusqu'au milieu du XVIIe siècle', *La musique instrumentale de la Renaissance: CNRS Paris 1954*, 327
'Notes sur Etienne Moulinié, maître de la musique de Gaston d'Orléans', *Mélanges d'histoire et d'esthétique musicales offerts à Paul-Marie Masson* (Paris, 1955), ii, 67
'A propos d'une Messe de Charles d'Helfer: le problème de l'exécution des messes réputées "a cappella" en France, aux XVIIe et XVIIIe siècles', *Le Baroque musical: Wégimont IV 1957*, 177
'Les motets à double choeur en France dans la première moitié du XVIIe siècle', *RdM*, xxxix–xl (1957), 173
with A. Verchaly: 'Les prolongements de la Renaissance (1600–1650)', *Précis de musicologie*, ed. J. Chailley (Paris, 1958), 214
'A propos de quelques motets polyphoniques en l'honneur de St Martin: contribution à l'histoire du motet aux XVIe et XVIIe siècles', *RdM*, xlvii (1961), 67
'La paraphrase des psaumes de A. Godeau et ses musiciens', *RdM*, l (1964), 30–75
'Essai d'un commentaire de Titelouze par lui-même', *RMFC*, v (1965), 27
'Les rapports de tempo entre mesures binaires et mesures ternaires dans la musique française, 1600–1650', *FAM*, xii (1965), 166
'A propos de deux manuscrits musicaux aux armes de Louis XIII', *FAM*, xiii (1966), 67
'Après le Concile de Trente, la Contre-Réforme en France'; 'Deux grands savants du temps de la Contre-Réforme: Mersenne et Kircher', *Encyclopédie des musiques sacrées*, iii, ed. J. Porte (Paris, 1970), 404; 646
'L'art du compositeur de musique, essai sur la composition musicale en France au temps d'Henri IV et de Louis XIII', *Musica antiqua Europae orientalis III: Bydgoszcz 1972*, 209–43
La Querelle des Bouffons [selection of documents with introduction and commentary] (Geneva, 1973)
'Church Music in France (1630–60)', *NOHM*, v (1975), 414

EDITIONS
Anthologie du motet latin polyphonique en France (1609–1661), PSFM, 1st ser., xvii (1963)
Anthologie du psaume français polyphonique, 1609–1663 (Paris, 1974–6)

CHRISTIANE SPIETH-WEISSENBACHER

Launis [Lindberg], **Armas (Emanuel)** (*b* Hämeenlinna, 22 April 1884; *d* Nice, 7 Aug 1959). Finnish composer and ethnomusicologist. After studying composition and the cello at the orchestra school of the Helsinki Philharmonic Society (1901–7) he was a pupil of Klatte at the Stern Conservatory, Berlin (1907–8), and of von Baussnern in Weimar (1909). He taught theory at his old Helsinki school (1906–14) and was a singing master at the Finnish Lyceum in that city (1916–29). In 1922 he founded the Helsinki Folk Conservatory, which he directed until 1930. Thereafter he lived in France. He was principally a composer of operas, in a rather unimaginative and derivative style drawing on Finnish and other folk music (he published several articles on and collections of Baltic peasant song).

WORKS
(*selective list*)
Operas: Seitsemän veljestä [The 7 brothers], 1913; Kullervo, 1917; Aslak Hetta, 1922; Noidan laulu [The sorcerer's song], 1932; Kesä jota ei koskaan tullut [The summer which never came], *c*1936; Karjalainen taikahuivi [the Karelian magic kerchief], 1937; Oli kerran [Once upon a time], *c*1939; Jeduhith, 1940; Jäiset liekit [The icy flames], ballet-opera, *c*1957
Inst pieces excerpted from operas, 2 orch suites, chamber pieces, choral/ solo songs, incidental music

MSS in *SF-Hyf*

Principal publishers: Ahjo, Choudens, Weinberger

BIBLIOGRAPHY
H. Tomasi: *Armas Launis: notes biographiques* (London, 1940)
Armas Launis: henkilötietoja 60-vuotispäivän johdosta (Helsinki, 1944)

HANNU ILARI LAMPILA

Laura, Great. Monastery on MOUNT ATHOS.

Laurencie, Lionel de la. *See* LA LAURENCIE, LIONEL DE.

Laurencinus Romanus. *See* LORENZINI.

Laurenti. Italian family of instrumentalists, singers and composers. Its members made significant contributions over a period of nearly 100 years (*c*1670–*c*1765) to the musical life of Bologna (where the family originated and continued in the main to live) and other Italian cities, notably Venice. The precise family relationship of different musicians bearing the surname of Laurenti is in several cases impossible to establish on information now available, and their occasional confusion in their own day (and in later musicological writings) has made some attributions to individuals hazardous.

(1) Bartolomeo Girolamo Laurenti (*b* Bologna, 1644; *d* 18 Jan 1726). Composer and violinist. Laurenti studied under the violinist E. Gaibara. He was one of the first members of the Accademia Filarmonica, founded in 1666, and joined the orchestra of S Petronio as a first violinist, at one stage sharing a first-violin desk with Torelli and taking some solos. He was also employed at other Bolognese churches and visited numerous Italian cities as a virtuoso. There seems to be no evidence to confirm (or refute) a belief that Corelli studied with him. In 1706 he retired from S Petronio on full pay (a rare privilege indicative of the esteem in which he was held). He had a small quantity of instrumental music published, all in Bologna: 12 *Suonate per camera a violino e violoncello* op.1 (1691); one sonata in C. Buffagnotti's collection of *Sonate per camera a violino e violoncello* (c1700); and a set of *Sei concerti a tre, cioè violino, violoncello ed organo* op.2 (1720) of which no example survives. The duo sonatas, pieces in the chamber idiom which dispense with keyboard continuo, are attractive examples of a neglected genre.

Two other musicians bearing the family name belonged to the same generation as Bartolomeo Girolamo and may have been his brothers. Rocco Laurenti (*d* Bologna, 1709) was Perti's organ teacher and was appointed organist at S Petronio in 1676. He was also one of the first members of the Accademia Filarmonica. Leonardo Laurenti (*b* c1650) was a trumpeter who, having already received occasional employment at St Mark's, Venice, was engaged there on a permanent basis in July 1689, remaining until at least 1708.

(2) Girolamo Nicolò Laurenti (*d* Bologna, Dec 1751). Composer and violinist, son of (1) Bartolomeo Girolamo. He replaced his father in the S Petronio orchestra when the latter retired. Instructed in violin-playing by his father as well as by Torelli and T. A. Vitali, Girolamo Nicolò enjoyed a similar career (and a similar longevity). In 1698 he was admitted to the Accademia Filarmonica. Evidently much in demand outside Bologna, he earned Quantz's praise for his direction of the orchestra of the opera house of S Giovanni Grisostomo at Venice in February 1726. He was rewarded with the directorship of the S Petronio orchestra, conferred on him by Perti in 1734. His published works comprise a trio sonata in the *Corona di dodici fiori armonici* (Bologna, 1706) and a set of six *Concerti a tre violini, alto viola, violoncello e basso* op.1 (Amsterdam, 1727). There are six of his concertos in manuscript (two in the Henry Watson Library, Manchester, four in the Sächsische Landesbibliothek, Dresden), and single concertos in the Archivio di S Petronio, Bologna (autograph) and the Österreichische Nationalbibliothek, Vienna. The Biblioteca del Conservatorio Benedetto Marcello, Venice, possesses 25 'ricercari' for unaccompanied violin and one violin sonata by him. The concertos in Dresden, probably dating from the 1720s or early 1730s, are attractive works in post-Vivaldian style.

(3) Pietro Paolo Laurenti (*b* Bologna, c1675; *d* Bologna, 25 March 1719). Composer, string player and singer, son of (1) Bartolomeo Girolamo. According to Fétis he was a Franciscan and managed to accommodate a great diversity of musical activities in both sacred and secular spheres. His first instrument was the violin; he then devoted himself to the cello; but it was as a viola player that he was engaged at S Petronio in December 1691. In the period 1695–1706 he was listed among the violinists but he returned to the ranks of the viola players, 1706–12. He was admitted to the Accademia Filarmonica as a cellist in 1698 and as a composer (having studied with Perti) in 1701. He was elected *principe* of the academy in 1701 and again in 1716. From 1703 he was *maestro di cappella* at the Collegio dei Nobili in Bologna. Pietro Paolo was noted as a singer in church when young, and was active as an opera singer in the last nine years of his life. He sang in Lotti's *Teuzzone* at Bologna in 1711–12 and made his final appearance in 1717–18 at Venice. His works reflect this many-sided career. The surviving instrumental works comprise a trio sonata in Peri's *Corona di dodici fiori armonici* (1706), two cello sonatas in the Musiksammlung des Grafen von Schönborn-Wiesentheid, Wiesentheid, and a Sinfonia *a 4* in the Österreichische Nationalbibliothek, Vienna. Six operas of his were performed in Bologna between 1701 and 1714; 11 of his oratorios are known, all but one performed in Bologna (the first nine are attributed to B. G. Laurenti in older reference works).

WORKS

OPERAS

Attilio Regolo in Africa, 1701; Esone ringiovenito, 1706; L'Iride dopo la tempestà, 1709; Sabella mrosa d'Truvlin, 1710; Li diporti d'amore in villa, 1710; Il teatro in festa, 1714

ORATORIOS

La conversione alla santa fede del rè di Bungo giapponese (1703); Sospiri del cuore umano, 1703; Santa Radegonda reina di Francia, Faenza, 1703; I pastori al presepio, 1704; La croce esaltata, 1704; L'eloquenza del mare, 1705; La fede consolata, 1705; Mosè infante liberato dal fiume, 1707; San Sebastiano, 1710; I Giuochi di Sansone, 1718; Il bambino Gesù in braccio al S Felice di Cantalice

(4) Antonia Maria Novelli Laurenti ['La Coralli'] (*fl* 1715–35). One of the most celebrated opera singers of her day. Her career began in 1715, when she appeared at the Formigliari Theatre in Bologna, and she appeared on many northern Italian stages thereafter. In 1719 F. M. Veracini engaged her for the Dresden opera. After her departure in 1720 we find her listed as 'virtuosa di camera di S Maestà il re di Polonia' (Friedrich August I of Saxony) for a Vivaldi opera staged at Venice in 1721. Her last known appearance was at Faenza in 1735.

(5) Angelo Maria Laurenti (*fl* early 18th century). Composer, string player and organist. He was apparently of the same generation as (2) Girolamo Nicolò; he joined the S Petronio orchestra in the same year (1706) as a viola player and held this appointment until 1742, when he became second and finally (in 1753) first organist of the Basilica. His oratorio *Attalia* was performed in Bologna in 1716.

(6) Lodovico Filippo Laurenti (*fl* early 18th century). Composer and string player. He was appointed as a viola player to the S Petronio orchestra in February 1712, replacing (3) Pietro Paolo, who was probably his elder brother. His only known instrumental compositions are a printed set of *Suonate da camera pel violoncello e basso* op.1, of uncertain date and place of publication. His oratorio *La morte di Maria Stuard* was performed at Bologna in 1718. In 1725 he reportedly left Bologna to enter the service of a nobleman.

Another Laurenti whose name, like Leonardo's, is not known from Bolognese sources, and whose connection with the family is therefore conjectural, was Saverio Laurenti, joint composer with Antonio Boroni of an opera, *La pupilla rapita*, staged at Venice in 1763. Nothing further is known of him.

BIBLIOGRAPHY

*Fétis*B; *Ricordi*E
G. B. Martini: *Serie cronologica* (Bologna, 1777)
F. Caffi: *Storia della musica sacra nella già cappella ducale di San Marco in Venezia dal 1318 al 1797* (Venice, 1854–5, repr. 1931)
C. Ricci: *I teatri di Bologna* (Bologna, 1888)
A. Schering: *Geschichte des Instrumental-Konzerts* (Leipzig, 1905, 2/1927/R1965)
F. Vatielli: *Arte e vita musicale a Bologna* (Bologna, 1927)
F. Giegling: 'Laurenti', *MGG*

MICHAEL TALBOT

Laurentius de Florentia [Laurentius Masii]. *See* LORENZO DA FIRENZE.

Laurentius von Schnüffis [Schnüfis, Schnifis] [Martin, Johannes] (*b* Schnifis [Schnüffis], Vorarlberg, 24 Aug 1633; *d* Konstanz, 7 Jan 1702). Austrian composer, poet, novelist, actor and friar, later resident in Germany. He used his baptismal name until 1665. He was probably taught Latin and singing at the school founded in 1612 by Count Caspar von Hohenems, and in 1644 he was still living at Schnifis. He left there about 1650, travelling as a 'student from Feldkirch' (which was near his home), down the Rhine to Strasbourg, Durlach and Cologne. Gross assumed that he joined the theatrical company of Joris Jolipous in Strasbourg or Cologne, and his earliest literary work, the *Tragico-Comoedia genannt Die Liebes-Verzweiflung*, dates from this period. In 1656 he joined Hans Ernst Hoffmann's theatrical company, and he later appeared as an actor in Vienna. In August 1658 he went with Hoffmann's company to Innsbruck, and when the Archduke-Regent Carl Ferdinand prepared a magnificent reception for his brother, the Archduke Sigismund Franz, on his return home in 1659, Martin was commissioned to celebrate the event in a laudatory poem. From 21 June 1659 he lived in Innsbruck with a clerk at the court, Veit Schechtl. When in 1661 he himself applied for a clerical post he referred to his successfully completed studies and to his three years of faithful service. But his application was in vain: a serious illness, during which everyone deserted him, induced him to leave the court and the theatre, and at the end of 1661 he returned home, where he was assisted by Count Carl Friedrich von Hohenems.

Martin now decided to become a priest, and he was ordained in Konstanz Cathedral on 24 March 1663. He became chaplain at the court of Count von Hohenems; there he wrote his first novel, *Philotheus, oder Des Miranten durch die Welt* (1665), which is autobiographical ('Mirant' is an anagram of 'Martin'). On 10 August 1665 he entered the Capuchin friary at Zug, Switzerland, as a novice and adopted the name Laurentius. In 1668, he moved to the Capuchin friary at Konstanz and produced there a series of miscellaneous works. *Mirantisches Flötlein* (1682) is a devotional book including 30 elegies, and he also reworked *Philotheus* into a devotional book. A second novel with melodies, *Mirantische Wald-Schallmey*, appeared in 1688. As a reward for his *Mirantische Mayen-Pfeiff* (1692), dedicated to the Empress Eleonora, he was crowned poet laureate by the Emperor Leopold I. In 1695, according to the dedication of his *Mirantische Maul-Trummel*, he was living at the Capuchin friary at Messkirch; the 30 melodies in that work are by Romanus Vötter of the monastery at Memmingen. As in his earlier works, he himself probably wrote the melodies for the last volume that he published, *Futer über die Mirantische Maul-Trummel* (1698).

Laurentius von Schnüffis was one of the foremost and most popular south German songwriters of the Baroque period. He probably composed about 100 melodies. All are simple, for he himself said that he wanted to put melodies of no great difficulty into his books so that even the common people could sing them. To this end the experience that he gained during his years as an actor stood him in good stead.

WORKS
(musical works only)

Philotheus, oder Des Miranten durch die Welt (Ems, 1665); contains 6 songs

Mirantisches Flötlein oder Geistliche Schäfferey (Konstanz, 1682; enlarged, rescored, Frankfurt, 1711/*R*1968); 1 ed. in Dörffel; 2 ed.

without bc, in Bäumker

Mirantisches Wald-Schallmey, oder Schul wahrer Weisheit (Konstanz, 1688)

Mirantische Mayen-Pfeiff, oder Marianische Lob-Verfassung (Dillingen, 1692)

Mirantische Maul-Trummel oder Wohlbedenckliche Gegen-Säze böser und guter Begirden (Konstanz. 1695, 3/1698/*R*1978) [music by R. Vötter]

Futer über die Mirantische Maul-Trummel (Konstanz, 1698)

BIBLIOGRAPHY

R. von Stockach: *Historiae provinciae Anterioris Austriae Fratrum Minorum Capucinorum* (Kempten, 1747)

A. Dörffel: 'Laurentius von Schnüffis', *MMg*, ii (1870), 97

W. Bäumker: *Das katholische deutsche Kirchenlied in seinen Singweisen*, iii (Freiburg, 1891), 356f

H. Kretzschmar: *Geschichte des neuen deutschen Liedes*, i (Leipzig, 1911), 134ff

W. Vetter: *Das frühdeutsche Lied* (Münster, 1928), i, 283ff

P. Nettl: *Das Wiener Lied im Zeitalter des Barock* (Leipzig, 1934), 16ff

H. Gross: *Laurentius von Schnüfis: Beitrag zur Geschichte der süddeutschen Barockliteratur* (diss., U. of Vienna, 1942)

H. Senninger: *Die Mayen-Pfeiff des Laurentius von Schnüffis* (diss., U. of Vienna, 1946)

N. Tschulik: *Laurentius von Schnüffis: ein Beitrag zur Geschichte des deutschen Sololiedes im 17. Jahrhundert* (diss., U. of Vienna, 1949)

E. Thurner: 'Laurentius von Schnifis, zum 250. Todestag 1702', *Vorarlberger Volkskalender* (Sornbirn, 1951), 65

N. Tschulik: 'Laurentius von Schnüffis, zu seinem 250. Todestag', *Musica Orans*, v (1952–3), 16

W. Senn: *Musik und Theater in Innsbruck* (Innsbruck, 1954), 278ff

G. Walser: 'Laurentius von Schnifis, OFMCap, 1633–1702', *Collectanea franciscana*, xxxii (1962), 56–88

T. Hoebers: 'Laurentius von Schnüffis: sein Leben, seine Werke und die Forschung', *Montfort: Vierteljahrsschrift für Geschichte und Gegenwartskunde Vorarlbergs*, xxiii (1971), 143

WALTHER LIPPHARDT

Laurenzi [Laurenti, Lorenzi], **Filiberto** [Filibertus de Laurentiis] (*b* Bertinoro, nr. Forlì, probably in 1619 or 1620; *d* after 1651). Italian composer. His birthdate may be deduced from the inscription 'aetatis ann. XXIIII' appended to the portrait in his 1644 book. It has been argued that the portrait and its inscription may date from earlier than 1644, though since in that year he was described (by F. M. Gigante in Strozzi) as a young man it is unlikely that he was born much earlier than 1619–20. In 1633 he was a soprano at S Luigi dei Francesi, Rome. Late in 1640 he moved to Venice together with the singer ANNA RENZI, who was his pupil and with whom he remained associated until at least 1644. The subsequent course of his career is uncertain, though he may have been the Filiberto Laurenti mentioned in connection with a performance at S Petronio, Bologna, in 1659. Laurenzi is not known to have held a post in Venice, though on 20 November 1641 he dedicated his *Concerti ed arie* to Giovanni da Pesaro, procurator-elect of St Mark's, perhaps in the hope of obtaining employment. This collection includes settings of texts both by contemporary Roman poets such as Domenico Benigni and Ottaviano Castelli and by poets such as Orazio Persiani and Giulio Strozzi who were working in Venice in the mid-17th century. The longest single work in the book is the serenata *Guerra non porta*, to a text by Giulio Strozzi, written for a celebration for Giovanni da Pesaro. The work, which is scored for various combinations of one to five voices and includes instrumental movements, opens with a short passage for solo soprano and two violins written in the *stile concitato*. The rest of the volume consists mainly of strophic arias but also includes sets of strophic variations, among them a very florid setting for solo voice of Persiani's sonnet *Già del sacro Leon*. Both Laurenzi's operas were written in collaboration with other composers. He did, however, contribute most of the music for *La finta savia* for which, according to Strozzi, he drew on the fine schools of Rome and Venice to create the best possible style 'both for the recitative and the arioso'.

WORKS

OPERAS

La finta savia (G. Strozzi), Venice, Teatro Novissimo, carn. 1643 (Venice, 1643); collab. A. Crivelli, B. Ferrari, A. Leardini, T. Merula, V. Tozzi; Laurenzi's arias pubd as Arie . . . raccolte da G. B. Verdizotti nel dramma della Finta savia, 1v, bc [op.2] (Venice, 1643)
L'esiglio d'Amore (F. Berni), Ferrara, Teatro di Cortile, 1651 (Ferrara, 1651); collab. A. Mattioli

OTHER VOCAL

Concerti ed arie, 1–3vv, con una serenata, 5vv, 2 vn, chit [op.1] (Venice, 1641)
Spiritualium cantionum, liber primus, 1v, op.3 (Venice, 1644)
Arie e siciliane, 1v; lost, cited in *Indice*

BIBLIOGRAPHY

G. Strozzi: *Le glorie della signora Anna Renzi romana* (Venice, 1644)
Indice di tutte le opere che si trovano nella Stampa della Pigna di Alessandro Vincenti (Venice, 1649); repr. in *MMg*, xiv (1882), suppl.
A. W. Ambros: *Geschichte der Musik*, iv (Leipzig, rev. 3/1909 by H. Leichtentritt), 883
E. Schmitz: *Geschichte der weltlichen Solokantate* (Leipzig, 1914, rev. 2/1955), 24, 29, 74ff
A. A. Abert: *Claudio Monteverdi und das musikalische Drama* (Lippstadt, 1954), 133
A. Ghislanzoni: *Luigi Rossi: biografia e analisi delle opere* (Milan, 1954), 29
W. Osthoff: 'Neue Beobachtungen zu Quellen und Geschichte von Monteverdis "Incoronazione di Poppea" ', *Mf*, xi (1958), 135
——: *Das dramatische Spätwerk Claudio Monteverdis* (Tutzing, 1960), 62, 115
C. Sartori: 'La prima diva della lirica italiana: Anna Renzi', *NRMI*, ii (1968), 430
A. Schnoebelen: 'Performance Practices at San Petronio in the Baroque', *AcM*, xli (1969), 49
W. Osthoff: 'Filiberto Laurenzis Musik zu "La finta savia" im Zusammenhang der frühvenezianischen Oper', *Venezia e il melodramma nel Seicento: Venezia 1972*, 173

JOHN WHENHAM

Laurenzini. See LORENZINI.

Lauri-Volpi [Volpi], **Giacomo** (*b* Rome, 11 Dec 1892; *d* Valencia, 17 March 1979). Italian tenor. He studied law, and then singing at the Accademia di S Cecilia with Antonio Cotogni, and later with Enrico Rosati. He made his début under the pseudonym Giacomo Rubini at Viterbo in 1919 as Arturo in *I puritani*, and in 1920 sang under his own name in Rome. Toscanini engaged him for La Scala as the Duke of Mantua in 1922, and he sang there regularly in the 1930s and 1940s. He was a member of the Metropolitan Opera from 1922 to 1933, singing in 232 performances of 26 operas; his roles included Calaf in the first American performance of *Turandot* (1926) and Rodolfo in the first Metropolitan *Luisa Miller* (1929). His only Covent Garden appearances were in 1925 and 1936. He was chosen to sing Boito's Nero to open the Teatro dell'Opera, Rome, in 1928 and to sing Arnold in the centenary production of Rossini's *Guillaume Tell* at La Scala in 1929. His repertory also included Raoul in *Les Huguenots*, Othello and Manrico. He made many records and continued to sing in public until 1959. In January 1972 he appeared at a Gala at the Teatro Liceo, Barcelona, and sang 'Nessun dorma' from *Turandot*. His bright, ringing tone and beautiful legato made him one of the finest lyric-dramatic tenors of his day. He was married to the Spanish soprano Maria Ros.

WRITINGS

L'equivoco (Milan, 1938)
Cristalli viventi (Rome, 1948)
A viso aperto (Milan, 1953)
Voci parallele (Milan, 1955)
Misteri della voce umana (Milan, 1957)

BIBLIOGRAPHY

C. Williams and T. Hutchinson: 'Giacomo Lauri-Volpi', *Record Collector*, xi (1957), 245 [with discography]
R. Celletti: ' "Il tenore eroico" del melodramma celeste', *Musica e dischi*, xiv (1958): May, 47; July, 47; Aug, 39
P. Caputo, ed.: 'Tre generazioni di artisti festeggiano Lauri-Volpi', *Musica e dischi*, xix (1963), Feb, 44

HAROLD ROSENTHAL

Lauro, Domenico [Laurus, Dominicus] (*b* Padua, 1540; *d* ?Mantua, after 1607). Italian composer and priest. The frequency of the name 'Lauro' among 16th-century Paduan musicians has led to confusion; it is unlikely that he was the 'Laurus Patavinus Mantuae' mentioned by Bernardino Scardeone (*De antiquitate Patavinis*, Basle, 1560). He was probably a student of Francesco Stivori, since the latter included four of Lauro's madrigals in his own first two books (*RISM* 1583[17] and 1585[33]) and they also collaborated on a book of three-part madrigals (*RISM* 1590[22]). Lauro apparently went to Mantua in 1598 to be *maestro di cappella* at the cathedral; Sartori stated (in *MGG*) that in 1598 he was *maestro di cappella* at Padua Cathedral, but his name does not appear in the chapel documents there and there seems to be no reason to doubt statements by Canal, Bertolotti and Zacco that Lauro was then working in Mantua. His extant works include three masses, one motet and 14 madrigals. The four-voice motet *Hodie Cristus* attributed to 'Laurus' must be the work of a much earlier composer, since the manuscript dates from about 1530; both Eitner and Sartori, however, listed the work as being by Domenico Lauro. Lauro's work is typically Venetian and his masses use the fully developed concerted style.

WORKS

Madrigali . . . libro primo, 3vv (Venice, 1590[22])
[3] Missae, 8vv, insts, org (Venice, 1607)
Works in 1583[17], 1585[33], 1590[17], 1592[3], 1594[8], 1611[12], 1629[8]

BIBLIOGRAPHY

EitnerQ
T. Zacco: *Cenni biografici di illustri scrittori e musica padovani* (Padua, 1851)
N. Pietrucci: *Biografia degli artisti padovani* (Padua, 1858), 69
P. Canal: *Della musica in Mantova* (Venice, 1881)
A. Bertolotti: *Musici alla corte dei Gonzaga in Mantova dal secolo XV al XVIII* (Milan, 1891/R1969), 74

PATRICIA ANN MYERS

Lauro, Hieronymo del [Alauro, Hieronymo] (*fl* 1514–17). Italian composer. 11 frottolas by him have survived in Petrucci's 11th frottola book (*RISM* 1514[2]) and Antico's fourth book (1517[2]). He set both the new, more refined verse forms and the established frottola types. His style matched his taste in verse, which avoided the frivolous and favoured the pains and torments of love. As in many frottolas of the second decade of the 16th century, the cantus parts are almost syllabic, while the inner parts provide a more florid and continuous accompaniment, supported by a simple harmonic bass. An exception is the more solemn Latin ode *Laura romanis*, a dedicatory piece, prompted perhaps by the opportunity it affords for play on words.

BIBLIOGRAPHY

A. Einstein: 'Das elfte Buch der Frottole', *ZMw*, x (1927–8), 613
K. Jeppesen: *La frottola*, i (Copenhagen, 1968)

JOAN WESS

Lausanne. Swiss town. In the Middle Ages Lausanne was a cathedral town and from the 10th century was influenced by the musical traditions of the monastery of St Gall. From 1536 to 1798 it was dominated by the

Bernese and accepted the Reformation and its musical ideas. The cathedral organ, constructed in 1411, was demolished in 1537; the Geneva Psalter by Loys Bourgeois was imposed and later replaced by that of François Gindron, who also composed 'Proverbs' and motets. Guillaume Franc, who came from Geneva, taught church music in the College of Lausanne from 1545 until his death in 1570. As in Geneva, secular music declined during the 16th century, and in the 17th and 18th centuries only church music was performed. Nevertheless, a few families played chamber music, and a number of famous musicians visited Lausanne (including Mozart in 1766).

In the 19th century musical life slowly gathered momentum after the foundation in 1812 of a Musical Society which established an orchestra in 1827 and presented adventurous programmes with some of the best soloists of the time. During the second half of the century local music was particularly influenced by German or German-speaking Swiss musicians who directed the Beau-Rivage Orchestra, founded in 1872 as a professional ensemble of 45 performers. Choral singing also became important, under the direction of Hugo de Senger, Rudolph Herfurth, Jean-Bernard Kaupert and Gustave-Adolphe Koëlla, founder of the conservatory (1861). During this period the town was visited by Liszt (1836), Mendelssohn (1842), Wagner and Gounod, and later Fauré, Skryabin and Paderewski.

At the beginning of the 20th century Emile Jaques-Dalcroze and Gustave Doret were the dominating personalities; they brought native works allied to the French school into the previously very Germanic repertory. In 1908 at the Théâtre du Jorat, Mézières (near Lausanne), René Morax founded a new type of musical theatre directed towards a wide public, and collaborated with Doret and, later, with Honegger. World War I ended the existence of the Lausanne SO, which had replaced the Beau-Rivage Orchestra, but brought about the meeting between Stravinsky and C. F. Ramuz and their collaboration in *The Soldier's Tale*, performed at the Théâtre de Lausanne in 1918. After the war musical life developed more swiftly, particularly through the excellence and variety of the subscription concerts given by the Orchestre de la Suisse Romande under Ernest Ansermet. This ensemble is based in Geneva but plays an essential role in Lausanne life. A rival orchestra was set up and supported by the Suisse Romande Radio (1935–8) and, though it could not survive, a need was felt after World War II for a local chamber orchestra to complement the Orchestre de la Suisse Romande. The group consequently founded in 1945 by the conductor Victor Desarzens has gained an international reputation and takes part in many European festivals. It gives ten subscription concerts a year and often plays on Radio Lausanne; its programmes are eclectic and do much to promote contemporary music, including works by Lausanne composers (Aloÿs Fornerod, Raffaele d'Alessandro, Hans Haug, Constantin Regamey, Julien-François Zbinden, Jean Perrin and Jean Balissat).

Lausanne has only 150,000 inhabitants but there are at least six large mixed choirs, of which two are professional. As well as the concerts of old and new works they present each year, there are chamber concerts organized by the Société pour l'Art, various recitals (though fewer now than in the past) and concerts of organ music. Many of the soloists are trained in the town's two academies, the conservatory and the Institut

de Ribaupierre. Several contemporary music groups have been formed (e.g. La Clarinette, the SIMC, Le Prestant), but the public is conservative.

Lausanne has always been visited by foreign opera companies, particularly from France, but has never had an opera house. The Lausanne International Festival (founded 1956), held in May and June, brings together opera companies from Belgrade, Prague and East Berlin, with the world's best orchestras, ballet companies and performers of serious music and jazz. The festival is complemented by a series of operettas in April and a festival of Italian opera in October, presented by the Bologna Opera and La Fenice from Venice.

Radio Lausanne has commissioned and performed new works by Honegger, Jean Binet, Jacques Ibert and Henri Sauguet and taken part in the performance of important works by Frank Martin.

BIBLIOGRAPHY

J. Burdet: *La musique dans le pays de Vaud sous le régime bernois (1536–1798)* (Lausanne, 1963)

P. Meylan: *René Morax et Arthur Honegger au Théâtre du Jorat* (Lausanne, 1966)

J. Burdet: *La musique dans le canton de Vaud au XIXe siècle* (Lausanne, 1971)

PIERRE MEYLAN

Lausch, Laurenz (*fl* late 18th century). Austrian music copyist and publisher. He began his career in Vienna on 27 March 1782 as a music copyist and subsequently developed a prominent copying business; by 13 August 1783, when he moved his premises to the Kärntnerstrasse, he was calling himself a music publisher (though the business at that time handled only the retail sale of printed and manuscript music). A few publications appeared between 1797 and 1801. The first printed edition of Haydn's *Volkshymne* was probably published by Lausch, although it does not bear his imprint. He advertised in the *Wiener Zeitung* only the many works of which he had made manuscript copies; among these were a complete set of parts of Mozart's *Le nozze di Figaro* (announced 1 July 1786) and a similar set for *Don Giovanni* (24 May 1788). The German war-song K539, written on 5 March 1788, was offered for sale by Lausch as early as 19 March in parts and vocal score.

BIBLIOGRAPHY

A. Weinmann: *Wiener Musikverleger und Musikalienhändler von Mozarts Zeit bis gegen 1860* (Vienna, 1956)

——: *Wiener Musikverlag "am Rande"* (Vienna, 1970)

ALEXANDER WEINMANN

Laute (Ger.). LUTE.

Lautenklavier [Lautenklavecimbel, Lautenwerk] (Ger.). LUTE-HARPSICHORD.

Lautenzug (Ger.). BUFF STOP.

Lauterbach, Johann Christoph (*b* Culmbach, Bavaria, 24 July 1832; *d* Dresden, 28 March 1918). German violinist. In 1850 he entered the Brussels Conservatory as a pupil of Bériot and Fétis, received the gold medal in 1851, and during Léonard's absence the next year took his place as professor of violin. In 1853 he became Konzertmeister and violin professor at the Munich Conservatory. He moved in 1861 to Dresden, where he was second Konzertmeister in the royal orchestra, succeeding to first place in 1873. There he led a string quartet whose members included the cellist Gützmacher, and taught at the conservatory. Lauterbach toured extensively in Europe and spent two seasons in England, appearing in London at the Philharmonic Society on 2 May 1864 and 15 May 1865. He published a few pieces for the violin.

DAVID CHARLTON

Lauto (It.). LUTE.

Lauverjat, Pierre (*b* ?last quarter of the 16th century; *d* ?Bourges, after 1625). French composer. At least from 1613 to 1625 he was chaplain of the Sainte-Chapelle, Bourges, and master of the choristers at its choir school. His masses were apparently highly esteemed: for example, in 1621–2 six were purchased for the choir school of Troyes Cathedral. Obeying the decrees of the Council of Trent he always took a Latin cantus firmus from liturgical sources – hymns, psalms and antiphons. He was an excellent contrapuntist and composed in the style usually employed in France for masses in the early 17th century: his counterpoint is very sparingly ornamented and written according to the traditional modal system, yet it is strongly marked by modern tonality. His melodic writing is rather stiff in his earliest works but becomes freer in those published in 1617 and even more so in those of 1623: his last works display solid musical qualities. It is noteworthy that his requiem mass (1623) contains, besides the Ordinary of the Mass for the Dead (with the two graduals, the Roman and the Parisian), the *Libera me* and the three nocturns.

WORKS

Missa 'Confitebor tibi', 5vv (Paris, 1613)
Missa 'Fundamenta ejus', 5vv (Paris, 1613)
Missa 'Ne morieris', 5vv (Paris, 1613)
Missa 'Tu es petrus', 5vv (Paris, 1613)
Missa 'Iste confessor', 4vv (Paris, 1617)
Missa 'Legem pone', 4vv (Paris, 1617)
Missa 'O gloriosa Domina', 4vv (Paris, 1623)
Missa pro defunctis, 4vv (Paris, 1623)

BIBLIOGRAPHY

A.-E. Prévost: *Histoire de la maîtrise de la cathédrale de Troyes* (Troyes, 1906/*R* in *Vie musicale dans les provinces françaises*, i, Geneva, 1972)

DENISE LAUNAY

Laux, Karl (*b* Ludwigshafen, 26 Aug 1896; *d* Dresden, 27 June 1978). German musicologist. He studied while a POW in England with Blume, and later at Heidelberg University, taking the doctorate in 1926 with a dissertation on Schleiermacher's theory of education. He worked in music publishing in Mannheim (1926–34) and Dresden (1934–45) and then as a music critic before being appointed rector of the Dresden Musikhochschule (1951–63). He was vice-president of the Gesellschaft für Musikforschung (1959–68) and in 1956 became president of the Robert-Schumann-Gesellschaft (Zwickau). His extensive publications on contemporary music stem from his ten years as a practising music critic; their emphasis is primarily on analysis and cultural history. As a music historian he concerned himself with a wide variety of periods, and particularly with Weber, Bruckner, Joseph Haas, Bach's sons and Schumann; his book on music in Russia and the Soviet Union (1958) was the first comprehensive work on the subject in German.

WRITINGS

Der Erziehungsgedanke bei Schleiermacher (diss., U. of Heidelberg, 1926)
Joseph Haas (Mainz, 1931, 2/1954)
'Orchester- und Kammermusik', *Atlantisbuch der Musik*, ed. F. Hamel (Zurich, 1934), 556–608

Carl Maria von Weber (Berlin, 1935)
Der Thomaskantor und seine Söhne (Dresden, 1939)
Anton Bruckner (Leipzig, 1940, 2/1947)
Musik und Musiker der Gegenwart, i (Essen, 1949)
Kleine Bach-Biographie (Berlin, 1950)
ed., with H. H. Draeger: *Bach-Probleme* (Leipzig, 1950)
'Dresden ist doch gar zu schön: der Aufenthalt Schumanns in Dresden: eine Ehrenrettung', *Robert Schumann: aus Anlass seines 100. Todestages* (Leipzig, 1956), 25
Joseph Haas: Leben und Werk (Leipzig, 1958)
Die Musik in Russland und in der Sowjetunion (Berlin, 1958)
ed.: *10 Jahre Musikleben der DDR* (Leipzig, 1959)
Ottmar Gerster: Leben und Werk (Leipzig, 1962)
Die Dresdner Staatskapelle (Leipzig, 1963; Eng. trans., 1967)
ed.: *Das Musikleben in der Deutschen Demokratischen Republik* (Leipzig, 1963)
'Carl Maria von Webers Münchner Beitrag zur deutschen Oper', *Festschrift Hans Engel* (Kassel, 1964), 221
Carl Maria von Weber (Leipzig, 1966)
'Wesen und Wandel des philharmonischen Gedankens', *Musa-mens-musici: im Gedenken an Walther Vetter* (Leipzig, 1969), 337
Kunstansichten, Ausgewählte Schriften Carl Maria von Webers (Leipzig, 1969)
Robert Schumann (Leipzig, 1972)
'Burkhard–Haas–Hindemith: eine schöpferische Freundschaft: ein Beitrag zur Geschichte der Donaueschinger Kammermusiktage und zur Joseph-Haas-Biographie', *Musicae scientiae collectanea: Festschrift Karl Gustav Fellerer* (Cologne, 1973), 363

BIBLIOGRAPHY

H. Schaefer: 'Karl Laux 75?', *Musik und Gesellschaft*, xxi (1971), 521

HORST SEEGER

Lauxmin, Zygmunt (*b* Żmudź district, Lithuania, *c*1596; *d* 11 Sept 1670). Polish writer on music. He was deputy provincial of the Jesuit order in Lithuania and was probably rector of the Jesuit college at Vilnius too. He published *Ars et praxis musicae in usum studiosae iuventutis in collegiis Societatis Jesu* (Vilnius, 1667, 2/1693; *PL-Kcz*, *Kc* and *WRol*), a practical handbook about basic musical principles, which was known to Brossard and has subsequently been widely mentioned in lexicographical writings on music.

BIBLIOGRAPHY

EitnerQ; *GerberNL*; *SMP*; *WaltherML*
S. de Brossard: *Dictionaire de musique* (Paris, 1703/*R*1964)
A. Sowiński: *Les musiciens polonais et slaves* (Paris, 1857), 372; Pol. trans. (1874), 222
K. Estreicher, ed.: *Bibliografia polska*, xxi (Kraków, 1906), 130
A. Chybiński: *Słownik muzyków dawnej Polski* [Dictionary of early Polish musicians] (Kraków, 1949), 69

MIROSŁAW PERZ

Lavallée, Calixa (*b* Ste Théodosie de Verchères [now Calixa-Lavallée], Quebec, 28 Dec 1842; *d* Boston, Mass., 21 Jan 1891). Canadian composer and pianist. Son of Augustin Pâquet dit Lavallée, an instrument builder and bandmaster, and of a mother partly of Scottish descent, Lavallée received his early musical training in St Hyacinthe and Montreal. Having become proficient on the piano, the violin and the cornet, he worked as a travelling theatre musician from about 1857. He won a musical competition in New Orleans and was asked by the Spanish violinist Olivera to accompany him on a tour that took him as far as Brazil. In 1861 and 1862 Lavallée was enrolled as a bandsman in a northern regiment during the American Civil War. There followed years as a teacher and travelling musician in Montreal, California, New Orleans and Lowell, Massachusetts, until he was appointed conductor and artistic director of the New York Grand Opera House (more minstrel show theatre than opera house) in about 1870. After the closing of the theatre in 1872, Lavallée returned for a time to Montreal, where friends raised money to enable him to complete his education at the Paris Conservatoire (1873–5). His teachers included Bazin, Boieldieu *fils* and Marmontel. He returned to Canada convinced of his mission to develop the latent talent of the young dominion through the foundation of a state-supported conservatory and opera company. He set up a studio (an embryonic conservatory) with Frantz and Rosita Jehin-Prume and became choirmaster at a Montreal church. Performances of Gounod's *Jeanne d'Arc* and Boieldieu's *La dame blanche* under Lavallée's direction enchanted the public but failed to convince the Quebec authorities that music education should be subsidized. Officials encouraged Lavallée to write a cantata for the welcome of a new governor-general in 1879 but failed to reimburse him for his expenses. In the following year the music committee for the Fête Nationale des Canadiens-français, an event planned to coincide with the St John the Baptist Day celebrations on June 24, invited Lavallée to set *O Canada* written by Judge Adolphe B. Routhier. The song, first performed at the Festival, has become the national anthem of Canada. The accepted English version of the text is substantially that written in 1908 by R. Stanley Weir. Soon after composing the anthem, Lavallée once again moved to the USA, where he received the recognition he had missed at home. He became music director of the Roman Catholic cathedral in Boston and a teacher at the Petersilea Conservatory there. His *opéra comique*, The Widow, was performed in several American cities in 1882, and many of his works were published including *Tiq*, a melodrama on the Indian question and its solution by the US government. He became active in the Music Teachers' National Association, organizing some of the first all-American concerts from 1884. He became the MTNA's president in 1886 and represented the USA at the London conference of the National Society of Professional Musicians in 1888. Lavallée died of tuberculosis. His remains were transferred to Montreal in 1933. Nearly all of his unpublished music is lost and, since the published works were those written for the broad public, it is easy to get the impression that Lavallée catered to popular taste. All accounts indicate however that he was a serious musician, at home in the classics as much as in the operetta music of his day. The piano piece *Le papillon* enjoyed popularity in Europe as well as North America for many decades. Lavallée's greatest talent lay in melodic invention. Logan summed up Lavallée's place in Canadian music: '. . . though others preceded him and were more effective than he as a formative force in promoting musical education and taste in Canada, Lavallée must be regarded as the first native-born Canadian creative composer – first in time, in genius, in versatility of achievement and in meritorious musicianship'.

WORKS

STAGE

Lou-Lou (comic opera, 3), 1872, not perf., lost
The Widow (opéra comique, F. H. Nelson), Springfield, Ill., 1882, vocal score (Boston, Mass., 1882)
Tiq, or Settled at Last (melodramatic musical satire, 2, W. F. Sage, P. Hawley), vocal score (Boston, Mass., 1883)

ORCHESTRAL AND CHORAL

Symphony, perf. Paris, 1874; Symphony, 4vv, orch, ded. City of Boston, c1885; 2 suites, orch: all lost
Le jugement de Salomon, oratorio; Cantata en l'honneur du Marquis de Lorne (N. Legendre), perf. Quebec, 11 June 1879; both lost
Hymne à la paix, lost; orch version by E. Lapierre, CBC Music Library, Montreal
Tu es Petrus, offertorium (Boston, Mass., 1883)
3 ovs., band (Boston, Mass., 1885–8): Bridal Rose, Golden Fleece, King of Diamonds

CHAMBER, PIANO, SONGS

2 str qts; Pf Trio; Sonata, vn, pf; Suite, vc, pf: all lost
Grande fantaisie, op.75; Meditation: both cornet, pf (Boston, Mass., c1880)
L'oiseau mouche, op.11, pf (Montreal, c1866)
Grande marche de concert, op.14; Souvenir de Tolède, op.17; Le papillon, étude de concert, op.18: all pf (Paris, c1875)
Marche funèbre, hommage à Pie IX, pf (Montreal, 1878)
Valse de salon, op.39; Mouvement à la pavane, op.41: both pf (Boston, Mass., 1886)
O Canada, chant national (Quebec, c1880)
Andalouse, bolero, op.38, lv, pf (Boston, Mass., 1886)
Many other pf pieces and songs, Eng. and Fr. texts, some lost

BIBLIOGRAPHY

D. J. Logan: 'Canadian Creative Composers', *Canadian Magazine*, xli (1913), 489
S. Salter: 'Early Encouragements to American Composers', *MQ*, xviii (1932), 76
E. Lapierre: *Calixa Lavallée* (Montreal, 1936/R1966)
H. Kallmann: *A History of Music in Canada 1534–1914* (Toronto, 1960), 132ff, 239ff

HELMUT KALLMANN

Laval University. The university of QUEBEC.

Lavaux, Nicolas [?Amable] (*fl* Paris, 1739–67). Oboist and composer. The preface to his op.1 contains an apology for his incomplete knowledge of French, indicating a foreign origin. The earliest mention of him is in a privilege of 1739 granted for his six sonatas op.1 and his *airs* for musettes and vielles: he is described as 'maître de musique et ordinaire de la musique' to the Prince of Carignan (Victor-Amédée of Savoy), Intendant of the Paris Opéra. Lavaux appeared at least twice in the Concert Spirituel, probably in his own compositions, in 1741 (a concerto) and 1749 (an oboe-violin duet). An Amable Lavaux listed as an oboist in the Concert Spirituel troupe of 1755 (and named by Fétis as a Parisian flute teacher) is probably the same person as Nicolas. Several of Lavaux's dance pieces were composed for the Théâtre de la Comédie Italienne (which may suggest an Italian origin). In July 1767 he testified on behalf of the Bureau d'Abonnement Musical when the legality of musical subscription series was in question.

Lavaux's instrumental duets enjoyed a long-lived popularity. His sonatas op.1 were listed in Bailleux's catalogue between 1767 and c1786, and the Bureau d'Abonnement Musical listed the sonatas op.7 from 1769 until c1782. When the Parisian music teacher Toussaint Bordet advertised his own new duets in 1758, he pointed out that they were in the style of the duets of Lavaux. Bordet's description of these as 'more interesting than difficult' equally fits those of Lavaux.

WORKS

(all printed works published in Paris unless otherwise stated)
6 sonates, 2 fl/other insts, op.1 (1739)
Airs, musettes/vielles (1739), cited in Privilège Général
[Premier](-Quatrième) Divertissement (c1740–50); nos.1, 3, dances for any insts; no.2, fl/ob/vn, inst acc.; no.4, 3 suites en duo
Sonates, 2 vn, op.7 (n.d.), ?lost
Transcriptions, hpd, *F-Pa*
Works in: Minuetti diversi (c1745); Vaudeville, menuets, contredances et airs détachés chantés (c1745); Deuxième livre ou recueil d'airs en duo (1755); Amusement des compagnies (The Hague, 1761); Recueil de contredanse, menuet et cotillon écrie par Caillat, 1767, *F-Pn*; Sixième recueil nouveaux d'airs (c1775)

BIBLIOGRAPHY

FétisB
M. Brenet: 'La librairie musicale en France de 1653 à 1790, d'après les Registres de privilèges', *SIMG*, viii (1906–7), 401–66
G. Cucuel: 'Quelques documents sur la librairie musicale au XVIIIe siècle', *SIMG*, xiii (1911–12), 385
M. Benoit: *Versailles et les musiciens du roi 1661–1733* (Paris, 1970)

PEGGY DAUB

Lavenu. English family of music publishers and musicians, established in London. Lewis Lavenu (*d* London, 17 Aug 1818), a flautist, was in business as a music publisher in London from early 1796. From 1802 to 1808 he was in partnership with Charles Mitchell, the firm being known as Lavenu & Mitchell. At Lavenu's death his widow Elizabeth Lavenu succeeded to the business. She married the violinist Nicolas Mori as her second husband in 1819, and he continued the firm as Mori & Lavenu from about 1827.

Mori was succeeded at his death in June 1839 by his stepson Louis Henry Lavenu (*b* London, 1818; *d* Sydney, 1 Aug 1859), who had studied at the RAM (composition with Bochsa and Potter) and had served as a cellist at the opera and for the Westminster Abbey Festival of 1834 before becoming a partner in the family firm. He maintained the firm until 1844 when it was taken over by Addison & Hodson. Lavenu also composed and published a few of his songs and short piano pieces; his operetta, *Loretta, a Tale of Seville*, on a libretto by Alfred Bunn, was successfully produced at Drury Lane Theatre on 9 November 1846. Dissatisfied with his position, Lavenu emigrated to Australia and became music director at the theatre in Sydney.

The house of Lavenu was among the most prolific music publishers of the early 19th century, with a wide range of new vocal and instrumental music in its catalogue. It also ran a circulating music library, and by 1808 had obtained royal patronage as music sellers to the Prince of Wales.

BIBLIOGRAPHY
C. Humphries and W. C. Smith: *Music Publishing in the British Isles* (London, 1954, 2/1970)

PETER WARD JONES

Lavergne [La Vergne, Delavergne], **Antoine-Barthélemy (de)** (*b* ?1670; *d* Paris, 1726). French organist and composer. He was organist of the church of St André-des-Arts in Paris from at least 1703, and held the same position at St Etienne-du-Mont from 1705 in succession to his teacher, Jean-Baptiste Buterne. He was assisted (in 1723) and replaced (in 1726) in that parish by Claude-Nicolas Ingrain. Lavergne composed an opera *La princesse d'Elide* to a libretto by Roy, based on Molière, intended for the Académie Royale de Musique but not performed. It was published by Ballard in 1706 and follows the model of Lully's *opéras-ballets*.

BIBLIOGRAPHY
EitnerQ
D. Launay: 'Lavergne, Antoine-Barthélemy', *MGG*
L. E. S. J. de Laborde: *Musiciens de Paris, 1535–1792*, ed. Y. de Brossard (Paris, 1965)
M. Benoit and N. Dufourcq: 'Documents du Minutier central: musiciens français du XVIIIe siècle', *RMFC*, viii (1968), 250; x (1970), 201

GUY BOURLIGUEUX

La Viéville, Jean Laurent le Cerf de. *See* LE CERF DE LA VIÉVILLE, JEAN LAURENT.

Lavigna, Vincenzo (*b* Altamura, nr. Bari, 21 Feb 1776; *d* Milan, 14 Sept 1836). Italian composer and teacher. From 1790 to 1799 he studied in Naples at the Conservatorio di S Maria di Loreto under Fenaroli and Valente. In 1801 he moved to Milan, where, thanks to the protection of Paisiello, his first opera, *La muta per amore, ossia Il medico per forza*, was performed at La Scala in 1802. In the same year he became *maestro al cembalo* at La Scala, and in 1823 teacher of solfège at the Milan Conservatory. Between 1802 and 1810 he wrote 11 operas and two ballets, with a fair degree of success, for La Scala and other north Italian opera houses.

After Verdi's application for admission to the Milan Conservatory was turned down, he studied counterpoint privately under Lavigna in 1832–5. In a letter to Florimo in 1871 Verdi wrote of him: 'He was very good at counterpoint, a little pedantic, and didn't care for any music but Paisiello's. ... In my three years with him I did nothing but canons and fugues, fugues and canons in all kinds of sauces. ... He was a learned man, and I wish all teachers were equally so'.

BIBLIOGRAPHY
G. De Napoli: 'Nel centenario verdiano: due musicisti altamuresi maestri a Verdi', *Rassegna pugliese* (1913), Oct
——: *La triade melodrammatica altamurana: Giacomo Tritto, Vincenzo Lavigna, Saverio Mercadante* (Milan, 1931)

GIOVANNI CARLI BALLOLA

Lavignac, (Alexandre Jean) Albert (*b* Paris, 21 Jan 1846; *d* Paris, 28 May 1916). French teacher and musicologist. He studied at the Paris Conservatoire with Marmontel, Bazin, Benoist and Ambroise Thomas, winning *premiers prix* in solfège (1857), piano (1861), harmony and accompaniment (1863) and counterpoint and fugue (1864), and a *second prix* for organ (1865). In 1871 he returned to the Conservatoire as a lecturer in solfège; four years later he was made a professor and from 1891 he taught harmony classes. In 1915 he was pensioned and named honorary professor. He wrote songs and light piano pieces, and made piano transcriptions of works of Bach, Beethoven, Berlioz, Gounod, Handel, Mendelssohn, Weber and others, but is better known for his writings, both pedagogical and historical. His numerous works for use in teaching solfège and harmony remain in wide circulation. The *Cours complet ... de dictée musicale*, written at the request of Thomas, then director of the Conservatoire, prompted the introduction of dictation courses in several European conservatories. Lavignac's *Ecole de la pédale*, a collection of material drawn from various piano methods, was apparently the first book devoted entirely to this subject. His most important historical project was the founding of the *Encyclopédie de la musique et Dictionnaire du Conservatoire* which he edited until his death. Publication was resumed in 1920 under the editorship of Lionel de La Laurencie, on whose death in 1933 the work was abandoned. The *Encyclopédie* covers both history and practical techniques of music and is noteworthy for its sizable portion on non-European music; the dictionary section never materialized.

WRITINGS
Cours complet théorique et pratique de dictée musicale (Paris and Brussels, 1882)
Preface to M. Simon: *Cours complet ... des principes de musique* (Paris, 1886)
Ecole de la pédale (Paris, 1889, ?2/1927)
La musique et les musiciens (Paris, 1895, rev., enlarged 1950; Eng. trans., 1899, with adds by H. F. Krehbiel, 4/1903)
Le voyage artistique à Bayreuth (Paris, 1897, rev. 1951 by H. Busser; Eng. trans., 1898, as *The Music Dramas of Richard Wagner*, 2/1904/R1968)
Les gaîtés du Conservatoire (Paris, 1899)
with 20 others: *Collection complète des leçons d'harmonie* (Paris, 1900)
L'éducation musicale (Paris, 1902, 4/1908; Eng. trans., 1903)
Notions scolaires de musique (Paris and Brussels, 1905–6)
Cours d'harmonie théorique et pratique (Paris, 1907)
Abrégé de la théorie des principes fondamentaux de la musique moderne (Paris, 1909, 2/1914)
Théorie complète des principes fondamentaux de la musique moderne (Paris and Brussels, 1909)
Solfège des solfèges (Paris, 1910–11; Eng. trans., 1924, as *Singing Exercises*)

ed.: *Encyclopédie de la musique et Dictionnaire du Conservatoire* (Paris, 1920–31) [vols.i–iii only, work continued by L. de La Laurencie]

BIBLIOGRAPHY
C. Pierre: *Le Conservatoire national de musique et de déclamation: documents historiques et administratifs* (Paris, 1900)

ELISABETH LEBEAU

Lavin, Carlos (*b* Santiago, 10 Aug 1883; *d* Barcelona, 27 Aug 1962). Chilean composer and ethnomusicologist. He studied music in Valparaiso and Santiago, but most of his early education was acquired independently. A Chilean government scholarship enabled him to study with Pénau and Caplet in Paris and with Hornbostel at Berlin University (1922–34), during which period he visited folk-music archives and institutes in Spain, France, Germany, Romania and Greece. His interest in folk music, that of the Araucanian Indians, had been stimulated largely by the achievements of Felix de Augusta, and he had begun fieldwork in 1907. After his return from Europe he was on the research staff of the institute of folklore at the University of Chile (1945–8) and he directed the folk-music archive of the Institute for Musical Research (1948–60). He published essays on indigenous music and other musical subjects, and he contributed entries on Spanish American musicians to the *Riemann Musik Lexikon* (Mainz, 1959).

WORKS
(*selective list*)
Ballets: La encantada, 1925; Danza blanca, 1936
Orch: Fiesta araucana, 1926; Lamentaciones huilliches, A, orch, 1928
Inst: Cadencias tehuelches, vn, pf, 1926; Suite andine, pf, 1926; Misiones, pf, 1930
5 film scores

BIBLIOGRAPHY
J. Urrutia-Blondel: 'Carlos Lavin compositor', *Revista musical chilena* (1967), no.99, p.61

JUAN A. ORREGO-SALAS

Lavirgen, Pedro (*b* Bujalance, 31 July 1930). Spanish tenor. He first worked as a schoolteacher, then studied singing with Miguel Barrosa in Madrid. He made his operatic début as Radamès in *Aida* in Mexico City in 1964, before making his first appearance in Spain, as Don José in *Carmen*, at the Teatro del Liceo, Barcelona. In 1966 he made his début at the Vienna State Opera in *Pagliacci*. His American début was with the Metropolitan Opera, New York (Cavaradossi, 1969), and he then went on to sing Manrico and other Verdi and Puccini roles in several American cities. Subsequent engagements included Buenos Aires (Manrico, 1970), Tokyo (Don José, 1973) and Verona (Radamès, 1973). He made his début at La Scala, Milan, as Radamès in 1975. He first appeared at Covent Garden in 1975 as Don José and returned there in 1978 to sing Pollione opposite Caballé's Norma. In the same year he sang Escamillo at the Edinburgh Festival opposite Teresa Berganza's Carmen. Lavirgen specializes in Italian lyric tenor roles, notably Verdi and Puccini, to which he brings a warm vibrancy and dramatic strength.

Lavolta. See VOLTA (i).

Lavotta, János (*b* Pusztafödémes, 5 July 1764; *d* Tállya, 11 Aug 1820). Hungarian composer and violinist. His title of nobility was 'izsépfalvi és kevelházi'. He was taught the violin by his father, János Lavotta sr, an official of the council of government at Pozsony (now Bratislava) and later at Buda. He attended secondary schools at Nagyszombat (Trnava) and Pozsony, and studied law at Pozsony and Pest. He continued his musical education in Pozsony with Bonaventura Sabodi, Ferenc Hossza, Joseph Zistler and the military bandmaster Glanz. After a short period of military service at Pozsony, Lavotta went to Vienna in 1784 for further musical studies, and in 1786 moved to Pest. From 1788 to 1791 he was an official of the council of government and in 1791–2 tutor to the sons of Count Károly Zichy. It was not until 1792 that Lavotta decided upon a musical career. In 1792–3 he conducted, as music director, the orchestra of the Hungarian Actors' Society in Pest and Buda. From about 1797 to 1799 he lived in Miskolc, and in 1802–4 in Kolozsvár (Cluj), where he was director of the theatre orchestra. From 1804 Lavotta led an unsettled life, wandering restlessly and seeking hospitality at the country houses of noblemen, although he had a music shop at Debrecen in 1816–17. While visiting his friend Fülep Eöri, a doctor in Tállya, he died, his health completely ruined by alcoholism.

Like János Bihari and Antal Csermák, Lavotta belonged to the generation of violin virtuosos and composers that was responsible for the creation of a new Hungarian national style, the classical *verbunkos*. Lavotta was the first member of the Hungarian upper class in that era to devote himself entirely to music, and he was also the first professional musician to be recognized as an equal by the upper class. As a composer he showed less refinement than Csermák, and lacked the powerful originality of Bihari. As well as displaying the new national style, his works also show the influence of the German and Polish music of his time. Apart from dances he composed various pieces of programme music, including *Nobilium hungariae insurgentium nota insurrectionalis hungarica* (1797), a suite in 18 movements. In this work Lavotta attempted for the first time to adapt the new Hungarian music to more advanced, cyclical forms. For these and similar attempts to combine the melodic and formal resources of eastern and western Europe Lavotta's contemporaries extolled him as a cultivated innovator, in contrast to Bihari, who was the instinctive, unrefined gypsy. Only two series of his compositions appeared in print during his lifetime, *Ungarische Werbungs Tänze* for two violins and bass (Vienna, 1810), and *Verbunkós nóták oder Aecht ungarische National-Tänze* for piano (Vienna, 1814). Shortly after his death some of his *verbunkos* dances were published in various collections, such as *Magyar nóták Veszprém vármegyéből* ('Hungarian dances from County Veszprém'), edited by Ruzitska (Vienna, 1822–4), and *Nemzeti Magyar tántzok* ('Hungarian national dances') edited by A. Mohaupt (Pest, 1823–4). His manuscripts, consisting chiefly of *verbunkos* dances, German dances, minuets, contredanses and polonaises, are in the music collection of the National Széchényi Library in Budapest (*H-Bn*).

BIBLIOGRAPHY
M. Bernáth: *A' bájoló hegedűs, vagy is A' híres virtuosus 's diletant hegedűs Lavotta János életének leírása* [The magic violinist, or A biography of the famous virtuoso and dilettante violinist Lavotta] (MS, 1818, *H-Bn*)
G. Bernáth: *Lavotta élete* [Lavotta's life] (Pest, 1857)
M. Markó: *Emlékkönyv izsépfalvi és kevelházi Lavotta János halálának századik évfordulójára* [Memorial album for the 100th anniversary of the death of Lavotta] (Budapest, 1920)
S. Szilágyi: *Lavotta János* (Budapest, 1930) [incl. list of Lavotta's MSS in *H-Bn*]
B. Szabolcsi: *A XIX. század magyar romantikus zenéje* [19th-century Hungarian Romantic music] (Budapest, 1951)
E. Major and I. Szelényi: *A magyar zongoramuzsika 100 éve* [100 years of Hungarian piano music] (Budapest, 1956)

B. Szabolcsi and F. Bónis: *Magyar táncok Haydn korából* [Hungarian dances from the time of Haydn] (Budapest, 1959)

FERENC BÓNIS

La Voye-Mignot, de (*d* 1684). French mathematician and theorist. His first name is not known. He was admitted as a junior member to the French scientific academy in 1666 and is known to have written on the disciplines of geometry and zoology as well as on music. His *Traité de musique* (Paris, 1656, enlarged 2/1666/*R*1972; It. trans., 1659; Eng. trans., 1972) is a systematic, practical guide, principally for beginners, to the elements of music and of composition in both simple and figural counterpoint. The second edition is provided with an additional part, which deals in large measure with aesthetics in music and includes definitions of musical terms. The author shows interest in elements of style characteristic of music from Italy and England, both of which he claims to have visited. An allemande attributed to 'la Voÿs' in MS sources (*D-Kl*; concordance in *S-Uu*) may be by him.

BIBLIOGRAPHY

M. J. A. N. de C. de Condorcet: *Oeuvres*, ii (Paris, 1847/*R*1968), 87f
J. Ecorcheville: *Vingt suites d'orchestre du XVIIᵉ siècle français* (Berlin and Paris, 1906/*R*1970)
J. J. S. Mráček: *Seventeenth-century Instrumental Dances in Uppsala, University Library IMhs 409* (diss., Indiana U., 1965)
Institut de France: index biographique des membres et correspondants de l'Académie des sciences (Paris, 1968)
H. Schneider: *Die französische Kompositionslehre in der ersten Hälfte des 17. Jahrhunderts* (Tutzing, 1972)

ALBERT COHEN

Lavra, Great. Monastery on MOUNT ATHOS.

Lavrangas, Dionyssios (*b* Argostolion, Kefallinia, 17 Oct 1860 or 1864; *d* Razata, Kefallinia, 18 July 1941). Greek composer, conductor and teacher. Fascinated as a child by the performances of visiting Italian opera companies, he studied the violin with Nazaro (alias Lazaro) Serao and harmony with Ghideon Olivieri and Metaxas-Tzanis. In 1882 he left for Naples, where he studied privately with Mario Scarano (harmony and counterpoint) and Augusto Ross (piano), later attending the composition courses of Lauro Rossi and Paolo Serao at the S Pietro a Majella Conservatory. After three years he moved on to Paris, and there he remained for about four years, studying for three months under Delibes and later under Massenet at the Conservatoire. He also took private lessons with Dubois (harmony), Anthiome (piano) and Franck (organ). During this time he returned occasionally to Kefallinia to conduct and, when his studies were over, it was as a touring opera conductor that he made his living. In 1894 he settled in Athens as director (until about 1896) of the Philharmonic Society. There, together with the conductor Ludovicos Spinellis, he founded the Helleniko Melodhrama (Greek Opera) company, which made its début with a performance of *La bohème* under Spinellis (1900). By 1935, when Lavrangas retired, the company had staged 13 Greek and 38 foreign (mainly Italian) operas in Athens, the provinces and abroad. Lavrangas was also active at the Athens Conservatory as a teacher of the piano, harmony and choral singing (1900–05), at the Piraeus League Conservatory (?*c*1905–10), at the Hellenic Conservatory as artistic director of the opera school (1919–24) and at the National Conservatory as a teacher of solfège and sight-reading (1926–34). In addition he became head of the music department of the publishing house of Fexis (*c*1900), and he wrote music

criticism for *Eleftheron vima* and *Ethnos* in the 1920s. He was awarded the Golden Cross of King George and the National Award for Arts and Letters, both in 1919.

Lavrangas's work with the Helleniko Melodhrama helped to establish opera in Greece, but he had less influence than Kalomiris on the development of Greek composition. His works make conservative use of folk elements, with a colourful orchestration, derived from Bizet and Delibes, which helps to compensate for the simplicity of harmony and development. In the operas he was substantially indebted to Massenet and other French composers, but he learnt from Italian opera his flowing melody, effective at moments of drama (e.g. the Puccinian touches at the conflagration scene of *Dido*) or comedy (e.g. the Rossinian *Fakanapas*). He took little care of his manuscripts, which are widely scattered; some works may have been destroyed during the 1953 earthquake in the Ionian Islands.

WORKS
(*selective list*)

OPERAS

Elda di Vorn (3, Guidi), ?1886, lost; Galatea (?5, Guidi, after S. Vassiliadis), ?1887, lost; La vita è un sogno (4, E. Golisciani), *c*1890, lost; Ta dyo adelfia [The two brothers] (3 scenes, I. Tsakassianos, Lavrangas), 1899–1900, Athens, 24 April 1900, vocal score extant; Mayissa [Sorceress] [after La vita è un sogno: Act 4] (1, Lavrangas), 1901, Athens, 8 Oct 1901; O lytrotis [The redeemer] (3, Z. Papantoniou), *c*1902, Corfu, 24 Feb 1934
Dido (4, P. Dimitrakopoulos), *c*1906, Athens, 10 April 1909; Mavri petalouda [Black butterfly] (1, S. Sperantzas), 1923, Athens, 25 Jan 1929, vocal score extant; Ena paramythi [A fairy tale] (comic opera, 3, D. Bogris), 1930, Athens, vocal score extant; Fakanapas (comic opera, 2, Lavrangas, after Scribe), 1935, Athens, 2 Dec 1950; Frosso (3, Lavrangas), 1938, unperf.

OTHER DRAMATIC WORKS

I aspri tricha [The white hair] (operetta, 3, N. Laskaris, H. Anninos), Athens, 22 March 1917, vocal score extant; Sporting Club (operetta, 3, Lavrangas, S. Vekiarellis), Athens, 4 Aug 1917, ?lost; Dipli fotia [Double flame] (operetta, 3, Dimitrakopoulos), Athens, 10 Jan 1918, ?lost; To dachtylidi tou Pierrotou [Pierrot's ring], film score, Athens, 22 March 1918, lost; Apollon ke Dafni, ballet, 8 scenes, A. Doxas, 1920, New York, 1927, ?lost
Satore [retrograde of erotas = love] (operetta buffa/vaudeville, 3, Doxas), 1927, unperf., vocal score extant; To agapitikos tis voskopoulas [The shepherdess's lover], score for 1st Gk. sound film, Athens, 25 Jan 1932; Kapia nychta sti Sevilli [A night in Seville], ballet, 6 scenes, Doxas, 1933, ?lost; O tragoudistis tou kazinou [The casino singer] (operetta, 3, Doxas, Sylvio), Athens, 7 July 1934, collab. 9 others; Persefoni, ballet, Z. Papamichalopoulos, 1936, part of vocal score extant

INSTRUMENTAL

Orch: 2 intermezzi lirici, G, D, str, harp, ?1885–7; Barcarolle, G, str, ?before 1900; Remvasmos [Rêverie], C, str, ?before 1900; Greek Suite no.1, ?1903; Prelude, E♭, 1905; Romanesca, after 1913, ?lost; Impressions religieuses, 1920; Capriccio sur deux thèmes grecs, vn, pf/orch, 1921; Jota navarra, perf. 1923; Greek Suite no.2, 1922; La vita è un sogno, suite [from opera], 1939; Introduzione e fuga; Ouverture orientale
Other pieces: Nanourisma (La berceuse de ma fille), A modal, vn, pf, 1910 or 1911; Sérénade grecque, G, vn, pf, 1937; Airs de ballet, pf; Nocturne, E modal, pf; Valse brillante, B♭, pf

VOCAL

Choral: O paedes Hellenon [Ye children of Greece], 2vv, orch, 1889, doubtful authorship; O naftis tou Ioniou [Sailor of the Ionian Sea] (barcarolle, Mavroyenis), F, (chorus, orch)/male 4vv, 1889; Pentathlon (I. Polemis), T, B, male vv, orch, 1896; Asmata tis Thias Liturgias [Chants of the Holy Liturgy], TTBB, 1913; Hymnos ton progonon [Hymn of the ancestors] (G. Drossinis), unison vv, orch, perf. 1924; Missa solemnis, D, S, T, B, chorus, org, orch, 1931
Vocal orchestral: Hymnos tis irinis [Hymn to peace] (Palamas), A♭, S, pf/orch
Songs for 1v, pf: Exotica (Polemis); Ela na yiris [Come, lie down] (G. Tsokopoulos); Dipli agapi [Double love] (Polemis), Xypna [Wake up] (A. Nikolaras); 3 hellenika tragoudia (Polemis, Papantoniou), ?before 1918; Elegion (Dimakopoulos), ?1921; Souroupo [Dusk] (K. Tsoukalas), 1930; Arapiki serenata (Lavrangas), ?1938; [14] Hellinika tragoudia [incl. 2 nos. from Exotica] (Polemis, G. Avazos, G. Athanas, V. Messolonghitis); Thymissi [Memory] (G. Markoras); Dya bouboukia [Two flower buds] (M. Hieropoulos)

Many other songs and choral pieces

Principal publishers: Fexis, Greek Ministry of Education, Konstantinidis, Union of Greek Composers

WRITINGS

Enchiridion harmonias [Harmony handbook] (Athens, 1903)
Stichia theoretikis ke praktikis anagnosseos ke diaeresseos tis moussikis [Rudiments of score-reading] (Athens, 1912)
Engolpion moussikis technis [Handbook of musical art] (Athens, 1937)
T' apomnimonevmata mou [My memoirs] (Athens, 1940)

BIBLIOGRAPHY

I. A. Tsitselis: 'Lavrangas Dionyssios', *Kefalliniaka symmikta*, i (Athens, 1904), 285
G. Sklavos: 'Dionyssios Lavrangas', *Pangefalliniakon imerologion*, i (1937), 114
A. Hadziapostolou: *Historia tou Hellinikou melodramatos* (Athens, 1949)
S. A. Evangelatos: *Historia tou theatrou en Kefallinia 1600–1900* (diss., U. of Athens, 1970; Athens, 1970)
G. S. Leotsakos: 'Dion. Lavrangas: Apomnimonevmata: apopira theorissis apo ti skopia tou 1972' [Lavrangas: Memoirs: an attempted survey from the standpoint of 1972], *Vima* (Athens, 8 July 1972), 2

GEORGE S. LEOTSAKOS

Lavrovskaya [Lawrowka], Elizaveta Andreyevna (*b* Kashin, Tver govt., 13 Oct 1845; *d* Petrograd, 4 Nov 1919). Russian mezzo-soprano. She studied at the Elizabeth Institute and at the St Petersburg Conservatory. In 1867 she made her début in Gluck's *Orfeo*; her performance greatly impressed the Grand Duchess Elena, who sent her to Paris to take lessons from Pauline Viardot. In 1871 she sang in Tchaikovsky's first concert, and in 1877 suggested the subject of *Eugene Onegin* to him. Tchaikovsky dedicated to her his Six Songs op.27. Lavrovskaya sang in opera in St Petersburg (1868–72, 1879–80) and appeared at the Bol'shoy during the 1890 season. In 1888 she was appointed professor of singing at the Moscow Conservatory. She undertook successful concert tours in Russia and western Europe, and in 1873 sang at the Monday Popular Concerts at Crystal Palace. Her dramatic performances of operatic arias and her sensitive interpretations of lieder were highly praised. In 1871 she married Prince Tsertelev.

BIBLIOGRAPHY

B. Yagolim: 'E. A. Lavrovskaya: k 30-letiyu so dnya smerti' [On the 30th anniversary of her death], *SovM* (1949), no.3, p.76
V. A. Bagadurov: *Ocherki po istorii vokal'noy pedagogiki* [Essays on the history of vocal training] (Moscow, 1956)

JENNIFER SPENCER

Lavrovsky, Leonid (1905–57). Russian choreographer; *see* DANCE, §VII, 1(iii).

Lavry, Marc (*b* Riga, 22 Dec 1903; *d* Haifa, 24 March 1967). Israeli composer and conductor of Latvian birth. He studied at the Riga and Leipzig conservatories and also privately with Glazunov. After various appointments as an opera and ballet conductor in Germany and Latvia he emigrated to Palestine in 1935. The new surroundings, the pioneering spirit of the settlers and the contact with oriental folk music profoundly influenced him, and in 1937 he wrote one of his most successful pieces, the symphonic poem *Emek*, which in song-like melody and dance rhythm expressed the joy of return to the homeland. It was also a work that achieved Lavry's aim of writing popular, unproblematic symphonic music. Further successes included the oratorio *Shir ha'shirim* ('The Song of Songs'), drawing on Jewish cantillation, and the folk opera *Dan ha'shomer* ('Dan the guard') on life in a collective settlement. Lavry conducted the Palestine Folk Opera (1941–7) and from 1950 to 1958 he directed the music department of the short-wave station Kol Zion LaGola, broadcasting to overseas Jewish communities. In 1955 he was commissioned by the Emanu-El congregation of San Francisco to compose a sacred service; he wrote other liturgical music while in the USA for two years in the mid-1960s. The most distinctive feature of Lavry's music is its diatonic-modal oriental melody. Nevertheless, his melodic invention was limited; aiming at popularity, he often failed to distinguish between simplicity and banality, and some of his work is marred by a quasi-orientalism. He was at his most effective in smaller forms, and was a gifted arranger and orchestrator. Although his music was a genuine expression of a certain period in Israeli history, it has not retained its popularity.

WORKS
(*selective list*)

Emek, sym. poem, 1937; Shir ha'shirim [The Song of Songs] (oratorio, Brod), 1940; Dan ha'shomer [Dan the guard] (opera, Brod), 1945; Horrah, chorus/many other versions, n.d.; Sym. no.2 'Ha'atzmaut' [Liberation], 1951; Yerushalayim, sym. poem, 1953; Avodat ha'-kodesh [Sacred service], 1955; Esther ha'malka [Queen Esther], oratorio, 1960; 3 other syms., 3 other sym. poems, concs. for harp, pf, vn; chamber pieces, piano music, songs, choral works

Principal publishers: Israeli Music Publications

BENJAMIN BAR-AM

Law, Andrew (*b* Milford, Conn., 21 March 1749; *d* Cheshire, Conn., 13 July 1821). American singing teacher and tune book compiler. He graduated from Rhode Island College (Brown University) in 1775 and was ordained as a Congregational minister in 1787. Active in music for half a century, Law was the most travelled American musician of his age, and the most prolific compiler. At first he remained in New England, based at the family home in Cheshire, teaching singing-schools and compiling tune books. After 1783 he travelled mostly outside New England, teaching from his tune books and hiring others to do the same, in an attempt to extend his influence southwards. Declaring a preference for European music in 1793, he organized his publications into a comprehensive vocal method, *The Art of Singing*, and worked to promote this method in New England (to 1798) and Philadelphia (1798–1802). He then devised a staffless shape-notation (1803), issued tune books using it, and worked towards its acceptance mostly from Philadelphia, where he lived from 1806 until 1813. After 1813 he resumed his travels and continued to teach and publish until his death. A contentious, self-righteous Calvinist, Law received little financial benefit from the ascendancy of his Reform views, partly because in his shape-note tune books he stubbornly refused to employ a staff.

WRITINGS

Select Harmony (Cheshire, 1779)
The Rudiments of Music (Cheshire, 1783, 4/1793)
The Art of Singing (Cheshire, 1794, 4/1810), [three-part work made up of the *Musical Primer, Christian Harmony* and *Musical Magazine*]
The Harmonic Companion (Philadelphia, 1807, 4/1819)
Essays on Music (Philadelphia, 1814)

BIBLIOGRAPHY

I. Lowens: *Music and Musicians in Early America* (New York, 1964), 58–88
R. Crawford: *Andrew Law, American Psalmodist* (Evanston, 1968)
See also PSALMODY (ii), §II and SHAPE-NOTE HYMNODY.

RICHARD CRAWFORD

Lawes, Henry (*b* Dinton, Wilts., 5 Jan 1596; *d* London, 21 Oct 1662). English composer and singer, elder brother of WILLIAM LAWES. He was the leading English songwriter of the mid-17th century.

1. Henry Lawes: portrait (c1642), artist unknown, in the Faculty of Music, Oxford

1. LIFE. Lawes may have been a chorister at Salisbury Cathedral, where his father was a lay vicar. He was employed by John Egerton, Earl of Bridgwater, to teach his daughters music; this may have been as early as 1615 or possibly after 1622 (when John Attey seems still to have held the position). He was sworn 'pistoler' of the Chapel Royal on 1 January 1626 and Gentleman on 3 November in the same year. His appointment as one of Charles I's musicians 'for the lutes and voices' dated from 6 January 1631. At about this time too his friendship with Milton must have begun, as he composed the songs for *Arcades* (c1630) and actually arranged for Milton to write *Comus*, which was performed at Ludlow Castle on 29 September 1634 to mark the Earl of Bridgwater's appointment as Lord President of the Council of Wales (Lawes brought out the first edition of the masque in 1637).

Undoubtedly Lawes took part in many of the court masques of the 1630s, although his brother William seems usually to have been employed to write the music. An ambiguous allusion on the title-page of Carew's *Poems* (1640) has been taken as indicating that Henry composed the songs for Carew's masque *Coelum Britannicum* (1634), but it is doubtful that he did so. He did, however, collaborate with his brother in providing songs for Davenant's masque *The Triumph of the Prince d'Amour* (23 February 1636). Another entertainment for which he may have composed music is Aurelian Townshend's Masque for Lady Hatton (1 March 1636). He supplied extensive musical episodes for plays put on at Oxford on 29–30 August 1636 for the king's visit: William Strode's *The Floating Island* and William Cartwright's *The Royal Slave*. His association with Cartwright led to his setting as recitative his lament of Ariadne, *Theseus, O Theseus, hark! but yet in vain* (in *Ayres and Dialogues*, 1653, and also in his autograph songbook).

In 1638 Lawes published settings of George Sandys's metrical psalms and ten years later *Choice Psalmes*. It was for the latter that Milton wrote his famous sonnet:

> To my Friend M^r. *Henry Lawes.*
> *Harry*, whose tunefull and well measur'd song
> First taught our English Music how to span
> Words with just note and accent, not to scan
> With *Midas* eares, committing short and long.

During the Commonwealth period Lawes was a much sought-after teacher 'for the Voyce or Viole'; among his pupils were Mary Harvey (Lady Dering) and the singer Mary Knight. Fashionable musical parties were held at his house: the Duchess of Newcastle 'went with my Lord's brother to hear music in one Mr. Lawes his house, three or four times'. Among his circle were his two erstwhile pupils, the daughters of the old Earl of Bridgwater, and to them he dedicated his first book of *Ayres and Dialogues* (1653), 'most of them being Composed when I was employed by Your ever Honour'd Parents to attend Your Ladishipp's Education in Musick'. The preface to this book condemns his fellow countrymen's predilection for foreign music and recounts the famous story of when his setting of the list of contents of Cifra's *Scherzi et arie* (1614) had been much acclaimed and hailed as 'a rare *Italian Song*'. In the preface to his *Second Book of Ayres, and Dialogues* (1655) he again mounted his hobby horse, complaining of the unthinking admiration with which Italian music was accepted in England (at, he felt, his own expense).

In 1656 Davenant's *First Dayes Entertainment at Rutland House* and *The Siege of Rhodes* were performed. A contemporary report of the former states that 'the first song was made by Hen: Lawes, ye other by Dr. Coleman who were the Composers'. For *The Siege of Rhodes*, which was apparently a proper opera with 'the Story sung in *Recitative* Musick', Lawes wrote the vocal music for the first and last acts, the other composers being Cooke and Locke; all the music is lost. A third book of *Ayres and Dialogues* by Lawes appeared in 1658, and John Playford published 43 more of his songs posthumously in 1669, 'transcribed from his Originals, a short time before his Death, and with his free consent for me to Publish them, if occasion offer'd'.

Lawes's anthem *Zadok the priest* was sung at the coronation of Charles II. He was reinstated in both his old positions in the King's Musick and the Chapel Royal. Portraits of him include one dated 1622 in the Choir Room at Salisbury Cathedral, another (roughly 20 years later) in the Faculty of Music, Oxford, and the engraving by Faithorne published in his collection of 1653.

2. WORKS. Although he wrote a quantity of church music it was as a songwriter that Lawes made his reputation. Apart from the three-part settings of *Choice Psalmes* and the simple hymn tunes published in 1638, only six anthems survive complete. The verse anthem *My song shall be of mercy* may be regarded as representative: the verse sections are somewhat after the declamatory style of his songs, the full sections are for the most part homophonic and rather dull.

Lawes's known songs number 434. The most important printed sources are his three books of ayres and dialogues and the collections published by Playford between 1652 and 1669. The autograph songbook (in *GB-Lbm*) containing 325 songs is also very important.

Although he may not have begun to compile it until after 1636 it probably represents the output of about 30 years, from the early 1620s (possibly even earlier) to the 1650s, arranged in roughly chronological order. In this manuscript there is clearly a gradual transition from the unsophisticated solemnity and rather stiff manner of the earlier songs to altogether freer settings with wonderfully flexible declamation and greater subtlety and variety of feeling. These latter are surely the songs of Lawes's maturity and probably date from the years following his appointment as a musician to the king in 1631, which seems to have brought him into contact with the circle of court poets. Among these he favoured most the exquisite Carew: there are 38 settings of his poems in the manuscript (concentrated mainly between ff.95v and 121), as well as 16 of Waller's, 14 of Herrick's and some of the most celebrated anthology pieces of Suckling and Lovelace.

Some of Lawes's settings, such as that of Herrick's *Bid me but live* (MB, xxxiii, no.53), are simple strophic songs in triple time, enlivened by syncopations and hemiola rhythms. On the other hand Suckling's *No, no, fair heretic* (no.50), though basically strophic, is set in the declamatory style. The music closely follows the argumentative nature of the verse, necessitating modification of detail in the second stanza to suit a different phraseology, but the final epigrammatic couplet of each stanza is in a tuneful triple time, thus giving shape and point to the song as a whole. The essentially rhetorical nature of Lawes's declamation is well illustrated in the through-composed setting of Carew's *When thou, poor*

2. A dialogue by Henry Lawes from 'Select Ayres and Dialogues' (1669⁵, vol.ii)

excommunicate (no.55). Vocal contour, rhythm, punctuation, phrasing and cadences are all perfectly adapted to the self-dramatizing manner of this type of poetry.

Early editions of Carew (1640), Waller (1645), Milton (1645), Suckling (1646) and Cartwright (1651) all advertised the fact that Lawes had set their songs, as did the titles of individual poems by Herrick and Lovelace. Burney suspected that such praise by poets for a composer could only mean that the music was in some way deficient and he duly found cause for censure. Even as to 'just note and accent' he pointed out certain faults, although a closer look at the particular instances he cites suggests that he was hasty as well as unsympathetic in his judgment. Undoubtedly sympathy is needed in approaching the songs of Lawes, for performance shows that details that look stiff and awkward on paper come vividly to life when properly performed. Indeed the decline in his reputation since his own day may be attributed to the fact that his songs became material for study and analysis rather than for performance. Any critical rehabilitation will therefore need to take into account the style required for their performance; there are signs that as this is done some former critical judgments will have to be reversed.

WORKS

Editions: *H. Lawes: 10 Ayres for Contralto (or Baritone) and Keyboard*, ed. T. Dart, English Songs, i (London, 1956) [D]
    English Songs 1625–1660, ed. I. Spink, MB, xxxiii (1971) [S]

(all published in London)

SACRED VOCAL

A Paraphrase upon the Psalmes of David: by G[eorge] S[andys]: set to New Tunes for Private Devotion, 1v, bc (1638)
Choice Psalmes put into Musick, 3vv, bc (1648⁴) [incl. 30 full anthems]
3 other full anthems (1 inc.) in J. Clifford: The Divine Services and Anthems (1663), *GB-Lbm*, *LF* (inc.)
6 verse anthems (2 inc.), *Ckc*, *Cu*, *DRc*, *GL*, *Lbm*, *Lcm*, *LF*, *Lsp*, *Ob*, *Och*, *Ojc*, *Y*, *US-BE*
11 anthems (texts only)

SECULAR

Ayres and Dialogues ... First Booke, 1–3vv (1653); 2 in D
The Second Book of Ayres, and Dialogues, 1–3vv (1655); 4 in D
Ayres and Dialogues ... Third Booke, 1–3vv (1658); 4 in D
239 songs in the above sources and in 1652⁸, 1652¹⁰, 1653⁷, 1659⁵, 1663⁶, 1667⁶, 1669⁵/R1966, 1673⁴, 1678⁵

325 songs, *GB-Lbm* Add.53723 (autograph) [incl. 148 printed in the above vols.]; 25 in S
17 songs, principal sources *F-Pn*, *GB-Lbm*, *Ob*, *US-NYp*; 2 in S

For plays containing songs by Lawes see Day and Murrie, Willetts and S
For some conflicting attributions *see* WILLIAM LAWES

Several inst works, *GB-Ob* Mus.Sch.D.220, 233–4, 236, E.451

BIBLIOGRAPHY

E. J. Dent: *Foundations of English Opera* (Cambridge, 1928/R1965)
C. L. Day and E. B. Murrie: *English Song Books, 1651–1702* (London, 1940)
W. McC. Evans: *Henry Lawes, Musician and Friend of Poets* (New York, 1941/R1966)
E. F. Hart: 'Introduction to Henry Lawes', *ML*, xxxii (1951), 217f, 328ff
V. Duckles: 'English Song and the Challenge of Italian Monody', in V. Duckles and F. B. Zimmerman: *Words to Music* (Los Angeles, 1967), 3–42
R. J. McGrady: 'Henry Lawes and the Concept of "Just Note and Accent"', *ML*, l (1969), 86
P. J. Willetts: *The Henry Lawes Manuscript* (London, 1969)
I. Spink: *English Song: Dowland to Purcell* (London, 1974)

IAN SPINK

Lawes, William (*b* Salisbury, baptized 1 May 1602; *d* Chester, 24 Sept 1645). English composer and musician, younger brother of Henry Lawes. He was a gifted, versatile and prolific composer. Unlike his brother, who wrote only vocal music, he also composed a wide range of instrumental music, most notably for consorts of viols and accompanied violins, and he was the leading

English composer of dramatic music before Purcell.

1. Life. 2. Works: introduction and sources. 3. Instrumental music. 4. Vocal and stage music. 5. Assessment.

1. LIFE. Lawes's father moved his family in 1602 from Dinton, Wiltshire, to the close of Salisbury Cathedral, where he had been appointed lay vicar. Lawes probably received his earliest education at the free grammar school in the close. Since the family was noted for its fine voices, and William was later a countertenor at court, it is probable that he was a chorister at Salisbury Cathedral. He probably received his first music lessons from his father. According to Fuller, he showed such talent in his early childhood that Edward Seymour, Earl of Hertford, a generous patron of Salisbury and its musicians, obtained him from his father and brought him up at his own expense under the tutelage of his own music master, John Coprario, at his estates at Amesbury and Wulfall, Wiltshire. It was probably here that William first met the future King Charles I, who studied the viola da gamba with Coprario in his youth, for Prince Charles, who was two years older than Lawes, was a frequent visitor to the Hertford estates. He and Lawes quite possibly played in consort together under Coprario, who, moreover, may have written his *Rules how to Compose* for Lawes's instruction at that time. Hatcher stated that Lawes was selected before he was 23 as one of the private musicians to Prince Charles and that when Charles became king in 1625 he continued in this post with additional marks of favour. Records show, however, that he did not receive his official court appointment as 'musician in ordinary for the lutes and voices' until 1635 (when he replaced John Lawrence, deceased), yet since he is known to have composed music for the court at least as early as 1633 it is indeed probable that he was a member of a select group of musicians, led by Coprario, in Charles's service both before and immediately after he became king. From this time until his death he regularly composed vocal and instrumental music for the court, especially for the elaborate masques and entertainments of Charles's reign and for the many plays performed by the King's Men at the Cockpit-in-Court and at Blackfriars. In this activity he appears to have succeeded such official court dramatic composers as Coprario, Alfonso Ferrabosco (ii), Robert Johnson (ii) and Nicholas Lanier.

When in 1642 the king moved his court to Oxford, Lawes, who was a staunch royalist, joined him, and shortly afterwards he enlisted in the royalist army. To shield him from danger he was made a commissary in the king's personal life guards. His whereabouts after about 1643 can thus be traced to the various campaigns in which the king accompanied his troops. He rode into Chester with Charles on 23 September 1645 in the attempt to relieve the beleaguered garrison there. During the battle, which took place on the following day, he evidently joined the garrison in what seemed for the moment a victorious rout of the rebel forces. But when the retreating rebels, who had been secretly reinforced from the rear, unexpectedly turned and charged their onrushing pursuers, Lawes – 'betrayed thereunto by his own adventurousness', in Fuller's words – was shot and killed. Of the king's reaction Fuller wrote that 'hearing of the death of his *deare servant William Lawes*, he had a particular Mourning for him when *dead*, whom he loved when living, and commonly called the *Father of Musick*'. Many of the poets whose words Lawes set to music mourned him in verse, for example Robert Herrick in his *Hesperides* (1648), Robert Heath in *Clarastella* (1650) and John Tatham in *Ostella* (1650). In the royalist ranks his death became a symbol of the excesses of the Puritan revolt: 'Will Lawes was slain by those whose wills were laws' is a play on words often found in royalist poetry. He was clearly a man of great personal attractiveness, in Fuller's words 'respected and beloved by all those who cast any looks towards virtue and honour'. His reputed portrait, showing him in the garb of a dashing cavalier, hangs in the Faculty of Music, Oxford (see illustration).

2. WORKS: INTRODUCTION AND SOURCES. None of Lawes's music was published during his lifetime. The first print to include any of it was *Choice Psalmes* (*RISM* 1648⁴), which Henry Lawes edited as a memorial to him. It contains 30 of his psalm settings for three voices with a thoroughbass, and ten of his sacred canons appear at the end. The volume also includes 30 of Henry Lawes's psalms and several musical elegies written by him and other famous court musicians, among them John Hilton (ii), Simon Ives, John Jenkins and John Wilson. At the head of the volume are several commendatory verses by leading poets and other notables, all bemoaning the loss of one of England's great musicians. In his introductory dedication to Charles I and to the reader, Henry Lawes penned one of the noblest testaments of fraternal devotion in any literature, and wrote of his brother's music that it was

too voluminous for the presse . . .; for, besides his Fancies of the Three, Four, Five and Six Parts to the Viols and Organ, he hath made above thirty severall sorts of Musick for voices and Instruments: Neither were there any Instrument then in use, but he compos'd to it so aptly, as if he had only studied that.

Many of Lawes's songs, catches and dance tunes appeared in miscellanies that John Playford published after 1650. Much of this music, however, is not truly representative, for many of the pieces are simplified two-part arrangements of works that survive in authentic form in manuscript sources. Such sources fully support Henry Lawes's description quoted above. At least 14 autograph volumes of William Lawes's music are extant, all similarly bound in brown calf with the arms of Charles I, some with initials W. L. or H. L. on the covers. In the Bodleian Library, Oxford, MSS Mus.Sch.B.2 and B.3 are the autographs of the consort suites, which include fantasias, pavans, In Nomines and ayres in four, five and six parts in score 'ffor yᵉ viols'. Mus.Sch.B.2 also contains the suites for two bass viols and organ, the suite for two lutes, several catches and most of Lawes's music for court masques; B.3 also includes scores of the large variation pavans of the 'Harpe' consorts and the autographs of most of the so-called 'Royall' consort for two violins and two bass viols with continuo for two theorbos. The partbooks MSS Mus.Sch.D.238–40 contain the autographs of the complete 'Harpe' consorts and the violin 'sonatas', of which there are two sets, one for one violin, bass viol and organ, the other for two violins, bass viol and organ. Mus.Sch.D.229 contains both the harp and organ parts to the 'Harpe' consorts and violin 'sonatas' as well as the organ parts (reductions) for the consort suites. In the British Museum, Add.31432 is the autograph source of many of the songs, and a single bass viol partbook of the consort suites, Add.17798, indicates that at least five volumes of autographs are still lacking. A curious set of partbooks, Add.40657–61, partly autograph and lack-

William Lawes: portrait (2nd quarter of the 17th century), artist unknown, in the Faculty of Music, Oxford

first-movement sonata design; without abandoning the established form he expanded and reworked it to suit his own romantic temperament. Thus his fantasias are much longer than previous examples and are in fewer and longer sections marked off with clear cadences; thematic material from the opening imitative section is often transformed and developed in a variety of ways in later sections. Most important, he wrote more idiomatically than his predecessors for the instruments, making many new demands on the virtuosity of his performers, modulating to new keys and exploring new sonorities and new textures. Variety and contrast in mood between the sections is a hallmark of his style. It is achieved by the use of interludes for fewer instruments, dissonant homophonic writing, shorter note values during a thematic transformation, bold contrapuntal lines and exciting crossing of the parts, with concertante interplay between some or all of them. In addition Lawes highlighted his drive to the final cadence, which became a veritable dissonant coda. The ayres of the consort suites are quite different; they are stylized dances, usually almans of two strains, in a much lighter vein, tuneful, concertante and rhythmically exciting. This is a style in which Lawes apparently wrote with great facility and for which he became popular at court. The ayres are an admirable foil to the more serious fantasias, pavans and In Nomines of the set.

While in his consorts for viols Lawes exhibited late Renaissance traits, in his violin music he was much more a child of the Baroque era. Indeed by far the larger part of his chamber music is written for violins in the concertante style of Italian early Baroque violin music with basso continuo. This is true, for instance, of so little understood a work as the 'Royall' consort, which consists of some 66 dance pieces arranged in large suites by key. It exists in several versions but was

ing a bass, includes 11 three- and four-part ayres by Lawes not found elsewhere. He apparently used it as a commonplace book since it includes several pieces by other composers, among them Coprario, Alfonso Ferrabosco (ii), Marenzio, Monteverdi, Benedetto Pallavicino, Vecchi and John Ward. Finally, a partial, but incomplete, autograph of Lawes's lyra viol music exists as MS Mus.70 in the Houghton Library, Harvard University. It is one of an original set of three partbooks and contains, among other things, most of the suites for three lyra viols in tablature.

3. INSTRUMENTAL MUSIC. In his chamber music Lawes is representative of the romanticism of the second generation of 17th-century English viol composers (c1625–50), rather than of the classic style of the previous generation (c1600–25). His instrumental writing in the five- and six-part fantasias of the consort suites is both original and striking – highly personal, introspective and often experimental. Not all the pieces are of equal merit. Endowed with a gift for warm, dramatic and flowing melody, Lawes sometimes used it to achieve an angularity of line approaching romantic mannerism. His harmonies are often bold and discordant, especially in works in minor keys (above all C minor) and in his slow, homophonic middle sections. Here he tended to exploit the augmented and diminished intervals of the mixed major–minor mode but always within the context of clear tonal direction. It is probably his use of unprepared and sometimes unresolved 7ths and augmented and diminished chords that prompted Anthony Wood's rather naive comment that his music 'broke sometimes yᵉ rules of mathematicall composition'. In fact his harmonies grow logically out of and intensify the dissonance practices of the late Renaissance Italian and English madrigal idiom as exploited by such men as Marenzio, Monteverdi, Weelkes and Wilbye (see ex.1).

In many respects Lawes's attitude towards the fantasia is analogous to that of Beethoven towards

Ex.1 Consort Suite in G minor a 6, 1st movt 'Fantazy'

probably composed originally in four parts (see Lefkowitz, 1960, p.74). Although the later arrangement is for six instruments, specified by Lawes himself, there are only four real parts: two concertante violins, an unfigured continuo for two theorbos, and a tenor part whose phrases alternate between the two bass viols, each of which retreats in turn to join the theorbos on the bass line. Moreover, even the tenor part is a dividing bass to the continuo part; in fact a trio setting for two concertante violins and continuo is also extant (in *GB-Lbm* Add.31431). The 'Royall' consort also exists under the title 'The Greate Consort' (in *GB-Och* 391–6). The suites are loosely ordered in the sequence of almans–corants–sarabands, sometimes preceded by a pavan or fantasia. They were probably written for revels and entertainments at court.

The stylized dance suite is the basic vehicle for Lawes's chamber music, and he used it in a variety of guises in which the violin figures prominently. Often the dances are preceded by a fantasia or pavan, as in the Italian canzona suite or in the later *sonata da chiesa*. One early and important English variety is the so-called fantasia-suite or trio sonata, of which Lawes left two sets of eight each, one in three parts and one in four. These are of unequal merit, but some, like nos.1, 7 and 8 of the three-part set and nos.1, 6 and 7 of the four-part set, are outstanding. All are in three movements, fantasia–alman–galliard. The keyboard parts for organ are remarkably independent, at least a century ahead of their time, and employ solo interludes of their own (see ex.2). The works are unified at the end of the galliard last movement by the addition of a large coda, which returns to the duple time of the opening movement and is in a slow, dissonant contrapuntal style. The influence of concertante interplay, lively dance rhythms and virtuoso variation techniques is specially pronounced in these works. Certainly the fantasias of these sets bear scant resemblance to those of the viol consorts and represent a marked advance over those of Coprario. The sonatas can also be seen as antecedents of those of three and four parts by Purcell, who may have known and learnt from them.

The dance suite appears in another guise in the 'Harpe' consorts, a unique collection of variation suites for a broken consort of violin, bass viol, theorbo and harp. It is one of the earliest collections of chamber music – possibly the only one – to employ the harp. It comprises extended sets of fully written-out paired variations on the dance strains which show exactly how variations were ordered and arranged and how they were performed. They show too that Lawes must have been a fine string player himself and a great practitioner of the art of improvisation as expounded in Christopher Simpson's *The Division Violist* (1659). The three large pavans in this collection are virtuoso works, especially for the bass violist, and are masterpieces of their kind. Playford later printed (in *Court Ayres*, 1655, and *Courtly Masquing Ayres*, 1662) several pieces in these consorts as short two-part 'lessons' or dances for a treble and a bass, minus the harp part and the variations. The suites for two division bass viols and organ and the suites for three lyra viols, of which there are three each, are similar in style to the 'Harpe' consorts. Both of these sets are of extremely high quality. Lawes was credited by Wood with being an 'approver and improver of the lyra viol'; he is in fact often mentioned in this regard. The suites are one of the few collections for a consort of

Ex.2 Violin Sonata in G minor a 3, 1st movt, Fantasia

number of dances for a single lyra viol. In the suites the three instruments continually switch roles as treble, tenor and bass. Lawes's favourite tuning for his lyra viols is that known as 'eights' (Ferrabosco-way): *d'–a–d–A–D–A'*.

It is doubtful whether Lawes wrote any original solo keyboard works. There are none in his autographs, and most of those that have survived in manuscripts and in Playford's publications have been identified as arrangements of his consort music. Nevertheless, the singular Suite in A minor (in *F-Pc* Rés.1185) must be mentioned as a particularly delightful variation set.

4. VOCAL AND STAGE MUSIC. Because of his own over-riding success as an instrumental composer and because after his death his brother Henry achieved such great popularity as a song composer, Lawes's vocal music has generally been overshadowed. Recent research, beginning with that of Dent, has greatly increased our knowledge of his activities and importance as a composer of both vocal and instrumental music for court masques and the theatre, but his many other songs, secular and sacred, are less known. Like his brother and with at least equal acclaim, he set the verses of a number of Caroline poets, among them Carew, Davenant, Herrick, Lovelace, Shirley and Suckling. Well over 200 of his songs are extant in manuscripts and early printed books, but only a handful have appeared in modern editions. They are thoroughly representative of Caroline song styles and as such are of several kinds: (1) those in ballad style, many of which are dance-songs, attractively tuneful strophic love-songs, usually in triple metre and using the lively rhythms and hemiola patterns of the popular corants and sarabands of the dance suite (in fact some – e.g. *O my Clarissa* – exist in both instrumental and dance-song versions; three fine examples of this type are *Deerest, all faire, Aske me noe more* and the celebrated *Gather ye rosebuds*; (2) those in declamatory style – usually set to dramatic texts and exploring such subjects as pathetic love, tragedy and mythological allegory – which were partly an attempt to imitate the contemporary Italian recitative but with an emphasis on intellectual rather than emotional content; they are through-composed and are concerned with expressing the prosody of the text through the use of such devices as word-painting, speech rhythm, voice inflection, poetic metres, word rhythm and verse punctuation; *Amarillis, Those lovers only hapye are* and *White though yee bee* are good examples; (3) those in a bipartite form beginning in declamatory style but with the last couplet set in ballad style; (4) dialogues, which are dramatic duets in declamatory or bipartite style employing pastoral or mythological themes, rather as in the dramatic secular cantata; a fine piece in this form is the setting of *Charon, O gentle Charon, Dialogue between Charon and Philomel*; (5) a few partsongs in late madrigal style, of which *Cease, warring thoughts* from Shirley's *The Triumph of Beautie* should be singled out; and (6) catches and drinking-songs, for which, to judge by Playford's songbooks, Lawes was very popular; the catch *The wise men were but seven* and the drinking-song *The catts as other creatures doe* are excellent examples. A few catches exploiting *double entendres* are particularly obscene; such a one is *See how in gathering*.

Lawes's best-known sacred work is his verse anthem *The Lord is my light*, one of the most distinguished examples of its period. The three-part psalms in *Choice*

Psalmes (1648) are akin to full anthems of the time, and they are among Lawes's finest vocal works; this is specially true of his settings of the *Lamentations of Jeremiah*. Some of his sacred canons and rounds are also of high quality, especially the four-part *She weepeth sore in the night*. There is also a unique collection of 12 three-part verse anthems 'to the common tunes' (*GB-Och* 768–70). They are early works and are particularly interesting in that they are complete settings of the psalms, of considerable length, in which the composed verses, set through-composed as solos, duets and trios, alternate with verses to the common tunes sung by either the choir or the congregation or perhaps even played by the organist. The composed verses are in the declamatory style and make much use of word-painting, so the works present a curious mixture of secular style and sacred *alternatim* practice.

Among the precursors of Purcell, Lawes left the largest single body of English stage music, including music for the theatre and for court masques and entertainments: at least 43 songs from some 25 dramatic productions have been identified as his. The record begins in 1633 with music for Jonson's *Entertainment at Welbeck* and Fletcher's play *The Faithful Shepherdess*. Then, in 1634, followed his music for Shirley's monumental masque *The Triumph of Peace*, the most spectacular of all English masques, in which he collaborated with Simon Ives (see Lefkowitz, 1965 and 1970); in the same year he wrote incidental music and songs for Davenant's play *Love and Honour*. In 1636 he collaborated with his brother on another court masque, *The Triumphs of the Prince d'Amour* by Davenant, and wrote music for at least three other productions: a revival of Jonson's *Epicoene, or The Silent Woman*, William Cartwright's *The Royal Slave* (at Oxford, with his brother) and Shirley's *The Duke's Mistress*. In 1637 he supplied songs for William Berkeley's *The Lost Lady*, Jasper Mayne's *The City Match*, John Suckling's *Aglaura* and a revival of Beaumont and Fletcher's *Cupid's Revenge*, and in 1638 he wrote the music for another large court masque, *Britannia triumphans* by Davenant, and for at least three more plays: Ford's *The Lady's Trial*, Davenant's *The Unfortunate Lovers* and Suckling's *The Goblins*. We have music by him for only two plays staged in 1639, Suckling's *The Tragedy of Brennoralt* and Henry Glapthorne's *Argalus and Parthenia*, and for only one in 1640, *The Country Captain* by Cavendish (or possibly Shirley). 1641 was the last year of his dramatic production: it was then that he wrote music for Shirley's *The Cardinal*, Sir John Denham's *The Sophy* and Richard Brome's *The Jovial Crew*. He also wrote music for at least three works for which the dates cannot be determined: Shirley's school masque *The Triumph of Beauty* and revivals of Fletcher's *The Mad Lover* and Middleton's *The Widow*. For all of these works we have songs by him but no complete scores. All were performed before the king and queen while he was employed at court, a record that supports the claim that he was in fact the official composer for the King's Men and for Beeston's Boys as well.

The music that Lawes wrote for court masques is a particularly impressive and historically significant part of his legacy. It paved the way for the work of such important dramatic composers as Locke, Blow and Purcell. Future evaluation may indeed credit Lawes with being the first English composer to create musical continuity within a dramatic work. It is already known that his masque music follows a preconceived and well balanced tonal plan from beginning to end. He also had a keen sense of the dramatic, for he sought musical variety and contrast through continually changing textures, sonorities, mood and action; instrumental symphonies and ritornellos alternate with solo songs, duets, trios and choruses in a mixture of declamatory, madrigal and ballad styles, the whole punctuated by dances. The recent identification of the music for *Britannia triumphans* and the discovery of the Longleat papers have added considerably to our knowledge of his role in the development of the court masque (for a more detailed discussion *see* MASQUE, §4).

5. ASSESSMENT. A revaluation of Lawes's musical production places him in the mainstream of English music. His influence on his contemporaries and those who followed him – Jenkins, Ives, Christopher Simpson, Christopher Gibbons, Locke and Purcell in particular – was considerable, especially in the areas of instrumental and dramatic music. The question of Italian influence on him is often raised. If there is Italianism in his music it is in the concertante writing for violins and in the use of the continuo, albeit unfigured. Yet these features were already in evidence in the previous generation. Did it come, then, via Coprario? It has still to be proved that Coprario visited Italy and that his music was Italian-influenced. That Lawes was familiar with Italian music, especially that of Marenzio and Monteverdi, is quite clear from the partbooks (*GB-Lbm* Add.40657–61) into which he copied it, apparently as a young man – almost the only clue, incidentally, towards establishing any chronology in his instrumental works. But direct influence from this source is also difficult to show. The warp and woof of Lawes's music seems firmly rooted in English musical practice. It is in fact in Coprario's music and *Rules how to Compose* that one finds his antecedents, whether in form, counterpoint or harmony, and he built upon what he learnt there, expanding the forms, intensifying the harmonies, demanding increased virtuosity and imbuing his music with more dramatic contrast to suit his own more romantic temperament. This is surely what Fuller meant when he stated that 'the *Schollar* in time did *Equal*, yea *Exceed* his Master'. Lawes's popularity lasted well into the Restoration period, and in 1676 Thomas Mace (*Musick's Monument*, 151) still accorded him first place among English composers of the recent past:

These last Ages have produc'd very many Able, and most Excellent Masters in Musick; Three only (of which) I will instance in, in this Particular; because they were so Voluminous, and very Eminent in Their Works; viz. Mr. William Lawes, Mr. John Jenkins and Mr. Christopher Simpson

After the age of Purcell, however, Lawes's music was laid aside, forgotten but happily not lost.

WORKS

Editions: *The Rounds, Catches and Canons of England*, ed. E. F. Rimbault (London, 1865) [R]

Masque of Comus (Milton), ed. F. Bridge (London, 1908/R1956) [B]

Songs and Dances for the Stuart Masque, ed. A. J. Sabol (Providence, Rhode Island, 1959; rev., enlarged 2/1978) [A]

W. Lawes: Select Consort Music, ed. M. Lefkowitz, MB, xxi (1963, 2/1971) [L]

Trois masques à la cour de Charles Ier d'Angleterre, ed. M. Lefkowitz (Paris, 1970) [M]

English Songs, 1625–1660, ed. I. Spink, MB, xxxiii (1971) [S]

W. Lawes: Consort Sets in Five and Six Parts, ed. D. Pinto (London, 1979)

For further source information see Lefkowitz, 1960

* – incl. autograph   † – incl. inc. copy

CONSORT SUITES
(*viols: 2 tr, 2 b*)
'ffor yᵉ viols': c, *Ob; C, *Ob, 1 movt in M

(*viols: 2 tr, a/t, t, b; org*)
'ffoy yᵉ viols': g 'on the playnesong', *Lbm*, *Ob, ed. in L; a, *Lbm*, *Ob [see also 'Keyboard'], 1 movt ed. in L; c, †*Lbm, *Ob, 1 movt ed. in L, 1 movt ed. in *MA*, i (1909–10); F, *Lbm*, *Ob; C, †*Lbm, *Ob, ed. H. Mönkemeyer (Wilhelmshaven, 1966)

(*viols: 2 tr, a/t, t, 2 b; org*)
'ffor yᵉ viols': c, *Lbm*, *Ob, ed. in L; C, *Lbm*, *Ob, ed. H. Mönkemeyer (Wilhelmshaven, 1966), 1 movt ed. in M; B♭, *Lbm*, *Ob, 1 movt ed. in L; g, *Lbm*, *Ob; F, *Lbm*, *Ob

(*2 vn, 2 b viols, bc [2 theorbos]*)
'Royall' consort: d, *Lbm*, *Ob; d, *Lbm*, *Ob, *Och*, ed. in L, 2 movts ed. in M; d, *Lbm*, *Ob, *Och*, 1 movt ed. in Meyer (1946), 1 movt ed. in Lefkowitz (1960); D, *Lbm*, *Ob, *Och*, 1 movt ed. in B; D, *Lbm*, *Ob, *Och*; D, *Lbm*, *Ob, *Och*, 1 movt ed. in B; a, *Lbm*, *Och*; C, *Lbm*, *Och*; F, *Lbm*, *Och*; B♭, *Lbm*, *Och*

(*vn, b viol, harp, bc [theorbo]*)
'Harpe' consort: g, *Ob, *Och*, ed. in L; g, *Ob, *Och*; G, *Ob, *Och*, 1663⁷ (2 movts) [see also 'Keyboard']; d, *Ob, *Och*, 1 movt ed. in M, 1 movt ed. in Lefkowitz (1960); D, *Ob, *Och*; D, *Ob, *US-NYp* (inc.) [see also 'Keyboard']; G, *GB-Ob, *Och*; G (pavan), *Ob, ed. in L, ed. in M; D (pavan on a bass theme by J. Cormacke), *Ob, ed. in L; g (pavan on a bass theme by Coprario), *Ob, ed. in L; d, *Ob

SONATAS/FANTASIA-SUITES
(*vn, b viol, org*)
g, *Lbm*, *Ob, *Och*, ed. in L; G, *Lbm*, *Ob, *Och*; a, *Lbm*, *Ob, *Och*; C, *Lbm*, *Ob, *Och*; d, *Lbm*, *Ob, *Och*; D, *Lbm*, *Ob, *Och*; d, *Lbm*, *Ob, *Och*, ed. in L, ed. in Poulos; D, *Lbm*, *Ob, *Och*, ed. in L, ed. in Lefkowitz (1960), ed. in Poulos

(*2 vn, b viol, org*)
g, *F-Pc*, *GB-Lbm*, *Ob, *Och*, ed. in L; G, *F-Pc*, *GB-Lbm*, *Ob, *Och*; a, *F-Pc*, *GB-Lbm*, *Ob, *Och*, 1 movt ed. in M; C, *F-Pc*, *GB-Lbm*, *Ob, *Och*; d, *F-Pc*, *GB-Lbm*, *Ob, *Och*; D, *F-Pc*, *GB-Lbm*, *Ob, *Och*, ed. in L; d, *F-Pc*, *GB-Lbm*, *Ob, *Och*, ed. in L; D, *F-Pc*, *GB-Lbm*, *Ob, *Och*, 1 movt ed. in Meyer (1946)

OTHER SUITES
(*2 b viols, org*)
g, *Ob [see also 'Dances']; C (on a bass theme by 'Alfonso' [Ferrabosco]), *Ob, ed. in L; C, *Ob

(*3 lyra viols*)
D, *Och*, *US-CA (inc.), 1 movt ed. in M; d, *GB-Och*, *US-CA (inc.), ed. in L; d, *GB-Och*, *US-CA (inc.)

DANCES
85 aires, almans, corants, sarabands, etc, tr viol/vn, b viol, *GB-Ob*, 1651⁶

29 aires, almans, corants, sarabands, etc, 2 tr viols/2 vn, b viol, *Lbm, *T*; 2 ed. in M

11 aires, almans, corants, saraband, 2 tr viols/2 vn, t viol, b viol, bc, *Lbm, †*Ob*

2 aires, 2 tr viols, 2 b viols, *Lbm

Suite, g, 2 tr viols/2 vn, t viol, b viol, bc, *Lbm*, *Ob*, *Och* [arr. from Suite, g, 2 b viols, org]

KEYBOARD
(*virginals/hpd*)
Suite, a, †*F-Pc*, †*GB-Lbm*, †*Och*, Roger Lancelyn Green's private collection, Poulton Lancelyn, Ches. (1 movt), 1651⁶ (1 movt); 1 movt ed. in B; 1 movt ed. in M*B*, xx (1962); complete edn. in M

The Golden Grove Suite, *Ob*, †*Och*, 1662⁸; 1 movt ed. in M

One of ye Symphonies, *Lbm*, *Ob (a 2), *US-NYp* [symphony no.1 in J. Shirley: *The Triumph of Peace*, 1634]; ed. in Dent, ed. in A and M

[Symphony], *GB-Lbm* (a 3), *US-NYp*, 1651⁶ (a 2); ed. in B and M

Temple Mask, *GB-Och* (a 3), *US-NYp*, 1655⁵ (a 2); ed. in M

A Maske, *GB-Lbm*, *Ob (a 2) [symphony no.2 in *The Triumph of Peace*, 1634]; ed. in Dent, ed. in A and M

Mr Laws flat tanz, *Lbm* (a 5), *Ob (a 5), *US-NYp* [arr. from 3rd movt of consort suite, a, a 5]

Alman, *GB-Ob (a 3), *Och*, *US-NYp* (inc.), 1655⁵ (a 2) [arr. from 'Harpe' consort, D]

Coranto, *GB-Lbm (a 4), †*Ob* (a 4), *Och* (a 4), *US-NYp*

Gigge, *NYp*, 1655⁵ (a 2)

Suite, G, *GB-Ob (inc.), *Och*, 1663⁷ [2 movts arr. from 'Harpe' consort, G]; 1 movt ed. in B

2 dances: Contry Daunce, saraband, *Och*, 1663⁷

OTHER INSTRUMENTAL
8 pieces: The Golden Grove Suite, songs, cithren, 1666⁴

28 pieces: almans, corants, jigge, preludium, sarabands, 'Countrey Coll', 'Jubeters Aire', 'The Trumpet', 1, 3 lyra viols, *Lbm, *Mp*, *Ob*,

R. Spencer's private collection, Woodford Green, Essex, *US-CA, 1652[7], 1661[4]

Suite, 2 lutes, GB-Ob

(incomplete)

83 pieces: aires, almans, corants, sarabands (incl. 23 similar to 'Royall' consort), some a 2, 3, *Ob

13 pieces: aires, almans, corants, pavens, sarabands, toy, thump, 3 lyra viols, *US-CA

SECULAR VOCAL

(dramatic works containing songs are given in parentheses)

A hall, a hall, to welcome our friend (J. Suckling: The Tragedy of Brennoralt, 1639), 3vv, *GB-Lbm

Ah cruel love [To Pansies] (R. Herrick: Hesperides, 1648), 1v, *Lbm

A health to the northerne lasse (Suckling; The Goblins, 1638), 3vv, *Lbm, US-NYp

A knot of good fellows, catch, 3vv, 1667[6]; M

All these lye howling (J. Fletcher: The Mad Lover, revived 1630s), glee, 2vv, NYp

Amarillis, teare thy haire, 1v, *GB-Lbm, 1669[5]; ed. in Lefkowitz (1960)

And may your language be of force (W. Davenant: The Triumphs of the Prince d'Amour, 1636), madrigal, 3vv, chorus 4vv, *Ob; A, M

A pox on our gaoler (W. Cartwright: The Royal Slave, 1636), catch, 4vv, 1667[6]; R

A round, a round, boys (R. Brome: A Jovial Crew, 1641), catch, 3vv, 1667[6]

Aske me noe more where Jove bestowes (text: T. Carew), 1v, *Lbm, 1678[4]; ed. in Lefkowitz (1960)

Behold how this conjunction thrives (Davenant: The Triumphs of the Prince d'Amour, 1636), 1v, chorus 4vv, Eu (inc.), *†Ob; A, M

Belina, shade your shining eyes, 1v, *Lbm

Be not proud, pretty one [Love's Affection], 1v, *Lbm, Ob (a 3), 1669[5] [also with text: I can love for an hour, Eu (inc.), Lbm, Ob (inc.)]

Bess black as a charcole, catch, 3vv, 1667[6]

Brisk clarett and sherry, catch, 3vv, *Ob (only incipit texted)

Britanocles the great and good appears (Davenant: Britannia triumphans, 1638), 5vv, *Ob; M

Call for the ale, catch, 4vv, Lbm, *Ob, 1652[10]; R

Can bewtye's spring admitt, 1v, *Lbm

Cease, warring thoughts (J. Shirley: The Triumph of Beautie, before 1645), madrigal, 3vv, Eu (inc.), *†Ob; ed. in Lefkowitz (1960)

Charon, O Charon, hear a wretch opprest [Charon and Amintor], dialogue, 2vv, 1669[5]; S

Charon, O gentle Charon, let me wooe thee [Charon and Philomel], dialogue (Herrick: Hesperides, 1648), 2vv, *Lbm, Ob, 1652[8]

Clorinda, when I go away [Elizium], 1v, †Ob, US-NYp, 1651[6]

Cloris, I wish that Envye were as just, 1v, *GB-Lbm

Come, Adonis, come away (J. Tatham: Ostella, 1650), 1v, US-NYp (a 3), 1659[5]; S

Come, Amarillis, now let us be merry, catch, 4vv, 1667[6]

Come away, see the dawning of the day (Shirley: The Triumph of Peace, 1634), ?4vv (?inc.), *GB-Ob; M

Come, Cloris, hye wee to ye bower (text: H. Reynolds), 3vv (inc.), Eu (inc.), Ob (inc.)

Come follow me brave hearts, catch, 3vv, 1663[6]

Come, heavy hart, whose sighs thy sorrowes shew, dialogue, 2vv, *Lbm

Come, let us cast the dice (Shirley, or W. Cavendish: The Country Captain, 1640), catch, 3vv, Lbm, 1663[6]

Come, let us have a merry heart, catch, 3vv, 1667[6]

Come, lovely Cloris, 3vv, Ob, 1673[4]

Come, my Daphne, come away [Strephon and Daphne] (Shirley: The Cardinal, 1641), dialogue, 2vv, *Lbm, 1652[8]

Come, my lads, catch, 6vv, *Ob (only incipit texted)

Come, quaffe apace this brisk Canary wine, catch, 3vv, 1652[10]

Come, shepherds, come, come away (Beaumont and Fletcher: The Faithful Shepherdess, 1607, revived 1633), 1v, US-NYp; ed. in Cutts (1963)

Come, take a carouse, 3vv, *GB-Lbm

Cupids wearie of the court, 1v, *Lbm, US-NYp, 1678[4]

Dainty fine aniseed water, catch, 3vv, 1652[10]

Damon, good morrowe, may ye morninge queene, ?3vv (?inc), GB-Eu (inc.), Ob (inc.)

Deere, leave thy home and come with me [A Sonnet] (text: W. Herbert), madrigal, 4vv (inc.), Eu (inc.), *†Ob

Deerest, all faire is in your browne, 1v, *Lbm, US-NYp; M

Doris, see the am'rous flame, 1v, *GB-Lbm

Dost see how unregarded now [Sonnet] (Suckling: Fragmenta Aurea, 1646), 1v, *Lbm

Drink tonight of the moonshine bright, catch, 3vv, Lcm, 1652[10]; R

Erly in the morne, 1v, *Lbm

Fair as unshaded light [To the Queene, entertained . . . by the Countesse of Anglesey] (Davenant: Madagascar, 1638), 1v, 1678[4]; ed. in Gibbs

Faith, be noe longer coy [A Motive to Love] (Wit's Interpreter, 1655), 1v, *Lbm, US-NYp, 1652[8]; S

Far well, faire sainct [On his mistress crossing the sea] (T. Cary, in R. Fanshawe: Il pastor fido, 1647), 1v, *GB-Lbm, 1678[4]

Feare not, deere love [Secresie Protested] (T. Carew, 1640), madrigal, 5vv (inc.), *Ob

Fill, fill ye bowele, glee, 2vv, US-NYp

Gather ye rosebuds while ye may (Herrick: Hesperides, 1648), 1v, *GB-Lbm, Ob, US-NYp, 1652[7]; S

Gather ye rosebuds while ye may (Herrick: Hesperides, 1648), 3vv, GB-Eu (inc.), Gu, Lbm, Ob (inc.), 1652[8] [arr. from above setting]; S

God of winds, thou art growne brethles, 1v, *Lbm

Goe, bleeding hart, before thou die, madrigal, 3vv (inc.), *Ob

Good morrow unto her (text: Shirley), 3vv, Eu (inc.), Ob (inc.), US-NYp

Goose law'd with Goose for cousin Gander's land, catch, 3vv, 1652[10]; R

Had you but herd her sing, 1v, *GB-Lbm, 1678[4]

Hang sorrow and cast away care, catch, 3vv, Lbm, 1652[10]; R

Harke, harke, how in every grove [Cupid's Call] (text: Shirley, 1646), 1v, US-NYp

Harke, jolly lads, catch, 3vv, *GB-Ob (only incipit texted)

Hast you, nimphs, make hast away [Nimph and Shepherd], dialogue, 2vv, 1669[5]

Ha we to the other world, catch, 4vv, 1652[10]; R

He that will not love [Not to Love] (Herrick: Hesperides, 1648), 1v, *Lbm, 1659[5]

Heark, faire one (R. Lovelace: Lucasta, 1649) (text only)

Hence, flatt'ring hopes, 1v, *Lbm

Hence, ye prophane, far hence away (Shirley: The Triumph of Peace, 1634), 1v, chorus 4vv, *Ob; ed. in Dent, A and M

Here's a jolly couple, 1v, US-NYp

I burne, and beg of you to quench or cool me [To the Deeres] (Herrick: Hesperides, 1648), 1v, *GB-Lbm

I can love for an hour [Love's Flattery] (Wit's Interpreter, 1655), 1v, US-NYp, 1653[7]; S

I can love for an hour [Love's Flattery] (Wit's Interpreter, 1655), 1v, GB-Eu (inc.), Lbm, Ob (inc.) [music as Be not proud, pretty one]

I doe confesse, catch, 3vv, *Ob (only incipit texted)

If you a wrinkle on the sea have seene, 1v (inc.), *Lbm

If you will drink Canary, catch, 3vv, Lbm, *Ob, 1652[10]; R

I keepe my horse, I keepe my whore [The Cuttpurse Song] (T. Middleton: The Widow), 1v, US-NYp

Ile tell you of a matter, catch, 3vv, 1652[10]

I'm sick of love [To the Sycamore] (Herrick: Hesperides, 1648), 1v, *GB-Lbm

In envye of the night (Shirley: The Triumph of Peace, 1634), 1v, *Lbm, US-NYp; ed. in Lefkowitz (1960), A and M

It is folly to be jolly, catch, 3vv, 1658[5]

It tis her voice, 1v, *GB-Lbm

I would the god of love would dye (text: Shirley), 1v, *Lbm

Lets cast away care, catch, 3vv *Ob, 1651[6]; R

Listen near to the ground, catch, 3vv, 1658[5]

Love, I obey, shoot home thy dart, 1v, *Lbm, 1678[4]

Love is lost and gone astray, glee, 2vv, in J. Playford: *A Brief Introduction to the Skill of Musick* (London, 4/1660)

Love throws more dangerous darts, 3vv (inc.), Eu (inc.), Ob (inc.)

Lovers rejoice, your paines shall be rewarded (Beaumont and Fletcher: Cupid's Revenge, revived 1637-9), 1v, *Lbm

Love's a child and ought to be won with smyles (H. Glapthorne: Argalus and Parthenia, 1639), 1v, *Lbm, 1678[4]

May our three gods so long conjoyne (Davenant: The Triumphs of the Prince d'Amour, 1636), 4vv, *Ob; A, M

Music, the master of thy art is dead [On the memory of my friend, John Tomkins] (text by ? W. Lawes), madrigal, 3vv, 1638, *Ob, 1648[4]

Never let a man take heavily, catch, 3vv, *Ob, 1652[10]; R

Noe, noe, faire heriticke (Suckling: Aglaura, 1638), 1v, US-NYp [also attrib. H. Lawes]; S

Now in the sad declenshion of my time, 1v, *GB-Lbm

Now, my lads, now let's be merry (catch), 3vv, 1667[6]

Now that the spring hath fill'd our veins (W. Browne in Merry Drollery, 1661), glee, 2vv, Lbm, 1652[8]

Now the sun is fled downe, dialogue (Cartwright: The Royal Slave, 1636), 2vv, chorus 5vv, F-Pc, US-NYp [also attrib. H. Lawes]; S

O draw your curtaynes and apeere (Davenant: Love and Honour, 1634), 1v, *GB-Lbm, US-NYp, 1678[4]; ed. in Gibbs

O love, are all those arrowes gone, 1v, *GB-Lbm

O my Clarissa, thou cruel faire, Och, US-NYp, 1652[10]

O my Clarissa, thou cruel faire, 3vv, GB-Gu, Lbm, 1653[7]; ed. in Lefkowitz (1960) [version for 4 insts], M

O tell me, Damon, canst thou prove (Wit's Interpreter, 1655), 1v, US-NYp, 1652[8] [probably by W. Webb]

O the fickle state of lovers (text: F. Quarles), glee, 2vv, GB-Ob, US-NYp, 1653[7] [also attrib. H. Lawes]

O thinke not Phoebe cause a cloud (text: Shirley, 1646), 1v, *GB-Lbm

On, on, compassion shall never enter heere, 1v, chorus 3vv, *Lbm

Orpheus, O Orpheus, gently touch thy Lesbian lyre [Trialogue between Alecto, Orpheus and Euridice], 3vv, *Lbm, 1678[4]

Perfect and endless circles are, 1v, *Lbm

Pleasures, bewty, youth attend yee [Love in the Spring] (J. Ford: The Lady's Trial, 1639), 1v, *Lbm, US-NYp, 1669[5]; S

Sacred love whose vertues power, dialogue, 2vv, NYp

See how Cawoods dragon looks, catch, 3vv, 1658[5]; R

See how in gathering of their may, catch, 3vv, *GB-Lbm*, 1652¹⁰

Sing out pent soules (Lovelace: Lucasta, 1649) (text only)

Singe, singe his praises that do keep our flocks (Fletcher: The Faithful Shepherdess, revived, 1633), 3vv (inc.), *Eu* (inc.), *Ob* (inc.); ed. in Cutts (1963)

Soe well Britanocles o're seas doth raigne [Song of Galatea] (Davenant: Britannia triumphans, 1638), 1v, choruses 3, 5vv, **Ob*; M

Some drink boy, some drink (Suckling: The Goblins, 1638), catch, 3vv, *Lbm*, **Ob*, 1667⁶

Somnus, the 'umble god (J. Denham: The Sophy, 1641), 1v, *US-NYp*

Stand still and listen, catch, 3vv, **GB-Ob*, 1652¹⁰

Stay, Phoebus, stay [Songe] (text: E. Waller), 1v, **GB-Lbm*

Still to bee neate, still to bee dresst (B. Jonson: Epicoene, or The Silent Woman, 1609, revived 1636), 1v, chorus 4vv, *US-NYp*; ed. in Lefkowitz (1960)

Sullen care, why dost thou keepe, 1v, *NYp*

Suppose her fair, suppose I know itt, 1v, *NYp*, 1678⁴ [also attrib. A. Coates]

Tell me noe more her eyes (H. Moody in Wit's Interpreter, 1655), 1v, **GB-Lbm*, *US-NYp*, 1652⁸

That flame is born of earthly fire [Love's Constancy], 1v, *F-Pc*, **GB-Lbm*, 1669⁵

The angry steed, the phyph and drum (Davenant: The Triumphs of the Prince d'Amour, 1636), 1v, chorus 4vv, **Ob*; A, M

The balmes rich swet, the myrrhs sweet teares (Davenant: The Triumphs of the Prince d'Amour, 1636), 2vv, chorus 4vv, **Ob*; A, M

The catts as other creatures doe, 3vv, **Lbm*, *US-NYp*

The larke now leaves his wattry nest (text: Davenant), dialogue, 2vv, *NYp*; ed. in Gibbs

The pot, the pipe, the quart, the can, catch, 4vv, *GB-Lbm*, 1658⁵; R

There can bee noe glad man (Wit and Drollery, 1661), 1v, chorus 3vv, *US-NYp*

The wise men were but seven, catch, 3vv, *GB-Lbm*, 1652¹⁰; ed. in Lefkowitz (1960) and R

Thinke not I could absent myself this night (Shirley: The Triumph of Peace, 1634), 2vv, chorus 4vv; ed. in Dent, A and M

Those lovers only hapye are, 1v, **Lbm*

Though I am not Bachus preist, catch, 3vv, **Ob* (only incipit texted)

Thou that excellest, 1v, **Lbm*, *US-NYp*

Tis no shame to yeild to beauty, 1v, chorus 3vv, *NYp*

Tis not, boy, thy amorous looke, dialogue, 2vv, **GB-Lbm*

To bed, to bed (Davenant: Britannia triumphans, 1638), 5vv, **Ob*; M

Tom, Ned and Jack, catch, 3vv, **Ob* (only incipit texted)

To whome shall I complaine, 1v, **Lbm*, *US-NYp*, 1678⁴; S

Upp, ladies, upp, prepare your loving faces [Cupid's Progress], 1v, **GB-Lbm*, *US-NYp*, 1669⁵; M

Virgins, as I advise, forbeare, 1v, **GB-Lbm*, 1678⁴

Vulcan, O vulcan, my love [Venus and Vulcan], dialogue, 2vv, 1653⁷

Warrs are our delight, catch, 6vv, *Lbm*, **Ob*, 1652¹⁰; M

Wee shoe noe monstrous crockadell (J. Mayne: The City Match, 1637), 1v, *US-NYp*

What hoe, wee come to bee merry (Ford: The Lady's Trial, 1639), 3vv, **GB-Lbm*

What if I die for love of thee, dialogue, 2vv, *Lbm*, *Och*

What should my mistresse doe with haire [One that loved none but deformed women] (Shirley, ? intended for The Duke's Mistress, 1636), glee, 1v, chorus, 2vv, *US-NYp*

What softer sounds are these [Joy and Delight] (Jonson: Entertainment at Welbeck, 1633), dialogue, 2vv, **GB-Lbm*

When by thy scorne foule murderess [The Apparition] (J. Donne, 1633), madrigal, 3vv (inc.), *Eu* (inc.), *Ob* (inc.)

When death shall snatch us from these kidds [Thirsis and Dorinda] (text: A. Marvell, 1681), dialogue, 2vv, *Lbm*

When each lynes a faithfull drinker, 3vv, **Lbm*, *US-NYp*

When I by thy faire shape (Lovelace: Lucasta, 1649), 1v, *NYp*

Where did you borrow that last sigh (W. Berkeley: The Lost Lady, 1637), 1v, **GB-Lbm*, *US-NYp*

Wherefore do my sisters stay? (Shirley: The Triumph of Peace, 1634), madrigal, 1v, chorus 3vv, **GB-Ob*, ed. in Dent, A and M

Whieles I this standing lake swathe up with ewe [Justicia Sacrum] (text: Cartwright, 1651), 1v, **Lbm*

White though yee bee [On the Lillyes] (Herrick: Hesperides, 1648), 1v, **Lbm*, 1669⁵

Whither goe yee?, catch, 3vv, **Ob*

Why doe you dwell soe longe in clouds (Shirley: The Triumph of Peace, 1634), 3vv (inc.), *Eu* (inc.), *Ob* (inc.); ed. in Cutts (1963), Walls and M

Why move these princes of his traine so slow? (Davenant: Britannia triumphans, 1638), 1v, choruses 2, 4, 5vv, **Ob*; M

Why should fond man be led about, 3vv (inc.), *Eu* (inc.), *Ob* (inc.)

Why should great bewty retaine fame desire (Davenant), 1v, **Lbm*, *US-NYp*, in H. Lawes: Second Book of Ayres and Dialogues, 1–3vv (London, 1655); ed. in Gibbs and S

Why soe pall and wan, fond lover (Suckling: Aglaura, 1637), 1v, *NYp*; ed. in Lefkowitz (1960) and S

Wise nature that the dew of sleep prepares (Davenant: Britannia triumphans, 1638), 1v, chorus 3vv, **GB-Ob*; M

Yee feinds and furies, come along (Davenant: The Unfortunate Lovers, 1638), 1v, **Lbm*, 1678⁴; ed. in Gibbs

SACRED VOCAL
(anthems; all full unless otherwise stated)

All people that on earth doe dwell, verse, 3vv, *Och*

All yee yt feare him, praise ye Lord, verse, 3vv, *Och*

Before the mountains were brought forth, *Lbm* (text only)

Behold how good and joyful a thing it is, 3vv, 1648⁴

Cast mee not, Lord, out from thy face, verse, 3vv, *Och*

Come sing the great Jehovah's praise, 3vv, *Lbm*, *Ob* (inc.), 1648⁴

Gloria Patri et filio, 3vv, 1648⁴

Have mercy on us, Lord, verse, 3vv, *Och*

How hath Jehovah's wrath, 3vv, *Lbm*, 1648⁴

How like a widow, 3vv, 1648⁴

How long wilt thou forget me, O Lord, *Ob* (inc.), 1648⁴

I am weary of my groaning, 3vv, *Ob* (inc.), 1648⁴

I to thy wing for refuge fly, 3vv (inc.), **Ob*

In resurectione, 3vv, 1648⁴

In the substraction of my yeares, 3vv, *Ob* (inc.), 1648⁴

Judah in exile wanders, 3vv, 1648⁴

Let all in sweet accord clap hands, 3vv, *Lbm*, *Ob* (inc.), 1648⁴

Let God arise, verse, 1v, *Lbm*, *Och*

Let God, the God of battell, rise, 3vv, *Lbm*, *Ob* (inc.), 1648⁴

Lord, as the hart imbost with heat, 3vv, *Lbm*, *Ob* (inc.), 1648⁴

Lord, in thy wrath reprove mee not, verse, 3vv, *Och*

Lord, thy deserved wrath asswage, 3vv, *Lbm*, *Ob* (inc.), 1648⁴

Memento, memento, Domine, 3vv, 1648⁴

My God, my rock, regard my cry, 3vv, *Ob* (inc.), 1648⁴

My God, O why hast thou forsook, 3vv, *Ob* (inc.), 1648⁴

Ne irascaris, Domine, 3vv, 1648⁴

Oft from my early youth, 3vv, *Ob* (inc.), 1648⁴

O God, my God, wherefore doest thou forsake me, verse, 3vv, *Och*

O God, my strength and fortitude, verse, 3vv, *Och*

O Lord, consider my distresse, verse, 3vv, *Och*

O Lord, depart not now from mee, verse, 3vv, *Och*

O Lord, in yee is all my trust [The Lamentation], verse, 3vv, *Och*

O Lord, of whom I doe depend [Humble Suite of a Sinner], verse, 3vv, *Och*

O Lord, turne not away thy face [The Lamentation of a Sinner], verse, 3vv, *Och*

O sing unto the Lord a new song, 3vv, 1648⁴

Out of the horrour of the deep, 3vv, *Ob* (inc.), 1648⁴

Praise the Lord enthron'd on high, 3vv, *Lbm*, *Ob* (inc.), 1648⁴

Sing to the king of kings, 3vv, *Lbm*, *Ob* (inc.), 1648⁴

The Lord is my light, verse, 4vv, *Lbm*, *Och*, W. Boyce, Cathedral Music (London, 1760–78), ii

They who the Lord their fortresse make, 3vv, *Ob* (inc.), 1648⁴

Thou mover of the rowling spheres, 3vv, *Ob* (inc.), 1648⁴

Thou that art inthron'd above, 3vv, 1648⁴

To thee I cry, Lord, hear my cries, 3vv, *Ob* (inc.), 1648⁴

To thee, O God, my God, 3vv, *Ob* (inc.), 1648⁴

To the God whom we adore, 3vv, *Ob* (inc.), 1648⁴

When man ffor sinne thy judgment feeles, verse, 1v, *Lbm*

Who is this that cometh out of the wildernesse, *Lbm* (text only)

Yee nations of the earth, 3vv, *Ob* (inc.), 1648⁴

(canons)

Gloria in excelsis Deo, 3vv, 1648⁴

Happy sons of Israel, 3vv, *Lbm*, **†Ob*, 1648⁴

Jesus is harmonius, 3vv, *Lbm*, 1648⁴

Lord, thou hast been favourable, 3vv, *Lbm*, **†Ob*, 1648⁴

Re, me, re, ut, sol, 3vv, **Ob*

Regi, regis, regum (2 versions), 4vv, **Ob*, 1648⁴

She weepeth sore in the night, 4vv, *Lbm*, *Ob* (inc.), 1648⁴

These salt rivers of mine eyes, 3vv, 1648⁴

Tis joy to see, 3vv, **Lbm*, 1648⁴

Why weepest thou, Mary, 3vv, 1648⁴

BIBLIOGRAPHY

BurneyH; HawkinsH

A. Wood: *Manuscript Notes on the Lives of English Musicians* (MS, *GB-Och* Wood D 19 [4], ?c1660), f.83v

T. Fuller: *A History of the Worthies of England* (London, 1662, repr. 1840)

H. Hatcher: *The History of Modern Wiltshire*, vi: *Old and New Sarum*, ed. R. C. Hoare (London, 1843)

[Anon.]: 'A Pavan by William Lawes', *MA*, i (1909–10), 113

E. J. Dent: *Foundations of English Opera* (Cambridge, 1928/R1965)

R. Erlebach: 'William Lawes and his String Music', *PMA*, lix (1932–3), 103

E. H. Meyer: *Die mehrstimmige Spielmusik des 17. Jahrhunderts in Nord- und Mitteleuropa* (Kassel, 1934)

D. H. Robertson: *Sarum Close* (London, 1938)

W. McC. Evans: *Henry Lawes, Musician and Friend of Poets* (London, 1941/R1966)

C. W. Hughes: 'John Gamble's Commonplace Book', *ML*, xxvi (1945), 215

E. H. Meyer: *English Chamber Music* (London, 1946, 2/1951)

V. Duckles: 'The Gamble Manuscript as a Source of *Continuo* Song in England', *JAMS*, i/2 (1948), 23

C. Arnold: 'Early 17th-century Keyboard Parts', *ML*, xxxiii (1952), 151

J. P. Cutts: 'British Museum Additional MS 31432: William Lawes' Writing for Theatre and Court', *The Library*, 5th ser., vii (1952), 225

V. Duckles: *John Gamble's Commonplace Book: a Critical Edition of New York Public Library MS Drexel 4257* (diss., U. of California, Berkeley, 1953)

W. L. Woodfill: *Musicians in English Society, from Elizabeth to Charles I* (Princeton, 1953/R1969)

M. C. Crum: 'Notes on the Texts of William Lawes' Songs in B.M. MS Add. 31432', *The Library*, 5th ser., ix (1954), 122

C. Arnold and M. Johnson: 'The English Fantasy Suite', *PRMA*, lxxxii (1955–6), 1

I. Spink: 'English Seventeenth-century Dialogues', *ML*, xxxviii (1957), 155

J. P. Cutts: 'Seventeenth-century Songs and Lyrics in Edinburgh University Library, Music MS Dc.1.69', *MD*, xiii (1959), 169

M. Lefkowitz: 'New Facts concerning William Lawes and the Court Masque', *ML*, xl (1959), 324

A. J. Sabol: *Songs and Dances for the Stuart Masque* (Providence, Rhode Island, 1959; rev., enlarged 2/1978)

I. Spink: 'English Cavalier Songs, 1620–1660', *PRMA*, lxxxvi (1959–60), 61

M. Lefkowitz: *William Lawes* (London, 1960)

J. P. Cutts: 'William Lawes's Writing for the Theater and the Court', *JAMS*, xvi (1963), 243

R. J. McGrady: *The English Solo Song from William Byrd to Henry Lawes* (diss., U. of Manchester, 1963)

J. P. Cutts: 'Drexel Manuscript 4041', *MD*, xviii (1964), 151–202

M. Lefkowitz: 'The Longleat Papers of Bulstrode Whitelocke: New Light on Shirley's *Triumph of Peace*', *JAMS*, xviii (1965), 42

A. J. Sabol: 'New Documents on Shirley's Masque "The Triumph of Peace" ', *ML*, xlvii (1966), 10

I. Spink: 'Sources of English Song, 1620–1660', *MMA*, i (1966), 117

P. le Huray: *Music and the Reformation in England 1549–1660* (London, 1967)

V. Duckles: 'The Music for the Lyrics in Early 17th-century English Drama: a Bibliography of the Primary Sources', in *Music in English Renaissance Drama*, ed. J. H. Long (Lexington, Kentucky, 1968), 117–60

J. H. Long: *Music in English Renaissance Drama* (Lexington, Kentucky, 1968)

M. Lefkowitz: *Trois masques à la cour de Charles Ier d'Angleterre* (Paris, 1970)

C. Field: *The English Consort Suite of the 17th Century* (diss., U. of Oxford, 1971)

J. T. Johnson: *The English Fantasia-Suite, ca. 1620–1660* (diss., U. of California, Berkeley, 1971)

H. Poulos: *Giovanni Coperario and William Lawes: the Beginnings of Pre-Commonwealth Violin Music* (diss., Indiana U., Bloomington, 1971)

A. M. Gibbs: *Sir William Davenant: The Shorter Poems and Songs from the Plays and Masques* (London, 1972)

D. Pinto: 'William Lawes' Consort Suites for the Viols, and the Autograph Sources', *Chelys*, iv (1972), 14

I. Spink: *English Song: Dowland to Purcell* (London, 1974)

P. Walls: 'New Light on Songs by William Lawes and John Wilson', *ML*, lvii (1976), 55

D. Pinto: 'William Lawes' Music for Viol Consort', *Early Music*, vi (1978), 12

MURRAY LEFKOWITZ

Lawrence, Ashley (Macdonald) (*b* Hamilton, New Zealand, 5 June 1934). British conductor. After graduating from Auckland University, he moved to London and studied at the RCM and with Rafael Kubelik, joining the conducting staff of the Royal Ballet in 1962. In association with the choreographer Kenneth MacMillan as director of ballet, Lawrence became music director for the ballet of the Deutsche Oper, Berlin, in 1967, and then for the Stuttgart Ballet at the Württembergische Staatstheater in 1969. He returned to Britain two years later as principal conductor of the BBC Concert Orchestra, and in 1972 became, in addition, principal conductor of the Royal Ballet (music director in 1973). He has made a special study of the needs of musical performance in relation to dance; his experience in a wide repertory from light to symphonic music has helped to set and maintain musical standards of unusual distinction in the dance performances he conducts at Covent Garden and elsewhere, notably in the major ballet scores by Stravinsky and Tchaikovsky, and in Mahler's *Das Lied von der Erde*.

NOËL GOODWIN

Lawrence, Marjorie (Florence) (*b* Dean's Marsh, nr. Melbourne, 17 Feb 1909; *d* Little Rock, Arkansas, 10 Jan 1979). Australian soprano, later American. After winning a local contest, on the advice of John Brownlee she went to Paris, studying with Cécile Gilly, and making her opera début at Monte Carlo in 1932, as Elisabeth. In 1933 she first appeared at the Paris Opéra (Ortrud, 25 February), returning until 1936 as Brünnhilde, Salomé (*Hérodiade*), Rachel, Aida, Donna Anna, Brunehild (*Sigurd*), Brangäne and Valentine. On 21 December 1935 she made her Metropolitan début as the *Walküre* Brünnhilde, appearing there for six seasons, mostly in the Wagnerian repertory but also as the heroines of *Alceste*, *Salome* and *Thaïs*. Although she had polio in 1941, she was able in 1943 to resume her career in a limited way, in specially staged performances during which she was always seated; later she appeared in concerts. She retired in 1952. Lawrence possessed a large, vibrant and expressive voice of mezzo-soprano quality. Her not always secure singing gave pleasure because of its physical impact and distinctive sound.

BIBLIOGRAPHY
M. Lawrence: *Interrupted Melody: the Story of my Life* (New York, 1949)

MAX DE SCHAUENSEE

Lawrowka, Elizaveta Andreyevna. *See* LAVROVSKAYA, ELIZAVETA ANDREYEVNA.

Lawton, Dorothy (*b* Sheffield, 31 July 1874; *d* Bournemouth, 19 Feb 1960). English music librarian. She was taken as a child to the USA, where her piano teachers included Sigismund Stojowski, and her theory teacher was Eduard Hermann. She taught and lectured in New York until 1920, when she joined the staff of the New York Public Library to organize and direct the newly established circulating music library. Despite her lack of formal training as a librarian, she did the task with distinction until 1945. In 1930 she organized a similar department for the American Library in Paris. She helped attract private funds to improve the New York collection of scores, parts and sound recordings, and helped establish the library's section on dance, as well as a course in music librarianship at the New York College of Music. In 1946 she returned to England, where she helped to organize the Central Music Library in London. She retired in 1950.

BIBLIOGRAPHY
Obituary, *New York Times* (21 Feb 1960), 92

RAMONA H. MATTHEWS

Lay, François. *See* LAYS, FRANÇOIS.

Lay clerk. A layman serving in the Anglican Church. *See* CATHEDRAL MUSIC AND MUSICIANS, ANGLICAN.

Layer (Ger. *Schicht*). In Schenkerian analysis (*see* ANALYSIS, §§II, 6; III, 2) one of a set of polyphonic representations of a tonal piece or movement which has been stripped of some or all of its ornament so that only the essentials of the part-writing remain. The fundamental, primary layer of a piece, represented by an URSATZ consisting only of the essential conjunct melodic descent supported by the chord progression I–V–I, is called the background (Ger. *Hintergrund*). The layer that most resembles the piece itself, lacking only some embellishments (note repetitions and certain non-harmonic notes), is called the foreground (Ger. *Vordergrund*); this is the only layer whose representation is rhythmic (i.e. corresponds to the piece bar for bar). Between the foreground and the background lies the middleground (Ger. *Mittelgrund*), which is made up of one layer or more (depending upon the complexity of the piece, as well as upon the detail of the analysis) that serve to link the foreground to the background; that is, the layers it comprises may be understood as successive polyphonic 'reductions' of the foreground (itself a reduction of the piece), the last of which is reducible to the *Ursatz*. Schenker saw this as the normal way of deriving the polyphonic layers of a piece, the exact shape of the *Ursatz* being determined only at the last step.

Schenker presented his layered analyses in reverse, beginning with a brief explanation of the *Ursatz* and then, in successively longer sections, describing the part-writing in each layer as growing out of that of the previous layer. In his account of the increased complexity from one layer to the next, he developed the theory of PROLONGATION, the linear (i.e. 'horizontal') elaboration of a basic contrapuntal idea by any number of methods, such as adding scale fragments, broken chords or non-harmonic notes, or repetition in a higher or lower octave. In each new layer of an analysis there are prolongations not previously accounted for, which have to be described. The number of new prolongations increases as one approaches the foreground, and for this reason the discussion of the foreground is usually the longest; Schenker, however, usually ended his analyses with some remarks on the details of the piece itself (i.e. the layer beyond the foreground called the *Ausführung*, or 'realization'). Since analysis is to a great extent the explanation of composition, it seems only logical that the layers are presented in the reverse order of their derivation: background (= *Ursatz*), middleground layer or layers, foreground, realization.

WILLIAM DRABKIN

Layolle, Alamanne de [Aiolli, Alamanno] (*b* ?Lyons, *c*1521–5; *d* Florence, 19 Sept 1590). Italian composer and organist. He grew up in Lyons, where his father, the Florentine composer Francesco de Layolle, settled in 1521. A Lyonnaise document of 1551 calls him 'a player of instruments'. According to Fétis, he was named organist at St Nizier, Lyons, in the preface to his volume of four-voice *Chansons et vaudevilles* published by Gorlier in 1561 (now lost). (Plantin's catalogue states that the same volume contained pieces for four to six voices.)

In 1565 Layolle emigrated to Florence, where he followed a career as a performer (organist at the Badia, 1570–75) and teacher (among his pupils was the daughter of Benvenuto Cellini, who mentioned him in the celebrated *Autobiography*). He also seems to have been associated with the Florentine printing firms of GIUNTA and MARESCOTTI, for frequent legal disputes among the three parties are recorded during the 1570s and 1580s. He may have collaborated with the latter in producing the 1582 collection of three-voice madrigals 'by the most excellent authors of our times' since he is represented by more works than any other composer in the volume. These madrigals, three of which use texts previously set by his father, and a five-voice setting of

the *Canticum Zachariae* are the only known vocal works by him. His most important surviving work is the *Intavolatura di M. Alamanno Aiolli*, a holograph volume (*I-Fl* 641) now much mutilated and reduced in content, discovered in 1961. This collection contains 16 keyboard arrangements (several incomplete) of some of the best-known works of the time, among them Janequin's *La guerre* and Lassus's *Susanne ung jour*, as well as selections from the sixth *intermedio* of the comedy *La pellegrina*, presented in Florence in 1589. The arrangements are distinguished by Layolle's aptitude for inventing and developing new material that greatly enhances the original pieces in their new settings, and by his ability to write sensitively and idiomatically for the keyboard.

BIBLIOGRAPHY

FétisB
G. Tricou: 'Les deux Layolles et les organistes lyonnais du XVIᵉ siècle', *Mémoires de la Société littéraire, historique et archéologique de Lyon* (1898), 229
F. A. D'Accone: 'The Intavolatura di M. Alamanno Aiolli', *MD*, xx (1966), 151
FRANK A. D'ACCONE

Layolle, Francesco de [Francesco dell'Aiolle, dell'Aiolli, dell'Ajolle, dell'Aiuola] (*b* Florence, 4 March 1492; *d* Lyons, *c*1540). Italian composer and organist. There has been some confusion about his identity because Einstein suggested that there were two musicians with this name. Recently, however, it has been confirmed that he was the first, and at that time the only, member of his family to become a professional musician. His musical career began shortly after his 13th birthday, when he was appointed a singer in the chapel of the Florentine church of the Ss Annunziata. There he became acquainted with the organist and composer Bartolomeo degli Organi, from whom he eventually received private instruction. The master–pupil relationship was evidently a close one, and in later years he married Maddalena Arrighi, a younger sister-in-law of Bartolomeo. He was a friend of Andrea del Sarto, who in 1511 painted Layolle's portrait, together with his own and that of the architect Jacopo Sansovino, in a fresco depicting the journey of the Magi in the atrium of the Ss Annunziata. Layolle remained in Florence until 1518. According to his pupil Benvenuto Cellini, he had by that time established a reputation as 'a fine organist and an excellent musician and composer'. In 1521 he settled in Lyons, where he lived until his death.

He also enjoyed the friendship of several Florentine men of letters, among them the poet Luigi Alamanni, who dedicated the sonnet *Aiolle mio gentil cortese amico* to him and spoke flatteringly of him in two other works (*Egloga prima* and *Selve*). The writer Antonio Brucioli introduced him, Alamanni and Zenobi Buondelmonte as interlocutors in one of his *Dialoghi della morale philosophia* (Venice, 1538, 2/1544). These men were among the principal figures in a group of Florentine republicans who unsuccessfully conspired to overthrow the Medici government in the spring of 1521. When the plot was discovered, Alamanni and Buondelmonte fled to Lyons, where Layolle gave them shelter. Although this and subsequent actions leave no doubt that Layolle's sympathies lay with the republicans, the records of the judicial proceedings, in which the conspirators were condemned *in absentia*, show that he was not directly involved in the plot.

In Lyons he was employed as the organist at the Florentine church of Notre Dame de Confort and also composed, collected and edited music for a few of the printing firms there. After a brief association with the bookseller Etienne Gueynard, marked by the publication in 1528 of the *Contrapunctus seu figurata musica*, he joined forces with JACQUES MODERNE. During the decade 1530–40 they worked in close collaboration; from the prefaces to the 1532 and 1540 editions of the *Liber decem missarum* it may be deduced that Layolle not only contributed to but also edited the various volumes of sacred music issued by Moderne. Possibly in the early 1530s Moderne also published the six volumes of his sacred works that are now lost. Their association continued until the composer's death, the date of which, although not documented, has generally been accepted as 1540, the last year in which new music of his appeared in dated publications of Moderne. Bibliographical evidence seems to confirm this date, for it was apparently in 1540 that Moderne issued Layolle's volume of the *Cinquanta canzoni*, which closes with a lament on the composer's death.

Layolle entered fully into the artistic and intellectual life of Lyons. In 1537 the poet Eustorg de Beaulieu published a rondeau in praise of 'a beautiful garden on the Saône in Lyons belonging to maistre François Layola, a most expert musician and organist'. He was also a close friend of the banker Luigi Sostegni, who in 1538 forwarded some of his compositions to Rome. In his letter of acknowledgment the poet Annibale Caro stated that they were well received.

Layolle cultivated all the principal forms of vocal polyphony current in his time. Although it would appear that he was primarily a composer of secular music, his church music must also have included the contents of the six lost volumes of motets, each of which (according to a contemporary catalogue of the Colombina Library in Seville) contained 12 works. Since at present only 11 of his extant motets can be assigned to these publications, some 61 remain lost. In addition there are three masses, one listed in the Colombina catalogue and two others mentioned by Zacconi in his *Prattica di musica* (Venice, 1592), which likewise seem not to have survived. Perhaps Layolle contributed more pieces to the *Contrapunctus* of 1528 than the three that are ascribed to him in that collection.

The extant sacred works illustrate his mastery of the most advanced techniques of his day and reveal that he was one of the first Italians to fuse successfully Italianate tonal-harmonic precepts with Franco-Netherlands contrapuntal techniques. *Missa 'Adieu mes amours'*, based on Mouton's chanson, uses both parody and cantus firmus techniques. Throughout the work only the first phrase of the chanson melody is used, employed as a tenor ostinato in various rhythmic patterns. Presentation of the entire melody is reserved for the last Agnus Dei, when in an expanded five-part texture, it is set out in the tenor beneath a freely composed canon for two altos. This mass also shares some thematic similarities with one of his motets, *Libera me, Domine*, which follows it in both editions of the *Liber decem missarum*. The parody technique is more fully exploited in *Missa 'O salutaris hostia'*, where several voices of the polyphonic model are drawn upon simultaneously. *Missa 'Ces fascheux sotz'*, composed between 1532 and 1540, is also a parody mass in which Gardane's two-part chanson is extensively reworked into a complex and spirited fantasy for four voices.

The variety of contrapuntal techniques and the beauty of the melodies and harmonies in the motets also confirm Layolle's place in the front rank of composers of his generation. It is possible that Layolle paraphrased a traditional melody in the first section of the lovely Christmas motet for four voices, *Noe, noe, noe*. The cantus firmus technique is prominent in *Media vita* and *Salve, virgo singularis*; in the four-voice *Ave Maria* an ostinato derived from the antiphon's first phrase, provides the basis of the structure. Canons are successfully interwoven into the fabric of *Ave virgo sanctissima*, *Libera me, Domine* and *Congregati sunt*. Another setting of *Ave Maria* is a three-part canon.

Apart from a few early works, the bulk of his secular Italian music survives in two collections, the *Venticinque canzoni a cinque voci* (1540) and the *Cinquanta canzoni a quatro voci*, published by Moderne. Entitled canzoni, these pieces are in fact madrigals. Their texts, drawn from a number of poets – among them, Petrarch (the most frequently represented), Alamanni, Machiavelli and the brothers Strozzi – are typical of those set by the earliest masters of the genre. They also display many of the general musical characteristics found in contemporary madrigals. Several of the four-voice canzoni were in fact published in some of Arcadelt's madrigal books; however, they were either omitted or ascribed correctly to Layolle in most later editions of the same volumes. One work, *Lasciar il velo*, was popular enough to be mentioned by Doni in his *Dialogo della musica* (Venice, 1554). It was also published in lute transcriptions by both Crema (1546) and Gintzler (1547), as well as in an ornamented vocal arrangement by Maffei (1562).

Two works in the collection of five-voice canzoni have French texts and are based on popular chansons. Another, *Sì ch'io la vo seguire*, makes use of a cantus firmus, unusual for madrigals of this period. The remaining works with French texts, published by Moderne in the first five volumes of *Le parangon des chansons*, display a diversity of styles. Notable among them are the canonic duo *Les bourguignons*, which celebrates the raising of the siege of Péronne in 1536, and *Ce me semblent*, written in the manner of the Parisian chanson made popular by Claudin.

WORKS

Edition: *Music of the Florentine Renaissance: F. de Layolle, Collected Works*, ed. F. A. D'Accone, CMM, xxxii/3–6 (1969–73) [D iii–vi]

SACRED

Missa 'Adieu mes amours', 4vv, D vi, 1 (on Mouton's chanson); Missa 'Ces fascheux sotz', 4vv, D vi, 41 (on Gardane's chanson); Missa 'O salutaris hostia', 4vv, D vi, 21
7 penitential psalms, 4vv, D vi, 60
35 motets (1 attrib.), 2–6vv, D v

SECULAR

Venticinque canzoni a cinque voci (Lyons, 1540) [includes 2 chansons], D iii
Cinquanta canzoni a quatro voci (Lyons, ?1540) [includes anon. lament], D iv
3 madrigals and 9 chansons in other collections, D iii
3 masses and c61 motets, lost

BIBLIOGRAPHY

G. Tricou: 'Les deux Layolles et les organistes lyonnais du XVIᵉ siècle', *Mémoires de la Société littéraire, historique et archéologique de Lyon* (1898), 229
R. Gandolfi: 'Intorno al codice membranaceo . . . N.2440', *RMI*, xviii (1911), 540
H. E. Wooldridge: *The Oxford History of Music*, ii (London, 1932), 101
A. Einstein: *The Italian Madrigal*, i (Princeton, 1949/R1971), 279
N. Bridgman: 'Giovanni Camillo Maffei e sa lettre sur le chant', *RdM*, xxxviii (1956), 22
C. W. Chapman: 'Printed Collections of Polyphonic Music Owned by Ferdinand Columbus', *JAMS*, xxi (1968), 34

D. Sutherland: *Francesco de Layolle (1492–1540): Life and Secular Works* (diss., U. of Michigan, 1968)

S. F. Pogue: *Jacques Moderne: Lyons Music Printer of the Sixteenth Century* (Geneva, 1969), 34

D. Crawford: 'Reflections on some Masses from the Press of Moderne', *MQ*, lviii (1972), 82

FRANK A. D'ACCONE

Layriz [Layritz], Friedrich (Ludwig Christoph) (*b* Nemmersdorf, Franconia, 30 Jan 1808; *d* Unterschwaningen, Franconia, 18 March 1859). German theologian and hymnologist. He studied theology, philosophy and philology at the universities of Leipzig (PhD 1829) and Erlangen, where he joined the theology faculty in 1833. In 1837 he became rector of Merkendorf and in 1842 of St Georgen, near Bayreuth. In 1846, as the result of a fierce controversy with Elias Sittig on the subject of hymnological reform, he was forced to leave for Unterschwaningen.

Layriz was an important figure in the early stages of the 19th-century revival and reform of Lutheran liturgy and music. He campaigned with energetic persistence for the polyrhythmic rather than the isometric form of the chorale, and for a return to the old melodies and the original manner of singing them. Although the effect of his work was felt mainly in Bavaria, it also helped to prepare for Johannes Zahn's later hymnological research. He worked with similar zeal for the restoration of the original hymn texts and for a revival of the old Lutheran liturgy. His hymn collections include *CXVII geistliche Melodien meist aus dem 16. und 17. Jahrhundert in ihren ursprünglichen Rhythmen* (Erlangen, 1839, enlarged 2/1844–50, 3/1862), *Kern des deutschen Kirchenlieds von Luther bis auf Gellert* (Nördlingen, 1844) and *CC Chorälen meist aus dem XVI. und XVII. Jahrhundert in ihren ursprünglichen Tönen und Rhythmen* (Nördlingen, 1844, enlarged in four vols., 2/1849–53, 3/1854–5). Among his numerous writings in support of his theories are *Offener Sendbrief an die protestantische Geistlichkeit Bayerns . . . in Betreff der Gesangbuchs-Reform* (Bayreuth, 1843), which prompted the disagreement with Sittig, and *Die Liturgie eines vollstimmigen Hauptgottesdienstes nach lutherischen Typus nebst Ratschlägen zu deren Wiederherstellung* (Nördlingen, 1849), as well as several essays and reviews. A number of his hymn melodies may be found in Zahn, while some of his poetry also came into regular congregational use.

BIBLIOGRAPHY

Beleuchtung des offenen Schriftenwechsels zwischen den Herren DD. Sittig und Layriz in Betreff der Gesangbuchs-Reform (Ansbach, 1844)

E. S. F. Sittig: *Offene Antwort auf den offenen Sendbrief des Herrn Dr. Fr. Layriz* (Nuremberg, 1844)

S. Kümmerle: *Encyklopädie der evangelischen Kirchenmusik* (Gütersloh, 1888–95/R1974)

J. Zahn: *Die Melodien der deutschen evangelischen Kirchenlieder* (Gütersloh, 1889–93/R1963), v, 485; vi, 434, 455, 463f and elsewhere

F. Blume: *Die evangelische Kirchenmusik*, HMw, x (1931, rev. 2/1965 as *Geschichte der evangelischen Kirchenmusik*; Eng. trans., enlarged, 1974, as *Protestant Church Music: a History*)

H. J. Moser: *Die evangelische Kirchenmusik in Deutschland* (Berlin and Darmstadt, 1954), 238f, 242, 298

based on *MGG* (xvi, 1097–8) by permission of Bärenreiter

FRANZ KRAUTWURST

Lays [Lai, Lay], François (*b* La Barthe de Nesthes, 14 Feb 1758; *d* Ingrande, nr. Angers, 30 March 1831). French tenor. He learnt music as a theology student in the monastery of Guaraison, but before he was 20 his fame as a singer had spread, and by April 1779 he was in Paris. His name, spelt Laïs, first appears in the role of Petrarch in Candeille's *Laure et Pétrarque*, 2 July 1780. He is next mentioned in Piccinni's *Iphigénie en Tauride*, 23 January 1781. (Fétis's statement that the title role of Floquet's *Seigneur bienfaisant* was written in 1780 for Lays is not corroborated by Lajarte.) Lays sang at the Opéra until October 1823. He also appeared regularly at the concerts of Marie Antoinette and the Concert Spirituel. He was professor of singing at the Conservatoire from 1795 until 1799, and was principal singer in the chapel of Napoleon from 1801 until 1814, when he was dismissed by Louis XVIII. From 1819 to his retirement in 1826 he was professor of singing at the Ecole Royale de Chant et de Déclamation.

Lays's violent partisanship of the Revolution led to quarrels with his colleagues, but with no further result than to cause him to write a pamphlet and to force him, after 9 Thermidor, to appear in parts distasteful to him and to sing before the Bourbons after the Restoration. He was a poor actor, except in parts specially written for him; Fétis pronounced him not even a good singer, saying that his taste was poor and that he had several bad tricks. Nevertheless he had warmth and animation, and the beauty of his voice so far atoned for everything that for a long time no opera could be successful in which he had not a part.

WRITINGS

Lays, artiste du théâtre des arts, à ses concitoyens (Paris, 1793)

BIBLIOGRAPHY

FétisB

T. Lajarte: *Bibliothèque musicale du Théâtre de l'Opéra* (Paris, 1878)

GEORGE GROVE/R

Layton, Billy Jim (*b* Corsicana, Texas, 14 Nov 1924). American composer. He studied composition with Cooke and McKinley at the New England Conservatory (BMus 1948), and with Porter at Yale (MMus 1950). His interest having been aroused by courses in the history of music, he began the PhD course in musicology at Harvard in 1951 under Gombosi and continued to study composition with Piston. He was awarded the Rome Prize in composition in 1954 and spent three years at the American Academy in Rome. On returning to Harvard in 1957 he completed a dissertation under Pirrotta on medieval Italian settings of the Mass Ordinary. He then remained at Harvard as assistant professor until 1966, when he was appointed professor of music at the State University of New York, Stony Brook. As chairman of the department until 1972 he had major responsibility for its development.

WORKS

5 Studies, op.1, vn, pf, 1952; An American Portrait, op.2, sym. ov., 1953; 3 Dylan Thomas Poems, op.3, chorus, brass sextet, 1954–6; Str Q, op.4, 1956; 3 Studies, op.5, pf, 1957; Divertimento, op.6, cl, bn, trbn, hpd, perc, vn, vc, 1958–60; Dance Fantasy, op.7, orch, 1964

BIBLIOGRAPHY

R. Browne: 'Billy Jim Layton: Dance Fantasy', *PNM*, iv/1 (1965), 161

B. J. Layton: 'The New Liberalism', *PNM*, iii/2 (1965), 137

AUSTIN CLARKSON

Layton, Robert (*b* London, 2 May 1930). English musicologist. He studied at Worcester College, Oxford (1949–53), taking the BA under Rubbra and Wellesz in 1953. He also studied with Moberg at the universities of Uppsala and Stockholm (1953–5). After three years of teaching he joined the BBC (1959) to take charge of music presentation. In 1960 he became responsible for music talks. His main preoccupation has been with Scandinavian music; he has written extensively on

Berwald and Sibelius. Layton is also concerned with other 19th- and 20th-century music, in particular with the symphonic process. He broadcasts regularly, both for the BBC and for Swedish Radio, and is a regular contributor to the *Gramophone* and a co-editor of the *Stereo Record Guide*.

WRITINGS
Franz Berwald (Swed. trans. Stockholm, 1956; Eng. orig., 1959)
'U.S.A.', *Twentieth Century Music*, ed. R. H. Myers (London, 1960), 197
Sibelius (London, 1965, rev. 2/1979)
'Franz Berwald'; 'Serge Prokofiev', 'Dmitri Shostakovich', 'Martinů and the Czech Tradition', 'Vagn Holmboe and the Later Scandinavians', *The Symphony*, ed. R. Simpson (Harmondsworth, 1966–7), i, 175; ii, 166, 197, 218, 230
Sibelius and his World (London, 1970)
with H. Searle: *Twentieth-Century Composers* (London, 1972) [chaps. 'Britain', 'Scandinavia', 'The Netherlands', 153–84]
trans. of E. Tawaststjerna: *Sibelius*, i: *1865–1905* (London, 1976)
'Berwald', 'Holmboe, Vagn', 'Sibelius, Jean', 'Wellesz, Egon', *Grove 6*

DAVID SCOTT

Lay vicar. A layman serving in the Anglican Church. *See* CATHEDRAL MUSIC AND MUSICIANS, ANGLICAN.

Lazăr, Filip (*b* Craiova, 6 May 1894; *d* Paris, 3 Nov 1936). Romanian composer and pianist. At the Bucharest Conservatory (1907–12) he studied theory with D. G. Kiriac, harmony and composition with Castaldi and the piano with Emilia Saegiu; his studies were continued at the Leipzig Conservatory (1913–14) under S. Krehl (harmony and composition) and Teichmüller (piano). As a concert pianist he toured Europe and the USA, introducing a great deal of new music in his recitals (he was a member of the ISCM). His dedication to modern music also found expression in his organizing activities as a founder member of the Romanian Composers' Society (1920) and as a founder and chairman of the Triton society in Paris (1928); in addition he worked as a piano teacher in France and Switzerland (1928–36). The variety of styles in Lazăr's music shows his breadth of outlook. In his first period (1919–28) Romanian folk elements were firmly asserted – gypsy-like urban folktunes appear in such works as the Concerto grosso and the instrumental suites and sonatas. Later Lazăr turned his attention to current musical developments, serialism and neo-classicism, but without losing sight of the peasant music of his native land. Despite its stylistic diversity, all of his music is distinguished by conciseness and vigour of form, a refined harmony that allows for freely treated dissonances and polytonal chords, generally polyphonic textures and a brilliant orchestration, with emphasis on the percussion and on percussive writing for the piano.

WORKS
(selective list)

Stage: La bouteille de Panurge, ballet, after A. Coeuroy, 1918; Les images de Béatrice, op.18 (opera-cantata, Coeuroy), 1928
Orch: Suita română, D, 1921; Suite valaque, 1925; Tziganes, 1925; Concerto grosso, op.17, 1927; Le ring, 1928; Muzică pentru radio, 1931; 4 pf concs., opp.18, 19, 23, 24, 1930–34
Inst: 2 pf sonatas, 1913, 1929; Sonata, vn, pf, e, 1919; 2 suites, pf, 1924–5; Două dansuri populare românești, pf, 1925; Trio, ob, cl, bn, 1934; Str Trio, 1935; Harp Trio, ?1936
Vocal: Dor de crîng (chorus, F. Lazăr), 1924; Paparudele [The rainmakers] (chorus, F. Lazăr), 1924; 3 pastorales, 1v, pf, 1927

Principal publishers: Durand, Oxford University Press, Universal

BIBLIOGRAPHY
G. Breazul: 'Lazăr, Filip', *MGG*
V. Tomescu: *Filip Lazăr* (Bucharest, 1963)
M. Jora: *Momente muzicale* (Bucharest, 1968), 179f

Z. Vancea: *Creaţia muzicală românească: sec. XIX–XX* (Bucharest, 1968), 382ff
V. Cosma: *Muzicieni români* (Bucharest, 1970), 273ff

VIOREL COSMA

Lazari, Alberto (*b* Perugia; *fl* 1635–7). Italian composer. He became a Carmelite friar and held the post of organist at the collegiate church at Massa Lombarda in 1635. He belonged to two cultural academies in nearby cities, the Accademia degli Spennati at Faenza and the Accademia degli Offuscati at Cesena (the latter in 1637). Lazari's publications were both of church music: *Armonia spirituale a 1–4 voci con letanie della Beata Vergine e una messa concertata a 3 voci* (Venice, 1635) and *Armonie spirituali a 1–6 voci con le lettanie della Beata Vergine a 4 e 8 se piace con il basso continuo, libro secondo* op.2 (Venice, 1637). He was one of many minor figures in northern Italy at the time to adopt the small-scale concertato motet for provincial use. His mass is in the same style, though the litanies of 1637 have an optional ripieno choir. He seems to have been less than competent when writing for larger forces, his partwriting and melodies lacking in invention. On the other hand the duet *In sanctitate fulgida* (1637) is a good example of the expressive type of small motet common at this time in which ornamentation, though elaborate, helps to shape melodies, and triple-time writing tends towards arioso style.

BIBLIOGRAPHY
J. L. A. Roche: *North Italian Liturgical Music in the Early 17th Century* (diss., U. of Cambridge, 1968)

JEROME ROCHE

Lazari, Ferdinando Antonio. *See* LAZZARI, FERDINANDO ANTONIO.

Lazarini, Scipione. *See* LAZZARINI, SCIPIONE.

Lazarof, Henri (*b* Sofia, 12 April 1932). American composer of Bulgarian origin. He graduated from the Sofia Academy in 1948 and then studied at the New Conservatory in Jerusalem (1949–52), with Petrassi at the Accademia di S Cecilia (1955–7) and at Brandeis University (1957–9, MFA 1959). In 1962 he joined the staff of the University of California at Los Angeles, where he was appointed professor of composition. His music is highly individual, atonal in harmony and, in some works, freely serial.

WORKS
(selective list)

Orch: Conc., pf, 20 insts, 1960–61; Va Conc., 1962; Structures sonores, 1966; Mutazione, 1967; Vc Conc., 1968; Omaggio, 19 insts, 1968; Ricercar, va, pf, orch, 1968; Textures, pf, 5 ens, 1970; Koncordia, str, 1971; Spectrum, tpt, orch, tape, 1972
Choral: Canti, 1971
Inst: Inventions, va, pf, 1962; Quantetti, pf, 3 pf on tape, 1963; Tempi concertati, vn, va, 7 insts, 1964; Rhapsody, vn, pf, 1966; Espaces, 2 fl, 2 cl, 2 va, 2 vc, 2 pf, 1967; Cadence II, va, tape, 1969; Cadence III, vn, 2 perc, 1970; Continuum, str trio, 1970; Partita, brass qnt, tape, 1971; Cadence V, tpt, tape, 1972

Principal publishers: Associated, Bote & Bock, Israeli Music Publications

W. THOMAS MARROCCO

Lazarus, Daniel (*b* Paris, 13 Dec 1898; *d* Paris, 27 June 1964). French conductor and composer. He studied at the Paris Conservatoire with Diemer, Leroux and Vidal; after this he was successively musical director at the Théâtre du Vieux Colombier (1921–5), artistic director of the Opéra-Comique (1936–9), choirmaster of the Paris Opéra (1946–56) and lastly professor at the

Schola Cantorum. His long association with the theatre as a conductor was complemented by his compositional activity.

WORKS

L'illustre magicien (opera, J. R. Bloch after Gobineau), 1924; La véritable histoire de Wilhelm Meister [from themes by Schumann] (opera), 1927; Trumpeldor (opera, 3), 1935; La chambre bleue (opera, Prunières after Mérimée), 1938

Pf Conc., 1929; Sym. no.1, 1933; Sym. no.2, 1934; other orch works

Pf music, incidental scores, 3 ballets, songs

Principal publishers: Durand, Eschig, Sénart

WRITINGS

Accès à la musique (Paris, 1960)

BIBLIOGRAPHY

G. Ferchault: 'Lazarus, Daniel', MGG

ANNE GIRARDOT

Lazarus, Henry (b London, 1 Jan 1815; d London, 6 March 1895). English clarinettist and basset-horn player. He held a unique position in the musical life of Victorian England, playing in every important festival and series of concerts during his 54-year career. He was educated at the Royal Military Asylum in Chelsea, where he studied the clarinet with the bandmaster John Blizzard. He then became assistant to Charles Godfrey, bandmaster of the Coldstream Guards. After ten years' service he bought his discharge and joined the Duke of Devonshire's private band.

Lazarus's first solo appearance was in a supporting role at Mme Dulcken's concert of 2 May 1838 at the Hanover Square Rooms. He soon became a prominent figure at all the regular chamber music concerts, and his many appearances as a soloist with the Philharmonic Society date from 1844. It was not until Joseph Williams retired from the society as the orchestra's first clarinet that Lazarus was able to take up this position; from 1841 to 1860 he had had to be content with that of second clarinet. However, he had long associations as principal with the Italian Opera (1838–83) and the Birmingham Festival (1840–85), and he also played for the Sacred Harmonic Concerts.

Lazarus was no less successful as a teacher, his most important pupil being Charles Draper. In 1854 he was appointed to the staff of the RAM and in 1858 to Kneller Hall, where his memory is still held in honour. His *New and Modern Method* was published in 1881, and when the RCM was opened in the following year he became its first clarinet professor. He retired from playing in 1891 and from teaching in 1894.

Lazarus used a variety of clarinets, beginning with a simple-system pair by Key, changing to ones by Fieldhouse to which he added ingenious Boehm improvements, and finishing with a pair by Albert. Although he never owned a Boehm clarinet he used a Boehm basset-horn and recommended the system to his pupils. His elegant style and pure tone were ideally suited to the occasional pieces in vogue at the time, but his more important contribution lay in the great number of larger-scale chamber works and obbligatos which he introduced to the public.

BIBLIOGRAPHY

G. B. Shaw: Music in London 1890–1894 (London, 1932), ii, 109f

J. Brymer: 'Henry Lazarus', The Clarinet (1950), no.2; (1956), no.24

P. Weston: Clarinet Virtuosi of the Past (London, 1971)

——: 'Lazarus' Instrument Collection', National Association of College Wind and Percussion Instructors' Journal, xxiii/2 (1974)

PAMELA WESTON

Łazarz, Andrysowicz (b Stryków; d Kraków, 1577). Polish printer who took over the printing house of HIERONIM WIETOR on the latter's death.

Lazzari [Lazari], **Ferdinando Antonio** (b Bologna, March 1678; d Bologna, 19 April 1754). Italian composer and organist. He entered the Franciscan order in Bologna on 29 September 1693. While still a novice he was pressed into service both as a singer and an organist; it seems probable that the absence of his name from the monastery registers for several years after this was due to his having been sent away to study music further, a supposition strengthened by the fact that on his return to the monastery in Bologna in 1702 he was immediately named *magistero della cappella* of S Francesco (31 May 1702). He retained this position until the end of 1705, when he became *maestro di cappella* at S Maria Gloriosa dei Frari in Venice. In 1712 Lazzari was invited to return to Bologna to participate in festivities on the elevation of S Caterina de' Vigri; his music for the occasion was performed on 12 July. He returned to his post in Venice, but after an illness which severely damaged his eyesight he sought and received permission to return to his native Bologna, where he remained until his death.

WORKS

Crudelissimi regnantis, motet for the Feast of Holy Innocents, 8vv, 2 tpt, 2 vn, violetta, vc, org, autograph I-Bc; 5 motets, chorus, orch A-Wn

Sonata a 6, I-Bsp

Oratorios: Mosè gittato nel Nilo, Foligno 1700; S Maria Maddalena de' Pazzi, Bologna, 1704; L'innocenza diffesa da S Antonio da Padova, Cremona, 1705; lost

BIBLIOGRAPHY

EitnerQ; La MusicaD

L. Busi: Il Padre G. B. Martini (Bologna, 1891/R1961), 232ff

NONA PYRON

Lazzari, Virgilio (b Assisi, 20 April 1887; d Castel Gandolfo, 4 Oct 1953). Italian bass, later naturalized American. He began his career with the Vitale Operetta Company, making his début as L'Incognito in Suppé's *Boccaccio* in 1908 and remaining a member of the company until 1911, when he began to study in Rome with Antonio Cotogni. He made his operatic début at the Teatro Costanzi, Rome, in 1914, then appeared in South America and in 1916 made his North American début at St Louis as Ramfis. He sang regularly with the Chicago Opera from 1918 to 1933; that year he joined the Metropolitan Opera and remained with it until 1950, taking more than 22 roles. From 1934 to 1939 he appeared regularly at the Salzburg Festival, where he sang Pistol in *Falstaff* under Toscanini, and Mozart's Bartolo and Leporello under Walter. It was as Leporello that he made his only Covent Garden appearances, in 1939 under Beecham. His most famous role was that of the blind king, Archibaldo, in Montemezzi's *L'amore dei tre re*, which he first sang in 1916 in Mexico City and as late as 1953 in Genoa. Although not blessed with a great voice (he was in any case more a light *basso cantante* than a deep-voiced bass like Pinza or Pasero), Lazzari was generally considered one of the best singing-actors in his particular repertory.

HAROLD ROSENTHAL

Lazzarini [Lazarini], **Scipione** (b Ancona, c1620; d in or after 1675). Italian composer and teacher. He was an Augustinian monk and teacher of theology at

Ancona, where he also ran a school of music; he was known chiefly as a teacher of composition. His earliest known work is a motet for three voices and continuo, *Si linguis hominum* (*RISM* 1646²). Nearly 30 years later he published two collections both called *Motetti a due e tre voci* (both Ancona, 1674) as his opp.1 and 2; the second of these (*RISM* 1674¹) includes one work by each of three of his pupils, A. G. Giamaglia, Filippo Giamaglia and M. F. Nascimbeni. In the following year he published *Salmi vespertini parte a cinque voci e parte a tre voci e due violini* op.3 (Ancona, 1675). The style of the motets is conservative and reflects the polyphonic tradition of the 16th century, which was still current at Ancona. The psalms, however, show some concessions to contemporary practice, particularly in the use of accompanying instruments.

Le. The sharpened submediant of the prevailing key (or, if this is minor, the sharpened submediant of its relative major) in TONIC SOL-FA.

Leach, James (*b* Wardle, nr. Rochdale, Lancs., 1762; *d* Blackley, nr. Manchester, 8 Feb 1798). English psalmodist. A handloom weaver by trade, with little education, he devoted his leisure hours to the singing and composition of psalmody for Methodist meetings. Soon after the publication of his first collection in 1789, he became a full-time musician and music teacher. As an alto singer he took part in the Handel Festivals in Westminster Abbey and in other festivals. He moved to Salford about 1795, and died three years later as the result of a stage-coach accident.

Leach was one of the best practitioners of the Methodist style of church music, consisting of florid psalm and hymn tunes and metrical 'anthems' or set pieces frankly based on the livelier secular and operatic music of the time. Some of his pieces have instrumental accompaniment (e.g. for two clarinets and figured bass). They have much word repetition, echo effects and so on, but never contain counterpoint with overlapping words; thus they observe Wesley's rule against obscuring the sense. His music was enormously popular, especially at class meetings, love feasts and revival meetings. The two collections, *A New Sett of Hymns and Psalm Tunes* (London, 1789) and *A Second Sett of Hymns and Psalm Tunes* (London, 1794), were drawn on in countless 19th-century publications, especially in America, and were reprinted in full as late as 1884, with a sketch of the composer's life and work by Thomas Newbigging.

BIBLIOGRAPHY
T. Newbigging: Memoir, in J. Leach: *Psalmody* (London, 1884)
J. C. Hadden: 'Leach, James', *DNB*

NICHOLAS TEMPERLEY

Leadbelly. *See* LEDBETTER, HUDDIE.

Leader [concertmaster] (Fr. *chef d'attaque*; Ger. *Konzertmeister*; It. *violino primo*). In modern orchestras, the principal first violinist, who sits immediately to the left of the conductor as viewed by the audience. He occupies the 'outside' chair – the chair nearer to the audience – of the first desk (or stand) of the first-violin section, and is responsible for executing the wishes of the conductor in all technical matters, such as the marking and bowing of parts. He is also responsible for playing solo violin passages and, if gifted in conducting, he may sometimes be called on to conduct in place of the regular conduc-

tor. The leader also acts as liaison between the members of the orchestra and the management and is responsible for section rehearsals.

This description is valid after the advent of the modern (baton-wielding) orchestral conductor early in the 19th century (see Spohr's account of his early use of the baton in a rehearsal of the Philharmonic Orchestra in London, 1820, and Carse: *The History of Orchestration*, London, 1925, 341f). Before then the function of leader in instrumental music was exercised either by the first violinist (comparable with the present leader) or by the organist, harpsichordist or even pianist, seated at the keyboard (*see* CONDUCTING).

DAVID D. BOYDEN

Leading note (Fr. [*note*] *sensible*; Ger. *Leitton*; It. [*nota*] *sensibile*; Lat. *subsemitonium*). The seventh degree of the major or harmonic minor scale, so called because it lies a semitone below the tonic and therefore has a strong tendency to lead up to it. In early medieval music leading-note resolutions were infrequent, being confined to pieces in the Lydian mode. With the development of polyphony in the late Middle Ages and Renaissance, however, the penultimate degree of a mode eventually became sharpened automatically, according to the principles of *musica ficta*, and leading-note motion became an identifying feature of the cadence. In the major–minor tonal system this resolution could itself imply a harmonic progression V–I; for this reason the leading note may be thought of as the most characteristic melodic scale degree.

Some writers use the term 'upper leading note' for the flattened supertonic, or the natural second degree when it lies a semitone above the tonic or final (e.g. in the Phrygian mode). One also encounters 'leading harmony', a term conceived by analogy with 'leading note' to mean any harmony that behaves like a dominant in its inclination towards resolution on the tonic.

League of Composers. An organization founded in 1923 in New York by members of the International Composers' Guild in order to promote the composition and performance of contemporary music. Before it merged with the ISCM in 1954, the league had commissioned 110 works by outstanding American and European composers, including Copland, Bartók and Barber, sponsored American stage premières of *The Rite of Spring*, *Oedipus Rex* and *The Wedding*, and mounted the first radio broadcasts of contemporary music. It also gave concerts and receptions honouring Schoenberg, Hindemith, Milhaud and other composers who had recently emigrated to the USA. Its quarterly *Modern Music* (1924–47), which contained critical reviews of new works and articles by leading composers, did much to increase awareness and appreciation of contemporary music. The executive chairmen were Claire R. Reis (1923–48) and Copland (1948–50).

BIBLIOGRAPHY
C. R. Reis: *Composers, Conductors and Critics* (New York, 1955)

RITA H. MEAD

Leal, Eleutério Franco (*b* ?Lisbon, c1758; *d* Lisbon, c1840). Portuguese composer. He taught in the *seminário* (choir school) of Lisbon Cathedral and was cathedral *mestre de capela* from about 1780 until 1819, when he was retired because of chronic illness. His surviving music is in a fluent Italianate style resembling that of David Perez. *Regras de acompanhar*, his treatise on accompanying for use in the Lisbon Cathedral *seminário*, consists mainly of examples and contrapuntal exercises progressing from two to four parts in all keys containing up to four sharps or flats.

WORKS

Mass, 4vv, org; 8 vesper psalms and Magnificat, 4vv, org; all *P-EVc*

In convertendo, 4vv, bc, *La*

3 masses, 4vv, org; 3 vesper psalms, 4vv, org; all *Lf*

Credo, 4vv, insts; Responsory for Matins of Our Lady, 4vv, 2 vc, org, 1817: both *Ln*

Regras de acompanhar: para uso do Real seminario da Santa Igreja Patriarchal, *Ln*

BIBLIOGRAPHY

DBP

M. A. Machado Santos: *Catálogo de música manuscrita*, iii (Lisbon, 1960), 23f

J. Augusto Alegria: *Arquivo das músicas da Sé de Évora: catálogo* (Lisbon, 1973), 25, 31

ROBERT STEVENSON

Lear [née Shulman], **Evelyn** (*b* Brooklyn, 8 Jan 1928). American soprano. She studied the piano and the horn (playing in the Tanglewood Orchestra under Bernstein); at the Juilliard School she studied singing, making her New York recital début in 1955. After further study in Berlin in 1957 she was engaged by Carl Ebert for the Berlin Städtische Oper, where she made her début in 1959 as the Composer. In 1961 she created the title role in Klebe's *Alkmene* at the rebuilt Deutsche Oper, Berlin, where she has since performed regularly. In 1963 she created Jeanne in Egk's *Die Verlobung in San Domingo* at the opening celebrations of the rebuilt National Theatre, Munich; her Metropolitan début was as Lavinia in the first performance of Levy's *Mourning Becomes Electra* (16 March 1967), during the first Lincoln Center season. Since her first performance as Berg's Lulu (in concert) in May 1960 she has been closely associated with the role, recording it under Böhm; she sang it in London with the Hamburg company in 1966 (her London opera début was a year earlier at Covent Garden, as Donna Elvira). Her repertory includes both Cherubino and the Countess, Fiordiligi, Pamina, Handel's Cleopatra, Mimì, Verdi's Desdemona, Tatyana and Octavian. From 1972 she began to undertake heavier roles, including Tosca and the Marschallin. She is a distinguished recitalist, singing in seven languages. Her voice, though not large, is of distinctively warm and affecting quality and is well produced and projected apart from occasional upper-register strain; her performances are marked by an intelligent treatment of the text and an appealing stage presence. She married the baritone Thomas Stewart in 1955.

HAROLD ROSENTHAL

Leardini, Alessandro (*b* Urbino; *fl* 1643–62). Italian composer. He wrote two intermezzos for the opera *La finta savia* (libretto by Giulio Strozzi; remainder of music by Laurenzi, Merula, G. B. Crivelli, B. Ferrari and V. Tozzi), performed at Venice in 1643. His *Argiope* (text by P. Micheli and G. B. Fusconi) was given there in 1649, but it may already have been composed for Carnival 1646. In one anthology (*RISM* 1648[1]) he is described as being in the service of 'Cavaliere Sforza', probably Francesco Maria Sforza (1612–80), a Knight of Malta from 1634 and later Marquis of Caravagio. The motet by him in that collection is representative of the new progressive style of Roman church music. He was *maestro di cappella* at the Mantuan court from at least 1649 to 1652; in 1649 his opera *Psiche* (libretto by D. Gabrielli; music in *I-Vnm*) was performed there on the occasion of the marriage of the Duke of Mantua. The occasional, courtly nature of *Psiche* accounts for its considerable use of the chorus, its instrumental writing for up to six parts and possibly also its wealth of arias. In 1651 Leardini's *Introduzzione al balletto dei dodeci Cesari Augusti* (text by A. Tarachia) was performed at Mantua, and in 1652 his *Festa della barriera* (devised by P. E. degli Obizzi; music lost) was given at the Teatro Grande there. Four solo cantatas, dated 1662 (?*recte* 1652), also survive (in *I-MOe*).

BIBLIOGRAPHY

EitnerQ

A. Tarachia: *Feste celebrate in Mantova alla venuta de' serenissimi archiduci Ferdinando Carlo e Sigismondo Francesco d'Austria, et arciduchessa Anna Medici* (Mantua, 1652)

A. M. Monterosso Vacchelli: ' "Psiche", tragicommedia di Alessandro Leardini', *Scritti in onore di Luigi Ronga* (Milan and Naples, 1973), 389

JEROME ROCHE

Le Bailly, Henry [Bailly, Henry de] (*d* Paris, 25 Sept 1637). French composer and singer. He worked at the court of Louis XIII. He is listed as 'musicien ordinaire du Roy' in 1617, and from 1625 until his death he was, jointly with Antoine Boësset, superintendent of the music of the royal chapel. He took part in several *ballets de cour*, at least up to 1622, and one or two songs that he wrote for them were printed in two volumes of Gabriel Bataille's *Airs mis en tablature de luth* (Paris, 1614–15), together with a few other songs by him. Bénigne de Bacilly in his *Remarques curieuses sur l'art de bien chanter* (Paris, 1668; Eng. trans., 1968) cited him as being best known for his ornamental variations of already existing melodies (example in E. T. Ferand: *Improvisation in Nine Centuries of Western Music*, Mw, xii, 1956; Eng. trans., 1961).

AUSTIN B. CASWELL

Lebano, Felice (*b* Palermo, 1867; *d* Buenos Aires, 1916). Italian harpist and composer. He completed his musical education at the Naples Conservatory, studying the harp under Alfonso Scotti (1805–89), whom he succeeded. He resigned to play in the principal cities of Europe, later extending his concert tours to include Brazil, Uruguay and Chile. He settled in Buenos Aires and accepted a professorship at the conservatory there. His compositions, all for harp, include *Serenata andalusa*, *Serenata*, *Pensiero poetico*, two polonaises and transcriptions.

BIBLIOGRAPHY

B. Bagatti: *Arpa e arpisti* (Piacenza, 1932), 65

M. G. Scimeca: *L'arpa nella storia* (Bari, 1938), 154

A. N. Schirinzi: *L'arpa* (Milan, 1961), 110

ALICE LAWSON ABER

Lebanon. A country of the Near East.

1. Historical outline. 2. Music in modern Lebanon.

1. HISTORICAL OUTLINE. Lebanon lies between Syria and Israel on the eastern shore of the Mediterranean Sea. In spite of its small area, Lebanon has been the centre of many different civilizations: what is now Lebanon formed the centre of Canaan–Phoenicia, which before 1500 BC extended from the Bay of Iskenderun in the north to Gaza in the south. Subsequently Hebrews occupied the southern part and Arameans from Mesopotamia settled in the northern part, the latter

mixing with the Phoenicians to make one people speaking the Aramaic language.

As a rich and civilized country (the biblical 'land of milk and honey') Phoenicia exerted an enormous influence on the surrounding peoples and attracted many invaders and conquerors including the Egyptians, Hittites, Assyrians, Babylonians, Persians, Greeks and Romans, and later the Arabs (AD 636) and Turks (AD 1516). These successive occupations, whether enforcing a subjugation against which the Phoenicians always revolted, or permitting an interior autonomy within the conqueror's kingdom, left a deep impression on the country and made Phoenicia a crucible of civilizations.

Modern knowledge of Phoenician music is scant and depends on what can be inferred from some remains of musical instruments, from scattered hints in the Bible and from the works of ancient writers. They suggest that Phoenician music was a highly developed facet of its cultural life. Historians no longer believe (as did Ambros, *Geschichte der Musik*, 3/1887) that its chief function was 'to drown the cries of the victims who burned in the glowing arms of Moloch'. It evidently had dignity as well as power and the Greeks themselves claimed to have learnt from it. Egypt welcomed the Phoenician female singers who introduced the Phoenician long-necked pandore (lute) and the arched harp; and Egyptian painters (*c*2000 BC) prove that the Semitic kithara (box lyre, known in Syriac as the *kennārā*) was also known in Egypt.

According to the Bible, Hiram, king of Tyre in Phoenicia, supplied Solomon with wood for the temple at Jerusalem and to make kitharas and pandores (*1 Kings* x.11–12) and Ezekiel's denunciation of Tyre includes the sentence 'And I will stop the music of your songs and the sound of your lyres will be heard no more' (*Ezekiel* xxxvi.13). During the establishment of Greek supremacy in Phoenicia the influence of the latter's culture on that of Greece was stronger than the reverse. According to Strabo (1st century BC) all Thracian music had oriental origins, and the Greeks borrowed many names of instruments from the Phoenicians: the *nablā* (a plucked chordophone), *sambūcā* (angular harp) and *kennārā* became in Greek *nablas*, *sambykē* and *kinyra*. The Romans showed a similar appreciation of oriental musicians. Plautus (*d* 184 BC) and Adrian (*d* AD 138) described Phoenician musicians playing the *sambūcā*, lyre and flute; Horace referred to *ambubaiae*, the female players of the *ambūbā* (the Phoenician flute); and Juvenal to flutes and harps (*sambūcā*). The *zamorā* (pipe) and the *tabolā* (drum) were used for popular songs and festivals.

Music was particularly important in Phoenician worship. Profane and sacred dances accompanied by music were performed in honour of Marqod, the god of dance. In the cult of Astarté, the divinity of love and fecundity, dances were accompanied by the flute (*ambūbā*) and the practice of obscene rites; Lucian (*d* AD *c*180) described the deafening noise of songs, flutes and cymbals accompanying the bloody dance of the priests (*De dea Syria*, x). But the cult of Adonis (Tammūz) was associated with a sentimental 'ballet' with restrained music and songs.

Until the 8th century AD Phoenicia supported two main cultures, the Hellenistic and the Aramaic, which influenced the balance of each other in varying degrees at different periods and places. Christian missionaries from Phoenicia spread into many countries and at the beginning of the 6th century Syrian monks went to Ethiopia (*see* ETHIOPIAN RITE, MUSIC OF THE) where the first bishop was a Phoenician. The Arabs, who conquered the plain of the Bekaa and entered the coastal towns in 636, failed to penetrate the mountain regions.

In the 7th and 8th centuries the Maronites came to northern Lebanon and their descendants form the preponderant element in the population of modern Lebanon. They were followers of St Maron (*d c*410) who lived in northern Syria and when they went to Lebanon they established a religious state in which secular and religious music was probably undifferentiated. In the early 11th century the Druze religion began to spread in the eastern mountains of Lebanon. During the period when the crusaders dominated Lebanon European music had apparently no influence, but the 400 years of Turkish rule saw a period of general decadence and sterility and a certain amount of Turkish influence on Lebanese secular music. The treatise *Al-Risāla al-shihābiyya fi al-ṣina 'a al-mūsīqiyya* ('Treatise on the art of music' for Emir Shihab) by the famous Lebanese–Syrian theorist Mikhā'īl Mashāqa (1800–88) deals with the quarter-tone system which, according to Collangettes (1904), was in general use.

2. MUSIC IN MODERN LEBANON. The successive immigrations and the continuous influence of music from abroad have given a heterogeneous quality to the music of Lebanon. This is reflected for instance in the number of differing Christian churches and rites and the rich repertory of old and new religious chants: they include Maronite, Syrian-Catholic and Jacobite (or Monophysite), Chaldean and Nestorian, Greek Catholic and Orthodox, Armenian Catholic and Monophysite, Roman Catholic and Protestant. There are also Shi'ite and Sunnite muslims. The Maronites and Druzes form the majority (for Druze chants *see* DRUZE MUSIC).

Because the Maronite Church is a branch of the Antiochian Church of the Syriac language, its traditional chants share a musical heritage with other churches of Antioch (*see* SYRIAN CHURCH MUSIC). Its melodies have always been simple and austere and the repertory comprises five groups distinguished by their origin, nature and traditional value: Syro-Maronite chant, Syro-Maronite-Arabic chant, improvised melodies of the soloists, personal or original melodies, and foreign melodies. The first named group is the finest and consists of about 150 melodies transmitted orally. The melodies are composed according to two methods: CENTONIZATION, and adaptation of melody-type. The archaic modality is defined by such elements as range, scale, principal notes, melodic contour and particularly the peculiar melodic formulae: it is related neither to the modes of Arab art music, nor to the system of eight modes used in several other churches. The chant is further characterized by its strophic and syllabic form, monodic setting, limited range, conjunct movement, varied rhythm and simple structure. It is related to traditional Lebanese folksong as well as to the chants of the Jacobite and Syro-Catholic church. Sometimes the chant is accompanied by metallic percussion instruments: the *nāqūs* (handbell), *marwaḥā* (rattle), small and large cymbals.

Traditional Arab art music, found also in other countries of the Near and Middle East (*see* ARAB MUSIC, §I), is taught in the oriental section of the National Conservatory at Beirut and the music school of the

1. 'Ūd (lute)

2. Qānūn (zither)

3. Mijwiz or arghūl (double clarinet), Baalbek

4. Rabāb (fiddle), Baalbek

University of the Holy Spirit at Kaslik. It is a fundamental element in modern oriental compositions and usually requires the accompaniment of various instruments such as the nāy (flute), 'ūd (unfretted lute; fig.1), qānūn (zither; fig.2), darabukka (single-membrane frustum-shaped drum) and daff (frame drum). Most mūwashshahāt (semi-popular songs) fall into this category.

In Lebanese popular music a distinction should be made between the traditional folk music and indigenous popular songs of recent date. The former is a homogeneous repertory based on Lebanese poetry in a metre of Syriac origin and a rhyme-scheme of Arab origin. The melodies generally resemble those of the Syro-Maronite chant. Some of these songs (for example the 'atābā) are common to a number of countries in the Near East (see ARAB MUSIC, §II), others seem to be purely Lebanese (e.g. the al-'aīn yā bū zuluf). They are characterized by rhymed four-line stanzas, the first three lines being sung by the soloist in a half-syllabic, half-melismatic style, the fourth being in strict metre and tempo and repeated in chorus. Instrumental accompaniment is limited to melodic instruments (the mijwiz or arghūl, a double clarinet, or sometimes the rabāb, a fiddle; figs.3 and 4), and percussion (the darabukka or daff drums, and hand-clapping or finger-clicking). On certain occasions other classical instruments are used.

In spite of diverse influences, modern popular song is rooted in traditional folksong and keeps its Lebanese identity. The popularity of modern Lebanese music has greatly increased since the 1950s because of the increasing number of music festivals, Baalbek being the oldest and most important.

Western art music is taught at the occidental section of the National Conservatory and in many schools and is played at concerts. Western popular music and jazz, which were not introduced into Lebanon until the 1950s, are imported and imitated in Lebanon; they are particularly popular with young people.

In the 20th century Beirut, the capital city, became the centre of a sudden musical renaissance. Prominent in this was the School of Music (Dār al-Mūsīqā), founded in 1910 by Wadī'Sabrá and adopted by the Lebanese government first as the National School of Music (1925) and then as the National Conservatory of Music (1929). The music school of the Lebanese Academy of Fine Arts, founded in 1943 by Alexis Botros, has particularly encouraged Western music. The American University in Beirut established a music school in 1923. The University of the Holy Spirit at Kaslik, near Beirut, has an Institute of Musicology (the only one of its kind in all the Arab countries), a School of Music (1970) and a Centre for Sacred Music (1972), all of which were founded and directed by Louis Hage.

The Jeunesses Musicales du Liban (JML), educational societies founded in the public interest in 1956, have consistently fulfilled their double aim of spreading occidental music in Lebanon and oriental music in both Lebanon and the West. Music festivals, especially that of Baalbek, have since 1956 popularized many compositions in a new style of Lebanese music, inspired mostly by native traditions.

Of the numerous composers who have promoted music in Lebanon in the first half of the 20th century the most notable include Wadī'Sabrā, first director of the National Conservatory, who was also famous as a musicologist; Paul Ashkar (1881–1962), who contributed greatly to the reform and progress of sacred music in Lebanon and to music education in general; and Bertrand Robillard (d 1964), an organist, composer and professor of composition, who made a special contribution to the musical renaissance by directing his students towards counterpoint rather than harmony.

Contemporary Lebanese composers and performers work in a number of different media and styles, both European and Near Eastern. Composers of art music using primarily a Western idiom include Salvador Arnita, an organist and founder of the chorus at the American University in Beirut, who has written three symphonies and four concertos for piano, organ and flute; and Boghos Gelalian (b 1927), a professor of piano at the National Conservatory in Beirut, who has written sonatas for piano and for other instruments, orchestral ballet music and organ works. An art music composer who has used both Western and Near Eastern idioms, Toufic Saba Succar, directed the National Conservatory (1964–9), where he became professor of solfège, harmony and counterpoint in 1953. He also directs the chorus Echo des Cèdres, which sings in Arabic in four-part harmony using quarter-tones; his compositions include chamber music, symphonies, choral works and ballet music and he has written and lectured on such subjects as the problems of harmonizing Arab music and the music of the Maronites. Georges Farah (b 1913), the head of the oriental section at the National Conservatory (appointed 1945), has written compositions in Near Eastern style, such as L'indépendance du Liban (1945) (an 'oriental musical poem'); he has also written on Arab music theory and on methods of learning the 'ūd.

An increasingly important area of composition has been popular music. Among the most prolific composers have been the Rahbani brothers, Assi (b 1923) and Mansour (b 1925); in collaboration they have composed over 300 songs and many operettas, mostly for Assi's wife, the singer Hoda Haddad ('Feyrouz') (b 1934) who has devoted her career to their performance. Elias ar-Rahbani (b 1938) has composed music for over 15 films. The singer and composer Wadi' as-Safi (Wadi' Bechara Francis, b 1921) has promoted the performance of traditional Lebanese folksongs and worked on opera productions at the Baalbek Festival. He has performed popular songs from Lebanese films and composed songs which have been recorded and sung on television.

BIBLIOGRAPHY

E. Smith: 'A Treatise on Arab Music, Chiefly from a Work by Mikhâil Meshâkah, of Damascus', Journal of the American Oriental Society, i (1847), 171–217

M. Collangettes: 'Etude sur la musique arabe', Journal asiatique, iv (1904), 365–422; viii (1906), 149–190

C. Sachs: The Rise of Music in the Ancient World, East and West (London, 1944)

H. G. Farmer: 'Syrian Music', Grove 5

J. Abdel-nour: Etude sur la poésie dialectale au Liban (Beirut, 1957, 2/1966)

S. Jargy: 'Libanaise, musique', Encyclopédie de la musique, ed. F. Lesure and V. Fédorov, iii (Paris, 1961), 965

S. F. A. al-Asmar: Al-Ghinā' al-kilasīkī al-'arabī [Arabian classical singing] (Beirut, 1963)

J. Chami: De la Phénicie (Beirut, 1967)

M.-H. Mainguy: La musique au Liban (Beirut, 1969)

S. Jargy: La poésie populaire traditionnelle chantée au proche-orient arabe, i: Les textes (Paris, 1970)

L. Hage: 'Music of the Maronite Church', Parole de l'orient, ii/1 (1971), 197

L. Hage: Le chant de l'Eglise maronite (Beirut, 1972)

LOUIS HAGE

Le Bé, Guillaume (b Troyes, 1525; d Paris, 1598). French type cutter. He became an apprentice at the age of 15 in the household of Robert Estienne, where he learnt from Claude Garamond the art of cutting punches. After a five-year stay in Italy he returned to Paris at the end of 1550. There he worked for Garamond and then in 1552 set up in business as one of the first independent type founders; his last type was cut in 1592.

Le Bé was well-known for his Hebrew types, but his Roman and Greek types were almost as popular. Between 1554 and 1559 he engraved three music types on commission from the firm of Le Roy & Ballard (illustrated on f.26 of his type specimen book, annotated in his own hand, F-Pn nouv.acq.fr.4528). A fourth music type attributed to Le Bé is listed in an 18th-century inventory of the successor firm of Ballard. A plainsong music type was cut by him but evidently not sold to Le Roy & Ballard, since it is listed as still a part of Le Bé's stock in an inventory drawn up at the time of his death. This inventory also lists music punches and matrices of all kinds designed by other makers; many of these are unidentified, but several are attributed to Attaingnant, Danfrie, Granjon, Villiers and Du Chemin.

After Le Bé's death his son Guillaume (c1563–1645) and subsequently his grandson, also Guillaume (d 1685), inherited the business. They were also type cutters but probably did not make any new music types; nevertheless they continued to sell from the stock of punches and matrices they inherited. The foundry was sold by the Le Bé heirs in 1730. A document in the hand of the second Guillaume Le Bé, with additions in a later hand, known as the Le Bé Memorandum, traces the history of type making, particularly in France. It contains references (not always accurate) to music types cut by Granjon, Sanlecque, Jean Jannon and Du Chemin.

BIBLIOGRAPHY

H. Omont: 'Spécimens de caractères hébreux, grecs, latins et de musique gravés à Venise et à Paris par Guillaume Le Bé (1546–1574)', Mémoires de la Société de l'historie de Paris et de l'Ile de France, xv (1888), 273

E. Howe: 'The Le Bé Family', Signature, viii (1938), 1

F. Lesure and G. Thibault: Bibliographie des éditions d'Adrian le Roy et Robert Ballard (Paris, 1955)

S. Morison: L'inventaire de la fonderie Le Bé (Paris, 1957)

H. Carter: Sixteenth-century French Typefounders: the Le Bé Memorandum (Paris, 1967)

D. Heartz: Pierre Attaingnant, Royal Printer of Music (Berkeley, 1969), 48ff

SAMUEL F. POGUE

Lebègue [Le Bègue], Nicolas-Antoine (b Laon, c1631; d Paris, 6 July 1702). French composer, organist and harpsichordist. He was of humble origin. Of his early musical education in Laon nothing definite is known, though it may be assumed that his uncle (and namesake), a *maître joueur d'instrument*, played some part in it. Hypotheses also surround the date and circumstances in which he moved to Paris. By 1661, however, he had clearly been there long enough to have established his reputation, for in the chapter records of Troyes Cathedral for that year he is called 'fameux organiste de Paris' (this, the earliest document to refer directly to Lebègue, relates to a payment for his playing at the cathedral when he was passing through Troyes). Although he must surely have held a Paris appointment by this time – Dufourcq (1954) suggested that it could have been at the church of the Mathurins in the rue St Jacques – the only such post he is known to have held was at St Merry from 18 December 1664 until his death. In 1678 he also became *organiste du Roi*, a duty and privilege that he shared with Nivers, Jacques-Denis Thomelin and Jean-Baptiste Buterne, attending the royal chapel during the October quarter.

To judge from the number of reprints of his keyboard works Lebègue enjoyed considerable success as a composer. No less considerable was his reputation as an expert on organ building: in this capacity he advised church authorities as far afield as Bourges, Blois, Chartres, Soissons and Troyes. In addition he must be reckoned one of the most influential teachers of the ensuing generation of French organists, numbering among his pupils Grigny, Dagincour and Nicolas Geoffroy and probably Gilles Jullien and Gabriel Garnier (the last-named succeeded him at court).

One volume of motets, a pseudo-plainchant hymn tune (of little interest) and many keyboard works are extant. There are five keyboard publications – two *livres de clavecin* and three *d'orgue* – and a number of MS pieces, notably in two sources at *US-BE*, one of which contains seven harpsichord pieces attributed by Curtis to Lebègue, the other 20 unique organ pieces.

Lebègue's harpsichord music owes much to that of Chambonnières and Louis Couperin. But there are notable differences: in his titles Lebègue eschewed picturesque elements and topical allusions; his pieces are correspondingly less personalized, more formal. The formality is reflected, furthermore, in the organization of his suites: the allemande–courante coupling became the standard opening, preceded only in his first book by unmeasured preludes. After the courante there follows a mixture of gavottes, minuets, canaris, gigues, sarabandes, chaconnes, ballets and bourrées, often with their *doubles*. Despite the censure in Pirro (1924), apropos of the first *livre de clavecin*, that 'the preludes seem to absorb in advance all the fantasy which might disturb the *ordre consacré* of these dances', Lebègue's harpsichord music contains his most poised and elegantly turned work for keyboard. Moreover, such pieces as the Chaconne in C (first book) and the *Chaconne grave* in G (second book) attain a stature fully worthy of Louis Couperin.

Lebègue's contribution to the organ repertory is substantial and correspondingly important. His first *livre d'orgue*, comprising eight suites, shows him as an innovator, rejecting the more severely contrapuntal style found in the organ music of Louis Couperin and Nivers (not to mention Roberday), evolving the *récit en taille* (which he considered the most beautiful of all the genres of organ music) and coining the *trio à deux dessus*, the *trio à deux claviers et pédalle* and the *dialogue entre le*

dessus et la basse. The independent pedal required in some of these genres marks a new departure in French organ technique. The exceptional nature of this first book, demanding an instrument of considerable resource and an organist no less well endowed, is highlighted by the character of Lebègue's second *livre d'orgue*, containing versets for the Mass and the *Magnificat*; it is much more modest in design and was intended for the organist of only 'une science médiocre'. His third book, comprising ten offertories, four *symphonies*, nine noëls, a picturesque piece entitled *Les cloches* and eight *élévations*, was published at the peak of his career and is unique in classical French organ literature. Dufourcq designated its contents as 'paraliturgical', which perhaps characterizes the secular spirit that dominates the collection. Although Lebègue's organ music is considerably less interesting than that of Grigny, for instance, it is to him that we owe the evolution of the musical language that his more illustrious pupil was to perfect.

WORKS

Editions: *N. Lebègue: Oeuvres de clavecin*, ed. N. Dufourcq (Monaco, 1956) [D]

    N. Lebègue, Archives des maîtres de l'orgue, ix, ed. A. Guilmant and A. Pirro (Paris, 1909) [G]

INSTRUMENTAL

Les pièces d'orgue (Paris, 1676), G
Les pièces de clavessin (Paris, 1677), D
Second livre d'orgue (Paris, ?1678), G
Troisième livre d'orgue (Paris, ?1685), G
Second livre de clavessin (Paris, ?1687), D
7 pieces, hpd, *US-BE* De La Barre 6
Several pieces, org, *F-Pn*, G appx; authorship questioned by Dufourcq (1972)
20 pieces, org, *US-BE* Lebègue MS

VOCAL

Motets pour les principales festes de l'année, 1v, bc, & plusieurs petits ritournelles, org/viols (Paris, 1687)
1 hymn, in Hymni sacri et novi (Paris, 1698)
Vespers, 2 choirs; lost, cited in De Fontenay, *Dictionnaire des artistes* (Paris, 1776)

BIBLIOGRAPHY

A. Pirro: biographical note in *Nicolas Lebègue*, Archives des maîtres de l'orgue, ix, ed. A. Guilmant and A. Pirro (Paris, 1909)
A. Tessier: 'L'oeuvre de clavecin de Nicolas Le Bègue', *RdM*, vii (1923), 106
A. Pirro: *Les clavecinistes* (Paris, 1924)
N. Dufourcq: *Nicolas Lebègue . . . étude biographique* (Paris, 1954)
——: 'A travers l'inédit: Nicolas Lebègue', *RMFC*, i (1960), 205
A. Curtis: 'Musique française classique à Berkeley: pièces inédites de Louis Couperin, Lebègue, La Barre, etc.', *RdM*, lvi (1970), 123–64
N. Dufourcq: *Le livre de l'orgue français, 1589–1789*, iv: *La musique* (Paris, 1972)

          EDWARD HIGGINBOTTOM

Le Bel, Barthélemy (*b* Anjou, Isère, *c*1483; *d* Geneva, 16 Oct 1553). French composer. After being ordained a priest in the early years of the 16th century he was appointed 'master of the boys of the vestment' at St Peter's Cathedral, Geneva, where Antoine Brumel had had a similar post some years before. He later held a similar position at the Sainte-Chapelle, Dijon. Having previously sought the patronage of the traitorous Duke of Guise, he announced that Charles V would be welcome at Dijon after his victory over François I at Pavia. He was arrested and interrogated on 17 March 1525 by the municipal judge. On 1 March 1552 he requested permission to reside in Geneva and to pursue his musical art. He died there at the age of 70. None of his compositions is known to have been printed during his lifetime, but a Latin motet for four voices was published in Geneva in 1554 (*RISM* 1554[13]) and in the following year there appeared a three-voice setting of the Ten

Commandments and three four-voice settings of prayers by Clément Marot (*RISM* 1555[16]), which, in spite of their French texts, were described as being 'in the form of motets'.

BIBLIOGRAPHY

P. Pidoux: *Le psautier huguenot du XVIe siècle*, ii (Basle, 1962), 175
F. Lesure: 'Some Minor French Composers of the 16th Century', *Aspects of Medieval and Renaissance Music: a Birthday Offering to Gustave Reese* (New York, 1966), 542

FRANK DOBBINS

Lebel, Firmin (*b* Noyon, early 16th century; *d* Rome, 27–31 Dec 1573). French choir director and composer active in Rome. The earliest known documents concerning his career indicate that he was a chaplain at S Maria Maggiore and the director of its Cappella Liberiana. As such, he may have had the young Palestrina in his charge. On 25 October 1545 Lebel became the seventh *maestro di cappella* at S Luigi dei Francesi (the French national church in Rome), a position that he retained for 16 years until September 1561, when he was succeeded by Annibale Zoilo. His directorship was an extremely successful one; he managed to enlarge the chapel from a group of two adults and two boys in 1548 to one of seven adults and two or three boys in 1552. On leaving S Luigi on 4 September 1561, he joined the papal chapel; so great was his reputation that Pius IV issued a *motu proprio* waiving the usual entrance examination and in 1563 Lebel was elected *puntatore annuale* of the chapel. His service was short-lived, for on 31 August 1565 he and 13 other singers were dismissed in the wake of reforms (drawn up by a commission headed by the Cardinals Borromeo and Vitelli) that aimed to reduce the size of the chapel. Lebel spent his remaining years in Rome where he held several benefices including one at S Maria Maggiore. On 4 March 1574 the papal singers sang a Requiem in his honour at S Luigi dei Francesi. Whether Firmin Lebel was related to Barthélemy Le Bel (1483–1553), a musician active in Geneva, is not known.

Three motets by him survive: *Ave verum corpus* for five voices (in *I-Rvat* C.S.38), *Puer natus est* for six voices (in C.S.38), and *Sancta Maria succurre miseris* for five voices (in C.S.17). (Both the works in C.S.38 are available in modern editions in *Psalterium*, ed. R. Casimiri, Rome, 1922.) Regardless of the merit of his compositions – and they show Lebel to be a competent composer – his importance rests on his activities as *maestro di cappella* of a number of the most important churches of Rome.

BIBLIOGRAPHY

R. Casimiri: *Giovanni Pierluigi da Palestrina: nuovi documenti biografici* (Rome, 1918)
——: 'Firmin Le Bel di Noyon', *NA*, i (1924), 64
A. Cametti: 'Firmino Lebel: maestro in S. Luigi dei Francesi a Roma', *RMI*, xxxii (1925), 196 [Fr. trans. in *ReM*, viii (1926), 21]
R. Casimiri: 'Firmin Lebel e la data di sua morte', *NA*, iii (1926), 46
H.-W. Frey: 'Die Kapellmeister an der französischen Nationalkirche San Luigi dei Francesi in Rom im 16. Jahrhundert (Teil I, 1514–1577)', *AMw*, xxii (1965), 272
F. Lesure: 'Some Minor French Composers of the 16th Century', *Aspects of Medieval and Renaissance Music: a Birthday Offering to Gustave Reese* (New York, 1966), 538
L. Perkins: 'Notes bibliographiques au sujet de l'ancien fond musical de l'église de Saint Louis des Français à Rome', *FAM*, xvi (1969), 57

ALLAN W. ATLAS

Lebendig (Ger.: 'lively'). See VIVACE.

Lebermann, Walter (*b* Karlsruhe, 23 Feb 1919). German musicologist. He studied at Karlsruhe and at the conservatory in Frankfurt am Main, and from 1936 to 1964 was a violin and viola player. From 1956 onwards he studied musicology. He has prepared a large number of editions of 18th-century music, including a volume of Mannheim flute concertos (EDM, li, 1964), many concertos for string instruments, especially violin and viola, and a large number of chamber works (e.g. by W. F. Bach, F. and G. Benda, Boccherini, Dittersdorf, J.-M. Leclair, G. B. Sammartini, A., C. and J. Stamitz, Telemann and Vivaldi). His articles, mostly published in *Die Musikforschung*, cover a considerable range of topics, for example the Toeschi family and other Mannheim composers, J. C. Fischer and I. J. Pleyel; he was the first to point out that the violin concerto in D attributed to Boccherini, and long thought to be the model for Mozart's K218, was a falsification.

Lebertoul, Franchois [Le Bertoul, François; Franchois] (*fl* 1409–10). Franco-Netherlands composer. An entry in a register of Cambrai Cathedral for the year 1409–10 describes him as *frequentanti chorum*; evidently he was employed at this time to sing with the choir on the major feast days of the liturgical year. Five chansons are currently attributed to him, all of which are in *GB-Ob* Canonici misc.213; the style suggests the late 14th or early 15th centuries. His most impressive work is the ballade *Au pain faitich* which is characterized by complex cross-rhythms, vocal flourishes and striking harmonic shifts. The triple ballade *O mortalis/O pastores/O vos multi*, which comments on the vanity of human endeavour, is somewhat unusual in that it has three separate texts, all in Latin.

WORKS

Editions: *Polyphonia sacra*, ed. C. van den Borren (Burnham, 1932/R1963) [B]
    Early Fifteenth-century Music, ed. G. Reaney, CMM, xi/2 (1959) [R]

BALLADES

Au pain faitich ne me veul plus tenir, 3vv, R 45
Depuis un peu un joyeux parlement, 3vv, R 43
O mortalis homo/O pastores/O vos multi, 3vv, B 273, R 47

RONDEAUX

Las, que me demanderoye, 3vv, R 42
Ma doulce amour et ma mestresse, 3vv, R 41

BIBLIOGRAPHY

E. Dannemann: *Die spätgotische Musiktradition in Frankreich und Burgund vor dem Auftreten Dufays* (Strasbourg, 1936), 26ff, 41
A. Pirro: *Histoire de la musique de la fin du XIVe siècle à la fin du XVIe* (Paris, 1940), 55
H. Besseler: *Bourdon und Fauxbourdon* (Leipzig, 1950), 38ff, 58f, 131

CRAIG WRIGHT

Lebeuf [Le Beuf], **Jean** (*b* Auxerre, 7 March 1687; *d* Auxerre, 10 Aug 1760). French ecclesiastic, archaeologist and historian. His early training was in religion and humanistic studies in his native city and in Paris (from 1701). In 1712 he returned to Auxerre as canon, and shortly afterwards as *sous-chantre*, at the cathedral – a post he held until 1743. His principal interests – church history, archaeology and music in the liturgy – manifested themselves early in his career, and he published over 200 essays on various aspects of these subjects throughout his life. He actively corresponded with leading church figures of the day and travelled widely in pursuit of knowledge. In 1740 he was named a member of the Académie des Inscriptions et Belles-Lettres.

Lebeuf's principal contributions to music relate to the history, theory and practice of plainchant. He was a proponent of reform in liturgical practice, and he played an active role in promoting revisions in the music for the Gallican service. Many of his ideas, first stated in letters and articles in the *Mercure de France*, reappear in his major work devoted to music, *Traité historique et pratique sur le chant ecclésiastique* (1741). This work resulted from his preparation (undertaken in 1734) of a revised antiphonary and gradual for the diocese of Paris. It is divided into two parts: 'Traité historique', which deals with the history, organization and forms of plain-chant; and 'Traité pratique', intended to serve as a hand-book for the teaching and performance of plainchant, the basic contents of which Lebeuf attributed to his former teacher, Claude Chastelain. Of interest in the treatise are his concern with retaining, in the face of church reforms, certain traditional characteristics of Gallican chant, such as ornate passage-work and *agré-ments*; his favouring of a revised system of solmization syllables to permit the singing of chromatically altered notes in chant (*ut, re, ma, mi, fa, fi, sol, la, sa, si, ut*); and his descriptions of the varied use of discant ('déchant') and fauxbourdon in the development of liturgical prac-tice in France.

WRITINGS
BOOKS
Traité historique et pratique sur le chant ecclésiastique (Paris, 1741/*R*1972)

ARTICLES
in historical studies
'De l'état des sciences dans l'étendue de la monarchie française, sous Charlemagne' (Paris, 1734); repr. in Leber, xiv, 338ff
'Dissertation sur l'état des sciences dans les Gaules depuis la mort de Charlemagne, jusqu'à celle du Roy Robert', *Recueil de divers écrits pour servir d'éclaircissemens à l'histoire de France, et de supplément à 'la notice des Gaules*, ii (Paris, 1738), esp. 95ff
'Dissertation sur l'état des sciences en France depuis la mort du roi Robert, jusqu'à celle de Philippe-le-Bel', *Dissertation sur l'histoire ecclésiastique et civile de Paris, suivies de plusieurs éclaircissemens sur l'histoire de France*, ii (Paris, 1741); repr. in Leber, xiv–xv, esp. xiv, 551ff

in academic journals
'Notice sommaire de deux volumes de poësies françoises et latines [de G. de Machaut], conservés dans la bibliothèque des Carmes-Déchaux de Paris, avec une indication du genre de musique qui s'y trouve', *Mémoires de littérature, tirés des registres de l'Académie royale des inscriptions et belles-lettres, depuis l'année 1744, jusques et compris l'année 1746*, xx (Paris, 1753), 377

in 'Mercure de France'
'Lettre éscrite de . . . en Brie, contenant quelques remarques sur le chant ecclésiastique' (Sept 1725), i, 1987
'Dessein d'un recueil d'hymnes nouvelles avec les plus beaux chants, selon chaque mesure' (Aug 1726), 1729–59
'Lettre sur le système de chant inventé depuis peu par un prêtre de S. Sulpice' (Feb 1728), 217; 'Continuation des remarques' (Nov 1728), 2350; (Dec 1728), i, 2571
'Observations sur la composition du chant ecclésiastique de plusieurs nouveaux bréviaires' (June 1728), i, 1162; ii, 1300
'Réponses aux questions proposées dans le Mercure du mois de Novembre dernier, à l'occasion de quelques contestations musicales, formées à Troyes en Champagne' (May 1729), 844
'Lettre . . . à M. H[erluyson] chanoine de l'église cathédrale de [Troyes] sur le choix que les musiciens ont fait de Ste. Cécile pour leur Patronne' (Jan 1732), 21; (June 1732), i, 1081
'Lettre sur les orgues' (Aug 1737), 1750

BIBLIOGRAPHY
FétisB
P. Papillon: *Bibliothèque des auteurs de Bourgogne* (Dijon, 1745/*R*1970), i, 388ff
J.-M. Quérard: *La France littéraire* (Paris, 1827–64), v, 13f
C. Leber: *Collection des meilleurs dissertations, notices et traités par-ticuliers relatifs à l'histoire de France*, xiv–xv (Paris, 1838)
P. Aubry: *La musicologie médiévale: histoire et méthodes* (Paris, 1900), 31ff
A. Cioranescu: *Bibliographie de la littérature française du dix-huitième siècle*, ii (Paris, 1969), 1055ff

ALBERT COHEN

Lebeuf d'Abbeville en Pontieu, Jehan. *See* JEHAN LEBEUF D'ABBEVILLE EN PONTIEU.

Lebhaft (Ger.: 'lively', 'sprightly', 'brisk'). A tempo mark. In the second movement of his A major Piano

Sonata op.101 Beethoven translated *lebhaft, marsch-mässig* as *vivace alla marcia*; but in the first movement *etwas lebhaft und mit der innigsten Empfindung* becomes *allegretto ma non troppo*. The introduction to Act 3 of *Lohengrin* is headed *sehr lebhaft*.

Lebič, Lojze (*b* Prevalje, Koroška, 23 Aug 1934). Yugoslav composer and conductor. He studied archaeology at Ljubljana University until 1957, then composition with Kozina and conducting with Švara at the Ljubljana Academy of Music. He conducted the Tone Tomšič chorus (1959–63) and the Radio-Televizije chamber chorus of Ljubljana (1962–71). In 1971 he became musical editor of Radio Ljubljana and in 1972 a professor at the Ljubljana Pedagogical Academy.

Lebič's music is strongly influenced by the Polish avant garde, but follows a separate line of development, with a strong feeling for melodic lines and a 'sym-phonic' interaction of the various elements used. This is well illustrated in the chamber works *Meditacija* and *Ekspresije*, in which the harmonic implications of the contrapuntal lines are carefully worked out, despite an apparently free coordination. The development of these characteristics in *kons* (*b*) shows a strong dramatic sense, while in *kons* (*a*) phonetic material is integrated into the delicate textures. In the cantata *Požgana trava* ('Scorched grass') the full orchestra is used with similar care to balance the recitative-like vocal lines. Lebič's orchestral masterpiece, *Korant*, reconciles on the one hand the huge orchestral tutti with the subtle sounds of the chamber works, and on the other static harmony with vigorous rhythmic activity and variety.

WORKS
(selective list)
Orch: Sinfonietta, 1962; Sentence, wind, 2 pf, perc, 4 vc, 2 db, 1967; Korant, 1969; Nicina, 1971; Glasovi [Voices], harp, pf, hpd, gui, mand, perc, str, 1974
Vocal: Požgana trava [Scorched grass] (D. Zajc), cantata, Mez, orch, 1965
Chamber: Sonata, vn, pf, 1959; Sonata, cl, pf, 1960; Conc. per 5, 1963; Inscriptiones, fl, cl, tpt, trbn, perc, harp, vc, 1965; Meditacija za 2, va, vc, 1965, rev. 1972; Impromptus, pf, 1967–74; Ekspresije, pf trio, 1968, rev. 1972; kons (b), 3 cl, perc, harp, str qt, 1968; kons (a), fl, cl, hn, perc, pf, harp, str trio, 1970; Atelier, vn, pf, 1973

Principal publishers: Društvo slovenskih skladateljev, Gerig

NIALL O'LOUGHLIN

Le Bienvenu, Fleurant. *See* BIENVENU, FLORENT.

Lébl, Vladimír (*b* Prague, 6 Feb 1928). Czech musicologist. He began studying medicine, but after three years he transferred to music and ethnography at the arts faculty of Prague University, where he was a pupil of Očadlík and Sychra. He took his doctorate with a dissertation on Janáček in 1953. He then became a lecturer at the department of music history at Prague University (1953–7), chief of the music section of the Prague Theatre Institute (1957–63), and research fellow at the musicology institute at the Czechoslovak Academy of Sciences in Prague (1963). He obtained his CSc degree in 1966 with a monograph on the life and work of Vítězslav Novák. From the late 1950s he has been active as a music critic (contributing to *Hudební rozhledy, Divadlo, Literární noviny* and other journals) and as an administrator, notably in the Czechoslovak Composers Union. Recently he has con-centrated on research into the history of music, par-ticularly Czech music in the 20th century and into acoustics, electronic music and *musique concrète*, taking his standpoint mainly from the work of the French experimental studio of Pierre Schaeffer. In the 1960s, with the music director and theorist Eduard Herzog, he was instrumental in propagating electronic music among Czech and Slovak composers, presenting before the public electronic works by Vostřák, Kopelent and others. Of particular value were the courses on electronic music that he organized in Prague and Plzeň jointly with Czechoslovak Radio and the Czechoslovak Composers Union (1965–7). In 1966 he became head of the sound research laboratory at the musicology institute of the Czechoslovak Academy of Sciences, a new department which he has built up largely by himself.

WRITINGS
Pět kapitol o Leoši Janáčkovi [Five chapters on Janáček] (diss., U. of Prague, 1953)

Cesty moderní opery [Paths of modern opera] (Prague, 1961)

Vítězslav Novák: život a dílo [Life and work] (CSc diss., U. of Prague, 1966; Prague, 1964)

with L. Mokrý: 'O současném stavu nových skladebných směrů u nás', [The present state of new directions of composition in Czechoslovakia], *Nové cesty hudby* (Prague, 1964), 11

Elektronická hudba (Prague, 1966)

'Příspěvek k morfologii zvukové struktury' [The morphology of sound structures], *HV*, viii (1971), 3

'Moderní hudba', [Modern Music], *Československá vlastivěda*, xi/3, ed. M. Očadlík and R. Smetana (Prague, 1971), 227–85

with others: *Dějiny české hudební kultury, i: 1890–1918* [The history of Czech musical culture] (Prague, 1972)

'Případ Vojcek' [The case of Wozzeck], *HV*, xiv (1977), 195–227

JOSEF BEK

Le Blan, Pierre-Joseph (*b* Zinnik [now Hennegau], baptized 18 July 1711; *d* Ghent, buried 25 May 1765). South Netherlands carillonneur, and composer. Known by 1729 as a carillonneur and clockmaker in his home town, Le Blan appeared from 1743 in Veurne exercising these two occupations, then succeeded Pierre Schepers as town carillonneur at Ghent, becoming town clockmaker in 1751. He is said to have invented around 1763 a kind of glass carillon upon which he gave a concert. One work is known, a *Livre de clavecin* (Ghent, 1752) containing six suites.

BIBLIOGRAPHY
E. vander Straeten: *La musique aux Pays-Bas avant le XIXᵉ siècle* (Brussels, 1867–88/R1969)

E. Closson and C. van den Borren, eds.: *La musique en Belgique* (Brussels, 1950)

DAVID FULLER

Leblanc [first name unknown] (*b* ?c1750; *d* Paris, March 1827). French composer and violinist. By 1767 he had published *La chasse*, a violin sonata; he wrote light works for the Paris stage, beginning with *La noce béarnaise* in 1787. He was director of the orchestra of the Théâtre-Française Comique et Lyrique until at least 1791, and was a composer of operas and pantomimes for the Théâtre d'Emulation until 1801. At least the overture and accompaniments for Beffroy de Reigny's extremely popular *Nicodème dans la lune* (1790) are by him, but it was his misfortune to compose for the short-lived, smaller theatres, and his successes were quickly forgotten. He composed much music, often anonymously, for the pantomimes, ballets and melodramas of the boulevard theatres. A fall in his fortunes obliged him to accept the position of second violin at the Théâtre sans Prétention, and he was later reduced to copying music to support himself.

WORKS
Stage works first performed in Paris; printed works published in Paris, n.d., unless otherwise stated.

La noce béarnaise (opéra comique, 3, Lutaine), Beaujolais, 14 Nov 1787; ov., entr'acte pubd, arr. for hpd/pf, vn by P. A. César; 2 ariettes pubd

Gabrielle et Paulin (vaudeville, 1), Beaujolais, 9 or 10 May 1788; 5 airs pubd, incl. 3 lost

Nicodème dans la lune, ou La révolution pacifique (opéra comique, 3, Beffroy de Reigny), Comique et Lyrique, 7 Nov 1790; ov. pubd, arr. for 2 vn by Anicot

La folle gageure (comédie, 1, F.-P.-A. Léger), Comique et Lyrique, 1790 (1790)

Le berceau de Henri IV (opéra comique, 2), Comique et Lyrique, 1790

Rosine et Zély, Comique et Lyrique, 1791

La mariage de Nanon, ou La suite de Madame Angot (opéra comique, A. F. Eve), Emulation, 1796

Gonzalve et Zuléma, ou La destruction des Maures (heroic pantomime, 3, Leblanc), Cité, 1797

Télémaque (pantomime), Emulation, 1797; only ov., entr'acte

La fausse mère, ou Une faute d'amour (operetta), Emulation, 1798

Rannucio (pantomime, 3), Emulation, 1798

La bergère de Saluces, ou La vertu à l'épreuve (4), Jeunes Artists, 29 Jan 1799

La forêt enchantée, ou Isaure et Florestan, Gaîté, 1800

Huon de Bordeaux, ou L'épreuve des amants fidèles (pantomime-féerie, 5, P. J. Noel), Gaîté, 28 Jan 1802

Les deux nuits (opéra comique, 2, ? A.-J. Coffin-Rosny, ? L.-F.-G. Béraud), Gaîté, 31 May 1802

Ecbert, premier roi d'Angleterre, ou La fin de l'heptarchie (mélodrame, 3, P.-A.-L.-P. Plancher [V. Valcour]), c1802

Esther (mélodrame, 3, Plancher), 1802 or 1803

La belle Milanaise, ou La fille-femme, page et soldat, Gaîté, 28 June 1804

Holkar et Palamys, ou Les anglais dans l'Hindoustan (pantomime, 2, ?Leblanc), Cité, 1805

L'isle flottant, ou Les voyageurs aériens (comédie-féerie, 1, R. Périn), Gaîté, 3 March 1806; ballets by Husjeune

Le sabot miraculeux, ou L'isle des Nains, Salle de Jeux Forains, 8 Jan 1811

Saphirine, ou Le réveil magique (mélo-féerie, 2, J.-T. Merle, E. T. M. Ourry), Gaîté, 25 July 1811

Riquet à la houpe (mélo-féerie, 2, ?A.-J.-B. Simonnin), Gaîté, 28 Sept 1811; ballets by ?J.-B. Hullin

L'armure, ou Le soldat moldave (mélodrame, 3, J.-G.-A. Cuvelier de Trie, Léopold [L. Chandezon]), Gaîté, 20 Oct 1821; adds. C. G. Alexandre, ballets by F. C. Lefevre

Azémire, ou Les réfugiés péruviens (mélodrame)

Elisa, ou Le triomphe des femmes (mélodrame)

Le sérail (mélodrame)

La chasse, vn, b (by 1767)

Sonates, vn, bc

BIBLIOGRAPHY
FétisB; *GerberNL*

P. L. Jacob, ed.: *Bibliothèque dramatique de Monsieur de Soleinne* (Paris, 1843–5)

F. Clément and P. Larousse, eds.: *Dictionnaire lyrique, ou Histoire des opéras* (Paris, 1867–9, 4 suppls. to 1881) [2/1897, ed. A. Pougin, suppl. 1904, 3/1905/R1969]

C. S. Brenner: *A Bibliographical List of Plays in the French Language 1700–1789* (Berkeley, 1947)

LELAND FOX

Le Blanc, Didier (*fl* ?Paris, 1578–84). French music editor and composer. His *Airs de plusieurs musiciens ... réduiz a 4 parties* (Paris, 1579; ed. in MMFTR, iii, 1925) contains 42 *airs* and is dedicated, in a sonnet signed by the composer, to the lutenist and printer Adrian le Roy. The *Second livre d'airs des plus excelants musiciens ... réduiz a 4 parties* (Paris, 1579) also contains 42 *airs* and a shorter dedicatory poem by Le Blanc to Pierre Dugué. The title-pages of the collections explain that the contents are four- and five-voice arrangements of *airs* by several composers to strophic poems by Desportes and others (Jamin, Baïf, Ronsard, Belleau and Du Bellay are acknowledged in the first book). Some of the tunes are those of the four-voice settings of the same texts by Caietain and Beaulieu published in 1576 and 1578. The style of the *airs* is generally homophonic and metrical, exploiting alternation of duple and triple metres and respecting the poetic prosody of *musique mesurée* without the strictly quantitative approach; a few *airs* have unusual concluding cadences with an anticipation of the final chord. Le Blanc also contributed eight contrapuntal duet arrangements of four- and five-voice chansons by Lassus to the second edition of Le Roy & Ballard's first book of bicinia (*RISM* 1578[17]), and a trio arrangement of Willaert's six-voice *A la fontaine* to the same publishers' second book of chansons for three voices (*RISM* 1578[15]). His only original composition is a four-voice *Te Deum* printed at the end of an anthology of *Magnificat* settings (*RISM* 1584[1]).

BIBLIOGRAPHY

F. Lesure and G. Thibault: *Bibliographie des éditions d'Adrian le Roy et Robert Ballard* (Paris, 1955)

FRANK DOBBINS

Le Blanc [Leblanc], **Hubert** (*fl* early 18th century). He was active in Paris as a jurist, churchman and devotee of the bass viol. In his *Défense de la basse de viole contre les entreprises du violon et les prétentions du violoncel* (Amsterdam, 1740/*R*1975; reprinted serially in *ReM*, ix, 1927–8, Eng. trans. in Jackson), he considered this instrument a special gift from the gods to French music, and championed it against the encroachments of the violin and the cello. Le Blanc envisaged an 'Empire de la viole' in which Marin Marais, Antoine Forqueray and Caix d'Hervelois occupied the first, second and third ranks. Although somewhat eccentric, Le Blanc provides valuable information concerning performing practices and Parisian cultural life during this period.

BIBLIOGRAPHY

J. W. von Wasielewski: *Das Violoncell und seine Geschichte* (Leipzig, 1889, enlarged 3/1925/*R*1970; Eng. trans., 1894/*R*1968)
G. R. Hayes: *The Viols, and Other Bowed Instruments* (London, 1930)
A. Erhard, ed. and trans.: *Verteidigung der Viola da Gamba gegen die Angriffe der Violine und die Anmassungen des Violoncells* (Kassel, 1951) [Ger. trans. of *Défense*]
N. Dolmetsch: *The Viola da Gamba* (London, 1962)
B. G. Jackson: 'Hubert Le Blanc's "Défense de la viole"', *Journal of the Viola da Gamba Society of America*, x (1973), 11, 69; xi (1974), 17; xii (1975), 14 [Eng. trans. and commentary]

CLYDE H. THOMPSON

Leblanc du Roullet, Marie François Louis Gand. *See* ROULLET, MARIE FRANÇOIS LOUIS GAND LEBLANC.

Leborne, Aimé (Ambroise Simon) (*b* Brussels, 29 Dec 1797; *d* Paris, 1 or 2 April 1866). French composer and teacher of South Netherlands birth. He attended the free school in Versailles, winning prizes in 1809 and 1810, and entered the Paris Conservatoire in 1811 where he studied harmony (with Berton and Dourlen) and composition and counterpoint (with Cherubini). In 1818 he won the second prize in the Prix de Rome contest, and in 1820 obtained the first prize with the cantata *Sophonisbe*, enabling him to travel in Italy and Germany for three years. On his return to Paris he taught solfège at the Conservatoire (an appointment which he had held since 1820), and gained recognition as an opera composer. He was named librarian of the Opéra in 1829 and of the royal chapel five years later. After Reicha's death in 1836 Leborne became professor of counterpoint and fugue at the Conservatoire, and from 1840 he taught composition, retaining this post until his death. He was named a Chevalier of the Légion d'honneur in 1853.

Leborne was a renowned teacher; several of his pupils won the Prix de Rome. He brought out a new edition of Catel's *Traité d'harmonie* with numerous practical additions (1848), and wrote his own treatise on harmony which was never published. His operas, which displayed much coloratura writing, were produced between 1827 and 1838 with little success.

WORKS

Sophonisbe (cantata, Vieillard), 1820
Les deux Figaro (opera, 3, V. Tirpenne), Paris, Odéon, 22 Aug 1827, collab. M. Carafa
Le camp du drap d'or (comic opera, 3, P. de Kock), Paris, Opéra-Comique (?Théâtre Feydeau), 23 Feb 1828, collab. Baton, Rifaut
Cinq ans d'entracte (comic opera, 2, A. Féréol), Paris, Opéra-Comique (Théâtre des Nouveautés), 15 June 1833
Lequel? (comic opera, 1, P. Duport, Ancelot), Paris, Opéra-Comique (Théâtre des Nouveautés), 21 March 1838
Finales to Acts 1, 2, Carafa's La violette (comic opera, 3, E. de Planard, after L. Lavergne, Compte de Tressan: Gerard de Nevers), Paris, Opéra-Comique (Théâtre Royal), 7 Oct 1828 (Paris, ?1829)
Songs

WRITINGS

Traité complet d'harmonie, de contrepoint, et de fugue (MS, n.d.)
ed.: C. Catel: *Traité d'harmonie* (Paris, 1848) [enlargement of original edn. (Paris, 1802)]

BIBLIOGRAPHY

FétisB
C. Pierre: *Le Conservatoire national de musique et de déclamation: documents historiques et administratifs* (Paris, 1900)
R. Vannes: *Dictionnaire des musiciens (compositeurs)* (Brussels, 1947)

MARIE LOUISE PEREYRA/JEFFREY COOPER

Le Boscu d'Arras [Le Bossy], **Adan.** *See* ADAM DE LA HALLE.

Le Bouteiller [Boutillier], **Jean** (*fl* Bourges, 1530–42). French composer. He was *maître des enfants* at the Sainte-Chapelle, Bourges, from November 1530 to October 1535 and then served in the same capacity at Chartres Cathedral until 1542. His only known works are two motets and four chansons, all for four voices, printed at Paris by Attaingnant between 1534 and 1540.

WORKS

2 Lat. motets, 4vv, 1534[3], 1534[4]; ed. A. Smijers and A. T. Merritt, *Treize livres de motets parus chez P. Attaingnant en 1534–1535*, i–ii (Paris, 1934)
4 chansons, 4vv, 1532[12], 1539[15], 1539[17], 1540[14]; 1 ed. H. M. Brown, *Theatrical Chansons of the Fifteenth and Early Sixteenth Centuries* (Cambridge, Mass., 1963)

BIBLIOGRAPHY

F. Lesure: 'Some Minor French Composers of the 16th Century', *Aspects of Medieval and Renaissance Music: a Birthday Offering to Gustave Reese* (New York, 1966), 543

FRANK DOBBINS

Le Bret (*fl c*1740). Composer of the only single-author 18th-century collection of French harpsichord music to have survived only in MS. The copy, by the Abbé Pingré (*F-Psg*), contains 17 pieces arranged in two suites, each beginning with an allemande. All bear titles and the point of departure is clearly Couperin and Rameau; but certain elements (notably a penchant for left-hand accompaniments consisting of repeated chords, rare in French music) point to the likelihood that Le Bret knew some sonatas of Scarlatti. The collection, entitled simply *Oeuvre de Mr. Le Bret*, is competent and even interesting.

DAVID FULLER

Le Breton. *See* BERTON, PIERRE-MONTAN.

Lebrun. German family of musicians.

(1) **Ludwig August** [Ludwig Karl Maria] **Lebrun** (*b* Mannheim, baptized 2 May 1752; *d* Berlin, 16 Dec 1790). Oboist and composer. He was the son of Jakob Alexander Lebrun, an oboist and répétiteur at the Mannheim court from 1747 until his death in 1771, who, according to Marpurg's Mannheim register of 1756, came from Brussels. Ludwig learnt from his father and was taken into the Mannheim orchestra as a 'scholar' in 1764 and three years later was appointed to

a full position which he held until his death. He was a member of the select group of chamber musicians at court and his high salary (recorded in court accounts of 1776 and 1778) shows that his distinction was acknowledged by the Elector Carl Theodor. Lebrun travelled extensively from about 1772, and after his marriage to Franziska Danzi in summer 1778 the couple were almost constantly on tour, to Milan (1778), Paris (1779), London (1779–81), Vienna and Prague (1785), Naples (1786–7) and finally Berlin (1789–90). His travels brought him great fame as perhaps the leading oboist of his day. He wrote a number of effective oboe concertos (many of which were arranged for flute) and published some chamber works and ballets. While in London he wrote ballet music for the King's Theatre, probably for operas in which his wife was performing. C. F. D. Schubart said he was the first oboist to reach *d'''* and *e'''*, praised his sweet tone in the upper range, and called his compositions 'as sweet as drops of nectar'.

WORKS

Dance music: The Celebrated Opera Dances, hpd, vn, insts, London, King's Theatre, 1782, arr. kbd (London, 1782); The Favourite Airs in the Grand Ballet of Adel de Ponthiew, arr. kbd (London, 1782); The Favourite Dances in the Opera of Armida, arr. kbd, vn (London, 1782); Kora und Alonzo (P. Crux), Munich, Nationalschaubühne, 25 Feb 1784, lost; Diana and Endimion, lost

Concs.: G, fl, op.1 (n.p., n.d.); ob, opp.2–4 (n.p., 1777); ob, op.5 (n.p., n.d.); fl, op.6 (n.p., 1778); F, ob, op.7 (Paris, 1787); 6, ob (Paris, after 1802); 6, ob (Offenbach, 1804), arr. fl by Ebers (Offenbach, 1804); C, ob, arr. B♭-cl, A-Wn; C, fl, listed in Breitkopf catalogues (1782–4)

Chamber: 6 trios, 2 vn, vc, op.1 (Mannheim, 1774; Paris, 1776), arr. ob/vn, vn, bc (Offenbach, after 1783), thematic catalogue in Riemann (1915); 6 trios, fl/vn, vn, bc, op.2 (Paris, 1776); 6 duos faciles, 2 fl (Paris, after 1777); 6 duos, vn, va, op.4 (Paris, 1783; Mannheim, 1784–5; London, c1790); 6 duos, 2 va, op.2 (Amsterdam, 1786); 6 duos (Augsburg, n.d.); Qt., C, ?ob, ?str, lost; Rondeau, D, ob, cembalo, lost

(2) Franziska [Francesca] **(Dorothea) Lebrun** [née Danzi] (*b* Mannheim, baptized 24 March 1756; *d* Berlin, 14 May 1791). Soprano, wife of (1) Ludwig August Lebrun and elder sister of Franz Danzi. She made her début in Sacchini's *La contadina in corte* at the 'little theatre' of the electoral court's country residence at Schwetzingen in 1772 (where Burney heard her on 9 August). She soon gained the leading position at the Mannheim court opera, and is described as a *virtuosa da camera* in the printed libretto to Salieri's *Fiera di Venezia* (1772). She sang in Anton Schweitzer's *Alceste* (1773) and created the role of the countess in Holzbauer's *Günther von Schwarzburg* (1777) which was written for her. In autumn 1777 she was granted a year's leave of absence by the Elector Carl Theodor, and went to London where she sang the lead in four *opere serie* (from 8 November). After her marriage to Lebrun she sang in the inaugural performance of Salieri's *Europa riconosciuta* that opened La Scala in Milan (3 August 1778), and in spring 1779 the couple performed at the Concert Spirituel in Paris. Münster mentioned her taking part with her husband in *symphonies concertantes*, singing the solo parts adapted to Italian words.

The couple were in London for two opera seasons (from November 1779). Burney remarked that her vocal abilities were superior to those of other women on the London stage but that, 'travelling with her husband, an excellent performer on the hautbois, she seems to have listened to nothing else ... [and has] copied the tone of his instrument so exactly, that when he accompanied her in divisions of thirds and sixths, it was

impossible to discover who was uppermost'. While in London she published two sets of six sonatas for keyboard and violin, opp.1 and 2 (which were issued in several editions in Paris, Offenbach, Mannheim, Berlin, Amsterdam and Worms; thematic catalogue in Riemann, 1915). Before the Mannheim court had moved to Munich, Franziska Lebrun had already commanded a prima donna's salary, but by 1782 it had increased by half as much again. In addition to her Munich obligations she travelled with her husband, sang as a guest artist in operas and concerts in Vienna and Verona, and spent a year at S Carlo, Naples (1786–7). She sang in Vogler's *Castore e Polluce* during Carnival 1787–8 in Munich, and in 1789–90 she was a guest artist in Berlin, performing twice there after her husband's death.

(3) Sophie Lebrun [Dülken] (*b* London, 20 June 1781; *d* after 1815). Pianist, daughter of (1) Ludwig August and (2) Franziska Lebrun. After studying music with Knechtl, a pupil of Vogler, she was taught the piano by Andreas Streicher, composition by Schlett in Munich and singing by her uncle Franz Danzi. She became the focal point of an early Romantic salon in Munich about 1810. After her marriage to the Munich piano maker J. L. Dülken on 27 December 1799, she won recognition as a pianist, touring Switzerland, Italy and France under her married name. Meyerbeer, Spohr and Weber mention her in their letters. None of her compositions (concertos and sonatas mentioned by Lipowsky) was published or survives. Her three daughters Louise (*b* 1805), Fanny (*b* 1807) and Violande (*b* 1810), all of whom married brothers from the Bohrer family of musicians, and a granddaughter Sophie were all musicians.

(4) Rosine Lebrun [Stentzsch] (*b* Munich, 29 April 1783; *d* Munich, 5 June 1855). Singer and actress, daughter of (1) Ludwig August and (2) Franziska Lebrun. Like her sister (3) Sophie, she studied the piano with Streicher and singing with her uncle Franz Danzi. She was successful as an opera singer, and after her marriage to the Munich actor K. A. A. Stentzsch (3 November 1800) she turned to acting, though she is still recorded as a singer in the printed libretto of Gyrowetz's *Der Augenarzt* (Munich, 1812). From 1801 to her retirement on 1 January 1830 she was a member of the Munich theatre company.

BIBLIOGRAPHY

BurneyH; GerberL; GerberNL

Court records (MS, D-KA 77/1657, 77/1665)

C. Burney: *The Present State of Music in Germany, the Netherlands and United Provinces* (London, 1773, 2/1775); ed. P. Scholes as *Dr. Burney's Musical Tours* (London, 1959)

Musikalische Real-Zeitung, iii (1789), no.52, col.415; iv (1790), no.1, col.7; no.4, col.30; no.17, col.128

Musikalische Korrespondenz der teutschen Filarmonischen Gesellschaft (6 Jan 1791; 16 Feb 1791)

C. F. D. Schubart: *Ideen zu einer Ästhetik der Tonkunst* (Vienna, 1806/R1969)

F. J. Lipowsky: *Baierisches Musik-Lexicon* (Munich, 1811/R1969)

F. Walter: *Geschichte des Theaters und der Musik am kurpfälzischen Hofe* (Leipzig, 1898/R1968)

H. Riemann: Introduction to DTB, xvi (1915)

R. Münster: 'Lebrun', MGG

ROLAND WÜRTZ

Lebrun [Le Brun, Brun, Braun], **Jean** (*b* Lyons, 6 April 1759; *d* Paris, c1809). French horn player. He went to Paris about 1780 to study with Punto, making his début at the Concert Spirituel in 1781; a *symphonie concertante* by him was performed there in 1785. In 1786 he was appointed principal horn at the Opéra, remaining there until 1792. When Palsa died that year in Berlin, Lebrun succeeded him as principal horn in the Prussian court orchestra in Bérlin and as first in the famous duo with Türrschmidt, with whom he toured until Türrschmidt's death in 1797. Homesickness eventually drove Lebrun to return to Paris, where he apparently reverted from the *cor alto* to the *cor basse* register, which formed the basis of all the great soloists' technique. Many sources state that Lebrun committed suicide by inhaling sulphurous fumes after a colleague had spoilt a double concerto performance in which Lebrun took part in 1806. The story cannot be entirely accurate, however, for the Leipzig *Allgemeine musikalische Zeitung* reports on his activity in Amsterdam as late as 1808.

Lebrun invented a lacquer for coating the inside of the horn's tubing, eliminating any irregularities of the inner surface, and preventing verdigris. Although he used a silver *cor solo* by Raoux, he recommended brass as the ideal material, and arrived at an optimum thickness for this metal which contributed to evenness of tone quality between stopped and open notes.

Gerber's appraisal of Lebrun's playing makes special mention of his voice-like tone quality, singing style and tasteful ornamentation, as well as his incomparable intonation and accuracy. A writer for the *Allgemeine musikalische Zeitung* summarized current critical opinion in 1799: 'I have never heard [Lebrun] spoil the tiniest detail. Every note, whether in passage-work or ornamentation, is sure and clear. His *allegro* is beautiful, his *andante* charming and his *adagio* moves one to tears every time'. Lebrun was an exceptional player, but these comments reveal the high general level of artistry and technical perfection which horn-playing had attained during the late 18th century.

Lebrun wrote a quantity of concertos for himself in nearly every key, but none was published and their whereabouts are unknown.

BIBLIOGRAPHY

FétisB; *GerberNL*

AMZ, i (1798–9), 621; ix (1806–7), 372; x (1807–8), 84, 265, 589, 814

G. Schilling: *Encyclopädie der gesammten musikalischen Wissenschaften oder Universal-Lexikon der Tonkunst* (Stuttgart, 1835–42/*R*1973)

C. von Ledebur: *Tonkünstler-Lexicon Berlin's* (Berlin, 1861/*R*1965)

R. Morley-Pegge: *The French Horn* (London, 1960, 2/1973)

C. Pierre: *Histoire du Concert spirituel 1725–1790* (Paris, 1975)

HORACE FITZPATRICK

Lebrun, Louis-Sébastien (*b* Paris, 10 Dec 1764; *d* Paris, 27 June 1829). French tenor and composer. At the age of seven he entered the *maîtrise* of Notre Dame, Paris, where he studied composition and received singing lessons, remaining there until 1783 when he became musical director of the church of St Germain-l'Auxerrois. Encouraged to take up theatrical singing, he made his début at the Paris Opéra in 1787 as Polynices in Sacchini's *Oedipe à Colone*. In the same period he appeared at the Concert Spirituel in the dual role of singer and composer of several *scènes* and an oratorio. Despite his limited acting ability he remained on the stage and transferred to the Théâtre Feydeau in 1791, leaving it in 1799. He then rejoined the Opéra as an understudy, becoming a singing tutor in 1803. In 1807 he was admitted as a tenor into the imperial chapel, where he was promoted to director of singing after three years. His responsibilities may also have lain outside the chapel, for Choron and Fayolle (1810–11) described

him as 'leader of the vocal division of the music of His Majesty'.

Among his stage works, most of which are *opéras comiques*, *Marcelin* (1800) and *Le rossignol* (1816) were quite successful. The former was presented in Madrid, Vienna, St Petersburg, Budapest, Prague and Stockholm. *Le rossignol* was famed for its virtuoso exchanges between the soprano and the solo flute, of which the original interpreters were Mme Albert-Hymm and J.-L. Tulou. It was performed 227 times in Paris up to 1852, though Clément and Larousse ascribed its longevity merely to the general shortage of operas brief enough to precede an evening of ballet. During its performance at the Théâtre Louvois on 13 February 1820, Charles-Ferdinand de Bourbon, the Duke of Berry and heir to the throne, was assassinated. *Le rossignol* was played in New York (1833) and London (Drury Lane, 1846).

WORKS

STAGE

All are opéras comiques, unless otherwise indicated; all were first performed in Paris.

L'art d'aimer, ou L'amour au village (1, [?L.-H.] Dancourt), Montansier, 1790; Ils ne savent pas lire (1), Montansier, 1791; Emilie et Melcour (1, L. Hennequin), Louvois, 3 July 1795; Le bon fils (1, Hennequin), Feydeau, 17 Sept 1795; L'astronome (1, Desfaucherets), Feydeau, 1798, *F-Po*, pubd, according to Fétis; Le menteur maladroit (1), Molière, 1798; Un moment d'erreur (1), Louvois, 1798; La veuve américaine (2), Louvois, 1799, Pc

Le maçon (1, C. A. B. Sewrin), Feydeau, 4 Dec 1799, Pc; Marcelin (1, F. Bernard-Valville), Feydeau, 22 March 1800, Pc, pubd according to Fétis, excerpts pubd separately; Eléonore et Dorval, ou La suite de la cinquantaine (1), Montansier, 1800; Les petits aveugles de Franconville (1, A. Croizette), Montansier, 1802; Le rossignol (opera or comic opera, 1, C. G. Etienne), Opéra, 23 April 1816 (n.d.), excerpts pubd separately; Zéloïde, ou Les fleurs enchantées (opéra-ballet, 2, Etienne), Opéra, 19 Jan 1818, Po; L'an II (genre unknown, 5), unperf., fragments, Pc

OTHER WORKS

Sacred: Te Deum for the victories of Wagram and Enzersdorf, perf. Paris, Notre Dame, 1809; Messe solennelle de Ste Cécile, perf. Paris, St Eustache, 1815; Messe en trio, with str, perf. Paris, St Maur, 1826.

Secular: oratorio, perf. Paris, Concert Spirituel, 1787; La mort d'Abel, scène, perf. Concert Spirituel, 1787, Pc; other scènes, perf. Concert Spirituel, 1788–9, lost; Recueil d'airs et romances (Paris, n.d.)

BIBLIOGRAPHY

FétisB

A. Choron and F. Fayolle: *Dictionnaire historique des musiciens* (Paris, 1810–11/*R*1971)

Castil-Blaze: *Chapelle-musique des rois de France* (Paris, 1832)

F. Clément and P. Larousse: *Dictionnaire lyrique, ou Histoire des opéras* (Paris, 1867–9, 4 suppls. to 1881) [2/1897, ed. A. Pougin, suppl. 1904, 3/1905/*R*1969]

J. Mongrédien: 'La musique du sacre de Napoléon 1er', *RdM*, liii (1967), 137–74

D. H. Foster: 'The Oratorio in Paris in the Eighteenth Century', *AcM*, xlvii (1975), 67-133, esp. 113

C. Pierre: *Histoire du Concert spirituel 1725–1790* (Paris, 1975)

DAVID CHARLTON

Le Brung [Le Brun, Lebrun], **Jean** (*fl c*1498–1513). French composer. He was a bass singer in the royal chapel, Paris, from about 1498 to at least 1513. Most of the sources of his music relate to the chapel's repertory. The motets are in the style prevalent at the chapel during the early years of the century, a style found in some of Josquin's late works. Le Brung frequently used the chant that was proper to the text as a basis for one voice, or as short points of imitation. Much of the writing is syllabic and clear in its harmonic direction. Even in a well-planned work, such as the *Magnificat*, there is little sense of form beyond the customary interchange of duos and tuttis. Most of the chansons are through-composed, with imitative entries and syllabic treatment of the text.

WORKS

Magnificat, 4vv, 1534[7]
10 motets, 1519[2], 1519[3], 1526[5], 1534[10], 1537[1], 1539[8], 1540[6], 1542[8]; *A-Wn* 18825, *D-Mbs* Art.401, *Mu* 34, *F-CA* 18(20), *I-Rvat* C.S. 46
5 chansons, 1540[6], 1545[15], 1549[25]; *A-Wn, D-Bds, F-Nd, O, Pn*

STANLEY BOORMAN

Le Caine, Hugh (*b* Port Arthur, Ontario, 27 May 1914). Canadian scientist and composer. He undertook graduate studies, specializing in nuclear physics, at Queen's University, Kingston, Ontario, and at the University of Birmingham; during World War II he worked on the development of radar. In 1954 he established the ELMUS Laboratory of the National Research Council, Ottawa, and thereafter gave his attention to designing electronic music instruments and to advising major Canadian studios. His design achievements include the Sackbut (1945), the Multitrack Tape Recorder (1953), the Serial Sound Structure Generator (1964) and the Sonde (1967). Among his compositions is *Dripsody* (1955), derived entirely from the sound of a falling drop of water.

BIBLIOGRAPHY
L. Cross: *A Bibliography of Electronic Music* (Toronto, 1967)

GUSTAV CIAMAGA

Le Camus, Sébastien (*b* *c*1610; *d* Paris, 24 March 1677). French viol player and composer. He was a musician of the king's household about 1640, by 1648 director of music to Gaston d'Orléans and in 1660 *surintendant de la musique* to Queen Marie-Thérèse. He played the viol and the theorbo and in 1661 shared with Hotman the position of viol player to the king, the position having been made vacant by the death of Louis Couperin. Though married, he lived with a mistress, surrounded by beautiful furniture and portraits of famous men and women of his age who admired his talents. The only volume devoted to his music is *Airs à 2 et 3 parties de feu M. Le Camus* (Paris, 1678), collected by his son Charles. These *airs*, which are settings of poems by Quinault and other, lesser poets, are in binary form. They are imaginative, with occasionally adventurous harmony and flexible, tuneful bass parts. Other *airs* by Le Camus are found in published anthologies of the late 17th and early 18th centuries and in MSS (at *F-Pa* and *F-Pn*).

NORBERT DUFOURCQ

Le Cerf de la Viéville, Jean Laurent, Seigneur de Freneuse (*b* Rouen, 1674; *d* Rouen, 10 Nov 1707). French author, poet and musical amateur. He was a student of law and in 1696 was appointed Keeper of the Seals of the parliament in Rouen. It was in response to the *Parallèle* of FRANÇOIS RAGUENET and to arguments in support of Italian music over French that Le Cerf produced his major work, the *Comparaison*. Made up of various 'dialogues', 'lettres', 'traités' and 'discours', it takes as its initial point of departure a reply to the attacks on French music by Raguenet, but it develops from this reply a series of essays that, taken together, describe the musical aesthetic prevalent in France during the late 17th century. It is an aesthetic that favours a simple, rational, 'natural' art over one based primarily on sensual beauty and that finds its expression in the ideals inherent in the music of Lully. The work of Le Cerf forms an important contribution to the development of musical criticism and aesthetics in the early 18th century.

WRITINGS
Comparaison de la musique italienne et de la musique française, 3 vols. (Brussels, 1704–6/*R*1972); repr. in P. Bourdelot and P. Bonnet-Bourdelot: *Histoire de la musique et de ses effets*, ed. J. Bonnet. ii iv (Paris, 1715/*R*1969, 7/1743); Ger. edns. in J. Mattheson: *Critica musica*, i (Hamburg, 1722/*R*1964) and F. W. Marpurg: *Kritische Briefe über die Tonkunst*, i (Berlin, 1759/*R*); Eng. trans. of extract from 6th dialogue in O. Strunk: *Source Readings in Music History* (New York, 1950), 489ff
L'art de décrier ce qu'on n'entend point, ou Le médecin musicien (Brussels, 1706)

BIBLIOGRAPHY
F. W. Marpurg: *Historisch-kritische Beyträge zur Aufnahme der Musik*, i (1754/*R*), 1–46
H. Prunières: 'Lecerf de la Viéville et l'esthétique musicale classique au XVIIe siècle', *BSIM*, iv (1908), 619–54
P.-M. Masson: 'Musique italienne et musique française: la première querelle', *RMI*, xix (1912), 519
H. de Curzon: *La musique* (Paris, 1914), 67ff
R. Wangermée: 'Lecerf de la Viéville, Bonnet-Bourdelot et l' "Essai sur le bon goust en musique" de Nicolas Grandval', *RBM*, v (1951), 132

ALBERT COHEN

Le Chevalier, Amédée (*b* Savoy, *c*1650; *d* Amsterdam, buried 5 Dec 1720). French musician, publisher and music printer. He set himself up in Amsterdam as 'muziekmeester' and on 1 December 1689 obtained a 15-year licence for music publication. On 24 July 1690 he made an agreement with D. Robethon, by which the latter promised to finance the production of 1000 copies of his first publication, *Les trios des opéra de Monsieur de Lully*. This was printed in Amsterdam by Blaeu, who worked for Le Chevalier until Le Chevalier himself became established as a printer in 1692. His publications are known from the catalogue at the end of J. de Gouy's *Airs à quatre parties sur la paraphrase des pseaumes* (1691) and from two advertisements in the *Amsterdamsche courant* (27 December 1691 and 1 July 1692). The second of these states that Le Chevalier sold not only his own publications but also music printed by A. Pointel. Le Chevalier's catalogue regularly included editions of *airs* and other compositions by C. Rosier, J. Schenck and others. In 1968 the magistrate in Ghent allowed him to establish himself in the city as a music printer without going through the prescribed period of apprenticeship. According to vander Straeten, he had returned to Holland by 1702. In 1716 he is mentioned in the *Album studiosorum* of Leiden University as 'musicus'. There are two manuscripts containing works of his in the Landesbibliothek at Karlsruhe.

BIBLIOGRAPHY
A. Goovaerts: *Histoire et bibliographie de la typographie musicale dans les anciens Pays-Bas* (Antwerp and Brussels, 1880/*R*1963)
E. vander Straeten: *La musique aux Pays-Bas avant le XIXe siècle*, v (Brussels, 1880/*R*1969), 243ff, 410f
D. F. Scheurleer: 'Eene Amsterdamsche uitgave van Lully en Colasse, 1690', *TVNM*, ix/4 (1914), 250
I. H. Van Eeghen: *De Amsterdamse boekhandel 1680–1725*, iii (Amsterdam, 1965), 202f

HENRI VANHULST

Lechler, Benedikt [Johannes] (*b* Füssen, 24 April 1594; *d* Kremsmünster, 18 Jan 1659). German composer, music copyist and lutenist, resident in Austria. He became a Benedictine monk and changed his first name from Johannes to Benedikt. From 1607 to 1615 he studied at the Jesuit College, Vienna, and then became director of the school at the abbey at Admont, Styria, where he also had charge of the music. In 1617 he went to the Benedictine monastery at Kremsmünster, where he remained for the rest of his life. He was first employed as a lutenist and administrative official. In 1628, after he had become a full member of the Benedictine order, he was given charge of the sacred music; the court music was in the hands of Alessandro Tadei, but after Tadei left, on 20 May 1629, Lechler directed that too. His desire to provide the chapel, school and theatre of the monastery with suitable compositions prompted him to undertake extensive travels in Italy in 1632–3, including a visit to Rome, where he became acquainted with Carissimi. As a result of this journey and of the purchase of many other printed works by Italian and German composers, he gradually compiled four large collections of mainly vocal works, which he copied in score between 1633 and 1650 (they are still at *A-KR*). Almost all the compositions are by composers of the time, including not only the foremost Italians but also many of the more progressive Austrian and south German composers such as Stadlmayr, Christoph Strauss, Pfendner and Kraf. Lechler included a number of his own works, among them masses, requiems, hymns and *Magnificat* settings, many of them dated 1632 or 1633 and thus composed while he was in Italy. As with his choice of transcriptions, they show a fondness for the colourful Venetian polychoral style, with essential use of instruments; the standard of performance demanded by this music shows that musical activity at Kremsmünster reached in his time a degree of supremacy that it probably did not attain again until the mid-18th century. The importance of his work, through his tireless efforts as a scribe, reached far beyond the confines of the abbey itself.

BIBLIOGRAPHY
G. Huemer: *Pflege der Musik im Stift Kremsmünster* (Wels, 1877), 17ff
A. Kellner: *Musikgeschichte des Stiftes Kremsmünster* (Kassel, 1956), 193ff

A. LINDSEY KIRWAN

Lechner, Konrad (*b* Nuremberg, 24 Feb 1911). German composer, conductor, cellist and teacher. He studied at the Munich Musikhochschule from 1929 to 1934 under Hugo Becker (cello), Karl Marx, Orff, J. N. David, Fortner (composition) and Krauss (conducting). He began his career as a cellist at the Bavarian National Theatre in Munich (1934–5); during the years 1941–5 he was a lecturer at the Salzburg Mozarteum, and he was conductor of the Bamberg SO from 1946 to 1948. Since then he has taught at the Freiburg Musikhochschule (1948–53 and from 1970) and at the Darmstadt Academy of Music (1953–70). Having devoted his attention for many years to medieval music (he was a founder-member of the Munich Fideltrio) he emerged as a composer in the 1950s. His music seeks a meaningful union of medieval means (e.g. modes) with modern techniques – at first classical dodecaphony, latterly further serial procedures. The sacred quality present in all of his work links it with Stravinsky's.

WORKS
(selective list)
Requiem, chorus, orch, 1952; Geistliches Konzert, chorus, orch, 1958; 3 Organ Pieces, 1962; Kontraste, chamber orch, 1963; Cantica I, 1v, ens, 1966; Cantica II, 1v, ens, 1971; 3 Stücke, fl, 1972; Studien, vc, 1972–3; Topoi, pf, 1973; Psalm in die paschae, S/T, 1975; 6 Fresken, vc, 1970–76; Perspektiven, fl, pf, 1975–6

Principal publishers: Peters, Gerig

BIBLIOGRAPHY
R. Lück, ed.: *Neue deutsche Klaviermusik* (Cologne, 1974)

RUDOLF LÜCK

Lechner, Leonhard [Lechnerus, Leonardus Athesinus] (*b* valley of the River Adige, South Tyrol, *c*1553; *d* Stuttgart, 9 Sept 1606). German composer and music editor of Austrian birth. He was the leading German composer of choral music in the later 16th century.

1. Life. 2. Character. 3. Works. 4. Reputation.

1. LIFE. The cognomen 'Athesinus', which Lechner always used on the title-pages of his printed volumes and manuscripts, shows that he came from the valley of the River Adige (Athesis). He is first heard of in the accounts of the Bavarian court for 1570 as a chorister in the Hofkapelle of the hereditary Prince Wilhelm at Landshut, which was founded in 1568. It had been disbanded by 1570, and one of those dismissed was Lechner, who received a severance payment of ten florins. The first director of the Landshut Kapelle was Ivo de Vento, previously court organist under Lassus at Munich, and he was followed by Antonius Gosswin. Lechner clearly learnt a great deal from both men, but it was always Lassus whom he later referred to, with gratitude and reverence, as his teacher. Up to 1568, and probably from about 1564, he must therefore have belonged to the Munich Hofkapelle, directed by Lassus, and have lived in Lassus's house with the other choristers. It is doubtful whether he was personally taught by Lassus, since he did not mention this in the preface to his first printed volume of music in 1575 (nor indeed in any other source): he simply stated that his passionate love of music was fired by great models and that he had tried not merely to learn how to sing but also to compose music himself. It is not known where he spent the early 1570s, but in the preface to his Latin motet volume of 1581 he wrote that he had once 'roved far and wide, visiting various places'. It is reasonable to assume that it was during these years of apprenticeship that he did so and, moreover, that he spent some time in Italy: Italian influences are discernible from his earliest compositions onwards, and his anthology *Harmoniae miscellae* (1583), which includes works by 12 Italian composers, some of them virtually unkown in Germany, shows a familiarity with Italian music that he could hardly have acquired without going to Italy.

It is clear from the 1575 preface that at that time Lechner was an assistant teacher at the St Lorenz school, Nuremberg, then the town's largest grammar school. This was a very junior position, which is no doubt why he insisted that he wished to be regarded and judged not as a schoolmaster but as a musician and composer. The town council soon honoured him with the title of 'archimusicus', and his salary, 90 florins a year, was now the same as the Kantor's 'because he is such an outstanding composer and musician'. A number of leading citizens became his patrons and friends during his ten years at Nuremberg; he dedicated to them nearly all the volumes of music that poured from his pen during these years, no doubt for performance in the flourishing musical societies to which they belonged. The works ranged from light three-part Italianate pieces, through German sacred and secular songs for four and five voices to Latin motets and liturgical works; and they included editions and reworkings too. Several of these publications went into more than one edition, while individual pieces appeared in anthologies or circulated in manuscript form. In this way Lechner soon became known as a leading composer far beyond the confines of Nuremberg. He often received commissions to write works for festive occasions, among them the ceremonial opening of Altdorf University in 1575 (the work was published in *Motectae sacrae*), and the magnificent wedding of the Augsburg patrician Sebald

Welser to the daughter of a Nuremberg councillor on 15 January 1582; on the latter occasion there were performances not only of a mass by Lechner – the *Missa prima* of the 1584 volume – but also of an epithalamium for three choirs totalling 24 voices, to a text by Lechner's friend the poet Paul Melissus Schede.

In spite of such honours and fruitful activity, in spite too of the ties of friendship and feelings of gratitude that bound him to Nuremberg, Lechner became increasingly dissatisfied with his subordinate position as an assistant schoolmaster. Having previously rejected a number of other offers, he accepted an invitation in the autumn of 1583 to present himself before Count Eitelfriedrich IV von Hohenzollern-Hechingen, who received him cordially and appointed him his Kapellmeister. Lechner thanked him by dedicating his 1584 volume to him, and he took up his appointment at Hechingen in the spring of that year. The Hofkapelle, though not large, was of a high standard and well equipped, and it seemed that Lechner could look forward to a period of activity no less satisfying than his years at Nuremberg. His salary was 160 florins a year, with additional income in kind, and his duties embraced music for the chamber and for mealtimes on the one hand and for the chapel and church on the other. Difficulties first began to make themselves felt in the matter of church services, for Count Eitelfriedrich was a fervent supporter of the Counter-Reformation, while Lechner was an equally fervent Lutheran (he was converted from Catholicism in his 18th year). The oration delivered at his funeral stated that he had

constantly and steadfastly supported . . . our true Christian religion . . . so that when, for the sake of his art, he was obliged to . . . eke out a living under the papacy he nevertheless expressly refrained from practising the [Catholic] religion and the exercise of its rites, as may be shown by the orders that were drawn up against him and still exist.

This can only refer to Hechingen, the only Catholic court that Lechner served. Denominational differences in Germany at that time had become increasingly polarized. Following the victory of the Catholic princes in the 'Cologne feud' over Archbishop Gebhard Truchsess von Waldburg, who had turned Lutheran, the Counter-Reformation gained ground, and further support came in the form of an endowment of 2000 florins made by Count Eitelfriedrich in 1584, the annual interest on which was intended to allow two boys from his county to study 'with our lords the Jesuits' and thus contribute towards combating 'the seductive and accursed heresies of the Lutherans and Calvinists and similar superstitious religious sects'. This suggests how passionately the count was prepared to persecute supporters of the Reformation, and it is easy to see why Lechner was unwilling to remain for long at his court and soon began looking for another post. In June 1585 he applied unsuccessfully to the Dresden court despite letters of recommendation from Lassus and Duke Wilhelm V of Bavaria.

Since Count Eitelfriedrich was reluctant to lose his Kapellmeister, Lechner soon took advantage of his absence to leave the court secretly. He fled to nearby Tübingen, which lay on Württemberg soil, and he was warmly welcomed there into the circle of the humanist scholar and poet Nikodemus Frischlin. Count Eitelfriedrich tried to persuade him to return in a letter of 25 July 1585 containing a friendly admonition and a promise to release him from his service 'without delay and with every honour and favour'. The following day

Lechner drafted a letter in reply in which he declined to return and threatened that he 'would enlist the help of men of learning' and 'publish details of how things stood at that court'; if the count were to cast aspersions upon him and if he, Lechner, were then forced to answer those charges, he would 'have the very devil to pay'. This letter is so unlike Lechner's other surviving writings – and so exceptional a response of a court servant to his master – that it seems reasonable to assume that the quarrelsome Frischlin, who later, in an academic address, violently attacked the aristocracy and lampooned the rulers of his own country, lent him his moral support in this uncompromising refusal. As a result of it the count became his bitter enemy and sent letters to several princes and to the Nuremberg town council, requesting them to hunt down his runaway Kapellmeister, take him into custody and return him to Hechingen. Lechner, however, sought refuge with Duke Ludwig of Württemberg, convincing him of his innocence and receiving an appointment as a tenor at the Stuttgart Hofkapelle, where he had to make do with a far smaller salary than he had been used to. The duke also supported him in other ways: he used his influence with the Nuremberg council on behalf of Lechner's family there and in January 1586 helped him settle his differences with Count Eitelfriedrich, as a result of which he was able to visit Nuremberg safely and bring his wife and son back with him to Stuttgart. Duke Ludwig authorized grants to cover his increased expenses and rewarded the numerous works he dedicated to him with honoraria of between 6 and 20 florins; there are records of payments to him nearly every year from 1586 to 1600. Some of these works are printed, but most remained in manuscript and are nearly all lost; consequently far less is known of the music of the last 20 years or so of Lechner's life than of that from the previous ten.

In the Stuttgart court records Lechner is described first as 'former Hohenzollern Kapellmeister', then as 'musician', 'tenor', 'member of the Kapelle' and, from 1586 onwards, 'composer'. He was assistant to the Hofkapellmeister, Ludwig Daser, who was succeeded on his death in 1589 by his son-in-law Balduin Hoyoul, by virtue of his seniority. It was only when Hoyoul himself died in November 1594 that Lechner became Hofkapellmeister, and he was officially installed in April 1595. At that time the Kapelle included 24 singers and 24 instrumentalists. The then ruler, Duke Friedrich, issued a service manual entitled *Staat und Ordnung eines Kapellmeisters*, which came into force on 10 May 1595. It contained precise instructions for the education, upkeep and instruction of the eight choristers, who were given board and lodging in the Kapellmeister's house, and much space was given over to strict orders enjoining the musicians, above all the instrumentalists, 'dutifully to obey the Kapellmeister in all musical matters'. It is clear that the achievements of the Kapelle had suffered from a lack of discipline, generally because the instrumentalists disputed the right of the Kapellmeister, who had risen from the ranks of the singers, to criticize their playing and dictate to them. Lechner was soon to discover that this was still true, for on 1 March 1596 he petitioned the duke to command the instrumentalists to perform their duties as he had ordered; otherwise he could accept no responsibility for the inadequacy of their performances. Duke Friedrich immediately issued a decree threatening severe punishments. Lechner was thus able to ensure that the standards of the Kapelle gradually improved and that court festivities once more gave them an opportunity to distinguish themselves. When an English legation came to Stuttgart in November 1603 with its own retinue of musicians in order to hand over to Duke Friedrich the Order of the Garter that had been conferred on him, the two groups of musicians organized a competition, which the Württembergers won, though narrowly.

The fact that Lechner brought about such an improvement in the Hofkapelle is all the more remarkable considering that he was frequently ill during the last years of his life; mention of this fact occurs in the funeral oration, and from 1586 onwards court accounts frequently contain entries relating to payments to him towards a spa tax, showing that he visited various resorts, including what is now Baden-Baden in 1593 and Bad Boll in 1605, in search of a cure. Yet in spite of his ill-health he continued to direct the Kapelle and write music up to the very end of his life. For the marriage of the Württemberg Princess Sibylle Elisabeth and Duke Johann Georg, later the Elector of Saxony, he wrote a large-scale psalm setting, *Laudate Dominum, quoniam bonus est*, for 15 voices divided into three choirs, which was performed at Dresden by members of the Stuttgart Hofkapelle on 16 September 1604. Lechner's illness probably prevented his travelling to Dresden, for by this time he was frequently obliged to hand over direction of the Hofkapelle to the alto Tobias Salomo. In 1604 Salomo described himself in a petition as vice-Kapellmeister, even though he had not officially been so designated; Lechner complained to the duke, but in vain. He died two years later and was buried with great ceremony in the upper Spitalkirche, close to the altar, where only members of the ruling house and the highest court officials were laid to rest.

2. CHARACTER. The oration at Lechner's funeral emphasized that he was 'not only well informed about all matters of religion and faith but was thoroughly versed in them too', for he was in the habit of reading all manner of histories and other books, particularly the Bible and 'works of pure theology'. Kade (1869) was typical of scholars of an earlier age when he saw him as a 'fickle and passionate character' and as an 'easily roused, hot-tempered artist in whom Germanic coarseness mingled with the fiery nature of his foreign blood'. A careful investigation of all relevant sources that have since come to light reveals an essentially different picture. Lechner's letters – except for the one of 1585 from Tübingen to Count Eitelfriedrich (see §1 above) – and the prefaces to his printed works reveal a well-bred, highly cultivated man of superior intellect and some discrimination, whose essential modesty was tempered by a justifiable self-assurance. Like all who hailed from South Tyrol, he was of pure German extraction; that he was not 'fickle' is shown by his ten years of uninterrupted activity at Nuremberg and his 22 years in the service of the dukes of Württemberg. Though a committed Lutheran, he remained tolerant and associated freely with Catholic musicians, performing their works and sending young musicians to advance their education at Catholic courts in Austria and Italy.

3. WORKS. Lechner's first published works, a collection of 30 Latin motets for four to six voices, appeared in 1575, when he cannot have been much more than 20, but they show that he was already a fully mature composer. They show too that he was unmistakably a product of the Lassus school, although there is a certain Italian influence too, particularly in the use of madrigalisms, which he employed more regularly than any of his German and Netherlands contemporaries. The volume also includes an eight-part psalm, which is one of the earliest German examples of Venetian double-choir polyphony. In his Latin sacred works Lechner continued to be heavily indebted to the Netherlands school, but he was always far more than an imitator of Lassus, though he was so regarded until recently.

The individuality of Lechner's style can be more clearly seen in his settings of vernacular texts. He generally based his German villanellas on Italian models which had been introduced to Germany by Ivo de Vento in 1573 and which came into fashion with the work of Jacob Regnart, some of whose three-part pieces he published in five-part versions in 1579. But he began to go his own way in this genre as early as 1576. He refined it by dispensing with obscene texts, while retaining its loosely structured form, and by adopting a solid contrapuntal technique and madrigal-inspired means of expression. By so doing he created a new type of Gesellschaftslied. His four- and five-part secular songs show similar characteristics. The title of his 1586 volume includes the words 'in the style of Italian canzoni'; here too he combined elements of the Netherlands style with those of the Italian madrigal in order to give more intense expression to the spiritual and intellectual content of the texts. This aim is particularly evident in the settings of sacred German texts that he included in his volumes of 1582 and 1589. Certain poems, for instance *Nun schein, du Glanz der Herrlichkeit* and *O Tod, du bist ein bittre Gallen*, exerted a particularly powerful influence on him. In setting them he created a new kind of German song motet and at the same time reached such a pitch of excellence in it that he himself was the only composer to surpass it, in his late works, such as the cycle *Deutsche Sprüche von Leben und Tod*. The late works, which survive in a manuscript of 1606, consist in the main of four- and five-part settings of German words which show that he pursued his own independent course and was in advance of his time and unique in the forms he used. He was the first composer to set a complete cycle of German poems. He collaborated with the leading poets of his day; in Nuremberg he worked with Schede and the goldsmith Paul Dulner, who both provided him with texts which in power of language and imagery were far superior to all other contemporary German verse. Some of the other texts in the 1606 manuscript are most probably by Georg Rudolf Weckherlin (1584–1653), the brother-in-law of Lechner's son, Gabriel, and are no less impressive.

With Lechner's four-part Passion of 1593, his most extensive work, the German motet Passion reached its peak. Its full title, given in a print cited in book fair catalogues but either lost or never published, emphasized that he had based it on 'the old Latin church tone'. This Passion tone moves from one voice to another, thus constantly repeating itself, whereas it is not used at all in other German motet Passions. In this respect Lechner revealed his debt to liturgical tradition, while at the same time using a particularly free form and introducing every stylistic means at his disposal so that the Gospel narrative is endowed with devotional fervour and compassion and impresses itself all the more poignantly upon the listener.

4. REPUTATION.

The rediscovery during the past 50 years of much of Lechner's work has revealed the extent to which he managed to reconcile a commitment to tradition with the freedom of artistic creativity. The personal style of his late works was known to few of his contemporaries. Christoph Demantius included these lines of verse in his first published volume of secular music in 1595: 'Orlandus valuit permultum cantibus olim, Langius et Lechner non valuere minus'. The comparison with Lassus was obviously intended to flatter Lechner; Gregor Lange seems then to have been overrated. Lechner's earlier works at least were widely known, and some of them were mentioned by theorists as models and examples, but his music soon fell into oblivion, mainly because of fundamental changes in style that coincided with the introduction of the continuo about 1600. The renewed interest in early music in the 19th century brought to light only a few of his minor works. His life was investigated, but prejudice, allied to inadequate knowledge of the sources, led to mistaken judgments and misinterpretations. It was not until his fine later works were rediscovered in 1926 that the way was open for a true evaluation of him. A complete edition was inaugurated in 1954 and has facilitated the appreciation of him at his true worth as a leading German composer of choral music.

WORKS

Edition: *L. Lechner: Werke*, ed. K. Ameln and others (Kassel, 1954–) [A]

(published in Nuremberg unless otherwise stated)

SACRED VOCAL

Motectae sacrae, 4–6vv, . . . addita est in fine motecta, 8vv (2 choirs) (1575); A i

Sanctissimae virginis Mariae canticum, quod vulgo Magnificat inscribitur, secundum octo vulgares tonos, 4vv (1578); A iv

Sacrarum cantionum, liber secundus, 5, 6vv (1581); [A vi]

Liber missarum . . . adjunctis aliquot introitibus in praecipua festa, ab Adventu Domini usque ad festum Sanctissimae Trinitatis, 5, 6vv (1584); A viii

Septem psalmi poenitentiales . . . additis aliis quibusdam piis cantionibus, 6 and more vv (1587); [A x]

3 motets, 1583² [see 'Editions']

Historia der Passion und Leidens Christi, 4vv, perf. Stuttgart, 1593, *D-Kl* [announced in Messkatalog of 1594 as pubd Nuremberg, 1594; edn. lost or possibly never pubd]; A xii

LIEDER

Neu teutsche Lieder, nach art der welschen Villanellen gantz kurtzweilig zu singen, auch auff allerley Seytenspil zu gebrauchen, 3vv (1576, 3/1586 as part of Der erst und ander Theil der teutschen Villanellen); A ii

Der ander Theyl neuer teutscher Lieder, nach art der welschen Villanellen, 3vv (1577, 2/1586 as part of Der erst und ander Theil der teutschen Villanellen); A ii

Neue teutsche Lieder, 4, 5vv (1577) [incl. sacred lieder]; A iii

Neue teutsche Lieder, erstlich durch . . . Jacobum Regnart . . . componirt mit drey Stimmen, nach art der welschen Villanellen, jetzund aber . . . mit fünff Stimmen gesetzet . . . con alchuni madrigali in lingua Italiana, 5vv (1579); A v

Neue teutsche Lieder, 4, 5vv (1582) [incl. sacred lieder]; A vii

Neue lustige teutsche Lieder nach art der welschen Canzonen, 4vv (1586); A ix

Neue geistliche und weltliche teutsche Lieder, 4, 5vv (1589); [A xi]

3 sacred and secular Lieder, 4vv, 1585³⁷

Neue geistliche und weltliche deutsche Gesänge samt 2 lateinischen, 4, 5vv, MS dated 1606, *D-Kl* (inc.); A xiii

SECULAR VOCAL

Madrigal, 5vv, 1585¹⁷

OCCASIONAL

Illustrissimo heroi ac domino . . . Ioachimo Ernesto, antiquissimi stemmatis Anhaldini . . . harmoniam hanc panegyricam composuit, 6vv (1582); [A xiv–xv]

Eadem epitaphia (Martini Crusii), musicis modis, 6vv, in Martini Crusii . . . De imp. rom. Friderico . . . Barbarossa . . . oratio (Tübingen, 1593); [A xiv–xv]

3 wedding works, 6, 15, 24vv, perf. Nuremberg, 1582–3, Dresden, 1604; motet in honour of August, Elector of Saxony, 6vv, 1585: *Dla, Ngm,* Welser-Archiv, Neunhof, nr. Nuremberg [A xiv–xv]

Wedding work, 5vv, Nuremberg, 1582, lost

EDITIONS

Harmoniae miscellae cantionum sacrarum, 5, 6vv (Nuremberg, 1583²)

O. de Lassus: Selectissimae cantiones, 6 and more vv [2 parts] (Nuremberg, 1579)

Lassus: Liber missarum, 4, 5vv (Nuremberg, 1581)

BIBLIOGRAPHY

EitnerQ; *WaltherML*

E. Grüninger: *Christliche Leichpredigt bey der Begraebnuss weylund des . . . Leonhardi Lechneri, fuerstlichen wuertembergischen Capellmeisters. Gehalten zu Stuttgarten in der Spitalkirchen den 11. Sept. Anno 1606* (Tübingen, 1607)

O. Kade: 'Leonhard Lechner und sein Streit mit dem Grafen Eitel Friedrich von Hohenzollern im Jahre 1585', *MMg*, i (1869), esp. 179

M. Fürstenau: 'Kurfürst August von Sachsen, Graf Eitel Friedrich von Hohenzollern-Hechingen und der Kapellmeister Leonhard Lechner', *Mitteilungen des Königlich Sächsischen Vereins für Erforschung und Erhaltung vaterländischer Geschichts- und Kunstdenkmäler*, xx (1870), 55

R. Eitner: 'Leonhard Lechner', *MMg*, x (1878), esp. 137

J. Sittard: *Zur Geschichte der Musik und des Theaters am württembergischen Hofe*, i (Stuttgart, 1890/*R*1970)

A. Sandberger: *Beiträge zur Geschichte der bayerischen Hofkapelle unter Orlando di Lasso*, i, iii (Leipzig, 1894–5)

P. Manns: *Geschichte der Grafschaft Hohenzollern im 15. und 16. Jahrhundert* (Hechingen, 1897)

K. Vossler: *Das deutsche Madrigal: Geschichte seiner Entwicklung bis in die Mitte des 18. Jahrhunderts* (Weimar, 1898)

G. Bossert: 'Die Hofkantorei unter Herzog Ludwig', *Württembergische Vierteljahrshefte für Landesgeschichte*, new ser., ix (1900)

A. Sandberger: Introduction to DTB, v/1 (1904/*R*)

G. Bossert: 'Die Hofkapelle unter Herzog Friedrich', *Württembergische Vierteljahrshefte für Landesgeschichte*, new ser., xix (1910)

R. Velten: *Das ältere deutsche Gesellschaftslied unter dem Einfluss der italienischen Musik* (Heidelberg, 1914)

T. W. Werner: 'Die im Herzoglichen Hausarchiv zu Zerbst aufgefundenen Musikalien aus der zweiten Hälfte des 16. Jahrhunderts', *ZMw*, ii (1919–20), 681–724

G. Müller: *Geschichte des deutschen Liedes vom Zeitalter des Barock bis zur Gegenwart* (Munich, 1925)

J. Neyses: *Studien zur Geschichte der deutschen Motette des 16. Jahrhunderts*, ii: *Die Motetten-Sammlungen Leonhard Lechners von 1575 und 1581* (diss., U. of Bonn, 1927)

H. J. Moser: 'Das deutsche Chorlied zwischen Senfl und Hassler als Beispiel eines Stilwandels', *JbMP 1928*, 43

F. Blume: *Die evangelische Kirchenmusik*, HMw (1931, rev. 2/1965 as *Geschichte der evangelischen Kirchenmusik*; Eng. trans., enlarged, 1974, as *Protestant Church Music: a History*)

M. Schreiber: *Leonhard Lechner Athesinus 1553–1606: sein Leben und seine Kirchenmusik* (Birkeneck, nr. Freising, 1932)

A. A. Abert: *Die stilistischen Voraussetzungen der 'Cantiones sacrae' von Heinrich Schütz* (Wolfenbüttel, 1935)

W. Scheer: *Die Frühgeschichte der Villanelle* (diss., U. of Cologne, 1935)

M. Schreiber: *Die Kirchenmusik des Kapellmeisters Leonhard Lechner Athesinus* (Regensburg, 1935)

H. Osthoff: *Die Niederländer und das deutsche Lied 1400–1640* (Berlin, 1938/*R*1967)

L. Hübsch-Pfleger: *Das Nürnberger Lied im deutschen Stilwandel um 1600* (diss., U. of Heidelberg, 1942)

B. P. Baader: *Der bayerische Renaissancehof Herzog Wilhelms V.* (Leipzig and Strasbourg, 1943)

K. Ameln: 'Herkunft und Datierung der Handschrift Mus. fol. 15 der Landesbibliothek Kassel: Leonhard Lechner, Johannes-Passion', *Mf*, vi (1953), 156

——: Lechners Lebenswerk und seine Beurteilung im Wandel der Zeit', *Hausmusik*, xvii (1953), 2

——: 'Leonhard Lechners Bekenntnis', *Musik und Kirche*, xxiii (1953), 19

G. Reichert: 'Martin Crusius und die Musik in Tübingen um 1590', *AMw*, x (1953), 185

U. Martin: 'Der Nürnberger Paul Dulner als Dichter geistlicher und weltlicher Lieder Leonhard Lechners', *AMw*, xi (1954), 315

K. Ameln: 'Leonhard Lechner', *Musik und Kirche*, xxvi (1956), 223

——: *Leonhard Lechner (um 1553–1606): Leben und Werk eines deutschen Komponisten aus dem Etschtal* (Lüdenscheid, 1957)

U. Martin: *Historische und stilkritische Studien zu Leonhard Lechners Strophenliedern* (diss., U. of Göttingen, 1957)

E. F. Schmid: 'Hohenzollern', §5, *MGG*

B. Smallman: *The Background of Passion Music* (London, 1957), 27, 118; (rev., enlarged 2/1970)

W. Boetticher: *Orlando di Lasso und seine Zeit (1532–1594)* (Kassel, 1958)

U. Martin: 'Die Nürnberger Musikgesellschaften', *Mitteilungen des Vereins für die Geschichte der Stadt Nürnberg*, xlix (1959), 185–225

K. Ameln: 'Lechner, Leonhard', *MGG*

——: 'Leonhard Lechner, ein eigenwüchsiger Meister der deutschen Chormusik', *Württembergische Blätter für Kirchenmusik*, xxvii (1960), 117

——: 'Leonhard Lechner, Kapellmeister und Komponist, um 1553–1606', *Lebensbilder aus Schwaben und Franken*, vii (1960), 69

H. Weber: *Die Beziehungen zwischen Musik und Text in den lateinischen Motetten Leonhard Lechners* (diss., U. of Hamburg, 1961)

E. F. Schmid: *Musik an den schwäbischen Zollernhöfen der Renaissance* (Kassel, 1962)

W. Boetticher: *Aus Orlando di Lassos Wirkungskreis: neue archivalische Studien zur Münchener Musikgeschichte* (Kassel, 1963)

H. Zirnbauer: *Musik in der alten Reichsstadt Nürnberg: Ikonographie zur Nürnberger Musikgeschichte* (Nuremberg, 1965)

K. Ameln: 'Leonhard Lechner in his Time', *Cantors at the Crossroads: Essays on Church Music in Honor of Walter E. Buszin* (St Louis, 1967), 75

——: ' "Ohn Gott muss ich mich aller Freuden massen": eine Villanellenweise von Leonhard Lechner als Gemeindelied', *Jb für Liturgik und Hymnologie*, xiv (1969), 190

W. Blankenburg: 'Zu den Johannes-Passionen von Ludwig Daser (1578) und Leonhard Lechner (1593)', *Musa–mens–musici: im Gedenken an Walther Vetter* (Leipzig, 1969), 63

C. Gottwald: 'Humanisten-Stammbücher als musikalische Quellen', *Helmuth Osthoff zu seinem siebzigsten Geburtstag* (Tutzing, 1969), 89

KONRAD AMELN

Leckingfield Proverbs. A collection of verses from *GB-Lbm* R.M.18.D.2, entitled 'The Proverbis in the Garet at the New Lodge in the Parke of Leckingfelde'. They are believed to have been inscribed on the walls and ceilings of the 'garet' (or gallery) of this building, part of the Yorkshire estate of Henry Percy, 5th Earl of Northumberland (1487–1527). There are 32 quatrains in rhyming couplets and irregular metre: ten refer to musical instruments; the remainder deal with the performing, composing, copying and criticizing of music, and with its philosophical aspects. A good selection was printed by F. M. C. Cooper: 'The Leckingfield Proverbs', *MT*, cxiii (1972), 547. The whole collection is invested with an allegorical significance; the quality of the verse is poor and the information imparted minimal.

JOHN CALDWELL

Leclair. French family of violinists and composers. Of the eight children of Antoine Leclair, master lacemaker and cellist, and Benoîte Ferrier, the musical careers of six can be traced. Four are separately noted below; Jeanne (1699–after 1762) was a player and teacher of the violin in Lyons, and François (1705–after 1762) was a professional musician there.

(1) Jean-Marie Leclair [*l'aîné*] (*b* Lyons, 10 May 1697; *d* Paris, 22 Oct 1764). French composer, violinist and dancer; considered the founder of the French violin school.

1. LIFE. Before his 19th year, Leclair mastered violin playing, dancing and lacemaking. He was then listed among the dancers at the Lyons opera, together with Marie-Rose Casthagnié whom he married on 9 November 1716. He may also have been active as a dancer and violinist in Rouen, where according to Gerber (1790) his patron was Mme Mezangère (La Laurencie however doubted the Rouen connection).

Leclair's earliest known music appears in a manuscript anthology of 1721 containing 69 violin sonatas by French and Italian composers (*US-CA*). He is represented by ten sonatas (later published in his opp.1 and 2). These are hardly the work of a neophyte, and the Parisian origin of the anthology suggests Leclair's presence in that city. He was in Turin in 1722 (if a 19th-century report of a now lost libretto is correct), where he may have been drawn by employment at royal wed-

1. Jean-Marie Leclair: engraving (1741) by Jean-Charles François after Alexis Loir

ding festivities; he was evidently active there as a ballet-master, though he did not hold an official position. Possibly he received violin lessons from G. B. Somis.

Going to Paris in 1723, Leclair came under the patronage of one of the richest men in France, Joseph Bonnier, while he prepared his op.1 for publication. These sonatas were recognized for their originality and, according to one contemporary, they 'appeared at first a kind of algebra capable of rebuffing the most courageous musicians'. Another wrote: 'Le Clair est le premier qui sans imiter rien, Créa du beau, du neuf, qu'il peut dire le sien'.

In June 1726 J. J. Quantz visited Turin where, he noted in his diary, Leclair was studying with Somis. Leclair provided ballets (now lost) as postludes to two operas at the Teatro Regio Ducale, Turin, in 1727. In Paris the following year he published a second book of violin sonatas and made his début with ten appearances at the Concert Spirituel, where he was vigorously applauded in performances of his own sonatas and concertos. He also travelled to London, where John Walsh issued a book of his sonatas, and to Kassel, where he performed at court with Pietro Locatelli. This performance may have been an enactment of the battle between the French and Italian styles which so interested writers of the period. J. W. Lustig recounted that Leclair played 'like an angel' and Locatelli 'like a devil'; that Leclair employed extreme rhythmic freedom and moved his listeners by the beauty of his tone, while Locatelli astonished his listeners with a deliberately scratchy tone and left-hand pyrotechnics. Leclair apparently worked with Locatelli at this time, perhaps returning to Amsterdam with him; 18th-century commentators noted Locatelli's influence in the sonatas of op.5.

Another of his teachers at this period was the Parisian composer, harpsichordist and conductor André Chéron, to whom he subsequently dedicated his op.7.

Leclair's first wife had died childless, and on 8 September 1730 he married Louise Roussel, who engraved his op.2 and all his subsequent works. Their only child, Louise, also an engraver, married the painter Louis Quenet.

Numerous performances and publications in Paris led to official recognition when late in 1733 Leclair was appointed by Louis XV *ordinaire de la musique du roi*. He responded by dedicating to the king his third book of violin sonatas, of which the sixth in C minor (later dubbed 'Le tombeau') is his best-known composition. In his new capacity Leclair associated with some of the best French musicians of the day, including his friend the viol player Antoine Forqueray and his rival Pierre Guignon. The court favoured older French music – Lully for the chamber, Lalande for the chapel – but Leclair was allowed at least once to perform one of his concertos for the queen's entourage, when 'his delicate and brilliant playing was greatly applauded'. This employment ended in 1737 when Leclair and Guignon quarrelled over the directorship of the king's orchestra. The two agreed to alternate monthly, with Leclair leading off; but after the first month he resigned and left Paris rather than sit second to Guignon.

Leclair next accepted an invitation to the court of Orange in the Netherlands from Anne, Princess of Orange and daughter of George II of England. Princess Anne had become an accomplished harpsichordist under Handel's tutelage; their mutual esteem may be surmised from his dedication to her of his op.9 and her decorating him with the Croix Néerlandaise du Lion. From 1738 to 1743 Leclair spent three months each year at the court. After July 1740 the remaining nine months were spent at The Hague, where he had become *maestro di cappella* to a wealthy commoner, François du Liz, who maintained an establishment of 20 musicians. This arrangement ended with Du Liz's bankruptcy in January 1743; Leclair returned to Paris to publish his fourth and final book of violin sonatas. In 1744 he spent some time in Chambéry playing for the Spanish Prince Don Philippe, to whom he subsequently dedicated op.10. He then returned to Paris, and remained there, apart from an occasional visit to Lyons.

Leclair spent the next few years in semi-retirement, on a pension from the Bonnier de la Mosson family, teaching the violin and composing. On 4 October 1746, in his 50th year, his only opera, *Scylla et Glaucus*, had its première at the Académie Royale de Musique. In his letter of dedication he wrote 'Today I enter upon a new career', surely an allusion to Rameau who similarly embarked on an operatic career in his 51st year. Leclair's opera, stylistically in the Rameau tradition, was well received and had 18 performances in two months but was then dropped from the repertory.

In 1748 Leclair was called into the service of his former pupil, the Duke of Gramont. He became composer and musical director of the duke's private theatre at Puteaux, a suburb of Paris, and held that position until his death. He wrote a variety of vocal and instrumental pieces for the duke's theatre, all now lost. About 1758 Leclair and his wife parted and set up separate households, Leclair buying a small house in a dangerous part of Paris. He was murdered late one evening in 1764 as he entered his house. The Paris police conducted a thorough investigation and found

2. *Opening of Sonata no.8 in D from Jean-Marie Leclair's 'Second livre de sonates' (c1728)*

three suspects: the gardener who found the body; Leclair's nephew, Guillaume-François Vial, with whom he had fallen out; and Mme Leclair herself. The murder is often said to be shrouded in mystery, but the evidence (in the French Archives Nationales) is so clearly against the nephew, who was a violinist and the author of *L'arbre généalogique de l'harmonie* (1767), that the only remaining mystery is that he was never brought to trial.

2. WORKS. Leclair's achievement as a composer lay in his modification of the Corellian sonata style to accommodate French taste. The result was the *goûts réunis* prophesied by Couperin, the *vermischter Geschmack* later recommended by Quantz. He imbued the Italian sonata style with elements drawn from the Lullian dance and from the *pièce* of the French viol players and harpsichordists. Leclair was often able to combine the two styles and to arrive at a new synthesis. In this he was a child of his time, for comparable syntheses were attempted by many of his contemporaries. Leclair was one of the most successful. In his concertos he stayed close to Vivaldian models in the fast movements, more often introducing the French taste in the slow movements.

In his melody Leclair ranged from the *détaché* style of the Lullian dances and French viol players to the cantabile melodies of the Italian violinists, with a moderately ornamented line, fully written out. His melodic style shows a preference for an accumulation of shorter phrases as compared with the seamless *Fortspinnung* of Bach; shorn of their overlay of Rococo ornamentation, his melodic lines show a basic structure and style close to that of such models as Corelli and Lully. His harmony is varied and colourful, and includes occasional bold strokes such as enharmonic modulations and intensely chromatic progressions. One cannot speak of an 'early' or 'late' style in Leclair's music. His remarkably consistent style was as advanced in 1723 as it was outmoded in 1753. Although none of his works can be dated other than by the *terminus ad quem* provided by their first appearance, there is some evidence that Leclair, like Corelli, composed the bulk of his music early in his career and published it little by little; the increase in harmonic complexity found by Preston in the four books of violin sonatas is probably due to Leclair's preferring to publish the less problematic works first. He handled the favourite forms of the period with mastery, though without introducing innovations or prefiguring the development of the 'sonata form' of the early Classical style.

Technically, Leclair made considerable demands. For the left hand there were excursions into high positions, multiple stops (for virtually entire movements), double trills, and left-hand tremolo (its earliest appearance). The bow arm had to master tied-bow staccatos, rapid string crossings and a variety of subtle articulations. In his own day Leclair was renowned for his brilliant and accurate performance of multiple stops. Insofar as he wrote out his ornaments and sometimes required the use of *notes inégales*, Leclair performed in the French tradition. But in most aspects of violin technique, including his use of the longer, so-called 'Tartini bow', his manner of performance was Italian. An account of 1738 praised his ability to play well in either style.

Leclair's pupils – leaving aside a number of noble dilettantes – included L'abbé *le fils*, Elisabeth de Haulteterre, Petit, Geoffroy, Guillaume-Pierre Dupont, Jean-Joseph Rudolphe and, perhaps, Gaviniès and Le Chevalier de Saint-Georges (but not, as erroneously claimed, Dauvergne or Mahoni dit Le Breton). Leclair is rightly considered the first great figure of the French violin school, and his influence on French violinists persisted to the end of the 18th century.

WORKS
(all published in Paris)

op.

[1] Premier livre de sonates (a, C, B♭, D, A, e, F, G, A, D, B♭, b), vn, bc (1723), 2 also for fl; ed. A. Guilmant and J. Debroux as op.3 (Paris, 1905/R)

[2] Second livre de sonates (e, F, C, A, G, D, B♭, D, E, c, b, g), vn, bc (c1728), 5 also for fl; ed. in PÄMw, xxvii (1903/R1966)

3 Sonates (G, A, C, F, e, D), 2 vn/tr viols (1730); ed. M. Pincherle (Paris, 1924); ed. S. Beck (New York, 1946); ed. Rost (Locarno, Wilhelmshaven and Amsterdam, 1963)

4 Sonates en trio (d, B♭, d, F, g, A), 2 vn, bc (c1731–3); ed. M. Pincherle (Paris, 1922)

5 Troisième livre de sonates (A, F, e, B♭, b, c, a, D, E, C, g, G), vn, bc (1734); ed. in RRMBE, iv–v (1968–9)

6 Première recréation de musique d'une exécution facile (D), 2 vn, bc (1736) [suite with ov.]; ed. H. Ruf (Kassel, 1976)

7 6 concertos (d, D, C, F, a, A), vn, str, bc (1737), no.3 for fl/ob, str, bc

8 Deuxième recréation de musique d'une exécution facile (g), 2 rec/vn, bc (c1737) [suite with ov.]; ed. H. Ruf (Kassel, 1967)

9 Quatrième livre de sonates (A, e, D, A, a, D, G, C, E♭, f, g, G), vn, bc (1743), 6 pubd as op.1 (London, c1755); ed. in RRMBE, x–xi (1969–72)

10 6 concertos (B♭, A, D, F, e, g), vn, str, bc (1745)

11 Scylla et Glaucus (opéra tragédie, prol, 5, d'Albaret), Paris, Académie Royale de Musique, 4 Oct 1746, MS with autograph corrections, *F-Po*; score pubd (1746); rev. Lyons, Concert de l'Académie des Beaux-Arts, c1755, see Vallas

12 Second livre de sonates (b, E, D, A, g, B♭), 2 vn/tr viols (c1747–9); ed. M. Pincherle (Paris, 1950)

13 [3] Ouvertures et [3] sonates en trio (G, D, D, b, A, g), 2 vn, bc (1753); ov. no.3 is arr. ov. to 1746 Scylla et Glaucus; sonata no.1 is arr. op.2 no.8; no.2 is arr. op.1 no.12; no.3 is arr. op.2 no.12

[14] Trio (A), 2 vn, bc (1766), posth. [suite with ov.]; ov. is ?arr. ov. to c1755 Scylla et Glaucus; 2nd movt arr. from op.9 no.11; 3rd movt arr. from prol to Scylla et Glaucus; 4th movt arr. from op.5 no.4

[15] Sonate (F), vn, bc (1767), posth.; ed. in RRMBE, xi (1972); see Preston (1967)

2 minuets, vn, bc, in [Ir](-IXe) Recueil de menuets nouveaux français et italiens tels qu'ils se dansent aux bals de l'Opéra (Paris, 1740s)

Other pieces by Leclair pubd in 18th-century anthologies are reprs. of movts from pubd works with op. nos.

Lost: ballet music for G. M. Orlandini's Semiramide, Turin, Regio, carn. 1722, lib also lost, ? same music as ballet music for D. Sarro's Didone abbandonata, Turin, Regio, carn. 1727, lib pubd; ballet music for Orlandini's Antigona, Turin, Regio, carn. 1727, lib pubd; Près des bois enchantés (cantata), poem pubd in *Mercure de France* (Jan 1736), music announced for publication, Paris, 1767; divertissement for Le danger des épreuves (comedy, 1, J. de La Porte or Senneterre), Paris, de Puteaux, 19 June 1749, lib pubd (Paris, 1749); Apollon et Climène, 2nd entrée of Amusements lyriques, Paris, de Puteaux, Feb 1750, lib pubd (Paris, 1750); arias and dances for several Fr. plays perf. in Paris, de Puteaux, 1751–64, unpubd, see La Laurencie, Pincherle; Tablature idéale du violon jugée par feu M. le Clair l'aîné être la seule véritable (Paris, 1766)

(2) Jean-Marie Leclair [*le second*; *le cadet*] (*b* Lyons, 23 Sept 1703; *d* Lyons, 30 Nov 1777). French violinist and composer. In 1732 the city councillors of Besançon engaged him as director of their Académie de Musique, but the city fathers of Lyons lured him back after less than a year with the offer of an annual pension. In return Leclair agreed to remain at Lyons as director of the Académie des Beaux-Arts and to teach the violin to anyone requiring lessons. In all this he was so successful that in 1741 the city fathers augmented his pension and passed an appreciative motion which read in part:

His talent for playing the violin, with a perfection which daily brings him approbation, leaves the public nothing to desire. Such a talent is of considerable importance in sustaining the concerts and the Opéra of this city, since by his efforts the instrumental music in both places is performed in a much more regulated manner. Besides, he daily trains youngsters of good family in the art of violin-playing, so that one can say that persons of all ages profit from Mr Leclair's ability.

The honour and financial rewards accorded Leclair by the people of Lyons were accompanied by a growing reputation elsewhere. In 1738 a report published in Paris listed him among French violinists who 'already have a great reputation', and the following year he published a book of 12 violin sonatas, dedicated to Camille Perrichon, Louis XV's commandant for Lyons. On 25 January 1748 he married Jeanne-Suzanne Crus de la Chesnée; they had a son in 1749 and a daughter in 1751. Around this time Leclair's op.2, six sonatas for two violins or viols, was published. The rest of his life was spent peacefully in Lyons. The syndics of the Lyons Concert named him secretary in perpetuity and from time to time performed his works. There is mention of such works as Le Rhône et la Saône, a 'Divertissement champêtre' (1736), and in 1768 a 'symphony', some arias and a motet, but all of these works are lost.

Leclair's published music suggests that he was an excellent violinist as well as an able composer. Many movements have a decided charm, but others are pedestrian. The style of the music is close to that of Jean-Marie *l'aîné*. According to Marpurg (1754) Jean-Marie *le second* was as great a virtuoso as Jean-Marie *l'aîné*; as a composer, however, he was but a pale reflection of his older brother.

WORKS

Premier livre de sonates (e, G, F, A, G, B♭, A, D, g, C, a, E), vn, bc, op.1 (Paris, 1739)

Sonates (A, D, E, G, F, D), 2 vn/tr viols, op.2 (Paris, c1750)

Le Rhône et la Saône (cantata, P. Dubruit de Charville), Lyons, 1730s; lost, see Vallas, 187

Divertissement champêtre (anon.), Lyons, 1736; lost, see Vallas

1 motet, 14 Dec 1768; 1 symphonie, 2 March 1768; ariettes avec orchestre, 13 July, 7 Sept, 23 Nov 1768: all lost, see Vallas, 195

(3) Pierre Leclair (*b* Lyons, 19 Nov 1709; *d* Lyons, 2 April 1784). French violinist and composer. He spent most of his life as a violinist in Lyons. He married on 30

January 1730. A certain 'Pr. Le Claire, of Lyons' was active as an engraver of music in Ghent around 1750; this may be the same man. In 1764 Pierre, living in Versailles, published his op.1, *Six sonates de récréation à deux violons*. His op.2, also violin duets, remained in manuscript (*F-LYm*). He died poor and was given a pauper's burial.

(4) **Jean-Benoît Leclair** (*b* Lyons, 25 Sept 1714; *d* after 1759). French *comédien*, violinist and composer. He appeared, with his father and two older brothers, among the musicians performing in the annual *Voeu du Roi* in Lyons on 8 August 1735. On 1 August 1736 the city of Moulins engaged him as director of its newly formed Académie de Musique and offered a position to his fiancée, Catherine (Pierrette) de la Porte: the couple married a fortnight later in Moulins. Their contract was to run 'until 1 January 1738 at least'; by July 1737, however, they had left Moulins, and by February 1739 were back in Lyons, where they had a daughter and were proprietors of a shop.

Nearly a decade later Leclair was head of a travelling troupe of actors, dancers and musicians. His troupe played at Louvain in 1748, at Brussels and Liège in 1749, at Ghent in 1750, at Liège again in 1750–51, at Utrecht in 1751 and finally at Liège once more in 1758–9. His activity as composer is known only from the libretto of a divertissement performed on 27 April 1749 in Brussels to celebrate the return of Duke Charles of Lorraine from the negotiation of a peace treaty. The work, a *ballet héroïque* entitled *Le retour de la paix dans les Pays-Bas* (B. de la Roche), was composed and directed by Leclair, and the dancers included three of his children.

BIBLIOGRAPHY
L. de La Laurencie: *L'école française de violon de Lully à Viotti* (Paris, 1922–4/*R*1971)
L. Vallas: *Un siècle de musique et de théâtre à Lyon 1688–1789* (Lyons, 1932/*R*1972)
E. Appia: 'The Violin Sonatas of Leclair', *Score* (1950), no.3, p.3
M. Pincherle: *Jean-Marie Leclair l'aîné* (Paris, 1952)
M. Lemoine: 'La technique violonistique de Jean-Marie Leclair', *ReM* (1955), no.225, p.117
R. E. Preston: 'The Treatment of Harmony in the Violin Sonatas of Jean-Marie Leclair', *RMFC*, iii (1963), 131
G. Nutting: 'Jean-Marie Leclair, 1697–1764', *MQ*, l (1964), 504
J.-F. Paillard: 'Les concertos de Jean-Marie Leclair', *Chigiana*, xxi (1964), 47
N. Zaslaw: 'Some Notes on Jean-Benoît Leclair', *RBM*, xix (1965), 97
R. E. Preston: 'Leclair's Posthumous Solo Sonata: an Enigma', *RMFC*, vii (1967), 155
N. Zaslaw: 'Handel and Leclair', *CMc* (1969), no.9, p.184
C. Pierre: *Histoire du Concert spirituel 1725–1790* (Paris, 1975)
N. Zaslaw: 'Leclair's "Scylla and Glaucus"', *MT*, cxx (1979), 900
NEAL ZASLAW

Le Clerc, Charles-Nicolas (*b* Sézanne en Brie, 20 Oct 1697; *d* Paris, 20 Oct 1774). French violinist and music publisher, brother of Jean-Pantaléon Le Clerc. The brothers have often been confused owing to the similarity of their activities and the infrequent use of Jean-Pantaléon's first name. Charles-Nicolas Le Clerc's name appears for the first time in the list of violinists of the Académie Royale de Musique in 1729 and in that of the 24 Violons du Roi in 1732. He held the former post until 22 May 1750 and the latter until 1761. His talents as a violinist were frequently mentioned during that period in accounts of concerts published in the *Mercure de France*.

Le Clerc began publishing music in 1736 and remained in the business until his death; the first privileges registered in his name date from 9 March

1736 and 17 November 1738; his first catalogue (1738) shows an impressive list of works. His shop was in the rue St-Honoré and bore the signs 'A la Ville de Constantinople' (1737–8), 'A l'Image Ste Geneviève' (1759–60) and 'A Ste Cecile' (1760–74). The fact that he specialized in music publishing indicates that he was something of a pioneer, and also distinguishes his career from that of his brother and the Boivin dealers (primarily commission agents). The only works he sold to the public were those he had commissioned and had engraved. After 1760 he became a commission agent. He was the first in France to have the idea of establishing a repertory of engraved works on which he had sole rights, following the principle which Ballard had been applying for generations with printed music. He published largely foreign music by well-known Italian, German and Flemish composers; some French composers (e.g. J.-M. Leclair and Guillemain) were also listed. Up to 1760 he published mainly instrumental music, later including *opéras comiques*, ariettas and *cantatilles*. His music stock was sold in lots by his widow a few months after his death. One lot was bought in December 1774 by Mathon de la Cour on behalf of the Bureau du Journal de Musique and another in February 1775 by the composer Taillart the elder.

BIBLIOGRAPHY
M. Brenet: 'Quelques musiciens français du XVIIIème siècle: les Le Clerc', *RHCM*, vi (1906), 291
G. Cucuel: 'Notes sur quelques musiciens, luthiers, éditeurs et graveurs de musique au XVIIIe siècle', *SIMG*, xiii (1911–12), 385
C. Hopkinson: *A Dictionary of Parisian Music Publishers 1700–1930* (London, 1954)
A. Devriès: *Edition et commerce de la musique gravée à Paris dans la première moitié du XVIIIe siècle: les Boivin, les Leclerc* (Geneva, 1976)
ANIK DEVRIÈS

Leclerc, Félix (*b* La Tuque, Quebec, 2 Aug 1914). Canadian songwriter, singer and writer. He began his career as a radio announcer in the late 1930s and then joined the CBC in Montreal as writer and producer. Although he had little musical training, he began to write songs to his own poems. He was heard in Montreal by Jacques Canetti, who brought him to Paris in 1950 to make a successful début at l'ABC where he remained for five weeks. Subsequently he toured in France and Switzerland. In 1951, his song *Moi, mes souliers* was awarded a Grand Prix du Disque by the Académie Charles Cros. He became known in Europe as 'le Canadien', and was the first French-Canadian chansonnier to achieve wide recognition in the French-speaking world. In his songs he follows no popular trends and avoids sophistication in both text and music. With a deep, robust baritone voice he sings of Quebec's landscape, people and customs. To one critic, his songs 'smacked of the rich damp earth, of the forests and lakes, of ripe apples and of new-mown hay'.

GILLES POTVIN

Le Clerc [Leclercq], Jacques (*b* Langres; *d* St Pierre de Melun, 1 Jan 1679). French writer on music. He was a Benedictine monk of the congregation of St Maur; he professed to the order at St Augustin, Limoges, on 20 April 1647. He served as sub-prior of the abbey of Sainte Trinité, Vendôme. He is chiefly known for the misattribution to him in early literature of P.-B. de Jumilhac's *La science et la pratique du plain-chant* (1673). Nevertheless, among MSS left by him and currently in *F-Pn* are original writings by him related to chant. Two are of note: *Méthode facile et accomplie pour apprendre le* *chant de l'église sans l'aide d'aucune gamme* (dated 1665, f.fr.20001) and *Règles du chant et de la prononciation grecque et latine* (an extended work, comprising five treatises, which is incomplete and is found in portions of f.fr.19103 and 20002).

BIBLIOGRAPHY

R. P. Tassin: *Histoire littéraire de la congrégation de Saint-Maur* (Brussels and Paris, 1770/*R*1965), 99, 274

A. Cohen: 'Survivals of Renaissance Thought in French Theory 1610–1670: a Bibliographical Study', *Aspects of Medieval and Renaissance Music: a Birthday Offering to Gustave Reese* (New York, 1966), 92

ALBERT COHEN

Le Clerc, Jean-Pantaléon (*b* ?Sézanne en Brie, before 1697; *d* after 1760). French violinist and publisher. He lived at the 'Croix d'Or', rue du Roule, Paris, from 1728 to 1758. Having entered the 24 Violons du Roi on 17 July 1720, he remained a member until 1760. A periodical advertisement dated October 1728 announced the start of his career as a music commission agent. Up to 1753 his name was often associated with that of Boivin, both on the title-pages of works and in music advertisements. There seems to have been a tacit agreement between the two dealers; they shared the Parisian music market and the same works are listed in their respective catalogues. Their trade was supplied by the composers themselves, mainly by those having had their works engraved at their own expense. They also represented French and foreign publishers such as Ballard, Charles-Nicolas Le Clerc and Michel-Charles Le Cène.

Three catalogues dated 1734, 1737 and 1742 provide an inventory of the music on sale at the 'Croix d'Or'; the list is supplemented by a further undated catalogue published in 1751. Some of the works listed were commissioned by Le Clerc himself; they are recorded in the 'Registres des Privilèges' and in an engraved catalogue (the French national archives contain the only surviving copy attached to a deed dated 13 April 1752). Composers listed in this catalogue include Quantz, Telemann, Bourgouin, Croes, Lavaux, Wiseman, Deltour, Noblet and Bourgeois; chamber music, dances (minuets, quadrilles, airs) and songs represent the works published by Le Clerc. The rights on these works were acquired by his younger brother Charles-Nicolas on 13 April 1752.

On 7 June 1751 Le Clerc retired and handed over the commission agency to his daughter Anne-Cécile on her marriage to the organist Claude Vernadé. He authorized her to run the business under the name of Le Clerc and this explains the alternation of the names of Le Clerc, Le Clerc-Vernadé and Vernadé on the title-pages of works sold between 1751 and 1758. In 1758 La Chevardière took over from Mme Vernadé and described himself as the successor of M. Le Clerc.

It is possible that Le Clerc was also a composer. Some dances signed Le Clerc are contained in contemporary anthologies entitled *Nouveaux menuets français et italiens . . . mis en ordre par M. Leclerc* (Paris, 1730), but this is not sufficient evidence that he was the author. The last known reference to Le Clerc is a deed drawn up by a notary in 1760 which mentions that at that time he kept a haberdashery in Paris.

For bibliography *see* LE CLERC, CHARLES-NICOLAS.

ANIK DEVRIÈS

Lecocq, (Alexandre) Charles (*b* Paris, 3 June 1832; *d* Paris, 24 Oct 1918). French operetta composer. One of five children, of a poor family, he was born infirm and from the age of five or six was forced to use crutches. He soon concentrated on music, playing first a flageolet and later the piano. By the age of 16 he was sufficiently accomplished a pianist to give lessons. After a period of instruction in harmony by Crèvecoeur, he entered the Paris Conservatoire in 1849, where he studied harmony with Bazin and composition with Halévy, and made friends with his fellow students Bizet and Saint-Saëns. At the end of his second year he gained *second prix* in counterpoint and was *primus accessit* in Benoist's organ class. But the weakness of his legs made organ playing tiring and difficult. He was forced to leave the Conservatoire prematurely, in 1854, to help support his parents by giving piano lessons and by playing at dances and for lessons of the dancing-master Cellarius. He first attracted attention as a composer in 1856 when, out of 78 entrants in a competition organized by Offenbach for the Théâtre des Bouffes-Parisiens, he and Bizet shared first place with their settings of an operetta libretto *Le docteur Miracle*.

In spite of this success, Lecocq had to wait for recognition. A few of his one-act operettas were performed during the 1860s, but it was not until 1868 that he enjoyed his first real success with *Fleur-de-thé*, an operetta with a Japanese setting, after the current fashion. He finally achieved prominence after the 1871 revolution. In Brussels, where Lecocq lived for several years from 1870, the popular acclaim accorded his operettas *Les cent vierges* (1872), *La fille de Madame Angot* (1872) and *Giroflé-Girofla* (1874), all of which were later produced in Paris and abroad, established him as a natural successor to Offenbach. Settling once again in Paris, he confirmed his international reputation with *La petite mariée* (1875) and *Le petit duc* (1878), both of which have remained in the French operetta repertory. After a lapse of more than a year caused by illness and domestic problems, his career resumed with *Janot* (1881), *Le jour et la nuit* (1881) and *Le coeur et la main* (1882), but these were his last real successes. He accepted that fashion had changed, and his output gradually decreased as he turned to other genres. *Plutus* (1886), an attempt to write in a more serious vein, was produced by the Opéra-Comique; it failed, and received only eight performances. He also composed a ballet *Le cygne* for the Opéra-Comique (1899). During the 1890s he took up the scores of his earlier works, wrote prefaces on their background and made critical comments on individual numbers. His last important operetta was *La belle au bois dormant* (1900); thereafter he composed little. He was made a Chevalier of the Légion d'honneur in 1900 and an Officier in 1910.

Much of Lecocq's music is characterized by a light touch, but he could also adopt a more lyrical and elevated style than Offenbach and termed several of his operettas *opéras comiques*. His greatest popular triumph, *La fille de Madame Angot*, has remained a classic among operettas, and demonstrates Lecocq's abundant flow of pleasing melodies, his deft exploitation of rhythm for a lively theatrical effect, impressive building up of extended numbers, and typically French shaping of phrases.

WORKS

(all printed works published in Paris)

STAGE

Unless otherwise indicated, all operettas published in vocal score, first performed in Paris.

Le docteur Miracle (1, L. Battu, Halévy), Bouffes-Parisiens, 8 April 1857 (1877)

Huis-clos (1, A. Guénée, A. Marquet), Folies-Nouvelles, 28 Jan 1859
Le baiser à la porte (1, J. de la Guette), Folies-Nouvelles, 26 March 1864 (c1890)
Liline et Valentin (1, de la Guette), Champs-Elysées, 25 May 1864 (?c1864)
Le myosotis (1, Cham, Busnach), Palais-Royal, 2 May 1866 (1866)
Ondines au champagne (1, H. Lefébvre, Pelissie, Merle), Folies Marigny, 5 Sept 1866 (1876)
Le cabaret de Ramponneau (1, Lesire), Folies Marigny, 11 Oct 1867 (?c1867)
L'amour et son carquois (2, Marquet, Delbès), Athénée, 30 Jan 1868 (1868)
Fleur-de-thé (3, Chivot, Duru) Athénée, 11 April 1868 (1868)
Les jumeaux de Bergame (1, Busnach), Athénée, 20 Nov 1868 (1876), orch score (1884)
Gandolfo (1, Chivot, Duru), Bouffes-Parisiens, 16 Jan 1869 (1869)
Deux portiers pour un cordon (1, Lucian), Palais-Royal, 19 March 1869 (?c1869)
Le rajah de Mysore (1, Chivot, Duru), Bouffes-Parisiens, 21 Sept 1869 (1869)
Le beau Dunois (1, Chivot, Duru), Variétés, 13 April 1870 (1870)
Le testament de M. de Crac (1, J. Moinaux), Bouffes-Parisiens, 23 Oct 1871 (1872)
Le barbier de Trouville (1, A. Jaime, Noriac), Bouffes-Parisiens, 19 Nov 1871 (1872)
Sauvons la caisse (1, de la Guette), Tertulia, 22 Dec 1871 (?c1871)
Les cent vierges (3, Clairville, Chivot, Duru), Brussels, Fantaisies-Parisiennes, 16 March 1872 (1872)
La fille de Madame Angot (3, Clairville, Koning, Siraudin), Brussels, Fantaisies-Parisiennes, 4 Dec 1872 (1873)
Giroflé-Girofla (3, Letterier, Vanloo), Brussels, Fantaisies-Parisiennes, 21 March 1874 (1874)
Les prés Saint-Gervais (3, Sardou, P. Gille), Variétés, 14 Nov 1874 (1874)
Le pompon (3, Chivot, Duru), Folies-Dramatiques, 10 Nov 1875 (1875)
La petite mariée (3, Letterier, Vanloo), Renaissance, 21 Dec 1875 (1876)
Kosiki (3, Busnach, Liorat), Renaissance, 18 Oct 1876 (1877)
La marjolaine (3, Letterier, Vanloo), Renaissance, 3 Feb 1877 (1877)
Le petit duc (3, Meilhac, Halévy), Renaissance, 25 Jan 1878 (1878)
La Camargo (3, Letterier, Vanloo), Renaissance, 20 Nov 1878 (1879)
Le grand Casimir (3, J. Prével, Saint-Albin), Variétés, 11 Jan 1879 (1879)
La petite mademoiselle (3, Meilhac, Halévy), Renaissance, 12 April 1879 (1879)
La jolie persane (3, Letterier, Vanloo), Renaissance, 28 Oct 1879 (1879)
Janot (3, Meilhac, Halévy), Renaissance, 21 Jan 1881 (1881)
La rousotte (3, Meilhac, Halévy, Millaud), Variétés, 28 Jan 1881, completed by Hervé (1881)
Le jour et la nuit (3, Letterier, Vanloo), Nouveautés, 5 Nov 1881 (1882)
Le coeur et la main (3, Nuitter, Beaumont), Nouveautés, 19 Oct 1882 (1883)
La princesse des Canaries (3, Chivot, Duru), Folies-Dramatiques, 9 Feb 1883 (1883)
L'oiseau bleu (3, M. Hennequin fils), Nouveautés, 16 Jan 1884 (1884)
La vie mondaine (3, E. de Najac, P. Ferrier), Nouveautés, 13 Feb 1885 (1885)
Plutus (opéra comique, 3, Millaud, Jollivet), Opéra-Comique, 31 May 1886 (1886)
Les grenadiers de Mont-Cornette (3, Daunis, Delormel, Philippe), Bouffes-Parisiens, 4 Jan 1887 (?c1887)
Ali-Baba (4, Vanloo, Busnach), Brussels, Alhambra, 11 Nov 1887 (1887)
La volière (3, Nuitter, Beaumont), Nouveautés, 11 Feb 1888 (?1885)
L'égyptienne (opéra comique, 3, Chivot, Nuitter, Beaumont), Folies-Dramatiques, 8 Nov 1890
Nos bons chasseurs (vaudeville, 3, P. Bilhaud, M. Carré), Casino de Paris, 10 April 1894
Ninette (3, Clairville, Hubert, Lebeau, C. de Trogoff), Bouffes-Parisiens, 28 Feb 1896 (1896)
Barbe-Bleu (ballet-pantomime), Olympia, 12 May 1898 (1898)
Ruse d'amour (comédie, 1, S. Bordèse), Boulogne, Casino, 26 June 1898 (1897)
Le cygne (ballet, 1), Opéra-Comique, 20 April 1899 (1899)
La belle au bois dormant (3, G. Duval, Vanloo), Bouffes-Parisiens, 19 Feb 1900 (2/c1905)
Yetta (opéra comique, 3, F. Beissier), Brussels, Galeries St-Hubert, 7 March 1903 (1903)
Rose Mousse (comédie-musicale, 1, A. Alexandre, P. Carin), Capucines, 28 Jan 1904 (1904)
La salutiste (opéra monologue, 1, F. Beissier), Capucines, 14 Jan 1905
Le trahison de Pan (opéra comique, 1, S. Bordèse), Aix-les-Bains, Casino, 1911 (1912)

Le chevrier (opéra comique, 2, C. Narre, M. Carré fils) (c1888)
Renza; Ma cousine; both unperf.

OTHER WORKS

2 choruses
Over 100 songs
Les clercs de la Basoche, orch
Deux morceaux religieux: Andante nuptial, Offertoire, vn, org/pf (1883), also arr. orch; Mélange sur La fille de Madame Angot, ob, pf (1884); Allegretto, vc, pf (1885); Sonata, vn, pf
c60 dances and salon pieces, pf, 2 pieces arr. orch

BIBLIOGRAPHY
L. Schneider: Les maîtres de l'opérette française: Hervé, Charles Lecocq (Paris, 1924), 125–283 [with detailed list of works]
G. Lebas, ed.: 'Lettres inédites de Lecocq à Saint-Saëns', ReM, v (1924), 119; vi (1925), 216
L. Schneider: Une heure de musique avec Charles Lecocq (Paris, 1930)
P. Landormy: La musique française de Franck à Debussy (Paris, 1943, 2/1948)
L. Oster: Les opérettes du répertoire courant (Paris, 1953)
                                                        ANDREW LAMB

Lecocq, Jean [Jehan] (*fl* 1540–60). Composer, who may be identifiable with JOANNES GALLUS.

Le Coincte, Louis. *See* LE QUOINTE, LOUIS.

Leçon de ténèbre (Fr.). A name applied during the Baroque period to French polyphonic settings of the Lamentations of Jeremiah, a text that forms the first three lessons of Tenebrae, the combined Offices of Matins and Lauds as sung on Thursday, Friday and Saturday of Holy Week. *See* LAMENTATIONS.

Le Conte, Pierre-Michel (*b* Rouen, 6 March 1921). French conductor. At the Paris Conservatoire he studied the bassoon with Gustave Dhérin and conducting with Eugène Bigot and Louis Fourestier. Throughout his career he has worked chiefly in French radio. He was conductor for radio in Nice from 1946 to 1949 and in Toulouse from 1950 to 1952, and in 1960 he was appointed resident conductor of the ORTF Opera Orchestra in Paris. He has also conducted other orchestras, both in France and elsewhere; he conducted the Paris Conservatoire Orchestra at the Aix-en-Provence Festival in 1947, and in 1972 he toured the USSR with a programme of French music.

Le Conte favours 19th-century symphonic works, but as a radio conductor he is also concerned with performing contemporary works, chiefly operatic. He has conducted several first performances, including those of *Les amants captifs* and *La fille de l'homme* by Pierre Capdeville. He also has a particular talent for conducting lighter music.

CHRISTIANE SPIETH-WEISSENBACHER

Lectionary (from Lat. *lectionarium*). A liturgical book of the Christian Church, either Western (Latin and derived rites) or Eastern, containing scriptural or other readings read or chanted by a deacon, sub-deacon or lector at the Eucharist or during the Divine Office (e.g. in the Latin rite after each nocturn at Matins). In the Latin rite some of the earliest lectionaries (e.g. the Luxeuil Lectionary, *F-Pn* lat.9427, 7th century, possibly for Paris for the Gallican rite, ed. P. Salmon, *Le lectionnaire de Luxeuil*, Rome, 1944) contain merely a table of incipits and *explicits* of the passages to be read. Such tables are known as capitularies (from Lat. *capitulare, liber capitularius*). The preferred medieval term for the Mass lectionary, until approximately the 9th century, was *comes* (*liber comicus, liber comitis*), used both for tables of incipits (as in the Murbach Comes, *F-B* 184, late 8th century, ed. A. Wilmart, *Revue bénédic-*

tine, xxiii, 1913, 25–69) and for collections of the complete passages or pericopes (as in the Würzburg Comes, *D-WÜu* mp.theol.f.62, early 7th century, ed. G. Morin, *Revue bénédictine*, xx, 1910, 41; and see 'Lectionnaire', *Dictionnaire d'archéologie chrétienne et de liturgie*). After the Carolingian renaissance, mere tables were used less often. From the 12th century, Mass and Office pericopes, with chants, were increasingly included in sacramentaries (*see* BREVIARY and MISSAL).

The term 'evangeliary' ('evangelistiary'; from Lat. *evangelarium, evangeliarium, evangelistarium*) denotes a book similar to the capitulary, listing texts to be used for the Gospel at Mass in liturgical order. Early examples have been classified by T. Klauser (*Das römische Capitulare evangeliorum*, Münster, 1935). (*See* GOSPEL, §2.) The homiliary (Lat. *homiliarium, homeliarius, homeliarium, homelium*) is a collection of patristic homilies, tracts or sermons, read probably since the 6th century during the night Office.

Lectionaries in both West and East were provided with systems of punctuation from an early date and, since the 8th or 9th century at latest, these systems were interpreted as musical notation, giving indications of the inflections to be adopted during the chanting of the lessons (*see* EKPHONETIC NOTATION; INFLECTION; BYZANTINE RITE, MUSIC OF THE, §2). The chief Byzantine lectionaries are termed, according to content, the *apostolos* (Epistles), *euangelion* (Gospels) and *prophetologion*.

See also LITURGY AND LITURGICAL BOOKS, §§II, 3; III, 3; MASS, §I, 2.

Lectionary notation. *See* EKPHONETIC NOTATION.

Lecuna, Juan Vicente (*b* Valencia, 20 Nov 1899; *d* Rome, 15 April 1954). Venezuelan composer and pianist. He studied the piano with Llamozas at the Caracas National School of Music and composition with Jaime Pahissa in Buenos Aires (1937–41), where he also received guidance from Falla. In 1941 he worked with Straube at the Peabody Conservatory, and he continued to travel extensively in the Americas and Europe. He was commissioned by the Venezuelan Ministry of Education in 1942 to study the state of public school music education in Argentina, Brazil, Uruguay and Chile; during the visit he was made an honorary member of the fine arts faculty at the University of Chile. His last years were spent as a member of the Venezuelan legation to the Vatican. Principal among his compositions are the piano pieces, the Alberti songs (1948) and the Harp Sonata (1941).

JUAN A. ORREGO-SALAS

Lecuona, Ernesto (*b* Guanabacoa, 7 Aug 1896; *d* S Cruz de Tenerife, 29 Nov 1963). Cuban composer. Born into a musical family, he played the piano from an early age and wrote his first song when he was 11. He graduated from the National Conservatory in Havana in 1913 and soon made his first appearance as a composer-pianist. Then, after further studies with Joaquín Nin, he made several tours of Latin America, Europe and the USA as the leader of a dance band, Lecuona's Cuban Boys, which became quite well known. For some years he lived in New York, where he wrote for musicals, films and the radio. In his concerts he usually performed his songs and dances for piano, as well as light pieces by other late 19th-century and early 20th-century Cuban composers. His salon piano pieces, using

'white' peasant and Afro-Cuban rhythms, found wide favour, and many of his songs, too, achieved great popularity.

WORKS
(*selective list*)

Zarzuelas: El Cafetal, Lola Cruz
Orch: Rapsodia negra, pf, orch, 1943; Suite
Songs: Andalucía, Aquella tarde, Canto Carabalí, Como arrullo de palmas, Dame tus dos rosas, El crisantemo, Malagueña, María la O, Mariposa, Rosa la china, Siboney, many others
Pf: Danza de los ñáñigos, Danza Lucumí, La comparsa, many other dances

Principal publisher: Marks

AURELIO DE LA VEGA

Ledang, Ola Kai (*b* Namsos, 25 July 1940). Norwegian musicologist. He studied the organ at the Trondheim School of Music (diploma 1962), civil engineering at the Norwegian Institute of Technology, Trondheim (1963), and musicology at the University of Oslo (MA 1966). After holding a scholarship at the Norwegian Folk Music Institute in Oslo (1964–70) he became a lecturer in musicology at the University of Trondheim; he has also been a music critic for the Oslo newspapers *Dagbladet, Verdens gang* and *Morgenbladet*. His research has been particularly concerned with Norwegian folk instruments and the social aspects of music.

WRITINGS

'Instrumentell analyse av einstemmig musikk', *Forskningsnytt*, no.3 (Oslo, 1966), 13
'Folkemusikk i Namdalen', *Namdal historielags årbok* (1967), 3
Song, syngemåte og stemmekarakter: samanliknande gransking av 28 lydbandopptak av ein norsk religiøs folketone (Oslo, 1967)
'Some Musicological Applications of the Sonagraph', *SMN*, i (1968), 21
'Seljefløyta – eit naturtoneinstrument?', *Spelemannsbladet*, no.3 (Oslo, 1971), 8
'Spelmann, forskar og komponist', *Eivind Groven: heiderskrift til 70-årsdagen 8. oktober 1971* (Oslo, 1971), 154
'On the Acoustics and the Systematic Classification of the Jaw's Harp', *YIFMC*, iv (1972), 95
with A. Holen and E. Diesen: 'Musikklivet i ei bygd', *Norsk musikktidsskrift*, x (1973), 7
'Folkemusikk i smeltedigelen', *I forskningens lys, Norges almenvitenskapelige forskningsråd 25 år* (Oslo, 1974), 311
'Instrument–Player–Music: on the Norwegian Langleik', *Festschrift to Ernst Emsheimer* (Stockholm, 1974), 107

KARI MICHELSEN

Ledbetter, Huddie ['Leadbelly'] (*b* Mooringsport, Louisiana, 21 Jan 1885; *d* New York, 6 Dec 1949). Black American songster, blues singer and guitarist. By the age of 15 he was well known in the Caddo Lake region of Louisiana as a musician. Early this century he learnt the 12-string guitar, and he later accompanied Blind Lemon Jefferson in Dallas. He was sentenced for murder in Texas but released in 1925. In 1930 he was sentenced to the Louisiana State Penitentiary at Angola for intent to murder; there he was discovered in 1933 by the folksong collector John A. Lomax, who recorded him for the Library of Congress and assisted in gaining his parole. He went to New York with Lomax in 1934, and from 1935 to 1940 was extensively recorded by him for the Library of Congress. His recordings, which are remarkable for their variety, include a beautiful version of Jefferson's *Match Box Blues* played with a knife on the guitar strings, and a haunting *If it wasn't for Dicky* (both 1935). His first commercial recordings included a powerful *Honey I'm all out and down* and the ballad *Becky Deem, she was a gamblin' gal* (both 1935), but they were anachronistic to the black audience and did not sell well.

In New York Ledbetter found a welcome audience among jazz supporters, who viewed him as the last of the blues singers, and he had a moderate success as a night club singer. His *Good Morning Blues* (1940), with a spoken introduction defining blues, was his most admired song. In his last years he made a large number of recordings; several were with the harmonica player Sonny Terry. In 1948 he recorded an extensive collection of traditional songs, many of them unaccompanied. Shortly before his death he performed in Paris.

Ledbetter was the most prolific of all songsters, with a repertory of perhaps 500 songs at ready recall. A notable custodian of the black song tradition, his work is distinguished for its wide range and variety, his full-throated singing with rough vibrato, and his accomplished, highly rhythmic playing of the 12-string guitar. His *Goodnight Irene* (1943) became a popular favourite after his death and his *Rock Island Line* (1942) was virtually an anthem of the 'skiffle' craze in England, resulting in a temporary devaluation of his reputation as a musician.

BIBLIOGRAPHY

J. Lomax: *Negro Folk Songs as Sung by Leadbelly* (New York, 1936, 3/1959)

'A Tribute to Huddie Ledbetter', *Jazz Music*, ed. M. Jones, A. J. McCarthy and F. Ramsey jr (London, 1946)

A. J. McCarthy and D. Carey, eds.: *Jazz Directory*, vi (London, 1957), 1039ff

M. Asch and A. Lomax, eds.: *The Leadbelly Songbook* (New York, 1962)

L. Cohn: 'Leadbelly: the Library of Congress Recordings', EKL-301/2 [disc notes]

P. Oliver: *The Story of the Blues* (London, 1969)

PAUL OLIVER

Ledenyov, Roman (Semyonovich) (*b* Moscow, 4 Dec 1930). Soviet composer. He studied under Rakov and Alexandrov at the Moscow Conservatory, completed his postgraduate training there and later joined the staff as a theory teacher. His music is marked by a delicate psychological approach, a general lyrical quality and an attractive Russian atmosphere.

WORKS
(selective list)

Choral: Oda radosti [Ode to joy] (Neruda), cantata, 1956–8; Pesni svobodï [Songs of freedom] (Asian and African verse), oratorio, 1960–61; Slovo o polku Igoreve [Lay of Igor's host] (10th-century Russ. verse), oratorio, 1952–74

Ballet: Skazka o zelyonïkh sharakh [Tale about green balls] (after V. Lugovskoy), 1963–4

Orch: Oda partii, 1961; Vn Conc., 1961–4; Kontsert-poema, va, orch, 1963–4; Kontsert-noktyurn, fl, orch, 1964

Chamber: Sonata, cl, pf, 1952; Sonata to the Memory of Prokofiev, pf, 1953–6; Str Qt, 1955–8; Children's Album, 98 pf pieces, 1959–61; Ballad, pf, 1961; 6 Pieces, str qt, harp, 1965–6; 10 eskizov, ens, 1967; 7 nastroyeniy [7 moods], ens, 1967; Popevki [Ditties], str qt, 1969; 4 zarisovki [4 sketches], ens, 1972; other pieces

Songs: Romansï (Nekrasov), 1972–3; others

Music for the theatre and cinema

BIBLIOGRAPHY

A. Shnitke: 'Navstrechu slushatelyu' [Meeting the listener], *SovM* (1962), no.1, p.16

A. N. Alexandrov: 'Neskol'ko slov o Romane Ledenyove' [A few words about Ledenyov], *SovM* (1969), no.1, p.10

S. Savenko: 'Novïye sochineniya R. Ledenyova' [New works of Ledenyov], *SovM* (1969), no.1, p.10

GALINA GRIGOR'YEVA

Lederer, Joseph [Anton] (*b* Ziemetshausen, Swabia, 15 Jan 1733; *d* Ulm, 22 Sept 1796). German composer. After an elementary education in Ulm, he entered the Augustinian seminary 'Zu den Wengen' and then the monastery, where he was a prebendary, teacher of theology and musician. According to Weyermann, 'he was talented, very industrious and studied harder than most of his fellow friars, but he was the most intolerant monk, and insulted the town's Protestants at every op-

portunity', for which he was reproached by his superiors. Lederer's works include numerous theological writings and a chronicle of the monastery (Augsburg, 1783). His compositions are mostly musical comedies and operettas written for the monastery's Gymnasium. He usually wrote his own texts, some of which are extant (*D-Us*), and he was given the honorary title 'kaiserlich und königlich gekrönten Dichter' for his activities as a poet. His stage works were occasionally performed outside Ulm, and Schikaneder presented his comedy *Der Chargenverkauf* several times in Salzburg in 1780–81. Most of Lederer's published output is sacred music. He described his six masses (1776) as 'short, light, and melodic', intended primarily 'for the use of country choirs and in nunneries'. In 1775, through his brother Ambrosius Lederer, he dedicated the masses and a poem to Prince Ernst of Oettingen-Wallerstein, indicating in the poem that his models as a composer were Gluck and Haydn. Lederer himself engraved his harpsichord concerto on copper. His only extant instrumental work, the *Apparatus musicus*, containing pieces for beginners, was a product of his teaching activities in the monastery, as was his treatise *Neue und erbauliche Art zu solmisiren* (Ulm, 1756, rev. 2/1796 as *Neue und erleichterte Art zu solmisiren*).

WORKS

Stage (most perf. Ulm, music lost, some libs in *D-Us*): 22 Singspiels, 1765–88; 4 Trauerspiels, 1761–75

Vocal: Stabat mater (Augsburg, 1752); Laus Dei (Augsburg, 1761); 6 masses, 2 solo vv, chorus, insts (Augsburg, 1776); 5 vespers, 5 psalms, Magnificat, Stabat mater, 4vv, insts (Ulm, 1780); cantata, S, insts, in Apparatus musicus (Augsburg, 1781); Offertory, 4vv, insts, *D-Tl*; 6 masses, op.4 (Augsburg, 1785), mentioned in Weyermann

Inst: Hpd Conc. (Ulm, n.d.), lost; Apparatus musicus oder Musikalischer Vorrath, incl. 18 versettes, 17 preambles, minuet, trio, 3 sonatas, rondo with 5 variations, cantata (Augsburg, 1781), 1 preamble ed. U. Siegel, *Musik des oberschwäbischen Barock* (Berlin and Darmstadt, 1952, 2/1954)

BIBLIOGRAPHY

A. Weyermann: *Neue . . . Nachrichten von Gelehrten und Künstlern . . . aus der vormaligen Reichsstadt Ulm*, ii (Ulm, 1829), 267ff [incl. list of writings and works]

E. Stiefel: 'Lederer, Joseph', *MGG*

ADOLF LAYER

Ledesma, Dámaso (*b* Ciudad Rodrigo, 3 Feb 1868; *d* Salamanca, 13 June 1928). Spanish composer, organist and folklorist. His talent as a musician was nurtured during his early childhood. He was ordained a priest in Salamanca, and after serving as organist at a local church (1889–96) became organist at the cathedral, a post he held until his death. He was a famous improviser and a prolific composer of organ and liturgical music, but he is best remembered for his *Folk-lore ó Cancionero salmantino* (Madrid, 1907/R1972), which contains approximately 400 melodies collected from the rich oral tradition of his native province. This was awarded a prize in an open competition and published by the Real Academia de Bellas Artes de San Fernando after several songs from the collection had been performed at the Ateneo Literario y Artistico de Madrid (9 May 1906); the collection remains one of the most outstanding in Spanish folklore.

BIBLIOGRAPHY

I. J. Katz: 'The Traditional Folk Music of Spain: Explorations and Perspectives', *YIFMC*, vi (1974), 6

ISRAEL J. KATZ

Ledesma, Mariano Rodríguez de. See RODRÍGUEZ DE LEDESMA, MARIANO.

Ledesma, Nicolás (*b* Grisel, Saragossa, 9 July 1791; *d* Bilbao, 4 Jan 1883). Spanish composer. He was a choir-boy at Tarazona Cathedral, where he was taught music by Francisco Javier Gibert and José Angel Martinchique. He later moved to Saragossa, where he studied the organ with Ramón Ferreñac. From an early age he was organist and choirmaster in various collegiate churches: Borja (1807), Tafalla (1809), Calatayud (where he is known to have been about 1824) and finally Bilbao (1830), where he remained until his death. Ledesma was a prolific composer of masses, Lamentations, motets and villancicos. Although his music reflects the bombastic and theatrical tendencies of his age, he had a sound technique and a certain nobility of invention. He was also active with Eslava in efforts to renew and purify religious music.

BIBLIOGRAPHY
J. López-Calo: *Catálogo musical del Archivo de la Santa Iglesia Catedral de Santiago* (Cuenca, 1972), 273ff [with addl bibliography]
JOSÉ LÓPEZ-CALO

Ledger, Philip (Stevens) (*b* Bexhill-on-Sea, Sussex, 12 Dec 1937). English organist whose many-sided musical achievements were recognized by his appointment as director of music at King's College, Cambridge, in January 1974. He made his mark as an organist while still in his teens and was awarded the Limpus and Read prizes when he took his Fellowship of the Royal College of Organists. At Cambridge, where he was a music scholar at King's, he gained first-class honours in both parts of the music tripos and a distinction in the MusB examination. His first appointment as master of the music at Chelmsford Cathedral in 1961 at the age of 24 made him the youngest cathedral organist in the country. He soon showed, however, that his potential ranged beyond the organ loft, and in 1965 he became director of music at the newly founded University of East Anglia at Norwich. For three years he was dean of the School of Fine Arts and Music, and he laid the foundations of a new Music Centre at the university, opened in 1973.

Ledger's all-round musicianship attracted the attention of Benjamin Britten and in 1968 he became closely associated with him as an artistic director of the Aldeburgh Festival. He conducted at the opening concert in the rebuilt Maltings at Snape and has participated in recordings of a number of Britten's works. He has also conducted at the Promenade Concerts in London, appeared as harpsichord soloist and continuo player, given organ recitals at the Festival Hall, and played as a pianist with the Melos Ensemble. His interest in the music of Purcell is reflected in a performing edition of *King Arthur* (with Colin Graham), in which he has conducted the English Opera Group in performances in Britain and abroad.

STANLEY WEBB

Ledger line. See LEGER LINE.

Leduc [Le Duc]. French family of musicians, composers and music publishers. The origins of the family are unclear, but musicians of this name lived in Paris at the beginning of the 17th century and probably earlier, in the neighbourhood where the Leduc publishing house has remained. A Pierre Le Duc, maker of musical instruments, lived in the rue St-Honoré from 1602 and died childless in about 1635. His relationship to other Leducs is unknown. (*See also* ALPHONSE LEDUC.)

(1) Simon Leduc [*l'aîné*] (*b* Paris, ? before 1748; *d* Paris, buried 22 or 25 Jan 1777). Violinist, composer and publisher, brother of (2) Pierre Leduc. A pupil of Gaviniès, he was a second violinist in the Concert Spirituel orchestra in 1759 and made his début as soloist in 1763. If the birthdate given in many early sources (1748) is to be believed, he was only 15 when he made his first solo appearance. While this is not impossible, it is strange that no contemporary report mentions his comparative youth, for journalists of that day seldom missed a chance to point out a prodigy. It therefore seems likely that he was born a few years earlier, perhaps in about 1745. In 1763 he was one of the first violins in the Concert Spirituel orchestra, and he continued to appear as an orchestral player and soloist until his death. He earned consistently favourable reviews in the Parisian press and received an understated compliment in Leopold Mozart's travel diary of 1763–4: 'He plays well'.

Despite his success, however, Leduc decided to devote the greater part of his efforts to pursuits other than virtuoso performance. He took great care in teaching his brother Pierre, whom he apparently considered a greater violinist than himself. He composed exceptionally fine orchestral and chamber music, publishing some of it under a privilege granted on 17 March 1768, retroactive from 16 December 1767. (Simon never published any works but his own, the general privilege of 1 September 1767 notwithstanding; it was Pierre who undertook to develop a fully-fledged publishing business.)

In 1773 Leduc assumed the directorship of the Concert Spirituel with Gaviniès and Gossec, and soon earned the applause of the press for a noticeable improvement in the quality of these concerts. He was clearly a well-loved director; shortly after his death, the orchestra, trying to prepare one of his symphonies for a forthcoming performance, was collectively so overcome with grief that the rehearsal had to be suspended. His friends paid tribute to his memory in a religious service on 22 March 1777, at which Gossec's *Messe des morts* was performed.

Leduc's compositions compare favourably with those of any other young composer of his time. The writing is skilful and idiomatic, particularly for the violin; the harmonies are inventive, expressive, and often unusually chromatic. Painstakingly notated nuances, frequent dynamic contrasts and expressive harmonic progressions contribute to a style which has been called a 'French Storm and Stress'.

WORKS
(printed works published in Paris)

Orch: 2 concertos, vn solo, op.7 (1771), announced in 1771; earliest extant edns. pubd separately (1775, 1776); Suite de noëls . . . mêlés de solo et d'echo concertants, perf. 1773, unpubd, lost; Simphonie concertante, 2 solo vn (1775), 1st edn. 'à 16 parties', lost; 2nd edn. 'à 10 parties' (1779); Sym. no.1 in 3 simphonies à 8 parties . . . by Leduc, C. Stamitz, Gossec (1776); Syms. nos.2–3 in 3 symphonies à 4 ou à 8 parties . . . by J. C. Bach and Leduc (1777); 3me concerto, vn solo (?1778–81); Symphonie concertante, 2nd vn part only, *F-AI*, Fonds Aiguillon (1st movt identical to Sym. no.2); 6 trios, op.2 (1768), 3 for 2 vn, b, 3 for orch

Chamber: 6 sonates, vn, acc. ?va, b/hpd, op.1 (1767); 6 trios, op.2 (1768), 3 for 2 vn, b, 3 for orch, 1st vn part lost; 6 duos, 2 vn, op.3 (1771) [incl. catalogue of all Leduc's works with op. nos.]; 2me livre de sonates, vn, ?bc, op.4 (1771); 6 trios, 2 vn, b, op.5 (1771); 6 petits duos, 2 vn, op.6 (1771); Sonate, vn, b acc., (1782); 1 op. of [?6] qts, lost [cited in P. Leduc's posth. catalogue of S. Leduc's works]; 5 divertimenti à 4, *D-Bds* according to *EitnerQ* [? = preceding work]

Sonate, vn solo, 1760, *F-Pc*

(2) Pierre Leduc [*le jeune*] (*b* Paris, 1755; *d* Netherlands, Oct 1816). Violinist and publisher, brother of (1) Simon Leduc. He made his début as a violin soloist at the Concert Spirituel in the spring of 1770 and appeared frequently thereafter, receiving consistently favourable reviews. He studied with his brother Simon, whose works made up the bulk of Pierre's concert repertory. The brothers sometimes appeared together, on which occasions Simon yielded the first violin part to Pierre.

In March 1775 Leduc first advertised as a publisher, not as his brother's partner but as an independent businessman. (Although Simon had published works under the Leduc name, these were exclusively his own.) Pierre published works by contemporary composers and thus founded the Leduc publishing house as an enduring enterprise. In 1780 or 1781 he enlarged the firm by acquiring the stock of Preudhomme; in 1784 or 1785 he took over La Chevardière. Many sources say that he also absorbed Venier in 1781 or 1782, but this is not correct; Venier was active until late 1782 at least, and his stock was acquired by Boyer in 1784. Leduc published a great variety of music, particularly orchestral and serious chamber music at first, then a quantity of less weighty material for amateurs during the 1790s. He did not completely stop playing the violin; his name continued to appear in the lists of violinists in the Concert Spirituel, although he seems to have devoted most of his attention to publishing from about 1776. In 1803 or 1804 he turned the business over to his son (3) Auguste Leduc; he disappeared from public life shortly thereafter.

Pierre Leduc composed nothing of consequence, although he may have contributed an occasional arrangement to his publication *Journal de harpe*. His wife, known only as Mme Leduc, wrote a few harp accompaniments for that periodical. An *Essai sur la mélioration de la guitare ou lyre-guitare à clavier* by Pierre Leduc survives (in *F-Pc*).

(3) (Antoine-Pierre) Auguste Leduc (*b* Paris, 1779; *d* Paris, 25 May 1823). Music publisher, son of (2) Pierre Leduc. He probably assumed the directorship of his father's publishing house at some time between April 1803 and January 1804. He established his business in Paris at 267 rue de la Loi; but in 1805–6 the house was renumbered 78, and in 1807 the street reverted to its pre-Revolutionary name of rue de Richelieu. After its death the firm was run by his second wife, Augustine-Julie Bernier, as Mme Veuve Leduc. In August 1830 one Pierrot advertised as her successor, and in 1831 she was bankrupted; but from 1835 to 1837 she was again in business, at 47 rue Neuve-Vivienne, before selling out to Janet Frères. Finally, in 1846, she was listed at 19 rue Vivienne.

Whereas Pierre Leduc had been active both in soliciting interesting new works and in reprinting from the plates acquired from other publishers, Auguste was comparatively unenterprising and not very prolific. He, and later his widow, published full scores of a handful of operas, including three by Carafa in the 1820s; each week he continued to issue (at least until 1821) the *Journal hebdomadaire*, a periodical collection of vocal music which had been started by La Chevardière in 1764. But the contents of the *Journal*, like most of Leduc's output, tended to be second-rate. Among his more significant publications were Choron's *Principes*

de composition des écoles d'Italie (1808) and a reprint of the full scores, edited by Choron, of the 26 Haydn symphonies which his father had published in 1802–3. He must also be credited with a rare flash of enlightenment for putting out the song *Le dépit de la bergère* (*c*1820), probably Berlioz's first appearance in print. Almost all Leduc's publications were printed from engraved plates, but in about 1807 he flirted briefly with lithography – one of the earliest publishers to do so.

BIBLIOGRAPHY

L. de La Laurencie: *L'école française de violon de Lully à Viotti* (Paris, 1922–4/*R*1971)
C. Hopkinson: *A Dictionary of Parisian Music Publishers 1700–1950* (London, 1954)
C. Johansson: *French Music Publishers' Catalogues of the Second Half of the Eighteenth Century* (Stockholm, 1955)
R. Cotte: 'Le Duc', *MGG*
B. S. Brook: *La symphonie française dans la seconde moitié du XVIIIe siècle* (Paris, 1962)
——: 'Simon Le Duc l'aîné, a French Symphonist at the Time of Mozart', *MQ*, xlviii (1962), 498
A. Devriès: 'Deux dynasties d'éditeurs et de musiciens: les Leduc', *RBM*, xxviii–xxx (1974–6), 195
A. Devriès and F. Lesure: *Dictionnaire des éditeurs de musique français*, i: *Des origines à 1820* (Geneva, 1979)

JEAN HARDEN (1, 2), RICHARD MACNUTT (3)

Leduc, Alphonse. French firm of music publishers. It was founded, in Paris, in about 1841 by Alphonse (*b* Nantes, 9 March 1804; *d* Paris, 17 June 1868), who was not a blood relation of Pierre and Auguste Leduc. He studied harmony at the Paris Conservatoire under Reicha and became an excellent player of the bassoon, flute and guitar as well as a prolific composer. Pougin estimated his output to be at least 1300 works, including an elementary piano method (op.130, frequently reprinted), 960 piano solos (632 of them in dance forms), 94 songs and 103 works for bassoon, flute or guitar. On his death he was succeeded by his son, Alphonse (*b* ?Paris, 29 May 1844; *d* Paris, 4 June 1892), whose widow, Emma, daughter of the pianist Henri Ravina, directed the firm from his death until 1904, when their son, Emile-Alphonse (*b* Paris, 14 Nov 1878; *d* Paris, 24 May 1951) took over. His two sons, Claude-Alphonse and Gilbert-Alphonse, became his partners in 1938 and succeeded to the business in 1951. Trade has been carried on under the name Alphonse Leduc except for a brief period (*c*1907–*c*1914) when the firm was styled 'Alphonse Leduc, Paul Bertrand & Cie'; about 1914 Bertrand (*d* 1953) left to join Heugel.

The firm's first premises were at 78 passage Choiseul. In 1846 or 1847 the business of Auguste Leduc was acquired, and by May 1847 the firm had moved to 18 rue Vivienne. In 1852 it moved to 2 rue de la Bourse, in 1862 to 4 rue Ménars, in about 1867 to 35 rue Le Peletier, and in November 1874 to 3 rue de Grammont; in February 1929 it moved to 175 rue St-Honoré. Although its output has probably amounted to some 50,000 publications over a period of 135 years, few significant works from notable composers have been acquired. The chief importance and pride of the firm lies rather in its contribution to music teaching in France by the publication of numerous elementary and advanced instrumental and vocal methods and studies as well as a vast quantity of instrumental music. In December 1883 Leduc took over the weekly journal *Art musical* from Girod (who had acquired it from its founder Léon Escudier); its final appearance was in September 1894, after which it was absorbed by Maurice Kufferath's *Guide musical*.

BIBLIOGRAPHY
C. Hopkinson: *A Dictionary of Parisian Music Publishers 1700–1950* (London, 1954), 74ff
RICHARD MACNUTT

Leduc, Jacques (*b* Jette, nr. Brussels, 1 March 1932). Belgian composer. He studied at the Brussels Conservatory and later took composition lessons with Absil; in 1961 he won the Belgian second Prix de Rome with the cantata *L'aventure* op.8. In 1968 he was appointed professor of harmony, and in 1972 of counterpoint, at the Brussels Conservatory. He has also taught at the Chapelle Musicale Reine Elisabeth. His works are conventional in style and highly elaborate in form.

WORKS
(*selective list*)
Stage: Nous attendons Sémiramis (comédie lyrique, G. Sion), op.38, 1972
Orch: Antigone, sym. poem, op.5, 1960; Ob Concertino, op.10, 1962; Divertissement, fl, str, op.12, 1962; Le printemps, sym. sketch, op.25, 1967; Ouverture d'été, op.28, 1968; Sym., op.29, 1969; Pf Conc., op.31, 1970; 5 croquis, op.34, 1971; Instantanés, op.37, 1972; Dialogue, cl, chamber orch, op.39, 1972
Choral works, songs, many chamber and inst pieces

Principal publishers: CeBeDeM, Leduc, Maurer, Schott
MSS in *B-Bcdm*
HENRI VANHULST

Le Duc, Philippe. *See* DUC, FILIPPO.

Lee, George Alexander (*b* London, 1802; *d* London, 8 Oct 1851). English composer. He began his career as a tenor singer and conductor at Dublin in 1822 and in 1826 returned to London, where his first engagement was at the Haymarket Theatre. The following year he began to write for the stage, contributing incidental music to several plays at Covent Garden; the opera *The Sublime and the Beautiful* was produced there in 1828, and another, *The Nymph of the Grotto, or A Daughter's Vow*, written in collaboration with Giovanni Liverati, in 1829. About this time Lee became involved in various managerial ventures, at the Tottenham Theatre (1829–30), Drury Lane (1831–2) and the Strand Theatre (1834), all of short duration. In 1835–6 he had a music shop in Frith Street; later he was conductor at the Olympic Theatre (1845) and Vauxhall (1849), and finally pianist at the 'Poses Plastiques' in Bow Street. Lee adapted two of Auber's operas for the English stage (*Fra Diavolo* as *The Devil's Brother*, Drury Lane, 1831, and *Le lac des fées* as *The Fairy Lake*, Strand Theatre, 1839) and wrote music for about 20 plays, burlettas and melodramas. He composed many songs and ballads, highly popular in their day (*Away, away to the mountain's brow*, *Come where the aspens quiver*, *The Macgregors' Gathering*), and was the author of a *Complete Course of Instruction in Singing* (London, repr. 1872).

About 1830 Lee established a liaison with the popular ballad singer Mrs Waylett, to whom he was devoted and whom he married about 1840, after Waylett died.

BIBLIOGRAPHY
R. F. Sharpe: 'Lee, George Alexander', *DNB*
ALFRED LOEWENBERG/R

Lee, Louis. German cellist and pianist, brother of SEBASTIAN LEE.

Lee, Maurice. German pianist and composer, brother of SEBASTIAN LEE.

Lee, Peggy [Egstrom, Norma Dolores] (*b* Jamestown, North Dakota, 26 May 1920). American popular singer, songwriter and actress. She began singing in a church choir, then on the radio, and from 1936 toured with dance bands. Her first hit was *Why don't you do right?* (1942) with Benny Goodman's band. In 1943 she married the guitarist Dave Barbour, with whom she wrote the song *Mañana* (1947), and in 1944 she left the swing bands and began a career on her own. She had a successful film début in a remake of *The Jazz Singer* (1953), and portrayed an alcoholic blues singer in *Pete Kelly's Blues* (1955). Lee's voice was small, with a compass of little more than an octave and a half; her distinction lay in her characterization of songs, achieved through vocal colour and inflection with careful attention to the subtleties of language, to musical arrangements and to stage manner and presentation. Though she was first a singer in the swing style, unlike many of her colleagues she did little improvisation. She wrote or collaborated on over 500 songs.
HENRY PLEASANTS

Lee, Samuel (*b* ?Dublin; *d* Dublin, 21 Feb 1776). Irish publisher, music seller and violinist. In 1745 he was admitted to the City Music or Corporation Band, of which he was appointed bandmaster in 1752 at a salary of £40, increased to £60 in 1753. During this period he was appearing regularly as a violinist, notably at the summer open-air concerts at Marlborough Green between 1750 and 1756. In July 1751 he became violinist and musical director in the syndicate which leased Crow Street Music Hall for the six years before it was taken over, rebuilt and opened as a theatre. The other members of the syndicate, who had quarrelled by 1753, were Signor Marella, Joseph de Boeck, Daniel Sullivan and the double-bass player Stefano Storace, who was listed as a musician in the Smock Alley Theatre Company for the 1756–7 season.

Samuel Lee was founder of the music shop and publishing firm which carried on business at Little Green, off Bolton Street (1752–63), the Harp and Hautboy, Fownes Street (1764–8), and 2 Dame Street (1769–1821). From Samuel's death in 1776 his widow Anne had charge of the firm, with their son Edmond as assistant; Edmond himself carried on the business thereafter until John Aldridge took it over in 1821. The business operated under the name Walker & Lee in 1781 and John Lee in 1789. John, another son of Samuel, traded as a publisher, music seller and instrument maker at 64 Dame Street (1775–8) and 70 Dame Street (1778–1803).
BRIAN BOYDELL

Lee, Sebastian (*b* Hamburg, 24 Dec 1805; *d* Hamburg, 4 Jan 1887). German cellist. He studied with J. N. Prell and made his début in Hamburg in 1831. He then travelled via Leipzig, Kassel and Frankfurt am Main to Paris, appearing with great success at the Théâtre des Italiens in April 1832. He spent the next five years touring, returning to Paris to become solo cellist at the Opéra. On retiring in 1868 he settled in his native town and devoted himself to teaching and composing. He published a cello method op.30 and four sets of solo and duo studies. His concert works are largely forgotten, but he produced useful editions of Classical works for the cello and an edition of the *Méthode* of Baillot, Levasseur, Catel and Baudiot.

Lee had two younger brothers who became musicians. Louis (*b* Hamburg, 19 Oct 1819; *d* Lübeck, 26 Aug 1896), a cellist and pianist, made his first tour at the age of 12, playing in northern Germany and Copenhagen, then settled in Hamburg, where he became a cellist in the theatre orchestra, organized chamber music recitals with Hafner (later with Boïe), taught at the conservatory 1873–84 and was principal cellist of the Philharmonic Society; he composed chamber music and symphonies and wrote incidental music to Schiller's *Die Jungfrau von Orleans* and *Wilhelm Tell*. Maurice (*b* Hamburg, ?Feb 1821; *d* London, 23 June 1895), a pianist, spent the latter part of his life teaching in London, where he won a reputation as a composer of popular salon music.

LYNDA LLOYD REES

Leeds. English city. It is one of the most active centres of music in Britain, and has become more widely known for the Leeds International Pianoforte Competition held there every three years since 1963, and the Leeds Musical Festival. In the 19th century the parish church became a focal point for reform and enterprise in sacred music. Citizens of Leeds have been involved in cultural activities at every level, and the wealth of musical opportunity that has developed testifies to a long tradition of community responsibility.

1. Concerts and oratorio in the 18th century. 2. Choral music. 3. Orchestral music. 4. Other institutions. 5. Music publishers and instrument makers. 6. Education.

1. CONCERTS AND ORATORIO IN THE 18TH CENTURY. The first public concert in Leeds to be documented (*Leeds Mercury*, 20 Sept 1726) took place in the Assembly Room in Kirkgate, after which there was a rapid proliferation of concerts, music meetings and ballad operas given mainly in the Assembly Room (seating 400) or in suitable rooms in inns. At the beginning, Handelian influence was strong, and in 1741 the Welsh harpist John Parry (i), a collaborator with Handel in London, visited the town. The direction and coordination of public music-making – from 1772 centred on the annual series of subscription concerts – was mainly the responsibility of the organists of the parish church, who included John Carr (appointed 1714), Crompton, R. Jobson and David Lawton. In the *Leeds Intelligencer* of 11 September 1770 the 'new-invented . . . Piano Forte' was advertised as on sale from Thomas Bullasse, cabinet maker and organ builder in Barnsley. A piano concerto was introduced into a subscription concert programme for the first time in 1795, the soloist being Lawton, who controlled the programmes until his death in 1807. It had long been clear that the Assembly Room was inadequate and a purpose-built New Music Hall was opened in Albion Street in January 1794. In 1827 an Amateur Society was formed for the purpose of 'cultivating a more extensive taste for music and ensuring the frequency and success of public concerts' (*The Harmonicon*, v, 1827, p.161). Paganini visited Leeds in 1832.

Singers from the Holbeck Chapel in 1767 celebrated the anniversary of the king's accession by performing Purcell's *Te Deum* and parts of *Messiah*, which was performed no fewer than 18 times in the next year. The popularity of Handel's music in Yorkshire at that time was enhanced by the publication of the oratorio texts by T. Lesson of Doncaster. On 24, 25 and 26 November 1784 there was a festival of Handel's works in which the star performer was Miss Harwood, a citizen of Leeds

and pupil of Jobson. After 1771, when the infirmary was opened, the fact that oratorio was thought by the sick to have a beneficial influence very much contributed to its popularity as a form. As the Assembly Hall was too small, and the interior of the parish church too awkward for the large-scale performances considered necessary, oratorio musicians of Leeds took part in the festivals in York which were organized primarily for the benefit of the hospitals of the county.

2. CHORAL MUSIC. In the early 19th century religious feeling was strong in and around Leeds, where Methodist adherents were both numerous and vocal, and where low church factions were dominant in the Established Church. Regarding the presence of a surpliced choir of men and boys in the parish church, it was said by way of protest in 1826 that 'the exhibition of these singing men and boys was doubtless a relic of popery'. Two years later Samuel Wesley, the most renowned English organist, visited Leeds to open a new organ in the Brunswick Methodist Chapel, the installation of which had also provided cause for bitter controversy. In 1837 W. F. Hook (1798–1875) became vicar of Leeds and immediately began a campaign of reform and reconstruction. Between 1839 and 1841 the parish church was rebuilt in Perpendicular style by a local architect, R. D. Chantrell, in accordance with the liturgical requirements of the high church party to which Hook belonged. Though unmusical, Hook was concerned for the proper performance of church music; he invited John Jebb to give a series of lectures on church music in the Church Institute, and on Jebb's advice appointed James Hill, a lay clerk from St George's Chapel, Windsor, to train the choir. In the following year Hook instituted a system of payment for men and boys and appointed Wesley organist. The standards sustained at Leeds parish church influenced the musical life of the whole community. After Wesley left Leeds his work was continued by William Spark, his former articled pupil, who followed him from Exeter, and Robert Burton, his successor at the parish church.

A Madrigal and Motet Society was founded on 17 April 1850; this was re-established as a choral society in 1864. There was a musical festival in 1858 conducted by Sterndale Bennett to mark the opening of the town hall (7 September 1858); the second festival (conducted by Costa) did not take place until 1874. Sullivan was appointed conductor of the next festival in 1880, after which date the festival was held every third year (from 1970 every second year). Sullivan conducted on seven occasions, and resigned the appointment only when his health no longer permitted him to perform the duties of the office. During the Sullivan era the Leeds Festival assumed international status on account of both the quality of the chorus and the new works commissioned from such composers as Raff, Dvořák, Massenet, Humperdinck, Parry, Stanford, Elgar and Sullivan himself; the tradition of commissioning new works has been maintained. Sullivan was responsible for the inclusion of unfamiliar works by the madrigalists, and by Palestrina, Bach, Handel and Mozart, and for their being interpreted according to the latest scholarly research into performing practice. At the 1880 festival the progress of science was marked by the lighting of the town hall for the first time by electricity and – even more – by the transmission of some of the performance to neighbouring towns by land-line by the National Telephone Company. After Sullivan's retirement Stanford conducted three festivals; he was followed by a succession of virtuoso conductors, none having the overall responsibility previously required. Elgar's *Caractacus* (1898) and Walton's *Belshazzar's Feast* (1931) both had their premières there, the latter conducted by Sargent. The Centenary Festival, directed by the Earl of Harewood, took place in 1958. The festival chorus, which draws members from all over West Yorkshire and on which much of the success of the festival has traditionally depended, has had many fine chorus masters, among whom Herbert Bardgett achieved a wide reputation. In his early days he had been successively deputy organist of the parish church, organist of All Souls' Church and St Bartholomew's, Armley (with a fine Schulze organ), and conductor of the Leeds New Choral Society.

3. ORCHESTRAL MUSIC. From its inception the Leeds Festival depended on London for its orchestra, a fact reflecting the somewhat chequered history of orchestral music in what was for so long a choral stronghold. An amateur West Riding Orchestral Union was active in the 1840s but after the town hall had been opened it was considered that the magnificent organ built by Gray & Davison to the specification of Spark (appointed civic organist in 1860 in preference to Walter Parratt and James Broughton), at a cost of £5000, should do all that an orchestra could do for normal occasions, and less expensively. The organists of Leeds, however, had their own ideas: Spark instituted Saturday evening concerts in the town hall, and Burton 'Saturday Pops' at the Coliseum. Both were conscious of the social necessity of musical recreation, to which general attention had been drawn in 1853 by the 'Rational Recreation Society'. This body had sought to arrange cheap concerts for the workers of the area, but in fact found that support came from the more prosperous middle class, and later provided Herbert Fricker, the city organist, with audiences for his Saturday Orchestral Concerts, begun in 1903. By that time competition for the talents of more modest music-makers came from the brass bands of the neighbourhood, prominent among which was the Leeds Forge Band, founded by Samson Fox of Harrogate, benefactor of the Royal College of Music. Fricker's organization merged into the Leeds Symphony Orchestra, and this became the Northern Philharmonic Orchestra (conducted 1933–7 by Barbirolli) in 1928. In 1945 the city council and certain neighbouring authorities began to consider the practicability of maintaining a full-time permanent professional orchestra at an estimated cost of £50,000 a year. Two years later the Yorkshire Symphony Orchestra (conductor Maurice Miles) was founded; despite high aims and promising beginnings, the enterprise came to an end in 1955, largely through local rivalries and loyalties to other organizations such as the Hallé Orchestra, which had a long involvement in Yorkshire musical life. Throughout that period the Leeds Symphony Society (founded in 1890), successor to the Amateur Orchestral Society, maintained a high standard of amateur competence.

4. OTHER INSTITUTIONS. In the late 19th century musical institutions became more numerous. The Leeds Philharmonic Society, founded by T. Dobbs in 1870, was first conducted by James Broughton and then by his brother Alfred (both were chorus masters for the festival at different times). In 1896 Adolph Beyschlag, previously engaged in Mainz, Frankfurt am Main, Belfast and Manchester, was appointed conductor of what the *Allgemeine musikalische Zeitung* at the time described as 'the famous Yorkshire choir'. He was succeeded by Stanford who conducted the society for 11 years during which time performances were given in London and Paris; later conductors included Fricker, Bairstow and Sargent. In 1895 there was a choral contest, adjudicated by C. H. Lloyd, under the aegis of the Leeds Prize Musical Union. Alfred Benton, organist of the parish church, assisted by H. C. Embleton, a wealthy amateur and friend of Elgar, formed in 1886 the Leeds Choral Union, which travelled widely in England and visited France and Germany, before being disbanded in 1939. Henry Coward, the most notable choral director of his day, was among the society's conductors. In 1950 Melville Cooke, organist of the parish church, established the Leeds Guild of Singers, comprising 26 members, so that the Bach bicentenary could be marked by performances bearing some relation to authentic standards.

In the 19th century chamber music soirées and musical evenings organized by Thomas Haddock provided the foundation for later chamber music enterprise. Recitals and concerts are regularly given in the art gallery and in the town hall under the aegis of the city council, and also in the summer in the Long Gallery of Temple Newsam House. In 1963 the International Pianoforte Competition was established through the enterprise of a local teacher, Fanny Waterman, and Marion Thorpe (then Countess of Harewood). Winners of the competition have included Michael Roll, Radu Lupu and Murray Perahia.

In 1978 Leeds became the home of the English National Opera North, a new company under the musical directorship of David Lloyd-Jones.

5. MUSIC PUBLISHERS AND INSTRUMENT MAKERS. From the early 18th century music publishers abounded in Leeds, and were at first strongly biassed towards the publication of sacred music. In 1700 John Penrose published *The Psalm-tunes in 4 Parts* (4th edn., rev. A. Barker), John Swale *A Collection of Psalm Tunes* in 1718 and Thomas Wright *A Book of Psalmody* by John Chetham (11/1787). The works of the Leeds composer Henry Hamilton were engraved by Christopher Livesley, who was active from about 1790 to 1810. Other publishers include: Joseph Ogle (c1736), Griffith Wright, father of Thomas, and in the 19th century, Joshua Mutt, W. Clifford, John Swallow and William Jackson; in the 20th century much educational music and music literature has been published by E. J. Arnold & Son. There were several string instrument makers active in Leeds during the 19th century, and the firm of J. & J. Hopkinson, piano makers, had its main branch there from about 1835. The organ in the town hall was renovated by Abbott & Smith in the 19th century, and rebuilt to the design of Donald Hunt, then organist of the parish church, by Wood & Wordsworth in 1971.

6. EDUCATION. Vocal music in schools grew out of religious instruction and from about 1850 led to marathon performances of 'sacred choruses'. After 1886 there were Leeds School Board Concerts in which the choir of 1000 voices was conducted by W. Goodson. The demands of more specialized musical education were met for a time by the Leeds College of Music. However, a new dimension was brought into the musical life of the city by the establishment of a music department in the university; this has prospered particularly during the vice-chancellorship of Lord Boyle. Through the initiative of Alexander Goehr, professor of music

from 1971 to 1975, works outside the conventional limits have been included within programmes given in the university. From 1975 to 1981 Ian Kemp was professor of music. In 1961 the education committee, having been served by able music advisers for many years, set up the Leeds Music Centre, which in 1965 came under the control of a full-time director and resumed the title of Leeds College of Music. The Brotherton Library of the university has the Cowden Clarke Collection; the music and local history sections of the City Library have valuable holdings which include manuscripts and early editions formerly the property of the Irwin family of Temple Newsam, and the City Museum has a collection of instruments.

BIBLIOGRAPHY
Order of Service for the Day of Public Thanksgiving by the Wesleyan Reformers (Leeds, 1850)
J. Hole: *The Working Classes of Leeds* (London, 1863)
Leeds Triennial Musical Festival Programmes (Leeds, 1880–)
W. Spark: 'Musical Services at (1) Parish Church, (2) All Souls' Church (Hook Memorial), (3) Holy Trinity Church, (4) St. Martin's Church', *Musical World*, lxii (1884), 450, 460, 507, 542
F. R. Spark and J. Bennett: *A Full History of the Leeds Musical Festivals, 1858–89* (Leeds and London, 1892)
Leeds College of Music Quarterly News (Leeds, 1897–1902)
'Elgar's Caractacus at Leeds Festival', *Neue Musik-Zeitung*, xx (1898), 260
Leeds Parish Church; History of Organs 1714–1899 (Leeds, 1899)
E. Hargrave: *Musical Leeds in the Eighteenth Century*, Thoresby Society Publications, xxviii (Leeds, 1928), 302
The Novello-Cowden Clarke Collection (Leeds, 1955)
L. Sprittles: *Leeds Musical Festivals*, Thoresby Society Publications, xiii/2 (Leeds, 1958), 102
Master Violins & Antique Stringed Instruments – Exhibition Catalogue (Leeds, 1958)
E. Bradbury: '100 Years of the Leeds Festivals', *MT*, xcix (1958), 540
Centenary Musical Festival Notes (Leeds, 1958)
E. Bradbury: 'Pen Portrait: Herbert Bardgett', *MT*, ci (1960), 424
G. Jackson: *First Flute* (London, 1968)
B. Rainbow: *The Choral Revival in the Anglican Church, 1839–72* (London, 1970)
P. M. Young: *Sir Arthur Sullivan* (London, 1971)
A. Goehr: 'The Study of Music at University', *MT*, cxiv (1973), 588
S. Lindley: *The Organs, Organists & Choir of Leeds Parish Church* (Leeds, 1976)

PERCY M. YOUNG

Leemans, Hébert [Aybert] **Philippe Adrien** (*b* Bruges; *d* Paris, 10 June 1771). Flemish cellist and composer, resident in Paris. According to Vannes he was 'fils probable d'Adrien Pierre', presumably referring to the Adrien Leemans who was organist at St Donatien in Bruges from about 1738 to 12 October 1750. Leemans probably arrived in Paris in the 1750s. In the dedication of his op.3 quartets (1769) to the Marchioness of Lestang, he stated that he had long been in the service of a Parisian patron; but his name appears in contemporary periodical literature only between 1765 and 1771, and all of his known compositions date from this brief period. In the *Mémoire signifié du Sieur Peters* (1767), he is listed as 'professeur de chant et de violoncelle', and a publication announcement in the *Mercure de France* of March 1769 referred to him as a virtuoso, but did not specify his instrument. The dedication to his ariette *Que l'attente me tourmente* (1768) indicates that he was music teacher to the Countess of Polignac; further dedications show that he frequented other fashionable salons, particularly that of the Marquis and Marchioness of Seignelai. He had no official position with any of the Parisian orchestras, nor is he ever mentioned as a soloist. In 1767 Leemans began to publish his works using movable type, a process which was rare in Paris, then the centre of engraving in Europe; it

resembled the system invented in Leipzig by J. G. I. Breitkopf and was equally unsuccessful.

Leemans devoted his talents to teaching titled students and composing works appropriate to their taste. His symphonies are well constructed, employing the prevailing Italo-Mannheim style infused with French lyricism; all but two contain four movements including a minuet. The smaller chamber pieces are charming works which, to expand their sales, allow for the substitution of instruments: this flexibility, which obviously inhibited idiomatic instrumental writing, reveals much about the nature of his clientèle. Leemans's modest gifts are seen to excellent advantage in his *ariettes*, attractive little songs with simple and deft orchestral accompaniments.

WORKS
All printed works published in Paris; detailed list with partial thematic catalogue in Brook, 1962

Inst: 6 sinfonie, op.1 (c1765); 3 simphonies [op.2] (1766); 1ère [–2e] symphonie à grand orchestre (1767); Trio, 2 vn, bc/vc (1767); 6 qts, op.3 (1769), 3 for fl, bn, vn, vc, 3 for ob, vn, bn, vc or 2 vn, 2 vc or 2 vn, va, vc; 3 simphonies à grand orchestre, op.4 (1771); 1er recueil de 6 quatuors d'airs choisis [Grétry, Philidor], str qt, op.5 (1771)
Vocal: Recueil de duos, 2vv (1765), lost: 1er[–2e] recueil d'airs (1771), lost; La constance, cantatille (1767), lost; La vaine promesse, romance (c1768); 14 ariettes with insts, pubd singly (1766–71); 5 airs, 2vv, *F-Pn*; Air, 1v, harp, *Pn*

BIBLIOGRAPHY
EitnerQ; *FétisBS*
E. G. J. Gregoir: *Documents historiques relatifs à l'art musical et aux artistes-musiciens* (Brussels, 1872–6)
E. vander Straeten: *La musique aux Pays-Bas avant le XIXe siècle*, iv (Brussels, 1878/*R*1969)
M. Brenet: 'Les débuts de l'abonnement de musique', *BSIM*, ii (1906), 256
R. Vannes: *Dictionnaire des musiciens* (*compositeurs*) (Brussels, 1947)
B. S. Brook: 'Leemans of Bruges and Paris', *RBM*, xv (1961), 47
——: *La symphonie française dans la seconde moitié du XVIIIe siècle* (Paris, 1962)
M. Benoit, N. Dufourcq and M. Rambaud: 'Documents du minutier central . . . actes recueillis', *RMFC*, vii (1967), 222
BARRY S. BROOK, RICHARD VIANO

Leero [leerow] *viol. See* LYRA VIOL.

Lees, Benjamin (*b* Harbin, China, 8 Jan 1924). American composer of Chinese birth and Russian parentage. When very young, Lees moved with his parents to the USA, taking American citizenship through his parents' naturalization. He was educated in California. After military service (1942–5), he studied at the University of Southern California (1945–8) under Halsey Stevens (composition), Ernst Kanitz and Ingolf Dahl. Impressed by his compositions, George Antheil undertook to teach him, and after some four years' study recognition came with a Fromm Foundation Award in 1953. In 1954 Lees received a Guggenheim Fellowship allowing him to work in Europe; he stayed there until 1962. His aim was to remain uninfluenced by the turbulent American scene and to create his own style. He worked away from the academic centres where many American composers had studied, living at Longpont-sur-Orge, France (1954–5 and 1957–62), Vienna (1955–6) and Helsinki (1956–7). His growing reputation resulted in a publisher's contract in 1956. He returned to the USA with many mature and impressive works, prepared for a career as a composer, dividing his time between composition and teaching, first at the Peabody Conservatory in Baltimore and later in New York. He has successfully fulfilled many commissions, with many works played by major American symphony orchestras.

Lees's music is basically traditional in approach; his musical development, comparatively free from the influence of avant-garde fashions and schools, has been steady and consistent. From an early interest in the bittersweet melodic style of Prokofiev and the bizarre and surrealist aspects of Bartók's music, he progressed naturally under the unconventional guidance of Antheil. Dissociating himself from fashions and cliques, particularly while in Europe, Lees extended the tonal system with semitonal inflections, both harmonic and melodic, around not only the 3rd, but the root, 5th and octave of the major and minor chords. Rhythmically his music is active, with frequent changes of time signature and shifts of accent. These features are shown even in his early works, particularly the award-winning String Quartet no.1 and Sonata for two pianos, and his masterly Second Quartet. Having refined his style, he embarked on a series of large-scale works in which his secure command of orchestral technique and form is everywhere apparent. The Second Symphony with its recurring motifs and slow-movement finale (also a feature of the Third Symphony) is particularly notable. Of comparable stature are the Concerto for Orchestra (influenced by Bartók's), the virtuoso Violin Concerto and the cantata–oratorio *Visions of Poets*. The ironic musical juxtapositions found occasionally in these earlier works dominate the Third Symphony, which together with the bizarre *Medea of Corinth* shows a refreshing restatement of Lees's artistic creed: to be original but comprehensible.

WORKS

VOCAL AND CHORAL
Operas: The Oracle (1, Lees), 1956; The Gilded Cage (3, A. Reid), 1970–72
Other works: Songs of the Night (J. R. Nickson), 1v, pf/orch, 1952; 3 Songs (Nickson, Blake), A, pf, 1959; Cyprian Songs (Nickson), Bar, pf, 1960; Visions of Poets (Whitman), S, T, chorus, orch, 1961; Medea of Corinth (R. Jeffers), S, Mez, Bar, B, wind qnt, timp, 1970; The Trumpet of the Swan (E. B. White), narrator, orch, 1972; Songs of Love and the Sea, 1v, pf, 1977

ORCHESTRAL
Profile, 1952; 3 syms., 1953, 1958, 1968; Declamations, str, pf, 1953; 2 pf concs., 1955, 1966; Divertimento-burlesca, 1957; Interlude, str, 1957; Vn Conc., 1958; Conc. for Orch, 1959; Concertante breve, 1959; Prologue, Capriccio and Epilogue, 1959; Ob Conc., 1963; Str Qt Conc., 1964; Spectrum, 1964; Conc., chamber orch, 1966; Labyrinths, band, 1974; Etudes, pf, orch, 1974; Passacaglia, 1975; Conc., wind qnt, orch, 1976; Variations, pf, orch, 1976; Va Conc., 1977

CHAMBER AND INSTRUMENTAL
Sonata, hn, pf, 1951; 2 str qts, 1952, 1955; Evocation, fl, 1953; Vn Sonata no.1, 1953; Movement da camera, fl, cl, pf, vc, 1954; 3 Variables, ob, cl, bn, hn, pf, 1955; Invenzione, vn, 1965; Duo, fl, cl, 1967; Study no.1, vc, 1969; Collage, wind qnt, perc, str qt, 1973; Dialogue, vc, pf, 1977; Sextet, wind qnt, pf, 1977
Pf: 4 sonatas, 1949, 1950, 1956 (Sonata breve), 1963; Sonata, 2 pf, 1951; Toccata, 1953; Fantasia, 1954; 10 Pieces, 1954; 6 Ornamental Etudes, 1957; Kaleidoscopes, 1959; Epigrams, 1960; 3 Preludes, 1962; Odyssey, 1970
Principal publisher: Boosey & Hawkes

BIBLIOGRAPHY
D. Cooke: 'The Music of Benjamin Lees', *Tempo* (1959), no.51, p.20
——: 'The Recent Music of Benjamin Lees', *Tempo* (1963), no.64, p.11
——: 'Benjamin Lees's Visions of Poets', *Tempo* (1964), no.68, p.25
N. O'Loughlin: 'Benjamin Lees's String Quartet Concerto', *Tempo* (1967), no.82, p.21
——: 'Two Works by Benjamin Lees', *Tempo* (1970), no.93, p.19
NIALL O'LOUGHLIN

Leeuw, Cornelis Janszoon (de) (*b* Edam, *c*1613; *d* Amsterdam, *c*1662). Netherlands publisher, composer and editor. He gave up his musical career for that of publisher, joining the Amsterdam booksellers' guild in about 1648. He edited and published both musical and non-musical books, often for the Remonstrant Church; after going bankrupt in 1660 he edited music for other publishers, although in some cases perhaps merely for publicity (possibly editions of Pers). He had little success with his choral settings of Camphuysen's *Stichtelycke rymen* or his own songbook *Christelycke plichtrymen*, but his editions of the psalms, with all melodies for the first time in the same (alto) clef, enjoyed great popularity.

WORKS
(printed works published in Amsterdam unless otherwise stated)
Een kindeken is ons gebooren, 3vv, 1644[3]
[12] Stichtelycke rymen (D. Camphuysen), 3–8vv, bc (1646)
Traen ooghen traen, 4vv, in D. Camphuysen: Stichtelycke rymen (1647); authorship doubtful
Wie kan die op aerde woonen, song, 3vv; 19 canons: in Christelycke plichtrymen (1648–9); song ed. in Enschedé (1903)
Psalm xli.7, 4vv, *c*1651; Psalms xxiii, cxxviii, 4vv; 12 canons, 1658–; 2 canons, 1661: in De CL Psalmen Davids (Datheen) (several edns., *c*1650–*c*1661)
Psalms i, viii, 4vv, in Uytbreydingh over de psalmen Davids (Camphuysen) (1652, 1662–97)
9 lofzangen, 4vv, in C. le Jeune: De CL Psalmen Davids (Schiedam, 1665)

LOST
[6] Wegh-wijser (Camphuysen), 4vv (1638)
Hollandtsche vreughd' (2 vols.), 4vv, bc (1642–*c*1644)
Vierdagen, 3vv, bc (1644 or earlier): Lofsangen op de geboorte Christi; 't Leven Christi; Christelycke betrachtinge op het lijden Christi op Goede Vrijdagh; Sondagh, ofte geestelijcke nut des verrijsenis Christi; Olijf-bergh, ofte vertooningh des hemelvaerts Christi; Pinxter, ofte zendingh des Heyligen Geestes op d'apostelen Christi
Christelycke gebeden [op] sangs voyse ghestelt, 3vv (1644 or earlier) [? part of Vierdagen]

EDITIONS
(all published in Amsterdam)
G. G. Gastoldi: Balletten met drie stemmen (1648) [with 4th voice part added by Leeuw]
Christelycke plichtrymen (1648–9)
De CL Psalmen Davids (Datheen) (several edns., *c*1650–*c*1661)
Uytbreydingh over de Psalmen Davids (Camphuysen) (1652, 1662–97)
Davids Psalmen (H. Bruno) (1656)
Davids Psalmen (J. Westerbaen) (The Hague, 1656); editorship doubtful
P. Pers: Bellerophon; Urania; Gesang der Zeden (1662–95); editorship doubtful

BIBLIOGRAPHY
Primeira parte do index da livraria de musica do muyto alto, e poderoso Rey Dom João o IV. nosso senhor (Lisbon, 1649/R1967), 162, 167f, 504; ed. J. de Vasconcellos (Oporto, 1874–6)
J. W. Enschedé: 'Cornelis de Leeuw', *TVNM*, vii/2 (1902), 89–148; vii/3 (1903), 157–232
D. F. Scheurleer: *Nederlandsche liedboeken* (The Hague, 1912–23)
R. A. Rasch: 'The Balletti of Giovanni Giacomo, Gastoldi and the Musical History of the Netherlands', *TVNM*, xxiv/2 (1974), 112–45
RANDALL H. TOLLEFSEN

Leeuw, Ton de (*b* Rotterdam, 16 Nov 1926). Dutch composer and teacher. He had his first composition lessons from Toebosch, studied next with Badings, and then worked under Messiaen and Hartmann in Paris; on returning to the Netherlands he studied ethnomusicology under Jaap Kunst for four years. There followed a period as a music producer for Dutch radio (1954–60). A teacher of composition at the Amsterdam Conservatory, he directed the institution between 1971 and 1973, and he also teaches modern music and ethnomusicology at the musicology institute of Amsterdam University.

Leeuw's first compositions, such as the Concerto grosso, the *Treurmuziek* and the Symphony for strings, appeared in the immediate postwar period; in structure and technique they relate to the music of Bartók and Hindemith. The Sonata for two pianos (1950) shows Pijper's influence, in that the germ-cell principle is applied to the rhythmic as well as the melodic structure. This first period closed with the radio oratorio *Job*, which won an Italia Prize in 1956; here a French text, compiled by the composer, is set for singing and speaking voices with orchestral and electronic sounds. The next phase in Leeuw's work began with the orchestral *Mouvements rétrogrades*, a highly concentrated piece governed by mirror relations. It is in ten short sections, which he described as ten different facets of a single structure, and the music makes use of harmonic and 12-note pitch serialism. Among the chamber works of the same period, the First Quartet is particularly notable, extending serial procedures to durations and dynamics. The music develops in four stages: the first is a disordered cloud of pitches, in the second small atonal units crystallize from the cloud, the third develops them to individual musical shapes, which, in the fourth stage, are mutually related according to principles drawn from the pitch series. Structures are clearly distinguished by means of dynamic nuances and performing techniques.

A first journey to India in 1961, made at the invitation of the Dutch Ministry of Education, brought Leeuw into closer contact with eastern thought, which from that time has exerted an important influence on his work. The orchestral pieces *Nritta* and *Ombres* indicate the first steps in the new direction, a direction towards open, asymmetrical structures, staticity and objective expression. In *Ombres* the music arises from statistical and serial techniques, manipulative methods borrowed from mathematics, and elements of chance. The Symphonies of Winds (1963), commissioned by the Pittsburgh Wind SO, are built from large banks of sound which merge with and overwhelm one another in a great number of different forms and timbre combinations. Based on a chord from Stravinsky's Symphonies of Wind Instruments, the composition is dedicated to that composer. In it Leeuw introduced an original proportional rhythmic notation intended not only to simplify performance, but to achieve a new, freer conception of rhythm. Another noteworthy piece from these years is the one-act opera *De droom*, in which the most important episode is a dream scene, a dance accompanied by choral singing of haiku in English translation; the final scene is a retrograde of the first.

In Leeuw's compositions after 1965 space has an important place, most particularly in the series *Spatial Music* (1966–71). The first of these works requires the 32–48 players to be spread about the hall as much as possible, the music performed by any individual depending on his position. *Spatial Music II* is for a spatially disposed percussion ensemble, and the third piece places an orchestra at four corners of the hall, with changes of position going on during the music. The live sounds of this work are heard in combination with the electronic composition *Syntaxis I*. In *Spatial Music IV* 12 players are in constant movement around nuclear points represented by a piano and two percussionists. *Haiku II* has a soprano soloist singing from six different points and accompanied on her journey by four wind players, while the orchestra is divided into five groups. The singer's ambulations, the antiphonal character of much of the music and the percussion writing all support a sense of affinity with oriental ritual music. Later works to employ spatial groupings include *Lamento pacis* and Music for Organ and 12 Players, the latter intended for performance in a church.

WORKS

ORCHESTRAL

Conc. grosso, str, 1946; Treurmuziek in memoriam Willem Pijper, 1946; Sym., str, perc, 1950; Sym., str, 1951; Plutos-suite, 1952; Vn Conc. no.1, 1953; Mouvements rétrogrades, 1957; Nritta, 1961; Ombres, 1961; Vn Conc. no.2, 1961; Symphonies of Winds, 1963;

Spatial Music I, 1966; Spatial Music III, 1967; Music for Str, 1970; Spatial Music V, 1971; Gending, gamelan, 1975

VOCAL

Dramatic: Alceste, television opera, 1963; De droom (opera, 1, Leeuw, after Chin. legend), 1963; Litany of our Time, television score, S, chorus, fl, harp, pf, db, perc, tape, elec, 1969

Other works: Job (radio oratorio, Leeuw, after Bible), 1956; The Magic of Music (after Indian book on music theory), chorus 2vv, 1958; Psalm cxviii, chorus, 3 trbn, 1966; Haiku II, S, orch, 1968; Lamento pacis (Erasmus), 16 solo vv, 9 insts, 1969; Cloudy Forms, male chorus, 1970

Songs: Die Weise von Liebe und Tod (Rilke), 1v, pf, 1948; Berceuse presque nègre (P. van Ostayen), 1v, pf, 1948; Goden en zangers (A. R. Holst), S, pf, 1948; Diablerie (J. Engelman), S, pf, 1948; 5 Songs (Lorca), 1v, pf, 1952; 2 Songs (Mistral), 1v, pf, 1953; De toverfluit (B. Aafjes), S, fl, vc, pf, 1954; 8 European Songs, 1v, pf, 1954; 4 Songs, 3 rec, 1v, 1955; Haiku I, S, pf, 1963; Vocalise, 1v, 1968

INSTRUMENTAL AND ELECTRONIC

Str Trio, 1948; Introduzione e passacaglia, org, 1949; Sonata, fl, pf, 1949; Sonata, vn, pf, 1951; Trio, fl, cl, pf, 1952; 5 Sketches, ob, cl, bn, va, vc, 1952; Sonatine, vn, pf, 1955; Str Qt no.1, 1958; Antiphony, wind qnt, 4-track tape, 1960; The Four Seasons, harp, 1964; Schelp, fl, va, gui, 1964; Str Qt no.2, 1964; Nightmusic, fl, 1966; Syntaxis I, tape, 1966; Music for Vn, 1967; Spatial Music II, perc ens, 1967; Spatial Music IV, 15 insts, 1968; Music for Ob, 1969; Music for Org and 12 Players, 1970; Reserved Night, fl, 1971; Midare, mar, 1972; Sweelinck-variaties, org, 1972–3; Canzone, 10 brass, 1973–4; Music for trbn, 1973–4; Mo-du, amp clavichord/hpd, 1974; Rime, fl, harp, 1974; Mountains, b cl, tape, 1976

Pf: Scherzo, 1948; Sonatine, 1949; Sonata, 2 pf, 1950; Variations sur une chanson populaire française, pf/hpd, 1950; 4 Preludes, 1950; 5 études, 1951; 4 Rhythmic Studies, 1952; 3 African Etudes, 1954; 6 Dances, 1955; Men Go their Ways, 1964; Linkerhand en rechterhand, 1976

Principal publisher: Donemus

BIBLIOGRAPHY

T. de Leeuw: 'Mouvements rétrogrades', *Sonorum speculum* (1961), no.8, p.24

W. Paap: 'A new String Quartet by Ton de Leeuw', *Sonorum speculum* (1965), no.25, p.24

E. Vermeulen: 'Lamento pacis by Ton de Leeuw', *Sonorum speculum* (1969), no.39, p.23

D. Manneke: 'Ton de Leeuw's Music for Strings', *Sonorum speculum* (1971), no.48, p.17

J. Wouters: 'Ton de Leeuw', *Dutch Composers' Gallery* (Amsterdam, 1971), 17–49

D. Manneke: 'Ton de Leeuw: Music for Organ and 12 Players', *Sonorum speculum* (1972), no.49, p.7   JOS WOUTERS

Leeuwen Boomkamp, Carel van (*b* Borculo, 11 Aug 1906). Dutch cellist and viola da gamba player. He studied with Gerard Hekking in Paris, among others, and was engaged as a cellist for some years with the Haarlem Orchestral Society, and the Concertgebouw Orchestra, Amsterdam, before devoting himself solely to playing chamber music and teaching. His special interest is 18th-century music, and he owns an important collection of old instruments. He came to be regarded as a virtuoso viola da gamba player and a sensitive stylist. In 1947 he published *De klanksfeer der oude muziek*. He has been a member of various outstanding chamber music groups, such as the Netherlands String Quartet and Alma Musica. Works were written for him by Badings and Escher, among others, and he has taught at the conservatories of Amsterdam, Utrecht and The Hague. He is a Knight of the Order of Oranje Nassau.

TRUUS DE LEUR

LeFanu, Nicola (Frances) (*b* Wickham Bishops, Essex, 28 April 1947). English composer, daughter of Elizabeth Maconchy. She was educated at St Hilda's College, Oxford, and the RCM. She also studied composition in master classes with Petrassi in Siena and Maxwell Davies at Dartington. After three years as a schoolteacher, she became a tutor at Morley College, London, in 1972, and a lecturer at King's College,

London University, in 1977. One of her earliest compositions, the Variations for oboe quartet, won her the first of several prizes and scholarships. Her music is distinguished above all by its linear qualities: the melodic line of the contrapuntal, serially organized earlier works and of the monodic pieces; and the splintered line, the complex instrumental gestures, of her later writing, as in *The Hidden Landscape*. The later style is particularly well suited to theatre pieces such as *Antiworld* and *The Last Laugh*.

WORKS

Music-theatre: Antiworld, dancer, ens, 1972; Magic Theatre, ens, tape, 1973; The Last Laugh, 1973; Dawnpath, S, Bar, dancer, ens, 1977
Orch: Preludio, chamber orch, 1968; The Hidden Landscape, 1973; Columbia Falls, 1975; Preludio II, 1976 [rev. of Preludio]
Choral: Christ Calls Man Home, SATB, 1971; The Valley Shall Sing, vv, brass, 1973, rev. as The Little Valleys, SSSS, 1975
Solo vocal: Il cantico dei cantici, S, 1968; Always New and Always Hidden, Mez, pf, 1969; But Stars Remaining, S, 1970; Rondeaux, T, hn, 1972; Paysage, Bar, 1973; The Same Day Dawns, S, fl + a fl, cl + b cl, perc, vn, vc, 1974; For we are the Stars, 16 solo vv, 1978; Verses from Ps xc, S, chorus, 1978
Chamber and inst: Soliloquy, ob, 1965; Trio, cl, vn, vc, 1966; Variations, ob qt, 1968; Chiaroscura, pf, 1969; Cl Qnt, 1971; Abstracts and a Frame, vn, pf, 1971; Omega, org, 1972; Collana, fl + a fl, cl + b cl, perc, vn, vc, db, 1976; Deva, solo vc, fl + a fl, cl, bn, hn, vn, va, db, 1979
Educational: Songs and Sketches, vcs, 1971

Principal publisher: Novello

BIBLIOGRAPHY
R. Cooke: 'Nicola LeFanu', *MT*, cxvi (1975), 961
                                        GERALD LARNER

Lefébure. *See* LEFÈVRE.

Lefebure, Louis Antoine [André]. *See* LEFEBVRE, LOUIS ANTOINE.

Lefebure, Yvonne (*b* Ermont, Seine-et-Oise, 29 June 1900). French pianist. Showing pronounced musical gifts at an early age, she won the *prix des petits prodigies* of the Paris Conservatoire at nine. Later she won there six *premiers prix*; her teachers were Maurice Emanuel, Georges Caussade, and (for fugue) Widor. She gave her first recital when she was 12, her earliest programmes including works like Liszt's Sonata and Schumann's *Etudes symphoniques*. Her main piano teacher was Cortot, in whose Ecole Normale de Musique she later held a master class; she was also a professor at the Paris Conservatoire from 1952 to 1967. An officer of the Légion d'honneur, she is also the wife of the musicologist Frederick Goldbeck. Lefebure's career has been divided between playing and teaching. Her acute musical ear and mind have made her an unusually authentic guide to the performance of French piano music of the first half of the 20th century, but her very catholic repertory includes the Diabelli Variations of Beethoven as well as those on a theme of Rameau by Dukas, all Ravel, and all the sonatas of her teacher, Maurice Emanuel, which she has recorded. In concertos she has been heard with Van Beinum, Boult, Furtwängler, Markevich, Mengelberg, Mitropoulos, Munch and Paray in many important musical centres.
                                        FELIX APRAHAMIAN

Lefebvre. *See* LEFÈVRE.

Lefebvre, Charles Edouard (*b* Paris, 19 June 1843; *d* Aix-les-Bains, 8 Sept 1917). French composer. A son of the celebrated painter Jules Lefebvre (1805–82), he studied law before enrolling at the Paris Conservatoire. In 1870 he won the Prix de Rome for his cantata *Le jugement de Dieu*. After his stay in Italy he toured Greece and the orient, returning to Paris in 1873. Twice awarded the Prix Chartier, in 1884 and 1891, he replaced Benjamin Godard in 1895 as professor of the ensemble class at the Conservatoire. He spent most of his life in Paris, where he devoted himself to composition as well as teaching.

As a composer Lefebvre was highly regarded by French critics during the late 19th century. Even they, however, recognized that his contribution, comprising virtually all the important musical genres, was not up to the level of the leading French composers of the time. He was not an innovator, and although he admired Wagner's music, his own instrumentation was never as dense as Wagner's. In his own words, he worked in pastels rather than oils. The style and texture of his instrumental pieces might be compared to those of Mendelssohn, whom he admired greatly. In *Judith* he anticipated the 20th-century French predilection for opera-oratorio typical of Les Six, particularly Milhaud and Honegger.

WORKS
(selective list; all printed works published in Paris)
STAGE
(all operas, unless otherwise stated)
Lucrèce (3, E. Blau), 1877–8
Le trésor (opéra comique, 1, F. Coppée), op.53, Angers, 1883 (?1884)
Zaïre (4, P. Collin, after Voltaire), op.66, Lille, 1887 (1887)
Djelma (3, C. Lormon), Paris, Opéra, 25 May 1894 (1894)

OTHER VOCAL
Solo vv, chorus, orch: Le jugement de Dieu, 1870, cantata [Prix de Rome]; Psaume xxiii [Domini est terra], op.25, 1871 (1876); Judith, biblical drama (Collin), op.31 (1877); Melka, fantastic legend (Collin), op.53 (1880); Eloâ, lyric poem (Collin, after A. de Vigny), op.70 (1888); Sainte-Cécile, lyric poem (E. Guinand), op.99 (1896); La fille de Jephté, lyric poem (de Vigny), op.120 (1908)
Unacc. chorus: Au bord du Nil (Hugo), op.49, 1879 (?c1879); Divine Hébé (Leconte de Lisle), op.69, 1886 (?c1886); Choeur d'Esther (Racine), op.74, 1888 (n.d.); Sombre nuit (Racine), op.127 (1912); Les anges gardiens (Collin) (n.d.); Isis (n.d.)

35 songs

INSTRUMENTAL
Orch: Sym., d, op.50, 1879 (?c1879); Ouverture de Fiesque, 1866; Ouverture dramatique, g, 1875; Ouverture Toggenburg (1905); Dalila, op.40 (1875); [2] Suites, opp.57, 59 (n.d.); Une sérénade, op.65 (1884); Cortège villageois, op.75, 1890 (n.d.); Suite, op.116 (n.d.); Andante et choral, harp, op.117 (1906); Prélude dramatique (1912); Cortège nuptial (1924); Esquisses pastorales, suite (n.d.)
Other works: Pieces for org, solo pf, pf 4 hands

WRITINGS
'Les formes de la musique instrumentale', *EMDC*, II/v (Paris, 1930), 3121

BIBLIOGRAPHY
H. Imbert: *Profils d'artistes contemporains* (Paris, 1897) [with catalogue of works]
Orbus: 'La vie intime d'un grand musicien: Charles Lefebvre', *Revue des deux mondes*, lviii (1930), 346–76
                                        ELAINE BRODY

Lefebvre, Denis (*fl* 2nd half of the 17th century). French composer. The only fact known about him is that he was *maître de musique* at Roye, Picardy, before going about 1660 to Paris, where he was perhaps associated with the Jesuits. He may have been related to the Denis Lefebvre, a native of Péronne, who was a singer and chaplain at the Sainte-Chapelle early in the century. His three sets of *Cantiques spirituels et hymnes de l'église* for two voices (Paris, 1660, 1666, 1674; 2/1710) have texts translated from the Latin (perhaps by Rotrou), and some of their melodies are paraphrased from Gregorian chant. Gastoué regarded these pieces as the real source of popular religious song in France. Lefebvre also published a book of 19 four-part *Airs à boire* and the *Premier livre d'airs à quatre parties* (both Paris, 1660).

BIBLIOGRAPHY
A. Gastoué: 'Sur quelques vieux cantiques', *Variations sur la musique d'église* (Paris, 1913)
——: *Le cantique populaire en France* (Paris, 1924)
DAVID TUNLEY

Le Febvre, Jacques. *See* FABER STAPULENSIS, JACOBUS.

Lefebvre [Le Fevre], Jacques (*fl* early 17th century). French composer. He was a composer to the king until 1619. The 36 vocal pieces constituting his *Meslanges de musique* are in the polyphonic tradition of the previous century. The one extant copy is incomplete, but to judge by the few works that can be restored from the four partbooks remaining he was a fine exponent of the light and witty Renaissance chanson. His few *airs* include one or two in the more progressive medium of voice with basso continuo. La Borde included two airs by Lefebvre in his *Essai sur la musique* (1780).

WORKS
Meslanges de musique, 2–6, 8vv (Paris, 1613)
2 airs in 1615[11], 1 in 1626[11]; 1 in *Airs de cour pour voix et luth* (*1603–1643*), ed. A. Verchaly (Paris, 1961)
Airs de cours et airs à boire, 1v, bc, *F-Pn*
Various edns. of individual songs in 18th- and 19th-century anthologies; 2 chansons, 3vv, ed. in Tunley

BIBLIOGRAPHY
D. Tunley: 'Jacques le Fevre and his "Meslanges de Musique"', *MT*, cxv (1974), 381
DAVID TUNLEY

Lefèbvre, Joseph (*b* Berlin, 20 July 1761; *d* ?Paris, after 1822). French composer. He was a brother of Mme Dugazon and wrote the music to two comic operas given in Paris at the Comédie-Italienne. The first, *Le prix, ou L'embarras du choix* (one act, 10 December 1788), was saved only by the presence of Mlle Renaud and Mme Dugazon in the cast, while *Caroline de Lichtfield* (Lichfield) (three acts, 2 December 1789) so displeased the audience that the performance had to be abandoned. Several songs from these operas were published separately. From 1790 to 1794 Lefèbvre was a violinist at the Comédie-Italienne. He then became first violinist at the Théâtre Feydeau, and in 1801, when the Feydeau and Favart troupes united to form the Opéra-Comique, he was made *chef d'orchestre*. He retired in 1822.

BIBLIOGRAPHY
J. J. Olivier: *Madame Dugazon* (Paris, 1917), 15
PHILIP ROBINSON

Lefebvre [Lefebure, Lefevre], Louis Antoine [André] (*d* La Ferté-sous-Jouarre, 20 July 1763). French composer. He was organist at the royal church of St Louis-en-l'Isle (Paris). He composed almost exclusively vocal music, mainly motets, *airs* and *cantatilles*, through which he seems to have made a considerable name in Paris, for when reporting the publication of his third *cantatille*, *L'absence*, the *Mercure de France* (June 1747, p.137) commented on his growing reputation. Lefebvre wrote 22 such works and a cantata *Atalante et Hippomène* (1759) in which, as in some of the *cantatilles* written towards the end of his life, the Rococo characteristics of the form give way to those of the nascent Classical style, not only in the phrase structure of the melodic lines but also in the instrumental writing of the accompaniments. His later *cantatilles* thus mark a new trend in French vocal chamber music; indeed the publisher Le Clerc contracted him to provide new ac-

companiments to some 60 *cantatilles* by Louis Lemaire, but he died before carrying this out. He also composed some sacred music, his motets being performed fairly regularly at the Concert Spirituel for a period from 1749 onwards.

WORKS
(all printed works published in Paris)
22 cantatilles, most for 1v, insts (*c*1745–59)
Atalante et Hippomène, cantata, 2vv, insts (1759)
Divertissements: L'amour justifié, 2vv, insts (?1761); Le réveil de Flore, 3vv, insts (n.d.)
12 motets, 4 pubd (n.d.), 8 in MS collections
airs, duos etc

BIBLIOGRAPHY
D. Tunley: *The Eighteenth-century French Cantata* (London, 1974)
DAVID TUNLEY

Lefèbvre, Louise-Rosalie. *See* DUGAZON, LOUISE-ROSALIE.

Lefebvre, Xavier. *See* LEFÈVRE, XAVIER.

Lefeure. *See* LEFÈVRE.

Lefèvre [Lefebvre, Fèvre, Lefeure, Lefébure]. French 16th- to 19th-century organ builders. The name belonged to at least 23 builders, mostly members of the same family.

Some of the early Lefèvres include: Antoine (*fl* Paris, 1524–51), who built an organ for Les Mathurins, Paris, in 1524 and made his will at Sens in 1528; Guillaume (*fl* 1572–81), his son, an organ builder of Rouen, who worked at Le Mans in 1572 and at Chartres from 1574 to 1581; Charles (i) (*fl* Rouen, 1573), another son of Antoine, who cleaned and repaired the organ at St Maclou, Rouen, in 1573; Léonard (*d* Angoulême, *c*1659), son of Guillaume, a native of Fresnay-sur-Sarthe who worked at Le Mans from 1603 to 1613, Angoulême in 1615, Mitry-Mory and the St Ausone Abbey; Nicolas (i) (*fl* 1606–10), son of Charles (i), both an organist and organ builder, who worked at Angoulême (1606–8), Rouen (1609), Mantes and then Chevreuse (St Martin, 1610); Nicolas (ii) (*fl* 1629–*c*1635), a grandson of Charles (i), who is known to have worked in Rouen about 1635.

Clément (*b* Rouen, *c*1630; *d* Rouen, 29 Sept 1709), son of Nicolas (ii), was organist of Notre-Dame-la-Ronde in 1663. He rebuilt the organ of St Nicaise, Rouen, in 1684. From 1681, he worked with his son Germain (baptized Rouen, 6 Oct 1656; *d* Rouen, 1694), until the latter's death; together they built a four-manual and pedal organ at St Herbland, Rouen (1685–8), and an almost identical organ at St Denis, Rouen (1688–97) (*Grand orgue*: Montre 8′, Bourdon 16′, Bourdon 8′, Prestant, Flûte 4′, Nazard, Doublette, Tierce, Fourniture IV, Cymbale III, Cornet V, Trompette, Clairon, Voix humaine; *Positif*: Montre 4′, Bourdon 8′, Flûte 4′, Nazard, Doublette, Quarte de nazard, Tierce, Fourniture III, Cymbale II, Larigot, Cromhorne; *Récit*: Cornet V, Trompette; *Echo*: Bourdon, Prestant, Nazard, Doublette, Tierce, Fourniture III, Cromhorne, Voix humaine; *Pédale*: Bourdon (open) 8′, Flûte (open) 4′, Trompette). The St Herbland organ is now at Bolbec. On the completion of this organ Germain became organist at St Herbland, remaining there until his death. Another son of Clément, Claude (baptized Rouen, 29 Dec 1667), crossed the Atlantic in 1707. His letters from Cartagenas, where he built three organs, and Caracas, where he built one or two others, are printed in Dufourcq (1934–5, p.394). Charles (ii) (baptized Rouen, 22 May 1670; *d* 8 Sept 1737), a third son of Clément, worked as an organ builder with his father after his brother Germain's death. He restored the organ of St Maclou (1696–1707) and built that at St Vivien (1710–12, enlarged 1719). His last organ was for St Nicolas, Rouen. He was organist of St Vivien from 1698 to 1735.

Jean-Baptiste Nicolas (baptized Rouen, 6 Feb 1705; *d* Rouen, 26 March 1784), son of Charles (ii), was the most famous of the Lefèvres, of comparable importance to F.-H. Clicquot and Riepp. Characteristics of his style were an extension of the manual compass up to *e′′′* but a curtailment of the upper range of the pedal from the old *e′* to *c′* only; an extension of some of the cornets from *c′* down to *f*; an increase in the number of ranks of the Fournitures and Cymbales, often up to five each; the addition of 8′ flutes to both *Grand orgue* and *Positif* of narrow-scale leaded metal from *c*; the addition of extra trumpets (frequently in large numbers), his normal arrangement being two on the *Grand orgue* and one each on the *Positif* and *Récit*, besides those on the *Pédale* and *Bombarde* (on organs having one); the use of a Bombarde 16′; up to five cornets, one on each manual; and the addition on the *Pédale* of a Nazard and a 16′ Trompette.

A list of the principal organs of Jean-Baptiste Nicolas Lefèvre is given in Dufourcq (1934–5, p.305f). Chief among these were the instruments at Caudebec-en-Caux (1738–40; including a new Flûte allemande dessus); St Etienne, Caen (1743–7); Abbaye de Montivilliers (1746); St Maclou, Rouen (1761); St Martin, Tours (1761; the largest French classical organ, it has the following specification: *Grand orgue*: 32, 32, 16, 16, 8, 8, two 8′ flutes, 4, 2, VI, V, IV, Gros nazard, Grosse tierce, Nazard, Quarte de nazard, Tierce, Larigot, Cornet, two Trompettes, two Clairons; *Positif*: 8, 16, 8, two 8′ flutes, 4, 2, V, IV, Nazard, Quarte, Tierce, Larigot, Cornet, Trompette, Cromhorne, Voix humaine, Clairon; *Bombarde*: 8, 4, Cornet, Bombarde, two Trompettes, Clairon; *Récit*: Cornet, Trompette; *Echo*: Cornet; *Pédale*, 36 notes: 16, 8, 8, 4, 4, Gros nazard, Grosse tierce, Nazard, Quarte, Tierce, Bombarde (24′), two Trompettes, two Clairons); Evreux Cathedral (1774); St Pierre, Caen (1753, 1778; including a new Bombarde on the *Grand orgue*, a new Flûte of three octaves, Quarte and Hautbois on the *Positif* and a new Bombarde on the *Pédale*); Verneuil (1779; including a Flûte allemande on the *Grand orgue* and Quarte, Cornet, Voix humaine and Hautbois de deux octaves on the *Positif*; recently restored). Jean-Baptiste Nicolas was also organist of St Nicaise, Rouen, in 1737, at which time he appears to have succeeded his father at St Vivien, Rouen, where he was organist until 1782.

Another son of Charles (ii), Louis (baptized 23 May 1708; buried Rouen, 23 Dec 1754), worked sometimes alone and sometimes with his brother Jean-Baptiste Nicolas. In 1739 he restored the organ of St Vivien, Rouen, and together with his brother he restored and reconstructed the organ of Notre Dame, Caudebec-en-Caux, Normandy (1738–40; four manuals and pedal, the keyboards with bone naturals and ebony accidentals). The inventory of his possessions made on 17 January 1755 is printed in Dufourcq (1934–5, pp.390–92).

Other Lefèvre organ builders were apparently not related to the main Lefèvre family. Jacques Liévin (*b* Hesdin, 1621; *d* ?Rouen, after 1665), son of a half-brother of the De Héman nephews, was their pupil in Paris and later their colleague. He married a sister of Pierre Desenclos, with whom he worked at Mitry and at St Médard, Paris. He later went to Rennes, where he built the organ of St Georges in 1654 (now in St Sauveur), and to Dôle (1657), and built the organ at the Église du Voeu, Cherbourg (1661). Jean (*fl* 1650–66) was an organist and Carmelite priest; as an organ builder he restored the instrument at St Vivien, Rouen. Pierre (*b* Troyes, *c*1670; *d* Paris, 1737) worked as an organ builder in Paris from 1692. Charles (iii) (*fl* Abbeville, mid-19th century) built the organ at St Sépulcre, Abbeville.

BIBLIOGRAPHY

N. Dufourcq: *Documents inédits relatifs à l'orgue français* (Paris, 1934–5)
——: *Esquisse d'une histoire de l'orgue en France* (Paris, 1935)
M. Vanmackelberg: 'Les orgues d'Abbeville', *Mémoires de la Société d'Emulation d'Abbeville* (Abbeville, 1967)
F. Douglass: *The Language of the Classical French Organ* (New Haven, 1969)

GUY OLDHAM

Lefevre, André. *See* LEFEBVRE, LOUIS ANTOINE.

Le Fèvre, François (*fl* Paris, 1558–60). French composer. He seems to have specialized in occasional pieces for the court. His chanson *Que dira l'on du noble advenement de ce vainqueur*, celebrating the return of Duke François de Guise after the capture of Calais from the English, was printed in 1558 along with panegyric verses by François Habert. Its musical style is reminiscent of Janequin's *Bataille*. Two years later Du Chemin's 14th book of chansons included a piece by Le Fèvre entitled *Le roy boit*; it is also possible that the same composer was responsible for an unascribed piece celebrating the siege and capture of Calais, *Hardis Français et furieulx Normans* from the same book. Eitner identified Le Fèvre with 'Lefe' to whom Attaingnant attributed two chansons – *Puisque ton dard m'a mis soubz ta puissance* and *Troys mois y a que j'attens ung bon jour* (1548[8–9]).

BIBLIOGRAPHY

EitnerS
D. Heartz: *Pierre Attaingnant, Royal Printer of Music* (Berkeley and Los Angeles, 1969)

FRANK DOBBINS

Le Fevre, Jacques. *See* LEFEBVRE, JACQUES.

Lefevre, Louis Antoine. *See* LEFEBVRE, LOUIS ANTOINE.

Lefèvre [Lefebvre, Lefevre, Lefévre], **(Jean) Xavier** (*b* Lausanne, 6 March 1763; *d* Paris, 9 Nov 1829). French clarinettist and composer of Swiss birth. He studied the clarinet with Michael Yost in Paris and joined the Gardes Françaises in 1778. He performed a concerto at the Concert Spirituel as early as 1783. From 1791 to 1817 he played in the Opéra orchestra and he was principal clarinettist in the imperial chapel (later the royal chapel) from 1807. He taught at the Paris Conservatoire from its foundation (1795) until 1824. His clarinet method was adopted there and used even after improvements to the clarinet had made the work obsolete; it was also translated into German and Italian. His compositions include concertos, symphonies concertantes and chamber music, all of which use the clarinet prominently. He added a *c#′/g#′′* key to the standard five-key clarinet but was not, as many sources state, the first to play a clarinet with six keys. Fétis praised his beautiful sound and clean execution.

WORKS
(*most published in Paris*)

Vocal: Vive le roi, 3vv; Canon; Les frères La Rochejaquelin, 1v, pf; La ronde anglaise

Orch: 7 cl concs., nos.4, 6 ed. S. Dudley (Paris, 1975); 2 symphonies concertantes, solo cl, bn (after 1801), lost; Symphonie concertante, solo ob, cl, bn (after 1801), lost

Wind band: many minor works, incl. marches, Pas de manoeuvre

Chamber: at least 3 qts, cl, vn, va, b; 6 trios, 2 cl, bn, mentioned by Fétis; at least 48 duos in 8 sets, 2 cl; 12 petits duos très faciles (in 2 sets), 2 cl; 80 airs en duo in 2 bks; 6 duos in 2 sets, cl, bn; ?7 sonates, cl, bc, op.12 [no.5, ed. R. Viollier (Geneva, 1949); no.3 ed. E. Borrel (Geneva, 1950)]

Pedagogical: Méthode de clarinette . . . adoptée pour le Conservatoire (1802/*R*1974), incl. 12 sonatas, cl, bc

BIBLIOGRAPHY
FétisB

C. Pierre: *Le Conservatoire national de musique et de déclamation: documents historiques et administratifs* (Paris, 1900)

G. Rendall: *The Clarinet* (London, 1954, rev. 2/1971 by P. Bate)

L. V. Youngs: *Jean Xavier Lefèvre, his Contributions to the Clarinet and Clarinet Playing* (diss., Catholic U., Washington, DC, 1970)

FRÉDÉRIC ROBERT

Leffloth, Johann Matthias [Löffeloth, J. Matthäus] (*b* Nuremberg, baptized 6 Feb 1705; *d* Nuremberg, buried 2 Nov 1731). German organist and composer. Leffloth was the son of Johann Matthias Leffloth, organist at St Margaretha in Nuremberg, from whom he received his first musical training; he probably also received some instruction from W. H. Pachelbel. Some time after 1722 he became organist at St Leonhard. The only noteworthy biographical sketch is by Schubart; it is an extravagant account praising Leffloth as a genius who might have changed the course of music but for his early death.

Leffloth's tonal and thematic materials are firmly rooted in Baroque tradition, but his keyboard style frequently calls for hand crossing and a degree of dexterity unusual for this period. Although he is often mentioned as a composer of keyboard concertos, only two of his works designated concerto remain, both written for solo violin and obbligato keyboard. They are more properly considered as early duo sonatas rather than as keyboard concertos in the usual sense. A sonata for viola da gamba and obbligato keyboard published in Handel's collected works, vol.xlviii, has often been attributed to Leffloth. The title-page of the MS (in *D-Bds*) indicates Leffloth as composer; Handel's name has been added in pencil and then crossed out by a different hand. Einstein described another MS in Darmstadt to which Leffloth's name has been added below Handel's, but he stated that this is a copy by Christoph Graupner of an original Handel sonata. Leffloth's keyboard style is generally much more progressive than that revealed here, and the sonata should not be counted among his works.

WORKS

Raths wahl in Wehrd, cantata, *D-Nst* (text only)

Divertimento musicale, consistente in una partita, hpd (Nuremberg, *c*1726)

2 concertos, D, F, vn/fl, hpd (Nuremberg, *c*1730, *c*1734)

Lost: Sonata e fuga, kbd (Nuremberg, *c*1726); 6 sonatas, vn/fl, bc (Nuremberg, *c*1729); Concerto, G, hpd, str; 2 sonatas, G, A, vn, hpd

BIBLIOGRAPHY
C. F. D. Schubart: *Ideen zu einer Ästhetik der Tonkunst* (Vienna, 1806)

M. Seiffert: *Geschichte der Klaviermusik* (Leipzig, 1899)

A. Einstein: 'Zum 48. Bande der Handel-Ausgabe', *SIMG*, iv (1902–3), 170

H. Daffner: *Die Entwicklung des Klavierkonzerts bis Mozart* (Leipzig, 1906)

DOUGLAS A. LEE

Lefkowitz, Murray (*b* Mineola, NY, 20 April 1924). American musicologist. He studied the violin at the University of South California and received the BMus in 1950; the following year he took the MMus in musicology, and in 1963 the PhD under Raymond Kendall and Pauline Alderman with a dissertation on Lawes. He taught in the school systems of Los Angeles and Hollywood from 1954 to 1964 and was on the staff of San Fernando Valley State College from 1964 to 1967. Since then he has been professor and chairman of the departments of musicology and theory at Boston University.

Lefkowitz has performed and taught as a violinist and viola da gamba player. His scholarly interests are 17th-century English chamber music and the music of the English masque and theatre; he is particularly noted for his publications on William Lawes, including a biography and editions of his masques and consort music.

WRITINGS
'New Facts Concerning William Lawes and the Caroline Masque', *ML*, xl (1959), 324

William Lawes (London, 1960)

William Lawes: his Life and Works (diss., U. of Southern California, 1963)

'The Longleat Papers of Bulstrode Whitelocke: New Light on Shirley's *Triumph of Peace*', *JAMS*, xviii (1965), 42

'Matthew Locke at Exeter', *The Consort*, xxii (1965), 5

Trois masques à la cour de Charles Ier d'Angleterre (Paris, 1970)

'Lawes, William', 'Locke, Matthew', 'Masque', *Grove 6*

EDITIONS
W. Lawes: Select Consort Music, MB, xxi (London, 1963, 2/1971)

Trois masques à la cour de Charles Ier d'Angleterre (Paris, 1970)

PAULA MORGAN

Le Flem, Paul (*b* Lezardrieux, Côtes-du-Nord, 18 March 1881). French composer. He studied at the Paris Conservatoire, where he attended Lavignac's harmony class in 1899. After spending some time in Russia, he continued his studies at the Schola Cantorum in 1904, taking lessons with d'Indy and Roussel. Concurrently he studied philosophy at the Sorbonne. He succeeded Roussel as professor of counterpoint at the Schola Cantorum, and on the death of Bordes he took over the direction of the St Gervais Choir. An enthusiastic choral conductor, using traditional training methods, he brought this choir up to a high standard, and it gave many successful concerts in France and abroad. Le Flem himself received the benefit of a close contact with 15th- and 16th-century polyphony. Later he was chorusmaster at the Opéra-Comique.

His early works have a gracious melancholy that reflects the landscape of his native Brittany; this quality continued to form an important constituent of his music, as in the choral fable *Aucassin et Nicolette* (1908) and the dramatic piece *Le rossignol de St Malo* (1938). He was also strongly influenced by the sobriety and technical mastery of d'Indy's music, and all of his work is marked by solid craftsmanship. Nonetheless, he also admitted something of the poetic spirit of Debussy. Although his music has remained tonal and cast in established forms and genres, he has always taken a keen interest in later developments, from dodecaphony to the innovations of the youngest French composers. This open-mindedness informs the criticism which he wrote for *Comoedia*.

WORKS

DRAMATIC

Endrymion et Sélémé (opera, Le Flem), 1903; Aucassin et Nicolette (chante-fable, Le Flem), 1908; La folie de Lady Macbeth, ballet, 1934; Le rossignol de St-Malo (opera, 1, Grandey-Rety), 1938; Les paralytiques volent, radio score, 1938; La clairière des fées, opera,

1, 1944; La magicienne de la mer (opera, 1, J. Bruyr), 1946; Macbeth, radio score, 1950; Côte de granit rose, film score, 1954

ORCHESTRAL

En mer, 1901; Scherzo, 1906; Sym., A, 1907; Les voix du large, 1911; Fantaisie, pf, orch, 1911; Danses, 1912, lost; Pour les morts, 1913; Le village, 1943; La ronde des fées, 1943; Sym. no.2, 1956; Concertstück, vn, orch, 1965; Sym. no.3, 1971

VOCAL

6 chants populaires grecs, 1902; Mandoline, Soleils couchants (Verlaine), 1v, pf, 1904; Ariettes oubliées (Verlaine), 1v, pf, 1904; Tu es Petrus, chorus, 1909; Le grillon au foyer (D. Thaly), 1v, pf, 1911; La neige, chorus, n.d.; Vray Dieu qui m'y confortera, chorus, n.d.; La procession, chorus, 1912

Invocation, 1v, orch, 1920; Lamento, chorus, 1920; Paysage, chorus, 1923; Le vin, chorus, wind orch, 1924; Crépuscule d'amour, chorus, n.d.; La fête de printemps, female chorus, orch, 1937; numerous Breton folksongs for chorus

CHAMBER AND INSTRUMENTAL

Rêverie grise, vc, pf, 1899; Sonata, vn, pf, 1905; Par landes, pf, 1907; Par grèves, pf, 1907; Pf Qnt, 1909; Le vieux calvaire, pf, 1910; Le chant des genêts, pf, 1910; Claire de lune sous bois, fl, harp, str, 1911; Danse désuète, fl, harp, str, 1911; Avril, pf, 1912; Pièce, hn, 1955

Principal publisher: Lemoine

BIBLIOGRAPHY

R. Dumesnil: *La musique contemporaine en France* (Paris, 1930)
P. Landormy: *La musique française après Debussy* (Paris, 1943)

ANNE GIRARDOT

Le Franc, Martin. *See* MARTIN LE FRANC.

Le Froid de Méreaux. *See* MÉREAUX family.

Le Gallienne, Dorian (Leon Marlois) (*b* Melbourne, 19 April 1915; *d* Melbourne, 29 July 1963). Australian composer and critic. His father was French, and his mother Australian. He studied composition at Melbourne University Conservatorium and at the RCM (1938–9). In 1951, as a British Council Commonwealth Jubilee Music Scholar, he returned to England to study with Gordon Jacob. In 1950 he became music critic for Melbourne's *Argus* and in 1957 for *The Age*. His career was marred by constant ill-health, from 1951 seriously affecting his heart, but he continued to compose. A slow worker, Le Gallienne was extremely critical and sensitive. He was subject to diverse influences: the English lyrical style popular in Australian instrumental music of the 1930s, light French wit and buoyancy, and the bitonality of early Stravinsky and later Bartók. This eclecticism is evident in the engaging Sinfonietta and the Symphony, a work of impressive drive and rigorous intellectual argument which Covell believed to be 'the most accomplished and purposive symphony written by an Australian'. From 1961 to his death Le Gallienne was working on a second symphony; only the first movement, known as the Symphonic Study, was completed. Its material, with its sparse ascetic lines, tonal friction, sharp colour and thin texture, shows the new direction in which he was moving.

WORKS

Unpublished works incl. Symphony, 1952–3, Symphonic Study [1st movt of inc. Sym. no.2], many orch sketches, some early completed orch works, film scores, ballet and incidental music, pf and other inst music, songs, partsongs; MSS in State Library of Victoria, Melbourne

Published works incl. Duo, vn, va, 1956 (1963); Sinfonietta, 1951–6; Four Divine Songs of John Donne (1967); Trio, ob, vn, va, 1957 (1976); several early inst works (1969)

Principal publisher: Allans

BIBLIOGRAPHY

M. R. Best: *Australian Composers and their Music* (Adelaide, 1961), 31ff
R. I. Downing: 'Dorian Le Gallienne', *Adult Education*, viii/1 (1963), 6
J. D. Garretty: *Three Australian Composers* (diss., U. of Melbourne, 1963), 144–82

F. Werder: 'The Music of Dorian Le Gallienne', *Adult Education*, viii/1 (1963),10
C. Brumby, ed.: 'Discography of Australian Music', *Australian Journal of Music Education*, i (1967), 51
R. Covell: *Australia's Music: Themes of a New Society* (Melbourne, 1967), 160ff
A. D. McCredie: *Musical Composition in Australia* (Canberra, 1969), 11
——: *Catalogue of 46 Australian Composers and their Works* (Canberra, 1969), 14f
N. Nickson: 'Dorian Le Gallienne', *The Composers and their Work* (Canberra, 1969), 12ff
——: 'Dorian Le Gallienne: Two Instrumental Works', *SMA*, x (1976), 25, suppl.
——: 'Dorian Le Gallienne', *Australian Composition in the Twentieth Century: a Symposium*, ed. D. Tunley and F. Callaway (Melbourne, 1976)

NOEL NICKSON

Legány, Dezső (*b* Szombathely, 19 Jan 1916). Hungarian musicologist. After completing his studies at the University of Pécs (LlD 1937) he studied with Kodály, Viski, Bartha and Szabolcsi at the Budapest Academy of Music, where he began teaching and became a research assistant at the musicology institute (1951). He was also a lecturer at the Free University courses (1954–8) and a teacher at the Bartók High School (from 1958) before being appointed to the musicology institute of the Hungarian Academy of Sciences (1972), where he became head of the department of Hungarian music history in 1974. His main areas of research are Hungarian music history and European Romanticism; he has written extensively and has translated much of the west European and Russian literature. In 1973 he took the *kandidátus* degree with a dissertation on Erkel's works in their historical context and joined the musicological committee of the Hungarian Academy of Sciences.

Legány's wife Erzsébet Hegyi (*b* Nagykanizsa, 4 Nov 1927) studied with Kodály, Bárdos, Forrai and Gárdonyi at the Budapest Academy of Music, where she has taught harmony and solfège from 1951; she is also visiting professor in harmony and form analysis at the Zoltán Kodály Education Institute for foreign music teachers in Kecskemét (opened in 1975), and in 1971 began giving regular summer courses at the Kodály Institute in Wellesley, Massachusetts. Her writings include a two-volume collection of examples from Bach's cantatas (Budapest, 1971–4), a book on solfège according to the concept of Kodály (Kecskemét, 1975) and *Énektanárképzés Kodály pedagógiai múvei alapján* ('The training of music teachers, based on Kodály's works', Budapest, 1976).

WRITINGS

'Népi és egyéni műalkotás a zenetörténetben' [Popular and individual creation in the history of music], *MTA nyelv- és irodalomtudományi osztályának közleményei* [Communications of the first department of the Hungarian Academy of Sciences], iv (1953), 294
'Tématípusok Bartók utolsó műveiben' [Thematic patterns in Bartók's last works], *Zenetudományi tanulmányok*, iii (1955), 505 [with Eng. and Ger. summaries]
Henry Purcell (Budapest, 1959)
A magyar zene krónikája: zenei művelődésünk ezer éve dokumentumokban [Chronicle of Hungarian music: 1000 years of documentation on musical culture] (Budapest, 1962)
'A zeneakadémia születése' [The founding of the Music Academy in Budapest], *Magyar zenetörténeti tanulmányok* (1968), 75
'Erkel és Liszt Zeneakadémiája' [Erkel's and Liszt's Academy of Music], *Magyar zenetörténeti tanulmányok* (1969), 247; (1973), 103 [with Eng. and Ger. summaries]
'Erkel Hunyadi Lászlója', *Magyar zene*, xi (1970), 97
Erkel Ferenc művei és korabeli történetük [Erkel's works and their contemporary history] (diss., Hungarian Academy of Sciences, 1973; Budapest, 1975)
'Kodály, Zoltán', *Sohlmans Musiklexikon* (Stockholm, 2/1975–9)

Liszt Ferenc Magyarországon [Liszt in Hungary 1869–73] (Budapest, 1976)
2500 entries in *ZL*
'Budapest', 'Erkel', 'Hungary 1500–1900', *Grove 6*

VERA LAMPERT

Legar [Legare, Legard], **John.** *See* LAGUERRE, JOHN.

Légat de Furcy [Furci, Fursy, Legal Defurcy], **Antoine** (*b* Maubeuge, *c*1740; *d* ?after 1790). French composer, harpsichordist and organist. Directed towards an ecclesiastical career, he studied philosophy in Paris, where he also took lessons in harmony and keyboard playing from Charles Noblet, befriended Rameau and took part in the concerts of the Prince of Conti. In 1761 he served as organist at St-Germain-le-Vieil. He was organist at the Carmelite monastery in the Place Maubert from 1770 at least until 1787, by which time he had also become organist at Sainte-Croix de la Bretonnerie. He was primarily active as a singing and harpsichord teacher and as a composer of charming keyboard pieces and of many light *cantatilles* and *ariettes*. Gerber, who wrote of him in 1790 as still living, praised the taste of his earlier works, which he attributed to the influence of the Prince of Conti, but which he found lacking in his more recent efforts. Légat de Furcy also attempted a career as a theatrical composer, but none of his several operas was performed or published. According to Choron and Fayolle, he collaborated with La Borde in his *Essai sur la musique* (1780), and the rather long notice of him in that work may be autobiographical.

WORKS

(all printed works published in Paris)

VOCAL

Les soirées de Choisy le roy, chansons, 3 vols. (1762, 1764, n.d.)
Mes loisirs, ariettes, etc (1774)
At least 13 cantatilles; ariettes with insts; numerous airs pubd singly, in *Mercure de France* (1757–78) and in contemporary anthologies
Solfèges (n.d.); Seconds solfèges (1784); Nouvelles solfèges (1787)
Operas, all unperf., lost: Philire (pastorale, 3, Poisinet de Sivry); Le saut de Leucade ou Les désespérés (opéra comique, Mentelle); Palmire ou Le prix de la beauté (opéra comique, after Voltaire); Les rendez-vous (opéra-comique); Le jardinier de Sidon (?comédie, 2, Pleinchesne); Apollon et Daphné (tragédie, 3, Saint Marc), inc.

INSTRUMENTAL

Les leçons de Minerve, ariettes, hpd, 2 vols. (1779, 1785)
Ovs. to Prati's L'école de la jeunesse, Grétry's Andromaque and Evénements imprévus, arr. pf/hpd, vn ad lib
Airs, arr. kbd/other insts, in contemporary anthologies
6 sonates en duo, 2 fl, lost; pf pieces, MS, cited by Fétis

BIBLIOGRAPHY

FétisB; *GerberL*; *GerberNL*
J.-B. de La Borde: *Essai sur la musique ancienne et moderne* (Paris, 1780/*R*1972)
Tablettes de renommée des musiciens (Paris, 1785)
A. Choron and F. Fayolle: *Dictionnaire historique des musiciens* (Paris, 1810–11)
G. Servières: *Documents inédits sur les organistes français* (Paris, 1924), 34f

ROGER COTTE

Legato (It.: 'bound'; Fr. *lié*; Ger. *gebunden*). A term meaning connected smoothly, with neither a perceptible break in the sound nor (ordinarily) special emphasis (the antonym of STACCATO). In notation, this effect might in early music be indicated by a LIGATURE or more recently by a curved line across a succession of notes thus smoothly intended, i.e. a SLUR. Where not notated, the same effect may be intended or desirable. In current usage it is normally presumed that notes neither slurred nor bearing dots or dashes are to be bound in continuous legato except for articulation (usually unmarked) between phrases. On the piano and on bowed string instruments this disposition is strong; on wind instruments a little less strong. The term used by violinists for notes not slurred yet taken smoothly and without audible separation is 'détaché', which is perhaps misleading, but means legato.

This assumption would be erroneous for music of the Classical period, the Baroque period or earlier. Daniel Gottlob Türk (*Clavierschule*, Eng. trans., 1804, p.36) wrote: 'If Notes are to be played in the common way; that is to say, neither staccato nor legato, the fingers must be lifted a little sooner than the Time of the length of the Note is expired'; and F. W. Marpurg (*Anleitung zum Clavierspielen*, 1755, 2/1765, i/7, p.29): 'Opposed to legato as well as to staccato is the ordinary movement which [in the absence of notated indications to the contrary] is always understood'.

The harpsichord, because of its relatively evanescent tone, requires greater attention to legato than most other instruments: 'it is necessary to sustain a perfect smoothness', wrote François Couperin (*L'art de toucher le clavecin*, 2/1717, p.61). This, of course, is a general recommendation, since any particular passage must have its own requirements; but it is a good basis, whereas violinists playing Baroque music need rather to be advised not to take successions of rapid or moderate notes with so legato a stroke as their modern *détaché*. A relaxed and lightly separated stroke in the upper half of the bow is a much more normal requirement. This is also true for cellists playing typical allegro basses; but the common mistake here is not too legato but too *marcato* an articulation, and a sense of melodic shape is the saving grace.

Legato may be, but is not necessarily, combined with slurring on bowed strings (notes taken in one bow) or on wind instruments (notes taken in one breath). In singing, notes sung to one syllable must be, and notes sung to more than one syllable may normally be thus brought within one breath; but only notes sung to one syllable have quite the smooth legato which slurring (marked or unmarked) entails. To change bow need not perceptibly interrupt the legato; to take new breath must do so, but in so slight a degree, given the necessary skill, that the musical continuity is barely broken. It would often be desirable, especially in Baroque wind and voice parts, to take new breath much more perceptibly for the sake of better and clearer phrasing. Legato is one of the main necessities for bel canto singing; but the proper interruption of this legato for making the phrase patterns clear needs no less attention.

ROBERT DONINGTON

Legatura (It.). LIGATURE (i).

Legendarius (Lat.). MARTYROLOGY.

Légende (Fr.). A title used in the 19th century for a piece intended to have a legendary character or to depict a legend. Liszt and Tchaikovsky are among the composers who used the term.

Le Gendre, Jean (*fl* 1533–57). French singer, composer and theorist. He was a member of the royal chapel of François I and Henri II of France. Glarean called him Fra Legendre Antuacensis, indicating perhaps that he was from Antuates, a region bordering the shores of Lake Geneva.

With the exception of *Laudate Dominum*, a motet appearing in Glarean's *Dodecachordon* (modern edition in MSD, vi/2, p.356), other compositions by Le Gendre are found only in Parisian editions. Between 1533 and 1547 Attaingnant printed five of his chansons in various collections and Du Chemin brought out eight more between 1549 and 1557. His many French settings of psalms and canticles were printed by Fezandat. A treatise, *Brieve introduction en la musique tant au plain chant que chose faites*, published by Attaingnant in 1545, is apparently lost. Le Gendre must have been well known in French circles by the middle of the 16th century, for Rabelais in the *Quart livre* listed him among the notable musicians, and in the *Discours* (1558) Gentillet praised the sweet sound of his motets.

BIBLIOGRAPHY

F. Lesure and G. Thibault: 'Bibliographie des éditions musicales publiées par Nicolas du Chemin (1549–1576)', *AnnM*, i (1953), 269–373

D. Heartz: *Pierre Attaingnant: Royal Printer of Music* (Berkeley and Los Angeles, 1969)

CLEMENT A. MILLER

Léger (Fr.: 'light'). As a tempo designation, particularly in its adverbial form *légèrement* (or *légérement*), it was widely used in the early 18th century by French composers. J. G. Walther (1732) defined it as a mark of expression to indicate a light performing style, but there can be little doubt that François Couperin, who used it along with *tres légérement*, *d'une légéreté modérée*, *d'une légéreté gracieuse* and *d'une légéreté tendre*, regarded it as a fairly precise indication of tempo as well as of mood. So did Rousseau (1768), who placed it between *gai* and *vite* as the equivalent of the Italian *vivace*.

For bibliography *see* TEMPO AND EXPRESSION MARKS.

DAVID FALLOWS

Leger [ledger] **line** (Fr. *ligne postiche, ligne supplémentaire*; Ger. *Hilfslinie, Nebenlinie*; It. *linea d'aiuto*). A short line drawn above or below the staff for notes that are too high or too low to be printed on the staff itself. Leger lines are occasionally found in manuscripts containing plainchant or early polyphony, but as clefs were placed on any line of the staff in the Middle Ages, scribes were usually careful to see that leger lines were unnecessary. M. A. Cavazzoni's *Recerchari motetti canzoni* for organ (1523) is an early example of their extensive use (see illustration).

Leger lines in M. A. Cavazzoni's 'Recerchari motetti canzoni' (1523)

Legge, Walter (*b* London, 1 June 1906; *d* St Jean, Cap Ferrat, 22 March 1979). English music administrator

and writer. He received no formal musical training but from 1925 spent all his time attending rehearsals and musical performances and acquiring a fine ear, understanding of style and unusual linguistic prowess (Frank Walker's *Hugo Wolf* is based on Legge's original research in Austria), as well as a capacious knowledge of the musical repertory. In 1927 the HMV record company engaged him to write literary material in connection with its classical records. Legge persuaded HMV to let him form subscription societies for producing limited recorded editions of important music, Haydn's string quartets, Sibelius's music, Wolf's songs and Beethoven's piano sonatas played by Schnabel being a few of his chief successes. In 1932 he had formed the London Lieder Club to build larger, more knowledgeable audiences for masterpieces of German song; from then until 1937 he worked regularly as a deputy music critic of the *Manchester Guardian*. In 1938–9 he was Beecham's assistant artistic director at the Royal Opera House, Covent Garden. During World War II he was in charge of ENSA concerts for troops and war workers, work in which his wide knowledge was able to bring music and musicians of highest quality to audiences many of whom remained devotees of music afterwards. Throughout these years Legge had been working for the Gramophone Company as manager for artists and repertory. In 1945 he toured Europe securing outstanding talent for this record company and in the following 19 years produced recorded performances of opera, song, orchestral and chamber music that have become classic examples of the medium, in 78 r.p.m. (coarse groove), monophonic LP and then stereophonic sound: Columbia's 1951 Bayreuth recordings, the *Tosca* conducted by de Sabata, Verdi's *Falstaff* and Strauss's *Der Rosenkavalier* conducted by Karajan, Maria Callas's many records, piano music played by Dinu Lipatti, the violin legacy of Ginette Neveu, the operetta series involving Elisabeth Schwarzkopf (Legge's second wife – he had formerly been married to the English mezzo-soprano Nancy Evans), and many records conducted by Klemperer, are particularly connected with Legge as producer.

Legge always worked to raise standards of musical execution and interpretative artistry. In 1945, to this end, he formed and coached unremittingly the Philharmonia String Quartet, then the eponymous string orchestra, and finally the Philharmonia Orchestra, an élite whose virtuosity transformed British concert life, at first under Beecham, later under Karajan, Cantelli, Toscanini, Klemperer and Giulini, and was admired on international concert tours, and constantly on records. To match this orchestra, Legge formed the Philharmonia Chorus in 1957, trained by Wilhelm Pitz, initially for Beethoven's Ninth Symphony under Klemperer; this too was immediately recognized as a choir without peer. All this activity was achieved without state subsidy; the Philharmonia's only grant came, for three years, from the Maharajah of Mysore. Legge was from 1946 one of the associate directors of the Gesellschaft der Musikfreunde in Vienna; from May 1958 to November 1963 he was a director of the Royal Opera House, Covent Garden. In 1964 he was obliged to dissolve the Philharmonia Orchestra and Chorus, and he left his record company, by then EMI Ltd, to live on the Continent, whence he continued to promote concerts and recitals and to produce records for other companies, as well as to write occasional articles about music.

There is no question that his activities have immensely benefited musical performance and appreciation all over the world. In 1974 he was awarded the Hugo Wolf medal of the International Hugo Wolf Society in Vienna.

BIBLIOGRAPHY

B. Dean: *The Theatre at War* (London, 1956)
V. Newman: *Ernest Newman: a Memoir* (London, 1963)
W. Mann: 'Walter Legge', *Gramophone*, lvi (1978–9), 1875

WILLIAM S. MANN

Leggermente. See LEGGERO.

Leggero [leggiero] (It.: 'light'). A performance direction which belongs characteristically to the 19th century and is also found in the adverbial forms *leggermente* and *leggiermente*, occasionally misspelt by Beethoven *leggeramente* (op.120) and *leggieramente* (opp.47, 74 and 95). Normally it called for a light, detached style of playing in rapid passages. But it can be interpreted more loosely: *legato* passages are marked *leggeramente* in the 25th of Beethoven's Diabelli Variations; the *forte* opening of the scherzo in Beethoven's E♭ Quartet op.74 is marked *leggieramente*; and Mendelssohn has *leggero* simultaneously with *forte* and *legato* in the finale of his G minor Piano Concerto. Verdi used the superlative form *leggerissimo*, e.g. for Alfredo in the 'Brindisi' from *La traviata* and for Preziosilla in Act 2 of *La forza del destino*; Elgar used the form *leggierissimo* in the second movement of his Cello Concerto.

See also TEMPO AND EXPRESSION MARKS.

DAVID FALLOWS

Leggiadro (It.: 'pretty', 'graceful'). A performance instruction found as early as the 18th century. J. G. Walther (*Musicalisches Lexicon*, 1732) gave for *leggiodro* (probably a misprint) and *leggiadramente* (the adverbial form) the entry: 'sehr schön, über die Massen annehmlich, mit einer artigen Manier' ('very beautiful, exceptionally charming, with a pleasing manner').

Leggiero [leggiermente]. See LEGGERO.

Leghorn. See LIVORNO.

Legley, Vic(tor) (*b* Hazebrouck, 18 June 1915). Belgian composer. His early musical studies were in Ieper; in 1934 he went to the Brussels Conservatory, where he won prizes in counterpoint, fugue, chamber music and viola (1937). After his demobilization in 1941 he became a composition pupil of Absil and took the Belgian second Prix de Rome in 1943. He played the viola in a string quartet and in the Belgian RSO (1936–48), activities which left their mark on his composition. On leaving the orchestra he became music producer for the Flemish department of Belgian radio; he was appointed head of serious music for the third programme in 1962, and this position has enabled him to propagate new music from Belgium and elsewhere. He has also been active as a teacher: he was appointed professor of harmony at the Brussels Conservatory in 1949, and of composition in 1959; he became professor of composition and analysis at the Chapelle Musicale Reine Elisabeth in 1950. Legley was made a member in 1965 and president in 1972 of the Belgian Royal Academy.

Although clearly influenced by Absil in his early music, Legley has steadily developed an individual style in which highly charged emotion is kept in check by firm technique and refined taste. Most of his pieces are instrumental: his string quartets contain some of his best work, and the six symphonies constitute landmarks in his career. The fourth and fifth were commissioned by the Festival of Flanders. Some of his works (e.g. *La cathédrale d'acier*) have been frequently performed outside Belgium; perhaps his best known piece (if not the most important) is the Violin Concerto no.2, which was used in the finals of the 1968 Queen Elisabeth Competition. After 1952 he made particular efforts to reach the public, but without sacrificing his dignity and his individuality. Typical of this approach are *Middagmuziek*, the Serenade for strings, the *Kleine carnavalouverture* and *La cathédrale d'acier*. Legley has often spoken and written in defence of Belgian music, has sat on several competition juries and has represented his country at conferences and festivals.

WORKS
(selective list)

Orch: Sym. Variations on an Old Flemish Song, 1941; 6 syms., 1942, 1947, 1953, 1964, 1965, 1976; Suite op.18, 1944; Symphonie en miniature, 1945; Vn Conc. no.1, 1947; Pf Conc., 1952; Kleine carnavalouverture, 1954; Timp Conc., 1955; Serenade, str, 1957; La cathédrale d'acier, 1958; Ouverture pour une comedie de Goldoni, 1958; Harp Conc., 1966; Vn Conc. no.2, 1966; Paradise Regained, 1967; Espaces, str, 1970; Va Conc., 1971; Conc. d'automne, op.85, a sax, orch, 1974; Conc. grosso, op.87, vn, a sax, str orch, 1976

Chamber: 4 String Quartets, 1941, 1947, 1956, 1963; Sextet, pf, wind qnt, 1945; Middagmuziek, fl, cl, bn, hn, str qt, db, 1948; Conc., 13 insts, 1948; Serenade, 2 vn, pf, 1954, rev. fl, vn, pf, 1957; 5 Miniatures, sax qt, 1958; 2 harp suites, 1968, 1972; Pf Qt no.1, 1973; several sonatas, other chamber and inst works

Vocal: The Veil, 1v, str qt, c1945; De boer die sterft [The dying peasant] (radio drama, H. Teirlinck), 1950; De gevallen vriend [The fallen friend] (J. de Haes), double chorus, 1951; La farce des deux nues (opera, 4 scenes, H. Closson), 1939–63; Mythologie, op.82, S, pf, 1973; La terra e la morte, op.83 (Pavese), female chorus, 1974; Mijn gegeven woord, op.90 (H. C. Pernath), T, pf, 1976

Principal publishers: Metropolis, CeBeDeM
MSS in B-Brtb

WRITINGS

'Muziek en radio', *Mededelingen van de Koninklijke Vlaamse academie voor wetenschappen, letteren en schone kunsten van België*, xxix/1 (1967)
'Actuele aspecten voor een compositieleer', *Mededelingen van de Koninklijke Vlaamse academie voor wetenschappen, letteren en schone kunsten van België*, xxxii/2 (1970)
'Muziek en traditie', *Mededelingen van de Koninklijke Vlaamse academie voor wetenschappen, letteren en schone kunsten van België*, xxxvi (1974)

BIBLIOGRAPHY

R. Wangermée: *Vic Legley* (Brussels, 1953)
K. de Schrijver: *Levende componisten uit Vlaanderen*, ii (Antwerp, 1955)
Music in Belgium (Brussels, 1964)
C. Mertens: *Hedendaagse muziek in België* (Brussels, 1967)

CORNEEL MERTENS

Legnani, (Rinaldo) Luigi (*b* Ferrara, 7 Nov 1790; *d* Ravenna, 5 Aug 1877). Italian guitar virtuoso, instrument maker and composer. Although trained from his earliest years as an orchestral string player, Legnani devoted himself to singing and especially to the guitar. In 1807, and again in 1816, he appeared in Ravenna as a tenor, performing arias by Cimarosa, Donizetti and Rossini. He launched his public career as a concert guitarist in Milan in 1819, and in the same year appeared to loud acclaim in Vienna soon after Mauro Giuliani had left (*AMZ*, xxi, 557). The city received Legnani with much praise again in 1822–3, 1833 and 1839. In the intervening years, besides touring Italy, Germany and Switzerland as a soloist, he struck up a friendship with Paganini. Together they gave concerts in the principal European courts (1836–8). In about 1840 Legnani retired to spend his remaining years in Ravenna constructing fine guitars and violins. His famous 'Legnani model' guitar, with a screw-adjusted neck, was widely copied by guitar makers in central Europe between about 1830 and 1880 (notably by Staufer of Vienna); similar guitars are still being manufactured by such firms as Klein of Koblenz.

About 250 works by Legnani were published with opus numbers, principally by Ricordi of Milan, Artaria of Vienna, B. Schotts Söhne of Mainz, and Hofmeister of Leipzig. Variations, fantasies and potpourris for guitar on well-known operatic themes account for most of his output. Of greater interest are the duets for flute (or violin) and guitar, such as the *Duetto concertante* op.23.

BIBLIOGRAPHY
G. Schilling: *Encyclopädie der gesammten musikalischen Wissenschaften*, iv (Stuttgart, 1837)
J. Zuth: 'Die Leipziger AMZ als gitarristische Quelle', *Die Gitarre*, i (Berlin, 1920), 84, 102
R. Ferrari: 'Luigi Legnani', *Der Gitarrenfreund*, xxvii (1926), 101, 119, 135; xxviii (1927), 7

THOMAS F. HECK

Legni (It.). WOODWIND INSTRUMENTS.

Legnica (Ger. Liegnitz). Town now in Poland, ruled for part of the 17th century by GEORG RUDOLPH.

Legno (It.: 'wood'). *Strumenti di legno*, or simply *legni*, are woodwind instruments. In string-instrument playing COL LEGNO means tapping the strings with the bowstick.

Legouix, (Isidore) Edouard (*b* Paris, 1 April 1834; *d* Boulogne, Seine-et-Oise, 15 Sept 1916). French composer. His father was the founder of a Parisian publishing house whose management later passed to Edouard's brother Gustave (1843–1916) and Gustave's son Robert. Edouard studied at the Paris Conservatoire with Henri Reber (harmony) and Ambroise Thomas (composition), winning the *premier prix* for harmony in 1855 and an honourable mention in the Prix de Rome in 1860. He soon devoted himself to a career in light opera and operetta; his one-act *Un Othello* (1863) was the first of several successes. The craftsmanship of his works is notable and, according to Feschotte, they survive in part in the French broadcast repertory. The operas tended to be fashionable and escapist; Clément and Larousse particularly noted the extravagance of the plot and incoherence of ideas in *Les dernières grisettes*.

WORKS
(stage works first performed in Paris unless otherwise stated)

Un Othello (?operetta, 1), Théâtre des Champs-Elysées, 1863, vocal score (Paris, ?n.d.)
Le lion de Saint Marc (opéra bouffe, 1, C. Nuitter, Beaumont [A. Beaume]), St Germain, 24 Nov 1864, vocal score (Paris, ?1866), excerpts pubd separately
Ma fille (operetta, 1, A. Bouvier), Délassements-Comiques, 20 March 1866
Malborough s'en va-t-en guerre (opéra bouffe, 4, P. Siraudin, W. Busnach), Athénée, 15 Dec 1867, collab. Bizet, Delibes, E. Jonas
Le vengeur (opéra bouffe, 1, Nuitter, Beaumont), Athénée, 20 Nov 1868, vocal score (Paris, ?1869), excerpts pubd separately
Deux portières pour un cordon (?operetta, 1), Palais-Royal, 19 March 1869, collab. F. Hervé, C. Lecocq, G. Maurice
L'ours et l'amateur de jardins (bouffonnerie musicale, 1, Busnach, Marquet), 1 Sept 1869, vocal score (Paris, ?1869)
Les dernières grisettes (operetta, 3, Nuitter, Beaumont), Brussels, Fantaisies-Parisiennes, 12 Dec 1874
Le mariage d'une étoile (operetta, 1, E. Grangé, V. Bernard), Bouffes-Parisiens, 1 April 1876, vocal score (Paris, ?1876)
Madame Clara, somnambule (?operetta, 1), Palais-Royal, March, 1877

Other operettas incl. Quinolette; La clef d'argent; La tartane; Une nouvelle Cendrillon (Paris, ?1885); La fée aux genêts
Other works: songs; pf works, many pubd (Paris)

BIBLIOGRAPHY
FétisB
F. Clément and P. Larousse: *Dictionnaire lyrique, ou Histoire des opéras* (Paris, 1867–9, 3/1905/*R*1969) [with suppls.]
J. Feschotte: 'Legouix, Isidore Edouard', *MGG*

DAVID CHARLTON

Legrand. A number of French 18th-century musicians bore this name (or 'Le Grand'), and the habit of omitting first names makes it difficult to distinguish one from another. The best-known is Jean-Pierre Legrand (*b* Tarbes, 8 Feb 1734; *d* Marseilles, 31 July 1809), organist and composer. A son of Pierre Legrand, organist of the Cathedral of Lescar (Béarn), he left Bordeaux for Paris, where he was appointed organist of St Germain-des-Prés (1 April 1758). The eccentricities that seem to have characterized his work there may also have caused his wife, whom he married in 1765, to leave him and sue for separate maintenance (1776–7). In 1770 he left Paris to return to his 'own country'. Certain documents connect him with Montpellier Cathedral in 1779; in 1780 he went to Marseilles, where he remained until his death, serving as *maître de musique* at the opera and the Concert. His career was crowned by his election to the Academy of Marseilles (1801).

A *premier livre* of six sonatas for harpsichord by 'J.-P. Legrand, m^e de clavecin & organiste de l'Abbaye de S. Germain-des-Prés', advertised in 1763–4, is almost certainly the work to which Leopold Mozart referred in a letter of 1 February 1764: 'M. Le Grand, a French harpsichordist, has completely abandoned his *goût*, and his sonatas are completely in our style'. No copy of the work has been found, nor has any of the other music attributed to Jean-Pierre Legrand been located: orchestral music, motets, masses, the cantata *L'hymne des Lys* (1783) and choruses for Racine's *Athalie* (1792).

Leopold Mozart's reference to a 'Le Grand' has drawn more attention to the name than it might otherwise have received. Louis-Alexandre Legrand (*b* ?Châlons-sur-Marne; *d* Paris, 30 Nov 1773) was a pupil of Daquin and his successor as organist of the convent of the Cordeliers (July 1772). He was also organist at St Côme (from before 1759), St Nicholas-des-Champs (*c*1761–5, again from 1771) and the Premonstratensians at the rue de Sèvres. Either he or a Louis Le Grand, an organist living in the rue de Grenelle on 28 November 1741 (Brossard), was probably the Legrand recommended as among the best harpsichord teachers in Paris by Pascal Taskin in a letter of 6 October 1765. Another Legrand, an organist at Bordeaux, was one of the experts invited to examine the new organ in Angoulême Cathedral in 1786. According to Fleury, 'The canons, charmed by the personal relations which they had with M. Legrand ... proposed that he should become their organist ... which he accepted'. Mathieu and Etienne Legrand were active as king's musicians in 1765. A Legrand performed organ concertos of his own on at least three occasions at the Concert Spirituel between February 1763 and April 1764; *petits* and *grands* motets by a Legrand were given there between 1771 and 1773.

The only substantial work bearing the name of Legrand is a set of six *Pièces de clavecin en sonates avec accompagnement de violon* (Paris, *c*1755), whose author is identified as organist of the abbey church of Sainte-Croix and the parochial church of St Rémy de Bordeaux. The music, certainly inspired by Mondonville's like-named collection of 1734, is of high quality with imaginative themes and an independent and active violin part which everywhere engages in imitative and canonic dialogue with the harpsichord. It is not impossible that the composer was Jean-Pierre; French keyboard music of this quality was rare at that period under any name, and the likelihood of two able Legrands is slim. The Legrand who composed *L'amour à la mode, cantatille à voix seule avec symphonie* (Paris, after 1754) was a harpsichord teacher living in the rue Geoffroy L'Angevin. Nothing in the style of the music prevents it from being by the composer of the *Pièces de clavecin en sonates* (*RISM* attributes both publications to Louis-Alexandre Legrand); but a long, busy, one-movement sonata by 'Legrand' in *20 sonate per cembalo* (Paris, c1760) would need its incessant Alberti basses explained away by the hypothesis of its having been an experimental work in a new style. Somewhat better are two manuscript sets of variations by a 'Legrand' (*F-Pc* D.14218). *Les trois roses, ou Les graces*, a three-act *comédie mêlée d'ariettes* with words by Rozoi and music by Legrand, performed at Versailles on 10 December 1779 (Paris, 1780), is known only through an advertisement in the *Mercure de France* (17 January 1780, p.48).

BIBLIOGRAPHY
M. P. de Fleury: 'Les anciens orgues de la cathédrale d'Angoulême', *Bulletin de la Société archéologique et historique de la Charente*, 5th ser., xi, année 1889 (Angoulême, 1890), 215–67
G. Servières: 'Documents inédits sur les organistes français des XVIIe et XVIIIe siècles', *Tribune de St Gervais*, xxiii (1922); pubd separately (Paris, 1924)
J. Bonfils and H. A. Durand: 'Legrand', *MGG* [incl. detailed bibliography]
L. E. S. J. de Laborde: *Musiciens de Paris, 1535–1792*, ed. Y. de Brossard (Paris, 1965)   DAVID FULLER

Legrand, Michel (*b* Paris, 24 Feb 1932). French composer and conductor. He studied with Henri Chaland (harmony) and Boulanger (conducting and score reading) at the Paris Conservatoire (1943–50). Very soon his activities as composer, conductor and arranger were directed towards jazz and light music. A brilliant orchestrator, he won a prize in 1953 from the Académie Charles Cros for his arrangements for a recital disc by Catherine Sauvage; his international career began in 1954–5 when he conducted at Maurice Chevalier's shows in Paris and New York. He has written scores for numerous films, winning Oscars for his contributions to *Les parapluies de Cherbourg* (1964), *The Thomas Crown Affair* (1968), *Les demoiselles de Cherbourg* (1968) and *Summer of 42* (1971).

DOMINIQUE AMY

Legrant [Lemacherier], Guillaume (*fl* 1418–56). French composer. His true name was Guillaume Lemacherier. He entered the chapel of Pope Martin V in October 1418 and remained as a Papal singer there until at least the summer of 1421. He possessed several church benefices in the diocese of Rouen, including one which he held as late as 1449. It is possible that the 'Guillaume le Grain' listed as a singer in the chapel of Duke Charles of Orleans in 1455–6 was identical with this composer. His Credo (no.2) was composed by 1426.

Guillaume Legrant's surviving compositions include sacred and secular works. His Gloria and two Credos are each alternately for two and three parts and are among the earliest compositions to distinguish between solo and choral polyphony. The three extant chansons by Legrant are all virelais and survive in only one source.

WORKS
Edition: *Early Fifteenth-century Music*, ed. G. Reaney, CMM, xi/2 (1959) [R]
3 single mass movements: Gloria, 3vv, R no.5; Credo, 3vv, R no.6 (dated 1426 in *GB-Ob* 213); Credo, 3vv, R no.7
3 virelais: Ma chiere mestresse, 3vv, R no.2; Or avant gentilz fillettes, 3vv, R no.3; Pour l'amour de mon bel amy, 3vv, R no.1
Lost composition, title unknown, keyboard arrangement in Paumann's 'Fundamentum organisandi', and in the Buxheim Organ Book, R no.4
Ct to Pierre Fontaine's rondeau, A son plaisir volentiers serviroye (ed. in J. Marix: *Les musiciens de la cour de Bourgogne au XVIe siècle*, Paris, 1938)

BIBLIOGRAPHY
E. Dannemann: *Die spätgotische Musiktradition in Frankreich und Burgund vor dem Auftreten Dufays* (Strasbourg, 1936), 49, 83
A. Pirro: *Histoire de la musique de la fin du XIVe siècle à la fin du XVIe* (Paris, 1940), 66
M. Schuler: 'Zur Geschichte der Kapelle Papst Martins V', *AMf*, xxv (1968), 30   CRAIG WRIGHT

Legrant, Johannes (*fl* c1420–40). French composer. Although there is no biographical information about Johannes Legrant, the style of his eight extant compositions and the dates of their sources suggest that he was active as a composer during the first half of the 15th century. His rondeau *Les mesdisans ont fait raport*, for example, exhibits points of imitation in all three voices and was probably written some time between 1420 and 1440. This chanson is notable also for its clearly directed melodies, extended sequences and purposeful harmonic movement at cadences. Imitative entries are also abundant in Legrant's two-voice Gloria, and in the concluding Amen of the movement a point of imitation is extended as a two-part canon. His music shows skill in structure and unification. His historical position will be difficult to assess until we know more precisely when and where he worked.

WORKS
Editions: *Dufay and his Contemporaries*, ed. J. F. R. Stainer and others (London, 1898/R1963) [S]
Sechs Trienter Codices, ed. G. Adler and O. Koller, DTÖ, xxii, Jg. xi/1 (1904/R) [A]
Early Fifteenth-century Music, ed. G. Reaney, CMM, xi/2 (1959) [R]
A 15th-century Repertory from the Codex Reina, ed. N. Wilkins, CMM, xxxvii (1966) [W]

SACRED
Gloria, 2vv, R (ed. in Wolf)
Gloria, 3vv, R (*I-Bc* Q15 has an 'alius Ct')
Credo, 3vv, R
Unicus dei filius [= Las, je ne puis oïr nouvelle], 3vv, *I-TRmn* 90

BALLADE
Entre vous, nouviaux mariées, 3vv, R, S

RONDEAUX
Las, je ne puis oïr nouvelle [= Unicus dei filius], 3vv, A, R
Layssies moy coy, 3vv, R, S
Les mesdisans ont fait raport, 3vv, A, R, W
Se liesse est de ma partie, 3vv, R, S

BIBLIOGRAPHY
J. Wolf: 'Eine neue Quelle zur Musik des 15. Jahrhunderts', *Juhlakirja Ilmari Krohn'ille* (Helsinki, 1927), 151   CRAIG WRIGHT

Legrense [Carthusensis, Gallicus, Mantuanus], Johannes [Jean de Chartreaux; Jean de Namur (i)] (*b* Namur, c1415; *d* Parma, 1473). French humanist and theorist. His extant writings provide the only information about his life; the birthdate was conjectured by Coussemaker. Legrense (commonly known as Gallicus) wrote that he was born at Namur and learnt to sing there, but studied formally under Vittorino da Feltre (1378–1446) at Mantua, where he later became a Carthusian monk. His primary treatise was written during the pontificate of

Pius II (1458–64). Some of the manuscripts are in the hand of his pupil Nicolaus Burtius, who recorded his date of death as 1473.

Legrense's three treatises begin *Libelli musicalis de ritu canendi vetustissimo et novo* (*CS*, iv, 298–396), *Praefationcula in tam admirabilem quam tacitam et quietissimam novorum concinetiam* (*CS*, iv, 396–409) and *Tacita nunc inchoatur stupendaque numerorum musica* (*CS*, iv, 409–421). They survive only in *GB-Lbm* Add.22315, ff.1–60 and Harl.6525, ff.1–96. Coussemaker, however, made them appear to be one continuous work by taking the obituary from f.60 to Add.22315 and placing it after the material transcribed from Harl.6525 (ff.77–96). The first part of the largest treatise, comparing the old and the new, covers the materials of music, proportions, the division of the monochord and the genera. Its second part, an introduction to singing, explains the modes and psalm tones, solmization and counterpoint; an interesting part of this section is concerned with secular music. The second treatise is taken up with arithmetic, while the third discusses musical proportions in terms of the Aristidean numbers.

Through his random remarks advocating a return to the ideals of an earlier era, Legrense established himself as the first 15th-century musician to indicate an awareness of the Renaissance. This humanist bent is reflected in his suggestions that a reading of Boethius and his own tenth chapter – to the neglect of all that came between – would suffice for the reader's education on a certain point, and that Marchetto da Padova and Guido of Arezzo, both of whom he cited frequently, erred in their respective innovations of tonal division and solmization. These ideas are directly attributable to Feltre, whose successor he became at Mantua and later at Parma. In turn, the rebirth was transmitted through his pupils Burtius, Gaffurius, Ramos de Pareia and Spataro to one of the most influential writers of the late 15th century, Johannes Tinctoris.

BIBLIOGRAPHY
C. Adkins: *The Theory and Practice of the Monochord* (diss., U. of Iowa, 1963)
L. Schrade: 'Renaissance: the Historical Conception of an Epoch', *IMSCR, v Utrecht 1952*, 19
                                                CECIL ADKINS

Legrenzi, Giovanni (*b* Clusone, nr. Bergamo, baptized 12 Aug 1626; *d* Venice, 27 May 1690). Italian composer and organist. He was one of the most gifted and influential composers of the latter half of the 17th century. Active in most fields of composition, he was an important force in the development of the late Baroque style in northern Italy.

1. LIFE. Legrenzi was a son of Giovanni Maria Legrenzi, violinist at the parish church in Clusone and a minor composer. Caffi's statement that he studied in Venice with Giovanni Rovetta and Carlo Pallavicino is neither supported by documentary evidence nor suggested by what is known about his early years. On 30 July 1645, newly arrived from Clusone, he became organist at S Maria Maggiore in Bergamo and was elected a resident chaplain there on 2 May 1651, having been ordained earlier that year. On 6 September 1653 he sought and was granted the title of first organist. On 30 December 1654 he failed for some unstated reason to be reconfirmed as organist. After several inconclusive votes by the governing body he was reinstated on 23

February 1655 but left at his own request on 31 December 1655. He was, however, still serving there in some capacity in April 1656. His published output from this period consists primarily of church music.

Legrenzi's years at S Maria Maggiore, Bergamo, coincided with the final period of its musical glory. The three *maestri di cappella* with whom he served, Giovanni Battista Crivelli, Filippo Vitali and above all Maurizio Cazzati, were handsomely supported in their endeavours, as is indicated by the huge sums spent annually on music for the most important feast, the Assumption of the Blessed Virgin Mary. But by far the largest expenditure was in 1665 and 1666, when Legrenzi returned as visiting *maestro*. Musicians were assembled from such distant points as Venice, Ferrara, Mantua and Lucca, the total forces in 1665 comprising 43 musicians, only 11 of whom were attached to the basilica. Legrenzi's other activities in Bergamo included membership of the Accademia degli Eccitati.

Later in 1656, probably with the assistance of Cazzati, he became *maestro di cappella* of the Accademia dello Spirito Santo at Ferrara, an institution devoted, like the Scuola Grande in Venice, to the performance of sacred music and oratorios. Ferrara was a more vital musical centre than Bergamo and provided him with both the incentive and the opportunity to write operas and oratorios. His first opera, *Nino il giusto*, dates from 1662. Ferrara also provided him with indispensable aristocratic connections, which he cultivated assiduously. The most important of these was with Hippolito Bentivoglio, who was active in the affairs of the academy, a supporter of opera, librettist for at least one of Legrenzi's dramatic works and a lifelong patron and friend, who appears to have assisted him in obtaining first performances in Venice in 1664 and Vienna in 1665. Except for three operas, one oratorio and several *sonate da camera* and dances, Legrenzi's output during these years continued to be devoted to church music. He appears to have left Ferrara in June 1665 after the completion of his third opera, *Zenobia e Radamisto*. But strong ties with Ferrara continued, as is seen from his numerous letters to Bentivoglio up to 1685 and in the performance of five oratorios there in 1677–8.

With his departure begins a period of almost 12 years in which there is no certain information on his positions, except for those he sought unsuccessfully or refused. These include many of the most important posts in northern Italy and several beyond. During these years he published only church music. From a letter of 14 April 1665 it is clear that he had been offered a post in Modena, probably as successor to Marco Uccellini as *maestro di cappella* at the cathedral. He refused it, as well as an offer he claimed in the same letter to have received from S Maria Maggiore, Bergamo, to return as *maestro di cappella* in succession to Giovanni Battista Pederzuoli. A letter of 17 July 1665 shows that Legrenzi had enlisted the help of Carlo II Gonzaga, Duke of Mantua, in a bold scheme to obtain the post of Kapellmeister at the Habsburg court in Vienna. His attempt was unavailing; the post was occupied by Antonio Bertali until 1669. According to his own account he was subsequently appointed a director of music at the court of Louis XIV but was unable to assume the position because of a grave illness that incapacitated him for a year. The post to which he had been named was probably that of *sous-maître* of the royal chapel, which since 1663 had been divided among four men, Henri du

1. Giovanni Legrenzi: anonymous 18th-century portrait in the Civico Museo Bibliografico Musicale, Bologna

Mont, Pierre Robert, Thomas Gobert and Gabriel Expilly. The appointment probably dated from 1668, the year in which Gobert retired. Legrenzi is next found in 1669 competing for the post of *maestro di cappella* at Milan Cathedral as successor to Michelangelo Grancini, but Giovanni Antonio Grossi was elected. In August 1670 he enlisted the aid of Cardinal Girolamo Buonvisi, a patron from his Ferrarese days, in obtaining a similar post with Ranuccio II Farnese, Duke of Parma; but there was no vacancy, the incumbent, Marco Uccellini, continuing in the post. His name next appears in September 1671 as a candidate for the post of *maestro di cappella* at S Petronio, Bologna, in succession to Cazzati. During the protracted deliberations, which included four different votes on the candidates, his prospects rose and fell and at one point in the balloting were better than those of the ultimate winner in 1674, Giovanni Paolo Colonna.

It is probable that by 1671 Legrenzi was living in Venice and that he began in that year his service at the Conservatorio dei Mendicanti, where he is found as *maestro di coro* in 1683. (Johann Philipp Krieger's encounter with him in Venice, mentioned by Mattheson, could not have occurred before 1673 at the earliest.) Between 1675 and 1678 Legrenzi turned for the first time for ten years to the writing of operas and oratorios and produced five of each; he also published then his only collections of secular music. In February 1677 he was *maestro* of the Oratorio at S Maria della Fava, a Venetian church under the direction of the Congregazione di S Filippo Neri. On 30 April 1676 he had made his first attempt at obtaining the post of *maestro di cappella* at St Mark's, as successor to Cavalli. He lost by one vote to Natale Monferrato, for long the *vice-maestro* and Legrenzi's superior at the Mendicanti. Given the closeness of the vote it is odd that he did not compete two weeks later for the vacant post of *vice-maestro*, since it was this post that he sought and obtained on 5 January 1681, succeeding Antonio

Sartorio; he was the only candidate and was elected unanimously.

On Legrenzi's appointment there was a marked increase in the number of singers and instrumentalists hired. The increase continued until his election as *maestro* on 16 April 1685, following Monferrato's death, at which time it appears the alarmed procurators of St Mark's acted to limit further expansion. In fact during Legrenzi's years at St Mark's both the *cappella* and the *concerto* attained their largest recorded size. On 23 April 1686 the procurators authorized a choir of 36 voices, nine to a part, but this balance was never achieved in Legrenzi's time: in 1687 the choir consisted of six sopranos, seven altos, thirteen tenors and ten basses. On 21 May 1685 they had moved to reduce the number of instrumentalists to 34: eight violins, eleven violettas (violas), two *viole da braccio* (?cellos), three violones, four theorbos, two cornetts, one bassoon and three trombones. But the procurators were eminently pleased with his service, as they unanimously granted him the highest recorded salary as both *vice-maestro* and *maestro*: his salary as *maestro* from 1687 amounted to 470 ducats, 'to the person and not to the office'.

Legrenzi's years as *vice-maestro* were his last and most prolific in the field of opera, two appearing in Venice each year between 1681 and 1684. As *maestro* he turned again to the composition of sacred music, writing responsories for Holy Week, a collection of motets (op.15) and a mass dedicated to the Madonna of Loreto, but none of the music he composed for the St Mark's *cappella* seems to have survived. He was also involved in the special services held in 1687 in celebration of the last victories of the Venetians in their costly wars with the Turks.

In his last years his house opposite S Lio, where he lived with his sister Giovanna, was a centre of musical life. At one concert held there early in 1688 three French sisters sang duets and trios by Lully, and some of his own instrumental works were performed. From 1687 he was also the moving force behind the foundation of the *sovvegno* (a mutual-aid society) of musicians in Venice. After 1687 his activities at St Mark's were curtailed by an illness that was to prove fatal. He was buried in S Maria della Fava. Of all the students he is reputed to have taught there is certain information on only one, his nephew Giovanni Varischino, to whom he bequeathed his unpublished works: Varischino subsequently published at least two collections (opp.16–17) and may have published a third (op.18), of which no copies are extant.

Legrenzi's rise to fame, honour and wealth was remarkable. As a young man from the provinces his resources were so meagre that he required a title of patrimony, granted in 1649, in order to be ordained. But by 1653 he was able to underwrite the costs of educating three boys (one of them his brother Marco) at the Accademia Mariana at Bergamo. At his death he owned property in Clusone.

2. WORKS. Legrenzi's music represents the final stage in the formation of the late Baroque style. It is characterized by clarity of design achieved through the coordination of well-defined tonal drives and incisive themes employed in various repetitive schemes; a contrapuntal style in which line is subordinated to harmony and rhythm is metrically conceived; integration of the bass into the thematic process; and skilful employment of the

new violin idiom without its more virtuoso special effects. Most of the means for creating the large-scale tonal forms of the late Baroque are present: the pervasive use of antecedent–consequent structures defined by half- and full closes; the coordination of thematic materials and textures to reinforce these structures; the resourceful use of sequences, deceptive cadences and internal repetitions to enhance tonal drive through the deferment of the full close; and adept modulations. Perhaps his most important contribution is found in his fugal writing (especially in the instrumental works), which displays a broad variety of approaches, ranging from that of the ricercare on several subjects, as developed by Frescobaldi and Giovanni Gabrieli, to the use of contrasting episodic materials (later so characteristic of Bach). Yet though most ingredients of the late Baroque style are present in his music, it lacks the breadth and expansiveness associated with this style; it is essentially shortwinded. His style, which remains virtually the same regardless of genre, displays little sign of development or change throughout his career, only of refinement.

In his sacred music, which shows the influence of Merula and Cazzati, he wrote in four of the stylistic categories cultivated by his predecessors: the concertato for few voices, which he used for motets and psalm settings for one to three voices, which often resemble his cantatas in their sectional form and use of recitative; the concertato for larger numbers of voices, which he employed in mass, vesper and compline settings, which call for solo voices, chorus and strings; massive Venetian polychoral works, used in his mass and psalm settings and a *Dies irae*; and several examples of the *stile antico*, including his five-part mass of 1689, which is, however, thoroughly infected with the new tonal procedures. One motet, *Intret in conspectu tuo*, exists only in a copy made by Handel, who drew on it for the section 'To thy dark servant' in the chorus 'O first created beam' in *Samson*.

Legrenzi's sonatas are his most forward-looking works. They show the strong influence of the ensemble canzonas of Merula, Neri and Cazzati in their themes and designs, yet there is in them a surer feeling for the development of dynamic form through the interplay of theme and key. They in turn exerted a strong influence, particularly in the handling of structure, on the sonatas and concertos of Torelli, Vivaldi and Bach. Most are either for two violins and continuo or violin, cello and continuo or are trio sonatas for two violins, cello and continuo. In op.8 there are two late examples of the Venetian polychoral sonata, reduced now to six parts, and in op.10 two for either viols or members of the violin family. Those for four and five parts in op.8 and op.10 appear to have been written with the possibility of orchestral performance in mind. Bach wrote a fugue BWV574 said to be on a subject by Legrenzi, but the source is yet to be identified.

Legrenzi's surviving operas and oratorios show a close connection with his sonatas and dances, eight movements from which appear as opening sinfonias in them. The operas are of the heroic–comic type, with complicated plots, and they employed large casts and marvellous machines. Like those of Pietro Andrea Ziani and Antonio Cesti they show the growing importance of the aria, of which Legrenzi wrote two basic types: those in fast common time with diatonic melodies and much use of dactylic rhythms; and those in slow triple time, which occasionally employ chromatic and diminished intervals for expressive effect. Both types range from simple syllabic settings to settings with extensive roulades, which, because of their unpredictable angularity, often lack the grace found in arias by his successors. Legrenzi employed a wide range of unifying procedures, often combining two or more in the same aria: a motto,

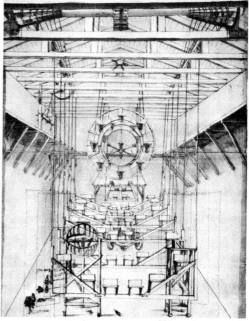

2. Moving cloud scene (with stage machinery, right) from Legrenzi's opera 'Germanico sul Reno', first performed at the Teatro S Salvatore, Venice, in 1676: pen and ink drawing, with wash, in the Bibliothèque de l'Opéra, Paris

ostinato, da capo form, strophic form and the *ABB* form associated with Cesti. Many of the characteristics of his aria style as found in his operas, oratorios, cantatas and motets are seen in ex.1. He also lavished care on his orchestral parts, both in ritornellos and in accompaniments to arias. His aria style was to prove a strong influence on Alessandro Scarlatti and Handel.

Ex.1 Legrenzi: *Giustino*, 1683, Act 1 scene xii

WORKS

OPERAS

Title	Librettist	Performances	Remarks
Nino il giusto	?H. Bentivoglio	Ferrara, Teatro S Stefano, 1662	lost
L'Achille in Sciro	?Bentivoglio	Ferrara, Teatro S Stefano, 1663; Venice, Teatro S Salvatore, 1664; Bologna, Teatro Formigliari, 1673	lost
Zenobia e Radamisto	?Bentivoglio	Ferrara, Teatro S Stefano, 1665; Brescia, Teatro degli Erranti, 1666; Macerata, Teatro di Macerata, 1669	*I-Nc*, Rari 6.5.10
Tiridate	N. Minato, after ?Bentivoglio	Venice, Teatro S Salvatore, 1668	adaptation of Zenobia e Radamisto; lost
Eteocle e Polinice	T. Fattorini	Venice, Teatro S Salvatore, 1675; Naples, 1680; Milan, Teatro Regio, 1684; Modena, Teatro Fontanelli, 1690	1675 arias, *I-Vnm*; 1680 score, *Nc*, copies, *B-Bc*, *US-Wc*; 1690 score, *I-MOe*; another score, *F-Pn*
La divisione del mondo	G. C. Corradi	Venice, Teatro S Salvatore, 1675	score, *Pn*
Adone in Cipro	G. M. Giannini or I. Teomagnini	Venice, Teatro S Salvatore, 1676	lost
Germanico sul Reno	Corradi	Venice, Teatro S Salvatore, 1676; Milan, Regio Palazzo, 1677; Modena, Teatro Ducale, 1677	1677 score, *I-MOe*
Totila	M. Noris	Venice, Teatro SS Giovanni e Paolo, 1677; Palermo, 1696	1677 score, *Vnm*; 1677 arias, *Vqs*; production described in *Le nouveau mercure galant* (Aug 1677)
Il Creso	Corradi	Venice, Teatro S Giovanni Grisostomo, 1681	arias, *Vqs, Bca*
Antioco il grande	G. Frisari	Venice, Teatro S Giovanni Grisostomo, 1681	arias, *Vqs, Bca*
Il Pausania	Frisari	Venice, Teatro S Salvatore, 1682	arias, *T, Vnm, Vqs*
Lisimaco riamato	G. Sinibaldi, rev. A. Aureli	Venice, Teatro S Salvatore, 1682; Bologna, Teatro Malvezzi, 1688; Florence Teatro degli Accademici Infuocati, 1690; Ferrara, Teatro Bonacossi, 1693	1682 arias, *Vqs*
L'Ottaviano Cesare Augusto	N. Beregan	Mantua, Teatro Ducale, 1682	lost
Giustino	Beregan	Venice, Teatro S Salvatore, 1683; Naples, Palazzo Regio, 1684; Milan, 1689; Genoa, 1689; Bologna, Teatro Malvezzi, 1691; Rome, Teatro di Tordinona, 1695; Verona, Teatro di Verona, 1696; Modena, Teatro Fontanelli, 1697; Vicenza, 1697	1683 score, *Vnm*; 1683 arias, *Vqs*; 1684 score, *Nc*; 1 aria ed. in GMB
I due Cesari	Corradi	Venice, Teatro S Salvatore, 1683; Milan, Teatro Regio, 1687	1683 arias, *Vqs*; production described in *Mercure galant* (March 1683)
L'anarchia dell'imperio	T. Stanzani	Venice, Teatro S Salvatore, 1684; Milan, Teatro Regio, 1688	lost
Publio Elio Pertinace	P. d'Averara	Venice, Teatro S Salvatore, 1684	lost
Ifianassa e Melampo	G. A. Moniglia	Pratolino, Villa, 1685	lost

ORATORIOS

Oratorio del giuditio (H. Bentivoglio), Vienna, Capella dell'Imperatrice, 1665; lost

Gli sponsali d'Ester, Modena, Palazzo Ducale, 1676; Ferrara, Accademia della Morte, 1677; lost

Il Sedecia, Ferrara, Accademia della Morte, 1676; score, *I-Rvat*

La vendita del core humano, Ferrara, Accademia della Morte, 1676; Vienna, Cappella dell'Imperatore, 1692, as Il prezzo del cuore humano; score, *Rvat, MOe*

Il Sisara, Ferrara, Chiesa di S Filippo Neri, 1678; lost

Decollatione di S Giovanni, Ferrara, Chiesa di S Filippo Neri, 1678; lost

La morte del cor penitente, Vienna, Cappella dell'Imperatore, 1705; score, *A-Wn*

SACRED

op.
1 Concerti musicali per uso di chiesa (Venice, 1654)
3 Harmonia d'affetti devoti, 2–4vv, libro primo (Venice, 1655)
5 [13] Salmi a 5 (Venice, 1657)
6 Sentimenti devoti, 2–3vv, libro secondo (Venice, 1660)
7 Compiete con le lettanie & antifone della BV a 5 (Venice, 1662)
9 Sacri e festivi concenti, messa e psalmi a due chori (Venice, 1667)
10 Acclamationi divote, 1v (Bologna, 1670)
11 [2nd edn. of op.10] (Venice, 1680), lost, see Sartori (1966); MS copy, *I-Vnm*
15 Sacri musicali concerti, 2–3vv, libro terzo (Venice, 1689)
17 Motetti sacri, 1v, ed. G. Varischino (Venice, 1692)

Missa, 5vv, 1689, *LT*; Missa, 4vv, insts, *D-Bds*; Ky, Gl, Cr, 1v, orch, *GB-Ob*

Compline, 5vv, *D-Bds*; Mag, 4vv, insts, *Bds*; Mag, 3vv, *Bds*; Laudate pueri, 5vv, insts, *Bds*; Intret in conspectu tuo, 6vv, bc, *GB-Lbm* (in Handel's hand); In nativitate Domini invitatorium, 8vv, insts, *I-Vnm*; Nolite timere, *Md*; Credidi propter, A, insts, *D-Bds*; Dies irae, prosa per mortuis, *F-Pn*; 30 other psalms and motets, *D-Bds*; 15 motets, *F-Pn* (copied by Brossard); 4 motets, *GB-T*; Spirate aurae serenae, S, 2 vn, org, in 1695[1]

SECULAR VOCAL

12 Cantate e canzonette, 1v (Bologna, 1676); ed. in RRMBE, xiv–xv (1972)

13 Idee armoniche, 2–3vv (Venice, 1678)

14 Echi di riverenza di cantate e canzoni, libro secondo (Bologna, 1678)

Son tutto furore, S, bc, in 1670³; Amor ti punge il seno, *I-Rvat*; Vuoi farmi piangere, *Rvat*; Cintia dolente, *Nc*; No, no, non ti dolor, in Arie e ariette, 1–2vv, bc, *Nc*; Disperarsi, 2vv, bc, *F-Pn*; Non può viver, aria, 1v, bc, *Pn*; Volo vivere, A, bc, *D-Bds*

Notte, madre d'orrori, serenade, S, bc, *Bds*; 12 cantatas, 1v, bc, *Bds*; 3 chamber cantatas, 1v, bc, *Mbs*; Voti di musicale plauso, cantata, 1662, MS in private collection of P. Camerini, Montruglio, nr. Vicenza

INSTRUMENTAL

2 [18] Sonate a 2–3, libro primo (Venice, 1655), incl. 1 sonata by Giovanni Maria Legrenzi; 1 sonata ed. in HM, xxxi (1949)

4 [30] Sonate da chiesa e da camera . . . a 3, libro secondo (Venice, 1656); 6 ed. in Le pupitre, iv (Paris, 1968)

8 [16] Sonate a 2, 3, 5, & 6, libro terzo (Venice, 1663); 4 ed. in Le pupitre, iv (Paris, 1968)

10 La cetra, sonate a 2–4, libro quarto (Venice, 1673) [*recte* op.11], no.13 and 4 ed. in HM, lxxxiii and lxxxiv (1951)

16 Balletti e correnti a 5, libro quinto, ed. G. Varischino (Venice, 1691)

18 Sonate, 2–7 insts con trombe e senza, overo flauti, ? ed. G. Varischino (Venice, ?1695), lost, see Sartori (1966)

BIBLIOGRAPHY

F. Caffi: *Storia della musica sacra nella già cappella ducale di San Marco in Venezia dal 1318 al 1797* (Venice, 1854–5/R1972)

A. Heuss: 'Die venetianischen Opern-sinfonie', *SIMG*, iv (1902–3), 404–77

E. Schmitz: *Geschichte der weltlichen Solokantate* (Leipzig, 1914, rev. 2/1955)

H. Nüssle: *Giovanni Legrenzi als Instrumentalkomponist* (diss., U. of Munich, 1917)

P. Camerini: *Piazzola* (Milan, 1925)

R. Haas: *Die Musik des Barocks* (Potsdam, 1928)

A. Schlossberg: *Die italienische Sonata für mehrere Instrumente im 17. Jahrhundert* (Paris, 1935)

G. Tebaldini: 'Giovanni Legrenzi', *Musica d'oggi*, xix (1937), 125

M. F. Bukofzer: *Music in the Baroque Era* (New York, 1947), 133f, 137f

P. Fogaccia: *Giovanni Legrenzi* (Bergamo, 1954)

S. T. Worsthorne: *Venetian Opera in the Seventeenth Century* (Oxford, 1954), 37, 43, 48, 105

R. Monterosso: 'Medaglioni di musicisti lombardi, ii: Giovanni Legrenzi', *Musicisti lombardi ed emiliani*, Chigiana, xv (1958), 55

W. S. Newman: *The Sonata in the Baroque Era* (Chapel Hill, North Carolina, 1959, rev. 2/1966/R1972), 128ff

S. Bonta: *The Church Sonatas of Giovanni Legrenzi* (diss., Harvard U., 1964)

J. A. MacDonald: *The Sacred Vocal Music of Giovanni Legrenzi* (diss., U. of Michigan, 1964)

C. Sartori: 'Un catologo di Giuseppe Sala del 1715', *FAM*, xiii (1966), 114

A. Meli: 'L'esordio di Giovanni Legrenzi da Clusone in Santa Maria Maggiore dal 1645 al 1655', *L'eco di Bergamo* (23 Aug 1970)

S. Bonta: 'A Formal Convention in 17th-century Italian Instrumental Music', *IMSCR, xi Copenhagen 1972*, 288

C. Sartori: 'Due Legrenzi ricuperati', *AcM*, xlvi (1974), 217

H. E. Smither: *A History of the Oratorio, i: The Oratorio in the Baroque Era: Italy, Vienna, Paris* (Chapel Hill, North Carolina, 1977), 308ff

STEPHEN BONTA

Legros [Le Gros], **Joseph** (*b* Monampteuil, Laon, 7 or 8 Sept 1739; *d* La Rochelle, 20 Dec 1793). French tenor and composer. A choirboy at Laon, he developed into a powerful, sweet-toned *haute-contre*, but was a stiff actor. He made his début at the Paris Opéra in 1764 in Mondonville's *Titon et l'Aurore*. He played title roles in Rameau's *Castor et Pollux*, *Zoroastre*, *Hippolyte et Aricie* and *Dardanus* and created Sandomir in Philidor's *Ernelinde*. He was the first Achilles in *Iphigénie en Aulide* and his popularity influenced the revision of the castrato role of Orpheus to the *haute-contre* range in the French version of this opera. In Gluck's later French operas he played Admetus (in *Alceste*), Renaud (in *Armide*), Pylades (in *Iphigénie en Tauride*) and Cynire (in *Echo et Narcisse*). For Piccinni he created Médor (in

Roland), Atys and Pylades. He left the stage in 1783 because of obesity.

Legros directed the Concert Spirituel from 1777 until 1790, when it was dissolved. There he promoted Haydn's music and in 1778 commissioned works from Mozart but too often let commercial interests outweigh his artistic judgment. With L.-B. Desormery he rewrote the second entrée of F. L. Grenet's opera-ballet *Le triomphe de l'harmonie* as *Hylas et Eglé* (performed at the Opéra in 1775). He also composed another opera, *Anacréon*, and some songs.

BIBLIOGRAPHY

FétisB

F. Serpa: 'Le Gros, Joseph', *ES*

B. S. Brook: *La symphonie française dans la seconde moitié du XVIIIᵉ siècle* (Paris, 1962)

C. Pierre: *Histoire du Concert spirituel 1725–1970* (Paris, 1975)

JULIAN RUSHTON

Leguar [Leguerre], **John.** See LAGUERRE, JOHN.

Leguerney, Jacques (Alfred Georges Emile) (*b* Le Havre, 19 Nov 1906). French composer. In early childhood he took the decision to compose, and he had considerable success with a cantata written when he was 14. He began formal training with Samuel-Rousseau and Boulanger at the Ecole Normale de Musique in 1927, but in 1932 his career was interrupted by the death of his father and the consequent need for him to support the family. It was only in the 1940s that he could devote himself to composition in earnest. He then produced a body of songs distinguished by a courtly elegance of line and supple, sophisticated harmony. At the time these were regarded as second only to those of Poulenc, and Souzay recorded several of them. Leguerney displayed the same exquisite taste in his few larger works, of which the ballet *Endymion* was produced at the Paris Opéra with choreography by Lifar.

WORKS

Ballets: Endymion (1, Doderet), 1948, Paris, 1949; La reine noire (2, Devillez, Leguerney), 1963

Vocal orch: Psalm lxxi, Bar, orch, 1954; orchd songs

Chamber: Sonatine, G, vn, pf, 1944; Str Qt, b, 1947

Songs: Signes (Tombeau), S, Bar, pf, 1943; Je vous envoie (Ronsard), Genvièvres hérissés (Ronsard), Je me lamente (Ronsard), Bel aubépin (Ronsard), Au sommeil (P. Desportes), Si mille oeillets (Ronsard), S, pf, 1944; A la fontaine billerie (Ronsard), Chanson triste (Ronsard), Villanelle (Desportes), S, pf/(fl, harp, str trio), 1945; Ciel, air et vents (Ronsard), Ode anacréontique (Ronsard), S, pf, 1946; Clotilde, L'adieu (Apollinaire), Mez, pf, 1947; Ah! bel accueil, A sa maitresse, A son page (Ronsard), Bar, pf/orch, 1949; Le présent (Laurencin), S, pf, 1950; Ma douce jouvence est passée, Epipsalmodie (Ronsard), Bar, pf, 1950; 7 poèmes de François Maynard, Bar, pf, 1951; La nuit (St Amand), 3 songs, Bar, pf, 1951; Le carnaval (St Amand), 3 songs, Bar, pf, 1951; La solitude (St Amand), 3 songs, Bar, pf/orch, 1951; De l'abîme profond (La Ceppède), S, Bar, pf, 1952; Le paysage du Port-Royal (Racine), 4 songs, Mez/Bar, pf, 1956; Come Away (Shakespeare), Bar, pf, 1964

Principal publishers: Durand, Salabert

PAUL GRIFFITHS

Lehár, Franz [Ferencz] (*b* Komáron, Hungary, 30 April 1870; *d* Bad Ischl, 24 Oct 1948). Austrian composer and conductor of Hungarian origin. He was the leading operetta composer of the 20th century, being primarily responsible for the revival of the genre as an international form of entertainment. At a time when the general musical standard of operetta was rapidly declining he achieved the distinction that his last work, *Giuditta*, was written for the Vienna Staatsoper. His most successful operetta, *Die lustige Witwe*, has established a place in the opera house as well as in the operetta theatre and, along with Offenbach and Johann

Strauss II, Lehár has remained one of the most popular composers of light music.

1. LIFE. The family came originally from the eastern Sudetenland, the name originally being Lehar. Lehár's father, also Franz (1838–98), received his music education in Sternberg, played the horn in the orchestra of the Theater an der Wien, and was for nearly 40 years a military bandmaster and composer of dances and marches. In 1869 he married the Hungarian Christine Neubrandt, and in the following years moved between various Hungarian garrison towns. The mother-tongue of their offspring was Hungarian and the family name acquired the accent to indicate a long vowel (the stress being on the first syllable). In 1880 the father's regiment moved to Budapest, but to improve his German the young Lehár was sent to Sternberg where his uncle was the town music director. During the summer Lehár played the violin in the spa orchestra at Bad Ullersdorf in Moravia, and at the age of 12 he went to the Prague Conservatory, studying the violin with Bennewitz and theory with Foerster. He also took some private lessons in composition from Fibich and received some advice from Dvořák.

In autumn 1888 Lehár took up a position as theatre violinist at Barmen-Elberfeld in the Rhineland. Then, called up for military service, he joined the band of the 50th Austrian infantry regiment, playing under his father and alongside his future colleague, Fall. In 1890 he was made bandmaster of the 25th infantry regiment in Losoncz and in 1894 of the naval corps in Pola. He gave up the position when his opera *Kukuška* was about to be performed, but its failure in Leipzig in November 1896 forced him to return to military service as bandmaster of the 87th infantry regiment in Trieste. On his father's retirement he took over his position with the 3rd Bosnian-Herzegovinan infantry regiment in Budapest, and finally in 1899 was appointed bandmaster of the 26th infantry regiment, a post which brought him to Vienna. He had been composing dances and marches and in Vienna achieved success with the march *Jetzt geht's los!* and the waltzes *Asklepios* (1901) and *Gold und Silber* (1902). In 1902 he finally left military service and in that year he conducted at the Venedig in Wien summer theatre in the Prater and then at the Theater an der Wien. There and at the rival Carltheater his operettas *Wiener Frauen* and *Der Rastelbinder* were performed within the space of a month, the latter being a particular success. Their successors, *Der Göttergatte* (1904) and *Die Juxheirat* (1904), were both failures, but in 1905 Lehár was called in to set *Die lustige Witwe*, a libretto originally intended for Heuberger. Its success in Vienna and abroad was the greatest in operetta history, heralding a new international era for Viennese operetta not only through Lehár's own works but through those of Straus, Fall and later Kálmán.

A relative failure followed, in *Der Mann mit den drei Frauen* (1908), but then three works were produced within the space of three months, of which *Der Graf von Luxemburg* and *Zigeunerliebe* both achieved wide international popularity. Lehár was by now building on his reputation and producing works which were more ambitious in both subject matter and musical style, but they failed to attract the same wide public. After the war (during which he conducted many concerts for the armed forces), the arrival of new styles of popular music from the USA increasingly made it appear that Lehár's period of greatest popularity was over. However, a new period of success arrived with a series of operettas written for Tauber. In particular, the tenor arias which Lehár wrote for Tauber caught the public fancy and ensured the lasting popularity of these late works. The series began with *Paganini* (though the tenor lead at the première was sung by Carl Clewing) and continued with *Der Zarewitsch* (1927) and *Friederike* (in which Tauber portrayed Goethe) before there came the most widely popular, *Das Land des Lächelns* (1929). This work, which was first produced in Berlin where Lehár's premières were now staged, was a revision of an earlier work, *Die gelbe Jacke* (1923), with the most famous of all the Tauber songs, 'Dein ist mein ganzes Herz', among the additions to the score.

At this time Lehár was occupied with film versions of his operettas, and he also composed some original film scores. Apart from some further revisions for Tauber, his next stage work was *Giuditta*, a still more ambitious work written for the Vienna Staatsoper where it was produced in 1934 with Tauber and Jarmila Novotna in the leading roles and with 120 radio companies relaying the performance. Lehár never again found the subject or the frame of mind for a new work. In 1935 he founded his own publishing house, Glocken Verlag, to take over the rights to many of his works from the bankrupt Karczag publishing house; he also added the rights to many published by other firms with the notable exception of *Die lustige Witwe*, the lucrative rights to which were retained by Doblinger. He concentrated mainly on these publishing activities, his most substantial piece of composition being the revision of *Zigeunerliebe* as the opera *Garabonciás diák* for Budapest (1943). During the war he remained in Vienna and Ischl, suffering the equivocal situation that, whereas his wife was Jewish and several of his friends and collaborators died in concentration camps, *Die lustige Witwe* was one of Hitler's favourite works. Always wrapped up in his music and unwilling to become involved in politics, his failure to protest against Nazi atrocities at first made him an object of suspicion after the war. Suffering ill-health, in 1946 he moved to Zurich where his wife died in September 1947; in summer 1948 he returned to Bad Ischl where he died soon afterwards. His villa in Bad Ischl is now a Lehár museum, and a memorial in front of the Kursaal was unveiled in 1958.

2. WORKS. The extent of the development of Lehár's musical style was unusually great, if not unique, for an operetta composer, and his works divide naturally into the early successes before World War I and the subsequent phase culminating in the Tauber successes. His earlier works, both independent pieces such as *Gold und Silber* and the early stage successes, show above all a natural and profuse flow of melody. Like Johann Strauss II he had the ability to make melodies take an unexpected but natural-sounding turn and to maintain interest through the contrasted shape and rhythm of succeeding melodies. Although he introduced the full range of social dance rhythms into his works, the centrepiece was of course the waltz, though a more tender, swaying type of waltz than that which typified those of the previous generations of waltz composers. His technical grasp, gained through a thorough theoretical and practical education, and his study of musical development in both serious and popular music, enabled him to give his fluent melodic output a substance that is not often found

Franz Lehár

in music of its type. His vocal writing was particularly sympathetic, with phrasing and melodic shaping disguising the underlying rhythm, and he was especially adept at using counterpoint for melodic, rhythmic and also dramatic purposes. His wide knowledge of instrumental capabilities made him a sympathetic orchestrator, making effective use of national instruments to bring out the local atmosphere of the settings of his stage works.

Nowhere is the freshness of his invention better displayed than in *Die lustige Witwe*, the work with which his name is most closely associated and one which shows remarkably little trace of the rather stereotyped patterns into which operetta was inclined to sink. Probably no leading pair of roles had had so individual and effective a pair of entrance songs as Hanna Glawari and Danilo Danilowitsch, and this originality is maintained throughout the score. Lehár was perhaps lucky that the Viennese operetta was at the time suffering something of an eclipse following the deaths of the leading practitioners of the previous generation such as Suppé, Johann Strauss II, Millöcker and Zeller, so that opportunities were there for new composers. He was lucky too that the Theater an der Wien company was composed of relative newcomers who were thus not in a position to demand show numbers to suit their own taste, and in particular he was able to avoid writing numbers for performers who were comics rather than singers. In fact the chief comic role, Njegus, has no solo singing. Lehár was thus more than usually free to follow his own inclination without extraneous influences. Above all, however, he was fortunate in having the good text on which an operetta, far more than an opera, is dependent. The waltzes, which were *de rigueur* in Viennese operetta, were able to occur as an integral part of the action, and the book strikes an

ideal balance between reality and fantasy, with a fine combination of romance and wit and a succession of interesting situations.

These factors were in varying degrees and combinations missing from his other works, obscuring the worth of individual numbers with no less melodic appeal. Even in the early works Lehár's aim to raise the standard of his work was evident, not least in the frequent revisions which he made at all stages of his career. In the years just before World War I his attempts to extend the scope of his operettas led to the use of more serious subjects. *Zigeunerliebe* contained elements of melancholy and fantasy, *Eva* was set in a factory and dealt with contemporary social problems, and *Endlich allein* (1914) included a whole act with the leading couple alone on a mountain top. Lehár gradually extended his harmonic language, showing an awareness of Puccinian, Straussian and Debussyan developments. Indeed he was taking Viennese operetta towards a Puccinian plane at a time when Puccini himself was flirting with Viennese operetta à la Lehár in *La rondine*. (The two composers were close friends and mutual admirers, and Lehár was even suggested as a candidate for completing *Turandot*.) However, these attempts at raising the quality of operetta brought with them suggestions of pretentiousness and sentimentality, heightened by the introduction of historical characters such as Paganini and Goethe. The incompatibility of his more serious aspirations and the traditional lightness of operetta was heightened further as Lehár began employing the new popular music styles of the time, such as the blues, foxtrot, onestep, tango and shimmy.

It was this lack of a focal point that was solved first by the advent of Tauber, who had the personality to draw audiences to Lehár's works and to do justice to the more ambitious vocal music which Lehár was able to compose for him from *Paganini* onwards. If Lehár's melodic flow was now less consistent, his shaping of vocal line was still exemplary. The typical Tauber song, with its virile initial upward thrust, became very popular but was apt to seem stereotyped when repeated in successive works ('O Mädchen, mein Mädchen' in *Friederike*, 'Dein ist mein ganzes Herz' in *Das Land des Lächelns* and 'Freunde, das Leben ist Lebenswert' in *Giuditta*) and when seized upon by hosts of tenor imitators. The final resolution of the conflict between Lehár's ambitions and the essential features of operetta came with *Giuditta*. Writing for an opera house and for opera singers, Lehár at last had the scope he needed, and the work perhaps does justice to the mature Lehár as *Die lustige Witwe* does to the younger man. It was a work for which Lehár had a particular affection and one which he arranged to have engraved in full score, though the fact that it falls uneasily between opera house and operetta theatre has restricted its subsequent acceptance.

In his last works Lehár produced his own unique style of operetta, more integrated than the revue manner then in fashion. After *Giuditta* the traditional relationship between opera and operetta finally disappeared, and Lehár, in pursuing his own course, has even been described as the destroyer of operetta. Yet it is fairer to suggest that, with the advent of new styles of popular music from the USA, operetta had already run its course as a truly international form of entertainment, and that in his final works Lehár gave the genre a final fling just as he had earlier given it new life with *Die lustige Witwe*.

WORKS

(for complete list see Czech (1957), and Peteani)

OPERETTAS

Fräulein Leutnant (1, Kolhapp), Vienna, 1901

Arabella, die Kubamerin (G. Schmidt), 1901, inc.

Das Club-Baby (V. Léon), 1901, inc.

Wiener Frauen (Der Klavierstimmer) (3, O. Tann-Bergler, E. Norini), Theater an der Wien, 21 Nov 1902

Der Rastelbinder (prelude, 2, Léon), Carltheater, 20 Dec 1902

Der Göttergatte (prelude, 2, Léon, L. Stein), Carltheater, 20 Jan 1904

Die Juxheirat (3, J. Bauer), Theater an der Wien, 22 Dec 1904

Die lustige Witwe (3, Léon, Stein, after H. Meilhac: L'attaché d'ambassade), Theater an der Wien, 30 Dec 1905

Der Schlüssel zum Paradies [rev. of Wiener Frauen] (3, Norini, J. Horst), Leipzig, Stadttheater, Oct 1906

Peter und Paul reisen im Schlaraffenland (Max und Moritz reisen im Schlaraffendland) (1, F. Grünbaum, R. Bodanzky), Theater an der Wien, 1 Dec 1906

Mitislaw der Moderne (1, Grünbaum, Bodanzky), Vienna, Die Hölle, 5 Jan 1907

Der Mann mit den drei Frauen (3, Bauer), Theater an der Wien, 21 Jan 1908

Das Fürstenkind (prelude, 2, Léon, after About), Johann Strauss Theater, 7 Oct 1909

Der Graf von Luxemburg (3, A. M. Willner, Bodanzky), Theater an der Wien, 12 Nov 1909

Zigeunerliebe (3, Willner, Bodanzky), Carltheater, 8 Jan 1910

Die Spieluhr (1, T. Zasche), Die Hölle, 7 Jan 1911

Eva (Das Fabriksmädel) (3, Willner, Bodanzky, E. Spero), Theater an der Wien, 24 Nov 1911

Rosenstock und Edelweiss (1, Bauer), Die Hölle, 1 Dec 1912

Die ideale Gattin [rev. of Der Göttergatte] (3, J. Brammer, A. Grünwald), Johann Strauss, 11 Oct 1913

Endlich allein (3, Willner, Bodanzky), Theater an der Wien, 10 Feb 1914

Der Sterngucker (3, F. Löhner-Beda, Willner), Theater in der Josefstadt, 14 Jan 1916

A Pacsirta (Wo die Lerche singt) (3, Willner, H. Reichert, after F. Martos), Budapest, Király-Szinház, 1 Jan 1918

Die blaue Mazur (2, Stein, B. Jenbach), Theater an der Wien, 28 May 1920

Die Tangokönigin [rev. of Der Göttergatte] (3, Brammer, Grünwald), Vienna, Apollo, 9 Sept 1921

Frühling (1, R. Eger), Die Hölle, 20 Jan 1922

La danza della libellule (Libellentanz, Die drei Grazien), Milan, Lirico, 3 May 1922

Frasquita (3, Willner, Reichert), Theater an der Wien, 12 May 1922

Die gelbe Jacke (3, Léon), Theater an der Wien, 9 Feb 1923

Cloclo (Lolotte) (3, Jenbach), Vienna, Bürgertheater, 8 March 1924

Paganini (3, P. Knepler, Jenbach), Johann Strauss, 30 Oct 1925

Gigolette [rev. of Der Sterngucker, La danza della libellule] (3, C. Lombardo, G. Forzano), Milan, Lirico, 30 Oct 1926

Der Zarewitsch (3, Jenbach, Reichert, after Zapolska-Scharlitt), Berlin, Deutsches Künstlertheater, 21 Feb 1927

Friederike (3, L. Herzer, F. Löhner), Berlin, Metropol, 4 Oct 1928

Das Land des Lächelns [rev. of Die gelbe Jacke] (3, Herzer, Löhner), Berlin, Metropol, 10 Oct 1929

Frühlingsmädel [rev. of Der Sterngucker, Frühling], Berlin, Theater des Westens, 29 May 1930

Schön ist die Welt [rev. of Endlich allein] (3, Herzer, Löhner), Berlin, Metropol, 3 Dec 1930

Der Fürst der Berge [rev. of Das Fürstenkind], Berlin, Theater am Nollendorfplatz, 23 Sept 1932

Giuditta (5, Knepler, Löhner), Vienna, Staatsoper, 20 Jan 1934

OPERAS AND FILMS

Der Kürassier (G. Ruther), 1891–2, inc.

Rodrigo (1, R. Mlčoch), 1893, inc.

Kukuška (3, F. Falzari), Leipzig, Stadttheater, 27 Nov 1896

Tatjana [rev. of Kukuška] (3, M. Kalbeck), Brünn, Stadttheater, 21 Feb 1905

Garabonciás diák [rev. of Zigeunerliebe] (3, E. I. Vincze), Budapest, Király Operaház, 20 Feb 1943

Film scores: Die grosse Attraktion, 1931; Es war einmal ein Walzer, 1932; Grossfürstin Alexandra, 1934; Die ganze Welt dreht sich um Liebe, 1936; Une nuit à Vienne, 1937

OTHER WORKS

Concert orch pieces: Eine Vision: meine Jugend, sym. fantasy; 2 other sym. poems; 2 vn concs., unpubd; other music

Dances: c65 waltzes incl. Stadtpark-Schönheiten, Asklepios-Walzer (Pikanterien-Walzer), Gold und Silber, Ballsirenen-Walzer [after Die lustige Witwe], Wilde Rosen (Chrysanthemum-Walzer); other dances

Over 50 marches incl. Jetzt geht's los!, Jupiter-Marsch [after Der Göttergatte], Piave-Marsch

c90 songs, pf sonatas, other pf pieces

BIBLIOGRAPHY

E. Decsey: *Franz Lehár* (Munich, 1924, 2/1930)

S. Czech: *Franz Lehár: sein Weg und sein Werk* (Lindau, 1948)

M. von Peteani: *Franz Lehár: seine Musik, sein Leben* (Vienna, 1950)

W. Macqueen-Pope and D. L. Murray: *Fortune's Favourite* (London, 1953)

S. Czech: *Schön ist die Welt: Franz Lehárs Leben und Werk* (Berlin, 1957) [incl. bibliography]

B. Grun: *Gold und Silver: the Life and Times of Franz Lehár* (London, 1970)

M. Schönherr: *Franz Lehár: Bibliographie zu Leben und Werk* (Vienna, 1970) [summary in 'Beiträge zu einer Franz-Lehár Bibliographie', *ÖMz*, xxv (1970), 330]

ANDREW LAMB

Lehel, György (*b* Budapest, 10 Feb 1926). Hungarian conductor. He studied privately with Pál Kadosa (composition) and László Somogyi (conducting), and made his début in 1946. After working for Hungarian radio he was appointed principal conductor and music director of the radio orchestra (the Budapest SO) in 1962. With this orchestra he made his British début at the 1968 Cheltenham Festival, where he conducted the first performances of Crosse's Chamber Concerto op.8, and Maconchy's *Three Cloudscapes*. He has also toured with the orchestra, and has been a guest conductor with others, in the USSR, USA, Japan and Europe; in 1974 he was appointed permanent guest conductor of the Basle RSO. His many records include much of Liszt, and Bartók (for the complete recorded edition), and new Hungarian music which he has consistently championed; many contemporary Hungarian composers have dedicated works to him. Lehel is one of the best Hungarian conductors, chiefly of contemporary and late Romantic music. He has received the Liszt Prize (1955, 1962) and the Kossuth Prize (1973) and was named Artist of Merit in 1967.

PÉTER P. VÁRNAI

Le Héman. *See* DE HÉMAN family.

Le Heurteur [Hurteur], **Guillaume** (*fl* 1530–45). French composer and choirmaster. The only known biographical information comes from the title-page of his book of motets published by Attaingnant in 1545. It states that Le Heurteur was a priest, serving as canon and preceptor of the choirboys at St Martin, Tours. Virtually all his music appeared in Parisian or Lyonnaise prints between 1530 and 1545.

Le Heurteur's surviving works include four masses, two *Magnificat* settings, 21 motets and 23 chansons. A lost Attaingnant book of settings of texts from the Song of Songs mentioned Le Heurteur on the title-page and would no doubt increase substantially the corpus of motets attributed to him. All the masses call upon pre-existent material: the *Missa 'Impetum'*, for example, is based on the anonymous motet *Impetum inimicorum ne timueritis* printed by Attaingnant in 1528 and the *Missa 'Ung jour Robin'* on Sermisy's chanson. The *Missa 'Osculetur me'* may well be based on one of Le Heurteur's lost motets on texts from the Song of Songs. His sacred music shows much variety in its contrapuntal style as well as reflecting the French predilection for harmonic orientation. In the masses and motets block-like chordal textures are interspersed with a host of contrapuntal procedures. Only rarely do these consist of relatively strict imitation; more often Le Heurteur's counterpoint brings voices together in homorhythmic groupings or combines a fast-moving melody with a slower-moving 'harmonic' support. A comparison of the two *Magnificat* settings shows the extent of the contrapuntal variety in his music. Both pieces include sections for two, three, four and six voices. The two-part sections resemble texturally the 16th-century bicinium in their combination of initial imitation with a mixture of homorhythmic passages and florid writing in semiminims. The six-part section of the *Magnificat primi toni* is essentially chordal whereas the analogous passage in the *Magnificat quarti toni* exemplifies in its canonic writing Le Heurteur's most conservative counterpoint.

The chansons for four voices are freely composed and reflect in their short phrases, concise formal structures, frequent cadences, transparent textures and melodic stereotypes, the style of the Parisian chanson. Their fabric, however, incorporates a somewhat greater measure of linear independence than is characteristic of a typical chanson by, for example, Sermisy. Le Heurteur's chansons for two or three voices are based on four-voice models by Sermisy, Gheerkin, Jacotin or Rocquelay. They are not mere arrangements of pre-existing chansons, for Le Heurteur transformed his borrowed material thoroughly, changing chordal four-voice chansons into linear duos or trios, while still retaining a recognizable image of the original.

WORKS

Edition: *Treize livres de motets parus chez Pierre Attaingnant en 1534 et 1535*, ed. A. Smijers and A. T. Merritt (Paris and Monaco, 1934–64) [S]

MASSES AND MAGNIFICAT

Missa 'Fors seulement', 4vv, 1534[1]
Missa 'Impetum', 4vv, 1532[7]
Missa 'Osculetur me', 4vv, 1532[4]; ed. in Stein
Missa 'Ung jour Robin', 4vv, 1534[1]
Magnificat primi toni, 4vv, 1534[7]; S vi
Magnificat quarti toni, 4vv, 1534[8]; S vi

MOTETS

Cantica canticorum Salomonis Guill. le Heurteur (Paris, 1541), lost
Operum musicalium liber primus (Paris, 1545) [17 motets]; 2 in S iii, iv
4 other motets, 2, 4, 5 vv, 1534[6], 1538[2], 1543[19], 1549[16]; 1 in S vii
Nisi Dominus aedificaverit domum, attrib. Le Heurteur in 1535[1], 1555[15], is by Johannes Lhéritier

CHANSONS

22 chansons, 2–4vv: 1530[3]; Chansons musicales a quatre parties (Paris, 1533); 1533[1]; 1534[12]; 1534[14]; Trente et une chansons musicales (Paris, 1535) (attrib. Janequin in 1541[13] and 1543[23]), 1 ed. M. Cauchie, *Trente chansons ... de Clément Janequin* (Paris, 1928); 1535[6]; 1538[14], 2 ed. in FCVR, viii (1929/R); 1539[19], also in *S-Uu* 87, ed. in Hambraeus; 1540[11] (attrib. Bon Voisin in 1538[13]); 1541[5–6]; 1553[22]

BIBLIOGRAPHY

E. Stein: *Twelve Franco-Flemish Masses of the Early 16th Century* (Rochester, NY, 1941)
F. Lesure: 'Les chansons à trois parties de Clément Janequin', *RdM*, xliv (1959), 193
E. Weber: 'Le Heurteur, Guillaume', *MGG*
B. Hambraeus: *Codex carminum gallicorum: une étude sur le volume musique vocale de manuscrit 87 de la Bibliothèque de l'Université d'Upsala*, Studia musicologica upsaliensia, vi (Uppsala, 1961)
F. Lesure: 'Latin Church Music on the Continent – 1: France in the Sixteenth Century (1520–1610)', *NOHM*, iv (1968), 237
D. Heartz: *Pierre Attaingnant, Royal Printer of Music* (Berkeley and Los Angeles, 1969)
——: '*Au pres de vous* – Claudin's Chanson and the Commerce of Publishers' Arrangements', *JAMS*, xxiv (1971), 193–225
LAWRENCE F. BERNSTEIN

Lehmann, Hans Ulrich (*b* Biel, canton of Berne, 4 May 1937). Swiss composer. He studied theory with Paul Müller and the cello with Rudolf Looser; from 1960 to 1963 he attended the master classes given by Boulez and Stockhausen at the Basle Academy of Music, concurrently studying musicology with Kurt von Fischer at Zurich University. He taught the cello and theory at the Basle Academy (1964–72), and in 1969 was appointed to the staff of the musicology department of Zurich

University. In 1972 he began to teach composition and theory at the Zurich Musikhochschule and Conservatory. Although he stresses the influence of Stockhausen on his early music, such pieces as *Quanti I* are clearly indebted to Boulez in their measured sonorities and serial organization. In the course of the 1960s Lehmann moved away from strict serial writing to a style that is rich in contrast and contains many playful elements. He was awarded the music prize of the C. F. Meyer-Stiftung in 1973.

WORKS
(*selective list*)

Structures transparentes, cl, va, pf, 1960; Cantata (L. Lüscher), S, fl, hn, va, harp, 1962; Quanti I, fl, ens, 1962; Régions, fl, 1963; Episoden, wind qnt, 1963–4; Mosaik, cl, 1964; Notenbüchlein, harp, 1965; Spiele, ob, harp, 1965; Komposition für 19, ens, 1964–5; Studien, va, 1966; Noten, org, 1964–6; Rondo (H. Heissenbüttel), S, orch, 1967; Instants, pf/pf, str, 1969; Conc., fl, cl, str, 1969; Dis-Cantus I, ob, str, 1971; Positionen, orch, 1971; bringen um zu kommen (F. Mon), S, 5 insts, 1972; gegen(-bei-)spiele, wind qnt, 1973; à la recherche, orgs, vv, 1973; quod libet, vn, pf, 1974; zu streichen, 6 str, 1975

Principal publisher: Schott (Mainz)

BIBLIOGRAPHY
I. Stoïanova: 'Hans Ulrich Lehmann', *SMz*, cxvi (1976), 80
JÜRG STENZL

Lehmann, Lilli (*b* Würzburg, 24 November 1848; *d* Berlin, 17 May 1929). German soprano. She studied with her mother, the singer Marie Loewe, in Prague, and made her début there on 20 October 1865 as the First Boy in *Die Zauberflöte*, later taking over the part of Pamina. In 1868 she was engaged at Danzig, and on 31 August 1869 she sang for the first time at the Court Opera, Berlin, as Marguerite de Valois in *Les Huguenots*. The following year, after appearances in Leipzig, she was engaged permanently in Berlin. She took part in the first complete *Ring* cycle at Bayreuth (1876), delighting Wagner with her singing as Woglinde, Helmwige and the Woodbird. She made her London début at Her Majesty's Theatre in June 1880 in *La traviata*, and also sang Philine in Thomas' *Mignon*. In 1882 she was heard in Vienna for the first time, and in 1884 she returned to London, appearing at Covent Garden as Isolde and as Elisabeth in *Tannhäuser*.

In 1885 Lehmann broke her contract with the Berlin Opera and went to New York, where she made her début at the Metropolitan on 25 November as Carmen. During her first season she also sang Brünnhilde in *Die Walküre*, Sulamith in the first American performance of Goldmark's *Die Königin von Saba* (2 November), Bertha in *Le prophète*, Marguerite in *Faust*, Irene in *Rienzi* and Venus in *Tannhäuser*. She took part in the first New York performances of *Tristan und Isolde* (1 December 1886), Goldmark's *Merlin* (3 January 1887), *Siegfried* (9 November 1887) and *Götterdämmerung* (25 January 1888), as well as the first complete *Ring* cycle given in the USA (March 1889). In 1891 she returned to Berlin and in 1896 she sang Brünnhilde at Bayreuth. During her final season at the Metropolitan (1898–9) she sang Fricka in *Das Rheingold*, and at Covent Garden, where she returned in 1899, her last appearances were as Isolde, Sieglinde, Ortrud, Leonore, Donna Anna and Norma. Between 1901 and 1910 she sang at the Salzburg Festival (Donna Anna and the First Lady in *Die Zauberflöte*) and also became the festival's artistic director. She continued to appear on the concert platform until 1920. She had started to teach in Berlin as early as 1891, and among her many famous pupils were Olive Fremstadt and Geraldine Farrar.

Lehmann's enormous repertory ranged from the light, coloratura parts of her youth to the dramatic roles which she sang with superb authority and technical skill during the middle and later years of her career. As it grew more powerful, her voice retained all its flexibility, and she could turn from Wagner or Verdi to Mozart or Bellini with astonishing ease; Henderson wrote that dramatically 'she was possessed of that rare combination of traits and equipment which made it possible for her to delineate the divinity in womanhood and womanhood in divinity, the mingling of the unapproachable goddess and the melting pitying human being'. However, not all of Lehmann's critics were unstinting in their praise. Hugo Wolf, writing in the *Wiener Salonblatt* of 25 January 1885, objected to her making a virago of Isolde, and he felt that her interpretation of the part was neither rounded nor fully worked out, though it contained many beautiful, even gripping details.

Lilli's younger sister, the soprano Marie Lehmann (*b* Hamburg, 15 May 1851; *d* Berlin, 9 Dec 1931), was also taught by their mother. She made her début in 1871 at Leipzig as Aennchen in *Der Freischütz* and then sang at Breslau, Cologne, Hamburg and Prague. In 1872 she sang in the performance of Beethoven's Ninth Symphony at the laying of the foundation stone of the Bayreuth Festspielhaus, and in 1876 took part in the first complete *Ring* cycle at Bayreuth, singing Wellgunde and Ortlinde. From 1882 to 1896 she was engaged at the Vienna Court Opera. Her repertory included Marguerite de Valois (*Les Huguenots*), Donna Elvira (*Don Giovanni*), Adalgisa (*Norma*) and Antonina in Donizetti's *Belisario*. She returned to Bayreuth in 1896 to sing the Second Norn in *Götterdämmerung*.

BIBLIOGRAPHY

A. Ehrlich: *Berühmte Sängerinnen der Vergangenheit und Gegenwart* (Leipzig, 1895)
L. Lehmann: *Meine Gesangskunst* (Berlin, 1902, 3/1922; Eng. trans., 1902, as *How to Sing*, rev., enlarged 3/1924/R1949)
——: *Mein Weg* (Leipzig, 1913, 2/1920; Eng. trans., 1914/R1977)
E. Newman: *The Life of Richard Wagner* (London, 1933–47/R1976)
J. Kapp: *Geschichte der Staatsoper Berlin* (Berlin, 1937)
W. J. Henderson: *The Art of Singing* (New York, 1938)
W. H. Seltsam: *Metropolitan Opera Annals* (New York, 1949)
I. Kolodin: *The Story of the Metropolitan Opera* (New York, 1951)
H. Fetting: *Die Geschichte der Deutschen Staatsoper* (Berlin, 1955)
H. Rosenthal: *Two Centuries of Opera at Covent Garden* (London, 1958)
G. Skelton: *Wagner at Bayreuth* (London, 1965)

ELIZABETH FORBES

Lehmann, Liza [Elizabeth] **(Nina Mary Frederica)** (*b* London, 11 July 1862; *d* Pinner, 19 Sept 1918). English soprano and composer. She was the daughter of Amelia Lehmann (widely known under the initials A. L. as a teacher, composer and arranger of songs) and Rudolf Lehmann, a German painter. She studied singing with Alberto Randegger and Jenny Lind in London, and composition with Raunkilde in Rome, Freudenberg in Wiesbaden and Hamish MacCunn in London. Realizing that despite her wide range (*a* to *b''*) she lacked the stamina and vocal power necessary for opera, she made her début as a recitalist at a Monday Popular Concert on 23 November 1885, and during the next nine years undertook many important singing engagements in England, receiving encouragement from Joachim and Clara Schumann. After a farewell concert at St James's Hall on 14 July 1894 she retired to marry Herbert Bedford, a painter and composer. She had already pub-

lished some songs, and in 1896 *In a Persian Garden* appeared, a cycle of selected quatrains from FitzGerald's version of the *Rubayyāt of Omar Khayyām*, for four soloists and piano; its exotic text and lyrical style appealed to contemporary taste, and it became popular. More song cycles and a number of musical comedies followed. In 1910 Lehmann undertook the first of two successful tours of the USA, accompanying her own songs in recitals. From 1911 to 1912 she was the first president of the Society of Women Musicians. She later became a professor of singing at the Guildhall School of Music and wrote *Practical Hints for Students of Singing*. Her memoirs, completed shortly before her death, make fascinating reading, giving a witty and humorous insight into the musical society of the period in London and the USA.

WORKS
(selective list; printed works published in vocal score in London)

STAGE
Sergeant Brue (musical farce, O. Hall [pseud. of J. Davis] and J. H. Wood), London, 14 June 1904 (1904); The Vicar of Wakefield (romantic light opera, 3, L. Housman, after Goldsmith), London, 12 Nov 1906 (1907); The Happy Prince (Wilde) (1908); Everyman (opera, 1), London, 28 Dec 1915 (1916); The Twin Sister (incidental music), unpubd

OTHER WORKS
Vocal with orch: Young Lochinvar (Scott), Bar, chorus, orch (1898); Once upon a Time, cantata (1903); The Golden Threshhold (S. Naidu), S, A, T, B, chorus, orch (1907); Leaves from Ossian, cantata
Song cycles: The Daisy Chain (A. P. Graves) (1893); In a Persian Garden (FitzGerald, after O. Khayyām), S, A, T, B, pf (1896); In memoriam (Tennyson) (1899); [10] Nonsense Songs (L. Carroll: Alice in Wonderland) (1908); Four Cautionary Tales and a Moral (H. Belloc) (1909); More Daisies; Prairie Pictures
Other vocal works, incl. 4 Shakespearean Partsongs (1911), 5 Tenor Songs (1913)

Chamber works, incl. Romantic Suite, vn, pf, Cobweb Castles, pf

BIBLIOGRAPHY
L. Lehmann: *The Life of Liza Lehmann, by Herself* (London, 1919)

STEPHEN BANFIELD

Lehmann, Lotte (*b* Perleberg, 27 Feb 1888; *d* Santa Barbara, 26 Aug 1976). German soprano, later naturalized American. She studied singing in Berlin, finding the most sympathetic and successful of her teachers to be Mathilde Mallinger, Wagner's original Eva. Lehmann began her career in 1910 with the Hamburg Opera, where her first solo role was Aennchen in Nicolai's *Die lustigen Weiber von Windsor*. By 1914 she had made enough of a name to be engaged for Beecham's season at Drury Lane, London, to succeed Claire Dux as Sophie in *Der Rosenkavalier*. In 1916 she moved to Vienna, and at once established herself as a prime favourite there in the role of the Composer in the revised version of *Ariadne auf Naxos*; widely recognized after the end of the war as one of the most eminent lyric–dramatic sopranos of her time, she retained her links with Vienna until the Anschluss and distaste for the Nazi regime drove her from Austria in 1938. During her Viennese years she sang many roles besides the German parts generally associated with her name; for example, several Puccini heroines (among which the composer specially esteemed her Suor Angelica), Massenet's Manon and Charlotte, Tchaikovsky's Tatyana and the heroines of Korngold's *Die tote Stadt* and *Das Wunder der Heliane*. Strauss was particularly charmed by her warm timbre and impulsive style, as exemplified in *Der Rosenkavalier* (Octavian, later the Marschallin) and in the title roles of *Ariadne* and *Arabella*; he chose her as his first Färberin (Dyer's Wife) in *Die Frau ohne*

Lotte Lehmann as the Marschallin in 'Der Rosen-kavalier'

Schatten (Vienna, 1919) and Christine in *Intermezzo* (Dresden, 1924)

Lehmann's brilliant English career dates from her appearance at Covent Garden in 1924 as the Marschallin (her first assumption of this part) under Bruno Walter; she returned nearly every year until 1938, singing Mozart's Countess and Donna Elvira, Beethoven's Leonore, Wagner's Elisabeth, Elsa, Eva, Sieglinde and Gutrune, Johann Strauss's Rosalinde, Richard Strauss's Ariadne, and – exceptionally – an Italian-language Desdemona which was singled out for high praise. Her American career began in Chicago (1930, as Sieglinde), and took her to several other cities as well as to New York, where she made her Metropolitan début as Sieglinde in 1934 and sang regularly until her farewell as the Marschallin in 1945; in October 1946 she gave two further performances in the same role at San Francisco. By that time her lieder recitals had won her a following no less devoted than her operatic public, and her final New York concert (16 February 1951) was marked by emotional scenes. She sang once again in public, on 7 August 1951, at Santa Barbara, where she made her home.

During her years of retirement Lehmann remained busy teaching, writing and painting; she also gave public master classes in opera and lieder in London and elsewhere. As a girl she had had literary ambitions, and these she was not altogether to renounce; she published verses and a novel as well as autobiographical writings and studies in interpretation.

Though Prussian by birth, Lotte Lehmann came to represent to the world the traditional Viennese qualities of charm, breeding and warm-heartedness. The vivid personality expressed by her voice was sometimes felt to overpower her characterizations; and while no-one in her time sang Sieglinde more beautifully, a certain assurance of ingratiation inseparable from her art introduced into Hunding's hut a note not purely primeval. She succeeded, however, in spite of an utterance that could not have been more feminine, in becoming a pre-eminently famous Leonore in *Fidelio*. Her voice was lovely, and generous enough in volume to carry fully formed words across a large space; and along with her rich vocal gift went a rare theatrical power of establishing herself from the first phrase of a part as ardently engaged and quiveringly sentient. Elsa's 'Mein armer Bruder!' never failed, as she uttered the words, to raise the action to a higher degree of vividness and pity. She continued to sing as Eva at a time when the experience of a magnificent career had begun rather to weigh upon the fresh girlishness of her delightful earlier interpretation; but the part of the Marschallin became more and more her own. The lyric stage of the time knew no performance more admirably accomplished; it seemed to embody a civilization, the pride and elegance of old Vienna, its voluptuousness, chastened by good manners, its doomed beauty.

The best of Lehmann's many records, made for various companies between about 1917 and 1946, convey a vivid impression of her voice and urgently dramatic style. The most valuable are the abridged *Der Rosenkavalier* of 1933 (made with her regular associates, Elisabeth Schumann and Richard Mayr) and the first two acts of *Die Walküre* (1934, with Lauritz Melchior and Bruno Walter); the saddest gap is a companion set from *Die Meistersinger*. Some of the later recordings of lieder made in the USA also repay attention.

WRITINGS

Anfang und Aufstieg (Vienna, 1937; Eng. trans., London, 1938, as *Wings of Song*; New York, 1938, as *Midway in my Song*)
More than Singing (New York, 1945)
My Many Lives (New York, 1948)
Five Operas and Richard Strauss (New York, 1964; London, 1964, as *Singing with Richard Strauss*)
Eighteen Song Cycles (London and New York, 1971)

BIBLIOGRAPHY

P. L. Miller: 'Lotte Lehmann', *Record News*, iv (1960), 391, 440; v (1960), 20, 45 [with discography]
B. W. Wessling: *Lotte Lehmann . . . mehr als eine Sängerin* (Salzburg, 1969)
M. von Schauensee: 'The Maestro's Singers: Lotte Lehmann', *The Maestro*, iii/1–2 (1971), 14 [with discography by H. P. Court]
RICHARD CAPELL/DESMOND SHAWE-TAYLOR

Lehms, Georg Christian (*b* Liegnitz, 1684; *d* Darmstadt, 15 May 1717). German poet and librettist. He was educated at the Gymnasium in Görlitz and at the University of Leipzig, where he became acquainted with Christoph Graupner. In 1710 he was appointed poet and librarian to the court of Darmstadt; by 1713 he had risen to the position of princely counsel. His works include a dictionary of German poetesses (1715); romances and occasional poems published under the name 'Palidor'; several dramatic librettos, few of which survive; and five cycles of sacred cantata texts (1711, 1712, 1714, 1715, 1716) intended for use by the two Darmstadt Kapellmeister, Graupner and Gottfried Grünewald. The cantatas of the first cycle, *Gottgefälliges Kirchen-Opffer*, received attention outside Darmstadt as well: J. S. Bach set two of the librettos while still in Weimar (BWV54 and 199) and eight more in Leipzig during the years 1725 and 1726 (BWV110, 57, 151, 16, 32, 13, 170, 35).

BIBLIOGRAPHY

F. Noack: *Christoph Graupners Kirchenmusik* (Leipzig, 1916)
——: *Christoph Graupner als Kirchenkomponist* (Leipzig, 1926/*R*1960)
E. Noack: 'Georg Christian Lehms, ein Textdichter Johann Sebastian Bachs', *BJb*, lvi (1970), 7
H. Streck: *Die Verskunst in den poetischen Texten zu den Kantaten J. S. Bachs* (Hamburg, 1971)
A. Dürr: *Die Kantaten von Johann Sebastian Bach* (Kassel, 1971)

JOSHUA RIFKIN

Lehotka, Gábor (*b* Vác, 20 July 1938). Hungarian organist. He began his studies at the age of nine. At the Liszt Academy of Music his teachers were Sebestyén Pécsi and Ferenc Gergely for organ, and Rezső Sugár and Endre Szervánszky for composition; he graduated in 1963. He made his début that year, and has since toured France, Belgium, the Netherlands, Sweden, Italy, Germany, the USSR and Poland. In 1968 he was appointed a professor at the Budapest Conservatory. One of Hungary's leading organists, he has an excellent technique, and his rhythmic playing and strong sense of style is particularly suited to the music of Bach, in which he specializes. He is a fervent advocate of mechanical action organs, and has chosen to record on historical Hungarian instruments. Among the first performances he has given is that of Ligeti's *Volumina*, and of several Hungarian works. He was awarded the Liszt Prize in 1974.

PÉTER P. VÁRNAI

Lehrstück (Ger.: 'teaching piece'). A 20th-century neologism closely associated with the work of BERTOLT BRECHT, who probably invented the term; he used it to describe a theatrical genre for amateur performance whose principal function was to teach the participants (through performance and discussion) rather than to engage the attention of an audience. Written at a time when the Nazis were gaining power in Germany, Brecht's Lehrstücke attempt in particular to teach political attitudes, often explicitly Marxist.

Brecht wrote his texts when he was experimenting with novel yet highly simplified forms of presentation derived from agit-prop drama, *Gebrauchsmusik* and his own theories of 'epic theatre'. Music plays an important part in all of them, and a dominant one in the Lehrstücke composed by Weill, Hindemith and Eisler. Their settings enlarged the boundaries of music-theatre by integrating a variety of techniques from conventional opera and theatre with elements from oratorio, revue, dance and film. The composers also underlined the didactic purpose of a Lehrstück, treating it as a means by which amateurs could be taught specific musical accomplishments and a new interpretative dimension added to the dialectic.

Brecht's attitude to his seven Lehrstücke was pragmatic, and he frequently revised them. The first three were revised extensively, with the result that their definitive texts do not correspond with those set to music. *Der Lindberghflug*, for example, was first published in 1929 as a play for radio. It was set jointly by Hindemith and Weill and presented at the Baden-Baden Festival in the same year, in a manner indicating that some parts of it were ideally to be supplied by the radio loudspeaker and some by the listener at home. Later in 1929 Weill alone composed a second setting, the published *Der Lindberghflug*, as a cantata for the concert

hall that revealed little of its origins in radio. In 1930 Brecht published an expanded version of his text under the title *Flug der Lindberghs*, describing it as a 'Radio Lehrstück for boys and girls' (in 1950 he altered the title to *Der Ozeanflug*, added a prologue and suppressed the name of Lindbergh, who had been a Nazi sympathizer; the title of Weill's cantata was also changed). This work contained no explicitly didactic content until Brecht made his 1930 version, and although suitable for amateurs Weill's cantata is thus not a true Lehrstück.

A work actually called *Lehrstück*, with music by Hindemith, was written for the same Baden-Baden Festival of 1929, and the vocal score was published in that year. Brecht later published a revised and expanded version of the text as *Das Badener Lehrstück vom Einverständnis*. *Der Jasager*, with music by Weill, was written and first performed in 1930. After criticism from the children who performed it, Brecht wrote a second version and a complementary Lehrstück, *Der Neinsager*. Weill set neither of these texts. Brecht's most important Lehrstück, *Die Massnahme*, was first performed with music by Eisler in 1930. Paul Dessau composed the music for *Die Aussnahme und die Regel* (1930) and Kurt Schwaen for *Die Horatier und die Kuriatier* (1934).

BIBLIOGRAPHY

S. Günther: 'Lehrstück und Schuloper', *Melos*, x (1931), 410
M. Esslin: *Brecht: a Choice of Evils* (London, 1959)
J. Willett: *The Theatre of Bertolt Brecht* (London, 1959)
H. Braun: *Untersuchungen zur Typologie die Schul- und Jugendoper* (Regensburg, 1963)
B. Brecht: 'Zu den Lehrstücken', *Gesammelte Werke*, xvii (Frankfurt, 1967), 1022
R. Steinweg: *Das Lehrstück* (Stuttgart, 1972)

IAN KEMP

Le Huray, Peter (Geoffrey) (*b* Norwood, London, 18 June 1930). English musicologist. In 1948 he won an organ scholarship to St Catharine's College, Cambridge; he took a double first in the Music Tripos (1951) and for his work for the MusB was awarded the Barclay Squire Prize (1952). After National Service he was a research fellow at St Catharine's, where his research on the English anthem was supervised by Thurston Dart. He was appointed first assistant lecturer at Cambridge (1958) and then full lecturer and Fellow of St Catharine's College (1961). In 1969–70 he was Barclay Acheson Professor of International Studies at Macalester College, Minnesota.

From 1962 to 1967 le Huray edited the *Proceedings of the Royal Musical Association*, and in 1969 he joined the editorial committee of Early English Church Music. His research has been principally concerned with church music in England from the Reformation to the Restoration and the conditions under which it developed. He supervises, with David Willcocks, the revisions of Fellowes's Tudor Church Music editions. As an organist he has frequently broadcast and has appeared as soloist at the Proms; he was president of the Incorporated Society of Organists (1970–72) and has written on aspects of performing practice and technique for *The Diapason* and the *Organists Review*.

WRITINGS

The English Anthem, 1603–60 (diss., U. of Cambridge, 1959)
'The English Anthem, 1580–1640', *PRMA*, lxxxvi (1959–60), 1
'Towards a Definitive Study of Pre-Restoration Anglican Service Music', *MD*, xiv (1960), 167
Music and the Reformation in England, 1549–1660 (London, 1967, 2/1978)
with R. T. Daniel: *The Sources of English Church Music, 1549–1660*, EECM, suppl.i (1972)

'English Keyboard Fingering in the 16th and Early 17th Centuries', *Source Materials and the Interpretation of Music: a Memorial Volume to Thurston Dart* (in preparation)

'Anthem', §I, 'Service', 'Tomkins', *Grove 6*

EDITIONS

The Treasury of English Church Music, ii [1545–1650] (London, 1965)

with D. Brown and W. Collins: *T. Weelkes: Collected Anthems*, MB, xxiii (1966)

M. Locke: Anthems and Motets, MB, xxxviii (1976)

DAVID SCOTT

Leibniz, Gottfried Wilhelm (*b* Leipzig, 3 July 1646; *d* Hanover, 14 Nov 1716). German philosopher. The significance of this great philosopher and all-round scholar for the history and theory of music is still not fully clear, since a modern edition of the relevant parts of his writings, especially his correspondence with Conrad Henfling, has not yet been published. (Some of his letters appear, ed. C. Kortholt, as *Epistolae ad diversos*, Leipzig, 1734, and some of them have been catalogued in E. Bodemann: *Der Briefwechsel des G. W. Leibniz in der königlichen öffentlichen Bibliothek zu Hannover*, Hanover, 1889.) As he lived in Hanover from 1678, he may well have met Handel when he was there in 1710–11 and 1716. Nothing, however, is known about this or as to whether his known contact there with Steffani concerned musical matters. He had a preference for church music and valued simple hymns above all, yet he also wrote an authoritative assessment of opera for Marci of the Hamburg Opera.

Leibniz's two letters to Christoph Goldbach (1712) show his profound knowledge of the theoretical basis of music. In the first he cited, among other things, the well-known definition 'musica est exercitium arithmeticae occultum nescientis se numerare animi' ('music is the hidden arithmetical exercise of a mind unconscious that it is calculating'), which expresses the idea that the unconscious realization of mathematical proportions is the ultimate cause of the sensuous effect of music; he associated this with a tradition going back to antiquity which has since been taken up scientifically in the theories of consonance formulated by HEINRICH HUSMANN. Leibniz also acknowledged the *senario* of GIOSEFFO ZARLINO and held that intervals divisible into seven were possible. In the theory of harmony, dissonances were as natural to him as shadows in the theory of light. He also thoroughly analysed temperament, as can be seen in the second letter, where he discussed in detail a system of temperament developed by CHRISTIAAN HUYGENS.

Leibniz's studies in the theory of music may have been stimulated by his correspondence with Henfling between 1705 and 1709. This mathematician from Ansbach, who is unknown as a music theorist, conveyed to him in detail his calculations of intervals and temperament, and the many notes that Leibniz appended to their correspondence show that he made intensive calculations of his own. Shortly afterwards he published in the *Miscellanea Berolinensia* for 1710 an essay of Henfling's called 'Epistola de novo suo systemate musico', a draft of which is found in a letter of 1706.

The above-mentioned definition of music places Leibniz's knowledge of music theory in a wider framework, within the tradition of Pythagorean harmony. The ancient idea of a harmony of the universe, a harmony of the spheres, was revived as a result of humanist thought but was more or less refuted by many thinkers, among them Robert Fludd, Athanasius Kircher and Marin Mersenne. Kepler alone pursued the idea scientifically and produced as evidence in his *Harmonices mundi libri V* (1619) intervallic proportions deriving from the orbit of the planets. Leibniz knew this tradition, revered Kepler above all such thinkers and often expressed markedly similar ideas. Harmony is a central concern of his philosophy, especially his system of 'prestabilized harmony', to which his concepts of analogy, representation, rhyme etc are related. His philosophical harmony is, however, more abstract and metaphysical than that of Pythagoras; above all, it lacks intervallic proportions as connected laws. Yet he was aware of these too, as many references make clear, and there are indications from his last years that he was planning a philosophical synthesis with harmonic content.

BIBLIOGRAPHY

C. Henfling: 'Epistola de novo suo systemate musico', *Miscellanea Berolinensia* (1710)

J. G. Meckenheuser: *Die so genannte Allerneueste Musicalische Temperatur . . . des Hochgelahrten Herrn Hof-Raths Hänflings zu Onoltzbach* (Quedlinburg, 1727)

H. Sievers: *Die Musik in Hannover* (Hanover, 1961)

R. Haase: 'Leibniz und die pythagoreisch-harmonikale Tradition', *Antaios*, iv (1963), 368

——: *Leibniz und die Musik* (Hommerich, 1963)

F. Vonessen: 'Reim und Zahl bei Leibniz', *Antaios*, viii/2 (1967), 99

R. Haase: *Geschichte des harmonikalen Pythagoreismus* (Vienna, 1969)

——: 'Leibniz und die harmonikale Tradition', *Kongressakten des II. Internationalen Leibniz-Kongresses Hannover 1972*, i

——: 'Korrespondenten von G. W. Leibniz: 3. Conrad Henfling', *Studia Leibnitiana*, viii/2 (1976)

RUDOLF HAASE

Leibowitz, René (*b* Warsaw, 17 Feb 1913; *d* Paris, 29 Aug 1972). French musicologist, teacher, composer and conductor of Polish origin. The decisive starting-point of his career was a period of study with Schoenberg and Webern in Berlin and Vienna (1930–33). He also studied orchestration under Ravel in Paris (1933), where he lived from 1945. After his début in 1937 he appeared as a conductor throughout Europe and the USA with the chamber ensemble of the Orchestre National de la RTF. In 1947 he founded the International Festival of Chamber Music, at which some of the works of Schoenberg, Berg and Webern were played in Paris for the first time. Indeed, Leibowitz's work on behalf of the Second Viennese School – through performances, teaching and writings – was his major contribution. Between 1945 and 1947, when 'Schoenberg and his school' were almost ignored in official French teaching circles, Leibowitz's private lessons (attended by Boulez among others) facilitated the explorations of a new generation, and in this, his book *Schönberg et son école* was similarly influential. This basic treatment was followed by the masterly *Introduction à la musique de douze sons*, containing a searching analysis of Schoenberg's Orchestral Variations op.31 that was to be closely studied by serial composers in France and abroad. But Leibowitz's emphasis on pitch-class organization was already regarded by those who had been his pupils as outmoded.

During the 1950s Leibowitz became increasingly remote from developments in composition and in music theory. Neither his other theoretical works – such as *L'artiste et sa conscience*, in which he used Sartrean existentialism to make a courageous refutation of Zhdanov's ideas – nor his research on opera and on interpretation enjoyed anything like the success of earlier publications. His compositions are close to Schoenberg and Berg in their classical serial procedures, displaying a certain intellectualism which also marked his work as a conductor (he advocated a conscientious faithfulness to the score based on close analysis). However, a new lyricism emerges in his last opera, *Les espagnols à Venise*, through a fusion of expressionism and rigorous method.

WORKS

STAGE

La nuit close, op.17, drame musical, 3 scenes, 1949; La rumeur de l'espace, opera, 1950; Circulaire de minuit, opera; Ricardo Gonfalano, opera, 1953; Les espagnols à Venise, opera, Grenoble, 1970

ORCHESTRAL

Sym., op.4, 1941; Chamber Conc., op.5, vn, pf, 17 insts, 1942; Chamber Conc., op.10, wind qn, str trio, db, 1944; Variations, op.14, 1944–5; Chamber Sym., op.16, 12 insts, 1948; 6 Pieces, op.31, 1958; Pf Conc., op.32, 1954; Va Conc., op.35, 1954; Fantaisie symphonique, op.39, 1956

VOCAL

Choral: 4 Pieces, op.13, 1944–6; The Grip of the Given, op.21, cantata, chorus, 6 insts, 1950; Träume vom Tod und vom Leben, op.33, sym. funèbre, solo vv, chorus, orch, 1955; Pieces, op.37, 1955; The Renegade, op.40, cantata, chorus, 8 insts, 1956; Sym. funèbre, solo vv, chorus, orch

Solo vocal: 6 mélodies, op.6, B, pf, 1942; Tourist Death, op.7, S, chamber orch, 1943; 3 mélodies, op.9 (Picasso), S, pf, 1942; L'explication des métaphores, op.15, speaker, 2 pf, harp, perc, 1947; Mélodies, opp.18, 25, 34; Perpetuum mobile 'The City', op.24, sym. dramatique, speaker, orch, 1951; Sérénade, op.38, Bar, 8 insts, 1955; Capriccio, op.41 (Hölderlin), S, ens, 1956

CHAMBER AND INSTRUMENTAL

10 Canons, op.2, ob, cl, bn, 1939; Str Qt no.1, op.3, 1940; Wind Qnt, op.11, 1944; Sonata, op.12, vn, pf, 1944–8; Pf Trio, op.20, 1950; Str Qt no.2, op.22, 1950; Duos, op.23, pf, vc; Str Qt no.3, op.26, 1952; 5 Pieces, op.29, cl, pf, 1952; Rhapsodie concertante, op.36, vn, pf; Str Trio, op.42; Humoresque, op.44, perc, 1958; Str Qt no.4, op.45; 3 poèmes, op.46, vn, 5 insts

Pf: Sonata no.1, op.1, 1939; 4 Pieces, op.8, 1943; Pieces, op.19, 1950; Fantaisie, op.27, 1952; Pieces, op.28, 1952; Sonata no.2, op.43

Principal publishers: Bomart, Universal

WRITINGS

Schönberg et son école (Paris, 1946; Eng. trans., 1949/R1975)
Introduction à la musique de douze sons (Paris, 1949/R1974)
L'artiste et sa conscience (Paris, 1950)
L'évolution de la musique, de Bach à Schönberg (Paris, 1952)
Histoire de l'opéra (Paris, 1957)
Schönberg (Paris, 1969)
Le compositeur et son double (Paris, 1971)
Les fantômes de l'opéra (Paris, 1973)

BIBLIOGRAPHY

J. Maguire: 'René Leibowitz (1913–1972)', Tempo (1979), no.131, p.6; (1980), no.132

DOMINIQUE JAMEUX

Leich. Middle High German for 'lai'; see LAI, §1(ii).

Leichnamschneider [Leichamschneider, Leichnambschneider, Leicham Schneider]. Austrian family of brass instrument makers, of Swabian origin. Working mainly in Vienna, they evolved the first specifically orchestral model of horn with crooks in 1700. Michael Leichnamschneider (*b* Osterberg, nr. Memmingen, 26 Aug 1676; *d* Vienna, after 1746) appears to have been the head of the firm. He took his oath as a citizen of Vienna in 1700 and married in 1701. In 1700 and 1703 he furnished horns with crooks and tuning-bits – the earliest of their kind – to the abbey of Kremsmünster, signing himself as a maker of horns before his brother on the bill of 1703. His brother Johannes (*b* Osterberg, 26 June 1679; *d* Vienna, after 1725) was also a maker of brass instruments, though Michael was the more prolific.

To the list of Michael's instruments given in Langwill may be added two horns with crooks of 1700 and a pair with crooks of 1703 (both for Kremsmünster); a pair of horns with crooks (Göttweig Abbey, 1709); and an orchestral horn with crooks, presumably one of a pair,

from 1721 (surviving in the Oettingen-Wallerstein collection, Harburg; only the bell-branch is authenticated, however). The pair of silver parforce horns with gold mounts made by Johannes Leichnamschneider in 1725 for Lord Tredegar, whose family still owns them, lend support to the theory that the brothers worked with Count Sporck, the first patron of artistic horn playing: Michael Heinrich Rentz, a copper engraver to the courts of Vienna and Prague and a protegé of Sporck, engraved the hunting scenes on the gold garlands of these horns.

The name of Franz Leichnamschneider, presumably the son of Michael, appears on a gold-mounted silver trumpet that Maria Theresia presented to the Viennese court orchestra in 1746. The instrument is associated with, but not part of, a set of five silver trumpets by Michael Leichnamschneider dated 1741, and is in the Kunsthistorisches Museum, Vienna. Johann Leichnamschneider, a copper engraver, appears in the parish records of St Stephen's Cathedral in 1747. The rarity of the name points to a relationship with the family of instrument makers; he probably worked as an associate, engraving garlands and collars.

BIBLIOGRAPHY

L. G. Langwill: *Index of Wind Instrument Makers* (Edinburgh, 1960, rev., enlarged 5/1977)
H. A. Fitzpatrick: *The Horn and Horn-playing, and the Austro-Bohemian Tradition from 1680 to 1830* (London, 1970)

HORACE FITZPATRICK

Leichner, Eckhardt. German musician who made several sacred contrafacta of secular works by JOHANN HERMANN SCHEIN.

Leichtentritt, Hugo (*b* Pleschen, Posen [now Pleszow, Poznań], 1 Jan 1874; *d* Cambridge, Mass., 13 Nov 1951). German musicologist, music critic and composer. At the age of 15 he was sent to the USA where he studied liberal arts at Harvard University (BA 1894) and music with John Knowles Paine; he continued his musical studies in Paris (1894–5) and at the Hochschule für Musik in Berlin (1895–8). Subsequently he studied music history, philosophy, aesthetics, classical and modern literature and art at Berlin University under Oscar Fleischer and Max Friedlaender (1898–1901), taking the doctorate there in 1901 with a dissertation on Keiser's operas. While lecturing in composition, music history and aesthetics at the Klindworth-Scharwenka Conservatory, Berlin (1901–24), he taught composition privately in Berlin and wrote music criticism for several journals, including the *Allgemeine Musik-Zeitung*, *Die Musik*, *Signale für die musikalische Welt* and the *Vossische Zeitung*, and was German correspondent of the *Musical Courier* and the *Musical Times*. In 1933 he left Germany to settle in the USA at the invitation of Harvard University, where he was a lecturer in music until his retirement in 1940; thereafter he lectured at Radcliffe College and New York University (1940–44). Concurrently he was a contributing editor of Oscar Thompson's *Cyclopedia of Music and Musicians* (1938), contributed articles to the *Musical Quarterly* and had four books published by the Harvard University Press. He composed music in all forms throughout his life, especially while he was in Europe, where much of it was performed.

Leichtentritt hoped to re-establish himself in the USA as a respected musicologist, writer on music and (especially) composer, and the failure of his music to gain acceptance greatly disappointed him. As a writer on music his hopes were only partly realized, and as a musicologist he suffered for his strong opinions and characteristic directness of expression. After his death his personal library was purchased by the University of Utah, and his manuscripts and personal papers were deposited in the Library of Congress.

Leichtentritt was an extremely thorough and painstaking scholar. For his monumental *Geschichte der Motette* (1908) he analysed over 600 motets in score. His book on Handel (1924), in addition to treating the known facts of Handel's life, gives a comprehensive survey of his works, discussing in some detail his operas and oratorios, most of which were unperformed at that time. The short volume *Geschichte der Musik* (1905) was intended as an outline history of music to guide the student and lay person interested in the evolution of Western music. Two works represent the culmination of Leichtentritt's writings and the synthesis of his thought: *Music, History, and Ideas* (1938), which he developed from his Harvard lectures, examines music as a part of general culture, expounding its relationship to the other arts, political and social conditions, philosophy and religion; and *Music of the Western Nations* (1956), in which music is viewed as an expression of the cultural status of the various nations.

WRITINGS
Reinhard Keiser in seinen Opern: ein Beitrag zur Geschichte der frühen deutschen Oper (diss., U. of Berlin, 1901; i; Berlin, 1901)
'Ein Urahne des Berliozschen Requiem', *AMz*, xxx (1903), 677
'Neue Ausgaben Bach'scher und Händel'scher Werke', *AMz*, xxx (1903), 697
ed.: L. Bussler: *Der strenge Satz in der musikalischen Kompositionslehre*
'Über Pflege alter Vokalmusik', *ZIMG*, vi (1904–5), 192
ed.: L. Bussler: *Der strenge Satz in der musikalischen Kompositionslehre* (Berlin, rev. 2/1905)
Frédéric Chopin (Berlin, 1905, 3/1949)
Geschichte der Musik (Berlin, 1905; Eng. trans., 1938 as *Everybody's Little History of Music*)
'Aufführungen älterer Musik in Berlin', *ZIMG*, vii (1905–6), 368
'Was lehren uns die Bildwerke des 14.–17. Jahrhunderts über die Instrumentalmusik ihrer Zeit?', *SIMG*, vii (1905–6), 315–64
Geschichte der Motette (Leipzig, 1908/*R*1967)
ed.: A. W. Ambros: *Geschichte der Musik*, iv (Leipzig, rev. 3/1909/*R*1968)
ed.: L. Bussler: *Kontrapunkt und Fuge im freien (modernen) Tonsatz* 5/1931)
Musikalische Formenlehre (Leipzig, 1911, 4/1948; Eng. trans., 1951 as *Musical Form*)
Erwin Lendvai (Berlin, 1912)
ed.: L. Bussler: *Kontrapunkt und Fuge im freien (modernen) Tonsatz* (Berlin, rev. 1912)
ed.: J. C. Lobe: *Katechismus der Musik* (Leipzig, rev. 1913, 2/1919)
'The Renaissance Attitude toward Music', *MQ*, i (1915), 604
Ferruccio Busoni (Leipzig, 1916)
'Die Quellen des neuen in der Musik', *Melos*, i (1920), 28
Analyse der Chopin'schen Klavierwerke (Berlin, 1921–2)
'Nationalism and Internationalism in Music', *Sackbut*, ii/12 (1922), 13
'Das moderne Händel Opernproblem', *Der Auftakt*, iii (1923), 211
'Philipp Jarnach', *Musikblätter des Anbruch*, v (1923), 258
'Das Händelsche Opernwerk', *Die Musik*, xvi (1923–4), 551
'German Music of the Last Decade', *MQ*, x (1924), 193
Händel (Stuttgart and Berlin, 1924)
Ignaz Waghalter (New York, 1924)
'Das Kieler Tonkünstlerfest des Allgemeinen Deutschen Musikvereins', *Die Musik*, xvii (1925), 819
'Musical Transmigrations', *MM*, iv/3 (1926–7), 3
'Harmonic Daring in the 16th Century', *MM*, v/1 (1927–8), 12
'Schönberg and Tonality', *MM*, v/4 (1927–8), 3
'Schubert's Early Operas', *MQ*, xiv (1928), 620
'On the Art of Bela Bartok', *MM*, vi/3 (1928–9), 3
'Arnold Schönbergs op.19', *Die Musik*, xxv (1932–3), 405
'Bartok and the Hungarian Folk-song', *MM*, x/3 (1932–3), 130
'Mechanical Music in Olden Times', *MQ*, xx (1934), 15
'Händel's Harmonic Art', *MQ*, xxi (1935), 208
'On Editing Netherlands Music', *Musical Mercury*, ii (1935), 5
'On the Prologue in Early Opera', *PAMS 1936*, 89
Music, History, and Ideas (Cambridge, Mass., 1938, 2/1947/*R*1964, 4/1954)
'The Reform of Trent and its Effect on Music', *MQ*, xxx (1944), 319

Serge Koussevitzky, the Boston Symphony Orchestra and the New American Music (Cambridge, Mass., 1946)
ed. N. Slonimsky: *Music of the Western Nations* (Cambridge, Mass., 1956)

EDITIONS
H. Praetorius: Ausgewählte Werke, DDT, xxiii (1905)
A. Hammerschmidt: Ausgewählte Werke, DDT, xl (1910)
The Complete Pianoforte Sonatas of Beethoven (New York, 1936) [with analytical notes]
J. Schenk: Scherzi musicali, UVNM, xxviii (1907)
Deutsche Hausmusik aus vier Jahrhunderten i (Berlin, 1907, 2/1921)

BIBLIOGRAPHY
C. E. Selby: *A Catalogue of Books and Music Acquired from the Library of Dr. Hugo Leichtentritt by the University of Utah Library* (Salt Lake City, 1954)
N. Slonimsky: 'Hugo Leichtentritt (1874–1951)', *Music of the Western Nations* (Cambridge, Mass., 1956)
J. E. Seiach: *Leichtentritt's 'History of the Motet': a Study and Translation (Chapters 7–15)* (diss., U. of Utah, 1958)
                                RODNEY H. MILL

Leiden. Dutch city. In about 1400 the city employed a number of pipers and trumpeters to take part in processions. There were three main churches, St Peter's (12th century with 14th century additions), St Pancras's (14th century, now Hooglandse Kerk) and the Onze Lieve Vrouwekerk (14th century) which has not survived. In the 15th century the municipality repeatedly tried to improve the singing, including the discant, in these churches. A choirbook from the Lopsterklooster near Leiden contains some examples of Christmas songs for two voices. An improvement in church singing was particularly fostered by the colleges of the Getijdenmeesters throughout the country and the St Peter Getijdencollege acquired an excellent reputation in the 16th century. The extant choirbooks of this college, dating from 1549 and subsequent years, include masses, motets, *Magnificat* settings and Passion settings by Clemens non Papa, Josquin Desprez, Willaert, Crecquillon and others. In 1572 Leiden accepted the Reformation and consequently secular forms of music-making became more prominent than ecclesiastical. In 1593 Cornelis Schuyt, who had just returned from Italy, was appointed city organist. The terms of his appointment are characteristic of the task of a Protestant organist at that time: to play the organ before and after service and at weekdays, and to restrain the citizens from visiting taverns. In 1636 it was decided that the organ should be used to accompany psalm-singing during services.

Towards the end of the 16th century music printing became important in Leiden: the first music print in the north Netherlands, the *Missale Trajectense*, was produced in 1514 by Jan Seversz. Works by Sweelinck and Schuyt were printed by Frans van Rathelingen, father and son, in the first decades of the 17th century. There is evidence of an early kind of music society, called the Broederschap en Gemeene Vergadering in de Muzyk, in a letter of 1578, in which the society tried to obtain the choirbooks of St Peter's. In the 17th century many musicians settled in Leiden, mainly lute and viol teachers, including Joachim van den Hove from Antwerp and Dudley Rosseter, son of Philip Rosseter. Instrument making flourished for some time, the most famous exponent being Hendrick Asseling. At the world-famous Leiden University, which attracted many foreign scholars from its foundation in 1575, the office of *musicus academiae* existed in 1686; the first to act as such was J. H. Weyssenbergh (Albicastro) from Vienna. C. F. Ruppe, who became a *kapelmeester* in 1790 and a lecturer in music in 1816, was the last official university musician. He composed cantatas and in 1800 founded the first choral society in Leiden.

In the 18th century the composers A. Groneman and P. Hellendaal studied at Leiden University. Musical life declined, however, with the declining economic conditions; it was revived in the 19th century through the activities of various music societies. The Gregorius Musis Sacrum, the oldest Leiden orchestra (founded 1826), gave eight concerts a year. The Leiden music society Maatschappij voor Toonkunst (founded 1834) established a music school which for over a century has greatly stimulated musical activities and which, in 1961, became the Stichting Leidse Streekmuziekschool. Between 1864 and 1879 several music festivals were organized by local choirs.

Leiden has no professional orchestra but several amateur ones, two of which are student societies. The main concert hall is the Stadsgehoorzaal, dating from the late 19th century and modernized in the 1960s. Concerts are given by the eight local choirs of various denominations, ensembles, and by the Hague Residentie Orkest and the Rotterdam PO. At Leiden University a chair of music history was established in 1950; J. van der Veen was appointed professor in 1970.

BIBLIOGRAPHY

G. W. Groen: *Ons eeuwfeest (1834–1934): Maatschappij voor toonkunst te Leiden* (Leiden, 1934)

E. H. Ter Kuile: 'Leiden en Westdijk Rijnland', *Nederlandsche monumenten van geschiedenis en kunst*, vii (The Hague, 1944)

E. Reeser, ed.: *Music in Holland: a Review of Contemporary Music in the Netherlands* (Amsterdam, 1953)

H. A. Bruinsma: 'The Organ Controversy in the Netherlands', *JAMS*, vii (1954), 205

C. C. Vlam: 'De werkplaats van Hendrick Asseling', *Mens en melodie*, viii (1954), 12

——: 'Sweelinckiana', *TVNM*, xviii/1 (1956), 37

C. C. Vlam and T. Dart: 'Rosseters in Holland', *GSJ*, xi (1958), 63

A. Annegarn: *Floris en Cornelis Schuyt* (diss., U. of Utrecht, 1973)

JAN VAN DER VEEN

Leider, Frida (*b* Berlin, 18 April 1888; *d* Berlin, 4 June 1975). German soprano. After vocal studies in Berlin, she made her début at Halle in 1915 as Venus in *Tannhäuser*. Between 1916 and 1923 she was engaged successively at Rostock, Königsberg and Hamburg; but her career took wing with her move in 1923 to the Berlin Staatsoper, where she was principal dramatic soprano for some 15 years. She appeared there in numerous Mozart, Verdi and Strauss operas as well as in the Wagner roles that were soon to bring her international fame; she also sang Dido in *Les troyens* and the Duchess of Parma in Busoni's *Doktor Faust*.

In 1924 Leider made her Covent Garden début as Isolde and Brünnhilde, and at once became the favourite Wagnerian soprano of the house, to which she returned every year until 1938; her other London roles were Senta, Venus, Kundry, the Marschallin, Gluck's Armide (in German), Donna Anna, and Leonora in *Il trovatore* (the last two in Italian). Between 1928 and 1938 she often sang at Bayreuth. In 1928 she made her first American appearance, in Chicago, as Brünnhilde in *Die Walküre*, and remained with the company for four seasons, singing not only in *Der Rosenkavalier* and the Wagner operas but also in *Fidelio*, *Die Zauberflöte* (First Lady), *La juive*, *Un ballo in maschera*, and *Mona Lisa* (Schillings). In 1933 she made her Metropolitan début as Isolde, followed by Brünnhilde and Kundry, but sang in New York only for two seasons and exclusively in the heavy Wagner repertory. Guest appearances took her to Vienna, to the Colón (Buenos Aires), to the Paris Opéra, and to La Scala (where she sang

Wagner in Italian). The fact that she had married the Jewish violinist Rudolf Deman (formerly leader of the orchestra at the Berlin Staatsoper) led to difficulties with the Nazis, but her career was not at first affected. After the outbreak of the war she gave some lieder recitals, and later won success in Berlin both as a teacher and as an operatic producer.

Frida Leider as Isolde

Leider was a splendid artist with a dark-coloured, ample and well-trained voice of lovely quality and a fine-spun legato and purity of phrase that enabled her to excel in Mozart and Italian opera as well as in the heaviest Wagner roles. These qualities, coupled with her dramatic fire, made her the most notable interpreter of Isolde and Brünnhilde between the retirement of Olive Fremstad and the arrival of Kirsten Flagstad. During her best years she made some treasurable records, many of them in company with Melchior, Schorr and her other regular Wagnerian associates.

BIBLIOGRAPHY

H. Burros: 'Frida Leider', *Record News*, ii (1958), 345 [with discography]

F. Leider: *Das war mein Teil* (Berlin, 1959; Eng. trans., 1966, as *Playing my Part*) [with discography by H. Burros]

DESMOND SHAWE-TAYLOR

Leidesdorf, Marcus (Maximilian Josef). Austrian music publisher, partner in the firm of Ignaz SAUER.

Leiding [Leyding], **Georg Dietrich** (*b* Bücken, nr. Nienburg, 23 Feb 1664; *d* Brunswick, 10 May 1710). German composer and organist. He was the son of a retired riding master of the French lifeguards. He showed a marked propensity for music at an early age. In 1679 he went to Brunswick to study with the organist Jacob Bölsche and in 1684 visited Hamburg and Lübeck to obtain further instruction from Reincken and

Buxtehude. Soon, however, he had to return to Brunswick, where he deputized for the ailing Bölsche. After Bölsche's death in the same year he succeeded him in the posts of organist of St Ulrich and St Blasius, and he later became organist of St Magnus as well. At the end of the 1680s he took composition lessons with Johann Theile, Hofkapellmeister at nearby Wolfenbüttel. According to Walther he was 'primarily a composer for the organ (to which ... his many extant keyboard pieces bear testimony)'. Only five of his works survive, however (all in later transcriptions in *D-B*). Among them are three preludes, in B♭, C and E♭ (the first ed. in Die Orgel, ii/15, Leipzig, 1957, the second and third in Organum, iv/7, Leipzig, 1930, and the third also in *Freie Orgelstücke alter Meister*, ed. A. Graf, ii, Kassel, 1971), which are noteworthy for the virtuosity of their pedal parts. The other two are a set of chorale variations, *Von Gott will ich nicht lassen*, and a setting, likewise for organ, of the chorale *Wie schön leucht' uns der Morgenstern*.

BIBLIOGRAPHY
GerberNL; *WaltherML*
A. G. Ritter: *Zur Geschichte des Orgelspiels, vornehmlich des deutschen, im 14. bis zum Anfange des 18. Jahrhunderts*, i (Leipzig, 1884), 183
M. Seiffert: 'Das Plauener Orgelbuch von 1708', *AMw*, ii (1919–20), 388
F. Dietrich: *Geschichte des deutschen Orgelchorals im 17. Jahrhundert* (Kassel, 1932), 84f
G. Frotscher: *Geschichte des Orgel-Spiels und der Orgel-Komposition*, i (Berlin, 1935, enlarged 3/1966)
E. Bruggaier: *Studien zur Geschichte des Orgelpedalspiels in Deutschland bis zur Zeit Johann Sebastian Bachs* (diss., U. of Frankfurt am Main, 1959), 98
HORST WALTER

Leier (Ger.). (1) LYRE.

(2) HURDY-GURDY, as in *Drehleier*, *Radleier* and *Bettlerleier*. A *Leierkasten*, on the other hand, is a BARREL ORGAN.

Leifs, Jón (*b* Sólheimer Farm, north Iceland, 1 May 1899; *d* Reykjavík, 1968). Icelandic composer, teacher, conductor and pianist. He studied at the Reykjavík College of Music and then in Leipzig (1916–22) with Teichmüller, Scherchen, Szendrei, Lohse and Graener. For about the next 30 years he lived in Germany, conducting various European orchestras, including the Hamburg PO on a tour of Iceland (1926). He founded the Union of Icelandic Artists (1928), the Icelandic Composers' Society (1945) and the Icelandic performing rights society, STEF (1948). Besides serving as president of these organizations, he was an adviser to Icelandic radio (1934–7). He was also interested in Icelandic folk traditions and made recordings of folksongs for Staatlicher Phonogram of Berlin in 1928. It was his belief, expressed in both music and essay, that Icelandic folk music might form the basis for larger compositions.

WORKS
(selective list)
Orch: Galdra-Loftur Suite, op.6; Org Conc., op.7; Iceland Ouvertüre, op.9, 1926; Sym. no.1, op.26; Baldur, op.34; 3 Abstract Pictures, op.44
Vocal: Kyrie, op.5, chorus; Iceland Cantata, op.13; The Song of Gudrun, op.22, A, T, B, chamber orch; Requiem, op.33b, chorus; Edda Oratorium I–II; hymns and other sacred pieces, many choral and solo songs
Kbd: Intermezzo, op.1/2, pf, 1950; 4 Pieces, op.2, pf; Chorale Prelude, op.5, org; 3 Chorale Preludes, op.16, org, 1951

Principal publisher: Musica Islandica

WRITINGS
Islands künstlerische Anregung (Reykjavik, 1951)
Tonlistarhaettir (Reykjavík, n.d.)

BIBLIOGRAPHY
B. Tobíasson: *Hver er madurinn?* (Reykjavik, 1944), 413
J. Gundson and P. Haraldsson: *Íslenzkir samtidarmenn* (Reykjavik, 1965), 405
A. Burt: *Iceland's Twentieth-century Composers and a Listing of their Works* (Fairfax, Virginia, in preparation)
AMANDA M. BURT

Leigh, Mitch (*b* Brooklyn, NY, 30 Jan 1928). American songwriter. He studied composition with Hindemith at Yale, and in 1954 began writing television commercials, founding the Music Makers (1957) for their performance. After composing the incidental music for a revival of Shaw's *Too True to be Good* (1963) and the Broadway play *Never Live over a Pretzel Factory* (1964) he had his first international success with the musical play *Man of La Mancha* (1965); the lyrics were by J. Darion, with whom he collaborated again in *Cry for All of Us* (1970).

Leigh, Walter (*b* London, 22 June 1905; *d* nr. Tobruk, Libya, 12 June 1942). English composer. He was educated at University College School, London, and in 1922 won an organ scholarship to Christ's College, Cambridge, where he graduated in 1926. From 1927 to 1929 he studied composition with Hindemith at the Berlin Hochschule für Musik, and his first published works date from this period. From 1931 to 1932 he was musical director of the Festival Theatre, Cambridge. He joined the army in World War II and was killed in action.

Leigh's work for amateurs and for the stage reflects Hindemith's concern for practical music-making. His style is simple but musicianly. Leigh's dramatic pieces helped to raise the standard of light music in England, since they combine a flair for popular melody with fine craftsmanship. The music for the Cambridge production of Aristophanes' *The Frogs* shows a talent for parody. Leigh's most successful stage work was the comic opera *Jolly Roger*, which ran for six months at the Savoy Theatre, London in 1933.

WORKS
(selective list)
Stage: Aladdin, or Love will find out the way (V. C. Clinton-Baddeley), 1931; The Pride of the Regiment, or Cashiered for his Country (Clinton-Baddeley), 1932; Jolly Roger, or The Admiral's Daughter (S. Mackenzie, Clinton-Baddeley), 1933; The Frogs (Aristophanes), 1936
Orch: 3 Pieces for Amateur Orch, 1929; Music for Str Orch, 1931; Agincourt, ov., 1935; Concertino, hpd/pf, str, 1936
Chamber: Str Qt, 1929; 3 Movts, str qt, 1930; Sonatina, va, pf, 1930; Trio, fl, ob, pf, 1936; Sonatina, tr rec/fl, pf, 1939
Music for plays, revues, ballets, films and radio; pf pieces, songs

Principal publishers: Boosey & Hawkes, Hansen, Hug (Zurich), Oxford University Press, Schott (London)

BIBLIOGRAPHY
R. Wimbush: 'Walter Leigh', *MRR*, lxviii (1938), 138
W. F. Williamson: 'Leigh, Walter', *MGG*
JACK WESTRUP

Leighton, Kenneth (*b* Wakefield, 2 Oct 1929). English composer and teacher. He studied classics (1947–50) and composition with Rose (1950–51) at Queen's College, Oxford. In 1951 he won the Mendelssohn Scholarship, which enabled him to study in Rome with Petrassi. Other awards have included the Royal Philharmonic Society Prize (1950 and 1951), the Busoni Prize (1956 for the *Fantasia contrappuntistica*), the Trieste Prize (1965 for the Symphony op.42), the Bernhard Sprengel Prize (1966 for the Trio op.46) and the Cobbett Medal (1968). In 1968 he was appointed lecturer in music and Fellow of Worcester College, Oxford, and he was made Reid Professor of Music at

Edinburgh University in 1970.

Leighton's music has a certain romanticism, expressed in highly lyrical melody, the liberal use of instrumental colour and a penchant for virtuoso solo writing. These qualities appear to best advantage in the concertos, and the last is consistently displayed in the piano music. His lyrical instinct has clearly shaped his attitude to 12-note composition, Leighton's serialism owing more to Berg and Dallapiccola than to Schoenberg. It is primarily the thematic possibilities of the technique that attract him, and particularly its capacity to achieve cohesion through the use of characteristic intervals. In this, 12-note writing was a straightforward development from the chromaticism of his earlier works. But much of his music, notably that for chorus, remains fundamentally diatonic. Another guiding tendency is a concern with taut organization, sometimes on Baroque models (these appeared first in the *Fantasia on the name BACH* for viola and piano, and in the *Fantasia contrappuntistica*).

WORKS
(selective list)

VOCAL

Columba (opera, 3), op.77, 1978
Veris gratia, op.6, cantata, 1950; A Christmas Caroll, op.21, Bar, chorus, str, pf/org, 1953; The Birds, op.28, S/T, chorus, str, pf, 1954; The Light Invisible, op.16, sinfonia sacra, T, chorus, orch, 1958; Crucifixus pro nobis, op.38, T, SATB, org, 1961; Missa Sancti Thomae, op.40, SATB, org, 1962; Mass, op.44, S, A, T, B, SSAATTBB, org, 1964; Communion Service, D, op.45, unison vv, SATB ad lib, org, 1965; Missa brevis, op.50, SATB, 1967; An Easter Sequence, op.55, boys'/female vv, org, tpt ad lib, 1968; Laudes animantium, op.61, solo vv, double chorus, boys' vv, 1971; The Second Service, op.62, SATB, org, 1971; 6 Elizabethan Lyrics, op.65, female vv, 1972; Sarum Mass, op.66, solo vv, chorus, org, 1972; Laudate pueri, op.68, 3 choirs, 1973; Laudes montium, op.71, Bar, chorus, semi-chorus, orch, 1975; Hymn to Matter, op.74, Bar, chorus, str, perc, 1976; Columba mea, op.78, solo vv, str, cel, hpd, 1978; Mass, op.81, treble vv, org, 1979
Motets, anthems, canticles, etc.

ORCHESTRAL

Sym., op.3, str, 1949; Veris gratia, op.9, ob, vc, str, 1950; Primavera romana, op.14, ov., 1951; Pf Conc. no.1, d, op.11, 1951; Conc., op.12, vn, small orch, 1952; Conc., op.15, va, harp, timp, str, 1952; Conc., op.23, ob, str, 1953; Conc., op.26, 2 pf, timp, str, 1954; Vc Conc., op.31, 1956; Passacaglia, Chorale and Fugue, op.18, 1957; Burlesque, op.19, 1957; Pf Conc. no.2, op.37, 1960; Conc., op.39, str, 1961; Festive Ov., 1962; Sym., op.42, 1964; Dance Suite, D, op.53, 1968; Pf Conc. no.3 'Estivo', op.57, 1969; Conc., op.58, org, timp, str, 1970; Dance Suite no.2, op.59, 1970; Dance Ov., op.60, 1971; Sym. no.2 'Sinfonia mistica', op.69, S, chorus, orch, 1974

CHAMBER AND INSTRUMENTAL

Sonata no.1, op.4, vn, pf, 1949; Elegy, op.5, vc, pf, 1949; Fantasia on the name BACH, op.29, va, pf, 1955; Str Qt no.2, op.33, 1957; Pf Qnt, op.34, 1959; Nocturne, vn, pf, 1959; 7 Variations, op.43, str qt, 1964; Pf Trio, op.46, 1965; Metamorphoses, op.48, vn, pf, 1966; Sonata, op.52, vc, 1967; Marcia capricciosa, fl, pf, 1969; Contrasts and Variants (Qt in 1 Movt), op.63, pf qt, 1972; Fantasy on an American Hymn-tune, op.70, cl, vc, pf, 1974; Improvisations, op.76, hpd, 1977; Es ist genug, op.80, vn, org, 1979
Pf: 2 Sonatinas, op.1, 1946; Sonata no.1, op.2, 1948; Sonata no.2, op.17, 1953; 5 Studies, op.22, 1953; Variations, op.30, 1955; Fantasia contrappuntistica, op.24, 1956; Jack-in-the-box, 1959; 9 Variations, op.36, 1959; Pieces for Angela, op.47, 1966; Conflicts, op.51, 1967; 6 Study-Variations, op.56, 1969; Sonata, op.64, 1972
2 pf: Scherzo, op.7, 1950
Org: Prelude, Scherzo and Passacaglia, op.41, 1963; Elegy, 1965; Fanfare, 1966; Paean, 1966; Et resurrexit, op.49, 1966; Festive Fanfare, 1968; Improvisation, 1969; 6 Fantasies on Hymn-tunes, op.72, 1975; Ode, 1977; Martyrs (Dialogues on a Scottish psalm-tune), 2 org, op.73, 1976

Principal publishers: Lengnick, Novello, Oxford University Press, Ricordi
MSS in *GB-Lmic*

BIBLIOGRAPHY

J. V. Cockshoot: 'The Music of Kenneth Leighton', *MT*, xcviii (1957), 193
E. Bradbury: 'Kenneth Leighton's "The Light Invisible" ', *MT*, xcix (1958), 426
A. Milner: 'An Organ Work by Kenneth Leighton', *MO*, lxxxviii (1964–5), 33
B. Hesford: 'Kenneth Leighton's Congregational Communion Service, Op.45', *MO*, lxxxix (1965–6), 745
R. Fulton: 'Robin Fulton talks to Kenneth Leighton', *New Edinburgh Review* (1970), no.5, p.25
G. Cox: *The Musical Language of Kenneth Leighton* (diss., Queensland U., 1972)

RICHARD COOKE

Leighton, Sir William (*b* ?Plash, Shropshire, *c*1565; buried London, 31 July 1622). English amateur poet, editor and composer. Leighton was probably born at Plash Hall near Cardington, Shropshire, about 1565. He attended Shrewsbury School from 1578 and married Winifred (or Willingford), daughter of Sir Simon Harcourt probably about 1590. They had one son, Harcourt, who fought at Naseby, and two daughters.

During the 1590s Leighton became involved in the familiar activities of the landed gentry, attaching himself to the court and public life of London and dealing in leases and mortgages. Richard Topcliffe in a letter to Sir Robert Cecil, 11 October 1600, stated that Leighton was 'sometime a follower of the Earl of Essex', to whom he was distantly related. In 1601 he was Member of Parliament for Much Wenlock, and on 11 December 1602 was sworn in as a member of the Honourable Band of Gentlemen Pensioners. Leighton was knighted at the coronation of James I, in honour of whom he wrote in 1603 a set of 221 stanzas entitled *Vertue Triumphant, or a Lively Description of the Foure Vertues Cardinall*.

The first record of his activities is that of an action he brought in Chancery, 27 June 1594, against Ralphe Marston for recovery of a debt incurred in 1589. He was in Chancery again in November 1596 seeking recovery of the deeds of properties in Walton, Sandon and High Offley in Staffordshire from three defendants. Various Public Records concern actions, indentures, deeds, fines etc, involving properties in Shropshire, Staffordshire and Derbyshire, including a long and bitter Star Chamber case involving Leighton, Topcliffe, Edward Bellingham, the Bishop of Coventry and Lichfield, Thomas Fitzherbert and others over the Fitzherbert lands in Derbyshire.

From about 1604 Leighton's financial position deteriorated. An increasing number of actions was brought against him for debt, and seemingly endless recognizances were recorded. In 1608 he was outlawed by letters patent, and sometime between 1606 and 1609 he appears to have left the Gentlemen Pensioners, due no doubt to the outlawry or even imprisonment. In 1609 the King's Bench repeatedly ordered him to surrender to the Marshalsea Prison; for some time he failed to comply, but he was in prison by 1612.

In 1612 Leighton wrote a collection of semi-religious poems to show 'the least part of my unfained and true repentance' under the title *The Teares or Lamentations of a Sorrowfull Soule*. It was entered at Stationers' Hall on 25 January 1612/13 and printed by Ralph Blower. The following year, as he promised, Leighton published through William Stansby a collection of 55 settings of many of these poems by 21 English composers. Leighton wrote the first eight of the 18 consort songs, which are all for four voices and broken consort. There follow 12 unaccompanied four-part and 25 unaccompanied five-part settings. The quality varies from the merely competent (Leighton) to the highly creditable (Byrd). In each case the first stanza is underlaid and the singers are recommended to sing the other stanzas from the book of poems. The volume is in double folio, as are contemporary lute-song books.

Leighton had left prison by 1615. On 11 January 1615/16 his wife was buried at St Dunstan's-in-the-West, where they had lived since 1613 or possibly earlier (their only other known place of residence was in Molestrand Oars Rents, Southwark, between 1605 and 1607). Nothing is known of him after that time, beyond the settlement of a recognizance to Randolph Groome in a Chancery report of 1623. This settlement might explain the lack of a will and the entry in the burial register of St Bride's, Fleet Street, for 31 July 1622 which reads 'William Layton: A pentioner'.

WORKS

The Teares or Lamentacions of a Sorrowfull Soule, ed. W. Leighton (London, 1614); ed. C. Hill, EECM, xi (London, 1970); consort songs in 4vv, unaccompanied songs, 4, 5vv

WRITINGS

Vertue Triumphant, or a Lively Description of the Foure Vertues Cardinall (London, 1603)
The Teares or Lamentations of a Sorrowfull Soule (London, 1613)

BIBLIOGRAPHY

P. le Huray: *Music and the Reformation in England, 1549–1660* (London, 1967), 388

CECIL HILL

Leimma. See LIMMA.

Leinati, Giovanni Ambrogio. See LONATI, CARLO AMBROGIO.

Leinbach, Edward William (*b* 1823; *d* 1901). American Moravian musician and composer; *see* MORAVIANS, AMERICAN.

Leinsdorf [Landauer], **Erich** (*b* Vienna, 4 Feb 1912). American conductor of Austrian birth. He took advanced studies, including composition with Paul Pisk, the piano and the cello, at the University and the State Academy in Vienna. His early experience included being rehearsal pianist (1932–4) for Webern's Singverein der Sozialdemokratischen Kunststelle, and he made his professional début with them as a pianist in Stravinsky's *The Wedding*. A quick learner, a fluent pianist, and gifted with an exceptional memory, he became Bruno Walter's assistant at Salzburg in 1934, playing in Vienna later that year when Toscanini needed a pianist for Kodály's *Psalmus hungaricus*, a work Leinsdorf had played for Webern. His association with Walter, Toscanini and Salzburg lasted until 1937. Leinsdorf was beginning to be known in Europe, having particular success in Italy; in 1937, on Lotte Lehmann's recommendation to Bodanzky, he went to the Metropolitan Opera as assistant conductor. He made his début with *Die Walküre* on 21 January 1938, impressing with his energy and technical assurance. He conducted more Wagner and Strauss's *Elektra*, and, despite opposition from Melchior (who disliked his insistence on rehearsals) and Flagstad (who wanted to establish Edwin McArthur in the house), he was put in charge of the German wing after Bodanzky's death in November 1939.

In 1943 he succeeded Rodzinski with the Cleveland Orchestra but during his army service (1944) Cleveland made other plans. He again worked at the Metropolitan, took guest engagements, and was conductor of the Rochester PO (1947–55). In 1956 he became musical director of the New York City Opera, but in spite of his energetic attempts to enliven its repertory and style of performance, the appointment was not well received. In

Erich Leinsdorf, 1970

1957 he returned to the Metropolitan as conductor and musical consultant. In 1962 he succeeded Münch as musical director of the Boston SO. He expanded the repertory and restored some of the technical finesse that had been lost in previous years. After some genuine excitement at the beginning (as Münch's personal and musical polar opposite, he had advantages as well as problems) it became evident that the arrangement was not a success, a situation it took the participants longer to admit than to observe. In 1969 he left Boston and began once more to travel. Except for conducting some Wagner at the Metropolitan, he has been more active in concert than in opera. His honours include a fellowship in the American Academy of Arts and Sciences, and degrees from several colleges and universities in the USA.

Leinsdorf is curious and informed about many matters in and out of music, and articulate to the point of virtuosity in his adopted as well as his mother tongue. Of quick intelligence, he has a remarkable capacity for recovering from difficult professional reverses. Because the restraint he has learnt to apply to his nervous, restless temperament is strong, he is often an inhibited performer. An impression of tightness, of insufficient breathing-space, is reinforced by a rhythmic weakness that leads him to rush the approach to the bar-line. Words, particularly German, inspire him, and some of his most memorable achievements have been with Schumann's *Szenen aus Goethe's 'Faust'*, the earlier versions of *Fidelio* and *Ariadne auf Naxos* (unfamiliar *ur*-versions being a special interest of his) and Brahms's *German Requiem*.

BIBLIOGRAPHY

A. Blyth: 'Erich Leinsdorf Talks', *Gramophone*, xlvii (1969), 740
E. Leinsdorf: *Cadenza: a Musical Career* (Boston, 1976) [autobiography]
——: *Lesen Sie Musik oder 'aimez-vous Beethoven'? Einige musikalische Gedenken für alle die Noten lesen* (Frankfurt am Main, 1976)

MICHAEL STEINBERG

Leinster School of Music. See DUBLIN, §10.

Leiper, Joseph. See RIEPEL, JOSEPH.

Leipp, Emile (*b* Ste Marie-aux-Mines, Haut-Rhin, 4 Dec 1913). French acoustician and musicologist. He trained for the 'Professorat de chant à la ville de Paris' and was apprenticed as a violin maker (1937–42) to the master violin maker Frédéric Carchereux in Paris. He later studied physics at the Sorbonne and in 1960 took the doctorate with a dissertation on the physics of string instruments. After teaching until 1956, he became scientific adviser to several instrument makers; he himself made violins, violas and cellos until 1962. He became *maître de recherche* at the CNRS in 1961 and concurrently director of the acoustic laboratory in 1962 which he founded at the University of Paris VI. Though he has always taken an interest in various aspects of acoustics (diapason, high fidelity, architectural acoustics, experimental music), Leipp has specialized in the study of string instruments; recently he has dealt with the problems of hearing and speech (especially its intelligibility in song and its synthesis). His double training as a violin maker and a physicist has made him the foremost exponent of musical acoustics in France. In 1962 he created the Groupe d'Acoustique Musicale (GAM), where various aspects of musicological research (e.g. ethnomusicology) are studied in the light of acoustics. Many of his prolific writings are published in GAM's bulletin.

WRITINGS

Essai sur la lutherie (Paris, 1946)
La sonorité du violon, de l'alto, du violoncelle (Paris, 1946)
Les paramètres sensibles des instruments à cordes (diss., U. of Paris, 1960)
'Un vocoder mécanique, la guimbarde', *Annales des télécommunications*, xviii (1963), 82
'Was ist ein Klarinettenklang?', *Das Musikinstrument*, viii (1964), 1
'Le problème de la perception des signaux d'avertissement par effet de contraste: les sifflets', *Annales des télécommunications*, xx (1965), 103
Le violon, historique, esthétique, facture et acoustique (Paris, 1965; Eng. trans., 1969)
Was ist ein Pianoklang? (Konstanz, 1965)
'Mécanique et acoustique de l'appareil phonatoire', *Bulletin du GAM* (1967), no.32, p.1
'L'intelligibilité de la parole', *Bulletin du GAM* (1968), no.37, p.1
'L'acoustique musicale moderne', *Revue d'acoustique* (1969), no.8, p.313
with L. Thevet: 'Le cor d'orchestre', *Bulletin du GAM* (1969), no.41, p.1
'Réflexions sur la mécanique et l'acoustique de l'oreille moyenne', *Bulletin du GAM* (1970), no.49, p.1
Acoustique et musique (Paris, 1971)
'Le violon de Savart', *Bulletin du GAM* (1971), no.57, pp.1–35
'Présentation de l'orgue expérimental Cantor', *Bulletin du GAM* (1971), no.56, p.1
'Un diapason électronique nouveau à l'Opéra de Paris', *Revue d'acoustique* (1971), no.16, p.1
'Le problème de l'audition stéréophonique', *Bulletin du GAM* (1972), no.62, p.1
'L'apport de l'acoustique musicale à l'étude digitale des musiques ethniques: une méthode d'étude des échelles musicales ethniques', *Journées d'étude informatique musicale: ERATTO Paris 1973*, 144
'Le timbre en musique', 'Le violon', *Encyclopedia universalis* (Paris, 1973)

CHRISTIANE SPIETH-WEISSENBACHER

Leipzig. City in the German Democratic Republic. One of the leading musical centres of Europe, it is first recorded in 1015, and the trade fairs held twice yearly since the 12th century instilled a lively sense of civic purpose, which in turn stimulated numerous cultural institutions. With no princes or bishops in residence the city's music has long been primarily bourgeois, with equally strong traditions of sacred and secular music and numerous amateur performing bodies. In the domain of education, the university and Thomasschule were active for many centuries, and the Hochschule für Musik, founded by Mendelssohn in 1843, brought Leipzig's musical importance and influence to a peak in the second half of the 19th century.

1. Church music. 2. Opera. 3. Concert life and the Gewandhaus. 4. Broadcasting. 5. Education. 6. Museums and libraries. 7. Instrument makers and publishers.

1. CHURCH MUSIC. A church Kapelle, possibly at the Jacobskirche, existed by 1017. The Nicolaikirche, the town church until it was superseded by the Thomaskirche in 1755, had the city's first grammar school, founded in 1512; it was rebuilt in 1746, and its buildings survive. The first monks in the city were the Dominicans, who built the Paulinerkirche (1240, later the Universitätskirche). The Franciscans used the Barfüsserkirche (later the Neukirche, renamed the Matthaeikirche in the 19th century and since destroyed). In all these churches Gregorian chant was sung. The Nicolaikirche had an organ by 1457; this was replaced in 1597–8 with a new instrument by Johann Lange, which was rebuilt in 1693–4. The Johanniskirche had a positive in 1533 and a small organ by T. G. Trost in 1695, rebuilt in 1745 by Johann Scheibe under J. S. Bach's supervision. The organ of the Paulinerkirche (1528) was described by Praetorius (*Syntagma musicum*, ii, 1618, p.116), and after several rebuildings it was replaced between 1710 and 1717 by a new instrument by Scheibe, also inspected by Bach.

The Thomaskirche, for long the centre of Leipzig's musical life, existed as a monastic institution by 1212, when it probably already included a song school, although the first documentary reference to such a school is a deed of foundation of 1254. It was not until the time of the Reformation, however, that it was organized under the leadership of a Kantor; until then music was led by one of the monks, the first known being Stefani von Orba (1435–66). The first Kantor of significance was Georg Rhau (1518–20), dismissed on account of his conversion to Protestantism and subsequently active as a printer. When Luther disputed with Johann Eck in the Leipzig Pleissenburg, Rhau was present with the Thomasschule choristers ('Thomaner') and the Stadtpfeifer to preface the debate with a *Veni Sancte Spiritus* and conclude it with a *Te Deum*. In 1539 the Kantor became a civic officer, but the post was not as highly regarded as that of Kantor at Meissen and J. Brückner, Ulrich Lange and Wolfgang Figulus remained in office only for brief periods.

In 1543 the monastic properties of the Thomaskirche were sold, and the school became a city grammar school. The Kantor, third in the hierarchy of teaching staff, was expected not only to direct musical studies but also to instruct in other disciplines; this principle was acceptable during the Renaissance but was later to prove a matter of contention. Sethus Calvisius, a distinguished mathematician and astronomer as well as an able composer, was Kantor from 1594; however, J. H. Schein (Kantor 1615–30) did not gladly fulfil his obligation to teach ten hours of Latin grammar weekly in addition to teaching singing and directing the choral music in the Thomaskirche and the Nicolaikirche. The separate post of organist at the Thomaskirche attracted a number of outstanding musicians, including E. N. Ammerbach (1561–95), Andreas Düben (1595–1625) and Georg Engelmann (i) (1625–32) and (ii) (1634–59).

In the early 17th century the importance of Leipzig was recognized in the dedication to the city council of works by Demantius, Praetorius, Scheidt and Schütz, all of whom were active elsewhere in Saxony. However, music in Leipzig, as elsewhere, was adversely affected by the Thirty Years War (1618–48); the city was besieged five times between 1631 and 1642 and the members of the Thomasschule reduced to near-starvation. The school's musical activity gradually revived under Tobias Michael (Kantor 1631–57), who contributed vigorously to the performance of music in

1. The Thomaskirche and Thomasschule (left), Leipzig: engraving

the city in addition to composing numerous sacred concertos. An extension of function is indicated by the title *director musices* held by Sebastian Knüpfer (Kantor 1657–76), who superintended the music of the whole city and raised the musical standards of student music and theatre, civic and state festivities; these standards were maintained by Johann Schelle (Kantor and *director chori musices* 1677–1701), under whom the duties of the post extended to include the supervision of music at the Paulinerkirche (on academic occasions) in addition to the Thomaskirche and Nicolaikirche. Schelle caused some controversy by diminishing the amount of Latin used in the Thomaskirche services, and nearly all of the cantatas of his successor Johann Kuhnau (Thomaskirche organist from 1684 and Kantor 1701–22) are in German. Although Kuhnau was antipathetic to the secularization of church music through operatic influence, he employed the concertante style and da capo aria in his cantatas and included chorales in only two of them. During his term of office the position of Kantor declined in stature, as is shown by the fact that the mayor granted the young Telemann permission to compose music for the Thomaskirche, an act that Kuhnau was powerless to prevent. From 1711 Kuhnau also directed music at the Petrikirche and, on important holidays, at the Johanniskirche; in later life he became dissatisfied with the declining standards at the Thomasschule.

J. S. Bach (Kantor and *director musices* 1723–50) was similarly beset by apathy and petty disputes with the officials of the town and the university. He was appointed only after Telemann and Graupner, the council's first and second choices and both regarded as progressive, had declined the position. He frequently found himself at variance with the demands of the new style of educational curriculum designed according to *Aufklärung* precepts by the Rektor, J. A. Ernesti. Bach's first years in Leipzig were among his most productive, particularly of cantatas; by 1730, however, he was looking for another post. His memorandum submitted to the council in that year indicates that church music was too dependent on inadequate student performers; even his modest requirements of 36 singers and 18 instrumentalists to provide music in the Thomaskirche, Nicolaikirche, Neukirche and Petrikirche could not be met. By 1739 he had become so disillusioned that, replying to the council's threat to refuse permission for the performance of Passion music, he could state that 'he did not care, for he got nothing out of it anyway, and it was only a burden'; his involvement in the collegium musicum (see §3 below) after 1729 may have been a result of his desire to maintain his independence and find another outlet for his creative energy.

Bach's successor was Gottlieb Harrer (1750–55), who introduced the practice of the unaccompanied performance of Bach's motets, virtually his only works to be performed in Leipzig in the years after his death. Several subsequent Kantors, all competent composers, contributed to the maintenance of the city's choral tradition while adapting the talents of the Thomaner to more modern requirements: Bach's pupil J. F. Doles (1756–89), J. A. Hiller (director of music at the Paulinerkirche 1778–85 and Neukirche 1783–5; Thomaskantor 1789–1804), A. E. Müller (Hiller's deputy 1800–04 and Thomaskantor 1804–10) and J. G. Schicht (1810–23).

In the 19th century the choir became closely associated with the Gewandhaus orchestra; Kantors included Wagner's teacher C. T. Weinlig (1823–42), Moritz Hauptmann (1842–68), founder of the Bach Gesellschaft, and Gustav Schreck (1892–1918), whose vocal works show the influence of Bach, Wagner and Reger. Karl Straube (1918–40) was a distinguished teacher who maintained the choir's tradition through a

2. Interior of the Neues Stadttheater, opened in 1867: engraving from the Leipzig 'Illustrirte Zeitung' (1869)

troubled period in German history, as did Günther Ramin, organist under Straube and his successor as Kantor. Postwar Kantors include Kurt Thomas (1955–61), Erhard Mauersberger (1961–72) and H.-J. Rotzsch (1972–). Motets are sung in the Thomaskirche on Fridays, Saturdays and Sundays. The buildings of the Thomasschule were demolished in 1903.

2. OPERA. Before the Thirty Years War there was little dramatic entertainment in Leipzig, though some impetus appears to have been given by visiting English actors and musicians, performing the works of Shakespeare and his contemporaries, with music, at the beginning of the 17th century. Development, however, was impeded by the war, and it was not until the end of the 17th century that drama of any sort began to play a part in the life of the city. Because of the lack of any princely establishment, expensive musical theatre was slow in developing, but eventually occasional works, composed locally and performed by local artists (mostly students at the university) augmented by professionals from Dresden, were offered during the fair. In 1693 N. A. Strungk, Kapellmeister at Dresden, was given electoral authority to open an opera house in Leipzig; the first production was of his own *Alceste*. Until his death in 1700 he was assisted in the supervision of the Leipzig opera, such as it was, by C. L. Boxberg, a pupil both of himself and of Schelle. After Strungk's death, Telemann took on the management of the theatre for a time, arranging librettos and, according to his autobiography, composing some 20 operas for Leipzig. The opera was similar to that in Hamburg, patronized by a prosperous middle class and orientated towards German rather than Italian music. In 1720 the enterprise came to an end. From 1744 Italian companies, such as those of Pietro Mingotti and G. B. Locatelli, paid regular visits to the

city. In 1752 the poet C. F. Weisse and the violinist J. G. Standfuss successfully presented *Der Teufel ist los*, an adaptation of *The Devil to Pay* by Charles Coffey. In 1766 the same piece, with new music by Hiller, provided the material for a Singspiel, which inspired further works in this genre; for at least a decade such pieces were in high favour.

In 1766 the Schauspielhaus was built, and operas were regularly performed there, mostly by guest companies such as those of Seyler and Bondini (from 1790 F. Seconda), under conductors such as Hiller, C. G. Neefe, F. L. Benda, F. I. Danzi and, briefly, E. T. A. Hoffmann. Bondini's troupe mounted the first Leipzig productions of *Don Giovanni* and *Le nozze di Figaro* in 1788. The Schauspielhaus was reconstructed in 1817, when it acquired a permanent company and became the Stadttheater; its repertory included works by Spohr, Marschner, Weber and Lortzing. In 1867 it was replaced by the Neues Stadttheater (capacity 1900; see fig.2) on the Augustusplatz (now Karl-Marx-Platz); the new theatre was designed by C. F. Langhans of Berlin. The old Stadttheater remained in use for the performance of plays, burlesques with music etc, and operettas were performed in the Carola Theater. The Gewandhaus Orchestra had close connections with opera in Leipzig from its foundation in 1781 and played regularly with the new company from 1817; and the city council formally contracted the orchestra to play at the Opera from 1840. Lortzing was conductor in 1844–5 and was succeeded by Julius Rietz (1847–54). In 1850 Schumann conducted the première of his *Genoveva* there, and in the second half of the 19th century the theatre flourished, attracting leading singers and conductors and producing new works, particularly those of Wagner, soon after their premières; *Tannhäuser* was given in 1853, followed by *Lohengrin* in 1854, and in 1878 Angelo Neumann, director of the theatre from 1876 to 1880, mounted the third complete production of the *Ring*. Conductors after Rietz included A. F. Riccius (1854–64), Gustav Schmidt (1865–76), Josef Sucher (1876–8), Anton Seidl (1878–80), Arthur Nikisch (1879–89), Gustav Mahler (1886–8) and Alfred Sendrey (1918–24).

Under Gustav Brecher, who was director of the Leipzig Opera from 1923 to 1933 but who subsequently fled from the Nazis, there were premières of such works as Krenek's *Jonny spielt auf* (1927) and Weill's *Aufstieg und Fall der Stadt Mahagonny* (1930). The latter created one of the worst scandals in German theatrical history, and the resulting tumult spread to the streets when the police cleared the house. Langhans's opera house was destroyed during World War II, and until a new building was ready Paul Schmitz (Generalmusikdirektor 1933–51) and Helmut Seydelmann (1951–62) mounted performances, including a notable production of Dessau's *Die Verurteilung des Lukullus* in 1951, in a temporary theatre. The new opera house, designed by K. Nierade, was opened on 8 October 1960. It is one of the best-equipped modern theatres, containing three small stages in addition to the main auditorium (capacity 1682). The activities of the Dreilindenhaus (devoted to light opera) were transferred to the Kleines Haus within the complex. First performances in Germany of Prokofiev's *War and Peace* and Shostakovich's *Katerina Izmaylova* were given at the theatre, and the ballet company associated with the complex has given a number of first performances, including those of Wolfgang Hohensee's *Das Fanal* (1961) and U. Ködderitzsch's *Till Eulenspiegel* (1965).

3. CONCERT LIFE AND THE GEWANDHAUS. From early times the municipal authority of Leipzig exercised much control over musical activities, which on the whole brought about a maximum use of available resources and a degree of cooperation between different groups (not always willingly given) hardly paralleled elsewhere. In the late Middle Ages and the Renaissance, public secular instrumental music was the domain of the Stadtpfeifer (city wind players) and Kunstgeiger (string players); the earliest recorded engagement of a city trumpeter is in 1479. In 1599 the practice of a group of brass players (Türmer) playing daily from the tower of the town hall began, but it was not until after the Thirty Years War (1618–48) that the civic instrumentalists achieved a significant status. They were engaged to perform at festival services, weddings and funerals or as directed by the Thomaskantor or as required by the city council. Because of their sometimes intemperate habits the town instrumentalists as a body were generally treated with some disdain, despite their usefulness. There were unflattering references by, among others, Johann Beer (*Musikalische Discurse*, 1719) both to them and to their humbler companions, the Bierfiedler and Music-Stümper, who led more vagrant lives. Such tensions were caused by indifferent management, lack of communication and consequent jealousies; matters improved when C. S. Scheinhardt understood how to conduct negotiations on behalf of the Bierfiedler with the two guilds of musicians. Otherwise the status of the Stadtpfeifer was considerably enhanced at that time by one of their members, Johann Pezel, whose collection of 40 five-part sonatas for brass or strings, *Hora decima musicorum Lipsiensium* (1670,

dedicated to the city council), and *Bicinia variorum instrumentorum* (1675) were outstanding additions to local secular music. A lively picture of various people engaged in Leipzig music is given in Keiser's Hamburg opera *Le bon vivant, oder Die Leipziger Messe* of 1710 (see Schering, 1926, p. 304).

The foundation of a real concert tradition was laid when the musical talents of the citizens were brought together through the institution of the collegium musicum. That students in particular formed groups for the cultivation of music in the early 17th century is clear from the nature of certain music (e.g. Schein's *Studenten-Schmaus*, 1626) and from the setting up of a Collegium Gellianum in 1641 and Pezel's collegium in 1672. It was not, however, until 1688 that the performances of chamber music by 'den Herren Studiosi' brought forth Kuhnau's collegium musicum, which was the real start of the tradition. In 1704 Telemann, who seduced some of Kuhnau's members from their first allegiance, founded another collegium, as did J. F. Fasch in 1708 while he was a student at the university. Meetings of musical amateurs, with professional assistance, took place in coffee houses in various parts of the city known for their provision of facilities for music lovers; of these the most famous were those of Zimmermann, where Bach directed performances from 1729 of the collegium founded by Telemann, and of E. Richter (father and, later, son), the headquarters for Bach's rival J. G. Görner. In 1743 an amalgamation of interests resulted in the establishment of a private music circle, the Grosses Concert, which soon moved to the inn Zu den drei Schwanen. The first director of the concerts was Doles, and a Herr Zehmisch, noted for the elegance of his taste, was probably the first conductor. After being suspended during the Seven Years War, the series was re-established in 1763 by J. A. Hiller, who had already begun a series of his own in 1762, and a high standard of performance was set, which, however, dropped after 1771 under Hiller's successors, G. S. Löhlein and G. F. Hertel; the society was dissolved in 1778. In 1765 the university launched a new society to provide a 'Gelehrte-Konzert', but the Musikübende Gesellschaft, founded by Hiller in 1775 and consisting largely of a student and amateur choir and orchestra, was far more important and gradually replaced the Grosses Concert. The society gave series of concerts on a subscription basis until 1781. Hiller also put on *concerts spirituels* during Lent, comprising performances of sacred music.

With the building of a new Gewandhaus ('Cloth Hall') in 1781 by J. C. F. Dauthe (who was also responsible for the reconstruction of the interior of the Nicolaikirche), Leipzig finally had an adequate concert room, and the Gewandhaus concerts soon assumed the central position in Leipzig's musical life. Hiller, who had become one of the city's most prominent musicians, conducted the first 'Gewandhaus Concert' on 25 November 1781 with an orchestra and chorus expanded from that of the Musikübende Gesellschaft. At that time the musical affairs of the Gewandhaus were controlled by Burgomaster Müller and leading lawyers of the city, and the season lasted from Michaelmas to Easter, concerts being given each Thursday, as had long been the custom.

Hiller was succeeded by three adequate musicians of the second rank: J. G. Schicht (1785–1810), J. P. C. Schulz (1810–27) and C. A. Polenz (1827–35). At that

3. The old Gewandhaus, c1840: engraving

4. The new Gewandhaus, opened in 1884: engraving from the Leipzig 'Illustrirte Zeitung' (1891)

time, however, the conductor was responsible only for the vocal items, and the Konzertmeister led overtures, symphonies and concertos. The orchestra's standards were maintained by a series of fine Konzertmeister, notably Bartolomeo Campagnoli (1797–1816) and Karl Matthäi (1817–35); the latter founded the Gewandhaus Quartet from the orchestra's leading string players. The orchestra's excellence in Classical music was established at that time; Mozart gave a concert of his works in the Gewandhaus in 1789, including two piano concertos and two symphonies, and Beethoven's First Symphony was played in 1801, only a year after its Vienna première, followed by the 'Eroica' in 1807 and the Fifth in 1809. Much vocal music was also included, with the participation of the Thomaner; Haydn's *The Creation* was given in 1800, followed a year later by *The Seasons*. From its inception the orchestra had close connections with church and theatre music; members were contracted to play for the visiting Italian opera troupes and from 1817 accompanied the permanent Leipzig company. The Stadtpfeifer played in the orchestra in the late 18th century, and in the early 19th the municipal musical posts were occupied by leaders of the Gewandhaus string sections, which resulted in a considerable improvement in the standard of church music.

Mendelssohn was conductor of the orchestra from 1835 until his death in 1847, and through his unrelenting zeal the ensemble became one of the finest in Germany. He broadened its repertory, increased the players' salaries and, conducting the instrumental works as well as the vocal, raised the standards of performance; he was the first Gewandhaus conductor to use a baton. Ferdinand David, a close friend, was his outstanding Konzertmeister. Working against the background of the Bach tradition and the pioneering criticism of Rochlitz and Schumann, Mendelssohn introduced the Leipzig public to many unfamiliar works – the *St Matthew Passion* was given in 1841, and there were regular series of historical concerts – as well as giving many important premières, including Schumann's First, Second and Fourth symphonies and *Das Paradies und die Peri*, Schubert's Ninth Symphony (brought by Schumann from Vienna) and his own Third Symphony, *Ruy Blas* Overture and Violin Concerto (with David as soloist). When Mendelssohn was obliged to work elsewhere he was replaced by two outstanding deputies, Niels Gade and Ferdinand Hiller; his intensive activity in Leipzig included significant contributions to music education, above all the foundation of the Leipzig Conservatory (see §5 below). The orchestra also worked with guest conductors and performers; Liszt played in 1840, and in 1843 Berlioz gave his *Symphonie fantastique* and other works.

After Mendelssohn's death it was difficult to find a worthy successor. Julius Rietz, who had just become conductor of the Leipzig Opera, was taken on, but after a number of years he found that holding both posts was too much for him and he gave up the Gewandhaus post. Gade and David substituted, but in 1854 Rietz was persuaded to give up the Opera post and conduct the Gewandhaus once more, which he did until his departure for Dresden in 1860. Rietz was an admirer of Mendelssohn but was antipathetic to newer music and regarded Liszt's symphonic poems as 'sins against art'. His successor, Carl Reinecke (1860–95), held similar views, so the orchestra's tradition of presenting a wide

spectrum of new music dwindled. But Brahms was welcomed; he first performed in Leipzig in 1853 and played his First Piano Concerto in the Gewandhaus in 1859. He also conducted the first Leipzig performances of his symphonies, and under Reinecke all four were often given in a season; in 1879 Joachim gave the première of the Violin Concerto. Other guest conductors were Wagner, who conducted the *Tannhäuser* and *Meistersinger* overtures in 1862, Richard Strauss, Grieg and Tchaikovsky. Clara Schumann frequently performed with the orchestra until 1889, and in 1885 she played with them in the last concert in the old Gewandhaus. A new building was erected in 1882–4 in what was then a suburb of the city; it included large and small halls (capacity 1700 and 640 respectively) and was designed by M. Gropius and H. Schmieder; it also was named the Gewandhaus, for although it never served as a cloth hall the name had become inseparably connected with the orchestra. Three festival concerts were given to mark the opening of the new building in 1884, but no contemporary composers were represented; the programmes ranged from Bach to Schumann and Spohr.

Reinecke was succeeded in 1895 by Arthur Nikisch, a conductor of international repute who contributed much to modern conducting techniques; he held the post until his death in 1922. By the turn of the century the number of players in the orchestra had increased from 24–30 in 1781 and 56 in 1850 to almost 100. Nikisch maintained the strong Brahms tradition but restored works by Berlioz, Liszt and Wagner to the repertory; he was a devoted champion of the works of Bruckner, then still a controversial figure outside Vienna and Linz, and gave a complete cycle of his symphonies in the 1919–20 season. Strauss, Reger, Tchaikovsky and even Schoenberg and Delius were supported by Nikisch, and some of their works were first performed there; he also gave evenings of 'old classics', which he directed from the harpsichord. The diverse guest conductors during his term of office included Fritz Steinbach, Mengelberg, Schuch, Muck, Reger, Strauss and Schillings.

Guest conductors such as Fritz Busch and Hans Pfitzner appeared immediately after Nikisch's death, and Furtwängler held the post of conductor from 1922 to 1929, when he resigned because of his commitments elsewhere; his frequent absences from Leipzig had begun to damage the orchestra's reputation. He was succeeded by Bruno Walter, who in 1933 was forced by the Nazis to resign, despite his enormous success and reputation in Leipzig. Neither Furtwängler nor Walter conducted all the concerts, and guest conductors, including Beecham, were still invited. In 1936 the music of Mendelssohn was banned in Germany, and the statue of him that stood in front of the Gewandhaus was removed; it was never recovered. Walter was succeeded by Hermann Abendroth in 1934, and the Gewandhaus concerts continued despite wartime difficulties, but presenting a repertory largely restricted to Classical works and to the idolized Bruckner and Wagner, until the hall was destroyed by aerial bombardment on 4 December 1943.

After the war the orchestra revived at first under Herbert Albert (1946–9), then under Franz Konwitschny (1949–62), who restored its international reputation. Concerts were given in the great hall of the zoo, rebuilt into a congress hall; the Gewandhaus had still not been reconstructed in the mid-1970s. The orchestra began to tour only in 1916 and now makes at least one tour each year. It numbers about 180 players, who play in the Gewandhaus concerts, the Opera orchestra and the Bach Orchestra. Many players also teach at the Hochschule für Musik and play in chamber groups, while the whole organization, like others in the DDR, has become concerned with the popularization of music through educational and industrial involvement. Konwitschny's successors have included Vaclav Neumann, Heinz Bongartz and Kurt Masur, and many famous guest conductors and soloists have performed with the orchestra.

There is a long tradition of popular classical concerts in Leipzig, and at the end of the 19th century the Philharmonic Orchestra, founded and conducted by H. Winderstein, was conspicuous in this respect. Music began to receive increasing consideration within formal adult education, and, through the agency of the Arbeiter-Bildungsinstitut, concerts for workers were given by the Gewandhaus Orchestra, conducted by Nikisch, as early as 1915. From these efforts came a Leipzig SO and Philharmonic concerts directed by Hermann Scherchen, which led directly to the organization of music within broadcasting in 1924 (see §4 below). A brief, but important series of historical concerts were the Akademische Orchesterkonzerte, initiated by Hermann Kretzschmar in 1890 and lasting until 1895.

There have been many choral societies in Leipzig. J. A. Hiller founded a song school in 1771, one of the important early choral societies in Germany. Some of the best known among subsequent societies were the Singakademie founded by Schicht in 1802 and conducted by Schulz (1817–27), Pohlenz (1827–43), E. F. E. Richter (1843–7) and Reitz (1847–51), the Leipziger Liedertafel, founded by Limberger in 1815, the Universitätsgesangverein Paulus (1822), the Musikverein Euterpe (1824), the Riedel-Verein (1854) and the Sängerschaft Arion (1909). The Riedel-Verein, whose conductors after Carl Riedel included Kretzschmar (1888–97) and Göhler (1897–1913), gave the first complete performance in Leipzig of Bach's B minor Mass, and sang in Beethoven's Ninth Symphony under Wagner's direction at a concert to celebrate the laying of the foundation stone of the festival theatre at Bayreuth in 1872. Choral institutions founded during the 19th century, like much of the music composed for them, frequently expressed nationalist aspirations, while from the beginning of the 20th century new institutions came into existence reflecting emancipatory resolution. Among such institutions the Arbeiter-Sängerband established in Leipzig soon after World War I, comprising 550 members belonging to 90 separate associations, was particularly significant, since it was involved in the preparation of broadcast music programmes at an early date. Other important choirs were those founded by and named after Otto Didem and Barnet Licht in the 1920s. In 1925 it was estimated that there were some 14,000 choral singers in Leipzig.

4. BROADCASTING. The foundation of the Mitteldeutsche Rundfunk AG in 1924 gave a new dimension to music in Leipzig, though without distorting the established pattern. The Leipzig SO became the radio orchestra, which from 1924 to 1932 was conducted by Alfred Sendrey and others. In addition to regular orchestral concerts, large-scale choral performances were undertaken in conjunction with the Arbeiter-Sängerband, which led in 1926 to an Arbeiter-Händelfest. The radio orchestra gave public concerts from 1930. It was conducted by Carl Schuricht from 1931 to 1933; in 1933 the organization suffered continual harassment, and during one of Schuricht's rehearsals in the Gewandhaus the SS intruded to arrest members of the orchestra. Hans Weisbach conducted from 1934 to 1939. After the war the orchestra was revived with a handful of players under the direction of Fritz Schröder on 1 July 1945. Subsequent directors of the orchestra have been G. Wiesenhütter (1946–8), Hermann Abendroth and G. Pflüger (1949–56) and Herbert Kegel (1960–). In 1947 a radio choir (successively directed by H. Werlé, H. K. Hessel and Kegel) was formed, followed in 1948 by a youth choir. In the mid-1970s the instrumental forces of Leipzig radio comprised the Rundfunk Sinfonieorchester (RSO), with about 100 players; the Grosses-Rundfunk Orchester Leipzig (GO), founded in 1946 and conducted by A. F. Guhl; an Unterhaltungsorchester, conducted by K. Wiese, for the performance of light music; a wind band (1950), conducted by E. Brandt; and a dance orchestra.

5. EDUCATION. Originally, music education was strictly divided into two sections: philosophical and theoretical, and practical. As far as the first of these was concerned, the place of music in the liturgy and its moral function demanded evaluation of philosophical and scientific propositions as soon as higher education became formalized. Thus, soon after the foundation of Leipzig University in 1409 Jehan des Murs' *Musica speculativa* (1323), edited by Conrad Norica, was issued in Leipzig. Early alumni of the university who made some mark in music included Lazarus Strasser (matriculated 1494), author of a treatise, Hermann Busch (1503), Johann Walther (i) (1517) and Nikolaus Lepparth (1553), who became *symphoniacorum puerorum praeceptor* of the Margrave of Brandenburg. The statutes of the university decreed the performance of music on ceremonial occasions, and instructors such as Udalricus Burchardi and Georg Rhau were engaged to develop practical music among the student body, whose private music studies in the mid-16th century were described by Christof Kress of Nuremberg. The rigorous musical training given in the schools of St Thomas and St Nicolai, the extension of the authority of the Kantor of the former to supervise the musical activities of the university, and a laudable desire to perform music led to a diminution in the music-teaching function of the university but to an increase in its importance as a focal point for practical experience. Indeed, the students of the university played a central role in the development of the various collegia musica in the late 17th and 18th centuries.

In 1736 L. C. Mizler von Kolof became a lecturer at the university and developed the Societät der musicalischen Wissenschaften, of which Bach, Handel, Telemann, and other prominent figures were members, but it was not until 1859 that musical science, in the wake of other sciences, was brought into the academic programme. In 1834 Mendelssohn refused an invitation to become professor of music. In 1867 Oscar Paul was engaged to give regular lectures on musical subjects. His pupil Hugo Riemann was a lecturer in music from 1878 to 1880 and returned in 1895, by which time Kretzschmar had been appointed director of music. Riemann was a leading figure in the development of musicology and was partly responsible for the establishment in 1899, in Leipzig and Berlin, of the Internationale Musikgesellschaft and wholly for the foundation of the Musikwissenschaftliches Institut at Leipzig in 1908. Directors of the institute since Riemann have included Hermann Abert (1920–23), Theodor Kroyer (1923–32), Heinrich Schultz (1933–45), Walter Serauky (1949–59) and Heinrich Besseler (1959–65; deputy director 1956–9). In 1952 the university was renamed the Karl Marx University.

A conservatory was founded at Leipzig on 2 April 1843, principally through the energies of Mendelssohn, who was its first principal. In 1876 it was designated a royal institution, and in 1887 new premises replaced the original cramped quarters in the Gewandhaus; the new building, in Grassistrasse, was designed by Hugo Licht. During the last part of the 19th century the conservatory attracted students from all parts of the world, especially from Britain, the USA and Scandinavia. In 1946 it was renamed the Mendelssohn Akademie, while remaining the Hochschule für Musik. In addition to the Kantors and organists of the principal churches and members of the Gewandhaus Orchestra, its teachers have included Schumann, Moscheles, Reger and Karg-Elert, while among its students the reputations of Gade, Grieg, Sullivan, Delius, Carl Rosa and Adrian Boult testify to the efficacy of their Leipzig instruction. After World War II Rudolf Fischer, a professor of the piano, served as Rektor of the Hochschule, and he was succeeded in 1974 by the violinist G. Schmahl. For the provision of specialist tuition for gifted young pupils there is a special division of the Hochschule at nearby Halle. Under Karl Straube a department of church music was incorporated within the school, and a number of notable musicians, including the Mauersberger brothers, were trained there.

6. MUSEUMS AND LIBRARIES. There is a fine collection of many kinds of musical instrument in the Museum des Kunsthandwerks Leipzig (Grassi-Museum); it was originally assembled at Cologne in 1902 and was brought to Leipzig and given to the university in 1926 through Kroyer, the publisher Henri Hinrichsen and the city administration. The museum is near the Musikwissenschaftliches Institut, of which the collection is a part. The Bach Archiv Leipzig was founded in 1950. The Museum für Geschichte der Stadt Leipzig, in the Altes Rathaus, contains material of musical interest and established a Mendelssohn Room in 1970. The Deutsche Bücherei, established in 1913 for the acquisition of all books published in the German language, is the largest library of its kind in Germany, with holdings of more than 3,500,000 items, among them a vast number of musical works. The Musikbibliothek der Stadt Leipzig, also of great importance, was formed in 1953 as an amalgamation of various music collections, the earliest of which was that of K. H. L. Pölitz, a musical amateur who assembled manuscript and printed copies of keyboard, chamber and vocal music between 1750 and 1820; it came into the city's possession in 1839. In 1856 the city acquired the fine library of C. F. Becker, organist and authority on musical bibliography, containing many old and rare items. From Kurt Taut came various manuscripts of 19th-century composers, and Rudolf Hagedorn's Wagner collection, comprising 2000 volumes, came into municipal care in 1920. Another important acquisition, in 1953, was the library begun by C. F. Peters.

7. INSTRUMENT MAKERS AND PUBLISHERS. The standing of Leipzig in the international commercial world has been reflected in the various commercial enterprises naturally attendant on music, notably instrument manufacture and publishing. There were well-known families of instrument makers in the 17th and 18th centuries: the Donats were prominent as organ builders, as also were Johann Scheibe (father of the critic J. A. Scheibe) and Zacharias Hildebrandt (whose son was a partner with Gottfried Silbermann); the Hoffmann family produced string instruments, exporting (especially lutes) to Holland, England and France; and the Bauermanns specialized in wind instruments. J. G. Irmler founded a firm of piano makers in 1818, A. Bretschneider established a similar enterprise in 1833, and J. F. Blüthner set up the most famous of all such Leipzig firms in 1853.

Leipzig was an important European centre of book publishing and from an early date musical works were also issued. Nicolaus Faber (i) was active there as a music printer from 1533. In the aftermath of the Reformation, church music in practical editions was published by or for V. Babst, T. and Z. Schürer and C. Klinger, but it was not until the 18th century that Leipzig moved into the forefront of music publishing. This was in large measure due to the initiative of J. G. I. Breitkopf, son of B. C. Breitkopf, a publisher who issued songbooks as early as 1719. About 1750 the younger Breitkopf undertook research to remedy defects in the use of movable types, and by 1754 he was able to make public a new and much improved fount in *Il trionfo della fedeltà*, a pastoral drama by Maria Anna Walpurgis, Electress of Bavaria. In 1795 G. C. Härtel became a partner in the firm, which as Breitkopf & Härtel became world-famous. In 1800 the firm of Hoffmeister & Kühnel was founded; it produced the first complete editions of Haydn and Mozart and the first authentic editions of the keyboard works of Bach. In 1814 it was sold to C. F. Peters and after passing through several hands eventually came into the possession of the Hinrichsen family. By the end of the 19th century there were at least 60 music publishing firms in Leipzig, including M. P. Belaieff, Bosworth & Co., August Cranz, Ernst Eulenburg, A. R. Forberg, F. Kistner, Merseburger, A. Payne and Gottlob Schuberth. C. G. Röder and F. M. Geidel were two engravers whose skill and inventiveness contributed greatly to the excellence of many Leipzig publications. Since World War II, publishing houses and associated businesses have been in public ownership, but (as they had done through many previous changes of ownership) the best-known names have been retained, while new firms have been established for particular specialist purposes; the most extensive is the Deutscher Verlag für Musik.

Important music journals issued in Leipzig have included the *Allegemeine musikalische Zeitung* (1798), the *Neue Zeitschrift für Musik* (1834), the *Signale für die musikalische Welt* (1843) and the *Zeitschrift der Internationalen Musik-Gesellschaft* (1899), as well as house journals and periodicals of specialist interest such as *Die Sängerhalle* (1861), *Musikalisches Wochenblatt* (1870), the *Zeitschrift für Instrumentenbau* (1880) and the *Deutsche Musikdirektoren-Zeitung* (1899).

BIBLIOGRAPHY
GENERAL
J. E. Kneschke: *Zur Geschichte des Theaters und der Musik in Leipzig* (Leipzig, 1864)
E. d'Harcourt: 'Leipsick', *La musique actuelle en Allemagne et*

Autriche-Hongrie, ii (Paris, 1908), 276–338

R. Wustmann: *Musikgeschichte Leipzigs*, i: *Bis zur Mitte des 17. Jahrhunderts* (Leipzig and Berlin, 1909/*R*1975)

A. Schering: *Musikgeschichte Leipzigs*, ii: *Von 1650 bis 1723* (Leipzig, 1926)

——: *Musikgeschichte Leipzigs*, iii: *Das Zeitalter Johann Sebastian Bachs und Johann Adam Hillers (von 1723 bis 1800)* (Leipzig, 1941)

R. Eller, G. Hempel and P. Rubhardt: 'Leipzig', *MGG*

F. K. Prieberg: *Musik im anderen Deutschland* (Cologne, 1968)

CHURCH MUSIC

K. C. E. Gretschel: *Kirchliche Zustände Leipzigs vor und während der Reformation im Jahre 1539* (Leipzig, 1839)

G. Stallbaum: *Die Thomasschule zu Leipzig* (Leipzig, 1839)

E. Dohmke: *Die Nikolaischule zu Leipzig im 17. Jahrhundert* (Leipzig, 1874)

A. Prümers: *Berühmte Thomaskantoren und ihre Schüler* (Langensalza, 1908)

O. Kaemmel: *Geschichte des Leipziger Schulwesens...(1214–1846)* (Leipzig and Berlin, 1909)

A. Schering: 'Über die Kirchenkantaten vorbachischer Thomaskantoren', *BJb*, ix (1912), 86

R. Sachse: *Die ältere Geschichte der Thomasschule zu Leipzig* (Leipzig, 1912)

A. Schering: 'Die alte Chorbibliothek der Thomasschule in Leipzig', *AMw*, i (1918–19), 275

H. Hofmann: 'Gottesdienst- und Kirchenmusik in der Universitäts-Kirche zu St. Pauli-Leipzig seit der Reformation (1543–1918)', *Beiträge zur sächsischen Kirchengeschichte*, xxxii (1919), 118

F. Kemmerling: *Die Thomasschule zu Leipzig: eine Kurzgeschichte von ihrer Gründung 1212 bis zum Jahre 1927* (Leipzig, 1927)

G. Hempel: 'Der Leipziger Thomanerchor im Vormärz', *Musik und Gesellschaft*, xii (1962), 350

R. Petzoldt: *Der Leipziger Thomaner Chor* (Leipzig, 1962; Eng. trans., 1962)

F. Ostarhild: *St. Nikolai zu Leipzig* (Leipzig, 1964)

B. Knick: *St. Thomas zu Leipzig, Schule und Chor: Bilder und Dokumente zur Geschichte der Thomasschule und des Thomanerchores* (Wiesbaden, 1968)

E.-H. Lemper, H. Magirius and W. Schrammek: *Die Thomaskirche zu Leipzig* (Berlin, 1974)

OPERA

H. Blümer: *Geschichte des Theaters in Leipzig* (Leipzig, 1818)

F. Berend: *Nicolaus Adam Strungk, 1640–1700: sein Leben und seine Werke. Mit Beiträgen zur Geschichte der Musik und des Theaters in Celle, Hannover und Leipzig* (Freiburg, 1915)

F. Schulze: *Hundert Jahre Leipziger Stadttheater* (Leipzig, 1917)

G. F. Schmidt: 'Die älteste deutsche Oper in Leipzig am Ende des 17. und Anfang des 18. Jahrhunderts', *Festschrift zum 50. Geburtstag Adolf Sandberger* (Munich, 1918)

F. Reuter: *Die Geschichte der deutschen Oper in Leipzig (1693–1720)* (diss., U. of Leipzig, 1922)

Festschrift zur Eröffnung des neuen Leipziger Opernhauses (Leipzig, 1960)

G. Braun: *Die Leipziger Allgemeine Theater-Chronik in ihrer Bedeutung für die Theaterkritik und Theatergeschichte des 19. Jahrhunderts* (diss., U. of Berlin, 1963)

G. Rudolff-Hille: *Das Theater auf der Ranstädter Bastei* (Leipzig, 1969)

CONCERT LIFE

A. Dörffel: *Geschichte der Gewandhausconcerte zu Leipzig* (Leipzig, 1884/*R*1972)

R. Kade: 'Die Leipziger Stadtpfeifer', *MMg*, xxi (1889), 194

P. Langer: *Chronik der Leipziger Singakademie zu Leipzig, 1802–1902* (Leipzig, 1902)

A. Göhler: *Der Riedel-Verein zu Leipzig* (Leipzig, 1904)

F. Schmidt: *Das Musikleben der bürgerlichen Gesellschaft Leipzigs im Vormärz (1815–48)* (Langensalza, 1912)

A. Schering: 'Die Leipziger Ratsmusik von 1650 bis 1775', *AMw*, iii (1921), 17–53

J. Hohlfeld: *Geschichte der Sängerschaft Arion (Sängerschaft in der D.♭ F.) 1909–1924* (Leipzig, 1924)

E. Creuzberg: *Die Gewandhaus-Konzerte zu Leipzig, 1781–1931* (Leipzig, 1931)

A. Werner: *Freie Musikgemeinschaften alter Zeit im mitteldeutschen Raum* (Wolfenbüttel, 1940)

H.-J. Nösselt: *Das Gewandhausorchester* (Leipzig, 1943)

H. Heyer, ed.: *Festschrift zum 175 jährigen Bestehen der Gewandhauskonzerte 1781–1956* (Leipzig, 1956)

G. Hempel: 'Das Ende der Leipziger Ratsmusik im 19. Jahrhundert', *AMw*, xv (1958), 187

F. Hennenberg: *Das Leipziger Gewandhausorchester* (Leipzig, 1962, rev. 2/1972; Eng. trans., 1962)

G. Hempel: 'Die bürgerliche Musikkultur Leipzigs im Vormärz', *BMw*, vi (1964), 3

R. Schmitt-Thomas: *Die Entwicklung der deutschen Konzertkritik im*

Spiegel der Leipziger Allgemeinen musikalischen Zeitung (1798–1848) (diss., U. of Frankfurt am Main, 1969)

D. L. Smithers: *The Music and History of the Baroque Trumpet before 1721* (London, 1973)

Rundfunk Sinfonieorchester Leipzig (Leipzig, 1974) [with introduction by F. Hennenberg]

OTHER STUDIES

J. Beer: *Musikalische Discurse* (Nuremberg, 1719)

A. Weizius: *Verbessertes Leipzig* (Leipzig, 1728)

Anon.: *Beschreibung der Stadt Leipzig* (Leipzig, 1784)

J. E. Kneschke: *Das Conservatorium der Musik in Leipzig* (Leipzig, 1868)

A. Göhler: *Verzeichnis der in den Frankfurter und Leipziger Messkatalogen der Jahre 1564 bis 1759 angezeigten Musikalien* (Leipzig, 1902/*R*1965)

A. Heuss: *Bach-Fest anlässlich der Enthüllung des Bach-Denkmals in Leipzig, 16. bis 18. Mai 1908* (Leipzig, 1908)

H. von Hase: 'Breitkopfsche Textdrucke zu Leipziger Musikaufführungen zu Bachs Zeit', *BJb*, x (1913), 69

P. Röntsch, ed.: *Bericht über die ersten 75 Jahre des Königlichen Konservatoriums zu Leipzig, erstattet zum 2 April 1918* (Leipzig, 1918)

M. Bruckner-Bigenwald: *Die Anfänge der Leipziger Allgemeinen musikalischen Zeitung* (Hilversum, 1965)

H. Lindlar: *C. F. Peters Musikverlag: Zeittafeln zur Verlagsgeschichte 1800–1867–1967* (Frankfurt am Main, London and New York, 1967)

R. Elvers, ed.: *Breitkopf und Härtel 1719–1968: ein historischer Überblick zum Jubiläum* (Wiesbaden, 1968)

J. Forner, H. Schiller and M. Wehnert: *Hochschule für Musik Leipzig (1843–1968)* (Leipzig, 1968)

Pasticcio auf das 250 jährige Bestehen des Verlages Breitkopf und Härtel: Beiträge zur Geschichte des Hauses (Leipzig, 1968)

H. C. Wolff: 'Die Geschichte der Musikwissenschaft an den Universitäten Leipzig und Berlin', *Sborník prací filosofické fakulty brněské university*, H4 (1969), 17

G. Pietzsch: *Zur Pflege der Musik an den deutschen Universitäten bis zur Mitte des 16. Jahrhunderts: Leipzig* (Hildesheim, 1971)

PERCY M. YOUNG

Leise (Middle High Ger. *Leis*). A devotional, Germanic song stanza in the nature of a refrain, found particularly in the later Middle Ages. Supposedly deriving its name from the words 'Kyrie eleison' as they appear repeatedly in the litany, the *Leise* is normally considered a part of the general category RUF and is distinguished within that category by being characteristically in a four-line form. The earliest known example is thought to be the 9th-century Freising song to St Peter, *Unsar trothîn hât farsalt* (*D-Mbs* clm 6260, f.158*v*). In the early stages of specifically German polyphony (beginning with the lost early 15th-century Strasbourg manuscript *F-Sm* 222) *Leisen* were often set; other examples include *Christ ist erstanden* (based on the opening of the sequence *Victimae paschali laudes* and traced to the mid-12th century) and *Nun bitten wir den heiligen Geist* (based on the sequence *Veni Sancte Spiritus* and traced to the mid-13th century).

BIBLIOGRAPHY

H. Teuscher: *Christ ist erstanden: Stilkritische Studie über die mehrstimmigen Bearbeitungen der Weise von den Anfängen bis 1600* (Kassel, 1930)

J. Riedel: *Leisen Formulae: their Polyphonic Settings in the Renaissance and Reformation* (diss., U. of Southern California, 1953)

H. Hucke: 'Die Neumierung des althochdeutschen Petruslieds', *Organicae voces: Festschrift für Joseph Smits van Waesberghe* (Amsterdam, 1963), 71

W. Lipphardt: 'Leisen und Rufe', *MGG* [incl. further bibliography]

DAVID FALLOWS

Leisentrit, Johannes [Johann] (*b* Olomouc, May 1527; *d* Bautzen, 24 Nov 1586). German theologian, hymnologist and composer of Moravian birth. He studied theology at Kraków and was ordained in 1549. After a short period spent teaching in Vienna and Prague, he was sent to the diocese of Meissen by the Archbishop of Prague. The last Catholic Bishop of Meissen appointed him canon of Bautzen Cathedral in 1551. In 1559 he became dean, and in 1560 official-general for the diocese of Lusatia. When the bishopric of Meissen became Protestant in 1561, the papal nuncio in Prague appointed him 'administrator and commissioner-general of the see of Meissen for Upper and Lower Lusatia'. The fact that Lusatia remained predominantly Catholic must be attributed to his pastoral endeavours, which were reflected in many catechetic and other writings, and to his astute and moderating ecclesiastical policy. He was one of the great reformers of the early years of the Counter-Reformation. The crowning achievement of his ministry was his great hymnbook *Geistliche Lieder und Psalmen* (Bautzen, 1567/R1966), which was only the second Catholic hymnbook to appear in the 16th century (the first was Michael Vehe's of 1537). It has 480 folios containing 250 hymns and 180 melodies and is magnificently adorned with woodcuts and marginal decorations. It is the largest and finest hymnal of the Counter-Reformation. Leisentrit fully explained his intentions in an extensive preface. Two further editions with different prefaces appeared during his lifetime, in 1573 and 1584; in the last of these, published as *Catholisch Gesangbuch voller Geistlicher Lieder und Psalmen*, the repertory of texts and melodies is considerably expanded. The hymnal was circulated not only in Leisentrit's own diocese of Lusatia but throughout Germany. At the instigation of the Bishop of Bamberg an abridged version was published at Dillingen in 1576; this was the first German Catholic diocesan hymnbook. Leisentrit used a number of Protestant hymnbooks, including Nikolaus Herman's *Sonntagsevangelia* (1561) and Valentin Triller's *Schlesisch Singebüchlein* (1555), as his sources; he also appears to have drawn on the repertory of the Bohemian Brethren. In addition to Vehe's hymnal his Catholic sources included hymns by his friend Christoph Hecyrus of Budweis that were first printed in the hymnal *Christliche Gebet und Gesäng* (Prague, 1581) but whose texts appeared in Leisentrit's hymnal in 1567; for the third edition he also used texts from R. Edlinguis's *Teutsche evangelische Messen, Lobgesange* (Cologne, 1572) and the Tegernsee hymnal (1577). He took over many of the melodies of Hecyrus, Herman and Triller and, as he stated in a letter to Hecyrus appended to the first edition, composed some of the others himself. Some 70 melodies appeared in his hymnbook for the first time.

BIBLIOGRAPHY

G. Rupertus: *Oratio funebris in obitum Johannes Leisentritii a Julisberg* (Bautzen, 1586)

F. Schnorr von Carolsfeld: 'Leisentrit, Johannes', *ADB*

J. Kehrein: *Katholische Kirchenlieder, Hymnen, Psalmen aus den ältesten deutschen gedruckten Gesangbüchern und Gebetbüchern zusammengestellt* (Würtzburg, 1859–63/R1965)

P. Wackernagel: *Das deutsche Kirchenlied von der ältesten Zeit bis zum Anfang des 17. Jahrhunderts* (Leipzig, 1864–77/R1964), ii–iii

W. Bäumker: *Das katholische deutsche Kirchenlied in seinen Singweisen*, i–ii (Freiburg, 1886, 1883/both R1962) [incl. several melodies]

W. Crecelius: 'Über die Quellen von Leisentrits Gesangbuche', *Archiv für die Geschichte deutscher Sprache und Dichtung*, i (1873), 337

W. Gerblich: 'Johann Leisentrit', *Neues Lausitzer Magazin*, cvii (1931), 1–78

W. Lipphardt: 'Johann Leisentrits Gesangbuch von 1567', *Studien zur katholischen Bistums- und Klostergeschichte*, v (1963)

J. Gülden: 'Johann Leisentrits Bautzener Messritus und Messgesänge', in *Leben und Kampfen im Zeitalter der Glaubensspaltung*, Vereinsschriften der Gesellschaft zur Herausgabe des Corpus Catholicorum (Münster, 1964)

W. Lipphardt: Afterword to facs. repr. of *J. Leisentrit: Geistlicher Lieder und Psalmen (1567)* (Kassel and Leipzig, 1966)

WALTHER LIPPHARDT

Leisring [Leissringk, Leisringus], **Volckmar** (*b* Gebstedt, Thuringia, 1588; *d* Buchfarth, nr. Weimar, 1637). German composer, theorist and clergyman. From 1605 to 1611 he studied theology at Jena. In 1611 he became Rektor, Kantor and town clerk of Schkölen, near Naumburg. Most of his known music dates from this period of his life, and according to the preface to the second edition of his *Cymbalum Davidicum* (1619) he resolved to give up composing when he became pastor at Nohra, near Erfurt, in 1618 (his *Taedae nuptiales*, however, appeared in 1624). From 1626 until his death he was pastor at Buchfarth and nearby Vollhardsroda. Leisring was a conservative composer. His *Cymbalum Davidicum* contains mainly homophonic motets, those for eight voices being double-choir works similar in style to those of Jacob Handl. His *Corona musices* is an encomium about the origin, nature and effects of music. *Breviarium artis musices*, which is similar in layout to Heinrich Faber's *Compendiolum musicae* (1548; many subsequent edns.), contains, like many other didactic books of the time, chapters on modes, clefs, voices, intervals, modulation, tactus and so on.

WORKS

Brautlied (Jena, 1609), lost
Cantio magnificus et prudentissimi, 6vv (Jena, 1609)
Canticum gratulatorium in Faustum (Jena, 1610)
Cymbalum Davidicum, 5–6, 8vv (Jena, 1611)
Strenophonia oder ein new Jahr Geschenck, 4–6, 8vv (Jena, 1615)
Taedae nuptiales, 4–8vv (Erfurt, 1624)
2 sacred songs in Cantionale sacrum, i (Gotha, 1646); 1 in Cantionale sacrum, ii (Gotha, 1655)
Trotz sei dem Teufel, 8vv, *D-Mbs*
Several other MS compositions listed in *EitnerQ*

WRITINGS

Corona musices (Jena, 1611)
Breviarium artis musices (Jena, 1615)

BIBLIOGRAPHY

WaltherML

E. Ulrici: *Chronologie von Schkölen* (Osterfeld, 1903)

A. Werner: *Städtliche und fürstliche Musikpflege in Weissenfels* (Leipzig, 1911)

——: 'Die alte Musikbibliothek und die Instrumentensammlung an St. Wenzel im Naumburg', *AMw*, viii (1926), 390

HORACE FISHBACK

Leitão de Avilez, Manuel. *See* AVILEZ, MANUEL LEITÃO DE.

Leite, António (Joaquim) da Silva (*b* Oporto, 23 May 1759; *d* Oporto, 10 Jan 1833). Portuguese composer. After studying for the priesthood he decided on a career in music instead. He probably studied with Girolamo Sertori, an Italian living in Oporto in the 1780s. He became well known as a teacher and in 1787 published at Oporto his own text, *Rezumo de todas as regras, e preceitos da cantoria* for his students. By 1788 he was a teacher at the Real Colégio dos Meninos Orfãos and organist at the convents of S Clara and S Bento da Ave-Maria, becoming *mestre de capela* of the latter by 1792. Most of his sacred compositions were written for the virtuoso singers attached to that convent. He was also a fine guitarist and published *6 sonatas de guitarra* (Oporto, 1792) and an *Estudo de guitarra* (Oporto, 1796), illustrated with numerous minuets, marches, contradanses and other pieces. A manual on accompanying techniques, *O organista instruido*, written about the same time, was not published. In 1806 he published in Oporto a *Novo directorio funebre*, which contained a translation of the reformed funeral liturgy as well as funeral hymns for use in the service. In 1807 his two operas, *Puntigli per equivoco* and *L'astuzie delle donne*, were produced at the Teatro de S João, and the next year his 'famous' Restoration Symphony was performed at Vila Nova de Gaia on 11 December. By 1808 he was *mestre de capela* of Oporto Cathedral.

As a composer of sacred music he vied with Jommelli. Notable among his sacred compositions are a *Tantum ergo* (London, 1815), for four voices and string orchestra with elaborate flute obbligato, and *Hora de Noa* (in *P-Ln*), for four sopranos, violin and organ, in which the highly ornamented voice lines are set in close, interweaving polyphony. In his *modinhas* and sonatas Leite showed singular gifts for captivating melody, piquant rhythm and colouristic instrumental effects.

WORKS

Operas, perf. Oporto, 1807: Puntigli per equivico; L'astuzie delle donne
Sacred: 6 masses, 23 motets, 33 other Lat. pieces, dated 1784–1829, *P-Ln*; Tantum ergo, 4vv, str, fl obbl (London, 1815)
Other: 6 sonatas, gui, vn and 2 hn ad lib (Oporto, 1792); Os génios premiados, cantata, Real Academia, Oporto, 1807; Restoration Sym., perf. 1808; Hymno patriotico, orch, for coronation of John VI (Paris, 1820); 6 pieces in *Jornal de modinhas* (1792–5)

BIBLIOGRAPHY

DBP, ii, 19ff
M. de Sampayo Ribeiro: *A música em Portugal nos séculos XVIII e XIX* (Lisbon, 1936), 39, 127
B. D. Rocha da Silva Guimarães: *Primeira esboço duma bibliografia musical portuguesa* (Oporto, 1957), 86f

ROBERT STEVENSON

Leitgeb, Joseph [Ignaz]. *See* LEUTGEB, JOSEPH.

Leitmotif (from Ger. *Leitmotiv*: 'leading motif'). A theme, or other coherent musical idea, clearly defined so as to retain its identity if modified on subsequent appearances, whose purpose is to represent or symbolize a person, object, place, idea, state of mind, supernatural force or any other ingredient in a dramatic work, usually operatic but also vocal, choral or instrumental. The leitmotif may be musically unaltered on its return, or altered in its rhythm, intervallic structure, harmony, orchestration or accompaniment, and also may be combined with other leitmotifs in order to suggest a new dramatic condition.

The term was coined by F. W. Jähns in his *Carl Maria von Weber in seinen Werken* (1871); but the device has a long ancestry, and it has subsequently been applied in ways not envisaged by Jähns. As its nature is to be extremely flexible, it is not always distinguishable in its action from comparable musical devices, such as, first, *Reminiszenzmotiv* or *Erinnerungsmotiv*, in which the same music returns more or less unaltered, purely as identification for the audience or to signify recollection of the past by a dramatic character, secondly IDÉE FIXE, and thirdly Liszt's thematic metamorphosis (*see* TRANS-FORMATION, THEMATIC). Whereas the potential value, for unification, of a significant theme in a full-scale opera had been recognized since the 18th century, the mature operas of Wagner were the first to elevate leitmotif to a position of paramount musical importance as themes for symphonic development. The technique is essentially musical, though it has been adapted for literary purposes, notably by George Moore, D. H. Lawrence and others. T. S. Eliot drew attention to the motivic technique of *The Waste Land* with actual Wagner quotations. The consciously Wagnerian use of leitmotif in literature however has on the whole revealed a misunderstanding of Wagner's use of it as a musical device, with the striking exception of that by Thomas Mann (especially in *Buddenbrooks*).

The systematic use of motifs for dramatic purposes first developed in France and Germany in late 18th-century opera, though earlier examples may be found (for example where one character quoted another's music allusively). With the weakening of the closed form of da capo aria, greater importance began to pass to other forms, such as arioso, recitative and scena; and the association of motifs with characters and events began now to provide not only a useful system of illustration but, gradually, the means of applying formal control through quasi-symphonic techniques. An early formulation of the principle of associating a musical idea with a character occurs in Lacépède's *La poétique de la musique*, ii (1785): a chapter on 'Des caractères des personnages considérés relativement à la tragédie lyrique' proposes for the musician that, in 'chaque morceau qu'il composera, il comparera ce sentiment qu'il aura, pour ainsi dire, créé, avec celui que le morceau devra montrer et faire naître' ('in each piece which he composes, he shall match this feeling which he will have, so to speak, created, with the person whom the piece is to show and bring to life').

Mozart's use of motif was generally confined to such straightforward devices as the recurrence of Figaro's 'Se vuol ballare' to re-emphasize his intentions towards the Count, but there are prefigurations of later leitmotif technique in *Idomeneo*, particularly in figures associated with Ilia's emotions. Other operas of the closing decades of the 18th century make effective use of reminiscence motifs. A celebrated instance is Blondel's song in Grétry's *Richard, Coeur de Lion* (1784); the device was also used by Méhul (*Ariodant*, 1799) and Catel (*Sémiramis*, 1801), among many others, to provide a reminder of a previous dramatic event. The quotation of a whole number for dramatic effect remained a familiar device, as with 'The Last Rose of Summer' in Flotow's *Martha* (1847) or 'La donna è mobile' in Verdi's *Rigoletto* (1851).

However, the action of leitmotif is essentially different. It is already suggested, and developed from simple 'reminiscence motif' to a considerable extent, by Méhul, Dalayrac and Catel. In Méhul's *Euphrosine* (1790), a motif symbolizes not only jealousy but its action, its object and the intention to implant it; and in his *Mélidore et Phrosine* (1794) a motto theme is identified with the words 'Love, be our guide' as the mainspring of the opera. The most important Romantic musician first to appreciate the significance of this development was Weber. Familiar with the work of Méhul and Catel, he also several times remarked on the effect of motif in French and German operas. In 1811 he commented on Dalayrac's use in *Macdonald* (as *Léhéman* was known in Germany) of the *romance* 'Ein Pilger irrt' as 'a consoling star', adding that 'such pieces are the delicate threads in the tissue of an opera which, spun as here by a true dramatic composer, must irresistibly bind the hearts of the listeners'. Having commented favourably on the use of motif in Poissl's *Athalia* (1816), he returned to his first metaphor in his review of Spohr's *Faust* in the same year: 'a few melodies, felicitously and aptly devised, weave like delicate threads through the whole, and hold it together artistically'. Another opera of 1816 significant for its use of motifs was Hoffmann's *Undine*, in which use is made of what Heuss identified as the 'Beseelungs-melodie', used however in a manner close to reminiscence motif.

Weber himself developed the technique in a manner that was to warrant Jähns's invention of the new term. In *Der Freischütz* (1821) he introduced Kaspar's piccolo trills and other quotations from previously heard music in the freely composed Wolf's Glen scene, and caused the diminished 7th chord identified with Samiel to recur both literally and in different orchestral and rhythmic guises, even making its four constituent notes provide the key structure of the Wolf's Glen scene. The real possibilities of leitmotif, however, are more fully outlined in *Euryanthe* (1823), in which Eglantine's theme of deceit is used in various guises and is also used to give structural coherence to freely composed scenes (see ex.1). Leitmotif remained valuable for opera in closed

Ex.1

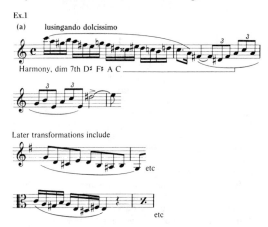

forms, as with Weber's own *Oberon* (1826; the three rising notes of Oberon's horn serve to unify widely separated numbers), with Marschner's *Der Vampyr* (1828), Lortzing's *Undine* (1845) and *Rolands Knappen* (1849), Schumann's *Genoveva* (1850), and in operas by Lindpaintner, Reissiger and others. In most of these, it proved particularly valuable for the representation of the supernatural. However, its full power was disclosed only with the loosening of operatic form into completely continuous composition that came with Wagner's *Der fliegende Holländer*.

Wagner did not himself use the term 'Leitmotiv', preferring various descriptions such as 'melodisches Moment', 'thematisches Motiv', 'Ahnungsmotiv', 'Hauptmotiv', 'Grundthema' and others, as in a passage outlining his intentions: 'the new kind of dramatic music *must* display the unity of a symphonic movement. . . . This unity is contained in an interlacing network of *Grundthemen* which, as in symphonic movements, contrast, develop, re-form, dissolve and unite'. As Wagner pointed out, the analogy is only partial, since in music drama of the kind he envisaged, the function of the motif is dramatic as well as structural; but there is a crucial point here for the understanding of how Wagner acted on his belief that the Ninth Symphony was 'music crying out for redemption by poetry'. It is in the dramatic handling of this newly expanded range of possibilities that an essential part of Wagner's greatness rests.

What Wagner did was to bring leitmotif into the forefront as a crucial element in his rethinking of the relationship between music and drama. Leitmotif could now assume many roles in the task of making meanings clear and of binding music more closely to drama. It could identify and define, as with the noble theme of the Meistersinger, in nimble diminution for the apprentices (ex.2). It could indicate a new condition, simply as when the perfect 4ths of Fafner and Fasolt as giants become augmented 4ths for Fafner as dragon, more subtly as with the growth of Siegfried from carefree young hero to his new maturity in his knowledge of Brünnhilde, still more complexly in its psychology as when Parsifal's theme is profoundly altered in the Act 3 prelude to suggest the depth of his experiences (exx.3 and 4).

Ex.3 Wagner: *Siegfried*

Ex.4 Wagner: *Parsifal*

Always referential, it could address the audience across the heads of the characters, as when the mysterious man in grey described by Sieglinde is revealed as Wotan by the Valhalla motif (*Die Walküre*, Act 1). It could replace words to reveal the working of the mind, as when Beckmesser's mental confusion in Sachs's workshop is shown by use of motifs associated with the riot, his serenade, the Prize Song and so forth, loosely and abruptly assembled to indicate the disarray that has overtaken him. Conjunctions or combinations of motifs, possibly altered and developed expressively, could reflect events on the stage, contradict them, or superimpose new shades of meaning upon them. In the handling of this subtlety, leitmotif takes on the condition of a new conceptual language.

Ex.2

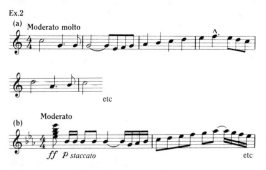

As early as 1871, Federlein had named some of Wagner's motifs. Jähns's term 'Leitmotiv' was first applied to Wagner by Hans von Wolzogen in 1876; and there followed much analysis and description, some of which, whether hostile or admiring, misunderstood Wagner's aims. For Debussy, the leitmotifs appeared but 'visiting cards'; for many enthusiasts, the interpretation stopped at literal identification subjected merely to suitable musical modification. Thus the so-called Spear Motif was misunderstood as representing simply Wotan's spear and not (as is the essence of Wagner's idea) the treaties engraved on it: since he rules by these, their infraction leads to his forfeiture of rule and thence to a whole range of experiences connected with his decline which it is the function of the motif to indicate. Wagner commentators have often felt obliged to warn listeners against taking the conventional labels of his motifs too literally: the essence of the power of leitmotif in Wagner resides in its suggestive adaptability to changed dramatic circumstances.

After Wagner, leitmotif was taken up by his own disciples, such as Cornelius and Humperdinck, and by others, including those in reaction to him. Strauss's use (e.g. the themes for different members of the family in the *Sinfonia domestica*) derives both from Wagner and from Liszt's technique of thematic metamorphosis. Leitmotif was used, despite his anti-Wagnerian strictures, by Debussy (*Pelléas et Mélisande*, 1902). It was also used by Fauré (*Pénélope*, 1913), Delius, Janáček (*Kat'a Kabanová*, 1921), Berg (e.g. the three-part fugue on the themes of the Doctor, the Captain and Wozzeck, in *Wozzeck*, 1925), and many others. Not only the reaction against Wagner, but also the ensuing rekindled interest in closed forms, has diminished interest in leitmotif as a basic dramatic device; but its lessons have been learnt and applied by contemporary composers in many ways.

BIBLIOGRAPHY

La Ville de Illon, Comte de Lacépède: *La poétique de la musique* (Paris, 1785)

F. W. Jähns: *Carl Maria von Weber in seinen Werken* (Berlin, 1871)

G. Federlein: ' "Das Rheingold" von Richard Wagner: Versuch einer musikalischen Interpretation', *Musikalisches Wochenblatt*, ii (1871)

——: ' "Die Walküre" von Richard Wagner: Versuch einer musikalischen Interpretation', *Musikalisches Wochenblatt*, iii (1872)

H. von Wolzogen: *Thematisches Leitfaden durch Musik zu Richard Wagners Festspiel 'Der Ring des Nibelungen'* (Leipzig, 1876)

——: 'Die Motive in Wagner's "Götterdämmerung" ', *Musikalisches Wochenblatt*, viii (1877); ix (1878); x (1879)

J. van Santen-Kolff: 'Erinnerungsmotiv-Leitmotiv', *Musikalisches Wochenblatt*, xiv (1883); xv (1884)

——: 'Geschichtliches und Aesthetisches über das Erinnerungs-motiv', *Bayreuther Blätter*, viii (1885), 248

E. Schmitz: *Zur Geschichte des Leitmotivs in der romantischen Oper* (Hochland, 1907)

G. Kaiser: *Sämtliche Schriften von Carl Maria von Weber* (Berlin and Leipzig, 1908)

R. Wagner: *Sämtliche Schriften und Dichtungen*, iii, iv, x (Leipzig, 1913–14) [incl. *Oper und Drama* (1851), *Eine Mitteilung an meine Freunde* (1851), *Über die Anwendung der Musik auf der Drama* (1879)]

E. Haraszti: 'Le problème du Leit-Motiv', *ReM*, iv/10 (1923), 35

A. Schaeffner: 'Richard Wagner et l'opéra français du début du XIXe siècle', *ReM*, iv/11 (1923), 111

G. Abraham: 'The Leit-motif since Wagner', *ML*, vi (1925), 175

K. Wörner: 'Beiträge zur Geschichte des Leitmotivs in der Oper', *ZMw*, xiv (1931–2), 151

R. Engländer: 'Zur Geschichte des Leitmotivs', *ZMw*, xiv (1931–2), 356

M. Lamm: *Beiträge zur Entwicklung des musikalischen Motivs in den Tondramen R. Wagners* (diss., U. of Vienna, 1932)

L. Sabanayev: 'Remarks on the Leit-motif', *ML*, xiii (1932), 200

T. Mann: 'Richard Wagner und der "Ring des Nibelungen" ', *Richard Wagner und unsere Zeit* (Frankfurt, 1936)

S. Goslich: *Beiträge zur Geschichte der deutschen romantischen Oper* (Leipzig, 1937, rev. 2/1975)

T. W. Adorno: *Versuch über Wagner* (Berlin and Frankfurt, 1952, 2/1964)

G. Knepler: *Musikgeschichte des 19. Jahrhunderts*, ii (Berlin, 1961)

J. Matter: 'La fonction psychologique du leitmotiv wagnérien', *SMz*, ci (1961), 312

G. Knepler: 'Richard Wagners musikalische Gestaltungsprinzipien', *BMw*, v (1963), 33

J. Rushton: 'An Early Essay in "Leitmotiv": J. B. Lemoyne's "Electre" ', *ML*, lii (1971), 387

D. Heartz: 'Tonality and Motif in Idomeneo', *MT*, cxv (1974), 382

H. Federhofer and others: 'Tonartenplan und Motivstruktur (Leitmotivtechnik?) in Mozarts Musik', *MJb 1973–4*, 82–143

D. Charlton: 'Motive and Motif: Méhul before 1791', *ML*, lvii (1976), 362

JOHN WARRACK

Leitner, Ferdinand (*b* Berlin, 4 March 1912). German conductor. At the Berlin Hochschule für Musik he studied composition with Schreker and conducting with Julius Prüwer (a pupil of Brahms and Richter). He worked first as a piano accompanist to well-known singers and instrumentalists (such as the violinist Georg Kulenkampff and the cellist Ludwig Hoelscher). In 1935 he was assistant to Fritz Busch at Glyndebourne. Leitner began his career as a conductor in 1943 at the Nollendorf Theatre in Berlin. In 1945 he went to the Hamburg Staatsoper as a conductor, and in 1946 to the Munich Staatsoper.

He first made a name for himself at the Stuttgart Opera, where he arrived in 1947 as director of opera, and took over as musical director from 1950 to 1969. In these two decades he made guest appearances with the Stuttgart Opera in the most important centres of Europe, and more than once in Vienna, Paris and Edinburgh. As well as many of Günther Rennert's productions, Leitner conducted 13 by Wieland Wagner in Stuttgart (the last being *Lulu* in 1966). A specialist in the music of Carl Orff, he gave at Stuttgart the first performances of *Oedipus der Tyrann* (1959) and *Prometheus* (1968).

In 1969 Leitner became principal conductor of the Zurich Opera. In addition he made frequent appearances as a guest conductor at the Munich and Hamburg Staatsopern and in Chicago. In 1972 he was for the tenth time conductor of the German season at the Teatro Colón, Buenos Aires. He has also made guest appearances as a concert conductor in many major cities throughout the world. He regularly conducts the three major orchestras of the Netherlands, the Concertgebouw, the Rotterdam PO and the Residentie Orchester (Bernard Haitink studied with him). His numerous gramophone records include complete recordings of Busoni's *Doktor Faust* and Orff's *Antigonae* and *Prometheus*.

Leitner's extensive and many-sided repertory is centred on the operas of Mozart, Wagner and Richard Strauss, but also includes both Berg's operas and works by younger contemporaries. He has a special affinity with the symphonies of Bruckner and of Karl Amadeus Hartmann. Leitner avoids emotional excess and manages to do without undue fervour even in Wagner. He has a particular mastery of the art of accompanying singers without sacrificing any of a score's symphonic demands.

WOLFRAM SCHWINGER

Leitton (Ger.). LEADING NOTE.

Leittonwechselklang (Ger.). In a major triad, the chord formed by keeping the 3rd and 5th fixed and lowering the tonic by a minor 2nd; in a minor triad, the chord formed by keeping the tonic and 3rd fixed and raising the 5th by a minor 2nd. Either of these formations may be rearranged as a triad in root position. Thus, for instance, each of the C major and E minor triads is *Leittonwechselklang* to the other. The 'leading note' (*Leitton*) effect of the chord is illustrated in ex.1.

Ex.1 Mozart: *Le nozze di Figaro*, 'Non so più'

Leiviskä, Helvi (Lemmikki) (*b* Helsinki, 25 May 1902). Finnish composer. After graduating from the Helsinki Music Institute in 1927, she took private lessons with Funtek and Madetoja. She was librarian of the Helsinki Academy (1933–66). In her music she followed the German romantic tradition, but with national features.

WORKS
(selective list)

Orch: 2 suites, 1934, 1938; Pf Conc., 1935; 2 intermezzos, 1945; 3 syms., Bb, 1947, d, 1954, 1971; Sinfonia brevis, 1962–72
Inst: Pf Qt, Vn Sonata, pf pieces
Vocal: Songs with pf/orch

Principal publisher: Finnish Broadcasting Corporation

HANNU ILARI LAMPILA

Le Jeune, Claude [Claudin] (*b* Valenciennes, 1528–30; *d* Paris, buried 26 Sept 1600). French composer. He was one of the most prolific and original composers of the second half of the 16th century and one of the chief exponents of *musique mesurée à l'antique*; his application of this and other theories of musical and textual relationships had a lasting influence on French sacred and secular music.

1. LIFE. Le Jeune probably received his early music education at or near Valenciennes, then part of the Imperial Low Countries. His name first appears in 1552 as the composer of four chansons in anthologies published at Louvain which also contain works by his older compatriots Clemens non Papa, Crecquillon and Waelrant. He was a Protestant and from 1560 enjoyed the protection of a group of Huguenot nobles that included William of Orange, Agrippa d'Aubigné, Henri de Turenne, Duke of Bouillon and Henri of Navarre (later Henri IV). By 1564 he had settled at Paris where his *Dix pseaumes* were published, dedicated to two more Huguenot patrons, François de la Noue and Charles de Téligny. He participated in the Académie de Poésie et de Musique established by Baïf and Courville in 1570, and became one of the leading exponents of *musique mesurée à l'antique*. Some time between the end of 1579 and January 1582 he succeeded the lutenist Vaumesnil as 'maistre des enfans de musicque' at the court of François, Duke of Anjou, brother of Henri III. In autumn 1581 he collaborated with Baïf, d'Aubigné and Ronsard in providing entertainments for the marriage of the Duke of Joyeuse to Marie de Lorraine, the queen's half-sister. Together with Nicolas de la Grotte he received from the king a special sum to devise a 'Guerre' to accompany a symbolic tournament; he also contributed an 'Epithalme' which was published, with the 'Guerre', in his posthumous *Airs* of 1608. After the death of François of Anjou in 1584 he made use of a royal privilege of January

1582 to have his *Livre de meslanges* published by Plantin at Antwerp; further editions appeared at Paris in 1586 and 1587.

According to Mersenne Le Jeune wrote a 'confession de foi' hostile to the Catholic League and was obliged to flee Paris during the siege of 1589. His *Dodécacorde* and other manuscripts were saved from burning at the hands of the guards at the St Denis gate only by the intercession of his Catholic friend Mauduit. He took refuge at La Rochelle, a Protestant stronghold, where the *Dodécacorde* was published in April 1598. However, in September 1596 and in May 1600 his name appeared in Henri IV's household records as 'maistre compositeur ordinaire de la musique de nostre chambre'. He was buried in the Protestant cemetery of La Trinité, Paris. Except for the printed collections mentioned above and a number of pieces in anthologies, his works were in manuscript at the time of his death; eight collections were published posthumously between 1601 and 1612 by Pierre Ballard. The dedications are mostly by his sister Cecile or his niece Judith Mardo and are addressed to his former Protestant friends, pupils and patrons.

2. WORKS. Le Jeune's surviving output includes 347 psalms, 146 *airs* (all but three are *mesurés*), 66 secular chansons, 38 sacred chansons, 43 Italian madrigals, 11 motets, a mass and three instrumental fantasias. His work shows the influences of both the school of Flemish composers living in Venice and the Parisian school which cultivated the harmonic *air de cour* with its lightly accompanied prosodic recitation embellished with melismas. Willaert's influence is particularly evident in the formal aspects of Le Jeune's Mass, *Magnificat* and motets. His three instrumental fantasias demonstrate his contrapuntal skill and are similar in style to the sonatas, sinfonias and ricercares of the Venetians; two are in four parts, and the third in five parts is based on Josquin's motet *Benedicta es coelorum regina*. There is no proof that Le Jeune visited Italy, and the chromatic madrigalisms that occur in some of his chansons and *airs* are of the type found in the works of his contemporaries Bertrand, Boni, Costeley, La Grotte, Du Caurroy and many who worked in southern and central France.

The four chansons attributed to Le Jeune in anthologies of 1552 (*RISM* 1552[12], 1552[13]) are settings of archaic texts in the outmoded polyphonic style of Crecquillon's generation. They may be student works or may have been misattributed to Le Jeune by the publishers; for example, *Bonjour m'amye* had appeared anonymously as early as 1531 (*RISM*, 1531[1]). By the 1560s he had gained international repute and his name appears with those of Clemens non Papa and Lassus among the 'musici praecipii et excellentissimi' listed in the manuscript of Lassus's Penitential Psalms (in *D-Mbs*). The ten four-voice psalms (1564) are free settings of De Bèze's translations in the light polyphonic motet style of Goudimel. A seven-voice dialogue *Mais qui es tu?* at the end of the collection anticipates Le Jeune's later mastery of the larger ensemble, as does his seven-voice setting of Guéroult's *Susanne un jour* (*RISM* 1572[2]).

In comparison with the northern chanson, in which a craftsmanlike exploitation of polyphonic techniques was more highly prized than subtleties of verbal expression, the Parisian chanson of the 1560s was lighter and freer, aiming at an intimate unity of text and music by charac-

Claude Le Jeune: engraving from his 'Dodécacorde' (1598)

terizing the spirit of the poem. This approach to word-setting undoubtedly contributed to Baïf's experiments, though it was subordinated to his new syllabic prosody, the rapid pace of which often disguised a lack of tunefulness. From the time that he joined Baïf's movement Le Jeune wholeheartedly embraced its ideals, to the extent that a certain esotericism cultivated by the group infected his work. The chief adverse effect of his membership, however, was the delay in the publication of his works caused by the ban on copying and circulating any works performed in the Académie. The introduction into poetry of a metrical scheme based on values doubled or halved was neither altogether new nor confined to the French language, since it had preoccupied first the troubadours and trouvères and then poets and musicians at the end of the 15th century. More important than VERS MESURES itself was the

2. Title-page of Le Jeune's 'Premier livre, contenant 50 pseaumes de David mis en musique' (1602)

Académie's revival of the humanist ideal, based on Greek music, of a setting subjected to its text, expressing its sense and avoiding any textural complexity (e.g. canon and imitation) that might obscure the words or the metre. Le Jeune's largely homophonic settings of *vers mesurés* faithfully reflect the quantitative metres prescribed by the Académie by equating the long syllables with minims and the short with crotchets, although both values are often varied by melismatic subdivision. The predetermined, extra-musical metres (elegiacs, sapphics etc) revolutionized the traditional rhythms of polyphony, often producing lilting patterns of great freedom and charm, while the simple vertical textures resulting from the strict alternation of two basic note values focussed attention on the harmonic structure and encouraged experiment. Though originally unrhymed, the texts of Le Jeune's *Airs* and *Pseaumes en vers mesurez* have rhymes added.

In 1583 the hitherto secret art of *musique mesurée à l'antique* developed by the Académie was made public by the printing of six *chansonettes mesurées* by Le Jeune to poems by Baïf (*RISM* 1583⁹). The novel rhythmic vitality and variety of these pieces are matched in the 36 madrigals, published in the *Livre de meslanges* (1585) but probably written much earlier under the influence of Nola, Ferretti and other Italian masters of the villanella. Another facet of the Académie's work was the attempted revival of the Greek genera; Le Jeune experimented in particular with the enharmonic tetrachord approximately reproduced by two semitones and a minor 3rd. The tetrachord formula is used in *Quelle eau* (1585) and in the multi-stanza psalms, and gave rise to Le Jeune's most remarkable chromaticisms, notably in his settings of Durand's elegy *Qu'est devenu ce bel oeil?* (from the second book of *airs*, 1608) and the *chanson spirituelle* by Guéroult *Hélas mon Dieu* (from *Second livre des meslanges*, 1612). According to his friend Artur Thomas, Le Jeune excelled his predecessors in his understanding of the modes, as illustrated by the alternate rousing and calming effects on a gentleman of two *airs* performed during the wedding festivities of the Duke of Joyeuse in 1581.

The 12 psalms of the *Dodécacorde*, like the two books of *airs* of 1608 and the *Octonaires* of 1606, are arranged in the order of the 12 modes prescribed by Zarlino, though all except the 5th and 6th modes (Phrygian) are effectively converted into major and minor keys by the liberal use of accidentals. The translations are by Marot and De Bèze and the orthodox Genevan tunes are always present in one of the voices; by varying the number of voices between two and seven for the different stanzas Le Jeune created extended structures alternating polyphony and homophony. Even larger forces are used in Psalms xxxv and cii which are set for 13 and 16 voices respectively. The second psalm in the collection follows a procedure typical of Le Jeune's larger works (e.g. *Le printemps*, no.13); the voices accumulate in successive stanzas so that the work ends with a grand sonorous climax. The numerous psalms for three to six voices, published posthumously, use the melodies of the Huguenot Psalter freely or strictly in a variety of ways: as a basis for note-against-note counterpoint in motet form, or with varying degrees of freedom in any of the voices. The many editions of the psalm collections printed at Paris, Geneva, Amsterdam, Leiden and London until the last quarter of the 18th century are proof of their great popularity. The *Pseaumes en vers mesurez* (1606) are settings of 23 French translations and three Latin paraphrases of the psalms by Baïf and Agrippa d'Aubigné for two to eight voices; the collection also includes a French translation of the *Te Deum* set for six voices. According to d'Aubigné, Eustache du Caurroy was converted to *musique mesurée* on hearing two of Le Jeune's psalms performed by over 100 singers at Paris in 1605. The *Octonaires de la vanité et inconstance du monde* (1606) consist of the 36 eight-line strophes by the Calvinist minister and moralist Antoine de la Roche Chandieu arranged in 12 groups of three settings in each mode (two for four voices and one for three); according to the preface by his sister, Le Jeune died before he could add a further group of settings for five and six voices.

The 'Préface sur la musique mesurée' to Le Jeune's settings of Baïf's *Le printemps* (1603) extols the composer as the first to revise the affective and subtle rhythmic skill of the ancients and to combine it with the harmonic perfection achieved during the previous two centuries; the accompanying ode by Artur Thomas praises his sweet harmony and counterpoint, his science and mathematical secrets, his melodic artifices and his fine sense of movement. Mersenne claimed that Le Jeune used an instrument when composing, and ascribed his popularity to the variety and vivacity of his rhythms, his talent for melody and his skill in handling large ensembles of voices and viols. Burney described Le Jeune as a learned and laborious composer, despite his lapses in contrapuntal technique (dissonances resolved by leap, crossing of parts, leaps of a major 6th etc) which were censured by the severe contemporary masters from Flanders and Italy. His music is distinguished by an instinctive choice of memorable motifs, rhythmic verve and élan and elegant forms and textures. His psalms remained widely popular throughout the 17th century, his sonorous ensembles inspired French sacred music of the next generation and his *musique mesurée* provided a model not only for the *air de cour* and *ballet de cour* but for Monteverdi's *Scherzi musicali*.

WORKS

Editions: *Clément Marot et le psautier huguenot*, ii, ed. O. Douen (Paris, 1879) [D]
C. Le Jeune: *Airs of 1608*, ed. D. P. Walker, AIM Miscellanea, i (1951–9) [W]
Anthologie de la chanson Parisienne au XVIᵉ siècle, ed. F. Lesure (Monaco, 1953) [L]
Chorals de la Réforme, ed. M. Honegger (Paris, 1953) [H]

(*published in Paris unless otherwise stated*)

PSALMS

Dix pseaumes de David, 4vv, en forme de motets avec un dialogue, 7vv (T. de Bèze) (1564); dialogue ed. in MMFTR, viii (1928)
Dodécacorde (12 psalms) (C. Marot, De Bèze), 2–7vv (La Rochelle, 1598); 3 ed. in MMRF, xi/1 (1900/R); 1 in D
Les 150 pseaumes, 4, 5vv (1601; La Rochelle, 2/1608; Paris, 3/1613; Amsterdam, 4/1629; Leiden, 5/1635; Paris, 6/1650; Schiedam, 7/1664; edn. entitled The First 12 Psalms . . . adapted to the English Version, London, ?1775); 2 in D [from an edn. Geneva, 1627], some in H
Premier livre, contenant 50 pseaumes de David mis en musique, 3vv (1602); some in D, some in H
Pseaumes en vers mesurez (26 psalms, Te Deum) (J. A. de Baïf, A. d'Aubigné), 2–8vv (1606); ed. in MMRF, xx–xxii (1905–6/R)
Second livre contenant 50 pseaumes de David, 3vv (1608); 2 in D, some in H
Troisièmc livre des pseaumes de David, 3vv (1610); some in D, some in H
2 psalms 5, 6vv, in Second livre des meslanges (1612) [also incl. other sacred and secular works, see below]; ed. in MMFTR, viii (1928)

OTHER SACRED VOCAL

Octonaires de la vanité et inconstance du monde (36 works) (A. de la Roche Chandieu), 3, 4vv (1606); ed. in MMFTR, i (1924), viii (1928); ed. and trans. A. Seay, as Reflections on the Vanity and Inconstancy of the World (New York, 1967–9)

Missa ad placitum, 4–7vv (1607); ed. M. Sanvoisin, Le pupitre, ii (Paris, 1967)
Second livre des meslanges (Magnificat, 3 motets, sacred chanson), 3–7, 10vv (1612) [also incl. psalms and secular works]; sacred chanson ed. in MMFTR, viii (1928)

Motet, 3vv, sacred chanson, 1565², 1572²

SECULAR VOCAL

Livre de meslanges (26 chansons, 36 madrigals, 5 motets, Lat. echo composition), 4–8, 10vv (Antwerp, 1585) [incl. 9 from 1572², 1583⁷, 1583⁹]; 13 chansons ed. in MMRF, xvi (1903/R); 2 madrigals ed. R. J. Maldeghem, Trésor musical, xxix (Brussels, 1893); 1 in L
[33] Airs mis en musique, 4, 5vv (1594) [incl. 20 from 1585¹³, 1585¹⁴]; 2 in L
Le printemps (33 airs mesurés, 6 chansons) (Baïf), 2–8vv (1603) [incl. 6 airs from 1594 edn.]; ed. in MMRF, xii–xiv (1900–01/R)
[68] Airs, 3–6vv (1608) [incl. works from 1594 and 1603 vols.]; W i–ii
Second livre des [59] airs, 3–6vv (1608) [incl. works from 1594 and 1603 vols.]; W iii–iv
Second livre des meslanges (30 chansons, 3 airs, 2 airs mesurés, 7 madrigals), 4–8vv (1612) [also incl. psalms, other sacred and instrumental works, and 9 chansons from 1572², 1575⁴, 1578¹², 1583⁸]; 2 in L

27 chansons, some 4, 5vv, 1552¹², 1552¹³, 1572², 1575⁴, 1577⁶, 1578¹², 1583⁷, 1583⁸, 1585¹³, 1597¹⁰; 20 airs, 4, 5vv, 1583⁹, 1585¹⁴; 3 in L

INSTRUMENTAL

3 fantasias in Second livre des meslanges (1612) [also incl. psalms, other sacred and secular works]
Canzonetta, sacred chanson, lute, 1592²²
7 other works, lute, 1601¹⁸

BIBLIOGRAPHY

BurneyH; RiemannL 12
M. Mersenne: *Harmonie universelle* (Paris, 1636–7/R1963; Eng. trans., 1957)
E. Bouton: *Esquisse biographique sur Claude Lejeune* (Valenciennes, 1845)
O. Douen: *Clément Marot et le psautier huguenot*, i–ii (Paris, 1878–9)
M. Cauchie: 'La mort de Claude le Jeune', *RdM*, xi (1927)
G. Thibault and L. Perceau: *Bibliographie des poésies de P. de Ronsard mises en musique au XVIᵉ siècle* (Paris, 1941)
D. P. Walker: 'The Aims of Baïf's Académie de Poésie et de Musique', *JRBM*, i (1946), 91
F. A. Yates: *The French Academies of the Sixteenth Century* (London, 1947)
——: 'Poésie et musique dans les "Magnificences" ', *Musique et poésie au XVIᵉ siècle: CNRS Paris 1953*, 241
D. P. Walker: 'The Influence of Musique mesurée à l'antique, particularly on the airs de cour of the Early Seventeenth Century', *MD*, ii (1948), 141
F. Lesure and D. P. Walker: 'Claude Le Jeune and Musique Mesurée', *MD*, iii (1949), 151
D. P. Walker: 'The Rhythm and Notation of Musique Mesurée', *MD*, iv (1950), 163
K. Levy: 'Le Jeune, Claude', *MGG*
P.-A. Gaillard: 'Chanson', *LaMusicaD*
F. Lesure: 'Le Jeune, Claude', *Dictionnaire de la musique*, ii (Paris, 1970)

PAUL-ANDRÉ GAILLARD, FRANK DOBBINS

Lekeu, Guillaume (Jean Joseph Nicolas) (*b* Heusy, nr. Verviers, 20 Jan 1870; *d* Angers, 21 Jan 1894). Belgian composer. He studied in Poitiers and then in Paris where he worked first with Franck and, after Franck's death, with d'Indy. He began to compose at the age of 15 with the *Andante et variations* for violin and piano (1885). D'Indy advised him to compete for the Belgian Prix de Rome; in 1891 he won a second prize with his cantata *Andromède*. Ysaÿe, on hearing parts of the work in Brussels, was so impressed that he commissioned what turned out to be Lekeu's most celebrated work, the Sonata for violin and piano (1892). Lekeu spent the remaining three years of his life in Paris, composing prolifically; thc orchestral *Fantaisie sur deux airs populaires angevins* and the Adagio for string quartet and string orchestra are generally considered the more important products of this brief final period. He died of typhoid fever. D'Indy completed the unfinished Cello Sonata and Piano Quartet (the former a student work dating from 1888).

Lekeu was greatly affected by the perfervid emotional temperature of the Franck circle, and the two great influences on his work, as on others of the circle, were late Beethoven and Wagner (of Franck's own music Lekeu tended to re-create the spirit rather than the letter). His credo is best summed up in his own words: 'Je me tue à mettre dans ma musique toute mon âme'. The Piano Sonata and the Violin Sonata are among those works suffused with a kind of feverish, almost preternatural intensity, and his weaknesses are the outcome of the then currently fashionable necessity to think, as well as to feel, in the grand manner. However, signs of an individual intelligence in the making are detectable on almost every page; for instance, in the 'Nocturne' (no.3 of the *Trois poèmes* for voice and piano to Lekeu's own words) the late Romantic afflatus gives place to early glimmerings of impressionism, and in the orchestral *Fantaisie sur deux airs populaires angevins* folksong proved to be (as with d'Indy) a revitalizing and purifying influence.

WORKS
(all printed works published in Paris unless otherwise stated)

STAGE
Les burgraves (drame lyrique, V. Hugo), 1887, inc., lost
Barberine (opera, A. de Musset), 1889, prelude to Act 2 and frags. only

VOCAL
Noël, 2 S, str qt, pf, 1888
Andromède (poème lyrique, J. Sauvenière), solo vv, chorus, orch, 1891, B-Bc, vocal score (Liège, ?1892)
Chant lyrique, chorus, orch, 1891, MS at Société Royale d'Emulation, Verviers
Fugue, double choir
Songs (for 1v, pf): La fenêtre de la maison paternelle (A. de Lamartine), 1887; Chanson de mai (G. Lekeu), 1891 (1900); 3 poèmes (Lekeu), 1892 (?1904): 1 Sur une tombe, 2 Ronde, 3 Nocturne; L'ombre plus dense (Lekeu), 1893 (Liège, n.d.); Quelque antique et lente danse (Lekeu) (Brussels, 1895); Les pavots (Lamartine) (1909)

INSTRUMENTAL
Orch: Marche d'Ophélie, 1887; Prelude for Act 3 of Racine: Phèdre, 1888; 1re étude symphonique: Chant de triomphale délivrance, 1889 (n.d.); 2me étude symphonique: 1 Hamlet, 1890, unpubd, 2 Faust (n.d.); Adagio, str qt, str orch, op.3, 1891 (1908); Fantaisie sur deux airs populaires angevins, 1892 (1909), also arr. pf 4 hands; Suite, with solo vc, 1892; Poème, with solo vn, inc.
Fantaisie contrapunctique sur un cramignon liégeois, ob, cl, bn, hn, str, 1890 (n.d.)
Epithalame, str qnt, 3 trbn, org, 1891
Introduction et adagio, brass, tuba obbl, 1891
Chamber: Andante et variations, vn, pf, op.1, 1885; Commentaire sur les paroles du Christ, str qt, 1887; Méditation, str qt, 1887; Minuet, str qt, 1887; Str Qt, d, 1887; Adagio, 2 vn, pf, 1889; Vc Sonata, F, 1888 (?1910), completed by d'Indy; Pf Qt, 1888 (1893), 2nd movt completed by d'Indy; Pf Trio, 1890 (1908); Vn Sonata, G, 1891 (1892); Str Trio; others
Pf: Lamento and Lento doloroso, 1887; Tempo di mazurka, 1887 (n.d.); Fugue in 4 pts., 1889; Morceau, pf 4 hands, 1889; Sonata, 1891 (?1900); 3 pièces (Liège, 1892): 1 Chansonette sans paroles, 2 Valse oubliée, 3 Danse joyeuse; others, lost

BIBLIOGRAPHY
O. G. Sonneck: 'Guillaume Lekeu', *MQ*, v (1919), 109–47, repr. in Sonneck: *Miscellaneous Studies in the History of Music* (New York, 1921/R1968)
M. Lorrain: *Guillaume Lekeu, sa correspondance, sa vie et son oeuvre* (Liège, 1923)
A. E. Hull: *A Dictionary of Modern Music and Musicians* (London, 1924/R1971)
V. Denis: 'Guillaume Lekeu (1870–1894) et Henri Evenepoel (1872–1899)', *Hommage à Charles van den Borren: Mélanges* (Antwerp, 1945), 163
P. Dukas: *Les écrits . . . sur la musique* (Paris, 1948)
A. vander Linden: 'Lettres de Guillaume Lekeu à Octave Maus', *RBM*, iii (1949), 155
M. Cooper: *French Music from the Death of Berlioz to the Death of Fauré* (London, 1951, 3/1969)
L. Davies: *César Franck and his Circle* (London, 1970)
CHRISTOPHER PALMER

Lelarge, Jacques-George (*b* Liège, baptized 15 April 1713; *d* ?Liège, after 1793). South Netherlands organist, teacher and ecclesiastic. He probably served his musical apprenticeship at the collegiate church of St Paul, and was appointed organist at St Martin's, Liège, in 1734; he was ordained priest at about that time. In 1745 he successfully competed against three other musicians for the position of organist at Liège Cathedral, where he served until 1793, although J.-P.-V. Lhoest assisted him from 1784 (with J.-J.-J. Lhoest 'en survivance'). In 1754 the prince-bishop Jean-Théodore of Bavaria granted him a living in the church of St Denis. Lelarge's manuscript treatise *Traité d'harmonie par demandes et réponses* is a practical teaching manual, probably written for the *duodenes* whom he taught the organ and harpsichord. It is based on Rameau's works, and thus shows the French bias of some Liège musicians in the second half of the 18th century. None of his organ compositions survives.

BIBLIOGRAPHY
A. Auda: *La musique et les musiciens de l'ancien pays de Liège* (Liège, Brussels and Paris, 1930), 251
A. vander Linden: 'Sur un manuscrit inédit: le Traité d'harmonie de J. G. Lelarge, organiste de la Cathédrale de Liège, 1782', *Association française pour l'avancement des sciences* (1939), no.63, p.1436
R. Vannes: *Dictionnaire des musiciens (compositeurs)* (Brussels, 1947)
A. vander Linden: 'Note sur l'abbé Lelarge', *RBM*, iv (1950), 72
JOSÉ QUITIN

Lelei, Georg Simon. See LÖHLEIN, GEORG SIMON.

Leleu, Jeanne (*b* St Mihiel, 29 Dec 1898). French pianist and composer. Her father was a bandmaster, her mother a piano teacher. At the age of nine she began studying at the Paris Conservatoire, where her teachers included Marguerite Long, Cortot and Widor. In 1923 she won the Prix de Rome with her cantata *Béatrix*. The Institut de France followed the Prix de Rome and two other prizes (Georges Bizet and Monbinne). She became a professor at the Paris Conservatoire in 1947, first for research, then for harmony. In style her compositions belong to no school. Clear, rhythmically alive, adventurous in harmony, her Symphonic Suite caused something of a sensation in Rome, where it was first heard. In 1937 she played her own Piano Concerto with success in Paris, at the Concerts Lamoureux. Her *Transparences*, with its imaginative orchestral textures, was described by Florent Schmitt as 'a marvel of freshness, finesse and feminine grace', showing a high degree of invention, sensibility, richness and knowledge. Her ballets, *Un jour d'été* and *Nautéos*, have been praised for their grace, wit and invention, and both have enjoyed considerable success in the theatre.

WORKS
(selective list)

Stage: Le cyclope (incidental music, Euripides), 1928, unpubd; Un jour d'été (ballet), Paris, Opéra-Comique, 1940, unpubd; Nautéos (ballet), Monte Carlo, 1947, unpubd
Orch: Esquisses italiennes, 1926; Sym. Suite, wind, 1926; 2 danses, 1927; Transparences, 1935, Pf Conc., 1935, unpubd; Femmes, suite, 1947, unpubd; Virevoltes, suite, 1950, unpubd
Other works: Pf Qt, 1922; pf pieces, songs

Principal publishers: Heugel, Leduc

DAVID COX

Leleu, Jehan [Jennot]. See LUPI, JOHANNES.

Lelyā. Office of the Syrian Churches corresponding to Matins; *see* SYRIAN CHURCH MUSIC.

Lemacher, Heinrich (*b* Solingen, 26 June 1891; *d* Munich, 15 March 1966). German teacher and composer. From 1911 to 1916 he studied conducting, composition and the piano at the Cologne Conservatory, as well as musicology at the University of Bonn. After military service in 1916–18 he continued to live in Cologne as a composer and critic for the *Rheinische Volkswacht*. He founded in 1924 the Seminar des Reichsverbandes deutscher Tonkünstler und Musiklehrer which he led until 1933. From 1925 until his retirement in 1956, he taught composition, theory and history at the Cologne Hochschule für Musik, where he was made professor in 1928. During this time he also taught at the Rheinische Musikschule and at the University of Cologne. He was co-founder of the Gesellschaft für neue Musik, Cologne (1921) and the Internationale Gesellschaft für neue katholische Kirchenmusik (1927). From 1956 he was a director of the Cäcilienverband. Lemacher's music reflects his lifelong concern with church music. He was greatly influenced by Bruckner, whose masses and motets he edited, but his work also harks back to Renaissance models, specifically Palestrina and Lassus, in its linearity and its use of parody and cantus firmus.

WORKS
(for complete list see Hammerschlag and Schneider)

Masses: 25 for chorus; 10 for high vv, org; 2 for chorus, org, wind
Other sacred pieces: 16 mass propers, 81 opp. of motets, 15 cantatas
Secular vocal: 68 choral opp., 4 cantatas, 28 opp. of lieder, 2 melodramas
Inst: 14 orch works, Pf Qnt, Str Qnt, 2 pf qts, 4 str qts, 4 pf trios, 4 str trios, other chamber pieces, music for pf, pf duet, org
Arrangements of Palestrina, Lassus, Haydn, Mozart, Bruckner

WRITINGS
Zur Geschichte der Musik am Hofe zu Nassau-Weilburg (diss., U. of Bonn, 1916)
Handbuch der Hausmusik (Regensburg, 1948)
ed., with K. G. Fellerer: *Handbuch der katholischen Kirchenmusik* (Essen, 1949)
Lehrbuch des Kontrapunkt (Mainz, 1952)
Generalbassübungen (Düsseldorf, 1954)
Harmonielehre (Cologne, 1957)
with H. Schmidt: *Almanach der Hausmusik* (Cologne, 1958)
with H. Schroeder: *Formenlehre der Musik* (Cologne, 1962; Eng. trans., 1967)

BIBLIOGRAPHY
P. Mies: 'Heinrich Lemacher: über das Verhältnis von Wort und Ton in seinen Werken', *NZM*, xcv/3 (1928), 146
——: 'Grundprinzipien der Messekompositionen bei H. Lemacher', *Musica sacra*, xxxiii (1932)
——: 'Heinrich Lemacher: sein Werk und Stellung in der Musik', *Sinfonia sacra*, ii (1948)
F. Oberborbeck: 'Heinrich Lemacher: zu seinem 60. Geburtstag am 26 Juni', *ZfM*, cxii (1951), 299
W. Hammerschlag and A. Schneider: *Musikalisches Brauchtum: Festschrift Heinrich Lemacher* (Cologne, 1956)
P. Mies: 'Lemacher, Heinrich', *MGG*
W. Thomson: Review of Eng. trans. of *Formenlehre*, *Notes*, xxiv (1967–8), 713
CHARLOTTE ERWIN

Lemacherier, Guillaume. *See* LEGRANT, GUILLAUME.

Le Maire, Jean (*b* Chaumont-en-Bassigny, Haute-Marne, *c*1581; *d c*1650). French mathematician, engineer and inventor. He lived in Toulouse and Paris. His widespread interests led to the development of novelties in such diverse areas as architecture, language, mnemotechnics and typography. In music he is credited with devising an equal-tempered scale, with adding a seventh syllable (*za*) to the hexachordal solmization system, with constructing a new type of lute called 'almérie' (an anagram of his name) and with proposing a novel musical notation ('musique almérique'). Although Mersenne (in *Harmonie universelle*, Paris, 1636–7, and in his correspondence) strongly supported Le Maire's

ideas, others did not, and controversy regarding his inventions spread throughout France and elsewhere in Europe.

BIBLIOGRAPHY
A. Pirro: 'Jean le Maire et l'*Almérie*', *BSIM*, iv (1908), 479
C. de Waard, ed.: *Correspondance du P. Marin Mersenne* (Paris, 1932)
A. Cohen: 'Jean Le Maire and La Musique Almérique', *AcM*, xxxv (1963), 175
J. R. Knowlson: 'Jean Le Maire, the Almérie, and the "musique almérique": a Set of Unpublished Documents', *AcM*, xl (1968), 86
ALBERT COHEN

Lemaire (de Belges), Jean (*b* Bavai, Hainaut, *c*1473; *d* after 18 March 1514). French poet and historiographer. He may have been a choirboy at Notre-Dame de Valenciennes, since he wrote that there, 'en ma premier jeunesse j'avoie chanté "Benedicamus" ' (Stecher, iv, 489). Between 1498 and 1503 he was employed by Duke Pierre II de Bourbon at Villefranche, and then by Pierre's brother-in-law, Count Louis de Ligny, who died the following Christmas eve. In June 1504 Lemaire took up a position at the court of Margaret of Austria, and he entered the service of Anne of Brittany and Louis XII in 1512. The last surviving document relating to his life is a letter of 18 March 1514.

La plainte du désiré, lamenting the death of Louis de Ligny, invokes Josquin, Agricola, Hilaire Penet, Evrart, Conrad and Pregent, and calls for the alliance of music and poetry. An allegory urging spiritual harmony between France and Italy, *La concorde des deux langages*, abounds in musical imagery, mingling old and new: monocords, psalteries and guitars, Sapphic odes and virelais, and includes the names of Amphion, Arion, Orpheus, Ockeghem, Josquin, Agricola and Compère. Not only did he use technical terms like 'pedal points' and 'alternating verses', but he attempted to characterize the different styles of contemporary composers with such phrases as 'entrebriser musicque' for Agricola, 'verbes coulourez' for Josquin, 'armonie tres fine' for Ockeghem and 'termes doulx' for Compère. A four-voice chanson, *Mille regretz de vous abandonner*, is ascribed to him in Attaingnant's *Vingt et sept chansons musicales desquelles les plus convenables à la fleuste* (*RISM*, 1533[1]). Later sources however attribute it to Josquin, who is generally accepted as being its composer.

BIBLIOGRAPHY
J. Stecher, ed.: *Oeuvres de Jean Lemaire de Belges* (Paris, 1882–91)
D. Yabsley, ed.: *La plainte du désiré* (Paris, 1932)
J. Frappier, ed.: *La concorde des deux langages* (Paris, 1947)
——, ed.: *Les épîtres de l'amant vert* (Paris, 1948)
G. Doutrepoint: *Jean Lemaire de Belges et la renaissance* (Brussels, 1934)
M. Françon, ed.: *La concorde des deux langages, et Les épîtres de l'amant* (Cambridge, Mass., 1964) [facs. edn. with commentary]
M. Picker: *The Chanson Albums of Marguerite of Austria* (Berkeley, 1965)
F. Dobbins: *The Chanson at Lyons in the Sixteenth Century* (diss., U. of Oxford, 1971), i, 18ff
FRANK DOBBINS

Lemaire, Louis (*b* 1693 or 1694; *d* Tours, *c*1750). French composer. Trained as a chorister at Meaux Cathedral and taught by Sébastien de Brossard, who was organist there, Lemaire became well known in Paris as a composer of vocal music. His name first appeared in an anthology of *airs* published by Ballard in 1712, followed two years later by a volume devoted to his own. (A retrospective catalogue issued by Le Clerc in 1742 lists eight such volumes, but only six survive.) A more substantial work, *Les quatre saisons*, appeared in 1724. This was a collection of four cantatas and his only contribution to the genre, for he preferred to cultivate the *cantatille*, a form best described as the Rococo version of the Baroque French cantata. Lemaire was the most prolific of all *cantatille* composers, publishing 66 of them between 1728 and 1750 and, together with Mouret and Lefebvre, he lifted this form to the height of its popularity. Between 1728 and 1736, 21 of his *cantatilles* were heard at concerts in the Tuileries, and many were included in the various anthologies of this kind of work that appeared frequently after 1730. Most of Lemaire's *cantatilles* were written for high voice with instrumental accompaniment, usually for violins and flutes and occasionally for musette and for vielle (or hurdy-gurdy). He also composed two books of motets (or *saluts*) which were sung at the Concert Spirituel between 1728 and 1733.

WORKS
(all published in Paris)

Airs à chanter (1714–19); 8 vols. mentioned in Le Clerc catalogue of 1742, only 6 extant
Les quatre saisons, 4 cantatas (1724)
Suite pour la vielle et la musette (c1725)
Recueils d'airs sérieux et à boire, vaudeville et ronde de table, 6 vols. (1725–30)
Motets, 1–2vv, some with insts, 2 vols. (c1728)
Concerts spirituels ou Recueil d'airs sur toutes sortes de sujets de piété (1729)
Recueil d'airs sérieux et à boire, mêlez de vaudeville, ronde de table, duo, récit de basse, airs tendres et chansons à danser (1738)
Recueil d'airs sérieux et à boire, mêlez de brunette, ronde de table, duo, récit de basse, musette et vaudeville (1740)
Fanfares ou Concerts de chambre, vn, fl, ob, musette, vielle, bn, tpt, perc (1743)
66 cantatilles (1728–50), 5 lost
Airs in Ballard's Recueil d'airs sérieux et à boire (1712–24), Nouveau recueil de chansons choisies (1723–36) and other anthologies
Sacred contrafacta in Nouvelles poésies spirituelles et morales (1730–37)

BIBLIOGRAPHY
D. E. Tunley: *The Eighteenth Century French Cantata* (London, 1974)
DAVID TUNLEY

Le Maistre [Meistre, Maystre], **Matthaeus** (*b* ?Roclengesur-Geer, Liège, *c*1505; *d* Dresden, before April 1577). Netherlands composer. Kade's early hypothesis that he had at one time been active in Milan, and was identical with Mathias Hermann Werrecore, also known as Mathias Fianergo, was refuted by F. X. Haberl ('Matthias Hermann Werrecorensis: eine bibliographische-kritische Studie', *MMg*, iii (1871), 197). A newly discovered manuscript (*A-Gu* 13), which was apparently taken to Graz from Munich in 1573, supports Sandberger's conjecture that the 'Mathesz Nidlender' reported in the Munich court chapel is Le Maistre. Furthermore, two Munich choirbooks are unique sources for several masses and motets by him. In 1554 he succeeded Johann Walter as Kapellmeister of the Dresden Kantorei, then consisting of 40 musicians. Since he had lost the patrimony of his old home on his conversion to Protestantism, the elector compensated him in 1565 with a grant for life. Additional income came from compositions dedicated to the authorities of Zwickau. He suffered from illness for some years before his retirement in June 1568, when he was given a pension of 195 florins; his successor, Antonio Scandello, had already taken over his duties five months previously. In January 1577 he wrote the foreword to his last work to be printed. His son, Valerian, was a musician in the imperial chapel.

Le Maistre was a conservative musician. On his conversion to Lutheranism he adopted the authentic Protestant tradition of Johann Walter and Georg Rhau. Their approach, however, was somewhat old-fashioned

and seemed to confirm Le Maistre's own Renaissance idea of music as 'ars'. Understandably therefore his works met with little appreciation in his lifetime, although musically and intellectually they were far above average standard. His masses were predominantly influenced by elements of post-1500 Netherlands style, and most are parody or cantus firmus masses. Not until his old age did he make a valuable contribution to the Protestant mass with his *Missa super 'Ich weiss mir ein fest gebauets Haus'*, which also makes use of *O du Lamm Gottes, das der Welt Sünde trägt* in the 'Qui tollis'. Most of the motets, too, show characteristics of an earlier style. The *Catechesis musicis inclusa*, consisting of seven motets in simple three- to four-part form, is intended primarily for didactic purposes and is a musical memorial to the Protestant re-latinization of texts in the second half of the 16th century. (Luther had previously translated the text into German.)

Le Maistre's most important compositions are his sacred and secular songs in German. They are a late echo of the tradition of the German partsong, which had reached its peak in the works of Ludwig Senfl. Le Maistre's pieces, however, could not give any new impetus to the genre, which was already regarded as out of date by mid-century. The *Geistliche und weltliche teutsche Geseng* (1566) owed much to the example of the fine collection *Neue deudsche geistliche Gesenge*, edited in 1544 by Georg Rhau. In his sacred pieces he made use of a wide range of compositional techniques, from simple homophonic songs to the great motets using cantus firmus and imitation. The texts of the more 'modern' compositions of his second collection (1577) were addressed more to the youth of his day. Didactic, declamatory texts, many of which were translated back into Latin, reveal his humanistic, pedagogic tendencies. In the secular songs he followed the earlier tradition of setting the cantus firmus in the tenor; however, some madrigalian influences can be seen in the part-writing of individual love-songs. He also composed two ingeniously constructed quodlibets.

WORKS

Editions: *Handbuch der evangelischen Kirchenmusik*, i–iii, ed. K. Ameln (Göttingen, 1933–40) [contains 13 pieces]
    Luthers Kirchenlieder in Tonsätzen seiner Zeit, ed. K. Ameln (Kassel, 1934) [contains 6 pieces]

Magnificat octo tonorum (Dresden, 1557)
Catechesis musicis inclusa, 3vv (Nuremberg, 1559) [7 motets]
Geistliche und weltliche teutsche Geseng, 4–5vv (Wittenberg, 1566) [91 pieces]; 2 ed. O. Kade in A. W. Ambros: *Geschichte der Musik*, v (Leipzig, 1881), 421, 424
Liber primus [15] sacrarum cantionum (Dresden, 1570)
Officia de nativitate et ascensione Christi (Dresden, 1574)
Schöne und auserlesene deudsche und lateinische geistliche Gesenge (Dresden, 1577) [20 German and 4 Latin pieces]
Missa super 'Ich weiss mir ein fest gebauets Haus', 5vv, 1568[1]; 7 motets in 1554[11], 1564[1], 1568[21], 1571[17]

Mass, 4vv, *D-Mbs* 43; Missa 'Doulce memoire', 6vv, inc., *Z* 100, 4; Missa 'Pis ne me peult', 5vv, *Mbs* 43; Missa 'Praeter rerum seriem', 6vv, *Mbs* 43; Missa 'Regnum mundi', vv, ed. in MAM, xiv (1965); Missa 'Wo der Herr nicht bauet das Haus', 5vv, inc., *Z* 100, 4
5 motets, *Mbs* 43; 22 proper motets, *Mbs* 28
Further masses and motets in libraries in Ansbach, Dresden and Zwickau

BIBLIOGRAPHY
O. Kade: *Mattheus le Maistre* (Mainz, 1862) [contains edns. of 20 pieces]
A. Sandberger: *Beiträge zur Geschichte der Bayerischen Hofkapelle unter Orlando di Lasso* (Leipzig, 1894–5) [1st and 3rd vols. only]
H. Osthoff: *Die Niederländer und das deutsche Lied* (Berlin, 1938, 2/1967)
H. Federhofer: 'Jugendjahre und Lehrer Rogier Michaels', *AMw*, x (1953), 223
W. Boetticher: *Orlando di Lasso und seine Zeit* (Kassel, 1958)
F. Blume: *Geschichte der evangelischen Kirchenmusik* (Kassel, rev. 2/1965; Eng. trans., enlarged, 1974 as *Protestant Church Music: a*

History)
D. C. Gresch: *Mattheus Le Maistre: a Netherlander at the Dresden Court Chapel* (diss., U. of Michigan, 1970)
R. Caspari: *Liedtradition im Stilwandel um 1600*, Schriften zur Musik, xiii (Giebing über Prien, 1971)
D. C. Gresch: 'Mattheus Le Maistre's Polyphonic *Officia*', *MQ*, lx (1974), 94   LOTHAR HOFFMANN-ERBRECHT

Lemberg (Ger.). L'VOV (i).

Lemblin, Lorenz. *See* LEMLIN, LORENZ.

Le Menu. French firm of music publishers. Christoph Le Menu de St Philbert (c1720–1780) began publishing in Paris in the 1740s by issuing his own compositions, including some *cantatilles*, motets and a *Méthode de musique*. In 1774 or 1775 he was succeeded by Mme Le Menu, who joined forces with Mme Boyer about 1776. In 1783 Mme Boyer was succeeded by her husband, who published works both with Mme Le Menu and alone and who acquired Venier's plates about 1784. In 1790 Mme Le Menu ceased her activities and the music publisher Lobry possibly took over her business; Boyer himself continued publishing until 1796, when he was succeeded by Naderman. At the beginning Le Menu had published mainly *cantatilles*, motets and *ariettes*. Later the number of instrumental works published grew, and included symphonies and concertos, but the firm's particular interest was in chamber music by contemporary French, Italian, German, Austrian and Bohemian composers.

BIBLIOGRAPHY
C. Hopkinson: *A Dictionary of Parisian Music Publishers, 1700–1950* (London, 1954)
C. Johansson: *French Music Publishers' Catalogues of the Second Half of the Eighteenth Century* (Stockholm, 1955)   CARI JOHANSSON

Lemeshev, Sergey (Yakovlevich) (*b* Knyazevo, Tver govt., 10 July 1902; *d* Moscow, 1977). Soviet tenor. In 1925 he graduated from Raysky's class at the Moscow Conservatory, then studied under Stanislavsky at the Bol'shoy Opera Studio. He made his début in 1926 in Sverdlovsk, and until 1931 sang there and in Tbilisi. In 1931 he joined the Bol'shoy Theatre. Lemeshev was among the most admired Soviet singers of his time. His lyrical voice, with its individual tone, and his heartfelt sincerity imbued his operatic heroes with special charm, and his performances were noted for their intelligence, fastidious detail and fine acting. His impressive gallery of roles included Lensky, Bayan (*Ruslan and Lyudmila*), Vladimir (*Prince Igor*), Berendey and Levko (*The Snow Maiden* and *May Night*), Vladimir in Nápravník's *Dubrovsky*, Gounod's Faust and Romeo, the Duke of Mantua and Count Almaviva. Lemeshev also enjoyed widespread popularity as a concert and recital artist and singing folksongs. As a director he produced *La traviata* in 1951 at the Malïy Theatre, Leningrad, and *Werther* in 1951 at the Bol'shoy. He also made successful films and published *Put' k iskusstvu* ('The path to art', Moscow, 1968). He was made People's Artist of the USSR in 1950.

BIBLIOGRAPHY
M. L'vov: *S. Ya. Lemeshev* (Moscow and Leningrad, 1947)
E. Grosheva: *S. Ya. Lemeshev* (Moscow, 1960)   I. M. YAMPOL'SKY

Lemière [Le Mière, Lemierre] de Corvey, Jean Frédéric Auguste (*b* Rennes, 1770; *d* Paris, 19 April 1832). French composer. He attended the *maîtrise* at Rennes and wrote his first compositions before receiving formal musical training; among his early works was an opera, *Constance*, allegedly produced at Rennes in 1790. In 1792 he moved to Paris, where he studied harmony with Berton and wrote *opéras comiques* with astonishing rapidity. His main career, however, was military, and though he was fortunate to work for several years under a music-loving commander, his participation in numerous campaigns (including the battle of Waterloo), severely interrupted his musical output; between 1798 and 1818 he wrote only two stage works. He returned to Paris in 1817 and composed more *opéras comiques*, none of which was particularly well received. His meagre military pension was not, however, enough to support his family, and though he gained some income by proofreading music, he died (of cholera) in a state of relative poverty. According to Fétis, Lemière de Corvey's best and most successful opera was *Andros et Almona* (1794). His other compositions include light chamber and piano works, and collections of romances.

WORKS
STAGE
(*all opéras comiques and produced in Paris, unless otherwise indicated*)
Constance (?opéra comique, 1), ? Rennes, 1790; Les chevaliers errants (1), Théâtre Montansier, 1792; Crispin rival (1), Théâtre Montansier, 1793; Le poëme volé (1), Théâtre Montansier, 1793; La reprise de Toulon par les français (1, A. Duval), Opéra-Comique (Théâtre Favart), 21 Jan 1974, ov. (Paris, 1793); Andros et Almona, ou Le français à Bassora (1, L. B. Picard, Duval), Opéra-Comique (?Théâtre Favart), 4 or 5 Feb 1794
Le congrès des rois (Desmaillots [A. F. Eve]), Opéra-Comique (Théâtre Feydeau), 26 Feb 1794, collab. Berton, Grétry, Méhul, Kreutzer, Cherubini, Dalayrac, Solié, Devienne, Jadin, Trial *fils*, Deshayes, Blasius; Scene patriotique, Théâtre Favart, 1794; Babouc (4), Opéra-Comique (Théâtre Feydeau), 1795; L'écolier en vacances (1), Opéra-Comique (Théâtre Favart), 1795 [doubtful attribution]; Les suspects (1). Théâtre Louvois, 19 May 1795; La blonde et la brune (1), Théâtre Feydeau or Théâtre Louvois, 1795; La moitié du chemin (3). Théâtre Louvois, 1796; La paix et l'amour (1), Lille, 5 Dec 1797
Les deux orphelines (1), Théâtre des Amis des Arts, 26 May 1798; Les deux crispins (1, Lemière de Corvey), Théâtre Molière, 16 June 1798; La maison changée (1), Théâtre Molière, 1798; Le porter d'eau (1), 'en provence', 1801; Henri et Félicie (3), 'en provence', 1808; La cruche cassée, ou Les rivaux de village (1/2, Lemière de Corvey), Opéra-Comique (Théâtre Feydeau), 24 Dec 1818 (Paris, ?c1819); La fausse croisade (2, Lepoltevin de St Alme, J.-B.-R.-B. V. d'Epagny), Opéra-Comique (Théâtre Feydeau), 12 July 1825
Les rencontres (3, J. B. Vial, Mélesville [A. H. J. Duveyrier]), Opéra-Comique (Théâtre Feydeau), 11 June 1828; Le testament (2, de Sauer, Saint-Geniez), Odéon, 22 Jan 1827, ?pasticcio of Rossini; arrs. of Fr. versions of Rossini's La donna del lago, 1825, Tancredi, 1827

OTHER WORKS
La bataille de Jéna gagnée sur les prussiens, orch, op.36 (Paris, ?1806), arr. pf (Paris, 1806)
Chamber: 3 duo concertants, harp, pf, opp.23–4, 28 (Paris, ?1805); Trio, harp, hn, bn (Paris, n.d.); 3 vn sonatas (Paris, n.d.); 2 pf sonatas, opp.3, 8 (Paris, n.d.); Sonata, pf 4 hands, op.9 (Paris, n.d.); other chamber, pf works, contredanses, studies
Romances, opp.17, 25, 32, 37; others in Le porte-feuille du troubadour, ed. Lemière de Corvey (Paris, ?1821)
Music for military band

BIBLIOGRAPHY
*Fétis*B
F. Clément and P. Larousse: *Dictionnaire lyrique, ou Histoire des opéras* (Paris, 1867–9, 3/1905/R1969)   JEFFREY COOPER

Lemlin [Lemblin, Lemlein], Lorenz (*b* Eichstätt, c1495; *d* after 1549). German composer. He probably attended the cathedral school in Eichstätt, receiving his first music instruction from the Kapellmeister Bernhard Adelmann. In 1513 he entered Heidelberg University, where he received the bachelor's degree on 13 November 1514. He was a priest, joining the Heidelberg court chapel, where he became Kapellmeister under Elector Ludwig V (*d* 1544). As the teacher of the choirboys

Jobst von Brandt, Georg Forster, Caspar Othmayr and Stephan Zirler he was at the head of the so-called 'Heidelberger Liedmeister', who were still in close contact in later years. Forster's song publications included the works of his colleagues and in 1549 he dedicated to Lemlin the *Dritte Theil schöner, lieblicher, alter und neuer deutscher Liedlein*.

Lemlin's creative powers were too limited for him to be considered the leader of a school of songwriting. Certainly the 'Liedmeister' were indebted to their teacher for many suggestions about composition, but these did not result in a homogenous style. Lemlin's output was relatively small and not widely circulated in the first half of the 16th century. The 15 surviving secular songs are conservative in their imitative pairing of parts at the beginning and in their rigid cantus firmus treatment. Such a technique shows appreciation of the considerably more inspired examples by Paul Hofhaimer and Heinrich Finck. His most popular work, the six-voice *Der Gutzgauch auf dem Zaune sass*, in its imitation of the cuckoo's call has the lightheartedness of a real folksong. His motets are more homophonic with shorter phrases, reflecting the influence of the humanist ode compositions and the new stylistic tendencies of the late Netherlands masters,

WORKS

Edition: *Georg Forster, frische teutsche Liedlein (1539–1556)*, I–II, ed. K. Gudewill and H. Siuts, EDM, 1st ser., xx (1942/R), lx (1969) [G i–ii]

SECULAR

Ach höchster Hort, vernimm mein Wort, 4vv, G i, 76; Ach höchste Zir, auff all mein Gir, 4vv, G i, 20; Der Gutzgauch auf dem Zaune sass, 6vv, G ii, 42; Der Mey wil sich mit Gunsten beweisen, 4vv, G i, 66; Des Spilens ich gar kein Glück nit han, 4vv, G i, 121; Ein Beumlein zart, 4vv, G i, 37; Ernstliche Klag, 4vv, G i, 155; Ich Armer klag, 4vv, G i, 38; Ich gwahrts noch gut, 4vv, G i, 162; Lust und Freud thet mich umbgeben gar, 4vv, 1549[37]; Mich jammert sehr, 4vv, G i, 128; Tag, Nacht ich ficht, 4vv, G i, 82; Von Herzen gern, on all Beschweren, 4vv, G i, 131; Was sterblich Zeyt, mir Freuden geyt, 4vv, 1549[37]

SACRED

Converte nos Deus, 2vv, 1545[6]; Deus adiuva me, 3vv, 1541[2]; Deus in adiutorum, 4vv, 1542[6]; Grates nunc omnes, 8vv, 1564[1]; In convertendo Dominus, 4vv, 1542[6]; In manus tuas, Domine, 4vv, 1538[1]; Memento mei, 5vv, 1540[7]; Nisi Dominus, 4vv, 1542[6]; Oramus Domine, 8vv, *D-Kl* 4° Mus.38, Nr.4; Vivo ego dicit Dominus, 3vv, 1542[8]

BIBLIOGRAPHY

C. P. Reinhardt: *Die Heidelberger Liedmeister des 16. Jahrhunderts* Heidelberger Studien zur Musikwissenschaft, viii (Kassel, 1939)
H. Albrecht: *Caspar Othmayr* (Kassel, 1950)
G. Reese: *Music in the Renaissance* (New York, 1954, rev. 2/1959)
G. Pietzsch: *Quellen und Forschungen zur Geschichte der Musik am kurpfälzischen Hof zu Heidelberg bis 1622* (Mainz, 1963)
LOTHAR HOFFMANN-ERBRECHT

Lemmens, Jaak Nikolaas [Jacques Nicolas] (*b* Zoerle-Parwijs, Antwerp, 3 Jan 1823; *d* Zemst, nr. Mechelen, 30 Jan 1881). Belgian organist, teacher and composer. He showed remarkable musical ability as a child, studying first with his father, an organist and verger at Zoerle. In 1839 he entered the Brussels Conservatory where he studied the piano, the organ (with Christian Girschner) and composition (with Fétis). Despite an interruption in his studies, during which he was a church organist at Diest, he won first prizes for piano in 1842 and for organ and composition in 1845. On a scholarship from the Belgian government he went to Breslau to study with Adolf Hesse (a pupil of Forkel who had studied with Bach), who taught him traditional German interpretations of Bach; after a year Hesse claimed that he had nothing more to teach Lemmens. On his return to Brussels in 1847 he won second prize in the Belgian Prix de Rome with his cantata *Le Roi Lear* and two

years later was named professor of organ at the conservatory. In 1857 he married Helen Sherrington (*see* LEMMENS-SHERRINGTON, HELEN), a British singer. He resigned from the conservatory and moved to London in 1869, after which he and his wife made several concert tours. He returned to Belgium in 1878 and spent his final years attempting to raise the musical standards of the Catholic church. Under the auspices of the Belgian bishops, he established the Ecole de Musique Religieuse (the Lemmens Institute) at Mechelen, and with Canon Van Demme he founded the Société de St Gregoire for the improvement of church music. His *Ecole d'orgue*, a method adopted at several conservatories, was based on plainsong and avoided the use of Protestant chorales.

As an organist and teacher, Lemmens had great influence in Belgium and France. He was particularly renowned for his pedal technique and skilful registration, which contributed to the creation of a new school of organ playing and an end to the primitive state of organ building in Belgium. His role in the introduction of Bach's organ works in France was continued by his pupils, among whom were Alphonse Mailly, Alexandre Guilmant and C.-M. Widor. His compositions, which include orchestral and sacred vocal works as well as many organ pieces, are seldom performed.

WORKS

Oeuvres inédites (Leipzig, 1883–7) [4 vols., incl. works for org, motets, masses, others]
Vocal: Te Deum, 4vv, orch; motets, acc. org; Le Roi Lear (A. Pujol), cantata, 1847; songs, 1v, pf
Orch: 2 syms.
Org: 3 sonatas (Paris, 1876); [10] Improvisations (Brussels, n.d.); offertories; studies; other pieces
Pieces for harmonium; pieces for pf, incl. 2 sonatas, mentioned in *FétisB*
Pedagogical: *Ecole d'orgue basée sur le plain-chant romain* (Brussels, 1862)

WRITINGS

Du chant grégorien, sa mélodie, son rythme, son harmonisation (Ghent, 1886)

BIBLIOGRAPHY

FétisB
J. Duclos: Introduction to J.-N. Lemmens: *Du chant grégorien* (Ghent, 1886), pp.xv–xlix [essay on Lemmens's life and works; incl. list of works]
R. Vannes: *Dictionnaire des musiciens (compositeurs)* (Brussels, 1947)
N. Dufourcq: 'La pénétration en France de l'oeuvre d'orgue de J. S. Bach', *ReM*, xiii (1932), 363

PATRICK PEIRE

Lemmens Institute. Belgian institute of church music founded by JAAK NIKOLAAS LEMMENS, opened in Mechelen in 1879; *see also* LOW COUNTRIES, §5.

Lemmens-Sherrington [née Sherrington], **Helen** (*b* Preston, 4 Oct 1834; *d* Brussels, 9 May 1906). English soprano, wife of Jaak Nikolaas Lemmens, whom she married in 1857. She came of a family who had lived for several generations at Preston. Her mother was a musician. In 1838 they emigrated to Rotterdam, and there Helen Sherrington studied with Verhulst. In 1852 she entered the Brussels Conservatory and took first prizes for singing and declamation. On 7 April 1856 she made her first appearance in London and soon rose to the position of leading English soprano, both in sacred and secular music; after the retirement of Clara Novello in 1860 she had no rival. She appeared in English opera from 1860 to 1865, and at Covent Garden in 1866, but found her place more in concert and oratorio. During the 1870s she formed part of the vocal quartet most in demand for festivals, with Janet Patey, Sims Reeves and Charles Santley. After her husband's death in 1881 she retired to Brussels, but continued to sing occasionally in England. Her last appearance was in 1894.

BIBLIOGRAPHY
Obituary, *MT*, xlvii (1906), 395
H. Davey: 'Lemmens-Sherrington, Helen', *DNB*
GEORGE GROVE/BRUCE CARR

Lemnitz, Tiana (Luise) (*b* Metz, 26 Oct 1897). German soprano. She studied music in Metz with Hoch and then for three years with Anton Kohmann in Frankfurt am Main. She made her début at Heilbronn in 1920 in Lortzing's *Undine*, and from 1922 to 1928 was at Aachen. She became leading lyric soprano at Hanover (1928–33) and then, after a year in Dresden, joined the Berlin Staatsoper in 1934, remaining there until she retired in 1957. In Berlin she sang lyric and lyric-dramatic parts in the German, Italian, French and Russian repertories. Her roles ranged from Mimì and Micaela to Aida and Desdemona, from Pamina and Mařenka to Sieglinde. Later she sang the Marschallin, Milada in Smetana's *Dalibor*, Jenůfa, and Nastasia in Tchaikovsky's *The Enchantress*.

Lemnitz made her Covent Garden début in 1936 as Eva and immediately established herself as one of the most sensitive and finished artists to have come out of Germany. Her Octavian was considered one of the best ever heard; and when she sang a deeply touching Pamina, in which her exquisite *pianissimo* was employed to the full, she was hailed as the finest interpreter of the part since Claire Dux. Apart from her London appearances before World War II and two appearances at the Teatro Colón in Buenos Aires, Lemnitz's career was mostly confined to central Europe. As a singer of lieder she was no less distinguished; her final appearance was in a concert of Brahms, Wolf and the Wagner Wesendonk Songs in Berlin on 7 April 1957.

BIBLIOGRAPHY
R. Seeliger: 'Tiana Lemnitz', *Record Collector*, xv (1963), 29 [with discography by R. Seeliger and B. Park]
HAROLD ROSENTHAL

Lemoine. French family of music publishers. The firm was founded in 1772 by Antoine Marcel Lemoine (*b* Paris, 3 Nov 1753; *d* Paris, April 1817); he was a guitarist, author of a guitar method, violist, theatre orchestra director and composer. His publications include Méhul's *Messe solennelle*, composed for Napoleon's coronation (1804). His eldest son François (*d* 1840) published independently under the name Lemoine aîné (1809–40, succeeded by his widow, 1841–51). Another son, Antoine Henry Lemoine (*b* Paris, 21 Oct 1786; *d* Paris, 18 May 1854), succeeded him in 1816. A successful piano teacher and a harmony student of Reicha, he published most of Chopin's music and firmly established the company's production of instructional materials with Berlioz's *Traité d'instrumentation* (1844) and his own methods for piano, harmony and solfège.

Achille-Philibert Lemoine (*b* Paris, 15 April 1813; *d* Sèvres, 13 Aug 1895), son of Antoine Henry Lemoine, became a partner in 1850 and was director from 1852 to 1895. In 1858 he added engraving and printing to the business and began publication of *Panthéon des pianistes* (about 600 compositions). He acquired Schönenberger's catalogue (1862) and in 1885 inaugurated a branch in Brussels with *Le chant classique*, edited by Gevaert. His four sons became partners in 1871. They were Henry-Félicien Lemoine (*b* Paris, 8 April 1848; *d* Paris, 24 April 1924), director from 1895 to 1924; Gaston Lemoine (*b* c1851); Léon Lemoine (*b* Paris, 1855; *d* Paris, 1916), who left the firm in 1900; and Achille Lemoine (*b* 1857).

Henry Jean Lemoine (*b* Paris, 10 April 1890; *d* Paris, 20 Nov 1970), son of Gaston and successor to Henry-Félicien, entered the firm in 1907. He became a partner (1920) and director (1924–70). He acquired the extensive theatrical and symphonic catalogue of Lucien Grus in 1932. André Lemoine (*b* Paris, 5 April 1907), son of Henry-Félicien, became a partner (1946) and later co-director. Max Lemoine (*b* Paris, 27 June 1922), son of Henry Jean, became a partner (1955) and later also a co-director. Publications by Editions Henry Lemoine have continued to emphasize instruction, ballet and opera.

ROBERT S. NICHOLS

Lemoyne, Gabriel. French pianist and composer, son of JEAN-BAPTISTE LEMOYNE.

Lemoyne [Moyne], Jean-Baptiste (*b* Eymet, Dordogne, 3 April 1751; *d* Paris, 30 Dec 1796). French composer. He was brought up by his uncle, the *maître de chapelle* at Périgueux. In 1770 he went to Berlin with a theatre company, and he held a minor appointment with the Crown Prince of Prussia while he studied under J. G. Graun, Kirnberger and J. A. P. Schulz. He then obtained a post in Warsaw, where his opera *Le bouquet de Colette* was produced with his pupil Antoinette Clavel (Mme de Saint-Huberty) in the cast; she was later to contribute much to his first Parisian success, *Phèdre*, by her performance in the title role. Lemoyne was in Paris by about 1780. His first serious opera, *Electre*, was dedicated to Marie-Antoinette with flattering references to Gluck, whose methods he claimed to follow. The work was poorly received; Gluck dissociated himself from Lemoyne, and the latter accordingly took Piccinni as a model for *Phèdre*. In 1787 he visited Italy, presumably to study the musical style then rapidly coming into vogue in Paris.

In spite of its universal critical rejection, *Electre* is Lemoyne's most interesting work. It makes striking use of free, short and abbreviated musical forms, and in the heroine's role uses a highly expressive recitative, seasoned with musical repetitions akin to the technique of leitmotif. The orchestration is frequently crude, but the quiet ending, as Orestes is pursued off the stage by the Furies, is noteworthy; Lemoyne repeated the effect, with more subtlety, in *Phèdre* and *Nephté*. The weakest parts of *Electre* are those in which purely musical invention is required, rather than declamation and orchestral effects; the dances are poor, and the longer arias weak in melody and design. *Phèdre* contains only a residue of the leitmotif technique, and although Lemoyne improved in aria writing and his operas became less uneven in quality, his originality became diluted. *Nephté* contains some fine scenes, and was his greatest success in tragedy – he was called on to the stage after the first performance, a favour then quite unusual at the Opéra – and it gave rise to the Abbé Toscan's pamphlet in which Lemoyne is considered to have surpassed Gluck by adding melodic sweetness to dramatic power. Lemoyne had less talent for comedy, but the slight charms of *Les prétendus*, enhanced by the unusual orchestral use of the piano, kept it in the repertory for 294 performances until 1827. Lemoyne's later works, including some with Revolutionary themes, are of decreasing interest and aroused little enthusiasm.

Lemoyne's son, Gabriel Lemoyne (*b* Berlin, 14 Oct 1772; *d* Paris, 2 July 1815) was a pianist and composer. He went to Paris as a boy with his father and studied the piano under C.-F. Clément and J. F. Edelmann. About 1800 he undertook a concert tour in France and the Netherlands with the violinist Lafont; but he lived chiefly by teaching the piano in Paris. He also edited a journal for the publication of rondeaux, *romances*, and similar small-scale compositions. He wrote three *opéras comiques*, one (*L'entresol*, 1802) in collaboration with L. A. Piccinni. His output consists mainly of vocal romances and instrumental music, which includes some chamber works, two piano concertos (Paris, 1813) and, for solo piano, sonatas, caprices, fantasias and a toccata. Tasteful rather than adventurous, his music is typical of a prolific and complicated period in the development of piano music.

WORKS

PO – *Paris, Opéra*   PF – *Paris, Théâtre Feydeau*

Le bouquet de Colette (French opera, 1), Warsaw, 1775

Electre (tragédie, 3, N. F. Guillard), PO, 2 July 1782 (n.d.)

Phèdre (tragédie lyrique, 3, F.-B. Hoffman), Fontainebleau, 26 Oct 1786 (n.d.)

Nadir, ou Le dormeur éveillé, 1787, unperf.

Les prétendus (comédie lyrique, 2, M. A. J. Rochon de Chabannes), PO, 2 June 1789 (n.d.)

Nephté (tragédie lyrique, 3, Hoffman, after T. Corneille: Camma), PO, 15 Dec 1789 (n.d.)

Les pommiers et le moulin (comédie lyrique, 1, Forgeot), PO, 22 Jan 1790 (n.d.)

Louis IX en Egypte (opera, 3, Guillard and Andrieux), PO, 15 June 1790, ballet in *F-Po*

Elfride (drame héroïque, 3, Guillard), Paris, Favart, 15 Dec 1792

Silvius Nerva, ou La malédiction paternelle (Beffroy de Régny), 1792, unperf., *Po*

Miltiade à Marathon (opera, 2, Guillard), PO, 3 Nov 1793

Toute la Grèce, ou Ce que peut la liberté (tableau patriotique, 1, Beffroy de Regny), PO, 5 Jan 1794

Le compère Luc (opéra comique, 2), PF, 19 Feb 1794

Le batelier, ou Les vrais sans-culottes (opéra comique, 1, Rézicourt), PF, 12 May 1794

Le mensonge officieux (1, N. J. Forgeot), PF, ?13 March 1795

L'île des femmes (opera, 2), 1796, unperf.

Other stage works: Storm scene for Gossec: Toinon et Toinette, Berlin, 1772; many airs de ballet for productions at PO, *Po*; many excerpts from above operas pubd separately; Ode sur le combat d'Ouessant, perf. Paris, Concert Spirituel, 1778; airs

BIBLIOGRAPHY

FétisB

G. L. G. Toscan: *De la musique et de Nephté: aux mânes de l'abbé Arnaud* (Paris, 1790)

F. M. Baron von Grimm: *Correspondance littéraire, philosophique et critique* (Paris, 1813); complete, uncensored edn., ed. M. Tourneux (1877–82)

J. Rushton: 'An Early Essay in "Leitmotiv": J. B. Lemoyne's "Electre"', *ML*, lii (1971), 387

JULIAN RUSHTON

Le Munerat, Jean (*fl* 1490). French scholastic active in Paris. He studied with two celebrated masters, Jean Raulin and Louis Pinelle, and described himself as *concentor* of the Collège Royal de Navarre. In 1490 he brought out for the clergy and students of the college a new *Martirologium* (based on that of Usard), to which he appended two short treatises. One gives the rules for reciting the Divine Office laid down by the Council of Basle (1431–49). The other is Le Munerat's own *De concordia grammatice et musice in ecclesiastico officio*, a short work throwing much light on plainsong performance in late 15th-century France, particularly in Paris, Bourges and Sens. Singers were clearly in disagreement over questions of rhythm and underlay. Le Munerat demonstrated the existence of several styles and advocated their use in different situations. One style (cantillation) involves the technique of speech recitation

with measured syllables, another for florid chant allows the music to be mistress of the words, and a third for psalmody combines recitation and measured syllables with fixed melodic formulae at intonations. Le Munerat's reputation lasted well into the 18th century; Lebeuf quoted him several times and mentioned his important editorial work, drawing attention to his fine edition of the Paris Breviary (1492).

BIBLIOGRAPHY

J. de Launoy: *Regii Navarrae gymnasii parisiensis historia* (Paris, 1677)

J. Lebeuf: *Traité historique et pratique sur le chant ecclésiastique* (Paris, 1741)

Sister Thomas More [M. Berry]: *The Performance of Plainsong in the Later Middle Ages and the Sixteenth Century* (diss., U. of Cambridge, 1968) [incl. text and Eng. trans of *De concordia*]

MARY BERRY

Lenaerts, René Bernard (Maria) (*b* Bornem, 26 Oct 1902). Belgian musicologist. He trained for the church and was ordained priest in 1927 and canon in 1955. While he was at the theological seminary at Mechelen he also studied at the Lemmens Institute, and took the doctorate in Germanic philology at Louvain in 1929 with a dissertation on Netherlands polyphonic song in the 16th century. He pursued further musicological studies under André Pirro in Paris (1931–2), and began his teaching career in secondary schools at Geel and Antwerp. He then taught at the Catholic University of Louvain, as junior lecturer (1944), lecturer (1946) and as full professor of musicology (1949–73); his great achievement there was to develop an excellent department of musicology. In 1953 he was visiting professor at Columbia University and the University of California at Berkeley. From 1958 to 1971 he was reader in Renaissance music history at Utrecht University (in succession to Smijers).

In 1955 he became a member of the committee of the IMS and an active member of the Royal Academy of Belgium. For a number of years he also served on the committees of the Belgian and Dutch associations for music history and was on the editorial staff of *Revue belge de musicologie*. In 1959 he became editor of Monumenta Musicae Belgicae. His numerous travels in Germany, England, Italy and Spain in search of unknown Netherlands polyphonic music in 15th- and 16th-century manuscripts resulted in several articles and editions and in the compilation of catalogues of old Netherlands polyphony. His perceptive and fluently written contributions, substantial despite their habitual brevity, to congress reports, Festschriften, periodicals and encyclopedias, are based on a thorough study of musical source material, long experience as a teacher and a wide knowledge of cultural history.

WRITINGS

Het Nederlands polifonies lied in de zestiende eeuw (diss., U. of Louvain, 1929; Mechelen and Amsterdam, 1933)

Oude Nederlandse muziek (Brussels, 1937)

'Notes sur Adrien Willaert', *Bulletin de l'Institut historique belge de Rome*, xv (1935), 107, 236

'La chapelle de Saint-Marc à Venise sous Adriaen Willaert (1527–1562)', *Bulletin de l'Institut historique belge de Rome*, xix (1938), 205–55

'Van Monteverdi tot Bach', *Algemene muziekgeschiedenis*, ed. A. Smijers (Utrecht, 1938), 167–247 (rev. 4/1947), 169–244

Johann Sebastian Bach (Diest, 1943)

'The 16th Century Parody Mass in the Netherlands', *MQ*, xxxvi (1950), 410

'Contribution à l'histoire de la musique belge de la Renaissance', *RBM*, ix (1955), 103

Belangrijke verzamelingen Nederlandse muziek uit de zestiende eeuw in Spanje (Brussels, 1957)

De Nederlandse muziek uit de vijftiende eeuw (Louvain, 1959)

'Paesi Bassi', *LaMusicaE*

'Erasmus en de muziek', *Erasmus plechtig herdacht* (Brussels, 1969), 75
'Musical Structure and Performance Practice in Masses and Motets of Josquin and Obrecht', *Josquin des Prez: New York 1971*, 619
'Die Kirchenmusik der Niederländer', *Geschichte der katholischen Kirchenmusik*, ed. K. G. Fellerer, i (Kassel, 1972), 438

EDITIONS

P. de la Rue: Missa de beata virgine; Missa de virginibus (O quam pulchra est); Missa de Sancta Anna, MMBel, viii (1960) [with J. Robijns]
Nederlandse polyfonie uit Spaanse bronnen, MMBel, ix (1963)
Die Kunst der Niederländer, Mw, xxii (1962; Eng. trans., 1964)
P. de Monte: New Complete Edition (Louvain, 1975–) [with others]

BIBLIOGRAPHY

AMe
J. Coppens and M.-L. Stockman: 'Lenaerts, René', *Katholieke Universiteit Leuven: Bibliographia Academica*, x, 1957–63 (Louvain, 1964), 417 [incl. list of publications]
Lovaniensia: Academisch nieuws (van de) Katholieke Universiteit Leuven (1967), no.1, p.80
J. Robijns, ed.: *Renaissance-Muziek 1400–1600: donum natalicium René Bernard Lenaerts* (Louvain, 1969), 7 [incl. J. Robijns: 'Professor Dr. René Bernard Lenaerts bij zijn 65ste verjaardag', 7 and full bibliography]

GODELIEVE SPIESSENS

L'Enclos [Lenclos, Lanclos, la Douardière], **Henri de** (*b* ?Touraine, 1592–3; *d* 1649). French lutenist and composer. He was probably a gentleman. He became skilled in arms and horsemanship as well as at music and played the lute. As an officer he was attached to the household of the Duke of Elbeuf and later to that of the Marshal of S Luc. Following his conversion to the ranks of the freethinkers he soon came to scorn music. In 1632 he killed a nobleman of the royal household in a duel and was obliged to go into exile. Mersenne spoke highly of him as a lutenist and ranked him equal to the Gaultiers and Blancrocher. Ennemond Gautier was his friend and composed *Tombeau de L'Enclos* in his memory. There are pieces by him in Lord Herbert of Cherbury's Lutebook (*GB-Cfm*) and in L. de Moy: *Le petit bouquet de frise orientale* (MS dated 1631, *D-ROu*). He also contributed to the lost *Suittes faciles pour une flute ou un violon et basse continue* (Amsterdam, 1703). His daughter was Ninon de l'Enclos, celebrated leader of Parisian society, to whom he taught singing and the lute.

BIBLIOGRAPHY

M. Mersenne: *Harmonie universelle* (Paris, 1636/*R*1963), book 2: 'Des instrumens'
C. Nuitter and E. Thoinan: *Les origines de l'opéra français* (Paris, 1886)
M. Brenet: 'Notes sur l'histoire de luth en France', *RMI*, vi (1899), 1
E. Mague: *Ninon de l'Enclos* (Paris, 1925)
T. Dart: 'Lord Herbert of Cherbury's Lute-book', *ML*, xxxviii (1957), 136

JOËL DUGOT

L'Enclos, Ninon de. French singer and lutenist, daughter of HENRI DE L'ENCLOS.

Lendvai, Ernő (*b* Kaposvár, 6 Feb 1925). Hungarian musicologist. He studied the piano at the Budapest Academy of Music (1945–9). He has been director of the Szombathely Music School (appointed 1949) and the Győr Conservatory (appointed 1954) as well as professor at the Szeged Conservatory (from 1957); he has also lectured on musical analysis at the Budapest Academy of Music (1954–6 and from 1973). After serving as a music producer for Hungarian radio (1960–65) he concentrated on music research.

Lendvai is an outstanding Bartók scholar who through his radical methods and searching analyses has transformed the previously accepted view of Bartók's style. His writings show a preoccupation with melodic, harmonic and formal structure and describe the syn-

thesizing character of Bartók's music, in which the traditions of European art music and eastern folk music are assimilated. Defining the proportions of its construction, he based his analysis on the golden section, the proportionate relationship found in natural objects and used particularly in classical architecture. Lendvai's first papers (in *Zenei szemle*, xx, 1947–8), published while he was a student, were analyses of Bartók's *Improvisations, Night Music* and Sonata for Two Pianos and Percussion, which he followed with a general study, 'Bevezetés a Bartók-művek elemzésébe' ('Introduction to the analysis of Bartók's works'), and a book on Bartók's style with detailed analyses of the Sonata for Two Pianos and Percussion and Music for Strings, Percussion and Celesta. He then turned to Bartók's stage works and *Cantata profana*; he has analysed nearly all Bartók's major works. In *The Poetic World of Bartók*, intended for the general reader, Lendvai discussed the *Two Portraits, Two Images*, Four Orchestral Pieces, Dance Suite, Violin Concerto, Divertimento and the six string quartets. He has also done some research on Kodály's compositions, and specializes in interpretative analysis; in 1967 he published a book on Toscanini's interpretations of Beethoven.

WRITINGS

'Bevezetés a Bartók-művek elemzésébe' [Introduction to the analysis of Bartók's works], *Zenetudományi tanulmányok*, iii (1955), 461–503; Fr. version in *Bartók: sa vie, son oeuvre* (Budapest, 1956, 2/1968), 88–161; Ger. version in *Bartók: Weg und Werk* (Budapest, 1957, 2/1972), 95–137
Bartók stílusa [Bartók's style] (Budapest, 1955)
'Bartók und die Zahl', *Melos*, xxvii (1960), 327
'A Kékszakállú herceg vára' [Prince Bluebeard's Castle], *Magyar zene*, i (1960–61), 339–87
'Der wunderbare Mandarin', *SM*, i (1961), 363–431
'Bartók pantomimja és táncjátéka' [Bartók's pantomime and ballet], *Zenetudományi tanulmányok*, x (1962), 69–187
'Duality and Synthesis in the Music of Béla Bartók', *New Hungarian Quarterly*, iii/7 (1962), 91; also in *Module, Proportion, Symmetry, Rhythm* (London, 1966), 174
Bartók's Dramaturgy: Stage Works and Cantata Profana (Budapest, 1964)
'A műalkotás egysége Verdi Aidájában' [The unity of the composition in Verdi's *Aida*], *Magyar zene*, v (1964), 490–522; Ger. trans. in 'Verdis Formgeheimnisse', *I° congresso internazionale di studi verdiani: Venezia 1966*, 157
'Bartók und der goldene Schnitt', *ÖMz*, xxi (1966), 607
Toscanini és Beethoven (Budapest, 1967); Eng. version in *SM*, viii (1966), 217–90
'Über die Formkonzeption Bartóks', *SM*, xi (1969), 271
Bartók költői világa [The poetic world of Bartók] (Budapest, 1971)
Béla Bartók: an Analysis of his Music (London, 1971)
'Allegro barbaro', *Magyar zenetörténeti tanulmányok* (Budapest, 1973), 257
Bartók és Kodály harmóniavilága [The harmonic world of Bartók and Kodály] (Budapest, 1975)

MÁRTA PAPP

Lendvay, Kamilló (*b* Budapest, 28 Dec 1928). Hungarian composer. He studied composition with Viski at the Budapest Academy of Music and appeared as a theatre conductor, notably as musical director of the State Puppet Theatre from 1960. His subsequent posts have included those of artistic director of the Hungarian People's Army Ensemble (1966–8), conductor (from 1970) and musical director (from 1973) of the Capital Operetta Theatre, and professor at the academy (from 1973). He has received two Erkel Prizes (1962, 1964).

Like many composers of his generation, Lendvay has followed the traditions of Bartók and Kodály. The most characteristic features of his earlier music, in melody, rhythm and harmony, were all derived from the former. In 1965, however, this style changed when he composed the Four Duos for flute and piano and the *Four Invocations* for orchestra. The change was not radical, but it did show the influence of contemporary trends; and the works he went on to compose in the mid-1970s, particularly, draw on the Second Viennese School and on modern Polish music. The Cello Concerto, for example, is very concise by comparison with his previous compositions, consisting of a single movement based on four themes. In another later piece, *Hangulatok* ('Dispositions') for cimbalom, he was able to discover new sound effects and technical solutions.

WORKS
(selective list)

Stage: A bűvös szék [The magic chair] (comic opera for television, 1), 1972
Orch: Tragikus nyitány [Tragic ov.], 1958; Mauthausen, 1958; Concertino, pf, wind, perc, harp, 1959; Vn Conc., 1961–2; 4 Invocations, 1966; Vc Conc., 1975
Choral: 3 Male Choruses, 1959; Téli reggel [Winter morning], unacc., 1966; Orogenesis, oratorio, 1969; Oratorium Rákócziensis, T, Bar, male vv, orch, 1975
Solo vocal: A rendíthetetlen ólomkatona [The indomitable tin soldier], narrator, orch, 1961; Kocsiút az éjszakában [Cart way in the night], A, ens, 1970
Chamber: Fantasy, vn, pf, 1951; Rhapsody, vn, pf, 1955; Str Qt, 1962; 4 Duos, fl, pf, 1965; Chamber Conc., 13 insts, 1969; Kifejezések [Expressions], 11 str/str orch, 1974; Hangulatok [Dispositions], cimb, 1975

Principal publisher: Editio Musica

ANTAL BORONKAY

Lenear. *See* LANIER family.

Lenepveu, Charles (Ferdinand) (*b* Rouen, 4 Oct 1840; *d* Paris, 16 Aug 1910). French composer and teacher. On his father's insistence he went to Paris to study law, but was also able to study music seriously there. After two years he submitted a cantata for the centenary of the Société d'Agriculture et de Commerce of Caen, which was accepted and performed there on 29 July 1862. He then entered the Paris Conservatoire and joined A. Thomas' composition class, winning the Prix de Rome in 1865.

While in Rome Lenepveu entered a competition organized by the minister of fine arts in 1867 and his opera, *Le Florentin*, was immediately accepted as the winner, but the war delayed its production and when it was finally given at the Opéra-Comique in 1874 it failed. Meanwhile Lenepveu had resumed studies in counterpoint with Chauvet. On 20 May 1871 he produced a requiem at Bordeaux, sections of which were played at the Concerts du Conservatoire on 29 May 1872; but he wrote little else. After the failure of *Le Florentin* he was unable to get his opera *Valléda* produced in France, and so brought it to London, where it was performed in Italian with Patti in the principal part at Covent Garden in July 1882.

Lenepveu taught harmony at the Paris Conservatoire from 1880 to 1894, and composition from 1894; he published *Cent leçons d'harmonie* (1896–8). Koechlin described him as an 'honest academic', which indicates both his increasing interest in teaching and his growing pedantry. Apparently he could not accept the harmonies that begin Fauré's *Le parfum impérissable* and opposed Florent Schmitt's winning the Prix de Rome. He was made Chevalier de la Légion d'honneur in 1887, and elected to the Institute in 1896.

WORKS
(all printed works published in Paris)

5 dramatic works, incl.: Le Florentin (3, M. de Saint-Georges), 1867, Paris, Opéra-Comique, 26 Feb 1874 (1874); Jeanne d'Arc (3, P. Allard), Rouen Cathedral, 1 June 1886 (1886); Valléda (4, A. Chal-

lamel, J. Chantepie, after Chateaubriand: Les martyrs), London, Covent Garden, 4 July 1882 (1883)
9 choral and orchestral works, incl.: 2 requiems, 1871, 1893; Scene from Hernani (Hugo), Act 5 (1881); Hymne funèbre et triomphale (Hugo), Rouen, 1889 (1895); Ode triomphale à Jeanne d'Arc (Allard), Rouen, 1892 (1895)
Other works for orch and for solo pf (1869–97)

BIBLIOGRAPHY
R. de Saint-Arroman: *Charles Lenepveu* (Paris, 1898)
A. Dandelot: *La Société des Concerts du Conservatoire* (Paris, 1923)
C. Koechlin: *Gabriel Fauré* (Paris, 1927, 2/1949; Eng. trans., 1945)
R. Dumesnil: *La musique française contemporaine* (Paris, 1949)

ADOLPHE JULLIEN, GUSTAVE FERRARI/
DAVID CHARLTON

Léner Quartet. Hungarian string quartet. Its members all studied at the Musical Academy of Budapest. Jenő Léner, the leader (1894–1948), Joseph Smilovits, the second violinist (*b* 1894), and Sandor Roth, the viola player (1895–1951), were pupils of Jenő Hubay; Imre Hartman, the cellist (*b* 1895), was a pupil of David Popper. At the outbreak of revolution in 1918 the four musicians, by this time members of the Budapest Opera orchestra, retired to a remote Hungarian village to study chamber music. A year later they made their début in Budapest. In 1920 they appeared in Vienna before an international gathering of musicians, among them Ravel, who invited them to Paris the following year. Within a few years they had established themselves throughout Europe and, after their New York début in 1929, in the USA, as one of the world's most distinguished ensembles. Their frequent recitals in London between 1922 and 1939 included complete performances of the Beethoven quartets, one of which formed part of the centenary celebrations in 1927, and a series illustrating the historical development of the string quartet.

Their playing was remarkable above all for rich and mellow tone-quality combined with an unusually homogeneous blend of the four instruments, finesse and beauty of phrasing, and immaculate ensemble. The extraordinary smoothness and finish of their performances were universally acknowledged; but there were critics who found them over-sophisticated at times – particularly in works demanding rugged strength. Their playing of Mozart won the most consistently high praise. Among their many gramophone records are the complete quartets of Beethoven, and works by Brahms, Debussy, Dvořák, Haydn, Mozart (including a famous recording of the Oboe Quartet with Leon Goossens), Ravel, Schubert, Schumann and Wolf. Works dedicated to them include Respighi's *Quartetto dorico* (1924), as well as a quartet by Eugene Goossens and a trio by Casella which, with other papers, were lost at the beginning of the war. Léner was the author of *Technique of String Quartet Playing* (London, 1935).

ROBERT PHILIP

Leng, Alfonso (*b* Santiago, 11 Feb 1894; *d* Santiago, 11 Nov 1974). Chilean composer. In 1905 he enrolled at the Santiago National Conservatory, but he remained there for less than a year. He then joined a group of self-taught musicians of the same generation, among them García-Guerrero, Lavin, Bisquertt and Cotapos, and together they began studies of music of the past and present. Leng's Piano Preludes (completed 1906) pointed to the development of a style deeply rooted in German late Romanticism, a style which reached a high level of maturity and individuality in the *Doloras* for piano (1914) and the symphonic poem *La muerte de Alsino* (1920). During this period he was studying at the dental school of the University of Chile, and he subsequently established himself as an odontologist of international repute. However, he continued to compose works of distinction, depth and originality, receiving the National Arts Prize in 1957. His songs are particularly outstanding.

WORKS
(selective list)
Orch: La muerte de Alsino, sym. poem, 1920; Canto de invierno, 1933; Fantasia, pf, orch, 1936
Vocal: Ps lxxvii, chorus, orch, 1967; songs to Fr., Ger. and Span. texts
Pf: Preludes, completed 1906; 5 doloras, 1914; 2 sonatas, 1950, 1973

Principal publisher: Instituto de Extensión Musical

BIBLIOGRAPHY
Revista musical chilena (1966), no.98 [Leng issue]
Composers of the Americas, xv (Washington, DC, 1968), 158
JUAN A. ORREGO-SALAS

Lengnick. English firm of music publishers. It was founded in 1893 by Alfred Lengnick (d 1904) in London. Lengnick had been appointed the British agent for the N. Simrock catalogue, and the company expanded quickly. After his death the company was acquired by Schott and was incorporated as a limited company in 1924. Although it was sole British agent for several European publishers, its main success lay with the promotion of the Simrock catalogue, especially the works of Brahms and Dvořák. But it did maintain its own publishing programme, first specializing in educational music and later expanding to include symphonic and chamber works by contemporary British composers, including Alwyn, Arnold, Maconchy, Reizenstein, Rubbra, Simpson and Wordsworth. Alfred Lengnick & Co. eventually bought the complete Simrock catalogue up to and including 1954; the firm acts as British Commonwealth agents for CeBeDeM and Donemus. In 1964 it moved to South Croydon.

BIBLIOGRAPHY
'Alfred Lengnick & Co', MO, xxxv (1911–12), 805
ALAN POPE

Leningrad. City in the Soviet Union. Founded in 1703, St Petersburg, as it was then called, was for much of the 18th and 19th centuries the capital city of Russia (only after the October Revolution was Moscow established as the permanent capital). On 31 August 1914 the German name was abandoned in favour of the Russian form Petrograd, and the city was renamed Leningrad on 26 January 1924.

1. General. 2. Theatres. 3. Court chapel. 4. Concerts and music societies. 5. Amateur music-making. 6. Music education. 7. Musicology and criticism. 8. Publishing and instrument making. 9. Libraries.

1. GENERAL. From its foundation St Petersburg was at the fore of Russian musical culture. Under Peter the Great a new national importance was attached to art: the role of music increased in the church, with *partesnoye peniye* (part-singing), and at court and in everyday urban life with the *kantï* and *psalmï*. The celebrations in honour of the capture of Schlüsselburg (1702), the founding of the new capital on the Neva (1703), the victory at Poltava (1709) and the signing of the Peace of Neustadt with the Swedes required new forms of community music-making: trumpets and kettledrums and large ensembles of wind instruments were used for open air festivals, and by a special *ukaz* (order) wind bands were established in military units in 1711. In 1718 string ensembles were also introduced for the 'assemblées' (court balls), of which there were about 30 a year. An *ukaz* of 1713 enlisted the services of a choir

of hand-picked singers for state celebrations; half a century later this choir was to serve as the basis of the Pridvornaya Pevcheskaya Kapella (court chapel choir). In 1729 an orchestra was organized at the court, in 1736 the first operatic productions were staged, and in 1750 the Czech Jan Mareš founded a unique horn band. Attendance at theatrical events became obligatory for the St Petersburg nobility, and prominent magnates (Menshikov, Stroganov, Yaguzhinsky and others) established their own instrumental ensembles and private theatres, mostly using their own serfs but also employing some foreign artists. Against this background the work of the native Russian composers centred on St Petersburg (including Pashkevich, Fomin, Bortnyansky, Trutovsky and Khandoshkin) began to develop. In 1759 the first Russian musical publication appeared: *Mezhdu delom bezdel'ye, ili sobraniye raznïkh pesen* ('Idleness in activity, or a collection of varied songs'), compiled by Grigory Teplov. Arrangements of Russian folksongs were also published (Trutovsky's in 1776–95 and Pratsch's in 1790), as well as collections of keyboard and guitar music. The first music library was opened in 1798. In the last third of the 18th century the musical life of St Petersburg became still more active: commercial concerts were given in the houses of the nobility (the first concert organizations had appeared in the 1770s), and operas by Russian, Italian and French composers were performed in the theatres. Folk festivals and celebrations were accompanied by choral singing, and Russian horn bands became a common feature along many of the canals and rivers of the capital.

In the first decades of the 19th century Russian music, with St Petersburg as its centre (musical Moscow developed later, from the second half of the century), entered a period of rich maturity. The work of Glinka is inseparable from the development of St Petersburg's artistic culture. His immediate predecessors all lived in St Petersburg: in the sphere of song there were Alyab'yev and Varlamov (a pupil of the court chapel choir), in stage music Verstovsky (who moved to Moscow in 1824), Davïdov (also a pupil of the choir) and Cavos; Kozłowski and others were all in St Petersburg, and Glinka's younger contemporary Dargomïzhsky spent his whole life there. At that time the repertory of the music theatres was governed by the conservative tastes of the imperial court, unlike concerts, which were directed to a wider circle of listeners. Thus, in the quarter-century of Alexander I's reign the Russian share of new operatic productions was less than a third. This situation deteriorated even further in the reign of Nicholas I (i.e. during the years when Glinka and Dargomïzhsky were flourishing), when Russian singers were forced to give up their theatre to an Italian opera company. However, the social developments of the late 1850s and early 1860s created a favourable climate for the consolidation of Russian art. Dargomïzhsky formed a connecting link between Glinka and the representatives of the St Petersburg-based Five – Balakirev, Borodin, Musorgsky and Rimsky-Korsakov, with Stasov as their literary champion. Serov, too, was a supporter of Russian music. At the same time Anton Rubinstein contributed much to the musical life of St Petersburg by organizing the concerts of the Russian Musical Society (from 1859) and by founding the Conservatory (1862); among its first graduates was Tchaikovsky, who lived in St Petersburg until 1866. The music and musical institutions (notably the Mariinsky Theatre) of St Petersburg won wide recognition abroad. Glazunov and Lyadov stood out among its composers in the 1880s, and Stravinsky and Prokofiev in the first decade of the 20th century. Among performers, the pianist Anna Esipova, the violinist Leopold Auer (a professor at the St Petersburg Conservatory from 1868), the cellists Karl Davïdov and Alexander Verzhbilovich and many others were notable. Strong ties with Moscow enriched the musical life of the capital. The first performances of many works by Moscow composers (for example Tchaikovsky, Skryabin and Rakhmaninov) took place in St Petersburg, and such well-known Moscow artists as Shalyapin, Sobinov and Koussevitzky were constantly performing there. Dyagilev's ballet company, which strengthened the world-wide renown of Russian art from 1907 onwards, was linked with St Petersburg.

The October Revolution of 1917 signalled the start of a new epoch in the musical culture of Petrograd–Leningrad. The organization of concert and theatre life was altered, and composers were given new ideals for their creative work: art was to serve the people, to satisfy the spiritual needs of the masses and to draw them into the building of a new culture. Theatres, schools, publishing houses and music shops were nationalized; music education was expanded, and a variety of amateur artistic enterprises developed. During World War II Leningrad's musical institutions were evacuated, but their work did not come to an end. For example, the Philharmonic Orchestra, evacuated to Novosibirsk, gave 538 concerts in three years, performing 1500 works, of which over 300 were being heard in Novosibirsk for the first time. Leningrad composers, scattered in different towns in the country, actively pursued their work, writing symphonies, concertos, a series of orchestral suites, operas, ballets and many songs and choruses. Nor was musical activity halted during the siege of Leningrad (Beethoven's Ninth Symphony was performed in October 1941, Shostakovich's Seventh in August 1942, etc).

In 1944 and 1945 the evacuees were able to return to Leningrad. The city had suffered severely in the war years: concert and theatre buildings were partly destroyed and needed repair, and losses in human terms were felt, too: some musicians had died, others had gone to Moscow (Asaf'yev, Sofronitsky, Shostakovich and others). The recovery did not take long, however. The ranks of composers and performers were strengthened by fresh forces, and concert and theatre life attained still greater breadth. Today Leningrad and Moscow are the most important centres of musical culture in the USSR.

2. THEATRES. The first theatre in St Petersburg was erected in 1722–3, at a time when Italian singers were beginning to visit the city. The first opera written in Russia, *Tsefal i Prokris* ('Cephalus and Procris'), by Francesco Araia, with a text by Sumarokov, was produced in 1755. After Araia, who lived in St Petersburg from 1735 to 1759, Manfredini (1758–69 and 1798–9), Galuppi (1765–8), Paisiello (1776–83), Sarti (1784–1802), Traetta (1768–75) and Cimarosa (1789–91) worked at the Russian court. Talented Russian composers of stage works (Sokolovsky, Pashkevich, Fomin and Bortnyansky) also began to emerge in the 1770s and 1780s. By the end of the 18th century St Petersburg had many theatres besides those at the imperial palaces of Tsarskoye Selo, Gatchina,

Peterhof and Oranienbaum. The Bol'shoy Kamennïy Teatr (Large Stone Theatre) was built in 1757 and continued until the 1880s, when it was rebuilt for the conservatory; also there were the Ermitazhnïy Teatr (Hermitage Theatre) at the Winter Palace (from 1783), the Derevyannïy or Malïy Teatr (Wooden or Small Theatre) on Kamennïy Ostrov, the Vol'nïy (Free) Theatre in the Field of Mars, etc. From 1783 they were governed by a specially established committee, and until the beginning of the 19th century drama and opera productions were staged alternately. The separation of opera from drama companies took place in 1803 under a new system for the imperial theatres. However, during the first half of the 19th century the Russian opera company had to face strong competition from Italian opera troupes on tour in St Petersburg. Even though the Russian opera could offer such outstanding singers as Osip Petrov and Anna Petrova-Vorob'yova, conductors of the calibre of Caterino Cavos (who directed the opera for over 40 years from 1798 to 1840) and artists like Andreas Roller, the nobility still showed a preference for the Italians. (The Russian ballet company, headed by the well-known choreographer Charles Didelot did, however, retain its popularity.) Yet the first performances of Glinka's *A Life for the Tsar* (1836) and *Ruslan and Lyudmila* (1842) at the Bol'shoy Theatre were events of great significance in the history of the nation's music.

In 1860 the Mariinsky Theatre (see illustration) was opened on the site of the former Teatr-tsirk (Theatre-circus) which had been burnt in 1859, and rebuilt by the architect Alberto Cavos, son of Caterino. It was here in the 19th century that the first performances of a series of operas by Russian composers were given, including Musorgsky's *Boris Godunov* (1874), Rimsky-Korsakov's *The Maid of Pskov* (1873) and *The Snow-maiden* (1882), and Tchaikovsky's *The Queen of Spades* (1890). Well-known singers regularly appeared there, among them Elizaveta Lavrovskaya, Yuliya Platonova, Fyodor Komissarzhevsky, Fyodor Stravinsky (father of Igor), Mariya Slavina, Medea and Nikolay Figner, Ivan Ershov (the best interpreter of Wagner in Russia), Shalyapin and Sobinov. Conductors included Konstantin Lyadov (father of the composer, working there until 1869), Nápravník (1863–1916) and Albert Coates (1910–19). As a result of the success of the Mariinsky Theatre, the Italian opera company, which had been active in St Petersburg for about 100 years, was disbanded at the beginning of the 1880s. The Russian theatre's fame (it was one of the most important theatres in Europe) was increased by its excellent ballet company, which Marius Petipa directed for many years (1869–1910); he had lived in Russia from 1847. Many of the ballet company's choreographers and soloists (above all Nizhinsky) later took part in Dyagilev's Ballets Russes in Paris. The opera company of the Mariinsky Theatre also put on public performances in the vast hall of the Narodnïy Dom (People's House) from 1909 until 1923. The experimental Teatr Muzïkal'noy Dramï (Musical Drama Theatre) came into being in 1912, but lasted for only a short time; productions were mounted in the great hall of the conservatory and conducted by Mikhail Bikhter.

After the October Revolution the Mariinsky Theatre was proclaimed a state institution; in 1920 it was termed 'academic' and in 1935 was renamed the Teatr imeni S. M. Kirova (Kirov Theatre). It seats 1621, and was re-equipped between 1963 and 1970. The repertory, too, has changed: alongside the classics of Russian and Western opera, new works by foreign composers were produced in the 1920s (e.g. Berg's *Wozzeck* in 1927), and later many works by Soviet composers were performed. The theatre's conductors have included Dranishnikov, Daniil Pokhitonov, Ary Pazovsky and Konstantin Simeonov. The theatre's opera company is one of the best in the USSR, and the Kirov Ballet, along with the ballet company of the Moscow Bol'shoy Theatre, is the pride of Soviet choreography.

Leningrad has three opera theatres. In addition to the Kirov, there is the Malïy Opernïy Teatr (Small Opera Theatre) which seats 1212; it was built by Alexander Bryullov to a plan by Karl Rossi in 1833 and rebuilt in 1859. Before the Revolution the theatre was known as the Mikhaylovsky; light entertainment was put on there, and Italian and French companies visited it. The character of the repertory of the Malïy finally took shape in the mid-1920s when intensive work on new productions by Soviet composers began; several important first performances took place there, including Shostakovich's *Lady Macbeth* (1934), Prokofiev's *War and Peace* (1946, 1955) and other operas by Dzerzhinsky and Kabalevsky. The theatre's conductors have included Samosud (1919–36) and Khaykin (1936–44). The third theatre is the Opernaya Studiya Konservatorii (Opera Studio of the Conservatory); it seats 1718, and was opened in 1923, occupying the site of the Teatr Muzïkal'noy Dramï (Musical Drama Theatre) which existed before the Revolution. The first operetta was produced in St Petersburg in 1859; this was Offenbach's *Orphée aux enfers*, given at the Mikhaylovsky Theatre. Operettas were produced at various theatres, mostly the drama theatres. Operetta artists were combined into a single company in 1924, and in 1927 the Teatr Muzïkal'noy Komedii (Musical Comedy Theatre), seating 1580, was formed; its repertory consists mostly of Soviet operettas and musicals.

3. COURT CHAPEL. A large role was assigned to music in the celebrations on the occasion of the victory over the Swedes and the founding of St Petersburg. For this purpose Peter the Great summoned from Moscow the choir of *gosudarevï pevchiye d'yaki* (ruler's singing clerks), who long before had become an essential part of the court ceremonial of Russian princes. The *ukaz* on the formation of such choirs is dated 1479, and was decreed by the founder of the Muscovite state Ivan III, who wanted to safeguard the worship in the Uspenskiy Sobor (Cathedral of the Assumption) in the Kremlin by employing professional singers. In 1713 Peter the Great ordered the choir to be augmented to 60. Thus a choral ensemble was formed in St Petersburg that took part in the liturgy, in official state ceremonies and in court entertainments, and later also in the first theatrical presentations. A 1753 *ukaz* increased its numbers to 100 and made its functions more specific, and in 1763 it was given the title Pridvornaya Pevcheskaya Kapella (court chapel choir). Its first director was Mark Poltoratsky, who held the post for 33 years. Singers underwent preliminary training at Glukhov in the Ukraine, and their singing was perfected in the chapel, where they received professional musical education. In the next century such outstanding musicians as Bortnyansky and Glinka, Balakirev and Rimsky-Korsakov were connected with the court chapel; the choir took part in the first performances in Russia of

The Kirov (formerly Mariinsky) Theatre, Leningrad

Mozart's Requiem (1805) and Berlioz's Requiem, and in the world première of Beethoven's *Missa solemnis* (1824). A boys' choir was also organized by the court chapel; this has given independent concerts since the end of the 18th century. In the 1840s the education of the singers was improved.

After the 1917 Revolution the court chapel's activities were revised and for a time it was called the Narodnaya Khorovaya Akademiya (People's Choral Academy); under its conductor Mikhail Klimov, the choir gave the first performances of Stravinsky's *The Wedding* and *Oedipus rex* and Honegger's *Le roi David*, and performed works by Handel and Bach. The Leningradskaya Gosudarstvennaya Akademicheskaya Kapella imeni M. I. Glinka (Leningrad State Glinka Academic Chapel Choir), as it is now called, is housed in a large building containing the Khorovoye Uchilishche (Choral College), extensive rehearsal accommodation and a concert hall seating 803. Another choir was founded in St Petersburg in the 1880s; with Alexander Arkhangel'sky as its conductor, it toured extensively in Russia and abroad. In the early 1920s it was merged with the chapel choir.

4. CONCERTS AND MUSIC SOCIETIES. The first notice of a public concert appeared in the *Sankt-Peterburgskiye vedomosti* in 1746; until that time concerts had been the privilege of the court and noblemen. From the time of Peter the Great's reforms concerts were frequently given with Russian (mostly serfs) and foreign artists taking part, but regular public concert life started later.

A great number of music lovers organized a Muzïkal'nïy Klub (Music Club) in 1772; later, professional musicians joined it as well and helped to organize the Novoye Muzïkal'noye Obshchestvo (New Music Society). Public chamber and symphony concerts took place in the hall of the Blagorodnoye Sobraniye (Assembly of the Nobility); they became popular, and in 1802 the Sankt-Peterburgskoye Filarmonicheskoye Obshchestvo (St Petersburg Philharmonic Society) was founded. This institution survived for 100 years, and gave 205 concerts in all, but only occasionally from the 1890s. It was on the initiative of this society that the première of Beethoven's *Missa solemnis* took place in St Petersburg in 1824. A wider audience attended the Sunday Muzïkal'nïye Uprazhneniya dlya Studentov Universiteta (musical exercises for students of the university), which took place from about the 1830s.

From the beginning of the 19th century the circle of those attending concerts in large private houses was increased: at Count Wielhorski's the first Russian performances of Beethoven's symphonies took place, at Count Kushelyov-Bezborodko's the Muzïkal'naya Akademiya L'vovïkh (L'vovs' Music Academy) was organized and at Prince Golitsïn's concerts were given from the end of the 18th century (this last venue was also known as the Salle Mme Engelhardt from the beginning of the 19th century until 1846). Among the foreign visitors who appeared at these concerts and in the hall of the Assembly of the Nobility were Liszt (1842, 1843), Clara and Robert Schumann (1844), Berlioz (1847, 1868) and Wagner (1862). In the summer months concerts were given in parks, particularly that of the St Petersburg suburb Pavlovsk (from 1838), where Johann Strauss appeared with his orchestra (first in 1849 and regularly between 1856 and 1865).

The Imperatorskoye Russkoye Muzïkal'noye Obsh-chestvo (Imperial Russian Musical Society), which gave up to 20 concerts a year, was founded in 1859 on the initiative of Anton Rubinstein. This society, which was disbanded in 1917, had branches in many towns in Russia, and the local conservatories came under its authority. As a counterweight to this official organization Balakirev and Lomakin organized the Besplatnaya Muzïkal'naya Shkola (Free Music School), which gave 50 concerts in its 25 years of existence, concentrating on Russian music, particularly the works of the Five. The wealthy benefactor Mitrofan Belyayev had the same aim, and from 1885 the Obshchedostupnïye Russkiye Simfonicheskiye Kontsertï (Russian Public Symphony Concerts) came into being at his expense; they ceased in 1918, but in their first 25 years 680 works by 48 composers were performed at 93 concerts. Belyayev also established the Glinkinskiye Premii (Glinka Prizes), which were awarded each year to Russian composers (between 1884 and 1917, 216 works were awarded prizes). An important role in the propagation of contemporary music was played by a new organization, the subscription Kontsertï A. Ziloti (Ziloti Concerts) at which, besides Ziloti himself, other well-known artists, including foreign ones, appeared in symphonic and chamber music programmes. From 1910 Koussevitzky with his Moscow orchestra, Richard Strauss, Mahler, Reger, Debussy, Schoenberg, Nikisch, Mottl, Mengelberg and others visited St Petersburg–Petrograd. Thus, by the beginning of the 20th century the concert life of St Petersburg was in no way inferior in artistic level and variety to that of other major European centres of musical culture, and in some respects was superior to them, as the Russian seasons organized in Paris by Dyagilev demonstrated.

Before 1917 St Petersburg had only one permanent concert orchestra (theatres, naturally, had their own orchestras). This was the court orchestra, founded in 1882 and conducted by Gugo Varlikh. Its main function was to provide music for ceremonial occasions at the tsar's court, but it also arranged private readings of new works. The Philharmonic (formed officially in 1921) came into being on the basis of this orchestra after the Revolution. Emil Cooper (1921–3), Nikolay Malko (1926–9), Alexander Gauk (1930–3), Fritz Stiedry (1934–7) and Evgeny Mravinsky (from 1938) have been in charge of the Philharmonic's orchestra. The orchestra occupies the building of the former Assembly of the Nobility (built 1834–9, with a façade designed by Rossi); this has a great hall (seating 1318) and (since 1949) a small hall, rebuilt from the former Salle Mme Engelhardt (seating 480). The Philharmonic has two orchestras: the first, the 'academic honoured ensemble', is conducted by Mravinsky; the second, the former orchestra of the Radio Committee (which has been combined with the Philharmonic since 1953), is conducted by Yury Temirkanov. From the members of these orchestras two chamber orchestras are formed as independent ensembles. From the first years of its existence the Philharmonic has done considerable work in cultural education: it publishes pamphlets of programme notes for concerts, arranges discussions with listeners, and plays in various institutions in the city, including factories. It has also arranged public lectures by such speakers as Sollertinsky, Vaynkop, Dolzhansky and Chernov. The repertory of the Philharmonic concerts is very wide: it encompasses all the Russian and world classics, and devotes much attention to contemporary, and above all Soviet, music. Thus it was that in

Leningrad the first performances of the majority of Shostakovich's symphonies took place; at various times Prokofiev, Schreker, Milhaud, Honegger, Casella, Hindemith, Stravinsky and Britten have given concerts of their own music. Special mention should be made of the interest in early music, which has grown in recent years, and, in particular, of the popularity of organ music. The first organ was installed in the city in 1737, and now there are three important organs: in the great hall of the Philharmonic, in the Academic Chapel, and in the small hall of the conservatory. Regular concerts are given in the small hall of the conservatory (with 576 seats), in the Leningrad Concert Hall (since 1967, 3734 seats) and elsewhere. Besides the two Philharmonic orchestras, there are other symphony and light music orchestras, an Orkestr Starinnoy i Sovremennoy Muzïki (Orchestra for Ancient and Modern Music), founded by the conductor Nikolay Rabinovich, and the Vasily Andreyev Orchestra of Folk Instruments, founded in 1886. Radio broadcasts of music have been given in Leningrad since 1925; television has broadcast music programmes since 1938.

During the years of the Soviet state, several other organizations have played an important part in the development of musical culture: the Leningrad branch of the Assotsiatsiya Sovremennoy Muzïki (Association for Contemporary Music) during the second half of the 1920s, the Obshchestvo Druzey Kamernoy Muzïki (Society of Friends of Chamber Music) during the 1920s and 1930s, and the Leningrad branch of the Soyuz Kompozitorov (Union of Composers) since 1932; this last is managed by an elected board and has over 150 members, including both composers and musicologists. The union has its own accommodation, the Dom Kompozitorov (House of Composers), where musical discussions are held and concerts are given.

5. AMATEUR MUSIC-MAKING. There have been gatherings of music lovers in the city since earliest times; usually they took place on the initiative of patrons or leading figures of musical society and satisfied the artistic needs of the educated classes. At the beginning of the 20th century educational activities directed to a wider range of listeners were extended with the so-called Obshchedostupnïye Kontsertï (Popular Concerts), and choral groups were formed in a working-class environment. However, the concept of amateur artistic enterprise itself was firmly established only after the October Revolution. The slogan under which Soviet music developed was 'Muzïka – Massam' (Music for the masses). Hence the huge range of cultural-educational work and the effective involvement of the masses in theatrical and concert activity. Elaborate open-air theatrical productions, such as the *Gimn osvobozhdyonnomu trudu* ('Hymn to liberated labour') and *Vzyatiye Zimnevo dvortsa* ('The capture of the Winter Palace'), were given in Petrograd from 1920, with large choral and instrumental ensembles taking part. Choral Olympiads, directed by the conductor Iosif Nemtsev, an enthusiast for such events, became very important: in 1927 6000 people took part, in 1930 12,000. Berlioz's *Grande symphonie funèbre et triomphale* was performed by combined wind orchestras at the 1932 Olympiad. Workers and students, soldiers and collective farm workers were all encouraged to take part in amateur music-making. For example, over 800 choral and instrumental ensembles took part in the 1956 review. Over 5000 Leningrad students participate in amateur organiza-

tions, the best known of which is the student choir of Leningrad University, which was formed in 1949. Operas are also staged by amateur ensembles, and in this field the Dvorets Kul'turï imeni S. M. Kirova (Kirov Palace of Culture) enjoys a special reputation. In Leningrad province there are over 500 clubs and palaces of culture, which have choral, ballet and orchestral ensembles. They receive great help with the organization of their activities from the Dom Khudozhestvennoy Samodeyatel'nosti (House of Amateur Artistic Enterprises), established in 1937, and by institutions of higher education, such as the Institut Kul'turï imeni N. K. Krupskoy (Krupskaya Institute of Culture), the conservatory and others.

6. MUSIC EDUCATION. The first music school to be established in Russia was the Tantseval'naya Shkola (Dancing School) (1783); Charles Didelot was in charge of it at the beginning of the 19th century, and Marius Petipa during the second half of the century; in Soviet times Agrippina Vaganova was for a long period head of the ballet school. Artists and ballet-masters of international repute (including Pavlova, Ulanova, Nizhinsky, Fokin, Balanchin and many others) have graduated from this school. Until the mid-19th century opera singers studied with actors at a school run by the directorate of the imperial theatres; also, from 1840 classes in various facets of the art of singing were held at the court chapel. Private schools also existed, but their activity was irregular.

A decisive turning-point in music education occurred when the music classes of the Russian Musical Society opened in 1860 on the initiative of Anton Rubinstein. Two years later the conservatory was founded on this basis, with Rubinstein as its director. The conservatory moved several times before settling in the building it occupies today, rebuilt in 1896 from the Bol'shoy Theatre by the architect V. Nikolya. The conservatory has had many renowned professors, including Rimsky-Korsakov (1871–1908), Glazunov (1899–1925; from 1905 he was also director), Lyadov (1878–1914), and in Soviet times Shteynberg, Vladimir Shcherbachov, Shostakovich and others. After the Revolution the conservatory was reorganized under Glazunov's directorship with the help of Ossovsky, Asaf'yev and the other professors. Among its graduates have been Shostakovich, Sviridov, Solov'yov-Sedoy, Dzerzhinsky, Balanchivadze, the musicologists Kushnaryov and Tyulin, the conductors Dranishnikov, Mravinsky and Melik-Pashayev, the organist Braudo, the pianists Sofronitsky, Yudina and Serebryakov and the singers Davïdova and Preobrazhenskaya. Many of these later became professors at the conservatory. There are 1500 students at the Leningrad Conservatory in the departments of piano and organ, orchestra, voice and stage production, conducting, theory and composition. The conservatory has had a special music school for particularly gifted children since 1936, and also has a separate music college. In addition Leningrad has 25 music schools, including the Uchilishche imeni Musorgskovo (Musorgsky College), the Muzïkal'no-Pedagogicheskoye Uchilishche (College of Musical Education), and the Institut Kul'turï imeni N. K. Krupskoy (Krupskaya Institute of Culture). This last has departments for conductors and choral trainers, stage producers and ballet directors; it also has a department for light music, and trains those intending to direct amateur societies.

7. MUSICOLOGY AND CRITICISM. The first writings on music appeared in the 18th century: academician Leonard Eiler published his research on acoustics in 1739, Jacob von Stählin his *Izvestiya o muzïke v Rossii* ('Report on music in Russia') in 1770. In the first half of the 19th century Odoyevsky (from 1824) and Senkovsky (1833–44) were prominent music critics; later in the century such major critics as Serov, Stasov, Cui and Laroche emerged. In the years before the Revolution Ossovsky, Karatïgin and Asaf'yev (Igor' Glebov), well-known figures in Soviet musicology, embarked on their careers; Sollertinsky played a particularly important role among Leningrad critics in the 1920s and 1930s. Critical articles were published in newspapers and magazines of a general sort, and there were also special journals: *Nuvellist* (1840–1905), *Russkaya muzïkal'naya gazeta* ('Russian musical gazette', edited by Findeyzen, 1894–1918), *Muzïkal'nïy sovremennik* ('Musical contemporary', edited by Andrey Rimsky-Korsakov, 1915–17) and others.

The study of music grew stronger and developed on the basis of music criticism. It won recognition and authority, established a new methodology and extended its range after the 1917 Revolution. Scholarly work in Leningrad is centred on the conservatory and the Institut Teatra, Muzïki i Kinematografii (Institute for the Theatre, Music and Cinematography). This institute was one of the first establishments for music research in Russia. In 1910 Count V. Zubov established a library of literature on the arts in his own house; three years later public courses started there, and from 1916 there were lectures on the history of music. The Institut Istorii Iskusstv (Institute for the History of the Arts), with its departments for music history and theory headed by Asaf'yev, was founded in 1920 on the basis of these courses. Renamed later the Institute for the Theatre, Music and Cinematography and partly changed in organizational structure, it remains one of the major centres of scholarship in the USSR. It has departments for music, the study of instruments, the study of sources and folklore, and its annual research journal *Voprosï teorii i estetiki muzïki* ('Questions of music theory and aesthetics') has been published since 1962. The Muzey Muzïkal'nïkh Instrumentov (Museum of Musical Instruments) at the institute was opened in 1951; founded in 1902, it possesses about 2500 instruments. Leningrad musicologists have made an important contribution to Soviet musicology as a whole. Besides Asaf'yev, Ossovsky and Sollertinsky, Leningrad's scholars include the theorists Kushnaryov and Tyulin, the historians Gruber, Druskin, Kremlyov and Orlova, and the folklorists Evgeny Gippius, Eval'd and Rubtsov.

8. PUBLISHING AND INSTRUMENT MAKING. Music printing began in earnest in St Petersburg in the 1730s, and the number of publications has steadily increased since the end of the 18th century. Towards the mid-19th century two music publishing houses became prominent – those of Bernard and Stellovsky (taken over by Gutheil in 1886); in 1869 the firm of Bessel was established, and in 1885 that of Belyayev. Since the Revolution there have been branches of the Gosudarstvennoye Muzïkal'noye Izdatel'stvo (State Music Publishing House) (now Muzïka), and of the Sovetskiy Kompozitor (Soviet Composer) publishing house (since 1957) in Leningrad. The cooperative publishing house Triton (1925–36) brought out novelties of contemporary music and books.

Until 1917 the Becker, Schrider, Diderichs, Offen-

bacher and Rönisch factories produced 80% of all the keyboard instruments (pianos) manufactured in Russia. In 1924 the Krasnïy Oktyabr' (Red October) factory took over production. In addition, there are factories making wind and plucked string instruments (including balalaikas, harps and so on). Some electrical musical instruments were also first produced in Leningrad: the termenvox invented by L. Termen in 1921, and later the emiriton invented by Alexander Ivanov.

9. LIBRARIES. The most important collection of books and music in Russia is in the Leningrad Gosudarstvennaya Publichnaya Biblioteka (State Public Library), formerly the Imperial Public Library. Stasov was in charge of the music section for many years. After the 1917 Revolution the printed and manuscript stock was greatly expanded, thanks to the nationalization of extensive private libraries, in particular those of the Yusupovs and Stroganovs. The library contains about 800 old Russian church documents, many 18th-century *psalmï* and *kantï*, a rich collection of music manuscripts and letters of Russian musicians. The stocks of books and music in the Leningrad Conservatory are also of great value: its record library contains over 13,000 discs and more than 2000 tape recordings. In addition there are important collections of music in the Tsentral'naya Teatral'naya Biblioteka (Central Theatre Library), which includes 18th-century manuscripts. Libraries have also existed at the Philharmonic since 1882, the chapel since its foundation, the Institute for the Theatre, Music and Cinematography since 1910 (it also has a manuscript archive) and the Radio Committee since 1924.

The folklore archive is concentrated in the Institut Russkoy Literaturï: Pushkinskiy Dom (Institute for Russian Literature: Pushkin House) of the USSR Academy of Sciences. This contains over 6000 cylinders, records and tapes, on which there are more than 30,000 recordings of the music of 70 nationalities of the Soviet Union and 17 foreign countries. The systematic recording of folksongs began in 1884, when on the initiative of Balakirev a song commission was established at the Imperatorskoye Russkoye Geograficheskoye Obshchestvo (Imperial Russian Geographical Society), though the first publications of Russian folksongs date from the second half of the 18th century. Subsequently, particularly during the Soviet period, these archives have multiplied, and folklore expeditions are still made today under the auspices of the conservatory and the Union of Composers.

BIBLIOGRAPHY

N. F. Findeyzen: *Ocherk deyatel'nosti Sankt-Peterburgskovo otdeleniya imperatorskovo russkovo muzïkal'novo obshchestva 1859–1909* [An outline of the activity of the St Petersburg branch of the Imperial Russian Musical Society 1859–1909] (St Petersburg, 1909)

——: *Pavlovskiy muzïkal'nïy vokzal: istoricheskiy ocherk 1838–1912* [The Pavlovsk musical pleasure garden: a historical sketch 1838–1912] (St Petersburg, 1912)

P. Stolpyansky: *Starïy Peterburg* [Old St Petersburg] (Leningrad, 1926)

N. F. Findeyzen: *Ocherki po istorii muzïki v Rossii s drevneyshikh vremyon do kontsa XVIII veka* [Essays on the history of music in Russia from earliest times to the end of the 18th century], ii (Moscow and Leningrad, 1929)

V. Muzalevsky: *Stareyshiy russkiy khor* [The oldest Russian choir] (Leningrad, 1938)

Ocherki istorii Leningrada [Essays on the history of Leningrad] (Leningrad, 1955–70)

M. S. Druskin and Yu. V. Keldïsh, eds.: *Ocherki po istorii russkoy muzïki 1790–1825* [Essays on the history of Russian music 1790–1825] (Leningrad, 1956)

V. M. Bogdanov-Berezovsky, ed.: *V godï velikoy otechestvennoy voynï*

[In the years of World War II] (Leningrad, 1959)
I. L. Gusin and V. M. Bogdanov-Berezovsky, eds.: *V pervïye godï sovetskovo muzïkal'novo stroitel'stva* [In the early years of Soviet musical composition] (Leningrad, 1959)
L. A. Barenboym and others, eds.: *100 let Leningradskoy konservatorii: istoricheskiy ocherk* [100 years of the Leningrad Conservatory: a historical sketch] (Leningrad, 1962)
V. M. Bogdanov-Berezovsky, ed.: *Muzïkal'naya kul'tura v Leningrada za 50 let* [Musical culture in Leningrad over 50 years] (Leningrad, 1967)
O. L. Dansker: 'Muzïkal'naya zhizn' Petrograda–Leningrada: kratkiy khronograf' [The musical life of Petrograd–Leningrad: a short chronicle], *Voprosï teorii i estetiki muzïki*, vi–vii, ed. L. N. Raaben (Leningrad, 1967), 306–47
V. Il'in: *Iskusstvo millionov: iz istorii muzïkal'noy samodeyatel'nosti Petrograda–Leningrada* [Art of the millions: from the history of amateur musical activity in Petrograd–Leningrad] (Leningrad, 1967)
L. A. Entelis, ed.: *Leningradskiy gosudarstvennïy ordena Lenina akademicheskiy teatr operï i baleta imeni S. M. Kirova 1917–67* [The Kirov Opera and Ballet Theatre 1917–67] (Leningrad, 1968)
Leningradskiy Malïy teatr operï i baleta [The Malïy Theatre] (Leningrad, 1968)
S. Volkov: *Molodïe kompozitorï Leningrada* [Young composers in Leningrad] (Leningrad and Moscow, 1971)
L. Grigoriev and Ya. Platek: *Leningradskaya gosudarstvennaya ordena trudovovo krasnovo znamenii filarmoniya: stat'i, vospominaniya, materialï* [The Leningrad Philharmonic: articles, reminiscences, materials] (Leningrad, 1972)

MIKHAIL DRUSKIN

Lenja, Lotte. *See* LENYA, LOTTE.

Lennon, John (Winston Ono) (*b* Liverpool, 9 Oct 1940). English pop singer and songwriter, member of the BEATLES.

Leno, Antonio [Antonius] de. *See* ANTONIUS DE LENO.

Lenox. Town in Massachusetts, site of the annual BERKSHIRE FESTIVAL; the Lenox Arts Center, a laboratory for experimental music-theatre, was founded there in 1971.

Lent. *See* LENTO.

Lentando (It.: 'becoming slower'). *See* RALLENTANDO and TEMPO AND EXPRESSION MARKS.

Lentement. *See* LENTO.

Lento (It.: 'slow'). One of the earliest tempo marks to be used in music. Mentioned in passing by Zarlino ('movimenti tardi e lenti'), it was used by Praetorius (*Polyhymnia caduceatrix*, 1619; *Puericinium*, 1621), Thomas Selle (1636) and Schütz. Praetorius (1619) gave the equation *lento vel adagio: tardè: mit langsamen Tact*, and in *Syntagma musicum*, iii (2/1619) equated *adagio: largo: lento: langsam*. The word never achieved the same popularity as *adagio*, *largo* and *grave*; but in French music from Lully onwards it became one of the major tempo marks in its adverbial French form *lentement*. *Sans lenteur* was a particular favourite of François Couperin. Rousseau (1768) gave the French adjective *lent* and its adverb *lentement* as being the same as the Italian *largo*, which he considered the slowest of all tempos; but there is no evidence that his opinion was generally held and he may well simply have been avoiding the dangers of translation by cognate. In the Polonaise of his B minor orchestral suite J. S. Bach marked *lentement* in the violin part but *moderato e staccato* in the flute part: even if this is an oversight it strongly suggests that he thought of *lentement* and *moderato* in the same way.

For bibliography *see* TEMPO AND EXPRESSION MARKS.

DAVID FALLOWS

Lenton, John (*b* mid-17th century; *d* London, ?1718). English violinist, singer, composer and editor. His career as a royal musician is fairly well documented; he was appointed 'musician for the violin' to Charles II on 2 August 1681, a position he retained under James II. In 1685 he joined the King's Private Musick and later that year became a Gentleman Extraordinary of the Chapel Royal. He was reappointed to the private music of William and Mary and in 1691 attended the king on his visit to Holland. He continued as a member of the royal band until 1718, when his name disappears from the records and he may be presumed to have died. Although he served as a violinist for many years the lack of references to him in concert announcements suggests that he was no outstanding performer.

Lenton's compositions include a good deal of incidental music for plays, but little of it is of value; the same may be said of his *Consort of Musick of Three Parts* as far as can be judged from the incomplete surviving copy. A single, incomplete copy is known of his violin tutor *The Gentleman's Diversion* (*GB-CDp*), probably the earliest extant violin tutor in any language. Containing some 30 solos and duets composed for Lenton by his English contemporaries, it is one of several publications reflecting the violin's increasing cultivation by amateurs at the time. Hawkins described its contents, noting its absence of reference to position changing and its warning to the player against holding the violin either under the chin or 'so low as the girdle'.

WORKS

A Consort of Musick of Three Parts (London, 1692), with T. Tollett, incomplete
A Three Part Consort of New Musick . . . Overture, Trios and Ayres, a 3 (London, 1697, 2/1699), with T. Tollett
2 vn pieces in The First Book of Apollo's Banquet (London, 1693[5])
Overtures and act tunes, 4 str, in Harmonia anglicana (London, 1701–5)
Songs and catches in A Third Collection of New Songs, ed. T. D'Urfey (London, 1685[7]), Catch that Catch Can (London, 1685[4]), The Theater of Music (London, 1685[5]–7[5]), The Catch Club or Merry Companions (London, 1720)
Wit and Mirth, ed. J. Lenton (London, 2/1707–9)
The Dancing Master, ii, ed. J. Lenton (London, 1710, 2/1713)
Dialogue: Awake fair Venus, tunes for vn/rec, incidental music for Shakespeare's Othello, overture, airs 'played before the King at his Returne' (1697), *GB-Lbm*
Incidental music for revival of Otway's Venice Preserved (1707), *Lcm*
Instrumental airs in 3 parts, *US-NYp*

WRITINGS

The Gentleman's Diversion, or the Violin explained (London, 1693, 2/1702 as *The Useful Instructor on the Violin*)

BIBLIOGRAPHY

HawkinsH
H. C. de Lafontaine: *The King's Musick* (London, 1909/R1973)
J. Pulver: *A Biographical Dictionary of Old English Music* (London, 1927)
S. Jeans: 'Seventeenth-century Musicians in the Sackville Papers', *MMR*, lxxxviii (1958), 184
M. Tilmouth: *Chamber Music in England, 1675–1720* (diss., U. of Cambridge, 1959), i, 252f
——: 'A Calendar of References to Music in Newspapers published in London and the Provinces (1660–1719)', *RMARC*, i (1961/R), 12, 14, 20, 41, 62, 75, 77

MICHAEL TILMOUTH

Lenya [Lenja], **Lotte** [Blamauer, Karoline Wilhelmine] (*b* Vienna, 18 Oct 1898). American singing actress of Austrian birth. An early ambition to become a dancer led her in 1914 to Zurich where she remained until 1920, studying classical dance and the Dalcroze method, and gaining experience in the opera-ballet at the Stadttheater. She also worked at the Schauspielhaus, and among the artists she encountered there was Frank Wedekind. She was greatly impressed by his stage personality, and in particular his style of ballad singing. She left Zurich for Berlin in 1920 with the intention of making a career there as a dancer. Two years passed before she turned to the spoken theatre, and among those who encouraged her was the distinguished expressionist playwright Georg Kaiser. Her marriage in 1926 to Kaiser's outstanding musical collaborator, Kurt Weill, was followed by her appearance at the 1927 Baden-Baden festival of modern music, where she sang one of the two females roles in Weill's and Brecht's short scenic cantata *Mahagonny*.

Lotte Lenya with Kurt Weill

Her international reputation dates from her creation in 1928 of Jenny in Weill's and Brecht's *Die Dreigroschenoper* at the Theater am Schiffbauerdamm, Berlin, and from the subsequent recordings and film (directed by G. W. Pabst). While continuing a notable career as an actress, she created three further roles in works by Weill, singing Anna in the choral ballet *Die sieben Todsünden* (Paris, 1933), Miriam in *The Eternal Road* (New York, 1937), and the Duchess in *The Firebrand of Florence* (New York, 1945).

Soon after Weill's death in New York she began to devote much of her time to the revival of some of his most important works from the German years. Her live and recorded performances won for her and for Weill a new or renewed reputation in many lands, and established as 'classical' a performing style whose characteristics of timbre and tessitura were markedly different from those of her Berlin years. But what had survived from those years, and most remarkably developed and matured, was that combination of dramatic insight and musical instinct, of intelligence, wit, coolness and passion which arises from a strictly inimitable and seemingly monogamous relationship to the music itself.

Although her tastes in both popular and classical music are broad, as a performer she confined herself almost entirely to the songs of her husband, and to the one extended work he composed especially for her, *Die sieben Todsünden*; this has been enough to establish her as one of the outstanding *diseuses* of the time.

BIBLIOGRAPHY

C. Osborne: 'Berlin in the Twenties: Conversations with Otto Klemperer and Lotte Lenya', *London Magazine*, i/2 (1961), 43

H. Marx, ed.: *Weill-Lenya* (New York, 1976)

DAVID DREW

Lenz, Wilhelm von (*b* Riga, 1 June 1809; *d* St Petersburg, 19 Jan 1883). Russian official and writer on music, of German descent. He was educated in Riga until 1827. The next year he continued his musical studies in Paris as a pupil of Liszt. This was followed by a year in London with Moscheles. After further travels he became Imperial Russian Councillor of State in St Petersburg, where he developed his writing on music, particularly on Beethoven.

Lenz was the first to elaborate the idea, originally suggested by Fétis, that Beethoven's works may be divided into three periods: early, middle and late. Although the book is entitled *Beethoven et ses trois styles*, the tripartite division is made on the arbitrary and unreliable order of opus numbers rather than solely on stylistic grounds. Lenz's biographical writing is based on Ries, Wegeler, and above all Schindler (to Schindler's disgust). His uncritical enthusiasm for Beethoven as both man and musician, along with his romantic bias towards portraying Beethoven as an artistic martyr, provides an example of the kind of writing against which Thayer reacted in his monumental biography. Less recognized, however, is the remarkable thoroughness of Lenz's 'Kritische Katalog' of Beethoven's collected works, including editions and revisions.

WRITINGS

Beethoven et ses trois styles: analyses des sonates de piano suivies de l'essai d'un catalogue critique chronologique et anecdotique de l'oeuvre de Beethoven (St Petersburg, 1852, 3/1855); ed. M. D. Calvocoressi (Paris, 1906)

Beethoven: eine Kunststudie, i–ii (Kassel, 1855); iii/1–2, iv–v: *Kritische Katalog sämtlicher Werke Ludwig van Beethovens mit Analysen derselben* (Hamburg, 1860); ed. A. Kalischer (Berlin, 1908, 3/1921)

Die grossen Pianoforte-Virtuosen unserer Zeit aus persönlicher Bekanntschaft: Liszt, Chopin, Tausig, Henselt (Berlin, 1872; Eng. trans., 1899) [Eng. trans. also in *MMR*, viii (1878), nos.88–91]

BIBLIOGRAPHY

A. F. Schindler: *Biographie von Ludwig van Beethoven* (Münster, 1840, rev. 3/1860; Eng. trans., 1966, as *Beethoven as I Knew him*)

A. Schmitz: *Das romantische Beethovenbild* (Berlin and Bonn, 1927), 18

ELLIOT FORBES

Leo, Magister (*fl* ?late 12th century). Composer or theorist. He was described by Anonymous IV (ed. Reckow, 1967, i, 22) as one of the earliest to have used (or to have written about – the passage is ambiguous) the *ordines* and *colores* of rhythmic modal notation as a means of ordering long and short note values. It is possible that Anonymous IV may have been referring to none other than LÉONIN, whom he discussed and at one point (i, 46) specifically called by this name ('a tempore Leonis'). The attribution of a 'lost' treatise to this Magister Leo rests on a misreading (by Dittmer, 1959; for correction see Waite, *JAMS*, xiv, 157).

See ORGANUM AND DISCANT: BIBLIOGRAPHY.

IAN D. BENT

Leo X, Pope. Patron of music and a member of the MEDICI family.

Leo, Leonardo [Lionardo] **(Ortensio Salvatore de** [di]**)** (*b* S Vito degli Schiavi [now S Vito de Normanni], 5 Aug 1694; *d* Naples, 31 Oct 1744). Italian composer and teacher. He was one of the leading Neapolitan composers of his day, especially of theatre and church music.

1. LIFE. The son of Corrado de Leo and Rosabetta Pinto, he went to Naples in 1709 and became a pupil of

Nicola Fago at the Conservatorio S Maria della Pietà dei Turchini. At the beginning of 1712 his *S Chiara, o L'infedeltà abbattuta*, a *dramma sacro*, was performed at the conservatory; from the fact that it was performed again in the viceroy's palace on 14 February it would seem that Leo's work attracted unusual attention. On finishing his studies he was appointed supernumerary organist in the viceroy's chapel on 8 April 1713 and at the same time was employed as *maestro di cappella* in the service of the Marchese Stella; he is also said to have been *maestro di cappella* at the church of S Maria della Solitaria.

As early as 13 May 1714 his first opera, *Il Pisistrato*, was staged. There followed commissions for opera arrangements, intermezzos and serenatas, and in 1718 a second opera, *Sofonisba*. From *Caio Gracco* (1720) the list of his opera commissions continues without a break up to his death. In 1723 he wrote his first opera for Venice, and in the same year, with *La 'mpeca scoperta*, he turned for the first time to the developing genre of Neapolitan *commedia musicale*; from then on he was regarded as one of the leading composers of comedy.

On Alessandro Scarlatti's death in 1725 Leo was promoted to first organist of the viceregal chapel. In the following years he lost his supremacy as a composer of serious opera in Naples to his rivals Vinci and Hasse, and between 1726 and 1730 he apparently received no commissions for opera at the Teatro S Bartolomeo in Naples. He did however write serious operas for Rome and Venice, and in Naples he pursued his career as a composer of comic operas. After Hasse's departure and Vinci's death in 1730, Leo became the dominant figure in Neapolitan musical life. He succeeded Vinci as *provicemaestro* and on Mancini's death in 1737 he became *vicemaestro* of the royal chapel. He was repeatedly given leave to fulfil commissions for operas elsewhere (1737 Bologna, 1739 Turin, 1740 Turin and Milan), and through the family connections of the Neapolitan royal family he received commissions from the Spanish court. Even greater than his reputation as an opera composer was the esteem he acquired as a composer of oratorios with his settings of Metastasio's *S Elena al Calvario* and *La morte di Abele*.

Leo also became prominent as a teacher: from 1734 to 1737 he taught as *vicemaestro* at the Conservatorio S Maria della Pietà dei Turchini, in 1739 he succeeded Feo as *primo maestro* at the Conservatorio S Onofrio and in 1741 he also took over the duties of *primo maestro* at the S Maria della Pietà dei Turchini in succession to his own teacher, Fago. The *Miserere* for double choir in eight parts and organ (March 1739) appears to be the first of his works aimed at the reform of church music, which are closely connected with his activities as a teacher. In both respects he was in competition with Francesco Durante, who taught at the two other conservatories in Naples. On Domenico Sarro's death (25 January 1744) Leo at last became *maestro di cappella* of the royal chapel. He immediately composed a series of *a cappella* compositions (with continuo) for the use of the royal chapel during Lent and reformed the orchestra of the royal opera, but he died after only nine months in office.

2. WORKS. Leo was the most versatile and technically the most accomplished among the Neapolitan composers of his time. But he lacked both the genius of Pergolesi and the facility of his rivals Vinci and Hasse

(a guard once had to be posted outside his door to force him to finish an opera in time). New versions of his own works play an important part in his output.

Leo's early works are comparatively conservative in character: chamber cantatas, mostly with only continuo accompaniment, still occupy an important place among them, and it was only gradually that he came to favour Metastasio's librettos for his operas. Leo helped to raise the musical standards of both *commedie musicali* and intermezzos. His comedy *Amor vuol sofferenze* (1739), with which he followed up Pergolesi's success in this genre, marks the end of the heyday of Neapolitan musical comedy. In the revivals of his operas *Il Ciro riconosciuto* and *Olimpiade* (1742–3) Leo introduced the chorus into Neapolitan opera. His opera overtures, whose opening movements are in the tradition of the march rather than that of the instrumental concerto, represent an important stage in the development of the pre-Classical symphony.

Leo's reforming activities in sacred music in his last years are seen both in the composition of *a cappella* works (with organ) for the church's times of penance (which, however, are by no means written in the 'old style') and in his use of choral cantus firmi and scholarly contrapuntal techniques in church music with orchestral accompaniment. It is clear that his *Istituzioni o regole del contrappunto* and *Lezioni di canto fermo* were also produced in his last years; he seems to have been in contact with G. O. Pitoni in Rome and Padre Martini in Bologna. Leo's pedagogical and theoretical work was of lasting importance for the Neapolitan school. He is said to have had a difference of opinion with Durante about the consonance of the interval of the 4th, from which the tradition of opposing 'Leisti' and 'Durantisti' schools seems to derive. His most important pupils were Piccinni and Jommelli. Towards the end of the 18th century his *Miserere* played an important role in the rediscovery of the 'church music of the old Italians' and was widely rated as comparable to the works of Palestrina.

WORKS

(presumed lost unless source given)

SERIOUS OPERAS

First performed in Naples unless otherwise stated; most Neapolitan works performed with intermezzos.

RP – *Naples, Real Palazzo*
SB – *Naples, Teatro S Bartolomeo*
SC – *Naples, Teatro S Carlo*

Il Pisistrato (D. Lalli), RP, 13 May 1714
Sofonisba (F. Silvani), RP, 22 Jan 1718
Caio Gracco (S. Stampiglia), RP, 19 April 1720
Arianna e Teseo (P. Pariati), SB, 26 Nov 1721
Baiazete, imperator dei Turchi (B. Saddumene), RP, 28 Aug 1722
Timocrate (Lalli), Venice, S Angelo, carn. 1723
Il Turno Aricino, 1724, collab. L. Vinci
Zenobia in Palmira (Zeno), SB, 13 May 1725, *I-Nc*
Il trionfo di Camilla, regina dei Volsci (Stampiglia), Rome, Capranica, 8 Jan 1726, *A-Wn, D-Dlb*
Il Cid (G. G. Alborghetti), Rome, Capranica, 10 Feb 1727
Argene (S. Biancardi), Venice, S Giovanni Grisostomo, 17 Jan 1728
Catone in Utica (Metastasio), Venice, S Giovanni Grisostomo, carn. 1729, *B-Bc*
Semiramide (Metastasio), 2 Feb 1730
Evergete (Biancardi), Rome, delle Dame, 1731
Demetrio (Metastasio), SB, 1 Oct 1732
Nitocri, regina d'Egitto (Zeno), SB, 4 Nov 1733
Il castello d'Atlante (T. Mariani), SB, 4 July 1734
Demofoonte (Metastasio), SB, 20 Jan 1735; Act 3 by Leo, Act 1 by D. Sarro, Act 2 by F. Mancini, intermezzos by G. Sellitti, *GB-Lbm, I-Nc*
La clemenza di Tito (Metastasio), Venice, S Giovanni Grisostomo, carn. 1735
Emira, SC, 12 July 1735, intermezzos by I. Prota, *I-Nc*
Demetrio (Metastasio), Castello di Torremaggiore, 10 Dec 1735 [different from 1732 setting]

Farnace (Biancardi), SB, 19 Dec 1736, *A-Wn, F-Pc*

Siface (?Metastasio), Bologna, Malvezzi, 11 May 1737; rev. as Viriate, Pistoia, 1740, collab. others

Olimpiade (Metastasio), SC, 19 Dec 1737, *B-Bc, F-Pc, I-Mc, Nc*

Demetrio (Metastasio), pasticcio, SC, 30 June 1738, collab. L. Fago, G. de Majo, N. Logroscino, R. Broschi, A. Amorevole

Il Ciro riconosciuto (Metastasio), Turin, Regio, carn. 1739, *D-Bds, F-Pc, I-Mc, Nc*

Achille in Sciro (Metastasio), Turin, Regio, carn. 1740, *D-Bds, I-Mc, Nc*

Scipione nelle Spagne, Milan, Ducale, carn. 1740

Demetrio (Metastasio), SC, 19 Dec 1741, *F-Pc, I-Mc* [different from previous settings]

Andromaca (A. Salvi), SC, 4 Nov 1742, *I-Nc*

Vologeso, re dei Parti, Turin, Regio, 1744

Prol, arias, comic scenes in F. Gasparini: Eumene, 1 Oct 1715; Arias in Gasparini: Sesostri, re d'Egitto, RP, 4 Nov 1717; Comic scenes in Handel: Rinaldo, RP, 1 Oct 1718; Prol to Vinci: Artaserse, Nuovo, 20 Jan 1738; Arias in G. A. Ristori: Temistocle, SC, 1738 or 1739; Arias in J. A. Hasse: L'Issipile, SC, 19 Dec 1742; Arias in D. Perez: Siroe, re di Persia, *B-Bc*; Aria in Andromeda, pasticcio, *A-Wn*

Doubtful works: Artaserse (Zeno), ?Rome, 1722; ?Carlo Calvo, Lisbon, Rua dos Condes, 1739; Ezio, Modena, 1739; Carlo in Alemagnia, Milan, Jan 1740; Lucio Papirio (Salvi), Venice, 1737, *B-Bc* [1 act], probably by F. Feo

COMIC OPERAS
(*unless otherwise stated, written for Naples*)

NO – *Naples, Teatro Nuovo*   FI – *Naples, Teatro dei Fiorentini*

La 'mpeca scoperta (F. Oliva), FI, 13 Dec 1723

L'ammore fedele (Oliva), FI, 25 April 1724

Lo pazzo apposta (Oliva), FI, 26 Aug 1724

Orismene, ovvero Dalli sdegni l'amore (C. de Palma), NO, 19 Jan 1726

La semmeglianza de chi l'ha fatta (D. Senialbo), FI, aut. 1726

Lo matrimonio annascuso, early 1727

La pastorella commattuta (T. Mariani), NO, aut. 1727

La schiava per amore (Mariani), NO, ? aut. 1729

Rosmene (B. Saddumene), NO, sum. 1730

Amor da' senno [? Amore mette sinno] (Mariani), NO, early 1733

Onore vince amore, FI, 1736

L'amico traditore, FI, carn. 1737

La simpatia del sangue (P. Trinchera), NO, aut. 1737, *F-Pc*

Il conte (G. Federico), FI, 1738

Amor vuol sofferenze [La frascatana; Il cioè] (Federico), NO, aut. 1739; rev. as La finta frascatana, NO, Nov 1744, adds M. Capranica, *A-Wgm, F-Pc, I-Nc*

L'Alidoro (Federico), FI, sum. 1740

L'ambizione delusa (D. Canicà), NO, early 1742, *F-Pc*

Il fantastico, od Il nuovo Chisciotte (Federico), NO, 1743; rev. FI, aut. 1748, adds P. Gomes

La fedeltà odiata, FI, 1744

Rev. of A. Orefice: Le ffente zingare, FI, wint. 1724; rev. of Orefice: La vecchia Travera, NO, 1732; rev. of L. Vinci: La festa di Bacco, NO, 1732; completion of Orefice: Rosilla, NO, aut. 1733

Doubtful works: Il Medo, *B-Bc*; Li mariti a forza (Latilla), NO, 1732; L'Alessandro (Federico), FI, 1741; L'impresario delle Isole Canarie (intermezzo), Venice, 1741; I viaggiatori, Paris, 1754, *F-Po* [identical with unknown work Il giramondo, ? Naples, 1741]; Camilla ed Emilio, *I-Nc*, cited by Eitner

SERENATAS, PROLOGUES, FESTE TEATRALI
(*selective list*)

Il gran giorno d'Arcadia (serenata), Naples, Royal Palace, 1716

Diana amante (serenata), Naples, Royal Palace, 4 Dec 1717

Le nozze di danza (serenata), Naples, Palace of the Principe di San Nicandro, 1718

Serenata commissioned by Nicola Grimaldi in praise of his admiral and officers, Naples, Grimaldi Palace, Jan 1719

Onore e Virtù (prol to Baiazete, imperator dei Turchi), Naples, S Bartolomeo, 1722

Serenata [characters: Speranza, Apollo, Dora, Lacone], for the birthday of Empress Elisabeth, Rome, ambassador's palace, 19 Nov 1733

Le nozze di Psiche con Amore (festa teatrale, G. Baldassare), for the wedding of Carlos III of Naples and Maria Amalia of Saxony, Naples, S Carlo, 23 June 1738, *D-Bds, I-Nc*

Festa teatrale for the wedding of Prince Philip, Madrid, 1739

Serenata del felice parto della regina di Napoli, 1743, collab. G. Manna and N. Logroscino, unperf.

Le nozze di Jole ed Ercole, *D-MÜp*

Flavio e Domizia (componimento pastorale), *D-Bds* (autograph, inc.)

Decebalo (festa teatrale), ? on birth of Princess Maria Elisabeth, 1743, *F-Pc* (inc.)

CHAMBER CANTATAS, ARIAS, DUETS

A complete list is not yet possible; see the catalogues (which differ) in Leo (1905) and Pastore (1957). The principal sources are *A-Wgm, D-Bds, Dlb, KA, Mbs, SWl, F-Pc, GB-Lbm, I-Bc, Mc, Nc*. Numerous

songs, including some from the operas, were published in 18th-century anthologies.

SACRED DRAMAS AND ORATORIOS

S Chiara, o L'infedeltà abbattuta, Naples, Conservatorio di S Maria della Pietà dei Turchini, carn. 1712; Royal Palace, 16 Feb 1712

Il trionfo della castità di S Alessio (C. de Petris), Naples, S Maria della Pietà dei Turchini, 4 Jan 1713, in *F-Pc* (?frag.)

Dalla morte alla vita di S Maria Maddalena, Atrani, nr. Amalfi, 22 July 1722

Oratorio per la Ss vergine del rosario, Naples, Cloisters of S Caterina a Formiello, 1 Oct 1730

S. Elena al Calvario (Metastasio), Bologna, 1734 [? Naples, 1732], *A-Wn, B-Bc, D-Bds, Dlb, GB-Cfm, I-Nc*; sinfonia ed. R. Engländer (London, c1955)

La morte di Abele (Metastasio), Bologna, 1738 [? Naples, 1732], *A-Wn, B-Bc, D-Bds, Dlb, Mbs, I-Bc, Nc*

S Francesco di Paola nel deserto, Lecce, S Maria degli Angeli, 1738

Il verbo eterno e la religione (C. F. Taviani), Florence, 1741

Saul et Gionata. doubtful

Choruses for Sofronia (sacred tragedy), in A. Marchese: *Tragedie cristiane*, ii (Naples, 1729)

OTHER SACRED VOCAL

See complete list in Pastore (1957); principal sources: *A-KR, Wgm, Wn, B-Bc, D-Bds, Dkh, Dlb, DS, Mbs, GB-Cfm, Lbm, I-Bc. Mc, Nc.*

Masses: 6 Neapolitan masses (Ky–Gl), 4 for SSATB, insts, 1 for SATB, insts, 1 for SATB a cappella; miscellaneous mass movts., incl. 5 Credos, vv, insts, 3 Cr–San–Ag, vv, insts

Introits, incl. Introit pel Dì delle Ceneri, 1744, SATB, bc, org; others for Holy Week

Graduals, incl. Laudate Dominum, SATB, insts; Benedicite et venerabilis es, virgo Maria, 2vv, insts; Laudate pueri (alleluia verse), double choir; others for Holy Week

Offertories and communions for Holy Week

2 Magnificat, 1 for SATB, insts, 1 for SSATB, insts

Te Deum, SATB, insts

c22 antiphons, incl. Alleluja, 4vv; 4 Christus factus est, S, insts; 7 Dixit Dominus 4–10vv, insts, 1 ed in *Opera omnia di Giovanni Battista Pergolesi*, xiii (1942); 2 Gloria, 2vv, insts; Haec regina virginum, SATB; 4 Miserere, 4–8vv, insts/org; Miserere, 1739, double choir, org; Salve regina, S, insts, ed. in Die Kantate, iv (Cologne, 1958)

Vesper psalms, incl. Confitebor tibi, Domine (Ps cx), 5vv

5 lessons, 1 responsory, for Holy Week

Litany, 4vv, viol, bc

c10 motets, incl. 2 Heu nos miseros, 1 ed. R. Ewerhart (Altötting, 1958); Praebe virgo, S, org, ed. in Cantio sacra, xv (Altötting, 1957); 1 for double choir

2 hymns, Pange lingua, double choir; A solis, 3vv, bc

Cantata per il miracolo di S Gennaro, 5vv

5 fugues, incl. Tu es sacerdos, SATB, bc, org

INSTRUMENTAL

Ov. in 6 ouverture a più stromenti composte da vari autori, op.5 (Paris, c1759)

Sinfonia a 6, 2 vn, 2 ob, 2 hn, hpd, in Ier recueil de sinfonies de différens autheurs italiens (Paris, c1760)

6 concs., vc, str orch, bc, 1737–8, *I-Mc, Nc* (incl. 1 as Sinfonia concertata, autograph); 1 in D, ed. F. Cilea (Milan, 1934), 1 in A, ed. E. Rapp (Mainz, 1938), 3 ed. in SEM, vii (1973)

Conc., D, 4 vn, bc, *D-Bds*, ed. in Musikschätze der Vergangenheit, xxiv (Berlin, 1952)

Duet in Scielta di 6 duetti . . . composte da vari autori, 2 fl/vn/bn (Paris, n.d.)

Trios in 6 Trios, fl, vn, bn/vc (London, c1795)

14 toccatas, hpd, *I-Mc*, ?1 pubd in The Lady's Entertainment or Banquet of Music, bks.1–2 (London, 1708): some ed. M. Maffioletti, *6 toccate per cembalo* (Milan, 1926); 3 ed. in Antologia di musica antica e moderna per pianoforte, xii (Milan, 1932)

Aria con variazioni, hpd, ?*D-Dlb, I-Nc*

DIDACTIC WORKS

Solfeggi, Partimenti, *A-Wn, D-Bds, I-Bc, Mc*; some pubd in Solfèges d'Italie avec la basse chiffrée (Paris, 1772); also in Nouveaux solfèges d'Italie avec la basse (Paris, c1784); 6 ed. G. F. Malipiero, *6 solfeggi di Leonardo Leo* (Milan, n.d.)

Fugues, 4, 6, 8vv

Istituzioni o regole del contrappunto

Lezioni di canto fermo

BIBLIOGRAPHY
EitnerQ

C. A. de Rosa, Marchese di Villarosa: *Memorie dei compositori di musica del regno di Napoli* (Naples, 1840)

F. Florimo: *La scuola musicale di Napoli e i suoi conservatorii* (Naples, 1880–83/R1969)

G. Leo: *Leonardo Leo, musicista del secolo XVIII e le sue opere musicali* (Naples, 1905)

E. Dent: 'Leonardo Leo', *SIMG*, viii (1906–7), 550

F. Piovano: 'A propos d'une récente biographie de Léonard Leo', *SIMG*, viii (1906–7), 70, 336

K. G. Fellerer: *Der Palestrinastil und seine Bedeutung in der vokalen Kirchenmusik des 18. Jahrhunderts* (Augsburg, 1929/*R*1972)

E. Faustini-Fasini: 'Leonardo Leo e la sua famiglia', *NA*, xiv (1937), 11

F. Walker: 'Cav. Giacomo Leo and his Famous "Ancestor" ', *MR*, ix (1948), 241

U. Prota-Giurleo: 'Breve storia del teatro di corte e della musica a Napoli nei secoli XVII–XVIII', *Il teatro di corte del palazzo reale di Napoli* (Naples, 1952)

F. Schlitzer, ed.: *Tommaso Traetta, Leonardo Leo, Vincenzo Bellini: noti e documenti raccolti da F. Schlitzer*, Chigiana, ix (1952)

G. A. Pastore: *Leonardo Leo* (Galatina, 1957)

H. Hell: *Die Neapolitanische Opernsinfonie in der ersten Hälfte des 18. Jahrhunderts* (Tutzing, 1971)

HELMUT HUCKE

Leo [Leone] **da Modena** (*b* Modena, ?1571; *d* ?1648). Italian writer on music. He was a member of the Jewish community at Mantua and a pupil of SALAMONE ROSSI. He founded the Accademia Musicale Ebraica at Venice, and it functioned between 1629 and 1639. In 1622 he edited Rossi's *Ha-shirim asher lish'lomo*. He also wrote a prefatory essay in which he defended and justified the gradual introduction of polyphony into the synagogue, citing various Talmudic and rabbinical sources in support. To the five traditional divisions of music he added a sixth, which aimed to 'approve music as a practical study, so that when we Jews sing to God we do not sound like dogs or ravens'.

BIBLIOGRAPHY

S. Bernstein: *The Divan of Leo Modena* (Philadelphia, 1932)

S. Simonsohn, ed.: *Leon da Modena: zikne yehuda* (Jerusalem, 1956)

——: *History of the Jews in the Duchy of Mantua* (Jerusalem, 1962–4)

Hebrew Writings concerning Music in Manuscripts and Printed Books from Geonic Times up to 1800, RISM, B/IX/2 (1975)

MARIA BERTUCCIOLI LOPRIORE

Leofric Collectar (*GB-Lbm* Harl.2961). See SOURCES, MS, §II, 3.

Leo Hebraeus [R. Levi ben Gershom [Gershon]; Gersonides; Magister Leon de Bagnols] (*b* Bagnols, *c*1288; *d* Provence, 1344). Jewish neo-Aristotelian philosopher, mathematician and astronomer. He lived in Provence, mostly at or near Avignon, which was one of the few regions to afford protection to Jews in this period of savage persecution. Generally he wrote in Hebrew, but most of his works were soon translated into Latin; these include theological treatises, studies on Averroes and Aristotle and basic treatises on the principles of algebra and geometry. His only work of interest to music historians, *De numeris harmonicis*, was written in 1343 at the request of Philippe de Vitry in order to demonstrate the mathematical validity of granting duple rhythm an equal place with triple rhythm in the Ars Nova mensural system. Mathematical proof was necessary because with four series of proportions, each of which could be ternary or duple, Vitry had to be assured that duplication could never occur among all the possible combinations of proportions; to do each by trial and error would be an enormous undertaking. The proof was simple: it showed that when dealing with the powers of 2 and 3 – except for the proportional pairs: 1, 2 $(3^0, 2^1)$; 2, 3 $(2^1, 3^1)$; 3, 4 $(3^1, 2^2)$; and 8, 9 $(2^3, 3^2)$ – the powers of 2 and 3 and their corresponding products differ from each other by more than unity. The products 9 and below are irrelevant, as for practical purposes the required products must fall between 16 (or 24 as binary *modus* was not used) and 81: *maxima* = 3 *longae* = 9 *breves* = 27 *semibreves* = 81 *minimae* (3^4); *maxima* = 2 *longae* = 4 *breves* = 8 *semibreves* = 16 *minimae* (2^4); between these two occur many products of the combina-

tion of these powers, e.g. 3.3.2.2 (36), etc. The proof followed from the theorem: if $m > 1$ and $n > 2$, $3^m + 1 \neq 2^n$, and if $m > 2$ and $n > 3$, $3^m - 1 \neq 2^n$ (m and n are integers).

Vitry wished to show that, within all possible combinations (even beyond 81), modifications such as points of addition or alteration would not cancel or confuse basic duple or triple divisions. In practical terms Leo's theorem meant that, even without signature, duple and triple time could be recognized in each mensural unit and that the sum total of the smallest units (*minimae*) would determine for each case one, and only one, of the possible basic rhythmic divisions. Leo was thus able to give irrefutable mathematical justification to one of the most complex musical systems ever propounded.

BIBLIOGRAPHY

Jewish Encyclopedia (1904), viii, 26

J. Carlebach: *Levi ben Gerson als Mathematiker* (Berlin, 1910) [incl. edn. of *De numeris harmonicis*, 129]

H. Riemann: *Geschichte der Musiktheorie im IX.–XIX. Jahrhundert* (Berlin, 2/1921), 235; (Eng. trans., 1962/*R*1974)

E. Werner and I. Sonne: 'The Philosophy and Theory of Music in Judeo-Arabic Literature', *Hebrew Union College Annual*, xvii (1943), 564

E. Werner: 'The Mathematical Foundation of Philippe de Vitri's *Ars Nova*', *JAMS*, ix (1956), 128

——: 'Leo Hebraeus', *MGG*

GORDON A. ANDERSON

León, Argeliers (*b* Pinar del Río, 7 May 1918). Cuban composer and ethnomusicologist. He studied composition at the Havana Municipal Conservatory with José Ardévol (1938) and in 1943 became a member of the Grupo de Renovación Musical. From 1938 to 1957 he taught music education, theory and history at the Havana Conservatory, and from 1948 to 1950 he studied Cuban folklore with Fernando Ortiz at Havana University. In 1951 a grant from the University of Chile took him to Santiago to study Chilean folklore; while in South America he lectured in Montevideo, Buenos Aires and Lima. He directed the music section of the Cuban National Library (1959–67) and, from its creation, the institute of ethnology and folklore of the Cuban Academy of Sciences (1961–9). In 1962 and 1969 he did ethnomusicological research in west Africa. He has composed a series of 12-note works, beginning with *Cánticos de homenaje* for orchestra (1958), exploiting Afro-Cuban rhythms. This piquant combination of the austere and the popular has earned him a particular niche in contemporary Cuban composition.

WORKS
(selective list)

Orch: Sinfonía, str, 1946; Suite cubana, str, 1946; Sym. no.1, 1946; Concertino, fl, pf, 1946; Canticos de homenaje, 1958; Sym. no.2, 1962; Sonatas para la Virgen de Cobre, pf, str

Choral: Creador del hombre nuevo, cantata, solo vv, narrator, chorus, ww, perc; 19 other pieces

Inst: Str Qt no.1, 1957; Wind Qnt, 1959; Str Qt no.2, 1961; 3 canciones lentas, gui, 1961; 5 piezas breves, fl, cl, gui, 1971; 7 other pieces

Principal publisher: Biblioteca Nacional José Martí (Havana)

WRITINGS

'Las obras para piano de Amadeo Roldán', *Revista de música*, i (Havana, 1960), 112

Música folklore: yoruba, bantú, abakuá (Havana, 1964)

Música folklórica cubana (Havana, 1964)

'Música popular de orígen africano en América latina', *América indigena*, xxix (1969), 627–64

ROBERT STEVENSON

Leon, Bayani Mendoza de (*b* Manila, 24 Nov 1942). Filipino composer and teacher. He took the BPhil at the University of Santo Tómas (1963), studied at the

Centro Escolar University (BMus in composition) and held a scholarship of the Music Promotion Foundation of the Philippines (1971). Among the various posts he has held as a teacher, writer (he is a gifted poet) and administrator are those of chairman of the Concert Philippines Society (1966–70) and resident composer of the Kalinangan Ensemble of the Philippine Educational Theatre Association (1968).

WORKS
(selective list)

Dramatic: The Golden Earth (dance drama), 1966; Ako [I am] (zarzuela, 3), 1971; film music
Orch: Batong buhay [Live stone], sym. poem, 1968; The Legend of the Sarimanok, 1968; Pag-asa [Hope], 1969; Vertigo Concertino, cl, orch, 1970
Vocal orch: Los penitentes, choral poem, 1967; Alamat ng lupa [Legend of the land], choral drama, 1968; Sisa, choral fantasy, 1968; Be Still my Heart, S, orch, 1971
Chamber: Perlas, vc, pf, 1971; Essay, fl, pf, 1972

LUCRECIA R. KASILAG

Leon, Felipe Padilla de (*b* Penaranda, Nueva Ecija, 1 May 1912). Filipino composer and conductor. He studied at the University of the Philippines Conservatory, where he received a teacher's diploma in composition and conducting (1939), and where he remained as a teacher of theory and composition. Thereafter he was director of the music school at Union College, Manila, and then, during the war, he founded his own music academy. He later taught at the Laperal Piano Academy and lectured on Philippine music in many parts of the country. A grant from the Music Promotion Foundation of the Philippines enabled him to make a study tour of the USA in 1959. Formerly music critic for the *Manila Times* and *Taliba*, he was director of cultural affairs for the city of Manila; he has also held appointments as regent of Manila University, state cultural adviser (1972), president of the National Music Council of the Philippines (until 1973), president of the Philippine Society of Composers, Authors and Publishers, president of the National Band Association, and trustee of the Music Promotion Foundation. Among the many honours he has received are the Rizal Pro-Patria Presidential Award of Merit, the Republic Cultural Heritage Award (1972) and the Araw ng Maynila Cultural Award (1972). An intensely nationalist composer, he employs native features in an impressionist style.

WORKS
(selective list)

Operas: Noli me tangere, opera, 3, 1957; El filibusterismo, opera, 3, 1970
Orch: Banyuhay [New life], sym. poem, 1v, orch, 1947; Cry of Balintawak, sym. poem, 1949; Manila Sketches, 1949; Rosa encantada, sym. poem, 1950; Muntawit [Short songs], 1v, orch, 1950; Concertstück, vn, orch, 1952; Divertimento filipino, 1967; Awit ng buhay [Song of life], sym. drama, Bar, orch, 1969; Rhapsodietta, tpt, perc, 1972; Bataan, sym. poem
Pf: Music Time, 61 educational pieces

LUCRECIA R. KASILAG

León Antiphoner. *See* SOURCES, MS, §II, 9.

Léonard, Hubert (*b* Bellaire, nr. Liège, 7 April 1819; *d* Paris, 6 May 1890). Belgian violinist, composer and teacher. He studied the violin with his father and with August Rouma (1802–74), a pupil of Pieltain active in Liège, and made his début at the Liège Theatre on 13 March 1832. He entered the Brussels Conservatory in 1832, where he studied briefly with François Prume and perhaps with Pieltain. Financial support from the Francotte-Pieltain family enabled him to go to Paris,

where he was a pupil of Habeneck at the Conservatoire (1836–9) and played the violin at the Théâtre des Variétés, the Opéra-Comique and the Académie Royale de Musique (until 1844). He became a friend of Henry Vieuxtemps in 1841.

From 1845 to 1848 Léonard made extensive concert tours throughout Europe, in particular Germany. He married Antonia Stiches de Mendi, a Spanish singer, in 1849 and toured with her in 1852. The following year he succeeded Bériot at the Brussels Conservatory; he remained there until 1866, when he moved to Paris and established himself as a virtuoso, chamber music player, composer and teacher. Except for a brief return to Liège, where he taught at the conservatory, during the Franco-Prussian War, he remained in Paris until his death.

As a virtuoso, Léonard lacked the temperament of Vieuxtemps and the bravura technique of Sivori. But his critics and pupils praised his intonation, his singing tone and his classical and noble style that made him an ideal chamber music player. He was among the first to play the chamber music of Brahms in Paris, and was an ardent champion of Saint-Saëns, Fauré, Lalo and d'Indy. His compositions, which include five violin concertos, fantasias on opera melodies, duos and salon pieces, are not original and did not survive their time; his editions of Baroque and Classical works and his cadenzas to concertos by Beethoven and Viotti were more lasting. His didactic works, highly praised during his lifetime, reveal the intellectual and musical gifts that made him a successful teacher; in the words of his pupil Ovide Musin: 'a great, if not the greatest of all pedagogues ... whose method was designed to develop equally and with uniformity the bowing, [left-hand] technique, style, musical knowledge and comprehension necessary to make a complete artist'.

BIBLIOGRAPHY
FétisB
J. Pazdírek: *Universal-Handbuch der Musikliteratur* (Vienna, 1904–10/*R*1967) [incl. list of works]
O. Musin: *My Memories* (New York, 1920)
E. van der Straeten: *The History of the Violin* (London, 1933/*R*1968), ii
J. Quitin: 'Hubert Léonard', *Bulletin d'information de la vie musicale belge*, viii/6 (1969)

ALBERT MELL

Leonarda, Isabella. *See* ISABELLA LEONARDA.

Leonardo da Vinci (*b* Vinci, nr. Empoli, 1452; *d* château of Cloux, nr. Amboise, 2 May 1519). Italian artist and scientist. Although his 'universal genius' has always been recognized, his musical thought and activities have received little serious attention and have never been treated systematically. It is significant that the standard works on Leonardo, even in the 20th century, either do not mention music at all, or merely quote remarks by Vasari, the author of the famous *Le vite de' più eccellenti pittori, scultori ed architetti* (Florence, 2/1568).

Leonardo was profoundly occupied with music. He performed and taught it, he was deeply interested in acoustics and made many acoustical experiments with immediate bearing on music, he wrestled with the concept of musical time, and he invented a considerable number of ingenious musical instruments and improved existing ones. He also had some highly original ideas about the philosophy of music that were intimately connected with his philosophy of painting. It is characteristic that in his *Paragone*, which forms an introduction to his treatise on painting, he accorded music the highest place, after painting, among the arts.

No details are known about Leonardo's musical education in Florence, but it is significant that Andrea del Verrocchio, in whose workshop he grew up, was also a musician. The earliest biographical source, the Anonimo Gaddiano (*I-Fn* Magl.XVII) of the early 16th century, mentions Leonardo as a musician:

he was an elegant speaker and an outstanding performer on the lira, and he was the teacher of Atalante Migliorotti, whom he instructed on this instrument. From Lorenzo il Magnifico, he was sent to the Duke of Milan, together with Atalante Migliorotti, to present to him a lira, for he was unique in playing this instrument.

The 'lira' was the *lira da braccio*, then the most fashionable instrument among improvisers. Vasari, whose famous biography of Leonardo in his *Le vite* is partly based on the Anonimo Gaddiano, recorded that Leonardo 'devoted much effort to music; above all, he determined to study playing the lira, since by nature he possessed a lofty and graceful mind; he sang divinely, improvising his own accompaniment on the lira'. Vasari also noted that after Lodovico Sforza became Duke of Milan, Leonardo, already famous, was brought to play for him

since the duke had a great liking for the sound of the lira; and Leonardo brought there the instrument which he had built with his own hands, made largely of silver but in the shape of a horse skull – a bizarre, new thing – so that the sound ['l'armonia'] would have greater sonority; with this, he surpassed all the musicians who met there to play. In addition, he was the best improviser of rhymes of his time.

The mathematician Luca Pacioli, for whose *De divina proportione* Leonardo drew geometric illustrations, also described him as a musician. The Milanese painter, Giovanni Paolo Lomazzo, extolled Leonardo as one of the outstanding masters of the lira. Among Milanese musicians, Gaffurius had close contact with Leonardo, lent him books, and is probably the subject of Leonardo's painting *Portrait of a Musician*, in the Ambrosiana. In a comparison between wind instruments and the larynx, Leonardo referred to a book 'delli strumenti armonici', possibly Gaffurius's *De harmonia musicorum instrumentorum*.

There are several reasons why Leonardo's musical significance has never been fully examined and evaluated. Art historians have understandably concerned themselves little with the musical situation of Leonardo's time and environment, considering neither the musical properties and intricacies of musical instruments then popular, nor the level reached by musical technology of the time. Music historians, on the other hand, have usually devoted little time to a man who did not leave any written compositions. However, musical improvisation, though not much discussed in musical treatises of the Renaissance, was in fact one of the most subtle and popular branches of performance, as attested by countless paintings and other works of art showing instruments of improvisation in the hands of angels, King David or the great mythological figures of antiquity such as Apollo, Orpheus, Amphion and the Muses.

Leonardo's ideas about music are scattered through many of his numerous notebooks; they range from passing thoughts, notes and marginal remarks, to ideas for planned research, results of experiments or hypotheses in various degrees of verification. Many of his remarks permit interpretation only on the basis of sufficient familiarity with the natural sciences and technology of his time. A systematic examination and correlation of

the enormous amount of material he left reveals an intensive occupation with music.

Leonardo, who regarded himself as 'uomo sanza lettere' was neither a humanist nor a philosopher in the strict sense. Of ancient theories of music only some echoes of Pythagoras and Boethius appear in his notebooks. He inquired into the origins of sound ('What is the nature of a sound produced by a blow?') and examined the sonorous impact of bodies upon bodies, expanding the age-old Pythagorean notions. He studied the phenomenon of vibration and sympathetic vibration, noting that the percussion of a body makes it oscillate and communicate its oscillation to the surrounding air or to other liquid or solid matter. He studied the propagation of sound waves as differing from that of light waves, the reflection and refraction of sound waves and the phenomenon of echo, the speed of sound and the factors that determine degrees of loudness. Especially characteristic of his approach in this context is his establishment of what can be called a 'perspective of sound', that is, the fading of sound in exact ratio to the distance of the ear from the source of sound, paralleling the laws of optical and pictorial perspective that were so important to him as a painter. His ideas about proportions in music go far beyond the traditional theory of intervals and the Pythagorean patrimony. Also, as a musician, he was naturally occupied with the factors that determine musical pitch and experimented with vases of different shapes and apertures. He anticipated by three centuries Chladni's discovery of the geometrical sand figures produced by setting the edge of a plate in vibration with a fiddle bow.

Leonardo's studies of anatomy and physiology, based on his own dissections, enabled him to examine the structure and function of the musician's hand. His dissection of the respiratory organs of animals gave him interesting ideas about voice production, although, lacking the preserving chemicals, he could not have had the necessary knowledge of the vocal cords. Probably for similar reasons he gave no description or discussion of the inner ear. He discussed the peripheric phonetic organs such as the facial muscles, the lips and the tongue, and their impact on pronunciation. His study of the tongue led him to an investigation of vocal pitch, comparing the function of the trachea to that of wind instruments such as organ pipes and the slide trumpet. His alleged authorship of a treatise on the voice, *De vocie*, is controversial.

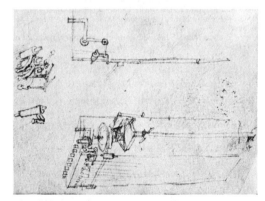

Sketch by Leonardo da Vinci for his 'viola organista' with its endless bow (F-Pi MS H, f.45v)

Leonardo's universal command of technology enabled him to construct novel musical instruments, and to improve existing ones radically. In his notebooks there are numerous drawings of such instruments, from rapid sketches, often not easily decipherable, to exact blueprints for their execution in the workshop. They reveal his systematic efforts to realize some basic aims: automation of certain instruments and the wider use of various types of keyboard to facilitate playing technique; increasing the speed of playing; extension of tonal range to play, for instance, melodies on drums; and overcoming the quickly fading sound of plucked strings. Among other instruments, he constructed glissando flutes, flutes with key systems anticipating Boehm's invention more than three centuries later, bells with variable pitch, drums of which the pitch could be changed during performance or which could produce chords, and above all, the 'viola organista' (see illustration), a keyboard instrument the strings of which were set into vibration by an endless friction band, and which permitted polyphonic playing with dynamic gradation – a virtual string orchestra under the control of ten fingers. Here, as in other cases, Leonardo tried to obtain from one instrument what could normally be produced only by several or by a whole set of instruments.

The sensational reappearance in 1967 at the National Library, Madrid, of two of Leonardo's notebooks, comprising 700 pages, substantially enriched our information about his novel ideas for the construction of musical instruments. The notebooks include drawings of new types of bellows for *organetti* and chamber organs, another drawing for the *viola organista*, and one for the *viola a tasti*, a keyed string instrument operated by segments of cogwheels.

The depth and originality of Leonardo's meditations on music can be perceived by his definition of music as the 'figurazione delle cose invisibili' ('shaping of the invisible').

BIBLIOGRAPHY

J. P. Richter: *The Literary Works of Leonardo da Vinci* (London, 1883)

G. Panconcelli-Calzia: *Leonardo als Phonetiker* (Hamburg, 1943)

A. Marinoni: *I rebus di Leonardo da Vinci* (Florence, 1954)

E. Magni-Dufflocq: 'Da Vinci's Music', *Leonardo da Vinci* (London, 1957), 227

E. Winternitz: 'Lira da braccio', *MGG*

——: 'Keyboards for Wind Instruments Invented by Leonardo da Vinci', *Raccolta Vinciana*, xx (Milan, 1964), 69

——: 'Leonardo's Invention of the Viola Organista', *Raccolta Vinciana*, xx (Milan, 1964), 1

——: 'Melodic, Chordal and other Drums Invented by Leonardo da Vinci', *Raccolta Vinciana*, xx (Milan, 1964), 49

——: 'Anatomy the Teacher – on the Impact of Leonardo's Anatomical Research on his Musical and other Machines', *Proceedings of the American Philosophical Society*, iii/4 (1967), 234

——: 'Strange Musical Instruments in the Madrid Notebooks of Leonardo da Vinci', *Metropolitan Museum Journal*, ii (New York, 1969), 115

——: 'La musica nel "Paragone" di Leonardo da Vinci', *Studi musicali*, i (1972), 79

——: 'Leonardo and Music', *The Unknown Leonardo* (New York, 1974), 110

EMANUEL WINTERNITZ

Leonardus Athesinus. *See* LECHNER, LEONHARD.

Leonardus Nervius. *See* NERVIUS, LEONARDUS.

Leonati, Carlo Ambrogio. *See* LONATI, CARLO AMBROGIO.

Leoncavallo, Ruggero (*b* Naples, 8 March 1857; *d* Montecatini, 9 Aug 1919). Italian composer and libret-

Ruggero Leoncavallo: lithograph by E. Fontana

tist. A member of the *verismo* school, his fame rests on a single work, *Pagliacci*.

1. LIFE. His christian name is properly Ruggero, not, as often given, Ruggiero. After preparatory lessons, Leoncavallo, the son of a police magistrate in Naples, was admitted to the conservatory there in 1866, studying composition under Lauro Rossi and graduating in 1876. Moving to Bologna University, from which he received a degree in literature in 1878, he assiduously attended the poet Carducci's lectures, becoming through them particularly interested in the literature and prosody of the Italian Renaissance. These lectures, coupled with his first exposure to Wagner's music, inflamed him with the notion of composing a Renaissance trilogy. To prepare himself he hastily completed the opera *Chatterton*, begun when he was a student. His hopes for a performance of this work were blasted when an unscrupulous impresario absconded with the money that Leoncavallo himself had provided for one. Falling on hard times, he became an itinerant café pianist, travelling across Europe, even in 1882 to Egypt. This cycle of vagabondage was broken when he made friends with Victor Maurel, who sensed his potentialities and introduced him to Giulio Ricordi.

Ricordi took options on *Chatterton* and on the libretto to *I Medici*. More impressed with Leoncavallo as a librettist than as a composer, Ricordi asked him late in 1889 to write *Manon Lescaut* for Puccini. But Puccini, dissatisfied with his efforts, had him removed from the project. Next, Leoncavallo finished the score of *I Medici*, but Ricordi disliked the opera. Angry now and desperate for fame, he determined to capture the public by surpassing the success of the hour, Mascagni's *Cavalleria rusticana*. 'I lost patience, knowing that Ricordi was doing nothing for me. I shut myself up in my house . . . and in five months I wrote the poem and music of *Pagliacci*.'

For his plot Leoncavallo drew on memories of one of

his father's law cases – a middle-aged actor had murdered his unfaithful young wife. To this sordid triangle he added complexities absent in *Cavalleria*: the *commedia dell'arte* playlet and the Zola-inspired prologue, with its rationale for naturalism. He took his score to Ricordi's rival, Sonzogno, who promptly arranged a performance. Given at the Teatro dal Verme in Milan on 21 May 1892 under Toscanini, it made Leoncavallo a celebrity overnight. Hoping to capitalize on the success of *Pagliacci*, Sonzogno arranged for performances of *I Medici*. This opera was the first part of the projected but never completed trilogy *Crepusculum*, the later parts of which were to have dealt with Savonarola and Cesare Borgia. After much advance publicity, *I Medici* was given at the Dal Verme on 9 November 1893. With few exceptions an undigested gallimaufry of Wagner and Meyerbeer, it was an embarrassing failure, the critics treating Leoncavallo's pretentiousness with pitiless irony.

In February 1893 two Milan newspapers carried announcements of operas to be composed on the subject of *La bohème*, one by Leoncavallo, one by Puccini. Although Leoncavallo claimed precedence, Puccini's opera reached the stage in 1896, while Leoncavallo's was performed at La Fenice in Venice on 6 May 1897, successfully at first, but losing ground as Puccini's version established itself. Hoping to offset Puccini, Sonzogno had also ill-advisedly produced the neglected *Chatterton*, entirely rewritten and reduced from four to three acts, at Rome on 10 March 1896, but even a subsequent revision in 1905 could not salvage it. After *La bohème* Leoncavallo turned again to a French subject, *Zazà*, based on a play by Simon and Berton. Conducted by Toscanini and with Storchio in the title role, it was enthusiastically received at the Teatro Lirico, Milan, on 10 November 1900. This opera ranks as his best work after *Pagliacci*, but a considerable distance separates them.

On *I Medici*'s première in Berlin in February 1894, the Kaiser had been so impressed by it that he had commissioned from Leoncavallo an opera glorifying the Hohenzollerns. Willibald Alexis's novel *Der Roland von Berlin* (1840), dramatized and translated into Italian, was arranged by Leoncavallo and retranslated into German. *Der Roland von Berlin* (Berlin, 13 December 1904) had a hollow triumph; even official patronage could win it no more than 38 performances. Up to this time Leoncavallo had written his own librettos; now he turned to Angelo Nessi for *Maia*, which failed at the Teatro Costanzi in Rome on 15 January 1910.

One of the first composers to become seriously involved with gramophone records, Leoncavallo wrote for the G&T Company the words and music to the song *Mattinata*, which was recorded in April 1904 by Caruso accompanied by the composer. In 1907 he conducted *Pagliacci*, also for G&T, the first complete opera to be recorded in Italy. He also did much travelling to promote his own works. In the USA he staged his first operetta, *La jeunesse de Figaro* (1906). His next work in that vein, *Malbrouck*, succeeded at Rome in 1910, its première following that of *Maia* by four days. On 16 September 1912 he was at the London Hippodrome for the première of *Zingari*, a return to the *verismo* vein of *Pagliacci*. In 1913 he brought to London another operetta, *Are you There?*. The entry of Italy into the war in 1915 caused him to abandon a projected opera, *Ave Maria*, to a libretto by Illica. The

posthumous *Edipo Re* (Chicago, 13 December 1920) employed Forzano's adaptation of Sophocles (not Leoncavallo's, as is usually stated). It was not given in Italy until 1958.

Leoncavallo's career after *Pagliacci* was anticlimactic. Too much of the time he was an unlucky opportunist. It is ludicrous that the man who had proposed to write a trilogy to rival Wagner's *Ring* should also have composed, shortly before he died, an operetta entitled *A chi la giarrettiera?* ('Whose garter is this?'). What he almost fatally lacked was a sense of proportion.

2. WORKS. More than any of Leoncavallo's other operas *Pagliacci* possesses the merits of economy and consistent impetus. The Prologue, revitalizing a convention of the 17th-century stage, combines the exposition of literary theory with a vocal showpiece. The offstage oboe solo lends local colour to the bagpipers' chorus. In contrast to the more formal design of Nedda's 'Ballatella' and her love duet with Silvio is the succinct arioso 'Vesti la giubba'; here Leoncavallo took what was once considered a transition between recitative and fully-fledged aria and converted it into a moment of climactic utterance.

Leoncavallo originally intended *Pagliacci* as a one-act opera (the autograph in the Library of Congress is headed 'dramma in un atto'), but the extended applause usual after 'Vesti la giubba' led to the division into two acts. The prelude to Act 2 was originally designed as an intermezzo (in imitation of *Cavalleria*). The autograph further shows that the famous line 'La commedia è finita!' should be uttered by Tonio. The tradition that it be spoken by Canio has been variously attributed to de Lucia and Caruso. However it began, it stands as an example of tenor vanity and destroys the logical relationship between that line and Tonio's explanatory function in the Prologue.

To produce its effect, *Zazà*, an unabashedly sentimental work, requires a soprano capable of vibrant climaxes, a telling projection of the text and great stage presence. Thus *Zazà* has succeeded with a Storchio, a Farrar or a Favero, and failed with less impressive artists. The opening act, set backstage in a French music hall, is a minor gem of atmosphere, a distillation of Leoncavallo's memories of his early vagabond years. The climax of Act 3, Zaza's encounter with her lover's young daughter, contains Leoncavallo's variant of Giordano's device in Act 2 of *Fedora* of accompanying the soprano's lines by a piano played onstage. Although the score contains passages of direct appeal, such as the baritone's two arias, it does not come alive unless performed with overwhelming conviction.

Leoncavallo's *La bohème* makes an interesting comparison with Puccini's. Leoncavallo used much of the same material – Act 1 (Café Momus), Act 2 (the courtyard, a scene sketched for Puccini and then suppressed), Acts 3 and 4 (the garret). Leoncavallo's assignment of voices to some of the roles differs from Puccini's; he made Musetta a mezzo, Marcello a tenor, Rodolfo a baritone. While an adroit balance between humour and pathos characterizes Puccini's *Bohème*, Leoncavallo's comedy seems raucous and capricious, and the emotionalism of the final acts even approaches violence in the scene where Marcello nearly strangles Musetta. A most striking episode, one with no counterpart in Puccini, is Schaunard's parody of Rossini, in which he discusses the influence of blue in the arts. Leoncavallo's score has attractive and moving moments, and occasionally it bursts into dramatic life; but it is a more uneven, less disciplined work than Puccini's.

It is ironical that the composer of two such popular tunes as 'Vesti la giubba' and the song *Mattinata* should have been on the whole unsuccessful. Except for his timely exploitation of the *verismo* trend of the early 1890s, Leoncavallo lacked the artistic vision and creative power to cope with a period of rapid transition in opera. Yet his career cannot be dismissed as a failure; *Pagliacci* will remain his monument.

WORKS
OPERAS

Chatterton (melodramma, 4, Leoncavallo, after A. de Vigny), c1876, not perf., lib pubd (Bologna, 1877); rev. (dramma lirico, 3), Rome, Argentina, 10 March 1896, vocal score (1896); rev., Nice, 7 April 1905
Pagliacci (dramma, prol, 2, Leoncavallo), Milan, Dal Verme, 21 May 1892; autograph *US-Wc* (1892)
Crepusculum (poema epico in forma di trilogia storica, Leoncavallo): I Medici (azione storica, 4), Milan, Dal Verme, 9 Nov 1893, vocal score (1893); pts.2, 3 not composed
La bohème (commedia lirica, 4, Leoncavallo), Venice, La Fenice, 6 May 1897, vocal score (1897); rev. as Mimi Pinson (3), Palermo, Massimo, 14 April 1913, vocal score (1913)
Zazà (commedia lirica, 4, Leoncavallo, after P. Berton and C. Simon), Milan, Lirico, 10 Nov 1900, vocal score (1900); rev. by R. Bianchi (1947)
Der Roland von Berlin (historisches Drama, 4, Leoncavallo, after W. Alexis, Ger. trans. by G. Droescher), Berlin, Opera, 13 Dec 1904; vocal score (1904)
Maia (dramma lirico, 3, A. Nessi, after P. de Choudens), Rome, Costanzi, 15 Jan 1910 (1908)
Zingari (dramma lirico, 2, E. Cavacchioli and G. Emanuel, after Pushkin), London, Hippodrome, 16 Sept 1912, vocal score (1912)
Edipo Re (grand opera, 1, G. Forzano, after Sophocles), Chicago, Opera, 13 Dec 1920; completed by G. Pennacchio
Prometeo, not perf., unpubd
Ave Maria (Illica and Cavacchioli), abandoned in 1915
Tormenta (3, G. Belvederi), not completed

OPERETTAS

La jeunesse de Figaro (after Sardou: Les premières armes de Figaro), USA, 1906
Malbrouck (fantasia comica medioevale, 3, Nessi), Rome, Nazionale, 19 Jan 1910, vocal score (1910)
La reginetta della rose (3, Forzano), Rome, Costanzi, 24 June 1912, vocal score (1912)
Are you There? (farce, 3, A. de Courville and E. Wallace), London, Prince of Wales, 1 Nov 1913
La candidata (3, Forzano), Rome, Nazionale, 6 Feb 1915
Prestami tua moglie (3, E. Corradi), Montecatini, Casino, 2 Sept 1916
Goffredo Mameli (3, Belvederi), Genoa, Carlo Felice, 27 April 1916
A chi la giarrettiera? (3), Rome, Adriano, 16 Oct 1919
Il primo bacio (1, L. Bonelli), Montecatini, Salone di Cura, 29 April 1923
La maschera nuda (3, Bonelli and F. Paolieri), Naples, Politeama, 26 June 1925; completed by S. Allegri

SONGS

Album Stecchetti: 4 poesie delle 'Postuma' (Olindo Guerrini) (1880): 1 October, fantasia, 2 Un organetto suona per la via, pensiero, 3 Donna vorrei morir, melodia, 4 Era d'inverno, pensiero; At Peace (Mrs A. Roberts) (1884); Lost Love (Roberts) (1884); 10 Songs (1893): 1 Dietro le nubi, 2 Addio, 3 Nulla so, 4 Suzon, adieu Suzon!, 5 Un sogno, 6 Non dirmi chi sei, 7, 8, 9 = Album Stecchetti nos.1, 2, 3, 10 Chitaretta (Leoncavallo); Déclaration (A. Silvestre) (1893); Tonight and Tomorrow (F. E. Weatherly) (1893); Serenata (1893)
Rapsodia primaverile (1893); Canzone della nonna (1894); A Summer Idyll (1895); Invocation à la Muse (1896); A Ninon: Si je vous le disais (1896); Vorrei dirvi che v'amo, serenatella (1897); C'est l'heure mystérieuse (Leoncavallo), serenade (1897); Aprile (1897); C'est bien toi (1898); Nuit de décembre (1900); Les deux sérénades (1903): Sérénade française, Sérénade napolitaine; La chanson de Don Juan (1904); Mattinata (Leoncavallo) (1904); Ninna nanna (Leoncavallo) (1904); Ave Maria, T, harp, harmonium ad lib (1905)
Barcarola, 1v, pf, vn (1905); Mai fleuri, rapsodie printanière (1905); Brise de mer (1906); Et nunc et semper (1906); Mandolinata (Leoncavallo) (1907); Se! (Leoncavallo) (1907); Vieni, amor mio (1907); Canzone d'amore (1912); Lasciate amar (1913); For I do love you so (A. de Courville) (1919); Ruit hora: frammento dell'ode barbara di Giosuè Carducci; Napuletana

Pantins vivants, danse de caractère (?1898); La joyeuse, waltz (?1898); Valse mélancolique (1901); Cortège de Pulcinella, petite marche humoristique (1903); Flirt-Walzer (1905); Papillon, scherzo (1906); Sarabande, danse ancienne (1906); Viva l'America, march (1906); Airs des ballets espagnols (?1904): Sevillana, Gitana-tango, Playeras ancienne, Granadinas; Nights of Italy, intermezzo (1914)
Undated: Romanesca, morceau de style ancien; Sous les palmiers; Valse coquette; Valse mignonne; Serenata d'Arlecchino; Tarantella

OTHER WORKS

Chorus, orch: Nuit de mai, c1895, not perf.; Requiem, for Umberto I, 1900, not perf.; Inno alla Croce rossa (1901); Inno della Lega nazionale (1913); Inno franco-italiana (1915)
Orch: Séraphitus-Séraphita, sym. poem after Balzac, Milan, 1894, programme pubd (Milan, 1894); La vita di una marionetta, ballet, c1900
Principal publishers: Sonzogno, Choudens

LIBRETTOS

Mario Wetter, A. Machado, 1898
Redenzione, G. Pennacchio, 1920

BIBLIOGRAPHY

R. Giani and A. Engelfred: '*I Medici*', *RMI*, i (1894), 86–116
F. Pfohl: *Die moderne Oper* (Leipzig, 1894)
R. A. Streatfeild: *Masters of Italian Music* (London, 1895)
E. Hanslick: 'Der Bajazzo von Leoncavallo', *Die moderne Oper*, vii: *Fünf Jahre Musik (1891–1895): Kritiken* (Berlin, 1896), 96
——: '*Die Bohème* von Leoncavallo', *Die moderne Oper*, viii: *Am Ende des Jahrhunderts (1895–1899): musikalische Kritiken and Schilderungen* (Berlin, 1899), 123
N. Tabanelli: 'La causa Ricordi–Leoncavallo', *RMI*, vi (1899), 833
O. Roux: *Memorie giovanili autobiografiche di Leoncavallo* (Florence, n.d.)
W. Pastor: 'Leoncavallos *Roland von Berlin*', *Die Musik*, xiv/7 (1904–5), 45
'Leoncavallo at the Hippodrome', *The Times* (13 Sept 1911)
C. Trevor: 'Ruggiero Leoncavallo', *MMR*, xlix (1919), 193
J. Korngold: 'Ruggiero Leoncavallo: *Zazà* (1909)', *Die romanische Oper der Gegenwart* (Vienna, 1922), 103
A. de Angelis: 'Il capolavoro inespresso di Leoncavallo? *Tormenta*: opera di soggetto sardo', *RMI*, xxx (1923), 563
G. Monaldi: *Ricordi viventi di artisti scomparsi* (Campobasso, 1927)
G. Fauré: 'Leoncavallo', *Opinions musicales* (Paris, 1930), 64
G. Adami: *G. Ricordi e i suoi musicisti* (Milan, 1933)
L. Kárpáth: 'Das Dioskurenpaar Mascagni–Leoncavallo', *Begegnung mit dem Genius* (Vienna, 1934), 365
G. Giachetti: 'Leoncavallo a Milano prima dei *Pagliacci*', *La sera* (Milan, 20 March 1942)
A. Baratti: *Profili di musicisti* (Milan, 1949)
R. de Rensis: *Per Umberto Giordano e Ruggiero Leoncavallo* (Siena, 1949)
A. Holde: 'A Little-known Letter by Berlioz and Unpublished Letters by Cherubini, Leoncavallo, and Hugo Wolf', *MQ*, xxxvii (1951), 350
E. Greenfield: 'The Other Bohème', *Opera Annual*, v (1958), 77
J. W. Klein: 'Ruggiero Leoncavallo (1858–1919)', *Opera*, ix (1958), 158, 232
G. Gualerzi: 'Ruggiero Leoncavallo: i suoi interpreti', *La Scala* (1959), April
M. Morini: 'Ruggiero Leoncavallo: la sua opera', *La Scala* (1959), April
R. Giazotto: 'Uno sconosciuto progetto teatrale di Ruggiero Leoncavallo', *NRMI*, ii (1968), 1162
T. Lerario: 'Ruggiero Leoncavallo e il soggetto dei "Pagliacci"', *Chigiana*, xxvi–xxvii (1971), 115
A. Marchetti: 'Lo smisurato sogno dell'autore di "Pagliacci"', *Rassegna musicale Curci*, xxv (1972), 23

WILLIAM ASHBROOK

Leon de Bagnols, Magister. *See* LEO HEBRAEUS.

Leone da Modena. *See* LEO DA MODENA.

Leonel [Leonelle, Leonellus] **(Power).** *See* POWER, LEONEL.

Leonetti, Giovanni Battista (*fl* 1604–17). Italian composer and organist. He was a pupil of G. B. Caletti at Crema and included two madrigals by him in his madrigal book of 1617. He became an Augustinian monk and was organist of S Agostino, Crema, in 1617. Three six-part madrigals by him appear in *RISM* 1604[19]. He published two collections of his own at Venice in 1617, *Il primo libro de' madrigali a 5 voci* (*RISM* 1617[15]), with harpsichord continuo and including two pieces by Caletti, and *Missarum octonis vocibus liber primus*, with organ continuo and consisting of three masses and an Elevation motet, all conventionally scored for double choir.

JEROME ROCHE

Leonhardt, Gustav (Maria) (*b* 's Graveland, Netherlands, 30 May 1928). Dutch harpsichordist, organist and conductor. After a classical education, he studied the organ and harpsichord with Eduard Müller at the Schola Cantorum in Basle from 1947 to 1950. He made his début in Vienna in 1950, performing Bach's *Die Kunst der Fuge* on the harpsichord. After a year of musicological study in Vienna, he served as professor of harpsichord at the Vienna Academy of Music from 1952 to 1955. Since 1954 he has occupied a similar post at the Amsterdam Conservatory, and is also organist of the Waalse Kerk there with its superb Christian Müller organ of 1733. In 1967 he acted the part of J. S. Bach and played both the organ and the harpsichord in Jean-Marie Staub's biographical film, *Die Chronik der Anna Magdalena Bach*. In 1969–70 he was visiting professor at Harvard University.

Each year Leonhardt tours Europe and North America, principally as a harpsichordist, performing an extensive repertory encompassing a catholic selection of keyboard music from the early 16th century to the late 18th. His interpretations of the great 17th-century keyboard composers, above all Frescobaldi, Froberger and Louis Couperin, are greatly admired, winning a wider audience for this music and setting a standard of interpretative style. Despite much subtle rhythmic nuance and tasteful ornamentation, Leonhardt's playing tends to be rather sober and at times even severe. He dislikes the consciously 'modern' type of harpsichord and prefers instruments constructed on historical principles. He has frequently performed and recorded on antique harpsichords linked historically to the music of specific periods and national schools. In chamber music, too, he has been associated with several distinguished ensembles, notably the Leonhardt Consort, which he founded in 1955, that seek to match the instrumental sound to the particular 17th- and 18th-century works being played. His appearances as a conductor of Baroque choral and operatic music have been marked by the same sensitivity and stylistic authority which characterize his solo and chamber playing. He edited Sweelinck's keyboard fantasias and toccatas in the complete critical edition issued by the Vereniging voor Nederlandse Muziekgeschiednis (Amsterdam, 1968–).

WRITINGS

The Art of Fugue: Bach's Last Harpsichord Work (The Hague, 1952)

HOWARD SCHOTT

Leoni, Franco (*b* Milan, 24 Oct 1864; *d* London 8 Feb 1949). Italian composer. He studied at the Milan Conservatory with Dominiceti and Ponchielli. His first opera, *Raggio di Luna*, was produced at Milan in 1890. Two years later he emigrated to England, where his operas *Rip van Winkle* (1897) and *Ib and Little Christina* (Savoy Theatre, 1901) were produced. His best-known work, the one-act *L'oracolo*, was produced at Covent Garden in 1905 with Antonio Scotti as the opium dealer Chim-Fen, and conducted by André Messager. However, the piece, musically rather a long way beyond Ponchielli and Puccini, did not achieve popular success until it was produced at the Metropolitan in 1915, when Scotti proved it an apt

vehicle for his vocal and dramatic abilities. He chose it for his farewell at that house in 1933, after which the work seems to have fallen out of the repertory. There were however revivals at the Curtis Institute (1949) and Philadelphia Opera (1952). A recording appeared with Tito Gobbi as Chim-Fen in 1977, when the 'Puccini-and-water' description of a contemporary critic seemed apt. His later operas were composed after he returned to Italy in 1917; from that date he appears to have shared his time between his own country, France and England. He also wrote several oratorios, among them *Golgotha* (1909), and light songs, many of them English settings. *Golgotha* was first given at the Queen's Hall by the Queen's Hall Choral Society, of which Leoni was the conductor. It appears to have been a tedious work.

WORKS
(selective list)

OPERAS

Raggio di Luna, Milan, 1890
Rip van Winkle, London, 1897
Ib and Little Christina, London, Savoy Theatre, 1901
L'oracolo, London, Covent Garden, 28 June 1905
Tzigana, Genoa, 1910
Francesca da Rimini (M. Crawford), Paris, Opéra-Comique, 1914
Le baruffe chiozzotte (after Goldoni), Milan, 1920
Falene, Milan, 1920
La terra del sogno, Milan, 1920
Massemarello, ?not perf.

The Prayer of the Sword (play, J. B. Fagan), incidental music, London, 1904

ORATORIOS

Sardanapalus, London, 1891
The Gate of Life, London, 1891
Golgotha, London, Queen's Hall, 1909

BIBLIOGRAPHY

LaMusicaD
G. Kobbé: *The Complete Opera Book* (New York, 1919 etc)
A. Loewenberg: *Annals of Opera* (Cambridge, 1943, rev. 3/1978)

ALAN BLYTH

Leoni, Giovanni Antonio (*b* ?late 16th century; *d* ?Rome, after 1652). Italian composer, violinist and teacher. For many years he enjoyed the patronage of Cardinal G. B. Pallotta in Rome, composing and playing music for the vocal and instrumental concerts promoted by the cardinal in the church of the Santa Casa di Loreto, Rome. By 1625 his reputation was such that a motet by him was included in Francesco Sammaruco's collection of *Sacri affetti* (*RISM* 1625[1]) by 'eccellentissimi autori', among them Frescobaldi and Monteverdi. He had many pupils, and his sonatas and sinfonias circulated widely in MS. So widespread, indeed, was the anonymous circulation with unauthentic alterations, ornamentations and arrangements that he felt obliged to print some solo violin sonatas that he had written some years before. Although its contents are by no means the first printed sonatas for solo violin and continuo, the *Sonate di violino a voce sola ... libro 1* op.3 (Rome, 1652) is the first publication devoted entirely to this scoring. Leoni's two earlier prints appear to be lost.

BIBLIOGRAPHY

W. S. Newman: *The Sonata in the Baroque Era* (Chapel Hill, 1959, rev. 2/1966/R1972)
W. Apel: 'Studien über die frühe Violinmusik, V', *AMw*, xxxiv (1977), 117–47, esp. 132

JOHN HARPER

Leoni, Leone [Leo] (*b* Verona, *c*1560; *d* Vicenza, 24 June 1627). Italian composer. Entries in the archives of Vicenza Cathedral and remarks in his dedications indicate that he was a native of Verona and received musical training and encouragement there at the 'academy' of Count Mario Bevilacqua. From 4 October 1588 until his death he was *maestro di cappella* of Vicenza Cathedral. He was also a member of the Accademia Olimpica in Vicenza.

Leoni is known to have written 130 madrigals, 89 of which are extant. He also made significant contributions to the motet form, keeping abreast of the rapid changes of style as polyphony and polychoral writing gave way to monody and concertato textures. There exist 144 motets by him, mainly in his six collections, and some 40 others have been lost.

In his handling of texture and form he emphasized aural contrasts, which are most evident in the volume called *Aurea corona*: here solo passages, obbligato instrumental trios and rapid polychoral alternations are combined in a musical unity which prefigures the later Baroque cantata. Leoni's treatment of melody, harmony and rhythm is simple: melodies adhere closely to the notes of the common chords implied by the continuo bass; the bass notes of chords (often 5-3 chords) are generally limited to movement in 4ths and 5ths; and the predominantly duple metre faithfully presents the rhythms of the words. His aim, in short, was the direct, expressive setting of his chosen texts. In this he was modern, and he was in fact one of the composers responsible for the new vocal style emerging at the beginning of the 17th century. His ability to keep pace with the rapid stylistic changes of the period ensured widespread performance of his music even after his death, and anthologists appear to have considered him one of the leading north Italian composers of his time.

WORKS
SACRED

Penitenza: primo libro de [21] madrigali spirituali, 5vv (Venice, 1596)
Sacri fiori: [20] mottetti [1 Magnificat], 2–4vv, org, libro primo (Venice, 1606)
[20] Sacrarum cantionum liber primus, 8vv, 2 org (Venice, 1608)
Sacri fiori: secondo libro de [31] mottetti, 1–3vv, org ... con una messa, 4vv (Venice, 1612)
Omnium solemnitatum psalmodia, 8vv (Venice, 1613), 15 psalms, 2 Magnificat
Aurea corona ingemmata d'armonici, concerti a 10, 4vv, 6 insts (Venice, 1615), 25 motets; survives in MS copy, D-F
Sacri fiori: quarto libro de [25] mottetti, 1–4vv, org (Venice, 1622)
Missa 'Ab austro veniet', 12vv, A-Wn 16707b; Falsobordone, 4–5vv, I-VId
Sacred works found only in anthologies: 1592[3], 1612[2], 1620[2], 1622[2], 1624[3], 1627[2]
Sacred works reprinted from his publications in anthologies: 1609[15], 1611[1], 1612[3], 1613[2], 1616[2], 1621[2], 1623[2], 1626[2], 1627[1], 1643[2]
In addition to a third book of Sacri fiori, a collection of motets pubd in 1602 appears to be lost. (The latter is cited in an early 17th-century inventory; see G. Turrini: *Atti e memorie ... di Verona*, 5th ser., xviii, p.205.)

SECULAR

Il primo libro de [21] madrigali, 5vv (Venice, 1588)
Bella Clori: secondo libro de [22] madrigali, 5vv (Venice, 1591); includes Quell'augelin, text from Guarini's Il pastor fido
Il terzo libro de [21] madrigali, 5vv (Venice, 1595), only T survives
Il quarto libro de [20] madrigali (Venice, 1598), only known copy destroyed in World War II
Bell'Alba: quinto libro de [21] madrigali, 5vv (Venice, 1602)
Secular works found only in anthologies: 1592[11], 1594[6], 1598[6], 1600[12], 1605[7]
Secular works reprinted from his publications in anthologies: 1606[5], 1613[13], 1619[16]
Chorus to Edipo Re, Vicenza, Teatro Olimpico, 1612, lost

MS copies of printed works in A-Wn, D-Bds, F, Lr, Mbs, Z, PL-WRu

BIBLIOGRAPHY

G. Mantese: *Storia musicale Vicentina* (Vicenza, 1956)
H. Wing: *The Polychoral Motets of Leone Leoni* (diss., Boston U., 1966)

HENRY J. WING JR

Leoni, Michael [Lyon, Myer] (*b* ?London, *c*1755; *d* Kingston, Jamaica, 1797). English tenor. He may have had some connection with Benedetto Leoni who published harpsichord lessons in London about 1768. Leoni's début was as Arbaces in Arne's *Artaxerxes* (Covent Garden, April 1775), and he had his greatest success the following October as Don Carlos in *The Duenna*. Sheridan wrote the part with Leoni in mind, and significantly gave him more to sing than anyone else and less to act. His voice was smoothly beautiful. Leoni made himself unpopular with his fellow-Jews in London by singing in *Messiah*; that may be why he went to Dublin in 1778. He and Tommaso Giordani tried to popularize opera at the theatre in Chapel Street, but went bankrupt. Back in London Leoni failed to find the favour he had enjoyed before. He sang briefly at the Royalty Theatre near the Tower (which was soon closed because it infringed the patents held by Drury Lane and Covent Garden), and there he introduced his pupil, John Braham, who was still a boy; Leoni is said to have been his uncle. He later went to Jamaica to be *hazzan* in Kingston synagogue. He composed a number of small pieces for Jewish ritual. A splendid hymn tune called 'Leoni' is to be found in both *Hymns Ancient and Modern Revised* (631) and *Songs of Praise* (398); the melody is an ancient Hebrew one which Leoni arranged and gave to a Church of England friend.

ROGER FISKE

Léonin [Magister Leoninus; ?Leo] (*fl* Paris, *c*1163–90). Composer of organum. He is credited by the theorist Anonymous IV with perhaps the greatest single achievement in the development of early polyphony: the creation of the MAGNUS LIBER. No works survive with ascriptions to him in musical sources. Anonymous IV's information implies that he wrote down organal settings for two voices of the solo portions of graduals, alleluias and responsories for principal feasts of the entire ecclesiastical year.

Léonin is usually associated with the cathedral of Notre Dame in Paris. This is because the *Magnus liber* as it now survives is liturgically designed for use in Notre Dame, and because Anonymous IV referred to the books of polyphony which were initiated by him and modified by Pérotin as remaining in use in the choir of the cathedral in the early 13th century. An attempt has been made to identify him with a 'Henricus Leonellus laicus' who was associated with the Abbey of St Victor in Paris, who is first encountered in archival records between 24 March 1163 and 11 April 1164, and who must have died some time between 1187 and 1192 (Birkner). The assumption that Léonin was choirmaster at Notre Dame is now no longer made. The footings of the cathedral were in any case laid only in 1163, the choir completed and the high altar consecrated not until 1182. Up to 1185 services continued in the church of St Stephen nearby on the same site. Indeed, Anonymous IV, as the sole testimony to Léonin's achievement, was writing a full century later: it is even possible that Léonin was more legendary than real.

Even if the theorist's words are to be taken as accurate, the nature of Léonin's achievement has still to be determined (Reckow, ii, p.46):

Magister Leoninus, according to what is said, was the best composer [or singer] of organum [*optimus organista*]; he made [*fecit*] the great book of organum for the gradual and antiphoner [*Magnus liber organi de gradali et antifonario*] for the amplification of divine service. And this was in use up to the time of Perotinus Magnus, who shortened it and made many better clausulas or *puncta* [*see* CLAUSULA], for he was the best composer [or singer] of discant [*discantor*], and better than Leoninus. But the same cannot be said for the subtlety of organum etc.

The verb *fecit* is unlikely to mean 'compose' in the modern sense of that word. The music of the *Magnus liber* is an extension of an essentially improvisatory polyphonic tradition. It came, however, at a point in that tradition when aesthetic considerations were playing an increasing role in the minds of singers, and in the writings of the theorists who prescribed the rules for this improvisatory technique. A feeling for the balance of a phrase, and for the structure of a larger span, was clearly emerging. Léonin's role in creating the *Magnus liber* was probably one of capturing and formalizing the inventiveness of singers – including perhaps his own inventiveness as a singer (?*organista*). The style which he represented was probably one of freely flowing melismatic organum with a tendency towards shapely phrasing and the recurrent use of certain melodic turns of phrase in the upper voice, as in ex.1.

Ex.1 *Alleluia Nativitas, D-W* 677, f. 42

Na - - - - - - - - - - - [tivitas]

In this sense, his role as a notator is highly significant. Waite (1954, p.8) said: 'It was Leonin's incomparable achievement to introduce a rational system of rhythm into polyphonic music for the first time, and, equally important, to create a method of notation expressive of this rhythm'. He was referring to the principles of modal rhythm (*see* RHYTHMIC MODES) on which his own transcription of the *Magnus liber* is based. This view has seriously been called in question as imposing a 13th- and 14th-century outlook upon 12th-century note patterns (for modal notation involved the redeployment of existing notational signs rather than the creation of new ones). Reckow (1967, ii, pp.49f), for example, has maintained that whereas theorists since Franco took the presence of modal rhythm in florid organum for granted, it is by no means the case that Léonin intended it thus. Indeed, certain remarks about organum by Johannes de Garlandia speak against this.

The problem is further aggravated, because the original form of the *Magnus liber* no longer exists. The book survives in three more or less reworked versions from the 13th century and the early 14th. The original can no longer be reconstructed. Hence it is impossible to know, for example, whether passages of COPULA – in which phrases of undoubtedly modal rhythm occur in the upper voice over sustained tenor notes – now present in the florid sections of the organum have been there since the original book or are later adaptations. The same is true of the sections of DISCANT – in which the two voices move together in modal rhythm approximately note against note – now present in the surviving versions. Husmann (*MGG*) cited a passage in Anonymous IV (ed. Reckow, i, p.46) in which the theorist seems to be saying that in the time of Léonin (*a tempore Leonis*) only the first rhythmic mode (long–short–long) was known and not the greater notational complexities of Pérotin's time. He deduced from this that passages of discant such as that in ex.2 were a feature of his style which contrasted with the

Ex.2 *Hec dies: Confitemini, D-W* 677, f. 31*v*

[Domi-no]

unmeasured rhythm of the organal sections. It is equally possible, however, that Anonymous IV was referring to passages of modal rhythm in the upper voice of organum, as in ex.3.

Ex.3 *Igitur dissimulata: Cui sacerdos, I-Fl* plut. 29.1, f. 92 *r-v*

sa - - - cer - - - - - - - dos

The contents of the original book have been established, though not conclusively, by Husmann (1963). We now have some idea of which items were included, for which feasts they were intended, and how much of each item was sung in polyphony (see the list in MAGNUS LIBER). The picture which emerges suggests an enterprise of great consistency and thoroughness. It may be that Léonin's principal contribution lies in the selection and ordering of the book, and in the skilful way in which he harnessed the available resources of highly trained solo organum singers.

BIBLIOGRAPHY
H. Tischler: 'New Historical Aspects of the Parisian Organa', *Speculum*, xxv (1950), 31
W. G. Waite: *The Rhythm of Twelfth-century Polyphony: its Theory and Practice*, Yale Studies in the History of Music, ii (New Haven, 1954) [contains edn. of *Magnus liber*]
H. Husmann: 'Leonin', *MGG*
——: 'The Origin and Destination of the Magnus liber organi', *MQ*, xlix (1963), 311
G. Birkner: 'Notre Dame-Cantoren und -Succentoren vom Ende des 10. bis zum Beginn des 14. Jahrhunderts', *In memoriam Jacques Handschin* (Strasbourg, 1962)
F. Reckow, ed.: *Der Musiktraktat des Anonymus 4* (Wiesbaden, 1967), i, 46, 98; ii, chap.2
For further bibliography *see* ORGANUM AND DISCANT: BIBLIOGRAPHY.
IAN D. BENT

Leonova, Dar'ya Mikhaylovna (*b* Vishniy Volochok, Tver govt., 21 March 1829; *d* St Petersburg, 6 Feb 1896). Russian contralto. Some authorities give 16 March 1834 as her date of birth, but this is unlikely. She studied at the imperial opera school in St Petersburg, and made her début in 1852 as Vanya in *A Life for the Tsar*. She had rehearsed the part with Glinka himself, and she continued to take lessons from the composer. It seems that by the summer of 1855 their relationship had become more than that of pupil and teacher: Glinka's letters to his sister are full of discreet remarks about the young singer, but it is not certain whether she was in fact his mistress. She sang in opera in St Petersburg and Moscow until 1874.

Throughout her career Leonova championed the cause of Russian music, and her best-known roles included the Princess in Dargomïzhsky's *Rusalka*, the title role in Serov's *Rogneda*, and the Hostess in Musorgsky's *Boris Godunov*, all of which she created. She was also praised for her interpretation of Azucena in *Il trovatore* and Ortrud in *Lohengrin*. Between 1875 and 1879 she toured Russia, China, America and western Europe. In 1879 she went to southern Russia and the Crimea where, with Musorgsky as her accompanist, she gave a series of concerts. She did much for Musorgsky during his last years, engaging him to supervise studies at her private singing academy and providing him with a home on her estate where he could continue to compose. At his memorial concert in November 1881 she sang two of his songs. She taught at the drama school in Moscow (1888–92), and her reminiscences were published in *Istoricheskiy vestnik* (1891, nos.1–4). Leonova had a bright, clear voice with a range of two and a half octaves (*g* to *c'''*). Her strong dramatic instinct and engaging simplicity of expression were often commended.

BIBLIOGRAPHY

N. Findeyzen, ed.: *Polnoye sobraniye pisem Mikhayla Ivanovicha Glinki* [Collected letters of Glinka] (St Petersburg, 1907)
B. Modzalevsky: 'K biografii Glinki: neskol'ko neizdannïkh pisem' [Towards a biography of Glinka: some unpublished letters], *Muzikal'naya letopis': stat'i i materialï*, ed. A. N. Rimsky-Korsakov (Leningrad, 1925)
A. Shteynberg: 'D. M. Leonova', *SovM* (1946), nos.2–3, p.121
J. Leyda and S. Bertensson: *The Musorgsky Reader* (New York, 1947/*R*1970)
V. Bagadurov: 'M. I. Glinka kak pevets i vokal'nïy pedagog' [Glinka as singer and singing teacher], *M. I. Glinka: sbornik materialov i stat'yey*, ed. T. Livanova (Moscow, 1950), 288

JENNIFER SPENCER

Leontovych, Mykola Dmytrovich (*b* Monastïryok, Podolia [now Vinnitsa province], 13 Dec 1877; *d* Markovka, nr. Tul'chin, 25 Jan 1921). Russian composer, ethnomusicologist, teacher and conductor. Born into the family of a priest, he studied at the seminaries of Stargorod and Kamenets-Podol'skiy. He had received no systematic education in music, but after graduating (in 1899) he worked as a singing teacher in primary and middle educational establishments and also as an organizer and director of amateur choirs and orchestras. In 1904 he completed as an external student the educational classes of the St Petersburg court chapel choir, and from 1909 to 1914 he had sporadic consultations with Boleslav Leopol'dovich Yavorsky on the recommendation of Taneyev. From 1918 he worked as a teacher at the Lisenko Music and Drama Institute in Kiev, as an organizer and director of the First Ukrainian State Chapel, and as an inspector of the Ukrainian State SO and of cultural and educational establishments.

Leontovych was the most brilliant of the immediate successors of Lisenko. Central to his output are the arrangements of Ukrainian folksongs for unaccompanied choral ensembles, a genre represented in much Ukrainian music of the early 20th century. His original method of arranging folk material, called by Nejedlý the 'characteristic method', definitively established the fun-

damental features of the national style and decisively influenced the further assimilation of the nation's folklore by professional composers. Leontovych was the first Ukrainian composer to abolish completely the stylistic contradiction between original folk material and arrangement: by means of a professional technique he brought about an organic synthesis, although in his early arrangements (1899–1908) he followed Lisenko's aesthetic, employing the latter's chordal-harmonic style of accompaniment, which was connected with the development of the traditions of the 17th- and 18th-century choral *kant*.

It was in his middle period (1908–18) that Leontovych departed radically from traditional notions of arrangement. The change is reflected in the selection of songs (those with a vividly expressed individual character) and themes (predominantly ritual), all within the boundaries of a single eastern Volhynian–Podolian musical dialect, and in the texture, an original fusion of Ukrainian folk polyphony (with its improvised inner parts) and the devices of contrasting and imitative counterpoint. The intensification of melodic self-sufficiency in the choral parts led to the creation of thematically striking counterpoints which sometimes outshine the original tunes in their figurative richness, especially at climaxes, where Leontovych freely dispensed with the couplet-variation form. All these features contributed to the consolidation of a distinctive genre: the folklore poem miniature. Between 1918 and 1920 Leontovych sought to create more extended original works, both unaccompanied choral and vocal instrumental. His unfinished opera *Na rusalchyn velykden'* surpasses in complexity and immediacy of expression all that had been achieved previously in Ukrainian music. *Shchedryk*, performed in December 1916 by a students' choir of Kiev University, won him fame among the whole people, and his position as the most popular Ukrainian composer has remained firm.

WORKS

Narodni pisni [Folksongs] (Kiev, 1921)
Ukrayins'ki narodni pisni (Lips'k, 1923)
ed. P. Kozytsky: *Muzychni tvory* [Musical works] (Kiev, 1925)
ed. Ya. Yurmas: *Muzychni tvory* (Kharkov and Kiev, 1930)
Khorovi tvory [Choral works] (Kiev, 1970)
Povnyy zbirnyk narodnïkh pisen' [Complete collection of folksongs] (Sask, n.d.)

WRITINGS

Zbirka statey ta materialiv [Collection of articles and materials] (Kiev, 1947)

BIBLIOGRAPHY

Z. Nejedlý: *Ukrayins'ka respublikans'ka kapela* (Lwów, 1922)
Svitova kontsertova podorozh ukrayins'kovo natsional'novo khoru [World concert tour of the Ukrainian national choir] (Paris, 1928)
V. Dyachenko: *M. D. Leontovych* (Kharkov, 1941)
M. Gordiychuk: *M. D. Leontovych* (Kiev, 1972)

BOGDAN LUKANYUK

Leopardi, Venanzio [Venantio] (*b* Camerino, Marche; *d* Jan 1658 or later). Italian singer, instrumentalist and composer. He was a contralto and tenor and was admired not only for his singing but also for his playing of the harpsichord and theorbo. According to a document of 1645 (in *I-MOs*; pr. in Culley, 237, 275) he had for long served Cardinal Colonna at Bologna as musician and valet and had also been in Germany, 'where he has served many princes'; he was said to be still young. From May to October 1646 he was on the payroll of the Collegio Germanico, Rome. He was in the service of the Duke of Modena when he was given leave of absence to sing in Luigi Rossi's opera *Orfeo* in Paris in 1647. He spent the early months of 1647 in Paris and sent a number of interesting letters to the duke about musical life there (they are in *MOs* and are printed in Prunières, 378ff). Not long afterwards he left the duke's service, but in a letter of 30 September 1653 he asked to be taken back again; it is not known if his request was granted. He is next heard of as a musician in the service of the Empress Eleonora at the Vienna court early in 1656, the year in which he also returned to Rome. He was again paid by the Collegio Germanico from April 1657 to January 1658. The above-mentioned document of 1645 states that he had composed theatre, church and (presumably vocal) chamber music. Four solo cantatas with continuo and a motet for three sopranos (in *I-Bc*, *MOe*, *Rc* and *TE*, *GB-Och* and *A-Wn*) are the only extant pieces known to be by him. *Di già dato il tributo* (transcr. in Prunières, appx, 7ff) is an extended cantata in several contrasting sections; it is of fair musical interest and may be taken as representative of his work.

BIBLIOGRAPHY

H. Prunières: *L'opéra italien en France avant Lulli* (Paris, 1913)
E. Schmitz: *Geschichte der weltlichen Solokantate* (Leipzig, 1914, rev. 2/1955), 135
H. Knaus: *Die Musiker im Archivbestand des kaiserlichen Oberst-hofmeisteramtes (1637–1705)*, i (Vienna, 1967), 68f, 129
T. D. Culley: *Jesuits and Music, i: A Study of the Musicians Connected with the German College in Rome during the 17th Century and of their Activities in Northern Europe* (Rome, 1970), esp. 237f, 275

NIGEL FORTUNE

Leopold I (*b* Vienna, 9 June 1640; *d* Vienna, 5 May 1705). Holy Roman Emperor, composer and patron of music, second son of the Emperor FERDINAND III. A member of the house of HABSBURG, he received a broad humanistic education under the tutelage of the Jesuit Neidhard to prepare him for intellectual and spiritual pursuits rather than for the succession to the throne. His training included extensive instruction in playing various instruments (notably the harpsichord, violin and flute) and in composition, probably at the hands of Antonio Bertali and Markus and Wolfgang Ebner, the last of whom kept a collection of his early works, *Spartitura compositionum sacrae regiae maiestatis Hungariae, Leopoldi I*, composed and copied between 1655 and 1657. When the first son and chosen successor to Ferdinand III died, however, Leopold succeeded to the royal thrones of Hungary (1655) and Bohemia (1656) and on the death of his father was crowned Holy Roman Emperor on 18–19 July 1658. To ensure the succession he entered into three marriages: in 1667 to Margaretha Theresia of Spain (1651–73), in 1673 to Claudia Felicitas of Tyrol (1653–76) and in 1676 to Eleonora Magdalena Theresia of the Palatinate (1655–1720), who gave birth to his successors, Joseph I and Charles VI.

Contemporary accounts of Leopold I stress the following aspects of his personality and habits: his deep religiosity, reflected in his tenacious defence of the Roman Catholic Church and penetrating the entire life of the court; his love of outdoor activities such as hunting and open-air entertainments of various kinds; his knowledge of at least four languages and skill in Italian poetry; and his love of, and excellence in, music. As a politician he relied heavily on the advice of his counsellors and was strongly influenced by the court clergy. Kann, comparing him with Louis XIV, characterized him as

irresolute in action but tenacious in the defense of the *status quo*, narrow and yet with an artistic mind, impecunious and splendor-loving, homely, unheroic, and unmartial, he was indeed the true antithesis of his more brilliant opponent and cousin.

For the history of music, Leopold I is significant both as a major patron and as a composer. Considering the severe internal as well as external political problems during his reign (including the siege of Vienna by Ottoman forces in 1683 and subsequent campaigns to alleviate the Turkish threat, the attempts to secure the western frontiers of the empire against French invasions, the artificially prolonged Counter-Reformation and the great plague of 1679–80), it is surprising to find an unprecedented cultural growth at the Habsburg court and in the heartland of the empire in general. Building on the foundations laid by his predecessors (especially Ferdinand III), Leopold considerably expanded the court musical establishment – the imperial Hofkapelle – by continuing to employ Italian musicians, among them the composers Antonio Bertali, G. F. Sances, Antonio Draghi, M. A. Ziani and Francesco Conti, but also by drawing on native talent, including the composers J. H. Schmelzer, J. K. Kerll, F. T. Richter and J. J. Fux. Although he did not neglect church music or independent instrumental music, his main interest was in dramatic music. Outside the court, this interest can be seen in his encouragement of Jesuit drama, probably for religious as well as artistic reasons. At court, secular and sacred dramatic music flourished. Generous financial support for opera productions, including the extravagant expenditure of about 100,000 florins for the performance of Antonio Cesti's *Il pomo d'oro* (as opposed to an average of about 20,000 florins per opera production and the average yearly salary of 2000 florins for the Kapellmeister); the judicious hiring of librettists, composers and stage designers, among them the dominating collaborators Nicolò Minato, Draghi, Schmelzer and L. O. Burnacini; participation in performances by members of the imperial family; the emperor's personal interest and support: these all resulted in a theatrical life at court not equalled at any other court during his reign. Thus, between 1658 and 1705 more than 400 dramatic compositions were presented there: operas and shorter secular dramatic works during Carnival and as celebrations of birthdays and name days of members of the imperial family as well as on other important occasions at court; and oratorios and *sepolcri* mainly in Lent, notably to commemorate the Passion on Maundy Thursday and Good Friday.

As a composer, Leopold I contributed a large number of works to the repertory performed at court. In style they follow the Venetian tradition as seen especially in composers active in Vienna, such as Bertali and Draghi. His sacred and secular Italian dramatic compositions evince a careful attention to the text, skilful manipulation of recitative and arioso sections rather than a regular alternation of clearly defined recitatives and arias, and a preference for a simple and deeply felt melodic style rather than vocal display by means of extensive use of coloratura. By contrast his ballet music and his contributions to the developing German-language comedy – mainly short songs and arias – are light and extremely simple and use folk music idioms; they are clearly influenced by Schmelzer. Leopold's most successful compositions are without question his liturgical works. In them he combined polychoral techniques, the concertato style, and effective melodic writing influenced by characteristics of monody to produce substantial works – especially the *Missa angeli custodis* and the three lessons for the burial of his second wife – that proclaim him as no mere aristocratic dilettante, but as a talented and successful composer.

WORKS

Edition: *Musikalische Werke der Kaiser Ferdinand III., Leopold I., und Joseph I.*, ed. G. Adler (Vienna, 1892–3) [A]

(*principal source A-Wn; for catalogue see Brosche*)

STAGE

Apollo deluso, dramma per musica (A. Draghi), Vienna, 1669, collab. G. F. Sances; excerpts in A ii
Giudizio d'amore, dramma musicale
Del silenzio profondo, serenata
Rimbomba mia tromba, serenata
L'amoroso giudizio, dialogo musicale

Die vermeinte Brueder- und Schwesterliebe (C. Schlegel), Linz, 7 Jan 1677; excerpts in A ii
Der thöreichte Schaffer, Vienna, 1683; arias in A ii
Die Ergetzungstund der Sclavinnen aus Samien, Vienna, 1685 [Comedy], Vienna, 1686
[Festa], Vienna, 1695; excerpts in A ii
[Comedy], Vienna, 1697; excerpts in A ii
Fineza contra fineza (P. Calderón); excerpts in A ii
Recitatives and arias, incl. those in works by A. Draghi, A. Cesti, G. F. Sances and J. H. Schmelzer; some in A ii

ORATORIOS, SEPOLCRI

Il sagrifizio d'Abramo (Conte Caldana), Vienna, 26 March 1660; scene in A ii
Il figliuol prodigo (G. P. Monesio), Vienna, 1663
Il lutto dell'universo (F. Sbarra), Vienna, 29 March 1668; excerpts in A ii
L'ingratitudine rimproverata (N. Minato), Vienna, 12 April 1675, music lost
Die Erlösung des menschlichen Geschlechts (J. A. Ruedolf), Vienna, 30 March 1679; 2 scenes in A ii
Il transito di Giuseppe (Minato), Vienna, 1680
Sig des Leydens Christi über die Sinnligkeit (Ruedolf), Vienna, 26 March 1682; excerpts in A ii; ed. E. Strache (Vienna, 1918)
S Antonio di Padova, Vienna, 1684; 4 scenes in A ii
L'amor della redentione, oratorio delli sette maggiori dolori della vergine (Minato), Vienna, 9 April 1677
Recitative, 2 arias in A. Draghi: La virtù della croce, A ii

SACRED VOCAL

Missa angeli custodis, 4vv, insts, A i; Missa pro defunctis, 5vv, insts (dated 1673); 3 lessons, 5vv, insts (1 dated 1676), A ii; 2 offertories, 4, 6vv, insts (1 dated, 1662); Magnificat, 5vv, insts; Dies irae, 4vv, insts (1673); Stabat mater, 4vv, insts; 5 Marian antiphons, 1–5vv, insts, 1 in A i; 1 other antiphon, 5vv, org, A i; 3 litanies, 4–6vv, insts; 6 motets, 1–5vv, insts, 1 in A i; 5 psalms, 1–4vv, insts, 2 in A i; 12 hymns, 2–6vv, insts, 3 in A i; masses and Stabat mater ed. M. Dietz (Vienna, 1891)

SECULAR

4 canzonettas, 1–3vv, insts, 1655–7; madrigal, 3vv, bc
Sonata, 4 va, bc, 1656; ritornello [sonata] (bc only extant); 102 dances [incl. 16 suites] (many inc., bc only extant), 28 in A ii

Lost works, incl. 2 masses, Dies irae, Stabat mater, Compline, 2 Magnificat, 11 antiphons, litany, 2 Miserere, 20 motets, cited in *Distinta specificatione dell'archivio musicale per il servizio della cappella e camera cesarea, A-Wn*, catalogue of Leopold's private collection

BIBLIOGRAPHY

E. Brown: *Ganz sonderbare Reisen durch Niederland, Teutschland* (Nuremberg, 1684; Eng. trans., 1685)
E. Vehse: *Geschichte des Oesterreichischen Hofes seit der Reformation* (Hamburg, 1856; Eng. trans., 1856, repr. 1896, as *Memoirs of the Court and Aristocracy of Austria*)
J. Fiedler: *Die Relationen der Botschafter Venedigs über Deutschland und Oesterreich im siebzehnten Jahrhundert* (Vienna, 1867)
L. von Köchel: *Die kaiserliche Hof-Musikkapelle in Wien von 1543 bis 1867* (Vienna, 1869)
——: *Johann Josef Fux* (Vienna, 1872/R1974)
M. Landau: *Die italienische Literatur am österreichischen Hofe* (Vienna, 1879)
G. Adler: 'Die Kaiser Ferdinand III., Leopold I., Joseph I. und Karl VI. als Tonsetzer und Förderer der Musik', *VMw*, viii (1892), 252
A. von Weilen: *Zur Wiener Theatergeschichte: die vom Jahre 1629 bis zum Jahre 1740 am Wiener Hofe zur Aufführung gelangten Werke theatralischen Charakters und Opern* (Vienna, 1901)
A. Schering: *Geschichte des Oratoriums* (Leipzig, 1911/R1966)
R. Kralik: *Oesterreichische Geschichte* (Vienna, 1913)
G. Renker: *Das Wiener Sepolcro* (diss., U. of Vienna, 1913)
E. Wellesz: 'Studien zur Geschichte der Wiener Oper, i: Cavalli und der Stil der venetianischen Oper von 1640–1660', *SMw*, i (1913), 1–58
G. Adler: 'Zur Geschichte der Wiener Messkomposition in der zweiten Hälfte des XVII. Jahrhunderts', *SMw*, iv (1916), 5–45
E. Wellesz: 'Die Opern und Oratorien in Wien 1660–1708', *SMw*, vi (1919), 5–138
P. Nettl: 'Die Wiener Tanzkomposition in der zweiten Hälfte des siebzehnten Jahrhunderts', *SMw*, viii (1921), 45–175
——: *Das Wiener Lied im Zeitalter des Barock* (Vienna, 1934)
M. Eisenberg: 'Studien zur Historiographie über Kaiser Leopold I', *Mitteilungen des Instituts für österreichische Geschichtsforschung*, li (1937), 359
E. C. Salzer: 'Teatro italiano in Vienna barocca', *Rivista italiana del dramma*, ii (1938), 47
——: 'Il teatro allegorico italiano a Vienna', *Rivista italiana del dramma*, iii (1939), 65
A. Liess: *Wiener Barockmusik* (Vienna, 1946)
G. Tauschhuber: *Kaiser Leopold I und das Wiener Barocktheater* (Mühldorf am Inn, 1947)
H. V. F. Somerset: 'The Habsburg Emperors as Musicians', *ML*, xxx (1949), 204
F. Hadamowsky: 'Barocktheater am Wiener Kaiserhof; mit einem Spielplan (1625–1740)', *Jb der Gesellschaft für Wiener Theaterforschung 1951–2* (1955)
R. A. Kann: *A Study in Austrian Intellectual History* (New York, 1960)
O. Wessely: 'Kaiser Leopolds I. "Vermeinte Bruder- und Schwesterliebe" ', *SMw*, xxv (1962), 586
C. D. Harris: *Keyboard Music in Vienna during the Reign of Leopold I, 1658–1705* (diss., U. of Michigan, 1967)
H. Knaus: *Die Musiker im Archivbestand des kaiserlichen Obersthofmeisteramtes (1637–1705)* (Vienna, 1967–9)
H. Seifert: 'Die Festlichkeiten zur ersten Hochzeit Kaiser Leopolds I', *ÖMz*, xxix (1974), 6
G. Brosche: 'Die musikalischen Werke Kaiser Leopolds I: ein systematisch-thematisches Verzeichnis der erhaltenen Kompositionen', *Beiträge zur Musikdokumentation: Franz Grasberger zum 60. Geburtstag* (Tutzing, 1975), 27–82
C. B. Schmidt: 'Antonio Cesti's *Il pomo d'oro*: a Reexamination of a Famous Hapsburg Court Spectacle', *JAMS*, xxix (1976), 381–412
J. P. Spielman: *Leopold I of Austria* (London, 1977)

RUDOLF SCHNITZLER

Leopolita [Lwowczyk, ze Lwowa], **Marcin** [Leopolitanus, Martinus] (*d* Lwów, 1589). Polish composer and ?poet. What little is known about him derives from Starowolski and Zimorowicz and is otherwise undocumented. He is said to have studied under Sebastian z Felsztyna and Jan Jeleń of Tuchola, and to have been a student at Kraków Academy; he was not, as has been claimed, organist at the court of King Sigismund August, but he has been identified with a 'Marcin' who was engaged in 1560 as a 'compositor cantus' at this court. His extant works are the *Missa Paschalis* (formerly in *PL-Kk*; ed. in Monumenta musicae sacrae in Polonia, iii, Poznań, 1889, and WDMP, xxxv, 1957), which is based on melodic material deriving from four Polish Easter hymns, four five-part motets, which survive only in organ transcriptions (in *PL-WRu*; two, one in a reconstruction of the original version, ed. M. Perz in *Muzyka w dawnym Krakowie*, ed. Z. M. Szweykowski, 1964; one, also reconstructed, ed. M. Perz in *Muzyka staropolska*, ed. H. Feicht, 1966; one ed. in AMP, xv, 1968), and another motet of which only two vocal parts are extant; two other masses, *Missa Rorate* and *Missa de Resurrectione*, were known as recently as the end of the 19th century (then in *PL-Kk*) but have since disappeared.

BIBLIOGRAPHY

SMP
S. Starowolski: *Scriptorum polonicorum Hecatontas* (Frankfurt am Main, 1625, 2/1627)
B. Zimorowicz: *Viri illustres civitatis Leopoliensis* (Lwów, 1671); ed. K. Heck (Lwów, 1890)
A. Chybiński: *Słownik muzyków dawnej Polski* [Dictionary of early Polish musicians] (Kraków, 1949)
H. Feicht: 'O mszy wielkanocnej Marcina Leopolity' [Concerning Marcin Leopolita's Easter mass], *KM*, ii/6 (1930), 109

M. Perz: 'Motety Marcina Leopolity', *Studia Hieronymo Feicht septuagenario dedicata* (Kraków, 1967), 155–89
——: 'Rękopiśmienne partesy olkuskie' [The contents of a manuscript from Olkusz], *Muzyka*, xiv/2 (1969), 18

ELŻBIETA ZWOLIŃSKA

Leotsakos, George S. (*b* Athens, 9 Aug 1935). Greek music critic, musicologist and composer. He studied music with Papaioannou at the Hellenic Conservatory, Athens (graduated 1964), and as a student began writing music criticism for the Athens morning newspaper, *Kathimerini*, succeeding Dounias as full-time critic in 1962. Subsequently he worked for several daily papers in Athens, including *Messimvrini* (1961–3), *Ta nea* (1965–75) and *To vima* (1975); he also served as music editor for the Greek edition of the *Encyclopaedia Britannica* (1971) and as a producer of Greek art music programmes for Hellenic Radio and Television (from 1975). From 1956 he developed an interest in ethnomusicology and has been responsible for introducing programmes of traditional Asian music to the Greek public. In later research he concentrated on the history of modern Greek music since 1830. His compositions, mostly Asian in character, are in a free atonal style, and were written between 1957 and 1966.

WRITINGS
'Protassis yia to noh' [Remarks about noh theatre], *Epoches*, (1965), no.29, p.33
'Bartok, génie discret', *Musique hongroise*, ed. M. Fleuret (Paris, 1972), 72
'Japan's Presence in Greek Musical Life and Creation', *Studies on Japanese Culture*, i, ed. S. Ōta and R. Fukuda (Tokyo, 1973), 576
'Greece', *Dictionary of Contemporary Music*, ed. J. Vinton (New York, 1974), 284
'Synchronoi ellines synthetes: Kyriakos Sfetsas' [Contemporary Greek composers: Kyriakos Sfetsas], *Theltio kritikis discographias* (1975), nos.14–17, p.312
'Yannis Christou (1926–1970), 1: Teleftea erga' [Jani Christou 1926–70, 1: Final works], *Theltio kritikis discographias* (1975), nos.14–17, p.328
Articles in *Grove 6*

DIMITRI CONOMOS

Leoz, Jesús García (*b* Olite, Navarre, 10 Jan 1904; *d* Madrid, 25 Feb 1953). Spanish composer. Born into a family of musicians, he began his career as cantor in his native village, and then studied in Pamplona, where he was a member of the Orfeón Pamplonés. When he was 17 he went to Argentina, earning his living as a teacher and pianist. On his return to Spain he studied composition with del Campo and the piano with Balsa; later he was the favourite pupil of Turina, whose nationalist style he followed in his own music, while keeping his individuality. He had many popular successes and was twice winner of the National Music Prize.

WORKS
(*selective list*)
Stage: La duquesa del Candil, zarzuela, 1947; La alegre alcaldesa, zarzuela, 1949; La zapatera y el embozado, ballet, 1950; Primavera del portal, retablo lírico navideño, 1952; Barataria, opera, inc.
Orch: 3 danzas, 1934; Homenaje a Manolete, gui, str, 1948; Sinfonia, 1950
Chamber: Sonata, vn, pf, 1932; Str Qt, 1940; Pf Qt, 1946
Pf: Giga en rondó, 1931; Sonatina, 1933, orchd
Many songs (Lorca, Machado, etc), film scores
Principal publisher: Unión Musical Española

BIBLIOGRAPHY
A. Fernández Cid: *Jesús Leoz* (Madrid, 1953)

CARLOS GÓMEZ AMAT

Le Petit, Johannes. *See* NINOT LE PETIT.

Le Picard. Northern French and Belgian family of organ builders. Philippe (i) (*fl* Amiens, 1667; *d* early 1702) built a new organ at Montdidier in 1667 and restored that in Amiens Cathedral in 1671. With his sons Antoine (*fl* 1685–1716) and Joseph he enlarged the organ at Liessies in 1693–5 and restored that in Noyon Cathedral in 1698. Antoine constructed a new organ with three manuals and 36 stops at St Hubert's Basilica in 1685 (case survives) and repaired that at Amiens Cathedral early in the 18th century. Philippe (ii) (*b* Noyon; *d* ? Liège, *c*1730), another son, married Marie-Anne Delaplace before 1701. A fine builder, he worked on the organs at St Pierre, Liège (1702); the Cathedral of St Lambert, Liège (1705; with French pedals); St Alexandre and St Hermes, Theux (1710 and 1716); and St Croix, Liège (1716).

Jean-Baptiste (baptized Liège, 23 May 1706; *d* *c*1760), son of Philippe (ii), spent his whole life in Liège where in 1755 he was a priest, probably at St Pierre. Also a fine builder in the French style, his organs were made with short compass divisions (*Récit, c'*, and *Echo, c*), and pedal pull-downs. His instruments include those at: St Jean-Baptiste, Namur (1731; restoration); Abbaye de Beaufais, Liège (1741–2; one manual, 13 stops, with pull-downs; still extant); Nunhem, near Roermond (1742; two manuals, with pull-downs; the *Positif* survives as the choir organ in the Martinikerk at Groningen); Houtain-l'Evêque (*c*1745; one manual, with pull-downs; extant); Roermond (*c*1745; now in the Gereformeerde Oosterkerk, Utrecht); Roermond, Groot-Seminarie (1745; case and seven stops survive); Abbaye St Michel, Torn (1745); Hodimont (1747); Roermond Cathedral (1750–52; three manuals, with pull-downs); Notre-Dame-aux-Fonts, Liège; St Loup, Namen; St Pierre, Liège (1739–41; four manuals, 39 stops, with pull-downs); the Abbaye, Herkenrode (1744–6); Onze Lieve Vrouwen, Tongeren (1750–52; case survives); Benedictine Abbey, St Truiden (1753–6).

BIBLIOGRAPHY
N. Dufourcq: *Esquisse d'une histoire de l'orgue en France* (Paris, 1935), 311
G. L. J. Alexis: 'Un facteur français établi à Liège', *Bulletin trimestriel des Amis de l'orgue*, x/34 (1938), 21
A. Bouman: *De orgels in de Groote of Martinikerk te Groningen* (Amsterdam, 1941), 98ff
M. Waltmans and M. Smeets: *Kerkorgels te Roermond* (Heythuysen, 1957)

GUY OLDHAM

L'Epine [Lépine, Lespine]. French family of organ builders. Adrian L'Epine (*fl* Bordeaux, 1711–31) worked on the organs of Bordeaux Cathedral (1711), St Jean-de-Luz (1724) and St Michel, Bordeaux (1731). Jean-François L'Epine (i) (*b* Abbeville, *c*1682; *d* Toulouse, 1762), brother of Adrian, settled in Toulouse about 1725 and worked at Albi, Rodez and Lodève. His son Jean-François L'Epine (ii) *l'aîné* (*b* Toulouse, 1732; *d* Pézenas, 1817) was a pupil and colleague of Bédos de Celles. He built the organs at Pézenas (1755–6; with an early example of a Hautboy on the *Récit*) and Montpellier Cathedral (in collaboration with Dominique Cavaillé-Coll). He worked for a long time with Isnard at Béziers and at Narbonne (1776–80). Another son of Jean-François L'Epine (i), Adrien (*b* Toulouse, 1735; *d* Paris), married F.-H. Clicquot's sister. He worked at Nantes (1767), Nogent-sur-Seine, Brie-Comte-Robert, the chapel of the Ecole Militaire, Paris (1772; three manuals, 31 stops including two Dessus de flûte), Montargis (1778) and St Médard, Paris (1778). He also built harpsichords and presented a combined piano and organ at the Académie des Sciences in 1772.

BIBLIOGRAPHY

F. Raugel: 'Autour de Jean-François l'Epine', *L'orgue*, nos.40–43 (1946–7)

F. Douglass: *The Language of the Classical French Organ* (New Haven, 1969)

GUY OLDHAM

L'Epine, (Francesca) Margherita de (*b* *c*1683; *d* London, 8 Aug 1746). Italian soprano, perhaps of Huguenot extraction. She sang with Durastanti in the pasticcio *L'oracolo in sogno* at Venice in 1700; the cast were described as virtuosos of the court of Mantua. She arrived in London in late 1702, probably from Tuscany with the German composer JAKOB GREBER, whose mistress she was (the poet laureate Nicholas Rowe satirized her as 'base Greber's Peg'), and her sister, also a singer (MARIA GALLIA). L'Epine sang at Lincoln's Inn Fields in a play called *The Fickle Shepherdess*, for which she received 20 guineas on 27 May 1703. She appeared twice with Greber at the same theatre in June, in works of his composition, and was singing at Southborough near Tunbridge Wells in the summer. She was courted by more than one peer of the realm and lived with Daniel Finch, Earl of Nottingham, at his seat, Burley, during the autumn and early winter of 1703. In these early years she danced as well as sang in public. From January 1704 she was employed regularly at Drury Lane until January 1708, when she moved with the rest of the opera company to the Queen's Theatre, remaining there until December 1714. For three years her repertory was confined to songs and cantatas in Italian and English, and included many by Purcell as well as Bononcini and Alessandro Scarlatti. She enjoyed the usual benefit each spring. It was at this period that the rivalry between her partisans and those of the English soprano Catherine Tofts grew notorious; on 5 February 1704 a former servant of the latter created a disturbance in the theatre by throwing oranges and hissing when L'Epine was singing. L'Epine's extramural activities inspired many an unheroic couplet in the press and more exalted circles; on 13 July 1706 an anti-theatrical writer in *The Observator* asked: 'Can we help Laughing and Weeping the same time, to see a Secretary retiring from the Great Affairs of State to an Allcove with Donna Margaritta de la Pin, alias Pegg Thorn, to hear her Sing "Colly my Cow", and "Uptails all"?'.

L'Epine returned to the Continent for a time late in 1704; during the following summer Greber, with whom she lived in Suffolk Street, left England. She sang occasionally at Chelsea College, York Buildings and Hickford's Room and on 5 February 1706 at court. On 13 April she introduced at Drury Lane a new English cantata 'written and compos'd after the Italian manner'. The first London opera in which she is known to have appeared was Haym's pasticcio *Camilla* at Drury Lane; she replaced Mrs Tofts as the heroine at the fourth performance (23 April 1706) and sang the part probably until 4 June. On 1 April 1707 she sang in the

'The Rehearsal of an Opera': painting (first half of the 18th century) by Marco Ricci (private collection). Nicolini and Catherine Tofts (dressed in white) sing a duet, accompanied by Haym at the harpsichord, Margherita de L'Epine (with a muff) stands to their right talking to Pepusch (extreme right), while her mother stands behind holding a fan; other characters include Heidegger (seated extreme right), the violinists John, James and Michael Festing (left) and the cellist Andrea Caporale

Pepusch pasticcio *Thomyris*, and from then until 1714 was in almost all the operas, most of them pasticcios, produced in London: a revival of *Camilla* (December 1707, in a male part), *Love's Triumph* (February 1708), A. Scarlatti's *Pirro e Demetrio* (December 1708 and later), *Clotilda* (March 1709), *Almahide* (January 1710 and later), Mancini's *Idaspe fedele* (March 1710 and later), Gasparini's *Antioco* (December 1711) and *Ambleto* (February 1712), Galliard's English opera *Calypso and Telemachus* (in which she played Calypso, May 1712), *Ernelinda* (February 1713 and later), *Dorinda* (the revival of January 1714), *Creso* (January 1714) and *Arminio* (March 1714 and later). In several of these L'Epine played male parts. At her benefit in *Arminio* on 1 May 1714 she inserted additional songs and played 'an Instrument of Invention entirely New, imitating the Harp and Lute'. She sang Goffredo in the revivals of Handel's *Rinaldo* on 23 January 1712 and 6 May 1713 and created the parts of Eurilla in his *Il pastor fido* (22 November 1712), Agilea in *Teseo* (10 January 1713) and probably Flavia in *Silla* (Burlington House, 2 June 1713).

Early in 1715 L'Epine joined Pepusch at Drury Lane, only returning to the King's for a royal command performance of *Idaspe fedele* on 27 August. She had sung in odes by Pepusch as early as 1707, and they gave a concert together at the Great Room, Peter's Court, on 14 June 1710; she was associated with him for the rest of her life. The date of their marriage, generally given as 1718, is uncertain; they had a son John (baptized at St Clement Danes, 9 January 1724), 'a child of very promising parts' according to Hawkins, who died prematurely, probably late in 1738. L'Epine sang in several masques by Pepusch at Drury Lane, including the popular *Venus and Adonis* (March 1715 and later), *Myrtillo* (November 1715), *Apollo and Daphne* (January 1716) and *The Death of Dido* (April 1716). In the first three she played leading male parts, as she did in English revivals of *Camilla*, *Calypso and Telemachus* and *Thomyris* early in 1717. Many of Pepusch's cantatas, especially those with Italian words, were probably written for her. Next season she made a single concert appearance at York Buildings on 5 March 1718, but the following winter was back with Pepusch at the rebuilt Lincoln's Inn Fields Theatre. She sang several of her old parts and in the first performance of Galliard's *Circe* (11 April 1719); five days later she introduced 'a new Trumpet Song' in *Camilla*. She retired at the end of this season and took up teaching; several of her pupils gave concerts in the next few years. In June 1720 she came out of retirement to replace Mrs Turner Robinson in one performance each of Domenico Scarlatti's *Narciso*, Handel's *Radamisto* and Porta's *Numitore* during the Royal Academy's first season at the King's. She sang once at Drury Lane by special request as late as 21 May 1733.

L'Epine was the leading female singer in the years just before and after the introduction of Italian opera to London, and the first Italian to establish a lasting reputation there. She was immensely popular; Downes in 1708 estimated that she had received 'by Modest Computation . . . by the Stage and Gentry above 10,000 Guineas', though this may be an exaggeration (her salary at the opera in 1707–8 and 1712–13 was £400). About 1710 she received £40 for singing in a private concert at the Duchess of Shrewsbury's house in Kensington. Burney was impressed by the difficulty of some of her songs: 'Indeed, her musical merit must have been very considerable to have kept her so long in favour . . . Our galleries would have made her songs very short, had they not been executed in such a manner as to silence theatrical snakes, and command applause'. The compass of the parts Handel composed for her is *d'* to *a''*. She was tall, with a fine stage presence, but according to Hawkins 'remarkably swarthy, and so destitute of personal charms, that Dr Pepusch, who afterwards married her, seldom called her by any other name than Hecate, which she answered to very readily'. She was a fine harpsichordist, and her performance of pieces from the Fitzwilliam Virginal Book, then owned by Pepusch, was much admired. She appears with her mother, Nicolini, Tofts, Pepusch, Heidegger and others in a conversation piece by Marco Ricci (see illustration).

BIBLIOGRAPHY

BurneyH; *HawkinsH*
E. L. Moor: 'Some Notes on the Life of Françoise Marguerite de L'Épine', *ML*, xxviii (1947), 341

WINTON DEAN

Leppard, Raymond (John) (*b* London, 11 Aug 1927). English conductor, harpsichordist and editor. He studied at the University of Cambridge from 1948 to 1952, where Hubert Middleton and Boris Ord were among his teachers. He made his London début as a conductor at the Wigmore Hall in 1952 and soon became known particularly for his lively interpretations of 17th- and 18th-century music and his inventive continuo playing. In 1957 he returned to Cambridge as lecturer in music and Fellow of Trinity College, remaining there until 1967. By then he had appeared at the leading English opera houses: he made his Covent Garden début in 1959 in the bicentenary production of Handel's *Samson* and first appeared at Glyndebourne in 1962 and at Sadler's Wells three years later. He also frequently conducted orchestral concerts, notably with the English Chamber Orchestra, specializing to some extent in 18th-century music; works by Handel, Haydn and Mozart were prominent in his programmes. From 1973 to 1980 he was principal conductor of the BBC Northern SO.

In 1962 Leppard conducted his own edition of Monteverdi's *L'incoronazione di Poppea* at Glyndebourne, inaugurating an important and influential series of revivals there and elsewhere of 17th-century Italian operas, among them Monteverdi's *L'Orfeo* and *Il ritorno d'Ulisse in patria* and works by Cavalli. Leppard's versions of these operas, particularly Cavalli's *L'Ormindo* and *La Calisto*, while successful with a wide public, have been criticized for their free attitude to the original texts, especially in such matters as transposition of voice parts, rich orchestral writing, cuts and insertions, and remodelling of the librettos. Leppard's attitude, defined in his paper 'Cavalli's Operas', *PRMA*, xciii (1966–7), p.67, and in several shorter essays, is essentially an empirical one, based on his keen sense of theatrical timing and effect. Several of his editions have been published (Faber) and a number of recordings have been made which originate from his Glyndebourne performances.

As a harpsichordist and pianist, Leppard's most marked qualities are his liveliness of rhythm and crispness of articulation. Light, dance-like rhythms, polished phrasing and a keen sense of colour characterize his conducting and lend a special charm to his readings of music by Couperin, Rameau and their contemporaries. His Handel performances are notable more for shapeliness of line and precision of detail than for rhythmic breadth. His recordings include Monteverdi madrigals, music by Bach and his sons, Handel concertos and many rare works by 18th- and early 19th-century composers.

STANLEY SADIE

Le Quointe [Le Quoynte, Le Quoint, Le Coincte], **Louis** (*b* Ieper, 19 Oct 1652; *d* St Omer, 9 June 1717). South Netherlands composer and organist. He was a chorister at St Martin, Ieper, from 8 October 1665. After his voice broke he enrolled in the seminary at Ieper and became a Jesuit on 30 September 1675. He spent the rest of his life in various houses of the Jesuit order in the southern Netherlands and northern France – notably at St Omer – generally as director of music and organist. He appears to have written a good deal of music, but only the set of *Psalmi concertati* (1704) and the *Bouquet de fleurs* seem to survive. The psalm collection suggests that he was a competent composer. The themes are often instrumental in nature, and the rhythms are well varied. There is also a wide range of vocal and instrumental textures, though there are too many duets in thirds.

WORKS

Psalmi concertati, 1–5vv, 4, 5 insts, op.6 (Antwerp, 1704)
Bouquet de fleurs, présenté aux âmes dévotes (14 songs), 1v, bc (Paris, 1722)

LOST WORKS
(all cited in catalogues)

Psalmi breves pro omnibus . . . vesperis, 1–4vv, 3, 4 insts, op.1
Airs spirituels nouveaux, 1–3vv . . . pour les violons, les flûtes, les hautbois, le clavecin et l'orgue en forme de duo, et de trio, op.2 (Valenciennes, 1696)
Pièces en trio . . . à la manière italienne et . . . française, vn, fl, ob, op.2 (Valenciennes, 1696) [presumably inst. arr. of Airs spirituels]
Psaumes, 1–5vv (Antwerp, 1704)
Missae, litaniae, motetti et Tantum ergo, 5vv/insts, op.3a
Sonates, 2 vn, va, b viol, bc, op.3a [sic]
Missa brevis, motetta, Te Deum et litania, 5vv/insts, op.5
Motetti, 1v, bc, op.7
Motetti, 1v, 3 insts, op.9
Compositione sacre de diversi, 1–5vv, op.11

BIBLIOGRAPHY

E. vander Straeten: *La musique aux Pays-Bas avant le XIXᵉ siècle*, i (Brussels, 1867/R1969), 205, 213, 218, 226
R. Vannes: *Dictionnaire des musiciens (compositeurs)* (Brussels, 1947)
R. Monseur: *Catalogue de la bibliothèque du Conservatoire royal de musique de Liège, Fonds Terry: musique religieuse* (Liège, n.d.)

JOSÉ QUITIN

Le Rat (*fl* 1549–57). French composer. He contributed seven four-voice chansons to anthologies published at Paris between 1549 and 1557 (*RISM* 1549²⁷, 1550¹¹, 1550¹², 1551⁹, 1553²⁰, 1557¹⁰). The texts are all amorous poems typical of the preceding generation; one is by Clément Marot and another by François I or his mentor St Gélais.

FRANK DOBBINS

Lerchenfels, Johann Sixt von [Lerchenfelsu, Jan Sixt z]. *See* SIXT Z LERCHENFELSU, JAN.

Lerethier, Isaac. *See* LHÉRITIER, ISAAC.

Le Riche, Antonius. *See* DIVITIS, ANTONIUS.

Lermontov, Mikhail Yur'evich (*b* Moscow, 15 Oct 1814; *d* Pyatigorsk, 27 July 1841). Russian poet and novelist of Scottish descent. A visit to the Caucasus

when he was nine left a lasting impression on him. In 1834 he became a Guards officer. His first published poem *Hajji Abrek* (1835) had a Caucasian setting; it attracted little attention. He became widely known for a poem attacking society in connection with the death of Pushkin (1837), which was circulated clandestinely; he was consequently expelled from the Guards and transferred to a regiment of the line in the Caucasus. He was pardoned and reinstated (1838) but, as a result of a duel, again posted to the Caucasus in 1840, where he was killed in a duel.

A typical Romantic in life as in art, Lermontov was influenced by such Western writers as Byron, Goethe and Schiller, yet his own Romanticism is specifically Russian, and his work also contains elements of realism which foreshadow Tolstoy and Chekhov. His rhythmically complex poetry, extremely mellifluous and rich in visual imagery, defies translation. His best-known poem *Dyemon* (1829–41) is a version of the Lucifer legend in a Caucasian setting. His fastidious prose also loses much in translation and is little appreciated outside Russia; yet his novel *Geroy nashevo vremeni* ('A hero of our own time', 1840) is one of the masterpieces of Russian fiction.

Many composers have been attracted both by Lermontov's lyric poetry and by the exotic element in much of his work. There are innumerable settings of his short poems, especially by Russian composers; operas, ballets and symphonic poems by such composers as Asaf'yev, Balakirev, Rakhmaninov and Ippolitov-Ivanov have also been based on his works, as well as Glinka's *Prayer* (1855) for solo voice, chorus and orchestra.

WORKS SET TO MUSIC

Geroy nashevo vremeni [A hero of our own time]: Krepost' u kamennovo broda, opera by V. Gaygerova, 1941; Knyazhna Meri [Princess Mary], opera by V. A. Dekhterev, Moscow, 1941; opera by A. N. Alexandrov, Moscow, 1946, rev. 1948; ballet by V. M. Deshevov, 1940; Knyazhna Meri, film score by L. A. Schvarts
Boyarin Orsha [The boyar Orsha]: opera by Kashperov, 1880; opera by K. D. Agrenev-Slavyansky, Tiflis, 1910; operas by G. Fistulari, P. Krotov
Dyemon [Satan]: opera by A. G. Rubinstein, 1875; Tamara, opera by Baron Vietinghof-Scheel, St Petersburg, 1886; lyric scenes by A. S. Yur'evich, St Petersburg, 1891; Thamara, opera by L. A. Bourgault-Ducoudray, 1891; Tamara, opera by L. Rogowski, 1918; Tamara, sym. poem by Balakirev, 1864; cantata by P. I. Blaramberg, 1869; oratorio by P. Gilson; Sym. no.3, op.18, and Tamara, 1v, orch, by E. Nápravník; ballet by S. F. Tsintsadze
Maskarad [The masked ball]: lyric–dramatic scenes by N. A. Kolesnikov, 1890s; incidental music by Glazunov, 1913, perf. 1917; incidental music by V. Ya. Shebalin, 1939; opera by A. V. Mosolov, 1940; opera by V. N. Denbsky, 1941; incidental music by Khachaturian, 1941; opera by Bunin, 1944; opera by B. A. Zeidman, 1945; opera by Nersesov, 1948; opera by A. P. Artamanov, Khar'kov, 1957; ballet by Yu. Lamputin, ?1960
Mtsïri: sym. poem by Catoire, 1899; sym. poem, op.8, by V. A. Senilov, 1906; sym. poem by O. V. Taktakishvili, 1956; ballet by A. Balanchivadze, Tbilisi, 1964; sym. poem, op.54, by Ippolitov-Ivanov, 1923–4

BIBLIOGRAPHY

M. Yu. Karatïgin: 'Lermontov i muzïka', *Sovremennik* (1914), nos.17–20, p.148
——: 'Kontsert Skryabina', *Rech* (1915), no.43, p.6
E. Kann and A. Novikov: 'Muzïka v zhizni i tvorchestve Lermontova', *SovM* (1939), nos.9–10, p.85
E. Kann: *M. Yu. Lermontov i muzïka* (Moscow, 1939)
——: *Romansï i pesnï russkikh kompozitorov XIX stoletiya na tekstï Lermontova* (Moscow and Leningrad, 1941)
I. Eyges: 'Muzïka v zhizni i tvorchestve Lermontova', *Literaturnoye nasledstvo*, xlv–xlvi (Moscow, 1948), 497–540
——: *M. Yu. Lermontov v romansakh i pesnyakh sovetskikh kompozitorov* (Moscow and Leningrad, 1951)
H. Troyat: *L'étrange destin de Lermontov* (Paris, 1952)
B. Glovatskiy: *Lermontov i muzïka* (Moscow and Leningrad, 1964)

APRIL FITZLYON

Lerner, Alan Jay (*b* New York, 31 Aug 1918). American song lyricist. He is noted for his musical plays, particularly those for FREDERICK LOEWE (e.g. *My Fair Lady*, 1956), with whom he worked from 1942; he also wrote for Kurt Weill, Burton Lane, André Previn, Leonard Bernstein and others.

Lerner, Edward R(obert) (*b* New York, 19 April 1920). American musicologist. After taking a PhD in musicology at Yale University, where he studied under Leo Schrade, he taught at Columbia University from 1958 to 1962. Since 1962 he has been on the faculty at Queens College of the City University of New York and was appointed professor of music in 1969. Lerner's writings concentrate on the music of the Renaissance and Middle Ages, particularly the sacred music of these periods and the works of Alexander Agricola. In addition he has edited the *Study Scores of Musical Styles*, an annotated anthology of pieces illustrating the course of music history from plainchant to Bach as an aid to undergraduate instruction.

WRITINGS

The Sacred Music of Alexander Agricola (diss., Yale U., 1958)
'Richard Wagner's Apostle to America: Anton Seidl (1850–1898)', *Columbia Library Columns*, viii (1959), 24
'The "German" Works of Alexander Agricola', *MQ*, xlvi (1960), 56
'Some Motet Interpolations in the Catholic Mass', *JAMS*, xiv (1961), 24
'The Polyphonic Magnificat in 15th-century Italy', *MQ*, l (1964), 44
'Historical Anthologies of Music – a Review and Critique', *College Music Symposium*, x (1970), 123
Articles in *Encyclopedia of World Biography* (New York, 1973)
'The Music of Noel Bauldewen', *JAMS*, xxvii (1974), 525

EDITIONS

A. Agricola: Opera omnia, CMM, xxii/1–5 (1961–70)
Study Scores of Musical Styles (New York, 1968)
Opera omnia Henrici Isaac, CMM, lxv (1974–)

PAULA MORGAN

Le Rochois, Marthe (*b* Caen, *c*1658; *d* Paris, 9 Oct 1728). French soprano and singing teacher. She may have studied with Michel Lambert, who brought her to the attention of his son-in-law, Lully. She entered the Paris Opéra in 1678 and retired in 1698. Lully chose her to create the major female roles in his *Proserpine*, *Persée*, *Amadis*, *Roland* and *Armide*; she was best known for her performance of Armide, the memory of which caused Le Cerf de la Viéville to 'shiver' with delight. Titon du Tillet called her the 'greatest actress and the best model for declamation to have appeared on the Stage' (*Le Parnasse françois*). He also wrote:

Although she was of mediocre height, dark complexioned and possessed a rather ordinary figure as seen off-stage, . . . On stage she made one forget all the most beautiful Actresses; she had the air of a Queen or Goddess, her head nobly placed, with an admirable sense of Gesture; all her actions were correct and natural. She knew what to do during the *Ritournelle* which played while an Actress came on-stage, and she was a master of pantomime. . . .

On her retirement she received a 1500-livre pension which was augmented by the Duke of Sully. She then purchased a small country house in Certrouville-sur-Seine (now Sartrouville), outside Paris, where she received important musicians, actors and actresses who profited from her 'pleasant conversation, her knowledge and her good taste' (Titon du Tillet). She died in an apartment on rue St Honoré and was buried at St Eustache.

JAMES R. ANTHONY

Lerolle, Jacques. *See* ROUART-LEROLLE.

Le Rouge, Guillaume. *See* ROUGE, GUILLAUME.

Le Roux, Gaspard (*b* 2nd half of the 17th century; *d* ?Paris, 1705–7). French composer and harpsichordist. The first mention of him is in the *Mercure de France* of March 1690, where, in connection with an *air spirituel*, there is a note stating that the figured bass was by 'M. le Roux, maistre de musique'. In the *Livre commode des adresses de Paris*, he is listed among the foremost harpsichordists, along with Lebègue, François Couperin, d'Anglebert and others. In a list of taxes paid by musicians in 1695 he appears among the very finest and best known. Nothing significant is then heard of him until 1705, when his one collection of harpsichord pieces was published. Internal evidence suggests that he must have composed them some years before this. Since there is no dedication it may be inferred that he did not need patronage. The tax records speak of him as an organist, but since the trios in the collection are subtle and imaginative we can assume that he was not only a keyboard player. It was surely his popularity with the public that led to the pirated Amsterdam edition of the pieces (without the trios) first advertised in Roger's catalogue of 1706. An inventory of 17 June 1707 proves that he died before that date. Sebastien de Brossard referred to him in 1725 as having been 'the celebrated master of the harpsichord and excellent musician'.

Le Roux's *Pièces de clavessin* (Paris, 1705; edn., New York, 1959) is arranged in what are in effect suites, although he did not use the term; pieces in the same tonality are grouped together, G minor being the commonest. There is an archaic quality in the preludes in that they revert to the most rhythmically ambiguous notation of simple semibreves, the practice of Louis Couperin, though they are much simpler than Couperin's. The allemandes and courantes are remarkably sophisticated examples of a well developed, lute-based French keyboard style. The sarabandes show a diversity not to be found in those of other composers of the period: two *sarabandes en rondeau* indicate connections with the chaconne-rondeau convention; the qualification merely describes a simple return, while a fuller and more traditional use of rondeau structure can be found in the first 54 bars of the F major chaconne. Two of the gigues are in the traditional French style, while the G major gigue is in the Italian manner: it is but a short step from this to François Couperin's celebrated union of the two styles and to the two *gigues en rondeau* in Rameau's E minor suite. Among the remaining dances minuets predominate, with five examples and three variations (one of which varies not the melody but the bass line); there are also three gavottes and two passepieds. Apart from the preludes only three pieces in the book are not dances, but these three – *La pièce sans titre*, *La favoritte* and *La bel-ebat* – pointed the way to a general broadening of what could be included in keyboard suites.

A unique feature of Le Roux's *Pièces* is that he also presented nearly every one of them in an arrangement for trio, with the usual figured bass and two melody parts. Although many French composers of the time suggested transcriptions of their works for instruments different from those for which they were originally intended, they neither gave examples nor described how to make them. Le Roux's transcriptions may be played not only by a normal string or wind trio but also by a single melody instrument, with the harpsichordist's right hand playing the other melodic line and his left hand the bass. The trios may also serve as a basis for versions of the pieces for two harpsichords: Le Roux himself suggested this procedure and for six of the pieces offered as a model his own version of a part arranged for a second harpsichord – a valuable and unique feature of his volume. Le Roux's work can very well be considered a summation of 17th-century French keyboard traditions.

Le Roux also composed three motets, and an *air sérieux* by him is in a *Recueil d'airs sérieux et à boire* (Paris, 1701; edn., *ReM*, v, 1924).

BIBLIOGRAPHY
A. Pirro: *L'esthétique de Jean-Sébastien Bach* (Paris, 1907)
A. Tessier: 'L'oeuvre de Gaspard Le Roux'. *RdM*, iii (1922), 168
——: 'Un claveciniste français: Gaspard Le Roux', *ReM*, v/5 (1924), 230
A. Pirro: *Les clavecinistes* (Paris, 1925)

ALBERT FULLER

Le Roux, Maurice (*b* Paris, 6 Feb 1923). French composer and conductor. He studied with Messiaen at the Paris Conservatoire (1946–52), during which period he made his first contributions to the ornamented violence typical of French serial music at the time. The *Cahier d'inventions* for piano has moments of Boulezian tempestuousness, but in general its counterpoint is more classically controlled and suavely lyrical; and, despite the surrealist exuberance that surrounds some of Michaux's images in *Au pays de la magie*, this song cycle is not so far removed from those of Poulenc. The graceful charm of these works is less obvious in *Le cercle des métamorphoses* for orchestra, where Le Roux approached the contemporary pieces of Nono in essential simplicity. At its première (Aix-en-Provence Festival, 1953) *Le cercle* brought an outburst from the audience, responding perhaps to its brash 'point'-style orchestration rather than to the passages of fine-spun harmony. Subsequently Le Roux gave more time to activities other than serious composition. He made a reputation as a composer for the cinema, and he was conductor of the Orchestre National de l'ORTF (1960–68), recording with them Messiaen's *Turangalîla-symphonie* and the first disc of music by Xenakis. His opera performances included *Don Giovanni* at the Paris Opéra (1961) and *Samson et Dalila* at the Liceo in Barcelona (1965). In 1968 he began a popular television series on music, 'Arcana'. He then took appointments as artistic adviser to the Paris Opéra (1969–73) and Inspecteur Général de la Musique (from 1973). His first important concert piece for some time, *Un koan*, was introduced at the 1973 La Rochelle Festival during the course of a day honouring his work as a composer and conductor. The composition takes its title and formal idea from the riddle offered by a Zen Buddhist teacher to his pupil, inviting him to contemplation and perpetual reinterpretation. It is not, however, a 'meditative' piece, but one that bounces from one bold idea to the next with unkempt vigour.

WORKS
(selective list)

Pf Sonata, 1946; Cahier d'inventions (à 2 voix), pf, 1948; Au pays de la magie (Michaux), Bar, pf, 1951; Le cercle des métamorphoses, orch, 1953; Un koan, orch, 1973

Film scores incl. Crin blanc, The Red Balloon, Amère victoire, A View from the Bridge, La chamade

Principal publishers: Choudens, Salabert

WRITINGS
Introduction à la musique contemporaine (Paris, 1947)
Monteverdi (Paris, 1951)

PAUL GRIFFITHS

Leroux, Xavier (Henry Napoléon) (*b* Velletri, Italy, 11 Oct 1863; *d* Paris, 2 Feb 1919). French composer. He was a pupil of Dubois and Massenet at the Paris Conservatoire, where in 1885 he took the Prix de Rome with the cantata *Endymion*. After his return to Paris from Rome he began to make a name as a composer of *verismo* operas; both *La reine Fiammette* (1903) and *Le chemineau* (1907) were eventually performed at the Metropolitan Opera in New York and in other foreign cities. In 1896 Leroux was appointed professor of harmony at the Conservatoire, a post he retained until his death. He also edited *Musica* and founded the Conservatoire Musica.

WORKS
(all vocal scores published in Paris unless otherwise stated)

THEATRICAL

All probably pubd; all first perf. in Paris and all publications indicated are vocal scores, unless otherwise stated.

Evangeline (L. de Gramont and others, after Longfellow), Brussels, Monnaie, 18 Dec 1885 (1895)
Cléopâtre (incidental music, Sardou, Moreau), Porte-St-Martin, 23 Oct 1890
Les Perses (incidental music, after Aeschylus), Odéon, 5 Nov 1896
La montagne enchantée (incidental music), Porte-St-Martin, 12 April 1897, collab. Messager (1897)
Astarté (de Gramont), Opéra, 15 Feb 1901 (1901)
La reine Fiammette (C. Mendès), Opéra-Comique, 23 Dec 1903 (c1910)
William Ratcliff (de Gramont, after Heine), Nice, 26 Jan 1906 (1906)
Théodora (Sardou, P. Ferrier), Monte Carlo, 19 March 1907, orch score (1907)
Le chemineau (J. Richepin), Opéra-Comique, 6 Nov 1907, orch score (1907)
Xantho chez les courtisanes (incidental music, Richepin), Bouffes-Parisiens, 17 March 1910, orch score (1910)
Le carillonneur (Richepin, after G. Rodenbach), Opéra-Comique, 20 March 1913 (1913)
La fille de Figaro, Apollo, 11 March 1914
Les cadeaux de Noël (E. Fabre), Opéra-Comique, 25 Dec 1915 (1915)
1814, Monte Carlo, 6 April 1918
Nausithoé, Nice, 9 April 1920
La plus forte, Opéra-Comique, 11 Jan 1924, orch score (1924)
L'ingénu (C. Méré, R. Gignoux, after Voltaire), Bordeaux, 13 Feb 1931 (1930)

OTHER WORKS

Endymion, cantata, 1885 (1885)
Vénus et Adonis (lyric scene, de Gramont), Concerts de l'Opéra, 1897 (1897)
Mass, 4vv, orch; motets
Harald, ov., orch; suite arr. from incidental music to Les Perses, orch (1897)
Song collections, incl. Les estampes, 10 mélodies (c1895), texts by de Gramont; Les [10] sérénades (1903), texts by Mendès; L'amour d'aimer, 10 mélodies (1913), texts by J. C. Mendès
Separate songs, pf pieces
Pf arr. of Audran's Le grand mogul (c1884)

BIBLIOGRAPHY
D. C. Parker: 'Xavier Leroux', *Musical Standard*, ix (1917), 198
P. Landormy: *La musique française de Franck à Debussy* (Paris, 1943, 2/1948), 8, 158f

GUSTAVE FERRARI,
MARIE LOUISE PEREYRA/BRUCE CARR

Le Roy, Adrian (*b* Montreuil-sur-mer, c1520; *d* Paris, 1598). French music printer, lutenist and composer. He was born into a wealthy merchant family from northern France. As a young man he entered successively the service of two members of the aristocracy close to the French throne. He became acquainted with the editor Jean de Brouilly in Paris, bought some properties from him in St Denis and married his daughter Denise (*d* before 1570). He moved to Brouilly's house at the sign of Ste Geneviève (later the sign of Mount Parnassus) in the rue St Jean-de-Beauvais – an address which was to become famous as the home of one of the greatest of the French music-printing establishments.

On 14 August 1551 Le Roy and his cousin Robert

Ballard obtained a privilege from Henri II to print and sell all kinds of music books. Their first publication appeared at the end of the same month. On 16 February 1553, the king gave Le Roy & Ballard the title of royal music printer, which had been vacant since Attaingnant's death in 1552. The title was renewed in 1568 and 1594. The history of the firm (*see* BALLARD) was brilliant and its successor firms continued to dominate French music printing until the middle of the 18th century. Le Roy was the artistic director, while Ballard, who was nevertheless knowledgeable in music, apparently handled the business side. Le Roy survived Ballard by ten years.

Some of the printing firm's success can be attributed to the entrée both Le Roy and Ballard had to court circles, including the king himself. Le Roy was a regular member of the salon of the Countess of Retz. There he met artists, musicians and the poets Ronsard, Baïf and Melissus, who wrote dedicatory verses for some items.

Le Roy himself wrote odes in dedications to Charles IX and the Count of Retz. Greater artistic success came to him, however, as a composer of chansons and music for lute, guitar and cittern, instruments on which he was an accomplished virtuoso. Some of the songs with guitar accompaniment use the instrument to double the vocal line (for illustration from *Cinquiesme livre de guiterre, see* BALLARD). He was also an important pedagogue; his instruction books written for the amateur lutenist, guitarist and performer on the cistre were so thorough and practical that they continued to be influential through most of the 17th century. He was in addition the author of a book on the rules and theory of music, which his firm published in 1583.

Le Roy's friendship with musicians helped assure the firm's pre-eminence. Certon, Arcadelt, Le Jeune, Costeley and Goudimel were personal acquaintances. The most valuable friendship of all was that with Orlande de Lassus, who stayed in Le Roy's house during a visit to Paris and whom Le Roy introduced at court. A letter dated 14 January 1574, from Le Roy to Lassus describes the delight that Charles IX took in Lassus's music and tells Lassus that the king wanted to make him composer of the royal chamber and that he had urged Le Roy to print his music as soon as possible for fear that it otherwise might be lost. Le Roy & Ballard was chiefly responsible for making Lassus's music well known in France and for disseminating his newest works to the rest of the musical world; much of his music appeared in print there for the first time.

After Ballard's death in July 1588 the firm did not publish anything until 1591, when three books of songs appeared under Le Roy's name alone. After another pause publishing began again in 1593 and continued until Le Roy's death. During this period 15 more books were published, this time under the name of Adrian Le Roy and the widow of Ballard. Le Roy died childless, turning over his interest to Ballard's heirs.

Although Le Roy was respected as a composer and pedagogue, perhaps his most lasting contribution to music history is the influence he exercised as a publisher on musical taste. His firm had very little competition in France; the favour of four kings, Henri II, Charles IX, Henri III and Henri IV, assured the dominance of Le Roy & Ballard. These conditions, together with Le Roy's discrimination and experience as a musician and artistic director of the firm, gave him a dominating role in moulding French musical taste.

BIBLIOGRAPHY

R. de Suvigny, ed.: *Les bibliothèques françoises de La Croix du Maine et de Du Verdier* (Paris, 1772), i, 8; iii, 25
A. Sandberger: 'Roland Lassus' Beziehungen zu Frankreich', *SIMG*, viii (1906–7), 355–401
L. de La Laurencie, A. Mairy and G. Thibault, eds.: *Chansons au luth et airs de cour français du XVIᵉ siècle* (Paris, 1934), p.xxi
F. Lesure and G. Thibault: *Bibliographie des éditions d'Adrian Le Roy et Robert Ballard (1551–1598)* (Paris, 1955; suppl., *RdM*, xl, 1957, p.166)
F. Lesure: 'Le Roy, Adrian', *MGG*
D. Heartz: 'Parisian Music Printing under Henry II', *MQ*, xlvi (1960), 448
J. Cain and P. Marot: *Imprimeurs et libraires parisiens du XVIᵉ siècle, d'après les manuscrits de Ph. Renouard*, ii (Paris, 1969)

SAMUEL F. POGUE

Le Roy [Roi], Bartolomeo. *See* ROY, BARTOLOMEO.

Leroy, Jehan. *See* REGIS, JOHANNES.

Le Sage de Richée, Philipp Franz (*fl c*1695). German lutenist and composer of French birth. In early sources he is stated to have been a pupil of Charles Mouton. In 1695 he seems to have been in the service of Baron von Neidhardt in Breslau. He was an aristocrat and must have travelled in a number of countries, gaining a broad knowledge of the lute repertory in Bohemia, Austria and France. One publication of his has survived, *Cabinet der Lauten, in welchem zu finden 12 neue Partien, aus unterschiedenen Tonen und neuesten Manier so aniezo gebräuchlich'* (n.p., n.d.; it must have appeared in Breslau and the copy formerly in Riemann's possession bore the date 1695). It contains 98 pieces engraved in French lute tablature and arranged in 12 suites. The preface mentions Dufaut, Mouton, Losy and Gaultier (though which one is unspecified). The following types of piece occur: praeludium, allemande, courante, sarabande, gigue, gavotte, minuet, bourrée, chaconne, passacaglia, ouverture and rondeau (with echo). One piece is attributed to 'Graf Logi' [Losy]; presumably Le Sage de Richée composed all the others himself. Surprisingly, he is seldom mentioned in MSS, but the sumptuous appearance of his volume bears witness to the outstanding esteem in which he was held.

BIBLIOGRAPHY

H. Riemann: 'Ein wenig bekanntes Lautenwerk', *MMg*, xxi (1889), 10
T. Wortmann: *Ph. F. Le Sage de Richée und sein Cabinet der Lauten* (diss., U. of Vienna, 1919)
W. Boetticher: *Studien zur solistischen Lautenpraxis des 16. und 17. Jahrhunderts* (Berlin, 1943), 169ff
E. Pohlmann: *Laute, Theorbe, Chitarrone* (Bremen, 1968, enlarged 4/1976)

WOLFGANG BOETTICHER

Lésbio, António Marques (*b* Lisbon, 1639; *d* Lisbon, 21 Nov 1709). Portuguese writer and composer. He spent his life in Lisbon. Seeing one of his juvenile compositions in 1653, João Soares Rebelo prophesied that he would become one of the best Portuguese contrapuntists. In 1660 he began publishing vilhancico texts in the annually printed booklets for the church festivals of 8 and 25 December and 6 January and remained a frequent contributor until 1708. On 9 December 1663 and on 5 February 1665 he presided over the seventh and 34th of the 36 sessions of the Academia dos Singulares and in 1665 and 1668 published two orations in Portuguese and 49 Spanish and Portuguese poems in the proceedings of the academy. On 10 October 1668 he became master of the royal chamber musicians. An ardent supporter of King Pedro II, he published in the following year an 80-octave panegyric,

Estrella de Portugal, on the birth of Princess Isabella. On 3 November 1679 he was appointed master of the boys in the choir school of the royal chapel; on 18 July 1670 he had been given a sinecure doubling his previous salary. He became curator of the royal music library on 2 November 1692 and royal choirmaster on 15 January 1698. His last publication – *Vilhancicos que se cantarão na Igreja de N. Senhora de Nazareth das Religiosas Descalças de S. Bernardo em as Matinas, e Festa do glorioso S. Gonçalo* (Lisbon, 1708) – crowned a lifetime spent writing festival verse for which he himself supplied the music. The music of only 16 Spanish villancicos and Portuguese vilhancicos by him has survived (in *P-EVp* and *Ln*; two ed. in Stevenson). They range from the delightful *Ayreçillos manços* for four voices (Christmas 1681) and *Es flor del campo el infante* for eight to the imposing eight-part *Quem vio hum menino bello*, which calls for both harp and organ accompaniment; all show that he was a composer of much grace and polish. His Latin works have all perished, apparently in the Lisbon earthquake of 1755. According to Barbosa Machado they included eight-part Vespers and Marian antiphons, Holy Week music in four, five, six, eight and 12 parts and responsories for the Office of the Dead in eight and 12 parts.

BIBLIOGRAPHY

DBP
D. Barbosa Machado: *Bibliotheca lusitana*, i (Lisbon, 1741), 321ff
F. M. Sousa Viterbo: *A livraria de musica de D. João IV e o seu index* (Lisbon, 1900), 6
E. Vieira: 'A conferencia de Ernesto Vieira', *A arte musical*, v (3 Jan 1903), 17
R. E. Horch: *Vilancicos da Coleção Barbosa Machado* (Rio de Janeiro, 1969), 130f
D. Damasceno: *Vilancicos seiscentistas* (Rio de Janeiro, 1970), 186f
R. Stevenson, ed.: *Vilancicos portugueses* (Lisbon, 1976), 49ff
ROBERT STEVENSON

Lesch, Albrecht (*b* Munich, not later than *c*1420; *d* Munich, 1478 or 1479). Meistersinger. He belonged to a family established in Munich by 1380. His profession is uncertain: from 1459 to 1471 he was in municipal service, among other things as a magistrate for petty offences. He must be distinguished from the 'professional' Meistersinger – the *gernde meister* like Muskatblüt and Michel Beheim, who made a living as travelling poet-musicians – and from members of the local Meistersinger guilds (of which the one in Munich existed only from about 1510 to 1530); yet he had similar artistic aims. He sang on a variety of occasions, and may even have performed at the Munich court, where he could perhaps have met Beheim around 1450. Beheim mentioned him in one of his poems (no.428, 54).

Some scholars (Brandis, Kiepe, Brunner) have attempted to identify him with the Albrecht Lesch born in Munich about 1380 (who may have been his father). They suggested a dating of 1425–35 for the section of *D-Mbs* cgm 351 containing poetry by Lesch, because its watermark is not documented after 1435; but this is insufficient evidence since the paper might easily have lain unused for some years. Moreover, the consciously elegant melodic style at the ends of stanzas suggests a dating in the middle decades of the century and has so far been found only in the work of Muskatblüt and Beheim, who were active in the mid-15th century.

Lesch's songs have not so far been thoroughly investigated. Like Beheim, he tended to restate part of a melody at the end of a stanza, unlike the non-repeating,

line-by-line setting of most Meisterlieder. He also occasionally rounded off a melody with a more expansive, shapely phrase which encompasses perhaps the last two or three lines of the text. He used formal elements with greater consistency than Beheim. His *Ton* 'Goldener Reien', like other examples of the medieval *Reien* or *Reigen* (*see* REIGENLIED), is a medium for the expression of joy – the basic emotion of its text. Yet it does not exhibit certain other features – regularity of structure, frequency of repetition – as consistently as do other *Reien*. Lesch still used lai technique ('Tageweise'), but it is modified by inserting an additional line of text and melody from time to time in order to stress a point of Christian ideology. His *Töne* were still being sung in Nuremberg as late as about 1600.

WORKS

Text edition: *Albrecht Lesch: ein Münchner Meistersinger des 15. Jahrhunderts*, ed. L. Koester (Schloss Birkeneck, 1937)
Music editions: *Die Sangesweisen der Colmarer Handschrift und die Liederhandschrift Donaueschingen*, ed. P. Runge (Leipzig, 1896/R1965) [R]
    Das Singebuch des Adam Puschman, ed. G. Münzer (Leipzig, 1906/R1970) [M]
    Die Colmarer Liederhandschrift: Faksimile-Ausgabe ihrer Melodien, ed. F. Gennrich, SMM, xviii (1967)

TÖNE
'Feuerweise' [or 'Mühlweise'], Ich lob die reinen frauen zart, R 125 [poem considered by Koester to be spurious; Abgesang of melody lost]
'Gekrönter Reien', Zukunft der wort, *D-Mbs* cgm 4997, f.842 [text only]
'Gesangweise' [or 'Sangweise'], Wer nimpt mit lieb das höchste gut, M 71, R 128 [also in *D-Nst* Will III 792, f.38]
'Goldener Reien', Ave Maria, dich lobet musica, R 6 [also in *D-DO* 120, p.219]
'Goldenes Schloss', Ich will von einer maget fron [text only; complete in *D-Mbs* cgm 5198 only]
'Hofweise', Das recht ist manigfeltig krumm, R 126 [Abgesang inc., and in a later hand]
'Kurzer Ton' [or 'Kurzer Reien'], Wolauf, mein sel, hin über mer [probably spurious, since only ascribed in *D-Dlb* M 13, f.11]
'Süsser Ton', Maria Keiserinne [ascribed only in *D-B* Mgq 414, text only]
'Tageweise', Zeuch durch die Wolken, mein gesang, R 129 [last two lines text only; preceding line has music added in a later hand; also in *D-Mbs* cgm 778 with empty staves]
'Zirkelweise', Got, herr, du ewikeite, R 124, M 73 [also in *D-Nst* Will III 792, f.38]

BIBLIOGRAPHY

C. Petzsch: 'Zu Albrecht Lesch, Jörg Schechner und zur Frage der Münchener Meistersingerschule', *Zeitschrift für deutsches Altertum*, xciv (1965), 121
——: 'Folgen nachträglich eingeführter Text-Form-Korrespondenz für Text und Lai-Technik', *Mf*, xxviii (1975), 284 ['Tageweise']
——: 'Lesch, Albrecht', *MGG*
For further bibliography *see* MEISTERGESANG.
CHRISTOPH PETZSCH

Leschenet [**Lachenet**], **Didier** (*d* Paris, *c*1603). French composer. In 1559 he became the assistant *maître de chapelle* at the royal chapel and in 1578 canon at St Quentin. Two years later he received another canonry at Meaux. Although he held the position of singer and composer-in-ordinary of the king's chapel in 1582, he resigned and moved to Meaux in 1584, accepting an additional canonry at Langres at this time. Two years later he became a member of the choir at the Sainte-Chapelle and was chosen as a cantor on 20 May 1589.

WORKS

Magnificat, 4vv, 1557[8]
A dieu gentil corsaige, 4vv, 1553[20]; En te contemplant je te prise, 4vv, 1553[20]; Est-il douleur cruelle, 5vv, 1572[2]; Gris et tanné me faut porter, 5vv, 1572[2]; Helas, pourquoy ne suis-je mariée, 6vv, 1572[2]; Je m'y plain fort qu'amours, 6vv, 1572[2]
Le cueur est mien, 6vv, 1572[2]; Les mesdisantz par leur, 4vv, 1553[20]; Pour vous ami tousjours, 4vv, 1553[20]; Puis que j'ai belle amie, 5vv,

1572[2]; Si par souffrir on peult, 6vv, 1554[27]; Souspirs ardens parcelles, 6vv, 1554[27]

RUTH K. INGLEFIELD

Leschetizky, Theodor [Leszetycki, Teodor] (*b* Łańcut, Galicia, 22 June 1830; *d* Dresden, 14 Nov 1915). Polish pianist, teacher and composer. He was first taught music by his father Józef, the music master of the Potocki family at Łańcut. When he was ten he made his first public appearance as a pianist in Lemberg (Lwów), and that year his family moved to Vienna, where he

Theodor Leschetizky

studied the piano with Czerny and composition with Sechter. By the age of 14 he was already in great demand as a piano teacher, and from 1845 until the 1848 Revolution he was also a philosophy student at the University of Vienna. In 1852 he moved to St Petersburg, where he soon attracted a large circle of pupils and, shortly after his début, was invited to appear before the tsar. He became a close friend of Anton Rubinstein, occasionally deputizing for him as teacher and conductor, and in 1862, at Rubinstein's request, he became director of piano studies at the conservatory. He returned to Vienna and private teaching in 1878; he organized a music society, which held regular meetings and concerts, and became an important figure in the city's musical activities.

Besides his teaching, Leschetizky toured Russia, Poland and Germany, both as a pianist and as a conductor. Of his conducting activities he said: 'Conducting is not difficult. It is harder to play six bars well on the piano than to conduct the whole of Beethoven's Ninth Symphony'. In 1880 he married his pupil and assistant Anna Esipova, with whom he gave a celebrated series of duet recitals until 1887. On their divorce in 1892 he married another pupil, Mrs Dawimirska (née Benisławska); earlier (1856–72) he was married to one of his singing pupils, Mlle de Friedebourg, lady-inwaiting to the Russian imperial court, and a fourth

marriage was to yet another pupil, Marie Gabriela Rozborska, who made public appearances as Mme Leschetizky in London in 1908, the year in which they were married. In Vienna a monument was raised to Leschetizky during his lifetime; there is a fine portrait of him by Dreger.

In his teaching methods, Leschetizky continued the school of Czerny, which he modified in his own way. He did not demand excessive technical practice from his pupils, but stressed complete concentration on the music and a thorough knowledge of it in every detail. An important feature of his teaching was a regular evening class, in which detailed criticism was made by the pupils under his supervision. His approach was practical rather than scientific; he taught chiefly by demonstration, handling technical and musical problems according to the needs of each pupil. A vigorous, strong-willed man and musician, with a formidable memory and an infallible ear, he was a hard master, and for the exacting demands he made was both feared and worshipped by his pupils. Among the most eminent of the hundreds of pianists he taught were Paderewski, Artur Schnabel, Elly Ney, Mark Hambourg, Ossip Gabrilovich, Ignaz Friedman and Benno Moiseivich.

Leschetizky's 49 compositions are chiefly nocturnes, romances, salon dances and other miniatures for the piano. They are distinguished by their virtuoso character and a careful attention to formal structure. He also composed two operas, the unperformed *Die Brüder von Marco* and *Die erste Falte*, which was produced at Prague in 1867.

BIBLIOGRAPHY

M. Unschuld von Melasfeld: *Die Hand des Pianisten* (Leipzig, 1901, 2/1903)
M. Brée: *Die Grundlage der Methode Leschetizky* (Mainz, 1902, 4/1914; Eng. trans., 1902)
A. Potocka: *Theodor Leschetizky* (New York, 1903)
M. Prentner: *The Leschetizky Method* (London, 7/1903)
A. Hullah: *Theodor Leschetizky* (London, 1906)
A. Schnabel: 'Theodor Leschetizky', *AMz*, xxxvii (1910), 599
W. Niemann: *Meister des Klaviers* (Berlin, 1919, rev. 2/1921)
E. Newcomb: *Leschetizky as I Knew him* (New York, 1921/*R*1967)
G. Woodhouse: 'How Leschetizky Taught', *ML*, xxxv (1954), 220
B. Moiseivich: 'Leschetizky', *Sunday Telegraph* (3 Sept 1961)
R. R. Gerig: 'The Leschetizky Influence', *Famous Pianists & their Technique* (Newton Abbot, 1976), 271ff

TADEUSZ PRZYBYLSKI

Lescot, C. François (*b* *c*1720; *d* *c*1801). French composer and violinist. He worked as a *maître de musique* at Auch Cathedral from 1747 to 1764, and at Nantes Cathedral probably from 1764 to 1768. His first three stage works, for which he wrote both librettos and music, were first performed at the Théâtre d'Auch, two in 1761 and the third in 1767. His motet *Exaltabo te* was twice performed at the Concert Spirituel in Paris in 1764. He moved to Paris and joined the orchestra of the Comédie-Italienne in autumn 1768; there he played in the first violin section until 1774 and second violin until 1785. He left the orchestra from 1785 until autumn 1787; he held the position of principal second violin from 1788 until his retirement with a pension in 1790.

Lescot's theatre works were suited to contemporary French taste and were well received. Many were later included in the repertories of the Parisian theatres in the late 18th century and the early 19th. His first stage work presented in Paris was *La négresse, ou Le pouvoir de la reconnaissance*, performed at the Comédie-Italienne in 1787 during his absence from the orchestra. The chronicler of the *Mercure de France* wrote: 'The *airs*, which are very well arranged by M. Lescot, were chosen with great intelligence and taste'. He used vaudevilles in all his Parisian stage works.

WORKS
(all printed works published in Paris unless otherwise stated)

STAGE

L'amour et l'hymen (opéra comique, 1, Lescot), Auch, 1761 (Auch, 1761)
La fête de Thalie (pastorale, 1, Lescot), Auch, 1761 (Auch, 1761)
La fête de Thémire (pastorale with vaudevilles and ariettes, 1, Lescot), Auch, 1767
La négresse, ou Le pouvoir de la reconnaissance (comédie with vaudevilles and divertissements, 2, P.-Y. Barré, J.-B. Radet), Paris, Comédie-Italienne, 15 June 1787 (1787)
Les solitaires de Normandie (opéra comique with vaudevilles, 1, A.-P.-A. de Piis, Barré), Paris, Comédie-Italienne, 15 Jan 1788 (1788)
Candide marié, ou Il faut cultiver son jardin (comédie with vaudevilles, 2, Barré, Radet), Paris, Comédie-Italienne, 20 June 1788 (1788)

OTHER WORKS

Sacred: Exaltabo te, motet, 1764; Requiem, 1766; De profundis, motet, 1766; other masses, lost
Other vocal: L'absence et le retour de Flore, cantatille, 1759, *F-Pn*; L'été, cantatille (1759); Iris, cantatille (1759); L'amitié, cantatille, acc. 2 vn, b, 1764, lost; Recueil portatif de chansons, airs, ariettes, et duo (1765); 2 collections of ariettes, duos, romances, acc. bc (1775, 1782); Recueil d'airs, romances, et duo, acc. 2 vn, bc (1782); other cantatilles, lost
Inst: 6 duos, 2 vn, op.1 (1777); 6 trios, 2 vn, b, op.2 (1781)

BIBLIOGRAPHY

FétisB
Almanach des spectacles (Paris, 1769–90)
Mercure de France (July 1764, Sept 1764, July 1787, Jan 1788, June 1788)
Almanach musical/Calendrier musical universel (Paris, 1782–9)
Babault: *Annales dramatiques, ou Dictionnaire général des théâtres* (Paris, 1808–12)
C. D. Brenner: *A Bibliographical List of Plays in the French Language, 1700–1789* (Berkeley, 1947)
E. Borrel: 'Lescot, C . . .-François', *MGG*
D. Tunley: *The Eighteenth-century French Cantata* (London, 1974)
ETHYL L. WILL

L'Escurel, Jehannot de. *See* JEHANNOT DE L'ESCUREL.

Lesczyński, Władysław. *See* LESZCZYŃSKI, WŁADYS-ŁAW.

Leslie, Henry (David) (*b* London, 18 June 1822; *d* Llansaintfraid, nr. Oswestry, 4 Feb 1896). English choral conductor and composer. He was a pupil of Charles Lucas, and played the cello at the Sacred Harmonic Society and other concerts. From 1847 he was associated with the Amateur Musical Society, first as honorary secretary and later as conductor. In 1855 he took charge of what became known as the Henry Leslie Choir; this celebrated *a cappella* ensemble, first heard at the Hanover Square Rooms on 22 May 1856, gained first prize in an International Choral Competition held at the Paris Exhibition in 1878. It was dissolved in 1880, but re-formed in 1882 under Alberto Randegger, with Leslie as conductor from 1885 to 1887. Leslie's London concert programmes were notable for the large amount of English choral music they contained, though they also featured one or two 19th-century French composers. In 1864 Leslie became principal of the National College of Music (dissolved in 1866). From 1863 to 1889 he conducted the Herefordshire Philharmonic Society, and in 1874 founded the Guild of Amateur Musicians. While living in the west country he interested himself in the training of village choirs; he was a founder of the Oswestry School of Music and the Oswestry Festival. Leslie's own compositions include symphonies, oratorios, operas, cantatas and partsongs; he edited *Cassell's Choral Music* (London, 1867) and

other collections intended to popularize partsongs from earlier periods. His work with local choral groups was continued by his son, W. H. P. Leslie (1860–1926), an able business man and a Master of the Musicians' Company (1924).

H. C. COLLES/E. D. MACKERNESS

Lesotho. Country in southern Africa, inhabited by the Sotho, whose music is stylistically similar to that of the other indigenous peoples of southern Africa. The Sotho have strong historical, cultural and linguistic links with the Tswana of Botswana and the Pedi of the northern Transvaal, but corporate and geographical separation of these peoples has differentiated their musical styles, especially those connected with social identity and occupations.

1. Musical types and instruments. 2. Song. 3. Traditional forms and recent developments.

1. MUSICAL TYPES AND INSTRUMENTS. Music is an integral part of Sotho social education and traditionally links hearing with the understanding of the natural and social worlds. The temporal arts (*lipapali*) of the Sotho are clearly separated from the graphic and plastic arts. Their four basic types include three connected with sound-making (*ho letsa*) and singing (*ho bina*).

There are two kinds of instrument, those sounded by the hand (*liletsa tsa matsoho*) and those sounded by the mouth (*liletsa tsa molomo*). Each group contains idiophones, chordophones and aerophones, but only those sounded by the hand include membranophones. All the instruments are played solo or in the accompaniment of songs, dances and other activities; ensemble performances rarely occur. While there is not a large variety of musical instruments, a wide range of game and topical songs can be performed on any one instrument, in addition to its characteristic songs. All the instruments have been described in detail by Kirby.

Hand-sounded instruments include both a single- and a double-headed drum, the *moropa* and the *sekupu*. The *moropa* is used to accompany girls' initiation songs and women's dancing, and the *sekupu* is used by certain healers. This group also includes the *sevuvu* (bullroarer), *morutlhoana* (shaken rattles), *setjoli* (rubbed rattles) and the *mangenengene* (metal bells). The principal string instruments in this group are the two monochord musical bows, the *thomo* which is beaten with a small stick and has a gourd resonator with a hole in the back which is stopped against the body; and the *sekhankula* which is also beaten, but which has a large, closed tin resonator at one end. A third important string instrument is the *masholo-sholo*, a bowed trough zither made of bamboo (Koole).

Mouth-sounded instruments include all that are blown, vocalized or mouth-resonated; mouth-resonance is an important feature in the Sotho classification of instruments and is regarded as a part of the instrument and not solely as a performing technique. These include aerophones (*lekhitlane*, megaphones; *liphala*, trumpets; *phalana* and *lekolilo* flutes), chordophones (*lekope* and *setolotolo*, simple and compound mouth-resonated bows) and idiophones (*sekebeku*, a jew's harp; *lesiba*, a mouth-resonated stick zither sounded by blowing, more commonly known by its Korana Hottentot name GORA; see figs.1 and 2).

Sotho musical instruments are used with specific functional objectives, e.g. the primary use of the *lesiba* is in cattle herding: birds' sounds and actions are seen to affect cattle; these sounds can be imitated on the *lesiba* and the instrument used to control the animals' behaviour.

2. SONG. Songs are divided into songs which are sung standing still (*ho engoe*) and songs involving coordinated movement which are sung 'with the feet' (*ka maoto*).

The former are used in girls' and boys' initiation ceremonies. The education of boys for initiation consists to a considerable extent of *likoma* (secret instructional songs). The texts of these songs, which have a special linguistic structure, are of two types. There are myth-like historical songs which trace origins and migrations, cite hardships and punishments, and establish the general continuity of the present with the past. Other song texts are concerned with customs, moral principles and with the dangers of life (Guma, 1967). Closely related, conceptually and musically, to the instructional songs are *mangae*, songs learned by the initiates to be presented publicly upon their return from isolation. The texts of these songs are a combination of farewells to the past, self-praises and the construction of a poetic image of one's identity and personality. While each initiate sings and recites praises, his fellow initiates respond by singing, and the audience responds with gifts which mark their acceptance of the boy. The instructional songs impress the significance of their ideas on the initiate, while he learns to express what he has absorbed through *mangae*.

The *ho engoe* type also includes a hymn, now confined to Christian churches (*sefela*), as well as the songs of spiritualist and prophetic churches. Other songs in this group are lullabies, responsorial laments for the dead sung by women (*koli ea malla*), songs of school choirs, a responsorial prayer for rain (*thapelo*), and songs sung during the arrangements preceding a marriage.

Songs which involve coordinated actions include work songs for threshing, tanning, grinding and hoeing. Herdboys sing mouse-hunting songs which praise mice and frighten them into being trapped and killed (Mokhali, 1967). Most work songs are responsorial and iterative, with texts which refer to the tasks performed and the hardships they involve (Guma, 1967).

Songs which serve as the motive force in dramatic dances are central to this type. The *mokhibo*, a group dance, is performed by women who dance on their knees while gesturing with the upper half of the body. They are supported by a group of singers who encourage them and explain the dance through topical and mundane song texts. The songs, sung by both men and women, are polyphonic and responsorial and are accompanied by a single drum and hand-clapping. The *mokorotlo* is a men's dance associated with warfare, and its stamping gestures dramatize the strategy and tactics of battle; long responsorial songs describe the fate of men who fall. It is performed, occasionally on horseback, to highlight the special activities of chiefs, to accompany the ritual hunting of wild animals, during boys' initiation, and in preparation for other dance performances. *Mokorotlo* performances are individualistic and competitive and, like *mangae*, they are interspersed with praises. The *mohobelo* is another men's dance supported by responsorial songs and characterized by uniform movements of the dancers punctuated by solo dancing. As in *mokhibo* these songs are topical and in combination with the dancing serve to maintain group

1. *Lesiba (mouth-resonated stick zither); detail showing placement on the lips*

cohesion. There were originally two basic styles of *mohobelo*, geographically and socially separate, one being more energetic and faster in tempo than the other; each style had its own corpus of songs.

There are few occasions when young men and women participate in the same dance. In one version of a dance called *moqoqopelo* or *motjeko*, boys and girls dance in a circle while one girl sings of her affection for a boy who responds by dancing (Mokhali, 1967). In another version young men dance and respond with a short refrain to witty and amusing texts sung by a leader (Guma, 1967). Men and women participate in the therapeutic songs and dances of the *mathuela*, a possession cult of Nguni origin.

3. TRADITIONAL FORMS AND RECENT DEVELOPMENTS. All the types of Sotho music discussed above are performed with specific objectives and derive their cultural significance more from the concrete social contexts in which they occur than from their musical form or style. Many forms are found in more than one context; for

2. *Lesiba (mouth-resonated stick zither); the instrument is normally played singly*

example the *mokorotlo* and the *mohobelo*, with a change of text, also provide the songs for communal work. In addition to these specific uses, many *lipapali* occur as forms of competition: this is especially so with the *linong*, the *mohobelo*, the *mokhibo* and school choir singing. These periodic competitions help to maintain the common musical traditions and at the same time define and maintain the social, regional and individual identity of performers and social groups.

Traditionally there was no professionalism in Sotho music though this has developed in response to changes in Sotho culture and as a result of the rise of patronage and a popular market. Broadcasting is also changing Sotho music: new forms of musical expression, especially those of instrumental groups, as well as extensive changes in interpretation and the loss of some of the more restricted and specialized types of music are a result of mass exposure to traditional styles as well as those of foreign music. Other factors that have contributed to change are the market that has emerged for popular music and new opportunities given to professional composers and performers.

Over 40 Sotho composers have been listed and their works span the Western classical, Sotho traditional and current popular fields (see Huskisson, 1969). One of these composers, J. P. Mohapeloa, has published a collection of 92 choral partsongs in three volumes entitled *Meloli lo lithallare tsa Afrika* ('Melodies and decorated songs of Africa', Morija, 1935, 1939, 1947). These are in Tonic Sol-fa notation, and they provided the first new Sotho school music since the hymnbook *Lifela tsa Sione* ('Hymns of Zion'; see Huskisson) was published. Another collection of composed songs, which includes a few transcriptions of traditional children's songs, is *Binang ka thabo: lipina tsa Sesotho tsa likolo le lihlopha tsa libini* ('Sing with joy: Sesotho songs for schools and choirs', Mazenod, 1963).

Recordings of Sotho music are held at the International Library of African Music, Grahamstown, South Africa.

BIBLIOGRAPHY

E. Casalis: *The Basutos; or, Twenty-three Years in South Africa* (London, 1861/R1965)
W. A. Norton: 'Sesuto Songs and Music', *South African Journal of Science*, vi (1910), 314
——: 'African Native Melodies', *South African Journal of Science*, xii (1916), 619
N. Scully: 'Native Tunes Heard and Collected in Basutoland', *Bantu Studies*, (1931), 247
P. R. Kirby: *The Musical Instruments of the Native Races of South Africa* (London, 1934; Johannesburg, rev., enlarged 2/1965)
H. Ashton: *The Basuto: a Social Study of Traditional and Modern Lesotho* (London, 1952; rev., enlarged 2/1967)
A. Koole: 'Report on the Inquiry into the Music and Instruments of the Basutos in Basutoland', *IMSCR, v Utrecht 1952*, 263
H. Tracey: 'Sotho Folk Music', *Basutoland Notes and Records*, ii (1960), 37
——: 'Folk Music in Basutoland', *Basutoland Notes and Records*, iii (1962), 26
S. M. Guma: *The Form, Content and Technique of Traditional Literature in Southern Sotho* (Pretoria, 1967)
A. G. Mokhali: *Basotho Music and Dancing* (Mazenod, Lesotho, 1967)
Y. Huskisson: *The Bantu Composers of Southern Africa/Die Bantoekomponiste van Suider-Afrika* (Johannesburg, 1969)
CHARLES R. ADAMS

Lespine. See L'EPINE family.

Lessard, John (Ayres) (*b* San Francisco, 3 July 1920). American composer. He studied with Boulanger and Dandelot at the Ecole Normale de Musique in Paris (1937–9) and received a Guggenheim Fellowship in 1946. A composer of French-orientated neo-classical pieces, he was grouped within the American 'Stravinsky school' in the years immediately following World War II. In 1963 he was appointed to teach at the State University of New York, Stony Brook.

WORKS
(selective list)

Orch: Vn Conc., 1941; Bos Hill, ov., 1946; Cantilena, ob, str, 1946; Sinfonietta concertante, 1961; Harp Conc., 1963
Vocal: Ariel, 1v, pf, 1941; Orpheus, 1v, pf, 1943; Bag of a Bee, 1v, pf, 1949; Interior, 1v, pf, 1951; When as in silk my Julia goes, 1v, pf, 1951; Rose-cheekt Laura, 1v, pf, 1960; 12 Mother Goose Songs, 1v, str trio, 1964; Fragments from the Cantos of Ezra Pound, cantata, Bar, fl, 2 tpt, 2 hn, trbn, vn, va, vc, 1969
Chamber and inst: Qnt, fl, cl, vn, va, vc, 1943; 2 pf sonatas, 1944, 1945; Toccata, hpd, 1951; Wind Octet, 1952; Str Trio, 1963; Trio in 6 parti, pf trio, 1966; Quodlibets, 2 tpt, trbn, 1967

Principal publishers: American Composers Alliance, Joshua

Lessel, Franciszek (*b* Warsaw, *c*1780; *d* Piotrków, 26 Dec 1838). Polish composer and pianist, son of Wincenty Ferdynand Lessel. He first studied music with his father, and then in December 1799 became a pupil of Haydn in Vienna. In 1809 he returned to Poland, where he gave concerts, first in Kraków (4 January 1809) and then in Warsaw (3 February 1810). It is known that he also gave concerts in Lwów before going to Vienna, and that he played the musical glasses. Lessel gave up musical activities in 1822 because of a personal tragedy. In 1823 he became agent on the estate of the Duchess Maria of Württemberg, in 1836 inspector of the school of rural economy at Marymont (now within the boundaries of Warsaw), and in 1837 inspector of a secondary school at Piotrków. Lessel's output consisted mainly of instrumental music. His music displays mastery of the technical means of the Classics and the principles of polyphony, combined with a feeling for the new Romantic trends in music. This is shown particularly in his use of colouristic effects in his piano music and in the piano accompaniments to his songs.

WORKS
INSTRUMENTAL

Orch: 5 syms., incl. no.5, g, 1805, finale in *PL-Wtm*; Ov., op.10 (Leipzig, 1842); 12 Ländler samt Posthorn und Coda (Vienna, 1806); Pf Conc., C, op.14 (Leipzig, 1813); Potpourri, pf, orch, op.12 (Leipzig, 1813)
Chamber: 3 Parthiae, 2 cl, 2 bn, 2 hn, *CS-Pnm*; Pf Qnt, f, op.25, perf. 1834, lost; 8 str qts, incl. no.1, A, 1800, no.6, D, frags. in *PL-Wtm*; Pf Qt, Eb, *Wtm*; Fl Qt, op.3 (Vienna, 1806); Fantaisie caractéristique, pf qt, op.31, 1822, *Wtm*; Pf Trio, E, op.5 (Leipzig, n.d.); 3 duos, 2 fl, op.1 (Bonn, n.d.); Adagio et polonaise, vn, pf, 1807, *Wtm*
Pf: 3 Sonatas, op.2 (Vienna, *c*1800); Variations on a Ukrainian song Jichaw kozak zza Dunaju, op.15 no.1 (Warsaw, 1810); Variations, a, op.15 no.2 (Warsaw, 1934); Adagio et rondeau à la polonaise, op.9 (Leipzig, 1810); 2 Fantaisies, op.8 (Leipzig, 1810), op.13 (Leipzig, 1813); Fugue, pf 4 hands, op.11 (Warsaw, 1812)

VOCAL

Sacred: Oratorium ku czci św. Cecylii [Oratorio in honour of St Cecilia], 1812, *CZp*; 3 masses, incl. Msza polska [Polish mass] (F. Wężyk), 1813, *CZp*; Requiem, 1837, lost; another Requiem, offertories and motets, all lost
Stage: Cyganie [The gypsies] (opera, 3, F. D. Kniaźnin), inc., lost; Les marchands de modes (ballet), lost; La dançomanie (ballet), lost
Songs: 10 songs for Śpiewy historyczne [Historical songs] (J. U. Niemcewicz) (Warsaw, 1816) [incl. Bogurodzica [Mother of God] (Warsaw, 1816)]

PEDAGOGICAL WORKS

Contrapuntal study, pf, *c*1805, *PL-Wtm*
Solfeggio nos.1 and 2, *c*1810, *ŁA*

BIBLIOGRAPHY
SMP

A. Nowak-Romanowicz, ed.: *Z dziejów polskiej kultury muzycznej* [A historical survey of Polish musical culture], ii (Kraków, 1966)
ALINA NOWAK-ROMANOWICZ

Lessel, Wincenty Ferdynand (*b* Jilové, nr. Prague, *c*1750; *d* Puławy or Warsaw, after 1825). Polish composer of Bohemian descent. He received his musical education in Germany, where his family settled in 1762. He studied composition, the keyboard, violin and viola in Dresden under J. G. Schürer and from 1762 to *c*1776 played the viola in the Dresden royal orchestra. By 1780 he was in Warsaw, and the next year he took the post of piano teacher at Prince Adam Kazimierz Czartoryski's establishment in Puławy. In 1787 he was appointed court Kapellmeister. By 1812 he was also music director of the theatre at Sieniawa (the other Czartoryski residence), and from 1814 he directed and taught at the organists' school at Puławy founded by Czartoryski. In 1825 he was living at Puławy and was a singing teacher. His works show technical competence, and, like those of many of his contemporary compatriots, are characterized by elements of Polish folk music.

WORKS
STAGE
(all first produced Puławy and all lost, except where otherwise indicated)
Matka spartanka [The Spartan mother] (opera, F. D. Kniaźnin), 1787
Troiste wesele [Triple wedding] (5-act opera, Kniaźnin), 1787
Dwaj strzelcy i mleczarka [Two huntsmen and the milkmaid] (operetta, L. Anseaumé, trans. J. Baudouin), 1787, rev. (trans. A. Hoffman), 1804; fragment of a duet, *PL-Wtm*
Cyganie [The gypsies] (opera, Kniaźnin), 1787
Piast (melodrama, J. U. Niemcewicz), 1800, rev. (L. A. Dmuszewski), Sieniawa, 27 Jan 1820
Pantomima, 1805
I plotka czasem się przyda [Even gossip is sometimes useful] (idyll, I. Tański), 1805; a sequel with the same title was performed at Sieniawa, 1818
Domek na gościńcu [Little house in the high-road] (1 act, Dmuszewski), Sieniawa, 1818
Pielgrzym z Dobromila [The pilgrim from Dobromil] (2 acts, A. Kłodziński), Sieniawa, 31 March 1819
Przyjazd pożądany [Wished-for arrival] (2 acts, Kłodziński), Sieniawa, 31 March 1820

OTHER WORKS
Cantata for the consecration of the Protestant church, Warsaw, 30 Dec 1781, lost
Symphony for his son's birthday, sinfonias, marches, polonaises, orch, all lost
Nuta z odmianami z Weledy [Melody of Weleda with variations], pf 4 hands, vn, lost
3 polonaises: pf, B♭, *PL-Wtm*; pf, E♭, ed. in Prosnak; vn, D; Ariette . . . variée, pf, 1797, *A-Wgm*: all ed. in Rudnicka-Kruszewska
Sonatas, polonaises, pf; preludes, org: all lost

BIBLIOGRAPHY
J. Prosnak: *Kultura muzyczna Warszawy XVIII wieku* (Kraków, 1955)
H. Rudnicka-Kruszewska: *Wincenty Lessel* (Kraków,)
S. Durski: 'Zabawy teatralne w Sieniawie' [Theatre amusements in Sieniawa], *Pamiętnik teatralny*, xix (Warsaw, 1970), 28
ALINA NOWAK-ROMANOWICZ

Lesser, Wolfgang (*b* Breslau, 31 May 1923). German composer. He studied composition under Wagner-Régeny, Eisler and Kochan at the Berlin Hochschule für Musik (1950–54). From 1954 to 1961 he was a teacher and composer with the German Democratic Republic's State People's Art Ensemble, and then he established himself as a freelance composer. In 1964 he became second secretary of the East German League of Composers and Musicologists, and in 1968 first secretary; his awards include the Vaterländischer Verdienstorden and the National Prize. He is best known for his strongly emotional songs which, in their concise and heavily optimistic expression, recall Eisler; and there is an equally lyrical expressiveness in the concertante works. All of Lesser's music is marked by a striving for simplicity and for freedom of form.

WORKS
(selective list)
Vn Conc., 1962; Sonata, vn, 1964; Ein Tag in unserer Stadt (M. Streubel), lv, pf, 1967; Das Jahr, children's chorus, insts, n.d.; Liederzyklus (G. Maurer), lv, pf, n.d.; Im Vogelflug (Streubel), lv, pf, n.d.; Oktoberkinder, children's opera, n.d.; mass songs, scores for theatre, cinema, radio, television

Principal publishers: Deutscher Verlag für Musik, Internationale Musikbibliothek

BIBLIOGRAPHY
L. Markowski: 'Wolfgang Lesser', *Musik und Gesellschaft*, xiii (1963), 296
H. Schaefer: '. . . gesellschaftlich konkret: Bemerkungen zum Violinkonzert von Wolfgang Lesser', *Musik und Gesellschaft*, xiv (1964), 331

Lesson. A term originally used in England to denote an exercise in performance or composition but eventually extended to cover almost the entire field of domestic keyboard music as well as some kinds of instrumental chamber music. The last meaning came into use as early as 1599 with Morley's *First Booke of Consort Lessons* for treble viol, flute in G, bass viol, lute, cittern and pandora, which was followed by Rosseter's *Lessons for Consort* for the same instruments (London, 1609). The word appears on the title-page of the second English version (London, 1574) of Le Roy's (now lost) *Instruction* for the lute of 1567 ('with a briefe instruction how to play on the lute by tablature, to conduct and dispose thy hand unto the lute, with certaine easie lessons for that purpose'). This clearly pedagogic meaning was quickly expanded, and in due course the word appeared as part of a main title, for example in Robert Dowland's *Varietie of Lute Lessons* (London, 1610). It does not occur on the title-page of *Parthenia* (London, *c*1613), the first collection of keyboard music to be printed in England, though it does occur in George Chapman's introductory sonnet. The earliest known application of the word to a single piece occurs in My Ladye Nevells Booke (1591), a manuscript collection of keyboard music by Byrd, no.29 of which is *A Lesson or Voluntarie*. An early 17th-century source (*GB-Lbm* Add.30485) contains 'A lesson of Mr Tallis: two partes in one'; but this wording may not be original, and the piece appears as 'Canon in subdiapente . . . with a running Base' (attrib. Bull, in Add.31403; MB, xiv, no.51).

The word is not found extensively in early 17th-century sources, but it must have continued in use, for after the Restoration it came to denote almost any kind of domestic keyboard piece. The keyboard suite had originated during the Commonwealth: such groups of dances, unified by key, became known as suites or sets of lessons, and a published 'collection of lessons' might consist entirely or partly of such suites. Thus we have, for example, Locke's *Melothesia . . . With a Choice Collection of Lessons* (London, 1673); Purcell's posthumous *A Choice Collection of Lessons* (London, 1696), which consists of eight suites and some separate movements; and two collections of *Suits of . . . Lessons* edited by William Babell (London, *c*1715 and 1717). Towards the end of the 18th century the educational connotation reappears in such phrases as 'lessons for beginners', 'progressive lessons' and so on, more ambitious works being labelled 'sonata'. The most frequent use of the term thus coincides with the era of the keyboard suite, roughly from 1660 to 1750; but the word normally applies to an individual movement. 'Lesson' was preferred to 'sonata' for solo, as opposed to accompanied, keyboard music.

The French word 'leçon' is found comparatively

rarely in this sense – in works such as Couperin's *Leçons de ténèbres* the reference is of course to the liturgical lesson. The normal French equivalent is simply 'pièce', as in the numerous collections of 'suites de pièces' published during the 18th century (including Handel's *Suites de pièces*, London, 1720, which, however, uses the word 'lesson' in its English preface). The *1re leçon* in Rameau's second collection (Paris, 1724) is merely an exercise for the five fingers, and most uses of the word are of this type. Italy had no generic name for a single keyboard piece other than the word 'sonata' when used in this sense. (30 of Domenico Scarlatti's sonatas were published, apparently in London (in 1738 or early 1739), as *Essercizi per gravicembalo*; subsequent English editions of his sonatas naturally used the title 'lessons'.) There is a closer parallel in the German word 'Übung', though this is a collective noun (as in Johann Krieger: *Anmuthige Clavier-Übung*, Nuremberg, c1698, and Bach: *Clavier-Übung*, 4 pts., 1731–c1742).

The use of the word 'lesson' in its educational sense was eventually superseded by 'STUDY', derived from the French 'étude', and 'exercise'. The latter generally corresponded to the stricter use of 'leçon', while 'étude' or 'study' came to mean a freer kind of instructive piece, culminating in the masterpieces of Chopin; but the use of the terms was subject to a good deal of variation.

JOHN CALDWELL

Lessoth, Troilus à. *See* TROILUS À LESSOTH, FRANCISCUS GODEFRIDUS.

L'Estocart, Paschal de (*b* Noyon, Picardy, ?1539; *d* after 1584). French composer. In his youth he visited Italy several times. On 15 September 1581 he received a ten year *privilège* from Henri III to publish his works: these were printed at Geneva by Jean de Laon and are exclusively religious in character. L'Estocart seems to have had connections with certain leading Protestant nobles (Guillaume de la Marck, Duke of Bouillon, his brother Jean, Count of la Marck, and the King of Navarre, who became Henri IV). He was also very friendly with Simon Goulart, a Protestant minister, as well as with a small Genevan literary circle of Huguenot refugees. All this indicates that L'Estocart was in close touch with Reformation ideologies. In 1581 he matriculated at the University of Basle and in the following year he went to the court at Nancy, where on 4 April 1582 he received a gratuity of 60 écus from Duke Charles III as a reward for the dedication of his *Quatrains du sieur de Pibrac*. In 1583 he was again in Basle. He is next heard of as a member of the Abbot of Valmont's chapel in the Catholic setting of the Puy d'Evreux, which organized an annual competition for composers. L'Estocart won the prize of the Harpe d'argent for a five-part Latin motet, *Ecce quam bonum et quam jucundum*.

One of the hallmarks of L'Estocart's style is his daring harmony, and this is particularly marked in his *Octonaires de la vanité du monde*. He liked harmonies that were used very little by his contemporaries, such as augmented 5ths and augmented 6ths in discords and unusual sequences, and he enlivened his melodic lines with many intervals which are difficult to pitch. His concern was to convey as vividly as possible the sense of the words and to evoke precise ideas. He was one of the most thoroughly Italianate of French composers in the

second half of the 16th century. Yet in that his works are exclusively religious L'Estocart remains an essentially Huguenot composer, and his music has a strength and austerity that well accords with this.

WORKS

Premier livre des octonaires de la vanité du monde, 3–6vv (Geneva and Lyons, 1582); ed. in MMFTR, x (Paris, 1929)
Second livre des octonaires de la vanité du monde, 3–6vv (Geneva and Lyons, 1582); ed. in MMFTR, xi (Paris, 1958)
126 quatrains du sieur de Pibrac, 2–6vv (Geneva and Lyons, 1582)
Sacrae cantiones, 4–7vv (Lyons, 1582)
150 pseaumes de David mis en rime françoise par Clément Marot et Théodore de Besze, 4–8vv, avec la mélodie huguenote (Geneva and Lyons, 1583/R1954)

BIBLIOGRAPHY

H. Albrecht: 'Musikdrucke aus den Jahren 1576–1580 in Wilster (Holstein)', *Mf*, ii (1949), 204
E. Droz: 'J. de Sponde et P. de L'Estocart', *Bibliothèque d'humanisme et Renaissance*, xiii (1951), 312
J. Chailley and M. Honegger: Introduction to MMFTR, xi (1958)
S. Fornaçon: 'L'Estocart und sein Psalter', *Mf*, xiii (1960), 188

MARC HONEGGER

L'Estrange [Le Strange; Lestrange]. English family of patrons of music and amateur musicians who lived in Hunstanton, Norfolk. The family account books show that Sir Hamon L'Estrange (1583–1654) encouraged his whole family to make music. Resident musicians at Hunstanton included John Jenkins and Thomas Brewer, and two of Sir Hamon's sons deserve special mention as amateur musicians. One of them, Sir Nicholas L'Estrange (1603–55), amassed a music library, several volumes from which still survive (in *GB-Lbm*, *Lcm*, *Och*, *US-Cn*). Apart from copying pieces himself, he fastidiously collated his music with other copies belonging to his acquaintances, provided indexes, commissioned scores and himself annotated the partbooks with directions for performance and other valuable information. His work has been of inestimable value to 20th-century scholars. The other son, Roger L'Estrange (1616–1704), taught by Thomas Brewer, was noted for his skill as a player of the bass viol: an anecdote in his *Truth and Loyalty Vindicated* (London, 1662) shows that he was able to play at sight with professional musicians such as John Hingeston. As Licenser of the Press he wrote commendations for the publications of Christopher Simpson.

BIBLIOGRAPHY

P. J. Willetts: 'Sir Nicholas Le Strange and John Jenkins', *ML*, xl (1961), 30
——: 'Sir Nicholas Le Strange's Collection of Masque Music', *British Museum Quarterly*, xxix (1965), 79
J. T. Johnson: 'How to "Humour" John Jenkins' Three-Part Dances: Performance Directions in a Newberry Library MS', *JAMS*, xx (1967), 197

ANDREW ASHBEE

Le Sueur [Lesueur], **Jean-François** (*b* Drucat-Plessiel, nr. Abbeville, 15 Feb 1760; *d* Paris, 6 Oct 1837). French composer and writer on music. He was one of the most prominent French musicians during the Revolution, the Empire and the Restoration, distinguishing himself primarily as a composer of operas and religious music.

1. Life. 2. Achievements and influence.

1. LIFE. He came from a background of modest Picardy peasants and seems to have had no family connections (despite his own claims) with the 17th-century French painter Eustache Le Sueur. He showed musical talent at an early age, which led his family to send him to the choir schools of Abbeville and Amiens. He left Amiens in 1776 and spent the next ten years as a choirmaster at various provincial choir schools. While in Sées, he was

summoned to Paris for a few months as assistant choirmaster at the church of the Holy Innocents. It was during his stay in the capital that he had lessons in harmony and composition with the Abbé Nicolas Roze, choirmaster at the church of the Holy Innocents and author of a harmony method, extracts of which were published by La Borde in the third volume of his *Essai sur la musique* (Paris, 1780). Thereafter, Roze remained one of his closest friends.

Jean-François Le Sueur: engraving

Le Sueur's first appointments were as choirmaster of St Etienne in Dijon, St Julien in Le Mans and St Martin in Tours. He aroused the hostility of the chapter in Tours by attempting to introduce novel musical practices in the church; shortly afterwards this involved him in still more serious difficulties at Notre Dame in Paris. He returned to the church of the Holy Innocents as choirmaster in 1784, and two years later became choirmaster of Notre Dame, though not (as has been claimed) as the result of a competition; he owed this position to his renown, the testimonials of his colleagues and masters and the patronage of Marie-Antoinette. He stayed at Notre Dame for only a year, during which time he provoked violent polemics resulting in his dismissal; he was reproached in particular for introducing large orchestras and opera singers in the cathedral, as well as for his theories of a novel kind of liturgy which involved, for instance, the inclusion of excerpts from the Prophets and Gospels in the Ordinary of the Mass (which he regarded as a theatrical representation).

At about the same time Le Sueur, who had hitherto restricted himself to sacred music, turned to opera. With the help and advice of Sacchini, then in Paris, he undertook the composition of *Télémaque*. The work was not performed until 1796, and then in a modified and adapted version with additional spoken dialogue.

After spending a number of years in seclusion not far from Paris, Le Sueur reappeared on the scene during the Revolution. He made his début as an opera composer at the Théâtre Feydeau in 1793 with *La caverne*, possibly his greatest work. Its success placed him, together with Méhul and Cherubini, firmly in the public's attention during the Revolution. At the same time he became equally well known for his ten hymns, performed at the great festivals of the Revolution. There followed two more operas, *Paul et Virginie* and *Télémaque*, which were also given successful performances at the Théâtre Feydeau. Le Sueur was associated with the Institut National de Musique (the forerunner of the Paris Conservatoire) from 1793; when the Conservatoire opened in 1795 he became one of the inspectors of teaching. After a disagreement with the Conservatoire's director, Bernard Sarrette, he left in 1802, though not before he had eloquently defended himself in his *Lettre en réponse à Guillard*.

In a difficult situation both materially and morally, Le Sueur was saved by Napoleon, who in 1804 appointed him Paisiello's successor as director of the Tuileries Chapel, which had been restored in 1802. He held this position on his own under the Empire; under the Restoration he shared it first with Martini (until his death in 1816) and then with Cherubini until 1830, when the royal chapel was closed down. It was at the start of this new period in his life that he gained his greatest triumph with *Ossian ou Les bardes*, one of the greatest operatic successes of the first half of the 19th century, a success which owed as much to circumstances and the tastes of the period as to the quality of the work itself. It has often been mistakenly asserted that Napoleon suggested the subject of this work to him as he was particularly fond of Ossian's poetry, but Le Sueur had already begun working on the opera at the end of the 18th century. Another opera, *La mort d'Adam*, adapted from Klopstock's play, failed at the Opéra in 1809. By 1807 two works written in collaboration with Persuis had been performed at the Opéra: *L'inauguration du temple de la Victoire* (an occasional work designed to flatter Napoleon) and *Le triomphe de Trajan*, which was recast several times and had a success that lasted into the years of the Restoration; it is difficult to determine the extent of Le Sueur's contribution to these two works but it was certainly minimal. His last opera, *Alexandre à Babylone*, was completed in 1815 but never performed.

From 1 January 1818 until his death Le Sueur taught composition at the Conservatoire. After the Tuileries Chapel was closed in 1830 he devoted himself to long labours of erudition and compilation, covering innumerable folios with his delicate, cramped handwriting; a few of these have survived, including numerous works on the history of ancient and medieval music, interspersed with moral, religious and philosophical thoughts. At this time, too, he resumed work on his vast *Histoire de la musique*, which had been announced as early as 1810 but was never published; the manuscript is lost.

2. ACHIEVEMENTS AND INFLUENCE. The substance of Le Sueur's ideas on theory and history is found in his four-volume *Exposé d'une musique* (1787). Here the young musician gave evidence of a resolute and sometimes bold intellect, showing himself a true successor to the great 18th-century theorists, above all Rousseau. He took up some of the major aesthetic problems of imitation. For Le Sueur, the essential aim of music is imitation of nature or human passions; divorced from a literary text, music loses nearly all its meaning. The

function of imitation is not, he considered, to make a literal copy of an object, but to evoke in the soul of the listener what he called 'the sensations which one experiences in looking at an object' (following along these lines, Rousseau had claimed that 'even silence could be depicted by sounds'). Thus in the 'Hymn of the Indian Savages' in Act 1 of *Paul et Virginie*, the depiction of the sunrise is achieved by a passage consisting almost exclusively of simple triads that produce a curious, almost religious effect of freshness and peace. This theory of imitation, when interpreted strictly, implies a condemnation of instrumental music which affected many French composers and may explain Le Sueur's exclusive interest in vocal music.

The discussion of Greek music in the *Exposé* went no further than the views of the 18th-century theorists, but Le Sueur attempted to discover the rhythms of ancient poetry in French versification, thus reviving an old idea of the poets of the Pléiade. He also claimed to have introduced Greek rhythms into his music (particularly in *Télémaque*), e.g. hexameters, in which a crotchet was equivalent to a long syllable and a quaver to a short.

Of Le Sueur's three operas performed at the Théâtre Feydeau, *La caverne* is undoubtedly the finest. It is a strong, dramatic work, whose harmonies are sometimes distinctly harsh, and its popularity during the Reign of Terror is easily understandable. Le Sueur proved himself a master of choral writing, particularly in the syllabic choruses of the brigands. But his most notable achievement in this work is his uniting of disparate stylistic elements from various operatic genres: *opera seria* (the heroine Séraphine's long recitative and grand aria at the beginning of Act 2), *opera buffa* (Léonarde's strophic aria to a mildly bawdy text), and *opéra comique* (spoken dialogues). (For the title-page *see* NADERMAN.)

Paul et Virginie developed along similar lines; conceived in the *opéra comique* tradition, it nevertheless moved towards the style of grand opera, especially in Act 3. *Ossian ou Les bardes* triumphed as much through circumstance (the presence of the Emperor Napoleon at its second performance, the current taste for · things 'Ossianic', the magnificence of the stage designs) as through the musical quality of the work itself, which is somewhat frigid and conventional; the most interesting passages are undoubtedly the choruses, notably those of Act 4 ('Le rêve d'Ossian'). There are also some fine passages in *La mort d'Adam*, for instance, Cain's curse; Le Sueur certainly managed to instil into the work some biblical colour and atmosphere, but as a whole it is much too static for an opera, and in spirit really lies closer to oratorio. In *Alexandre à Babylone* there is a development away from the traditional forms and structure of 18th-century opera towards a more modern style, heralding the continuous melody of later 19th-century opera.

For 25 years Le Sueur was considered one of the masters of French church music. At a time when opera was suffering a period of decline, the Tuileries Chapel, as even foreign writers agreed, shone with exceptional brilliance, due to the work of Le Sueur and Cherubini. Le Sueur's sacred music is extremely simple in style. There are few modulations (he claimed that frequent modulations could not be distinctly perceived in cathedral acoustics), few fugues, and a deliberate use of simple, sometimes barren harmonies, with the voices often doubled at the octave. Nevertheless, there is enormous power and skill in his choral writing and much

charm in his melodies; it is music which was not designed to be studied, but to be heard in the surroundings for which it was intended. Between 1826 and 1841, 17 volumes of Le Sueur's church music were published; unfortunately, these scores do not accurately reflect the form in which they were performed at the Tuileries Chapel. In preparing these volumes, he combined several of his own works, and recomposed by stringing the works together end to end. The manuscripts of his works, in their original form, are extant, however, and reveal that there were 29 major sacred works (masses, oratorios, motets) and 30 shorter pieces, including some sections not in the printed volumes.

Le Sueur's musical influence on his pupils was less than has sometimes been maintained, certainly by Fouque as far as Berlioz is concerned. That his effect was certainly strong, however, is shown in the fact that between 1822 and 1839, 12 of the 18 winners of the Prix de Rome were, or had been, his pupils; these included Berlioz, Ambroise Thomas and Gounod. His support and encouragement of Berlioz in the early years was received gratefully and always remembered, but once Berlioz had matured and gained command over his talent, he seems to have been vividly conscious of his former teacher's limitations and the weaknesses of his instruction: Le Sueur, in fact, played only a modest part in forming Berlioz's musical personality.

Although Le Sueur was not a prolific composer and limited himself virtually to opera and sacred music, he was able to forge a strong personal style. He had been a modernist in his youth, before the years of the Revolution, but subsequently allowed himself to become confined within unduly narrow principles. Persuaded by Berlioz to hear Beethoven's Fifth Symphony, he was on his own admission 'moved and disturbed'; by the next day he had recovered the balance that he regarded as a fundamental artistic canon and declared that 'music like that ought not to be written'. He remained essentially untouched by the Romantic movement, except in its early and specifically French aspect, and suspected little of the vast musical revolution that had already been set in motion in Germany.

WORKS

Catalogue: *J.-F. Le Sueur: a Thematic Catalogue of his Complete Works*, ed. J. Mongrédien (New York, 1980)

STAGE
(all printed works published in Paris)

La caverne (drame lyrique, 3, Palat-Dercy, after Lesage: Gil Blas), Paris, Théâtre Feydeau, 16 Feb 1793 (1793)

Paul et Virginie (drame lyrique, 3, A. Dubreuil), Paris, Théâtre Feydeau, 13 Jan 1794 (?1794)

Télémaque (tragédie lyrique, 3, Palat-Dercy), Paris, Théâtre Feydeau, 11 May 1796, vocal score (?n.d.)

Ossian ou Les bardes (opera, 5, Palat-Dercy, rev. E. Deschamps), Paris, Opéra, 10 July 1804 (?1804)

L'inauguration du temple de la Victoire (intermède, 1, L. P. Baour-Lormian), Paris, Opéra, 2 Jan 1807, unpubd, collab. L. Loiseau de Persuis

Le triomphe de Trajan (opera, 3, J. A. Esménard), Paris, Opéra, 23 Oct 1807, unpubd, collab. Persuis

La mort d'Adam (tragédie lyrique et religieuse, 3, H. F. Guillard, after Klopstock), Paris, Opéra, 21 March 1809 (1822)

Alexandre à Babylone (opera, 5, Baour-Lormian), 1815, unperf.

OTHER WORKS
c60 sacred pieces, incl. oratorios, masses, motets, psalms and cantatas, 17 bks pubd (Paris, 1826–41), other works, F-Pn
c10 hymns and odes for Revolutionary celebrations, 1794–1802
A few songs and solfège exercises

WRITINGS
Exposé d'une musique une, imitative et particulière à chaque solemnité (Paris, 1787)
Lettre en réponse à Guillard (Paris, 1801)

'Observations sur les grandes parties de la musique et de la poésie chantée', *Odes d'Anacréon*, trans. J.-B. Gail (Paris, 3/1799)

BIBLIOGRAPHY

H. Berlioz: *Mémoires* (Paris, 1870; Eng. trans., 1969) [see particularly edn. by P. Citron, 1969]

F. Lamy: *Jean-François Le Sueur (1760–1837)* (Paris, 1912)

W. Buschkötter: 'Jean François Le Sueur', *SIMG*, xiv (1912–13), 58–154

M. Herman: *The Sacred Music of Jean-François Le Sueur: a Musical and Biographical Source Study* (diss., U. of Michigan, 1964)

J. Coutts: *Jean-François Le Sueur: a Study of the Composer and Five of his Operas* (diss., U. of Cardiff, 1966)

W. Dean: 'Opera under the French Revolution', *PRMA*, xciv (1967–8), 77

J. Mongrédien: 'La musique du sacre de Napoléon', *RdM*, liv (1968), 137–74

——: 'La musique aux fêtes du sacre de Charles X', *RMFC*, x (1970), 87

O. Saloman: *Aspects of "Gluckian" Operatic Thought and Practice in France: the Musico-dramatic Vision of Le Sueur and La Cépède (1785–1809) in Relation to Aesthetic and Critical Tradition* (diss., Columbia U., 1970)

——: 'The Orchestra in Le Sueur's Musical Aesthetics', *MQ*, lx (1974), 616

——: 'La Cépède's "La poétique de la musique" and Le Sueur', *AcM*, xlvii (1975), 144

D. Charlton: 'Ossian, Le Sueur and Opera', *SMA*, xi (1977), 37

JEAN MONGRÉDIEN

Lesur, Daniel Jean Yves. *See* DANIEL-LESUR.

Lesure, François(-Marie) (*b* Paris, 23 May 1923). French musicologist and librarian. He took a degree in history at the Sorbonne (1946) and also studied at the Conservatoire, at the Ecole des Chartes (diploma as an archivist-palaeographer, 1950), and at the Ecole Pratique des Hautes-Etudes (diploma, 1948). He was a librarian in the music department of the Bibliothèque Nationale in Paris for 20 years before becoming its head keeper in 1970, and was responsible for arranging several exhibitions at the Bibliothèque Nationale (Mozart, 1956; Debussy, 1962; Berlioz, 1969) and at the Opéra (Deux Siècles d'Opéra Français, 1972). In 1965 he became professor of musicology at the Free University, Brussels, and in 1973 he succeeded Solange Corbin as director of studies at the Ecole des Hautes-Etudes.

Lesure's research has been concerned principally with the sociology of music, 16th-century French music, Debussy and bibliography in all periods; he is co-author (with G. Thibault) of the bibliographies of the 16th-century musical editions brought out by the French publishers Du Chemin and Le Roy & Ballard, and author of the bibliography of the 18th-century musical editions of the publishers Estienne Roger and M.-C. Le Cène. He was in charge of the secretariat of RISM (1953–67) and edited the volumes devoted to printed collections of the 16th and 17th centuries, the printed collections of the 18th century and printed writings about music. He is editor of Le Pupitre, a collection of pre-1800 music published by Heugel (Paris, 1967–), and of the series of books Iconographie Musicale. All his work bears the mark of his training both as a historian and as an archivist, a training which ensures his punctiliousness with documents and the value of his research. He was president of the Société de Musicologie Française from 1971 to 1974.

WRITINGS

'Claude Goudimel: étudiant, correcteur et éditeur parisien', *MD*, ii (1948), 225

with D. P. Walker: 'Claude Le Jeune and Musique mesurée', *MD*, iii (1949), 151

'Pierre Attaingnant: notes et documents', *MD*, iii (1949), 33

'Réflexions sur l'origine du concert parisien', *Polyphonie*, v (1949), 47

'La guitare en France au XVIe siècle', *MD*, iv (1950), 187

'Autour de C. Marot et de ses musiciens', *RdM*, xxx (1951), 109

'C. Janequin: recherches sur sa vie et son oeuvre', *MD*, v (1951), 157–93

with G. Thibault: 'Bibliographie des éditions musicales publiées par Nicolas Du Chemin (1549–1576)', *AnnM*, i (1953), 269–373; iv (1956), 251

'Eléments populaires dans la chanson française', *Musique et poésie au XVIe siècle: CNRS Paris 1953*, 169

'La communauté des joueurs d'instruments au XVIe siècle', *Revue historique de droit français et étranger* (1953), 79–109

'Marin Marais: sa carrière – sa famille', *RBM*, vii (1953), 129

'Musicologie et sociologie', *ReM* (1953), no.221, p.4

'La facture instrumentale à Paris au XVIe siècle', *GSJ*, vii (1954), 11–52

'La musique religieuse française au XVIe siècle', *ReM* (1954), no.222, p.61

ed.: *La Renaissance dans les provinces du nord: CNRS Entretiens d'Arras 1954*

'Les orchestres populaires à Paris vers la fin du XVIe siècle', *RdM*, xxxvi (1954), 39

with G. Thibault: *Bibliographie des éditions d'Adrian Le Roy et Robert Ballard (1551–1598)* (Paris, 1955; suppl., *RdM*, xl, 1957, p.166)

'Danses et chansons à danser au début du XVIe siècle', *Recueil de travaux offerts à M. Clovis Brunel* (Paris, 1955), 176

'Le recueil de ballets de Michel Henry', *Les fêtes de la Renaissance I: CNRS Abbaye de Royaumont 1955*, 205

'Le Traité des instruments de musique de Pierre Trichet', *AnnM*, iii (1955), 283–387; iv (1956), 175–248

Mozart en France (Paris, 1956) [exhibition catalogue]

'Mozartiana gallica', *RdM*, xxxviii (1956), 115

Musicians and Poets of the French Renaissance (New York, 1956)

ed.: P. Trichet: *Traité des instruments de musique* (Neuilly-sur-Seine, 1957)

Introduction to G. Morlaye: *Psaumes de Pierre Certon réduits pour chant et luth*, ed. R. de Morcourt (Paris, 1957)

'Recherches sur les luthistes parisiens à l'époque de Louis XIII', *Le luth et sa musique: CNRS Neuilly-sur-Seine 1957*, 209

'Un musicien d'Hippolyte d'Este: Pierre Sandrin', *CHM*, ii (1957), 245

'La musicologie en France depuis 1945', *AcM*, xxx (1958), 3

with R. de Morcourt: 'G. P. Paladino et son "Premier livre" de luth (1560)', *RdM*, xlii (1958), 170

'XVIe siècle', *Précis de musicologie*, ed. J. Chailley (Paris, 1958), 191

with N. Bridgman: 'Une anthologie "historique" de la fin du XVIe siècle: le manuscrit Bourdeney', *Miscelánea en homenaje a Monseñor Higinio Anglés* (Barcelona, 1958–61), 151

ed.: *Recueils imprimés du XVIe et XVIIe siècles*, RISM, B/I/1 (1960)

'Une querelle sur le jeu de la viole en 1688: Jean Rousseau contre Demachy', *RdM*, lxvi (1960), 181

'Pour une sociologie historique des faits musicaux', *IMSCR, viii New York 1961*, i, 333

ed.: *Claude Debussy* (Paris, 1962) [incl. 'Debussy de 1883 à 1885 d'après la correspondance de Paul Vidal à Henriette Fuch', p.98; 'Bibliographie debussyste', p.129]

Introduction to *M. Mersenne: Harmonie universelle* (Paris, 1636) (Paris, 1963) [facs. edn.]

'L'"affaire" Debussy-Ravel: lettres inédites', *Festschrift Friedrich Blume* (Kassel, 1963), 231

ed.: *Recueils imprimés du XVIIIe siècle*, RISM, B/II (1964)

Musica e società (Milan, 1966; Ger. trans., 1966; Eng. trans., 1968)

Bibliographie des éditions musicales publiées par Estienne Roger et M. C. Le Cène (Amsterdam, 1696–1743) (Paris, 1969)

ed.: *Ecrits imprimés concernant la musique*, RISM, B/VI/1–2 (1971)

ed.: *Mr. Croche et autres écrits* (Paris, 1971) [Debussy's writings]

'Archival Research: Necessity and Opportunity', *Perspectives in Musicology*, ed. B. S. Brook, E. O. D. Downes and S. van Solkema (New York, 1972), 56

L'opéra classique français (Geneva, 1972)

'L'affaire Fétis', *RBM*, xxviii–xxx (1974–6), 214

Claude Debussy (Geneva, 1975)

'Ebauche d'un répertoire des éditeurs de musique dans les provinces françaises', *Beiträge zur Muzikdokumentation: Franz Grasberger zum 60. Geburtstag* (Tutzing, 1975), 233

Maurice Ravel, 1875–1975 (Paris, 1975)

Musique et musiciens français du XVIe siècle (Geneva, 1976) [repr. of articles pubd 1950–69]

Catalogue de l'oeuvre de Claude Debussy (Geneva, 1977)

ed., with C. Sartori: *Bibliografia della musica italiana vocale profana pubblicata dal 1500 al 1700* (Geneva, 1977) [based on *VogelB*]

with A. Devriès: *Dictionnaire des éditeurs de musique français, i: Des origines à environ 1820* (Geneva, 1979)

EDITIONS

Anthologie de la chanson parisienne au XVIe siècle (Monaco, 1953)

with T. Merritt: *C. Janequin: Chansons polyphoniques* (Monaco, 1965–71)

CHRISTIANE SPIETH-WEISSENBACHER

Leszczyński [Lesczyński], **Władysław** [Aleksander] (*b* 1616; *d* Częstochowa, 24 Sept 1680). Polish composer and organist. His father, Izydor Leszczyński, who was a painter, entered the Pauline monastery of Jasna Góra, Częstochowa, after his wife's death, and he soon followed him: he became a monk on 8 September 1632, taking the name Władysław in place of his baptismal name, Aleksander. He spent the rest of his life in this monastery, where he was conductor, organist and cantor. During his lifetime he enjoyed a wide reputation as a composer. He left a large number of his own works, a library of scores and a collection of instruments, which were partly dispersed after his death, in spite of the efforts of a special monastic commission set up to ensure their preservation, and those that remained intact perished in a fire in 1690. Only two of his works are known to survive: the four-part *Missa per octavas* (in two copies at *PL-Kk*, one of them, in the hand of G. G. Gorczycki, incomplete) and *Mandatum novum* for five voices with violone (in *PL-CZp*). Six other works (now lost) are mentioned in a contemporary inventory from the Carmelite monastery at Kraków.

BIBLIOGRAPHY

SMP
A. Chybiński: 'Aleksander Władysław Leszczyński, 1616–1680', *Spiewak* (1927), no.1
——: *Słownik muzyków dawnej Polski* [Dictionary of early Polish musicians] (Kraków, 1948–9), 71f
P. Podejko: 'Nieznani muzycy polscy, kompozytorzy, dyrygenci, instrumentaliści, wokaliści (1572–1820)' [Unknown Polish musicians – composers, conductors, instrumentalists, singers (1572–1820)], *Z dziejów muzyki polskiej*, xi (1966), 57f
——: 'Na marginesie dotychczasowych wzmianek o życiu muzycznym na Jasnej Górze w Częstochowie' [Marginalia about the details of musical life of Jasna Góra Monastery in Częstochowa], *Muzyka*, xii/1 (1967), 37
——: 'Źródła do dziejów muzyki polskiej w archiwum zakonu paulinów w Częstochowie' [Sources for the history of Polish music in the archive of the Pauline monastery in Częstochowa], *Z dziejów muzyki polskiej*, xiv (1969), 33
——: *Kapela wokalno-instrumentalna zakonu paulinów na Jasnej Górze w Częstochowie* [The vocal and instrumental establishment of the Pauline monastery of Jasna Góra in Częstochowa] (diss., U. of Warsaw, 1971)
T. Maciejewski: 'Inwentarz muzykaliów kapeli karmelickiej w Krakowie na Piasku z lat 1665–1684' [Inventory of the Carmelite chapel at Kraków on the Piasek, 1665–1684], *Muzyka*, xxi/2 (1976), 77

MIROSŁAW PERZ

Leszetycki, Teodor. *See* LESCHETIZKY, THEODOR.

Letania (Lat.). LITANY.

Le Tansur, William. *See* TANS'UR, WILLIAM.

Letelier(-Llona), Alfonso (*b* Santiago, 4 Oct 1912). Chilean composer. He studied with Hügel for the piano and Allende for composition at the Santiago National Conservatory (1930–35), simultaneously reading agriculture at the University of Chile. In 1938 and 1946 he travelled to Europe for the University of Chile to lecture on and promote contemporary Chilean music. He was a founder-director of the Escuela Moderna de Música in Santiago (1940), and he conducted its madrigal ensemble (1940–48). His other appointments have included those of professor at the National Conservatory (from 1946), president of the Chilean National Association of Composers (1950–56), dean of music at the University of Chile, president of the executive board of the Instituto de Extensión Musical (1953–62) and vice-rector of the University of Chile (1958–62). He made further visits to Europe in 1947 (Spain), 1958 (Germany and Austria, attending the performance of his Piano Variations at the ISCM Festival) and 1962. In 1967 he was elected to permanent membership of the Chilean Academy of Fine Arts, and in 1969 he was appointed head of the music department at the Chilean Ministry of Public Education. He has served on the juries of international composition competitions and has received numerous prizes and commissions, most notably the Chilean National Arts Prize (1968). His early compositions show the influences of French impressionism and Chilean folk music, and he has also been drawn to the music and mysticism of the Spanish Renaissance, as well as to Gregorian chant. From the early 1950s his music became less attached to nationalism and more to the aesthetics and methods of the Second Viennese School, using these with great freedom and individuality. He has published over 50 articles in the *Revista musical chilena*.

WORKS
(*selective list*)

Choral: Mass, op.1, SATB, org, orch, 1929; 8 canciones, op.9, 1934–9; 3 Motets, SATB, 1939; Vitrales de la Anunciación (Claudel), cantata, SSA, orch, 1950; La historia de Tobías y Sara, part 1, op.26 (Claudel), opera-oratorio, 1955; O sacrum convivium, SATB, 1969; 3 madrigales campesinos (O. Castro), SATB, ens, 1970; Mass, SATB, org, chamber orch, 1972

Orch: La vida del campo, op.14, pf, orch, 1937; Suite grotesca, 1946; Divertimento, op.25, 1955; Suite Aculeo, op.17, 1956; Gui Conc., 1961; Preludios vegetales, op.35, 1968; Conc., str, 1972

Solo vocal: Ballad and Song, S, pf, 1935; Canciones de cuna, op.13, Mez, chamber orch, 1939; Sonetos de la muerte, op.18 (Mistral), S, orch, 1948; Canciones antiguas, Mez, pf, 1951; Estancias amorosas, op.34 (Valdes), Mez, str orch, 1966; 2 canciones, op.36 (George), 1v, chamber orch, 1971

Chamber: Str Qt, 1939; Sonata, op.19, va, pf, 1949; Sonatina, vn, pf, 1953; Sax Qt, 1958

Pf: Variations, op.22, 1948; 4 Pieces, op.33, 1964

Principal publisher: Instituto de Extensión Musical

BIBLIOGRAPHY
Composers of the Americas, ii (Washington, DC, 1956), 104
D. Santa Cruz: 'El compositor Alfonso Letelier', *Revista musical chilena* (1967), no.100, p.8

JUAN A. ORREGO-SALAS

Letra (Sp.: 'letter'). (1) The words of a song or a libretto.

(2) From the 15th century to the 17th the term was used, along with 'mote', 'pie', 'cabeza', 'villancico' (in its restricted sense), 'estribo' and 'estribillo', to designate the refrain of a song or poem, especially a given or traditional refrain. As with 'villancico' it was sometimes used to refer to the song as a whole, both refrain and stanza. By the 17th century the diminutive 'letrilla' came to be more favoured by poets and sometimes musicians to designate a jocular or satirical refrain song.

JACK SAGE

Leuckart. German firm of music publishers. It was founded in 1782 in Breslau by Franz Ernst Christoph Leuckart (1748–1817) and Johann Daniel Korn (the younger) as a fine-art and music shop. As F. E. C. Leuckart, the firm was notably successful in the third generation, when Constantin Sander (1826–1905) took over its management (1849). He made agreements with talented young composers (Robert Franz, Bruch), worked with Liszt, Ferdinand Hiller, Bülow and Thuille, and encouraged the music historian A. W. Ambros to write his *Geschichte der Musik*. The firm published organ works, instructional literature and dramatic works (including Bruch's *Loreley*), and encouraged the work of Eduard Kremser (*Altniederländisches Dankgebet*) and Thomas Koschat, the Carinthian folksong collector. In 1870 the firm moved to Leipzig, where it was active in promoting individual compositions by Richard Strauss (*Ein Heldenleben* op.40; *Eine Alpensymphonie* op.64), Pfitzner and Reger. After the death of Constantin Sander, his son Martin (1859–1930) expanded the catalogue to include Catholic liturgical music, contemporary orchestral and chamber music, the collection *Leuckarts Hausmusik* and choral music (e.g. by Richard Trunk, Armin Knab and Hugo Kaun). For several decades the hospitable Sander home was a meeting-place for distinguished musicians visiting Leipzig for world and local premières. In 1930 Martin Sander's son Horst (1904–45) inherited the firm and increased its output to almost 10,000 items. It suffered war damage and moved from Leipzig in 1945, remaining in the family's possession and resuming its activities on the same lines in Munich in 1948.

BIBLIOGRAPHY

175 Jahre Musikverlag F. E. C. Leuckart: Verlagsgeschichte und Gesamtkatalog (Munich, 1957)

HANS-MARTIN PLESSKE

Leutgeb [Leitgeb], **Joseph** [Ignaz] (*b* ?Salzburg, *c*1745; *d* Vienna, 27 Feb 1811). Austrian horn player. (According to the 1770 Salzburg court calendar he was also a violinist.) In 1770, shortly after becoming first horn in the archbishop's orchestra at Salzburg, he travelled to Paris, where he appeared twice, in April and May, at the Concert Spirituel as soloist in three concertos of his own composition (now lost). On the first occasion the *Mercure de France* praised his superior talent, on the second his ability to 'sing an adagio as perfectly as the most mellow, interesting and accurate voice'. Leutgeb was the first in Paris to perform a solo concerto using the new hand-stopping technique, 15 years after Hampel's first experiments in developing it in Dresden. During other periods of leave from Salzburg he played in Vienna and Milan. In 1777 he moved from Salzburg to Vienna, where he set up or, more likely, inherited a cheesemonger's shop; he received financial help from Leopold Mozart. W. A. Mozart's concertos K417, 447 and 495 were composed for him, and probably also the two separate movements in D K412/386*b* and 514, the incomplete Rondo K371 and the Quintet K407/386*c*, as well as horn parts in various other works; in the autographs many of the horn parts contain jocular remarks at Leutgeb's expense. Leutgeb remained a friend to the end of Mozart's life, and is mentioned in his last letter; he apparently retired from playing in 1792.

BIBLIOGRAPHY

P. R. Bryan: 'The Horn in the Works of Mozart and Haydn', *Haydn Yearbook*, ix (1970), 189–256

H. Fitzpatrick: *The Horn and Horn-playing* (London, 1970)

K. M. Pisarowitz: 'Mozarts Schnorrer Leutgeb', *Mitteilungen der Internationale Stiftung Mozarteum*, xviii (1970), 21

REGINALD MORLEY-PEGGE/R

Leuthon, Karl. *See* LUYTHON, CARL.

Leuto (It.). LUTE.

Leuttner, Georg Christoph (*b* Tölz, Bavaria, 12 Aug 1644; *d* Altötting, Bavaria, 26 April 1703). German composer and clergyman. After completing the usual studies he was ordained priest in 1671 and in 1682 was called to the Freising court of the Prince-Bishop Albert Sigismund as chaplain and vice-Kapellmeister. In 1688, he was the bishop's spiritual adviser and a canon and scholar at the collegiate church of St Zeno, Isen, Upper Bavaria. Although the administrators of the Kapelle at Altötting had already considered him as a possible director of their choir in May 1683, it was not until 30 September 1694 that he was finally employed there as Kapellmeister. Among his contemporaries he had a notable reputation as a composer, but an assessment of him is impossible, since only one piece survives, *Mein Seel ist betrübt*, a sacred song for solo voice and continuo found in four different settings in *D-Mbs* Mus.92. Apart from a number of other MS pieces two printed collections by him are known: *Cithara Davidica, sive psalmi per annum consueti, cum duabus lytaniis lauretanis*, for four and five voices, organ, two violins and two violas (Munich, 1682), and *Apollo seraphicus, sive sacri concentus, mottae, psalmi, antiphonae*, for one to five voices, organ, two violins and two violas (Munich, 1688).

BIBLIOGRAPHY

M. Moesmang: *Geschichte der Altöttinger Stifts- und Kapellmusik* (Altötting, n.d.)

K. G. Fellerer: *Beiträge zur Musikgeschichte Freisings* (Freising, 1926)

AUGUST SCHARNAGL

Leuven (Flemish). LOUVAIN.

Levant, Oscar (*b* Pittsburgh, 27 Dec 1906; *d* Beverly Hills, 14 Aug 1972). American pianist, composer and writer. After training with local teachers in Pittsburgh he moved to New York, where he studied with the pianist Sigismund Stojowski; later he briefly studied composition with Schoenberg. He was active as a pianist with jazz bands and as a composer of popular songs, but achieved prominence as a sympathetic interpreter of Gershwin's music. His works for the Broadway stage brought his talents to the attention of Hollywood, and after moving to the west coast he wrote the scores for several films (including *Street Girl* and *Tanned Legs*) and also appeared in some (including *Dance of Life* and *An American in Paris*). Among his compositions are a piano concerto, which he played with the NBC SO in 1942, a *Nocturne* for orchestra (1937), two string quartets and many popular songs. His writings include two books of autobiographical reminiscences, *A Smattering of Ignorance* (New York, 1940) and *The Memoirs of an Amnesiac* (New York, 1965), which are caustic in content and conversational in tone.

GEORGE GELLES

Levarie, Siegmund (*b* Vienna, 24 July 1914). American musicologist and music educationist of Austrian birth. He took a diploma in conducting at the New Vienna Conservatory in 1935 and a PhD in musicology from the University of Vienna in 1938. Moving to America, he joined the faculty of the University of Chicago, where he taught from 1938 to 1952. There he organized a collegium musicum, one of the first in the USA, and directed the group in performances of early music. He was dean of the Chicago Musical College from 1952 to 1954, when he was appointed professor at Brooklyn College of the City University of New York; he served as chairman of the music department there from 1954 to 1962. In addition to his academic duties he was executive director of the Fromm Music Foundation from 1952 to 1956 and directed the Brooklyn Community SO from 1954 to 1958.

Levarie's interests include music theory and analysis, Machaut and Goethe. His writings cross disciplinary lines, drawing on the fields of education, psychology and physics.

WRITINGS

Fugue and Form (Chicago, 1941)
'Music in the Education of the Whole Man', *The Educational Forum*, xiii (1949), 449
with H. Kohut: 'On the Enjoyment of Listening to Music', *Psychoanalytic Quarterly*, xix (1950), 64
Mozart's 'Le Nozze di Figaro': a Critical Analysis (Chicago, 1952/R1977)
Fundamentals of Harmony (New York, 1954, 2/1962)
Guillaume de Machaut (New York, 1954, 2/1970)
Review of F. Sternfeld: *Goethe and Music* (New York, 1954), *MQ*, xlii (1956), 105
Review of *W. A. Mozart: Sonatas and Fantasies for the Piano*, ed. N. Broder (Bryn Mawr, Penn., 1956), *MQ*, xlii (1956), 252
' "Solitario bosco ombroso" – eine musikalische Kindheitserinnerung Goethes', *Goethe*, xix (1957), 196
Musical Italy Revisited (New York, 1963)
'The Italian Province', *Opera News*, xxviii/23 (1964), 6
with E. Levy: *Tone: a Study in Musical Acoustics* (Kent, Ohio, 1968)
'La musique d'Ernst Lévy', *SMz*, cviii (1968), 178
'The Closing Numbers of *Die Schöpfung*', *Studies in Eighteenth-century Music: a Tribute to Karl Geiringer* (New York and London, 1970), 315
with E. Levy: *A Dictionary of Musical Morphology* (Brooklyn, 1977)
ed.: *Lucy Van-Jung Page (1892–1972): Recollections of Pupils and Friends* (Oxford, 1977)

EDITIONS

S. Rossi: Sinfonie a tre voci (1608) (Vienna, 1937)

PAULA MORGAN

Levashova, Ol'ga Evgen'yevna (*b* Blagoveschchensk-na-Amure, Siberia, 30 March 1912). Soviet musicologist. She graduated from the department of theory and composition at Moscow Conservatory, taking her *Kandidat* degree in 1948 and her doctorate in 1964 under K. A. Kuznetsov. Since 1946 she has taught at the conservatory in the department of Russian musical history; in 1951 she was appointed lecturer, and in 1966 professor. Since 1951 she has also been a senior research fellow at the Institute for the History of the Arts in Moscow. Levashova is the author of a series of substantial books on the history of Russian and west European music of the 18th and 19th centuries, and also of documentary publications designed as educational material for the conservatory. Other interests include contemporary Soviet chamber music and ballet, about which she wrote in *Istoriya russkoy sovetskoy muzïki* ('The history of Soviet Russian music'), and Italian and French opera.

WRITINGS

'Romans i pesnya' [Ballad and song], *Ocherki po istorii russkoy muzïki 1790–1825*, ed. M. S. Druskin and Yu. V. Keldïsh (Leningrad, 1956)
'Sovetskaya kamernaya muzïka'; 'Sovetskiy balet', *Istoriya russkoy sovetskoy muzïki*, ed. Institut Istorii Iskusstvo, ii–iv (Moscow, 1959–63)
Edvard Grig [Grieg] (Moscow, 1962)
'Frantsuzskoye muzïkovedeniye 18–19 vekov' [French musicology of the 18th and 19th centuries], *Istoriya evropeyskovo iskusstvoznaniya*, (Moscow, 1963–9)
ed.: *E. Grig: izbrannïye stat'i i pis'ma* [Collected articles and letters] (Moscow, 1966)
'Opernaya estetika Gretri', *Klassicheskoye iskusstvo za rubezhom* (Moscow, 1966)
'Sovetskiy balet posle 1945g' [Soviet ballet after 1945], *Istoriya muzïki narodov SSSR*, ed. Yu. V. Keldïsh (Moscow, 1970–)
with Yu. Keldïsh and A. Kandinsky: *Istoriya russkoy muzïki*, i (Moscow, 1972)

EDITIONS

Russkaya vokal'naya lirika XVIII veka [18th-century Russian lyrical songs], Pamyatniki russkovo muzïkal'novo iskusstva, i (Moscow, 1972)

YURY KELDÏSH

Levasseur, Jean Henri (*b* Beaumont-sur-Oise, 29 May 1764; *d* Paris, *c*1826). French cellist, brother of Pierre François Levasseur. He studied with J. B. Cupis and J. L. Duport. In 1782 he joined the orchestra of the Paris Opéra, where he was solo cellist from 1789 until 1820. A professor at the Paris Conservatoire, 1795–1826, he was co-author, with Baudiot, Catel and the violinist Baillot, of the *Méthode de violoncelle et de basse d'accompagnement* (Paris, 1804), which was adopted by the Conservatoire. Lamarre, Norblin and Franchomme were among his pupils. He was appointed imperial musician to Napoleon I and to the royal chapel of Louis XVIII. He published sonatas, duets and studies for the cello.

E. VAN DER STRAETEN/LYNDA LLOYD REES

Levasseur, Nicholas (Prosper) (*b* Bresles, 9 March 1791; *d* Paris, 6 Dec 1871). French bass. He entered the Paris Conservatoire in 1807 and made his début at the Opéra in Grétry's *La caravane du Caire* (14 October 1813). However, the Opéra's repertory lacked deep bass roles, and for two seasons he sang in Italian opera at London, making his début at the King's Theatre in Mayr's *Adelasia ed Alderano* (10 January 1815). He returned to the Opéra as an understudy but in 1819 joined the Théâtre-Italien, first appearing as Almaviva in *Le nozze di Figaro* (5 October). The following year he appeared at La Scala, Milan, in the première of Meyerbeer's *Margherita d'Anjou* (14 November). At the Théâtre-Italien Levasseur sang in many Rossini operas new to Paris, notably in the title role of *Mosè* (20 October 1822), a role he repeated when Rossini revised the work for the Opéra (26 March 1827). In 1828 he rejoined the Opéra as one of its leading singers, and over the next 12 years he created virtually every important new bass role in the Opéra's repertory, including Bertram in *Robert le diable* (1831), Brogni in *La juive* (1835), Marcel in *Les Huguenots* (1836) and Balthazar in *La favorite* (1840). He left the Opéra in 1845, but at Meyerbeer's request returned to sing in the première of *Le prophète* (16 April 1849), and finally retired in 1853. Levasseur taught at the Conservatoire from 1841 to 1869, and on his retirement he was made a Chevalier of the Légion d'honneur. He became blind shortly before his death.

PHILIP ROBINSON

Levasseur [Le Vasseur], Rosalie [Marie-Rose-[Claude-]Josephe] (*b* Valenciennes, 8 Oct 1749; *d* Neuwied am Rhein, 6 May 1826). French soprano. She made her début at the Paris Opéra in 1766 as Zaide in Campra's *L'Europe galante* and appeared there regularly until 1785. Known as Mlle Rosalie during her first ten years at the Opéra, she took only minor roles until, in 1776, she was entrusted with Eurydice and Iphigenia in revivals of Gluck's first French operas. She was then preferred over her rival, Sophie Arnould, to create the title role in the French *Alceste*. Her lover, Count Mercy-Argentau, the Austrian ambassador, used his influence to promote her career. She became Gluck's close friend and favourite interpreter, creating the title roles in *Armide* (1777) and *Iphigénie en Tauride* (1779). She was successful in the title role of Philidor's *Ernelinde* during its 1777 revival, but less so in Piccinni's works, relinquishing his Angélique (*Roland*) to Mme de Saint-Huberty and Sangaride (*Atys*) to Marie Joséphine Laguerre. Of unattractive features (in contrast to Arnould), she was a powerful rather than flexible singer, with a good stage presence. Although never undisputed mistress of the Opéra, she negotiated for herself a special salary of 9000 livres.

BIBLIOGRAPHY

FétisB

J. G. Prod'homme: 'Rosalie Levasseur, Ambassadress of Opera', *MQ*, ii (1916), 210–43

H. Boschot: 'Levasseur, Rosalie', *ES*

JULIAN RUSHTON

Levé (Fr.). UPBEAT; *see also* ANALYSIS, §II, 2.

Leveridge, Richard (*b* 1670–71; *d* London, 22 March 1758). English bass and composer. For more than half a century Leveridge was a leading singer on the London stage and a popular composer of songs. He emerged as a soloist in April 1695, when the division of London's one theatre company left him as the leading bass in the company with which Henry Purcell worked until his death in November. Leveridge's first part was the magician Ismeron in *The Indian Queen*, where he sang the impressive 'Ye twice ten hundred deities', and the first incidental song published as sung by him was Purcell's *Take not a woman's anger ill*. He probably also sang the bravura bass solos in *The Tempest*. After Purcell's death the company's composers were Daniel Purcell, Jeremiah Clarke and Leveridge himself. In 1698 all three provided music for *The Island Princess*, in which Leveridge's performance of his own *Enthusiastic Song* was immensely popular. Regular revival performances, sung by him, were advertised until 1739. Two handsome books of his songs were published in 1697 and 1699 and his popular theatre songs were already appearing on single sheets. In 1699 he moved to the theatre in Dublin; one of Vanbrugh's letters states: 'Liveridge is in Ireland, he Owes so much money he dare not come over, so for want of him we han't had one Opera play'd this Winter'. He returned in 1702 to a revival of *The Island Princess* and a new production of *Macbeth* with music 'Vocal and Instrumental, all new Compos'd by Mr Leveridge'. He was to sing Hecate in this version for nearly 50 years.

He continued to sing both songs and dramatic operas but a new element was added with the introduction of operas in the Italian style. Between 1705 and 1708 he was the leading bass, generally with a comic role, in *Arsinoe*, *Camilla*, *Rosamond*, *Thomyris* and *Love's Triumph*. At first the operas were performed in English, but soon the Italian singers and language took over. After a lean period Leveridge sang in the English opera *Calypso and Telemachus* (1712) and then had a season with Handel's company. He was in the first performances of *Il pastor fido* and *Teseo* and played Argantes in a revival of *Rinaldo*. He never sang for Handel again, but in 1731 was Polypheme in the first public performance of *Acis and Galatea*, and a few of Handel's Italian airs were published with English words by Leveridge.

In 1714 he moved to the new theatre at Lincoln's Inn Fields, which was managed by John Rich, with whom he was to work for the rest of his career. He returned to his English repertory and a new form, the musical afterpiece. These lightweight works were often comic, and for his benefit in 1716 Leveridge produced his own afterpiece, *Pyramus and Thisbe*. It is an amusing and good-natured parody of Italian opera, and Leveridge wrote the music, adapted the libretto from Shakespeare and sang Pyramus to the Thisbe of the tenor George Pack. His music is lost but the libretto was published and Lampe reset it in 1745. By 1720 Lincoln's Inn Fields was in financial difficulties and Leveridge retired from the stage to the coffee shop in Tavistock Street, Covent Garden, which he had opened in about 1716.

He returned to the stage in 1723 and for the next 28 years was the leading bass at Lincoln's Inn Fields and later at Covent Garden. His repertory expanded to include parts in Rich's phenomenally successful series of pantomime afterpieces. Seven of these works, from *The Necromancer*, introduced in 1723, to *Orpheus and Eurydice* (1740), were given between 60 and 90 performances a season. Leveridge generally sang impressive roles as gods and magicians and his voice, if no longer as flexible as when Purcell wrote for it, remained firm and powerful. He was rarely a performer in the ballad operas but his own compositions were often in the ballad style and included *The Roast Beef of Old England* and a number of convivial drinking-songs. He was a favourite with audiences and his very individual annual benefits were generously supported. He enjoyed remarkably good health and reduced his appearances only in his last few seasons. In 1751 he was forced to leave the stage because of the 'infirmities incident to his great age' and in his retirement his friends organized a subscription for 'honest Dick Leveridge, the Father of the English Stage'.

WORKS
SONG COLLECTIONS

A New Book of Songs (London, 1697)
A Second Book of Songs (London, 1699)
A Collection of Songs (London, *c*1725)
A Collection of Songs (London, 1727)
A New Book of Songs (London, 1730)

STAGE MUSIC

The Island Princess, with D. Purcell, J. Clarke (Motteux, after Fletcher), London, ?Nov 1698, 4 songs by Leveridge in *GB-Lbm*

Title-page of 'A New Book of Songs' (1697) by Leveridge

Add.15318, Songs in the New Opera, call'd The Island Princess (London, 1699) and song sheets

Macbeth (after Shakespeare), London, 21 Nov 1702; the music pubd in 1770 by Boyce as The Original Songs Airs and Choruses ... in Macbeth and attrib. Locke is almost certainly by Leveridge

Britain's Happiness, musical interlude also set by Weldon (Motteux), London, 7 March 1704, music lost, libretto pubd London, 1704

The Mountebank or The Humours of the Fair, musical interlude in Farewell Folly (Motteux), London, 18 Jan 1705, 2 songs by Leveridge

The Mountebank or The Country Lass, London, 21 Dec 1715, 2 songs by Leveridge

Pyramus and Thisbe (Leveridge, after Shakespeare), London, 11 April 1716, music lost, libretto pubd London, 1716

Jupiter and Europa, with Colston and Galliard, London, 23 March 1723, Lbm Add.31518 and song sheets

Numerous single songs sung in plays (especially earlier in his career) or performed as entertainment between acts; among the most frequently performed were:

The Fisherman's Song from The Famous History of the Rise and Fall of Massinello (D'Urfey), London, May 1699

Come fair one be kind from The Recruiting Officer (Farquhar), 8 April 1706

The Tippling Philosophers, first performed at Rich's benefit, London, 19 March 1720

The Cobbler's End, first performed at Leveridge's benefit, London, 28 March 1728

The Roast Beef of Old England, first performed at Leveridge's benefit, London, 15 April 1735

The Anacreontic Song, first performed in 1735, also performed at Leveridge's benefit, London, 12 April 1736

Leveridge's theatre songs were published mainly as separate sheets, but also in miscellaneous collections including editions of Wit and Mirth: Pills to Purge Melancholy (London, 1700⁴) and Thesaurus musicus (London, 1744)

BIBLIOGRAPHY

BurneyH; HawkinsH

Anon.: 'An Account of Richard Leveridge', European Magazine, xxiv (1793), 243, 363

W. C. Smith: A Bibliography of the Musical Works published by John Walsh during the years 1695–1720 (London, 1948)

R. E. Moore: 'The Music to Macbeth', MQ, xlvii (1961), 22

R. Fiske: 'The Macbeth Music', ML, xlv (1964), 114

W. C. Smith and C. Humphries: A Bibliography of the Musical Works published by the Firm of John Walsh during the years 1721–1766 (London, 1968)

O. Baldwin and T. Wilson: 'Richard Leveridge, 1670–1758', MT, cxi (1970), 592, 891, 988

OLIVE BALDWIN, THELMA WILSON

Lévesque, Elisabeth de Hauteterre. See HAULTETERRE, ELISABETH DE.

Levey [O'Shaughnessy]. Irish family of musicians.

(1) **Richard Michael Levey** (b Co. Meath, 25 Oct 1811; d Dublin, 28 June 1899). Violinist and conductor. After an apprenticeship under James Barton he joined the Theatre Royal orchestra. As leader (from 1834) he composed much music for plays and pantomimes. He went on tour in 1829 with Mme Catalani, and in 1839 with Balfe's opera company; he took part in many opera seasons in Dublin and on 20 April 1876 celebrated the 50th anniversary of his association with the Theatre Royal. With Joseph Robinson and others he helped to establish the (Royal) Irish Academy of Music, at which he was professor of violin; he also assisted in chamber music performances. He compiled a Collection of the Dance Music of Ireland (1858), and with J. O'Rorke the Annals of the Theatre Royal, Dublin (1880).

(2) **Richard C. Levey** (b Dublin, 1833; d ?1904). Son of (1) Richard Michael Levey. He was a violinist of some distinction who appeared at Musard's concerts in Paris. He later devised an 'act' in which he posed as 'Paganini Redivivus', having, it was said, a Svengali-like appearance which could be made to resemble Paganini's 'ghost'. On tour he enthralled audiences with his imitations of other musical instruments; he could perform the 'most extraordinary tricks without using the bow' (The Orchestra, 28 October 1865). He even presented a version of the William Tell overture played on one string with the wood of the bow. Some authorities refer to him as Richard M. Levey jr; but in an advertisement in The Orchestra (30 September 1865) 'Paganini Redivivus' gives his name as 'Mr Richard C. Levey'.

(3) **William Charles Levey** (b Dublin, 25 April 1837; d London, 18 Aug 1894). Composer and conductor, brother of (2) Richard C. Levey. He studied with his father, and then in Paris. He was for some years musical director at the Drury Lane, Covent Garden and Adelphi theatres. His operettas Fanchette (Covent Garden, 1864) and Punchinello (Her Majesty's, 1864) were followed by a 'musical folly', The Girls of the Period (Drury Lane, 1869). Levey also wrote music for pantomimes and for a production of Antony and Cleopatra; his other works include songs, drawing-room operettas, a Triumphal March composed for the Dublin International Exhibition of 1865 and a descriptive fantasia, The Man of War, for chorus, military band and orchestra (1874).

WILLIAM HENRY GRATTAN FLOOD, ALEXIS CHITTY/
E. D. MACKERNESS

Levi, Giuseppe. See ALLEVI, GIUSEPPE.

Levi, Hermann (b Giessen, Upper Hesse, 7 Nov 1839; d Munich, 13 May 1900). German conductor. The son of a rabbi, he attended the Mannheim Gymnasium and had his first music lessons with Vinzenz Lachner; he studied with Hauptmann and Julius Rietz at the Leipzig Conservatory (1855–8). After a short stay in Paris he became the musical director of Saarbrücken (1859), and two years later was made assistant Kapellmeister of the Mannheim National Opera, on Lachner's recommendation, and Kapellmeister of the Rotterdam Opera (1861–4). As Hofkapellmeister in Karlsruhe (1864–72), he became a friend of Clara Schumann (in nearby Baden-Baden) and Brahms, and this led him to produce Schumann's Genoveva; he also became interested in Wagner's operas, and in 1869 he gained Wagner's recognition with his performances of Die Meistersinger and Rienzi. From 1872 to 1890 he was Hofkapellmeister in Munich, and was made general music director of the city in 1894.

A distinguished and serious-minded artist of great personal qualities and musical gifts, Levi was universally recognized as one of the greatest conductors of his time. He was an esteemed interpreter of Brahms, and his modern, flowing, declamatory translations of Mozart's operas (Le nozze di Figaro, Don Giovanni and Così fan tutte), to which he also made alterations in the score, were great successes. But it was at Bayreuth that he made his strongest mark; he must be ranked with Richter, Mottl and Seidl as one of the greatest of the first generation of Bayreuth conductors. Cosima Wagner regarded him as 'a most excellent person, with real delicacy of feeling', and for Wagner he was 'the ideal Parsifal conductor'. However, Wagner had made a clumsy and unsuccessful attempt to convert Levi to Christianity, and his attitude, especially in connection with the idea of a Jew conducting Parsifal with its representation of the central Christian mystery, compounded by an anonymous letter complaining of this and also accusing Levi of being Cosima's lover, drove Levi to attempt to withdraw from conducting the work. Eventually Wagner, largely impelled by King Ludwig's insistence, made peace with Levi, who conducted the première on 26 July 1882. In 1888 Cosima replaced Levi as *Parsifal* conductor with Mottl, but Levi was recalled for the performances in 1889–94. He retired in 1896, but was persuaded to conduct Beethoven's Ninth Symphony in 1897; however, the effort precipitated a nervous breakdown, and Hans von Bülow had to step into the breach. By this time, Levi was already mortally ill.

The 'spiritual' quality of Levi's interpretations was widely admired, and the economy of his gestures, as well as his masterly technique, exercised an influence on a number of conductors of the following generation, especially Weingartner. For a photograph of Levi *see* RICHTER, HANS.

BIBLIOGRAPHY

C. F. Glasenapp: *Das Leben Richard Wagners* (Leipzig, 1894–1911)
E. von Possart: *Erinnerungen an Hermann Levi* (Munich, 1901)
F. Gräflinger: *Anton Bruckner* (Berlin, 1927)
R. Du Moulin Eckart: *Cosima Wagner* (Munich, 1929–31)
J. Kniese: *Der Kampf zweier Welten um das Bayreuther Erbe* (Leipzig, 1931)
M. Millenkovich-Morold: *Cosima Wagner* (Leipzig, 2/1937)
C. Schünemann: 'Mozart in deutscher Übertragung', *JbMP 1940*, 62
E. Newman: *The Life of Richard Wagner* (London, 1933–47/R1976)
H. Schonberg: *The Great Conductors* (New York, 1970)
P. Gay: 'Hermann Levi and the Cult of Wagner', *Times Literary Supplement* (11 April 1975), no.3814, p. 402

FRIEDRICH BASER

Levi, Jul (*b* Saloniki, 19 June 1930). Bulgarian composer and operetta conductor. While still a pupil at the Sofia Music Gymnasium he worked for the children's drama section of Bulgarian radio. He was then composer to the army ensemble (1950–58) and conductor and composer for the State Satirical Theatre, Sofia (1958–63). In 1956 he graduated from the Sofia State Academy of Music and in 1963 he was appointed conductor of the State Music Theatre (operetta theatre) in the same city. His music is conventional and straightforward.

WORKS
(*selective list*)

Stage: Momicheto, koeto obichah [The girl I love], musical, 1963; Panaïr v Sofia [Fair in Sofia], ballet, 1968; Svetat e malak [The world is small], musical, 1969; 6 other theatre works, 3 pieces for puppet theatre
Orch: Vn Conc., 1953; 3 syms., 1955–8, 1969–70, 1975; Ouvertüre-Poem, 1962; Divertimento concertante, tpt, orch, 1963; Divertimento concertante, fl, orch, 1971
4 film scores, more than 60 solo/choral songs, folksong arrs.

Principal publisher: Nauka i izkustvo

LADA BRASHOVANOVA

Levi ben Gershom [Gershon], **R.** *See* LEO HEBRAEUS.

Levidis, Dimitrios (*b* Athens, 8 April 1885 or 1886; *d* Palaeon Phaleron, nr. Athens, 29 May 1951). Greek composer, later naturalized French. He studied at the Lottner Conservatory, Athens; at the Athens Conservatory (1898–1905) with Boemer, Lavrangas, Mancini and Choisy; at the Lausanne Conservatory (1906–7) with Denéréaz and at the Munich Academy (1907–8) with Klose (fugue), Mottl (orchestration) and Strauss (composition), winning the Franz Liszt Prize for his Piano Sonata op.16. After a short period in Greece he settled in France (1910), served in the French army during World War I and took French nationality. His music was often performed at the Colonne, Straram,

Pasdeloup and Touche concerts, and he was decorated by the French Academy for a paper on the nature of sound. He returned to Athens in around 1932 to teach at the Hellenic Conservatory and at the Music Lyceum. In 1934 he founded the Phaleron Conservatory, later subsumed into the Hellenic Conservatory, and he was president of the Union of Greek Composers (1946–7). He was in Paris again in 1947–8.

A composer of refined technique, Levidis combined a Straussian harmony with Ravelian impressionism, also exploiting Greek modes, in a style of greater homogeneity than that of Kalomiris. However, his elegance was sometimes achieved at the expense of vigour. More expansive in love songs, he could yet be penetrating in dramatic and epic outbursts such as *O yirismos stin xesklavomeni patrida* ('The return to the liberated homeland'). Most successful are his orchestral works, where subtle contrasts of texture often achieve impressive dramatic effects. He was a notable experimenter with novel combinations and new instruments: he was among the first to write for the ondes martenot (his *Poème symphonique* was given on the occasion of the first public appearance of the instrument) and he also provided music for the polychord, a chromatic harp invented by the Greek piano tuner Evangelos Tsamourtzis (1888–1965); the 'dixtuor (éolien) d'orchestre' (possibly identical with the 'Aeolian orchestra') for which he wrote consisted of strings, piano, celesta, two harps and percussion. Levidis's MSS are dispersed in private collections and the following list is tentative.

WORKS
(*selective list*)

STAGE AND ORCHESTRAL

O voskos ki i neraida [The shepherd and the fairy], op.39 (ballet, 1, Levidis), 1923; To fylachto ton theon [The talisman of the gods] (ballet, 3, ?Levidis), solo vv, chorus, orch, 1925; 4 tableaux en un acte, op.45, ?ballet, n.d.; Symphonie mystique, vv, orch, ?dancers, 1928–?, inc.
Little Suite, D, str, 1902–3 or 1904–5, parts arr. pf and str qt; Pour une poupée bien sage, Aeolian orch, 1904; Divertissement, op.25, eng hn, dixtuor éolien, 1911; Variations, a, op.27, chamber orch, ?1911, arr. 3 polychords, 8 wind, 4 perc, perf. 1937; Chant païen, op.37, ob, str, harp, perc, 1921, arr. fl, polychord, n.d.; Poème symphonique, op.43, vn, orch, 1926, arr. as op.43b, ondes martenot, orch, perf. 1928; Stances (Stances symphoniques), orch/Aeolian orch, 1932

VOCAL

Tristesse, op.5 (J. Lemaire), S/T, pf/orch, 1899 or 1902; L'amour de l'amour, op.13 (P. d'Amor), S, pf, 1906, ?orchd, arr. vn, pf; Eolienne, op.14 (d'Amor), S/T, SMez ad lib, orch, 1906, arr. small orch/1v, pf/pf/chorus/others; Nazmi, op.19 (d'Amor), S, pf, 1909, ?orchd; A Hilda, op.20 (Lemaire), S, pf/orch, 1910; Lorsque tu ne m'aimeras plus, op.29 (L. Fortolis), T, pf/orch, 1911; 4 roubaïyat perses, opp.30–32, 40 (Khayam, Hafiz, trans. Levidis), S, orch, 1912–14, arr. 1v, pf/ondes martenot, pf/ondes martenot/others
Se ymnoumen [We praise thee] (Gk, liturgy), T, chorus, 1925; Sirène (Marine), op.42 (Levidis), S, orch, 1926; Hommage, op.44 (Levidis), S, pf (1927); De profundis, T, 2 ondes martenot, orch, 1929, arr. 3 polychords; To kyparissi [The cypress], op.47 (Palamas), Mez/Bar, orch, 1934 or 1935, arr. 1v, pf (1960); Offrande, op.48 (Levidis), A/B, orch, n.d., arr. 1v, pf (1933); Tes yeux, op.50 (Levidis), 1v, pf/orch, 1932; Lelita, op.51 (Levidis), 1v, pf/orch, 1932; Ta pallikaria tis Pindou [The heroes of Pindos] (V. Pezopoulou), chorus, orch, 1940; Nekriki pombi [Funeral procession], op.56 (?Gk liturgy), chorus, orch, ?1941
Ta hellenika ta pelaga [Greek seas] (G. Ikonomidis), 1v (?vv), orch, 1941, ?arr. 1v, pf; O yirismos stin xesklavomeni patrida [The return to the liberated homeland], op.61 (I. Polemis), Mez/Bar, orch, 1941; The Iliad (trans. Y. Lignadis), narrator, T, orch, 1942–3, ?lost; O levendis ki o haros [The young man and death] (K. Velmyras), S, Mez, T, orch, 1944; La tour d'honneur, narrator, orch, 1947; La vache burlesque, Mez, pf, 1948, ?orchd; Lullaby (Polemis), 1v, ?pf, 1948; Love (P. Magnis), 1v, ?pf, 1948; 3 Songs (A. Simiriotis), 1v, ?pf, 1950; 2 Songs (G. Delis), 1v, ?pf, n.d.

INSTRUMENTAL

Lacrimae, pf/vn, pf, 1898; Study, a, pf, 1898; Menuet, pf, 1898; Impromptu no.1, b, op.6, pf, 1902 or 1903, arr. str orch, c1913; Pf

Sonata, f, op.16, 1907, ?orchd; Fugue, e, str qt, 1908; Boîte à musique, hpd, 1908; Preludes, C, op.21, d, op.22, org, 1910, orchd, n.d.; Flûte de Pan, fl, pf, 1914

Pièce chromatique (Piècette chromatique), C, polychord, 1936; Etude chromatique, a, polychord, 1936; Etude romantique (Pièce pour polycorde), e, n.d.; Variations sous forme de choral, a, vn, polychord, n.d.; Carillon, 3 polychords, 1v ad lib, n.d.; Méthode spéciale destinée à l'enseignement du polycorde, op.57, 3 vols., ?1940

Principal publishers: Darimont, Durand, Durdilly-Hayet, Hayet, Ricordi (Paris), Tsamourtzis

WRITINGS

Techniki ftis moussikis technis [Treatise on the technique of the art of music] 1935–49, ?inc., unpubd
'Ai tasseis tis neohellenikis moussikis dimiourgias' [Tendencies in modern Greek composition], *Helleniki dimiourgia*, vii (1951), 785

BIBLIOGRAPHY

P. K. Bouboulidis: *Neohellines moussourgoi: I. Dimitrios Levidis: symvoli eis tin historian tis neohellenikis moussikis* (Athens, 1949)
S. K. Spanoudi: 'I exelixis tis hellenikis moussikis apo tou 1821 mehri ton imeron mas' [The development of Greek music from 1821 to the present], *Helios*, vii (Athens, c1950), 1035
——: 'Levidis, Dimitrios', *Helios*, xii (Athens, c1950), 168
I. Boukouvala-Anagnostou: 'Hellenikes synthesseis ya piano', *Helleniki dimiourgia*, vii (1951), no.79, p.796
G. Sklavos: 'Dimitrios Levidis', *Helleniki dimiourgia*, viii (1951), no.82, p.67
A. S. Theodoropoulou: 'Dimitrios Levidis', *Nea estia*, xlix (1951), no.575, p.819
F. Anoyanakis: 'I moussiki stin neoteri Hellada', in K. Nef: *History of Music* (Gk. trans., Athens, 1958), 590ff

GEORGE S. LEOTSAKOS

Levine, James (*b* Cincinnati, 23 June 1943). American conductor and pianist. He was ten when he made his début as a piano soloist with the Cincinnati SO. He studied analysis and style with Walter Levin, leader of the LaSalle Quartet, then went to the Juilliard School, New York, where he worked with Rosina Lhévinne for piano and with Jean Morel for conducting. Later he had periods of study with Rudolf Serkin, Alfred Wallenstein, Max Rudolf and Fausto Cleva. In 1964 Szell invited him to be assistant conductor of the Cleveland Orchestra, where he stayed for six years (he was also music director of the University Circle Orchestra and chairman of the department of orchestral training at the Cleveland Institute). He conducted and taught at the Aspen Music School and Festival, as well as at Meadow Brook, the summer activity of the Detroit SO, and Oakland University. In 1971 he made his début at the Metropolitan Opera with *Tosca* and in 1973 was appointed principal conductor; the post was renamed music director in 1975. In 1973 he assumed the directorships of the Ravinia (Chicago SO) and Cincinnati May festivals. Because of his success at the Metropolitan Levine has become best known as an opera conductor, and his first recordings included Verdi's *Giovanna d'Arco* and Bellini's *Norma*. In Britain he has worked with the Welsh National Opera, making his début with *Aida* in 1970 (he made his concert début with the LSO in 1973), and in Germany he conducted *Otello* at Hamburg in 1975. He is, however, a strikingly versatile musician. He remains active as a pianist, in chamber music, with singers, and in concertos, particularly by Bach and Mozart, which he directs from the keyboard. His conducting has ranged from the 18th-century classics to Xenakis and Cage. Mozart and Verdi are special strengths, and he quickly established himself as an outstanding Mahler interpreter. Vitality and architectural clarity are the hallmarks of his pleasingly unmanipulated performances.

MICHAEL STEINBERG

Levolto. *See* VOLTA (i).

Levy, Alexandre (*b* São Paulo, 10 Nov 1864; *d* São Paulo, 17 Jan 1892). Brazilian composer of French descent. Belonging to a family of musicians, he received early teaching in the piano and later in composition from European immigrants. He was largely responsible for the foundation of the Haydn Club in São Paulo in 1883, sponsoring and conducting concerts of the symphonic repertory. He went to Europe in 1887 but stayed only for a few months: after a period in Milan, he went to Paris where he studied harmony with Emile Durand at the Conservatoire. On his return he tried to organize a regular symphony orchestra in his native city, but did not find enough support.

Levy was the first important figure in Brazilian musical nationalism. But his most typically nationalist works are based less on folk music traditions than on popular music of the time: *modinhas*, tangos, *maxixes* and early urban sambas. Such works include the tone poem *Comala*, the *Tango brasileiro* for piano and the *Suite brésilienne* for orchestra, all written in 1890. The last movement of the suite, 'Samba', attempts to describe the frenzy of this dance by using its characteristic syncopations together with the basic rhythmic patterns of the habanera. The melodic material of the movement is based on two traditional urban tunes. Although Levy had no great influence on the later development of the nationalist trend in Brazil, he remains an important figure for his receptiveness to the most characteristic aspects of urban popular music.

BIBLIOGRAPHY

DBP [with list of works]
'Alexandre Levy', *Gazeta musical*, ii/4 (1892), 58
G. Pimenta: *Alexandre Levy* (São Paulo, 1911)
G. Béhague: *The Beginnings of Musical Nationalism in Brazil* (Detroit, 1971)

GERARD BÉHAGUE

Lévy, Emile. *See* WALDTEUFEL, EMILE.

Lévy, Ernst (*b* Basle, 18 Nov 1895). Swiss composer, pianist and writer on music. He studied in Basle and Paris, his teachers including Hans Huber, Petri and Pugno, and then at Basle University under Nef and others. He taught briefly at Basle Conservatory, then moved to Paris. In 1941 he went to the USA and taught successively at New England Conservatory, Bennington College (Vermont), Chicago University, Massachusetts Institute of Technology and Brooklyn College, New York. He returned to Switzerland in 1966. A man of wide culture, he is noted as a pianist and writer on music (he wrote, with S. Levarie, *Tone: a Study in Musical Acoustics*, 1968, and articles in *SMz* and the Nef Festschrift) as well as a composer. His works, marked by an emphasis on melody and the retention of various forms of tonality (he has experimented with non-diatonic scales), include 15 symphonies, four orchestral suites, five cantatas and much chamber and keyboard music as well as smaller vocal pieces. His son, Frank Levy (*b* Paris, 15 Oct 1930), is a cellist and composer; he studied at the Juilliard School and Chicago University, has played in various orchestras and ensembles, and has written chamber music, orchestral music and works for organ.

BIBLIOGRAPHY

Baker 6; RiemannL 12
N. Slonimsky: 'Lévy, Ernst', MGG
S. Levarie: 'La musique d'Ernst Lévy', SMz, cviii (1968), 178

Levy, Jules. See LEVI, JUL.

Levy, Kenneth J(ay) (b New York, 26 Feb 1927). American musicologist. He studied music history at Queens College, New York, with Sachs and theory with Karol Rathaus and took the BA in 1947. At Princeton, where his professors included Strunk and Hertzmann, he took the MFA in 1949 and the PhD in 1955. He taught at Princeton from 1952 to 1954 and at Brandeis University from 1954 to 1966, when he returned to Princeton as a professor.

Levy's interests include Gregorian, Byzantine and Old Slavonic liturgical chant, medieval polyphony and the 16th-century French chanson. In his chanson research he has concentrated on the composers and secular forms of the latter 16th century, and has drawn on social and political background for a comprehensive view. More recently he has worked on liturgical chant, publishing important articles in this area. He has investigated Byzantine and Western chant, including the Old Roman, Ambrosian, Beneventan and Ravennate repertories, and by careful comparison he has been able to draw tentative conclusions regarding the relationships of certain Western chants to Byzantine models and between modal patterns and performing practices common to East and West. He has also approached the problem of transcription of Slavonic kondakarion notation by proposing 'counterpart transcriptions', which relate Slavonic melodic formulae to those occurring in transcribable Byzantine melodies.

WRITINGS

'New Material on the Early Motet in England: a Report on Princeton Ms. Garrett 119', JAMS, iv (1951), 220
'Chanson in der 2. Hälfte des 16. Jahrhunderts', MGG
' "Susanne un jour": the History of a 16th Century Chanson', AnnM, i (1953), 375–408
'Vaudeville, vers mesurés et airs de cour', Musique et poésie au XVIe siècle: CNRS Paris 1953, 185
The Chansons of Claude Le Jeune (diss., Princeton U., 1955)
'Costeley's Chromatic Chanson', AnnM, iii (1955), 213–63
'The Byzantine Sanctus and its Modal Tradition in East and West', AnnM, vi (1958–63), 7–67
'An Early Chant for Romanus' Contacium trium puerorum?', Classica et mediaevalia, xxii (1961), 172
Review of Contacarium Paleoslavicum Mosquense, ed. A. Brugge, MMB, main ser., vi (Copenhagen, 1960) and Byzantine Elements in Early Slavic Chant, ed. M. Velimirović, MMB, Subsidia, iv (Copenhagen, 1960), MQ, xlvii (1961), 554
Review of A History of Byzantine Music and Hymnography, ed. E. Wellesz (Oxford, 2/1961), Speculum, xxxvii (1962), 467
'A Hymn for Thursday in Holy Week', JAMS, xvi (1963), 127–75
'Die slavische Kondakarien-Notation', Anfänge der slavischen Musik: Symposia I: Bratislava 1964, 77
'The Byzantine Communion cycle and its Slavic Counterpart', XIIe congrès international d'études byzantines: Ochride 1961, ii, 571
'The Slavic Kontakia and their Byzantine Originals', Queens College Twenty-fifth Anniversary Festschrift (Flushing, NY, 1964), 79
'Three Byzantine Acclamations', Studies in Music History: Essays for Oliver Strunk (Princeton, 1968), 43
'Idiomelon', 'Russia. I', Harvard Dictionary of Music (Cambridge, Mass., 2/1969)
'The Italian Neophytes' Chants', JAMS, xxiii (1970), 181–227
'Lux de luce: the Origin of an Italian Sequence', MQ, lvii (1971), 40
'The Trisagion in Byzantium and the West', IMSCR, xi Copenhagen 1972, 761
'A Dominican Organum Duplum', JAMS, xxvii (1974), 183
'Italian Duecento Polyphony: Observations on an Umbrian Fragment', RIM, x (1975), 10
The Byzantine Chants of the Mass-Ordinary (in preparation)
'Byzantine rite, music of the', 'Liturgy and liturgical books', §III, 'Plainchant', §I, Grove 6

EDITION

with F. Lesure and others: Anthologie de la chanson parisienne au XVIe siècle (Monaco, 1953)
                                                  PAULA MORGAN

Levy, Marvin David (b Passaic, NJ, 2 Aug 1932). American composer. He studied at New York University under Philip James, under Otto Luening at Columbia University and in Europe. His music, theatrical by predisposition, is atonal and flexible in its treatment of rhythm. His Mourning Becomes Electra is one of the few operas by an American to have been commissioned for the Metropolitan Opera, New York, where it remained in the repertory for several seasons.

WORKS

Operas: Sotoba Komachi (after noh play), New York, 1957; The Tower, Santa Fe, 1957; Escorial (M. de Ghelderode), New York, 1958; Mourning Becomes Electra (3, after E. O'Neill), New York, 1967
Orch: Caramoor Festival Ov., 1959; Sym., 1960; Pf Conc., 1970
Chamber: Str Qt, 1955; Rhapsody, vn, cl, harp, 1956; Chassidic Suite, hn, pf, 1956
Choral: For the Time Being, Christmas oratorio, 1959; Sacred Service (Park Avenue Synagogue, New York), 1964

Lévy, Roland Alexis Manuel. See ROLAND-MANUEL.

Levy [née Itzig], **Sara** (b 1761; d 1854). German musical amateur and patroness of music. She was a pupil of W. F. Bach and a patroness of C. P. E. Bach, and a figure in the German Bach revival; a friend of Zelter's, she presented him with valuable Bach manuscripts. She was Mendelssohn's great-aunt and was probably influential in his becoming a pupil of Zelter. Her salon was a meeting-place for the musical intellectuals of Berlin in her time. Her music collection passed after her death to the Singakademie and eventually to the Preussische Staatsbibliothek.

based on MGG (viii, 684) by permission of Bärenreiter
                                                  ERIC WERNER

Lewandowski, Leon Leopold (b Kalisz, 14 March 1831; d Warsaw, 22 Nov 1896). Polish violinist, composer and bandmaster. Born into a Jewish intellectual family, he started learning to play the violin at an early age and gave public performances as a child. After leaving secondary school in Kalisz, he studied the violin under K. Baranowski and J. Hornziel in Warsaw. From 1850 he played in the orchestra of the Grand Theatre in Warsaw. Then, with the cooperation of A. Kühn, he organized his own orchestra and gave concerts at Nowa Arkadia. He also gave performances at the Mineral Water Institute in the Saski Gardens, and from 1857 until his death he performed in the Rozmaitości Theatre, playing mainly dances, of which he composed many. He also organized popular symphony concerts at the Resursa Obywatelska (Citizens' Club) and played in chamber music concerts. For a time he was a member of the string quartet founded by Baranowski. Lewandowski left about 350 compositions, which were published from 1855 by numerous Polish and foreign houses. His pieces, most of them in dance genres (mazurkas, polkas, contredanses, polonaises, obereks, kujawiaks, quadrilles, galops, etc), were extremely popular. He also composed interludes to the ballets Wedding at Ojców (J. Stefani, J. Damse, K. Kurpiński), Pan Twardowski (A. Sonnenfeld) and Coppélia (Delibes). Other compositions include a Nocturne for orchestra, a concert mazurka for violin, cello, oboe, trumpet and orchestra, and choral songs.

BIBLIOGRAPHY

SMP

J. Reiss: 'Polska muzyka taneczna 19 wieku' [Polish dance music of the 19th century], *Muzyka*, iv/9–10 (1953), 36

JERZY MORAWSKI

Lewenthal, Raymond (*b* San Antonio, Texas, 29 Aug 1926). American pianist. He studied with Olga Samaroff at the Juilliard School, then with Cortot and spent a year teaching in Rio de Janeiro. His career has been marked by special concern for neglected composers of the early 19th century, among them Hummel, Dušek, Henselt, Thalberg and, notably, Alkan (he has edited an Alkan collection). He has recorded Etudes and parts of Alkan's Symphony for piano, the solo version of the *Hexameron* by Liszt and others, and concertos by Henselt and Rubinstein. He is an articulate spokesman on behalf of his chosen repertory. At his recitals, he achieves atmosphere by means of low lights, high temperatures and quasi-period costume. His performances tend to be marked more by generalized flair than by specific pianistic skills of the first order.

MICHAEL STEINBERG

Lewis, Sir Anthony (Carey) (*b* Bermuda, 2 March 1915). English musicologist, conductor, music administrator and composer. He went to Peterhouse, Cambridge, in 1932 as an organ scholar and held the John Stewart of Rannoch scholarship in sacred music (1933). Dent guided his studies at Cambridge, and a grant from his college enabled him to study with Nadia Boulanger in 1934. In 1935 he took the BA and the MusB (with the Barclay Squire Prize for musical palaeography) and joined the BBC music department. There he organized the 'Foundations of Music' series, and later became responsible for all broadcast chamber music and recitals. In 1938 he planned a memorable series under the title 'Handel in Rome'. During the war he served abroad and in 1945 returned to the BBC to plan the Third Programme, which gave its first broadcast in the following year. Lewis was then put in charge of the organization and general direction of all Third Programme music, and was responsible for broadcasting many unfamiliar works.

In 1947 he was elected Peyton and Barber Professor of Music at Birmingham University, where he continued his pioneering activities. During his 21-year professorship he conducted many revivals of orchestral, choral and stage works, particularly Handel operas, collaborating with other members of the university in preparing the musical texts and making English singing translations of the librettos. These performances are remembered not only for their considerable success but also for the high standards they established for revivals of Handel operas. During this time Lewis was also active in the recording studio and made the first English gramophone recordings of such works as Monteverdi's *Vespro della beata vergine*, Lully's *Miserere*, Purcell's *The Fairy Queen* and *King Arthur* and Handel's *Semele* and *Sosarme* (which he had conducted and broadcast in 1948).

In 1950 Lewis became honorary secretary of the Purcell Society, a position he held until he became chairman in 1976. About 1950 he proposed the initiation of a national edition of British music to the Royal Musical Association council; this idea resulted in the inception of Musica Britannica in 1951. Lewis has since the beginning been its general editor; with Thurston Dart, its first secretary, he supervised the production of over 30 volumes in the first 20 years of the series. From 1963 to 1969 he was president of the RMA, and in 1968 was appointed principal of the Royal Academy of Music, where he had studied as a junior student (piano, composition) in 1928. As well as his tireless efforts on behalf of musicology (his first editions, for L'Oiseau-Lyre, were published in 1936), and of the stylish performance of the music itself, Lewis has also composed; his works include a Choral Overture (1938), an Elegy and Capriccio for trumpet and orchestra (1947), a Trumpet Concerto (1950), *A Tribute of Praise* (1953) and a Horn Concerto (written for Dennis Brain and published in 1959). He has also worked on music committees of the Arts Council. He was knighted in 1972 for his services to music.

WRITINGS

'Matthew Locke: a Dynamic Figure in English Music', *PRMA*, lxxiv, (1947–8), 57

'A Newly-discovered Song by Purcell' [*The Meditation* zD71], *The Score* (1951), no.4, p.2 [incl. edn.]

'Handel and the Aria', *PRMA*, lxxxv (1958–9), 95

'Purcell's Music for *The Tempest*', *MT*, c (1959), 321

'Purcell and Blow's "Venus and Adonis" ', *ML*, xliv (1963), 266

'Notes and Reflections on a New Edition of Purcell's "The Fairy Queen" ', *MR*, xxv (1964), 104

The Language of Purcell (Hull, 1968)

'Student Performers and Musicologists: Partners or Strangers?', *ISME*, xi *Perth, W. Australia 1974*

'Some Notes on Editing Handel's *Semele*', *Opera and English Music: Essays in Honour of Sir Jack Westrup* (Oxford, 1975), 79

ed., with N. Fortune: *Opera and Church Music 1630–1750*, NOHM, v (1975) [incl. 'English Church Music', 493–556]

EDITIONS

J. *Blow: Venus and Adonis* (Paris, 1939); *Coronation Anthems and Anthems with Strings*, MB, vii (1953, rev. 2/1969) [with W. Shaw]

G. F. *Handel: Apollo and Daphne* (London, 1956); *Athalia* (London, 1967); *Semele* (London, 1971) [with C. Mackerras]

H. *Purcell: Miscellaneous Odes and Cantatas*, Works, xxvii (London, 1957) [with T. Dart, D. Arundell and A. Goldsbrough]; *Sacred Music, Part IV, Part V, Part VI, Part VII*, ibid, xxviii (London, 1959, rev. 2/1967), xxix (1960, rev. 2/1967), xxx (1965), xxxii (1962, rev. 2/1967) [with N. Fortune]; *The Fairy Queen*, ibid, xii (London, rev. 2/1968) [with N. Fortune]

BIBLIOGRAPHY

T. Dart: 'A Background for *Musica Britannica*', *Music 1952*, ed. A. Robertson (Harmondsworth, 1952), 24

DAVID SCOTT

Lewis [Zeno], George (Louis Francis) (*b* New Orleans, 13 July 1900; *d* New Orleans, 31 Dec 1968). Black American jazz clarinettist. He played the clarinet from the age of 16 and began his professional career shortly thereafter with Buddy Petit, Kid Ory, Kid Rena and other New Orleans groups. In 1933 he joined the Eureka Brass Band, and in the same year began to lead his own groups. He made his first recording in 1942 with Bunk Johnson and worked with him intermittently until 1946. From 1952 he often performed outside Louisiana, making a tour of Japan and several of Europe. Lewis was a leading figure in the New Orleans revival. When playing in a traditional New Orleans setting he showed a limited technique that could disguise his debt to popular clarinettists of the 1930s (he was often mistakenly regarded as an unspoilt example of his local idiom). Nevertheless, the sincerity of his performances of simple pieces was widely appreciated, and he acquired many imitators (mostly outside the USA).

BIBLIOGRAPHY

D. Mangurian: 'George Lewis: a Portrait of the New Orleans Clarinettist', *Down Beat* (29 Aug 1963)

J. Stuart [D. Tate]: *Call him George* (London, 1963)

M. Williams: *Jazz Masters of New Orleans* (New York, 1967), 233ff

T. Bethell: *George Lewis: a Jazzman from New Orleans* (Berkeley, 1978)

J. R. TAYLOR

Lewis, Henry (*b* Los Angeles, 16 Oct 1932). Black American conductor. As a boy, Lewis studied the piano and the double bass, and at 16 became a double bass player in the Los Angeles PO. In 1956 he was conductor of the 7th US Army SO in Stuttgart. After his return, he founded the Los Angeles Chamber Orchestra, then became assistant conductor of the Los Angeles PO, making his professional début with that orchestra in 1963. In 1968 he became music director of the New Jersey SO. He conducted at La Scala in 1965, and at the Metropolitan Opera in 1972, and has been a guest conductor with most major American orchestras, including those in Boston, Chicago, Cleveland and New York. He has appeared extensively in Europe and has made a number of recordings, some with his wife, the mezzo-soprano Marilyn Horne. He holds honorary doctorates from six colleges and universities.

Although Lewis works with singers and in opera with special sympathy, he is also active in other fields. By temperament thoughtful rather than fiery, his broadly paced Metropolitan Opera performances of *La bohème* and *Carmen* were notable for what they revealed in orchestral detail. In New Jersey, with an organization designed to serve a region rather than one particular city, he has strikingly broadened the orchestra's repertory, audience and scope of operations.

MICHAEL STEINBERG

Lewis, Houston & Hyde. English music publishers, successors to JOHN BLAND.

Lewis, John (Aaron) (*b* LaGrange, Ill., 3 May 1920). Black American jazz composer, small-group leader and pianist. He studied anthropology and music at the University of New Mexico and in 1945 joined Dizzy Gillespie's first big band as pianist and arranger; Gillespie gave the premières of his Toccata for trumpet and orchestra at Carnegie Hall in 1947 and his *Period Suite* in 1948. In 1949–50 he took part in Miles Davis's recordings, and thereafter was a freelance performer, writer and teacher in New York until he became the pianist and music director of the MODERN JAZZ QUARTET about 1952. He accompanied Ella Fitzgerald for several months in 1954, but otherwise remained with the quartet throughout its career, making several world tours and many recordings.

A capable though not extraordinary pianist, Lewis is among the most significant jazz composers. After his somewhat orthodox work for Gillespie he struck an independent path with *Rouge*, recorded by Davis's Capitol Band (1949), and particularly the contrapuntal *Afternoon in Paris* for J. J. Johnson (1949). In his work for the Modern Jazz Quartet he continued, in such pieces as *Concorde* (1955), to adapt fugal texture to jazz, this process culminating in the remarkable triple fugue *Three Windows* (1957). The brass piece *Three Little Feelings* (1956) points to directions he never fully explored, for his main contribution was the large and unusually consistent output of the Modern Jazz Quartet, notably his extended work *The Comedy* (1960–62). Unusually versatile for a jazz musician, Lewis directed the summer jazz courses at Lenox, Massachusetts, from 1957, was musical director of the Monterey Jazz Festival (1958–64) and from 1962 presented concerts by Orchestra USA, a large ensemble of jazz and classical musicians with a repertory of works by himself, Gunther Schuller, Harold Farberman and others.

WORKS

Selective list; dates refer to earliest recorded version; many works appeared later in arrs. for the Modern Jazz Quartet, brass etc.

Stage: Original Sin (ballet), San Francisco, 1961; Natural Affection (incidental music, E. Inge), New York, 1963

Film scores: Sait-on jamais (No Sun in Venice; One Never Knows), 1957, incl. The Golden Striker, One Never Knows, The Rose Truc, Cortege, Venice, Three Windows; Odds against Tomorrow, 1959, incl. Skating in Central Park, No Happiness for Slater, Social Call, Cue no.9, A Cold Wind is Blowing, Odds against Tomorrow; Exposure, 1959; A Milanese Story

Jazz qt; Vendôme, 1952; Django, 1954; Concorde, 1955; La ronde, 1955; Two Degrees East, Three Degrees West, 1956; Fontessa, 1956; Versailles, 1956; Midsömmer, 1957; The Comedy, 1960–62, incl. Spanish Steps, Columbine [orig. pf], Pulcinella, Pierrot [orig. pf], La cantatrice, Harlequin [orig. pf], Piazza Navona

Other works: Minor Walk, jazz orch, 1947; Toccata, tpt, orch, 1947; Period Suite, 1948; Rouge, jazz orch, 1949; Afternoon in Paris, jazz qnt, 1949; Sketch 1, jazz sextet, 1953; Three Little Feelings, brass, 1956; Da Capo, jazz septet, 1960; Sketch, jazz qt, str qt, 1960

Principal publisher: MJQ Music

BIBLIOGRAPHY

N. Hentoff: 'John Lewis', *Down Beat* (20 Feb 1957), 15

M. Harrison: 'The *Sait-on jamais* Music', *Jazz Monthly*, iv (1958), Aug, 25

——: 'Looking back at the Modern Jazz Quartet', *The Art of Jazz*, ed. M. Williams (New York, 1959), 219

M. James: *10 Modern Jazzmen* (London, 1960), 65ff

N. Hentoff: *John Lewis: a List of Compositions Licenced by B. M. I.* (New York, 1961)

——: *The Jazz Life* (New York, 1961), 170ff

F. Postif: 'John Lewis à Coeur Ouvert', *Jazz Hot*, xxxvi (1969), April, 16

M. Williams: *The Jazz Tradition* (New York, 1970), 156ff

T. Owens: 'Fugal Pieces of the Modern Jazz Quartet', *Journal of Jazz Studies*, iv (1976), aut, 25

MAX HARRISON

Lewis, Meade (Anderson) ['Lux'] (*b* Chicago, 4 Sept 1905; *d* Minneapolis, 7 June 1964). Black American jazz pianist. Influenced by 'Fats' Waller and the Chicago blues pianist Jimmy Yancey, he played in Chicago bars and clubs before recording his celebrated masterpiece *Honky Tonk Train Blues* (1927), which was not issued until 18 months later. Rediscovered by the entrepreneur John Hammond in late 1935, he again recorded this work and issued a number of other pieces in boogie-woogie style over the next few years, most notably the influential *Yancey Special* (1936), *Bear Cat Crawl*, *Tell Your Story* and *Bass on Top*. His technical ability, energetic cross-rhythms and remarkable invention made him one of the most important figures of the boogie-woogie craze of the late 1930s. In 1939 he formed a short-lived piano trio with two other important pianists of this school, Albert Ammons and Pete Johnson, but he soon returned to working alone in New York and California night clubs. He also performed with such jazz musicians as Sidney Bechet, and was occasionally recorded playing the celesta and harpsichord. He grew increasingly dissatisfied with being identified exclusively as a blues and boogie-woogie player, and his later playing was often rushed and perfunctory.

BIBLIOGRAPHY

W. Russell: 'Boogie Woogie', *Jazzmen*, ed. F. Ramsey and C. Smith (New York, 1939), 183

M. Harrison: 'Boogie Woogie', *Jazz*, ed. N. Hentoff (New York, 1959), 105–137

W. Russell: 'Three Boogie Woogie Pianists', *The Art of Jazz*, ed. M. Williams (New York, 1959), 104

MARTIN WILLIAMS

Lewis, Richard (*b* Manchester, 10 May 1914). English tenor. His studies with Norman Allin, both at the Royal Manchester College of Music and later at the Royal Academy of Music, were interrupted by World War II, but he began his career in 1946 with several concert engagements in Denmark and Norway. In Britain he made his concert début early in 1947 at Brighton, singing Britten's Serenade; his operatic début was at Glyndebourne that summer as the Male Chorus in *The Rape of Lucretia* and his Covent Garden début as Peter Grimes was that November. The same season he made guest appearances with the Sadler's Wells company as Ferrando in *Così fan tutte*; he sang that role for several seasons from 1950 at Glyndebourne, where between 1951 and 1974 he also sang Don Ottavio, Admetus (*Alceste*), Idomeneus, Tom Rakewell, Bacchus, Florestan, Monteverdi's Nero and Eumetus. At Covent Garden his roles include Don José, Hoffmann, Tamino, Hermann and Alfredo. During the 1954–5 season there, he created Troilus in Walton's *Troilus and Cressida* and Mark in Tippett's *The Midsummer Marriage*; in 1962 he sang Achilles in Tippett's *King Priam*. In 1965, in the first British stage performance of Schoenberg's *Moses und Aron* at Covent Garden, he sang Aaron, a part he sang in concert performances with Solti in the USA during 1972 and at the Paris Opéra in 1973–4.

Lewis made his American operatic début at San Francisco, singing Troilus (Walton) and Don José in 1953. His roles there include Pinkerton, Dmitry, Jason, Jenik, Des Grieux, Tom Rakewell and the Drum Major (*Wozzeck*). He has also sung in opera in Buenos Aires, Geneva, Zagreb and in West Berlin, where he created Amphitryon in Klebe's *Alkemene* in 1961. Lewis has shared his time between the opera house and the concert platform, and has been a leading exponent of the tenor parts in the regular oratorio repertory; he is particularly admired for his interpretation of Gerontius and his performances of *Das Lied von der Erde*. He has never shirked new or difficult works, and he took part in the first performance of Stravinsky's *Canticum sacrum* at Venice in 1956.

Lewis's voice is mellifluous and distinguished by great flexibility. All his work is notable for intelligence and understanding, which have contributed to his interpretation of certain parts that were heavy for his natural resources. His Idomeneus, Troilus, Achilles and Gerontius are particularly memorable.

ALAN BLYTH

Lewis, Robert Hall (*b* Portland, Oregon, 22 April 1926). American composer. After receiving the MM degree (1951) from the University of Rochester, he went to Paris for further studies at the Conservatoire and private lessons with Nadia Boulanger. He also studied composition at the Vienna Academy of Music and with Hans Erich Apostel. Lewis is professor of music at Goucher College and Johns Hopkins University. His musical style owes allegiance to no particular trend: although his earlier works were concerned with linear developmental processes using serial methods, he has abandoned this approach in favour of larger and more varied gestures. Textural invention, subtle contrasts of timbre and rhythm, structural flexibility and the interaction between continuity and discontinuity are features of his present style. His major orchestral works include two symphonies (1964 and 1971), Three Pieces (1966) and *Intermezzi* (1974). He has written two string quartets and other pieces for less conventional chamber ensembles. His *Monophonies* form a series of works for solo wind instruments.

SAM DI BONAVENTURA

Lewis, Thomas Christopher (*fl c*1861–*c*1900). English organ builder and bellfounder. Lewis was an architect before setting up as an organ builder in London in about 1861. His style of organ building, modelled on that of Edmund Schulze and Aristide Cavaillé-Coll, is characterized by a bold and powerful chorus on the Great organ, the blend being attributable to the mixture (15, 19, 22 and sometimes 26). The manual double is normally a bourdon, the quieter flutes are of particularly good voicing, and there is usually a good mixture (15, 19, 22) on the Swell. His custom was to use spotted metal in his pipework. His instruments suffer from a certain lack of blend between individual chorus stops on the Great, very poorly developed Choir organs, uneven and nasal manual reeds (too loud in the bass because of an exaggerated scale) and badly designed specifications. They are well built and impressive in their big effects, with some beautiful soft tones, but are unsuitable for the performance of much of the organ repertory.

Lewis organs survive at St Mary the Virgin, Beddington, Surrey (1869; original); All Saints, Hatcham Park, Surrey (1871); St Matthew's, Croydon (1882); All Saints, Ilkley, Yorkshire (1882; rebuilt); St George's, Jesmond, Newcastle upon Tyne (1886; rebuilt); Holy Trinity, Bramley, Surrey (1894); Southwark Cathedral (1896); Hatfield House Chapel, Hertfordshire; St Anne's, Brondesbury, Middlesex (originally at Hanover Square (London) Rooms); St Matthias, Richmond, Surrey.

BIBLIOGRAPHY

G. Benham: 'Interesting London Organs XXXII: Southwark Cathedral', *The Organ*, xii (1932–3), 90

——: 'Interesting London Organs XXXIII: St. Mary's, Kennington Park Road, S.E.', *The Organ*, xii (1932–3), 172

——: 'Interesting London Organs XXXIV: St. John-the-Evangelist, Wilton Road, Victoria', *The Organ*, xii (1932–3), 218

H. Snow: 'A Lewis Residence Organ at Frodsham, Cheshire', *The Organ*, xiv (1934–5), 116

A. Niland: 'The Lewis Organ at St. Peter's Church, Eaton Square, Revisited', *The Organ*, xxvii (1947–8), 155

GUY OLDHAM

Lewisohn Stadium. New York stadium, site of outdoor summer concerts from 1918 to 1966; *see* NEW YORK, §5.

Lewkovitch, Bernhard (*b* Copenhagen, 28 May 1927). Danish composer. He was a choirboy at the Roman Catholic church of St Ansgar; after his schooling he was admitted to the Royal Danish Conservatory to study the organ, theory and music history. In 1948 he graduated in theory, in 1949 he received a degree as an organist, and in 1950 he took lessons in composition and orchestration with Schierbeck and Jersild. Later he studied for a short while in France. From 1947 to 1963 he was organist at St Ansgar, and also precentor from 1953. He founded and directed the mixed chorus Schola Cantorum and the all-male Schola Gregoriana; these groups, besides singing Lewkovitch's own compositions, did a great deal to make the sacred music of the Middle Ages and Renaissance better known in Denmark, notably through numerous broadcasts. As a composer, Lewkovitch is strongly attached to the liturgy of the Catholic Church and its music. Even such early works as *Mariavise* op.1 (1947) display the influence of Gregorian chant, together with a free exploitation of the church modes. In the early 1950s this manner was developed in sacred music (including the Three Psalms op.9 and the Mass op.10) and also in secular pieces to texts by contemporary Danish writers.

In around 1955 there was a change of style brought about by Lewkovitch's interest in the works of Stravinsky (particularly the Mass) that he was then writing about in the *Dansk musiktidsskrift*. With the Three Madrigals (1954–5) he abandoned modality to experiment with bi- and polytonality, and eventually to employ 12-note serial methods in the *Cantata sacra* (1959) and the *Improperia per voci* (1961), a work that combines dodecaphonic sections with spoken and improvised passages. This adventurous phase brought Lewkovitch considerable renown in Denmark and abroad; his music was performed at the ISCM festivals in Cologne (1960) and Amsterdam (1963). The period culminated in *Il cantico delle creature* (1962–3), where there is no conventional notation and no specification of pitch. The piece progresses from barely audible whispering to a rhythmically strict but melodically free declamation, in which words are loosened into syllables, and the syllables recombined. After writing this work Lewkovitch resigned his official connections with the Church, and during the next four years he completed only a few works. When he returned to sustained composition, it was again to write liturgical works in his style of the mid-1950s, although developed in a new direction under the influence of his intervening work.

WORKS
(selective list)

SACRED VOCAL

Mariavise, op.1 (J. Jørgensen), chorus, 1947; 3 Psalms, op.9, chorus, 1952; Mass, op.10, chorus, 1952; 3 Motets, op.11, chorus, 1952; Mass, op.15, chorus, wind, harp, 1954; Missa brevis, male chorus, 1955; 10 Latin Motets, male chorus, 1957; 3 orationes, T, ob, bn, 1957–8; Cantata sacra, T, fl, eng hn, cl, bn, trbn, vc, 1959; Improperia per voci, chorus, 1961; Il cantico delle creature, 8 male vv, 1962–3; Veni Creator Spiritus, chorus, 6 trbn, 1967; Laudi a nostra signora, chorus, 1969; Stabat mater, chorus, 1970; Sub vesperum, chorus, 1970

SECULAR VOCAL

Sommeren, op.6 (O. Sarvig), chorus, 1951; Grønne sange, op.7 (Sarvig), male chorus, 1951; 6 Songs, op.8 (Jørgensen), Bar, pf, 1952; 5 danske madrigaler, op.12 (F. Jaeger), chorus, 1952; 3 Madrigals, op.13 (Tasso), chorus, 1954–5; 3 canzonetter (G. Chiabrera, J. Vittorelli), Bar, pf, 1956; 8 børnesange [8 Children's Songs] (H. Rasmussen), 3vv, 1957; 3 Songs (Rasmussen), 3vv, 1958; 3 Songs (Sarvig), male chorus, 1965; Sangvaerk after Danish folksongs, 3vv/1v, pf, 1968; 8 børnesange (Lewkovitch), 1v, pf, 1970

INSTRUMENTAL

Sonatine, pf, 1947; 4 pf sonatas, opp.2–5, 1948, 1949, 1950, 1950; Dansesuite no.1, op.16, pf/orch, 1955; Dansesuite no.2, op.17, pf, 1960; 65 Organ Chorales, 1972; 6 Partitas, org, 1973

Principal publisher: Hansen

WRITINGS

'Strawinskys klagesang', *Dansk musiktidsskrift*, xxxiv (1959), 37
'Interviews med Strawinsky', *Dansk musiktidsskrift*, xxxiv (1959), 149
'Strawinsky igen', *Dansk musiktidsskrift*, xxxv (1960), 242
'Hvorfor og til hvad', *Dansk musiktidsskrift*, xxxvii (1962), 69 [on *Improperia*]
'Ord og toner uden noder', *Nutida musik*, xii (1968–9), 1
Numerous other articles and reviews in *Berliner tidsskrift* (1955–) and *Dansk musiktidsskrift* (1952–62)

BIBLIOGRAPHY

B. Wallner: *Vår tids musik i Norden* (Stockholm, 1968)

JENS BRINCKER

Ley, Henry George (*b* Chagford, 30 Dec 1887; *d* nr. Ottery St Mary, 24 Aug 1962). English organist. As a choirboy at St George's, Windsor, and at the Royal College of Music he studied the organ with Walter Parratt. He won an organ scholarship to Keble College, Oxford, and while still an undergraduate was appointed organist of Christ Church (1909). He was made chor-

agus of the University, and joined the staff of the RCM. In 1926 he became precentor at Eton College, where his remarkable playing and genial personality left a lasting impression on generations of schoolboys, and where he persuaded such artists as d'Arányi, Dupré and Harold Samuel to perform. He retired in 1945 but continued to examine for the RCO and to give recitals.

STANLEY WEBB

Ley, Salvador (*b* Guatemala City, 2 Jan 1907). Guatemalan composer and pianist. After piano and theory studies with Herculano Alvardo and Louis Roche in Guatemala (1917–22) he moved to Berlin, where he remained until 1934. There he attended the Hochschule für Musik, took private piano lessons from George Bertram (1922–30), and studied theory and composition with Wilhelm Klatte (1923–5) and Hugo Leichtentritt (1928–9). He also studied the piano with Petri at Zakopane in 1931, though his public career had already begun in 1926. In 1934 he returned to Guatemala and was appointed director of the National Conservatory, a post he held until 1937 and again from 1944 to 1953, when he settled in the USA. He has since been active as a soloist, accompanist, teacher (at the Westchester Conservatory, New York, 1963–70) and participant in international congresses. His music has been influenced by the cultural climate he found in Berlin – in particular by Busoni's ideas and by his contacts with Schnabel, Walter, Furtwängler, Klemperer and Fischer.

WORKS
(selective list)

Opera: Lera (2, G. Campbell), 1960
Orch: Serenade, str, 1949; Obertura jocosa, 1950; Concertante, va, str, 1962
Songs for 1v, pf: 5 Songs (E. González Martínez), 1940; 6 Songs (Rilke), 1942; Der Krieg (Claudius), 1950; Chamber Music 1 and 5 (Joyce), 1958; 6 Songs (Campbell), 1958; Hymn to Being (Campbell), 1962; Yo pienso en ti (J. Batres Montúfar), 1963; Tarde del trópico (R. Dario), 1969; We face each other (Campbell), 1969; The Serpent (Roethke), 1970
Inst: Danza fantástica, pf, 1950; Piece, va, pf, 1956; Danza exotica, pf, 1959; Semblanza, pf, 1959; Suite, fl, pf, 1962; 4 Pf Pieces, 1966

Principal publishers: Elkan-Vogel, Peer

BIBLIOGRAPHY

Composers of the Americas, xii (Washington, DC, 1966), 90

DONALD THOMPSON

Leybach, Ignace Xavier Joseph (*b* Gambsheim, Alsace, 17 July 1817; *d* Toulouse, 23 May 1891). French composer, organist and pianist. He studied first in Strasbourg and later in Paris with Pixis, Kalkbrenner and Chopin. In 1844 he became organist at Toulouse Cathedral. He was a noted pianist and teacher as well as a remarkably prolific composer of superficial works designed for popular consumption, publishing well over 200 operatic fantasias and salon pieces for piano, of which several, notably nocturnes, were often included in anthologies. Among his other works are *L'organiste pratique* (*c*1880–90), *Le nouvel organiste* (1881–3), methods for piano (1888) and harmonium (1864) and several volumes of songs and motets with organ.

SUSAN THIEMANN SOMMER

Leyden, John (*b* Denholm, Roxburghshire, 8 Sept 1775; *d* Batavia, now Jakarta, Indonesia, 28 Aug 1811). Scottish antiquarian, folksong collector, editor, poet and orientalist. He was a powerful force in Edinburgh's intellectual life from the mid-1790s until his departure for India in 1802. His two outstanding contributions to

Scottish folksong scholarship were in helping Walter Scott to collect material for the *Minstrelsy of the Scottish Border* (1802) and editing the 16th-century political tract *The Complaynt of Scotland*, adding to it a *Preliminary Dissertation* which, though prone to irrelevance, is a mine of indispensable material about Scottish folk music and Border customs. Leyden also edited the *Scots Magazine* for a short period, did pioneering philological work on the Scots dialect and on oriental languages, wrote poetry prolifically and was a qualified surgeon.

BIBLIOGRAPHY

J. Morton: 'Memoir', *Poetical Remains of the late Dr John Leyden* (London, 1819)

M. R. Dobie: 'The Development of Scott's "Minstrelsy" ', *Transactions of the Edinburgh Bibliographical Society*, ii (1946), 67

DAVID JOHNSON

Leyding, Georg Dietrich. *See* LEIDING, GEORG DIETRICH.

Leyrac [Tremblay], **Monique** (*b* Montreal, *c*1930). Canadian singer and actress. She studied elocution with the singer Jeanne Maubourg and made her radio début as an actress in 1943 in Werfel's *Le chant de Bernadette*. Her singing début, followed by her first recording, was in 1948 in Montreal, at 'Au Faisan Doré', a popular *boîte*. In 1952 she married the French actor Jean Dalmain and retired. She resumed her acting career in 1955 with the Théâtre du Nouveau-Monde in Montreal and Paris and sang Polly in *L'opéra de quat'sous* in 1961 with noted success. In 1965 she was awarded first prize for interpretation at competitions in Sopot and Ostend. Since then she has widely toured Canada, France, North Africa, the Soviet Union and the USA. She is a gifted *chanteuse* and comedienne with a haunting, husky voice and a compelling stage presence.

GILLES POTVIN

L. H. Left hand (also Ger., *linke Hand*).

Lhéritier, Antoine (*fl* 1508–32). French singer. The earliest archival notice referring to him indicates that after an examination he was accepted as a singer at the Sainte-Chapelle on 22 December 1508; the length of his service there is not known. From 1520 to 1532 he served in the musical chapel of Emperor Charles V. Since official documents call him a 'clericus morinensis', like Jean Lhéritier, he must have come from the former diocese of Thérouanne (Pas-de-Calais) and the two may be related. Brenet suggested that some of the compositions attributed in 16th-century sources only to Lhéritier may be by Antoine, but this is unlikely. Most works attributed to 'Lhéritier' are signed 'Jo.' (or 'Joan.') in some other source, whereas neither the name 'Antoine' nor the initial 'A.' is found in any of the contemporary anthologies and MSS.

BIBLIOGRAPHY

M. Brenet: *Les musiciens de la Sainte-Chapelle du Palais* (Paris, 1910), 50

J. Schmidt-Görg: *Nicolas Gombert, Kapellmeister Kaiser Karls V: Leben und Werk* (Bonn, 1938), 52f

L. Perkins: *The Motets of Jean Lhéritier* (diss., Yale U., 1965), 52f

LEEMAN L. PERKINS

Lhéritier [Lerethier], **Isaac** (*fl* *c*1540). French composer. The Lyons publisher Moderne printed three of his chansons: *De loing travail* and *O vous omnes par trop aventureulx* (in *Le parangon des chansons, neuf-*

viesme livre, 1541[8], and *dixiesme livre*, 1543[14], respectively) and, in a lute intabulation by Francesco Bianchini, *Quant tu vouldras* (1547).

BIBLIOGRAPHY

L. Perkins: *The Motets of Jean Lhéritier* (diss., Yale U., 1965), 53ff

S. Pogue: *Jacques Moderne, Lyons Music Printer of the Sixteenth Century* (Geneva, 1969), 171, 179, 197, 334

LEEMAN L. PERKINS

Lhéritier [Lheretier, Lhiretier, Lirithier], **Jean** [Johannes] (*b* *c*1480; *d* after 1552). French composer.

According to notarial documents drawn up in Avignon in the 1540s, 'Johannes Lhéritier' was a 'clericus morinensis diocesis', a native of the former diocese of Thérouanne (in the present-day Pas-de-Calais). A contemporary, Tomaso Cimello, called him a disciple of Josquin Desprez. The influence of Franco–Netherlands style discernible in Lhéritier's early motets and a mass based on a chanson by Févin suggest that the contact with Josquin probably took place at the French court in about 1501 or later.

The archives of the Estense court show that a 'Metregian leretier' arrived in Ferrara towards the end of 1506 and remained there until 5 June 1508 when Duke Alfonso I gave him leave to return to France. Some 13 years later, between 28 July 1521 and 8 August 1522, he received payments from St Louis-des-Français in Rome as *capellanus* and *maestro di cappella*. Perhaps he had already been in the city for a time before obtaining his position at St Louis since one of his motets was included in the so-called Medici Codex of 1518 (*I-Fl*) and three others in *Rvat* C.S.26, an MS copied during the papacy of Leo X (1513–21). Indirect evidence also suggests that Lhéritier may have had connections with Florence in the late 1520s.

After a hiatus of 18 years in the archival records, on 28 April 1540, the first of a series of notarial instruments was drafted. These documents refer to five separate benefices awarded to Lhéritier within the ecclesiastical jurisdiction of his patron, Cardinal François de Clermont, the papal legate in Avignon. From the cumulation of remunerative appointments it can be inferred that Lhéritier enjoyed the cardinal's protection considerably longer than the year separating the earliest recorded date and Clermont's death on 2 March 1541. The latest indicates that Lhéritier was still alive in 1552, but gives no clue concerning where and how he was then employed. Scotto's publication of the *Moteti de la fama* under Lhéritier's name in 1555 may point to a period of residence in Venetian territories. This hypothesis is also supported by Pietro Gaetano's treatise (written between 1566 and 1574). Gaetano, a singer at St Mark's, affirmed that Lhéritier had been his *praeceptor* but provided no information about the date and place of his studies.

Lhéritier's compositions survive in 42 MSS and 45 printed collections of the 16th century. The majority originated in Italy, but France, the Netherlands, Spain, Germany, Austria, and even Poland and Czechoslovakia are also represented. His *Missa 'On a mal dit de mon amy'* is of the type that began to be cultivated by Mouton and Févin around 1500 and best designated *ad imitationem*. Lhéritier extracted from Févin's three-voice chanson the four points of imitation that constitute its substance and used them at key structural points in the mass as the starting-point for his own composition. His *Magnificat* settings are more traditional in that the liturgical reciting-tone occurs in each of them, at times in extended values and carried by the tenor, but more often migrating from voice to voice or permeating imitatively the entire texture. The only chanson unequivocally his, *Jan, petit Jan*, is in the light, declamatory style that became current in France in the 1520s.

At the focal point of Lhéritier's compositional activity, clearly, was the motet. In choice of texts he favoured antiphons, psalms, responsories and devotional verse, although he also set other sacred texts and one erotic secular poem. A little over half of his motets are in a single section; the remainder are divided into two *partes*. In many, some sort of structural repetition is used to articulate the formal design. This is done most consistently in the responsory settings where the reiteration of the respond practised in the liturgical chant is retained in the polyphony, but a similar effect is also achieved by the refrain-like repetition of distinctive material, a dual statement of the concluding phrase or some analogous procedure. Lhéritier consistently employed the liturgical plainsong traditionally associated with a given text only in setting the Marian antiphons sung at Compline. It provides the essential melodic material which, treated imitatively, pervades the entire musical fabric. Only occasionally did he cast a cantus firmus in extended note values or generate one voice from another in strict canon, and then only in motets for five or six voices. He adopted these traditional techniques primarily to enhance the seriousness of a work and, particularly where a second text is involved, to gain a depth of expression because of their associative value.

The compositional procedure basic to all of Lhéritier's works is syntactic imitation relieved by homophonic writing where appropriate for textual or formal reasons, or simply for variety, but the entries of the separate voices tend to be more closely and evenly spaced in the later works, resulting in a generally fuller texture. His melodies present nicely balanced arches with smooth profiles resulting from predominantly stepwise motion with the leaps usually filled. They are generally contrived to provide for a syllabic declamation of the text at the beginning of a phrase, but may be continued melismatically. That modal consistency was an important consideration is evident from Lhéritier's use of final and confinal as orientation points within the melodic line and his selection for internal cadences of pitches conforming to the usage described by the theorists and exemplified by liturgical chant. Also contributing to a sense of coherence and unity in many of his works is the elaboration and transformation of significant melodic material in a manner much like that of Mouton. In his carefully regulated counterpoint and suave melodic writing, Lhéritier clearly anticipated essential characteristics of the style associated with Palestrina. His historical significance derives in large measure from the role he played not only in the shaping of those stylistic norms, but also in their dissemination in Italy.

WORKS

(only sources not in modern edition listed)

Edition: *J. Lhéritier: Opera omnia*, ed. L. L. Perkins, CMM, xlviii/1–2 (1969) [P]

SACRED

Moteti de la fama, libro primo, 4vv (Venice, 1555)

Missa 'On a mal dit de mon amy', 4vv (on Févin's chanson), P 1, *DK-Kk* Ny.Kgl.Saml.1848–2° (anon.), *I-CMac* P (olim E)

Alma Redemptoris mater, 4vv, P 218; Alma Redemptoris mater, 5vv, P 84; Angelus Domini descendit, 4vv, P 225; Ascendens Christus in altum, 4vv, P 139, *CMac* D (olim F) (anon.); Ave domina mea, 4vv, P 66; Ave Maria, gratia plena, 4vv, P 240; Ave mater matris Dei,

4vv, P 95; Ave regina celorum, 4vv, P 79; Ave verum corpus natum, 5vv, P 321; Ave virgo gloriosa, 3vv, P 330; Ave virgo gloriosa, 4vv, P 285, Rome, Palazzo Massimo VI. C.6.23–4

Beata Dei genetrix, 4vv, P91, *CMac* D (olim F), inc. (anon.; also attrib. Willaert and Conseil); Beata es, virgo Maria, 4vv, P 235 (also attrib. Verdelot); Benedicat te Dominus, 4vv, P 276; Cum rides mihi basium negasti, 4vv, P 248; Deus, in nomine tuo, 5vv, P 149 (also attrib. Willaert); Dum complerentur dies penthecostes, 4vv, P 52, *CMac* P (olim E) (anon.); Hodie salvator mundi, 4vv, P 60, *CMac* D (olim F) (anon.; also attrib. Mouton); In te, Domine, speravi, 4vv, P 130; In te, Domine, speravi, 4vv, P 209 (also attrib. Verdelot); Locutus est Dominus, 9vv, P 336

Miserere mei, Domine, 6vv, P 171; Magnificat quarti toni a voce pari, 4vv, P 20; Magnificat quarti toni, 4vv, P 25; Magnificat octavi toni, 4vv, P 37, *CMac* N (anon.); Nigra sum sed formosa, 4vv, P 297; Nigra sum sed formosa, 5vv, P161, *CMac* D (olim F) (anon.), Rome, Palazzo Massimo VI. C. 6. 23–4; Nigra sum sed formosa, 6vv, P 254; Nisi Dominus edificaverit, 4vv, P 198, attrib. Sermisy in *F-CA* 125–8 (olim 124) (also attrib. Le Heurteur); O clemens, o pia, 4vv, P 99, *I-CMac* D(olim F)(anon.); O beatum pontificem, 4vv, *TVca(d)* 4, lost; O quam magnificum, 4vv, *TVca(d)* 4, lost; Petrus apostolus, 5vv, P 333; Qui confidunt in Domino, 4vv, P 108, *CMac* N (anon.); Redde mihi letitiam, 6vv, P 183; Regnum mundi, 5vv, P 166; Repleatur os meum, 5vv, P 324

Salvator mundi, salva nos, 4vv, P 72, *CMac* D (olim F) (anon.; also attrib. Mouton); Salve mater Salvatoris, 4vv, P 300; Salve regina, 6vv, P 262; Sancta Maria, succurre miseris, 4vv, P 69, *CMac* D (olim F) (anon.); Senex puerum portabat, 4vv, P 308; Si bona suscepimus, 4vv, P 314, Rome, Palazzo Massimo VI. C. 6. 23–4; Sub tuum presidium, 4vv, P 119, Rome, Palazzo Massimo VI. C. 6 23–4; Sub tuum presidium, 6vv, P 190; Surrexit pastor bonus, 6vv, P 291; Te matrem Dei laudamus, 4vv, P 46; Usquequo, Domine, oblivisceris me, 4vv, P 123 (also attrib. Mouton); Virgo Christi egregia, 4vv, P 244

CHANSON

Jan, petit Jan, P 347

DOUBTFUL WORKS

Domine exaudi me, 5vv, attrib. Lhéritier in Rome, Palazzo Massimo VI. C. 6. 23–4; attrib. Jacquet in 1539[5], *Primo libro di motetti di Jachet*, 5vv (Venice, 1540), 1542[6]

Visita quesumus, Domine, 4vv, attrib. 'Iritier' in *E-Tc* 17; attrib. Jacquet in *GB-Lcm* 2037, *I-Bc* Q20; attrib. Jacquet and Willaert in 1538[5]

En l'ombre d'ung buissonet, 4vv, attrib. Lhéritier in 1535[8]; attrib. Lasson in *c*1528[9]

BIBLIOGRAPHY

P. Aaron: *Toscanello in musica* (Venice, 2/1529/R1969; Eng. trans., 1970), ff.Hiv, Ii

S. Vanneo: *Recanetum de musica aurea* (Rome, 1533/R1969), f.93r

A. P. Coclico: *Compendium musices* (Nuremberg, 1552/R1954), chap. 'De musicorum generibus'

F. Lesure: 'Notes pour une biographie de Jean Lhéritier', *RdM*, xlii (1958), 219

L. L. Perkins: *The Motets of Jean Lhéritier* (diss., Yale U., 1965)

H.-W. Frey: 'Die Kapellmeister an der französischen Nationalkirche San Luigi dei Francesi in Rom im 16. Jahrhundert', *AMw*, xxii (1965), 272, xxiii (1966), 32

LEEMAN L. PERKINS

Lhévinne, Josef (*b* Orel, nr. Moscow, 13 Dec 1874; *d* New York, 2 Dec 1944). Russian pianist. The son of a trumpeter in the Royal Opera orchestra, he entered the Moscow Conservatory in 1885, and attended Safonov's piano class until his graduation with the gold medal in 1891. Among his fellow students at the conservatory were Rakhmaninov and Skryabin, and he also benefited from the acquaintance of Anton Rubinstein. After graduation he began giving concerts abroad, but was recalled to Russia for military service. In 1898 he married Rosina Bessie (*b* Kiev, 28 March 1880; *d* Glendale, Calif., 9 Nov 1976), also a pianist. She had recently graduated from the Moscow Conservatory with the gold medal, but for the rest of her husband's life she devoted much of her energy to supervising his career, appearing with him only occasionally in two-piano performances. Lhévinne taught in Tiflis (1900–02), and then became a professor at the Moscow Conservatory (1902–6). Between 1907 and 1919 the Lhévinnes lived principally in Berlin, where they were interned during World War I because

Josef Lhévinne

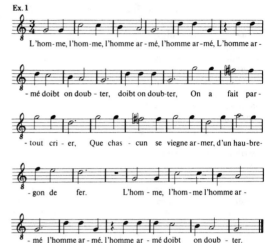

Ex.1

they were Russian; this experience played a large part in their decision to move to New York after the war. In 1922 Lhévinne joined the staff of the new Juilliard School of Music; his wife did so too, and came to be regarded as one of the great teachers of her time. Her pupils included John Browning, Arthur Gold, James Levine and Van Cliburn.

Lhévinne's few gramophone records clearly reflect the prodigious technique that was one of the most famous of his day. But the success of his playing lay in his ability to combine this technique with a firm control of tone and phrasing. His playing of Chopin was noted for its firm lines within rubato, and he performed even the most exhibitionist 19th-century works with a compelling musicianship. He was shy and almost without competitive impulse, and in his later years would have made fewer appearances than he did but for his wife's virtual management of his career. He wrote *Basic Principles in Pianoforte Playing* (Philadelphia, 1924/*R*1972, with foreword by Rosina Lhévinne).

BIBLIOGRAPHY

G. Sherman: 'Josef Lhévinne', *Recorded Sound*, xliv (1971), 784 [with discography by H. L. Anderson]

R. R. Gerig: *Famous Pianists and their Technique* (Newton Abbot, 1976), 300ff

JERROLD NORTHROP MOORE

L'homme armé. A melody of the 15th century which became the basis for a long series of polyphonic elaborations, particularly masses, dating from about 1450 to the early 17th century. The melody appears with what seems to be its original text in a late 15th-century MS at Naples (*I-Nn* VI-E-40) which contains a cycle of six anonymous masses based on the melody; this source was first described by Dragan Plamenac in 1925. The melody and text as given in complete form in the tenor of the sixth mass in the Naples MS are shown in ex.1.

The single stanza of text supplied in the Naples MS can be briefly translated as follows: 'Fear the armed man; word has gone out that everyone should arm himself with a hauberk of mail'. That this may refer to a crusade against the Turks is suggested by a further text in an anonymous three-voice setting in the Mellon Chansonnier (*see* SOURCES, MS, §IX, 8); the textual history of the poem has yet to be fully investigated. On the

musical side it is clear that this famous melody is, in its symmetry and clarity of structure, ideally suited as a subject for elaboration, and especially for canonic treatment. Its normal modal final is G and most of its elaborations are in this mode, some with a signature of one flat and some without. Since the earliest chanson settings are on G and without a flat, this may be the original mode for the tune. Whether it was originally a monophonic song or a tenor of a lost three-voice chanson is an unsolved problem (see Plamenac and Gombosi).

The earliest chanson settings are the anonymous one in the Mellon Chansonnier and those by Robert Morton, Basiron, Japart and Josquin Desprez. Pietro Aaron in *Thoscanello* (1523) suggested that the author of the tune was Busnois, but this is otherwise uncorroborated and may only reflect the authority of Busnois' mass on this melody (Strunk).

The repertory of *L'homme armé* includes at least 31 settings which can be provisionally divided into several groups. Perhaps the earliest are the masses by Dufay, Ockeghem and Busnois; a second, slightly later group, may be formed by the masses of Caron, Faugues, Regis, Tinctoris, the six settings of the Naples MS, Basiron and Vaqueras; a third group embraces the late 15th and early 16th centuries, and includes masses by Obrecht (shown by Strunk to be structurally dependent on the mass by Busnois), Pierre de La Rue (2), Josquin (2), Orto, Vitalier (lost), Pipelare, Brumel and Jean Mouton (also attributed to Forestier); a fourth group, all of the 16th century, is made up of the settings by De Silva, Carver, Morales (2) and Palestrina (2). A special use of the tune in the early 16th century is found in Costanzo Festa's *Missa diversorum tenorum*, which quotes *L'homme armé* along with other famous melodies. The end of the tradition is marked by a 12-voice mass by Carissimi. About half the known mass settings belong to the period from 1450 to 1500 and form the largest group of rival settings of a single antecedent in the period, substantially larger than the groups of settings of such popular contemporary subjects as *Fors seulement*, *De tous biens plaine*, and *J'ay pris amours*. See HAM, i, nos.66, 73, 89, 92. *See also* MASS.

BIBLIOGRAPHY

M. Brenet: 'L'homme armé', *MMg*, xxx (1898), 124

O. Gombosi: *Jacob Obrecht* (Leipzig, 1925)

D. Plamenac: 'La chanson de L'homme armé et MS VI. E. 40 de la

Bibliothèque Nationale de Naples', *Fédération archéologique et historique de Belgique: Annales*, xxv (1925), 229

O. Gombosi: 'Bemerkungen zur 'L'homme armé'-Frage', *ZMw*, x (1927–8), 609

——: reply to Plamenac, *ZMw*, xii (1929–30), 378

O. Strunk: 'Origins of the 'L'homme armé' Mass', *BAMS*, ii (1937), 25

W. Apel: 'Imitation Canons on L'homme armé', *Speculum*, xxv (1950), 367

L. Lockwood: 'Aspects of the *L'homme armé* Tradition', *PRMA*, c (1973–4), 97

D. Fallows: *Robert Morton's Songs* (diss., U. of California, Berkeley, 1978), 202ff

LEWIS LOCKWOOD

L'Hoste da Reggio. *See* HOSTE DA REGGIO.

Lhotka, Fran (*b* Mlada Vožice, Budejovice, 25 Dec 1883; *d* Zagreb, 26 Jan 1962). Yugoslav composer and conductor of Czech origin. He studied the horn and composition in Prague under Stecker, Klička and Dvořák. His teaching career began in Jekaterinoslav (now Dnepropetrovsk) and in 1909 he joined the Zagreb Opera orchestra. From 1920 to 1961 he was a professor at the Zagreb Academy of Music, and dean during the years 1923–40 and 1948–52. In his music Lhotka often used Croatian folk materials. He wrote in a late Romantic style, strong in contrasts and brilliant in instrumentation. A vivid rhythmic sense distinguished his work for the ballet, as well as a gift for the musical reflection of a wide range of emotions and dramatic effects. His most popular work, *Đavo u selu*, encompasses scenes of rowdy carousing and banal everyday life, hellish and grotesque moments, and a wedding finale. Lhotka's conducting activities included the direction of the Zagreb chorus Lisinski (1912–20) and of the orchestral society of the Croatian Institute of Music. He also wrote textbooks.

WORKS
(selective list)

Ballets: Đavo u selu [The devil in the village], Zurich, 18 Feb 1935; Balada o jednoj srednjovjekovnoj ljubavi [Ballad on a medieval love story], Zurich, 6 Feb 1937; Luk [The arc], Munich, 13 Nov 1939

Other works: Str Qt, G, 1911; Vn Conc., 1913; Conc., str qt, 1924; 2 hrvatske rapsodije, vn, chamber orch, 1928; choruses, songs

Principal publishers: Schott (Mainz), Društvo Hrvatskih Skladatelja

BIBLIOGRAPHY

K. Kovačević: *Hrvatski kompozitori i njihova djela* [Croatian composers and their works] (Zagreb, 1960), 242ff

P. Mlakar: 'Značajan i plodonosan susret' [A significant and productive encounter], *Zvuk* (1962), no.54, p.401

K. Kovačević: *Muzičko stvaralaštvo u Hrvatskoj 1945–1965* [Musical creation in Croatia 1945–1965] (Zagreb, 1966)

KREŠIMIR KOVAČEVIĆ

Lhotka-Kalinski, Ivo (*b* Zagreb, 30 July 1913). Yugoslav composer and singer, son of Fran Lhotka. He studied composition with his father and solo singing at the Zagreb Academy of Music until 1937, when he went to Rome for two years of composition study with Pizzetti. After holding various teaching posts (1939–51) he became a professor of singing at the Zagreb Academy.

Lhotka-Kalinski's early works, of which the most important are *Jutro* ('Day') and the Symphony in E♭, were mainly romantic and programmatic. An intense study of folksong resulted in his making numerous arrangements for vocal and instrumental groups, and also influenced the melodic patterns of his original music. Lhotka-Kalinski gradually abandoned this folk style for a less nationalistic neo-classical idiom which incorporated elements of 12-note and atonal techniques. An excellent singer with a well-developed dramatic sense, he is a natural operatic composer. He gained an enviable reputation with the four brilliant one-act radio and television operas to texts by Branislav Nušić written between 1954 and 1958. This style was greatly expanded in the atonal opera *Svijetleći grad* ('The shining city'), a bitter indictment of what is worthless in society, mirrored musically by a coarse harmonic intensity.

WORKS
(selective list)

DRAMATIC

Pomet, meštar od ženidbe [Pomet, the marriage maker] (opera, after M. Držić: Dundo Maroje), 1944

Matija Gubec (opera, Lhotka-Kalinski, M. Fotez, T. Prpić), 1947

Velika coprarija [The great sorcery] (children's opera), 1952

Analfabeta [The illiterate] (radio opera, B. Nušić), 1954

Legenda o pjesmi [Legend of a song] (ballet), 1955

Putovanje [The journey] (television opera, Nušić), 1956

Dugme [The button] (television opera, Nušić), 1957

Vlast [Political power] (opera, Nušić), 1958

Svijetleći grad [The shining city] (opera, P. Šegedin), 1967

Tko će svima da ugodi (musical tale), 1968

VOCAL

Cantatas: Verba fili David, 1940; Hrvatska kronika [Croatian chronicle], 1952; Kerempuhova pesem [Kerempuh's song] (Krleža), 1959

Other works: Srebrna cesta [The Srebreno road], 1v, orch, 1937; Ples smrti [Dance of death], Bar, orch, 1940; 2 popevke Gorana Kovačića, 1v, pf, 1947; 3 pjesme Mate Balote, 1v, chamber orch, 1949; Bugarštice, 1v, pf, 1951; 3 pjesme Dobriše Cesarića, 1v, pf, 1953; Ojađena svirala [Unhappy flute], 1v, cl, 1957; Žalobna muzika [Mournful music], 1v, orch, 1961; 4 epitafa, 1v, ens, 1961; Pjesme moga vremena, 1v, orch, 1963; 3 Krležine, 1v, orch, 1964; Meditacije XX, Bar, chamber orch, 1965; other solo and choral songs, folksong arrs.

INSTRUMENTAL

Orch: Sym., E♭, 1937; Plesna suita [Dance suite], 1937; Rimske impresije [Roman impressions], 1938; Zemlja [The land], sym. variations, 1939; Jutro [Morning], sym. poem, 1941–2; Vedri prizori [Gay scenes], 1947; Baletni prizori u starom stilu [Ballet scenes in the old style], 1950; Komendrijaši [The comedians], chamber orch, 1952; Simfonijeta, G, 1953; 7 Bagatelles, ob, bn, str, 1954; Omladinska simfonijeta, chamber orch, 1956; Mala balkanska suita [Little Balkan suite], 1961; Misli [Thoughts], cl, str, 1963; 6 eseja [Essays], 1964

Inst: Dijalozi, fl, cl, 1966; 5 Monologues, vc, 1969; Little Suite, va, pf, 1969

Pf: Stari dalmatinskih plesovi [Old Dalmatian dances], 1942; Međimurje malo, suite, 1946; 2 plesa na istarske motive [Dances on Istrian motifs], 1946; Male priče [Little stories], 1949; 2 sonatinas, 1950; Iverije, 1957; Mala balkanska suita, 1961; Mikroforme, 1964

Principal publisher: Udruženje Kompozitora Hrvatske

WRITINGS

Tehnika pjevanja [The techniques of singing] (Zagreb, 1940)

Umetmost pjevanja [The art of singing] (Zagreb, 1953)

BIBLIOGRAPHY

I. Kirigin: 'I. Lhotka-Kalinski *Matija Gubec*', *Muzičke novine* (1948)

D. Gostučki: 'Ivo Lhotka-Kalinski *Analfabeta*', *Zvuk* (1955)

NIALL O'LOUGHLIN

L'Huyllier [L'Huillier, Luiller] (*fl* 1539–50). French composer. His 14 surviving chansons were published in Paris at a time when this form was at the height of its popularity. Like most of his contemporaries, he preferred to set texts with four-line stanzas, usually serious love-songs. He was able to balance skilful imitation with homophonic writing, and used brief phrases in triple metre to contrast with the prevailing duple metre. The tenor parts are particularly ornate, but all four voices have considerable melodic interest.

WORKS
(all for 4vv)

Au monde estoint douleur, 1546[14]; Avecqes vous mon amour finira, 1540[14]; Hélas, amy, 1547[8]; Je me veulx tant à son vouloir, 1550[11]; Le cueur loyal, 1543[8]; O doulx raport, 1541[6]; O ma Vénus, 1547[8]; Pareille au feu, 1546[14]; Si je voy, 1550[9]; Si l'amytié voire, 1543[11–12]; Si me voyez face triste, 1550[11]; Toy seul sans plus peulx, 1539[17]; Ung si grand bien, 1544[7]; Vous me laissez pour ung aultre, 1545[8]

CAROLINE M. CUNNINGHAM

Liadov, Anatol [Anatoly] **Konstantinovich.** *See* LYADOV, ANATOL KONSTANTINOVICH.

Liaison (Fr.). LIGATURE (i).

Liban, Jerzy (*b* Liegnitz, 1464; *d* after 1546). Polish humanist, theorist and composer. He belonged to a German family in Silesia and his true name was probably Wiehrauch. In 1494 he began his studies at Kraków University, and later went to Cologne for a time before returning to Kraków in 1501. From 1506 he was probably associated with the Gymnasium of the church of St Mary, Kraków, first as a cantor and from 1514 as rector. In 1511, 1513 and 1520 Liban lectured at Kraków University. Among his many writings are two music treatises: *De accentum ecclesiasticorum exquisita ratione* (Kraków, *c*1539) and *De musicae laudibus oratio* (Kraków, *c*1539). There are also passages on music in his *De philosophiae laudibus oratio* (Kraków, 1537). *De accentum* is a lengthy treatise on the use of accentuation in reciting liturgical texts: it shows his humanist inclinations, including among the authorities cited Pico della Mirandola and Erasmus. The other treatise, *De musicae*, although incorporating the views of Gaffurius, was devoted primarily to ancient music; Liban appended a glossary of Greek musical terms in order to demonstrate that Latin music theory was derived from Greek. He also attempted to relate Greek theories on the ethical aspects of music to the church modes, insisting that attention should be paid to the verbal character of the text when choosing a mode.

The treatises contain some music by Liban. A four-voice hymn *Ortus de Polonia Stanislaus* (ed. Z. Szweykowski, *Muzyka w dawnym Krakowie*, Kraków, 1964) written in 1501 and published in *De accentum* uses note-against-note technique. Eight *Magnificat* settings and one psalm, *In exitu Israel*, all for four voices, were printed as music examples in *De musicae*. They are all based on chant melodies and use imitative counterpoint.

The two musical treatises and *De philosophiae* are reprinted in MMP, ser.D, vi–viii (1975–6).

BIBLIOGRAPHY

J. Reiss: 'Georgius Libanus Lignicensis als Musiker', *ZMw*, v (1922–3), 17
——: *Przyczynki do dziejów muzyki w Polsce* [Contributions to the history of music in Poland] (Kraków, 1923)
——: *Książki o muzyce od XV do XVII wieku w Bibliotece Jagiellońskiej* [Books on music from the 15th to 17th centuries in the Jagellonian Library] (Kraków, 1924)
H. Barycz: *Historia Uniwersytetu Jagiellońskiego w epoce humanizmu* [History of the Jagellonian University in the age of humanism] (Kraków, 1935)
——: *Ślązacy na Uniwersytecie Jagiellońskim od XV do XVIII wieku* [Silesians at the Jagellonian University from the 15th to 18th centuries] (Katowice, 1935)
Z. Jachimecki: *Muzyka polska w rozwoju historycznym* [Polish music in its historical development] (Kraków, 1948)
Z. Szweykowski, ed.: *Z dziejów polskiej kultury muzycznej* [From the history of Polish musical culture] (Kraków, 1958), 1

ELŻBIETA WITKOWSKA-ZAREMBA

Liber, Joseph Anton (*b* Sulzbach, Upper Palatinate, 1732; *d* Regensburg, 1809). German violinist and composer. He studied the violin and composition with Riepel at Regensburg. In 1766 his name appeared on the salary list of the court of Thurn und Taxis, and he remained a member of the orchestra there until it disbanded in 1806. His extant works (in the Thurn und Taxis library) include a symphony, a divertimento for nine instruments and a mass in A; six trio sonatas were published at Mannheim (*c*1775). Numerous masses, symphonies and violin concertos are lost. His son Wolfgang Liber (*b* Donauwörth, 31 Oct 1758; *d*

Regensburg, 23 July 1839) was a monastic musician (from 1779) and priest (1784) at the Benedictine abbey of Michelfeld, and at its dissolution in 1803 became organist at Regensburg.

BIBLIOGRAPHY

EitnerQ
F. J. Lipowsky: *Baierisches Musik-Lexikon* (Munich, 1811/*R*1971)
D. Mettenleiter: *Musikgeschichte der Oberpfalz* (Amberg, 1867)
Musikalisches Conversations-Lexikon, ed. H. Mendel and A. Reissmann (Berlin, 1870–80)
S. Färber: *Das Regensburger fürstliche Thurn und Taxissche Hoftheater und seine Oper* (Regensburg, 1936)

AUGUST SCHARNAGL

Liberati, Antimo (*b* Foligno, 3 April 1617; *d* Rome, 24 Feb 1692). Italian theorist and composer. He studied law and fine arts and became a notary in his native town. From 1637 to 1643 he was at the Viennese court in the service of the Emperor Ferdinand III and Archduke Leopold. On 6 February 1644 he took minor orders at Foligno. About 1650 he moved to Rome, where he became a pupil of Gregorio Allegri and, after the latter's death in 1652, of Orazio Benevoli. On 20 November 1661 he was engaged as an alto in the papal choir, to which he belonged until his death; in 1674 and 1675 he was chosen as *maestro di cappella*. Besides these duties he was organist and *maestro di cappella* of the German church in Rome, S Maria dell'Anima, and at Ss Trinità del Pellegrini and Ss Stimate di S Francesco.

Although Liberati's music was frequently mentioned in earlier literature, little of it survives, mostly single arias in contemporary manuscripts. He is much more important for his theoretical writings, in which he unequivocally declared himself a champion and adherent of the Roman tradition. His *Epitome della musica*, which he presented to Pope Alexander VII in 1666, and his *Lettera* of 1684 clearly show that in his view the only ideal church music was that of Palestrina; therefore any reform must take place within the Palestrina tradition. Liberati's attitudes to musicians of his day are particularly interesting for the light they throw on musical life at that period, the best-known example being his defence against G. P. Colonna of the so-called parallel 5ths in Corelli's Violin Sonata op.2 no.3. In his *Lettera* he expressed exhaustive opinions on 17th-century composers of the Roman school, such as Allegri, Benevoli, Cifra and Nanino. Characteristically, however, he never mentioned such celebrated Roman opera and oratorio composers as Landi, Marazzoli, the Mazzocchi brothers and Luigi Rossi, for he disapproved of the *stile nuovo* and the *seconda prattica*. He also opposed the new interpretation of music in the Sistine Chapel. Traditionalism and musical purism are indeed as much the hallmarks of his personality as his uncompromising commitment to the Roman tradition in church music. He was thus one of those who initiated the Palestrina revival in the second half of the 17th century.

WRITINGS

Lettera . . . in risposta ad una del Signor Ovidio Persapegi, 15 Ottobre 1684 (Rome, 1685)
Epitome della musica (MS, *I-Bc*, *Rvat*, ?1666)
Ragguaglio dello stato del coro de' cantori nella cappella pontificia (MS, *Rvat*)
Due lettere a Giovanni Paolo Colonna in difesa d'un passo dell'opera Seconda Sonata terza d'Arcangelo Corelli (MS, *Bc*)

WORKS
SACRED

Laudate Dominum, 4vv, bc, 1683[1]
Aita, ò numi, aita, oratorio, 5vv, vns; lost, mentioned in Mischiati

SECULAR

Amanti non va così, *I-Nc*, *Rvat*; Amore che cosa sarà, *Nc*; Amor è un laberinto, *Rdp*; Con atroce martire, *Rc*; Con rauco mormorio, *Gi(l)*; D'un' erma spiaggia, *Nc*, *F-Pthibault*; Era la notte, *I-Rn*; Gioite o miei pensieri, *Nc*; Impari ogn' amante l'amore da me, *F-Pthibault*; La mia vita è una canzone, *I-Rn*; No non mi tenete, *Nc*; Non ve lo posso dire, *Rc*, *F-Pthibault*; Ove tra sponde d'oro, *I-Nc*; Quanto godo e quanto rido, *Nc*; Sentite l'amore, *Rc*; Sò ben io quel che dico, *Rn*

BIBLIOGRAPHY

EitnerQ; *FétisB*; *HawkinsH*; *SchmidlD*

A. Adami: *Osservazioni per ben regolare il coro dei cantori della cappella pontificia* (Rome, 1711), 206

G. Baini: *Memorie storico-critiche della vita e delle opere di Giovanni Pierluigi da Palestrina* (Rome, 1828/R1966), 50f

F. X. Haberl: 'Giovanni Maria Nanino', *KJb*, vi (1891), 81

F. Vatielli: 'Le "Quinte" del Corelli', *Nuova musica* (1913), April

——: 'Le "Quinte seguite" di Corelli', *Arte et vita musicale a Bologna*, i (Bologna, 1927), 184ff

K. G. Fellerer: *Palestrina* (Regensburg, 1930), 16, 26

P. Kast: 'Antimo Liberati: eine biographische Skizze', *KJb*, xliii (1959), 49

O. Mischiati: 'Per la storia dell'oratorio a Bologna', *CHM*, iii (1963), 131–70

SILKE LEOPOLD

Liber capitularius (Lat.). A LECTIONARY of the Latin rite.

Liber comicus [comitis] (Lat.). A lectionary of the Latin rite; *see* LECTIONARY and LITURGY AND LITURGICAL BOOKS, §II, 3.

Liber gradualis (Lat.). *See* GRADUAL (ii).

Liberia. West African republic. The population of Liberia consists of the indigenous peoples and the descendants of English-speaking repatriated Africans who settled on the coast during the 19th century. The country owes its political origin to the latter groups. Indigenous peoples include the Belle, Gbande, Gio (Dan), Kpelle (Guerzé), Loma (Toma), Mandingo (Malinke), Mano, Mende and Vai of the Mande language sub-family; the Bassa, Dei, Grebo, Jabo, Krahn and Kru of the Kwa language sub-family; and the Gola and Kissi of the west Atlantic language sub-family. These subfamilies are part of the Niger–Congo language family. Certain peoples, including the Gio, Kissi, Kpelle, Loma, Mandingo and Vai, are also in adjoining countries, so the music of Liberia shares some features with that of neighbouring territories and should be considered in relation to the music of GUINEA, IVORY COAST and SIERRA LEONE.

1. Historical background and research. 2. Types of music. 3. Concepts and occasions. 4. Instruments. 5. Styles.

1. HISTORICAL BACKGROUND AND RESEARCH. While Liberian music is created by peoples of diverse language backgrounds, it is often performed by and for individuals who are multi-lingual and have interacted extensively with those in other groups. This interaction goes back at least to the 15th century, when the Mande migrations towards the coast began, continuing on a smaller scale into the 19th century. Throughout these migration periods, and into the 20th century, shifting political alliances have also facilitated contact; and there has been interaction through trade between peoples within Liberia and those living beyond its borders, as well as intergroup interaction promoted by the Poro secret societies acting as pan-group institutions of traditional authority.

The earliest written accounts of music in Liberia are contained in the observations of 19th-century travellers, missionaries and scholars. On a journey in 1868, Benjamin Anderson observed a chief travelling from Totaquella to Boporu accompanied by an entourage of praise-singing musicians playing drums, horns and an iron percussion idiophone. Johann Büttikofer, who began his travels in 1879, described music and dance performances and included drawings of drums, rattles, a *sanza* (lamellaphone) and a triangular frame zither. The first detailed ethnomusicological work was George Herzog's study of Jabo music in south-east Liberia (1930, published 1934) which focussed on signalling music and the relationships between language and music. In later literature, Warren d'Azevedo has been concerned with the behaviour of musicians, dancers and other artists in Gola society, and with Gola aesthetic concepts. Bai T. Moore has described categories of songs in Liberian music, and Agnes von Ballmoos has examined music of the descendants of the 19th-century settlers.

Films and recordings of musical performances date from the 1920s. In 1923 H. Schomburgk made a silent film of dance in women's secret society rituals; Paul Germann filmed Gbande masked and stilt dances (1928, 1929). Early recordings include Herzog's 226 cylinder recordings of Jabo music (1930), and Robert Morey's recordings (1935) of Loma, Gbande and Mandingo music. Packard L. Okie, an Episcopalian missionary, collected music in various places (1947–54). Arthur Alberts, on his 1949 west African recording trip, collected music of the Loma and Mano, of the Fanti community on Marshall Island and songs in Monrovia from the community descended from settlers.

Hans G. Himmelheber made six extended ethnographic research trips to Liberia and the Ivory Coast (1949–65) during which he recorded Gio, Krahn and Mano music; many of his short research films include sound recordings of musical performances. Leo Sarkisian and Bai T. Moore (under-secretary of information and cultural affairs for Liberia) travelled extensively throughout Liberia in 1965–6 and collected a wide variety of music. Many field recordings made in Liberia have been deposited at the Archives of Traditional Music, Indiana University, Bloomington. Films incorporating music and dance performance are available in the Institut für den Wissenschaftlichen Film, Göttingen.

2. TYPES OF MUSIC. The music of Liberia can tentatively be categorized as that performed by indigenous peoples, by descendants of repatriated Africans, and urban popular music performed by both. Yet such distinctions are difficult to maintain as interaction provides a mixture of elements between all types of music. Herzog has noted that a large number of the Jabo signalling texts are in the languages of the more powerful neighbouring peoples, the Grebo and Kru. Radio programmes and recordings also promote this interchange, and the national dance troupe incorporates elements of various types of Liberian music.

Before concentrating on the music of the indigenous peoples, mention must be made of the two other types of music, neither of which has been studied extensively. The music of settler descendants has been explored by Agnes von Ballmoos, who studied the Johnsonville Singers, a group organized in the early 1950s. They perform chiefly religious music, and their songs bear some relationship to spirituals. She has also discussed the Greenwood Singers, a group with a mainly secular repertory; it was founded in 1949 and recorded that year by Alberts, but no longer exists. The music of both the Johnsonville and Greenwood Singers draws heavily on Western rhythmic, melodic and harmonic styles. The urban popular music reflects aspects of HIGHLIFE, jazz and American popular music, as well as indigenous music. It is important in Monrovia and is increasingly widespread elsewhere.

3. CONCEPTS AND OCCASIONS. Most Liberian peoples seem to incorporate 'music' within a broader term that describes an event involving music sound, dancing and celebration. The Kpelle term for this type of event is *pêlee*. When narration and drama are also included, it is called *meni-pêlee* (*chantefable*). Related terms are *măla* for dance and *wule* for song. Music sound for the Gio, Gola and Kpelle is the voice or speech of instruments and singers. The voice is termed *mié* by the Gola and *wóo* by the Kpelle and Gio. *Wóo* for the Kpelle may mean the voice of a group of performers, of an individual singer or instrument, or of an individual part of an instrument, such as a string.

There are professional musicians who are socially accepted and publicly recognized for their special skill among the various Liberian peoples, though most of them work part of their time as subsistence rice farmers or wage labourers. Singers are called *ayun gbembe* among the Gola and *ngulei-sîyge-nuu* ('the song-raising person') among the Kpelle. Gola professional singers are thought to be endowed by their *neme*, or guardian spirit, and given the ability to invent new songs. Indeed it is widely believed among the Gola that singers are unfaithful to their spouses and lovers because their true lovers are their spiritual guardians. Throughout Liberia singers are in demand to perform at festivals, funerals and receptions. Virtuoso performance is intensely appreciated, and ensembles spend much time touring. Solo singers are often women, but male professional storytellers, and instrumentalists playing the pluriarc, the lamellaphone and the triangular frame zither, are also singers.

Kpelle performing ensembles show parallels to the Kpelle political organization. For instance, the drum-dominated ensembles are usually headed by the *pêlee-kalong* ('chief of the play'), who is the group's liaison with the town chief and the manager who negotiates playing engagements. The *posîa*, as master of ceremonies, calls for pauses in the music, interprets speeches of praise to the players, and keeps the crowd from pressing too close to the players. The musical leader of the group, the master drummer (*fêli-ygále-nuu*), plays the single-headed goblet drum (see illustration); he plays the most varied and complex part, and knows all other parts and how they fit together. Also in the ensemble are the *gbùng-gbùng* drummer, who gives the ensemble a steady background beat, vocal soloists, dancers and the audience, which may also act as a chorus. A performance incorporates not only music sound, but also intermittent pauses during which the performance is explained or commented on, and token gifts are presented to performers with elaborate speeches. The phases of a Kpelle performance are co-ordinated by many cues. The master drummer plays specific rhythmic patterns that cue dancers to execute particular choreographic movements, and gives other players cues for tempo, coordination or dynamics. The vocal soloist may also signal to the ensemble that she

Fêli (goblet drum) and gbùng-gbùng (double-headed cylindrical drum) of the Kpelle people in a pêlee

wants a pause in the music, by inserting certain verbal phrases in her melodic line. Herzog has reported that among the Jabo a musical phrase is played to mock a dancer who stumbles or falls, and another phrase to indicate the end of a musical segment.

Music is performed on various occasions. Those connected with the life cycle include the initiation of young people into the Poro and Sande secret societies. The extent and elaboration of music for a death depends on the age and status of the deceased. But birth and marriage are relatively minor musical occasions among most Liberian peoples. Music-making may also relate to the annual cycle. It is especially prominent after the rice harvest and on such holidays as Liberian Independence Day, 26 July. Music is performed for cooperatives working on clearing bush, planting and harvesting. The full moon often coincides with musical entertainment. Social occasions such as games may incorporate music. In the games played by Jabo men gossip, anecdotes and nicknames are communicated by xylophone playing, with the meaning veiled so that only a few understand the signalling.

Masked dancers appear at various musical occasions. The Kpelle have a masked dancer who is the public manifestation of the Poro and is known as *gbetû*. The Mano and Gio have a masked dancer on stilts whose face is covered with a black net and who dances for entertainment or in honour of distinguished guests. The Mano also have a masked clown dancer (*domia*) who carries a rope and pretends to beat those who cannot sing; he tries to show them how to sing, but is himself incompetent.

4. INSTRUMENTS. The Kpelle and Gio divide instruments into two categories: blown (Kpelle *fée*) and struck (Kpelle *ygále*). Instrument names within Kpelle ensembles sometimes reflect their social organization.

For instance, in an ensemble of three hand-held slit idiophones, the largest and therefore lowest pitched is *kóno-lee* ('mother *kóno*'), the medium-sized *kóno-sama* ('middle *kóno*') and the smallest *kóno-long* ('child *kóno*').

The Liberian peoples also have names for the various pitch registers of the instruments. The Jabo use the terms 'ke' (a small bird with a high-pitched voice) and 'dolo' (a larger bird) to distinguish higher from lower pitches. By compounding these terms with the words for 'large' and 'small' the Jabo designate four pitch registers for a variety of instruments. The Kpelle, with some variation in terminology, designate strings or other individual parts of instruments by the sound they produce. On one pluriarc the strings, in ascending pitch order, are named as follows: *ṅee*, 'the mother'; *ṅee ṅóng*, 'the mother's child'; *ṅee ṅóng ngo ṅóng*, 'the mother's child's child'; *nêyge*, 'the younger sibling' (of the third string); *ṅóng*, 'the child' (of the fourth string); *ṅóng*, 'the child' (of the fifth string); *gbe-ngâ*, 'end'. Many Liberian instruments have, in addition to the timbre of the basic instrument, a metallic rattle consisting of loose metal pieces often attached to drums, lamellaphones, struck idiophones and chordophones.

Membranophones include goblet and conical single-headed drums, hourglass and cylindrical double-headed drums, and footed drums. Master drummers beat the goblet drum (Kpelle *fêli*) or the conical drum (Vai *samgba*) with the hands, both drums having laced skins and attached metal rattles. The HOURGLASS DRUM (Kpelle *daniṅg*; Mano *tama*; Gio *dama*) is also widespread in Liberia. The player uses a hooked stick and can produce a wide range of glides. A cylindrical, stick-beaten drum (Vai *gbemgbem*; Kpelle *gbùng-gbùng*) usually provides the ensemble with a steady rhythmic background. Large footed drums, 2 to 4½ metres long, have been reported among the Gio, Jabo and Mano. When the drums are exceptionally large platforms may be built in order to play them. Among the Jabo, the large footed drum has the honorary title of 'God's wife' and is the official signalling instrument of the village.

Idiophones are struck, plucked and shaken. Struck idiophones include slit-drums, xylophones, pieces of iron and the glass bottles that have occasionally replaced the iron percussion idiophones. Slit-drums are of two types. The first is a relatively large wooden drum played horizontally (Kpelle *kéleng*). Among the Jabo such drums have single slits, the lips of varying thicknesses producing different pitches; among the Mano and Gio they have one or two longitudinal slits. Where there are two slits, the tone produced in the area between them is known as the 'son's piping voice'; the lower tone of the outer lip is the 'mother's resonant response'. A drum with a single slit has a 'man's voice only'. The Jabo use these instruments for dance performances, to send messages, and to organize meetings of local policing groups. Praise titles may be incorporated into these performances. The second type of slit-drum is a smaller bamboo or wooden idiophone (Kpelle *kóno*) held vertically and played in ensembles when bush is being cleared for rice farms. Among the Kpelle tortoise-shells are also played as slit idiophones in the Sande women's secret society.

Xylophones (Gio *blande*; Kpelle *bala*; Mano *balau*) are found throughout Liberia and often consist of free logs resting on banana stalks. They are played by boys on rice farms to drive away birds, and are used for signalling. Lamellaphones appear in several varieties.

One has seven to nine lamellae with a hemispherical gourd or enamel bowl resonator (Kpelle *gbelee*). It is played as a solo instrument, the player also singing. A larger two- or three-tongued instrument with a box resonator is known as a *kónggoma* (*see* SIERRA LEONE, §2) among the Vai and Kpelle, as a *bonduma* among the Gola. It usually accompanies a vocal ensemble that may also include other instruments. Shaken idiophones, which include basket rattles and gourd rattles with external networks of beads, are played chiefly by women. Dancers often wear leg rattles of seed-pods or bells.

Chordophones include the triangular frame zither, the pluriarc and the musical bow. The triangular frame zither (Kpelle *konîng*) consists of eight or nine strings spanning the triangular wooden frame. The strings are tuned by moving them up or down the frame to change their tension. An attached half-gourd resting on the player's chest acts as a resonator. Melodic motifs played by this instrument may illustrate an implied text depicting, for instance, a leopard stalking prey, or women sowing rice seed. The pluriarc (Kpelle *gbegbetele*) has piassava bows attached to a round gourd resonator. Metal or rattan strings are stretched across each bow, which has metal rattles attached to its underside. The musical bow (Kpelle *gbong-kpala*) is played by striking the string with a stick held in one hand, while the other hand stops the lower end of the string at various points. The mouth encircles the string at the upper end, without touching it, to amplify the sound.

Side-blown horns (Kpelle *túru*) made of wood, ivory or horn are the most common aerophones. They are played in ensembles of four to six horns using hocket technique and voice disguise. Horns are also used in signalling. Globular pottery flutes are used in the secret society for creating the Poro spirit's voice.

5. STYLES. Melody is generally syllabic and percussive. Ostinato is common, appearing as short, repeated melodic patterns either to accompany a more extended melody or in combination to form a complex ostinato, the patterns of which may be simultaneous, alternating or overlapping. In the latter case, for instance in bush-clearing songs, hocketing sometimes also occurs. A striking example of hocket occurs in the music of side-blown horn ensembles: in a typical group of four to six horns, each instrument plays only one or two notes of the melody. Melody sometimes approaches a type of recitative that reflects the rhythm, pitches and nuances of speech. The storyteller of a *chantefable* uses recitative during the musical sections of the story. Vocal glissandos and other melodic devices suggest subtleties of speech. Phonemic pitches in these tone languages do not completely govern melodic pitches, or even melodic direction, although speech tone is clearly reflected in the music, especially at semantically crucial points.

The range of pitches used in Liberian music varies, and may include five, six, seven or more notes. Performance is frequently focussed within a pentachord, the voice or instrument shifting from one pentachord to another. The Kpelle have songs that use a pentatonic scale within an octave. This includes a minor 3rd, which is often closer to a major 2nd, implying a tendency towards isotonicism. However, there also appear to be 3rds and 2nds of various sizes, including neutral ones.

Both instrumental and vocal polyphony are important in Liberian music. Of the various harmonic intervals used, 3rds, 4ths, 5ths and 6ths are prominent. Parallel 4ths may form opening or closing patterns on the lamellaphone or triangular frame zither. Contrapuntal motion is prominent in songs with an overlapping complex ostinato. Herzog described canonic xylophone songs, performed by two men, with the form built on repetition, imitation and transposition.

Much of the music is based on rhythms of unequal beats, as in ex.1, and thus belongs to a broad stylistic area extending through parts of Africa, the Middle East, Mediterranean Europe and India. An idiophonic accompaniment to a pluriarc entertainment song has a 12/8 pattern shown in ex.2, also composed of unequal beats. This rhythmic pattern appears in a *fêli* (goblet drum) signal pattern of the Kpelle, where the mnemonic syllables name a bird by imitating its voice.

Ex.1 Metre of Kpelle *chantefable;* rec. and transcr. R. Stone

$\frac{9}{8}$ ♩ ♩ ♩ ♩. |

(Units = 2 + 2 + 2 + 3)

Ex.2 Idiophonic accompaniment to pluriarc song; rec. and transcr. R. Stone

Rhythm: $\frac{12}{8}$ ♩ ♩ ♪♩ ♩ ♪♩ |

(Units =   2 + 2 + 3 + 2 + 3)

Performances are typically by ensembles rich in contrasting timbres: voices, drums, rattles and metal idiophones. Entries are usually staggered, giving an accumulation of textures. The metal rattles attached to many instruments add variety to the timbre. Horn players and singers delight in voice disguise to produce animal and bird imitations. Master drummers playing membranophones imitate the sound of a slit-drum or other drums to demonstrate their skill. They even imitate the sound of side-blown horns with their voices, placing their mouths close to the drumhead for resonance.

Men sing primarily in the upper vocal register, women in the lower. Both mostly use mouth resonance. There is some tightness in vocal production, which is pronounced in the men's voices when they sing bush-clearing songs. Tempo in all music is quite fast. Responsorial singing is widespread. The Kpelle call the soloist *ngulei-sîyge-nuu* ('song raiser') and the chorus the *faa-ma-nuai* ('answering people'). Litany and strophic forms are both prominent, a variation being the narrative *chantefable* with recurring musical chorus and narrated story verses.

In every aspect of Liberian musical style there appears to be logic and consistency amid variety and richness. But further detailed research is needed to understand this logic more fully as it is perceived and ordered by Liberian musicians and audiences.

BIBLIOGRAPHY

B. J. K. Anderson: *Narrative of a Journey to Musardu, the Capital of the Western Mandingoes* (New York, 1870), 31
J. Büttikofer: *Reisebilder aus Liberia,* ii (Leiden, 1890), 334ff
H. H. Johnston: *Liberia* (London, 1906)
D. Westermann: *Die Kpelle: ein Negerstamm in Liberia* (Göttingen, 1921), 34, 47, 286
M. J. Herskovits: 'Kru Proverbs', *Journal of American Folklore,* xliii (1930), 225–93 [with transcr. by G. Herzog of 2 Kru melodies]
R. P. Strong, ed.: *The African Republic of Liberia and the Belgian Congo,* i (Cambridge, Mass., 1930), 64ff, 90
P. Germann: 'Musik', *Die Völkerstämme im Norden von Liberia* (Leipzig, 1933), 62
G. Herzog: 'Speech-melody and Primitive Music', *MQ,* xx (1934), 452
——: 'Drum-signaling in a West African Tribe', *Word,* i (1945), 217
G. Schwab: 'Tribes of the Liberian Hinterland', *Papers of the Peabody Museum of American Archeology and Ethnology,* xxxi (1947), 149, 270
G. Herzog: 'Canon in West African Xylophone Melodies', *JAMS,* ii (1949), 196
G. W. Harley: 'Masks as Agents of Social Control in Northeast Liberia', *Papers of the Peabody Museum of American Archeology and Ethnology,* xxxii/2 (1950), 3–41
P. L. Okie: 'Folk Music of Liberia', FE 4465 (1954) [disc notes]
H. and U. Himmelheber: *Die Dan: ein Bauernvolk im westafrikanischen Urwald* (Stuttgart, 1958)
W. L. d'Azevedo: 'Some Historical Problems in the Delineation of a Central West Atlantic Region', *Annals of the New York Academy of Sciences,* xcvi (1962), 512
R. Brandel: 'Polyphony in African Music', *The Commonwealth of Music, in Honor of Curt Sachs* (New York, 1965), 26
A. N. von Ballmoos: 'Liberian Music', *Liberian Research Association Journal,* iii/2 (1970), 30
B. T. Moore: 'Categories of Traditional Liberian Songs', *Liberian Studies Journal,* ii (1970), 117
R. M. and V. L. Stone: 'Music of the Kpelle of Liberia', FE 4385 (1970) [disc notes]
R. M. Stone: 'Meni-Pêlee: a Musical-dramatic Folktale of the Kpelle', *Liberian Studies Journal,* iv (1971), 31
H. Zemp: *Musique Dan: la musique dans la pensée et la vie sociale d'une société africaine* (Paris, 1971)
R. M. Stone: *Music of the Kpelle People of Liberia* (diss., Hunter College, NY, 1972)
V. L. Stone: *A Survey of Recorded Materials Available for the Study of Traditional Music of Liberia* (MS, 1975)
A. N. von Ballmoos: *The Role of Folksongs in Liberian Society* (diss., Indiana U., 1975)

RUTH M. STONE

Libero Castro, Heinricus de. Composer, possibly identifiable with HEINRICH LAUFENBERG.

Libert, Gualterius [Liberti, Gualtero] (*fl* 1423–8). French composer. A work of his in *GB-Ob* 213 is dated 1423; whether this is the date of composition or of copying is unknown. It is recorded that he received four florins as a singer (tenth on the list) in the papal chapel in 1428. No link is known between Gualterius and Reginaldus Libert. The opinion that Gualterius was the same man as the English composer Walter Frye is no longer accepted.

Three works are known to be his: *Se je me plains, Belle, plaisant que nulle autre née*/*Puisque je suis* and *De tristesse, de dueil.* All appear uniquely in *GB-Ob* 213, where the last is dated 1423. Another work, *Comment pourray,* is attributed to 'C. Libert' in Coussemaker's copy of *F-Sm* 222; 'C' may have been a misreading of 'G'.

BIBLIOGRAPHY
F. X. Haberl: 'Wilhelm Dufay', *VMw,* i (1885), 60
G. Reaney, ed.: *Early Fifteenth-century Music,* CMM, xi/2 (1959)

TOM R. WARD

Libert, Reginaldus [Liebert] (*fl* c1425–35). French composer. He is sometimes identified with a Reginaldus who was *magister puerorum* in Cambrai in 1424. Stylistically his works belong to the period around 1430. The most interesting of these is the Marian mass (in *I-TRmn* 92). It resembles the earlier *Missa Sancti Jacobi* of Dufay in including settings of both Ordinary and Proper. All the movements except the Gloria and Credo are based on an ornamented form of the appropriate chant melody. Musical unification is achieved through the use of similar mensuration patterns throughout.

Two rondeaux are attributed to him, *Mourir m'envoy* and *Mon cuer s'en va.* Both are set for three voices, with only the highest voice texted. He also wrote a Kyrie (in *I-TRmn* 92). The work has four written voices, only three of which can be performed together.

BIBLIOGRAPHY
G. Adler and O. Koller, eds.: *Sechs Trienter Codices . . . I. Auswahl,* DTÖ, xiv–xv (1900/*R*1959)

R. von Ficker and A. Orel, eds.: *Sechs Trienter Codices . . . 4. Auswahl*, DTÖ, liii (1920/*R*1960), 1
R. von Ficker: 'Die Kolorierungstechnik der Trienter Messen,' *SMw*, vii (1920), 5ff

TOM R. WARD

Liberti, Gualtero. *See* LIBERT, GUALTERIUS.

Liberti, Hendrik (*b* ?Groningen, *c*1600; *d* ?Antwerp, *c*1661). Dutch composer and organist. He was in the service of Antwerp Cathedral by 1620 and was organist there from 17 March 1628 to 1661 in succession to John Bull. He primarily composed vocal music, but this and his one instrumental collection are either lost or incomplete.

WORKS
[Symphonies and motets], 6–8vv, op.1 (n.p., n.d.), lost
Cantiones sacrae et suavissimae, 4–5vv (Antwerp, 1621), inc.
Paduanes et galiardes, 6 insts (Antwerp, 1632), inc.
Vocal compositions in 1634², 1648², 1650⁷, 1651³, and Fasciculus missarum diversorum autorum, 2–5vv (n.p., n.d.), lost

BIBLIOGRAPHY
J. de Vasconcellos, ed.: *Catalogo da livraria de musica d'el-Rey D. João IV*, i (Oporto, 1874), 140, 153
E. vander Straeten: *La musique aux Pays-Bas avant le XIXᵉ siècle*, iv (Brussels, 1878/*R*1969), 274ff
F. Noske: 'The *Cantiones natalitiae*', *Essays in Musicology: a Birthday offering for Willi Apel* (Bloomington, Ind., 1968), 123

RANDALL H. TOLLEFSEN

Liberti, Vincenzo (*b* ?Spoleto; *fl* 1598–1609). Italian composer and organist. He was organist of Spoleto Cathedral from 1598 to about 1600, and he is probably the 'Don Vincenzo' who was *maestro di cappella* there in 1602; in the latter position he would no doubt have succeeded Antonio Liberti, who held it until 1602 and who may well have been his brother. He published at Venice in 1608 a collection of 21 five-part madrigals, *Il primo libro de madrigali*, and he produced *Il secondo libro* there in the following year. On their title-pages he is not described as holding any position.

BIBLIOGRAPHY
L. Fausti: *La cappella musicale del duomo di Spoleto* (Perugia, 1916), 31, 63

Liber usualis (Lat.: 'Book of common practice'). The short title of a book first issued by the monks of SOLESMES in 1896, *Liber usualis missae et officii pro dominicis et festis duplicibus cum cantu gregoriano* ('Book of common practice for Mass and Office for Sundays and double feasts, with Gregorian chant'). It is a compendium, though not comprehensive, of prayers, lessons and chants for the more important services of the Roman Catholic Church as prescribed between the Council of Trent and the Second Vatican Council. It includes the kyriale; Mass, Vespers and Compline for Sundays and feast days; Prime, Terce, Sext and None for Sundays and feasts of the First and Second Class; Matins for four festivals – Christmas, Easter, Whitsun (Pentecost) and Corpus Christi; Lauds for feasts of the First Class; the liturgy for Holy Week; sundry litanies; and votive Masses.

The *Liber usualis* represents the culmination of a tendency, specially noticeable in the Western church, to combine in one volume for practical use selections from liturgical books hitherto kept separate; such combinations had earlier appeared in the BREVIARY, MISSAL and Anglican Book of Common Prayer. These multi-purpose, non-comprehensive volumes differ somewhat from early compendia such as those made for the master-general of the Dominican order, Humbert of Romans, in the 13th century (*I-Rss* XIV lit.1, *GB-Lbm* 23935), which contain the entire Dominican liturgy: these consist of entire books – the gradual, antiphoner etc – bound together, rather than of conflated selections like the *Liber usualis*, and were used during visitations to check the accuracy of local books.

The *Liber usualis* is not an official Vatican liturgical book, but since certain chant books have not yet appeared in official editions, it is useful in providing some chants not easily accessible elsewhere. It is adequate to the musical needs of churches without resident choirs, and has become a standard teaching aid in university music departments and other seminaries. Its usefulness as a source book for medieval chant is severely limited, however, by the fact that it contains chants from a wide variety of period and provenance, some post-medieval, usually without distinction.

See also LITURGY AND LITURGICAL BOOKS.

Libon, Philippe [Felipe] (*b* Cádiz, 17 Aug 1775; *d* Paris, 5 Feb 1838). Spanish violinist and composer. For six years he studied in London with Viotti, with whom he appeared in concerts. He studied composition with Cimador and subsequently held positions as court violinist at Lisbon (1796), Madrid (1798) and Paris (1800), where he worked until his death, in the service of the empresses Josephine and, from 1810, Marie-Louise. His compositions include six violin concertos, trios for two violins and cello, violin duos, variations and 30 caprices for solo violin.

Libraries.
I. Introduction. II. Europe. III. North America. IV. Latin America, Caribbean. V. Africa, Asia, Australasia.

This article provides a survey of institutional libraries containing source materials of Western music; the list is organized alphabetically by country within the regions listed above. It does not deal with libraries containing only secondary material; with libraries of recorded sound; with privately owned libraries; with collections of instruments; or with collections of non-Western materials (which are referred to in entries on the cultures concerned). *See also* COLLECTIONS, PRIVATE; SOUND ARCHIVES; INSTRUMENTS, COLLECTIONS OF; RÉPERTOIRE INTERNATIONAL DES SOURCES MUSICALES.

I. Introduction
1. Definition. 2. Early history of music libraries. 3. Types of music library: (i) Monasteries (ii) Cathedrals (iii) Other ecclesiastical institutions (iv) Universities (v) National libraries (vi) Public libraries, museums (vii) Conservatories (viii) Music information centres (ix) Composers' associations (x) Opera houses (xi) Music publishers (xii) Radio stations (xiii) Private societies (xiv) Private libraries. 4. New functions: (i) Recordings and sound archives (ii) Musicology and libraries (iii) Supplementary services.

1. DEFINITION. The English term 'library', related to the Latin *liber* for book (the words in most Western languages, Fr. *bibliothèque*, Ger. *Bibliothek* and It. *biblioteca*, derive from the Greek *biblos* for book and *thēkē* for container), generally stands for a collection or repository of books. In contradistinction, an archive (often used in the plural) is defined as an organized body of records, usually of an official or governmental nature, or the place where they are stored. The traditional dichotomy between the terms has become increasingly tenuous, however, as historical accident and the quantities

and varieties of material collected have expanded the mutual encroachment. In any case, since many institutions bearing the title 'archive' include not only official records but also material more directly musical in nature (e.g. letters or contracts concerning musicians, and manuscript or printed compositions), they are included in the discussion here. Even the term 'music library', which could long be taken to refer specifically and restrictively to a collection of music and books about music, now encompasses a much more diversified group of materials, with their accompanying and often very complicated service equipment.

2. EARLY HISTORY OF MUSIC LIBRARIES. Little is known about early music libraries: in part because so little is known of the early history of libraries in general, and in part because it is not known whether early libraries contained music (although recent research suggests that some did). In addition, the many functions of music and its widespread use conspired to make it a part of everyday life and thus of a kind inappropriate to preservation in libraries. Even if this were so, however, early libraries would certainly have contained documents on musicians (in archives) and theoretical writings. This latter thesis is supported by the widely documented connection between theoretical music and the sciences of the Quadrivium, and by the equally general theories as to the ethical and physical virtues of music.

Among the earliest known libraries was the collection of cuneiform tablets assembled in the 7th century BC at Nineveh by King Ashurbanipal for the education of his subjects. It contained religious texts and histories as well as other documents. Similar collections of tablets, from Assur (9th century BC) and Tell Harmal, have been thought to contain musical notation; and recently Richard Crocker drew attention to what may be music on a tablet from Ras Shamra (c1800 BC). These would, if correctly interpreted, confirm that some of these early libraries held musical documents.

Libraries were cultivated in both Greek and Roman cultures, particularly in the former, when the library at Alexandria was perhaps the most extensive collection in antiquity. Although it probably included writings on music, there is no positive evidence that it did so and most of the collection was destroyed during the Roman campaign of 47 BC. While such classical collections were either universal collections or were based on the works of the principal authors, their successors in medieval times, the monastic libraries, were concerned primarily to collect sacred texts, commentaries on the scriptures or patristic writings. Thus few classical manuscripts were preserved in them. Despite this – and the fact that they were closed institutions, the contents read and copied only by members of the monastery – they were the guardians of Western culture.

Three medieval scholars in particular are often cited, both for their encouragement of libraries and for their encyclopedic knowledge. Cassiodorus (d 577), Boethius (d 524) and Isidore of Seville (d 636) all published comprehensive works which included large sections on music. Cassiodorus's *Institutiones* was important in transmitting classical musical theory, and the *Etymologiae* of Isidore (who owned one of the richest libraries of his time, some still extant at the University of Madrid) defined many musical terms, especially those used in connection with the liturgy. Other famous continental monastic libraries came into existence about this time, often through the work of Irish monks under the leadership of St Columba. Particularly important for music is that at St Gall (founded 613) because of the concern for Gregorian chant and for musical theory expressed by its leaders (e.g. Notker Balbulus, d 912, and Notker Labeo, d 1022). The monastery was famous for its scriptorium, and the collection there still includes among its important holdings of practical and theoretical music 20 volumes of the 9th to 12th centuries with neumatic notation, some of them Irish in origin. The monastery at Fulda, founded by the English, developed a famous scriptorium, library and school of chant, although little of the library survived the Thirty Years War. Charlemagne, through his efforts to establish general adoption of Roman chant, founded reading schools and made provision for advanced education at cathedral schools (Lyons, Orleans) or monastic schools (Tours, Corbie, Metz) with associated scriptoria. Rome remained an important centre for manuscripts as late as 855, but the collection seems to have passed into disuse soon after; apparently it was destroyed during the 14th century, so it is not known whether it contained music.

In the Byzantine Empire similar patterns of development can be traced, beginning with the important collection established by Constantine the Great. Musical studies flourished, particularly in St Sabas during the 8th century and later at the Studium monastery in Constantinople. Among the existing monastic libraries, there are important musical collections at St Catherine, at the foot of Mount Sinai, and in the 20 monasteries of Mount Athos. The function of Islam and Arab libraries in disseminating the culture of the Eastern Empire through western Europe, and particularly Spain, should not be underestimated. Toledo, for example, which boasted a famous choir school at the cathedral, had one of the most famous scriptoria in Spain, from which Latin translations of Arab works, many descended from Greek thinking and often including musical philosophy, spread throughout Europe.

3. TYPES OF MUSIC LIBRARY. Although some of the information provided in this discussion reappears in the entries below on individual institutions, it is here placed in a more general setting, providing an overview of the subject. It may serve to remind those seeking source material of the broad range of avenues open for their exploration.

(i) *Monasteries*. During the late Middle Ages some monastery collections fell into neglect or were ravaged by war or insurrection; others avoided or overcame such disasters and grew in importance and wealth. Among the latter were many of the Benedictine order, which retained among its tenets rules for the organization, cataloguing and enlargement of their libraries and their performing repertory. Important Benedictine collections included Monte Cassino (the principal abbey, founded 529), St Germain (590), St Gall (616), Metz (662), St Peter in Salzburg (700), St Emmeram in Regensburg (739; since suppressed), Montserrat (888), Einsiedeln (934) and Göttweig (1070). Archives of mendicant orders, although tending to exclude secular music, also had sizable collections as at Assisi (Franciscan), Bologna (Dominican), the Escorial, Klosterneuburg and St Victor in Paris (Augustinian). The Jesuit order, not founded until 1539, differed from other mendicant orders in its special cultivation of school-drama, particularly during the era of the Counter-Reformation: somewhere between a Singspiel and an opera, these plays were performed by students, sometimes with professional musicians, in both the vernacular and Latin. Unfortunately only a small proportion of scores and librettos survived the order's suppression in 1773 by Pope Clement XIV. (E. Tittel, *Oesterreichische Kirchenmusik*, 1961, discusses early musical treasures of Austrian monasteries and contemporary evidence concerning their libraries.)

A wave of suppression and secularization of religious houses swept through Europe, beginning in the 1530s with Henry VIII's abolitions and continuing until the Swiss persecutions of 1838–47. The motives were often economic gain or the issue of state supremacy, but sometimes such movements as agnosticism, materialism or rationalism provided the incentive. Despite the loss of many treasures, numerous books survived because governments provided for the distribution of religious libraries among public institutions, where many still remain. During the French Revolution, for example, the libraries of émigrés and the condemned were added to those of religious houses to form the *biens nationaux* (national property) – an elaborate scheme both saving the libraries and using their books for the instruction of the uneducated; it involved the establishment of regional distribution depots, a plan for uniform cataloguing and a national union catalogue, but it eventually had to be abandoned (see P. Riberette, *Les bibliothèques françaises pendant la Révolution*, 1970). It is nevertheless to this type of programme that we owe the survival of many important theoretical treatises, liturgical works and other genres of music still being discovered in unlikely corners of municipal libraries, particularly in France, Italy and Spain. Some monasteries, especially in Austria, Italy and Spain, have been restored to their orders, and the care of books and music once more undertaken by the monks (e.g. St Florian, St Peter at Salzburg, the Escorial, Montserrat, Monte Oliveto, Subiaco and S Maria del Monte near Cesena). The last three are supported by the Italian government as national monuments.

(*ii*) *Cathedrals*. From the 10th century onwards, cathedral libraries gradually became more important than those of monasteries. The former were usually closer to the centres of population and more often were linked with schools for the training of priests and for secular education. Their book collections tended to be broader in content, more modern and better organized. In addition, as headquarters for bishops or archbishops, cathedrals often maintained trained performers to provide the service music. From these origins, and often from the personal possessions of the attached musicians, important musical archives remain in many cathedrals (e.g. Aachen, Bologna, Cologne, Évora, Faenza, Florence, Milan, Salzburg and Tarragona). Non-Catholic cathedrals similarly own valuable music collections (e.g. Canterbury, Durham and Worcester). Some rich collections of cathedral music have been incorporated into governmental archives (e.g. the many works from the Prague Loreta Cathedral, now in the state archives at Zitenice, and the neumed manuscript of the Metropolitan Cathedral deposited in the Zagreb National Library).

(*iii*) *Other ecclesiastical institutions*. Interesting music collections often belong to parish and diocesan churches and offices: for example Pfarramt St Peter in Görlitz, Diözesanarchiv in St Pölten, the Proskesche Musikbibliothek in Regensburg (belonging to the Bischöfliches Ordinariat) and the Bistumsarchiv in Trier. Others may belong to church music societies (St Gregorius Vereniging, Utrecht), to seminaries (Bischöfliches

Priesterseminar, Münster; Grand Séminaire, Strasbourg; Seminario Maggiore, Aosta), to the archives of particular orders or denominations (Brüder-Unität, Herrnhut; Biblioteca Oratoriana, Naples), to chapter or bishopric archives kept in or close to cathedrals (Cuenca, Granada, Lisbon, Modena, Piacenza), to museums, of which many are also attached to cathedrals (Évora, Huesca, St Ambrose in Milan), and to schools of sacred music (Pontificio Istituto di Musica Sacra, Rome; Institut Supérieur de Musique Liturgique, Paris).

(*iv*) *Universities*. The 12th century saw the rise of the first universities, formed from loosely-knit groups of students and designed, like the monasteries, with faculties (e.g. Bologna, Montpellier, Oxford and Paris). For many years the separate colleges or nations maintained their own libraries, each with its own organization, rules and subject emphases; outsiders were usually permitted to use the books. Central university libraries began to appear two centuries later. Oxford, after several false starts, finally centralized in 1411, Cambridge in 1415. At Prague the Charles University formed a central library soon after its founding in 1348, and before the end of the century Coimbra, Kraków and Orleans had university libraries. With over 50 individual college and school libraries, Paris did not form a central library until the 19th century, basing it on the Sorbonne nucleus.

In addition to works donated by members of the university community and those acquired from defunct monasteries, universities have often received gifts from kings, nobles, bishops and other collectors, and holdings have been increased with the help of endowments and the exchange of duplicates with other libraries. G. Pietzsch (*Zur Pflege der Musik an den deutschen Universitäten bis zur Mitte des 16. Jahrhunderts*, 1971) discusses early holdings of musical material at the universities of Prague (*c*1370), Heidelberg (1396–1432), Erfurt (1412), Cologne (1474–94) and Greifswald (*c*1482); at Trier University (founded in 1473), students may have had to use books from the abbey and cathedral (he could locate no early library inventory). In countries where historic geographical divisions have prevented establishment of a single national library, large regional or city libraries have merged with university libraries in function and administration (e.g. Frankfurt am Main Stadt- und Universitätsbibliothek, Dessau Universitäts- und Landesbibliothek and Basle Öffentliche Bibliothek der Universität). In smaller countries, university libraries have often merged with national libraries (e.g. Lisbon, Oslo, Prague and Stockholm). In countries requiring copyright deposit of more than one example, extras are usually given to universities (e.g. Oxford, Cambridge, and Trinity College, Dublin).

(*v*) *National libraries*. These are a special class of public library (including central governmental libraries, whatever the form of government: e.g. the Royal Library of Belgium, Denmark or Sweden). Regardless of their present titles, they are virtually all descended from collections maintained by ruling houses for the use of their families, their chapels, their private theatres or other musical establishments (Lisbon, Madrid, Paris and Vienna). In some instances a national museum rather than a library houses the central music collection (e.g. The Hague Gemeente Museum, Prague National Museum, London British Museum – recently given autonomy from the museum under the title British

Library). The music divisions of national libraries are almost always administered independently; this step was taken only recently in Belgium (by a law of 1965) and in Canada (1969). Some divisions are separated physically from other departments (Paris, Vienna) but most are in the same building. The most prolific source for the building of national collections is material received on obligatory copyright deposit (but there is no such law in, for example, the Netherlands; many countries lack one with respect to recordings).

Cataloguing connected with *RISM* and other projects has stimulated national libraries into increasing their bibliographical activity. Many maintain central union catalogues of music holdings throughout the country; some assist small libraries that lack qualified personnel for the proper cataloguing of music and retain photocopies of unique items held in remote areas of the country. Several national centres have begun to issue series of printed catalogues of the country's important music collections (e.g. Czechoslovakia, Italy, Poland). Recent years have seen a further extension of this centralizing process, with increasing numbers of ecclesiastical and private collections being absorbed into national libraries, where they are more easily available to users and where trained personnel are available to catalogue and care for the treasures (notably the Prague State and University Library and National Museum, which received the collections of many churches and cathedrals, as well as of private collectors, among them the important princely Lobkowitz library from Roudnice; and music from various small parish churches of the area have been deposited at the Bayerische Staatsbibliothek in Munich, where printed catalogues are being prepared – although the institution nominally belongs to the Bavarian area it comes close to being a national library by virtue of its long history and rich holdings). A less typical amalgamation, demonstrating the same trend towards centralization, is the absorption of the former Landesbibliothek in Weimar by the city's Zentralbibliothek in 1969.

(*vi*) *Public libraries, museums.* Collections open to the public have existed in Europe for at least four centuries. They were originally established by social, religious, commercial or benevolent societies and were limited in appeal and access. Probably the earliest of those supported directly by cities were the council libraries or *Ratsbüchereien* of 14th-century Germany. Like the others mentioned, it was in fact used mainly by the 'Bürger' class of established citizens, although theoretically open to all.

Two factors were chiefly responsible for the development on a much broader scale of truly public libraries: the invention of printing in the late 15th century, and the social, cultural and religious changes brought about by the Reformation in the early 16th. Despite the positive influence of Luther's 1524 appeal to German mayors, urging them to spare no pains to procure good libraries in large cities, negative forces were at work and reformist zeal caused the destruction of thousands of European monastery libraries. Among the earliest municipal libraries are several in Germany – at Nuremberg (founded 1429), Ulm (1516), Magdeburg (1525) and Strasbourg (1531). City halls in other countries had small reference libraries or collections (often little used) received as gifts or taken over from monasteries; but the first real advance towards the more general availability of library facilities occurred during the French Revolution, when public libraries received the possessions of clergy and nobility. But the real public library used freely by a broad segment of the population is a phenomenon of the late 19th and the 20th centuries.

In the modern municipal or regional public library, music usually forms a part of much broader holdings. Some music collections are run as semi-autonomous organizations, physically separate from other branches; several have become famous for their research funds (e.g. Biblioteca Musicale Andrea della Corte in Turin, Henry Watson Music Library in Manchester, Musikbibliothek der Stadt Leipzig and New York Public Library of Performing Arts). Besides government support for administration and growth, these institutions frequently have to depend on gifts from private donors and from commercial, performing or other types of organization (e.g. the library of the Allgemeine Musikgesellschaft in the Zurich Zentralbibliothek, collections of orchestral societies in the public libraries of Lucca, Milan and Turin, and recordings from defunct USA Information Service libraries deposited in various Italian institutions).

Museums devoted to topics more or less closely related to music, like the arts, church history, dance, folklore, general history or instruments, often have valuable music holdings (e.g. Carolino Augusteum in Salzburg, Musée Guimet in Paris, Museum für Geschichte der Stadt Leipzig, Smithsonian Institution in Washington, DC, Victoria and Albert Museum in London and the Museo del Risorgimento in Vicenza).

(*vii*) *Conservatories.* Many conservatory libraries originally had a largely practical function, their collections of modern editions and textbooks having been assembled for teaching or performance; over the years such collections have often become historic treasures, forming important research materials in their own right. The foundation of some conservatories, however, in the late 18th and early 19th centuries, coincided with the foundation of libraries, in which earlier sources – representing a national or local musical tradition – were gathered and preserved. Such is the case with Stockholm (founded 1771), Prague (1811), Parma (1818), Madrid (1830), Brussels (1832), Lisbon (1835) and the various institutions of Naples. The Paris Conservatoire, founded in 1784 to train opera singers, formerly held one of the world's richest collections of source material; in 1964 these holdings were transferred to the Music Department of the Bibliothèque Nationale, in the interest of better preservation and public service. In the USA a trend towards the amalgamation of conservatory and university has resulted in the development of large libraries that serve the dual needs of performance and research (e.g. at the Eastman School of Music of the University of Rochester, or the School of Music of Indiana University).

(*viii*) *Music information centres.* A relatively new type of music library has developed in the various national music information centres, usually financed by the government, sometimes jointly with the music publishing industry. The centres have as their chief purpose the promotion at home and abroad of their national music (with emphasis generally on contemporary music), and collect scores, parts, recordings, books, articles, analyses of compositions, interviews and press clippings. In London a centre was established in 1967 by the Composers' Guild of Great Britain as a showroom for 20th-century music, particularly of living composers; by 1972 it housed 10,000 scores in addition to many tapes and discs. The Scottish Music Archive, founded in 1968 at the University of Glasgow, differs from most others in its emphasis on documentation for Scottish composers of all periods. The following is a list of such centres.

Australia: Australian UNESCO Committee for Music, PO Box 826, Canberra City, Australian Capital Territory 2601
Austria: Österreichische Gesellschaft für Musik, Hanuschgasse 3, 1010 Vienna
Belgium: CeBeDeM, Centre Belge de Documentation Musicale, 31 rue de l'Hôpital, Brussels 1
Canada: Canadian Music Centre, 33 Edward Street, Toronto 101, Ontario
Czechoslovakia: Ceskoslovenské Hudební Informacní Stredisko, Besedni 3, Prague 1 – Malá Strana
Denmark: Samfundet til Udgivelse af Dansk Musik, Gråbrødretorv 7, 1154 Copenhagen
Finland: Musiikin Tiedotuskeskus, Runeberginkatu 15A, Helsinki 10
France: Centre National d'Information et de Documentation Musicale, a/s Bibliothèque Musicale de l'Office de Radiodiffusion-Télévision Française, 116 avenue Président Kennedy, Paris 16
Germany (Federal Republic): Internationales Musikinstitut, Nieder-Ramstädterstrasse 190, Darmstadt
Great Britain: British Music Information Centre, 10 Stratford Place, London W1
Iceland: Islensk Tonverkamidstod, Laufásvegur 40, Reykjavik
Israel: Israel Music Institute, PO Box 11253, 4 Chen Boulevard, Tel-Aviv
Netherlands: Stichting Donemus, Jacob Obrechtstraat 51, Amsterdam Z
Norway: Norwegian Music Information Centre, c/o Norsk Komponistforening, Klingenberggate 5, Oslo 1
Poland: Polskie Centrum Muzyczne, Rynek Starego Miasta 27, Warsaw
Portugal: Fundação Calouste Gulbenkian, Parque de S Gertrudes, avenida de Berna 45, Lisbon 1
Sweden: Svenska Tonsättares Internationella Musikbyrå (STIM), Tegnérlunden 3, 11185 Stockholm
Switzerland: Schweizerisches Musik-Archiv, Bellariastrasse 82, 8038 Zurich
USA: American Music Center Inc., 2109 Broadway (15–79), New York, NY 10023

(*ix*) *Composers' associations.* In most countries there exist organizations for the protection of valuable artistic properties and to provide their creators with aid and information concerning copyright, performance and other legal rights. These societies may preserve in their archives letters and contracts concerning composers, as well as autographs and early editions of their works. For example, the archives of Broadcast Music Inc. (BMI) in New York contain the Carl Haverlin collection of autographs, printed music, letters, iconography etc begun in 1949 and by the mid-1970s containing 6000 items from the 16th century to the present. Associations in other countries include the Société des Auteurs, Compositeurs et Editeurs de Musique, founded in Paris in 1850, the Composers' Guild of Great Britain, the Society of Norwegian Composers in Oslo, the Sociedad General de Autores de España in Madrid, and the Verband Deutscher Komponisten und Musikwissenschaftler in Berlin (which also operates a music lending library). In some cases the composers' associations are related in function or administration to Music Information Centres.

(*x*) *Opera houses.* Besides the theatrical collections deposited in governmental libraries, many theatres preserve the documents (scores and orchestral material, librettos, programmes, scenic designs, costumes etc) of their careers virtually intact in annexed libraries or museums. Among the most valuable are those of the Deutsche Staatsoper in Berlin, La Fenice in Venice, La Scala in Milan and the Paris Opéra. In Parma the Archivio Storico of the Teatro Regio is kept at the theatre but administered as a section of the city's Biblioteca Municipale.

(*xi*) *Music publishers.* Although the archives of some important defunct or reorganized firms have been deposited in public institutions (e.g. Artaria in the Vienna Stadtbibliothek, Peters in the Leipzig Stadtarchiv), long-established firms with long histories have often retained autographs of works they have published, their early editions (and sometimes actual printing plates), letters and contracts with composers, or publication records that may supply missing dates or other important data. For some of these houses, catalogues or other descriptive literature concerning earlier periods have been issued: André in Offenbach, Breitkopf & Härtel in Wiesbaden and Leipzig (although some of that collection was dispersed or lost during World War II), the Plantin firm in Antwerp, Ricordi in Milan and Schott in Mainz. Some firms whose records are not open to the public are nevertheless prepared to provide information to scholars.

(*xii*) *Radio stations.* Radio and television libraries, which generally preserve both commercial material and their own recordings of broadcast programmes, often have in addition excellent facilities for music reference work as well as collections of manuscripts of unpublished works or arrangements that have been commissioned for particular occasions. Outstanding among these organizations are the BBC in London, the ORTF in Paris, Sveriges Radio in Stockholm, the CBC in Toronto and the several Deutsche Rundfunken. In the USA live radio broadcasting is the exception rather than the rule, and good collections are rare. In tune with the prevailing tendency towards centralization, part of the CBS library has lately passed to the New York Public Library. Through the International Association of Music Libraries, radio librarians are seeking to encourage the mutual exchange of performance materials and recordings as well as cooperative cataloguing of their rich holdings.

(*xiii*) *Private societies.* This category includes a variety of institutions not otherwise catered for. The archives of many such bodies have already been deposited in large libraries, but enough remain to warrant listing here.

(*a*) Societies for the propagation of a single composer's works. Such centres usually also collect documents concerning the composer's contemporaries. Many of them pursue programmes of research and issue publications (complete works, yearbooks, journals, congress reports); some are intended for staff use rather than for a visiting public, but will usually respond to inquiries. Among the active institutions are the Istituto di Studi Verdiani in Parma, the Joseph-Haydn-Institut in Cologne, the Mozarteum in Salzburg (which is also a conservatory), the Bach-Archiv in Leipzig, the Beethoven-Haus in Bonn and the Centro di Studi Donizettiani in Bergamo.

(*b*) Organizations dedicated to a particular genre or geographical area of musical activity. The Moravian Music Foundation maintains rich libraries at its branches in Winston-Salem, North Carolina, and Bethlehem, Pennsylvania. Fraternal lodges frequently have small music collections which may be related to their rites or members (e.g. the library of Freemasonry in Washington, DC). Other societies in this category are the Archive of New Orleans Jazz (at Tulane University), the English Folk Dance and Song Society in London and the Instituto del Teatro in Barcelona.

(c) Artistic, historical or scholarly societies. These include the following (titles are self-explanatory): American Antiquarian Society in Worcester, Massachusetts, the Academia das Ciências in Lisbon, the Accademia Virgiliana di Scienze, Lettere ed Arti in Mantua, the Hispanic Society of America in New York, the Literary and Historical Society of Quebec and the Royal Norwegian Scientific Society.

(d) Societies of friends of music or the arts. These organizations sometimes consist solely of a group of persons joined together for promotion or philanthropic purposes. This is often the case in the USA, where associations called 'Friends of the Library' or 'Friends of Music' help support the library with donations or fund-raising activities. Such societies may however have a headquarters office and some of these have libraries (e.g. the Academia de Amadores de Música in Lisbon, the Société des Amis des Arts de Strasbourg). Even the famous Gesellschaft der Musikfreunde, Vienna, dedicated to the furtherance of music by the establishment of various concert series and a conservatory, justified its name, in 1815, soon after its foundation, by making an appeal to 'friends of music' to donate worthwhile musical works in their possession to the society's library. The subsequent gifts of Czerny, Köchel, Brahms and many others testifies to the success of the solicitation.

(xiv) *Private libraries.* Although private libraries may be available to only a single individual, many of them eventually come into the public domain through gift, purchase or default. Because of the care usually bestowed on the selection of items, private libraries tend to be more homogeneous and complete in their chosen subject areas than other types of collection. Music collectors fall into two main types, the first choosing items with a scholarly purpose or for the sheer joy of collecting, the second with the more immediate, utilitarian aim of having them performed. Some collectors combine both aims. For fuller discussion and a list of important collections, historical and present-day, and information on the present whereabouts of historical collections, *see* COLLECTIONS, PRIVATE.

4. NEW FUNCTIONS.
(i) *Recordings and sound archives.* The technological revolution that may be said to have begun after World War II with the appearance of long-playing discs and magnetic tape has since introduced into music libraries a variety of film (audio- and micro-, on cards, strips, reels and cassettes), computer printouts and elaborately designed audio-visual systems controlled by hidden monitors or tied into local radio or television broadcasts and requiring only the flick of a switch for instant reception. For a fuller account of the development and role of this kind of library, *see* SOUND ARCHIVES.

The enormous popularity of recordings and their increased availability to a much broader segment of the population has changed the character of many music libraries by the demands made upon their administration, organization and personnel. As recorded music has become a pervasive cultural and recreational interest for a large segment of library users, the demand for information about composers and performers, as well as about such subjects as opera, instruments, acoustics, aesthetics, forms, history and psychology of music, has intensified. The resultant plethora of more or less popular books and journals comprises chiefly bio-graphy, discography, analysis, methods and self-help books.

(ii) *Musicology and libraries.* The worldwide growth of musicology since World War II has been a powerful stimulus to the growth of music libraries. Taking as its chief area of investigation the history of music, although not excluding other aspects of musical research (e.g. theory, acoustics, psychology, aesthetics), the discipline is naturally more dependent on library resources than any other type of musical activity. The growth in number and size of university departments and independent institutes of musicology has necessitated the creation and enlargement of collections of reference and source materials in order to provide the tools for student and faculty research. Newer institutions must frequently rely on reprint editions and various types of photocopy to build up their holdings of rare or early works.

The close relationship between musicology and music libraries is reflected in the long-standing tradition of appointing trained musicologists as librarians of important music collections. Despite the spread of library science education, many library schools remain unaware of or choose to ignore the highly technical nature of music and the consequent necessity of specialized musical training for librarians handling music. With research libraries, the need for musicological training is even greater, since librarians in such institutions bear additional responsibilities beyond the usual ones of acquisition, classification and preservation of their materials, including at least a minimal understanding of the contents of the entire collection and the compilation of bibliographical aids for the use of its particular clientèle. F. Lesure ('Librarians and Musicologists', *Notes*, xxiv (1967–8), 665) has suggested that the research librarian should also locate and evaluate documentary evidence to lighten the load of the musicologist, both by personal service and by annotated bibliographies; that he should serve a role of liaison among scholars, notifying them when material is already being used by others, or between music and another field such as literature, folklore, ethnology, aesthetics or drama; and that he should facilitate the flow of material among libraries and among countries.

Finally, the research library must produce . . . The librarian's function will not be completed until he has classified, placed where it may be consulted, identified, dated, and even published and had performed the works under his guardianship . . . To guide a researcher one must be a researcher . . . A specialized library that does not make itself known, that does not diffuse the riches which it guards, gravely fails in its cultural duty.

Scholar-librarians today also carry the burdensome responsibility of participation and contribution to the several important international cooperative projects dependent on their aid. These enterprises, jointly sponsored by the International Association of Music Librarians and the International Musicological Society, facilitate the location of important source materials (early prints and eventually manuscripts) in RÉPERTOIRE INTERNATIONAL DES SOURCES MUSICALES, of current published literature on music, in RÉPERTOIRE INTERNATIONAL DE LITTÉRATURE MUSICALE, and musical iconography in RÉPERTOIRE INTERNATIONAL D'ICONOGRAPHIE MUSICALE.

(iii) *Supplementary services.* Beyond the reference and the circulation of music, books and recordings minimally expected today, some music libraries are able to offer certain additional services.

(a) The collecting of musical instruments, particularly those of historic or ethnic interest, or of common instruments that may be borrowed.

(b) The circulation of performing parts for orchestra, band, choir or glee club, not normally a function of libraries serving the public. Many municipal libraries make this a special feature of their services (e.g. the Westminster Central Music Library in London, or the Free Library of Philadelphia with the Fleischer Collection of orchestral music and the Drinker Collection of choral music).

(c) The administration of live or recorded concerts on the library premises or elsewhere (e.g. in a park in summer), sometimes broadcast, with the double purpose of service and publicity.

(d) Participation in regional or national networks for inter-library loan, to broaden the scope and depth of their resources while avoiding the necessity for expensive duplication of materials. Some libraries are interconnected by telex or video-screen communication, making possible the immediate transmission or the imminent mailing of the desired material.

BIBLIOGRAPHY

H. F. Conover: *Current National Bibliographies* (Washington, DC, 1955/*R*1968) [describes music indexing in most countries]

A. Esdaile: *National Libraries of the World: their History, Administration and Public Services* (London, rev. 2/1957) [lists 32 countries]

International Association of Music Libraries: *Code international de catalogage de la musique* (Frankfurt, 1957–71) [i *The Author Catalog of Published Music*, ed. F. Grasberger; ii *Limited Code*, ed. Y. Fedoroff; iii *Rules for Full Cataloging*, ed. V. Cunningham]

K.-H. Köhler: 'Zwei Grundtypen historischer Musiksammlungen', *IMSCR, vii Cologne 1958*, 162

Music Library Association: *Code for Cataloging Music and Phonorecords* (Chicago, 1958)

E. T. Bryant: *Music Librarianship: a Practical Guide* (London, 1959)

V. H. Duckles: *Music Libraries and Librarianship* [*Library Trends*, viii/4 (1960)]

L. Brummel and E. Egger: *Guide to Union Catalogues and International Loan Centers* (The Hague, 1961) [lists *c*200 union catalogues, some printed, in *c*50 countries]

HMYB, xi (1961) [*Music, Libraries and Instruments*]

E. D. Johnson: *A History of Libraries in the Western World* (New York, 1965, 2/1970)

L. R. McColvin and H. Reeves: *Music Libraries* (London, 1965)

C. Bradley, ed.: *Manual of Music Librarianship* [Music Library Association] (Ann Arbor, 1966)

B. Redfern: *Organizing Music in Libraries* (London, 1966, rev. 2/1978)

F. Riedel: 'Zur Geschichte der musikalischen Quellenüberlieferung und Quellenkunde', *AcM*, xxxviii (1966), 3

R. Benton, ed.: *Directory of Music Research Libraries, including Contributors to the International Inventory of Musical Sources* (*RISM*) (Iowa City, 1967–72; Kassel, 1975) [i *Canada and the United States*; ii *Thirteen European Countries*; iii *Spain, France, Italy, Portugal*; iv *Australia, Israel, Japan, New Zealand*; now = *RISM* Series C)

A. Veinstein, ed.: *Bibliothèques et musées des arts du spectacle dans le monde* (Paris, 2/1967)

V. H. Duckles: 'Music Literature, Music and Sound Recordings', *Library Trends*, xv (1967), 494

Guide to National Bibliographical Centers (Paris, 3/1970) [lists aims, resources, addresses, publications etc of centres in 77 countries]

Music Librarianship and Documentation: Report of the 1970 Adelaide Seminar (Adelaide, 1970)

F. Lesure: 'Archival Research: Necessity and Opportunity', *Perspectives in Musicology*, ed. B. S. Brook, E. O. D. Downes and S. van Solkema (New York, 1972), 56

C. Bradley, ed.: *Reader in Music Librarianship* (Washington, DC, 1973) [previously (with one exception) published articles, from 1897 onwards, with many from *Notes* and *FAM*; bibliographies]

International Council on Archives: *International Directory of Archives, Archivum*, xxii–xxiii (Munich, 1975)

II. Europe

AUSTRIA (A)

The Österreichische Akademie der Wissenschaften issues a series of catalogues of archival holdings and composers' works under the title *Tabulae musica austriacae* (Vienna, 1964–). Addresses, hours, personnel, history and catalogues for a variety of music institutions are listed in brief and convenient form in H. Goertz: *Österreichisches Musikhandbuch* (Munich, 1971) with a section on documentation and research on pp.82–114. Two publications deal with particular genres and give information on the location of relevant source material: J. Klima: 'Lautentabulaturen in Niederösterreich', *Kulturberichte aus Niederösterreich*, i (1958), and J. Kock: *Handschriftliche Missalien in Steiermark* (Vienna, 1961). Publications particularly valuable for their listings of and information on monastery collections are E. Tittel: *Österreichische Kirchenmusik: Werden, Wachsen, Wirken* (Vienna, 1961) and *Musical MSS Filmed in Austrian Monastic Libraries for the Monastic MS Microfilm Library, St. John's University, Collegeville, Minnesota* (Collegeville, 1967). The latter names liturgical works, secular music, treatises on music, and fragments of parchment and paper, all dating from before 1600, found in 16 Austrian monasteries.

ADMONT. Benediktinerstift, 8911 Admont (*A*). The monastery was founded in 1074. Some of its library, including much music, was destroyed by fire in 1865; there remain about 700 works by 180 composers and liturgical works dating back to the 11th century (including an early Passion, a psalter, a beautifully decorated missal, antiphoners, breviaries and fragments of hymns and Offices).

J. Wichner: 'Zur Musikgeschichte Admonts', *Mitteilungen des Historischen Vereines für Steiermark*, xl (Graz, 1892), 3–57; A. Krause: 'Zur Musikgeschichte Admonts (ab 1865)', *Zeitschrift des Historischen Vereines für Steiermark* (Graz, 1962); A. Krause: *Die Stiftsbibliothek in Admont* (Linz, enlarged 7/1969)

BREGENZ. Kapuzinerkloster, Kirchstrasse 36, 6901 Bregenz. The monastery (founded in 1636) contains some medieval music.

——. Vorarlberger Landesarchiv, Kirchstrasse 28, 6900 Bregenz (*BRa*). The archive has MS fragments of the 14th–16th centuries, and the *Mehrerauer Zinsbücher* (early 17th century), with St Gall neumes, as well as printed missals of the 16th and 18th centuries and a large collection of Vorarlberg folksongs.

J. Bitsche: *Liederschatz der Vorarlberger: Liedkatalog der Bestände des Vorarlberger Landesarchivs in Bregenz* (Lustenau, 1969); *ÖMz*, xxv/8 (1970) [special issue on music in Vorarlberg]

——. Zisterzienserstift, Wettingen-Mehrerau, 6901 Bregenz (*BRwm*). The monastery, founded in Switzerland in the 13th century, moved to Bregenz in 1854. Music holdings include chant MSS of the 12th–14th centuries, MS scores dating from about 1770 to 1820, and printed music of the 19th and 20th centuries.

E. Bernhauer: 'Zur Musikpflege in der Zisterzienserabtei Mehrerau bei Bregenz', *ÖMz*, xxv (1970), 478

BREITENAU. Wallfahrtskirche St Erhard, Pfarramt Breitenau, 8615 Breitenau. The church has a collection of uncatalogued MS and printed music, chiefly of the 17th and 18th centuries.

EISENSTADT. Burgenländisches Landesmuseum, Museumgasse 5, 7001. The museum library has music books, printed music (including first editions) and autographs.

——. Dompfarre zum Heiligen Martin, Pfarrgasse, 7000 Eisenstadt. The church archive has MS sacred music (including autographs) of the 18th century and printed music of the 17th–20th centuries.

——. Esterházy-Archiv, Schloss, Esterházyplatz 5, 7001 Eisenstadt (*Ee*). The collection belongs to Prince

Paul Esterházy, a descendant of Haydn's patron. Most of the former music holdings are now in the National Széchényi Library in Budapest, but about 2000 MS performing copies of sacred works of the 18th and 19th centuries remain, including small works by Haydn (but no autographs) and C. P. E. Bach. Among the remaining material are documents concerning musicians and performances (such as account books and correspondence) dating back to Haydn's time.

K. Geiringer: 'The Small Sacred Works by Haydn in the Esterházy Archives in Eisenstadt', *MQ*, xlv (1959), 460; J. Harich: 'Haydn Documenta', *Haydn Yearbook*, ii (1963–4), 2; iii (1966), 122; iv (1968), 39; vii (1970), 47

——. Haydn Museum, Haydngasse 21, 7000 Eisenstadt (*Eh*). The museum is in the building Haydn occupied from 1766 to 1778. It houses the Sandor Wolf Collection, consisting mainly of paintings of Haydn, his patrons, friends and fellow musicians and letters and general iconography; it also contains first editions, MS copies and early prints of Haydn and his contemporaries.

A. Csatkai and E. F. Schmidt: *Joseph Haydn: Katalog der Gedächtnisausstellung in Eisenstadt* (Eisenstadt, 1932)

GÖTTWEIG. Benediktinerstift, 3511 Furth bei Göttweig (*GÖ*). Founded in 1072 by the Augustiner-Chorherren, the abbey became Benedictine at the beginning of the 12th century. Early MSS include a 10th-century German psalter, a 12th-century *Ambrosiuskodex*, a 15th-century *Missale ecclesiae bambergensis* and an antiphoner and gradual from the Upper Rhine region. The music archive also has Meistersinger MSS and lute tablatures (including a French MS of c1710) as well as many early MS copies of Haydn works. The monastery acquired part of the library of Aloys Fuchs (d 1853), containing correspondence of Raphael Kiesewetter, autographs and 17th- and 18th-century editions.

H. Wondratsch: *Katalog der Musikalien des Stiftes Göttweig* (Göttweig, 1830); L. Koller: 'Inventar der Göttweiger Kantorei 1612', *Das Waldviertel*, iv (1955), 6; F. W. Riedel: 'Die Bibliothek des Aloys Fuchs im Stift Göttweig', *Hans Albrecht in memoriam* (Kassel, 1962), 207 [with index to writings on music in Fuchs collection at Göttweig; errata and addenda in *Mf*, xvi (1963), 270]; F. W. Riedel: 'Die Libretto-Sammlung im Benediktinerstift Göttweig', *FAM*, xiii (1966), 105; F. W. Riedel and E. Ritter: *Musik, Theater, Tanz vom 16. Jahrhundert bis zum 19. Jahrhundert in ihren Beziehungen zur Gesellschaft* (Göttweig, 1966) [exhibition catalogue]

GRAZ. Diözesan Archiv, Bischofplatz 4, 8010 Graz (*Gd*). The archive has a large collection of music from Styrian parish churches and monasteries.

——. Dominikanerkonvent, Münzgrabenstrasse 61, 8011 Graz. The library of the convent, founded in 1466, has music books, autographs and MSS of the 16th–18th centuries.

——. Landesmusikschule and Hochschule für Musik und Darstellende Kunst, Nikolaigasse 2, 8023 Graz (*Gk*). The libraries of these institutions, housed in the same building, contain the private library of Baron H. E. J. Lannoy, with 1256 musical and theoretical works, chiefly of the first half of the 19th century, but also including some Haydn material and autographs of works mainly by Lannoy. There is also part of Ferdinand Bischoff's collection, containing 17th-century guitar–lute tablature, 18th-century editions, numerous first editions of the Viennese Classics, copies by Aloys Fuchs of Mozart material and composers' letters, and works by Karl Mikuli.

W. Suppan: 'Die Musiksammlung des Freiherrn von Lannoy', *FAM*, xii (1965), 9 [lists 1256 musical works]; H. Federhofer: 'Mozartiana im

Musikaliennachlass von Ferdinand Bischoff', *MJb 1965–6*, 15; H. Federhofer: 'Eine Angelica- und Gitarrentabulatur aus der 2. Hälfte des 17. Jahrhunderts', *Festschrift für Walter Wiora* (Kassel, 1967), 313; I. Becker-Glauch: 'Die Haydniana der Lannoy-Sammlung', *Haydn-Studien*, iii (1973), 46

——. Musikwissenschaftliches Institut, Mozartgasse 3, 8010 Graz (*Gmi*). The library holds bequests from several local composers, the collection of the St Jakobskirche in Leoben and part of the old collection of the Steiermärkische Musikverein.

H. Federhofer: 'Die Musikpflege an der St. Jacobskirche in Leoben', *Mf*, iv (1951), 333

——. Steiermärkisches Landesarchiv, Bürgergasse 2a, 8010 Graz. The archive has a large collection of MS music, chiefly folksong and folkdance material and sacred music, as well as printed music from numerous private and family archives, with emphasis on Styrian composers.

F. Posch: *Gesamtinventar des Steiermärkischen Landesarchiv* (Graz, 1959), esp. 21–76, 83f

——. Universitätsbibliothek, Universitätsplatz 3, 8010 Graz (*Gu*). Founded in 1573, the library has MSS dating back to the 13th century, including a 14th-century treatise, liturgical works and 16th-century polyphonic music. Some are from the Cistercian monastery in Neuberg and the Augustinians in Seckau.

A. Kern: *Die Handschriften der Universitätsbibliothek Graz* (Leipzig and Vienna, 1942–67); W. Irtenkauf: 'Das Seckauer Cantionarium vom Jahre 1345 (Hs. Graz 756)', *AMw*, xiii (1956), 116; H. Federhofer: 'Alte Liederdrucke in der Universitätsbibliothek', *Jb des österreichischen Volksliedwerkes*, vi (1957), 39; Z. Falvy and L. Mezey: *Codex Albensis: ein Antiphonar aus dem 12. Jahrhundert* (Graz *UB 211*) (Graz, 1963); W. Lipphardt: *Hymnologische Quellen der Steiermark und ihre Erforschung* (Graz, 1974)

——. Wiener Franziskanerprovinz in Graz, Franziskanerplatz 14, 8010 Graz. The library has a collection of uncatalogued MS and printed sacred music dating from the 17th century.

GÜSSING. Franziskaner Kloster, 7540 Güssing (*GÜ*). The library has medieval liturgical MSS as well as printed and MS music of the 16th–19th centuries.

H. Federhofer: 'Musikdrucke von Ottaviano Petrucci in der Bibliothek des Franziskanerklosters Güssing', *Mf*, xvi (1963), 157

HERZOGENBURG. Chorherrenstift, 3130 Herzogenburg (*H*). Founded in 1551, the monastery has late Renaissance partbooks; its Baroque sacred music, mostly MS copies of works by local composers, comes in part from the Donberg court, and there are symphonies and smaller works dating from the 18th century.

INNSBRUCK. Prämonstratenser-Chorherrenstift Wilten, Klostergasse 7, 6020 Innsbruck (*Iw*). The archive of the monastery (founded in 1138) has collected music since 1945: its holdings include organ music, oratorios and sacred music from the 18th and 19th centuries.

KLOSTERNEUBURG. Augustiner-Chorherrenstift, Stiftsplatz 1, 3400 Klosterneuburg (*KN*). Founded in the 12th century, the monastery has rich MS holdings of the 12th–16th centuries, and 16th-century printed editions. Among the sacred music used for performance are many 18th-century works, including authentic parts for Haydn's *Missa in tempore belli* and Nelson Mass, as well as MS copies of all his masses.

KREMS. Stadtpfarre St Veit, 3500 Krems. The music collection includes MSS by 155 composers of the 18th and 19th centuries.

F. W. Riedel: 'Beiträge zur Geschichte der Musikpflege an der Stadtpfarrkirche St Veit zu Krems', *950 Jahre Pfarre Krems* (Krems, 1964), 301

KREMSMÜNSTER. Benediktinerstift, 4450 Kremsmünster (*KR*). Founded in 777, the monastery has rich holdings of theoretical works and unique MS and printed music, including the so-called Codex 309 (a neumed MS from the 11th century) and other medieval MSS and fragments, sacred and secular German song from the 8th century on, and instrumental works from 1550 to 1780. There are autographs and copies of works by Michael Haydn and Süssmayr, early MS copies of Joseph Haydn's works, and a wide variety of chamber music, symphonies, Singspiels and church music.

A. Kellner: *Musikgeschichte des Stiftes Kremsmünster* (Kassel, 1956) [describes Codex 309 on pp.37–47; acquisitions from 1739 to 1747 listed on pp.347–56]; R. Flotzinger: *Die Lautentabulaturen des Stiftes Kremsmünster: thematischer Katalog* (Vienna, 1965) [describes 9 MS and 2 printed Fr. and It. lute tablatures]

LAMBACH. Benediktinerstift, 4650 Lambach (*LA*). Founded in 1056, the monastery has medieval liturgical MSS and treatises, and 18th-century sacred and secular MSS. It is rich in works of Michael Haydn (including the Flute Concerto in D) and Lindemayr, and also has MSS of Joseph Haydn, including a copy of his Second Symphony, as well as symphonies by Mozart and his father.

MS catalogue prepared in 1768 available in library; W. Luger: 'Lambach', *MGG*

LINZ. Bundesstaatliche Studienbibliothek, Schillerplatz 2, 4020 Linz (*LIs*). The music holdings, collected from Upper Austrian monastery and court libraries, include an anonymous mandora tablature, early neumed MSS, and printed theoretical works of the 16th–18th centuries.

——. Oberösterreichisches Landesarchiv, Anzengruberstrasse 19, 4020 Linz (*LIm*). The small music collection of the archive includes lute and organ tablatures, missals and antiphoners.

MELK. Benediktinerstift, 3390 Melk (*M*). Founded during the 12th century, the monastery has liturgical and theoretical MSS dating from the 13th–16th centuries, as well as partbooks by Lassus and his contemporaries. Among the rich holdings of sacred and secular vocal and instrumental music are printed and MS works of the 18th–20th centuries, in which the Viennese Classics are well represented. Sacred and secular works by Haydn include a unique copy of his Violin Concerto in A.

MICHAELBEUERN. Benediktinerabtei, 5152 Michaelbeuern (*MB*). The abbey, founded *c*977, has medieval sacred music MSS and printed and MS works of the 18th and 19th centuries.

H. Federhofer: 'Zur Musikpflege im Benediktinerstift Michaelbeuern', *Festschrift Karl Gustav Fellerer* (Regensburg, 1962), 106; R. Federhofer-Königs: 'Ein anonymer Musiktraktat aus der 2. Hälfte des 14. Jahrhunderts in der Stiftsbibliothek Michaelbeuern', *KJb*, xlvi (1962), 43

SALZBURG. General literature: R. Angermüller: 'Libraries, Archives and Musicological Research in Salzburg', *CMc* (1962), no.16, p.26

——. Dom, Domplatz, 5010 Salzburg (*Sd*). The cathedral's music collection is in the charge of the Musikwissenschaftliches Institut of the University of Salzburg, and most of the secular music is in the library of the Mozarteum. There remain operas, instrumental music and a rich collection of 17th- and 18th-century sacred music including masses by Biber and authentic performance material of works by Michael Haydn and Mozart.

W. Senn: 'Der Catalogus musicalis des Salzburger Doms (1788)', *MJb 1971–2*, 182

——. Mozarteum, Schwarzstrasse 26, 5020 Salzburg (*Sm*). The library and archive were begun in 1842 by the so-called 'Dommusikverein und Mozarteum', founded the previous year. The secular collection was taken over by the Mozarteum on its establishment in 1880. Holdings concentrate on Mozart (autograph scores and letters, early editions, MS copies, critical writings and documents), but also include letters and works by and about other composers, particularly of the 18th and 19th centuries. In 1974 C. B. Oldman's widow presented many items from her husband's collection, including 25 letters from Constanze Mozart to the publisher André.

E. Valentin: 'Das Handschriften-Archiv der Internationalen Stiftung Mozarteum', *ÖMz*, xiii (1958), 347; G. Rech: 'Aus dem Briefarchiv der Internationalen Stiftung Mozarteum', (Kassel, 1963), 159; G. Rech: 'Die Bibliotheca Mozartiana der Internationalen Stiftung Mozarteum', *ÖMz*, xxiv (1969), 641; R. Angermüller: 'Zeitschriftenrara in der Bibliothek der Internationalen Stiftung Mozarteum', *Mitteilungen der Internationalen Stiftung Mozarteum*, xx (1972), 11; R. Angermüller: 'Zur Bibliotheks-Ausstellung der Internationalen Stiftung Mozarteum', *ÖMz*, xxix (1974), 29; R. Angermüller: *Bibliotheks-Ausstellung in Mozarts Geburtshaus vom 27.I. – 10.II.1974: Einführung in die Geschichte der Sammlung und Verzeichnis der Ausstellungsstücke* (Salzburg, 1974) [exhibition catalogue]; J. H. Eibl: 'Zu den Autographen aus dem Nachlass von C. B. Oldman', *Mitteilungen der Internationalen Stiftung Mozarteum*, xxii (1974), 16

——. Museum Carolino Augusteum, Museumplatz 6, 5010 Salzburg (*Sca*). The museum was founded in 1834 and has works by Salzburg composers and others, including autographs of Adlgasser, Biber, Diabelli, Michael Haydn, Leopold and W. A. Mozart and Weber. It has many Viennese editions of the early 19th century.

J. Gassner: *Die Musikaliensammlung im Salzburger Museum Carolino Augusteum* (Salzburg, 1962) [orig. in *Museum Carolino Augusteum: Jahresschrift*, vii (1961), 119–365]

——. Musikwissenschaftliches Institut der Universität Salzburg, Getreidegasse 9/IV, Postfach 505, 5020 Salzburg (*Smi*). After its foundation in 1966 the institute, in the Mozarthaus, received many gifts, including O. E. Deutsch's extensive and valuable Mozart collection and reference items from the Richard Engländer estate. The private collection of Alfred Orel was purchased in 1969.

ÖMz, xx (1966), 497 [5 forewords announcing foundation of institute]; G. Croll: 'Ein Jahr Musikwissenschaftliches Institut in Salzburg', *ÖMz*, xxi (1967), 742; G. Croll: 'Zwei Jahre Aufbauarbeit im Salzburger Musikwissenschaftlichen Institut', *ÖMz*, xxiv (1969), 456; G. Croll: 'Neues aus dem Musikwissenschaftlichen Institut der Universität Salzburg', *ÖMz*, xxv (1970), 408

——. St Peter Benediktiner-Erzabtei, St Peter Bezirk 1, 5010 Salzburg (*Ssp*). Founded *c*700, the abbey owns Latin theoretical MSS and polyphonic liturgical works of the 12th–15th centuries. MS works of Leopold and W. A. Mozart and of Joseph and Michael Haydn include some autographs. Besides 18th-century vocal and instrumental music, there is also a large and important collection of dance music including a unique set of minuets by Joseph Haydn.

M. H. Schmid: *Die Musiksammlung der Erzabtei St Peter in Salzburg: Katalog, erster Teil: Leopold und Wolfgang Amadeus Mozart, Joseph und Michael Haydn* (Kassel, 1970)

ST FLORIAN. Augustiner-Chorherrenstift, 4490 St Florian (*SF*). Founded in 1071, the monastery has a rich collection of MS and printed sacred and secular music, including Latin theoretical MSS of the 11th–15th centuries, many incunabula and first editions of pre-Classical and Classical composers. MS III, 222A, partly in St Gall neumes, is the oldest choral document in Austria.

A. Czerny: *Die Handschriften der Stiftsbibliothek St Florian* (Linz, 1871); A. Czerny: *Die Bibliothek des Chorherrenstiftes St Florian* (Linz, 1874, 5/1962)

SECKAU. Benediktinerabtei, 8732 Seckau (*SE*). The abbey was founded in 1240 by the Augustinians and taken over by a Benedictine order in 1883. There is an extensive collection of church music, mostly uncatalogued. Two MS choirbooks, dating from the late 16th and early 17th centuries, one containing masses and *Magnificat* settings by Lassus, Stadlmayr, Gatto and Zweiller, are at the University of Graz.

H. Federhofer and R. Federhofer-Königs: 'Mehrstimmigkeit in dem Augustiner-Chorherrenstift Seckau (Steiermark)', *KJb*, xlii (1958–9), 98

SEITENSTETTEN. Benediktinerstift, Am Klosterberg 1, 3353 Seitenstetten (*SEI*). Music holdings of the monastery, founded in 1112, include medieval MSS and songbooks, Haydn and Bruckner autographs, 500 first editions of Schubert works, and several thousand printed and MS sacred and secular works from the 18th century onwards.

STAMS. Zisterzienserstift, 6422 Stams (*ST*). The monastery was founded in 1273. There is an illuminated gradual of 1432 in the music archive, but the strength of the collection is chamber music, mainly from 1750 to 1910. There is a large number of unica by people connected with the monastery (particularly Jan Zach) and many works by late 18th- and early 19th-century south German, Tyrolean and Swiss composers, Haydn, and Leopold and W. A. Mozart.

A. Gottron and W. Senn: 'Johann Zach, Kurmainzer Hofkapellmeister', *Mainzer Zeitschrift*, 1 (1955), 81 [discusses 39 previously unknown MSS by Zach]; W. Senn: 'Stams', *MGG*

TULLN. Pfarrkirche St Stephan, Wienerstrasse 20, 3430 Tulln (*TU*). The church has a collection of about 500 sacred works, chiefly MS, used for performance from about 1765 to 1900.

K. Schnürl: *Das alte Musikarchiv der Pfarrkirche St Stephan in Tulln* (Vienna, 1964) [gives incipits for works not listed elsewhere]

VIENNA. General literature: R. Haas: 'Die Wiener Musiksammlungen', *Musikblätter des Anbruch*, vi (1924), 369; L. Nowak: 'Kirchenmusikschätze aus Wiener Bibliotheken', *Singende Kirche*, i (1954), 10; F. Grasberger: *Die Handschriften der Meister: berühmte Werke der Tonkunst im Autograph* (Vienna, 1966) [exhibition catalogue with items chiefly from Viennese libraries]; F. Grasberger: 'Beethoven-Handschriften in Wien', *ÖMz*, xxvi (1971), 41; D. Whitwell: 'Early Small Wind Ensemble MSS in Vienna', *Instrumentalist*, xxviii (1973), Aug, 44 [lists works for fewer than 8 insts in *A-Wgm* and *Wn*]

——. Gesellschaft der Musikfreunde, Bösendorferstrasse 12, 1010 Vienna (*Wgm*). Founded in 1812, the society's collection has become one of the richest in the world, with musicological studies, theoretical works, early editions, 2500 autographs, MS copies, letters of musicians, folksongs, coins, medals, portraits and programmes. The large collection of Austrian music of the 18th and early 19th centuries is based on the estate of Archduke Rudolph, whose legacy included MS autographs of Beethoven and his contemporaries and 130

letters from Beethoven. The library also holds the collection of E. L. Gerber (received in 1819 and containing books and music prints from the 17th and 18th centuries), Czerny (complete works), Johann Strauss, Ludwig von Köchel, Aloys Fuchs (autographs) and a large number of Schubert autographs from the estate of his brother Ferdinand. Brahms bequeathed most of his private collection, which contained many of his own and other valuable autographs, including Beethoven sketches, a volume of Haydn quartets and works by Mendelssohn, Schubert, Schumann and Wagner.

E. Mandyczewski: *Zusatz-Band zur Geschichte der Gesellschaft der Musikfreunde in Wien* (Vienna, 1912) [summary listing of contents of archive, library and museum, arranged systematically]; E. Mandyczewski: 'Die Sammlungen der Gesellschaft der Musikfreunde', *Musikblätter des Anbruch*, iii (1921), 240; K. Geiringer: 'Wie die Sammlungen der Gesellschaft der Musikfreunde entstanden', *Musikblätter des Anbruch*, xix (1937), 276; H. Kraus: 'The Society of the Friends of Music in Vienna and World War II', *Notes*, iii (1945–6), 395; H. Kraus: 'Die Sammlungen der Gesellschaft der Musikfreunde in Wien', *ÖMz*, x (1955), 69; *Notendrucke des 16. und 17. Jahrhunderts* (Vienna, 1965) [exhibition catalogue]; W. Deutsch and G. Hofer: *Die Volksmusiksammlung der Gesellschaft der Musikfreunde in Wien* (Vienna, 1969); K. and I. Geiringer: 'The Brahms Library in the "Gesellschaft der Musikfreunde", Wien', *Notes*, xxx (1973–4), 7

——. Männergesangverein, Bösendorferstrasse 12, 1010 Vienna. Founded in 1843, the society has many printed and MS music works, including Bruckner autographs, about 50 Schubert MSS and some of Johann Strauss. Three versions of the MS by Heinrich Kreissle von Hellborn of his Schubert biography are in the library and about 7400 letters from noted musicians from 1843. There are also copies of Schubert songs once thought to be lost.

C. Landon: 'New Schubert Finds: Hitherto Unknown MSS in the Archive of the Wiener Männergesang-Verein', *MR*, xxxi (1970), 215 [inventory]

——. Minoritenkonvent. Alserstrasse 17, 1080 Vienna (*Wm*). The convent has a collection of 17th- and 18th-century theoretical works, masses, motets, keyboard works and instrumental ensembles (including autographs and sketches by Poglietti). Performance copies of about 600 sacred works of the late 18th and early 19th centuries are listed in an MS inventory of 1934, available in the archive.

F. W. Riedel: *Das Musikarchiv im Minoritenkonvent zu Wien: Katalog des älteren Bestandes vor 1784* (Kassel, 1963)

——. Österreichische Nationalbibliothek, Musiksammlung, Albertina Museum, Augustinerstrasse 1, 1014 Vienna (*Wn*). During the early 1820s the former Hofbibliothek began to receive music from the archives of the court chapel and opera, and from the private library of Emperor Franz I. In 1826 Anton Schmid took charge of this musical material and gave the initial impetus to the organized collection of music. The Musiksammlung has collected very rich holdings of music from all periods, the emphasis being on music of Austrian origin.

Among the initial holdings were 16th- and 17th-century choirbooks (including the Kuttenberger Cantionale), opera scores from the time of Charles VI and the Fugger Collection (purchased and brought from Augsburg to Vienna in 1656; it contains 19 individual MSS of 16th-century choirbooks, partbooks, lutebooks and theoretical works, with compositions by Lassus, Josquin, Mouton, Melchior Schramm, Ockeghem and J. A. Reuss). Further valuable early material includes 14th-century songs by the Benedictine monk Hermann of Salzburg, some Petrucci editions, the discantus and altus partbooks of the first printed edition of Oeglen's

Liederbuch (Augsburg, 1512), a 15th-century MS of Minnelieder by Frauenlob and an organ MS of John Bull.

During the 19th century the Musiksammlung was expanded by various purchases, gifts and bequests, including numerous MSS of Viennese Classical composers, among which the most important are Haydn's *Volkshymne* ('Emperor's Hymn'), *Theresienmesse* and Nelson Mass, Mozart's Requiem and several smaller sacred works, Beethoven's 'Spring' Sonata, Violin Concerto and some letters, and in 1898 a group of Schubert MSS, found in the church of St Peter. Salieri's estate, most of Raphael Kiesewetter's extensive private collection and Bruckner's estate (bequeathed in 1893 and received in 1897), including most of his major works in autograph, also came to the Musiksammlung.

The beginning of the 20th century saw the acquisition of numerous valuable MSS and printed works, including the estate of Cornelius and autographs of Brahms, E. A. Förster, Michael Haydn, Reger, Richard Strauss, Wolf and further works by Bruckner. The archives of the Kärntnertor-Theater, the Haydn-Verein, the Suppé-Museum, the Carl-Theater, the Theater an der Wien, the Josefstädtertheater, the remains of the Haslinger music publishers' archive, and various private collections, in particular those of the theatre director Schreiber and the music historian A. W. Ambros, all came to the Musiksammlung (expanding the large collection of material related to music theatre, librettos, stage and costume designs and ballet scenarios). The collection of the Obizzi branch of the Este family of Modena, including MS and printed music and instruments, came to the library early in the 20th century; it comprises a very large collection of Italian music from the 17th and 18th centuries, including works by (among others) Albinoni, Ariosti, G. and A. M. Bononcini, Caldara, Corelli, Locatelli, Marini, Veracini and Vivaldi.

The Photogramm Archiv, founded in August 1927 by Anthony van Hoboken and presented to the Musiksammlung in 1957, gave an enormous impetus to the library's collection with its photographic and microfilm copies of autographs. The library has also collected Austrian folk music and music of all levels and genres. It is responsible, with the Internationale Bruckner-Gesellschaft, for the Bruckner Gesamtausgabe, edited by Haas and Orel. In 1968 the music collection of the church of St Peter was acquired by the Musiksammlung and in 1974 the private collection of Anthony van Hoboken. As a copyright depository the Musiksammlung receives one copy of every work published or printed in Austria; it also collects contemporary autographs.

R. G. Kiesewetter: *Catalog der Sammlung alter Musik des K. K. Hofraths Rafael Georg Kiesewetter* (Vienna, 1847); C. Rouland: *Katalog des Musik-Archivs der St. Peterskirche in Wien* (Vienna, 1908); R. Haas: 'Die Musiksammlung an der Nationalbibliothek in Wien', *Musikblätter des Anbruch*, iii (1921), 236; R. Haas: *Die Estensischen Musikalien: thematisches Verzeichnis* (Regensburg, 1927); R. Lach: 'Aus dem Handschriftenschätze der Musikaliensammlung der Wiener Nationalbibliothek', *Festschrift zur 200. Jahrfeier der Wiener Nationalbibliothek* (Vienna, 1929), 553; R. Haas: 'Die Musiksammlung der Nationalbibliothek', *JbMP 1930*, 48; L. Nowak: 'Die Musiksammlung', *Festschrift . . . Josef Bick* (Vienna, 1948), 119; L. Nowak: 'Die Musikhandschriften aus Fuggerschem Besitz', *Festschrift . . . Josef Bick* (Vienna, 1948), 505; F. Grasberger: 'Musikhandschriften in der österreichischen Nationalbibliothek', *ÖMz*, x (1955), 100; L. Nowak: 'Das Bruckner-Erbe der Österreichischen Nationalbibliothek', *ÖMz*, xxi (1966), 526; A. Ziffer: *Katalog des Archivs für Photogramme musikalischer Meisterhandschriften, Widmung Anthony van Hoboken* (Vienna, 1967); F. Grasberger: *Die Musiksammlung der Österreichischen Nationalbibliothek* (Vienna, 1970; Eng. trans., 1972); D. Whitwell: 'Early Flute MSS in the Austrian

National Library', *Instrumentalist*, xxvii (1972), Sept, 39; W. Szmolyan: 'Hoboken-Sammlung an die Nationalbibliothek', *ÖMz*, xxix (1974), 625

——. Pfarrkirche St Karl Borromäus, Kreuzherrengasse 1, 1040 Vienna (*Wk*). Music holdings consist of sacred works in MS and 19th- and 20th-century printed editions.

T. Antonicek: *Das Musikarchiv der Pfarrkirche St. Karl Borromäus* (Vienna, 1968–) [complete catalogue of prints and MSS]

——. Stadtbibliothek, Neues Rathaus, 1082 Vienna (*Wst*). Besides its large holdings of printed and MS music works, the library has a collection of autograph letters, theatre and concert programmes, posters and periodical clippings, all indexed. Its special strength lies in autographs and printed works by Austrian composers from the pre-Classical period to the 20th century, including early works by Wolf and MSS of Brahms and Lanner. The library received bequests from the Johann Strauss family, Wilhelm Kienzel, Karl Millöcker, Adolf Müller (i), Suppé and others. Special collections include: Viennese folk music; that of the publishing firm of Artaria; that of the Vienna Tonkünstler-Sozietät; and a collection of Schubert material gathered by Nikolaus Dumba, O. E. Deutsch and Ignaz Weinmann.

A. Orel: 'Die Musikaliensammlung der Wiener Stadtbibliothek', *Denkschrift zu den Meisteraufführungen Wiener Musik*, ed. D. J. Bach (Vienna, 1920), 66; F. Racek: 'Die Musiksammlung der Wiener Stadtbibliothek', *ÖMz*, x (1955), 171

——. Schottenstift, Benediktinerabtei Unserer Lieben Frau au den Schotten, Freyung 6, 1010 Vienna (*Ws*). The abbey's collection is strongest in 18th-century sacred music, although it also has some early liturgical MSS and printed and MS works from the 16th century.

A. Hübl: *Catalogus codicum manuscriptorum* (Vienna, 1899)

ZWETTL. Zisterzienserstift, 3534 Zwettl (*Z*). The monastery was founded in 1138 and its early holdings include 12th- and 13th-century antiphoners, graduals and psalteries, some 16th-century choral fragments and early 18th-century sacred and chamber works. There are many works by Joseph and Michael Haydn and Mozart, and first and early editions of sacred and secular works of the 18th and 19th centuries by Austrian, German and Italian composers.

S. Holzhauser: 'Zwettl', *MGG* [lists many composers represented]

BELGIUM (*B*)

For information on archival and obscure collections, E. vander Straeten: *La musique aux Pays-Bas avant le XIXe siècle* (Brussels, 1867–88/R1969) remains a reliable source. Collections in Antwerp, Brussels, Ghent, Liège, Mechelen and Louvain (the last-named since destroyed) are covered in J.-G. Prod'homme: 'Les institutions musicales (bibliothèques et archives) en Belgique et en Hollande', *SIMG*, xv (1913–14), 458–88, and collections in Brussels, Liège, Mechelen and Tournai (the last-named destroyed in 1940) are described in C. van den Borren: 'Inventaire des MSS de musique polyphonique qui se trouvent en Belgique', *AcM*, v (1933), 66, 120, 177, and vi (1934), 23, 65, 116. Other valuable references are S. Clercx: 'Le problème des bibliothèques musicales en Belgique', *Alumni*, xvi (1947), 227, and B. Huys: 'Belgische en buitenlandse muziekbibliotheken', *Archives et bibliothèques de Belgique*, xxxvii (1966), 172, which discusses musicological research in Belgium and the organization of the music section of the Bibliothèque Royale. MSS of music for wind instruments in the conservatories of Brussels and Liège are listed in D. Whitwell: 'Early Wind MSS in Belgium',

Instrumentalist, xxvii (1973), Jan, 37. The issue of *FAM*, xxiii/3 (1976), is devoted to Belgian music libraries.

ANTWERP. Collegiale en Parochiale Kerk St-Jacob, Lange Nieuwstraat 73, 2000 Antwerp (*Asj*). Apart from the 18th- and 19th-century repertory, the library has music of the 16th–19th centuries published by Plantin, Paisiello MSS and compositions written for this church.

——. Museum Plantin-Moretus, Vrijdagmarkt 22, 2000 Antwerp (*Amp*). In 1876 the city purchased the building (and its contents), occupied since 1576 by the printer Christophe Plantin and his descendants, the Moretus family; it opened as a museum in 1877. The archives contain documents relating to music printing, and the library has about 500 musical works of the 15th–18th centuries issued by various publishers, as well as some MSS. The museum has a collection of punches, matrices and other equipment used in the early printing of music.

J. Denucé: *Inventaris van het Plantinsch Archief* (Antwerp, 1926); J. A. Stellfeld: 'Het muziekhistorisch belang der catalogi en inventarissen van het Plantinsch Archief', *Vlaamsch jaarboek voor muziekgeschiedenis*, ii–iii (1940–41), 5–50; J. A. Stellfeld: *Bibliographie des éditions musicales plantiniennes*, Académie royale de Belgique, Classe des beaux-arts: Mémoires, v/3 (Brussels, 1949) [with historical introduction based on museum's archival documents]

——. Onze-Lieve-Vrouwkathedraal, Groenplaats 21, 2000 Antwerp (*Ak*). The contents of the cathedral's music library are described in the appendix of the work listed. The library contains the private collections of Kennis and Callaerts.

W.-J.-J. Kennis and others: *Muziekcultuur in de Onze-Lieve-Vrouwkathedraal van Antwerpen* (Antwerp, 1968; *Kapittelschriften*, vii)

BRUSSELS. Archives de la Ville, Hôtel de Ville, Grand'Place, 1000 Brussels (*Ba*). The city archives contain a collection of 18th- and 19th-century scores (some autograph) of operas, ballets, musical comedies and vaudevilles, as well as librettos from the city's theatres, in particular the Théâtre de la Monnaie (founded in 1700). There are also theatre programmes, artists' contracts and documents on the administration of the royal theatres.

J. Isnardon: *Le Théâtre de la monnaie depuis sa fondation jusqu'à nos jours* (Brussels, 1890); J. Salès: *Théâtre royal de la monnaie 1856–1970* (Nivelles, 1971) [based on documents in city archives]

——. Bibliothèque Royale Albert Ier/Koninklijke Bibliotheek Albert I, Boulevard de l'Empereur 4, 1000 Brussels (*Br*). After a period from 1886 during which no copyright existed, the royal library became Belgium's only copyright depository in 1965. In the same year the music section was created as a separate division and it receives books and printed music on copyright deposit, but not recordings. The library's collection is based on the royal collections, especially Burgundian and Austrian, and many of the musical treasures in the music section stem from this source. One of the richest royal collections belonged to Margaret of Austria, ruler of Belgium from 1506 to 1530: her library has many masses and motets of the late 15th and early 16th centuries, and her book of *basses danses* (MS 9085). During the late 18th century monastic libraries were dispersed and from this source came many liturgical MSS of which the earliest is the Mont Blandin antiphoner (end of the 8th century). Among the MSS, many types of neume are represented, including Metz, St Gall, Aquitanian and German; there are also early printed liturgical works and theoretical

treatises. The largest part of the library's music holdings was received between 1837 and 1877 from several private collectors. The massive library of the historian Charles van Hulthem was purchased in 1837; among its 30,000 volumes are 250 printed items on music and dance. In 1847 about 20 books of Netherlands polyphonic chansons were purchased from the collection of J.-F. Willems and in 1872 about the same number of books of Netherlands sacred songs from the collection of Serrure. The library was greatly enriched by the purchase, in 1872, of the entire private library of F.-J. Fétis, consisting of over 7000 volumes, almost exclusively on music: printed music from the 16th–19th centuries and books on numerous musical topics (including ancient music and ethnomusicology) in many languages. In 1877 the library acquired 200 musicological works, lute and keyboard tablatures and liturgical music from the collection of Charles de Coussemaker. A collection of 17th- and 18th-century opera librettos and a large number of composers' letters are also in the library.

Bibliotheca Hulthemiana ou Catalogue méthodique de la ... collection ... délaissés par M. Ch. Van Hulthem (Ghent, 1836–7) [music items in vol.ii, nos.9701–834; dance items in vol.ii, nos.9921–44; 3 music MSS in vol.vi, nos.166–8]; *Catalogue de la bibliothèque de F.-J. Fétis acquise par l'Etat belge* (Brussels, 1877/R1969); *Exposition de documents musicaux: manuscrits, imprimés, estampes* (Brussels, 1955) [exhibition catalogue]; A. van der Linden: 'Contribution à l'histoire de la formation d'une bibliothèque musicale [Collection F.-J. Fétis]', *RBM*, xix (1965), 101; B. Huys: *Catalogue des imprimés musicaux des XVᵉ, XVIᵉ et XVIIᵉ siècles, fonds général: Bibliothèque royale de Belgique* (Brussels, 1965) [446 items], suppl. (1974) [445 items]; B. Huys: *De Grégoire le Grand à Stockhausen: douze siècles de notation musicale* (Brussels, 1966) [exhibition catalogue, describes c100 works]; B. Huys: 'La section de musique', *Bibliothèque royale: memorial 1559–1969* (Brussels, 1969), 312; *François-Joseph Fétis et la vie musicale de son temps 1784–1871* (Brussels, 1972) [253-page illustrated catalogue of exhibition celebrating centenary of Belgian government's purchase of Fétis collection]; B. Huys: 'Liturgica met muzieknotatie voor 1800 gedrukt, en bewaard in de Koninklijke bibliotheek van Belgie', *Archives et bibliothèques de Belgique*, xli (1970), 22 [lists 117 liturgical works with musical notation, printed before 1800, specifying type of notation]; B. Huys: *Catalogue des imprimés musicaux du XVIIIᵉ siècle, fonds général: Bibliothèque royale Albert Iᵉʳ* (Brussels, 1974) [754 items]; P. Hooreman: *Catalogue des lettres autographes des musiciens* (in preparation)

——. CeBeDeM, Bibliothèque Royale Albert Ier, Boulevard de l'Empereur 4, 1000 Brussels (*Bcdm*). The Belgian Centre for Music Documentation is an independent organization, supported by the Ministry of Culture, for the propagation of contemporary Belgian music. It holds MS scores and parts of works by contemporary Belgian composers, and has a large collection of programme notes and reference literature on its composer members.

——. Conservatoire Royal de Musique, rue de la Régence 30, 1000 Brussels (*Bc*). Founded in 1832, the conservatory has a diverse collection totalling about 450,000 volumes. It is especially rich in 18th-century works, most notably in the music of the Bach sons (many from the collection of the organist J. J. H. Westphal), and also has many librettos of 17th-century Italian dramas. Among the important private collections are those of Wagener (purchased in 1902), Hollenfeltz (autographs, MSS and first editions of W. A. Mozart and son), Marchot, Piron and documents amassed by Bergmans. Some secular music as well as sacred works were received from the churches of Ste Elisabet in Mons and, in 1929, from the Brussels Cathedral of St Michael and Ste Gudule. The Fonds Ste Gudule consists of about 450 MS works, most of them unknown masses and motets, chiefly by Belgian and Italian composers of the period from about 1675 to 1800.

A. Wotquenne: *Catalogue de la Bibliothèque du Conservatoire royal de musique de Bruxelles* (Brussels, 1898–1912), suppl.: *Libretti d'opéras et d'oratorios italiens du XVIIᵉ siècle* (Brussels, 1901); J. Bacq: *Le fonds Ste Gudule: son origine, sa composition, son importance* (Louvain, 1953); R. B. Lenaerts: 'The "Fonds Ste Gudule" in Brussels: an Important Collection of Eighteenth Century Church Music', *AcM*, xxix (1957), 120

GHENT. Rijksuniversiteit, Centrale Bibliotheek, Rozier 9, 9000 Ghent (*Gu*). The university library has some MS psalters, missals and antiphoners of the 10th–14th centuries, early theoretical works, numerous 16th- and 17th-century editions and a collection of MS and printed music (mainly Flemish) from the 19th century. It also has opera and ballet scores from the Grand-Théâtre and Italian librettos of the late 17th and early 18th centuries, purchased in 1875 from the collection of François du Bus.

J. de Saint Genois: *Catalogue méthodique et raisonné des MSS de la Bibliothèque de la ville et de l'Université de Gand* (Ghent, 1849–52) [music entries described briefly in *MMg*, v (1873), 62]; P. Bergmans: 'Une collection de livrets d'opéras italiens (1669–1710) à la Bibliothèque de l'Université de Gand', *SIMG*, xii (1910–11), 221 [inventory of Du Bus' 32 libs, most of them perf and pubd in Vienna]; A. Derolez: *Beknopte catalogus van de middeleeuwse handschriften in de Universiteetsbibliotheek te Gent* (Ghent, 1971)

LIÈGE. Conservatoire Royal de Musique, rue Forgeur 14, 4000 Liège (*Lc*). The library's collection of old music is based on MSS and printed editions from the 17th and 18th centuries, gathered at the time of the foundation of the conservatory in 1826. This was supplemented by the Debroux Collection (printed scores formerly owned by 18th-century French and Italian violinists, and late 18th-century opera MSS, especially *airs séparés*), and in 1886 the Léonard Terry Collection was placed in the library. Of the approximately 8000 volumes in this collection, about half concern music. The collection was gathered from Terry's music-printer ancestors, from the valuable library of the cathedral (destroyed during the French Revolution) and from Terry's private purchases. There are sacred and secular MSS and printed works by well-known and otherwise unknown composers, publications of Ballard, 16th- to 18th-century treatises and liturgical works, and 19th-century French and Walloon folksongs. The conservatory also has a collection of modern music and composers' letters, including MSS of Franck and Ysaÿe.

E. Monseur: *Catalogue de la Bibliothèque du Conservatoire royal de musique de Liège: Fonds Terry* (Liège, ?1960–)

ZOUTLEEUW. St Leonarduskerk (*Z*). The church has about 50 printed and MS works of the late 18th century.

A. van der Hallen: 'Le fonds musical de l'église Saint-Léonard à Zoutleeuw', *FAM*, iii (1956), 203 [lists all works, with incipits for anon. compositions]

CZECHOSLOVAKIA (*CS*)

A general historical introduction and specific information on current holdings are provided by Z. E. Fischmann: 'Report on Czechoslovakia: some Musicological Sources', *CMc* (1970), no.10, p.44; D. Plamenac: 'Music Libraries in Eastern Europe: a Visit in the Summer of 1961', *Notes*, xix (1961–2), 590, is also still generally informative. A lavish description of several hundred collections in Bohemia is presented by J. Kouba: *Průvodce po pramenech k dějinám hudby: fondby a sbírky uložené v Čechách* [Guide to sources of music history: Czech holdings and collections] (Prague, 1969). The annual music acquisitions of ten important libraries are listed in Z. Zouhar: *Přírůstky hudebnin v československých knihovnách* [Music acquisitions of

Czech libraries] (Brno, 1956–). J. Racek: 'Hudební inventáře a jejich význam pro hudebně-historické bádáni' [Music inventories and their meaning for musicological research], *Časopis moravského musea*, xlvii (1962), 135, discusses inventories in courts, convents and chapels. Thematic catalogues of two collections in Bratislava and Martin are printed in M. J. Terrayová: 'Súpis archívnych hudobných fondov na Slovensku' [Inventory of archival music holdings in Slovakia], *Hudobnovedné študie*, iv (1960), 197–328, and M. Svobodová: 'Tschechoslowakische Musikbibliotheken und Archive', *Musiknachrichten aus Prag*, x (1965), provides an informal survey. Information on polyphonic music is in K. von Fischer: 'Repertorium der Quellen tschechischer Mehrstimmigkeit des 14. bis 16. Jahrhunderts', *Essays in Musicology in Honor of Dragan Plamenac* (Pittsburgh, 1969/R1977), 49, and on lute music in A. Simpson: 'The Lute in the Czech Lands: an Historical Survey', *Journal of the Lute Society of America*, iv (1971), 9, which gives locations and further literature. The State Library in Prague (*Pu*) has begun a series of catalogues which systematically records music collections in the whole country: *Catalogus artis musicae in Bohemia et Moravia cultae* (Prague, 1973–), beginning with early music: *Artis musicae antiquioris catalogorum*.

BANSKÁ ŠTIAVNICA. Farský Rímsko-Katolický Kostol, Archív Chóru, Banská Štiavnica, District of Žiar nad Hronom (*BSk*). The choir archive of the parish Roman Catholic church includes MSS (some autograph) once owned by Ján Jozef Richter and František Hrdina, 18th-century organists at the church.

E. Muntag: *Súpis hodobním z rímsko-katolického kostola v Banskej Štiavnici* [Catalogue of music in the Roman Catholic church in Banská Štiavnica] (Martin, 1969–) [incl. incipits, description of autographs, and index]

BĚLÁ POD BEZDĚZEM. Městské Muzeum, Bělá pod Bezdězem, District of Mladá Boleslav (*BEL*). The collection of the Municipal Museum, inherited primarily from the city's Augustinian church of St Václav, contains a small number of printed and MS (some autograph) compositions from the late 18th and early 19th centuries.

BEROUN. Okresní Archív, 24 budova děkanství, Beroun (*BER*). The District Archive has more than 1200 music items of the 18th and early 19th centuries from the estates of Joseph Anton Seydl and the singer Tekla Podleská-Batková, the latter estate containing vocal material, particularly opera and cantata scores, and church music from the curate church of St Jakub.

J. Holeček: *Hudební sbírky děkana J. A. Seydla* [A musical collection from the estate of Dean J. S. Seydl] (Prague, 1975) [thematic catalogue]; J. Holoček: *Hudební sbírky Tekly Podlesk-Batkov* [A musical collection from the estate of Tekla Podleská-Batková] (Prague, in preparation)

BRATISLAVA. Slovenské Národné Muzeum, Hudobné Oddělenie, Vajanského nábř. 2, Bratislava (*BRnm*). The music division of the Slovak National Museum contains music holdings formerly in Kežmarok and Svedlár; the division, a centre for Slovak music research, has compiled since 1966 a catalogue of material in Slovakia that relates to Slovak music history. The sources are predominantly of the 18th and early 19th centuries; as many are anonymous, incipits are included in the catalogue.

——. Štátny Ústredný Archív Slovenskej Socialistickej Republiky, Krížkova 5, 80100 Bratislava

(*BRsa*). Among the holdings of the Central Slovak State Archive are compositions and MS fragments from Slovakia. The Bratislava capitular library, administered by the archive, has volumes of sacred medieval music.

——. Univerzitná Knižnica, Michalská ulica 1, 88517 Bratislava (*BRu*). Founded in 1919, the university library is based on the collections of several 17th-century libraries and on the bequest of the conductor and teacher Miloš Ruppeldt. It serves as a central research library for Slovakia, receiving legal deposits for Czechoslovakia and collecting literature in all languages. The music collection of some 100,000 items is broad in scope but strongest in Czech and Slovak material.

V. Dvořák: 'Hudobné fondy Univerzitnej knižnice' [Music collections of the University Library], *Univerzitná knižnica v Bratislave 1914–1919–1959* (Martin, 1959), 121 [basic information about music department in jubilee yearbook]; V. Dvořák: *Hudobná pozostalosť' Miloša Ruppeldta v Univerzitnej knižnici v Bratislave* [Miloš Ruppeldt's music bequest to the University Library in Bratislava] (Bratislava, 1967) [describes the bequest of 300 MS and printed works, chiefly Slovak, with incipits and various indexes]

BRNO. General literature: O. Settari: 'Musikalische Drucke und Handschriften in Brünn', *Sborník prací filosofické fakulty brněnské university*, H5 (1970), 151 [describes 34 printed and MS songbooks of various denominations and dating from 1564 to 1784, in either Moravian Provincial Museum or University Library]

——. Státní Vědecká Knihovna, Universitní Knihovna, Leninova 5–7, Brno (*Bu*). The university was founded in 1919 and at that time it absorbed into its library the collection of the Moravian Provincial Museum. Serious collecting of music was begun by the musicologist Leoš Firkušný in 1941, when a separate music section was organized. The collection includes all European style periods. Among the rare MSS and early editions are theoretical works, opera and oratorio librettos and first editions of 18th- and 19th-century composers, including Haydn, Mozart, Beethoven, Schubert and Chopin.

V. Telec: *Erste Drucke der Werke von J. Haydn, W. A. Mozart und L. v. Beethoven in der Universitätsbibliothek in Brno* (Brno, 1966); V. Telec: *Hudební úsek Universitní knihovny v Brně: průvodce hudební fondy* [Music section of University Library in Brno: guidebook to music collections] (Brno, 1968); V. Telec: *Alte Drucke der Werke von tschechischen Komponisten des 18. Jahrhunderts in der Universitätsbibliothek in Brno* (Prague, 1969); V. Telec: *Erstausgaben der Werke von F. Schubert und F. Chopin in der Universitätsbibliothek in Brno* (Brno, 1975); V. Dokopuil: *Hudební staré tisky ve fondech Universitní knihovny v Brně* [Early books on music in the University Library in Brno] (Brno, 1975); V. Telec and V. Dokoupil: *Soupis tisků hudební povahy do r. 1800 z fondů Universitní knihovny v Brně* [Catalogue of printed music to 1800 in the collection of the University Library in Brno] (in preparation)

——. Ústav Dějin Hudby Moravského Musea, Hudebněhistorické Oddělení, Smetanova 14, Brno (*Bm*). In 1919 Vladimir Helfert established a music archive within the then Moravian Museum, which in 1948 became the Institute of Music History of the Moravian Museum. Music from about 150 Moravian churches (such as St Jakub's in Brno) and monasteries (such as the large Benedictine collection of Rajhrad), and private castle collections from Náměšt', Lipník, Petrov (Brno) and elsewhere, were then deposited in the museum. There is a rich collection of material from the 18th and the first half of the 19th centuries and some earlier MSS (e.g. lute, guitar and mandora tablatures), but the institute's principal activity lies in collecting and cataloguing 20th-century sources. The institute houses the separately organized Janáček Archive, with basic

sources for the composer's life and work. It also has Helfert's library and the estates of various Moravian composers. The institute maintains a register of activities related to Moravian music, and inventories of Bohemian and Moravian material held in Czechoslovakia and abroad.

V. Helfert: *Katalog výstavy hudebního archivu Zemského musea v Brně* [Catalogue of the exhibition in the music archive of the regional museum in Brno] (Brno, 1930); M. Krejčí: *Inventař* hudebnin kostel sv. *Jakuba v Brně z r.1763* [Inventory of the music in St Jakub's Church in Brno c1763] (Brno, 1957); T. Straková and others: *Průvodce po archivních fondech: Ústavu dějin hudby Moravského musea* [Guide to archival collections: Institute of Music History of the Moravian Museum] (Brno, 1971) [with Eng., Ger. and Russ. résumés; detailed list of music, writings on music, librettos, instruments, programmes, posters and other iconography, cuttings, microfilms]

ČESKÁ LÍPA. Okresní Archív and Okresní Vlastivědné, Muzeum, Komenského nám. 297, Česká Lípa (*LIa*). The District Archive has a collection of about 3000 printed and MS works from the late 18th–20th centuries, from church choirs in the region. The archive also maintains files of archival material (programmes, inventories, histories) from local musical societies, parish and city offices, and schools.

The District Local History Museum has a collection of early MSS and printed editions of sacred works, the most important being a *Missale romanum* (1515), two psalters (1604 and 1623), two cantionals (1610 and 1712), a MS Latin gradual of the 17th century and another dated 1738.

ČESKÝ KRUMLOV. Pracoviště Státního Archívu Třeboň, Hudební Sbírka, Zámek [Castle], Český Krumlov (*K*). This branch of the State Archive in Třeboň has 6621 sacred and secular works, chiefly German, Czech and Italian, from the estate of Count Philipp Karl von Oettingen-Wallerstein and from the family archive of Prince Ernst zu Schwarzenberg, the Schwarzenberg palace in Vienna and the repertory of its chapel, the Schwarzenberg castle and other branches of the Schwarzenberg family. Catalogued in 1890–91, the collection is rich in works of all genres from the 18th and early 19th centuries and theoretical works. There are Mozart editions and important Haydn MS sources not listed in Hoboken, mostly of Viennese origin and especially rich in wind-band music. In 1967 about 4000 Czech compositions, collected mainly from south Bohemian churches, were deposited in the library.

J. Záloha: 'Díla českých skladatelů 18. a 19. století v česko-krumlovské hudební sbírce' [Works of 18th- and 19th-century Czech composers in the music collection of Český Krumlov], *HV*, ii (1965), 310, 333; J. Záloha: 'Drei unbekannte Autographe von Karl Stamitz in der Musikaliensammlung in Český Krumlov', *Mf*, xix (1966), 408 [relates history and outlines library holdings]; J. Záloha: 'Díla českých skladatelů v dodatcich českokrumlovské hudební sbírky' [New acquisitions by Czech composers in the music collection of Český Krumlov], *HV*, v (1968), 458; J. Záloha: 'Rossica v hudební sbírce v Českém Krumlově [Russian items in the music collection of Český Krumlov], *HV*, vi (1969), 102 [incl. works on Russian themes by Dussek, Steibelt and others]; J. Záloha: 'Über die Herkunft der Musikalien mit der Signatur "C.d'Oetting" in der Schlossmusikaliensammlung in Český Krumlov, ČSSR', *Mf*, xxvi (1973), 55

HRADEC KRÁLOVÉ. Muzeum, Nábořeží protifašistických bojovníků 465, Hradec Králové (*HK*). The museum has MS Latin and Czech graduals, antiphoners and cantionals (notably the *Kancionál Franusův* of 1505) from the 15th–19th centuries, primarily of local provenance. There are also liturgical and vocal polyphonic works printed in the 15th–18th centuries, 18th- and 19th-century compositions inherited from church curates and choir directors in the area, early

19th-century theoretical works, correspondence of musicians, and archival material on musical activities.

D. Orel: *Kancionál Franusův* (Prague, 1922); *Výstava památek hudebního života v Hradci Králové v městském museu od 1. do 21. září 1932* [Exhibition of documents of musical life in Hradec Králové in the Municipal Museum 1–21 September 1932] (Hradec Králové, 1932); J. Černý: 'Soupis hudebních rukopisů muzea v Hradci Králové' [Catalogue of music MSS in the Museum of Hradec Králové], *MMC*, xix (1966), 9–240 [describes 56 MSS of the 15th–18th centuries; in Czech, with Ger. preface]; *Pearls of Old Parchments: Musical MSS of East Bohemia* (Hradec Králové, 1967) [exhibition catalogue]

HRONOV. Muzeum Aloise Jiráska. Hronov, District of Nachod (*H*). The museum has a collection of printed works of the late 18th and early 19th centuries, including autographs by Jiří Jan Novák, Antonín Novák and František Xaver Novák. It also has printed songbooks of 1710.

JINDŘICHŮV HRADEC. Státní Archív, Zámek [Castle], Jindřichův Hradec (*JIa*). This branch of the State Archive in Třeboň possesses two Latin graduals, one dated 1491 and the other also from the second half of the 15th century, and printed and MS works from the 16th–18th centuries. Among the family and institutional archives in the collection are letters, signatures and fragments of autographs by Haydn, Grétry, Kozeluch, Robert and Clara Schumann, Vitásek etc.

——. Vlastivědné Muzeum, Balbinovo nám. 19, Jindřichův Hradec (*JIm*). The Local History Museum has a 16th-century MS gradual, a Czech cantional printed in 1808, and 300 pieces of MS and printed music of the 17th–20th centuries.

KOLÍN. Muzeum Města Kolína, Kolín. The Kolín City Museum has a Czech MS cantional from the first half of the 16th century and fragments of three Latin neumed MSS. There are also MSS of sacred works for voices and instruments and works for piano and flute duet from the first half of the 19th century, and 36 printed compositions and 22 MSS of František Kmoch.

KRALUPY NAD VLTAVOU. Pobočka Okresního Archivu Mělník, Kralupy nad Vltavou, District of Mělník. This is a branch of the Mělník District Archive with material from the Society of the Dvořák Museum of Kralupy, including autograph sketches, compositions and letters by Dvořák. It also has a collection of works (chiefly for piano) from the first half of the 19th century and documents and correspondence regarding musicians and musical societies of the 19th and early 20th centuries.

KŘIVOKLÁT. Zámecká Knihovna, Křivoklát, District of Rakovník. The castle library formerly belonging to Prince Fürstenberg has been entirely catalogued, with a copy deposited in the Národní Muzeum in Prague. The collection includes early missals and psalters, MS German and Italian arias of around 1700, 18th-century opera and oratorio librettos, and some 18th- and 19th-century theoretical works.

KROMĚŘÍŽ. Státní Zámek a Zahrady, Historicko-Umělecké Fondy, Hudební Archív, Sněmovní nám. 1, Kroměříž (*KRa*). In 1927 the music archive of the State Castle and Gardens Art Historical Collection received music holdings from the church of St Mořic, including the collection of Karl Liechtenstein-Kastel-korn, Prince-Bishop of Olomouc. The archivist Antonín Breitenbacher organized this material into three sections, the first comprising 415 printed works of 1545–1891; the second containing over 1000 items

from the Liechtenstein collection, most notable for its 17th-century instrumental works (e.g. autographs of H. I. F. Biber and Vejvanovský; and the third made up of 700 MS sacred works, chiefly of 1770–1900 and predominantly by Viennese composers. The archive also has part of the library of Archduke Rudolph, Beethoven's patron. Among the late 18th- and early 19th-century works are several Beethoven autographs, compositions by the archduke, Mozart, Caldara and Salieri, and important Haydn source material. Music from the Marienkirche and the Piarist college has also been deposited in the archive. A MS thematic catalogue of 1759 is in the Moravian Museum in Brno.

K. Vetterl: 'Das musikalische Nachlass des Erzherzogs Rudolf im erz-bischöflichen Archiv zu Kremsier', *ZMw*, ix (1926–7), 168; A. Breiten-bacher: *Hudební archív kolegiátního kostela sv. Mořice v Kroměříži* [The music archive of the collegiate church of St Mořic in Kroměříž], *Časopis Vlasteneckého spolku musejního v Olomouci*, xl (1928), suppl.; xli–xlii (1929), suppl.; addns in xiii (1930), 1–23; xlviii (1935), 1–9; A. Breitenbacher: *Hudební archív z bývalé piaristické koleje v Kroměříž* [The music archive of the former Piarist college in Kroměříž] (Kroměříž, 1937); E. H. Meyer: 'Die Bedeutung der Instrumentalmusik am fürstbischöflichen Hofe zu Olomouc (Olmütz) in Kroměříž (Kremsier)', *Mf*, ix (1956), 383, repr. in E. H. Meyer: *Aufsätze über Musik* (Leipzig, 1957), 180–221; J. Sehnal: *Hudební literatura zá-mecké knihovny v. Kroměříži* [Music literature in the castle library in Kroměříž] (Gottwaldov, 1960); J. Sehnal: 'Die Musikkapelle des Olmützer Bischofs Karl Liechtenstein-Castelcorn in Kremsier', *KJb*, li (1967), 79–123 [esp. 'Die Musikaliensammlung', 114]; G. Croll: 'Die Musiksammlung des Erzherzogs Rudolph', *Beethoven-Studien*, ed. E. Schenk (Vienna, 1970), 51; J. Sehnal: 'Die Kompositionen Heinrich Bibers in Kremsier (Kroměříž)', *Sborník prací filosofické fakulty brněnské university*, H5 (1970), 21

KUTNÁ HORA. Oblastní Muzeum, Barborská 28, Kutná Hora (*KU*). The District Museum has works collected from the Voršilek monastery, St Jakub's church, and various city and church offices. They include over 1000 MSS from the second half of the 18th to the early 20th century (including Scarlatti, Gluck, Haydn and many others), and about 500 printed works from the 16th–19th centuries, including Handl's *Opus musicum* (Prague, 1586).

H. Oplatková: *Musica kutnohorských archivů* [Music in the Kutná Hora Archive] (Prague, 1960)

LITOMĚŘICE. Státní Archiv, Krajská 1, Litoměřice (*LIT*). The 'monastery collection' comes from Dominican, Augustinian, Cistercian, Capuchin and Minorite houses. It includes MS liturgical compositions of the 17th and 18th centuries.

LOUNY. Okresní Archív, Mírové nám. 57, Louny. The District Archive has a small collection of Latin and Czech graduals of the late 14th–early 17th centuries and sacred works by Cherubini, Haydn, Mozart and Vanhal, copied or printed in the early 19th century. The municipal archive has documents relating to musical activities dating back to the 15th century.

MARTIN. Matica Slovenská, Oddělenie Hudobných Pamiatok, Mudroňova 35, Martin (*Mms*). The library of the Slovak Association's division of musical monuments was founded in 1863 and now serves as the national library of Slovakia. The music holdings were received from private estates, music societies, churches and monasteries (including the Premonstratensian monastery in Jasov). There are MS and printed works of all periods, correspondence, musicological literature, documents concerning Slovak musical culture, Slovak folksongs (including recordings made by Bartók) and Gesellschaftslieder from the beginning of the 18th century to the present. The Szirmay-Keczer collection of folksongs and -dances written between 1625 and 1630 was received by the Literary Archive in 1867.

J. Kresánek: 'Die Sammlung von Szirmay-Keczer', *SM*, vi (1964), 39; B. Ormisová-Záhumenská: *Soupis hudobnín z bývalého premonštratského kláštora v Jasove* [Inventory of printed and MS music from the former Premonstratensian monastery in Jasov] (Martin, 1967) [thematic catalogue]; M. J. Terrayová-Dokulilová: 'Ein Dokument zur Geschichte der Orgelmusik in der zweiten Hälfte des 18. Jahrhunderts', *Sborník prací filosofické fakulty brněnské university*, H2 (1967), 107 [thematic catalogue of a 144-page organ MS from monastery of Malacky]

MĚLNÍK. Okresní Archív, Gottwaldova 246, Mělník (*ME*). The District Archive has a 12th-century evangeliary and a 14th-century missal from the city's chapter library, and various documents, correspondence and iconography from the 19th century (especially relating to Dvořák) and the 20th.

MILEVSKO. Městské Muzeum, Milevsko, District of Pisék. The Municipal Museum has two parchment fragments with neumes, printed liturgical songbooks of the 17th and 18th centuries, and a collection of popular ballads and early 19th-century waltzes in MS.

MLADÁ BOLESLAV. Okresní Archív, Staroměstské nám. 71, Mladá Boleslav (*MB*). Music holdings of the District Archive come from local sources, including the city archive, literary and musical societies, the city Gymnasium, the Piarist library, parish office and private estates. The collection has 17th- and 18th-century cantionals, opera librettos and several hundred MSS of the second half of the 18th and first half of the 19th centuries.

——. Vlastivědné Muzeum, Českobratrské nám. 69, Mladá Boleslav. The Local History Museum has two MS 16th-century graduals and MS Czech cantionals of the 16th and early 18th centuries, as well as printed cantionals and other liturgical books of the same period. Secular works include early editions of operas by Benda and instrumental works of the 18th and late 19th centuries, MS and printed.

MNICHOVO HRADIŠTĚ. Vlastivědné Muzeum, Zámek [Castle], Mnichovo Hradiště, District of Mladá Boleslav (*MH*). The music collection includes printed and MS cantionals from the 17th–19th centuries, early 19th-century MSS from the cathedral, and 19th-century printed works from the synagogue. The separate Castle Library consists of 22,000 items from the Waldstein collection. This contains mainly printed material including two missals (1499 and 1711), 18th-century opera and oratorio librettos, 17th- and 18th-century theoretical works (Burney, Fabricius, Noverre), 18th-century periodicals and music literature of the 17th and 18th centuries.

OLOMOUC. Státní Oblastní Archív v Opava, Pobočka Olomouc, Wurmova ul. č.11, Olomouc (*OLa*). The Olomouc branch of the State Archive in Opava has a small music collection of 11th- to 18th-century MSS from the municipal chapter. The MSS comprise liturgical works and songs. The special archbishopric collection comprises 100 MS and printed scores mainly from the early 19th century.

J. Bistrický, F. Drkal and M. Kouril: *Státní archiv v Opave: průvodce po archivních fondech 3: Pobočka v Olomouci* (Prague, 1961) [guide to archive, listing MSS]

——. Státní Vědecká Knihovna, Bezručova 2, Olomouc (*OLu*). Established in 1566 as the library of a Jesuit College, the present State Scientific Library is the oldest research library in Moravia. It became a university library in 1778 and although most of the music was transferred to Kroměříž before World War II it still holds Baroque works by Biber and others, as well as late medieval MSS with Latin church songs and the St Wenzel Song.

PLZEŇ. Městský Archív, Veleslavínova 19, Plzeň (*PLa*). The music collection of the Municipal Archive derives from several monasteries (including Cheb), gymnasia and private libraries, and comprises liturgical works of the 15th–18th centuries, printed and MS vocal and instrumental works from the 18th–20th centuries, 19th-century MSS of theoretical works, and autograph compositions and letters. There are early and later inventories and catalogues, some with incipits.

M. Belohlávek: *Městský archív v Plzni: průvodce po archivu* (Plzeň, 1954) [guide to archive, pp.190–96 list music]; M. Belohlávek: 'Prámeny k literární historii a dějinám hudby v Městském archivu v Plzni' [Literary and music historical sources in the Municipal Archive in Plzeň], *Archivní časopis*, xi (1961), 37

——. Západočeské Muzeum, Uměleckoprůmyslové Oddělení, Kopeckého sady 2, Plzeň (*PLm*). The Artistic–Industrial Division of the Western Bohemian Museum has a MS Latin gradual of 1531 from the Archdeacon of Plzeň, a MS Latin antiphoner of the 17th century, and MS fragments of 14th- to 16th-century liturgical songbooks, chiefly of foreign provenance. There are printed songbooks and liturgical works dating from 1490 to the 18th century.

PRAGUE. General literature: J. Bužga: 'Kantional (tschechisch)', *MGG* [lists locations in Prague]; J. Bužga: 'Prag', *MGG*; J. Bužga: 'Prager Handschriften', *MGG*

——. Československý Rozhlas, Vinohradská 12, Prague 2-Vinohrady (*Pr*). The Central Archive of Czech Radio in Prague maintains a union catalogue of material in all provincial studios and has a rich collection of Czech and Slovak music.

——. Knihovna Josefa Dobrovského, Maltézské nám. 471, Prague 1-Malá Strana (*Pdobrovského*). The Josef Dobrovský library of 16,000 volumes was formerly owned by Count Nostitz. Now administered by the Národní Muzeum, it includes printed and MS musical and theoretical works of the 16th to the 18th centuries. Among them is a copy (probably the only complete copy extant) of the oldest printed collection of Italian organ music, Antico's *Frottole intabulate da sonore organi* (Rome, 1517).

J. V. Simák: *Rukopisy majorátní knihovny hrabut z Nostitz a Rhienecka v Praze* [MS possessions of the library of Count Nostitz-Rhieneck in Prague] (Prague, 1910)

——. Státní Konservatoř, Dům umělců, Prague 1-Staré Město (*Pk*). The conservatory archive's earliest music holdings consist of printed and MS cantionals and similar vocal works of 1571–1764. MS opera scores of the 18th century include works by Scarlatti, Leo and Mozart. Among the 15,000 items of the 18th and 19th centuries sacred printed works predominate, although there is a considerable number of 17th- and 18th-century orchestral parts (largely MS) from Czech theatres and concerts. 19th- and 20th-century autographs include works by Dvořák, Fibich, Suk and Martinů, as well as by foreigners. There are letters by Wagner, Reinecke and other composers.

R. Prochaszka: *Aus fünf Jahrhunderten: Musikschätz des Prager Konservatoriums, zur Ausstellung anlässlich der Anstalt, Mai 1911: Katalog* (Prague, 1911)

——. Kostel Sv Jakuba, Malá Štupartská 6, Prague

l-Staré Město (*Psj*). St Jakub's church, formerly a Minorite monastery, has a collection of about 900 works of the 18th and early 19th centuries, mainly MSS and including 80 works by F. X. Brixi.

E. Trolda: 'Hudební archív minoritského kláštera u Sv. Jakuba v Praze' [The music archive of the Minorite monastery of St Jakub in Prague], *Cyril*, xliv (1918)

——. Národní Muzeum, Hudební Oddělení, Velkopřevorské nám. 4, Prague l-Malá Strana (*Pnm*). The National Museum began collecting music in the 1860s. An independent music division was formed in 1946 and separate quarters were established in the Velkopřevorský (Grand Prior) Palace in 1950–51. The collection has been enlarged by gifts, bequests and purchases from Jan Pohl, O. Horník, E. E. Homolka, K. Hůlka and others, musical societies (the Bohemian Artists' Organization [Umělecká Beseda], the Mozart Society of the ČSSR) and publishers. More recent acquisitions by the National Cultural Commission include collections from Bohemian castles and monasteries, including part of the large castle library of the Lobkowitz family in Roudnice and others from Doksy (Schloss Hirschberg, from the Waldstein family), Frýdlant (Friedland, of the Counts Clam-Gallas), Kačina (the Counts Chotek) and Rychnov (Kolovrat-Krakovský). There are monastery collections from the Benedictines of Broumov and Břevnov, Premonstratensians of Strahov and Želiv, Cistercians of Osek and many others. The museum's music holdings of over 100,000 works, some of them still uncatalogued, are strongest in compositions of the central European Baroque, pre-Classical and Classical periods, with emphasis on sacred works, chamber and orchestral music. There are many first editions and contemporary MS copies of works by Gluck, Haydn and Mozart. Among the autographs are 39 compositions and 274 letters of Dvořák to Simrock and Hans Richter, bought in the 1930s; other notable autographs of the 19th and 20th centuries include those of Smetana, Fibich, Suk, Janáček and Martinů. Among earlier works in the collection are lute tablatures, 17th-century Czech cantionals and liturgical songbooks of the 17th and 18th centuries. The museum (not the music division) also administers former private libraries still in their original settings (e.g. Mnichovo Hradiště and the Prague Nostitz library). The museum's theatre division (Divadelní Oddělení) has the collection of Oskar Nedbal (*d* 1930) with his own and other compositions, iconography, correspondence and programmes.

P. Nettl: *Beiträge zur böhmischen und mährischen Musikgeschichte* (Brno, 1927), chap. 'Musicalia der fürstlich Lobkowitzschen Bibliothek in Raudnitz'; Z. Blažek: *Bohemica v lobkovickém zámeckém archivu v Roudnici* [Bohemica in the Lobkowitz Castle archive in Roudnice] (Prague, 1936) [thematic catalogue of works by Paul and Anton Wranitzky]; A. Buchner: *Hudební sbírka Emiliána Troldy* [The music collection of Emilian Trolda] (Prague, 1954) [thematic catalogue of 520 Czech sacred vocal works of 1550–1820 in *Pnm*]; O. Pulkert: 'The Musical Department of the National Museum in Prague', *FAM*, ii (1955),112; R. Quoika: 'Über die Pflege weltlicher Musik in der Benediktiner Abtei Braunau in Böhmen', *Musik des Ostens*, i (1962), 198 [with catalogue of abbey library, now in *Pnm*]; J. Tichota: 'Tabulatury pro loutnu a přibuzné nástroje na území ČSSR' [Tablatures for the lute and related instruments in Czech territory], *Acta Universitatis Carolinae*, ii (1965), 139; O. Pukl: 'Zpráva o průzkumu pramenů k dějinámčeské hudby' [News about research into the sources for Czech music], *HV*, iv (1967), 506; A Buchner: *Oskar Nedbal: soupis pozůstalosti* [Oskar Nedbal: catalogue of the bequest] (Prague, 1964–8]; M. Poštolka: 'Libreta strahovské hudební sbírky' [Librettos in the Strahov music collection], *MMC* (1973), nos.25–6, pp.79–124; M. Poštolka: 'Musikerbriefe in der Musikabteilung des Nationalmuseums in Prag', *Beiträge zur Musikdokumentation: Franz Grasberger zum 60. Geburtstag* (Tutzing, 1975), 363

——. Památník Národního Pisemnictví na Strahově, Strahovské nádvoří 132, Prague l-Hradčany (*Ppp*). The library of Strahov monastery, founded in the 12th century by the Premonstratensian order and abolished in 1950, formed the basis of the present National Literature Memorial. The collection has been augmented by the deposit of libraries from other dissolved monasteries, chiefly in central and western Bohemia. Most of the music holdings have been transferred to the Národní Muzeum but some items, particularly those related to Czech literature, have remained here. They include liturgical books of the 16th–19th centuries; theoretical works of the 16th–18th centuries; musical documentation from the estate of B. J. Dlabač (*d* 1820), the monastery's librarian and choirmaster; and correspondence of composers, musicologists and literary figures. The late 15th-century MS DG IV 47, described by Plamenac (*JAMS*, xiii (1960), 102), is now in the Národní Muzeum.

B. Pražáková: 'Bohumír Jan Dlabač ve Strahovské knihovně' [Bohumir Jan Dlabač in the Strahov library], *Strahovská knihovna*, i (1966), 133–71 [inventory of estate]; J. Loužil: 'Literární archív Památníku národního písemnictví' [The literary archive of the National Literature Memorial], *Archivní časopis ročenka* (1968), 79 [with summary of archive contents and further bibliography]

——. Pražský Hrad. [Prague Castle] (*Pp*). The Prague Castle archive, supervised by the president of the republic, has on deposit MSS from the metropolitan chapter (*Pak*), including a troper of 1235 and later liturgical works; 1600 sacred works of the 18th and early 19th centuries, primarily MS; and documents concerned with the operation of the chapter chapel from the 15th century to the 18th. From the chapel of the church of St Kříže the archive has 350 MS and printed sacred works, mainly 19th-century. The archive also has documents concerning the music for 18th-century coronations.

A. Podlaha and A. Patera: *Soupis rukopisů metropolitní kapituly pražské* [Catalogue of MSS in the metropolitan chapter of Prague] (Prague, 1910–22); see also catalogue listed for *Pak*

——. Pražské Metropolitní Kapituly, Hradčanské nám. 10, Prague l-Hradčany (*Pak*). The MSS from the library of the metropolitan chapter of St Vitus Cathedral are in the archive of Prague Castle (*Pp*); the printed works remaining in the library include books of masses by Luython and Monte, psalters, cantionals and other sacred songs (1567–1789), 16th- and 17th-century theoretical works and opera and oratorio librettos (Vienna, 1696–1723).

A. Podlaha: *Catalogus collectionis operum artis musicae quae in bibliotheca capituli metropolitani Pragensis asservantur* (Prague, 1926)

——. Státní Knihovna ČSSR, Universitní Knihovna, Klementinum 190, Prague l-Staré Město (*Pu*). The State Library of the ČSSR was formed after World War II by the amalgamation of the National Library, the State Library of Social Sciences, the Slavonic Library and the important University Library, which dates back to 1348. A separate music division (Hudební Oddělení) of the University Library was created in 1918. Early music MSS and printed works are kept in the department of MSS and rare printed works (Oddělení Rukopisů a Vzácných Tisků). The library has also received, in the 20th century, the collections of many dissolved monasteries, as well as the oldest part of the Lobkowitz Castle collection of Roudnice and private bequests including that of the singer Emmy Destinn. Early music holdings include medieval MSS, theoretical treatises (Listenius and Fux), liturgical works, opera and oratorio librettos and lute tablatures. Since 1782 the

University Library has received on deposit one copy of all Prague publications, and later of all material published in the country. It is also establishing a collection of works by Czech composers published abroad. Many compositions by Dvořák are among the autographs, with fewer works by Smetana, Suk, Fibich and Foerster. Letters from these and many foreign composers are also held. The 'Mozart Memorial' collection, founded in 1837, assembles documents and early editions of the composer's works. The music section is developing a catalogue of the music holdings of all Czech libraries.

R. Eitner: 'Die K. K. Universitäts-Bibliothek in Prag', *MMg*, ix (1877), 171; P. Nettl: *Beiträge zur böhmischen und mährischen Musikgeschichte* (Brno, 1927), chap. 'Musicalia der fürstlich Lobkowitzschen Bibliothek in Raudnitz'; E. Urbánkova': *Rukopisy a vzácné tisky pražské Universitní knihovny* [MSS and early editions in Prague University Library] (Prague, 1957); M. Sovbodová: 'Le département de la musique de la Bibliothèque universitaire de Prague', *FAM*, iv (1957), 7; M. Svobodová: 'Das "Denkmal Wolfgang Amadeus Mozarts" in der Prager Universitäts-Bibliothek', *MJb 1967*, 353–86 [with detailed description of Mozart's works in the memorial]; V. Plocek: 'Nejstarší dvojhlasy v rukopísech Universitní knihovny' [The oldest 2-part settings in MSS of the University Library], *Ročenka Universitní knihovny v Praze 1960–61*, 129; V. Plocek: *Catalogus codicum notis musicis instructorum qui in Bibliotheca publica rei publicae Bohemicae socialisticae in Bibliotheca universitatis Pragensis servantur* (Prague, 1973) [catalogue with 2989 incipits for 243 Lat. and Lat.–Cz. sacred works of the 12th–18th centuries from monastery and university libraries]

ŽITENICE. Pobočka Státního Archivu v Litoměřicích, Žitenice, District of Litoměřice. This branch of the State Archive in Litoměřice (*LIT*) contains the collection of the Prague Loreta church, consisting of sacred music from the late 18th and early 19th centuries, mostly MS copies and contemporary transcriptions. In 1921 the collection was absorbed into the Lobkowitz collection at Roudnice; it was moved to Litoměřice in 1956.

O. Pulkert: *Domus lauretana pragensis: catalogus collectionis operum artis musicae*, Catalogus artis musicae in Bohemia et Moravia cultae: Artis musicae antiquioris catalogorum, i/1 (Prague, 1973) [lists 801 inventoried items; introductory material also in Eng.]

DENMARK (DK)

The office of the national librarian issues an annual catalogue entitled *Music in Danish Libraries: a Union Catalogue* (Copenhagen, 1970–), listing printed music acquisitions in 94 Danish research and major public libraries.

ÅRHUS. Statsbiblioteket, Århus Universitet, Universitetsparken, 8000 Århus (*A*). The library has received depository copies since 1902, when it opened as a state library: in 1937 it took on the added function of university library. The music division was founded in 1904 with a gift from the organist R. C. Rasmussen, which has been supplemented by other gifts. In 1922 the publisher Wilhelm Hansen presented the remains of the lending libraries of the 18th- and 19th-century music publishing firms Lose–Delbanco and Hornemann–Erslev. In 1920 and 1930 the library received valuable additional material from the Society for the Purchase of Foreign Music. The music holdings, about 50,000 items, include standard literature and various 18th-century works. There are also some earlier works, and international folk music material.

Musik, Statsbiblioteket i Aarhus: fagkataloger, iv (Århus, 2/1946) [books about music]; *Musikalier*, Statsbiblioteket i Aarhus: fagkataloger, iii (Århus, 2/1951–70) [music of all types]

COPENHAGEN. Det Kongelige Bibliotek, Christians Brygge 8, 1219 Copenhagen (*Kk*). Denmark's national library has received copyright deposits since 1697. The

music section contains over 100,000 works, including about 3000 from before 1800. Among these are Scandinavian liturgical songbooks of the 11th–19th centuries; lute, guitar and keyboard tablatures; and many autographs of Danish and foreign composers. In 1842 the music department received the bequest of the Danish composer C. E. F. Weyse, with 74 of his own autograph works, other Danish autographs, and early editions of Danish and foreign composers. The department acquired Heinrich Panofka's books of autographs (Beethoven, Schubert, Brahms, Gade and Liszt) in 1972, and has a fragment of the diary written by Wolfgang and Nannerl Mozart in 1780 as well as the 15th-century Copenhagen Chansonnier.

P. Hamburger: 'Ein handschriftliches Klavierbuch aus der 1. Hälfte des 17. Jahrhunderts', *ZMw*, xiii (1930), 133; H. Neeman: 'Laute- und Gitarren handschriften in Kopenhagen', *AcM*, iv (1932), 129; S. Lunn: 'Det Kgl. biblioteks danske musikautografer', *Bogens verden*, xxiii (1941), 353; C. S. Petersen: *Det kongelige bibliotheks håndskriftsamling* (Copenhagen, 1943); S. Lunn: 'Orkesterbiblioteket på Det kongelige bibliotek', *Bogens verden*, xlviii (1966), 517; *Music in Denmark: Summer Exhibition 1972* (Copenhagen, 1972)

——. Det Kongelige Danske Musikkonservatorium, H. C. Andersens Boulevard 36, 1553 Copenhagen (*Kmk*). The library's instructional collection is supplemented by about 100 works printed before 1800 and by about 200 MSS, including one letter each from Beethoven, Mendelssohn, Schumann and Weber and letters of contemporary Danish composers.

Katalog over Det kongelige danske musikconservatoriums musikbibliotek (Copenhagen, 1907)

——. Københavns Universitet, Musikvidenskabeligt Institut, Klerkegade 2, 1308 Copenhagen (*Kv*). The library has a small collection of printed and MS music dating from before 1800, formerly owned by the Danish collector Christian Barnekow.

——. Musikhistorisk Museum, Åbenrå 32–34, 1124 Copenhagen (*Km(m)*). The museum's collection includes the music from the Carl Claudius Musikhistoriske Samling. Made up chiefly of instruments, the collections also contain several hundred MS and printed works from before 1800, including liturgical MSS of the 11th–17th centuries, and two lute tablatures and one organ tablature from the 17th century.

A. Hammerich: *Das Musikhistorische Museum: beschreibender Katalog* (Copenhagen, 1911); *Carl Claudius' samling af gamle musikinstrumenter* (Copenhagen, 1931) [catalogue of insts and early MSS]

FINLAND (SF)

The data from the *Directory of Special Libraries in Finland* (Helsinki, 1958) have been incorporated into, and are superseded by, M. Liinamaa, ed.: *Suomen tieteellisten kirjastojen opas* [Guide to the research and special libraries of Finland] (Helsinki, enlarged 4/1971). It describes 399 libraries and gives their names (and some indexes) in English. The audio-visual aspects of music library service are emphasized in R. Piispanen: 'Music Libraries in Finland 1967', *FAM*, xv (1968), 49. Also helpful is the *Samkatalog över handskriftssamlingar i vetenskapliga bibliotek i Finland*, Helsingfors universitetsbiblioteks stencilserie, iv, vi (Helsinki, 1971–2).

HELSINKI. Helsingin Yliopiston Kirjasto, Unioninkatu 36, 00171 Helsinki 17 (*Hy*). The Helsinki University Library serves also as the country's national library, and has received deposit copies of all material printed in Finland since 1707. From 1820 to 1917 it also received on deposit copies of material published in Russia; those publications are held in the Slavonic collection. The Faltin collection of scores and books on music is in the foreign department; holdings of MS works by Finnish composers and medieval MS fragments of missals and other liturgical works are in the MS department. Music of Finnish origin printed abroad and music published in Finland is in the library's department of Finnish music.

T. E. Haapanen: *Verzeichnis der mittelalterlichen Handschriftenfragmente in der Universitätsbibliothek zu Helsingfors* (Helsinki, 1922–32); T. E. Haapanen: *Die Neumenfragmente der Universität Helsingfors* (diss., U. of Helsinki, 1924)

TAMPERE. Tampereen Yliopiston Kansanperinteen Laitos, Tampere (*TA*). The library of Tampere University has about 20,000 pieces of vocal and instrumental folk music of Finnish origin, some of it primary source material.

TURKU [Åbo]. Sibelius Museum, Piispankatu 17, 20500 Turku 50 (*A*). The museum functions as the Musicological Institute of Åbo Akademi (the Swedish University of Åbo). The collection consists of music, books, letters, iconography and instruments, mostly received as gifts from individuals and institutions, such as the Åbo Musikaliska Sällskapet (founded in 1790). Its valuable library includes 18th-century orchestral and chamber music, especially editions of Hummel, André and Schmitt.

Acta musica: källskrifter och studier (1937–) [museum journal, lists acquisitions]; O. Andersson: *Musikaliska sällskapet i Åbo, 1790–1808*, Skrifter utgivna av svenska litteratursällskapet i Finland, cclxxxiii (Helsinki, 1940) [history of Åbo Musical Society, with account of library on pp.94–126; list of musical works in collection on pp.350–406]; *Svenskt musikhistoriskt arkiv bulletin* (Stockholm, 1966–) [activities and acquisitions of museum regularly mentioned]; G. Reimers: 'Sibelius-museum i Åbo', *Musikkultur*, xxxiii/7 (1969), 8; *Sibelius Museum* (Turku, 1973) [brochure describing activities; lists 473 insts in collection; periodically rev.]; I. Tolvas: 'Sibeliusmuseet i Åbo', *Musikrevy*, xxx (1975), 120

FRANCE (F)

French law requires four copies of music and six copies of books and periodicals published in the country to be deposited at the Bibliothèque Nationale. Publishers are also required to deposit three copies in the regional depository library (for further information see M.-T. Dougnac and M. Guilbaud: 'Le dépôt légal: son sens et son évolution', *Bulletin des bibliothèques de France*, v (Paris, 1969), 283.

Catalogues: *Catalogue général des manuscrits des bibliothèques publiques de France: Départements* (Paris, 1849–85/R1968), *Paris* (Paris, 1885–), new ser. (Paris, 1886–) [includes music MSS]; A. Gastoué: *Catalogue des manuscrits byzantines de la Bibliothèque nationale de Paris et des bibliothèques publiques de France* (Paris, 1928) [in *Pn, B, C, CHR*]; A. Gastoué and others: *La musique française du moyen âge à la Révolution* (Paris, 1934) [many libraries, chiefly Fr.]; *Répertoire des bibliothèques et organismes de documentation* (Paris, 1971, suppl.1973)

Articles: A. Tessier: 'Quelques sources de l'école française de luth au 17e siècle', *IMSCR, i Liège 1930*, 217 [MSS in Aix, Besançon and Paris]; F. Lesure: 'Richesses musicologiques des bibliothèques provinciales', *RdM*, xxxii (1950), 109; N. Bridgman: 'Musique profane italienne des 16e et 17e siècles dans les bibliothèques françaises', *FAM*, ii (1955), 40; P. Chaillon: 'Les fonds musicaux de quelques bibliothèques provinciales de France', *FAM*, ii (1955), 151; V. Fédorov: 'Les bibliothèques musicales françaises', *FasquelleE*; E. Lebeau: 'La recherche musicologique dans les bibliothèques et archives', *Précis de musicologie*, ed. J. Chailley (Paris, 1958), 13; F. Lesure: 'Les bibliothèques des conservatoires en France', *FAM*, xxii (1975), 119

ABBEVILLE. Bibliothèque Municipale, Jardin d'Emonville, place Clemenceau, 80100 Abbeville (*AB*). The library has liturgical MSS of the 11th–18th centuries. A

typewritten supplement to the *Catalogue général des manuscrits ... de France* was prepared by M. Agache-Lecat in 1957.

AGEN. Archives Départementales de Lot-et-Garonne, 3 place de Verdun, B.P. 342, 47000 Agen (*AG*). In 1913 the Bibliothèque Municipale transferred to this library its collection of about 350 Italian, French and German 17th- and 18th-century instrumental and vocal works from the library of the dukes of Aiguillon.

G. Tholin: 'Bibliothèque d'ouvrages de musique provenant du château des ducs d'Aiguillon', *Inventaire-sommaire des archives communales antérieurs à 1790*, 2nd ser. (Paris, 1884), suppl.; J. Robert: 'La bibliothèque musicale du chateau d'Aiguillon', *RMFC*, xiii (1973), 56

AIX-EN-PROVENCE. Bibliothèque Municipale (Méjanes), Hôtel de Ville, 13100 Aix-en-Provence (*AIXm*). The library was originally owned by the Marquis of Méjanes, an 18th-century bibliophile, and was opened to the public in 1810. Among its early sources the library has liturgical MSS of the 13th–19th centuries, 14th-century troubadour songs (including an MS of *Le jeu de Robin et Marion* by Adam de la Halle), and a lute MS (Reynaud MS, no.147) with songs of the 16th and 17th centuries (see A. Tessier: 'Quelques sources de l'école française de luth au 17e siècle', *IMSCR, i Liège 1930*, 217). There are also 18th-century operas, the Boissy collection of theatrical material, and autographs of Félicien David and Milhaud. The Bibliothèque Municipale now has on deposit the collection of the music school of St Sauveur Cathedral (*AIXmc*). The school was founded in the 13th century and its library contains MSS by former *maîtres de chapelle* (including Campra, Gilles and Poitevin). Printed and MS masses and motets by Campra, Lalande, David, Pergolesi and others have not yet been fully catalogued.

F. Raugel: 'La bibliothèque de la maîtrise de la Cathédrale d'Aix-en-Provence', *IAML, ii Lüneburg 1950*, 33

AJACCIO, CORSICA. Bibliothèque Municipale, Palais Fesch, rue Fesch, 20000 Ajaccio, Corsica (*AJ*). Founded in 1801, the library was enriched by Napoleon's deposit of 50,000 early books collected elsewhere. Among them are music and theoretical works of Mersenne, Rameau, Rousseau, Le Sueur and others.

AMIENS. Bibliothèque Municipale, 50 rue de la République, 80000 Amiens (*AM*). The library was founded in 1791 with works from Corbie Abbey (including an early parchment polyphonic MS; see H. Hofmann-Brandt: 'Eine neue Quelle zur mittelalterlichen Mehrstimmigkeit', *Festschrift Bruno Stäblein*, Kassel, 1967, p.109) and elsewhere. Other holdings include operas of 1688 to 1787 (by Campra, Grétry, Monsigny, Quinault and Rameau) and 17th-century theoretical works and liturgical MSS. Works of local composers include operas and sacred MSS by Le Sueur.

J. Garnier: *Catalogue méthodique de la Bibliothèque communale de la ville d'Amiens*, iv (1859), 596

ANGERS. Bibliothèque Municipale, 10 rue du Musée, 49000 Angers (*AN*). Holdings include a 9th-century illuminated MS with a psalter, a 15th-century collection of *prosae* from a Dominican convent and another from Paris, early theoretical works, 17th- and 18th-century music, and piano scores of operas by local composers.

A. Lemarchand: *Catalogue des manuscrits de la bibliothèque d'Angers* (Angers, 1863); A. Lemarchand: *Catalogue des imprimés de la bibliothèque d'Angers* (1871–5); X. Barbier de Montault: 'Antiphonaires et lectionnaires manuscrites de la Bibliothèque publique d'Angers', *Revue d'Anjou*, ii (1897), 241

ANNECY. Bibliothèque Municipale, Hôtel de Ville, 74000 Annecy (*ANN*). The library was founded in 1744 and later received the library of the cathedral chapter of St Pierre. The Martin collection contains about 200 works of the Classical period.

APT. Cathédrale Ste Anne, 84400 Apt (*APT*). The chapter library holds two 11th-century tropers, a 14th- or 15th-century mass and an important polyphonic MS of the late 14th century.

J. Sautel: 'Catalogue descriptif des manuscrits liturgiques de l'église d'Apt', *Annales d'Avignon et du Comtat venaissin* (1919), 53; P. L. Neveux and E. Dacier: *Les richesses des bibliothèques provinciales de France* (Paris, 1932), i, 32f; H. Besseler: 'Apt', *MGG*

ARLES. Bibliothèque Municipale, 35 place de la République, 13200 Arles (*AR*). 17th- and 18th-century works include an autograph and papers of Destouches, *ariettes* and *airs*, *cantiques spirituels* from Provence and other French regions, and a unicum of Vivaldi.

ARRAS. Bibliothèque Municipale d'Arras, Palais St Vaast, 20 rue Paul-Doumer, 62000 Arras (*AS*). The collection (based on the library of the Benedictines of St Vaast) includes an 11th-century collection of *prosae*, two 13th-century polyphonic MSS, and some music from the 17th–19th centuries that was not destroyed in the bombing of July 1915. There are also several works related to the trouvère repertory.

Z. Caron: *Catalogue des manuscrits de la Bibliothèque de la ville d'Arras* (Arras, 1860)

AUTUN. Bibliothèque Municipale, Hôtel de Ville, place du Champ de Mars, 71400 Autun (*AUT*). The library was founded in 1792 with works from various religious communities, including a 7th–8th-century Visigothic MS, a 9th–10th-century Aquitanian sequence and a 12th–13th-century parchment MS with monodic and polyphonic works.

AUXERRE. Bibliothèque Municipale, 9 place du Maréchal Leclerc, 89000 Auxerre (*AU*). The library has several 18th-century song MSS and early 19th-century scores. Important collections are those of Claude (chamber music), Leblanc-Duvernoy (chamber music and musicology), H. Brochet (theatre) and Corte (scores and musicology).

Collection Le Blanc Duvernoy, musique instrumentale et vocale, livres de biographie et d'esthétique musicale: catalogue (Auxerre, 1907)

AVIGNON. Bibliothèque Municipale, Musée Calvet, 65 rue Joseph-Vernet, 84000 Avignon (*A*). The library has its origins in the 1810 bequest of Esprit Calvet. Among its rarities are liturgical MSS of the 9th–13th centuries, sacred and secular music of the 17th and 18th centuries from the city's former Académie de Musique, and late 17th–early 19th-century operas from the library of Castil-Blaze and the city's early theatres. The Requien collection includes autograph works of Adolphe Adam, Berlioz, Cherubini, Liszt, Rossini and others. Various records of the city's musical activities (including those of the Société Ste Cécile) have been deposited here from the notarial archives.

MSS à la Bibliothèque d'Avignon (*F-Pn* Vmd. 1) [compiled early 20th century incl. printed works]

AVRANCHES. Bibliothèque Municipale, Hôtel-de-Ville, place Littré, 50300 Avranches (*AVR*). The collection includes two 12th-century parchment MSS from the monastery of Mont-St-Michel.

J. Martin: *La Bibliothèque d'Avranches: ses origines et ses richesses* (Caen, 1933)

BERNAY. Bibliothèque Municipale, Hôtel de Ville, 27300 Bernay (*BER*). A collection of 17th- and early 18th-century works comprises operas of Collasse, Lully and others, as well as cantatas of Clérambault.

Catalogue de la Bibliothèque de Bernay (Bernay, 1877)

BESANÇON. Bibliothèque Municipale, 1 rue de la Bibliothèque, 25000 Besançon (*B*). The rich collection of early works includes medieval liturgical works with musical notation, theoretical treatises of Besard, Mersenne, Rousseau and Zarlino, 16th-century sacred music, 17th-century lute and theorbo music (by Jacquesson, Visée and others), and 17th- and 18th-century works (ballets, cantatas, divertissements, motets, operas) by Campra, Charpentier, Collasse, Destouches, Lully and others. There is also a collection of works by local composers.

Catalogue des livres imprimés de la Bibliothèque de Besançon: sciences et arts (1842–75), i, 366ff; C. Becker: 'Besançon', *MGG*, suppl. [list of holdings]

BORDEAUX. Bibliothèque Municipale, 3 rue Mably, 33075 Bordeaux (*BO*). Music of the 16th–19th centuries was received in the bequests of Clapisson, Ferroud and the widow of Spontini. The library received on deposit 1227 scores and librettos of the 18th and 19th centuries from the Grand Théâtre of Bordeaux.

I. Delas: *Catalogue des livres composant la bibliothèque de Bordeaux*, ix (1856) [list of 1000 musical items]; J. Delpit: *Catalogue des manuscrits*, i (1880), 37ff, 235ff

CADOUIN. Bibliothèque de l'Abbaye, 24480 Cadouin (*CAD*). The Cistercian monastery has 24 MSS, including antiphoners, sacramentaries, and graduals with musical notation.

S. Corbin: 'Le fonds manuscrit de Cadouin', *Bulletin de la Société historique et archéologique du Périgord*, lxxxi (1954), suppl., 1–33

CAEN. Bibliothèque Municipale, place Louis-Guillouard, 14037 Caen (*CN*). The origins of the library are in the former university library, which had as its basis an 18th-century Jesuit collection. Among the musical items are MSS by Léopold Bossy, a local composer of the 19th century.

J. Carlez: 'Liste des oeuvres musicales et des ouvrages relatifs à la musique qui se trouvent à la bibliothèque de la ville de Caen', *Bulletin de la Société des beaux-arts*, iv (1868), 244

——. Conservatoire National de Musique, place Louis-Guillouard, 14037 Caen (*CNc*). The conservatory has works by 18th-century French composers (Berton, Bury, Dauvergne, Francoeur, Saint Georges, etc).

CAMBRAI. Bibliothèque Municipale, 37 rue St Georges, 59400 Cambrai (*CA*). Among the library's rich holdings of early works are 12th-century theoretical works and 15th-century choirbooks from the cathedral that was destroyed in 1793. There are also *airs profanes et sacrés* in 16th-century MSS, sacred works of the Flemish–Burgundian school and 18th-century masses.

C. E. H. de Coussemaker: *Notice sur les collections musicales de la Bibliothèque de Cambrai* (Paris, 1843/R1970, 1972 and 1975); G. Reese: 'Maldeghem and his Buried Treasure', *Notes*, vi (1948–9), 75–117

CARCASSONNE. Bibliothèque Municipale, 1 rue de Verdun, 11012 Carcassonne (*CC*). A collection of 16th-century Italian madrigals includes rare Venetian editions of Alessandro Gabrieli, Marenzio and Nanino. The library has received gifts (including personal papers) from the family of the poet André Chenier.

CARPENTRAS. Bibliothèque Municipale (Inguimbertine), 234 boulevard Albin-Durand, 84200 Carpentras (*C*). The library was founded by Inguimbert, Bishop of Carpentras, who opened his collections to the public in 1747. The J.-B. Laurens collection comprises autographs of Bach, Schumann and others, vocal and instrumental music of the 17th–19th centuries, letters, portraits and other materials. There are also sacred works of the 12th and 13th centuries.

R. Caillet: *Catalogue de la collection musicale J.-B. Laurens* (Carpentras, 1901); R. Caillet: *Trésors des bibliothèques de France*, iii (Paris, 1930), chap. 'Les portraits des musiciens par Bonaventure Laurens à la bibliothèque de Carpentras'; R. Caillet and E. Göpel: 'Ein Brahmsfund in Südfrankreich', *ZMw*, xv (1932), 371

CHÂLONS-SUR-MARNE. Archives Départementales de la Marne, 1 rue des Buttes, 51000 Châlons-sur-Marne. A set of nine parchment bifolia, dating from the second quarter of the 13th century and containing music of the Notre Dame school, has been removed from its binding.

R. Gandilhon and J. Hourlier: *Inventaire sommaire de fragments de manuscrits . . . conservés aux Archives de la Marne* (Châlons-sur-Marne, 1956)

———. Bibliothèque Municipale, 1 passage Henri-Vendel, 51000 Châlons-sur-Marne (*CSM*). The library has motets of the Notre Dame school and some 16th-century sacred music.

CHANTILLY. Musée Condé, Château de Chantilly, 60500 Chantilly (*CH*). The library is part of the Institut de France and specializes in art and history. There is a precious Ars Nova MS (564; formerly 1047), a collection of chansons and noëls and music of the 15th–18th centuries.

H. d'Aumale and G. Macon: *Chantilly, le cabinet des livres: manuscrits* (Paris, 1910–11), ii, 277ff; G. Reaney: 'The MS Chantilly, Musée Condé 1047', *MD*, viii (1954), 59–114, and x (1956), 55

CHARTRES. Bibliothèque Municipale, 35 rue St Michel, 28000 Chartres (*CHR*). Although most of the library's treasures (early liturgy and theoretical works, 18th-century MS operas, ballets and cantatas) were destroyed in 1944, some fragments survive and copies of others are available.

Y. Delaporte, ed.: *Les manuscrits de chant liturgique de la Bibliothèque municipale de Chartres*, PalMus, 2nd ser., xvii (1959); V. Fédorov: 'Chartres', *MGG*

CHERBOURG. Bibliothèque et Archives Municipales, 13–15 rue Thiers, 50100 Cherbourg (*CHE*). In addition to operas by the 19th-century composers Adam, Aubert, Halévy and others, the library has an 18th-century collection of *airs, menuets*, marches and rondeaux (1749) and *Tendresses bachiques* (1711–18).

CLERMONT-FERRAND. Bibliothèque Municipale et Universitaire, 1 boulevard Lafayette, B.P. 27, 63001 Clermont-Ferrand (*CF*). The university library (founded in 1880) was joined to the city library in 1905. Holdings include many liturgical MSS (no.73 described by M. Huglo in 'Trois anciens manuscrits liturgiques d'Auvergne', *Bulletin historique et scientifique de l'Auvergne*, lxxvii, 1957, p.100) and the Grenier–Haynl collection of 19th-century scores. The library of the city's Académie des Sciences, Belles-Lettres et Arts is on deposit.

COLMAR. Bibliothèque Municipale, 1 place des Martyrs de la Résistance, 68000 Colmar (*CO*). Among the liturgical MSS are missals, graduals and antiphoners of the 11th–15th centuries. The Charles Sandherr collection of music history and theory was received during the period 1876 to 1885. Since 1972 the library has held the collection of the Consistoire de l'Eglise de la Confession d'Augsbourg à Colmar, rich in early 16th-century psalters, in many languages, that contain music.

A. Roth: 'En marge d'une exposition "La musique religieuse en Alsace au moyen âge" ', *Caecilia*, lxii (1954), 135 [lists liturgical works in the library]; P. Bolchert: *Catalogue de la bibliothèque du Consistoire de l'Eglise de la confession d'Augsbourg à Colmar* (Strasbourg and Colmar, 1955–60); F. A. Göhlinger: 'Die Stadtbibliothek von Colmar und ihre reichen Schätze an Gradualien, Antiphonarien, Psalterien, Hymnarien vom 11. bis 15. Jahrhundert', *Caecilia*, lxv (1957), 243

DIEPPE. Bibliothèque Municipale, boulevard Général de Gaulle, 76200 Dieppe (*DI*). The library possesses the private collection of Saint-Saëns, with his own works and those of others, as well as letters, documents and other items. These may be found in the museum, in the Vieux-Château. An inventory of the collection is being prepared by Yves Gérard.

DIJON. Bibliothèque Municipale, 5 rue de l'Ecole-de-Droit, 21000 Dijon (*Dm*). The library was founded in the early 18th century at what had been a Jesuit school. It holds a number of musical MSS, including a 15th-century chansonnier (no.517) with about 160 works of Barbingant, Busnois, Ockeghem and others (see review by M. Picker in *JAMS*, xxvi (1973), 336, for contents, and *Veröffentlichungen–mittelalterlicher Musikhandschriften*, xii (1971), for a facsimile edition; another 15th-century MS, no.2837, is described by C. Wright in 'A Fragmentary Manuscript of Early 15th-century Music in Dijon', *JAMS*, xxvii (1974), 306). Among its imprints is a copy of Rameau's *Traité de l'harmonie* annotated by the author.

———. Ecole Nationale de Musique et d'Art Dramatique de Dijon, 5 rue de l'Ecole-de-Droit, 21000 Dijon (*Dc*). Housed in the same building as the public library but independent from it, the school's largest collection is the bequest of Count Kerveguen in 1897 of about 11,500 musical works.

DOUAI. Bibliothèque Municipale, rue de la Fonderie, 59500 Douai (*DOU*). A collection of liturgical works from the 10th–12th centuries includes a hymnary, missal and two-part sequence with Metz neumes, some coming from the abbey of Anchin.

EPERNAY. Bibliothèque Municipale, 13 avenue de Champagne, 51200 Epernay (*EP*). From various religious houses the library has acquired liturgical MSS of the 9th–13th centuries. There are also some musical works of the 17th and 18th centuries.

L. Paris: *Bibliothèque d'Epernay: catalogue des manuscrits et imprimés*, ii (1894), 270 [list of musical works]

EPINAL. Bibliothèque Municipale, 2 rue de Nancy, 88000 Epinal (*E*). The library has secular works of the 16th–18th centuries, especially chansons.

E. Martin: 'En marge des vieux livres de la bibliothèque d'Epinal', *Bulletin de la Société d'émulation des Vosges* (1928), 61, 72

GRENOBLE. Bibliothèque Municipale, 3 boulevard Maréchal Lyautey, 38000 Grenoble (*G*). Founded in 1772, the library received works from the abbeys of St Antoine of Viennois and of the Grande Chartreuse. Holdings include a 13th-century plainsong MS (no.124), 17th-century sacred MSS, the Salette collection of 18th-century MS and printed works, autograph and printed works of Berlioz, and *c*150 scores of Dauphinois composers. There are also letters of Stendhal and the Ulysse Chevalier collection of the history and bibliography of liturgy.

P. Vaillant and J. Leymarie: *Exposition Hector Berlioz* (1953) [catalogue]

LAON. Bibliothèque Municipale, rue du Bourg, 02000 Laon (*LA*). The library was founded in 1794 and received liturgical MSS of the 9th–13th centuries from the city's Notre Dame cathedral and from other religious establishments. There is also a collection of 19th-century autographs.

LE MANS. Bibliothèque Municipale, 102 rue Gambetta, 72000 Le Mans (*LM*). The library was founded during the Revolution with works from various sacred archives. Among its holdings are a 9th-century evangeliary, 16th-century French sacred works, sonnets of Ronsard set to music by Guillaume Boni (1576), and vocal and instrumental works of 17th- and 18th-century composers (Lully, Lebègue, La Barre, Bataille, Blavet, Marais).

F. Guérin: *Catalogue de la Bibliothèque du Mans: sciences et arts* (1879), 474ff

LILLE. Bibliothèque Municipale, 32–4 rue Edouard Delesalle, 59000 Lille (*Lm*). The library was opened in 1726 with works from the chapter of St Pierre, including a 13th-century parchment MS. It later received the material confiscated in the Revolution and the archives of the Académie de Musique, Société des Concerts and Théâtre Municipal. Other holdings include autographs of Rousseau's *Dictionnaire de la musique* and Béranger's chansons, as well as *opéra comique* from the 17th–19th centuries and operas (especially librettos) of the 18th and 19th centuries.

Catalogue de la Bibliothèque de la ville de Lille: sciences et arts (1879), 515–1225 [suppl.]

LIMOGES. Bibliothèque Municipale, 6 place de l'Ancienne-Comédie, 87032 Limoges (*LG*). Among the works received from former religious institutions are a 13th-century antiphoner from the chapter of St Jumien and a 14th-century parchment gradual containing sequences (see L. Guibert: 'Le graduel de la Bibliothèque communale de Limoges', *Bulletin historique et philologique du Comité des travaux historiques et scientifiques* (Paris, 1887), 323–65).

LYONS. Bibliothèque Municipale, 30 boulevard Vivier-Merle, 69431 Lyons (*LYm*). The library originally belonged to the Collège de la Trinité, which had received gifts from Richelieu, Mazarin, Henry IV and others, and became public in 1765. Among its valuable holdings are the autograph of Rousseau's *Le devin du village* and editions of Jacques Moderne (1557). Its special collections include those of Georg Becker (1500 French and German works of music history); Vautier (19th-century scores, including works by Berlioz); the Académie du Concert (18th-century works); and the Académie d'Opéra (18th-century operas and cantatas).

MÂCON. Bibliothèque Municipale, place des Carmélites, 71000 Mâcon (*MAC*). Holdings include operas of Collasse, Destouches and Lully in Ballard editions, and early editions of works by Rameau and Caix d'Hervelois.

MARSEILLES. Conservatoire de Musique et de Déclamation, 1 rue de la Bibliothèque, 13013 Marseilles (*Mc*). In addition to works by Provençal composers, the library has MSS of 17th-century cantatas and other vocal works of the 17th and 18th centuries.

MELUN. Bibliothèque Municipale, 5 rue du Franc-Murier, 77000 Melun (*MEL*). The library holds ten early works by Campra, Marais and Nivers, as well as the Vincent collection of autographs.

METZ. Bibliothèque Municipale, 2 rue du Haut-Poirier, 57036 Metz (*MZ*). Most of the music MSS owned by the library were destroyed in World War II. Among the works received from Metz Cathedral and other religious and private sources are 11th- and 12th-century theoretical works and a troper dated 878 from the St Arnould abbey in Metz.

MONTAUBAN. Bibliothèque Municipale, square du Générale Picquart, 82000 Montauban (*MON*). There is a rich fund of 18th-century opera and chansons of La Borde. The Lacroix collection contains 18th-century music.

MONTPELLIER. Bibliothèque de la Ville et du Musée Fabre, 37 boulevard Bonnes Nouvelles, 34000 Montpellier (*MOv*). Founded with archives confiscated during the Revolution, the library is named after F.-X. Fabre, who donated works in 1825. In addition to liturgical works of the 10th–13th centuries, the collection is rich in folksongs and literature of France, Spain and Italy, and particularly Catalonia, Provence and Languedoc.

Catalogue de la Bibliothèque de la ville de Montpellier (Montpellier, 1875–98)

——. Université de Montpellier, Bibliothèque Universitaire, Section Médecine, 2 rue de l'Ecole de Médecine, B.P. 1135, 34060 Montpellier (*MO*). The library has a small but valuable collection of music MSS which includes the 400-page MS H196, the most important source of 13th-century motets; an 11th-century MS of Gregorian chant from St Bénigne Abbey in Dijon (H159); and a 12th-century organum treatise on two pages of H384. Cardinal Albani's collection of letters from Queen Christina of Sweden includes some to musicians.

Y. Vidal: 'La bibliothèque de la Faculté de médecine de Montpellier', *Montpellier médical*, 3rd ser., liv (1958), July–Aug, 77 [bibliography]; G. Reaney: 'Montpellier-Handschriften', *MGG*

MULHOUSE. Bibliothèque Municipale, 19 Grand'rue, 68100 Mulhouse (*MH*). The library has a 15th-century antiphoner and a parchment gradual from the early 16th century. There are also MS works of Boccherini and a considerable collection of musicological literature. In 1950 the conservatory library was incorporated into the collection.

Catalog der Stadtbibliothek von Mülhausen (1890–93)

NANTES. Bibliothèque Municipale, 37 rue Gambetta, 44000 Nantes (*Nm*). The library is based on the collection ceded to the city in 1753 by the Oratorians. In addition to liturgical works acquired during the Revolution, the library has 17th- and 18th-century vocal and instrumental music.

E. Péhant: *Catalogue méthodique de la Bibliothèque de Nantes: arts*, ii (1861), 646; A. Bloch-Michel and others: *Richesses de la Bibliothèque municipale* (1965) [exhibition catalogue]

——. Musée Thomas Dobrée, place Jean-V, 44000 Nantes (*Nd*). In the encyclopedic collection left to the city by the businessman Dobrée in 1895 are 16th-century chanson collections published by Du Chemin and Attaingnant, 17th-century *airs de cour* and ballets, and 18th-century operas.

Catalogue de la bibliothèque du Musée Th. Dobrée (1903–4); P. de Lisle du Dréneuc: *Catalogue sommaire de la bibliothèque du Musée Th. Dobrée: sciences et arts* (1905), 57, 122, suppl. (1908), 30

NARBONNE. Bibliothèque Municipale, Hôtel de la Ville, rue Jean-Jaurès, 11100 Narbonne (*NAR*). The collection includes a 13th-century antiphoner and some printed and MS music of the 17th and 18th centuries.

J. Tissier: *Catalogue de la Bibliothèque publique de la ville de Narbonne* (Narbonne, 1891)

NICE. Bibliothèque Municipale, 21*bis* boulevard Dubouchage, 06047 Nice (*NI*). The library has its origin in the archive of the cathedral chapel and was later enriched with works from local convents and from the former library of the princes of Monaco. It holds 16th-century editions of treatises by Aaron and Gaffurius, a collection of 17th-century opera programmes and, in the bequests of the Count of Falicon and President Tardieu, 488 scores (including 18th- and 19th-century operas and chansons).

NÎMES. Bibliothèque Municipale (Séguier), 19 Grand'rue, 30000 Nîmes (*NS*). The library was opened to the public in 1794 with collections from local convents and private holdings. There is a 16th-century choirbook, works by Boismortier, Corelli and Grétry and parts to 17th- and 18th-century cantatas and operas. The Sabatier collection comprises 18th- and early 19th-century operas.

ORLEANS. Bibliothèque Municipale, 1 rue Dupanloup, 45043 Orleans (*O*). There is a collection of sacred and secular works of the 16th century, including poems of Ronsard set to music by Regnard (see IMa, 1st ser., ii, for an edition of MS 201, which contains *rappresentazioni sacre*, and S. Corbin: 'Le MS 201 d'Orléans, drames liturgiques dits de Fleury', *Romania*, lxxiv (1953), 1–45). The library also has 12th-century mystery plays and a 13th-century collection entitled *Sermons et tragédies* containing music.

C. Cuissard: *Bibliothèque publique d'Orléans: catalogue des incunables et des éditions rares* (1895); *Bulletin des bibliothèques de France*, viii (1963), 103 [report of a Debussy–Massenet exhibition]

PARIS. General literature: J.-G. Prod'homme: 'A Musical Map of Paris', *MQ*, xviii (1932), 607; F. Lesure: 'Musique et musicologie dans les bibliothèques parisiennes', *Bulletin des bibliothèques de France*, iii (Paris, 1958), 259

——. Bibliothèque de l'Arsenal, 1 rue de Sully, 75004 Paris (*Pa*). A public institution since 1797, the library became a branch of the Bibliothèque Nationale in 1926. The collection is rich in missals, breviaries, graduals, psalters and other sacred books of the 9th–16th centuries, some of them confiscated during the Revolution. The MS department also has early secular works, including 13th-century collections of chansons, 18th-century anthologies of various kinds of songs and instrumental pieces mostly from the period 1770–80, as well as operas and keyboard works. The department of printed works has a few items of the 16th and 17th centuries (polyphonic works of Conversi, Monte and Striggio) and collections of *airs* by Lambert, Bousset and Gillier as well as ballets and operas by Collasse, Lully and Marais. 18th-century operas, *opéras comiques* and cantatas constitute the largest part of the vocal holdings, but there are also printed *airs*, *ariettes*, *cantiques* and hymns. There are also several hundred instrumental works (chiefly for chamber ensembles) of the 17th and especially the 18th century. The library's collection of theatre material is exceptional and includes the collections of August Rondel (formerly at the Comédie Française), Georges Douay, Edward Gordon Craig, Gabriel Germinet-Vinot, and that of the Théâtre des Variétés. Among the purely dramatic items are scores, librettos and iconography related to music.

L. de La Laurencie and A. Gastoué: *Catalogue des livres de musique (manuscrits et imprimés) de la Bibliothèque de l'Arsenal à Paris*, *PSFM*, 2nd ser., vii (1936); J. von Gardner: 'Altrussische Musik-Handschriften der Bibliothèque de l'Arsenal', *AcM*, xxxviii (1966), 189, xlii (1970), 221–55; M. Bernard: *Répertoire de manuscrits médiévaux contenant des notations musicales*, iii: *Bibliothèques parisiennes, Arsenal* (Paris, 1974)

——. Bibliothèque Mazarine, 23 quai de Conti, 75006 Paris (*Pm*). Cardinal Mazarin's personal library was opened to scholars in 1643, making it the oldest public library in France. In 1926 it was attached to the Bibliothèque Nationale, but it has been part of the Institut de France since 1945. Rare items include a 15th-century missal and evangeliary and a 13th-century parchment MS containing a motet. There are also printed 16th-century works (some published by Attaingnant) of Colin, Janequin, Sermisy and others.

M. Bernard: *Répertoire des manuscrits médiévaux contenant des notations musicales*, ii: *Bibliothèque Mazarine* (Paris, 1966)

——. Bibliothèque–Musée de l'Opéra, 1 place Charles Garnier, 75009 Paris (*Po*). The most important holdings are the scores and parts of works performed at the Opéra since 1671, many of them autographs; the Silvestri collection is rich in librettos. In 1952 the library received from Rolf de Maré his archive of international dance documentation from the 15th century and later. Books and papers belonging to the former librarian Charles Nuitter, and more recently, the collections of Jules Barbier and Jacques Rouché have been deposited. The library has works on the history of opera and ballet, as well as on costume and stage design.

T. Lajarte: *Bibliothèque musicale du théâtre de l'Opéra: catalogue historique, chronologique, anecdotique* (Paris, 1878); C. Malherbe: 'Archives et bibliothèque de l'Opéra', *RHCM*, iii (1903), 269; J.-G. Prod'homme: 'Etat alphabétique sommaire des archives de l'Opéra', *RdM*, xiv (1933), 193; P. Tugal: 'Un centre de documentation unique: les archives internationales de la danse', *ReM* (1937), no.175, p.71; J.-G. Prod'homme: 'Two Musical Libraries of Paris', *MQ*, xxv (1939), 34; J. Corday: *Le Musée de l'Opéra* (Paris, 1945)

——. Bibliothèque Nationale, 75002 Paris (*Pn*). There are many important music MSS in the Department of Manuscripts in the main building (59 rue de Richelieu): liturgical and theoretical works from the 9th century and later; 13th-century troubadour songs; French and Italian polyphonic music from the 13th–16th centuries; 15th- and 16th-century chansonniers; and the James de Rothschild collection of 16th-century imprints.

The Music Department of the library (at 2 rue Louvois) is based on the former Royal Library, to which many later gifts and bequests were added, among them the Brossard collection of 16th- and 17th-century works. When the valuable holdings of the Conservatoire were moved to the department in 1964, the following were incorporated: part of the Philidor collection of 17th-century music; works of the Menus-Plaisirs du Roi (17th–19th centuries); the Blancheton gift of pre-1750 instrumental works; Handel materials in the Schoelcher collection; autographs of Beethoven, Berlioz, Mozart and others from Charles Malherbe; MS copies of works from the 14th–16th centuries owned by Bottée de Toulmon; and a collection of 17th-century English MSS of Coprario, Jenkins, Lawes and others. The library also collects musical iconography, concert programmes and memorabilia, and musicological literature of all periods.

J.-B. Weckerlin: *Bibliothèque du Conservatoire national de musique et de déclamation: catalogue bibliographique* (Paris, 1885); J. Ecorcheville: *Catalogue du fonds de musique ancienne de la Bibliothèque nationale*, i–viii (Paris, 1910–14); L. de La Laurencie: *Inventaire critique du Fonds Blancheton de la bibliothèque du Conservatoire de Paris*, PSFM, 2nd ser., i–ii (1930–31); A. Gastoué: 'Manuscrits et fragments de musique liturgique à la bibliothèque du Conservatoire', *RdM*, xiii (1932), 1; E. Lebeau: 'L'entrée de la collection musicale de Séb. de Brossard à la bibliothèque du Roy d'après des documents inedits', *RdM*, xxix (1950), 77, xxx (1951), 20; R. Girardon: 'Exposition des trésors du Département de la musique de la Bibliothèque nationale', *IAML*, iii *Paris 1951*, 73; S. Wallon: 'Les acquisitions de la Bibliothèque du Conservatoire à la vente de la collection Van Maldeghem', *RBM*, ix (1955), 36; E. Lebeau: 'Un fonds provenant du Concert spirituel à la Bibliothèque nationale', *RdM*, xxxvii (1955), 187, xxxviii (1956), 54; S. Wallon: 'Le fonds Coirault de la Bibliothèque nationale', *RdM*, xlix (1963), 108; N. Bridgman: 'La typographie italienne (1475–1630) dans les collections de la Bibliothèque nationale', *FAM*, xii (1966), 24; C. Massip: 'La collection musicale Toulouse–Philidor à la Bibliothèque nationale', *Bulletin de la Bibliothèque nationale*, iv (1979), 147

——. Bibliothèque Ste Geneviève, 10 place du Panthéon, 75005 Paris (*Psg*). The library originated in the Middle Ages at the abbey of Ste Geneviève, the chancellory of the University of Paris. In 1790 it was nationalized and took the name Bibliothèque du Panthéon; during the Restoration it assumed its present name. In 1926 it became affiliated with the Bibliothèque Nationale, but in 1930 was reattached to the university. Among its rare musical materials are 11th-century MSS, Latin theoretical treatises of the 13th–15th centuries, and theoretical works, airs, madrigals, harpsichord pieces, motets, psalms and other music from the 16th–18th centuries.

M. Bernard: *Répertoire des manuscrits médiévaux contenant des notations musicales: Bibliothèque Sainte-Geneviève* (Paris, 1965); M. Garros and S. Wallon: *Catalogue du fonds musical de la Bibliothèque Sainte-Geneviève de Paris*, CaM, iv (1967) [lists MSS of all periods, but printed works to 1801 only]

——. Institut de Musicologie de l'Université de Paris, Bibliothèque Pierre Aubry, 3 rue Michelet, 75006 Paris (*Pim*). When the institute was created in 1951, the library comprised works formerly in the library of the Sorbonne, including the collection of medieval works and folklore formerly owned by Pierre Aubry (*d* 1910). Various other private collections have since been added: Alexandre Guilmant (organ music); Théodore Reinach (17th- and 18th-century works); P.-M. Masson (18th- and 19th-century music literature and criticism); Emil Haraszti (Liszt biographical material); Chaillez-Richez (Classical piano music); Institut Autrichien (works by Austrian composers); Société des Auteurs et Compositeurs (17th- and 18th-century works). The library has a 14th-century mass MS from Besançon.

——. Office de Radiodiffusion-Télévision Française (ORTF), Bibliothèque Centrale Musicale, Maison de la Radio, 116 avenue du Président Kennedy, 75016 Paris (*Prt*). Originally a library of performing material for broadcasting, the collection now serves the function of a national centre for the documentation of contemporary music, with holdings of about 100,000 compositions.

——. Société d'Histoire du Protestantisme Français, 54 rue des Saints-Pères, 75007 Paris (*Pshp*). The society owns a number of psalters from the 16th and 17th centuries and has unique 17th-century editions of madrigals by Bernardi, Cifra, De Metrio and Ugolini.

POITIERS. Bibliothèque Municipale, 43 place Charles-de-Gaulle, 86000 Poitiers (*PO*). Formed during the Revolution with books from religious houses and of émigrés, the library owns about 130 liturgical MSS, most of them fragmentary and chiefly of the 10th–17th centuries.

D. Smoje: *Les manuscrits médiévaux notés conservés à Poitiers* (diss., U. of Poitiers, 1967)

ROUEN. Bibliothèque Municipale, 3 rue Jacques Villon, 76000 Rouen (*R(m)*). In addition to works confiscated during the Revolution, the library has received materials from T. Bachelet (printed and MS sacred music of the 16th–19th centuries and 18th-century cantatas and operas); Baudry (orchestral parts for 560 operas); Jumièges cloister (40 liturgical MSS); Mme Sanson-Boieldieu (documents and music of François-Adrien Boieldieu and his son Adrien-Louis-Victor); the Société Philharmonique (18th- and 19th-century sacred music); and the Théâtre des Arts (18th- and 19th-century ballet and opera).

T. Licquet and A. Pottier: *Catalogue de la Bibliothèque de la ville de Rouen: belles-lettres, sciences et arts*, ii (Rouen, 1833), 477; R.-J. Hesbert: *Les manuscrits musicaux de Jumièges*, Monumenta musicae sacra, ii (Mâcon, 1954) [annotated catalogue]

SALINS. Bibliothèque Municipale, place Emile-Zola, 39110 Salins (*SA*). Among the small collection of 17th- and 18th-century editions and MSS are four operas by Lully. The Charles Magnin collection includes autographs of Grétry, d'Alembert, Quicherat and others, from the 17th–early 19th centuries.

B. Prost: 'Catalogue des manuscrits de la bibliothèque de Salins', *Cabinet historique*, xxiv (Paris, 1878), 1–35

STRASBOURG. Archives de la Ville, 8 place de l'Hôpital, 67000 Strasbourg (*Sm*). The archive was established in 1399. Documents from the church of St Thomas include MSS of Walliser and Hausmann dated 1605, and there is a collection of early hymns, chansons and other works. Eugène Wagner's MS volumes concerning 16th- and 17th-century Protestant church music in Strasbourg include copies of documents he acquired elsewhere. Strasbourg's municipal library, founded in 1765 and housed with the archives, was moved to a new building in 1974.

P. Ristelhuber: 'Catalogue des manuscrits de la Bibliothèque municipale de Strasbourg', *Bibliographie alsacienne* (Strasbourg, 1872), 130

——. Grand Séminaire, 2 rue des Frères, 67000 Strasbourg (*Sg(sc)*). The Catholic seminary has liturgical music of the 15th–17th centuries, as well as a sizable collection of MS and printed works of F. X. Richter.

J. Victori: 'Bibliothek des Strassburger Priester-Seminars', *MMg*, xxxiv, suppl. (1902), 1; F.-X. Mathias: 'Thematischer Katalog der in Strassburg Münsterarchiv aufbewahrten kirchenmusikalischen Werke Fr. X. Richters', *Riemann-Festschrift* (Leipzig, 1909), 394

——. Institut de Musicologie de l'Université des Sciences Humaines de Strasbourg, 22 rue Descartes, 67084 Strasbourg (*Sim*). The institute acquired the library of Gustav Jacobsthal, including items from that of Otto Jahn. Holdings include autographs of Gabrieli, Galuppi, Gluck, Haydn and Scarlatti; 16th-century theoretical works; printed music of the 16th–18th centuries, including first editions of Lully and others; and 17th- and 18th-century editions of operas.

F. Ludwig: *Die älteren Musikwerke der von Gustav Jacobsthal begründeten Bibliothek des Akademischen Gesang-Vereins* (Strasbourg, 1913)

TOULOUSE. Bibliothèque Municipale, 1 rue de Périgord, 31000 Toulouse (*TLm*). Since 1967 the library has held all the early or unusual material (including the collection of Lefranc de Pompignan) formerly in the city's conservatory. Combined holdings include 16th-century motets, psalms of Marot (1563) and

Le Jeune (1611), 18th-century brunettes, and theatre music of the 18th–20th centuries.

TOURS. Bibliothèque Municipale, place Anatole France, 37042 Tours (*TO*). The library is rich in liturgical works of the 9th–18th centuries which include antiphoners, responsories, processionals and a 13th-century Easter play 'Office of the Resurrection'. There are also 17th-century motets, early Lully operas and 18th-century organ pieces.

Catalogue méthodique de la Bibliothèque de la ville de Tours (Tours, 1891–6) [lists works destroyed in the fire of 1940]

TROYES. Bibliothèque Municipale, 21 rue Chrestien de Troyes, 10000 Troyes (*T*). The library has a rich store of theoretical and religious MSS from the 7th century and later. There are also sacred and instrumental works of the 16th–18th centuries, including organ music by d'Anglebert, Lebègue and Nivers and vocal works of Lassus, Arbeau and Caroso.

Les richesses de la Bibliothèque de Troyes (Troyes, 1951)

VALENCIENNES. Bibliothèque Municipale, 2–6 rue Ferrand, 59300 Valenciennes (*VAL*). The library is chiefly constituted of the former Jesuit College library, but has also received works from various nearby religious houses (including a 9th- or 10th-century theoretical MS from the St Amand abbey). From the library of the Duke of Croy came a lute tablature of *c*1600 and works of Lully, Grétry, Mondonville and Philidor printed between 1709 and 1753.

VERSAILLES. Bibliothèque Municipale, 5 rue de l'Indépendance Américaine, 78000 Versailles (*V*). The library's music collection is based on the Royal Library, with books and music (MS and printed) of the 17th and 18th centuries, including a large part of Philidor's MS copies. Other collections include those of Gouget (16th-century printed works), Augusta Holmès (19th-century music and criticism), and the Institut St Louis at St Cyr (vocal music). There are also some 16th-century works, including collections published by Attaingnant.

Manuscrits musicaux de la Bibliothèque de Versailles (Versailles, 1884); E. H. Fellowes: 'The Philidor MSS', *ML*, xii (1931), 116; A. Tessier: 'Un catalogue de la bibliothèque de la musique du Roi au château de Versailles', *RdM*, xv/38 (1931), 106, 172; A. Tessier: 'Un fonds musical de la bibliothèque de Louis XIV: la collection Philidor', *ReM* (1931), nos.111–15, p.295

GERMANY, DEMOCRATIC REPUBLIC OF (*D-ddr*)
Of very general interest are the two library lists, H. A. Knorr: *Handbuch der Museen und wissenschaftlichen Sammlungen in der Deutschen demokratischen Republik* (Halle, 1963) and *Jahrbuch der Bibliotheken, Archive und Informationsstellen der Deutschen demokratischen Republik 1968–9*. Collections devoted to a single composer are described by H.-M. Plesske: 'Musikergedenkstätten in der DDR', *FAM*, xiii (1966), 161. The Democratic Republic of Germany section of the International Association of Music Libraries and the Music Division of the Deutscher Bibliotheksverband sponsored *Musikbibliotheken und Musikaliensammlungen in der Deutschen demokratischen Republik*, ed. P. Thüringer, J. Theurich and R. Hebenstreit (Berlin, 1969). Libraries in both the Democratic Republic and the Federal Republic of Germany are included in R. Schaal: *Führer durch deutsche Musikbibliotheken* (Wilhelmshaven, 1971).

BAUTZEN. Domstift, An der Petrikirche 6, Bautzen (*BAUd*). Among its holdings of sacred music the cathedral chapter library has many 18th- and 19th-century

masses and Vespers. There is also literature about sacred music.

——. Stadt- und Kreisbibliothek, Schloss-strasse 10, 86 Bautzen (*BAUk*). Founded in 1596, the library possesses a MS lute tablature among its early printed and MS music.

BERLIN. Akademie der Künste der Deutschen Demokratischen Republik, Robert-Koch-Platz 7, 104 Berlin (*Ba*). The library is rich in 20th-century music, and the archives document the compositions of prominent East German composers. The Hanns-Eisler-Archiv, based on the private bequest of Eisler, is publishing a complete edition of his works. There is also a Paul-Robeson-Archiv and an Arbeiterlied-Archiv with workers' songs of the period from 1844 to 1945, and their documentation.

W. Steinitz: *Deutsche Volkslieder demokratischen Charakters aus sechs Jahrhunderten* (Berlin, 1954–62); N. Notowicz and J. Elsner: *Hanns Eisler: Quellennachweis* (Leipzig, 1966); *Bibliographie der deutschen Arbeiterliedbücher 1833–1945* (Leipzig, 1973); *Bibliographie der deutschen Arbeiterliedblätter 1844–1945* (Leipzig, 1975)

——. Berliner Stadtbibliothek, Breite Strasse 32–4, 102 Berlin (*Bs*). The collection of early music and theoretical works includes about 50 items from the Graue Kloster collection (*Bgk*) which were not destroyed in World War II.

F. Bellermann: 'Verzeichniss der grösstentheils von Sigismund Streit dem Grauen Kloster geschenkten Musikalien', *Wohltäterfestprogramm des Grauen Klosters 1856*, 5

——. Deutsche Staatsbibliothek, Unter den Linden 8, 108 Berlin (*Bds*). Founded in 1661 as the Kurfürstliche Bibliothek, the library has been known successively as the Königliche Bibliothek, Preussische Staatsbibliothek, and the Öffentliche Wissenschaftliche Bibliothek until the present name was taken in 1954. The separate music section, founded in 1824, is one of the world's great collections. Among the many private collections in the library are those of J. F. Naue (1824), Pölchau (1841; comprising 250 MS volumes with works of the 16th–18th centuries and 50 autograph Bach cantatas), Schindler (1843; including the MS on Beethoven), J. N. Forkel (1845), the Voss-Buch Collection (1851; music from 1680 to 1750), Joseph Fischhof and L. Landsberg (1859), Otto Jahn (1869), Johann André (1873), Richard Wagener (1874; containing autographs of Bach, Mozart and Schubert), F. A. Grasnick (1879; including much of Aloys Fuchs's collection of MSS), Friedrich Jähns (1881; with nearly 4000 Weber items), Artaria (1901), F. Hauser (1904) and others. The collection has also been enriched by many institutional libraries, including those of the Michaeliskirche, Erfurt, the Joachimsthaler Gymnasium (which contained the library of Princess Anna Amalia of Prussia, and the Thulemeier and Spiker collections of music books), the Königliche Hausbibliothek (the private library of the Hohenzollern family), and the photocopy collection of the former Reichsinstitut für Musikforschung. From the private collections, the library acquired many autograph MSS of musicians and other musical figures including Bach, Beethoven, Busoni, Cherubini, E. T. A. Hoffmann, Lendvai, Lilli Lehmann, Mendelssohn, Mozart, Schumann and Weber. There are also the collections of such scholars as Franz Commer, Ernst Flade, J. G. Kastner, Wilhelm Tappert and Carl von Winterfeld. The collection now numbers some 500,000 music works, books and periodicals; 76,000 MSS and autographs (including musicians' letters); and extensive collections of portraits, recordings, microfilms and photocopies. About 1940 many of the MSS in the Preussische Staatsbibliothek were moved for safe-keeping. Those that were not lost or destroyed during the war were later divided between the Deutsche Staatsbibliothek and the Staatsbibliothek Preussischer Kulturbesitz in West Berlin; missing items continued to be returned to the Deutsche Staatsbibliothek more than 30 years after the war, but many important autograph MSS were still (in 1980) missing, believed stored in Poland.

Die Handschriften-Verzeichnisse der Königlichen Bibliothek zu Berlin (Berlin, 1853–1919); R. Eitner: *Katalog der Musikalien-Sammlung des Joachimsthalschen Gymnasiums (Amalien-Bibliothek)*, *MMg*, xvi (1884/R), suppl.; G. Thouret: *Katalog der Musiksammlung auf der Königlichen Hausbibliothek im Schlosse zu Berlin* (Leipzig, 1895) [see also *MMg*, xxxv (1903), suppl.]; R. Jacobs: *Thematischer Katalog der von Thulemeier'schen Musikalien-Sammlung in der Bibliothek des Joachimsthal' schen Gymnasiums*, *MMg*, xxx–xxxi (1899/R), suppl.; E. Noack: 'Die Bibliothek der Michaeliskirche', *AMw*, vii (1925), 65–116; W. Virneisel: 'Die Musikabteilung der Deutschen Staatsbibliothek', *FAM*, ii (1955), 108; P. Kast: *Die Bach Handschriften der Berliner Staatsbibliothek* (Trossingen, 1958); K.-H. Köhler: 'Die Musikabteilung', *Deutsche Staatsbibliothek 1661–1961* (Leipzig, 1961), 241–74; R. Blechschmidt: *Die Amalien-Bibliothek: Musikbibliothek der Prinzessin Anna Amalie von Preussen (1727–1787): historische Einordnung und Katalog* (Berlin, 1965); R. Schaal: *Quellen und Forschungen zur Wiener Musiksammlung von Aloys Fuchs* (Vienna, 1966); R. Schaal: 'Dokumente zur Wiener Musiksammlung von Joseph Fischhof', *MJb 1967*, 339; R. Schaal: 'Zur Musiksammlung von Richard Wagener', *MJb 1968–70*, 387; E. Bartlitz: *Die Beethoven-Sammlung in der Musikabteilung der Deutschen Staatsbibliothek: Verzeichnis, Autographe, Abschriften, Dokumente, Briefe* (Berlin, 1970); H. Kümmerling: *Katalog der Sammlung Bokemeyer* (Kassel, 1970) [collection of sacred and secular works of 16th–18th centuries, now divided between *Bds* and *B*]; R. Schaal: *Die Tonkünstler-Porträts der Wiener Musiksammlung von Aloys Fuchs* (Wilhelmshaven, 1970) [most of this collection now in *Bds*]; D. Johnson: 'The Artaria Collection of Beethoven MSS: a New Source', *Beethoven Studies* (New York, 1973), 174–236; K.-H. Köhler: '150 Jahre Musikabteilung der Deutschen Staatsbibliothek', *Beiträge zur Musikdokumentation: Franz Grasberger zum 60. Geburtstag* (Tutzing, 1975), 203

——. Deutsche Staatsoper, Unter den Linden 7, 108 Berlin (*Bdso*). Besides reference material on music, theatre and literature, the opera library has MS performance material from the old opera library. There is archival material from the estates of Padilla, Pittschau, Taubert and Wolff.

——. Humboldt-Universität, Clara-Zetkin-Strasse 27, 108 Berlin (*Buh*). The university library maintains the catalogue of the large collection of German and international dissertations and *Habilitationsschriften*, which includes many on musicological topics. Besides a collection of early opera librettos (part of the Hirschberg library), there are some early music works. The university's separate musicological division (at Universitätsstrasse 7) also has a collection of early music.

Catalogus librorum bibliotheca universitatis litterariae Fridericae Guilelmae Berolinensis adservantur (Berlin, 1839) [lists early music]

——. Internationale Musikbibliothek, Leipziger-Strasse 26, 108 Berlin (*Bmb*). The collection contains predominantly 20th-century works, including 1000 autographs. The library is administered by the Verband der Komponisten und Musikwissenschaftler der DDR and lends performance materials in the DDR and abroad.

——. Komische Oper, Unter den Linden 41, 108 Berlin (*Bko*). Founded in 1953, the library contains performance material of every sort, as well as programmes and iconographic documentation from this and other theatres.

——. Märkisches Museum, Abteilung Berliner Literatur- und Theatergeschichte, Am Köllnischen Park

5, 102 Berlin (*Bmm*). The musical theatre of the 18th and 19th centuries is especially well documented in the collection of printed and MS music and music books. The bequests of Hauptmann, Hitzig, Fontane, Doering and Vollmer include pre-1800 music.

——. Rundfunk der Deutschen Demokratischen Republik, Nalepa-Strasse 18–50, 116 Berlin (*Br*). Although not open to the public, the music archive is one of the richest radio collections in Germany, consisting of all the pre-World War II Berlin radio material.

——. St Marien–St Nikolai-Gemeinde, Sprachenkonvikt, Borsigstrasse 5, 104 Berlin (*Bn*). The music in the church library dates from the 16th century and liturgical works are especially well represented.

BRANDENBURG. Bibliothek der Katharinenkirche, Katharinenkirchplatz 2, 18 Brandenburg (*BD*). The church library has printed and MS partbooks of 16th- and 17th-century sacred works. There are also MS and printed vocal and instrumental compositions of the 18th and 19th centuries.

J. F. Täglichsbeck: 'Die musikalischen Schätze der St. Katharinenkirche zu Brandenburg a.H', *Programmschrift des Brandenburgischen Gymnasiums* (Brandenburg, 1857), 1–50

DESSAU. Stadtbibliothek, Strasse der DSF 10, 45 Dessau (*DEl*). Founded in 1897, the Stadtbibliothek amalgamated in 1970 with the Dessau branch of the Universitäts- und Landesbibliothek Sachsen-Anhalt (formerly the Anhaltische Landesbibliothek, founded in 1922). The collection covers the 15th–20th centuries, including the estates of the composers August Klughardt and Johann Friedrich Schneider (d 1853), and holdings from the former ducal Hoftheater.

A. Seidl: 'Kirchenmusikalisches in der Musikbibliothek des Herzoglichen Hoftheaters zu Dessau: eine Einführung', *Blätter für Haus- und Kirchenmusik*, xiv (1909); A. Seidl: 'Aus der Musikbibliothek des Herzoglichen Hoftheaters zu Dessau', *Musikalisches Wochenblatt*, xl (1909), 281

DRESDEN. Sächsische Landesbibliothek, Marienallee 12,806 Dresden (*Dlb, Dl*). The music department of the library has a very rich collection, including about 10,000 MSS, of which 1700 are autographs. The holdings are especially strong in the areas of Protestant church music of the 17th century, German and Italian opera of the 18th century, and German instrumental music of the 18th century. The entire collection of 19th-century printed music was destroyed in World War II. Music archives incorporated in the source collection include those of Schloss Oels, the Kantoreien of Glashütte, Pirna, Schellenberg, and Schwarzenberg, the Ratsbibliotheken of Kamenz and Löbau (*Dl*), Oberschule (formerly Landesschule) Grimma, all MSS from the Dresden Katholische Hofkirche, the Dresden State Opera, and the Sammlung Exner from Zittau. Among the private estates now in the collection are those of Robert Volkmann, Felix Draeseke, J.-L. Nicodé, Otto Reinhold, Johann Paul Thilman and Rudolf Mauersberger.

O. Kade: 'Die musikalischen Schätze der Landesschule zu Grimma', *Serapeum*, xvi (1855), 305 and 321; O. Kade: 'Die Musikalien der Stadtkirche zu Pirna', *Serapeum*, xviii (1857); N. M. Petersen: *Verzeichnis der in der Bibliothek der Königlichen Landesschule zu Grimma vorhandenen Musikalien aus dem 16. und 17. Jahrhundert* (Grimma, 1861); M. Fürstenau: 'Die Königliche Musikaliensammlung in Dresden', *MMg*, x (1878), 113; *Katalog der Handschriften der Königlichen öffentlichen Bibliothek zu Dresden* (Leipzig, 1882–1923) [esp. A. Reichert: 'Die Original-Handschriften der Musikabteilung', vol.iv, 196–250; list incomplete]; P. Fischer: 'Zittauer Konzertleben vor 100 Jahren', *VMw*, v (1889), 582 [describes Exner collection]; R. Eitner and O. Kade: *Katalog der Musik-Sammlung der Königlichen öffentlichen Bibliothek zu Dresden, MMg,* xxi–xxii (1890/*R*), suppl.; [covers only a small part of the source collection]; L. Hoffmann-Erbrecht: 'Die Chorbücher der Stadtkirche zu Pirna', *AcM,* xxvii (1955), 121; H. R. Jung: 'Die Dresdner Vivaldi-MSS', *AMw,* xii (1955), 314; F. Krummacher: 'Zur Sammlung Jacobi der ehemaligen Fürstenschule Grimma', *Mf,* xvi (1963), 324; W. Steude: *Die Musiksammelhandschriften des 16. und 17. Jahrhunderts in der Sächsischen Landesbibliothek zu Dresden* (Leipzig and Wilhelmshaven, 1974); *Sächsiche Landesbibliothek Dresden: die Musikabteilung* (in preparation)

——. Staatstheater, Julian-Grimau-Allee 27, 801 Dresden (*Ds*). The theatre music archive has large holdings of complete performance material connected with opera and concerts. An archive with historical data concerning the theatre is annexed. There is also material from the Staatsoper, Staatskapelle and Staatsschauspiel. The collections are well catalogued.

——. Stadt- und Musikbibliothek, Elsa-Fenske-Strasse 11, 801 Dresden (*Dmb*). The large music collection has various special holdings, such as the collection of music from East Germany and other Socialist countries. The separate music section was founded in 1925, and later received the libraries of the city's Händel-Verein, Mozart-Verein, Tonkünstlerverein, Dreyssigsche Singakademie and Konservatorium. The book collection was destroyed in the war.

R. Hebenstreit: '40 Jahre Musikbibliothek Dresden', *Der Bibliothekar,* xx (1966), 170

EISENACH. Bachmuseum, 59 Eisenach (*EIb*). The museum has a collection of MSS, printed works and iconography related to J. S. Bach and his family.

C. Freyse: *Eisenacher Dokumente um Sebastian Bach* (Leipzig, 1933); C. Freyse: 'Das Bach-Haus zu Eisenach', *BJb,* xxxvi (1939), 66, and xxxvii (1940–48), 152; C. Freyse: '50 Jahre Bach-Haus', *BJb,* xliv (1957), 168; pubd separately (Berlin, 1958)

ERFURT. Wissenschaftliche Allgemeinbibliothek Erfurt, Michaelisstrasse 39, 50 Erfurt (*EF*). Founded in 1392, the library was known as the Königliche Bibliothek until 1908, later as the Stadt- und Hochschulbibliothek and the Wissenschaftliche Bibliothek der Stadt. The music division is rich in medieval theoretical tracts and liturgical works, including a *Hymnus francogallus* in a 1147 bible, a 12th-century Italian antiphoner, and a parchment antiphoner of 1530 from Erfurt Cathedral. There are also valuable printed works. Some of the holdings are from former monastery libraries (in particular the Benedictine monastery of St Peter), and there are 14th- and 15th-century polyphonic works from the MS collection built up by Amplonius, rector of Erfurt University at the end of the 14th century.

W. Schum: *Beschreibendes Verzeichnis der Amplonianische Handschriftensammlung zu Erfurt* (Berlin, 1887); J. Theele: *Die Handschriften des Benediktinerklosters St. Petri zu Erfurt, Zeitschrift für Bibliothekswesen,* xlviii (1920), suppl.; R. Hernried: 'Erfurter Notenschätze', *Neue Musikzeitung,* xlvi (1925), 226; J. Handschin: 'Erfordensia', *AcM,* vi (1934), 97; B. Wirtgen: *Die Handschriften des Klosters St. Peter und Paul zu Erfurt* (Leipzig, 1937)

FREIBERG (Saxony). Erweitete Oberschule Geschwister Scholl, Geschwister-Scholl-Strasse 1, 92 Freiberg (*FBo*). The school library was founded in 1565 and later incorporated monastery collections (from the Collegiat-Stift zu St Marien and the Barfüss Predigermönchen). The music holdings include MS and printed works by Demantius, Kantor of the city's cathedral, and by other German (Eberlin, Hammerschmidt, Schürt, Schütz) and foreign (Gaffurius, Lassus, Rogier, Zanotti) composers.

O. and R. Kade: *Die älteren Musikalien der Stadt Freiberg in Sachsen, MMg,* xx (1888/*R*1960) suppl.; E. Flade: 'Freiberg', *MGG*

GLASHÜTTE. Evangelisch-Lutherisches Pfarramt, Markt 6, 8245 Glashütte (*GLA*). The parish archive has valuable holdings of partbooks, including works of Schütz, Schein, Seidel, Vulpius and others. Some of the collection was moved to the Dresden Landesbibliothek before 1920.

W. Schramm: 'Der Musikalienbestand der Kirche zu Glashütte', *AMf,* iii (1938), 58

GÖRLITZ. Oberlausitzische Bibliothek bei den Städtischen Kunstsammlungen, Neiss-strasse 30, 89 Görlitz (*GÖs*). The library of the former Oberlausitzische Gesellschaft der Wissenschaften (1779–1945) contains a small music section; most of the works were previously owned by the Görlitzer Singverein and were handed on to the Gesellschaft between 1841 and 1851, together with several printed works. Most of the collection consists of MS copies of a wide variety of 18th- and 19th-century works.

GOTHA. Forschungsbibliothek Gotha, Methodisches Zentrum für Wissenschaftliche Bibliotheken, Schloss Friedenstein, 58 Gotha (*GOl*). The library was founded in 1647 as the Herzogliche Bibliothek and, until 1968, was known as the Landesbibliothek. The collection of 7540 titles includes over 800 music MSS and a considerable number of early printed works, especially of the 18th and 19th centuries (C. P. E. Bach, Georg Benda, Dussek). The collection is also strong in hymnological works and in compositions by Thuringian composers.

exhibition catalogues for Spohr (1959) and J.-L. Böhner (1960); M. Pulst: *Kompositionen der böhmischen Musikeremigranten in der Landesbibliothek Gotha* (Gotha, 1967)

——. Superintendentur Gotha, Myconlusplätz 2, 58 Gotha. The ministry holds the archive of the Augustinerkirche (*GOa*), with some 200 music MSS of the 18th and 19th centuries. The library's holdings of early printed and MS works are recorded at the Deutsche Staatsbibliothek, Berlin.

GREIFSWALD. Ernst-Moritz-Arndt-Universität, Universitätsbibliothek, Rubenowstrasse 4, 22 Greifswald (*GRu*). The library has a rich hymnological collection, especially in German songbooks of the Evangelical church.

W. Rust: *Die Chansons-Sammlung der Universitätsbibliothek Greifswald* (Greifswald, 1929)

HALLE. Händel-Haus, Grosse Nikolai-Strasse 5, 402 Halle (*HAh*). The collection specializes in Handel research, also musical instruments and the city's musical history. There are MSS of Robert Franz, Carl Loewe, J. F. Reichardt and Scheidt.

K. Sasse: *Das Händel-Haus in Halle, Geburtshaus Georg Friedrich Händels: Geschichte und Führer durch die Ausstellung* (Halle, 1958) [exhibition guide]; K. Sasse: *Katalog zu den Sammlungen des Händel-Hauses* (Halle, 1961–)

——. Marienbibliothek, An der Marienkirche 1–3, 402 Halle (*HAmk*). Founded in 1560, the church library has a collection of about 1600 songbooks, and works dating from the 16th and 17th centuries, including compositions by Lassus, Hammerschmidt, Schein, Schütz and Rosenmüller.

R. Eitner: 'Mitteilungen', *MMg,* xxvi (1894), 42 [lists 16th- and 17th-century partbooks]

——. Martin-Luther-Universität, Sektion Germanistik und Kulturwissenschaften, Heinrich- und Thomas-Mann Strasse 26, 402 Halle (*HAmi*). The former Institut für Musikwissenschaft (founded in 1913) has

MS and printed works dating back to the 16th century. Among them are MS opera scores of the 18th century. Works have been received from the libraries of the Akademischer Gesangverein, Friedrich Rust and Robert Franz.

——. Martin-Luther-Universität, Universitäts- und Landesbibliothek Sachsen-Anhalt, August-Bebel-Strasse 13 and 50, 402 Halle (*HAu*). The university library contains about 700 MSS and many printed musical and theoretical works, many acquired from provincial libraries during the period of agrarian reform. There are also works from the private collection of Arno Werner.

HERRNHUT. Archiv der Brüder-Unität, Zittauer-Strasse 24, 8709 Herrnhut (*HER*). The archive was founded in 1765 as the central church archive of the Evangelische Brüder-Unität. The library was annexed in 1820 as a reference collection. The holdings are mainly MS and printed sacred music used in all branches of the order and are especially strong for the late 18th and early 19th centuries. The collection has been extended by music from the archives of neighbouring districts.

JENA. Friedrich-Schiller-Universität, Universitätsbibliothek, Goetheallee 6, 69 Jena (*Ju*). Founded in 1549, the library has among its musical treasures 18 choirbooks with Burgundian–Netherlands repertory and 63 printed partbooks from the 16th century. There are also liturgical MSS from the 14th–16th centuries and the famous Minnesinger song collection of the 13th and 14th centuries.

G. Holz and others: *Die Jenaer Liederhandschriften* (Leipzig, 1901/*R*1966); K. E. Roediger: *Die geistlichen Musikhandschriften der Universitätsbibliothek Jena* (Jena, 1935); U. Aarburg: 'Jenaer Liederhandschrift', *MGG*; L. Hoffmann-Erbrecht: 'Jenaer Musikhandschriften', *MGG*; H. Tervooren und U. Müller, eds.: *Die Jenaer Liederhandschrift in Abbildung* (Göppingen, 1972)

KINDELBRÜCK. Evangelisch-Lutherisches Pfarramt, Puschkinplatz 4, 5233 Kindelbrück (*KIN*). The parish archive has some 160 musical works, chiefly sacred vocal music of the 18th century.

LEIPZIG. General literature: P. Hauschild: 'Leipzig Musikhandschriften', *MGG* [lists MSS in *LEm* and *LEu*]; *Führer durch die Bibliotheken der Stadt und des Bezirks Leipzig* (Leipzig, 1963)

——. Bach-Archiv, Göhliser Schlösschen, Menekestrasse 23, 7022 Leipzig (*LEb*). The archive was founded in 1951 and is the central repository for all material related to Bach research or history, including practical and scholarly editions of his music, autographs, literature, iconography, recordings and so on. Sections of the estates of Martin Falck and Karl Straube have been added.

E. Creuzberg: 'Das Bach-Archiv', *Musica*, ix (1955), 187; E. Creuzberg: 'Zehn Jahre Bach-Archiv', *Musica*, xv (1961), 511; F. Zschoch: 'Zehn Jahre Wirken im Dienste der Bach-Forschung', *Das Musikalienhandel*, vii (1961), July, 25; W. Neumann: 'Das zwanzigjährige Bach-Schlösschen', *Musik und Gesellschaft*, xxi (1971), 329

——. Breitkopf & Härtel Musikverlag, Karlstrasse 10, 701 Leipzig (*LEbh*). The firm's archive suffered severe losses during World War II. Some of its former autograph material has been acquired by the Darmstadt Hessische Landesbibliothek; a few items were given to the Leipzig Staatsarchiv in 1962. The remaining holdings total about 3000 books and 22,000 musical works, many of great value. The archive functions in co-operation with the Hofmeister and Deutscher Verlag für Musik archives.

W. Hitzig: *Katalog des Archivs von Breitkopf & Härtel* (Leipzig, 1925–6) [lists autograph scores and letters]

——. Deutsche Bücherei, Deutscher Platz 1, 701 Leipzig (*LEdb*). Established in 1942, the music division of the Deutsche Bücherei (founded in 1912) is the central music bibliographical institution for the Democratic Republic; it has issued the *Deutsche Musikbibliographie* and the *Jahresverzeichnis der Musikalien und Musikschriften* since 1943, and consequently has an enormous collection of publications issued after that date. It collects works in the German language on an international scale, also translations of German works, foreign-language works appearing in Germany, and works in any language concerning German music and personalities.

H.-M. Plesske: 'Musikbibliographie und Deutsche Bücherei', *Deutsche Bücherei 1912–1962* (Leipzig, 1962), 141; *Die Musikaliensammlung der Deutschen Bücherei*, Neue Mitteilungen aus der Deutschen Bücherei, xxiv (Leipzig, 1965)

——. Karl-Marx-Universität, Beethovenstrasse 6, 701 Leipzig (*LEu*). The university library's music holdings include the collections of the Nikolaikirche and the Thomaskirche, containing valuable partbooks and theoretical MSS of the 11th–16th centuries. Since 1973 the library of the Institut für Musikwissenschaft has been incorporated into the university library.

——. Museum für Geschichte der Stadt Leipzig, Im Alten Rathaus, Markt 1, 701 Leipzig (*LEsm*). The museum's reference collection possesses about 2500 books concerned with the history of music in the city and especially with Wagner, the choir of the Thomaskirche and the Gewandhausorchester (for which it has complete programmes since 1781). It also has other theatre programmes, 500 musical works and 2000 further MSS of musical interest.

——. Musikbibliothek der Stadt Leipzig, Ferdinand-Lassalle-Strasse 21, 701 Leipzig (*LEm*). The rich collection was formed between 1951 and 1953 from the former Musikbibliothek Peters (founded 1894) and the music holdings of the Stadtbibliothek and Städtische Musikbücherei (founded 1914). Among private collections incorporated in the library are those of C. F. Becker (especially 18th-century material, some from Aloys Fuchs), K. H. L. Pölitz (chamber and vocal music of 1750 to 1820), Kurt Taut (autographs of minor 19th-century composers), Rudolf Hagedorn (2000 volumes on the life and work of Wagner), Ernst Rudorff, Heinrich Besseler and the Leipzig Singakademie. The library holds considerable source material of J. S. Bach, including MSS, first editions and early prints from the 19th century. There is a large collection of musical periodicals from the 18th–20th centuries and rich holdings of MS and printed keyboard and lute tablatures, many autographs (especially of the 18th and 19th centuries), theoretical works, librettos, first and early editions, and iconographical works.

K. F. Becker: *Alphabetisch und chronologisch geordnetes Verzeichnis einer Sammlung von musikalischen Schriften* (Leipzig, 1843); *JbMP* 1894–1940; E. Vogel: *Katalog der Musikbibliothek Peters* (Leipzig, 1894) [section on books and writings rev. R. Schwartz (Leipzig, 1910)]; *Bibliographische Veröffentlichungen der Musikbibliothek der Stadt Leipzig*, i: *Erst- und Frühdrucke von Robert Schumann* (1960); ii: *Zeitgenössische Drucke und Handschriften der Werke Joseph Haydns* (1963); iii: *Handschriften und ältere Drucke der Werke Johann Sebastian Bachs* (1964); iv: *Handschriften und ältere Drucke der Werke Georg Friedrich Händels* (1966); v: *Originalausgaben und ältere Drucke der Werke Johann Sebastian Bachs* (1970); v: *Autographen, Erst- und Frühdrucke der Werke Felix Mendelssohn-Bartholdys in Leipziger Bibliotheken und Archiven* (1972); vii: *Musikperiodika: Zeitschriften, Jahrbücher, Almanache, Bestandsverzeichnis* (1974); *Autographe,*

Handschriften, Erstausgaben und Faksimiles der Werke Ludwig van Beethovens in der Musikbibliothek der Stadt Leipzig (Leipzig, 1970)

——. Staatsarchiv Leipzig, Georgi-Dimitroff-Platz 1, 701 Leipzig. The archive holds the international correspondence of the music publishers Breitkopf & Härtel, C. F. Peters and Friedrich Hofmeister. This correspondence covers the period from the early 19th century to 1935 and comprises original letters and copies of publishers' letters to and from composers, performers, writers and other publishers.

H.-M. Plesske: 'Der Bestand Musikverlag C. F. Peters im Staatsarchiv Leipzig', *Jb der Deutschen Bücherei*, vi (1970), 1

LUCKAU. Kantorei St Nikolai, Schulstrasse 1, 796 Luckau (*LUC*). The music collection of the diocese includes about 500 MS cantatas and partbooks of the 17th and 18th centuries.

K. Paulke: *Musikpflege in Luckau* (Guben, 1918) [esp. 'Die Handschriften und altern Drucke im Archiv von St Nikolai']; F. Krummacher: *Die Überlieferung der Choralbearbeitungen in der frühen evangelischen Kantate· Untersuchungen zum Handschriftenrepertoire evangelischer Figuralmusik im späten 17. und beginnenden 18. Jahrhundert* (Berlin, 1965), 254ff

MEININGEN. Staatliche Museen, Schloss Elisabethenburg, 61 Meiningen (*MEIr*). Besides the separate Reger-Archiv with an extensive collection of Reger's works and documents concerning him, the museum has material related to the city's musical history and personalities (especially Brahms, Bülow, Richard Strauss and the Hofkapelle), and 18th-century printed and MS music.

MÜGELN. Evangelisch-Lutherisches Pfarramt St Johannis, Johanniskirchhof 5, 412 Mügeln (*MÜG*). Noteworthy items among the several hundred MS and printed works of the 17th–19th centuries include a motet collection of the early 17th century and cantatas by Dedekind, Hassler, Lassus, Praetorius, Römhild, Schütz, Telemann and Vulpius.

E. A. Fischer: 'Eine Sammelhandschrift aus dem Anfang des 17. Jahrhunderts', *AMw*, viii (1926), 420; F. Krummacher: *Die Überlieferung der Choralbearbeitungen in den frühen evangelischen Kantate* (Berlin, 1965)

MÜHLHAUSEN (Thuringia). Pfarrarchiv Divi Blasii, Johann-Sebastian-Bach-Platz 4, Mühlhausen (*MLHb*). The parish music collection numbers 700 printed and MS compositions, sacred and secular, many dating from before 1800.

ORANIENBAUM. Landesarchiv–Historisches Staatsarchiv, Schloss, 4407 Oranienbaum (*ORB*). Until 1945 it owned late 16th-century prints and MSS (including a Luther setting of Psalm lxiv) from the princely house of Anhalt formerly held by the Anhaltisches Staatsarchiv and Hausarchiv in Zerbst. The archive now contains a small collection of MSS from the 18th century (Fasch, Wetzke, Rolle) from the Musikstube of Zerbst castle.

T. W. Werner: 'Die im Herzoglichen Hausarchiv zu Zerbst aufgefundenen Musikalien aus der zweiten Hälfte des 16. Jahrhunderts', *ZMw*, ii (1919–20), 681–724; H.-J. Moser: 'Der Zerbster Lutherfund', *AMw*, ii (1920), 337; H. Ross: 'Entwicklung, Aufbau und Aufgaben des Landesarchivs Oranienbaum', *Archivmitteilungen*, xiii (1963), 59

ROSTOCK. Universitätsbibliothek, Universitätsplatz 5, 25 Rostock (*ROu*). The university was founded in 1419 and the library of the arts faculty came into general use as the university library in 1659. The collection of the Marienkirche was incorporated in 1842, and that of the Landesbibliothek Rostock in 1924. The large music collection is strongest in 18th- and 19th-century works, but also has about 1000 printed and MS works from before 1800, including the famous Rostock Liederbuch (*c*1465–87), rare organ and lute tablatures, and MS

copies of 16th- and 17th-century German polyphonic music (Agricola, Heinichen, Hasse, Keiser).

F. H. Dunckelmann: *Katalog der Landesbibliothek ... Mecklenburg* (Rostock, 1905–9); W. T. Gaehtgens: 'Die alten Musikalien der Universitätsbibliothek und die Kirchenmusik in Alt-Rostock', *Beiträge zur Geschichte der Stadt Rostock*, ii (1941); W. Salmen: 'Rostocker Liederbuch', *MGG*

RUDOLSTADT. Staatsarchiv, Schloss Heidecksburg, 682 Rudolstadt (*RUl*). The archive has printed works, MSS and archival records for music of the 17th–19th centuries, including the collections of the princely chapels of Rudolstadt and Sondershausen, and the private libraries of Caroline Louise and Ernst Wollong, with a wide variety of secular and sacred music.

B. Baselt: 'Die Musikaliensammlung der Schwarzburg-Rudolstädtischen Hofkapelle unter Ph. H. Erlebach (1657–1714)', *Traditionen und Aufgaben der Hallischen Musikwissenschaft* (Halle, 1963), 105; H. Eberhardt: *Übersicht über die Bestände des Landesarchivs Rudolstadt* (Weimar, 1964); H. Tzschöckell: 'Die Notenbestände der ehemaligen Hofkapellen Rudolstadt und Sondershausen im Staatsarchiv in der Heidecksburg', *Rudolstädter Heimatshefte*, xii (1966), 6

SCHWERIN. Wissenschaftliche Allgemeinbibliothek, Am Dom 2, 27 Schwerin (*SWl*). Until 1969 the library was known as the Mecklenburgische Landesbibliothek. It was founded in 1779 as the Regierungsbibliothek and established a separate music section in 1891. The collection of printed and MS music is particularly strong in music of the 18th and 19th centuries, including almost all genres, and of Mecklenburg composers. Collections making up the holdings include those of the cathedral school of Güstrow, and of the royal chapels of Schwerin and Ludwigslust. The private estates of Carl Fuchs, Robert A. Kirchner, E. F. Rohloff and several 20th-century composers are also in the collection. There are compositions from the Landesbibliothek in Neustrelitz and many works from the theatre archive of the Staatstheater in Schwerin.

O. Kade: *Die Musikalien-Sammlung des Grossherzoglichen Mecklenburg-Schweriner Fürstenhauses aus den letzten zwei Jahrhunderten* (Schwerin, 1893); O. Kade: *Der musikalische Nachlass der ... Frau Erbgrossherzogin Auguste von Mecklenburg-Schwerin* (Schwerin, 1899); C. Meyer: 'Die Musikaliensammlung in der Mecklenburgischen Landesbibliothek', *Monatshefte für Mecklenburg*, xiv (1938), 495; C. Meyer: 'Die Musikaliensammlung der Mecklenburgischen Landesbibliothek im Blickfeld der Musikwissenschaft', *Zentralblatt für Bibliothekswesen*, lxvi (1952), 359; R. Dempe: 'Die Musikaliensammlung der Schweriner Landesbibliothek', *BMw*, xi (1969), 207

SONDERSHAUSEN. Stadt- und Kreisbibliothek, Schloss, 54 Sondershausen (*SHsk*). The library (formerly the Thüringische Landesbibliothek) has a collection of about 600 MSS from the former castle church, with works by Stölzel, Telemann and others, mainly of the 18th and 19th centuries, including composers of the Berlin school.

UDESTEDT. Evangelisch-Lutherisches Pfarramt, 5101 Udestedt über Erfurt (*UDa*). The parish office owns a small collection of MS and printed works of the period from 1615 to the end of the 18th century.

F. Krummacher: 'Motetten und Kantaten der Bachzeit in Udestedt', *Mf*, xix (1966), 402

WEIMAR. Deutsches Nationaltheater, Theaterplatz, 53 Weimar (*WRdn*). Known earlier as the Grossherzogliches Theater, the institution has a collection of musical theatre works, most still in MS, performed there since 1784 (some were destroyed in 1945).

——. Franz-Liszt-Hochschule, Platz der Demokratie 2–3, 53 Weimar (*WRh*). The large music collection is especially strong in material relating to Liszt and to Thuringian musicians. The library administers the music, books and archival material of the former Allgemeiner Deutscher Musikverein. The school houses the Institut für Volksmusikforschung, founded in 1951 to promote folk music research, especially in relation to performance and education. The institute's library also has a large collection of printed and MS music including folk music of Thuringia and elsewhere. The private collections of Arno Werner, H. Möller and Franz-Magnus Böhme have been incorporated into the library.

——. Nationale Forschungs- und Gedenkstätten, Zentralbibliothek der Deutschen Klassik, Platz der Demokratie 1, 53 Weimar (*WRz*). Since 1969 the Thüringische Landesbibliothek (founded in 1691 as the Grossherzogliche Bibliothek) has been joined with the central library of German classicism to form a rich music collection (not maintained in a separate music division). Besides the works found in the private libraries of Duchess Anna Amalia and Archduchess Maria Pavlovna (1786–1859), important holdings are Goethe's collection of 18th- and 19th-century music, the Nietzsche collection (60 compositions in MS), and the Liszt collection (early editions of his works and his own music library). There are also liturgical works from former monasteries and sacred music of the 16th century. The library specializes in literature and culture of the period 1750–1850.

P. von Bojanowski: *Anna Amalie und die Weimarer Bibliothek* (Weimar, 1907); R. Münnich: 'Aus der Musikaliensammlung der Weimarer Landesbibliothek, besonders dem Nachlass der Anna Amalie', *Aus der Geschichte der Landesbibliothek zu Weimar und ihrer Sammlungen: Festschrift zur Feier ihres 250-jährigen Bestehens* (Jena, 1941), 168

WITTENBERG. Evangelisches Predigerseminar, Collegienstrasse 54, 46 Wittenberg (*WGp*). The library was founded in 1817 and has theological and related material from the former university library and from the private collection of Dr Heubner, one of the seminary's early directors.

O. Dibelius: *Das Königliche Predigerseminar zu Wittenberg 1817–1917* (Berlin, 1917)

ZITTAU. Stadt- und Kreisbibliothek 'Christian-Weise-Bibliothek', Strasse der Einheit 10–12, 88 Zittau (*ZI*). The library was founded in 1607 with books from a former Franciscan monastery. Later acquisitions included works from the church of SS Peter and Paul. Holdings include MS liturgical works and music of the 16th and 17th centuries (Gabrieli, Hammerschmidt, Lassus) and many printed works.

'Zittau: Stadtbibliothek', *MMg*, iv (1872), 37 [lists holdings]; J. G. Kraner: 'Zittau', *MGG*

ZWICKAU. Ratsschulbibliothek, Lessingstrasse 1, 95 Zwickau (*Z*). The library was founded in the early 16th century and contains rich holdings of the 16th–18th centuries (especially 1520–1680). Many of the pre-1546 works come from the bequest of Stephan Roth, and the Italian madrigals (in particular Venetian imprints) from the physicist Peter Poach. There are also various liturgical works and a collection of symphonies written about 1800.

H. Schulz: 'Zur alten musikalischen Literatur', *AMZ*, xlv (1843), 689 and 705 [lists partbooks printed in 16th and 17th centuries]; O. Kade: 'Noch einmal die musikalischen Schätze des 15. bis 17. Jahrhundert aus der Ratsschulbibliothek', *MMg*, viii (1876), 17; R. Vollhardt: *Bibliographie der Musik-Werke in der Ratsschulbibliothek zu Zwickau*, *MMg*, xxv–xxviii (1893–6/*R*), suppl.

——. Robert-Schumann-Haus, Hauptmarkt 5, 95 Zwickau (*Zsch*). The house was established in 1956 in the composer's birthplace, incorporating the Schumann-Museum founded in 1910. The library has a small number of important Schumann MSS, but its main strength lies in its collection of writings by Schumann, including diaries, sketchbooks and articles, largely unpublished. It also holds the composer's personal library of books and scores, and iconographical items.

G. Eismann: 'Das Robert-Schumann-Museum zu Zwickau', *NZM*, cxvii (1956), 425; M. Schoppe and G. Nauhaus: *Das Robert-Schumann-Haus in Zwickau* (Zwickau, 1973) [guide]

GERMANY, FEDERAL REPUBLIC OF (and West Berlin) (*D-brd*)

A valuable guide for music library holdings in both the Federal Republic and the Democratic Republic of Germany is R. Schaal: *Führer durch deutsche Musikbibliotheken* (Wilhelmshaven, 1971). In 1965 the Bayerische Staatsbibliothek undertook its *Kataloge bayerischer Musiksammlungen* series which is planned to catalogue all Bavarian music collections not under state control (i.e. primarily church and monastic libraries). Already published or in preparation in the series are catalogues of the collections at Bad Tölz, Benediktbeuren, Berchtesgaden, Frauenwörth, Indersdorf, Laufen, Neumarkt/St Veit, Tegernsee, Teisendorf, Tittmoning, Wasserburg and Weyarn, and the Munich churches St Kajetan and the Frauenkirche (also a thematic catalogue of the Hofkirchenmusik based on an inventory of 1810). Scattered throughout the Federal Republic are seven central catalogues (called Gesamtkataloge) which carry cards of all printed books available in the area (excluding MSS and printed music). Those attached to libraries are at the Freie Universität Berlin (for West Berlin only, excluding the collection of the Staatsbibliothek Preussischer Kulturbesitz), the Bayerische Staatsbibliothek Munich (for Bavaria), the Stadt- und Universitätsbibliothek Frankfurt am Main (for Hesse) and the Staats- und Universitätsbibliothek Hamburg (for all libraries in the north of the Federal Republic). The other Gesamtkataloge are in Stuttgart (for Baden-Württemberg, the Saarland and Rheinland-Pfalz), in Göttingen (for Lower Saxony) and in Cologne (for Nordrhein-Westfalen). Precise information on the Gesamtkataloge can be found in *Zeitschrift für Bibliothekswesen*, viii (1968).

AACHEN. Domarchiv, Domhof 6, 51 Aachen (*AAm*). The cathedral choir school was founded in 805 and the cathedral has liturgical MSS of the 12th–18th centuries.

O. Gatzweiler: *Die liturgischen Handschriften des Aachener Münsterstiftes* (Münster, 1926)

AMORBACH. Fürstlich Leiningische Bibliothek, Konventgebäude, 8762 Amorbach (*AB*). This is the private family library of Prince Leining; the music collection includes 18th- and 19th-century printed works.

F. J. Bendel: *Die Handschriften und Inkunabeln der ehemaligen Abtei Amorbach* (Salzburg, 1912–13); C. Valentin: *Theater und Musik am Fürstlich Leiningischen Hofe* (Würzburg, 1921); P. Lehmann: *Die Bibliothek des Klosters Amorbach* (Salzburg, 1930)

ANSBACH. Regierungsbibliothek, Schloss, Ansbach (*AN*). The library has music works of the 15th–18th centuries, in particular sacred vocal music of Clemens non Papa, J. F. Franck and Lassus. There are also librettos and opera scores from the Hofkapelle of the Margrave of Ansbach. The former collection of the Sing- und Orchesterverein includes printed and MS copies of 65 Haydn symphonies, and other works of the late 18th century.

Katalog der Regierungsbibliothek in Ansbach (Ansbach, 1913); G. Schuhmann: 'Die Regierungsbibliothek Ansbach', Jb des Historischen Vereins für Mittelfranken, lxxix (1960–61), 315

AUGSBURG. Domikanerkloster Heilig-Kreuz, Heilig-Kreuz-Strasse 3, 89 Augsburg (Ahk). Music holdings include works of Gruber, Haydn and Müller, and there are especially rich Mozart holdings from the Leopold Mozart bequest.

E. F. Schmid: 'Mozart und das geistliche Augsburg, insonderheit das Chorherrenstift Heilig-Kreuz', Augsburger Mozartbuch, lv–lvi (1942–3), 40–202; W. Senn: 'Die Mozart-Uberlieferung im Stift Heilig-Kreuz zu Augsburg', Zeitschrift des Historischen Vereins für Schwaben, lxii–lxiii (Augsburg, 1962), 333–68

——. Staats- und Stadtbibliothek, Schaezlerstrasse 25, 89 Augsburg (As). Holdings are particularly rich for the years 1580 to 1620, many of the works coming from nearby monasteries during the period of secularization (1802–3). There is sacred vocal music by Lassus, Hassler, Handl, the Gabrielis, Agazzari, Ingegneri and Marenzio, and the collection also includes theoretical and liturgical works, autograph letters, documents and iconography. The library is now adding only works by local composers and editions of Augsburg publishers.

H. M. Schletterer: Katalog der in der Kreis- und Stadtbibliothek, dem städtischen Archive und der Bibliothek des Historischen Vereins zu Augsburg befindlichen Musikwerke (Augsburg, 1879/R1960); R. Schaal: Das Inventar der Kantorei St. Anna in Augsburg (Kassel, 1965); C. Gottwald: Die Musikhandschriften der Staats- und Stadtbibliothek Augsburg (Wiesbaden, 1974)

BAMBERG. Staatsbibliothek, Neue Residenz, Domplatz 8, 86 Bamberg (BAs). The library was founded in 1611 by the Jesuits, became part of the university in 1773 and in 1789 was combined with the Fürstbischöfliche Hofbibliothek. The libraries of many secularized religious institutions were added in 1802, including the cathedral and the former abbeys of Michelsberg and Banz. Music holdings are rich in liturgical MSS of the 11th–13th centuries (including the important Bamberg MS, a 13th-century motet collection) and there are some 17th-century printed works. There are also autograph compositions and letters (E. T. A. Hoffmann), and iconographical material.

F. Leitschuh and H. Fischer: Katalog der Handschriften der Königlichen Bibliothek zu Bamberg (Bamberg, 1887–1912) [repr. with corrections and revised (Wiesbaden, 1966)]; H. Husmann: 'Bamberger Handschrift', MGG

BENEDIKTBEUREN. Pfarrkirche, 8174 Benediktbeuren (BB). The collection consists of 226 MSS and 34 printed works, chiefly sacred music by south German composers of the late 18th and early 19th centuries.

R. Münster and R. Machold, eds.: Thematischer Katalog der Musik-Handschriften der ehemaligen Klosterkirchen Weyarn, Tegernsee und Benediktbeuren (Munich, 1971)

BERCHTESGADEN. Katholisches Pfarramt, Stiftskirche, 8240 Berchtesgaden (BGD). The parish office possesses about 300 sacred works of the late 18th and early 19th centuries, both MS and printed.

Katalog der Musikhandschriften der Pfarrkirchen Laufen, Tittmoning, Teisendorf, Berchtesgaden und Neumarkt/St. Veit (in preparation)

BERLEBURG. Fürstlich Sayn-Wittgenstein-Berleburgsche Bibliothek, Schloss, 592 Berleburg (BE). The music collection of some 2000 works spans from 1550 to the end of the 19th century, but contains predominantly orchestral and chamber music from the years 1750–1850 (from the princely Hauskapelle).

BERLIN (see also under D-ddr). General literature: H. Lullies: Verzeichnis der Bibliotheken in Berlin (West) (Berlin, 1966) [lists 612 libraries; with subject index]

——. Amerika-Gedenkbibliothek, Blücherplatz 2, 1 Berlin 61 (Ba). The music section specializes in contemporary music and in documentation concerning contemporary musical life, with emphasis on the USA and eastern European countries.

E. Breitenbach: 'The American Memorial Library in Berlin', Libri, iv (1954), 281; H. Schermall: 'Die Musikabteilung der Amerika-Gedenkbibliothek', Die Musikbücherei, ii (1955), 113; F. Moser: Die Amerika-Gedenkbibliothek Berlin (Wiesbaden, 1964)

——. Das Deutsche Musikarchiv, Rüdesheimerstrasse 54–56, 1 Berlin 33. This is a separate branch of the Deutsche Bibliothek, Frankfurt am Main, created by statute in 1969; it was based on the former Deutsche Musik-Phonotek in Berlin and is responsible for collecting and cataloguing legal depository copies of music and recordings from German-speaking countries. These titles are listed in the Deutsche Bibliographie, issued by the Deutsche Bibliothek; since 1974 the archive has issued an independent bibliography of recordings.

E.-L. Berz: 'Das Deutsche Musikarchiv', Quellenstudien zur Musik: Wolfgang Schmieder zum 70. Geburstag (Frankfurt, 1972), 28

——. Staatliche Hochschule für Musik und Darstellende Kunst, Fasanenstrasse 1, 1 Berlin 12 (Bhm). Although many MSS and early prints were lost in World War II the library has about 243,000 printed musical works of the 16th–20th centuries, 30,000 books and 150 MSS. In 1894 the collection of Philipp Spitta was added and later that of Joseph Joachim. The library has also acquired works from the former Staatliche Akademie für Schul- und Kirchenmusik.

——. Staatliches Institut für Musikforschung Preussischer Kulturbesitz, Stauffenbergstrasse 14, 1 Berlin 30 (Bim). The library maintains a reference collection of some 25,000 volumes, especially strong in theoretical literature on instruments, acoustics, the psychology of music, European music ethnology and music bibliography; it also includes large parts of the ethnomusicological collection from the former Staatliches Institut für Deutsche Musikforschung. There is some rare printed music of the late 18th and early 19th centuries, and among the MSS are letters and the diaries of Meyerbeer and also a large group of letters written to Joseph Joachim.

A. Berner: 'Neuerwerbungen des Staatlichen Instituts für Musikforschung', Jb der Stiftung Preussischer Kulturbesitz (1964–5)

——. Staatsbibliothek Preussischer Kulturbesitz, Musikabteilung, Archivstrasse 33, 1 Berlin 33 (B). Most of the library's holdings were once part of the former Preussische Staatsbibliothek, which was dispersed in Germany and Poland during World War II. After the war some of the holdings were retrieved and housed at the Westdeutsche Bibliothek in Marburg and Tübingen University Library until the mid-1960s; the rest was returned to the Deutsche Staatsbibliothek in East Berlin (D-Bds). The collection of some 200,000 printed works spans the 16th–20th centuries, but is strongest for the 18th and 19th centuries. 18,000 MSS, dating back to the 13th century, include 800 autograph compositions and 20000 letters; the collections of Bach and Mozart autographs and Beethoven sketchbooks are among the largest and most important in the world. The Mendelssohn-Archiv is housed and administered separately and includes books, printed and MS music, letters and iconography relating to the composer. The library also has the collection of Ferruccio Busoni and many other important musical figures. The Pretlack collection of 1079 18th-century works (mainly MS arias, concertos, sonatas and symphonies) was acquired in 1969, and in 1975 the bequest of Raoul von Koczalski (*d* 1948), which includes some of his unpublished works, was transferred here from the Staatliches Institut für Musikforschung Preussischer Kulturbesitz (*Bim*).

P. Gehring and W. Gebhardt: 'Signaturenverzeichnis abendländischer und Musikhandschriften der ehemaligen Preussischen Staatsbibliothek, die jetzt in der Westdeutschen Bibliothek (WDB) in Marburg und der Universitäts-Bibliothek Tübingen aufbewahrt werden', *Scriptorium*, xiii (1959), 127 [all items now returned to *B*]; *Jb der Stiftung preussischer Kulturbesitz* (1962–) [lists new acquisitions in all departments]; R. Elvers: *Felix Mendelssohn Bartholdy: Dokumente seines Lebens* (Berlin, 1972); J. Jaenecke: *Die Musikbibliothek des Ludwig Freiherrn von Pretlack (1716–1781)* (Wiesbaden, 1973); R. Elvers, ed.: *Kataloge der Musikabteilung* (Berlin, 1975–) [the 1st series of 9 vols. lists MSS]

BEUERBERG. Pfarramt, Stiftskirche, 8191 Beuerberg (*BG*). The monastery parish office has a collection of works (mainly MS) of the late 18th and early 19th centuries.

R. Münster: 'Die Musik im Augustinerchorherrenstift Beuerberg von 1786 bis 1803 und der thematische Katalog des Chorherrn Alipius Seitz', *KJb*, liv (1970), 47–76 [lists pre-1800 works still extant]

BONN. Beethoven-Haus und Beethoven-Archiv, Bonngasse 18–20, 53 Bonn (*BNba*). The Beethoven-Haus contains a valuable collection of MSS and early editions and the bequests of several Beethoven researchers; the Beethoven-Archiv is an independent foundation within the Verein Beethoven-Haus, created as a research institute and devoted to the publication of a *Beethoven-Jahrbuch* (*BeJb*, 1953–) and collected editions of Beethoven's works, letters and sketches. Many of the autographs come from private collections, including the estate of Anton Schindler; the estate of Theodore von Frimmel (*d* 1928), acquired probably in 1929 and comprising numerous notes for his work on Beethoven, and letters (the books, periodicals and facsimiles have been absorbed into the collection of the Archiv); the collection of Beethoveniana from H. C. Bodmer (*d* 1956), including contemporary letters and documents, first editions, and extensive secondary literature on Beethoven and his circle; and the Max Unger estate, acquired in 1961, consisting of books and periodicals and all Unger's notes.

J. Schmidt-Görg: *Katalog der Handschriften des Beethoven-Hauses und Archivs* (Bonn, 1935); M. Unger: *Eine schweizer Beethovensammlung* (Zurich, 1939) [catalogue of Bodmer's collection, which was later extended]; D. Weise: 'Schweizer Vermächtnis für das Beethoven-Haus', *NZM*, cxxi (1960), 410; J. Schmidt-Görg: 'Anton Schindlers musikalischer Nachlass im Beethoven-Archiv', *Sbornik praci filosofické fakulty brněnské university*, F9 (1965), 263; H. Schmidt: 'Die Beethoven-Handschriften des Beethovenhauses in Bonn', *BeJb 1969–70*, 1–443, suppl. in *BeJb 1973–4*

——. Musikwissenschaftliches Seminar der Universität, Am Hof 34, 53 Bonn (*BNms*). The collection has rare items from the libraries of the organist Christian Benjamin Klein (*d* 1825) and of Ludwig Schiedermair (early printed works); the former numbers about 600 MSS and 150 early prints, mainly works of the 18th and early 19th centuries.

M. Marx-Weber: *Katalog der Musikhandschriften im Besitz des Musikwissenschaftlichen Seminars der Rheinischen Friedrich-Wilhelms-Universität zu Bonn* (Cologne, 1971)

——. Universitätsbibliothek, Adenauerallee 37–41, 53 Bonn (*BNu*). Besides the theoretical and printed music works from the C. B. Klein collection the university has 567 musical autographs, mainly from the private collections of Otto Jahn, Franz Gehring and others. There are letters of Brahms, Bruch, Chrysander, Czerny, Theodor von Frimmel, George Grove, Ferdinand

Hiller, Liszt, Franz Ries, Clara Schumann, A. W. Thayer and others.

T. Clasen: 'Die musikalischen Autographen der Universitätsbibliothek Bonn', *Festschrift Joseph Schmidt-Görg zum 60. Geburtstag* (Bonn, 1957), 26–65; M. Marx-Weber: *Katalog der Musikhandschriften im Besitz des Musikwissenschaftlichen Seminars . . . zu Bonn* (Cologne, 1971) [preface refers to Klein collection in university]

BRUNSWICK. Stadtarchiv und Stadtbibliothek, Steintorwall 15, 33 Brunswick (*BS*). The collection is rich in literature related to the theatre (including musical theatre and puppet plays). The city library holds about 800 librettos of the 18th century and early printed works, especially of the 16th and 17th centuries, while the archive contains letters of musicians and a large collection of theatre posters of the 18th–20th centuries. Some items are from the churches, monasteries and city halls of the region.

H. Nentwig: *Die mittelalterlichen Handschriften in der Stadtbibliothek zu Braunschweig* (Wolfenbüttel, 1893); F. Hamel and A. Rodemann: 'Unbekannte Musikalien im Braunschweiger Landestheater', *Gedenkschrift für Hermann Abert* (Halle, 1928/R1974), 72; W. Wöhler: 'Handschrift der Komponisten', *Braunschweig: Berichte aus dem kulturellen Leben* (1960–61), 22; M. Ehrhorn: 'Alte Motetten neu entdeckt', *Braunschweig: Berichte aus dem kulturellen Leben* (1961–2), 12

CLAUSTHAL-ZELLERFELD. Universitätsbibliothek, Leibnizstrasse 2, 3392 Clausthal-Zellerfeld (*CZu*). The Calvörsche Bibliothek, private library of Caspar Calvör (1650–1725), though primarily theological, also contains music and theoretical works.

COBURG. Landesbibliothek, Schloss Ehrenburg, Schlossplatz, 8630 Coburg (*Cl*). The library's holdings of early music (17th–19th centuries) and music literature come from various court, public and private collections, including the Bibliotheca Casimiriana, the Bibliotheca Mauritiana, the court and state library, the music from the castle library, the Ernst-Albert-Oratorio Society, the court theatre library, and private collections of Max Hellmuth, Franz Peters-Marquardt and Paul von Ebart. Of particular importance are the works in the court theatre library, including opera performance material and concert music mostly of the 19th century.

F. G. Kaltwasser: *Die Handschriften der Bibliothek des Gymnasium Casimirianum und der Scheres-Zieritz-Bibliothek* (Coburg, 1960); F. G. Kaltwasser: 'Die Schlossbibliothek des Herzogs Johann Casimir von Sachsen-Coburg', *Jb der Coburger Landesstiftung* (1961), 13; I. Hubay: *Die Handschriften der Landesbibliothek Coburg* (Coburg, 1962)

COLOGNE. Erzbischöfliche Diözesan- und Dombibliothek, Gereonstrasse 2–3, 5 Cologne 1 (*KNd*). The library's Leibl collection comprises 18th- and 19th-century choral music from the cathedral chapel. MS holdings come from the monastery of the Kreuzbrüder of Hohenbusch.

G. Göller: *Die Leiblsche Sammlung: Katalog der Musikalien der Kölner Domkapelle* (Cologne, 1964), suppl. in *Mitteilungen der Arbeitsgemeinschaft für rheinische Musikgeschichte*, xxxiii (1968), 33, and xxxiv (1969), 55; G. Göller: 'Die Kreuzbrüderhandschriften aus Hohenbusch', *Beiträge zur Musikgeschichte der Stadt und des Kreises Erkelenz*, ed. G. Göller (Cologne, 1968), 13

——. Universitäts- und Stadtbibliothek, Universitätsstrasse 33, 5 Cologne 41 (*KNu*). The library has 16th-century editions of works by Clemens non Papa, Jean de Castro, Lassus and François Sale, and various 17th- and 18th-century prints. There are several tablatures, autograph letters of musicians and MS holdings from the library of Ernst Bücken. The Bäumker collection has almost 2000 volumes (source material and literature) on German Catholic song.

W. Kahl: *Katalog der in der Universitäts- und Stadtbibliothek Köln vorhandenen Musikdrucke des 16., 17. und 18. Jahrhunderts* (Cologne, 1958); W. Kahl: 'Musikhandschriften aus dem Nachlass Ernst Bückens in der Universitäts- und Stadtbibliothek Köln', *Aus der Welt des Bibliothekars: Festschrift für Rudolf Juchoff* (Cologne, 1959), 159; M. Härting: 'Die Sammlung Bäumker der Universitäts- und Stadtbibliothek Köln', *Beiträge zur Musikgeschichte der Stadt und des Kreises Erkelenz*, ed. G. Göller (Cologne, 1968), 91 [lists 87 items of the 16th and 17th centuries]

DARMSTADT. Hessische Landes- und Hochschul-bibliothek, Schloss, 61 Darmstadt (*DS*). Since the loss of about 90% of its collection during World War II, the music section has accumulated rich holdings of some 4000 MSS and 4000 printed works of the 16th–19th centuries (with particular emphasis on the Baroque period), and composers of the Darmstadt area (Mangold, Rinck, Vogler) are well represented. There is also an important collection of musicians' letters (many from the estate of C. H. Rinck and from Breitkopf & Härtel), also liturgical MSS, librettos and iconographical material. The library has absorbed works from the monasteries of Seligenstadt, St Kunibert of Cologne and Wimpfen and from the private libraries of Ludwig I of Hessen-Darmstadt, Karl Anton, Franz Hauser, Breitkopf & Härtel, R. G. Kiesewetter, H. Heiss and others.

P. A. F. Walther: *Die Musikalien der Grossherzoglichen Hofbibliothek in Darmstadt* (Darmstadt, 1874); F. W. E. Roth: 'Musikhandschriften der Darmstädter Hofbibliothek', *MMg*, xx (1888/*R*), 64, 82; F. W. E. Roth: 'Zur Bibliographie der Musikdrucke des XV. bis XVII. Jahrhunderts in der Darmstädter Hofbibliothek', *MMg*, xx (1888/*R*), 134, 154; H. Kretzschmar: *Katalog der Bibliothek Hauser, Karlsruhe: wertvolle Musiksammlung* (Leipzig, 1905) [auction catalogue]; F. Noack: 'Die Tabulaturen der Hessischen Landesbibliothek', *Kongressbericht: Basel 1924*, 276; W. Schmieder: *Musikautographen: Auktion am 10. Oktober 1951 im Stuttgarter Kunstkabinett: beschreibendes Verzeichnis* (Eutin, Stuttgart, 1951) [auction catalogue of the firm J. A. Stargardt; Breitkopf archive was acquired by *DS*]; F. Noack: 'Eine Briefsammlung aus der 1. Hälfte des 19. Jahrhunderts', *AMw*, x (1953), 323 [describes Rinck collection of 581 letters and documents]; L. Eizenhöfer and H. Knaus: *Die liturgischen Handschriften der Hessischen Landes- und Hochschulbibliothek in Darmstadt* (Wiesbaden, 1968); O. Bill: 'Unbekannte Mendelssohn-Handschriften in der Hessischen Landes- und Hochschulbibliothek Darmstadt', *Mf*, xxvi (1973), 245; F. Kaiser: 'Zur Geschichte der Darmstädter Musiksammlung', *Durch der Jahrhunderte Strom: Beiträge zur Geschichte der Hessischen Landes- und Hochschulbibliothek* (Frankfurt am Main, 1967), 108–40

———. Internationales Musikinstitut Darmstadt, Nieder-Ramstädter Strasse 190, 61 Darmstadt (*DSim*). The institute was founded in 1947 by Wolfgang Steinecke (*d* 1961) to function as a centre for the Darmstadt Internationale Ferienkurse für Neue Musik; the library serves as an information centre for contemporary music.

Katalog der Abteilung Noten (1966, suppls. 1967, 1968, 1969–70, 1971–3); *Katalog Bücher-Periodica* (1970)

DETMOLD. Lippische Landesbibliothek, Hornsche Strasse 41, 493 Detmold (*DT*). The music section has rich holdings of early printed and MS music, also theoretical works and librettos. The Lortzing-Archiv has most of the composer's works and many other theatre compositions. The library received music from the former Fürstliche Hofkapelle, from local institutions (the Richard-Wagner Schule, the Oratorioverein, the Lehrerseminar), and from several private collections (W. Schramm, G. R. Kruse). The library of Freiherr Josef von Lassberg, received in 1855, includes a 14th-century liturgical music MS.

W. Schramm: 'Notenbestand der früheren Fürstlichen Hofkapelle', *Gesellschaft für Musikforschung: Mitteilung*, iv (1948), 20; H. Haxel: 'Die Musikbestände der Lippischen Landesbibliothek', *Verband der Bibliotheken des Landes Nordrhein-Westfalen: Mitteilungsblatt*, new ser., iv (1954), 62

DONAUESCHINGEN. Fürstlich Fürstenbergische Hof-bibliothek, Haldenstrasse 5, 771 Donaueschingen (*DO*). The library's large collection of early printed and MS music (including many autographs) is especially rich in chamber music of the 18th century, with many symphonic and operatic works of the 18th and early 19th centuries (including early ornamented texts of some Mozart operas). There are also liturgical works and some Mozart letters.

K. A. Barack: *Die Handschriften der Fürstlich Fürstenbergischen Hofbibliothek zu Donaueschingen* (Tübingen, 1865); C. Valentin: 'Mozartbriefe der Donaueschinger Bibliothek', *MMg*, xxxi (1899/*R*), 26; F. Schnapp: 'Neue Mozart-Funde in Donaueschingen', *Neues Mozart-Jb*, ii (1942), 211; H. C. R. Landon: *The Symphonies of Joseph Haydn*, suppl. (London, 1961), 33; C. Schoenbaum: 'Vzácná bohemika v Donaueschingen' [Important Bohemian works in Donaueschingen], *Zprávy Bertramky* (1961), no.29, p.1

DÜSSELDORF. Goethe-Museum, Hofgärtner-Haus, Jägerhofstrasse 1, 4 Düsseldorf (*DÜk*). The museum was opened in 1956 and contains holdings from the collection of the Anton and Katharina Kippenberg Foundation, formerly in Leipzig. It includes printed music (especially first and early editions of songs), documents, letters and iconography related to song and to the theatre of Weimar in Goethe's time. There is also autograph material from the estate of Zelter.

Jb der Sammlung Kippenberg (1921–35, 1963–); *Katalog der Sammlung Kippenberg* (Leipzig, 2/1928); *Johann Nepomuk Hummel, Komponist der Goethe-Zeit, und sein Sohn Carl, Landschaftsmaler des späten Weimar* (Düsseldorf, 1971) [exhibition catalogue]; *Felix Mendelssohn Bartholdy zum 125. Todestag* (Düsseldorf, 1972) [exhibition catalogue]

———. Landes- und Stadtbibliothek, Grabbeplatz 7, 4 Düsseldorf (*DÜl*). Rarities include autographs (music and letters) of Burgmüller, Mendelssohn, Schumann and others of the 19th and 20th centuries, some of them in the Heine-Archiv. The library also has some liturgical MSS.

E. Jammers: *Die Essener Neumenhandschriften der Landes- und Stadtbibliothek Düsseldorf* (Ratingen, 1952); E. Jammers: 'Die Bedeutung der Handschriften Düsseldorf D 1–3 aus Essen für die Musik- und Geisteswissenschaft', *Beiträge zur Geschichte von Stadt und Stift Essen*, lxvii (1952), 7; *Musik in Düsseldorf* (Düsseldorf, 1960) [exhibition catalogue]

EICHSTÄTT. Staats- und Seminarbibliothek, Am Hofgarten 1, 8833 Eichstätt (*Es*). The collection contains liturgical works and 16th- to 18th-century printed music (including an Attaingnant collection of 1530), some of it from former religious institutions of the area.

R. Schlecht: 'Ein Beitrag zur ältesten Klavier-Literatur', *MMg*, ii (1870/*R*), 122 [describes Attaingnant collection]; D. Heartz: 'A New Attaingnant Book and the Beginnings of French Music Printing', *JAMS*, xiv (1961), 9

ERLANGEN. Musikwissenschaftliches Seminar der Universität Erlangen-Nürnberg, Bismarckstrasse 1, 852 Erlangen (*ERms*). The institute holds the private collection (including the files) of Jacques Handschin and others; it also has the library of the Altdorf Lehrerseminar. There are first and early editions of music from 1770–1830 and theoretical works. A valuable microfilm collection concentrates on medieval MSS, especially monophonic music.

———. Universitätsbibliothek, Universitätsstrasse 4, 852 Erlangen (*ERu*). The holdings of early printed and MS music have been collected from the former Heilsbronn monastery, the library of the Margrave of Ansbach, the university library of Altdorf and the gymnasial library of Neustadt an der Aisch. There are also valuable portrait and graphic collections.

Katalog der Handschriften der Universitätsbibliothek Erlangen (1928–73); F. Krautwurst: *Die Heilsbronner Chorbücher der Universitätsbibliothek Erlangen* (Habilitationsschrift, U. of Erlangen-Nürnberg, 1956); A. Dietzel: *Die Universitätsbibliothek Erlangen-Nürnberg: Geschichte, Gliederung, Benutzung, Schätze* (Erlangen, 1966)

EUTIN. Kreisbibliothek, Stolbergstrasse 20, 242 Eutin (*EU*). The library has 18th-century printed and MS music from the former Eutin Hofkapelle, including works by C. P. E. Bach and composers and musicians from the Eutin district. There is a card file of the holdings in the library.

G. Eilers: *Bücherverzeichnis der Grossherzogl. öffentlichen Bibliothek* (Eutin, 1911, suppls. 1926, 1936); T. Holm: 'Eutin', *MGG*

FRANKFURT AM MAIN. Deutsche Bibliothek, Zeppelinallee 8, 6 Frankfurt am Main. This is the national archival library and bibliographic centre of the Federal Republic of Germany and is active in most areas of general library science. Since 1947 it has issued the *Deutsche Bibliographie*, listing legal depository copies of all publications from the German-speaking world (including the German Democratic Republic). Since 1969 music and recordings have been included in the *Bibliographie*, this being the task of the documentary centre Das Deutsche Musikarchiv, Berlin, which was specially created for the purpose.

——. Stadt- und Universitätsbibliothek, Bockenheimer Landstrasse 134–8, 6 Frankfurt am Main (*F*). This extensive collection comes from several sources, including the former Stadtbibliothek, the F. N. Manskopfisches Museum für Musik- und Theatergeschichte, the Bibliothek für Neuere Sprachen und Musik (formerly the Carl von Rothschildsche Öffentliche Bibliothek), the libraries of the Peterskirche and Barfüsserkirche, the earlier holdings of the opera library, and many literary estates (including Humperdinck's). The library is especially rich in autograph letters; autographs and MS copies of 17th- and 18th-century German church music (Telemann and others); 18th- and 19th-century opera music and opera archival material; MSS of the 18th–20th centuries; and printed music in early editions. Since 1948 the library has maintained the Gesamtkatalog for Hesse.

K. Israel: 'Die musikalischen Schätze der Gymnasialbibliothek und der Peterskirche aus Frankfurt a.M.', *MMg*, xxxiii (1901/*R*), 181, 197, and xxxiv (1902), 1, 23 [describe 16th–18th-century church books]; K. Süss: 'Die Manuskripte protestantischer Kirchenmusik zu Frankfurt am Main', *Festschrift . . . Rochus Freiherrn von Liliencron* (Leipzig, 1910), 350; K. Süss and P. Epstein: *Stadtbibliothek Frankfurt am Main: kirchliche Musikhandschriften des 17. und 18. Jahrhunderts: Katalog* (Berlin and Frankfurt am Main, 1926); K. Ohly and V. Sack: *Inkunabelkatalog der Stadt- und Universitätsbibliothek und anderer öffentlicher Sammlungen in Frankfurt* (Frankfurt am Main, 1967); G. Powitz: *Die Handschriften des Dominikanerklosters und des Leonhardstiftes in Frankfurt am Main* (Frankfurt am Main, 1968); G. Powitz and H. Buck: *Die Handschriften des Bartholomäusstifts und des Karmeliterklosters in Frankfurt am Main* (Frankfurt am Main, 1974)

FREIBURG IM BREISGAU. Deutsches Volksliedarchiv, Silberbachstrasse 13, 78 Freiburg i.Br. The archive collects and promotes research on folksongs in all languages, with the emphasis on German song. Besides a collection of some 300,000 songs, there are 30,000 books on folksong and folklore, ethnomusicology and German philology. The archive sponsors the publication of the *Jahrbuch für Volksliedforschung* (Berlin, 1928–41, 1951, 1964–).

R. W. Brednich: *Das Deutsche Volksliedarchiv* (Freiburg, 1951, 4/1970)

——. Universitätsbibliothek, Rempartstrasse 15, 78 Freiburg i.Br. (*FRu*). The library has valuable MSS

from former monasteries, and a collection of musicians' letters.

H. Wachtel: 'Die liturgische Musikpflege im Kloster Adelhausen seit der Gründung des Klosters 1234 bis zum 1500', *Freiburger Diözesan-Archiv*, new ser., xxxix (1938), 1–96; G. Seifert: *Die Choralhandschriften des Predigerklosters zu Freiburg i.Br. um 1500* (diss., U. of Freiburg, 1957)

FREISING. Dom, Domberg 34, 805 Freising (*FS*). The cathedral music collection came from the monasteries of Neustift, Straubing and Weihenstephan, the diocesan library of Munich (acquired in 1857) and the private library of Benedikt Werner, abbot of Weltenburg (received in 1827). In 1964 the important collection from the parish church of Weyarn, mainly of works of the late 18th and early 19th centuries, was deposited here (other portions of the collections were transferred to *Mbs* in 1803).

A. Mitterweiser: 'Die Freisinger Domkapitelbibliothek zu Ausgang des Mittelalters', *Zeitschrift für Bücherfreunde*, ii (1918), 227; E. Abele and G. Lill: *Der Dom zu Freising* (Freising, 1951), 70ff; R. Münster: 'Weyarn', *MGG* [with list of composers in the collection]; R. Münster and R. Machold: *Thematischer Katalog der Musikhandschriften der ehemaligen Klosterkirchen Weyarn, Tegernsee und Benediktbeuren* (Munich, 1971)

FULDA. Hessisches Landesbibliothek, Heinrich-von-Bibra-Platz 12, 64 Fulda (*FUl*). The library owns MS copies of Mozart's works formerly held by the publishing firm of Johann André in Offenbach and Johann Henkel (*d* 1851), Kantor of Fulda. There are also 25 liturgical works, dating back to the 9th century, from former religious institutions.

K. Christ: *Die Bibliothek des Klosters Fulda im 16. Jahrhundert: Die Handschriftverzeichnisse* (Leipzig, 1933); H. Hettenhausen: *Die Choralhandschriften der Fuldaer Landesbibliothek* (diss., U. of Marburg, 1961); W. Plath: 'Mozartiana in Fulda und Frankfurt am Main', *MJb 1968–70*, 333

GÖTTINGEN. Niedersächsische Staats- und Universitätsbibliothek, Prinzenstrasse 1, 34 Göttingen (*Gs*). The MSS consist mainly of vocal music from the years 1695–1833, including a collection of works by Bach. The university's separate musicological seminar (at Kurze Geismarstrasse 40) holds the private library of Friedrich Ludwig.

A. Quantz: *Die Musikwerke der Königlichen Universitätsbibliothek in Göttingen* (Berlin, 1883/*R*1960); W.-M. Luther: *Johann Sebastian Bach Documenta* (Kassel, 1950) [exhibition catalogue]; W.-M. Luther: 'Die nichtliturgischen Musikinkunabeln der Göttinger Bibliothek', *Libris et litteris: Festschrift für Hermann Tiemann* (Hamburg, 1959), 130; A. Dürr: 'Eine Handschriften-Sammlung des 18. Jahrhunderts in Göttingen', *AMw*, xxv (1968), 308

HAMBURG. Staatsarchiv, ABC-Strasse 19, 2 Hamburg 36 (*Ha*). The archive contains some early music and important material from the city's musical history, including church, civic and private records of the 16th–19th centuries. It also has part of the private libraries of C. P. E. Bach and of other musical figures.

Die Musik Hamburgs im Zeitalter Sebastian Bachs: Ausstellung (Hamburg, 1921) [exhibition catalogue; esp. 'Musikgeschichtliche Akten des Hamburgischen Staatsarchiv']; H. Meisner: 'Philipp Emanuel Bachs musicalischer Nachlass', *BJb*, xxxv (1938), 103, xxxvi (1939), 81–112, xxxvii (1940–48), 161

——. Staats- und Universitätsbibliothek, Moorweidenstrasse 40, 2 Hamburg (*Hs*). The library is an important centre for music, literature and documents relating to composers active in Hamburg (including Handel and Telemann). The music collection spans the 16th–19th centuries, but is strongest in 18th-century opera. The Brahms-Archiv has autographs, MS copies and printed works of the composer and his circle. The library of Friedrich Chrysander, of which the largest part is in this collection, contains Handeliana (notably

Handel's annotated conducting scores) and 18th-century theoretical works. The university has a separate theatre collection (the Theatersammlung at Rothenbaumchaussee 162), containing valuable librettos, theoretical works and 2000 autographs of composers, singers, conductors and other artists, as well as some music. A handwritten catalogue by A. Dommer, available in the library, indicates the collection's wartime losses (which comprise mainly 16th- to 19th-century printed works and collective MSS). The library holds the Gesamtkatalog for the north German region.

Musikalisches Schaffen und Wirken aus drei Jahrhunderten: sein Fortleben in der Gegenwart: Ausstellung musikgeschichtlicher Drucke, Handschriften und alter Musikinstrumente (Hamburg, 1925) [exhibition catalogue]; W. Schulze: *Die Quellen der Hamburger Oper 1678–1738: eine bibliographisch statistische Studie* (Hamburg, 1938); G. Fock and K. Richter: *Johannes Brahms-Ausstellung* (Hamburg, 1958) [exhibition catalogue]; H. C. Wolff: *Die Barockoper in Hamburg 1679–1738* (Wolfenbüttel, 1957)

HANOVER. Kestner-Museum, Trammplatz 3, 3 Hanover. The collection, founded in 1884 with a gift from Hermann Kestner (*d* 1890), is one of general cultural history, but it has some liturgical works and an autograph sketch of Beethoven's *Egmont*, also two of his letters.

A. Fecker: 'Die Beethoven-Handschriften des Kestner-Museums in Hannover', *ÖMz*, xxvi (1971), 336

——. Arbeitsstelle für Gottesdienst und Kirchenmusik der Evangelisch-Lutherischen Landeskirche Hannovers, Am Markt 4–5, 3 Hanover (*HVk*). In 1972 the Kirchenmusikschule of Hanover was closed and its library went to the Arbeitsstelle. Besides its other holdings of music and books, the library has an archive of about 1600 songbooks and a special collection of publications concerning the development of the liturgy since 1965.

K. F. Müller: 'Gesangbucharchiv der Evangelisch-Lutherischen Landeskirche Hannovers in der Kirchenmusikschule Hannover', *FAM*, xiv (1967), 119, repr. in *BJb*, liv (1968), 104

——. Niedersächsische Landesbibliothek, Am Archive 1, 3 Hanover (*HVl*). The library has a large collection of librettos of the 17th and 18th centuries and many rare items of printed music of the Baroque period.

E. Bodemann: *Die Handschriften der Königlichen öffentlichen Bibliothek in Hannover* (Hanover, 1867); K.-H. Weinmann: *Die niedersächsische Landesbibliothek Hannover: Führer durch ihre Geschichte, Bestände und Einrichtungen* (Hanover, 3/1972)

——. Stadtbibliothek, Hildesheimerstrasse 12, 3 Hanover (*HVs*). The collection has the printed works from the library of Hermann Kestner (*d* 1890) and the MSS formerly in the Stadtarchiv, consisting of Italian and English partbooks, cantatas of the 17th and 18th centuries, a collection of 18th-century harpsichord pieces and arias with accompaniment. The attached Niedersächsisches Handschriften-Archiv has music autographs of Heinrich Marschner, Joseph Joachim, Hans Stieber and others.

O. Jürgens: *Katalog der Stadtbibliothek Hannover* (Hanover, 1901, suppls. 1903–16); T. W. Werner: 'Die Musikhandschriften des Kestnerschen Nachlasses im Stadtarchiv zu Hannover', *ZMw*, i (1918–19), 441; T. W. Werner: 'Katalog der Musikhandschriften des Kestnerschen Nachlasses im Stadtarchiv zu Hannover', *Hannoversche Geschichtsblätter*, xxii (1919), 241–372; J. Hennies: 'Die Musikabteilung der Stadtbibliothek Hannover', *Die Musikbücherei*, iv (1957), 286

HARBURG. Fürstlich Oettingen-Wallerstein'sche Bibliothek, Schloss, 8856 Harburg (*HR*). The collection, which was in Maihingen until 1948, contains music from the princely court and various monastery libraries. It is especially rich in instrumental music of

the second half of the 18th century; there is also an 8th-century evangeliary.

G. Grupp: *Oettingen-Wallersteinsche Sammlungen in Maihingen: Handschriften-Verzeichnis* (Nördlingen, 1897); L. Schiedermair: 'Die Blütezeit der Oettingen-Wallerstein'schen Hofkapelle', *SIMG*, ix (1907–8), 83–120; A. Layer: 'Wallerstein', *MGG*; J. R. Piersol: *The Oettingen-Wallerstein Hofkapelle and its Wind Music* (diss., U. of Iowa, 1972); G. Haberkamp, ed.: *Thematischer Katalog der Musikhandschriften der Fürstlich Oettingen-Wallerstein'schen Bibliothek Schloss Harburg* (Munich, 1976)

HEIDELBERG. Universitätsbibliothek, Plöck 107–9, 69 Heidelberg (*HEu*). The library has some valuable early MSS, including a late 13th-century parchment (Heid.2588) of the Notre Dame school with seven two- and three-voice pieces in conductus form; a 14th-century gradual and a two-part 15th-century Kyrie from the Cistercian cloister of Salem (together in Sal.IX 67); an 11th-century copy of *Musica enchiriadis* (Sal.IX 20); Minnesinger MSS, most of which are purely text although melodies are included to the texts of Hugo von Montfort and Michael Beheim; and various chant MSS.

Katalog der Handschriften der Universitätsbibliothek in Heidelberg (Heidelberg, 1887–1903); R. Sillib: *Zur Geschichte der grossen Heidelberger (Manesseschen) Liederhandschrift* (Heidelberg, 1921); J. T. Krug: *Quellen und Studien zur oberrheinischen Choralgeschichte: Die Choralhandschriften der Universitätsbibliothek Heidelberg* (Freiburg, 1937) [introduction and pt.i]; E. Jammers: *Das Königliche Liederbuch des deutschen Minnesangs: eine Einführung in die sogenannte Manessische Handschrift* (Heidelberg, 1965)

HEILBRONN. Stadtarchiv, 71 Heilbronn am Neckar (*HB*). Then Gymnasium library now in the city archive contains 16th- and 17th-century sacred and secular vocal music, fugues and dances from Germany, France, Italy and the Netherlands, as well as theoretical works.

E. Mayser: *Alter Musikschatz der Lehrerbibliothek* (Heilbronn, 1893) [library of the teachers at the Gymnasium]; M. Seiffert: 'Rarissima in Heilbronn', *TVNM*, v (1897), 242; U. Siegele: *Die Musiksammlung der Stadt Heilbronn: Katalog mit Beiträgen zur Geschichte der Sammlung und zur Quellenkunde des 16. Jahrhunderts* (Heilbronn, 1965)

HELMSTEDT. Ehemalige Universitätsbibliothek, Juleum, Postfach 84, 333 Helmstedt (*HSj*). The Juleum holds items from the library of the former university (1490–1810), including music works and some autographs (the rest is in *W*). There are also old parchment music MSS from the bindings of other books.

Katalog der im Juleum verbliebenen Teile der ehemaligen Universitätsbibliothek Helmstedt (Helmstedt, 1958) [music listed in vi, 'Mathematics']

KARLSRUHE. Badische Landesbibliothek, Lammstrasse 16, 75 Karlsruhe (*KA*). Before World War II, the library had a rich music collection derived from gifts of the conductor Josef Strauss (*d* 1866), the book dealer Max Müller, the Bachverein and the Grand Duchess Sophie, but those collections were destroyed in 1942 as was the collection of archival material and music from the Hoftheater library. The collections from the Baden-Durlach court at Karlsruhe and from monastary libraries incorporated during the secularization remain, and holdings are especially strong for the mid-18th century, particularly Italian composers. There are about 160 medieval MSS, and the collection of J. W. and Wilhelm Kalliwoda is on deposit.

Katalog der Grossherzoglich Badischen Hof- und Landesbibliothek (Karlsruhe, 1876–1927) [music in vii, nos.30503–837]; *Die Handschriften der Grossherzoglich Badischen Hof- und Landesbibliothek in Karlsruhe*, i–ix (Karlsruhe, 1891–1932/R1969), x (1969); H. Ferdinand: *Das Ordinarium Missae in den Handschriften der Badischen Landesbibliothek* (diss., U. of Bonn, 1952); R. Euhrmann: *Mannheimer Klavier-Kammermusik* (diss., U. of Marburg, 1963) [indicates library's holdings]

KASSEL. Deutsches Musikgeschichtliches Archiv, Schloss Bellevue, Schöne Aussicht 2, 35 Kassel (*Kdma*). Founded in 1954, the archive is a centre for the documentation of music by German composers, and foreign composers who worked in Germany, whose works were issued by German publishers or whose compositions are found in MSS of German provenance. The sources (MSS and early printed practical and theoretical works) are kept in film copies, numbering in 1975 about 10,000 titles covering the period 1450–1700.

F. Blume: 'Deutsches Musikgeschichtliches Archiv', *FAM*, i (1954), 90; H. Heckmann and J. Kindermann: *Deutsches Musikgeschichtliches Archiv: Katalog der Filmsammlung* (Kassel, 1955–); H. Heckmann: 'Archive of German Music History', *Notes*, xvi (1958–9), 35; H. Heckmann: 'Musikgeschichtliche Quellen auf Mikrofilmen', *Nachrichten für Dokumentation*, x (1959), 152; J. Kindermann: 'Musikalien auf Filmen', *Musica*, xxvii (1973), 380; J. Kindermann: 'The "Deutsche Musikgeschichtliche Archiv"': Microfilm Archives as Institutions for Documentation and Information', *FAM*, xxi (1974), 11

——. Louis-Spohr-Gedenk- und Forschungsstätte, Brüder Grimm Platz 4A, 35 Kassel (*Ksp*). The centre collects all material related to Louis Spohr, to violinists and violins, to literature for the violin and violin methods. The collection numbers over 3000 printed works, about 400 autograph scores and letters, 500 books and brochures, 14,000 microfilm frames and a large collection of newspaper clippings, programmes and portraits.

——. Murhardsche Bibliothek der Stadt Kassel und Landesbibliothek, Brüder Grimm Platz 4A, 35 Kassel (*Kl*). The special department of MSS contains early music autographs and prints (from presses in Venice, Nuremberg and elsewhere) formerly in the Landgräfliche Hofkapelle (16th and 17th century), many of them unique. There are 19th-century MS holdings, including about 150 autographs and first editions and 3222 letters from Spohr's estate.

C. Israel: *Übersichtlicher Katalog der Musikalien der ständischen Landesbibliothek zu Cassel* (Kassel, 1881); W. Hopf, ed.: *Die Landesbibliothek Kassel 1580–1930* (Marburg, 1930); F. Blume: *Geistliche Musik am Hofe des Landgrafen Moritz von Hessen* (Kassel, 1931); C. Engelbrecht: *Die Kasseler Hofkapelle im 17. Jahrhundert und ihre anonymen Musikhandschriften aus der Kasseler Landesbibliothek* (Kassel, 1958) [lists 65 vocal works thought to be by Schütz, Scheidt, Praetorius, G. Gabrieli and others]; H. Heckmann: *Musikalische Kostbarkeiten aus der Murhard- und Landesbibliothek 11. bis 19. Jahrhunderts* (MS, 1962) [unpubd exhibition catalogue of 28 items]

KIEL. General literature: K. Hortschansky: *Katalog der Kieler Musiksammlungen: die Notendrucke, Handschriften, Libretti und Bücher über Musik aus der Zeit bis 1830* (Kassel, 1963)

——. Schleswig-Holsteinische Landesbibliothek, Schlossgarten, Oslokai, 23 Kiel (*Kll*). The library has 103 MS and printed works by C. P. E. Bach, the complete collection of sacred songs edited by Johann Rist (1641–64), opera librettos (including many published in Denmark) from about 1750 to 1830, and items bought at the Wolffheim sale (including a unique Schütz item). The collection of Prince van Noer contains many works of the Viennese Classical school, and that of the Salzau Count Blome contains about 300 prints and MSS of the 19th century. The library also has the private collection of Bernhard Engelke, and in 1970 it received the estate of the folk-music researcher Max Kuckei. There is a collection of about 6000 folksong books from the Lehmann collection. The Schleswig-Holsteinische Musiksammlung, opened in Neumünster in 1920, has also been transferred to Kiel; it holds about 5000 works of composers connected with Schleswig-Holstein.

——. Universitätsbibliothek, Olshausenstrasse 29, 23

Kiel (*KIu*). The largest part of the music collection (including printed music works of the 16th and 17th centuries from the Stadtkirche in Heide and the librettos and works on theatre history from the Uhde collection) was destroyed in April 1942. Remaining are some hymnbooks, psalmbooks and choirbooks, folksong collections (especially Scandinavian), early theoretical works and periodicals, and some music printed after 1780.

——. Musikwissenschaftliches Institut der Christian-Albrecht Universität, Neue Universität, Haus 11 und 15, 23 Kiel (*KImi*). The institute's extensive working library includes a large number of operatic piano reductions of the late 18th and early 19th centuries, and many early 19th-century string quartets, formerly owned by the Harmonie-Gesellschaft of Rendsburg.

LAUFEN. Stiftsarchiv Laufen, 8229 Laufen an der Salzach (*LFN*). The Stift's MS collection includes 18th-century works and 17th-century hymns and psalms.

R. Münster: 'Seltene Musikdrucke des 17. Jahrhunderts im Stiftsarchiv Laufen an der Salzach', *Mf*, xx (1967), 284; *Katalog der Musikhandschriften der Pfarrkirchen Laufen, Tittmoning, Teisendorf, Berchtesgaden und Neumarkt/St Veit* (in preparation).

LÜBECK. Bibliothek der Hansestadt Lübeck, Hundestrasse 5–7, 24 Lübeck (*LÜh*). The library's music division has printed works from the 16th century, many of them received as private gifts (for example from the organist Stiehl-Reval, the composer Jimmerthal and from Lübeck families). The library also holds the collection of the Lübeck Musikverein (dissolved *c*1850) and 16th- to 18th-century works from the church libraries of St Peter, the Marienkirche, the Catharinen-Gymnasium, the cathedral, the Aegidienkirche and the Katharinenkloster. There are many MSS of Buxtehude and Franz Tunder.

C. Stiehl: 'Die Stadtbibliothek in Lübeck', *MMg*, xvi (1884/R), 113; C. Stiehl: *Katalog der Musik-Sammlung auf der Stadtbibliothek zu Lübeck* (Lübeck, 1893); W. Stahl: *Musik-Bücher der Lübecker Stadtbibliothek* (Lübeck, 1927) [classified catalogue of 19th- and 20th-century literature]; W. Stahl: *Die Musik-Abteilung der Lübecker Stadtbibliothek in ihren älteren Beständen* (Lübeck, 1929) [music and books from the 12th–19th centuries]; W. Stahl: 'Verzeichnis der in Lübeck noch vorhandenen Kirchenmusik aus dem 16., 17. und 18. Jahrhundert', *Musikgeschichte Lübecks*, ed. J. Hennings and W. Stahl, ii (Kassel, 1952), 194; G. Karstädt: *Die extraordinairen Abendmusiken D. Buxtehudes* (Lübeck, 1962) [describes Buxtehude's works in the Stadtbibliothek]; G. Karstädt: *Der Lübecker Kantatenband Dietrichs Buxtehudes: eine Studie über die Tabulatur Mus A 373* (Lübeck, 1971)

LÜNEBURG. Ratsbücherei, Am Marienplatz 3, 314 Lüneburg (*Lr*). The music section holds 596 volumes of early music, notable for keyboard tablatures and choral music of the 17th century, especially of north German composers.

F. Welter: *Katalog der Musikalien der Ratsbücherei Lüneburg* (Lippstadt, 1950) [lists early music]; K. G. Hartmann: 'Die Handschrift KN 144 der Ratsbücherei in Lüneburg', *Mf*, xiii (1960), 1; M. Reimann: 'Lüneburger Orgel- und Klavier-Tabulaturen', *MGG*

MAINZ. B. Schott's Söhne, Archiv, Weihergarten 5, 65 Mainz (*MZsch*). The archive of the publishing firm founded in 1770 has about 50,000 printed and 5000 MS compositions, of the 18th century (Beethoven, Haydn and Mozart), the 19th century (notably Chopin, Liszt, Wagner and Reger) and the 20th (Hindemith, Stravinsky, Schoenberg, Orff, Henze, Ligeti and others). There are also numerous letters (of Beethoven, Tchaikovsky, Mahler, Bartók and many contemporary composers) and documents relating to the firm's history.

M. Seiffert: 'Das Haus Schott', *AMz*, xx (1893), 557; *RiemannL 12*; E. Laaff: 'B. Schott's Söhne', *MGG*; E. Helm: '200 Years of B. Schott's

Söhne', *High Fidelity*, xxi (1971), Jan, 55; H. C. Müller: *Die Frühgeschichte des Verlagshauses Schott bis 1797* (Mainz, 1976)

——. Stadtbibliothek und Stadtarchiv, Rheinallee 3B, 65 Mainz (*MZs*). Some printed music of the 15th–18th centuries comes from the former university library. The holdings also include the estate of Peter Cornelius and some 600 letters written to the firm of B. Schott's Söhne, including some from Beethoven.

F. W. E. Roth: 'Zur Bibliographie der Musikdrucke des 15.–18. Jahrhunderts der Mainzer Stadtbibliothek', *MMg*, xxi (1889/R), 25; G. Stephenson: 'Zeugnisse aus dem Leben und Schaffen eines Mainzer Komponisten: der Peter-Cornelius-Nachlass der Stadtbibliothek Mainz', *Mainzer Zeitschrift*, lix (1964), 103; H. Federhofer: 'Zwei Mainzer Sammlungen von Musikerbriefen des 19. Jahrhunderts', *Mainzer Zeitschrift*, lx–lxi (1965–6), 1–33

MANNHEIM. Wissenschaftliche Stadtbibliothek und Universitätsbibliothek, Schloss, Ostflügel, 68 Mannheim 1 (*MH*). In January 1971 the municipal and university libraries were combined and, although this is a general scholarly collection without a separate music section, the library has MS and early printed music, including many works published in Mannheim. The former library of the national theatre (but not including the music from it, which was destroyed) was taken over before World War II and includes many librettos and writings about theatre music.

F. Walther: *Archiv und Bibliothek des Grossherzoglichen Hof- und Nationaltheaters in Mannheim 1779–1839* (Leipzig, 1899)

METTEN. Abtei, Abteistrasse 3, 8354 Metten (*MT*). The abbey library has many liturgical works and sacred music of the 17th and early 18th centuries by local composers. There is also printed and MS instrumental and vocal music of the 18th and 19th centuries, especially works by Mannheim and Viennese Classical composers.

A. Scharnagl: 'Metten', *MGG*

MUNICH. Bayerische Staatsbibliothek, Ludwigstrasse 16, 8 Munich 34 (*Mbs*). The music section is especially noteworthy for its holdings of medieval liturgical MSS and 16th-century polyphony. There are also strong collections of sacred songbooks, opera scores and chamber music of the 18th century, first editions, and sources of Bavarian music history. Writings on music date from the 15th century. The collection was built up from monastery holdings, private Augsburg collections of the 16th century, the Bavarian Hofmusikintendanz, the Collectio Musicalis Maximilianea (containing Italian sacred music of the 16th–18th centuries), the Her collection of German librettos of the 18th and 19th centuries, and the private collections of Michael Haydn, Lachner, Rheinberger, Sandberger, Schafhäutl, Thibaut and others. The library maintains the Gesamtkatalog for Bavaria.

J. J. Maier: *Die musikalischen Handschriften der Kgl. Hof- und Staatsbibliothek in München* i: *Die Handschriften bis zum Ende des 17. Jahrhunderts* (Munich, 1879; corrected and enlarged new edn., with tablatures and partbooks by M.-L. Göllner and choral books by M.-L. Göllner and M. Bente, in preparation); J. von Gardner: 'Die altrussischen neumatischen Handschriften der Bayerischen Staatsbibliothek', *Die Welt der Sklaven*, ii (Wiesbaden, 1957), 322 [describes 17th-century MSS]; H. Zirnbauer: *Der Notenbestand der Reichsstädtischen Nürnbergischen Ratsmusik* (Nuremberg, 1959) [collection formerly in Nuremberg, in *Mbs* since 1894]; R. Schlötterer: 'Münchener Handschriften', *MGG* [lists works in *Mbs* and *Mu*]; I. Bezzel: *Bayerische Staatsbibliothek München, Bibliotheksführer: Geschichte und Bestände* (Munich, 1967) [pp.69ff on the music division]; M.-L. Göllner: 'Die Augsburger Bibliothek Herwart und ihre Lautentabulaturen: ein Musikbestand in der Bayerischen Staatsbibliothek', *FAM*, xvi (1969), 29; R. Münster: 'Nikolaus Lang und sein Michael-Haydn-Kopien in der Bayerischen Staatsbibliothek', *ÖMz*, xxvii (1972), 25; R. Münster: 'Zur Geschichte der handschrift-

lichen Konzertarien W. A. Mozarts in der Bayerischen Staatsbibliothek', *MJb 1971–2*, 157; R. Münster: 'Die Nachlässe in der Musiksammlung der Bayerischen Staatsbibliothek', *Beiträge zur Musikdokumentation: Franz Grasberger zum 60. Geburtstag* (Tutzing, 1975); *Münchener Bibliotheken: Bestände und Benützung* (Wiesbaden, 1975)

——. Frauenkirche Sammlung, Bibliothek des Metropolitankapitels, Maxburgstrasse 2, 8 Munich 2 (*Mbm*). The chapter holds 700 sacred music MSS of the 16th–19th centuries and some 16th- and 18th-century printed works.

Katalog der Musikhandschriften des Doms zu Unser Lieben Frau München (in preparation)

——. Städtische Musikbibliothek, Salvatorplatz 1, 8 Munich 1 (*Mmb*). A branch of the city's public library system, the collection contains valuable printed and MS items of the 19th and 20th centuries, including autographs of Munich composers and documentation on the city's musical life and composers connected with the city (such as autographs and first editions of Reger and Richard Strauss). There is a large folksong collection and an iconographical archive.

——. Theatermuseum der Clara-Ziegler-Stiftung, Galeriestrasse 4*a*, 8 Munich 22 (*Mth*). Opened in 1910 with the collection of the actress Clara Ziegler, the museum has early librettos, iconography, clippings, programmes and autograph letters. There are also some printed works of the 17th and 18th centuries and writings about music from the 18th century to the present.

R. Schaal: *Die vor 1801 gedruckten Libretti des Theatermuseums München* (Kassel, 1962); orig. in *Mf*, x–xiv (1957–61)

——. Universitätsbibliothek, Geschwister-Scholl-Platz 1, 8 Munich 22 (*Mu*). Although not now collecting music, the library has a number of music MSS dating from the 14th–18th centuries, and printed collections and individual works of the 16th–18th centuries. Some of the items (especially theoretical tracts) belonged to Heinrich Glarean (*d* 1563); the largest number came from south German monasteries. Among the holdings are chant MSS, partbooks by Senfl, Hofhaimer, Gombert, Josquin and others, a lute-violin tablature of the 16th century, and organbooks.

R. Schlötterer: 'Münchener Handschriften', *MGG*; C. Gottwald: *Die Musikhandschriften der Universitätsbibliothek München* (Wiesbaden, 1968) [with detailed contents and references for each MS]

MÜNSTER. Bibliothek des Bischöflischen Priesterseminars, Überwasserkirchplatz 3, 44 Münster (*MÜp*). The library has the collection of Abbé Fortunato Santini (formerly in *MÜu*), with over 5900 MS and printed works (500 were destroyed in World War II); besides autographs, the collection includes copies made by Santini. Italian sacred music of the 16th–18th centuries is well represented; there are also operas and instrumental music and important Handel items.

J. Killing: *Kirchenmusikalische Schätze der Bibliothek des Abbate F. Santini* (Düsseldorf, 1911); K. G. Fellerer: 'Fortunato Santini als Sammler und Bearbeiter Händelscher Werke', *HJb 1929*, 25; K. G. Fellerer: 'Verzeichnis der kirchenmusikalischen Werke der Santinischen Sammlung', *KJb*, xxvi–xxxii (1931–8) [incomplete inventory]; R. Ewerhart: 'Die Bischöfliche Santini-Bibliothek', *Das schöne Münster*, xxxv (1962); W. Wörmann: *Katalog der Santini-Bibliothek* (MS, n.d.)

——. Universitätsbibliothek, Krummer Timpen 3–5, 44 Münster (*MÜu*). The library's holdings of early printed and MS music include liturgical works received from monasteries during the secularization. In 1964 the collection was enriched by the Bürgsteinfurt library of the Prince of Bentheim and in 1966 by the Rheda music library of the Prince of Bentheim-Tecklenburg. Together these two collections contain about 4000 printed and MS works, mainly secular vocal and instrumental chamber music (with many works for flute) of 18th-century composers of the Mannheim school, Neapolitan operas, and songs and keyboard pieces of the Berlin school.

J. Domp: *Studien zur Geschichte der Musik an Westfälischen Adelshöfen im 18. Jahrhundert* (Regensburg, 1934) [list of works at Rheda, pp.14–34]; E. Kruttge: *Geschichte der Bürgsteinfurter Hofkapelle 1750–1817* (Hagen, 1973)

NEUBERG. Staatliche Bibliothek, Karlsplatz A17, 8858 Neuburg (*NBsb*). The library has printed music of the 17th and 18th centuries and some liturgical MSS. The holdings stem from various secularized monasteries, also from the collections of Prince Ott-Heinrich and of the humanist Heinrich Wolf.

NUREMBERG. General literature: H. Zirnbauer: *Geistliche Musik des Mittelalters und der Renaissance: Handschriften und frühe Drucke in Nürnberger Bibliotheken* (Nuremberg, 1963)

——. Germanisches National-Museum, Kornmarkt 1, 85 Nuremberg 1 (*Ngm*). The museum library has printed music of the 16th–18th centuries, music incunabula, and MSS dating back to the 9th century. The collection is especially strong in organology, but also includes lute tablatures and vocal music of the 16th and 17th centuries, and autographs of Lortzing (*Hans Sachs*) and Wagner (*Die Meistersinger*).

Bibliothek des Germanischen National-Museums zu Nürnberg (Nuremberg, 1855) [catalogue]; E. Rücker and W. Schadendorf: *Bibel und Gesangbuch im Zeitalter der Reformation* (Nuremberg, 1967) [exhibition catalogue]

——. Stadtbibliothek, Egidienplatz 23, 85 Nuremberg (*Nst*). The municipal library holds many early prints of Nuremberg composers and printers of the 16th–18th centuries, and theoretical treatises of the same period, also MS liturgical works. There is rich archival documentation for local music history. The material is derived from the collection of the municipal theatre and from the music scholar Rudolf Wagner. Photocopies of the Ratsmusik collection are in the library, although the collection was transferred to Munich (now in *Mbs*) in 1894.

Liste der 1952 und 1953 erworbenen Autographen (Nuremberg, 1954–5); H. Zirnbauer: *Der Notenbestand der Reichstädtischen Nürnbergischen Ratsmusik* (Nuremberg, 1959); H. Zirnbauer: *Nürnberger Musik zwischen Gotik und Barock* (Nuremberg, 1959) [exhibition catalogue]; *Die Handschriften der Stadtbibliothek Nürnberg* (Wiesbaden, 1965–7)

OFFENBACH. Johann André Verlag, Archiv, Frankfurterstrasse 28, 605 Offenbach (*OF*). The publishing firm has been in the André family for seven generations and among the collection of archival material are some 5000 examples of works published by the firm, a number of MSS that served as models for printing, musicians' letters, record books and other documentation on its activities.

W. Matthäus: *Johann André Musikverlag zu Offenbach am Main: Verlagsgeschichte und Bibliographie 1772–1800* (Tutzing, 1973); M. Thomas-André: *Johann André 1774–1974* (Offenbach, 1974) [Festschrift for 200th anniversary of firm]; catalogue of collection in preparation

OTTOBEUREN. Benediktiner-Abtei, 8942 Ottobeuren (*OB*). The abbey's MS collection includes medieval works and 17th-century keyboard suites by Froberger,

Kerll, Muffat and others. The abbey archive and the library of the attached Stiftskirche contain early printed works. Some of the early MSS from the abbey (which was founded in 764) were transferred to Munich (*Mbs*) in 1802.

W. Pfänder: 'Das Musikleben der Abtei Ottobeuren vom 16. Jahrhundert bis zur Säkularisation', *Studien und Mitteilungen zur Geschichte des Benediktiner-Ordens und seiner Zweige*, ed. R. Bauerreiss, lxxiii (1962), 45; W. Irtenkauf: 'Zur mittelalterlichen Liturgie- und Musikgeschichte Ottobeurens', *Ottobeuren: Festschrift zur 1200-Jahrfeier der Abtei* (Augsburg, 1964), 141–79; T. Wohnhaas: 'Ottobeuren', *MGG* [lists MSS transferred to *Mbs*]

PASSAU. Staatliche Bibliothek, Michaeligasse 11, 839 Passau (*Ps*). The collection derives primarily from the Fürstbischöfliche Bibliothek and the former Jesuit college. There are 15th- to 18th-century prints and some MSS.

POMMERSFELDEN. Graf von Schönborn'sche Schlossbibliothek, Schloss, 8602 Pommersfelden. Although most of the music in this private library is at Wiesentheid (*WD*), there are some important items here, including 11th- and 12th-century parchments with tracts of Guido and Aurelian of Réôme, 70 liturgical works printed in the 15th–17th centuries, a few liturgical MSS (one from the 11th century), several music works printed in the 16th–18th centuries, and 100 librettos.

REGENSBURG. General literature: E. R. Hauschka: *Regensburger Bibliotheken* (Regensburg, 1961)

——. Fürstlich Thurn und Taxis'sche Hofbibliothek, Schloss, Emmeramsplatz 5, 84 Regensburg (*Rtt*). The collection is based on the Thurn und Taxis Fürstliche Hofkapelle and Hoftheater, but also received material from the Neresheim and Obermarchtal monasteries. Besides chant MSS and tablatures, the library is notable for its 18th-century holdings, especially opera and instrumental music.

R. Freytag: 'Aus der Geschichte der Fürstlich Thurn und Taxisschen Hofbibliothek', *Zeitschrift für Bibliothekswesen*, xl (1923), 323; S. Färber: *Das Regensburger Fürstlich Thurn und Taxissche Hoftheater und seine Oper 1760–1786* (Regensburg, 1936) [catalogue of operatic works in Hofbibliothek, pp.1–154]; E. Tscheuschner: *Die Neresheimer Orgeltabulaturen der Fürstlichen Thurn und Taxisschen Bibliothek* (Kassel, 1963)

——. Bischöfliche Zentralbibliothek, Proske-Musikbibliothek, St Petersweg 13, 84 Regensburg (*Rp*). The library contains the collection built up by Karl Proske (d 1861), comprising chiefly his own copies of works in Italian libraries. There is a collection of Antiquitates Ratisbonenses, a collection of theoretical writings and of sacred and secular vocal music as well as acquisitions from the collections of Dominikus Mettenleiter (d 1868; 18th- and 19th-century prints and MSS), F. H. Witt (d 1888; the music of the Cäcilienverein), F. X. Haberl (d 1910) and the library of Karl Weinmann (d 1929).

K. Weinmann: 'Die Proskesche Musikbibliothek', *Festschrift... Rochus Freiherrn von Liliencron* (Leipzig, 1910), 387, repr. in *KJb*, xxiv (1911), 107; B. Stäblein: 'Choralhandschriften der Regensburger Bibliotheken', *Musica sacra*, lxii (1932), 198; W. Brennecke: *Die Handschrift A.R. 940/41 der Proske-Bibliothek zu Regensburg* (Kassel, 1953); P. Mohr: *Die Handschrift B211–215 der Proske-Bibliothek zu Regensburg mit kurzer Beschreibung der Handschriften B216–219 und B220–222* (Kassel, 1955); A. Scharnagl: 'Die Orgeltabulatur C11 der Proske-Musikbibliothek', *Festschrift Bruno Stäblein* (Kassel, 1967), 206; A. Scharnagl: *Die Proske-Musikbibliothek in Regensburg* (in preparation)

——. Staatliche Bibliothek, Gesandtenstrasse 13, 84

Regensburg (*Rs*). Music published in the 18th century is well represented in the library's collection, which also has chorales and songbooks of the 16th–18th centuries. There are autographs of local composers, including Max Reger. Many works came from neighbouring monasteries (notably St Emmeram), as well as from the city library (Ratsbibliothek), the ministerial library of the evangelical church and the Kammerer estate (1964).

Oberpfälzische Komponisten zur Zeit Mozarts: Ausstellung vom 10. bis 29. Juni 1963 (Regensburg, 1963) [exhibition catalogue]

——. Universitätsbibliothek, Universitätsstrasse 33, 84 Regensburg (*Ru*). Since 1968 the library has absorbed the collection of the former Institut für Musikforschung, with its material on folksong, including valuable field recordings. The library also includes a part of the ethnomusicological collection of the former Staatliches Institut für Deutsche Musikforschung in Berlin.

F. Hoerburger: *Katalog der europäischen Volksmusik im Schallarchiv des Institutes für Musikforschung* (Regensburg, 1952)

STUTTGART. Staatliche Hochschule für Musik und Darstellende Kunst, Urbansplatz 2, 7 Stuttgart (*Sh*). Besides its general holdings of 19th- and 20th-century editions (much 19th-century music was lost in World War II, however), the conservatory has some 150 works printed in the 17th and 18th centuries and 50 MSS copied in the 18th–20th centuries.

——. Württembergische Landesbibliothek, Konrad-Adenauer-Strasse 8, 7 Stuttgart (*Sl*). The collection is noteworthy for its medieval chant MSS, 16th-century songbooks, MS opera, cantata and ballet scores, and printed piano reductions of the 18th and 19th centuries. There is also a large collection of hymnbooks. Many of the works came from secularized monasteries, from the Hofkapelle and Hoftheater, and from bequests of Württemberg composers.

A. Halm: *Katalog über die Musik-Codices des 16. und 17. Jahrhunderts auf der Kgl. Landesbibliothek in Stuttgart* (Leipzig, 1902–3); A. Kriessmann: 'Die Choralhandschriften der Württembergischen Landesbibliothek', *KJb*, xix (1934), 41; *Die Handschriften der Württembergischen Landesbibliothek Stuttgart*, 1st ser., i, ed. C. Gottwald (Wiesbaden, 1964), 2nd ser., vi/1, ed. C. Gottwald (Wiesbaden, 1965); C. Gottwald and W. Irtenkauf: 'Stuttgarter Musikhandschriften', *MGG*

TEGERNSEE. Pfarrkirche, Katholisches Pfarramt, 818 Tegernsee (*TEG*). The collection consists of sacred music from 1700 to about 1840, chiefly MS.

R. Münster and R. Machold: *Thematischer Katalog der Musikhandschriften der ehemaligen Klosterkirchen Weyarn, Tegernsee und Benediktbeuren* (Munich, 1971)

TRIER. Stadtbibliothek, Weberbach 25, 55 Trier (*TRs*). The library has a notable collection of chant MSS that date back to the 10th century.

P. Bohn: 'Eine Trierer Liederhandschrift aus dem Ende des 15. bis Anfang des 16. Jahrhunderts', *MMg*, xxix (1897), 37; *Die liturgischen Handschriften, Beschreibendes Verzeichnis der Handschriften der Stadtbibliothek Trier*, iv, x (Trier, 1897, 1931); R. Ewerhart: *Die Handschrift 322/1994 der Stadtbibliothek Trier als musikalische Quelle* (diss., U. of Cologne, 1953); R. Ewerhart: 'Trier', *MGG*

TÜBINGEN. Musikwissenschaftliches Institut der Eberhard-Karls-Universität, Schulberg 2, 47 Tübingen (*Tmi*). At its founding the institute was given most of the early music collection of the Evangelisches Stift (*Tes*). Besides the considerable collection of medieval and Renaissance theoretical works, 16th-century music and works of J. S. Bach and his circle, the institute has held the collection of the Schwäbisches Landesmusikarchiv

(*Tl*) since 1963. This archive was founded in 1935 and contains 3000 MS and printed works, primarily sacred music (masses, motets, cantatas, liturgical books and chorale books) of the 18th century from Swabian monasteries, seminaries and other religious foundations.

W. Gerstenberg: *Schwäbisches Landesmusikarchiv am Musikwissenschaftlichen Institut der Universität Tübingen: Inventar* (Tübingen, 1963)

——. Universitätsbibliothek, Wilhelmstrasse 32, 74 Tübingen (*Tu*). Music holdings deposited during World War II for safe-keeping have been returned to Berlin (*B*). The university has a collection of early prints and MSS, including theoretical works, and some rare music items have been transferred from the city's Evangelisches Stift (*Tes*).

A. Bopp: *Das Musikleben in der freien Reichstadt Biberach: Katalog der Kickschen Notensammlung* (Kassel, 1930) [catalogue of library's Kick collection on pp.100–179]; W. Virneisel: *Musikhandschriften und Musikdrucke aus 5 Jahrhunderten ... beschreibendes Verzeichnis* (Tübingen, 1957)

WEYARN. Some portions of the collection from the parish church of Weyarn were transferred to Munich (*Mbs*) in 1803, and in 1964 the music was placed on deposit at Freising (*FS*).

WIESBADEN. Breitkopf & Härtel, Archiv, Walkmühlstrasse 52, 62 Wiesbaden (*WIbh*). The firm's archive still possesses MS and printed music and theoretical works from the Classical period to the present. Some of the collection, however, was dispersed during World War II, the private collection of Härtel went to the Staatsbibliothek Preussischer Kulturbesitz in Berlin (*B*), and some portions (in particular many musicians' letters) were bought by the Hessische Landes- und Hochschulbibliothek, Darmstadt (*DS*), in 1951.

W. Hitzig: *Katalog des Archivs von Breitkopf & Härtel* (Leipzig, 1925–6)

——. Hessische Landesbibliothek, Rheinstrasse 55–7, 62 Wiesbaden (*WIl*). The library's early music holdings are especially rich in 16th-century works. Copies are received on deposit from the music publishers in the city.

F. W. E. Roth: 'Musikalisches aus Handschriften der K. Landesbibliothek zu Wiesbaden', *MMg*, xx (1888), 48 [describes MSS of 10th–16th centuries, including a 13th-century 'Reisencodex' of St Hildegard]; G. Zedler: *Die Handschriften der Nassauischen Landesbibliothek zu Wiesbaden* (Leipzig, 1931); H. J. Moser: 'Eine Musikaliendruckerei auf einer deutschen Ritterburg', *ZMw*, xvii (1935), 97 [describes 4-voice masses by Senfl, Josquin, Mouton, Fevin, Janequin and Richafort, printed 1557–60 by the Count of Büdingen]

WIESENTHEID. Graf von Schönborn-Wiesentheid Musiksammlung, Schloss, 8714 Wiesentheid (*WD*). The contents of this private library are divided between Pommersfelden and Wiesentheid. Although the collection possesses works of the period from 1670 to 1825, its greatest strength lies in sacred and chamber music (in particular cello music) of the 18th century. There are also letters and other documentation of musical activity at the count's court.

F. Zobeley: 'Werke Händels in der Gräfl. von Schönbornschen Musikbibliothek', *HJb 1931*, 98; F. Zobeley: *Rudolf Franz Erwein Graf von Schönborn und seine Musikpflege* (Würzburg, 1949); F. Zobeley: *Die Musikalien der Grafen von Schönborn-Wiesentheid*, i/1 (Tutzing, 1967) [review of catalogue by W. G. Marigold, *Notes*, xxiv (1967–8), 715]

WILSTER. Stadtarchiv, Doos'sche Bibliothek, Rathaus, 2213 Wilster (*WILd*). There are partbooks for 13 works printed in Antwerp, Lyons and Venice from 1576 to 1582 (works of L'Estocart, Ingegneri,

Massaino, Gabucci, Lassus, Balbi, Pordenon, Merulo and Vecoli).

H. Albrecht: 'Musikdrucke aus den Jahren 1576–1582', *Mf*, ii (1949), 204

WOLFENBÜTTEL. Herzog August Bibliothek, Lessingplatz 1, 334 Wolfenbüttel (*W*). A first ducal library was collected from 1550 by Duke Julius of Brunswick-Wolfenbüttel (whose first librarian from 1571–2 was the composer Leonhard Schroeter) and his son Duke Heinrich Julius; that collection was given to the University of Helmstedt in 1618. The second and more famous founder was Duke August (*d* 1666) who built up the library: among contemporary composers and theorists he collected were Praetorius, Schütz, Demantius, Franck, Gastoldi, Vecchi, Hassler, Lassus, Palestrina, Marenzio, Frescobaldi and Kircher. There are also four Petrucci editions (1504–5) and an important tablature collection (Vallet, Neusidler, Besard and others). The collection from the former university library in Helmstedt was returned to Wolfenbüttel by the early 20th century; it comprises theoretical works by major 16th- and 17th-century writers. In 1960 the library acquired printed and MS music, chiefly sacred, from the Cantorei Sancti Stephani of Helmstedt. There are also 18th-century editions of Handel, Hasse, Haydn, Mozart, Beethoven (first editions) and their contemporaries, and about 1750 librettos of the period from 1568 to 1800. The library's most famous possession is the 13th-century parchment 'W' with the earliest extant Notre Dame repertory, from the estate of Matthias Flacius, acquired in 1597.

E. Vogel: *Kataloge der Herzog-August-Bibliothek Wolfenbüttel*, viii: *Die Handschriften nebst den älteren Druckwerken der Musik-Abteilung* (Wolfenbüttel, 1890); W. Schmieder and G. Hartwieg: *Kataloge der Herzog-August-Bibliothek Wolfenbüttel*, xii, xiii: *Musik: alte Drucke bis etwa 1750* (Frankfurt am Main, 1967); E. Thiel and G. Rohr: *Kataloge der Herzog-August-Bibliothek Wolfenbüttel*, xiv: *Libretti: Verzeichnis der bis 1800 erschienenen Textbücher* (Frankfurt am Main, 1970); L. A. Dittmer, H. M. Brown and A. Main: 'Wolfenbütteler Handschriften', *MGG*

WÜRZBURG. Universitätsbibliothek, Domerschulstrasse 16, 87 Würzburg (*WÜu*). Most of the rich early chant MSS and the incunabula collection of the library survived World War II, although much of the later printed material was destroyed. The university has since acquired printed and MS parts for early 19th-century compositions.

H. Beck: 'Alte Musikbestände der Hofkirche zu Würzburg', *Mf*, xvii (1964), 45 [on masses and a *Te Deum* by Haydn, Danzi, Diabelli, J. E. Brandl, J. A. André, Hummel and V. Maschek]; *Die Handschriften der Universitätsbibliothek Würzburg* (Wiesbaden, 1970–) [vol.i describes MSS of Cistercian and Benedictine origin]

GREAT BRITAIN (*GB*)

The locations of many important private British collections now in libraries are given in J. H. Davies: 'Principal Music Collections, formerly in Private Hands and now to be found in Institutions and Libraries of Great Britain', *Musicalia: Sources of Information in Music* (Oxford, 1966, 2/1969), 127, and in A. H. King: *Some British Collectors of Music, c.1600–1960* (Cambridge, 1963). Two handbooks issued by the Library Association are M. W. Long: *Music in British Libraries: a Directory of Resources*, Library Association Research Publications, vii (London, 1971, 2/1974), and M. W. Long: *Musicians and Libraries in the United Kingdom*, Library Association Research Publications, viii (London, 1972). The half-yearly jour-nal *Brio*, issued by the British branch of the International Association of Music Libraries, has printed useful information about various library acquisitions since 1964. The most valuable union catalogues devoted to Great Britain are W. H. Frere: *Bibliotheca musico-liturgica: a Descriptive Handlist of the Musical and Latin-liturgical MSS of the Middle Ages preserved in the Libraries of Great Britain and Ireland* (London, 1901 [dated 1894]–1932/R1967), E. B. Schnapper: *The British Union-catalogue of Early Music printed before the year 1801: a Record of the Holdings of over One Hundred Libraries throughout the British Isles* (London, 1957) and, with mostly British locations, R. T. Daniel and P. le Huray: *The Sources of English Church Music, 1549–1660*, EECM, suppl.i (1972). There are also listings in A. Simpson: 'A Short-title List of Printed English Instrumental Tutors up to 1800, found in British Libraries', *RMARC*, vi (1966), 24, and a list of film copies in British libraries of which the originals are in foreign locations is given in D. Charlton: 'A National Catalogue of Music Microfilms', *RMARC*, xi (1973), 1–70.

With the Copyright Act of 1911 six libraries became entitled to receive copies of all books and music published in Great Britain: the British Library (formerly British Museum), Bodleian Library (Oxford), Cambridge University Library, National Library of Scotland (Edinburgh), National Library of Wales (Aberystwyth), and Trinity College Library (Dublin). Recordings are not covered by the 1911 act.

ABERDEEN. University Library, King's College, Old Aberdeen AB9 2UB (*A*). The Macbean Historic Collection includes songs of the Stuart and Jacobite periods. The W. L. Taylor Collection, acquired in 1910, contains complete and partial versions of the psalms.

Catalogue of the Taylor Collection of Psalm Versions, University of Aberdeen Studies, lxxxv (Aberdeen, 1921); M. D. Allerdyce: *Aberdeen University Library Macbean Collection*, University of Aberdeen Studies, cxxvi (Aberdeen, 1949) [catalogue of books, pamphlets, broadsides and portraits gathered by Macbean]

ABERYSTWYTH. National Library of Wales, Aberystwyth SY23 3BU (*AB*). Founded in 1909, the library has rich holdings of works by Welsh composers, Welsh ballads and songs, and documents concerning Welsh music. There is a volume of 16th- and 17th-century lute pieces. As a copyright library it receives annually a considerable amount of new and other music.

Bibliotheca celtica (1910–) [lists Welsh music and literature in the library]

BIRMINGHAM. University Music Library, Barber Institute, PO Box 363, Birmingham B15 2TS (*Bu*). A 17th-century collection of songs, odes and anthems includes autographs of Blow and Purcell. There is also a representative collection of mainly 18th-century music in pre-1801 editions, as well as the Gloria Rose collection of transcriptions of 17th-century Italian works. Granville Bantock's collection includes his own MSS. The library has many works by Elgar, the university's first music professor.

W. Shaw: 'A Collection of Musical MSS in the Autograph of Henry Purcell and other English Composers *c* 1665–85', *The Library*, xiv (1959), 126; I. Fenlon: *A Catalogue of Printed Music and Musical MSS before 1801 in the Music Library of the University of Birmingham* (London, 1976)

BOURNEMOUTH. Central Library, Dorset County Library, Bournemouth BH1 3DJ (*BO*). The John B. M. Camm bequest (1912) of about 4000 items consists principally of orchestral scores including first editions of works by Dvořák, Glazunov and Tchaikovsky.

BRISTOL. Central (Public) Library, College Green, Bristol BS1 5TL (*BRp*). The bequests to the music library of George Riseley (1930) and Basil Harwood (1935–6) include early editions of 18th-century music. The Russell Collection (1968) contains 1100 Victorian songs. The library is now Avon County Library.

Catalogue of Music Scores (Bristol, 1959) [dictionary catalogue, imprints not given]

CAMBRIDGE. General literature: H. W. Tillyard: 'Some Byzantine Musical MSS at Cambridge', *Annual of the British School at Athens*, xxii (London, 1916–18), 133; V. Duckles: 'Some Observations of Music Libraries at Cambridge', *Notes*, 2nd ser., ix (1952–3), 388–94; A. N. L. Munby: *Cambridge College Libraries* (Cambridge, 1960, 2/1962)

——. Cambridge Union Society, Bridge Street, Cambridge CB2 1UB (*Cus*). The bequest of the Victorian composer Erskine Allon (1897) included many scores, some of which were damaged during World War II.

——. Clare College, Cambridge CB2 1TL (*Cclc*). In 1924 the college received Cecil Sharp's bequest of his MSS of British and American folksongs.

——. Corpus Christi College, Cambridge CB2 1RH (*Ccc*). The Parker Library, the private library of the Master and Fellows of the college, contains liturgical and theoretical MSS of the 9th to 15th centuries, including the famous Winchester Troper and treatises by Hucbald, Odo of Cluny and the MS of Walter Odington's *De speculatione musices*.

M. R. James: *A Descriptive Catalogue of the MSS in the Library of Corpus Christi College Cambridge* (Cambridge, 1912)

——. Fitzwilliam Museum, Trumpington Street, Cambridge CB2 1RB (*Cfm*). The collection was founded in 1816 with the bequest of Richard Fitzwilliam, 7th Viscount Fitzwilliam of Meryon. Besides the well-known Fitzwilliam Virginal Book, Lord Herbert of Cherbury's Lutebook and 15 volumes of Handel autograph material, the museum library includes MS and printed Italian cantatas, French operas and motets and 18th-century English harpsichord music. Among the museum's important accessions are MS copies of Handel's works made by J. C. Smith, owned by Thomas Greatorex, sold in 1832 and presented in 1902 by the son of Henry Barrett-Lennard. It also holds some of E. J. Dent's library, which includes English and Italian music (lutenists, Purcell) bequeathed to him in 1947 by Gerald M. Cooper. There are autographs of two Mozart duet sonatas (K497 and K521) and of works by Bach, Beethoven, Storace and Wesley. Charles Fairfax Murray's gifts contained 18th- and 19th-century music. The museum also owns a number of liturgical MSS of the 10th to 16th centuries, many of foreign provenance. It was decided in 1925 to transfer the modern works in the museum, including music presented to it by Richard Pendlebury between 1880 and 1902, to the Pendlebury Library of the music faculty; the museum has since acquired autograph MSS of 20th-century composers including Berkeley, Bliss, Britten, Gerhard, Holst, Tippett and Vaughan Williams.

J. A. Fuller Maitland and A. H. Mann: *Catalogue of the Music in the Fitzwilliam Museum, Cambridge* (London, 1893) [lists works to

*c*1800]; C. Cudworth: 'Richard, Viscount Fitzwilliam, and the French Baroque Music in the Fitzwilliam Museum, Cambridge', *FAM*, xiii (1966), 27; *Handel and the Fitzwilliam* (Cambridge, 1974) [essays and exhibition catalogue]

——. Gonville and Caius College, Cambridge CB2 1TA (*Cgc*). Among several 12th- to 16th-century liturgical MSS with music the library owns an early 16th-century choirbook (MS 667/760, at the University Library) compiled by Edward Higgons (*b c*1475; *d* before 16 Jan 1538) and containing a *Magnificat* 'regali' by Fayrfax and five- and six-voice masses and motets by English composers including Cornysh, Fayrfax and Ludford.

M. R. James, ed.: *A Descriptive Catalogue of the MSS in the Library of Gonville and Caius College* (Cambridge, 1907–8, suppl. 1914); G. Chew: 'The Provenance and Date of the Caius and Lambeth Choirbooks', *ML*, li (1970), 107

——. King's College, Cambridge CB2 1ST (*Ckc*). The collection of Louis Thompson Rowe, particularly rich in 18th-century chamber music, was received by the college in 1928. Nearly 600 volumes from the library of A. H. Mann were acquired in 1930. They are chiefly librettos and early editions of Handel, early keyboard and theoretical works, and 18th-century songbooks. The library also has the Torpyn book of lute-songs (bequeathed by J. M. Keynes in 1939), the collections of Lawrence Haward, part of that of Boris Ord, and letters and compositions written by E. J. Dent.

W. B. Squire: *Catalogue of the King's Music Library* (London, 1927); J. Vlasto: 'The Rowe Music Library, King's College, Cambridge', *MR*, xii (1951), 72

——. Magdalene College, Cambridge CB3 0AG (*Cmc*). Samuel Pepys's library was received by the college in 1724. The collection includes some works of Pepys's period (music for recorder or flageolet, songs, guitar music, Italian operas and writings on theory and instruments), a MS of about 1490 that is an important source of English church music, a late 15th-century collection of motets and chansons by French and Flemish composers and a MS of Machaut songs. The college also owns several liturgical MSS of the 13th–16th centuries.

Pepys MSS at Magdalene College, Cambridge, 1485–1703, HMC 70; *Bibliotheca Pepysiana*, ii–iii (London, 1914–40) [describes music]

——. Pembroke College, Cambridge CB2 1RF (*Cpc*). A set of partbooks assembled for the college by Henry May (*d* 1634) contains psalms and anthems. There is also some 18th-century chamber music and volumes of the collected writings of W. B. Squire.

——. Pendlebury Library of Music, University Music School, West Road, Cambridge CB3 9DP (*Cpl*). The music collected by Richard Pendlebury and originally presented to the Fitzwilliam Museum between 1880 and 1902 was received at the music faculty in 1929. The library has several research collections, which include many MSS (over 100 of them pre-1800), several hundred pre-1800 editions of music and theoretical works, E. J. Dent's transcriptions of 17th- and 18th-century Italian music and J. B. Trend's of Spanish music, Laurence Picken's collection of first editions of J. S. Bach, and the diaries and other archives of R. J. S. Stevens and W. H. Weiss.

——. Peterhouse, Cambridge CB2 1RD (*Cp*). A collection of partbooks, now at the University Library, was assembled about 1635 by John Cosin, Bishop of Durham and later Master of Peterhouse, and is probably the most valuable liturgical source of the period; known as the 'Caroline' set, the collection also includes organ pieces by Cambridge composers. The 'Henrician' set of partbooks, which is lacking the tenor, dates from about 1540 and includes masses and motets by Aston, Fayrfax and Taverner.

A. Hughes: *Catalogue of the Musical MSS at Peterhouse Cambridge* (Cambridge, 1953) [with historical account of MSS and inventory of contents]

——. Trinity College, Cambridge CB2 1TQ (*Ctc*). The college possesses a roll of 15th-century English carols, published in 1891 by Fuller Maitland and Rockstro, two 15th-century Greek MSS with music, lute tablatures of Bacheler, Greaves, Robert Johnson and Robert Taylor, 17th-century lute-songs by Handford and anthems of George Loosemore. There are autographs of Alan Gray, Parry, Stanford (composition treatise) and T. A. Walmisley, early printed music of Byrd, Mace, Morley, Playford and Purcell and theoretical works by Zarlino.

M. R. James: *Catalogue of Western MSS in the Library of Trinity College, Cambridge* (Cambridge, 1900–04)

——. University Library, 1 West Road, Cambridge CB3 9DR (*Cu*). The university established a library during the second decade of the 15th century; the music collection has grown as an integral part of the whole and contains rich holdings of medieval MSS (breviaries, missals, gospel-books) and of printed works from the late 15th century onwards. Printed music was first acquired in quantity under the terms of the Copyright Act of the 1790s, and since then a considerable collection of British music has accrued. There are several noteworthy collections: a rich store of 16th- and 17th-century tablatures, mainly for lute (and lyra viol); ten volumes of autograph song MSS by James Hook from the library of A. H. Mann, donated by his family in 1929; 486 volumes of 17th- and 18th-century chamber music, together with rare books mainly on thorough-bass, bequeathed in 1940 by F. T. Arnold; 552 items (books, early editions, portraits and relics) bequeathed by Marion Scott in 1953 from her Haydn collection; autograph MSS of Peter Warlock, mainly his transcriptions of 16th- and 17th-century music. The Paul Hirsch Library, housed in the University Library from 1936 to 1946, now forms part of the British Library collection. The music MSS of Ely Cathedral, some 600 works in 38 volumes, were deposited in the library in 1970. The collection consists principally of English music gathered by James Hawkins, organist at Ely from 1682 to 1739. It also has on deposit the Peterhouse collection of 17th-century partbooks and the Gonville and Caius College Choirbook.

C. Hardwick and H. R. Luard: *A Catalogue of the MSS Preserved in the Library of the University of Cambridge* (Cambridge, 1856–67), i, v; W. E. Dickson: *A Catalogue of Ancient Choral Services and Anthems Preserved among the MS Scores and Partbooks in the Cathedral Church of Ely* (Cambridge, 1861); C. E. Sayle: *Early English Printed Books in the University Library Cambridge, 1475 to 1640* (Cambridge, 1900–07) [with index to music items]; D. R. Wakeling: 'An Interesting Music Collection', *ML*, xxvi (1945), 159 [describes the Arnold Collection]; I. Harwood: 'The Origin of the Cambridge Lute MSS', *LSJ*, v (1963), 32; A. E. B. Owen: *Summary Guide to Accessions of Western MSS, other than Medieval, since 1867* (Cambridge, 1966) [music on pp.28f]; N. Nordstrom: 'The Cambridge Consort Books', *Journal of the Lute Society of America*, v (1972), 70–103

CANTERBURY. Cathedral Archives and Library, Canterbury CT1 2EG (*CA*). The library contains about 80 volumes of MS partbooks of the 18th and early 19th centuries. Apart from the large collection of music for the cathedral the library houses the music of the former Canterbury Catch Club, including many volumes of glees and choral works.

CARDIFF. Central (Public) Library, The Hayes, Cardiff CF1 2QU (*CDp*). In 1919 R. Bonner Morgan presented the library with about 500 items amassed by Herbert Mackworth between 1761 and 1788. Consisting mainly of English and French chamber music, Italian operas, and English, French and Spanish songs, the collection also includes several hundred single-sheet songs. About 60 MS volumes contain complete scores of operas by Alessandro Scarlatti, Bononcini, Capelli, Porpora and other Italians, and there are several volumes of Italian chamber cantatas, including 18 by Scarlatti. The composers best represented are Handel and Hasse. The library has rich holdings of Welsh music.

M. Boyd: catalogue of the collection with indexes (MS, *CDp*, 1969); M. Boyd: 'Music MSS in the Mackworth Collection at Cardiff', *ML*, liv (1973), 133 [with summary of MS contents, some incipits and list of items not in *BUCEM*]; D. Stefanović: 'Unknown Russian Music Mss at Cardiff', *Musica slavica*, ed. E. Arro and F. Steiner (Wiesbaden, 1976)

DUNDEE. Public Libraries, Albert Institute, Dundee DD1 1DB (*DU*). In 1884 the Dundee Town Council received the bequest of Andrew John Wighton (*d* 1866). Consisting of about 700 titles, most of them collected on the Continent although strongly Scottish in origin or association, the set includes copies made by Wighton of early MSS or rare printed works.

H. M. Willsher: 'The Wighton Collection of National Music', *Review of the Activities of the Dundee Public Libraries*, ii (1948), July, 12

DURHAM. Cathedral Library, The College, Durham DH1 3EH (*DRc*). The bequest of Philip Falle, Canon of Durham until his death in 1742, consists of more than 400 items, about half being instrumental music and the rest secular and sacred vocal music and writings on music. There are many editions by Phalèse, Playford, Roger and Walsh. In 1958 the cathedral received on indefinite loan the music portion of the Bamburgh Library, formed by the Sharp family in the 17th and 18th centuries at Bamburgh Castle, Northumberland: it consists of 384 items of which 150 are single-sheet copies of songs and arias, predominantly printed, and MSS largely of instrumental works, many for violin. The cathedral also has an extensive collection of MS English church music, mainly from the 17th century.

P. Evans: '17th-century Chamber Music MSS at Durham', *ML*, xxxvi (1955), 205; A. I. Doyle: 'Unfamiliar Libraries IV: the Bamburgh Library', *Book Collector*, viii (1959), 14; R. A. Harman: *A Catalogue of the Printed Music and Books on Music in Durham Cathedral Library* (London, 1969) [lists works printed to 1825]; B. Crosby: 'Durham Cathedral's Music MSS', *MT*, cxv (1974), 418; B. Crosby: *Durham Cathedral MS Music* [catalogue in preparation]

EDINBURGH. National Library of Scotland, Music Department, George IV Bridge, Edinburgh EH1 1EW (*En*). Known until 1925 as the Advocates Library, the institution has functioned since 1709 as a copyright depository for music printed anywhere in Great Britain. In 1927 the library received from Lady Dorothea Ruggles-Brise the 900 items constituting the Glen Collection; gathered by John Glen (*d* 1904), music publisher, dealer and bagpipe maker, it consists principally of printed Scottish music and works on the subject. In 1929 the holdings were enriched by the bequest of A. W. Inglis, consisting of about 740 items of English and Scottish music of the 18th and early 19th centuries, and by the Alexander Cowan Collection of over 1000 liturgical works of the 16th to 20th centuries. The late Earl of Balfour's Handel collection was given in

1938. In 1952 Cecil Hopkinson donated his collection of Berlioz autographs, early editions and literature and in 1969 he added his valuable Verdi material. In 1973 the library received by bequest the John Murdoch Henderson Collection of Scottish music, comprising 786 items, mainly 18th- and 19th-century printed editions. Apart from the Scottish collections, the library has substantial holdings of 18th-century music, particularly instrumental. Works by modern central European, Russian, French and American composers are represented; other fields of interest are 20th-century opera and chamber music, and instrumental tutors of all periods. Among additional items of interest are the MSS of Percy Grainger and the Scone Antiphoner (or Carver Choirbook), the earliest and most extensive collection of sacred polyphony in Scotland and an important source of the music of the 16th-century Scottish composer Robert Carver.

H. W. Meikle and M. R. Dobie: *Catalogue of the MSS acquired since 1925* (Edinburgh, 1938–68); D. Stevens: 'The MS Edinburgh, National Library of Scotland, Adv.Ms.5.1.15', *MD*, xiii (1959), 155; K. Elliott: 'The Carver Choir-book', *ML*, xli (1960), 349; G. Beechey: 'A New Source of 17th-century Keyboard Music', *ML*, l (1969), 278 [Inglis 94 MS 3343, with works by Blow, Hart, Lully, Purcell; article gives incipits]; *Hector Berlioz, 1803–1869* (Edinburgh, 1969) [exhibition catalogue]; *Summary Catalogue of the Advocates MSS* (Edinburgh, 1971); detailed catalogue of MSS, typescript, available in library

——. New College Library, University of Edinburgh, Mound Place, Edinburgh EH1 2LU (*Enc*). Serving the university's divinity faculty, the library has the James Thin Collection of about 7500 items of hymnology, some containing music.

J. Laing: *Catalogue of the Printed Books and MSS* (Edinburgh, 1868) [excluding the Thin Collection]

——. Public Library, George IV Bridge, Edinburgh EH1 1EG (*Ep*). Besides its collection of Scottish music the library has several others of interest, including the archive of the Edinburgh Musical Society, and bequests of R. C. Marr, comprising chiefly 18th-century printed music, and of Friedrich Niecks.

——. Reid Music Library, University of Edinburgh, Alison House, Nicolson Square, Edinburgh EH8 9BH (*Er*). Founded in 1838 with the bequest of John Reid (*d* 1807), the library has had numerous other gifts since then, including the private collections of John Donaldson, Herbert S. Oakeley, Friedrich Niecks and Donald Tovey, and Paul Weiss's collection of Beethoveniana. The holdings are rich in theoretical works from the 17th and 18th centuries and first editions of music from the 17th–19th centuries, and there are five volumes of Lassus's *Patrocinium musices* (1573–89). The library is a department of the main University Library and serves the music faculty.

H. Gál: *Catalogue of MSS, Printed Music and Books on Music up to 1850 in the Library of the Music Department of the University of Edinburgh (Reid Library)* (Edinburgh, 1941); J. M. Allan: 'The Reid Music Library, University of Edinburgh: its Origin and Friends', *Library World*, li (1948), 99

——. School of Scottish Studies Library, 27 George Square, Edinburgh EH8 9LD. The school is a department of the arts faculty of the University of Edinburgh and was established in 1951. Its library contains a general collection of Scottish MSS, including 18th- and 19th-century fiddlers' tune books, a number of early 20th-century collections of pipe music (an important source for pibroch music), the Lady Doyle MS (1811), which is one of the earlier extant MSS of Scots Gaelic song and instrumental music, and the Lucy Broadwood MS collection of Scottish material.

——. University Library, George Square, Edinburgh EH8 9LJ (*Eu*). From William Mure of Rowallan the library has a lute tablature book, a treble partbook and his 17th-century MS copies of English and Scottish songs, as well as early 18th-century French books. There are also treble, tenor and bass parts of a Scots metrical psalter (*c*1566), a 16th-century collection of lute-dances, a music book of Louis de France (*c*1680), John Squyer's music book (*c*1700) and some organ pieces and a treatise on music by William Herschel. Printed works include 16th-century French masses and late 17th- and early 18th-century English and Italian madrigals and English songsheets. Marjorie Kennedy-Fraser's records (MS transcriptions from wax cylinders) of Gaelic song collected in the Highlands are in the library; there are also the late 18th-century Angus Fraser MS of Scots Gaelic tunes, arranged for harp or keyboard, and Joseph MacDonald's *Compleat Theory of the Scots Highland Bagpipe* (*c*1762).

J. Cutts: '17th-century Songs and Lyrics in Edinburgh University Library Music MS Dc.1.69', *MD*, xiii (1959), 169; *Index to MSS, Edinburgh University Library* (Boston, 1964)

EXETER. Cathedral Library, Bishop's Palace, Exeter EX1 1HX (*EXc*). The archives of the dean and chapter contain about 30 letters and papers of S. S. Wesley (1840–45) and one letter of Purcell (1686). There are 18 volumes of MS choir parts (one late 18th century, the rest 19th).

——. Central Library, Castle Street, Exeter EX4 3PQ (*EXcl*). The Burnet Morris Index contains references to printed and MS sources concerning musical figures connected with Devon (including Christopher Gibbons, Locke, S. S. Wesley and other musicians).

——. East Devon Area Record Office, Castle Street, Exeter EX4 3PQ (*EXed*). The office has a 15th-century four-voice *Magnificat* setting from the borough archives of Dartmouth, the archive of the Exeter Oratorio Society and a letter from J. L. Dussek to his publisher dated 1807.

T. Dart: 'The Dartmouth Magnificat', *ML*, xxxix (1958), 209

——. University Library, Prince of Wales Road, Exeter EX4 4PT (*EXu*). The collection has much literature on American music. There are many ethnic, national and local folksong collections.

GLASGOW. Mitchell Library, North Street, Glasgow G3 7DN (*Gm*). The library has many private collections including most of Frank Kidson's (over 3000 items comprising his 57-volume index of airs, works with his bibliographical annotations, and 17th- and 18th-century British dance and vocal music), and those of Russell Fergusson (photographs of harps), G. B. Gardiner (folksongs of 18 European countries and literature of folk music), Fanny Moody and Charles Manners (opera scores with conductor's annotations, orchestral and choral parts) and Robert Turnbull (opera scores and other general music and literature, including his own critical writings).

The Mitchell Library: Catalogue of Additions 1915–1949 (Glasgow, 1959); H. G. Farmer: 'The Kidson Collection', *The Consort*, vii (1950), 12; G. H. Rolland: 'The Music Collection in the Mitchell Library', *HMYB*, xi (1961), 95

——. University Library, Glasgow G12 8QE (*Gu*), incorporating the Euing Musical Library (*Ge*). William Euing (*d* 1874) bequeathed his rich collection to Anderson's University, from where it passed to Glasgow University in 1936. Among its treasures are a MS lute tablature (c1620), over 2000 theoretical works (dating back to the 15th century), early editions of Byrd, Frescobaldi and Praetorius, a large number of English psalters and hymnbooks and autographs and other MSS of British and foreign composers (including Asola, Callcott, Pergolesi and Wesley). In addition to strong general holdings the University Library has the Zavrtal Collection (Mozart relics, including his last letter, and works by the Zavrtal family), the collection of H. G. Farmer (relating to Arabic, Jewish, Persian and Turkish music and to military music), the Stillie Collection (760 volumes with many operas, partly from the library of G. F. Graham), material on Scottish popular music, a collection of the published music of Hugh Roberton, the library of W. G. Whittaker and a collection of autographs of Scottish musicians (Drysdale, MacCunn, Lamond, McEwen and Moonie).

The library of Trinity College, Glasgow (Gtc), was presented to the university by the Church of Scotland in 1974. It includes the Mearns Hymnology Collection. The Scottish Music Archive (Gsma), housed at the university, was founded in 1968 to provide a national centre for the collection and documentation of Scottish composers of all periods, and their music.

Catalogue of the Musical Library of the Late Wm. Euing (Glasgow, 1878) [inadequate listing, with many errors]; A. Hubens: 'La Bibliothèque Euing à Glasgow', *RMI*, xxiii (1916), 243–72 [selective holdings list]; H. G. Farmer: 'The Euing Musical Collection', *MR*, viii (1947), 197; H. G. Farmer and H. Smith: *New Mozartiana: the Mozart Relics in the Zavertal Collection*, Glasgow University Publications, xxxvii (Glasgow, 1936); F. Rimmer: 'Report from Glasgow: Scottish Music Archive', *CMc* (1969), no.9, p.39; *Scottish Music Archive Catalogue of Printed Music* (Glasgow, 1970, suppl. 1972); F. Rimmer: 'The Scottish Music Archive (Glasgow)', *FAM*, xxi (1974), 12

GLOUCESTER. Cathedral Library, 6 College Green, Gloucester GL1 2LX (*GL*). The library has a small collection of 17th-century church music, including incomplete choirbooks with anthems by Davies, Henstridge, Jefferies, Parsons, Rogers, Tye, Wise and others and an anthem by Purcell that is ascribed to him in only one other source. There is a fragment from a single leaf of medieval music, and other fragments recovered from book bindings.

HEREFORD. Cathedral Library, The Cathedral, Hereford HR1 2NG (*H*). The library has several hundred music items including 18th- and 19th-century MS sacred music, glees and madrigals. There are also piano pieces and songs formerly owned (and autographed) by Fanny Kemble and others. Notable items include the Hereford Breviary (c1270), Roger North's autographs of his *Musicall Grammarian* and *Memoires of Musick* and MSS of S. S. Wesley and Elgar.

A. T. Bannister: *Descriptive Catalogue of the MSS in the Hereford Cathedral Library* (London, 1927) [details only the medieval MSS; excludes Hereford Breviary]; F. C. and P. E. Morgan: *Hereford Cathedral Libraries . . . and Muniments* (Hereford, 1975)

LANCASTER. District Central Library, Market Square, Lancaster LA1 1HY (*LA*). The library holds most of the valuable Fuller Maitland Collection, bequeathed to the City of Lancaster in 1936: it comprises about 7000 volumes of music and music literature, including some MSS.

——. University Library, Bailrigg, Lancaster LA1 4YH (*LAu*). The library purchased part of the Hans F. Redlich Collection in 1970, consisting of annotated scores and books; the collection left by Edward Lockspeiser, strong in books of the *fin de siècle* era, was acquired in 1973.

LEEDS. Brotherton Library, University of Leeds, Leeds LS2 9JT (*LEbc*). The library has the Herbert Thompson Collection and chamber music from F. H. Fulford's library. There are 70 letters from Mendelssohn to Moscheles (c1824–7), some early printed theoretical works and 30 MSS of Charles Dibdin.

J. A. Symington: *Brotherton Library: a Catalogue of Ancient MSS and Early Printed Books* (Leeds, 1931); *The Brotherton Collection: a Brief Description* (Leeds, 1953)

——. Central Library, Calverley Street, Leeds LS1 3AB (*LEc*). The library acquired 123 of the 876 lots sold in 1905 from the collection of T. W. Taphouse, of which some items had belonged to Crotch, Rimbault and Sterndale Bennett. The library also owns MS catalogues and the folk music notebooks of Frank Kidson, a native of Leeds. Holdings of 18th-century music number about 600 items.

'Dotted Crotchet': 'The Musical Library of Mr. T. W. Taphouse', *MT*, xlv (1904), 629

LICHFIELD. Cathedral Library, The Close, Lichfield WS13 7LD (*LF*). The library contains a collection of 18th-century partbooks written by the vicar-choral John Barker. There are also seven parts of Barnard's *First Book of Selected Church Musick* (printed in 1641) with MS additions made from about 1662 to 1700. Among the MSS are works by John Alcock and anthems by Blow, Croft, Purcell and other 17th-century composers; the printed music includes a French volume with an otherwise unknown mass by d'Helfer (1658).

A Catalogue of the Printed Books and MSS (London, 1888, suppl. 1911) [neither lists music]; D. Franklin: 'Five MSS of Church Music at Lichfield', *RMARC*, iii (1963), 55; detailed catalogue in preparation

LINCOLN. Cathedral Library, Lincoln LN2 1TJ (*LI*). The chapter library (designed by Wren) has a MS of a 13th-century Gilbertine missal, several MS fragments of a 15th-century Sarum antiphoner, MSS of an Italian gradual book (dated 1500) and an Italian antiphoner (dated 1527), and autograph copies of works by Purcell, Blow, Wise and Lawes. There are early editions of songs by Byrd, Dowland and G. D. Montella and of some printed by Phalèse. Of interest are fragments of Anglo-Saxon notation removed from choirbook bindings and now bound in books.

R. W. Woolley: *Catalogue of the MSS of Lincoln Cathedral Chapter Library* (London, 1927); A. L. Kirwan: *The Music of Lincoln Cathedral* (London, 1973)

LIVERPOOL. Public (Music) Library, William Brown Street, Liverpool, Merseyside L3 8EW (*LVp*). Since its destruction in World War II the library has received many gifts, including the Booth Collection of Catholic church music, Carl Rosa's opera library and the Earl of Sefton's collection of early English editions of Haydn and Pleyel. The collection also includes autographs of Handel, Haydn, Rossini and Schubert.

Liverpool Public Libraries: Catalogue of the Music Library (Liverpool, 1954) [dictionary catalogue, most entries lack imprint]

LONDON. General literature: *Union List of Periodicals in Music in the Libraries of the University of London and some other London Libraries* (London, 1969)

——. BBC Central Library, Yalding House, 156 Great Portland Street, London W1N 6AJ (*Lbbc*). The library's function is to provide music for broadcast performances. Within the enormous collection of performing material, much with annotations of timing, cues, translations or conductors' markings, a large proportion comprises MS scores and parts for works composed or adapted for BBC performances. There is a reference collection of the standard scholarly editions and bibliographical tools.

J. H. Davies: 'Die grösste musikalische Aufführungsbibliothek', *Musica*, iv (1950), 331; *Piano and Organ Catalogue* (1965); *Chamber Music* (1965); *Song Catalogue* (1966); *Choral and Opera Catalogue* (1967)

——. **British Library, Great Russell Street, London WC1B 3DG (*Lbm*, *Lbl*).** The musical resources of the Reference Division of the British Library (formerly part of the British Museum) are contained in the departments of (1) Manuscripts, (2) Printed Books and (3) Oriental Manuscripts and Printed Books. They were transferred to the British Library Board by Act of Parliament in July 1973 though the departments continue to be housed in the premises of the British Museum.

(1). *Department of Manuscripts*. The foundation collections of the British Museum (the Cotton, Harley and Sloane collections) and the Old Royal Library (presented in 1757 by George II) included a small number of music MSS of which the most important are *Sumer is icumen in* (Harl.978), a collection of anthems transcribed by Thomas Tudway (Harl.7337–42) and a number of medieval treatises. A few music MSS were also acquired when the Lansdowne, Burney (the library of the younger Charles Burney), King's (the library of George III), Arundel and Stowe collections came to the museum between 1807 and 1883.

Additions by gift or bequest (numbered in the two continuing series of Additional and Egerton MSS) have been many, beginning with a group of treatises (presented by John Hawkins in 1778) and a collection of Italian and English music transcribed by Henry Needler (bequeathed by James Mathias in 1782). Important gifts in the 1840s included those of Vincent Novello (MS works by Dragonetti and Samuel Wesley, and many volumes of 17th- and 18th-century vocal music); the Marquis of Northampton (chiefly 18th-century Italian vocal music collected by Gasparo Selvaggi) and Dragonetti (MSS of 17th- to 19th-century Italian operas). In 1896 Eliza Wesley, daughter of Samuel, bequeathed many volumes of her father's music and the famous MS (mostly autograph) of Bach's *Das wohltemperirte Clavier*, book 2. In 1907 the autographs of Mozart's last ten quartets and Beethoven's Violin Sonata op.30 no.3 were bequeathed by Harriet Chichele Plowden, and in 1928 E. Perry Warren presented the collection formed by Ernst Perabo of Boston which included autographs of Michael Haydn, Beethoven and Schubert, and many letters. In 1952 E. H. W. Meyerstein bequeathed to the museum his musical and literary collections containing autographs of Haydn, Mozart, Beethoven, Schubert, Weber, Chopin and others.

Presentations and bequests of modern music, chiefly by relatives of composers, have brought to the department several extensive collections of autograph MSS. The composers represented include Bax, Dohnányi, Elgar, Grainger, Holst, Ireland, Ethel Smyth and Vaughan Williams. Other collections include MSS of Denis ApIvor, William Baines, Rutland Boughton and Havergal Brian, and letters and papers of Peter Warlock and Henry Wood. In 1975 K. H. Roth presented the autograph score of Stravinsky's *Capriccio* (Add. 58431).

During the 19th and 20th centuries the collections have been supplemented by the purchase of transcripts made by Burney in preparation for his *General History of Music*; many MSS of 16th- and 17th-century English music, including the Mulliner Book and a volume owned

and partly compiled by Thomas Tomkins; Julian Marshall's large collection, chiefly of English and Italian music; the source for the medieval *Play of Daniel*; several Beethoven sketchbooks; large quantities of music by Dibdin, Bishop, Balfe and Pearsall; the Granville Collection of Handel's works; several autograph volumes of works by Purcell, Blow and Croft; papers of F. G. Edwards, editor of the *Musical Times* from 1897 to 1909 (including material relating to Mendelssohn), and the papers and journals of George Smart. More recent purchases include the Windsor Carol Book (Eg.3307); one of the Tregian anthologies (Eg.3665); letters by musicians to Edward Clark, music director of the BBC from 1924 to 1936 (Add.52256–7); music MSS of Peter Warlock (Add.52904–12); the autograph songbook of Henry Lawes (Add.53723); scores of Tippett's *The Midsummer Marriage* (Add.53771) and *King Priam* (Eg.3786); scores of Gilbert and Sullivan's *Patience* and *The Gondoliers* (Add.53777, 53779); the Old Hall MS (Add.57950); and the Mozart–Attwood MS (Add.58437).

Also in the department on permanent loan are MSS and correspondence of the Royal Philharmonic Society, Mozart and Bach autographs from the Stefan Zweig Collection, and MSS of Richard Strauss, Kodály and Delius lent by Universal Edition. The collection of music MSS of the RCM, formerly on 'permanent loan', was returned in 1961.

(2). *Department of Printed Books*.

(i) *Printed music*. The quantity of printed music stood in 1974 probably between a million and one and a quarter million items, most of it music received by deposit under successive copyright acts; it includes extensive holdings of European and American imprints and numerous works published in France and Germany during the late 19th century. The policy of acquisition has remained broadly the same as that which Panizzi laid down for the General Library in the 1840s, namely to aim at the best representative collection of music published in any country outside that country itself. The results of this policy are particularly apparent in the music of earlier periods. The collection is rich in partbooks of the 16th to 18th centuries and in first and early editions of the Classical and Romantic composers.

There are several important special collections. The Paul Hirsch Music Library, housed from 1936 in the Cambridge University Library, was acquired in 1946; it comprises some 20,000 items of printed music and music literature of all periods, including a few MSS, but its great wealth lies in music theory, opera full scores and first editions of the Viennese Classics. The Royal Music Library, deposited on indefinite loan by George V in 1911, was presented outright by Elizabeth II in 1957. It is notable for the splendid collection of Handel autographs in 97 volumes and also includes the Baldwin MS (*c*1600), the Benjamin Cosyn Virginal Book (1612), the William Forster Virginal Book (1624), a magnificent volume of autograph scores of Purcell, autograph operas of Steffani, and numerous other important MSS. More than 90 MS volumes from the Chapel Royal were added in 1926 and 1968. The library of Church House, Westminster, presented in 1949, comprises several thousand books of hymns and psalms, many with music. The library of the Noblemen's and Gentlemen's Catch Club was presented in 1952 and includes both printed and MS material. John Barbirolli's conducting scores were presented by his widow in 1971. The library of the Madrigal Society, including some important MS part-books of the early 17th century, was deposited on loan in 1953.

(ii). *Music literature.* The foundation collections contained a small number of books on music theory. They were augmented in 1776 by a valuable collection purchased from John Hawkins, and in 1814 over 250 volumes were purchased from the library of Charles Burney. The library now contains an extensive range of music literature, housed in the General Library of the Department of Printed Books.

(3). Department of Oriental Manuscripts and Printed Books. This department possesses comprehensive collections of oriental MS music. Among the many Hebrew and Christian Near Eastern liturgical MSS there is an Armenian hymnbook (Or.1418) in which a few musical notes or neumes have been added by the rubricator. Musical instruments are depicted in a number of Ethiopian miniatures. The Arabic MS collection includes some extremely important items, among them the Ibn al-Munajjim MS (Or.2361), one of the principal sources for the study of old Arabian music. The Persian MSS include treatises and miniatures showing musical instruments, dancing and the like, and the Turkish MSS include *şarkılar* (folksongs and poems set to music), some with musical notation. The north Indian collections contain standard editions of Sanskrit texts on Indian music, albums of paintings of the ragas of Indian music with texts in Hindi, and a large collection of Indian miniatures in which musical instruments are depicted. The Dravidian collection has material relating to south Indian musicians and singers, together with the most important written compositions. The Burmese section contains books on music and instruments and texts of classical Burmese dance-dramas and songs. Some folding books in the MS collection illustrate scenes with Burmese orchestras and dance troupes. Examples of songs without musical notation but written for well-known tunes and music of Dutch people born in Indonesia are included in the Malay and Indonesian collections. The Chinese collection has scores, standard reference works and reprints of early texts on Chinese music. The Stein Collection has several T'ang dynasty MSS of musical importance. Some early Japanese printed books describe musical instruments and court- and folkdancing.

Department of Manuscripts: *Catalogue of Additions to the MSS in the British Museum 1783–1945* (London, 1843–1970); A. Hughes-Hughes: *Catalogue of MS Music in the British Museum* (London, 1906–9/R1964–6); *Catalogue of the Musical MSS Deposited on Loan in the British Museum by the Royal Philharmonic Society of London* (London, 1914); B. Schofield: 'Perabo Collection of Musical Autographs', *British Museum Quarterly [BMQ]*, iii (1928–9), 56; B. Schofield and C. E. Wright: 'The Meyerstein Bequest', *BMQ*, xvii (1953), 97; P. J. Willetts: 'Autographs of Musicians', *BMQ*, xx (1955–6), 3; P. J. Willetts: 'Autograph Music MSS of Sir Arnold Bax', *BMQ*, xxiii (1960–61), 43; P. J. Willetts: 'The Ralph Vaughan Williams Collection', *BMQ*, xxiv (1961), 3; P. J. Willetts: 'Recent British Museum Acquisitions', *MT*, cii (1961), 287; P. J. Willetts: 'The Dohnányi Collection', *BMQ*, xxv (1962), 3; P. J. Willetts: 'The Percy Grainger Collection', *BMQ*, xxvii (1963–4), 65; P. J. Willetts: 'The Rutland Boughton Collection', *BMQ*, xxviii (1964), 67; J. M. Backhouse: 'Delius Letters', *BMQ*, xxx (1966), 30; P. J. Willetts: *The Henry Lawes MS* (London, 1969); P. J. Willetts: *Beethoven and England: an Account of Sources in the British Museum* (London, 1970); P. J. Willetts: *Handlist of Music MSS acquired 1908–67* (London, 1970); H. Cobbe: 'Papers of Sir Henry Wood', *BMQ*, xxxvi (1971–2), 11; H. Cobbe: 'British Musical Autographs', *MT*, cxiv (1973), 793

Department of Printed Books: W. B. Squire: *Catalogue of Printed Music published between 1487 and 1800, now in the British Museum* (London, 1912/R1968) [incl. suppl.i]; W. B. Squire: *Catalogue of the King's Music Library* (London, 1927–9); K. Meyer and P. Hirsch:

Katalog der Musikbibliothek Paul Hirsch, i, ii (Berlin, 1928–30), iii (Frankfurt, 1936), iv (Cambridge, 1947); K. Meyer: 'The Liturgical Music Incunabula in the British Museum, Germany, Italy and Switzerland', *The Library*, 4th ser., xx (1939), 274; W. C. Smith: *Catalogue of Printed Music published before 1801 now in the British Museum* (London, 1940/R1968) [suppl.ii]; A. Loewenberg: 'Early Dutch Librettos and Plays with Music in the British Museum', *Journal of Documentation*, ii (1947), March, 210; *Catalogue of Printed Music in the British Museum*, liii (London, 1951) [music in the Hirsch Library]; A. H. King: 'The Hirsch Library: Retrospect and Conclusion', *Notes*, ix (1952–3), 381; A. H. King: 'The Music Room of the British Museum, 1753–1953', *PRMA*, lxxix (1952–3), 65; A. H. King: 'English Royal Music-lovers and their Library, 1600–1900', *MT*, xcix (1958), 311; *Catalogue of Printed Books in the British Museum*, 3rd ser., pt.291*b* (London, 1959) [books in the Hirsch Library, with suppl. list of music]; C. B. Oldman: 'Panizzi and the Music Collections of the British Museum', *HMYB*, xi (1961), 62; U. Sherrington: *Hand-list of Music Published in some British and Foreign Periodicals between 1787 and 1848, now in the British Museum* (London, 1962); A. H. King: 'The History and Growth of the Catalogues in the Music Room', *Festschrift Otto Erich Deutsch* (Kassel, 1963), 303; A. H. King and O. W. Neighbour: 'Printed Music from the Collection of Alfred Cortot', *BMQ*, xxxi (1966–7), 8; D. Poulton and D. Mitchell: 'A List of Printed Lute Music in the British Museum', *LSJ*, xiii (1971), 40, and xiv (1972), 42; R. Bray: 'British Museum MS Royal 24.d.2 (John Baldwin's Commonplace Book): an Index and Commentary', *RMARC*, xii (1974), 137; A. H. King: 'Music in the British Library', *FAM*, xxiii (1976); A. H. King: *Printed Music in the British Museum: an Account of the Collections, the Catalogues and their Formation, up to 1920* (London, 1979)

——. City of London Guildhall Library, Guildhall, Aldermanbury, London EC2P 2EJ (*Lgc*). The library holds the archives of the Worshipful Company of Musicians, most from 1770 and later. In 1958 the music items from the Gresham College Library were deposited in the library: the collection, begun by the singer and Gresham Professor of Music Edward Taylor about 1838, consists mainly of works printed in the 18th and early 19th centuries, but there are also 17th-century imprints and MSS, notably a volume of songs in Purcell's hand and another of odes and other works signed by Blow; there is also a collection of glees written for performance at the Concentores Society (from 1817).

A Catalogue of the Printed Books and MSS Deposited in Guildhall Library (London, 1965) [describes Gresham collection]

——. Lambeth Palace Library, London SE1 7JU (*Llp*). The archiepiscopal library has MS and printed psalters, missals and breviaries, as well as early printed psalters and hymnbooks. There are also MS treatises collected by William Chelle, a volume of MS English, French and Italian lute-songs in tablature and another of harpsichord dances and airs by R. Ayleward and others.

M. R. James: *A Descriptive Catalogue of the MSS in the Library of Lambeth Palace* (Cambridge, 1932)

——. Royal Academy of Music, York Gate, Marylebone Road, London NW1 5HT (*Lam*). Among the more important gifts to the library are Henry Wood's collection of orchestral scores and parts; Angelina Goetz's score library; the collections of R. J. S. Stevens (with many catches and glees, and MSS of 17th- and 18th-century Italian operas and cantatas), G. D. Cunningham (organ music), H. Prendergast (church music), Ferdinand Ries and the English Bach Society; and Otto Klemperer's library of scores and parts, as well as his archival material. There are many autographs by British composers. The library has a copy of Mendelssohn's music for *A Midsummer Night's Dream* inscribed by the composer and dated 1829 (this is no longer considered to be an autograph) and a MS full score of Purcell's *The Fairy Queen*, with a few pages in the composer's hand, said to be the copy he used in the theatre. There are many early 19th-century autograph letters. Printed works include 16th- and 17th-century partbooks, first editions of later works, and a collection of Promenade Concert programmes to 1927. The archive of the Delius Trust Fund contains originals and photocopies of the composer's autograph compositions and letters.

A. Rosenkranz: *A Catalogue of the Angelina Goetz Library* (London, 1904); J. Harington: 'The Academy's New Library', *RAM Magazine* (1968), no.194, p.5; R. Lowe: 'The Delius Trust MSS', *Brio*, v (1968), 5; R. Lowe: *Frederick Delius 1862–1934: Catalogue of the Music Archives of the Delius Trust* (London, 1974)

——. Royal College of Music, Prince Consort Road, London SW7 2BS (*Lcm*). The RCM has two separately organized libraries, the main working collection and the Parry Room Library. The rich collection in the latter was acquired from a variety of sources, the most important of which was the library of the Sacred Harmonic Society, purchased in 1883. Queen Victoria later presented the library of the Concert of Ancient Music and subsequent additions include the library of George Grove (*d* 1900), the library of the Musical Union (transferred from the Victoria and Albert Museum in 1900), duplicates from the British Library and material from the Library of Congress, Franz Ries, Edward Dannreuther, Arthur Sullivan, Augustus Hughes-Hughes, W. B. Squire and many others. The MS collection (until 1961 on loan to the British Museum) includes autographs of Haydn, Mozart and Schubert.

W. B. Squire: *Catalogue of Printed Music in the Library of the Royal College of Music, London* (London, 1909); W. B. Squire: *Catalogue of the MSS in the Library of the Royal College of Music, with Additions by Rupert Erlebach* (typescript, 1931, copies in *Lbm, Ob, Cu*)

——. Sion College, Victoria Embankment, London EC4Y 0DN (*Lsc*). The college has a York breviary (*c*1400) and a 15th-century York hymnal. There is also some late 16th- and 17th-century printed music.

——. Trinity College of Music, Mandeville Place, London W1M 6AQ (*Ltc*). The Bridge Memorial Library was opened in 1924 and contains some early editions of works by Piccinni, Gluck, Monsigny and others, a first edition of Purcell's *Orpheus britannicus* and two short piano pieces in autograph of Sterndale Bennett. There are also some 16th- and 17th-century printed editions and MSS.

——. University of London Music Library, Senate House, Malet Street, London WC1E 7HU (*Lu*). The library was established in 1926 and the initial holdings came from bequests by George Elvey (*d* 1893) and Alma Haas (*d* 1932) among others. The holdings include the Littleton Collection (15th- to 17th-century printed music and treatises) and the Tudor Church Music Collection (photostats of MS and printed Tudor and Jacobean music), both presented by the Carnegie United Kingdom Trust. There are also the libraries of the Oxford and Cambridge Musical Club (on permanent loan), the Plainsong and Mediaeval Music Society (formerly on loan, acquired in 1967), the Royal Musical Association (on permanent loan) and the United States Information Service. Among the 30 or so MSS there is a copy of the first and third parts of Handel's *Messiah* (formerly part of Newman Flower's Handel collection) and a score of Donizetti's *Gabriella di Vergy*.

Catalogue of the Society's Library (Burnham, Bucks., 1928) [describes the Plainsong and Mediaeval Music Society Collection]; [M. A. Baird]: *University of London Library: a Guide to the Music Library* (typescript, 1973) [describes history and facilities]

——. Vaughan Williams Memorial Library, English Folk Dance and Song Society, Cecil Sharp House, 2 Regent's Park Road, London NW1 7AY (*Lcs*). The library constitutes the country's most comprehensive collection of folksong, -dance and -lore, and is based on the large Cecil Sharp Collection. It also incorporates items from the personal collections of Janet Blunt, Lucy Broadwood, George Gardiner, R. A. Gatty, Anne Gilchrist, Percy Grainger, H. E. D. Hammond, Peter Kennedy, E. M. Leather, Alan Lomax and E. H. White.

M. Dean-Smith: 'The Gilchrist Bequest', *JEFDSS*, vii (1955), 218; P. N. Shuldham-Shaw: 'The James Duncan MS Folk Song Collection', *Folk Music Journal*, i (1966), 67, 181, 267; F. Purslow: 'The George Gardiner Folk Song Collection', *Folk Music Journal*, i (1967), 128; *The Vaughan Williams Memorial Library Catalogue* (London, 1973); *The Vaughan Williams Memorial Library: Contents and Services*, English Folk Dance and Song Society Leaflet, iii (London, rev. 2/1974)

——. Victoria and Albert Museum, Cromwell Road, London SW7 2RL (*Lva*). In 1974 the Theatre Section of the Department of Prints and Drawings became part of the Theatre Museum, administered by the Victoria and Albert Museum although from 1976 housed in new premises in Somerset House, Strand. It includes many items relevant to music, documenting the history of entertainment (including opera and ballet) in London and elsewhere from about 1700 to the present. Besides sheet music, programmes and posters there is a collection of reference books on all aspects of stage history, costume, scenery and biography. The Theatre Reference Section was a gift of Gabrielle Enthoven (*d* 1950). Recent acquisitions include the extensive private collection of Harry R. Beard (*d* 1969), containing material on the history of the British stage, prints and portraits of composers and musicians, and programmes and librettos from the major European opera houses and theatres. The London Archives of the Dance are also housed in the Theatre Museum.

'The Theatre, and the Enthoven Theatre Collection', *Victoria and Albert Museum: a Handbook to the Departments of Prints and Drawings and Paintings* (London, 1964)

——. Westminster Abbey, The Cloisters, London SW1P 3PE (*Lwa*). The chapter library has 17th- and 18th-century Italian and English MSS and late 16th- and early 17th-century madrigals.

W. B. Squire: *Musik-Katalog der Westminster-Abtei*, *MMg*, xxxv (1903), suppl.

MANCHESTER. Chetham's Library, Long Millgate, Manchester M3 1SB (*Mch*). In 1851 a collection of about 3000 proclamations, broadsides, ballads and poems was presented to the library by James O. Halliwell-Phillipps (*d* 3 Jan 1889), who also prepared a privately printed catalogue of the set dated 1851; a copy is available in the library. Popular songs of the 16th to 18th centuries include catches and odes by Purcell, Croft, Pepusch, Carey and Weldon and many single-sheet songs published from 1680 to 1740.

——. Central Public Library, St Peter's Square, Manchester M2 5PD (*Mp*). The Henry Watson Music Library contains the private collection of Henry Watson (*d* 1911), given to the city on 24 January 1902. It consisted of some 16,700 volumes which form the nucleus of the present music library. Since that time this has grown to what may be the largest provincial public music library in Britain: it contains about 400 MS volumes and an extensive collection of printed material and sheet music. In 1965 Manchester Public Libraries acquired Newman Flower's valuable collection of Aylesford Handel MSS, which also included MS volumes by early 18th-century Italian composers. The library holds a 17th-century MS volume of music for viola da gamba, and there is a volume of organ parts to Purcell anthems, possibly in the hand of John Blow.

J. A. Cartledge: *List of Glees, Madrigals, Part-songs, etc. in the Henry Watson Music Library* (Manchester, 1913/*R*1970); L. W. Duck: 'The Henry Watson Music Library', *MT*, xciii (1952), 155; L. Ring: 'Some Observations on the Contents of the Henry Watson Music Library', *The Consort*, ix (1952), 23; L. W. Duck: 'Henry Watson Music Library', *Library World*, lxiii (1961), 132; L. W. Duck: *The Henry Watson Music Library: a Survey of its Resources* (Manchester, 1961, 2/1964); Anon.: 'Henry Watson Music Library: MSS [*recte* prints] Available in Microform', *FAM*, xiii (1966), 167; A. D. Walker: *George Frideric Handel: the Newman Flower Collection in the Henry Watson Music Library: a Catalogue* (Manchester, 1972); L. W. Duck: 'Handel: Early Printed Editions in the Henry Watson Music Library', *Manchester Review*, xii (1972–3), 73; M. Talbot: 'Some Overlooked MSS in Manchester', *MT*, cxv (1974), 942 [describes the 18th-century Italian music in the Newman Flower collection]

——. John Rylands Library, University of Manchester, Deansgate, Manchester M13 9PL (*Mr*). The library has liturgical MSS of the 11th to 18th centuries (including missals and antiphoners) and some early theoretical books among the 600 volumes on music from the 16th to 20th centuries.

OXFORD. Bodleian Library, Oxford OX1 3BG (*Ob*). The library was founded by Sir Thomas Bodley in 1598, after an earlier university library had been closed in 1550 and its books dispersed. The earliest medieval monodic MSS in the library include 11th-century tropers from Winchester (Bod.775) and Heidenheim (Selden Supra 27). There are many liturgical MSS from the 11th and 12th centuries, and MSS of secular and sacred polyphony from the 12th to 16th centuries, mostly fragments recovered from book bindings. This includes leaves of the Worcester fragments, dating from the 13th century (Lat.liturg.d.20), and fragments from Bury St Edmunds dating from the 14th century (e Mus.7). There is an important collection of chansons by Dufay, Binchois and others compiled by 1436 (Canonici misc.213) and an early 15th-century English collection of carols (Arch.Seld.B26).

Many of the 17th- and 18th-century MSS in the Bodleian Library formerly belonged to the university music school, and were transferred in 1885. The original nucleus included the Forrest–Heyther Partbooks (part of one book is in the hand of John Baldwin), containing masses by Aston, Fairfax, Taverner and others (Mus.Sch.E.376–81), and also a fine collection of printed partbooks of English and Italian motets and madrigals. Later acquisitions include autograph works of William Lawes and of Boyce, as well as a good collection of music for strings collected or copied for use in the music school, and instrumental sonatas, suites and vocal music by Italian, French and German composers.

Apart from an isolated gift (*c*1656) from John Wilson of a folio MS of his own lute music and songs, the library owned little music until 1800, when Osborne Wight bequeathed his collection of late 17th- and 18th-century English and Italian music, with 18th-century copies of earlier material and printed books including editions of Handel, Boyce and Arnold. Wight's earliest possession was an incomplete set of 28 vocal partbooks copied by a 17th-century amateur, Thomas Hamond, mainly from printed sources, but including pieces by Kirbye, Peerson, Ramsay and Ravenscroft, and others not then available in print. Additions have been made to Wight's collection, the first substantial acquisition being the Sadler partbooks, containing motets by Byrd, Tallis, Taverner and others, bought in 1885 (e Mus.1–5). The library has acquired MSS of Elgar, Holst,

Sullivan, Vaughan Williams, Bax, Delius and Ethel Smyth, some of which were given by the Friends of the Bodleian. Other gifts include the papers of Parry, Howard Ferguson, George Butterworth and Gerald Finzi. The library of T. W. Bourne, bequeathed in 1947, contains contemporary printed editions of 18th-century composers including J. C. Bach, Corelli, Geminiani, Handel, Leclair, Vivaldi and others.

Through Margaret Deneke, Mendelssohn MSS and papers from the collections of two of the composer's grandchildren (Paul Benecke and Maria Wach) came to the library between 1950 and 1974. Benecke had Mendelssohn's music library, which includes rarities such as first editions of Chopin's works and the score of Bach's *St Matthew Passion*, and the Green Books in which Mendelssohn had bound about 6500 letters received between 1821 and the year of his death. From Wach came Mendelssohn's sketchbooks, three albums containing autograph music by Mozart, Haydn and Beethoven, as well as contributions from many friends, and family papers. Further MSS from Deneke's own collection, including the autograph of Schubert's Grand Duo, were presented by her sister.

In 1974 the library received the collection of Walter Harding of Chicago (*d* 1973), the musical portion of which includes English, American and French songs and opera scores from the 17th to 20th centuries totalling some 100,000 items.

As a copyright depository, the library has received copies of British printed material since 1610, though music has been regularly included only since about 1790.

R. Hake: *Catalogue of Music belonging to the Music School* (MS, 1854, available in library); F. Madan: *Summary Catalogue of Western MSS in the Bodleian Library* (Oxford, 1895–1953); H. G. Farmer: 'The Arabic Musical MSS in the Bodleian Library: a Descriptive Catalogue', *Royal Asiatic Society Journal*, iv (1925), 1; A. Hughes: *Medieval Polyphony in the Bodleian Library* (Oxford, 1951) [catalogue]; *Latin Liturgical MSS and Printed Books* (Oxford, 1952) [exhibition guide]; D. Stevens: '17th-century Italian Instrumental Music in the Bodleian', *AcM*, xxvi (1954), 67; J. A. Westrup and others: *English Music* (Oxford, 1955) [exhibition guide]; D. Stevens: 'Unique Italian Instrumental Music in the Bodleian Library', *CHM*, ii (1957), 401; M. Crum: 'A 17th-century Collection of Music Belonging to Thomas Hamond, a Suffolk Landowner', *Bodleian Library Record*, vi/1 (1957), 373; G. Reaney: 'Oxforder Handschriften', *MGG*; N. G. Wilson and D. I. Stefanović: *MSS of Byzantine Chant in Oxford* (Oxford, 1963); M. Crum: 'Early Lists of the Music School Collection', *ML*, xlviii (1967), 23; M. Crum: 'Working Papers of 20th-century British Composers', *Bodleian Library Record*, viii/2 (1968), 101; [M. Crum]: *Felix Mendelssohn Bartholdy* (Oxford, 1972) [Bodleian picture book illustrating the collection]; P. Ward Jones: 'Music at the Bodleian', *Brio*, x (1973), 1; D. W. Krummel: 'A Musical Bibliomaniac', *MT*, cxv (1974), 301 [describes Walter Harding's collection]; S. J. P. Van Dijk: typed catalogue of liturgical MSS in the Bodleian library [available in library]

——. Christ Church, Oxford OX1 1DP (*Och*). The rich holdings of MSS and early printed music are mostly from the bequests of Henry Aldrich (1710) and Richard Goodson (1718): the works are mainly anthems, motets, madrigals, canzonets and cantatas by English and Italian composers, and there are many anonymous instrumental MSS. Handwritten catalogues of the Aldrich and Goodson collections, prepared in 1787 by J. B. Malchair, are in the RCM.

G. E. P. Arkwright: *Catalogue of Music in the Library of Christ Church Oxford* (London, 1915–23) [i: MSS of ascertained authorship (*R*1971: also lists microfilms held up to March 1970); ii: thematic catalogue of anon. vocal MSS; iii: thematic catalogue of anon. instrumental MSS (unpubd, available in the library)]; A. Hiff: *Catalogue of Printed Music published prior to 1801 now in the Library of Christ Church Oxford* (London, 1919)

——. Faculty of Music Library, 32 Holywell Street, Oxford OX1 3SL (*Ouf*). Although primarily a working and reference collection, the library has been enriched with various gifts and bequests from Henry Hadow, Ernest Walker and J. H. Mee. The collections of Edward Heron-Allen (books on the violin) and C. S. Terry (Bach), formerly on loan from the RCM, have now been returned. The collection that remains comprises medieval and Byzantine music, 16th- and 17th-century editions of English music, and early printed treatises.

——. Oriel College, Oxford OX1 4EW (*Ooc*). The library has about 200 items of concertos, sonatas and opera, printed in the 17th and 18th centuries and bequeathed to the college at the end of the 18th century by Lord Leigh of Stoneleigh. The collection also includes the only known copy of Purcell's march for the funeral of Queen Mary.

——. Queen's College, Oxford OX1 4AW (*Oqc*). The library has about 200 music volumes, including some early English items by Blow, Purcell and others. There is also a half-page anonymous lute MS.

——. St John's College, Oxford OX1 3DY (*Ojc*). The library has two bass partbooks of church music written by Michael East between 1625 and 1632. There is also an organbook (*c*1637), bass-part fragments of four anthems (*c*1600) and a MS part by Purcell found in the partbooks of Lawes's *Choir Psalms* (1648).

J. B. Clark: 'A Re-emerged 17th-century Organ Accompaniment Book', *ML*, xlvii (1966), 149

RIPON. Cathedral Library, Ripon HG4 2LA (*RI*). The library has about 100 works printed in the late 18th and early 19th centuries. Some 16th-century items formerly in the library have been sold. A few parchment fragments with music have been recovered from the bindings of other books.

J. T. Fowler: 'Ripon Minster Library and its Founder', *Yorkshire Archaeological Journal*, ii (1871), 371–402

ST ANDREWS. University Library, North Street, St Andrews KY16 9AD (*SA*). The library has a collection of British music copyrighted from about 1780 to 1837. In 1966 it received the library of Gerald Finzi (*d* 1956) which comprises chiefly 18th-century English music (both MSS and photocopies of MSS and printed editions of Boyce, Stanley and others, as well as Cavalli).

catalogue in preparation

TENBURY WELLS. St Michael's College Library, Tenbury Wells WR15 8PH (*T*). The library consists of the valuable collection of Frederick Ouseley (*d* 1889), containing some 3000 volumes, of which about 1000 are on the theory and history of music. The collection has many rarities, including English and Italian madrigal partbooks, polyphonic MS partbooks of about 1600 with sacred and secular works of English and Continental composers, Adrian Batten's organbook, autographs of Blow, Boyce, Burney, Wesley and other English composers, Handel's annotated score of *Messiah* used at the 1742 Dublin première, and printed and MS operas and sacred works of the 17th to 19th centuries (including many in the hand of André Philidor *l'aîné*, which formed part of the French royal music library). In 1934 an additional group of 61 volumes, also from the Toulouse–Philidor Collection, was purchased from Arthur Rau. This and the other Toulouse–Philidor material, however, was sold at Sotheby's in 1978 (see sale catalogue, 26 June 1978); most of it went to *F-Pn* and *V*.

E. H. Fellowes: 'The Philidor MSS: Paris, Versailles, Tenbury', *ML*, xii (1931), 116; E. H. Fellowes: *Catalogue of the MSS in the Library of St. Michael's College, Tenbury* (Paris, 1934); J. Morehen: 'The Southwell Minster Tenor Partbook in the Library of St Michael's College, Tenbury (1382)', *ML*, l (1969), 352; C Massip: 'La collection musicale Toulouse-Philidor à la Bibliothèque nationale', *Bulletin de la Bibliothèque nationale*, iv (1979), 147

WINDSOR. Eton College Library, Windsor SL4 6DB (*WRec*). The Provost and Fellows' library contains the Eton Choirbook, a valuable MS volume of 16th-century English sacred music, and a set of nine MS organbooks dating from 1686–1732. The collection contains 25 services (settings of the evening canticles) and about 150 anthems by Aldrich, Clarke, Greene, Humfrey, Turner and local composers.

R. Williams: 'MS Organ Books in Eton College Library', *ML*, xli (1960), 358

——. St George's Chapter Library, The Cloisters, Windsor Castle, Windsor SL4 1NJ (*WRch*). The chapter library has a fragment of a late 13th-century antiphoner and a considerable collection of partbooks used by the chapel choir, including some from the 17th century (Child, Tallis, Croft and Goldwin). There are also a few printed anthems, oratorios and other sacred works by 18th-century composers.

C. Mould: *The Musical MSS of St. George's Chapel Windsor Castle* (Windsor, 1973) [printed works listed in appx iii]

WORCESTER. Cathedral Library, 8 College Precincts, Worcester WR1 2LG (*WO*). The library contains a 13th-century Benedictine antiphoner, a 14th-century Hereford missal and some partbooks of Barnard's *First Book of Selected Church Musick* (1641) and of Tomkins's *Musica Deo sacra* (1668). Its most renowned possession is a set of parchment fragments (the earliest from about 1280) of sacred Latin polyphonic music, recovered from the bindings of later books. Parts of the same collection (known as the Worcester fragments) are in the Bodleian Library and the British Library, the whole providing a repertory of 109 compositions and forming the most important source for English polyphonic music of the period 1200–1350.

L. Dittmer: 'The Dating and Notation of the Worcester Fragments', *MD*, xi (1957), 1; L. Dittmer: 'Worcester Fragments', *MGG*

YORK. Minster Library, Dean's Park, York YO1 2JD (*Y*). The cathedral library has MS and printed works, both sacred and secular, from the 17th century to the present, including music by Purcell, Walmisley and Stanford, as well as a 15th-century York missal (Add.30), the Gostling Partbooks, and the Dunnington-Jefferson MS (a bass partbook with anthems and services, originating at Durham Cathedral and dating from about 1632. Most of the Purcell MSS were lost in the 1829 fire, but the library has copies made by Vincent Novello.

W. H. Frere: *The York Service Books* (York, 1927, repr. 1940 as *A Collection of Papers on Liturgical and Historical Subjects*, ed. J. H. Arnold and E. G. R. Wyatt); J. Pilgrim: 'The Music of the York Minster Library', *MT*, xcix (1958), 100; W. K. Ford: 'An English Liturgical Partbook of the 17th Century', *JAMS*, xii (1959), 144 [describes the Dunnington–Jefferson MS]; P. Aston: *The Music of York Minster* (London, 1972); R. Charteris: 'Matthew Hutton (1638–1711) and his MSS in York Minster Library', *GSJ*, xxviii (1975), 2 [description of 11 MSS of chamber and organ works by Purcell, Simpson, Bassani, Jenkins, Ward and Ferrabosco]; D. Griffiths: *A Catalogue of the Printed Music Published before 1850 in York Minster Library* (York, 1977)

GREECE (*GR*)

A good source for Byzantine MSS, especially those in Greece, is Index 2, 'Byzantine Musical MSS Cited', an appendix to each issue of *Studies in Eastern Chant* (London, 1966–).

ATHENS. Akadímia Athinon, Hodos Venizelou, Athens. The Athens Academy has an archive of Greek folklore gathered from all over Greece, and from other regions where Greeks have settled. The material includes over 60,000 folksong texts, as well as tales, ceremonies, proverbs etc. In 1951 a National Music Collection was established; it has some 4500 items of folk music on disc or tape, and is rapidly expanding. The recordings are being transcribed into western European notation.

G. Spyridakis: 'The Folklore Archive of the Athens Academy', *JIFMC*, xii (1960), 75

——. Ethnike Biblioteke tes Hellados, Hodos Venizelou, Athens (*Ae*). Founded in 1828, the National Library receives depository copies of everything published in Greece. Among its treasures is MS 2147, a 14th-century work with 16 folios containing 22 stichera with musical notation. It was one of the MSS transferred during World War I from the Gymnasium in Salonica. A catalogue of all the MSS in the National Library is in preparation.

D. Serruys: 'Catalogue des manuscrits conservés au Gymnase grec de Salonique', *Revue des bibliothèques*, xiii (1903), 12–89; M. Velimirović: 'Unknown Stichera for the Feast of St. Athanasios of Mount Athos', *Studies in Eastern Chant*, i (1966), 108 [discusses MS 2147]; M. Velimirović: ' "Persian Music" in Byzantium?', *Studies in Eastern Chant*, iii (1973), 179 [discusses a composition in MS 2401, a large anthology of Byzantine chants]

MOUNT ATHOS. The peninsula of Mount Athos has 20 monasteries, many of them with rich holdings of Byzantine musical MSS. For details *see* ATHOS, MOUNT.

S. Lambros: *Catalogue of the Greek MSS on Mount Athos* (Cambridge, Mass., 1895–1900); H. J. W. Tillyard: 'Fragment of a Byzantine Musical Handbook in the Monastery of Laura on Mt. Athos', *Annual of the British School at Athens*, xix (1912–13), 95; S. Eustratiadis: *Catalogue of the Greek MSS in the Library of the Monastery of Vatopedi on Mt. Athos*, Harvard Theological Studies, xi (Cambridge, Mass., 1924); S. Eustratiadis and Monk Spyridon: *Catalogue of the Greek MSS in the Library of the Laura on Mount Athos*, Harvard Theological Studies, xii (Cambridge, Mass., 1925); M. Richard: *Répertoire des bibliothèques et des manuscrits grecs* (Paris, 1948) [lists liturgical MSS with musical notation]; M. Adamis: 'Katalogos ton cheirographon tes bibliothekes P. Gritsane apokeimenes nyn en te hiera metropolei Zakynthou' [Catalogue of the MSS in the Library of P. Gritsane now in the sacred chapter of Zakynthos], *Epetiris Etairias Byzantinon Spoudon*, xxv (1966), 313–65; A. Jakovljević: *Slavic and Byzantine Musical MSS at Mount Athos*, i: *Catalogue of MSS in Chilander*, Monumenta musicae slavicae (Munich, in preparation)

HUNGARY (*H*)

There are 727 hymns (in 146 MSS) listed in P. Radó: *Répertoire hymnologique des MSS liturgiques dans les bibliothèques publiques de Hongrie* (Budapest, 1945); and P. Radó: *Libri liturgici manuscripti bibliothecarum Hungariae* (Budapest, 1947) has an index listing 24 MSS with musical notation (mainly 11th- to 15th-century missals). Gregorian sources in Hungary and in several other eastern European cities are cited in K. Szigeti: 'Denkmäler des Gregorianischen Chorals aus dem ungarischen Mittelalter', *SM*, iv (1963), 129–72. Works by Hummel, Gassmann, Krommer, Pichl, Reicha and many other Czech composers are listed in M. Poštolka: 'Bohemika 18. stoleti v Mad'arsku' [18th-century musical Bohemica in Hungary], *HV*, ii (1965), 683, and iii (1966), 151. The history, function and holdings of various libraries are briefly described in I. Péthes: 'Musikbibliotheken in Ungarn', *FAM*, xv (1968), 114. Beethoven sources are described in F. Gyímes and V. Vavrinecz: *Ludwig van Beethoven a magyar könyvtárakban és gyűjteményekben* [Ludwig van Beethoven in Hungarian libaries and collections] (Budapest, 1970–71).

BUDAPEST. Bartók Béla Zeneművészeti Szakközépiskola Könyvtára, Semmelweis utca 21, 1052 Budapest V (*Bb*). The library of the Béla Bartók Conservatory is the oldest public institution of music instruction in contemporary Hungary (founded in 1836). Although partly destroyed in World War II, it is now the country's third largest music library. The autographs and some early printed works (including the *verbunkos* collection) were transferred to the National Széchényi Library in 1936; remaining works include MS copies, 18th- and early 19th-century Viennese editions and early Hungarian editions. There are rich holdings of 18th- and 19th-century Hungarian composers.

——. Egyetemi Könyvtár, Károlyi Mihály utca 10, Budapest V (*Bu*). The library of Loránd Eötvös University was founded in 1561 as part of a Jesuit college; when the order was disbanded in 1774, the library became of national importance. After 1785 many books were received from abolished monasteries, including MSS and early prints containing liturgical books with music.

L. Mezey: *Codices latini medii aevi Bibliothecae universitatis Budapestinensis* (Budapest, 1961) [describes 132 Latin MSS]

——. Liszt Ferenc Zeneművészeti Főiskola, Liszt Ferenc-tér, Budapest (*Bl*). The Academy of Music was founded by Liszt in 1875 and received his MSS, letters and other documents, as well as early editions of his music. The collection of about 100,000 volumes is Hungary's largest music library. It collects mostly music and literature for teaching purposes.

A 233-page catalogue was published in the academy's *Annuaire 1884–5* (Budapest, 1885); M. Prahács: 'A Zeneművészeti főiskola Liszt-hagyatéka' [The bequest left by Liszt to the Academy of Music], *Zenetudományi tanulmányok*, vii (1959)

——. Magyar Tudományos Akadémia Zenetudományi Intézet Könyvtára, Országház utca 9, 1014 Budapest (*Ba(mi)*). The present library of the Institute of Musicology of the Hungarian Academy of Sciences was founded in 1974 with the fusion of the Bartók Archive (founded 1961) and the Folk Music Research Group (founded 1953). The library collects books, MSS, printed scores and reviews, with the emphasis on Hungarian music. A MS of 1711, Paul Esterházy's *Harmonia caelestis*, contains 55 sacred compositions with Latin text. The Bartók Archive contains documents relating to the life and works of the composer, and the archive is editing *Documenta Bartókiana* (1964–). The Folk Music Research Group collection comprises about 100,000 Hungarian folksongs, partly collected and ordered by Bartók and Kodály, and about 80,000 recorded folktunes.

——. Néprajzi Múzeum Népzenei Osztálya, Könyves Kálmán krt.40, Budapest (*Bnm*). The Folk Music Department of the Ethnological Museum was founded in 1872 and holds one of Europe's oldest folk collections. This includes the early folk material collected by Bartók, Kodály, Lajtha, Veress, Vikár and others, totalling 35,000 pieces of music and about 5000 recordings. There are also over 2000 Hungarian and foreign folk instruments.

——. Országos Széchényi Könyvtár, Pollack Mihály-tér 10, 1827 Budapest (*Bn*). The National Széchényi Library was founded in 1802 by Count Ferenc Széchényi; in 1949 it was made independent from the Hungarian National Museum. The music division's 10,000 MSS and 70,000 printed works comprise the world's largest collection of musical Hungarica, with special holdings of Dohnányi, Goldmark, Kodály and Liszt. The Bártfa collection, until 1915 in the church of St Aegidius in Bártfa (now Bardejov in Czechoslovakia), comprises MS and printed partbooks of 16th- and 17th-century works. The music collection of the former Esterházy Archives contains Haydn autographs, contemporary MS copies, first editions and personal belongings, as well as autographs and other works by J. J. Fux, G. J. Werner, Michael Haydn, Albrechtsberger, Dittersdorf and Süssmayr; there is also a rich MS collection of operas by contemporary composers. There are plans to move the library to new quarters in the former Royal Palace in Buda. It organizes the distribution of copyright deposit books, sending copies to the University of Debrecen, the Central Statistical Office in Budapest and other large libraries.

O. Gombosi: 'Die Musikalien der Pfarrkirche zu St. Aegidi im Bártfa', *Musikwissenschaftliche Beiträge: Festschrift für Johannes Wolf* (Berlin, 1929), 38; *Zenei kéziratok* [Musical MSS], A Magyar nemzeti múzeum könyvtárának címjegyzéke, vi (Budapest, 1924, 1940) [i, ed. K. Isoz, lists 1449 autograph musicians' letters; ii, ed. R. Lavotta, lists 1937 music MSS]; A. Valko: 'Haydn magyarországi működése a levé tári akták tükrében' [Haydn's activity in Hungary as reflected in the archival material], *Zenetudományi tanulmányok*, vi (1957), 627–67, viii (1960), 527–668 [register of Haydn documents in the Esterházy Archives, divided between Bn and Hungarian State Archives in Budapest]; D. Bartha and L. Somfai: *Haydn als Opernkapellmeister: die Haydn-Dokumente der Esterházy-Opernsammlung* (Budapest, 1960); J. Vécsev: *Haydn Compositions in the Music Collection of the National Széchényi Library* (Budapest, 1960) [catalogue]; L. Somfai: 'Albrechtsberger-Eigenschriften in der Nationalbibliothek Széchényi, Budapest', *SM*, i (1961), 175; iv (1963), 179; ix (1967), 191 [with thematic catalogue]; I. Kecskeméti: 'Musikhandschriften österreichischer Meister in der Ungarischen Nationalbibliothek', *ÖMz*, xxi (1966), 594; *The National Széchényi Library* (Budapest, 1972)

——. Ráday-Gzüjtemény, Ráday utca 29, Budapest (*Br*). Founded in 1711 by Calvinists, the Ráday collection has MS and printed psalters of the 16th–18th centuries and collections of student songs.

Z. Péter: *A jubiláló Ráday Könyvtár 1711–1961* (Budapest, 1962)

KESZTHELY. Országos Széchényi Könyvtár Helikon Könyvtára, Szabadság utca 1, Keszthely (*KE*). The holdings of the Helikon library include first editions of Italian operas, MS works from the city's former music school, and a collection of autographs, printed works and mementos of the composer Karl Goldmark (d 1915).

PANNONHALMA. Szent Benedekrend Központi Fökönyvtára, Fömonostor, Pannonhalma (*PH*). The Benedictine abbey which administers the library was founded by St Stephen in 1001. Available to male researchers only, the collection is the oldest in Hungary and possesses incunabula and music MSS. It also has 18th-century works (acquired from the Jesuit order in Györ in 1773), late 18th- and 19th-century music from Pannonhalma Cathedral and material related to the Cecilian movement.

SOPRON. Berzsenyi Dániel Gimnázium Könyvtára, Sopron (*Sg*). The Gymnasium library has some medieval liturgical parchment fragments, 18th-century French and German plays with music, and works from its former Singing and Music Circle.

——. Liszt Ferenc Múzeum, Május 1-tér 1, Sopron (*Sl*). The museum has documents concerning the city's former Music Society (1829) and other musical and theatrical activities in the region; it also holds the Wohlmut Virginal Book (1689).

IRELAND, REPUBLIC OF (*EIRE*)

There are chapters in A. Fleischmann, ed: *Music in Ireland: a Symposium* (Cork and Oxford, 1952) which describe the collections in the National Library, Dublin (with a separate chapter on the Plunkett Collection), Trinity College, Archbishop Marsh's Library and the Royal Irish Academy, and several other smaller libaries.

CORK. University College Library, Western Road, Cork (*C*). In 1949 the library received the estate of J. C. Sperrin-Johnson, including collections of chamber music of all periods, and folk music of many countries. It also holds the Lloyd collection of harp music, the Arnold Bax collection of MSS and printed works, and the Gulbenkian bequest of music scores and recordings. There is an extensive collection of Irish folk and traditional music.

DUBLIN. Archbishop Marsh's Library, St Patrick's Close, Dublin 8 (*Dm*). Otherwise known as the St Sepulchre Library, the institution was founded by Narcissus Marsh in 1701 and became the first free public library under the 1707 Act of Parliament. The collection includes about 100 MS and printed works of the late 16th and the 17th centuries, chiefly by English and Italian composers. The printed works include madrigal partbooks and theoretical treatises. The MSS comprise early 17th-century instrumental fantasias and lute and virginal pieces; a set of 18th-century MS scores presented by Jacob Stone in 1934 includes works by Purcell, Croft and Handel.

J. R. Scott: *Catalogue of the Manuscripts Remaining in the Library* (Dublin, 1913); N. J. D. White: *An Account of Archbishop Marsh's Library* (Dublin, 1926); J. Deedy: 'An Account of Marsh's Library', *Library Review*, xcii (1949), wint., 219; J. M. Ward: 'The Fourth Dublin Lute Book', *LSJ*, xi (1969), 28; R. Charteris: 'Consort Music Manuscripts in Archbishop Marsh's Library, Dublin', *RMARC*, xiii (1976), 27–63; R. Charteris: *A Catalogue of the Printed Books on Music and Music Manuscripts in Archbishop Marsh's Library, Dublin* (in preparation)

——. National Library of Ireland, Kildare Street, Dublin 2 (*Dn*). The library concentrates on Irish music and its history, as well as on Irish composers (Stanford, Harty, Wood). There are many MS collections of Irish airs. In 1863 Jasper Joly presented his library, which included some 18th-century operas and a rich store of songs and country dances issued in the 18th and 19th centuries by Irish, English and Scottish publishers. In 1942 the library received about 400 volumes from the collection of George Noble Count Plunkett, consisting of 18th- and early 19th-century keyboard music by continental composers, English country dances, songs, glees, catches and ballad operas, Irish dance music printed in Dublin in the second half of the 18th century, works by Irish composers (Cogan, Cooke, Geary, Stevenson), and music printed during the 18th century in Cork, Dublin and Limerick. Since 1927 the library has received under Irish copyright law a copy of everything published in the country.

C. F. Hegarty: *Thematic Index and Analytical Investigation of the Joyce Manuscripts* (Nat. Libr. nos.2982–3) (diss., National U. of Ireland, 1965–6)

——. Royal Irish Academy, 19 Dawson Street, Dublin 2 (*Da*). The collection of Irish music in the library comprises 19 MSS containing only Irish music and seven MSS which, in addition to other material, contain some Irish airs and historical articles on Irish music. One MS dates from the 18th century and the others from the 19th, but the airs recorded date from the

17th. The largest collection is the Forde–Pigott collection of over 4000 airs (some repeated in differing versions), compiled by William Forde and John Edward Pigott in the years 1840–50, and received by the Academy about 1910. There is a one-page autograph of a Thomas Moore melody.

——. Royal Irish Academy of Music, 36–8 Westland Row, Dublin 2 (*Dam*). The Academy's Monteagle Library was opened in 1939. Besides a comprehensive collection of performing scores, it includes the collections of the Ancient Concerts' Society (1834–63) and some printed music of the late 18th century.

——. Trinity College Library, College Street, Dublin 2 (*Dtc*). In addition to the collection of British printed music received since 1801 under the copyright acts, the library contains the Ebenezer Prout collection, acquired in 1910 (comprising many 19th-century scores), the Townley Hall collection (including an early copy of *Messiah*, late 18th-century Neapolitan operas, and other 18th- and early 19th-century music – much of it popular in nature), and early editions of Tallis, Byrd and Merbecke's *Booke of Common Praier Noted*. MSS include liturgical music from the 11th–18th centuries, the Ballet and Dallis lutebooks (16th–17th century), the 16th-century Dublin Virginal Book, John Travers's *De arte musica*, and other theoretical works from the 17th and 18th centuries. There are MS collections of 20th-century Irish composers and some Irish folk music collected by Petrie, Goodman and Moeran.

T. K. Abbott: *Catalogue of the Manuscripts in the Library of Trinity College* (Dublin, 1900); T. Dart: 'New Sources of Virginal Music', *ML*, xxxv (1954), 93; H. W. Parke: *The Library of Trinity College: a Historical Description* (Dublin, 1961); *Treasures of Trinity College Dublin* (Dublin, 1961) [exhibition catalogue]; J. Ward: 'The Lute Books of Trinity College Dublin', *LSJ*, ix (1967), 17, and x (1868), 15 [with detailed inventories of MSS]

——. University College Library, Earlsfort Terrace, Dublin 2 (*Duc*). Besides the standard collection, the library has large holdings of Irish folk music. In 1945 the bequest of the tenor John McCormack was acquired. The library receives depository copies of everything published in the country.

ITALY (*I*)

The central office for musical research in Italy is the Ufficio Ricerca Fondi Musicali (at Via Clerici 5, 20121 Milan), which was founded in 1966 as a special section of the Biblioteca Nazionale Braidense. It supervises the cataloguing of all pre-1900 MS and printed sources, files of which may be consulted until the publication of a general catalogue (see M. Donà: 'Joint Session of Music Research Libraries and Music Information Centres', *FAM*, xxi, 1974, p.8).

The national libraries in Florence and Rome receive copies of everything published in the country. In each province, the most important general public library in the capital city receives a copy of every publication (including music) issued in the province. In Milan music is transferred from the Biblioteca Nazionale Braidense to the Conservatorio di Musica 'Giuseppe Verdi', and in Rome from the Biblioteca Nazionale Centrale 'Vittorio Emanuele II' to the Conservatorio di Musica 'S Cecilia'.

Government-sponsored publications: *Inventari dei manoscritti delle biblioteche d'Italia*, ed. G. Mazzatinti and others (Forlì, 1890–, rev. 1962–); *Accademie e biblioteche d'Italia: annali della Direzione generale* (Rome, 1927–42, 1950–); *Guida delle biblioteche italiane* (Rome, 1969); *Annuario delle biblioteche italiane* (Rome, 1949, 3/1970–)

Other series: Associazione dei musicologi italiani (Parma, 1911–38/part *R*1969–) [catalogues]; *NA*, i–xx (1924–43) [with descriptions and catalogues of many archives]; *Bibliotheca musicae: collana di cataloghi e bibliografie* (Milan, 1962–)

General bibliography: W. Rubsamen: 'Music Research in Italian Libraries', *Notes*, vi (1948–9), 220, 543, and viii (1950–51), 70, 513; C. Sartori: 'Le biblioteche musicali italiane', *FAM*, xviii (1971), 93–157 [many sections written by librarians of those collections]

ALBENGA. Biblioteca Capitolare, Cattedrale S Michele, Piazza S Michele, 17031 Albenga (*AL*). The sacristy contains 22 illuminated liturgical MSS of the 13th–15th centuries.

ANCONA. Biblioteca Comunale Luciano Benincasa, Via Ascoli Piceno 10, 60100 Ancona (*AN*). The library has imprints and MSS of the 16th–19th centuries, including works by Anerio, Boccherini, Corelli, Nenna, Palestrina, Tartini and Zarlino.

AOSTA. Seminario Maggiore, Viale Xavier de Maistre 17, 11100 Aosta (*AO*). The seminary owns the famous 15th-century Aosta MS and, among others, MSS from the 11th century with neumatic and diastematic notation.

H. Besseler: 'Aosta', *MGG*; R. Amiet: *Repertorium liturgicum augustanum*, ii (Aosta, 1974), 9ff

AREZZO. Biblioteca Consorziale, Via dei Pileati, 52100 Arezzo (*ARc*). The library was formed in 1953 by joining several public and private collections. Among its musical treasures are liturgical MSS of the 11th–15th centuries, a Kapsberger chitarrone tablature (1604) and various treatises of Aaron, Gasparini, Grétry, Tartini and Zarlino.

——. Duomo, Piazza del Duomo, 52100 Arezzo (*ARd*). The capitular archive has two illuminated choirbooks of 1511 and some printed music of the 16th–18th centuries (works of Bononcini, Colonna, Morales and others).

F. Coradini: *L'archivio musicale del duomo di Arezzo nel secolo xvi* (Arezzo, 1922) [list of holdings]

ASSISI. Biblioteca Comunale, Via S Francesco 12, 06081 Assisi (*Ac*). The library holds part of the rich archive of the convent of S Francesco, including MSS of its former *maestri di cappella* Ferrari, Martini, Porta and Vallotti, and sacred works of the 15th and 16th centuries. There are also Italian MSS of the 18th century and 16th- and 17th-century imprints of musical and theoretical works, including some Petrucci editions.

F. Pennacchi: *Catalogo delle opere musicali*, Associazione dei musicologi italiani, xi (Parma, 1921); C. Sartori, ed.: *Assisi: la cappella della basilica di S. Francesco: catalogo del fondo musicale nella Biblioteca comunale di Assisi*, Bibliotheca musicae, i (Milan, 1962)

——. Cattedrale S Rufino, Piazza S Rufino, 06081 Assisi (*Ad*). The library of the cathedral chapel contains liturgical MSS of the 13th–18th centuries, as well as printed antiphoners, graduals, missals and breviaries of the 16th–18th centuries. There are also printed works of Giovanni Giudetti and theoretical treatises of Gasparini and Ghezzi. The largest portion of the collection dates from the 19th century, but there are also numerous works by 18th-century composers.

BERGAMO. Biblioteca Civica Angelo Mai, Piazza Vecchia 15, 24100 Bergamo (*BGc*). The library acquired a collection of MS choirbooks from the church of S Maria Maggiore in Bergamo. Other important items include autograph MSS and other music of Mayr and his contemporaries, a 15th-century parchment MS, nine Petrucci imprints, 16th- and 17th-century printed madrigals and 18th-century MSS. The library was founded in 1768.

A. Gazzaniga: *Il fondo musicale Mayr della Biblioteca civica Angelo Mai*, Monumenta bergomensia, xi (Bergamo, 1963)

——. Civico Istituto Musicale Gaetano Donizetti, Via Arena 9, 24100 Bergamo (*BGi*). The library owns the collection of the cellist Alfredo Piatti, containing many MS and printed cello works, and has acquired many early English editions, including Handel oratorios. It received three 15th-century MSS of polyphonic music and other sacred MSS (many of them autographs) from the archive of S Maria Maggiore. The Donizetti museum, which forms part of the institute, holds many of the composer's autographs, printed works and letters, as well as related materials.

G. Donati-Petteni: *L'istituto musicale G. Donizetti, la cappella musicale di S. Maria Maggiore, il museo Donizettiano* (Bergamo, 1928); J. Roche: 'An Inventory of Choirbooks at S. Maria Maggiore, Bergamo, January 1628', *RMARC*, v (1965), 47; V. Sacchiero: *Il museo Donizettiano* (Bergamo, 1970) [chiefly a catalogue]

BOLOGNA. General literature: A. Bonora and E. Giani: *Catalogo delle opere musicali ... città di Bologna*, Associazione dei musicologi italiani, ii (Parma, 1910–38) [incl. *Baf, Bam, Bsp*]

——. Accademia Filarmonica, Via Gerrazzi 13, 40125 Bologna (*Baf*). Masseangelo Masseangeli gave the library a large collection of musicians' autographs. Other holdings include a number of Petrucci editions, opera librettos, music documentation and iconography.

F. X. Haberl: 'Drucke von O. Petrucci auf der Bibliothek des Liceo filarmonico in Bologna', *MMg*, v (1873), 49, 92; E. Colombani: *Catalogo della collezione d'autografi lasciata alla R. Accademia filarmonica di ... Masseangeli* (Bologna, 1881/*R*1969); F. A. Gallo: 'L'Accademia filarmonica e la teoria musicale attraverso i testi conservati nell'archivio', *Quadrivium*, viii (1967), 51

——. Biblioteca Universitaria, Via Zamboni 35, 40126 Bologna (*Bu*). The university owns important liturgical MSS from the Nonantola abbey and from S Salvatore in Brescia, including an 11th-century missal (see H. Besseler: 'The Manuscript Bologna Biblioteca Universitaria 2216', *MD*, vi (1952), 39, and L. Gherardi: 'Il codice Angelica 123 monumento della chiesa bolognese nel sec. XI', *Quadrivium*, iii (1959), 5–114). Other rarities include MS music of the 15th–18th centuries, MS scores of A. Scarlatti's *Scipione nelle Spagne* and *Carlo, re d'Allemagna*, librettos, and editions of works by Merulo, Perti, Porta, Ruffo and Vitali.

F. Liuzzi: 'I codici musicali conservati nella R. Biblioteca universitaria di Bologna', *Rinascita musicale*, i/2 (1909), 10; L. Frati: 'Codici musicali della R. Biblioteca universitaria di Bologna', *RMI*, xxiii (1919), 219; R. Strohm: 'Neue Quellen zur liturgischen Mehrstimmigkeit des Mittelalters in Italien', *RIM*, i (1966), 86

——. Civico Museo Bibliografico Musicale, Piazza Rossini 2, 40126 Bologna (*Bc*). The nucleus of this rich collection is part of the library of Padre Martini, to which later works were added from the libraries of Mattei, Gaspari, Torchi, Vatielli and others. The entire collection formerly belonged to the Liceo Musicale, a city institution that became a state conservatory in 1942. The library has been separate since 1959, although it is still housed in the conservatory building. One of the richest in Italy, its holdings include illuminated and medieval MSS, autographs of important composers, madrigals, rare 18th-century editions, about 10,000 opera librettos and many first editions of the 19th century.

G Gaspari: *Catalogo della biblioteca del Liceo musicale di Bologna*, i–iv (Bologna, 1890–1905/*R*1961), v, ed. U. Sesini (Bologna, 1943/*R*1970); P. O. Kristeller: *Iter italicum: a Finding List of Uncatalogued or Incompletely Catalogued Humanistic MSS of the Renaissance* (London, 1963–7), i, 28ff [inventory of theoretical MS

works]; S. Paganelli: 'Il fondo Rossiniano del Museo bibliografico musicale', *Almanacco dei bibliotecari italiani* (Rome, 1968), 149

——. Convento di S Francesco (dei Frati Minori Conventuali), Piazza Malpighi 9, 40123 Bologna (*Bsf*). The convent library holds the part of Martini's collection not in the Civico Museo, as well as others of his MSS. There are also MS works from the library of the Abbé Fortunato Santini (the remainder being in the Bischöfliches Priesterseminar in Münster), a number of early choirbooks (some parchment) and 200 autographs of Stanislao Mattei.

G. Zanotti: *Biblioteca del Convento di S. Francesco di Bologna: catalogo del fondo musicale* (Bologna, 1970)

——. S Petronio (Basilica), Piazza Galvani 5, 40124 Bologna (*Bsp*). The church archive has important MS holdings: polyphonic works of the 15th–17th centuries, sacred vocal works of the 17th–19th centuries, 17th- and 18th-century instrumental works, and 18th- and 19th-century secular vocal works. There are also about 200 printed works of the 16th–18th centuries.

L. Frati: *I libri corali della Basilica di S. Petronio* (Bologna, 1896); J. Berger: 'Notes on some 17th Century Compositions for Trumpet and Strings in Bologna', *MQ*, xxxvii (1951), 354; C. Hamm: 'Musiche del quattrocento in S. Petronio', *RIM*, iii (1968), 215; A. Schnoebelen: 'Performance Practice at San Petronio in the Baroque', *AcM*, xli (1969), 37

CASALE MONFERRATO. Archivio Capitolare (S Evasio), Casa Parrochiale, Via Liutprando 22, 15033 Casale Monferrato (*CMac*). The archive has choirbooks copied in the first quarter of the 16th century containing works by anonymous composers, as well as Josquin, La Rue, Mouton and others (see D. Crawford: *16th-century Choirbooks in the Archivio capitolare at Casale Monferrato*, RMS, ii, 1975). There are also 15th-century illuminated MSS and an MS of 1594 copied by Francesco Sforza containing works by Jacquet of Mantua and Victoria (see D. Crawford: 'The Francesco Sforza MS at Casale Monferrato', *JAMS*, xxiv, 1971, p.457).

P. Guerrini: 'I codici musicali dell'Archivio capitolare di Casale Monferrato', *Rivista di storia, arte e archeologia della provincia di Alessandria*, xlii (1933), 599

CESENA. Badia S Maria del Monte, Via del Monte 999, 47023 Cesena (*CEb(sm)*). The library was founded in the Middle Ages and reconstituted by the Benedictine order after the Napoleonic dispersions in 1819. During World War II more than half of its holdings were destroyed by bombing. It now owns a 16th-century Ambrosian antiphoner and a variety of masses, psalms, *laudi*, hymns, litanies, motets and oratorios. There are 16th-century editions of Zarlino and Vicentino and secular works of the 18th and early 19th centuries by Bellini, Donizetti, Haydn, Martini and others.

——. Biblioteca Comunale Malatestiana, Piazza Bufalini 1, 46023 Cesena (*CEc*). The library was founded in 1452 by Malatesta Novello in the convent of the Frati Minori. Music holdings include 15th-century illuminated choirbooks, 16th- and 17th-century theoretical works, and 18th-century instrumental and sacred vocal music.

S. Paganelli: 'Catalogo delle opere musicali a stampa dal '500 al '700 conservato presso la Biblioteca comunale di Cesena', *CHM*, ii (1957), 311

CIVIDALE DEL FRIULI. Museo Archeologico Nazionale, Piazza del Duomo 1c, 33043 Cividale del Friuli (*CFm*). Founded in 1725, the museum library has not acquired materials since c1830. It has, however, an important collection of missals, graduals, antiphoners,

Passions and other sacred works of the 13th–15th centuries, some from the city's cathedral.

P. Petrobelli: 'Nuovo materiale polifonico del medioevo e del rinascimento a Cividale', *Memorie storiche Forogiuliesi*, xlvi (1965), 213

CREMONA. Biblioteca Statale, Via Ugolani Dati 4, 26100 Cremona (*CR*). The music room is named after the musicologist Gaetano Cesari, whose library was given to the city by his widow in 1934. Besides his own MS notes and transcriptions, the collection comprises early editions of madrigals and motets, theoretical works, compositions by Cremona composers, and letters and correspondence of various musicians (e.g. Paganini). 18th- and 19th-century opera is well represented in two further collections of MSS and printed scores received from the Pia Istituzione Musicale and the library of Della Corna Mainardi.

R. Monterosso: 'Guida alla biblioteca di G. Cesari, musicologo cremonese', *Annali*, i (1948), 35; R. Monterosso: 'Mostra bibliografica dei musicisti cremonesi, dal rinascimento all'ottocento: catalogo', *Annali*, ii (1949), 107–50 [journal issued by library]

FAENZA. Archivio Capitolare (Duomo), Piazza della Liberia, 48018 Faenza (*FZac(d)*). The archive has a collection of MSS and printed works of the 16th–19th centuries. 16th- and 17th-century editions include works by Asola, Ingegneri, Lassus, Merulo and Moraies.

E. Hilmar: 'Die Musikdrucke im Dom von Faenza', *Symbolae historiae musicae: Hellmut Federhofer zum 60. Geburtstag* (Mainz, 1971), 68 [catalogue chiefly of 16th- and 17th-century sacred works]

——. Biblioteca Comunale, Via Manfredi 14, 48018 Faenza (*FZc*). Besides various early antiphoners (some illuminated), the library owns the famous 15th-century Faenza MS, copied by Bonadies (see D. Plamenac: 'Faenza, Codex 117', *MGG*). Autographs and printed works by Giuseppe Sarti, Paolo Alberghi and other local composers are in the collection, and there are also a large number of librettos, some early printed theoretical works, sacred music, and iconographic material relating to singers.

FERRARA. Biblioteca Comunale Ariostea, Via Scienze 17, 44100 Ferrara (*FEc*). The library has Italian vocal music printed in the 16th–18th centuries, much of it related to local musical activities.

E. Davia and A. Lombardi: *Catalogo delle opere musicali . . . città di Ferrara*, Associazione dei musicologi italiani, ix (Parma, 1917)

FLORENCE. General literature: B. Becherini and others: 'Florenz', *MGG* [incl. discussion of MSS in Florence libraries]; M. Picker: 'Notes and Queries', *Notes*, xxiii (1966–7), 633; M. Picker: 'Communications', *JAMS*, xx (1967), 147, 515

——. Biblioteca Marucelliana, Via Cavour 43, 50129 Florence (*Fm*). The library was privately owned by Francesco Marucelli in the 17th century. Enlarged with other gifts and works from dispersed convents of the region, it is now a public library. The Bonamici collection, formerly in Livorno, was purchased in 1904; it consists of 10,000 opera and oratorio librettos, including 500 from the 17th century. The library also owns MS works by Doni, and among its printed music of the 16th–18th centuries are four Petrucci editions.

R. Lustig: 'Saggio di catalogo della collezione di melodrammi della R. Biblioteca Marucelliana', *La bibliofilia*, xxv (1923–4), 239, 305, and xxvi (1924), 67 [lists 17th- and early 18th-century librettos in the Bonamici collection]

——. Biblioteca Medicea-Laurenziana, Piazza S Lorenzo 9, 50123 Florence (*Fl*). The library was opened to the public in its present building (constructed by Michelangelo) in 1571. Music forms only a small part of the collection, but among its treasures are a 13th-century *Antiphonarium medicaeum* containing Pérotin's *Magnus liber organi*, the Squarcialupi MS (works by Landini and other 14th-century Italian composers), some of the Ashburnham MSS (see C. Paoli and others: *I codici Ashburnhamiani della R. Biblioteca Mediceo-Laurenziana*, Indici e cataloghi, viii, Rome, 1887–1948), and the magnificent 16th-century Medici MS, a gift from Alida Varzi (see E. E. Lowinsky: 'The Medici Codex', *AnnM*, v (1957), 61–178). There are also some 18th-century cantatas.

A. M. Bandini: *Catalogus codicum manuscriptorum Bibliothecae Mediceae Laurentianae* (Florence, 1764–70/*R*1961)

——. Biblioteca Nazionale Centrale, Piazza Cavalleggeri 1, 50122 Florence (*Fn*). Italy's largest and richest library, the Biblioteca Nazionale (which has included the Magliabechiana and Palatina libraries since 1861) has been the copyright depository since 1886 and issues the national bibliography. The department of MSS and rare items holds among other important sources Banco rari 18 containing *laudi*, and Panciatichiano 26 with works of the Florentine Ars Nova. The collection also includes 16th- and 17th-century editions of theoretical works, tablatures, secular polyphony and early liturgical works. In 1945 the library received the Landau–Finaly memorial collection.

D. Fava: *La Biblioteca nazionale centrale di Firenze e le sue indigini raccolte* (Milan, 1939); *Catalogo dell'Esposizione nazionale dei conservatori musicali e delle biblioteche* (Florence, 1950); B. Becherini: *Catalogo dei manoscritti musicali della Biblioteca nazionale di Firenze* (Kassel, 1959)

——. Biblioteca Riccardiana e Moreniana, Via dei Ginori 10, 50129 Florence (*Fr*). Among its MSS the library has theoretical works of the 15th–17th centuries; French, Italian and Spanish songs of the 15th–18th centuries; and guitar sonatas of the 17th century. Printed works of the 16th–18th centuries include anthologies and single-composer editions of Monte, Lassus, Martini, Monteverdi, Palestrina, Rore, Striggio and Vecchi, as well as a number of early librettos. The library consists of two separate institutions sharing functions and services and specializing in works from ancient cultures.

S. Morpurgo: *I manoscritti della Biblioteca Riccardiana*, Indici e cataloghi, xv (Rome, 1893–1900); C. Nardini and others: *I manoscritti della Biblioteca Moreniana* (Florence, 1903–)

——. Conservatorio Statale di Musica 'Luigi Cherubini', Piazza Belle Arti 2, 50122 Florence (*Fc*). Formerly the R. Istituto Musicale, the library was founded in 1862 with the archives of the ducal court of Tuscany and the Accademia di Belle Arti. Of the many donations it subsequently received, the two largest are the Pitti and Basevi collections. There are compositions and theoretical works of the 15th–17th centuries, as well as important 18th- and 19th-century operatic and instrumental works. Autographs include compositions and letters of Cherubini, Donizetti, Monteverdi, Rossini and Verdi.

R. Gandolfi: *Indice de alcuni cimeli esposti appartenenti alla biblioteca del R. Istituto musicale* (Florence, 1911); R. Gandolfi and C. Cordara: *Catalogo delle opere musicali . . . città di Firenze*, Associazione dei musicologi italiani, iv/1 (Parma, 1910–11); A. Damerini: *Il R. Conservatorio di musica 'Luigi Cherubini' di Firenze* (Florence, 1941); B. Becherini: 'I manoscritti e le stampe rare della biblioteca del Conservatorio L. Cherubini', *La bibliofilia*, lxvi (1964), 255–99 [16th- and 17th-century partsongs]

FORLI. Biblioteca Comunale 'Aurelio Saffi', Corso della Repubblica 72, 47100 (*FOc*). The music section has 15th-century sacred music and printed works of the

16th and 17th centuries. The 1937 gift of Carlo Piancastelli included early editions of works by Geminiani, Mozart, Tartini and others, but is especially rich in MSS and printed works of Corelli.

A. Servolini: 'I corali e gli offizi miniati della Biblioteca comunale di Forlì', *Gutenberg Jb* (1949), 18; F. Walker: 'Rossiniana in the Piancastelli Collection', *MMR*, lxxx (1960), 138, 203; *Catalogo della mostra delle edizioni e manoscritti nelle raccolte Piancastelli della Biblioteca comunale di Forlì* (Fusignano, 1967)

GENOA. General literature: G. Piersantelli: *Storia delle biblioteche civiche genovesi* (Florence, 1964)

——. Biblioteca Universitaria, Via Balbi 3, 16126 Genoa (*Gu*). The library has lute tablatures (see A. Neri: 'Un codice musicale del secolo XVI', *Giornale storico delle letteratura italiana*, vii (1886) for a description of lute MS F.VII) and troubadour songs, in addition to imprints of the 16th–18th centuries.

R. Bresciano: *Catalogo delle opere musicali ... città di Genova*, Associazione dei musicologi italiani, vii (Parma, [1929])

——. Conservatorio di Musica 'Nicolò Paganini', Via Albaro 38, 16145 Genoa (*Gi(l)*). The conservatory was formerly called the Istituto or Liceo Musicale. Its library has letters, documents and iconography related to Paganini. Other valuable holdings include MS anthologies of 17th- and 18th-century vocal music, 18th-century editions of theoretical works (Arteaga, Martini, Sala and others), and numerous 18th-century French imprints. There are also MSS of Abel, Anfossi, J. C. Bach, Cimarosa, Galuppi (autographs), Hasse, Haydn, Piccinni, Sarti and many other Italian (and some foreign) composers.

S. Pintacuda: *Genova, Biblioteca dell'Istituto musicale N. Paganini: catalogo del fondo antico*, Bibliotheca musicae, iv (Milan, 1966); G. Piumatti: *Catalogo delle opere di musicisti liguri esistenti presso la biblioteca del Conservatorio di musica Nicolò Paganini di Genova* (Genoa, 1975)

GROTTAFERRATA. Badia Greca, 00046 Grottaferrata (*GR*). Founded in 1004, the abbey has a collection of Byzantine MSS from the 11th–14th centuries.

L. Tardo: 'La musica bizantina e i codici melurgici della biblioteca di Grottaferrata', *Accademie e biblioteche d'Italia*, iv (1930–31), 355

IVREA. Biblioteca Capitolare, Piazza del Duomo, 10015 Ivrea (*IV*). The library has about 130 MSS of the 7th–15th centuries, some with Gregorian notation. There are also 11th-century copies of treatises by Boethius and St Augustine. The famous Ivrea MS of the second half of the 14th century has 81 compositions by Vitry, Machaut, Loys and others (see M. H. Johnson: *The 37 Motets of the Codex Ivrea* (diss., Indiana U., 1955) and G. Reaney: 'Codex Ivrea', *MGG*).

LIVORNO. Biblioteca Comunale Labronica F. D. Guerrazzi, Piazza Matteotti 19, 57100 Livorno (*LI*). The Autografoteca Bastogi contains letters and compositions by famous musicians of the 18th and 19th centuries; Mascagni is represented by mementos as well as autographs. The gift of the Delle Sedie family consists of about 2000 piano scores of operas and other vocal works of the 17th–19th centuries. The library also has a collection of 18th-century librettos. The music collection is to be transferred to the city's music school.

LORETO. Archivio Storico della Cappella Lauretana, Piazza della Madonna, 60025 Loreto (*LT*). The music section of the library has printed and MS works by former *maestri di cappella* of the Cappella Lauretana and other composers (including Cifra, Porto and Rossi).

G. Tebaldini: *L'archivio musicale della Cappella lauretana: catalogo storico-critico* (Loreto, 1921); F. da Morrovalle: *L'archivio storico della Santa Casa di Loreto: inventario* (Vatican City, 1965)

LUCCA. General literature: A. Bonaccorsi: 'Catalogo con notizie biografiche delle musiche dei maestri lucchesi esistenti nelle biblioteche di Lucca', *CHM*, ii (1957), 73 [lists works in *Lg*, *Li* and *Ls*], and 'Catalogo delle musiche esistenti nelle biblioteche di Lucca', *Maestri di Lucca*, ed. A. Bonaccorsi (Florence, 1967)

——. Archivio di Stato, Piazza Guidiccioni 5, 55100 Lucca (*La*). The archive has MS and printed choirbooks, including 18 leaves of the famous Mancini MS containing 14th- and early 15th-century vocal music with French and Italian texts (see K. von Fischer: 'Lucca, Codex', *MGG*) and the Strohm MS containing sacred music of *c*1485 (see R. Strohm: 'Ein unbekanntes Chorbuch des 15. Jh.', *Mf*, xxi, 1968, p.40).

——. Biblioteca Statale, Via S Maria Corte Orlandini 12, 55100 Lucca (*Lg*). The library's MS and printed works of the 11th–19th centuries include a lute tablature, some theoretical treatises, liturgical works, and 17th- and 18th-century librettos.

——. Istituto Musicale 'Luigi Boccherini', Piazza S Ponziano, 55100 Lucca (*Li*). Formerly called the Istituto Pacini, the library holds about 630 volumes by the Puccinis and other Lucca composers, about 660 volumes of MS and printed sacred music of the 18th–20th centuries (mostly by Lucca composers), and the Bottini collection of about 1200 MS and printed works (mostly secular) from the time of Rossini.

——. Seminario Vescovile, Via Monte S Quirico, 55100 Lucca (*Ls*). The music section of the seminary library has a good collection of 17th-century sacred works, imprints of the 17th and 18th centuries, works by Lucca composers of the 18th and 19th centuries, and some theoretical works.

C. Sartori: 'Il fondo di musiche a stampa della biblioteca del Seminario di Lucca', *FAM*, ii (1955), 134; E. Maggini: *Lucca, biblioteca del Seminario: catalogo delle musiche stampate e manoscritti del fondo antico*, Bibliotheca musicae, iii (Milan, 1965)

MANTUA. Accademia Virgiliana di Scienze, Lettere ed Arti, Via dell'Accademia 47, 46100 Mantua (*MAav*). Founded in 1768, the library has 426 vocal and instrumental works, chiefly MSS of the 18th and 19th centuries, including several operas and a cantata by Traetta as well as shorter works by Anfossi, Galuppi, Jommelli, Paisiello, Sacchini and others.

G. G. Bernardi: *La musica nelle R. Accademia Virgiliana* (Mantua, 1923), chap. 'Catalogo dell'Archivio musicale'

MESSINA. Biblioteca Universitaria, Via dei Verdi 71, 98100 Messina (*ME*). The library has Greek MSS of the 7th–12th centuries with Byzantine music. The music section has liturgical MSS (12th–18th centuries) from various monasteries, treatises and printed music (16th-century), and librettos. The Gaetano La Corte-Callier collection contains 19th-century works.

'La collezione La Corte-Callier della BU di Messina', *Accademie e biblioteche d'Italia*, i (1927), iii; O. Tiby: 'I codici musicali italo-greci di Messina', *Accademie e biblioteche d'Italia*, xi (1937), 65; L. Tardo: 'I MSS greci di musica bizantina nella Biblioteca universitaria di Messina', *Archivio storico per la Calabria e la Lucania*, xxiii (1954), 187

MILAN. General literature: G. Tintori: 'Mailänder Handschriften', *MGG* [lists MSS in *Ma*, *Md*, *Mc* and *Mt*]; M. Donà: *La musica nelle biblioteche milanesi: mostra di libri e documenti* (Milan, 1963)

——. Archivio della Cappella Musicale del Duomo,

Palazzo Reale, Piazza del Duomo, 20122 Milan (*Md*). The music treasures kept in the cathedral museum (administered by the Veneranda Fabbrica del Duomo) consist of works (mostly autograph) by former *maestri di cappella*, works performed by the chapel, and works submitted by candidates for the position of *maestro di cappella*. The material has been organized into three groups: 51 large volumes with heavy bindings, including the Gaffurius autographs and works of the 16th–18th centuries; works written by *maestri di cappella*; and works written for the chapel services by other composers.

C. Sartori: *La cappella musicale del duomo di Milano: catalogo delle musiche dell'archivio* (Milan, 1957); G. De Florentiis: *Sei secoli di musica nel duomo di Milano: raccolta di documenti d'archivio riguardanti la cappella musicale* (Milan, 1969)

——. Biblioteca Ambrosiana, Piazza Pio XI 2, 20123 Milan (*Ma*). Important early items in the collection are Latin, Greek and Byzantine liturgical MSS and fragments of the 9th and 10th centuries, various liturgical MSS of the 10th–13th centuries, a troubadour MS (R 71), and a 16th-century MS containing masses by Josquin, La Rue and Morales; Gaffurius, Rore, Zarlino and others are represented by autographs. Printed works include Italian editions of the late 16th and early 17th centuries, theoretical works and other musical writings of all periods, and opera and oratorio librettos (printed chiefly for local performances). 18th-century works include popular Italian lute-songs and 30 MSS mainly of Milanese composers.

G. Cesari: *Biblioteca Ambrosiana: opere teoriche manoscritti*, Associazione dei musicologi italiani, indice e cataloghi, iii (Parma, 1910–11); M. L. Gengaro: *Codici decorati e miniati dell'Ambrosiana* (Milan, 1959); R. Cipriani: *Codici miniati dell'Ambrosiana* (Vicenza, 1968)

——. Biblioteca Nazionale Braidense, Palazzo di Brera, Via Brera 28, 20121 Milan (*Mb*). The library founded by Empress Maria Theresia was opened to the public in 1773. Later many works were received from the archives of suppressed religious orders, and liturgical books (e.g. antiphoners and missals) of the 12th–18th centuries were acquired from the duchy of Parma. The library owns several lute tablatures. Its collection of opera and oratorio librettos of the 16th–19th centuries acquired from Count Corniani-Algarotti of Treviso includes many texts prepared for Milan performances, and there is a collection of musicians' letters (63 from Verdi). A special section of the library catalogues the country's musical resources (see introductory section for Italy).

F. Carta: *Codici corali e libri a stampa miniati della Biblioteca nazionale di Milano*, Indice e cataloghi, xiii (Rome, 1891); *La biblioteca liturgica dei duchi di Parma* (Milan, 1934) [catalogue]; M. Donà: 'Musiche a stampa nella Biblioteca braidense', *FAM*, vii (1960), 66 [lists some of the most important works]

——. Biblioteca Teatrale Livia Simoni, Via Filodrammatici 2, 20121 Milan (*Ms*). Situated in La Scala's theatrical museum, the library holds many autographs (including works by Bellini, Berlioz, Cilea, Donizetti, Jommelli, Mascagni and Paganini) as well as 16th- and 17th-century librettos. In 1930 a collection of Verdiana was added, and in 1954 the library of Renato Simoni. Holdings also include stage designs and costumes, iconography, instruments, choreography and the related literature.

S. Vittadini: *Catalogo del Museo teatrale alla Scala* (Milan, 1940, suppl. 1959); S. Vittadini: 'La biblioteca di Renato Simoni al Museo teatrale alla Scala', *Accademie e biblioteche d'Italia*, xxii (1954), 579; T. Rogledi Manni: 'La biblioteca Livia Simoni', *Il Museo teatrale alla Scala, 1931–1963* (Milan, 1964)

——. Conservatorio di Musica 'Giuseppe Verdi', Via del Conservatorio 12, 20122 Milan (*Mc*). One of the richest music collections in Italy, the library was founded in 1809 with a gift of a dozen volumes from the Paris Conservatoire. By a decree of 1850 the library was enriched by 5000 volumes from the University of Pavia and by a large portion of the music collection of the Biblioteca Nazionale Braidense. Almost 300 MS and printed volumes of the 16th and 17th centuries (including the precious Sforza MS with works of Gastoldi) were received from the chapel of the ducal church of S Barbara in Mantua. The scores of operas performed in Milan from 1816 to 1850 were received from the city's theatres and a large opera collection from La Scala. The Noseda archive, owned by the city but placed here on deposit, consists of 10,000 MS and printed works of the 18th and 19th centuries, including many autographs. The library also owns 15th-century French and Italian songs, 16th-century printed sacred vocal music, operatic arias and 18th- and 19th-century sacred works of unknown provenance. The private library of Giacomo Benvenuti was bought in 1951, and the Polo collection of violin music was given by his daughter in 1954.

E. de Guarinoni: *Indice generale dell'Archivio musicale Noseda* (Milan, 1897); *Catalogo della biblioteca: letteratura musicale e opere teoriche*, i: *Manoscritti e stampe fino al 1899* (Milan, 1969) and *Catalogo della biblioteca: fondi speciali*, i: *Musiche della cappella di Santa Barbara in Mantova* (Florence, 1972) [2 parts of library's new catalogue, to contain about 20 vols.]

——. Ricordi, Via Salomone 77, 20138 Milan (*Mr*). The firm's archive holds autographs and printed works by composers on its roster. The works are chiefly operatic, but include chamber, orchestral and other vocal music, as well as letters from composers, singers and musicologists. In 1888 the collection of the Milanese publisher Francesco Lucca was incorporated.

Catalogo (in ordine numerico) delle opere pubblicate . . . di Gio. Ricordi (Milan, 1857); *Internationale Musik- und Theater-Ausstellung, Wien 1892* (Milan, 1892), 145 [list of autographs in the archive]; C. Sartori: *Casa Ricordi, 1808–1958: profilo storico* (Milan, 1958); T. F. Heck: 'Ricordi Plate Numbers in the Earlier 19th Century', *CMc* (1970), no.10, p.117

MODENA. Accademia Nazionale di Scienze, Lettere ed Arti, Corso Vittorio Emanuele II 59, 41100 Modena (*MOa*). The library of the academy was founded in the 18th century. During the 1960s two groups of musical material were received from the family of the musicologist Vincenzo Tardini. One was a collection of about 500 scores, chiefly reductions of 19th-century stage and sacred works, but also including theoretical works, instrumental methods and instrumental music. The second gift consisted of 950 librettos (mostly 19th-century), of which 160 were published in Modena; many of these are not available elsewhere.

G. Roncaglia: *Della raccolta musicale di Vincenzo Tardini donata dagli eredi alla Accademia nazionale di scienze, lettere e arti di Modena*, Atti e memorie della Accademia nazionale di scienze, lettere e arti di Modena, 6th ser., iii (1961); G. Roncaglia: *Elenco degli spartiti della 'Biblioteca musicale' Tardini e della 'Raccolta musicale' Righi Molinari*, ibid, 6th ser., iv (1962); G. Pistoni: *Della raccolta di libretti musicali donata dalla famiglia Tardini all'Accademia nazionale di scienze, lettere e arti di Modena*, ibid, 6th ser., xi (1969)

——. Biblioteca Estense e Universitaria, Piazza S Agostino 309, 41100 Modena (*MOe*). The Biblioteca Estense was founded in Ferrara by the Este family in the late 14th century and transferred to Modena in 1598; it was opened to the public in 1761 and moved to its present location in 1883. The Biblioteca Universitaria, founded in 1772 by Francesco II, was opened to the public in 1844 and became part of the Estense in 1892.

It is now the copyright deposit library for the province. Its music section is especially rich in French and Italian works of the 15th and 16th centuries (including printed madrigals of Monte, Festa, Gastoldi, Lassus, Palestrina and Wert); 17th-century operas, oratorios and cantatas of Stradella and others; instrumental works from the 17th–19th centuries (by Haydn, Cambini, Corelli, Torelli, Vitali and others); theoretical works of the 16th–19th centuries; and choirbooks of the 15th and 16th centuries.

A. Catelani: 'Delle opere di Alessandro Stradella esistenti nell'archivio musicale della R. Biblioteca Palatina di Modena', *Atti e memorie della RR. Deputazioni di storia patria per le provincie modenesi e parmensi*, iii (?Modena, 1865), 319–54; V. Finzi: 'Bibliografia delle stampe musicali della R. Biblioteca Estense', *Rivista delle biblioteche e degli archivi*, iii–v (1892–5) [describes 321 works]; P. Lodi: *Catalogo delle opere musicali . . . città di Modena*, Associazione dei musicologi italiani, viii (Parma, 1916–24/R1967); D. Fava: *La Biblioteca Estense nel suo sviluppo storico con il catalogo della mostra permanente* (Modena, 1925); D. Fava: *Catalogo degli incunaboli della R. Biblioteca Estense di Modena* (Florence, 1928); E. J. Luin: 'Repertorio dei libri musicali di S. A. S. Francesco I d'Este', *La bibliofilia*, xxxviii (1936), 418; G. Roncaglia: 'Le composizioni strumentali di Alessandro Stradella esistenti presso la R. Biblioteca Estense di Modena', *RMI*, xliv (1940), 81, 337; C. V. Aubrun: 'Chansonniers musicaux espagnols du XVIIe siècle: les recueils de Modène', *Bulletin hispanique*, li (1949), 269, lii (1950), 313; D. Fava and M. Salmi: *I manoscritti miniati della Biblioteca Estense di Modena* (Florence, 1950), vol.ii ed. E. Pirani (Milan, 1973)

——. Duomo, Via Lanfranco 6, 41100 Modena (*MOd*). The cathedral library has 16th-century MS and printed sacred music and a number of 17th-century imprints.

A. Catelani: 'L'archivio della cattedrale di Modena', *Gazzetta musicale di Milano*, xix (1861), 168–203; A. Dondi: *Notizie storiche ed artistiche del duomo di Modena* (Modena, 1896), 159ff; D. E. Crawford: *Vespers Polyphony at Modena's Cathedral in the First Half of the 16th Century* (diss., U. of Illinois, 1967) [discusses 13 MS vols.]

MONTE CASSINO. Abbazia, 03043 Monte Cassino (*MC*). The abbey was founded in the 6th century, and although its library passed to the state in 1866, it is still affiliated with the Benedictine monks who occupy the abbey. The books were sent to Rome for safe-keeping during World War II and were subsequently returned to the reconstructed abbey. The abbey received the Rignani bequest of 18th-century operas and oratorios as well as the city's music archive. Among the rarities are 11 MSS of Gregorian chant, 67 choirbooks from the cathedral's basilica (some richly illuminated), and various 16th–18th-century editions of works by J. C. Bach, Cerone, Corelli, Frescobaldi, Jommelli, Lassus, Lully, Piccinni, Porpora, Vitali and many others.

P. M. Ferretti: 'I manoscritti musicali gregoriani dell'archivio di Montecassino', *Casinensia: miscellanea di studi cassinensi*, i (1929), 187; A. Pirro: 'Un manuscrit musical du 15e siècle au Mont-Cassin', ibid, i (1929), 206; E. Dagnino: 'L'archivio musicale di Montecassino', ibid, i (1929), 273

MONZA. Duomo (Basilica di S Giovanni Battista), Via Duomo 8, 20052 Monza (*MZ*). The capitular archive contains some liturgical MSS of the 10th–14th centuries and various compositions by little-known pre-1900 composers (especially Francesco Pezzoli).

R. Dalmonte: *Catalogo musicale del duomo di Monza*, BMB, 6th ser., ii (1969) [with detailed descriptions of early works in the library]

NAPLES. Biblioteca Nazionale 'Vittorio Emanuele III', Piazza del Plebiscito, 80132 Naples (*Nn*). The library was formerly called the Reale Biblioteca Borbonica. The music collection includes Byzantine and other liturgical MSS of the 12th–18th centuries, some printed works of the 16th and 17th centuries, and a large collection of opera, oratorio and cantata librettos of the 17th–19th centuries. The separate theatre and music section called

the Biblioteca Lucchesi-Palli was given to the city in 1888 by Count Lucchesi Palli and contains some 60,000 volumes valuable for the documentation of opera activity in the city. Among the MSS are 17th- and 18th-century sacred works of the Neapolitan school (some autograph), 18th- and 19th-century opera and salon music, 19th- and 20th-century Neapolitan popular songs and librettos of the 17th–19th centuries.

E. Nobile: 'Inediti verdiani nella Biblioteca Lucchesi Palli', *Accademie e biblioteche d'Italia*, xix (1951), 111; R. Arnese: 'Codici di origine francese della Biblioteca Lucchesi Palli', *Etudes grégoriennes*, iii (1959), 27; A. Mondolfi: 'Il fondo musicale cinquecentesco della Biblioteca nazionale di Napoli', *CHM*, ii (1957), 277; R. Arnese: *I codici notati della Biblioteca nazionale di Napoli*, Biblioteca di bibliografia italiana, xlvii (Florence, 1967) [lists mainly liturgical works, especially pre-1700 graduals and antiphoners]

——. Conservatorio di Musica 'S Pietro a Majella', Via S Pietro a Majella 35, 80138 Naples (*Nc*). The library was founded in 1791 with a donation from Saverio Mattei. Its rich holdings of 50,000 MSS and many printed works are particularly valuable for autographs of operas by Jommelli, Paisiello, Cimarosa, Piccinni and others; madrigals printed from 1550 to 1728 in Naples, theoretical treatises of all periods; opera librettos from the 17th century to the present; and a collection of musicians' letters.

G. Gasparini and F. Gallo: *Catalogo delle opere musicali . . . città di Napoli*, Associazione dei musicologi italiani, x/2 (Parma, [1918]–1934); F. Bossarelli: 'Mozart alla biblioteca del Conservatorio di Napoli', *AnMc*, no.5 (1968), 249, no.7 (1969), 180–213, and no.9 (1970), 336; A. Mondolfi-Bossarelli: 'La biblioteca del Conservatorio di Napoli', *Accademie e biblioteche d'Italia*, xxxviii (1970), 286

OSTIGLIA. Biblioteca Musicale Greggiati, Palazzo del Municipio, 46035 Ostiglia (*OS*). The collection was originally a bequest of Canon Giuseppe Greggiati, a musician, to the commune. The library holds some fragments of the Rossi MS (of the Vatican), 17th-century collections of arias, 16th-century editions of all Zarlino's works, and various works by Artusi, Faber, Gaffurius, Galilei, Vicentino and others. The largest part of the collection comprises works from the late 18th and early 19th centuries.

Descrizione e stima delle opere musicali raccolte nel gabinetto di casa Greggiati che formano parte della sostanza caduta in eredità al comune di Ostiglia (Rovere, 1874); C. Sartori: 'Nascita, letargo e risveglio della Biblioteca Greggiati', *FAM*, xxiv (1977)

PADUA. General literature: A. Garbelotto and others: 'Padua und Paduaner Handschriften', *MGG* [describes MSS in *Pc*, *Pca*, *Ps* and *Pu*]

——. Biblioteca Antoniana, Cappella Antoniana, Basilica del Santo, Piazza del Santo, 35100 Padua (*Pca*). The chapel was founded in 1487 by the minorite monks of St Francis, and access to the collection is difficult, though possible. There are 40 choirbooks (some illuminated); autograph concertos and sonatas of Tartini, who led the basilica orchestra from 1721 to 1770; and MS vocal music of Bononcini, Gasparini, Scarlatti and other 18th-century composers.

G. Tebaldini: *L'archivio musicale della Cappella Antoniana* (Padua, 1895); A. Garbelotto: *La cappella musicale di S. Antonio in Padova* (Padua, 1966)

——. Biblioteca Capitolare, Curia Vescovile, Via dietro al Duomo 3, 35100 Padua (*Pc*). Founded at the end of the 15th century, the library owns MSS of the 11th–13th centuries, sacred music of the 15th and 16th, and printed works of the 16th–18th centuries.

A. Garbelotto: 'Codici musicali della Biblioteca capitolare di Padova', *RMI*, liii (1951), 289; liv (1952), 218, 289

——. Biblioteca Universitaria, Via S Biagio 7, 35100 Padua (*Pu*). Founded in 1629, the library is Italy's oldest university library. The music collection includes liturgical MSS of the 12th–18th centuries, French and Italian songs of the 14th, MS organ tablatures of Hassler, Sweelinck and others, some printed works of the 16th and 17th centuries, and a large number from the 19th. In the rich collection from the Benedictine abbey of S Giustina in Padua are 14th-century MS fragments with works by Ciconia, Landini, Jacopo da Bologna and others.

PALERMO. Conservatorio di Musica 'Vincenzo Bellini', Via Squarcialupo 45, 90133 Palermo (*PLcon*). The library owns 16th-century editions (including a number of theoretical treatises), imprints from the 17th and 18th centuries, MS intermezzos, symphonies, madrigals, canzoni, harpsichord sonatas, operas and other works of the same period (including 130 autographs).

PARMA. General literature: G. Gasparini and N. Pelicelli: *Catalogo delle opere musicali . . . città di Parma*, Associazione dei musicologi italiani, i/1 (Parma, 1911) [lists works in *PAac*, *PAas*, *PAc* and *PAst*]

——. Archivio Storico del Teatro Regio, Via della Repubblica 41, 43100 Parma (*PAt*). A section of the city's public library, the historical archive of the theatre keeps the librettos and scores of works performed there since its founding in 1829. There are autographs and musical iconography.

——. Conservatorio di Musica 'Arrigo Boito', Via del Conservatorio 27, 43100 Parma (*PAc*). The conservatory houses the music section of the Biblioteca Palatina. Many of the works came from the library of Queen Marie Louise and from the Bourbon court in Parma. Important holdings include a 14th-century parchment, treatises of Aaron, Artusi, Gaffurius, Mersenne, Zarlino and others, over 400 MS sonatas of Domenico Scarlatti, some 7000 librettos, 18th- and 19th-century operas, and instrumental works of the 18th and early 19th centuries.

R. Allorto: 'La biblioteca del Conservatorio di Parma e un fondo di edizioni dei sec. XVI e XVII non comprese nel catalogo a stampa', *FAM*, ii (1955), 147 [catalogue of the partbooks]; M. Medici: 'Osservazione sulla Biblioteca musicale di Parma', *Aurea Parma*, xlviii (1964), 119–65 [cites many rare MS and printed works]

——. Istituto di Studi Verdiani, Strada della Repubblica 57, 43100 Parma (*PAi*). The institute has a collection of early printed works of Verdi and his contemporaries, as well as material related to him and 19th-century theatre in general.

PESARO. General literature: E. Paolone: 'Codici musicali della Bibl. Oliveriana e della Bibl. del R. Conservatorio di musica, di Pesaro', *RMI*, xlvi (1942), 186

——. Biblioteca Oliveriana, Via Mazza 96, 61100 Pesaro (*PESo*). The library was founded in 1793 and is administered by the Olivieri Society. Its music treasures incude a 15th-century illuminated psalter, a lute tablature of c1500 (probably the earliest extant document of lute notation; see W. H. Rubsamen: 'The Earliest French Lute Tablature', *JAMS*, xxi, 1968, p.286), and theoretical MSS of the 16th and 17th centuries (including a treatise of Paolo Luchini and a choirbook compiled between 1278 and 1326 that documents the musical life of the order of S Decenzio; see L. Bellonci and A. Pierucci: 'Un libro corale fra i codici della

oliveriana', *Studia oliveriana*, xviii (1970), 21–85 and A. J. Dirks: 'Note su un graduale domenicano fra codici della Biblioteca oliveriana', *Studia oliveriana*, xix–xx (1971–2), 9–39).

——. Conservatorio di Musica 'Gioacchino Rossini', Piazza Olivieri 5, 61100 Pesaro (*PESc*). Formerly called the Liceo Musicale, it was founded in 1882 with Rossini's gift to the commune. It is the headquarters for the Centro Rossiniano di Studi. In addition to autographs and early editions of the works of Rossini, Spontini and Meyerbeer, the collection includes the MS score of Carlo Pallavicino's *Massimo Puppieno*, the autograph of Morlacchi's opera *Il Simoncino* (1809) and many operatic excerpts published in the 18th century by Marescalchi and Barberis. There are also three lute tablatures, a guitar tablature of c1600, and secular vocal music in editions from the 16th–18th centuries. A set of parts for string quartet contains 680 works of Haydn, Beethoven, Mozart, Boccherini and others in early or first editions. Editions of theoretical works date from the early 16th century onwards.

'Inediti rossiniani acquistati dal Conservatorio di Pesaro', *Accademie e biblioteche d'Italia*, xxi (1953), 277; F. Schlitzer: 'Il fondo francese dell'Archivio rossiniano di Pesaro', *RaM*, xxiv (1954), 220; G. Macarini-Carmignani: 'La musica per pianoforte di G. Rossini negli autografi pesaresi', *RaM*, xxiv (1954), 229; various articles in the *Bollettino* of the Centro Rossiniano di Studi (1954–)

PIACENZA. General literature: F. Bussi: *Due importanti fondi musicali di Piacenza: la Biblioteca-archivio capitolare del duomo e la biblioteca del Conservatorio statale di musica 'Giuseppe Nicolini'* (Piacenza, 1972)

——. Conservatorio di Musica G. Nicolini, Via S Franca 35, 29100 Piacenza (*PCcon*). Printed works include early editions of Haydn quartets, 18th-century theoretical works and 19th-century librettos. Among the MSS are operas of Rossini, Cimarosa, Paisiello, Spontini and others, and works by local composers. The conservatory (formerly called the Liceo Musicale) received a gift of 19th-century Italian operas and other material in 1928 from the former Turin publishers Guidici e Strada.

C. Censi: *Il Liceo musicale 'Giuseppe Nicolini' di Piacenza* (Florence, 1952)

——. Duomo, Piazza del Duomo, 29100 Piacenza (*PCd*). The capitular archive (in the Curia Vescovile) holds some 80 MSS of the 11th–16th centuries, including 12th- and 13th-century parchments with theoretical treatises. There are many unica among the 125 volumes in the collection published from 1561 to 1710. 16th-century works include 149 motets (many by Willaert), masses by Févin, Jacquet of Mantua, Jacquet de Berchem and Festa, and hymns by Willaert.

C. Sartori: 'L'archivio del duomo di Piacenza', *FAM*, iv (1957), 28 [with catalogue]; F. Bussi: *Piacenza, archivio del duomo: catalogo del fondo musicale*, Bibliotheca musicae, v (Milan, 1967); J. B. Weidensaul: 'Early 16th-century Manuscripts at Piacenza: a Progress Report', *CMc* (1973), no.16, p.41

PISA. General literature: P. Pecchiai: *Catalogo delle opere musicali . . . città di Pisa*, Associazione dei musicologi italiani, xiii (Parma, 1932–5) [incl. collections in *PIa*, *PIc*, *PIca*, *PIcc*, *PIp* and *PIu*]

——. Archivio di Stato, Lungarno Mediceo 30, 56100 Pisa (*PIa*). Besides parchment fragments of the 11th–13th centuries, the archive contains 271 printed sacred vocal works of the 17th century from the church of S Stefano. There are also MS vocal works by Delvimare, Rossini and others.

——. Biblioteca Cateriniana, Seminario Vescovile, Piazza S Caterina 4, 56100 Pisa (*PIca*). The seminary owns ten large volumes containing chant MSS of the 14th and 15th centuries. There are also some Latin theoretical MSS and liturgical music of the 18th and 19th centuries.

——. Biblioteca Universitaria, Via XXIX Maggio 15, 56100 Pisa (*PIu*). The university's 200 musical works are chiefly writings about music, including two 15th-century MSS with Latin treatises (by Ciconia, Marchetto da Padova and Jehan des Murs) and theoretical works of the 17th and 18th centuries.

——. Duomo, Piazza Duomo 3, 56100 Pisa (*PIp*). The archive of the Opera della Primaziale has many MSS by Brunetti and Clari (some autograph). There are also imprints of the 16th–19th centuries, many Italian.

P. Pecchiai: *Alcune notizie sull'Archivio musicale del duomo di Pisa* (Pisa, 1930); E. C. Saville: 'Liturgical Music of Giovanni Clari', *FAM*, xv (1968), 17 [catalogue of MSS, most in the cathedral]

PISTOIA. Archivio Capitolare del Duomo, Via Sozomeno 3, 51100 Pistoia (*PS*). The capitular archives have a 12th-century MS with works by Guido of Arezzo and some fragments of the Lucca MS. Sacred works from the 16th–19th centuries preserved in the library were written mainly for the cathedral services; many oratorios, however, come from the city's S Filippo oratory. Operatic and symphonic music was a gift of the Filarmonica Pistoiese, and chamber music and other instrumental and vocal music were received from the Gherardeschi and Rospigliosi families (the latter collection also containing theoretical works and librettos). The library is to move to new quarters and is receiving material from the Baldi-Papini family (operatic, sacred and instrumental works) which have not yet been catalogued.

U. de Laugier: *Catalogo delle opere musicali ... città di Pistoia*, Associazione dei musicologi italiani, iv/2 (Parma, 1936–7) [inc. with many errors; new catalogue by U. Pineschi not yet pubd]; G. Savino: 'Gli incunaboli dell'Archivio capitolare del duomo di Pistoia', *Bollettino storico pistoiese*, new ser., vii (1965), 97; M. Fabbri: 'Una preziosa raccolta di musica sacra cinquecentesca: il codice 215', *CHM*, iv (1966), 1013

RAVENNA. Biblioteca Comunale Classense, Via Baccarini 3, 48100 Ravenna (*RAc*). The library was founded in the 18th century by the Abbé Canneti and now occupies the building of the former monastery of Classe. MS holdings include 13th- and 14th-century fragments, organ tablatures of Frescobaldi, Merula, Pasquini, Zipoli and others, and 18th-century masses. There are also imprints and MSS from the 19th century.

REGGIO EMILIA. General literature: G. Gasparini and N. Pelicelli: *Catalogo delle opere musicali ... città di Reggio-Emilia*, Associazione dei musicologi italiani, i/2 (Parma, 1911/R1970) [lists works in *REas*, *REd*, *REm* and *REsp*]

——. Archivio di Stato, Corso Cairoli 6, 42100 Reggio Emilia (*REas*). The archive owns printed 16th-century canzonettas, madrigals and motets by Corteccia, Jehan, Luzzaschi and Tresti from dispersed monasteries, 18th-century MS compositions, and parchment fragments from the bindings of other books.

——. Biblioteca Municipale, Via Farini 3, 42100 Reggio Emilia (*REm*). Founded in 1797 by Napoleon's order, the library has illuminated choirbooks from local churches, printed music and theoretical works of the 16th–18th centuries, and a theatre collection.

V. Ferrari: *La miniatura dei corali della Ghiari e di altre chiese di Reggio Emilia* (Reggio Emilia, 1923)

RIMINI. Biblioteca Civica 'Gambalunga', Via Gambalunga 27, 47037 Rimini (*RIM*). This library and the palace in which it is situated were given to Rimini in 1619 by Alessandro Gambalunga. Source materials include 17 large choral MSS and MS scores of cantatas, oratorios and sonatas of the 17th–19th centuries (Bianchelli, Caruso, Hofmeister, Gyrowetz, Pleyel and others). The library has recently acquired the important Mattei-Gentili collection of music and theoretical works (about 1000 in MS and about 3000 printed) from the 17th–20th centuries. It also owns the MS scores and writings of Amintore Galli.

ROME. General literature: E. E. Lowinsky: 'The State of Musical MSS [in Postwar Rome]', *JAMS*, i (1948), 47; A. Holschneider and others: 'Römische Handschriften', *MGG*

——. Accademia Filarmonica Romana, Via Flaminia 118, 00196 Rome (*Raf*). The library was founded in 1822 with MSS (some autograph) of 19th-century operas, choral and orchestral music. Holdings also include 16th-century motets and madrigals, editions of the 18th and 19th centuries, letters and documents.

——. Archivio del Vicariato di Roma, Via Amba Aradam 3, Rome. The musical items of S Maria in Trastevere were transferred to this library when the basilica archive was closed. These include sacred works (masses and Vespers) of composers working in Rome and of the Bologna school, as well as some 250 works of Berardi.

B. C. Cannon: 'Music in the Archives of the Basilica of Santa Maria in Trastevere', *AcM*, xli (1969), 199 [checklist of works dated 1650–1710]

——. Biblioteca Angelica, Piazza S Agostino 8, 00186 Rome (*Ra*). Rome's oldest public library, the Angelica was founded in 1614 by the Augustinian Bishop Angelo Rocca. There are 44 MSS of the 11th–18th centuries, chiefly antiphoners and graduals, some beautifully illuminated and others only fragments of antiphons and responses with neumatic notation. The library also has some printed works of the 16th–18th centuries, opera librettos donated by Nicola Santangelo of Naples, and some ten incunabula containing music. The remainder of the music collection has been transferred to the Conservatorio S Cecilia.

L. Gherardi: 'Il codice Angelica 123 monumento della chiesa bolognese nel sec. XI', *Quadrivium*, iii (1959), 5–114

——. Biblioteca Apostolica Vaticana, Vatican City, 00120 Rome (*Rvat*). The rich library of the Vatican is made up of many separate collections, the first three of which contain only musical sources: (1) Cappella Giulia, deposited in 1941 from the chapel of St Peter's, with many works by its *maestri di cappella*, but also secular and sacred works of the 16th–18th centuries (see J. Wolf: 'Die Musikbibliothek der Cappella Giulia', *KJb*, xxi, 1908, p.176; J. M. Llorens: *Le opere musicali della Cappella Giulia*, i: *Manoscritti e edizioni fino al '700*, Studi e testi, cclxv, Vatican City, 1971); (2) Cappella Liberiano di S Maria Maggiore, containing MS and printed sacred works; (3) Cappella Sistina (or Pontificia), with MS and printed works transferred from the papal chapel in 1870 (see F. X. Haberl: *Bibliographischer und thematischer Musikkatalog des päpstlichen Kapellarchives im Vatikan*, *MMg*, xix (1887), xx (1888), suppls.; J. M. Llorens: *Capellae Sixtinae codices musicis notis instructi sive manuscripti sive praelo excussi*, Rome, 1960); (4) Archivio di S Pietro, containing antiphoners and missals dating from the 11th century onwards and 15th-century masses and motets (some works listed in G. Stornajolo: *Inventarium codicum manuscriptorum latinorum archivii basilicae S. Petri*, Rome, 1968); (5) Barberiniani Latini, with MS treatises and polyphonic masses (some by Morales and Palestrina) of the 14th–17th centuries, as well as MS arias and cantatas of the 17th and 18th centuries; (6) Borgia Latini, containing an 11th-century gradual from Besançon; (7) Borghese codices, with liturgical MSS of the 12th–16th centuries (see A. Maier: *Codices Burghesiani Bibliothecae vaticanae*, Studi e testi, clxx, Vatican City, 1952); (8) Chigi Collection, bought by the Italian government in 1918 and part of the Vatican library since 1923. It contains 12th- and 13th-century breviaries, 16th-century masses and motets, Italian Baroque vocal music, popular Italian religious songs, a 14th-century mystery of St Agnes, and works for organ and harpsichord (see H. Besseler: 'Chigi-Kodex', *MGG*; H. B. Lincoln: 'I manoscritti chigiani di musica organo-cembalistica', *L'organo*, v, 1967, p.63); (9) Oratorio di S Marcello, containing librettos and other works from the oratory (see A. Liess: 'Materialen zur Römischen Musikgeschichte des Seicento: Musikerlisten des Oratorio San Marcello 1664–1775', *AcM*, xxix, 1957, pp.137–71; A. Liess: 'Die Sammlung der Oratorienlibretti (1679–1725) und der restliche Bestand des Fondo San Marcello', *AcM*, xxxi, 1959, p.63); (10) Ottoboniani Latini, which originated in the 16th century, but has no catalogue or inventory as yet. It contains liturgical MSS of the 9th–13th centuries (including hymnals and a sacramentary from St Denis in Paris and a Beneventan missal), 14th- and 15th-century polyphony for the Ordinary of the Mass, Byzantine music, and vocal music of the 16th–18th centuries by Anerio, Mouton, Nanino and others (see J. M. Llorens: 'Felice Anerio: compositor pontificio en los codices Ottoboniani', *AnM*, xix, 1964, p.95); (11) Palatini Latini, containing Gregorian neumatic MSS of the 9th–14th centuries, an 11th-century Berne tonary, and pre-1600 polyphony by Brumel, Compère, Josquin, La Rue, Mouton and others; (12) Reginenses Latini, containing hymnals of the 8th–10th centuries, Gregorian MSS with neumes, a 10th-century troper, the Le Mans missal, 12th-century treatises of Guido of Arezzo, the Arras Chansonnier, 14th- and 15th-century polyphony, and medieval court music; (13) Rossiani codices, including 11th-century Moissac hymns, 12th- and 13th-century graduals, and works by Giovanni da Cascia and Magister Piero; (14) Urbinati Latini, containing a 10th- or 11th-century hymnary-troper and works by Binchois, Dufay and others; (15) Vaticani Greci, with MSS of Byzantine and polyphonic 14th-century music; (16) Vaticani Latini, containing medieval theoretical treatises, works of the 14th–16th centuries (including motets of Isaac, Josquin and La Rue) and MSS of the 18th–20th centuries; and (17) Vaticani Musicali, comprising some MSS formerly in the Vaticani Latini collection as well as 18th- and 19th-century works given to the papal successors of Leo XIII.

H. M. Bannister: *Monumenti vaticani di paleografia musicale latina* (Leipzig, 1913); L. Feininger: 'The Music MSS in the Vatican', *Notes*, iii (1945–6), 392; R. J. Schuler: 'The Music Collections in the Vatican Library', *Caecilia*, lxxxiv (1957), 25; H. Anglès: 'El tesoro musical de la Biblioteca vaticana', *Collectanea vaticana* (Vatican City, 1962), 23–53

——. Biblioteca Casanatense, Via di S Ignazio 52,

00186 Rome (*Rc*). Founded in 1698 with the testament of Cardinal Gerolamo Casante, the library later received the bequest of Giuseppe Baini, consisting chiefly of 16th- and 17th-century works. The collection of Baroque MS arias, duets, chamber cantatas and operas is one of the richest in the country. There are also choirbooks from the Dominican convent of Santo Spirito in Siena, a theatrical collection with many librettos and other musical works, and a 15th-century chansonnier (see A. S. Wolff: *The Chansonnier Biblioteca Casanatense 2856*, diss., North Texas State U., 1970). Recent acquisitions include 90 MSS (some autograph) of Paganini and a group of 18th- and 19th-century works from the library of Compagnoni-Marefoschi.

A. de la Fage: *Essais de la diphthérographie musicale* (Paris, 1864/R1964), chap. 'Notes sur la vie et les ouvrages de Joseph Baini'; *Catalogo dei manoscritti della Biblioteca Casanatense*, Indici e cataloghi, new ser., ii (1949–58)

——. Biblioteca Corsiniana, Accademia Nazionale dei Lincei e Corsiniana, Via della Lungara 10, 00165 Rome (*Rli*). The library was founded in the 18th century by Cardinal Corsini and received later gifts from his family and from Girolamo Chiti. It has belonged to the academy since 1883. It owns MS oratorios of Alessandro Scarlatti, MS works by Palestrina, printed music of the 16th–18th centuries, and a large collection of oratorio librettos.

V. Raeli: 'La collezione Corsini di antichi codici musicali e Girolamo Chiti', *RMI*, xxv (1918), 345–76, xxvi (1919), 112, and xxvii (1920), 60; V. Raeli: 'La Biblioteca Corsini dei Lincei e l'annessavi collezione musicale', *Accademie e biblioteche d'Italia*, iii (1930), 427; A. Bertini: *Catalogo dei fondi musicali Chiti e Corsiniano*, Bibliotheca musicae, ii (Milan, 1964)

——. Biblioteca Musicale Governativa del Conservatorio di Musica 'S Cecilia', Via dei Greci 18, 00187 Rome (*Rsc*). Although not founded until 1877, the conservatory has its roots in the Congregazione dei Musici di Roma (definitively established in 1585). The library has grown rapidly not only through the transference of materials from general libraries and the dispersed archives of monasteries and churches (e.g. Santo Spirito in Sassia and the Chiesa Nuova), but also through donations and since 1879 by copyright deposit of all music published in Italy. Notable among the extensive holdings of works of all types are the many librettos, 16th-century editions of church music, and 17th-century editions of operas (especially of the Roman school). Also important are printed theoretical and historical works from before 1500 to the 19th century, autographs and other MSS of Italian and foreign composers, editions of French, Italian and Spanish stage works of the 16th–18th centuries, and theatrical treatises. Complete or partial collections incorporated into the library include those of the singing teacher Alessandro Orsini, Queen Margherita of Savoy, Prince Paolo Borghese, V. Carotti (4000 librettos of the 17th–19th centuries), Manoel Pereira Peixoto d'Almeida da Carvalhoes (21,000 opera, cantata and oratorio librettos), the tenor Mario di Candia (many English editions, particularly of vocal music of the 17th and 18th centuries, known as the Fondo Mario), and much of the Silvestri collection of librettos (6000 from theatres of Milan and Monza, published from 1670 to 1885; the remainder are owned by the Bibliothèque Nationale in Paris). Since 1912 the library has been divided into two large sections: the Biblioteca Musicale Governativa and the section added in 1911 belonging to the Accademia Nazionale di S Cecilia.

Catalogo delle opere di musica o ad essa relative che dall'anno 1836 all'anno 1846 sono state depositate nell'archivio della Congregazione ed Accademia di Santa Cecilia (Rome, 1846); E. Vogel: 'Schicksal der Borghese-Musiksammlung', *JbMP 1896*, 73; A. Berwin: *Notizie storiche, bibliografiche e statistiche sulla Biblioteca musicale della R. Accademia di S. Cecilia* (Rome, 1900); O. Andolfi: *Catalogo delle opere teoriche anteriori all'800: Roma Conservatorio di musica S. Cecilia*, Associazione dei musicologi italiani, v (Parma, 1912–13)

——. Biblioteca Vallicelliana, Piazza della Chiesa Nuova 18, 00186 Rome (*Rv*). The library was founded in the 16th century by S Filippo Neri's order, the Oratorians. When it became state-controlled in 1873, most of the music collection was transferred to the Conservatorio S Cecilia. The remaining works are chiefly MSS and imprints of the 16th and 17th centuries (including a 16th-century motet MS; see E. E. Lowinsky: 'A Newly Discovered 16th Century Motet MS at the Biblioteca Vallicelliana', *JAMS*, iii, 1950, pp.173–232), but there are some *laudi spirituali* of the 15th century and several Latin theoretical treatises of the 10th–16th centuries.

A. M. Giorgetti Vichi and S. Mottironi: *Catalogo dei manoscritti della Biblioteca Vallicelliana*, i, Indici e cataloghi, new ser., vii (Rome, 1961); a catalogue of the musical holdings is being prepared

——. Congregazione dell'Oratorio San Filippo Neri di Roma, Via del Governo Vecchio 134, 00186 Rome (*Rf*). The collection consists principally of MS originals and copies of the 18th and 19th centuries, but it also has works from the 17th century. The journal *Oratorium* was published from 1970 to 1974.

D. Alaleona: *Storia dell'oratorio musicale in Italia* (Milan, 1945); A. Bertini: 'La musica all'Oratorio dalle origini ad oggi', *Quaderni dell'Oratorio*, xi (1966); A. Bertini: *Inventario del fondo musicale dell'Oratorio* (Rome, 1968–71) [lists works from before 1900]

——. S Luigi de' Francesi, Piazza S Luigi dei Francesi 5, 00186 Rome (*Rslf*). The French church has a collection of musical works of the 17th–20th centuries both printed and MS (some autograph).

L. L. Perkins: 'Notes bibliographiques au sujet de l'ancien fonds musical de l'Eglise de Saint Louis des Français à Rome', *FAM*, xvi (1969), 57; M. Staehelin: 'Zum Schicksal des alten Musikalien-Fonds von San Luigi dei Francesi', *FAM*, xvii (1970), 121

SIENA. Accademia Musicale Chigiana, Via di Città 89, 53100 Siena (*Sac*). The academy was founded in 1932 by Count Guido Chigi Saracini, and its library owns about 1000 autograph letters and scores. There is also a large collection of early editions from the 16th–18th centuries, especially strong in chamber music and Italian opera. The academy issued *Quaderni* from 1942 to 1961 and a *Bollettino* from 1948 to 1962, which often contained information about the library's holdings.

——. Biblioteca Comunale degli Intronati, Via della Sapienza 5, 53100 Siena (*Sc*). The library owns 13th-century trouvère songs (see C. P. S.: 'An Ancient Manuscript of French Minstrel Songs', *MT*, xxvii, 1886, p.648), some 15th-century treatises, printed music of the 16th–18th centuries (some from the city's cathedral) and about 16,000 MS sacred works of the 18th and 19th centuries.

A. Castan: 'Le missel du cardinal de Tournay à la bibliothèque de Sienne', *Bibliothèque de l'Ecole de Chartes*, 4th ser., xlii (1881), 442; O. Mischiati and L. F. Tagliavini: 'Appunti di organaria in un manoscritto del XVII secolo della Biblioteca comunale di Siena', *L'organo*, iv (1963), 201

TURIN. Archivio Musicale del Duomo (S Giovanni Battista), Via Arcivescovado 12, 10121 Turin (*Td*). Although the property of the cathedral, the capitular library is housed in the archepiscopal archive for safe-keeping. There are seven antiphoners from Milan dated 1450–55 (lacking their illuminations), works published in the 16th century by Du Chemin, Ballard, Le Roy and others, a few editions of the late 17th century and many printed works by Beethoven, Haydn and Mozart, especially symphonies. Sacred MSS dating from 1630 to 1900 include works by the cathedral's *maestri di cappella* and by musicians of the Sardinian court.

C. Segre-Montel: 'I manoscritti e i libri a stampa dell'Archivio capitolare', *Bollettino della Società piemontese di archeologia e belle arti*, new ser., xviii (1964), 27, and xx (1966), 78; M. T. Bouquet: *Musique et musiciens à Turin de 1648 à 1775* (Turin, 1968), chap. 'Répertoire des oeuvres composées par les maîtres de chapelle du dôme . . . qui se trouvent . . . aux archives capitulaires'

——. Biblioteca Civica Musicale Andrea della Corte, Via Roma 53, 10123 (*Tci*). The 35,000-volume collection includes a number of 18th-century editions. Opera and ballet librettos of the 17th–20th centuries, which document stage performances in Piedmont, were received from Valentino Carrera; 19th- and 20th-century orchestral works (MSS and imprints) from the Società di Concerti del Teatro Regio; and choral music from the municipal Scuola di Canto Corale. In 1968 it received the 15,000-volume library of Andrea della Corte, rich in letters and MSS.

M. G. Delleani: 'La civica biblioteca musicale', *Torino*, xxix/12 (1953), 30

——. Biblioteca Nazionale Universitaria, Via Po 19, 10124 Turin (*Tn*). Among its treasures are eight medieval MSS from Bobbio monastery (see P. Damilano: 'Sequenze Bobbiesi', *RIM*, ii, 1967, pp.3–35), early 17th-century German organ tablatures (see O. Mischiati: 'L'intavolatura d'organo tedesca . . . catalogo ragionato', *L'organo*, iv (1963), pp.1–154, which inventories a 16-volume MS compiled between 1637 and 1640 containing 1770 works), 17th-century ballets, 16th-century editions of madrigals, and many works by Stradella and Vivaldi.

A. Gentili: 'La raccolta Mauro Foà nella Biblioteca nazionale di Torino', *RMI*, xxiv (1927), 356; A. Gentili and A. Cimbro: *Catalogo delle opere musicali: città di Torino*, Associazione dei musicologi italiani, xii (Parma, 1928); A. Gentili: 'La raccolta di antiche musiche Renzo Giordano alla Biblioteca nazionale', *Accademie e biblioteche d'Italia*, ix (1930), 117; P. Damilano: 'Inventario delle composizione musicali manoscritti di Antonio Vivaldi esistenti presso la Biblioteca nazionale di Torino', *RIM*, iii (1968), 109–79; G. G. Verona: 'Le collezioni Foà e Giordano', *Vivaldiana*, i (1969), 31

VENICE. General literature: G. Concini and others: *Catalogo delle opere musicali: città di Venezia*, Associazione dei musicologi italiani, vi/1 (Parma, 1914–42) [incl. *Vc, Vnm, Vqs*]; F. Fano and others: 'Venedig und venezianische Handschriften', *MGG* [incl. *Vc, Vnm, Vqs, Vcg, Vmc, Vt*]

——. Biblioteca Nazionale Marciana, Piazzetta S Marco 7, 30124 Venice (*Vnm*). The library has several thousand instrumental and vocal works by composers who worked at the basilica of St Mark's in the 18th and 19th centuries. Rare items include medieval theoretical MSS and Venetian editions of madrigals, as well as many autographs (Marcello, the Scarlattis, Cavalli, Monteverdi, Haydn and others). The Contarini collection contains 17th-century Venetian operas, early theoretical works, and 700 MSS (chiefly of 18th- and early 19th-century Italian opera, oratorio, chamber music and sacred polyphony). In 1961 the library received the musical MSS of S Maria Formosa.

Biblioteca musicale del Prof. P. Canal in Crespano Veneto (Bassano, 1885); T. Wiel: *I codici musicali contariniani del secolo xvii nella R.*

Biblioteca di San Marco (Venice, 1888/*R*1969); L. Ferrari: 'La collezione musicale Canal alla Marciana', *Accademie e biblioteche d'Italia*, i (1927–8), 140, and iii (1929–30), 279

——. Conservatorio di Musica 'Benedetto Marcello', Campo Pisani 2809, 30121 Venice (*Vc*). The school received some 2000 Venetian MSS of the 18th century in the Wiel, Pascoluto and Contin bequests. Music from the Civico Museo Correr was transferred there in 1941 (leaving fewer than 1000 pieces of music in the museum's collection). A. Giustiniani donated 200 late 18th-century editions in 1949.

——. Fondazione Ugo Levi, Rio di S Vidal 2893, 30100 Venice (*Vlevi*). The library owns madrigals and sacred music in Italian editions of the 16th and 17th centuries, as well as 18th-century editions of operas of Gluck, Rousseau, Philidor and others.

S. Cisilino: *Stampe e manoscritti preziosi e rare della biblioteca del palazzo Giustinian Lolin a San Vidal* (Venice, 1966) [lists 70 selected items]

——. Istituto di Lettere, Musica e Teatro, Fondazione Giorgio Cini, Isola di S Giorgio Maggiore, 30124 Venice (*Vgc*). Founded by the Cini Foundation in 1952, the library contains about 35,000 librettos from the collection of Ulderico Rolandi. There are also editions of music and theoretical works published in the 16th–18th centuries and many thousands of copies of Venetian and other Italian music located elsewhere.

U. Rolandi: 'Unici, rari e curiosi nella biblioteca musicale Rolandi', *Accademie e biblioteche d'Italia*, xix (1951), 118; F. A. Gallo: 'Da un codice italiano di mottetti del primo trecento', *Quadrivium*, ix (1968), 25

——. S Marco (Basilica), Ponte Canonica, 30100 Venice (*Vsm*). The music archive of the Procuratoria di S Marco contains 14 16th-century MSS, as well as many MSS (and a few printed editions) of the late 17th and 18th centuries with works by Asola, Cifra, Galuppi and others.

J. Bastian: 'The Cappella musicale at San Marco in the Late 16th Century', *American Choral Review*, xii (1970), 3

——. S Maria della Consolazione detta Della Fava, Castello 5503, 30122 Venice (*Vsmc*). The church library has 166 anonymous MSS by former members of the Filippini fathers (in residence from 1661 to 1912). The library owns three 14th-century MSS of the Neri school, 29 oratorio MSS (and about 10,000 librettos) from the 18th century, and 729 MSS of the 18th and 19th centuries. There are 61 printed editions (chiefly masses) from the 16th–19th centuries.

P. Pancino: *Venezia, S. Maria della Consolazione, detta 'Della Fava', già sede della Congregazione di S. Filippo Neri: catalogo del fondo musicale*, Bibliotheca musicae, vi (Milan, 1969)

NETHERLANDS (*NL*)

Medieval sacred works in the archives of Arnhem, Groningen and Leiden are described by J. P. N. Land: 'Middeneeuwsche kerkmuziek in Nederlandsche archieven', *TVNM*, iii/4 (1891), 231. Public and private collections in Amsterdam, The Hague, Leiden and Rotterdam are reported in J.-G. Prod'homme: 'Les institutions musicales (bibliothèques et archives) en Belgique et en Hollande', *SIMG*, xv (1913–14), 488. The documentary compilation by E. Reeser: *Music in Holland* (Amsterdam, 1959) has a section on libraries, archives and museums (pp.206–12). 16th-century organum MSS are listed in J. Volkestijn: 'Organa-Handschriften uit de XVIe eeuw in Nederlandsche bibliotheken', *Gregoriusblad*, lxxxviii–xc (1964–6). The loose-

leaf guide *Gids van muziekbibliotheken en fonotheken in Nederland* (The Hague, 1972) and its annual supplements, issued by the Studiecentrum voor Muziekbibliotheken en Fonotheken, list addresses and hours, and give brief characterizations of collections. The special Netherlands issue of *FAM*, xxi (1974), describes several important collections in the country. There is no obligatory copyright deposit law in the Netherlands.

AMSTERDAM. Ethnomusicologisch Centrum Jaap Kunst, Kloveniersburgwal 103, Amsterdam (*Aec*). The centre is a branch of the University of Amsterdam and holds a scholarly collection of literature, sound documentation and photographic material concerning all music other than Western classical music, specializing in the music of Indonesia (in particular Java). There is a large indexed collection of offprints and clippings, a few old Javanese MSS, all the publications of E. M. von Hornbostel, and the library formerly owned by Jaap Kunst.

'News of Institutions', *Society for Ethnomusicology Newsletter*, vii (1973), May–June

——. Stichting Donemus, Paulus Potterstraat 14, Amsterdam (*Ad*). Established in 1947, the foundation promotes the works of contemporary Dutch composers and as part of its activities maintains a library of MS and printed scores, tape recordings and literature relating to contemporary music. It also holds the library of the music publisher Johan A. Alsbach (*d* 1961), with about 13,000 Dutch compositions from the mid-19th century to about 1920.

——. Toonkunst-Bibliotheek, Prinsengracht 587, Amsterdam C (*At*). The library has about 5000 early printed works, including a large number of unica, and is especially rich in partbooks of motets and madrigals by Arcadelt, Lassus and Palestrina, and in psalms by Sweelinck. It also has 350 songbooks and 2500 autographs of 19th-century Dutch composers. There are many editions by Amsterdam music publishers, including some 300 Hummel prints. In 1960 the library received the collection of the Vereeniging voor Nederlandse Muziekgeschiedenis, formerly held by the University of Amsterdam. The library also holds the collection of 18th-century operas and symphonies from the scholarly and cultural society for dillettantes called Felix Meritis (1777–1889), and 18th- and 19th-century sacred music from the Amsterdam church of Moses and Aaron. The latter collection of 375 MS and early printed works includes some late 18th-century editions of J. J. Lotter of Augsburg.

J. P. Heije: 'Lijst van boek- en muziekwerken' [in the Bibliotheek der Maatschappij tot Bevordering der Toonkunst], *Bouwsteenen: JVNM*, i (1869–72), 123, and ii (1872–4), 230; H. C. Rogge: *Catalogus van de Bibliotheken der Maatschappij tot bevordering der toonkunst* (Amsterdam, 1884, suppl. 1895); S. Bottenheim: *Catalogus van de Bibliotheek der Vereeniging voor Nederlandsche muziekgeschiedenis* (Amsterdam, 1919); P. van Reijen: 'De Toonkunst-Bibliotheek', *Mens en melodie*, xxiv (1969), 323

DEVENTER. Stads- of Athenaeumbibliotheek, Klooster 3, Deventer (*D*). The music section has MS fragments from the late Middle Ages and early 16th century, printed music from 1800–50, and autographs of 19th-century local composers. The collection of the Deventer Muziek-Collegie was acquired in the 1830s.

THE HAGUE. Gemeentemuseum, Stadhouderslaan 41, The Hague (*DHgm*). The music collection of the museum contains one of the largest research and source music libraries in the Netherlands, and has an extensive collection of musical instruments. There are 16th- to 20th-century compositions and publications on music, including the opera repertory from the city's Théâtre Français, and music from the royal chapel, as well as the greater part of the Scheurleer collection; 18th- and 19th-century opera librettos; and an archive of 19th- and 20th-century Dutch composers (MSS and documents). It also has a collection of 19th- and 20th-century letters and concert programmes. The iconographical collection contains prints, drawings and paintings with musical subjects (from the 16th–19th centuries) and photographs of musicians.

Muziekhistorisch museum van Dr. D. F. Scheurleer: catalogus van de muziekwerken en de boeken over muziek (The Hague, 1923–5); exhibition catalogues on: Dutch musical life 1600–1800 (1936); The Mozart family in Holland (1965); Telemann (1967); Schoenberg, Webern and Berg (1969); 100 years of music and science in the Netherlands (1969); C. C. J. von Gleich, ed.: *The Hague Gemeentemuseum: Catalogues of the Music Library and the Musical Instrument Collection* (Amsterdam and New York, 1969–); A. Verveen and M. Klerk: 'The Gemeentemuseum at The Hague', *FAM*, xxi (1974), 106

——. Koninklijke Bibliotheek, Lange Voorhout 34, The Hague (*DHk*). There are 500 early printed music works and 200 early books, as well as the MS collections of the composer Willem Pijper and the musicologist Julius Hijman. The songbooks from the Scheurleer collection were deposited there when the remainder of the library went to the Gemeentemuseum.

Catalogus van schoone kunsten en kunstnijverheid (The Hague, 1905); *Muziekhistorisch museum van Dr. D. F. Scheurleer: catalogus van muziekwerken en de boeken over muziek* (The Hague, 1923–5) [ii, pp.1–273, refer to works in *DHk*]

——. Koninklijk Huisarchief, Noordeinde 74, The Hague (*DHa*). Music holdings consist of 18th- to 20th-century music composed for or given to the royal family. The family archive of the House of Orange-Nassau includes over 1000 volumes of military, sacred, operatic, piano, string, orchestral and vocal works, partly in MS, written for celebrations of the royal house.

M. de Smet: *La musique à la cour de Guillaume V, Prince d'Orange, d'après les archives de la maison royale des Pays-Bas* (Utrecht, 1973)

'S-HERTOGENBOSCH. De Illustre Lieve Vrouwe Broederschap, Hinthamerstraat 94, 's-Hertogenbosch (*'sH*). Founded in 1318 by the Bishop of Liège as a brotherhood of clerics and scholars, the society became half Protestant by a decree of 1642, at which time it also lost its musical significance. The archive has a valuable collection of 15th- and 16th-century Gregorian chant and partbooks, chiefly MS, with *Magnificat* settings, masses, sequences and other liturgical works by Monte, Hellinck and Mouton, and many anonymous works.

P. J. R. van der Does de Bije: *Catalogus van het archief der Illustre lieve vrouwe broederschap te 's-Hertogenbosch* ('s-Hertogenbosch, 1874); A. Smijers: 'Meerstemmige muziek van de Illustre lieve vrouwe broederschap te 's-Hertogenbosch', *TVNM*, xvi/1 (1940), 1–30 [with inventory of collections nos.72–7]

LEIDEN. Bibliotheek de Rijksuniversiteit, Rapenburg 70–74, Leiden (*Lu*). The library holds the Bibliotheca Thysiana, the famous 17th-century Thysius lute collection of over 1000 pages, and works by composers of many nationalities. There are also 15th-century MSS, *Souterliedekens*, and a small collection of important 18th-century editions with many unica. The latter comprises chiefly Dutch composers, although there is a group of Dutch editions of works by Locatelli.

J. P. N. Land and H. C. Rogge: 'Muziekwerken in de Universiteitsbibliotheek te Leiden', *Bouwsteenen: JVNM*, iii (1874–81), 111; J. P. N. Land: 'Het luitboek van Thysius beschreven en toegelicht', *TVNM*, i/3 (1884), 129–95; i/4 (1885), 206–64; ii/1 (1885), 1–56;

ii/2 (1886), 109–74; ii/3 (1887), 177–94; ii/4 (1887), 278–350; iii/1 (1888), 1–57

ROTTERDAM. Gemeentebibliotheek, Nieuwe Markt 1, Rotterdam 3001 (*R*). The music section of the library has some early partbooks and a collection of early Rotterdam imprints, including 13 editions published by Barth and 310 by Plattner.

UTRECHT. Instituut voor Muziekwetenschap, Drift 21, Utrecht (*Uim*). The university institute of musicology has the collection (partly also in the city's Openbare Muziekbibliotheek) of the musicologist Hans Brandt Buys, including two 17th-century keyboard MSS, and the library of the St Gregoriusvereeniging (mainly songbooks and Catholic church music). Other holdings include 17th- and 18th-century MSS and printed music and books, as well as film material (including a duplicate of the Phonogramm-Archiv in *A-Wn*).

J. du Saar: 'Uit de geschiedenis van het Collegium musicum ultrajectinum', *Vlaamsch jaarboek voor muziekgeschiedenis*, iv (1942), 112 [with list of works in the library, 126f]

——. Bibliotheek der Rijksuniversiteit, Wittevrouwenstraat 9–11, Utrecht (*Uu*). The university library has a number of liturgical and secular MSS with music of the 12th–17th centuries, some probably from the city's church of St Mary (including the 13th-century Utrecht Prosarium). There is also a collection of 80 letters from English and Scandinavian musicians, from 1822 to 1940. The Lerma MS, now in this library, contains compositions (some unpublished) of Lassus, Clemens non Papa, Crecquillon, Josquin and others.

P. A. Thiele and A. Hulsof: *Catalogus codicum manuscriptorum bibliothecae Universitatis Rheno-Trajectinae* (Utrecht, 1887–1909); N. de Goede: *The Utrecht Prosarium* (Amsterdam, 1965) [preface]; W. Elders: 'The Lerma Codex: a Newly Discovered Choirbook from Seventh-century Spain', *TVNM*, xx/4 (1967), 187

NORWAY (N)

Occasional information about music collections is presented in the journal *Information om nordisk musikforskning* (Copenhagen and Oslo, 1967–).

BERGEN. Offentlige Bibliotek, Strømgaten 6, 5000 Bergen (*Bo*). In 1907 the public library inherited the extensive collection of Grieg, containing 110 of his MSS and his collection of 2762 printed scores, both his own works and those of his contemporaries. There are an estimated 34,000 first editions and reprints of first editions of Grieg compositions, 340 of Grieg's letters and about 5000 letters to him. The collection contains diaries, sketchbooks, account books, pictures etc. From 1975 the music department of the library has acted as the National Music Library for Norway.

J. Bygstad: 'Edvard Grieg og musikksamlingen i Bergen offentlige bibliotek', *Bibliotek og forskning årbok*, viii (1959), 55 [with Eng. summary; statistics based on approximations]; *Katalog over Griegutstillingen 1962 i Bergen Offentlige bibliotek* (Bergen, 1962) [lists autographs]; J. Horton: *Grieg* (London, 1974) [appx E, 245, lists autographs]

OSLO. Norsk Musikksamling, Observatoriegaten 1, Oslo 2 (*Oum*). Founded in 1927, the Norwegian music collection is a branch of the university library and has served as the national depository of Norwegian printed music. In addition to printed music of Norwegian origin, there is a wide representation of foreign composers, including early MS and printed works. The MS collection numbers some 10,000 items and includes autographs by several Norwegian composers. There are photocopies of music from other important collections and an extensive collection of Norwegian folk music. Among the special collections are the bequest of the Schubert scholar Odd Udbye (*d* 1960), which includes MSS and first editions of Schubert lieder, and N. H. Knudtzon's large collection of Beethoven literature.

H. Kragemo: 'Norsk musikksamling 1927–52', *Norsk musikkgranskning årbok* (1951–3), 16; H. Kragemo: 'Musikkhåndskriftene i norsk musikksamling', *Bibliotek og forskning årbok*, vi (1957), 31 [with list of Norwegian composers represented; with Eng. summary]; Ø. Gaukstad: 'Franz Schubert og hans snager', *Bibliotek og forskning årbok*, xii (1963), 181 [with Eng. summary]; Ø. Gaukstad: 'Norsk musikksamling 1927–1977', *Studia musicologica norvegica*, iii (1978), 9

——. Riksarkivet, Bankplass 3, Oslo (*Ora*). The Royal Archive has fragments of Catholic liturgical MSS, some from the 12th century.

TRONDHEIM. Det Kongelige Norske Videnskabers Selskab, Universitets-Biblioteket, Erling Skakkes Gate 47c, Trondheim (*T*). Norway's oldest scientific library was founded in 1767. It has a collection of 6000 printed works and 250 MSS of the late 18th and 19th centuries.

H. Midbøe: *Det Kongelige norske videnskabers selskab* (Trondheim, 1960)

POLAND (*PL*)

The history of Polish music libraries is stressed by M. Prokopowicz: 'Les bibliothèques de musique en Pologne', *FAM*, vii (1960), 7. Library discoveries made since the 1957 inventory of sources undertaken by the Musicological Institute of the University of Warsaw are reported by H. Feicht: 'Neue Quellen zur Geschichte der alten polnischen Musik', *FAM*, xiv (1967), 11. Also informative are H. Feicht: 'Quellen zur mehrstimmigen Musik in Polen vom späten Mittelalter bis 1600', *Musica antiqua Europae orientalis I: Bydgoszcz 1966*, 281–333, and J. Wecowski: 'Catalogue des symphonies du 18e siècle conservées en Pologne', ibid, 334. M. Prokopowicz, ed.: *Katalog mikrofilmów*, xii: *Muzykalia* (Warsaw, 1956–65) is an inventory of the microfilm collection in the National Library in Warsaw, and lists MS and printed music of the 12th–19th centuries in Polish libraries (including *Kc*, *Kj*, *GD*, *PE*, *SA*, *Wtm* and *WRu*). Two series of catalogues are in progress: W. Hordyński and K. Michałowski, eds.: *Katalog polskich druków muzycznych 1800–1863* [Catalogue of Polish music printed 1800–63] (Kraków, 1968–) and Z. M. Szweykowski: *Katalog tematyczny rękopiśmiennych zabytków dawnej muzyki w Polsce/Thematic Catalogue of Early Musical MSS in Poland* (Kraków, 1969–), with English synopses. A list of hymnbooks, songbooks and other musical works published in the 15th–18th centuries, with library locations, appears in M. Przywecka-Samecka: *Drukarstwo muzyczne w Polsce do końca XVIII wieku* [Music printing in Poland to the end of the 18th century] (Kraków, 1969). Of specialized interest is J. Gołos: 'MS Sources of Eastern Chant before 1700 in Polish Libraries', *Studies in Eastern Chant*, iii (1973), 74.

CZĘSTOCHOWA [Tschenstochau]. Klasztor OO. Paulinów na Jasnej Górze, ulica Kordeckiego 2, Częstochowa (*CZp*). The monastery of the Reverend Pauline Fathers is on Jasna Góra mountain; its archives have over 300 works by Polish composers and 1200 by foreign composers, dating mainly from the 18th and early 19th centuries. There are many works by Haydn and Dittersdorf, five early MSS by Mozart and 13 others attributed to him. There are liturgical MSS of the 15th–18th centuries.

P. Podejka: 'Na marginesie dotychczasowych wzmianek w życiu muzycznym na Jasnej Górze' [On the margin of musical life in extant records in Jasna Góra], *Muzyka*, xii (1967), 37 [reports results of an inventory of the monastery's musical material]; K. Musiol: 'Mozartiana im Paulinenkloster zu Tschenstochau', *Mitteilungen der Internationalen Stiftung Mozarteum*, xv/3–4 (1967), 5; P. Podejka: 'Źródła do dziejów muzyki polskiej w archiwum zakonu paulinów w Częstochowie' [Sources of Polish music in the archives of the Pauline monastery in Częstochowa], *Z dziejów muzyki polskiej*, xiv (1969), 33; K. Musiol: 'Bohemika v hudebním archívu Čenstochové' [Bohemica in the music archives in Częstochowa], *Zprávy z Bertramky* (1969), 6 [with complete list of all MSS by 18th- and 19th-century Bohemian composers]

GDAŃSK [Danzig]. Biblioteka Polskiej Akademii Nauk, ulica Wałowa 15, Gdańsk (*GD*). The collection of the Polish Academy of Sciences in Gdańsk came from the Municipal Library (Biblioteka Miejska), which was founded in 1596 and administered the important music from the local churches of St Catherine and St John. Some 1200 music works survived World War II. They comprise sacred music of the 16th–19th centuries, mainly cantatas (in particular by Gessel and C. G. Tag), and secular MSS (16th-century Italian madrigals and French chansons). There are 165 MS and printed works by Telemann, and church cantatas, Passions and similar works by 18th-century musicians active in Gdańsk and the neighbourhood.

O. Günther: *Die musikalischen Handschriften der Stadtbibliothek und der in ihrer Verwaltung befindlichen Kirchenbibliotheken von St. Katharinen und St. Johann in Danzig* (Gdańsk, 1911); M. Prokopowicz, ed.: *Katalog mikrofilmów*, xii: *Muzykalia*, i (Warsaw, 1956), 11–74, and ii (Warsaw, 1962), 20–88; K.-G. Hartmann: 'Musikgeschichtliches aus der Danziger Stadtbibliothek', *Mf*, xxvii (1974), 387 [lists corrections to and omissions from Günther and Prokopowicz]

GNIEZNO [Gnesen]. Archiwum Archdiecezjalne Gniezno, Cathedral, Gniezno (*GNd*). The Archdiocesan Archive (also called Capitular Library) has some 1000 musical works, including missals of the 11th and 12th centuries with cheironomic monody, and 18th- and early 19th-century MSS of works (especially symphonies and masses) by Brixi, Dankowski, Dittersdorf, Haberl, Haydn, Pichl, Richter, Vanhal and others.

T. Trzcinski: *Catalogus codicum manuscriptorum usque ad initium saeculi XVI, qui in bibliotheca ecclesiae metropolitanae gneznensis asservantur* (Poznań, 1910); W. Zientarski: 'O XVIII wiecznych muzykaliach gnieźnieńskich' [18th-century Gniezno music], *Z dziejów muzyki polskiej*, vii (1964), 64; D. Idaszak: 'Autografy Antoniego Habla w zbiorach gnieźnieńskich' [Autographs of Anton Haberl in the Gniezno collection], *Z dziejów muzyki polskiej*, vii (1964), 83; D. Idaszak: 'Rękopisy symfonii Józefa Haydna w zbiorach Archiwum Gnieźnieńskiego' [MSS of Haydn symphonies in the Gniezno Archives], *Studia Hieronymo Feicht septuagenario dedicata* (Kraków, 1967), 307

KÓRNIK. Biblioteka Kórnicka, Polskiej Akademii Nauk, ulica Zamkowa, Kórnik (*KO*). The Kórnik branch of the Polish Academy of Sciences holds the castle collection formerly owned by the Działyński family. There are a number of valuable 16th- and 17th-century MS and printed monophonic cantionals and hymn collections.

W. Hordyński and K. Michałowski: *Katalog polskich druków muzycznych 1800–1863* [Catalogue of Polish music printed 1800–63], i (Kraków, 1968), 54

KRAKÓW. General literature: A. Chybiński: 'Die Musikbestände der Krakauer Bibliotheken von 1500–1650', *SIMG*, xiii (1911–12), 382; J. Pieniążek: *Informator o bibliotekach krakowskich* (Kraków, 1961) [lists 152 libraries]

——. Archiwum Państwowe Miasta Krakowa i Województwa Krakowskiego, ulica Sienna 16, Kraków (*Kpa*). The State Archive of the city and province of Kraków has MS partbooks for 16th- and 17th-century motets and other liturgical works by Polish and foreign composers.

Z. M. Szweykowski: *Katalog tematyczny rękopiśmiennych . . . Polsce/Thematic Catalogue of Early Musical MSS in Poland* (Kraków, 1969–) [vol. on *Kpa* in preparation]

——. Biblioteka Czartoryskich, Muzeum Narodowe, św. Marka 17, Kraków (*Kc*). The Czartoryski Library of the National Museum possesses Polish and foreign MS and printed music works from the 14th–19th centuries. Among printed works are Polish theoretical treatises of the 16th and 17th centuries, early foreign editions of works by Maria Szymanowska, several Ballard editions, and first editions of Beethoven works published in Vienna. MSS include antiphoners, graduals and hymnbooks, collections of Polish dance-melodies (with many polonaises written in the early 19th century), texts of 19th-century operas and other theatrical pieces (in Polish or translated from foreign authors), and harpsichord pieces and excerpts from large vocal works of the early 19th century. The library owns the autograph of Chopin's Krakowiak op.14, a Haydn autograph and several of Józef Elsner. There are also sketches or letters of Haydn, Beethoven, Cherubini, Hummel, Salieri and Weber.

W. Hordyński: 'Zbiór muzyczny w Bibliotece XX. Czartoryskich' [The music collection in the Czartoryski Library], *Przegląd biblioteczny*, iii (1937); M. Prokopowicz, ed.: *Katalog mikrofilmów*, xii: *Muzykalia*, iii (Warsaw, 1965), 17–77; K. Zawadzki: *Katalog mikrofilmów*, x: *Rękopisy Biblioteki Czartoryskich w Krakowie* [MSS in the Czartoryski Library in Kraków] (Warsaw, 1965); xi: *Katalog rękopisów Biblioteki Czartoryskich w Krakowie*, ii (Warsaw, 1966)

——. Biblioteka Jagiellońska, Uniwersytet Jagielloński, Aleja Mickiewicza 22, Kraków (*Kj*). The university was founded in 1364 and the library built up from royal or professional donations; then, after 1559 (with the establishment of the Benedict of Koźmin endowment), also by purchase. A copyright depository institution, the library collects and stores the entire body of Polish literature, in particular items published in Poland before 1800. A special music collection was begun in 1869 and the library established a separate music division in 1958. The Manuscript Department and the Department of Old Printed Books hold several early MSS with medieval theoretical treatises, an Ambrosian antiphoner and other liturgical works, and 17th-century songs, while the Music Division has a collection of documents relating to music in society (posters, programmes, librettos etc). Its 19th- and 20th-century collection includes MSS of Józef Elsner, Chopin, Maria Szymanowska, M. K. Ogiński, Szymanowski, Lutosławski and others. The collection survived World War II almost intact.

W. Wisłocki: *Katalog rękopisów Biblioteki uniwersytetu Jagiellońskiego* [Catalogue of MSS in the Jagiellonian University Library] (Kraków, 1877–81) [lists MSS 1–4176]; J. Reiss: *Książki o muzyce w Bibliotece Jagiellońskiej* [Books about music in the Jagellonian Library] (Kraków, 1924–38) [lists 15th- to 18th-century books]; A. Jałbrzykowska and others: *Inwentarz rękopisów Biblioteki Jagiellońskiej* (Kraków, 1938–72) [lists MSS 4175–9000]; M. Prokopowicz, ed.: *Katalog mikrofilmów*, xii: *Muzykalia*, i (Warsaw, 1956), 208; Z. M. Szweykowski: *Katalog tematyczny rękopiśmiennych . . . Polsce/Thematic Catalogue of Early Musical MSS in Poland*, ii (Kraków, 1972) [collections from the Kraków area, 17th-century pieces now in *Kj*]

——. Biblioteka Prowincji OO. Bernardynów, ulica Bernardyńska 2, Kraków. The central library of the Reverend Fathers of the Bernardine Order holds in its MS collection 105 musical works, mainly graduals, psalters and cantionals of the 15th–18th centuries.

——. Kapituła Metropolitalna, Wawel 3/3, Kraków (*Kk*). The Metropolitan Chapter archive on Wawel Hill contains several hundred liturgical works with music. A 15th-century parchment MS known as the 'Gosławski Cantional' contains monophonic Lamentations, Passions, antiphons, hymns, responsories and masses, and a four-part *liber generationis* notated in Gothic neumes.

Archiwum do dziejów literatury i oświaty w Polsce, iii (1884), 1–168 [catalogue of MSS in *Kk* by J. Polkowski]; Z. M. Szweykowski: *Katalog tematyczny rękopiśmiennych . . . Polsce/Thematic Catalogue of Early Musical MSS in Poland*, i/1 (Kraków, 1969) [music copied for use at Wawel Castle]

ŁANCUT. Muzeum, ulica Zamkowa 1, Łancut (*ŁA*). The museum archive, in Łancut castle, was begun about 1780 by Izabela Lubomirska and enlarged during the 19th century by the Potocki family, owners of the castle until 1944. The library's 2637 music items comprise MSS (some autograph) dating from 1700 to 1820 and printed works from 1730 to 1900, especially 18th-century chamber music, harp music to 1830, and French opera.

K. Biegański: *Biblioteka muzyczna zamku w Łancucie: katalog* [The music library of the castle in Łancut: catalogue] (Kraków, 1968)

LEGNICA [Liegnitz]. Biblioteka Towarzystwa Przyjaciół Nauk w Legnicy, Legnica (*LEtpn*). The library of the Society of the Friends of Science holds 135 printed works and some MSS (bound in 44 volumes) from the Bibliotheca Rudolphina, the only surviving part of the collection of the former Ritter-Akademie in Legnica.

E. Pfudel: *Mittheilungen über die Bibliotheca Rudolfina der Königlichen Ritter-Akademie zu Liegnitz* (Legnica, 1876–8); A. Kolbuszewska: muzykalia w Bibliotece Towarzystwa przyjaciół nauk w Legnicy' [Precious musical items in the library of the Society of the Friends of Science in Legnica], *Szkice legnickie*, vii (1973), 245

PELPLIN. Biblioteka Seminarium Duchownego, Pelplin (*PE*). The library of the Diocesan Seminary has printed and MS liturgical music, most of it from the former Cistercian abbey in Pelplin. Among the MSS is the six-volume Pelplin Tablature, a late Renaissance and early Baroque tablature compiled about 1620–40 by Felix Trzcinski, a Pelplin monk. Its 900 compositions are mainly by Italian composers, with Austrian, German, Polish, English, Dutch and Spanish composers also represented. Other liturgical music includes antiphoners, graduals and processionals of the 13th–17th centuries.

A. Sutkowski and O. Mischiati: 'Una preziosa fonte manoscritta di musica strumentale: l'intavolatura di Pelplin', *L'organo*, ii (1961), 53; M. Prokopowicz, ed.: *Katalog mikrofilmów*, xii: *Muzykalia*, ii (Warsaw, 1962), 91; E. Hinz: 'Tablatura organowa cystersów z Pelplina', *Studia pelplińskie 1969*, 199

POZNAŃ. Uniwersytet im. Adama Mickiewicza, Biblioteka Główna, ulica Ratajczaka 30–40, Poznań (*Pu*). Within the main library of the Adam Mickiewicz University is the Adolf Chybiński Archive, which holds fragments of late 13th-century motets from Stary Sącz, 16th-century partbooks for masses, motets and other sacred works by Polish and foreign composers, and partbooks from Kraków Cathedral (the oldest polyphonic MSS from the Rorantist chapel of the 16th century). The principal music holdings, totalling over 20,000 items, are 19th-century German and Polish music and 20th-century Polish works, including autographs, correspondence and other material relating to the composer Mieczysław Karłowicz.

W. Hordyński and K. Michałowski: *Katalog polskich druków muzycznych 1800–1863* [Catalogue of Polish music printed 1800–63], i (Kraków, 1968); Z. M. Szweykowski: *Katalog tematyczny rękopiśmiennych . . . Polsce/Thematic Catalogue of Early Musical MSS in Poland,* i/4 (Kraków, 1975)

SANDOMIERZ. Seminarium Duchownego, ulica Żeromskiego 2, Sandomierz (*SA*). The library of the Diocesan Seminary antiphoners, graduals and other vocal and instrumental works (mainly sacred vocal MSS) of the 16th–19th centuries.

M. Prokopowicz, ed.: *Katalog mikrofilmów,* xii: *Muzykalia,* ii (Warsaw, 1962), 97 [lists 103 MSS and 3 printed works]; Z. M. Szweykowski: 'Katalog rękopiśmiennych zabytków muzycznych Biblioteki Seminarium duchownego w Sandomierzu' [Catalogue of old music MSS in the library of the Diocesan Seminary in Sandomierz], *Archiwa, biblioteki i muzea kościelne,* x (1965); Z. M. Szweykowski: *Katalog tematyczny rękopiśmiennych . . . Polsce/Thematic Catalogue of Early Musical MSS in Poland* (Kraków, 1969–) [vol. on *SA* in preparation]

TORUŃ [Thorn]. Biblioteka Uniwersytecka im. Mikołaja Kopernika, ulica Gagarina 13, Toruń (*Tu*). Founded in 1945, the library of the Nicolaus Copernicus University received its collection of early music works from the city's Municipal Library in 1947. Holdings include incomplete sets of 16th-century editions of works of Lassus, and music by other 16th- and 17th-century composers. Most of the works probably came from the church of St Mary in Elbląg. There is also extensive hymnological material, and sacred monophonic songs, psalmbooks and canticles.

T. Carstenn: 'Katalog der St. Marienbibliothek zu Elbing', *KJb,* xi (1896), 40

WARSAW. Biblioteka Narodowa, Plac Krasińskich 3–5, 00-207 Warsaw (*Wn*). The National Library was founded in 1928 and since then has received depository copies of all Polish music. After almost total destruction of the collection in World War II, the Music Department was re-established in 1951. The music collection (divided between the Music Department and the departments of MSS, old books, 19th- and 20th-century books and periodicals) includes single liturgical MSS of the 11th century, a few 15th- and 16th-century polyphonic works and theoretical treatises, the oldest Polish record of organ music of the 16th century, old musical printed material, autographs of Chopin and other Polish composers (including Józef Elsner) from the end of the 18th century up to the present (Lutosławski, Grażyna Bacewicz), and a large number of rare Polish printed music editions from the beginning of the 19th century to 1928. The Microfilm Department has copies of musical treasures held elsewhere in the country, and of some rare Polonica held in foreign libraries. Since 1961 the library has also received depository copies of all recordings produced in Poland.

Katalog wystawy zbiorów teatralnych i muzycznych Biblioteki narodowej w Warszawie [Exhibition catalogue of theatre and music collections of the National Library in Warsaw] (Warsaw, 1934) [see esp. 103–38; contains information about MSS and prints destroyed in World War II]; M. Prokopowicz, ed.: *Katalog mikrofilmów,* xii: *Muzykalia* (Warsaw, 1956–65); B. Frydrychowicz, M. Prokopowicz and W. Bogdany: *Muzyka polska/Polish Music: Manuscripts and Prints from the 11th to the 20th Century: Guide to an Exhibition* (Warsaw, 1966) [most items from *Wn*]; M. Prokopowicz: 'Zbiory muzyczne Biblioteki narodowej/Music Collections of the National Library', *Rocznik Biblioteki narodowej,* v (Warsaw, 1969), 293; B. Frydrychowicz: 'Augustiański fragment organowy i jego środowisko macierzyste', *Muzyka,* xvi/2 (1971), 3–33

——. Biblioteka Uniwersytecka, Oddział Zbiorów Muzycznych, ulica Krakowskie Przedmieście 32, Warsaw (*Wu*). The Department of Music Collections of the University Library, founded in 1954 and housed with the Musicological Institute of the university (at ulica Żwirki i Wigury 93), includes 1700 works printed before 1800 (from the former Musicological Institute in Wrocław), 4500 MSS from before 1850 and almost 3000 MSS of contemporary Polish composers; there is also a large general research collection. The library holds about 11,000 letters, programmes, posters, photographs and other musical documents.

E. Kirsch: *Die Bibliothek des Musikalischen Instituts bei der Universität Breslau* (Berlin, 1922) [many items now in *Wu*]; J. Mendysowa: *Katalog druków muzycznych XVI–XVIII w. Biblioteki Uniwersytetu Warszawskiego* [Catalogue of printed music of the 16th–18th centuries in the library of the University of Warsaw] (Warsaw, 1970) [i: 16th-century works, introduction also in Fr.]

——. Biblioteka, Muzeum, Archiwum Warszawskiego Towarzystwa Muzycznego im. S. Moniuszki, ulica Zakroczymska 2, 00-225 Warsaw (*Wtm*). The Warsaw Music Society library was founded with the society in 1871. It collects autographs, documents, mementos and printed editions of works by Polish composers active in the 19th and 20th centuries. The library possesses over 3500 musical autographs (including some of Chopin, Józef Elsner, Karol Kurpiński, Stefani and Szymanowski, and complete collections of MSS of Moniuszko, Noskowski and Karłowicz). It also collects programmes, posters and iconography. A 16th-century organ tablature burnt in 1944 now remains in a copy.

M. Prokopowicz, ed.: *Katalog mikrofilmów,* xii: *Muzykalia,* i (Warsaw, 1956), 75–201, and iii (Warsaw, 1965), 78; I Chomik and A. Spóz: *Katalog wystawy: Polska kultura muzyczna w XIX wieku* [Exhibition catalogue: Polish music culture in the 19th century] (1966) [historical introduction also in Fr.]; A. Spóz: *Warszawskie Towarzystwo Muzyczne 1871–1971* [Warsaw Music Society 1871–1971] (Warsaw, 1971)

——. Towarzystwo im. Fryderyka Chopina, ulica Okólnik 1, Warsaw. The Fryderyk Chopin Society was founded in 1934 and revived in 1945. The world centre for Chopin research, it comprises a museum, library and archive. The museum has some of the composer's autographs, personal effects and portraits, totalling 1450 items. In the library are about 6000 books and 4000 items of music, mostly concerning Chopin and other 19th-century Polish composers. The archive contains photocopies of all documents concerning Chopin. The society administers Chopin's birthplace at Żelazowa Wola, and sponsors international competitions, congresses and research projects, such as the annual research journal *Annales Chopin* (1956–).

S. Golańska: 'La Société Frédéric Chopin à Varsovie', *La musique en Pologne,* v (1970), 11; Z. Jaźwińska: 'The Frederic Chopin Society in Warsaw', *Polish Music/Polnische Musik* (1970), no.4; Z. Lissa: 'Chopin Gesellschaft', *MGG*

WROCŁAW [Breslau]. Biblioteka Uniwersytecka, Oddział Zbiorów Muzycznych, ulica św. Jadwigi 3–4, Wrocław (*WRu*). The Music Department Collection of the University Library has a valuable collection of printed music of the 16th and 17th centuries, containing many unique prints of early 17th-century Italian music. The collection comprises that part of the former Stadtbibliothek that survived World War II; the collection from the Gymnasium at Brzeg (Brieg), transferred to the University Library in 1899; and prints from various Silesian libraries. The music MS collection was destroyed during World War II, and the collection from the former Akademisches Institut für Kirchenmusik (later known as the Musikalisches Institut bei der Universität Breslau) is in the University Library, Warsaw. The present collection of MSS includes mostly instrumental music of the 18th and 19th centuries. Liturgical music MSS are also in the library's Department of Manuscripts. The microfilm collection includes copies of 44 volumes of the Bibliotheca Rudolphina of Legnica.

E. Bohn: *Bibliographie der Musik-Druckwerke bis 1700, welche in der Stadtbibliothek, der Bibliothek des Academischen Instituts für Kirchenmusik und der Königlichen und Universitätsbibliothek zu Breslau aufbewahrt werden* (Berlin, 1883/R1969); E. Bohn: *Die musikalischen Handschriften des XVI. und XVII. Jahrhunderts in der Stadtbibliothek zu Breslau* (Berlin, 1890) [all MSS destroyed in World War II]; F. Kuhn: *Beschreibendes Verzeichnis der alten Musikalien – Handschriften und Druckwerke – des Königlichen Gymnasiums zu Brieg* (Leipzig, 1896–7); W. Schenk: 'Rękopisy liturgiczne od XIII do XV wieku w Bibliotece uniwersyteckiej we Wrocławiu' [Liturgical MSS from the 13th–15th centuries in the University Library in Wrocław], *Archiwa, biblioteki i muzea kościelne*, ii (1961), 185, and vi (1963), 191; A. Kolbuszewska: *Katalog muzycznych dzieł teoretycznych XVI i XVII wieku: Biblioteka uniwersytecka we Wrocławiu* [Catalogue of books on music theory of the 16th and 17th centuries: University Library, Wrocław] (Wrocław, 1973)

PORTUGAL (*P*)

Locations for MS and printed polyphonic works are provided by A. T. Luper: 'Portuguese Polyphony in the 16th and Early 17th Centuries', *JAMS*, iii (1950), 93. MSS in Arouca, Aveiro, Braga, Coimbra, Guimarães, Lisbon, Ponte de Lima, Oporto, Refajos de Lima and Viana do Castelo are described in S. Corbin: *Essai sur la musique religieuse portugaise au moyen âge* (Paris, 1952) [see chap. on 'L'état des sources']. All aspects of library history, administration, collections and publications are treated by S. Skorge: *Das portugiesische Bibliothekswesen der Gegenwart* (Cologne, 1967). R. M. Stevenson: 'Some Portuguese Sources for Early Brazilian Music History', *Yearbook, Inter-American Institute for Musical Research*, iv (1968), 1–43, mentions 17th-century masses at Arouca, Brazilian *modinhas* at Lisbon's Biblioteca da Ajuda, Biblioteca Nacional and Cathedral, and villancicos at Évora, as well as archival documents and their locations.

Since 1931 Portuguese law has required that 13 copies of books and periodicals be deposited at various national and municipal libraries. Three copies of music and recordings are deposited at the Biblioteca Nacional, Lisbon, and the conservatories of Lisbon and Oporto.

AROUCA. Museu Regional de Arte Sacra do Mosteiro, Arquivo, Arouca (*AR*). The archive of the monastery (founded in 716) has the country's richest collection of medieval sacred music. Among the treasures are choirbooks from before 1124, a 12th-century collectarium, early antiphoners and processionals, and a volume of 17th- and 18th-century sacred music.

J. Leclercq: 'Les MSS cisterciens du Portugal', *Analecta sacri ordinis cisterciensis*, vi (1950), 135; M. Joaquim: 'O colectário de Arouca e os seus textos musiciais', *Douro Litoral*, 8th ser., v/6 (Oporto, 1957), 413–81; Andrew Hughes: 'Medieval Liturgical Books at Arouca, Braga, Evora, Lisbon, and Porto: some Provisional Inventories', *Traditio: Studies in Ancient and Medieval History, Thought, and Religion*, xxxi (New York, 1975), 369

AVEIRO. Museu de Aveiro, Mosteiro de Jesus, rua Santa Joana princesa, Aveiro (*AV*). The library of the monastery (founded in 1461) is important for the history of liturgy and of Latin poetry in Portugal. The collection includes five 15th-century antiphoners, two sets of 16th- and 17th-century processionals and several later choirbooks.

S. Corbin: 'Les livres liturgiques d'Aveiro', *Arquivo do distrito d'Aveiro*, viii (1942)

BRAGA. Biblioteca Pública e Arquivo Distrital, Palácio dos Arcebispos, praça do Município, Braga (*BRp*). The public library (founded in 1841) and the district archive were joined in 1917. Among the archive's collections were those of the local cathedral and of extinct monasteries; of particular note is the collection of S Bento. Rarities in the holdings include

leaves from early choirbooks, 16th-century editions of the Braga liturgy, and 17th- and 18th-century sacred and secular MSS. There is an important 17th-century four-line organ tablature (MS 694) formerly belonging to the cathedral organist, comprising mainly works by Spanish and Portuguese composers.

M. S. Kastner: 'Tres libros desconocidos con música orgánica en las bibliotecas de Oporto y Braga', *AnM*, i (1946), 143, and ii (1947), 77; A. do Rosário: 'Noticia de alguns MSS e impressos na Biblioteca pública e Arquivo distrital de Braga', *Arquivos do Centro cultural português*, iv (1972), 679 [lists liturgical works]; Andrew Hughes: 'Medieval Liturgical Books at Arouca, Braga, Evora, Lisbon, and Porto: some Provisional Inventories', *Traditio: Studies in Ancient and Medieval History, Thought, and Religion*, xxxi (New York, 1975), 369

COIMBRA. Biblioteca Geral, Universidade de Coimbra, Coimbra (*C*). The rare book department of the university library (the country's largest and most important) has music from the city's cathedral and the monasteries of Santa Cruz and Celas. Its holdings include 16th- to 18th-century MSS and printed choirbooks; 15th- and 16th-century European sacred polyphony; mostly anonymous 15th- to 17th-century sacred works; 16th- and 17th-century Portuguese vocal and instrumental music; and 17th- and 18th-century organ music and organ intabulations of vocal works. The university was founded in 1290 in Lisbon and moved to Coimbra in 1537.

E. Donato: 'Os vilancicos da Biblioteca geral da Universidade de Coimbra', *Boletim bibliográfico da Biblioteca geral da Universidade de Coimbra*, ix (1930), 94–144, 384–439; *Catálogo de manuscritos* (Coimbra, 1935–40); *Inventário dos inéditos e impressos musicais: subsidios para um catálogo* (Coimbra, 1937) [esp. preface by M. S. Kastner]; U. Berti: *Ensaio com notas biográficas de um catálogo dos manuscritos musicais da Biblioteca da Universidade de Coimbra* (Coimbra, 1940); M. de Sampayo Ribeiro: *Os manuscritos musicais nos 6 e 12 da Biblioteca geral da Universidade de Coimbra: contribução para um catálogo definitivo* (Coimbra, 1941); M. S. Kastner: *Los manuscritos musicales núms. 48 y 242 de la Biblioteca general de la Universidad de Coimbra* (Barcelona, 1950); *Catálogo da Colecção de misceláneas* (Coimbra, 1967–72); *Catálogo dos reservados da Biblioteca geral da Universidade de Coimbra* (Coimbra, 1970); E. G. de Pinho: *Santa Cruz de Coimbra, centro de actividade musical nos seculos XVI e XVII* (Lisbon, 1972)

ÉVORA. Biblioteca Pública e Arquivo Distrital, largo do Conde de Vila Flor, Évora (*EVp*). The library has MS and printed music of the 15th–18th centuries, with works by the Portuguese composers Mendes and Cardoso, and the Évora Cancioneiro. Many works were received from former religious houses in the district. The library holds the 18th-century MS of José Mazza's *Dicionário biográfico de músicos portugueses*.

A. Joaquim Lopes da Silva Junior: *Os reservados da Biblioteca pública de Évora* (Coimbra, 1917); Andrew Hughes: 'Medieval Liturgical Books at Arouca, Braga, Evora, Lisbon, and Porto: some Provisional Inventories', *Tratitio: Studies in Ancient and Medieval History, Thought, and Religion*, xxxi (New York, 1975), 369

LISBON. Biblioteca da Ajuda, Palácio Nacional da Ajuda, Lisbon 3 (*La*). The former royal library has strong opera holdings, in particular of the 17th and 18th centuries, and works by Jommelli, Almeida, Portugal and Lima. The library also has the 13th-century Ajuda Cancioneiro (without musical notation) and a collection of works by Giorgi.

M. A. Machado Santos: *Catálogo de música manuscrita* (Lisbon, 1958–68); G. Béhague: 'Biblioteca da Ajuda: MSS 1595/1596: Two Anonymous 18th-century Collections of Modinhas', *Yearbook, Inter-American Institute for Musical Research*, iv (1968), 44–81

——. Biblioteca Nacional, rua Ocidental do Campo Grande 83, Lisbon 5 (*Ln*). Another former royal library (1796–1836), it now serves as university and national library. Many of its musical works were formerly owned by religious establishments, particularly the

Cistercian abbey of S Maria in Alcobaça and the Dominican monastery of Jesus in Aveiro. In 1969 the library received the private collection of the musicologist and journalist Mario Sampayo Ribeiro, and in 1971 that of the composer and former director of the conservatory Ivo Cruz. Holdings include early MS and printed works by Portuguese and foreign composers, and theoretical works.

E. Vieira: 'A música na Biblioteca nacional de Lisboa', *Arte musical*, iii (1901), 134, 142, 150, 158, 174; G. Pereira: *Biblioteca nacional de Lisboa: colecção dos livros de côro dos conventos extinctos* (Lisbon, 1904)

——. Fábrica da Sé Patriarcal, largo de S António da Sé, Lisbon (*Lf*). The cathedral's sacred works are chiefly by Portuguese and Italians. Among them is a four-voice motet by John IV, the monarch whose own rich musical library was destroyed during the 1755 earthquake. The cathedral archive has become the central depository for MS and printed music formerly held by several other churches in the Lisbon diocese. It also received as donations some private collections, which include piano and chamber music of the 18th and 19th centuries.

L. de Freitas Branco: *D. João IV, músico* (Lisbon, 1956); L. Feininger: *Catalogus thematicus et bibliographicus Joannis de Georgiis operum sacrorum omnium*, ii (Trent, 1971)

——. Fundação Calouste Gulbenkian, Musical Division, avenida de Berne 45, Lisbon 1 (*Lcg*). The division is in charge of cataloguing Portugal's MS and printed musical resources and has catalogues of works in progress. There is also a modest library, to which has been added the collection of the composer–pianist José Vianna da Motta (*d* 1948), the former head of the Lisbon Conservatory.

exhibition catalogues on Beethoven (1960); early instruments (1961); Debussy (1962); Richard Strauss (1964); Rameau (1965); Britten (1967); Monteverdi (1967); Vianna da Motta (1968); Milhaud (1968); Francisco de Lacerda (1969); Berlioz (1969); Gluck (1970)

——. Teatro Nacional de S Carlos, Biblioteca e Museu, largo de S Carlos, Lisbon (*Lt*). There is a collection of early opera librettos, scores, MSS, scenic designs and iconography related to opera performances since the founding of the theatre in 1793.

MAFRA. Palácio Nacional, Biblioteca, Terreiro de D. João V, Mafra (*Mp*). The palace and its attached monastery and basilica were inaugurated in 1733. The library has French and Portuguese 18th-century theoretical works, and works by Portuguese and foreign composers. A large group of sacred works for male voices and four to six organs was written by M. A. Portugal about 1807 for performance in the basilica.

J.-P. Sarraute: 'Les oeuvres de Marcos Portugal à la basilique de Mafra', *Arquivos do Centro cultural português*, ii (1970), 486

OPORTO. Biblioteca Pública Municipal, Jardim de S Lázaro, Oporto (*Pm*). Founded in 1833, the library received MSS from the Santa Cruz monastery in Coimbra, including 12th- and 13th-century liturgical works. There is a MS (no.714) dating from about 1450 which is the earliest source of polyphonic music in Portugal, and MSS 1577 and 1607 are important sources for 17th-century Iberian organ music.

M. S. Kastner: 'Tres libros desconocidos con música orgánica en la bibliotecas de Oporto y Braga', *AnM*, i (1946), 143; ii (1947), 77; Andrew Hughes: 'Medieval Liturgical Books at Arouca, Braga, Evora, Lisbon, and Porto: some Provisional Inventories', *Traditio: Studies in Ancient and Medieval History, Thought, and Religion*, xxxi (New York, 1975), 369

VILA VIÇOSA. Casa de Bragança, Museu-Biblioteca, Paço Ducal, Vila Viçosa (*VV*). The palace library is administered by the Fundação da Casa de Bragança. Music holdings include 20 MS and printed polyphonic choirbooks of the 16th–18th centuries, with sacred works by Portuguese and foreign composers. There are many secular MSS of Portuguese and Italian origin, most dating from the reign of King John V.

M. Joaquim: 'A propósito dos livros de polifonia existentes no Paço ducal de Vila Viçosa', *AnM*, ii (1947), 69; M. Joaquim: *Vinte livros de música polifónica do Paço ducal de Vila Viçosa catalogados, descritos e anotados* (Lisbon, 1953)

ROMANIA (*R*)

A publication of general value is *Libraries in the Rumanian People's Republic* (Bucharest, 1961), which also includes music libraries.

ALBA IULIA. Biblioteca Batthyaneum, Strada Filimon Sîrbu 1, Alba Iulia. The library, now a branch of the Central State Library in Bucharest, was founded in 1794 and contains MSS relating to Catholic church music, mainly of the 14th–16th centuries; most are illuminated.

BRAŞOV [Kronstadt]. Biblioteca Municipală, Bulevardul Gheorghe Gheorghiu-Dej 33, 2200 Braşov (*BRm*). The municipal library has part of the music collection formerly in the Honterusgymnasium, including cantatas and other sacred vocal works by German and Czech composers of the 17th and 18th centuries.

E. H. Müller: *Die Musiksammlung der Bibliothek zu Kronstadt* (Braşov, 1931) [lists about 1000 MS and printed books and musical works from the 16th century on]

——. Biserica Neagră, Curtea Bisericii Negre 2, 2200 Braşov. The archive of the Black Church has works of the 16th and 17th centuries including Daniel Croner's organ tablatures.

A. Porfetye: 'Daniel Croner und die Orgelmusik in Siebenbürgen vom 15. bis 18. Jahrhundert', *Musica antiqua Europae orientalis III: Bydgoszcz 1972*, 551–88

BUCHAREST. Academiei Republicii Socialiste România, Calea Victoriei 125, Bucharest (*Ba*). Founded in 1867, the library of the Academy of Sciences has about 35,000 musical works, including over 300 Byzantine music MSS of the 15th–19th centuries, but mainly of the 18th and early 19th.

S. Sava: 'Die altrussischen Neumen-Handschriften in der Bibliothek der Rumänischen Akademie der Wissenschaften zu Bukarest', *Musik des Ostens*, vi (1971), 126 [with detailed description of 11 items, and facsimiles]

——. Biblioteca Centrală de Stat, Strada Ion Ghica 4-Sector 4, Bucharest (*Bc*). The music division of the Central State Library was set up in 1956. Being a copyright library and responsible for the national bibliography of music and recordings, it collects a large amount of music and musical literature. There is a general catalogue of musical MSS in Byzantine notation for the whole territory of Romania before 1820. The music division also has MSS of Orthodox church music from the 17th and 18th centuries and a complete photocopy collection of all Byzantine MSS from the 9th–16th centuries extant in Romanian archives. MSS in Western notation include Haydn's Kyrie and Christe from the *Missa Cellensis* (1766) and more recent MSS of Enescu, Bartók, Lipatti, Ionel Perlea and others related to Romanian music.

——. Conservatorul de Muzică 'Ciprian Porumbescu', Strada Stirbei Vodă 33, Bucharest. The conservatory library was established in 1910, and contains 150,000 volumes (MSS, books, printed scores and periodicals), some 1400 of them in a Museum of Romanian Music.

M. Curcăneanu and V. Tenciu: 'O bibliotecă muzicală: Biblioteca conservatorului Ciprian Porumbescu din Bucureşti', *Revista biblio-tecilor*, xii (1969), 283; V. Cosma: 'Manuscrise muzicale româneşti in Biblioteca Conservatorului Ciprian Porumbescu din Bucureşti', *Studii de muzicologie*, v (1969), 266–309

CLUJ-NAPOCA. Biblioteca Centrală Universitară, Strada Clinicilor 2, Cluj-Napoca (*Cu*). Founded in 1872, the library receives depository copies of all Romanian publications. It has about 16,000 musical works.

——. Conservatorul de Musică 'George Dima', Strada 23 August 25, Cluj-Napoca. The conservatory library has 18th- and 19th-century printed and MS works by Czech, German, Romanian and Hungarian composers (Dussek, Gyrowetz, Romberg, Rossetti, Caudella, Dima, Farkas and others).

I. Lakatos: 'Alte tschechische Musikalien in der Bibliothek der Musikhochschule von Klausenberg', *SM*, vi (1964), 144

IAŞI. Biblioteca Universitară 'Mihail Eminescu', Strada Păcurari 4, 6600 Iaşi (*J*). The university library has early 16th-century MS Byzantine music of the Putna school which complements the holdings at Putna and Dragomirna monasteries. The library also has 19th-century printed and MS works by Romanian composers.

G. Ciobanu: *Studii de etnomuzicologie şi bizantinologie* (Bucharest, 1964), esp. 265ff

SIBIU. Muzeul Brukenthal, Piaţa Republicii 4, Sibiu (*Sb*). The present museum library was founded in the 18th century by Samuel Brukenthal, incorporating later collections from the city's Dominican library (founded in the 15th century) and the former municipal library. Items related to music are mainly concerned with music drama and folklore.

——. State Archives, Strada Arhivelor 3, 2400 Sibiu (*Sa*). The archive has printed and MS works of the 16th–19th centuries by Transylvanian composers including Ostermayer, Reilich, Sartorius, Boer and Caudella.

——. Institutul Teologic Protestant, Strada General Magheru 4, 2400 Sibiu. The church library contains the 16th-century polyphonic collection *Odae cum harmoniis* on humanist texts, attributed to Honterus.

R. Ghircoiaşiu: 'O colecţie de piese corale din sec. XVI: "Odae cum Harmoniis" de Johannes Honterus', *Muzica*, x (1960), 22

SPAIN (*E*)

A general introduction is offered in R. Stevenson: 'Music Research in Spanish Libraries', *Notes*, x (1952–3), 49. Valuable lists of composers whose works are found in specific collections appear in H. Anglès: 'Biblioteca y archivos musicales: España', *LaborD*. Locations and contents of some important MSS are given by M. Querol and others: 'Spanien', *MGG*. Also informative are J. Garcia Morales: 'Spanische Musikbibliotheken', *Die Musikbücherei*, ii (1955), 371; M. Querol: 'Lista de las catálogos musicales publicados en España', *FAM*, xiii (1966), 103; and, on Spanish conservatory libraries, M. Querol: 'España', *FAM*, xxii (1975), 116.

Spanish copyright law requires that three copies of everything printed in the country be sent to the legal depository offices. One copy of printed music goes to the Madrid Conservatory, while the other two go to the Instituto Bibliografico Hispánico, which deposits them at the Biblioteca Nacional, Madrid. Three copies of provincial book publications go to the legal depository offices in the capitals of all Spanish provinces. The offices send one copy to the main public library in their localities and the other two copies are forwarded to the Instituto Bibliografico Hispánico, which deposits them at the Biblioteca Nacional.

ÁVILA. Archivo de la Catedral, calle del Tostado, Ávila (*Ac*). Part of the cathedral archive was moved to the Archivo Histórico Nacional, Madrid, in the latter half of the 19th century. Among the works remaining in Ávila are MS choirbooks of the 12th–18th centuries with numerous masses (by Juan del Vado, Morales and others), as well as *Magnificat* settings (by Aguilera), villancicos, hymns and psalms.

J. López-Calo, ed.: *Catálogo del archivo de música de la catedral de Ávila* (Santiago de Compostela, 1978)

BADAJOZ. Archivo de Musica de la Catedral, plaza de la Constitución, Badajoz (*BA*). The archive has MS and printed sacred works by 16th-century Spanish composers, and some symphonies by Haydn.

BARCELONA. Archivo de la Corona de Aragón, plaza del Rey, Barcelona 2 (*Bac*). The archive of the Aragonese Crown has some 100 MSS on musical subjects, dating from the 11th–15th centuries, acquired, according to the archive's records, from S Cugat del Vallès and S María de Ripoll monasteries. There are also miscellaneous documents concerning music, and loose MS leaves.

J. M. Madurell Marimón: 'Documentos de archivo, MSS e impressos musicales (siglos XIV–XVIII)', *AnM*, xxiii (1968), 199 [discusses *Bac* and three other Barcelona archives]

——. Biblioteca de Cataluña, calle del Carmen 47, Barcelona 1 (*Bc*). The Central Library was founded in 1907, and a separate music section was created in 1917, primarily on the basis of the private collections of Pedrell and Carreras Dagas, and on the music holdings of the Diputación Provincial of Barcelona (founded 1892). In 1939 the Biblioteca de Cataluña of the Institut d'Estudis Catalans was deposited here, and the central library has since adopted this name. There are rich holdings of Gregorian MSS, fragments and entire liturgical works of the 11th–18th centuries, early theoretical works, MS and printed works of Spanish and foreign composers of the 15th and 16th centuries, guitar, vihuela and organ works of the golden Spanish era, autographs of famous Spanish composers, and a modern collection. The library has an archive of copies of Spanish music held elsewhere. Gifts received include the 6000-volume Wagner collection of Joaquín Pena, the library of Luis Sedo Paris-Mencheta, acquired in 1969, and the outstanding musicological collection of Higini Anglès, acquired in 1971.

F. Pedrell: *Catàlech de la Biblioteca musical de la diputació de Barcelona* (Barcelona, 1908–9); H. Anglès: *Catáleg dels manuscrits musicals de la Colleció Pedrell* (Barcelona, 1921)

——. Catedral, Archivo, plaza de Cristo Rey, Barcelona 2 (*Bca*). The cathedral archive has fragments of Gregorian MSS from the 11th–14th centuries, other liturgical MSS (including a rich collection of 16th- and 17th-century *cantorales gregorianos*), and other polyphonic MSS and printed organ music.

——. Instituto del Teatro, calle del Conde del Asalto 3, Barcelona 1 (*Bit*). Formerly known as the Museo del Arte Escénico, the Theatre Institute collects documentation of the 16th–20th centuries relating to the theatre, including MS and printed scores of theatrical compositions, in particular ballet and zarzuela. It has received the extensive theatrical collection of Arturo Sedó, which has been supplemented by the private collections of José Canals, Cotarelo and Guerra.

J. Montaner: *La colleción teatral de Don Arturo Sedó* (Barcelona, 1951) [catalogue]

——. Instituto Español de Musicología, calle de la Egipciacas 15, Barcelona (*Bim*). The small but valuable collection of the institute includes early printed and MS works, as well as the library of Anselmo González del Valle, rich in piano music. There are film copies of early Spanish music in several Spanish cathedral archives, and of regional Spanish folksongs.

——. Instituto Municipal de Historia, calle de Santa Lucía 1, Barcelona 2 (*Bih*). The Historical Institute has a collection of 25,000 *goigs*, religious songs dedicated to various Catalonian patron saints. There are also further items of Spanish folklore.

——. Orfeó Català, calle Amadeo Vives 1, Barcelona 3 (*Boc*). Founded with the choral society in 1891, this private members' library possesses a 13th-century organum MS and 15th- to 18th-century printed music and theoretical works. There are also autographs of recent Spanish composers (Albéniz, Granados, Vives and others).

——. Universidad, avenida de José Antonio Primo de Rivera 585, Barcelona 7 (*Bu*). The university library has some polyphonic MSS and MS organ and piano sonatas, as well as printed theoretical works of the 16th–18th centuries.

BURGOS. Archivo de la Catedral, plaza de S María, Burgos (*BUa*). The chapter archive contains Mozarabic MSS, 16th-century polyphonic MS choirbooks and MS quartets by Boccherini.

——. Monasterio de Las Huelgas, Burgos (*BUlh*). The Cistercian monastery, founded about 1180, has the famous 14th-century Las Huelgas MS, with important polyphonic works. It also holds Gregorian MSS of the same period.

L. Dittmer: 'Codex Las Huelgas', *MGG*

——. Parroquia de S Esteban, Burgos (*BUse*). The church's library has ten 13th-century parchment fragments (from bindings) containing monodic sequences and polyphony for two to three voices in diastematic Aquitanian notation.

CÓRDOBA. Catedral, Archivo de Música, calle Torrijos 10, Córdoba (*C*). The cathedral music archive, in the Episcopal Palace, has two Mozarabic MSS, the Codex de Córdoba, a collection of MSS copied in the 17th and 18th centuries, and several masses, motets and *Magnificat* settings printed in the 16th and early 17th centuries.

La miniatura en la catedral de Córdoba (Córdoba, 1973)

CUENCA. Catedral, Archivo Capitular, plaza Mayor, Cuenca (*CU*). The chapter archive has Gregorian chant MSS, and 16th- to 19th-century MS and printed polyphonic works (by Morales, Palestrina, Victoria etc).

R. Navarro Gonzalo and J. López Cobos: *Catálogo musical del Archivo de la Santa Iglesia Catedral basílica de Cuenca* (Cuenca, 1965, rev. 2/1973)

EL ESCORIAL. Real Monasterio de S Lorenzo, El Escorial, Madrid (*E*). The monastery has a separate library and music archive. Among the holdings are the famous 13th-century cantigas of Alfonso X, ten MSS with Byzantine notation, 15th-century choirbooks (with works by Binchois, Dufay, Dunstable and others), 16th-

century printed works, 17th- and 18th-century vocal and organ music, and theoretical works from the 16th century on.

C. J. de Benito: MS catalogue of the collection (1875) [copy available in *Mn*, Department of MSS]; R. B. Lenaerts: 'Nederlandse polyphonische liederen in die Bibliotheek van El Escorial', *RBM*, iii (1949), 134; S. Rubio: 'MSS musicales de la liturgia bizantina que se conservan en la Biblioteca del Monasterio de El Escorial', *I° congresso internazionale di musica sacra: Roma 1950*, 119

GERONA. Biblioteca Catedralicia, plaza de la Catedral, Gerona (*G*). The cathedral library contains Gregorian and other MSS, including a volume of polyphony copied by Pujol in 1618. The cathedral received the bequests of Francisco Soler, with all his compositions, and of José Gaz, a 17th-century *maestro de capilla*, who left his music and instruments to the cathedral.

GRANADA. Capilla Real, Gran-via de Colón, Granada (*GRcr*). The music archive of the royal chapel has 40 volumes of Gregorian chant, eight volumes of masses and motets printed 1567 to 1608, and 16th- to 18th-century polyphonic MSS (masses, motets, Vespers, Passions etc). There are also many documents concerning music.

J. López Calo: 'El archivo de música de la Capilla real de Granada', *AnM*, xiii (1958), 103; xxvi (1971), 213 [catalogue]

——. Catedral, Archivo, plaza de Alonso Cano, Granada (*GRc*). The chapter archive has printed and MS choirbooks and partbooks, including many from the 16th century.

GUADALUPE. Real Monasterio de S María, Archivo de Música, Guadalupe (*GU*). The music archive has about 700 sacred music works, many from the 18th century; the monastery museum has a collection of 16th-century choirbooks copied at the monastery.

A. Barrado Manzano: *Catálogo del archivo musical del monasterio de Guadalupe* (Badajoz, 1947)

HUESCA. Catedral, Archivo, plaza de la Catedral, Huesca (*H*). The cathedral archive has a 12th-century troper (with Aquitanian notation) from the monastery of S Juan de la Peña, and other liturgical MSS of the 11th–13th centuries. There are also 16th-century polyphonic MSS.

R. del Arco: 'Libros corales, códices y otros MSS de la catedral de Huesca', *Linajes de Aragón*, vi (1915), 242

LAS PALMAS. Catedral de Canarias, plaza de Santa Ana, Las Palmas de Gran Canarias (*LPA*). The cathedral archive has works used for services since the cathedral's foundation in the late 15th century, the largest part written by its *maestros de capilla*. The works include masses, *Magnificat* settings, motets, villancicos, Lamentations and psalms, some with accompanying instruments. There are also a few MS and printed 18th-century symphonies.

L. de la Torre de Trujillo: 'El archivo de música de la Catedral de Las Palmas', *El museo Canario*, xxv (1964), 181–242; xxvi (1965), 147–203 [with historical introduction]

LEÓN. Catedral, Archivo, plaza de la Catedral, León (*La*). The chapter archive is famous for its 10th-century Mozarabic antiphoner. There are also later works, including some by the 17th-century composer Juan Pérez Roldán.

——. Colegiata de S Isidoro, plaza de S Isidoro, León (*Lc*). The church's library has 12th- and 13th-century liturgical MSS. There are also sacred MSS of the 15th–18th centuries.

J. Pérez Llamazares: *Catálogo de los incunables y libros antiguos raros y curiosos de la Real colegiata de San Isidoro* (Madrid, 1943)

MADRID. Archivo Histórico Nacional, calle de Serrano 115, Madrid 6 (*Mah*). The National Historical Archive has music MSS from the 11th century on, but especially of the 15th–17th centuries. Some of the works were transferred from Avila Cathedral in the 19th century.

N. Alvarez Solar-Quintes: 'La musicología en el Archivo histórico nacional', *Revista de archivos, bibliotecas y museos*, lxv (1958), 113

——. Biblioteca y Archivo Municipal, plaza Mayor 27, Madrid (*Mm*). The city library and archive owns works from the Teatro de la Cruz and Teatro Principe, especially *tonadillas* and music for 18th-century Spanish plays by Calderón, Lope de Vega and others. The Sbarbi collection consists of 18th-century sacred music. The library also has operas, symphonic works, and guitar music by Soler and others.

J. Subirá: *Catálogo de la sección de música de la Biblioteca municipal de Madrid* (Madrid, 1965–) [i: *Teatro menor: tonadillas y sainetes*]

——. Biblioteca Musical Circulante, calle Imperial 8, Madrid 5 (*Mam*). Otherwise known as the Biblioteca Municipal de Música, the library was founded in 1919 by the municipal administration as a public music library. Its source material spans the 12th–20th centuries, but is notable for the 18th-century *tonadillas* and a collection of musical works inspired by Cervantes's *Don Quixote*, beginning with a work by Purcell (1694). The library received the collections of the Casa Real de las Sicilias and of Alfonso de Bourbon y Braganza.

J. Espinós Orlando: *Catálogo general ilustrado de la Biblioteca musical* (Madrid, 1946, suppls. 1954, 1973); V. Espinós Moltó: *El Quijote en la música* (Barcelona, 1947)

——. Biblioteca Nacional, paseo de Calvo Sotelo 20, Madrid 1 (*Mn*). The National Library was founded in 1712 and a separate music section was established in 1875, although musical material is still held by the departments of MSS, rare books and incunabula. It receives copyright deposit copies of all Spanish publications. The library holds music MSS and autographs from the 9th century on, including Mozarabic chant, and examples of many musical genres up to the 19th century, including works by Ruperto Chapí and Gerardo Gombau, and several other 19th- and 20th-century Spanish composers. The holdings of printed works span the 16th–18th centuries and are rich in the writings of early theorists and organ, guitar and vihuela tablatures. Among the private libraries incorporated are those of Francisco Asenjo Barbieri, with many 17th- and 18th-century books on dance, and of Francisco de Paula Antonio de Bourbon.

J. Subirá and H. Anglès: *Catálogo musical de la Biblioteca nacional de Madrid* (Barcelona, 1946–51); J. Moll Roqueta: *Exposición de música sagrada española: catálogo* (Madrid, 1954) [lists 120 MS and printed 9th- to 18th-century works]; *Guía de la exposición de música antigua española: siglos IX a XVIII* (Madrid, 1958); H. Anglès: 'La música española para órgano de los siglos XVI–XVII conservada en la Biblioteca nacional de Madrid', *AnM*, xxi (1966), 141; J. Janini, J. Serrano and A. Mundó: *Manuscritos litúrgicos de la Biblioteca nacional* (Madrid, 1969); M. de Castro: *Manuscritos franciscanos de la Biblioteca nacional de Madrid* (Madrid, 1973) [includes music MSS]

——. Conservatorio Superior de Música, plaza de Isabel II, Madrid 13 (*Mc*). The conservatory library was founded with the school in 1830 and reorganized in 1872, when early music works were received from disbanded monasteries. An exceptional collection of printed 16th-century polyphony came from the monastery of Santiago de Uclés in Cuenca in 1873. Gifts from

members of the royal family (in particular Amadeo of Savoy, Isabel Francisca de Bourbon y Asis, and José Eugenio de Baviera y Bourbon) have included opera MSS and zarzuelas, many of them performed at the royal theatre, and a valuable portrait collection. Another set of (mainly MS) zarzuelas was the gift of the Sociedad General de Autores de España. Further noteworthy gifts include the chamber music received in 1952 from John Milanés, English consul to Madrid, unusual dance music in the bequest of José María Moreno Gil de Borja, the libraries of the composers Gerardo Gombau and Rogelio del Villar, and the music library of America House. The library also has the music works and administrative records of the Concert Society of Madrid; and there are first editions of Classical composers and autographs of famous 19th-century Spanish composers. As a copyright depository the conservatory receives copies of all music printed in Spain.

H. Anglès: 'Una col.leció de polifonia del segle XVI', *Estudis universitaris catalans*, xii (1927), 388 [lists works not in *EitnerQ*]

——. Palacio Real, plaza de Armería, Madrid (*Mp*). The most famous possession of the palace library is the Cancionero Musical de Palacio (*c*1500), which contains 458 accompanied Spanish songs, mostly villancicos. There are over 4000 opera MSS of the 18th century. The library also has 18th-century editions of chamber and symphonic works, collections of works for flageolet and *tambour de Basque*, and other Spanish folk music. The separate palace music archive, reorganized in 1914, contains further MSS and printed works.

J. Garcia Marcellán: *Catálogo del Archivo de música de la Real capilla de Palacio* (Madrid, 1938) [list does not indicate whether works are MS or printed; most titles in Sp. trans.]; J. Subirá: *El Teatro del Real palacio (1849–1851)* (Madrid, 1950) [pp.91–109 list music in *Mp*]

——. Real Academia de Bellas Artes de S Fernando, calle de Alcalá 13, Madrid (*Ma*). The Academy of Fine Arts was opened in 1752 but had no music section until 1873. The library has MS and printed works dating back to the 16th century but is strongest in chamber music of the 18th and early 19th centuries. There are some early music dictionaries and theoretical works, as well as some folkloric material.

J. Subirá: 'La música en la biblioteca de la Real academia', *AnM*, xi (1956), 111 [lists 18th- and early 19th-century works and the dictionaries]

MÁLAGA. Catedral, Archivo, calle de Molina Larios, Málaga (*MA*). The chapter archive has MSS of the 16th–19th centuries (Aguilera, Brito, Jommelli, Morales, Palestrina and others) and printed choirbooks of the 16th–18th centuries.

MONTSERRAT. Monasterio de S María, Montserrat, Barcelona (*MO*). The various libraries and archives of the monastery have some 8000 printed and 6000 MS volumes of music. Among them are 11th- to 15th-century choirbooks with Aquitanian, Catalan and German notation; polyphonic MSS of the 14th–18th centuries with works by Flemish, Spanish and Italian composers; keyboard MSS with several thousand pieces, most of them copied in the 18th century; theoretical treatises, and some autographs of famous Spanish composers.

R. B. Lenaerts: 'Niederländische polyphone Musik in der Bibliothek von Montserrat', *Festschrift Joseph Schmidt-Görg zum 60. Geburtstag* (Bonn, 1957), 196; M. Querol: 'Montserrat', *MGG* [lists important chant, keyboard and polyphonic MSS]

ORENSE. Catedral, Archivo, plaza del Trigo, Orense (*OR*). The cathedral archive has 35 choirbooks of 1737 to 1802 and later volumes for Offices and masses.

PALMA DE MALLORCA. Catedral, plaza de General Goded, Palma de Mallorca (*PAc*). The chapter archive has rich parchment volumes with Gregorian chant, early editions of major polyphonic composers, and MS works of the 17th and 18th centuries, many of them incomplete.

PAMPLONA. Catedral, Archivo, calle de Dormiteleria 5, Pamplona (*PAMc*). The cathedral archive has some 2000 musical items, including early masses, motets and other sacred works, chiefly by Spanish composers. There are also some *gozos*.

J. Goñi Gaztambide: 'Catálogo del Archivo catedral de Pamplona', *Príncipe de Viana*, xxii (1961)

PLASENCIA. Catedral, Archivo de Música, Plasencia (*P*). The music archive has MS partbooks of the 16th–18th centuries with masses, motets, villancicos, *Magníficat* settings and psalms, and a few printed works of the same genres.

S. Rubio: 'El archivo de música de la catedral de Plasencia', *AnM*, v (1950), 147 [catalogue]

SALAMANCA. Biblioteca Universitaria, plaza de la Universidad, Salamanca (*SAu*). The University Library has about 3000 music MSS, mainly of the 18th century. Among them are masses, *Magníficat* settings, arias and villancicos, some with accompanying instruments.

C. Gómez: 'Fondo musical de la capilla de la Universidad de Salamanca', *Música*, v (Madrid, 1953), 112 [catalogue]

——. Catedral, Archivo, plazuela de Anaya, Salamanca (*SA*). The archive has parchment Gregorian chant MSS and MS motets, villancicos and polyphonic masses. There are also MS works by the cathedral's *maestros de capilla* of the 17th–19th centuries.

SANTIAGO DE COMPOSTELA. Catedral, Archivo de Música, plaza de España, Santiago (*SC*). The cathedral archive and library have rich music holdings, including the famous 12th-century Calixtine MS.

L. Dittmer: 'Santiago de Compostela', *MGG*; J. López-Calo: *El archivo musical de la catedral de Santiago* (Cuenca, 1972; orig. in *Compostellanum*, iii–xi, 1958–66) [catalogue]

SARAGOSSA. Catedral, Archivo de Música, plaza de la Seo, Saragossa (*ZA*). The chapter and music archives have many MS and printed volumes of Spanish composers of the 16th and early 17th centuries. Most of the collection from the music archive of the Iglesia Metropolitana de la Virgen del Pilar (*Zvp*), consisting of MS and printed works of the 16th–18th centuries, has been combined with that of the cathedral.

P. Calahorra: *La música en Zaragoza en los siglos XVI y XVII* (Saragossa, 1972)

SEGOVIA. Catedral, Archivo, plaza del Generalísimo Franco, Segovia (*SE*). The chapter archive has a cancionero from the Real Alcazar of Segovia, with Flemish and Spanish repertory. There are also 16th-century MSS mainly by Spanish composers, and printed masses, motets and other works of the 16th–early 18th century.

H. Anglès: 'Un MS inconnu avec polyphonie du XVe siècle conservé à la cathédrale de Segovie', *AcM*, viii (1936), 6 [with detailed list of contents]

SEVILLE. Catedral, Biblioteca Capitular y Colombina, avenida de Queipo de Llano, Seville (*Sc*). The chapter library was founded in the 13th century and enlarged in the 16th century with the library of Ferdinand

Columbus (Sp. Hernando Colón). Most of this collection is no longer extant. The cathedral possesses the Seville cancionero of the second half of the 15th century, theoretical works copied in the 15th century, and other MSS of the 15th and 16th centuries. There are also 16th-century printed works, some by Attaingnant and Petrucci. The cathedral's Biblioteca del Coro has MS and printed works by Morales, Josquín, Willaert and others.

A. M. Huntington: *Catalogue of the Library of Ferdinand Columbus Reproduced in Facsimile from the Unique MS in the Columbine Library* (New York, 1905); H. Anglès: 'La musica conservada en la Biblioteca Colombina y en la catedral de Seville', *AnM*, ii (1947), 3–39; C. W. Chapman: 'Printed Collections of Polyphonic Music owned by Ferdinand Columbus', *JAMS*, xxi (1968), 34–84

SILOS. Monasterio Benedictino (Abadia) de S Domingo, Archivo, Silos, Burgos (*SI*). Founded in the 6th century, the monastery has 11th-century Mozarabic MSS with music for the Mass and Office. Research into Gregorian chant, especially that of the Visigothic period, is conducted by the monks. During the 1835 suppression of the monastery, many of the treasures were dispersed (some finally reaching *GB-Lbm* and *F-Pn*).

W. M. Whitehall: *Santo Domingo de Silos and Mozarabic Liturgy* (New York, 1938)

TARAZONA. Catedral, Archivo, Tarazona (*TZ*). The chapter archive has a 13th-century lectionary with Aquitanian notation, three parchment 15th-century missals, and 12 volumes of sacred works by Spanish and foreign composers, published in the 16th and early 17th centuries.

J. Sevillano: 'Catálogo musical del Archivo capitular de Tarazona', *AnM*, xvi (1961), 149

TOLEDO. Biblioteca Pública Provincial y Museo de la Santa Cruz, calle de Cervantes, Toledo (*Tp*). The collection of the public library includes liturgical MSS dating back to the 11th century. Among the early printed works are *El Delphin* by Narvaez (1538) and Esteban's *Reglas de canto piano* (1410). The chapter library has several Mozarabic MSS, some from the Parroquia S Justa y Rufina. Among the treasures are 34 polyphonic choirbooks with masses, *Magníficat* settings and many other works, by Guerrero, Josquin, Morales, Ribera, Torrentes, Victoria and others.

F. Rubio Piqueras: *Códices polifónicos toledanos* (Toledo, 1925); R. B. Lenaerts: 'Les MSS polyphoniques de la Bibliothèque capitulaire de Tolède', *IMSCR, v Utrecht 1952*, 276; R. Stevenson: 'The Toledo MS Polyphonic Choirbooks and some other Lost or Little Known Flemish Sources', *FAM*, xix (1973), 4 [detailed description of contents]

VALENCIA. Catedral, Archivo y Biblioteca, plaza de la Almoina, Valencia (*VAc*). The rich holdings of the cathedral archive and library include early chant MSS from the monastery of S Miguel de los Reyes and many sacred works of Spanish origin from the 16th–18th centuries.

J. B. Guzman and O. Badas: *Inventario de las obras musicales de la catedral de Valencia* (1881) [MS copy of catalogue also available in *Mn*, Department of MSS]; V. Ripollés: *El villancico i la cantata del segle XVIII a Valencia* (Barcelona, 1935) [lists works in *VAc*]; J. Climent: 'Obras vocales inéditas de Juan Cabanilles conservados en la catedral de Valencia', *AnM*, xvii (1962), 121; J. Climent: 'La música en Valencia durante el siglo XVII', *AnM*, xxi (1966), 211–41 [lists works in *VAc* and *VAcp*]; M. Palau: 'Valencia', *MGG*

——. Colegio y Seminario del Corpus Christi del Patriarca, calle de la Nave 1, Valencia (*VAcp*). The collection was founded with the chapel (1604) by Juan de Ribera and is one of the richest in Spain for sacred music, particularly 16th-century printed polyphonic works with 17th-century MSS, by Spanish and foreign composers. Various inventories dating from 1625 to the present are available in the college.

V. Ripollés: 'Fragmentos del epistolario de Pedrell (el tesoro musical de la Real capilla de Corpus Christi)', *Boletin de la Sociedad castellonense de cultura*, vi (1925), 278, vii (1926), 18, 125 [series of articles quoting from Pedrell's letters describing the music collection of *VAcp*]; J. Climent: 'La musica en Valencia durante el siglo XVII', *AnM*, xii (1966), 211–41 [lists works in *VAc* and *VAcp*; incl. some items from early inventories]; M. Palau: 'Valencia', *MGG*

VALLADOLID. Catedral Metropolitana, Archivo, Valladolid (*V*). The cathedral's music archive has a large collection of MS and early printed vocal and instrumental works, primarily of the 16th and early 17th centuries. There are also printed theoretical works by Bermudo, Cerone, Heyden, Santa María and others.

H. Anglès: 'El archivo musical de la catedral de Valladolid', *AnM*, iii (1948), 59–108 [lists MS and printed works mainly of the 16th century]; J. López-Calo: catalogue of the archive's 17th- to 19th-century holdings (in preparation)

VICH. Museo Episcopal, Biblioteca Capitular y Archivos Historicos, Palacio Episcopal, Vich (*VI*). The museum has liturgical books (sacramentaries, antiphoners, missals, prosaria etc) with music, and music treatises.

J. Gudiol: *Catàleg dels MSS anteriors al segle XVIII del Museu episcopal de Vich* (Barcelona, 1834, suppl. by E. Junyent, 1936)

SWEDEN (*S*)

Locations of instrumental music in Swedish and several foreign libraries are given in C. Nisser: *Svensk instrumentalkomposition 1770–1830: nominalkatalog* (Stockholm, 1943); 16th- and 17th-century printed music in Swedish libraries is well described in Å. Davidsson: *Catalogue critique et descriptif des imprimés de musique des XVIe et XVIIe siècles conservés dans les bibliothèques suédoises (excepté la Bibliothèque de l'Université royale d'Upsala)* (Uppsala, 1952); theoretical works from the same period are covered in the subsequent volume, Å. Davidsson: *Catalogue critique et descriptif des ouvrages théoriques sur la musique imprimés au XVIe et XVIIe siècles et conservés dans les bibliothèques suédoises* (Uppsala, 1953). Of particular interest are Å. Davidsson: 'Utländsk musiklitteratur från, 1700-talet i svenska bibliotek', *STMf*, xxxv (1953), 117, and xxxviii (1956), 153, and Å. Davidsson: *Studier rörande svenskt musiktryck före år 1750* (Uppsala, 1957) [with Ger. synopsis]. Informal but informative are F. Lindberg: 'A Survey of the Musical Resources of Scandinavia', *FAM*, iii (1956), 109, and Å. Davidsson: 'Cultural Background to Collections of Old Music in Swedish Libraries', *FAM*, xi (1964), 21. A rich source of information on music research material is the annual *Bulletin* (Stockholm, 1966–) of the Svenskt Musikhistoriskt Arkiv in Stockholm.

JÖNKÖPING. Per Brahegymnasiet, Residensgatan, 55590 Jönköping (*J*). Some 2000 printed chamber and orchestral works of the 18th and 19th centuries derive from the school's own concerts, the Musical Society (1817–39), the People's Choral Society (1853–c1864), and the band and chorus of the local Rifle Club (founded 1861).

G. Ruuth: *Katalog över äldre musikalier i Per Brahegymnasiet i Jönköping* (Stockholm, 1971); G. Ruuth: *Musikaliska Sällskapet i Jönköping 1779–1839* (Jönköping, 1973)

KALMAR. Stifts- och Gymnasiebiblioteket, Kalmar Kommun, Box 18, 38101 Kalmar 1 (*K*). The city library holds a small collection of 18th-century music MSS, including works by Corelli and Gluck and a group of anonymous chansons, mostly French; there are also several Lassus MSS.

KARLSTAD. Stadsbiblioteket, Musikavdelningen, Box 358, 65105 Karlstad (*KA*). The former Stifts- och Läroverksbibliotek was dispersed in 1970 and most of its collection went to the public library, including the Fryxell collection, which contains five 16th-century MSS and two gradual fragments of about 1475. There is a small chamber music collection formerly belonging to Count Carl Gustav Löwenhielm (1790–1858), which contains some interesting editions for basset-horn.

N. Lindahl: *Katalog över Fryxellska samlingen i Karlstads Stifts- och Läroverksbibliotek* (Karlstad, 1930)

LINKÖPING. Stifts- och Landsbiblioteket, Hunnebergsgatan 8, 58003 Linköping (*LI*). Among 16th-century works are several volumes of sacred songs, a set of partbooks for Neapolitan songs printed in Venice by Scotto (1565–6), and an MS collection of 42 chansons, madrigals and motets by Noë Faignient.

T. Noske: 'The Linköping Faignient-MS', *AcM*, xxxvi (1964), 152

LUND. Universitetsbiblioteket, Helgonabacken, Box 1010, 22103 Lund (*L*). Founded in 1671, the library has received depository copies since 1698. The collection includes the bequests of Baron Barnekow (printed 18th-century instrumental music) and the organist Hinrich Engelhart (early 18th-century works), and late 17th- and early 18th-century chamber, orchestral and vocal works from the conductor Friedrich Kraus. The bequest of the organist Emanuel Wenster included musical treatises and printed and MS music, with 35 cantatas by Boxberg and organ music by Buxtehude; in 1969 the library received the famous Schubert collection (many items of which are cited in Deutsch) owned by Otto Taussig, consul of Malmö.

NORRKÖPING. Stadsbiblioteket, Södra Promenaden 105, 60181 Norrköping (*N*). The library's collection was formerly kept by the De Geer family at Finspång Castle, and in 1904 it was acquired by the city of Norrköping. The holdings comprise many 17th-century works for solo instrument, especially lute and clavier, and many specimens of dance music. Rarities include a unique copy of a guitar tablature by R. Médard (1676) and early 17th-century French and English lute-songs.

B. Lundstedt: *Katalog öfver Finspongs bibliotek* (Stockholm, 1883)

SKARA. Stifts- och Landsbiblioteket, Biblioteksgatan 3, 53200 Skara (*SK*). The library of the diocese comprises an archive as well as public and research divisions. The collection includes some early sacred songbooks, and an organ or guitar tablature of 1659.

J. O. Ruden: 'Ett nyfunnet komplement till Dübensamlingen', *STMf*, xlvii (1965), 51 [inventory (with incipits) of organ–guitar tablature]

STOCKHOLM. Kungliga Biblioteket, Humlegården, 10241 Stockholm (*Sk*). The National Library also serves as the university library and has large holdings of Swedish printed music, much of it received since 1661 on deposit. There are also early liturgical MSS and rare printed works of the 16th–18th centuries, mainly French and German. In 1959 and 1969 some autographs of the composer Karl-Birger Blomdahl were acquired.

C.-G. Mörner: 'Rariteter ur en okatalogiserad notsamling i Kungl. biblioteket', *STMf*, xliii (1961), 273 [with Ger. summary]

——. Kungliga Musikaliska Akademiens Bibliotek, Nybrokajen 11, 11148 Stockholm (*Skma*). The library of the Royal Music Academy (founded in 1771) contains Sweden's richest music collection. It has works from the 16th century to the present but is especially rich in 18th-century music. The oldest printed works are 103 sacred and secular pieces of the 16th and 17th centuries, formerly in the possession of the German St Gertrude Church and the German School in Stockholm, and presented to the library in 1874. The collections of Baron Patrick Alströmer (one of the founders of the academy), of the Swedish society Utile Dulci (founded in 1766) and of the postmaster J. F. Hallardt (1726–94) all contain printed and MS instrumental and vocal music from the late Baroque to the early Classical period. In 1858 Duke P. A. d'Otrante donated his library of 18th-century printed music and MSS, consisting almost entirely of operas, arias and ensembles. Printed and MS operas, arias and ensembles from 1700 to 1858 were also donated to the library in 1860 by Count Gustaf Göran Gabriel Oxenstierna. In 1847 Johan Mazer (1790–1847) presented orchestral, choral and chamber music, chiefly of the 19th century. C. O. Boije af Gennäs's collection of guitar music was donated in 1924 and the library of Daniel Fryklund, formerly housed in Hälsingborg, has been divided between the academy and Stockholm Musikmuseet. The Berwald family archive was presented to the library in 1969. The academy's autographs are mainly by Swedish composers and those active in Sweden, from the Swedish Baroque composer J. H. Roman to the present day. Other Scandinavian and foreign composers are also represented (Nielsen, Albrechtsberger, Joseph and Michael Haydn). There is a collection of 15,000 letters.

M. Boheman and C. F. Hennerberg: *Katalog öfver Kungl. musikaliska akademiens bibliotek* (1905–10); C. F. Hennerberg: *Brevsamlingen i Kungl. musikaliska akademiens bibliotek* (Stockholm, 1927); C. Johansson: 'Något om Mazers musiksamling', *STMf*, xxxiii (1951), 142; C. Johannson: 'Studier kring Patrik Alströmers musiksamling', *STMf*, xliii (1961), 195 [with Eng. summary]; C. Johansson: Något om de äldre samlingarna i Kungl. musikaliska akademiens bibliotek', *Svenska musikperspektiv: minnesskrift vid Kungl. musikaliska akademiens 200-årsjubileum 1971* (Stockholm, 1971), 88 [with Eng. summary]

——. Kungliga Teaterns Bibliotek, Gustav Adolfs Torg, 11152 Stockholm (*St*). The library of the Royal Opera has a collection of vocal music, mostly operas, and some orchestral works, mostly ballets. Of particular note are the French 18th-century printed *opéras comiques* and the autographs of Swedish and foreign composers from the repertory of the Royal Orchestra, Stockholm's leading concert organization for many centuries. The older material of the theatre collection was deposited in the library of the Kungliga Musikaliska Akademien in 1965, but has since been returned.

——. Musikmuseet, Slottsbacken 6, 11130 Stockholm (*Sm*). The Music Museum (formerly Musikhistoriska Museet) centres its activities on folk instruments, but there are also holdings of printed and MS music, some of the latter from the Fryklund collection (most of which is in *Skma*), autographs of Swedish composers and letters of other musicians. The museum holds collections of Swedish folk music; literature on instruments, folk music and ethnomusicology; and the Archive of the Swedish Folk Music Commission.

'Inventeringar, Musikhistoriska Museet', *Svenskt musikhistoriskt arkiv bulletin*, i (1966), 11 [lists composers' names only, for holdings of MMS and Swed. printed music]

——. Stiftelsen Musikkulturens Främjande, Torstenssonsgatan 15, 11456 Stockholm (*Smf*). The Foundation for Furthering Musical Culture owns the collection of Rudolf Nydahl of Stockholm, consisting of about 1200 autograph compositions and MS copies, and some 4800 items of correspondence and other biographical documents. Besides many Swedish MSS from the 18th century on, a large part of the collection has considerable international significance. It also contains printed music and books of various periods, old instruments, souvenirs of musicians and iconography.

G. Holst: 'Stiftelsen musikkulturens främjande; förteckning över musikhandskrifter: musikalier, brev och biografica', *Svenskt musikhistoriskt arkiv bulletin*, viii (1972), 1–51

——. Stims Informationscentral för Svensk Musik, Tegnérlunden 3, 11185 Stockholm (*Sic*). The Swedish Music Information Centre was founded in 1962 to promote all types of music originating from the country. Its library has MS Swedish works from the mid-19th century on, and a large collection of Swedish popular music since 1900.

——. Svenskt Musikhistoriskt Arkiv, Strandvägen 82, 11527 Stockholm. The archive is a general documentation and information centre for Swedish music history. Besides collecting documents (concert programmes, copies of inventories and rare musical works), the centre assists scholars in locating sources, indexes current literature, makes systematic inventories of archival source material in Sweden and other Scandinavian countries and experiments with the retrieval of historical data by computer. The archive disseminates information on its own and other archival holdings by an annual *Bulletin* (1966–) and by a monographic series of documents, catalogues and studies entitled *Musik i Sverige* (1969–).

A. Helmer: 'The Swedish Archive of Music History', *FAM*, xiv (1967), 101; A. Helmer: 'Från källorna till forskarna' [From sources to researchers], *Svenska musikperspektiv: minnesskrift vid Kungl. musikaliska akademiens 200 årsjubileum 1971* (Stockholm, 1971), 308 [with Eng. summary]

——. Sveriges Radio, Oxenstiernsgatan 20, 10510 Stockholm (*Ssr*). Founded in 1925, the broadcasting library has amassed an extensive collection of autographs of Swedish composers as a result of commissioning works for radio and television performance. The library also has scores of 18th- and 19th-century dramatic works, as well as late 19th-century performance material for opera, operetta, vaudeville and revues. The musical property of several Swedish composers, including Karl-Birger Blomdahl, is held by the library. The general archives contain correspondence with composers, performers and other musical figures.

F. Lindberg: 'Sveriges radios musikbibliotek', *STMf*, xliii (1961), 227; F. Lindberg: 'Broadcasting Libraries and Archives as Music Research Centres', *FAM*, xiii (1966), 76; B. Wallner: 'Om Blomdahlarkivet', *Nutida musik*, iii (1972–3), 40

STRÄNGNÄS. Roggebiblioteket, Box 167, 15200 Strängnäs (*STr*). The library's collection stems from the former city Gymnasium and comprises 16th- and 17th-century printed music, with works by Lassus, Lechner, Kaspar Othmayr and others.

Å. Davidsson: 'En hoop discantzböcker i godt förhwar … någöt om Strängnäsgymnasiets musiksamling under 1600-talet', *Från biskop Rogge till Roggebiblioteket: studier utgivna till Strängnäs gymnasiums 350-årsjubileum*, ed. R. Lundström (Nyköping, 1976) [lists 25 music prints of the 17th century]

UPPSALA. Universitetsbiblioteket, Box 510, 75120 Uppsala (*Uu*). The largest library in Sweden, founded in 1620, it has received depository copies since 1692. Among the collections are printed and MS 16th-century music taken by King Gustavus Adolphus from Braniewo (Poland) in 1626 and from Mainz in 1631; the Düben collection donated in 1732, consisting of over 1500 17th-century MSS, among them 100 by Buxtehude, including autographs; the bequest of Fredrik Samuel Silverstolpe (1852), including in particular works by J. M. Kraus, partly autograph, together with autographs of W. A. Mozart and his son; the Gimo collection of Italian MS music of about 1760, donated by Gustaf Brun in 1971; Hugo Alfvén's musical autographs, received in 1960, and Gösta Nystroem's autographs, received in 1968. In addition the MS department has medieval MSS containing liturgical music, and letters of musicians.

R. Mitjana and Å. Davidsson: *Catalogue critique et descriptif des imprimés de musique des XVIe et XVIIe siècles conservés à la Bibliothèque de l'Université royale d'Upsala* (Uppsala, 1911–51); R. Engländer: 'Die Mozart-Skizzen der Universitätsbibliothek Uppsala', *STMf*, xxxvii (1955), 98; Å. Davidsson: *Musical Treasures in the University Library of Uppsala: Exhibition* (Uppsala, 1962); Å. Davidsson: *Catalogue of the Gimo Collection of Italian MS Music in the University Library of Uppsala* (Uppsala, 1963); B. Grusnick: 'Die Dübensammlung: ein Versuch ihrer chronologischen Ordnung', *STMf*, xlvi (1964), 27–82; xlviii (1966), 63–186 [detailed inventory]

VÄSTERÅS. Stadsbiblioteket, Biskopsgatan 2, Box 717, 72120 Västerås (*V*). One of Sweden's richest music collections during the 17th century, the city library (formerly the Stifts- och Landsbiblioteket) is now notable primarily for its 16th- and early 17th-century vocal works, especially by German composers.

W. Molér: *Förteckning över musikalier i Västerås Högre allmänna läroverks bibliotek t.o.m. 1850* (Västerås, 1917)

VÄXJÖ. Landsbiblioteket. Västra Esplanaden 7B, 35101 Växjö (*VX*). The library has a small music collection comprising 11 MSS of works from the 16th–18th centuries (by composers such as Crüger, Handl, Hassler, Lully and Volpius) and printed works from the 16th and 17th centuries, most anonymous though identified works are by Dressler, Lassus, Praetorius, Scheidt, Schütz and others.

VISBY. Landsarkivet, Visborgsgatan 1, 62101 Visby, Gotland (*VIl*). The archive contains about 100 autographs of the 19th century, mostly local folk music, and the collections of various city music societies comprising 19th-century printed works and documents from about 1836 onwards concerning local music activities.

SWITZERLAND (*CH*)

Brief general descriptions of Swiss music libraries are presented in E. Refardt: 'Musik in schweizerischen Bibliotheken', *AcM*, v (1933), 142, and in H. P. Schanzlin: 'Musik in schweizerischen Bibliotheken', *Musica*, xiii (1959), 475. Works listed in connection with preparations for *RISM* are given in H. P. Schanzlin: 'Musiksammeldrucke des 16. und 17. Jahrhunderts in schweizerischen Bibliotheken', *FAM*, iv (1957), 38 and 'Musiksammeldrucke des 18. Jahrhunderts in schweizerischen Bibliotheken', *FAM*, vi (1959), 20, and viii (1961), 26 [incl. suppl. to 16th- and 17th-century list]. Some assistance is afforded by the general compilation (with an index of subject specialities and text in Fr., Ger. and It.) of R. Wyler: *Archive, Bibliotheken und Dokumentationsstellen der Schweiz* (Berne, 3/1958); and liturgical MSS are presented in J. Stenzl: *Repertorium der liturgischen Musikhandschriften der Diözesen Sitten, Lausanne und Genf* (Fribourg, 1972–) [i: *Diözese Sitten*].

BASLE. Öffentliche Bibliothek der Universität Basel, Schönbeinstrasse 20, 4000 Basle (*Bu*). This is the country's richest music collection, with medieval treatises, 13th- to 15th-century liturgical MSS, and many 18th-century works. It holds the private libraries of the Schweizerische Musikforschende Gesellschaft, with an extensive collection of works by Swiss composers; the Lucas Sarasin library and the holdings of the Basle Collegium Musicum, with 18th-century symphonic MSS; part of the K. Geigy-Hagenbach autograph collection; and the library of B. Amerbach.

J. Richter: *Katalog der Musik-Sammlung auf der Universitätsbibliothek in Basel* (Leipzig, 1892); *Catalog der Schweizerischen Musikbibliothek*, i: *Musikgeschichte und theoretische Werke* (Basle, 1906) [no further vols. pubd]; E. Refardt: *Katalog der Musikabteilung der Öffentlichen Bibliothek der Universität Basel und der in ihr enthaltenen Schweizerischen Musikbibliothek*, i: *Musikalische Kompositionen* (Basle, 1925) [no further vols. pubd]; R. Sondheimer: 'Sinfonien aus dem 18. Jahrhundert in den Basler Sammlungen Lucas Sarasin und Collegium musicum', *Kongressbericht: Basel 1924*, 321; H. Zehntner: 'Die handschriftlichen Nachlässe von schweizer Komponisten in der Universitätsbibliothek Basel', *Festschrift Karl Schwarber* (Basle, 1949), 297; H. Zehntner: 'Handschriftliche Musiknachlässe in Schweizer Bibliotheken', *IAML*, ii *Lüneburg 1950*, 41 [discusses 19th-century composers' MSS]; E. Refardt: *Thematischer Katalog der Instrumentalmusik des 18. Jahrhunderts in den Handschriften der Universitätsbibliothek Basel* (Berne, 1957); H. Zehntner: 'Musikerbriefe in der Universitätsbibliothek Basel', *FAM*, xiii (1966), 140; M. Walter: *Miszellen zur Musikgeschichte* (Berne, 1967) [see chaps. 'Musikalische Seltenheiten' and 'Musikalische Erst- und Frühdrucke der Universitätsbibliothek Basel']

BERNE. Bürgerbibliothek, Münstergasse 63, 3000 Berne 7. In 1951 the Bürgerbibliothek separated from the Stadt- und Universitätsbibliothek Bern with the entire MS collection of the former combined library. There are many medieval MSS from the 9th century (including missals, psalters, antiphoners etc), some with neumes, and a small collection of 17th- and 18th-century MS copies, mostly works of Italian and French chamber music and symphonies.

H. Hagen: *Catalogus codicum bernensium* (Berne, 1875); *Schätze der Bürgerbibliothek* (Berne, 1953); *Bibliotheca bernensis 1974: Festgabe* (Berne, 1974)

——. Schweizerische Landesbibliothek, Hallwylstrasse 15, 3003 Berne (*BEl*). The Swiss National Library (founded in 1895) collects all material published in Switzerland and all Helvetica published abroad; this programme includes music titles. The library received the collection of the composer and Gluck scholar Josef Liebeskind, consisting of operas and symphonic works, with some works of Gluck and Dittersdorf; it also holds a collection of printed and unpublished compositions by members of the Schweizerischer Tonkünstlerverein. The MS collection includes autographs by Ernest Bloch and Othmar Schoeck.

K. Joss: *Katalog der Schweizerischen Landesbibliothek: Musik, Werke der Mitglieder des Schweizerischen Tonkünstlervereins veröffentlicht von 1848 bis 1925* (Berne, 1927); E. Wissler: *Verzeichnis der handschriftlichen Musikalien* (Berne, 1938); *Fünfzig Jahre Schweizerische Landesbibliothek 1895–1945* (Berne, 1945) [see esp. chaps. 'Die Musikalien' and 'Die Musik-Sammlung Liebeskind']; I. Lauterberg: *L'établissement du catalogue des oeuvres musicologiques de la collection Liebeskind à la Bibliothèque nationale à Berne: Sammlung Liebeskind* (Berne, ?1970)

——. Stadt- und Universitätsbibliothek, Münstergasse 61, 3011 Berne (*BEsu*). The library has its origins in the Chorherrenstift school library (founded in 1528), and until 1951 was connected with the city's Bürgerbibliothek, which now holds all the MSS of the former joint collection. The university's collection is rich in Swiss hymnbooks, particularly from Berne (printed in the 17th and 18th centuries), and leaflets with sacred and secular folksongs.

Bibliotheca bernensis 1974: Festgabe (Berne, 1974)

EINSIEDELN. Benediktinerkloster, Musikbibliothek, 8840 Einsiedeln (*E*). Founded in the 10th century, the monastery holds MSS from its own and from other Benedictine houses. The collection includes many liturgical works (including a 10th-century gradual), and sacred and secular works of the 18th–20th centuries; much of the music (oratorios, symphonies, concertos and even operas) was performed in the monastery.

G. Meier: *Catalogus codicum manuscriptorum* (Leipzig, 1899); P. Vetter: 'Einsiedeln', *MGG*

GENEVA. Bibliothèque Publique et Universitaire, Promenade des Bastions, 1211 Geneva 4 (*Gpu*). The library's notable holdings include several early missals, a collection of works by Geneva composers, and the library of R.-A. Mooser, whose collection is rich in Russian music and musicological writings, including works by foreigners resident in Russia. Rarities include editions issued in Moscow and St Petersburg in the 18th century.

Catalogue de la Bibliothèque publique de Genève (Geneva, 1875–99, continuing suppls.) [see section on 'Beaux-arts']

LAUSANNE. Bibliothèque Cantonale et Universitaire, place de la Riponne 6, 1005 Lausanne (*LAcu*). Since 1938 the library has received depository copies of everything published in the Vaud canton. In 1965 the library acquired the large collection of the composer François Olivier (*d* 1948) which includes his own works and many by other composers.

J.-L. Matthey: *Inventaire du fonds musical François Olivier* (Lausanne, 1971)

LUCERNE. Zentralbibliothek, Sempacherstrasse 10, 6002 Lucerne (*Lz*). The Central Library consists of the combined Kantonsbibliothek and Bürgerbibliothek. It has 100 works (in 300 partbooks) from the former monastery of St Urban, including ten early antiphoners and graduals, 18th-century sacred music chiefly by Bavarian monastic composers, and printed 18th-century symphonic music. It also holds the collection of the Allgemeine Musikgesellschaft Luzern.

W. Jerger: 'Die Musikpflege in der ehemaligen Zisterzienserabtei St. Urban (mit Katalog neu aufgefundener Musikdrucke des 18. Jahrhunderts)', *Mf*, vii (1954), 386; *Katalog der Musikalien der Allgemeinen Musikgesellschaft* (MS, 1958); catalogue of printed music (in preparation)

NEUCHÂTEL. Bibliothèque Publique, place Numa-Droz 3, 2000 Neuchâtel (*N*). The library has a collection of 18th-century Italian MSS, chiefly opera and symphony. The bequest of Felix Bover contained about 400 16th- to 19th-century psalters in many languages. From P.-A. du Peyrou came autographs of J.-J. Rousseau (forming part of the library's large Rousseau collection).

Catalogue de la Bibliothèque de Neuchâtel (1861, continuing suppls.); Z. Estreicher: 'Le fonds de musique ancienne de la Bibliothèque', *Bibliothèque et musées de la ville de Neuchâtel* (Neuchâtel, 1949); J. M. Bonhôte: 'La collection de psautiers de la Bibliothèque de la ville', *Jb für Liturgik und Hymnologie*, vii (1962), 182 [partial catalogue]

RHEINFELDEN. Christkatholisches Pfarramt, 4310 Rheinfelden (*R*). The parish office owns the library of the former Chorherrenstift St Martin, with about 150 MS and printed sacred and secular vocal and instrumental works, including symphonies of Gyrowetz, Haydn, Holzbauer, Stamitz and others.

W. Mahrer: 'Musikalische Funde in der Stiftsbibliothek zu St. Martin', *Christkatholisches Kirchenblatt*, lxxvii (1954), 186; H. P. Schanzlin: 'Kirchenmusik in der Stiftsbibliothek zu St. Martin', *KJb*, xliii (1959), 84 [lists about 75 sacred MSS of 1750–1850]

ST GALL. Stiftsbibliothek, Klosterhof 6, 9000 St Gall (*SGs*). The splendid library of the former monastery has about 200 MSS of musical importance, spanning the 8th–18th centuries. Among them are liturgical works, treatises, and church and folksong books chiefly of the 15th and 16th centuries.

G. Scherrer: *Verzeichnis der Handschriften der Stiftsbibliothek von St Gallen* (Halle, 1875); J. M. Clark: *The Abbey of St. Gall as a Centre of Literature and Art* (Cambridge, 1926) [with list of MSS]; D. J. Rittmayer-Iselin: 'St. Gallen', *MGG*; J. Duft: *Gesangskunst – Buchkunst: Handschriften aus dem 8. bis 18. Jahrhundert in der Stiftsbibliothek St. Gallen* (St Gall, 1971) [exhibition catalogue]

ZURICH. Zentralbibliothek. Zähringerplatz 6, 8025 Zurich (*Zz*). The library (also known as the Kantons-, Stadt- und Universitätsbibliothek), was founded in 1919. Its department of MSS has liturgical music MSS of the 10th–15th centuries, some from the Rheinau monastery. The music collection includes organ treatises, 16th-century organ music, 18th-century editions, hymnbooks, Swiss songbooks of the 19th and 20th centuries, and autographs of Swiss composers. On deposit is the collection of the Allgemeine Musikgesellschaft Zürich (founded in 1812 from organizations existing since the end of the 16th century). Its holdings are rich in first and early editions of German and Italian Baroque composers, including psalms, masses, orchestral works, trios, sacred concertos, and sacred and secular cantatas and oratorios of the 17th century and the first half of the 18th. In 1973 the library began administering the extensive collection of Bernhard Päuler, containing many first and early editions of chamber music of the Classical and Romantic periods. The collection of Erwin R. Jacobi, with 15th- to 20th-century music and writings (including autographs and other MSS), was purchased in 1974. The holdings of the Czesław Library and Foundation will also be deposited in the library.

E. Gagliardi: *Katalog der HSS der Zentralbibliothek Zürich, ii: Neuere Handschriften seit 1500* (Zurich, 1931–49); L. C. Mohlberg: *Katalog der Handschriften der Zentralbibliothek Zürich, i: Mittelalterliche Handschriften* (Zurich, 1932–52); E. Schenk: 'Die österreichischer Musiküberlieferung der Züricher Zentralbibliothek', *Festschrift Josef Bick* (Vienna, 1948), 576; P. Sieber: 'Die Bibliothek der Allgemeinen Musikgesellschaft Zürich', *IAML*, ii *Lüneburg 1950* [with partial list of works]; G. Walter: *Katalog der gedruckten und handschriftlichen Musikalien des 17. bis 19. Jahrhunderts im Besitze der Allgemeinen Musikgesellschaft Zürich* (Zurich, 1960) [omits works by composers born after 1850 and writings about music]; M. Bircher: 'Von Boethius bis Hindemith: eine Zürcher Sammlung von Erstausgaben zur Geschichte der Musiktheorie', *Librarium*, xiii (1970), 134 [description of the Jacobi collection]; R. Puskás: *Musikbibliothek Erwin R. Jacobi ... The Music Library of Erwin R. Jacobi: Rare Editions and Manuscripts: Catalogue* (Zurich, rev., enlarged 3/1973)

UNION OF SOVIET SOCIALIST REPUBLICS (*USSR*)
Information about holdings is included in M. Elmer: 'Notes on Catalogs and Cataloging in some Major Music Libraries of Moscow and Leningrad', *Notes*, xviii (1960–61), 545. Liturgical musical MSS are included in A. I. Rogov: *Svedeniya o nebol'shikh sobraniyakh slavyano-russikikh rukopisey v SSSR* [Information about a small collection of Slavonic–Russian MSS in the USSR] (Moscow, 1962). A collection of articles surveying theatrical and musical MS materials in various Soviet repositories is in A. D. Alexeyev and I. F. Petrovskaya: *Teatr i muzïka: dokumentï i materialï* (Moscow and Leningrad, 1963). MSS, printed material, instruments and documents concerning musical life are described in

L. Korabel'nikova: 'Materialy muzyczne w zbiorach ZSSR (archiwa, muzea, biblioteki)' [Musical material in Soviet collections (archives, museums, libraries)], *Muzyka*, xii/3 (1967), 71. Among other rich source data, a list of 51 musical MSS (11th–15th centuries) in libraries of Kiev, Leningrad and Moscow is provided by M. Velimirović: 'The Present Status of Research in Slavic Chant', *AcM*, xliv (1972), 235. Besides offering much general and useful information, an index with many references to music is in P. K. Grimsted: *Archives and MS Repositories in the USSR: Moscow and Leningrad*, Studies of the Russian Institute, Columbia University (Princeton, 1972). An informal account of music collections in Moscow and Leningrad appears in B. Schwarz: *Music and Musical Life in Soviet Russia, 1917–1970* (New York, 1972), 406ff. 335 institutions (with data about their services, collections and relevant literature) are listed in I. Koltypina, ed.: *Muzïkal'nïye biblioteki i muzïkal'nïye fondï v bibliotekakh SSSR: spravochnik* [Music libraries and music collections in Soviet libraries: a guide] (Moscow, 1972), issued by the Lenin State Library.

KIEV. Tsentral'naya Naukova Biblioteka, Akademiya Nauk URSR, ulitsa Vladimirska 62, Kiev 17 (*Kan*). The Central Scientific Library of the Ukrainian Academy of Sciences receives depository copies of everything published in the Ukrainian Republic and has the right to purchase all Soviet publications. The separate music section has a wide assortment of foreign, Russian and Ukrainian music, the last being most numerous. The collection assembled by the Counts Razumovsky comprises over 2500 works of the 18th and early 19th centuries: operas, oratorios, cantatas, masses, symphonic and chamber music. The library also has publications of the Soviet period, including works of the early Revolutionary period, contemporary music, musicological works and periodicals. There are special catalogues for the Razumovsky collection, Ukrainian folklore, and works for *bajan*, among others.

Biblioteka Akademii nauk URSR (Kiev, 1971)

LENINGRAD. General literature: I. V. Golubovsky, ed.: *Muzïkal'nïy Leningrad 1917–1957* (Leningrad, 1958) [esp. 'Biblioteki i muzei', pp.351–428, which briefly describes MS and printed musical material in 28 libraries and museums]; A. S. Mïl'nikov: *Rukopisnïye fondï leningradskikh khranilishch: kratkiy spravochnik po fondam bibliotek, muzeyev nauchno-issledovatel'skikh i drugikh uchrezhdenii* [MS collections of Leningrad repositories: brief guide to collections of libraries, museums, scientific investigatory and other institutions] (Leningrad, 1970)

——. Biblioteka Akademii Nauk SSSR, Birzhovaya liniya 1, Leningrad V-164 (*Lan*). Founded in 1714, the library has been part of the USSR Academy of Sciences since 1725. The MS and Rare Book Division grew out of the personal library of Peter the Great and his family. MSS include early Greek and Latin as well as 12th- to 18th-century MSS from western Europe. Among important music holdings is a 17th-century keyboard MS (QN 204) acquired in the first quarter of the 18th century, a unique source for three pieces by Sweelinck. The library receives national depository copies.

A. Curtis: preface to *Dutch Keyboard Music of the 16th and 17th Centuries*, MMN, iii (1961), xi–xvii; E. P. Faidel' and others: *Biblioteka Akademii nauk SSSR, 1714–1964: bibliograficheskiy ukazatel'* (Leningrad, 1964) [complete bibliography of books and articles related to the library]

——. Biblioteka Leningradskoy Gosudarstvennoy Konservatoriy imeni N. A. Rimskovo-Korsakova, ulitsa Brodskiy 2, Leningrad 190000 (*Lk*). The library has many early theoretical treatises and 18th-century musical works. The MS Division (Rukopisnïy Otdel), at Teatral'naya ploshchad' 3, has rich holdings of autograph and copied music, as well as correspondence of musicians of the 19th and early 20th centuries, both Russian and foreign. There are also a few items of the 18th and early 19th centuries. Composers most richly represented are Borodin, Glazunov, Musorgsky and Rimsky-Korsakov. The MS Division also houses the large archive of the late 19th-century Patronage Council for the Encouragement of Russian Composers and Musicians.

'Biblioteka ordena Lenina Konservatorii imeni N. A. Rimskovo-Korsakova', in I. V. Golubovsky: *Muzïkal'nïy Leningrad* (Leningrad, 1958), 359; V. G. Putsko: 'Maloizvestnïye rukopisnïye sobraniya Leningrada', *Trudï Otdela drevnerusskoy literaturï AN SSSR*, xxv (1970), 346 [mentions the library's lesser-known early MSS]

——. Tsentral'naya Muzïkal'naya Biblioteka Gosudarstvennovo Akademicheskovo Teatra Operï i Baleta imeni S. M. Kirova, ulitsa Zodchevo Rossi 2, Leningrad (*Ltob*). Founded in 1870, the library originated with the scores of the St Petersburg Imperial Theatre. The collection is now one of the largest for Russian MS music, especially opera and ballet. There are autograph scores of almost all important Russian composers and a vast collection of letters and other personal papers of musicians. The library also contains some old and new printed works, especially theatre music. A collection of 18th-century Italian works, chiefly MS, stems partly from contemporary operatic performances given in Russia, but also includes some sacred works.

R.-A. Mooser: 'Catalogue d'oeuvres italiennes du 18e siècle, conservées à Léningrad', *RdM*, xxv (1946), 29; 'Tsentral'naya muzïkal'naya biblioteka ordena Lenina Akademicheskovo teatra operï i baleta imeni S. M. Kirova', in I. V. Golubovsky: *Muzïkal'nïy Leningrad* (Leningrad, 1958), 366

——. Gosudarstvennaya Ordena Trudovovo Krasnovo Znameni Publichnaya Biblioteka imeni M. E. Saltïkova-Shchedrina, Sadovaya ulitsa 18, Leningrad D-69 (*Lsc*). Originally established in the 18th century by Catherine the Great, the library was opened in 1814, since when it has received depository copies of everything published in the country. The collection was also built up from gifts (including many from important composers), since 1850 by purchasers, and by exchange of duplicates with foreign libraries. Among its holdings of printed music, three-fifths were published in the USSR since the Revolution, but remaining works include 18th-century Russian imprints, French, Italian and other works published in the 16th and 17th centuries, French and Italian opera collections of the 17th and 18th centuries, and French Revolutionary works of Gossec, Méhul and others. The MS Division (Otdel Rukopisei, earlier known as the Depo Manuskriptov) is the largest in the nation. Besides important early liturgical works, the division has the personal archives of Borodin, Glinka, Musorgsky, Rimsky-Korsakov, Rubinstein and other composers, as well as other material for documentation and musicological research. A large collection of the personal papers of Diderot is kept in the division, while the extensive personal library of Voltaire and the material he collected for Catherine the Great form a special collection in the library.

J.-B. Thibaut: *Monuments de la notation ekphonétique et hagiopolite de l'église grecque ... conservés à la Bibliothèque impériale de Saint-Pétersbourg* (St Petersburg, 1913/R1976); A. N. Rimsky-Korsakov:

Muzïkal'nïy sokrovishcha rukopisnovo otdeleniya Gosurdarstvennoy publichnoy biblioteki imeni M. E. Saltïkova-Shchedrina: obzor muzkal'nïkh fondov [Musical treasures of the Department of MSS of the Leningrad M. E. Saltïkov-Shchedrin Public Library: survey of music collections] (Leningrad, 1938); A. S. Lyapunova: *Rukopisi M. I. Glinki: katalog* (Leningrad, 1950) [supersedes the 1898 catalogue of Glinka MSS by N. Findeyzen]; O. Golubeva: 'The Saltykov-Shchedrin Library, Leningrad', *Book Collector*, iv (1955), sum., 99 [devoted mainly to the MS Division, with helpful bibliography]; V. Baresenkov: 'The Saltykov-Scedrin State Public Library', *UNESCO Bulletin for Libraries*, xi (1957), 32; L. N. Pavlova-Sil'vanskaja and A. A. Rackova: 'Le département de la musique de la Bibliothèque publique de Léningrad', *FAM*, viii (1960), 1; V. M. Barashenkov and others: *Istoriya Gosudarstvennoy ordena Trudovovo Krasnovo Znameni publichnoy biblioteki imeni M. E. Saltïkova-Shchedrina* (Leningrad, 1963) [history for 150th anniversary of the library, with summary of major acquisitions and activities, and lists of catalogues and documents]

——. Leningradskiy Gosudarstvennïy Institut Teatra, Muzïki i Kinematografii, Arkhiv Rukopisnïkh i Pervopechatnïkh Materialov [Archive of MS and Early Printed Materials], Isaakiyevskaya ploshchad' 5 (*Lit*). The rich music MS material of the archive comes from a variety of sources and has a complicated history dating back to 1902, when plans for a museum were formulated. In 1921 it came under the administration of the Leningrad PO and took the name Music History Museum (Muzïkal'no-istoricheskiy Muzei), also incorporating holdings of the former memorial museums for Glinka and Rubinstein. In 1932 it was put under the administration of the Hermitage but in 1940 was reorganized under the Scientific Research Institute of Theatre and Music (Nauchno-Issledovatel'skiy Institut Teatra i Muzïki). Holdings related to musical history and culture date from the 18th century to the present, with large amounts of material devoted to Rimsky-Korsakov, Glinka and Borodin. There is an interesting collection of 18th-century opera, operetta and ballet MSS, some autograph, by former court composers. A comprehensive reference collection in many languages is concerned with music, drama and cinema. The institute's Museum of Musical Instruments houses some 2500 instruments, a large quantity of iconographic materials, music and literature on the history of instruments. A full description of the institute's archival holdings is in preparation.

I. V. Golubovsky: *Muzïkal'nïy Leningrad* (Leningrad, 1958), 400ff [describes the former Historiographical Cabinet and Rimsky-Korsakov Museum and Archive, both consolidated in the institute's present archive]; O. Seaman: 'An Unknown Leningrad Museum', *Tempo* (1961–2), no.60, p.17

——. Leningradskiy Gosudarstvennïy Teatral'nïy Muzey, Rukopisnïy Otdel [MS Division], ploshchad' Ostrovskovo 6 (*Lt*). Since its foundation in 1918 the museum has become the nation's largest and most important collection of holdings related to the history of theatre and musical culture in the USSR and abroad. The museum collections of the Aleksandrinsky, Mariinsky and Mikhaylovsky theatres form the basis, but there are also many private papers of people active in theatre and music, and other related documents dating from the 1780s to the present. The museum also has a collection of many different types of theatrical and musical recordings.

——. Notnaya Biblioteka Leningradskovo Komiteta po Radioveshchaniyu i Televideniyu, Malaia Sadovaia 2, Leningrad D-11. Since 1924 the library has been collecting original scores of Leningrad composers, but its present large store dates chiefly from World War II.

MOSCOW. Gosudarstvennaya Ordena Lenina Biblioteka SSSR imeni V. I. Lenina, Prospekt Kalinina 3, Moscow (*Ml*). The library was founded in 1862, since which time it has been collecting music. A separate music department was opened in 1960, but some musical works (MSS with 12th-century hook notation, autographs of most important Russian composers, etc) remain in the MS Division (ulitsa Frunze 6). The library holds foreign editions from the 17th century on and Russian music published since the 18th century. There are vast folklore holdings and first editions of Bach, Beethoven, Schumann and many others. This foremost national library, constituting the country's largest collection of printed works, receives three depository copies of everything published in the USSR.

I. M. Kudryavtsev: *Sobraniya D. V. Razumovskovo i V. F. Odoyevskovo: arkhiv A. V. Razumovskovo: opisaniya* [Collections of D. V. Razumovsky and V. F. Odoyevsky and the Razumovsky archive] (Moscow, 1960) [catalogue of 170 MSS, chiefly sacred music of the 15th to the 19th centuries, and of the biographical material, papers, letters etc in the archive]

——. Gosudarstvennïy Tsentral'nïy Muzey Muzïkal'noy Kul'turï imeni M. I. Glinki, Georgiyevskiy pereulok 4, Moscow K-9 (*Mcm*). Founded in 1948, the museum is one of the largest and richest repositories in the world for MSS related to music. Many of the MSS were transferred after 1960 from the Moscow Conservatory, and the museum also absorbed the holdings of the Nikolay Rubinstein Museum. Personal archives, both compositions and papers, include those of Tchaikovsky, Musorgsky, Skryabin, Prokofiev, Shostakovich and many other composers, conductors, critics, folklorists, historians and theoreticians. The museum has the Beethoven sketchbooks known as the 'Wielhorski' and the 'Moscow'. The archives of the Moscow Conservatory and of the Russian Musical Society are among many other institutional collections. The museum also collects folk and historical instruments, books on music, programmes, clippings, periodicals, printed music (some with composers' annotations), and microfilms and photostats of rare music held elsewhere. The recording department is being developed as the national archive and holds chiefly recordings made in the USSR or foreign recordings of Russian composers. A new building is under construction. The museum has issued centenary exhibition catalogues of Haydn, Handel, Chopin and Mozart; catalogues of autographs of individual composers contained in the collection: Balakirev, Tchaikovsky, Rakhmaninov and Rimsky-Korsakov; and a catalogue of all Beethoven autographs in various USSR libraries.

——. Gosudarstvennaya Konservatoriya imeni P. I. Chaykovskovo, Nauchnaya Muzïkal'naya Biblioteka imeni S. I. Taneyeva, ulitsa Gertsena 13, Moscow 103871 (*Mk*). The library was opened in 1860 with the personal collections of Anton and Nikolay Rubinstein. In 1869 the widow of V. F. Odoyevsky donated his collection of folk material, works on ancient Russian church music, 18th- and early 19th-century French and German writings on composers and acoustics, French works on the philosophy and aesthetics of music, and musical dictionaries. Taneyev's music theory library was acquired in 1924. The conservatory regularly receives foreign editions and is notable for its excellent reference collection of all periods and in all languages. There are also many first editions and composers' annotated copies, as well as autographs of such composers as Beethoven, Berlioz, Rossini and Mozart.

Nauchnaya muzïkal'naya Biblioteka imeni S. I. Taneyeva (Moscow, 1966); B. Krader: 'Folk Music Archive of the Moscow Conservatory', *Folklore and Folk Music Archivist*, x (1967–8), 13–46

YUGOSLAVIA (*YU*)

The article 'Music Libraries and Collections in Yugoslavia', *Muzička enciklopedija*, ii (Zagreb, 1963), 251, was prepared by S. D. Klajn (for Serbian libraries), V. Bonifačić (for Croatian libraries) and L. Zepič (for Slovenian libraries). Musical material in Koper (Capodistria), Ljubljana, Maribor, Novo Mesto and Ptuj is listed in J. Höfler and I. Klemenčic: *Glasbeni rokopisi in tiski na Slovenskem do leta 1800: Katalog/Music MSS and Printed Music in Slovenia before 1800: Catalogue* (Ljubljana, 1967); and material in Dubrovnik, Hvar, Split, Zadar and Zagreb is inventoried in V. Bonifačić: 'Music Libraries and Collections in Croatia', *Arti musices* (1970), 47 [special issue].

According to law the national library of each republic receives two copies of each work published within that republic. One copy is sent to the national libraries of the other republics and to autonomous provinces. A tenth copy is sent to the Belgrade Jugoslovenski Bibliografski Institut.

BELGRADE. Narodna Biblioteka N. R. Srbije, ul. Knez Mihailova 56, Belgrade (*Bn*). The Serbian National Library (founded in 1832) was completely destroyed in 1941, and during 1973 it was installed in a new building.

L. Stojanović: *Katalog Narodne biblioteke u Beogradu: rukopisi i stare stampene knjige* [Catalogue of the National Library in Belgrade: MSS and old printed books] (Belgrade, 1903); D. Stefanović: 'Izgoreli neumski rukopis br. 93 beogradske Narodne biblioteke–jedini poznati musička spomenik iz srpskog srednjeg veka' [The burnt neumed MS 93 in the Belgrade National Library – the only known Serbian musical document of the Middle Ages], *Bibliothekar*, xiii (1961), 379

DUBROVNIK. Knjižnica Samostana Dominikanaca, Vrata Ploča 1, Dubrovnik (*Dsd*). The library of the Dominican monastery has some medieval neumed MSS, and music incunabula of Boethius and Gaffurius.

T. Kaeppeli and H. Schooner: *Les manuscrits médievaux de St. Dominique de Dubrovnik: catalogue sommaire* (Rome, 1965), esp. 11ff

——. Franjevački Samostan 'Mala Braća', Biblioteka, Dubrovnik (*Dsmb*). The library of the monastery of the Franciscans Minor has over 6000 items of MS and printed secular and sacred music, some of it received from Dubrovnik aristocracy and citizens during the 19th century. Secular works include compositions by local musicians, some of them members of the Sorkočević family.

A. Vidaković: 'Uredenje glazbenog arhiva Male braće u Dubrovniku' [The music archive of the Franciscans Minor in Dubrovnik], *Ljetopus JAZU*, lxiii (1959), 535

HVAR. Kaptol, Hvar. The cathedral chapter library has several liturgical fragments of the 12th–14th centuries, some theoretical treatises of the 16th and 17th centuries, and a group of compositions of figural music by Josip Raffaelli.

LJUBLJANA. Narodna in Univerzitetna Knjižnica, Turjaška 1, Ljubljana (*Lu*). The National and University Library was founded in 1774; during the reforms of Joseph II (1781) it received collections from dissolved monasteries (the Jesuits of Ljubljana, monasteries of Bistra and Sticna), including Gregorian chant MSS. The library also received gifts from private scholars and collectors, and after World War II from the Federal Collection Centre for confiscated national property. The music collection has more than 50,000 items, including a collection of Renaissance music assembled in the early 17th century by the Bishop of Ljubljana; MS and printed instrumental music of the Classical period (including first editions of Haydn and Mozart); theatre music connected with performances of German and Italian opera companies; and the archives of the former Academia Philharmonicorum (founded in 1701), donated by its successor the Glasbena Matica. The library has all the works (some in photocopy) of the composer J. G. Carniolus.

——. Semeniska Knjižnica, Dolnicarjeva 4, Ljubljana. The Seminary Library was founded in 1701 as a public library by the members of the Academia Operosorum. It possesses many contemporary editions of the librettos of Baroque operas and oratorios.

PTUJ. Ljudska in Študijska Knjižnica, Trg. Svobode 1/II, 62250 Ptuj. Founded in 1948, the reference library has over 60 MSS of early Classical harpsichord music, including 30 concertos. The collection probably originated with the Attems family, owners of Wurmberg Castle outside Ptuj. Among the composers represented are Hasse, Monn, Scheibl, Sennft, Steinbacher, Wagenseil and Zechner.

ZAGREB. Hrvatski Glazbeni Zavod, Gundulićeva ul. 6, 41000 Zagreb (*Zha*). The Croatian Music Institute was founded in 1827 as the 'Musikverein', and took its present name in 1925. The library possesses many important autographs of Croatian composers, as well as books and an archive of documents for the study of Croatian music history, in particular of the 19th and 20th centuries. In 1935 some 3000 MS and printed works were received from the collection of Nikola Udina Algarotti (*d* Vienna, 1838), including first editions and MSS of Viennese composers. Holdings of Yugoslav composers include works of Giornovichi, Lukačić, Zajc, Kunc and Papandopulo.

——. Jugoslavenska Akademija Znanosti i Umjetnosti, Arhiv, Strossmayerov trg 2, 41000 Zagreb (*Za*). The archive of the Yugoslav Academy of Sciences and Arts has MSS and fragments of the 13th–15th centuries in neumatic and square choral notation. There is also a collection of old Slavonic (Glagolithic) texts written in 1556 according to earlier models, some with neumes. The MS collection of works (dating from about 1625) by Dalmatian authors contains one of the seven existing European violin tablatures. The academy also owns one of the earliest records of Croatian folk melodies, compiled by Hektorović and published in Venice in 1568.

——. Nacionalna i Sveučilišna Biblioteka, Marulićev trg 21, 41000 Zagreb (*Zu*). Founded in 1606, the university library established a separate music division in 1942. The collection comprises some 1500 MSS and 14,000 printed works, including song collections of the 17th and 18th centuries, various early printed works, an MS of the first 19th-century Croatian opera, and individual MSS and complete estates of some 19th- and 20th-century Croatian composers (Pintarić, Zajc, Kuhač, Bersa, Širola and Padovec). The largest proportion of the collection is devoted to music by Croatian and other Yugoslav composers. In 1916 the Bibliotheca Metropolitana was deposited in the library for safe-keeping. It is one of the country's oldest libraries, dating from the 11th century, and contains 35 neumatic MSS. After World War II, the library became a national copyright depository. The National Phonotheque was founded in 1965 as part of the Music Division.

III. North America

CANADA (C)

The growth of music libraries in Canada is a relatively recent development, characterized by the acquisition of current musicological publications and Canadian rather than European source material. The first Canadian imprints – volumes of plainchant, instruction manuals and songbooks – date from the early 19th century. Music publishers had established themselves in urban areas by about 1845, but were unable to compete with European publications and have generally limited themselves to popular music, items for specific local occasions and French Canadian works.

The Canadian Music Library Association, a subsection of the Canadian Library Association, operated from 1956 to 1971, when it was superseded by the Canadian Association of Music Libraries.

Canadian Library Association: 'Music in Libraries', *Bulletin*, xii (1956), 169; K. F. Dean: *Four Canadian Music Libraries: their History and Objectives* (diss., Catholic U. of America, 1961); National Library of Canada: *Research Collections in Canadian Libraries*, i: *Universities* (Ottawa, 1972); M. L. and H. C. Young and A. T. Kruzas, eds.: *Directory of Special Libraries and Information Centers* (Detroit, 3/1974)

LONDON. University of Western Ontario, Faculty of Music Library, London, Ont., N6A 3K7 (*Lu*). First established as a reading room in 1962 and as a divisional library a year later, the library (sometimes referred to as the Lawson Memorial Library) acquired an important collection of late 19th-century sacred music and other materials assembled by G. B. Sippi, organist at St Paul's Cathedral for 37 years. In 1972 the library purchased the entire catalogue of Richard Macnutt entitled 'Opera, 1751–1800', comprising 300 operas, books on opera, letters and autographs. A similar Macnutt catalogue of another 300 volumes, 'Opera, 1597–1750', was more recently acquired. Also in 1972 a collection of 38 letters written by or to Gustav Mahler was purchased from the composer's nephew, Alfred Rosé.

'Notes for Notes', *Notes*, xxxi (1974–5), 767

MONTREAL. Canadian Broadcasting Corporation, Music and Record Library, 1400 Dorchester Boulevard East, Montreal, Quebec, H3C 3A8. The CBC music libraries in Montreal, Toronto, Winnipeg, Vancouver and Halifax all act as regional copyright administrators for music.

——. Conservatoire de Musique et d'Art Dramatique, Bibliothèque, 1700 rue St Denis, Montreal, Quebec, H2X 3K4 (*Mc*). Under the auspices of the provincial ministry of cultural affairs, the conservatory and its library were established in 1942. The S. N. Gallini collection contains MSS of works by Guglielmi, L. Capotorti, Paer, Antonio Bazzini, Giovanni Bottesini and Paolo Serrao. Other important Italian MSS include the opera *La caduta dei decemviri* (1697) by Alessandro Scarlatti, a Sinfonia in D by Bellini, and parts of works by Ponchielli and Mercadante. A French MS of note is Clérambault's *Cantates françoises*. Autographs include works by Rossi, an aria by Paisiello, an excerpt from Spontini's opera *Nurmahal* (1822), and the full score of Marenco's ballet *Amore ed arte*. The early 17th-century lute MS cited in *Notes*, xviii (1960–61), 38, can no longer be traced, and the MSS and letters of Berg and Webern mentioned in the same article belong to a private collector.

——. McGill University, McLennan Library, 3459 McTavish Street, Montreal, Quebec, H3A 1Y1. The Department of Rare Books and Special Collections houses the earliest of the library's European sacred works, a single folio from a neumed 13th-century gospel in Greek. Larger items include a German *Missale romanum* (c1440) and a Dutch or German breviary of the 15th century, both with neumes; a 15th-century missal; three Italian choirbooks of the same period; and an Italian book of Latin hymns of c1700. There are numerous pages from 14th- and 15th-century Italian choirbooks and a few from antiphoners and hymnals of the 16th century. The Lawrence M. Lande Collection of Canadiana contains about 200 musical items, half of which are pre-Confederation (1867) works. Much of the personal library of the Montreal singer Pauline Donalda [Lightstone] was transferred to the music library. (The Redpath Library (*Mm*) at the same address houses the undergraduate library of the university; the Faculty and Conservatorium of Music Library became independent of the Redpath Library in 1964.)

S. DeRicci: *Census of Medieval Manuscripts in the US and Canada*, ii (New York, 1937); L. M. Lande: *The Lawrence Lande Collection of Canadiana in the Redpath Library* (Montreal, 1965, suppl. 1971)

OTTAWA. National Library of Canada, Music Division, 395 Wellington Street, Ottawa, Ont., K1A ON4 (*On*). In 1970 a separate Music Division of the National Library was established. As the national depository, it holds about two-thirds of the music published in Canada before 1953 (when the National Library Act was passed, establishing copyright deposit regulations) and practically all works from that date onwards. The library collects autograph scores, papers and memorabilia of Canadian composers. In 1969 it acquired the papers of Healey Willan and, more recently, those of Claude Champagne, Alexis Contant, Hector Gratton and others. The sheet music collection includes a few thousand pieces transferred from the Library of Parliament, representing deposits since 1867, and more than 19,000 French songs acquired in 1970. In the same year the library began to collect concert programmes and now maintains information files on Canadian musicians and musical subjects. The scrapbooks of the founder of the McGill Conservatorium, C. A. E. Harris, and the music notebooks of the early 19th-century Quebec organist Frederick Andrews are also there. The library maintains a national union catalogue.

'The Music Division/Division de la Musique', *National Library News/Nouvelles de la Bibliothèque nationale*, iii (1971), 3

QUEBEC. Petit Séminaire de Québec, Bibliothèque, 3 rue de l'Université, Quebec, G1R 4R7. The history of the music collection, founded in 1663, is intertwined with that of the Université Laval, but the two collections have been separate since 1964. The Seminary has retained all materials acquired before 1910, including the major portion of a collection dating from the late 18th century that passed from Jonathan Sewell through various hands to the university. The 330 or so volumes are chiefly contemporary London prints of quartets and overtures by Haydn, Mozart, Abel, J. C. Bach, Gossec, Pleyel, Stamitz, Viotti and others; this part of the collection has not yet been catalogued. The seminary also contains the Joseph Vézina collection of late 19th-century military music for brass or wind band (prints and MSS).

H. Kallmann: *A History of Music in Canada, 1534–1914* (Toronto, 1960), 60f

——. Université Laval, Cité Universitaire, Quebec, G1K 7P4 (*Qul*). Although the university was founded in 1852, the School of Music was not established until 1922. Its music collection was housed in the Petit Séminaire de Québec until 1964, when all items purchased since 1910 with university funds were placed with the university library's general collections. The 45,000 volumes of music include a large number of French works of the 19th century and books on music education.

The department of special collections contains Catholic liturgical music and motets dating from 1542, and the remainder of the Sewell collection (about 170 volumes, catalogued) of late 18th-century chamber music. The collection of Sophia Desbarats-Sheppart includes excerpts and arrangements of early 19th-century European operas.

TORONTO. Canadian Broadcasting Corporation, Music and Record Library, 354 Jarvis Street, Toronto, Ont., M4Y 2G6 (*Tb*). Of chief interest are MS scores of works commissioned by the CBC and about 7000 MS arrangements of orchestral scores and parts. The library issues at intervals catalogues of its holdings by category.

——. University of Toronto, Edward Johnson Music Library, 86 Queen's Park Crescent, Toronto, Ont., M5S 2C5 (*Tu*). The Faculty of Music library officially dates its establishment in 1947, although some of its holdings belonged to the Royal (formerly Toronto) Conservatory of Music, founded in 1886. The music library was greatly enriched when musical material previously held in the main library was transferred to the new Edward Johnson Music Building in 1961. It is now Canada's largest general music collection, owning some 60,000 volumes and 15,000 items of sheet music. The Rare Book Room contains about 150 pre-1800 editions, about half of which are theoretical works and the rest printed music, and an extensive collection of 18th-century editions of Italian, French and English operas. Important acquisitions include the Fisher Collection of historical books, music and instruments, and the entire chamber music collection of W. W. Cobbett (1847–1937).

UNITED STATES OF AMERICA (*US*)

The establishment of American libraries, as opposed to European collections, generally occurred in institutions imbued with a belief in mass education; music libraries, under the influence of *Dwight's Journal of Music* (1852–81) and the Mason family, emerged in this same spirit. Of the three major historical collections established before 1900, two were in the public libraries of New York and Boston and the third in a private library open to the public (the Newberry Library in Chicago).

During the first half of the 20th century public library collections expanded through the financial impetus of the Carnegie endowments. The extensive and unexpected growth of college and university collections since the 1950s has been the result of government policy in two areas: a brief but massive effort to upgrade libraries through direct grants for materials, equipment and buildings, and changes in taxation of individual incomes that made gifts to non-profit-making institutions financially attractive. A burst of postwar vigour and new production techniques quickly fattened the catalogues of music publishers, but the inflated budgets could absorb the flow of new material. Of the libraries described below, those of the universities of California, Indiana and Michigan were particularly fortunate during these years.

Many important musical sources formerly in European collections are now in American libraries. The chief goal of American music libraries however has not been to vie for important primary sources but rather to include representative samples in research collections often rich in microforms; service, rather than conservation, has been the guiding principle. Only a very few collections (notably the Eastman School of Music and the New York Public Library) can aim for complete coverage of current publications. Even the Library of Congress depends on gifts and on copyright deposits, having a surprisingly limited budget for imprints earlier than the current year.

No discussion of American music libraries would be complete without mention of the music librarians who in the first half of the 20th century created the standards of scholarship and service we find today: Oscar Sonneck, the first director of the Music Division at the Library of Congress, whose classification scheme has been widely adopted by almost all American music libraries; Otto Kinkeldey and Carleton Sprague Smith (New York Public Library); Barbara Duncan (Boston Public Library and the Eastman School of Music); H. Dorothy Tilly (Detroit Public Library); Eva Judd O'Meara (Yale University); and George Sherman Dickinson (Vassar College). After World War II, contributions were made by Vincent Duckles (University of California at Berkeley), Ruth Watanabe (Eastman School of Music), Elizabeth R. Hartman (Philadelphia Free Library), Hans Lenneberg (University of Chicago) and James Pruett (University of North Carolina).

O. E. Albrecht: *A Census of Autograph Music Manuscripts of European Composers in American Libraries* (Philadelphia, 1953, suppl. in preparation); R. Benton: *Directory of Music Research Libraries*, i (Iowa City, 1967); D. Seaton: 'Important Library Holdings at Forty-one North American Universities', *CMc* (1974), no.17, pp.7–68

ANN ARBOR. University of Michigan, Music Library, 3239 School of Music Building, Ann Arbor, Mich. 48105 (*AA*). Established in 1941 to provide specialized services to the recently incorporated School of Music, the library consolidated its dispersed holdings in the School of Music building in 1964 and now contains over 48,000 volumes. Its research resources were greatly strengthened in 1954 with the purchase of the collection of the Belgian musicologist J.-A. Stellfeld (1881–1952). Of some 10,000 items in the Stellfeld Collection, about 1600 are pre-1800 imprints and MSS of the 18th century, particularly rich in 18th-century opera. Other notable collections in the library include materials related to the composer and conductor F. A. Stock and letters from Gerhard, Carter, Riegger and others regarding the Stanley Quartet commissions. Schoenberg's family recently donated letters from Wallenstein, Schnabel, Furtwängler and others to the composer, and Eva Jessye donated an archival Afro-American music collection.

L. E. Cuyler and others: 'The University of Michigan's Purchase of the Stellfeld Music Library', *Notes*, xii (1954–5), 41

——. William L. Clements Library, South University Avenue, Ann Arbor, Mich. 48104. The library of early Americana and the building which houses it were presented to the university in 1922 by W. L. Clements (1861–1934). The music collection, now numbering some 22,000 items, embraces American printed music and books about music up to 1900. A large collection (143 items) of early tune books includes 20 shape-note volumes; to complement the 25 tune books and other publications of Andrew Law the library purchased about 1200 documents of Law and his brother William. There is a collection of music in honour of Lafayette, including a volume of some 29 printed and MS songs of 1824–5. Books include 45 songbooks and 83 discourses on early American church music.

BALTIMORE. Enoch Pratt Free Library, 400 Cathedral Street, Baltimore, Maryland 21201 (*BAep*). The Fine Arts and Music Department, established in 1921, has an uncatalogued collection of American popular songs since 1850 containing about 16,000 items.

——. Peabody Institute of the City of Baltimore, Conservatory of Music Library, 21 Mt Vernon Place, Baltimore, Maryland 21202 (*BApi*). In 1966 the music collections were reorganized and now contain about 8000 books and 45,000 scores, including musical MSS of Beethoven, Asger Hamerik, Theodor Hemberger, John Itzel, Gustav Strube and Efrem Zimbalist and letters of Beethoven, Bloch, Falla, Grieg, Landowska, Liszt and Messager.

Catalog of the Library of the Peabody Institute (1883–92); Second Catalog . . . including Additions made since 1882 (1896–1905)

BEREA. Riemenschneider Bach Library, Baldwin-Wallace College, Berea, Ohio 44107 (*BER*). The Riemenschneider Bach Library (part of the Ritter Library) owns about 5000 volumes and comprises three distinct collections. The Riemenschneider Collection of works by and related to Bach was presented to the college in 1950 and contains early editions of his works. The Emmy Martin Collection contains first editions from the 17th–20th centuries (notably of Beethoven); in April 1970 the Hans T. David Collection of Renaissance and Baroque material was acquired. The library continues to collect works of the Baroque period. The Riemenschneider Bach Institute, established in 1969 to promote the collections, issues a quarterly journal called *Bach*.

S. W. Kenney: *Catalog of the Emilie and Karl Riemenschneider Memorial Bach Library* (New York, 1960; suppls. by J. B. Winzenburger)

BERKELEY. University of California, Music Library, Morrison Music Building, Berkeley, Calif. 94720 (*BE*). Although the general library of the university purchased collected editions as early as 1912, the real impetus for a separate and expanded music library began in 1941 when Manfred Bukofzer joined the faculty. The library was formally established six years later and moved to its present quarters in 1958, where its reference collections expanded under the direction of Vincent Duckles.

The first major purchase was the Harris D. H. Connick Collection of some 5000 18th- and 19th-century opera scores in 1950. It was strengthened three years later by the acquisition of the Sigmund Romberg Collection of 4000 scores of 18th- to early 20th-century operas, and in 1965 by about 285 scores and some 300 librettos, chiefly 18th-century French, from the collection of Alfred Cortot (1877–1962). Other operatic materials include 25 MS volumes of mid-18th-century English arias and ensembles, a 900-volume collection of operas from the 17th–20th centuries performed in Sicily, about 4400 Italian opera librettos from the 17th–19th centuries and 45 letters by Jommelli. The private

libraries of Alfred Einstein (excluding madrigals and instrumental music in *US-Nsc*) and Manfred Bukofzer were acquired in 1954 and 1956 respectively.

The library has acquired an important representative body of rare sources, including the 11th-century Wolfheim Antiphoner, treatises (notably a late medieval MS, formerly no.4450 in the Phillipps Collection), 16th- and 17th-century partbooks from Cortot's library, 17th- and 18th-century English and French keyboard music, Beethoven sketches, and Schoenberg's corrected first edition of his *Gurrelieder*. Some 990 MSS representing the violin school of Tartini, containing works by 82 composers (chiefly Tartini himself and his pupil Michele Stratico), were purchased in 1958. Other special collections include the Alice Lawson Aber Collection of Harp Music (early 19th-century MSS and editions), the A. P. Berggreen Collection (all editions of the composer's works as well as Danish folksong material), and the archives of Ernest Bloch (including holographs and sketches of about 35 of his works) and Andrew Imbrie.

Additional List of Holdings which Supplement the RISM Recueils imprimées XVIe–XVIIe siècles (1960); V. Duckles: 'William F. Herschel's Concertos for Oboe, Viola and Violin', Festschrift Otto Erich Deutsch (Kassel, 1963), 66; V. Duckles and M. Elmer: Thematic Catalog of a Manuscript Collection of Eighteenth-century Italian Instrumental Music in the University of California, Berkeley Music Library (Berkeley and Los Angeles, 1963); A. Curtis: 'Musique classique française à Berkeley', RdM, lvi (1970), 123–64 [includes inventory of 11-vol. MS collection copied by De la Barre]; F. Traficante: 'Dispersal of the Cortot Collection: 290 Treatises in Lexington', Notes, xxvi (1969–70), 713; J. Ladewig: 'University of California, Berkeley', CMc (1974), no.17, p.33

BETHLEHEM. The Moravian Music Foundation, Archives, P.O. Box 1292, Bethlehem, Penn. 18018 (*BETm*). The archives date from the organization of the Moravian Church in Bethlehem in 1741 and include important special collections of church music from Bethlehem, Lancaster, Lititz and Nazareth, Pennsylvania, and from Dover, Ohio, as well as instrumental music of the Philharmonic Societies of Bethlehem and Lititz. The library also has many hymnals and other choral music of the Moravian Church, the earliest from 1545.

A. G. Rau and H. T. David: *Catalogue of Music by American Moravians, 1742–1842* (Bethlehem, 1938)

BLOOMINGTON. Indiana University, Bloomington, Ind. 47401. The School of Music Library (*BLu*) holds about 285,000 items, including material associated with the Latin American and Black Music Centers, established in 1960 and 1968 respectively. The library is especially interested in opera scores and recently received substantial additions from the estate of Bernardo Mendel. Most of the rare musical items, acquired since 1960, are housed in the Lilly Library (*BLl*). They include duplicates of Handel scores and related material from the collections of William C. Smith and Gerald Coke, annotated scores of the German conductor Fritz Busch, a collection of first edition opera scores and librettos purchased and donated from Mendel's library and, from Mendel's estate, a collection of more than 100,000 items of vocal and instrumental American sheet music from 1750 onwards. Mendel also donated his collection of Latin Americana, including four 16th-century Guatemalan MSS of music by Spanish and Flemish composers. The library owns a copy of Navarro's *Liber in quo quatuor passiones Christi Domini continentur* (Mexico City, 1604), believed to be the oldest example of printed music composed in the Americas. The Ege, Poole and Ricketts MS collections of chiefly medieval and Renaissance material contain several liturgical works. Musical MSS and correspondence of Hoagy Carmichael are also housed here.

The Apel Collection of Early Keyboard Sources in Photographic Reproduction in the Indiana University Music Library (Bloomington, 1961) [revision in preparation]; J. Orrego-Salas: *Music from Latin America Available at Indiana University: Scores, Tapes and Records* (Bloomington, 1964, 2/1971); J. O. Falconer: 'Music in the Lilly Library: Handel, Opera, and Latin Americana', *Notes*, xxix (1972–3), 5; D.-R. de Lerma: *The Fritz Busch Collection* (Bloomington, 1972)

BOSTON. Public Library, Music Department, Copley Square, Boston, Mass. 02117 (*Bp*). In 1859 the library's principal early benefactor, Joshua Bates, purchased the nucleus of the music department's research collections in Berlin: the 400-volume library of Joseph Koudelka (1773–1850), mainly historical and theoretical works of the 15th and 16th centuries, and 100 volumes from the library of A. W. Thayer (1817–97). Collections acquired from notable musicians include autograph works by John Barnett, scrapbooks of Arthur Foote and Philip Hale, letters, scrapbooks and Latin Americana of Nicolas Slonimsky, organ music of Florence Rich King and the library of Serge Koussevitzky. Holographs include items by minor 19th-century German composers, and by A. W. Bach, Samuel Wesley, Franck, Tosti, Coleridge-Taylor (*Hiawatha's Wedding Feast*) and the Boston organist and composer G. E. Whiting (1840–1923), and collections of works by Mabel Daniels and Gardner Read. There are also autograph fragments of works by Mozart, Schubert, Shostakovich and Virgil Thomson.

In the 1970s the library acquired two important collections. One contains incidental music from the Haymarket Theatre (from 1888) and Her Majesty's Theatre (1897 to 1916) including several autograph scores of Coleridge-Taylor, among them his music for Israel Zangwill's *The God of War*; also included are stage works of Edward German, Bantock, Adolf Schmid, Raymond Roze, George Henschel and Mascagni. The other contains the library of the Boston Handel and Haydn Society (founded 1815) (which includes material from the earlier Massachusetts and Old Colony musical societies and of its founder members Johann Graupner and George K. Jackson), rich in early annotated performing editions of Handel and Haydn, as well as holographs of a few commissioned works by New England composers (notably Randall Thompson).

Catalogue of the Allen A. Brown Collection of Music (Boston, 1910–16); B. Duncan: 'The Allen A. Brown Libraries', *Bulletin*, 4th ser., iv (1922), 121 [*Bp* publication]; G. K. Hall: *Dictionary Catalogue of the Music Collection* (1972); J. Sheveloff: *Rare Old Music and Books on Music in Boston* (1972) [MS catalogue of the most interesting holdings of the Handel and Haydn Society of Boston]

——. Harvard Musical Association, 57a Chestnut Street, Boston, Mass. 02108 (*Bh*). The association was formed in 1837. Sporadic purchases and gifts through the years, frequently reported in *Dwight's Journal of Music* (Boston, 1852–81), form an 18th- and 19th-century repertory of some 10,000 volumes. The collection has letters of Beethoven, Liszt, Mendelssohn, Berlioz, Schumann and Verdi, 18th- and early 19th-century imprints and MSS from the publisher Johann Graupner, material on the piano manufacturers Chickering & Sons and autograph MSS of the Boston composer Arthur Foote (1853–1937). A *Library of the*

Harvard Musical Association Bulletin was published irregularly from 1934 to 1959.

——. New England Conservatory of Music, Harriet M. Spaulding Library, 290 Huntington Avenue, Boston, Mass. 02115 (*Bc*). In 1870 the private library of the conservatory's founder and director, Eben Tourjée, became the nucleus of a small collection. The library now holds a fairly extensive autograph MS collection of scores and parts by the 'Boston classicists' (Paine, Foote, Chadwick and Loeffler), and earlier Americana include 18th-century books on singing, psalmody and glees, and letters and memorabilia of Boston musicians. There are autographs of songs by Franz, and Debussy's first draft of *Pelléas et Mélisande*. The John A. Preston Collection of letters and documents represents 55 19th-century musicians (including Beethoven, Berlioz, Liszt, Mendelssohn, Schumann and Wagner). The library also has numerous 19th-century first editions, early treatises, partbooks and pre-1800 publications. An autograph MS collection of French saxophone music is on deposit.

BUFFALO. Buffalo and Erie County Public Library, Lafayette Square, Buffalo, NY 14203 (*BU*). Formed in 1954, the library includes the former Grosvenor Reference Library collection of popular Americana, with sheet music, volumes of 18th- and 19th-century songs and piano pieces, songbooks, hymnals and broadsides.

——. State University of New York at Buffalo, Music Library, Baird Music Hall, Buffalo, NY 14214. The music library expanded rapidly in the 1960s. It has MSS of works by avant-garde composers (as well as correspondence and scrapbooks) written in conjunction with the Center for the Creative and Performing Arts established at the university by Lukas Foss; rare items are about a dozen MS copies of Lully operas and librettos, MSS and early prints of works by Clari and Paer, and early editions of 18th-century operas and chamber music.

CAMBRIDGE. Harvard University, Cambridge, Mass. 02138 (*CA*). Musical material is found in five libraries. The collections were started in 1870; the music department library started its own collection in 1898, which absorbed others and is now the Eda Kuhn Loeb Music Library. Associated with this collection is the Isham Memorial Library which includes a large quantity of microfilm. The college library (the Widener Memorial) holds material related to A. B. Lord's folklore studies and the Divinity School has a collection of hymns and hymnology.

The Houghton Library is the chief repository of rare materials. Its earliest MS, recently acquired, is a 14th-century eastern Mediterranean sticherarion in Middle Byzantine notation; another recent purchase is the long-lost autograph of Gaffurius's *Practica musicae*, ii, dated 1480. An anonymous *Speculum exemplorum* of 1481 containing fragmentary works by Dunstable, song MSS of Byrd, anonymous Italian cantatas, French *airs* on political texts, French guitar tablature and lyra viol dances in the hand of William Lawes are among the library's notable pre-1700 possessions.

The 18th-century MS holdings are extensive, including autographs of J. S. and J. C. F. Bach, Durante, G. B. Martini, Haydn and Rousseau; MS copies include a collection of 70 French and Italian violin sonatas copied by Dublicq in 1721 and works by Boccherini. Popular British ballads of the late 18th and early 19th centuries are contained in several MS anthologies compiled by Thomas Moore and others. Major 19th-century composers represented by autographs are Beethoven, Bellini, Elgar, Franz, Liszt, Mahler, Mendelssohn, Puccini, Reger, Rossini, Anton Rubinstein, Schubert, Schumann and Wagner. In 1970 the library purchased an important collection of Italian materials including 58 MSS from Rossini's *Péchés de vieillesse* and letters of Bellini, Verdi and Puccini. There is a collection of printed music by 19th- and 20th-century Russian composers, with autographs and letters (described by Miloš Velimirović in *Notes*, xvii, 1959–60, p.539). 20th-century autographs include works of Berg, Berger, Fauré, Holst, Kirchner, Migot, Pinkham, Satie (discussed by N. Wilkins in 'The Writings of Erik Satie', *ML*, lvi, 1975, p.288), Schoenberg, Sessions, Sibelius, Strauss, Varèse and Webern.

The Houghton Library Theatre Collection holds MSS, printed works, scrapbooks, programmes and memorabilia relating to stage productions, including operas. Letters of 18th- and 19th-century opera composers in the John Benjamin Heath volumes (London, 1865) are selectively described and translated by Hans Nathan and listed by Frances Fink (*Notes*, v, 1947–8, p.461).

N. Pirrotta: 'The Eda Kuhn Loeb Music Library', *Harvard Library Bulletin*, xii (1958), 410; C. Wright: 'Report from Cambridge: Rare Music Manuscripts at Harvard', *CMc* (1970), no.10, p.25; S. Youens: 'Harvard University', *CMc* (1974), no.17, p.17

CHAPEL HILL. University of North Carolina, Music Library, Hill Hall, Chapel Hill, North Carolina 27514 (*CHH*). Founded in 1932, this music library is the largest in the south-eastern USA with about 70,000 volumes. The collection is particularly strong in Renaissance music and includes representative early prints and many microfilms. The Early American Music Collection contains about 5000 items, chiefly pre-Civil War imprints and some MSS.

CHARLOTTESVILLE. University of Virginia, Music Library, 113 Old Cabell Hall, Charlottesville, Virginia 22903. The library houses the Monticello Music Collection of material relating to the Jefferson family (*CHum*). About half the vocal music from Jefferson's own library is there and a small part of the instrumental; these are mostly London imprints of 1740–80. Also in the collection are imprints from the 1780s, from Paris and London. American items include a rare copy of Hopkinson's songs, and MS copies of contemporary popular items made by Jefferson's children and grandchildren. The Alderman Library (*CHua*) houses the John Fawcett collection of librettos from London theatres, the Alfred Swan collection of books, MSS, letters and other material relating to Russian studies, and collections of 19th-century American sheet music and of American folk material.

C. G. Nolan: *Thomas Jefferson: Gentleman Musician* (diss., U. of Virginia, 1967); H. Cripe: *Thomas Jefferson and Music* (Charlottesville, 1974) [incl. catalogue]

CHICAGO. Newberry Library, 60 West Walton Street, Chicago, Ill. 60610 (*Cn*). Founded in 1887, the Newberry Library is a privately supported research library whose music collection numbers some 200,000 items. It is particularly strong in material of the European Renaissance and Baroque and in Americana to 1918. In 1889 the library purchased some 751 items from Count Pio Resse, a Florentine collector, including a first edition of Peri's *Euridice*. The library received many private collections during subsequent decades, among them those of the Beethoven Society of Chicago, Julius Fuchs, Otto Lob, Theodore Thomas (including personal papers and a Wagner autograph), the music publisher Hubert P. Main, T. Le Carpentier-Morphy, G. P. Upton, W. J. Wollfheim (17th- and 18th-century scores), Frederick Stock (including many of his own compositions), Bernhard Ziehn (1845–1912) and Yuri Arbatsky. The J. Francis Driscoll collection of about 83,000 items of American sheet music, acquired in 1960, is rich in negro minstrelsy and songs of Boston and New England. In 1966 the library purchased 315 items from the library of Alfred Cortot, comprising early hymnology sources and theoretical treatises. From the opera singer Claire Dux (*d* 1967) came two of the library's four Mozart autographs.

The strength of the collection lies particularly in medieval and Renaissance treatises: they include a 12th-century MS of Boethius's *De musica*, a 15th-century MS of works by Marchetto da Padova and Jehan des Murs, an *Ars perfecta in musica* ascribed to Vitry, and works of Gaffurius, Zarlino, Agricola, Glarean and Praetorius. Renaissance and Baroque items include early service music, many sacred and secular partbooks, and much lute music. The 18th and 19th centuries are represented primarily by treatises and a small number of MSS by master composers. A strong Americana collection includes 18th-century copies of the Bay Psalmbook and tune books of Billings and Law, and extends into the 20th century with documents on Chicago musical life.

D. W. Krummel: 'The Newberry Library, Chicago', *FAM*, xvi (1969), 119; F. Traficante: 'Dispersal of the Cortot Collection: 290 Treatises in Lexington', *Notes*, xxvi (1969–70), 713

——. University of Chicago, Music Collection, Joseph Regenstein Library, 1100 East 57th Street, Chicago, Ill. 60637 (*Cu*). The library has sought to acquire MSS and first editions to complement those in the Newberry Library, particularly of music of the 18th and 19th centuries. The papers of John and Elinor Castle Nef contain unpublished letters of Schnabel and Schoenberg. The total collection now numbers about 50,000 volumes and contains many microfilms.

Music in the University of Chicago Library Selected for an Exhibition at the Joseph Regenstein Library July–October 1972 (Chicago, 1972)

CINCINNATI. Hebrew Union College, Jewish Institute of Religion, Klau Library, 3101 Clifton Avenue, Cincinnati, Ohio 45220 (*CIhc*). The nucleus of the music holdings (about 10,000 items) is the Eduard Birnbaum Collection, particularly strong in cantorial music of the 19th century and including a thematic catalogue of Jewish music. An important MS compilation of 1791 by the Berlin Kantor Aaron Baer contains 447 compositions arranged in a cycle for the year's 53 Sabbath services.

E. Werner: *MSS of Jewish Music in the Eduard Birnbaum Collection* (Cincinnati, 1944); *Dictionary Catalogue* (Boston, 1963)

——. University of Cincinnati, College-Conservatory of Music, Gorno Memorial Music Library, Cincinnati, Ohio 45221 (*CIu*). The Cincinnati Conservatory of Music (founded in 1867) and the College of Music (1878) merged in 1955 and became part of the university in 1962. The holdings of both libraries were combined in 1967 and moved to the Corbett Center for the Performing Arts. The collections include 19th-century 'singing skewl' books, about 3000 items from the library of Everett Helm (including early editions of 18th- and 19th-century scores, particularly French music, 1750–1850) and the Anatole Chujoy Memorial Dance Collection.

DENTON. North Texas State University, Music Library, Denton, Texas 76203 (*DN*). This library of about 40,000 volumes and a large microfilm collection is particularly strong in music of the 20th century. It has acquired two important contemporary collections: 33 MSS by Schoenberg and his letters to Hans Nachod written between 1909 and 1949 (described by D. Newlin in *MQ*, liv, 1968, p.31) and material relating to Duke Ellington. In 1966 it received the library of the medievalist Lloyd Hibberd, including many 18th-century French and English stage works.

A. H. Heyer: *A Bibliography of Contemporary Music in the Music Library of North Texas State College* (Denton, 1955); Seminar in Musicology: *An Annotated Bibliography of Rare Materials contained in the Music Library of the North Texas State University* (1969, suppl. 1970)

DETROIT. Public Library, Music and Performing Arts Department, 5201 Woodward Avenue, Detroit, Mich. 48202 (*Dp*). The library's notable collections include the E. Azalia Hackley Memorial Collection, documenting black achievements in music, drama and dance, the Michigan Collection of autograph works by Michigan composers, early American hymnals and songbooks, and much popular American sheet music. Musical life in Detroit is richly documented.

K. Myers: *The Music and Drama Department of the Detroit Public Library* (Detroit, 1957)

EVANSTON. Northwestern University, Music Library, Evanston, Ill. 60201 (*Eu*). This library specializes in 20th-century MSS and editions, the most notable being those items acquired from the Moldenhauer Archives in Spokane. All the MSS collected and catalogued by John Cage in his *Notations* (New York, 1969), as well as the related correspondence, are on deposit here. The libraries of Fritz Reiner and Boris Goldovsky have been acquired but not yet transferred. The library has published *1810 Overture* bi-monthly since 1972.

IOWA CITY. University of Iowa, School of Music, Library, Eastlawn, Iowa City, Iowa 52240 (*IO*). The collection has leaves of Gregorian chant (the earliest from a 13th-century English gradual) and a few 16th- and 17th-century treatises; its greatest strength lies in printed 18th- and 19th-century keyboard works, chamber music and treatises. The University Library holds the Edward Ford Piper Collection of ballads, folksongs and other musical materials relating to local and Midwestern history.

A. T. Luper: *An Exhibit of Music and Music Materials, Early and Rare* (Iowa City, 1953); F. K. Gable: *An Annotated Catalog of Rare Musical Items in the Libraries of the University of Iowa* (1963) [addns from 1963 to 1972 by G. S. Rowley, 1973]; G. S. Rowley: 'University of Iowa', *CMc* (1974), no.17, p.46

ITHACA. Cornell University, Music Library, Lincoln Hall, Ithaca, NY 14850 (*I*). Otto Kinkeldey, the renowned musicologist and university librarian from 1930 to 1946, was responsible for the early growth of the music collection. The library of Donald J. Grout, containing microfilms of Renaissance MSS and early prints and of MSS and librettos of Baroque operas, forms a special collection, which supplements the library's particular strength in opera and 20th-century music. In 1970 Vaughan Williams's widow donated microfilm copies of his MSS as well as printed proof copies, published scores with his annotations and correspondence.

LOS ANGELES. Arnold Schoenberg Archives, California State University, 5151 State University Drive, Los Angeles, Calif. 90032. California State University is the temporary home of the Schoenberg Archives, a gift of his heirs, until a building can be completed for the Schoenberg Institute at the University of Southern California. Included are almost all the composer's original musical sketches, autographs, unpublished works and writings.

J. Meggett and R. Moritz: 'The Schoenberg Legacy', *Notes*, xxxi (1974–5), 30

——. Public Library, Art and Music Department, 630 West Fifth Street, Los Angeles, Calif. 90017. This large collection contains about 1000 Spanish South American songs in addition to strong holdings in opera, song anthologies, musical comedy and jazz.

A Bibliography of Early Music (c1240–c1725) in the Music Department of the Los Angeles Public Library (Los Angeles, 1941)

——. University of California, 405 Hilgard Avenue, Los Angeles, Calif. 90024. The Walter H. Rubsamen Music Library (at Schoenberg Hall; *LAu*) was founded in 1942 when the Southern California Federal Music Project was transferred to the university. It now holds MSS of works by Paul Chihara, Henry Leland Clarke, Roy Harris, Henri Lazarof, Roy Travis, John Vincent, Boris Kremenliev, Mantle Hood and others. The compositions and Balinese materials of Colin McPhee were acquired in 1974. There are special collections of holographs, sketches and letters, including those of Ernst Toch and Rudolf Friml. The Meredith Willson Library contains both the Stanley Ring Collection of popular American sheet music (from 1800 onwards) received in 1965 and the Music Mart Collection, together numbering some 600,000 items.

Earlier music is also well represented. Of particular interest is the 117-volume set of 1215 opera librettos printed in Venice and Padua between 1635 and 1769. There are also 170 English and German librettos of 1750 to 1820 and librettos of 100 French comic operas of the later 18th century and of 1150 *comédies-vaudevilles* performed at the Théâtre de Vaudeville and the Théâtre de Gymnase from 1792 to 1855; French opera is further documented by the Paris Opera Roll containing MS receipts of 1780–91. Recent acquisitions of theatre music include scores of late 18th-century English composers. The library has early editions of French motets and operas (as well as MS copies of Lully's *Isis* and *Thésée*), and Dutch psalmbooks and secular songbooks of the 17th and 18th centuries. Instrumental works include an early 17th-century Italian keyboard MS (described by R. Hudson in *JAMS*, xxvi, 1973, p.345) and printed works (catalogued by M. S. Cole in *Notes*, xxix, 1972–3, p.215). Recently the library has begun to collect treatises from the 16th century onwards.

The Department of Special Collections in the Research Library specializes in early American hymns, folksongs and broadside ballads; the film composer Eugen Zador presented more recent Americana, consisting of the MS music and other memorabilia of the actor Lionel Barrymore (1878–1954). Dance manuals and histories of the 17th–19th centuries are also well represented.

The William Andrews Clark Memorial Library (at 2520 Cimarron Street, West Adams Boulevard, Los Angeles, Calif. 90018; *LAuc*), was given to the university in 1934 as a memorial to Senator Clark. It specializes in English life and thought between 1640 and 1750 and is rich in original editions of dramatic works in many forms (librettos, full scores, songs and arias from English and Italian operas, masques, ballad operas and other musical plays from 1728 to 1810); composers represented include Blow, Carey, Handel, Henry Lawes, Leveridge, Morley, Purcell, Ravenscroft, Reggio, Rousseau and Vanbrughe. About 40 collections of quarto sheets represent English and Scottish songs of the 17th and 18th centuries. MSS include contemporary copies of dance-tunes, chamber music (fancies, solo motets and continuo songs), four Genoese operas of 1754, Cecilian odes, a Campra ballet, an anonymous Italian mass and Italian arias and cantatas. The collection has some Baroque treatises, psalms and hymns. There are also letters of Haydn, Mendelssohn, Liszt, Wagner, Berlioz, Gounod and Saint-Saëns, two essays by Gounod, and MSS of minor compositions by Grieg and Mendelssohn.

Southern California Historical Records Survey Project: *List of the Letters and Manuscripts of Musicians in the William Andrews Clark Memorial Library* (Los Angeles, 1940); W. H. Rubsamen: 'Unusual Music Holdings of Libraries on the West Coast', *Notes*, x (1952–3), 546; P. J. Revitt: *The George Pullen Jackson Collection oj̇ Southern Hymnody: a Bibliography* (Los Angeles, 1964); F. Freedman: *A Bibliography of Baroque Materials in the UCLA Music Library* (Los Angeles, 1966); W. Salloch: 'Joseph Stone (1758–1837), his Music Autographs, Tune Books, Manuscripts and Diaries', *Catalogue 237: the World of Music* (Ossining, NY, 1966), 7; S. M. Fry: *Directory and Index of Special Music Collections in Southern California Libraries and in the Libraries of the Campuses of the University of California* (Los Angeles, 1970), 8f

NEW HAVEN. Yale University, New Haven, Conn. 06520 (*NH*). Although the university collected music from its foundation, it was not until 1917 that a separate music library was established. About 10,000 items from the Lowell Mason Library were transferred to the new music library (at 98 Wall Street). It was enlarged in 1956 through a memorial gift in honour of a 1934 alumnus, John Herrick Jackson, after whom the library was then named. It has about 16,000 MSS or early imprints from before 1820 in a section devoted to special collections. The Mason Library includes about 700 MSS and early imprints, as well as Lowell Mason's own works and those of the organist and pedagogue Johann Christian Heinrich Rinck (1770–1846), from whose son Mason had bought the bulk of the collection in 1852. Rinck had studied with J. C. Kittel (1732–1809), one of Bach's last pupils, and his library is thus rich in contemporary MS copies acquired from sources close to the composers. Notable among these is the Lowell Mason Codex, an important source of keyboard music of the late 17th and early 18th centuries with unique works by Buxtehude, Poglietti, Radex, Strunck and Weisthoma (described by F. W. Riedel, *Quellenkundliche Beiträge zur Geschichte der Musik für Tasteninstrumente in der zweiten Hälfte des 17. Jahrhunderts*, Kassel, 1960, pp.99ff). Part of Mason's library is a group of 66 theoretical treatises he had purchased from S. W. Dehn of the Royal Library in Berlin. Most of the collection however reflects Mason's own professional interests – chiefly sacred vocal music, hymnals and methods published mainly in the USA between 1750 and 1850. A MS catalogue was compiled 1874–7 by J. S. Smith.

The library has continued to specialize in music of the 18th century, particularly members of the Bach family, and now owns a holograph of Bach's *Clavier-Büchlein vor Wilhelm Friedemann Bach* and a first edition of his *Clavier-Übung*. There are early printed editions of C. P. E. Bach and Clementi, about 20 operas by Lully in 18th-century editions and a recently acquired MS score of Hasse's *Leucippo*, dated 1747.

Among the library's other notable collections is a comprehensive group of theoretical treatises amassed through systematic purchase. The Filmer Collection of 40 MSS and a few printed works was deposited in 1946 and contains Elizabethan madrigals and motets, lutesongs, solo works for lute and harpsichord, consort pieces, solo anthems and madrigals from the press of Vincenti. The library has Ellsworth Grumman's collection of early editions of Beethoven piano sonatas and (since 1972) a collection of about 150 MSS and 25 editions, dating 1810–40, from the descendants of Francesco Galeazzi (1758–1819), Italian violinist, composer and theorist (largely operatic material, and some chamber music). Miscellaneous MSS of particular interest include several medieval illuminated MSS; the 16th-century Wickhambrook Lute MS; vocal works of Alessandro Scarlatti, J. F. Agricola, Salieri, Hasse, Beethoven (sketches for *Die Weihe des Hauses*), Berg, Bax and Dello Joio; autograph MSS of Clementi, Chopin (op.18 and op.70 no.1), Schubert (D317, 318 and 650), Schumann (op.83 no.1), Brahms (op.76 no.1), Mendelssohn and Sibelius.

Beginning with the acquisition in 1955 of the complete MSS and papers of Charles Ives and more recently with those of Carl Ruggles and Leo Ornstein, the library has become an important repository of 20th-century musical sources. It is now the American branch of the Hindemith Archives and holds nine of the composer's holographs and some sketches. Other Yale composers represented include Gustave Stoeckel (1819–1907), Horatio Parker (1863–1919) and his pupil David Stanley Smith (1877–1970). There are also autograph scores of contemporary harpsichord music from the library of Ralph Kirkpatrick.

The diaries and letters of Lowell Mason were presented to the library from the estate of his grandson. A collection of about 1500 letters concerns the activities of the Kneisel Quartet from 1886 to 1917, and there are also letters from Myra Hess and some in the hand of Rossini's wife, Olympe, describing her husband's final illness.

The Sterling Memorial Library (120 High Street), Yale's general library, holds a number of important musical items, especially American songbooks, folksongs and the carol collection of Edward Bliss Reed, secretary of the Carol Society in New Haven from its foundation in 1923 until his death in 1940, during which time volumes of carols of various nationalities were issued annually. With a gift from Robert Barlow in 1954, the library has made a special collection of literature of the American Musical Theatre. A group of Cole Porter's MSS and papers was received in 1964.

The Beinecke Rare Book and Manuscript Library (Wall and High Streets) contains a number of musical items: a Cistercian gradual of *c*1300, a group of medieval antiphoners and graduals, many late medieval MS leaves (some containing *prosae* attributed to Notker) and the late 15th-century Burgundian chansonnier known by the name of its donor, Paul Mellon (described by Bukofzer in *MQ*, xxviii, 1942, pp.14–49). The William A. Speck Collection of Goethe material (in the German literature collection) includes autographs and early editions of music connected with Goethe.

Most notable is the James Marshall and Marie-Louise Osborn Collection, mainly of 17th- and 18th-century English verse but containing important musical MSS from the 16th–20th centuries. In particular it includes the Braye Lutebook of c1560, autograph scores by Alessandro Scarlatti, Britten, Dohnányi, Holst, Mahler (Symphonies nos.1 and 2 and other works) and Vaughan Williams, and variations on an Elizabethan round by six British composers, dated 1953. Included also are about 900 of Burney's letters, notebooks and MSS as well as letters to him from Haydn and others.

R. Barlow: 'A University Approach to the American Musical Theatre', *Notes*, xii (1954–5), 25; B. Shepard: 'A Repertory of 17th-century English House Music', *JAMS*, ix (1956), 61 [Filmer Collection]; B. Shepard: 'Yale's Music Library Revised', *Notes*, xiii (1955–6), 421; H. C. Fall: *A Critical Bibliographical Study of the Rinck Collection* (diss., Yale U., 1958); J. Kirkpatrick: *Temporary Mimeographed Catalog of Music MSS and Related Materials of C. E. Ives, 1874–1954* (New Haven, 1960); D. Boito: 'MS Music in the James Marshall and Marie-Louise Osborn Collection', *Notes*, xxvii (1970–71), 237; E. J. O'Meara: 'The Lowell Mason Library', *Notes*, xxviii (1971–2), 197 [rev. edn. of an earlier article]; V. Perlis: 'Ives and Oral History', *Notes*, xxviii (1971–2), 629; V. Perlis: 'The Futurist Music of Leo Ornstein', *Notes*, xxxi (1974–5), 735 [catalogue of works at Yale]

NEW YORK. Columbia University, Broadway at 116th Street, New York, NY 10027. The Music Library (at 701 Dodge Hall; *NYcu*) is strong in late 18th- and early 19th-century opera scores, as well as first and early editions (chiefly from the Bass Collection) of composers of this period. Erich Hertzmann donated his large film collection of Beethoven materials.

In the division of special collections (at 654 Butler Library) are the papers of Edward MacDowell, Daniel Gregory Mason, Nicolai Berezowsky and Douglas Moore. There are 68 autograph letters of composers and performers of the 18th–20th centuries, and Jacques Barzun's assemblage of correspondence and material forms the Hector Berlioz Collections. The Anton Seidl Collection of Musical Autographs, acquired in 1905 from his estate, contains material relating to his activities as a conductor. Other collections include Eda Rothstein Rappaport's holographs and the Isidore Witmark Collection of MS scores and 43 letters to American publishers from popular song composers.

An important collection of early liturgical MSS was assembled by George A. Plimpton, and ranges from a 10th-century neumed German lectionary to an 18th-century collection of Greek hymns, including a large group of antiphoners. The largest single collection (some 300,000 items) was assembled by Arthur Billings Hunt and purchased through a gift by Alfred C. Berol; it is chiefly noted for its early musical Americana. The library's autograph scores include works by 19th-century composers (e.g. Brahms, Bruckner and Richard Strauss) and works by Babbitt, Copland, Holst, MacDowell and others. Bartók gave the library MSS of his Romanian, Turkish and Serbo-Croatian folk material in 1943.

——. Juilliard School, Lila Acheson Wallace Library, Lincoln Center, Broadway and 65th Street, New York, NY 10023 (*NYj*). The Institute of Musical Art (founded in 1904 by Frank Damrosch) opened its music library in 1906 and merged with the Juilliard Graduate School 20 years later; together they were chartered as the Juilliard School of Music in 1927. A few holograph scores and letters are owned by the library and its special collections section includes early

editions of Liszt's piano music.

——. Library and Museum of the Performing Arts, Music Division, New York Public Library at Lincoln Center, 111 Amsterdam Avenue, New York, NY 10023 (*NYp*). The nucleus of the library is a collection of music, books on music and autographs assembled by H. F. Albrecht in Europe between 1845 and 1858 and purchased by the Philadelphia financier Joseph Drexel. By 1871 Drexel had acquired the libraries of R. la Roche and E. F. Rimbault. He issued a catalogue (Philadelphia, 1869) of the musical writings and compiled MS catalogues of the other material. The collection of some 6000 items was bequeathed to the Lenox Library (founded in 1870) in 1888; it included incunabula, theoretical works (especially Italian of the 15th–18th centuries) and the only known copy of *Parthenia inviolata or Mayden-Musicke for the Virginalls and Bass-viol* (*RISM* c1614[23]). It was especially famous for its English MSS for virginals (one Gibbons autograph), instrumental consort and voices (the Sambrooke MS, *NYp* Drexel 4302).

The libraries of John Jacob Astor (about 4000 music items), Lenox, and the Tilden Foundation were opened to the public in 1854, 1877 and 1887 respectively. The Music Division of the Reference Department was established in 1911 when the new building opened at 42nd Street. The Music Division, together with the theatre and dance collections, were moved to Lincoln Center in 1965 and collectively renamed the Library and Museum of the Performing Arts.

The library's special collections hold a number of incunabula, items by Boethius, Aristides, Glanvilla and Gaffurius. 16th-century publications include works by Agricola, Galilei, Fuenllana, Lassus and Beaujoyeux; important 17th-century imprints besides the Drexel items mentioned above include works by Lassus, Schadaeus, Besard and Vallet, as well as many theoretical works. Early and rare editions of Beethoven's works were received from the Beethoven Association when it dissolved in 1940.

A few autograph MSS had been acquired by the time the library opened in 1911, including works by Beethoven, Haydn and Mozart (K318); by 1915 holograph compositions by Mercadante, Paganini, Liszt and Glinka had been added. A 1932 gift in memory of Lizzie Bliss and Christian A. Herter included MSS by Bach, Handel, Haydn (H XVIII:6), Mozart (K296/315g), Schubert and Schumann. In 1950 the pianist Angela Diller presented the autographs of Stravinsky's *Symphony of Psalms* and *Capriccio*. Seven Brahms autographs were bequeathed by Paul Wittgenstein as well as music for the left hand he had commissioned from Ravel, Prokofiev and others. There are Liszt MSS and documents in the Carl Lachmund collection, and a Duke Ellington autograph. An unusual set of MSS, known as the Chirk Castle partbooks after their Welsh origin, was acquired in 1970 and contains 65 pre-Restoration Anglican services and anthems which survived the English Civil War in their original bindings. In 1975 the Columbia Broadcasting System presented about 200,000 pieces of MS music from its library (founded in 1929); the hundreds of commissioned compositions and arrangements for musical broadcasts include holographs of Antheil, Copland, Gould, Milhaud, Vittorio Giannini, Deems Taylor and Alex Wilder.

A substantial number of autograph letters was

received in the Drexel collection, in the Bliss–Herter gift of 1932 and in the donation of Howard van Sinderen in 1929, which contained the papers of the pianist William Mason. Numerous autograph letters, photographs and MS fragments were received in the estate of the pianist Alexander Lambert. The Hufstaders presented some correspondence and photographs of well-known musicians in 1965, and five years later the library purchased a collection of about 700 unpublished letters of Mendelssohn and the correspondence of Giuditta Pasta (containing letters from Bellini, Donizetti, Pacini, Rossini, Liszt, Malibran, Mazzini, Stendhal, Nicolini and Paer).

The Americana Collection grew out of a memorial to the composer and conductor Henry Hadley (1871–1937); MS collections include works by Ruggles, Varèse and Harris. All known MSS of the works of Gottschalk were acquired through purchases in 1948 and 1967. The archive of the League of Composers, containing many letters and other documents, was presented in 1966 by Claire R. Reis and musical scores of young Americans performed monthly at the Composers' Forums (sponsored jointly with Columbia University) became the property of the Americana Collection. There are 350,000 titles of American sheet music. The library is known for its special indexes (e.g. instrumental music published in the USA, 1830–70).

The Music Division has been responsible for a number of publications. During the 1930s and up to just after World War II editions were issued of works in its collections, including the Ozalid Print Series of early American sacred and secular music, a number of early symphonies, concertos and chamber works, and 16th- and 17th-century consort music.

A *Bulletin* of the New York Public Library, noting acquisitions, has been published quarterly since 1897. H. Botstiber: 'Musicalia in der NYPL', *SIMG*, iv (1902–3), 738; K. Brown: 'A Guide to the Reference Collections of the NYPL, *Bulletin*, xliii (1939), 53 [lists important gifts]; F. C. Campbell: 'The Music Division of the NYPL', *FAM*, xvi (1969), 112; New York Public Library Reference Department: *Dictionary Catalog of the Music Collection* (Boston, 1964); *Dictionary Catalog of the Research Libraries* (1971–)

——. National Broadcasting Company, Music Library, 30 Rockefeller Plaza, New York, NY 10020. Founded in 1926 by Julius Mattfeld (1893–1968), the library contains about 500,000 items, including works commissioned by the TV Opera Theater, and the Lewis Lane Music Collection of biographical material and programme notes.

——. Pierpont Morgan Library, 29–33 East 36th Street, New York, NY 10016 (*NYpm*). This important, privately endowed library was founded in 1924, and until recently contained only a few musical items. In 1971 it owned some 200 printed books on music, an equal number of printed scores and about 300 music MSS.

Important items in the original collection are a 13th-century Provençal chansonnier, an early 15th-century MS with four chansons of Machaut, the unique complete copy of Antico's *Motetti e canzoni* (1521; part of the Toovey Collection, acquired in 1899), autograph MSS of short vocal works by Rousseau, Haydn, Zingarelli, Vaccai and Rossini, and autograph scores of Beethoven (op.96), Gounod and Frederick Converse's opera *The Pipe of Desire* (the first American work to be performed by the Metropolitan Opera Company, 1910) and Sixth Symphony. There was also a collection of letters, including a document signed by Palestrina, Mozart's

two earliest surviving letters (both dated 13 December 1769) and important groups of letters by Mendelssohn and Wagner.

In 1949 Reginald Allen presented the first of many gifts from his collection of the works of Gilbert and Sullivan, which have been subsequently augmented by other gifts and purchases. In 1962 the library received a group of books and MSS collected by the financier Dannie N. Heineman. Important items are fragments and parts of works by Bach (Cantata 197*a*), Haydn (H XV:30), Mozart, Mendelssohn and Wagner; sketches of works by Beethoven (op.73) and Strauss (*Die ägyptische Helena*); and complete works by Mozart (K112, 467 and 537), Schubert (several songs), Schumann, Chopin, Brahms, Strauss and Wagner. There are two Wagner imprints heavily annotated by the composer: the proof of the full score of *Die Meistersinger von Nürnberg*, with thousands of corrections, and his own copy of the 1853 edition of *Der Ring des Nibelungen*, interleaved with his revisions. The Heineman Collection also contains a small but distinctive group of letters, notably from Haydn, Beethoven, Mozart and Rossini.

Mrs Janos Scholz has presented several important autograph MSS from the library of Ernest Schelling (including works by Chopin and Schumann). Gifts from the distinguished private collection of Robert Owen Lehman (now in the library) have been received annually from 1968 until the whole was eventually deposited; of particular interest is a large group of French autograph MSS formerly owned by Alfred Cortot, including works by Fauré, Massenet (piano concerto), Saint-Saëns (piano concerto), Franck (*Les béatitudes*) and Honegger (*Jeanne d'Arc au bûcher*). Four Chausson autographs, and others by Berlioz, Gounod, Hahn, d'Indy, Koechlin, Milhaud, Offenbach, Ropartz and Florent Schmitt, supplement the Cortot items. There are autograph full scores of works by Johann Strauss (ii), Moscheles and Paderewski. Recent gifts include autographs of nine Berg songs and several Webern MSS and a previously unknown self-portrait by Schoenberg.

The large gift of some 60 German, 9 Italian, 6 French and 15 other autograph MSS of great distinction was received in 1968 from Mary Flagler Cary; two years after her death in 1967 the trust established in her name added over 60 more. The earliest MS in the archive is a neumed 13th-century gradual from Germany. The Cary Collection is rich in autograph and holograph scores, notably Bach's Cantata 112, Beethoven's op.70 no.1, Schubert's *Winterreise* and *Schwanengesang*, Cherubini's sonata for two organs, Brahms's op.34*b*, Liszt's *Glanes de Woronince* and three versions of *Am Grabe Richard Wagners*, and Strauss's *Don Juan* and *Tod und Verklärung*, as well as works by Mozart, Weber, Chopin, Ponchielli and Mahler. Also in the collection are Beethoven sketches, the autograph voice part and annotated engraver's copy of Schumann's *Frauenliebe und -leben* and part of Berlioz's *Mémoires*. 19th-century Italian composers further represented by autograph works include Bellini, Giordano, Mascagni, Mercadante, Puccini, Rossini and Spontini; also present are minor compositions in the hand of Busoni, Catalani, Cimarosa, Crescentini, Pacini, Salieri and Verdi. Elaborate written-out embellishments occur in a collection of bel canto cadenzas for some 30 operas, as sung by Barbara Marchisio (1833–1919) and her sister Carlotta (1835–72), pupils of Luigi Fabbrica.

There is an autograph MS of Spohr's *Violinschule*, dated 1832. Because the collection was not strong in works by French composers, the Cary trustees later sought out such works and it now includes autograph full scores of two operas by Offenbach, *Les contes d'Hoffmann* and *La permission de dix heures*, Gounod's *Mireille*, Lecocq's *Le petit duc* and Massenet's *Manon*, as well as autographs of works by Debussy and Fauré (op.50).

Most interesting among the few 20th-century works is Dyagilev's copy of a full score of Stravinsky's *Firebird*, containing many revisions in the hand of the composer and various conductors who directed the work, as well as 76 MS and printed orchestral parts. The first draft of parts of Schoenberg's *Moses und Aron* and of his *Gurrelieder* are also in the library's possession.

By far the largest part of Mrs Cary's collection are the 3000 autograph letters of composers and musicians collected by her father, Harry Harkness Flagler, many of which are addressed to the Flaglers and the Carys themselves. A large number of letters (and some scores) were originally owned by the Leipzig publishers C. F. Peters, confiscated in World War II, then released to Walter Hinrichsen who took them to the USA. Other letters were acquired from Alfred Cortot and the English music critic Joseph Bennett. The earliest is from Nicolas Gombert (1547). 20th-century composers are represented by Schoenberg (with 43 letters), Berg (69) and Webern (14); from the 19th century are letters from Berlioz (33), Schumann (10), Wagner (25), Wolf (11), Richard Strauss (22), Chabrier (34), Verdi (31), Julius Benedict (22), Arthur Sullivan (34) and George Grove (22). Other musical documents include a group relating to the Vienna Court Orchestra, 1781–1810, and contemporary portraits (notably of Brahms, Mendelssohn and Schubert).

E. N. Waters: 'The Music Collection of the Heineman Foundation', *Notes*, vii (1949–50), 181–216 [incl. facs. of unpubd MSS]; *Books and Manuscripts from the Heineman Collection* (1963) [catalogue]; *The Mary Flagler Cary Music Collection* (1970); O. Albrecht: 'Musical Treasures in the Morgan Library', *Notes*, xxviii (1971–2), 643 [suppl. to the last-named]; Pierpont Morgan Library: *Sixteenth Report to the Fellows, 1969–1971* (New York, 1973)

NORTHAMPTON. Smith College, Werner Josten Music Library, Center for the Performing Arts, Northampton, Mass. 01060 (*Nsc*). The library received Alfred Einstein's MS transcriptions of 15th- and 16th-century Italian vocal music and 16th- and 17th-century instrumental music, and in 1965 the music collection of Henry S. and Sophie Drinker was deposited there. Much of the material has been published in the *Smith College Music Archives* (1935–).

OAKLAND. Mills College, Margaret Prall Music Library, Oakland, Calif. 94613 (*OAm*). Milhaud gave the Music Library some facsimiles of his works (not all published) while he was a teacher at the college; that gift augmented an already large collection of materials by and about him, including letters and autographs. Early MSS include dances of c1600 by Alison, Bacheler, Philips and others, arranged for cittern, and a collection of 18th-century English songs and dance tunes.

W. Rubsamen: 'Unusual Music Holdings of Libraries on the West Coast', *Notes*, x (1952–3), 546

OBERLIN. Oberlin College Conservatory of Music, Mary M. Vial Library, Oberlin, Ohio 44074 (*OB*). The conservatory and the college maintained separate music libraries until 1964, when both collections were moved into the new conservatory building. Recent additions to the library, which was founded in 1867, include a late 16th-century antiphoner and the holograph of Stravinsky's *Threni* (given by the composer in 1964). The C. W. Best Collection, bequeathed to the library in 1948, contains letters and autographs. In 1974 the library purchased from Félix Raugel some 500 volumes of early French theoretical treatises.

Mr. and Mrs. C. W. Best Collection of Autographs (Oberlin, 1967); W. Warch: *Our First 100 Years: a Brief History of the Oberlin Conservatory of Music* (Oberlin, 1967)

PHILADELPHIA. Curtis Institute of Music, 1726 Locust Street, Philadelphia, Penn. 19103 (*PHci*). Mary Louise Curtis Bok Zimbalist founded the institute in 1925 and was a benefactor of the library from its opening a year later until her death in 1970. Notable among her many gifts are autograph MSS by Mozart (K85/73*f*), Liszt, Strauss and the Czech composer Karel Navrátil. In 1931 she purchased from the heirs of Mary Banks Burrell (*d* 1898) a collection of 500 letters, music MSS and memorabilia of Wagner, including autograph short scores of *Rienzi* and *Tannhäuser*. A MS source of three-part organ tablature, containing the first known indication for the use of pedal (dated 1448), and the Jarvis Collection of 18th- and 19th-century printed music are important holdings.

M. B. Burrell: *Catalog of the Burrell Collection of Wagner* (London, 1929); J. N. Burk: *Letters of Richard Wagner: the Burrell Collection* (New York, 1950)

——. Free Library of Philadelphia, Logan Square, Philadelphia, Penn. 19103 (*PHf*). The first planned purchase of music occurred in 1897, five years after the founding of the library, and a separate Music Department was created in 1927. The Musical Fund Society, established in 1820, has supported the library through gifts and deposits. The collections are strong in Americana, with special emphasis on the music of Philadelphia from colonial times (including imprints, MSS and memorabilia of Benjamin Carr, Raynor Taylor, Alexander Reinagle, Francis Johnson, William Wallace Gilchrist, Charles Jarvis, Charles Zeuner, Samuel Laciar, Domenico Brescia and Frances McCollin). Other important Americana include 150,000 items of sheet music (including the Edwin I. Keffer Collection of about 1000 pre-1850 imprints); similar material from the collections of Edith A. Wright and Josephine A. McDevitt, Harry Dichter and Theodore Presser; songbooks, broadsides, psalms and hymns; American music periodicals dating from the early 19th century; and diaries, correspondence and pictures relating to Gottschalk. The Edwin A. Fleisher Music Collection of orchestral music contains much rare performing material.

The Edwin A. Fleisher Music Collection in the Free Library of Philadelphia: a Descriptive Catalog, i (1935, rev. 2/1965), ii (1945), suppl. (1966); B. B. Larrabee: 'The Music Department of the Free Library of Philadelphia', *Library Trends*, viii (1960), 574; Musical Fund Society: *Catalog of Orchestral & Choral Compositions Published and in MS between 1790 and 1840* (Philadelphia, 1974)

——. Historical Society of Pennsylvania, Library, 1300 Locust Street, Philadelphia, Penn. 19107 (*PHhs*). Founded in 1824, and occupying its present site since 1883, the library has a few European autograph MSS but is chiefly noted for its American music of the colonial and federal periods.

——. University of Pennysylvania, Philadelphia, Penn. 19104. The libraries of the University of Pennsylvania acquired some 1800 items of early music in print and MS while Otto Albrecht was music curator (1937–69). The strength of the music collection (now called the Otto E. Albrecht Music Library at 201 South 34th Street; *PHu*) lies in music of the 18th and early 19th centuries. French and English operas, librettos and instrumental music are represented by first and early editions.

The Rare Book Division of the Van Pelt Library (at 3420 Walnut Street) contains musical items. Its most notable collection is the library of Francis Hopkinson, which includes three MS volumes (a fourth is in the Library of Congress) containing songs and music for the harpsichord, the earliest dated 1759, a MS partbook of four-part psalms by Farnaby (possibly holograph), and 18th-century editions of Italian and German concertos. Other distinguished items include a 14th-century volume of poems containing works by Machaut and others, many unpublished, 15th- and 16th-century treatises, Haydn first editions, letters and papers of the Boston music journalist John Rowe Parker (1800–40) and some 25 cartons of letters and journals of Alma Mahler Werfel, which contain letters from Mahler, Berg, Webern and Schoenberg.

A *Library Chronicle of the University of Pennsylvania* has been published since 1933.

O. Sonneck: *Francis Hopkinson and James Lyon* (Washington, 1905/*R*1967); O. E. Albrecht: '18th-century Music in the University Libraries', *Library Chronicle of the University of Pennsylvania*, v (1937), 13; O. E. Albrecht: 'Francis Hopkinson, Musician, Poet and Patriot', ibid, vi (1938); N. P. Zacour and R. Hirsch: *Catalog of the Manuscripts in the Libraries of the University of Pennsylvania to 1800* (Philadelphia, 1966); C. Richards: *An Eighteenth-century Music Collection* (diss., U. of Pennsylvania, 1968)

PITTSBURGH. Carnegie Library of Pittsburgh, 4400 Forbes Avenue, Pittsburgh, Penn. 15213 (*Pc*). This public library, opened in 1895, has a collection from Karl Merz, founder of the Conservatory of Music at what was then the University of Wooster. Most of the library's musical MSS are related to musical life in Pittsburgh: the sketches for Emil Pauer's symphony *In der Natur*, the draft of Gardner Read's *Pennsylvania*, and MSS by Dallapiccola, Ross Lee Finney, Isadore Freed, Ginastera, Villa-Lobos and others, of works commissioned for the Pittsburgh ISCM Festival (1952) and the Pittsburgh Bicentennial (1958). There are autograph letters from Saint-Saëns, Herbert, Ives, Varèse, Damrosch and others, and documents relating to the early 19th-century singing-school conductor William Evens. The library of the Pittsburgh organist and scholar Charles N. Boyd was purchased in 1938 and includes material on Pittsburgh music.

Catalog of the Karl Merz Music Library (Pittsburgh, 1892); M. Emich: *Catalog of Music Books and Scores published before 1801 located in Carnegie Library of Pittsburgh* (diss., Western Reserve U. School of Library Science, 1952); T. M. Finney: *A Union Catalogue of Music and Books on Music Printed before 1801 in Pittsburgh Libraries* (Pittsburgh, 1959, 2/1963, suppl. 1964); I. Millen: 'Andrew Carnegie's Music Library', *Notes*, xxii (1965–6), 681

———. University of Pittsburgh, Theodore Finney Music Library, School of Music Building, Pittsburgh, Penn. 15213 (*Pu*). This library, organized in 1966 and named after the chairman of the music department, 1936–68, has Finney's private collection, rich in early editions of 17th- and 18th-century music as well as English and early American popular ballads and hymnbooks. Finney's MS collection, now in the special collections of the Hillman Library (the university's general library), includes, besides works by the 19th-century composer Fidelis Zitterbart, about 25 folios of mono-

phonic chant fragments from the 11th–15th centuries (the earliest in St Gall notation), a 17th-century collection of English liturgical music with works by Matthew Locke, a Haydn holograph, and works by the Pittsburgh composers Adolphe Foerster (1845–1927) and Ethelbert Nevin (1862–1901). The Foster Collection, amassed by J. K. Lilly, contains about 10,000 items relating to Stephen Collins Foster.

F. Hodges: 'A Pittsburgh Composer and his Memorial', *Western Pennsylvania Historical Magazine*, xxi/2 (1938), 3; T. M. Finney: *A Union Catalogue of Music and Books on Music Printed before 1801 in Pittsburgh Libraries* (Pittsburgh, 1959, 2/1963, suppl. 1964); T. M. Finney: 'A Group of English Manuscript Volumes at the University of Pittsburgh', *Essays in Musicology in Honor of Dragan Plamenac* (Pittsburgh, 1969), 21

POUGHKEEPSIE. Vassar College, George Sherman Dickinson Music Library, Poughkeepsie, NY 12601 (*PO*). The library owns a special collection of material (including MSS) by women composers, and modest collections of other MSS, mainly of former faculty members, but also 18th-century works and letters. Notable private collections acquired include chamber music parts from Edward Dannreuther, who was a pupil of F. L. Ritter (1834–91), the first music teacher at the college, the library of the Venezuelan musician Teresa Carreño (1853–1917), and MSS of the Russian violinist and composer Boris Koutzen (1901–66). A catalogue of the library's holdings is available on microfilm.

PRINCETON. Princeton University, Harvey S. Firestone Memorial Library, Princeton, NJ 08540 (*PRu*). Important holdings are spread among several collections particularly rich in medieval and Renaissance music and later autograph MSS. The Music Collection was established in 1935 and shares some early editions with other collections administered by the Department of Rare Books and Special Collections, notably works by Palestrina, Wilbye, Purcell, Bach, Handel, Haydn, Mozart and Brahms. The department holds the private collection of William H. Scheide which includes medieval liturgical MSS (including a 9th- or early 10th-century evangeliary with ekphonetic notation, an 11th-century French antiphoner with neumes on a primitive staff, an early 14th-century Franciscan antiphoner for Rome Use, a Rhenish *Psalterium feriale* of the same period and a 15th-century English gradual for Sarum Use); musical incunabula (including the earliest known example of Gerson's *Collectorium super Magnificat*, 1473; Niger's *Grammatica brevis*, 1480; and a *Missale romanum*, c1482); autograph MSS (e.g. the full score of Bach's motet BWV118, Mozart's K332/300k, a Beethoven sketchbook of 1815 and other unbound sheets, a Schubert song and a full score of Wagner's *Das Rheingold*).

Other notable music collections are the Robert Garrett Collection (including 13th-century English psalters, an important group of English motets from c1300, early 15th-century fragments of Latin treatises and 15th- and 16th-century Byzantine, Armenian, Slavonic, French, Italian and Spanish liturgical books), the Greenville Kane Collection (early French, German and Italian psalters, 14th- and 15th-century German and Italian choirbooks and an early 13th-century English copy of a Boethius treatise), the Princeton Collection (whose liturgical works include a 12th-century French *Missale plenum* with Aquitanian neumes, a 13th-century English troper, and German, Spanish and northern Italian MSS up to the 17th century); and the James S. Hall Handel Collection (nearly all the published 18th-century editions of Handel's works and important contemporary MSS).

The *Princeton University Library Chronicle* has been published three times yearly since 1939.

M. R. Bryan and P. Morgan: 'Music Exhibition', *The Princeton University Library Chronicle*, xxviii (1967), 106; J. M. Knapp: 'The Hall Handel Collection', *The Princeton University Library Chronicle*, xxxvi (1974–5), 3

PROVIDENCE. Brown University, Providence, Rhode Island 02912 (*PROu*). Music may be found in the Music Department and the John D. Rockefeller jr Library, but the John Hay Library holds the special collections and MSS. The Harris Collection of American Poetry and Plays, presented in 1884, has since been considerably enlarged through the acquisition of parts of the libraries of H. T. Burleigh, Jerome Kern and Ewen McColl. It contains many music imprints of 1820–60, including dramatic music, songbooks, broadsides and material relating to Boston music publishing (particularly the Graupners). The Hamilton C. MacDougall Collection of about 3000 hymnals and psalters is noted for its early 18th-century Moravian and Shaker works, and there is sheet music of the Civil War period in the McLellan Lincoln Collection. American music printed before 1801 is collected (and indexed) by the John Carter Brown Library, which is strong in music of the Americas. It owns a Navarro edition (1604) and a 12th-century MS gradual from Ottobeuren for Benedictine Use. The Annmary Brown Memorial Library collects pre-1500 imprints, including theoretical treatises and liturgical works.

A. C. Morril: *Civil War Ballads in the Harris Collection* (Providence, 1928); D. Laurent: *Secular Music Published in America before 1830 in the Harris Collection* (diss., Brown U., 1953); T. D. Roy: *Study and Catalogue of Presidential Campaign Songsters in the Harris . . . and McLellan Lincoln Collection* (diss., Brown U., 1964); Brown University Libraries: *Dictionary Catalog of the Harris Collection of American Poetry and Plays* (Boston, 1972)

ROCHESTER. University of Rochester, Eastman School of Music, Sibley Music Library, 44 Swan Street, Rochester, NY 14604 (*R*). The school was founded in 1921, and the library's first important purchase was the archive of the French music critic and pedagogue known as Pougin (1834–1921) in 1923, which contained some 3000 items related to French theatre and opera from the 17th–19th centuries. The 11th-century Reichenau MS and the 12th-century Admont–Rochester MS 494 were acquired in 1929 and 1936 respectively, containing treatises by Hermannus Contractus, William of Bernon, Wilhelm of Hirsau, Grutolf of Michelsberg, Aribo (*De musica*) and Guido of Arezzo (*Micrologus*). A MS collection illustrating musical notation from the 10th century to the 16th, amassed by Oskar Fleischer and purchased in 1935, has 35 volumes of music and treatises. The library has continued to collect theoretical works of all periods, and has incunabula by Niger and Keinspeck.

During the early 1930s some 16th-century partbooks were acquired, including unique copies of Italian madrigals, and early editions of Palestrina, Josquin, Morales, Pietro Vinci and Lassus. The Leo S. Olschki Collection of 17th-century sacred partbooks was purchased in 1940, consisting of sacred works by Angeleri, Beria, Cima and others (described by Einstein, *La bibliofilia*, xl, 1933, p.38). Autograph scores include trio sonatas by Purcell, fragments of works by Haydn, Mozart and Beethoven, songs by Schubert and Brahms, Liszt piano arrangements of Weber overtures, and items

by Saint-Saëns, Debussy, Fauré and Krenek.

During the 1950s, collections of Italian songs, ballets and comic operas of late 18th-century London and Paris, as well as nearly 1000 operas (mostly French, 1880–1930), were acquired. Howard Hanson presented 23 of his holograph MSS in 1949 and others later. The library also owns MS material by Weldon Hart and Parks Grant.

A *Library Bulletin* has been published since 1945.

B. Duncan: 'The Sibley Music Library', *Library Bulletin*, i (1946), 26; R. Watanabe: 'Historical Introduction to the Sibley Music Library', *Library Bulletin*, xvii (1962), 43

SALEM. Essex Institute, James Duncan Phillips Library, Salem, Mass. 01970 (*SA*). The library has a small but distinguished collection of Americana, of tune books, partbooks and early instruction books, printed and MS copies. Later MSS and publications are restricted to Essex County musicians (A. W. Foote, P. S. Gilmore, the Hutchinson family and H. K. Oliver). Most of the uncatalogued music referred to by H. E. Johnson in 'Notes on Sources of Musical Americana', *Notes*, v (1947–8), 169, was sold in 1971. The library has published *Historical Collections* quarterly since 1859.

SAN FRANCISCO. Public Library, Fine Arts Department, Music Division, Civic Center, San Francisco, Calif. 94102 (*SFp*). This library, founded in 1878, inaugurated a separate Music Department in 1917. Among the special collections are nearly 200 volumes of popular sheet music from after 1800, materials relating to the music of the Gold Rush era (*c*1849), San Francisco and California.

——. San Francisco State College Library, Frank V. de Bellis Collection, 1630 Holloway Avenue, San Francisco, Calif. 94132 (*SFsc*). From 1952 until his death in 1968 De Bellis amassed 10,000 early editions and MSS of Italian music and arranged performances of these works, primarily in the San Francisco area. He donated most of his incunabula in 1963 to the trustees of the California State Colleges, who housed the collection there. The earliest MSS include part of a northern Italian choirbook of *c*1380 and an antiphoner of 1497. The 16th century is represented by a MS requiem mass, a *cantorinus* (Venice, 1513) containing music for liturgical offices and instructions for choral singing, and a number of printed partbooks (which contain works by Corteccia, Palestrina, Striggio, Raimondi and others). 17th-century partbooks contain madrigals, motets and psalms by Agazzari, Anerio, Asola, Dembolencio, Gesualdo, Giovanelli, Giovanni del Turco, d'India, Maschera, Miniscalchi, Montella, Nanino and Zoilo. There is a lute MS of 1615 containing about 60 airs and dances (described by G. Reese in 'An Early Seventeenth-century Italian Lute Manuscript at San Francisco', *Essays in Musicology in Honor of Dragan Plamenac* (Pittsburgh, 1969), 253) and two volumes of continuo songs and duets. The collection is strong in 18th-century music, with a holograph MS by Alessandro Scarlatti, dated 1707, of his oratorio *Il primo omicidio*, and many first editions, including Benedetto Marcello's *Estro poetico-armonico* (1724–6), cantatas and 100 Italian orchestral works in contemporary parts. Italian opera is represented by several hundred full and vocal scores and librettos, many of them first editions. There are also many pre-1600 theoretical works. De Bellis also acquired a number of autograph letters and 18th- and 19th-century contemporary portraits of composers and performers.

The Frank V. de Bellis Collection in the Library of San Francisco State College (1964, 2/1967)

SAN MARINO. Henry E. Huntington Library and Art Gallery, 1151 Oxford Road, San Marino, Calif. 91108 (*SM*). Before his death in 1927 Huntington amassed a collection strong in English and American history and literature of some 175,000 volumes, about 5500 of which are musical items. Most are English or American works of the 16th–18th centuries, and come principally from the Bridgewater House Library (founded in the time of Elizabeth I by Thomas Egerton and rich in Renaissance and 17th-century materials), the Britwell Court Library (founded by W. H. Miller, 1789–1848, and noted for its English madrigals, American broadside ballads and early songbooks in fine editions), and the library of Henry Huth (containing liturgies, psalters and a few madrigals in MS, as well as printed English and Italian madrigals of the 16th century, popular songs and theatre music). There are 106 musical items relating to George Washington in the collection of W. U. Lewisson and early American music in the collection of R. A. Brock. The few recent additions include some 300 engraved 18th-century English broadsides and much 19th- and early 20th-century American sheet music.

Of the 129 musical incunabula, about two-thirds are theoretical works without notation. About 900 of the musical items published between 1500 and 1640 are English madrigals, lute-songs and instrumental works, Reformation Dutch, English, French, German and Italian psalters and English theoretical works (supplemented by a few Italian ones). The only complete set of partbooks of Thomas Whythorne's *Songes* (London, 1571) is found here. Music of the late 17th century is represented by a large collection of Playford's songbooks, numerous vocal works by Henry and William Lawes, one of two known copies of *Tripla concordia* (London, 1677[4]), treatises of Simpson and Mace, rare publications of the pioneer Aberdeen printer John Forbes, and early broadside melodies.

The greatest quantity of music is of 18th-century origin. The Huth Collection is augmented by 40 ballad operas, the John Larpent Collection (18th- and 19th-century English and Italian MS plays and librettos), the J. P. Kemble-Devonshire Collection (printed English plays), a large collection of British magazine music published between 1740 and the early 1770s, some French operettas and musical comedies and American hymnbooks and anthems.

A large quantity of American sheet music of the 19th century is related to the war of 1812, the 1840 Whig Convention, the Civil War and Harriet Beecher Stowe's influence. There are early Afro-American and minstrel songs, ballads by Henry Russell, John L. Hewitt and Stephen Foster, theatre music and American hymnbooks. Most of the library's few autograph MSS are from this period; they include works by Gounod, Liszt and Mendelssohn. Among the other MSS are 18 early liturgical ones, which are supplemented by a 14th-century theological miscellany (Gwysaney 19914); there is also a fine MS collection of Italian madrigals copied for Sir John Egerton, an autograph collection of airs by J.-J. Rousseau and a group of 28 anthems by Charles Wesley.

The *Huntington Library Bulletin*, published irregularly from 1931 to 1937, was superseded by the *Huntington Library Quarterly* in 1937.

D. MacMillan: *Catalogue of the Larpent Plays in the Huntington Library* (San Marino, 1939); E. N. Backus: 'The Music Resources of the Huntington Library', *Notes* (1942), no.14, p.27; E. N. Backus: *Catalogue of Music in the Huntington Library Printed before 1801* (San Marino, 1949)

STANFORD. Stanford University, Stanford, Calif. 94305. The Memorial Library of Music (in the special collections section of the main library) was presented by George Keating and his wife in 1950 and collects chiefly autograph MSS (especially of living composers) and autographed copies of first editions from the late 17th century. It holds autograph MSS of Blow, Purcell, Alessandro Scarlatti (*La sposa de cantici*), Bach, Handel, Schubert (*Zauberharfe* overture, generally known as that to *Rosamunde*), Schumann, Mendelssohn, Mascagni (*Cavalleria rusticana*), Stravinsky (*Danses concertantes*) and Irving Berlin. The library has recently acquired material including MSS from composer Dane Rudyhar.

The Music Library (*STu*) (in the Division of Humanities and Social Sciences, at The Knoll) specializes in 18th-century theoretical works, early 19th-century chamber music, opera and materials concerning performing practice. The Hoover Institution on War, Revolution and Peace contains materials relating to music and politics.

The university's Archive of Recorded Sound is second only to that of the Library of Congress in size and scope.

N. Almond and H. H. Fisher: *Special Collections in the Hoover Library of War, Revolution and Peace* (Stanford, 1940); N. van Patten: *Catalog of the Memorial Library of Music* (1950)

URBANA. University of Illinois, Urbana, Ill. 61801 (*U*). The Music Library (220 Smith Music Hall), founded in 1944, now contains over 200,000 items, as well as the stock of 500,000 items in the Hunleth Music Store in St Louis acquired in 1974 (mostly American imprints from 1900), and a separate performing collection. The John Philip Sousa collection of more than 3000 instrumentations and sets of parts is administered by the University Band Department. Special collections include the library of the pianist Rafael Joseffy, containing 19th-century piano music, with his annotations, Joseph Szigeti's collection of editions and MSS (chiefly violin music) and the Dichter collection, originally of 3300 items of American sheet music of 1830–76 and now much expanded with more recent material.

The special collections of the University Library include American music, notably a collection of over 800 items in 15 volumes printed in Chicago before the 1871 fire, and Confederate imprints including the sheet music collection of R. Harwell. There is English material printed before 1700, a late 15th-century MS book of chants and Lamentations for the Office, a contemporary copy of Gluck's *Alceste* and an autograph score of Stravinsky's *Mavra*.

J. Allen: 'The Music Library at the University of Illinois', *Notes, Supplement for Members*, vi–vii (1949), 3; R. Harwell: *More Confederate Imprints*, i (Richmond, 1957), 225ff; Andrew Hughes: 'New Italian and English Sources of the 14th to 16th Centuries', *AcM*, xxxix (1967), 171; 'Recent Acquisitions', *Notes*, xxxi (1974–5), 282

WASHINGTON, DC. Folger Shakespeare Library, 201 East Capitol Street NW, Washington, DC 20003 (*Ws*). The Folger collection (opened in 1932) and the Leicester Harmsworth collection (acquired 1937) include copies of about half of all known Elizabethan printed music as well as MSS and historical and theoretical works of the period, and is now administered by the trustees of Amherst College. Notable among the MSS are autographs by Dowland, Robert Jones and John Playford (his own copy of songs in *The Tempest* set by John Wilson). Two MS collections include madrigals by Weelkes, Wilbye and Morley and liturgical music. Rare printed items include a unique copy of Thomas Morley's *First Booke of Ayres* (1600) and works by Byrd, East and Leighton. From later periods the library has amassed a large MS collection of operas based on Shakespearean plays, as well as incidental music and individual song settings. Holographs include John Hatton's incidental music to *Henry VIII, Macbeth* and *Richard II* and Niccolò Zingarelli's *Romeo e Giulietta*, dated 1796.

Catalog of Printed Books of the Folger Shakespeare Library, Washington, D.C. (Boston, 1970); *Catalog of Manuscripts of the Folger Shakespeare Library* (Boston, 1971)

——. Library of Congress, Music Division, Washington, DC 20540 (*Wc*). The Music Division is a service and custodial division in the Reference Department of the Library of Congress. It was established officially in 1897 under Walter Rose Whittlesey. Its director from 1902 to 1917, Oscar Sonneck, displayed extraordinary skill and energy in developing and organizing the archive. Early in his administration Sonneck devised a classification system which, revised and amplified by his successors, has been adopted by many other libraries. It divides the collection into three main categories: Music, Musical Literature and Musical Theory or Teaching. His work was continued by his successors (Carl Engel, 1922–34; Oliver Strunk, 1934–7; Harold Spivacke, 1937–72; Edward N. Waters, from 1972), and the resources of the division have helped to make the collection one of the richest in existence.

In 1976 the total holdings of the Music Division numbered approximately 4,500,000 items, and about 55,000 are added annually through copyright deposit, gift, purchase, transfer and exchange. This largely accounts for the rapid growth of the collections and gives special significance to the holdings of contemporary publications. The Copyright Office, which is a part of the Library of Congress, regularly publishes lists of titles deposited. Notable acquisitions used to be announced in the annual reports of the librarian of Congress from 1903 to 1942 and are now announced in the *Quarterly Journal of the Library of Congress*.

Outstanding features of the collections are early books on music, estimated at about two-thirds of all such books printed before 1800; dramatic, symphonic and chamber works, both pre- and post-1800; more than 50,000 librettos; early Americana, including hymnbooks, patriotic and popular music; and autograph scores and letters (including probably the largest collection of Brahms MSS as well as those of American composers from the 18th century to the present).

The division is rich in MS materials of many kinds, including thousands of autograph letters and other papers of musicians such as Antheil, Beethoven, Berg, Brahms, Bridge, Casella, Damrosch, Liszt, MacDowell, Paganini, Rakhmaninov, Loeffler, Schoenberg and Webern. Notable special collections of MSS are the Martorell Collection of 18th-century opera excerpts, the 20th-century transcripts of operatic full scores and the Albert Schatz Collection of opera librettos (shelved with subject-related matter). The following musical autographs warrant special mention: Bach's Cantatas nos.9 and 10; Bartók's Concerto for Orchestra and String

Quartet no.5; Beethoven's Piano Sonata op.109 and part of String Quartet op.130; Berg's *Wozzeck*; Brahms's Handel Variations and Fugue op.24, String Sextet op.18, Symphony no.3 and Violin Concerto; Chausson's *Poème*; Debussy's *Nocturnes*; Hindemith's *Hérodiade*; Leoncavallo's *Pagliacci*; Liszt's *Festpolonaise* and *Soirées de Vienne*; Prokofiev's String Quartet op.50; Rakhmaninov's Paganini Rhapsody, Piano Concerto no.4, Symphony no.3 and *Symphonic Dances*; Ravel's *Chansons madécasses*; Schoenberg's *Verklärte Nacht*, *Pierrot lunaire*, *A Survivor from Warsaw* and all the string quartets; Schumann's Symphony no.1; Stravinsky's *Apollo Musagetes*, *The Fairy's Kiss*, Mass and *Oedipus rex*; and Webern's String Quartet op.28. American composers represented by autograph MSS include John Alden Carpenter, George Chadwick, Frederick Shepherd Converse, Gershwin, Victor Herbert, Loeffler, MacDowell, David Stanley Smith, Sousa and most important 20th-century composers.

With the acquisition of the Cummings, Weckerlin, Prieger and Landau collections the division greatly increased its holdings of primary sources and research materials. It holds only a few medieval sources, however. Items notable for their rarity and importance are John Cotton's 12th-century *De musica*; the late 15th-century MS Laborde Chansonnier, many early editions including several by Petrucci (notable are works by Mouton, Josquin, Gombert, Palestrina, Victoria, Byrd, Peri and Caccini); and a large representation of theoretical writings from the early 16th century onwards.

Other departments of the library include the Archive of Folk Song, which since 1928 has assembled a national collection of folk music and folklore, with recorded items and many thousands of MSS, international but concentrating on the USA; the archive also coordinates and disseminates information about the subject. There is also a Recorded Sound Section, which under a 1972 amendment to the USA copyright statutes receives published recordings in the obligatory classification long applicable to books and musical scores; attached to the Recorded Sound Section is the Recording Laboratory, which makes original recordings for the collections and conducts research into the preservation and reproduction of recorded sound (its work resulted in the report *Preservation and Storage of Sound Recordings* by A. G. Pickett and M. M. Lemcoe, Washington, 1959).

Within the Music Division are several foundations and activities created by private philanthropy; these enable the Library of Congress to exert an influence in the world of music rarely associated with library institutions.

The Elizabeth Sprague Coolidge Foundation, established by Mrs Coolidge in 1925, has commissioned many significant chamber works. It has acquired a fine collection of 20th-century musical autographs, including many of those mentioned above as well as others by Barber, Bloch, Britten, Chávez, Copland, Cowell, Dallapiccola, Dello Joio, Finney, Ginastera, Hanson, Harris, Honegger, Malipiero, Martinů, Mennin, Menotti, Milhaud, Nono, Piston, Pizzetti, Porter, Poulenc, Respighi, Roussel, Saygun, Schuller, Schuman, Sessions, Thompson, Thomson, Villa-Lobos and Wellesz. Mrs Coolidge also had an auditorium built in the library.

During 1935–6 Gertrude Clarke Whittall presented

to the Library of Congress five magnificent Stradivari instruments and five Tourte bows, creating a foundation to care for the instruments and to give public concerts in which they would be heard. The foundation has provided the Music Division with the means of acquiring a distinguished group of autographs.

The Serge Koussevitzky Music Foundation was established in 1949 to commission new works; their MSS are added to the autograph collections and include items by Bernstein, Blackwood, Britten, Copland, Crumb, Diamond, Fine, Ginastera, Harris, Kay, Kirchner, Klebe, Ligeti, Matsudaira, Mennin, Mennini, Messiaen, Moore, Orrego-Salas, Riegger, Somers, Stockhausen, Takemitsu, Tippett, Varèse, Walton, Wuorinen and Xenakis. The McKim Fund (1970) is one of the endowments in the Music Division devoted to commissioning and performance; among the commissioned MSS thus far received are works for violin and piano by Blackwood, Kupferman, Laderman, Rorem and Siegmeister. To bring Coolidge Auditorium concerts to a larger audience, the Katie and Walter Louchheim Fund (1968) supports recording and broadcasting. The Norman P. Scala Memorial Fund financially assists performances, lectures and research on the music of the Francis M. Scala's era (the mid-19th century), the acquisition of relevant material for the collections, and exhibits of special items; the library has Francis M. Scala's collection of documentary material. The Louis Charles Elson Memorial Fund (1945) provides for the delivery and publication of lectures on music and musical literature. The Nicholas Longworth Foundation was established after the death of the statesman Nicholas Longworth (1869–1931) to assure concerts in his memory. He was the first president of the Friends of Music in the Library of Congress, a national organization founded in 1928 to assist the Music Division in purchasing rarities. The Sonneck Memorial Fund, an endowment established by the Beethoven Association of New York, is used to subsidize the publication of original research in American musical history. The library houses the Dayton C. Miller Flute Collection, with instruments, music, literature and works of art, and its endowment provides concerts and other activities in connection with the flute and its music.

WINSTON-SALEM. Moravian Music Foundation, 20 Cascade Avenue, Salem Station, Winston-Salem, North Carolina 27108 (WS). The purpose of the foundation when it was created by Donald M. McCorkle in 1956 was to preserve and encourage the study of Moravian music in Germany and America; its scope now covers the related areas of American music, Protestant hymnody and European music of the 18th and 19th centuries (particularly orchestral and chamber works). One of its special collections is the Moravian Music Archives of sacred vocal and secular instrumental music (mainly in MS) used in the Moravian communities of North Carolina. It contains the Salem Congregation Collection (parts for about 1200 arias and anthems accompanied by small orchestra composed by Moravians and others, c1760–1830), the Johannes Herbst Collection (arias, anthems and larger choral works, chiefly in score, c1760–1810), the Collegium Musicum Salem Collection (over 500 orchestral and chamber works by 18th- and 19th-century European composers, nearly half in MS), the Salem Band

Collection (partbooks containing 18th-century German chorales and American Civil War music) and miscellaneous copybooks and documents. Other collections of the foundation are the Irving Lowens Musical Americana Collection of over 2000 volumes (chiefly tune books), the Richard A. Kurth Collection of compositions and arrangements by members of the Kurth family in Germany and America from c1840 to the early 20th century, and the Peter Memorial Library containing reference works, miscellaneous 18th- and 19th-century editions and MSS. Many Moravian works have been published in modern editions, and a half-yearly *Bulletin* has been issued since 1956.

D. M. McCorkle: 'The Moravian Contribution to American Music', *Notes*, xiii (1955–6), 597; M. Gombosi: *Catalog of the Johannes Herbst Collection* (Chapel Hill, 1970)

WORCESTER. American Antiquarian Society, 185 Salisbury Street, Worcester, Mass. 01609 (*WOa*). Founded by the publisher Isaiah Thomas in 1812 as the first national historical society in the USA, the library has amassed near-complete collections of published works on US history and culture up to 1876, including music. The collection of sacred American tune books issued before 1820 is the largest in the country, and there are many hymnals of 1821–80. There are interesting collections of instrumental instruction books issued before 1820, early manuals for vocal instruction, and patriotic and popular songs up to the war of 1812.

IV. Latin America, Caribbean. Early Western polyphony survives in at least 12 colonial cathedrals of Hispanic America: Mexico City, Puebla, Oaxaca, Morelia, Guadalajara, Guatemala City, Santiago (Cuba), Bogotá, Lima, Cuzco, Sucre and Santiago (Chile). The only extant early music in other cathedrals known to have been once rich in polyphonic music (such as those at Quito, Ecuador and Ayacucho, Peru) is volumes of plainchant. In Brazil, the cathedrals at Rio de Janeiro and São Paulo (though not the oldest one at Bahia) still have important historic music holdings.

With the exception of Brazil, the national libraries of Latin America did not fund separate music divisions in the 1970s, though those of Mexico, Peru, Bolivia (at Sucre), Chile and Argentina all owned a certain amount of music in that year. The difficulty of estimating accurately the music holdings of any Latin American library or archive, national or provincial, is demonstrated by the article on libraries and archives in the leading Spanish-language lexicon, *Diccionario de la música Labor* (1954), which omits Latin America. Several scholars collaborating in that work lived in Latin America and owned personal music collections; the best music libraries other than those in ecclesiastical institutions of restricted access are in private hands.

In the 1970s Latin American conservatories, except in Brazil, kept little more than a few elementary texts and dictionaries. Essentially nothing has changed since 1954, when a survey conducted by the Pan American Union in Washington of all Latin American music schools showed how meagre their collections were (*Conservatorios, academias y escuelas de música y orquestas sinfónicas*).

R. Stevenson: *Renaissance and Baroque Musical Sources in the Americas* (Washington, DC, 1970)

The archival heritage of the Caribbean Islands is small: what once existed has been largely destroyed by pirate attacks, during the colonial period, and by the natural elements in a tropical climate. There are no catalogues of the music collections in any libraries of the area, except those in Cuba; the many publications by scholars who have surveyed the island libraries do not include music.

R. Stevenson: *A Guide to Caribbean Music History* (Lima, 1975)

ARGENTINA

Two historical events contributed to the loss of so many of Argentina's musical sources: the violent expulsion in 1767 of the Jesuits, who had contributed much to the development of Argentine music since the early 1600s, and the destruction for political reasons of the oldest Catholic churches in Buenos Aires in 1955. It is significant that no MSS of Domenico Zipoli, who died in Argentina in 1726 and was the greatest of the Jesuit composers, have been found in Argentine libraries, although some exist in neighbouring countries. The oldest surviving musical material dates from the 19th century, and even here there are few MSS. The following libraries contain musical sources: in Buenos Aires, the Museo Historico Nacional (at Defensa 1600; it owns five MS volumes from the 19th century known as the 'Albums of Manuelita', which contain works by Juan Pedro Esnaola and other Argentine composers as well as copies of European works); the Archivo General de la Nacion (Leandro N. Alem 246; autograph MSS of Esnaola and his contemporaries); the Biblioteca Nacional (México 564; a large number of printed works by Argentine composers as well as a book of lute tablature, compiled in Prague between 1720 and 1730); the Biblioteca y Archivo del Teatro Colón (Libertad 611); the Facultad de Artes y Ciencias Musicales de la Universidad Católica Argentina (Humberto I° 656; more than 1000 volumes of Argentine music from the 19th and 20th centuries, the complete collection of the musicologist Carlos Vega, and a vocal score of *Huemac* by Pascual de Rogatis dated 1916, one of the most important operas of the Argentine nationalist school); the Biblioteca del Instituto Nacional de Estudios de Teatro (Avenida Córdoba 1199; MSS and early printed editions of music for various 19th- and 20th-century farces); in La Plata, the Universidad Nacional de la Plata, Coleccion Azzarini (19th-century MSS and first editions); and in Mendoza, the Escuela Superior de Música de la Universidad de Cuyo (San Lorenzo 110; 20th-century MSS and printed editions of Argentine works).

BOLIVIA

LA PAZ. Biblioteca del Congreso, Avenida Mariscal Santa Cruz, La Paz. There is a collection of about 300 17th- and 18th-century villancicos, which originated in Sucre (presumably from the disestablished monastery of St Philip Neri) and was formerly owned by Julia Elena Fortún; apart from Galuppi and José Sanz, the composers named in her published lists (Juan de Araujo, Ceruti, Antonio Durán de la Mota, Pablo Grandón and Manuel Mesa) lived in the areas now constituting Bolivia and Peru.

J. E. Fortún: 'La navidad en el ámbito chuquisaqueño', *Cuaderno de la Sociedad folklórica de Bolivia*, i (Sucre, 1952), 13; J. E. Fortún: 'La navidad en Bolivia', *Universidad de San Francisco Xavier*, xvii (Sucre, 1953), 194–248; J. E. Fortún: *Antología de navidad* (La Paz, 1956); R. Stevenson: *Renaissance and Baroque Musical Sources in the Americas* (Washington, DC, 1970), 107ff

MOXOS, BENI. S Ignacio, Moxos, Beni. The church was staffed by Jesuit missionaries until 1768 and contains works attributed by Indian scribes to Zipoli and Araujo.

S. Claro: *La música en las misiones Jesuitas de Moxos* (Santiago de Chile, 1969)

SUCRE. Catedral, Sala Capitula, Plaza 25 de Mayo, Sucre. What is now Sucre was from 1609 the seat of the archbishopric of La Plata, which, rivalling Spain's great city Toledo in wealth, attracted many of the best composers in Spanish dominions, including Araujo and Gutierre Fernández Hidalgo. Among more than 600 MSS from the 16th century to the beginning of the 19th are 119 works by Araujo; other composers well represented include Theodoro de Ayala, Manuel Carrizo, Agustín Cavezas, Andrés Flores, Eustachio Franco Rebollo, Blas Tardio and Julián de Vargas. There are also MSS from nearby Potosí, including works by Durán de la Mota, Vargas and an otherwise unknown mass by Zipoli (copied in 1784). The library holds a number of works by European composers, mainly Spanish. New World representatives include Toribio del Campo y Pando, Ceruti, Miguel Mateo de Dallo y Lana, Bartolomé Massa, José de Orejón y Aparicio and J. M. Tirado.

C. García Muñoz and W. Axel Roldán: *Un archivo musical americano* (Buenos Aires, 1972) [part catalogue]; R. Stevenson: *Renaissance and Baroque Musical Sources in the Americas* (Washington, DC, 1970), 222ff

——. Biblioteca Nacional, Casa de la Libertad, Sucre. The library owns more than 500 works by 19th- and early 20th-century Bolivians, including Simeón Roncal and Mariano and Luis Pablo Rosquellas. M. M. Mercado's *Ilustraciones gráficas del Potosí Colonial* (Colección Rück 486–8) is the most important music MS there.

BRAZIL (BR)

The public archives and those of orchestras and bands maintain valuable collections of MSS but have yet to be fully organized. Nor have the rich collections of cathedrals, churches and religious orders been properly catalogued. Three collections in Minas Gerais deserve mention for their important holdings. The Palácio do Arcebispado, the Pão de S. Antônio (a home for the elderly) in Diamantina and the Arquivo de Música da Arquidiocese in Mariana hold more than 300 MSS, including works by José Mauricio Nunes Garcia (the most important Brazilian composer of the late 18th century), José Joaquim Emerico Lobo de Mesquita, Marcos Coelho Netto, Francisco Manuel da Silva, José Maria Xavier, Henrique Alves de Mesquita, Antônio Leal Moreira and João de Deus. The Centro de Ciências, Letras e Artes (at Rua Bernardino de Campos 989, Campinas, São Paulo) holds MSS of works by Carlos Gomes, J. M. Nunes Garcia and others.

PETRÓPOLIS. Museu Imperial, Avenida 7 de Setembro 94, 25600 Petrópolis. The historical archive of the museum contains about 100 documents relating to music. Originally belonging to the royal family, the collection was taken to France when the Republic of Brazil was founded and not returned to the country until 1948. Of particular interest are the letters to Emperor Pedro II from Brazilian and foreign composers offering their compositions or thanking him for special favours. Other composers represented include Sigismund Neukomm, Rossini, Ambroise Thomas, Saint-Saëns, Dubois, Patti, Fiorito, Fachinetti, Itiberê da Cunha, Carlos Gomes, Leopoldo Miguez and João Gomes de

Araujo. Four holograph scores of operas by Gomes (*Il Guarany*, *Fosca*, *Salvator Rosa* and *Maria Tudor*) were donated by the Milanese publisher Ricordi, and 26 of his songs and other material by the composer's daughter.

RIO DE JANEIRO. Arquivo do Cabido Metropolitano, Catedral Metropolitana, 20000 Rio de Janeiro. When Brazil became independent in 1822, the archive of the royal chapel, which contained music composed by royal *maestros de capilla* for important events and also works by other composers, became known as the Archive of the Imperial Chapel. Now kept by the Cabido, it contains about 70 MSS of 18th- and 19th-century composers, such as the Brazilians J. M. Nunes Garcia, F. M. da Silva, Pedro I (the country's first emperor), H. Alves de Mesquita, Damião Barbosa de Araujo, José Joaquim dos Santos, Francisco da Luz Pinto and Luciano Xavier dos Santos, as well as M. Portugal, Neukomm, Fortunato Mazziotti and David Perez.

R. Stevenson: *Renaissance and Baroque Musical Sources in the Americas* (Washington, DC, 1970), 310ff

——. Biblioteca Nacional, Seção de Música e Arquivo Sonoro, Avenida Rio Branco 219, 20000 Rio de Janeiro (*Rn*). The music section of the National Library was founded in 1952 on the basis of the Real Biblioteca and the Teresa Cristina Maria collection. The Royal Library was brought to Brazil by John VI of Portugal and his family in 1808. It is curious that although music had been important to the Portuguese emperors (John IV owned a famous music collection, lost in the earthquake of 1755), there are no compositions in the collection. John VI may have taken the musical works back with him to Lisbon in 1821, as he had done with a number of historical MSS. More than 100 of his MSS are extant in Brazil, but in the Cabido and the Escola de Música. Another part of the Royal Library surviving in Brazil was originally owned by the abbot Diogo Barbosa Machado (1682–1772). It contains documents relevant to the history of music in Portugal and Brazil, and a large number of dramatic texts and villancicos. Particulary valuable in the Royal Library are volumes of Catholic liturgical music, the incunabulum *Missale bracarense* (1498) and the only complete copy of Johannes de Garlandia's treatise *Introductio musice* (1486).

The collection named after the second Empress of Brazil, Teresa Cristina Maria, was donated by her husband Pedro II to the Brazilian government in 1889. The largest part of the collection, about 1000 imprints brought to Brazil in 1817, had once belonged to Leopoldina, the Austrian wife of Pedro I. Among the more important items are first editions of piano music by 18th- and 19th-century composers and some of Breitkopf & Härtel's early *Oeuvres complettes*. Surprisingly, there are no MSS of Garcia and only a few vocal compositions by Portugal, who was greatly respected by the Portuguese royal family and who followed them to Brazil in 1811. During the reign of Pedro II (1841–89), the collection was gradually enriched with holograph scores customarily dedicated to the emperor. Giovanni Pacini's lyric drama *Niccolò de' Lapi* and his cantata *L'alleanza*, Cécile Chaminade's opera *La sévillane* and the *Suite d'orchestre* by the Brazilian composer Henrique Oswald were acquired at this time, as well as a large number of marches and vocal works celebrating royal occasions. Also in the Teresa Cristina Maria col-

lection are a large number of vocal and piano works, which illustrate the musical taste during the imperial reign.

Three other collections acquired by the Biblioteca Nacional should also be mentioned for their 16th- and 17th-century source material: the Conde de Barca collection (which includes Zarlino's *De tutte l'opere*), the Marques collection (containing *Manuali chori*, 1564; *Processionarum*, 1589; Martínez de Bizcargui's *Arte de canto*, 1515; Fernandez's *Arte de musica*, 1626; and Nunes da Silva's *Arte minima*, 1685) and the Salvador de Mendonça collection (including a 16th-century MS gradual).

The acquisition in 1953 of the Abrahão de Carvalho library of more than 17,000 items established the Biblioteca Nacional as an important music research archive. Literature on music (including treatises on music theory, history, organology, dramatic and religious music, biographies and essays) is the strongest part of this collection. Notable items include treatises of Aaron, Zarlino, Fux, Rameau and Tartini; 17th-century Portuguese and Italian plainchant manuals; and the MS *Pontificale ad usum Monasterii Sanctae Crucis* of Coimbra (1781). Also in 1953 the Biblioteca Nacional purchased the collection of the Brazilian musician and folklorist Luciano Gallet, who had received most of Glauco Velasquez's works on the composer's death. The National Library also contains one of the largest collections of scores by Villa-Lobos.

R. Stevenson: *Renaissance and Baroque Musical Sources in the Americas* (Washington, DC, 1970), 259–300; various catalogues of the library's exhibitions and special collections (1954–67)

——. Escola de Música, Universidade Federal do Rio de Janeiro, Biblioteca Alberto Nepomuceno, Rua do Passeio 98, 20000 Rio de Janeiro (*Rem*). The founder of the original national conservatory, Francisco Manuel da Silva, created the school's library in 1855. After the reorganization of the conservatory in 1889 as the Instituto Nacional de Música, its first director, Leopoldo Miguez, donated to the library a large number of rare books (including treatises of Artusi, Descartes and Bontempi, and graduals of 1551 and 1583). The archive of the Imperial Teatro S. Pedro de Alcantra was also acquired by bequest, containing more than 100 early copies of operas by Donizetti, Rossini, Pacini, Mercadante, Bellini, Cimarosa, Jommelli, Auber, Aspa, Battista, Foroni, Flotow, Meyerbeer, Ricci, Rossi and Verdi, and other MSS of both native and European composers. In 1898 the library received 112 MSS (including many autographs) of J. M. Nunes Garcia. About 300 works, including MSS of the Brazilian composers Francisco Braga, Carlos Gomes, Leopoldo Miguez, Alberto Nepomuceno and Henrique Oswald, were left to the library by the Sociedade de Concertos Sinfônicos. Under the administration of Nepomuceno (1906–16) a librarian was appointed and proper cataloguing undertaken. A new building was erected in 1922 and the library installed there ten years later. In 1934 the school began to publish its journal, *Revista brasileira de música*, whose musical supplements print modern editions of unknown and rare Brazilian works in the library's possession. In 1957 the library was again moved and renamed the Biblioteca Alberto Nepomuceno.

R. Stevenson: *Renaissance and Baroque Musical Sources in the Americas* (Washington, DC, 1970), 301ff; various catalogues of the school's exhibitions (1952–67)

SÃO JOÃO D'EL REI. Lira Sanjoanense, 36300 São João d'el Rei. Founded in 1776, this music institution in the state of Minas Gerais has a library of about 500 chiefly sacred MSS and prints by composers of the 18th and 19th centuries from Minas Gerais. Composers represented include J. M. Xavier, J. M. Nunes Garcia, F. M. da Silva, Carlos Gomes, J. J. E. Lobo de Mesquita, J. de Deus, Pedro I, M. Portugal, João José Chagas and Jeronimo de Souza Lobo.

SÃO PAULO. Arquivo da Curia Metropolitana, Avenida Higienopolis 890, 01333 São Paulo. The library holds MSS of many Brazilian composers, including 76 works by André da Silva Gomes.

R. Duprat: *A música na matriz e na sé da São Paulo colonial, 1611–1822* (diss., U. of Brazilia, c1966)

——. Conservatório Dramático e Musical, Avenida S João 269, 01333 São Paulo. The library of the conservatory contains about 12,000 works, including a number of important Brazilian MSS of the 18th–20th centuries (including works by J. M. Nunes Garcia, A. da Silva Gomes, Giannini, Manuel Joaquim de Macedo, Francisco Libânio Colas, J. P. Gomes Cardim, the younger João Gomes and Francisco Mignone). The printed music in the archive consists chiefly of Brazilian works of the 20th century. There are a few early treatises, such as Meibom's *Antiquae musicae* (1652) and works by Rameau, Rousseau, Gerbert, Solano, Eximeno and Forkel.

——. Universidade de São Paulo, Instituto de Estudos Brasileiros, Parque Universitario, 01333 São Paulo. Although not housed in a self-contained music library, the institute's Coleção Mário de Andrade contains a few rare 18th-century editions by Martini, Rameau, Frezza dalle Grotte, Rousseau, Buonanni, Roussier, Arteaga and Cataneo, as well as early Handel, Haydn and Beethoven scores. There is a substantial amount of 19th-century popular music (e.g. *modinhas* and *lundús*) and material relevant to the musical taste of the country in the 19th century. The Coleção Lamego contains the earliest surviving Brazilian music MS with Portuguese text (MS 3117).

R. Duprat: 'A música na Bahia colonial', *Revista de história*, xxx/61 (1965), 106

CHILE

The organization of source material in the country's music libraries is still at an early stage; material in cathedral, monastery and church libraries outside Santiago, in particular, is little investigated. Other than the libraries discussed below, Santiago's Archivo Municipal de Ballet 'Elena Poliakova' (at Casilla 2844) documents ballet and opera in Chile from 1827, and the Museo-Archivo del Teatro Municipal (San Antonio 149) gathers material relevant to the Municipal Theatre, which opened in 1857 and has served both as a concert hall and as an opera house.

SANTIAGO. Archivo Musical de la Catedral de Santiago, Plaza de Armas 444, Santiago. The library of the cathedral contains more than 400 MSS, including works by José de Campderros (the most important colonial Chilean composer), José Bernardo Alzedo, Cristóbal Ajuria, José Maria Filomeno, José Antonio González and José Zapiola.

R. Stevenson: *Renaissance and Baroque Musical Sources in the Americas* (Washington, DC, 1970), 315–46; S. Claro: *Catálogo del Archivo musical de la Catedral de Santiago de Chile* (Santiago de Chile, 1974)

——. Biblioteca Americana José Toribio Medina, Alameda B. O'Higgins y E. Mac-Iver, Santiago. The Fondo Histórico y Bibliográfico José Toribio Medina, one of the most important collections for Latin American studies in the Americas, contains valuable material for musical research, including a copy of Navarro's *Liber in quo quatuor passiones Christi Domini continentur* (Mexico City, 1604), one of the earliest examples of printed music composed in the Americas.

——. Biblioteca Nacional, Alameda B. O'Higgins y E. Mac-Iver, Santiago. As the national copyright depository, the library is rich in Chilean music. The Colección José Miguel Besoain is part of the lending library and contains imprints of 19th-century composers such as Federico Guzmán (a leading Chilean composer of piano music, 1837–85), Eleodoro Ortiz de Zárate and José Soro Sforza. The composers' section, founded in 1971, collects music MSS of Chilean composers, and holds the complete works of Acario Cotapos (1889–1969) and Carmela Mackenna (1879–1962), as well as a number of works by Alfonso Leng (1884–1974).

——. Universidad de Chile, Santiago. The Faculty of Music has two separate music libraries: the Biblioteca y Discoteca Central de la Facultad de Ciencias y Artes Musicales (Companía 1264) is a large reference library with some 20th-century MSS, and the Archivo Musical del Instituto de Extensión Musical (Casilla 14050), established in 1940 as an independent institution and part of the Faculty of Music since 1962, is a working library with much modern Chilean material. The Biblioteca Central (Alameda B. O'Higgins 1058) contains most of the publications of members of the university since 1843; printed editions of Guzmán, Guillermo Frick and other composers of the 19th and 20th centuries may be found in the Colección Domingo Edwards Matte.

COLOMBIA (CO)

Other than the Cathedral Archive of Bogotá, Colombia has no important music libraries. The settlements of the missionaries and the old dioceses of Cartagena, Santa Marta, Panamá and Popayán had a strong musical tradition but most of their books and MSS have been lost or dispersed.

BOGOTÁ. Archivo de la Catedral, Bogotá (*B*). The archive has some of the earliest printed and MS music surviving in Latin America; of its 400 MSS and books, 250 are anonymous. Particularly noteworthy are 32 atlas-size plainchant choirbooks (1606–8) and unique MSS of Gutierre Fernández Hidalgo (c1553–1620), *maestro de capilla* from 1585 to 1588, Rodrigo de Ceballos (c1530–71) and Juan Navarro. There are also works by the Spanish composers Manuel Blasco, Miguel Mateo Dallo y Lanas and Cristobal de Bersayaga and rare sacred printed editions by Sebastián Aguilera de Heredia, Domenico Massentio, Nicasio Zorita, Antonio Burlini, and the Colombians José Cascante (*d* 1704) and Juan de Herrera (c1665–1738).

R. Stevenson: 'The Bogotá Music Archive', *JAMS*, xv (1962), 292; R. Stevenson: *Renaissance and Baroque Musical Sources in the Americas* (Washington, DC, 1970); J. I. Perdomo Escobar: *El archivo musical de la catedral de Bogotá* (Bogota, 1976)

CUBA (CU)

HAVANA. Biblioteca Nacional José Marti, Apdo Oficial 3, Plaza de la Revolución José Marti, Havana (*Hn*). The library has a copy of the earliest Cuban imprint, a Christmas villancico by the Cuban composer Esteban Salas (Santiago de Cuba, 1793).

SANTIAGO. Archivo de Música de la Catedral, Santiago. The library holds Salas's copies of works by 17th-century composers (including Sebastián Durón, Juan Francisco de Barrios and Juan del Vado) as well as works by Salas himself and the 19th-century composers Pedro and Silvano Boudet, Laureano Fuentes Matons, Cratilio Guerra and Antonio Raffelin.

P. Hernández Balaguer: *Catálogo de música de los archivos de la Catedral de Santiago de Cuba y del Museo Bacardi* (Havana, 1961)

——. Archivo de Música del Museo Municipal 'Emilio Bacardí', Aguilera y Pío Rosado, Santiago. The archive, founded in 1899 and named after the historian and magnate Emilio Bacardí Moreau (1844–1922), has copies of works by Salas and many MSS of other Cuban composers of the 19th and 20th centuries, including Francisco J. Hierrezuelo (1763–1824), Juan París (1759–1845), Fuentes Matons (1825–98), Cratillio Guerra (1834–96), Silvano Boudet (1825–63), Rafael Salcedo (1844–1917), Ramón Figueroa (1862–1928) and Rodolfo Hernández (1856–1937).

P. Hernández Balaguer, op cit

GUATEMALA

GUATEMALA CITY. Catedral, Palacio Arzobispal, 7a Avenida 6–21, Guatemala City. Although Guatemala was created a diocese in 1534 and an archdiocese in 1743, the present cathedral was built after 1776. The extremely rich colonial music archive consists of four polyphonic choirbooks (containing works of both European and New World composers) and about 120 17th-century and 760 18th-century works in loose sheets. This sheet-music archive, which has works by more than 40 European composers, is extremely rich in Portuguese and Italian as well as Spanish, Mexican and Guatemalan music. The two Guatemalan musicians Manuel José de Quiros and Rafael Castellanos are best represented, and other local composers included in the archive are Francisco de Aragón, Nicolás Espinosa, Pedro Nolasco, Mariano Estrada Aristondo and Pedro Antonio Roxas. Also in the collection are works by the New World composers Miguel Mateo Dallo y Lana, J. Gavino Leal, Juan Gutiérrez de Padilla, Juan Mathías, Tomás de Torrejón y Velasco, Matheo Vallados and Manuel de Zumaya. For geographic and chronological breadth, the cathedral's archive ranks with those in Bogotá, Cuzco, Lima, Mexico City, Puebla and Sucre.

D. Pujol: 'Polifonía española desconocida conservada en el Archivo capitular de la Catedral de Guatemala', *AnM*, xx (1967), 3; R. Stevenson: *Renaissance and Baroque Musical Sources in the Americas* (Washington, DC, 1970), 65–106

HAITI

PORT-AU-PRINCE. Ecole Sainte Trinité, rue de Msr. Guilloux, B. P. 857, Port-au-Prince. In the library of the Orchestre Philharmonique Sainte Trinité there is a MS collection of music by Haitian composers, including Onikel Augustin (*b* 1954), Lina Blanchet-Mathon (*b* 1904), Justin Elie (1883–1931), Werner Jaegerhuber (1900–53), Occide Jeanty (1860–1936), Férère Laguerre (*b* 1935), Ludovic Lamothe (1882–1954), Hector Lominy (*b* 1930), Michael Mauléart Mouton (1855–98) and Jacques Roussel (*b* 1939).

MEXICO

The earliest music to be printed in the Americas was at Mexico City in 1556, and 13 books containing music

were published before 1600. In 1604 Juan Navarro published a book of Passions, the largest and most sumptuous edition of music printed before 1800 in the Americas; only two copies survive in Mexico, the others having found their way to the USA, England and Chile. Many other sacred works have been moved and some lost, for example the *Libro de coro 21*, formerly at the Museo del Carmen in Villa Obregón (S Angel), but now known only from a microfilm (*US-Wc*). A copy of Alonso Lobo's *Liber primus missarum* (Madrid, 1602) is in the National Museum of History at Chapultepec Castle.

MEXICO CITY. Biblioteca Nacional, Calle Uruguay e Isabel la Católica, Mexico 1, DF. Established in 1867, the National Library has no separate music division. Its oldest Mexican imprint is a *Graduale dominicale* printed in Mexico City by Antonio de Espinosa before 1572; other notable items are the only printed libretto of the first North American opera, Zumaya's *La Partenope* (Mexico City, 1711), the *Cantares en idioma mexicano*, one of the most valuable MS sources for the study of pre-Conquest Mexican music, and an early Mexican tablature, MS 1560 (olim 1686), which includes numerous early 18th-century anonymous dances ciphered for guitar, as well as violin music by, among others, the (apparently) local violinist Bartolomé Gerardo.

R. Stevenson: *Music in Aztec and Inca Territory* (Berkeley and Los Angeles, 1968), 46ff

——. Conservatorio Nacional de Musica, Candelario Huízar Library, Avenida Presidente Masaryk 582, Mexico 5, DF. The library, established in 1878 (ten years after the school itself was founded), has sheet music of the 19th and 20th centuries and 300 rare books from the Sánchez Garza collection (see the Instituto Nacional de Bellas Artes below). The best-represented Mexican composer is Melesio Morales (1838–1908), five of whose operas exist in holographs. The earliest Mexican MS is by José Manuel de Aldana (1758–1810).

C. Dorronsoro de Roces: *Catálogo de obras de compositores del continente americano* (Mexico City, 1959) [lists the 572 works of New World composers acquired before 1958]

——. Catedral Metropolitana, Mexico, DF. The library holds 72 large volumes of plainchant copied between c1600 and 1852; valuable for their illuminations, the books (mostly copied in Mexico City) contain chants in mensural notation and some part-music. There are nine atlas-size polyphonic choirbooks containing works of Palestrina, Victoria, Guerrero, Duarte Lobo and eight *maestros de capilla* at the cathedral active between 1575 and 1715 (F. López Capillas, F. Franco, A. Rodríguez de Mata, L. Coronado, F. Ximeno, Loaysa y Agurto, A. de Salazar and Zumaya). There are 800 sacred works in MS, over a third by 18th-century composers active in Mexico City (e.g. Ignacio Jerusalem, M. Tollis de la Rocca, Antonio Juanas and Aldana) and the rest by Europeans (e.g. Ripa, Rutini, Sarti and Cimarosa) and 19th-century Mexican composers (e.g. M. Manterola, L. Baca, A. Caballero, L. Beristain, J. A. Gómez and J. I. Triugeque). (A microfilm catalogue, prepared by E. T. Stanford in the mid-1960s, is at the National Institute of Anthropology and History Library in Mexico City.) The cathedral archive also contains first editions of sacred and secular works by 18th- and 19th-century composers.

L. D. Spiess and E. T. Stanford: *An Introduction to Certain Mexican Musical Archives* (Detroit, 1969), 25 [reviewed by H. Cobos in *Notes*, xxvii (1970–71), 491]; R. Stevenson: *Renaissance and Baroque Musical Sources in the Americas* (Washington, DC, 1970), 137ff, 146ff

——. Instituto Nacional de Bellas Artes, Sección de Investigaciones Musicales, Londres 6, Mexico 6, DF. In 1967 the institute purchased 276 Baroque MSS from the heirs of Jesús Sánchez Garza, whose collection originated at the now extinct Holy Trinity convent in Puebla founded in 1619. Many Spanish and Portuguese composers are represented in the collection as well as seven *maestros de capilla* active at the cathedrals in Mexico City and Puebla between 1629 and 1726.

R. Stevenson: *Renaissance and Baroque Musical Sources in the Americas* (Washington, DC, 1970), 166ff; R. Stevenson: *Christmas Music from Baroque Mexico* (Berkeley and Los Angeles, 1974), 10ff [incl. transcrs.]

MORELIA. Conservatorio de Santa Rosa, Morelia, Michoacán. Though the archive holds 40 volumes of plainchant, most of the 600 other MSS in loose sheets are 18th- and 19th-century works. The 28 composers represented include Patiño (the only 17th-century composer in the collection), 11 local musicians, 11 Europeans (Cayetano Echeverria, Mir y Llussá, D. de las Muelas, Nebra and J. de Torres Martínez Bravo from the Iberian Peninsula; Galuppi, Jommelli and four others from Italy), and five others who worked in Mexico City. The best-known unica in this collection are the three-movement *oberturas* by Antonio Rodil and Antonio Sarrier.

M. Bernal Jiménez: *Morelia colonial: el archivo musical del Colegio de Santa Rosa de Santa Maria de Valladolid* (*siglo XVIII*) (Mexico City, 1939), 37ff; L. B. Spiess and E. T. Stanford: *An Introduction to Certain Mexican Musical Archives* (Detroit, 1969), 29

OAXACA. Catedral Metropolitana, Independencia 50, Oaxaca. The cathedral was begun in 1553 and completed in 1730. About 1640 it acquired the large Gaspar Fernandes collection of villancicos, *chanzonetas*, *negros* and other popular music of 1609–20, perhaps the single most important collection of early New World music with vernacular texts. The loose sheet music MSS in the archive include works by Spanish composers (including Victoria and Torres Martínez Bravo) and at least five local musicians, of whom Zumaya is the best represented. The oldest printed polyphonic choirbook is Alonso Lobo's book of masses (1602).

PUEBLA. Catedral Metropolitana, 5 Oriente 4, Puebla. The cathedral in Puebla, one of the most important cultural centres in the viceroyalty of New Spain, was consecrated in 1649. The 375 masses, *Magnificat* settings, motets, hymns, psalms, Lamentations and other liturgical works in its archive make it musically the most important in Mexico, comparable to the richest libraries of Spain. There are 128 atlas-size volumes of plainchant, 20 large polyphonic choirbooks, including compositions by musicians who worked in Mexico (e.g. Manuel Arenzana, Francisco Atienza, Pedro Bermúdez, Fructos del Castillo, Miguel Mateo de Dallo y Lana, Hernando Franco, Juan García de Zéspedes, Juan Gutiérrez de Padilla, Juanas, Jerusalem, Antonio de Salazar and Fabián Ximeno), and a wide range of important European works.

R. Stevenson: 'Sixteenth- and Seventeenth-century Resources in Mexico', *FAM*, i (1954), 69 [amplified in *Renaissance and Baroque Musical Sources in the Americas* (Washington, DC, 1970), 208ff]; A. R. Catalyne: 'Music Manuscripts of the Sixteenth, Seventeenth and Eighteenth Centuries in the Cathedral of Puebla de los Angeles, Mexico', *Yearbook, Inter-American Institute for Musical Research*, ii (1966), 80

——. Museo de Arte 'José Luis Bello y González', Avenida 3 Poniente 302, Puebla. Founded in 1944, the museum holds 30 plainsong choirbooks known for the beauty of their illuminations as well as their mensural chants, and four music imprints, the earliest of which is Hernando de Issasi's *Quatuor passiones Domini cum Benedictione Cerei* (Salamanca, 1582).

——. Biblioteca Palafoxiana, Puebla. Once the richest library in Mexico, it was founded by Bishop Juan de Palafox y Mendoza in 1646 and has occupied its present site since 1773. In 1836 it held 78 liturgical books containing music.

E. de la Torre Villar: *Reseña histórica de la Biblioteca Palafoxiana* (Puebla, 1957), 30ff

TEPOTZLÁN. Museo Virreinal, Tepotzlán, Estado de Mexico. The Viceregal Museum, occupying part of a Jesuit church built in *c*1680, acquired six polyphonic choirbooks from Mexico City Cathedral: four European imprints of 1584–1621, a copy of Franco's *Magnificat* settings (1611) and a Mexican MS (1717). European composers represented are Guerrero, Aguilera de Heredia and Duarte Lobo, and there are also works by the Mexicans López Capillas, Salazar and Zumaya.

R. Stevenson: *Renaissance and Baroque Musical Sources in the Americas* (Washington, DC, 1970), 134ff

NETHERLANDS ANTILLES

ORANJESTAD, ARUBA. Departamento de Cultura, Juan Enrique Irausquinplein, Oranjestad, Aruba. The library holds MSS by 20th-century Aruban composers such as Padu Lampo and Rufo Wever.

PERU

CUZCO. Catedral, Cuzco. According to early inventories, Cuzco Cathedral (built in 1560) once contained a large amount of printed polyphonic music, but little remains. There are 45 huge plainchant choirbooks, mostly copied between 1599 and 1605.

——. Seminario de S Antonio Abad, Cuzco. The seminary received the unbound works of Cuzco Cathedral earlier this century. 143 of the approximately 370 pieces are anonymous Latin or Spanish works of the middle and late Baroque. The 17th-century Spanish and Portuguese villancico composers in the collection include Diego Casseda, Agustín de Contreras, Manuel Correa, Sebastián Durón, Vicente García, Gerónimo González, Bernardo de Medina, Murillo, C. Patiño and José Sanz. Peru and Bolivia are represented by José de Araujo, Durán de la Mota, Pancorbo, Esteban Ponce de León, Tomás de Torrejón y Velasco, Pedro Villalobos and Pedro Ximenes. There are also works by the Italian composers Ceruti (in Peru for most of his life) and Tarditi.

R. Vargas Ugarte: 'Un archivo de música colonial en la ciudad del Cuzco', *Mar del Sur*, v/26 (1953), 1; S. Claro: 'Música dramática en el Cuzco durante el siglo XVIII', *Yearbook, Inter-American Institute for Musical Research*, v (1969), 1–48; R. Stevenson: *Renaissance and Baroque Musical Sources in the Americas* (Washington, DC, 1970), 31ff

LIMA. Archivo Arzobispal, Arzobispado de Lima, Carabaya, Lima. The original cathedral was destroyed by an earthquake in 1746, but some music survived. Most works in the library date from after the completion of the new cathedral in 1758 and have been in the adjacent Archivo Arzobispal since 1945. The earliest publication is Guerrero's *Liber vesperarum* (Rome, 1584). About half of the 200 catalogued pieces are Latin sacred works, the rest villancicos and other festival music with vernacular texts. The European composers represented include D. Arquimbau, F. J. García Fajer, F. García Pacheco, J. M. Gaytán y Arteaga, J. Mir y Llussá, M. de Moraes Pedroso, D. de las Muelas, A. Ripa (with more works here than in Seville), A. Rodriguez de Hita, G. Romero de Ávila, J. de San Juan and J. de Torres Martínez Bravo. Among the Peruvian composers are J. de Ampuero, J. de Beltrán, T. del Campo y Pando, R. Ceruti (from Italy), M. de Dávalos y Chauca, B. Llaque, P. Montes de Oca, J. de Orejón y Aparicio, M. Tapia y Zegarra, J. M. Tirado and E. Zapata.

R. Holzmann and C. Arróspide de la Flor: 'Catálogo de los manuscritos de música existentes en el Archivo arzobispal de Lima', *Cuaderno de estudio*, iii/7 (Lima, 1949), 36; R. Stevenson: *Renaissance and Baroque Musical Sources in the Americas* (Washington, DC, 1970), 114ff [amplification of the Holzmann catalogue]

——. Biblioteca Nacional, Avenida Abancay, Lima. The library was founded in 1821 and plundered of all but 700 of its volumes 60 years later; its rebuilt collection was destroyed by fire in 1943. The present music holdings in the MSS division were obtained by Jorge Basadre, Alberto Tauro and Graciola Sánchez Cerro, and include the holograph of Torrejón y Velasco's *La púrpura de la rosa*, dated 1701 (the earliest extant New World opera), a *Libro de musica instruccion española sobre la guitarra* with music attributed to Gaspar Sanz, and a MS *Cuaderno de musica* for vihuela.

C. Raygada: 'Guía musical de Perú', *Fénix*, xii (1956–7), 21 [catalogue of Alzedo's works in the library]

——. Escuela Nacional de Música, Avenida de la Emancipación, Lima. The library of the Escuela Nacional (until 1962 the Conservatorio Nacional de Música) has the score of Valle-Riestra's *Ollantay* and a number of works by early directors of the conservatory.

——. S Agustín, 225 Jiron Ica, Lima. The church archive in 1960 contained the complete works of Alberto Villalba Muñoz, and may possess works of earlier composers, but there is no music section, nor any catalogue.

——. S Francisco, Jirón Lampa, Lima. In 1966 the church owned only a small remnant of its once-rich music library. Its oldest MS is a Madrid copy of five Palestrina masses dated 1729.

PUERTO RICO

SAN JUAN. Archivo General de Puerto Rico, 500 Avenida Ponce de León, Apartado 4184, San Juan. Called the Archivo General del Estado until it was destroyed by fire in 1926, the library was reopened in 1955, moved in 1973, and is now the central depository. The music division houses over 5000 MSS (the earliest dated 1859), sketchbooks and first editions by Puerto Rican composers. Important collections include the Colección Alfredo Romero (c400 items by Romero and Baulio Dueño Colón), Colección Antonio Otero (works by José Ignacio Quintón and R. Retena), Colección Braulio Dueño Colón (donated by the composer's daughter in 1973 and containing about 200 MSS of his works), Colección Herminio Brau (donated in 1974, containing about 700 MSS, first editions and rare sheet music of 1880–1930), Colección Juan F. Acosta (containing 150 MSS of his danzas), and the Colección Villavicencio (containing MSS of Simón Madera). Among the other composers represented are Rafael Balseiro Dávila (1867–1929), Fernando Callejo

Ferrer (1862–1926), Domingo Delgado, Monsita Ferrer Otero (1882–1966), Juan Morel Campos (1857–96), Heraclio Ramos (1837–91), Juan Rios Ovalle, Luis R. Miranda, Angel Mislán, Arturo Pasarell, Jaime Pericas and, represented in several separate collections, José Ignacio Quintón (1881–1925). A photocopy of the complete list of MSS is in the Inter-American Institute of Indiana University.

T. Mathews: 'Documentacion sobre Puerto Rico en la Biblioteca del congresso', *Historia*, vi/2 (1966), 89–142

——. Ateneo Puertorriqueño Biblioteca, Avenida Ponce de León, Apartado 1180, San Juan. Founded in 1876, this cultural organization sponsors contests for artists, writers and composers, and houses the prizewinning music MSS. Puerto Rican composers represented include José Agullo y Prats, Balseiro Dávila, Hector Campos Parsi (*b* 1922), Jack Delano (*b* 1914), Monsita Ferrer Otero (1882–1966), Juan Morel Campos (1857–96) and Manuel Gregorio Tavárez (1843–83).

——. Conservatorio de Música de Puerto Rico, Avenida F. Roosevelt y Lamar, Hato Rey, Apartado 2350, San Juan 00936. Founded in 1962 and affiliated with the Festival Casals, the library contains a collection of Puerto Rican and Latin American music. The Pablo Casals Museo (at Plaza S José) houses documents and memorabilia of Casals donated by his widow.

——. Instituto de Cultura Puertorriqueña, Avenida Norzagary cor. Calle del Cristo, Apartado 4184, San Juan 00905. A small collection of 16th-century Spanish choirbooks, three printed, are in the institute's library. The Casa del Libro (at Calle del Cristo 255, Apartado 2265, San Juan 00903) has a small but valuable collection including two processionals (1494 and c1500), a Spanish MS choirbook of 1556, the only copy in the Western hemisphere of Guillermo de Podio's theoretical treatise *Ars musicorum* (1495) and a neumed Ethiopian MS.

R. Stevenson: *Spanish Music in the Age of Columbus* (The Hague, 1960), 73ff

——. Seminario de Estudios Hispanicos 'Federico de Onis', Universidad de Puerto Rico, Facultad de Humanidades, Recinto de Río Piedras, San Juan 00931. The library contains books, periodicals, bulletins, and journals published in and about Spain and Hispanic America, including folklore, music, a collection of zarzuelas, and Spanish folksongs.

——. Universidad de Puerto Rico, José M. Lazaro Memorial Library, Recinto de Río Piedras, San Juan 00931. The Salón de Música contains over 25,000 volumes, some of which are sources of Puerto Rican, Caribbean and other Latin American music. The Puerto Rican Collection (1940) includes books on music relating to the Caribbean area, essays on music instruction, information on Puerto Rican folklore, folk music and festivals, and printed music by Puerto Rican composers. The Caribbean Regional Library, founded in 1946, has been housed in the General Library since 1975 but is not connected with the university. It is the focal point for the development of a current national bibliography by region. The basic collection of the library was inherited from the Caribbean Commission (1946–60) and the Caribbean Organization (1961–5). It includes books on the music of the Caribbean islands, especially folklore and folk music, and has published *Caribbean Regional Library* annually since 1966.

PORT-OF-SPAIN. Central Library of Trinidad and Tobago, 20 Queens Park East, Box 547, Port-of-Spain. The library was established by the Andrew Carnegie Foundation in 1941 and is a national depository of MSS. It has published the *Trinidad and Tobago West Indian Bibliography in Monthly Accessions* since 1965.

URUGUAY

Uruguay's musical sources have been centralized in Montevideo since the mid-1930s through the efforts of the Musicological Division of the National Historical Museum and F. C. Lange, president of the Inter-American Institute of Musicology. Materials documenting music history since the early 19th century have been acquired and preserved, though they have not yet been adequately classified. The National Library has not to date established a separate music division. The Instituto de Estudios Superiores owns many MSS of the composer León Ribeiro (1854–1931; the MSS are discussed by F. C. Lange in 'León Ribeiro', *Boletín latino-americano de música*, iii, Montevideo, 1937, p.519), and the Casa de la Cultura in Minas is notable for its Eduardo Fabini archive, containing 35 MSS of the composer.

MONTEVIDEO. Museo Histórico Nacional, Sección Musicología, Calle Rincón 437, Montevideo. In addition to the materials acquired from private estates (e.g. those of Lauro Ayestarán and the Copetti, Vitelli and Grasso families), the library has acquired large amounts of material from the collections of the composers Francisco José Debali (including 900 of his MSS), Manuel Ubeda (who composed the first Uruguayan mass, 1802), Carmelo Calvo (1842–1922), Tomás Giribaldi (1847–1930), Alfonso Broqua (1876–1946), Ramón Rodriguez Socas (1886–1957), Eduardo Fabini (1882–1950), Vicente Ascone (*b* 1897), Ismael Cortinas (1892–1918), Luis Cluzeau Mortet (1889–1957) and the Giucci family. Other collections acquired by the museum include the archives of the Verdi Conservatory, the church of St Francis (including 194 MSS of Spanish, Italian and Brazilian composers), and 24 MSS from S Felipe Neri in Sucre (anonymous Baroque composers and works by José Nebra, Juan de Araujo and Antonio Leyseca).

L. Ayestarán: *La música en el Uruguay*, i (Montevideo, 1953), 123ff; L. Ayestarán: 'El barroco musical hispano-americano', *Yearbook, Inter-American Institute for Musical Research*, i (1965), 55

VENEZUELA

CARACAS. Archivo de Música Antigua Venezolana, Conservatorio José Angel Lamas, Veroes a Santa Capilla, Caracas. The archive has a large number of MSS by Venezuelan composers from the late 18th and early 19th centuries. There are works by José Angel Lamas (1775–1814), Juan Manuel Olivares, José Francisco Velásquez the elder and many other composers of the colonial period.

V. Africa, Asia, Australasia

AUSTRALIA

CANBERRA. National Library of Australia, Canberra, Australian Capital Territory 2600. Music was collected rather sporadically until 1969, but after the Music and Sound Recordings section was established in 1973, the library increased its activities as a national depository. It now houses the valuable archive of Kenneth Hince, a book dealer who collected material relating to Australian

music, and the papers of Dame Nellie Melba.

MELBOURNE. Grainger Museum, University of Melbourne, Parkville, Victoria 5052. In 1935 the Australian composer Percy Grainger founded a museum in the grounds of the University of Melbourne to hold his own materials as well as those of Delius and others of his friends. Since his death in 1961, his widow has continued to acquire material and catalogue the collection.

——. State Library of Victoria, Swanston Street, Melbourne, Victoria 3000. The library holds a 10th-century copy of Boethius's *De musica*, a French choirbook of *c*1350 (a rare example of antiphony from the school of Jean Pucelle), the Hildesheim missal from Nuremberg dated 1499, and MSS of Schumann, Mendelssohn and Wieniawski. Two special collections are the Dyer Collection of works by modern English composers and the Thomas Collection of lieder, art songs and national songs.

PERTH. Wigmore Music Library, Department of Music, University of Western Australia, Nedlands, W. Australia 6009. The library has a unique collection of French cantatas resulting from the specialized research of David Tunley.

SYDNEY. Australian Broadcasting Commission, 1459 Elizabeth Street, Sydney, NSW 2000. The Federal Music Library of the Commission feeds the professional orchestras and ensembles of the country and holds a fair amount of 19th-century Australian music.

——. Library of New South Wales, Macquarie Street, Sydney, NSW 2000. The Mitchell Library, devoted to Australian works, receives all publications in New South Wales under copyright deposit.

——. University of New South Wales, Kensington, NSW 2033. The library began to acquire musical works in 1966, and a buying policy gives priority to electronic music, native Australian works and musical theatre of all kinds.

——. University of Sydney, NSW 2006. The T. H. Kelly Music Library belonging to the Department of Music is rich in music of earlier centuries. The university's main library, the Fisher Library, houses the collection of the Australian scholar Robert Dalley-Scarlett, including editions of works by Handel and other 18th-century composers.

ISRAEL (*IL*)

Two libraries, the Patriarchal Library (*Jp*) in Jerusalem and the Monastery of St Catherine in Sinai, are notable for their Byzantine MSS and literature.

JERUSALEM. Jewish National and University Library, Music Department, Gizat Ram Campus, Jerusalem (*J*). The library specializes in European, Jewish and Near Eastern music, numbering about 40,000 musical items and 18,000 books and periodicals in 1975. Special collections include the Jakob Michael Collection of Jewish Music, the Alex Cohen Collection of Mozartiana (containing a few MSS and about 100 first editions and early imprints) and about 50 first editions of French operas of the 18th and 19th centuries. The library holds the scholarly papers of Abraham Zvi Idelsohn, Joseph Achron, Friedrich Gernsheim, Robert Lachmann, Fernando Liuzzi and Georg Alter (whose papers included those of the Prague Society for Contemporary

Music, relating to Schoenberg and his circle; they are discussed by A. Ringer in 'Schoenbergiana in Jerusalem', *MQ*, lix (1973), 1).

JAPAN (J)

The literary arts were certainly known in Japan by the 6th century when the Buddhist priests arrived from continental Asia. The earliest known libraries were the Zushoryō and the Isonokaminoyakatsugu collections of *c*700, which served the imperial court, and the privately owned public library called the Unteiin, founded *c*770. From the 10th century to the mid-19th, Japan was dominated by military clans, who built schools with libraries, such as the Kanagawa Bunko (*c*1270). After an isolationist period under the Tokugawa clan from the early 17th century to 1868, there was a movement towards Westernization and many libraries were built along the lines of European institutions. The Imperial Library (now part of the National Diet Library) was built in 1872 and became the first national copyright depository three years later. The first music library was founded in 1890 at the music college in Ueno Park, Tokyo.

Three national laws affecting the growth of libraries were enacted after World War II. The National Education Act (1947) made funds available for universities and their libraries (emphasis on European music is characteristic of Japan's university libraries, which generally contain modern editions and recordings rather than early Japanese sources). The National Diet Library Act (1948) established that library as the national copyright depository and compiler of the national bibliography. The Japanese Library Act (1950) was passed so that funds could be allocated to local public libraries, which acquired old and new regional archives. About 25 public libraries were founded or reorganized as performing arts centres, with theatres, libraries and museums. The government has also helped Buddhist temples and Shintō shrines preserve their archives. Japan's recent prosperity has made it possible for foundations, individuals and religious groups to maintain private collections, which contain some of the most precious native and foreign musical sources in the country.

The Japan Library Association (Nihon Toshokan Kyōkai) and the Japan Music Library Association (Ongaku Toshokan Kyōgikai) were founded after World War II. The membership of the Music Library Association is confined to libraries, numbering eight in 1973.

Most of the libraries in Japan are devoted to sources of traditional music, such as music for the theatre (e.g. kabuki, bunraku and *jōruri* music), early chant MSS (e.g. noh texts and Shingon chant) and other, more recent vocal and instrumental works (e.g. gagaku and *kagura* music). Many valuable collections are found in university libraries: Kōya University (noted for its MSS of Shingon chant), Okayama University (gagaku, shamisen and koto scores of the 18th and 19th centuries), Tenri University (one of the most important sources of imperial court music), Tokyo University (koto music, vocal music and musical theatre), Hosei University in Tokyo (various sources, 1423–*c*1850), Waseda University in Tokyo (13th- to 19th-century scores and music histories, as well as noh and *jōruri* works), Osaka University in Toyonaka (17th- to 19th-century editions of vocal music, shamisen and koto scores). Other types of library also contain ethnomusicological sources: museums and government archives (e.g. the Gotō Art Museum, the Department of Archives and Mausolea in the Imperial Household Agency, the Tōyō Library and the National Archives, all in Tokyo), public libraries (e.g. the Chikamatsu collection of the Osaka Prefectural Library, the Central Public Library in Tokyo, the Min-Bunka Kaikan in Toyohashi and the Public Library in Ueda), as well as the libraries of foundations (e.g. the Yōmei Archive in Kyoto), professional associations (e.g. the Bunraku Association in Osaka, the Nagauta Association in Tokyo and the Japan Broadcasting Corporation) and individuals (e.g. the Kōzan Archive, the personal library of Ejima Iheri).

Ongaku tenrakai shuppin mokuroku [Music exhibition catalogue] (Tokyo, 1933); K. T. Kokuritsu, ed.: *Ongaku bunka shiryo tenrankai mokuroku* [Catalogue of an exhibition of musical source material] (Tokyo, 1950); *National Diet Library Newsletter* (1958–); Japan Music Library Association: *Union List of Periodicals* (Tokyo, 1972); E. Harich-Schneider: *A History of Japanese Music* (London, 1973); Special Libraries Association of Japan: *Directory of Special Libraries* (Tokyo, 1973); J. Siddons: 'Japan', *Directory of Music Research Libraries*, ed. R. Benton (Kassel and Basle, 1976)

NISHINOMIYA.   Kōbe   Jogakuin   University, Okadayama 4–1, Nishinomiya. In the library of this private women's university is the Allchin collection of Methodist hymns in Japanese translation, dating for the most part from 1880 to 1912. About 20 Japanese and American evangelists, including the missionary George Allchin (1851–1935), are represented.

TOKYO. Musashino Music College, Hazawa-chō 1–13, Nerima Ward, Tokyo (*Tm*) and *Tma* (*Tmc*). Also known in the West as Musashino Academia Musicae, the library of this private college has collected some 1000 MSS, letters, and first or rare editions of European (and particularly German) origin. Most of the major composers of the late 18th and the 19th centuries, as well as a number of others outside that period (e.g. Rameau and Berg), are represented. The library holds the first editions of important treatises by Fux, Morley, Kircher and others.

Litterae rarae: liber secundus (Tokyo, 1969) [catalogue of authors, in Ger.]

——. Nanki Music Library, Nippon Kindai Museum, Komaba 4–3–55, Meguro Ward, Tokyo (*Tn*). The founder of this collection was Marquis Yorisada Tokugawa, a descendant of the Tokugawa clan that ruled Japan for 250 years. Having studied music at Cambridge University in the late 1890s, the marquis envisaged a library in Japan in which the classics of European music might be studied. In 1914, he organized a library at his own expense to collect both native and foreign works, and started construction of a building that would house not only the collection, but also a concert hall with a pipe organ (apparently the first in Japan since the early 17th century). He purchased almost half (450 volumes) of the former library of the English musicologist W. H. Cummings in 1917, and in the following three years added portions of the libraries of Joseph Hollmann and Max Friedlaender. By the early 1920s the collection included about 1000 early and first editions (particularly of German and English composers and theorists), autograph letters and MS scores and sketches dating from the 17th–19th centuries. The building, however, was destroyed in the 1923 earthquake, and the collection transferred to Keiō University in Tokyo, where it was not made available to readers. In 1946 the marquis sold it to a private individual, Kyūbei Ohki, who made it public again only in 1966. It was then named the Ohki Collection after its beneficent owner, and a temporary home was found in the Nippon Kindal Museum until a new building complete with concert hall like the original could be built. In spite of its precarious history, the collection still contains such treasures as the best-preserved MS of Purcell's *Dido and Aeneas*, two letters by Beethoven to C. F. Peters, Zarlino's *Le istitutione harmoniche* (1562), two copies of Morley's *A Plaine and Easie Introduction* (1597), a large MS book of anthems by John Blow (1683) and many Playford and Walsh editions.

Nanki bunko gaiyō [Brief guide to the Nanki Library] (Tokyo, 1914); *Catalogue of the Nanki Music Library* (Tokyo, 1916, 4/1970); *Catalogue of the Famous Musical Library of Books, Manuscripts, Autograph Letters, Musical Scores, etc., the Property of the Late W. H. Cummings* (London, 1917); K. Kanetsune and S. Tsuji: *On the W. H. Cummings Collection in the Nanki Music Library* (Tokyo, 1925); *Catalogue of the W. H. Cummings Collection in the Nanki Music Library* (Tokyo, 1925/R1974); K. Kanetsune and S. Tsuji: *Die geschichtlichen Denkmäler der japanischen Tonkunst* (Tokyo, 1930); *Nanki ongaku bunko tokubetsu kōkai* [Nanki Music Library special exhibition] (Tokyo, 1967)

——. Sonkei Kaku Archive, Komaba 4–3–55, Meguro Ward, Tokyo. This collection contains the libraries of the aristocratic Maeda family of Kanazawa and is now administered by the Maeda Foundation (Maeda Ikutoku-kai).

——. Toyama Music Library, 4–19–6 Nishi Azabu, Minato Ward, Tokyo. Founded in 1962 by Kazuyuki Tōyama, a professor of Tōhō Music College in Tokyo, the library contains MSS, letters and other materials relating to the composer Kosaku Yamada (1886–1966).

——. Ueno Gakuen University, Higashi Ueno 4–24–12, Taitō Ward, Tokyo. The library of this private university has a collection of MS scores by modern Japanese composers (especially Yoritsune Matsudaira), a MS of J. S. Bach (BWV998), and a number of early editions of European composers (Purcell, Rameau, Rousseau and Beethoven).

NEW ZEALAND (NZ)

AUCKLAND. Auckland Public Library, PO Box 4138, Auckland (*Ap*). The library has two antiphoners of the 15th century, as well as works by a number of European composers in pre-1800 editions. New Zealand composers represented in MS include John Maughan Barnett, Edwin Carr, Barry Coney, Vernon Griffiths, John Grigg, Te Rangi Hikiroa, Alfred Hill, Llewellyn Jones, R. S. Mitchell, J. H. Phillpot, Alice Rowley, John Tait, Baron Charles de Thierry, William Thomas and John Joseph Woods.

——. University Library, University of Auckland, Private Bag, Auckland (*Au*). In addition to a number of MSS of New Zealand composers, a few early prints (including works by Rameau and Zarlino) may be found in the collection. The Archive of Maori and Pacific Music is administered by the Anthropology Department of the university.

WELLINGTON. Alexander Turnbull Library, The National Library of New Zealand, Private Bag, Wellington (*Wt*). All music printed in New Zealand is deposited in this branch of the National Library. The Archive of New Zealand Music, created in 1974 when the Composers' Association of New Zealand asked the Turnbull Library to become a repository for unpublished music by New Zealand composers, contains various kinds of research material (e.g. scores, programmes, photographs, letters, diaries and archives of musical organizations).

D. Freed: 'Union List of Music Manuscripts in New Zealand Libraries', *Continuo*, ii/2 (1972)

SOUTH AFRICA

CAPE TOWN. Music Library, South African College of Music, Main Road. Rosebank, Cape Province 7700. The library became a branch of the University of Cape Town libraries in 1943 and owed much to Erik Chisholm, a principal of the college, for widening its scope, and for the bequest of his music on his death in 1965. It has a large collection of South African printed music, popular and classical, and of autographs of South African composers and foreign composers who have lived and worked in the country, especially W. H. Bell, Erik Chisholm and Victor Hely-Hutchinson. The collection also includes programmes, clippings and unpublished theses on aspects of musical life in South Africa. The J. W. Jagger Library holds letters from South African composers, including Joubert, concerning their music.

L. E. Taylor: *Catalogue of the Music Manuscripts of William Henry Bell* (Cape Town, 1948)

GRAHAMSTOWN. International Library of African Music, Rhodes University, Grahamstown 6140. It was established by Hugh Tracey in Roodepoort in 1953 as an offshoot of the African Music Society for the purpose of research into African music. The library holds about 10,000 unpublished and 3000 published recordings of traditional African music.

JOHANNESBURG. Public Library, Market Square, Johannesburg 2001. Material of South African interest is held both in the Music Library and in the Strange Library of Africana, including autographs of South African composers, a large collection of South African printed music of all types, concert programmes and archival material covering local musical life.

Catalogue of Music in the Strange Collection of Africana (Johannesburg, 1944, suppl. 1945); M. de Lange: *Catalogue of the Musical Instruments in the Collection of Professor Percival R. Kirby* (Johannesburg, 1967)

——. South African Broadcasting Corporation Music Library, PO Box 4559, Johannesburg 2000. The library has a collection of autographs of South African composers and of South African printed music, chiefly vocal.

PRETORIA. Merensky Library, University of Pretoria, Pretoria 0002. The library acquired, on his death in 1968, the collection of F. Z. van der Merwe, consisting of some 2300 items of MS and printed music, serious and ephemeral, by South African composers of all races. Housed separately from the working stock of the Music Library, the collection is being expanded.

STELLENBOSCH. Music Branch Library, University of Stellenbosch, Private Bag 5036. The library's most important collection is that presented in 1952 by Albert Coates, consisting mainly of 19th-century orchestral works, autographs and editions of his own compositions, and letters, programmes and other subsidiary material concerning Coates and his wife Vera de Villiers. The library also holds autographs of Arnold van Wyk and has a collection of South African printed music.

RITA BENTON (I, II), MARY WALLACE DAVIDSON (III)
SAMUEL CLARO, CATHERINE DOWER, JOSÉ
IGNACIO PERDOMO ESCOBAR, NORMA GONZÁLEZ,
FRANCISCO CURT LANGE, MERCEDES REIS PEQUENO,
ROBERT STEVENSON, POLA SUÁREZ URTURBEY (IV),
DOROTHY FREED, WERNER GALLUSSER, DON HARRAN
KATHARINE A. HASLAM, JAMES SIDDONS (V)

Libretto (It.: 'small book'; Fr. *livret*; Ger. *Textbuch*). A printed book containing the words of an opera, oratorio or other extended vocal work in dialogue; by extension,

38

Torni di Tito a lato,
   Torni e l' error passato
Con riplicate amendi
Prove di fedeltà.
L' acerbo suo dolore
E segno manifesto
Che di virtù nel core
L' immagne gli stà.   [*Parte.*

SCENA IV.

Vitellia che affretta ansiosamente Sesto, indi
Publio con guardie.

SES. Vive Lentulo ancora!
   Alfin posso, o crudele....
VIT. Oh Dio ! l' ore in querele
Non perdiamo così ; fuggi, conserva
La mia vita, e il tuo onor: tu sei perduto
Se alcun ti scopre : e se scoperto sei
Pubblico è il mio segreto. SES. In questo
      seno
Sepolto resterà ; nessuno il seppe,
Tacendolo morrò. VIT. Mi fiderei
Se minor tenerezza
Per (Tito in te vedessi. Il suo rigore
Non temo già, la sua clemenza io temo
Questa ti vincerà.
            [*Entra Publio con guardi.*
PUB. Sesto? SES. Che chiedi.
PUB. La tua spada. SES. E perchè ? PUB. Per
      tua sventura
Lentulo non morì: già il resto intendi,
Vieni. VIT. Oh colpo fatale !
                  [*Sesto dà la spada.*
SES. Alfin tiranna....

39

Let him return to Titus, and amend his past errors
by repentance and sorrow. His bitter sorrow is
a sincere mark, that virtue's image is still engraved on his heart.   {*Exit.*

SCENE IV.

Vitellia, hastening Sextus with anxious fear ; then Publius,
with guards.

SEX. Lentulus yet alive ! At length I may, thou
barbarous. . . . .
  VIT. Oh Gods ! forbear ; let us not waste our
time in vain contest ; fly, Sextus, and preserve my
life, and thy honour—thou art lost, if betrayed by any of
thy accomplices ; and if thou art discovered, my secret
guilt is known.
  SEX. Buried within this breast thy secret lies ;
none shall from hence unroot it, nor death itself, shall
wrest it from me.
  VIT. I might trust thee, but that I see thy fond
affection for Titus. His rigour I dread not ; but his cle-
mency, I fear, may conquer thee.

            Enter Publius.

PUB. Sextus.
SEX. What wouldst thou ?
PUB. Thy sword.
SEX. Ha ! wherefore—speak ?
PUB. For thy misfortune, Lentulus yet lives : the
rest is plain—away.
VIT. Oh fatal blow !
                  [*Sextus gives his sword.*
SEX. At length, inhuman....

Opening of Act 2 scene iv of the libretto for Mozart's 'La clemenza di Tito' as printed for the first English performance of the opera, at the King's Theatre, Haymarket, in 1806; the parts of Vitellia and Sextus were sung by Elizabeth Billington and John Braham

the text itself. (For a historical survey of opera texts *see* OPERA, §VII.)

The earliest opera librettos were produced at the expense of the prince for whose entertainment the works were composed; they were often printed in a dignified style and were mostly a little over 20 cm in height. When opera became a public spectacle the height was reduced to about 14 cm, as in the case of Busenello's *L'incoronazione di Poppea* (1642), so that the diminutive form of the word became appropriate. The size of these wordbooks and the style of their typography have varied considerably at different periods and in different countries. For special performances they were sometimes printed on a sumptuous scale with numerous engravings of the scenic designs, but most early librettos were produced for the immediate performance and not for posterity; they use inferior paper and, partly because of the necessity of meeting performance deadlines, often abound in typographical errors. In the 17th and 18th centuries librettos were much more read during performances than they can be now, in darkened theatres, and they sometimes bear interesting and even valuable annotations, as well as spots of candle grease from the wax tapers used to read them.

The sale of librettos was often a perquisite of the author, and the poets regarded them as literary works in their own right, though usually as a sideline to seemingly more important activities. Giovanni Francesco Busenello, whose texts were set by Cavalli and Monteverdi, published his opera librettos collectively in 1656 as *Delle ore ociose*, and Benedetto Marcello's

satire *Il teatro alla moda* (c1720) advises librettists to disclaim serious responsibility for their texts by saying that they were hasty and youthful productions. With a number of significant exceptions (notably Pietro Metastasio), librettists have not on the whole enjoyed much esteem in literary circles; during the 17th and 18th centuries especially, their works were constantly adapted for performance in a different city and sometimes supplemented by texts borrowed from other works or written to order by a local hack. So that the poet's work could be used in its entirety, passages which were either not set to music or were discarded before performance were often printed; in Italy such passages were commonly indicated by double commas, and are therefore known as *versi virgolati*. Mozart's correspondence with his father in late 1780 and early 1781, regarding the preparation of *Idomeneo*, throws an interesting light on such procedures and the attitudes of librettists.

The study of librettos was for a long time neglected by historians of opera and oratorio, and it has generally been taken for granted that the vast majority of them are as literature beneath contempt. But there has been a growing awareness of the importance of the libretto itself in the musicological and sociological study of the two genres. Scores are often deficient in the kind of information that librettos contain, including stage directions, spoken dialogue and lists of characters. It was the practice until the 19th century to print a fresh libretto for each new production of an opera, and it is often necessary to consult a libretto in order to determine what was performed on a particular occasion. In many cases a libretto provides the main (sometimes the only) evidence of a performance or even of a composition, and the value of a libretto in identifying untitled, incomplete or anonymous scores, as well as isolated arias, has been proved over and over again. Title-pages, dedications, prefatory essays and names of singers all supply valuable information, and collectively librettos can help to build up a picture of opera and oratorio in particular places and periods: the size of companies, the activity and mobility of leading singers, the make-up of repertories, local customs, censorship and so on.

Three factors contributed materially to a decline in the printing of librettos after about 1800. One was the introduction of gas lighting into theatres early in the 19th century; this made it easy to dim the lights in the auditorium, which in the days of candlelight had remained illumined throughout the performance. Another factor was the greater uniformity of performance; although cuts were frequently made in 19th-century productions, the substitution of one aria or ensemble for another became much less common. The third factor was the more widespread publication of complete works in full or vocal score. Except for the earliest Italian works (e.g. Monteverdi's *Orfeo*, 1607) and the courtly French operas (Lully, Rameau), 17th- and 18th-century scores existed almost exclusively in manuscript. The overtures and 'favourite airs' from the operas and oratorios of Handel and his contemporaries were published in London, but with few exceptions it was not until after Handel's death that the works began to appear in complete form. The value of the libretto declined as operas and oratorios became available in complete and reasonably cheap editions.

Librettos have continued to be printed in the 19th and 20th centuries, often in anticipation of a first performance, but they are of less interest to scholars than earlier librettos because the information they contain is usually readily available elsewhere. Among the largest libretto collections are those formed by Albert Schatz (now in the Library of Congress, Washington), Ulderico Rolandi (Cini Foundation, Venice) and Manoel de Carvalhoes (Accademia di S Cecilia, Rome). Other libraries with important holdings include the British Library, London, the Biblioteca Marciana, Venice, the Österreichische Nationalbibliothek, Vienna, the State Library, Leningrad, the conservatory libraries in Paris, Brussels, Milan, Bologna and Naples, and the university libraries of Texas and California. Catalogues have been published of a number of these and other collections, the most valuable being Oscar Sonneck's Library of Congress catalogue.

BIBLIOGRAPHY

P. Bergmans: 'Une collection de livrets d'opéras italiens 1669–1710', *SIMG*, xii (1910–11), 224

O. G. T. Sonneck: 'Italienische Opernlibretti des 17. Jahrhunderts in der Library of Congress', *SIMG*, xiii (1911–12), 392

——: *Catalogue of 19th Century Librettos* [*US-Wc*] (Washington, DC, 1914)

——: *Catalogue of Opera Librettos Printed before 1800* [*US-Wc*] (Washington, DC, 1914/*R*1968)

R. Haas: 'Zur Bibliographie der Operntexte', *Kongressbericht: Leipzig 1925*, 59

V. Raeli: 'Catalogazione statistica delle collezioni di libretti per musica', *Musica d'oggi*, xii (1930), 356

A. A. Abert: 'Libretto', *MGG*

R. Schaal: 'Die vor 1801 gedruckten Libretti des Theatermuseums München', *Mf*, x (1957), 388, 487; xi (1958), 54, 168, 321, 462; xii (1959), 60, 161, 299, 454; xiii (1960), 38, 164, 299, 441; xiv (1961), 36, 166

A. Caselli: *Catalogo delle opere liriche pubblicate in Italia* (Florence, 1969)

E. Thiel and G. Rohr: *Kataloge der Herzog August-Bibliothek Wolfenbüttel*, xiv: *Libretti: Verzeichnis der bis 1800 erschienenen Textbücher* (Frankfurt am Main, 1970)

P. J. Smith: *The Tenth Muse: a Historical Study of the Opera Libretto* (New York, 1970)

For further bibliography *see* OPERA, §VII.

EDWARD J. DENT/PATRICK J. SMITH

Libya. North African Arab republic; *see* ARAB MUSIC and NORTH AFRICA.

Licenza (It.: 'licence'). (1) In the 17th and 18th centuries a passage or cadenza inserted into a piece by a performer.

(2) In the same period, an epilogue inserted into a stage work (opera or play) in honour of a patron's birthday or wedding, or for some other festive occasion. This usually consisted of recitatives and arias but choruses were sometimes included. The *licenza* could be an integral part of the main work (as in Fux's *Costanza e fortezza*, 1723) or it could be written later by a different composer and librettist; in 1667 the Emperor Leopold I composed his own *licenza* for the Viennese performances of Cesti's *Le disgrazie d'amore*.

(3) The directions 'Con alcuna licenza' or 'con alcune licenze' indicate either that a piece is to be performed somewhat freely in the matter of tempo or expression (the slow movement of Tchaikovsky's Fifth Symphony is marked 'Andante cantabile, con alcuna licenza') or that in its composition some liberty has been taken with strict forms and procedures (e.g. the fugue in Beethoven's Hammerklavier Sonata op.106).

WILLIAM C. HOLMES

Licette, Miriam (*b* Chester, 9 Sept 1892; *d* Twyford, 11 Aug 1969). English soprano. She studied under Marchesi, Jean de Reszke and Sabbatini, making her début in Rome as Cio-cio-san (1911). After further successful European appearances, she returned to England, where she became one of the leading lyric sopranos of her day, joining the Beecham Opera Company in 1915, the British National Opera Company in 1922, and singing at Covent Garden from 1919 to 1929. Her roles included Mimì, Desdemona, Eva and Louise, and she was specially admired in Mozart. Her voice was pure and steady, with firmly placed tone and a remarkably even scale, well represented in a complete recorded *Faust* under Beecham.

J. B. STEANE

Lichfild, Henry (*fl* 1613). English madrigalist. The preface of Lichfild's only publication, *The First Set of Madrigals of 5. Parts, Apt both for Viols and Voyces* (London, 1613/14; ed. in EM, xvii, 1969/*R*1972), reveals that he was in the service of Lady Cheyney (Cheney) of Toddington, near Luton. He was not employed primarily as a domestic musician but possibly, as Edmund Fellowes suggested, as a household steward. In her will Lady Cheyney, who died in 1614, left £20 to Lichfild.

Lichfild's madrigals were composed in his leisure hours under the encouragement of Lady Cheyney, and were first performed by the 'instruments and voyces' of her family. They are unpretentious pieces that take no account of the technical and expressive elaboration of the form already displayed in the work of Weelkes and Wilbye, but return to the simplest canzonet manner that

Morley had established in England 20 years earlier. Lichfild handled this undemanding manner cleanly but without enterprise, and his music is acceptable, though lacking in individuality.

BIBLIOGRAPHY

E. H. Fellowes: *English Madrigal Verse, 1588–1632* (Oxford, 1920, rev., enlarged 3/1967)
——: *The English Madrigal Composers* (Oxford, 1921, 2/1948/R1975)

DAVID BROWN

Lichnowsky. Aristocratic family, several members of whose Austrian branch supported the arts in the late 18th century and early 19th.

(1) Prince Karl [Carl] (Alois Johann Nepomuk Vinzenz Leonhard) von Lichnowsky (*b* Vienna, 21 June 1761; *d* Vienna, 15 March 1814). He lived mostly in Vienna but also maintained an estate near Troppau. In 1788 he married Maria Christiane (1765–1841), daughter of Countess Maria Wilhelmine of Thun-Hoherstein. Countess Thun, an accomplished musician and pupil of Haydn, was a good friend to both Mozart and Beethoven, and presided over evening gatherings of the most cultivated people in Vienna. Prince Karl was a pupil and patron of Mozart; they belonged to the same masonic lodge. A year after his marriage he invited Mozart to accompany him on a trip to Prague, Dresden, Leipzig and Berlin. When Beethoven arrived in Vienna in late 1792, he was introduced to the Lichnowskys by Haydn, and it was in their house on the Alserstrasse that he had his first quarters. The prince reserved Friday mornings for music-making; for this purpose he hired four young string players, led by Schuppanzigh, to form a nucleus of performers. Beethoven's early chamber works were played as soon as they were composed. Haydn was present when the three trios op.1 (dedicated to the prince, whose subscription helped make their publication possible) were given their first performance. In 1800 Prince Karl offered Beethoven 600 florins as support until he should receive a suitable post. It was at the Lichnowskys' house on the Mölkerbastei that a group of concerned musicians gathered with Beethoven in 1805 to play through the first version of *Fidelio*, with Princess Christiane at the piano, in an attempt to cut and revise the opera.

(2) Countess Henriette von Lichnowsky (*b* Vienna, 10 May 1769; *d* after 1829). Sister of (1) Karl von Lichnowsky. She also befriended Beethoven in Vienna. After her marriage to the Marquis of Carneville she moved to Paris, where she was associated with musicians, including Chopin.

(3) Count Moritz (Josef Cajetan Gallus) von Lichnowsky (*b* Vienna, 17 Oct 1771; *d* Vienna, 17 March 1837). Pianist and composer, brother of (1) Karl von Lichnowsky. He was also a patron and friend of both Mozart and Beethoven, and a constant promoter of Beethoven's interests. His involvement with the latter was at its height in the 1820s when he tried to secure him a position as court composer, tried to bring him and the poet Grillparzer together for an opera text, offered advice in Beethoven's business affairs and participated vigorously in the arrangements for the first performance of the Ninth Symphony. He was a fine amateur musician and published a set of seven piano variations on Paisiello's 'Nel cor più non mi sento' (Vienna, 1798). In his last years he became acquainted with Chopin.

(4) Prince Felix von Lichnowsky (*b* Vienna, 5 April 1814; *d* Frankfurt am Main, 18 Sept 1848). Son of the poet Eduard Maria and grandson of (1) Karl von Lichnowsky. He was a member of the National Assembly at Frankfurt, and became a friend of Franz Liszt, with whom he corresponded.

BIBLIOGRAPHY

'Franz Liszts Briefe an den Fürsten Lichnowsky', *Bayreuther Blätter*, xxx (1907), nos.1–3
T. Frimmel: *Beethoven-Handbuch*, ii (Leipzig, 1926/R1968), 345ff
C. Preihs: 'Mozarts Beziehungen zu den Familien von Thun-Hohenstein', *Neues Mozart-Jb*, iii (1943), 63
P. Nettl: *Beethoven Encyclopedia* (New York, 1956), 120f
R. Schaal: 'Lichnowsky', *MGG*
E. Forbes, ed.: *Thayer's Life of Beethoven* (Princeton, 1964, 2/1967)
A. F. Schindler: *Beethoven as I knew him*, ed. D. W. MacArdle and C. S. Jolly (London, 1966)

ELLIOT FORBES

Lichtenauer, Paul Ignaz (*fl* 1736). German composer. He was cathedral organist at Osnabrück in 1736, when he published a set of offertories for four voices, violins and continuo with Lotter of Augsburg. He was one of the few composers from northern Germany to write in the simple parish-church style favoured by his south German contemporaries.

ELIZABETH ROCHE

Lichtenegger, Mathilde. *See* MALLINGER, MATHILDE.

Lichtenfeld, Monika (*b* Düsseldorf, 16 Sept 1938). German musicologist. She studied musicology, philosophy and art history from 1957 in Cologne, Florence and Vienna until 1963, when she took the doctorate at Cologne with a dissertation on Hauer's 12-note technique. During the same period she attended the Darmstadt summer courses. Since 1959 she has written extensively for radio, record companies, newspapers, periodicals and encyclopedias in Germany and abroad. Her research deals chiefly with style, experiment and innovation in contemporary music and with the social and philosophical aspects of 19th-century music.

WRITINGS

Untersuchungen zur Theorie der Zwölftontechnik bei Josef Matthias Hauer (diss., U. of Cologne, 1963; Regensburg, 1964)
'Gesamtkunstwerk und allgemeine Kunst: das System der Künste bei Wagner und Hegel', *Beiträge zur Geschichte der Musikanschauung im 19. Jahrhundert*, ed. W. Salmen (Regensburg, 1965), 171
'Triviale und anspruchsvolle Musik in den Konzerten um 1850', *Studien zur Trivialmusik des 19. Jahrhunderts*, ed. C. Dahlhaus (Regensburg, 1967), 143
'Zur Geschichte, Idee und Ästhetik des historischen Konzerts', *Die Ausbreitung des Historismus über die Musik*, ed. W. Wiora (Regensburg, 1969), 41
'Zur Technik der Klangfächenkomposition bei Wagner', *Das Drama Richard Wagners als musikalisches Kunstwerk*, ed. C. Dahlhaus (Regensburg, 1970), 161
'Das "grosse Konzert": Entstehung, Form, Programm', *Die Welt der Symphonie*, ed. U. von Rauchhaupt (Hamburg, 1972), 35
'Über Schönbergs Moses und Aron', *Arnold Schönberg Gedenkausstellung 1974*, ed. E. Hilmar (Vienna, 1974), 125
'Hauer, Josef Matthias', 'Zimmermann, Bernd Alois', *Grove 6*

ALFRED GRANT GOODMAN

Lichtenfels, Hainrich. *See* FABER, HEINRICH.

Lichtenhahn, Ernst (*b* Arosa, canton of Graubünden, 4 Jan 1934). Swiss musicologist. He studied musicology at Basle University with Schrade and Arnold Schmitz, and German literature with Walter Muschg; at the same time he completed a course at the Basle Academy for school music (1959). In 1966 he took a doctorate at Basle with a dissertation on Schumann. In 1961 he became an assistant lecturer at Basle University

Musicology Institute, becoming lecturer on instruments in 1968. In 1969 he was appointed to the chair of musicology at Neuchâtel University, where he teaches both historical musicology and ethnomusicology. In addition to studying European music history, particularly that of the 19th century, Lichtenhahn has done extensive work on African music, notably that of the Tuareg. In 1973 he was appointed president of the Basle section of the Schweizerische Musikforschende Gesellschaft.

WRITINGS
'Über einen Ausspruch Hoffmanns und über das Romantische in der Musik', *Musik und Geschichte: Leo Schrade zum sechzigsten Geburtstag* (Cologne, 1963), 178
Die Bedeutung des Dichterischen im Werk Robert Schumanns (diss., U. of Basle, 1966; Basle, 1974)
ed.: L. Schrade: *De scientia musicae studia atque orationes* (Berne, 1967) [Schrade's collected articles and bibliography]
'"Ars perfecta": zu Glareans Auffassung der Musikgeschichte', *Festschrift Arnold Geering* (Berne, 1972), 129
'Die Popularitätsfrage in Richard Wagners Pariser Schriften', *Schweizer Beiträge zur Musikwissenschaft*, i (1972), 143
'Begegnung mit "andalusischer" Praxis', *Basler Jb für historische Musikpraxis*, i (1977), 137
JÜRG STENZL

Lichtenstein, Karl August, Freiherr **von** (*b* Lahm, Franconia, 8 Sept 1767; *d* Berlin, 10 Sept 1845). German composer, theatre manager, poet, conductor, producer and singer. After spending his childhood in Gotha, where his father was a government official, and further education at Göttingen, he served for a while with the English army before entering Hanoverian service; his opera *Glück und Zufall*, to his own libretto, was performed at Hanover in 1793. A Singspiel, *Knall und Fall*, was given at Bamberg in 1795. In 1797 he was appointed manager of the Dessau Opera, whose new house opened on 26 December 1798 with a performance of his opera *Bathmendi*. Apart from his administrative responsibilities and the works he wrote, he and his wife frequently performed in operas. His Singspiel *Die steinerne Braut* proved very successful in 1799; a duet from it was published in the *Allgemeine musikalische Zeitung*. In 1800, following financial difficulties after an ambitious and artistically successful guest season at Leipzig, Lichtenstein left Dessau for Vienna, where he became Kapellmeister and artistic director under Baron von Braun, Intendant of the court theatre, for three years. *Bathmendi* was a failure when, newly revised, it was given on 16 April 1801. In 1806 he gave up theatrical activities and returned to diplomacy, as minister to the Duke of Saxe-Hildburghausen, but in 1811 he went to Bamberg and in 1813 became director of the theatre. He also took up composing again, with *Die Waldburg* (1811), *Imago* (1813–14) and a considerable number of other stage works; he continued to write operas until the late 1830s. In 1814 Lichtenstein moved from Bamberg to Strasbourg, as musical director. He returned to Bamberg in 1817 and in 1823, after a brief stay in Dresden, he settled in Berlin, where his opera *Der Edelknabe* was given on 27 May. After a period of responsibility for the spoken theatre, he took up an appointment at the opera in 1825. He was pensioned in 1832 though he continued to adapt, translate and even compose stage works; and his official retirement did not prevent him from continuing to work in the administration of the opera house.

Lichtenstein wrote some 17 stage works, four librettos for other composers (including *Die Hochzeit des Gamacho* for Mendelssohn in 1825 and a revision of

Agnes von Hohenstaufen for Spontini in 1837). He translated or arranged nearly 20 operas by some of the leading composers of the day (Adam, Auber, Bellini, Boieldieu, Donizetti, Halévy, Hérold, Rossini (*Guillaume Tell*, adapted as *Andreas Hofer* for Berlin in 1830, after the Tyrolese national hero) and Thomas.

BIBLIOGRAPHY
GerberNL
G. Schilling: *Das musikalische Europa* (Speyer, 1842), 210
J. Schladebach and E. Bernsdorf: *Neues Universal-Lexikon der Tonkunst*, ii (Dresden, 1856), 757
C. von Wurzbach: *Biographisches Lexikon des Kaiserthums Oesterreich*, xv (Vienna, 1866), 84
R. Eitner: 'Lichtenstein, Karl August', *ADB*
C. Schäffer and C. Hartmann: *Die königlichen Theater in Berlin: statistischer Rückblick* (Berlin, 1886)
F. Leist: 'Geschichte des Theaters in Bamberg', *Bericht des historischen Vereins zu Bamberg*, iv (Bamberg, 1893)
M. von Prosky: *Das herzogliche Theater zu Dessau* (Dessau, 2/1894)
G. Fischer: *Musik in Hannover* (Hanover, 2/1903)
F. Schnapp, ed.: *E. T. A. Hoffmanns Briefwechse*, iii (Munich, 1969)
——: *E. T. A. Hoffmann: Tagebücher* (Munich, 1971)
PETER BRANSCOMBE

Lichtenstein, Ulrich von. See ULRICH VON LIEHTEN-STEIN.

Lichtenthal, Peter [Pietro] (*b* Pressburg, 10 May 1780; *d* Milan, 18 Aug 1853). Austrian amateur composer and writer on music. A doctor of medicine by profession, having earned his degree in Vienna, he settled in Milan in 1810 as a censor for the government. He was a close friend of Mozart's son Karl, and an ardent proponent of Mozart's chamber music. He composed about 50 works, including seven ballets for the Teatro alla Scala, church music, chamber music, songs, piano and organ works. A number of these were published; most of his MSS are in the Conservatorio Giuseppe Verdi, Milan.

Lichtenthal's importance lies in his writings, in particular his four-volume *Dizionario e bibliografia della musica* (1826), which although full of factual errors, and being in significant measure a translation of the dictionaries of Gerber (1790–92) and Koch (1802) and the bibliography of Forkel (1792), is nevertheless a landmark in the development from dilettantism to modern, systematic bibliographic method.

WRITINGS
Harmonik für Damen (Vienna, 1806)
Der musikalische Arzt, oder Abhandlung von dem Einflusse der Musik auf den menschlichen Körper (Vienna, 1807; It. trans., 1811)
Orpheik, oder Anweisung, die Regeln der Komposition auf eine leichte und fassliche Art gründlich zu erlernen (Vienna, 1816)
Cenni biografici intorno al celebre maestro W. A. Mozart (Milan, 1816)
Dizionario e bibliografia della musica (Milan, 1826)
Estetica ossia Dottrina del bello e delle belle arti (Milan, 1831)
Mozart e le sue creazioni (Milan, 1842)
BIBLIOGRAPHY
EitnerQ; *FétisB*; *SchmidlD*
C. Sartori: 'Lichtenthal, Peter', *MGG*
ALFRED LOEWENBERG/BRUCE CARR

Lichtenwanger, William (John) (*b* Asheville, North Carolina, 28 Feb 1915). American music librarian. He attended the University of Michigan, where he took the BM in 1937 and the MM in 1940; he also did postgraduate work at Indiana University. From 1937 to 1940 he was music librarian at the University of Michigan. He then joined the staff of the Library of Congress, where he was head of the reference section in the music division from 1960 to 1974.

Lichtenwanger's particular interests as a librarian are music reference problems and services and musical lexicography. He has also been active as an editor of reference works and *Notes of the Music Library Association*, which he supervised from 1960 to 1963. As co-compiler of the checklist of instruments in the Dayton C. Miller Collection he was responsible for providing a guide to the large collection of flutes housed in the Library of Congress. Lichtenwanger has been general editor of the 'Bibliography of Asiatic Musics' in *Notes* (1947–51), editor and contributor to *Church Music and Musical Life in Pennsylvania in the 18th Century*, iii, pt 2 (Philadelphia, 1947) and music editor and a contributor to *Collier's Encyclopedia* (New York, 1947–51), *Dictionary of American Biography*, suppl.2–3 (New York, 1958–73) and to *Notable American Women, 1607–1950* (Cambridge, Mass., 1971). He was chairman of the MLA committee compiling the *Directory of Musical Instrumental Collections in the U.S. and Canada* (1974) and was joint editor of the analytical index (1976) to *Modern Music*.

WRITINGS

with L. E. Gilliam: *The Dayton C. Miller Flute Collection: a Checklist of the Instruments* (Washington, DC, 1961)

'Another Treble Flute d'Allemagne by P.-J. Bressan', *GSJ*, xv (1962), 45

'Walter Hinrichsen, 23 Sept. 1907–21 July 1969', *Notes*, xxvi (1969–70), 491

'Star-spangled Bibliography', *College Music Symposium*, xii (1972), 94

'The Music of "The Star-spangled Banner"', *Library of Congress Quarterly Journal*, xxxiv/3 (1977), 136–70

PAULA MORGAN

Licino, Agostino (*fl* 1545–6). Italian composer. His only known works are two volumes of canonic duos, *Primo libro di duo cromatici ... da cantare et sonare* (Venice, 1545) and *Il secondo libro di duo cromatici ... da cantare et sonare* (Venice, 1546). All that is known about his life is stated in these volumes: he was from Cremona, he worked in the service of Benedetto Guarna of Salerno, and he intended his duets for the instruction and enjoyment of his patron's sons and their friends. Together the two volumes contain examples of canons at various intervals of time and pitch in each of the eight modes. Though printed without text, they were intended either to be sung or played. The 'cromatici' of the titles refers to their many black notes and hence fast passages, rather than to accidentals.

HOWARD MAYER BROWN

Lickl. Austrian family of musicians.

(1) **Johann Georg Lickl** (*b* Korneuburg, Lower Austria, 11 April 1769; *d* Fünfkirchen [now Pécs], Hungary, 12 May 1843). Composer and conductor. Orphaned at an early age, he studied music under Witzig, the Korneuburg church organist. In 1785 he went to Vienna, teaching music and himself studying with Albrechtsberger and Haydn. He was appointed organist at the Carmelite Church in the Leopoldstadt, where Eybler was choirmaster. From about 1789 (or later) he was on the music staff of Schikaneder's Freihaus-Theater auf der Wieden, from 1793 contributing complete or partial scores to a series of popular Singspiels, including *Der Zauberpfeil*, *Das Zigeunermädchen*, *Die Haushaltung nach der Mode*, *Der Bruder von Kakran*, *Der Kampf mit dem Fürsten der Finsternis*, *Fausts Leben, Taten und Höllenfahrt*, *Der vermeinte Hexenmeister*, *Der Orgelspieler* and *Der Durchmarsch*. For the new Theater an der Wien he wrote *Der Brigitten-Kirchtag* in 1802, and in 1812 he supplied the Leopoldstadt Theatre with a comic opera,

Slawina von Pommern. Despite these successes, church music was his particular interest, and in 1804 he composed a mass for Empress Maria Theresia, followed by one for Princess Esterházy. In 1805 he was appointed *regens chori* at Fünfkirchen Cathedral, where he lived and worked for nearly 40 years. During this period he wrote a quantity of church music, including 24 masses, two requiems and many smaller pieces, and a number of keyboard works.

(2) **Karl Georg Lickl** (*b* Vienna, 28 Oct 1801; *d* Vienna, 3 Aug 1877). Physharmonica player and composer, son of (1) Johann Georg Lickl. He became a civil servant but was a talented amateur musician who gained particular fame as a virtuoso on, and composer and theorist for, the physharmonica.

(3) **Aegidius** [Ferdinand] **Karl Lickl** (*b* Vienna, 1 Sept 1803; *d* Trieste, 22 July 1864). Composer and conductor, son of (1) Johann Georg Lickl. After study with his father and gaining some eminence as a pianist he moved to Trieste in the 1830s, where he became a popular teacher, conductor and composer. His opera *La disfida di Berletta* was staged in February 1848, the oratorio *Der Triumph des Christentums* was performed in Vienna in 1855, and he wrote a quantity of church music.

BIBLIOGRAPHY

GerberNL

A. Gross: Obituary, *Allgemeine Wiener Musik Zeitung*, no.84 (15 July 1843), 349

J. Schladebach and E. Bernsdorf: *Neues Universal-Lexikon der Tonkunst*, ii (Dresden, 1856), 759

C. von Wurzbach: *Biographisches Lexikon des Kaiserthums Oesterreich*, xv (Vienna, 1866), 89 [with work-lists for all 3 composers]

R. Eitner: 'Lickl', *ADB*

PETER BRANSCOMBE

Lidarti, Christian Joseph [Cristiano Giuseppe] (*b* Vienna, 23 Feb 1730; *d* ?Pisa, after 1793). Austrian composer of Italian descent. He studied at a Cistercian monastery in Klagenfurt and afterwards at the Jesuit seminary in Leoben. He then studied philosophy and law at the University of Vienna. He had meanwhile studied the harpsichord and harp and had begun to teach himself composition. In Vienna the Kapellmeister Giuseppe Bonno, his uncle, reproached him for his dilettantism and directed him to study the classic theorists. In 1751 he went to Italy to complete his musical education. After short stays in Venice and Florence, he spent five years in Cortona as a music teacher and composer. He studied with Jommelli in Rome in 1757 and from then until at least 1784 was a player in the chapel of the Cavalieri di S Stefano in Pisa. In 1761 he became a member of the Accademia Filarmonica in Bologna and later in Modena. His last dated composition is from 1793. Five letters to Martini are in the Bologna Conservatory library.

Lidarti's instrumental music is marked by a certain felicity of invention: each instrument, including the cello, moves with a songlike and agile grace. His compositions are bipartite in structure, showing a preference for forms like the minuet, even in sonata finales. Their thematic ideas tend towards homogeneity, particularly in the continual recurrence of a few rhythmic figures, removing all possibility of dramatic contrast. As a result, Lidarti's compositions, especially the instrumental ones, maintain an unbroken and serene songlike quality, interrupted only by occasional fugal or canonic passages.

WORKS

Inst: Sonata, 2 vn, bc, in 6 Sonatas . . . by Salvatore Galleotti and . . .
Lidarti (London, 1762); 6 sinfonie, 2 vn, va, b, other insts ad lib, op.2
(Paris, *c*1768); 6 trii, 2 vn, b, op.3 (Paris, *c*1770); 6 Sonatas, 2 fl/vn,
bc (hpd) (London, *c*1770); 6 Duetts, vn, vc (London, *c*1795); others,
A-Wgm (incl. sonata, viola pomposa, bc, attrib. in *EitnerQ*) *B-Bc*;
D-Hs, *MÜs*; *GB-Lbm*; *I-Mc*, *MOe*, *Nc*, *Pls*
Vocal: La tutela contrastata fra Giunone, Marte e Mercurio, col giudizio
di Giove, componimento drammatico, 1767, *A-Wn*; arias, *D-Dlb*;
I-MTventuri; sacred works, *Baf*, *Fc*, *PAc*, *PIst*

BIBLIOGRAPHY
C. G. Lidarti: *Aneddoti musicali di C. G. Lidarti* (MS, *I-Bc*)
C. Burney: *The Present State of Music in France and Italy* (London,
1771, 2/1773); ed. P. Scholes as *Dr. Burney's Musical Tours*
(London, 1959)
E. van der Straeten: *History of the Violoncello* (London, 1915/*R*1971)
R. Meylan: 'La collection Antonio Venturi, Montecatini-Terme
(Pistoia), Italie', *FAM*, v (1958), 31
L. F. Tagliavini: 'Lidarti, Christian Joseph', *MGG*

GUIDO SALVETTI

Lidel, Andreas. *See* LIDL, ANDREAS.

Lidholm, Ingvar (Natanael) (*b* Jönköping, 24 Feb
1921). Swedish composer. In 1940 he entered the
Stockholm Music High School to study the violin with
Barkel, the piano with Brandel and conducting with
Mann, but in 1943 he broke off his studies to join the
royal chapel as a viola player. He stayed there until
1946, also studying composition with Rosenberg during
this period. Later he was to be associated with other
Rosenberg pupils (Blomdahl, Bäck, Johanson and
others) in the influential Monday Group. He conducted
the partly amateur Örebro Orchestra from 1947 to
1956, during which period he visited France,
Switzerland and Italy (1946–7), the Darmstadt summer
courses (1949) and England for further composition
studies with Seiber (1954). He has also served as director of chamber music for Swedish Radio (1956–65),
professor of composition at the Stockholm Music High
School (from 1965) and director of planning for the
radio music department (from 1974).

Lidholm's early works, especially the often performed *Toccata e canto* for chamber orchestra, the
songs and piano pieces, reveal a Nordic tone and an
affiliation to Nielsen and Hindemith. Of the Monday
Group composers he was at first the most concerned
with Stravinsky and early vocal polyphony, as is evident
from the very successful choral *Laudi* (1947); but subsequent contacts with new tendencies in Europe
profoundly altered his thinking. As early as 1949 he
took up 12-note serialism in the *Klavierstück*, and this
was followed by his adoption of later serial practices
and of improvisatory sequences, as in the orchestral
Poesis (1963), with its central piano cadenza. However,
within this development he has maintained and even
emphasized certain distinctive characteristics, such as
his marked sensitivity to choral scoring (his major
works holding a pre-eminent place in modern Swedish
choral music), his colourful orchestral language and his
lyricism, which permeates even the large-scale works
and brings to them a formal neatness.

Although Lidholm has composed in most genres, he
is at his best in vocal works, in which he has evolved a
style often at variance with those of his colleagues, such
as Blomdahl and Bäck. If the earlier pieces lie within the
middle ground of modern music, the pedagogical *A
cappella-bok*, begun in 1956, raises all manner of artistic 'problems' and seeks their solution. Its basis is a
single 12-note series with tonal associations (to assist
singers), but gradually a whole range of techniques is

brought into play, culminating in the great *Canto
LXXXI*. The symphonic cantata *Skaldens natt* ('The
poet's night') uses words as symphonic elements, while
in *Nausikaa ensam* textless vocal effects are skilfully
applied. All of Lidholm's vocal techniques are brought
to a masterly integration in . . . *a riveder le stelle*.

WORKS
(*selective list*)

Dramatic: Riter (ballet, E. Lindegren), orch, tape, 1960; Holländarn
(television opera, H. Grevenius, after Strindberg), 1967; Inga träd
skall väcka dig (television drama), 1974
Orch: Toccata e canto, chamber orch, 1944; Conc. [after Str Qt], str,
1945; Vn Conc., 1951; Musik för stråkar, 1952; Ritornell, 1955;
Mutanza, 1959; Motus-colores, 1960; Poesis, 1963; Greetings from
an Old World, 1976
Vocal: Laudi, chorus, 1947; 6 Songs, 1v, pf, 1946–48; Cantata, Bar,
orch, 1949; 4 Choruses, unacc., 1953; A cappella-bok, 1956–, incl.
Canto LXXXI (Pound), 1956; Skaldens natt [The poet's night] (C. J.
L. Almqvist), S, chorus, orch, 1957–8; Nausikaa ensam (E. Johnson),
S, chorus, orch, 1963; . . . a riveder le stelle (Dante), 1v, chorus,
1971–3
Chamber and inst: Str Qt, 1945; Sonata, fl, 1946; Pf Sonata, 1947; 10
miniatyrer, pf, 1948; Klavierstück, 1949; Pf Sonatina, 1950; Little
Str Trio, 1953; Invention, cl + b cl/va + vc/pf, 1954; 4 Pieces, vc,
pf, 1955; Stamp Music, score on postage stamp, 1971

Principal publishers: Gehrman, Nordiska Musikförlaget, Universal

BIBLIOGRAPHY
I. Bengtsson: 'Sven-Erik Bäck und Ingvar Lidholm', *Melos*, xxiii
(1956), 345
I. Lidholm: 'Tankar kring Ritornell för orkester', *Modern nordisk
musik*, ed. I. Bengtsson (Stockholm, 1957), 204
——: 'Rörelser, färger', *Nutida musik*, iv/2 (1960–61), 23
——: 'Poesis for Orchestra', *Three Aspects of New Music* (Stockholm,
1968), 55; Ger. trans. in *Melos*, xxxvi (1969), 63
B. E. Johnson: 'Ingvar Lidholm', *Nutida musik*, xii/2 (1968–9), 36

HANS ÅSTRAND

Lídl. Czech instrument makers. Joseph Lídl (*b* Manětín,
1 July 1864; *d* Brno, 11 Jan 1946) founded the first Moravian music instrument factory. He was apprenticed to a
wind instrument maker in Brno, where in 1892 he was
an agent for piano and harmonium factories. Later he
started making his own instruments, and in 1909 he
opened a factory manufacturing brass and string
instruments and accordions. Because the instruments
manufactured by the factory were of a very high quality
the firm was given the title 'Supplier to the Imperial and
Royal Household', together with the right 'to use the
Imperial eagle in the sign of the firm'. His son Václav
(*b* Brno, 31 Oct 1894) took over the management of his
father's firm in 1918, having served his apprenticeship
in his father's factory, and later worked in Vienna. His
instruments were popular, and Václav established a
second factory in Olomouc, and in 1921, together with
his partner Velík, he founded a piano and harmonium
factory in the town of Moravský Krumlov. Lídl's
instruments, particularly the brass instruments, were of
very high standard and quality, and had a number of
improvements in their construction and design. His
double horn was widely used and appreciated, at home
and abroad. This was the result of cooperation with the
acoustician and mathematician Čupr. In 1948 the
factory was nationalized, but Lídl continued to manage
it until 1957.

BIBLIOGRAPHY
ČSHS
Bericht der Handels- und Gewerbekammer in Brünn (1900–01)
'Erste Mährische Musikinstrumenten-Fabrik Josef Lídl, k. und k. Hof-
und Heeres-Lieferant Brünn', *Musikalische Anzeiger* (1912–13)

ALEXANDR BUCHNER

Lidl [Lidel], **Andreas** (*b* ?Vienna; *d* London, ?before
1789). Austrian baryton and viola da gamba player. He

was in the Eszterházy *Kapelle* from 1769 or 1771 to 1774, and Pohl who, incidentally, called him 'ein Deutscher', said that Schubart heard him in Augsburg in 1776 and that he went to London in 1778. In Pohl's lists (1867) of virtuosos in London Lidl is given as baryton player in 1776 and viola da gamba player in 1778. Fétis said 'il brillait encore à Berlin, 1784'; and Burney said that he was dead by 1789. To Pohl (1878) we owe the information that his performance enchanted through 'sweet grace, with German strength unexpectedly linked with most harmonious melody', and also that he increased the wire understrings to 27 so that the self-accompaniment could be fully chromatic. Burney's reference to Lidl includes an amusing account of what he considered to be the outlandishness of the baryton.

WORKS
(all published in London)

op.
1 6 Trios, vn/fl, vn, vc (1776)
2 6 Quartettos (1777); 3 for 2 vn, va, vc; 3 for fl, vn, va, vc
3 6 Duettos, vn, va/vc/vn (1778)
4 6 Sonatas, vn, va, vc (1778)
5 3 Quintettos, fl, vn, 2 va, vc (c1780)
6 A 2nd Sett of 6 Duettos (c1780); 3 for vn, va; 3 for vn, vc
7 A 2nd Sett of 6 Quartettos (c1785); 5 for 2 vn, va, vc; 1 for ob, vn, va, vc
8 A 3rd Sett of 6 Duettos, vn, vn/vc (1781)

Songs pubd singly and in 18th-century anthologies

BIBLIOGRAPHY
BurneyH; *EitnerQ*; *FétisB*
C. F. Pohl: *Mozart und Haydn in London* (Vienna, 1867/*R*1970), i, 52; ii, 96, 374
——: *Joseph Haydn*, i (Berlin, 1875, 2/1878), 251; ii (Leipzig, 1882), 16, 18
S. Gerlach: 'Die Chronologische Ordnung von Haydns Sinfonien zwischen 1774 und 1783', *Haydn-Studien*, ii/1 (1969), 50
J. Harich: 'Haydn Documenta IV', *Haydn Yearbook*, vii (1970), 67, 84
PETER PLATT

Lidón, José (*b* Béjar, nr. Salamanca, 1746; *d* Madrid, 11 Feb 1827). Spanish organist and composer. He was trained in the Real Colegio de Niños Cantores in Madrid and then served as organist at Orense Cathedral. In 1768 he returned to Madrid as fourth organist of the royal chapel, becoming first organist in 1787. In 1805 he succeeded Ugena as master of the royal chapel and rector of the Real Colegio, remaining at these posts until his death. His pupils included his nephews Alphonso and Mariano, both active in the royal chapel, and Pedro Carrera y Lanchares.

An inventory of the numerous works of Lidón is needed; some credited to him by earlier scholars have not been found. The extant works reveal a style relatively conservative for its period, restrained, solid and competent. His organ music uses the figurations typical of the late 18th century, but shows a penchant towards counterpoint, with melodic interest distributed throughout the texture. His more numerous sacred vocal works with orchestra, written for forces from solo voice to eight-part double chorus, seem austere and relatively simple, displaying neither polyphonic complexity nor theatrical coloratura. His *drama heroico Glaura y Coriolano* is a number opera with overture, recitatives (both simple and accompanied), arias and ensembles; it is of interest as an example of *opera seria* in Castilian, but its musical style varies little from that of the typical Italian opera of the period. His chamber music, a genre rarely attempted by native Spanish composers, seems relatively primitive both in form and texture for its time.

WORKS
Stage: Glaura y Coriolano (drama heroico, 2), Madrid, Príncipe, 1791, *E-Mn*; El baron de Illescas (zarzuela), lost
Vocal: more than 57 sacred works, some acc., incl. at least 4 masses, vespers, complines, hymns, Lamentations, Misereres, lits, *Mp*, Convento de la Encarnación, Madrid; villancicos, *Mn*, *Mp*
Organ: 6 fugas para el organo con sus intentos formados sobre el canto de 6 himnos (Madrid, ?1778, 2/?1781), lost; 6 piezas, ó sonatas ... en forma de versos grandes de octavo tono (Madrid, ?1798), lost, MS in *Mn*; 12 Pange lingua, *Mn*; 12 glosas sobre el Tantum ergo, *Mn*; Juego de versos, *MO*; 3 intentos ed. S. Rubio, *Organistas de la Real capilla*, i (Madrid, 1973)
Chamber: 2 vn sonatas, *Mp*; Qt, tpt, str, *Mp*
Theoretical: Colección de bajetes, in F. M. López: *Escuela de acompañar al órgano o al clave* (MS, *Mn*); Reglas muy útiles para todo organista y aficionado al pianoforte, para acompañar, lost, ?identical with preceding work; Tratado de la fuga, lost; Compendio theórico y práctico de la modulacion, *Bc*

BIBLIOGRAPHY
LaborD
M. Soriano Fuertes: *Historia de la música española*, iv (Madrid and Barcelona, 1859), 297 [incl. list of works in *E-Mp*]
B. Saldoni: *Diccionario biográfico-bibliográfico de efemérides de músicos españoles*, i (Madrid, 1868), 247ff
J. García Marcellán: *Catálogo del archivo de música de la real capilla de palacio* (Madrid, 1938)
H. Anglés and J. Subirá: *Catálogo musical de la Biblioteca nacional de Madrid*, i (Barcelona, 1946) [with additional bibliography]
J. Subirá: *Historia de la música española e hispanamericana* (Barcelona, 1953), 486
W. S. Newman: *The Sonata in the Classic Era* (Chapel Hill, 1963, rev. 2/1972)
ALMONTE HOWELL

Lié (Fr.). LEGATO.

Lie, Sigurd (*b* Drammen, 23 May 1871; *d* Vestre Aker, 30 Sept 1904). Norwegian composer. He was first taught music by August Rojahn, the organist of Kristiansand Cathedral. He studied the violin with Gudbrand Bøhn and theory and composition with Iver Holter at Lindeman's conservatory in Christiania, where he was also a violinist in a theatre orchestra. In 1891 he went to Leipzig, where for two and a half years he studied theory and composition with Reinecke and Rust and the violin with Arno Hilfs at the conservatory. His first music was published in 1892 – six songs to texts by his friend Vilhelm Krag. A piano quintet written at Leipzig was performed in 1894 after his return to Christiania, and its acclaim led to a state stipend. He went to Berlin and studied composition with Heinrich Urban (1894–5), writing, among other things, a suite for strings and a concert piece for violin and orchestra based on the folksong *Huldra aa'n Elland*.

In 1895 Lie was invited to become the leader of the musical society˙Harmonien in Bergen. He soon added to his duties the conductorship of the Musikforening, which in 1897 performed his *Erling Skajalgson*, a large work for baritone solo, male chorus and orchestra. During the winter of 1898–9 he was conductor of the orchestra of Fahlstrøm's Centre Theatre in Christiania and in October 1899 he gave a concert of his own works which established him as one of the most promising Norwegian musical talents. He divided the next two years between periods of study in Berlin and engagements in Bergen, where in October 1901 he conducted the first three movements of his Symphony in A minor. In the following year his health deteriorated seriously; he was forced to defer taking up a conducting appointment in Christiania and to spend the winter of 1902–3 in a sanatorium. There he tried to finish his symphony for performance in Christiania, but in order to meet the deadline he required the assistance of his friend and former teacher Iver Holter, who also conducted the first complete performance in February

1903. His health improved during 1903 and in spring 1904 he took the Handelsstandens Sangforening of Christiania on a successful tour of northern Norway; but after a concert in the autumn he collapsed and died shortly after.

In a short working life plagued by illness, Lie produced a sizable output, including a String Quartet in D minor, a violin sonata, a number of orchestral pieces, character-pieces for piano, choral pieces and some 80 songs, of which about 60 (but few of his other works) have been published. Undoubtedly his prominence in Norwegian musical life of the ambitious nationalistic period was as much an investment in his promise of future achievements as it was a reward for his actual accomplishments. Nevertheless, a number of his songs, including the famous Sne ('Snow', text by Helge Rode), choral pieces (especially those for male voices) and, among his instrumental works, the two fine Norwegian dances for violin and piano, have deservedly maintained a firm place in the repertory.

BIBLIOGRAPHY

O. M. Sandvik and G. Schjelderup: *Norges musikkhistorie* (Christiania, 1921)

J. Arup: 'Lie, Sigurd', *NBL*

N. Grinde: *Norsk musikkhistorie* (Oslo, 1971)

JOHN BERGSAGEL

Liebe [Lieben, Lieber], **Christian** (*b* Freiberg, Saxony, 5 Nov 1654; *d* Zschopau, Saxony, 3 Sept 1708). German composer, organist and schoolmaster. He received his earliest musical training at Freiberg, where Christoph Frölich was cathedral Kantor and schoolmaster; he also acquired a wide knowledge of ancient languages. In 1676 he became a theology student at the University of Leipzig. At Leipzig he was probably encouraged to compose church music by Johann Schelle, who was appointed Kantor at the Thomaskirche early in 1677. From 1679 Liebe was employed as music master in an aristocratic household at Dresden. His reputation as a keyboard player led in 1684 to his appointment as organist at Frauenstein, Erzgebirge, where he also became Rektor of the school. From 1690 until his death he was Rektor of the school at Zschopau, where in addition to his teaching duties he devoted himself to music and the musical life of the town, as composer, organist and organizer of church musical events. His sacred works were known about 1700 as far afield as Gottorf, Stettin and Strasbourg, as well as more locally at Freyburg, Grimma and Leipzig; he may have had direct connections with some of these towns. Nearly 40 sacred works survive in manuscript (in *D-Bds*, *D-Dlb* and *F-Ssp*). They comprise settings for one to six voices, sometimes with accompaniment for up to nine instruments, including rich wind scoring. Among them are a Latin mass and Gloria, a German *Magnificat* and some motets, but the majority are cantatas. The aria cantatas contain aria sections with several verses, or, in place of a straightforward sequence of arias, chorale verses and short concertato passages with or without simple concluding chorales. Krummacher (1965, pp.533ff) listed 20 chorale-based works by Liebe, with detailed information about their scoring, forms and textual sources and about the melodies used. Of the 22 compositions by Liebe at Strasbourg, 16 form a sequence from the liturgical year. According to Mattheson the funeral aria *Es ist nun aus mit meinem Leben* was still widely known and used towards the mid-18th century.

BIBLIOGRAPHY

EitnerQ; GerberL

J. Mattheson: *Grundlage einer Ehren-Pforte* (Hamburg, 1740); ed. M. Schneider (Berlin, 1910/*R*1969), 170f, suppl. p.8

C. A. Bahn: *Das Amt, Schloss und Städtgen Frauenstein* (Friedrichstadt, nr. Dresden, 1748), 109

E. F. W. Simon: *Kurze historisch-geographische Nachrichten von den vornehmsten Denkwürdigkeiten der . . . Berg-Stadt Zschopau im erzgebürgischen Kreise* (Dresden, 1821), 130

G. Erler: *Die jüngere Matrikel der Universität Leipzig, ii: 1634–1709* (Leipzig, 1909), 260

A. Schering: 'Die alte Chorbibliothek der Thomasschule zu Leipzig', *AMw*, i (1918–19), 275

——: *Musikgeschichte Leipzigs, ii: 1650–1723* (Leipzig, 1926), 332

E. Müller: *Musikgeschichte von Freiberg*, Mitteilungen des Freiberger Altertumsvereins, lxviii (Freiberg, 1939), 31ff

W. Braun: 'Die alten Musikbibliotheken der Stadt Freyburg (Unstrut)', *Mf*, xv (1962), 125, 130, 139

F. Krummacher: 'Zur Sammlung Jacobi der ehemaligen Fürstenschule Grimma', *Mf*, xvi (1963), 340, 346

——: *Die Überlieferung der Choralbearbeitungen in der frühen evangelischen Kantate* (Berlin, 1965), 292ff

H. Kümmerling: *Katalog der Sammlung Bokemeyer* (Kassel, 1970), 119

KARL-ERNST BERGUNDER

Liebermann, Rolf (*b* Zurich, 14 Sept 1910). Swiss composer and opera manager. He studied law at Zurich University and took music lessons at the José Berr Conservatory there. In 1937–8 he was private secretary and music assistant to his composition teacher, Scherchen, in Budapest and Vienna. He returned to Switzerland as a music critic, studying composition (particularly 12-note technique) further with Vogel in Ascona. Appointments followed as producer at the Schweizerische Rundspruchgesellschaft Studio in Zurich (1945–50) and as manager of the Beromünster RO until 1957. In that year he was made musical director of North German Radio, Hamburg, and two years later he became general manager of the Hamburg Staatsoper, which he made into one of the centres of modern music theatre, giving many works their world première. He occupied a similar position with the Paris Opéra from 1973 to 1980. Honours he has received include an honorary doctorate from the University of Spokane, Washington, an honorary professorship from the Hamburg Senate (1963), membership of the Berlin and Hamburg fine arts academies, and honorary membership of the Royal Society of Arts, London. As a composer he made an international reputation through his operas and, more sensationally, through the Concerto for Jazzband and Symphony Orchestra – an early attempt to bring jazz and conventional performers together – and the *Concert des échanges* for machines. Liebermann used 12-note technique in a free and individual way, with a predilection for bitonality and with tonal references. The structures are clear, and the vocal lines of the operas are eminently singable. On taking up his Hamburg appointment he withdrew almost completely from composition. He has published *Actes et entractes* (Paris, 1976).

WORKS

(selective list)

Dramatic: Das neue Land (Festspiel, A. Ehrismann), Basle, 1946; Leonore 40/45 (opera semiseria, Strobel), Basle, 1952, suite, S ad lib. orch (1952); Penelope (opera semiseria, Strobel, after Molière), Salzburg, 1954; Die Schule der Frauen (opera buffa, Strobel), as The School for Wives, Louisville, USA, 1955, orig., Salzburg, 1957; incidental music, radio scores

Vocal: Une des fins du monde (cantata, Giraudoux), Bar. orch. 1944; Chinesische Liebeslieder (Li-tai-pe, trans. Klabund), T, harp, str (1945); Musik (Baudelaire, Verlaine), speaker, orch, 1948; Chinesisches Lied (Klabund, Leeb), A, T, pf, 1949; Streitlied zwischen Leben und Tod (cantata, after R. Kothe), 4 solo vv, chorus, orch, 1950; Capriccio, S, vn, wind orch, perc, db, 1959

Orch: 5 polyphone Studien, chamber orch (1943); Furioso, 1947;

Suite über 6 schweizerische Volkslieder (1947); Sinfonie, 1949. 1949; Conc., jazz band, orch (1954); Geigy Festival Conc., Basle drum, orch (1958)

Other works: Pf Sonata, 1951; Concert des échanges, machines, perf. Lausanne, 1964

Principal publishers: Ars Viva, Universal

BIBLIOGRAPHY
H. H. Stuckenschmidt: 'Rolf Liebermann', *SMz*, xcii (1952), 137
J. Müller-Marein and H. Reinhardt, eds.: *Das musikalische Selbstporträt* (Hamburg, 1963)
H. Liepman: '195 Sekunden alle 15 Minuten 6 Monate lang', *Melos*, xxx (1963), 357
H. J. Pauli: 'Liebermanns Konzert für Maschinen', *Melos*, xxx (1963), 363
I. Scharberth and H. Paris, eds.: *Rolf Liebermann zum 60. Geburtstag* (Hamburg, 1970)
C. Riess: *Rolf Liebermann, 'Nennen Sie mich einfach Musiker'* (Hamburg, 1977)

PETER ROSS

Liebert. See LIBERT, REGINALDUS.

Liebesgeige (Ger.). VIOLA D'AMORE.

Liebes-Oboe (Ger.). OBOE D'AMORE.

Liebhold [Liebholdt] (*fl* Udestedt, nr. Weimar, early 18th century). German composer. According to Walther, writing in 1740, Liebhold was 'found a few years ago, frozen to death on the highway not far from Weimar'. This and other details of his life – such as a change of name and his refusal of the sacraments – point to a rejected composer, perhaps an organist or Kantor, who became an itinerant musician, playing the oboe, horn and violin in taverns. His cantatas and motets, which considerably enriched the repertory of village choirs, are based on a variety of miniature forms, both homophonic and polyphonic. Liebhold's predilection for writing 'utility music' for the church year, and particularly for Christmas and New Year, is shown by most of the cantatas and motets (including several cycles) so far ascribed to him, whose distribution from Königsberg (now Kaliningrad) to Brussels is proof of their popularity. Walther wrote that he sent to a friend Liebhold's cantata cycles rather than Telemann's and made a fair copy of them. According to J. N. Forkel, however, Telemann referred to 'a certain Liebhold, of no fixed abode', who 'collected musical snippets and glued them together into an unfortunate hotch-potch'. This opinion (shared by Moser) is contradicted by Liebhold's actual music, which is always technically assured, contains programmatic and symbolic details and is representative of the Thuringian choral tradition of his time.

WORKS
(cantatas for 4vv, insts, unless otherwise stated)

Auf, ihr ernstlichen Gemüter, 10 March 1735; Ist mir aller Trost entschwunden, B solo, insts: *B-Bc*
Alle, die gottselig Leben wollen; Der jüngste Tag wird bald sein Ziel erreichen; Gott hat uns selig gemacht; Ihr seid alle Gottes Kinder; Ihr Völker, bringet her dem Herrn; Mein Kind, willst du Gottes Diener sein; Mein Jesu, ist dirs denn verborgen; Mein Jesus bleibet mir ein Heil und Hülfs-Panier; Wie lieblich sind deine Wohnungen: all *D-Bds*
Ich will meinen Geist ausgiessen; Preise, Jerusalem: Mücheln
Des Menschen Sohn ist kommen, B solo, insts; Mein ganzes Wissen soll Jesus sein, B solo, insts: *D-MÜG*
In Deo ist salus et gloria mea: Gdańsk, St John's Church
22 motets a 4: Befiehl dem Herrn; Da die Zeit erfüllet war; Das ist meine Freude [2 settings]; Das ist das ewige Leben; Das Wort ward Fleisch; Der Herr wird sein Volk; Ehre sei Gott in der Höhe; Es ist keinem andern Heil; Freuet euch, ihr Gerechten; Gott, du krönest das Jahr; Gott, gib Fried; Güldner Fried uns sehr ergötzet; Habe deine Lust; Ich bin arme und elend; Ich verlasse mich auf Gott; Jauchzet ihr Himmel; Kommt herzu und lasset; Kündlich gross ist das gottselige; Lobe den Herrn, meine Seele; Uns ist ein Kind geboren [2 settings]: *USSR-KAg*, ed. in DDT, xlix–l (1915/*R*1960)

BIBLIOGRAPHY
K. Schmidt: 'Beiträge zur Kenntnis des Kantatenkomponisten Liebhold', *AMw*, iii (1921), 247
G. Schünemann: 'J. G. Walther und H. Bokemeyer', *BJb*, xxx (1933), 86–118
O. Brodde: 'Von dem thüringer Motettenmeister Liebhold', *ZMw*, vi (1934), 248
H. J. Moser: *Die evangelische Kirchenmusik in Deutschland* (Berlin, 1954)

G. KRAFT

Lieblich gedackt (Ger.). An ORGAN STOP.

Lied (Ger.: 'song'). A song in the German vernacular. I. The polyphonic lied. II. The Generalbass lied, *c*1620–*c*1750. III. Lieder, *c*1750–*c*1800. IV. The Romantic lied. V. The 20th century.

I. The polyphonic lied

1. Introduction. 2. 14th and 15th centuries. 3. 1500–*c*1630. 4. German choral song, 1630–1950.

1. INTRODUCTION. The term 'polyphonic lied' is generally used in German to describe a polyphonic composition for any combination of forces, with or without the human voice, which is either songlike in character or derives its particular identity from the technical elaboration of a pre-existing lied melody, for instance as a cantus firmus. In the terminology of musical history this wide definition in fact applies only to the heyday of the polyphonic lied in the 15th and 16th centuries. German partsongs were first written down in about 1400, and were the earliest specifically German contribution to Western polyphony. This genre reached the climax of its historical development in 1500, and for several decades thereafter it continued to compete successfully, even with the extraordinarily popular French chanson. After 1570 it fell under foreign, especially Italian, influence, and from the mid-17th century it was found concealed within other forms of vocal and vocal–instrumental chamber music, so that the term 'polyphonic lied' ceased to have a defining function. Only towards 1800 did one kind of polyphonic lied – the choral song – achieve some degree of independent significance, particularly from a musico-sociological point of view.

2. 14TH AND 15TH CENTURIES. Whoever the legendary monk (the MONK OF SALZBURG) may have been (today he is usually identified as Hermann von Salzburg), his six two-part German songs in the Mondsee-Wiener Liederhandschrift were presumably composed before 1400 and are the oldest written examples of the polyphonic lied. In both text and melody they are successors of the late MINNESANG and apparently return to the practices of polyphonic improvisation rather than following the brilliant technical achievements of the Ars Nova and the Italian trecento. In the song *Das Nachthorn* the lower part consists almost entirely of tonic and dominant, to be blown on the 'pumhart' (pommer, or lower-register shawm). The *Tagelied* is more decisively developed: its lower part is sung by the 'Wächter' (watchman), while the upper part consists of a trumpet prelude followed by a love dialogue between 'him' and 'her'.

The songs of Oswald von Wolkenstein, a knight from the Tyrol, surpass those of the monk in quantity and quality. Among his 120 or more songs (including love-songs, sacred songs and songs with biographical and political texts), are 36 in two or three parts in which the diction of the later Minnesang mingles with popular themes. The widely travelled Oswald, who was both poet and composer, was not only familiar with the original practice of two-part organum (as witness his frequent use of parallel octaves and 5ths), but also with the melodically and rhythmically varied cantilena style of the western chanson. In fact some of his polyphonic songs were originally French compositions to which he contributed only a new German text. Thus, for instance, his *Der may mit lieber zal* is Jehan Vaillant's three-part virelai *Par maintes foys*, and *Die Minne füget niemand* is the French canon *Talent mes prus*, but the canon *Gar wunniklaich* is probably an original composition. Though eclectic in some respects, the works of this 'edler und vester Ritter' ('noble and perfect knight') do not lack warmth and sentiment. His best-known song, *Wach auff, myn hort*, was sung throughout the German-speaking world until the end of the 15th century. As in some of Oswald's other works, its vocal line is set against an instrumental upper part (ex.1).

Ex.1 Oswald von Wolkenstein: *Wach auff, myn hort*

1. Wach auff, myn hort, — es leucht dort her von

o - ri - ent der liech - te tag, plick durch die

praw, ver - nim den glanz, wie gar rein plaw des

hi - mels kranz sich mengt durch graw von rech - ter

schanz. Ich fürcht ein kürz - lich ta - - gen.

While Oswald left several personally supervised copies of his works, polyphonic songs from the second half of the 15th century have survived only anonymously in civic manuscript collections. The Lochamer Liederbuch (*c*1452–60), which probably originated in Nuremberg, contains 35 monophonic, two two-part and seven three-part compositions. Of the 128 works collected in the Schedelsches Liederbuch, mostly copied out personally in the 1460s by Hartmann Schedel (a Nuremberg doctor and historian), 68 are polyphonic lieder, 18 are textless and the rest are chansons and

Latin or Italian pieces. The Glogauer Liederbuch (*c*1480) is even more varied, including 70 German songs along with 224 other compositions of every kind, though mainly of western origin. These collections demonstrate on the one hand how strongly the musical repertory of the cultured German middle classes had been penetrated by Franco-Flemish and Burgundian influence, and on the other the unmistakable identity of the specifically German song, now known as the Tenorlied. The characteristics of the Tenorlied first appear clearly in the three-part *Der wallt hat sich entlawbet* from the Lochamer Liederbuch. Its distinctive feature is that a pre-existing vocal line used as a cantus firmus (*Liedweise* or Tenor, often in the highest voice) forms the axis of the polyphonic construction. Clear musical caesurae mark the divisions between the lines of the text, and the melodic and rhythmic movement is usually well balanced, although declamation of the words is sometimes emphasized by a change from simple to compound time. Texturally these songs move between a simple three-part note-against-note or 'contrapunctus simplex' construction, and a two-part 'framework' form, with soprano and tenor contrapuntally independent and a countertenor filling in between them. In many cases the character of the Tenor and the text will have determined the choice of form; thus the elegant Easter hymn *Du Lenze gut*, to a text by Conrad von Queinfurt (*d* 1382), is notably more elaborate contrapuntally than the simple popular song *Elslein, liebstes Elslein* (both from the Glogauer Liederbuch). Unadulterated folksongs are rare in polyphonic collections, where most melodies have obviously been modified to fit polyphonic settings, or were originally composed. Although usually the cantus firmus is to be sung by a solo voice accompanied by instruments, purely instrumental performance is nevertheless a legitimate alternative. Thus the keyboard arrangements surviving in early tablatures like the Buxheimer Orgelbuch may also be included in the repertory of the polyphonic lied.

3. 1500–*c*1630. Soon after 1500 the polyphonic lied became an established genre through the printing of the first books by Erhard Oeglin (Augsburg, 1512), Peter Schoeffer (Mainz, 1513) and Arnt von Aich (Cologne, *c*1519). Although these do not give the composers' names, later editions do mention famous musicians, among them Adam von Fulda, Erasmus Lapicida, Isaac, Heinrich Finck and Hofhaimer. A new stylistic standard evolved under the influence of these masters: four-part compositions became the norm, and while in the 15th century the Tenor frequently lay in the highest sounding part it now appeared almost without exception in the highest male part (tenor), while the soprano, alto and bass were distinguished from this melodic cantus firmus by their livelier rhythms and often more disjunct, instrumental melodic lines. The so-called 'Hofweisen-tenores' (courtly tenors) in particular were set to polyphony in this style (ex.2) (*see* HOFWEISE). The lyrical texts, faintly reminiscent of the Minnesang, place them in a more sophisticated social context and their melodies, many of which were original, sometimes tend towards the formal style of the mastersingers. Hofweise settings represent the apogee of the Tenorlied and determined the style contained in the early printed editions.

The best-known example of the early German polyphonic lied, Isaac's four-part *Isbruck, ich muss dich lassen*, is actually in no way typical of this style; with its soprano cantus firmus and chordal accompani-

Ex.2 Hofhaimer: *Zvcht eer vnd lob*

ment, it tends more in the direction taken by Isaac's pupil Ludwig Senfl in his popular songs. In this versatile composer's 260 or so songs, every type of poetic verse deemed appropriate in his day for musical setting is represented – coarse ditties and delicate love-lyrics, popular dance-songs and sophisticated morals, sacred songs and political diatribes. Senfl explored and developed the stylistic potential of the Tenorlied in every conceivable way, drawing on his thorough knowledge of Netherlands polyphony. When he introduced the thematic material of the cantus firmus into all the contrapuntal parts in through-imitation ('Durchimitation') he had already reached the limits of traditional treatment of the Tenorlied, as when, in his five- and six-part compositions, he had doubled the Tenor canonically or combined two or three different Tenors to be sung simultaneously. On the whole, however, Senfl's compositions, like those of his contemporaries Thomas Stoltzer, Arnold von Bruck, Balthasar Resinarius, Sixt Dietrich and Benedictus Ducis, are firmly within the tradition of the Tenorlied.

The traditional Tenorlied style is also evident in the works of the younger composers attracted to Heidelberg around 1530 by the teacher Laurenz Lemlin – Othmayr, Jobst vom Brandt, Georg Forster and Stephan Zirler. Their assignment of texts to melodies and their cantabile accompaniment style were new, however, indicating the lied's changing social function, a change outwardly shown by the large-scale publications of lieder after 1530. In contrast to the courtly repertory of earlier publications, the collections of Hans Ott (1534 and 1544), Christian Egenolff (1535), Peter Schoeffer and Mathias Apiarius (1536), Hieronymus Formschneider (1536), Georg Forster (1539–56) and others look towards the wider circles of the musical middle class and the student world with their Gesellschaftslieder or community songs. Everything points to an attempt to satisfy the needs of communal music-making in all possible situations: varying numbers of parts (from two to eight; the general instruction for performance by any

combination of voices and instruments ('zum Singen und auf allerlei Instrumenten dienlich'); and even the fact that from 1536 all the parts of a polyphonic composition were usually supplied with words (albeit clumsily) in reprints of older Tenorlieder which originally had instrumental accompaniments. Georg Forster gave the most comprehensive survey in his five-volume collection *Ein Ausszug guter alter und neuer teutscher Liedlein*, parts of which were reprinted several times, and which contains 380 songs by at least 50 different composers. The quodlibets collected by Wolfgang Schmeltzl in 1544 should be mentioned in this context as curiosities (*see* QUODLIBET).

With Othmayr's death in 1553 the heyday of the secular Tenorlied came to an end; the compositions of Paul Kugelmann (1558), Matthaeus Le Maistre (1566), Antonio Scandello (1568, 1570 and 1575) and Caspar Glanner (1578 and 1580) were only echoes. At the same time, however, the sacred cantus firmus song had found a lasting foothold in Protestant church music, as witnessed by outstanding works such as the Wittenberg songbooks of Johann Walter (i) (1524, with an introduction by Martin Luther) and Georg Rhau (1544). Divergent stylistic trends were already apparent in these collections: on the one hand the influence of Latin florid counterpoint which led to the motivic through-imitation found in the song motet; on the other the development of simple, chordal hymn settings ('Cantionalsatz', 'Cantionalstil') with the melody in the highest part (e.g. those by Lucas Osiander, 1586). In Protestant church music the old cantus firmus principle has remained important, because, like plainchant, it is particularly well suited to preserving the sacred vocal line as an invulnerable liturgical basis. The Lutheran church was for a long time the mainstay of the sacred polyphonic lied, with important contributions by Rogier Michael, Johannes Eccard, Seth Calvisius, H. L. Hassler and Michael Praetorius, while Catholic and Calvinist composers such as Lassus, Aichinger and Mareschall used this form relatively little.

In about 1570 the secular polyphonic song received a decisive new impetus from Lassus who, although he did still occasionally set old texts to music, did so in a freer form, often like a motet or chanson and without using the old cantus firmi. While Lassus was enriching his lieder with the elaborate modes of expression of the madrigal, Jacob Regnart, in 1576 and after, very successfully sowed the seeds in Germany of the popular three-part villanella. Lassus's pupils (Ivo de Vento, Johannes Eccard and Leonhard Lechner) also sought a stylistic synthesis of madrigal, villanella and canzonetta in their lieder, as did such minor German musicians as Christian Hollander, Alexander Utendal, Jacob Meiland, H. G. Lange, Thomas Mancinus and the Fleming Lambert de Sayve. The highpoint of this later period of polyphonic lied was indisputably reached in the works of Hans Leo Hassler of Nuremberg. He studied in Italy under Andrea Gabrieli, and wrote about 60 lieder to his own texts, beginning in 1596 with *Neue teutsche Gesang nach Art der welschen Madrigalien und Canzonetten* for four to eight voices. His perfect synthesis of Italian style (e.g. that of Gastoldi's ballettos) with German lyricism influenced virtually all musicians who devoted themselves to the polyphonic lied in this period (J. C. Demantius, Melchior Franck, Valentin Haussmann, Johann Staden and Daniel Friderici).

4. GERMAN CHORAL SONG, 1630–1950. On the threshold of the high Baroque period, polyphonic lieder in canzonetta style for a few performers quickly gave place to the solo lied over a figured bass accompaniment (the so-called Generalbass lied; see §II below). Meanwhile, the first experiments with other stylistic innovations of the *seconda prattica* occurred in the more heavily scored lied derived from the madrigal. Concertante vocal parts with obbligato instruments, interludes in recitative style and instrumental ritornellos gave this polyphonic vocal chamber music an almost unlimited stylistic potential, beside which the principle of the strophic lied relying entirely on its cantabile melody hardly survived. Throughout the secular works of Schein the true polyphonic lied figured only slightly (*Venuskränzlein*, 1609), and thereafter it appeared virtually only in company with cantatas or dramatic quodlibets, as, for example, in the works of Sebastian Knüpfer, Johann Theile, W. C. Briegel and Daniel Speer, and also in J. V. Rathgeber's multi-volume *Augsburgische Tafelkonfekt* (1733–46). Almost the only exception is Heinrich Albert, whose 'Arien' (in collections published from 1638 to 1650) adhere to the strong Königsberg tradition of polyphonic lieder. Relatively untouched by current trends, however, the sacred polyphonic lied developed on the stylistic basis of simple chordal hymns in cantional style (Schein, 1627, Schütz, 1628 and later Johannes Crüger), and numerous ad hoc wedding and funeral songs were written by, for instance, Hammerschmidt, Rosenmüller and Adam Krieger. It reached its climax in the 400 or so choral compositions of Bach, received an additional impulse from C. F. Gellert's *Geistliche Oden und Lieder* set polyphonically by C. P. E. Bach, J. F. Doles and J. A. Hiller, and finally died out in about 1800 in occasional works of the simplest hack variety. More demanding forms of vocal–instrumental cantus firmus technique survived in chorale concertos and cantatas (*see* CHORALE SETTINGS) and in settings of the Passion. Towards 1800 J. A. P. Schulz made one of the first

attempts to revive the secular polyphonic song. Any hope of its sustained success, however, lay only in a new awakening of communal interest. Polyphonic songs for freemasons had already led the way, but in Austria the political situation left little scope for communal gatherings and Vienna's contribution was confined to a few unimportant four-part choruses by the Haydns. The new choral song was, however, well nurtured in Berlin by the members of C. F. Zelter's exclusive Liedertafel (1809) and in Zurich, where from 1810 H. G. Nägeli tried with his male-voice choir to improve popular musical education on a broad basis. The members of the Liedertafel were committed to artistic collaboration: Zelter himself wrote 100 choral songs, some to texts by Goethe; Nägeli, too, promoted his ideas by compiling eight collections of his own songs. Early attempts to form male-voice choirs, often with patriotic motives, were encouraged by compositions such as Weber's settings of Theodor Körner's poems. Schubert's polyphonic songs, mostly with piano accompaniments, stand apart from this line of development; they were largely written as household music for solo voices, and rank with many of his classic solo lieder in their imaginative, expressive style. Their artistic quality excels not only that of the works of his contemporaries Konradin Kreutzer, Spohr and H. A. Marschner, but even that of Mendelssohn's and Schumann's choruses. The male-voice choir movement spread fast, though no great 19th-century composer was closely connected with it; P. F. Silcher satisfied the growing demand for new repertory with his 144 successful *Volkslieder* (1826–60). In the hands of minor composers, German choral song sank into the abyss of kitsch. Brahms, however, wrote his *a cappella* choruses, mostly for mixed voices, with dedicated seriousness and discrimination, creating a synthesis of old folksong and its more studied counterpart, on occasion even relying directly on medieval sonority. Liszt, Cornelius, Bruckner and in particular Wolf and Reger, who all worked with demanding late Romantic harmonies, partially blurred the line between the true part-song and large-scale choral composition. Reger was also responsible for reviving the sacred choral song. After the great masters came a long line of worthy composers of *Volkslieder*, such as Franz, Schreck and Jenner, while Arnold Mendelssohn began the renaissance of the choral madrigal.

Although the beginning of the 20th century saw a great stimulus to the male-voice choir tradition through the publication of the *Kaiserliederbuch* in 1907, it was the youth movement, begun in 1918 and led by Fritz Jöde and Walther Hensel with their song circles (the Finkensteiner Bund and the Musikantengilde), which guided the choral song into new channels. Enthusiastic reverence for the rediscovery of old folksongs and art songs gave composers the task of forging a new type of choral song, uniting the modern tendency away from tonality with a strongly historical stylistic pattern, while respecting as far as was possible the technical limitations of amateur music. In the Protestant church a similar problem was posed by the revival of evangelical church music, especially from Luther's time. A large number of composers have made a significant contribution to 20th-century polyphonic song, both sacred and secular, including Schoenberg, Krenek, Hindemith, Pepping, J. N. David, Kurt Thomas, Distler, Günther Raphael, H. F. Micheelsen, E. L. von Knorr, Armin Knab, Hermann Grabner, Kurt Hessenberg, Hans

Lang, Günther Bialas, Helmut Bornefeld, Hermann Reutter and Cesar Bresgen. Most of them worked within the framework of a very free tonality in a strongly contrapuntal style, and often with recourse to historical forms. Because the song – and especially the polyphonic song – is essentially a traditional genre, it has been unable to lend itelf to the post-1950 musical avant garde.

II. The Generalbass lied, c1620–c1750

1. Introduction. 2. The Opitz lied (to c1660). 3. The late Baroque lied.

1. INTRODUCTION. The German Generalbass or continuo lied of the 17th and early 18th centuries is a secular, strophic song for one or occasionally more voices, with an instrumental bass accompaniment and sometimes with additional instruments playing obbligatos or ritornellos. The musical style varies from simple, syllabic, homophonic dance-songs to relatively ornate, more melismatic, contrapuntal art songs, but in all cases there is a careful synchronization of musical and poetic prosody. The genre flourished especially from the mid-1630s to the 1670s, but there are a few earlier and numerous later examples; its locale was mostly Protestant Germany. While it was an outgrowth of traditional German 16th-century songs, there were clear influences of Dutch, French and Italian songs. The lieder survive almost exclusively in prints in score or choirbook format; there are only a few manuscripts.

The history of the continuo lied is inextricably linked with the history of its poetry. Many lieder collections were compiled by poets who determined the nature of the collection and invited minor composers to write music to fit the texts. When a composer compiled the collection, the music was usually more ornate, although from 1640 to 1670 nearly all lieder conformed to established patterns of simplicity. The collections were written for the amusement of literati, students, the cultivated middle classes of such cities as Hamburg and Leipzig, and a few noblemen; German continuo lieder thus were similar to Dutch solo songs, but simpler and often cruder than the solo songs of France, Italy and Spain, which were designed exclusively for aristocratic audiences.

2. THE OPITZ LIED (TO c1660). The continuo lied before 1660 was dominated by Martin Opitz, whose *Buch von der deutschen Poeterey* (1624) established firm rules for High German poetry. Under the influence of French and Netherlands poets (e.g. Ronsard and Heinsius), Opitz preached clarity and consistency in diction, metre and rhyme, and advocated moral or pastoral subject matter.

Contrast between the older, earthy German dialect texts and the reform texts can be seen in Johann Nauwach's *Teutscher Villanellen* (1627), the first collection of German continuo lieder. It contains both the old and new kinds of verse, both set syllabically. The long, gangling, asymmetrical, falsely-rhymed, traditional verse had awkward musical rhythm which upsets both poetic and musical metre. Opitz's symmetrically structured, concise, rhyming verses, on the other hand, have music with a strong metre that does not contradict the strict, heavily accented iambs of the poetic metre. This same contrast can be seen in the only two earlier isolated continuo lieder: Schein's *Jocus nuptialis* (1622) foreshadows the Opitzian lied, while the anonymous *Ein ... Kipp [Wipp] und Münster Lied* (1623) has poetically awkward metre with Italianate music typical of songs of the decades immediately preceding Opitz.

Thomas Selle's two collections *Deliciarum juvenilium* (1634) and *Mono-phonetica* (1636), the next continuo lied publications, have little to do with the mainstream of the genre. Selle's lieder use long melismas, frequent word-painting, echoes and other expressive devices which link them more to Italian than German tradition. The absence of any reform verse denies them the historical importance achieved by the lieder included in Kaspar Kittel's *Cantade und Arien* (1638), for Kittel, despite clearcut Italianisms in the music, set exclusively Opitz's poems. He introduced Italian strophic variations ('cantade') to Germany, and here as well as in his simple homophonic strophic arias he followed Opitz's verse metre, rhyme and phraseology concisely and without contradiction.

The most important composer of the early continuo lied is Heinrich Albert, whose eight collections (1638–50) had more influence during the 1640s and 1650s than any others. The collections include solo and polyphonic lieder, sacred and secular. Only a few texts are actually by Opitz; the rest are by a group of lesser-known but in many cases more gifted poets, all of whom were indebted to Opitz's reforms. A few texts are translations from French. The solo songs are strophic and syllabic, with strict adherence to correct poetic accent and only occasional Italian expressive devices such as word-painting or echoes. Ex.3 shows how the structure of Albert's music corresponds to Opitz's text: the alexandrine line has a regular caesura after the sixth syllable which is clearly stressed in the music, and the German iambs are strictly maintained within a regular musical metre.

Ex.3 H. Albert: *Arien*, iii (1640), no. 16

Was zwingt mich auf der Welt mich al-so hin-zu-ge-ben?

During the 1640s many collections of continuo lieder were compiled and composed by different men in different places. (Kretzschmar has classified these works by locale, e.g. Hamburg, Saxony.) The most important collections, besides Albert's, are those by Andreas Hammerschmidt (*Oden*, 1642–9), and that by Johann Rist (*Des Daphnis aus Cimbrien Galathee*, 1642, 7/1677). Hammerschmidt, who is also well known for his dances, is the more interesting musically. He included polyphonic madrigals in the third volume, and the more ornate style of his strophic continuo lieder shows both his skill as a composer and his independence from Albert. Occasionally Hammerschmidt included a violin obbligato and recast a solo song polyphonically. He generally followed the reform verse, though in a few instances he purposely used *plattdeutsch* phrases. A few lieder are dance-songs incorporating the musical rhythms of the saraband or the courante. Rist, on the other hand, was primarily a poet, and his texts are set very simply by minor composers living in or near Hamburg, such as Heinrich Pape and Johann Schop (i). There is no polyphony, no ornamentation of any kind, no use of obbligato instruments; he stood completely in the shadow of Opitz and Albert. Perhaps because of the simplicity of its text and music, Rist's collection was exceptionally popular.

Other collections of the 1640s continued the new

tradition of continuo lied established by the above composers. J. E. Kindermann devoted his two-volume *Opitianischer Orpheus* (1642) exclusively to the poems of Opitz. Like Hammerschmidt he was a composer of dances and included dance-like lieder and some more ornate musical flourishes. In general, however, he followed the simple Albert–Rist pattern. There is one dialogue, which introduces an unusual recitative-like passage, and elsewhere Kindermann used some imitation between the continuo and the voice. Gabriel Voigtländer's large collection, *Allerhand Oden* (1642), also of the Albert–Rist type, contains 100 poems and 95 melodies with both old German verse and reform verse. There are other collections by Christoph Antonius, Göring and Johann Weichmann.

The influence of Albert and Opitz continued in the 1650s with collections by Grefflinger (1651), J. A. Gläser (1653), C. C. Dedekind (1657) and Rist. Rist published another collection, *Florabella* (1651, enlarged 1656) and also school plays with continuo lieder. Similar lieder appeared in other plays, ballets, pastorals and romans, most notably those by Harsdorffer with music by Johann Staden (i). The latter also published the isolated continuo lied *Poetische Vorstellung* (1658), which is rich in symbolism. Löwe and J. J. Weiland's *Tugend und Schertz Lieder* (1657) includes a strophic madrigal and use of echo, both of which demonstrate a superficial Italian influence on the basically Albert–Rist type. Georg Neumark's two lied collections (1652 and 1657) are probably the most significant of the decade. They include dialogues, dance-songs (some apparently of Polish origin) and violin obbligatos. Despite these and other interesting features the songs are still in the Albert–Rist style and do not approach Hammerschmidt's ornateness. Filador's *Die geharnischte Venus* (1660) is another large collection following Rist's models; Ex.4, *Die ernstliche Strenge*, shows how dance-songs fit a reform scheme. The typical courante rhythm in no way contradicts the poetic amphibrachic metre, with phrases and rhymes neatly coinciding.

Ex.4 Filador: from *Die geharnischte Venus* (1660), i, 6

Die ernst - li-che Stren-ge sieht end-lich ver-süs-set/Die

quee-len-de See-le wird eins - ten ge-sund.

Adam Krieger stands out as the greatest of all continuo lied composers. He himself published only one collection of *Arien* (1657), which is incomplete and survives only in a sacred contrafactum. The lieder were for one to three voices with violin obbligato and may have resembled Neumark's collections. Much more can be said about the later, posthumous collection of *Arien* (1667, enlarged 1676). The compiler, David Schirmer, was a distinguished poet who supplied Krieger with many texts. The songs, mostly solos with continuo and with ritornellos for five instruments, vary from pastoral love-songs or tragedy songs to frivolous and lascivious dance-songs and drinking-songs for the entertainment of

Krieger's student friends. The influence of Opitz and Neumark is offset by the introduction of expressive dramatic Italian vocal contours.

Perhaps the best poet of the continuo lieder was Philip von Zesen, who expanded on Opitz's verse forms with clever dexterity and whose poetry shows greater aesthetic and human insight. His principal collections span several decades, the most important being *Dichterische Jugendflammen* (1651) and *Rosen- und Lilientahl* (1670). The music is often borrowed from Dutch lieder; Zesen had close ties with the Netherlands and even wrote some Dutch verse. Since the poet is far superior to the composer, Zesen's very simple melodies and accompaniment are too easily ignored by literary historians, but they clearly were popular and are fine examples of the continuo lied. The influence of Rist is especially pronounced in the music, though Zesen's style owes little or nothing else to Rist.

3. THE LATE BAROQUE LIED. Just as the earlier continuo lied followed Opitz, so from the 1660s Caspar Ziegler's treatise *Von den Madrigalen* (1653, rev. 1685) played an ever-increasing role. Ziegler introduced and adapted into German the concepts of Italian madrigal verse; poems were no longer strophic or in the set number of lines of sonnets and other types, but could be of any length, while the lengths of individual lines had to be either the shorter type, seven or eight syllables, or the longer, eleven or twelve. From Opitz, Ziegler accepted the rules of High German spelling, accent and rhyme, the regularity of metre, and the lofty subject matter. Sebastian Knüpfer applied this theory in *Lustige Madrigalien und Canzonetten* (1663), and David Schirmer composed numerous madrigals in this fashion. Ziegler's madrigal ideas were still applied in the 18th century, most notably in the recitatives of cantata texts set by, among others, Bach.

By the 1670s there were two important new musical stimuli to the lied that changed it in a way that led to its virtual disappearance as a genre. The Italian cantata and German opera became much more popular, and when collections of German songs appeared they were full of either opera and cantata arias or imitations of such arias. No longer was the text of paramount importance, and the Albert–Rist tradition still maintained by Krieger and, to a lesser extent, even by Knüpfer gave way to an operatic style. Only Laurentius von Schnüffis's four more conservative collections (1688–95) and a few others had links with the earlier lied. After 1670 the music became more florid, more melismatic and more difficult, as can be seen, for example, in P. H. Erlebach's *Harmonische Freude musicalischer Freunde* (1697). Da capo form replaced the strophic forms and the vocal line was operatic. Similar arias were written by Jakob Kremberg in *Musikalische Gemuths-Ergötzung* (1689) alongside more traditional strophic types, and the songs in *Musicalischer Ergetzigkeit* (1684) contain echoes and other musical repetition which distort the order of the text. Such songs were in general too difficult for the amateur, who had relished the Generalbass lied before 1670, and as a result they did not have the popularity of the earlier lieder. Amateurs continued to sing the older songs, or turned to the new collections of sacred music in similar style. The professional singer concerned himself with the opera and the cantata and, though capable of singing the more complicated arias in the new collections, would probably have had little use for them.

As a result, there was a drastic decline in the number of Generalbass lied collections during the last quarter of the century. At the beginning of the 18th century sacred collections of solo songs with continuo accompaniment were popular, beginning with J. A. Freylinghausen's *Neue geistreiche Gesangbuch* (1704), but these songs belong more to the history of chorales and church music than to that of the continuo lied. A few collections of secular continuo lieder appeared sporadically. Christian Schwartz's *Musae teutonicae* (ii, 1706), for example, contains strophic folklike love-songs for tenor or bass and accompaniment. The rather mediocre poetry was set by J. A. Schope. In many cases the tunes were taken from other sources and words were fitted to them. Whereas in the mid-17th century borrowed melodies were adjusted to fit new poetry, in the first half of the 18th the new poetry was usually forced to fit the existing metre of the borrowed music, often resulting in serious conflict between the prosody of the text and the music. Albrecht Kammerer's manuscript book (1715) includes keyboard dances with added texts; the texts might be well-known folksongs or newly composed, but in any case they seem to be optional and arbitrary.

A new upsurge in the lied began in the 1730s, but at first the collections were primarily for keyboard with incidental texts. A collection of strophic dance-songs and drinking-songs by J. V. Rathgeber, *Augsburgische Tafelkonfekt* (1733–46), includes solo songs and duets as well as polyphonic quodlibets or parodies of earlier instrumental works. The work has special importance for its folk melodies, but as lieder the pieces are crudely constructed. The same borrowing occurs in J. S. Sperontes's *Singende Muse an der Pleisse* (1736–45, enlarged 1747), where the author added words to dances and marches. This very ornate printed collection was the most popular in the 18th century, and because of its longevity as household music it is an important milestone in the social history of German music. It contains about 250 songs for one voice and keyboard accompaniment. Although in later editions the accompaniment is fully written out and the text appears with the top part, in the first editions the accompaniment is still a basso continuo and the text appears only by itself, after the music, seemingly as an afterthought.

J. F. Gräfe's *Samlung* (1737–43), written in competition with Sperontes's collection, contains 144 old poems with new music by various composers (including C. P. E. Bach), all for solo voice and continuo. Telemann's collections, which seem not to have been as popular as his other works, and J. V. Görner's *Sammlung*, consisting of 70 songs mostly on texts by F. von Hagedorn, resemble the mid-17th-century lied in care of setting and in musical form. Görner's long preface, an aesthetic treatise on poetry, links the volume to the tradition of Opitz and his followers. Both represent a resurgence of the continuo lied in the 1740s which continued into the second half of the century.

III. Lieder, *c*1750–*c*1800

1. The First Berlin School. 2. The Second Berlin School. 3. Lieder in Vienna.

1. THE FIRST BERLIN SCHOOL. Berlin was a principal centre of lied composition during the second half of the 18th century. Its rise to cultural prominence began when Frederick the Great, a leading patron of the arts, ascended the Prussian throne. A significant result of his patronage was the establishment of the 'First Berlin Lied

School'. The self-appointed founder of this school of lied composition was Christian Gottfried Krause (1719–70), a lawyer in Prussia's high court. In his book *Von der musikalischen Poesie* (Berlin, 1752), he outlined his concept of a lied aesthetic, noting that the lied should be folklike (*Volkstümlich*), easily singable even by the non-professional, should express the mood and meaning of the text, and should have an accompaniment simple and independent enough for the lied to be singable without it. The resulting lieder were diatonic, harmonically and rhythmically uncomplicated and relatively short. Krause pointed to French *airs à boire* and *brunettes* as models.

In 1753, in collaboration with the Anacreontic poet Karl Wilhelm Ramler, Krause published a lied collection entitled *Oden mit Melodien*, a volume which marked the beginning of a new style of lied composition, effectively laying the groundwork for the great lieder of the 19th century. No composers were mentioned in Krause's collection, but some were later identified, including several of Berlin's leading musical figures, F. Benda, J. F. Agricola, C. H. Graun and C. P. E. Bach. In 1755 Krause published a second volume, and in 1768 collected and edited 240 lieder, publishing them in four volumes as *Lieder der Teutschen*.

Sacred lieder were also written by the composers of the First Berlin School, for example *Geistlichen Oden in Melodien gesetzt von einigen Tonkünstlern in Berlin* (1758), which contained sacred lieder by Agricola, Graun (whose *Auferstehung* is still widely sung in Germany) and Krause, all three of whom had contributed to the 1753 *Oden mit Melodien*. Another important collection of sacred lieder published in 1758 was C. P. E. Bach's *Geistlichen Oden und Lieder*, containing 54 settings of sacred poems by Christian Gellert, the Leipzig professor of literature who had been called to the Prussian court. The lied *Bitten* from this collection is one of Bach's better works in this genre, although its use of ornamentation is not specifically in the style of the First Berlin School. The independent accompaniments of some of his lieder reflect his activity as a keyboard composer and accompanist as well as indicating the decline of the Baroque continuo lied style and the near ascendancy of the keyboard-accompanied lied style. Bach's lieder range from the simple, folklike idiom of the First Berlin School to the more stylized one of operatic or keyboard music, but are nearly always lyrical. He composed lieder throughout his life, writing nearly 200; his last lied collection was published posthumously, in 1789.

The lied was further propagated during this period through the inclusion of numerous newly composed lieder in such music journals as *Der Freund* (Berlin), *Wochentlichen musikalischen Zeitvertrieb* (Leipzig) and *Musikalisches Wochenblatt* (Vienna). Lieder were published in increasing numbers during the second half of the 18th century; in the half century before Krause's 1753 *Oden mit Melodien* only 40 lied collections had been published; in the half century that followed, more than 750 collections appeared.

Three volumes of secular lieder were published in Berlin in 1756, 1759 and 1763 respectively, under the title *Berlinische Oden und Lieder*. The theorist Marpurg published and edited these, and was also a contributor. Two important features of the songs are keyboard interludes (for the most part simply descriptive keyboard pieces) and closing choruses (in the so-called

'Chorlieder'). With these volumes, Marpurg was in effect criticizing the stylistic dictates of the First Berlin School, which he considered too simple. Krause's 1768 collection *Lieder der Teutschen* had been prompted partly by a desire to counter Marpurg's critical collections.

Other significant collections of this period include the Magdeburg organist A. B. V. Herbing's *Musikalischer Versuch in Fabeln und Erzählungen des Herrn Professor Gellerts* (1759), in which fables and stories by Gellert are set in a style like the operatic scena (creating a form not unlike, and perhaps a precursor of the ballade; *see* BALLAD), and J. P. Kirnberger's set of lieder published between 1762 and 1782. His are melodically static and rhythmically monotonous in most cases; but their excellent harmonic structure marks a significant move away from the simple harmonies of the First Berlin School.

Another significant departure from the simplicity of the First Berlin School composers was made by C. G. Neefe, Beethoven's first important teacher in Bonn. Neefe began to introduce and to encourage a modification of the usual strophic form of lied composition, a principle which was to free the lied from the self-imposed restrictions of the Berlin School. Neefe's technique allowed the original setting to be altered wherever it did not fit the text of succeeding strophes, a technique which effectively deals with the awkward declamation which occasionally occurs in strophic lied style.

Some of the best examples of Neefe's 'modified-strophic' lieder can be found in his *Serenaten beim Klavier zu singen* (Leipzig, 1777). The changes are usually dictated by the text, and can appear in the melodic line, the rhythmic structure or (as often in Neefe's lieder) the accompaniment; the last technique marked an important move back to the use of accompaniments as integral parts of the lied, rather than being adjuncts, as often with the First Berlin School.

2. THE SECOND BERLIN SCHOOL. The composers of the Second Berlin Lied School, which arose around 1770, wrote lieder with more complex melodic, rhythmic and harmonic structures, more important keyboard accompaniments, and in modified strophic as well as strophic formats, even proceeding beyond modified strophic to through-composed writing (in which new musical material is composed for each succeeding strophe). The three leading figures of this Second Berlin School were J. A. P. Schulz, J. F. Reichardt and C. F. Zelter. The composers of the Second Berlin School further recognized the need for lied texts which were good poetry. Schulz in particular insisted on the avoidance of trite and tasteless texts and began to use the works of better poets, from the members of the Göttinger Hainbund, such as Bürger, Stolberg and Voss, to the literary giants of the time, including Goethe and Schiller.

Schulz stands as a transitional figure between the First and Second Schools, for although he decried the trite poetry used by the earlier composers he adhered to their principle of *Volkstümlichkeit*, writing lieder which are often more like folksongs than art songs. His three main collections are all entitled *Lieder am Volkston* (1782, 1785, 1790), a further indication of his commitment to this folklike style of lied composition; and his lieder show the development of periodic phrase structure, a prominent aspect of music of the Classical era.

An equally important member of the Second Berlin School was the Prussian Kapellmeister Reichardt, one of the most prolific composers in the history of the genre; he wrote hundreds of lieder, although the quality of his work was uneven. He gave increased importance to his accompaniments and occasionally wrote long, declamatory works with extensive middle sections. Like Schulz, Reichardt was aware of the need for better poetry, and some of his best lieder are settings of Goethe; his 1794 collection *Goethe's lyrischen Gedichten mit Musik von Reichardt* includes settings of both *Erlkönig* and *Heidenröslein*.

A third important figure of the Second Berlin School was C. F. Zelter, many of whose several hundred lieder are settings of Goethe, a close friend. Goethe preferred Zelter's settings of his poetry above those of any other composer. Zelter's best lied writing is to be found in his shorter, lyrical songs, although he wrote numerous varied strophic and through-composed lieder, as well as several extensive cantata-like works. His conviction that the accompaniment should be given more importance is shown in the title of his earliest published collection, *Lieder am Klavier zu singen*. He used many different keys, metres, harmonies and declamatory styles, but never achieved a prominent position among lied composers despite his continued, prolific and often distinguished work in the genre.

Other important composers of the Second Berlin School were the Singspiel composer Johann André, Schulz's successor in Denmark, A. K. Kunzen, Peter Grönland (who composed a striking setting of Goethe's *Heidenröslein*), the Berlin music publisher J. G. K. Spazier and the Berlin organist Friedrich Seidel.

The Swabian School, which included J. R. Zumsteeg and C. F. Schubart, was influenced by the Berlin schools, and in turn was to influence 19th-century composers. Zumsteeg's interests lay chiefly in setting rambling, multi-strophic ballades, such as those of the poet Bürger. Influenced by the 'Sturm und Drang' literary movement, he did not set them in the simple strophic form usually given them in folksong literature, but chose to set them as elaborate, complex, through-composed works more like solo cantatas than lieder. His influence on the young Schubert has often been noted, and indeed Schubert's first experiments in the lied seem to have been imitative of these Zumsteeg ballades. Schubart, on the other hand, was interested in writing lieder which sounded more like folksongs, much like his Berlin predecessor J. A. P. Schulz. A writer and a controversial political figure, Schubart expounded his *volkstümlich* lied aesthetic in his writings and composed numerous folklike lieder himself. The chief difference between Schubart's lieder and those of the First Berlin School is that his often have more independent accompaniments, a stylistic trait more closely allied with the Second Berlin School than the First.

3. LIEDER IN VIENNA. Although Vienna was one of the major centres of musical activity in Europe during this period, and the home of some of the greatest lied composers, it was not a centre of lied composition in the 18th century. If an 18th-century Viennese lied school were to be identified as such, it would include – besides of course, Gluck, Haydn and Mozart – J. A. Steffan, Karl Friberth and Leopold Hoffmann, none of whom wrote lieder of significant quality. Steffan was Vienna's *Klaviermeister* and as such wrote lieder which are orientated towards the keyboard part rather than the vocal one, with numerous embellishments, preludes, interludes

and postludes, a style which recalls that of Sperontes in Leipzig earlier in the century (see §II,3 above). The two Kapellmeisters Friberth and Hoffmann also wrote keyboard-orientated lieder like Steffan's, perhaps preferring this somewhat archaic lied style because keyboard music was then so prominent in Vienna.

Gluck's lied output was small. His work in operatic reform had a significant parallel in the lied: just as he espoused a simpler, more compact operatic form, so did many 18th-century lied composers encourage the writing of simpler, more folklike art songs. Gluck's few lieder, chiefly settings of the Klopstock odes, are lyrical and well constructed.

Haydn's work in the genre of the lied was limited to a dozen 'canzonettas' written to English texts, acquired during his two visits to London, and about 25 German lieder. His choice of texts was often from inferior literature; he once complained that German poets did not write in a musical language, that they were not particular enough in their choice of vowel sounds, and that their verses lacked uniformity of mood. He was nearly 50 when he wrote his first lieder, the 1781 collection *XII Lieder für das Clavier*, which includes an example of his humour in *Lob der Faulheit*, a satirical song in praise of laziness. Frequently performed songs from Haydn's English collections include *The Mermaid's Song*, *A Pastoral Song* ('My mother bids me bind my hair') and *The Sailor's Song*, as well as *The Spirit's Song*, which foreshadows some of the aspects of the 19th-century lied.

Like Gluck and Haydn, Mozart seems to have had only a passing interest in the lied (he wrote about 40 songs), but his great gift for lyrical expression led him to write some of the first masterpieces before Schubert. He wrote songs in French and Italian, as well as in German, and they range in style from strophic to through-composed, and from folklike to intensely dramatic. He wrote his first song with keyboard at the age of 11, a setting of Uz's *An die Freude*. In his late teens and early 20s he wrote songs in languages other than his native German, including the Italian canzonetta *Ridente la calma* and two *ariettes* in French, *Oiseaux, si tous les ans* and *Dans un bois solitaire*. In 1785, at the age of 29, he first encountered the poetry of Goethe and wrote his first German lied masterpiece, *Das Veilchen*, in which he effectively captured the subtle philosophical nuances of the text, creating a lied very much like a miniature dramatic piece. In 1787 he again turned to the lied, writing nine more songs, including his humorous setting of Weisse's *Die Alte*, a poem dealing with an older woman's criticism of youth and indicated by Mozart to be sung 'a little through the nose'; the very dramatic *Unglückliche Liebe* ('As Louise burned the letters of her unfaithful lover'), complete with fire music in the accompaniment; and his second great masterpiece, in the field of the lied, his setting of *Abendempfindung*, the text of which is involved with thoughts of death. He wrote more lieder in his last year, when he set three children's songs, full of hope and the joy of nature, and almost forming a lied trilogy. All his songs show his lyrical gift, and his lied accompaniments are subtly executed. Perhaps more important, as regards the development of the lied, was his keen sense of the word–note relationship so vital to good lied writing: he expressed the mood and meaning of the texts he set with remarkable effectiveness, and was one of the first great masters of the genre.

IV. The Romantic lied. In the 19th century the German vernacular song developed into an art form in which musical ideas suggested by words were embodied in the setting of those words for voice and piano, both to provide formal unity and to enhance details; thus in Schubert's *Gretchen am Spinnrade* (1814) the image of the spinning wheel in the title evokes the recurrent circling semiquavers of the accompaniment, while the text later suggests (by its exclamation and repetition) the cessation and resumption of the semiquaver figure at the climax of the song. The genre presupposes a renaissance of German lyric verse, the popularity of that verse with composers and public, a consensus that music can derive from words, and a plentiful supply of techniques and devices to express that interrelation.

1. Intellectual, social and musical sources. 2. Schubert. 3. Loewe and Mendelssohn. 4. Schumann and Franz. 5. Wagner, Liszt and Cornelius. 6. Brahms. 7. Wolf.

1. INTELLECTUAL, SOCIAL AND MUSICAL SOURCES. The lied thus defined essentially began with its greatest poet, Goethe. But minor poets like Hölty and Müller and even gifted amateurs like Mayrhofer had their importance. The seminal quality of the new verse was not its literary merit but its emotional tone, which blended both higher and lower lyric styles. The former expressed mid-18th-century sentiment in classical metres, in such poems as Klopstock's *Die Sommernacht* (1776). At the same time Claudius and others of peasant stock were writing simple popular lyrics like *Abendlied* in rhymed folksong couplets or quatrains. Primitive, national or traditional verse of all kinds and from all lands was a growing influence strongly fostered by Herder (*Volkslieder*, 1778–9) and a source of resurgent interest in the BALLAD. Classical and popular styles, metres and themes are found together in the verses of Hölty (*d* 1776), who wrote fluently in either style and could also combine the two, as in his Anacreontic or elegiac verses. All these styles and forms were practised by Goethe and Schiller, who both added a further dramatic dimension to lyric verse by writing songs for plays (e.g. *Faust* and *Wilhelm Tell*).

This lyric renaissance, though multi-faceted, has a discernible central theme: personal, individual feeling is poignantly confronted with and affected by powerful external forces, whether of nature, history or society. The human being and the human condition are typically conceived as isolated yet significant (as in the landscape painting of Caspar David Friedrich). The idea had Protean and far-reaching applications and implications, and it was readily adaptable to the expression of national and social aspirations as well as the traditional subjects of lyric verse, both religious and secular. It made a particular appeal to the rapidly expanding German-speaking educated classes, whose feelings it embodied, and to whom the cultural journals and almanacks of the time, where much of the new poetry was published, were specifically addressed. A middle class was well placed to appreciate not only the new personal and emotional content of this poetry but also its stylistic blend of elevated courtly style with popular lyric.

The Romantic lied directly mirrored these literary developments by combining the styles and themes of opera, cantata or oratorio with those of folk or traditional song, and reducing the result to terms of voice and keyboard. The poetry of individual feelings could thus ideally be expressed by one person who might, in theory at least, be poet, composer, singer and accompanist simultaneously. The piano (from about 1790 the titles of songbooks refer to 'Fortepiano' rather than 'Klavier') had so evolved that it could render orchestral sound-effects in addition to the homelier lilt or strumming of the fiddle or guitar. Thus string tremolandos were reproduced at the keyboard to symbolize the sights and sounds of nature, from thunder and lightning to brooks and zephyrs, symbols that could then be used as images of human feeling in the lyric mode. Recitative and arioso could be enriched by the simpler movement and structure of popular song melody and the directness of its syllabic word-setting, and these, too, could in turn be used as symbols of emotional immediacy.

Yet the new art lay dormant for some decades. The intellectual climate was unpropitious to further growth, which though fostered by the popularity of poetry was retarded by the denial of equal rights to music. Many 18th-century songs were entitled simply 'Gedichte' for voice and piano. Gluck's *Oden und Lieder beim Klavier zu singen in Musik gesetzt* exemplify his famous dictum (preface to *Alceste*, 1769) that music in mixed forms was ancillary to poetic expression. This doctrine, evidently unconducive to the development of the lied as an independent art form, was warmly espoused by the north German songwriters Reichardt, Schulz, Zelter and Zumsteeg.

They were all composers of opera or Singspiels, and imported the expressive devices of those forms into their songs. But as Gluckians they did so only sparingly and with restraint. Not surprisingly, this attitude was approved by Goethe, whose texts they often set. But he knew instinctively that a new art was about to be born, remarking in a letter to Zelter (21 December 1809) that no lyric poem was really complete until it had been set to music. 'But then something unique happens. Only then is the poetic inspiration, whether nascent or fixed, sublimated (or rather fused) into the free and beautiful element of sensory experience. Then we think and feel at the same time, and are enraptured thereby.'

The process had been anticipated by Mozart in *Das Veilchen* (Goethe) and *Abendempfindung* (anon.). Each poem anticipated aspects of Romantic individualism; each setting is musically varied yet unified, in response to the poetic mood, by use of vocal recitative and keyboard symbolism (light staccato for the tripping shepherdess, sighing 6ths for the evening winds). These and other Mozart songs were published in Vienna in 1789, and hence were readily available to Schubert, who used analogous motifs (staccato in the pastoral *Erntelied*, wind-effects in *Abendbilder* etc).

Another precursor was Beethoven, who can plausibly be claimed to have created the lied. Though his songs remain in the 18th-century tradition of self-effacing enhancement of the words, his inventive genius often restored the balance, partly by the detail of his illustrative writing (e.g. not just birdsong but nightingales, larks, doves and quails) but also by the variety and imagination of his more conceptual musical equivalents (from the welling of tears in *Trocknet nicht* to the crushing of fleas in *Aus Goethes Faust*). Each such motivic usage is integrated into a prevailing unity of musical mood, for example in the song cycle *An die ferne Geliebte*, where such purely musical elements as folksong melody, harmony, variation form, and cyclic unity are themselves used as expressive devices. A typical example of the conceptual lied-motif would be the repeated chords which for Beethoven the songwriter signify 'stars' (*Adelaide*, bar 33; *Die Ehre Gottes aus der Natur*, bar 19ff; *Abendlied unter gestirntem Himmel*, bars 10ff and 44f). This idea has a precursor in Haydn's *The Creation*, at the moment when stars were created.

In these ways Beethoven (and to some extent Haydn, as in *The Spirit Song*, a setting of English words) asserted the composer's right to independence, a right further implicit in Beethoven's familiar phrase 'durchkomponiertes Lied', that is, a continuous musical structure often superimposed on a strophic poem. In contrast, Weber favoured, both by precept (letter to F. Wieck, 1815) and by example, a consistently 18th-century attitude; form as well as declamation were to derive from the poem, and the music was to forego autonomy.

2. SCHUBERT. It was Schubert who, by fusing the verbal and musical components of the lied, first synthesized in significant quantity the new element predicted by Goethe. His essential apparatus was a mind infinitely receptive to poetry, which he must have read voraciously from early boyhood on. His 610 settings demonstrate familiarity with hundreds of textual sources, including novels and plays as well as poems, and ranging from the complete works of acknowledged literary figures to the amateur verses of himself and his friends. His passionate response to imaginative writing impelled him to bring the musical component of song to a level of expressiveness and unity never since surpassed.

It is arguable that Schubert made no innovation; even the continuous narrative unity of *Die schöne Müllerin* and *Winterreise* was already inherent in Müller's verses. All Schubert's infinite variety of styles and forms, melodic lines, modulations, and accompaniment figures are essentially the result of responsiveness to poetry. Equally notable is his evident sense of responsibility. His revisions confirm that he was actively seeking to recreate a poem, almost as a duty; he would rewrite, rethink, give up and start again, rather than fail a poem that had pleased him, and his aim was to find an apt expressive device that could also be used as a structural element. Each such device occurs, at least in embryo, in his predecessors, whether the quasi-operatic techniques and popular elements of the north German school or the inspired motivic ideas of Haydn, Mozart and Beethoven. From the former he absorbed the ideas of simplified folklike melody, interpolated recitative, a range of forms from miniature strophic or modified strophic to extended cantatas, and expressive sound-effects. Thus the 'typically Schubertian' brooks and rivers that flow so effortlessly through his piano parts took their rise in north Germany. So did the musical metaphors of human motion and gesture: walking or running rhythms; tonic or dominant inflections for question and answer; the moods of storm or calm; the major–minor contrasts for laughter and tears, sunshine and shade; the convivial or melancholy melodies moulded to the shape and stress of the verse. All these abound in Schubert's precursors, notably Zumsteeg, on whose work his own is often closely and deliberately modelled.

Schubert's debt to the musical resources of Zumsteeg's generation is so evident in his earliest surviving song, *Hagars Klage*, as to suggest a set composition exercise. The music, though manifestly immature, rises fresh from deep springs of feeling about human fate, here a mother's concern for her dying child. The composer identifies with poet, character, scene and singer and strives to concentrate lyric, dramatic and graphic ideas into an integrated whole. It was this concentration that distilled the whole essence of the Schubertian lied, but the process was a gradual one and took time to master. Long diffuse ballads or cantatas on Zumsteegian lines continued for some years, as in *Die Bürgschaft* and *Die Erwartung*. They seek with varying success to unify disparate elements such as melody, often inset for dramatic purposes to indicate a song within a song (as at 'Ich singe wie der Vogel singt' in *Der Sänger*), recitative, and interpolated descriptive or narrative music (the interludes in *Der Taucher* or *Die Bürgschaft*). It is no coincidence, however, that Schubert's earliest masterpieces are settings of shorter and more readily unifiable lyrics on his favourite theme of intense personal concern, whether of a girl for her absent lover (*Gretchen am Spinnrade*), a father for his doomed son (*Erlkönig*) or an awestruck observer for the immensities of nature (*Meeres Stille*). Each is imagined against a background of moods and scenes suitable for quasi-dramatic re-creation in sound. Further, all three poems are by Goethe, whose genius lay in making the universal singable, and these songs were selected by Schubert for earliest publication as reflecting the greatest poet and the most modern spirit of the new age.

They made an instant and intense appeal to an intellectual avant garde, the apostles of Romantic individualism. Thus 300 copies of *Erlkönig* were sold within 18 months; the correspondence of Schubert's own circle and its adherents (comprising lawyers and civil servants as well as musicians and artists) is full of excited references to new songs; the Schubertiads in his honour were staunchly supported by his numerically few but culturally influential devotees. This professional middle-class audience was the musical segment of the wider public for the poetic renaissance described earlier. The musical components of the songs corresponded to the new poetry of which they were the setting and hence the equivalent: a blend of classical and popular, dramatic and lyric, complex and simple. The music of the palace had united with the music of the people to produce the music of the drawing room. In the process the focus of artistic attention had shifted from the larger scale to the smaller, and from the plot or scene to the individual. So the musical motive power of each of these songs, and of Schubertian lied in general, comes from a dramatic source condensed into lyric terms. It is opera with orchestra reduced to voice and keyboard, with scenery and costumes thriftily expressed in sound, transported from the theatre to the home, and economically entrusted to one or two artists rather than to a company. And one stylistic source of the keyboard accompaniment effects and motifs in Schubert's songs is the piano scores of opera and oratorio (which may help to explain why Schubert's keyboard writing is sometimes held to be unpianistic). Thus the ominous figure of the night ride in *Erlkönig* recalls the dungeon scene of *Fidelio*, while the becalmed semibreves of *Meeres Stille* have their counterparts in Haydn's *Creation*. Each such sonorous image is set vibrating by verbal ideas, and the increasing range and resonance of response from these early masterpieces, through the Rückert songs of 1823 to the final year of *Winterreise* and the Heine settings, is the history of Schubert's development as a songwriter.

In addition to obvious onomatopoeic devices and other self-evident equivalences, there are hundreds of deeper, more personal and less readily explicable verbo-musical ideas, corresponding, for example, to springtime, sunlight, evening, starlight, sleep, love, grief, innocence and so on, and occurring in infinitely variable permutation. Songs in which such expressive motifs are embodied in musical permutation represent the apotheosis of Schubert's lieder, whether the linking force is rhythm (*Geheimes*), harmony (*Dass sie hier gewesen*), melody (all strophic songs), tonality (*Nacht und Träume*), variation form (*Im Frühling*), imitation (*Der Leiermann*), quasi-impressionism (*Die Stadt*), or incipient leitmotif used either for dramatic (*Der Zwerg*) or descriptive ends (the river music of *Auf der Donau* or the brook music of *Die schöne Müllerin*). The 'star' chords already noted in Beethoven, to take just one instance out of hundreds, can be observed in a wide range of illustrative or structural use, as in *Adelaide*, *Die Gestirne*, *Der Jüngling auf dem Hügel*, *Todesmusik*, *Abendstern*, *Die Sterne*, *Der liebliche Stern*, *Totengräberweise*, *Im Freien* and many other songs.

3. LOEWE AND MENDELSSOHN. By comparison with those of Schubert, the approximately 375 songs of Carl Loewe lack the dimension of musical independence. Loewe maintained the 18th-century tradition of subordination to words designedly, because he was above all a musical raconteur without the emotional range needed to match the great German lyrics (although his 30 Goethe settings include many of the better-known poems). In search of the narrative ballads that best suited him, he used no fewer than 80 different poets, including many in translation. Loewe ran little risk of allowing over-concentrated dramatic and scenic invention to impede the action, nor, conversely, was he usually content with a strophic repetition that relied overmuch on the poem to provide variety and development. In both respects he improved on his mentor Zumsteeg, and indeed even on Schubert, whose treatment of *Edward*, though much later than Loewe's op.1, is far less telling. Instead of condensed drama or formular narrative Loewe offered a storybook with pictures – expository melody with descriptive accompaniments. His harmony, though mainly monochrome, adds an occasional surprising splash of colour. The vocal line adopts the style appropriate to the reciter of the poem, ranging from monotone (as for the century-long sleep of the hero of *Harald*) to a free cantilena (in songs about singing, such as *Der Nöck*). The voice can further be put to illustrative use to suggest a harp (*Der Nöck*) or a bell (*Des Glockentürmers Töchterlein*), as well as by the skilful exploitation of other techniques and styles, including bel canto. Developed preludes and postludes are rare because the piano accompaniments tend to begin and end with the voice, as the narrative form requires. But there are often extended interludes, exploiting particularly the upper register, which are especially effective in illustrating narratives of the supernatural, such as the elves and sprites of *Die Heinzelmännchen* or *Hochzeitslied*. So broad was Loewe's command of expressive vocabulary that any song is likely to offer a thesaurus of such devices; *Die verfallene Mühle* is a typical if rarely heard example. But his practice of stringing such effects on the narrative thread of the poem was not conducive to change and development. His earliest songs include some of his best (in op.1 not

only *Edward* but *Erlkönig* bears comparison with Schubert). On the other hand, his abundant and continuous invention, and its clear relation to the texts, make Loewe an exemplary if neglected master of the lied, understandably admired by Wolf and Wagner and influential for both.

Mendelssohn is Loewe's antithesis. His approximately 90 songs include no true ballads; indeed, there is rarely any hint of drama, character or action. The music is autonomous in most, and one can readily imagine them arranged as 'Lieder ohne Worte' (which may have been the origin of that title). Although Mendelssohn was taught for many years by the doyen of the north German school, Carl Zelter, only the very earliest songs (such as *Romanze*) show any influence of opera or Singspiel, or any hint of musical subordination to the words. On the contrary, the texts seem almost to have been chosen to be dominated by the music; thus the most frequent of Mendelssohn's 30 poets was his versifying friend Klingemann, with eight settings – twice as many as Goethe. Songs and sketches alike suggest that the main aim was formal perfection, normally conceived as strophic with a varied last verse or coda. The piano offers unobtrusive accompaniment in arpeggios or four-part harmony; the tonality is diatonic with occasional altered chords, often diminished 7ths over a bass pedal. But none of these effects seems clearly related to the poems; and in general there are few overt equivalents for verbal ideas, as though the music had no deep roots in language. Yet Mendelssohn was both original and influential, especially on Brahms. His genius for expressive melody, well exemplified by *Auf Flügeln des Gesanges* (one of five Heine settings), was manifest from the first. Indeed, publication of his earliest songs in Paris in 1828 may have stimulated the development of the MÉLODIE there. His aim of formal perfection was both salutary and timely; and there are many German poems of the period for which melodic and formal beauty are in themselves close equivalents. In such settings, where the musical expression relies on vocal lilt and cadence, structural pattern and design – Lenau's *An die Entferne* or Geibel's *An den Mond* – Mendelssohn excels.

4. SCHUMANN AND FRANZ. Mendelssohn's praxis compared with Loewe's suggests that the Schubertian compound of words and music was still unstable and could readily split into its narrative and lyric components, losing some energy in the process. Schumann was well placed to reunite them. Like Mendelssohn he was a melodist; like Loewe he was literary. But he too began with the 18th-century notion that the music of a song should just express the poem, which implied not only that songwriting was an inferior art (as he believed, according to a letter of June 1839 to Hirschbach) but also that the composer had a secondary role – whereas Schumann was by temperament a dominant innovator and leader. Hence perhaps his own tentative début as a songwriter at 18. The following decade as a pianist and composer gave him the necessary foundation of independent musicianship; the emotional crisis of his betrothal to Clara Wieck heightened his receptivity to poetry. The mixture was explosive: his total of 140 songs written in the 12 months beginning February 1840 is unmatched even by Wolf or Schubert for quality and quantity of output in a single year, and it includes most of the best and best known of his nearly 260 lieder.

These recombine the two basic elements of the lied, the verbal equivalence exploited by Loewe and the musical independence stressed by Mendelssohn, thus revealing Schumann as the true heir of Schubert, with whose quasi-verbal expressive style he had always felt the deepest affinity (according to passages in the *Jugendbriefe* and *Tagebücher*) and whose immense legacy of songs was increasingly available for study throughout the 1830s. Schumann had complete command of the musical metaphor exploited by Schubert. His introduction of contrasting sections in related keys (such as the mediant minor) without genuine modulation in particular yielded new and subtle contrasts. But his personal innovation was a new independence, to the point of dominance, in the piano part. The paradigm of a Schumann song is a lyric piano piece, the melody of which is shared by a voice. As Mendelssohn played songs on the piano and called them *Lieder ohne Worte*, so Schumann sang piano pieces and turned them back into lieder. Thus the preludes and postludes to his songs tend to be self-expressive solos rather than merely illustrative as were Loewe's.

This piano style, together with Schumann's literary leanings and his personal feelings, led him to write love-songs in groups or cycles arranged by poet, often with a deliberately unified tonality. Heine (*Dichterliebe* op.48 and *Liederkreis* op.24) and Eichendorff (*Liederkreis* op.39), both master lyricists of intense and changing moods, were Schumann's favourite poets in early 1840, with 41 and 14 settings respectively. Later in the same year his songwriting became more objective, beginning with the 16 Chamisso songs, including *Frauenliebe und -leben*, lyrics that reflected his lifelong social concern.

Schumann's second songwriting phase began with the Rückert and Goethe songs of 1849. His harmonic language had become more intensely chromatic, and the consequent absence of diatonic tensions and contrasts meant that a new principle of organization was needed. In the Wielfried von der Neun songs of 1850 Schumann sought a solution through use of the short adaptable motif, already adumbrated by Schubert and Loewe, which could be changed and developed to match the changing thoughts of the verses; but his increasing illness inhibited his further development of such ideas, which later became the province of Wagner in opera and of Wolf in the lied.

With Schumann songwriting was conscious, even cerebral; he was the first theorist of the lied, which he described as the only genre in which significant progress had been made since Beethoven (*NZM*, xix, 1843, p.34f). This he attributed to the rise of a new school of lyric poets – Eichendorff and Rückert, Heine and Uhland – whose intensity of emotion and imagery had been embodied in a new musical style. As example he chose the op.1 of Robert Franz, himself a notable theorist of the lied as well as a practitioner with about 285 songs. For Franz, musical expression of poetry in the 18th-century tradition was a *sine qua non*. He was explicit, too, about his aims and methods: 'In my songs the accompaniment depicts the situation described in the text, while the melody embodies the awareness of that situation'. He claimed that in addition to all the techniques developed by previous songwriters he (and he alone) had deliberately sought to draw on the resources of Bach and Handel, the Protestant chorale, and traditional folksong; and it is true that Franz included modal as well as chromatic harmony.

His own invention, however, especially of melody, was not quite abundant enough to give his songs the musical autonomy characteristic of the best 19th-century lieder, so that his work seems old-fashioned by comparison with that of his contemporaries. As in Mendelssohn's songs, a deliberate limitation of scope resulted in the absence of dramatic or narrative songs. The piano parts are unobtrusive to a fault, and there are few independent preludes or postludes because the musical material is so economically tailored to the poem. Mendelssohnian too is Franz's extensive use of the undistinguished verses of a close friend (Osterwald, with 51 settings). There are also certain palpable defects, such as an over-reliance on the sequential treatment of melody (as in *Für Musik*) and an over-insistence on formal perfection, with sometimes contrived effects. The compensation is a Schubertian devotion to lyric verse, typified in his passionate identification with Heine (67 settings, the greatest concentration in the lied repertory). Thus in *Aus meinen grossen Schmerzen* the piano part is itself a small-scale song because the poem is about the fashioning of small songs; the illustrative arpeggios at 'klingend' are woven into the texture with unobtrusive dexterity; and the slight divergence of vocal and instrumental lines at the end makes the poetic point most tellingly. The craftsmanship is self-effacingly immaculate. Though a minor composer, Franz is a major lied writer, greatly admired by Schumann, Liszt and Wagner; his work is long overdue for reappraisal.

5. WAGNER, LISZT AND CORNELIUS. The admiration of both Liszt and Wagner is relevant because they too belong to lied history, even though their creative gestures were generally too wide and sweeping for the lyric form. Their early songs are rather inflated in style, as in Wagner's 1840 setting of Heine's *Die Grenadiere* in French. Liszt himself later acknowledged this aspect of his own early songs (letter to Josef Dessauer, *Franz Liszts Briefe*, ed. La Mara, ii, 1893, p.403), and although he stood far nearer than Wagner to the lyric mode (writing 83 songs as against Wagner's 20), he was not a native German speaker, which caused him some uncertainty of style and scansion (see the first versions of *Wanderers Nachtlied* and *Die Lorelei*). In general Liszt's songs are eclectic and experimental, and their inspiration seems to have been social or personal rather than literary, drawing on 44 poets in five languages, with texts ranging from acknowledged masterpieces to trivial salon verses. They are treated with musical unity and fidelity to the text, and they tend to be dominated by local colour or sound-effects. Thus even the late *Die drei Zigeuner* illustrates the surface rather than the substance of Lenau's poem.

Liszt was well aware of these problems, as his revisions show. His integrity as well as his development can be measured by comparing various versions of a single song, as, for example, the three settings of Goethe's *Kennst du das Land?*; his perseverance was comparable only with Schubert's and was equally motivated by genuine devotion. He may also have been fired by Schumann's songwriting, for his own 62 German settings began in 1840 (when the two met) with a Heine poem set by Schumann in that year, *Im Rhein, im schönen Strome*. Although lack of deep knowledge and response to language may leave Liszt as only a tributary to the lied, he was nevertheless a powerful influence in the mainstream, and through several channels. He was an active propagandist, both in his prose writing

(essay on Franz in *Gesammelte Schriften*, iv, 1855–9) and more generally through his piano transcriptions of lieder (Beethoven, Schubert, Schumann, Mendelssohn and Franz as well as his own songs). His keyboard techniques were a source of new effects and sonorities, and his harmonic originality was also seminal (for example, some passages in *Die Lorelei* of 1840 and *Ich möchte hingehn* of 1847 are strikingly predictive of *Tristan*). Finally, his gift for simple but refined melody, especially in his late settings of unpretentious texts, enabled Liszt to achieve unusual effects of poignancy and even irony, with altered chords and semitonal clashes (as in *Es muss ein Wunderbares sein*), which look forward to the 20th century, in particular to the songs of Richard Strauss.

Wagner's later songs, notably the five *Wesendonk-Lieder* of 1857, are also forerunners of *Tristan* (avowedly so in the third and fifth, implicitly in the rest). Despite their voice and piano scoring they were clearly conceived in broad orchestral terms rather than as re-creations of lyric poetry. In a small, intimate genre like the lied, it is often the minor master like Franz or Peter Cornelius who excels. Cornelius, too, was praised by Liszt and Wagner, and for much of his life he fell directly under their shadow, since he worked for each in turn as an amanuensis. If they were turbulent tributaries, he was a mainstream backwater, receiving multiple influences but contributing little. Yet his very receptivity, to plainsong and Baroque traditions as well as to the latest developments in harmony and declamation, gave him, like Franz, a broad-based originality. Cantus firmus (in the *Paternoster* cycle) and chorale (in the *Weihnachtslieder*) appear as unifying devices. Free tonal fluctuations are used for colour or contrast within a diatonic style or, as in the juxtaposition of E major within Db major at the word 'Jubel' in op.2 no.2, as a deliberate equivalent for a verbal image. Vocal melodies often linger on one note or move by step, as though the words were recited. Such devices and many more, including meaningful motifs, are put at the service of lyric verse.

Alone among lied composers Cornelius was his own favourite poet, with 50 settings of his approximately 100 songs. This was both strength and weakness. Its advantage was that Cornelius had a genuine if slender poetic gift, and as a composer he was well placed to know what musical equivalence was appropriate and how it could be achieved. But the essence of the lied was diluted by using his own poetry: pre-existing familiarity must inevitably lessen the impact of verse on the musical mind. Further, his lyrics themselves tended to be rather wistful and colourless, and hence not especially striking or memorable when wearing their matching music. The rather repetitive or limited emotional content, form and metre of the verses is often reflected in repeated rhythms and melodies of restricted range. Thus the well-known *Ein Ton* (op.3 no.3), in which the voice part has but a single note, in its way symbolizes not only the poem but the whole Cornelian approach to the lied. Yet this quietly inward and spiritual work in music and poetry, based on domestic scenes of worship (*Weihnachtslieder*) or betrothal (*Brautlieder*) and often grouped, like Schumann's songs, into sequences or cycles, has its own enduring value.

6. BRAHMS. In his approximately 200 songs Brahms was both more and less objective than Cornelius. He was neither poet nor connoisseur, and never set any verse of his own, but his choice of texts regularly reflects

his own inner moods and needs. Hence his comparative neglect of such major poets as Goethe (only five settings) and Mörike (three) and his devotion to such minor lyricists as Daumer (19) and Groth (11) whose specialities were erotic and nostalgic sentiment respectively. Similarly, Brahms had a predilection for anonymous texts, notably so-called folksongs, whether originally German or translated (46 solo settings, including four from the Bible). Such verses have no identifiable creative personality of their own, and are thus easily adapted for autobiographical purposes. In that sense Brahms departed radically from the 18th-century tradition of re-creating the poem, but in that sense only. In other respects he was both by temperament and by training the supreme traditionalist. He received perhaps the most thorough grounding of all great lied composers, and was a practised songwriter at an early age: *Heimkehr* (1851) and *Liebestreu* (1853) are already mature in their grasp of word–tone relations and synthesis. Apart from some essays in the extended Schubertian ballad style, the *Magelone-Lieder*, almost all Brahms's songs are carefully unified formal structures consciously elaborated from certain basic ideas by a process described by the composer in a discussion with Georg Henschel (M. Kalbeck, *Johannes Brahms*, 1904–14, ii/1, p.181ff). In his insistence on craftsmanship he reverted to the practice of Mendelssohn, whom he much admired and whose influence is apparent in even the earliest songs. He felt that a strophic poem should be set in verse-repeating forms, and in fact nearly half his own songs are strophic, most of the rest being simple ternary forms. Even Brahms's expressive devices are academic and formular. Like Franz and Cornelius, Brahms had assimilated the forms and techniques of early music, including the modality of folksong (*Sonntag*) and the four-part texture of chorale (*Ich schell mein Horn*), together with such devices as augmentation (*Mein wundes Herz*), inversion and contrary motion (*Vier ernste Gesänge*). Like Schubert, of whose songs he was editor, collector and orchestrator as well as general devotee, Brahms preferred a song texture of melody plus bass, and indeed he advocated this approach not only as a procedure but as a criterion. The essential Brahms song model is the instrumental duo, the violin or clarinet sonata, whence the typical long-breathed melodies (*Erinnerung*), some of which are embodied in the violin sonatas (for example, *Regenlied* in the finale of op.78).

Brahms's song melodies rarely have purely vocal inflections, and thus it is rare in Brahms to find a syllable prolonged or shifted in response to its poetic significance or proper scansion. Similarly, the use of harmonic or textural colouring for analogous reasons is as rare in Brahms as it is common in Schubert or Wolf. The tonal schemes are usually long-range, much as in instrumental forms. Though often complex, the piano parts are essentially integrated with or subordinate to the vocal lines, rather than being dominant or independent. They are mainly accompaniment figurations (arpeggios or broken chords) altered and disguised; textural and rhythmic variety are cultivated as deliberately yet unobtrusively in the songs as in the duo sonatas.

Against this background Brahms's expressive vocabulary tends to sound so purely musical that its quasi-verbal significance may not be readily apparent. Thus the favourite hemiolas used at cadence points had for Brahms the idea of a calming and broadening finality, as of a river reaching the sea (*Auf dem See*) or, more metaphorically, eternal love (*Von ewiger Liebe*). His other motivic elements tend to be similarly unobtrusive and predictably related to personal feeling rather than to the poem as such; thus the descending octaves that signify death in *Auf dem Kirchhof* and *Ich wandte mich* are almost incongruous in *Feldeinsamkeit*. This autobiographical element gives Brahms's lieder a special and unique development over 40 years of personal and musical experience, with heights of nostalgia and longing scaled by no other songwriter, culminating in the *Vier ernste Gesänge* of 1896.

7. WOLF. Hugo Wolf represented the opposite end of the spectrum of lied composition; hence, no doubt, his fanatical anti-Brahmsian, pro-Wagnerian, stance as a critic. His procedures in his own 300 songs were intuitive and poetry-orientated. As an originator rather than a traditionalist he had to create his own models by assimilating the wide variety of vocal and keyboard techniques and devices needed to express the deep emotive content of verse. In one sense this involved a return to the 18th-century concept of poetic dominance; like Schumann, Wolf published songbooks devoted to particular poets (Mörike, Goethe, Eichendorff) under the title 'Gedichte von . . .'. Far more vital, however, were the 19th-century metamorphoses of poetic elements into musical substance. Wolf was no theorist, but his descriptions of the word–tone relation instinctively drew on metaphors of organic unity and symbiosis: music absorbs and thrives on the essence of poetry like a child on milk, or a vampire on blood. These similes are pertinent to Wolf's own creative function. From the first he battened on poetry and language, absorbing their rhythms, overtones and cadences. In several ways his development as a songwriter is reminiscent of Schumann's career. Like Schumann, he acquired relevant linguistic disciplines through his years as a critic. By composing in all forms he gradually accumulated a personal compendium of expressive device designed to subserve compositional ends which – again like Schumann's – were essentially associated with words and ideas. The parallel is completed by Wolf's choice of texts (the early Heine and Chamisso settings strongly under the Schumann influence, later independent treatments of translations from the Spanish) and most spectacularly by Wolf's delayed and Schumannesque outburst of concentrated songwriting in 1888 – as if the word–music hybrid compensated for its slow germination and growth by a sudden and profuse flowering.

The basic Wolf song style is keyboard writing enriched by vocal and instrumental counterpoint. As with Franz, Wolf's years of training and practice in choral music yielded a four-part piano texture that could be used expressively in its own right for religious songs (*Gebet*) and also serve as background material on which to embroider expressive motifs. In the depiction of individual emotion (as distinct from the re-creation of great poetry) towards which Wolf evolved in the Spanish, Italian and Michelangelo songs, the four parts can become so independent as to suggest string quartet writing (*Wohl kenn ich Euren Stand*). Such linear thinking also yields a variety of counterpoints for expressive purposes, like the duet between voice and piano in *Lied eines Verliebten*, or within the piano part itself in the postlude to *Fühlt meine Seele* (the latter a frequent image in the love-songs generally). Wolf's keyboard style is related to that of the contemporary piano reductions of Wagner operas by Klindworth and others, including such masters of expressive techniques as Liszt and Rubinstein. His own pianistic prowess disposed him to add bravura illustrative interludes (*Die Geister am Mummelsee*) like those found in Loewe, and to write songs the piano parts of which are in effect independent solos, as so often in Schumann. To this basic concept Wolf often added a voice part that was not only itself independent, as in Brahms, but was also moulded to the words in their every inflection, whether of sound or sense; *Auf dem grünen Balkon* is an example. This characteristic fluidity of melodic line is wholly Wolfian, differing from its Wagnerian equivalent as poetry recitation differs from stage declamation. Thus, the sustained notes Wagner gave Isolde in *Tristan* (Act 1 scene iii) express the feeling of the character, while the same effect in Wolf's *Die ihr schwebet* expresses the beauty of the individual word 'geflügelt'. The same distinction applies to Wolf's use of the extended harmonic language of Wagner and Liszt: for Wolf harmonic complexity expressed the symbolic connotations of poetry. Wolf regarded the development of his own detailed motivic language as his most significant contribution; it is a language that varies, in ways too detailed to summarize, from the illustration of a single word (such as 'traurig', in *Alles endet*, with a deliberately altered minor chord) to the development and contrast of motifs throughout a whole song (*Auf einer Wanderung*). It includes local colour effects, instrumental imitations and a Debussian sensitivity to the placing and spacing of chords and tones. It offers musical equivalents not only for the subject matter of poetry but also for its technical devices such as dialogue and irony. All this is further enhanced by the extremes of his emotional range – hilarity and desperation, comedy and tragedy. Finally he added a new dramatic dimension within the lyric frame, for his songs encompass dance and incidental music as well as lighting, costume and scenery. The Wolfian lied thus continued the Schubertian tradition, culminating in a complete theatre of the mind, a *Gesamtkunstwerk* for voice and piano.

Wolf's creative maturity was perhaps too brief to permit radical change or development; the four-part textures of the Italian songs, for example, are already outlined in the Mörike volume. But there is a discernible trend: the dramatic or theatrical element became more rarefied, more generalized. The Spanish songs, and more particularly the Italian, are a musical *comédie humaine*. Social life is conceived as a stage, with ordinary men and women the players. In this respect the Romantic lied ended as it had begun, with individual concern set against a broader social background as its principal theme. But the element of conflict had evaporated. Neither nature nor society was conceived as puzzling or hostile in the Wolfian lied. Rather, in the poems Wolf chose, the human heart and mind increasingly engender their own delight and despair, without reference to an external cause. Increasingly, too, Wolf turned to translations for his texts, and not to original German verse (as Brahms had similarly had recourse to the Bible in German translation). The end of the century seems to signal an end of the German poetic renaissance, and hence a decline in the power of the lied.

The same may apply to audiences. The Schubert song had become accredited and established; Schumann and his successors, especially Brahms, had come to command a wide public for their songs. But Wolf was offering a new genre. Just as Schubert had reduced

Mozart and Beethoven operas and Haydn oratorios to the miniature domestic frame, so Wolf adopted Wagner. That allegiance and that idiom imposed difficulties of appreciation, further restricting the appeal of an art already limited to the poetry lovers among music lovers. So Wolf's work took longer to gain ground and find adherents. As before, dissemination of the new art was through friends and admirers and their immediate circle. The Wolf Society in Vienna corresponded to the Schubertiads of 70 years earlier, but with fewer active members (a relation that persists in posterity). It is as if the springs that had powered the early years of the lied had, for whatever reason, relaxed. An art of strong direct expressiveness culminated in an art of refinement, nuance, subtlety, and perfection within limitations.

The high road had narrowed and arguably reached an impasse. So had some earlier byways, such as accompanied recitation, despite one example from Schubert (*Abschied von der Erde*), three from Schumann (e.g. *Die Flüchtlinge*) and six from Liszt (e.g. *Lenore*). A much more rewarding development was the addition of vocal lines, as in the duets and partsongs with or without accompaniment written by all the major masters of the lied, and still, despite neglect, an essential aspect of their art. But most significant of all was the addition of extra instruments. Schubert had used instrumental obbligato for quasi-verbal effect (e.g. the pastoral sound of the clarinet in *Der Hirt auf dem Felsen*). Schumann orchestrated his song *Tragödie*, presumably in order to enhance its dramatic content. Liszt's song orchestrations and Wagner's *Wesendonk-Lieder* pointed clearly along that road; so, less demonstratively, did Brahms's songs with viola obbligato, op.94. A crucial stage was reached with Wolf's 20 orchestral versions, including one (*Der Feuerreiter*) for chorus instead of solo. But these new departures meant a farewell to the lied as here considered, namely as a musical expression of the poetry of individual or social concern within the framework of domestic music-making. At the same time, poetry and its musical setting were losing their power to unify and stimulate any special segment of European society, German or other. The hegemony of the lied was in decline.

V. The 20th century. The lied was essentially a 19th-century genre, and its history in the 20th century is that of a brief and rapid continued development followed by a sudden decline. Schoenberg and Strauss, to take two representative composers, both wrote many lieder before 1918 and few thereafter: Schoenberg's opp.1–22 (1897–1916) include 45 lieder, his subsequent works only three. The reasons for this falling of interest have certainly as much to do with public tastes and requirements as with compositional techniques and aesthetics. Hindemith, the 20th-century composer of practical music *par excellence*, recognized that there was little call for lieder from the amateurs of his time. In general, the lied after World War I has been the province of specialist composers (Kilpinen, Schoeck, Reutter), or else it has been cultivated to meet commissions from those few lieder artists interested in the 20th-century repertory (notably Fischer-Dieskau in the 1960s and 1970s).

1. 1900–1918. 2. After 1918.

1. 1900–1918. Before World War I the genre was flourishing, even if many lied composers were in thrall to the examples of Brahms and Wolf. Reger was proving

himself the heir of Brahms, though he was not a naturally lyrical musician and his lieder suffer more than his instrumental works from clogged counterpoint and a resurrection of Baroque devices and attitudes. Strauss, on the other hand, was cultivating a dramatic, declamatory style, with a free use of melisma and opulent accompaniments; his allegiances were to Wolf, Wagner and Liszt. The possibility of a novel departure in the lied was offered by the new symbolist poetry, concentrating on the significant moment rather than on narrative, and in particular by the work of Richard Dehmel. Dehmel's poems were set by Reger and Strauss around the turn of the century, and also by Schoenberg (in opp.2, 3 and 6, 1899–1905), who remarked in a letter to the poet that his verses had helped him 'to find a new tone in the lyrical mood'. This 'new tone' involved a floating harmonic stasis and an exquisiteness of texture, a sumptuous clarity illuminating the instant, and it contrasts with that of the rhetorical monologue lieder which were Strauss's great strength and which were being composed by Schoenberg at the same time. It is to be found most clearly and purely in the Dehmel settings of Schoenberg and his pupil Webern (*Fünf Dehmel Lieder*, 1906–8).

If a modern poet was thus encouraging composers to press forward the expressive possibilities of the lied, another contemporary, Mahler, had already found his stimulus in the quasi-folk poetry of *Des Knaben Wunderhorn*. In fact, the *Lieder eines fahrenden Gesellen* (1883–5), to his own words, had displayed his mature lied style before he had composed his first settings from that collection, but it was there that he found the qualities – observation of nature, religious feeling and a Romantic sense of apartness, all expressed without selfconsciousness – which most appealed to him as a song composer in the 1890s. Where others found new subject matter for the lied in symbolist verse, Mahler took up the old Romantic themes, but presented them with a new nakedness of expression. The set of *Lieder aus 'Des Knaben Wunderhorn'* was conceived with orchestral accompaniment, as were the later settings of Rückert (the cycle *Kindertotenlieder* and five other songs, 1901–4) and Hans Bethge's Chinese translations (the symphony–song cycle *Das Lied von der Erde*, 1907–9), for only with a full and sensitively used instrumental ensemble could Mahler bring to his texts the weight, exactitude and complexity of response that made possible the extremely subjective character of his lieder. With Mahler the lied was taken from the drawing room or recital platform to the concert hall: it was no longer a polite genre.

Mahler's favouring of the orchestra, as well as his choice of texts from *Des Knaben Wunderhorn* and *Die chinesische Flöte*, was not without effect on his contemporaries. Strauss was least influenced, for he had established both his song style and his orchestral brilliance before 1890; his lieder, even – or perhaps especially – those with orchestra, remained more comfortable, smoother and richer than those of Mahler. Schoenberg, however, produced a quite Mahlerian work in his *Sechs Orchesterlieder* op.8 (1904), two of which are to Wunderhorn poems, and he developed the Mahlerian orchestra of varied chamber ensembles to a culmination in the *Vier Lieder* op.22 (1913–16). (His other set of orchestral songs, the *Gurrelieder*, 1901–11, is almost an oratorio.) The influence of Mahler is also present in the lieder of Zemlinsky and of Schoenberg's two principal

pupils, particularly in Berg's *Sieben frühe Lieder* (1905–8, orchestrated 1928) and Webern's *Vier Lieder* op.13 for voice and small orchestra (1914–18), which include two settings from *Die chinesische Flöte*. Webern, however, distilled Mahler's style to produce the fine lyricism and urgency that characterize many of his lieder from after World War I as well.

Alongside the influence of Mahler on the Second Viennese School must be placed their continuing interest in new poetry. For Schoenberg and Webern, Dehmel was succeeded by Stefan George, whose still more rarefied images brought atonality to birth in Schoenberg's cycle *Das Buch der hängenden Gärten* op.15 (1908–9) and Webern's opp.3–4 (1907–9), both for voice and piano. Rilke, Altenberg, Mombert, Trakl and Kraus were all set by Schoenberg, Berg and Webern during the next decade, the intense, visionary and often brief poems fitting well with the qualities of early atonal music, delicate, erratic and adrift.

Strauss has already been mentioned as relatively unaffected by the means and matter introduced by contemporary poets and composers. He was not alone. Metner wrote lieder in a somewhat Brahmsian manner, and Wolf had a direct follower two decades after his death in Joseph Marx, who even set those poems from Heyse's *Italienisches Liederbuch* which his model had omitted. Pfitzner, with his conscientious respect for Schumann, Eichendorff and the spirit of German high Romanticism in general, went on composing lieder essentially in the old mould throughout the first four decades of the century, contributing some fine examples to close a rich tradition.

2. AFTER 1918. It was perhaps no accident that the lied tradition as Pfitzner might have seen it was also perpetuated after 1918 by two composers from outside the Austro-German territories, the Swiss Othmar Schoeck and the Finn Yrjö Kilpinen; for they were able on occasion, despite their ties with the tradition (Schoeck was a pupil of Reger), to produce something new and distinctive in conventional modes. Their works contrast markedly with the lieder of composers who, in the 1920s, attempted to recapture the 19th-century manner from the perspective of later experiences. Krenek, for example, made such a deliberate effort in his Schubertian *Reisebuch aus den österreichischen Alpen* op.62 (1929), and the cycle has a feeling of irony, of stylistic displacement, which is quite lacking from the lieder of Pfitzner or Schoeck. In general, however, the neo-classical movement had little effect on the lied: most composers associated with it were looking to periods well before the early Romantic. Hindemith's *Das Marienleben* op.27 (1922–3, controversially revised in 1936–48) is a rare instance of an important song cycle composed on neo-Baroque lines.

Nor did Schoenberg and Berg pay much attention to the lied after World War I. For Schoenberg words had given a framework in the atonal period of opp.15 and 22; the development of 12-note serialism provided once more the means for elaborating independent musical structures, and it was not until 1933 that he returned, for the last time, to song composition with the Three Songs op.48. Berg, who had been a compulsive writer of lieder in his youth, produced only one song in his last 20 years. Webern, however, cultivated the lied almost to the exclusion of other genres between 1914 and 1925. Most of his works of this period are accompanied by a small group of instruments, enhancing his nervously mobile and intensely lyrical responses to the texts. The influence of *Pierrot lunaire* in this (though it is noteworthy that Webern's Two Songs op.8 for voice and eight instruments antedate Schoenberg's work) is particularly clear in the Six Songs op.14 (1917–21), setting Trakl poems for voice, two clarinets and two strings. Hindemith also drew something from *Pierrot* in his Trakl cycle, *Die junge Magd* op.23 no.2 (1922) for contralto, flute, clarinet and string quartet.

Pierrot lunaire itself has not been considered here, since its use of Sprechgesang perhaps disqualifies it from classification as a cycle of lieder; though it could be regarded as the tradition's culmination, remaining unique despite imitation, exacerbating the expressive possibilities of both voice and accompaniment. One source of the work, the cabaret song (a genre to which Schoenberg had contributed in 1901), was developed in a quite different direction by the composers associated with Brecht: Weill, Eisler and Dessau. Their lieder, often using popular dance rhythms, tinges of jazz and a dance-band instrumentation, were explicitly designed to appeal widely and to encourage activism in the socialist cause. Eisler, a Schoenberg pupil, was the greatest exponent of this style, and notable examples of his work include the *Solidaritätslied* op.27 (1930) and the *Einheitsfrontlied* (1934), both to Brecht texts. The genre originated in the 'Songspiel' version of the Brecht–Weill *Mahagonny* (1927) and persisted after World War II as an important part of musical life in the German Democratic Republic.

In the 1930s, therefore, one might distinguish three categories of lied composition: the mass-directed political style; the direct continuation of the 19th-century tradition by Pfitzner and others, and also by new composers such as Hermann Reutter; and the beginning of an exploration of lyricism on 12-note serial lines. Webern, like Schoenberg and Berg, had turned away from the lied on mastering the new technique, but he returned to it for two final sets with piano accompaniment, opp.23 and 25 (1934–5). During the next 20 years some of the finest serial lieder were composed by musicians from outside Austria and Germany: Martin in his *Drei Monologe aus 'Jedermann'* for baritone and piano or orchestra (1943), Babbitt in his Stramm setting *Du* for soprano and piano (1951) and Dallapiccola in his *Goethe-Lieder* for female voice and three clarinets (1953). These last two works are among the few significant additions to the repertory since World War II. Most German-speaking composers born after 1920 have given little attention to the lied; even Henze, with the abundant lyrical gift displayed in his operas and cantatas, has contributed only the *Fünf neapolitanische Lieder* for voice and chamber orchestra (1956) and a few numbers in *Voices* for two soloists and small orchestra (1973) which might be counted as lieder. Other composers have written lieder for particular singers, notably Aribert Reimann for Fischer-Dieskau. But the tradition of the lied as an intimate, personal, confessional mode of expression appears to have been lost: Strauss's *Vier letzte Lieder* (1948) may well be said to bear their epithet for the genre.

BIBLIOGRAPHY
POLYPHONIC LIED
W. Gurlitt: 'Burgundische Chanson und deutsche Liedkunst des 15. Jahrhunderts', *Kongressbericht: Basel 1924*, 153
L. Nowak: 'Das deutsche Gesellschaftslied in Österreich von 1480–1550', *SMw*, xvii (1930), 21–52

O. A. Baumann: *Das deutsche Lied und seine Bearbeitungen in den frühen Orgeltabulaturen* (Kassel, 1934)
H. Osthoff: *Die Niederländer und das deutsche Lied (1400–1640)* (Berlin, 1938/*R*1967)
G. Reese: *Music in the Middle Ages* (New York, 1940), 376ff
H. Rosenberg: 'Frottola und deutsches Lied um 1500', *AcM*, xviii (1946), 30–78
K. Gudewill: 'Zur Frage der Formstrukturen deutscher Liedtenores', *Mf*, i (1948), 112
K. Gudewill, F. Noack, H. Osthoff: 'Chorkomposition', *MGG*
G. Reese: *Music in the Renaissance* (New York, 1954, rev. 2/1959), 632ff, 676ff, 705ff
K. Gudewill: 'Beziehungen zwischen Modus und Melodiebildung in deutschen Liedtenores', *AMw*, xv (1958), 60
C. Petzsch: ' "Hofweisen": ein Beitrag zur Geschichte des deutschen Liederjahrhunderts', *Deutsche Vierteljahresschrift für Literaturwissenschaft und Geistesgeschichte*, xxxiii (1959), 414–45
W. Salmen: 'European Song (1300–1530)', *NOHM*, iii (1960), 349–80
H. Besseler: 'Renaissance-Elemente im deutschen Lied 1450–1500', *SM*, xi (1969), 63
H.-J. Feurich: *Die deutschen weltlichen Lieder der Glogauer Handschrift (ca. 1470)* (Wiesbaden, 1970)
R. Caspari: *Liedtradition im Stilwandel um 1600* (Munich, 1971)
W. Wiora: *Das deutsche Lied: zur Geschichte und Ästhetik einer musikalischen Gattung* (Wolfenbüttel and Zurich, 1971)
N. Böker-Heil: *Das Tenorlied*, CaM, ix (1979)

GENERALBASS LIED c1620–c1750
C. F. Becker: *Die Hausmusik in Deutschland in dem 16., 17. und 18. Jahrhunderte* (Leipzig, 1840)
K. Goedeke: *Grundrisz zur Geschichte der deutschen Dichtung*, iii (Hanover, 1859, 2/1887)
W. Niessen: 'Das Liederbuch des Leipziger Studenten Clodius von Jahre 1669', *VMw*, vii (1891), 579
J. Boltz: 'Das Liederbuch der Prinzessin Luise Charlotte von Brandenburg', *Zeitschrift für deutsche Philologie*, xxv (1892), 32
P. Spitta: 'Die Anfänge madrigalischer Dichtung in Deutschland', *Musikgeschichtliche Aufsätze* (Berlin, 1894)
K. Vossler: *Das deutsche Madrigal* (Weimar, 1898/*R*1972)
M. Friedlaender: *Das deutsche Lied im 18. Jahrhundert* (Stuttgart, 1902/*R*1962)
M. Breslauer: *Das deutsche Lied* (Berlin, 1908/*R*1966)
H. Kretzschmar: *Geschichte des neuen deutschen Liedes* (Leipzig, 1911/*R*1966)
A. Einstein: 'Ein unbekannter Druck aus der Frühzeit der deutschen Monodie', *SIMG*, xiii (1911–12), 286
G. Müller: *Geschichte des deutschen Liedes* (Munich, 1925, 2/1959)
W. Vetter: *Das frühdeutsche Lied* (Münster, 1928)
H. Abert: 'Entstehung und Wurzeln des begleiteten deutschen Sololieds', *Gesammelte Schriften und Vorträge* (Halle, 1929/*R*1968)
H. J. Moser: *Corydon* (Brunswick, 1933/*R*1966)
E.-F. Callenberg: *Das obersächsische Barocklied* (Freiburg, 1952)
H. C. Worbs: 'Die Schichtung des deutschen Liedgutes in der zweiten Hälfte des 17. Jahrhunderts', *AMw*, xvii (1960), 61
R. T. Hinton: *Poetry and Song in the German Baroque* (Oxford, 1963)
J. H. Baron: *Foreign Influences on the German Secular Solo Continuo Lied of the Mid-seventeenth Century* (diss., Brandeis U., 1967)

c1750–c1800
A. Reissmann: *Das deutsche Lied in seiner historischen Entwicklung* (Kassel, 1861)
E. Lindner: *Geschichte des deutschen Liedes im 18. Jahrhundert* (Leipzig, 1871)
M. Blumner: *Geschichte der Singakademie zu Berlin* (Berlin, 1891)
M. Friedlaender: *Das deutsche Lied im 18. Jahrhundert* (Stuttgart, 1902/*R*1962)
W. von Jolizza: *Das Lied und seine Geschichte* (Vienna, 1910)
H. Kretzschmar: *Geschichte des neuen deutschen Liedes* (Leipzig, 1911/*R*1966)
I. Pollak-Schlaffenberg: 'Die Wiener Liedmusik von 1778 bis 1789', *SMw*, v (1918), 97–151
E. Alberti-Radanowicz: 'Das Wiener Lied: 1789–1815', *SMw*, x (1923), 37–78
G. Müller: *Geschichte des deutschen Liedes* (Munich, 1925, 2/1959)
O. Bie: *Das deutsche Lied* (Berlin, 1926)
E. Bücken: *Das deutsche Lied* (Hamburg, 1939)
F. Blume: *Goethe und die Musik* (Kassel, 1948)
H. J. Moser: *Das deutsche Sololied und die Ballad*, Mw, xiv (1957)
A. Sydow: *Das Lied* (Göttingen, 1962)
H. Schwab: *Sangbarkeit, Popularität und Kunstlied: Studien zu Lied und Liedästhetik der mittleren Goethezeit* (Regensburg, 1965)
R. Barr: *C. F. Zelter: a Study of the Lied in Berlin during the Late 18th and Early 19th Centuries* (diss., U. of Wisconsin, 1968)
W. Wiora: *Das deutsche Lied: zur Geschichte und Ästhetik einer musikalischen Gattung* (Wolfenbüttel and Zurich, 1971)

FROM 1800

E. Schure: *Geschichte des deutschen Liedes* (Berlin, 1870)

A. Reissmann: *Geschichte des deutschen Liedes* (Kassel, 1874)

W. K. von Jolizza: *Das Lied und seine Geschichte* (Vienna, 1910)

H. Kretzschmar: 'Das deutsche Lied seit Robert Schumann', *Gesammelte Aufsätze über Musik und anderes*, i (Leipzig, 1910)

——: *Geschichte des neuen deutschen Liedes* (Leipzig, 1911/R1966)

O. von Hazay: *Entwicklung und Poesie des Gesanges* (Leipzig, 1911–15)

G. Müller: *Geschichte des deutschen Liedes vom Zeitalter des Barock bis zur Gegenwart* (Munich, 1925)

O. Bie: *Das deutsche Lied* (Berlin, 1926)

F. E. Pamer: 'Deutsches Lied im 19. Jahrhundert', *Handbuch der Musikgeschichte*, ed. G. Adler (Berlin, rev. 2/1930/R1961)

H. J. Moser: *Das deutsche Lied seit Mozart* (Zurich, 1937/R1966)

E. Bücken: *Das deutsche Lied* (Hamburg, 1939)

M. Castelnuovo-Tedesco: 'Music and Poetry: Problems of a Songwriter', *MQ*, xxx (1944), 102

G. Baum: 'Wort und Ton im Romantischen Kunstlied', *Das Musikleben*, iii (1950), 136

J. Müller-Blattau: *Das Verhältnis von Wort und Ton in der Geschichte der Musik* (Stuttgart, 1952)

J. H. Hall: *The Art Song* (Norman, Oklahoma, 1953)

M. Beaufils: *Le Lied romantique allemand* (Paris, 1956)

H. J. Moser: *Das deutsche Sololied und die Ballade*, Mw, xiv (1957)

K. Gudewill: 'Lied', §A, *MGG*

P. Radcliffe: 'Germany and Austria', *A History of Song*, ed. D. Stevens (London, 1960 /R1971)

M. Bortolotto: *Introduzione al Lied romantico* (Milan, 1962)

H. W. Schwab: *Sangbarkeit Popularität und Kunstlied: Studien zu Lied und Liedästhetik der Mittleren Goethezeit 1770–1814* (Regensburg, 1965)

F. A. Stein: *Verzeichnis deutscher Lieder seit Haydn* (Berne and Munich, 1967)

D. Ivey: *Song: Anatomy, Imagery and Styles* (New York, 1970)

H. J. Moser: 'Lied', *LaMusicaE*

J. M. Stein: *Poem and Music in the German Lied from Gluck to Hugo Wolf* (Harvard, 1971)

W. Wiora: *Das deutsche Lied: zur Geschichte und Ästhetik einer musikalischen Gattung* (Wolfenbüttel and Zurich, 1971)

E. F. Kravitt: 'Tempo as an Expressive Element in the Late Romantic Lied', *MQ*, lix (1973), 497

W. Oelmann: *Reclams Liedführer* (Stuttgart, 1973)

E. F. Kravitt: 'The Orchestral *Lied*: an Inquiry into its Style and Unexpected Flowering around 1900', *MR*, xxxvii (1976), 209

NORBERT BÖKER-HEIL (I), JOHN H. BARON (II), RAYMOND A. BARR (III), ERIC SAMS (IV), PAUL GRIFFITHS (V)

Liederbuch (Ger.: 'songbook'). A term applied to certain 15th- and 16th-century German collections of polyphonic songs or short lyric poems that were usually sung. F. W. Arnold was perhaps the first to use it in an article, 'Das Locheimer Liederbuch nebst der Ars organisandi von Conrad Paumann' (*Jahrbücher für musikalische Wissenschaft*, ii, 1867, pp.1–234), although the term 'Liederhandschrift' was more common, particularly when referring to the sources of Minnesang. It is not at all clear, however, the extent to which the term 'Liederbuch' was used during or before the 19th century. It does not appear in the MSS of those collections most commonly associated with it such as the Lochamer Liederbuch and the Glogauer Liederbuch; moreover, 15th- and 16th-century MSS and publications frequently use in their titles 'Lied', 'Liedlein', 'Gesänge', 'geistliche Gesänge', etc, but not 'Liederbuch'.

The term is also applied to collections of poetry that could be sung or were likely to have been sung (e.g. Das Liederbuch des Jakob Kebitz) or collections that contained some poetry with music and some without (e.g. Das Liederbuch des Hartman Schedel).

'Liederbuch' as used today refers to those MSS of polyphonic music found in partbooks, of which the earliest is thought to be the Glogauer Liederbuch. Not all the pieces found in these 'songbooks' are to be sung;

many are obviously intended for instruments or for a combination of voices and instruments.

BIBLIOGRAPHY

RiemannL 12

H. Rupprich: *Die deutsche Literatur vom späten Mittelalter bis zum Barock*, Geschichte der deutschen Literatur, iv/1 (Munich, 1970), 193ff [contains list of MSS now known by term 'Liederbuch']

See also SOURCES, MS, §IX.

WESLEY K. MORGAN

Liederkreis [Liederkranz, Liederzyklus] (Ger.: 'song circle'). (1) A term used to mean a circle (or cycle) of songs, for example Schumann's *Liederkreis* op.24. (*See* SONG CYCLE.)

(2) A circle or club of people dedicated to the cultivation of popular song. Examples are the 'Mittwochskränzchen' ('Cour d'amour') that met during the early 1800s in Goethe's Weimar home, the Stägemann circle in Berlin, 1815–18, that included the young poet Wilhelm Müller, the Dresden Liederkreis ('Dichtertee'), c1804–24, in which Weber met the poet Kind, and the 'Schubertianer' or friends of Schubert in Vienna, who held regular meetings during the 1820s. Liederkreis activities were varied, recreational as well as creative. They included singing simple group songs, playing charades and other games with songs, and listening to song performances staged with costumes, 'attitudes' or elaborate 'living pictures'. To supply the demand parody texts were often set to song melodies from, for example, *Das Mildheimische Liederbuch* (ed. R. Z. Becker, 1799, 4/1810); either the melodies were rearranged or the verse newly set. Collections that reflected the work of a Liederkreis were titled accordingly, like J. H. C. Bornhardt's *Liederkranz für Freunde des leichten Gesanges* (Hamburg, c1810) and similar publications by F. Methfessel, A. E. F. Langbein and G. Weber, or collections of texts and parodies by F. A. Tiedge, *Das Echo oder Alexis und Ida: ein Zyklus von Liedern* (Halle, 1812) or F. W. Gubitz, *Abends-Atemzüge: ein Liederkreis* (Berlin, c1815, 2/1859).

LUISE EITEL PEAKE

Liederspiel (Ger.: 'song-play'). A kind of dramatic entertainment developed in Germany in the early 19th century in which songs are introduced into a play. It differs from the older Singspiel principally in its inclusion of songs that as lyric poems already enjoyed some currency; the melodies (normally with simple instrumentation) were new, though some of the songs from such works later came to be regarded as folksongs. Ensembles and choruses were not at first admitted, and the music had an almost entirely lyrical rather than a dramatic character. Despite statements to the contrary, the Liederspiel differs generically from the French vaudeville and the British ballad opera, in both of which the melodies were normally familiar airs specially provided with new words, whereas normally in the Liederspiel the words were pre-existing and the melodies new.

The first Liederspiel was *Lieb und Treue*, by J. F. Reichardt, staged at the Berlin Royal Opera House on 31 March 1800 with text by the composer, using poems by Goethe, Herder and Salis, as well as folksongs. The somewhat enlarged second edition of the libretto (Berlin, 1800) contains 12 songs, including the Swiss folksong 'Wenn ich ein Vöglein wär', Goethe's 'Heidenröslein' and three other poems, and two each by Herder and Salis. An afterword by the author mentions that the songs are reproduced as they were set for the piano, without preludes and interludes; and that the complete score (suitable also for domestic performance) could be obtained from the composer at a cheap price.

Reichardt was the principal theoretician and apologist for the Liederspiel as well as being its best-known author and composer. The Leipzig *Allgemeine musikalische Zeitung* for 22 July 1801 contains his article about the Liederspiel, which he says was born of the desire to encourage simple, pleasant songs as opposed to brilliant and difficult operatic music. *Lieb und Treue* was written for a domestic occasion; the idea came to Reichardt when he so often found himself invited to perform the song 'Ach was ist die Liebe' from his own Singspiel *Die Geisterinsel* (a version of *The Tempest*, first given at Berlin in 1798). As *Lieb und Treue* drew from certain quarters criticism that its tone was too sentimental, Reichardt followed it with a comic and gay example, *Juchhey* (later known as *Der Jubel*) which included military songs. In the *Allgemeine musikalische Zeitung* article, Reichardt chided Himmel for the inappropriately heavy orchestration of his Liederspiel *Frohsinn und Schwärmerey* (libretto by C. A. Herklots, Berlin, 1801), though it enjoyed considerable popularity. Eberwein, Bergt and Lindpainter were among other successful exponents of the genre.

Mendelssohn's *Die Heimkehr aus der Fremde* and Schumann's *Spanisches Liederspiel* are examples of later works misleadingly entitled 'Liederspiel'. Schletterer in his valuable study (1863) of the Singspiel is not strictly accurate in his statement that the Liederspiel led to the racy vaudeville developed in Germany and Austria by Angely and others.

BIBLIOGRAPHY

J. F. Reichardt: 'Etwas über das Liederspiel', *AMZ*, iii (Leipzig, 1801), col.709

——: *Liederspiele* (Tübingen, 1804)

——: *Musik zu J. F. Reichardts Liederspielen* (Strasbourg, 1804)

H. M. Schletterer: *Das deutsche Singspiel von seinen ersten Anfängen bis auf die neueste Zeit* (Augsburg, 1863/*R*1975)

L. Kraus: *Das deutsche Liederspiel in den Jahren 1800–1830* (diss., U. of Halle, 1921)

PETER BRANSCOMBE

Liedertafel (Ger.: 'song-table'). Originally a society of men who met together on fixed evenings for the practice of vocal music in four parts, drinking forming part of the entertainment. These clubs arose during the political depression caused by Napoleon's rule in Germany. The first, consisting of 24 members only, was founded by Zelter in Berlin on 28 December 1808; others soon followed at Frankfurt am Main, Leipzig (1815), Magdeburg (1818) and elsewhere, gradually relaxing the rules as to numbers. Bernhard Klein founded the Jüngere Berliner Liedertafel, which aimed at a higher standard of art. These societies gave an immense impetus to men's part-singing throughout Germany. After the establishment of the *Männergesangvereine*, male singing societies proper, the word Liedertafel came to mean a society gathering, i.e. of invited ladies and gentlemen for whom the members performed pieces previously learnt. These were in fact informal concerts; guests moved about, ate, drank and talked as they pleased, provided they kept silence during the singing. The Liedertafeln of the large male singing societies of Vienna, Munich and Cologne were pleasant and refined entertainments, though not without a musical significance of their own.

In 1810 H. G. Nägeli founded a male singing society in Zurich, devoted to maintaining the humanistic and social ideals of Pestalozzi. A number of similar organizations were established in south German towns including Schwäbisch Hall (1817), Heilbronn (1818), Stuttgart (1824) and Ulm (1825).

BIBLIOGRAPHY

H. Kuhlo: *Geschichte des Zelterschen Liedertafels* (Berlin, 1909)

H. Dietel: *Beiträge zur Frühgeschichte des Männergesanges* (diss., U. of Berlin, 1938)

FRANZ GEHRING/R

Liederzyklus. See LIEDERKREIS.

Liedform (Ger.). Song form. A term proposed by A. B. Marx (*Allgemeine Musiklehre*, 1839; *Die Lehre von der musikalischen Komposition*, 1837–47) for BINARY FORM and TERNARY FORM; it is more often applied to the latter. Its usefulness (and that of the English equivalent) has been questioned since the lied is by no means tied to these particular structures, and the forms concerned appear no less often in instrumental music than in vocal.

BIBLIOGRAPHY

RiemannL 12

C. H. H. Parry: 'Lied-Form', *Grove 1–4*; 'Song Form', *Grove 5*

Lied ohne Worte (Ger.). SONG WITHOUT WORDS.

Liège [Liége] (Flemish Luik). City, Belgian since 1830; the capital of an independent episcopal principality until 1793, when it was annexed by France (until 1815) and the Netherlands (1815–30). Its cathedral school flourished during the 9th and 10th centuries, as did music in the convents and abbeys, where many scholars and plainsong composers were active. Towards the end of the 13th century the choirs of the cathedral and collegiate churches were enlarged by the addition of 12 choir-boys (known as *duodeni*) to the existing adult singers. In 1630 string instruments came into use in the churches. The tradition of church music led by *maîtres de chant* who were natives of Liège continued until 1797.

Many distinguished church musicians were born in, or were associated with, Liège. One of the earliest was the canon Jacques de Liège, whose *Speculum musicae* is the largest surviving medieval treatise on music. The motets in a manuscript at Turin (*I-Tr* Vari 42) were copied, if not composed, at the abbey of St Jacques, Liège. The leading composer of Netherlands polyphony in the 14th century, Johannes Ciconia, was born in Liège (*c*1335) and was a canon at the collegiate church of St Jean l'Evangéliste, a position he maintained for most of his life, despite his numerous journeys to Italy and elsewhere. His treatise *Nova musica* was written in Liège. Johannes Brassart was also connected with the church of St Jean from 1422, and he became a succentor at the cathedral in 1430; Johannes de Lymburgia worked at the church in the first quarter of the 15th century. Of the many musicians associated with the city or the prince-bishops' court in the 16th century Jean de Castro, Jean Guyot, Johannes de Fossa, Matthaeus le Maistre, Hubert Naich and the de Sayve family were outstanding; however, the most famous member of the latter, Lambert de Sayve, left as a boy to become a chorister in Vienna.

Little is known of early secular music in Liège or of activity at the courts of the prince-bishops before 1550. In the 17th and 18th centuries, church music continued to prosper in Liège, a situation that ended only with the downfall of the *ancien régime* and the annexing of the principality to France in 1793. The cathedral, seven collegiate churches, 32 parish churches and numerous monasteries supported a large number of musicians. The most representative composers of the city in the 17th century were Andreas d'Ath, Pierre Bonhomme, Gilles Hayne, Léonard de Hodemont and Lambert Pietkin; outstanding, however, were Mateo Romero, who worked at the Spanish court, and Henry Du Mont, educated in Liège from 1631 and later *maître de chapelle* to Louis XIV.

In the 18th century, besides the continuing church music tradition, secular music also developed. Opera, introduced about 1740 by a travelling troupe performing *opera buffa*, became popular in the form of burlesque operas in Walloon dialect (1756–7) by J.-N. Hamal and, after 1780, of French *opéras comiques*, above all those of Grétry (born at Liège in 1741). Instrumental chamber music flourished through the presence of several composer-performers: the violinists C.-N. Rosier and H.-F. Delange, the cellist J.-F. Decortis, the harpsichordists J.-J. Robson and Hubert Renotte and the organists Jean Buston, Lambert Chaumont and Thomas Babou; like Grétry, several natives of Liège, such as the composer F. A. Gresnick, the violinists Chartrain and D.-P. Pieltain and the singers Andrien and Gérard, pursued their careers in Paris. After 1738 numerous concerts were organized by various societies, among which the Société d'Emulation and the Société Philharmonique were pre-eminent. In the summer months concert activity was transferred to Spa, where a rich cosmopolitan clientèle took the waters.

The annexing of the principality of Liège to France (1793) and the abolition of the *maîtrises* (1797) brought all this musical activity to an end, and it was only with the establishment of the Ecole Royale de Musique (1826) that the city's musical life revived. Renamed the Conservatoire Royal in 1831, this institution was important both for its teaching and for its concerts and was the centre of the renowned Liège school of violin playing, with such teachers as Henry Vieuxtemps, Hubert Léonard, Lambert Massart, Eugène Ysaÿe, César Thomson, Ovide Musin and Martin Marsick.

César Franck was born (1822) and educated in Liège, and was the dominating influence on the work of such local composers as Eugène and Théophile Ysaÿe, Jean Rogister, Guillaume Lekeu, Albert Dupuis and Victor Vreuls. However, the fine teaching at the conservatory helped other composers such as Joseph and Léon Jongen and Désiré Pâque to develop more individual styles. Following World War I Debussy and Ravel became the main influences on René Defossez and others, and after 1945 Pierre Froidebise and his followers used serial techniques, as did Henri Pousseur, who founded the Centre de Recherches Musicales de Wallonie in 1970.

Several important musicologists have been active in Liège, including Antoine Auda, Suzanne Clercx-Lejeune (professor of musicology at the university from 1966), Maurice Barthélemy and José Quitin, who refounded the Société Liégeoise de Musicologie (1909) in 1972. Other associations for the study of old music have been the Association pour la Musique de Chambre, the A Cappella Liégeois (director Lucien Mawet) and, from 1970, Musique en Wallonie, which produces recordings of unpublished Walloon music.

Many performing groups and musical associations have been active in the city since World War II, including the Liège SO, the Liège Chamber Orchestra, the Walloon Opera, the choir of the cathedral of St Paul and several choral societies. The main concert halls are those of the conservatory (1887, capacity 1900), the Palais de Congrès (four halls, capacity from 300 to 1000), the Société d'Emulation (500), the Maison de la Culture (150) and the Chapelle de Vertbois (150). The 'Nuits de Septembre' festival, held annually, lasts between a week and ten days and is usually planned round a central theme or historical period.

BIBLIOGRAPHY

J. Daris: *Histoire du diocèse et de la principauté de Liège* (Liège, 1868–90)

J. Martiny: *Histoire du Théâtre de Liège depuis son origine jusqu'à nos jours* (Liège, 1887)

A. Auda: *La musique et les musiciens de l'ancien pays de Liège* (Liège, 1930)

J. Smits van Waesberghe: 'Some Music Treatises and their Interrelations: a School of Liège', *MD*, iii (1949), 95

C. van den Borren, S. Clercx and E. Closson: *La musique en Belgique* (Brussels, 1950)

J. Quitin: 'Les maîtres de chant de la cathédrale Saint-Lambert à Liège aux XVe et XVIe siècles', *RBM*, viii (1954), 5

S. Clercx: 'Mille ans de tradition musicale', *Liège et l'occident* (Liège, 1958), 253

——: 'Lüttich', *MGG*

J. Quitin: *Les maîtres de chant et la maîtrise de la collégiale Saint-Denis, à Liège, au temps de Grétry* (Brussels, 1964)

——: 'Orgues, organistes et organiers de l'église cathédrale Notre-Dame et Saint-Lambert à Liège aux XVIIe et XVIIIe siècles', *Bulletin de l'Institut archéologique liégeois*, lxxx (1967), 5–58

J. Quitin and H. Pousseur: 'Le Conservatoire Royal de Musique de Liège hier, aujourd'hui et demain', *150e anniversaire du Conservatoire royal de musique de Liège* (n.p., 1977), 35–80

JOSÉ QUITIN

Liegnitz (Ger.). Town, now Legnica in Poland, ruled for part of the 17th century by GEORG RUDOLPH.

Liehtenstein, Ulrich von. *See* ULRICH VON LIEHTENSTEIN.

Lienas, Juan de (*b* ?Spain; *fl* Mexico, ?c1620–50). Mexican composer possibly of Spanish birth. The only information about him is suggested by the manuscripts of his compositions. His name almost invariably includes the aristocratic title 'Don', which, in view of its extremely restricted usage in the 17th century, seems to indicate that he was a Spanish *hidalgo* or an Indian *cacique* who had taken the name of his sponsor at baptism (when the Spanish crown granted coats-of-arms to Indian princes it conferred the title 'Don'). He was evidently a married man with an unfaithful wife, for the manuscripts refer to him three times as 'el cornudo'. All his known works are contained in the manuscript of the Convento del Carmen, near Mexico City, and in the Newberry Choirbooks, Chicago (in *US-Cn*), which contain indications of performances by women's voices. The Newberry Choirbooks were apparently designed for use in the Encarnación convent, founded in Mexico City in 1595 and socially the most élite convent there, the colonial near-equivalent of the Descalzas Reales in Madrid. Other works in the Newberry Choirbooks are by Fabián Ximeno, organist and later choirmaster of Mexico City Cathedral from 1623 to 1654 and probably Lienas's contemporary. Lienas's compositions rank among the finest and most technically fluent in the large colonial repertory. The lines are smooth and melodious, textures are transparent and subtly varied, and the techniques of imitative counterpoint are handled with ease and skill. The *prima prattica* is invariably employed, and the rhythmic flow is unusually even for this period. The style shows only slight traces of 17th-century tendencies, such as the use of double choirs.

WORKS

Edition: *El Códice del Convento del Carmen*, ed. J. Bal y Gay, Tesoro de la música polifónica en México, i (Mexico City, 1952) [B]

Mass, 5vv, B
Magnificat primi toni, 8vv, *US-Cn*
Magnificat tertii toni, 5vv, *Cn*; B
Requiem, 5vv, B
2 Lamentations, 4vv, *Cn*, B; 5vv, B
Coenantibus autem, 4vv, B; Credidi propter, 8vv, *Cn*; Dixit Dominus, 4vv, *Cn*, B; Dixit Dominus, 8vv, *Cn*; Domine ad adiuvandum, 8vv, *Cn*; Laudate nomen Domine, 8vv, *Cn*; Miserere, 3vv, *Cn*; Nunc dimittis, 8vv, *Cn*; Salve, 4vv, *Cn*, B; Salve, 8vv, *Cn*; Tu lumen, 6vv, *Cn*

BIBLIOGRAPHY

S. Barwick: *Sacred Vocal Polyphony in Early Colonial Mexico* (diss., Harvard U., 1949)
——: 'A Recently Discovered Miserere of Fernando Franco', *Yearbook for Inter-American Musical Research*, vi (1970), 77
R. Stevenson: *Renaissance and Baroque Musical Sources in the Americas* (Washington, DC, 1970)
——: 'Mexican Colonial Music Manuscripts Abroad', *Notes*, xxix (1972–3), 203
E. A. Schleifer: 'New Light on the Mexican Choirbooks at the Newberry Library', *Notes*, xxx (1973–4), 231
R. M. Stevenson: 'El "Carmen" reivindicado', *Heterofonia*, vii/3 (1974), 17

ALICE RAY CATALYNE

Lienau. German firm of music publishers. Emil Robert Lienau (*b* Neustadt, Holstein, 28 Dec 1838; *d* Neustadt, 22 July 1920) studied philosophy and music under Moscheles and Rietz in Kiel and Leipzig. In 1863 he joined the publishing business of SCHLESINGER in Berlin, bought it in 1864 and continued it under the old firm name, adding 'Robert Lienau'; in 1875 he bought the Viennese firm of Haslinger. He retired from the business in 1898 and handed the management of the firms to his sons, first to Robert Heinrich Lienau (*b* Neustadt, 27 July 1866; *d* Berlin, 8 Nov 1949), and from 1907 to Friedrich Wilhelm Lienau (*b* Berlin, 6 Jan 1876; *d* Vienna, 15 Nov 1973) as well. In 1910, when the firm owned more than 25,000 titles, the brothers acquired the Viennese publishing firm of Rättig, and later also the Berlin firms of Krentzlin (1919), Wernthal (1925) and Köster (1928). Friedrich Wilhelm Lienau withdrew from the Berlin business in 1938 and directed sections of Haslinger in Vienna as an independent firm. The business in Berlin is managed by Robert Heinrich Lienau's children, Rosemarie (from 1949) and Robert Lienau (from 1958).

The elder Robert Lienau carefully continued the classical tendency of the firm of Schlesinger (Beethoven, Weber, Chopin) with Bruckner's Eighth Symphony and expanded the catalogue considerably (from the purchase of Haslinger) with works by Schubert, Johann Strauss (father and son), Lanner and Ziehrer. His sons followed with Sibelius (opp.46–57), Paul Juon and Philipp Jarnach, also including modern composers such as Hauer and Berg (opp.1–2). The firm specializes in neglected operas (Cimarosa, Donizetti), music for recorder and guitar, musicological literature and school music.

BIBLIOGRAPHY

Verzeichnis des Musik-Verlags der Schlesingerschen Buch- und Musikhandlung (Rob. Lienau) Berlin und des Carl Haslinger qdm. Tobias (Rob. Lienau) Wien (Berlin and Vienna, 1890)
W. Altmann, ed.: *J. Brahms: Briefwechsel*, xiv (Berlin, 1920)
R. Lienau: *Erinnerungen an Johannes Brahms* (Berlin, 1934)
O. E. Deutsch: *Music Publishers' Numbers* (London, 1946; Ger. trans., rev., 1961)
R. Elvers: *A. M. Schlesinger – Robert Lienau: 150 Jahre Musik-Verlag* (Berlin, 1960)
Musikverlage in der Bundesrepublik Deutschland und in West-Berlin (Bonn, 1968)

RUDOLF ELVERS

Lienike. *See* LINIKE family.

Liepmannssohn, Leo (*b* Landsberg, 18 Feb 1840; *d* Berlin, May 1915). German antiquarian music dealer. At the time when Liepmannssohn joined A. Asher & Co. (one of the best-known retail and second-hand booksellers in Europe) as an apprentice, the trade included a relatively small amount of music. He was thus prompted to develop his own strong musical interests into an independent business, which he ultimately established at Paris as Liepmannssohn & Dufour in January 1866. By the summer of 1872, when he disposed of the concern, he had issued no fewer than 37 catalogues, all of which included a section of music, while ten were entirely devoted to this subject. After a brief partnership in A. Asher & Co. following his return to Berlin, Liepmannssohn opened his own business there in 1874. In 1903 he sold it to Otto Haas, who had joined him early in that year, and who continued to trade under the name of Liepmannssohn.

Besides its own famous series of stock catalogues, the firm became widely known for the over 70 auction sales of music held between 1881 and 1934. Many notable collections of rare music and musical literature passed through its hands and the catalogues themselves are monuments of scholarship. Some, compiled by scholars such as Johannes Wolf and Georg Kinsky, have become reference works. The sales included the libraries of Spohr, Riemann, Commer, Eitner, André's heirs, J. E. Matthew and Wolffheim.

ALEC HYATT KING

Lier, Bertus van (*b* Utrecht, 10 Sept 1906; *d* Groningen, 14 Feb 1972). Dutch composer and conductor. He studied the cello with Orobio de Castro at the Amsterdam Conservatory, composition with Pijper (1926–32) and conducting with Scherchen (1933). For many years he worked as a critic, and in 1960 he began research work in music history at Groningen University, where he received an honorary doctorate in 1964. As a conductor he was particularly well known for his performances of the *St Matthew Passion* and his work with the Groningen student orchestra.

Van Lier's early compositions, strongly influenced by Pijper, include the Piano Sonatina no.2 and the First Symphony, a piece of remarkable (and, for the composer, typical) formal structure, in that the three short movements are motivically related. A polyrhythmic structure in the last movement combines duple and triple forms of the basic rhythmic formula. The Symphony no.2 (1931) is also formally characteristic: the opening prelude and fugue set out all of the material, a second-movement passacaglia is built on a modification of the fugue subject, and the rondo finale contrasts different elements from the various themes. Such procedures remained principal features of Van Lier's writing even when the direct influence of Pijper disappeared. His incidental music for the *Ajax* and *Antigone* of Sophocles met with great interest; both were for his own Dutch translations, which preserved the rhythms of the original (the *Antigone* translation won the Nijhoff Prize for literature in 1955). Van Lier's most important composition is *Het hooglied* for solo voices, chorus and orchestra, a work based on *The Song of Songs*. After thorough-going research he developed his own theory of the text, in which the king represents worldly power and the shepherd heavenly power, while the shepherdess (Shulamite) is seen as bound to the world but trusting in heaven; the choir, standing for the women and the people, fulfils the function of a Greek chorus. The whole work is conceived as a symbolic-mystical hymn, in which the solo parts consist mostly of melodic recitative. Between 1950 and 1957 Van Lier composed further large-scale orchestral works, but thereafter he wrote very little.

WORKS
(selective list)

Orch: 3 syms., 1928, 1931, 1939; Vc Concertino, 1933; Aias (incidental music, Sophocles, trans. Van Lier), 1933; Katharsis, ballet, 1945; Bn Conc., 1950; Antigone (incidental music, Sophocles, trans. Van Lier), 1952; Sinfonia, 2 str orchs, ww, hn, perc. 1954; Divertimento facile, 1957; Concertante muziek, ob, vn, orch, 1959; Intrada reale e sinfonia festiva, 1964; Suite, 1966

Choral: Canticum (P. H. Damstè), female vv, pf, str orch, 1929; 2 poésies de Ronsard, 1931; Psalm xxiii, 1940; O Nederland let op uw saeck, chorus, str, perc, 1945; Ik sla de trom (J. Greshoff), male vv, orch, 1948; Het hooglied (Song of Songs), solo vv, chorus, orch, 1949; Cantate voor Kerstmis (J. J. Thomson), chorus, orch, 1955; 4 hollandse kwartijnen (P. C. Boutens), 1956; Vijf het: zij (K. de Josselin), boys' chorus, chorus, orch, 1962; Psalm cxxxvi, Bar, chorus, orch, 1964

Solo vocal: 4 verzen van Leopold, S, orch, 1933; De dijk (J. Engelman), narrator, orch, 1937; 3 oud-persische kwartijnen (Boutens), S, a fl, ob d'amore, pf, 1956

Inst: Sonate pour une poupée, pf, 1925; 2 pf sonatinas, 1927, 1930; Str Qt, 1929; Sonata, vc, 1931; Suite, vn, pf, 1935; Liedje in canon, pf, 1944

Principal publisher: Donemus

BIBLIOGRAPHY
H. Badings: 'Bertus van Lier', *De hedendaagse nederlandse muziek* (Amsterdam, 1936), 95

J. Wouters: 'Bertus van Lier: Sonatine no.2 and Three Ancient Persian Quatrains', *Sonorum speculum* (1962), no.13, p.9

——: 'Bertus van Lier', *Sonorum speculum* (1966), no.29, p.1

W. Paap: 'Bertus van Lier', *Mens en melodie*, xxvii (1972), 99

JOS WOUTERS

Liera viol. See LYRA VIOL.

Liess, Andreas (*b* Klein Kniegnitz, Silesia [now Ksiéginice Małe], 16 June 1903). Austrian musicologist and journalist of German descent. After studying with Max Schneider at the University of Breslau (1922–5), he moved to Vienna, where he attended lectures in musicology by Adler, von Ficker and Wellesz, with archaeology as a subsidiary subject (1925–8). He took the doctorate in 1928 with a dissertation on Debussy's harmony and continued his studies in Paris (1927–33). He made his living at first as a freelance journalist, but in 1952 he was appointed lecturer in music history at the Vienna City Conservatory. From 1958 he was reader and from 1972 professor at the Vienna Academy (now Hochschule für Musik). His essential concern as a historian has been to present music history in its broadest cultural-historical aspects, its personalities as well as epochs and styles. He has done much for the understanding of French music in German-speaking countries.

WRITINGS
Die Grundelemente der Harmonik in der Musik von Claude Debussy (diss., U. of Vienna, 1928)
Claude Debussy (Strasbourg, 1936, 2/1977)
Joseph Marx (Graz, 1943)
Wiener Barockmusik (Vienna, 1946)
Johann Joseph Fux (Vienna, 1947)
Die Musik im Weltbild der Gegenwart (Lindau and Vienna, 1949)
Deutsche und französische Musik in der Geistesgeschichte des 19. Jahrhunderts (Vienna, 1950)
Franz Schmidt (Graz, 1951)
J. M. Vogl, *Hofoperist und Schubertsänger* (Vienna, 1954)
'Debussy, Claude Achille', 'Fux, Johann Josef', *MGG*
Carl Orff: Idee und Werk (Zurich, 1955, 2/1975; Eng. trans., 1965, 2/1971)

'Neue Zeugnisse für Corellis Wirken in Rom', *AMw*, xiv (1957), 130
Die Musik des Abendlandes im geistigen Gefälle der Epochen (Vienna, 1970)
Protuberanzen: zur Theorie der Musikgeschichte (Vienna, 1970)
'Musikgeschichte an der Epochenwende', *Beiträge 1970/71 der Österreichischen Gesellschaft für Musik* (Kassel, 1971), 21
'Zum Ursprung der Orchestra', *Symbolae historiae musicae: Hellmut Federhofer zum 60. Geburtstag* (Mainz, 1971), 19
Der Weg nach innen: Ortung ästhetischen Denkens heute (Zurich, 1973)
'Carl Orffs De temporum fine Comoedia: zu Zentstehung und Werk', *Studi musicali*, ii (1973), 341
'Claude Debussy und der Art Nouveau', *Studi musicali*, iii (1974)
Articles in *AMw*, *AcM*, *TVNM*, *NZM* and other periodicals

BIBLIOGRAPHY
A. Orel: 'Andreas Liess zur Vollendung seines 60. Lebensjahres', *NZM*, cxxiv (1963), 227

G. Berger: 'Die historische Dimension im musikphilosophischen Denken von Andreas Liess und Th. W. Adorno', *IRASM*, ii (1971), 5–35

RUDOLF KLEIN

Lieto, Bartolomeo. *See* PANHORMITANO, BARTOLOMEO LIETO.

Lieto fine (It.: 'happy ending'). A term used, in discussion of serious opera particularly of the 17th and 18th centuries, to refer to the situation at the end, signifying a sudden change for the better (often involving the appearance of a *deus ex machina*). A pejorative tinge is attached to its current use, since in some cases, like Gluck's *Orfeo ed Euridice* (1762), the ending is clearly not integral to the preceding. Many such endings were supplied because the festive nature of the original performance precluded a tragic ending. The *lieto fine* however had more significance than that: the intervention of the gods was possible because of their innate power, and their intervention for good denoted the working of a supreme morality. It was used by Metastasio as a logical outgrowth of the plot. In certain earlier librettos, notably several by Busenello (e.g. *L'incoronazione di Poppea*, 1642), the convention was used ironically; and in France its use was much parodied.

PATRICK J. SMITH

Lieurance, Thurlow Weed (*b* Oskaloosa, Iowa, 21 March 1878; *d* Boulder, Colorado, 9 Oct 1963). American composer noted for his use of Indian themes. Lieurance first encountered the music and customs of the plains Indians as a child. He served as a bandmaster during the Spanish-American War, then attended the Cincinnati Conservatory of Music. In 1903 the US government employed him to study and record the music of the American Indian; the results of this work constitute one of the more extensive collections of Indian music to date. Lieurance continued to devote most of his time to this and similar studies and was one of several composers who attempted to develop an indigenous American music based on Indian melodies. He wrote works for piano and for orchestra, one opera (*Drama of the Yellowstone*) and many songs, one of which is the famous *By the Waters of the Minnetonka* (also known as *Moon Deer*).

WRITINGS
'The Musical Soul of the American Indian', *The Etude*, xxxviii (1920), 655; repr. with essays by C. W. Cadman and A. Nevin as *Indian Music* (Philadelphia, 1928)

BIBLIOGRAPHY
Anon. [?T. W. Lieurance]: 'Legend of a Famous Lieurance Song', *The Etude*, xxxix (1921), 94

Anon. [?T. W. Lieurance]: 'From Broadway to the Pueblos', *The Etude*, xli (1923), 231

E. Reinbach: *Music and Musicians in Kansas* (Topeka, Kansas, 1930)

DOUGLAS A. LEE

Lifar, Serge (*b* 1905). French dancer of Russian birth; *see* DANCE, §VII, 1(ii).

Ligata. *See* FUGA LIGATA.

Ligature (i). A notational symbol that combines within itself two or more pitches and by its shape defines their rhythm. It is in fact a rhythmicized neume of two or more notes. Between the 12th and 16th centuries the ligature had a variety of causes, meanings and uses. Several of its ambiguities arise from its attempt to serve both as a neume (denoting several notes to be sung to a single syllable) and as a part of the rhythmic system; others arise because it was often merely a calligraphical flourish with no meaning beyond that of the note values it represented.

Its rhythmic implications follow a system that is historically logical but somewhat complicated in practice. Once established, around 1300, the system remained unchanged in principle but was used more and more selectively until by the 16th century only a single form of ligature was in common use. With the advent of type-set music the ligature eventually became extinct.

The earliest ligatures derive directly from the rising and falling two-note neumes of chant notation, the *pes* and the *clivis* (ex.1a). By the 12th century these had taken in central French notation the forms shown in ex.1b. How often these signs had any rhythmic impli-

Ex.1

(a) [musical notation] (b) [musical notation]

cations in monophonic chant is still much discussed; but there seems to be general agreement that when they had rhythmic meaning they implied some kind of a drive towards the second note, which would become more accented and longer (*see* NEUMATIC NOTATIONS).

With the advent of modal notation for polyphony some time around 1200 the two signs in ex.1b became fundamental building-blocks of the system (*see* RHYTHMIC MODES). The number of notes in each neume and the combination of such neumes in *ordines* defined the rhythms in the modal system; but in a surprisingly large proportion of cases these two neume shapes were to be interpreted as *brevis–longa* (as in ex.2).

Ex.2

(a) [musical notation] (b) [musical notation]

When the fully-fledged system of ligatures was described for the first time by Franco of Cologne and Johannes de Garlandia these two basic shapes retained their most common meanings, as in ex.2. Both shapes were described as being *cum proprietate* ('with propriety', that is, with the first note in its standard form) and *cum perfectione* ('with perfection', that is, with the last note in its standard form).

Alterations were made to these fundamental patterns by the addition or subtraction of stems, by turning notes round, or (for final notes only) by changing the shape of the ligature to become an oblique. Thus to turn round the last note of ex.2a as in ex.3a was to make it *sine perfectione* and to change its value from *longa* to *brevis*;

and then to add a descending stem to that note would restore its propriety, restoring therefore its original *longa* value (ex.3b).

Ex.3

(a) [musical notation] (b) [musical notation]

Exx.3b and 2b are the two shapes best remembered when attempting to understand the remaining world of ligatures. Any of the changes just mentioned had the effect of turning a *longa* to a *brevis* or equally – and this is perhaps the confusing point – turning a *brevis* to a *longa*. Thus to add a descending stem to the first note of ex.3b would have exactly the same effect as subtracting the descending stem from the first note of ex.2b – changing the value of that note from a *brevis* to a *longa* (ex.4).

Ex.4

[musical notation]

Similarly with the final notes: the subtraction of the stem from the second note of ex.2b changed it from a *longa* to a *brevis*. For a descending ligature, however, a different technique was used. Here, to avoid confusion with liquescent neumes, the ligature was altered by conversion to the oblique form (ex.5). In all other cases the

Ex.5

[musical notation]

oblique form was identical in meaning with the normal square form of ligature: it changed only the final note, and then only when the ligature descended to that note.

This system, deriving directly from the concepts of propriety and perfection in the basic ligature forms in exx.3b and 2b, has two important characteristics: the scheme in the rising form of ligature is different from that in the falling form; and it applies only to the first and last notes of ligatures. Ex.6 shows all the possibilities.

Ex.6

	Rising ligatures	
	First note	Last note
cum proprietate	[notation] = □	[notation] = ⌐
sine proprietate	[notation] = ⌐	[notation] = □
	Falling ligatures	
cum proprietate	[notation] = □	[notation] = ⌐
sine proprietate	[notation] = ⌐	[notation] = □

Two further features complete the system. A rising stem denotes the beginning of a ligature *cum opposita proprietate* ('with opposed propriety'): this is a ligature of two notes, each worth a *semibrevis* (ex.7a). Whatever else may be happening in the ligature the two notes immediately following that rising stem are always *semibreves* (ex.7b). All other notes – that is to say, notes other than the first and last in a ligature and ones not covered by the *cum opposita proprietate* convention – have the value of a *brevis* (ex.8), though a descending stem after any such note can turn it into a *longa* (ex.9).

Ex.7

(a) ... = ...   (b) ... = ...

Ex.8

... = ... = ...

Ex.9

... = ...

It is perhaps worth adding two points to the above explanation. First, while exx.2–9 are all in full-black notation they apply equally in the void notation that became customary in the 15th century. Second, the values of notes in ligature are of course subject to the same modifications as any other notes when used within the mensural system (see NOTATION, §III).

This system grew up in the notation of melismatic tenors in the motet repertory of the late 13th century (though it is as well to bear in mind that many early motets are written in modal notation, an earlier system that works rather differently). In the 14th century it was used particularly in the untexted lower voices of secular songs and in the more melismatic sections in sacred music. Here, and in later music, scribes seem to have avoided placing ligatures so that more than one syllable must be sung to the ligature; and indeed the few discussions of texting in the theorists of the 15th and 16th centuries specifically forbid the singing of more than one syllable to a ligature. Yet there are many cases where there is no alternative to breaking the ligature for texting; and this rule should therefore be taken only as the norm, not as of universal application. As early as the 13th century the conflicting meanings of a neume (to denote several pitches for a single syllable) and of a ligature (to denote a particular rhythmic configuration) can often be seen leading to notational confusion.

In the 15th century ligatures became increasingly rare. Some theorists of the time suggested that a ligature should be written whenever possible, and that to do otherwise would be to insult the musician. But there is very little evidence of this precept being followed at all rigorously. On the other hand that state of mind may well explain why there is relatively little agreement among the spasmodic ligatures that appear in 15th-century sources. Several scholars have attempted, for example, to trace relationships between manuscripts by charting the ligature variants; but while such variants have often been recorded in the critical commentaries to editions, the findings in terms of manuscript filiation have in general led nowhere and have not normally been published.

By the end of the 15th century there was in any case considerably less opportunity to write ligatures. As the *minima* and the *semiminima* became the most common note values there were fewer and fewer occasions where a delightful ligature of *brevis* and *longa* note values (as in exx.8 and 9) could be used. The *cum opposita proprietate* ligature of two *semibreves* therefore became al-

most the only form to appear; and this can be found even in the 17th century. But long before that the ligature was in most cases only a scribal flourish, a more elegant way of writing notes. That ligatures were included in many printed editions of the 16th century – and even, occasionally, of the 17th – is no more significant than the retention of printer's ligatures for normal letter-press typography.

For bibliography *see* NOTATION.

Ligature (ii). The metal band with two screws by which the reed of a clarinet or saxophone is secured to the mouthpiece. It replaces the earlier method of binding the reed with a wool or silk cord, still regarded as the correct method in Germany.

Ligendza, Catarina [Beyron, Katarina] (*b* Stockholm, 18 Oct 1937). Swedish soprano. Daughter of the soprano Brita Hertzberg and the tenor Einar Beyron, both former members of the Stockholm Opera, she studied at the Würzburg Conservatory, Vienna, and in Saarbrücken with Josef Greindl. She made her début at Linz in 1965 as Countess Almaviva. After engagements in Brunswick and Saarbrücken (1966–9), when she sang Elisabeth de Valois, Desdemona, Arabella and her first Brünnhilde, she began to sing regularly in Berlin, Hamburg and Stuttgart, as well as in Switzerland and Italy; she first appeared at La Scala as Arabella in 1970. That year she sang the First Norn at the Salzburg Easter Festival and in 1971 made her débuts at Bayreuth (as Brünnhilde) and the Metropolitan Opera (as Beethoven's Leonore). In 1972 she sang Senta at Covent Garden and that autumn made her first appearances in Stockholm. Ligendza returned to Bayreuth from 1972 as Brünnhilde and Isolde and was highly praised for her fresh, even and beautiful voice, gleaming tone and expressive acting. Although she was not at first considered a true Wagnerian dramatic soprano, her characterizations of Wagner's heroines are unusually credible.

HAROLD ROSENTHAL

Ligeti, György (Sándor) (*b* Dicsöszentmárton [Diciosânmartin, now Tîrnăveni], Transylvania, 28 May 1923). Austrian composer of Hungarian birth. His music became more widely known after the first performance of the orchestral *Apparitions* at the 1960 ISCM Festival in Cologne. In his next work, *Atmosphères*, he went still further in annihilating distinct pitch and rhythm as primary formal elements in favour of chromatic sound complexes of different volume, density and timbre. This technique was refined in the dense polyphonic writing of subsequent pieces, and at the same time Ligeti moved away from chromaticism to definite interval combinations, also using deviations from the tempered scale.

1. LIFE. Ligeti was born of Hungarian Jewish parents; shortly after his birth the family moved to Kolozsvár where he spent his school years. He studied composition with Farkas at the Kolozsvár Conservatory (1941–3) and took private lessons with Kadosa in Budapest during the summers of 1942 and 1943. After the war he resumed his composition studies with Farkas, Veress and Járdányi at the Budapest Academy of Music. He graduated in 1949 and then pursued field research in Romanian folk music. In 1950 he was appointed professor of harmony, counterpoint and formal analysis at the

Budapest Academy, where he remained until leaving Hungary in 1956. During these years he published some pieces in Hungary and Romania, most of them rather simple folksong arrangements or works based on peasant music. For political reasons his more daring scores could be neither printed nor performed, and most of his experiments failed for lack of information about international developments.

Reaching Vienna in December 1956, Ligeti was soon brought into contact with leading figures of the west European avant garde, including Stockhausen, Eimert and Koenig. He was invited by Eimert to work at the West German Radio electronic studios in Cologne, where he realized two pieces and planned another. *Artikulation*, the only one of these compositions to be published, was first heard in Cologne in March 1958; later in that year his First Quartet, composed in 1953–4, received its first performance in Vienna. Ligeti resumed work on some projects begun in Hungary, among them *Víziók* ('Visions') which, through several intermediate versions, became *Apparitions*, the work that caused a stir at the 1960 ISCM Festival and brought him almost immediate international recognition. Until that time Ligeti had been little known beyond a small circle of avant-garde musicians, and his reputation had been principally as an astute theorist. From 1959 he lectured at most of the annual Darmstadt summer courses, and from 1961 he went regularly to the Stockholm Academy of Music as visiting professor of composition. Ligeti moved from Vienna to West Berlin in 1969, holding a one-year DAAD scholarship. In spring 1972 he was visiting lecturer and composer-in-residence at Stanford University, California, and in 1973 he was appointed professor of composition at the Hamburg Musikhochschule. He was elected to the Royal Swedish Academy of Music in 1964 and is also a member of the West Berlin Academy of Arts and of the Hamburg Free Academy of Arts. In 1971 he was made vice-president of the Austrian section of the ISCM. In 1975 he was awarded the German decoration 'Pour le mérit' and the Bach Prize of the City of Hamburg.

2. WORKS. Ligeti's output may be divided into three distinct categories: juvenilia, the extensive oeuvre produced between 1944 and his move from Hungary in 1956, and the works written in the west. The original compositions of the first group, of which the earliest extant MSS date from 1938, are in the main piano pieces, songs and chamber works with piano, among them a short Piano Trio (1941–2) which was Ligeti's first publicly performed work (Kolozsvár, 1942). In the same year the rather Musorgsky-like song *Kineret* (1941) became his first published piece.

During the period 1944–8 Ligeti began to develop an individual style, but the political changes of 1948 brought difficulties for adventurous artists and, in order to retain his position as a professional composer, Ligeti was forced to produce simple folksong arrangements, mostly for chorus. Even so, his 'radical ideas' put his academy appointment in doubt, but Kodály's help and authority did much to guard him from direct persecution. After Stalin's death (1953) the most severe cultural restrictions were relaxed, and Ligeti's attempts at the subsequent style of *Apparitions* and *Atmosphères* may be found among the sketches and incomplete scores from this period onwards. Most characteristic of the finished works of the early 1950s are the choruses

Éjszaka ('Night') and *Reggel* ('Morning'), the very Bartókian Quartet no.1 'Métamorphoses nocturnes' and the 11 piano pieces *Musica ricercata*. All use a free tonal language far from his post-1956 work, though there are glimpses of the later style in the formal solutions and the ingenuities of vocal and instrumental writing.

With *Apparitions* (1958–9), *Atmosphères* (1961) and the organ piece *Volumina* (1961–2) Ligeti introduced and developed his technique of chromatic complexes, taking it almost to its ultimate consequence: the removal of melody, harmony and rhythm as distinct features. However, the two orchestral works are meticulously notated in conventional terms, and it was the more general aspects of Ligeti's work that had a decisive influence on the widespread cluster composition of the 1960s and early 1970s. Ligeti himself went on to write two vocal chamber pieces, later adapted for stage performance with texts by the composer: *Aventures* (1962) and *Nouvelles aventures* (1962–5). Here the use of an invented 'language' – drawing on a wide variety of speech sounds and inflections in a kaleidoscopic polyphony – goes back to the electronic *Artikulation* (1958). On the other hand, the *Pièce électronique* no.3 (1957–8), which remained unfinished, greatly resembles *Atmosphères* and was originally given that title. The two *Aventures* pieces and *Artikulation* represent one extreme; *Atmosphères* and *Volumina* the other. On one side a highly disjunct style, fast moving in its succession of ideas; on the other a calm and static music, a dim shadow of events far beyond view. Elements of both are present in *Apparitions*, well described in Ligeti's words: 'States, events, changes' (1960).

In the Requiem (1963–5) the first two movements, Introitus and Kyrie, further develop the style of *Atmosphères* contrapuntally: the Kyrie is a huge five-part fugue in which each part is a canon in four voices. The third movement, the Dies Irae, employs conventional word-painting to summon an oppressive and ceremonial representation of Death, while the final Lacrimosa, separated by a pause, retains only the two soloists for an utterly simple lament, sung to a diaphanous chamber accompaniment which gradually assumes a dreamlike spirit of comfort at 'Judicando homo reus', introduced by a *pppppp* harp *bisbigliando* and continued by processional harpsichord music. The Requiem made an enormous impression at its first performance in Stockholm in March 1965, and two years later it brought Ligeti the Bonn Beethoven Prize.

Ligeti's next work, the choral *Lux aeterna* (1966), is built entirely in strict canon, further developing the nonchromatic interval combinations that first appeared as a feature of his music in the last section of the Requiem. The slow first movement of the Cello Concerto (1966) sounds almost like an instrumental paraphrase of *Lux aeterna*, as does the orchestral *Lontano* (1967). The concerto's second movement, however, is completely different and aptly sub-titled 'Aventures ohne Worte': in many ways it is close to the *Aventures* style, but it is also a free variation on the first movement. The coherence and manifold complexity of Ligeti's musical thinking could not better be demonstrated.

In 1968 Ligeti composed the Second Quartet and the Ten Pieces for wind quintet. The five-movement quartet is one of his most profound works, somewhat resembling the combined variation and arch form of Bartók; but the Ten Pieces are brief, diverting and virtuoso sketches, every other number featuring one of the players in a

György Ligeti

produce sound of perpetual change in rhythm and colour, related to a scheme of interval changes. This was the formal principle in *Continuum* (1968) for harpsichord, in the second organ study, *Coulée* (1969), and also in several movements from larger works. The obsession with time-counting is evident in *Clocks and Clouds* (1972–3), where metronomic sounds are gradually transformed into misty images.

During his years in the West Ligeti has developed rapidly through a range of aesthetic positions, outstripping many superficial imitators. His real importance as an influence on others has been in opening vistas other than post-Webernian serialism.

WORKS
(*for complete list of pre-1956 works see Nordwall, 1971*)

WORKS WRITTEN IN HUNGARY

Idegen földön [In foreign land], 4 songs (B. Balassa, Hungarian trad., Slovak trad. trans. Balázs), female chorus 3vv, 1945–6, unpubd
Magány [Loneliness] (S. Weöres), chorus 3vv, 1946, unpubd
2 songs (Weöres), 1v, pf, 1946–7, unpubd; 3rd song lost, 4th inc.
2 capriccios, pf, 1947, unpubd
Invention, pf, 1948, unpubd
Tavasz [Spring] (17th-century Hungarian), chorus 5vv, 1948, lost
Musica ricercata, 11 pieces, pf, 1951–3, unpubd; no.11 'Omaggio a Frescobaldi' arr. org, 1953, unpubd; nos.3, 5, 7–10 arr. wind qnt as 6 Bagatelles, 1953
Pápainé (Hungarian trad.), chorus 8vv, 1953, unpubd
String Quartet no.1 'Métamorphoses nocturnes', 1953–4
Mátraszentimrei dalok [Mátraszentimre songs], 4 folksong arrs., children's chorus 2–3vv, 1955, unpubd
Éjszaka [Night], Reggel [Morning] (Weöres), chorus 8vv, 1955

LATER WORKS

Glissandi, 1-track tape [WDR, Cologne], 1957, unpubd
Pièce électronique no.3, 4-track tape, 1957–8, unrealized, score pubd in *Ligeti-dokument* (1968)
Artikulation, 4-track tape [WDR, Cologne], 1958 [see Wehinger (1970)]
Apparitions [from Víziók, 1956–7, inc.], orch, 1958–9
Atmosphères, orch, 1961
Fragment, chamber orch, 1961, rev. 1964
Trois bagatelles, pianist, 1961, pubd in *Ligeti-dokument* (1968)
Die Zukunft der Musik (The Future of Music), lecturer, audience, 1961, bilingual text pubd in *Dé/Collage* (Cologne, 1962), no.3
Volumina, org, 1961–2, rev. 1966
Poème symphonique, 100 metronomes, 1962
Aventures (Ligeti), 3 solo vv, 7 insts, 1962, arr. stage, 1966
Nouvelles aventures (Ligeti), 3 solo vv, 7 insts, 1962–5, arr. stage, 1966
Requiem, S, Mez, 2 choruses, orch, 1963–5
Concerto, vc, orch/chamber orch, 1966
Lux aeterna, 16 solo vv/chorus 16vv, 1966
Lontano, orch, 1967
Organ Study no.1 'Harmonies', 1967
Continuum, hpd, 1968; arr. 2 harps, 1974
String Quartet no.2, 1968
Ten Pieces, wind qnt, 1968
Ramifications, 12 str/str orch, 1968–9
Organ Study no.2 'Coulée', 1969
Chamber Concerto, 13 insts, 1969–70
Horizont, rec, 1971, collab. Vetter
Melodien, orch/chamber orch, 1971
Double Concerto, fl, ob, orch, 1972
Clocks and Clouds (Ligeti), female chorus 12vv, orch, 1972–3
San Francisco Polyphony, orch, 1973–4
Monument, Selbstporträt, Bewegung, 2 pf, 1976
3 Objekte, 2 pf, 1976
Le grand macabre (music-theatre, M. Meschke, after Ghelderode), Stockholm, Royal Opera, 12 April 1978

Principal publishers: Peters, Schott, Universal

WRITINGS
(*for complete list to 1970 see Nordwall, 1971*)

Klasszikus összhangzattan [Classical harmony] (Budapest, 1954)
A klasszikus harmóniarend (Budapest, 1956)
'Pierre Boulez: Entscheidung und Automatik in der Structure Ia', *Die Reihe* (1958), no.4, pp.33–63; Eng. trans. in *Die Reihe* (1960), no.4, pp.32–62
'Über die Harmonik in Weberns erster Kantate', *Darmstädter Beiträge zur neuen Musik* (1960), no.3, p.49
'Zustände, Ereignisse, Wandlungen', *blätter + bilder* (Würzburg and Vienna, 1960), no.11, p.50 [repr. in *Melos*, xxiv (1967), 165]

miniature concerto. However, both works give a sense that each part contains the seed of the whole, that past, present and future are equally accessible to experience. The Chamber Concerto (1969–70) – composed, like many other pieces, for particular performers: Cerha's Die Reihe ensemble – demonstrates Ligeti's knowledge of and feeling for instrumental characteristics. It is gay and straightforward, almost a sinfonia concertante for the 13 soloists. By contrast the next work was the stern and enigmatic *Melodien* for small orchestra, a wealth of swarming melodic shapes where no figure can be grasped before it has slipped away. The Double Concerto (1972) for flute, oboe and orchestra resembles *Apparitions* and the Cello Concerto in form, its second movement being a free variation of the first. This work also uses micro-intervals and intentionally 'false' harmonic and melodic relations; deviations from the tempered scale had already been introduced in the Second Quartet and in *Ramifications* (1968–9) for two string ensembles tuned a quarter-tone apart.

In the early 1960s some minor pieces arose from the simultaneous interest and distaste that Ligeti felt for the 'happening'. Of two 'music ceremonials', the *Trois bagatelles* (1961) for pianist satirized the Cage school and the *Poème symphonique* for 100 metronomes (1962) took an ironic look at the composer–performer–audience situation in mechanical music, electronic or otherwise. In *Fragment* (1961) he composed a self-persiflage, and in the 'musical provocation' *Die Zukunft der Musik* (1961) a lecture, commissioned for a symposium on the future of the arts, became a practical demonstration of the futility of such speculation, as well as an explosion of the 'happening' idea itself. But at least the metronome piece proved fruitful in a later stylistic development: the superposition of different metres to

'Wandlungen der musikalischen Form', *Die Reihe* (1960), no.7, p.5; Eng. trans. in *Die Reihe* (1965), no.7, p.5
'Neue Notation: Kommunikation oder Selbstzweck?', *Darmstädter Beiträge zur neuen Musik* (1965), no.9, p.35
'Requiem', *Wort und Wahrheit* (Vienna, 1968), no.4, p.308
'Über neue Wege im Kompositionsunterricht', *Three Aspects of New Music* (Stockholm, 1968)
'Was erwartet der Komponist der Gegenwart von der Orgel?', *Orgel und Orgelmusik*, ed. H. Eggebrecht (Stuttgart, 1968), 167
'Auf dem Weg zu "Lux aeterna" ', *ÖMz*, xxiv (1969), 80
'Auswirkungen der elektronischen Musik auf mein kompositorisches Schaffen', *Experimentelle Musik: Schriftenreihe der Akademie der Künste*, vii (Berlin, 1970)
'Apropos Musik und Politik', *Darmstädter Beiträge zur neuen Musik* (1973), no.13, p.42
'Musikalische Erinnerungen aus Kindheit und Jugend', *Festschrift für einen Verteger: Ludwig Strecker* (Mainz, 1973), 54

BIBLIOGRAPHY

H. Kaufmann: 'Strukturen im Strukturlosen', *Melos*, xxxi (1964), 391
E. Salmenhaara: 'György Ligetin "Atmosphères" ja siinä ilmenevä uusi esteettinen ja strukturalinen ajattelu' [Ligeti's 'Atmosphères' and the new aesthetic and structural thought it expresses], *Musiikin vuosikirja* (Helsinki, 1964), 7
D. Schnebel: 'Bericht von neuer Orgelmusik', *Walter Gerstenberg zum 60. Geburtstag* (Wolfenbüttel and Zurich, 1964), 151
O. Nordwall: *Det omöjligas konst: anteckningar till György Ligetis musik* [The art of the impossible: notes on Ligeti's music] (Stockholm, 1966)
——: 'Alice im Streichquartett', *Stuttgarter Zeitung* (2 Nov 1968)
——: 'Der Komponist György Ligeti', *Musica* (1968), 173 [incl. discarded middle movt of early version of *Apparitions*]
O. Nordwall, ed.: *Ligeti-dokument* (Stockholm, 1968) [incl. letters, sketches, scores, lectures, etc]
H. Kaufmann: 'Ein Fall absurder Musik', *Spurlinien* (Vienna, 1969), 130
H. Keller: 'The Contemporary Problem', *Tempo* (1969), no.89, p.25
O. Nordwall: 'György Ligeti', *Tempo* (1969), no.88, p.22
E. Salmenhaara: *Das musikalische Material und seine Behandlung in den Werken 'Apparitions', 'Atmosphères', 'Aventures' und 'Requiem' von György Ligeti* (Helsinki and Regensburg, 1969)
U. Dibelius: 'Reflexion und Reaktion: über den Komponisten György Ligeti', *Melos*, xxxvii (1970), 89
J. Häusler: 'György Ligeti: wenn man heute ein Streichquartett schreibt', *NZM*, lxxxi (1970), 378 [interview, repr. in Nordwall (1971)]
——: 'Interview mit György Ligeti', *Melos*, xxxvii (1970), 496 [on *Lontano*, repr. in Nordwall (1971)]
H. Kaufmann: 'Ligetis zweites Streichquartett', *Melos*, xxxvii (1970), 181
R. Wehinger, ed.: *György Ligeti: Artikulation* (Mainz, 1970) [listening score with disc and analysis]
H.-M. Beuerle: 'Nochmals Ligetis "Lux aeterna" ', *Musica* (1971), 279
C. Gottwald: 'Lux aeterna: zur Kompositionstechnik György Ligetis', *Musica* (1971), 12
H. Kaufmann: 'Betreffend Ligeti's Requiem', *Protokolle 71* (Vienna, 1971), no.1, p.158
O. Nordwall: *György Ligeti: eine Monographie* (Mainz, 1971) [incl. interviews, essay by H. Kaufmann, lists of works and writings]
U. Stürzbecher: 'György Ligeti', *Werkstattgespräche mit Komponisten* (Cologne, 1971), 32
M. Lichtenfeld: 'György Ligeti oder das Ende der seriellen Musik', *Melos*, xxxix (1972), 74
——: '10 Stücke für Bläserquintett von György Ligeti', *Melos*, xxxix (1972), 326
I. Fabian: 'Jenseits von Tonalität und Atonalität', *ÖMz*, xxviii (1973), 233
U. Urban: 'Serielle Technik und barocker Geist in Ligetis Cembalo-Stück "Continuum"', *Musik und Bildung*, v (1973), 63
A. Jack: 'Ligeti', *Music and Musicians*, xxii/11 (1974), 29 [interview]
S. Plaistow: 'Ligeti's Recent Music', *MT*, cxv (1974), 379
Musik und Bildung, vii/10 (1975) [special Ligeti no.]
Nutida musik, xix/2 (1975) [special Ligeti no.]
Artes (1976), no.3 [special Ligeti no.]   OVE NORDWALL

Light, Edward (*c*1747–*c*1832). English composer and inventor. He created seven plucked, fretted chordophones compounded from lute, lyre and harp structures. In 1798 he invented the harp-guitar, and later also invented a harp-lute-guitar. Between 1810 and 1813 he invented a harp-lute, which was patented in 1818, and at some time he invented an apollo lyre with 12 strings. In 1815 a harp-lyre was advertised in the *Caledonian*

Mercury, and in 1816 he patented a British lute-harp and a dital harp. Extant examples of his work are sometimes labelled as being made by A. Barry (18 Frith Street, Soho) and Wheatstone & Co. The title-page of his undated *Collection of Psalms &c.* indicates that he was organist of Trinity Chapel, St George's, Hanover Square, and 'Lyrist to H.R.H. The Princess [Charlotte] of Wales'. His teaching activity required his presence in London; and instrument labels and title-pages show that at various times he lived at 16 Harley Street; 34 Queen Anne Street, Portland Chapel; 3 and 8 Foley Place; 43 Portland Place (where his partner Angelo Ventura also lived) and 38 Berners Street.

He arranged, composed and published much of his own teaching material: four instrument tutors, two instrumental collections, five song collections (of which only one is not arranged for his own inventions). These are mostly binary pieces or strophic works, simple in harmony and texture, and of short duration, and reflect the short-term need for simple instruments and music as an alternative to the pedal harp and its music before the piano became widely available.

For an instrument by Light *see* HARP-LUTE, fig.2.

WORKS
(all published London)

Vocal: The Ladies' Amusement, 1v, gui (1783); 6 English Songs, 1v, 1/2 hpd, op.1 (*c*1800) [with 6 It. and Fr. songs]
Ensemble music: A Collection of Songs and Instrumental Pieces, harp-lute, pf (*c*1805); A Collection of Songs, arr. harp-lute, lyre, gui (*c*1810); A Collection of Psalms, Hymns, etc, arr. harp-lute, lyre (?1814)
Harp-lute solo: Preludes, Exercises and Recreations (*c*1810); National Airs, Songs, Waltzes, etc (*c*1810); Divertimentos, i (?1817)

THEORETICAL WORKS

The Art of Playing the Guitar (London, ?1785)
A First Book, or Master and Scholar's Assistant, Being a Treatise on, and Instructor for, Learning Music (London, 1794)
A Tutor, with a Tablature, for the Harp-lute-guitar (London, *c*1810)
New and Compleat Instructions for Playing on the Harp-lute (London, ?1812)
A New and Complete Directory to the Art of Playing on the Patent British Lute-harp (London, *c*1816)

BIBLIOGRAPHY

T. Busby: *Concert Room Anecdotes*, ii (London, 1825), 275f
R. B. Armstrong: *Musical Instruments*, ii (Edinburgh, 1908)
L. Fryklund: *Förteckning över Edward Lights musikaliska verk* (Hälsingborg, 1931)
A. Baines: *Non-keyboard Instruments*, Victoria and Albert Museum Catalogue of Musical Instruments, ii (London, 1968)
                                        STEPHEN BONNER

Lightstone, Pauline. *See* DONALDA, PAULINE.

Ligne, Charles-Joseph (Emmanuel) Prince de (*b* Brussels, 23 May 1735; *d* Vienna, 13 Dec 1814). South Netherlands writer. Son of Prince Claude Lamoral II and Princess Elizabeth von Salm, he was active in the military and later envoy to France. Frequent visits to Versailles evidently helped to shape his literary style. Travelling throughout Europe, he met many writers, musicians and actors, as well as the most important political figures; his voluminous published correspondence, particularly with Rousseau and Voltaire, is of great significance for the study of 18th-century culture. He wrote at least 16 stage works for his private theatre in Baudour, including *Céphalide* (1777), an *opéra comique* set to music by Vitzthumb. Grétry composed several songs to his texts. His son Charles de Ligne (*b* Beloeil, 1769; *d* Champagne, 14 Sept 1792) published three collections of French *airs* arranged for piano or harpsichord (Vienna, ?1791). Another de Ligne (first name unknown) played in the orchestra of the Antwerp theatre in 1790.

BIBLIOGRAPHY

EitnerQ; *FétisB*
A. Wauters: 'Ligne (le prince Charles-Joseph de)', *BNB*
Annales Prince de Ligne, ed. F. Leuridant, i–xix (Brussels, 1920–38)
M. Oulié: *Le Prince de Ligne, un grand seigneur cosmopolite* (Paris, 1926)
L. Dumont-Wilden: *La vie de Charles-Joseph de Ligne* (Paris, 1927)
E. Benedikt: *Karl Josef Fürst von Ligne: ein Genie des Lebens* (Vienna, 1936)
F. van den Bremt: 'Ligne, Charles-Joseph, Prince de', *MGG*

PHILIPPE MERCIER

Ligne postiche [supplémentaire] (Fr.). LEGER LINE.

Ligniville, (Pierre) Eugène (François), Marquis of, Prince of Conca (*b* nr. Nancy, 1730; *d* Florence, 10 Dec 1788). Italian composer and music organizer of French birth. From a noble family of Lorraine, he studied at the university of Pont-à-Mousson but lived most of his mature life in Italy. From 1757 he was at Mantua, going to Bologna in July 1758 for the examination to enter the Accademia Filarmonica (test piece in *I-Bc*). In 1761 he moved to Florence (where the House of Lorraine ruled the grand duchy of Tuscany) as a court chamberlain and postmaster general. He very soon also became director of the court music and was thus able to have important musical works performed, including cantatas and oratorios by Handel (according to a letter to Martini dated 30 May 1772). On 2 April 1770 he received Mozart at the grand-ducal palace; Leopold Mozart, in a letter dated 3 April, called him 'the best contrapuntist in all Italy' and reported that 'he presented Wolfgang with the most difficult fugues and themes, which Wolfgang played and worked out as easily as one eats a piece of bread'. Under the direct influence of Ligniville's *Stabat mater* (Florence, 1768) Mozart composed his own five-part Kyrie κ89/73*k* and copied out nine of its 30 canonic movements (κAnh.238/Anh. 109ᴵᴵ). Martini wrote to Ligniville about this work on behalf of the Accademia Filarmonica: 'Your excellency makes flourish again in this century that study that had somewhat declined, by spreading through your *Stabat* the most singular and artful canons, which have been practised by the most celebrated masters of centuries gone by'. Ligniville also published two canonic settings of the *Salve regina* (Bologna, *c*1760–62; Florence, *c*1770). A three-part madrigal by him is in the Fitzwilliam Museum, Cambridge, and a *Dixit* for four voices and orchestra at Tenbury.

BIBLIOGRAPHY

FétisB
C. Burney: *The Present State of Music in France and Italy* (London, 1771, 2/1773); ed. P. Scholes as *Dr. Burney's Musical Tours* (London, 1959)
E. Anderson, ed.: *The Letters of Mozart and his Family* (London, 1938, 2/1966)

FERRUCCIO TAMMARO

Lilburn, Douglas (Gordon) (*b* Wanganui, 2 Nov 1915). New Zealand composer. He studied journalism and music, under J. C. Bradshaw, at Canterbury University College (1934–6). In 1936 Percy Grainger awarded him the Grainger Prize for his overture *In the Forest*, which committed him to music rather than literature, for which he had decided gifts. At the Royal College of Music, London (1937–40), his teacher Vaughan Williams made a lifelong impression, through both his personality and his music. He was appointed part-time lecturer in music at Victoria University of Wellington (1947), lecturer (1949), associate professor (1963) and professor and director of the university's electronic music studio (1970). Visits to studios in Toronto and Europe in 1963 had led him shortly afterwards to establish the first electronic music studio in Australasia, since when he has trained a generation of young composers, some of whom have won international recognition.

Lilburn is a New Zealand composer with an authentic voice, an individual utterance and the power to evoke both a real and visionary landscape. He has overcome the at times crippling difficulties of working on the outer fringe of European musical culture and forged from unpromising material (a negligible folk inheritance, a pastiche English church and pastoral tradition) a highly articulate, unmistakable personal style that has undergone metamorphosis through three principal periods. The first, rhapsodic and astringently romantic, absorbed influences of Sibelius and Vaughan Williams and culminated in the Second Symphony (1951). The second traversed Bartók, Stravinsky, contemporary Americans and the Second Viennese School to end in the Third Symphony (1961). The third phase, still evolving, is concerned with electronic music.

Lilburn's early works include the Phantasy String Quartet, which won the Cobbett Prize (1939), and the overture *Aotearoa* (1940), first performed by Warwick Braithwaite at a New Zealand centenary matinée concert at His Majesty's Theatre, London. (*Aotearoa*, 'land of the long white cloud', is the Maori name for New Zealand; the title was given by Braithwaite.) This work projected a shimmering impression of a sea-spumed coast with the pure light that floods Katherine Mansfield's short stories when she writes of the sea. Lilburn's gift for the nuances and character of landscape found further telling expression in the string interludes in *Landfall in Unknown Seas* (1942), a setting for speaker and strings of Alan Curnow's poem, composed as a tercentenary celebration of Tasman's discovery of New Zealand.

Sensitive to the visual world as much as to words and music, Lilburn responded to the work of a group of young poets and painters working in Christchurch after his return to New Zealand. They included the poet Denis Glover and the artists Leo Bensemann and Rita Angus. Thenceforth a number of works were to have their origin in poems and paintings, and he gradually transmuted early influences of Sibelius and Vaughan Williams into his own lyrical and tersely energetic style. Quick to appreciate individual performers' abilities and to improvise where a sparse musical context provided few opportunities, he wrote effective chamber works, such as the Chaconne for piano (1946) and the Violin Sonata (1950). *Diversions* (1947) was written for the visit of the Boyd Neel String Orchestra. His feeling for the work of a group of young poets who emerged in the late 1940s brought about the fine song cycle *Elegy* (1951) to poems of Alistair Campbell, evoking the harsh, dramatic Clutha Valley of central Otago, a region with which he has a particular sympathy. The South Island back country permeates another cycle, *Sings Harry* (1953), in which Glover celebrated a solitary, idiosyncratic New Zealand character. Lilburn's work in the traditional media virtually came to an end in his Symphony no.3 (1961), a beautifully crafted, epigrammatic work in a single movement; the long melodic sweep has yielded to an explosive, disturbingly spiky style in a work of the utmost cohesion and unity.

Always a practical composer, Lilburn has a strong dramatic sense when writing for film and theatre, owing much in this respect to Ngaio Marsh and other producers. A sense of occasion is also to be found in his electronic work, which includes music for the ballet, theatre and television, all fresh explorations of the sound sources of a uniquely Pacific world. In *The Return* (1965), for instance, he used Campbell's haunting poem, a merging of classical and Polynesian imagery. Behind *Three Inscapes* (1972) lie those same insights that throughout his career have enabled him to project an essence of the New Zealand landscape.

Lilburn's forceful, generous personality has made him an important advocate of composers' rights, as when, almost single-handed, he led a successful campaign in 1960 against the government's proposed regressive copyright legislation. He has persevered amid much ignorant commentary. Composition in New Zealand has a continuity, commitment and purpose it would signally have lacked but for him.

WORKS
(selective list)

Orch: In the Forest, ov., 1936; Aotearoa, ov., 1940; Allegro, str, 1942; Diversions, str, 1947; Sym. no.1, 1948; Sym. no.2, 1951; Suite, 1955; A Birthday Offering, 1956; 3 Poems of the Sea, 1958; Sym. no.3, 1961

Vocal: Landfall in Unknown Seas (A. Curnow), speaker, str orch, 1942; Song of the Antipodes, chorus, 1946; Elegy (A. Campbell), song cycle, 1v, pf, 1951; Sings Harry (D. Glover), song cycle, 1v, pf, 1953; 3 Songs, Bar, va, 1958

Chamber: Phantasy Str Qt, 1939; Str Trio, 1945; Sonata, vn, pf, 1950; Duo, 2 vn, 1954; Wind Qnt, 1957

Pf: Chaconne, 1946; Sonatina no.1, 1946; Sonata, 1949; Sonatina no.2, 1962; 9 Short Pieces, 1966

Tape: The Return (Campbell), 1965; Poem in Time of War, 1967; Summer Voices, 1969; 3 Inscapes, 1972

Principal publisher: Price Milburn

J. M. THOMSON

Lilien, Ignace (*b* Lwów, 29 May 1897; *d* The Hague, 10 May 1964). Dutch composer and pianist of Polish birth. He moved to the Netherlands in 1914 where he trained as an engineer at the Technical University in Delft. He had previously studied the piano with Theodor Pollak, harmony with H. Ehrlich and orchestration with Suk. From 1918 he became known as a pianist in Europe and South America, principally as a performer of his own compositions. The influence of South American folk music is evident, for example, in the symphonic poem *Les palmes dans le vent*. His works, technically conventional, were performed fairly frequently during his lifetime.

WORKS
(selective list)

Orch: 4 syms.; Conc., vn, pf, orch, 1954; Les palmes dans le vent, sym. poem, 1955; Conc. da camera, fl, str, 1962

Vocal: Beatrijs (opera, Teirlinck), 1928; Great Catherine (opera, after Shaw), 1932; Nyuk tsin, oratorio, 1961; many songs, some to South American texts

Inst: Sonatine apollonique, wind, 1939; Voyage au printemps, wind qnt, 1950–52; 24 hiéroglyphes, pf, 1956

Principal publisher: Donemus

BIBLIOGRAPHY

W. Paap: 'Concert voor viool, piano en orkest van Ignace Lilien', *Mens en melodie*, x (1955), 54

——: 'De opera Beatrijs van Ignace Lilien', *Mens en melodie*, xi (1956), 392

——: 'Nyuk Tsin, dramatisch oratorium van Ignace Lilien', *Mens en melodie*, xix (1964), 124

——: 'Ignace Lilien †', *Mens en melodie*, xix (1964), 174

ROGIER STARREVELD

Liliencron, Rochus Freiherr **(Traugott Ferdinand) von** (*b* Plön, Holstein, 8 Dec 1820; *d* Koblenz, 5 March 1912). German musicologist. He was educated at Plön

and Lübeck before studying theology, law and philology at the universities of Kiel and Berlin, receiving the doctorate in 1846 for a dissertation entitled *Über Neidharts höfische Dorfpoesie*. After a short period of Old Norse studies at Copenhagen and qualifying as a lecturer at the University of Bonn, he entered the diplomatic service during the first Schleswig-Holstein war. He taught Old Norse language and literature at the University of Kiel in 1851 and philology from 1852 at Jena. From 1855 to 1858 he was at the court of the Duke of Saxe-Meiningen, where he conducted the court orchestra, supervised the library and was also privy-councillor. The newly founded historical commission of the Royal Bavarian Academy of Science commissioned him in 1858 to collect German folksongs. This work resulted in the publication of *Die historischen Volkslieder der Deutschen* (1865–9). Subsequently he settled in Munich as editor of the *Allgemeine deutsche Biographie* (with F. X. von Wegele), which was his life's work until 1907. He became prelate and prior of the monastery of the Order of St John in Schleswig in 1876 and continued his activity as a scholar and writer there before moving his family to Berlin in 1909 and Koblenz in March 1911. His many distinctions included an honorary doctorate from the University of Kiel (1890), membership of the Munich Academy of Science (1869) and the presidency of the editorial commission of the Denkmäler deutscher Tonkunst.

Liliencron was one of the pillars of German musicology. His importance rests mainly on his editorial, organizational and cultural-historical work. With his expertise in philology and literature and training in theology, he contributed much as editor of *ADB* (Leipzig, i–liii, 1875–1907). He also supervised the publication of some 45 volumes of the Denkmäler deutscher Tonkunst.

WRITINGS

with W. Stade: *Lieder und Sprüche aus der letzten Zeit des Minnesangs* (Weimar, 1854)

Die historischen Volkslieder der Deutschen vom 13. bis 16. Jahrhundert (Leipzig, 1865–9/*R*1966)

Deutsches Leben im Volkslied um 1530 (Berlin and Stuttgart, 1885/*R*1966)

Die horazischen Metren in deutschen Kompositionen des XVI. Jahrhunderts (Leipzig, 1887)

Liturgisch-musikalische Geschichte der evangelischen Gottesdienste von 1523 bis 1700 (Schleswig, 1893)

Die Aufgaben des Chorgesanges im heutigen evangelischen Gottesdienste (Oppeln, 1895)

Chorordnung für die Sonn- und Festtage des evangelischen Kirchenjahres (Gütersloh, 1900)

Volksliederbuch für Männerchöre (Leipzig, 1906)

BIBLIOGRAPHY

A. Biese: 'Rochus Freiherr von Liliencron', *Biographische Blätter*, ed. A. Bettelheim, ii (Berlin, 1896), 388

R. von Liliencron: *Frohe Jugendtage, Lebenserinnerungen, Kindern und Enkeln erzählt* (Leipzig, 1902)

H. Kretzschmar, ed.: *Festschrift zum 90. Geburtstag Sr. Exzellenz . . . Freiherrn von Liliencron* (Leipzig, 1910)

F. W. Franke: *Liturgische Kirchenmusik und Rochus von Liliencrons neue 'Chorordnung'* (Gütersloh, 1911)

E. Schröder: 'Rochus Freiherr von Liliencron', *Bettelheims Biographisches Jahrbuch und deutscher Nekrolog*, xvii (1915), 185

A. Bettelheim: *Leben und Wirken des Freiherrn Rochus von Liliencron* (Berlin, 1917)

O. von Hase: *Breitkopf und Härtel: Gedenkschrift* (Leipzig, 4/1917–19)

H. J. Moser: *Die evangelische Kirchenmusik in Deutschland* (Berlin and Darmstadt, 1953)

GAYNOR G. JONES

Lilius [Gigli]. Family of musicians of Italian origin resident in Poland. Their family relationships with each other are unknown.

(1) **Wincenty** [Vincentius] **Lilius** [Gigli, Vincenzo] (*b*

Rome; *d* ?Warsaw, *c*1640). Composer. In the 1590s he was active at the archducal court at Graz, then from about 1600 until his death in King Sigismund III's chapel at Kraków and Warsaw. He edited a collection of polychoral motets, *Melodiae sacrae* (Kraków, 1604²), containing works for five to eight and 12 voices by members of the royal chapel, among them a 12-part motet of his own, *Congratulamini mihi omnes*.

(2) Szymon [Simon] Lilius [Liliusz, Lilio, Lelia] (*d* ?Warsaw, after 1652). Organist and organ builder. He was connected with the court and active in Warsaw before 1622, when he settled at nearby Kazimierz Dolny. He built, among others, the famous organ in this town.

(3) Franciszek [Franciscus] Lilius (*d* ?Gromnik, nr. Tarnów, Aug or Sept 1657). Composer. He was for a time active as a musician and composer in King Sigismund III's chapel in Warsaw and then from 1630 to 1657 was director of music at Kraków Cathedral. About 1636 he took holy orders and in later years received a number of benefices. He left Kraków in 1655, when during the war with Sweden the enemy threatened the city: he went to Tarnów or, more probably, to Gromnik and died in one of these places. For 25 years he was the leading musician in Kraków. His works in the concertato style, only a few of which survive, were very popular, and although not printed some were also performed in Wrocław, Gdańsk and as far afield as Lüneburg. One polychoral piece and a number of *a cappella* works in the *prima prattica* style that are also extant are chiefly for male voices and were thus intended for the Rorantists' chapel at Kraków Cathedral.

WORKS

4 songs, 4vv, in Nabożne pieśni [Religious songs], ed. B. Derej (Kraków, 1645)
10 masses (8 inc.), *PL-Pu*
7 motets: Confitebor tibi, Domine, 4vv, *Pu*; Dextera Domini, formerly *USSR-KA*, extant only in pre-war transcr. by A. Chybiński; Domine rex Deus, 5vv, *PL-Kpa*; Haec dies, 2vv, bc, formerly *GD*, ed. Z. M. Szweykowski, *Muzyka w dawnym Krakowie* (Kraków, 1964); Jubilate Deo, 5vv, 2 vn, va, 2 trbn, bn, bc, formerly *USSR-KA*, ed. in WDMP, xl (2/1963); Recordare Domine, 4vv, *PL-Kpa*; Tua Jesu dilectio, 2vv, bc, formerly *GD*, ed. in WDMP, lvi (1965)
4 sacred works, formerly *WRu*, lost; 3 sacred works, formerly *D-Lm*, lost

BIBLIOGRAPHY

S. Chodyński: *Organy, śpiew i muzyka w kościele katedralnym włocławskim* [Organ, voices and music at Włocławek Cathedral] (Włocławek, 1902)
A. Chybiński: 'Muzycy włoscy w krakowskich kapelach katedralnych (1619–1657)' [Italian musicians at Kraków Cathedral (1619–57)], *Przegląd muzyczny*, iii (1927), nos.2–5, 7–8 [incl. list of works]
H. Feicht: 'Przyczynki do dziejów kapeli królewskiej w Warszawie za rządów kapelmistrzowskich Marka Scacchiego' [Contribution to the history of the royal chapel in Warsaw under the musical directorship of Marco Scacchi], *KM*, i (1928–9), 20
Z. Szweykowski: 'Franciszek Lilius i jego twórczość na tle współczesnego baroku w Polsce' [Franciszek Lilius and his music in the context of the contemporary Baroque period in Poland], *Muzyka*, v/1 (1960), 78; vii/4 (1962), 51
K. Parfianowicz: 'Szymon Liliusz organmistrz kazimierski', *Ruch muzyczny*, xiii/3 (1969), 12

ZYGMUNT M. SZWEYKOWSKI

Liljefors, Ingemar (Kristian) (*b* Göteborg, 13 Dec 1906). Swedish composer and pianist, son of Ruben Liljefors. He studied at the Stockholm Conservatory (1923–7, 1929–31) and in Munich (1927–9); in 1933 he passed the organists' examination. He taught the piano (1938–43) and then harmony at the Stockholm Musikhögskolan. In 1933 he participated in the founding of the Fylkingen concert society, which he chaired until 1946; from 1947 to 1963 he was chairman of the

Society of Swedish Composers. He was assistant music critic of the *Stockholms-tidningen* (1941–54). His early compositions combined Swedish folk elements with Stravinskian rhythm; later he made moderate use of new techniques in music of meditative and lyrical expressiveness.

WORKS
(*selective list*)

Orch: Suite, op.2, 1935; Rhapsody, op.5, pf, orch, 1936; Berget, op.6, tone poem, 1937; Pf Conc., op.11, 1940; Sym., op.15, 1943; Lyric Suite, op.18, small orch, 1942; 2 divertimentos, opp.21, 23, str, 1945, 1946; Pf Concertino, op.22, 1949; Sinfonietta, op.30, 1961
Inst: 2 pf trios, op.12, 1940, op.29, n.d.; Sonatine, C, pf, 1954; Sonatine, D, vn, pf, 1954; Trio, vn, va, pf, 1961; Str Qt, 1963; pf pieces
Vocal: En tijdh-spegel, chorus, orch, 1959; songs

Principal publisher: Föreningen Svenska Tonsättare

WRITINGS

Harmonilärans grunder, med ackordanalys enligt funktionsteorin (Stockholm, 1937)
Harmonisk analys enligt funktionsteorin (Stockholm, 1951)
Romantisk harmonik ur pedagogisk synvinkel (Stockholm, 1967)

BIBLIOGRAPHY

Å. Brandel: 'Kring trettitalisterna' [On the musicians of the 1930s], *Musikrevy* (1959), 267

ROLF HAGLUND

Liljefors, Ruben (Mattias) (*b* Uppsala, 30 Sept 1871; *d* Uppsala, 4 March 1936). Swedish composer and conductor. In the years 1895–6 and 1897–9 he studied composition with Jadassohn in Leipzig and with Draeseke and Reger in Dresden, and conducting with Kutzschbach. He was conductor of the Göteborgs Filharmoniska Sällskap (1902–11) and was then active principally in Gävle as a music teacher at the graduate school and conductor of the Gävleborgs Orkesterförening (1912–31). His works reveal a technically skilled composer rooted in the Scandinavian tradition (particularly Sjögren and Grieg) and in certain respects also influenced by Brahms, Reger and others; the choral works and solo songs were especially admired.

WORKS
(*selective list*)

Orch: Pf Conc., 1899; Sym., E♭, 1906; Concert Ov., 1908; Romans, vn, orch
Vocal: Blomsterfursten [The flower king], chorus, orch, 1907; Bohuslän, cantata, chorus, orch, 1908; pieces for male chorus, songs
Inst: Pf Sonata, f (1938); Vn Sonata, e

Edn.: *Upländsk folkmusik* (Stockholm, 1929)

Principal publishers: Gehrman, Raabe & Plothow

BIBLIOGRAPHY

K. Håkanson: 'Ruben Liljefors', *Ur nutidens musikliv*, iii (1922), 65

AXEL HELMER

Lill, John (Richard) (*b* London, 17 March 1944). English pianist. He studied at the RCM (1955–64) and privately with Kempff at Positano. A respectable career, with débuts at the Festival Hall (1963, in Beethoven's 'Emperor' Concerto) and at Carnegie Hall, New York in 1969, was given considerable impetus after he won the 1970 Tchaikovsky Competition in Moscow; since then he has appeared with orchestras and in recital throughout the world, and on television, in addition to recording concertos by Brahms and Beethoven. His commanding physical power and technique in the Chopin, Liszt, Rakhmaninov and Prokofiev works that form part of his large repertory are not always complemented by an equivalent care for atmosphere and tone-colour; however, particularly in Beethoven, the vigour and large scale of his playing are often greatly impressive. He was made an OBE in 1978.

MAX LOPPERT

Lille. Town in northern France, formerly the capital of

Flanders. The first documents to mention musical life date from the 11th century. The foundation charter of St Peter's collegiate church (1066) provided for the maintenance of a *maître de chapelle* and of a school for choirboys. Several 13th-century MSS record the activities of the trouvères of Lille; they include songs by Pierre li Borgnes, Maroie de Dregnau, Jehan Fremaus and Li Tresoriers de Lille. In 1306 an organ was built in St Peter's. It was in Lille that the famous 'Feast of the Pheasant' took place (in 1454, on the occasion of a projected crusade against the Turks), during which motets and songs by Dufay and Binchois were performed. Three songs and a *Missa 'O admirabilis'* have preserved the names of two 15th-century composers: Francus de Insula (i.e. from Lille) and Simon de Insula. In the 16th century the choir school attached to the collegiate church was evidently held in high repute, for the Emperor Charles V asked the chapter to send him choirboys for his own chapel (1543).

In 1667, Lille was conquered by Louis XIV, and operas and ballets began to be performed in the town. The composer Pascal Collasse was granted a privilege to have an opera house built, but in November 1700 it was burnt down after a performance of Charpentier's *Médée*. A new house was opened two years later; in a single year (1720) more than ten operas were performed (by Lully, Collasse, Charpentier, Destouches, Campra etc). At this period the Company comprised six actors, four actresses, 12 singers and dancers of both sexes and an orchestra of 13 (the composer Mondonville was the first violinist between 1734 and 1737). Grétry, staying in Lille in 1783, stated that the orchestra could compare favourably with that of the Italian Theatre in Paris. At the same period several musical societies flourished: the Concerts d'Amateurs, Concerts de M.M. les Abonnés, Concerts Spirituels, etc. In 1787, the Lille-born architect Lequeux built a new opera house. In 1800 the Société du Concert (founded 1798) gave the first performance in France of Haydn's *The Creation*. The following year a singing school was founded for 12 boys and 12 girls; in 1816 it became a music school, a branch of the Paris Conservatoire. The Lille public first heard Berlioz's Requiem in 1838, when Habeneck conducted a performance of the Lacrymosa. On 4 June 1846, under the direction of Berlioz, the orchestras of Lille, Douai and Valenciennes (150 performers) gave his *Chants des chemins de fer*, a cantata composed on the occasion of the Northern Railways inauguration. Composers born in Lille in the 19th century include Lalo (1823), E. Mathieu (1844) and Grovlez (1879).

St Peter's no longer exists; it was destroyed during the Revolution. The new cathedral, Notre Dame de la Treille, has a plainsong school. Concerts of sacred music are usually given at St Maurice's, a Gothic church in the centre of the town; but the best organ (built by Muller in 1958) is in the church of SS Peter and Paul. There are two playhouses in Lille, both built at the beginning of the 20th century: the Théâtre de l'Opéra (1500 seats) and the Théâtre Sébastopol (1450 seats). The musical season lasts from October to May, and concerts are given by the symphony orchestra of Lille Broadcasting House, the chamber orchestra of the conservatory, and the band of the 43rd Regiment of Infantry. The Academy of Music, Drama and Dance (Conservatoire National de Région) is one of the most important in the provinces.

GEORGES DOTTIN

Lillo, Giuseppe (*b* Galatina, Lecce, 26 Feb 1814; *d* Naples, 4 Feb 1863). Italian composer and pianist. Having received his first music lessons from his father, the conductor Giosuè Lillo, he studied counterpoint with L. Carnovale in Lecce. He completed his studies at the Reale Collegio di Musica (after 1826 the Conservatorio di S Pietro a Majella) in Naples, where he studied harmony and counterpoint with Furno, the piano with Francesco Lanza, and composition with Zingarelli. He made a successful début as a composer with a mass for four voices and orchestra. In 1834 he staged his first opera, *La moglie per 24 ore ossia L'ammalato di buona salute*; after this success he dedicated himself mainly to music for the theatre, winning much popularity with the Naples public; this first period of his career culminated with *L'osteria di Andujar* (1840), which was a great success and remains his most celebrated work. Various failures followed, and for a few years he abandoned composing for the theatre and began teaching the piano. In 1845 he became *ispettore dei partimenti* of the schools attached to the Naples Conservatory, and professor of harmony the following year. He visited Paris in 1847–8, and received support from Spontini. In 1859 he succeeded Carlo Conti as professor of counterpoint and composition at the Naples Conservatory, but in 1861 the first symptoms appeared of the insanity that later led to his death.

Lillo's theatrical works show him to be a faithful follower of Rossini, with a rich melodic vein in which the vocal virtuosity is always subjected to expressive aims; his piano music, which seems outdated, is of less significance.

WORKS

OPERAS

La moglie per 24 ore ossia L'ammalato di buona salute (A. Passaro), Naples, Reale Collegio di Musica, 1834
Il gioiello (L. Tarantini), Naples, Teatro Nuovo, aut. 1835
Odda di Bernaver (E. Bidera), Naples, Teatro S Carlo, 1837
Rosmunda in Ravenna (L. A. Paladini), Venice, Teatro La Fenice, 1837
Alisa di Rieux (G. Rossi), Rome, Teatro Valle, 1838
Il conte di Chalais (S. Cammarano), Naples, Teatro S Carlo, 1839
La modista, Florence, Teatro della Pergola, 1839
L'osteria di Andujar (Tarantini), Naples, Teatro del Fondo, Sept 1840
Le disgrazie di un bel giovane ossia Il zio e il nipote (Tarantini), Florence, Teatro della Pergola, 1840
Cristina di Svezia (Cammarano), Naples, Teatro S Carlo, 1841
Lara (Tarantini), Naples, Teatro S Carlo, 1842
Il cavaliere di S Giorgio ossia Il mulatto, Turin, 1846
Caterina Howard (G. Giachetti), Naples, Teatro S Carlo, 1849
La delfina (M. d'Arienzo), Naples, Teatro Nuovo, March 1850
La gioventù di Shakespeare ossia Il sogno d'una notte estiva (G. S. Giannini), Naples, Teatro Nuovo, 1851
Il figlio della schiava (Giannini), Naples, Teatro del Fondo, 1853
Ser Babbeo (E. Bardare), Naples, Teatro Nuovo, 1853

OTHER WORKS

Sacred choral works, incl. mass, 4vv, orch; syms., other orch works; str qt; qt, pf, fl, vn, vc; pf trio; pf solo works, incl. variation sets on opera themes

BIBLIOGRAPHY

FétisB; *RicordiE*; *SchmidlD*
F. Florimo: *La scuola musicale di Napoli e i suoi conservatorii* (Naples, 1880–83/R1969)
L. A. Villanis: *L'arte del pianoforte in Italia* (Turin, 1907)
G. Saponaro: 'Lillo, Giuseppe', *ES*

FRANCESCO BUSSI

Lilly [Lillie], John (*b* early 17th century; *d* London, 25 Oct 1678). English theorbo and division viol player, music copyist and composer. At the Restoration he joined the King's Private Musick, and remained active in court service until his death. Previously he had lived in Cambridge, where he was patronized by the North family, and at some time taught Roger North the theorbo. The latter wrote of him *c*1730 as being an old man, and as 'having a great expensive family, hardly maintaining them'. He was also a friend of the composer John Jenkins. He was active in the Westminster Corporation at least from 1664. His viol playing is praised in a poem 'To Mr. Lilly, Musick-Master in Cambridge' in Nicholas Hookes's collection *Amanda* (1653). Several MSS in his hand have been identified, among them sets of parts written for Edward Lowe of Oxford, and Christopher, 1st Baron Hatton. A few of his compositions in tablature for lute or viol are found in John Playford's *A Musicall Banquet* (London, 1651) and *Musick's Recreation on the Lyra Viol* (London, 1652, 1661 and 1669 edns.) and in MSS at *GB-Cu*, *Mp* and *Ob*.

BIBLIOGRAPHY
P. J. Willetts: 'John Lilly, musician and music copyist', *Bodleian Library Record*, vii (1967), 307

RICHARD M. ANDREWES

Lilt. Originally a Scots word meaning to sing in a low clear voice, with sweetness of tone and light, cheerful rhythm, or to sing a song without the words, particularly at a solitary task such as milking. Lilts were usually sung by women; in *The Flowers of the Forest* Scott wrote: 'I've heard them lilting at the ewes milking, *Lasses* a-lilting before dawn of day'; Robert Fergusson, in *Poems*, wrote: 'Nae mair ... shepherds ... wi' blytheness skip, Or lasses lilt and sing', and James Hogg, in *The Jacobite Relics of Scotland*, gave the word a note of sadness, with 'A lilt o' dool and sorrow'. The lilt of a song or tune may mean its proper air and characteristic expression; thus, in J. G. Lockhart's *Memoirs of the Life of Sir Walter Scott*, i, p.197: '... auld Thomas o' Tuzzilehope, ... celebrated in particular for being in possession of the real lilt of *Dick o' the Cow*'.

Another occasional meaning of lilt is to play a tune on a shepherd's pipe or stock-and-horn: 'The beastes ... which soberly they hameward drive, With pipe and lilting horn' (A. Hume: *Hymns*, 1594).

Richard de Holand's *Buke of the Howlat* (1450) mentions, among a list of other musical instruments, the lilt-pipe, a term having obvious affinity with the Dutch *lullepijp*, a bagpipe or shepherd's pipe.

The Skene MS (*GB-En* Adv.5.2.15, *c*1630) contains six short pieces for lute, called 'lilts'. These do not appear to possess any common musical factor of rhythm, tempo or mode which could suggest a musical definition of the word. It would seem that here 'lilt' is simply a fanciful name for a tune.

FRANCIS COLLINSON

Lima. Capital of Peru, called 'City of the Kings', founded in 1535 by Pizarro, who laid the cornerstone of the cathedral. In Peru as in Mexico, the Indians took immediately to the music of the friars sent to evangelize them. Pedro de la Gasca (1492–1565), Peru's first law-giver, summoned representatives of all three mendicant orders to Lima in 1549 and told them that they must learn Quechua, set up schools and teach the Indians such 'good things' as how to sing according to the rules of art and how to sol-fa (*dezir el sol, fa, mi, re*). Gasca's precise instructions were strengthened by the ruling of the Third Lima Council (1583) requiring systematic music instruction at every Indian mission. By 1622 Bernabé Cobo could cite the music of the Jesuit Indian church at Lima, Santiago del Cercado, as equal to that heard in most Spanish cathedrals. In that year the parish church owned two organs, four sets of shawms, two trumpets, viols of various sizes and other instruments for feast-day use.

The first polyphony printed in the New World was a Quechua four-part chanzoneta in sprightly march time, *Hanacpachap cussicuinin* (Juan Pérez Bocanegra, *Ritual formulario*, Lima, 1631, pp.708f; copies in the National Library of Peru and *US-Wc*). The earliest extant New World opera was mounted in the vice-regal palace at Lima (19 October 1701): Tomás de Torrejón y Velasco's setting of Pedro Calderón de la Barca's *La púrpura de la rosa*.

Lima Cathedral, the seat of an archbishop from 1549, had a distinguished succession of *maestros de capilla* during the vice-regal epoch (to 1821). Domingo Álvarez signed the first Lima Council constitutions (20 February 1552). The succentor Cristóbal de Molina (*fl* 1534–64), teacher of Pizarro's mestizo daughter Francisca, arrived in Peru already 'known in Italy and France'. The cathedral organist and *maestro de capilla* of the years 1612–14, Estacio de la Serna, had been royal chapel organist at Lisbon; and he and his successors Cristóbal de Belsayaga (1622–30), Pedro Ximénez (1657–68), Juan de Araujo (1670–76), Tomás de Torrejón y Velasco (1676–1728), Roque Ceruti (1728–60), José de Orejón y Aparicio (1760–65), and Juan Beltrán (1799–1807) left extant music which is generally of excellent technical quality. As at Mexico City, the Lima *maestro de capilla* ran a cathedral choir school, directed musical forces that always included at least six adult professional singers and an equal number of instrumentalists, maintained a choral library and composed new music for the chief annual festivals. Outside the cathedral the best music in Lima during the vice-regal period was at Encarnación Convent.

Lima exceeded even Mexico City in its lavish support of drama. The plays presented by contracted troupes from 1613, especially the Calderonian *autos sacramentales* (from 1670 to the end of the century) nearly always included solo songs, vocal ensembles, instrumental music and accompanied dances. With Ceruti and Bartolomé Mazza (*c*1725–99) the Lima lyric stage began to be dominated by emigrant Italian composers; Mazza composed nearly all the extant Lima stage music for two decades. His company was famous and notorious for its singing actresses.

The Peruvian national anthem, first performed in the Lima Teatro on 24 September 1821, was composed by the native of Lima José Bernardo Alcedo (Alzedo) (1788–1878); until 1946 the National Academy of Music bore his name. As early as 1748 blacks imported from the coasts of Guinea and Senegal and from the Congo to Lima numbered some 10,000, and in 1791 their music formed the subject of an article published in *Mercurio Peruano*, xlviii and xlix. Alcedo, Manuel de la Cruz Panizo (*d* 20 March 1889) and several other leading locally born 19th-century composers were of partly African descent. However, Lima concert and operatic life continued to be controlled mainly by European emigrants including Francesco Paolo Francia (1834–1904), Anton Neumann (Neumane) (1818–71), Carlo Enrico Pasta (1817–98), Claudio Rebagliatti (1833–1909) and his brother Reynaldo.

Pasta composed the first opera on an Inca subject to be presented at Lima, *Atahualpa* (libretto by Antonio Ghislanzoni), first performed at the Teatro Principal on

11 January 1877 and repeated eight times. A new Teatro Principal seating 1400 was inaugurated (11 December 1889) with the zarzuela *El hermano Baltasar*, to be replaced by still another theatre, now called the Municipal, authorized by the Peruvian Congress in 1901 and opened in 1904. The first native of Lima to compose an opera on a national subject was José María Valle Riestra (*b* 9 Nov 1859; *d* 25 Jan 1925), whose *Ollanta* was repeated 12 times after its première at the Teatro Principal on 26 December 1900.

The Orquesta Sinfónica Nacional was established by decree on 11 August 1938 and gave its first concert that year with 70 members in the Teatro Municipal under the Austrian Theo Buchwald. He was succeeded by the German Hans-Günther Mommer (1960–63), the native Peruvian Armando Sánchez Málaga (1963–4), the Mexican Luis Herrera de la Fuente (1964–6 and 1969–70), and the Peruvians José Belaúnde Moreyra (1966–9), Carmen Moral and Leopoldo la Rosa Urbani (1970–74).

The Academia Nacional de Música Alzedo, founded on 12 January 1929, was renamed the Conservatorio Nacional de Música on 30 March 1946 and the Escuela Nacional de Música on 11 January 1972, when it became associated with the newly-formed Instituto Nacional de Cultura. Its directors have included Carlos Sánchez Málaga (1960–68), José Malsio (1968–73) and the composer Enrique Iturriaga (*b* 1918). There were 160 students in 1970 and 600 by 1973.

In 1973 Victoria Santa Cruz directed the Conjunto Nacional de Folklore, Mildred Merino de Cela the Escuela Nacional de Folklore, Arndt von Gavel the recording chorus of the Asociación Artística y Cultural 'Jueves' (founded 17 August 1964) and Manuel Cuadros Barr the other chief recording chorus in Lima, the Camerata Vocale Orfeo Perú. On 1 July 1973 Armando Sánchez Málaga became executive director of the National Institute of Culture, the government department responsible for all subsidized orchestras, choruses, art and music schools, libraries and museums in the country.

The chief collection of pre-Hispanic Peruvian musical instruments is housed at the Museum of Anthropology and Archaeology, Plaza Bolívar, Pueblo Libre. The largest collection of colonial music MSS belongs to the Archivo Arzobispal, adjacent to Lima Cathedral. S Marcos University, founded in 1551, is the oldest in the continent.

BIBLIOGRAPHY

O. Mayer-Serra: *Música y músicos de Latinoamérica* (Mexico City, 1947), i, 3; ii, 710f, 765–72

R. Barbacci: 'Apuntes para un Diccionario Biográfico Musical Peruano', *Fénix*, vi (1949), 414–510

C. Raygada: 'Guía musical del Perú', *Fénix*, xii (1956), 3–77; xiii (1963), 1–82; xiv (1964), 3–95

R. Stevenson: *The Music of Peru* (Washington, 1960)

A. Sas: 'La vida musical en la Catedral de Lima durante la colonia', *Revista musical chilena* (1962), nos.79–82, pp.8–53

R. Stevenson: 'Lima', *Renaissance and Baroque Musical Sources in the Americas* (Washington, 1970), 110

A. Sas: *La música en la Catedral de Lima durante el Virreinato* (Lima, 1970–72)

R. Stevenson: *Foundations of New World Opera with a transcription of the earliest extant American opera, 1701* (Lima, 1973)

ROBERT STEVENSON

Lima, Braz Francisco de [Bras Francisco de, Biaggio Francesco] (*b* Lisbon, ?3 May 1752; *d* Lisbon, 25 Sept 1813). Portuguese composer. On 15 January 1761 he entered the Conservatorio di S Onofrio at Naples, along with his elder brother Jeronymo Francisco de Lima. He

then distinguished himself in his studies at the Seminário Patriarcal in Lisbon, and on 19 March 1785 his oratorio *Il trionfo di Davidde* was performed at the royal palace at Ajuda (score in *P-La*). From 1785 he also composed sacred works, some of which are in the Lisbon Cathedral archives. He went to Italy in about 1790 for further music study, but upon returning to Lisbon he abandoned music in favour of a business career.

For bibliography *see* LIMA, JERONYMO FRANCISCO DE.

ROBERT STEVENSON

Lima, Candido (*b* nr. Viana do Castelo, 22 Aug 1939). Portuguese composer. He studied at the conservatories of Braga, Lisbon and Oporto and then, on a Gulbenkian Foundation scholarship, travelled abroad to attend courses given by Stockhausen, Xenakis, Kagel, Ligeti and others. His compositional style has evolved from impressionism through 12-note serialism to embrace later techniques. Besides composing he has done important educational work, both as a teacher at the Oporto Conservatory and as a writer.

WORKS
(*selective list*)

STAGE AND ORCHESTRAL

Stage: Morte de um caixeiro viajante (incidental music, A. Miller), 1974; Histoire d'un enfant (teatro musical, Lima), fl, cl, pf, perc, vn, 1973–5; Liberdade de dizer não (teatro coreográfico, P. Barbosa, J. Martins, J. Coimbra), perc, org, 2 pf 8 hands, 1975

Orch: Epitáfio para Franz Kafka, orch, pf obbl., 1970; Canções estáticas, orch, vn obbl., 1971; Visões geométricas, chamber orch, 1972, full orch version as Oceanos cósmicos, 1973

VOCAL

Choral: Bailado do vento (A. Lopes Vieira), 1v, 5vv, pf, 1962; Canção lenta (Pessoa), 5vv, 1965; 2 poemas novos (M. Alegre), vv, pf, drums, 1974; 3 canções livres (Alegre), vv, pf, drums, 1974; Sol (Lima), 12vv, 1975

Solo vocal: Cristo (S. da Gama), 1v, pf, 1963; Manhã (da Gama), 1v, pf, 1963; Caminho (da Gama), 1v, pf, 1964; Nevoeiro (da Gama), 1v, pf, 1964; Tão vago é o vento (Pessoa), 1v, pf, 1964; Não quero mais que um som de água (Pessoa), 1v, pf, 1964; Começa a haver meia-noite (Pessoa), 1v, pf, 1965; Magnificat (Pessoa), 1v, perc, 1965, also for 1v, pf, 1970, 1v, orch, 1973; Impressões do crepúsculo (Pessoa), 1v, fl, vn, pf, 1967, orchd 1973; Desfraldando (Pessoa), 1v, pf, 1967; Música para 2 sonetos de Camões, 1v, fl, cl, pf, 1973; Poema (Lima), 4vv, pf, 1975

Arrs.: Espirituais negros, 1v/4 solo vv, pf, 1969

CHAMBER AND INSTRUMENTAL

Chamber: Canzoni liriche, vn, pf, 1964–5; Sonata litúrgica, vc, pf, 1964–9; Miniaturas, fl, ob, vn, 1969; Projecções, org, pf, (speaker, lights and mime ad lib), 1970; Andante (mosso), vn, pf, 1971; Enigma I–II, perc, 1974; 3 peças breves, str qt, 1974; Str Qt, 1974–5; Trio, fl/vn, cl/va, vc/pf, 1975

Pf: Burlesca, 1963; Dança exótica, 1963; Tocata, 1964; Estudos impressionistas, 1964; Suite infantil, 1964; Meteoritos I, 1973; Meteoritos II, pf, synth, 1974; Breves estudos dodecafónicos para jovens, 1975

Gui: Esboços, 1969

EDUCATIONAL

Ritos d'África, 1966–7: Missa mandinga, solo vv, chorus, perc, Ave Maria d'África, 12vv, Dança; Missa medieval (Kyrie para um jovem), 4 male vv, 1967; Canções para a juventude, (1v, pf)/chorus, 1967; Contradanças do Auto da Floripes (teatro popular), 2 pf 8 hands, 1972

WRITINGS

A música e o homem na reforma do ensino (Lisbon, 1972–4)

Conceito de história no pensamento musical português (Lisbon, 1973)

Bases para uma estética musical (Lisbon, 1974–5)

O ensino da música e as correntes do século XX (Lisbon, 1974–5)

JOSÉ CARLOS PICOTO

Lima, Jeronymo Francisco de [Girolamo Francesco] (*b* Lisbon, 30 Sept 1743; *d* Lisbon, 19 Feb 1822). Portuguese composer and organist, elder brother of Braz Francisco de Lima. He entered the Seminário Patriarcal, Lisbon, on 20 November 1751, and on 15

January 1761 along with his younger brother he entered the Conservatorio di S Onofrio in Naples. He returned to Lisbon in 1767, joined the Brotherhood of St Cecilia (15 December 1767) and became a music teacher at the Seminário Patriarcal. In 1785 he became *mestre* there and in 1798 succeeded Carvalho as *mestre de capela* of Lisbon Cathedral. During this period he produced much sacred music and also several serenatas, including *Le nozze d'Ercole e d'Ebe*, which was performed at the Spanish ambassador's palace in Lisbon for the double marriage of the future John VI with Carlota of Spain and of the Spanish crown prince Gabriel with Mariana Victoria of Portugal. From 1800 to 1822 he was organist of the royal chamber.

WORKS

(all in MS in P-La, unless otherwise indicated)

Lo spirito di contradizione (dramma giocoso, 3, G. Martinelli), Lisbon, Salvaterra, carn. 1772
Gli orti esperidi (serenata, Metastasio), Lisbon, 31 March 1779
Enea in Tracia, 1781
Teseo (serenata, 1, Martinelli), Lisbon, Queluz, 21 Aug 1783
La vera costanza (drama, 3, F. Puttini), Lisbon, Salvaterra, carn. 1785
Le nozze d'Ercole e d'Ebe (serenata, 1), Lisbon, residence of Count F. Nuñez, 13 April 1785

La Galatea, cantata, 5vv, insts; 2 other cantatas, only libs extant
Dixit Dominus, 8vv, *P-EVc*
Numerous sacred works, *P-Lf* (see Pereira Leal)

BIBLIOGRAPHY

DBP

M. de Sampayo Ribeiro: *A música em Portugal nos séculos XVIII e XIX* (Lisbon, 1938), 76f
M. A. Machado Santos: [*Biblioteca da Ajuda:*] *Catálogo de música manuscrita* (Lisbon, 1960), iii, 28ff; ix, pp.xlviii, lvi
L. Pereira Leal: Introduction to PM, ser.B, xxiii (1973)

ROBERT STEVENSON

Lima Sequeiros, Juan de. *See* SEQUEIROS, JUAN DE LIMA.

Limenius (*fl* 128 BC). Athenian composer of paeans and processionals. An inscription found at Delphi which can be dated precisely to 128 BC contains a lengthy composition, embodying both of these forms, provided with instrumental notation. A separate but related inscription testifies that it was performed in the same year. Two introductory lines identify it as a 'paean and processional to the god [Apollo] which was composed and provided with kithara accompaniment by Limenius of Athens, son of Thoenus'. An inscription made ten years earlier contains a paean and hyporcheme to Apollo; it has vocal notation. Although the name of the composer is effaced and only the adjective 'Athenian' remains, strong epigraphical and musicological grounds justify attributing this composition as well to Limenius. The two works have the common name of the Delphic Hymns. Their melodic structure emphasizes the fixed outer notes of the tetrachords which make up the Greater Perfect System. Dorian *mesē* clearly functions as a tonic, but at various points modality is difficult to determine. The second hymn, which uniquely illustrates a normal use of the chromatic genus, modulates frequently and obviously between Lydian and Hypolydian. The text and melody of both show a careful correlation between tonemic accent and musical pitch that probably represents an archaizing approach. They also show a high degree of what may be thought banality.

A separate inscription from Delphi identifies Limenius as a performer on the kithara. As a professional musician taking part in the *Pythaïs* (the *theōria*, or liturgical embassy, to the cult centre of Pythian Apollo at Delphi), he was required to belong to one of the guilds of 'Dionysiac artists' (*hoi peri ton Dionyson technitai*, Lat. *Dionysiaci artifices*); among these, the Athenian company had a high reputation. Membership meant that he was freeborn and enjoyed the civic rights of an Athenian wherever he might be – it was a highly itinerant life. The various guilds sometimes honoured the Muses and Pythian Apollo, not merely their divine patron. They existed to bring together all those who had any connection whatsoever with the musical competitions; Limenius's membership was based on his professional status as a kitharist concerned with agonistic performance. He himself wrote of the sacred 'swarm of artists' ('hesmos ... technitōn')' in the second hymn (l.20f), which gives an unusually detailed impression of the place of music in the liturgy, and it is virtually certain that the identical phrase occurs in the companion piece (l.16f).

BIBLIOGRAPHY

A. Müller: 'Die Vereine der dionysischen Künstler', *Lehrbuch der griechischen Bühnenalterthümer* (Freiburg, 1886), 392ff
P. Foucart: 'Dionysiaci artifices', *Dictionnaire des antiquités grecques et romaines*, ed. C. Daremberg and E. Saglio, ii/1 (Paris, 1892), 246ff
R. P. Winnington-Ingram: *Mode in Ancient Greek Music* (Cambridge, Mass., 1936/R1968), 32ff, 45
E. Pöhlmann, ed.: *Denkmäler altgriechischer Musik* (Nuremberg, 1970), 58ff

WARREN ANDERSON

Limma [leimma] (Gk.: 'remainder'). Diatonic semitone in the Pythagorean system of intervals, the difference between three pure octaves and five pure 5ths, amounting to 90.2 cents and with a theoretical ratio of 256:243. Theorists in the Pythagorean tradition, such as Claudius Ptolemy (i, 10), Gaudentius (p.342, ed. Jan) and Adrastus as quoted by Theon (p.66ff, ed. Hiller), defined the limma as the amount that the 4th is in excess of the Pythagorean ditone or major 3rd, i.e. (4:3) : (81:64) (*see also* DIESIS (ii)).

Limondjian, Hambardzum (1768–1839). Reformer of the *khaz* notation of the MUSIC OF THE ARMENIAN RITE.

Linceo. *See* COLONNA, FABIO.

Linck, Johannes (*b* Züllichau, Silesia, 1561; *d* Görlitz, Silesia, 20 July 1603). Silesian Kantor and poet. He succeeded Wolfgang Rauch as Kantor at the Lutheran school and church in Linz, upper Austria, on 8 July 1586, and although repeatedly censured for bad behaviour towards the students, he retained this post until 1600. On 12 September 1602 he left Linz for Görlitz, where he taught from 24 October 1602 until his death. He was crowned *poeta laureatus* in 1602. He is known for his collection of spring poems *Eacina sive carminum vernorum praecidanea* (Görlitz, 1603) and for many Latin poems either on music or on composers or persons connected with music. The *Deliciae poetarum germanorum huius superiorisque aevi illustrium*, iii (Frankfurt, 1612, pp.1092ff) contains two poems by him entitled *De musica* (edited in Wessely, 1954). In addition he wrote an elegy on the death of the Silesian poet Georg Calaminus, a poem in praise of the composer Valentin Haussmann for the latter's *Newe Teutsche Weltliche Lieder mit fünff Stimmen* (Nuremberg, 1592) and another praising the composer Andreas Raselius for his *Teutsche Sprüche aus den Sontäglichen Euangeliis* (Nuremberg, 1594).

BIBLIOGRAPHY
O. Wessely: 'Linz und die Musik', *Jb der Stadt Linz 1950* (1951), 122
——: 'Die Pflege der Musik an der evangelischen Landschaftsschule in Linz', *Festschrift zum 400jährigen Jubiläum des humanistischen Gymnasiums in Linz* (Linz, 1952), 57
J. Schmidt: 'Lateinisches Linz', *Mitteilungen des Instituts für österreichische Geschichtsforschung*, lx (1952), 213
O. Wessely: 'Tubingensia', *Mf*, vii (1954), 398

OTHMAR WESSELY

Lincke, Joseph (*b* Trachenberg, 8 June 1783; *d* Vienna, 26 March 1837). Silesian cellist and composer. He was taught the violin by his father and the cello by Oswald. Orphaned at the age of ten, he supported himself by copying music until in 1800 he was appointed violinist in the Dominican monastery at Breslau. There he continued to study the cello, and eventually became first cellist at the theatre at Breslau, where Weber was then Kapellmeister. In 1808 he went to Vienna and was invited by Ignaz Schuppanzigh to join Count Razumovsky's private string quartet; he consequently played many of Beethoven's works under the direct guidance of the composer, including the two cello sonatas op.102, which were written for him. Lincke seems to have been particularly successful in interpreting Beethoven's music and was on intimate terms with the composer. He also took part in Schuppanzigh's public concerts and in 1816 became chamber musician to the Countess Erdödy at Pancovecz, near Zagreb. In 1818 he returned to Vienna as first cellist at the Theater an der Wien, and from 1831 he played in the Hofoper orchestra. His compositions include concertos, variations and capriccios, but only three sets of variations were published.

BIBLIOGRAPHY
T. von Frimmel: *Beethoven-Handbuch*, i (Leipzig, 1926/R1968)
J. Herrmann: 'E. A. Förster, Joseph Lincke: zwei schlesische Musiker in Lebenskreis Beethovens', *Schlesien*, xi (1966)

C. F. POHL/R

Lincke, (Carl Emil) Paul (*b* Berlin, 7 Nov 1866; *d* Clausthal-Zellerfeld, Harz, 3 Sept 1946). German composer. He studied with Rudolf Kleinow in Wittenberge (1880–84), and learnt to play the bassoon, horn and percussion. Back in Berlin he played in dance orchestras and was bassoonist, occasional conductor and house composer at several variety theatres. He enjoyed success with popular songs including *Wenn die Blätter leise rauschen*, *Ach Schaffner, lieber Schaffner* and *Die Gigerlkönigin*, and from 1893 to 1897 he was conductor and resident composer at Berlin's main variety theatre, the Apollo. After a period when Lincke was conductor at the Folies-Bergère, Paris (1897–9), his operetta *Frau Luna* made his name and also his fortune through his own publishing company, Apollo-Verlag. The march song *Das ist die Berliner Luft*, waltzes, and other popular compositions of the next decade – such as the 'Glühwürmchen-Idyll' from *Lysistrata* (1902), popularized by Pavlova – made Lincke's name as much a symbol of Berlin as Offenbach's of Paris or Johann Strauss's of Vienna. In the 1920s and 1930s *Frau Luna*, *Im Reiche des Indra* and *Lysistrata*, originally written as items on variety programmes, were revised and expanded, incorporating music from *Berliner Luft* and other works. His music retained its popularity, in due course to be exploited by the Nazis. He was made a freeman of Berlin in 1941 and named professor in 1942.

WORKS
(selective list)

Operettas (pubd in vocal score in Berlin at time of first production):
Venus auf Erden (1, H. Bolten-Baeckers), Berlin, Apollo, 6 June 1897; Frau Luna (1, Bolten-Baeckers), Apollo, 1 May 1899; Im Reiche des Indra (1, Bolten-Baeckers), Apollo, 18 Dec 1899; Fräulein Loreley (1, Bolten-Baeckers), Apollo, 15 Oct 1900; Lysistrata (1, Bolten-Baeckers), Apollo, 1 April 1902; Nakiris Hochzeit (2, Bolten-Baeckers), Apollo, 6 Nov 1902; Berliner Luft (2, Bolten-Baeckers), Apollo, 28 April 1904; Grigri (2, Bolten-Baeckers, J. Chancel), Cologne, Metropol, 25 March 1911; Casanova (3, J. Glück, W. Steinberg, after Lebrun), Chemnitz, Stadtheater, 5 Nov 1913; Ein Liebestraum (3, A. O. Erler, Neumann), Berlin radio, 20 July 1940, Hamburg, Reeperbahn, 1940; over 20 other short operettas and revues
Orch: Folies-Bergère Marsch, Geburtstagsständchen, other light pieces
Many popular songs, choruses and light orch music, pubd Berlin

BIBLIOGRAPHY
E. Nick: *Paul Lincke* (Hamburg, 1953)
O. Schneidereit: *Operette von Abraham bis Ziehrer* (Berlin, 1966)
——: *Paul Lincke und die Entstehung der Berliner Operette* (Berlin, 1974)

ANDREW LAMB

Lincoln, Harry B(arnard) (*b* Fergus Falls, Minn., 6 March 1922). American musicologist. He graduated at Macalester College in 1946 and received his PhD from Northwestern University in 1951. Since then he has been on the faculty at the State University of New York at Binghamton. Lincoln has edited and written about Italian secular music of the 16th and early 17th centuries. His edition of the madrigal collection *L'amorosa Ero* makes available in a practical modern transcription a group of pieces by some of the major madrigal composers of the late 16th century; since all of these pieces used the same text and mode they provide an interesting comparison of the ways in which different composers approached text setting in madrigals. Lincoln is also one of the principal exponents of the application of computer technology to musical research, particularly to thematic indexing.

WRITINGS
Annibale Zoilo: the Life and Works of a Sixteenth-Century Italian Composer (diss., Northwestern U., 1951)
'I manoscritti chigiani di musica organo-cembalistica della Biblioteca apostolica vaticana', *L'organo*, v (1964–7), 63
ed.: *Directory of Music Faculties in Colleges and Universities, U.S. and Canada* (Binghamton, NY, 1967, 3/1970)
'Musicology and the Computer: the Thematic Index', *Computers in Humanistic Research*, ed. E. A. Bowles (Englewood Cliffs, NJ, 1967), 184
'Some Criteria and Techniques for Developing Computerized Thematic Indices', *Elektronische Datenverarbeitung in der Musikwissenschaft*, ed. H. Heckmann (Regensburg, 1967), 57
'The Thematic Index: a Computer Application to Musicology', *Computers and the Humanities*, ii (1968), 205
'The Computer and Music Research: Prospects and Problems', *Council for Research in Music Education, Bulletin*, xviii (1969), 1
'A Computer Application in Musicology: the Thematic Index', *Information Processing 68*, ed. A. J. H. Morrell (Amsterdam, 1969), 957
ed.: *The Computer and Music* (Ithaca, NY, 1970)
'The Current State of Music Research and the Computer', *Computers and the Humanities*, v (1970), 29
Index to Graduate Degrees in Music, U.S. and Canada (Binghamton, NY, 1971)
'Uses of the Computer in Music Composition and Research', *Advances in Computers*, xii (1972), 73–114

EDITIONS
The Madrigal Collection 'L'amorosa Ero' (Brescia, *1588*) (Albany, NY, 1968)
Seventeenth-Century Keyboard Music in the Chigi Manuscripts of the Vatican Library, CEKM, xxxii (1968)

PAULA MORGAN

Lincoln Center for the Performing Arts. New York arts complex opened during the 1960s; *see* NEW YORK, §2.

Lincolniensis. *See* GROSSETESTE, ROBERT.

Lincoln's Inn. One of the London Inns of Court; *see* LONDON, §III.

Lincoln's Inn Fields Theatre. London theatre opened in 1661; *see* LONDON, §IV, 3.

Lind [Lind-Goldschmidt], **Jenny** [Johanna Maria] (*b* Stockholm, 6 Oct 1820; *d* Wynds Point, Herefordshire, 2 Nov 1887). Swedish soprano. She was nicknamed 'the Swedish nightingale'. In 1830 she was enrolled as a pupil at the Royal Opera School, Stockholm, and made her first stage appearance on 29 November that year, when she was only ten. She studied with Isak Berg, meanwhile taking part in numerous comedies and melodramas and singing such roles as the Second Boy in *Die Zauberflöte*. Her formal operatic début was on 7 March 1838 as Agathe in *Der Freischütz*, and later that year she sang Pamina and the title role of *Euryanthe*. During the next three seasons she appeared in Spontini's *La vestale*, *Robert le diable* (1839), *Don Giovanni* (as Donna Anna), *Lucia di Lammermoor* (1840), *La straniera* and as Norma, which she sang for the first time on 19 May 1841. Although she was not yet 21, her voice showed signs of fatigue, the middle register being particularly worn. On the advice of Giovanni Belletti, the Italian baritone with whom she frequently sang in Stockholm, she went to Paris to consult the eminent singing teacher Manuel García (ii). After imposing upon her a period of rest and silence, Garcia took her as a pupil at the end of August 1841, and she studied with him for ten months. When she returned to the Royal Theatre, Stockholm, in *Norma* on 10 October 1842, a great improvement in both her voice and her technique was immediately apparent. The middle register remained veiled in tone and relatively weak for the rest of her career, but the notes from c'' to a'' had become marvellously strong and flexible, and her range extended to g'''.

Jenny Lind as Amina in Bellini's 'La sonnambula'

Lind's new roles included Valentine in *Les Huguenots*, Ninetta in *La gazza ladra*, the Countess in *Le nozze di Figaro* and Amina in *La sonnambula*, which she sang for the first time on 1 March 1843. During the next season she added *Il turco in Italia*, Gluck's *Armide*, and *Anna Bolena* to her repertory. In the autumn of 1844 she went to Berlin to sing Vielka in the first performance of *Ein Feldlager in Schlesien*, composed for her by Meyerbeer, but the Berlin soprano Tuczec created the role on 7 December; Lind made her début on 15 December in *Norma* and did not sing Vielka until 5 January 1845. In March she appeared at Hanover, and in April at Hamburg, expanding her repertory as quickly as she could re-learn her roles in German. Returning to Stockholm, on 9 June she sang Marie in *La fille du régiment* for the first time. After brief appearances in Frankfurt, Darmstadt and Copenhagen, she paid a second visit to Berlin, remaining there five months; on 4 December she sang at a Leipzig Gewandhaus concert, conducted by Mendelssohn.

Lind's Viennese début was at the Theater an der Wien on 22 April 1846 in *Norma*. She took part, with Mendelssohn, in the 1846 Lower Rhine Music Festival at Aachen, singing in Haydn's *The Creation* (31 May) and Handel's *Alexander's Feast* (1 June). For the rest of the year she continued to tour Germany, appearing at Munich, Stuttgart, Karlsruhe, Mannheim and Nuremberg. In January 1847 she returned to Vienna, where she scored an immense success as Marie. Her London début was at Her Majesty's on 4 May 1847 when, in the presence of Queen Victoria, Prince Albert and a large and distinguished audience, she sang (in Italian) Alice in *Robert le diable*. 'The great event of the evening', wrote the queen in her diary that night, 'was Jenny Lind's appearance and her *complete* triumph. She has a most exquisite, powerful and really quite peculiar voice, so round, soft and flexible and her acting is charming and touching and very natural'.

The queen's subjects endorsed her verdict, and London succumbed to the Jenny Lind fever. The new prima donna sang *La sonnambula* (13 May) and *La fille du régiment* (27 May) with even greater success, but her Norma (15 June), acclaimed in Sweden and Germany, was not popular in London. She also created the role of Amalia at the première of Verdi's *I masnadieri* (22 July) and sang Susanna in *Le nozze di Figaro* (17 August). After the opera season she went on a tour of the provinces, singing at Birmingham, Manchester, Liverpool, Edinburgh, Glasgow, Norwich, Bristol, Bath and Exeter. Having decided to give up the theatre, she sang in Stockholm during the winter, and her final operatic appearance there was on 12 April 1848, as Norma. The tour of Great Britain after her second season at Her Majesty's (1848) included a visit to Dublin in October, and she sang in Mendelssohn's *Elijah* at the Exeter Hall, London, on 15 December. Persuaded to give six farewell performances at Her Majesty's, she was not yet 29 when she made her last stage appearance as Alice in *Robert le diable* on 10 May 1849.

In 1850, accompanied by the conductor Julius Benedict and the baritone Giovanni Belletti, Lind sailed from Liverpool to the USA, where she was to make a concert tour managed by Phineas T. Barnum. She gave her first concert in New York on 11 September 1850, and the 93rd and last in the series at Philadelphia in

May 1851, having meanwhile visited Boston, Baltimore, Washington, Richmond, Charleston, Havana, New Orleans, Louisville, Cincinnati and other cities. Benedict then returned to England and Otto Goldschmidt became her accompanist and, in February 1852, her husband. She continued to sing in concert and oratorio, both in Germany and in England, where she lived from 1858 until her death. In 1883, the year of her last public performance, she became professor of singing at the Royal College of Music, London.

The greater part of Lind's career was as a recitalist and oratorio singer; outside Sweden, her operatic work lasted less than five years and was virtually restricted to Germany and England, where her repertory was limited by the necessity of re-learning her roles, first in German, then in Italian. Her stage reputation was based largely on her performances in four operas, *La sonnambula*, *Robert le diable*, *La fille du régiment* and *Norma*. Her *Norma* failed because of a temperamental inability to realize the character fully; thus Amina, Alice and Marie were probably her most satisfying artistic achievements (though her own preference was for Julia in *La vestale*). 'She impresses me as a remarkable Swedish type', wrote Chopin in a letter on 4 May 1848, 'surrounded not by an ordinary halo, but by a kind of northern lights. She produces an extraordinary effect in *La sonnambula*. She sings with amazing purity and certainty and her *piano* is so steady – as smooth and even as a thread of hair'.

BIBLIOGRAPHY

B. Lumley: *Reminiscences of the Opera* (London, 1864)

H. S. Holland and W. S. Rockstro: *Memoir of Madame Jenny Lind-Goldschmidt: her Early Art-life and Dramatic Career* (London, 1891)

S. Dorph: *Jenny Linds triumphtåg genom nya världen och övriga levnadsöden* (Uppsala, 1918)

J. M. C. Maude: *The Life of Jenny Lind* (London, 1926)

M. Pergament: *Jenny Lind* (Stockholm, 1945)

B. E. Sydow: *Korespondencja Fryderyka Chopina* (Warsaw, 1955; Eng. trans., abridged, 1962)

R. Godden: *Hans Christian Andersen* (London, 1955)

J. Bulman: *Jenny Lind* (London, 1956)

ELIZABETH FORBES

Lindberg, Armas. *See* LAUNIS, ARMAS.

Lindberg, Oskar (Fredrik) (*b* Gagnef, Dalarna, 23 Feb 1887; *d* Stockholm, 10 April 1955). Swedish composer, church musician and teacher. He served as organist in Gagnef from the age of 14 and studied at the Stockholm Conservatory, where he graduated as church musician (1906) and music teacher (1908), and where he studied composition with Ellberg and Hallén. Subsequently he conducted at Sondershausen and made other journeys abroad. He was organist at the Trefaldighetskyrka, Stockholm (1906–14), and then until his death at the Engelbrektskyrka. At the same time he taught music in Stockholm high schools and harmony at the conservatory (from 1919, as professor from 1936). In 1926 he was made a member of the Swedish Royal Academy of Music, of which he was a board member from 1937 to 1939 and from 1945 to 1955.

Lindberg came from a family with deep roots in Dalarna: several of his ancestors had been peasant violinists, and he himself was steeped in folk music, from which he took many of his themes. He became prominent in the Young Swedes group (*c*1910–20; other members were Rangström and Atterberg) and developed a rich late Romantic orchestral style, where the influences of Rakhmaninov and Sibelius were balanced with those of folk music, most successfully in his slightly impressionist nature scenes. One of his most noteworthy achievements was helping to compile the 1939 hymnbook, largely his work and containing 14 hymns of his own composition.

WORKS
(selective list)

Opera: Fredlös, 1936–42; Stockholm, 1943

Orch: Sym., F, op.16, 1909; Ov., E♭, 1909; Ov., b, 1911; Från de stora skogarna, sym. poem, 1918; Vår, ov., D, 1924; Per spelman, han spelte, op.32, rhapsody, 1930; 4 other sym. poems, 5 suites

Choral: Requiem, op.21, 1920–22; 5 large choral orch works, incl. 11 cantatas

Org: Sonata, op.23, 1924; several chorale preludes

Other works: songs with orch/pf/org, chamber music, pf pieces

Principal publisher: Nordiska Musikförlaget

HANS ÅSTRAND

Lindblad, Adolf Fredrik (*b* Skenninge, 1 Feb 1801; *d* Löfvingsborg, nr. Linköping, 23 Aug 1878). Swedish composer. He was adopted as a child by a merchant who gave him his name and tried to teach him his trade; however he showed an early interest in music, played the flute and piano and composed. In Hamburg (1818–19) he came into contact with the contemporary German culture led by Goethe, Jean-Paul, Tieck and Beethoven, who became his idol. Through his future wife he met P. D. A. Atterbom, the leading Swedish Romantic poet and teacher at Uppsala University, in 1822. While studying music at Uppsala (1823–5) he was welcomed into the group of older artists and humanists including the professor and composer Erik Gustaf Geijer. From 1825 to 1827 he travelled in Germany and went to Paris. He studied for a time with Zelter in Berlin, where he became a close friend of Zelter's young pupil, Mendelssohn (their correspondence, 1825–47, is in the Mendelssohn archives of *D-B*; other letters in *S-Sk*).

Back in Sweden, Lindblad directed a music and piano school from 1827 to 1861 using the Logier method. His pupils included Crown Prince Oscar I and his son Prince Gustaf, Ludvig Norman and other Swedish composers. His opera *Frondörerna* ('The rebels'), performed in 1835, was less successful than Lindblad had expected, but his Symphony in C won him membership of the Royal Swedish Academy of Music in 1831 and was played to great acclaim at a Leipzig Gewandhaus concert in 1839. The symphony and other instrumental works as well as several volumes of his songs were printed by German publishers. Jenny Lind, who had lived with Lindblad's family when young and can be considered his pupil, sang his songs all over the world. Lindblad's strong attachment to her was expressed in his 1845 collection of songs, which gave rise to a controversy in the press. He was criticized for the harmonic boldness of the songs, an element foreign to Swedish taste at the time. The battle ended with a laudatory article by Ludwig Spohr in Kassel, but wounded by this publicity and the poor reception of his instrumental works, Lindblad withdrew into a small, close-knit circle of fellow musicians and writers for the rest of his life, and wrote only chamber music and the kind of song that appealed to contemporary Swedish taste.

Lindblad's chief historical significance lies in his 215 songs (a complete edition was published in nine volumes by Hirsch, Stockholm, between 1878 and 1890), which began a new tradition in Swedish lieder; he also wrote the texts for about a third of them. He had published *Der Nordensaal*, a collection of 12 folksong arrangements, in Berlin as early as 1826. His own songs were often modelled on Swedish folk melodies, especially his simple and concentrated settings of the poems of his friend, Atterbom. Genuine folk ballads and later pastiches of these also inspired two dramatic songs, *Bröllopsfärden* ('The wedding journey', c1830) and *Den skeppsbrutna* ('Shipwrecked', c1840). In a number of colourful narrative songs, such as *Sotargossen* ('The chimney-sweep'), *Krigsinvaliden* ('The war veteran') and the popular *Skjutsgossen på hemväg* ('The driver on his way home'), he painted a realistic and humorous picture of daily life in town and country. The songs are often strophic or built on a pattern of two contrasting stanzas which return more or less varied. A good example of strophic variations is the self-revealing *Nattviolen* ('The night violet', c1860), in which the recitative develops into ecstatic melody. The finest of all are his nature songs, including *En sommardag* ('A summer's day'), *Aftonen* ('Evening'), *I dalen* ('In the valley'), *Måntro, jo jo* ('Perhaps, oh yes!') or *Nära* ('Nearby'); a few have German texts: *Am Aarensee*, *Der schlummernde Amor* (Claudius) and eight Heine songs (c1860), among them *Morgen steh ich auf und frage*, *Still ist die Nacht* and *Asra*. The opera *Frondörerna* and the Symphony in C show an uncommon talent for orchestration. Among his other works, mostly in manuscript (*S-Skma*), are a Symphony in D, two string quintets, seven string quartets, a trio for piano, violin and viola, a sonata and short pieces for piano, and two works for soloists, chorus and piano, *Om vinterkväll* ('In the winter evening') and *Drömmarne* ('The dreams', also orchestrated).

BIBLIOGRAPHY

C. R. Nyblom: *Adolf Fredrik Lindblad: minnesteckning* [Lindblad: reminiscences] (Stockholm, 1881); repr. in *Svenska akademiens handlinger*, lvii (1882)

L. Norman: 'Adolf Fredrik Lindblad som instrumentalkompositör', *Svensk musiktidning*, iii (1883), 178

L. Dahlgren, ed.: *Brev till Adolf Fredrik Lindblad fran Mendelssohn* (Stockholm, 1913) [letters from Mendelssohn and others]

F. H. Törnblom: 'Adolf Fredrik Lindblad som operakompositör', *STMf*, xvii (1935), 108

——: 'Adolf Fredrik Lindblad och Jenny Lind', *STMf*, xxiii (1941), 43

K. Linder: *Den unge Adolf Fredrik Lindblad (1801–27)* (diss., U. of Uppsala, 1973)

KERSTIN LINDER

Lindblad, Otto Jonas (*b* Karlstorp, Småland, 31 March 1809; *d* Norra Mellby, Skåne, 24 Jan 1864). Swedish composer, choral director and violinist. During his ten years as a pupil at Växjö Cathedral school he devoted much time to playing the violin and singing in male-voice trios and quartets. In 1829 he entered Lund University, where he studied humanities while earning a living as a private teacher. He received his essential musical training from Mathias Lundholm, Ole Bull's teacher, who lived in Lund from 1832 to 1836. In 1836 Lindblad played in the orchestra of the Heuser opera company and toured with part of it as orchestra leader. He also directed the Lund University Male Chorus (founded 1831) for more than ten years, soon making it famous abroad and stimulating the organization of similar choruses in Copenhagen and Christiania. In 1841 Lindblad took part in the music festival in Hamburg as an honorary guest. There he also had a few composition lessons from K.-A. Krebs. In 1846 he made a long tour through Sweden with his male quartet, which was received with great enthusiasm. His musical activities and long illnesses had prolonged his studies, but in 1844 he eventually graduated as *filosofie magister*. He received some money from the university for his

work with the student chorus and earned more through the famous musical soirées, at which he and his friends gave a small concert and then played for dancing. But his economic situation was still so bad that he became a parish clerk in Norra Mellby, 40 miles north of Lund. From 1847 to his death he was leader of the congregational singing in the two parish churches, both without an organ, and was one of the first in the country to organize a parish church choir. He was elected a member of the Academy of Music in Stockholm in 1857. Monuments to him have been erected in Lund and in Sösdala near Norra Mellby.

Lindblad's compositions are nearly all vocal. His solo songs with piano accompaniment do not attain the level of his many male-voice *a cappella* songs; one of these, *Ur svenska hjärtans djup* ('From the depths of the Swedish heart'), to a text by C. W. A. Strandberg, is the hymn for the King of Sweden. The lyrical *Orfeus sjöng* (C. A. Hagberg's translation of Shakespeare's 'Orpheus with his lute') and *Till skogs en liten fågel flög* ('A small bird flew towards the forest'), on a theme resembling that of the second movement of Beethoven's Piano Sonata op.13, are also often sung. Lindblad's setting of Sätherberg's *Vintern rasat ut* ('Winter raged out') is among the best-known Swedish spring songs, while *Ångbåtssång* ('Steamship song'), to Lindblad's own words, is a memory of the close contacts between the universities of Lund and Copenhagen. The Lund University library has a collection of Lindblad's manuscripts and printed compositions as well as his autobiography and letters.

BIBLIOGRAPHY

G. A. Feuk: *Otto Lindblad och hans sångare 1840–1846* [Otto Lindblad and his singers] (Lund, 1882) [incl. list of works]

T. Nerman: *Otto Lindblad: ett sångaröde* (Uppsala, 1930)

B. Möller: *Lundensisk studentsång under ett sekel* [A century of student singing at Lund] (Lund, 1931)

E. Danell: 'Bidrag till Otto Lindblads biografi', *STMf*, xxii (1940), 64

FOLKE BOHLIN

Linde, (Anders) Bo (Leif) (*b* Gävle, 1 Jan 1933; *d* Gävle, 2 Oct 1970). Swedish composer. After theory lessons with Bengtsson he studied composition with Larsson and the piano with Wibergh at the Stockholm Conservatory (1948–52). In 1953–4 he studied conducting in Vienna and travelled in Italy and Spain. He taught music theory at the Stockholm Borgarskola (1957–60) and then lived in Gävle as a composer and music critic. Linde was associated with a group of young composers characterized as '50-talisterna' ('belonging to the 1950s'), a group which looked back to the 1930s, particularly to Larsson, and to composers such as Britten and Shostakovich. He wrote with great facility and technical skill, notably in the vocal pieces.

WORKS
(selective list)

Orch: Sinfonia fantastica, op.1, 1951; Preludio e finale, op.16, str, 1955; Vn Conc., op.18, 1957; Sinfonia, op.23, 1960; Conc. for Orch, 1962; Vc Conc., op.29, 1965

Chamber: Str Qt, op.9, 1953; Vn Sonata, op.10, 1953; Divertimento, op.25, fl, vc, pf, 1962; Str Trio, op.37, 1968; Sonata a 3, op.38, pf trio, 1968

Choral: Symfoni i ord, op.33, 1966

Songs: 4 ballader, op.6; 2 naiva sånger, op.20; Sånger om våren, op.40; 4 allvarliga sånger

HANS ÅSTRAND

Linde, Hans-Martin (*b* Werne, nr. Dortmund, 24 May 1930). Swiss recorder player, flautist and composer of German birth. He studied the flute with Gustav Scheck and conducting with Konrad Lechner at the Staatliche

Hochschule für Musik, Freiburg (1947–51), then became solo flautist of the Cappella Coloniensis of West German radio at Cologne. A chance meeting with August Wenzinger in Cologne led to his appointment to the Schola Cantorum at Basle in 1957 and his joining the Schola Cantorum Basiliensis. He directs the vocal ensemble and in 1971 became joint director of the concert group. His high international reputation as a recorder player and flautist (he plays modern and Baroque flutes), is founded on an impeccable virtuoso technique and a scholarly sense of style. He tours widely and his extensive and important recordings include flute concertos by Leclair, Mozart, Stamitz and Dittersdorf, and recorder concertos by Sammartini, Vivaldi and Naudot. He has recorded early English consort music and Italian chamber music from 1600 with his own Linde-Consort. He and Frans Brueggen make an effective partnership. His compositions have been published, and he has written *Kleine Anleitung zum Verzieren alter Musik* (1958), and *Handbuch des Blockflötenspiels* (1962).

BIBLIOGRAPHY
J. M. Thomson: *Recorder Profiles* (London, 1972), 43ff
J. M. THOMSON

Lindegren, Johan (*b* Ullared, 7 Jan 1842; *d* Stockholm, 8 June 1908). Swedish organist, teacher, composer and scholar. He attended the Stockholm Conservatory from 1860 to 1865, studying composition with the elder Behrens, the piano with van Boom and the violin with Randel. From 1861 he directed the chorus of the Stockholm Opera and from 1876 he taught counterpoint at the conservatory; he became a music teacher at the Jacobshögskolan in 1881 and cantor of the Storkyrkan in 1884. In addition to his official duties he was increasingly active from the 1870s as a private teacher of counterpoint and composition. As a musicologist his chief interest was in church music; he edited the journal *Tidning för kyrkomusik* (1881–2), took part in the preparation of the music for the Swedish church handbook (1895) and published an edition (1905, 2/1906) and a study (1907) of Swedish chorales.

Lindegren was known during his lifetime mainly as a contrapuntist and teacher, and his pupils included a number of notable Swedish composers, among them Beckman, Alfvén, Melchers, Bäck, Håkanson and Wiklund. One of the best of his own compositions is the string quintet (*c*1870); in his piano works, such as the *Fuga uti fri stil* (1866) and the canon *Stor sonat* in B minor, op.2 (1869), he combined his contrapuntal mastery with idiomatic, virtuoso writing for the instrument. In 1903 he was made a member of the Kungliga Musikaliska Akademien.

BIBLIOGRAPHY
O. Blom: 'Johan Lindegrens lif och verksamhet', *Kyrkomusik och skolsång*, iv (1910), 111, 115
C.-A. Moberg: 'Johan Lindegren', *Kyrkosangförbundet*, xvii (1942), 39
H. Alfvén: 'Min lärare Johan Lindegren', *Musikmänniskor*, ed. F. H. Törnblom (Uppsala, 1943)
——: *Första satsen* (Stockholm, 1946), chap. 'Johan Lindegren'
ROBERT LAYTON

Lindelheim, Joanna Maria (*fl* 1703–17). German soprano. According to Burney and Hawkins she sang at many German courts before her arrival in England; Burney added that she was trained in Italy. She studied under Haym in London and first appeared there in public in concerts at Drury Lane Theatre on 23 January and 1 February 1703, accompanied by Saggione and Gasparo Visconti. Only one advertisement mentions her surname (and misspells it Lindelheim); elsewhere she is 'the Famous Signiora Joanna Maria'. She was probably 'la Signiora Maria, as of late taught by Signior Nicolini Haym', who sang between the acts of a play at the Queen's Theatre on 17 November 1705. She made her operatic début at Drury Lane in Haym's arrangement of Bononcini's *Camilla* on 30 March 1706 as 'Mrs Joanna Maria'. The contemporary Walsh score calls her the Baroness, the title under which she made all her subsequent appearances. These included a concert at Hickford's Room on 2 April 1707, the revival of *Camilla* in November 1707 (and perhaps January 1709), the pasticcios *Love's Triumph* (26 February 1708) and *Tomiri* (10 April 1708), and Haym's arrangement of A. Scarlatti's *Pirro e Demetrio* (14 December 1708), the last three at the Queen's Theatre. Lindelheim had benefits in *Pirro e Demetrio* on 29 March 1709 and 12 May 1711. On 24 April 1713 she took part with Haym and another of his pupils in a concert at Hickford's, and she had five further benefits there, on 27 May 1713, 17 March 1714, 6 April 1715, 21 March 1716 and 12 April 1717. She became a singing teacher; Anastasia Robinson studied with her for a time.

WINTON DEAN

Illustration Acknowledgments

We are grateful to those listed below for permission to reproduce copyright illustrative material, and those contributors who supplied or helped us obtain it. Every effort has been made to contact copyright holders; we apologize to anyone who may have been omitted. Brian and Constance Dear prepared the maps and technical diagrams, and Oxford Illustrators the typographic diagrams (except where otherwise stated). Photographs acknowledged to the following sources are Crown copyright: Her Majesty the Queen, the Victoria and Albert Museum (including the Theatre Museum), the Science Museum and the National Monuments Record. The following forms of acknowledgment are used where the copyright of an illustration is held by a contributor:

photo John Smith – John Smith is contributor and photographer
John Smith – John Smith is contributor and copyright holder
photo John Smith, London – John Smith is a contributor (not of the article concerned) and photographer
John Smith, London – John Smith is a contributor (not of the article concerned) and copyright holder.

Where illustrations are taken from books out of copyright, the full title and place and date of publication are given, unless in the caption.

Kern, Jerome Archive Department, Chappell International Music Publishers Ltd, London

Kettledrum Trustees of the British Museum, London

Keyboard *1* Antikvarisk-Topografiska Arkivet, Stockholm / photo Nils Lagergren; *2* British Library, London; *3* Smithsonian Institution, Washington, DC

Keyed bugle *1* Horniman Museum, London; *2* Music Division, Library of Congress, Washington, DC

Kircher, Athanasius Staatsbibliothek Preussischer Kulturbesitz, Musikabteilung, Berlin

Kirckman *1* Victoria and Albert Museum, London

Kirnberger, Johann Philipp Deutsche Staatsbibliothek, Berlin

Kit *1* Bildarchiv Preussischer Kulturbesitz, Berlin; *2a, 2d* Victoria and Albert Museum, London; *2b–c* Royal College of Music, London; *3* Conservatoire National Supérieur de Musique, Paris

Kithara Museum of Fine Arts (J. M. Rodocanachi Fund), Boston

Kjerulf, Halfdan Kunstforeningen i Oslo / photo Universitetsbiblioteket, Oslo

Kleiber, Erich Decca Record Co. Ltd, London

Klemperer, Otto photo Godfrey MacDomnic, Stanmore, London

Kodály, Zoltán *1, 3* Sarolta Kodály, Budapest; *2* Universal Edition (Alfred A. Kalmus Ltd), Vienna

Koechlin, Charles United Music Publishers Ltd, London / photo Edmund Joaillier, Paris

Kōmos Martin-von-Wagner Museum der Universität, Würzburg

Kondrashin, Kirill Novosti Press Agency, London

Konstanz Zentralbibliothek, Lucerne / photo Schweizerisches Landesmuseum, Zurich

Kora *1* photo Anthony King; *2* photo Gilbert Rouget, Paris; *3* after A. King

Korea *1–9* photo Byong Won Lee

Koussevitzky, Sergey Keystone Press Agency Ltd, London

Krauss, Clemens Clemens Krauss-Archiv, Vienna / photo Felicitas Timpe, Munich

Kreisler, Fritz Francis Hauert, New York / photo Roger Hauert

Krenek, Ernst Universal Edition (Alfred A. Kalmus Ltd), Vienna

Kubelík, Jan Royal College of Music, London

Kubelík, Rafael photo Erich Auerbach, London

Kuhnau, Johann British Library, London

Kurdish music *2* Iranian Embassy, London; *3, 4* International Institute for Comparative Music Studies and Documentation, Berlin / photo Joachim Wenzel

Kwela photo Gerhard Kubik

La Barre, Michel de *1* Trustees of the National Gallery, London; *2* Bibliothèque Nationale, Paris / photo J. Colomb-Gérard

Lablache, Luigi Royal Opera House, Covent Garden, London

La Chevardière, Louis Balthazard de Richard Macnutt, Tunbridge Wells

Lai *1, 3, 4* Bibliothèque Nationale, Paris; *2* Corporation of London Records Office

Lalande, Michel-Richard de *2* Fitzwilliam Museum, Cambridge

Lalo, Edouard Georges Sirot, Paris

Lambert, Constant Elliott & Fry (Bassano & Vandyk Studios), London

Lamellaphone *1, 2* Gerhard Kubik / (*1*) photo M. Djenda; *4* African Music Society, Grahamstown: from A. Tracey, 'The Original African Mbira?', *African Music*, v/2 (1972); *5* E. Stiglmayr, Vienna: from G. Kubik, 'Carl Mauch's Mbira Musical Transcriptions of 1872', *Review of Ethnology*, iii (1971)

Lamoureux, Charles Bibliothèque Nationale, Paris / photo R. Lalance

Lampe, John Frederick Richard Macnutt, Tunbridge Wells

Landi, Stefano Institut für Theaterwissenschaft, University of Cologne

Landini, Francesco Biblioteca Medicea Laurenziana, Florence

Ländler Österreichische Nationalbibliothek, Vienna

Landowska, Wanda Francis Hauert, New York / Roger Hauert

Lanier Kunsthistorisches Museum, Vienna

Laos *1–5* Terry E. Miller; *6* Musée de l'Homme, Paris / photo Mission Pavie

Lassus *1, 2* British Library, London; *3, 4* Bayerisches Staatsbibliothek, Munich; *5* from *O. de Lassus: Sämtliche Werke*, xii, plate XLIX (Leipzig, 1894–1926)

Lawes, Henry *1* Faculty of Music, University of Oxford; *2* Richard Macnutt, Tunbridge Wells

Lawes, William Faculty of Music, University of Oxford

Lebanon *1, 2* Louis Hage; *3, 4* International Institute for Comparative Music Studies and Documentation, Berlin / photo Joachim Wenzel

Leclair *1, 2* Bibliothèque Nationale, Paris

Leger line British Library, London

Legrenzi, Giovanni *1* Civico Museo Bibliografico Musicale, Bologna; *2* Service International de Microfilms, Paris

Lehár, Franz H. Roger-Viollet, Paris

Lehmann, Lotte Harold Rosenthal, London

Leider, Frida Stuart-Liff Collection, Tunbridge Wells

Leinsdorf, Erich RCA Records, London / photo Marvin Lichtner

Leipzig *1–3* Museum für Geschichte der Stadt Leipzig; *4* Bildarchiv Preussischer Kulturbesitz, Berlin

Le Jeune, Claude *2* British Library, London

Leningrad Novosti Press Agency, London

Lenya, Lotte CBS Records, London

Leonardo da Vinci Bibliothèque de l'Institut de France, Paris / photo J. Colomb-Gérard

Leoncavallo, Ruggero Archivio Storico Ricordi, Milan

L'Epine, Margherita de photo Sotheby Parke Bernet & Co., London
Leschetizky, Theodor Royal College of Music, London
Lesotho *1, 2* photo Charles R. Adams
Le Sueur, Jean-François Bärenreiter-Verlag, Kassel
Leveridge, Richard Richard Macnutt, Tunbridge Wells
Lewis, Richard Harold Rosenthal, London / photo Guy Gravett, Hurstpierpoint

Lhévinne, Josef Harry L. Anderson, San Diego, California
Liberia Ruth M. Stone / photo Verlon L. Stone, Bloomington, Indiana
Libretto British Library, London
Ligeti, György photo Clive Barda, London
Lind, Jenny Stuart-Liff Collection, Tunbridge Wells